A NAVAL

BIOGRAPHICAL DICTIONARY:

Vol. 2

COMPRISING

THE LIFE AND SERVICES OF

EVERY LIVING OFFICER IN HER MAJESTY'S NAVY,

FROM THE RANK OF

ADMIRAL OF THE FLEET TO THAT OF LIEUTENANT,

INCLUSIVE.

Compiled from Authentic and Family Documents.

BY WILLIAM R. O'BYRNE, ESQ.

LONDON:
JOHN MURRAY, ALBEMARLE STREET,
PUBLISHER TO THE ADMIRALTY.
1849.

TO

HER MOST GRACIOUS MAJESTY

THE QUEEN,

This Biographical Dictionary

OF THE OFFICERS OF THE ROYAL NAVY

IS,

BY HER MAJESTY'S AUTHORITY,

MOST DUTIFULLY DEDICATED,

BY HER MAJESTY'S LOYAL AND DEVOTED SERVANT AND SUBJECT,

WILLIAM R. O'BYRNE.

PREFACE.

At length, after six years of unremitting toil, mental and physical, I have succeeded, to the entire exclusion of every other pursuit, in accomplishing an undertaking deemed by all most arduous, by many impracticable; disheartening truly in the perspective, but in the retrospect, a source to me of sincere gratification and, I hope I may add, of honourable pride.

That any apology will be considered necessary for the publication of the present work I cannot believe: it was due to the Service—it was due also to the country. To the country, it was due that it should be made acquainted with the merits, individually, of men to whose collective efforts it is, in the main, indebted for its proud pre-eminence in the scale of nations; and upon whom it must, in days to come, rely in a great measure for its permanent security. To the Profession, it was due that some exertion should be made to furnish a public memorial of the services performed, the dangers braved, the honours attained, and the disappointments suffered, by those who have fought and bled in support of England's greatness, and who, during a long period of peace, have equally maintained her dignity, afforded protection to her commerce, and in every way guarded her interests.

Should any explanation, however, be looked for of the causes which have induced a civilian, previously unconnected with the Service, to embark in such an undertaking, the only excuse I have to offer is, that I perceived the necessity that existed for a book of the kind, and that I determined to attempt to supply it. The degree of success I may have achieved in the performance of my self-imposed task, it is not for me to estimate; but I can venture to claim credit for the most earnest zeal, the most unwearied industry, and the most undeviating impartiality in the prosecution of my labours.

The following pages will be found to comprise an account, more or less detailed, of nearly *five thousand* officers, including all those now deceased, (in number upwards of six hundred,) whose names are contained in the 'Navy List' for January, 1845. I have not the presumption to anticipate that I have, in every case, afforded satisfaction. He would, indeed, be over confident, and possess but a slight knowledge of human nature, who could for a moment believe that it was in his power to please so vast a number of persons as those who must of necessity be more or less interested in these records. All I can fairly hope, is that the result of my labours may be received with general favour, and that the desire I have felt to do entire justice to my subject may have proved successful to as great an extent as I could be warranted in expecting. A work of this character could not have been compiled without an extensive intercourse with the individuals to whose professional biography it is devoted; and it is with pride I confess my belief that no public writer was ever more honoured with the confidence of a profession than I have been with that of the Navy. With many, however, especially of the younger members, owing to their absence on foreign service, I have not been able to communicate; and some there are who, from a too fastidious feeling of modesty, or from accidental causes, have left me to my own resources. Whenever such difficulties have arisen, I have endeavoured, I trust not unsuccessfully, to overcome them so far as increased activity and perseverance could enable me so to do; and to obtain, from sources hardly less authentic, the materials of which fortuitous circumstances had deprived me. In all cases I have endeavoured to be as correct in my statements and as copious in my details as circumstances would permit.

For whatever errors may have crept, unconsciously on my part, into the memoirs of those who have afforded me information, I can only express my regret, and suggest as an excuse the impossibility, in a work embracing so immense a body of facts, of guarding against occasional inaccuracies. But these I trust and believe will be found to be of rare occurrence. I shall be equally sorry if faults of commission (and faults there must also be of omission) should present themselves in the histories of those who have disregarded the applications which I felt myself bound to make, in duty to them as well as to myself. In the prosecution of my task I have avoided adulation, and I hope that I have in no case rendered myself liable to the charge of having bestowed unmerited praise. I have, indeed, as a general rule, confined myself, in awarding commendation, to the language adopted in public despatches or other official documents; and in accordance with this principle, as well as with a view to rigid accuracy, I have, at no small pains, carefully examined the 'London Gazettes;' affixing in every instance to a memoir, by way of note, the date and page of the Gazette in which the officer's name stands recorded; with the single exception of occasions on which the captain of a comparatively large ship has obtained mention through the capture of privateers and letters-of-marque. With regard to Courts-martial, I have, whenever I have found it possible to do so, avoided any reference to them; the advantage to be derived from reviving the details of inquiries of this nature appearing to me anything but obvious; and I hope, for the credit of the Service, there are few, if any, of its members who would desire to enhance their reputation by recalling the errors, often trivial, of their brother officers.

Important as have been the communications I have received from members of the Naval Service, the work would have fallen far short of its present dimensions and completeness had it not been for the cordial support and countenance with which I have been honoured by the Board of Admiralty, who have most obligingly afforded me access to every record in their possession which appeared at all likely to facilitate its progress.

I have but little more to add: few besides myself can conceive the anxiety I feel for the success of an undertaking that has absorbed so many years of labour, and upon which so large an amount of capital has been expended; but I commit it with confidence to the leniency and consideration of the Service, trusting that my readers, mindful of the pains I have taken to satisfy all reasonable expectations in regard to it, and of my earnest endeavour to perform my task conscientiously and correctly, will rather give me credit for what I have achieved than censure me for what I have not.

I cannot conclude this notice without offering, in the most unequivocal terms, my acknowledgments to the present estimable Secretary of the Admiralty, Captain W. A. B. Hamilton, for the public-spirited manner in which he entered, from the date of my earliest application to him, into my views; and for the kindness with which he made known my intentions to his venerable predecessor Sir John Barrow, and after his own accession to office extended to me every facility for acquiring information. The memory of Sir John Barrow, too, I must ever revere, for the attention I experienced from him during the latter part of his official life, and for the sympathy he expressed, and the interest he appeared personally to take, in my labours. To my valued friend John Barrow, Esq., Keeper of the Records of the Admiralty, I owe more than I can well express. I could indeed scarcely find words adequate to convey my sense of the indefatigable assistance I have received at his hands throughout the progress of the work, and of the benefits I have at all times derived from his experience and his highly-prized advice.

Independently of the Admiralty, I have reason to feel gratified by the courtesy which has been exhibited towards me by members of other departments of the public service; and to no one am I more bound by obligation, and it is with heartfelt pride and pleasure I record it, than I am to William George Anderson, Esq., the Assistant Paymaster-General, both for the aid which his official position has enabled him to render me, and for the acts of personal kindness by which they have been accompanied.

It would be unjust to terminate this series of grateful acknowledgments without mentioning the aid I have received from a member of my own family, my brother, Robert Henry O'Byrne, author of the 'Representative History of Great Britain and Ireland;' to whose affectionate zeal and energetic exertions I am indebted not only for the compilation of the greater part of the Appendix, but for the collection of a large portion of the details on which the work is founded.

ABBREVIATIONS, ETC.

G.C.B. . . .	Denotes the officer to be a Knight Grand Cross of the most Honourable Order of the Bath.
K.C.B. . . .	,, ,, Knight Commander of the most Honourable Order of the Bath.
C.B.	,, ,, Companion of the most Honourable Order of the Bath.
G.C.M.G. . .	,, ,, Knight Grand Cross of the most distinguished Order of St. Michael and St. George.
K.C.M.G. . .	,, ,, Knight Commander of the most distinguished Order of St. Michael and St. George.
G.C.H. . . .	,, ,, Knight Grand Cross of the Royal Hanoverian Guelphic Order.
K.C.H. . . .	,, ,, Knight Commander of the Royal Hanoverian Guelphic Order.
K.H.	,, ,, Knight of the Royal Hanoverian Guelphic Order.
Fst.-Cl. Vol. . . Sec.-Cl. Vol. . .	First and Second Class Volunteer.
A.B.	Able Seaman.
Ordinary . . .	Ordinary Seaman.
L.M.	Landman.
F.P.	Full pay, or time actually served.
H.P.	Half pay, or time unemployed.
R. M.	Royal Marines.
Captain . . .	Denotes that the Officer has accepted the Retirement.

*** The signification of the other abbreviations used at the head of a memoir will be found in general detailed in the body of the memoir itself.

The ratings of A.B., Ordinary, L.M., Captain's Servant, Lieutenant's Servant, &c., were often during the war nominally given to young gentlemen on entering the service, owing to there not being at the time vacancies for them among the Volunteers and Midshipmen.

The Full-pay and Half-pay are computed up to the year 1847.

HAMLEY. (Commander, 1846.)

Wymond Hamley is youngest brother of Capt. Wm. Hamley, R.N.

This officer entered the Navy 1 April, 1811; passed his examination in 1817; and obtained his first commission 29 June, 1826. His subsequent appointments were, 30 Sept. 1837, and 20 Aug. 1841, as First Lieutenant, to the Edinburgh and Malabar, of 72 guns each, Capts. Wm. Wilmott Henderson and Sir Geo. Rose Sartorius, in the former of which ships he participated in the operations of 1840 on the coast of Syria, including the bombardment of St. Jean d'Acre. He was paid off from the Malabar in the early part of 1844; and on 9 Nov. 1846 was advanced to the rank of Commander. He is now on half-pay.

HAMMET. (Lieutenant, 1846.)

Lacon Ussher Hammet passed his examination 28 Feb. 1840; served as Mate of the Bellerophon 80, Capt. Chas. John Austen, at the bombardment of St. Jean d'Acre in Nov. 1840; and from the close of 1841 until the attainment of his present rank, 7 Feb. 1846, was employed on the North America and West India station in the Illustrious 72, flag-ship of Sir Chas. Adam, and Eurydice 26, Capt. Geo. Elliot. He has been attached, since 30 of the following March, to the Spartan 22, commanded in the Mediterranean by Capt. Thos. Matthew Chas. Symonds.

HAMMOND. (Lieut., 1805. f-p., 18; h-p., 32.)

Charles Hammond entered the Navy, 10 May, 1797, as Midshipman, on board the Havock, Capt. Philip Bartholomew, lying in Hamoaze; and, from the close of the same year until the summer of 1802, was employed, on the African, Home, and West India stations, in the Hornet 18, Capt. Jas. Nash. In 1803, on his return from the West Indies, where he had continued to serve, as Master's Mate, in the Excellent 74, Commodore Hon. Robt. Stopford, he joined the Topaze 36, Capts. Willoughby Thos. Lake, Anselm John Griffiths, Henry Hope, and Edw. Harvey, to which frigate he continued attached, on the Cork and Mediterranean stations, the greater part of the time as Lieutenant (commission dated 23 March, 1805), until Jan. 1812. During that period, among other dashing services, Mr. Hammond, on 12 March, 1809, took part, near Corfu, in a very spirited action which terminated in the beating off by the Topaze of the two French 40-gun frigates *Danaé* and *Flore;* and about the same period he received a severe wound, which nearly deprived him of the use of his right hand, at the cutting out of two vessels on the coast of Italy. Notwithstanding this misfortune, he again, on 31 of the following May, took command of the boats, and, by dint of sterling gallantry, succeeded, with a loss of only 1 man killed and another wounded, although encountered by a galling fire from the enemy and many severe obstacles, in capturing nine vessels lying at anchor in the road of Demata, behind a reef of rocks under the fortress of Santa Maura. The prizes on the occasion were loaded with timber and brandy on Government account, and were bound to Corfu, where their cargoes were much needed. They consisted, besides four trabacolos, of a xebec of 8 carriage-guns, 6 swivels, and a crew of 55 men; of one cutter of 4, and one felucca of 3 guns; and of two gun-boats of 1 gun each. So great was the admiration entertained of this exploit by Capt. Griffiths, that we find him recommending Mr. Hammond, who was at the time his First Lieutenant, in the very strongest manner to notice.* The next occasion on which we perceive mention of our valiant but ill-rewarded officer was on 31 Oct. 1809, when he took charge of the boats of the Topaze, and, in unison with those of a squadron under Lieut. John Tailour, contributed to the capture and destruction, in the Bay of Rosas—despite a fierce opposition from the crews, and a fire from the batteries inflictive of a loss on the British of 15 men killed and 55 wounded—of the French armed store-ship *Lamproie*, of 16 guns and 116 men, bombards *Victoire* and *Grondeur*, armed xebec *Normande*, and a convoy of seven merchantmen.* His last appointment was, 11 Aug. 1812, to the Nimrod sloop, Capts. Nathaniel Mitchell, Vincent Newton, and Geo. Hilton, stationed off the coast of North America, whence he returned in May, 1815. On 21 of the ensuing June he again presents himself to our notice as commanding the boats of the Topaze, and effecting the capture, in conjunction with those of the Alceste under Lieut. Andw. Wilson, of two vessels in the Bay of Martino, in the island of Corsica, where a 3-gun battery which protected the entrance of the bay was carried by a detachment of seamen and marines, and the guns rendered unserviceable; the enemy in the affair being occasioned a loss of several men killed and wounded, and the British 1 man killed and 2 wounded.† Agents—Messrs. Ommanney.

* *Vide* Gaz. 1809, p. 1238.

HAMMOND. (Lieutenant, 1827.)

Robert Hammond served on board the Hebrus 36, Capt. Edm. Palmer, at the forcing of the Gironde in 1814. He passed his examination in 1818; was made Lieutenant, 23 June, 1827, into the Glasgow 50, commanded in the Mediterranean by Capt. Hon. Jas. Ashley Maude; and, on 23 Aug. following, removed to the Gannet sloop, Capts. Lord Ingestrie and Hon. Wm. Edwardes. That vessel being paid off in 1828, he next joined, 24 Jan. 1835, the Dublin 50, bearing the flag in South America of Sir Graham Eden Hamond. He was superseded at his own request 12 April, 1836, and has not since been afloat.

Lieut. Hammond married, in 1836, Sophia, daughter of John Musters, Esq., of Colwick Hall, co. Nottingham (a Magistrate and Deputy-Lieutenant for that shire), by Mary, only daughter and coheiress of Wm. Chaworth, Esq., of Annesley, Notts.

HAMOND. (Captain, 1846.)

Andrew Snape Hamond, born 3 Oct. 1811, is eldest son of Admiral Sir Graham Eden Hamond, Bart., K.C.B.

This officer entered the Navy 5 Aug. 1824; served as Midshipman of the Talbot 28, Capt. Hon. Fred. Spencer, at the battle of Navarin, 20 Oct. 1827; passed his examination in 1830; and, obtaining his first commission 25 May, 1831, was successively appointed—30 Sept. 1831, to the Melville 74, flag-ship in the East Indies of Sir John Gore—and, 2 Oct. 1834, to the Dublin 50, as Flag-Lieutenant to his father, on the South American station. He was presented with a second promotal commission 19 May, 1838, and, on 24 June, 1842, was invested with the command of the Salamander steam-sloop in the Pacific. He has been on half-pay since the attainment of his present rank, 8 June, 1846.

Capt. Hamond married Mary, second daughter of Edw. Miller, Esq., co. Cambridge, and niece of General Miller, Her Britannic Majesty's Consul-General for the islands in the Pacific.

HAMOND, Bart., K.C.B., K.C.T.S. (Admiral of the Blue, 1847. f-p., 28; h-p., 34.)

Sir Graham Eden Hamond, born 30 Dec. 1779, in London, is only son of the late Sir Andw. Snape Hamond, Bart., F.R.S., Captain R.N.,‡ by Anne,

* *Vide* Gaz. 1809, p. 1907. † *V.* Gaz. 1810, p. 1205.

‡ Sir Andrew Snape Hamond was born in 1738, and entered the Navy in 1753. He served as Lieutenant of the Magnanime 74, in the action off Quiberon, 20 Nov. 1759; was in the same ship throughout a great part of the Seven Years' War; attained Post-rank 7 Dec. 1770; and, for the distinguished nature of his conduct as Captain of the Roebuck 44, during the hostilities with America, was awarded the honour of Knighthood in 1778. From 1780 until 1783, towards the close of which year he was created a Baronet, he officiated as Lieutenant-Governor and Commander-in-Chief of Nova Scotia, and Commodore and Resident Commissioner at Halifax. He afterwards, between 1785 and 1788, discharged the duties of Commodore and Commander-in-Chief

daughter and heiress of Henry Graeme, Esq., of Hanwell, co. Middlesex, a Major in the Army, who was severely wounded at the battle of Minden, when a Captain in the 37th Regt., in 1759, and died Lieutenant-Governor of St. Helena in 1786. He is uncle of the present Viscount Hood; and succeeded his father as second Baronet 12 Sept. 1828.

This officer entered the Navy, 3 Sept. 1785, as Captain's Servant, on board the IRRESISTIBLE 74, on the books of which ship, bearing the broad pendant of his father in the river Medway, his name appears to have been borne until March, 1790. In Jan. 1793, after a further servitude with Sir A. S. Hamond, as Midshipman, in the VANGUARD and BEDFORD 74's, and DUKE 98, he joined the PHAETON 38, commanded by his cousin Sir Andw. Snape Douglas, on the Channel station, where, in the course of the same year, he assisted at the capture of *Le Général Dumourier*, of 22 guns and 196 men, having on board 2,040,000 dollars; her prize, the *St. Jago*, laden with a cargo worth nearly 300,000*l.*; *La Prompte*, frigate, of 28 guns and 180 men; another privateer, of 16 guns and 60 men; and *La Blonde* national corvette, of 24 guns. Accompanying the last-mentioned officer, in April, 1794, into the QUEEN CHARLOTTE 100, flag-ship of Earl Howe, Mr. Hamond, besides witnessing the capture of H.M. late ship CASTOR, and of other vessels, had an opportunity of sharing in the triumph achieved by the British on 1 of the ensuing June. In June, 1795, having previously acted for a short period as Lieutenant of the AQUILON 32, Capt. Robt. Barlow, and ZEALOUS 74, Capt. Christ. Mason, he proceeded overland to the Mediterranean, and there got on board the BRITANNIA 100, bearing the flag of Admiral Wm. Hotham, just in time to behold the destruction of *L'Alcide*, a 74-gun-ship taken in the action of 13 July. Being confirmed a Lieutenant in the BRITANNIA, by commission dated 19 Oct. in the same year, he subsequently joined, in that capacity, 20 July, 1796, and 11 March, 1797, the AIGLE 38, bearing the flag, also in the Mediterranean, of Sir Hyde Parker, and NIGER 32, commanded on the Lisbon and Home stations by Capt. Edw. Jas. Foote. While afterwards in the ECHO 18, of which sloop he obtained command 20 Oct. 1798, Capt. Hamond destroyed a French cutter privateer, contributed to the capture of 30 large Dutch fishing-vessels, conveyed Prince Frederick of Orange from Yarmouth to Cuxhaven, was for some time employed at the blockade of Havre, and was intrusted on different occasions with the charge of convoys. After a continuance of about 12 months in the ECHO, he was made Post, 30 Nov. 1798, into the CHAMPION of 24 guns; in which ship we find him successively engaged in convoying a fleet of merchant-vessels to the Elbe; guarding the mouths of that river and the Weser, to prevent the enemy's gun-boats from entering; cruizing off Norway; carrying specie from the river Thames to the British army in Holland; and watching the return of the trade from Archangel. He likewise, on 28 June, 1799, effected the capture of *L'Anacréon*, a notorious French privateer, of 16 guns and 125 men, and was employed during the early part of 1800 in conveying to Minorca the officers and crew of the captured French ship of the line *Le Guillaume Tell*, as also at the blockade of Malta, where he occasionally served on shore at the siege of La Valette. In July of the latter year, owing to the state of his health, Capt. Hamond exchanged into the LION 64, and returned with despatches to England, but he had scarcely arrived when he was appointed to commission the BLANCHE 36; in which frigate, previously to participating in the battle of 2 April, 1801, he embarked at Copenhagen Mr. Drummond, H. B. Majesty's Minister, and the whole British Factory. On the Sunday following the action, Capt. Hamond had the peculiar satisfaction of holding the Prayer-Book from which Lord Nelson read thanks to Almighty God for the signal victory the British had obtained over their enemies. The BLANCHE ultimately returned to England with the flag of Sir Hyde Parker, but was not paid off until 22 Sept. 1802, by which period she had been further employed with activity in the Channel, and had been for many weeks in attendance on George III. off Weymouth. From 21 Feb. to 12 Nov. 1803, Capt. Hamond next commanded the PLANTAGENET 74, in which ship he contrived to capture *Le Courier de Terre Neuve*, a French brig privateer of 16 guns and 54 men, and three days afterwards *L'Atalante*, a beautiful corvette of 22 guns and 120 men. After an interval of half-pay, occasioned by ill health, he joined, 30 July, 1804, the LIVELY 38. In that frigate, on 5 of the following Oct., he distinguished himself, and had 2 of his men killed and 5 wounded, at the capture, off Cape St. Mary, of three Spanish frigates laden with treasure, and the destruction of a fourth.* During a subsequent cruize off Cape St. Vincent, Capt. Hamond captured, on 7 Dec., the *San Miguel*, a Spanish merchant-ship having on board 196,639 dollars, four cases of wrought plate, 2064 bales of indigo, and other valuable property; and in the course of the same day he was in company with the POLYPHEMUS 64, at the taking of the *Santa Gertruyda*, a frigate of 36 guns, laden, besides a cargo of the most costly merchandise, with 1,215,000 dollars in specie. All this treasure being however disposed of as droits of Admiralty, not more than a fourth of their proceeds was given to the captors. In March, 1805, the whole of the specie and bullion that had been taken, amounting to 5,000,000 dollars, was intrusted to the sole charge of Capt. Hamond, who brought it all in safety to England, but unfortunately just at a period when the payment of freight-money had been suspended; and he consequently received no remuneration whatever for the tremendous responsibility to which he had been subjected. Not long after this, being off Cadiz, the LIVELY, on 29 May, 1805, alone, and of her own accord, endured a very spirited skirmish with the Spanish 74-gun ship *Glorioso*, whom she sorely galled. She next, towards the close of 1805, embarked Gen. Sir Jas. Craig, and accompanied an expedition having for its object the defence of Naples against the threatened and eventually successful invasion of the French. Quitting the LIVELY in June, 1806, Capt. Hamond was subsequently appointed—22 Dec. 1808, to the VICTORIOUS 74, the command of which ship, after she had assisted at the reduction of Flushing, he resigned in Sept. 1809—14 May, 1813, to the RIVOLI 74, employed in the Mediterranean, whence he invalided in March 1814—and 30 March, 1824, to the WELLESLEY 74, stationed at first as a guard-ship at Portsmouth, and next employed in conveying to the Brazils the present Lord Stuart de Rothesay. Being advanced to the rank of Rear-Admiral, while on the latter station, by commission dated 27 May, 1825, he was ordered home in the SPARTIATE 74, charged with the delivery, *en route*, of the treaty of separation between Brazil and Portugal to the King of Portugal, who, on its reception, created him a K.C.T.S.; an order, however, which, as it was not obtained for war-service, he has not been permitted to wear. In 1828 Sir Graham Eden Hamond was selected by the Lord High Admiral to succeed the then Commander-in-Chief in the East Indies, but the resignation of office of H.R.H. did not allow the arrangements to mature. His last employment was on the South American station, where, with his flag successively in the SPARTIATE 76, and DUBLIN 50, he commanded in chief from 16 Sept. 1834, until 17 May, 1838. His attainment of the rank of Vice-Admiral took place 10 Jan. 1837, and of that of Admiral 22 Jan. 1847.

Sir Graham Eden Hamond (a Deputy-Lieutenant for co. Norfolk and the Isle of Wight) was nominated a C.B. 4 June, 1815; and a K.C.B. 13

on the river Medway; and in 1793-4 was successively appointed a Commissioner of the Navy Board and Deputy Comptroller and Comptroller of the Navy. He resigned the latter post with a retiring pension of 1500*l.* per annum in 1806. He died at Lynn, co. Norfolk, in the 90th year of his age, 12 Sept. 1828; at which period, had his previous tenure of office permitted his acceptance of Flag-rank, he would have been Admiral of the Fleet.

* *Vide* Gaz. 1804, p. 1[illegible]9.

Sept. 1831. He married, 30 Dec. 1806, Elizabeth, daughter of John Kimber, Esq., of Fowey, co. Cornwall, by whom he has had issue two sons (the present Capt. A. S. Hamond, R.N., and the late Commander G. E. W. Hamond, R.N.) and three daughters, of whom the second is married to her first-cousin Lieut.-Col. Hon. Fras. Grosvenor Hood, of the Grenadier Guards. AGENTS—Messrs. Ommanney.

HAMOND. (COMMANDER, 1843. F-P., 14; H-P., 5.)

GRAHAM EDEN WILLIAM HAMOND was born 3 March, 1814, at Fowey, co. Cornwall, and died 23 Jan. 1847, at Woolwich, while in command of the MEDEA steam-sloop. He was second and youngest son of the present Admiral Sir Graham Eden Hamond, Bart., K.C.B.

This officer entered the Navy, 22 Feb. 1828, as Fst.-cl. Vol., on board the BLONDE 46, Capt. Edm. Lyons, to whom, in the following Oct., after having for some time blockaded the port of Navarin, he officiated as Aide-de-Camp at the bombardment and storming of the Morea Castle. In the summer of 1829 he accompanied Sir Robt. Gordon as British Ambassador to Constantinople, where, during an audience with the Sultan, he was presented with a cloak by that potentate. He next visited the Black Sea, and in the spring of 1830 was employed in partially surveying and wholly sounding of the Bosporus, the Golden Horn of Constantinople, and many places in the Sea of Marmara. In Feb. 1831, shortly after he had escorted Sir John Malcolm from Alexandria to Malta, Mr. Hamond became Midshipman of the MADAGASCAR 46, also commanded by Capt. Lyons, in which ship he had an opportunity, in May, 1832, of witnessing Ibrahim Pacha's bombardment of St. Jean d'Acre. We subsequently find him, in the early part of 1833, attending King Otho and the Bavarian Regency from Trieste to Greece, and for several months in that year employed in the MADAGASCAR's barge as steersman to His Majesty. On the paying off of the latter frigate in Jan. 1835 Mr. Hamond (who, previously to passing his examination in Feb. 1834, had had charge of a watch for 12 months) sailed for South America in the ACTÆON 26, Capt. Lord Edw. Russell, for the purpose of joining the flag-ship of his father, by whom he was transferred to the RAPID 10, Lieut.-Commander Fred. Patten. Being awarded the rank of Lieutenant by commission dated 1 Feb. 1835, he was afterwards appointed in that capacity—29 June, 1835, to the NORTH STAR 28, Capt. Octavius Vernon Harcourt, under whom he surveyed in part several harbours on the N.W. coast of North America—23 July, 1836, to the BLONDE 46, bearing the broad pendant in the Pacific of Commodore Fras. Mason—4 July, 1837, to the IMOGENE 26, Capt. Hen. Wm. Bruce, employed among the South Sea Islands—17 Jan. 1838, to the ROVER 18, Capt. Chas. Eden, in which sloop he returned to England in the following summer—23 Feb. 1839, to the IMPLACABLE 74, Capt. Edw. Harvey, attached to the force in the Mediterranean, whence he invalided in May, 1840—and, 13 Jan. 1842, to the HOWE 120, as Flag-Lieutenant to Sir Fras. Mason, on the same station. He attained the rank of Commander 5 June, 1843, and was lastly appointed, 5 Nov. 1846, to the MEDEA steam-sloop. He died as above.

Commander Hamond married, 7 Dec. 1843, Lucia, only daughter of Luke Dodds, Esq., of Hythe House, Hythe, near Southampton, co. Hants, by whom he has left issue. AGENTS—Messrs. Ommanney.

HANCOCK. (LIEUTENANT, 1844.)

GEORGE HANCOCK entered the Navy 3 March, 1834; passed his examination 12 Dec. 1840; and after an intermediate servitude as Mate, in the Mediterranean and Home stations, in the VERNON 50, and EXCELLENT gunnery-ship, Capts. Wm. Walpole and Sir Thos. Hastings, was promoted to the rank of Lieutenant 1 July, 1844. He has been employed, since 5 of the following Nov., in the EAGLE 50, Capt. Geo. Bohun Martin, bearing the flag at first of Rear-Admiral Sam. Hood Inglefield on the S.E. coast of America, and now stationed in North America and the West Indies.

This officer obtained his commission as a reward for having passed the best examination at the Royal Naval College.

HANCOCK. (LIEUTENANT, 1843.)

JAMES KINNEER HANCOCK is son of the late Rear-Admiral Rich. Turner Hancock.

This officer entered the Royal Naval College 7 June, 1832; and embarked, in 1834, as a Volunteer, on board the NORTH STAR 28, commanded in South America by Capt. Octavius Vernon Harcourt. Becoming Midshipman, in Nov. 1836, of the SAMARANG 26, Capts. Wm. Broughton and Jas. Scott, he eventually, after a continued servitude on the latter station, where he passed his examination in the summer of 1839, proceeded to China. He came home in Aug. 1841, but being again ordered to China towards the close of the same year in the BELLEISLE troop-ship, Capt. John Kingcome, arrived there in time to witness the final operations in the Yang-tse-Kiang. For a short time previous to the receipt of his commission, which bears date 20 Sept. 1843, and which was given to him in consequence of the recommendation of Capt. Kingcome, we find Mr. Hancock successively employed in the STARLING surveying-vessel, Capt. Hen. Kellett, and CORNWALLIS 72, flag-ship of Sir Wm. Parker. He then joined the MINDEN, Capt. Michael Quin, Hospital-ship at Hong Kong, whence he returned to England in Jan. 1845 on board the PELICAN 16, Capt. Philip Justice. He has been serving on the coast of Africa since 26 May, 1845, as First of the HECATE steam-sloop, Capt. Joseph West.

HANCOCK. (LIEUT., 1811. F-P., 18; H-P., 34.)

JOHN HANCOCK (*a*) entered the Navy, 8 April, 1795, as A.B., on board the BRITANNIA 100, Capt. John Holloway, bearing the successive flags of Admirals Lord Hotham, Sir Hyde Parker, Chas. Thompson, and Sir Peter Parker; in which ship he participated in the actions of 13 July, 1795, and 14 Feb. 1797, off Capes Rioux and St. Vincent. In Feb. 1798 he removed to the ALARM 32, Capts. Edw. Fellowes and Robt. Rolles, on the West India station, where, during a continuance of three years, he appears to have been instrumental to the capture of a large number of the enemy's vessels. He then became Master's Mate of the GALGO 14, Capts. Rich. Hawkins and Michael Dodd, employed in the Channel and off Newfoundland, but, being discharged in Dec. 1802, he did not again go afloat until Jan. 1806, when he joined, in a similar capacity, the LION 64, commanded at first by Capt. Rolles, and afterwards by Capt. Hen. Heathcote, with whom he served in the East Indies until the early part of 1808. In April, 1809, after an intermediate attachment to the COQUETTE, Capt. Robt. Forbes, and ROYAL WILLIAM, Capt. Hon. Courtenay Boyle, Mr. Hancock was nominated Acting-Lieutenant of the RHODIAN 10, Capts. Geo. Moubray and John Geo. Boss. His appointment to that sloop being confirmed by commission dated 24 April, 1811, he continued to serve in her on the West India station—participating intermediately in the capture of two French privateers and of upwards of 20 American merchantmen—until wrecked, off Port Royal, Jamaica, in Feb. 1813. His subsequent appointments were—15 Oct. 1813, to the DASHER sloop, Capt. Wm. Henderson, also in the West Indies, whence he invalided in March, 1815—and, 24 Feb. 1829, to the Coast Blockade, in which service, with his name on the books of the RAMILLIES and TALAVERA 74's, Capt. Hugh Pigot, he remained until 1830. He has since been on half-pay.

HANCOCK. (LIEUTENANT, 1841.)

JOHN HANCOCK (*b*) entered the Navy 1 Feb. 1827; passed his examination in 1833; and was promoted, for his services on the coast of China, to the rank of Lieutenant 6 May, 1841. His appointments have since been—28 May, 1841, as Additional, to the Wellesley 72, Capt. Thos. Maitland, in the East Indies—17 March, 1842, to the Excellent gunnery-ship at Portsmouth, Capt. Sir Thos. Hastings—27 April, 1843, to the Pique 36, Capt. Hon. Montagu Stopford, attached to the force in North America and the West Indies—and, 25 Nov. 1844 and 28 April, 1845, again as Additional, to the Illustrious 72, and Vindictive 50, flag-ships of Sir Chas. Adam and Sir Fras. Wm. Austen, on the same station, where he is now employed in surveying. Agents—Messrs. Ommanney.

HANCOCK. (Rear-Admiral of the Blue, 1841. f-p., 29; h.p., 38.)

Richard Turner Hancock was born 23 June, 1764, and died 5 March, 1846, at Weymouth.

This officer entered the Navy, 24 July, 1779, as Midshipman, on board the Formidable 98, Capt. John Stanton, in which ship, under the flag of Sir Geo. Rodney, he took part in the actions of 9 and 12 April, 1782. Returning home from the West Indies in the course of the same year in the Ardent 64, Capt. Rich. Lucas, he next, until promoted to the rank of Lieutenant 26 Aug. 1789, served, in the Channel and at Portsmouth, on board the Orestes, Capt. Jas. Ellis, Expedition cutter, Lieut.-Commander Chas. C. Crooke, and Triumph and Barfleur, bearing the flags of Admirals Lord Hood and R. Roddam. His first commission was presented to him in consequence of his having been sent to attend on George III., on the occasion of a visit made by that monarch to Weymouth. His succeeding appointments, we find, were—11 May, 1790, to the Saturn 74, Capt. Robt. Linzee, in the Channel—21 Feb. 1792, to the Hussar 28, Capts. Rupert George, John Poo Beresford, Chas. Wemyss, and Chas. Rowley, on the Halifax station—7 Oct. 1796, to the Unité 38, commanded in the Channel and West Indies by Capts. C. Rowley, Wm. Shield, and J. P. Beresford—and, 5 Jan. 1800, to the Prince of Wales 98, bearing the flag on the latter station of Lord Hugh Seymour. In all but the first of those ships Mr. Hancock officiated as Senior-Lieutenant; and while in the Hussar he contributed, in company with the Thetis 36, to the defeat, 17 May, 1795, of five sail, two of which, *La Prévoyante* of 24, and *La Raison* of 18 guns, were captured after a close action of more than an hour's duration. He also, when in the Unité, assisted at the reduction of the Devil's Islands, near Cayenne. Being at length (on the earnest and repeated application of Capt. Beresford, under whom he had served on the two latter occasions) awarded a Commander's commission, dated 4 Sept. 1800, Capt. Hancock was next appointed, 27 May, 1803, to the Plover 18, in which sloop he cruized on the Channel station until posted 25 Sept. 1806. He afterwards served as Flag-Captain, in the 80-gun ships Tonnant and Foudroyant, to Hon. Michael De Courcy, from July, 1807, until Dec. 1812; during which period, besides pursuing a French squadron to the West Indies, he escorted the army home after the battle of Corunna, and was for a long time employed on the Brazilian station. While there Don John, the Regent, offered to invest him with a Portuguese order of knighthood; but, as Capt. Hancock did not conceive he had performed any military service deserving of the honour, it was modestly declined. The Regent, persisting, however, in his resolution of conferring on the Captain some mark of his regard, presented him with his portrait set with diamonds in a valuable gold box. Rear-Admiral Hancock, who had not been afloat since the period of his leaving the Foudroyant, attained Flag-rank 23 Nov. 1841.

He married, first, 1 Jan. 1813, Jane Love, daughter of Rear-Admiral Kinneer; and secondly, 21 Sept. 1826, Elizabeth, daughter and co-heiress of the late John Harwood, Esq., who died 11 Dec. 1843. By his first marriage the Rear-Admiral has left issue three children, one of whom, James Kinneer, is a Lieut. R.N.

HAND. (Commander, 1841.)

George Sumner Hand entered the Navy 1 Feb. 1821; and bore a part in the hostilities in Ava, where, in 1825, he commanded a boat at the capture of the formidable fortress of Donoobew, and the Alligator's two cutters at the taking of Melloone.* He passed his examination in 1827; obtained his first commission 14 July, 1829; and was afterwards appointed—8 Aug. in the same year, to the Shannon 46, Capt. Benj. Clement, in the West Indies—13 Sept. following, to the Grasshopper 18, Capt. John Elphinstone Erskine, in which sloop he returned to England, and was paid off 6 Sept. 1831—and 20 Jan. 1834, and 23 Nov. 1838, as Senior, to the Racehorse 18, Capt. Sir Jas. Everard Home, and Vestal 26, Capts. Thos. Wren Carter and John Parker, both on the North America and West India station. He attained his present rank, while serving in the latter ship, 23 Nov. 1841; and since 14 Dec. 1844, has been in command of the Espoir 10, on the coast of Africa. Agents—Messrs. Stilwell.

HANDLEY. (Lieut., 1815. f-p., 10; h-p., 32.)

John William Henry Handley entered the Navy, 2 March, 1805, as Third-cl. Vol., on board the Puissant 74, Capt. John Irwin, lying at Portsmouth; and on 4 of the following Nov., having joined the Namur 74, Capt. Lawrence Wm. Halsted, was present in Sir John Strachan's action off Ferrol. After that event he served, until July, 1807, in the West Indies, and on the African and American stations. He then removed, as Midshipman, to the Valiant 74, Capts. Young, Alex. Robt. Kerr, John Bligh, John Nash, and Robt. Dudley Oliver; in which ship, under Capt. Bligh, he assisted at the destruction of the French squadron in Aix Roads in April, 1809, and at the capture, near Belleisle, 3 Feb. 1810, of the French 40-gun frigate *Cannonière*, laden with the spoil of the principal prizes which the enemy had taken in the East Indies during the three preceding years. He also, while borne on the books of the Valiant, commanded a gun-boat during the operations of 1809 against the island of Walcheren. On leaving the last-mentioned ship, Mr. Handley, in Dec. 1811, joined the Bellerophon 74, bearing the flag of Rear-Admiral John Ferrier off the Texel, where he served until Nov. 1812. Becoming Master's Mate, in March, 1813, of the San Josef 110, flag-ship in the Mediterranean of Sir Rich. King, he there, on 5 Nov. in the same year, and 13 Feb. 1814, witnessed Sir Edw. Pellew's two actions with the Toulon fleet; after which, on being transferred to the Cyane, of 32 guns and 171 men, Capt. Gordon Thos. Falcon, he was on board that vessel when captured, 20 Feb. 1815, together with her consort, the Levant, of 20 guns and 131 men, by the United States frigate *Constitution*, of 54 guns and 469 men, at the close of a desperate conflict in which the Cyane sustained a loss of 6 men killed and 13 wounded. He was soon, however, restored to liberty, and, on his arrival in England, found that he had been promoted to the rank of Lieutenant by commission bearing date 7 Feb. 1815. He has since been on half-pay. Agents—Hallett and Robinson.

HANHAM. (Lieut., 1818. f-p., 9; h-p., 29.)

William Hanham entered the Navy, 29 Aug. 1809, as Fst.-cl. Vol., on board the Royal William, Capt. John Irwin, bearing the flag of Sir Roger Curtis, at Spithead, where, in April, 1810, he accompanied the same officers into the Puissant 74. In Aug. 1811, after serving for some time on the Jersey station with Capt. Corbet Jas. D'Auvergne of the Albacore sloop, he joined the Nijaden 36, commanded by Capt. Farmery Predam Epworth, with whom, and latterly with Capt. Hugh Pigot, he continued actively employed, off the coasts of Por-

* *Vide* Gaz. 1825.

tugal and America, and also in the West Indies, on board the same frigate and the NYMPHE 38, until Aug. 1815. He then removed in succession to the PRINCE and QUEEN CHARLOTTE, flag-ships at Portsmouth of Sir Edw. Thornbrough, but being soon again ordered to the West Indies, was there appointed Acting-Lieutenant, 24 March, 1816, of the SALISBURY 50, bearing the flag of Rear-Admiral John Erskine Douglas. In May, 1817, he was transferred, in the latter capacity, to the RIFLEMAN brig, Capts. Robt. Rochfort Felix and Norwich Duff, in which vessel (being confirmed to her by commission dated 15 May in the following year) he remained until paid off in Aug. 1818. He has not been since employed. AGENTS—Case and Loudonsack.

HANKEY. (COMMANDER, 1846. F-P., 17; H-P., 4.)

FREDERICK THOMAS BARNARD HANKEY, born 3 April, 1813, is third son of John Barnard Hankey, Esq., of Fetcham Park, co. Surrey, by the Hon. Elizabeth De Blaquiere, daughter of John, first Lord De Blaquiere. He is brother of Lieut. Henry Barnard Hankey, R.N.; nephew of General Lord De Blaquiere; and a connexion of Sir Hugh Dillon Massy, Bart.

This officer entered the Navy, in March, 1826, as Fst.-cl. Vol., on board the GANGES 84, Capt. Sam. Hood Inglefield, bearing the flag in South America of Rear-Admiral Robt. Waller Otway; became Midshipman, in the autumn of 1829, of the WINCHESTER 52, flag-ship in the West Indies of Sir Edw. Griffith Colpoys; and from Aug. 1831 until the receipt of his first commission, bearing date 11 April, 1833, was employed in the Mediterranean, the last twelve months as Mate, on board the ALFRED 50, Capt. Robt. Maunsell, and ST. VINCENT 120, flag-ship of Hon. Sir Henry Hotham. He continued to serve for some months, on the latter station and off Oporto, in the BELVIDERA 42, Capt. Hon. Rich. Saunders Dundas, and was afterwards appointed—9 June, 1834, to the ORESTES 18, Capts. Henry John Codrington, Julius Jas. Farmer Newell, and Wm. Holt, which sloop, also attached to the force in the Mediterranean, he fitted, during a violent gale, with a temporary rudder, and by that means enabled her to proceed 200 miles under close-reefed sails—2 Feb. 1839, as First, to the ACORN 16, Capt. John Adams, with whom he served for three years on the coast of Africa—and 7 May, 1844, in a similar capacity, to the COLLINGWOOD 80, flag-ship in the Pacific of Sir Geo. Fras. Seymour. During the period of his continuance in the ACORN, Mr. Hankey was instrumental to the liberation of about 1500 negroes, and the condemnation of about 3300 tons of shipping. On one occasion he was strongly recommended to Rear-Admiral Fred. Warren, the Acting-Commander-in-Chief at Plymouth, for his conduct in having intrepidly boarded, with a party of volunteers, during a passage made by the ACORN to England, and in the midst of a heavy gale, a schooner which had been utterly abandoned, and to which, having lost her own, he fitted a new rudder. He subsequently, on 6 July, 1841, after a running-fight, assisted in capturing the *Gabriel*, a notorious piratical vessel, well armed, and equally well defended. His previous services as interpreter during a negociation carried on between his Captain and the Governor-General of Mozambique, had obtained Mr. Hankey a very complimentary letter from the latter personage, as well as a flattering appeal in his behalf to the British and Portuguese Governments. He ultimately left the ACORN in consequence of fever contracted on board a slave-vessel of which he had been placed in charge. He was promoted to his present rank, while serving in the COLLINGWOOD, 26 June, 1846; and is now on half-pay.

Commander Hankey, we must not omit to record, had distinguished himself when a Lieutenant in the ORESTES, by voluntarily going ashore for assistance in the jolly-boat, during a tempest which had dismasted that vessel in the Mole of Malaga. AGENTS—Messrs. Stilwell.

HANKEY. (LIEUTENANT, 1845.)

HENRY BARNARD HANKEY is a younger brother of Commander F. T. B. Hankey, R.N.

This officer entered the Navy in 1832; passed his examination 6 March, 1839; and, after serving as Mate in the BRITANNIA 120, and, for three years, in the AGINCOURT 72, flag-ships of Sir John Acworth Ommanney and Sir Thos. John Cochrane, on the Mediterranean and East India stations, was promoted, 2 July, 1845, to a Lieutenancy in the HAZARD 18, Capts. Fras. Philip Egerton, under whom he is still employed. During an expedition conducted in July, 1846, by Sir T. J. Cochrane, against the Sultan of Borneo, Mr. Hankey officiated as Beach-Master, and assisted at the capture and destruction of the enemy's forts and batteries up the river Brune.*

HANMER. (LIEUT., 1813. F-P., 11; H-P., 32.)

DAVID HANMER entered the Navy, in Aug. 1804, as Fst.-cl. Vol., on board the AJAX 74, Capts. Lord Garlies, Christopher Laroche, and Wm. Brown, one of Sir Robt. Calder's fleet in the action of 22 July, 1805. From the following Sept. until Dec. 1808, he served in the Mediterranean and off Lisbon in the APOLLO frigate, and CONQUEROR 74, both commanded by Capt. Edw. Fellowes; and he was afterwards, until promoted to the rank of Lieutenant, 7 April, 1813, employed, off the coasts of Portugal, France, and America, chiefly as Master's Mate, in the SEMIRAMIS 36, Capt. Wm. Granger, UNICORN 32, Capts. Alex. Robt. Kerr and Geo. Burgoyne Salt, ACASTA 40, Capt. A. R. Kerr, and ST. DOMINGO 74, flag-ship of Sir John Borlase Warren. He then joined the STATIRA 38, Capts. Hassard Stackpoole and Spelman Swaine, also attached to the force on the American station, whence he returned home and was paid off in April, 1815. He has not been since afloat. AGENTS—Hallett and Robinson.

HANNANT. (LIEUTENANT, 1842.)

HENRY HANNANT entered the Navy 13 Sept. 1828; passed his examination 13 Feb. 1837; was for some time employed as Mate in the TERMAGANT brigantine, Lieut.-Commander Henry Frowd Seagram, on the coast of Africa; and on 16 Sept. 1842, was promoted to his present rank. His appointments have since been—18 May, 1843, to the RACER 16, Capt. Arch. Reed, on the Brazilian station—and 1 Aug. 1844, to the AMERICA 50, Capts. Hon. Wm. Gordon and Sir Thos. Maitland, with whom he has been successively employed in the Pacific and Mediterranean. AGENTS—Messrs. Ommanney.

HANSARD. (LIEUTENANT, 1844.)

ALFRED OGLE HANSARD passed his examination 4 Oct. 1836; and was for a long time employed in the Mediterranean on board the IMPLACABLE 74 Capt. Edw. Harvey, and GEYSER steam-vessel, Capt. Edw. John Carpenter. He obtained his commission 19 Dec. 1844; and since 11 March, 1845, has been serving on the coast of Africa in the FLYING FISH 12, Capt. Peché Hart Dyke.

HARCOURT, formerly VERNON. (Captain, 1814.)

FREDERICK EDWARD VERNON HARCOURT, born in 1790, is fourth son of the Right Hon. Edw. Harcourt, D.D., D.C.L., P.C., Archbishop of York, Primate of England, and Lord High Almoner to the Queen, by Anne, third daughter of Granville, first Marquess of Stafford. He is brother of G. G. V. Harcourt, Esq., M.P. for the co. of Oxford; of the Rev. L. V. Harcourt, Chancellor of York; of Capt. O. V. Harcourt, R.N.; of H. V. Harcourt, Esq., a Lieut.-Colonel in the army; and of Lieut.-Colonel Fras. Harcourt, of the Grenadier Guards, Equerry to the Duchess of Kent. He is cousin of the present Lord Vernon; and is closely connected with the Earls of Lucan, Oxford, Liverpool, Harcourt, and Leicester.

* *Vide* Gaz. 1846, pp. 3441–42.

This officer entered the Navy, in Feb. 1803, as Midshipman, on board the CALCUTTA 50, *armée en flûte*, Capt. Dan. Woodriff. On his return from a voyage round the world, performed by that ship in the short period of 10 months and three days, he joined, in July, 1804, the LATONA 38, Capt. Thos. Le Marchant Gosselin, with whom, on removing to the AUDACIOUS 74, he went in pursuit of Jerome Buonaparte to the West Indies. Being ultimately promoted, from the CENTAUR 74, bearing the flag of Sir Sam. Hood, to a Lieutenancy, 29 April, 1809, in the IMPLACABLE 74, commanded in the Baltic by Capts. Thos. Byam Martin and Geo. Cockburn, he took part in the boats of that ship in numerous detached services under Lieut. Joseph Hawkey, and on 7 of the ensuing July was especially mentioned for his highly exemplary conduct in a brilliant cutting-out affair, the particulars of which have been detailed in our narrative of the present Capt. Chas. Allen.* He was in consequence, as soon as he had completed his two years' servitude as Lieutenant, advanced to the rank of Commander, by commission dated 29 April, 1811. Previously, however, to the consummation of that event, he appears to have been further employed in making a voyage to the Havana, and assisting at the defence of l'Isla de Leon. In Sept. 1813, Capt. Harcourt, who had assumed command, on 25 of the preceding May, of the CHALLENGER 16, took part in the siege of St. Sebastian; and on 13 of the following Oct. we find him contributing to the capture of *Le Flibustier* French national brig, mounting 16 guns, a brass howitzer, and 4 swivels, and laden with treasure, arms, ammunition, and salt provisions. He next, in March, 1814, co-operated with the force under Rear-Admiral Chas. Vinicombe Penrose in forcing the passage of the Gironde. Attaining Post-rank on 7 June in the same year, he was afterwards employed in command of the BLOSSOM 24, and DORIS frigate, on the South American station. He accepted the Retirement 1 Oct. 1846.

Capt. Harcourt married Martha, daughter of the late Vice-Admiral John Richard Delap Tollemache (grandson of Lionel, third Earl of Dysart), by Lady Elizabeth Stratford, daughter of John, third Earl of Aldborough. He has issue. AGENTS—Messrs. Halford and Co.

* *Vide* Gaz. 1809, p. 1210.

HARCOURT, formerly VERNON. (CAPTAIN, 1827. F-P., 18; H-P., 23.)

OCTAVIUS VERNON HARCOURT, born 25 Dec. 1793, at Rose Castle, co. Cumberland, is eighth son of the Archbishop of York; and brother of Capt. F. E. V. Harcourt, R.N.

This officer entered the Navy, in Aug. 1806, as Midshipman, on board the TIGRE 74, Capt. Benj. Hallowell, and, on attending the expedition of 1807 to Egypt, witnessed the surrender of Alexandria, and was much employed on boat-service up the river Nile. After assisting at the blockade of Toulon, and contributing to the destruction, towards the close of Oct. 1809, of the French ships of the line *Robuste* and *Lion*, he accompanied Capt. Hallowell, on his promotion to the rank of Rear-Admiral, into the MALTA 80, and continued to serve with him in that ship, on the Mediterranean station, until the receipt of his first commission, bearing date 11 Jan. 1814—co-operating intermediately with the troops on the south-east coast of Spain, and serving in the batteries at the siege of Tarragona. He next joined the MULGRAVE 74, Capt. Thos. Jas. Maling, and, while cruizing in that ship off the coast of Italy, landed with a party of seamen and marines near Piombino, where he captured a martello tower, and brought out or destroyed a convoy anchored under its protection. During the war of a Hundred Days, Mr. Harcourt, then belonging to the AMELIA 38, Capt. Hon. Granville Proby, served at the blockade of Elba, and, on the intelligence arriving of the surrender of Buonaparte after the battle of Waterloo, he was sent with a Major of the Tuscan army to summon the town of Porto Ferrajo. Quitting the latter vessel in 1816, he remained on half-pay until appointed, 2 Feb. 1818, to the SIR FRANCIS DRAKE, flag-ship of Sir Chas. Hamilton at Newfoundland; where he obtained command, 3 Feb. 1820, of the DRAKE sloop, and, for a short time in the same year, of the CARNATION 18. He afterwards joined, 5 June, 1824, and 30 May, 1825, the BRITOMART 10, and PRIMROSE 18, both employed in the West Indies, from which station he returned to England, with upwards of a million of dollars, in July, 1827. He was promoted to his present rank on 7 of the following month, and, about the same period, was selected by the Lord High Admiral to act as his Aide-de-Camp, in the ROYAL SOVEREIGN yacht, on the occasion of a visit of inspection to the various seaports. Capt. Harcourt's last appointment was, 26 March, 1834, to the NORTH STAR 28, in which vessel he took out H. Hamilton, Esq., the British Minister, to Buenos Ayres, was then employed in surveying the coast of central America and California, and ultimately returned home with a large freight. He has been on half-pay since 27 Oct. 1836.

Capt. Harcourt, during the year 1820, discharged the duties of Surrogate at Newfoundland. He married, 22 Feb. 1838, Anne Holwell, daughter of Wm. Guter, Esq., and relict of Wm. Danby, Esq., of Swinton Park, Yorkshire.

HARDING. (CAPT., 1841. F-P., 20; H-P., 15.)

FRANCIS HARDING, born 28 April, 1799, is fifth son of the late Wm. Harding, Esq., of Baraset House, Stratford-on-Avon, co. Warwick, a gentleman of the Privy Chamber to George III.; and brother-in-law of Capt. Geo. Baker, R.N.

This officer entered the Navy, 24 Jan. 1812, as Fst.-cl. Vol., on board the AMAZON 38, commanded in the Channel by his patron, the present Sir Wm. Parker. Removing, in a few weeks, to the NORTHUMBERLAND 74, Capt. Hon. Henry Hotham, he assisted, on 22 May in the same year, at the destruction, near L'Orient, of the 40-gun frigates *L'Arienne* and *L'Andromaque*, and 16-gun brig *Mamelouck*, whose united fire, conjointly with that of a heavy battery, killed 5 and wounded 28 of the British. On being afterwards ordered to the Mediterranean, in the PEMBROKE 74, Capt. Jas. Brisbane, he shared, 5 Nov. 1813, in a partial action with the Toulon fleet, and, in the course of the next April, was present at the capture of a large convoy under the guns of Porto Maurizio, and also at the surrender of Genoa. Between Aug. 1814 and Aug. 1821, Mr. Harding (who passed his examination in 1818) was successively employed, as Midshipman and Mate, on the South American, Home, Newfoundland, and East India stations, in the VALIANT 74, flag-ship of Sir Manley Dixon, ALBION 74, Capts. Philip Somerville and Jas. Walker, PERSEUS 22, and TAMAR 28, both commanded by Capt. Thos. Rich. Toker, DAUNTLESS 26, Capt. Hon. Valentine Gardner, LIVERPOOL 50, Capt. Fras. Augustus Collier, and LEANDER 50, bearing the flag of Hon. Sir Henry Blackwood. He then became Acting-Lieutenant of the TOPAZE 46, Capts. Chas. Richardson and Price Blackwood, and in that vessel (being confirmed to her by commission dated on 30 of the following March) he continued to serve until Oct. 1822. His next appointment was, 7 April, 1824, to the GRIPER discovery-ship, Capt. Geo. Fras. Lyon, whom he accompanied in the same year in a disastrous attempt made to reach Repulse Bay, an enterprise, the harassing and distressing nature of which nearly ruined the constitutions of all those who were connected with it. He went on half-pay at the close of 1824, and remained thenceforward unemployed until 22 May, 1827, when he joined the ESPOIR 10, Capt. Henry Fras. Greville, and sailed for the Cape of Good Hope. In Nov. 1809 he assumed the acting command of the HECLA surveying-vessel, vacant by the death of Capt. Thos. Boteler, who, with the greater part of his crew, had been swept away by African fever. Immediately on his arrival home in the latter vessel, with such hands as had been left to navigate her, Capt. Harding was confirmed, 23 July, 1831, into the JASEUR 18, in which sloop he returned to the Cape. He was transferred, 16 Sept. following, to the Second-Captaincy of the WARSPITE 76, bearing the flag in South America of Sir Thos. Baker, with whom he remained until paid off in March, 1833. He was lastly, from 21 Jan. 1837 until Aug. 1839, employed in command of the PELORUS 16, on the East India station; during which period we find his services eliciting the thanks of the Governor-General in Council, also of Sir Jas. Stirling, the Governor of Western Australia, and of Sir John Franklin, the Governor of Van Diemen's Land. At the expiration of the above period, nine months whereof he had acted as Senior naval officer in the Australian colonies, Capt. Harding's health obliged him to seek a temporary cessation from the active duties of his profession. He acquired his present rank 23 Nov. 1841.

Capt. Harding married, 23 Oct. 1833, Davidona Eleanor, daughter of Gen. Chas. Dallas, Governor of St. Helena, by whom he has issue one son and one daughter.

HARDING. (LIEUT., 1815. F-P., 31; H-P., 10.)

GEORGE HARDING entered the Navy, 5 March, 1806, as Fst.-cl. Vol., on board the ISIS 50, Capt. John Laugharne, successive flag-ship at Newfoundland of Vice-Admirals Sir Erasmus Gower and John Holloway. He afterwards, on removing to the STORK 18, Capt. Geo. Le Geyt, contributed, as Midshipman, to the capture and destruction, 12 and 13 Dec. 1808, of *Le Cygne* corvette of 18 guns, and two schooners, near St. Pierre, Martinique. Quitting the latter vessel in Jan. 1811, he next, between that period and March, 1816, served, on the North Sea, Mediterranean, Cape of Good Hope, Channel, and Leith stations, in the EDINBURGH 74, EURYALUS, THAMES, LAUREL, and STAG frigates, SWIFTSURE 74, and DRIVER 16, Capts. Robt. Rolles, Rowland Mainwaring, Jeremiah Coghlan, John Strutt Peyton, Hon. Granville Proby, Phipps Hornby, Wm. Henry Webley, and John Ross. While attached with Capt. Proby to the THAMES, Mr. Harding served on shore with the patriots at the siege of Tarragona in 1813. He was presented, on leaving the DRIVER, with a commission dated back to 20 March, 1815; and, since 28 Feb. 1826, has been employed in the Coast Guard.

HARDING. (COMMANDER, 1846. F-P., 23; H-P., 19.)

JOHN HARDING entered the Navy, 19 Dec. 1805, on board the FOUDROYANT 80, Capt. John Chambers White, in which ship, until Nov. 1812, he continued, chiefly as Midshipman, to serve, on the Home, Lisbon, and Brazilian stations, under the successive flags of Admirals Sir John Borlase Warren, Albemarle Bertie, Sir Wm. Sidney Smith, and Hon. Michael De Courcy. Returning then to England he joined the DÆDALUS 38, Capt. Murray Maxwell, under whom, on eventually arriving in the East Indies, he was wrecked, off the island of Ceylon, 2 July, 1813. In consequence of that catastrophe he was received on board the MINDEN 74, bearing the flag of Sir Sam. Hood, in which ship he remained until Sept. 1814, when he became Acting-Lieutenant of the HECATE 18, Capt. John Allen. Being confirmed, 11 Feb. 1815, into the SPHYNX 10, Mr. Harding, during a continuance of a few months in that vessel, and prior to the arrival of the proper Captain, the Hon. Arthur Turnour, appears to have discharged the duties of sole commander. He was subsequently appointed—7 Jan. 1824 and 5 March, 1825, to the Coast Blockade, as Supernumerary-Lieutenant of the RAMILLIES 74, and HYPERION 42, Capts. Wm. M'Culloch and Wm. Jas. Mingaye—21 April, 1832, to the ROYAL CHARLOTTE yacht, Capt. Edw. Galwey, lying at Dublin—29 Sept. 1832 and 5 Sept. 1835, to the SAN JOSEF 110, and ROYAL ADELAIDE 104, flag-ships at Plymouth of Sir Manley Dixon and Sir Wm. Hargood—14 Dec. 1842 (after seven years of half-pay), to the command of the COLUMBIA steam surveying-vessel, employed, until the close of 1844, on the North American station—4 April, 1845, to the CYCLOPS steam-frigate, Capt. Wm. Fred. Lapidge, on the S. E. coast of America—and, 1 Dec. 1845, to the CROCODILE 8, Capt. Gower Lowe. With the exception of the COLUMBIA, Mr. Harding was attached as an Additional-Lieutenant to all the above ships, and was employed the whole time on surveying service. Since his promotion to the rank of Commander, which took place 9 Nov. 1846, he has been on half-pay.

HARDMAN. (LIEUTENANT, 1845.)

HENRY BOWMAN HARDMAN passed his examination 1 June, 1839; and from the latter part of 1841 until promoted to the rank of Lieutenant, 30 Dec. 1845, was employed as Mate, on the Mediterranean and East India station, in the FORMIDABLE 84, Capts. Sir Chas. Sullivan and Geo. Fred. Rich, flag-ship latterly of Sir Edw. W. C. R. Owen, and ESPIÈGLE 12, Capt. Thos. Pickering Thompson. He has since been on half-pay.

HARDWICK. (LIEUT., 1815. F-P., 8; H-P., 31.)

JOHN HARDWICK died 8 March, 1846.

This officer entered the Navy, 23 May, 1807, as Fst.-cl. Vol., on board the ISIS 50, Capt. John Laugharne, in which ship, and the ANTELOPE 50, bearing each the flag of Vice-Admiral John Holloway, he served at Newfoundland, the greater part of the time as Midshipman, until May, 1810. During the next two years we find him continuously employed with Capt. John Allen, in the FRANCHISE 36, RODNEY 74, and PERLEN 38, on the Greenland, Mediterranean, and Channel stations. He was then transferred to the MAGNIFICENT 74, Capt. Willoughby Thos. Lake, and in the course of the following summer was very actively employed in co-operation with the patriots on the north coast of Spain, where he witnessed the reduction of Castro, Puerta Galletta, Quetaria, St. Ano, &c. He was promoted, after making a voyage in the same ship to the West Indies, to the rank of Lieutenant by commission dated 8 March, 1815; but he did not again go afloat.

HARDWICKE, EARL OF. (CAPTAIN, 1825. F-P., 15; H-P., 19.)

THE RIGHT HONOURABLE CHARLES PHILIP YORKE, EARL OF HARDWICKE, born 2 April, 1799, is son of the late Admiral Sir Joseph Sydney Yorke,* K.C.B., M.P. (whose father and grandfather were each Lord High Chancellor of Great Britain), by his first wife, Elizabeth Weake, daughter of Jas. Rattray, Esq., of Atherstone; and nephew of the Right Hon. Chas. Philip Yorke, who filled the office of First Lord of the Admiralty from Nov. 1809 to March, 1812. One of his grand-uncles, the late Lord Dover, K.B., held high rank in the Army, and acted as Aide-de-Camp to H.R.H. the Duke of Cumberland at the battle of Fontenoy; and another, James, died Bishop of Ely in 1808. His Lordship succeeded to his titles on the demise of his uncle Philip Yorke, third Earl of Hardwicke, formerly Lord-Lieutenant of Ireland, 18 Nov. 1834.

* Sir J. S. Yorke was born 6 June, 1768. Entering the Navy 15 Feb. 1780, he acted as Aide-de-Camp to Sir George Rodney in the actions of 9 and 12 April, 1782; and he afterwards, between the period of his Post-promotion, 4 Feb. 1793, and of his advancement to Flag-rank, 31 July, 1810, commanded in succession the CIRCE 28, STAG 32, JASON 36, CANADA 74, PRINCE GEORGE and BARFLEUR 98's, and CHRISTIAN VII. 80; in the second-named of which ships, the STAG, he captured 22 Aug. 1795, after a close and spirited action, the Dutch 36-gun frigate ALLIANCE. In 1811 we find him commanding a squadron and escorting a large body of troops in transports to the Tagus for the reinforcement of Lord Wellington's army. He had been awarded, in the preceding year, a seat at the Board of Admiralty, and he continued to hold it until April 1818. From 1790 until drowned, in consequence of the upsetting of a yacht in Stokes Bay 5 May, 1830, Sir J. S. Yorke, with the exception of an interval of two years in 1810–12, had the honour of being uninterrupted representative in Parliament for the towns of Reygate, St. Germans, Sandwich, and, again, for Reygate. He was nominated a K.C.B. in 1815, and died an Admiral of the Blue.

This officer entered the Royal Naval College 4 Feb. 1813, and, after carrying off the second medal, embarked, 15 May, 1815, as Midshipman, on board the PRINCE 98, Capt. Geo. Fowke, flag-ship at Spithead. In the course of the same and the following year he successively joined the SPARROWHAWK 18, and LEVIATHAN 74, commanded in the Mediterranean by Capts. Fred. Wm. Burgoyne and Thos. Briggs, the QUEEN CHARLOTTE 100, flag-ship of Lord Exmouth, by whom he was intrusted with the charge of a gun-boat at the bombardment of Algiers, and the LEANDER 60, bearing the flag of Sir David Milne on the North American station, where he appears to have had command of the JANE, a small vessel employed in carrying despatches between Halifax and Bermuda. After acting for a few months as Lieutenant of the GRASSHOPPER 18, Mr Yorke was confirmed in that rank by commission dated 14 Aug. 1819; and on 29 of the following Oct. he joined the PHAETON 46, Capt. Wm. Augustus Montagu; in which frigate he served, on the Halifax station, until advanced another step in his profession 18 May, 1822. His next appointment was, 8 Aug. 1823, to the command of the ALACRITY 10, fitting for the Mediterranean, where, prior to the receipt of his Post-commission, which bears date 6 June, 1825, we find him very actively employed in the suppression of piracy, and in watching the movements of the Turco-Egyptian forces. While subsequently officiating as Captain, from 20 Nov. 1828 until the summer of 1831, of the ALLIGATOR 28, on the same station, Capt. Yorke further assisted in settling the affairs of Greece. He lastly, in 1844-5, assumed the command, for short periods, of the BLACK EAGLE steam-yacht, and ST. VINCENT 120; in the former of which he conveyed the Emperor of Russia from England, and was presented on the occasion with a snuff-box, bearing a highly-finished portrait of His Imperial Majesty, studded with a profusion of brilliants, valued at 1000 guineas.

The Earl of Hardwicke, who was lately a Lord-in-Waiting on the Queen, is Lord-Lieutenant and Custos Rotulorum of co. Cambridge. He married, 4 Oct. 1833, Susan, sixth daughter of Lord Ravensworth, and by that lady has issue three sons and four daughters.

HARDY. (LIEUTENANT, 1843.)

EDWARD HARDY entered the Navy, 13 Nov. 1824; passed his examination 28 Aug. 1832; and after serving for some time as Mate, in the Mediterranean, of the INDUS 78, Capt. Sir Jas. Stirling, and AIGLE 24, Capt. Clarence Edw. Paget, was presented with a commission dated 16 Feb. 1843. He then, for a brief period, became Additional-Lieutenant of the QUEEN 110, bearing the flag on the same station of Sir Edw. W. C. R. Owen; whom, however, he rejoined, 23 April, 1844, on board the FORMIDABLE 84. Since 30 Dec. 1845 he has been serving in the VERNON 50, flag-ship in the East Indies of Rear-Admiral Sam. Hood Inglefield.

HARDY. (LIEUTENANT, 1815. F-P., 9; H-P., 32.)

ROBERT WILLIAM HALE HARDY entered the Navy, 8 June, 1806, as Sec.-cl. Boy, on board the GANGES 74, Capt. Peter Halkett, lying at Portsmouth, where he shortly afterwards joined the ROYAL WILLIAM, flag-ship of Admiral Montagu. Between Sept. 1807 and Sept. 1813 we find him serving on the East India station, chiefly as Midshipman, in the MONMOUTH 64, and RUSSEL 74, bearing each the flag of Rear-Admiral Wm. O'Brien Drury, CAROLINE 36, Capt. Christopher Cole, and BUCEPHALUS 32, Capt. Barrington Reynolds. While in the CAROLINE he appears to have assisted at the celebrated capture of Banda Neira, in Aug. 1810, as also, in Aug. 1811, of the island of Java. He afterwards, from Jan. 1814 until his promotion to the rank of Lieutenant 20 Feb. 1815, served in the ASIA 74, Capt. John Wainwright, and TONNANT 80, flag-ship of Sir Alex. Cochrane, both on the North American station, where, among other operations, he attended the expedition to New Orleans. He has not since been afloat. AGENT—Joseph Woodhead.

HARDY. (LIEUTENANT, 1821. F-P., 17; H-P., 23.)

THOMAS HARDY entered the Navy, in May, 1807, as L.M., on board the CONQUEROR 74, Capts. Israel Pellew and Edw. Fellowes, successively employed in the Channel and in blockading the Russian Rear-Admiral Seniavin's squadron in the Tagus. In Aug. 1808, two months after he had attained the rating of Midshipman, he removed to the PLANTAGENET 74, Capts. Wm. Bradly and Thos. Eyles, with whom he actively served on the Lisbon and Baltic stations until 1811; in the course of which year he joined the STROMBOLI, commanded in the Downs by Capts. Thos. Cuthbert Hichens and Sam. Grove, and ARETHUSA 38, Capt. Fras. Holmes Coffin. On his return in June, 1813, from the West Indies, where he had been serving two years, and had been twice engaged in boat-actions with the enemy's privateers, Mr. Hardy became attached to the KANGAROO 16, Capt. Wm. Sumner Hall, and in that sloop he was continuously employed in the protection of convoys in the Baltic and Channel until Aug. 1815. The next six years were passed by this officer on the East India, Plymouth, West India, and Irish stations, as Admiralty-Midshipman, Acting-Lieutenant, and Chief Mate, in the BACCHUS 16, Capts. Wm. Hill and John Pengelly Parkin, FAVORITE 20, Capt. Hon. Jas. Ashley Maude, SPENCER 74, Capt. Wm. Robt. Broughton, RALEIGH 18, Capt. Wm. Augustus Baumgardt, and CASTLE COOTE Revenue-cruizer, Lieut.-Commander John Elwin. During a servitude of more than a year and a half in the latter vessel he contributed to the capture of two smuggling schooners; and on 20 Sept. 1820, while pursuing in the boats a Dutch lugger of 12 guns and 42 men, he had the misfortune to have his eyes severely injured by the flash from a blunderbuss fired by one of his men close to him. He received in consequence the thanks of the Commander-in-Chief at Cork, and of the Collector of Customs for Londonderry. Attaining the rank of Lieutenant 19 July, 1821, he was next appointed, 18 Dec. 1824 and 18 March, 1836, to the GENOA 74, Capts. Wm. Cumberland and Walter Bathurst, and, as First, to the CORNWALLIS 74, Capt. Robt. Worgan Geo. Festing. He was superseded from the former ship at his own request in Oct. 1826; and he left the CORNWALLIS, in consequence of the impaired state of his sight from the injury above alluded to, in the Oct. following his appointment to her. He has since been on half-pay.

Lieut. Hardy married, 31 July, 1821, Miss Eliza Phillips, of Kinsale, in Ireland.

HARE. (LIEUTENANT, 1810. F-P., 15; H-P., 31.)

CHARLES HARE is son of Capt. Rich. Hare, R.N., who commanded the VULCAN fire-vessel, with distinction, at the destruction of the French shipping at Toulon in 1793, and died in 1801 while commanding the MADRAS. He is brother-in-law of the late Admiral Alexander; and cousin of the present General of that name, a very gallant officer, who served as Aide-de-Camp to the late Lord Lynedoch. Mr. Hare, who has lost two brothers of his own rank in the Navy, is also cousin of Lieut. Rich. Hare, R.N.

This officer entered the Navy, in Feb. 1801, as Fst.-cl. Vol., on board the MADRAS, commanded by his father, Capt. Chas. Hare, whom he attended in the ensuing expedition to Egypt. In Feb. 1803, after having served for some time in the MINOTAUR 74, and AMPHION 32, Capts. Rich. Henry Alex. Bennett, Alex. Frazer, and Thos. Masterman Hardy, he joined LA MINERVE, of 48 guns, Capt. Jahleel Brenton; and, on 2 July, 1803, he was on board that frigate when she took the ground under the batteries of Cherbourg, and was compelled, in spite of a desperate and sanguinary resistance, to strike her colours. Being in consequence taken prisoner, he remained in captivity until 1809, when, contriving to escape, he was received on board the

Royal Oak 74, Capt. Lord Amelius Beauclerk. During the early part of 1810, we next find him (with his name successively on the books of the Circe, Atlas, Ville de Paris, and San Josef) employed at the siege of Cadiz. On 8 June in the same year, having for a few weeks acted as Lieutenant of the Cyane 20, Capt. Thos. Forrest, he was confirmed to that rank in the Porcupine 24, Capt. Robt. Elliot, stationed in the River Plate. He removed, in Nov. 1811, to the Barbadoes 28, Capts. Edw. Rushworth and Thos. Huskisson, stationed in the Channel and West Indies; and was lastly, from Oct. 12 until Sept. 1815, employed in command of the Bream and Manly schooners, and Picton brig. In those vessels he appears to have cruized with great activity in the Bay of Fundy, where he effected the capture of several privateers of superior force. On 9 June, 1811, in particular, when off Cape Forchu, in the Bream, he fell in with the American private armed sloop *Wasp*, mounting 2 6-pounder carriage-guns, with a crew of 33 men, which did not surrender until after a chase of seven hours and a half and a smart running action.* Agents—Coplands and Burnett.

* *Vide* Gaz. 1813, p. 1090.

HARE. (Lieutenant, 1815. f-p., 17; h-p., 22.)

Marcus Theodore Hare died in 1846.

This officer entered the Navy, 27 Nov. 1807, as Fst.-cl. Vol., on board the Nymphe 36, commanded by his cousin, Capt. Conway Shipley, with whom he continued until the death of the latter in a gallant but unsuccessful endeavour to cut out an enemy's vessel in the river Tagus in April, 1808. He then joined the Centaur 74, bearing the flag in the Baltic of Sir Sam. Hood, and, after attending the expedition to the Walcheren, he successively followed that officer into the Hibernia 120, Tigre 74, Owen Glendower 36, and Illustrious 74, and was employed with him, latterly as Midshipman, on the Mediterranean, Home, and East India stations. In Nov. 1812 he removed to the Malacca 36, Capt. Donald Hugh Mackay, also in the East Indies, where, on accompanying the same Captain into the Minden 74, he received an order, 1 March, 1815, to act as Lieutenant of that ship. He was confirmed to her by commission dated on 20 of the following Sept., and, being paid off in the early part of 1816, was next appointed—22 Dec. 1817, to the Erne 20, Capt. Timothy Scriven, which vessel was wrecked off the Cape de Verde Islands 1 June, 1819—31 Oct. 1823, to the Pelorus 18, Capt. Wm. Hamley, stationed, until 1826, off the coast of Ireland—7 June, 1828, to the Crocodile 28, Capt. John Wm. Montagu, in the East Indies—in Dec. 1830 (in consequence of his having been placed on the Lord High Admiral's list for promotion), to the acting-command of the Southampton 52, flag-ship on the same station of Sir Edw. W. C. R. Owen—and, 12 May, 1831, to the acting-command of the Satellite 18. He brought that sloop home and paid her off in May, 1832, but, a change of ministry having in the mean time taken place, he was, to his great mortification, allowed to remain unpromoted. He did not again go afloat.

Lieut. Hare married, 24 Sept. 1833, Lucy, daughter of Lord Stanley of Alderley, and by that lady has left issue three children.

HARE. (Lieutenant, 1814. f-p., 9; h-p., 32.)

Richard Hare, born 20 Nov. 1793, in the parish of St. Pancras, co. Middlesex, is son of Rich. Hare, Esq., of the same place; and first-cousin of Lieut. Chas. Hare, R.N.

This officer entered the Navy, 25 March, 1806, as Fst.-cl. Vol., on board the Medusa 32, Capt. Hon. Duncombe Pleydell Bouverie, and removed soon afterwards to La Chiffonne 36, Capt. John Wainwright, in which frigate he was occasionally in action with the Spanish batteries and gun-boats in the Mediterranean, and, on proceeding to the East Indies, accompanied an expedition against the pirates of the Persian Gulf, where he assisted, as Midshipman, at the destruction of the strong town of Ras-al-Khyma, and of more than 80 vessels In Nov. 1810 he was transferred to the Belliqueux 64, Capt. Hon. Geo. Byng, then at China; and, on his subsequent return to England in La Chiffonne, he further joined, in Aug. 1811 and Dec. 1813, the Bulwark and Venerable 74's, flag-ships of the late Sir Philip Durham in the Channel and West Indies. On his passage to the latter station, Mr. Hare contributed, in company with the Cyrené sloop, to the capture, not without opposition, of the French 44-gun frigates *Iphigénie* and *Alcmène*, 16 and 20 Jan. 1814. On 28 of the following month he was appointed Acting-Lieutenant of the Spider 12, Capt. Robt. Jas. Gordon, employed off Antigua; and, on 16 Sept. in the same year he was confirmed into the Orontes 36, Capt. Nathaniel Day Cochrane, also in the West Indies. He has been on half-pay since March, 1815.

Lieut. Hare married, 18 June, 1835, Mary Combe, daughter of John Maddison, Esq., of Bath, formerly of Little Grimsby, co. Lincoln, by whom he has issue two sons and a daughter. Agents—Coplands and Burnett.

HARE. (Lieutenant, 1815. f-p., 17; h-p., 25.)

Thomas Hare entered the Navy, 25 Jan. 1805, as A.B., on board the Fervent 12, Lieut.-Commander John Edw. Hare, whom he accompanied to the Mediterranean. He there removed, as Midshipman, in Nov. 1806, to the Morgiana sloop, Capt. Thos. Landless; and he next, from Aug. 1807 until promoted to the rank of Lieutenant 4 Feb. 1815, served uninterruptedly on the Home station in the Snake, Capt. Thos. Young, Namur, Capt. Rich. Jones, Starling, Lieut.-Commander Chas. Fred. Napier, Exertion, Lieut.-Commander Jas. Murray, Raisonnable 64, Capt. Edw. Sneyd Clay, and Impregnable, flag-ship for some time of Admirals Wm. Young, and of H. R. H. the Duke of Clarence, and afterwards commanded by Capts. John Wentworth Loring, Robt. Hall, and Jas. Nash. On 2 Aug. 1811, while Sub-Lieutenant of the Exertion, Mr. Hare assisted in the boats of a squadron, 10 in number, and carrying 116 men, under the command of Lieut. Sam. Blyth, at the cutting-out, from within the island of Mordeney, near the Texel, of four Danish gun-vessels, each armed with 1 long-12, and 2 long 6 or 8 pounders, and 25 men, including 5 soldiers, and commanded by a Lieutenant-de-Vaisseau of the French Navy; an exploit that was not accomplished until the enemy had sustained a loss of 4 men killed and 12 wounded, and the British, after an exposure to a fire of grape and canister, and a hard struggle, of 2 killed and 9 wounded, independently of 19 persons who were killed and wounded in the early part of the contest by an accidental explosion on board one of the gun-boats. Mr. Hare subsequently, when in the Impregnable under the Duke of Clarence, escorted the Emperor of Russia and the King of Prussia to England. He was lastly employed in command, from 26 Oct. 1836 until 1844, of a station in the Coast Guard. Agent—J. Hinxman.

HARGOOD. (Captain, 1837. f-p., 16; h-p., 18.)

William Hargood, born 22 June, 1801, is nephew of the late Admiral Sir Wm. Hargood, G.C.B., G.C.H.,*

* Sir Wm. Hargood bore a part, when a Lieutenant of the Magnificent 74, in Sir Geo. Rodney's action with the Comte de Grasse 12 April, 1782. He commanded the Hyæna 24, when that vessel was captured by the French in May, 1793; and between 1794 and his attainment of Flag-rank 31 July, 1810, he successively officiated as Captain of the Iris frigate, Leopard 50, Nassau and Intrepid 64's, Belleisle 80 (part of the victorious fleet in the action off Trafalgar 21 Oct. 1805), and Northumberland 74. In April, 1808, he was appointed a Colonel of Marines. From the close of 1810 until made a Vice-Admiral in 1814, we find him discharging the duties of Admiral Superintendent at Portsmouth, and of Commander-in-Chief on the Jersey and Guernsey station; in which latter capacity he was subsequently employed at Plymouth from April, 1833, until April, 1836. He was created a K.C.B. in 1815, and in 1831 a G.C.B. and G.C.H. He died at Bath, an Admiral of the White, 12 Dec. 1839.

and is descended in the male line from the ancient and noble family of Harcourt, the last of whose Earls died in 1830, at which period the title became extinct. Capt. Hargood's father, a gentleman in the law, was an elder brother of the Admiral.

This officer entered the Navy, 19 June, 1813, as Fst.-cl. Vol., on board the Fylla 22, Capt. Wm. Shepheard, bearing the flag of his uncle on the Jersey and Guernsey station, where he accompanied the Admiral into the Alonzo sloop, and continued until June, 1814. During the next three years we find him employed as a student at the Royal Naval College. On leaving that institution he re-embarked, as a Volunteer, on board the Blossom 24, Capts. Fred. Hickey and Fred. Edw. Vernon, and sailed for South America, where he appears to have been employed, the last 20 months as Midshipman, until Sept. 1820. He then joined the Sybille 44, of which ship, bearing the flag in the West Indies of Sir Chas. Rowley, he was created a Lieutenant 5 Oct. 1822. Being paid off in June, 1823, Mr. Hargood was next appointed—6 Dec. following, to the Tweed 28, Capt. Fred. Hunn, with whom he was once more ordered to South America—27 Oct. 1825 (after seven months of half-pay), to the Hyperion 42, Capt. Wm. Jas. Mingaye, lying at Newhaven for the purposes of the Coast Blockade—and, 5 Dec. 1826, again to the Sybille, bearing the broad pendant of Sir Fras. Augustus Collier on the coast of Africa, where, on one occasion, while officer of the watch, he received so severe a contusion of the fore-finger of the left hand as to render its immediate amputation necessary. He remained in the Sybille until promoted to the rank of Commander 15 Jan. 1828; after which he procured an appointment, 20 July, 1832, to the Scout 18. In that sloop he proceeded to the North Sea, whence, in the following year, after having been intermediately employed in imposing an embargo on the ships belonging to the subjects of the King of the Netherlands, he was ordered to the Mediterranean. Exchanging, in Dec. 1833, into the Scylla 16, Capt. Hargood soon afterwards returned to England, and on 8 March, 1834, was paid off. He has not been since afloat. His present rank was conferred on him 10 Jan. 1837.

Capt. Hargood married, 1 Oct. 1828, Catherine, eldest daughter of Henry Harison, Esq., of Seaford, co. Sussex, by whom he has issue two sons and two daughters. Agents—Coplands and Burnett.

HARLEY. (Retired Commander, 1837. f-p., 26; h-p., 39.)

Edward Harley died in Aug. 1846, in the 71st year of his age.

This officer entered the Navy, in 1781, as A.B., on board the Warspite 74, Capt. John Reynolds, lying at Portsmouth, where, in the following year and in 1785-6, he became Midshipman of the Diligente and Queen, flag-ships of Sir Thos. Pye and Admiral Montagu, and Hector, Capt. Sir John Collins. Between 1787 and Nov. 1794, he was employed, on the West India and Home stations, as Midshipman, in the Alert, Capt. Geo. Burdon, Active, Capt. Peter Rainier, Vanguard and Bedford, both commanded by Sir Andrew Snape Hamond, and Duke, Glory, and Resolution, bearing each the broad pendant of Commodore Geo. Murray. He was then appointed Acting-Lieutenant of the Thisbe, Capt. John Okes Hardy, on the Halifax station, and in Jan. 1795 he removed in a similar capacity to L'Espérance sloop, Capt. Jonas Rose, also employed off the coast of America. Being confirmed in the latter vessel by commission dated 8 Oct. 1796, Mr. Harley was subsequently appointed—in Jan. 1798, to the Isis 50, Capt. Wm. Mitchell, with whom he made a voyage to St. Helena—1 Aug. 1799, to the Andromache frigate, Capt. Sir Robt. Laurie, employed, until Feb. 1804, on the North American and Jamaica stations—14 Oct. 1807, to the Centurion 50, Capt. Chas. Webb, in which ship he proceeded to Gibraltar—2 June, 1808, to the Gorgon 44, Capt. Robt. Brown Tom, successively stationed at Woolwich and the Nore—and, 9 July, 1808, to the command of the Ildefonso, at Spithead. He went on half-pay in July, 1814; and became a Retired Commander on the Junior List 26 Nov. 1830. His promotion to the Senior List took place 26 Dec. 1837. Agents—Hallett and Robinson.

HARNAGE, Bart., formerly Blackman. (Commander, 1820. f-p., 12; h-p., 28.)

Sir George Harnage, born 19 July, 1792, is eldest son of the late Sir Geo. Harnage, Bart., by Mary, eldest surviving daughter of Henry Harnage, Esq., of Belswardyne, co. Salop, Lieut.-Colonel in the Army, who served as Major of the 62nd Regt., under General Burgoyne, during the first American war, and was severely wounded at the battle of Freeman's Farm 19 Sept. 1777. Sir George (whose brother, Capt. John Lucie Blackman, of the Coldstream Guards, fell at Waterloo) assumed the name of Harnage in 1821; and succeeded his father, as second Baronet, 19 Nov. 1836.

This officer entered the Navy, 1 May, 1807, as Midshipman, on board the Hibernia 120, flag-ship in the Channel and off Brest of Sir Jas. Saumarez. Removing, in July following, to the Penelope 36, Capt. John Dick, he was for some time employed at the blockade of Ferrol; after which he visited North America and the West Indies, and in Feb. 1809 was present at the capture of Martinique. Having been further attached for three years to the Defiance 74, commanded in the North Sea and Baltic by Capt. Rich. Raggett, he had the fortune, on 12 Aug. 1813, to be awarded a Lieutenant's commission. His subsequent appointments were—4 Feb. 1814, to the Hamadryad 36, Capt. Edw. Chetham, stationed off Newfoundland, where, in the following Sept., that vessel suffered so severely from the effects of a hurricane as to necessitate her being in a few months broken up—11 April, 1815, to the Boyne 98, as Flag-Lieutenant to Sir Israel Pellew, Captain of the Mediterranean fleet, in which capacity he officiated until 29 June, 1816—and, 4 Aug. 1818, to the Salisbury 58, bearing the successive flags in the Leeward Islands of Rear-Admirals Donald Campbell and Wm. Chas. Fahie. While in the latter ship, in Sept. 1819, Mr. Blackman, being at the time at anchor in the harbour of the island of St. Thomas, was again present in a hurricane of so fearful a nature that on the following morning the wrecks of 96 vessels were counted, independently of numerous others which had foundered—the Salisbury, indeed, out of 115 sail, being the only ship left afloat. He obtained command of the Raleigh sloop 16 Aug. 1820, and continued to serve in the West Indies until the close of 1821, when he returned to England with a freight of 320,000 dollars. He was paid off 14 Jan. 1822, and has not since been afloat.

Sir Geo. Harnage married, 26 Jan. 1826, Caroline Helena, youngest daughter of Bartlett Goodrich, Esq., of Saling Grove, Great Saling, co. Essex, and by that lady has issue an only son. Agent—J. Chippendale.

HARNESS. (Commander, 1814. f-p., 9; h-p., 33.)

Richard Stephens Harness, born in July, 1792, at Wickham, co. Hants, is son of the late Dr. John Harness, F.L.S., many years a Commissioner of the Transport Board; a gentleman who was twice married, the second time to the widow of Admiral Robt. Linzee.

This officer entered the Navy, 24 July, 1805, as Fst.-cl. Vol., on board the Diadem 64, Capt. Sir Home Riggs Popham, and in the course of 1806 attended the expeditions to the Cape of Good Hope and Buenos Ayres. In Dec. of the latter year he became Midshipman of the Sampson 64, Capt. Wm. Cuming, from which ship, on her return to England, he removed to the Inflexible 64, Capt. Joshua Rowley Watson, part of the force employed at the bombardment of Copenhagen in Sept. 1807. After that event he joined the Volontaire 38,

Capts. Chas. Bullen and Joseph Nourse, and proceeded to the Mediterranean; where, on the night of 31 Oct. 1809, he served with the boats of a squadron at the capture and destruction, in the Bay of Rosas—despite a fierce opposition from the crews, and a galling fire from the batteries, inflictive on the British of a loss of 15 men killed and 55 wounded—of the armed store-ship *Lamproie*, of 16 guns and 116 men, with three armed and seven merchant vessels.* In the course of 1809 he appears to have been also present in the VOLONTAIRE's boats under Lieut. Isaac Shaw at the capture—with a loss to the enemy of 5 men killed and 8 wounded, and to the English of 2 wounded—of Fort Rioux, near Cape Croisette, mounting 14 guns; and, under Lieut. Dalhousie Tait, at the destruction, near Marseilles, of the fort of Cassis, and the bringing out thence of several merchant-vessels, in July and Oct. 1811. Mr. Harness next joined the CUMBERLAND 74, Capt. Robt. Waller Otway, and MALTA 84, flag-ship of Rear-Admiral Benj. Hallowell. On the receipt of his first commission, bearing date 18 Feb. 1812, he removed to the FAME 74, Capt. Walter Bathurst, with whom he continued to serve (assisting intermediately, in 1813, at the defence of Tarragona) until advanced to his present rank, 27 Aug. 1814. He has since been on half-pay.

Commander Harness is a widower with two children.

HARPER. (LIEUTENANT, 1841.)

FRANCIS HENRY HARPER entered the Navy 1 June, 1826; passed his examination 11 Sept. 1833; and on 23 Nov. 1841 (while serving as Mate, in the Mediterranean, of the RODNEY 92, Capt. Robt. Maunsell) was promoted to the rank of Lieutenant. His subsequent appointments were—31 Jan. 1842, to the DAPHNE 18, Capt. John Windham Dalling, in the Mediterranean—4 June, 1842, to the TALBOT 26, Capt. Sir Thos. Raikes Trigge Thompson, lying at Sheerness—23 July, 1842, again to the DAPHNE, Capt. John Jas. Onslow, whom he accompanied to the Pacific—and, 20 June, 1844, to the SATELLITE 18, Capt. Robt. Hibbert Bartholomew Rowley, stationed on the south-east coast of America. He left the latter vessel in Aug. 1846. AGENT—Joseph Woodhead.

HARPER. (LIEUTENANT, 1837.)

GEORGE HARPER passed his examination in 1830; and obtained his commission 6 June, 1837. His appointments have since been—on 12 of the same month, to the EXCELLENT gunnery-ship at Portsmouth, Capt. Thos. Hastings—14 April, 1838, to the MALABAR 74, Capt. Edw. Harvey, on the North America and West India station—1 Feb. 1839, to the IMPLACABLE 72, commanded in the Mediterranean by Capt. Edw. Harvey—and, 3 June, 1842, as First-Lieutenant, to the TALBOT 26, Capt. Sir Thos. Raikes Trigge Thompson, attached to the force in the Pacific, whence he returned in 1847. AGENTS—Messrs. Stilwell.

HARPER. (LIEUT., 1815. F-P., 18; H-P., 24.)

JAMES HARPER entered the Navy, 27 Nov. 1805, as Fst.-cl. Vol., on board the ACTIVE 38, Capt. Rich. Hussey Moubray, with whom, in the same ship, and, as Midshipman, in the MONTAGU and REPULSE 74's, he continued to serve, on the Cork and Mediterranean stations, until June, 1814. He was present during that period, in the ACTIVE, at the passage of the Dardanells and the destruction of the redoubt at Point Pesquies in Feb. 1807; on shore, while belonging to the MONTAGU, at the reduction of Santa Maura in April, 1810; and, in the REPULSE's boats, in conjunction with those of the VOLONTAIRE and UNDAUNTED frigates, at the annihilation of two important batteries and the capture of a convoy near the port of Morjean 2 May, 1813. He next, on leaving the REPULSE, joined the LATONA 38, flag-ship of Sir Wm. Johnstone Hope at Leith, where he remained until promoted to the rank of Lieutenant, 1 Feb. 1815. From the latter date Mr. Harper remained unemployed until 12 Jan. 1839, when he was appointed to the NIAGARA 20, Capt. Williams Sandom, in which ship, stationed on the lakes of Canada, he continued to serve, the greater part of the time as First-Lieutenant, until the early part of 1843. While so attached he appears to have had charge of a steamer in action with the rebels at Prescott, in Upper Canada. He has been in successive command, since 16 Dec. 1843 and 1 Aug. 1846, of the EXPERIMENT and MINOS steam-vessels, on Lakes Huron and Erie. AGENT—Fred. Dufaur.

* *Vide* Gaz. 1809, p. 1907.

HARPER, C.B., K.L.A. (Captain, 1814. F-P., 35; H-P., 31.)

JOHN HARPER, born 18 Sept. 1772, at Chatham, co. Kent, is son of an officer in the Navy, who was mortally wounded on board the BRITANNIA, in Lord Howe's partial action with the combined forces of France and Spain, off Cape Spartel, 20 Oct. 1782. His younger brother attained the rank of Lieutenant at an early age, and was drowned in LA LUTINE frigate 9 Oct. 1799.

This officer entered the Navy, in March, 1781, as Captain's Servant, on board the BELLONA 74, Capt. Rich. Onslow, and, on removing in the following year to the BRITANNIA 100, bearing the flag of Hon. Sam. Barrington, fought in that ship in the action in which his father received his death-wound. During the six first years of the ensuing peace he appears to have been successively employed on the Portsmouth station, chiefly as Midshipman, in the EDGAR 74, Capt. Chas. Thompson, and TRIUMPH 74, and BARFLEUR 98, flag-ships of Sir Sam. Hood. He then proceeded to the coast of Africa in the POMONA 28, Capt. Henry Savage; and in Nov. 1793, after a further servitude in the Channel on board the DUKE 98, bearing the flag of Admiral Robt. Roddam, SPRIGHTLY cutter, and EDGAR 74, Capt. Albemarle Bertie, he was ordered to the West Indies in the BOYNE 98, flag-ship of Sir John Jervis. For his conduct at the proximate reduction of Martinique, where he had command of a flat-bottomed boat, Mr. Harper was promoted, 21 Feb. 1794, to a Lieutenancy in the AVENGER 20, Capts. R. Griffiths and Chas Ogle. Soon after that event, while rowing guard one night in a six-oared boat off the Carenage, during the siege of Ste. Lucie, he entered the harbour and, under the veil of a shower of rain, boarded, carried, and brought out a French schooner privateer, mounting 10 guns, fully manned, and perfectly ready for sea. He subsequently, on the surrender of Ste. Lucie, landed and co-operated with the army in the reduction of Guadeloupe. Removing, in Oct. of the same year, to the DEFENCE 74, Capts. Thos. Wells, John Peyton, and Lord Henry Paulet, Mr. Harper, during a continuance of five years under those officers, was present in Hotham's partial action 13 July, 1795, and, as Second Lieutenant, in the battle of the Nile, 1 Aug. 1798, besides participating in much boat-service off Cadiz in the summer of 1797. He once, from having volunteered, while watering at Syracuse, to superintend the performance of that fatiguing duty, contracted, in consequence of alternate exposure to the sun and dews, a fever so severe that his life was for a long time despaired of. On leaving the DEFENCE in Dec. 1799, he joined the GLORY 98, Capt. Thos. Wells, with whom he served in the Channel until April, 1802. In the summer of 1803 he was placed by Rear-Admiral Bartholomew Sam. Rowley, Commander-in-Chief at the Nore, to whom he had been recently appointed Flag-Lieutenant, in charge of the ADMIRAL MITCHELL hired cutter, and sent on a secret service of importance to the coast of France, where his gallant conduct, in an almost immediate action with the Boulogne flotilla, procured him the thanks of Rear-Admiral Robt. Montagu. After commanding for many months the DUKE OF CLARENCE, another hired cutter, on the Jersey and Guernsey station, Mr. Harper was further appointed—27 Oct.

1804, to the WASP 18, Capts. Hon. Fred. Wm. Aylmer and John Simpson, which vessel, in Aug. 1805, effected a very wonderful escape from a pursuing squadron of French ships—4 Oct. in the latter year, to the STAR 18, commanded by Capt. Simpson, on the coast of Portugal, where, with two boats containing about 20 men, he boarded and captured, in Jan. 1806, a Spanish lugger privateer, of 1 long 6-pounder, 6 swivels, and 45 men—and, 28 Jan. 1807, to the EXCELLENT 74, Capts. Thos. West and R. Griffiths, under the former of whom he assisted at the defence of the citadel of Rosas, when besieged by the French in Nov. 1808. During the period of his attachment to the EXCELLENT, Mr. Harper saw a great deal of detached service, and on every occasion he displayed the character of a most experienced and enterprising officer. He particularly, however, on 29 July, 1809, excited the admiration of his beholders by the prompt, gallant, and determined manner in which, under a covering fire from the ACORN and BUSTARD sloops, he boarded and carried, with the EXCELLENT's boats, six Italian gun-vessels, armed with long 18 and 24-pounders, and each manned with 20 men; the whole of them, together with a convoy of 10 laden trabacolos, being brought out, with but trifling loss to the British, from the harbour of Duino, near Trieste.* In the following Sept. he again presents himself to our notice as destroying, with only two boats under his orders, a large armed schooner lying aground under some heavy batteries in the neighbourhood of Brindisi. He soon after this received the thanks of the Admiralty for his valorous conduct in the affair at Duino; but it was not until 17 April, 1810, that he had the satisfaction of being promoted by their lordships to the rank of Commander. On 19 Aug. 1812, Capt. Harper obtained command of the SARACEN 18, in which sloop he remained for a period of two years, and performed a train of brilliant services. In the first place, he contrived, on 23 of the month following his appointment, having at the time but his marines and a few harbour-duty men on board, to capture, near Beachy Head, one of two fugitive privateers, *Le Coureur*, mounting 14 guns, with a crew of 50 men, commanded by an able and experienced Captain.† He next, in the early part of 1813, proceeded to the Adriatic, where, on the night of 17 June following, he landed with his boats, containing 40 men, in a storm on the island of Zupano, of which, after a difficult march of three miles, he succeeded in obtaining possession, although the whole of his ammunition had been rendered unserviceable, and he had to contend with a garrison of about 60 men.‡ Encouraged by this good fortune, Capt. Harper, in the course of the next month, determined, in unison with Capt. Jas. Black of the WEASEL sloop, to make a similar attempt on the adjoining island of Mezzo; and in this instance also the same happy issue crowned his endeavours; the castle, after an investment of several days, being compelled to surrender, and the troops taken prisoners of war.§ As a reward for these achievements he was intrusted by the Commander-in-Chief with the entire direction of the blockade of Ragusa and Boco di Cattaro, where his activity and vigilance kept the whole coast in a constant state of alarm. On one occasion, in Sept. 1813, he landed near the former place with his Master, Boatswain, and 20 men (all he had on board, the rest of the crew being employed on detached service), and intercepted a convoy of 50 oxen, the whole of which were embarked in fishing-boats, and brought safe alongside the SARACEN. In Oct. 1813, the BACCHANTE frigate, Capt. Wm. Hoste, having arrived off Ragusa, Capt. Harper handsomely volunteered the command of her launch and barge, together with two Sicilian gun-vessels and the boats of his own sloop; with which force he not only took four heavy gun-boats lying between the island of St. Giorgio and the town of Cattaro, but also gallantly made himself master of the former place, the Commandant and garrison

* *Vide* Gaz. 1809, p. 1931. † *V.* Gaz. 1812, p. 1937.
‡ *V.* Gaz. 1813, p. 2010. § *V.* Gaz. 1813, p. 2340.

(139 in number) surrendering at discretion. The capture of St. Giorgio was an event of the utmost importance, and was so highly esteemed by Capt. Hoste, that he declared himself unable in too warm terms to characterize the conduct which had led to it.* Its subjugation was followed by that of Castelnuovo and Fort Espagnol, mounting 6 brass guns, 19 iron ditto, and 7 swivels, and garrisoned by 299 officers and men. Capt. Harper afterwards, by his indefatigable zeal, contributed in a very signal manner to the arduous reduction of the towns of Cattaro and Ragusa, both which places fell in Jan. 1814.† His successful career in the Adriatic closed with the blockade and surrender of Venice. He attained Post-rank 7 June, 1814, and was subsequently appointed, in the course of that year and of 1815-16, to the command, on the East India and North American stations, of the TYNE 24, WELLESLEY 74, DORIS 36, and WYE 28. He went on half-pay in Dec. 1818; and accepted the Retirement 1 Oct. 1846.

Capt. Harper was nominated a C.B. 4 June, 1815. He had been previously presented by the Emperor of Austria with the Order of Leopold, as a reward for his distinguished conduct at Cattaro and Ragusa. He has been twice married—the second time, 30 Oct. 1834, to Susannah Maria, widow of the late H. Young, Esq., of Soldens, co. Surrey. His eldest son, John Horatio Harper, was educated at the Royal Naval College, and perished on board the ARAB.

HARRIES. (LIEUTENANT, 1833.)

EDWARD THORNBOROUGH HARRIES was born 5 June, 1804, and died towards the close of 1845.

This officer entered the Navy 15 June, 1815, and, between that period and his promotion to the rank of Lieutenant, which took place 11 March, 1833, nine years after he had passed his examination, served on board the FERRET 12, PHAETON 38, RAMILLIES 74, TAMAR 24, QUEEN CHARLOTTE 100, STARLING cutter, and HYPERION 42. He was appointed, 9 Nov. following, to the SPARROWHAWK 16, Capt. Chas. Pearson, under whom he was employed for nearly three years on the South American station; and he lastly, from 23 June, 1837, until the period of his death, commanded a station in the Coast Guard.

Lieut. Harries married, first, Anna Maria, youngest daughter of Hercules Jenkings, Esq., of Braganza Lodge, co. Cornwall; and, secondly, 17 Nov. 1840, Elizabeth Ann, only daughter of John Hill, Esq., of the same county. He has left issue two children.

HARRIOTT. (LIEUT., 1815. F-P., 10; H-P., 37.)

THOMAS HARRIOTT is brother of Wm. Harriott, Esq., Master R.N. (1828), now Superintendent of Convicts at Bermuda.

This officer entered the Navy, in 1800, on board the HANNIBAL 74, Capt. Solomon Ferris, which ship, having grounded under the enemy's batteries, was compelled, after a long and deadly resistance, inflictive on her of a loss of 81 men killed and 62 wounded, to strike her colours, in the action off Algeciras, 6 July, 1801. Being soon, however, restored to liberty, Mr. Harriott returned to England, and in the following Nov. was discharged. He re-embarked, in Oct. 1803, on board the TERRIBLE 74, Capt. Lord Henry Paulet, fitting at Portsmouth; and in May, 1804, and March, 1805, we find him joining the TIGRE and RENOWN 74's, Capts. Benj. Hallowell and Sir Rich. John Strachan; in the last-mentioned of which ships he came home from the Mediterranean, immediately after his removal to her, and was paid off. He did not again go afloat until Jan. 1808, when he succeeded in obtaining a berth on board the EREBUS 18, Capts. Wm. Autridge, Henry Lyford, Geo. Brine, John Forbes, and David Ewen Bartholomew, under whom he thenceforward served, on the Home, Baltic, and North American stations, until Sept. 1814.

* *Vide* Gaz. 1814, p. 83. † *V.* Gaz. 1814, p. 700.

During the closing portion of that period Mr. Harriott bore a warm part in the different Potomac operations connected with Sir Jas. Alex. Gordon's brilliant expedition against Alexandria, in the course of which the EREBUS particularly signalised herself and incurred a loss of 17 men killed and wounded. He was afterwards employed for nearly 12 months, latterly on the coast of France, in the EURYALUS 36, Capts. Chas. Napier and Thos. Huskisson. He then took up a commission bearing date 28 Feb. 1815, and has since been on half-pay.

Lieut. Harriott is married and has issue three children.

HARRIS, M.P. (CAPTAIN, 1841. F-P., 13; H-P., 13.)

THE HONOURABLE EDWARD ALFRED JOHN HARRIS, born 20 May, 1808, in London, is second son of Jas. Edw., second Earl of Malmesbury, by Harriet Susan, daughter of Fras. Bateman Dashwood, Esq., of Well Vale, co. Lincoln. He is brother and heir-presumptive to the present Earl of Malmesbury; and brother of the Hon. and Rev. Chas. Amyand Harris, Prebendary of Salisbury.

This officer entered the Royal Naval College 6 Sept. 1821; and embarked, in March, 1823, as Midshipman, on board the ISIS 50, Capt. Gordon Thos. Falcon, fitting for the flag of Sir Geo. Eyre, Commander-in-Chief in South America; where, until 1827, he further served with the Admiral in the SPARTIATE 76, and with Capts. John Macpherson Ferguson and Henry Prescott in the MERSEY 26, and AURORA 46. In the course of the latter year, in the June of which he passed a distinguished examination, Mr. Harris cruised experimentally in the PYRAMUS 42 and GALATEA 46, Capts. Geo. Rose Sartorius and Sir Chas. Sullivan. He then rejoined the ISIS, commanded at the time by Capt. Sir Thos. Staines, and, after attending an expedition against the pirates of Grabusa in the Grecian Archipelago, was promoted to the rank of Lieutenant 28 Feb. 1828. Between that period and the attainment of the next step in his profession 21 Nov. 1833, Mr. Harris was successively employed, on the Mediterranean, Home, and Lisbon stations, in the OCEAN 80; as Flag-Lieutenant to Sir Edw. Codrington, in the ASIA 84; for some time as First-Lieutenant in the PELICAN 18, Capts. Wm. Alex. Baillie Hamilton and Geo. Hutchison; and in the STAG 46, Capt. Nich. Lockyer. His last appointment was to the command, 29 April, 1839, of the RACEHORSE 18, in which sloop he served in North America and the West Indies until March, 1841. He was advanced to the rank he now holds on 23 Nov. in the latter year.

Capt. Harris has been in Parliament, since 1844, as member for Christchurch. He married, 4 Aug. 1841, Emma Wylly, youngest daughter of the late Capt. Sam. Chambers, R.N., by whom he has issue two sons.

HARRIS. (LIEUT., 1815. F-P., 30; H-P., 12.)

FRANCIS HARRIS is half-brother of Retired Commander John Read Bindon, R.N.

This officer entered the Navy, 12 July, 1805, as Fst.-cl. Vol., on board the TÉMÉRAIRE 98, Capts. Eliab Harvey and Sir Chas. Hamilton, in which ship he fought in the ensuing battle of Trafalgar, and (with an exception of 15 months in 1806-7) was afterwards employed, under the flags of Rear-Admirals Manley Dixon and Fras. Pickmore, on the Baltic and Mediterranean stations, and at the defence of Cadiz, until Feb. 1811—two years and four months of the time as Midshipman. He then joined the ROYAL SOVEREIGN 100, Capt. Joseph Spear, and on removing to the UNITÉ 36, Capt. Edwin Henry Chamberlayne, assisted at the capture, 31 March, 1811, of the French 800-ton store-ship *Dromadaire*. On 1 of the following May he was further present in the same frigate, and in company with the POMONE 38, and SCOUT 18, at the destruction of two vessels of the like description, the *Giraffe* and *Nourrice*, each mounting from 20 to 30 guns, and both protected by a 5-gun battery, a martello-tower, and a body of about 200 regular troops; and on 29 Nov. he contributed to the capture, after a severe running-fight of four hours, of the 26-gun store-ship *La Persanne*, supposed, until the moment of her surrender, to be a frigate. Mr. Harris, who subsequently participated in many boat affairs in the Adriatic, and witnessed the UNITÉ's capture of three Turkish ships, was transferred, in Oct. 1814, to the DEE 24, Capt. John Wm. Andrew, on the Leith station, and advanced, 1 March, 1815, to the rank of Lieutenant. With one slight interval, he has been continuously employed in the Coast Blockade and Coast Guard since March, 1826.

HARRIS. (RETIRED COMMANDER, 1845. F-P., 12; H-P., 36.)

HENRY HARRIS entered the Navy, 3 Dec. 1799, as Fst.-cl. Vol., on board the ARIADNE 20, Capt. Jas. Bradley, with whom, after serving for some time in the North Sea, he removed to the ANDROMEDA frigate, and proceeded to the West Indies, where he continued to serve under Capts. Edw. Durnford King and Chas. Fielding, latterly as Midshipman, until Oct. 1802. In March, 1803, a few days after he had been appointed Midshipman of the DÉTERMINÉE 24, *armée en flûte*, Capt. Alex. Becher, he had the misfortune to be wrecked off the island of Jersey; owing to which event he next joined the DREADNOUGHT 98, flag-ship off Brest of the Hon. Wm. Cornwallis, commanded subsequently by Capt. John Child Purvis, and also by Capt. Robt. Carthew Reynolds, whom we find him accompanying into the PRINCESS ROYAL 98. Proceeding in 1805 to the East Indies on board the GREYHOUND 32, Capt. Chas. Elphinstone, Mr. Harris, in July of the following year, assisted at the destruction of a Dutch armed brig under the fort of Manado, as also of a similar vessel off the island of Tidore; and on 28 of the same month he participated in a sharp action which terminated in the surrender, to the GREYHOUND and HARRIER sloop, of the *Pallas* frigate and two armed and richly-laden Indiamen. On 10 Jan. 1807, having been for the last four months Master's-Mate of the BLENHEIM 74, flag-ship of Sir Thos. Troubridge, he was nominated Sub-Lieutenant of the HARRIER brig, Capt. Justice Finley; which vessel, on 5 of the ensuing month, was in company with the BLENHEIM and JAVA frigate in the hurricane which, it is supposed, proved so fatal to those ships. Prior to his official promotion, which took place 16 Aug. 1808, Mr. Harris appears to have been further employed, as Acting-Lieutenant, in the MALABAR, Capt. John Temple, and DEFIANCE 74, Capt. John M'Kerlie. His succeeding appointments were—12 Sept. 1808, to the ARETHUSA 38, Capt. Robt. Mends, in the Channel —11 Jan. 1809 and 2 June, 1810, to the VIRGINIE 38, and ENDYMION 40, commanded on the Irish station by Capts. Edw. Brace, Hon. Thos. Bladen Capel, and Sir Wm. Bolton—and, 2 Feb. 1813, to the HAMADRYAD 36, Capt. Edw. Chetham, employed in the Baltic. He went on half-pay 18 Feb. 1814; and accepted his present rank 6 Nov. 1845. AGENTS—Messrs. Stilwell.

HARRIS. (RETIRED COMMANDER, 1845. F-P., 13; H-P., 34.)

ISAAC HARRIS entered the Navy, 1 Jan. 1800, as A.B., on board the BRAVO, commanded on the Jersey station by Capt. Philip d'Auvergne, Duc de Bouillon. In the following year he became Midshipman of the INSOLENT gun-brig, Lieut.-Commanders Bevan, Kortwright, Smith, and Morris; from which vessel, successively employed off the coasts of Wales and Bermuda, he removed, in 1805, to the PIKE, Lieut.-Commander Duncan M'Donald, and sailed for Jamaica; where, towards the close of the same year, he joined the VETERAN 64, Capt. Andrew Fitzherbert Evans, flag-ship subsequently of Vice-Admiral Jas. Rich. Dacres. He attained the rank of Lieutenant 5 June, 1808, and was next appointed—on 12 of the same month, to the HEBE frigate, Capt. John Fyffe—11 July, 1809, as First, to the FAVORITE sloop, Capt. Benj. Clement, under whom, while soon afterwards returning with the Jamaica trade to England, he was nearly lost in a hurricane—and, 14 Sept. 1810, in a similar capacity, to the HELENA sloop, Capts. Jas. Andrew Worth, Henry Haynes, and Henry Montresor, in which vessel he thrice escorted convoy to the West Indies. Having been on half-pay since 1813, at which period the state of his health had caused him to invalid, Commander Harris, on 30 April, 1845, was induced to accept the rank he now holds. AGENT—J. Chippendale.

HARRIS. (COMMANDER, 1815. F-P., 12; H-P., 32.)

JAMES HARRIS, born 15 April, 1791, is second son of Joseph Harris, Esq., solicitor, of Leominster, co. Hereford, by Elizabeth, daughter of Wm. Hooper, Esq., a descendant of the celebrated Bishop of that name.

This officer entered the Navy, in Aug. 1803, as Fst.-cl. Vol., on board LA VIRGINIE 38, Capt., afterwards Admiral, Sir John Poo Beresford, in which ship, until she was paid off in Aug. 1804, he was employed cruizing in the North Sea and Downs, and was on one occasion all but lost during a three weeks' gale. From Dec. in the latter year until advanced to the rank of Commander 23 June, 1815, Mr. Harris further served, under the command of Sir J. P. Beresford, on the Halifax, West India, Home, and North and South American stations, in the CAMBRIAN 38, THESEUS and POICTIERS 74's (of which latter ship he was created a Lieutenant 26 Feb. 1810), and, as Signal-officer, in the DUNCAN 74. While in the CAMBRIAN, Mr. Harris assisted at the capture of three privateers carrying in the whole 40 guns and 225 men; and on one occasion, while serving in the boats, he was not only wounded, but so distinguished himself as to be noted for early promotion. He subsequently, when in the THESEUS, commanded the pinnace belonging to that ship, and was employed covering the retreat of the officers and men who had been engaged in the attack on the French squadron in Aix Roads, 11 April, 1809. During the operations of the following day against the enemy, Mr. Harris, then on board the THESEUS, received a splinter-wound in the left leg; the injury he had formerly received having been in the right one. The THESEUS being next attached to the force at the siege of Flushing, our officer, on the surrender of that place, was sent on shore, with the carpenter and a party of shipwrights and seamen, for the purpose of completing a frigate and two brigs, and of taking to pieces the frame of a 74. In the POICTIERS, after having participated in many boat-attacks on the coast of France, Lieut. Harris proceeded off the Tagus; up which river he was sent, in command of that ship's barge and two cutters, as far as Alhandra, the extreme right of Lord Wellington's army, then at the lines of Torres Vedras, where he remained until Marshal Masséna's retreat; on which occasion he followed the troops to Santarem, and rendered much valuable service. He subsequently, when on the North American station, commanded the POICTIER's launch in an attack made in 1812 on Lewis Town, at the entrance of Delaware river; and a few days after that event he had the good fortune, with a single boat's crew, to effect the capture of an East Indiaman of 20 guns, which within a week was ransomed at 45,000*l*. Commander Harris has not been afloat since the attainment of his present rank.

He married, 31 July, 1821, Elizabeth Anne, only daughter of the Rev. Henry Beavan, Rector of Whitton, co. Radnor, Vicar of Llanguullo, and Rural Dean of the Diocese of St. David's, by whom he has issue one son.

HARRIS. (COMMANDER, 1841. F-P., 19; H-P., 6.)

ROBERT HARRIS, born 9 July, 1809, is son of Jas. Harris, Esq., of Wittersham Hall, co. Kent; and grandson of Mrs. Trimmer, the authoress.

This officer entered the Navy, 26 Jan. 1822, as a Volunteer, on board the EURYALUS 42, Capt. Augustus Wm. Jas. Clifford, and in the course of the year 1824 was employed at the blockade of Algiers. In June, 1825, after having served for a few months in the ALGERINE 10, Capt. Hon. Montagu Stopford, he joined the CAMBRIAN 48, Capt. Gawen Wm. Hamilton, under whom we find him enacting a part in the battle of Navarin, sharing also in the capture of numerous pirates in the Grecian Archipelago, and ultimately suffering shipwreck during an attack on a nest of those marauders at Carabusa, 31 Jan. 1828. In Jan. 1829, on his return to England, Mr. Harris was received, as Mate, on board the FERRET 10, Capt. Thos. Hastings, through whose agency he soon succeeded in obtaining an appointment to the ROYAL GEORGE yacht, Capts. Geo. Mundy and Lord Adolphus FitzClarence. During the four years his name was borne on the books of that vessel, he appears to have been continuously employed, as officer in charge of a watch, on board the ONYX and PANTALOON tenders, in which vessels he visited South America, the West Indies, and the coasts of Spain and Portugal, was employed in surveying the coast of Ireland, and cruized in the Channel. Attaining the rank of Lieutenant 21 May, 1833, he subsequently joined—28 Dec. 1833, the EXCELLENT, Capt. Thos. Hastings, gunnery-ship at Portsmouth, where his scientific attainments procured him the highest awardable certificate—and 19 Jan. 1836, the MELVILLE 72, Capts. Peter John Douglas and Hon. Rich. Saunders Dundas, in which ship, bearing the flags for some time of Sir Peter Halkett and Hon. Geo. Elliot, he served for four years as Gunnery-Lieutenant in North America and the West Indies, at the Cape of Good Hope, and on the China coast. While on the latter station, Mr. Harris, besides participating in the capture, 26 Feb. 1841, of the forts at the Boca Tigris, commanded a rocket-boat in the operations against the various defences in the Canton river, between the "First Bar" and Napier's Fort. He was advanced, in consideration of the action at the Boca Tigris, to the rank of Commander 8 June, 1841. In the following Aug. he was paid off. His last appointment was, 7 Sept. 1844, to the FLYING FISH 12, fitting for the coast of Africa, whence he returned in May, 1846.

Commander Harris, who has acquired a knowledge of steam machinery, was employed as a student at the Royal Naval College from Jan. to Dec. 1842. In 1841, on his return from China, he published, under the title of 'Remarks on Heaving-down a 72-gun Ship,' an account of the peculiar circumstances which had attended that operation as regarded the MELVILLE, when at Chusan; touching at the same time upon some nautical subjects previously but little noticed. This work attracted the favourable notice of the Admiralty, and was ordered to be supplied to the different seamen's libraries. Its author married, 10 Jan. 1843, Priscilla Sophia, daughter of Capt. Penruddocke, of the Fusilier Guards, and granddaughter of the late Chas. Penruddocke, Esq., of Compton Park, M.P. for North Wilts. AGENTS—Hallett and Robinson.

HARRIS. (LIEUT., 1811. F-P., 25; H-P., 22.)

WILLIAM CLARK HARRIS entered the Navy, 6 Jan. 1800, as a Volunteer, on board the ALARM frigate, Capt. Robt. Rolles, on the Jamaica station, where, from the following Oct. until Feb. 1806, he served, as Midshipman, in the APOLLO frigate, Capt. Peter Halkett, HUNTER and GOELAN sloops, Capts. Sam. Hood Inglefield and John Ayscough, and PITT schooner, Lieut.-Commander Michael Fitton. He then, for the purpose of returning home, joined LE BRAVE, Capt. Edm. Boger, which ship, however, one of those taken in the action off St. Domingo, unfortunately foundered during her passage in a gale between the Western Islands and the banks of Newfoundland, 12 April, 1806, just affording time for her officers and crew to be rescued by the DONEGAL 74, Capt. Pulteney Malcolm, then in company. Owing to the consequent loss of his certificates and other papers, and to the PITT's books not being sent to England, Mr. Harris, although he had served his time, was unable to pass his examination at Somerset House until the summer of 1808, by which period he had been further employed for two years, chiefly as Master's Mate, and on various stations, in the GANGES 74, Capt. Peter Halkett, and HIBERNIA 120, flag-ship of Sir Chas. Cotton. From the latter date, until officially promoted, 18 April, 1811, we find him successively officiating as Acting-Lieutenant, on the Lisbon and Mediterranean stations, of the HINDOSTAN 50, *armee en flûte*, Capts. Geo. Skinner and John Pasco, MEROPE, Capts. John Houstoun and Edw. Flinn, PELORUS 18, Capt. Thos. Huskisson, THALIA 36, Capt. Jas. Giles Vashon, and SHARK receiving-ship, Capt. Nicholas Pateshall. He was afterwards re-appointed to the SHARK, but, being obliged to invalid in Feb. 1812 from a severe affection of the eyes, was next employed, from 13 of the following Oct. until 4 Oct. 1814, in the KRON PRINCESSINN MARIA, prison-ship at Portsmouth, Lieut.-Commander Thos. Burdwood, and ENTERPRIZE, Impress service-ship, on the river Thames, Capt. Thos. Richbell. His appointments have since been—3 Sept. 1825, to the command of the DOVE Revenue-vessel—15 July, 1829, to be Agent for Transports Afloat, the duties of which office he continued to fill, with the exception of a few months in 1830, until 1834—and 21 May, 1842, again to the Transport service, in which he is still employed. AGENTS—Pettet and Newton.

HARRISON. (LIEUTENANT, 1834.)

GEORGE HARRISON entered the Navy 21 July, 1816; passed his examination in 1824; and obtained his commission 6 Jan. 1834. He has since been on half-pay. Lieut. Harrison, the Senior of his rank on the List of 1834, is a Magistrate at Van Dieman's Land. AGENT—J. Hinxman.

HARRISON. (LIEUT., 1814. F-P., 21; H-P., 22.)

JOHN HARRISON entered the Navy, 26 Jan. 1804, as L. M., on board the IEFLEXIBLE 64, Capt. Thos. Bayley, stationed in the Downs. He became Midshipman, in June, 1805, of the ELEPHANT 74, Capt. Geo. Dundas, and in Sept. 1807, after an intermediate servitude in the North Sea and West Indies, he was appointed Master's Mate of the STATIRA 38, Capts. Robt. Howe Bromley and Edwin Henry Chamberlayne, under whom he cruized on the American and Spanish coasts until Feb. 1809. Joining, then, the VALIANT 74, Capts. John Bligh, Thos. Geo. Shortland, and Robt. Dudley Oliver, he witnessed the ensuing attack on the French shipping in Basque Roads, and was present, in the course of the same year, at the siege of Flushing. The VALIANT being ultimately ordered to North America, Mr. Harrison there removed, in Aug. 1813, to the ST. DOMINGO 74, bearing the flag of Sir John Borlase Warren. He obtained his commission 27 June, 1814, four years after he had passed his examination, and was subsequently, from 1817 until 1827, employed in command of different Telegraph stations on the Chatham and Portsmouth lines. He has not since held any official occupation.

HARRISON. (COMMANDER, 1842. F-P., 19; H-P., 5.)

JOHN GUSTAVUS HARRISON, born 19 Nov. 1810, is son of the Rev. Wm. Harrison, Vicar of Fareham, and Prebendary of Winchester Cathedral.

This officer entered the Navy, 13 March, 1823, as Fst.-cl. Vol., on board the RAMILLIES 74, commanded on the Home station by Capt. Edw. Brace, with whom he was afterwards employed for some time in the West Indies as Midshipman of the GANGES 84. While next attached, from Nov. 1824 until Jan. 1827, to the BOADICEA 42, Commodore Sir Jas. Brisbane, we find him serving in the East Indies and participating in many of the operations connected with the Burmese war. He then for a few months joined the JAVA 52, bearing the flag of Rear-Admiral Wm. Hall Gage, on the same station; where, until the close of 1829, he further served in the RAINBOW 28, Capt. Hon. Henry John Rous, and again in the JAVA, Capt. Wm. Fairbrother Carroll. In Feb. 1830, immediately on passing his examination, Mr. Harrison was appointed Mate of the VICTORY 104, flag-ship at Plymouth of Hon. Sir Robt. Stopford. He was next transferred in succession to the ST. VINCENT 120, and ASIA 84, bearing each the flag of Sir Thos. Foley, Commander-in-Chief at Portsmouth; and for several months of 1831 he cruized in the Channel on board the BRISK 3, Lieut.-Commander Edw. Harris Butterfield. During the four following years he appears to have been again employed in the East Indies, for twelve months of the time as Acting-Lieutenant, in the MELVILLE 74, flag-ship of Sir John Gore. Being at length promoted (from the BRITANNIA 120, bearing the flag at Portsmouth of Sir Philip Durham) to the rank of Lieutenant, by commission dated 3 April, 1837, he was appointed, on 10 of that month, to the LARNE 18, Capt. Patrick John Blake, and again ordered to the East Indies. He afterwards took part in the hostilities on the coast of China, where, in command of the LARNE's pinnace, he contributed, with much credit to himself, to the capture, 7 Jan. 1841, of the enemy's forts at Chuenpee, and the destruction of 11 powerful junks, forming the flower of the Celestial Navy—a service for which he was recommended to the notice of the Admiralty.* Mr. Harrison's next and last appointment was, 16 Oct. 1841, to the First-Lieutenancy of the CALLIOPE 26, Capt. Augustus Leopold Kuper, in which vessel he shared in the operations of 1842 up the Yang-tse-Kiang. His advancement to the rank he now holds took place on 23 Dec. in the latter year. It was made the reward of his services in China.†

Commander Harrison married, first, in 1836, Jane, daughter of the late W. Hindmarch, Esq., of Bishop-wearmouth; and, secondly, 19 July, 1843, a daughter of the late J. Pooke, Esq., of Fareham. AGENTS—Messrs. Stilwell.

HARRISON. (CAPTAIN, 1832. F-P., 24; H-P., 24.)

JOSEPH HARRISON is son of the late Lieut. Harrison, R.N., who died Agent for Transports at Plymouth in 1808.

This officer entered the Navy, 25 July, 1799, as Fst.-cl. Vol., on board the SPIDER, Lieut.-Commander Rich. Harrison, of which vessel, successively stationed in the Channel and Mediterranean, he became Midshipman 1 Jan. 1800. During several months of the short-lived peace we find him again employed in the Channel on board the OISEAU, Capt. John Philips. He afterwards, in March, 1803, joined the AURORA frigate, Capts. Micajah Malbon and John Wentworth Loring, with whom he served on the Newfoundland station until transferred, in Jan. 1805, to the PALLAS 42, Capt. Lord Cochrane. Proceeding subsequently to the West Indies in the MERLIN sloop, Capt. John Parkinson, he was there, after a short attachment to the NORTHUMBERLAND 74, flag-ship of Hon. Sir Alex. Cochrane, appointed Sub-Lieutenant, 11 Sept. 1806, of the GROUPER gun-brig. Attaining the full rank of Lieutenant 10 May, 1807, he afterwards joined, in that capacity—11 May, 1808, the EPERVIER brig, Capts. Hon. Michael De Courcy, John Bowker, Thos. Tudor Tucker, Alex. Nesbitt, Thos. Barclay, and Jas. Pattison Stewart, also in the West Indies—16 Nov. 1809, the ACHILLE 74, Capts. Sir Rich. King, Hon. Geo. Heneage Lawrence Dundas, and Aiskew Paffard Hollis, during an attachment of nearly six years to which ship, besides commanding a Spanish gun-vessel at the defence of Cadiz, he served off Toulon, on the coast of Sicily, in the Adriatic, off Cherbourg, and on the South American station—and, 22 Sept. 1815, and 23 Oct. 1817, to the INCONSTANT and SEMIRAMIS frigates, respectively employed off the coast of Africa and at Portsmouth, and both commanded by Sir Jas. Lucas Yeo. On the occasion of his promotion to the rank of Commander 14 Sept. 1818, Capt. Harrison was invested, *pro tem.*, with the charge of the CHALLENGER 28. He afterwards obtained command, 6 May, 1829, of the FAVORITE sloop, fitting for the coast of Africa,

* *Vide* Gaz. 1841, pp. 1221-2. † *V.* Gaz. 1842, p. 3821.

whence he returned home and was paid off in Aug. 1833—having been elevated to Post-rank on 9 of the previous Oct. He has not been since afloat.

Capt. Harrison married, 15 April, 1820, Catherine, daughter of Mr. Mottley, of Portsmouth.

HARROP. (LIEUT., 1815. F-P., 14; H-P., 25.)

DAVID HARROP entered the Navy, 9 Jan. 1808, as Fst.-cl. Vol., on board the SULTAN 74, Capt. Edw. Griffith, employed off Cadiz and in the Mediterranean; and in Aug. 1809 became Midshipman of the FORMIDABLE 98, Capts. Fras. Fayerman and Jas. Nicoll Morris. In Dec. 1811, after having served for some time on the Baltic and North Sea stations, in the latter ship and in the CHRISTIAN VII. 80, bearing the flag of Admiral Wm. Young, he joined the MANILLA 36, Capt. John Joyce, in which frigate he had the misfortune, on 28 of the following January, to be wrecked, on the Haak Sands, near the Texel. He was in consequence detained a prisoner of war until the peace of 1814, when, on his return to England, he was received on board the IMPREGNABLE 104, flag-ship at the time of H.R.H. the Duke of Clarence, but subsequently commanded off Lisbon by Capt. John Wentworth Loring. Mr. Harrop was next transferred in succession to the NIOBE 40, *armée en flûte*, Capt. Henry Collins Deacon, and CENTURION 50, and BULWARK 74, bearing each the flag of Rear-Admiral Edw. Griffith on the Halifax station; where, being created a Lieutenant of the last-mentioned ship, by commission dated 1 May, 1815, he continued to serve until paid off in Aug. of the same year. His succeeding appointments were—19 Oct. and 4 Dec. 1818, to the BRITOMART and WOLF sloops, both commanded by Capt. Bernard Yeoman, under whom, in 1821, he escorted George IV. to Ireland—early in 1822, to the HELICON 10, Capt. Wm. Robt. Dawkins, in which vessel he sailed for the West Indies—and, 4 Feb. 1824, to the VALOROUS 26, Capt. Jas. Murray. Since the paying off of the latter vessel, on her return from Jamaica to England, Mr. Harrop has been unemployed. AGENTS—Goode and Lawrence.

HARROW. (LIEUT., 1814. F-P., 9; H-P., 32.)

HENRY HARROW entered the Navy, 30 Sept. 1806, as Fst.-cl. Vol., on board the ADAMANT 50, Capts. John Stiles, John Fyffe, and Micajah Malbon, of which vessel, successively employed on the African and West India stations, he soon became Midshipman. From Dec. 1807 until Oct. 1813, we find him serving, chiefly in the West Indies, Baltic, and Channel, on board the GOELAN and FAVORITE sloops, both commanded by Capt. Benj. Clement, ROVER 18, Capt. Justice Finley, CRESCENT frigate, Capt. John Quilliam, and BOYNE 98, and VILLE DE PARIS 110, bearing each the flag of Sir Harry Burrard Neale. During his attachment to the FAVORITE, a period of nearly two years, he appears to have been very arduously employed, and to have passed through scenes of great mortality. On one occasion, we believe, he assisted by his indefatigable exertions in subduing an alarming fire which had broken out at Falmouth, on the north side of the island of Jamaica; and he was afterwards, while returning with convoy to England, present in a desperate hurricane, in which the same vessel lost her topmasts and sustained considerable injury. On leaving the VILLE DE PARIS, as above, he was appointed Acting-Lieutenant of the FERRET brig, commanded on the north coast of Spain by Capt. Wm. Ramsden, but he went back to the former ship in Feb. 1814, and continued to serve in her until promoted to the rank of Lieutenant 27 June following. Mr. Harrow, who was subsequently employed for 10 months in the West Indies and Channel on board the SWIFTSURE 74, Capt. Wm. Henry Webley, has been on half-pay since Aug. 1815.

He married, in April, 1834, Ann, youngest daughter of the late E. D. Bridger, Esq., of Barton Farm.

HARSTON. (COMMANDER, 1845.)

HENRY COOKE HARSTON entered the Navy 16 Aug. 1826; passed his examination in 1832; and, on his promotion to the rank of Lieutenant, 26 Oct. 1840, was appointed to the ALBERT steamer, Capt. Henry Dundas Trotter, employed on an expedition up the river Niger. Quitting the latter vessel towards the close of 1841, he was subsequently appointed First, 15 April, 1842, and 25 Jan. 1845, of the PHILOMEL surveying-vessel, and ECLAIR steam-sloop, commanded on the Brazilian and African stations by Capts. Bartholomew Jas. Sulivan and Walter Grimston Bucknall Estcourt. Having the good fortune to survive the ravages of the fearful disease which, in Sept. 1845, swept away the Captain and nearly the whole of the crew belonging to the ECLAIR, Mr. Harston, on his arrival home, was promoted to his present rank by commission bearing date 6 Dec. in the same year. He has since been on half-pay.

HART. (LIEUT., 1815. F-P., 9; H-P., 31.)

BENJAMIN HART entered the Navy, 9 Jan. 1807, as Clerk, on board the PETEREL sloop, Capt. John Lamborn, employed on the Jamaica station, whence he returned in Nov. 1808. Becoming Midshipman, in April, 1809, of the MINOTAUR 74, Capt. John Barrett, he continued to serve under that officer, on the Baltic station, until 22 Dec. 1810, when he had the misfortune to be wrecked, on the Haak Sands, near the Texel, and taken prisoner. On his release from captivity in May, 1814, he joined the LEVIATHAN 74, Capts. Adam Drummond and Thos. Briggs, in which ship we find him employed, off Lisbon and Cork and in the Mediterranean, until Nov. 1815. He then took up a commission, dated on 6 of the previous March, and has since been on half-pay.

HART. (COMMANDER, 1830.)

FRANCIS HART died in March, 1845.

This officer entered the Navy, 1 June, 1808, as Fst.-cl. Vol., on board the NIOBE 40, Capts. John Wentworth Loring and Wm. Augustus Montagu, in which frigate he served on the coasts of Ireland, Spain, Portugal, and France, also in the West Indies, and off Greenland and the Western Islands, until Dec. 1813; participating during that period, as Midshipman, in an attack made, 15 Nov. 1810, by Capt. Chas. Grant of the DIANA, upon the two French frigates *Amazone* and *Eliza*, protected by the fire of several strong batteries near Cherbourg, as likewise in the subsequent destruction of one of the same ships, near Barfleur, 25 March, 1811. Joining, next, the SAN JOSEF 110, bearing the successive flags of Rear-Admirals Edw. Jas. Foote and Sir Rich. King, he witnessed, on proceeding to the Mediterranean, the two partial actions with the Toulon fleet of 5 Nov. 1813 and 13 Feb. 1814. Towards the close of the latter year he sailed for the East Indies in the CORNWALLIS 74, bearing the flag of Sir Geo. Burlton, from which ship, commanded latterly by Capt. Robt. O'Brien, he removed, 9 April, 1816, as Acting-Lieutenant, to the LEDA 36, Commodore Geo. Sayer. He was officially promoted 20 Jan. 1818, and subsequently appointed—6 Oct. and 3 Dec. following, to the MINDEN 74, flag-ship of Sir Rich. King, and CONWAY 26, Capt. Edw. Barnard, also in the East Indies—3 Dec. 1821, to the SEMIRAMIS frigate, bearing the flag at Cork of Lord Colville—22 Sept. 1825, to the VOLAGE 28, Capts. Hon. Rich. Saunders Dundas and Michael Seymour, on the South American station—and, 22 Aug. 1829, to the ALLIGATOR 28, Capt. Chas. Philip Yorke, in the Mediterranean. He attained the rank of Commander 26 Nov. 1830, but was not afterwards employed. AGENTS—Goode and Lawrence.

HART. (LIEUT., 1827. F-P., 11; H-P., 16.)

GEORGE VAUGHAN HART is son of the late Gen. G. V. Hart, M.P. for co. Donegal, and Military Governor of Londonderry and Culmore forts.

This officer entered the Navy, in 1820, as Midshipman, on board the ROCHFORT 80, Capt. Chas.

Marsh Schomberg, bearing the flag of Sir Graham Moore on the Mediterranean station, where, until 1825, he also served in the MEDINA 20, Capt. Hawkins, and DISPATCH 18, Capt. Edw. Hinton Scott. He then became attached to the BRISK 10, Capt. Chas Hope, and, after cruizing for some time in the North Sea, was appointed to the CALLIOPE 10, Lieut.-Commander John Powney, tender to one of the Royal yachts, in which vessel, we believe, he attended the Lord High Admiral and his consort in their visit to the different dockyards in 1827. Being in consequence promoted to the rank of Lieutenant on 11 Aug. in the same year, he afterwards served in that capacity on board the GLOUCESTER 74, Capt. Henry Stuart, PRINCE REGENT 120, Capt. Hon. Geo. Poulett, and VICTOR 18, commanded on the Lisbon station by Capt. Alex. Ellice. He has been on half-pay since 1832.

Lieut. Hart is a Magistrate for co. Donegal. He married, in 1835, his cousin, Jane Maria, daughter of the Rev. G. V. Hart, Rector of Castlebar, and granddaughter of the late Very Rev. Dean Hume, of Derry, by whom he has issue six children. AGENTS—Messrs. Ommanney.

HART, Kt., K.C.H. (REAR-ADMIRAL, 1846. F-P., 21; H-P., 30.)

SIR HENRY HART, born in 1781, is son of Rich. Hart, Esq., of Uckfield, co. Sussex, and belongs to an ancient and very respectable family, being a descendant of Sir Percival Hart, of Lullingstone Castle, co. Kent, and a distant relative of the present Sir Percival Hart Dyke, Bart., of the same place.

This officer entered the Navy, in March, 1796, as Fst.-cl. Vol, on board the INDEFATIGABLE 46, Capt. Sir Edw. Pellew, and on 13 of the following Jan., being at the time in company with the AMAZON 36, took part in a very gallant engagement of 10 hours, which ended in the loss of the French 74-gun ship *Les Droits de l'Homme*, whose opposition had had the effect of wounding 19 of the INDEFATIGABLE'S people. Being next transferred with Sir Edw. Pellew to the IMPÉTUEUX 74, he had an opportunity of distinguishing himself during the blockade of Belleisle, besides attending the expedition of 1800 to Ferrol, where he commanded a flat-bottomed boat, and assisted at the cutting out from under the batteries in Vigo Bay of *La Guêpe*, a vessel of 22 guns, desperately defended. On 2 April, 1802, having just completed his time, Mr. Hart was appointed by ord Keith to a Lieutenancy in the MEDUSA 32, Capt. Sir John Gore—an act which the Admiralty confirmed on 12 of the next June. On becoming Senior of that frigate we find him making prize, in one of her boats, of a French privateer off Gibraltar; and afterwards contributing to the capture of three Spanish frigates laden with treasure, and the destruction of a fourth, near Cape St. Mary, 5 Oct 1804; as also, in Nov. following, to the detention of the *Matilda* 36, a ship laden with a cargo of quicksilver worth 200,000*l*. He ultimately accompanied Lord Cornwallis, as Governor-General, to India, where, in July, 1805, he became Flag-Lieutenant, in the CULLODEN 74, to his old friend Sir Edw. Pellew; by whom, in the course of 1807, he was successively appointed Acting-Captain of the TERPSICHORE, DUNCAN, CAROLINE, and FOX frigates. While in the CAROLINE, Capt. Hart (independently of the cutting out from the coast of Java, in open day, of a Dutch sloop-of-war of 14 guns and 75 men) was instrumental to the annihilation at Griessee, 11 Dec. 1807, of the dockyard and stores, and of all the men-of-war remaining to Holland in the East Indies; being on that occasion intrusted with the duty of landing the troops and of commanding the seamen on shore. He subsequently, in the same frigate, partook of an engagement with the batteries and gun-boats at the entrance of Manilla Bay. Being superseded in the Fox in 1808, Capt. Hart, whose second promotal commission had been dated 12 Oct. 1807, was next appointed, in 1810, to the command of the THRACIAN 18, in which sloop he cruized off Cherbourg until posted 1 Aug. 1811. His subsequent appointments were—10 Dec. 1813, to the CYRUS 20, in the Mediterranean—for some months in 1814, to the REVENGE 74, bearing the flag of his former Captain, Sir John Gore—27 Aug. 1818, to the SAPPHIRE 26, in which vessel, prior to invaliding in Aug. 1820, we find him watching, with high credit to himself, the British interests at Porto Bello, at a time when that place was attacked by a force under Sir Gregor M'Gregor in unison with the Mexican patriots, and next intrusted with a mission to the Governor-General of South America, who had been driven from Mexico to Carthagena—and, 30 Sept. 1831, to the MELVILLE, 74, again as Flag-Captain to Sir J. Gore, then just appointed Commander-in-Chief in the East Indies. While on that station Capt. Hart was placed in temporary command of the IMOGENE 28, and specially deputed to conduct an important negotiation with the Imaum of Muscat; on the happy issue of which he went to Bombay with a ship of 74 guns, intended as a present from that potentate to William IV., who added her to the British Navy under the name of IMAUM. The MELVILLE returned to England with the Earl of Clare, and was paid off 22 July, 1835; a few months after which period, on 25 Jan. and 23 Feb. 1836, Capt. Hart, in acknowledgment of his services, was invested with the insignia of a K.C.H., and awarded the honour of Knighthood. He obtained the Captain's Good-Service Pension 12 April, 1842; and on 1 Oct. 1846 he accepted the rank he now holds.

The Rear-Admiral was appointed, in 1845, a Commissioner of Greenwich Hospital. He married, in 1808, a daughter of Andrew Williams, Esq., of Southampton, sister of the present Lady Page Turner. AGENTS—Messrs. Halford and Co.

HARVEY. (COMMANDER, 1814. F-P., 16; H-P., 35.)

CHARLES BERNHARD HARVEY entered the Navy, in March, 1796, as Fst.-cl. Vol., on board the DIAMOND 38, Capts. Sir Wm. Sidney Smith and Sir Rich. John Strachan; the former of whom, after a servitude of more than two years in the Channel, he rejoined, in July, 1798, as Midshipman, in the TIGRE 74, on the Mediterranean station; where, during a continuance of four years, he witnessed the defence of Acre, and attended the expedition to Egypt. While next attached, between the summer of 1802 and the spring of 1806, to the MEDUSA 32 (of which vessel, commanded by the late Sir John Gore, he was confirmed a Lieutenant 13 Jan. 1803), Mr. Harvey, besides much active service in the Gut of Gibraltar, and ultimately escorting Lord Cornwallis as Governor-General to India, assisted at the capture of three Spanish frigates laden with treasure, and the destruction of a fourth, near Cape St. Mary, 5 Oct. 1804; as he also did at the detention, in the following month, of the *Matilda* 36, a frigate laden with a cargo of quicksilver worth 200,000*l*. He subsequently, on leaving the MEDUSA, joined, for a short period, the AIMABLE 32, Capt. Clotworthy Upton, lying at Portsmouth, and then the POMPÉE 74, in which ship, under the successive flags of Sir W. S. Smith and Hon. Hen. Edwin Stanhope, he attended the expeditions of 1807 to the Dardanells (where he contributed to the destruction of the Turkish shipping at Point Pesquies) and Copenhagen. With the exception of an interval in 1809-10, and of a few months in 1811 and again in 1812, during which he served with Capts. Hon. Anthony Maitland and Leveson Gower in the PIQUE 36 and ELIZABETH 74, Mr. Harvey was further employed with Sir W. S. Smith, from Feb. 1808 until promoted to the rank of Commander 19 July, 1814, in the FOUDROYANT 80 and HIBERNIA 120, on the Brazilian and Mediterranean stations—participating, in the latter ship, in Sir Edw. Pellew's partial actions with the Toulon fleet of 5 Nov. 1813 and 13 Feb. 1814. He has since been on half-pay. AGENTS—Messrs. Halford and Co.

HARVEY. (Captain, 1811. f-p., 24; h-p., 30.)
Edward Harvey, born 3 March, 1783, is third and youngest son of Capt. John Harvey, R.N. (who was mortally wounded in command of the Brunswick 74 on the glorious 1 June, 1794, and whose services are recorded by a public monument in Westminster Abbey), by Judith, daughter of Hen. Wise, Esq., of Sandwich, co. Kent. He is brother of the late Admiral Sir John Harvey, K.C.B.;* brother-in-law, as well as first-cousin, of the late Vice-Admiral Sir Thos. Harvey, K.C.B.; and uncle of Commanders Thos., Hen., and John Harvey, R.N., and of Commander Hen. Boteler, R.N.

This officer entered the Navy, in 1793, as Fst.-cl. Vol., on board the Brunswick 74, commanded by his father, on the books of which ship his name continued until 1794. Re-embarking, in April, 1796, on board the Prince of Wales 98, bearing the flag of his uncle, Rear-Admiral Hen. Harvey, and commanded by his brother, Capt. John Harvey, he proceeded to the West Indies, where, in Feb. 1797, we find him assisting, as Midshipman, at the capture of Trinidad, and the seizure and destruction of four line-of-battle ships and a frigate in Chaguaramas Bay. On his ensuing return to England in the Zebra sloop, Capt. John Hurst, he was received on board the Beaulieu 40, Capt. Fras. Fayerman, under whom, on 11 Oct. in the same year, he shared in the action off Camperdown. In 1798 he rejoined his brother in the Southampton 32, and, proceeding again to the West Indies, was present in that frigate, of which he soon became Acting-Lieutenant, at the reduction of the Danish and Swedish islands in March, 1801. He was confirmed, shortly after accompanying his relative into the Amphitrite 28, by commission dated 24 July, 1801, and afterwards appointed—14 Oct. following, to the Iris 32, Capts. Hon. Philip Wodehouse and David Atkins, stationed in the North Sea—21 Nov. 1802, to the Apollo 36, Capt. John Wm. Taylor Dixon, which frigate, with her Captain and 60 of the crew, was lost on the coast of Portugal 1 April, 1804, the remainder of the men being in a great measure saved through the instrumentality of Mr. Harvey—next, to the Amethyst 36 and Amaranthe 18, Capts. John Wm. Spranger and Edw. Pelham Brenton, on the Home station—17 Aug. 1805, to the Intrepid 64, Capt. Hon. P. Wodehouse, under whom he commanded a detachment of seamen and marines at the capture of the island of Capri, and was also present at the defence of Gaeta—and, 24 Nov. 1807, to the Trident 64, Capt. Campbell, lying at Chatham. Being promoted to the command, 7 Jan. 1808, of the Cephalus 18, and re-ordered to the Mediterranean, Capt. Harvey there succeeded in capturing four privateers and several small merchant-vessels, and, while, co-operating in the defence of Sicily, came frequently into contact with the gun-boats on the Calabrian shore. After having acted for a short time in command of the Cumberland 74, he was officially posted, 18 April, 1811, into the Topaze 36, which frigate he brought home from the Mediterranean and paid off 30 Jan. 1812. His succeeding appointments were—3 Nov. 1830, to the Undaunted 46, successively employed, until put out of commission in Feb. 1834, on the Cape of Good Hope, African, and East India stations, during which period he commanded a squadron at the time of an insurrection in the Isle of France—14 Feb. 1838, to the Malabar 74, attached to the force in North America and the West Indies—and, 1 Feb. 1839, to the Implacable 74 in the Mediterranean, where his services in 1840, on the coast of Syria and at the blockade of Alexandria, procured him a gold medal, sabre, and decoration from the Grand Turk. He has not been afloat since he was paid off, 31 Jan. 1842.

Capt. Harvey married Miss Cannon, of Sandwich, and by that lady has had issue six children. Agents—Messrs. Ommanney.

* Obtaining his first commission in 1790, Sir John Harvey served as a Lieutenant of the Iphigenia 32, at the hard-wrought capture, by the latter ship and the Penelope 32, of the French 36-gun frigate *Inconstante* 25 Nov. 1793. He commanded L'Actif sloop when that vessel foundered in Nov. 1794, and, being shortly afterwards posted, in honour of his father's valour in the action of the 1st of June, he subsequently officiated as Captain of the Prince of Wales 98 (employed, as above, at the reduction of Trinidad), Southampton 32, Agamemnon 64 (one of Sir Robert Calder's most distinguished ships in the action of 22 July, 1805), Canada 74, Leviathan 74 (part of the squadron under Sir George Martin at the destruction, in Oct. 1809, of the *Robuste* 80 and *Lion* 74), and Royal Sovereign 100. As a Rear-Admiral, which rank he attained in Dec. 1813, he commanded in chief in the Leeward Islands from 1816 until 1819. He was nominated a K.C.B. 6 June, 1833, and died an Admiral of the Blue, at Upper Deal, 17 Feb. 1837, in the 65th year of his age.

HARVEY. (Lieut., 1826. f-p., 15; h-p., 17.)
Edward Harvey was born 7 April, 1801.

This officer entered the Navy, 5 March, 1815, as Fst.-cl. Vol., on board the Pompée 74, commanded in the Mediterranean by Sir Jas. Athol Wood; and from the close of the same year until June, 1821, when he passed his examination, was chiefly employed as Midshipman in the Childers 16, Capts. Rich. Wales and Amos Freeman Westropp, and in the Wye and Dover, of 26 guns each, Capts. Geo. Wickens Willes and Arthur Batt Bingham, on the West India and Home stations. He next, until promoted to the rank of Lieutenant, 27 Oct. 1826, served off the coast of Ireland, at Plymouth, and in the West Indies, on board the Sappho 18, Capts. Hen. Wm. Bruce, Hon. Hen. John Rous, and Jenkin Jones, Britannia 120, flag-ship of Sir Alex. Cochrane, Diamond 38, Capt. Lord Napier, and Dartmouth and Hussar frigates, Capts. Hon. Jas. Ashley Maude and Geo. Morris. He continued for a further period of 12 months in the West Indies on board the Britomart 10, Capt. Fred. Chamier; and was lastly, from April, 1833, until April, 1838, employed in the Coast Guard.

Lieut. Harvey married, in 1836, Jane, daughter of the Rev. Jas. Morewood, of co. Antrim, by whom he has issue four children.

HARVEY. (Commander, 1846.)
Gillmore Harvey entered the Navy 5 March, 1817; passed his examination in 1823; and was promoted to a Lieutenancy, 27 Aug. 1828, in the Druid 46, Capt. Gawen Wm. Hamilton. He invalided from that frigate in 1829, and afterwards joined, on the Mediterranean station—23 Nov. 1836, the Minden 74, Capt. Alex. Renton Sharpe—26 Aug. 1840, as First, the Medea steam-sloop. Capt. Fred. Warden—and 19 June, 1845, in a similar capacity, the Hibernia 104, bearing the flag of Sir Wm. Parker. He served in those ships for a period of nearly 10 years, and on 9 Nov. 1846 was advanced to his present rank. Commander Harvey is now on half-pay. Agents—Messrs. Chard.

HARVEY. (Commander, 1841. f.p., 16; h-p., 9.)
Henry Harvey, born 28 April, 1812, is a younger brother of Commander Thos. Harvey, R.N.

This officer entered the Navy, 15 Dec. 1822, as Fst.-cl. Vol., on board the Gloucester 74, bearing the broad-pendant of Sir Edw. W. C. R. Owen on the West India station, where, previously to his return home in Jan. 1825, he was for some time lent, we believe, to the Hyperion 42, Capt. Geo. Fred. Rich. In Oct. 1826, after having been attached for three months to the Prince Regent 120, flag-ship of Sir Robt. Moorsom at the Nore, he joined the Asia 84, bearing the successive flags of Sir Edw. Codrington and Sir Pulteney Malcolm, under the former of whom he officiated as Signal-Midshipman at the battle of Navarin, 20 Oct. 1827. Removing in Nov. 1830 to the Undaunted 46, Capt. Edw. Harvey, he served for upwards of two years in that frigate at the Cape of Good Hope and on the coast of Africa—the last nine months (having passed his examination 9 May, 1831) as Mate in charge of a watch. We next, from March to Aug. 1833, find him acting in a similar capacity on board the Favorite 18, Capt. Joseph Harrison, also on the African station. He obtained his first commission 26 Feb. 1834, and was subsequently appointed—30 April, and 20 Dec. 1834, to the SALAMANDER steamer and VICTOR 16, Capts. Wm. Langford Castle and Rich. Crozier, from the latter of which vessels he invalided, at Sydney, N.S. Wales, in Feb. 1837—15 Jan. 1838, to the Coast Guard—and 18 March, 1839, to the WINCHESTER 50, bearing the flag of his father, Sir Thos. Harvey, on the North America and West India station. He was sent home from Halifax towards the close of 1840, in acting-command of the SERPENT 16, but then went back to the WINCHESTER, and continued in that ship as Additional and Flag-Lieutenant until promoted to the rank he now holds 28 May, 1841. He has since been unemployed.

Commander Harvey married, 19 July, 1838, Jane, daughter of Dr. Denison, of Margate. He was left a widower 9 May, 1842. AGENTS—Hallett and Robinson.

HARVEY. (LIEUTENANT, 1834.)

HENRY JOHN HARVEY is second son of Major-Gen. Sir John Harvey, K.C.B., Governor of Newfoundland.

This officer entered the Navy 4 Nov. 1824; served as Midshipman of the TALBOT 28, Capt. Hon. Fred. Spencer, at the battle of Navarin, 20 Oct. 1827; passed his examination in 1830; and obtained his commission 6 Jan. 1834. He was appointed, 5 July following, Supernumerary-Lieutenant of the WINCHESTER 52, flag-ship of Hon. Sir Thos. Bladen Capel, on the East India station; where, from 12 April, 1836, until paid off, at the close of 1838, he further served, in the RALEIGH 18, Capt. Michael Quin. He has since been on half-pay.

Lieut. Harvey has been for a long time private secretary to his father. He married, 1 Sept. 1842, Ella Louisa, eldest daughter of the Right Rev. Aubrey George, then Bishop of Newfoundland, and now of Jamaica.

HARVEY. (LIEUT., 1819. F-P., 8; H-P., 28.)

HENRY WISE HARVEY is youngest brother of Commander John Harvey, R.N.

This officer entered the Navy, 21 Sept. 1811, as Fst.-cl. Vol., on board the BELLEROPHON 74, Capt. Geo. Halsted, bearing the flag in the North Sea of Rear-Admiral John Ferrier, with whom he was transferred, in Feb. 1813, to the SCARBOROUGH 74. In March, 1814, he became Midshipman of the SPENCER 74, commanded in North America by Capt. Rich. Raggett; and he next, from Sept. 1815, until promoted to the rank of Lieutenant, 21 April, 1819, served in the ANTELOPE 50, flag-ship of his uncle Rear-Admiral John Harvey on the West India station. He has not been since afloat.

He married first, in July, 1821, Alice Holness, only daughter of Jas. Simpson, Esq., of London; and, secondly, Elizabeth, daughter of the late Geo. Leith, Esq , of Walmer, co. Kent. AGENTS—Messrs. Ommanney.

HARVEY. (COMMANDER, 1819. F-P., 15; H-P., 28.)

JOHN HARVEY, born 31 Dec. 1793, is eldest son of Henry Wise Harvey, Esq., of Harnden, co. Kent, whose father, the gallant Capt. John Harvey, R.N., was mortally wounded in command of the BRUNSWICK 74, in the action of 1 June, 1794. He is brother of Lieut. H. W. Harvey, R.N.; nephew of the present Capt. Edw. Harvey, R.N.; and brother-in-law of Commander Geo. Hilton, R.N.

This officer entered the Navy, 6 Sept. 1804, as Fst.-cl. Vol., on board the AGAMEMNON 64, commanded by his uncle Capt. John Harvey. In Sept. 1805, after having served on the north coast of Spain, and participated in Sir Robt. Calder's action, he accompanied his relative into the CANADA 74, and sailed for the West Indies, where he remained, until transferred, about Jan. 1808, to the ORION 74, commanded in the Baltic by Sir Archibald Collingwood Dickson. From June, 1809, until Dec. 1811, he again served with Capt. Harvey in the LEVIATHAN 74, and ROYAL SOVEREIGN 100, both attached to the force in the Mediterranean; on which station he aided in the LEVIATHAN in causing the self-destruction of the French ships-of-the-line *Robuste* and *Lion*, between Cette and Frontignan, 25 Oct. 1809. Until Sept. 1813, we next find Mr. Harvey employed on the North Sea and North American stations in the SCEPTRE and MARLBOROUGH 74's, Capts. Thos. Harvey and Robt. Honyman, and ST. DOMINGO 74, flag-ship of Sir John Borlase Warren. He was then appointed Acting-Lieutenant of the SUCCESS 32, *armée en flute*, Capt. Thos. Barclay, to which vessel the Admiralty confirmed him by commission dated 13 Nov. 1813. Joining next the EPERVIER, of 18 guns and 117 men, Capt. Rich. Walter Wales, Mr. Harvey continued to serve on the American coast until 29 April, 1814, when that vessel, after a severe action of an hour, and a loss of 23 men killed and wounded, became a shattered prize to the United States sloop *Peacock*, of 22 guns and 185 picked seamen, two only of whom appear to have been hurt. On regaining his liberty he was appointed, 22 Aug. 1815, to the ASTRÆA 36, Capt. Edw. Kittoe; and from 22 Aug. 1815, until advanced to his present rank, 2 April, 1819, he further served in the ANTELOPE 50, as Flag-Lieutenant to his uncle Rear-Admiral John Harvey, Commander-in-Chief in the Leeward Islands. He has since been on half-pay. AGENTS—Messrs. Ommanney.

HARVEY. (LIEUTENANT, 1841.)

ROBERT BEAZLEY HARVEY entered the Navy 2 March, 1827; passed his examination 27 July, 1833; and obtained his first commission 23 Nov. 1841. He has been serving since 10 June, 1842, in the WOLF 18, Capts. Courtenay Osborn Hayes, Arthur Vyner, Geo. Evan Davis, and Jas. Alex. Gordon, on the East India station. AGENTS—Messrs. Halford and Co.

HARVEY. (COMMANDER, 1840. F-P. 17; H-P., 8.)

THOMAS HARVEY, born in Dec. 1810, at Walmer, co. Kent, is eldest son of the late Vice-Admiral of the White Sir Thos. Harvey, K.C.B.,* by Sarah, youngest daughter of his grand-uncle Capt. John Harvey, R.N., who was mortally wounded in command of the BRUNSWICK 74, in the action of 1 June, 1794. He is grandson of the late Admiral Sir Henry Harvey, K.B.;† brother of Commander Henry Harvey, R.N.; nephew, maternally, of Capt. Edw. Harvey, R.N.; and first-cousin of Commander John Harvey, R.N.

This officer entered the Navy, 16 Dec. 1822, as Fst.-cl. Vol., on board the GLOUCESTER 74, bearing the broad pendant in the West Indies of Sir Edw. W. C. R. Owen. He continued to serve on that station, part of the time in the TYNE 28, and HELICON 10, Capts. John Walter Roberts and Wm. Robt. Dawkins, until Feb. 1824; and from the following May until Dec. 1825, he was employed as a student at the Royal Naval College. Re-em-

* Sir Thomas Harvey served as Master's Mate of the RAMILLIES 74, in Lord Howe's action 1 June, 1794, and as Lieutenant of the PRINCE OF WALES in Lord Bridport's engagement 23 June, 1795. Immediately after the reduction of Trinidad, where he had commanded the PELICAN sloop, he was advanced to Post-rank 27 March, 1797; subsequently to which he officiated as Captain of the PRINCE OF WALES 98, CONCORDE, LAPWING, and UNITÉ frigates, STANDARD 64, and MAJESTIC, SCEPTRE, and NORTHUMBERLAND 74's. He was present in the PRINCE OF WALES at the attack on Puerto Rico in April, 1797; in the LAPWING in the expedition of 1799 against the Dutch colony of Surinam; in the UNITÉ at the reduction of the Danish and Swedish islands in 1801; and in the STANDARD at the passage of the Dardanells in Feb. 1807. He was nominated a C.B in 1815, a Colonel of Marines and a Rear-Admiral in 1821, a K.C.B. in 1833, and a Vice-Admiral in 1837. He died Commander-in-Chief on the North America and West India station 28 May, 1841, in his 66th year, and was buried at Bermuda.

† Sir Henry Harvey commanded the RAMILLIES 74, on the 1st of June, 1794; captured, in conjunction with Sir Ralph Abercromby, the Spanish island of Trinidad in Feb. 1797; and died an Admiral of the White 28 Dec. 1810.

barking, then, as Midshipman, on board the Dryad 42, Capts. Hon. Robt. Rodney and Hon. Geo. Alfred Crofton, he proceeded, after cruizing for a period on the Channel and Irish stations, to the Mediterranean, where, and in South America, he further, until Dec. 1829, served on board the Isis 50, Commodore Sir Thos. Staines, Camelion 10, Capt. Christ. Wyvill, Philomel 10, Capt. Edw. Hawes, Seringapatam 46, Capt. Hon. Wm. Waldegrave, and Warspite 76, flag-ship of Rear-Admiral Thos. Baker. On 24 of the month last-mentioned we find him promoted to a Lieutenancy in the Tribune 42, Capt. John Alex. Duntze, with whom he served, latterly in the North Sea, until paid off in Dec. 1831. He subsequently joined—4 Dec. 1833, the Asia 84, flag-ship of Rear-Admiral Parker, off Lisbon, whence he returned in June, 1834—28 July, 1835, the Russell 74, Capt. Sir Wm. Henry Dillon, employed on the latter station, and also in the Mediterranean, where, on one occasion, he took charge of the Ariadne from Malta to Alexandria, and on another was lent to the Portland 50, Capt. David Price — and, in the course of 1839, the Inconstant 36, and Winchester 50, as Flag-Lieutenant, in each ship to his father, on the North America and West India station. He was there promoted to the command, 6 Nov. 1840, of the Racer 16, in which sloop he remained until put out of commission in Oct. 1842. He has not been since afloat.

Commander Harvey married, 9 April, 1844, Christian Bargreve, eldest daughter of Wm. Bridger, Esq., of Eastry Court, co. Kent. Agents—Hallett and Robinson.

HARWARD. (Capt., 1809. f-p., 14; h-p., 36.)

Richard Harward died 2 May, 1845, at Geneva.

This officer entered the Navy, 5 June, 1795, as Fst.-cl. Vol., on board the Cæsar 80, Capts. Chas. Edm. Nugent and Roddam Home, of which ship, successively employed in the Channel and North Sea, he soon became Midshipman. Proceeding in 1798 to the Mediterranean in the Perseus, Capts. Jas. Oswald and Henry Compton, he assisted in the following year at the bombardment of Alexandria, and served in the ship's launch in action with an enemy's flotilla in the Bay of Naples. He subsequently became Acting-Lieutenant of the Blanche 36, Capt. Graham Eden Hamond, and, on 3 Sept. 1801, after participating in the victory gained by Lord Nelson at Copenhagen, was officially promoted. His next appointments were—26 March, 1803, to the Plantagenet 74, Capts. E. Hamond, Hon. Michael De Courcy, and Fras. Pender, on the Home station—17 Sept. 1804, to the Endymion 40, Capt. Hon. Chas. Paget—in 1805, to the command of the Netley schooner and Swinger gun-brig, in the former of which vessels he conveyed despatches to the West Indies—and, in Nov. 1805, to the Northumberland 74, bearing the flag of Rear-Admiral Hon. Alex. Cochrane. For his conduct as First-Lieutenant of the latter ship in the action off St. Domingo, Mr. Harward was promoted to the rank of Commander 2 April, 1806. He subsequently joined, 2 March, 1808, the Delphinen 18, but, that sloop being unfortunately wrecked off the coast of Holland 4 Aug. following, he was next appointed, in Oct. of the same year, to the Parthian 10; in which vessel we find him capturing *La Nouvelle Gironde*, a notorious privateer of 14 guns and 58 men,* and ultimately attending the expedition to the Walcheren. Capt. Harward, whose Post-commission bore date 31 July, 1809, was lastly employed, from June, 1810, to June, 1812, as Flag-Captain to Sir Edw. Pellew in the Christian VII. 00, and Caledonia 120, on the Mediterranean station.

Capt. Harward was Deputy-Lieutenant for co. Gloucester. He married, first, 11 Jan. 1810, Julia, youngest daughter of Admiral the late Lord Exmouth; and, that lady dying in 1831, secondly, in 1834, Julia, daughter of Admiral Sir Lawrence Wm. Halsted, G.C.B., and granddaughter of the above nobleman.

---

* *Vide* Gaz. 1809, p. 659.

HASKOLL. (Commander, 1841. f-p., 16; h-p., 22.)

William Haskoll was born 9 Oct. 1792.

This officer entered the Navy, 1 March, 1809, as Fst.-cl. Vol., on board the Victorious 74, Capts. Graham Eden Hamond and John Talbot, under whom he served on the Home, Mediterranean, and North American stations, chiefly as Midshipman, until Aug. 1814. He attended, during that period, the expedition to the Walcheren; was much employed against the enemy's flotilla and batteries at the defence of Sicily, where, on 18 Sept. 1810, a large body of troops having landed and been defeated near Stefano, he succeeded in the ship's pinnace in capturing, after some resistance, a boat with 15 soldiers besides the crew; partook, next, of many active operations in the Adriatic, omitting however the celebrated capture of the French 74-gun ship *Rivoli*, at which period he was in temporary charge of a Signal station on the island of Lissa; commanded, on proceeding to the American station, a tender in Hampton Roads and up James River; was captured in a prize by a privateer, in May, 1814, and detained for a short time in captivity; and on one or two occasions was very nearly wrecked. From Aug. 1814 until Jan. 1817, Mr. Haskoll further served, as Midshipman and Master's Mate, in the Sultan 74, Capt. John West (which ship lost her mizenmast, fore and main topmasts, mainyard, and quarter and stern boats, in a heavy gale on the south bank of Newfoundland 16 Feb. 1815), and Horatio 38, commanded on the Channel and East India stations by Capt. Wm. Henry Dillon. His health then obliging him to remain on shore, he did not again go afloat until April, 1824, when he rejoined his old Captain, Hamond, in the Wellesley 74. In the early part of 1825 he was transferred to the Owen Glendower 42, bearing the broad pendant at the Cape of Good Hope of Rear-Admiral Hood Hanway Christian, by whom, on 20 June, 1826, he was invested, as Acting-Supernumerary-Lieutenant, with the command of the colonial brig Wizard, in which vessel we find him cruizing on the coast of Madagascar and among the Seychelle Islands. He was subsequently lent for a short time to the Sparrowhawk 18, Capt. Jas. Polkinghorne, employed on the same station; and, on 18 Dec. 1826 (upwards of 11 years after he had passed his examination), he was officially promoted to the rank of Lieutenant. On leaving the Owen Glendower, about April, 1828, Mr. Haskoll served for a term of five months, until he was again compelled to invalid, on board the Helicon 10, Capt. Robt. Henry Stanhope. His next and last appointment was, 17 Feb. 1838, as First, to the Cruizer 16, Capts. Rich. Henry King and Henry Wells Giffard, fitting for the East India station, where, besides attending an expedition to the mouths of the Indus, he assisted at the capture of Aden. He afterwards, in 1840, accompanied the armament to China, and in the course of the same year was present at the capture of Chusan and the blockade of Ningpo. On the return of the Cruizer with Sir Hugh Gough to China, after having been sent in charge of despatches to Calcutta, Mr. Haskoll, it appears, commanded the second division of boats at the taking of Fort Macao 13 March, 1841, and assisted in the two series of operations against Canton—having charge, during the second, of the gun-boats at the capture, on 25 May, of the fort below the Folly.* He invalided 30 June, 1841, and on his arrival in England found that he had been promoted to the rank of Commander by commission dated 8 of that month. Agent—W. H. B. Barwis.

HAST. (Lieut., 1826. f-p., 18; h-p., 10.)

Philip Hast entered the Navy 11 April, 1819; passed his examination in 1825; and was promoted, 10 July, 1826, to a Lieutenancy in the Pylades sloop, Capt. Geo. Vernon Jackson, on the West India station. His subsequent appointments were, 11 Aug. 1827, to the Procris 18, Capts. Hon. Wm.

* *Vide* Gaz. 1841, pp. 1503-5, 2505.

Waldegrave and Chas. Henry Paget, employed off the coast of Ireland—16 March, 1830, to the WELLESLEY 74, Capt. Fred. Lewis Maitland—16 Aug. 1831, to the WARSPITE 76, Capt. Chas. Talbot, in South America—4 June, 1832, to the RATTLESNAKE 28, Capt. Chas. Graham, in which vessel he came home from the latter station and was paid off in Nov. 1833—17 Nov. 1834 and 20 April, 1835, as First, to the PIQUE 36, and CHAMPION 18, Capts. Hon. Henry John Rous, Robert Fair, and Geo. St. Vincent King, employed off Lisbon and in the West Indies—and, 18 July, 1837, to the command of the PICKLE schooner, on the North America and West India station. He was superseded from the last-named vessel in March, 1839, and has since been on half-pay.

Lieut. Hast has for several years been in command of a steamer belonging to the Royal West India Mail Packet Company. He married, 22 Aug. 1840, Mary, daughter of John Warrington, Esq., by whom he has issue. AGENT—John P. Muspratt.

HASTINGS. (CAPTAIN, 1840. F-P., 19; H-P., 21.)

FRANCIS DECIMUS HASTINGS entered the Navy, 19 Aug. 1807, as Third-cl. Vol., on board the TÉMÉRAIRE 98, Capts. Sir Chas. Hamilton and Edw. Sneyd Clay, successively stationed in the Channel and Baltic. In June, 1809, having attained the rating of Midshipman a few months previously, he removed to the AMETHYST 36, Capt. Jacob Walton, with whom he appears to have been employed on Home service until wrecked in Plymouth Sound 16 Feb. 1811. He then joined, for a short period, the ACASTA 40, Capt. Alex. Robt. Kerr; after which we find him, until Aug. 1815, employed, on the Spanish, North American, Jamaica, and Home stations, latterly as Master's Mate, in the IRIS 38, Capt. Hood Hanway Christian, ST. DOMINGO 74, flag-ship of Sir John Borlase Warren, EMULOUS brig, Capt. Wm. M'Kenzie Godfrey, and ARGO 44, and VILLE DE PARIS 110, bearing the flags of Rear-Admiral Wm. Brown and Lord Keith. With the exception of a few months in 1818-19, and until officially promoted on 18 Nov. in the latter year, Mr. Hastings next served, alternately as Acting-Lieutenant and Admiralty Midshipman, on board the CHARWELL sloop, Capt. Allen Otty, ICARUS 10, Capt. Hon. Chas. Orlando Bridgeman, and CARNATION 18, Capts. Henry Shiffner, Wm. Nugent Glascock, and Roger Hall. His succeeding appointments were, as First-Lieutenant—14 April, 1831, to the STAG 46, Capts. Sir Edw. Thos. Troubridge and Nich. Lockyer, on the Lisbon station, where he remained until superseded in Aug. 1834—and 31 Jan. 1835, to the EXCELLENT gunnery-ship at Portsmouth, Capt. Thos. Hastings. Being awarded a second promotal commission 10 Jan. 1837, he was nominated, 25 July following, Second-Captain of the EDINBURGH 72, Capt. Wm. Wilmott Henderson, with whom, after again serving with the force off Lisbon, he proceeded to the Mediterranean. For his conduct in the operations on the coast of Syria, where he displayed the greatest coolness and gallantry in command of the boats of the latter ship and of the HASTINGS 72, in an attempt made to remove the powder from the castle at Beyrout, and was slightly wounded at the bombardment of St. Jean d'Acre, Capt. Hastings was advanced to the rank he now holds 4 Nov. 1840.* He has since been unemployed.

Capt. Hastings was left a widower 31 July, 1846.

HASTINGS. (CAPTAIN, 1845. F-P., 18; H-P., 5.)

THE HONOURABLE GEORGE FOWLER HASTINGS, born 28 Nov. 1813, is second son (by Frances, third daughter of the Rev. Rich. Chaloner Cobb, Rector of Great Marlow, co. Bucks) of Hans Francis, 11th Earl of Huntingdon, a Captain in the R.N. (1824), who was for some time Governor of Dominica, and died 9 Dec. 1828. He is brother of the present Earl; and brother-in-law of Commanders Henry Parker and Chas. Calmady Dent, R.N.

* *Vide* Gaz. 1840, pp. 2609, 2901.

This officer entered the Navy 3 Sept. 1824; passed his examination 7 Jan. 1832; and was promoted, 7 Jan. 1833, to the rank of Lieutenant. His appointments in the latter capacity were—25 June, 1832, to the EXCELLENT gunnery-ship at Portsmouth, Capt. Thos. Hastings—13 May, 1834, to the REVENGE 74, commanded in the Mediterranean by Capt. Wm. Elliott—and, 8 Sept. 1837, as First, to the RHADAMANTHUS steam-vessel, Capt. Arthur Wakefield, on the same station. Obtaining a second promotal commission 30 June, 1838, he was nominated, 5 Jan. 1839, to an Inspectorship in the Coast Guard, and, 16 Aug. 1841, to the command of the HARLEQUIN 16. While in that sloop, Capt. Hastings, besides sharing in the closing operations of the Chinese war, acquired the public thanks of the Commander-in-Chief for his conduct in leading her boats, in conjunction with those of the WANDERER and DIANA, in an attack on the piratical towns of Murdoo and Quallo Batto, in the island of Sumatra. He was promoted to the rank of Captain, on the paying off of the HARLEQUIN, 31 Jan. 1845; and has since been unemployed. AGENTS—Coplands and Burnett.

HASTINGS, Kt. (CAPTAIN, 1830. F-P., 32; H-P., 12.)

SIR THOMAS HASTINGS, born 3 July, 1790, is eldest son of the Rev. Jas. Hastings, Rector and Impropriator of the living of Martley, and Patron of Areley Regis, co. Worcester. His family, of which the celebrated Warren Hastings was the head, is a branch of that of Hastings of Dalesford, in the latter shire, and of Yelford Hastings, co. Oxford.

This officer entered the Navy, in Sept. 1803, as Fst.-cl. Vol., on board the PRINCESS ROYAL 98, commanded in the Channel by Capts. Jas. Vashon, Herbert Sawyer, Dan. Oliver Guion, and Robt. Carthew Reynolds; and, from Oct. 1804 until Sept. 1807, served, as Midshipman, on the latter and on the north coast of Spain, Cadiz, and West India stations, in the ILLUSTRIOUS 74, Capts. Sir Chas. Hamilton, Michael Seymour, Wm. Shield, and Wm. Robt. Broughton. His name, during the two following years, was successively borne on the books of the SALVADOR DEL MUNDO, Capt. Isaac Wolley, lying at Plymouth, TEXEL and ARDENT 64's, flag-ships at Leith of his former Captain, the late Admiral Vashon, and LEYDEN 64, Capt. Thos. Ussher. As a reward for his conduct in command of a gun-boat at the siege of Flushing, Mr. Hastings was promoted, 17 Jan. 1810, to a Lieutenancy in the BADGER 10, Capt. John Lampen Manley, under whom we understand he assisted, as First of that vessel, in causing the destruction, off the river Ems, of the French privateer *La Comtesse d'Emerieau* of 11 guns and 110 men. His succeeding appointments were—7 June, 1811, to the HYACINTH 26, Capts. Thos. Ussher and Alex. Renton Sharpe—7 April, 1813, to the UNDAUNTED 38, Capts. Thos. Ussher and Chas. Thurlow Smith, in which frigate he continued until Nov. 1815—28 June, 1817, to the ICARUS 10, Capt. Hon. Chas. Orlando Bridgeman, fitting for the South American station, whence he invalided in Jan. 1819—and 27 Oct. 1821, as Senior, to the EURYALUS frigate, Capt. Augustus Wm. Jas. Clifford, attached to the force in the Mediterranean. On the night of 29 April, 1812, we find Mr. Hastings commanding the HYACINTH's pinnace, under Capt. Ussher, and acquiring the greatest praise for his undaunted courage, in a brilliant boat-attack on the enemy's privateers and batteries in the mole of Malaga; an enterprise which, although partially successful, terminated in a loss to the British, out of 149 officers and men, of 15 killed and 53 wounded. He also, in the course of the following month, assisted at the reduction of the strong castle of Almuñecar; and, on 18 Aug. 1813, he served in the boats of the UNDAUNTED and of a small squadron in a very gallant attack made on the batteries at Cassis, where, after sustaining a loss of 4 men killed and 16 wounded, the British, in four hours, succeeded in capturing three heavy gun-boats, and 26 vessels laden with merchandise.

On 9 Nov. 1813 he was again in the boats at the taking of a vigorously-defended tower at Port Nouvelle, and the destruction of 7 French vessels lying there under the protection of several batteries; after which, in April, 1814, he participated, as First-Lieutenant, in the honour of conveying Napoleon Buonaparte from Frejus to Elba. On the latter occasion, and when within four or five miles of the harbour of Porto Ferrajo, Mr. Hastings went on shore with the foreign ministers, as one of the commissioners for taking possession of the island, and making the proper arrangements for the reception of its future sovereign. During the war of a Hundred Days this officer further presents himself to our notice by his conspicuous exertions in the Undaunted's boats in preventing supplies from being thrown into Ancona; in destroying different armed towers; in capturing a Neapolitan flotilla, consisting of two schooners and nine gun-boats, protected by the fortress of Barletta; and in erecting, with wonderful celerity, a battery on the island of Tremiti, in the Adriatic, which his prompt and skilful measures soon forced to surrender. When subsequently in the Euryalus, Mr. Hastings was employed at the blockade of Algiers, preparatory to the concessions made by the Dey to Sir Harry Burrard Neale in 1824. On 9 May, 1825, having earned a reputation for merit of a very high order, he was at length advanced to the rank of Commander; and on 4 Nov. 1828 he was appointed to the Ferret sloop; in which vessel he appears to have been again employed for a period of 10 weeks off Algiers, with the view of observing and reporting to the British Government the proceedings of the French in their preparations for the attack and capture of that place; a delicate and important service, of which he acquitted himself to the high satisfaction of his Commander-in-Chief, Sir Pulteney Malcolm. Capt. Hastings, who continued in the Ferret until posted, 22 July, 1830, afterwards, from 13 April, 1832, until Aug. 1845, commanded the Excellent gunnery-ship at Portsmouth, where, during the last six years, he simultaneously discharged the duties of Captain Superintendent of the Royal Naval College.

In compliment to the professional and scientific attainments of Capt. Hastings, the honour of Knighthood was, at the request of the Admiralty, conferred on him 5 June, 1839. On leaving the Excellent he was appointed Storekeeper to the Ordnance; and he is also a Magistrate and Deputy-Lieutenant for co. Hereford. He married, 12 May, 1827, Louisa Elizabeth, sister of the Dean of Exeter, and daughter of Thos. Humphrey Lowe, Esq., of Bromsgrove, by Lucy, eldest daughter and co-heir of Thos. Hill, Esq., of Court of Hill, co. Salop, M.P. for Leominster. Agents—Messrs. Ommanney.

HASWELL. (Lieutenant, 1827.)

Charles Symes Haswell passed his examination in 1821; obtained his commission 4 April, 1827; and was appointed, 7 Aug. following, to the Bustard sloop, commanded in the West Indies by Capt. Geo. Sidney Smith. With the exception of a command, from 6 Oct. 1840 until Sept. 1845, of the Fox Revenue-vessel, Mr. Haswell has had charge, since 13 Sept. 1832, of a station in the Coast Guard.

He is married, and has issue.

HASWELL. (Lieut., 1815. f-p., 11; h-p., 31.)

Edward Haswell entered the Navy, in Feb. 1805, as Ordinary, on board the Centaur 74, bearing the broad pendant in the West Indies of Sir Sam. Hood. Being appointed Midshipman, in the early part of the following year, of the Indefatigable 46, Capts. John Tremayne Rodd, Henry Edw. Reginald Baker, John Broughton, and Edw. Tucker, he continued to serve in that frigate, on the Bay of Biscay and Channel stations, until June, 1812; in the course of which, and of the following year, he was successively transferred with Capt. Tucker to a Master's Mateship in the Cornwall 74, and Inconstant 36—the latter ship attached to the force in South America. He became Acting-Lieutenant, 18 June, 1814, of the Elk 18, Capt. John Bartholomew Hoar Curran, on the East India station, where he was confirmed 10 Feb. 1815. He went on half-pay in 1816, and has not been since afloat.

HASWELL. (Lieut., 1815. f-p., 12; h-p., 32.)

John Dawes Haswell entered the Navy, 15 July, 1803, as Fst.-cl. Vol., on board the Dreadnought 98, Capts. Edw. Brace, John Child Purvis, Robt. Carthew Reynolds, Geo. Reynolds, Edw. Rotherham, and John Conn, flag-ship for some time of Admirals Hon. Wm. Cornwallis and Cuthbert Collingwood, in which he fought at Trafalgar in the capacity of Midshipman. Between Aug. 1806 and his promotion to the rank of Lieutenant, 10 Feb. 1815, he served, chiefly as Master's Mate, in the Révolutionnaire 38, Capt. Chas. Fielding, Defiance 74, Capt. Hon. Henry Hotham, Royal George 100, bearing the flag of Sir John Duckworth, San Josef 110, Hibernia 120, Armide 38, and Dublin 50, all commanded by Capt. Rich. Dalling Dunn, and Statira 38, Capts. Jas. Nash and Thos. Brown, on the Channel, Spanish, and Halifax stations. He has since been on half-pay.

HASWELL. (Commander, 1830.)

William Henry Haswell is son of Mr. Haswell, R.N., who died suddenly, in the 77th year of his age, 5 Jan. 1831.

This officer entered the Navy, 1 Feb. 1800, as Ordinary, on board the Royal William, guard-ship at Spithead, and in the course of the following year was employed off Cadiz in the Dreadnought 98, Capt. Jas. Vashon. In Nov. 1802, after an employment of nearly 12 months, as Midshipman, in the Hydra 38, Capt. Hon. Chas. Paget, he joined the Phœbe 36, Capts. Hon. Thos. Bladen Capel and Jas. Oswald, under the former of whom it was his fortune to be present at the battle of Trafalgar, 21 Oct. 1805. Removing, in March, 1806, to the Endymion 40, Capts. Edw. Durnford King, and Hon. T. B. Capel, he accompanied the expedition of 1807 to the Dardanells, where, we believe, he was taken prisoner, and detained on board the Turkish Admiral's ship until he had participated in two general actions with the Russian fleet, by which he was re-captured. He was ultimately, on 28 Feb. 1809, promoted to a Lieutenancy in the Impétueux 74, Capt. John Lawford, and, being shortly afterwards appointed to the Revenge 74, Capts. Hon. C. Paget and John Nash, was attached to the force sent against Flushing; during the operations connected with the siege of which place he appears to have had charge of an armed transport. We afterwards, until Aug. 1814, find him commanding the Landrail, and serving, again with Capt. Paget, on board the Superb 74, off the coasts of Ireland, France, and America. He obtained an appointment in the Coast Guard 1 Nov. 1820; the command of the Bramble 10 May, 1827; the rank he now holds 22 July, 1830; a three-years' Inspectorship in the Coast Guard 20 March, 1832; and the command, 31 Oct. 1846, of the Poictiers 72, guard-ship at Chatham—an appointment he still enjoys.

Commander Haswell has been twice married—the second time, 9 Feb. 1839, to Frances Maria, third daughter of Lieut. Wm. Taylor, R.N. (1794), of Greenwich Hospital, who died in 1835. He has issue. Agents—Hallett and Robinson.

HASWELL. (Lieutenant, 1845.)

William Henry Haswell entered the Navy in 1830; passed his examination 2 May, 1838; and served, as Mate, on the Mediterranean, Home, and South American stations, in the Talbot 26, Capt. Hon. Robt. Fanshawe Stopford (under whom he was slightly wounded at the bombardment of St. Jean d'Acre, 3 Nov. 1840*), Agincourt 72 (fitting for the flag of Sir Thos. John Cochrane), St. Vincent 120, flag-ship of Sir Chas. Rowley, and Dolphin

* *V.* Gaz. 1840, p. 2901.

brigantine, Lieut.-Commanders Wm. O'Bryen Hoare and Reginald Thos. John Levinge. He was appointed, on being advanced to the rank of Lieutenant, 8 Aug. 1845, Additional of the VERNON 50, bearing the flag on the station last named of Rear-Admiral Sam. Hood Inglefield; and, since 3 Aug. 1846, has been employed on the coast of Africa in the DEVASTATION and PENELOPE steamers, Commodore Sir Chas. Hotham.

HATHORN. (CAPTAIN, 1840.)

GEORGE HATHORN, born 17 Nov. 1803, is son of Geo. Hathorn, Esq., of Brunswick Square, London, and is of the family of Hathorn, of Castle Wigg, co. Wigtoun, N.B. He is brother-in-law of Commander Matt. Dixon, R.N.

This officer entered the Navy, 9 Aug. 1817, on board the ACTIVE 46, Capt. Sir Jas. Alex. Gordon; passed his examination in 1824; obtained his first commission 30 April, 1827; and was afterwards appointed, 22 Jan. 1829, and 25 Nov. 1833, to the VANGUARD 76, Capts. Wm. Henry Shirreff, Sam. Burgess, and Chas. Talbot, and CANOPUS 84, Capt. Hon. Josceline Percy, on the South American and Mediterranean stations. Having officiated for a considerable time as First-Lieutenant of those ships, he was advanced, 10 Jan. 1837, to the rank of Commander; and, on 9 April, 1839, he was nominated Second-Captain of the BENBOW 72, Capt. Houston Stewart; his services in which ship on the coast of Syria and at the bombardment of St. Jean d'Acre procured him a Post-commission dated 4 Nov. 1840. He has since been on half-pay.

Capt. Hathorn married, 28 Sept. 1843, Mary Isabella, eldest daughter of the Rev. Wm. M'Douall, Vicar of Luton and Canon of Peterborough, and grand-niece of the late Earl of Dumfries, by whom he has issue. AGENTS—Messrs. Ommanney.

HATTON, M.P. (CAPTAIN, 1812. F-P., 11; H-P., 37.)

VILLIERS FRANCIS HATTON, born 20 Aug. 1787, at Dromana, co. Waterford, is eldest son of Geo. Hatton, Esq., formerly M.P. for Lisburne, co. Antrim, by Lady Isabella Rachel Seymour Conway, sixth daughter of Francis, first Marquess of Hertford. He is brother of Commander Henry John Hatton, R.N. (1815), a Gentleman Usher of the Privy Chamber, who died 21 Dec. 1831; nephew of the late Major-General John Hatton; and cousin of the present Marquess of Londonderry. His uncle, the late Henry Hatton, Esq., of Clonard, co. Wexford, married the eldest daughter of the second Earl of Arran; which lady espoused, a second time, the first Marquess of Abercorn.

This officer entered the Navy, in 1799, as Fst.-cl. Vol., on board the SANS PAREIL 80, Capt. Chas. Vinicombe Penrose, bearing the flag in the Channel and West Indies of his uncle, Lord Hugh Seymour. In 1801 he removed, as Midshipman, with Capt. Penrose to the CARNATIC 74; and he next, between 1802 and 1805, served, on the Home and East India stations, in the ST. FIORENZO 36, Capt. Joseph Bingham, and TRIDENT 64, flag-ship of Vice-Admiral Peter Rainier, by whom he was then appointed Lieutenant of the GRAMPUS 50, Capt. Thos. Gordon Caulfeild. Returning home shortly after his official promotion, which took place 31 Jan. 1806, he joined, on 3 Oct. in that year, the SEAGULL, of 16 guns and 94 men, Capt. Robt. Cathcart, and proceeded to the North Sea station, where he displayed great zeal for the public service, and often cruized, for days at a time, in an open boat for the suppression of smuggling. On 19 June, 1808, being at the time First of the SEAGULL, Mr. Hatton participated, off the coast of Norway, in a desperate and heroic action of two hours and a half, which, after the British had sustained a loss of 8 men killed and 20 wounded, and had been actually reduced to a sinking state, terminated in the surrender of that vessel to the Danish sloop *Lougen*, of 20 guns and 160 men, and six gun-boats, each armed with 2 long-24-pounders, and manned with from 60 to 70 men. During the contest Mr. Hatton lost an arm, and received two other wounds, one of which, in the knee, nearly deprived him of the use of his right leg; yet, although he was so dangerously wounded, he continued to give his support and encouragement to the last.* So distinguished indeed was his conduct that it not only called forth the highest approbation of the court-martial which assembled to try the officers and crew of the SEAGULL for the loss of their ship, but procured for him a Commander's commission dated back to the day of the action. From 3 March, 1810, until posted, 7 Feb. 1812, Capt. Hatton served in the PORT MAHON brig, on the Portsmouth station and on the north coast of Spain. He has not been since afloat.

Capt. Hatton, who is M.P. for co. Wexford, enjoys a pension of 300*l.* in consideration of his wounds. He married, 24 May, 1817, Harriet, second daughter of the Right Hon. David La Touche, M.P. for co. Carlow, by Lady Cecilia Leeson, daughter of the first Earl of Miltown; and by that lady has issue one son, in the Army, and two daughters. AGENTS—Messrs. Ommanney.

HAULTAIN, K.H. (COMMANDER, 1814. F-P., 13; H-P., 33.)

CHARLES HAULTAIN was born, in Dec. 1787, in London, and died 4 June, 1845, at Fairford, co. Gloucester. He was eldest son of Lieut.-Colonel Theodore Haultain, of the Commandry, in the city of Worcester, who served as Captain of the 37th Regt. at the battles of Minden, Warburg, Fillinghausen, &c., and saw much other service, both in Germany and North America. He was brother of Capt. Fras. Haultain, of the Royal Artillery; of Capt. Arthur Haultain, of the Hon. E. I. Co.'s service; and of Fred. Haultain, Esq., a Midshipman R.N., who died on board the THETIS frigate, in the West Indies, of yellow fever, in 1809.

This officer entered the Navy, 2 Jan. 1800, as A. B., on board the AGINCOURT 64, Capts. John Bligh and Geo. Fred. Ryves, bearing the flag of his patron, the late Sir Chas. Morice Pole, in which ship, after serving for some time at Newfoundland, he proceeded to the North Sea, and ultimately conveyed the 25th Regt. to Egypt. In 1801-2, having previously attained the rating of Midshipman, he successively joined the BONNE CITOYENNE and VINCEJO sloops, both commanded in the Mediterranean by Capt. Jas. Prevost; after which, on removing to the CERBERUS 32, bearing the flag of Sir Jas. Saumarez, he assisted at the bombardment of Granville 14 Sept. 1803. On leaving the latter ship, Mr. Haultain became attached to the SPEEDWELL schooner, Lieut.-Commander W. Robinson, THISBE 28, *armée-en-flûte*, Capt. Lewis Shepheard, and GLORY and OCEAN 98's, flag-ships of Sir John Orde, Rear-Admiral Chas. Stirling, and Lord Collingwood, under the second-named of whom he was present, in the GLORY, in Sir Robt. Calder's action, 22 July, 1805. On 26 April, 1806, we find him promoted to a Lieutenancy in the PRINCE 98, Capt. Wm. Lechmere, off Cadiz, where, until 1809, he further served in the QUEEN 98, Capt. Fras. Pender, EXCELLENT 74, Capt. John West, and QUEEN again, Capt. Thos. Geo. Shortland. He then cruized for a short period on the Irish station as Senior of the DECADE 36, Capt. John Stuart; and in the course of the same year, 1809, he proceeded to the Adriatic in the ACTIVE 38, Capt. Jas. Alex. Gordon. On 29 June, 1810, Mr. Haultain commanded the ship's launch, and assisted at the capture and destruction of a convoy of 25 vessels near the town of Groa. He took part in many other boat operations, and was employed on so much harassing service that his health in the end became seriously affected, and he was in consequence obliged to invalid. His next appointments were, 3 Sept. 1811, and 23 May, 1812, to the SAN JOSEF 110 and EGMONT 74, flag-ships of Sir Chas. Cotton and the late Sir Geo. Hope; under the latter of whom he escorted a Russian fleet from the Baltic to England. Volunteering about June,

* *Vide* Gaz. 1808, p. 1285.

1813, to serve with the force employed on the German rivers under the command of Capt. Arthur Farquhar, Mr. Haultain was nominated for that purpose the Senior officer of a flotilla of 12 gun-boats; in discharging the duties of which post he underwent for several months many very severe hardships. During that period he frequently came into close contact with the enemy, but especially on one occasion in the month of Sept., when he made a vigorous, although, from unforeseen circumstances, an unsuccessful attack on eight Danish vessels lying at Busum, a small and intricate harbour near the mouth of the Elbe—a service which procured him the thanks of Capt. Farquhar. He afterwards co-operated and displayed great merit at the reduction of the strong forts of Blexen and Bremerlehe in the Weser, and of Cuxhaven in the Elbe;* besides serving as a volunteer at the head-quarters of the Crown Prince of Sweden; and subsequently on shore at the siege of Gluckstadt.† As a reward for his conduct on the latter occasion he was advanced to the rank of Commander 15 June, 1814, and, in 1819, presented with the Swedish gold medal. The K.H. was conferred on him 1 Jan. 1833, but he was never able to procure further employment.

Commander Haultain was the originator and compiler of the 'New Navy List'—the editorship of which, since his decease, has passed into the hands of the talented Mr. Allen, of Greenwich Hospital. He married, 13 Aug. 1814, Eliza, daughter of — Saward, Esq., of Thorp Hall, Prittlewell, co. Essex. Agents—Coplands and Burnett.

HAWES. (Commander, 1828. f-p., 20; h-p., 19.)

Edward Hawes entered the Navy, 15 July, 1808, as Fst.-cl. Vol., on board the Alonzo sloop, Capt. Wm. Buckley Hunt, fitting at Deptford. In the following month he removed with the same officer to the Britomart 10, and in that vessel (with the exception of an attachment of a few months in 1813-14 to the Orion 74, Capt. Sir Arch. Collingwood Dickson) he continued to serve, latterly with the present Capt. Robt. Riddell Carre, until Oct. 1816. During that period Mr. Hawes, who at the early age even of 13 was intrusted with the charge of a prize, attended as Midshipman the expedition to the Scheldt, and saw a vast deal of active service on the North Sea and Baltic stations. Among the numerous detached operations in which he bore an active and prominent part, we may enumerate the destruction of several privateers and gun-vessels, in the Vlie Passage, in May, 1810; the proximate cutting out, by two of the Britomart's boats, of *L'Intrépide* privateer of about 8 guns and 40 men, from under the fire of an enemy's battery, and within sight of several armed ships; and the boarding and carrying, off Heligoland, 17 July, 1812, of *L'Eole*, another privateer, pierced for 14, but carrying only 6 guns, with a complement of 31 men, which vessel did not surrender until she had sustained a loss of 2 slain and 7 wounded, and had killed 3 and wounded 10 of the crews belonging to the British boats. In the summer of 1811 we find Mr. Hawes, while in the execution of his duty, receiving so severe an injury in the right eye that its effects have since nearly deprived him of the sight. For his subsequent services, as Master's Mate, at the battle of Algiers he was promoted to the rank of Lieutenant by commission dated 16 Sept. 1816; and he was afterwards appointed—1 Nov. 1821, to the Andromache frigate, bearing the broad pendants at the Cape of Good Hope of Commodores Joseph Nourse and Constantine Richard Moorsom—6 Oct. 1825, to the Beagle 10, Capt. Pringle Stokes, attached to the force in South America, whence he invalided in Aug. 1826—and 9 March, 1827, as Senior, to the Weasel 10, Capts. John Burnet Dundas, and Hon. Wm. Wellesley, on the Mediterranean station. While under Commodore Moorsom Mr. Hawes was despatched from the Cape in charge of the York, a small tender of only 30 tons, for the purpose of ascertaining the fate of a party who had gone some time before to form a settlement on the east coast of Africa, and who had not since been heard of. By dint of steady perseverance, and the exercise of the most seamanlike conduct, he overcame the obstacles offered to his progress by a succession of south-east gales, accompanied by heavy seas and strong currents, and contrived, in his mere epitome of a ship, fully to carry out the object of his mission—having the good fortune ultimately to find those of whom he had been sent in quest at Port Natal, where, owing to the loss of their vessel, they had been cut off from all means of communication. The York then returned to the Cape, which she reached in safety, long after every hope had disappeared of her having been able to survive the tempestuous weather she had encountered. The Andromache was at the time on the eve of sailing for England, and the vacancy supposed to have been occasioned by the death of Mr. Hawes had actually been filled up. On 18 Aug. 1828 our officer was promoted to the command of the Philomel 10, in which sloop he served in the Mediterranean until paid off, 15 June, 1829. From the latter date he appears to have remained unemployed until 23 April, 1842, when we find him receiving the appointment of Principal Agent for Transports in China; the harassing, and in some cases the delicate duties attached to which office (until the transport shipping had been all finally disposed of) he continued to discharge, with a zeal for the service, and a degree of activity, prudence, and judgment, that elicited the warmest thanks of his Commander-in-Chief, Sir Thos. John Cochrane. He returned to England in Sept. 1843, and since 21 May, 1844, has been Superintendent of the Packet Service at Portpatrick, with his name on the books of the Royal Sovereign yacht.

Commander Hawes married, 6 Oct. 1829, Mary Ann Cornelius, daughter of his old Captain, Wm. Buckley Hunt, who died in Nov. 1812, by whom he has issue five children. Agents—Hallett and Robinson.

* *Vide* Gaz. 1813, p. 2437. † *V.* Gaz. 1814, p. 126.

HAWKE. (Lieutenant, 1844.)

Bladen Edward Hawke, born 14 March, 1820, is second and youngest son of the Hon. Martin Bladen Edw. Hawke, by Hannah, only daughter of Thos. Nisbet, Esq., of Mersington; and first-cousin of the present Lord Hawke.

This officer entered the Navy 4 Nov. 1833; passed his examination 18 Nov. 1839; studied next for many months at the Royal Naval College; and from the early part of 1842, until promoted to the rank of Lieutenant, 24 Feb. 1844, served as Mate of the Thalia 42, Capt. Chas. Hope, on the East India station. He then, until the following summer, officiated as Additional of the Agincourt 72, flag-ship of Sir Thos. John Cochrane; but has since been on half-pay.

HAWKER. (Rear-Admiral of the Red, 1837.

Edward Hawker is son of Capt. Jas. Hawker, R.N., who commanded the Hero 74, and was with the squadron under Commodore Johnstone when attacked by M. de Suffrein, at Porto Praya, in 1781.

This officer (whose name had been borne since 28 May, 1786, on the books of the Pegasus 28, commanded by H. R. H. Prince Wm. Henry, Powerful 74, and Impregnable 98, Capt. Sir Thos. Byard) successively became Midshipman, in 1793, of the Pegasus, and of the Swiftsure 74, each commanded by Capt. Chas. Boyles, under whom he was nominated, 14 July, 1796, Lieutenant of the Raisonnable 64. His other appointments, in the latter capacity, were—22 July. 1799, and 2 Oct. 1800, to the Spitfire sloop, Capt. Michael Seymour, and Garland 28, Capt. Robt. Honyman, both on the Channel station—13 June, 1801, as Senior, to the Thames 32, Capt. Aiskew Paffard Hollis, in which frigate, after witnessing, we believe, Sir Jas. Saumarez' action of 12 and 13 July following in the Gut of Gibraltar, and commanding her boats at the very spirited capture, 21 Sept. 1801, of a Spanish privateer called the *Sparrow*, carrying 2 4-pounders, 2 brass swivels, and 31 men,* he visited the shores of Egypt —30 June, 1803, to the command of the SWIFT cutter, employed off Martinique and Jamaica—and, 22 Aug. in the same year, again as First, to the BELLEROPHON 74, Capt. John Loring. He was promoted, on 29 of the latter month, to the command of the PORT MAHON brig, also on the Jamaica station, where he was shortly afterwards transferred to the MIGNONNE. Attaining Post-rank, 6 June, 1804, he joined, on 15 of the following month, the THESEUS 74, bearing the flag of Rear-Admiral Jas. Rich. Dacres; from which ship, after experiencing a very dreadful hurricane, he removed, in the next Dec., to the TARTAR 32. In that vessel Capt. Hawker cruized for nearly two years in the West Indies and off the coast of America, and captured, on 9 June, 1806 (in company with the BACCHUS cutter), *L'Observateur*, French national brig, of 18 guns and 104 men.† The TARTAR being then ordered to England, in consequence of the damages she had sustained in a recent hurricane, he exchanged into the MELAMPUS 36; in which frigate we find him, in Jan. 1809, convoying a fleet of transports from Halifax to Barbadoes; and, on 16 of that month, capturing *Le Colibri*, a French brig-of-war mounting 16 guns, with a complement of 92 men, having on board 570 barrels of flour and a large quantity of gunpowder for the relief of St. Domingo.‡ On 14 of the ensuing Dec. he intercepted *Le Beauharnais*, of 16 guns and 109 men, laden with flour and warlike stores, from Bayonne bound to Guadeloupe; § after assisting at the reduction of which island, and capturing, in company with the DRIVER sloop-of-war, *La Fantôme*, French letter-of-marque, pierced for 20 guns, with a complement of 74 men, he returned to the Halifax station, where he continued until Jan. 1812. From 6 March, 1813, to Dec. 1815, he appears to have next commanded the BELLEROPHON 74, and SALISBURY 58, bearing each the flag of Sir Rich. Goodwin Keats at Newfoundland; on his passage whither in the former ship he captured *Le Génie* French privateer, of 16 guns and 73 men. His last appointments were, 30 April, 1827, and 7 Sept. 1829, to the BRITANNIA and ST. VINCENT 120's, flag-ships at Plymouth of the Earl of Northesk. He went on half-pay 30 April, 1830; and attained Flag-rank 10 Jan. 1837.

The Rear-Admiral is married, and has issue.

HAWKER. (COMMANDER, 1846.)

HENRY SAMUEL HAWKER obtained his first commission 6 March, 1838; and then joined for a short period the PEARL 20, Capt. Lord Clarence Edw. Paget, lying at Sheerness. He was afterwards appointed—14 Aug. 1839, to the EDINBURGH 72, Capt. Wm. Wilmott Henderson, in which ship (besides commanding her launch and covering in a very excellent manner a party who had landed for the purpose of destroying a train which had been laid between the town and one of the castles at Beyrout containing 200 barrels of gunpowder ‖) he witnessed the fall of St. Jean d'Acre, 3 Nov. 1840—7 Sept. 1841, to the AIGLE 24, Capt. Lord C. E. Paget, on the Mediterranean station—and, 11 Dec. 1845, to the SAMPSON steam-frigate, Capt. Thos. Henderson, attached to the force in South America, whence he came home in the spring of 1846. He was promoted to his present rank on 9 of the following Nov., and is now on half-pay. AGENTS—Messrs. Ommanney.

HAWKEY. (LIEUTENANT, 1843.)

CHARLES HAWKEY entered the Navy 31 Aug. 1831; passed his examination 4 June, 1838; and, we are informed, served as Mate on board the STROMBOLI steam-vessel, Capt. Woodford John Williams, in the operations of 1840 against Beyrout, Sidon, and Acre. He afterwards rejoined the latter vessel when she was commanded by Capt. Wm. Louis; and, obtaining a commission 20 Nov. 1843, was next appointed, 27 Dec. following, to the HECATE steam-sloop, Capt. Jas. Paterson Bower, employed, until 1845, in the execution of various particular services. He has been successively attached, since 13 April, 1846, to the RETRIBUTION steam-frigate, and VENGEANCE 74, both commanded by Capt. Stephen Lushington.

Lieut. Hawkey married, 9 June, 1844, the Hon. Christabella De Moleyns, eldest daughter of Lord Ventry. AGENTS—Hallett and Robinson.

HAWKINS. (CAPT., 1835. F-P., 25; H-P., 24.)

ABRAHAM MILLS HAWKINS, born at Kingsbridge, co. Devon, is second son of Rich. Hawkins, Esq., of that place, and enumerates amongst his ancestors the celebrated Sir John Hawkins, who was knighted for the conspicuous part he had enacted, as Rear-Admiral, in the defeat of the Spanish Armada; and Sir Rich. Hawkins, his son, an officer also distinguished in the naval annals of those days. Queen Elizabeth, in consideration of the important services rendered to his country by Sir John Hawkins, granted honourable augmentations to the family arms, which are still borne by Capt. Hawkins.

This officer entered the Navy, 23 March, 1798, as Fst.-cl. Vol., on board the BARFLEUR 98, Capt. Jas. Rich. Dacres, employed in the Channel and off Cadiz; and in Jan. 1799 became Midshipman of the PRINCE 98, bearing the flag of Sir Roger Curtis, whom he soon accompanied to the Cape of Good Hope in the LANCASTER 64. He there removed for a few months in 1800 to the RATTLESNAKE, Capt. Roger Curtis, but afterwards rejoined the LANCASTER, and continued to serve in that ship until Nov. 1803. He was then transferred to the TRIDENT 64, flag-ship of Admiral Rainier on the East India station; where, from July, 1804, until his return to England towards the close of 1806 in the WOOLWICH *armée-en-flûte*, Capt. Fras. Beaufort, he was further employed, as Acting-Lieutenant, on board the VICTOR sloop, Capt. Jas. Johnstone, SHEERNESS 44, Capt. Lord Geo. Stuart (under whom he was wrecked, in a gale of wind, off Trincomalee, 7 Jan. 1805), PSYCHE frigate, Capt. Wm. Woolridge, and DUNCAN 38, Capt. Lord Geo. Stuart. On being officially promoted, 11 June, 1807, Mr. Hawkins was appointed to the AIMABLE 32, in which frigate, and the HORATIO 38, both commanded by the last-mentioned officer, he served on the North Sea station, principally as First-Lieutenant, until Sept. 1812. While in the former ship he assisted at the capture, on 3 Feb. 1809, of *L'Iris* French national ship, pierced for 32 guns, but mounting only 24, after a short running-fight in which the latter sustained a loss of 2 men killed and 8 wounded, and the AIMABLE (besides being materially damaged in her masts, spars, sails, and rigging) of 2 wounded; and in the course of the following July we find him earning the thanks of his Captain for his indefatigable exertions at the reduction of the batteries of Cuxhaven and Bremerlehe, and the expulsion of the enemy from Gessendorf. On 2 Aug. 1812, being then in the HORATIO, he took command of four boats belonging to that ship, and, in a manner indescribably gallant, succeeded, at the end of a most sanguinary combat, in which the assailants suffered a loss of 9 men killed and 16 wounded, and their opponents of 10 killed and 13 wounded, in capturing a Danish schooner and cutter, mounting 10 guns between them, lying at anchor in a position of extraordinary strength near a village on an arm of the sea, 35 miles inland, on the coast of Norway.* He unfortunately, however, received a severe wound in the right hand while advancing to the attack, and another in the left arm when in the act of boarding; in consideration whereof he was awarded a pension of 150*l.*, and presented with a gratuity from the Patriotic Society. The valour of his exploit was also acknowledged by a Commander's commission dated

* *Vide* Gaz. 1801, p. 1339. † *V.* Gaz. 1806, p. 952.
‡ *V.* Gaz. 1809, p. 326. § *V.* Gaz. 1810, p. 176.
‖ *V.* Gaz. 1840, p. 2609.

* *Vide* Gaz. 1812, p. 1710.

on 12 of the following Dec. Capt. Hawkins' subsequent appointments were—18 March, 1814, to the CONFLICT sloop, in which vessel he served on the Home station until Sept. 1815—30 Aug. 1819, to a five-years' Inspectorship in the Water Guard—and 13 July, 1830, to the RALEIGH 18, fitting for the Mediterranean, whence he returned and was paid off 31 May, 1834. He was advanced to his present rank 6 Feb. 1835, but has not since been afloat.

Capt. Hawkins married, in 1819, Mary Wise, only daughter of Christopher Savery, Esq., of South Efford, co. Devon, and by that lady has issue two sons, of whom the eldest is an officer in the Army.

HAWKINS. (LIEUT., 1807. F-P., 22; H-P., 28.)

CHARLES HAWKINS entered the Navy, 24 Dec. 1797, as A.B., on board the CHAPMAN hired armed ship, Capt. Robt. Keen, with whom he continued to serve, principally as Midshipman, in the same vessel, and in the SPITFIRE sloop, until April, 1803; being much employed in the former in co-operation with the King's troops, in the neighbourhood of Wexford, during the rebellion of 1798. On leaving the SPITFIRE he joined the PICKLE schooner, of 10 guns and 35 men, Lieut.-Commanders John Richards Lapenotiere and Daniel Callaway, in which vessel he had an opportunity of rendering much assistance to the MAGNIFICENT 74, when that ship was wrecked, near Brest, 25 March, 1804; of also participating in the battle of Trafalgar 21 Oct. 1805, with the despatches announcing the glorious result of which the PICKLE was sent home; and of participating, as Sub-Lieutenant, in the capture, 3 Jan. 1807, of *La Favorite* privateer, of 14 guns and 70 men. Mr. Hawkins, who on the latter occasion received a slight wound, and distinguished himself by his activity and exertions in boarding and afterwards getting the prize clear, was for his conduct made Lieutenant, by commission dated on 7 of the same month, into the HUMBER armed ship, Capt. John Hill.* He afterwards joined—26 Nov. 1807, the HERCULE 74, Capt. Hon. John Colville, off Lisbon—8 Nov. 1808, the NORGE 74, Capt. John Sprat Rainier, which ship, employed on the same and Cadiz stations, he left in Aug. 1811—11 Sept. 1812, the CORDELIA 10, Capt. Thos. Fortescue Kennedy, attached to the force in the Downs—and, 21 July, 1813, the COLOSSUS 74, Capt. Thos. Alexander, stationed in the North Sea, whence he invalided in Feb. 1814. He assumed command, 12 Aug. 1839, of the ROMNEY receiving-ship at the Havana; and since 9 Oct. 1841 has been in charge of a Semaphore station.

HAWKINS. (LIEUTENANT, 1845.)

FRANK KEENE HAWKINS served as Midshipman of the PIQUE 36, during the operations of 1840 on the coast of Syria, and was mentioned in the highest terms by his Captain, Edw. Boxer;† passed his examination 7 July, 1841; and served as Mate, on the Mediterranean and American stations, in the QUEEN 110, and FORMIDABLE 84, flag-ships of Sir Edw. W. C. R. Owen, WARSPITE 50, Capt. Provo Wm. Parry Wallis, and EAGLE 50, Capt. Geo. Bohun Martin. He obtained his commission 9 Dec. 1845; joined, a few days afterwards, the GLADIATOR steam-frigate, Capt. John Robb, lying at Woolwich; and since 8 May, 1846, has been successively employed with Capt. Woodford John Williams in the AVENGER and AMPHION steam-frigates, on the Home station.

HAWKINS. (COMMANDER, 1842.)

HENRY CÆSAR HAWKINS, born 19 March, 1809, is second surviving son of the present Sir John Cæsar Hawkins, Bart., by Charlotte, eldest daughter of Wm. Surtees, Esq., of Hedley, co. Northumberland. One of his brothers is a Captain in the Indian, and three others are officers in the Queen's Army.

This officer entered the Navy 2 May, 1822; passed his examination in 1828; was employed on

* *Vide* Gaz. 1807, p. 34. † *V.* Gaz. 1840, p. 2001.

shore in Oct. of that year in constructing batteries and otherwise co-operating with the French army during the siege of Morea Castle;* and obtained his first commission 6 Sept. 1838. Being appointed, 11 April, 1839 (after a short servitude as Additional-Lieutenant in the DONEGAL 78, flag-ship at Lisbon of Sir John Acworth Ommanney), to the BLENHEIM 72, Capts. Sir Humphrey Fleming Senhouse and Sir Thos. Herbert, he ultimately proceeded to China, where he went through the whole campaign, including the storming of Chinghae,† on which occasion he served on shore in command of a party of seamen. He was in consequence advanced to his present rank 23 Dec. 1842,‡ but has not been since employed. AGENTS—Messrs. Stilwell.

HAWKSHAW. (LIEUT., 1819. F-P., 12; H-P., 25.)

HUGH HAWKSHAW is son of the late Rev. Rich. Hawkshaw, Rector of Fahan, co. Londonderry.

This officer entered the Navy, 24 Dec. 1810, as Fst.-cl. Vol., on board the FORTUNÉE 36, Capt. Henry Vansittart, on the Home station, where he assisted at the capture, 11 Oct. 1811, of *Le Vice-Amiral Martin*, a notorious privateer, of 18 guns and 140 men, and where he afterwards followed the same Captain into the CLARENCE 74. While next attached, between Sept. 1813 and Feb. 1817, to the PACTOLUS 38, and SEVERN 50, both commanded by Capt. Hon. Fred. Wm. Aylmer, we find him accompanying the Duke of Cambridge to Cuxhaven and his late Majesty to the Scheldt, serving for some time also on the North American station, and (besides attending an eminently successful expedition sent in the summer of 1815 to the Gironde in support of the French king) enacting a part in the memorable battle of Algiers 27 Aug. 1816. He was subsequently for nearly twelve months employed on the African and West India stations in the SEMIRAMIS 42, Capts. Sir Jas. Lucas Yeo and Joseph Harrison; after which he successively joined the SEVERN 50, NEWCASTLE 60, and LEANDER 50, commanded on the Home and Bermuda stations by Capts. Wm. M'Culloch, Arthur Fanshawe, and Edw. Chetham. He was promoted, 12 July, 1819, to a Lieutenancy in the NEWCASTLE, bearing the flag at the time of Rear-Admiral Edw. Griffith, Commander-in-Chief at Halifax; but since the paying off of that ship in 1822 has not been afloat.

Lieut. Hawkshaw, who is an Inspector of the Carlow Constabulary Force, married Catherine Eliza, fourth daughter of Robt. Miller, Esq., of Blackheath Park, co. Kent.

HAWTAYNE. (REAR ADMIRAL OF THE WHITE, 1841. F-P., 18; H-P., 36.)

CHARLES SIBTHORPE JOHN HAWTAYNE is second son of the Rev. Wm. Hawtayne, 34 years Rector of Elstree, co. Hertford, in the early part of his life an Ensign in the 3rd Regt. of Foot Guards; and brother of the Rev. John Hawtayne, D.D., Archdeacon of Bombay.

This officer entered the Navy, 19 July, 1793, as Captain's Servant, on board the DEFENCE 74, Capt. Jas. Gambier, of which ship his father was then Chaplain. In Oct. 1794, after having shared in the action of 1 June, he accompanied Capt. Gambier into the PRINCE GEORGE 98, commanded subsequently by Capt. Sir John Orde, in the river Medway. With the exception of an attachment of a few months in 1798-9 to the ZEALAND 64, flag-ship at the Nore, he next, from April, 1795, until Aug. 1799, served with Capt. Wm. Grenville Lobb, on the Home and West India stations, in the MARTIN and BABEL sloops, and AIMABLE and CRESCENT frigates. Being made Lieutenant, on 24 of the latter month, into the ESPIÈGLE sloop, Capts. Jas. Boorder and Jas. Slade, Mr. Hawtayne attended the ensuing expedition to Holland. He was afterwards appointed—11 July, 1800, to the GREYHOUND 32, Capts. Chas. Ogle and Wm. Hoste, on the Mediterranean station, where his services under the

* *Vide* Gaz. 1828, p. 2201. † *V.* Gaz. 1842, p. 396.
‡ *V.* Gaz. 1842, p. 3821.

former officer on the coast of Egypt procured him the Turkish gold medal—and 18 May, 1803, and 26 May, 1804, to the ISIS 50, and CULLODEN 74, flag-ships at Newfoundland and in the East Indies of Vice-Admiral Gambier and Sir Edw. Pellew. In the early part of 1805, we find him successively nominated Acting-Captain of the DUNCAN frigate, and Governor, *pro tempore*, of the Royal Naval Hospital at Madras; the latter of which posts he resigned about Sept. in the same year. On 31 Jan. 1806, Mr Hawtayne was promoted to the rank of Commander, and in that capacity he was next appointed, 6 May, 1807, to the CEPHALUS 18, in which sloop he conveyed Mr. Gambier, as Consul-General, to Lisbon, and then proceeded to the Mediterranean. He was posted, at the request of Lord Gambier, on 13 of the following Oct., but he does not appear to have again gone afloat until March, 1810, when he succeeded in obtaining an appointment to the QUEBEC 32, on the North Sea station, where he captured the privateers *L'Impératrice* of 14 guns and 60 men, *Le Renard* of 6 guns and 24 men (taken in company with the KITE sloop), and *L'Olympia*, of 10 guns and 78 men. The QUEBEC being paid off in Feb. 1812, Capt. Hawtayne next joined, 15 Jan. 1816, the SCAMANDER 42, fitting for the West India station. He exchanged, however, in the ensuing April, into the FLORIDA 24, and until placed out of commission in Dec. 1818, was chiefly employed in superintending the Revenue-cruisers in the North Sea. This was his last service afloat. He attained Flag-rank 23 Nov. 1841.

The Rear-Admiral married, first, Elizabeth, second daughter of the late Geo. Griffin Stonestreet, Esq., of Clapham, High Sheriff for co. Surrey, in 1800; and secondly, in Feb. 1820, Anne, sister of the present Rear-Admiral Henry Hope, C.B. He was again left a widower in 1825.

HAY. (CAPTAIN, 1846.)

GEORGE JAMES HAY is second son of the late Lieut.-General Hay, Lieut.-Governor of Edinburgh Castle.

This officer entered the Navy, 13 Dec. 1806, as Fst.-cl. Vol., on board the THAMES 32, Capt. Bridges Watkinson Taylor, with whom, and with Capt. Edwards Lloyd Graham, he continued to serve, in the same ship and the APOLLO 38, on the West India and Mediterranean stations, principally as Midshipman, until July, 1814. He assisted, in the latter vessel, in capturing, 13 April, 1812, the French frigate-built store-ship *Mérinos*, of 20 guns and 26 men, under the batteries of Corsica, and, on 20 of the following Sept., the National xebec *Ulysse*, of 6 guns. Participating also in nearly every one of the numerous affairs in which the APOLLO's boats were engaged when in the Adriatic, he was in consequence present at the reduction of the islands of Augusta and Curzola 29 Jan. and 3 Feb. 1813; the capture, on 11 April, of the Devil's Island, near the north entrance of Corfu; and the cutting-out, 13 days later, after a body of the enemy's troops had been defeated, of a felucca from under the batteries of St. Cataldo. On 6 July, 1815, while next serving on board the EUROTAS 38, Capts. Jas. Lillicrap and Robt. Bloye, Mr. Hay was promoted to the rank of Lieutenant. Being appointed, on 7 of the following Nov., to the ALCESTE 38, Capt. Murray Maxwell, he sailed in that ship with Lord Amherst for China, and continued in her until wrecked, in the Straits of Gaspar, on her passage home, 18 Feb. 1817, soon after the occurrence of which disaster he appears to have acquired honourable mention for his gallant conduct in pursuing with a single boat, and capturing, a Malay proa, whose crew defended themselves with so much desperation, that the vessel went down as soon as she had been taken. Mr. Hay's succeeding appointments were—24 April, 1819, to the MENAI 26, Capt. Fairfax Moresby, by whom his exertions on proceeding to the coast of Africa were often noticed, particularly when in command of the WIZARD tender, and once when cutting-out in the boats the piratical slaver *Industry* from under the batteries of Zanzibar—10 Dec. 1823, to the MAIDSTONE 42, bearing the broad pendant of Commodore Chas. Bullen, also on the African station, whence, although on the Admiralty List for promotion, his health obliged him to invalid—and, 4 Dec. 1827, to the command of the METEOR steam-vessel. He obtained a second promotal commission 18 Sept. 1828, but did not again go afloat until 14 Dec. 1844, when he obtained command of the RACEHORSE 18, and sailed for the East Indies. In Dec. 1845, being at the time at New Zealand, he landed in command of a detachment of seamen and marines, and on the 11th of the following month, after having participated for three weeks in a series of the most trying operations (more fully alluded to in our memoir of Capt. Chas. Graham), during which his zeal and exertions were very conspicuous, stormed and carried, notwithstanding a desperate resistance of four hours, a strongly fortified pah, belonging to a rebel chieftain, named Kawiti.* He was in consequence advanced to his present rank by commission bearing date the day of the action, 11 Jan. 1846, and nominated a C.B. 27 July following. He is now on half-pay.

Capt. Hay married, 24 June, 1830, Georgiana Middleton, fourth daughter of Sir John R. Whiteford. AGENTS—Messrs. Halford and Co.

HAY. (**Captain**, 1819. F-P., 16; H-P., 32.)

JAMES HAY is son of the late Jas. Hay, Esq., of Belton; great-grandson of John, first Marquess of Tweeddale; and a distant relative of the present Lord John Hay, Capt. R.N.

This officer entered the Navy, 13 Oct. 1799, as Fst.-cl. Vol., on board the ANSON 44, Capt. Philip Chas. Durham, on the Home station, where, until Nov. 1804, he further served with the same Captain, as Midshipman, in the ENDYMION 40, and with Capts. Jas. Athol Wood and Jas. Oswald in the ACASTA 40. He then rejoined Capt. Durham in the DEFIANCE 74, and on 1 March, 1806, after having participated in that ship in Sir Robt. Calder's action, and in the battle of Trafalgar, was promoted to a Lieutenancy in the ELECTRA 18, Capt. Geo. Barne Trollope, on the Leith station. Being next appointed, 11 May, 1807, to the AMARANTHE 18, Capt. Edw. Pelham Brenton, he proceeded to the West Indies, where, on 13 Dec. 1808, he took command of the boats of a small squadron, and much distinguished himself by the gallant manner in which, although under a heavy fire from the enemy's batteries and troops on the beach, he boarded and carried the French 18-gun brig *Le Cigne*, lying aground to the northward of St. Pierre's, Martinique.† On the subjugation of the latter island, during the operations connected with which he acted as Commander of the AMARANTHE, in consequence of Capt. Brenton's absence on shore, Mr. Hay became Signal-Lieutenant to the present Sir Geo. Cockburn in the BELLEISLE 74, and immediately returned to England. On again proceeding to the West Indies, in the RACOON, he joined the GLOMMEN sloop, Capt. Chas. Pickford, under whom he continued until wrecked, and saved by the GLOIRE frigate, in Carlisle Bay, Barbadoes, in Nov. 1809. He was nominated, on 29 of the following Dec., to the Acting-command of the PAPILLON 16, and in that vessel (being confirmed to her by commission dated 2 May, 1810) we find him uninterruptedly employed, on the West India, Cadiz, and Lisbon stations, until 24 April, 1815. He attained his present rank 12 Aug. 1819, and accepted the Retirement 1 Oct. 1846.

Capt. Hay is a Lieutenant of Yeomanry Cavalry, and Deputy-Lieutenant for co. Haddington. He is married and has issue three sons and one daughter. AGENTS—Hallett and Robinson.

HAY. (CAPTAIN, 1841. F-P., 23; H-P., 14.)

JAMES BECKFORD LEWIS HAY, born 25 Nov. 1797, is son of Capt. John Baker Hay, R.N. (1798) who fought under Lord Rodney in his various actions,

* *Vide* Gaz. 1846, pp. 2346, 2348.
† *V.* Gaz. 1809, p. 146.

and was Midshipman of his flag-ship in the battle of 12 April, 1782; who was afterwards present as a Lieutenant in the actions of 29 May, and 1 June, 1794, and in the mutiny at the Nore in 1797; and who ultimately died while commanding the QUEEN CHARLOTTE, flag-ship at Portsmouth of Sir Jas. Hawkins Whitshed, 13 May, 1823, in his 63rd year.

This officer entered the Navy, 1 April, 1810, as Fst.-cl. Vol., on board the PUISSANT 74, Capt. John Irwin, lying at Spithead. From the following June until June, 1814, we find his name successively borne on the books of the CLYDE 38, INCONSTANT 36, and CORNWALL 74, all commanded, principally on the Home station, by Sir Edw. Wm. Campbell Rich Owen, by whom, during four months in the winter of 1813-14, he was employed on shore with the army at South Beveland, where, on one occasion, six French brigs were driven aground by a battery mounting only one 18-pounder. While next cruizing in the ESK 20, Capt. Geo. Gustavus Lennock, Mr. Hay participated in the capture of the *Sine quà non* American privateer, and in a smart action, off Teneriffe, with two other American vessels, the *Grampus* and *Terpsichore*. In Oct. 1815 he removed to the BULWARK 74, flag-ship at the Nore of Sir Chas. Rowley; and on his being subsequently transferred to the QUEEN CHARLOTTE 100, bearing the flag of Lord Exmouth, he assisted, as a passed Midshipman, at the bombardment of Algiers 27 Aug. 1816; after which event he served for a short period in the PROMETHEUS sloop, Capt. Wm. Bateman Dashwood, and for two years as Master's Mate in the CONQUEROR 74, flag-ship at the Cape of Good Hope of Rear-Admiral Robt. Plampin. Being confirmed a Lieutenant 10 April, 1819, in the TEES 26, Capt. Geo. Rennie, Mr. Hay, who continued to serve in that vessel on the station last-mentioned until Aug. 1821, was further, until April, 1831, employed, at home and in the West and East Indies, on board the RAMILLIES 74, Capt. Edw. Brace, GLOUCESTER 74, Commodore Sir Edw. W. C. R. Owen, TYNE 28, Capt. John Walter Roberts, GLOUCESTER again, ARACHNE 18, Capt. Wm. Robt. Ashley Pettman (in which sloop he served as First-Lieutenant from Nov. 1826 until Jan. 1828), MONKEY and NIMBLE schooners, commanded by himself, and SOUTHAMPTON 52, bearing the flag of Sir Edw. W. C. R. Owen, under whom he officiated as Signal-Lieutenant for upwards of two years. When First of the TYNE, of which ship he acted for some time as Captain, Mr. Hay, in 1823, was recommended by his patron Sir E. Owen, to the Admiralty for his conduct during a successful expedition against the pirates of Cuba. The same officer ultimately, in April, 1831, appointed him to the command of the CRUISER 18, and, in the course of the following month, of his own flag-ship, the SOUTHAMPTON, to which the Admiralty confirmed him by commission dated 14 Oct. 1832. He went on half-pay in Jan. 1833, and on 23 Nov. 1841, a few weeks after his rejunction of his friend in the QUEEN 110, was advanced to the rank he now holds. He has not been since afloat.

Capt. Hay married, 14 Dec. 1842, Clotilda Henrietta, second daughter of Rear-Admiral Edw. Wallis Hoare, R.N.

HAY, LORD, C.B., G.C.C. (CAPTAIN, 1818. F-P., 23; H-P., 20.)

THE RIGHT HONOURABLE LORD JOHN HAY, born 1 April, 1793, is third son of Geo., seventh Marquess of Tweeddale, by Lady Hannah Charlotte Maitland, daughter of Jas., seventh Earl of Lauderdale. His eldest brother, the present Marquess of Tweeddale, K.T., a Major-General in the Army, and Lord-Lieutenant of co. Haddington, served as Aide-de-camp to the Duke of Wellington in the Peninsular War, and was wounded in that capacity at the battle of Busaco, 27 Sept. 1810. Two other of his brothers, Lords Jas. and Edw. Geo. Hay, are officers of high rank in the Army. His Lordship, who is a distant relative of the present Capt. Jas. Hay, R.N., is brother-in-law of John Henry Ley, Esq., Clerk to the House of Commons; and of Sir John Cam Hobhouse, Bart., President of the Board of Control.

This officer entered the Navy, 4 Dec. 1804, as Fst.-cl. Vol., on board the MONARCH 74, Capt. John Clarke Searle, bearing the flag in the Downs of Lord Keith, whom he followed, in Aug. 1805, into the EDGAR 74. After a further servitude on the Home station in the EGYPTIENNE frigate, and REVENGE 74, both commanded by Hon. Chas. Elphinstone Fleeming, PHŒBE 36, Capt. Jas. Oswald, and PUISSANT 74, Capt. John Irwin, he joined, in Dec. 1806, the SEAHORSE, of 42 guns and 281 men, Capt. John Stewart, attached to the force in the Mediterranean, where he continued until June, 1811. During that period Lord John Hay, besides being in attendance on various diplomatic personages, bore an ample part in many gallant operations against the enemy. Among other services, he was employed in the boats, and lost his left arm at the cutting out of some vessels in Hières Bay; and on the night of 5 July, 1808, he contributed to the capture, after a memorably furious engagement, and a loss to the SEAHORSE (30 of whose crew were absent) of 5 men killed and 10 wounded, of the Turkish man-of-war *Badere Zaffer*, mounting 52 guns, with a complement of 543 men, of whom 170 were slain and 200 wounded. The *Alis Fezan*, of 26 guns and 230 men, a ship which had been also opposed to the SEAHORSE, was at the same time put to flight. Obtaining a commission 1 May, 1812, Lord John Hay was next appointed, 1 June following, and 31 May, 1814, to the PIQUE 36, Capt. Hon. Anthony Maitland, and VENERABLE 74, bearing the flag of the late Sir Philip Durham, both on the West India station. On 15 Nov. in the latter year, having been advanced to the rank of Commander on 15 of the previous June, his Lordship joined the BUSTARD 10, off Lisbon, and he next, in the course of 1815, obtained command of the OPOSSUM 10, in which sloop he served on the Channel and North American stations until paid off 5 Aug. 1818. He attained Post-rank 7 Dec. following, and was subsequently appointed, 24 Sept. 1832, 19 Nov. 1836, and 8 March, 1837, to the CASTOR 36, PHŒNIX steamer, and NORTH STAR 28, which vessels he commanded until 1840. He had charge of a battalion of marines, during that period, and acted as Commodore of a small squadron on the north coast of Spain, where the importance of his services as connected with the civil war, especially at the siege of Bilbao, procured him, in 1837, the Grand Cross of the Order of Charles III., and the Companionship of the Bath. Lord John Hay, who next, from 17 Aug. 1841 until Oct. 1843, commanded the WARSPITE 50, on the coast of North America (whither he conveyed Lord Ashburton) and in the West Indies, was successively appointed in 1846, Acting-Superintendent of Woolwich Dockyard, Chairman of the Board of Naval Construction, and a Lord of the Admiralty —which latter office he still retains.

His Lordship, a Deputy-Lieutenant for co. Haddington, sat in Parliament for that shire in 1826 and 30. In 1833, he received a large silver medal from the "Society for the Encouragement of Arts," &c., for his invention of a telescope-holder for the use of a person with only one hand. AGENTS—Messrs. Stilwell.

HAY. (COMMANDER, 1841. F-P., 22; H-P., 8.)

JOHN HAY, born 23 March, 1804, is second son, we believe, of Jas. Hay, Esq., of Seggieden, co. Perth, and of Killicranky Cottage, in the pass of Killicranky, a Deputy-Lieutenant for that shire, by Margaret, daughter of John Richardson, Esq., of Pitfour. One of his brothers, Jas. Richardson, is a Captain in the Army; and another, Patrick, is a Lieutenant in the Bengal Native Infantry.

This officer entered the Royal Naval College in Jan. 1817, and embarked 12 Oct. 1819, as Fst.-cl. Vol., on board the PHAETON 46, Capts. Wm. Henry Dillon and Sir Wm. Augustus Montagu, of which frigate, employed on the Home and Halifax stations, he soon became Midshipman. On his removal, in 1822, to the REDWING 18, Capt. Hon. Geo. Rolle

Walpole Trefusis, we find him sharing in the boats of that sloop in an expedition against the pirates in the West Indies, and compelled, during a period of eight days, to subsist on the provisions of two. He afterwards served for about four years in South America, latterly as Mate, on board the MERSEY 26, Capt. John Macpherson Ferguson, JASEUR 18, Capt. Thos. Martin, and CAMBRIDGE 80, Capt. Thos. Jas. Maling; and he next, in 1827-8, joined the PRINCE REGENT 120, flag-ship at the Nore of Sir Robt. Moorsom, MARTIAL 14, commanded on the coast of Scotland by Lieut. Robt. M'Kirdy, and BLONDE 46, Capt. Edm. Lyons; under whom, towards the close of 1828, he was employed on shore in constructing batteries, and otherwise co-operating with the French army during the siege of Morea Castle.* Attaining the rank of Lieutenant 12 Nov. 1829, Mr. Hay, until June, 1831, served in that capacity on board the METEOR bomb, Capt. David Hope, BRITANNIA 120, bearing the flag of Sir Pulteney Malcolm, and SAMARANG 28, Capt. Wm. Fanshawe Martin. His next appointment was, 27 March, 1837, to the TALAVERA 74, Capt. Wm. Bowen Mends, stationed, as were the three ships last-mentioned, in the Mediterranean; on his return whence he became, 4 Jan. 1840, First-Lieutenant of the PYLADES 18, Capt. Talavera Vernon Anson. Proceeding in that vessel to China, he there commanded her boats, 29 July, 1840, in a severe action with three piratical junks, one of which he succeeded in capturing after a loss of 2 men killed and 8 wounded. With the exception of the attack on the forts at the Boca Tigris, Mr. Hay afterwards shared, and was particularly recommended for the ability he displayed in all the operations which led to the first and second capture of the city of Canton;† and on one occasion he rendered himself particularly conspicuous by his exertions at night in cutting through a raft which had been moored across the river, and had effectually obstructed the passage of the shipping. He was advanced to his present rank by commission dated 6 May, 1841; and since 15 May, 1844 (some months previously to which period he had been admitted a student at the Royal Naval College), has been in command of the PROMETHEUS steam-sloop, on the coast of Africa. AGENTS—Messrs. Halford and Co.

HAY. (LIEUTENANT, 1814. F-P., 9; H-P., 32.)

JOHN HAY (*a*) is second son of the late John Hay, Esq., of Morton, by Jane, daughter of Provost Wyllie, of Glasgow.

This officer entered the Navy, 9 Dec. 1806, as L. M., on board the TEXEL 64, Capt. Donald Campbell, bearing the flag at Leith of Rear-Admiral Jas. Vashon. On his removal, as Midshipman, in 1807, to the DICTATOR 64, also commanded by Capt. Campbell, he attended the expedition of that year to Copenhagen; after which we find him, while stationed in the Great Belt, sharing, 26 June, 1808, in an action with several Danish gun-boats, whose fire killed 1 and wounded 2 of the DICTATOR'S people. In Aug. 1809, having followed the same Captain into the AUDACIOUS 74, Mr. Hay assisted, as Master's Mate, at the bombardment of Flushing. On the evacuation of the Walcheren he returned to England in one of the prizes, but he subsequently rejoined the AUDACIOUS, and, proceeding off the Tagus, was sent up that river with a flotilla, commanded by the present Capt. Maurice Fred. Fitzhardinge Berkeley, for the purpose of co-operating with the troops occupying the lines of Torres Vedras. Between Nov. 1811 and the date of his promotion to the rank of Lieutenant, 1 July, 1814, he further served, on the North Sea and Mediterranean stations, in the WARRIOR and RIVOLI 74's, Capts. Hon. Geo. Byng and Graham Eden Hamond. With the exception of an attachment, from 8 Oct. 1823 until June, 1824, to the PRINCE REGENT 120, flag-ship of Sir Benj. Hallowell at the Nore, he has not been since afloat.

Lieut. Hay married, 1 June, 1824, his cousin, Marion, eldest daughter of the late David Carrick Buchanan, Esq., of Drumpilear, Lancashire, by whom he has issue.

* *Vide* Gaz. 1828, p. 2201.

† *V.* Gaz. 1841, pp. 1503, 1505, 2505, 2510.

HAY. (LIEUTENANT, 1832. F-P., 26; H-P., 9.)

JOHN HAY (*b*), born 22 March, 1802, is brother of Lieut. Wm. Hay, R.N.

This officer entered the Navy, 20 April, 1812, as Fst.-cl. Vol., on board the UNION 98, Capt. Sam. Hood Linzee and Robt. Rolles, in which ship he served at the blockade of Toulon and the reduction of Genoa. In Aug. 1815, after having been employed for a period of 12 months on the coasts of Ireland and France in the SCYLLA 18, Capt. Allen, and PHŒBE 36, Capt. Jas. Hillyar, he was nominated Midshipman of the PODARGUS 14, Capt. Jas. Wallis, under whom he further served, at the Cape of Good Hope, latterly in the RACOON 26, until Dec. 1818. In July, 1820, we next find him joining the PIGMY schooner, Lieut.-Commander Thos. Hills, in which vessel he cruized for three years with much success against the smugglers of the Channel, the greater part of the time as a passed Midshipman. He then, in Aug. 1820, became attached to the SUPERB 74, Capt. Adam Mackenzie, in whose tender, the LYRA 10, he was for many months employed; and he subsequently, from March, 1825, until promoted to the rank of Lieutenant 4 April, 1832, officiated as Chief Mate of the ROSE, DOLPHIN, and HARPY Revenue-cutters, Lieut.-Commanders Thos. Strong, Jas. Giffard, John Roche, and Sam. Grandy. Mr. Hay's commission was presented to him at the especial recommendation of the Board of Customs, for the daring conduct he had evinced in the previous October, in taking a hawser on board H.M. steamer ECHO, and thereby enabling that vessel to be hove off from a perilous position under the Hoe at Plymouth, where she had been driven on shore in the night during a violent gale. His last appointments were—10 Oct. 1832, to the Coast Guard, in which service he continued until 1838—and, 5 Nov. 1840, to the HOWE 120, Capts. Sir Watkin Owen Pell and Robt. Smart, flag-ship for some time of Sir Fras. Mason, on the Mediterranean station. He has been on half-pay since March, 1843.

Lieut. Hay married, 26 Aug. 1824, Miss Mary James Lawrence, and by that lady has issue three children.

HAY. (CAPTAIN, 1842.)

JOHN BAKER PORTER HAY entered the Navy, 28 Dec. 1811; and, obtaining his first commission 24 April, 1824, was afterwards appointed Lieutenant—12 March, 1827, of the ROMNEY 50, *armée en flûte*, Capt. Nicholas Lockyer, which ship was paid off 12 Oct. following—in 1828, of the WASP 18, Capts. Rich. Dickinson, Hon. Wm. Wellesley, Thos. Edwd. Hoste, Orlando Geo. Sutton Gunning, and Brunswick Popham, on the Mediterranean station, whence he invalided 15 June, 1831—4 May, 1836, of the CORNWALLIS 74, Capts. Robt. Worgan Geo. Festing, Sir Joshua Ricketts Rowley, and Sir Rich. Grant, stationed at first off Lisbon, but afterwards employed as flag-ship of Hon. Sir Chas. Paget, Commander-in-Chief in North America and the West Indies. On the death of the latter officer, Mr. Hay, who for upwards of three years had officiated as First of the CORNWALLIS, was advanced to the command, by commission dated 30 Jan. 1839, of the SNAKE 16, which sloop he brought home and paid off towards the close of the same year. His last appointment was, 26 Nov. 1841, to the Second-Captaincy of the QUEEN 110, fitting for the flag of Sir Edw. W. C. R. Owen; in honour of Her Majesty's visit to which ship, when lying at Spithead, and on the eve of her departure for the Mediterranean, he was advanced to his present rank 7 March, 1842. AGENTS—Case and Loudonsack.

HAY. (COMMANDER, 1846.)

JOHN CHARLES DALRYMPLE HAY served as Midshipman of the BENBOW 72, Capt. Houston Stewart, during the operations of 1840 on the coast of Syria, where, previously to assisting at the bombardment of St. Jean d'Acre, he commanded a boat, and was officially reported as deserving of every credit for his spirited conduct in the attack on Tortosa.* Passing his examination 17 Feb. 1841, he subsequently, until his attainment of the rank of Lieutenant, 15 Aug. 1844, officiated as Mate, on the Mediterranean and East India stations, of the same ship, and of the AGINCOURT 72, bearing the flag of Sir Thos. John Cochrane, and SPITEFUL steam-sloop, Capt. Wm. Maitland. His succeeding appointments were—12 Nov. 1844, again to the AGINCOURT, as Flag-Lieutenant—and, 1 March, 1846, to the VESTAL 26, Capt. Chas. Talbot, also in the East Indies. He attained his present rank on 28 Aug. in the latter year.

HAY. (CAPTAIN, 1833. F-P., 16; H-P., 26.)

PATRICK DUFF HENRY HAY entered the Navy, 16 June, 1805, as Fst.-cl. Vol., on board the ROEBUCK 44, Capt. Geo. M'Kinley, on the Leith station; and, in the early part of 1806, became attached, in the North Sea and at Halifax, to the MAJESTIC 74, bearing the flag of Vice-Admiral Thos. Macnamara Russell, and MILAN 38, Capt. Sir Robt. Laurie; in which frigate he attained the rating of Midshipman, 2 July, 1808, and continued to serve until Sept. 1810. In Dec. of the latter year he joined the BARFLEUR 98, flag-ship of Hon. Geo. Cranfield Berkeley on the Lisbon station, whence, in June, 1812, he returned to England as Acting-Lieutenant of the REGULUS, *armée en flûte*, Capt. John Tailour. Being confirmed on 31 of the next month, Mr. Hay, towards the close of 1812, was appointed a Lieutenant of the RAMILLIES 74, Capt. Sir Thos. Masterman Hardy, under whom, on proceeding to North America, he served at the blockade of New London, the capture of the islands in Passamaquoddy Bay, and the bombardment of Stonington. As a Commander, a rank he attained 31 Aug. 1815, Capt. Hay appears to have joined—10 Nov. 1820, and 3 Dec. 1821, the REDPOLE and MEDINA sloops, both on the Mediterranean station—and, 6 March, 1828, the PYLADES 18, which vessel he paid off 21 May, 1831. He attained the rank he now holds 15 Nov. 1833, but has not since been employed. AGENTS—Case and Loudonsack.

HAY. (LIEUTENANT, 1815. F-P., 22; H-P., 24.)

PETER HAY entered the Navy, about April, 1801, as A. B., on board the CAMBRIDGE 74, Capt. Rich. Lane, bearing the flag at Plymouth of Sir Thos. Pasley. In Oct. following he became Midshipman of the CENTAUR 74, Capt. Bendall Robt. Littlehales, stationed in the Channel; where, in April, 1803, after an unemployed interval of 12 months, he joined the SPITFIRE sloop, Capt. Robt. Keen. While next attached, between June in the latter year and Nov. 1812, to the FOUDROYANT 80, successive flag-ship, on the Home, Lisbon, and Brazilian stations, of Admirals Sir Thos. Graves, Sir John Borlase Warren, Albemarle Bertie, Sir Wm. Sidney Smith, and Hon. Mich. De Courcy, we find Mr. Hay, who during a great portion of the period bore the rating of a Master's Mate, assisting at the capture, 13 March, 1806, of the *Marengo* 80, bearing the flag of Admiral Linois, and 40-gun frigate *Belle Poule;* and next, in 1807, witnessing the departure for South America of the Royal Family of Portugal. He subsequently, from Dec. 1812 until within a few weeks of his promotion to the rank of Lieutenant, which took place 20 Sept. 1815, served under Sir Jas. Lucas Yeo on the Canadian lakes, and participated in many acts of hostility with the American enemy. His after-appointments were—2 March, 1827, to the Coast Blockade, in which service he remained, with his name on the books of the RAMILLIES and TALAVERA 74's, both commanded by Capt. Hugh Pigot, until Nov. 1830—and, 1 Nov. 1833, to an Agency for Transports afloat. He resigned the duties of the latter office in the spring of 1834, but, resuming them in Oct. 1835, continued in discharge of them until the close of 1839. He has since been on half-pay.

* *Vide* Gaz. 1840, p. 2607.

HAY. (COMMANDER, 1827. F-P., 23; H-P., 12.)

ROBERT SINCLAIR HAY is second son of Robt. Hay, Esq., of Charterfield, East Lothian, N.B.

This officer entered the Navy, 1 Sept. 1812, as Fst.-cl. Vol., on board the PIQUE 36, Capt. Hon. Anth. Maitland, and sailed for the West Indies, where, we believe, he attained the rating of Midshipman 20 Dec. 1813, and served until Aug. 1815. From 1816 until 1818 we next find him employed, in the Mediterranean, on board the SATELLITE 16, Capt. Jas. Murray, and GLASGOW 50, Capt. Hon. Anth. Maitland. In May, 1820, he became Master's Mate of the ROCHFORT 74, flag-ship on the same station of Sir Graham Moore. He was promoted, 4 Oct. 1823, to a Lieutenancy in the CAMBRIAN 48, Capt. Gawen Wm. Hamilton, and he subsequently, in the course of the same month, and on 6 Sept. 1825, joined the ROSE 18, Capt. Henry Dundas, and TALBOT 28, Capt. Hon. Fred. Spencer. Being Senior of the last-mentioned ship at the battle of Navarin, where he was slightly wounded,* Mr. Hay was advanced to the rank of Commander, by commission dated 22 Oct. 1827. He afterwards, from 28 March, 1832, until 1835, and again from 24 June, 1836, until 1839, officiated as an Inspecting Commander in the Coast Guard; in which capacity he has been re-employed since 29 Dec. 1841.

Commander Hay married, in Jan. 1831, Jane, eldest daughter of Andw. Knox, Esq., of Prehen, co. Derry.

HAY. (LIEUTENANT, 1830.)

WILLIAM HAY is brother of Lieut. John Hay (*b*), R.N.

This officer entered the Navy 2 Nov. 1809; passed his examination in 1817; and was promoted to the rank of Lieutenant 22 July, 1830. His appointments have since been—22 July, 1831, to the Coast Guard, which he left in 1834, and rejoined 26 April, 1837—16 Jan. 1841, as First, to the PELICAN 16, Capt. Chas. John Elers Napier, fitting at Portsmouth—16 Aug. 1841, again to the Coast Guard—and, 2 July, 1844, to the command of the LIVELY Revenue-cutter, in which he is still serving.

HAYCOCK. (LIEUT., 1813. F-P., 10; H-P., 31.)

CHARLES HAYCOCK entered the Navy, 18 May, 1806, as Fst.-cl. Vol., on board the DILIGENCE sloop, stationed in the North Sea; served next, from May, 1807, until April, 1811, chiefly as Midshipman, in the COSSACK 24, commanded in the Great Belt, off the north coast of Spain, and in the Mediterranean, by Capts. Geo. Digby and Thos. Garth; rejoined Capt. Digby, then, in the LAVINIA frigate, on the latter station; and, after having acted for 11 months as Lieutenant of the ONYX 10, Capts. Philips, Squire, Cobb, and Julian, and for a short time also in command of the VESTA schooner, off Cadiz and Lisbon, was confirmed, 6 Dec. 1813, into the SAN JUAN, flag-ship at Gibraltar of Rear-Admiral Sam. Hood Linzee. He was lastly, from 22 June, 1814, until 4 Dec. 1815, employed in the Mediterranean, on board the VOLONTAIRE 38, Capt. Hon. Wm. Waldegrave.

HAYDON. (LIEUT., 1810. F-P., 17; H-P., 27.)

CHARLES HAYDON was born 30 June, 1793, at Shute House, near Axminster, Devon, the seat of Sir John Wm. Pole, Bart.

This officer entered the Navy, 16 Oct. 1803, as Fst.-cl. Vol., on board the NORTHUMBERLAND 74, Capt., afterwards Rear-Admiral, Hon. Alex. Inglis Cochrane, with whom he was for several months employed in watching a French squadron in the port of Ferrol. He then accompanied the same officer to the West Indies, where, in 1805, he joined Lord Nelson in his celebrated pursuit of the combined fleets. Removing, in Sept. of the latter year, to the RAMILLIES 74, Capt. Fras. Pickmore, he witnessed, as Midshipman of that ship, the capture, 13 March, 1806, of the *Marengo* 80, bearing the flag of Admiral Linois, and 40-gun frigate *Belle Poule;* after which, on being transferred, in 1807, to the

* *Vide* Gaz. 1827, p. 2325.

EPERVIER brig, Capts. John Bowker and Thos. Tudor Tucker, he saw a good deal of boat-service, and assisted at the reduction of the islands of St. Thomas and Ste. Croix. While next employed with Capt. Tucker, as Master's Mate and Acting-Lieutenant, from Nov. 1808 to Sept. 1809, in the CHERUB 18, Mr. Haydon, besides contributing to the cutting-out of an American sloop protected by a very heavy fire from the enemy's batteries at Martinique, and participating in the destruction of one of those means of defence, served on shore at the capture of the above island, and was present in the CHERUB's yawl in a frustrated attempt made, in May, 1809, to annihilate the French frigates *Furieuse* and *Félicité*, lying in Basseterre, Guadeloupe. On leaving the CHERUB, our officer, whose conduct in that sloop had been marked by a very conspicuous degree of gallantry, zeal, and energy, became successively Master's Mate of the NEPTUNE 98, and POMPÉE 74, bearing each the flag of his old Commander, Hon. Sir Alex. Cochrane, under whom, previously to sharing in the operations which led to the surrender of Guadeloupe, he beheld the destruction, 18 Dec. 1809, of the 40-gun frigates *Loire* and *Seine*, laden with stores and provisions, moored in Ance la Barque, and defended by numerous batteries. Being ultimately obliged, from the impaired state of his health, to return to England in the CURIEUX sloop, Capt. Colin Campbell, Mr. Haydon had the satisfaction, on his arrival, of being presented, as a reward for his services, with a commission bearing date 28 Dec. 1810. He almost immediately afterwards sailed, in the STATELY 64, Capt. Edw. Stirling Dickson, for Cadiz, where, with a view to assisting in its defence, he joined the flotilla, and was for nearly two years incessantly employed in a gun-boat. During that period, one of more than ordinary fatigue and excitement, he frequently landed for the purpose of storming the enemy's batteries, under whose immediate fire he appears to have been not less than 16 times personally in action. For many days at a time he was compelled to subsist upon raw salt meat; and, although an extraneous fact, it may not be uninteresting to add that he was instrumental to the embarkation of the mortar which now stands, an object of curiosity, in St. James' Park. Proceeding, in Dec. 1812, to the Mediterranean, in the BARFLEUR 98, Capt. Sir Edw. Berry, Mr. Haydon was there successively appointed, in the course of 1813, to the TREMENDOUS 74, Capt. Robt. Campbell, PRINCE OF WALES 98, Capt. John Erskine Douglas, and GUADELOUPE 16, Capts. Arthur Stow, Chas. Hole, and Chas. Pengelly; which latter vessel, after having served as her First-Lieutenant at the reduction of Genoa and its dependencies, he left in Aug. 1814. His subsequent appointments were—26 June, 1815, to the CEPHALUS 18, Capt. John Furneaux, under whom, during the war of 100 days, he was employed in co-operation with the Royalists, on the coast of France and up the Gironde—6 Nov. 1815, to the RAMILLIES 74, flag-ship at Leith of Sir Wm. Johnstone Hope—and, 5 June, 1818, to the CARRON 20, commanded by his former Captain, J. Furneaux, at whose especial request, it appears, he was selected to fill the office of First-Lieutenant. He proceeded in the latter vessel to the East Indies, escorting *en route* Sir Ralph Darling, Governor of the Mauritius, and continued to serve on that station until wrecked, in the Bay of Bengal, and with difficulty saved, 6 July, 1820. He then, after encountering many perils, inflictive of serious injury to his health, returned to England, and has since been on half-pay.

Lieut. Haydon has for many years resided at Axminster, and there discharged, with credit, the various duties of Churchwarden, Overseer, Collector of Taxes, Assessor, Guardian, &c. He married, 12 March, 1822, Miss Sarah Lincoln, of Crin Chard, Chard, co. Somerset, and by that lady has issue two sons and three daughters. AGENTS—Messrs. Chard.

HAYDON. (LIEUT., 1807. F-P., 13; H-P., 34.)

GEORGE HAYDON is brother of Capt. Wm. Haydon, R.N.

This officer entered the Navy, 1 Sept. 1800, as a Boy, on board the ROYAL GEORGE 100, Capt. Wm. Domett, stationed in the Channel. In Feb. 1801 he became Midshipman of the BELLEISLE 74, commanded by the latter officer, and subsequently by Capts. Chas. Boyles, John Whitby, and Wm. Hargood; under the latter of whom, on proceeding to the Mediterranean, he fought at Trafalgar, 21 Oct. 1805. On 9 June, 1807, after having been for 18 months employed on the coasts of Ireland and of the north of Spain on board the AMETHYST 36, and WARRIOR 74, both commanded by Capt. John Wm. Spranger, Mr. Haydon was promoted to a Lieutenancy in the ROSAMOND sloop, Capt. Jas. Whitley Deans, and Benj. Walker, on the North Sea station. His last appointment was, 1 Feb. 1808, to the MEDUSA 32, Capt. Hon. Duncombe Pleydell Bouverie, in which frigate, besides assisting at the capture of three heavy privateers, he experienced great hardships during a fruitless pursuit of two French frigates to the coast of Labrador, and was actively employed in 1812 in co-operation with the patriots on the north coast of Spain. He left the MEDUSA 30 May, 1813.

HAYDON. (CAPTAIN, 1841. F-P., 16; H-P., 38.)

WILLIAM HAYDON is brother of Lieut. Geo. Haydon, R.N.

This officer entered the Navy, 14 July, 1793, as Admiral's Servant, on board the ROYAL GEORGE 100, Capt. Wm. Domett, bearing the flag on the Channel of the late Lord Bridport; and, from the following Sept. until his promotion to the rank of Lieutenant 26 Sept. 1799, was successively employed on the Home station in the NIGER, LATONA, and CAMBRIAN frigates, all commanded by Capt. Hon. Arthur Kaye Legge; under whom, in the NIGER, one of Vice-Admiral Graves' repeaters, he officiated as Signal-Midshipman in the action of 1 June, 1794. Until he invalided in Nov. 1801, Mr. Haydon next served on the Irish and West India stations in the HAZARD 18, and CERBERUS 32, Capts. Wm. Butterfield and Jas. Macnamara. He was subsequently, on 4 April, 1803, appointed First of the MERCURY 28, in which frigate, and in L'AIMABLE 32, and MEDUSA, of similar force, he uninterruptedly served for five years with Capt. Hon. Duncombe Pleydell Bouverie. He was at first employed, during that period, on the Jersey and Guernsey station; next, under Lord Nelson in the Mediterranean; and ultimately in South America, where, in Feb. 1807, he served on shore with a brigade of seamen and marines under Capt. Ross Donnelly, and obtained the high eulogiums of Sir Sam. Auchmuty for his conduct at the storming of Monte Video. On the return of the MEDUSA to England, Mr. Haydon was sent with a strong recommendation to Sir Wm. Sidney Smith, then at Rio de Janeiro, where, in July, 1808, he was invested by that officer with the command of the Hospital Island, and the rank of Commander. The Admiralty, however, refusing to confirm the appointment, he returned to England, and was not promoted until 1 Aug. 1811, from which period, with the exception of three months' acting-command (from Dec. 1811 to March, 1812), of the CRANE 18, he remained on half-pay until nominated, 15 May, 1828, Second Captain of the WINDSOR CASTLE 76, flag-ship in the Mediterranean of his friend Hon. D. P. Bouverie. In May, 1830, his private affairs requiring his presence in England, Capt. Haydon was obliged to resign his appointment; and he has not since been afloat. His elevation to the rank he now holds took place 23 Nov. 1841.

HAYDON. (LIEUT., 1809. F-P., 12; H-P., 32).

WILLIAM PHIPPARD HAYDON entered the Navy, 12 April, 1803, as Master's Mate, on board the WINCHELSEA, Lieut.-Commander Pope, lying at Sheerness. In Aug. following he removed to the

ROMNEY 50, Capts. Wm. Brown and Hon. John Colville, under the latter of whom, on his return from a voyage to the coast of Africa, he was wrecked, in a fog, on the Haaks, near the Texel, 19 Nov. 1804. He was then received on board the VESTAL 28, Capt. Stephen Thos. Digby, and after participating, during the summer of 1805, in many warm engagements with the enemy's flotilla and batteries near Calais, he accompanied that officer into the ARGO 44, and again sailed for the African station. In the course of 1808 we find him successively transferred to the BELLEISLE 74, and NEPTUNE 98, bearing each the flag of Hon. Sir Alex. Cochrane, by whom, subsequently to the fall of Martinique, he was nominated, 29 June, 1809, Acting-Lieutenant of the ALCMÈNE frigate, Capt. Wm. Maude. He was confirmed, 8 Dec. following, into the GUADELOUPE 16, Capt. Michael Head, also attached to the force at the West Indies; on his return whence, he joined, 6 Sept. and 20 Nov. 1810, the HIBERNIA 120, and CENTAUR 74, both commanded by Capt. John Chambers White. In the latter ship Mr. Haydon, after serving for some time with the inshore squadron off Toulon, co-operated in the defence of Tarragona, and, in April, 1814, witnessed the destruction, up the Gironde, of a French line-of-battle ship, three brigs of war, several smaller vessels, and of all the ports and batteries on the north side of the river. He was superseded from the CENTAUR at his own request 24 Dec. 1814, and has since been on half-pay.

HAYE. (CAPTAIN, 1829. F-P., 20; H-P., 26.)

GEORGE HAYE was born 15 April, 1788, at Callington, co. Cornwall.

This officer entered the Navy, 1 Aug. 1801, as Fst.-cl. Vol., on board the HERCULE 74, Capt. Wm. Luke, stationed in the Channel. From May, 1802, until April, 1807, he was next employed, as Midshipman and Master's Mate, chiefly in the East Indies, in the ST. FIORENZO 36, Capts. Joseph Bingham, John Batt, Henry Lambert, and Geo. Nicholas Hardinge. He then rejoined Capt. Bingham for a short time on board the SCEPTRE 74, and was afterwards, between July, 1807, and his promotion to the rank of Lieutenant, 9 Aug. 1808, transferred in succession to the GRAMPUS 50, Capt. Jas. Haldane Tait, ST. ALBANS 64, Capt. Fras. Wm. Austen, and IPHIGENIA 36, Capt. Henry Lambert. In the latter frigate he made a voyage to Quebec; on his return whence he was appointed, 11 Feb. and 26 June, 1809, to the VULTURE 16, Capt. Martin White, and ACTIVE 46, Capt. Jas. Alex. Gordon. Accompanying the last-mentioned officer to the Adriatic, Mr. Haye there, on 3 Feb. 1811, commanded the barges of his own frigate and of the CERBERUS, at the capture of four Venetian trabaccolos, under a heavy fire of musketry from a body of troops quartered at Pestichi; nine days after which event we find him conspicuously assisting in the boats of the same ships, under Lieut. Jas. Dickinson, at the cutting-out, near the town of Ortano (where two important magazines were at the same time destroyed), and in the face of a teasing fire, which was kept up for five hours, of a convoy of 10 sail, protected by a trabaccolo of 6 guns.* On 13 of the following March Mr. Haye had the fortune to participate in the memorable action off Lissa, where a British squadron, carrying in the whole 156 guns and 879 men, completely routed, after a conflict of six hours, and a loss to the ACTIVE of 4 men killed and 24 wounded, a Franco-Venetian armament, whose force amounted to 284 guns and 2655 men. At the close of the action he was placed on board the *Corona*, one of the prize-frigates, and for his exertions in extinguishing a fire which soon afterwards threatened the destruction of that ship, he appears to have elicited the warmest thanks of Capt. Wm. Hoste, the senior officer of the British squadron, and to have been strongly recommended by him to the Commander-in-Chief.† On 27 July, 1811, Mr. Haye, who had been se[illegible]rnt on the latter occasion, and had not yet recovered, very handsomely volunteered to assist, which he accordingly did, at the capture of a convoy of 28 merchantmen, defended, in a creek of the island of Ragosniza, by 300 troops and three gun-vessels.* He subsequently, on 29 Nov. in the same year (Capt. Gordon and the First-Lieutenant, Mr. Wm. Bateman Dashwood, having been put *hors-de-combat*), succeeded to the command of the ACTIVE, and was himself slightly hurt in the course of a hard-fought action of an hour and 40 minutes, which in rendering that frigate captor of *La Pomone*, of 44 guns and 332 men, 50 of whom were killed and wounded, occasioned her a loss of 8 killed and 27 wounded.† As a reward for his highly-lauded gallantry in these and other instances, Mr. Haye was ultimately, on 19 May, 1812, promoted to the rank of Commander. His last appointments were, 17 Feb. 1814, to the PELTER 12, employed, until Sept. 1815, on the North American station—1 Jan. 1821, to the Coast Guard service in Ireland, where his conduct in soon after effecting the destruction of the *Dandy*, a large smuggling cutter, procured him the particular notice of the Lords of the Treasury—8 Dec. 1827 (having left the Coast Guard in the previous Jan.), to the EREBUS bomb, attached to the force in the Mediterranean—and, 8 July, 1828, to the RALEIGH, 18, on the same station. He returned to England on being advanced to his present rank 4 March, 1829.

Capt. Haye married, 15 May, 1834, Nanny, youngest daughter of Wm. Davey, Esq., of Redruth, co. Cornwall, by whom, who died 6 June, 1843, he has issue two sons and one daughter. AGENTS—Coplands and Burnett.

HAYES. (CAPTAIN, 1846.)

COURTENAY OSBORN HAYES is eldest son of that distinguished seaman and able naval architect the late Rear-Admiral John Hayes, C.B.,‡ who died 7 April, 1838; brother of Commander John Montagu Hayes, R.N.; and nephew of Capt. Geo. Hayes, R.N.

This officer entered the Navy, 30 Nov. 1826; passed his examination in 1833; and obtained his first commission 17 Feb. 1835. His appointments as Lieutenant were—13 April and 28 Nov., in the latter year to the PELORUS 16, Capt. Rich. Meredith, and HASTINGS 74, flag-ship of Sir Wm. Hall Gage, on the African and Lisbon stations—and, 2 Sept. 1836, to the INCONSTANT 36, Capts. John Hayes (his father), and Dan. Pring, employed on Particular Service. Attaining the rank of Commander 20 Sept. 1839, he afterwards, from 8 June, 1842, until the receipt of a Post commission bearing date 9 Nov. 1846, served in the East Indies on board the WOLF 18 and DRIVER steam-sloop.

Capt. Hayes married, 14 May, 1840, Caroline Anne, only daughter of the late Alfred Slocock, Esq., of Donnington Cottage, Berks, by whom he has issue. AGENTS—Messrs. Ommanney.

HAYES. (CAPTAIN, 1829. F-P., 33; H-P., 30.)

GEORGE HAYES, born 13 May, 1769, is grand-nephew of the late Adam Hayes, Esq., Master Shipwright of Deptford Dockyard; brother of the late Rear-Admiral John Hayes, C.B.; and uncle of Capt. C. O. and Commander J. M. Hayes, R.N.

This officer entered the Navy, 17 April, 1784, as Fst.-cl. Vol., on board the THISBE 28, Capt. Geo. Robinson, on the Newfoundland station, whence he returned in March, 1786. He was next, between 1787 and the early part of 1793, employed in the Channel with Capts. Rowley Bulteel and John Salisbury, as Midshipman, Master's Mate, and Acting-Lieutenant, in the TERMAGANT 18, NARCISSUS 20, and ANDROMEDA 32; in the boats belonging to which frigates he appears to have arduously cruized, and not unsuccessfully, for the protection of the Revenue. On leaving the ANDROMEDA he was for

* *Vide* Gaz. 1811, p. 997.

* *Vide* Gaz. 1811, p. 2193. † *V.* Gaz. 1812, pp. 566-7.

‡ Rear-Admiral Hayes was the constructor of the 36-gun f[illegible]ate INCONSTANT, now on the list of the Navy.

a short time borne on the books of the CAMBRIDGE, guard-ship at Plymouth, for the purpose of inspecting the building of the EXPERIMENT lugger. On 25 May, 1793, Mr. Hayes was made Lieutenant into the ADVENTURE 44, Capt. Edw. Buller, from which ship we find him removing to the command, in the following June, of the above-named EXPERIMENT. In that vessel, one of 10 guns, he accompanied Sir John Borlase Warren on his expedition of 1795 to Quiberon Bay in support of the Royalist cause. After a subsequent attendance of some time on William Pitt, off Walmer Castle, and experiencing several skirmishes with the enemy's gun-boats in the Channel, Mr. Hayes proceeded, off Toulon, with despatches for Sir John Jervis, by whom he was sent with others for Sir Gilbert Elliot, the Viceroy of Corsica. On his passage to that island he had the gallantry to beat off a French brig of 12 guns, together with two gun-boats, mounting each 1 gun—an exploit whose importance procured him a very flattering testimonial from the Viceroy. When afterwards on his way to England, again in charge of despatches, the EXPERIMENT had the misfortune, on 2 Oct. 1796, to be captured by a Spanish fleet in a calm off the Cape de Gata. On being exchanged, in Jan. 1797, for the Captain of the *Mahonesa*, a frigate which had been recently taken by Capt. Rich. Bowen of the TERPSICHORE, Mr. Hayes, whose pecuniary loss by the above catastrophe had been great, joined the LIVELY 32, Capt. Lord Garlies, under whom, on 14 of the next Feb., he fought in the action off Cape St. Vincent. His subsequent appointments were to the command, on the Home station—10 April, 1798, of the REDBRIDGE schooner —11 Dec. 1800 and 6 Feb. 1803, of the GEORGE cutter and AGGRESSOR gun-brig, which vessels he respectively left in Oct. 1801 and Dec. 1803—19 Nov. 1805, of the DARING gun-brig, part of the force employed in the expedition to the Walcheren, where he exhibited a conspicuous degree of courage and conduct, and obtained a vigorous letter of recommendation from Capt. Philip Carteret, who commanded the gun-boats, to Commodore Owen, not only for his distinguished share in the siege of Flushing, but also for the means he had been of saving the REYNARD and CRACKER brigs-of-war from destruction, after they had grounded within point-blank shot of the enemy—11 Dec. 1810, for eight months of the BRAAVE, prison-ship at Plymouth—and, 5 Jan. 1813, of the WHITING schooner. Obtaining a second promotal commission 15 June, 1814, Capt. Hayes was next, from 1817 to 1824, employed as an Inspecting Commander in the Water Guard; the very arduous and harassing duties attached to which office he discharged with so much zeal, activity, and ability, that upon being superseded, he received from the Comptroller General a spontaneous offer of recommending his merits to the notice of the Admiralty. His last appointment was, 4 Dec. 1826, to the WOLF 18, the command of which sloop he retained, on the Mediterranean station, until Feb. 1830. He then went on half-pay, having been advanced to his present rank on 2 of the preceding Dec.

During the term of his servitude as Lieutenant, Capt. Hayes was employed for six months in the Sea Fencibles at Exmouth; for five months with a boat's crew at the Isle of Wight for the purpose of detecting deserters from the fleet; and for a year and five months at Torpoint, in command of a party of Marines for the apprehension of deserters and the entering of men for the Service. He married, 4 March, 1802, Phoebe, relict of Lieut. Chas. Henry Haswell, R.N., daughter of Capt. Wm. Starr, of Dover, and daughter-in-law of the late Admiral Robt. Haswell. By that lady he has issue two sons (one, the present First-Lieutenant Geo. Jas. Hayes, R.M.) and two daughters. AGENTS—Messrs. Ommanney.

HAYES. (COMMANDER, 1841. F-P., 13; H-P., 5.)

JOHN MONTAGU HAYES, born 23 March, 1816, is brother of Capt. C. O. Hayes, R.N.

This officer entered the Navy, 20 March, 1829, as Fst.-cl. Vol., on board the MELVILLE 74, Capt. Alex. Wilmot Schomberg, stationed in the Mediterranean; removed as Midshipman, in July, 1830, to the DRYAD 42, commanded on the western coast of Africa by his father, Capt. John Hayes; and at the commencement of 1833 sailed for South America in the SPARTIATE 76, successive flag-ship of Sir Michael Seymour and Sir Graham Eden Hamond. Being lent in July, 1834, to the SPARROWHAWK 16, Capt. Chas. Pearson, he made a voyage from Rio de Janeiro to Falkland Islands, and on 9 Aug. anchored in Berkeley Sound. On 6 Sept. he was thence sent with Lieut. Sam. Fielding Harmer and four men in a whale-boat for the purpose of endeavouring to save the crew of a merchant brig, which had been wrecked on the western point of the East Falkland Island, a distance of nearly a hundred miles along a most dangerous coast. Owing to contrary winds and stormy weather, sixteen days elapsed before the boat reached the point near which the wreck lay. At the end of that period, being unfortunately caught in a heavy snow-storm, she upset and was lost, together with 1 man and the whole of her provisions and arms, a misadventure which rendered it necessary for the survivors, now in a state of perfect destitution, to trace their way back to Berkeley Sound, as best they could, across a difficult and unknown country, and in the most inclement weather. The hardships and sufferings they underwent it is not easy to describe. The first two days were passed without food of any kind; on the third they contrived to catch a wild calf, whose raw flesh for ten days formed their scanty and only subsistence. Lieut. Harmer and two of the men by that time had become so weak that they were unable to proceed; and it was not until after a further lapse of six days that Mr. Hayes and his only remaining companion, supported *en route* by the carcass of a half-starved dog, were enabled in a deathlike state to reach the settlement, and despatch assistance to their wretched associates, all of whom, as was subsequently the case with the crew of the merchantman, were found and happily preserved from what had long appeared inevitable destruction. In Nov. 1834 Mr. Hayes, whose health continued for many months in a very impaired state, rejoined the SPARTIATE, and on 12 of the following May he passed his examination. He was ultimately, after having further served for two years in the Mediterranean as Mate of the RODNEY 92, Capt. Hyde Parker, promoted to the rank of Lieutenant by a commission bearing date 21 Oct. 1837. Being next appointed, 13 Feb. 1838, to the CRUIZER 16, Capts. Rich. Henry King and Henry Wells Giffard, he sailed in that sloop for the East Indies, where, besides attending an expedition to the mouths of the Indus, he assisted at the capture of Aden. He afterwards, in 1840, accompanied the armament to China, and in the course of the same year was present at the capture of Chusan and the blockade of Ningpo. On the return of the CRUIZER with Sir Hugh Gough to China, after having been sent in charge of despatches to Calcutta, Mr. Hayes, we find, was in the boats at the capture of several of the forts in the Canton river, and had charge of one of those forming the western division in the first attack on the outworks of that city. During the second series of operations against it, he was successively employed, in a manner that gained him the highest praise, on board the brig, then in the boats, and ultimately on shore at the capture of the French Folly.* On 26 Aug. 1841 he was in acting-command of the CRUIZER at the capture of Amoy, and in the course of the next Oct. he served in the boats and with the small-arm men at the recapture of Chusan, and was also present at the storming of Chinghae and the occupation of Ningpo. From 1 Nov. in the same year until 20 Jan. 1842, Mr. Hayes was again entrusted with the charge of the CRUIZER. He then returned home, having been rewarded for his services by a Commander's com-

* *Vide* Gaz. 1841, pp. 1505–2505.

mission dated 8 Oct. 1841;* and has since been on half-pay. AGENTS—Messrs. Ommanney.

HAYMES. (CAPTAIN, 1846. F-P., 14; H-P., 30.)

PHILIP GEORGE HAYMES entered the Navy, 1 June, 1803, as Fst.-cl. Vol., on board the ROMULUS, Capt. Woodley Losack, and after serving for some time with the same officer as Midshipman in the HELENA sloop on the Home station, joined, in 1806, the PRINCE GEORGE 98, Capt. Geo. Losack, and sailed for the West Indies. Between 1807 and 1812, he was next employed, on the Guernsey, Baltic, and Mediterranean stations, in the DIOMEDE 50 and VICTORY 100, flag-ships of Sir Jas. Saumarez, PHŒBE 36, Capts. Hassard Stackpoole and Jas. Hillyar, and SAN JOSEF 110, bearing the flag of Sir Chas. Cotton. He then rejoined Sir Jas. Saumarez on board the VICTORY, and on 23 July in the same year, 1812, was appointed, with the rank of Acting-Lieutenant, to the command of a gun-boat, in which we find him co-operating with the Russian flotilla in the defence of Riga, and participating in a successful expedition against the French and Prussians at Mittau, on the river Aa. Being rewarded for his services with a commission dated on 20 of the following Nov., Mr. Haymes was subsequently, after an intermediate attachment to the Russian Admiral's flag-ship, appointed, 30 Dec. 1812, to the ROYAL OAK 74, bearing the successive flags, on the Home and American stations, of Lord Amelius Beauclerk and the late Sir Pulteney Malcolm. On 13 March, 1815, having acted as Naval Aide-de-Camp to Major-Generals Ross and Gibbs during the expeditions against Washington, Baltimore, and New Orleans, he was advanced to the rank of Commander. Capt. Haymes' only appointment in the latter capacity appears to have been, 18 Dec. 1841, to the FANTOME 16, in which sloop he returned home from South America, and was paid off towards the close of 1843. He attained Post-rank 9 Nov. 1846.

Capt. Haymes is married and has issue. AGENTS—Messrs. Halford and Co.

HAYTER. (LIEUT., 1818. F-P., 14; H-P., 30.)

BENJAMIN HAYTER entered the Navy, 7 June, 1803, as Third-cl. Vol., on board the MAGNIFICENT 74, Capt. Wm. Hen. Jervis, under whom he was wrecked, on a sunken rock, near Brest, 25 March, 1804. From that period he remained a prisoner in France until the peace of 1814, when, being restored to liberty, he joined the SCIPION 74, Capt. Hen. Heathcote, in which ship, and in the SLANEY 20, Capt. Geo. Rose Sartorius, he served on the Mediterranean and Home stations until Aug. 1815—witnessing, in the latter vessel, the surrender of Napoleon Buonaparte. Joining, next, the IMPREGNABLE 98, he fought in that ship under the flag of Rear-Admiral David Milne at the bombardment of Algiers. Being, however, discharged in Oct. 1816, Mr. Hayter did not again go afloat until nominated Admiralty-Midshipman, in Jan. 1818, of the DRAKE sloop, Capt. Hen. Shiffner. He returned to England in Feb. 1819, having been advanced to the rank of Lieutenant by commission bearing date 19 of the previous Sept., and has not been since employed.

HEA. (LIEUTENANT, 1815. F-P., 10; H-P., 31.)

ROBERT HEA entered the Navy, 25 April, 1806, as Fst.-cl. Vol., on board the BOADICEA 38, Capt. John Maitland, with whom, and with Capt. John Hatley, he continued to serve, in the same ship, and in the RAISONNABLE 64, on the Cork, Newfoundland, Channel, and Cape of Good Hope stations, principally as Midshipman and Master's Mate, until July, 1810. He then became attached, for a short period, as a Supernumerary, to the NAMUR 74, flag-ship at the Nore of Vice-Admiral Thos. Wells; after which he served, until Dec. 1815, in the CRANE sloop, Capt. Jas. Stuart, SEINE frigate, Capt. John Hatley, and HORATIO 38, and NEWCASTLE 60, both commanded by Lord Geo. Stuart. He was employed, in the first mentioned of those vessels, on the West India station; and was present, in the HORATIO, after re-visiting the Cape, at the capture of the islands of Schouwen and Tholen, in the North Sea. While in the NEWCASTLE, of which ship he was confirmed a Lieutenant 11 March, 1815, he cruized with activity on the North American station. Since Dec. of the latter year he has been on half-pay.

Lieut. Hea has for a long time held the office of Inspector of Convicts at Norfolk Island. AGENTS—Collier and Snee.

* *Vide* Gaz. 1841, p. 2539.

HEAD. (COMMANDER, 1819. F-P., 22; H-P., 25.)

RICHARD JOHN HEAD was born at Helston, co. Cornwall.

This officer entered the Navy, 20 May, 1800, as a Volunteer, on board the CONQUEST gun-brig, Lieut.-Commander Green, attached to the force in the Channel, where, on his removal to the PELICAN 18, Capt. John Thicknesse, he was in the following winter cast away. He then, until the peace of Amiens, served on board the HERCULE 74, Capt. Wm. Luke; on leaving which ship he successively joined the CHILDERS and DASHER sloops, both commanded by Capt. J. Delafons; whom, in the latter vessel, he accompanied to the East Indies. Being there confirmed, 12 June, 1807, a Lieutenant (after having acted as such for a period of nine months) in the SIR FRANCIS DRAKE 32, Capt. Hon. Pownoll Bastard Pellew, he had the misfortune, during a continuance of three years in that ship, to be twice severely wounded, once at the destruction of six pirate vessels in the straits of Malacca, and again when beating off an attack made by the French frigate *Piedmontaise* on the SIR FRANCIS DRAKE and a convoy of Chinamen. Returning to England in 1810, Mr. Head was next, until Aug. 1814, employed, on the Channel, Baltic, and Mediterranean stations, in the DREADNOUGHT 98, Capt. Sam. Hood Linzee, and VENERABLE, MARS, and PEMBROKE 74's, Capts. Sir Home Popham, Hen. Raper, and Jas. Brisbane. While in the last-mentioned ship he participated, 5 Nov. 1813, in a partial action with the Toulon fleet, and in the course of the following April, besides commanding the boats at the capture of a large convoy under the guns of Porto Maurizio, served at the reduction of Genoa and the taking of Corsica. From Sept. 1814, until his promotion to the rank of Commander 15 May, 1819, he was employed in the QUEEN and ALBION 74's, chiefly as Flag-Lieutenant to Sir Chas. Vinicombe Penrose, by whom he was sent on a secret service to Rome, whence he brought away and delivered to the British Government all the valuable papers of the Cardinal de York, the last of the Stuart family. Commander Head's only other appointment was to the Coast Guard, in which service he continued from 1824 to 1827. On his retirement he was entertained at a dinner given to him by the officers of his district, who at the same time presented him with a snuff-box, of heart of oak, manufactured from a beam of St. Mawe's Castle, of 200 years standing, suitably ornamented, with an inscription commemorative of their feelings of respect and attachment to him.

He married, 16 Oct. 1832, Sarah Vigurs, daughter of the Rev. F. L. Bluett, Vicar of Mullion, by whom he has issue three sons.

HEALES. (LIEUT., 1827. F-P., 16; H-P., 22.)

THOMAS HEALES was born 23 April, 1794, and died 22 Nov. 1846 at Dalston, co. Middlesex.

This officer entered the Navy, 12 June, 1809, as a Volunteer, on board the ROTA 38, Capt. Philip Somerville. In the boats of that frigate, after attending the expedition to the Walcheren, he served at the siege of Cadiz, and assisted, 22 May, 1812, at the capture, with great loss to the British, of *L'Espardon* privateer, of 3 guns and 45 men. He subsequently, during a cruize off the Western Islands, participated, as Midshipman, in an unsuccessful attempt made on 26 Sept. 1814 to cut out from the road of Fayal the American privateer *General Armstrong*, a vessel whose resistance killed 34, and wounded 86 of her assailants, consisting originally of about 180 seamen and marines. In the course of 1815 Mr. Heales joined the ALBION and QUEEN 74's, Capts. P. Somerville and Jas. Walker; from the latter of which ships he volunteered, in July, 1816, into the INFERNAL bomb, Capt. Hon. Geo. Percival, for the purpose of attending the expedition against Algiers, where he fought as Master's Mate, having at the time the charge of a Lieutenant's watch. For his conduct on the occasion Mr. Heales was to have been promoted, but the commission, we understand, which had been actually intended for him being by some fatality given to another person, a Mr. Geo. Hales, he did not succeed in effecting his advancement until after a lapse of nearly 11 years; during which period he appears to have been employed, on the North and South American, St. Helena, Irish, East India, and Home stations, as Admiralty-Midshipman, in succession, of the PACTOLUS 38, Capt. Hugh Dobbie, BLOSSOM 18, Capts. Fred. Hickey and Fred. Edw. Vernon, BRAZEN 18, Capt. Wm. Shepheard, ALLIGATOR 28, Capt. Thos. Alexander, PRINCE REGENT 120, flag-ship of Sir Robt. Moorsom, and RAMILLIES Coast-Blockade-ship, Capt. Hugh Pigot. He was then at length created a Lieutenant by commission bearing date 28 April, 1827; and in that capacity he afterwards, from 10 Jan. 1838 until Feb. 1839, served at Sheerness on board the HOWE 120, and OCEAN 80, Capts. Chas. Hen. Paget and Sir John Hill.

Lieut. Heales married Maria, daughter of Mr. Butler Wm. Mountain, coach proprietor, of the Saracen's Head, Snow Hill, London, and of Whetstone House, Whetstone, near Barnet, co. Middlesex, by whom he has left issue.

HEALY. (RETIRED COMMANDER, 1839. F-P., 14; H-P., 35.)

JOHN HEALY died 27 April, 1846, at Bordeaux, aged 70.

This officer entered the Navy, 8 July, 1797, as A. B., on board the MONMOUTH 64, Capts. Lord Northesk, Jas. Walker, Robt. Deans, and Geo. Hart, and on 11 of the following Oct. fought as Midshipman in the action off Camperdown. After attending the expedition of 1799 to the Helder, he again, from Aug. 1800 until April, 1802, served with Capts. Walker and Lord Northesk, in the PRINCE 98. Proceeding then to the Cape of Good Hope in the IMOGENE 18, Capt. Hen. Vaughan, Mr. Healy served on that and the Indian stations for a period of five years on board the LANCASTER 64, CENTURION 50, and TRIDENT 64, bearing the flags of Sir Roger Curtis and Vice-Admiral Rainier, GRAMPUS 50, Capt. Thos. Gordon Caulfeild (of which ship he was created a Lieutenant 26 Feb. 1805), and SCEPTRE 74, Capt. Joseph Bingham. He was lastly, from Aug. 1808 until he invalided in Oct. 1812, employed, at home and in the West Indies, chiefly as First-Lieutenant, in the NEPTUNE 98, Capt. Sir Thos. Williams, LATONA frigate, Capts. Jas. Athol Wood and Hugh Pigot, YORK 74, Capt. Robt. Barton, VESUVIUS bomb, Capt. Saunders, ABOUKIR 74, Capt. Geo. Parker, and VESTAL 28, *armée en flûte*, Capt. Sam. Bartlett Deeckar. He accepted the rank of Retired Commander 12 Sept. 1839. AGENTS—Messrs. Ommanney.

HEARD. (LIEUTENANT, 1840.)

THOMAS HEARD entered the Navy 9 April, 1826; passed his examination in 1832; and on 4 Nov. 1840 was promoted to the rank of Lieutenant as a reward for the services he had rendered on the coast of Syria and at the bombardment of St. Jean d'Acre. His appointments have since been—15 Dec. 1840, to the POWERFUL 84, Capts. Sir Chas. Napier, Geo. Mansel, and Michael Seymour, in the Mediterranean—26 May, 1842, as First, to the ALBATROSS 16, Capt. Reginald Yorke, fitting at Portsmouth—29 Nov. 1842, to the SAMARANG 26, Capt. Sir Edw. Belcher, employed as a surveying-vessel in the East Indies—next, as a Supernumerary, to the AGINCOURT 72, flag-ship of Sir Thos. John Cochrane, Commander-in-Chief on the latter station, where it appears he had charge of a gun-boat and was wounded at the capture and destruction, 19 Aug. 1845, of Maloodoo, a strong fortification in the possession of Scheriff Osman, a rebel Borneo chieftain*—and, 27 Nov. 1845, as Senior, to the WOLF 18, Capt. Jas. Alex. Gordon, in which sloop he still serves in the East Indies. AGENTS—Messrs. Chard.

HEARLE. (RETIRED COMMANDER, 1840. F-P., 26; H-P., 30.)

ROBERT HEARLE entered the Navy, in 1791, as A.B., on board the FLY sloop, Capt. Jas. Drew, on the Newfoundland station; served, next, in the HANNIBAL 74, commanded at Plymouth by Capt. John Colpoys; and in July, 1792, became Midshipman of the PORCUPINE 24, Capts. Edw. Buller and Robt. Barlow, employed off the coast of Ireland and in the Channel. From July, 1793, until promoted to the rank of Lieutenant 9 May, 1797, he further served with Capt. Barlow on the Home station, the last two years as Master's Mate, in the PEGASUS 28, AQUILON 32, and PHŒBE 36. He then joined the POMONA armed brig, Capt. Joseph Eyles, and, in Feb. 1798, the NEMESIS 28, Capts. Robt. Dudley Oliver, Thos. Baker, Edw. W. C. R. Owen, and Philip Somerville; under the second named of whom he shared, 25 July, 1800, in a smart conflict of 25 minutes, which terminated in the capture of the Danish frigate *Freija*. From Aug. 1802, the date of his quitting the NEMESIS, until 1817, Mr. Hearle commanded a cutter under the Board of Customs. He was placed on the Junior List of Retired Commanders 26 Nov. 1830, and on the Senior 14 Jan. 1840.

Commander Hearle was left a widower 21 June, 1837. One of his daughters is married to the present Lieut. B. Hooper, R.N.

HEASLOP. (COMMANDER, 1817. F-P., 11; H-P., 31.)

JOHN COLPOYS HEASLOP entered the Navy, in April, 1805, as Fst.-cl. Vol., on board the DRAGON 74, Capt. Edw. Griffith, one of Sir Robt. Calder's fleet in the ensuing action of 22 July. In 1807 he successively became Midshipman of the TOPAZE 38, Capt. Anselm John Griffiths, and SULTAN 74, commanded by his former Captain, Griffith, under whom, on 26 Oct. 1809, he assisted in causing the self-destruction, between Frontignan and Cette, of the French ships of the line *Robuste* and *Lion*. While afterwards serving with Capt. Chas. Bullen in the VOLONTAIRE and CAMBRIAN frigates, Mr. Heaslop was much employed in co-operation with the patriots on the coast of Catalonia, particularly at the capture of Palamos and the siege of Tarragona. On 6 Nov. 1813, having been further attached for short periods to the BULWARK, QUEEN, and BELLONA 74's, Capts. Thos. Brown, Lord Colville, and Geo. M'Kinley (in the latter of which ships he had made a voyage to St. Helena), he was promoted to the rank of Lieutenant; a capacity in which he subsequently joined—4 May, 1814, the DIADEM 64, Capt. John Martin Hanchett, on the American station, where, previously to invaliding in the following Sept., he accompanied the boats of a squadron up St. Mary's river, and was present in the attacks on Washington and New Orleans—28 Oct. 1815, the AKBAR 50, bearing the flag at Halifax of his patron, Rear-Admiral Griffith—21 June, 1816, the NIGER 38, Capt. Sam. Jackson—and, in Nov. of the same year, the FORTH frigate, as Flag-Lieutenant to Rear-Admiral Griffith. He attained his present rank 24 June, 1817; but has not been since afloat. AGENTS—Messrs. Chard.

HEASTEY. (LIEUT., 1810. F-P., 14; H-P., 32.)

GEORGE HEASTEY was born 19 June, 1788, at Devonport.

This officer entered the Navy, 1 July, 1801, as A.B., on board the VILLE DE PARIS 110, bearing the flag in the Channel of Hon. Wm. Cornwallis; proceeded to the Mediterranean in 1802 as Midship-

* *Vide* Gaz. 1845, p. 6536.

man of the Belleisle 74, Capts. John Whitby and Wm. Hargood; rejoined the Ville de Paris in 1805 (after having gone in pursuit of the Franco-Spanish fleet to the West Indies); and between Nov. 1806 and Oct. 1808, was again employed in the Mediterranean on board the Royal Sovereign 100, and Ocean 98, flag-ships of Vice-Admirals Edw. Thornbrough and Lord Collingwood. Being then appointed Acting-Lieutenant of the Montagu 74, Capts. Rich. Hussey Moubray and John Halliday, he was much employed in the boats of that ship up the Adriatic, and commanded a battery at the reduction of Santa Maura in April, 1810. He was officially promoted on 4 May in the latter year, but he did not leave the Montagu until May, 1811; on 25 Sept. in which year we find him joining the Recruit 18, Capts. Humphrey Fleming Senhouse, John Evans, Geo. Rich. Pechell, Thos. Sykes, and John Lawrence, on the North American station, where, prior to his being paid off in Jan. 1815, he served as First-Lieutenant at the taking of Washington, and of other places in the Chesapeake. His last appointment was, 28 Feb. 1818, to the Carnation 18, Capts. Hon. John Gordon and Wm. Nugent Glascock, with whom he served as Senior on the Newfoundland and Halifax stations, until Sept. 1815, at which period he invalided.

Lieut. Heastey married, 23 Aug. 1821, and has issue four children. Agent—J. Hinxman.

HEATH. (Lieutenant, 1840.)

Leopold George Heath entered the Navy, 24 Dec. 1831; passed his examination in 1836; and obtained his commission 22 Dec. 1840. He then joined the Impregnable 104, Capt. Thos. Forrest, on the Mediterranean station; and on 19 Oct. 1843, he was appointed to the Iris 26, Capt. Geo. Rodney Mundy, whom he accompanied to the East Indies. During an expedition conducted in July, 1846, by Sir Thos. John Cochrane against the Sultan of Borneo, we find Mr. Heath, on 8 of that month, assisting, as second in command of the rocket-party, at the capture and destruction of the enemy's forts and batteries on the river Brune. On the ensuing ascent of a branch of that stream, by a force under Capt. Mundy, he led the boats, and by his efficient command of a body of pioneers proved of the greatest utility in clearing the passage of the many overhanging trees and other obstructions with which its navigation was beset. After the disembarkation of the British at the village of Mallout, he accompanied them in their arduous and fruitless pursuit of the Sultan to a place called Damuan, and again performed valuable service.* He has been in acting-command, since Jan. 1847, of the Wolf 18, on the same station.

HEATH. (Lieutenant, 1844.)

William Andrew James Heath entered the Navy in 1832; passed his examination 4 Dec. 1839; and served for nearly five years, on the Mediterranean and North American stations, as Mate of the Pique 36, Capts. Edw. Boxer, Rich. Augustus Yates, Henry Forbes, and Hon. Montagu Stopford; under the first-named of which officers (by whom his conduct was mentioned in the highest terms †) he took part, during the operations of 1840 on the coast of Syria, in the capture of Caiffa and Tsour, and the bombardment of St. Jean d'Acre. He obtained his commission 26 Nov. 1844; was appointed, 13 Dec. following, Additional-Lieutenant of the Illustrious 72, flag-ship of Sir Chas. Adam in North America and the West Indies; and since 27 Jan. 1845, has been employed on the same station in the Hyacinth 18, Capt. Fras. Scott.

HEATHCOTE. (Lieutenant, 1840.)

Edmund Heathcote entered the Navy 19 Dec. 1828; passed his examination in 1833; and attained his present rank 10 Jan. 1840. His appointments have since been, at first as Additional, but latterly as Senior Lieutenant—19 March, 1840, to the President 50, flag-ship in South America of Rear-Admiral Chas. Bayne Hodgson Ross—25 Feb. 1841, and 27 June, 1844, to the Electra 18, Capts. Edw. Reeves Philip Mainwaring, Philip Gostling, and Arthur Darley, and Eurydice 26, Capt. Geo. Elliot, both on the North America and West India station—and 8 July, 1846, to the Constance 50, Capt. Sir Baldwin Wake Walker, with whom he is now serving in the Pacific.

He married, in 1844, Elizabeth Lucy, eldest daughter of Lieut.-Colonel Law, K.H., commanding the Royal Newfoundland Companies.

* *Vide* Gaz. 1846, pp. 3441, 3444, 3446.

† *V.* Gaz. 1840, p. 2601.

HEATHCOTE. (Lieutenant, 1824.)

George Henry Heathcote was born 13 May, 1798.

This officer entered the Navy, in the winter of 1812, on board the Medina 20, Capt. Henry Bourchier, whom he accompanied to Newfoundland. In 1813 he proceeded, with the consent of Sir Josiah C. Coghill, to the West Indies in the Ister 36; and we afterwards, in 1815, find him employed at St. Helena on board the Conqueror 74, flag-ship of Rear-Admiral Robt. Plampin. In Aug. 1816, he fought and was wounded at Algiers in the Glasgow 40, Capt. Hon. Anthony Maitland. The next ship he joined was, we believe, the Liffey 50, Capt. Hon. Henry Duncan, fitting at Chatham. From 1820 until within a short period of his promotion to the rank of Lieutenant 31 March, 1824, Mr. Heathcote was lastly employed, on the Mediterranean station, in the Révolutionnaire 46, Capt. Hon. Fleetwood Broughton Reynolds Pellew, and Rochfort 80, flag-ship of Sir Graham Moore. Agents—Hallett and Robinson.

HEATHCOTE, Kt. (Admiral of the Blue, 1846. f-p., 18; h-p., 39.)

Sir Henry Heathcote, born 20 Jan. 1777, is fourth son of the late Sir Wm. Heathcote, Bart., of Hursley Park, near Winchester, M.P. for co. Hants, by Frances, daughter and co-heir of John Thorpe, Esq., of Embley, co. Hants; and brother of the late Capt. Gilbert Heathcote, R.N. (1806).

This officer entered the Navy, 3 July, 1790, on board the Captain 74, Capt. Arch. Dickson, stationed in the Channel, where, and in the West Indies and Mediterranean, he was employed, during the six following years, in the Colossus 74, Capt. Henry Harvey, Proserpine frigate, Capt. Jas. Alms, America 74, Capt. Hon. John Rodney, Inconstant 36, Capt. Augustus Montgomery, Egmont 74, Capt. Arch. Dickson, Princess Royal 98, flag-ship of Vice-Admiral Sam. Cranston Goodall, Cyclops frigate, Capt. Wm. Hotham, Windsor Castle 98, bearing the flag of Rear-Admiral Robt. Mann, Amphion 32, Capt. Israel Pellew, Goliath 74, Capt. Sir Chas. Henry Knowles, and Victory 100, flag-ship of Sir John Jervis. He served on shore, while in the Egmont, at the reduction of Corsica in 1794; and on 14 March and 13 July, 1795, he was present, as Midshipman of the Princess Royal, and Master's Mate of the Cyclops, in Admiral Hotham's partial actions. On 19 Sept. 1796 Mr. Heathcote was confirmed a Lieutenant in the Britannia 100, Capt. Thos. Foley, in which ship, and the Meleager frigate, he further served in the Mediterranean, until nominated, 5 June, 1797, Acting-Commander of the Alliance storeship—an appointment sanctioned by the Admiralty on 11 of the following Aug. From the latter vessel, then at Lisbon, he was removed, 7 Nov. 1797, to the Captaincy, by an order from his Admiral, of the Romulus 36, which frigate he paid off shortly after his official advancement, 5 Feb. 1798, to Post-rank. Capt. Heathcote's subsequent appointments were—4 April, 1803, to the Galatea 32, employed at first on the coast of Ireland, and then in convoying a fleet of 150 sail to the West Indies, where, during a continuance of many months, he performed much valuable service, and gave proofs not only of great seamanship, but of more than ordinary gallantry, always seeking opportunities of distinction, and on one occasion actually bidding defiance to two first-class French frigates, lying in Basseterre, Guadeloupe—19 April, 1805, by exchange, to the Désirée 36, for a passage to England, whither he escorted a convoy of 101 sail—21 March, 1807, to the Sea Fencibles in the Isle of Wight—and, 13 Feb. 1808, and 28 April, 1812, to the Lion 64, and Scipion 74. In the former of those ships he immediately sailed, in charge of 14 Indiamen, for Bengal and China, and in many instances during his sojourn in the East did he again display the character of an efficient and spirited officer. On his first arrival there, after having parted company with the Bengal division of the convoy, he volunteered to conduct the remainder to their destination, notwithstanding that a French squadron, consisting of three sail of the line, had been reported (although, as it was subsequently discovered, erroneously) to have just before passed through the straits of Malacca into the China sea. After remaining for some time at Chuenpee with two frigates under his orders, and arranging, by his firmness, a dispute which had arisen between the natives and a select committee of Hon. Company's supercargoes, Capt. Heathcote returned with the trade to England. As soon as his ship had been re-fitted, he was again ordered to India, and directed to convey to Persia their Excellencies Sir Gore Ouseley and Mirza Abdul Hassan, the Persian ambassador. When afterwards at Bombay, in June, 1811, Capt. Heathcote, owing to the absence of Commodore Broughton, the Commander-in-Chief, on the expedition to Java, was induced to open a set of despatches from England, from whose contents he learnt that a large force from France might reasonably be expected to be on its way to Java, for the purpose of defeating any attack on that settlement. From a feeling of zeal for the public service, which was subsequently approved by court-martial, Capt. Heathcote at once left his station for the purpose of communicating the intelligence to Commodore Broughton, and, in so doing, actually surrendered his right to a freight from China to India, worth the sum to him of at least 10,000*l*. On his return to England, after the subjugation of Java, and his appointment to the Scipion, our officer joined the fleet in the Mediterranean, where, in the autumn of 1813, he assumed command of the in-shore squadron off Toulon, and conspicuously participated, on 5 Nov. in that year, in Sir Edw. Pellew's skirmish with the enemy's fleet. On the conclusion of the war he was sent with four sail of the line to Marseilles, for the purpose of thence conveying the British prisoners of war to Port Mahon. He was paid off in Oct. 1814, and has not been since employed. He became a Rear-Admiral 27 May, 1825; a Vice-Admiral 10 Jan. 1837; and a full Admiral 9 Nov. 1846.

Sir Henry Heathcote (upon whom, at the joint request of the diplomatic personages he had formerly conveyed to Persia, the honour of Knighthood was conferred 20 July, 1819) had the satisfaction, during the term of his career afloat, frequently to receive the thanks of the Directors of the Hon. E. I. Co., the Governor in Council of Bombay, the West India merchants, and the Committee at Lloyd's. In 1823 he took out a patent for an improvement of the stay-sails between the masts of ships and other square-rigged vessels, and the better security of the masts; and in 1824 he published a treatise on the subject, which was by permission dedicated to the King. The plan, we understand, was tried on board two frigates, and reported to the Admiralty as worthy of its acceptance. Sir Henry Heathcote married, 10 Nov. 1799, Sarah Elizabeth, daughter of Thos. Guscott, Esq., many years Naval Storekeeper afloat at Sheerness, by whom he has issue, living, three sons (the eldest in the army) and seven daughters. His second son, Henry, a Major in the 88th Foot, died in 1829. Agents—Coplands and Burnett.

HEDDINGTON. (Commander, 1806.)

Thomas Heddington entered the Navy, previously to the year 1786, as a Boy, on board the Invincible 74, and, after an intermediate servitude in the Pegase and Castor frigates, Capts. Sam. Marshall and John Sam. Smith, became Midshipman, in Feb. 1791, of the Chatham, Lieut.-Commanders Wm. Robt. Broughton and Peter Puget, under whom he made a voyage of discovery round the world, and was for a considerable time engaged in surveying the coast of America. He was promoted, on his return home, to a Lieutenancy, 6 Nov. 1795, in the Kangaroo 18, Capt. Hon. Courtenay Boyle; and, between July, 1796, and the early part of 1802, he was next employed, on the Channel and Irish stations, in the Dryad 36, Capt. Lord Amelius Beauclerk, Havock, Capt. Philip Bartholomew, Saturn 94, Capts. Jacob Waller and Thos. Totty, Venus frigate, Capt. Thos. Graves, and Orion 74, Capt. Robt. Carthew Reynolds. Attaining the rank of Commander, after having for two years and a half had charge of a Signal-station at Hawkesley Point, 25 Sept. 1806, he was subsequently, between Feb. 1808 and April, 1814, employed at various places as Regulating Captain, and Agent for Prisoners of War. He has since been on half-pay.

HELBY. (Commander, 1847. f-p., 38; h-p., 2.)

John Hasler Helby entered the Navy, 1 June, 1807, as Fst.-cl. Vol., on board the Success 32, Capt. John Ayscough; during an attachment of nearly four years to which frigate he cruized off Havre de Grace, attended the expedition of Dec. 1807 to Madeira, afforded protection for some time to the Greenland fisheries, assisted in 1809 at the reduction of Ischia and Procida, and co-operated, as Midshipman, in the defence of Sicily against the threatened invasion of Murat. He also, among other boat-services, contributed, 4 April, 1810, to the destruction, with a loss to the British of 2 men killed, of two vessels laden with oil, and protected by a heavy fire of great guns and musketry, on the beach, near Castiglione; and, on 25 of the same month, he assisted at the capture of an armed ship and three barks, under the castle of Terracina. On the Success being ordered to England in 1811, Mr. Helby volunteered to continue in the Mediterranean, and he was therefore received on board the Cerberus 32, Capts. Henry Whitby and Thos. Garth. By those officers he appears to have been again employed on many cutting-out affairs, some of them of a very dashing nature, on the coasts of Corfu and Italy. On one occasion, however, while absent in a prize, he had the misfortune to be wrecked on the Calabrian shore, and taken prisoner, although he was happily not detained beyond a period of three months. He ultimately, in July, 1814, returned to England and was paid off, but, before he had been many weeks at home, he again sailed for the Mediterranean, in the Phœnix 36, Capt. Chas. John Austen; under whom, after having been very actively employed, in particular at the port of Pavos, where he had served in the boats in a sharp action which had preceded the capture of two pirate vessels, he was once more wrecked, near Smyrna, 20 Feb. 1816. On the occurrence of the latter catastrophe, Mr. Helby, we find, distinguished himself in an especial manner by his daring conduct in swimming on shore through a violent surf with a hauling-line, for the purpose of receiving a hawser to save the ship's company. Volunteering again to remain in the Mediterranean, our officer there became successively attached to the Boyne 98, and Queen Charlotte 100, both flag-ships of Lord Exmouth, whose favourable notice he had the good fortune to attract by the extreme gallantry of his behaviour at the ensuing battle of Algiers. Towards the close of 1816 he joined the Conqueror 74, bearing the flag of Rear-Admiral Robt. Plampin at St. Helena, where, on 19 Sept. 1818, he was appointed Acting-Lieutenant of the Eurydice 24, Capt. Robt. Wauchope. He was, however, superseded in the next December, and in a fortnight afterwards was compelled from the state of his health to invalid. In May, 1819, he obtained an appointment, as Admiralty-Midshipman, to the ALBION 74, commanded at Portsmouth by Capt. Rich. Raggett, with whom he continued until Sept. 1821, when he was nominated to a similar rating in the IPHIGENIA 42, bearing the broad pendant of Sir Robt. Mends on the coast of Africa. He was there again, on 4 March, 1822, appointed an Acting-Lieutenant of the PHEASANT 18, Capt. Douglas Chas. Clavering, to which sloop the Admiralty at length confirmed him on 1 of the following July. Since his return to England in Feb. 1823, Mr. Helby's appointments appear to have been—19 Oct. 1824, and 5 March, 1825, as a Supernumerary-Lieutenant, to the RAMILLIES and HYPERION, Capts. Wm. M'Culloch and Wm. Jas. Mingaye, employed on the Coast Blockade—5 Nov. 1828, to the Coast Guard—18 March and 20 May, 1835, to the successive command of the HOUND and CAMELION Revenue-vessels—and, 15 June, 1838, again to the Coast Guard, in which he continued until advanced to the rank he now holds 1 Jan. 1847.

Lieut. Helby is married, and has issue.

HELLARD. (CAPT., 1839. F-P., 33 ; H-P., 16.)

SAMUEL HELLARD entered the Navy, 7 Sept. 1798, as a Volunteer, on board the DIRECTOR 64, Capt. Wm. Bligh, from which ship, on his return from a voyage to St. Helena, he removed to the GLADIATOR, Lieut.-Commander John Bell Conolly, lying at Portsmouth. Joining, in 1802, the BLENHEIM 74, Capts. Henry Matson, Thos. Graves, Wm. Ferris, and Loftus Otway Bland, bearing the broad-pendant at first of Sir Sam. Hood, he proceeded to the West Indies, where, on 16 Nov. in the following year, he assisted at the cutting-out, from the harbour of Marin, Martinique, of the *Harmonie*, a notorious privateer, of 8 guns and 66 men, after a gallant conflict in which the enemy had 2 men killed and 14 wounded, and the British, out of 74, 1 killed and 5 wounded. In the spring of 1805, he accompanied Capt. Bland, as Midshipman, into the FLORA 36, in the boats of which frigate, commanded by Lieut. Thos. Furber, we find him contributing, off Oporto, to the capture, 25 Nov. 1806, at the end of a row of six hours, of the Spanish privateer *El Espedarte*, of 6 guns, 6 swivels, and 41 men. The FLORA being wrecked on the coast of Holland 19 Jan. 1808, Mr. Hellard next, in the course of the same and of the following year, joined the MAJESTIC 74, flag-ship in the North Sea of Vice-Admiral Thos. Macnamara Russell, PODARGUS sloop, commanded in the Downs and off Lisbon by Capt. Wm. Hellard, and CASTOR 32, Capt. Wm. Roberts. While in the latter frigate he took part, as Master's Mate, in a gallant action which preceded the capture, 17 April, 1809, of the French 74-gun ship *D'Haupoult;* was present as Acting-Lieutenant, on 18 of the following Dec., at the destruction of the 40-gun frigates *Loire* and *Seine*, laden with stores and provisions, moored in Ance la Barque, Guadeloupe, and defended by numerous strong batteries; and in Feb. 1810, commanded a detachment of seamen on shore at the reduction of Guadeloupe. After serving for a few months as Acting-Lieutenant also of the NEPTUNE 98, Capt. Volant Vashon Ballard, he was officially promoted by commission dated 29 Oct. 1810, and re-appointed to the PODARGUS 14, Capts. John Lloyd, John Bradley, George Rennie, and Wm. Robilliard; under the latter of whom, when in company with the DICTATOR 64, CALYPSO 18, and FLAMER gun-brig, he shared, as First-Lieutenant, 6 July, 1812, in the capture and destruction, within the rocks of Mardoe, on the Norwegian coast, of a Danish squadron, consisting of the *Nayaden* of 48 guns, the *Laland*, *Samsoe*, and *Kiel* sloops, and several gun-boats. The PODARGUS, whose loss on the latter gallant occasion amounted, we find, to 9 men wounded, was subsequently present at the relief of Danzig. Quitting her in Dec. 1813, her First-Lieutenant next, until April 18, served, on the West India and Home stations, in the BENBOW 74, Capt. Rich. Harrison Pearson, and SCOUT 18, Capt. Jas. Arthur Murray; after which he successively joined—31 Oct. 1820, and 31 May, 1823, the SEVERN and RAMILLIES Coast Blockade ships, both commanded by Capt. Wm. M'Culloch—28 April, 1824, the DOVER 28, Capt. Sam. Chambers, lying at Leith—9 Dec. 1824, the RAMILLIES again, Capts. W. M'Culloch and Hugh Pigot—and 15 Sept. 1829, the TALAVERA 74, Capt. Hugh Pigot, also attached to the Coast Blockade service. Attaining the rank of Commander 22 July, 1830, he was afterwards employed in that capacity in the Coast Guard from 13 April, 1831, until 1836, and again from 1 March, 1838, until advanced to his present rank 1 Jan. 1839. He has since been on half-pay.

Capt. Hellard is Senior of 1839.

HELPMAN. (LIEUTENANT, 1841.)

BENJAMIN FRANCIS HELPMAN entered the Navy 16 Dec. 1829; passed his examination 3 Jan. 1834; and was promoted from the WELLESLEY 72, bearing the broad pendant on the China station of Sir Gordon Bremer, to the rank of Lieutenant 22 Oct. 1841. He has not been since officially employed.

Lieut. Helpman has been in command for a considerable time of the CHAMPION Colonial schooner, in Western Australia. AGENT—J. Hinxman.

HELPMAN. (COMMANDER, 1842.)

PHILIP AUGUSTUS HELPMAN entered the Navy, 19 July, 1821; passed his examination in 1828; obtained his first commission 26 March, 1839; became, 3 Jan. 1840, Additional-Lieutenant of the WELLESLEY 72, Capt. Thos. Maitland, on the East India station; and on 19 Jan. 1841, was there appointed to the COLUMBINE 16, Capts. Thos. Jordaine Clarke and Wm. Henry Anderson Morshead. For his services during the campaign in China, where, besides sharing in the hostilities of May, 1841, against Canton, he served on shore in those of March, 1842, against Tsekee, and further participated in the attack of 16 June on the batteries at Woosung, Mr. Helpman was advanced to the rank of Commander on 23 Dec. in the same year.* Since 20 Feb. 1846, he has been employed in the Coast Guard. AGENT—J. Hinxman.

HEMER. (LIEUT., 1815. F-P., 27; H-P., 15.)

ROBERT HEMER entered the Navy, 13 Oct. 1805, as Fst.-cl. Vol., on board the AJAX 74, Acting-Capt. John Pilfold, under whom he fought at the ensuing battle of Trafalgar. In Dec. 1806, after having served for some time off Cadiz as Midshipman of the PRINCE 98, Capt. Wm. Lechmere, he accompanied the latter officer into the DREADNOUGHT 98, bearing afterwards the flag of Rear-Admiral Thos. Sotheby, in the Channel, where he continued until 26 July, 1809; on which date he was taken prisoner in an attempt to cut out a brig lying inside the Ile d'Aix. On his restoration to liberty at the peace of 1814, he joined the TELEGRAPH 12, Capt. Timothy Scriven, and cruized for a period of nearly 12 months on the Channel and American stations. In the capacity of Lieutenant, a rank he attained 9 Feb. 1815, Mr. Hemer's appointments, we find, were, in succession—20 Sept. 1827, to the Coast Blockade, as a Supernumerary of the HYPERION 42, Capt. Wm. Jas. Mingaye—19 Sept. 1829, to the Coast Guard—13 June, 1839, to the command of the LIVELY Revenue vessel—and 2 July, 1844, again to a station in the Coast Guard. AGENTS—Messrs. Chard.

HEMMANS. (LIEUTENANT, 1813.)

SAMUEL HOOD HEMMANS entered the Navy, 10 July, 1806, as Fst.-cl. Vol., on board the BOREAS 22, Capt. Robt. Scott, which vessel, after having effected the capture of *La Victoire* privateer, of 8 swivels and 28 men, was lost, together with her Commander

* *Vide* Gaz. 1841, p. 2506, and Gaz. 1842, pp. 2391, 3400, 3821.

and all but 68 of her crew, on the Hannois rocks, near Guernsey, 5 Dec. 1807. Mr. Hemmans, who previously to that catastrophe had attained the rating of Midshipman, was subsequently, until promoted to the rank of Lieutenant 5 Feb. 1813, employed, on the Home, Baltic, and Mediterranean stations, in the RESOLUTION and POMPÉE 74's, Capts. Geo. Burlton and Geo. Hope, VICTORY 100, flag-ship of Sir Jas. Saumarez, and VOLAGE 22, and RESISTANCE 36, Capts. Philip L. J. Rosenhagen, Chas. Hole, Wm. Hamilton, and Hon. Fleetwood Broughton Reynolds Pellew. Being then appointed to the UNDAUNTED 38, Capts. Thos. Ussher and Chas. Thurlow Smith, he assisted in that frigate in conveying Napoleon Buonaparte from Frejus to Elba in 1814, and was present in her at the capture of the Tremiti islands in 1815. He afterwards joined—22 Sept. 1815, the BULWARK 74, bearing the flag of Sir Chas. Rowley in the river Medway—27 Feb. 1818, the CURLEW 10, Capts. Wm. Walpole and Geo. Cornish Gambier, under the former of whom he was actively employed, in Jan. 1820, against the pirates of the Persian Gulf, where Ras-al-Khyma, their principal resort and head-quarters, was taken, the fortifications destroyed, all their vessels burnt or sunk, and a large quantity of treasure seized—7 Feb. 1824, the BLANCHE 46, Capt. Wm. Bowen Mends, fitting for the South American station, whence he returned to England and was paid off 25 Oct. 1827—and 6 April, 1829, the HERALD yacht, Capt. Geo. Berkeley Maxwell, which vessel, employed in attendance on various diplomatic personages, he left about Aug. 1830. He has not been since afloat.

Lieut. Hemmans has for some time, we believe, filled the post of Emigration Agent at Greenock. AGENTS—Goode and Lawrence.

HEMPSTED. (LIEUTENANT, 1845.)

EDMUND HEMPSTED entered the Navy in 1831; passed his examination 2 May, 1838; and was employed, as Mate, on the Mediterranean, Home, and Pacific stations, in the HOWE 120, Capts. Sir Watkin Owen Pell, Robt. Smart, and Thos. Forrest, bearing the flag for some time of Sir Fras. Mason, EXCELLENT gunnery-ship, Capt. Sir Thos. Hastings, and AMERICA 50, Capt. Hon. John Gordon. He obtained his commission 1 Dec. 1845, and has been since serving, also in the Pacific, as Additional of the COLLINGWOOD 80, flag-ship of Sir Geo. Fras. Seymour.

HEMSWORTH. (LIEUTENANT, 1815. F-P., 19; H-P., 28.)

WILLIAM GLASSFORD HEMSWORTH entered the Navy, 1 Nov. 1800, as Fst.-cl. Vol., on board the FORMIDABLE 98, Capt. Rich. Grindall, with whom he cruized in the Channel and West Indies until Sept. 1802. He re-embarked, 22 May, 1805, on board the BRILLIANT 28, Capts. Robt. Barrie, Rich. Budd Vincent, and Smyth, in which vessel he served for two years and a half on the Irish and Guernsey stations, and was on one occasion wounded while in charge of some French prisoners. From Nov. 1807 until Aug. 1808, Mr. Hemsworth officiated, we find, as Midshipman of the NEPTUNE 98, Capt. Sir Thos. Williams, both in the Channel and West Indies. In June, 1809, he joined the AJAX 74, Capts. Robt. Waller Otway, Robt. Clephane, and Sir Robt. Laurie, on the Mediterranean station, where (besides commanding, as Master's Mate, a boat in an attack on a French brig of war in the Piombino passage, and participating in a very gallant skirmish, in which the British with a slender force beat back a powerful division of the French Toulon fleet) he received a slight injury in a spirited but unfortunate attempt made by the boats of a squadron under Capt. Fras. Wm. Fane upon the enemy's shipping in the Mole of Palamos, on which occasion the British sustained a loss, out of 600 seamen and marines, of at least 200 killed, wounded, and taken prisoners. He also, we understand, contributed to the capture, 31 March, 1811, of *Le Dromadaire* store-ship, of 20 guns and 150 men. Being discharged from the AJAX in Dec. 1811, Mr. Hemsworth, during the next two years served, in the Mediterranean, off Lisbon, and at Spithead and Plymouth, on board the YORK 74, Capt. Robt. Barton, ANDROMEDA 24, Capt. Rich. Arthur, and PUISSANT and SATURN 74's, Capts. Benj. Wm. Page and J. Nash. He then proceeded to the East Indies in the MINDEN 74, bearing the flag of Sir Sam. Hood, and on 28 Feb. 1815, after having further served for a short time on board the HECATE 18, Capt. John Allen, was there appointed Acting-Lieutenant of the WELLESLEY 74, Capt. Mich. Matthews. He was officially promoted on 20 of the following Sept, and in July, 1816, he returned home in the SALSETTE 36, Capt. John Bowen. His appointments have since been—in 1840, to an Agency for Transports Afloat—17 Nov. 1842, to the post of Admiralty Agent on board a contract mail steam-vessel—and, 9 July, 1844, to the command of the CRESCENT receiving-ship at Rio de Janeiro, where he is at present employed. AGENTS—Messrs. Stilwell.

HENDERSON. (LIEUTENANT, 1815. F-P., 9; H-P., 32.)

DAVID HENDERSON entered the Navy, 16 Nov. 1806, as Fst.-cl. Vol., on board the SPEEDY brig, Capt. Rich. Henry Muddle, on the Newfoundland station; removed, in March, 1808, to the THETIS 38, Capt. Geo. Miller, with whom he visited St. Helena, and cruized in the Bay of Biscay; became Midshipman and Master's Mate, in March, 1809, and April, 1813, of the COMET sloop, Capts. R. H. Muddle, Wm. Shepheard, and Geo. Wm. Blamey, again at Newfoundland; and was next, in March, 1814, transferred to the PRINCE 98, flag-ship of Sir Rich. Bickerton at Spithead. He went on half-pay on the receipt of his commission, which bears date 3 March, 1815, and he has not been since afloat.

Lieut. Henderson married, 23 Feb. 1819, Anne, daughter of the late G. Brettell, Esq., of Baker Street. He was left a widower 18 July, 1836.

HENDERSON. (REAR-ADMIRAL, 1846. F-P., 14; H-P., 39.)

GEORGE HENDERSON is son of the late John Henderson, Esq., many years Secretary to Admiral Lord Bridport; and brother-in-law of Capt. W. W. Henderson, R.N., C.B.

This officer entered the Navy, 1 March, 1794, as part of the Admiral's retinue, on board the ROYAL GEORGE 100, Capt. Wm. Domett, on the books of which ship, bearing the flag in the Channel of the late Lord Bridport, then Sir Alex. Hood, he was borne until Dec. 1795. In May, 1799, he rejoined the ROYAL GEORGE, still the flag-ship of his patron, Lord Bridport, from which, in Nov. 1800, he removed, as Midshipman, to the BELLEISLE 74, Capts. Wm. Domett and Chas. Boyles, bearing the flag afterwards of Hon. Wm. Cornwallis. Proceeding, in the summer of 1802, to the West Indies as Master's Mate of the ULYSSES 44, Mr. Henderson served in that frigate, under the broad pendant of Sir Sam. Hood, at the capture of Tobago, 1 July, 1803. On rejoining the last-mentioned officer, after having gone to England for the purpose of passing his examination, he was promoted by him to the rank of Lieutenant 28 Jan. 1804, and appointed to the ALLIGATOR 28, *armée-en-flûte*, Capt. Chas. Richardson, part of the force employed at the ensuing reduction of the Dutch colony of Surinam, where he was severely wounded.* During the year 1805 Mr. Henderson presents himself to our notice as serving with Capt. Murray Maxwell, on board the CENTAUR 74, and GALATEA and HYÆNA frigates, in the first named of which ships he accompanied Rear-Admiral Hon. Alex. Cochrane in his pursuit of the celebrated Rochefort squadron. On his rejunction, in the early part of 1806, of Sir Sam. Hood in the CENTAUR, he cruized for some time off Rochefort, where, on

* *Vide* Gaz. 1804, p. 759.

25 Sept. 1806, he assisted, in company with the MARS and MONARCH 74's, at the capture of four heavy French frigates, whose resistance was not overcome until the Commodore had lost an arm. Mr. Henderson, who was sent with the despatches announcing the latter event to the fleet off Brest, next accompanied Lord Gambier's expedition to Copenhagen. On the surrender of Madeira in Dec. 1807, being at the time the CENTAUR's First-Lieutenant, he was again entrusted with Sir Sam. Hood's despatches,* and sent with a strong recommendation to England, where, on his arrival, he was presented with a Commander's commission bearing date 22 Jan. 1808. After an interval of half-pay he was appointed, 13 July, 1809, to the fire-vessel division of the expedition then fitting for the Walcheren, during the operations connected with which we find him frequently distinguishing himself, in particular, however, by the highly satisfactory nature of his conduct, at the destruction, under Capt. Nicholas Tomlinson, of the basin, arsenal, and sea-defences of Flushing on its evacuation by the British.† Capt. Henderson, it appears, next, in the course of 1810, joined the ECLIPSE and HECATE sloops, and NÉRÉIDE frigate; the latter of which vessels he brought home, after having assisted at the reduction of the Isle of France, and put out of commission in May, 1811. Attaining Post-rank on 1 of the following Aug., he was further appointed, on the East India station—23 June, 1813, to the ACORN 20—20 April, 1814, to the MINDEN 74, bearing the flag of his friend Sir Sam. Hood—and 14 Jan. 1815, to the MALACCA 42. The latter ship, the last he commanded, he paid off in the ensuing July. He accepted Flag-rank 1 Oct. 1846.

The Rear-Admiral married, first, 26 Nov. 1817, Frances, eldest daughter of Edm. Walcott, Esq., of Winkton, near Christchurch, Hants, and sister of Capt. J. E. Walcott, R.N., by whom (who died 1 Dec. 1836) he has issue four sons and two daughters; and, secondly, in 1842, Rachel, relict of R. P. Cazalet, Esq., and only daughter of the Rev. H. Davies, of Ringwood.

* *Vide* Gaz. 1808, 102. † *V.* Gaz. 1809, p. 2006.

HENDERSON. (LIEUTENANT, 1815. F-P., 10; H-P., 31.)

JOHN HENDERSON (*c*) entered the Navy, 1 Oct. 1806, as Fst.-cl. Vol., on board the MAJESTIC 74, Capt. Geo. Hart, bearing the flag of Vice-Admiral Thos. Macnamara Russell on the North Sea station, where, and on the Baltic, he served in the same ship, chiefly as Midshipman, until Jan. 1810. He then in succession joined the IMPÉRIEUSE 38, Capts. Thos. Garth and Hon. Henry Duncan, RODNEY 74, and VILLE DE PARIS 110, both commanded by Capt. Geo. Burlton, COSSACK 22, Capts. Thos. Garth and Geo. Price, VIGO 74, flag-ship of Sir Jas. Nicoll Morris, ILLUSTRIOUS 74, Capt. Alex. Skene, PRINCE 98, Capt. Geo. Fowke, ARIEL 16, Capt. Dan. Ross, and ST. LAWRENCE 98, bearing the broad pendant of Sir Edw. W. C. R. Owen, on the Mediterranean, Baltic, Portsmouth, African, and Canadian Lake stations. He was promoted to the rank of Lieutenant 10 March, 1815, and on leaving the ST. LAWRENCE was appointed to the PRINCE REGENT 56, in which vessel, commanded by Capt. Wm. Fitzwilliam Owen, he remained on the Lakes of Canada until Nov. 1816. He has since been on half-pay.

HENDERSON. (LIEUTENANT, 1822. F-P., 16; H-P., 24.)

JOHN HENDERSON (*d*) entered the Navy, 23 Oct. 1807, as Fst.-cl. Vol., on board the EXPERIMENT packet, Lieut.-Commander Fegen, employed on the Falmouth station. On being appointed, early in 1809, Midshipman of the MERCURIUS sloop, Capt. Thos. Renwick, we find him, in the course of that year, cruizing in the North Sea and Baltic, then visiting the north coast of Spain, and finally attending the expedition to the Walcheren. From Feb. 1810 until Sept. 1815 Mr. Henderson, besides making a voyage to Rio de Janeiro and the Cape of Good Hope, served on the stations above alluded to, principally as Master's Mate, in the IMPÉTUEUX 74, Capts. John Lawford, David Milne, Chas. Inglis, and Chas. Philip Butler Bateman, and NIGER 38, Capt. Peter Rainier. He was then employed for nearly two years in North America as Admiralty-Midshipman of the PACTOLUS 38, Capt. Wm. Hugh Dobbie, and was afterwards appointed, in a similar capacity—10 Aug. 1817, to the RAMILLIES 74, Capt. Thos. Boys, on the Home station—12 Sept. 1818, to the SEVERN frigate, Coast Blockade depôt, Capt. Wm. M'Culloch—and, 11 Feb. 1821, to the FURY bomb, Capt. Wm. Edw. Parry, whom he accompanied in his second north-west passage explorative mission, returning with him to England in the autumn of 1823. Since that date Mr. Henderson, who had been advanced to his present rank on 26 Dec. in the preceding year, has been on half-pay.

HENDERSON. (CAPT., 1840. F-P., 27; H-P., 10.)

THOMAS HENDERSON, born in June, 1795, in Scotland, is brother of Jas. Henderson, Esq., Master-Attendant at Plymouth Dockyard.

This officer entered the Navy, 10 May, 1810, as a Volunteer, on board the POMONE 38, Capt. Robt. Barrie, under whom, prior to being wrecked on the Needles Point, 14 Oct. 1811, we find him sharing, as Midshipman, in a gallant action of an hour and a half in Sagone Bay, where the POMONE, in company with the UNITÉ 36, and SCOUT 18, effectually destroyed, after incurring an individual loss of 2 men killed and 19 wounded, the two armed store-ships *Giraffe* and *Nourrice*, each mounting from 20 to 30 guns, and protected by a 5-gun battery, a martello tower, and a body of about 200 regular troops. We may add that he was also present at the capture, among other vessels, of one from Salem, the *Hercules*, on board of which were Lucien Buonaparte and his family. Joining next the FURIEUSE 36, Capt. Wm. Mounsey, Mr. Henderson served, as Midshipman and Master's Mate of that frigate, at the blockade of Toulon, the reduction of the island of Ponza and of the town of Via Reggio, the unsuccessful attack upon Leghorn, the occupation of Santa Maria and of the enemy's other forts in the Gulf of Spezia, and the capture of Genoa and its dependencies. Among the numerous boat affairs in which it was his fortune to participate we may enumerate the cutting-out of a bombard from Sagone Bay; of a xebec, mounting 2 six-pounders, from under the tower and batteries of Orbitello, 7 May, 1813; and, 4 Oct. following (with a loss to the British of 12 men killed and wounded) of a large convoy, protected by the galling fire of two gun-vessels and several batteries in the harbour of Marinelo. The FURIEUSE being ultimately ordered to North America, Mr. Henderson had the ill luck to be there captured, while detached in a small schooner in the Bay of Fundy, and detained a prisoner-of-war during the winter of 1814-15. In Aug. of the latter year, a few months after he had rejoined the FURIEUSE, he was received by his old Captain, Robt. Barrie, on board the DRAGON 74, from which ship, however, he almost immediately removed to the ROCHFORT 74, Capt. Sir Arch. Dickson, lying at Portsmouth, where he continued until he was enabled, in June, 1816, to pass his examination. He then served for three months in the Channel, as Mate of the SNAPPER cutter, Capt. Rich. Steel, on leaving which vessel in the following Oct. he joined, in a similar capacity, and was for more than 13 years employed in, the PRINCE OF WALES Revenue-vessel, Capt. Benj. Oliver. As a reward for the activity of his services during that period, both in the PRINCE OF WALES herself, and in her tender and boats, Mr. Henderson, in Dec. 1829, was appointed, on promotion, to the WINCHESTER 52, flag-ship of Sir Edw. Griffith Colpoys on the North America and West India station. He was accordingly advanced to the rank of Lieutenant on 2 of the next April, and appointed, about the same period, to the SHANNON 46, Capt. Benj. Clement, attached to the force in the West Indies, whence, however, he invalided in the ensuing month of July. On that occasion he took a passage home in the *Prospect* merchantman, of London, and was wrecked in her in the Gulf of Florida. After an interval of half-pay he succeeded, on 16 March, 1831, in obtaining an appointment to the Coast Guard, during his continuance in which service he once, on 22 Feb. 1832, came into conflict with an armed party of smugglers, and was severely wounded. From 27 June, 1832, until the spring of 1834, he successively commanded the VICTORINE, SYLVIA, and SPEEDY Revenue-cutters, and while in the second named of those vessels he was employed on the river Suir, and obtained the acknowledgments of the Lord-Lieutenant for his exertions in suppressing a combination which had been entered into by the lightermen for the purpose of preventing the colliers from proceeding above the bridge of Waterford. Being advanced, for his services and wounds in the Customs department of the Navy, to the rank of Commander 12 Feb. 1834, and appointed, 2 June following, to the COLUMBINE 18, Capt. Henderson sailed for the Mediterranean, and in the early part of 1835 accompanied the Euphrates expedition, under Lieut.-Colonel Chesney, from Malta to the mouth of the river Orontes. While engaged in superintending its debarkation, his boat upset on the bar of the stream, and, the strength of the current carrying him into the surf beyond all power of assistance from the shore, he was compelled to swim to sea, in the hope that the ships at anchor outside might have observed the accident, and have sent their boats to his rescue, which providentially proved to be the case. The COLUMBINE being paid off in April, 1838, on her return from a successful anti-slavery cruize on the coast of Africa, Capt. Henderson was next appointed, 31 Aug. 1840, to the VESUVIUS steam-vessel, and again ordered to the Mediterranean, whither he proceeded, carrying out a detachment of troops to Gibraltar and Malta. For the part he subsequently took in the bombardment of St. Jean d'Acre he was advanced to Post-rank by commission dated 4 Nov. 1840, but he did not resign the command of the VESUVIUS until 25 March, 1841, previously to which period he had further rendered himself useful to the Commanders of the British and Turkish forces by his transportance of their troops, guns, and stores, and by the assistance he had afforded in filling up the breaches formed in the battlements of Acre. He had also, during the same period, it appears, been of signal aid to the PIQUE when dismasted off Caiffa, and had conveyed to Malta the despatches announcing the evacuation of Syria by the Egyptians. Since 8 Dec. 1845 Capt. Henderson has been in command of the SAMPSON steam-frigate, in the Pacific.

He married, first, Jane, only daughter of the late John M'Cormick, Esq., of the firm of Stirling and Sons, Glasgow, by whom he has issue one daughter; and secondly, 30 Oct. 1841, Frances Maria, eldest daughter of the late Jas. Day, Esq., Captain in the Royal Horse Artillery. By the latter lady Capt. Henderson also has issue. AGENTS—Coplands and Burnett.

HENDERSON, C.B., K.S.F. (CAPTAIN, 1838. F-P., 26; H-P., 13.)

WILLIAM HONYMAN HENDERSON is son of the late Alex. Henderson, Esq., of Sempster, Caithness, N. B.

This officer entered the Navy, 25 Dec. 1808, as Fst.-cl. Vol., on board the HERO 74, Capt. Jas. Newman Newman, employed on the North Sea and Baltic stations, where, and in South America, he afterwards, until Oct. 1814, served, as Midshipman and Master's Mate, in the ARDENT 64, Capt. Robt. Honyman, and AQUILON and CERES frigates, Capts. Wm. Pakenham and Wm. Bowles. He was then for some time employed at Newfoundland in the PLOVER sloop, Capt. John Skekel; after which he joined the TONNANT 80, bearing the flag of Hon. Sir Alex. Cochrane, and on 14 Dec. 1814, previously to participating in the expedition against New Orleans, assisted in the boats of that ship and of a squadron at the capture, on Lake Borgne, of five American gun-boats under Commander Jones, who did not surrender until, in a severe conflict, he had occasioned the British a loss of 17 men killed and 77 wounded. Between June, 1815, and Jan. 1820, Mr. Henderson, we find, was next employed, on the Home, and again on the South American stations, as Master's Mate and Admiralty Midshipman, in the ROYAL SOVEREIGN 100, Capt. Broughton, CHILDERS 16, Capt. Rich. Wales, RIVOLI 74, Capts. Chas. Ogle and Aiskew Paffard Hollis, DOVER 28, Capts. John Ross and Chas. Hope Reid, CREOLE 42, Capts. Wm. Bateman Dashwood and Wm. Bowles, and SUPERB 74, Capt. Thos. White. On leaving the latter ship he rejoined Capt. Bowles as Acting-Lieutenant on board the CREOLE, which frigate, however, he quitted soon after his official promotion, which took place on 10 of the following May. His next appointments were—in the course of 1824, to the SERINGAPATAM frigate, ALBION 74, and TRIBUNE frigate, Capts. Chas. Sotheby, Sir Wm. Hoste, and Gardiner Henry Guion, on the Portsmouth and Lisbon stations—20 Feb. 1826, to the FORTE 44, Capt. Jeremiah Coghlan—22 March, 1826, to the BLONDE 42, Capt. Lord Byron, in the Pacific—14 Sept. 1827, to the COLUMBINE sloop, Capts. Chas. Crole and John Townshend, on the Halifax station, whence he returned home and was paid off 1 June, 1830—in March, 1831, to the BARHAM 50, Capt. Hugh Pigot—and 7 May, 1831, as First Lieutenant, to the DUBLIN 50, Capt. Lord Jas. Townshend, with whom he served, again in South America, until 1834, on 2 Oct. in which year the DUBLIN was put out of commission. Being advanced to the rank of Commander 19 Dec. following, Capt. Henderson, on 9 Sept. 1835, was placed in charge of the PHŒNIX steamer, and immediately ordered to the coast of Spain, where the importance of his services during the civil war was ultimately acknowledged by his investiture with the second class of the order of San Fernando. He was superseded from the PHŒNIX on being awarded a Post-commission, dated 27 June, 1838. His next appointment was, 19 June, 1839, to the GORGON, another steam-vessel, in which he was for three years employed in the Mediterranean—participating during that period in the operations on the coast of Syria, including those against Sidon and St. Jean d'Acre.* He was in consequence nominated a C.B. 18 Dec. 1840. He has been in command, since 25 Aug. 1846, of the SIDON steam-frigate.

Capt. Henderson married, 4 Sept. 1844, Elizabeth Martha, relict of his old Captain, Lord Jas. Townshend. AGENTS—Goode and Lawrence.

HENDERSON, C.B., K.H. (CAPTAIN, 1815. F-P., 24; H-P., 24.)

WILLIAM WILMOTT HENDERSON is brother of Lieut. John Henderson, R.N., who was lost in command of the MARIA schooner in a hurricane among the Leeward Islands, 16 Oct. 1807; of Benj. W. Henderson, Esq., Admiralty-Midshipman of the LEVEN, who died on board that ship's tender, in Delagoa Bay, while employed in surveying the east coast of Africa, in March, 1823; and of Lieut. Rich. Wilmott Henderson, R.N. (1823), who died in 1836. He is nephew, further, of the gallant Capt. David Wilmot, R.N., who was eight times wounded in battle, and closed a distinguished career at St. Jean d'Acre, where he fell in command of the ALLIANCE 36; and cousin of Lieut. John Blackmore, R.N.

This officer entered the Navy, in May, 1799, on board the ROYAL GEORGE 100, Capt. Wm. Domett, bearing the flag in the Channel of Lord Bridport; removed, in Oct. 1800, to the VILLE DE PARIS 110, flag-ship on the Mediterranean station of his patron Earl St. Vincent; was subsequently employed for three years and a-half on board the BELLEISLE 74, Capts. John Whitby and Wm. Hargood, under the latter of whom he accompanied Lord Nelson to the West Indies in pursuit of the combined squadrons, and, on his return to the Mediterranean, fought at Trafalgar; and on 26 March, 1806, was promoted,

* *Vide* Gaz. 1840, p. 2603.

from the HIBERNIA 110, bearing the flag of Lord St. Vincent, to an Acting-Lieutenancy in the NIOBE 40, Capt. John Wentworth Loring—to which vessel, after having assisted at the capture of *Le Néarque* national brig, of 16 guns and 97 men, he was confirmed on 11 of the following April. On the capture of Oporto by the French in March, 1809, Mr. Henderson, who had been sent thither with despatches, and for the purpose of superintending the landing of supplies, unfortunately fell into their power. He was accordingly placed in confinement, and ultimately obliged to accompany them in their retreat as far as the vicinity of Amaranta, where, however, he succeeded, on 16 May, in effecting his escape. Having contrived to get back to Oporto, in spite of many severe difficulties and privations, he there took a passage home in the NAUTILUS brig, Capt. Thos. Dench; and on his arrival he was immediately appointed First of the ACTIVE 46, Capt. Jas. Alex. Gordon. Continuing to serve under that officer, principally in the Adriatic, until 1 Aug. 1811, Mr. Henderson, besides assisting at the capture of many of the enemy's vessels, was present, on 13 March, 1811, in the celebrated action off Lissa, where a British squadron, carrying in the whole 156 guns and 879 men, completely routed, after a conflict of six hours, and a loss to the ACTIVE of 4 men killed and 24 wounded, a Franco-Venetian armament, whose force amounted to 284 guns and 2655 men. As a reward for his gallantry, which was described by Capt. Gordon in the warmest terms, Mr. Henderson had the satisfaction of being promoted to the rank of Commander by a commission ante-dated to the day of victory. Prior, however, to the receipt of the intelligence, we again, on 27 of the ensuing July, find him signalizing and recommending himself in the strongest manner to notice, by his conduct at the capture and destruction of a convoy of 28 sail, defended, in a creek in the island of Ragosniza, by 300 troops and 3 gun-vessels; on which occasion, while the boats were left to attack the enemy from without, he landed with the small-arm men and marines, stormed and carried a hill which commanded the creek, and, having put the military to flight with great loss, annihilated in a great measure the difficulties of the enterprise. When subsequently on his voyage home in the POMONE 38, Capt. Robt. Barrie, Capt. Henderson, it appears, had the misfortune to be wrecked, on a sunken rock, near the Needles Point, 14 Oct. 1811. He was next, on 3 April, 1812, appointed to the ROSARIO brig, from which vessel, after cruizing for some months in the Downs, and conveying the Duke of Brunswick Oels from Harwich to the Elbe, he removed, 7 June, 1813, to the DASHER sloop. In the following Oct. he accompanied the outward-bound trade to the West Indies, and during his continuance on that station he co-operated in the reduction of Guadeloupe in Aug. 1815. He attained Post-rank on 9 Oct. in the same year, but did not leave the DASHER* until May, 1816, and on 13 Jan. 1835, was created a K.H. Capt. Henderson's last appointments were, 25 July, 1837, and 2 Sept. 1841, to the EDINBURGH 72, and VICTORY 104, on the Mediterranean and Portsmouth stations; his services in the former of which ships in the operations on the coast of Syria and at the bombardment of St. Jean d'Acre were acknowledged by his nomination to the C.B. 18 Dec. 1840. He was superseded in the command of the VICTORY in Sept. 1844.

Capt. Henderson married, in June, 1817, a sister of the present Rear-Admiral Geo. Henderson, R.N.

HENDRY. (Captain, 1822. F-P., 25; H-P., 27.)

WILLIAM HENDRY was born 16 Aug. 1777, at Paisley, N. B.

This officer entered the Navy, 26 April, 1795, as Midshipman, on board the ALCMÈNE 32, Capt. Wm. Brown, with whom, in the same frigate, and in the DEFENCE 74, he served, in the North Sea and off Lisbon and Cadiz, until May, 1798. He then removed to the VILLE DE PARIS 110, bearing the flag of Earl St. Vincent, by whom, we believe, he was appointed, in Feb. 1799, Acting-Lieutenant of the TRANSFER brig, Capt. Geo. Mundy, on the Mediterranean station. In the following Aug. he rejoined Capt. Brown, as Midshipman, on board the VANGUARD 74, in which ship, and in the AURORA 28, Capt. Thos. Gordon Caulfeild, and ROBUST 74, and HUSSAR 38, both commanded by his friend Capt. Brown, he further served, on the Lisbon, Newfoundland, Channel, and Irish stations, until promoted, immediately on passing his examination, to a Lieutenancy, 11 July, 1801, in the HAZARD sloop, Capts. Wm. Butterfield and Rich. John Neve. Joining next (after a prolonged employment of four years off the coast of Ireland and in the Channel) the HERO 74, Capt. Hon. Alan Hyde Gardner, Mr. Hendy fought in that ship in Sir Rich. Strachan's action off Ferrol 4 Nov. 1805, and was also present, 13 March, 1806, at the capture of the French 80-gun ship *Marengo*, bearing the flag of Rear-Admiral Linois, and 40-gun frigate *Belle Poule*. In the course of the latter year, he was again placed under the orders of Lord St. Vincent, in the HIBERNIA 110; and while next attached, between Aug. 1807, and March, 1810, to the STATIRA 38, Capts. Robt. Howe Bromley, Chas. Worsley Boys, and Geo. Paris Monke, he attended, as First-Lieutenant, the expedition to the Walcheren (where, with the frigate-squadron under Lord Wm. Stuart, he assisted in forcing the passage between the batteries of Flushing and Cadsand), and co-operated in the reduction of Guadeloupe. From the period of his leaving the STATIRA until that of his advancement to the rank of Commander, 27 April, 1814, Mr. Hendy successively officiated as Senior and Flag-Lieutenant, in the West Indies and at home, on board the BLONDE 38, Capt. Thos. Huskisson, TONNANT 80, Capt. Sir John Gore, and ULYSSES and ARGO 44's, flag-ships of Rear-Admiral Wm. Brown. Being appointed, on 19 of the ensuing July, to the FORESTER 18, our officer, who retained command of that vessel on the Jamaica station until Aug. 1816, had the good fortune, although four other Captains had failed in the attempt, to obtain the liberation at Santa Martha of the officers and crews belonging to some vessels which had been confiscated by the authorities of Carthagena. Capt. Hendry's only other appointments were, 5 Jan. 1819, and 21 July, 1821, to the ROSARIO 10, and DOTEREL 18, on the St. Helena and North American stations, from the former of which he was selected to carry home, in the HERON 18, Capt. Job Hanmer, the despatches announcing the death of Napoleon Buonaparte. On the morning immediately after the decease of the unfortunate Emperor, 6 May, 1821, Capt. Hendry appears to have formed one of the three naval Captains who were admitted to view the body.* He attained Post-rank 19 July, 1822, and accepted the half-pay of Retirement 1 Oct. 1846.

On the first opening, in 1829, of the College in Portsmouth Dockyard for the instruction of officers in subjects connected with their profession, Capt. Hendry was the Senior of those admitted. The FROLIC 16, a sloop constructed by him, was launched 23 Aug. 1842.

HENN. (LIEUT., 1815. F-P., 10; H-P., 31.)

RICHARD HENN was born in March, 1791.

This officer entered the Navy, 17 June, 1806, as Sec.-cl. Vol., on board the CENTAUR 74, Capt. Wm. Henry Webley, bearing the broad pendant of Sir Sam. Hood. On 25 of the following Sept. he assisted, in company with the MARS and MONARCH 74's, at the capture, off Rochefort, of four heavy French frigates, whose complete subjugation was not effected until Sir Sam. Hood had lost an arm; and he subsequently, it appears, besides attending the expedition against Copenhagen, and witnessing the surrender of Madeira, contributed, in conjunction with the IMPLACABLE 74, to the taking, 26

* It is due to Capt. Henderson to state, that during the two years and a half the DASHER remained on the West India station she did not lose a single man from the effects of the climate.

* *Vide* Gaz. 1821, p. 1409.

Aug. 1808, in sight of the whole Russian fleet near Rogerswick, of the 74-gun ship *Sewolod*, after a close and furious conflict in which the CENTAUR lost 3 men killed and 27 wounded, and the enemy 180 killed and wounded. From 1810 until 1812 we find Mr. Henn serving under the successive flags of Sir S. Hood and Sir Rich. Goodwin Keats, as Midshipman and Master's Mate of the HIBERNIA 120, on the Mediterranean station. In 1813, being at the time in the STIRLING CASTLE 74, Capt. Sir Home Popham, he escorted the Marquess of Hastings as Governor-General to India, where, on his arrival, he rejoined Sir S. Hood, who had been recently nominated Commander-in-Chief, on board the MINDEN 74. On 27 Sept. 1814 he was appointed Acting-Lieutenant of the SALSETTE 36, Capt. John Bowen, with whom he continued to serve until paid off, on his return to England, in July, 1816. Mr. Henn, whose commission bears date 2 March, 1815, has not been since afloat.

He is married, and has issue a son and one daughter. AGENT—J. Hinxman.

HENNAH. (LIEUT., 1821. F-P., 14; H-P., 19.)

EDWARD HENNAH, born 12 Aug. 1800, is only son of Capt. Wm. Hennah, R.N., C.B. (1806), who died in 1832; grandson of the Rev. Rich. Hennah, Vicar of St. Austle, and Rector of St. Michael Penkirell, both in the county of Cornwall, and domestic Chaplain to Viscount Falmouth; and cousin of the Rev. Wm. Veale Hennah, Retired Chaplain, R.N.

This officer entered the Navy, 10 April, 1814, as Midshipman, on board the RIPPON 74, commanded in the Channel by Capt. Sir Christopher Cole. From Sept. 1814 until July, 1815, he was employed on the American coast in the BEDFORD 74, Capt. Jas. Walker; and he afterwards, until promoted to the rank of Lieutenant, 27 Nov. 1821, served, on the Home, Halifax, and Mediterranean stations, in the PUISSANT, ALBION, QUEEN, and NORTHUMBERLAND 74's, Capts. Benj. Wm. Page, Philip Somerville, and Jas. Walker, and ACTIVE 46, Capt. Sir Jas. Alex. Gordon. He then received an appointment to the Ordinary on the Canadian Lakes, under Capt. Sir Robt. Barrie, but, returning home in the spring of 1822, was not again employed until 1841, on 27 Aug. in which year he joined the Coast Guard, in which service he still continues.

Lieut. Hennah married, 28 Oct. 1825, Anne, daughter of Sam. Jewel, Esq., Surgeon, of Tregony, co. Cornwall, a descendant of John Jewel, Bishop of Salisbury, the celebrated Anglican Reformer. By that lady he has issue five children.

HENNAH. (LIEUTENANT, 1829.)

FREDERICK HENNAH died in 1845.

This officer entered the Navy in Jan. 1821; passed his examination in 1827; and obtained his commission 8 Aug. 1829. He then obtained command of the SPEEDWELL schooner, on the Jamaica station, and was afterwards appointed—26 Oct. 1830, to the REVENGE 78, Capts. Jas. Hillyar and Donald Hugh Mackay, employed on particular service and on the Lisbon station—30 Oct. 1832, to the SPARTIATE 76, flag-ship of Sir Michael Seymour in South America —5 Sept. 1835, for a few days, to the PYLADES 18, Capt. Wm. Langford Castle, fitting for the Cape of Good Hope—18 March, 1836, 26 Sept. 1839, and 31 Oct. 1840, to the TALAVERA 74, Capts. Thos. Ball Sulivan and Wm. Bowen Mends, PEMBROKE 72, Capt. Fairfax Moresby, and MONARCH 84, Capt. Sam. Chambers, all on the Jamaica station, where, with the exception of a few months in the last mentioned year, he served until the close of 1843—and 27 April, 1844, to the command of a station in the Coast Guard, which he retained until the period of his death.

HENNING. (LIEUT., 1815. F-P., 8; H-P., 31.)

ALEXANDER HENNING entered the Navy, 17 May, 1808, as Fst.-cl. Vol., on board the CHRISTIAN VII. 80, Capts. Sir Joseph Sydney Yorke, Woodley Losack, and Rich. Harward, of which ship, employed on the Home station, he became Midshipman 7 Aug. following. While in her he served for some time under the flag of Sir Edw. Pellew; and on two separate occasions, 20 Jan. and 13 Feb. 1810, he was employed in boat affairs of considerable gallantry; assisting, on the first, at the capture and destruction of part of a convoy of 30 sail, under a heavy fire of grape and musketry, and within a stone's throw of the batteries, in the Maumusson passage; and, on the second, at the destruction, with a loss to the British of 2 men killed and 3 wounded, of three deeply-laden chasse-marées, which had grounded on a reef between Rochelle and Ile d'Aix, and were protected by nine French boats, each carrying a 12-pounder carronade and 6 swivels, and rowing from 20 to 30 oars. The British, who in the latter instance succeeded in capturing one and dispersing the rest of the boats, were in both cases commanded by Lieut. Gardiner Hen. Guion. From Sept. 1810 until May, 1814, Mr. Henning again, we find, served with Capt. Woodley Losack, chiefly as Master's Mate, in the GALATEA 42, on the Cape of Good Hope, Channel, and West India stations; during which period he shared, 20 May, 1811 (while cruizing off Madagascar, in company with the ASTREA and PHŒBE, frigates about equal in force to the GALATEA, and 18-gun brig RACEHORSE), and was slightly wounded in the left arm, in a long and trying action with the French 40-gun frigates *Renommée*, *Clorinde*, and *Néréide*, in which the GALATEA, besides being cut to pieces in her hull, masts, and rigging, sustained a loss of 16 men killed and 46 wounded.* Between the date of his discharge from the GALATEA and that of his promotion to the rank of Lieutenant, 11 Sept. 1815, Mr. Henning was lastly employed in the West Indies on board the VENERABLE 74, flag-ship of Rear-Admiral Philip Chas. Durham, and SPIDER sloop, Capt. Robt. Caulfeild.

He married, 11 Dec. 1838 (while in command of the *Earl of Hardwicke* Indiaman), Melina, only surviving daughter of the late E. W. Smith, Esq.

HENRI. (LIEUTENANT, 1812. F-P., 41; H-P., 1.)

ALPHONSO HENRI entered the Navy, 28 Nov. 1805, as Fst.-cl. Vol., on board the ASTREA 32, Capt. Jas. Carthew; in which frigate, and in the CRESCENT 36, commanded by the same officer, he was for many months employed with the in-shore squadron off Brest, and off the Texel. In Aug. 1807 he was sent, as Midshipman, with only 1 man, to navigate into Yarmouth Roads a prize under Kniphausen colours, on board of which were 15 prisoners, who, on the wind suddenly shifting, and blowing hard on the Dutch coast, rose and retook their vessel. The latter being soon, however, chased by a British cruizer, ran on shore and was wrecked, owing to which catastrophe several of the crew were drowned. Mr. Henri, we may add, was himself saved by the intrepidity of a gendarme, who, witnessing his peril, swam off on horseback to his rescue. After nine months of imprisonment he joined, 27 May, 1808, the ROEBUCK 44, flag-ship at Yarmouth of Vice-Admiral Billy Douglas, but removing in a few days to the GLOIRE 38, commanded by his old Captain, Jas. Carthew, he was for some time employed in that frigate at the blockade of Cherbourg, and then at the reduction of Martinique. Immediately after the latter event Mr. Henri was appointed Master's Mate of the FROLIC 18, Capt. Thos. Whinyates, part of the force engaged in the ensuing capture of the Saintes. Rejoining the GLOIRE, a few months subsequently, he assisted at the taking of Guadeloupe in Feb. 1810, and continued to be borne on her books until June, 1811. During that period, while Mr. Henri had charge of an American prize, the watch below, it appears, subjected themselves to the stupification of opium, and thereby afforded the enemy an opportunity of making an attack upon the watch on deck, and, after a fierce struggle, of regaining their ascendancy. Being allowed the option of either going to

* *Vide* Gaz. 1811, p. 2191.

America or of taking his chance in the long-boat, Mr. Henri accepted the latter, and, accompanied by some others, had the good fortune, with no other shelter than that yielded by a blanket, to make the island of Barbuda, and in the end reach Antigua, where lay the Gloire. He was ultimately, while in the Dragon 74, flag-ship of Sir Fras. Laforey, promoted, 20 Dec. 1811, three days after he had passed his examination, to an Acting-Lieutenancy in the Amaranthe 18, Capt. Geo. Pringle. He was superseded at Antigua 30 June, 1812, but on his ensuing return to England found that, by a strange coincidence, he had been that very day promoted by the Admiralty. His appointments have since been—13 Dec. 1812, to the Cumberland 74, Capt. Thos. Baker, with whom he again sailed for the West Indies—27 Jan. 1813, to the Grampus 50, bearing the flag on that station of Sir F. Laforey—14 Feb. 1813, to the Tribune 36, Capt. Geo. Reynolds—18 Sept. 1813, to the Raven 16, Capts. Geo. Gustavus Lennock and Edw. Lloyd, during his continuance in which vessel he was employed on a branch of the Scheldt in the campaign of 1813-14, and commanded a division of boats on special service up the Gulf of Paria—27 Oct. 1815, to the Hope 10, Capt. Hen. Fyge Jauncey, employed in the Channel, where he served until superseded at his own request in March, 1817—17 Feb. 1818, to the Ramillies 74, flag-ship at Leith of Sir Wm. Johnstone Hope—11 Sept. 1818, to the command of the Viper cutter, in which he cruized very successfully against the Channel smugglers, and was on one occasion so nearly murdered that the Treasury offered a reward of 200*l*. for the apprehension of the offenders—and, 17 Dec. 1821, to the Coast Guard, in which service he still continues.

While on the books of the Hope, but detached in some other vessel, Lieut. Henri was wrecked on the coast of Devon, on which occasion, out of eight persons, himself and another, whom he had the good fortune to rescue, were the only persons saved. He has been in the commission of the peace for co. Mayo since Dec. 1834. Agents—Hallett and Robinson.

HENRY. (Lieutenant, 1842. f-p., 15; h-p., 1.)

Arthur Robert Henry entered the Navy, 20 Feb. 1831, as a Volunteer, on board the Pallas 42, Capt. Manley Hall Dixon, with whom he served in the West Indies, latterly as Midshipman, until May, 1834. In the following Sept. he joined the Tyne 28, Capt. Lord Viscount Ingestrie, on the Mediterranean station, where, for some months in 1837, he was further employed on board the Rodney 92, Capt. Hyde Parker. Having passed his examination on 15 Aug. in the latter year Mr. Henry, in May, 1839, was appointed Mate of the Childers 16, Capt. Edw. Pellew Halsted, and ordered to India, whence he ultimately, in June, 1841, carried, in the capacity of temporary Commander, the Plover 12 to China. During his continuance in that vessel, which was latterly commanded by Capt. Rich. Collinson, he assisted at the reduction of Amoy, was present at the re-capture of Chusan, witnessed the storming of the fortified heights and citadel of Chinghae, commanded a party on shore in the attack on Chapoo, and co-operated in the reduction of Chin-Kiang-Foo. He was promoted for his services to the rank of Lieutenant 23 Dec. 1842,* and has been since appointed—18 March, 1843, to the Pylades 18, Capt. Louis Symonds Tindal, with whom he returned to England from the East Indies, and was paid off in the following Oct.—18 Dec. 1844, to the Ranger 6, Capt. Jas. Anderson, fitting for the coast of Africa—and, 17 March, 1845, to the Racehorse 18, Capts. Geo. Jas. Hay and Edw. Southwell Sotheby, in which vessel he is now again serving in the East Indies. In Dec. 1845, being at the time at New Zealand, Lieut. Henry landed in command of a division of small-arm men, and on 11 of the following month, after having most usefully participated for three weeks in a series of the most trying operations (more especially alluded to in our biography of Capt. Chas. Graham), assisted, and was officially mentioned for his conduct, at the storming and capture, notwithstanding a desperate resistance of four hours, of a strongly fortified pah, belonging to a rebel chieftain named Kawiti.* Agents—Messrs. Stilwell.

* *Vide* Gaz. 1842, p. 3821.

* *Vide* Gaz. 1846, p. 2346.

HENRY. (Commander, 1841. f-p., 16; h-p., 8.)

George Augustus Henry, born 6 Oct. 1809, in Dublin, is brother of Capt. Hastings R. Henry, R.N.

This officer entered the Navy, 27 Aug. 1823, as a Volunteer, on board the Prince Regent 120, Capt. Wm. Hen. Webley Parry, flag-ship at the Nore of Sir Benj. Hallowell. In 1825, having previously attained the rating of Midshipman, he joined the Cambrian 48, Capt. Gawen Wm. Hamilton, in the boats belonging to which frigate he appears to have been very often employed in the suppression of piracy in the Mediterranean; where, on removing to the Talbot 28, Capt. Hon. Fred. Spencer, he bore a part in the battle of Navarin, 20 Oct. 1827. Passing his examination in 1829, he was next, for upwards of two years, employed again at Chatham, and then in South America, on board the Prince Regent 120, flag-ship of Hon. Sir Hen. Blackwood, and Druid 46, Capt. G. W. Hamilton. Attaining the rank of Lieutenant 24 Jan. 1832, Mr. Henry was in that capacity appointed—27 Feb. and 23 Nov. 1832, to the Warspite 76, bearing the flag of Sir Thos. Baker, and Clio 18, Capt. John Jas. Onslow, both on the station last mentioned, whence he returned home and was paid off in June, 1833—6 June, 1834, to the Winchester 52, flag-ship of Sir Thos. Bladen Capel in the East Indies, where he remained about four years—and, 16 May, 1840, as First, to the Southampton 50, bearing the flag of Sir Edw. Durnford King, at the Brazils and Cape of Good Hope. He acquired his present rank 23 Nov. 1841, and is now on half-pay.

Commander Henry for four months held the acting-command of the Lily 16, on the coast of Africa. He married, 30 Oct. 1845, Etheldreda Lucy Emily, only daughter of the late Lieut.-Colonel Ferris, Treasurer of the Island of Mauritius. Agents—Messrs. Stilwell.

HENRY. (Captain, 1843. f-p., 17; h-p., 7.)

Hastings Reginald Henry, born in March, 1808, is son of the late John Joseph Henry, Esq., of Straffan, co. Kildare, by the Lady Emily Elizabeth Fitzgerald, daughter of the late and sister of the present Duke of Leinster. Capt. Henry, whose brother, Geo. Augustus, is a Commander R.N., has several other relatives in the service.

This officer entered the Navy, 20 Aug. 1823, as Fst.-cl. Vol., on board the Sybille 48, Capt. Sam. John Brooke Pechell, and, proceeding to the Mediterranean, was present, 18 June, 1826, in a desperate action with some pirates off Candia, in which the British sustained a loss of 12 men killed and 29 wounded. He afterwards served on the Home station, as Midshipman and Mate, in the Columbine sloop, Capt. Wm. Symonds, Undaunted 46, Capt. Augustus Wm. Jas. Clifford, and St. Vincent 120, Capt. Hyde Parker; and, subsequently to his promotion to the rank of Lieutenant, which took place 18 Dec. 1830, was appointed—7 Sept. 1831, to the Asia 84, flag-ship off Lisbon of Rear-Admiral Wm. Parker—and, 20 Dec. 1834, to the Rattlesnake 28, Capt. Wm. Hobson, on the East India station. Capt. Henry, whose second promotal commission bears date 28 June, 1838, next joined in succession, between 14 Sept. 1840 and his advancement to Post-rank 5 Sept. 1843, the Salamander, Styx, and Devastation steamers, and, as Acting-Captain, the Queen 110, and Aigle 24, on the Channel and Mediterranean stations. Since the latter date he has been on half-pay.

Capt. Henry married, in 1845, the Dowager Marchioness of Hastings, Baroness Grey de Ruthyn.

HENRY. (Lieutenant, 1823. f-p., 21; h-p., 18.)

John Henry entered the Navy, 8 June, 1808, as a Volunteer, on board the Iphigenia 36, Capt. Hen. Lambert, in which ship, after making a voyage to Quebec, he proceeded to India, where he witnessed the conquest of Ile Bourbon in July, 1810, and in the course of the following month assumed a share, as Midshipman, in a series of gallant but unfortunate operations, which, by the 28th, terminated in the self-destruction of the British frigates Sirius, bearing the broad pendant of Commodore Sam. Pym, and Magicienne, the capture of the Nereide, and the surrender to a powerful French squadron of the Iphigenia herself, after incurring an individual loss of at least 5 men killed and 13 wounded, at the entrance of Port Sud-Est, Isle of France. From the date last mentioned Mr. Henry remained subject to the horrors of a loathsome captivity, until released at the subsequent reduction of the Mauritius, when he was re-appointed to the Iphigenia, Capt. Thos. Gordon Caulfeild, with whom he returned to England and was paid off in May, 1811. He then served for three years in the Baltic and Channel, part of the time as Master's Mate, on board the Pyramus 36, Capts. Chas. Dashwood and Jas. Whitley Deans Dundas; which frigate, towards the close of 1812, brought Sir Jas. Saumarez from Gottenborg to England. Between May, 1814, and Aug. 1824, Mr. Henry was employed, on the West India, Mediterranean, Home, and African stations, in the Sultan 74, Capt. John West, Euphrates 36, Capt. Robt. Preston, Tagus 38, Capt. J. W. D. Dundas, Active 46, Capt. Jas. Alex. Gordon, Ramillies 74, Capt. Edw. Brace, Owen Glendower 42, Commodore Sir Robt. Mends, and Driver sloop, Capt. Chas. Bowen. While in the latter vessel, of which he was confirmed a Lieutenant 22 Oct. 1823, we find him co-operating with the troops engaged in the Ashantee war. His last appointment afloat was, 6 Nov. 1828, to the Challenger 28, Capt. Chas. Howe Fremantle, with whom he served in the East Indies, as First Lieutenant, until he returned home and was paid off 12 June, 1833.

Lieut. Henry, who has long officiated as an Emigration Agent, is now employed in that capacity at Dublin.

HENRY. (Lieut., 1815. f-p., 14; h-p., 26.)

William Henry entered the Navy, 19 Nov. 1807, as Fst.-cl. Vol., on board the Neptune 98, Capt. Sir Thos. Williams, bearing the flag afterwards of Hon. Sir Alex. Cochrane, with whom he also served for some time in the Pompée 74, and Statira 38. During the term of his attachment to the two former of those ships he assisted as Midshipman at the reduction of Martinique and the Saintes, aided on shore at the taking of Guadeloupe, witnessed the capture of the French 74-gun ship *D'Haupoult*, and was at the destruction of the 44-gun frigates *Loire* and *Seine*, in L'Ance la Barque. In Feb. 1811, after having served for a short time with Sir Fras. Laforey in the Dragon 74, Mr. Henry joined the Castor 32, Capt. Chas. Dilkes, and proceeded to the Mediterranean, where, on 23 June, 1813, he contributed, in the boats, to the cutting-out, from under the protection of a strong fort, on the coast of Catalonia, of *La Fortune*, French privateer, of 2 guns, 2 swivels, and 48 men—an exploit which occasioned the British a loss of 4 men killed and 9 wounded. In 1814 Mr. Henry, we find, participated in another affair of the same description. Quitting the Castor in April, 1815, he next, for short periods, joined the Tonnant 80, flag-ship of Hon. Sir Alex. Cochrane, and Royal Sovereign 100; and on 13 of the following June he was promoted to the rank of Lieutenant. Since 21 Dec. 1841 he has been in charge of a station in the Coast Guard. Agents—Hallett and Robinson.

HENSLEY. (Lieut., 1813. f-p., 9; h-p., 32.)

Charles Hensley entered the Navy, 31 Jan. 1806, as Third-cl. Boy, on board the Nassau 64, Capt. Robt. Campbell. After serving for some time at the blockade of the Texel, and attending, as Midshipman, the expedition to Copenhagen, he assisted, 22 March, 1808 (on the Nassau's hard-wrought extrication from a mass of ice in which she had been blocked up during the whole winter), at the capture and destruction, when in company with the Stately 64, of the Danish 74-gun ship *Prindts Christian Frederic*—an achievement accomplished at the close of a long running fight in which the Nassau sustained a loss of 2 men killed and 16 wounded. While next attached, between Nov. 1809 and Aug. 1813, to the Eagle 74, Capt. Chas. Rowley, Mr. Hensley served with great activity on the Mediterranean and Adriatic stations, contributing, during that period, to the capture, 27 Nov. 1811, of *La Corceyre* French frigate, pierced for 40 but mounting only 28 guns, and the reduction, in July, 1813, of the town of Fiumé. On leaving the Eagle he became Master's Mate of the Union 98, Capt. Robt. Rolles, in which ship (being confirmed to her by commission dated 20 Oct. 1813) he further served in the Mediterranean until July, 1814. His last appointment was, 4 May, 1815, to the Towey 24, Capt. Hew Steuart, with whom, during a continuance of three months in that ship, he served at Falmouth and off Havre de Grace.

HENSLOW, K. W. (Lieutenant, 1829.)

Frederick John Francis Henslow entered the Navy 22 Aug. 1811; passed his examination in 1819; and was made Lieutenant, 16 March, 1829, into the Java 52, flag-ship in the East Indies of Rear-Admiral Wm. Hall Gage, with whom, in 1830, he returned to England. From 19 Sept. 1833 until Oct. 1836, he commanded the Rose, Revenue-vessel; and in 1841 he was appointed one of the Naval Knights of Windsor. Agents—Goode and Lawrence.

HERBERT. (Lieutenant, 1846.)

Douglas Herbert served for some time as Midshipman of the Edinburgh 72, Capt. Wm. Wilmott Henderson, on the Mediterranean station, where, including the bombardment of St. Jean d'Acre, he shared in the operations of 1840 on the coast of Syria, and was officially mentioned for his services.* Having passed his examination, 6 Oct. 1843, he was promoted, after an employment of some months, as Mate, on board the Excellent gunnery-ship, Capt. Henry Ducie Chads, and Victoria and Albert steam-yacht, Capt. Lord Adolphus FitzClarence, to the rank of Lieutenant 7 Oct. 1846. He has since been on half-pay.

HERBERT. (Lieut., 1844. f-p., 15; h-p., 1.)

Frederick Charles Herbert, born 25 Feb. 1819, at Spofforth, near Wetherby, co. York, is second son of the Hon. and Very Rev. Wm. Herbert, LL.D., Dean of Manchester, by Letitia Dorothea, second daughter of Joshua, fifth Viscount Allen; nephew of the late, and first-cousin of the present, Earl of Carnarvon; and nephew of Capt. Hon. Chas. Herbert, R.N., a gallant seaman who was accidentally drowned in 1808.

This officer entered the Royal Naval College 4 Aug. 1831; and embarked, 17 Aug. 1833, as Fst.-cl. Vol., on board the Forte 44, Capt. Watkin Owen Pell, with whom, latterly as Midshipman, he served on the North America and West India station, until Aug. 1836. He then joined the Pincher schooner, Lieut.-Commander Geo. Byng, and, after an employment of some months in that vessel on the coast of Africa, removed successively, on the Home station, to the Britannia 120, flag-ship of Lord Amelius Beauclerk, Modeste 18, Capt. Harry Eyres, and Royal Adelaide 104, bearing the flag again of Lord A. Beauclerk. His health obliging him to leave the latter ship in Aug. 1838, he remained on shore for a period of 10 months, and became an under-graduate at Trinity College, Cambridge. He re-embarked, in June, 1839, on board the Howe 120,

* *Vide* Gaz. 1840, p. 2610.

bearing the flag at Sheerness of Sir Robt. Waller Otway; and on passing his examination 27 Sept. 1839, proceeded, in the FIREFLY steamer, Lieut.-Commander Wm. Winniett to the Canadian Lakes, where, until his promotion to the rank of Lieutenant 2 March, 1844, he served with great activity, chiefly on board the NIAGARA 20, Capt. Williams Sandom, MOHAWK steam-vessel, Lieut.-Commander John Wm. Bedford, and MONTREAL schooner, commanded by Lieut. John Tyssen, and, for some time also, by himself. Since 9 Sept. 1844 Mr. Herbert has been occupied on the Home and on the North America and West India stations in the DARING 12, Commanders Henry Jas. Matson and Wm. Peel.

HERBERT. (COMMANDER, 1828. F-P., 25; H-P., 19.)

GEORGE FLOWER HERBERT is eldest son of Joseph Herbert, Esq., President of the island of Montserrat.

This officer entered the Navy, 11 Sept. 1803, as Fst.-cl. Vol., on board the GANGES 74, Capt. Thos. Fras. Fremantle, of which ship, employed on the India station and off Ferrol, he almost immediately became a Midshipman. Between Dec. 1804 and Jan. 1811 he served, on the Home, Cadiz, and West India stations, latterly as Acting-Lieutenant, in the BARFLEUR, NEPTUNE, and DREADNOUGHT 98's, Capts. Geo. Martin, T. F. Fremantle (under whom he fought in the NEPTUNE at Trafalgar, and took part, while for a time detached, in several actions with the Spanish gun-boats near Gibraltar), and Wm. Lechmere, ROYAL GEORGE 100, and SAN JOSEF 110, flag-ships of Sir John Thos. Duckworth, NIJADEN 36, Capt. Fred. Cottrell, NEPTUNE 98, and STATIRA 38, bearing each the flag of Hon. Sir Alex. Inglis Cochrane, and PORT D'ESPAGNE 18, Capt. Geo. Grey Burton. On 28 Feb. 1811 (after having been for a few weeks borne as a Supernumerary on the books of the DRAGON 74, Rear-Admiral Sir Fras. Laforey) he rejoined the NIJADEN, in the capacity of Acting-Lieutenant; and, being confirmed to her 16 May following, was subsequently, in March, 1812, present, when, under Capt. Farmery Predam Epworth, she contrived, during her passage home from Lisbon, to effect an escape from a pursuing squadron of five French line-of-battle ships. Mr. Herbert's subsequent appointments were—30 April, 1812, with Capt. Epworth, to the NYMPHE 38, from which vessel, fitting at Portsmouth, an attack of illness obliged him at once to invalid—21 April, 1813, to the SAN JOSEF 110, flag-ship of Sir Rich. King in the Mediterranean, where he witnessed, 5 Nov. 1813 and 13 Feb. 1814, two partial actions with the Toulon fleet, and was present at the capture of Genoa in April, 1814—28 Sept. 1814, to the ULYSSES 44, Commodore Thos. Browne, on accompanying whom to the coast of Africa, he assisted at the destruction of a slave-factory—in the course of 1816, to the IMPREGNABLE, BERWICK, and IMPREGNABLE again, flag-ships at Plymouth of Sir John Thos. Duckworth and Lord Exmouth—6 April, 1820, after 17 mouths of half-pay, to the command of the HARPY Revenue-cutter — 25 Oct. 1824, to the HERALD yacht, Capt. Henry John Leeke—7 June, 1825, to the ALBION 74, Capt. John Acworth Ommanney, lying at Portsmouth—and 22 Aug. 1825, 4 Aug. 1826, and 18 Jan. 1827, to the WARSPITE 76, BOADICEA 46, and JAVA 52, all flag-ships in the East Indies of Rear-Admiral Wm. Hall Gage. He attained his present rank 7 July, 1828; and, with the exception of a command, from 18 May, 1837, until Aug. 1840, of the TÉMÉRAIRE 104, OCEAN 80, and POICTIERS 72, guard-ships at Sheerness and Chatham, has since been on half-pay.

Commander Herbert married Mary, youngest daughter of the late Capt. Harding, R.N., and niece of Rear-Admiral Jas. Bowen, formerly a Commissioner of the Navy. AGENTS—Messrs. Stilwell.

HERBERT. (LIEUT., 1819. F-P., 12; H-P., 30.)

JOHN FLETCHER HERBERT entered the Navy, 15 May, 1805, as Fst.-cl. Vol., on board the THUNDERER 74, Capts. Wm. Lechmere, John Stockham (Acting), and John Talbot; which ship, after serving in Sir Robt. Calder's action, and the battle of Trafalgar, passed the Dardanells with Sir John Duckworth in Feb. 1807, and assisted on that occasion at the destruction of a Turkish squadron near Point Pesquies. In Nov. 1808 Mr. Herbert became Midshipman of the CHEERFUL cutter, Lieut.-Commander Carpenter, with whom he cruized off Yarmouth and in the Baltic until April, 1810. He was then for three years employed in the THESEUS 74, Capt. Wm. Prowse, both in the North Sea and at St. Helena; and, from April, 1816, until promoted to the rank of Lieutenant, 29 June, 1819, he further served, the last two years and a half as Master's Mate, on board the MARTIAL gun-brig, commanded at Leith by Lieut. Robt. M'Kirdy. He has since been on half-pay.

HERBERT, K.C.B. (CAPTAIN, 1822. F-P., 20; H-P., 24.)

SIR THOMAS HERBERT, born in Feb. 1793, is son of the late Rich. T. Herbert, Esq., of Cahernan, co. Kerry, where the Herbert family has been seated since the reign of Charles II. Among the early ancestors of Sir Thomas we discover the name of Sir Rich. Herbert, of Coldbrook, who, with his brother William, Earl of Pembroke, was beheaded at Banbury, the day after the battle of "Danes Moor," 26 July, 1469.

This officer entered the Navy, 23 July, 1803, as Fst.-cl. Vol., on board the EXCELLENT 74, Capt. Frank Sotheron, and, on proceeding to the Mediterranean, was there invested with the rating of Midshipman 1 Jan. 1804. After assisting at the defence of Gaeta and the capture of Capri, he removed to the BLONDE 38, Capt. Volant Vashon Ballard, whom he accompanied to the West Indies, on which station we find him witnessing the reduction, in Dec. 1807, of the Danish West India Islands, and contributing to the capture of five privateers, carrying in the whole 58 guns and 515 men. On 1 Aug. 1809, as a reward for the conduct he had in particular exhibited as prize-master of *L'Alert* of 20 guns and 149 men, Mr. Herbert, on the recommendation of his Captain, was nominated by Sir Alex. Cochrane to a Lieutenancy in his flag-ship the NEPTUNE 98. Being officially promoted on 10 of the following Oct., he was next, between March, 1810, and June, 1814, employed, as a Lieutenant, in the POMPÉE 74, Capt. Sir Jas. Athol Wood, on the West India, Home, and Mediterranean stations. He then became First of the EURYALUS 36, Capt. Chas. Napier, in which frigate he served until the close of the American war, and obtained the official mention of Sir Jas. Alex. Gordon for the ability and the conspicuous exertions he displayed throughout the operations on the river Potomac, including the capture of Fort Washington, and of the city of Alexandria.* On 19 Oct. 1814, Mr. Herbert, who by that period had been upwards of 20 times engaged with the enemy, in cutting-out affairs and otherwise, and had been thrice wounded, was advanced to the rank of Commander. He did not, however, take up his commission until Feb. 1815; from which period he appears to have remained on half-pay until 6 Sept. 1821. He then obtained an appointment to the ICARUS 10, fitting for the Jamaica station, where he removed, 6 May, 1822, to the CARNATION 18, and was posted, 25 Nov. following, to a death vacancy in the TAMAR 26. Continuing to serve in the latter vessel until paid off in Aug. 1823, Capt. Herbert succeeded during that period in destroying three piratical vessels on the coasts of Cuba and Yucatan. On 10 Nov. 1837, not having been afloat for a period of 14 years, he was next appointed to the CALLIOPE 26, and ordered to the Brazils. Until the arrival there from the Pacific of Commodore Thos. Ball Sulivan, Capt. Herbert, we find, conducted in person the duties of Senior Officer. He was subsequently directed to assume the command of the naval force in the Rio de la Plata for the protection of the British interests at

* *Vide* Gaz. 1814, p. 2081.

Buenos Ayres and Monte Video, during the blockade of the former place by a French squadron; and, while in discharge of the duties which were thus imposed upon him, he had the satisfaction of being twice officially assured of the entire approbation of the Admiralty at his proceedings. In Jan. 1840 Capt. Herbert went round Cape Horn, and joined Rear-Admiral Chas. Bayne Hodgson Ross at Valparaiso, whence, in the ensuing June, he sailed for China *viâ* St. Bernardin's Passage, encountering *en route*, while among the Philippine Islands, a typhoon, which the CALLIOPE was only enabled to survive through the extreme exertions of her officers and crew. Arriving in the Canton river on 10 Oct., Capt. Herbert immediately assumed, and, until the advent of Rear-Admiral Hon. Geo. Eliot on 20 Nov., retained, the command of the blockading force. The important nature of his services, as one of the chief actors in the scenes of hostility that followed, demands our particular attention. On 7 Jan. 1841, having been placed by the Rear-Admiral in charge of the advanced squadron off the Boca Tigris, he conducted the attack made on the enemy's forts at Chuenpee, where were annihilated 11 powerful junks, the flower of the Chinese navy;* and on 23 Feb., being at the time on board the NEMESIS, he effected the destruction of a 20-gun battery at the back of the island of Anunghoy.† Three days after the latter event we find him, in the CALLIOPE, heading the operations against the celebrated Bogue Forts, and on the 27th (with the CALLIOPE, HERALD 26, ALLIGATOR 26, MODESTE 18, SULPHUR 8, and NEMESIS and MADAGASCAR steamers, under his orders), attacking the enemy's camp, fort, and ship *Cambridge*, bearing the Chinese admiral's flag, at their position below Whampoa Reach, where 98 guns were on the whole destroyed.‡ After capturing, on 13 March, the last fort protective of the approaches to Canton, Capt. Herbert's squadron advanced towards the city, and on the 18th attacked all the batteries and flotilla in its immediate vicinity; the former of which, in the course of two hours and a half, were in succession destroyed, and the latter either burnt or dispersed; thus enabling the British to plant the Union-Jack on the walls of the factory, and placing totally in their power the huge capital of Quang-tong.§ On the renewal, in the following May, of the hostilities against Canton, the Chinese, on the night of 21 of that month, made a vigorous attack, with fire-rafts and armed boats, and from several masked and newly raised batteries, on the British shipping there located, and still commanded by Capt. Herbert. They were, however, totally defeated, and on the next day their batteries were dismantled, and their floating armament ruined. On 26 the water-defences between the Factories and Howqua's fort, mounting 64 guns, were levelled, and forcible possession taken of their naval arsenal and war-junks.‖ In the month of June Capt. Herbert, who until then had directed, as we have stated, the movements of the advanced squadron on the Canton river, succeeded, owing to the death of Sir Humphrey Fleming Senhouse, to the command of the whole force employed on that stream. On the arrival, a few weeks afterwards, of Rear-Admiral Sir Wm. Parker, as Commander-in-Chief, he was removed to the BLENHEIM 72; in which ship, in the course of the following Aug. and Oct., he assisted, with great distinction, at the capture of Amoy, the retaking of Chusan, and the reduction of Chinghae.¶ On the latter occasion, after the necessary breachings had been accomplished, he landed in command of the light column of attack, consisting of a body of upwards of 700 seamen, marines, and troops, and stormed and carried the citadel, situated on the left bank of the Tinghae river; while the General, Sir Hugh Gough, with the land forces, made himself equally master of the extensive and formidable works on the right bank. Capt. Herbert, who was next present at the surrender of Ningpo, and subsequently accompanied several reconnoitring parties up the Tinghae, returned to Hong-Kong from off Ningpo and Chusan in Feb. 1842, and resumed command of the squadron in the Canton river. In the month of July he left Hong-Kong in a steamer, for the Yang-tse-Kiang, for the purpose of visiting Nanking, where he remained until H. M. Plenipotentiary, in Oct., took leave of the Imperial Commissioner. Sir Thos. Herbert, whose brilliancy of service had been rewarded, 14 Oct. 1841, with the dignity of a K.C.B.,* returned to England by the Cape of Good Hope—thus accomplishing a circumnavigation of the globe—and paid the BLENHEIM off in March, 1843. Since 11 Jan. 1847 he has been employed on the south-east coast of America, with a broad pendant in the RALEIGH 50.

Sir Thos. Herbert, a Magistrate and Deputy-Lieutenant for Kerry, was High Sheriff for that co. in 1829.

* *Vide* Gaz. 1841, pp. 1162, 1222, 1424, 1496.
† *V.* Gaz. 1841, p. 1498. ‡ *V.* Gaz. 1841, p. 1500.
§ *V.* Gaz. 1841, pp. 1503-4-5. ‖ *V.* Gaz. 1841, pp. 2502-5.
¶ *V.* Gaz. 1842, pp. 82, 389, 393, 395, 396.

* He had been nominated a C B. on 29 of the previous June.

HERBERT. (LIEUT., 1845. F-P., 12; H-P., 0.)

WILLIAM GEORGE HERBERT entered the Navy in 1835; acquired official mention for his services as Midshipman of the EDINBURGH 72, Capt. Wm. Wilmott Henderson, during the operations of 1840 on the coast of Syria; passed his examination 20 Jan. 1841; and (until promoted to the rank of Lieutenant 1 Dec. 1845) served, as Mate, on the Home and Mediterranean stations, in the EXCELLENT gunnery-ship, Capt. Sir Thos. Hastings, and QUEEN 110, and FORMIDABLE 84, bearing each the flag of Sir Edw. W. C. R. Owen. He rejoined the EXCELLENT 17 Jan. 1846; and since 9 of the following May has been employed, with the Channel squadron, in the RODNEY 92, Capt. Edw. Collier.

HERRICK. (LIEUT., 1815. F-P., 21; H-P., 21.)

EDWARD HERRICK is brother of Commander Wm. Henry Herrick, R.N.

This officer entered the Navy, 18 June, 1805, as Fst.-cl. Vol., on board the REVENGE 74, Capts. Robt. Moorsom, Hon. Chas. Elphinstone Fleeming, John Gore, Hon. Chas. Paget, and John Nash. After participating, as Midshipman, in the action off Trafalgar, witnessing also Lord Cochrane's destruction of the French shipping in Basque Roads, and serving in the batteries during the operations against Flushing, he sailed in 1811 for the East Indies, on board the DROMEDARY store-ship, Master-Commander Pritchard. On his arrival on that station he joined the ILLUSTRIOUS 74, bearing the broad pendant first of Commodore Wm. Robt. Broughton and the flag afterwards of Rear-Admiral Sir Sam. Hood. He returned to England in March, 1813, in the MODESTE 38, Capt. Jas. Coutts Crawford, and, between May, 1814, and June, 1815, was next employed, latterly as Master's Mate, in the PRESIDENT frigate, Capt. Arch. Duff, on the Cork station. He then took up a commission bearing date 3 Feb. 1815, but did not again go afloat until appointed, 6 Aug. 1830, to the PRINCE REGENT 120, bearing the flag of Rear-Admiral Wm. Parker in the river Tagus. The latter ship being paid off 21 Feb. 1832, he subsequently joined—29 June, 1832, as First-Lieutenant, the CHAMPION 18, Capt. Hon. Arthur Duncombe, with whom he served in the Mediterranean until 16 Dec. 1834—18 March, 1836, in a similar capacity, the MINDEN 74, Capt. Alex. Renton Sharpe, from which ship, fitting at Plymouth, he was immediately superseded—13 July, 1838, the ASTRÆA 6, Capt. Jas. Hanway Plumridge, employed as a packet on the Falmouth station—and, 4 Jan. 1840, the EXPRESS, another Falmouth packet, which he himself commanded, with the exception, we believe, of some months in 1843-4, until June, 1846. He has since been on half-pay.

Lieut. Herrick married, in 1836, Charlotte, only daughter of the late Capt. Thos. Alexander, R.N.,

C.B., and niece of Commander Nicholas Alexander, R.N. AGENTS—Messrs. Ommanney.

HERRICK. (COMMANDER, 1813. F-P., 15; H-P., 34.)

WILLIAM HENRY HERRICK, born 13 Feb. 1784, is eldest son of the late Thos. Bousfield Herrick, Esq., of Shippool, near Innishannon, co. Cork, by Anne, only daughter of Henry Moore, Esq., of Frankfort House, co. Cork; brother (with the present Lieut. Edw. Herrick, R.N.) of Capt. Henry Moore Herrick, of the 45th Regt., who was killed at the storming of Badajos; and brother-in-law of the late Capt. Rich. Plummer Davies, R.N. His grand-uncle, Edw. Herrick, Esq., Lieutenant R.N., himself a nephew of the first Sir Riggs Falkiner, Bart., of Anne Mount, co. Cork, was killed on board the DORSETSHIRE in Sir Edw. Hawkes' action 20 Sept. 1759.

This officer entered the Navy, 20 May, 1798, as A.B., on board the DRYAD 36, Capt. Lord Amelius Beauclerk, under whom he very soon attained the rating of Midshipman. With the exception of a few months during the peace of Amiens, he was next, until the autumn of 1805, employed in the DORIS, FORTUNÉE, and AIGLE frigates, Capts. Lord Viscount Ranelagh, Lord A. Beauclerk, and Geo. Wolfe, MAJESTIC 74, Capt. Lord A. Beauclerk, and LEDA 38, Capt. Robt. Honyman. Mr. Herrick, who had hitherto served on the Irish and Channel stations, and had been frequently engaged with the boats in destroying the enemy's convoys on the coast of France, was then appointed Acting-Lieutenant of the DIADEM 64, Commodore Sir Home Popham, to which ship, after assisting on shore at the reduction of the Cape of Good Hope, he was confirmed by commission dated 5 Feb. 1806. In the course of the same and of the following year he presents himself to our notice, while attached to the DIADEM and to the RAISONNABLE, another 64, Capt. Josias Rowley, as further employed with the land forces in the operations against Buenos Ayres, Maldonado, and Monte Video. At the period, however, of the re-capture of the former place by the Spaniards in Aug. 1806, he was in the temporary command of the DOLORES, an armed schooner, and obtained the favourable notice of Sir Home Popham for the very creditable manner in which he worked out of the harbour, and thereby escaped capture.* Mr. Herrick, whose conduct, indeed, during the whole term of his sojourn in South America appears to have been much above the average, attracted the attention also of Rear-Admiral Geo. Murray, by the infinite service he rendered in piloting the squadron, immediately prior to the unfortunate attempt made by Lieut.-General Whitelocke to regain possession of Buenos Ayres in June, 1807.† His appointments, on leaving the RAISONNABLE, were, on the East India station—23 Feb. 1808, to the PROCRIS sloop, Capt. Jas. Murray Gordon, of which vessel he acted as Commander for nearly eight months—25 Jan. and 28 Feb. 1809, to the MODESTE 36, Capt. Hon. Geo. Elliot, and RUSSELL 74, bearing the flag of Rear-Admiral Wm. O'Brien Drury—1 March, 1810, to the acting-command, for upwards of two months, of the BLANCHE 28—then again, we presume, to the RUSSELL—28 Feb. 1812, to the HECATE sloop, Capt. Henry John Peachy—and, 4 Aug. 1812, to the acting-command of the ARROGANT guard-ship at Bombay, whence he invalided home in Jan. 1813. He was advanced to his present rank on 17 Aug. in the latter year, and has not been since afloat.

Commander Herrick is in the Commission of the Peace for co. Cork. He married, 8 Sept. 1814, Mary, only daughter of Robt. de la Cour, Esq., of Bear Forest, by whom he has issue four sons and five daughters. AGENTS—Messrs. Ommanney.

HERRINGHAM. (CAPT., 1837. F-P., 18; H-P., 26.)

WILLIAM ALLAN HERRINGHAM entered the Navy, 6 Nov. 1803, as Fst.-cl. Vol., on board the LEOPARD 50, Capt. Jas. Nicoll Morris, on accompanying whom, after having served off Dungeness and Boulogne, into the COLOSSUS 74, he fought, as Midshipman, and was wounded, at the battle of Trafalgar, 21 Oct. 1805.* Joining then the ADAMANT 50, Capts. John Stiles, John Fyffe, and Micajah Malbon, he escorted in that ship a valuable fleet of Indiamen to the Cape of Good Hope, accompanied another home from St. Helena, and was subsequently, until the autumn of 1808, employed on the African and Jamaica stations. The time which intervened between the date last mentioned and that of his official promotion, 2 Nov. 1810, was passed by Mr. Herringham in the Mediterranean and Channel, latterly in the capacity of Acting-Lieutenant, on board the THAMES 32, Capt. Hon. Granville Geo. Waldegrave, and CALEDONIA 120, flag-ship of Admirals Lord Gambier, Fras. Pickmore, and Sir Harry Burrard Neale. On 30 Sept. 1811, he joined the YORK 74, Capt. Robt. Barton, with whom he served, again in the Mediterranean and on the North Sea station, until next appointed, 17 Aug. 1812, to the JAVA, of 46 guns and 377 men; as Second-Lieutenant of which frigate he had the misfortune, on 29 of the following Dec., to be captured, while on his passage to India, by the American ship *Constitution*, of 55 guns and 480 men, after a close and fierce action sustained by the British for a period of 3 hours and 40 minutes, and until they had had 22 of their men killed and 102, including their Captain, Henry Lambert, mortally, wounded. On his restoration to liberty Mr. Herringham (whose able exertions during the conflict had obtained for him the highest commendation of his commanding officer)† was appointed, 8 Oct. 1813, to the TIGRIS 36, Capt. Robt. Henderson, under whom he served for four years on the Irish, West India, and Channel stations. Attaining the rank of Commander 16 Jan. 1818, he was subsequently, on 8 Sept. 1831, and 12 June, 1833, nominated to the Second Captaincy of the TALAVERA 74, commanded on particular service by Capts. David Colby and Thos. Brown, and of the FORTE 44, Capt. Watkin Owen Pell, employed on the North America and West India station. He left the former ship, for the recovery of his health, in Dec. 1832, and was paid off from the FORTE a few weeks after his advancement, 10 Jan. 1837, to Post-rank. He has not since been afloat.

Capt. Herringham, in consideration of his wound, was presented, after the battle of Trafalgar, with a gratuity from the Patriotic Fund. In 1817 he had the honour of steering H.R.H. the Duke of Gloucester when on a visit to the flag-ship at Plymouth.

HESELTINE. (COMMANDER, 1846.)

ALBERT HESELTINE passed his examination in 1832; obtained his first commission 28 Sept. 1837; and on 14 of the following Nov. joined the ELECTRA 18, Capt. Wm. Preston, fitting for the South American station, where he became, 3 April, 1839, First Lieutenant of the GRECIAN 16, Capt. Wm. Smyth. He was afterwards appointed, in the latter capacity, on the Brazilian and the Cape of Good Hope station—19 July, 1840, to the STAG 46, bearing the broad pendant of Commodore Thos. Ball Sulivan—22 March, 1843, after nearly two years of half-pay, to the SAPPHO 16, Capt. Hon. Geo. Hope—and, 12 March, 1844, to the CONWAY 26, Capt. Wm. Kelly. He was advanced to his present rank 9 Nov. 1846, and has since been unemployed.

Commander Heseltine, in the earlier part of his career, served in the ANDROMEDA frigate, in the East Indies, and was frequently engaged in her boats against the pirates of Malacca. He married, 28 Sept. 1840, Georgina, only daughter of Lieut. J. O'Reilly, R.N. AGENTS—Messrs. Stilwell.

HETHERINGTON. (LIEUTENANT, 1810. F-P., 10; H-P., 34.)

RICHARD HETHERINGTON entered the Navy, in 1803, as Fst.-cl. Vol., on board the MONTAGU 74, Capt. Robt. Waller Otway. During five years of

* *Vide* Gaz. 1807, p. 113. † *V.* Gaz. 1807, p. 1210.

* *V.* Gaz. 1805, p. 1484. † *V.* Gaz. 1813, p. 771.

servitude in that ship he assisted at the blockade of the enemy's ports from Brest to the Dardanells; was present, 22 Aug. 1805, in Admiral Hon. Wm. Cornwallis' attack on the French fleet close in with Brest harbour, on which occasion the Montagu exchanged fire with *L'Alexandre*, of 80 guns; aided, in the winter of 1807, at the evacuation of Scylla, a fortified rock in the Faro of Messina, the garrison of which was embarked under a smart fire from the enemy on the Calabrian shore; and co-operated with the patriots on the coast of Catalonia. In 1808 he removed with Capt. Otway to the Malta 80, off Toulon; and in the course of 1809 we find him joining the Ville de Paris 110, and Neptune 98, flag-ships in the Mediterranean and West Indies of Lord Collingwood and Hon. Sir Alex. Cochrane. On 8 Nov. 1810, nearly four months after he had been appointed to act as Lieutenant, Mr. Hetherington was confirmed to that rank in the Bellette 18, Capt. David Sloan, under whom he continued to serve, still in the West Indies, until 1 May, 1811, when, we believe, he was taken prisoner in a cutting-out affair. His subsequent appointments, it appears, were—30 Oct. 1811, to the Princess Caroline 74, Capt. Hugh Downman, employed in cruizing among the Western Islands—14 Sept. 1812, to the Arab sloop, Capts. John Wilson, Robt. Standley, and Geo. Elliott, from which vessel, successively stationed in the West Indies and off Passages, he invalided in March, 1813—and 31 Jan. 1814, to the Martial 12, Capts. Edw. Collins and Henry Forbes, lying at Plymouth. He went on half-pay in the following Aug., and has not been since employed.

HEWES. (Retired Captain, 1842. f.p., 16; h-p., 37.)

Thomas Oldacres Hewes entered the Navy, 2 Sept. 1794, as Fst.-cl. Vol., on board the Ruby 64, Capts. Hon. Henry Edwin Stanhope, John Wm. Spranger, and Jacob Waller, in which ship he was present, as Midshipman, at the detention of five Dutch men-of-war, and of a large convoy, in Plymouth Sound, 19 Jan. 1795—also at the reduction of the Cape of Good Hope—and, on 17 Aug. 1796, at the surrender of the Dutch squadron in Saldanha Bay. From Aug. 1797, until promoted to the rank of Lieutenant, 15 Oct. 1800, Mr. Hewes served, chiefly with Capt. Stanhope, although likewise with Sir Erasmus Gower and Capt. Geo. Murray, in the Neptune 98, and Achille 74, on the Home station. He was then employed for upwards of three years on board the Snake sloop, Capts. John Mason Lewis, Chas. Tinling, and Wm. Roberts, in the Channel, off the coast of Africa, and in the West Indies; after which he served, until Oct. 1808, with Capt. Zachary Mudge, in the Blanche and Phœnix frigates, on the Jamaica station, and again in the Channel. While in the former of those vessels Mr. Hewes, on 19 July, 1805, participated, as First Lieutenant, in an action of 45 minutes, which terminated in her surrender, after a loss of 8 men killed and 15 wounded, and when on the verge of sinking, to a powerful French squadron, consisting of *La Topaze* frigate, of 44 guns and 410 men, one ship of 22 guns and 236 men, a corvette of 18 guns and 213 men, and a brig of 16 guns and 123 men. His last appointments were—10 April, 1809, to the Heroine 32, Capt. Hood Hanway Christian, part of the Walcheren expeditionary armament, and one of the 10 frigates which, under Lord Wm. Stuart, forced the passage between Flushing and Cadsand—and, 2 March, 1810, as First, to the Edgar 74, Capt. Stephen Poyntz. On 7 of the following July he took command of the boats of the Edgar and Dictator, and captured three Danish row gun-boats, each mounting 1 long gun and 4 brass howitzers, with a complement of 28 men—an exploit which so won the approbation of Rear-Admiral Manley Dixon that to one of the prizes he gave the name of Hewes. The British on the occasion sustained a loss of 1 man killed and 3 wounded; the enemy, who were under the protection of a fire of guns and musketry from the shore near Granna, of 6 men killed and 16 wounded.* Lieut. Hewes, who left the Edgar in Dec. 1810, acquired the rank of Commander 1 Aug. 1811, and accepted that he now holds 10 Feb. 1842.

HEWETT. (Commander, 1845.)

Graham Hewett entered the Navy 22 Feb. 1808; passed his examination in 1814; obtained his first commission 27 May, 1825; and was afterwards appointed—10 June, 1826, to the Coast Blockade, in which he was for upwards of three years employed as Supernumerary-Lieutenant of the Ramillies 74, Capt. Hugh Pigot—and 18 Feb. 1832, to the Coast Guard. He left the latter service on advancement to his present rank, 16 Jan. 1845, and has since been on half-pay.

HEWETT. (Retired Commander, 1843. f-p., 16; h-p., 34).

James Hewett is the son of a Captain in the Navy, and has many relations in both services.

This officer entered the Navy, 17 July, 1797, as A.B., on board the Plumper, Lieut.-Commander M. T. Hewett; served next for a year and a half with Capt. David Milne in the Seine 36, on the coast of Africa and in the West Indies; and on 8 July, 1800, was appointed Midshipman of the Queen 98, Capt. Man Dobson. Between the close of the latter year and the peace of Amiens, he was further employed under the flag of Sir Hyde Parker on board the Royal George 100, and London 98, and during that period was present in the latter ship at the battle of Copenhagen, 2 April, 1801. In 1802 he sailed in the Glatton 50, Capt. Jas. Colnett, for New Holland, on his return whence, in 1803, he successively joined the Utrecht 64, Capt. John Wentworth Loring, Fortunée 36, Capt. Henry Vansittart, and Inconstant 36, Capt. Edw. Stirling Dickson. On the night of 7 March, 1804, immediately previous to the capture of the African island of Goree, we find Mr. Hewett assisting in the boats of the last-mentioned frigate at the cutting-out of a ship under a heavy fire from its batteries, which, however, although it sank one of the boats, wounded but one man. In Nov. 1804, he became Acting-Lieutenant of L'Aimable 32, Capts. Clotworthy Upton, Hon. Duncombe Pleydell Bouverie, and Lord Geo. Stuart, under whom (his appointment being confirmed by a commission dated 8 March, 1805) he continued successively to serve until April, 1809. He was chased, during that period, by a French squadron under M. Richery, when proceeding to join Lord Nelson's fleet off Cadiz, and (after having escorted Sir Arthur Wellesley's army from Cork to Vimeira, and been an eye-witness, as we understand, of the battle of Vimeira) was present at the capture, on 3 Feb. 1809, of *L'Iris* French National ship, pierced for 32, but mounting only 24 guns, which did not surrender until she had herself sustained a loss of 2 men killed and 8 wounded, and the *Aimable*, besides being materially damaged in masts, spars, sails, and rigging, of 2 wounded. Removing, in April, 1809, to the Sceptre 74, Capts. Joseph Bingham and Sam. Jas. Ballard, Lieut. Hewett accompanied the ensuing expedition to the Walcheren, and on being ordered to the West Indies contributed, antecedently to a participation in the operations against Guadeloupe, to the destruction, 18 Dec. 1809, of the French 40-gun frigates *Loire* and *Seine*, lying under the protection of several strong batteries in L'Ance la Barque. Quitting the Sceptre in March, 1811, he next and lastly, in the course of 1812, joined the Asia 74, Capt. Geo. Scott, and Crocodile 28, Capt. Wm. Elliott. He invalided home from the Mediterranean in 1814; and accepted the rank he now holds 18 April, 1843—exactly a week after he had been admitted to the out-pension of Greenwich Hospital.

Commander Hewett is agent for Beachy Head Lights.

* *Vide* Gaz. 1810, p. 1162.

HEWETT. (LIEUT., 1815. F-P., 12; H-P., 32.)

WILLIAM HEWETT (c) died 16 Feb. 1845, at Exeter.

This officer entered the Navy, 7 July, 1803, as Midshipman, on board the IMPÉTUEUX 74, Capts. Thos. Byam Martin, John Lawford, and David Milne, bearing the flag afterwards of Vice-Admiral Geo. Martin, in which ship he served for nearly 10 years — the last four as Master's Mate. Besides attending the expedition of 1809 to the Walcheren, he was much employed, during that period, off Brest, Ferrol, and Corunna, as also in the Baltic and Tagus. In the course of 1813 he successively accompanied Vice-Admiral Martin into the STATELY and RUBY 64's, also on the Lisbon station; and on 17 June, 1814, he was promoted from the SAN JUAN 74, flag-ship at Gibraltar of Hon. Chas. Elphinstone Fleeming, to an Acting-Lieutenancy in the PAPILLON 16, Capt. Jas. Hay. He returned home from the Mediterranean on the occasion of his official promotion, 1 April, 1815, and did not afterwards go afloat.

HEWITT. (LIEUT., 1828. F-P., 11; H-P., 27.)

THOMAS HEWITT was born 10 Jan. 1796.

This officer entered the Navy, 9 Aug. 1809, as Fst.-cl. Vol., on board the FYLLA 20, Capt. Hon. Edw. Rodney, with whom, after an intermediate servitude in the Channel, he ultimately proceeded to the East Indies, as Midshipman of the AFRICAINE 38. On his return to England in the early part of 1816, he passed his examination, but in the following year, being unable to procure an appointment in any way desirable, he joined the Merchant service, and again sailed for India, where he remained until the close of 1823. In March, 1824, having applied for re-employment in the Navy, he was appointed Admiralty-Mate of the PRINCE REGENT 120, flag-ship at the Nore. On 24 of next June he removed to the BRISK 10, Capt. Chas. Hope, and on being subsequently transferred to the DORIS 42, Capt. Sir John Gordon Sinclair, he was ordered to South America, whence he invalided home in March, 1826, on board the BRITON 46, Capt. Sir Murray Maxwell. Between the ensuing Aug. and Nov. 1828, we find Mr. Hewitt employed on the Home, Lisbon, and Mediterranean stations, in the VICTORY 104, TERROR bomb (which vessel was wrecked on the coast of Portugal), and OCEAN 80, Capt. Patrick Campbell. He was then nominated by Sir Pulteney Malcolm Acting-Lieutenant of the WOLF 18, Capt. Geo. Hayes—an appointment which the Admiralty confirmed. He left the Mediterranean, an invalid, in June, 1829, and has since been on half-pay.

Lieut. Hewitt married, 25 Nov. 1829, Miss Barlow, and by that lady has issue four children.

HEWLETT. (COMMANDER, 1845.)

RICHARD STRODE HEWLETT is son of John Valentine Hewlett, Esq., of Barnstaple, Devon, by Admonition, youngest daughter of Rich. Strode, Esq., of Boterford and Newnham Park, in the above shire. He is nephew of the present Geo. Strode, Esq., of Newnham Park, a magistrate and Deputy-Lieutenant for Devon, who served as High Sheriff of the co. in 1825.

This officer passed his examination in 1829; and obtained his first commission 10 Jan. 1837. His appointments, in the capacity of Lieutenant, were —27 Jan. 1837, to the ASIA 84, commanded in the Mediterranean by Capt. Wm. Fisher—3 April, and 16 Aug. 1837, as Additional, to the CALEDONIA 120, and PRINCESS CHARLOTTE 104, bearing the flags of Sir Josias Rowley and Hon. Robt. Stopford, on the same station—9 Oct. 1837, again in the ASIA, still commanded by Capt. Fisher, under whom he participated in the operations of 1840 on the coast of Syria, and served at the blockade of Alexandria—and 10 Aug. 1841, to the ILLUSTRIOUS 72, flag-ship in North America and the West Indies of Sir Chas. Adam. He was advanced, a few months after he had been paid off, to the rank of Commander, by commission dated 23 Sept. 1845, and, since 7 Jan. 1846, he has been officiating as Second Captain of the EXCELLENT gunnery-ship at Portsmouth, Capt. Henry Ducie Chads.

HEWLETT. (LIEUTENANT, 1825.)

WILLIAM HEWLETT, born 1 Jan. 1795, is son of the late Wm. Hewlett, Esq., Master R.N. (1799).

This officer entered the Navy, 20 July, 1807; and while attached to the ULYSSES 44, commanded in succession by Capts. Christ. John Williams Nesham, Wm. Maude, and Hon. Warwick Lake, was present, in 1808-9, at the reduction of Marie-galante, Deseada, Martinique, and Flushing. He passed his examination in 1814, and was promoted to the rank of Lieutenant, while serving in the Coast Blockade, 10 Jan. 1825. His appointments since that period have been to the command—29 Aug. 1833, of a station in the Coast Guard—17 March, 1835, to the SPRIGHTLY Revenue-vessel—17 March, 1838, again to a Coast-Guard station—6 Oct. 1840, of the CHEERFUL, another Revenue-cruizer—and 21 July, 1842, once more of a station in the Coast Guard, which he still retains.

Lieut. Hewlett married, in June, 1829, Rebecca, only daughter of W. Atkins, Esq., of Gosport, Hants, by whom he has issue three sons and three daughters.

HEWSON. (Captain, 1817. F-P., 22; H-P., 37.)

GEORGE HEWSON, born 26 July, 1776, is second son of the late Rev. Fras. Hewson, M.A., of Woodford, near Listowel, co Kerry, by Margaret, daughter of Lancelot Sandes, Esq., of Kilcavan, Queen's Co. He is brother of John Fras. Hewson, Esq., of Ennismore, a Deputy-Lieutenant for Kerry, and of the present Lieut. Maurice Hewson, R.N.; first-cousin of the Right Hon. Maurice Fitzgerald, the Knight of Kerry; and second-cousin of Lord Monteagle.

This officer entered the Navy, in Feb. 1788, as Fst.-cl Vol., on board the RACEHORSE 18, Capts. Thos. Foley and Mackay, under whom he served for four years on the Home station, latterly as Midshipman. In Nov. 1792 he became attached to the KINGFISHER 18, Capt. Thos. Graves, lying at Portsmouth; and on 19 March, 1793, he rejoined Capt. Foley, on board the ST. GEORGE 98, bearing the flag of Rear-Admiral John Gell, and fitting for the Mediterranean, on his passage whither he witnessed the capture of *Le Gén'ral Dumourier* privateer, and her prize the *St. Iago*, a galleon, with treasure on board to the value of a million sterling. On the occupation of Toulon by Lord Hood, Mr. Hewson was employed on shore with a party of seamen at Fort Mulgrave; after which we find him uniting in the operations of 1794 against Corsica, and—immediately on passing his examination, which he did before Nelson—appointed (through the instrumentality of Sir Hyde Parker, who had succeeded Rear-Admiral Gell) to the BRITANNIA 100, bearing the flag of Admiral Hotham; from which ship, subsequently to that officer's first partial action with the French fleet, he was promoted, 16 March, 1795, to the rank of Lieutenant, and placed on board *Le Censeur* 74, Capt. Thos. Boys, one of the prizes taken on that occasion. His next appointments were—18 April, 1795, to the INCONSTANT 36, Capt. Thos. Fras. Fremantle, also in the Mediterranean, where he assisted at the capture, 20 April, 1796, of the French 28-gun frigate *Unité*—in Oct. 1797, to the IMPÉTUEUX 74, Capt. John Willet Payne, in the Channel—1 March, 1799, as First, to the BOADICEA 38, Capts. Rich. Goodwin Keats and Chas. Rowley, by whom, as he had been by Capt. Payne, he was frequently employed on boat expeditions, on one of which occasions, we are informed, he contributed to the destruction of a convoy in the passage du Raz, and on another was officially noticed for his conduct at the cutting-out of a lugger of 6 guns from under the batteries of St. Matthew—13 June and 19 Oct. 1803, also as First, to the RUBY and GELYKHEID 64's, Capts. Hon. Fras. Farington Gardner and Isaac Wolley, both on the

Home station—28 Feb. 1805, as Second, to the ROYAL SOVEREIGN 100, Capts. Mark Robinson and John Conn, flag-ship for some time of Sir Rich. Hussey Bickerton on the east coast of Spain—11 Oct. 1805, to the DREADNOUGHT 98, Capt. Conn, under whom he fought at Trafalgar, virtually we believe as First-Lieutenant, but was left unpromoted, owing to the circumstances of his position not being known at the Admiralty, and to his inability to enter into an explanation—and, 17 June, 1806, again as Senior, to the SUPERB 74, commanded by his friend Capt. Keats. Being at length, after having attended the expedition to Copenhagen, presented with a second promotal commission bearing date 13 Oct. 1807, he further joined, in the capacity of Commander—15 July, 1809, LA FLÈCHE 14, in which vessel he assisted at the reduction of Flushing, and, on its evacuation by the British, covered their retreat—22 Oct. 1810 (having lost LA FLÈCHE off the mouth of the river Elbe on 24 of the previous May) the COQUETTE 18, employed at Portsmouth and Leith until Jan. 1812—and 7 June, 1814, the GRIFFON 14, in the Downs, where he served until his health obliged him to invalid in May, 1816. Capt. Hewson attained Post-rank 1 Jan. 1817; and accepted the Retirement 1 Oct. 1846.

He married, in 1808, Grace, daughter of W. Marshall, Esq., of Great Grimsby, co. Lincoln, second-cousin of the Duke of St. Albans, and first-cousin of Sir J. M. Brackenbury, late Consul at Cadiz, and of Colonel Sir Edw. Brackenbury, K.T.S. By that lady he has issue three sons, all in the medical profession, and one daughter.

HEWSON. (LIEUT., 1809. F-P., 18; H-P., 33.)

MAURICE HEWSON, born 5 Nov. 1786, is youngest brother of Capt. Geo. Hewson, R.N.

This officer entered the Navy, 27 May, 1796, as A. B., on board the SAVAGE sloop, Capt. Geo. Winckworth, in which vessel, and in the OVERYSSEL 64, bearing each the flag of Admiral Peyton, he served for twelve months in the Downs, latterly as Midshipman. He was then obliged to invalid from an attack of fever, and, when afterwards on his passage to Ireland in a merchant-vessel, he was captured by one of the enemy's row-boats and taken to Calais, whence, however, through the generous interference of the Prussian Consul, who claimed him as a relative, he was soon allowed to return home. Re-embarking, 18 March, 1798, on board the NEMESIS 28, Capts. Robt. Dudley Oliver and Thos. Baker, he made a voyage with convoy to Quebec, and was for some time employed in watching the movements of the enemy off Boulogne and Calais. On his subsequent rejunction of Capt. Oliver in the MERMAID 32, we find him visiting the Mediterranean, where, after many months of active boat and other service off Toulon, and assisting at the capture of *La Cruelle* French brig of war, he accompanied Lord Hutchinson, the conqueror of Egypt, to various places in Sicily and Naples. On the return of the MERMAID with that nobleman to England, Mr. Hewson, who for sixteen months had held the rating of Master's Mate, was received on board the DIAMOND 38, Capt. Thos. Elphinstone, with whom he served on the Home station until shortly after the renewal of hostilities, when he was sent into port in charge of a prize. While next awaiting off Brest, in the PICKLE schooner, Lieut.-Commander John Richards Lapenotiere, an opportunity (which, however, never presented itself) of rejoining the DIAMOND, he was at times intrusted with the sole management of that vessel, and often commanded her boats in operations against the enemy's coasting trade—a species of service in which he so attracted the attention of Rear-Admiral Collingwood as to obtain from him a promise of early recommendation to the Admiralty. On the evening of 4 Sept. 1803, the boats of the EMERALD frigate having been placed under his orders by direction of the Admiral, for the purpose of procuring intelligence from Brest in regard to a report then afloat of a counter-revolution at Paris, Mr. Hewson, while the rest of his force took the direction of Ushant, landed with one boat's crew on a projecting rock in Le Goulet passage. While engaged in reconnoitring his position, the keepers whom he had left in charge of the boat deserted with it, and, being thus cut off from all chance of escape, he had no alternative but to surrender himself and his men as prisoners of war. After five years of captivity, during which he had once escaped from Verdun, but had been recaptured, and had undergone all the sufferings that tyranny could suggest and barbarity enforce, he contrived, in company with the present Capt. Donat Henchy O'Brien and two others, to effect a miraculous flight from the renowned fortress of Bitche—the details of which have been published by the latter gentleman. On ultimately arriving at Trieste, after having traversed on foot more than 3000 miles of country, and been exposed for a month to a series of the most trying privations, Mr. Hewson and his companions, in March, 1808, contrived to get on board a boat belonging to the AMPHION frigate, Capt. Wm. Hoste, which had been sent inshore on the look-out under the command of Lieut. Geo. Matthew Jones. Previously, however, to reaching the ship, it was his fortune to participate in a desperate attack made by that officer on two powerful vessels, whose successful resistance killed 2 and wounded 5 of the boat's crew. Lieuts. Jones and O'Brien being among the latter, the command of the boat was thereupon conferred on Mr. Hewson, who soon afterwards obtained a passage in the SPEEDY to Malta, where he eventually, in Jan. 1809, joined Lord Collingwood on board the OCEAN 98. On 11 of the following April (having passed his examination 25 Jan. 1803) he was nominated Acting-Lieutenant of the MAGNIFICENT 74, Capt. Geo. Eyre—an appointment which received the sanction of the Admiralty by a commission dated 15 July in the same year. When again off Malta, during a violent gale which occurred soon after he had taken up his quarters on board the last-mentioned ship, Mr. Hewson was intrusted by his Captain, who happened to be a total stranger to the harbour of Valetta, with the sole duty of conducting her into port. In Oct. 1809 we find him contributing to the reduction of Zante, Cephalonia, &c.; and in March and April, 1810, serving on shore in command of the naval brigade during nearly the whole of the arduous operations which preceded the fall of Sta. Maura. Owing to the paucity of officers on board the MAGNIFICENT he was recalled a few hours only previous to the surrender of the fortress—a circumstance which had the mortifying effect of precluding his name from appearing as it otherwise would in the Gazette announcing the conquest. While subsequently attached, between July, 1812, and June, 1814, to the CLARENCE 74, Capt. Henry Vansittart, he was very actively employed off the coast of France, and on one occasion, when in command of the boats, he displayed so much skill and gallantry in an affair with a powerful division of the enemy's gun-vessels, that on his return to the ship the Captain on the quarter-deck presented him, in testimony of his regard, with a sword which had been given to himself on his first going to sea. He was frequently also sent on shore with flags of truce for the purpose of sounding the loyalty of the authorities, and of inducing them to join the standard of Louis XVIII.; and in every instance he had the satisfaction of seeing his exertions crowned with the most flattering and complete success. The only other appointment which Mr. Hewson was ever able to procure was, on 29 May, 1815, to the PROMETHEUS sloop, Capt. Wm. Bateman Dashwood, which vessel, on Napoleon Buonaparte's surrender, formed part of his escort into Plymouth. He left her 9 Sept. 1815.

Lieut. Hewson, we believe, was the very first person who established the practicability of a double-engine to the purposes of steam navigation, as he was also to navigate a steam-vessel on the Atlantic. He married Anna, daughter of John Hunt, Esq., of Dublin, Barrister-at-law.

HEXT. (Captain, 1841. f-p., 22; h-p., 34.)

William Hext, born 5 July, 1780, at Bodmin, co. Cornwall, is second and only surviving son of the late Fras. John Hext, Esq., Attorney-at-law, of Tredethy, by Margaret, daughter of Elias Lang, Esq., Surgeon, of Plymouth. One of his brothers, Samuel, a Major in the Army and a C.B., served with distinction, both in Egypt under Abercromby, and throughout the peninsular war, and died 24 July, 1822, aged 40; and another, George, Lieutenant of H.M.S. Barrosa, was killed by a rifle-shot while leading a boat-attack in the Chesapeake in 1813, aged 29.

This officer entered the Navy, 9 April, 1791, on board the Scout 14; and in Aug. 1793 joined the Russell 74, Capts. John Willet Payne and Thos. Larcom, part of the force under Lords Howe and Bridport in the actions of 28 and 29 May and 1 June, 1794, and 23 June, 1795. With the exception of a year in 1797-8, during which he was lent to the Phaeton 38, Capt. Hon. Robt. Stopford, he next, between Oct. 1796 and the peace of Amiens, served with Capts. Payne, Sampson Edwards, and Sir Edw. Pellew, on board the Impétueux 74, of which ship, employed on the Home station, he was created a Lieutenant, 8 Aug. 1799, as a reward for the conduct he had displayed on the occasion of a recent mutiny. In June, 1802, Mr. Hext became Second of the Clyde 38, Capt. John Larmour, under whom he shortly afterwards conveyed Sir John Borlase Warren as British Ambassador to St. Petersburg, whence he had the honour of being sent home in personal charge of his Excellency's despatches. In Jan. 1803 he was sent with an armed boat into the port of Leith for the purposes of impressment, and, although exposed for many hours to the attacks of a furious mob, he succeeded in fully effecting the service with which he had been entrusted. The prudence and forbearance manifested in this instance by Mr. Hext, notwithstanding the severe bruizes inflicted upon him and many of his men by the volley of stones incessantly kept up by the populace, were so marked as to elicit the warm plaudits of his Captain. In the following Nov. we find the Clyde employed in removing from Cronstadt the valuables (estimated at about 300,000*l.*) belonging to the King, which had been saved from the palace at Hanover when entered by the French. On her passage to England she took the ground, and remained in a state of jeopardy until at length righted through the instrumentality of Mr. Hext, who, having been sent for assistance, seized a British barque, and anchored her in such a position as enabled her to heave the frigate off. In the early part of 1804, while detached in a six-oared cutter, our officer appears, on his own responsibility, and with much difficulty and danger, to have detained and brought out from the river Ems a neutral laden with masts supposed to be for the use of the enemy. On reaching his ship the next day he had the satisfaction of learning that his Captain had just received orders for the apprehension of the very same vessel. In May, 1804, he assumed command of the Sheerness hired cutter, off Brest, from which station he was ultimately driven in a violent gale, which occasioned the necessity of all his guns being thrown overboard, and of his making the best of his way to Ireland, where he only arrived after a week of consummate exertion. On leaving the Sheerness in Jan. 1805, Mr. Hext was appointed Senior of the Santa Margarita 36, Capt. Wm. Rathborne, under whom, on 4 of the ensuing Nov., he fought in Sir Rich. Strachan's action off Ferrol. During the long chase which preceded the battle, the Santa Margarita, from the unwearied attention bestowed by her First-Lieutenant on the trimming of her sails, left the British squadron far astern. On the achievement of the victory the Commodore, while hailing Capt. Rathborne, availed himself of the opportunity of making particular mention of Mr. Hext, and in so especial a manner as to lead the latter to imagine that immediate promotion awaited him. This however he did not obtain until 28 April, 1809, by which time he had further served on the East India station in the Barracouta 18, Capt. Geo. Harris, Culloden 74, and Blanche frigate, both commanded by Capt. Geo. Bell, Culloden again, Capt. Hon. Pownoll Bastard Pellew, and, as Acting-Commander, in the Wilhelmina hospital-ship at Poulo-Pinang, where his exertions in suppressing two fires which endangered the public stores procured him the thanks of the Governor. Being superseded in the Wilhelmina by her proper Captain in Feb. 1810, Capt. Hext returned home in an Indiaman, and was not again employed until June, 1813, when he obtained an appointment to the Vesuvius bomb, but was ordered to assume the command, *pro tempore*, of the Unicorn 32, and to assist Capt. John Hancock, of the Nymphen 36, in escorting the outward-bound trade to Portugal; after which he proceeded, with some merchantmen under his convoy, to Gibraltar. When off St. Andero, on the north coast of Spain, in the Vesuvius, Capt. Hext, at the commencement of 1814, had the fortune, although at great personal risk, of saving the crew of a Spanish merchantman, and also a transport with Spanish troops on board. During the subsequent operations in the river Gironde he behaved in a very conspicuous manner, and was for several days engaged, amidst great difficulties of situation, in throwing shells into the fortress of Blaye. His services, in the whole, called forth the warm acknowledgments of Admiral Penrose. Capt. Hext, who left the Vesuvius in Sept. 1814, and has since been on half-pay, was not advanced to Post-rank until 23 Nov. 1841.

The subject of the foregoing narrative is a Magistrate, as was also his father, for co. Cornwall. He married, 15 Sept. 1812, Barbara, youngest daughter and last-surviving child of the late Jas. Read, Esq., M.D., of Tremear, near Bodmin, and sister of Lieut. John Read, R.M., who was killed in Sir Jas. Lucas Yeo's attack on Cayenne in 1809. By that lady he has issue two sons (the eldest of them, Fras. John, a Lieutenant in the 83rd Regt.) and one daughter.

HEYLAND. (Lieut., 1814. f-p., 11; h-p., 31.)

James Heyland, born 29 Sept. 1790, is son of a gentleman (himself the son of the Rev. Robt. Heyland, D.D., Rector of Coleraine) who lost his right leg when Midshipman of H.M.S. Thetis—was afterwards attached to the Ordnance service in Ireland—and in 1798 was killed by the rebels while commanding a division of gun-boats for the relief of New Ross. He is first-cousin of the present Capt. Wm. Cuppage, R.N.—that gentleman's father, Lieut.-General Cuppage, having married his paternal aunt.

This officer entered the Navy, 24 May, 1805, as Third-cl. Boy, on board the Helena sloop, Capts. Woodley Losack and Jas. Andrew Worth, in which vessel he served for nearly five years on the Cork station, and was instrumental to the capture, during that period, of many of the enemy's privateers and merchantmen. From the early part of 1810 until the summer of 1812 he was next actively employed with Capt. Fras. Beaufort, as Midshipman, in the Blossom sloop, Ville de Paris 110, and Frederickstein frigate, chiefly on the Mediterranean station, where he took part in the survey of the coast of Karamania. He then joined the Salsette and Endymion frigates, both commanded by Capt. Henry Hope, under whom he served, latterly on the coast of North America, until Nov. 1814. The number of prizes he there assisted in making was extremely great. He was also for some time engaged in the blockade of New London; and on one occasion, 8 April, 1814, he served in the boats under Capt. Rich. Coote, at the gallant destruction, near Pettipague Point, on the Connecticut River, with but trifling loss to the British, of 27 of the enemy's vessels, three of which were heavy privateers, and the aggregate burden of the whole upwards of 5000 tons. He left the Endymion, as above, having been advanced to the rank of Lieutenant by commission dated 19 July, 1814, and has since been on half-pay.

Lieut. Heyland married, 19 April, 1819, Miss Mary Matilda Barrett, and by that lady has issue a son and daughter. AGENTS—Pettet and Newton.

HEYSHAM. (LIEUT., 1827. F-P., 17; H-P., 18.)

JAMES HEYSHAM entered the Navy 17 May, 1812, and was for 15 years employed as Fst.-cl. Vol., Midshipman, and Mate, on board the PRINCE OF WALES 98, BOMBAY and BERWICK 74's, and other ships, on the North Sea, Mediterranean, Western Island, West India, English Channel, South American, and African stations. Having passed his examination in 1818, he was at length, on 4 May, 1827, promoted to the rank of Lieutenant. His last appointments were—21 April, 1831, to the PEARL 20, Capts. Wm. Broughton and Robt. Gordon, at first employed in protecting the British interests in the Western Islands, during the disputes between Don Pedro and Don Miguel, and then attached to the force in the West Indies—and, 29 Oct. 1832, to the WINCHESTER 52, Capt. Hon. Wm. Wellesley, on the latter station. He invalided home 15 March, 1833.

HIATT. (RETIRED COMMANDER, 1834. F-P., 19; H-P., 33.)

JOHN HIATT was born 3 April, 1784, at Portsea.

This officer entered the Navy, 24 March, 1795, as Fst.-cl. Vol., on board the NAMUR 98, Capts. Jas. Hawkins Whitshed, Thos. Sotheby, and Wm. Luke. After serving as Midshipman in the action off Cape St. Vincent, and for some time at the blockade of Cadiz, he rejoined his former Captain, then Rear-Admiral Whitshed, in July, 1799, on board the BARFLEUR 98, and in the course of the same year followed him into the TÉMÉRAIRE 98, flag-ship subsequently of Rear-Admiral Geo. Campbell, with whom he served on the Channel and Irish stations until March, 1802. On 29 of the following month, in consideration of his having been thrown down the fore cockpit during a mutiny, and as a reward for his general services, he was promoted to a Lieutenancy in the THESEUS 74, Capt. John Bligh. Soon after the commencement of hostilities, being then in the West Indies, Mr. Hiatt, in command of the boats of the latter ship and of the TARTAR 32, cut out from the port of Jeremie, St. Domingo, with but little loss to the British, not fewer than three ships, two brigs, and 11 schooners—a service for which the thanks in general orders of the Commander-in-Chief were on the quarter-deck communicated to him. He also assisted at the capture of *Le Duquesne* 74, and of *La Créole*, of 44 guns, with the French General, Morgan, and 530 troops on board; was present at the reduction of Port Dauphin, where two forts, and a 28-gun-ship, *La Sagesse*, were taken from the enemy; witnessed the capture of a French squadron with the remains of General Rochambeau's army from Cape François; and took part in the unsuccessful attack upon Curaçoa. Mr. Hiatt's subsequent appointments, we find, were—8 April, 1804, to the FORTUNÉE 36, Capt. Henry Vansittart, during his continuance in which vessel he made frequent descents upon the island of Curaçoa, and succeeded in the boats in capturing several privateers—16 June, 1805, to the REINDEER of 18 guns (16 32-pounder carronades and 2 long sixes), Capt. John Fyffe, under whom, on 24 March, 1806, he participated, off Puerto Rico, in a single-handed and very gallant action of many hours with the French corvettes *Phaëton* and *Voltigeur*, of 16 long 6-pounders and 115 men each—next, to the command of the LADRONE 4, fitted as a tender, which vessel, while in the conveyance of despatches from Curaçoa to Jamaica, was boarded and taken, 28 Oct. 1806, by a large French privateer, after a conflict of four hours and a half, and carried into Santiago de Cuba, where she sank a few hours subsequently to her arrival—8 March, 1808, to the Sea Fencibles at Poole, in Dorset—18 June, 1810, to the EXPERIMENT 44, Capt. Jas. Slade, on the Falmouth station—and in July, 1811, to the command of a Signal-station near Mount Edgecumbe, which he retained until the end of the war. He accepted the rank he now holds 25 Jan. 1834.

Commander Hiatt married, first, Ann, eldest daughter of Hugh Fishley, Esq., Master-Builder of H. M. Dockyard, Jamaica, by whom he had issue; and, secondly, 11 March, 1843, Elizabeth, eldest daughter of John Avery, Esq., of the Customs, Southampton, and sister of the Rev. John Symons Avery, of Efford House, Cornwall.

HIBBS. (LIEUTENANT, 1796. F-P., 25; H-P., 34.)

ROBERT JOHN HIBBS entered the Navy, 22 Nov. 1788, as a Volunteer, on board the PORCUPINE 24, Capts. Brabazon, Geo. Martin, and Edw. Buller. With the exception of an attachment of three months, towards the close of 1790, to the NASSAU 64, Capt. Andw. Sutherland, he continued to serve, in the above vessel, on the Channel and Irish stations, until 1793, when, accompanying Capt. Buller into the ADVENTURE 44, he proceeded with him to Quebec and Halifax, and was afterwards nearly captured by a French squadron while in escort home of a valuable fleet of merchantmen. On his ultimate arrival with the same officer at the Cape of Good Hope as Acting-Lieutenant of the CRESCENT 36, Mr. Hibbs there joined in succession the MONARCH 74, bearing the flag of Sir Geo. Keith Elphinstone (under whom he witnessed the surrender of the Dutch squadron in Saldanha Bay), MOSELLE sloop, Capt. Chas. Brisbane, and STATELY 64, Capts. Billy Douglas, Patrick Campbell, and John Osborne—of which latter ship he was confirmed a Lieutenant 29 Dec. 1796. He continued to serve on the Cape station, in L'OISEAU 36, Capt. Sam. Hood Linzee, and JUPITER 50, Capt. Geo. Losack, until the end of the French revolutionary war. He then returned home in the DIOMEDE 50, and, after serving for some time in that ship on the Jersey and Guernsey station under the flag of Sir Jas. Saumarez, was further employed, between 1803 and 1809, in the MALTA 84, Capt. Edw. Buller, AJAX 74, Capt. Lord Viscount Garlies, SAN JOSEF 110, flag-ship of Sir Chas. Cotton, LA FLÊCHE sloop, Capt. Thos. White, and DEFIANCE and BULWARK 74's, Capts. Chas. Ekins and Hon. Chas. Elphinstone Fleeming—off Cadiz and Ferrol, in the Channel, off Cherbourg and Madeira, and in the Mediterranean. Until Dec. 1813, Lieut. Hibbs next held an Admiralty appointment at Greenock. He has since been on half-pay.

This officer, who is the Senior of his rank in the Navy, was admitted to the out-pension of Greenwich Hospital 11 Feb. 1830. AGENTS—Goode and Lawrence.

HICKES. (LIEUT., 1811. F-P., 12; H-P., 31.)

AUGUSTUS THOMAS HICKES entered the Navy, 16 Aug. 1804, as Fst.-cl. Vol., on board the DEFIANCE 74, Capts. Philip Chas. Durham and Hon. Henry Hotham. During a continuance of nearly six years in that ship, he served, in 1805, in Sir Robt. Calder's action and the battle of Trafalgar, and, on 24 Feb. 1809, at the destruction of three French frigates under the batteries of Sable d'Olonne, on which occasion the DEFIANCE, besides being much cut up in her masts and rigging, sustained a loss of 2 men killed and 25 wounded. He was also much employed in co-operation with the patriots on the north coast of Spain. After a further attachment of some months with Capt. Hotham to the NORTHUMBERLAND 74, and a short servitude in the BARFLEUR 98, bearing the flag at Lisbon of Hon. Geo. Cranfield Berkeley, he was promoted, 8 March, 1811, to the rank of Lieutenant, and appointed, for passage home, to the FORMIDABLE 98, Capt. Jas. Nicoll Morris. He next, from 8 of the following Oct. until April, 1815, served in the Bay of Biscay and at the Cape of Good Hope on board the DANNEMARK 74, Capts. Jas. Bissett and Henry Edw. Reginald Baker; and he was lastly appointed, 17 April, 1818, to the FALMOUTH sloop, Capt. Geo. Fred. Rich, successively stationed in the North Sea and off the coast of Iceland. He has been on half-pay since March, 1819. AGENT—Joseph Woodhead.

HICKLEY. (LIEUTENANT, 1846.)

VICTOR GRANT HICKLEY passed his examination 18 Aug. 1842; served for some time in North America and the West Indies as Mate of the VINDICTIVE 50, flag-ship of Sir Fras. Wm. Austen; and obtained his commission 2 Jan. 1846. He continued to serve in the VINDICTIVE, as Additional-Lieutenant, until the receipt, 3 Oct. following, of his present appointment in the VESUVIUS steam-sloop, Capts. Geo. Wm. Douglas O'Callaghan and Ashley La Touche, in which vessel he is still employed on the above station.

HICKMAN. (LIEUT., 1812. F-P., 19; H-P., 24.)

JOHN HICKMAN, born in Jan. 1787, at Islington, co. Middlesex, is son (and one of 11 children) of the late Geo. Hickman, Esq., a gentleman who originally possessed considerable landed property, but afterwards endured great losses.

This officer (having cut and run from the merchant service, after three years of wearisome employment in it) entered the Navy, in March, 1804, on board the DEPTFORD tender, Lieut.-Commander Geo. Antram, lying in the river Thames. Becoming Midshipman, in April, 1805, of the RAMILLIES 74, Capts. Fras. Pickmore and Robt. Yarker, he witnessed, 13 March, 1806, the capture of the French 80-gun ship *Marengo*, bearing the flag of Rear-Admiral Linois, and 40-gun frigate *Belle Poule*, besides aiding in the boats at the cutting-out, in the course of the same year, of a schooner protected by a battery at Martinique, and serving on shore, in Dec. 1807, at the reduction of the Danish West India islands. Towards the close of 1808 he sailed in the CORNELIA 36, Capt. Henry Folkes Edgell, for the East Indies, where, in 1810, he joined the RUSSELL 74, bearing the flag of Rear-Admiral Wm. O'Brien Drury, and became Acting-Lieutenant of the EMMA armed ship, Capt. Benj. Street. In 1811, having been slightly wounded in the arm during the operations connected with the capture of Ile de Bourbon and the Isle of France, at the latter of which he was the officer who landed and first hoisted the British colours on Fort Cannonier, Mr. Hickman returned home on board the ENTREPRENANTE brig, Capt. Edw. Brazier. Being, however, unable to procure his commission, he was under the necessity of again going afloat as Midshipman, in which capacity, and that of Master's Mate, he was for a further period of 17 months borne on the books of the ONYX sloop, Capt. Hamilton, THUNDER bomb, Capt. Watkin Owen Pell, and REVENGE 74, flag-ship of Hon. Arthur Kaye Legge. As a reward for the services he had during that period rendered in command of a gun-boat at the defence of Cadiz, he was then advanced to the rank of Lieutenant by commission dated 21 Nov. 1812. He continued off Cadiz, in the STATELY 64, Capt. Philip Chas. Butler Bateman, until May, 1813; between which period and Aug. 1814, we find him serving with the flotilla in the North Sea, and attached to the ILLUSTRIOUS 74, and REDWING 18, Capts. Alex. Skene, and Sir John Gordon Sinclair, on the Portsmouth and Mediterranean stations. He next, from 5 April to 12 Aug. 1815, held command of a gun-boat in the Downs; and he was afterwards appointed—10 Oct. 1829, to the Coast Blockade, in which service, with his name on the books of the HYPERION 42, Capt. Wm. Jas. Mingaye, he continued until March, 1831—12 July, 1832, to the Ordinary at Sheerness, where he remained until 2 Aug. 1835—and 9 March, 1843, to the VICTORY 104, bearing the flag at Portsmouth of Rear-Admiral Hyde Parker. Since the summer of 1846 he has been again on half-pay.

While in the Coast Blockade in 1831 Lieut. Hickman's exertions in extinguishing a fire which had broken out in a rick-yard proved so valuable that they were reported to the Admiralty. He married, in 1814, Miss Mary Boyle Holt, of Islington, by whom he has issue two sons (William and George, both Clerks in the R.N.) and two daughters. AGENTS—Coplands and Burnett.

HICKS. (LIEUTENANT, 1812. F-P., 11; H-P., 29.)

EDWARD BULLER HICKS was born, 15 Sept. 1792, in Devonshire, and died 9 Feb. 1845, at Newport, Isle of Wight. He was youngest son of the late Admiral Thos. Hicks; brother of the late Commander Thos. Bickerton Ashton Hicks, R.N.; and godson of Vice-Admiral Sir Edw. Buller, Bart. Paternally he was descended of an old Gloucestershire family; and through his mother he claimed kindred with Lord Chancellor Hyde. Among his ancestors was the distinguished Capt. Jasper Hicks, who, in conjunction with the equally gallant Capt. Jumper, in the barges of their respective ships, attacked and took the Mole of Gibraltar.

This officer entered the Navy, 28 Feb. 1805, as Midshipman, on board the FOUDROYANT 80, commanded by his brother-in-law, Capt. Edw. Kendall, with whom, until the following Oct., he served in the Channel under the flag of Sir Thos. Graves. In June, 1806, he re-embarked on board the MALTA 84, Capt. Edw. Buller, in which ship, after witnessing the capture, on 27 of the next Sept., of the French 44-gun frigate *Le Président*, he proceeded to the Mediterranean; where, in the summer of 1807, he removed to the QUEEN 98, bearing the flag of Rear-Admiral Geo. Martin. Between Oct. 1808 and Aug. 1812 we find him successively employed at home, off Cadiz (during the siege of which place he aided in the boats at the defence of Fort Matagorda), again in the Mediterranean, and at Newfoundland, on board the SALVADOR DEL MUNDO and SAN JOSEF, flag-ships of Admirals Wm. Young and Sir John Thos. Duckworth, HIBERNIA 110, Capt. Rich. Dalling Dunn, and ANTELOPE 50, bearing also the flag of Sir J. T. Duckworth. He then became Acting-Lieutenant of the ELECTRA sloop, Capt. Wm. Gregory, in which vessel (being confirmed to her by commission dated 2 Dec. 1812) he continued to serve on the Newfoundland station until April, 1814, contributing during that period to the capture, after a short running fight, of the American privateer *Growler*, of 5 guns and 60 men. His last appointments were, in July and Sept. 1815, to the TIGRE and SPENCER 74's, Capts. John Halliday and Wm. Robt. Broughton, both lying at Plymouth. The latter ship was paid off 31 Aug. 1818.

Lieut. Hicks married, 1 June, 1820, Sarah, only daughter of the late Thos. Atkinson, Esq., of Berry House, co. Hants.

HICKS. (LIEUTENANT, 1815. F-P., 9; H-P., 33.)

JOHN HICKS was born 6 Nov. 1792.

This officer entered the Navy, 29 Sept. 1805, as a Volunteer, on board the POWERFUL 74, Capts. Robt. Plampin, Rich. Buck, Fleetwood Broughton Reynolds Pellew, and Chas. Jas. Johnston. Proceeding in that ship to the East Indies, he there (besides assisting at the capture of the privateers *La Henriette*, of 20 guns and 124 men, and *La Bellone*,* of 30 guns and 194 men) served as Midshipman in the boats at the capture and destruction, 27 Nov. 1806, of a Dutch frigate, seven brigs-of-war, and about 20 armed and other merchant-vessels lying in Batavia Roads. On 11 Dec. 1807 he similarly contributed to the annihilation, at Griessee, of the dockyard and stores, and of all the men-of-war remaining to Holland in the East Indies. On his ultimate return to Europe Mr. Hicks accompanied the expedition to the Walcheren, where, during the bombardment of Flushing, he commanded a gun-boat under the very walls of that city, and was in the end towed out with the loss of his mast, and of 1 man killed and 1 wounded. His conduct on the occasion, we may add, was deservedly marked by the approbation of his Captain. From Oct. 1809 to Feb. 1812 he again served with Capt. Plampin on board the

* *La Bellone* was not taken until after a running fight of considerable length, in which 1 of her men was killed and 6 or 7 wounded. The POWERFUL on the occasion had 2 killed and 61 wounded.

Courageux 74, and Gibraltar 84; and while in the latter ship he was for nearly two years constantly employed as a volunteer in her boats in operations against the enemy's coasting trade, and was in frequent action with their batteries and gun-vessels. In March, 1812, he joined the Stirling Castle 74, Capt. Jahleel Brenton, lying at Chatham, but before he had been many weeks in that ship he was appointed Master's Mate of the Tenedos 38, Capt. Hyde Parker, and ordered to North America. While on the latter station he assisted at the capture of some of the finest privateers belonging to the United States, and in particular of *L'Invincible Napoléon*, of 16 guns, which he cut out, when in command of the frigate's boats, from under the heights of Gloucester, near Cape Anne, in Boston Bay, in April, 1813, although exposed to a most galling fire from the enemy's field-pieces and musketry. As a reward for his conduct in this affair Mr. Hicks was ultimately, on 27 May, 1814, appointed Acting-Lieutenant of the Victorious 74, Capt. John Talbot, with whom he made a voyage to Davis Strait, and remained until the following Aug. He was officially promoted 21 Feb. 1815, but has not been since afloat.

He married 10 May, 1826.

HICKS. (Lieutenant, 1815. f-p., 20; h-p., 22.)

William Hicks entered the Navy, 10 May, 1805, as Midshipman, on board the Theseus 74, Capt. Fras. Temple, on the Jamaica station. While next attached, between the following Sept. and Oct. 1809, to the Powerful 74, Capts. Plampin, Buck, Pellew, and Johnston, he went through much active service in the East Indies, where he assisted in the boats at the destruction of a Malay pirate, and co-operated (as alluded to in our memoir of Lieut. *John* Hicks) in the capture and destruction of *La Henriette* and *La Bellone*, the shipping in Batavia Roads, and the dockyard, &c., at Griessee. He was also present, as Master's Mate, at the bombardment of Flushing. After that event he joined the Milford 74, commanded at first, as a private ship, by Capt. Hen. Wm. Bayntun, and next employed under the flag of Sir Rich. Goodwin Keats, with whom he for some time participated in the defence of Cadiz, and then proceeded to the Mediterranean. From Aug. 1811 until July, 1812, Mr. Hicks further served on the latter station with his former Captain, Buck, on board the Franchise frigate. In the spring of 1813 he joined the Wolfe 24, bearing the broad pendant of Sir Jas. Lucas Yeo on Lake Ontario, where, in May of the same year, he took part in an attack made by that officer and Sir Geo. Prevost upon the Americans at Sacket's Harbour. He subsequently commanded a division of gun-boats at the defeat of the American army at La Cole; and officiated as Acting-Lieutenant in command of the Finch schooner in an attack on the squadron at Plattsburg. He returned to England in Aug. 1815, having been confirmed in the rank he now holds on 15 of the previous March; and since 12 July, 1837, has been employed in command of a station in the Coast Guard.

HIGGINS. (Lieutenant, 1814. f-p., 7; h-p., 33.)

Thomas Higgins entered the Navy, 16 May, 1807, as Sec.-cl. Vol., on board the Cæsar 80, Capt. Chas. Richardson, successive flag-ship of Rear-Admirals Sir Rich. John Strachan, Hon. Robt. Stopford, and Wm. Albany Otway. In the course of 1809, previously to which he had made a voyage to the Mediterranean, we find him assisting in the destruction of three heavy French frigates under the batteries of Sable d'Olonne, also of the shipping in Basque Roads, and in the expedition to Flushing. In April, 1810, he removed with Capt. Richardson to the Semiramis frigate, and was for upwards of two years employed in that ship on the Lisbon and Channel stations. During the rest of the war he served, on the coast of North America, in the Ardent 64, Capt. Bell, and St. Domingo 74, bearing the flag of Sir John Borlase Warren. He obtained his commission 3 June, 1814; but has not been since afloat.

HIGGINSON. (Lieutenant, 1839.)

Francis Higginson entered the Navy, 15 Nov. 1813; and on 25 Feb. 1814, while serving, as we are informed, on board the Eurotas, of 46 guns and 320 men, Capt. John Phillimore, was present in an engagement of two hours and 10 minutes, which rendered captive to that ship, after she had incurred a loss of 20 men killed and 40 wounded, the French frigate *La Clorinde*, mounting 44 guns and 12 brass swivels, with a complement of 360 picked men, of whom 120 were killed and wounded. He subsequently (when in the Severn 40, Capt. Hon. Fred. Wm. Aylmer) shared in the bombardment of Algiers, 27 Aug. 1816; and on 1 Jan. 1839, having passed his examination in 1828, he was promoted to the rank of Lieutenant. He obtained an appointment in the Coast Guard 27 Feb. following; but has been on half-pay since the autumn of 1845.

Lieut. Higginson, who is Senior of 1839, has been presented with a medal by the Royal Humane Society. Agents—Messrs. Chard.

HIGGINSON. (Retired Commander, 1835. f-p., 23; h-p., 40.)

George Montagu Higginson entered the Royal Naval Academy in 1784; and embarked, in 1787, as Midshipman, on board the Adventure 44, Capts. Parry and John Nicholson Inglefield. After two years of servitude on the coast of Africa in that vessel, he was next, until the commencement of the French revolutionary war, employed, on the Home and West India stations, in the Chichester store-ship, Lieut.-Commander Chas. Papps Price, Triton 20, Capt. Geo. Murray, and Hector 74, Capt. Geo. Montagu. Under the latter officer he witnessed the unsuccessful attack of 1793 upon Martinique. He then became Master's Mate of the Alert 16, Capt. Chas. Smith, and in May, 1794, while on his passage out to America, he had the misfortune to be captured by the French 36-gun frigate *Unité*, after an action of an hour and 40 minutes, in which the British vessel sustained a loss of 3 men killed and 15 wounded. On his arrival at Rochefort Mr. Higginson, by a decree of the National Convention, was sentenced to death, together with the rest of his companions. They were thereupon all committed to a bare hulk, and for the space of three weeks were forced to subsist upon an allowance of one pound of black bread and a pint of sour wine each a-day, with the addition of some horse-bean broth, and of 14 ounces, per man, of meat in 10 days. Their sentence being at the expiration of that time commuted, they were marched to Cognac, without any alteration, however, being made in their rations. Medical aid, too, was totally denied to them, and in the course, in consequence, of 13 months, a full third of their number fell helpless victims to the ravages of sickness. Mr. Higginson himself was so inveterately attacked by fever that the upshot was a liver complaint, whose effects, continuing to be felt for many years, frequently incapacitated him from service. In July, 1795, having at length effected his escape, he joined the Prince 98, bearing the flag at Spithead of Admiral Harvey; from which ship he was soon, on 1 Sept. in the same year, promoted to a Lieutenancy in the Topaze 36, Capt. Stephen G. Church. When afterwards on the coast of North America, Mr. Higginson, about the close of 1797, was compelled, owing to injury received in the execution of his duty, to go to sick-quarters at Norfolk, in Virginia, where he suffered a relapse of his liver complaint. He ultimately found himself under the necessity, at a personal expense of 30*l.*, of returning to England. During a few months in 1798, and again of a few in 1799, we find him employed at the Nore and in the Mediterranean on board the Hecla bomb, and Defiance 74. Capts. Jas. Oughton and Thos. Revell Shivers, appointments which his health obliged him in each case to resign. At the commencement of the late war, being at the time in France for change of air, he was a second time made prisoner of war, and detained for a period of 14 months at Valenciennes, from which place he then had the fortune to contrive a flight. His next and last appointments were—in 1804-5, to the command of the HAPPY RETURN and FLY hired cutters, and ENCHANTRESS 10, on the Channel station—29 March, 1806, to the ROYAL WILLIAM, bearing the flag of Admiral Montagu at Spithead—and, 23 June, 1806, to the command of the PIGMY 14, which vessel, through the ignorance of her pilot, and at a moment when he himself was confined by illness to his bed, he lost, off Ile d'Oléron, 2 March, 1807. He remained thenceforward a captive in France until the peace of 1814. Unable afterwards to procure employment, our unlucky officer accepted the rank of Retired Commander on the Junior List 17 Jan. 1831; and on 19 March, 1835, he was promoted to the Senior List. AGENT—J. Hinxman.

HIGGON. (LIEUT., 1828. F-P., 28; H-P., 8.)

HENRY MILLER HIGGON was born 22 Jan. 1796.

This officer entered the Navy, 17 Aug. 1811, as Midshipman, on board the ABERCROMBY 74, Capt. Wm. Chas. Fahie, stationed in the Channel; and was next, between Feb. 1814 and Sept. 1821, employed, chiefly in the West Indies, on board the HALCYON sloop, Capt. John Houlton Marshall, ULYSSES 44, Capt. Thos. Browne, LARNE 20, Capt. Abraham Lowe, and SAPPHIRE 26, Capt. Henry Hart. He then joined the BANN 20, Capt. Chas. Phillips, and sailed for the western coast of Africa, where that vessel cruized with success against the slave-trade, and lost, when at Ascension in 1823, the greater part of her crew from the effects of the climate. In Oct. 1823 Mr. Higgon, who had passed his examination in Jan. 1818, and had for the last six months acted as First-Lieutenant, was superseded from the BANN; nor was he promoted until 6 April, 1828, by which period he had further served for four years and a half as (Admiralty) Midshipman, almost continuously on the African coast, in the JASPER 10, Capt. Alex. Dundas Young Arbuthnott, BLANCHE 46, Capt. Wm. Bowen Mends, BLONDE 42, Capt. Lord Byron, and SYBILLE 48, Commodore Sir Fras. Augustus Collier. He returned to England in May, 1828, after having been further attached for a few weeks to the NORTH STAR 28, Capt. Septimus Arabin; and, with the exception of a period of two years in 1840-2, has been employed in the Coast Guard since 7 Oct. 1833.

Lieut. Higgon, during his servitude afloat, was eight times attacked with yellow fever and once with cholera. His testimonials for character and conduct are of a very high order.

HIGGS. (CAPTAIN, 1846. F-P., 27; H-P., 24.)

WILLIAM HENRY HIGGS entered the Navy, 1 Jan. 1796, as a Volunteer, on board the DAPHNE hired armed lugger, employed in keeping up a communication with the French Royalists on the coast of Normandy. From Sept. following until April, 1797, he served on the Jersey station, on board the BRAVO 16, Capt. D'Auvergne, Prince de Bouillon; and he then became in succession Midshipman of the MONARCH 74, Capt. John Elphinstone and QUEEN CHARLOTTE 100, flag-ship of Lord Keith. In June, 1798, he joined the MAIDSTONE frigate, Capt. Ross Donnelly, attached to the force in the West Indies, where, during a continuance of rather more than two years, he was thrice attacked by the yellow fever. Arriving in the Mediterranean, about the commencement of 1801, in the CHICHESTER storeship, Capt. John Stephens, Mr. Higgs was there received, first on board the SALAMINE brig, Capt. Thos. Briggs, and then in the FOUDROYANT 80, bearing the flag of Lord Keith, and, as Master's Mate, in the PETEREL sloop, Capts. Chas. Inglis and John Lamborn. While in the latter vessel, which he left in March, 1802, he participated, as he likewise did in the FOUDROYANT, in the operations of the Egyptian campaign; but it was not until 7 May, 1804 (by which period he had further served, chiefly on the Home station, in the CAMBRIDGE 80, flagship of Sir Thos. Pasley, HUNTER sloop, Capts. Geo. Jones and Sam. Hood Inglefield, CONQUEROR 74, Capt. Thos. Louis, and MONARCH 74, bearing the flag of his friend Lord Keith), that he succeeded in obtaining his promotion to the rank of Lieutenant. He then joined the SULPHUR bomb, Capts. Donald M'Leod and Matt. Forster, in which vessel he witnessed, 2 Oct. 1804, the celebrated "Catamaran" attack made upon the Boulogne flotilla; and he was next, it appears, appointed—in the course of the same month, to the CYGNET sloop, Capts. D. M'Leod and Robt. Bell Campbell, with the latter of whom he again proceeded to the West Indies—in Aug. 1806, as First, to the ALLIGATOR 26, Capt. R. B. Campbell, in which ship he returned to England—in the spring of 1807, to the BARFLEUR 98, Capt. Sir Joseph Sydney Yorke, employed in the Channel—and, in June of the same year, as Senior, to L'ESPOIR sloop, commanded, on the Mediterranean station, by Capts. Henry Hope, Robt. Mitford, and Hon. Robt. Cavendish Spencer, and occasionally, *pro tempore*, by himself. During nearly seven years of employment in L'ESPOIR, Mr. Higgs saw a great deal of active service in the Mediterranean, where he assisted, in 1809, at the reduction of the islands of Ischia and Procida; in April, 1810, at the capture and destruction of several Neapolitan vessels on the coast of Italy; and on 8 Aug. 1813, at the taking, in a gallant attack on the town of Cassis, near Toulon, of five land-batteries, three heavy gun-boats, and 25 sail of merchant-vessels. On 25 July, 1814, five months after he had left L'ESPOIR, the subject of this narrative, who had acquired the highest reputation for his ability and zeal as an officer, became First-Lieutenant to Capt. Hon. Henry Duncan, in the GLASGOW 50, in which ship he cruized in the Western Ocean until paid off at Chatham, 1 Sept. 1815. He rejoined Capt. Duncan, 27 June, 1818, in a similar capacity, on board the LIFFEY 50; and on 11 Oct. 1819, after having made a voyage to the Mediterranean, he was at length promoted to the rank of Commander, in honour of the Prince Regent's visit to that ship. His next and last appointments were—11 June, 1831, to the Second-Captaincy of the REVENGE 78, Capt. Jas. Hillyar, an appointment he was induced to resign on 20 of the same month—and, 5 Feb. 1839, as Additional-Commander, to the ROYAL SOVEREIGN yacht, for the purpose of superintending the Packet Service at Pembroke, where he remained until June, 1845. His elevation to Post-rank took place 9 Nov. 1846.

We may here add that Capt. Higgs' appointments to the CYGNET, ALLIGATOR, ESPOIR, GLASGOW, and LIFFEY were all made at the especial request of their respective Captains. AGENTS—Collier and Snee.

HIGMAN. (Captain, 1817. F-P., 18; H-P., 35.)

HENRY HIGMAN entered the Navy, 28 Dec. 1794, as A. B., on board the CHARON, hospital ship, Capt. Walter Locke, attached to the Channel fleet. In Sept. 1795, after having participated in Lord Bridport's action, he removed, as Midshipman, to the TRIUMPH 74, Capts. Sir Erasmus Gower, Wm. Essington, and Thos. Seccombe, with whom he served for upwards of four years in the Channel, North Sea, and Mediterranean, latterly under the flag of Rear-Admiral Cuthbert Collingwood. He consequently had an opportunity of sharing with Capt. Essington in the glories of Camperdown 11 Oct. 1797, on which occasion he performed the duties of Master's Mate. On leaving the TRIUMPH, Mr. Higman joined the RAISONNABLE 64, Capt. Chas. Boyles, at Chatham, for the purpose of awaiting a passage to the West Indies, where, on his arrival in the following June, in the SEVERN 44, Capt. John Whitby, he was received by Lord Hugh Seymour, to whom he had been recommended by Sir Erasmus Gower, on board his flag-ship the SANS PAREIL 80. In Aug. of the same year—seven months, indeed, before he had passed his examination—he was appointed Acting-Lieutenant of the Calypso sloop, Capts. Joseph Baker and Robt. Barrie, on the Jamaica station; and in Dec. 1801 he joined, in a similar capacity, the Goliath 74, to which ship, commanded at first by Capt. Wm. Essington, and afterwards by Capts. Chas. Brisbane and Robt. Barton, he was in the end confirmed by commission dated 3 Sept. 1803. Mr. Higman (who on 28 June in the latter year had contributed, while in escort of a homeward-bound convoy, to the capture of *La Mignonne* French corvette, of 16 guns and 80 men) subsequently took command of the boats of the Goliath, and in a very seamanlike manner brought out a gun-brig from under a most destructive fire of the batteries at Sable d'Olonne, on the coast of France. Being next, on 28 May, 1805, allowed, on the application of Capt. Brisbane, to rejoin that officer, as his First-Lieutenant, in the Arethusa 38, he assisted, in company with the Anson 44, at the capture, 23 Aug. 1806, near the Havana, after a spirited action, in which the Arethusa had 2 men killed and 32 wounded, of the *Pomona* Spanish frigate, of 38 guns and 347 men, laden with specie and merchandize, and defended by a castle mounting 11 36-pounders, and a flotilla of 10 gun-boats, all of which were destroyed. A slight wound received by Mr. Higman on the occasion procured him a pecuniary grant from the Patriotic Society.* He was promoted, as a reward for the share he had borne at the brilliant reduction of Curaçoa, to the rank of Commander, 23 Feb. 1807; subsequently to which we find him joining—18 Aug. 1809, the Rattler 16, on the Newfoundland station—13 Jan. 1810, the Gluckstadt 18, employed in the conveyance of despatches to and from Gottenborg and Heligoland—11 Feb. 1811, the Fly 16, which vessel, through the obstinacy of her pilots (although Capt. Higman's exertions were so great as to elicit the plaudits of the subsequent court-martial), was lost on a reef near the island of Anholt 29 Feb. 1812—and, 6 Dec. 1813, the Brisk 16. In the latter sloop he served for some time on the Irish station, where he contrived by stratagem to recapture a prize belonging to the American privateer *Prince de Neufchâtel*. He then proceeded with convoy to the coast of Africa, on which station he cruized for nearly twelve months, and took four slavers having between 700 and 800 negroes on board. Owing, however, to a suspension in the payment of the ordinary bounty, neither the officers nor crew of the Brisk (the first vessel that felt the effects of the regulation) received any reward for their exertions; and in consequence Capt. Higman was deprived of nearly 4000*l.* He was paid off 31 Aug. 1815, but it was not until 1 Jan. 1817 that he was advanced to Post-rank. Unable from that period to procure employment, he at length, on 1 Oct. 1846, accepted the half-pay of Retirement.

Capt. Higman is a widower with five sons, the eldest of whom, a Midshipman R.N., was lately serving with Capt. Glascock on board the Tyne 26. Agent—J. Hinxman.

HILL. (Lieutenant, 1815. f-p., 10; h-p., 32.)

Charles Hill entered the Navy, 1 Oct. 1805, as Fst. cl. Vol., on board the Plantagenet 74, Capts. Wm. Bradley, Thos. Eyles, and Robt. Lloyd, in which ship he was for six years and a half employed, chiefly on the Home station. During that period, however, he witnessed the departure, in 1807, of the royal family of Portugal for the Brazils, and was for some time prior to the convention of Cintra engaged in blockading the Russian squadron in the Tagus. From March, 1812, until Oct. 1814, he was next employed, in the Baltic and Mediterranean, as Midshipman† and Master's Mate, on board the Bristol troop-ship, Capts. Wm. Kent, John Thompson, and Geo. Wyndham, besides serving in a gun-boat at Cadiz. He was ultimately promoted to the rank of Lieutenant, 6 Feb. 1815, while attached to the Lightning 20, Capt. Geo. Rennie, on the Irish station; but he has not, to our knowledge, been since afloat.

Lieut. Hill's eldest daughter is married to a son of Lieut. John Skinley, R.N.

* *Vide* Gaz. 1806, p. 1535.

† A rating he had attained in Oct. 1808.

HILL. (Lieutenant, 1833. f-p., 19; h-p., 19.)

Charles Thomas Hill, born 4 July, 1796, is fourth and eldest surviving son of the late West Hill, Esq., M.D., Deputy Inspector of Hospitals, who accompanied Lord Cornwallis to America, was at the head of the Medical Staff during several campaigns in the War of Independence, and died in 1834 in the 93rd year of his age. Three of the Lieutenant's brothers, West Tertius, John Hildebrand, and Justly, died officers in the Army; the first being a Lieutenant in the 5th Regt. Madras N.I.—the second a Captain and D. A. A. General in H. M. 27th—and the third a Lieutenant R.A. His youngest brother, Henry, is now serving in India as a Captain of the 57th. Lieut. Hill is first-cousin of the present Vice-Admiral Hill.

This officer entered the Navy, 13 July, 1809, as Fst.-cl. Vol. (under the auspices of his last-named relative), on board the Cæsar 80, Capt. Chas. Richardson, bearing the flag of Rear-Admiral Wm. Albany Otway; and, on attending the ensuing expedition to the Walcheren, was employed on shore with the Naval Brigade during the bombardment of Flushing. He subsequently became Midshipman of the Naiad 38, commanded at first by Capt. Hill and afterwards by Capt. Philip Carteret, under whom he participated, 20 and 21 Sept. 1811, in two actions with divisions of the Boulogne flotilla. On the last-mentioned occasion the Naiad sustained a loss of 2 men killed and 14 wounded, but succeeded in taking one of the enemy's prames, *La Ville de Lyon;* which vessel, of whose people upwards of 30 were either slain or wounded, Mr. Hill was the second officer to board. After further assisting at the capture and destruction of three privateers, he removed, in 1812, to the Impregnable 98, successive flag-ship of Admirals Wm. Young and H.R.H. the Duke of Clarence on the Home station, where, in June, 1814, he served in attendance on the Allied Sovereigns during their visit to England. He was next for two years employed in the West Indies and America on board the Araxes 38, Capt. Geo. Miller Bligh, and Tanais, of similar force, Capt. Joseph James; and he subsequently (having passed his examination 7 Nov. 1815) officiated as Admiralty-Midshipman, on the Plymouth, Mediterranean, and Portsmouth stations, of the Sealark schooner, Capt. Philip Helpman, Rochfort 80, flag-ship of Sir Thos. Fras. Fremantle and Sir Graham Moore, Glasgow 50, bearing the broad pendant of Hon. Anthony Maitland, Racehorse 18, Capt. Hon. Chas. Abbot, and Albion 74, Capt. Sir Wm. Hoste. In 1823 Mr. Hill, when at Portsmouth, volunteered to fit out a small schooner of 28 tons, designed as a tender to the flag-ship at Newfoundland; for his conduct and exertions in further navigating her to which place he elicited the approbation of the Admiralty. After an interval of eight years he re-embarked, in 1831, on board the Victory 104, in which ship he served at Portsmouth under the flags of Sir Thos. Foley and Sir Thos. Williams, until promoted to the rank of Lieutenant, 21 Aug. 1833. His after appointments afloat were—14 Feb. and 27 Aug. 1834, to the President 52, and Vernon 50, both commanded by Capt. John M'Kerlie, at Halifax and in the Mediterranean—20 July, 1835, to the command of the Alban steam-vessel, on the latter station—and, for a short time at the commencement of 1836, to the Howe 120, Capt. Alex. Ellice, lying at Sheerness. With the exception of a few months spent in 1841-2 in raising volunteers at Glasgow and Greenock, he has not held any additional employment.

Lieut. Hill married, 16 June, 1828, Mary Romman, third daughter of John Holmes, Esq., an opulent merchant of Kingston-upon-Thames, by whom he has issue three sons and one daughter.

HILL. (Lieutenant, 1815. f-p., 21 ; h-p., 23.)

Edward Hill (*a*) entered the Navy, 12 Nov. 1803, as Fst.-cl. Vol., on board the Aimable frigate, Capt. Wm. Bolton, stationed in the North Sea and Channel. In 1805 he removed to the Mercury 28, Capt. Chas. Pelly, and, on his return from a voyage with convoy to Quebec, he proceeded off Lisbon. From 1806 to 1809 he again served in the Channel, the last two years as Midshipman, on board the Pallas frigate, Capt. Geo. Miller, and Champion 24, Capts. Kenneth Mackenzie, Jas. Coutts Crawford, and Robt. Henderson. He then joined the Eagle 74, Capt. Chas. Rowley, with whom, after attending the expedition to the Walcheren and cruizing for some time in the latitude of the Western Islands, he proceeded to the Mediterranean, where, among other performances, he witnessed, 27 Nov. 1811, the capture of *La Corceyre* French frigate, pierced for 40 guns, but mounting only 28, with a complement of 170 seamen and 130 soldiers, laden with 300 tons of wheat and a quantity of military and other stores. Between 1813 and the date of his official promotion, 11 Feb. 1815, Mr. Hill was next employed, as Acting-Lieutenant, in the Niger 38, Capt. Peter Rainier, and Laurel and Amelia frigates, both commanded by Capt. Hon. Granville Proby, in South America (whither he escorted convoy), at the Cape of Good Hope, off the coast of Africa, and at home. He has been in charge, since 14 July, 1838, of a station in the Coast Guard. Agent—Fred. Dufaur.

HILL. (Lieutenant, 1843.)

Edward Hill (*b*) is youngest son of Vice-Admiral Hill.

This officer entered the Navy 15 Aug. 1833; passed his examination 21 May, 1840; and served as Mate on board the Herald 26, Capt. Jos. Nias, Childers 16, Capt. Geo. Greville Wellesley, and Cornwallis 72, flag-ship of Sir Wm. Parker—all on the East India station, where he fought during the war in China. He obtained a commission 16 Sept. 1843; and from 11 April, 1844, until paid off, on his return to England, in the autumn of 1845, was employed, still in the East Indies, in the Cambrian 36, Capt. Henry Ducie Chads. Since 28 Nov. 1845 he has been serving on the coast of Africa in the Nimrod 20, Capt. Jas. Rich. Dacres.

HILL. (Vice-Admiral of the Red, 1841. f-p., 22 ; h-p., 38.)

Henry Hill, born about 1775, is son of the late Colonel Wm. Hill, of St. Boniface, in the Isle of Wight, who served during the German war as Aide-de-Camp to Count de Lippe, and was afterwards for some time Governor of Berwick-upon-Tweed. He is brother of Lieut.-Colonel Chas. Fitzmaurice Hill, who commanded the 10th Regt. of Foot, and died in 1811; and first-cousin of the present Lieut. Chas. Thos. Hill, R.N.

This officer entered the Navy, 10 Nov. 1787, as a Volunteer (under the auspices of Sir John Jervis), on board the Vestal 28, Capt. Sir Rich. John Strachan, with whom he proceeded on an embassy to China, and removed as Midshipman, about Aug. 1791, to the Phœnix 36. On 19 of the following Nov., while cruizing off the Malabar coast, he took part, in company with the Perseverance frigate, in an obstinate action (produced by a resistance on the part of the French Captain to a search being imposed by the British upon two merchant-vessels under his orders) with *La Résolue*, of 46 guns, whose colours were not struck until she had herself sustained a loss of 25 men killed and 40 wounded, and had occasioned one to the Phœnix of 6 killed and 11 wounded. On his return to England in the autumn of 1793, Mr. Hill joined the Boyne 98, bearing the flag of Sir John Jervis, through whom he was promoted, on 17 Dec. in the same year, to a Lieutenancy in the Zebra bomb, Capts. Robt. Faulknor, Geo. Bowen, Geo. Vaughan, and Lancelot Skynner. In 1794 he was present in every distinguished operation connected with the reduction of the French West India islands, and in particular at the capture of Fort Royal, Martinique, where, landing with Capt. Faulknor, he participated in the heroic attack which, to the admiration of all who witnessed it, accomplished the premature fall of that stronghold. In March, 1795, he was again sent on shore, with a detachment of seamen and a 6-pounder, to co-operate with the British forces on the island of St. Vincent in their endeavours to suppress an insurrection which had there broken out among the Charibs. On the 14th, the insurgents having taken possession of Dorchester Hill, an eminence immediately commanding the town of Kingston, which they were preparing to cannonade, Mr. Hill suggested the propriety of driving them from their position; and accordingly, at midnight, his plan being adopted, he placed himself at the head of a storming-party, commanded by Capt. Skynner, and, commencing a furious assault, succeeded in utterly routing the enemy—thereby restoring confidence to the inhabitants of the colony, and saving its fall. In this brilliant affair, however, so desperate a wound was inflicted on his right shoulder, that he was obliged, as soon as the victory had been achieved, to retire to his ship, and soon afterwards to return home. Previously to his final departure from the island Mr. Hill had the satisfaction of receiving the thanks of the Governor and the House of Assembly, together with the most marked attention and the strongest expressions of gratitude from all classes. He was promoted to the rank of Commander on 24 of the following July; and in Feb. 1797 he had the further honour of being mentioned with Capt. Skynner in a letter of thanks from the agents for the colony of St. Vincent. Continuing long to feel the effects of his wound, Capt. Hill remained on half-pay until the spring of 1798, when he was appointed to the Sea-Fencibles in the Isle of Wight. From 27 June, 1799, until posted, 1 Jan. 1801, he commanded the Gorgon 44, *armée-en-flûte*, in the Mediterranean; and also the Megæra fire-vessel on the Channel station, where he had a narrow escape from capture while reconnoitring the French fleet in Camaret Bay, with a view to ascertaining the practibility of burning it. His next appointments were—3 Jan. 1801, for a very brief period, to the Princess Royal 98—8 March, and 14 June, 1802, to the Ruby 64, and Camilla 24, in the latter of which ships he went to Newfoundland—29 April, 1803, to the Orpheus 32, employed at first in escorting convoy to Newfoundland, and then in very successfully cruizing on the coast of France—14 Dec. 1805, to the Agincourt 64, stationed in the North Sea and off St. Helena—and 1 Sept. 1809, after 18 months of half-pay, to the Naiad 38. In the latter ship Capt. Hill, besides visiting the West Indies, was much employed, until superseded in the summer of 1811, in blockading the enemy's ports on the French coast. On one occasion, when in a gale off Cherbourg, the pilot, in attempting to pass through the Monkey Passage, by the island of Alderney, failed, and, by his ignorance, placed the Naiad in a state of great jeopardy, from which she was only extricated by dint of the greatest exertion and skill, and by a hitherto unknown outlet being found in the rocks called the Casketts. This accident occurred in 1810; in the course of which year the Naiad appears to have been in constant action with the enemy's batteries, and to have destroyed much of their coasting-trade. Capt. Hill's last appointments were, 20 Dec. 1825, and 31 March, 1826, to the Superb 78, guard-ship at Portsmouth, and Melville 74; in the latter of which he served, on the coast of Portugal and at Gibraltar, until shortly previous to her being paid off, 28 Feb. 1829. He became a Rear-Admiral 22 July, 1830; and attained his present rank 23 Nov. 1841.

In every ship commanded by the Vice-Admiral when afloat he won the approbation of the Admiralty. In the Melville he was particularly fortunate in eliciting that of H.R.H. the Lord High Admiral. On 26 Feb. 1845 he was granted the Good Service pension; and he is also in the receipt of a pension of 250*l*. for his wound.

He married, first, Anne, daughter of the late Rev. Jas. Worsley, of Gatcombe, in the Isle of Wight; and secondly, Caroline, daughter of the late Joseph Bettesworth, Esq., of Ryde, in the same island. He has issue, with four daughters, six sons, all of whom are in the service of their country—the eldest, Henry Worsley, a Commander, and the youngest, Edward, a Lieutenant, R.N. AGENTS — Messrs. Halford and Co.

HILL. (LIEUTENANT, 1825. F-P., 24; H-P., 17.)

HENRY JOSEPH HILL, born 3 Sept. 1780, is eldest son of the late Thos. Hill, Esq., of Gough Square, Fleet Street, London.

This officer (who had previously been in the Hon. E. I. Co.'s service) entered the Navy, 8 July, 1806, as Midshipman, on board the SPEEDWELL 14, Lieut.-Commander Wm. Robertson, on the Home station, where, on 24 of the following Dec., having been appointed Prize-Master of a Danish brig, he was captured by a French privateer and sent to Calais. He did not in consequence regain his liberty until the peace of 1814, when he returned to England and joined the guard-ship at Plymouth. He was soon afterwards removed into the RESOLUTE 12, Lieut.-Commander Wm. Pringle Green; while serving with whom he passed his examination, 2 Nov. in the same year. From Jan. 1815 until Feb. 1818, Mr. Hill served at Liverpool, Gibraltar, and Portsmouth, a great part of the time as Admiralty Midshipman, in the PRINCESS, Capt. Wm. Simpson, SERAPIS store-ship, Capt. Wm. Lloyd, QUEEN CHARLOTTE 108, flag-ship of Sir Edw. Thornbrough, and ROCHFORT 80, Capt. Sir Archibald Collingwood Dickson; and he was next for upwards of seven years employed, as Chief Mate, in the HAWKE Revenue cruizer, Lieut.-Commander Rich. Ward. He at length attained his present rank 27 May, 1825, and, after three years and four months' servitude in the Coast Guard, was appointed, 26 Nov. 1830, to the Coast Blockade, as Supernumerary-Lieutenant of the HYPERION 42, Capt. Wm. Jas. Mingaye. He was paid off in March, 1831, and has not been since able to procure employment. AGENTS — Messrs. Ommanney.

HILL. (COMMANDER, 1841.)

HENRY WORSLEY HILL is eldest son of Vice-Admiral Henry Hill.

This officer entered the Navy 24 March, 1810; obtained his first commission 13 July, 1824; and was afterwards appointed—20 Dec. 1825, and 31 March, 1826, to the SUPERB 78, and MELVILLE 74, both commanded by his father—18 Jan. 1828, to the TRIBUNE 42, Capts. John Wilson and John Alex. Duntze, employed on the South American station, whence he returned to England and was paid off 16 Dec. 1831—21 Sept. 1833, as First, to the ANDROMACHE 28, Capts. Bernard Yeoman and Henry Ducie Chads, in which vessel he sailed for the East Indies—1 Dec. 1834, to the MELVILLE 74, bearing the flag of Sir John Gore, with whom he came home and was put out of commission in July, 1835—and 14 April, 1837, to the command of the SARACEN 10, on the coast of Africa, where he served until a few months after his promotion to the rank he now holds, which took place 15 March, 1841.

Commander Hill, since 6 March, 1843, has filled the office of Lieut.-Governor of Her Majesty's Forts and Settlements on the Gold Coast. He married, 1 July, 1845, Amelia Jane, eldest daughter of Henry Pytches Boyce, Esq., and the late Lady Amelia Sophia Boyce, daughter of George third Duke of Marlborough. AGENTS—Messrs. Halford and Co.

HILL, Kt. (CAPTAIN, 1815. F-P., 51; H-P., 15.)

SIR JOHN HILL entered the Navy, 25 Sept. 1781, as Fst.-cl. Vol., on board the INFERNAL bomb, Capt. Jas. Alms, on the books of which vessel he was borne until March, 1783. On 20 April, 1788, he joined the NAUTILUS sloop, Capt. Thos. Boulden Thompson, stationed at Newfoundland; and he next, between 1789 and his promotion to the rank of Lieutenant, 28 July, 1794, served in the Channel and West Indies, as Midshipman and Master's Mate, on board the GOLIATH and BEDFORD 74's, Capts. Archibald Dickson and Robt. Mann, and PORCUPINE 24, Capt. Jas. Alms. In the course of the latter, and the following year, he was successively appointed to the INVINCIBLE 74, and JUSTE 80, both commanded by Capt. Hon. Thos. Pakenham, on the Channel station, where, for a few months in 1797, he again served with Capt. Alms, in the REPULSE 64. He then joined the PRINCESS ROYAL 98, bearing the flag in the Mediterranean of Sir John Orde, with whom he remained until transferred, in May, 1798, to the MINOTAUR 74, Capt. Thos. Louis, part of the victor-fleet at the ensuing battle of the Nile; for his conduct as Senior Lieutenant on which occasion, he was advanced to the rank of Commander by commission dated 8 Oct. in the same year. From 2 Feb. 1800, to 6 March, 1802, and from 31 March, 1804, until 27 Oct. 1808, we next find Capt. Hill commanding the HEROINE, and HUMBER, in the Mediterranean and Channel. On 24 March, 1813, he was appointed to an Agency for Transports—the duties of which post he continued to discharge, in the Baltic, and on the coasts of Holland and France, for a period of nearly six years. Having attained Post-rank 28 Oct. 1815, he was subsequently, from 1820 until 1838, employed as Captain-Superintendent of Deptford Victualling Yard. He was appointed, on 9 March in the latter year, Superintendent of the Dockyard at Sheerness; and, since 11 Dec. 1841, he has been again officiating in a similar capacity at Deptford.

The honour of Knighthood was conferred on Capt. Hill 31 Aug. 1831. His only son is a Captain in the Army; and one of his daughters, now deceased, was the wife of the present Capt. W. L. Castle, R.N.

HILL. (LIEUT., 1810. F-P., 26; H-P., 23.)

JOHN HILL (*a*) entered the Navy, 6 March, 1798, as Fst.-cl. Vol., on board the EUROPA 50, Capt. Jas. Stevenson, under whom he attained the rating of Midshipman 1 Jan. 1799, and continued to serve, in the same ship, and in L'EGYPTIENNE 50, and L'AFRICAINE 38, on the Channel and Mediterranean stations, until Feb. 1802. Attending, during that period, the expedition of 1801 to Egypt, he served in a launch with a carronade, and had two men wounded, while engaged, on 8 March, in covering the debarkation of the troops; and he was afterwards for six months employed on shore with the army. In May, 1803, he re-embarked on board the LEYDEN 64, Capt. John Seater, lying in the river Thames, whence, however, he soon sailed for the West Indies, with Capt. John Ayscough, in the CAMEL store-ship. In the course of 1804-5 Mr. Hill there accompanied the same Captain in the REYNARD, SHARK, and GOELAN sloops; in the first and last mentioned of which we find him frequently coming into contact with the enemy's privateers. From the GOELAN, which during the last two years and four months had been commanded by Capts. Arth. Lysaght, Benj. Clement, and Fred. Hoffman, he removed, in June, 1808, to the HEBE frigate, Capt. John Fyffe. On 4 April, 1809, he became Acting-Lieutenant of the PELICAN 18, Capt. Edw. Henry A'Court, also attached to the force in the West Indies, where, being confirmed to that vessel by commission dated 4 May, 1810, he continued to serve for a further period of 17 months. During nearly the whole of 1811 Mr. Hill was employed off North Cape in the TRINCULO sloop, Capt. Alex. Rennie. His subsequent appointments were, to the command—26 Aug. 1812, of the LANDRAIL 10, in which vessel he performed a service of some importance connected with the restoration of Louis XVIII.—in June, 1814, of the PIONEER 10, on the Newfoundland and Downs stations—18 May, 1816, after a few months of half-pay, of the SURLY 10, employed, until paid off in Sept. 1818, on Home duty—2 March, 1829, of the RINALDO Falmouth packet, which he put out of commission 19 Aug. 1834—and, 20 Aug. 1839, of the CRANE, another packet, also on the Falmouth station. On 11 of the following Sept., while fitting at Woolwich, Lieut. Hill had the honour, owing to the absence on leave of the Captain-Superintendent, of receiving their Majesties the Queen and Queen Dowager, the King and Queen of the Belgians, and the Duke of Saxe Coburg, and conveying them on board the LIGHTNING steamer, on the occasion of the departure of the latter personage from this country. He had likewise, a few days previously, received the King and Queen of the Belgians on their arrival in the *Véloce* French steamer. He has been on half-pay since May, 1842. AGENTS—Hallett and Robinson.

HILL. (LIEUTENANT, 1815. F-P., 34; H-P., 17.)

JOHN HILL (*b*), born 5 Oct. 1789, is a relative of John Hill, Esq., Purser and Paymaster, R.N. (1808).

This officer entered the Navy, in 1796, on board the GOLIATH 74, Capts. Sir Chas. Henry Knowles and Thos. Foley. After sharing in the action off Cape St. Vincent, and in the battle of the Nile, he accompanied Capt. Foley, in Dec. 1799, into the ELEPHANT 74, in which ship, commanded latterly by Capt. Geo. Dundas, he fought at Copenhagen 2 April, 1801, and served, in the Channel and West Indies, until Jan. 1804. He then became Midshipman in succession of the RACOON and DILIGENCE sloops, both under the orders of Capt. Jas. Alex. Gordon, with whom he continued on the West India station until appointed Master's Mate, in Sept. 1805, of the SAVAGE 16, Capt. Jas. Wilkes Maurice, attached to the force on the coast of Ireland. He next, towards the close of 1806, joined the SNAKE 18, Capt. Edw. Crofton, from which vessel, however, he was soon transferred to the LINNET 12, Lieut.-Commander John Tracey, part of the armament employed in 1809 in the expedition to the Walcheren. From Jan. 1810 until March, 1813, Mr. Hill officiated, on the Home station, as Midshipman, and alternately as Acting-Lieutenant and Master's Mate, in the TROMP 12, Lieut.-Commander Michael M'Carthy, EXPERIMENT 12, Capt. Jas. Slade, FYLLA 20, Capt. Hon. Edw. Rodney, MONMOUTH 64, bearing the flag of Admiral Foley, PHIPPS 14, Capt. Thos. Percival, CADMUS 10, Capt. Thos. Fife, MONMOUTH again, and CORDELIA 10, Capt. Thos. Fortescue Kennedy. For five months of 1813, he was next employed with Sir Jas. Lucas Yeo on the Canadian Lakes. Between Jan. 1814 and Aug. 1815, we further find him employed on the Home and East India stations in the EXPERIMENT, Capt. Jas. Slade, once more in the MONMOUTH, and in the TERMAGANT 20, Capt. Chas. Shaw.* He lastly served—in 1828, in the Coast Guard—from 2 March, 1830, to March 1833, in command of the CAMELION and BADGER Revenue-cruizers—and from 26 Aug. 1834 until 1845, again in the Coast Guard.

* He then took up a commission, dated 7 Feb. 1815.

HILL. (LIEUTENANT, 1825.)

JOSEPH AUGUSTUS WITHAM HILL entered the Navy 10 Dec. 1811; passed his examination in 1818; obtained his commission 4 Oct. 1825; and from that date until June, 1827, was employed with Capt. Hugh Patton in the IRIS frigate. His last appointments afloat were—23 July, 1832, as First-Lieutenant, to the ROVER 18, Capt. Sir Geo. Young—and, 2 Sept. 1833, to the PELICAN 16, Capt. Joseph Gape, both on the Mediterranean station, whence he returned home and was paid off in March, 1834.

The Lieutenant, who has been for some time employed under the Commissioners of Public Works, married, 23 July, 1831, Mrs. Heslop, widow of Capt. Heslop, formerly of the 60th Regt., and daughter of Jacob Owen, Esq., of Landport.

HILL. (LIEUTENANT, 1812. F-P., 6; H-P., 36.)

SAMUEL HILL entered the Navy, in Oct. 1805, as Fst.-cl. Vol., on board the MONMOUTH 64, Capt. Geo. Hart, bearing the flag in Yarmouth Roads of Admiral Thos. Macnamara Russell. In Jan. 1806, he became Midshipman of the STATELY 64, Capt. Geo. Parker, under whom, when in company with the NASSAU 64, he assisted at the capture and destruction, after an obstinate running fight, and a loss to the STATELY of 4 men killed and 28 wounded, of the Danish 74-gun ship *Prindts Christian Frederic* off the coast of Zealand, 22 March, 1808. He was next, between May, 1809, and Aug. 1812, employed, at first with Capt. Parker, and then with Rear-Admiral Thos. Byam Martin, on board the ABOUKIR 74, on the Baltic and Channel stations. Until promoted to the rank of Lieutenant 20 Nov. 1812, Mr. Hill further served with the flotilla at the siege of Riga. He has since been on half-pay.

HILL. (LIEUTENANT, 1833.)

THOMAS SHARP HILL died in 1845, on board the INCONSTANT.

This officer entered the Navy 22 May, 1822; passed his examination in 1828; and obtained his commission 21 Nov. 1833. His subsequent appointments were—15 Feb. 1834, as First, to the SALAMANDER steam-vessel, Capt. Wm. Langford Castle, employed on Home service—2 March, 1835, as a Supernumerary, to the THALIA 46, Capt. Robt. Wauchope, at the Cape of Good Hope—11 Feb. 1836, as Senior, to the PYLADES 18, Capt. W. L. Castle, an active anti-slaver—29 Oct. 1838, in a similar capacity, to the ROSE 18, Capt. Peter Christie, employed on the Spanish and Brazilian stations—21 Aug. 1841, to the Acting command of the SOUTHAMPTON 50, which ship, after having borne the flag at the Cape of Sir Edw. Durnford King, was paid off in Dec. 1842—and 5 Oct. 1843, again as First, to the INCONSTANT 36, Capt. Chas. Howe Fremantle, attached to the force in the Mediterranean, where he died, as above. AGENTS—Messrs. Halford and Co.

HILLDRUP. (LIEUT., 1815. F-P., 8; H-P., 32.)

JOHN HILLDRUP entered the Navy, 23 June, 1807, as Ordinary, on board the MEDIATOR 32, Capts. Wm. Furlong Wise and Jas. Rich. Dacres, on the Jamaica station; served from the following Dec. until March, 1809, in the TALBOT sloop, Capt. Hon. Alex. Jones, off Oporto; and was employed during the next two years in the Baltic and off the coast of Africa as Midshipman and Master's Mate of the NEMESIS 28, Capt. Wm. Ferris. After a further attachment of 11 months to the NAMUR 74, flag-ship of Sir Thos. Williams at the Nore, he returned to the Baltic and there served, between Feb. 1812, and Sept. 1813, on board the DAPHNE 20, Capts. Philip Pipon and Jas. Green. He then sailed with Capt. Pipon to South America in the TAGUS 36, in which ship, when subsequently cruizing among the Cape de Verde Islands, in company with the NIGER 38, he assisted at the capture, 6 Jan. 1814, of the French 40-gun frigate *Cérès*. He obtained his commission 21 Sept. 1815, but has not been since afloat.

HILLIER. (COMMANDER, 1814. F-P., 22; H-P., 35.)

CURRY WILLIAM HILLIER, born 6 Jan. 1778, is the son of a superannuated Warrant-officer who died at Devonport, 13 March, 1829, aged 89.

This officer entered the Navy, in 1790, as a Servant, on board the ALFRED 74, Capts. Harvey and John Bazely, under the latter of whom he fought as Midshipman in Lord Howe's action 1 June, 1794. While next attached, during a period of three years, to the BLENHEIM 98, successively commanded by Capts. Bazely, Thos. Lennox Frederick, and Wm. Bowen, we find him participating in one of Hotham's engagements in 1795, sharing also in the victory gained by Sir John Jervis off Cape St. Vincent 14 Feb. 1797, and witnessing the ensuing bombardment of Cadiz by Sir Horatio Nelson. After further figuring in many boat encounters with the enemy's flotilla at the latter place, he removed, in Sept. 1797, to the EMERALD 36, Capts. Lord Proby and Thos. Moutray Waller, on the Mediterranean station, where he was for a long time employed at the blockade of Alexandria and Malta, and where, on 3 Sept. 1798, he managed, in one of the ship's boats, to rescue the Captain and 7 men belonging to the French cutter *L'Animona* from the fury of the Arabs, who put to death all the remainder of the crew, originally 60 in number. Once, while on detached service in the CRUCIFIX, an armed tender, Mr. Hillier had the misfortune to be wrecked, on the Maltese coast. For his subsequent conduct as Master's Mate of the POMPÉE 74, Capt. Chas. Stirling, in Sir Jas. Saumarez' action off Algeciras 6 July, 1801, on which occasion he received a severe wound,* he was eventually promoted to an Acting-Lieutenancy in the *San Antonio* 74, Capt. Hon. Geo. Heneage Lawrence Dundas, one of the prizes taken in the battle fought six days afterwards in the Gut of Gibraltar. Being confirmed, 8 Oct. following, into the VANGUARD 74, he served for four years in that ship on the West India station under Capts. Sir Thos. Williams, Jas. Walker, Lord Wm. FitzRoy, Andrew Fitzherbert Evans, and Jas. Newman Newman—two years of the time as First-Lieutenant. He was consequently present at the capture, in 1803, of the French 74-gun ship *Le Duquesne*, and of *La Créole*, of 44 guns, with the French General Morgan and 530 troops on board; and he was for some time employed on shore at St. Marc's, St. Domingo, where General de Henen and 1100 troops surrendered to him. On landing the latter at St. Nicolas Mole, he was sent with the General and a few prizes to Jamaica. On 4 June, 1806, Mr. Hillier was appointed to the ARGO 44, Capt. Stephen Thos. Digby, in whose boats, during a servitude of nearly two years on the Coast of Africa, he was very constantly engaged. In May, 1808, on his arrival at Jamaica, he was under the necessity of going to the hospital at Port Royal, from which he was soon invalided and sent to England, where for a prolonged period of 10 weeks he was confined to the hospital at Deal. On his recovery, he was appointed, 21 Feb. 1809, First of the ROYALIST 18, Capts. John Maxwell and Geo. Downie; in the boats of which vessel, after attending the expedition to the Walcheren, he served off Calais, Boulogne, Estaples, Dieppe, and Havre, and proved instrumental to the capture of not fewer than 11 privateer luggers and a cutter. The manner in which he once, in Dec. 1811, destroyed a gun-boat, procured him the mention of Capt. Downie in two official letters. So extreme was the exertion undergone by Mr. Hillier while in the ROYALIST, that in the month of June, 1812, he was again obliged to be sent to the hospital. During the three years and a half he had been employed in her, she had had as many as six Second-Lieutenants, nearly all of whom had been obliged to leave from the same cause as was ultimately himself; and both her Captains, for service in which he participated, were promoted to Post-rank. His next and last appointments were to the command—29 April and 30 Dec. 1813, of the EL CORSO and DEFIANCE, lying (the latter as a prison-ship) at Gravesend and Chatham. His advancement to the rank he at present holds took place 7 June, 1814.

Commander Hillier's health during the war became so shattered, that he has never since ceased to feel the effects of what he then underwent. During the whole term of his career afloat, he was never off duty, except when actually compelled to be so by illness. He was left a widower 19 June, 1844. AGENTS—Collier and Snee.

* *Vide* Gaz. 1801, p. 931.

HILLIER. (COMMANDER, 1824. F-P., 18; H-P., 42.)

GEORGE HILLIER is brother of Commander C. W. Hillier, R.N.

This officer entered the Navy, in 1787, as a Volunteer, on board the ALFRED 74, Capts. West, Harvey, and Bazely, employed on the Home station, where, on 1 June, 1794, he was present, as Midshipman, in Lord Howe's action. Removing in the following Aug. to the RÉUNION 36, commanded in the North Sea by Capt. Jas. Alms, he took part in that ship, when in company with several others, in an obstinate fight, which terminated in the capture, 22 Aug. 1795, of one of three Dutch vessels—the *Alliance* 36. He continued to serve on the German Ocean in the ARDENT 64, Capts. Rich. Rundell Burgess (under whom, who was killed, he shared in the glories of Camperdown) and Thos. Bertie, until Jan. 1798, on 16 of which month he was promoted to the rank of Lieutenant, and appointed to the ALLIANCE, *armée-en-flûte*, Capts. Davis, John Baker Hay, and David Wilmot. After participating with much credit in the defence of St. Jean d'Acre he became, 7 June, 1799, First Lieutenant of the TIGRE 80, bearing the broad pendant of Sir Wm. Sidney Smith.* On the 8th, 13th, and 21st of March, 1801, Mr. Hillier was attached to the army under General Abercromby, and on those occasions he conducted himself to the entire satisfaction of Sir Sidney, who was in command of the seamen on shore. At the close of the Egyptian campaign he was presented with the Turkish gold medal. In March, 1803, having quitted the TIGRE in the previous Sept., he rejoined Sir W. S. Smith, again as Senior, on board the ANTELOPE 50, stationed in the North Sea, where, on 16 May, 1804, he was present in a gallant attack made by a British squadron upon a division of the enemy's flotilla passing along shore from Flushing to Ostend. Although at the time he was in an ill state of health, he afforded Sir Sidney, on the quarter-deck, all the assistance and support in his power.† He continued in the ANTELOPE until June, 1805, and was lastly employed, as a Volunteer, with the fire-ships under Capt. Nicholas Tomlinson in the expedition of 1809 to the Scheldt. His promotion to the rank of Commander did not take place until 21 Jan. 1824.

HILLS. (Captain, 1814. F-P., 23; H-P., 32.)

GEORGE HILLS, born 8 Nov. 1777, is only surviving son of Lieut. Wm. Hills, R.N., of Buckland, co. Kent, who perished when in command of H.M. cutter MUTINE, in a heavy gale of wind, in Dec. of the same year; grandson of the late Admiral John Barker; and nephew of Capt. John Hills, R.N., who lost his life from yellow fever, at Jamaica, in 1794, while commanding the HERMIONE 32.

This officer entered the Navy, 13 June, 1792, as Captain's Servant (under the auspices of his uncle, Capt. John Hills), on board the BULLDOG 16, Capt. Geo. Hope, on the Mediterranean station. Accompanying the same Captain, in Aug. 1793, into L'ECLAIR 18, commanded next by Capt. Geo. Henry Towry, he served in that vessel at the ensuing occupation of Toulon; after which we find him (until promoted to the rank of Lieutenant, 17 July, 1798) employed for a few months in the LEVIATHAN 74, Capt. Lord Hugh Seymour, and for four years, as Midshipman and Master's Mate, in the RANGER 18, commanded on the Home station by Capts. Jas. Hardy and Chas. Campbell. He then joined L'ATALANTE 18, Capts. Digby Dent and Anselm John Griffiths, and was afterwards appointed, on the Channel, Irish, and Halifax stations—6 May, 1799, to the AMETHYST 36, Capts. John Cooke, Henry Rich. Glynn, Alex. Campbell, John Wm. Spranger, and Thos. Alexander—in the autumn of 1804 to the DRYAD 36, Capts. John Giffard and Adam Drummond—7 Dec. 1807, to the SWIFTSURE 74, bearing the flag of Sir John Borlase Warren—and, 28 Jan. 1808, to the ATALANTE 18, Capt. John Evans. During an attachment of more than five years to the AMETHYST, Mr. Hills (besides assisting at the debarkation of the troops in the expedition of 1800 to Ferrol, and being employed in the conveyance of royal and diplomatic personages) contributed to the capture of three privateers, carrying 34 guns and 270 men, and was present at the taking, 28 Jan. and 9 April, 1801, of the French 36-gun frigate *La Dédaigneuse*, and national corvette *Le*

* In June, 1800, Lieut. Hillier accompanied Sir W. S. Smith on a visit to the Holy City. A journal of his excursion from Jaffa to Jerusalem is given in the 'Naval Chronicle,' vol. xxiii., p. 297 *et seq.*

† *Vide* Gaz. 1804, p. 641.

Général Brune, of 14 guns. He also, on the night of 29 Aug. 1800, fought in the boats of a squadron, 20 in number, commanded by Lieut. Henry Burke, at the cutting-out, close to the batteries in Vigo Bay, of *La Guêpe* privateer, of 18 guns and 161 men, which vessel, 25 of whose people were killed and 40 wounded, was in 15 minutes boarded and carried, with a loss to the British of 3 seamen and 1 marine killed, 3 Lieutenants, 12 seamen, and 5 marines wounded, and 1 seaman missing. When in the DRYAD, in 1806-7, Mr. Hills was for six weeks employed, in company with H.M.S. DIANA, in a fruitless quest of two French frigates among the ice-bergs on the coast of Greenland and in Davis' Strait. He was ultimately advanced, 20 April, 1808, to the command of the COLUMBINE sloop, on the North American station, whence he returned home and was paid off in March, 1810. He attained Post-rank 7 June, 1814, and was last employed as an Inspecting Commander in the Preventive Water-Guard, from Dec. 1820 to Nov. 1825. He accepted the half-pay of retirement 1 Oct. 1846.

Capt. Hills married, 10 March, 1815, Diana, third daughter of the late Thos. Hammersley, Esq., by whom he has issue eight children. AGENTS—Messrs. Halford and Co.

HILLS. (COMMANDER, 1841. F-P., 36; H-P., 3.)

JOHN HILLS entered the Navy, 6 Feb. 1808, as Fst.-cl. Vol., on board the NORTHUMBERLAND 74, Capt. Wm. Hargood; and during the two following years was often under the fire of the enemy's batteries in the Adriatic. From Aug. 1810 until Dec. 1814 he was employed in the Channel, off the north coast of Spain, and on the Brazilian station, as Midshipman and Master's Mate, in the IRIS 36, Capts. Thos. Geo. Shortland and Hood Hanway Christian. While on the Spanish coast he was frequently entrusted with the hazardous duty of landing arms for the use of the Guerillas. He figured also as a volunteer in two cutting-out expeditions, and, besides otherwise coming into contact with the enemy, assisted in the bombardment and capture of Bermeo and Castro. On leaving the IRIS Mr. Hills, who had passed his examination 7 June, 1814, successively joined the NAMUR 74, Capt. Geo. M'Kinley, and FORTH 44, Capt. Sir Wm. Bolton, in which latter ship he escorted the Duchesse d'Angoulême from Portsmouth to Dieppe, and on the occasion of her arrival and departure was each time selected to attend her at the side of the vessel. Between Sept. 1815 and Dec. 1817 we find him serving on board the DÉSIRÉE and ACTIVE frigates, commanded in the West Indies by Capt. Philip Carteret, and QUEEN CHARLOTTE 100, flag-ship of Sir Edw. Thornbrough at Portsmouth. After a subsequent servitude of six years in the Coast Blockade as Admiralty Midshipman and Mate of the SEVERN frigate, and RAMILLIES 74, both under the command of Capt. Wm. M'Culloch, Mr. Hills at length obtained a commission dated 21 Jan. 1824. Rejoining the Coast Blockade, however, in the following April, he continued in it until its abolition in March, 1831, from which period until advanced to the rank of Commander, 23 Nov. 1841, he officiated as a Chief Officer in the Coast Guard. Since 15 May, 1844, he has been again employed in that service.

During the term of his original servitude in the Coast Blockade and Coast Guard, Commander Hills was five times engaged in conflict with smugglers. In one of them his arm was broken, and in some of the others he had the misfortune to receive permanent injury.

HILLS. (LIEUTENANT, 1806.)

THOMAS HILLS entered the Navy, in Dec. 1794, as Fst.-cl. Vol., on board the VICTORY 100, Capt. John Knight, in which ship he was present under the flag of Rear-Admiral Robt. Mann in Hotham's action of 13 July, 1795, and under that of Sir John Jervis in the battle fought off Cape St. Vincent 14 Feb. 1797. He continued to serve with the last-mentioned officer as Midshipman of the VILLE DE PARIS 110, on the Mediterranean and Channel stations, until Jan. 1801, between which period and the date of his promotion to the rank of Lieutenant, 7 Nov. 1806, he was further, it appears, employed on board the EURYDICE 24, Capts. Walter Bathurst and Chas. Malcolm, SEAHORSE and AMPHITRITE frigates, both commanded by Capt. Hon. Courtenay Boyle, BELLONA 74, Capts. Chas. Dudley Pater and John Erskine Douglas, and HIBERNIA 110, bearing the flag of Earl St. Vincent. He made a voyage in the EURYDICE to the East Indies, and on his return to the Mediterranean in the SEAHORSE he served in the boats at the destruction of a convoy in Hyères Bay in 1804. From 28 Nov. 1806 until 27 May, 1811, Lieut. Hills was employed on board the PHILOMEL sloop, Capts. Geo. Crawley, Geo. Downie, Geo. Davies, Spelman Swaine, and Gardiner Henry Guion, under the first named of whom, besides witnessing the surrender, in 1809, of the island of Ithaca, he assisted, on 31 Oct. in that year, in covering the boats of a squadron during a desperate and successful attack made by them on a convoy in the Bay of Rosas. In Sept. 1811 he was appointed to the LEYDEN 64, *armée-en-flûte*, Capts. Edw. Chetham and John Davie, also in the Mediterranean, where he remained until Dec. 1814. He afterwards assumed command, in Feb. 1818 and June, 1820, of the INDUSTRY Revenue-cutter, and PIGMY schooner, on the Home station; and, since 8 March, 1837, he has been in charge (with a brief interval between 9 Oct. and 13 Dec. 1841) of the Semaphore Station at Holder Hill, Mildhurst.

Lieut. Hills is married and has issue.

HILLYAR. (LIEUTENANT, 1842.)

CHARLES FARRELL HILLYAR is son of the late Rear-Admiral Sir Jas. Hillyar, K.C.B., K.C.H.;* brother of Lieut. H. S. Hillyar, R.N.; and nephew of Capt. Wm. Hillyar, R.N.

This officer entered the Navy 18 March, 1831; passed his examination 17 March, 1837; served for some time in South America as Mate of the PRESIDENT 50, Capt. Wm. Broughton; and was promoted to the rank of Lieutenant 24 March, 1842. He was then employed for several months at Portsmouth on board the CALEDONIA 120, flag-ship of Sir David Milne; and from 12 May, 1843, until paid off at the commencement of 1847, he officiated as a Lieutenant of the TYNE 26, Capt. Wm. Nugent Glascock, on the Mediterranean station. AGENTS—Messrs. Ommanney.

HILLYAR. (LIEUTENANT, 1842.)

HENRY SHANK HILLYAR is brother of Lieut. C. F. Hillyar, R.N.

This officer entered the Navy 24 Dec. 1831; passed his examination 14 May, 1838; and was employed, as Mate, during the latter part of the hostilities in China, on board the CORNWALLIS 72, flag-ship of Sir Wm. Parker. He attained his present rank 23 Dec. 1842; and since 18 March, 1843, has been serving in the WOLF 18, Capt. Arthur Vyner, and WOLVERENE 16, Capts. Wm. John Cavendish Clif-

* Sir James Hillyar was created a Lieutenant 8 March, 1794, and a Commander 16 April, 1800. He soon afterwards distinguished himself, when in command of the NIGER troop-ship, by his gallantry, in cutting out, with the boats of that vessel and the MINOTAUR 74, two Spanish corvettes, lying in the road of Barcelona; and in 1801 he bore a conspicuous part in the operations of the Egyptian campaign. On the recommendation of Lord Nelson, and in consideration of his services, he was advanced to Post-rank 29 Feb. 1804. When subsequently in command of the PHŒBE frigate, he contributed to the reduction of the Isle of France in Dec. 1810; participated, off Madagascar, in an action fought 20 May, 1811, between a British squadron under Commodore Charles Marsh Schomberg, and a French force under Commodore François Roquebert; co-operated next in the capture of the Island of Java; and on 28 May, 1814, succeeded, in company with the CHERUB sloop, in making prize of the American frigate *Essex*, of 46 guns and 265 men. In acknowledgment of the importance of his professional career Capt. Hillyar was nominated a C.B. 4 June, 1815; a K.C.H. 1 Jan. 1834; and a K.C.B. 4 July, 1840. He acquired Flag rank 10 Jan. 1837; and died a Rear-Admiral of the White, at Tor House, Torpoint, 10 July, 1843, aged 73.

ford and John Chas. Dalrymple Hay, both on the East India station. On 19 Aug. 1845, as Senior of the latter vessel, he took command of her pinnace, and served with the boats of a squadron, carrying altogether 530 officers, seamen, and marines, at the destruction, under Capt. Chas. Talbot, of the piratical settlement of Malloodoo, on the north end of the island of Borneo, where the British encountered a desperate opposition, and sustained a loss of 6 men killed and 15 wounded.* AGENTS—Messrs. Ommanney.

HILLYAR. (CAPTAIN, 1836. F-P., 26; H-P., 26.)

WILLIAM HILLYAR, born 3 June, 1788, is son of Jas. Hillyar, Esq., Surgeon R.N.; brother of the late Rear-Admiral Sir Jas. Hillyar, K.C.B., K.C.H., and of the present Dr. Robt. Purkis Hillyar, K.H., K.T.S., Inspector of Hospitals and Fleets, who served as Surgeon of the ROEBUCK and APOLLO in the expeditions of 1801 and 1807 to Egypt, and was Surgeon of the ALBION 74, at the battle of Navarin; and uncle of Lieuts. C. F. and H. S. Hillyar, R.N.

This officer entered the Navy, in Dec. 1795, as Fst.-cl. Vol., on board the PHAETON 38, Capts. Hon. Robt. Stopford and Jas. N. Morris, of which frigate his brother, the late Sir Jas. Hillyar, was then Second-Lieutenant. During the five following years he presents himself to our notice as being very actively employed—a great part of the time as Midshipman—off the coast of France, also in cruizing to the westward, and ultimately in the Mediterranean, where he co-operated for several months with the Austrian army on the northern shores of Italy, and beheld the surrender of Genoa. Towards the close of 1800 he joined the NIGER troop-ship, under the orders of his brother, with whom he continued uninterruptedly to serve, chiefly on the Mediterranean station, until Jan. 1808. On the 18th of Aug. 1803, while at the blockade of Genoa, Mr. Hillyar was sent with a prize felucca and a small boat, under the command of Lieut. Jones, to effect the capture of a large Greek ship steering for that port. Determined, apparently, to reach their destination, and availing themselves of a light breeze which had sprung up and retarded the advance of the British, the enemy maintained a stern and fierce resistance. Lieut. Jones, at the commencement of the conflict, was mortally wounded, but, although they were at first repulsed, the crew of the felucca, now led by Mr. Hillyar, returned to the charge, and in a few minutes gained possession of the ship's deck, the Greeks being compelled either to run below or jump overboard. To evince his estimation of this exploit, Lord Nelson, on the 27th of the same month, promoted Mr. Hillyar to the vacancy created by the death of Lieut. Jones, and as he had but just accomplished his 15th year, his Lordship further obtained an Order in Council to confirm this mark of extraordinary favour. Of the NIGER, which ship was afterwards employed for a long time, as an active frigate, at the blockade of Toulon and Cadiz, our officer eventually became First-Lieutenant. His appointments on leaving her were —18 March and 18 Nov. 1808, to the WOOLWICH *armée-en-flûte*, and HIND 28, Capts. Fras. Beaufort and John Rich. Lumley, also in the Mediterranean, where he officiated for 20 months as Senior Lieutenant of the last-mentioned vessel—and 16 Aug. 1810 and 8 May, 1811, to the CHRISTIAN VII. 80, and CALEDONIA 120, bearing each the flag, off the Scheldt and again in the Mediterranean, of the late Lord Exmouth, under whom, besides witnessing the partial actions of 5 Nov. 1813 and 13 Feb. 1814, with the Toulon fleet, he was again, in April, 1814, present at the fall of Genoa—we believe as First-Lieutenant. Being advanced to the rank of Commander by commission dated 27 Aug. 1814, Capt. Hillyar was subsequently appointed in that capacity—6 July, 1824, to the Coast Guard at Merazion, where he remained three years—and, 14 March, 1834, to the REVENGE 78, Capt. Wm. Elliott, in which ship, successively employed on the Lisbon and Mediterranean stations, he remained until posted 20 Jan. 1836. During the preceding year he had been ordered to observe and report upon the sailing-trials between H.M. ships VERNON, BARHAM, and COLUMBINE, and so completely did the report he made win the approbation of the Sea Lords of the Admiralty, that in the June following his promotion he was nominated Secretary (in the BELLEROPHON 80) to Hon. Sir Chas. Paget, for the purpose of making all the observations and reports required in a series of experimental cruizes then about to take place. He left the BELLEROPHON in Dec. 1836; and was lastly employed, from 15 May, 1840, until he resigned 7 Aug. 1841, on board the SOUTHAMPTON 50, as Flag-Captain to Sir Edw. Durnford King, Commander-in-Chief at the Cape of Good Hope.

Capt. Hillyar is married and has issue. AGENTS—Messrs. Ommanney.

* *Vide* Gaz. 1845, p. 6536.

HILTON. (COMMANDER, 1814. F-P., 19; H-P., 33.)

GEORGE HILTON, born 18 Feb. 1782, is brother of Retired Commander Stephen Hilton, R.N.

This officer entered the Navy, 1 April, 1795, as Fst.-cl. Vol., on board the ANDROMACHE 32, Capt. Chas. John Moore Mansfield, with whom he served, in the same ship, and in the DRYAD 36, until April, 1801. While in the ANDROMACHE, he participated, as Midshipman, in three sharp encounters with the enemy—the first time, on 31 Jan. 1797, when, in a mistaken engagement of 40 minutes with an Algerine of similar force, 66 of whose people were killed and 50 badly wounded, the British sustained a loss of 3 men killed and 6 wounded; the second, in an action fought, in the same year, off Cadiz between the ANDROMACHE and three British ships on the one side, and a Spanish 74 on the other; and the third, in an affair with some Spanish gun-boats near the batteries of Algeciras, in which the ANDROMACHE, while in escort of a convoy, had 4 men killed and 19 wounded. When in the DRYAD, in the summer of 1800, Mr. Hilton assisted in taking captive a small Swedish frigate, the *Ulla Fersen*, a step rendered necessary by opposition the latter had offered to being detained. He was ultimately (while serving in the Channel on board the VILLE DE PARIS 110, flag-ship of Hon. Wm. Cornwallis) made Lieutenant, 29 July, 1801, into the ROYAL GEORGE 100, Capt. John Child Purvis, with whom he continued until paid off in April, 1802. On 23 of the following July he rejoined the DRYAD, then commanded by Capt. Robt. Williams, on the Irish station. On the renewal of hostilities in 1803, Commodore Wm. Domett having hoisted his broad pendant on board that frigate, Mr. Hilton was sent by him in a Revenue-cutter for the purpose of raising seamen, of whom the Navy was at the time in great need. Having put into a small harbour, to the south-west of the Cove of Cork, he landed with a party of men and proceeded towards Skibbereen with a view to the impressment of some sailors known to be at that place. On his way, however, he sustained a furious attack from a body of peasantry, who, besides more or less beating his men, inflicted upon him two severe cuts in the head, and all but deprived him of life. Being again, in Aug. 1804, placed under the orders of Admiral Cornwallis in the VILLE DE PARIS, Mr. Hilton had an opportunity, on 22 Aug. 1805, of joining in that officer's pursuit of the French fleet into Brest, and of afterwards acting for five months as his First-Lieutenant. His next appointment, we find, was, in Feb. 1807, to the ORION 74, Capt. Sir Arch. Collingwood Dickson, whom he accompanied in the ensuing expedition to Copenhagen, whence, on the surrender of the Danish shipping, he was sent home in command of the PERLEN, one of the largest of the enemy's frigates. While subsequently attached, between July, 1808, and May, 1810, in the capacity of First-Lieutenant, to the ATLAS 98, bearing the flag of his old Captain, Purvis, he witnessed many of the operations connected with the defence of Cadiz, and was for a considerable time charged, in addition to his other duties, with the province of translating all the public, as well as private, Spanish correspondence. In Oct. 1810, Mr. Hilton became First of the AFRICA 64, bearing the flag of the late Sir Herbert Sawyer on the Halifax station; where, from 14 Sept. 1813, until 7 June, 1814, he further served as Flag-Lieutenant to the same officer in the TRENT 36. He was then invested with the command of the NIMROD 18, which he retained, on the North American and Cork stations, until paid off in Sept. 1815. He has not been since afloat.

Commander Hilton married, 23 April, 1816, Elizabeth, eldest sister of the present Commander John Harvey, R.N., and was left a widower 25 Feb. 1819. AGENTS—Messrs. Stilwell.

HILTON, K.F.M. (COMMANDER, 1814. F-P., 15; H-P., 33.)

JOHN HILTON entered the Navy, 12 July, 1799, as Fst.-cl. Vol., on board the HECLA sloop, Capt. Peter Turner Bover, part of the force employed in the ensuing expedition to the Helder. After further serving for a short time with the same officer as Midshipman in the MEGÆRA fire-vessel, he joined Sir Andrew Mitchell, in Sept. 1800, on board the WINDSOR CASTLE 98, in which ship and in the BLENHEIM 98, bearing the flag of Rear-Admiral Manley Dixon, he did duty, in the Channel and North Sea, until Nov. 1802. Between April, 1803, and Dec. 1805, we find him employed off the coast of Ireland, and again in the Channel, on board the THUNDERER 74, Capt. Wm. Bedford, and HIBERNIA 110, flag-ship of Lord Gardner; and participating, during that period, in the capture, by the THUNDERER and other vessels, of the French frigate *La Franchise*, of 36 guns. In Feb. 1806 he became Acting-Lieutenant of the TOPAZE frigate, Capts. Wm. Luke and Anselm John Griffiths, attached to the force on the coast of Ireland, where he remained until the period of his official promotion, which took place 15 Aug. following. His subsequent appointments were—15 Oct. 1806, to the GLORY 98, Capt. Wm. Albany Otway, off Cadiz—21 Oct. 1807 and 15 Feb. 1808, to the SULTAN 74, and CHIFFONNE frigate, Capts. Edw. Griffith and John Wainwright, fitting at Woolwich and Portsmouth—and, 6 June, 1808, 16 Nov. 1811, and 7 June, 1813, to the BUSTARD 10, GANYMEDE 26, and MINSTREL 20, Capts. John Duff Markland, John Brett Purvis, and Robt. Mitford, all on the Mediterranean station. On 24 July, 1809, he received four wounds while attempting to burn an armed felucca under Cape del Arme; and, on 23 Sept. 1811, he obtained the royal authority to accept and wear the insignia of a K.F.M., which his Sicilian Majesty had been pleased to confer on him "as a testimony of his royal approbation of the great courage and intrepidity displayed by him in various actions with the enemy's vessels near Messina." His promotion to the rank of Commander took place 15 June, 1814; since which period he has not been employed. AGENTS—Coplands and Burnett.

HILTON. (RETIRED COMMANDER, 1839. F-P., 21; H-P., 31.)

STEPHEN HILTON, born 9 Aug. 1785, is brother of Commander Geo. Hilton, R.N.

This officer entered the Navy, 13 Aug. 1795, as Third-cl. Vol., on board the BRISTOL, Lieut.-Commander Hutchison, lying at Chatham; and, from July, 1796, until Jan. 1798, was borne at Sheerness on the books of the GRANA, Lieut.-Commander Dixon. Re-embarking, in Aug. 1799, on board the PEARL 32, Capt. Sam. Jas. Ballard, he proceeded to the Mediterranean, where, during a continuance of two years, he participated as Midshipman in various cutting-out affairs in the vicinity of Toulon, and attended the expedition of 1801 to Egypt. Between Feb. 1802 and March, 1805, he served on the Home station in the ACASTA 40, Capts. Edw. Fellowes and Jas. Athol Wood, REVOLUTIONNAIRE frigate, Capt. Walter Lock, and QUEEN 98, Capts. Thos Jones and Manley Dixon. He then became Master's Mate of the MINOTAUR 74, Capt. Chas. John Moore Mansfield, and, after sharing in the glories of Trafalgar, was promoted to the rank of Lieutenant 22 Jan. 1806. Being appointed, on 14 of the following June, to the REVENGE 74, Capts. Sir John Gore, Hon. Chas. Paget, and Alex. Robt. Kerr, he witnessed, 25 Sept. in the same year, the capture of four heavy French frigates by a squadron under Sir Sam. Hood, off Rochefort, and was further present, in 1809, at the destruction of the French shipping in Basque Roads, and the siege of Flushing. On the latter occasion he was sent on shore with a party of 80 seamen, and while employed in a battery was slightly wounded by the explosion of a cartridge, which killed 3 of his men and seriously injured a Midshipman.* His subsequent appointments were, always as First-Lieutenant—in 1810-11, to the PRIMROSE 18, Capts. Thos. Burton and Chas. Geo. Rodney Phillott, SOPHIE 18, Capt. Nicholas Lockyer, and PIQUE 36, Capt. Hon. Anthony Maitland, on the Home station—14 March, 1812, to the LEOPARD 50, *armée en flûte*, Capt. Wm. Henry Dillon, under whom he was actively employed in the Mediterranean and on the coast of Spain in the conveyance of troops and provisions for Lord Wellington's army—28 April, 1814, to the DÉSIRÉE 36, Capt. Wm. Woolridge, in which frigate he made a voyage to the Cape of Good Hope, and was next stationed in the Downs and off the Scheldt—and, 19 Sept. 1815 and 11 March, 1816, to the SPENCER 74, and MALTA 80, Capts. Wm. Robt. Broughton and Thos. Gordon Caulfeild, guard-ships at Plymouth. He went on half-pay 28 Feb. 1817; and accepted the rank he now holds 7 Jan. 1839.

Commander Hilton married in 1818, and has issue nine children.

HINDE. (LIEUTENANT, 1844.)

EDWIN THOMAS HINDE entered the Navy 24 July, 1829; and in 1831, while Midshipman of the DRYAD 42, Capt. John Hayes, was officially reported for the conduct he displayed in her tender, the BLACK JOKE, at the capture, by boarding, of a slave-vessel of superior force. He passed his examination 6 July, 1836; was employed, from 1841 until the close of 1843, in the Mediterranean, as Mate of the MONARCH 84, Capt. Sam. Chambers; obtained his commission 10 June, 1844; and since 9 Sept. 1844, has been stationed in the East Indies on board the CRUIZER 16, Capts. Edw. Gennys Fanshawe, Wm. Maclean, and Edw. Peirse.

HINDMARSH, K.H. (CAPTAIN, 1831. F-P., 22; H-P., 32.)

JOHN HINDMARSH entered the Navy, in May, 1793, as Fst.-cl. Vol., on board the BELLEROPHON 74, Capts. Thos. Pasley, Wm. Hope, Lord Cranstoun, John Loring, and Henry D'Esterre Darby, in which ship he was employed for the long period of seven years, and was consequently present in Lord Howe's action of 1 June, 1794, in Cornwallis' retreat of 16 and 17 June, 1795, and at the battle of the Nile, besides sharing, as Midshipman, in most of Nelson's boat-operations off Cadiz in 1797, and contributing, in 1799, to the capture of the forts at Naples and Gaeta. During the action off the Nile he was for some time the only person left on the BELLEROPHON's quarter-deck, and being so at the moment her opponent, *L'Orient*, caught fire, he ordered the cable to be cut and the spritsail to be set, a measure which, in the opinion of Capt. Darby (who returned to the quarterdeck from the Surgeon's hands immediately afterwards), saved the ship from destruction. For his conduct on that glorious day Mr. Hindmarsh had the honour of eliciting the public thanks of Lord Nelson, to whom, as subsequently to Earl St. Vincent, and to all the Nile Captains, he was personally presented by Capt. Darby. Although, on the occasion, he received so severe a contusion as ultimately to lose the sight of an eye (a misfortune for which he never obtained

* *Vide* Gaz. 1809, p. 1327.

any pension), yet, to his honour be it recorded, nothing could induce him to leave his station. Accompanying Capt. Darby, in May, 1800, into the SPENCER 74, he had an opportunity, in July, 1801, of sharing both in the action off Algeciras, and in the victory gained by Sir Jas. Saumarez in the Gut of Gibraltar; where he also came into frequent boat-contact with the Spaniards, and was once in particular engaged in repelling a serious attack made by their flotilla upon H.M.S. NORTHUMBERLAND, of 74 guns. The SPENCER being paid off in Sept. 1802, on her return from a voyage to the West Indies, Mr. Hindmarsh next, in April, 1803, joined the VICTORY 100, bearing the flag in the Mediterranean of Lord Nelson, through whose influence he was promoted, on 1 of the following Aug., to a Lieutenancy in the PHŒBE 36, Capt. Hon. Thos Bladen Capel. During a servitude of more than two years in that frigate, he commanded her boats at the capture of many of the enemy's vessels, and in one instance, having successfully stormed some batteries in the neighbourhood of Toulon, he brought out a ship which had been lying under their protection. After participating in the battle of Trafalgar, 21 Oct. 1805, he contributed, at its close, to the preservation of two of the prizes, the *Swiftsure* and the *Bahama*, and was subsequently placed in charge, first of the *Fougueux*, and then of the *Bahama*. On leaving the PHŒBE he was appointed, in Nov. 1805, Senior of the BEAGLE 18, Capts. Geo. Digby and Fras. Newcombe, under whom he was for a long time employed on the coast of France, and proved instrumental to the capture of many very heavy privateers. During the operations connected with the destruction of the French squadron in Aix Roads, in April, 1809, the BEAGLE, with a degree of gallantry that procured her general admiration, took up a position between H. M. ships and the enemy, and remained on the quarters of the *Aquilon* 74, and *Ville de Varsovie* 80, until they successively struck their colours. She then followed the *Océan* 120, up the river Charente, and, having moored across the stern of that ship, continued in hot action with her for a period of five hours, when the turning of the tide compelled her to desist. After assisting at the reduction of Flushing, Mr. Hindmarsh was nominated First-Lieutenant of the NISUS 38, Capt. Philip Beaver, and ordered to the Isle of France, where he arrived in time to aid in its subjugation, and to command a large detachment of boats sent to take possession of its coast batteries. He next, in Sept. 1811, beheld the fall of Java, and in May, 1813, he invalided home. His promotion to the rank of Commander took place 15 June, 1814, but it was not until 8 March, 1830, that he succeeded in obtaining another appointment. He was then placed in command of the SCYLLA 18, fitting for the Mediterranean, from which station, on advancement to Post-rank 3 Sept. 1831, he returned home. On 21 April, 1836, Capt. Hindmarsh (who had been allowed, previously to joining the SCYLLA, to study at the Royal Naval College) was next appointed to the BUFFALO 6, for the purpose of founding the colony of South Australia—a settlement of which he became the first Governor. He left the BUFFALO in June, 1837, and has not since held any employment afloat.

On 4 May, 1836, Capt. Hindmarsh had the honour of being invested with the insignia of a K.H. His nomination to the Lieutenant-Governorship of Heligoland, which he still retains, was effected on 28 Sept. 1840. Capt. Hindmarsh's only son, John, now a Barrister, was formerly in the Navy, having entered the College in 1833 (where he continued two years and carried off the first medal) and been subsequently employed for six months with Capt. Thos. Brown in the CALEDONIA 120. One of his daughters, Mary, is married to G. M. Stephen, Esq., son of Judge Stephen, and brother of Sir Alfred Stephen, Chief Justice of New South Wales; and another, Jane, is the wife of A. M. Mundy, Esq., Colonial Secretary for South Australia, nephew of Admiral Sir Geo. Mundy, G.C.B., brother of E. M. Mundy, Esq., M.P., of Shipley Hall, co. Derby, and brother-in-law of the Duchess of Newcastle.

HINGSTON. (LIEUTENANT, 1825.)

GEORGE HINGSTON entered the Navy 28 April, 1807; passed his examination in 1814; and obtained his commission 10 Jan. 1825. He has not been since employed.

HIPPISLEY. (LIEUT., 1836. F-P., 30; H-P., 6.)

CHARLES JAMES HIPPISLEY, born 23 Sept. 1798, is third son of the late Gustavus Mathias Hippisley, Esq., by Ellen, third daughter of Thos. Fitzgerald, knight of Glin, of Glin Castle, co. Limerick; and grandson of the late Robt. Hippisley Trenchard, Esq., of Abbot's Leigh Court, co. Somerset, Cutteridge, co. Wilts, and Mount Trenchard, Ireland. One of his brothers, Robt. Fitzgerald Hippisley, now deceased, was also a Lieutenant in the Navy.

This officer entered the Navy, 5 Aug. 1811, as Fst.-cl. Vol., on board the AUDACIOUS 74, Capt. Donald Campbell, stationed in the North Sea, and from the following Dec. until July, 1814, was employed in the PRINCE OF WALES 98, Capts. Thos. Burton and John Erskine Douglas, on the Mediterranean station, where, in April of the latter year, he was present, as Midshipman, at the capture of Genoa. Prior to Oct. 1815, he next, we find, served in the West Indies on board the RINALDO 10, Capts. Arch. Tisdall and John Undrell, but, being then paid off, he did not again go afloat until April, 1822, on 14 of which month he was nominated Master's Mate of the PIGMY 10, Lieut.-Commander Thos. Hills, with whom he cruized on the Channel and Irish stations until March, 1823. His name was then borne for two years on the books of the BULWARK 76, from which ship, commanded at Plymouth and Portsmouth by Capt. Thos. Dundas, he was lent as Mate in July, 1824 (having passed his examination on 4 of the preceding Feb.) to the HERALD yacht, Capt. H. J. Leeke, for the purpose of making a voyage to St. Petersburg. After a further employment of 2 years at Plymouth and off Lisbon in the WINDSOR CASTLE 74, Capts. Hugh Downman and Edw. Durnford King, Mr. Hippisley, in June, 1827, was appointed Chief Mate of the HORNET Revenue cutter, Lieut.-Commanders Henry Nevill Eastwood, Henry Crocker, and Dan. M'Neale Beatty, on the coast of Ireland. In July, 1831, and May, 1832, he successively removed to the SPRIGHTLY and HARPY, other Revenue vessels, commanded, on Channel service, by Lieut. Thos. Holloway Holman and Edw. Youel. He left the HARPY on the ultimate attainment of his present rank, 15 Jan. 1836, and since 9 of the following March has been in charge of a station in the Coast Guard.

Lieut. Hippisley, who is Senior of 1836, is in possession of testimonials that do him much credit. He married, 14 Dec. 1826, Mary Eliza Temple, second daughter of the late John Wills, Esq., Purser and Paymaster, R.N. (1797.)

HIRE. (LIEUTENANT, 1815. F-P., 36; H-P., 6.)

FREDERICK HIRE was born 15 Jan. 1796, and died in 1846. He was brother of the present Lieut. Henry Hire, R.N.

This officer entered the Navy, in Jan. 1805, as Fst.-cl. Vol., on board L'AIGLE 36, Capt. Geo. Wolfe. He was present, in the course of the same year, in Admiral Hon. Wm. Cornwallis' pursuit of the French fleet into Brest, and also in an action off Vigo, in which the British frigate captured one and defeated the rest of a flotilla of nine gun-boats by whom she had been attacked. In March, 1808, he enacted a Midshipman's part, and was wounded in a very gallant engagement fought by L'AIGLE with two French frigates and the enemy's batteries on Ile de Groix, where, besides having 3 of her guns split and dismounted, a bower-anchor cut in two, and her mainmast and bowsprit irreparably injured, the former ship had two-and-twenty of her people more or less severely hurt. One of her antagonists was compelled to take shelter under a fort; and the other to run on shore on Pointe des Chats. In April, 1809, immediately prior to the destruction of the shipping in Aix Roads, Mr. Hire served in the boats under Lieut. Rich. Devonshire at the destruction of the works on the Boyart Rock, a hazardous achievement, which elicited the thanks of Lord Gambier; and he subsequently, on becoming attached to the Walcheren armament, assisted in forcing the passage between Flushing and Cadsand; on which occasion L'Aigle, in consequence of a shell bursting in her after-gun-room, sustained a loss of 5 men wounded, and had her stern-frame greatly damaged. Continuing in the same ship until Nov. 1810, our officer had an opportunity, during a cruize to the westward, of contributing to the capture of *Le Phœnix* privateer, of 18 guns and 120 men. In Feb. 1811 he joined the Prince Frederick 64, Capt. Peter Fisher, lying at Plymouth, where he remained until the ensuing Oct.; between which period and the date of his promotion to the rank of Lieutenant, 11 Feb. 1815, he presents himself to our notice as employed on the Channel, Mediterranean, and Irish stations, chiefly as Master's Mate, in the Pelorus 18, Capts. Joshua Ricketts Rowley, Hon. Robt. Cavendish Spencer, Robt. Gambier, Lord Algernon Percy, Chas. Hole, and John Gourly; and as assisting at the capture, during that period, of a convoy off Rochefort in Jan. 1811, and of Genoa and its dependencies in April, 1814. From 8 May to 31 Dec. 1815, Mr. Hire was again employed under the orders of Capt. Gambier on board the Myrmidon 20, which vessel, being part of the squadron present at the surrender of Napoleon Buonaparte, was charged with the conveyance to England of a portion of the unfortunate Emperor's suite. His subsequent appointments were—for a short time in 1818, to the Water Guard—4 July, 1823, to the same service—10 Feb. 1824, to the Coast Blockade, in which he continued, as Supernumerary-Lieutenant of the Ramillies 74 and Hyperion 42, Capts. Wm. M'Culloch and Wm. Jas. Mingaye, until its abolition in March, 1831—on 16 of the latter month, to the Coast Guard—23 March, 1835, to the command of the Adelaide Revenue cutter—and, 17 March, 1838, again to the Coast Guard, in which service he died.

Lieut. Hire married a daughter of the late Capt. Wm. Stephens, R.N., by whom he has left issue. Agents—Messrs. Halford and Co.

HIRE. (Lieutenant, 1846.)

George Augustus Hire passed his examination 4 Jan. 1831; obtained an appointment in the Coast Guard 4 Dec. 1839; and continued in that service until advanced to his present rank, 1 July, 1846. He has since been on half-pay.

HIRE. (Lieutenant, 1808.)

Henry Hire is brother of the late Lieut. Fred. Hire, R.N.

This officer entered the Navy, 29 July, 1801, as Midshipman, on board the Prince George 98, Capt. John Tremayne Rodd, bearing the flag in the Channel of Sir Chas. Cotton, with whom he continued until April, 1802. Re-embarking, in Feb. 1803, on board the Boadicea 38, Capt. John Maitland, he took part, in the following Aug., while on his return from Ferrol, in a self-sought and very gallant skirmish fought by that frigate with the French 74 *Le Duguay Trouin*. Towards the close of the same year he rejoined Sir C. Cotton in the San Josef 110, flag-ship afterwards of Sir Jas. Saumarez, in which he remained until June, 1807. He then removed to the Ville de Paris 110, bearing the flag of Lord Gambier, but in May, 1808, was again placed under the orders of Sir C. Cotton, on board the Hibernia 110, part of the force employed on the Lisbon station, where, on 16 of the following Oct., he was confirmed a Lieutenant in the Primrose 18. He removed soon afterwards to the Audacious 74, Capts. Thos. Le Marchant Gosselin and Donald Campbell, on the North Sea station. On leaving that ship he served with great activity, from March, 1810, to Aug. 1813, in the Nautilus 18, commanded in the Mediterranean by Capt. Thos. Dench (*whom see*); and he then cruized for 15 months with Capts. Benj. Crispin and Jas. Arthur Murray in the Scout 18, also in the Mediterranean. We believe he has been in command, ever since Oct. 1823, of the Convict ship at Bermuda.

Lieut. Hire is married and has issue. One of his children, Henry William, is a Lieutenant, R.N.; and another, Unity Isabella, the wife of John Scott Tucker, Esq., third son of the late Joseph Tucker, Esq., Surveyor of the Navy. Agents—Messrs. Halford and Co.

HIRE. (Lieutenant, 1841.)

Henry William Hire is son of Lieut. Henry Hire, R.N.

This officer entered the Navy 9 Feb. 1830; passed his examination 6 April, 1836; and, during the latter portion of his servitude as Mate, was employed in North America and the West Indies on board the Pilot 16, Capt. Geo. Ramsay. Being made Lieutenant, 15 Sept. 1841, into the Racehorse 18, Capt. John Coghlan Fitzgerald, attached to the force on the same station, he there continued to serve, both in the last-mentioned vessel and in the Cleopatra 26, Capt. Christ. Wyvill, until the spring of 1842. His next appointments, it appears, were, in the Mediterranean—20 June, 1842, as Additional, to the Queen 110, bearing the flag of Sir Edw. W. C. R. Owen—and, 21 Jan. 1843 and 25 Oct. and 16 Nov. 1844, as First, to the Snake 16, Bonetta surveying-vessel, and Hecla steam-sloop, Capts. Hon. Walter Bourchier Devereux, Thos. Saumarez Brock, John Duffill, and Chas. Starmer. He has been employed, since 13 March, 1847, in the Rattler steam-sloop, Capt. Rich. Moorman, on Particular Service.

HIRTZEL. (Commander, 1842. f-p., 22; h-p., 13.)

George John Hirtzel, born at Exeter, is son of the late Geo. Hirtzel, Esq., of that place.

This officer entered the Navy, 8 Dec. 1812, as Fst.-cl. Vol., on board the Andromeda 24, Capt. Rich. Arthur, with whom he served on the Lisbon and Mediterranean stations, for some time as Midshipman, until Dec. 1815. Until Jan. 1821 he was next employed in the Comus 22, Capt. Thos. Tudor Tucker, also in the Berwick 74 and Impregnable 104, both flag-ships at Plymouth, and in the Spartan 46, commanded on Particular Service by Capt. Wm. Furlong Wise. While under the latter officer he passed his examination, 4 June, 1819; and on leaving him he was for upwards of ten years continuously employed in North America and the West Indies on board the Niemen 28, Capt. Edw. Reynolds Sibly, Jupiter 50, Capts. David Dunn, Sir Wm. Saltonstall Wiseman, and Wm. Webb, Hussar 46, and Winchester 52, flag-ships of Sir Chas. Ogle and Sir Edw. Griffith Colpoys (under the latter of whom he officiated as Acting-Signal-Lieutenant from May to Oct. 1830), and Grasshopper 18, Capt. John Elphinstone Erskine. After he had also acted for nine months as Lieutenant of the latter sloop, Mr. Hirtzel was at length officially promoted by commission dated 7 June, 1831. His subsequent appointments were—8 July, 1836, to the Dublin 50, bearing the flag at the Brazils of Sir Graham Eden Hamond—28 Dec. 1836, as Senior, to the Harrier 18, Capt. Wm. Henry Hallowell Carew, of which vessel, stationed until 1839 in the Pacific, he acted for some time as Commander—and, 1 Dec. 1841, as First, to the Alfred 50, fitting for the broad pendant of Commodore John Brett Purvis. He was promoted to his present rank in honour of Her Majesty's visit to Portsmouth, 7 March, 1842, but has not been since afloat.

When a Mate in North America, Commander Hirtzel appears to have had frequent charge of small vessels. He is married and has issue.

HITCHINS. (Retired Commander, 1836. f-p., 16; h-p., 34.)

Joseph Hitchins entered the Navy, in Aug. 1797, as Midshipman, on board the Royal George 100, Capt. John Draper, bearing the flag off Cadiz of Sir John Orde. In June, 1799, he joined La Loire frigate, Capt. Jas. Newman Newman; and after a servitude of nearly two years and a half with that officer in the Channel he removed, in Nov. 1801, to the Theseus 74, Capt. John Bligh, and sailed for the West Indies, where, on 4 Nov. 1803, he was promoted to a Lieutenancy in the Æolus frigate, Capt. Andrew Fitzherbert Evans. His subsequent appointments were—3 July, 1804, to the Veteran 64, Capts. J. N. Newman and A. F. Evans, also in the West Indies—29 July, 1806, and 6 Feb. 1807, to the Blonde 38 and Leyden 64, Capts. Volant Vashon Ballard and Wm. Cumberland, on the Home station—21 March, 1807, to the Surveillante 38, Capt. Sir Geo. Ralph Collier, with whom he accompanied the expedition to Copenhagen and then made a voyage to the Brazils—in Oct. 1809 and May, 1810, to the Echo 18, Capt. Robt. Keen, and Fylla 20, Capts. Hon. Edw. Rodney and Henry Prescott, both in the Channel—and, 29 Sept. 1812, to the Duncan 74, Capts. Robt. Lambert, Smith, and Thos. Ussher. He left the latter ship on her return home from the Mediterranean in Aug. 1814; and on 4 May, 1836, accepted the rank of Retired Commander. Agents—Hallett and Robinson.

HOAR. (Lieutenant, 1803. f-p., 15; h-p., 36.)

Balch Nun Hoar entered the Navy, in Oct. 1796, as A. B., on board the Prince 98, Capt. Thos. Larcom. In that ship, which afterwards bore the flag of Sir Roger Curtis, he continued to serve as Midshipman on the Channel, North Sea, and Irish stations, until 1798, when he removed to the Incendiary 14, Capt. Geo. Barker, and sailed for the Mediterranean. In 1799 he rejoined Sir Roger Curtis at the Cape of Good Hope on board the Lancaster 64, from which vessel he was promoted, 6 Jan. 1803, to an Acting-Lieutenancy in the Tremendous 74, Capt. John Osborn—an appointment officially sanctioned on 15 of the following April. On 21 April, 1806, while on her passage with a homeward-bound convoy from India, where she had been employed for upwards of three years, the latter ship pursued and fought a close action of an hour and a quarter with the French 40-gun frigate *Cannonière*, who in the end effected her escape, with a loss, besides being greatly damaged, of 7 men killed and 25 wounded. Mr. Hoar's appointments, after he left the Tremendous, were—9 Aug. 1806, to the Illustrious 74, Capt. Wm. Shield and Wm. Robt. Broughton, in the Mediterranean—8 Aug. 1808, to the Pelorus sloop, Capt. Hon. Jas. Wm. King—7 April, 1809, to the Diomede 50, Capt. Hugh Cook, for passage to the East Indies—11 July, 1809, to the Lion 64, Capt. Henry Heathcote, at St. Helena—18 May, 1810, to the Leda 36, Capt. Geo. Sayer, under whom he witnessed the earlier operations connected with the reduction of Java—and lastly, 17 May, 1813, after one-and-twenty months of half-pay, to the Grasshopper sloop, Capt. Henry Robt. Battersby, again on the Mediterranean station, whence he invalided in Jan. 1814.

For many years prior to 1838 Lieut. Hoar was one of the Naval Knights of Windsor. Since 28 June in that year he has been on the out-pension of Greenwich Hospital.

HOARE. (Captain, 1810. f-p., 21; h-p., 36.)

Edward Wallis Hoare, born 4 May, 1779, in the city of Cork, is son of the late Sir Edw. Hoare, Bart., of Annabelle, M.P. for Carlow, and a Captain of Dragoons, by Clotilda, second daughter and coheir of Wm. Wallis, Esq., of Ballycrenan Castle. He is brother of the present Sir Joseph Wallis Hoare, Bart., and uncle of Commander Wm. O'B. Hoare, R.N.

This officer entered the Navy, in May, 1790, as Fst.-cl. Vol. (under the auspices of Sir John Colpoys), on board the Squirrel 24, Capt. Wm. O'Brien Drury, employed at first on the Irish station, and then off the coast of Africa, where, in 1793 or 4, he took part, as Midshipman, in an engagement with a Portuguese fort on the island of Pines. In May of the latter year he removed to the Ruby 64, Capt. Sir Rich. Hussey Bickerton; and on next joining Sir John Colpoys in the London 98 (of which ship he was confirmed a Lieutenant 4 Aug. 1796), he shared, 23 June, 1795, in Lord Bridport's action with the French fleet off the Ile de Groix. During the famous mutiny at Spithead in 1797, Mr. Hoare, who was at the time Signal-Lieutenant of the London, was condemned to death by the delegates. In Dec. of the same year, a few months after he had been transferred to the Nymphe 36, Capt. Percy Fraser, he had the misfortune to be wounded and taken captive by the enemy, in an attempt to obtain possession of a cutter on the coast of France. While filling next, from April, 1798, to Sept. 1802, the post of Senior Lieutenant on board the Northumberland 74, Capt. Geo. Martin, he served at the reduction of Malta—was present, during its blockade, at the surrender of the French 74-gun ship *Le Généreux* and frigate *La Diane*—and attended the expedition of 1801 to Egypt, where he assisted at the landing of the troops. In June, 1803, Mr. Hoare rejoined Capt. Martin as his First-Lieutenant in the Colossus 74; and on 25 Oct. 1804, while officiating in a similar capacity on board the Glory 98, flag-ship of Hon. Wm. Cornwallis, he was at length advanced to the rank of Commander. His succeeding appointments appear to have been, 29 July, 1806, 19 May, 1807, and 18 Aug. 1809, to the Goshawk 16, Amsterdam 20, and Hesper 18; in which vessels we find him continuously employed on the African, Irish, and East India stations, until nominated, 5 March, 1810, Acting-Captain of the Blanche frigate. In the following summer he was further invested with the acting-command of the Cornwallis 50, and Russel 74; which latter ship, bearing the flag of Rear-Admiral W. O'B. Drury, was employed in the earlier portion of the operations that preceded the fall of the Isle of France. Capt. Hoare, whose promotion to Post-rank was confirmed 16 Oct. 1810, next, on 31 Jan. 1811, joined the Minden 74. In the ensuing spring he was despatched from Madras to the coast of Java, with two companies of troops on board, in order to await the arrival of the expedition then fitting out at the different ports of India for the attack of that island. After performing much arduous service in the Strait of Sunda, he landed on the 5th of June, and, with not more than 200 seamen and soldiers, succeeded in utterly routing a chosen body of the enemy's troops, 500 strong, whose close and desperate mode of fighting occasioned the gallant British a loss of 2 men killed and 23 wounded. The enemy had upwards of 50 killed and 100 wounded.* Capt. Hoare has been on half-pay since 13 Aug. 1812.

He married, in June, 1803, Mary, third daughter of Col. Robt. Uniacke Fitzgerald, M.P. for co. Cork, by whom he has issue two daughters, one of whom is married to Lieut. Thos. Burton Maynard, R.N., and the other to Capt. J. B. L. Hay, R.N. Agents—Messrs. Stilwell.

HOARE. (Captain, 1827. f-p., 17; h-p., 25.)

Richard Hoare, born 1 Sept. 1793, is third son of the late Sir Henry Hugh Hoare, Bart., F.S.A., F.R.S., of Stourhead, co. Wilts, by Maria Palmer, daughter of Arthur Acland, Esq., of Fairfield, co. Somerset. He is brother of the present Sir Hugh Rich. Hoare, Bart.

This officer entered the Navy, 5 July, 1805, as Fst.-cl. Vol., on board the Tribune frigate, Capt. Rich. Henry Alex. Bennett, with whom he served in the Channel and North Sea until compelled by sickness to be sent on shore in Jan. 1806. Re-embarking, 25 July, 1807, on board the Powerful 74, bearing the flag of the late Lord Gambier, he ac-

* *Vid.* Gaz. 1811, p. 2106.

companied that officer in the ensuing expedition to Copenhagen; on his return whence, he was for four years employed with Capt. Edw. Fellowes in the APOLLO 38, and CONQUEROR 74, chiefly on the Mediterranean station. Between Feb. 1812, and July, 1813, he served in the Channel on board the SAN JOSEF 110, and QUEEN CHARLOTTE 100, flag-ships of Lord Keith, by whom he was then appointed Lieutenant of the SPARROW sloop, Capt. John Campbell. While employed, soon afterwards, in rowing guard in a 6-oared cutter off St. Jean de Luz, Mr. Hoare, in spite of all the resistance he could offer, was captured by four French gun-boats and taken to Bayonne. On his exchange and return to England, he was at once, by a commission dated 13 Nov. 1813, officially advanced to the rank of Lieutenant, and on 30 of the same month nominated to the DRAGON 74, Capt. Robt. Barrie, under whom he enacted a prominent part in the after-scenes of the American war. His succeeding appointments were—30 Aug. and 27 Oct. 1815, to the MADAGASCAR and PHAETON frigates, commanded by Capt. Fras. Stanfell, at Sheerness and at the Cape of Good Hope—7 June, 1818, as First-Lieutenant, to the BLOSSOM 26, Capts. Fred. Hickey and Fred. Edw. Venables Vernon, in South America—and 9 Feb. 1821, in a similar capacity, to the NIEMEN 28, Capt. Edw. Reynolds Sibly, fitting for service at Halifax. He was promoted, on the latter station, to the command, 19 July, 1822, of the DOTEREL 18, which sloop he brought home and paid off in 1825. He acquired his present rank 7 July, 1827, but has not been since afloat.

Capt. Hoare married, first, 15 March, 1823, Mary Offley, youngest daughter of the late Admiral Sir Wm. Chas. Fahie, K.C.B., by whom (who died 27 Sept. 1826) he had issue; and secondly, in 1834, Elizabeth, eldest daughter of Wm. Praed, Esq., of Tyringham, Bucks, and of Trewithon, Cornwall.

HOARE. (COMMANDER, 1846. F-P., 12; H-P., 14.)

WILLIAM O'BRYEN HOARE, born 23 March, 1807, is second son of Sir Joseph Wallis Hoare, Bart., of Annabelle, co. Cork, by Lady Harriet O'Bryen, sister of the present Marquess of Thomond, Vice-Admiral of the Red, G.C.H. He is brother of John Willoughby Hoare, Esq., of the 13th Bombay Native Infantry; nephew of Capt. Edw. Wallis Hoare, R.N.; and brother-in-law of Commander Matthew Chas. Foster, R.N.

This officer entered the Navy 28 Feb. 1821; passed his examination in 1827; obtained his first commission 30 Aug. 1828; and was afterwards appointed — 6 Nov. 1829, to the DRUID 46, Capt. Gawen Wm. Hamilton, in South America—14 April, 1831, to the STAG 46, Capt. Sir Edw. Thos. Troubridge, employed on particular service, which vessel he left in January, 1832—and 25 May, 1843, to the command of the DOLPHIN brigantine, on the Brazilian station, where he continued until superseded in Feb. 1845. He attained his present rank 9 Nov. 1846, and has since been on half-pay.

Commander Hoare married, 2 May, 1834, Caroline, daughter of John Hornby, Esq., of the Hook, Hampshire, by whom he has issue.

HOBART. (LIEUTENANT, 1845.)

AUGUSTUS CHARLES HOBART entered the Navy in 1835; passed his examination 28 Dec. 1842; and served, as Mate, on board the EXCELLENT gunnery-ship at Portsmouth, Capt. Sir Thos. Hastings—also in the DOLPHIN brigantine, commanded on the Brazilian station by Lieut. Wm. O'Bryen Hoare—and in the VICTORIA and ALBERT steam-yacht, Capt. Lord Adolphus FitzClarence. He obtained his commission 25 Sept. 1845; joined, 11 Nov. following, the RATTLER steam-sloop, Capts. Henry Smith and Rich. Moorman, on the Channel station; and since 11 March, 1847, has been borne, as Additional-Lieutenant, on the books of the HIBERNIA 104, flag-ship of Sir Wm. Parker, Commander-in-Chief in the Mediterranean.

HOCKIN. (COMMANDER, 1846.)

CHARLES LUXMORE HOCKIN passed his examination in 1831; attained the rank of Lieutenant 2 March, 1838; was employed in the Mediterranean, from 8 of the following May until paid off in the summer of 1841, on board the DIDO 18, Capt. Lewis Davies; and on 18 Oct. 1842 was appointed Senior of the WASP 16, Capts. Andrew Drew, Henry Bagot, and Sidney Henry Ussher. After serving for nearly four years in the latter vessel on the North American, West India, and African stations, he was advanced to the rank he now holds 5 Aug. 1846. He has since been on half-pay.

HOCKIN. (LIEUT., 1815. F-P., 17; H-P., 24.)

HENRY HOCKIN was born 21 April, 1794. His father was a banker; and his mother a sister of the late Sir Wm. Adams.

This officer entered the Navy, 10 June, 1806, as Fst.-cl. Vol., on board the SUPERB 74, Capt. (subsequently Rear-Admiral) Rich. Goodwin Keats, under whom, after serving at the blockade of Rochefort, he attended the expedition to Copenhagen in Aug. and Sept. 1807, was present at the embarkation from Nyeborg of the Marquis de la Romana and his army, 11 Aug. 1808, and assisted as Midshipman at the bombardment of Flushing in Aug. 1809. He was next, from Nov. 1809 to Aug. 1810, borne at Spithead on the books of the PUISSANT 74, Capts. Robt. Hall and John Irwin; after which he rejoined Rear-Admiral Keats on board the MILFORD 74, and continued to serve with him in that ship and in the HIBERNIA 120, at the defence of Cadiz (where he participated in the duties of the flotilla) and off Toulon, until Sept. 1812. During the two following years we find him attached to the FRANCHISE 36, Capt. Rich. Buck, by whom, with a view to co-operating with the Spanish patriots, he was intrusted with the command of a boat, armed with a brass 6-pounder, for the purpose of annoying the French land-convoys on their way from the foot of the Pyrenees to Barcelona. On leaving the FRANCHISE, Mr. Hockin successively joined the MÆANDER 38, Capt. John Bastard, and ELIZABETH 74, bearing the flag of Hon. Chas. Elphinstone Fleeming, on the Gibraltar and Cadiz stations. In June, 1815, after having cruized for five months off Lisbon as Acting-Lieutenant of the JASPER 10, Capt. Thos. Carew, he took up a commission dated on 17 of the previous Feb. With the exception of an appointment in the Coast Guard, which he held from 13 Nov. 1833 until 1841, he has since been on half-pay.

Lieut. Hockin married Miss Elizabeth Dodd, of Cheshire, and by that lady has issue one son.

HOCKINGS. (Captain, 1821. F-P., 19; H-P., 38.)

ROBERT HOCKINGS, born 1 May, 1776, at Gibraltar, is eldest son of the late Thos. Hockings, Esq., a gentleman who held an appointment for nearly fifty years in the Civil department of the Ordnance at that place, and was severely wounded during its siege. He is nephew of Major Rich. Hockings, who died of yellow fever at Trinidad while commanding the Royal Engineers; brother of Lieut. Geo. Hockings, of the 10th Regt., who lost a leg in Egypt under Sir Ralph Abercromby, and ultimately died of fever at Gibraltar; and uncle of Robt. Hockings, Esq., First-Lieutenant R.M., of —— Hockings, Esq., of the 40th Regt., and of Thos. Hockings, Esq., Purser and Paymaster R.N.

This officer entered the Navy, 26 Oct. 1790, as A.B. (under the auspices of H. R. H. the late Duke of Kent), on board the AMBUSCADE 32, Capt. Robt. Devereux Fancourt, stationed in the Mediterranean, where, until Feb. 1793, he further served, part of the time as Midshipman, in the EURYDICE 24, Capt. Geo. Lumsdaine, ZEBRA 18, Capt. Wm. Brown, PEARL 32, Capt. Geo. Wm. Augustus Courtenay, MUTINE cutter, Lieut.-Commander Henry West, and ROMNEY 50, bearing the flag of Rear-Admiral Sam. Cranston Goodall. During the next four years he was employed in the Channel, and again in the Mediterranean, on board the LAPWING 28, and PALLAS 32, both commanded by Capt. Hon. Henry Curzon, under whom, in the latter frigate, he shared in Cornwallis' celebrated retreat of 16 and 17 June, 1795. The PALLAS having on one occasion captured a merchant-brig, Mr. Hockings was sent with her as Prize-Master to Elba. While on his way thither, and when in the Piombino Passage, he was attacked by two large row-boats containing about 50 or 60 men, whom, however, he beat off after a conflict of an hour, although he had but 5 hands on board, and only 2 rusty 4-pounder guns. This achievement was considered so gallant that on reaching Porto Ferrajo, where lay the BLANCHE frigate, Capt. Hon. Henry Hotham, he was highly complimented by that officer, and recommended by him to Earl St. Vincent, the Commander-in-Chief, by whom he was received on board his flag-ship the VILLE DE PARIS 110, and at once appointed, 29 April, 1797, First-Lieutenant of the HAMADRYAD 36, Capt. Thos. Elphinstone—an act which the Admiralty confirmed by a commission dated on 10 of the following June. Being wrecked on 25 Dec. in the same year during a violent gale in the Bay of Algiers, Mr. Hockings, who on the occurrence of the catastrophe was so seriously bruised that he still feels the effects, became First of the AURORA 28, Capts. Henry Digby, Thos. Gordon Caulfeild, and Micajah Malbon. With those officers he served uninterruptedly on the Lisbon, Mediterranean, and Newfoundland stations until March, 1803; participating intermediately in the capture of many privateers, also in several cutting-out affairs (in one of which he was slightly wounded), in the destruction, too, of the French 20-gun ship *Egalité*, and in the land-operations at the reduction of Minorca. On 12 June, 1803, he was appointed Senior of the PHAETON 38, Capts. Geo. Cockburn and John Wood, and ordered to North America in escort of Mr. Merry, the British Minister Plenipotentiary. He then proceeded to the East Indies, and, while on a subsequent cruize in the China Seas, he shared in an action with the French frigate *Sémillante*, and in the capture of a ship of immense value on her annual passage from Manilla to Lima. In Jan. 1807 Mr. Hockings' health compelled him to invalid, and he in consequence returned home, where, in May and Aug. 1808, he successively became Signal-Lieutenant to Lord Gambier in the VILLE DE PARIS 110, and CALEDONIA 120. As a reward for his subsequent conduct in command of a fire-ship during the celebrated attack made by the gallant Cochrane on the enemy's shipping in Basque Roads, he was presented with a second promotal commission dated 11 April, 1809—previously to which period, as has been seen, he had been for nearly ten years First-Lieutenant of a frigate. Although not included in the list of the wounded on the last-mentioned occasion, Capt. Hockings was severely hurt by the explosion of his vessel. Not wishing to remain idle on shore, he obtained permission soon after his promotion to rejoin the CALEDONIA, then the flag-ship of his friend Sir Harry Neale, with whom he served as a volunteer until the close of 1810. From 25 May, 1811, until driven home by the effects of the yellow fever in Oct. 1812, we find him in command of the DOMINICA 14, in the Channel and West Indies, and on 11 Sept. in the latter year effecting the capture of the *Providence* American privateer schooner, of 4 guns (pierced for 12) and 60 men. Capt. Hockings' next and last appointment was, 26 Dec. 1820, to the MEDINA 20, in which sloop he appears to have afforded protection to the European consuls and merchants at Smyrna during the fearful outrages which were there perpetrated by the populace in June, 1821. He was advanced to Post-rank on 19 of the following month; and on 1 Oct. 1846, awarded, at his own request, the half-pay of Retirement.

Capt. Hockings married, 13 March, 1821, Magdalena, eldest daughter of the late Gerard Montagu, Esq., formerly of Burlingham, co. Norfolk, grandniece of Admiral John Montagu, and a relative of the Duke of Manchester. By that lady he has issue two daughters. AGENTS—Messrs. Halford and Co.

HOCKLEY. (LIEUTENANT, 1837.)

JOHN BAKER HOCKLEY passed his examination in 1831; obtained his commission 21 July, 1837; and on 29 of the same month was appointed Additional-Lieutenant of the PRINCESS CHARLOTTE 104, flag-ship of Hon. Sir Robt. Stopford on the Mediterranean station, where he removed, 1 Dec. following, to the BARHAM 50, Capt. Armar Lowry Corry. With one or two slight interruptions he has been employed in the Coast Guard since 19 Nov. 1838.

HODDER. (LIEUT., 1815. F-P., 10; H-P., 30.)

MICHAEL HODDER—born at Fountainstown, co. Cork, the seat of his father—is brother of Lieut. Peter Hodder, R.N.

This officer entered the Navy, 14 March, 1807, as Fst.-cl. Vol., on board the DÆDALUS 32, Capt. Fred. Warren, whom he accompanied with convoy to the West Indies. He then proceeded to Bermuda in the LAURA, Lieut.-Commander Robt. Yates, and on his arrival at that place he took a passage home in the PRINCE GEORGE 98, Capt. Geo. Losack. From Sept. in the same year until Dec. 1813 he was employed, in the capacity of Midshipman, chiefly on the Home and Baltic stations, in the ALEXANDRIA 32, Capts. Nathaniel Day Cochrane, John Quilliam, and Robt. Cathcart. During that period, besides being at the blockade of many ports on the coast of Holland, he served in a boat at the cutting out of a Dutch guard-vessel from the river Elbe, was present at the capture of two armed vessels and of a convoy of 27 sail in a calm at sea, came frequently into contact with the enemy's gun-boats, and was concerned in the cutting out on different occasions of at least 150 vessels, many of them well armed. In most cases Mr. Hodder had the personal command of a boat. On the return of the ALEXANDRIA from Greenland, where she had arrived just in time to prevent the British whalers from falling into the hands of the American Commodore Rodgers, he rejoined Capt. Cochrane on board the ORONTES 36, and went with him in protection of a large convoy to the West Indies. On the ORONTES being recommissioned by the same Captain in the spring of 1815, Mr. Hodder, whose promotion to the rank of Lieutenant took place on 18 Feb. in that year, was again appointed to her. Continuing on her books until paid off in March, 1817, he was first employed in forwarding troops to Flanders, next in bringing the wounded and prisoners over after the battle of Waterloo, then in carrying out an Austrian commissioner to St. Helena for the security of Buonaparte, and finally in the suppression of the slave-trade at Madagascar. Since the date last named the Lieutenant has not held any official occupation.

HODDER. (LIEUT., 1812. F-P., 8; H-P., 35.)

PETER HODDER is son of Geo. Hodder, Esq., of Fountainstown, co. Cork, an extensive landed proprietor; and brother of Lieuts. Michael and Robt. Hodder, R.N.

This officer entered the Navy, 18 Aug. 1804, as Fst.-cl. Vol., on board the AMETHYST 36, in which ship, and in the WARRIOR 74, both commanded by Capt. John Wm. Spranger, he served on the North Sea, Irish, Channel, and Mediterranean stations, until April, 1811. He held, during the four last years, the rating of Midshipman, and in Oct. 1809 he was consequently present in that capacity at the surrender of the islands of Zante, Cephalonia, &c. On leaving the WARRIOR he joined the COLOSSUS 74, Capt. Thos. Alexander, stationed off the coast of France, where, on 27 Dec. 1811, he was taken prisoner in an attack on a flotilla near the Ile d'Aix. His promotion to the rank of Lieutenant took place 21 March, 1812, since which period—with the exception of an attachment of a few months in 1815 to the LEVANT 20, commanded on Home service by Capts. Jonathan Christian and John Theed—he has been on half-pay.

HODDER. (Lieut., 1817. f-p., 8; h-p., 30.)

Robert Hodder is brother of Lieut. Peter Hodder, R.N., and ninth son of Geo. Hodder, Esq., of Fountainstown.

This officer entered the Navy, 19 June, 1809, as Fst.-cl. Vol., on board the JAMAICA 26, Capt. Arthur Lysaght, stationed at Newfoundland. In Nov. 1810 he joined the SOUTHAMPTON 32, Capt. Jas. Lucas Yeo, lying at Spithead; and in the following Feb. he removed to the DEFIANCE 74, Capt. Rich. Raggett. During his servitude in the latter ship, which bore the flag for some time of Rear-Admiral Geo. Hope, we find him employed at the blockade of Flushing and the Texel, and superintending the transport of troops from Carlskrona to Swedish Pomerania. Between Oct. 1813 and June, 1814, he was borne on the books of the DEVONSHIRE 74, Capt. Ross Donnelly, and HARLEQUIN 18, Capt. Wm. Kempthorne, both fitting at Sheerness; and in the next Nov. he was received on board the ETHALION 36, Capt. Wm. Hugh Dobbie. On a subsequent occasion, while in escort of a convoy from Gibraltar to Cork, he very courageously volunteered, in company with Mr. Lane, another Midshipman, to take charge of one of the merchantmen which had been dismasted in a gale and abandoned by her master and crew. He accordingly went on board the vessel with his friend, and, having rigged jury-masts, retained possession of her for a period of 12 days, when they were both burnt out by the effects of a spontaneous combustion which took place in the hold. In Oct. 1815 Mr. Hodder was appointed Master's Mate of the CONGO sloop, Capt. Jas. Hingston Tuckey, for the purpose of exploring the river of that name on the coast of Africa. Being ultimately the only officer spared by the ravages of the climate, he assumed, in Oct. 1816, the rank of Acting-Lieutenant, although he had not yet passed his examination. He brought the CONGO home from Bahia in the spring of 1817, and on 24 May in that year, as soon as he had passed, was officially promoted. He has not been since afloat.

Lieut. Hodder has been employed in the Customs since Aug. 1819. He married, in March, 1834, Ellen Jane, eldest daughter of Capt. Wm. Henry Craig, R.M.

HODDER. (Lieutenant, 1824.)

Thomas Eyre Hodder is third son of the late Wm. Henry Moore Hodder, Esq., of Hoddersfield, co. Cork, by Harriet, daughter of the Right Hon. Henry Theophilus Clements, brother of the first Earl of Leitrim. He is grandson of the late Capt. Henry Moore, of the 48th Foot; and brother of the present Wm. Henry Moore Hodder, Esq., of Hoddersfield, Colonel of the North Cork Militia, and a Magistrate and Deputy-Lieutenant for that county.

This officer entered the Navy 26 Jan. 1811; was made Lieutenant, 19 June, 1824, into the EDEN 26, Capt. John Lawrence, on the West India station; and from 24 April, 1828, until paid off in April, 1829, was employed, on Home service, in the CLIO sloop, Capt. Robt. Deans. With the exception of a brief attachment in 1836 to the VANGUARD 80, Capt. Hon. Duncombe Pleydell Bouverie, fitting at Portsmouth, he has not been since afloat.

Lieut. Hodder is at present Emigration Agent at Liverpool.

HODGE. (Commander, 1846. f-p., 33; h-p., 9.)

Stephen Hodge was born 12 Jan. 1792.

This officer entered the Navy, in 1805, as Fst.-cl. Vol., on board the AUTUMN sloop, Capt. Thos. Searle; and in the course of the same year he partook, as Midshipman, of an action with the Boulogne flotilla. He next joined the REGULUS 44, Capt. Chas. Worsley Boys, with whom he served, on the Home station, until April, 1806, when he was again placed under the orders of Capt. Searle, in the FURY bomb. On subsequently accompanying the same officer to the Mediterranean in the GRASSHOPPER, of 18 guns and 120 men, he shared, 11 Dec. 1807, in a gallant action with three Spanish vessels-of-war, carrying in the whole 30 guns and 226 men, the largest of which, the *San Josef*, of 12 24-pounders and 99 men, was in 15 minutes compelled to strike her colours. He was also, on 4 April, 1808, present, in company with the MERCURY frigate, in a successful attack made off the town of Rota upon a Spanish convoy passing alongshore under the protection of about 20 gun-boats, and a numerous train of flying artillery on the beach; on which occasion the GRASSHOPPER, who sustained very serious damage, actually silenced the batteries at the above place, and attracted general admiration by her noble conduct. Nineteen days after the latter event we find him participating in the capture, at the end of a severe action of two hours and a half, fought among shoals and within grape-shot distance of a battery, of two Spanish vessels laden with cargoes worth 30,000*l.* each, and further protected by four gun-boats, two of which were forced to surrender, and the remainder driven on shore. The collective loss of the GRASSHOPPER in the three engagements above recorded amounted to 1 man killed and 10 wounded. In Sept. 1809 (the GRASSHOPPER having been latterly commanded by Capt. Henry Fanshawe) Mr. Hodge rejoined Capt. Searle for a short time as Master's Mate on board the FREDERICKSTEIN 32. He next served for 18 months on the Channel station in the COQUETTE 18, Capts. Robt. Forbes and Geo. Hewson; and on then removing to the DRUID 32, Capts. Thos. Searle, Fras. Stanfell, and Wm. King (of which vessel he was created an Acting-Lieutenant 17 July, 1811), he was successively employed at the defence of Cadiz and Tarifa. On the night of 17 Sept. in the latter year he was severely wounded during a mutiny of his boat's crew in Cadiz Harbour, where he was stripped of his clothes, and thrown overboard in a state of insensibility. On recovering his senses in the water, he swam a distance of nearly four miles, and was ultimately picked up by some Spanish fishermen on the beach in a state of great exhaustion. He was confirmed in the rank of Lieutenant 16 Feb. 1813, and, leaving the DRUID in the ensuing July, was next appointed, 5 Oct. 1813, and 18 Oct. 1814, to the WOLVERENE and BITTERN sloops, Capts. Chas. Kerr and Geo. Augustus Hire, both in the Channel. After nearly six years of half-pay Mr. Hodge, on 3 Oct. 1821, obtained an appointment to the GENOA 74, Capt. Sir Thos. Livingstone; in command of a tender belonging to which ship it fell to his lot to form part of George IV.'s escort, on the occasion of His Majesty's visit to Ireland. Having been in the Coast Guard since 19 March, 1823, he was at length advanced to the rank of Commander 5 Jan. 1846. He has since been on half-pay.

Commander Hodge married, in June, 1821, Miss Trout, of East Looe, Cornwall, and by that lady has issue five children.

HODGKINSON. (Lieutenant, 1841.)

Thomas Hodgkinson entered the Navy 18 Dec. 1828; passed his examination in 1833; and obtained his commission 4 May, 1841. His appointments have since been—30 Aug. 1841, to the EXCELLENT gunnery-ship at Portsmouth, Capt. Sir Thos. Hastings—14 June, 1842, to the PIQUE 36, Capts. Henry Forbes and Hon. Montagu Stopford, in which frigate he served for two years on the North America and West India station—23 May, 1845, as Additional, to the CALEDONIA 120, Capt. Manley Hall Dixon, lying at Devonport—and, 29 Jan. 1847, as Senior, to his former ship, the EXCELLENT, Capt. Henry Ducie Chads, with whom he is now serving.
AGENTS—Messrs. Stilwell.

HODGSKIN. (Lieutenant, 1841. f-p., 13; h-p., 7.)

James Archibald Hodgskin is son of the late John Arundel Hodgskin, Esq., Lieutenant R.N. (1793.)

This officer entered the Navy, 3 Aug. 1827, as A.B., on board the ALBION 74, Capt. John Acworth Ommanney. After participating in the battle of Navarin, he joined, in March, 1828, the CHANTICLEER 2, Capt. Henry Foster, with whom he served, on a scientific mission, as Fst.-cl. Vol. and Midshipman, until Dec. 1829, when, being in the West Indies, his health obliged him to return to England. In April, 1831, he joined the DUBLIN 50, Capt. Lord Jas. Townshend, fitting for the South American station, whence he returned home in the capacity of Mate in Oct. 1834. Between Feb. 1835 and Oct. 1837, and again between April, 1838, and the date of his promotion to the rank of Lieutenant, 23 Nov. 1841, we find Mr. Hodgskin employed in the MEDEA steam-frigate, Capt. Horatio Thos. Austin, and ANDROMACHE 26, Capt. Robt. Lambert Baynes, on the Mediterranean, North America and West India, and Cape of Good Hope stations. His last appointments were, 28 March, 1843, and 8 Sept. 1846, to the CYCLOPS and DEVASTATION steamers, Capts. H. T. Austin and Sir C. Hotham, to which vessels, stationed off the coasts of Ireland and Africa, he was but for a very short time attached.

HODGSKIN. (RETIRED COMMANDER, 1846. F-P., 12; H-P., 35.)

THOMAS HODGSKIN entered the Navy, in March, 1800, as a Volunteer, on board the ACTIVE 38, Capts. Chas. Sydney Davers and Rich. Hussey Moubray, in which frigate he served for upwards of six years on the North Sea and Mediterranean stations. The next five years and a half were passed by this officer, as Lieutenant, in the STAR sloop, Capt. John Simpson, NYMPHE frigate, Capts. Edm. Heywood, Conway Shipley, and Hon. Josceline Percy, SATURN 74, Capt. Cumberland, NEMESIS 28, Capt. Wm. Ferris, and MENELAUS 38, Capt. Sir Peter Parker. While in the NYMPHE, besides attending the expedition of 1807 to Copenhagen, he took partial command of the boats of that frigate, and on the night of 23 April, 1808, participated in a valorous but unsuccessful attack made by Capt. Shipley (who was killed in the act of boarding) upon a French corvette, *La Gavotte*, of 22 guns and 150 men, lying at anchor in a bight above Belem Castle, in the river Tagus. In the same ship, under Capt. Percy, we find Mr. Hodgskin escorting General Junot to Rochelle, after the convention of Cintra. He subsequently, when in charge of the boats of the NEMESIS, in company with those of the BELVEDERA 36, contributed to the spirited capture, on the coast of Norway, of two Danish gun-vessels, the *Bolder* and *Thor* (carrying each 2 long 24's, 6 6-pounder howitzers, and 45 men), and the destruction of a third, 23 July, 1810.* If we mistake not, he was present in the MENELAUS, at the reduction of the Isle of France. He was placed on half-pay 25 April, 1812; and awarded the rank of Retired Commander 27 Jan. 1846.

HODGSON. (REAR-ADMIRAL OF THE RED, 1838. F-P., 27; H-P., 33.)

BRIAN HODGSON entered the Navy, in 1787, as Fst.-cl. Vol., on board the SALISBURY 50, Capt. Erasmus Gower, on the Newfoundland station, where he continued until 1789. From 13 Dec. 1794 until Oct. 1802 he served uninterruptedly with Capt. Edw. Jas. Foote in the NIGER 32, and SEAHORSE, of 46 guns and 292 men; in the former of which ships he assisted, as Midshipman and Master's Mate, at the capture of a French convoy, near Granville, 9 May, 1795—the destruction, 27 April, 1796, off the Penmarcks, of *L'Ecureuil* national corvette, of 18 guns and 105 men—and the battle off Cape St. Vincent 14 Feb. 1797. When in the SEAHORSE, of which frigate he was created a Lieutenant 11 Dec. 1799, Mr. Hodgson, besides witnessing the capture of *Le Belliqueux* privateer, of 18 guns and 120 men, was present, off the island of Pantellaria, at the taking, 27 June, 1798, after a close action of eight minutes, a loss to the British of 2 men killed and 16 wounded, and to the enemy of 18 killed and 37 wounded, of the French frigate *La Sensible*, of 36 guns and 300 men. In 1799, during the absence of Lord Nelson, we find the SEAHORSE blockading the Bay of Naples; and, in July of the same year, escorting their Sicilian Majesties from Palermo to the latter place. Being shortly afterwards driven on shore in a violent gale near Leghorn, she was under the necessity, from the injuries she received, of returning to England, whence, in May, 1800, she was again ordered to the Mediterranean with Rear-Admiral Sir Rich. Bickerton and Sir Ralph Abercromby on board. During the ensuing summer she was employed in attendance upon the King and Queen off Weymouth; after which she was sent in escort of 10 sail of Indiamen to Calcutta. While on the Indian station her officers and crew succeeded by great exertion in rescuing the stores of *La Sensible*, a frigate that had been wrecked a few miles to the southward of the Molliwally shoal. The SEAHORSE being paid off in Oct. 1802, Mr. Hodgson was next, in Jan. 1805, appointed to the TOPAZE 38, Capt. Willoughby Thos. Lake, on the Cork station, where he remained until appointed, in Jan. 1805, Flag-Lieutenant to Lord Gardner, in the HIBERNIA 110, part of the Channel fleet. He obtained his second promotal commission on 8 of the following April; and, on 22 Jan. 1806, after having commanded, for very short periods, the INSPECTOR and PYLADES sloops, he was made Post into the TRUSTY 50. In that ship, in Aug. 1807, he accompanied the expedition sent against Copenhagen. He left her in May, 1809, and was lastly, in April, 1810, and July, 1811, appointed to the command of the BARBADOES 24, and OWEN GLENDOWER 42, both on the East India station. The latter ship returned to England in May, 1816; and, on 28 June, 1838, her Captain was advanced to Flag-rank.

Rear-Admiral Hodgson, who has issue, was left a widower 11 Nov. 1824. AGENT—J. Hinxman.

HODGSON. (LIEUT., 1842. F-P., 14; H-P., 1.)

GEORGE HENRY HODGSON entered the Navy, 14 June, 1832, as Midshipman, on board the REVENGE 78, Capt. Donald Hugh Mackay, employed off Lisbon. In the summer of 1834 he proceeded to South America in the NORTH STAR 28, Capt. Octavius Vernon Harcourt. On his return to England, towards the close of 1836, he joined the DIDO 18, Capt. Lewis Davies, in which sloop, and in the PEMBROKE 74, Capt. Fairfax Moresby, we find him, until Feb. 1840, employed on the Mediterranean station—the last 16 months in the capacity of Mate. In Oct. 1840 he was appointed to the EXCELLENT gunnery-ship at Portsmouth, Capt. Sir Thos. Hastings; and in June, 1842, he sailed for China, on board the CORNWALLIS 72, bearing the flag of Sir Wm. Parker. Joining subsequently in the hostilities in progress against the Celestial empire, Mr. Hodgson participated in the attack on the enemy's entrenched camp on the heights of Segoan (where he displayed very spirited conduct and was slightly wounded in a personal encounter with a Chinese), and was present at the capture of Chapoo, Woosung, Shanghae, and Chin-Kiang-Foo, as also at the pacification of Nanking.* At Chin-Kiang-Foo, having landed, he distinguished himself by the manner in which, with three other officers, he rushed into the Imperial Canal for the purpose of ascertaining its fordability.† Being rewarded for his services with a commission bearing date 23 Dec. 1842,‡ and appointed to the WANDERER 16, Capt. Geo. Henry Seymour, he served in the boats of that sloop, in company with those of H.M.S. HARLEQUIN, and Hon. E. I. Co.'s steamer DIANA, in an attack upon some pirates at Murdoo, on the Pedir coast, 12 Feb. 1843. On 27 Nov. 1844, five months after he had returned to England, he obtained a re-appointment to the EXCELLENT. Since 4 March, 1845, he has been employed on board the TERROR discovery-ship, Capt. Fras. Rawdon Moira Crozier, in

* *Vide* Gaz. 1810, p. 1342.

* *Vide* Gaz. 1842, pp. 2386, 2390, 3400, 3405, 3694.
† *V.* Gaz. 1842, p. 3389. ‡ *V.* Gaz. 1842, p. 3821.

a renewed attempt to explore the N.W. passage through Lancaster Sound and Behring Strait.

HODGSON. (Retired Commander, 1843. f-p., 16; h-p., 48.)

James Hodgson was born 24 Oct. 1766.

This officer entered the Navy (into which he was impressed from the merchant-service), in 1783, on board the Mohawk sloop, Capts. R. Tripp and J. Sutton, from which ship, on her return from the West Indies, he was paid off. In Oct. 1793 he was again impressed, and placed on board the Bellona 74, Capts. Geo. Wilson and Thos. Boulden Thompson. Under the former of those officers we find him present, as Master's Mate, at the capture, in Jan. 1795, of *Le Duras*, a French ship of 20 guns, having on board 400 troops; and also of *Le Duquesne* frigate of 44 guns. In Feb. 1797 he further served with Capt. Wilson at the reduction of Trinidad by the forces under Rear-Admiral Harvey and Lieut.-General Sir Ralph Abercromby; and in the following April he was likewise with him in the unsuccessful attack made by those commanders on Puerto Rico. Obtaining, 11 April, 1799, a Lieutenancy in the Nereide 36, Capts. Fred. Watkins, Henry Wm. Bayntun, and Robt. Mends, he assisted in that frigate at the capture, 2 and 3 March, 1800, of *La Vengeance* privateer of 16 guns and 174 men, and of an American ship with a cargo on board worth 30,000*l*. In the next Sept. he was present in her at the surrender of Curaçoa, where the character he had won for zeal, bravery, and ever-steady conduct, so gained him the confidence of his Captain, that the latter was induced to place him in command of the principal fortress commanding the town. He had previously been of the utmost service in a newly-erected battery in annoying the enemy, and had been a principal cause of their retreat.* On 11 Aug. 1801, a few weeks after his junction of the Lowestoffe 32, Capt. Robt. Plampin, Mr. Hodgson had the misfortune to be wrecked on the island of Heneaga. His last appointment was, 15 May, 1804, to the Barryhead Signal station, in Ireland, the charge of which he retained until superseded, at his own request, 9 April, 1812. He accepted the rank of Retired Commander on the Senior List 8 May, 1843.

Commander Hodgson is married, and has issue.

HOFFMAN. (Retired Captain, 1840. f-p., 14; h-p., 40.)

Frederick Hoffman entered the Navy, 18 Oct. 1793, as Midshipman, on board the Blonde 32, Capt. John Markham, with whom, after co-operating in the reduction of the French West India islands, he removed, in 1794, to the Hannibal 74, commanded subsequently by Capts. Joseph Bingham, Lewis, and Edw. Tyrrell Smith. In that ship he was present with Capt. Markham at the capture, 11 April, 1795, of the French frigate *La Gentille* of 42 guns, and also of several privateers. In 1798 he joined the Queen 98, bearing the flag of Sir Hyde Parker, by whom, on 17 Oct. in the following year, he was appointed to a Lieutenancy in the Volage frigate, Capt. Fras. Vesey. At the peace of Amiens Mr. Hoffman, after many years of servitude in the West Indies, returned to England. His next appointments were—14 March, 1803, to the Minotaur 74, Capt. Chas. John Moore Mansfield, from which ship, employed off the coast of France and in the Channel, he soon invalided—28 Feb. 1805, to the Tonnant 80, Capt. Chas. Tyler, under whom he fought and was wounded at Trafalgar — and, 8 March, 1806, to the Diamond 38, Capt. Geo. Argles, employed off Havre de Grace and the coast of France. He was promoted, 22 Feb. 1808, to the command of the Favourite sloop, in which vessel, and in the Goelan, he again served on the West India station until the ensuing Oct. Capt. Hoffman's last appointment was, 19 Dec. 1810, to the Apelles, another sloop. In that vessel, at the commencement of May, 1812, he was unfortunately run on shore to the westward of Boulogne, where himself and 19 of his people were obliged to surrender as prisoners of war. The remainder of his officers and crew contrived to effect their escape. He accepted his present rank 12 Sept. 1840.

In consideration of the wound he received at Trafalgar, Capt. Hoffman was at the time presented with a gratuity by the Patriotic Society.

* *Vide* Gaz. 1800, p. 1331.

HOFFMEISTER. (Lieutenant, 1841. f-p., 18; h-p., 2.)

Charles John Hoffmeister was born 31 March, 1813, at Portsmouth.

This officer entered the Navy, 7 Nov. 1827, as Fst.-cl. Vol., on board the Victory 104, Capt. Hon. Geo. Elliot, bearing the flag at Portsmouth of Hon. Sir Robt. Stopford. In Feb. 1828 he became Midshipman of the Revenge 78, Capt. Norborne Thompson, on the Mediterranean station, where, until the close of 1833, he continued to serve, in the Actæon 26, Capt. Hon. Fred. Wm. Grey. He then joined the Belvidera 42, Capt. Chas. Borough Strong, fitting for the West Indies; on which station he removed, in Nov. 1834, a few months after he had passed his examination, to a Mateship in the Fly 18, Capt. Peter M'Quhae. Joining, next, in Nov. 1835, the Quail cutter, Lieut.-Commander Philip Bisson, he was Senior Mate of that vessel in April, 1836, when she was dismasted 50 leagues S.W. of Ushant, lost 17 of her men, and was reduced to so pitiable a condition, that nine days of the greatest privation and suffering elapsed before the surviving crew were enabled to get her into Jersey. Being appointed, soon after the catastrophe, to the Pembroke 74, Capt. Sir Thos. Fellowes, Mr. Hoffmeister served off Lisbon until Aug. 1837, when his health obliged him to invalid. While next borne on the books, from Oct. 1837 until June, 1839, of the Melville 74, bearing the flag of Hon. Geo. Elliot at the Cape of Good Hope, we find him lent in succession to various small vessels for service on the coast of Africa. During the 11 months immediately antecedent to his promotion to the rank of Lieutenant, which took place 23 Nov. 1841, Mr. Hoffmeister presents himself to our notice as employed, on the Home and Mediterranean stations, in the Impregnable 104, Capt. Thos. Forrest. He was then appointed to the Belleisle troop-ship, Capt. John Kingcome, and ordered to China, where he arrived in time to witness the storming of Chin-Kiang-Foo, and to participate in the different operations on the Yang-tse-Kiang, terminating with the pacification of Nanking. He returned to England, an invalid, in Oct. 1842; and, on 5 June, 1843, was appointed to the Excellent gunnery-ship at Portsmouth, Capt. Sir Thos. Hastings, with whom he served for a period of 19 months. He has been employed, since 13 Nov. 1844, latterly as First-Lieutenant, in the Amazon 19, Capt. Jas. John Stopford, part of the force stationed in the Mediterranean. Agents—Messrs. Stilwell.

HOGGE. (Lieutenant, 1841.)

Edward Martin Hogge entered the Navy 9 April, 1823; passed his examination 5 May, 1829; and, while serving, as Mate, in the Seaflower cutter, Lieut.-Commander Nicholas Robilliard, was promoted to the rank of Lieutenant 17 Aug. 1841. His succeeding appointments were—31 Aug. 1841, to the Belvidera 38, Capt. Hon. Geo. Grey, in the Mediterranean—14 Oct. 1842, to the Impregnable 104, Capt. Thos. Forrest, on the same station—29 March, 1843, to the Howe 120, also commanded by Capt. Forrest, with whom he returned to England —11 Aug. 1843, to the Coast Guard—and, 19 April, 1845, to the Rodney 92, Capt. Edw. Collier, on the Home station. He has been on half-pay since Sept. 1846.

Lieut. Hogge is married, and has issue.

HOGHTON. (Lieut., 1815. f-p., 11; h-p., 31.)

William Hoghton entered the Navy, 20 May, 1805, as Fst.-cl. Vol., on board the St. Albans 64,

Capt. John Temple, lying in the Downs, where, in the following Aug., he accompanied the same officer, as Midshipman, into the UTRECHT 64. He was afterwards employed for several years in the Mediterranean, on board the GLATTON 50, Capt. Thos. Seccombe, and SPIDER, Lieut.-Commander Wm. Olliver. With the latter and another officer he further served, from Dec. 1811 to Sept. 1812, in the MARSHAL 12, on the Channel station. He then sailed for the West Indies in the ISTER 36, commanded by the present Sir Josiah Coghill Coghill, and, until his return to England in the summer of 1815, was there employed, as Master's Mate and Acting-Lieutenant. On the paying off of the ISTER at the latter period, he took up a commission bearing date 24 Feb. 1815; but he has not been since afloat. AGENTS—Goode and Lawrence.

HOLBECH. (COMMANDER, 1830. F-P., 13; H-P., 28.)

GEORGE HOLBECH, born 24 Dec. 1793, is son of the late Wm. Holbech, Esq., of Mollington, M.P. for Banbury from 1792 to 1796, by Anne, daughter of Wm. Woodhouse, Esq., M.D., of Lichfield; and uncle of the present Sir John Mordaunt, Bart., M.P., of Walton, near Stratford-on-Avon. One of his brothers, Edward, is an officer in the Army.

This officer entered the Navy, 19 Aug. 1806, as Fst.-cl. Vol., on board the SPENCER 74, Captain (afterwards Rear-Admiral) Hon. Robt. Stopford. In Aug. 1807, on his return from the Cape of Good Hope, he accompanied the expedition to Copenhagen; and from Jan. 1809 (11 months previously to which period he had attained the rating of Midshipman) until Nov. of the same year we find him stationed off the north coast of Spain in the AMAZON 38, Capt. Wm. Parker. He then rejoined Rear-Admiral Stopford on board the SCIPION 74, and, continuing to serve with that officer for upwards of three years in the same ship, and in the LION 64, and PRESIDENT 38, was present with him, in the former, at the reduction of Java in 1811. From July, 1813, until Aug. 1814, he was further employed on board the STATELY 64, and RODNEY 74, bearing each the flag of Vice-Admiral Geo. Martin on the Lisbon station, where he was created a Lieutenant of the last-mentioned ship by commission dated 16 June, 1814. His succeeding appointments were—in Oct. 1814, to the CLORINDE 40, Capt. Sam. Geo. Pechell, fitting for the purpose of attending the Princess of Wales during her visit to the Mediterranean, whence he returned in July, 1816—and, 9 Nov. 1823, to the MENAI 26, Capt. Houston Stewart, with whom he served on the Halifax station until paid off, about Jan. 1827. He assumed his present rank 22 July, 1830, but has not been since afloat.

Commander Holbech married, 2 June, 1846, Ellen Catherine, eldest daughter of Chas. M. Ricketts, Esq., of Alverton, Stratford-on-Avon.

HOLBERTON. (LIEUTENANT, 1816.)

JOHN HOLBERTON entered the Navy, 16 Dec. 1809, as Fst.-cl. Vol., on board the IMPLACABLE 74, Capt. Thos. Byam Martin, lying at Plymouth. In Feb. 1810 he joined the SCIPION 74, bearing the flag of Hon. Robt. Stopford, with whom, after sharing in the reduction of Java, he removed as Midshipman, in Jan. 1812, to the LION 64. From 1813 to July, 1816, he was employed on board the AJAX 74, Capts. Robt. Waller Otway and Geo. Mundy; and he assisted, during that period, at the siege of St. Sebastian, also at the capture of *L'Alcyon* corvette, of 16 guns and 120 men, and in many active operations in the Mediterranean, where he visited Algiers, Tunis, and Tripoli, for the purpose of obtaining the liberation of the Christian slaves in bondage at those places. For his subsequent conduct at the battle of Algiers in the IMPREGNABLE 104, flag-ship of Rear-Admiral David Milne, Mr. Holberton was promoted to the rank of Lieutenant by commission dated 16 Sept. 1816; but, with the exception of some time passed in the Coast Blockade as a Supernumerary-Lieutenant of the RAMILLIES 74, Capt. Wm. M'Culloch, he has since been on half-pay.

HOLBROOK. (COMMANDER, 1842. F-P., 19; H-P., 22.)

CHARLES HOLBROOK, born in 1795, is brother of Commander Thos. Holbrook, R.N.

This officer entered the Navy, 18 Aug. 1806, as Midshipman, on board the VESTAL 28, Capt. Edwards Lloyd Graham, with whom, after witnessing the first trial made with the Congreve rockets against the Boulogne flotilla, and being very actively employed on the Home and Newfoundland stations, he removed, in May, 1810, to the PALLAS 32, commanded subsequently by Capt. Geo. Paris Monke. Previously, however, to joining that frigate we find him assisting, in particular, at the capture, 19 Nov. 1809, of *L'Intrépide*, French brig-of-war, pierced for 20 guns. He afterwards, during a cruize off the Naze of Norway, contributed, in the boats of the PALLAS, to the capture of four Danish privateers. Of one of these, which had offered a spirited resistance, Mr. Holbrook was constituted Prize-Master, and sent with her into Leith. On his passage he encountered a severe gale, and, as his vessel was *minus* an anchor, he found himself under the necessity, when in the Frith of Forth, of supplying its place with two of her guns. The PALLAS being wrecked off St. Abb's Head, 18 Dec. 1810, he was next, in Jan. and Feb. 1811, received on board the SOUTHAMPTON 32, and ALCMÈNE 38, commanded by his friend Capt. Graham. On arriving in the Adriatic Mr. Holbrook there saw much detached service; and on one occasion, 22 May, 1812, he was present in a most gallant but sanguinary attack made by four boats under Lieut. Edw. Saurin upon an enemy's convoy, the result of which was the capture of one of their principal vessels, after nearly the whole of the crew had been either killed or wounded. The slaughter on the part of the British was likewise dreadful—the pinnace alone sustaining a loss of at least 20 officers and men killed and wounded. Among the latter was Mr. Holbrook, who received a shot through the body, and suffered in consequence a protracted illness of four months. On being eventually transferred with Capt. Graham to the CALEDONIA 120, bearing the flag of Lord Exmouth, he shared in the partial action fought with the French fleet off Toulon 13 Feb. 1814; and during the ensuing siege of Genoa he was employed with a battering-party on shore. After serving for a few months at Plymouth on board the PRINCE FREDERICK receiving-ship, and MALTA 84, Capts. Rich. Pridham and Wm. Chas. Fahie, he was presented with a commission dated 16 Feb. 1815. In the summer of 1827 Lieut. Holbrook joined the BLONDE 46, Capt. Hon. Wm. Gordon, from which frigate, after cruizing for a short time in the Atlantic, he was transferred to the command of the COCKBURN schooner, bearing the broad pendant of Commodore Robt. Barrie on the Canadian Lakes, where he continued for the long period of seven years, during 18 months of which, owing to the absence of the latter officer in England, he had the supreme direction of naval affairs. He ultimately, in Sept. 1834, returned home, in consequence of the establishment on the lakes being broken up; but it was not until after a lapse of another seven years, namely, on 7 Feb. 1842, that he succeeded in obtaining the rank of Commander. During the three years immediately preceding that event he had been further employed on board the SAN JOSEF 110, bearing the flag of Rear-Admiral Fred. Warren, Admiral-Superintendent at Plymouth. In 1839, during the conflagration which broke out in the dockyard at that place, his exertions proved of pre-eminent utility—the preservation, indeed, of two line-of-battle ships, the MINDEN and CANOPUS, being alone attributable, as officially asserted, to the energetic conduct he displayed, and to the judgment with which he placed and used the engines of which he had charge. His promotion was at length conferred upon him in consideration of his having been in command of the state barge in which the King of Prussia embarked at Woolwich on the occasion of His Majesty's departure from England. He has since been on half-pay.

In reference to the wound Commander Holbrook received while belonging to the ALCMÈNE, it may be further remarked, as indicative of its severity, that the ball entered before the left shoulder, passing under the shoulder-blade and out at the spine, and injuring, in its course, the clavicle bone—that, four years afterwards, the wound broke out afresh, and many pieces of bone were extracted from it—that an extraneous substance, frequently productive of pain, has been, in consequence, deposited in his left breast—and that the free use of his left arm has been lastingly affected. Not only has he never received any pay or remuneration for his sufferings, but even was his application refused for the repayment of his surgical expenses. Commander Holbrook is married, and has numerous issue.

HOLBROOK. (LIEUT., 1815. F-P., 24; H-P., 24.)

JAMES HOLBROOK entered the Navy, 30 Oct. 1799, as Midshipman, on board the ABUNDANCE storeship, Master-Commander Wm. Price; and in June, 1801, on his return from the Cape of Good Hope, he removed to the UNICORN 32, Capts. Chas. Wemyss and Chas. Stuart, attached to the force on the Home station; where, between Jan. 1803 and May, 1805, we find him employed on board the ETHALION and MELAMPUS frigates, Capts. Chas. Stuart and Stephen Poyntz. In the course of the latter year he proceeded to the East Indies in the WOOLWICH 44, *armée-en-flûte*, Capt. Fras. Beaufort, with whom, we believe, he remained until April, 1807. From Nov. 1809, until Jan. 1813, he served on board the MAGNIFICENT 74, Capts. Geo. Eyre and Willoughby Thos. Lake, in the Mediterranean, and also on the north coast of Spain, where, in co-operation with the patriots, he assisted at the reduction of Castro, Puerta Galletta, Guetaria, St. Ano, &c. Until Sept. 1814, Mr. Holbrook was further occupied on the Channel station, in the WHITING schooner, Lieut.-Commander Geo. Hayes, and INSOLENT brig, Capts. Edw. Brazier and Wm. Kelly. He obtained his commission 15 Feb. 1815, but, with the exception of an appointment in the Coast Blockade, which he held as Supernumerary-Lieutenant of the HYPERION 42, Capt. Wm. Jas. Mingaye, from 4 Sept. 1826, until Aug. 1827, he was not again employed until 27 Jan. 1837; since which period he has been in charge of a station in the Coast Guard. AGENTS—Messrs. Chard.

HOLBROOK. (COMMANDER, 1828. F-P., 16; H-P., 25.)

THOMAS HOLBROOK, born in Dec. 1792, at Ledbury, co. Hereford, is son of Wm. Holbrook, Esq., a solicitor at that place; brother of Commander Thos. Holbrook, R.N.; and brother-in-law of Capt. J. W. Gabriel, R.N., K.H.

This officer entered the Navy, 24 Feb. 1806, as Fst.-cl. Vol., on board the OCEAN 98, Capt. Fras. Pender, in which ship, and the VILLE DE PARIS 110, bearing each the flag of Lord Collingwood, he served off Cadiz and in the Mediterranean, until April, 1809—the last 20 months in the capacity of Midshipman. After further attachment with Capt. John Rich. Lumley to the HIND frigate, he joined, in April, 1810, the POMONE 38, Capt. Robt. Barrie, under whom, until wrecked, on the Needles Point, 14 Oct. 1811, he cruized with activity, also on the Mediterranean station, where—besides assisting at the destruction of *L'Etourdie* national brig of 18 guns and 200 men, and being on many occasions employed in the boats—he participated, 1 May, 1811, in a gallant action of an hour and a half in Sagone Bay, in which the POMONE, in company with the UNITÉ 36, and SCOUT 18, accomplished the annihilation, with a loss to herself of 2 men killed and 19 wounded, of the two armed store-ships *Giraffe* and *Nourrice*, each mounting from 20 to 30 guns, and defended by a 5-gun battery, a martello tower, and a body of about 200 regular troops. Being appointed, soon after the loss of the POMONE, to the ALCMÈNE 38, Capt. Edwards Lloyd Graham, he proceeded in that ship to the Adriatic; on which station, in the course of 12 months, he came at least 10 times into conflict with the enemy, either in the boats or on shore. On 22 May, 1812, while the boats under Lieut. Saurin, as alluded to in our memoir of Commander Chas. Holbrook, went in pursuit of an armed convoy, the subject of the present narrative was left with the launch at a neighbouring island for the protection of some prizes already taken. Immediately on hearing the report of firing he hastened to the assistance of his friends, and was of great service in securing their dearly-purchased capture, in towing her during the night, and in attending to the wounded. On 23 Sept. 1812, a few months after he had been appointed Acting-Lieutenant of the ALCMÈNE, Mr. Holbrook was nominated to a death-vacancy in the EAGLE 74, Capt. Chas. Rowley. In the following April he obtained warm mention for his conduct in the boats of that ship and the ELIZABETH 74, at the capture of one and destruction of another of an armed convoy, who had run themselves on shore into a tremendous surf, under the protection of a galling fire from a 2-gun battery, two schooners, and three gun-boats, near Goro.* He also, on 8 June, 1813, contributed to the destruction, close to Omago, of a battery of 2 guns, and the bringing off of four scuttled vessels, loaded with wine; and he was next, between the latter period and May, 1814, present at the reduction of Fiumé, Trieste, Boca Ré, and nearly all the towns and forts on the coast of Istria, and at the mouths of the Po. During his continuance in the EAGLE, Mr. Holbrook was likewise concerned in the capture and destruction of about 150 sail of the enemy's vessels. His subsequent appointments were—25 July, 1814, to the WANDERER 20, Capts. Fras. Newcombe, John Palmer, and Wm. Dowers, with whom he served in the Channel until Dec. 1815—5 Sept. 1818, as Senior Lieutenant, to the FLY 18, Capts. Jas. Tomkinson and John Townsend Coffin, in which sloop he was employed for three years and a half on the West India and Irish stations, where he contributed to the capture of several contraband traders—and, 22 Aug. 1825, to the DRYAD 42, Capts. Hon. Robt. Rodney and Hon. Geo. Alfred Crofton. During the protracted illness of the former of those officers, he thrice had command of the DRYAD at sea; and on his demise he again had temporary charge of her on the western coast of Ireland. In Dec. 1827 we find him escorting Mr. Stratford Canning, H. M.'s Ambassador at Constantinople, from the Dardanells to Vorla, Corfu, and Ancona. He was promoted to the rank of Commander, on the representation made of his services by the last-mentioned personage, 6 May, 1828; but he has not been since employed.

Commander Holbrook was a student at the R. N. College, from the summer of 1829 until Dec. 1831. He married, in 1832, Mary, widow of the late Lieut. Wm. Stock, R.N. (1807).

HOLBURNE, Bart. (LIEUTENANT, 1813. F-P., 10; H-P., 32.)

SIR THOMAS WILLIAM HOLBURNE is only surviving son of the late Sir Fras. Holburne, Bart. (whom he succeeded as fifth Baronet 13 Sept. 1820), by Alicia, daughter of Thos. Brayne, Esq., of co. Warwick; grandson of Fras. Holburne, Esq., Admiral of the White, Rear-Admiral of Great Britain, Governor of Greenwich Hospital, and M.P. for Plymouth; and cousin of Sir Alex. Holburne, Bart., a Captain in the R.N., who died 22 Jan. 1772. His elder and only brother, Francis, an officer in the 3rd Foot Guards, died of a wound he received before Bayonne, 14 April, 1814.

This officer entered the Navy, in July, 1805, as Fst.-cl. Vol., on board the ORION 74, Capts. Edw. Codrington and Sir Archibald Collingwood Dick-

* *Vide* Gaz. 1813, p. 1793.

son, under the former of whom he fought at Trafalgar. In Feb. 1807, after having been for some time employed at the blockade of Toulon, he became Midshipman of the TONNANT 80, bearing the flag of Hon. Michael de Courcy; in which ship we find him, in 1808, accompanying Sir John Duckworth to the West Indies in pursuit of a French squadron from Rochefort; and, in Jan. 1809, assisting at the embarkation of the army after the battle of Corunna. Until Nov. 1812 he next presents himself to our notice as serving with Rear-Admiral De Courcy on the Brazilian station in the FOUDROYANT 80. He was made Lieutenant, 5 Feb. 1813, into the STROMBOLI bomb, Capts. John Stoddart and Rich. Croker, with whom he cruized in the Mediterranean until the autumn of 1814; and he was lastly, from April to Oct. 1815, employed in the Channel on board the EUPHRATES 36, Capt. Robt. Preston. AGENTS—Messrs. Stilwell.

HOLE. (REAR-ADMIRAL, 1846. F-P., 17; H-P., 37.)

LEWIS HOLE, born 16 Jan. 1779, at Strodeley, in Devonshire, is son of the late Rev. W. Hole, of Kuscott Hill, Surrogate of Barnstaple, by a lady descended from Sir John Berry, Knt., who was a Captain in the R.N. in 1665. He is brother of Capt. Henry Hole, R.M. (1812), who died in 1838; and of Commander Chas. Hole, R.N. (1812), a very excellent officer, who died 8 Sept. 1844, in his 64th year. One of his nephews, Wm. Hole, is a Lieutenant R.N.

This officer entered the Navy, at the commencement of 1793, as A.B., on board the SAMPSON 64, Capt. Geo. Montagu; and was soon afterwards ordered to Quebec in the SEVERN 44, Capt. Paul Minchin. Being next, on his return, appointed Midshipman of the BELLIQUEUX 64, Capt. Jas. Brine, he assisted in that ship at the capture of Port-au-Prince, 4 June, 1794; after which event, and until promoted to the rank of Lieutenant 6 July, 1798, he served on the Home station in the SANDWICH, Capt. Moss, CAMILLA 20, Capts. Dacres, Rotheram, and Poyntz, ASTRÆA frigate, Capt. R. Dacres, and KENT 74, Capt. Wm. Johnstone Hope. He was then employed for two years on board the EXPLOSION bomb, in the Channel; and at the expiration of that time he joined the RAMILLIES 74, Capts. Rich. Grindall, John Wm. Taylor Dixon, Sam. Osborn, and Henry Nicholls, bearing the flag for some time of Sir Chas. Morice Pole. Continuing in the latter ship until 1802, he accompanied the expedition sent in 1801 to act against the Northern Confederacy. Previously to the attack made upon the Danish line of defence before Copenhagen, he had the fortune to be placed in command of a division of boats attached to Lord Nelson's squadron; and on the memorable 2 April he served as a volunteer on board the POLYPHEMUS 64. Mr. Hole's next appointments were, 9 March, 1804, and 18 April, 1805, to the TRUSTY, 50, and REVENGE 74, Capts. Geo. Argles and Robt. Moorsom. In the former ship he cruized off Boulogne; and in the REVENGE he was fiercely engaged, as First-Lieutenant, at Trafalgar; for his conduct on which occasion he was promoted to the rank of Commander 24 Dec. 1805. The ships he last joined were—2 Dec. 1807, the HINDOSTAN 50, lying at Plymouth—10 March, 1808, the EGERIA, in which sloop he served on the Channel and Leith stations until Aug. 1812—and 21 April, 1813, the BACCHUS 16, on the coast of Ireland. While in the EGERIA, he captured the *Naesois* privateer, of 10 guns and 26 men, the *Aalborg* cutter, of 6 guns and 25 men, and the *Alvor* privateer, of 14 guns and 38 men. He became a Post-Captain 4 Dec. 1813; left the BACCHUS in the following Feb.; and assumed his present rank 1 Oct. 1846.

Rear-Admiral Hole married a daughter of the late Wm. Finch, Esq., Barrister-at-Law, and Master of the Grocers' Company, by whom he has issue

---

HOLE. (LIEUTENANT, 1815. F-P., 30; H-P., 12.)

WILLIAM HOLE, born 10 Nov. 1792, is only son of the late W. B. Hole, Esq., of the island of Jamaica; and nephew of Rear-Admiral Lewis Hole.

This officer entered the Navy, 5 Oct. 1805, as Fst.-cl. Vol., on board the STAR sloop, Capt. John Simpson; on accompanying whom, after an active servitude on the Lisbon, Channel, and Newfoundland stations, into the WOLVERENE 18, he co-operated as Midshipman in the reduction of Martinique in Feb. 1809. While next attached, between March in the latter year and June, 1811, to the BACCHUS schooner, Lieut. Commander Chas. Dayman Jermy, he commanded one of the boats of a squadron at the cutting-out, 12 Dec. 1809, of *Le Nisus*, a French 16-gun brig-corvette, lying, vigorously defended, under the protection of a fort in the harbour of Hayes, Guadeloupe—shared, also, in a gallant action, in which the BACCHUS, with a loss of 5 men badly wounded, beat off two French schooner-privateers—and contributed, in Feb. 1810, to the reduction of the island of Guadeloupe. He was likewise twice engaged with French row-boats who had designedly approached the BACCHUS; and was on more than one occasion invested with the navigation of prizes into port. In June, 1811, Mr. Hole, who had been for nearly two years in discharge of the duties of Acting-Master, was transferred, as Master's Mate, to the GANYMEDE 26, Capts. Robt. Preston and John Brett Purvis. During the two following years we find him employed both in the West Indies and Mediterranean; at the expiration of which period he assumed the charge of a watch on board the BACCHUS sloop, commanded by his uncle, Capt. Lewis Hole, on the Cork station. Being subsequently, in April, 1814, appointed to the TRAVE *armée-en-flûte*, Capts. Rowland Money and John Codd, he proceeded in that vessel to North America, where, after having commanded a boat at the destruction of Commodore Barney's flotilla up the Patuxent, he landed and served with the army in the attack upon Baltimore. On 14 Dec. 1814 he next commanded one of the boats of a squadron at the capture, on Lake Borgne, of five American gun-boats under Commodore Jones, which did not surrender until the British, after a stern conflict, had endured a loss of 17 men killed and 77 wounded. Joining then in the hostilities against New Orleans, he again had charge of a boat, an 8-oared cutter, on the river Mississippi, and bore an active part in all the scenes which were there enacted, including the storming and capture of a heavy battery. During six whole weeks he was in consequence exposed, in his unsheltered boat, to the inclemency of the season which then prevailed, undergoing the greatest hardships, and being often, with his men, severely frost-bitten. Having passed his examination in Sept. 1812, Mr. Hole was at length, on 3 Feb. 1815, rewarded with a Lieutenant's commission. Since 3 March, 1827, he has been continuously employed in the Coast Guard—a service in which his exertions have been of a very signal nature, as testified by numerous high testimonials from his superior officers, as well as by various letters of thanks addressed to him by Lloyd's for salvage of property in cases of shipwreck. He has been instrumental, we understand, in the conviction of an extraordinary number of smugglers.

Lieut. Hole married, 28 Oct. 1816, Eliza, daughter of the late Rich. Mallard Herbert, Esq., of co. Somerset, by whom he has issue a son and a daughter.

HOLLAND. (COMMANDER, 1840.)

EDWARD HOLLAND entered the Navy 31 Jan. 1814; passed his examination in 1820; and from 26 July, 1826, the date of his promotion to the rank of Lieutenant, until he invalided in Dec. 1830, was in successive command, on the West India station, of the MONKEY schooner, NIMBLE cutter, and UNION, MINX, and FIREFLY schooners. He became Flag-Lieutenant, 31 March, 1836, to Hon. Chas. Elphinstone Fleeming, on board the HOWE 120, at Sheerness; was transferred, 8 Oct. following, to the command, on particular service, of the SCORPION brig, in which vessel he remained for a period of three months; from 2 Aug. 1838 until the spring of 1840 commanded the DOLPHIN brigantine, of 36 guns, on the coast of Africa, whence he removed early in 1840; and on 3 of the next July was advanced to his present rank. He has been employed in the Coast Guard since 10 July, 1845. AGENTS—Hallett and Robinson.

HOLLAND. (COMMANDER, 1846.)

FREDERICK HOLLAND obtained his first commission 13 Aug. 1836; joined, on 24 Oct. following, the SATELLITE 18, Capt. John Robb, on the North America and West India station; and on 9 March, 1839, was there removed to the command of the PICKLE schooner. He was superseded from the latter vessel in Dec. 1840; and advanced to the rank he now holds 9 Nov. 1846. He is at present on half-pay.

Commander Holland married, first, 14 Sept. 1842, Susan, eldest daughter of Sam. Christian, Esq., of Malta; and (having been left a widower 11 July, 1844) secondly, 18 Aug. 1846, Anne, fifth daughter of Lord Denman, Chief Justice of the Court of Queen's Bench. AGENT—Joseph Woodhead.

HOLLINWORTH. (LIEUTENANT, 1843.)

HENRY AUGUSTUS HOLLINWORTH entered the Navy 14 Feb. 1834; passed his examination 15 July, 1840; served on board the THUNDERER 84, Capt. Maurice Frederick Fitzhardinge Berkeley, during the proximate operations on the coast of Syria, including the bombardment of St. Jean d'Acre; and on proceeding to China as Mate of the CORNWALLIS 72, flag-ship of Sir Wm. Parker, was there employed in 1842, at the capture of Chapoo, Woosung, and Chin-Kiang-Foo.* He acquired his present rank, on his return to England, 20 Sept. 1843; since which period his appointments have been—28 Dec. 1844, to the EXCELLENT gunnery-ship at Portsmouth, Capts. Sir Thos. Hastings and Henry Ducie Chads—and 29 Jan. 1847, as Additional, to the CALEDONIA 120, flag-ship of Sir John Louis, Admiral-Superintendent at Devonport.

HOLLINWORTH. (REAR-ADMIRAL, 1846. F-P., 15; H-P., 37.)

JOHN HOLLINWORTH is son of M. Hollinworth, Esq., many years a clerk of the Admiralty; and brother of Thos. Hollinworth, Esq., formerly Naval Storekeeper at Devonport.

This officer entered the Navy, in June, 1795, as Midshipman, on board the REPULSE 74, Capt. Wm. Geo. Fairfax, employed on the Home station, where he removed, in March, 1797, to the DÆDALUS 32, Capt. Hall. Towards the close of the same year he sailed for the Cape of Good Hope in the GARLAND 28, Capts. John Clarke Searle and Jas. Athol Wood; under the latter of whom he had the misfortune to be wrecked, while in pursuit of an enemy's vessel, off Madagascar, 26 July, 1798. On his return to England, in 1799, on board the SPHYNX 20, Capt. Lord Augustus Fitzroy, he became attached in succession to the TÉMÉRAIRE, BARFLEUR, and TÉMÉRAIRE again, 98's, in which ships we find him serving until May, 1800, in the Channel, under the flag of Rear-Admiral Jas. Hawkins Whitshed. Joining, then, the ENDYMION 40, Capt. Sir Thos. Williams, he proceeded to the Mediterranean, where—being appointed on his arrival Acting-Lieutenant of the VESTAL *armée-en-flûte*, Capt. Valentine Collard—he accompanied the expedition to Egypt in 1801. On 10 June, 1802, he was confirmed a Lieutenant in the CARRÈRE, Capt. Maitland. Between Feb. 1803 and April, 1806 (on 22 Jan. in which latter year he was promoted to the rank of Commander), he presents himself to our notice as next serving, in the Channel and West Indies, on board the VENERABLE 74, flag-ship of Rear-Admiral Cuthbert Collingwood, MERMAID 32, Capt. Aiskew Paffard Hollis, and HERCULE 74, bearing the flags of Sir John Duckworth and Rear-Admiral Jas. Rich. Dacres. His succeeding and last appointments were, on the Mediterranean station—25 March, 1807, to the MINSTREL 18, in which sloop he captured, 16 July, 1808, the Italian schooner *Ortenzia*, pierced for 16 guns, but carrying only 2 long 24-pounders, 6 long 9-pounder and 2 3-pounder swivels, with a complement of 56 men, who effected their escape*—and, 22 Nov. 1809, and 7 April and 12 July, 1810, to the Acting-Captaincy of the INVINCIBLE 74, and RESISTANCE and SALSETTE frigates. He returned to England soon after his official advancement to Post-rank, which took place 3 April, 1811; and on 1 Oct. 1846 he became a Rear-Admiral.

He married, in 1808, a daughter of John Jackson, Esq., Master-Attendant at Portsmouth; by whom he has, with other issue, a daughter, Marianne, who married, in 1844, a son of Colonel Shadforth. AGENTS—Messrs. Stilwell.

* *Vide* Gaz. 1842, pp. 3400, 3405, 3694.

* *Vide* Gaz. 1808, p. 1556.

HOLLINWORTH. (LIEUTENANT, 1837.)

JOHN HOLLINWORTH entered the Navy 21 Nov. 1818; obtained his commission 10 Jan. 1837; and from 4 of the following March until paid off in the summer of 1842 was employed, a great part of the time as First-Lieutenant, in the SAPPHO 16, Capts. Thos. Fraser and Edw. Iggulden Parrey, on the North America and West India station. He has not been since afloat. AGENTS—Messrs. Stilwell.

HOLLOWAY. (LIEUT., 1812. F-P., 9; H-P., 32.)

THOMAS HOLLOWAY entered the Navy, in Jan. 1806, as Fst.-cl. Vol., on board the UTRECHT 64, Capt. Thos. Seccombe. With that officer, after having served a few months in the Downs under the flag of Rear-Admiral John Holloway, he removed to the GLATTON 50, and proceeded to the Mediterranean, where, until the close of 1808, he was actively employed with Capt. Robt. Waller Otway on board the MONTAGU 74, and MALTA 84. During the next 12 months we find him serving, on the Downs and Newfoundland stations, in the ISIS 50, Capts. Laugharne and D. M'Leod, and ANTELOPE 50, flag-ship of Vice-Admiral Holloway. He then rejoined Capt. Otway in the AJAX 74, and on 20 July, 1810, was on board that ship in a very gallant skirmish, in which the British, with a slender force, beat back a powerful division of the French flotilla. After an attachment of some time to the CUMBERLAND 74, commanded on the Home station by Capt. Thos. Baker, Mr. Holloway was made Lieutenant, 10 March, 1812, into the FAME 74, Capt. Walter Bathurst, under whom he long co-operated with the patriots on the coast of Spain, and came into frequent contact with the French. Since he was paid off, in Oct. 1814, he has not been afloat.

HOLMAN, K.W., F.R.S. (LIEUTENANT, 1807.)

JAMES HOLMAN is brother of Capt. Wm. Holman, R.N.

This officer entered the Navy, 7 Dec. 1798, as Fst.-cl. Vol., on board the ROYAL GEORGE 100, Capt. Chas. Morice Pole, bearing the flag in the Channel of Lord Bridport; served, from Sept. 1799 until April, 1805, in the CAMBRIAN 40, Capts. Hon. Arthur Kaye Legge, Geo. Henry Towry, Wm. Bradley, and John Poo Beresford, on the Home and North American stations; then joined in succession the LEANDER 50, Capts. John Talbot and Henry Whitby, and CLEOPATRA 32, of which frigate, commanded by Capts. John Wight, Love, and Simpson, he was created a Lieutenant 27 April, 1807; and from Oct. 1808 to Nov. 1810, when he invalided, was employed in the GUERRIÈRE frigate, Capts. Alex. Skene, Robt. Lloyd, and Sam. John Pechell, stationed, as was also the CLEOPATRA, on the coast of North America. He has since been on half-pay.

Lieut. Holman (who is totally deprived of sight, and whose extensive peregrinations have procured him the title of the "Blind Traveller") has been a Naval Knight of Windsor since the commencement of the peace. He is the author of 'A Narrative of a Journey taken in the years 1819-20-21 through France, Italy, Savoy, &c.,' published in 1822; and also of 'A Voyage round the World, including Travels in Africa, Asia, Australia, and America,' published in 1834-5, in 4 volumes.

HOLMAN. (Lieut., 1810. f-p., 19; h-p., 28.)

Robert Holman is brother of Capt. Wm. Holman, R.N.

This officer entered the Navy, 1 Sept. 1800, as Fst.-cl. Vol., on board the Royal George 100, Capts. Wm. Domett and Robt. Waller Otway, bearing the flag for some time of Sir Hyde Parker in the Channel. On accompanying that Admiral, as Midshipman, in Feb. 1801, into the London 98, he witnessed the ensuing memorable conflict off Copenhagen; after which event he was for three years and a half employed with Capt. John Hancock on board the Cruizer sloop. He assisted, during that period, at the capture, 14 June, 1803, when in company with L'Immortalité 36, and Jalouse 18, of the French gun-brigs *L'Inabordable* and *La Commode*, after an hour's engagement with the batteries on the east side of Cape Grisnez; participated also in a skirmish fought by the Cruizer, in March, 1804, with 13 armed vessels full of troops, which had come out of Flushing apparently for the purpose of carrying her by boarding; and on 16 May, 1804, was present in a gallant action of six hours and a half with a division of the French flotilla, consisting of 59 sail, passing alongshore from Flushing to Ostend, whose fire occasioned the Cruizer a loss of 1 man killed and 4 wounded. He further shared, 23 Oct. following, in the Cruizer's close action with a praam, which was completely silenced in less than an hour and a half; and he contributed to the destruction, among other privateers, of a very notorious one, *Le Contre Amiral de Magon*, of 17 guns and 84 men, 17 Nov. 1804. On 22 July, 1805, having joined the Prince of Wales 98, we find Mr. Holman acting as Aide-de-camp to Sir Robt. Calder in his action with the combined squadrons off Cape Finisterre. He subsequently, in Jan. 1806, rejoined Capt. Otway on board the Montagu 74, in which ship, on his return from a visit to the West Indies, he proceeded to the Mediterranean; where, in Feb. 1808 (nearly 12 months after he had passed his examination), he served in the boats at the evacuation of Scylla, a fortified rock in the Faro of Messina, the garrison whereof was embarked under a heavy fire from the enemy on the Calabrian shore. While on the books of the Montagu, Mr. Holman succeeded on one occasion, when in charge of two boats, in cutting out, close in with the town of Reggio, a vessel laden with wine, in tow of a gun-boat. On being removed to the Canopus 80, bearing the flag of Rear-Admiral Geo. Martin, he had an opportunity, in 1809, besides witnessing the annihilation of a flotilla of gun-boats on the coast of Italy, of aiding in the capture of the islands of Ischia and Procida, and of joining in the pursuit which led to the self-destruction of the French ships of the line *Robuste* and *Lion*. From Nov. 1809 to July, 1812, he was employed as Acting-Lieutenant and Lieutenant (commission dated 11 Aug. 1810) in the Bombay 74, Capts. Wm. Cuming and Norborne Thompson. In the boats of that ship, which was stationed the whole time in the Mediterranean, Lieut. Holman, in the year 1811, had the fortune and gallantry, at noonday, to bring out several vessels laden with wine from under Fort Trinidad, in the Bay of Rosas. With the exception of a cruize, during the latter months of 1813, off Cherbourg, in the Eridanus 36, Capt. Henry Prescott, he was uninterruptedly employed at Plymouth, from Sept. 1812 until Nov. 1819, on board the Salvador del Mundo, Impregnable, St. George, Impregnable again, Berwick 74, and a third time in the Impregnable, under the flags of Sir Robt. Calder, Sir Wm. Domett, and Sir John Thos. Duckworth. In Oct. 1814, on the occasion of an official visit made by the Lords of the Admiralty to the above port, it was the honourable lot of Lieut. Holman, then in temporary command of the Impregnable, to hoist their Lordships' flag. He has been on half-pay since 1819.

In June, 1838, he was appointed Superintendent of the Plymouth Police—a post he still continues to fill. He married, 2 Nov. 1824, Mary, daughter of the late Wm. Holman, Esq., of Hayne House, co. Devon, and by that lady, who died 4 Nov. 1840, has issue six children. Agents—Case and Loudonsack.

HOLMAN. (Commander, 1841.)

Thomas Holloway Holman is first-cousin of Capt. Wm. Holman, R.N.

This officer entered the Navy, 3 Feb. 1804, as Midshipman, on board the Tisiphone sloop, Capt. Wm. Williams Foote, employed on the Home station; and on removing, in May, 1806, to the Theseus 74, Capts. Geo. Hope, Rich. Turner Hancock, and John Poo Beresford, was for some time employed at the Cape of Good Hope and on the coast of Spain. While afterwards attached, between May, 1808, and March, 1812, to the Egeria sloop, Capt. Lewis Hole, he served on the Channel and Leith stations, and assisted at the capture of three privateers, carrying altogether 30 guns and 89 men. Being then appointed Master's Mate of La Minerve frigate, Capt. Rich. Hawkins, we find him cruizing, during the next two years, in the West Indies and along the American shores. He then joined for a few months the Namur 74, bearing the flag of Sir Thos. Williams at the Nore; and between Aug. 1814 and his promotion to the rank of Lieutenant, 6 Feb. 1815, he served, in the Channel and among the Western Islands, on board the Leyden 64, *armée-en-flûte*, Capts. John Davie and Henry Bazely. On 9 April, 1832, having previously had charge of a station in the Coast Guard, Mr. Holman obtained command of the Harpy Revenue-vessel. He returned to the Coast Guard 30 June, 1834, and continued in that service until advanced to his present rank 15 Jan. 1841. Since 16 Feb. 1842 he has been again attached to it in the capacity of Inspecting-Commander.

HOLMAN. (Retired Captain, 1844.)

William Holman is brother of Lieuts. Jas. and Robt. Holman, R.N.; and first-cousin of Commander T. H. Holman, R.N.

This officer entered the Navy 30 Dec. 1790, and was Midshipman of the Royal George 100, flag-ship of Lord Bridport, in the action off Ile de Groix, 23 June, 1795. Having attained the rank of Lieutenant by commission dated 26 Sept. 1797, and been appointed to the Regulus 44, Capt. Geo. Eyre, we find him, in the course of that year, serving in the boats at the capture of several vessels from under the fort of Guadilla, on the island of Puerto Rico; and again, on 11 July, 1798, ably contributing to the cutting-out of three others, beneath an incessant fire from the batteries in Aguada Bay, on the same island.* When afterwards in the London 98, flag-ship of Sir Hyde Parker, Mr. Holman was present at the victory achieved off Copenhagen 2 April, 1801. He obtained his second promotal commission 20 Feb. 1812, and accepted the rank of Captain 26 March, 1844.

Capt. Holman is married and has issue. His second daughter, Emily, is married to J. Kersey, Esq., of the Madras Medical Service. Agents—Pettet and Newton.

HOLMES. (Lieutenant, 1841.)

Edward Holmes entered the Navy 20 Aug. 1826; passed his examination 28 Jan. 1833; and at the period of his promotion to the rank of Lieutenant, which took place 23 Nov. 1841, was serving on the North America and West India station as Mate of

* *Vide* Gaz. 1798, p. 947.

the RACEHORSE 18, Capt. John Coghlan Fitzgerald. His appointments have since been—26 Dec. 1841, again to the RACEHORSE, Capt. Edm. Peel—14 Sept. 1843 (after about 12 months of half-pay), as First, to the HYACINTH 18, Capt. Fras. Scott, fitting at Sheerness—19 Oct. 1843, and 14 June, 1844, to the WINCHESTER 50, flag-ship of Hon. Josceline Percy, and BITTERN 16, Capt. Edm. Peel, both at the Cape of Good Hope—and, 23 July, 1845, to the CALLIOPE 26, Capt. Edw. Stanley, with whom he is now serving in the East Indies. AGENTS—Messrs. Stilwell.

HOLT. (CAPTAIN, 1838. F-P., 18; H-P., 26.)

WILLIAM HOLT entered the Navy, 4 July, 1803, as a Volunteer, on board the SAN JOSEF 110, Capts. John Tremayne Rodd and Tristram Robt. Ricketts, bearing the flag of Sir Chas. Cotton off Brest. On removing, in Jan. 1806, to the MINERVA frigate, Capt. Geo. Ralph Collier, stationed off Cape Finisterre, he frequently distinguished himself in the boats against the enemy, particularly on one occasion, 3 Oct. 1806, when, led by Capt. Collier in person, they boarded and carried, after a row of seven hours, a Spanish gun-boat, mounting 1 long 24-pounder and 2 short brass 4's, with a complement of 30 men, besides soldiers, together with a launch armed with a brass 4-pounder.* In Aug. 1807, having followed the same Captain into the SURVEILLANTE 38, he accompanied the expedition against Copenhagen, during the bombardment of which city he was more than once intrusted with the command of a rocket-boat. On 7 Nov. 1810, after he had acted for some time as Lieutenant of the NAUTILUS sloop, Capt. Thos. Dench, and BARFLEUR and SAN JOSEF, flag-ships in the Tagus and Mediterranean of Hon. Geo. Cranfield Berkeley and Sir Chas. Cotton, we find him appointed First of the BLOSSOM sloop, Capt. Wm. Stewart. During an attachment of three years to that vessel, from which he was lent for a short period at the close of 1811 to the TÉMÉRAIRE 98, flag-ship of Admiral Fras. Pickmore at Port Mahon, Mr. Holt assisted at the capture of upwards of 20 French and American merchantmen in the neighbourhood of Marseilles, where he also came into frequent affray with the enemy's batteries and naval force. At the commencement of Sept. 1811 he served on shore at the reduction of a French fort on the smaller Medis Island, mounting 1 mortar, 2 long 18-pounders, and 2 sixes—an achievement performed in the presence of a formidable force assembled on Cape Begu, on the coast of Catalonia. He next, on 23 Feb. 1812, aided at the capture of a schooner privateer, *Le Jean Bart*, of 7 guns and 106 men; and, on 29 of the following April, he commanded the boats of the BLOSSOM, in conjunction with those of the UNDAUNTED and VOLONTAIRE frigates, in an attack upon 26 vessels near the mouth of the Rhone, 7 of which were brought out, and 12, including a national schooner of 4 guns and 74 men, left stranded on the beach. When subsequently in the SAN JOSEF, with Sir Rich. King, Mr. Holt presents himself to our notice as co-operating, in April, 1814, in the reduction of Genoa. On 18 July in the following year, having become First-Lieutenant of the FERRET sloop, Capt. Jas. Stirling, he served with the boats of that vessel and a squadron, and enacted a distinguished part, at the cutting-out of a convoy and several armed vessels lying under the protection of a fort at Corrijou, near Brest. On that occasion his exertions called forth the warmest approbation, especially the promptness he displayed in taking possession of a French man-of-war brig, and bringing her to an anchor when she attempted to run for the rocks. Equally conspicuous was his conduct in the following year, when the FERRET, with only 8 12-pounder carronades mounted, captured, after a running fight of two hours, and a loss of 3 men killed and 2 wounded, the American-built brigantine *Dolores*, having on board nearly 300 slaves, armed with 1 long 32-pounder on a pivot, 4 long 9-pounders, and 2 12-pounder carronades, a vessel by whom she had been at first attacked. Quitting the FERRET in June, 1816, Lieut. Holt next, on 2 April, 1823, joined the HUSSAR frigate, Capt. Geo. Harris, fitting for the West India station, where his gallantry and perseverance in exterminating (during 67 days of absence from the ship in open boats) a horde of pirates who had taken possession of the Isle of Pines procured him the rank of Commander by commission dated 20 Aug. 1824. His succeeding and last appointments were, on the Mediterranean station—21 July, 1834, to the SCOUT 18, which sloop he paid off 8 Oct. 1835—and, 22 March, 1836, to the Second-Captaincy of the ASIA 84, Capt. Wm. Fisher. He continued in the latter ship until advanced to his present rank 28 June, 1838.

Capt. Holt, who has several children, was left a widower in 1839.

* *Vide* Gaz. 1806, p. 1379.

HOME, Bart., C.B., F.R.S. (CAPTAIN, 1837.)

SIR JAMES EVERARD HOME, born 25 Oct. 1798, in London, is son of the late Sir Everard Home, Bart., F.R.S., Sergeant-Surgeon to the King, and Physician to the Royal Hospital at Chelsea, by Jane, daughter and heiress of Jas. Tunstall, Esq., D.D., and widow of Stephen Thompson, Esq.; nephew of Capt. Wm. Home, E.I.C.S., and of John Hunter, Esq., Surgeon-General to the Army; and brother-in-law of Capt. Henry Forbes, R.N., and of the late Capt. Bernard Yeoman, R.N. He succeeded his father, as second Baronet, 31 Aug. 1832.

This officer entered the Navy, 10 April, 1810, as Midshipman, on board the EURYALUS frigate, Capt. Hon. Geo. Heneage Lawrence Dundas. Proceeding in that ship to the Mediterranean, he there joined, in Aug. 1812, the MALTA 80, bearing the flag of Sir Benj. Hallowell, with whom, subsequently to the peace, he served at Cork on board the TONNANT 80. On his ultimate arrival in the West Indies in the SYBILLE frigate, bearing the flag of Sir Home Popham, he was promoted, 14 July, 1814, to a Lieutenancy in the LARNE 20, Capt. Abraham Lowe, and next appointed to the PIQUE 36, Capt. John Mackellar. After a further servitude of eight months on the Home station in the HELICON 10, Capt. Wm. Robt. Dawkins, he succeeded in obtaining a second promotal commission, dated 28 Jan. 1822, but he did not again go afloat until Feb. 1834, on 1 of which month we find him assuming command of the RACEHORSE 18, fitting for the West Indies.* He acquired his present rank soon after he had been paid off, 5 Dec. 1837; and he was lastly, from 30 Aug. 1841, until the summer of 1846, employed in the East Indies on board the NORTH STAR 26. During the period he commanded the latter ship Sir Jas. Everard Home contributed to the capture of Woosung and Shanghae, and participated in the operations on the Yang-tse-Kiang†—services for which he was nominated a C.B. 24 Dec. 1842. In Dec. 1845, when Senior Naval Officer at New Zealand, he originated the instructions which were afterwards adopted by Capt. Chas. Graham, during whose siege of Kawiti's stronghold, as detailed in our memoir of that officer, he was intrusted with, and behaved with unwearied zeal, exertion, and attention at, the defence of a pah situated at the point of debarkation, six miles up the river and 12 from the pah destroyed.‡

Sir J. E. Home was elected a F.R.S. in 1825.

HONYMAN. (ADMIRAL OF THE BLUE, 1847. F-P., 29; H-P., 36.)

ROBERT HONYMAN is son of the late Patrick Honyman, Esq. (a descendant of Robert, first Earl of Orkney, natural son of James V. of Scotland), by his second wife, Margaret, daughter of Patrick Sinclair, Esq., of Durwin; half-brother of the late Lord Armadale, one of the Lords of Session, and Justiciary in the Supreme Courts of Scotland; and

* The RACEHORSE took an active part in the siege of Paria in 1835, and was for several days in contest with the batteries, in company with a Brazilian squadron.

† *Vide* Gaz. 1842, pp. 3391, 3404.

‡ *V.* Gaz. 1846, pp. 2345, 2317.

uncle of the present Sir Ord Honyman, Bart., Lieut.-Colonel of the Grenadier Guards, who married a daughter of Admiral Geo. Bowen, of Coton Hall, Salop.

This officer entered the Navy, 20 April, 1782, as Captain's Servant, on board the QUEEN, Capt. Patrick Sinclair, stationed in the North Sea, where he removed, with the same Captain, to the TERMAGANT sloop. In Sept. 1783, after he had served for six months with Capt. Benj. Archer in the UNICORN 32, he rejoined him as Midshipman on board the HYÆNA 24, on the Irish station; and he was next, from Oct. 1785 until promoted to the rank of Lieutenant 21 Oct. 1790, employed, chiefly at home, in the POWERFUL 74, Capt. Andrew Sutherland, LOWESTOFFE frigate, Capt. Edm. Dod, ORION 74, Capts. A. Sutherland and Chas. Chamberlayne, IPHIGENIA frigate, Capt. P. Sinclair, and REGULUS 44, Capt. Wm. Mitchell. On the renewal of hostilities in 1793 he obtained an appointment to the DIADEM 64, Capts. A. Sutherland and Wm. Smith, and sailed for the Mediterranean, where, after witnessing the occupation of Toulon, he removed in succession to the BERWICK 74, Capts. A. Sutherland and Wm. Smith, and ST. GEORGE 98, flag-ship of Sir Hyde Parker, under whom he was wounded in Hotham's first partial action, 14 March, 1795.* Being awarded (while serving in the Channel on board the DEFIANCE 74, Capt. Theophilus Jones) a second promotal commission 13 Aug. 1796, Capt. Honyman, on 4 May, 1797, assumed command of the TISIPHONE sloop, in which, in the course of the same year, he captured the French privateers *Le Prospère*, of 14 guns and 73 men, and *Le Cerf Volant*, of 14 guns, 6 swivels, and 63 men. He attained Post-rank in the DORTRECHT, on the Home station, 10 Dec. 1798, and was subsequently appointed—16 Oct. 1800, to the GARLAND 28, in which ship he conveyed Rear-Admiral Robt. Montagu to Jamaica—19 Oct. 1801, to the TOPAZE frigate, employed on the latter station, whence he returned towards the close of 1802—21 Dec. 1802, to the LEDA 38—14 March, 1809, to the ARDENT 64, attached to the force in the Baltic, on which station he continued until April, 1812—1 Jan. and 28 June, 1813, to the SCEPTRE and MARLBOROUGH 74's, both in North America—and, 11 June, 1814, to the office of Regulating Captain at Portsmouth. When in the LEDA, at the commencement of the late war, we find Capt. Honyman stationed on the coast of France, with a small squadron under his orders, for the purpose of obstructing the progress of the enemy's flotilla from the eastward towards Boulogne. On 29 Sept. 1803 part of his force attacked a division of gun-boats, and drove two on shore, where they were bilged; and on 24 April, 1805, having discovered 26 of the enemy's vessels rounding Cape Grisnez, he succeeded, during an engagement of about two hours, in cutting off seven schuyts, carrying altogether 18 guns, 1 howitzer, and 168 men, from Dunkerque, bound to Ambleteuse.† The LEDA afterwards assisted in a conspicuous manner at the reduction of the Cape of Good Hope in Jan. 1806 ‡—was present at the capture, 21 Feb. and 4 March following, of the *Rolla* brig and *Volontaire* frigate in Table Bay—took an active and zealous share, on accompanying Sir Home Popham to the Rio de la Plata, in all the operations which preceded the evacuation of Spanish America in 1807 §—formed part of the ensuing expedition to Copenhagen—effected the capture, 4 Dec. 1807, of *L'Adolphe* privateer, of 18 guns and 70 men—and was finally wrecked, near the entrance of Milford Haven, 31 Jan. 1808. The subject of the present narrative, whom a court-martial acquitted of all blame in the catastrophe, and who has been unemployed since Jan. 1816, became a Rear-Admiral 27 May, 1825, a Vice-Admiral 10 Jan. 1837, and a full Admiral 19 Feb. 1847.

Admiral Honyman was elected M.P. in 1802 for the shires of Orkney and Shetland. He is married.

---

* *Vide* Gaz. 1795, p. 306. † *V.* Gaz. 1805, p. 554.
‡ *V.* Gaz. 1806, p. 258.
§ *V.* Gaz. 1807, pp. 112, 113, 126.

HOOD. (LIEUTENANT, 1846.)

ARTHUR WILLIAM ACLAND HOOD, born 14 July, 1824, is second son of Sir Alex. Hood, Bart., of Tidlake, co. Surrey, by Amelia Anne, youngest daughter and co-heir of Sir Hugh Bateman, Bart., of Hartington Hall, co. Derby; grandson of the gallant Capt. Alex. Hood, R.N., who accompanied Capt. Cook in one of his voyages round the world, and, after much distinguished service, fell in command of the MARS 74, during a tremendous yard-arm-and-yard-arm conflict which preceded the surrender to the latter ship of the French 74 *L'Hercule*, 21 April, 1798; and grand-nephew of that excellent officer, the late Vice-Admiral Sir Sam. Hood, K.B., K.F.M.* His elder and only brother, Alex. Bateman Periam Hood, is a Lieutenant in the Royal Horse Guards.

This officer passed his examination 2 Aug. 1843; and, after serving for nearly two years, as Mate, in the EXCELLENT gunnery-ship, at Portsmouth, Capt. Sir Thos. Hastings, and for a short time in the PRESIDENT 50, fitting for the flag of Rear-Admiral Jas. Rich. Dacres, was promoted to the rank he now holds 9 Jan. 1846. He was then re-appointed to the PRESIDENT, in the capacity of Additional-Lieutenant, and is at present serving in her at the Cape of Good Hope.

HOOD. (COMMANDER, 1815. F-P., 15; H-P., 32.)

SILAS THOMSON HOOD, born in 1789, at Devonport, is elder and only brother of Captain W. J. T. Hood, R.N.

This officer entered the Navy, 1 May, 1800, as Fst.-cl. Vol., on board LA SUFFISANTE 14, Capts. Joseph Whitman, Jonas Rose, and Christopher John Williams Nesham, attached to the force in the Channel, where he served until Aug. 1802, and assisted at the capture of several privateers and merchantmen. In March, 1803, he re-embarked on board the PLANTAGENET 74, Capts. Graham Eden Hamond, Hon. Michael de Courcy, Fras. Pender, and Wm. Bradley, in which ship he was for five years actively employed on the Channel, St. Helena, and Lisbon stations, chiefly as Midshipman and Master's Mate. Being then, in March, 1808, ap-

* Sir Samuel Hood was born in 1762, and entered the Navy at the age of 14, on board the COURAGEUX 74, commanded by his father's first-cousin, the first Viscount Hood. He commanded the RENARD sloop on the glorious 12 April, 1782; and in 1784 he was advanced, for his services, to Post-rank. In Dec. 1793, being then in the JUNO frigate, he entered Toulon, unapprized of its evacuation, but succeeded, with consummate skill and presence of mind, in effecting his escape. He was next employed at the reduction of Corsica, and in command of a small squadron in the Archipelago. As Captain of the ZEALOUS 74, he accompanied Nelson to Teneriffe in 1797, and fought with him at the Nile, where he captured *Le Guerrier* 74, and, until called off by signal, was singly in combat with four French ships. His valour on the occasion procured him the thanks of Parliament, and a sword from the City of London. In 1799 his conduct in expelling the French from Naples was acknowledged with the order of St. Ferdinand and Merit from the King of the Two Sicilies. He subsequently commanded the COURAGEUX 74, in Sir John Borlase Warren's expedition to Ferrol; enacted a conspicuous part in the VENERABLE 74, in Sir James Saumarez' actions of 6 and 12 July, 1801, off Algeciras and in the Gut of Gibraltar; and in 1803, on being appointed Commodore of the West India squadron, with his broad pendant in the CENTAUR 74, won the distinction of a K.B. for his capture of the Dutch settlements of Demerara, Essequibo, and Berbice. In Sept. 1806, being still in the CENTAUR, and in command of a squadron off Rochefort, Sir Samuel Hood made prize of four heavy French frigates. Having on that occasion lost his right arm, he was awarded, in consideration of the wound and of his numerous services, a pension of 500*l.* In 1807 he was elected M.P. for Westminster, and in the ensuing Oct., on his return with Lord Gambier from Copenhagen, he was promoted to Flag-rank. In Dec. of the same year we find him obtaining possession, with Major-General Beresford, of the island of Madeira; and next, when in company with the IMPLACABLE 74, effecting the destruction, in Aug. 1808, of the 74-gun ship *Sewolod*, after a close and furious conflict fought in sight of the whole Russian fleet near Rogerswick. In 1809 he received the thanks of Parliament for his services at Corunna. He was created a Baronet on 13 of the following April; and on 24 Dec. 1814, a few months after his assumption of the rank of Vice-Admiral, died, on the East India station, where he had been appointed Commander-in-Chief.

pointed Sub-Lieutenant of the CONFLICT 12, Lieut.-Commander Joseph B. Batt, he witnessed Lord Cochrane's destruction of the French shipping in Basque Roads in April, 1809; and on one occasion, when in command of a single boat belonging to that vessel, had the good fortune and gallantry to effect the capture, during a heavy gale of wind, of *La Grande Décidée* letter-of-marque, armed with 1 long 18-pounder and 2 nines, and having on board a crew of 45 men. As a reward for this service, as also for the conduct he displayed in cutting out two sloops laden with naval stores from under the battery of St. Nicholas, near Sable d'Olonne, Mr. Hood was appointed, 28 July, 1809, Acting-Lieutenant of the DREADNOUGHT 98, to which ship, bearing the flag in the Channel of Rear-Admiral Thos. Sotheby, he was confirmed by commission dated on 19 of the next Dec. During his continuance in her we find him, on the night of 8 Sept. 1810, commanding one of her boats, under Lieut. Robt. Pettman, at the re-capture of the *Maria Antonia* Spanish merchantman among the rocks on the west side of Ushant, a desperate exploit, which was not achieved without a loss to the British of 6 men killed, 31 wounded, and 6 missing. The behaviour manifested in this affair by Mr. Hood led to his being appointed, in Dec. 1811 (after many months of servitude in the VALIANT 74, Capt. Robt. Dudley Oliver), Second-Lieutenant of the BACCHANTE 38, Capts. Wm. Hoste and Fras. Stanfell. On 18 Sept. 1812, the BACCHANTE having chased a convoy of 18 sail between the islands of Tremiti and Vasto, he was sent with her boats, six in number, containing 72 officers and men, the whole under the orders of Lieut. Donat Henchy O'Brien (whom he most ably seconded), to assist in bringing them out.* Although the merchantmen had been hauled on shore, and lay under the protection of eight armed vessels, carrying in all 8 long 12-pounders, 6 swivels, and 104 men, yet were they unable to withstand the impetuosity of the valiant seamen, who, rushing like lions to the attack, pushed through a heavy fire of grape and musketry, and boarded and carried each opponent, driving the crews over the sides in every direction; while the marines, under Lieut. Wm. Haig, landing, forced the fugitives from a neighbouring wood, where they would have had complete command of the coast, and thereby secured possession of the whole of the convoy and armed vessels. On 6 Jan. 1813 he was further present in the boats with Lieut. O'Brien at the capture of five gun-vessels near Otranto;† and, on the consequent promotion of that officer, he became the BACCHANTE's First-Lieutenant. On 14 of the following month we find him receiving a severe contusion, by a fall, while commanding the barge of the same ship, at the capture of *L'Alcinous*, a national vessel mounting 2 long 24-pounders, with a complement of 45 men—his own party not consisting of more than 23. The injuries he then received were so severe as to result in the loss of the use of both his legs, for which, in 1815, he was granted a pension of 200*l.* On 15 May, 1813, having somewhat recovered, Lieut. Hood was enabled to land with a detachment of seamen, and blow up the castle of Karlebago, whence, after destroying all the public works, he brought off 2 12-pounders, 4 nines, and 2 brass sixes.‡ His next achievement was the capture, 12 June, 1813, from under the town of Gela Nova, on the coast of Abruzzo, of seven large gun-boats, mounting each 1 long 18-pounder in the bow, three smaller gun-vessels, with a 4-pounder in the bow, and 14 sail of merchantmen, four of which also had guns in the bow. The British, as they advanced, were exposed to a heavy fire of grape and musketry; and it was not until they were fairly alongside the gun-boats that the crews of the latter slackened their fire: they were then driven from their vessels with great loss. The shore astern of the assailed was at the commencement lined with 100 troops, who, however, fled on the first fire, leaving behind them two field-pieces, which were destroyed by the marines under Lieut. Haig. In performing this brilliant exploit the boats of the BACCHANTE sustained a loss of 2 seamen and 1 marine killed, and 5 seamen and 1 marine wounded.* The gallant conductor of the enterprise was justly recommended by Capt. Hoste in the strongest manner to the notice of the Commander-in-Chief. After witnessing the reduction, in the early part of 1814, of the fortress of Cattaro and the town of Ragusa, he proceeded to North America, where he served at the capture of Castine, Belfast, and Machias. He was at length made Commander, 27 April, 1815, into the PORTIA 14, in which vessel he was employed, chiefly off Bermuda, until April, 1816, when he invalided. He has since been on half-pay.

In reviewing Commander Hood's services in the BACCHANTE, it may be observed that, in the space of two years, he assisted in making at least 1000 prisoners, and in capturing 27 national gun-vessels, 87 sail of merchantmen, and one privateer. He married, in Feb. 1822, Catharine, eldest daughter of the late Rev. Wm. Hamilton, D.D., Rector of Clondavadog, co. Donegal, and a Magistrate, who lost his life in the service of his country in 1797.

* *Vide* Gaz. 1813, p. 164. † *V.* Gaz. 1813, p. 626. ‡ *V.* Gaz. 1813, p. 1793.

* *Vide* Gaz. 1813, p. 1795.

HOOD. (LIEUTENANT, 1846.)

WILLIAM HENRY HOOD passed his examination 27 Feb. 1840; and, after officiating for some time as Mate of the VULCAN Revenue-steamer and SEA-FLOWER cutter, Lieut.-Commanders Wm. Crispin and Nicholas Robilliard, was appointed to a station in the Coast Guard 28 Feb. 1842. He left that service, on advancement to his present rank, 21 May, 1846; and, since 17 of the following June, has been employed on the coast of Africa in the CONTEST 12, Lieut.-Commander Arch. M'Murdo.

HOOD. (CAPTAIN, 1843.)

WILLIAM JOHN THOMPSON HOOD was born 6 Nov. 1794. He is younger brother of Commander S. T. Hood, R.N.

This officer entered the Navy 16 April, 1805. He served on board the ACHILLE 74, Capt. Rich. King, at the battle of Trafalgar; was in the DAPHNE 20, Capt. Fras. Mason, at the capture of Monte Video in Feb. 1807, and during the operations on the Rio de la Plata; assisted, when in the PLOVER and SHELDRAKE sloops, at the capture of several privateers, and the blockade of the French and Danish coasts; and, on being appointed Master's Mate of the MALTA 80, bearing the flag of Rear-Admiral Benj. Hallowell, commanded the Spanish gun-boat No. 5, in co-operation, during the latter part of the war, with the patriots on the north coast of Spain. Being advanced to the rank of Lieutenant 25 Feb. 1815 (nearly two years after he had passed his examination), he was successively appointed Senior—24 May, 1821, of the HELICON 10, Capt. Wm. Robt. Dawkins, stationed in the Channel—and, 24 July and 24 Dec. 1824, of the ROMNEY and HYPERION Coast Blockade ships, both commanded by Capt. Wm. Jas. Mingaye. He was promoted to the rank of Commander in the HYPERION, 9 Jan. 1828, and continued on the books of that frigate until paid off in Dec. 1829. His next and last appointment was, 27 April, 1842, to the CALEDONIA 120, flag-ship of Sir David Milne at Plymouth, where he remained until advanced to his present rank 25 Sept. 1843.

Independently of the thanks of the Board of Longitude, Capt. Hood, on 26 May, 1824, received from the Society for the Encouragement of Arts, &c., its gold Vulcan medal for his improved screen-glasses for quadrants and sextants for naval use. He has also been voted the silver medal of the same body for his invention of an ice-saw, for facilitating the progress or escape of ships navigating the high Polar latitudes, when surrounded by field-ice. In 1828 he obtained a similar honorary reward for his method of constructing a floating bridge, from the materials to be found on board all ships of war and vessels generally. In 1830 he again received the Society's medal for his invention of an improved rocket-shaft. Capt. Hood has also invented a rotatory lifting and forcing pump. He married, 16 Dec. 1830, Sophia Janet, second daughter of the late Robt. Henderson, Esq., Physician and Inspector of the Forces. AGENTS—Messrs. Stilwell.

HOOKEY. (LIEUT., 1828. F-P., 17; H-P., 16.)

JAMES HOOKEY, born 31 Dec. 1798, at Portsea, is son of Wm. Hookey, Esq., late Timber Master of H.M. Dockyard at Deptford.

This officer entered the Navy, 17 Feb. 1814, as Fst.-cl. Vol., on board the NEWCASTLE 60, Capts. Lord Geo. Stuart, Sam. Roberts, and Henry Meynell, in which ship we find him employed, on the North America and West India stations, half the time as Midshipman, until Jan. 1816. From the following Aug. until Sept. 1817 he served on Lake Erie in the CONFIANCE, Capt. Dan. Pring. He was next, during the summer-months of 1818, engaged on Home duty, in the WEYMOUTH 12, Master-Commander Turner; after which he was borne, between May, 1819, and Jan. 1823, on the books of the SWAN 6, Lieut.-Commanders Thos. Dilnot Stewart and Benj. Aplin. In 1822 he elicited the thanks of Capt. John Toup Nicolas, the Senior officer, and of the Mayor of Newcastle-upon-Tyne, for his conduct in command of the boats of that vessel during a severe dispute which had there broken out between the keelmen and the shipmasters and shipowners. After a servitude of three years on the Home and Mediterranean stations on board the TRIBUNE 42, Capt. Gardiner Henry Guion, Mr. Hookey, in Feb. 1826, joined the PRINCE REGENT 120, bearing the flag at the Nore of Sir Robt. Moorsom. Early in the following year he became Admiralty Midshipman of the BARHAM 50, bearing the flag of Hon. Chas. Elphinstone Fleeming in the West Indies, where (having passed his examination in March, 1822) he was constituted, 14 Sept. 1828, First-Lieutenant of the SLANEY 20, Capt. Joseph O'Brien. He invalided home in May, 1829, but, returning to the same station in the next Dec., was further appointed to the MAGNIFICENT receiving-ship at Port Royal, Jamaica, Capts. Smith and Gill. On 21 March, 1831, he was transferred to the command of the KANGAROO schooner. He came home and was paid off in Aug. 1833, and has not been since afloat.

Lieut. Hookey was presented, in 1827, by the "Society for the Encouragement of Arts, &c.," with a large silver medal for his invention of an improved log-ship. He married, 15 Jan. 1839, Mary, third daughter of John M'Coy, Esq., of the Royal Artillery, and sister of Capt. John M'Coy, of the same corps. AGENTS—Pettet and Newton.

HOOPER. (LIEUT., 1809. F-P., 37; H-P., 12.)

BENJAMIN HOOPER was born 18 Feb. 1789, at Torpoint, co. Cornwall.

This officer entered the Navy, in May, 1798, as Fst.-cl. Vol., on board the FOUDROYANT 80, Capt. Sir Thos. Byard. In that ship, after witnessing the capture, in the following Oct., of a French squadron under Commodore Bompart, destined for the invasion of Ireland, he sailed with the flag of Lord Keith for the Mediterranean; where, on Lord Nelson shifting his flag to the FOUDROYANT, he was employed in affording escort to King Ferdinand and the Neapolitan Court; and, in particular, in personally ministering, with Messrs. Walpole and Smith, Midshipmen, to the entertainment of the young princes on board. Continuing attached to the same ship under Sir Edw. Berry, Mr. Hooper, while at the blockade of Malta, assisted, as Midshipman, at the capture, on 18 Feb. 1800, of *Le Généreux* 74, and *Ville de Marseilles* armed store-ship, and on 31 March, after a desperate conflict, in which the FOUDROYANT (then in company with the LION 64, and PENELOPE 36) sustained a loss of 8 men killed and 64 wounded, of *Le Guillaume Tell*, of 84 guns and 1000 men, flag-ship of Rear-Admiral Decrès. He came home with Sir Edw. Berry at the commencement of 1801 in the PRINCESS CHARLOTTE frigate, but, returning to the Mediterranean on the renewal of hostilities in 1803 on board the CANOPUS 80, bearing the flag of Rear-Admiral Geo. Campbell, was for some time engaged at the blockade of Toulon, off which port he once participated in a brush with a powerful division of the enemy's fleet. Being again ordered to England in 1805 in the DILIGENT store-ship, Master-Commander Wm. Lloyd, he was appointed, on his arrival, to the LONDON 98, Capts. Sir Robt. Barlow, Robt. Rolles, Sir Harry Burrard Neale, Edw. Oliver Osborn, and Thos. Western; in which ship, under Sir H. B. Neale, we find him, on 13 March, 1806, aiding, in company with the AMAZON 38, at the capture of the French 80-gun ship *Marengo*, bearing the flag of Admiral Linois, and 40-gun frigate *Belle Poule*, whose fire, in the course of a long running action, occasioned the LONDON a loss of 10 men killed and 22 wounded. In Sept. 1808, after having accompanied the Royal Family of Portugal to the Brazils, and been for several months employed on that station, Mr. Hooper became Sub-Lieutenant of the ALBAN cutter, Lieut.-Commander Henry Weir, with whom he returned home and then proceeded to the Baltic, where he appears to have seen a good deal of boat service, and to have carried into Prussia secret despatches from the Commander-in-Chief, Sir Jas. Saumarez. On 27 Oct. 1809 he was appointed an Acting, and on 13 of the following Dec. a confirmed, Lieutenant of the PRINCESS CAROLINE 74, Capts. Chas. Dudley Pater and Hugh Downman. In 1810, during a cruize in the Gulf of Finland, he was intrusted with the command of the boats employed among the rocks and small islands inshore; and in 1811 we again discover him serving in the boats, and sharing in a cutting-out affair off the island of Zealand, in which they endured a loss of 1 man killed and 1 severely wounded. Rejoining Capt. Weir, in Oct. 1811, on board the CALYPSO 18, he had an opportunity, on 6 July, 1812, of enacting a part, in company with the DICTATOR 64, PODARGUS 14, and FLAMER gun-brig, at the gallant capture and destruction, within the rocks of Mardoe, on the coast of Norway, of an entire Danish squadron, consisting of the *Nayaden*, of 48 guns, the *Laland*, *Samsoe*, and *Kiel* sloops, and several gun-boats, at the close of a long conflict, productive of a loss to the CALYPSO of 3 men killed, 1 man wounded, and 1 missing, and to the enemy of 300 killed and wounded. Although Capt. Weir was made Post for this exploit, and the First-Lieutenant of the DICTATOR was advanced to the rank of Commander, Lieut. Hooper, who was himself Senior of the CALYPSO, and was officially praised for his exertions,* received no reward—an act of neglect he the more felt from the fact of the Acting-Lieutenant on board the latter vessel, and of course his inferior, being confirmed to the vacancy created in the DICTATOR. To add to his mortification he was even superseded in his post as First-Lieutenant, and another officer appointed over him. Continuing in the CALYPSO under Capts. Thos. Groube and Chas. Hope Reid until Aug. 1814, he was further employed in conveying Lord Walpole to St. Petersburg, and in co-operating in the siege of Danzig. On the occasion of the Grand Naval Review held at Portsmouth in 1814, he was again Senior of the CALYPSO. His last appointment afloat was, 20 Jan. 1815, to the PENELOPE 36, *armée en flûte*, Capt. Jas. Galloway, which vessel was lost, with part of her crew, in the gulf of St. Lawrence, on 30 of the ensuing April. Since 10 April, 1826, Lieut. Hooper has been in charge of a station in the Coast Guard.

He married, first, in 1829, Miss M. Webb, daughter of a naval officer; and secondly, 5 Jan. 1831, a daughter of Commander Robt. Hearle, R.N. By his first wife the Lieutenant has issue three children, and by his second he has had a further family of six children.

HOOPER. (LIEUT., 1815. F-P., 7; H-P., 31.)

JOHN SACKETT HOOPER was born 27 Dec. 1792.

This officer entered the Navy, 22 Feb. 1809, as

* *Vide* Gaz. 1812, p. 1362.

Midshipman, on board the STANDARD 64, Capt. Thos. Harvey, with whom he was for some months employed in the MAJESTIC 74, on the Baltic station; where, in the course of 1810, he joined the RUBY and DICTATOR 64's, both commanded by Capt. Robt. Williams. During the action of 6 July, 1812, with the Danish squadron, alluded to in our narrative of Lieut. Benj. Hooper, he is represented to have been on board the latter ship, whose loss on the occasion amounted to 4 persons killed and 24 (including himself*) wounded. The three years preceding his promotion to the rank of Lieutenant, which took place 20 Sept. 1815, were passed by Mr. Hooper on the North Sea, North American, West India, and Newfoundland stations, in the SCEPTRE and MARLBOROUGH 74's, Capts. Thos. Harvey and Robt. Honyman, and PERSEUS 22, Capt. Edw. Henry A'Court. He has since been on half-pay.

HOOPER. (LIEUT., 1810. F-P., 16; H-P., 31.)

RICHARD HOOPER entered the Navy, in 1800, as L.M., on board the SEVERN 44, Capts. John Whitby and Geo. Barker, employed in the West Indies; where, and in the Channel, he served, from Dec. 1803 until Aug. 1809, as A.B., Midshipman, Master's Mate, and Acting-Lieutenant, in the PORT MAHON brig, Capt. Sam. Chambers. During the three first years of that period he assisted at the capture, re-capture, and destruction of at least 50 vessels; among which were *El Galgo* Spanish packet, the *Aranzana* letter-of-marque, and *El Courier* privateer. In 1808 the PORT MAHON took two other privateers—*Le Furet*, of 16 guns and 47 men, and *Le Général Paris*, of 3 guns and 38 men. After an attachment of nearly 12 months to the SAN JOSEF 110, under the flags of Sir John Thos. Duckworth and Sir Chas. Cotton, Mr. Hooper was made Lieutenant, 4 July, 1810, into the TÉMÉRAIRE 98, flag-ship of Rear-Admiral Fras. Pickmore in the Mediterranean. His last appointments were—10 Sept. 1812, to the INSOLENT 14, Capts. Edw. Brazier and Wm. Kelly, with whom he served in the Channel and Baltic until compelled by illness to invalid in Sept. 1814—and, 3 Feb. 1816, to the DEE 24, commanded by Capt. Sam. Chambers on the Halifax station. The latter vessel was paid off 8 Dec. 1818.

HOOPER. (LIEUT., 1824. F-P., 11; H-P., 25.)

WILLIAM HOOPER (*b*) entered the Navy, 3 May, 1811, as Fst.-cl. Vol., on board the FISGARD frigate, Capt. Fras. Mason; and on removing, after serving for some time in the Baltic, to the NIOBE 40, Capts. John Wentworth Loring and Wm. Augustus Montagu, sailed for North America. In 1813 he became Midshipman of the PRESIDENT 38, Capts. F. Mason and Archibald Duff, in time, we believe, to witness the fall of St. Sebastian. Between Oct. 1815 and April, 1816, he was employed in the North Sea on board the FLORIDA 20, Capts. Wm. Elliott and Chas. Sibthorpe John Hawtayne. He then proceeded to the West Indies, where, for a period of two years and a half, he served under Capt. Elliott in the SCAMANDER 36. In 1820 he returned to the same station in the FORTE 44, Capt. Sir Thos. John Cochrane; on quitting which ship he successively joined, in 1822-3, the PHAETON 46, Capt. Henry Evelyn Pitfield Sturt, GLOUCESTER 74, Commodore Sir Edw. Owen, and TYNE, Capt. Roberts. He obtained his commission 12 Jan. 1824, and has since been on half-pay.

Lieut. Hooper married Elizabeth, youngest daughter of the late Thos. Gardiner Bramston, Esq., of Skreens, M.P. for co. Essex; and sister of the present Thos. Wm. Bramston, Esq., of Skreens, who married a daughter of the late Admiral Sir Eliab Harvey, G.C.B., M.P. He was left a widower 6 Aug. 1839.

HOOPS. (LIEUTENANT, 1840.)

RICHARD HOOPS entered the Navy 11 June, 1823; passed his examination in 1829; and for his services on the coast of Syria and at the bombardment of St. Jean d'Acre was promoted to the rank of Lieutenant 5 Nov. 1840. His appointments have since been—15 Dec. 1840, as Additional, to the PRINCESS CHARLOTTE 104, flag-ship in the Mediterranean of Hon. Sir Robt. Stopford—24 Jan. 1841, to the RODNEY 92, Capt. Robt. Maunsell, on the same station—and, 2 Feb. 1844, to the TORTOISE 12, Capts. Wm. Finlaison, Arthur Morrell, and Fred. Hutton, store-ship at Ascension, where he is at present employed.

* *Vide* Gaz. 1812, p. 1363.

HOPE. (CAPTAIN, 1826. F-P., 20; H-P., 16.)

CHARLES HOPE, born in 1798, is second son of the Right Hon. Chas. Hope, Lord President of the Court of Session in Scotland, by Charlotte, daughter of John, second Earl of Hopetoun; nephew of Lieut.-General Sir John Hope, G.C.H., and of Vice-Admiral the Right Hon. Sir Wm. Johnston Hope, G.C.B.;* brother of Wm. Hope, Esq., a Major in the Army and Captain in the 7th Foot; and first-cousin of the late Capts. Wm. James, Chas. Jas., and Geo. Jas., Hope, R.N.

This officer entered the Navy, 24 June, 1811, as Sec.-cl. Vol., on board the SARPEDON 10, Capt. Jas. Green, on the Leith station, where he removed, in the following Nov., to the ADAMANT 44, flag-ship of Rear-Admiral Wm. Albany Otway. In April, 1812, he became Midshipman of the SEMIRAMIS 36, Capt. Chas. Richardson, bearing the flag afterwards of Rear-Admiral Chas. Tyler at the Cape of Good Hope. On his return home in Aug. 1814 he joined the CHATHAM 74, Capt. David Lloyd, lying at Portsmouth, whence, towards the close of the same year, he sailed for North America in the ERNE 20, commanded by the late Lord Napier. In the course of 1815 he was successively received on board the ENDYMION, TAGUS, and ALCESTE frigates, Capts. Henry Hope, Jas. Whitley Deans Dundas, and Murray Maxwell; under the latter of whom he accompanied Lord Amherst on his embassy to China, and was wrecked, while returning home with that nobleman, in the Straits of Gaspar, 18 Feb. 1817. Obtaining his first commission on 20 of the following Oct., he was next, 22 Feb. 1818, appointed Lieutenant of the LIFFEY 50, Capt. Hon. Henry Duncan, in which ship he visited the Mediterranean and cruized for some time off Lisbon. After serving with Capt. Chas. Adam in the ROYAL SOVEREIGN yacht he was invested, 15 Oct. 1822, with the rank of Commander, and on 28 Feb. 1824 nominated to the BRISK 10. In the month of Sept. following he captured, off Flamborough Head, a large smuggling lugger, with a cargo of considerable value. Capt. Hope, whose advancement to Post-rank took place 26 Jan. 1826, was subsequently appointed—21 Oct. 1830, to the TYNE 28, a vessel in which he served on the South American station, and, prior to being paid off in Jan. 1834, passed over 82,000 miles, a greater distance than had been traversed by any vessel since the war—24 Jan. 1835, to the DUBLIN 50, fitting at Plymouth, where he was superseded in the ensuing July—and, 28 Aug. 1841, to the THALIA 42. He was employed in the latter frigate on the East India and Pacific stations until the close of 1845, when she returned to England and was put out of commission. He has since been on half-pay.

Capt. Hope married, 12 Sept. 1826, Anne, eldest

* Sir W. J. Hope was born 16 Aug. 1766, and entered the Navy in 1776. He commanded the BELLEROPHON 74, as Flag-Captain to Rear-Admiral Thomas Pasley, and obtained a gold medal for his services, in the actions of 28 and 29 May and 1 June, 1794. He afterwards served on board the KENT 74, bearing the flag of Lord Duncan, during the expedition to Holland in 1799. With the despatches announcing the results of that enterprise he was sent to England; and he was in consequence presented with a purse of 500*l*. In Dec. 1800, being still in the KENT, he conveyed Sir Ralph Abercromby from Gibraltar to Egypt. He was nominated a Colonel of Marines in 1811; advanced to the rank of Rear-Admiral in 1812; appointed to the chief command at Leith in Nov. 1813; created a K.C.B. in 1815; re-appointed to Leith in 1816; made a Vice-Admiral in 1819; invested with the dignity of a G.C.B. in 1825; and sworn a Privy Councillor about the close of 1830. Sir W. J. Hope, who was for a long time one of the Lords of the Admiralty, and sat for many years in Parliament for Dumfries, died 2 May, 1831.

daughter of the late Rear-Admiral Wm. Henry Webley Parry, C.B., by whom, who died 24 Dec. 1836, he has issue. AGENTS—Hallett and Robinson.

HOPE. (CAPTAIN, 1830. F-P., 20; H-P., 31.)

DAVID HOPE, born 9 July, 1787, in Edinburgh, is third son of Wm. Hope, Esq., of Newton, near that city, and descends from Sir Thos. Hope, Bart., of Edminstone and Cauld Coats, in co. Mid Lothian. One of his brothers, James, a Lieutenant in H.M. 1st Regt. of Foot, was severely wounded in Holland, and died from extreme fatigue during the campaign in Egypt; and another, William, an officer in the 19th Regt. of Foot, was massacred at Candy, in the island of Ceylon. A third brother of Capt. Hope was in the 89th.

This officer entered the Navy, 25 May, 1796, as Fst.-cl. Vol., on board the KITE sloop, Capt. Wm. Brown, and in May, 1798, accompanied, as Midshipman, an expedition under Sir Home Popham, having for its object the destruction of the locks and sluice-gates of the Bruges Canal, during the operations connected with which he was employed on shore. After witnessing, in the TISIPHONE sloop, Capt. Chas. Grant, the surrender to Sir Andrew Mitchell of the Dutch fleet under Rear-Admiral Story, Mr. Hope proceeded to the West Indies, where he successively followed Capt. Grant, as Master's Mate, into the ABERGAVENNY 54, and QUEBEC 32. Between Nov. 1802 and June, 1803, we find him employed on the Irish station in the DRYAD frigate, Capts. Robt. Williams and Wm. Domett; and on his removal to the PRINCE OF WALES 98, flag-ship of Sir Robt. Calder, sharing in the action with the combined squadrons of France and Spain, off Cape Finisterre, 22 July, 1805. Being confirmed a Lieutenant, 30 Aug. 1806, in the SIR FRANCIS DRAKE 36, Capts. Jas. Haldane Tait and Pownoll Bastard Pellew, on the East India station, he continued in that frigate until March, 1807, when he joined the WILHELMINA, Capt. Chas. Foote, whom, it appears, he accompanied, as his First-Lieutenant, into the PIEDMONTAISE. Towards the close of 1808 he invalided home on board the POWERFUL 74, Capt. Chas. Jas. Johnstone. In Sept. 1809, a few months after his arrival, he had the fortune to be appointed to the FREIJA frigate, Capt. John Hayes, fitting for the West Indies, where, in the next Dec. and Feb., he witnessed the destruction of the French 44-gun frigates *Loire* and *Seine*, in L'Ance-la-Barque, and the surrender of Guadeloupe. During the operations which led to the latter event Lieut. Hope commanded the boats of a small squadron at the capture and destruction of all the sea batteries on the N.W. side of the island; and on the night of 20 Jan. 1810,* with four of the ship's boats, and 83 officers, seamen, and marines under his orders, he entered Bay Mahaut under a most galling fire from the enemy in every direction, and, besides making prize, by boarding, of a brig mounting 6 guns, and setting fire to two other vessels, one of them a fine national schooner, pierced for 16, but carrying only 12 guns, stormed and took two batteries. The first of these was found to consist of 1 24-pounder, in addition to 6 howitzers, which had been dragged to the beach to oppose the landing of the British; and the second, of 3 24-pounders. To add to the lustre of this valorous exploit, successful in its every detail, it was effected with no greater loss than 3 persons wounded. Among them, however, was the gallant leader, whose conduct impressed the Commander-in-Chief with so high a sense of his bravery and merit as to elicit from him a declaration that he was deserving the notice of the Lords Commissioners of the Admiralty. On 24 Nov. 1810 Lieut. Hope was appointed First of the MACEDONIAN, of 48 guns and 254 men, Capts. Lord Wm. FitzRoy, Hon. Wm. Waldegrave, and John Surman Carden, in which frigate he was very actively employed on the coasts of Portugal and France, and came often into contact with the batteries in the neighbourhood of Ile d'Aix. On 25

* *Vide* Gaz. 1810, p. 388.

Oct. 1812 it was his lot to be on board the MACEDONIAN, when, after a glorious resistance of 2 hours and 10 minutes, in which she had been reduced to a perfect wreck, with a loss of 36 of her crew killed and 68 wounded, she was forced to strike to the American ship *United States*, of 56 guns and 474 men, of whom the killed and severely wounded do not appear to have exceeded the united amount of 12. At the commencement of the conflict Lieut. Hope was severely wounded in the leg, and towards the close he was still more seriously injured in the head, and taken below; but he was soon again upon deck, displaying that greatness of mind and exertion which, though it may be equalled, can never be surpassed.* At the subsequent trial, indeed, of the surviving officers and crew of the MACEDONIAN, the Court declared itself unable to dismiss Lieut. Hope without expressing its highest approbation of the support given by him to his Captain, and of his courage and steadiness during the contest. In June, 1813, within a few days of this honourable acquittal, he was appointed by Sir John Borlase Warren to the command of the SHELBURNE schooner, of 14 guns. In the course of the next 12 months he drove on shore and destroyed a number of the enemy's small privateers and merchantmen; and on 20 April, 1814, he was the instrument, through great exertion, of rendering the U.S. sloop-of-war *Frolic* a captive to the British frigate ORPHEUS. Continuing in the same vessel until Dec. 1814, Capt. Hope, whose commission as Commander was at length signed on 15 June in that year, was for about four months employed in blockading New Orleans, and in occasionally affording assistance to our allies, the Creek Indians, on the Apalachicola river. In Oct. 1814 we find him, with a zeal for the service highly honourable to him, voluntarily relanding a large sum of money which had been consigned to him for conveyance from New Providence to the Havana, for the sole purpose of affording to a newly-arrived squadron under Sir Jas. Alex. Gordon the benefit of his experience in navigating the Gulf of Florida. On leaving the SHELBURNE he assumed the duties of aide-de-camp to Sir Alex. Cochrane on board the TONNANT 80, and proved of much assistance to him throughout the arduous campaign against New Orleans. On one occasion, while so employed, he was near losing his life by jumping into the Pearl river to save a soldier of the 95th Regt., who would have been drowned but for his humane efforts. Capt. Hope, who left the TONNANT in March, 1815, did not again go afloat until 12 Jan. 1828, when he obtained an appointment to the TERROR bomb, in which he sailed with stores for the Mediterranean, but was wrecked on his passage out, under very awful circumstances, on the coast of Portugal, near Villa-Nova-de-mille-fuentes, 19 Feb. following. Although a survey held by the officers of a frigate and brig sent to the assistance of the TERROR announced it as impossible for her to be saved, and recommended her being sold, she was nevertheless got off by the extraordinary exertions of her officers and crew, and placed in a condition to return to England. On her arrival the Senior Lieutenant, Chas. Hotham, and Midshipman Robt. Cleugh, were rewarded for their labours by immediate promotion, and Capt. Hope himself, to whom every prospect of early advancement was held out by the Lord High Admiral, was at once, 26 July, appointed to the METEOR, another bomb. In that vessel he was at first employed in blockading the port of Tangier, for the purpose of obtaining the restoration of two merchantmen captured by Barbary cruizers. He returned home from the Mediterranean, on attaining his present rank, 4 Feb. 1830, and has since been on half-pay.

HOPE. (CAPTAIN, 1845. F-P., 17; H-P., 6.)

THE HONOURABLE GEORGE HOPE, born 12 April, 1811, is fourth son of John, fourth Earl of Hopetoun (a General Officer in the Army, Colonel of the

* *Vide* Gaz. 1812, p. 2595.

42nd Regt., and a G.C.B.), by his second wife, Louisa Dorothea, third daughter of Sir John Wedderburn, Bart. He is brother of Hon. Jas. Hope Wallace, of Featherstone Castle, co. Northumberland, Captain and Lieutenant-Colonel 2nd Foot Guards, and Deputy-Lieutenant for co. Linlithgow; and uncle of the present Earl of Hopetoun.

This officer entered the Navy 1 April, 1824, and obtained his first commission 20 Nov. 1830. His appointments as Lieutenant were—25 Nov. 1830, to the ACTÆON 26, Capt. Hon. Fred. Wm. Grey, on the Mediterranean station, whence he returned home and was paid off in Sept. 1834—and, 5 April, 15 July, and 2 Sept. 1836, to the BELLEROPHON 80, Capt. Sam. Jackson, INCONSTANT 36, Capt. John Hayes, and FLY 18, Capts. Russell Elliott and Granville Gower Loch. In the latter vessel he served for nearly four years in South America, and on her being put out of commission was advanced to the rank of Commander 26 Oct. 1840. His last appointment was, 18 March, 1843, to the SAPPHO 16, on the Cape station, where he continued until within a short period of his advancement to Post-rank, 24 July, 1845.

Capt. Hope married, 23 April, 1845, Katherine Frances, daughter of Wm. Leveson Gower, Esq. AGENTS—Hallett and Robinson.

HOPE. (COMMANDER, 1828.)

GEORGE HOPE, born in 1801, is youngest brother of Rear-Admiral Henry Hope, C.B.

This officer entered the Navy, 14 Nov. 1813, as Third-cl. Boy, on board the LATONA 38, Capt. Andrew Smith, bearing the flag at Leith of his cousin, the late Sir Wm. Johnstone Hope. In Aug. 1814 he became a Student at the Royal Naval College at Portsmouth, where he remained until June, 1816. He then re-embarked on board the GRANICUS 36, Capt. Wm. Furlong Wise, and, after serving for a short time in the Channel, joined the LEANDER 60, bearing the flag of Sir David Milne at Halifax, from which station he returned to England in July, 1819. Until Sept. 1821 Mr. Hope, who had attained the rating of Midshipman in Feb. 1817, was next employed on Home duty in the LIFFEY 50, Capt. Hon. Henry Duncan, and ROYAL SOVEREIGN yacht, Capt. Chas. Adam. He acquired the rank of Lieutenant 29 Jan. 1822, but did not again go afloat until 23 June, 1823, when he procured an appointment to the SPARTIATE 76, Capt. Gordon Thos. Falcon, and sailed for South America. He there removed, 14 May, 1825, to the JASEUR sloop, Capts. Thos. Martin and Edw. Handfield, and on 5 March, 1828, was advanced to his present rank.

Commander Hope married, in 1833, Charlotte, daughter of Vice-Admiral Delap Tollemache, and by that lady, who died 14 April, 1837, has issue.

HOPE, C.B. (REAR-ADMIRAL OF THE BLUE, 1846. F-P., 17; H-P., 32.)

HENRY HOPE, born in 1787, is eldest son of the late Commissioner Chas. Hope, R.N. (son of Hon. Chas. Hope Vere, by Ann Vane, eldest daughter of Henry, first Earl of Darlington, and grandson of the first Earl of Hopetoun), by Susan Anne, daughter of Admiral Herbert Sawyer. He is brother of Fred. Hope, Esq., a Major in the Army, and of the present Commander Geo. Hope, R.N.; brother-in-law of Rear-Admiral C. S. J. Hawtayne; nephew of Henry Hope, Esq., who was Lieut.-Governor of Canada, and died in 1789; and cousin of the late Rear-Admiral Sir Geo. Hope, K.C.B., and the late Vice-Admiral the Right Hon. Sir Wm. Johnstone Hope, G.C.B.

This officer entered the Navy, 2 April, 1798, as Third-cl. Vol., on board the PRINCESS AUGUSTA yacht, employed on the river Thames. Being discharged, as Midshipman, in May, 1800, into the KENT 74, commanded by his relative Capt. Wm. Johnstone Hope, he proceeded to the Mediterranean, where we find him, in the following Dec., escorting Sir Ralph Abercromby from Gibraltar to Egypt. After serving at the blockade of Alexandria, he removed to the SWIFTSURE 74, Capt. Benj. Hallowell, and on 24 June, 1801, was on board that ship in a desperate engagement of more than an hour's duration, which reduced her to a wreck, and rendered her a prize to a French squadron of four sail of the line under Rear-Admiral Ganteaume. In the ensuing Sept., on his restoration to liberty, Mr. Hope joined the LEDA frigate, Capts. Geo. Hope, Thos. Masterman Hardy, and Robt. Honyman, with whom he served on the Mediterranean and Home stations until June, 1803; between which period and his attainment of Lieutenant's rank, 3 May, 1804, he was further employed with Capts. George and Wm. J. Hope, in the North Sea, on board the DEFENCE and ATLAS 74's. After he had next cruized with Capt. Geo. Burlton in the ADAMANT 50, and had aided, in the NARCISSUS 32, Capt. Ross Donnelly, at the reduction of the Cape, Lieut. Hope was promoted, 22 Jan. 1806, to the command of the ESPOIR sloop; in which vessel he served in the Channel and Mediterranean, and off the coast of Portugal, until made Post, 24 May, 1808, into the GLATTON 50. His subsequent appointments were—17 Nov. 1808, 4 May, 1809, and 17 May, 1810, to the LEONIDAS, TOPAZE, and SATELLITE* frigates, all on the Mediterranean station, where he assisted Capt. Hallowell, in Oct. 1809, in making the preparations which led to the capture and destruction of a convoy in the Bay of Rosas, as detailed in our memoir of Sir Augustus Clifford—and, 18 May, 1813, to the ENDYMION, of 48 guns and 319 men. In that frigate Capt. Hope won perpetual fame by his ardour in pursuing, his intrepidity in bringing to close action, and his undaunted spirit in maintaining for two hours and a half a conflict with the American ship *President*, of 56 guns and 465 men, who at length hauled down her colours, after a loss to herself of 35 killed and 70 wounded, and to the British of 11 killed and 14 wounded.† Previously to this brilliant affair, which took place 15 Jan. 1815, Capt. Hope had taken the *Perry* letter-of-marque, had also served at the blockade of New London, and had contributed, during an expedition up the Penobscot, to the capture of the town of Castine, 1 Sept. 1814. On reaching Bermuda, after the capture of the *President*, the magistrates, merchants, and inhabitants, deputed a committee to wait upon him with a complimentary address, and with a request that he would accept a piece of plate as a token of their esteem; they also presented his officers with a goblet, to "be considered as attached to that or any future ship which might bear the gallant name of ENDYMION." On arriving with his prize at Spithead, Capt. Hope was presented by the Admiralty with a gold medal in acknowledgment of his gallant conduct; and on 4 June, 1815, he was nominated a C.B. He was put out of commission in the following Sept., and has since been on half-pay. His advancement to Flag-rank took place 9 Nov. 1846.

During the fifteen years immediately previous to his last promotion Rear-Admiral Hope filled the appointment of extra and full Aide-de-Camp to William IV. and to Her present Majesty. He married, 21 July, 1828, Jane Sophia, youngest daughter of Admiral Sir Herbert Sawyer, K.C.B., which lady died in 1829.

HOPE, C.B. (CAPTAIN, 1838. F-P., 18; H-P., 9.)

JAMES HOPE, born 8 March, 1808, is son of Rear-Admiral Sir Geo. Hope, K.C.B., by his first wife, Lady Jemima Hope Johnstone, fifth daughter of James, third Earl of Hopetoun; brother-in-law of Sir Harry Verney, Bart.; and cousin of the present Rear-Admiral Henry Hope, C.B.

This officer entered the R. N. College 1 Aug. 1820; embarked about June, 1822; and, after serving in the West Indies and Mediterranean on board the FORTE and CAMBRIAN frigates, was promoted to the rank of Lieutenant 9 March, 1827. His next

* The SATELLITE, on 21 April, 1812, effected the capture of *La Comète* privateer, of two 18-pounders and 45 men; and on 13 of the following Nov. she took, on her passage home, *Le Mercure*, a similar description of vessel, carrying 16 guns and 70 men.

† *Vide* Gaz. 1815, p. 281–2.

appointments were, 16 Sept. and 3 Oct. 1827, to the MAIDSTONE 42, Capt. Wm. Skipsey, and UNDAUNTED 46, Capt. Augustus Wm. Jas. Clifford, in the latter of which ships he escorted Lord Wm. Bentinck as Governor-General to India, and brought home Major-General Bourke, late Lieut.-Governor of the Cape. He became, in Aug. 1829, Flag-Lieutenant to Lord Northesk, Commander-in-Chief at Plymouth; and, obtaining a second promotal commission 26 Feb. 1830, Capt. Hope was, from 13 July, 1833, until paid off in 1838, employed on the North America and West India station in command of the RACER 16. He acquired his present rank on 28 June in the latter year; and, since 13 Dec. 1844, has been Captain of the FIREBRAND steam-frigate, on the south-east coast of America. On 20 Nov. 1845, Capt. Hope enacted a conspicuous part in the battle of the Parana, where a hard day's fighting resulted in the destruction, by the combined squadrons of England and France, of four heavy batteries belonging to General Rosas at Punta Obligado, also of a schooner-of-war carrying 6 guns, and of 24 vessels chained across the river. On that occasion, having volunteered, he gallantly pulled up in his boat and cut the chain which impeded the upward progress of the allies. At the close of the action he landed as Aide-de-Camp to Capt. Chas. Hotham, the Senior British officer, and assisted in giving the *coup-de-grace* to the defeat of the enemy, whose numbers originally consisted of 3500 men, in cavalry, infantry, and artillery, and whose batteries had mounted 22 pieces of ordnance.* As a reward for his conduct he was nominated a C.B. 3 April, 1846.

Capt. Hope is a Magistrate and Deputy-Lieutenant for co. Linlithgow. He married, 16 Aug. 1838, the Hon. Frederica Kinnaird, daughter of Charles, eighth Lord Kinnaird. AGENTS—Hallett and Robinson.

HOPE. (CAPTAIN, 1840. F-P., 22; H-P., 11.)

SACKETT HOPE is brother of the present John Minter Hope, Esq., Paymaster and Purser, R.N. (1814); and of Lieut. Thos. Hope (*a*), R.N. (1825), an officer who entered the service in 1809, and was in almost constant employment from that period until 1838, when he was lost in command of H.M. schooner PINCHER, with all on board, while working into Spithead.

This officer entered the Navy, 2 Nov. 1814, as Fst.-cl. Vol., on board the ICARUS 10, Capt. Thos. Barker Devon, which vessel, after serving in the Channel, escorted Napoleon Buonaparte to St. Helena, and was then sent with despatches to the Isle of France and Calcutta. On joining the LIVERPOOL 50, Capt. Fras. Augustus Collier, he accompanied an expedition sent, in 1819, against the pirates of the Persian Gulf, where he assisted at the bombardment and destruction of Ras-al-Khyma, their principal stronghold, and was very actively employed both in the gun-boats and on shore. After visiting China and various parts of India, and passing through scenes of great mortality, he returned to England in 1822 on board the GANGES 84, a new teak-built ship. Having passed his examination in Nov. of the previous year, he was then appointed Mate of the GLOUCESTER 74, bearing the broad pendant of Sir Edw. W. C. R. Owen in the West Indies, on which station we find him cruizing in a tender, off the island of Cuba, for the suppression of piracy and the slave-trade. On his arrival home, Mr. Hope attended the Duke of Clarence on a summer cruize in the ROYAL SOVEREIGN yacht, Capt. Chas. Adam, and went with the Lords of the Admiralty on a visit of inspection to Plymouth. While next attached, during a period of a few months, to the BRISK 10, Capt. Chas. Hope, he served in the North Sea and Channel, and was occasionally detached in the boats of that vessel for the suppression of smuggling. Between Feb. 1825 and Oct. 1826, he again served in the West Indies on board the FERRET and SCYLLA sloops, both commanded by Capt. Wm. Hobson. In the boats of the former vessel he once assisted in taking a slaver; and he was in her at a period of so much sickness that 12 out of 75 were all who were enabled to remain on board. During the whole term of his attachment to the SCYLLA, a period of seven months, Mr. Hope had charge of a watch, and was twice invested with the rank of Acting-Lieutenant. On 11 Dec. 1826, shortly after his rejunction to the FERRET, he was promoted to be her First-Lieutenant—a rank in which he was afterwards appointed—25 May, 1828, to the ARACHNE 18, Capt. Henry Smith—30 Aug. in the same year, to the FERRET again, Capt. Chas. Deare, with whom he returned home from the West Indies, much impaired in health, and was paid off in the following Nov.—11 July, 1832 (after many ineffectual attempts to procure employment) to the BEACON surveying-vessel, Capt. Rich. Copeland, on the Mediterranean station—and, 15 July, 1836, to the INCONSTANT 36, Capts. John Hayes and Dan. Pring. In April, 1833, Lieut. Hope took command of the boats of the BEACON, manned by 36 officers and men, and of a gun-boat with 5 Turks on board, and contrived to effect the capture, near the island of Thasos, not, however, without opposition, of 140 out of a notorious band of 200 armed pirates, who had become the terror of the Grecian Archipelago. Prize was at the same time made of seven of their vessels. In consequence of the detention of Capt. Copeland at Malta from ill health, Lieut. Hope, in the spring of 1836, was entrusted with the duty of navigating the BEACON to England. On his arrival he was immediately ordered to Greenock to volunteer men for the fleet. After that service had been accomplished he was paid off 4 June, 1836; and on the next day he received instructions to recommission the BEACON. On his removal, as above, to the INCONSTANT, we find him employed in experimentally cruizing, also in performing Particular Service, and in carrying troops to North America. In Dec. 1838, having attained the rank of Commander on 28 of the previous June, he went on half-pay, on which he continued until appointed, 10 May, 1839, Second Captain of the REVENGE 76, Capt. Hon. Wm. Waldegrave. In that ship he was at first stationed off Lisbon, and then sent to the Mediterranean, where he partook of the operations on the coast of Syria, and was present at the bombardment of St. Jean d'Acre. He was in consequence advanced to Post-rank 4 Nov. 1840; and, since Jan. 1841, when he left the REVENGE, has been on half-pay.

Capt. Hope is in the receipt of a pension of 6*l.* per annum for a very severe injury he sustained in the left hand, attended with the loss of a finger, while endeavouring, in H.M.S. LIVERPOOL, to clear a seaman, who by some accident had been jammed.

HOPE. (COMMANDER, 1841. F-P., 15; H-P., 7.)

THOMAS HOPE, born 10 July, 1810, is third son of Sir John Hope, Bart., of Craighall, co. Fife, by Anne, fourth daughter of the late Sir John Wedderburn, Bart., of Blackness and Ballindean; brother of Lieut. Wm. Hope, of the 71st Regt., and of Jas. Wedderburn Hope, Esq., an officer in the 26th Bombay Native Infantry; and nephew of Wm. Hope, Esq., Master-Attendant at Calcutta, who died in 1837.

This officer entered the Navy 16 Feb. 1825; passed his examination in 1831; obtained his first commission 6 July, 1832; and was successively appointed—20 Feb. 1833, as Supernumerary-Lieutenant, to the MELVILLE 74, flag-ship in the East Indies of Sir John Gore—9 Oct. 1833, to the HYACINTH 18, Capt. Fras. Price Blackwood, on the same station—and 14 March, 1837, as First, to the SAPPHO 16, Capt. Thos. Fraser. He served in the latter sloop in North America and the West Indies until promoted to his present rank 23 Nov. 1841; but has not been since employed. AGENTS—Messrs. Stilwell.

HOPKINS. (LIEUT., 1827. F-P., 18; H-P., 18.)

CHARLES HOPKINS (*b*) was born 7 July, 1796, at Milford, co. Pembroke.

* *Vide* Gaz. 1846, pp. 816-17.

This officer entered the Navy, 13 April, 1811, as a Boy, on board the NIEMEN 38, Capt. Sir Michael Seymour, employed in the Bay of Biscay, where, accompanying the same officer as Midshipman in May, 1812, into the HANNIBAL 74, he assisted, in March, 1814, at the capture, we believe, of the French 40-gun frigate *Sultâne*. Soon after that event he rejoined the NIEMEN, then commanded by Capt. Sam. Pym; and cruized until May, 1815, on the North American station. During the next six months we find him employed off the coast of Ireland in the MYRTLE 20, Capt. Arthur Batt Bingham. He then served for a period of three years with Capt. Jas. Rich. Dacres of the TIBER 38, on the Channel and Newfoundland stations; after which he became in succession attached to the NORTHUMBERLAND 74, Capts. Sir Michael Seymour and Thos. Harvey, SEVERN 40, Capt. Wm. M'Culloch, NORTHUMBERLAND again, Capts. Thos. Harvey and Thos. Jas. Maling, and BRITON, BLONDE, and SYBILLE 38's, Capts. Murray Maxwell, Lord Byron, and Fras. Augustus Collier. The three latter ships were employed on the South American, Pacific, and African stations; the others on the Home. On 30 April, 1827, Mr. Hopkins, who had passed his examination in June, 1817, and had served for a considerable time in the capacities of Admiralty-Midshipman and Mate, was at length promoted to the rank of Lieutenant; but he did not leave the SYBILLE until the following Oct. His last appointment was, 23 April, 1830, to the PRINCE REGENT 120, bearing the flags of Admirals Hon. Sir Henry Blackwood, Sir John Poo Beresford, and Wm. Parker. In that ship he served at the Nore, then took part in an experimental cruize under Sir Edw. Codrington, and eventually proceeded off Lisbon, whence he returned home and was paid off in Feb. 1832.

Lieut. Hopkins married, 18 Dec. 1832, Miss Sarah Ledsam, of Birmingham, co. Warwick.

HOPKINS. (LIEUTENANT, 1826.)

EDWARD JERVIS HOPKINS entered the Navy 26 Sept. 1809; passed his examination in 1815; was made Lieutenant, 10 July, 1826, into the TWEED 28, Capt. Fred. Hunn, on the Jamaica station, whence he invalided; and on 18 Sept. 1828, joined the SHANNON 46, Capt. Benj. Clement, from which ship he was superseded at his own request.

He married, in 1838, Elizabeth, widow of the late Isaac Field, Esq. AGENT—J. Chippendale.

HOPKINS. (LIEUT., 1842. F-P., 17; H-P., 1.)

ROBERT HOPKINS entered the Navy 12 Feb. 1829; passed his examination 20 Aug. 1835; and, until promoted to the rank of Lieutenant 15 Oct. 1842, served as Mate on board the CASTOR 36, and NORTH STAR 28, both commanded by Lord John Hay, SAVAGE 10, Lieut.-Commander John Harrison Bowker, CALEDONIA 120, bearing the flag at Plymouth of Sir Graham Moore, and WARSPITE 50, Capt. Lord John Hay. He was employed in the three former ships on the coast of Spain, during the operations connected with the civil war in 1835-40; and in the WARSPITE, he was attached to the force in North America and the West Indies. His appointments, subsequently to his promotion, were, on the last mentioned and the Mediterranean stations—29 April, 1843, and 24 July, 1844, as Additional Lieutenant, to the ILLUSTRIOUS 72, and FORMIDABLE 84, flag-ships of Sir Chas. Adam and Sir Edw. W. C. R. Owen—1 Oct. 1845, as Senior, to the SIREN 16, Capt. Harry Edm. Edgell—and 10 April, 1846, to the TYNE 26, Capt. Wm. Nugent Glascock. He was paid off from the latter vessel in the early part of 1847.

HOPKINSON. (COMMANDER, 1821. F-P., 22; H-P., 34.)

SIMON HOPKINSON entered the Navy, in June, 1791, as A.B., on board the MAGNIFICENT 74, Capt. Rich. Onslow, lying at Spithead, from which ship he was discharged in the following Sept. In June, 1795, he re-embarked on board the LYNX 20, Capt. Chas. Rowley, with whom, after serving, as Master's Mate, in the RAISON and HUSSAR, he sailed for the West Indies in the UNITÉ 38. From that frigate, on the books of which his name was borne for four years, he removed, in Sept. 1800, with Capt. John Poo Beresford, who had latterly commanded her, to the DIANA 38, also on the West India station, where, subsequently to the reduction of St. Bartholomew, St. Martin, &c., he joined the LEVIATHAN 74, bearing the flag of Sir John Thos. Duckworth. He was made Lieutenant, 18 July, 1801, into the HAWK sloop, Capt. Benj. Walker, and, leaving her in Sept. 1802, was afterwards appointed—16 Aug. 1803, to the ST. ALBANS 64, Capt. John Temple—14 Sept. 1804, to the RUBY 64, Capts. Chas. Rowley, John Temple, Thos. Masterman Hardy, John Draper, and Robt. Hall, in which ship he served off the ports of Cadiz and Lisbon, attended the expedition to Copenhagen, and, until he invalided in April, 1810, was further employed in the Baltic, under the flag of Rear-Admiral Manley Dixon—27 Aug. 1810, to the VENGEUR 74, Capt. Thos. Brown, attached to the force in the Channel—28 Dec. 1810, to the command of the TICKLER cutter, off Flushing, where he continued until Aug. 1815—and 13 Aug. 1818, to the PIKE. He retained the command of the latter vessel, on the Home station, until advanced to his present rank, 19 July, 1821; and has since been on half-pay.

Commander Hopkinson has a daughter, Caroline, who married, 29 Aug. 1836, Lieut.-Colonel Bowyer, C.B. AGENT—J. Hinxman.

HORE. (LIEUTENANT, 1846.)

CAVENDISH BRADSTREET HORE is youngest son of Walter Hore, Esq., of Harperstown, Wexford (who is a magistrate for that county, and served the office of High Sheriff in 1828), by the Hon. Mary Elizabeth Thornton Ruthven, daughter of the late Lord Ruthven. Two of his brothers, William and Walter, are officers in the Royal and Indian armies; and his uncle, Samuel Bradstreet Hore, a Commander R.N.

This officer passed his examination 7 Feb. 1843; and after an intermediate servitude, on the North American, West India, and Channel stations, on board the ILLUSTRIOUS 72, flag-ship of Sir Chas. Adam, and VANGUARD 80, Capt. Geo. Wickens Willes, was promoted to the rank of Lieutenant 15 Jan. 1846. Since 25 of the following month he has been employed in the Pacific on board the CARYSFORT 26, Capt. Geo. Henry Seymour.

HORE. (LIEUTENANT, 1846.)

EDWARD GEORGE HORE, born 17 Sept. 1823, is second son of Commander Herbert Wm. Hore, R.N. (1814), who died 10 Jan. 1823, by Eliza, daughter and co-heir of Geo. Curling, Esq., of West Hatch, co. Essex. He is brother of the present Herbert Fras. Hore, Esq., of Pole Hore, co. Wexford, and is the descendant of a very ancient family.

This officer (who was officially noticed for his services on the coast of Syria, where, as Midshipman of the CASTOR 36, Capt. Edw. Collier, he assisted in planting the Ottoman flag, and in destroying the guns on the ramparts of Caiffa*) passed his examination in Aug. 1842. Between that date and his promotion to the rank he now holds, which took place 15 Jan. 1846, we find him employed as Mate, on the Mediterranean and North America and West India stations, in the QUEEN 110, flag-ship of Sir Edw. W. C. R. Owen, DEVASTATION steam-sloop, Capt. Wm. Hewgill Kitchen, and VINDICTIVE 50, bearing the flag of Sir Fras. Wm. Austen. He continued in the VINDICTIVE, in the capacity of Additional Lieutenant, until appointed, 13 Oct. 1846, to the VIPER brigantine, which vessel he is now commanding on the station last-mentioned.

He married, 17 June, 1847, at Barbadoes, Maria second daughter of Lieut.-Colonel Reid, Governor of the Windward Islands.

* *Vide* Gaz. 1840, p. 2601.

HORE. (LIEUT., 1811. F-P., 15; H-P., 29.)

HENRY CAVENDISH HORE, born 31 March, 1790, is brother of Commanders S. B. and J. S. Hore, R.N.

This officer entered the Royal Naval Academy, in July, 1803, and, having gone through a distinguished course of studies, embarked, in March, 1807, as Midshipman, on board the DIAMOND 38, Capt. Thos. Elphinstone. Removing, in the following month, to the NAIAD 38, Capt. Thos. Dundas, he served in the boats of that frigate on two successful cutting-out affairs; after which, while under the late Sir Robt. Stopford in the SPENCER, CÆSAR, and SCIPION, ships-of-the-line, he attended the expedition to Copenhagen, witnessed the destruction of the French fleet in Aix Roads, served on shore during the operations against Flushing, and ultimately proceeded to the Cape of Good Hope; where, a few days after his promotion to the rank of Lieutenant, which took place 29 March, 1811, he removed to the HARPY sloop, Capt. Henderson Bain. In the proximate attack upon the island of Java we find him commanding a detachment, and receiving a slight wound in the left knee, at the storming and capture of Fort Cornelis. Between Jan. 1812 and March, 1814, he again served at the Cape as First of the LION 64, flag-ship of Rear-Admirals Stopford and Chas. Tyler. His next appointment was, in Oct. of the latter year, to the CRESCENT 38, Capt. John Quilliam, on the West India station, whence, after he had for some time officiated as Aide-de-Camp to Lieut.-General Sir Jas. Leith, the military Commander-in-Chief, he came home and was paid off in Sept. 1815. In 1821, Lieut. Hore entered the Water Guard Service, in which he continued three years, and particularly signalized himself by his efforts in the cause of the Revenue. His health at the expiration of that period being materially impaired from the effects of over-exertion, he resigned his appointment. He has not been since employed.

He married, 15 Sept. 1835, Clarissa Isabella, daughter of John Christopher Beauman, Esq., of Hyde Park, co. Wexford, and niece of Rear-Admiral Fras. Beauman, by whom he has issue three children.

HORE. (COMMANDER, 1828. F-P., 18; H-P., 21.)

JAMES STOPFORD HORE, born in April, 1795, is brother of Commander S. B. and of Lieut. H. C. Hore, R.N.

This officer entered the Navy, 10 Feb. 1808, as Midshipman, on board the MELPOMÈNE 38, Capt., afterwards Sir Peter, Parker, and was present in a desperate action in the Belt, in which that frigate beat off a flotilla of 19 Danish gun-boats by whom she had been attacked. Among the numerous cutting-out affairs in which he bore a part, during his continuance in the MELPOMÈNE, was the brilliant capture, 7 July, 1809, of the six Russian gun-vessels mentioned in our history of the services of Capt. Chas. Allen. Between Oct. in the latter year and May, 1810, he cruized on the Irish station in the ROTA 38, Capt. Philip Somerville; and he was then re-employed for upwards of four years with Sir Peter Parker in the MENELAUS 38. On proceeding in that ship to the Mediterranean, after having assisted in her at the reduction of the Isle of France, and been there employed in one of the blockading boats, Mr. Hore again contributed to the cutting-out of many of the enemy's vessels, one of them a brig pierced for 14 guns, and conducted four prizes in safety into port. In May, 1812, he was on board the MENELAUS when she pursued a frigate and brig close in with the batteries of Toulon, and then effected a masterly retreat from the French fleet, by passing through their line a-head of one 74, and astern of another. On being ordered to America, with the rating of Master's Mate, he frequently went on shore with armed parties of seamen and marines for the purpose of dislodging the enemy and destroying their stores, and on every occasion he evinced the greatest zeal and gallantry—qualities which were in particular displayed on 30 Aug. 1814, when a detachment of the British, 134 in number, having landed at Bellair, near Baltimore, succeeded in gallantly routing an overwhelming number of the Americans, whose resistance, however, occasioned the former a loss of 14 killed, including Sir Peter Parker, and 27 wounded. About the close of 1814, Mr. Hore became Acting-Lieutenant of the THAIS 20, Capt. Henry Weir, by whom he was soon afterwards, when off Madeira, sent home in charge of a French ship for adjudication, with discretionary power to liberate her or not, as might prove expedient from the state of hostilities at the time with France. On reaching Lisbon, deeming it unwise to risk a longer detention, he accordingly released the prize, and returned himself to England on board L'AIGLE frigate. He was officially promoted on his arrival by commission dated 7 March, 1815, and was afterwards appointed—in April, 1818, to the PHAETON 38, Capt. Wm. Henry Dillon, whom he accompanied to the East Indies—25 Dec. 1819, to the TAMAR 26, Capts. Arthur Stow, Sir Wm. Saltonstall Wiseman, John Theed, and Thos. Herbert, on the Jamaica station, where he obtained the honourable official mention of the last-mentioned officer for his conduct in the ship's boats in effecting the capture and destruction of four piratical vessels—and 2 Sept. 1824, to the OWEN GLENDOWER 42, bearing the broad pendant of Commodore Hood Hanway Christian at the Cape of Good Hope. He was promoted, on being paid off, to the rank of Commander 28 Aug. 1828; but has not been since afloat. AGENTS—Messrs. Ommanney.

HORE. (COMMANDER, 1813. F-P., 17; H-P., 30.)

SAMUEL BRADSTREET HORE, born in April, 1791, is third son (by Eleanor Catherine, daughter and heiress of Sir Simon Bradstreet, Bart., and niece of the Right Hon. Sir Henry Cavendish, Bart.) of Wm. Hore, Esq., of Harperstown, High Sheriff in 1788, and a Magistrate for co. Wexford, who was killed during the rebellion of 1798 while serving with the militia on the bridge of Wexford. He is brother of Commander Jas. Stopford, and of Lieut. Henry Cavendish, Hore, both of the R.N.; also of Major Wm. Hore, of the 67th Foot, who died in 1830, and of Capt. Thos. Hore, of the R.E.; and uncle of Lieut. Cavendish Bradstreet Hore, R.N.

This officer entered the Navy, in 1800, as Midshipman, on board the SANTA MARGARITA 36, Capt. Geo. Parker, on the North American station; became Midshipman, in March, 1801, of the EXCELLENT 74, Capt., afterwards Rear-Admiral, Hon. Robt. Stopford; and (with the exception of a brief attachment, in 1803, to the ENDYMION 40, Capt. Hon. Chas. Paget) continued to serve with that officer, until July, 1807, in the CASTOR frigate, and SPENCER 74. The latter ship, during the time he was in her, formed part of Lord Nelson's force in his pursuit of the combined squadrons to the West Indies, and of Sir John Duckworth's in the action off St. Domingo. On being appointed Master's Mate of the PRINCE OF WALES 98, bearing the flag of Admiral Gambier, Mr. Hore accompanied the expedition to Copenhagen, where he served with the flotilla, and was appointed Acting-Lieutenant of the LEYDEN 64, Capt. Wm. Cumberland. He was confirmed, on 19 Oct. in the same year, in his old ship the SPENCER, in which he continued with Rear-Admiral Stopford until Dec. 1808. On again joining his friend in the CÆSAR 80, we find him present at the destruction of three heavy French frigates under the batteries of Sable d'Olonne, and also of the shipping in Basque Roads. In the summer of 1809, he assumed command of a gun-boat, and shared in all the operations connected with the Walcheren expedition. Being subsequently appointed Flag-Lieutenant to Rear-Admiral Stopford in the SCIPION 74, Mr. Hore proceeded with him to the Cape of Good Hope; on his return from which station, after having participated in the reduction of the island of Java, he was promoted, 26 Jan. 1812, to the acting-command of the HARPY sloop.

On the breaking out of war with the United States, he conveyed the despatches announcing that event to the Mauritius—encountering on his passage a very fearful hurricane, which rendered it necessary for his guns to be thrown overboard. Commander Hore, who left the HARPY in March, 1813, and was officially promoted on 13 of the following May, held an appointment in the Coast Guard from 1821 to 1825. He has since been on half-pay.

Commander Hore has been 25 years a Magistrate for cos. Wicklow and Wexford. He married, 8 Sept. 1821, Jane Caroline, daughter of Rich. Solly, Esq., of Walthamstow, by Frances, only daughter of Sir Fred. Flood, Bart., LL.D., M.P.

HORNBY. (LIEUTENANT, 1846.)

FREDERICK JOHN HORNBY passed his examination 5 May, 1841; and, until March, 1845, was employed, as Mate, in the BELLEISLE 72, and VINDICTIVE 50, both commanded by Capt. John Toup Nicolas, MAGNIFICENT 72, Commodore Hon. Henry Dilkes Byng, and FORMIDABLE 84, Capts. Sir Chas. Sullivan and Geo. Fred. Rich, flag-ship for some time of Sir Edw. W. C. R. Owen—on the Home, Jamaica, and Mediterranean stations. He has been since serving in the TERROR discovery-ship, Capt. Fras. Rawdon Moira Crozier, in an attempt to ascertain the existence of a north-west passage through Lancaster Sound and Bering Strait. His commission bears date 21 May, 1846.

HORNBY, C.B. (REAR-ADMIRAL OF THE BLUE, 1846. F-P., 34; H-P., 16.)

PHIPPS HORNBY, born 27 April, 1785, is fifth son of the Rev. Geoffrey Hornby, Rector of Winwick, Lancashire, by the Hon. Lucy Stanley, sister of Edward, 12th Earl of Derby; brother of Lieut.-Colonel Charles Hornby, of the Scots Fusileer Guards; brother-in-law of the present Earl of Derby; and uncle both of Capt. W. W. Hornby, R.N., and of Edm. Geo. Hornby, Esq., late M.P. for Warrington, who married a cousin of the Right Hon. Sir Robert Peel, Bart., M.P.

This officer entered the Navy, 19 May, 1797, as Midshipman, on board the LATONA frigate, Capt. John Bligh, bearing the flag of Hon. Wm. Waldegrave at Newfoundland, where, removing successively to the ROMNEY 50, and AGINCOURT 64, he served with the same officers until 1800. He next cruized for several months in the Channel on board the ACTIVE frigate, Capt. John Giffard, and on then rejoining Capt. Bligh in the THESEUS 74, was for upwards of two years employed with him in the West Indies, on which station we find him repeatedly engaged in cutting out armed and other vessels from the enemy's different ports and harbours in St. Domingo. In July, 1803, he returned home in the SANTA MARGARITA 36, Capt. Wilson Rathborne, and in the spring of the following year he sailed in the LEVIATHAN 74, Capt. Henry Wm. Bayntun, for the Mediterranean, where, on 1 Aug. 1804, he was promoted from the VICTORY 100, flag-ship of Lord Nelson, to an Acting Lieutenancy in the EXCELLENT 74, Capt. Frank Sotheron—an appointment which the Admiralty confirmed by a commission dated on 16 of the ensuing Nov. In May, 1806, besides serving on shore at the defence of Gaeta, Mr. Hornby was entrusted with the command of the seamen and marines during the operations connected with the capture of the island of Capri. He soon afterwards joined the SWIFTSURE 74, Capt. Wm. Geo. Rutherford, and on 15 Aug. 1806 was promoted to the command of the DUCHESS OF BEDFORD of 16 guns. In that vessel, when in the Gut of Gibraltar, he succeeded in beating off two Spanish privateers who had endeavoured to carry her by boarding. Capt. Hornby's next appointment was, about Feb. 1807, to the MINORCA 18, in which sloop, previously to visiting the Adriatic, he came into frequent contact with the enemy's gun-boats and batteries, both in the vicinity of Cadiz and while employed in the blockade of Ceuta, a port on the coast of Morocco. On 31 March, 1810, he was appointed (having been advanced to Post-commission on 16 of the preceding month) to the temporary command of the FAME 74, off Toulon. On his proximate removal to the VOLAGE 22, he co-operated for some time in the defence of Sicily against the threatened invasion of Murat; and on 13 March, 1811, he had the honour of enacting a conspicuous part in the celebrated action off Lissa, when a British squadron, carrying in the whole 156 guns and 879 men, gloriously defeated, after a shattering battle of six hours, and a loss to the VOLAGE of 13 killed and 33 wounded, a Franco-Venetian armament, whose force amounted to 284 guns and 2655 men.* The brave and gallant conduct displayed on the occasion by Capt. Hornby, who himself received a slight wound, was rewarded by the Admiralty with a gold medal. He continued in the VOLAGE until Oct. 1811, and was next, on 6 Aug. 1812, and 3 Dec. 1814, appointed to the command of the STAG 36, and SPARTAN 38. In the former of those frigates he made a voyage to the Cape of Good Hope; and on returning, in the latter, to the Mediterranean, he was employed as Senior officer, in conjunction with a Tuscan land-force, to secure the accomplishment of a treaty stipulative of the surrender to Tuscany of the island of Elba by the French. For this service Capt. Hornby was presented by the Tuscan Government with the Cross of the Imperial Order of St. Joseph of Wurtzbourgh. He paid the SPARTAN off in July, 1816, and from that period remained unemployed until 1832, when he was appointed Superintendent of the Royal Naval Hospital and Victualling Yard at Plymouth. He removed, 6 Jan. 1838, to the command of the WILLIAM AND MARY yacht, and the superintendentship of the Dockyard at Woolwich; and from 16 Dec. 1841, until promoted to flag-rank, 9 Nov. 1846, he filled the office of Comptroller-General of the Coast Guard.

The Rear-Admiral was nominated a C.B. 4 June, 1815. He married, 22 Nov. 1814, Sophie Maria, eldest daughter of the late Right Hon. General Burgoyne, by whom he has issue eight children. His second daughter, Caroline Lucy, is married to Lieut. W. T. Denison, R.E. AGENTS—Messrs. Halford and Co.

HORNBY. (LIEUTENANT, 1825.)

WILLIAM HORNBY entered the Navy 21 Aug. 1811; passed his examination in 1818; and obtained his commission 4 Oct. 1825. He does not appear to have been since employed. AGENT—Joseph Woodhead.

HORNBY. (CAPT., 1846. F-P., 15; H-P., 7.)

WILLIAM WINDHAM HORNBY, born 23 July, 1812, at Huyton, in Lancashire, is eldest son of the Rev. Geoffrey Hornby, Rector of Bury, in that co., by the Hon. Georgiana Byng, sister of the late Vice-Admiral Viscount Torrington; and nephew of Rear-Admiral Phipps Hornby, C.B.

This officer entered the Royal Naval College 1 Dec. 1825; and embarked, in June, 1827, as a Volunteer, on board the GALATEA 42, Capt. Sir Chas. Sullivan, with whom he was for some time employed on particular service. On proceeding in 1828 to the Mediterranean as Midshipman of the RATTLESNAKE 28, Capt. Hon. Chas. Orlando Bridgeman, he assisted at the blockade of Navarin, and took part in several boat affairs with pirates. In 1831, after an attachment with Capt. Bridgeman to the REVENGE 78, he joined the GANNET 18, Capt. Mark Halpen Sweny, and sailed for the West Indies, where he was present at Jamaica during the insurrection of 1832. Passing his examination in the course of that year, he became Mate of the RANGER 28, Capt. Manley Dixon. Prior to his advancement to the rank of Lieutenant, which took place 9 Sept. 1833, Mr. Hornby was further employed in the SATELLITE 18, Capt. Robt. Smart, at the blockade of the Dutch coast, and in the CALEDONIA 120,

* *Vide* Gaz. 1811, p. 894.

flag-ship of Sir Josias Rowley in the Mediterranean. His next appointments were—25 Nov. 1833, and 20 Aug. 1836, to the CANOPUS 84, Capt. Hon. Josceline Percy, and BEACON surveying-vessel, Lieut. Commander Thos. Graves, both on the latter station, whence his health obliged him to return in June, 1838—10 April, 1839, to the BENBOW 72, Capt. Houston Stewart, from which ship also in the Mediterranean, he was again under the necessity of invaliding in June, 1840—and 21 Aug. 1841, as First-Lieutenant, to the WARSPITE 50, Capt. Lord John Hay, fitting at Portsmouth. He obtained a second promotal commission 23 Nov. following; and on 9 Nov. 1846, having been in command from 7 Feb. 1845 until April of the former year, of the STYX sloop, on the coast of Africa, he was promoted to Post rank. He is at present on half-pay. AGENT —Joseph Woodhead.

HORNSBY. (LIEUT., 1811. F-P., 14; H-P., 34.)

WILLIAM HORNSBY entered the Navy, in Sept. 1799, on board the EXPERIMENT 44, *armée en flûte*, Capts. John G. Saville and Geo. Chas. Mackenzie; to which ship (attending intermediately the expedition of 1801 to Egypt) he continued attached until the close of 1805. He afterwards joined the MEGÆRA fire-vessel, Capt. Arch. Duff, and ROSE 18, Capts. Lucius Curtis and Philip Pipon, in the Channel; served, from June, 1807, to July, 1810, in the RESOLUTION and RODNEY 74's, each commanded by Capt. Geo. Burlton, under whom he was present, as Midshipman of the RESOLUTION, at the bombardments of Copenhagen and Flushing; then became Acting-Lieutenant, for a short time, of the TONNANT 80, Capt. Sir John Gore; and, after a further employment, off Havre and Lisbon, in the CYANE 22, and ABERCROMBY 74, Capts. Fras. Augustus Collier and Wm. Chas. Fahie, was officially promoted, 26 Sept. 1811, into the CANOPUS 80, Capt. Chas. Inglis. His last appointments were—to the ROSE 18, Capt. Robt. Maunsell, and VILLE DE PARIS 110, and BOYNE 98, both under the orders of Capt. Burlton. He served in the ROSE on the Baltic station; and was a participator, in the BOYNE, in Sir Edw. Pellew's partial actions of 5 Nov. 1813 and 13 Feb. 1814, with the Toulon fleet. He has been on half-pay since Sept. of the latter year.

HORTON. (COMMANDER, 1844. F-P., 13; H-P., 2.)

FREDERICK WILMOT HORTON is a relative of Sir Robt. J. W. Horton, Bart.

This officer entered the Navy 6 Nov. 1832; passed his examination in 1838; obtained his commission 9 May, 1839; and was successively appointed—on 22 of the same month, to the JASEUR 16, Capt. Fred. Moore Boultbee, stationed in the Mediterranean—and, 31 Oct. 1840, and 29 Aug. 1842, to the ENDYMION 44, and, as Senior-Lieutenant, to the DIDO 18, Capts. Hon. Fred. Wm. Grey and Hon. Henry Keppel, both in the East Indies. For his spirited and zealous exertions in command of the boats of the latter vessel at the destruction of the forts and settlements belonging to the pirates in the Sarebus river, on the coast of Borneo, he obtained the expressed approbation of the Commander-in-Chief, Sir Wm. Parker, and of the Board of Admiralty, and was promoted to the rank of Commander 6 Jan. 1844. He was appointed, 17 Feb. 1846, to the CYGNET 6, on the African station, where, since 24 of the following April, he has been serving in the KINGFISHER 12. AGENTS—Messrs. Stilwell.

HORTON. (LIEUTENANT, 1842.)

WILLIAM HORTON is son (by Grace, daughter of —— Treacher, Esq., and widow of Henry Whorwood, Esq., of Headington House, co. Oxford) of Joshua Sydney Horton, Esq., Rear-Admiral of the White (1830), who died 24 Nov. 1834, at Boulogne-sur-mer, aged 67. His grandfather's first wife was a daughter of Geo. Clarke, Esq., Lieut.-Governor of New York; and his uncle, the late Thos. Horton, Esq., of Howroyde, co. York, married the Lady Mary Gordon, youngest daughter of George, third Earl of Aberdeen. The Lieutenant is nephew of Geo. Wm. Horton, Esq., a Lieut.-Colonel in the Army.

This officer entered the Navy 7 Dec. 1832; passed his examination 13 Dec. 1839; and served, as Mate, on board the TALBOT 26, Capts. Henry John Codrington and Robt. Fanshawe Stopford (under the former of whom he participated in the bombardment of St. Jean d'Acre), and QUEEN 110, and ST. VINCENT 120, flag-ships at Portsmouth of Sir Edw. Codrington. He obtained his commission 7 March, 1842, but, rejoining the ST. VINCENT soon afterwards, continued in that ship until appointed, 6 Dec. following, to the GORGON steamer, Capt. Chas. Hotham, on the South American station. On 25 Nov. 1844, after about 12 months of half-pay, he went back to the ST. VINCENT, then bearing the flag of Sir Chas. Rowley, with whom, however, he continued but a few months. Lieut. Horton, whose next appointment was, 25 July, 1846, to the QUEEN, Commodore Sir Jas. John Gordon Bremer, has been attached, since 14 Oct. in that year, to the THETIS 36, commanded by his former Captain, Codrington.

He married, 18 Feb. 1846, Agnes Jane, second daughter of the late J. Jeddere Fisher, Esq., of Great Culberden, Tunbridge Wells.

HOSEASON. (LIEUT., 1816. F-P., 8; H-P., 30.)

ANDREW HOSEASON died about the commencement of 1847.

This officer entered the Navy, 13 Oct. 1809, as A. B., on board the STRENUOUS gun-brig, Lieut.-Commander John Nugent, employed on the Leith station. Removing, in the next Dec., to the LEDA 36, Capt. Geo. Sayer, he sailed in that ship with a convoy for the East Indies, where we find him, in Aug. 1811 and Jan. 1813, assisting, as Master's Mate, at the reduction of Java, and in a very desperate attack made upon the pirates of Sambas, in the island of Borneo. In the spring of 1816 he was for a short time transferred to the PHILOMEL 10, Capt. Jas. Hanway Plumridge, but he then went back, in a similar capacity, to the LEDA, and continued in her until confirmed by a commission dated on 30 Dec. in the same year.

HOSEASON. (COMMANDER, 1844.)

JOHN COCHRANE HOSEASON entered the Navy 20 July, 1823; passed his examination in 1829; and obtained his first commission 10 Jan. 1837. His succeeding appointments were—12 Jan. and 24 April, 1837, and 18 Jan. 1838, to the DUBLIN 50, flag-ship of Sir Graham Eden Hamond, ROVER 18, Capt. Chas. Eden, and IMOGENE 26, Capt. Henry Wm. Bruce, all on the South American station, whence he returned to England, and was paid off at the close of 1839—and, 3 Feb. 1840, to the CAMBRIDGE 78, Capt. Edw. Barnard, with whom he served for nearly two years, and was present in the operations on the coast of Syria, and at the blockade of Alexandria. He acquired the rank he now holds 6 Sept. 1844; and, since 10 June, 1846, has been in command of the INFLEXIBLE steam-sloop, on the East India station. AGENTS—Hallett and Robinson.

HOSEASON. (COMMANDER, 1846.)

WILLIAM HOSEASON entered the Navy 24 May, 1811; passed his examination in 1818; and was made Lieutenant, 28 Dec. 1826, into the BUSTARD 10, Capt. Chas. Elliot, on the Jamaica station. He returned home in 1827, on board the PRIMROSE 18, Capt. Octavius Vernon Harcourt; and was afterwards appointed—17 Feb. 1831, to the NIMROD 20, Capt. Sam. Radford, on the Cork station—14 April, 1832, to the EXCELLENT gunnery-ship at Portsmouth, Capt. Thos. Hastings—15 Oct. 1833, to the THUNDERER 84, Capt. Wm. Furlong Wise, in the Mediterranean—and, 31 May and 4 Aug. 1837, 26 Oct. 1839, and 9 April, 1846, to the successive command of the PIGMY, PROSPERO, ALECTO, and TORCH steamers. He attained his present rank 9 Nov. 1846; and is now on half-pay. AGENTS—Messrs. Stilwell.

HOSKEN. (LIEUT., 1828. F-P., 24; H-P., 15.)

JAMES HOSKEN entered the Navy 23 Feb. 1808; passed his examination in 1816; and, between that period and 1824, was employed on the West India and Home stations, in the PIQUE 36, Capts. Fanshawe, John M'Kellar, and Jas. Haldane Tait, WOLF sloop, Capt. Bernard Yeoman, and BULWARK 74, Capt. Dundas. On 9 Aug. 1828, as a reward for four years of very active servitude, as Mate of the SCOUT Revenue-cutter, Lieut.-Commanders Cook and Fitzmaurice, he was promoted to his present rank. He was then, until paid off in May, 1830, employed on the Mediterranean station in the ÆTNA bomb, Capt. Stephen Lushington; and he afterwards, until put out of commission in Oct. 1832, had charge of the PRINCESS ELIZABETH and TYRIAN packets, in the West Indies and South America. He has since been on half-pay.

On leaving the TYRIAN, Lieut. Hosken took command of a merchant-ship; and, in July, 1836, he assumed that of the celebrated steamer the *Great Western*, in which he made 33 voyages, or 66 passages to and from New York. In Jan. 1844 he was appointed to that leviathan of the deep the *Great Britain* steam-ship.

HOSKINS. (COMMANDER, 1814. F-P., 11; H-P., 33.)

SAMUEL HOSKINS entered the Navy, 10 July, 1803, as A.B., on board the AMAZON 38, Capt. Wm. Parker. Continuing to serve with that officer for a period of nearly seven years, he in consequence commanded a boat at the cutting-out of a brig from under the batteries of Palma—accompanied Lord Nelson in his celebrated pursuit of the combined squadrons to the West Indies—assisted, on 13 March, 1806, in company with the LONDON 98, at the capture, after a long running fight, and a loss to the AMAZON of 3 men killed and 6 wounded, of the French 80-gun ship *Marengo*, bearing the flag of Rear-Admiral Linois, and 40-gun frigate *Belle Poule*—and co-operated with the patriots on the coast of Gallicia, where many of the enemy's batteries were destroyed. On 4 April, 1810, he was promoted to the rank of Lieutenant in the ROTA 38, Capt. Philip Somerville; in the boats belonging to which frigate he appears to have been wounded at the capture of a privateer, off the island of Ushant, in 1812. He was advanced—after having officiated for 18 months, on board the SAN JUAN 74, as Flag-Lieutenant at Gibraltar to Rear-Admiral Sam. Hood Linzee—to the rank of Commander 4 July, 1814; but he has not been since afloat.

Commander Hoskins married, in 1820, Mary Anne, youngest daughter of the late Commander Folliott, R.N. (1790), and by that lady has issue.

HOSTE, BART. (COMMANDER, 1843. F-P., 14; H-P., 3.)

SIR WILLIAM LEGGE GEORGE HOSTE, born 19 March, 1818, is son of that distinguished officer, the late Capt. Sir Wm. Hoste, Bart., K.C.B.,* by Harriet, third daughter of Horatio, second Earl of Orford; and nephew of Sir Geo. Chas. Hoste, C.B., Colonel of the Royal Engineers.

This officer entered the Navy, 1 Aug. 1830, as a Volunteer, on board the BRITON 46, Capt. John Duff Markland, employed on the Home station; became Midshipman, in Feb. 1833, of the VICTORY 104, Capt. Edw. Rich. Williams, guard-ship at Portsmouth; and proceeded soon afterwards to South America, in the CONWAY 28, Capt. Henry Eden. Between March, 1834, and his promotion to the rank of Lieutenant 27 June, 1838, we find him employed in the Mediterranean, the last 15 months as Mate, on board the THUNDERER 84, Capt. Wm. Furlong Wise, ASIA 84, Capt. Wm. Fisher, and PRINCESS CHARLOTTE 104, bearing the flag of Hon. Sir Robt. Stopford. Being then, however, reappointed to the latter ship, he continued attached to her, on the same station, until Nov. 1839. He subsequently, from 12 April, 1841, until paid off in Dec. 1842, served in the SOUTHAMPTON 50, under the flag of Sir Edw. Durnford King, Commander-in-Chief at the Cape of Good Hope and Brazils, and assisted during that period in taking possession of Port Natal. Being next, on 1 July, 1843, appointed to the VICTORIA AND ALBERT yacht, Capt. Lord Adolphus FitzClarence, Sir Wm. Hoste was present in the ensuing Sept. at the meeting which took place at Tréport between the Sovereigns of France and England. He was advanced to his present rank, at the request of H.R.H. Prince Albert, 5 Nov. 1843; and, since 17 Dec. 1845, has been in successive command of the RINGDOVE and SPITEFUL steam-sloops, on the East India station.

Sir Wm. Hoste received in 1845 the appointment of Gentleman Usher to the Queen Dowager.

* Sir Wm. Hoste entered the Navy at the commencement of the French revolutionary war, was with Nelson at Teneriffe in 1797, and attained Post-rank in 1802. On 13 March, 1811, being at the time in the AMPHION 32, and in command (including that ship) of four frigates, carrying, in the whole, 156 guns and 879 men, he effected the brilliant defeat, after a battle of six hours, and a loss to the AMPHION of 15 killed and 47 wounded, of a Franco-Venetian armament, whose force amounted to 284 guns and 2655 men. When in the BACCHANTE, in 1813, he commanded the Naval force employed at the reduction of the important fortresses of Cattaro and Ragusa. For the above and other dashing services, Capt. Hoste was raised to the dignity of a Baronet in 1814. In the same year he obtained an honourable augmentation to the family arms; and in 1815 he was nominated a K.C.B. In consideration of his services at Cattaro and Ragusa, the Emperor of Austria also conferred on him the insignia of a K.M.T. He died 6 Dec. 1828.

HOTCHKIS. (RETIRED COMMANDER, 1833. F-P., 9; H-P., 60.)

JOHN HOTCHKIS was born 28 Aug. 1766. One of his brothers, Adam, was killed in India, in the Medical Service of the Company, in 1780; another, Alexander, a Lieutenant of Marines, perished in the same year on board the STIRLING CASTLE 64, on the coast of America; and a third, David, lost his left leg while serving as a Lieutenant of the PRESTON 50, in the action off the Dogger Bank in 1781.

This officer entered the Navy, in Oct. 1778, as Captain's Servant, on board the CRESCENT 28, Capt. Chas. Hope, with whom he continued to serve as Midshipman of the IPHIGENIA 32, and LEOCADIA 36, on the Home and Newfoundland stations, until the peace of 1783. Re-embarking, in 1793, as Master's Mate, on board the GIBRALTAR 80, Capts. Thos. Mackenzie and John Pakenham, he had an opportunity, under the former officer, of witnessing Lord Howe's action of 1 June, 1794, on which occasion he was sent into port as Acting-Master of the NORTHUMBERLAND 74, one of the prizes taken by the British. On proceeding to the Mediterranean Mr. Hotchkis was there promoted, 17 June, 1795, to a Lieutenancy in the ÇA IRA 80, Capt. Chas. Dudley Pater. He remained in that ship until burnt out, in consequence of her having accidentally caught fire, in San Fiorenza Bay, 11 April, 1796; after which we find him employed, from 26 Sept. in the same year until May, 1797, on board the MONMOUTH 64, Capt. the Earl of Northesk, in the North Sea. He then invalided, from badness of sight, and did not again go afloat. He became a Retired Commander on the Junior List 26 Nov. 1830, and on the Senior 21 Dec. 1833.

Commander Hotchkis married, first, 9 Nov. 1800, Mary, daughter of Rich. Pearce, Esq., co. Westmeath. That lady dying in 1830, he espoused, secondly, in 1832, a daughter of Thos. Hart, Esq., a Major in the Hon. E. I. Co.'s service, by whom he has issue one son.

HOTHAM, K.C.B. (CAPTAIN, 1833. F-P., 19; H-P., 10.)

SIR CHARLES HOTHAM, born in 1806, is eldest son of the Rev. Fras. Hotham, Prebendary of Rochester (second son of the second Lord Hotham, one of the Barons of the Court of Exchequer), by Anne Elizabeth, eldest daughter of Thos. Hallett Hodges, Esq., of Hemsted Place, Kent; and first cousin of Capt. Hon. Geo. Fred. Hotham, R.N. Sir Charles, who is brother-in-law of Lieut.-Colonel Grieve of the 75th Regt., has also a brother, Augustus Thomas Hotham, in the Army.

This officer entered the Navy 6 Nov. 1818; and on the night of 23 May, 1824, when Midshipman of the NAIAD 46, Capt. Hon. Robt. Cavendish Spencer, served in the boats under Lieut. Michael Quin at the gallant destruction of a 16-gun brig, moored in a position of extraordinary strength alongside the walls of the fortress of Bona, in which was a garrison of about 400 soldiers, who, from cannon and musket, kept up a tremendous fire, almost perpendicularly, on the deck. He was made Lieutenant, 17 Sept. 1825, into the REVENGE 76, flag-ship of Sir Harry Burrard Neale in the Mediterranean; and next appointed—15 May, 1826, to the MEDINA 20, Capts. Timothy Curtis and Wm. Burnaby Greene, on the same station—and, 8 Dec. 1827, and 26 July, 1828, as First, to the TERROR and METEOR bombs, Capts. Wm. Fletcher and David Hope. As a reward for his distinguished exertions on the occasion of the wreck of the TERROR, more particularly alluded to in our memoir of Capt. Hope, Mr. Hotham was promoted by the Lord High Admiral to the rank of Commander 13 Aug. 1828. After an interval of half-pay he obtained an appointment, 17 March, 1830, to the CORDELIA 10, and returned to the Mediterranean, whence he ultimately came home and was paid off in Oct. 1833—having been raised to Post-rank on 28 of the preceding June in compliment to the memory of his uncle the late Vice-Admiral Hon. Sir Henry Hotham, G.C.B., G.C.M.G. His next appointment was, 25 Nov. 1842, to the GORGON steam-sloop, stationed on the S.E. coast of America. In Nov. 1845, having assumed command of a small squadron, he ascended the river Parana, in conjunction with a French naval force under Capt. Trèhouart, and on 20 of that month, after a hard day's fighting, succeeded in effecting the destruction of four heavy batteries belonging to General Rosas at Punta Obligado, also of a schooner-of war carrying 6 guns, and of 24 vessels chained across the river. Towards the close of the action he landed with 180 seamen and 145 marines, and accomplished the defeat of the enemy, whose numbers had originally consisted of at least 3500 men, in cavalry, infantry, and artillery, and whose batteries had mounted 22 pieces of ordnance, including 10 brass guns, which latter were taken off to the ships, the remainder being all destroyed. The loss of the British in this very brilliant affair amounted to 9 men killed and 24 wounded. In acknowledgment of the gallantry, zeal, and ability displayed throughout its various details by Capt. Hotham, he was recommended in the most fervent terms of admiration by his Commander-in-Chief, Rear-Admiral Sam. Hood Inglefield, in his despatches to the Admiralty, and he was in consequence nominated a K.C.B. 9 March, 1846. Since 13 May in that year he has been employed as Commodore on the coast of Africa, with his broad pendant successively flying in the DEVASTATION and PENELOPE steamers.

While Sir Chas. Hotham was in the GORGON, that vessel was blown far on shore in a hurricane at Colonia, and it was only by the most indomitable and procrastinated exertion on the part of himself and his crew that she was saved. AGENTS—Messrs. Halford and Co.

HOTHAM. (CAPTAIN, 1828. F-P., 12; H-P., 25.)

THE HONOURABLE GEORGE FREDERICK HOTHAM, born 20 Oct. 1799, is son of the late Hon. Beaumont Hotham (eldest son of the second Lord Hotham, one of the Barons of the Court of Exchequer), by Philadelphia, daughter of Sir John Dixon Dyke, Bart. Capt. Hotham, who is only brother of the present Lord Hotham, is nephew of Vice-Admiral Hon. Sir Henry Hotham, G.C.B., G.C.M.G. (who died Commander-in-Chief in the Mediterranean in 1833, aged 56), and of Admiral Sir John Sutton, K.C.B.; and cousin both of the present Admiral Sir Wm. Hotham, G.C.B., and of Capt. Sir Chas. Hotham, K.C.B.

This officer entered the Navy, 16 Sept. 1810, as Fst.-cl. Vol., on board the NORTHUMBERLAND 74, commanded by his uncle Capt. Hon. Henry Hotham. On 22 May, 1812, when in company with the GROWLER gun-brig, we find him contributing to the gallant destruction, at the entrance of L'Orient, of the French 40-gun frigates *L'Arienne* and *L'Andromaque*, and 16 gun-brig *Mamelouck*, whose united fire, conjointly with that of a destructive battery, killed 5 of the NORTHUMBERLAND'S people, and wounded 28. Becoming Midshipman, in Jan. 1813, of the RAMILLIES 74, Capts. Sir Thos. Masterman Hardy and Chas. Ogle, he sailed for the coast of North America, where he continued until the termination of hostilities, and, independently of the blockade of New London, participated in the operations against Moose Island, Baltimore, and New Orleans. After a brief re-employment under the orders of his uncle in the SUPERB 74, stationed off the coast of France for the interception of Napoleon Buonaparte, Mr. Hotham, in Oct. 1815, joined the PACTOLUS 38, Capts. Hon. Fred. Wm. Aylmer and Wm. Hugh Dobbie, the latter of whom he accompanied into the SEVERN 40. On next joining the MINDEN 74, Capt. Wm. Paterson, he assisted in that ship at the bombardment of Algiers, 27 Aug. 1816, and then sailed for the East Indies, on which station he served until after his promotion to the rank of Lieutenant, which took place 7 Dec. 1819. On 22 Oct. 1821, he obtained an appointment to the EURYALUS 42, Capt. Augustus Wm. Jas. Clifford, fitting for the Mediterranean, whence he returned to England on his advancement to the rank of Commander 25 March, 1822. On 16 May, 1828, Capt. Hotham had the misfortune, when off the coast of Egypt, to lose the PARTHIAN 10, a sloop of which he had been awarded the command 28 April, 1827. He attained the rank he now holds 7 June, 1828, and has since been on half-pay.

Capt. Hotham married, 12 Aug. 1824, Lady Susan Maria O'Bryen, eldest daughter of William, second Marquess of Thomond, by whom he has issue.

HOTHAM. (LIEUTENANT, 1832.)

JOHN WILLIAM HOTHAM, born in 1809, is third son of Admiral Sir Wm. Hotham, G.C.B., by his first marriage.

This officer passed his examination in 1830, and was made Lieutenant, 13 March, 1832, into the ALFRED 50, Capt. Robt. Maunsell, on the Mediterranean station. He was paid off on his return to England 28 July, 1834, and has since been unemployed.

Lieut. Hotham married, 29 April, 1838, Sarah Eliza, eldest daughter of Wm. Hawkesley, Esq., of the Circus, Bath.

HOTHAM, G.C.B. (ADMIRAL OF THE RED, 1837. F-P., 22; H-P., 46.)

SIR WILLIAM HOTHAM, born in Feb. 1772, is second son of Geo. Hotham, a General in the Army, and Colonel of the 14th Regt. of Foot, by Diana, youngest daughter of Sir Warton Pennyman, Bart.; brother-in-law of the late Lord Edw. O'Bryen, Capt. R.N.; and nephew of the first Lord Hotham, who commanded the EDGAR 74, at the relief of Gibraltar in 1782, fought the well-known actions of 14 March and 13 July, 1795, with the French fleet, was raised for his services to the peerage, and died 2 May, 1813.

This officer (whose name had been borne on the books of different ships since 21 Dec. 1779) went to sea from Westminster School, in the autumn of 1785, on board the GRAMPUS 50, Capt. Edw. Thompson. On his return home from the African station in the following spring, he entered the Royal Naval Academy at Portsmouth, but he re-embarked in

Sept. 1786 on board the SOLEBAY 32, Capt. John Holloway, and sailed for the Leeward Islands, where he remained until the close of 1789. In 1790 we find him cruizing in the Channel in the HEBE 36, Capt. Alex. Hood, and also in the PRINCESS ROYAL 98, bearing the flag of his uncle Rear-Admiral Hotham. Attaining the rank of Lieutenant on 27 Oct. in the same year, and being shortly afterwards appointed in that capacity to the ALLIGATOR 28, Capt. Isaac Coffin, he proceeded to Halifax, whence, in 1791, he returned home with Lord Dorchester, the Governor-General. In 1792 he was again ordered to Halifax, in the WINCHELSEA 32, Capt. Fisher; and in June, 1793, subsequently to his removal to the DUKE 98, Commodore Geo. Murray, he shared in the unsuccessful operation against Martinique. In January, 1794, on his arrival off Toulon in the INCONSTANT 36, Capt. Augustus Montgomery, Mr. Hotham was appointed Seventh Lieutenant of the VICTORY 100, bearing the flag of Lord Hood, by whom, during the siege of Bastia, he was allowed to serve on shore as a Volunteer with the brigade of seamen employed under the orders of Capt. Nelson. On 11 Aug. 1794, when before Calvi, which place also surrendered to the British arms, he was invested (being at the time First of the VICTORY) with the command of L'ECLAIR sloop; and on 7 Oct. in the same year he was made Post into the CYCLOPS 28, previously to his actual junction of which frigate he acted for a short time as Captain of the BEDFORD 74, lying in Leghorn Roads. After she had spent some time in blockading the port of Smyrna, in unison with a force under Capt. Sam. Hood, the CYCLOPS went to Gibraltar, and was thence ordered with despatches to England, where, on her arrival after an extraordinary passage of six days, she was paid off in March, 1796. Owing to this unexpected departure from the Mediterranean, Capt. Hotham appears to have lost the command of LA MINERVE, one of the finest frigates in the service, to which the Commander-in-Chief, we are informed, had in ignorance of his absence appointed him. With the exception of the command, held for a very brief period, of LA RÉUNION 36, he did not succeed in again procuring employment until Jan. 1797, when he received instructions to join the ADAMANT 50. In that ship, which, to the credit of her Commander, was the only two-decker that preserved its loyalty intact during the mutiny at the Nore, Capt. Hotham was stationed with Lord Duncan off the Texel, and, besides occasionally bearing the flag of that nobleman, was with him in the memorable victory achieved over the Dutch, off Camperdown, 11 Oct. 1797. On that occasion he took charge of the HAERLEM, a captured 64, and succeeded, after a great deal of blowing and unsettled weather, in carrying her through the Cockle Gatway into Yarmouth Roads. The share borne by Capt. Hotham in the engagement was recompensed with a gold medal, and his First-Lieutenant was promoted to the rank of Commander. After several months of employment on the coast of France, the ADAMANT proceeded to the Cape of Good Hope, and was ultimately sent on a cruize off the Isle of France. On 11 Dec. 1799, being at the time in company with the TREMENDOUS 74, she drove the French frigate *La Preneuse* on shore, under a heavy fire from the batteries in the neighbourhood of Port Louis, which harbour, with his own ship, and the LANCASTER, RATTLESNAKE, and EUPHROSYNE under his orders, Capt. Hotham was subsequently sent to blockade. Having returned with convoy to England, and been paid off, Capt. Hotham, in March, 1803, procured command of the RAISONNABLE 64. He at first served off the Dutch coast, and for a short time carried the flag of Admiral Thornbrough, as he afterwards did, in the Downs, of Admiral Montagu. He was also engaged in watching the movements of the enemy off Boulogne, at a moment when an invasion of England was anticipated; and during a very tempestuous winter, in which the YORK 64, was lost, he was stationed in the North Sea. His health obliging him to resign the command of the RAISONNABLE in 1804, he remained on half-pay until appointed to the Liverpool district of Sea Fencibles, which, however, he only joined a short time previously to the disbandment of the corps in 1810. He then acquired command of the ROYAL SOVEREIGN yacht, and remained in that vessel until advanced to the rank of Rear-Admiral 4 Dec. 1813. He has since been on half-pay. He was created a K.C.B. 2 Jan. 1815; a Vice-Admiral 19 July, 1821; a full Admiral 10 Jan. 1837; and a G.C.B. 4 July, 1840.

Sir Wm. Hotham married, first, in June, 1804, Anne, daughter of Sir Edw. Jeynes, Kt., of Gloucester, and sister-in-law of the late Admiral Sir Edw. Thornbrough, G.C.B., who died in 1827; and secondly, in 1835, Jane Seymour, widow of Roger Pettiward, Esq., formerly of Great Finborough, Suffolk. By his first marriage he had issue, with one daughter, four sons, of whom the eldest, Augustus, is in the Army, and the third, John William, a Lieutenant R.N.

HOTHAM, K.H. (Captain, 1825. F-P., 13; H-P., 31.)

WILLIAM HOTHAM, born in 1794, is eldest son of Lieut.-Colonel Geo. Hotham (elder brother of Admiral Sir Wm. Hotham, G.C.B.), by his first wife, Caroline, daughter of Robt. Gee, Esq., of Bishop Burton; and brother-in-law of Sir John Wm. Lubbock, Bart., the eminent banker. One of Capt. Hotham's brothers, George, is a Captain in the Royal Engineers; a second, Charles, Prebendary of York; and a third, John, an officer in the East India Company's Artillery.

This officer entered the Navy, in June, 1803, on board the RAISONNABLE 64, commanded by his uncle, Capt. Wm. Hotham, in the North Sea. With the exception of a few weeks towards the close of 1811, during which he served as Acting-Lieutenant of the UNITÉ 36,* Capt. Edwin Henry Chamberlayne, he appears to have been continuously, from 1804 until 1814, employed under the orders of Capt. Chas. Rowley, as Midshipman, Master's Mate, and Lieutenant (commission dated 12 Feb. 1812), on board the RUBY 64, and EAGLE 74. While in the latter ship he assisted at the defence of Gaeta, and the storming of Capri in 1806; attended the expedition of 1809 to the Walcheren; was employed at the siege of Cadiz in 1810; and participated, in 1813, in the operations against Fiumé, Rovigno, and Trieste, during the siege of the citadel at which latter place he served on shore, and manifested an admirable degree of courage and activity.† He also, on 8 June, 1813, had partial command of the boats at the destruction, close to Omago, of a 2-gun battery, and the capture of four scuttled vessels loaded with wine; and on 7 of the following month accompanied a party that stormed, carried, and levelled the fortress of Farasina, mounting 5 long 18-pounders.‡ From Aug. 1813 until Jan. 1814 Lieut. Hotham commanded a flotilla employed, in the River Po, in co-operation with the Austrian army; and honourable mention is made of him in several official letters from Capt. Rowley to Admiral Fremantle, as well as in a despatch from Count Nugent to Earl Bathurst, then H.M. Secretary of State for the War Department. The EAGLE formed part of the squadron which accompanied Louis XVIII. to France in April, 1814; and was paid off at Chatham in the course of the following month. A few days after his promotion to the rank of Commander, which took place 15 June, 1814, we find Capt. Hotham appointed to the FERVENT sloop. After witnessing the grand naval review held before the Allied Sovereigns at Spithead, he proceeded to Bermuda and the West Indies. In June, 1815, the FERVENT was put out of commission; and on 27 April, 1824, Capt. Hotham obtained command of

* While in this ship, Mr. Hotham was creditably noticed for his cool and steady conduct at the capture, after a severe running fight of four hours, of the 26-gun store-ship, *Persanne*, who, until the moment of her surrender, had been taken for a frigate.—*Vide* Gaz. 1812, p. 567.

† *Vide* Gaz. 1813, p. 2478. ‡ *V.* Gaz. 1803, p. 2010.

the SAPPHO 18, fitting for the Halifax station, whence he returned on his advancement to Post-rank 4 April, 1825. He accepted the half-pay of Retirement 1 Oct. 1846.

Capt. Hotham was nominated a K.H. 25 Jan. 1836.

HOUGH. (COMMANDER, 1827. F-P., 20; H-P., 28.)

JOHN JAMES HOUGH was born about Feb. 1785.

This officer entered the Navy, in Sept. 1799, as Fst.-cl. Vol., on board the MARS 74, Capt. John Monckton, bearing the flag in the Channel of Hon. Geo. Cranfield Berkeley. He served next, from Jan. 1801 to Aug. 1805, part of the time as Midshipman, in the ANSON 44, Capt. Wm. Edw. Cracraft, on the Mediterranean station; then joined, for short periods, the SATURN 74, Capt. Lord Amelius Beauclerk, KENT 74, Capt. Henry Garrett, and HIBERNIA 110, flag-ship of Earl St. Vincent, all engaged on Home service; and on 2 Oct. 1807 was nominated Acting-Lieutenant, after an unemployed interval of 17 months, of the BELLONA 74, commanded at Halifax by Capt. John Erskine Douglas, to which ship he was confirmed by commission dated 19 Nov. following. His next appointments, until paid off in Aug. 1814, were, on the last mentioned, and on the Lisbon, West India, and Home stations—18 Nov. 1808, to the HORATIO, of 46 guns and 270 men, Capt. Geo. Scott—27 Nov. 1810, to the FORMIDABLE 98, Capt. Jas. Nicoll Morris—9 March, 1811, to the BARFLEUR 98, bearing the flag of Hon. G. C. Berkeley—27 July, 1812, to the ASIA 74, Capt. Geo. Scott—and, 5 Feb. 1814, to the EGMONT 74, Capt. Joseph Bingham. Of the above ships the HORATIO appears, when in company with the LATONA 38, and SUPÉRIEURE and DRIVER sloops, to have effected the capture, 10 Feb. 1809, off the Virgin Islands, of *La Junon* French frigate, of 46 guns and 323 men, after a close and sanguinary action of nearly three hours, a loss to herself of 7 men killed and 33 wounded, and to her antagonist of 130 killed and wounded. We also, on 21 Feb. 1810, find her making prize, at the close of a long chase, and of a running fight of one hour, of *La Nécessité*, pierced for 40 guns, but not mounting more than 28, with a complement on board of 186 men, and laden with naval stores and provisions from Brest bound to the Isle of France. Mr. Hough, who on the latter occasion officiated as the HORATIO's First-Lieutenant, was in both instances the officer sent to take possession of the French ships, and he each time likewise conducted the prizes into port. He subsequently, on joining the EGMONT, served in that ship under the flag of Rear-Admiral Chas. Vinicombe Penrose at the forcing of the passage of the Gironde, in the spring of 1814. His last naval appointments were to the command, 3 May, 1817, 1 March, 1824, and 21 March, 1826, of the ACTIVE, BASILISK, and CRACKER cutters; in which vessels he effected the capture of several smugglers, twice conveyed large amounts of specie from London to Dublin, sailed on two occasions with squadrons of observation under the flag of H.R.H. the Duke of Clarence, and was employed as Senior officer in protecting the fisheries off Jersey. He attained his present rank 29 Sept. 1827.

In May, 1834, Commander Hough was nominated one of the six stipendiary magistrates appointed at Barbadoes under the Slavery Emancipation Act; and when he resigned that situation in Oct. 1838 he was presented with a sum for the purchase of a piece of plate, as a mark of the satisfaction he had afforded by the just and impartial manner in which he had administered its duties. He was afterwards employed in the Indian Navy, as Captain, from 7 April, 1840, until 29 July, 1846, of the *Proserpine* war-steamer. During the operations of 21 July, 1842, against Chin-Kiang-Foo, he was stationed on the Yang-tse-Kiang and blockaded an entrance to the Grand Canal.* He married, 28 Aug. 1815, a daughter of Geo. Thos. Tracey, Esq., Purser and Paymaster R.N. (1805), and sister of Lieut. Benj. Wheatley Tracey, R.N. By that lady he has issue a son and three daughters. AGENT—Joseph Woodhead.

* *Vide* Gaz. 1842, p 3104.

HOUGHTON. (RETIRED COMMANDER, 1838. F-P., 11; H-P., 39.)

CHARLES EVELYN HOUGHTON, born 20 Sept. 1784, is eldest son of Major Houghton, of the 69th Regiment, who lost his life in exploring the interior of Africa; grandson of Capt. Wm. Houghton, of the 3rd Light Infantry, who was wounded at the battle of Bunker's Hill; and great-grandson of Sir Wm. Houghton, Bart., of Hoghton Tower, Lancaster. Maternally, Commander Houghton is nephew of the present Sir Hugh Evelyn, Bart., of Wotton Place; grand-nephew of the late Gen. Wm. Evelyn, Colonel of the 29th Regt., and M.P. for Helston, in Cornwall; and a descendant of the learned and distinguished John Evelyn, F.R.S., who was a Commissioner of the Navy, also Treasurer of Greenwich Hospital (to which institution he was a donor of 3000*l.*), and the last joint Sheriff for cos. Surrey and Sussex. One of the Commander's brothers, Frederick, a Lieutenant R.N., was lost with Capt. F. Moore Maurice in the MAGNET sloop, in 1812; and another, Ralph, a Lieutenant in the Army, died in the West Indies.

This officer entered the Navy, 9 Aug. 1797, as Fst.-cl. Vol., on board the STANDARD 64, Capts. Thos. Parr and Thos. Revell Shivers, stationed in the North Sea; removed, in April, 1798, to the BLONDE 32, *armée-en-flûte*, commanded by Capt. Dan. Dobree, in the Baltic, off the Texel, and on the Irish coast; and in Nov. 1799 rejoined Capt. Shivers on board the DEFIANCE 74, flag-ship afterwards of Rear-Admiral Thos. Graves. Under the latter officer he bore a warm part, as Midshipman, in the action off Copenhagen 2 April, 1801; and at its close, when the *Dannebrog*, bearing the Danish Admiral's flag, caught fire, and was drifting towards the DEFIANCE, he was sent with the boats to tow her head round, and had actually hold of the tow-rope at the moment she blew up. Between Oct. 1801 and Jan. 1805 Mr. Houghton was employed, on the West India, Home, and Mediterranean stations, in the AUDACIOUS 74, Capt. Shuldham Peard, JUNO 32, Capt. Henry Richardson, TRIUMPH 74, Capt. Sir Robt. Barlow, and DRAKE 10, Capt. Drury. Having passed his examination in 1804, and been for six months in charge of a watch, he was then appointed Sub-Lieutenant of the LOCUST gun-brig, Lieut.-Commander John Lake; which vessel, in Feb. 1805, took the ground off Boulogne, while endeavouring to cut off a boat, and lay exposed for some time to a very heavy fire from 11 of the enemy's batteries, and several thousands of their troops. Although the sails and rigging of the LOCUST were cut to pieces, and she was otherwise damaged, the only person hurt on board was Mr. Houghton, who received a musket-ball in the right leg. On 24 of the following April we find the same vessel uniting with the RAILLEUR and STARLING gun-brigs in an attack upon a powerful division of the invasion flotilla. Six schuyts were on that occasion captured, after a spirited resistance; and in boarding one of them Mr. Houghton was again wounded by a bayonet under the left arm. He was made full Lieutenant, on 14 Sept. in the same year, into the REGULUS 44, *armée-en-flûte*, Capt. Boys, lying at Portsmouth, but continued only a few weeks in that ship, and was lastly, from 3 July, 1807, until 26 Feb. 1810, employed, in the Channel, off the coast of Portugal, and in the North Sea and Baltic, on board the PLANTAGENET 74, Capts. Wm. Bradley and Thos. Eyles. He accepted his present rank 17 Jan. 1838.

Commander Houghton married, in 1806, Charlotte, youngest daughter of the late Fras. Dancer, Esq., of the Treasury, and of Wealdstone House, Harrow, co. Middlesex, by whom he has issue three sons and two daughters. AGENTS—Messrs. Chard.

HOULTON. (Retired Commander, 1840. f-p., 10; h-p., 47.)

Robert Houlton is second son of the late Joseph Houlton, Esq., of Farley Castle, co. Somerset, a Captain in the Army, by Dorothea Sarah, daughter of Chas. Torriano, Esq., Capt. R.A.; and brother (with the present Sir Geo. Houlton, Kt., late Capt. 43rd Regt.) of John Houlton, Esq., Colonel of the 1st Regt. of Somerset Militia, and a Deputy-Lieutenant for that co., who died 17 Feb. 1839—of Lieut. Joseph Houlton, of the 40th Regt. of Infantry, who died in 1795—and of Capt. Sam. Houlton, of the 11th Regt. of Native Infantry, who died at Dinapore, in the East Indies, in 1827.

This officer entered the Navy, in 1790, as a Volunteer, on board the Bellona 74, Capt. Fras. John Hartwell, guard-ship at Spithead, and after serving with Capt. Thos. Elphinstone, in the Swan and Atalanta sloops, joined, in 1792, the Courageux 74, Capt. Hon. Wm. Waldegrave. After that ship had assisted in the occupation of Toulon, and had been disabled in an engagement at Corsica, Mr. Houlton, while she was being hove down, was sent in the Moselle sloop to Gibraltar for ammunition. On his return to Toulon he was unfortunately captured by the enemy, who detained him in France until 1796. He was then appointed Master's Mate of the Glenmore 36, Capt. Geo. Duff, stationed in the North Sea; and on 18 May, 1797, he was made Lieutenant into the Triton 32, Capt. John Gore, attached to the force on the French coast. Invaliding, however, in the following year, he did not again go afloat until Dec. 1805, on 15 of which month he obtained an appointment to L'Impétueux 74, Capt. John Lawford, off Brest. In 1806 he joined the Irish Sea Fencibles; and in 1807 he assumed charge of a Signal tower in co. Donegal. The latter, his last appointment, he held but a few months; a serious attack of asthma compelling him to invalid. He became a Retired Commander on the Junior List 26 Nov. 1830, and on the Senior 18 Jan. 1840. Agents—Coplands and Burnett.

HOUSTOUN. (Commander, 1842. f-p., 18; h-p., 5.)

Wallace Houstoun entered the Navy 2 Dec. 1824; passed his examination in 1830; obtained his first commission 3 March, 1832; and was appointed —8 Dec. 1832, to the Childers 18, Capt. Robt. Deans—10 Jan. 1833, to the Spartiate 76, flag-ship of Sir Michael Seymour in South America—10 March, 1834, to the Conway 28, Capt. Henry Eden, with whom he returned to England and was paid off in Oct. 1835—9 June, 1836, to the Madagascar 44, Capts. Sir John Strutt Peyton and Provo Wm. Parry Wallis, in which ship he served on the North America and West India station, latterly as First-Lieutenant, until put out of commission in the summer of 1839—23 July and 27 Oct. 1840, to the Impregnable 104, and Caledonia 120, flag-ships of Sir Graham Moore at Plymouth—and, 17 Aug. 1841, to the Illustrious 72, as Flag-Lieutenant to Sir Chas. Adam, in North America and the West Indies. Attaining his present rank 7 May, 1842, he was invested with the command, 3 Aug. following, of the Pilot 16, on the station last named; and on 4 March, 1843, was transferred to that of the Imaum 72, bearing the broad pendant at Jamaica of Commodore Alex. Renton Sharpe. He has been on half-pay since June, 1844.

HOWARD, M.P. (Captain, 1838. f-p., 12; h-p., 12.)

The Honourable Edward Granville George Howard, born 23 Dec. 1809, is fourth son of the present Earl of Carlisle, K.G., by Georgiana, eldest daughter of William, fifth Duke of Devonshire, K.G.; brother of Lord Morpeth, M.P., Chief Commissioner of Woods and Forests, of Hon. C. W G. Howard, M.P., and of Hon. Fred. Geo. Howard, an officer in the Army, who was accidentally killed in Nov. 1834; brother-in-law of the Duke of Sutherland and of the Earl of Burlington; and nephew of Hon. Fred. Howard, Major of Hussars, who was killed at Waterloo, and of the late Duchess of Rutland.

This officer entered the Navy 5 April, 1823; obtained his first commission 19 Sept. 1829; and, from 15 April, 1830, until promoted to the rank of Commander, 3 June, 1833, served in the Mediterranean on board the Pelican 18, Capt. Joseph Gape. His next appointments were, 24 Sept. and 13 Oct. 1836, to the Serpent and Wolverene, of 16 guns each; in the latter of which sloops he was again employed on the Mediterranean station until advanced to the rank he now holds 27 Dec. 1838. He has since been on half-pay.

Capt. Howard has been in Parliament, since 1840, as Member for Morpeth. He married, in 1842, Diana, only daughter of Hon. Geo. Ponsonby, and niece of the present Viscount Ponsonby, G.C.B., and of the late Major-General Sir Wm. Ponsonby, K.C.B. Agents—Messrs. Stilwell.

HOWARD. (Lieut., 1828. f-p., 18; h-p., 19.)

Richard Howard entered the Navy, 1 Jan. 1810, as Fst.-cl. Vol., on board the Diana 38, Capts. Chas. Grant and Wm. Ferris, employed on Channel service. In May, 1812, he became Midshipman of the Colossus 74, Capt. Thos. Alexander, also on the Home station; and between Dec. 1813 and June, 1815, he was employed in North America on board the Saturn 56, Capt. Jas. Nash. Until the early part of 1817 he again served at home in the Surprise 38, and Malta 84, Capts. Sir Thos. John Cochrane and Thos. Gordon Caulfeild. Towards the close of 1818 he joined the Coast Blockade, in the capacity of Admiralty-Mate, having passed his examination in Oct. 1816; and after an attachment of three or four years to it he was successively appointed, with the same rank, to the Rifleman 18, Capts. Jas. Montagu, Wm. Webb, and Wm. Carleton, Briton 46, Capts. Geo. Fras. Seymour and Hon. Wm. Gordon, and Asia 84, flag-ship of Sir Edw. Codrington, on the Halifax and Mediterranean stations. He was made Lieutenant, 5 June, 1828, into the Ocean 98, Capt. Patrick Campbell; but since May, 1830, when he returned from the Mediterranean, and was put out of commission, has been unemployed.

HOWAT. (Commander, 1846.)

William Howat passed his examination in 1820; and was made Lieutenant, 13 Nov. 1826, into the Cyrené 20, Capt. Alex. Campbell, on the East India station, whence he came home with that officer in the Bombay 84, in Sept. 1828. His subsequent appointments were—4 Jan. 1832, to the Talavera 74, Capts. Thos. Brown and Edw. Chetham, with the latter of whom he returned to England from the Mediterranean and was paid off 12 Feb. 1835—25 March, 1836, to the Pembroke 74, Capts. Sir Thos. Fellowes and Fairfax Moresby, in which ship he was for nearly four years employed, part of the time as Midshipman, on the Lisbon and Mediterranean stations—27 Nov. 1841, in the latter capacity, to the Vanguard 80, off Lisbon, where he continued until the summer of 1843—and, 14 Feb. 1845, again as Senior, to the same ship, then commanded by Capt. Geo. Wickens Willes as part of the Channel squadron. He attained his present rank 9 Nov. 1846; and is now on half-pay.

HOWE. (Lieut., 1803. f-p., 35; h-p., 17.)

Alexander Burgoyne Howe, born 30 June, 1783, is second son of Alex. Howe, Esq., of Annapolis Royal, Nova Scotia; and grandson of Edw. Howe, Esq., of Annapolis, who was treacherously murdered while under a flag of truce and in parley with a French officer in New Brunswick in 1752.

This officer entered the Navy 6 Jan. 1795 (under the patronage of H.R.H. Prince Edward) as Midshipman, on board the Africa 64, Capt. Roddam Home; and in March, 1796, was present in the unsuccessful attack made by the forces under Rear-Admiral Wm. Parker and Major-General Forbes on the town of Leogane, St. Domingo. After serving for upwards of three years in the Channel and on the coast of Ireland in the UNITÉ frigate, Capt. Chas. Rowley, and CÆSAR 80, Capts. R. Home and Sir Jas. Saumarez, Mr. Howe joined the AMERICA 64, which ship, bearing the flag of Sir Wm. Parker, struck, 13 Dec. 1800, upon the Formigas rocks, and was rendered unfit for further service. He then became attached in succession to the ST. ALBANS 64, Capt. John Okes Hardy, flag-ship at Halifax, and PHEASANT 16, Capt. Henry Carew; and in the latter vessel he was employed throughout the summer of 1801 in blockading an enemy's ship, *Le Berceau*, lying in the port of Boston. From May, 1802, until Dec. 1805, we find him serving on board the LEVIATHAN 74, at first under Sir John Duckworth in the West Indies (where he beheld the capture of the national vessels, *La Mignonne* and *La Supérieure*), and then under Capt. Henry Wm. Bayntun in the Mediterranean; on which station he had the fortune to participate in the battle of Trafalgar. In Jan. 1806 Mr. Howe, who had been promoted to the rank of Lieutenant 28 May, 1803, was appointed to the RENOWN 74, Capt. Philip Chas. Durham. Towards the close of the same year, having been intermediately employed in blockading the port of Rochefort, he returned to the Mediterranean, and was there very actively employed until March, 1810. In Oct. 1809 he united in the pursuit which led to the self-destruction, near Cape Cette, of the French ships of the line *Robuste* and *Lion*. On leaving the RENOWN, Lieut. Howe became First of the THESEUS 74, Capt. Wm. Prowse, under whom, with the exception of a voyage made to St. Helena for the purpose of bringing home an East India convoy, he served on the North Sea station until Dec. 1813. The ship he next joined was the NEWCASTLE 50, Capt. Lord Geo. Stuart, stationed off the coast of North America, where he further served as Senior Lieutenant, from Feb. 1814 until compelled to invalid from the effects of rheumatism in Jan. 1815. His last appointments were—2 Oct. 1827 and 27 March, 1828, to the successive command of the SPRIGHTLY and GREYHOUND Revenue-vessels, the latter of which he left in Oct. 1830—16 Sept. 1831, to the command of the ONYX, on the Cork station, where he remained until paid off in Nov. 1832—and 13 Nov. 1833, to an Agency for Transports Afloat. He left the latter service in June, 1844.

Lieut. Howe married, 15 April, 1815, Elizabeth, relict of Robt. Carpenter, Esq., of Bradford, co. Somerset, by whom he has issue two sons and one daughter. AGENTS—Hallett and Robinson.

HOWELL. (COMMANDER, 1816. F-P., 16; H-P., 32.)

JOSEPH BENJAMIN HOWELL is brother-in-law of Capt. Wm. Blight, R.N.

This officer entered the Navy, in April, 1799, as Fst.-cl. Vol., on board the SUCCESS 32, Capt. Shuldham Peard. Continuing in that frigate until captured, 13 Feb. 1801, by a French squadron under M. Ganteaume, he was for nearly the whole of the time employed at the blockade of Malta, and assisted at the taking, 18 Feb. and 24 Aug. 1800, of the French 74-gun ship *Le Généreux*, and 40-gun frigate *La Diane*. On his release from captivity in March, 1801, he was nominated Midshipman of the HECTOR 74, Capts. Thos. Elphinstone and Wm. Skipsey, and after participating in the operations connected with the Egyptian expedition, he successively joined the WOOLWICH 44, Capt. Rich. Bridges, GLADIATOR, flag-ship of Rear-Admiral John Holloway, BLENHEIM 74, Capt. Bouverie, and PRÉVOYANTE store-ship, Master-Commander Wm. Brown; and he was next, between May, 1803, and Sept. 1805, employed under Lords Northesk and Gardner, in the BRITANNIA 100, HIBERNIA 110, and TRENT frigate, on the Channel and Irish stations. On 21 Oct. 1805 Mr. Howell was confirmed to the rank of Sub-Lieutenant in the TURBULENT gun-brig, Lieut.-Commander Thos. Spearing Osmer, lying at Plymouth. The 22 of the following Jan. was marked by his promotion to a full Lieutenancy in the GIBRALTAR 80, Capts. Wm. Lukin, Willoughby Thos. Lake, John Halliday, Jas. Johnstone, and Henry Lidgbird Ball, with whom we find him continuously serving on the Channel station until appointed, 27 April, 1808, to the DRYAD 36, Capts. Adam Drummond and Edw. Galwey. During the whole of the siege of Flushing in 1809, he officiated on shore in command of a party of seamen attached to General Houston's brigade. On that occasion he superintended the erection of a battery of 6 24-pounders, and while in command of it had one Master's Mate and more than half his men killed. The exertions of Mr. Howell on this service were so conspicuous as to obtain for him an earnest recommendation to notice.* When afterwards on the north coast of Spain, he was detached for a period of 21 days in an open Spanish boat with 25 men, for the purpose of stopping the enemy's supplies. While on the same station he contrived, with the boats of a squadron under his orders, to effect the destruction of 20 large guns mounted on different batteries. On 26 Feb. 1814 he witnessed the capture of the French frigate *La Clorinde*, of 44 guns. The DRYAD, of which he had been three years First-Lieutenant, being paid off in April, 1814, he was next, in Oct. 1815 and March, 1816, appointed in a similar capacity to the ERIDANUS 36, and MINDEN 74, both commanded by Capt. Wm. Paterson. The part taken by Mr. Howell in the latter ship at the bombardment of Algiers, was rewarded with a Commander's commission dated 16 Sept. 1816. He has since been on half-pay.

Commander Howell married, 1 Oct. 1823, Patience Blackburrow, youngest daughter of the Rev. Wm. George, M.A., Vicar of North Petherton, co. Somerset, by whom he has issue two sons and three daughters. AGENT—Joseph Woodhead.

HOWES. (COMMANDER, 1847. F-P., 34; H-P., 6.)

GEORGE HOWES entered the Navy, 23 Jan. 1807, as Fst.-cl. Vol., on board the MAJESTIC 74, Capt. Geo. Hart, bearing the flag in the North Sea of Vice-Admiral Thos. Macnamara Russell. Between the following summer and March, 1809, we find him cruizing, part of the time on the Baltic station, in a small vessel commanded by Lieuts. C. C. Dobson and Thos. Mitchell. He was then employed for nine months off Greenwich under the flag of Hon. Sir Henry Edwin Stanhope; and from Dec. 1809 until Aug. 1814, he again served in the North Sea, as Midshipman of the PROSPERO sloop. The two following years were passed by Mr. Howes (whose first commission bears date 24 Feb. 1815) in the West Indies, as Master's Mate, Acting-Master, and Supernumerary-Lieutenant, on board the FORESTER 18, Capt. Wm. Hendry. His subsequent appointments were—9 June, 1821, 31 May, 1823, and 13 Feb. 1829, in the capacity last-mentioned, to the SEVERN, RAMILLIES, and HYPERION Coast Blockade ships, Capts. Wm. M'Culloch, Hugh Pigot, and Wm. Jas. Mingaye—16 March, 1831, to the Coast Guard —and 22 June, 1843, and 17 Jan. 1846, to the command of the MERMAID and RANGER Revenue-vessels. He was advanced to his present rank 1 Jan. 1847; and is now on half-pay.

Commander Howes is married and has issue.

HOWNAM. (LIEUT., 1809. F-P., 11; H-P., 33.)

JOSEPH ROBERT HOWNAM entered the Navy, 13 March, 1803, as Fst.-cl. Vol., on board the AFRICAINE 38, Capt. Thos. Manby, stationed in the North Sea; and in the early part of 1804 became Midshipman of the LIVELY 38, Capt. Graham Eden Hamond. On 5 of the following Oct. the latter frigate had 2 of her men killed and 5 wounded, at the capture, off Cape St. Mary, of three Spanish frigates, laden with treasure, and the destruction of a fourth; and in the course of 1805 we find her sustaining a self-sought and very spirited skirmish with the Spanish 74-gun ship *Glorioso*. On next

* *Vide* Gaz. 1809, p. 1327.

joining the CENTAUR 74, bearing the broad pendant of Sir Sam. Hood, Mr. Hownam was present, 25 Sept. 1806, at the capture, by that ship and the MARS and MONARCH 74's, of four heavy French frigates from Rochefort, on which occasion the British Commodore lost his arm. He also attended the expedition of 1807 to Copenhagen, and in Dec. of the same year was at the surrender of Madeira. After an attachment of more than 12 months to the BARFLEUR 98, flag-ship off Lisbon of Rear-Admirals Wm. Albany Otway and Chas. Tyler, and LAVINIA 40, Capt. Lord Wm. Stuart, he was made Lieutenant, 4 May, 1809, into the RESISTANCE 38, Capts. Chas. Adam, Philip L. J. Rosenhagen, and Fleetwood Broughton Reynolds Pellew, stationed in the Mediterranean; where, from 22 July, 1813, until he invalided in Jan. 1814, he was further employed, as Senior, in the UNDAUNTED 38, Capt. Thos. Ussher. On 9 Nov. 1813 Mr. Hownam commanded a detachment of seamen and marines, and distinguished himself by the gallant manner in which he effected the capture of a vigorously defended tower, 30 feet high, together with several batteries in the harbour of Port Nouvelle, where lay seven French vessels, whose destruction was at the same time accomplished.* Since he left the UNDAUNTED he has been on half-pay.

HUBBARD. (COMMANDER, 1838.)

WILLIAM HUBBARD entered the Navy, 24 April, 1808, as Fst.-cl. Vol., on board the TRIUMPH 74, Capt. Sir Thos. Masterman Hardy, in which ship, and as Midshipman, in the BARFLEUR 98, he served with the same officer, on the American and Lisbon stations, until March, 1811. Being then appointed Master's Mate of the MANILLA 36, Capts. Geo. Fras. Seymour and John Joyce, he was in that frigate wrecked, on the Haak sand, near the Texel, 28 Jan. 1812; from which period until the peace of 1814, it was his misfortune to be detained a prisoner of war. After again serving for a few months with Sir T. M. Hardy in the RAMILLIES 74, Mr. Hubbard took up a commission dated 4 March, 1815. His succeeding appointments were—in July, 1816, and Feb. 1817, to the PERSEUS 22, and TAMAR 28, both commanded by Capt. Thos. Rich. Toker, on the Newfoundland station—about April, 1822, to the ARIADNE 26, Capts. Constantine Rich. Moorsom and Isham Fleming Chapman, at the Cape of Good Hope—25 Feb. 1826, to the PRINCE REGENT 120, flag-ship of Sir Robt. Moorsom at the Nore, where he was paid off in July, 1827—9 Oct. 1829, as Senior Lieutenant, to the VOLAGE 28, Capt. Lord Colchester, under whom he escorted the ex-Emperor and Empress of Brazil to Cherbourg in April, 1831, and was employed during the winter of 1832 in enforcing the Dutch embargo—and 28 Jan. 1837 (after four years of half-pay), in a similar capacity, to the MALABAR 74, Capt. Sir Wm. Augustus Montagu, off Lisbon. He was promoted to the rank of Commander 28 June, 1838—a few months after the latter ship had been put out of Commission—but has not been since afloat.

HUBBARD. (LIEUTENANT, 1828.)

WILLIAM HUBBARD (*b*) entered the Navy 1 Jan. 1810; passed his examination in 1817; and was made Lieutenant, 13 Nov. 1828, into the RATTLESNAKE 28, Capt. Hon. Chas. Orlando Bridgeman, on the Mediterranean station, whence he invalided in Feb. 1829. His next and last appointments were —18 Nov. 1834, to the charge of the Semaphore station on Putney Heath—and, 23 Nov. 1835, to the Directorship of Police at Chatham Dockyard. He has been on half-pay since Sept. 1841.

Lieut. Hubbard was granted, 10 April, 1829, a pension of 103*l*. 5*s*. for wounds.

HUDSON. (COMMANDER, 1831. F-P., 23; H-P., 13.)

JOHN HUDSON is second son of the Rev. J. Hudson, late Vicar of Stanwie.

* *Vide* Gaz. 1814, p. 124.

This officer entered the Navy in Aug. 1811, as Fst.-cl. Vol., on board the AMERICA 74, Capt. Josias Rowley. He soon removed to the ALFRED 74, Capt. Joshua Sydney Horton, employed at the time at the siege of Cadiz, where he was transferred to the DRUID 32, Capts. Thos. Searle and Fras. Stanfell. While in that frigate, besides actively co-operating in a flat-bottomed boat in the defence of Tarifa, he visited Egypt, and thence escorted the Prince of Morocco to Tangier. Following Capt. Stanfell, as Midshipman, in Dec. 1812, into the COSSACK 22, he sailed with convoy for Jamaica, and was employed for many months off that island in cruizing against the American enemy. In June, 1814, having returned to the Mediterranean, he was for a short period appointed to the INDUS 74, Capt. Wm. Hall Gage; after which we find him serving for 12 months in the Channel on board the SHELDRAKE 16, Capt. Geo. Brine; and again with the same officer from Sept. 1815 to Nov. 1818, as Master's Mate, in the MOSQUITO 18, on the African and South American stations. During the latter period he cruized with much success against the slave trade, part of the time in command of a tender; and he was for nine months stationed off St. Helena for the security of Buonaparte. In Nov. 1820, Mr. Hudson, who had passed his examination in 1817, again proceeded to the coast of Africa, where, as Master's Mate of the TARTAR 42, Commodore Sir Geo. Ralph Collier, he assisted in the boats in effecting the capture of numerous vessels up the different rivers. Volunteering, on the return home of the TARTAR in June, 1821, to continue on the same station, he joined the PHEASANT 18, Capt. Benedictus Marwood Kelly, with whom he remained until appointed Acting-Lieutenant, 4 Dec. following, of the MYRMIDON 20, Capt. Henry John Leeke. In Feb. 1822, on the arrival from England of Commodore Sir Robt. Mends in the IPHIGENIA 42, he was superseded and nominated Admiralty Midshipman of the latter frigate. During a cruize of six weeks in the Bights of Biafra and Benin, he contributed to the taking of many more slave-vessels; and on one occasion, when in the river Bonny, he distinguished himself in the boats of the IPHIGENIA and MYRMIDON, under Lieut. G. W. St. J. Mildmay, at the capture, after a desperate resistance, of five vessels, having on board upwards of 1800 negroes. For this service he was promoted by the Commodore to a Lieutenancy, 14 June, 1822, in the BANN 20—an act which the Admiralty confirmed by a commission signed on 26 of the next Aug. Invaliding home in May, 1823, Lieut. Hudson was subsequently appointed—20 April, 1826, to the Coast Blockade, as Supernumerary-Lieutenant of the RAMILLIES 74, Capt. Hugh Pigot—and 16 June, 1829, and 26 Jan. 1831, to the PHILOMEL 10, and RATTLESNAKE 28, both commanded by Capt. Chas. Graham on the Mediterranean station, whence he returned to England, and was paid off in April, 1831. He attained his present rank on 5 Dec. in the same year; and was afterwards, from 6 June, 1833, until 1836, and again from 13 July, 1838, until 1843, employed on the Coast Guard.

Commander Hudson, since 1843, has been Governor of the Queen's Bench Prison. He married, 12 April, 1832, Emily, only child of the late Rev. Patrick Keith, Rector of Ruckinge and Stalisfield, co. Kent, by whom, who died 9 Oct. 1844, he has issue six children.

HUDSON. (LIEUT., 1813. F-P., 14; H-P., 30.)

JOHN HUDSON entered the Navy, 6 April, 1803, as A.B., on board the DRYAD 36, Capts. Wm. Domett, John Giffard, and Adam Drummond, stationed off the coast of Ireland. In July, 1805, he removed to the ORION 74, Capts. Edw. Codrington and Sir Arch. Collingwood Dickson, in which ship he fought at Trafalgar, assisted at the capture of Copenhagen, and was altogether for more than seven years employed, as Midshipman and Master's Mate, on the Mediterranean and Baltic stations. He next, in Oct. 1812, joined the BARFLEUR 98, Capt. Sir Edw. Berry; and on 31 March, 1813, having returned to the Mediterranean, he was there made Lieutenant into the REPULSE 74, Capt. Rich. Hussey Moubray. He was paid off, on his arrival home with convoy, in June, 1814; and was lastly employed in command, from 22 Oct. 1828 until Oct. 1831, of the SKYLARK Revenue-vessel, on the coast of Ireland.

HUDSON. (LIEUTENANT, 1846.)

PHILIP HUDSON passed his examination 28 Sept. 1840; and served, as Mate, in the CALEDONIA 120, flag-ship of Sir Graham Moore, CHAMPION 18, Capt. Rich. Byron, DOLPHIN and SPY brigantines, Lieut.-Commanders Philip Bisson and Sam. Otway Wooldridge, and ST. VINCENT 120, bearing the flag of Sir Chas. Ogle—on the Plymouth, South American, African, and Portsmouth stations. He obtained his commission 31 Jan. 1846; and since 2 of the following month has been employed in the Mediterranean on board the HARLEQUIN 12, Capts. Douglas Curry and John Moore.

HUGGINS. (COMMANDER, 1814. F-P., 18; H-P., 33.)

JAMES EDWARD HUGGINS was born in Aug. 1782, at Nevis.

This officer (who had previously been in the East India Company's service) entered the Navy, in Nov. 1796, as A.B., on board the VINDICTIVE frigate, Capts. Dan. Oliver Guion, Gardner, and Aiskew Paffard Hollis, stationed at the Cape of Good Hope; and on his return to England in 1798, appears to have been employed for upwards of seven months off Woolwich as Midshipman in command of the EXPERIMENT fire-vessel. After an attachment of some time to the ZEALAND 74, flag-ship at the Nore of Vice-Admirals Skeffington Lutwidge and Sir Andw. Mitchell, he joined the AMAZON 38, Capt. Edw. Riou, under whom he was severely wounded on the occasion of that ship running foul of *Le Bourgainville* French 18-gun privateer, in Feb. 1800. From the following April until April, 1802, he again served with Capt. Guion, on board the EURUS 36, and TRUSTY 50. In the former of those ships he attended the expeditions to Ferrol and Cadiz, and also the one to Egypt, where he was in command of a flat-boat during the battles of 8, 13, and 21 March, 1801, at the destruction of Rosetta Castle, and at the surrender of Grand Cairo and Alexandria. On the night of 29 Aug. 1800, he had served with the boats of a squadron, 20 in number, commanded by Lieut. Henry Burke, at the cutting-out, close to the batteries in Vigo Bay, of *La Guêpe* privateer, of 18 guns and 160 men; which vessel, 25 of whose people were killed and 40 wounded, was boarded and carried in 15 minutes, with a loss to the British of 3 seamen and 1 marine killed, 3 Lieutenants, 12 seamen, and 5 marines wounded, and 1 seaman missing. From June, 1802, to Oct. 1803, we find Mr. Huggins serving at Newfoundland as Admiralty-Midshipman of the CAMILLA 20, Capts. Edw. Brace, Henry Hill, and Bridges Watkinson Taylor. In March, 1804, having joined, as Master's Mate, the INCONSTANT 36, Capt. Edw. Stirling Dickson, he assisted at the re-capture of the African island of Gorée; with the despatches relative to which event he was sent to England. He was then, after having passed his examination, ordered to the West Indies, where he frequently distinguished himself in command of the tenders of the HERCULE and VETERAN flag-ships—particularly when in the GRACIEUSE, in which vessel, while in the act of boarding a French national schooner, off St. Domingo, he received a wound so severe as to deprive him of the entire use of his arm, and to elicit the presentation of a sword from the Patriotic Society.* In March, 1806, in consequence of the injury he had sustained, he was sent home to Haslar Hospital; but in the summer of the following year he returned to the West Indies, and joined the WOLF 16, Capt. Wm. Sumner Hall. Between May, 1808, and the date of his official promotion, which took place 27 Sept. 1810, Mr. Huggins was further employed on the same station, chiefly as Acting-Lieutenant, in the SHARK, GRIFFON, ELK, and PERT sloops, Capts. Edw. Henry A'Court, H. S. Jones, Jeremiah Coghlan, and W. S. Hall. In the GRIFFON, he also for some months discharged the duties of Acting-Commander. Obtaining an appointment, 16 Oct. 1810, to the ROVER 18, Capt. Justice Finley, he served in that vessel in co-operation with the patriots on the north coast of Spain until Aug. 1812, when he was again obliged to be sent to Haslar in consequence of a serious hurt he had received while engaging the batteries at Bilboa. He next, on 3 March, 1813, joined the MAJESTIC, a cut-down 74, Capt. John Hayes, under whom, during a cruize in the North American station, he contributed, 3 Feb. 1814, to the capture, after a running-fight of two hours and a-half, of the *Terpsichore* French frigate, of 44 guns. Since his advancement to his present rank, 15 June, 1814, Commander Huggins has been unable to procure employment.

He was awarded a pension of 150*l.* for his wounds, 28 May, 1816. AGENT—Fred. Dufaur.

* *Vide* Gaz. 1805.

HUGHES. (LIEUTENANT, 1846.)

JOHN CONSTANTINE HUGHES passed his examination 5 June, 1833; was employed for some time, as Mate, in the BADGER Revenue-cruizer, Lieut.-Commander Rich. Percival; obtained an appointment in the Coast Guard 8 June, 1842; and continued in that service until advanced to the rank of Lieutenant 3 July, 1846. He has since been on half-pay.

HUGHES. (RETIRED COMMANDER, 1842. F-P., 17; H-P., 33.)

ROBERT HUGHES entered the Navy, 1 Dec. 1797, as A.B., on board L'AIGLE 38, Capt. Chas. Tyler, and on 18 July, 1798, was wrecked, near Tunis, on which occasion he suffered many severe hardships. In the ensuing Sept. he became Midshipman of the MARLBOROUGH 74, Capt. Thos. Sotheby; but that ship being also lost, off Belleisle, 4 Nov. 1800, he next, in Jan. 1801, joined the TRENT 36, commanded at first by Sir Edw. Hamilton, and afterwards by Capt. Chas. Brisbane, whom he successively followed, as Master's Mate, into the GOLIATH 74, and ARETHUSA 38; assisting, in the GOLIATH, at the capture, 28 June, 1803, of *La Mignonne* French national corvette of 16 guns and 80 men. In June, 1805, he removed to the ASTREA 32, Capt. Jas. Carthew, at the Nore; and on 25 Aug. in the same year, he was appointed Acting-Lieutenant of the COMBATANT sloop, Capt. Alex. Robt. Kerr, in the Downs. In about a month afterwards, however, he went back to the ARETHUSA, still commanded by Capt. Brisbane; in which ship we find him present at the capture, 23 Aug. 1806, near the Havana, after a spirited action, in which the ARETHUSA had 2 men killed and 32 wounded, of the *Pomona* Spanish frigate, of 38 guns and 347 men, laden with specie and merchandize, and defended by a castle, mounting 11 36-pounders, and a flotilla of 10 gun-boats, all of which were destroyed. After further sharing in the memorable capture of Curaçoa, Mr. Hughes was promoted to the rank of Lieutenant, by commission dated 23 Feb. 1807. With the exception of a brief command, in June and July, 1812, of the MEROPE 10, he next, from Aug. 1808 until May, 1813, served with the same Captain and the present Sir Edw. Codrington on board the BLAKE 74. He took, during that period, a warm part in the hostilities of 1809 in the Scheldt, served at the siege of Cadiz, and, among other operations on the coast of Spain, united in the defence of Tarragona. On the night of 26 Sept. 1812, some time after the latter place had fallen into the hands of the French, we find Mr. Hughes, who was then First of the BLAKE, assuming command of her boats, and sweeping the mole of all the vessels and boats which had there sought protection, notwithstanding an angry discharge of shot and shells from the town. In the execution of this service, which was conducted simultaneously with a land-operation under the Baron d'Eroles, he greatly acquired the approbation of his Captain, Codrington.* His last appointment was,

* *Vide* Gaz. 1812, p. 2295.

20 Sept. 1813, to the RIPPON 74, Capt. Sir Christopher Cole, on the Channel station, where he assisted in capturing, 21 Oct., the French frigate *Le Weser*, of 44 guns, and, in Feb. 1814, a Spanish treasure-ship of immense value. He went on half-pay in Aug. of the latter year; and accepted his present rank 4 Feb. 1842.

HUGHES. (LIEUTENANT, 1815.)

ROBERT ANDREW HUGHES obtained his commission 2 March, 1815; and has since been on half-pay.

HUGHES. (RETIRED COMMANDER, 1839.)

THOMAS HUGHES died 29 Jan. 1845, at Brompton, co. Middlesex.

This officer entered the Navy, 24 Dec. 1796, as Midshipman, on board the MADRAS 54, Capt. John Dilkes, in which ship he continued to serve as Midshipman and Master's Mate, on the West India, Mediterranean, and Home stations, until Feb. 1804. He then removed to the AGINCOURT 64, Capt. Thos. Briggs; and on 22 Jan. 1806, after a servitude of some months, as Sub-Lieutenant, in the MERCATOR, Capt. Jas. Welch, and SNIPE, Lieut.-Commander Champion, he was presented with a commission conferring on him the rank of full Lieutenant. He joined, about the same period, the SPITFIRE sloop, Capt. Henry Sam. Butt, employed in the North Sea and Channel, but in Oct. following was obliged to go on shore in consequence of a wound in the side. In the course of 1807 he obtained appointments to the BELLEROPHON and ELIZABETH 74's, Capts. Edw. Rotheram and Hon. Henry Curzon, under the latter of whom he served for a short time at the blockade of Lisbon. He again went on half-pay in Dec. 1807, and owing to the effects of his wound, was unable, we believe, to accept further employment afloat. During a few months in 1815-16, and for some time subsequent to Oct. 1822, he appears to have had charge of the Telegraph at Chelsea Hospital. He became a Retired Commander 5 Jan. 1839.

HUGHES. (RETIRED CAPTAIN, 1840. F-P., 16; H-P., 36.)

WILLIAM JAMES HUGHES, born 15 Aug. 1783, at Halifax, Nova Scotia, is son of Mr. Hughes, who died Builder of the Naval Yard at that place. His eldest brother died Purser of a line-of-battle ship; and two others, also deceased, were Lieutenants in the R.N.

This officer entered the Navy, 16 April, 1795, as A.B., on board L'ESPÉRANCE 18, of which sloop, commanded on the Halifax station by Capt. Jonas Rose, he became Midshipman 10 June, 1796. Removing, in June of the following year, to the ROVER 18, Capt. Geo. Irvine, he assisted, under that officer, at the capture of *Le Jean Bart*, a noted privateer, and continued with him until wrecked, in the Gulf of St. Lawrence, in Aug. 1798. He then joined the ASIA 74, bearing the flag of Vice-Admiral Vandeput, from which ship he was transferred, in Oct. 1799, to the CLEOPATRA 32, Capt. Israel Pellew. He was afterwards detached in charge of a prize-schooner, and when in the Gulf of Mexico had the misfortune to be captured by a Spanish letter-of-marque. On being retaken by the ACASTA frigate, he was received, in April, 1801, on board the SANS PAREIL 80, flag-ship at Jamaica of Lord Hugh Seymour; who, on 31 Aug. following, appointed him Lieutenant of the TISIPHONE sloop, Capts. John Hayes and John Thompson—an act which the Admiralty confirmed 24 Feb. 1802. Soon after the renewal of hostilities, being at the time on leave of absence at Halifax, Mr. Hughes took a passage for England on board the LADY HOBART. That vessel having, three days subsequently to her departure, effected the capture of a French fishing-schooner, he volunteered, with five others, to navigate her into Liverpool, and he accordingly went on board, leaving all his effects, for better security, in the LADY HOBART. The latter, however, was unluckily wrecked, the very next morning, on an island of ice, and he thus, as he had before done in the ROVER and the CLEOPATRA's prize, lost everything he possessed. Reaching England in safety, he was appointed, 12 Aug. 1803, to the SCOURGE 18, Capt. Wm. Woolridge; as Senior Lieutenant of which vessel we find him, with 2 boats and 20 men, distinguishing himself at the boarding and recapture, in Jan. 1804, of a large English ship, of 20 men, mounting 8 guns, and lying close under the batteries in the Vlie Passage.* He invalided in March, 1804, but was appointed, for a short time in the same year, to the SWIFT 18, Capt. John Wright, and on 2 July, 1806, to the command of the PHOSPHORUS fire-brig, of 4 12-pounder carronades and 24 men. On 14 of the ensuing Aug., Lieut. Hughes displayed a very high degree of valour in beating off a French lugger privateer, *L'Elize*, mounting about 12 guns, with a crew of between 70 and 80 men, after a brave and determined action on the part of the British of an hour and 10 minutes; 45 minutes of which period the enemy, who attempted to carry the PHOSPHORUS by boarding, lay close alongside. Among the wounded on the occasion, eight in number, was Lieut. Hughes himself.† The gallantry of his exploit, indeed, was so fully appreciated, that, besides attracting the notice of H. R. H. the Duke of Kent and eliciting a letter of approbation from the Lords of the Admiralty, it obtained for him a sword from the Patriotic Society valued at 100*l*., also the same sum in money, and, more than all, a Commander's commission dated 25 Sept. 1806. His subsequent appointments were—11 June, 1807, to the office of Agent for Prisoners of War and Transports at Jamaica—4 July, 1808, to the command of the EPHIRA 10, in the North Sea and Downs, on which stations he continued until May, 1809—19 March, 1813, to the duties of Transport Agent in a secret expedition to the Baltic under Rear-Admiral Hope—21 May, 1813, to act as Port-Admiral at Carlskrona—and in Sept. 1813 (after having brought a body of Russian seamen from Kronstadt to England), to the Governorship of the Naval Hospital at Halifax. The latter appointment he accepted under the impression that it was a permanent one; an error he only discovered in June, 1816, when he was superseded, and found that it had only served to debar him from such chance as the war might have afforded of his obtaining further promotion. Unable to procure re-employment, he suffered his name to be added to the list of Retired Captains 10 Sept. 1840.

Capt. Hughes, in consideration of his wound, which was in the left hand and considered equivalent to the loss of a limb, obtained a pension of 150*l*. 2 Dec. 1815. He married, 7 March, 1804, Elizabeth Frances, daughter of the late Thos. Clay, Esq., a merchant in London, and granddaughter of the late Capt. Adler, in the Swedish service; by whom he has issue 10 children. AGENT—Fred. Dufaur.

HUGO. (LIEUTENANT, 1815. F-P., 14; H-P., 30.)

GEORGE HUGO, born 13 Jan. 1789, at Newton, is sixth son of the late Rev. Thos. Hugo, Rector of Newton, Dunchidiock, and Shillingford, all in co. Devon.

This officer entered the Navy, 3 April, 1803, as Midshipman, on board the FOUDROYANT 80, Capt. Peter Spicer, bearing the flag of Sir Thos. Graves in the Channel, where, and in the Baltic and Mediterranean, he served—for two years in the DISPATCH 18, Capt. Edw. Hawkins—for three years and eight months in the ST. GEORGE 98, flag-ship of Rear-Admirals Eliab Harvey and Fras. Pickmore—and for two years and nine months in the SAN JOSEF 110, bearing the flags of Sir Chas. Cotton and Lord Keith. In March, 1813, Mr. Hugo, who had passed his examination in Feb. 1810, and had been for the last two months employed under Lord Keith on board the QUEEN CHARLOTTE 100, at Plymouth, sailed with Sir Jas. Lucas Yeo in the WOOLWICH 44, Capt. Thos. Ball Sullivan, for the Lakes of Canada. In the following May he accompanied the

* *Vide* Gaz. 1804, p. 112. † *V.* Gaz. 1806, p. 1065.

unsuccessful expedition to Sackett's Harbour; and in July of the same year we find him commanding one of several gun-boats in an action with the enemy at Goose Creek. On that occasion he received a rifle-ball through the left elbow, which destroyed the joint and disabled two fingers. He was also present, 28 Sept. 1813, in a partial action fought with the Americans on Lake Ontario; and on 6 May, 1814, at the capture of Fort Oswego. During the remainder of the war he was employed, as Acting-Lieutenant of the Charwell, in conveying troops from one part of the lakes to another, and in serving on shore with them. When Sir Edw. W. C. R. Owen superseded Sir J. L. Yeo, Mr. Hugo was sent to Quebec for the purpose of raising men to supply the places of those whose time had expired. On the breaking up of the establishment on the lakes in Oct. 1816, he was ordered to take command of the Diana, a merchant-ship laden with spars for the Dockyard at Portsmouth, and to return with a party of men to England. He was placed on half-pay in Feb. 1817, having been awarded a commission dated 20 Sept. 1815, and has not been since employed.

On his arrival in England, Lieut. Hugo was presented by the Patriotic Society with a sword, valued at 50*l.*, in consideration of his wounds. He is married, and has issue two daughters.

HULL. (Lieutenant, 1811. f-p., 10; h-p., 33.)

William Hollamby Hull entered the Royal Naval College 23 May, 1804; and embarked, 3 June, 1807, as Midshipman, on board the Niobe 40, Capt. John Wentworth Loring. After participating in an attack made, 15 Nov. 1810, by Capt. Chas. Grant of the Diana, on the two French frigates *Amazone* and *Eliza*, under the fire of several formidable batteries in the neighbourhood of Cherbourg, he joined the Milford 74, bearing the flag of Sir Rich. Goodwin Keats off Cadiz—with the flotilla at the defence of which place he was for some time employed. In July, 1811, having been advanced to the rank of Lieutenant on 1 of the previous May, he removed in that capacity to the Comus 22, Capts. Matthew Smith and Fras. Geo. Dickins. He served in the latter vessel on the Mediterranean and Channel stations until May, 1814; and has since been on half-pay.

HUME. (Lieutenant, 1813. f-p., 10; h-p., 31.)

Joseph Hume entered the Navy, in April, 1806, as a Volunteer, on board the Theseus 74, Capt. Geo. Hope, whom he accompanied to the Cape of Good Hope. From June, 1807, until Oct. 1812, we find him successively employed with Capt. Henry Hope, as Midshipman, in the Espoir sloop, Glatton 50, and Leonidas, Topaze, and Satellite frigates, all on the Mediterranean station; where, until he invalided in March, 1814, he further served in the Goshawk sloop, Capt. Napier, Stromboli, Capt. Stoddart (of which vessel he was confirmed a Lieutenant 22 Jan. 1813), and Alcmène frigate, Capts. Edwards Lloyd Graham and Jeremiah Coghlan. On the night of 31 Oct. 1809, while in the Topaze, he assisted in her boats, with those of a squadron under Lieut. John Tailour, at the capture and destruction, after a desperate struggle and a loss to the British of 15 men killed and 55 wounded, of the French store-ship *Lamproie* of 16 guns and 116 men, bombards *Victoire* and *Grondeur*, and armed xebec *Normande*, with a convoy of seven merchant-vessels, defended by numerous strong batteries in the Bay of Rosas.* In the Alcmène, Mr. Hume, in Dec. 1813, contributed to the capture of *La Flèche* national schooner, of 12 guns and 99 men. His last appointments were, 16 June, 1815, and 19 Feb. 1816, to the Eurotas and Firth frigates, Capts. Jas. Lillicrap and Sir John Louis. He returned home from North America in July, 1817, having been superseded at his own request. Agents—Hallett and Robinson.

* *Vide* Gaz. 1809, p. 1907.

HUNGATE. (Lieut., 1815. f-p., 13; h-p., 31.)

William Hungate was born 7 Sept. 1786. He was presented to William IV. by the Earl of Denbigh, as a Baronet, 27 April, 1831.

This officer entered the Navy, 10 July, 1803, as Ordinary, on board the Pique 36, Capts. Wm. Cumberland and Chas. Bayne Hodgson Ross. In the course of the same year he witnessed the evacuation of Aux Cayes, St. Domingo, the capture, with other vessels, of *Le Goelan* 18, and the surrender of three French frigates with the remains of General Rochambeau's army from Cape François on board. He was also, in Jan. 1804, present in the unsuccessful attack on the island of Curaçoa; and in Dec. 1804 and Feb. 1805, we find him assisting at the capture of the Spanish ships of war *Diligentia* and *Orquijo*. On 26 March, 1806, he further contributed to the taking of the French corvettes *Phaeton* and *Voltigeur* of 16 guns and 115 men each; the former of which vessels offered so fierce a resistance that 9 of the British were killed, and 14 of them (including Mr. Hungate in the knee) wounded, while in the act of boarding. For their gallantry on the occasion the officers were each presented by the Patriotic Society with the sum of 100*l.* for the purchase of a sword, and the men with 20*l.* a-piece. In Aug. 1807, on his return with a large convoy to England, Mr. Hungate removed to the Elizabeth 74, Capts. Hon. H. Curzon, Thos. Searle, and Edw. Leveson Gower. In that ship, in which he served as Midshipman, Master's Mate, and Second Master, until June, 1812, he witnessed the departure of the Royal Family of Portugal for the Brazils, aided in blockading the Russian Rear-Admiral Seniavin's squadron in the Tagus, was employed in embarking the troops after the battle of Corunna, and was for some time stationed in South America. From June, 1812, until Feb. 1816, Mr. Hungate officiated as Second Master of the Minden 74, bearing the flag at first of Sir Samuel Hood, and afterwards commanded by Capt. Donald Hugh Mackay, on the East India station. He then, having passed his examination in Dec. 1809, took up a commission bearing date 2 March, 1815; and has since been on half-pay.

Lieut. Hungate married, 27 Aug. 1818, Jane, daughter of the late Lieut. Wm. Avery, R.N., and by that lady, who died 21 June, 1845, has issue six sons and four daughters. Agents — Goode and Lawrence.

HUNGERFORD. (Lieut., 1815. f-p., 15; h-p., 28.)

John Hungerford entered the Navy, 22 Jan. 1804, as Master's Mate, on board the Sandwich, Lieut.-Commander Emanuel Hungerford, lying in the river Medway; where, and in the North Sea, Baltic, and Channel, he served, from Sept. 1805, until Nov. 1811, in the Virginie 38, Capt. Edw. Brace, Imogene sloop, Capt. Thos. Garth, Sandwich again, Procris 18, Capt. Fras. Beauman (in which vessel he attended the expedition of 1807 to Copenhagen), Sandwich once more, Warspite 74, Capt. Hon. Henry Blackwood, Princess of Orange 74, Capt. Fras. Beauman, and St. Domingo 74, bearing the flag of Sir Rich. John Strachan. Prior to the receipt of his first commission, which bears date 4 Feb. 1815, he was further employed on board the Cumberland 74, Capt. Thos. Baker, under whom, besides serving on the coast of Holland, he escorted convoy to and from the West Indies and the Cape of Good Hope. With the exception of the command of the Hound Revenue-vessel, which he held from 20 March, 1829, until April, 1832, Lieut. Hungerford, since 1815, has been on half-pay.

HUNGERFORD. (Lieutenant, 1826.)

Thomas Hungerford entered the Navy, in 1809, on board the Fortunée 36, Capt. Henry Vansittart. In the boats of that ship, during a cruize on the coast of Ireland, he united in an attack upon an enemy's schooner, in which the British were repulsed with a loss of 21 men killed and wounded. Towards the close of 1810 he escorted Rear-Admiral Thos. Fras. Fremantle to the Mediterranean; and on 11 Oct. 1811, after having returned with an Algerine Ambassador to England, he assisted at the capture of a most notorious privateer, *Le Vice-Amiral Magon*, of 18 guns and 140 men. During the last two years of the war, Mr. Hungerford further served with Capt. Vansittart on board the CLARENCE 74, at the blockade of the Texel, Brest, and Rochefort. He then joined the TRENT, flag-ship of Sir Herbert Sawyer at Cork; where he remained until paid off in Nov. 1815. In 1819 he entered the Coast Guard; and in 1823, as a means of procuring his promotion, he again went afloat, in the HARLEQUIN 18, Capt. John Weeks. His commission was at length signed on 27 March, 1826; from 29 Nov. in which year until the close of 1843, he again served in the Coast Guard. He has not since been employed.

Lieut. Hungerford married, in Sept. 1835, Caroline, daughter of the late W. H. Trotter, Esq., of Downpatrick, and niece of a gentleman who was formerly private secretary to the Right Hon. Chas. Jas. Fox. He has issue three children. AGENT—Joseph Woodhead.

HUNN. (Captain, 1822. F-P., 18; H-P., 26.)

FREDERICK HUNN is son of the late Mr. Hunn, formerly of Exeter, by a lady nearly related to the Sheridan family, who had been twice before married—the first time to Geo. Canning, Esq., Barrister-at-law, the father of the future Prime Minister.

This officer entered the Navy, in Dec. 1803, as Fst.-cl. Vol., on board the DOLPHIN sloop, Capt. John Shortland, with whom he continued to serve in the TROMPEUSE and SQUIRREL, on the Irish, African, and North American stations until Nov. 1808. After cruizing for 12 months in the Channel as Midshipman and Master's Mate of the SURVEILLANTE 38, Capt. Sir Geo. Ralph Collier, he joined the CALEDONIA 120, bearing the flag of Rear-Admiral Fras. Pickmore off Cadiz, where, on 2 May and 1 June, 1810, he was successively appointed Acting-Lieutenant of the ZEALOUS and ACHILLE 74's, Capts. Thos. Boys and Sir Rich. King. In Jan. 1811 he removed in a similar capacity to the LAVINIA frigate, Capt. Geo. Digby, stationed in the Mediterranean; and on 5 April, 1811, he was confirmed into his former ship, the ACHILLE, then commanded by Capt. Aiskew Paffard Hollis, under whom we find him employed for 18 months at the blockade, in Venice, of three line-of-battle ships and a frigate ready for sea. His next appointment was, 10 April, 1813, to the ROYAL GEORGE 100, bearing the flag of Vice-Admiral Pickmore, also on the Mediterranean station. Obtaining a second promotal commission 27 Aug. 1814, Capt. Hunn, on 14 Aug. 1818, and 25 June, 1822, was awarded the command of the REDWING and PANDORA sloops, of 18 guns each, on the St. Helena, Cork, and Newfoundland stations. He acquired Post-rank 26 Dec. 1822; and from 28 Nov. 1823, until May, 1827, had the further command of the TWEED 28, on the South American, Irish, and Jamaica stations; on which last he captured, in 1826, a fine schooner with 276 slaves on board. He accepted the retirement 1 Oct. 1846.

Capt. Hunn married, in Oct. 1814, Emma, only daughter of Vice-Admiral Pickmore. AGENTS—Messrs. Chard.

HUNT. (LIEUT., 1830. F-P., 18; H-P., 19.)

EDWARD HUNT entered the Navy, 8 June, 1810, as Fst.-cl. Vol., on board the LEVERET 10, Capts. Jas. Andrew Worth, Geo. Wickens Willes, and Jonathan Christian, on the books of which vessel he was borne until Aug. 1815. He came frequently into contact, during that period, with the enemy's batteries on the coast of Norway and Denmark; assisted at the capture of four privateers, carrying in all 27 guns and 117 men; was in the gale in which the HERO, ST. GEORGE, and DEFENCE were lost; and, in the severe winter of 1813-14, saw a good deal of active night-service in the boats while engaged in protecting the fleet stationed in the Scheldt under Admiral Young from being attacked by the enemy's fire-rafts. He was also frequently sent in charge of captured vessels into port; and on the first of those occasions he was of such tender age and diminutive stature as to attract the peculiar notice and praise of the Commander-in-Chief. After having taken part in the grand naval review held at Spithead at the termination of hostilities in 1814, the LEVERET proceeded with convoy to Gibraltar, and soon after her arrival anchored, in company with the SAN JOSEF 110, bearing the flag of Sir Rich. King, off Ceuta, on the coast of Morocco. While there Mr. Hunt, as Midshipman in charge of a boat's crew, proceeded on shore, accompanied by the Second-Lieutenant, Master, Purser, and Mate, for the purpose of bathing and of procuring a supply of sand for the use of the ship. On landing, the British were suddenly, and without parley, assailed by a large party of Moors, who, riding down, opened a murderous fire upon such as had approached within a few paces with a view of speaking them; and indeed their evident intention of sacrificing the whole party was only arrested by the appearance of an aged man, unarmed, who was seen rushing down a hill calling upon them to desist. By this time, however, Mr. Hunt had received numerous wounds in the head, body, and arms, and several stabs from their scimitars and daggers. He was in consequence sent to the hospital at Gibraltar, where he remained until careful treatment had enabled him to recover. Rejoining the LEVERET at Portsmouth in Feb. 1815, he was employed in that vessel during the war of 100 days in conveying despatches and specie for the use of the army in Belgium; and, being at Ostend when the British army advanced from Brussels to meet the French at Waterloo, he had an opportunity of accompanying home the despatch which reported that fact, and announced the commencement of the glorious battle of the 18th of June. In Nov. 1815 he joined the FALMOUTH 20, Capt. Robt. Wergan Geo. Festing, which vessel appears, in the early part of 1816, to have co-operated with the fleet under Sir Edw. Pellew in procuring the release of the Christian slaves in bondage at Algiers, and to have been assigned an honourable post in the order of battle instituted before Tunis pending the accomplishment of the negotiations instituted for the same object at that place. On being ordered to the St. Helena station, Mr. Hunt assisted, in the FALMOUTH, in establishing a settlement at Tristan d'Acunha; as he did, on his temporary removal to the RACOON sloop, Capt. Geo. Fred. Rich, on the island of Ascension. Passing his examination in 1817, in the course of which year he returned to England and left the FALMOUTH, Mr. Hunt was subsequently employed as Mate—from Aug. 1820 to April, 1822, of the SEVERN, Coast Blockade ship, Capt. Wm. M'Culloch—from April, 1822, until July, 1825, of the PROTECTOR, Capt. Wm. Hewett, engaged as a surveying-vessel on the east coast of England, where, in Oct. 1824, she was extricated from a perilous position on a lee-shore during a violent storm, which proved fatal to all the ships and their crews in the vicinity—from July, 1825, until Nov. 1829, of the BADGER, Revenue cruizer, on the Irish station—and, from Nov. 1829 until Jan. 1831, of the WINCHESTER 52, flag-ship of Sir Edw. Griffith Colpoys, and SHANNON 46, Capt. Benj. Clement, in the West Indies. He then took up a commission dated 22 July, 1830; and has since been on half-pay. AGENT—Joseph Woodhead.

HUNT. (COMMANDER, 1846.)

HENRY SAMUEL HUNT passed his examination in 1832; obtained his first commission 10 Dec. 1835; and was appointed—13 Jan. 1836, to the RACER 18, Capt. Jas. Hope, on the North America and West India station—14 June, 1839, as First, to the CLIO 16, Capt. Stephen Grenville Fremantle, in South

America—25 Sept. 1839 and 26 Oct. 1840, to the ORESTES 18, Capt. Peter Sampson Hambly, and PRESIDENT 50, Capt. Wm. Broughton, both on the same station—and, 26 Nov. 1841, to the command of the BASILISK 6, which vessel, employed in the Pacific, he left towards the close of 1845. He was advanced to his present rank 10 March, 1846; and is at present on half-pay.

HUNT. (LIEUT., 1841. F-P., 13; H-P., 1.)

JAMES HUNT was born 27 Oct. 1817, at Oxford.

This officer entered the Navy, 23 July, 1833, as Fst.-cl. Vol., on board the WASP 18, Capts. Jas. Burney and John Sam. Foreman, stationed in the West Indies, whence, in April, 1836, he returned home as Midshipman of the PRESIDENT 52, flag-ship of Sir Geo. Cockburn. In the following Sept. he joined the HERCULES 74, Capts. Maurice Fred. Fitzhardinge Berkeley and John Toup Nicolas, with whom he cruized experimentally, and served on the coasts of Spain and Portugal until transferred, in April, 1838, to the NAUTILUS 10, Lieut.-Commander Geo. Beaufoy, on the African station. Joining, in Aug. 1840, after an interval of four months, the STROMBOLI steamer, Capt. Woodford John Williams, Mr. Hunt shared in that vessel in the whole of the ensuing operations on the coast of Syria, including the storming of Sidon and the bombardment of St. Jean d'Acre. On the former occasion he evinced a degree of zeal, activity, cool determination, and courage, most animating to the men, and not to be surpassed. He was intrusted with the colours, and ran a complete race with an Austrian officer as to who should be the first to display his national flag on the walls of the Castle—an honourable rivalry in which he had the good fortune to come off successful. From April to June, 1841, Mr. Hunt served in the Mediterranean on board the BELLEROPHON 80, Capt. Chas. John Austen; and on 12 of the following Aug., immediately after he had passed his examination, he was promoted to the rank of Lieutenant. His next appointment being, 2 Sept. 1841, to the DIDO 18, Capt. Hon. Henry Keppel, he sailed in that sloop for China, where he beheld the capture of Woosung and Shanghae, and the other operations on the Yang-tse-Kiang. On 21 May, 1843, when off Point Datou, on the coast of Borneo, in command of a native-built boat armed with a brass 6-pounder and 2 swivels, and manned with 18 officers, seamen, and marines, he simultaneously effected the destruction of one, and the utter defeat of another, of two piratical proas, each carrying about 2 guns and 50 men, by whom he had been attacked. His spirited and zealous exertions in this affair drew forth letters of approbation both from the Commander-in-Chief, Sir Wm. Parker, and from the Board of Admiralty. He continued on the books of the DIDO until he invalided in Feb. 1845; but appears, previously to that date, to have been allowed, from 1 Aug. to 1 Oct. 1843, to command the STARLING surveying-vessel, and to have been lent, from 6 June, 1844, to 15 Oct. 1844, to the DRIVER steamer, Capt. Courtenay Osborn Hayes. He has been employed, since 12 Nov. 1845, on the south-east coast of America, as First of the ALECTO steam-sloop, Capts. Fras. Wm. Austen and Vincent Amcotts Massingberd.

HUNT. (RETIRED COMMANDER, 1830.)

WILLIAM HUNT entered the Navy, 9 May, 1790, as Fst.-cl. Vol., on board the OTTER sloop, Capt. Thos. Williams, employed in the North Sea, where, in the course of the same month, he became Midshipman of the SPEEDY sloop, Capt. Geo. Maude, and afterwards of the LORD MULGRAVE 20, Capt. Robt. Rolles, and SUPERB 74, Capt. John Sutton—of which latter ship he was created a Lieutenant 24 Jan. 1799. Prior to the peace of Amiens he further served on the Home station on board the SALLY armed ship, Capt. Wolfe, VENGEANCE and IRRESISTIBLE 74's, Capts. Geo. Duff and Wm. Bligh, and AGAMEMNON 64, Capt. Robt. Devereux Fancourt. On the renewal of hostilities he obtained an appointment in the Impress service at Hull. He became a Retired-Commander on the Junior List 26 Nov. 1830; and on the Senior, 15 Dec. 1842. AGENTS—Halford and Co.

HUNTER. (COMMANDER, 1844.)

GEORGE MARTIN HUNTER is fourth son of General Sir Martin Hunter, G.C.M.G., G.C.H., of Medomsley, co. Durham, and Anton's Hill, co. Berwick, a Deputy-Lieutenant for the latter shire, and Governor of Stirling Castle, by Jean, only daughter and heiress of Jas. Dickson, Esq., of Anton's Hill. One of his brothers, James, is a Major in the Army; and two others, Robt. M'Keller and Thos. Harvey, are officers in the Military Service of the Hon. E. I. Co.

This officer was made Lieutenant, 8 Dec. 1828, into the HARPY sloop, Capt. Chas. Rich; and afterwards appointed—3 Aug. 1831, to the RACEHORSE 18, Capts. Chas. Hamlyn Williams and Fras. Vere Cotton, in the West Indies—1 May, 1834, to the PORTLAND 52, Capt. David Price, on the Mediterranean station—and, 7 Nov. 1838, to the command of the CAMELION 10, employed in South America and the East Indies. He paid the latter vessel off towards the close of 1843; and has since been on half-pay. His promotion to the rank of Commander took place 3 May, 1844. AGENTS—Hallett and Robinson.

HUNTER. (LIEUT., 1815. F-P., 8; H-P., 31.)

HUGH HUNTER entered the Navy, 25 March, 1808, as Fst.-cl. Vol., on board the ACHATES 10, Capt. Hugh Cameron; on accompanying whom into the HAZARD 18, he assisted, as Midshipman, at the capture, in Jan. and April, 1809, of the French 40-gun frigate *Topaze*, the Saintes Islands, and the *D'Haupoult* ship of the line. He also, on 17 Oct. in the same year, served in the boats of the HAZARD and PELORUS, under Lieut. Jas. Robertson, when they succeeded, after having incurred a loss of 6 men killed and 9 wounded, in gallantly blowing up a privateer, of 1 gun and 2 swivels, lying within 10 yards of 2 field-pieces and a long line of musketry on the beach, defended too by a heavy fire of grape from a battery, and moored to the shore with a chain from the mast-head and from each quarter; and on 18 of the following Dec. we find him contributing in the boats of a squadron under the personal command of Capt. Cameron, who was killed, to the destruction, in L'Ance la Barque, of the 40-gun frigates *Loire* and *Seine*, laden with stores, and protected by numerous batteries. After witnessing the fall of Guadeloupe, Mr. Hunter successively joined the POMPÉE, NEPTUNE, and STATIRA, flag-ships of Hon. Alex. Cochrane; and in Dec. 1810, the CASTOR 32, Capt. Chas. Dilkes. On 23 June, 1813, being still in the latter ship, he served in her boats, under the directions of Lieuts. Bassett, Loveless, and Edwyn Fras. Stanhope, at the boarding and bringing out from under the protection of a strong fort, on the coast of Catalonia, of *La Fortune* French privateer of 2 guns, 2 swivels, and 48 men; a service in the performance of which the British had 4 men killed and 9 wounded. In May, 1814, Mr. Hunter proceeded to North America in the PYLADES sloop, Capt. John Chas. Gawen Roberts, and on arriving on that station joined the TONNANT 80, flag-ship of Hon. Sir Alex. Cochrane, from which, on 9 of the ensuing Nov., he was transferred, as Acting-Lieutenant, to the ROTA 38, Capts. Philip Somerville and John Pasco. The boats of the latter ship he commanded at the taking of St. Mary's, on the coast of Georgia. He went on half-pay in Aug. 1815, having been officially promoted on 24 of the previous Feb.; and has since been unemployed. AGENTS—Hallett and Robinson.

HUNTER. (LIEUT., 1815. F-P., 9; H-P., 31.)

JAMES HUNTER was born 21 July, 1794.

This officer entered the Navy, 20 Jan. 1807, as Fst.-cl. Vol., on board the THALIA frigate, Capt. Jas. Walker, with whom, in the same ship and in the BEDFORD 74, he continued to serve for the space of eight years, principally as Midshipman and Master's Mate, on the Home, South American, North Sea, West India, and North American stations. Towards the close of 1807 he escorted the Royal Family of Portugal to the Brazils; and on 14 Dec. 1814 he served with the boats of a squadron at the capture, on Lake Borgne, of five American gun-boats under Commodore Jones, which did not surrender until the British, after a desperate struggle, had sustained a loss of 17 men killed and 77 wounded. On the occasion Mr. Hunter, while in the act of boarding one of the enemy's vessels, received a musket-ball through his left hand, a grape-shot wound in his right cheek, and one over the left eye.* In consideration of his gallantry and sufferings he was appointed to act as Lieutenant and Commander of one of the prizes, the *Harlequin*, which, with the remainder, was paid off at Bermuda in the following June. He has not since been employed. His commission bears date 27 Feb. 1815.

Lieut. Hunter never obtained any gratuity for his wounds. Since the peace he has had a command in the Merchant Service. He married 14 Dec. 1832; and has issue four children.

HUNTER. (Lieut., 1811. f-p., 23; h-p., 31.)

Robert Hunter, born 2 Dec. 1779, is a relative of the late Admiral W. Hunter.

This officer entered the Navy, in 1793, as a Boy, on board the Santa Margarita 36, Capt. Eliab Harvey, and in 1794 assisted at the reduction of the French West India Islands. Being discharged from the service in 1795, at which period he was employed in the Mediterranean in the Saturn 74, Capt. Jas. Douglas, he re-entered it, in April, 1802, as A.B. on board the Venus 32, Capts. Thos. Graves and Henry Matson. After an attachment of twelve months to the Nimrod sloop, Capts. Orde and Bennett, he removed, in Sept. 1805, to the Unicorn 32, Capts. Lucius Ferdinand Hardyman and Alex. Robt. Kerr, in which frigate he continued for four years, and was employed on shore during that period in the operations against Buenos Ayres and Monte Video, besides witnessing Lord Cochrane's destruction of the French shipping in Basque Roads. On rejoining Capt. Hardyman, on board the Armide 38, he was frequently sent in the boats to cooperate with the patriots on the coast of Spain, where in effecting on one occasion the capture of several *chasse-marées*, he received a severe splinter-wound in the breast, and by extreme exertion brought on a violent hemorrhage, with which he has ever since been periodically affected. He was next transferred, for short periods, to the St. Domingo and Milford 74's, flag-ships in the Downs and off Cadiz of Sir Rich. Strachan and Sir Rich. Goodwin Keats; and from Dec. 1810 until confirmed, 26 Sept. 1811, we find him discharging the duties of Acting-Lieutenant on board the Thunder bomb, Capt. Watkin Owen Pell, and the Milford and Hibernia, bearing each the flag of Sir R. G. Keats. He continued in the latter ship under Sir Wm. Sidney Smith until Oct. 1812; after which he served, from Feb. 1813 to Feb. 1814, on board the Resistance 36, Capt. Fleetwood Broughton Reynolds Pellew, and from July, 1830, until April, 1839, in the Coast Blockade and Coast Guard—the latter of which services he left from ill health. He has since been unemployed.

Being at Paris when Buonaparte arrived there from Elba in 1815, Lieut. Hunter brought to England the despatches communicating that event. He was then repeatedly charged by Mr. Hamilton, one of the Under Secretaries of State, with the conveyance of despatches to and from France; which service he continued to perform in a private vessel, at a period when no other British ship would venture, until the said vessel was at last detained at Havre, whence she was only liberated after the battle of Waterloo. For the loss he thus incurred, Lieut. Hunter declined receiving any compensation from the Admiralty other than his mere expenses, in order that he might thereby establish a claim (which has never been met) to future consideration. He married, in 1810, Miss Caroline Burton, and by that lady has issue four children. Agents—Messrs. Chard.

* *Vide* Gaz. 1815, p. 448.

HUNTER. (Lieut., 1815. f-p., 20; h-p., 24.)

Valentine Peter Hunter was born 21 Aug. 1794.

This officer entered the Navy, in Oct. 1803, as Fst.-cl. Vol., on board the Raisonnable 64, Capts. Wm. Hotham, Robt. Barton, Josias Rowley, and John Hatley; in which ship, under Capt. Rowley, he participated in Sir Robt. Calder's action, was present at the reduction of the Cape of Good Hope, of Buenos Ayres, and Monte Video, served at the blockade of the Isles of France and Bourbon, and assisted, as Midshipman, at the capture of the town of St. Paul's. Returning home in July, 1810, he was next, in March, 1811, received on board the Laurel 38, Capt. Sam. Campbell Rowley. In the following May he rejoined Capt. Josias Rowley in the America 74, and, continuing to serve with him until Oct. 1814, was most actively employed during that period on the Mediterranean station, where, besides enacting a part in numerous cutting-out affairs, and other detached services against the enemy's towns and batteries, he witnessed the unsuccessful attack upon Leghorn, and co-operated in the reduction of Genoa. Proceeding in the autumn of 1814 to New Orleans in the Vengeur 74, Capt. Tristram Robt. Ricketts, he served on shore with the army, and was wounded in the legs in the battle which proved so disastrous to the British. He was also present at the capture of Fort Bowyer, Mobille, on which occasion he took the American Colonel, Lawrence, a prisoner to Sir Alex. Cochrane, and had the honour, we believe, of firing the last shot of the war. In April, 1815, he received a commission dated on 7 of the previous Feb.; and he was afterwards, with the exception of an interval of three months in the autumn of 1832, employed, from 27 Dec. 1830 until 31 May, 1839, in the Coast Blockade (as Supernumerary-Lieutenant of the Talavera 74, Capts. Hugh Pigot and David Colby) and Coast Guard. He has since been unemployed.

Lieut. Hunter married Miss M. Gibbs, by whom he has issue a son and four daughters.

HUNTLEY, Kt. (Commander, 1838. f-p., 23; h-p., 15.)

Sir Henry Vere Huntley is third son of the late Rev. Rich. Huntley, A.M., of Boxwell Court, Gloucestershire, by Anne, daughter and sole heiress of the Venerable Jas. Webster, LL.B., Archdeacon of Gloucester; and brother of Major Wm. Warburton Huntley, who fought at Waterloo, was afterwards Captain of the 3rd Dragoon Guards, and died in 1844, while serving in India with the 9th Lancers.

This officer entered the Navy, 10 March, 1809, as Fst.-cl. Vol., on board the Thalia 36, Capt. Jas. Giles Vashon, of which ship, stationed in the West Indies, he became Midshipman 17 Sept. following. From Aug. 1812 until the receipt of his first commission, 10 Oct. 1818, he served, part of the time as Acting-Lieutenant, in the Victorious 74, Capt. Sir John Talbot, Albion and Northumberland 74's, flag-ships of Sir Geo. Cockburn (under whom, after serving on the coast of North America, he escorted Napoleon Buonaparte to St. Helena), Havannah 36, Capt. Gawen Wm. Hamilton, Spey 20, Capt. John Lake, and Queen Charlotte 100, flag-ship at Portsmouth of Sir Geo. Campbell. He then joined the Forth frigate, Capt. Sir John Louis, at Halifax, and was afterwards appointed—10 Nov. 1820, to the Redpole 10, Capt. Pat. Duff Henry Hay—28 March, 1826, as Senior, to the Parthian 10, Capts. Henry Byam Martin and Hon. Geo. Fred. Hotham, on the Mediterranean station, where he actively co-operated in the suppression of piracy, and was eventually wrecked, off the coast of Egypt, 15 May, 1828—in 1829-30. to the Childers 18, and Ganges 80, Capts. Wm. Morier and John Hayes—24 May,

1830, again as First, to the DRYAD 42, bearing the broad pendant of the last-named officer on the coast of Africa—and, 23 Sept. 1833, to the command, on the same station, of the LYNX brigantine of 3 guns. While in the DRYAD, Mr. Huntley had successive charge of the SEAFLOWER, FAIR ROSAMOND, and BLACK JOKE tenders, in the second of which, mounting but 1 gun, and having only 21 effective men on board, he very gallantly took, on 10 Sept. 1831, the *Regulo* and *Rapido* slavers, carrying between them 13 guns and 140 men. In the LYNX, which vessel he paid off in 1837, we also find him making several captures. Since the attainment of his present rank, 28 June, 1838, he has been on half-pay.

Sir Henry Vere Huntley, who afterwards received the honour of Knighthood, 9 Oct. 1841, very ably assisted Capt. Robt. Craigie, R.N., in conducting a difficult negotiation with the King and Chiefs of Bonny in the early part of 1837, on which occasion he was sent home with intelligence of the proceedings. In 1839 he was appointed Lieut.-Governor of the settlements on the river Gambia; and, while there, he repelled an irruption made into Cartabar by the barbarous chiefs of Dunkasseen. Since Aug. 1841 Sir Henry has filled the office of Lieut.-Governor of Prince Edward's Island. He married, 20 Sept. 1832, Anne, eldest daughter of the late Lieut.-General John Skinner, and sister both of Lieut.-Col. Thos. Skinner, C.B., of the 31st Regt., who figured in Affghanistan, and died from the effects of the hardships he there underwent, and of the late Capt. Jas. Skinner, chief Commissariat officer at Cabul, who had the good fortune, through his interest with Akbar Khan, to preserve Lady Sale and her friends from destruction in the disastrous retreat from Affghanistan. He has issue two sons and a daughter. AGENT—J. Hinxman.

HURDIS. (RETIRED CAPTAIN, 1840. F-P., 20; H-P., 44.)

GEORGE CLARKE HURDIS is son of the late Jas. Hurdis, Esq. of Seaford, co. Sussex; and brother-in-law of Lieut. John Reddie Black, R.N.

This officer entered the Navy, 1 Nov. 1783, on board the GRIFFIN cutter, Lieut.-Commander Jas. Cook, from which vessel, employed in the Channel, he was discharged 12 July, 1786. On 4 May, 1791, he re-embarked, as Midshipman, on board the ILLUSTRIOUS 74, Capt. Chas. Morice Pole; and, from the following Sept., until promoted to the rank of Lieutenant 16 June, 1795, he served with Capts. Rich. Goodwin Keats, Edw. Jas. Foote, and Hon. Arthur Kaye Legge, in the NIGER and LATONA frigates, on the Home station; where, while lent, we believe, to the BRUNSWICK, he was wounded in Lord Howe's action,* and escorted, in the LATONA, the Princess Caroline of Brunswick to this country. He then joined the LEANDER 50, Capt. Thos. Boulden Thompson, under whom he accompanied Sir Horatio Nelson's expedition to Teneriffe, and then visited the North Sea, Baltic, and Mediterranean; and on 27 April, 1798, and 15 March, 1801, he was appointed to the DIOMEDE 50, Capt. Hon. Chas. Elphinstone Fleeming, and WILHELMINA, Capt. Jas. Lind, both on the East India station. He attained the rank of Commander 29 April, 1802; was employed in that capacity in the Galway district of Sea Fencibles from March, 1804, to March, 1810; and accepted his present rank 10 Sept. 1840.

HURST, K.W. (LIEUT., 1810. F-P., 17; H-P., 32.)

GEORGE HURST entered the Navy, in Dec. 1798, as Ordinary, on board the DIANA 38, commanded at Cork by Capts. Jonathan Faulknor and Alex. Fraser; proceeded to Lisbon, towards the close of 1799, as Midshipman of the IMPREGNABLE 98, Capt. J. Faulknor; and, from Oct. 1799, until June, 1802, served, on the Home station, in the GLORY 98, Capt. Thos. Wells, and ACHILLE 74, Capts. Sir Edw. Buller and John Okes Hardy. He then accompanied Capt. Hardy into the COURAGEUX 74, in the boats of which ship he assisted at the reduction of Ste. Lucie in 1803; and he was subsequently, until July, 1807, employed, in the Channel, and off Cork and Cadiz, in the BRITANNIA 100, Captain (afterwards Rear-Admiral) the Earl of Northesk, VIRGINIE 38, Capt. Edw. Brace, and ATLAS 74, flag-ship of Rear-Admiral John Child Purvis. The next three years were passed by Mr. Hurst, as Acting-Lieutenant, in the ILLUSTRIOUS 74, Capt. Wm. Robt. Broughton, MINORCA 18, Capt. Phipps Hornby, and EXCELLENT and BOMBAY 74's, Capts. John West and Wm. Cuming, chiefly on the Mediterranean station. In Nov. 1808 we find him serving on shore in command of a party of the EXCELLENT's seamen, and uniting in the defence of Rosas, a citadel on the north-eastern extremity of Spain. Being confirmed 4 Dec. 1810, and appointed a few days afterwards to the GUADELOUPE of 16 guns and 102 men, Capts. Joseph Swabey Tetley, Geo. Rose Sartorius, and Arthur Stow, he served in that vessel, on 27 June, 1811, in a close and spirited action of an hour and 35 minutes, fought by her, off the town of Vendré, with the French corvette *Tactique* of 18 guns and at least 150 men, and armed xebec *Guêpe* of 8 guns and 65 or 70 men; both of whom were in the end beaten off with great slaughter to themselves, and with a loss to the British (who for some time had been simultaneously opposed by the fire of two heavy batteries) of 1 man killed and 12 or 13 wounded. On 9 Nov. 1813 Mr. Hurst commanded the boats of the GUADELOUPE, in conjunction with those of the UNDAUNTED, and distinguished himself by the gallant manner in which he aided at the capture of a vigorously defended tower, 30 feet high, together with several batteries in the harbour of Port Nouvelle, where lay 7 French vessels, whose destruction was fully effected.* After further contributing, in the boats of the same sloop and of the SALSETTE frigate, to the capture of a French privateer in the Archipelago, he removed, 24 Nov. 1813, to the GANYMEDE 20, Capts. John Brett Purvis and Wm. M'Culloch, with whom he served, as First-Lieutenant, in the Mediterranean and at Bermuda, until 5 Aug. 1815. He was next employed, in a like capacity, from 15 Oct. 1832 until he invalided in March, 1833, on board the RHADAMANTHUS steamer, Capt. Geo. Evans, with whom, during that period, he served in the North Sea, and made a voyage to Lisbon. He has not since been afloat.

Lieut. Hurst was appointed a Naval Knight of Windsor in 1838.

HUSKISSON. (CAPT., 1811. F-P., 15; H-P., 32.)

THOMAS HUSKISSON was born 31 July, 1784, at Oxley, near Wolverhampton, co. Stafford, and died 21 Dec. 1844. He was brother of Geo. Huskisson, Esq., formerly an officer of the Royal Marines, who died Collector of the Customs at the island of St. Vincent in Feb. 1844, having held that appointment since 1820; and half-brother of the late Right Hon. Wm. Huskisson, one of H.M. Principal Secretaries of State, as also of Major-General Sam. Huskisson. One of his sisters married the Rev. Jas. Walhouse, uncle to the present Lord Hatherton.

This officer entered the Navy, 22 July, 1800 (under the patronage of Admiral Mark Milbanke), as A.B., on board the BEAVER sloop, Capt. Christopher B. Jones, lying at Portsmouth; and, on removing, in the following Oct., to the ROMNEY 50, Capt. Sir Home Popham, proceeded to the Red Sea, where he was detached, as Midshipman, during a few months of 1802, in a small hired brig, to assist in surveying the coast of Arabia. After visiting other parts of India he returned home, and joined, in June, 1803, the DEFENCE 74, Capt. Geo. Hope, under whom we find him enacting a warm part in the action off Cape Trafalgar, 21 Oct. 1805. Being next transferred to the FOUDROYANT 80, successive flag-ship of Admirals Sir John Borlase Warren and Albemarle Bertie, he had an opportunity, on 13 March, 1806, of witnessing the capture of the *Ma-*

* *Vide* Gaz. 1794, p. 567.

* *Vide* Gaz. 1814, p. 124.

rengo of 80 guns, having Rear-Admiral Linois on board, and 40-gun frigate *Belle Poule*. On 9 Aug. in the same year Mr. Huskisson was nominated Acting-Lieutenant of the FOUDROYANT; an appointment which the Admiralty sanctioned by a commission signed on 15 of the ensuing Nov. In July, 1807, he was ordered to join the PRINCE OF WALES 98, bearing the flag of Admiral Gambier, to whom he officiated as Flag-Lieutenant during the operations which led to the subsequent fall of Copenhagen. In Jan. 1808 he obtained an appointment to the HYPERION 36, Capt. Thos. Chas. Brodie, fitting at Chatham, whence, in the spring, he sailed for Jamaica in the MELPOMENE 38, with Vice-Admiral Bartholomew Sam. Rowley, who, on their arrival, placed him in charge, on 5 July, of the FLEUR DE LA MER schooner, in which vessel he appears to have been for some time employed at the blockade of St. Domingo. Being advanced, 18 Jan. 1809, to the command of the PELORUS 18, Capt. Huskisson, on 17 Oct. in that year, distinguished himself by the very gallant style in which he supported Capt. Hugh Cameron of the HAZARD 18, at the destruction of a battery near Pointe-à-Pitre, Guadeloupe, while the boats of the two sloops were effecting the annihilation of a privateer in the manner alluded to in our memoir of Lieut. Hugh Hunter. The loss of the PELORUS on this occasion amounted to 2 men killed and 6 wounded. After assisting at the reduction of Guadeloupe, Capt. Huskisson was appointed Acting-Captain of the BLONDE frigate, and directed to escort home a valuable fleet of merchantmen. The vacancy which he had been selected to fill not being of a nature to entitle him to confirmation, he rejoined the PELORUS, and continued to serve in her, on the Jamaica station, until posted, 14 March, 1811, into the GARLAND 28. In June, 1812, being still in the West Indies, he was removed by Vice-Admiral Chas. Stirling to the BARBADOES 24; in which ship he succeeded, while in protection of a convoy, in capturing, at the close of a seven hours' chase, the U. S. Revenue-cruizer *James Maddison*, pierced for 14, but carrying only 10 guns, with a complement of 65 men. A few days after this event the BARBADOES was separated from the convoy in a violent gale, during which she lost her top-masts and main-yard. Having refitted at Bermuda, Capt. Huskisson took charge of three small vessels bound to Halifax, and was proceeding thither with 60,000 dollars on board for the dockyard, when, on the night of 28 Sept. 1812, the BARBADOES and two of her consorts were unfortunately wrecked on the N.W. bar of Sable Island. The specie, however, was saved by being thrown overboard with a buoy attached to each of the cases; and at the expiration of 12 days the sufferers were released from their unpleasant position by the advent of a frigate and schooner sent to their assistance. Capt. Huskisson, who was most fully acquitted by court-martial of all blame for the loss of his ship, was next employed, from 12 June to 28 Nov. 1815, in the EURYALUS 42, and PERSEUS 22; in the former of which ships he cruized in command of a small squadron off Havre and the mouth of the Seine, until the surrender of Napoleon Buonaparte. Rejoining the EURYALUS in July, 1818, he sailed in that frigate for the West Indies, where, on 18 Nov. 1819, in consequence of the death of Rear-Admiral Donald Campbell, he became Senior officer of the squadron in the Caribbean seas, and hoisted a broad pendant. On the arrival of Rear-Admiral Fahie from England in May, 1820, Capt. Huskisson was instructed to repair to Jamaica, and place himself under the orders of Sir Home Popham; and on 10 June, eight days only after he had reached his destination, he again hoisted a broad pendant, and assumed the chief command on the station, owing to the health of the Admiral necessitating his return to England. On being relieved by Sir Chas. Rowley in Dec. 1820, Capt. Huskisson himself invalided. His last appointment afloat was to the SEMIRAMIS 42, flag-ship at Cork of Lord John Colville, the command of which he retained from 1 Sept. 1821 until superseded, at his own request, in March, 1822. He was admitted into Greenwich Hospital 15 Oct. 1830.

Capt. Huskisson filled the office of Paymaster of the Navy from 28 March, 1827, until its abolition in Oct. 1830. He married, 22 Aug. 1813, Miss E. Wedge, daughter of an agriculturist eminent in the west of Staffordshire, by whom he had three sons and two daughters. His eldest son, Thomas, died at Malta, 16 May, 1833, while serving as Midshipman of H.M.S. CORDELIA. His second son, Wm. Milbanke, holds an appointment in the Foreign Office; and his youngest, John, is a First-Lieutenant, R.M.

HUSSEY. (LIEUT., 1822. F-P., 35; H-P., 4.)

RICHARD HUSSEY was born 24 Oct. 1796.

This officer entered the Navy, 1 July, 1808, as Fst.-cl. Vol., on board the PERUVIAN sloop, Capts. Fras. Douglas, Berkeley, Dickinson, Robt. Winthrop, and Geo. Kippen, stationed at first in the Channel, and next in the West Indies, where he attained the rating of Midshipman in Sept. 1810, and continued to serve until Nov. 1814. He then accompanied Capt. Kippen into the DIOMEDE troopship, and on 14 Dec. following served with the boats of a squadron at the capture, on Lake Borgne, of five American gun-boats under Commodore Jones, whose capture was not accomplished until the British, after a severe conflict, had sustained a loss of 17 men killed and 77 wounded. In the summer of 1815 he successively joined the HAVOCK sloop, and PIQUE frigate, Capts. Geo. Truscott and Hon. Anthony Maitland, on removing with the latter of whom to the GLASGOW 50, it was his fortune to share, as Master's Mate, in the bombardment of Algiers 27 Aug. 1816. During the next seven years Mr. Hussey, we find, served as Admiralty Midshipman and Mate in the PROMETHEUS 22, Capt. Constantine Rich. Moorsom, QUEEN CHARLOTTE 100, flag-ship of Sir Edw. Thornbrough, SPEY 20, Capt. Jas. Kearney White, and GANYMEDE 26, and HYPERION 42, both commanded by Capt. Hon. Robt. Cavendish Spencer, on the Home, Mediterranean, and South American stations. On 26 Dec. 1822, he was created a Lieutenant in the SPARROWHAWK 18, Capts. Edw. Boxer, Hon. Rich. Saunders Dundas, and Robt. Stuart, which sloop, after having for a length of time had charge of her, he brought home from the Mediterranean (she had previously been on the Halifax station) and paid off in 1825. Lieut. Hussey's next appointments were, 29 April, 1828, and 1 March, 1829, to the SAMARANG 28, and MADAGASCAR 46, Capts. Wm. Fanshawe Martin and Hon. Sir R. C. Spencer, also in the Mediterranean. He invalided in Aug. 1829; and, since 3 April, 1831, has been employed in the Coast Guard.

He married, in Dec. 1825, Sophia, third daughter of Jas. Cockrell, Esq., by whom he has issue four children.

HUTCHESON. (CAPTAIN, 1841.)

FRANCIS DEANE HUTCHESON entered the Navy 13 Oct. 1813; and, while serving on board the AMERICA 74, Capt. Josias Rowley, was present at the unsuccessful attack upon Leghorn, also at the occupation of Santa Maria, and of the enemy's other forts in the Gulf of Spezia, and at the reduction of Genoa and its dependencies. In 1815, being at the time in the UNDAUNTED 38, he assisted at the capture of a convoy at Barletta, and at the taking of the Tremiti islands. When afterwards with Rear-Admiral David Milne in the IMPREGNABLE 98, Mr. Hutcheson had an opportunity of sharing in the bombardment of Algiers, 27 Aug. 1816. He was made Lieutenant, 19 Jan. 1822, into the PYRAMUS 42, Capt. Fras. Newcombe, on the West India station, and next appointed, 15 June, 1826, and 8 Dec. 1827, to the HYPERION 42, Coast Blockade ship, Capt. Wm. Jas. Mingaye, and ÆTNA bomb, Capts. Thos. Edw. Hoste and Stephen Lushington, on the Mediterranean station. He was promoted, 9 Aug. 1828, to the command of the PELICAN sloop, and, having paid that vessel off 14

April, 1830, was lastly, from 20 March, 1832, until 1836, employed in the Coast Guard. His advancement to Post-rank took place 23 Nov. 1841.

We are informed that Capt. Hutcheson, in Oct. 1828, co-operated with the French Army in the reduction of the Morea Castle. AGENT—J. Hinxman.

HUTCHINSON. (COMMANDER, 1814. F-P. 17; H-P., 30.)

CHARLES HUTCHINSON entered the Navy, 16 Nov. 1800, as Fst.-cl. Vol., on board the TRENT 36, Capt. Sir Edw. Hamilton, stationed in the Channel; proceeded, towards the close of 1801, to Madeira, in the ARETHUSA 38, Capt. Thos. Wolley; and served, from Jan. 1802 until July, 1806, on the Jamaica station, chiefly as Midshipman and Master's Mate, in the ÆOLUS frigate, Capts. John Wm. Spranger and Andrew Fitzherbert Evans, VANGUARD 74, Capt. A. F. Evans, and VETERAN 64, flag-ship of Sir John Thos. Duckworth. He then came home with convoy in the PENGUIN sloop, Capt. Smith, and on 16 April, 1807, was confirmed a Lieutenant in the VALIANT 74, Capts. Jas. Young, Alex. Robt. Kerr, John Bligh, John Nash, Thos. Geo. Shortland, and Robt. Dudley Oliver, in which ship we find him assisting at the bombardment of Copenhagen, witnessing Lord Cochrane's destruction of the French shipping in Basque Roads, and attending the expedition to Flushing. From 3 May, 1811, until within three weeks of his promotion to the rank of Commander 21 July, 1814, Mr. Hutchinson further served on the Home station as Flag-Lieutenant to Admirals Wm. Young and to H.R.H. the Duke of Clarence in the CHRISTIAN VII. 80, IMPREGNABLE 98, and MAGICIENNE 36. He was consequently on board the IMPREGNABLE when she brought the Allied Sovereigns to England, and likewise at the grand naval review held on the occasion at Spithead. His next and last appointment was to the Coast Guard, in which he continued from 6 July, 1831, until 1834.

Commander Hutchinson is married and has issue.

HUTCHINSON. (RETIRED CAPTAIN, 1840. F-P., 26; H-P., 39.)

EDWARD HUTCHINSON was born 16 March, 1771.

This officer entered the Navy, in May, 1782, as a Servant, on board the NIMBLE, Lieut.-Commander Gabriel Bray, on the Home station, where, and in the East Indies, he continued to serve until March, 1793, chiefly as Midshipman and Mate, in the CLEOPATRA 32, Capt. Henry Harvey, SPEEDWELL 14, Lieut.-Commander Rich. Willis, and BUSY 14, SCOUT 16, and SWAN and ATALANTA 18's, all commanded by Capt. John Elphinstone. He then joined the BERWICK 74, Capts. Sir John Collins, Wm. Shield, Geo. Campbell, Geo. Henry Towry, Chas. Tyler, and Wm. Smyth, attached to the force in the Mediterranean, on which station, after a brief servitude in the BRITANNIA 100, bearing the flag of Vice-Admiral Wm. Hotham, he was successively appointed Acting-Lieutenant, at the commencement of 1795, of the ST. GEORGE 98, flag-ship of Sir Hyde Parker, and INCONSTANT 36, Capts. Thos. Fras. Fremantle and Geo. Oakes. On 13 March in the latter year, the day preceding Admiral Hotham's first partial action with the French fleet, the INCONSTANT particularly distinguished herself by the gallant manner in which she attacked, raked, and harassed one of the enemy's line-of-battle ships, the *Ça Ira*, of 80 guns. Mr. Hutchinson, who on the occasion performed the duties of Senior Lieutenant, did not obtain his first commission from the Admiralty until 30 Dec. 1796. He was, however, on 14 Oct. 1797, a few weeks after he had left the INCONSTANT,* promoted to the rank of Commander. He was lastly, from 1 June, 1803, until 5 Nov. 1814, and from 26 June, 1815, until 20 Feb. 1816, employed as Agent for Prisoners-of-War at Chatham and Plymouth. He accepted his present rank 10 Sept. 1840. AGENT—J. Hinxman.

* The INCONSTANT took, 20 April, 1796, the corvette *L'Unité*, of 34 guns and 218 men. The enemy had made an attempt to set her on fire, but by the exertions of Lieut. Hutchinson it was soon extinguished.—*Vide* Gaz. 1796, p. 528.

HUTCHINSON. (LIEUT., 1833. F-P., 14; H-P., 9.)

JOSHUA HUTCHINSON is son of a veteran naval officer, now deceased, who had been wounded in the service of his country; and only brother of Wm. Hutchinson, Esq., R.N., who died while employed under Capt. Wm. Fitzwilliam Owen in the survey of the coast of Africa. One of his uncles, Commander Joshua Kneeshaw, R.N. (1814), lost his right arm in the service, received a gold medal for the capture of Glückstadt, and died 1 Nov. 1843, aged 70; and another, the late Lieut. Sam. Kneeshaw, R.N., died while Agent of a Transport on the African coast.

This officer entered the Navy, 12 June, 1824, as Fst.-cl. Vol., on board the PRINCE REGENT 120, Capt. Wm. Henry Webley Parry, guard-ship at Chatham, and in the following year proceeded to the West Indies as Midshipman of the BUSTARD 10, Capt. Williams Sandom. After having there served for a short time with Capt. Hugh Patton on board the ISIS 50, he returned home in Jan. 1827, and rejoined the PRINCE REGENT, then commanded by Capt. Constantine Rich. Moorsom. He was next, for upwards of three years, employed in the ESPOIR 10, Capt. Henry Fras. Greville, at the Cape of Good Hope; and in Feb. 1831, having passed his examination on 20 of the previous Oct., he was appointed Mate of the ST. VINCENT 120, flag-ship in the Mediterranean of Hon. Sir Henry Hotham. Removing, in Nov. of the same year, to the PHILOMEL 10, Capt. Wm. Smith, Mr. Hutchinson, on 4 of the ensuing March, had the misfortune to be very severely wounded by two musket-balls passing through his left hand and arm while he was in the act of boarding, from a boat, a Spanish smuggler near Gibraltar. He continued in the PHILOMEL until Nov. 1832; and, on 11 Feb. 1833, as a reward for the gallantry he had evinced in the above affair, he was presented with a Lieutenant's commission. His subsequent appointments were—6 June, 1834, to the TALBOT 28, Capt. Follett Walrond Pennell, with whom he served on the South American and East India stations until June, 1837—26 Jan. 1839, as Senior, to the ZEBRA 16, Capt. Robt. Fanshawe Stopford, on the Mediterranean station—and, 5 Oct. 1839, to the BELLEROPHON 80, Capt. Chas. John Austen. During the operations of 1840 on the coast of Syria, Lieut. Hutchinson volunteered with another officer to guard a mountain pass of great importance, called the Dog River, a very arduous service, which imposed upon him the necessity of being on the alert from sun-set to sun-rise for the purpose of burning blue lights in the event of an attempt made by the Egyptian troops to pass the bridge. His zeal, attention, and ability in this, and in every other instance throughout the campaign, including the bombardment of St. Jean d'Acre, gained him the warm plaudits of Capt. Austen, as did his seamanlike conduct on the occasion of the BELLEROPHON being caught, 2 Dec. 1840, in a dreadful tempest, on a lee shore and iron-bound coast. He was paid off in June, 1841, and has not since been employed.

Lieut. Hutchinson is Senior of 1833. He married, in Aug. 1837, Hannah, daughter of J. Lacy, Esq., of Upleatham, Yorkshire.

HUTCHINSON. (COMMANDER, 1827. F-P., 24; H-P., 33.)

WILLIAM HUTCHINSON (*b*) entered the Navy, in Aug. 1790, as A.B., on board the NASSAU 64, Capt. Andrew Sutherland, from which ship, after serving in the Channel, he was discharged, as Midshipman, in Feb. 1791. Between the commencement of the French revolutionary war in 1793 and Aug. 1804, he appears to have been employed on the Home station, chiefly as Master's Mate, Second Master, Pilot, and Acting-Lieutenant, in the BELLEROPHON 74, Capt. (afterwards Rear-Admiral) Thos. Pasley (one of Lord Howe's victorious fleet on the memorable 1 June), CAROLINE gun-brig, Capt. Benj. Butler, GARLAND 28, Capt. John Erskine Douglas, ROBERT gun-brig, and UNION schooner, each commanded by himself, WOOLWICH, Lieut.-Commander John Cox, GALIKHEID 64, bearing the flag of Rear-Admiral Edw. Thornbrough, and RUBY 64, and EAGLE 74, both under the orders of Capt. David Colby. He was officially promoted to the rank of Lieutenant, and appointed to the command of the EL CORSO, 9 Feb. 1805; and he was afterwards employed—in 1807, as an Agent for Transports in the North Sea and Baltic, on the coasts of Spain and Portugal, and in the Mediterranean—from Oct. to Dec. 1809, in command of the BREVDRAGEREN 12, off Heligoland—from 14 May to 5 June, 1810, as First-Lieutenant, in the THISBE 28, flag-ship of Hon. Sir Henry Edwin Stanhope in the river Thames—during the next 13 months in command of various small vessels on the rivers Elbe, Weser, and Ems—from Aug. 1811 until Aug 1814, and from April to Oct. 1815, in command of the HOPE, PIGMY, and EARNEST gun-brigs, on the Irish, Channel, Baltic, Mediterranean, and North Sea stations—from 21 March, 1816, until March, 1819, in the Ordinary at Chatham—and, we believe, from 14 Sept. 1820 until advanced to his present rank 1 Dec. 1827, in command of the PLUMPER gun-brig, on the Cork station. His last appointments were—21 July, 1829, to the Coast Guard, in which he served for a period of nearly three years—and, 20 Oct. 1840, to the command of the VICTORY 104, Capts. Fras. Erskine Loch and Wm. Wilmott Henderson, guard-ship at Portsmouth. He has been on half-pay since Oct. 1843.

HUTCHISON. (COMMANDER, 1821. F-P., 22; H-P., 29.)

GEORGE HUTCHISON entered the Navy, 1 March, 1796, as Midshipman, on board a small vessel lying at Sheerness under the command of Lieut. Thos. Hutchison; removed for a short period in 1798 to the NASSAU 64, Capts. Wm. Hargood and Geo. Tripp, stationed at the Nore; and during the four following years was employed in the Baltic, North Sea, and Mediterranean, under Admiral John Peyton and Capt. John Larmour, with the latter of whom, in the DIADEM 64, we find him attending the expedition of 1801 to Egypt. From June, 1802, until the same month in 1806, he served with Sir Rich. John Strachan in the DONEGAL and RENOWN 74's, and CÆSAR 80; and he was thus afforded an opportunity of assisting at the DONEGAL's capture, in 1804, of the Spanish 44-gun frigate *Amfitrite*, and of a ship with a cargo on board worth 200,000*l.*, and of contributing in the CÆSAR to the capture, 4 Nov. 1805, of the four line-of-battle ships which had effected their escape from the battle of Trafalgar. He was confirmed a Lieutenant (after having acted for nearly five months as such) in the BELLONA 74, Capt. John Erskine Douglas, 11 Nov. 1806, and was afterwards appointed—12 Jan. 1807, to the TRIUMPH 74, Capt. Sir Thos. Masterman Hardy, in the Chesapeake, whence he returned in March, 1808—30 March, 1809, to the DEFIANCE 74, Capts. Hon. Henry Hotham and Rich. Raggett, employed on the coasts of Spain and France, and in the North Sea—19 Oct. 1811, to the ST. DOMINGO 74, flag-ship on the latter and on the North American stations of Sir J. Strachan and Sir John Borlase Warren—31 Aug. 1814, to the BRISEIS 10, Capt. Wm. Rush Jackson, which vessel he left in May, 1815—and, 10 April, 1818, and 18 May, 1821, to the VENGEUR and GENOA 74's, Capts. Thos. Alexander and Fred. Lewis Maitland, on the Home and South American stations. He assisted, while in the BELLONA, at the destruction, 14 Sept. 1806, off Cape Henry, of the French 74-gun ship *L'Impétueux;* co-operated, in the DEFIANCE, with the patriots on the north coast of Spain, and partially commanded her boats at the cutting-out of three chasse-marées laden with wine and rosin from under two batteries at Belleisle, and the fire of some field-pieces and armed vessels, in 1810;* and commanded for some time the DOLPHIN and HIGHFLYER, tenders† to the ST. DOMINGO, on the coast of America, where he was taken prisoner 30 March, 1814. He attained his present rank 9 Nov. 1821, and has since been on half-pay.

HUTCHISON. (LIEUT., 1813. F-P., 21; H-P., 26.)

WILLIAM HUTCHISON entered the Navy, 3 May, 1800, as Sec.-cl. Boy, on board the WINDSOR CASTLE 98, Capts. Albemarle Bertie and Jas. Oughton, in which ship, bearing for some time the flag of Sir Andrew Mitchell, he continued to serve as Midshipman, on the Channel and Irish stations, until April, 1804. From June, 1805, until taken prisoner in Jan. 1808, he performed the duties of Master's Mate in the Mediterranean and Channel on board the ROSE 18; and on regaining his liberty in March, 1811, he joined the NORGE 74, Capts. John Sprat Rainier and Wm. Waller. Being promoted from the ST. DOMINGO 74, bearing the flag of Sir John Borlase Warren, to a Lieutenancy, 28 May, 1813, in the MOHAWK 16, Capts. Hon. Henry Dilkes Byng and Henry Litchfield, he appears to have been much employed in that vessel up the rivers and along the shores of North America, and to have commanded a boat at the capture of the United States schooner *Asp*, mounting 1 long 18-pounder gun, and 2 18-pounder carronades, with swivels, &c., and having 25 men, which vessel, although she had been hauled close to the beach under the protection of a large body of militia, was boarded and carried with cool and determined bravery, the British sustaining a loss of 2 men killed and 6 wounded, and the enemy of their Commander (a Lieutenant) killed and several men drowned.‡ Mr. Hutchison, who invalided home in Dec. 1813, was lastly employed—from 5 Sept. 1822 until Sept. 1826, in the Coast Blockade, as Supernumerary Lieutenant of the SEVERN and RAMILLIES, Capts. Wm. M'Culloch and Hugh Pigot—and, from 24 July, 1829, until the early part of 1834, in the Coast Guard.

HUTCHISON. (LIEUT., 1815. F-P., 10; H-P., 31.)

WILLIAM HUTCHISON (*b*), born 26 May, 1793, in Dublin, is youngest son of the late Ephraim Hutchison, Esq. (great-grandson of an officer who served as Major of Cavalry at the battle of the Boyne, and to whose family King William III. made a grant of the extensive district of Cooliskrane, otherwise Quinsborough, in the Barony of Ophaly, in co. Kildare, free from quit and crown rent), by Elizabeth, daughter of Redmond Morres, Esq., a King's Counsel, and for many years M.P. for the city of Dublin in the Irish Parliament, and sister of the first Viscount Frankfort de Montmorency.

This officer entered the Navy, in Sept. 1806, as Fst.-cl. Vol., on board the DELIGHT 16, Capt. Philip Cosby Handfield, and in the course of the following year was employed as Midshipman in scouring the Calabrian shore, and destroying the enemy's coasting-trade. On 30 Jan. 1808, the DELIGHT, in an endeavour to re-capture four Sicilian gun-boats, unfortunately took the ground near Reggio, and was obliged to surrender, after losing, from an exposure of 15 hours to a galling fire from the enemy's batteries and troops, two-thirds of her crew, together with her Commander and Capt. Thos. Secombe of the GLATTON, who was serving on board at the time. Escaping in the boats, Mr. Hutchison got on board the BITTERN sloop, from which, in a short period, he was transferred to the MALTA 84, Capt. Wm. Shield. In May of the same year, he again joined a sloop named the DELIGHT, commanded by Capt. John Brett Purvis, with whom he remained until Jan. 1810, when he was received on board the ATLAS 74, bearing the flag off Cadiz of Rear-Admiral John Child Purvis. After assisting in the boats of the latter ship at the defence of Fort Matagorda, Mr. Hutchison removed to the APOLLO 38, Capts. Bridges Watkinson Taylor and Edwards

* *Vide* Gaz. 1810, p. 858. † *V.* Gaz. 1814, p. 1332.
‡ *V.* Gaz. 1813, p. 1767.

Lloyd Graham, to which frigate he continued attached, in the capacities of Master's Mate and Acting-Lieutenant, until June, 1814—a period of rather more than four years. On 29 Jan. and 3 Feb. 1813, we find him serving with credit at the reduction of the islands of Angusta* and Curzola; and on 28 of the following May uniting in a brilliant attack made by four of the boats belonging to the APOLLO and CERBERUS, under Lieuts. John Wm. Montagu and Wm. Henry Nares, upon a convoy, protected by 11 gun-boats, near Otranto, where the cliffs were covered with French troops. Upon this occasion, Mr. Hutchison, who commanded the APOLLO's gig, and had only seven men with him, actually boarded and carried a gun-vessel mounting one 12 and two 4-pounders, with a complement of 40 men, besides similarly making prize of four armed merchantmen.† In the month of June he further assisted at the capture of a gun-boat mounting 2 long guns, and the driving of another vessel on shore.‡ He attained his present rank 18 Feb. 1815, nearly three years after he had passed his examination; and was next, from 6 of the following May until 30 Nov. 1816, employed on the Channel and West India stations, in the PLUMPER, BRISEIS, and SABINE sloops, Capts. Geo. Domett and Geo. Campbell. He has since been on half-pay.

Lieut. Hutchison has for many years filled, with pre-eminent zeal and spirit, the post of Harbour-Master at Kingstown, Dublin. His exertions in the preservation of life at different periods have been of a singularly humane and intrepid character. The first instance of the kind was on 23 April, 1818, when he was the means of saving H.M. sloop PANDORA from destruction, during a violent gale and tremendous sea, by his voluntary efforts and example in manning a life-boat for the purpose of enabling pilots to be put on board—a service which procured him the approbation of the Admiralty, and the sum of 100*l*. from the Navy Office. The heroic manner in which he afterwards, under the most awful circumstances, rescued the crews of the schooner *Curwin* of Carlisle, and the brigs *Ellen* of Liverpool and *Duke* of Maryport, was such as to obtain the thanks of the Ballast-Office at Dublin, the presentation from the Corporation of a piece of plate of the value of 50 guineas, a recommendation in his favour to the Admiralty from the Viceroy of Ireland, the Duke of Northumberland, and the gold medallion of the London Shipwreck Institution. On 25 Jan. 1838, during a heavy gale from the east, he received a very severe wound, which totally deprived him of the sight of one eye, while in the act of bringing to anchor an Indiaman which he had boarded outside the harbour. The Lieutenant married, 25 Nov. 1818, Elizabeth, daughter of the late John Knox, of Warringsford, co. Down, by whom he has issue six sons and four daughters.

* At Angusta he had charge of one of several boats which were mentioned for their great exertions in drawing upon themselves the fire of a fort and battery.—*Vide* Gaz. 1813, p. 1307.

† *V.* Gaz. 1813, p. 1795. ‡ *V.* Gaz. 1813, p. 1795.

HUTTON. (CAPTAIN, 1844. F-P., 29; H-P., 5.)

FREDERICK HUTTON, born in 1801, is son of the Rev. Jas. Harriman Hutton, Vicar of Leckford, co. Hants.

This officer entered the Navy, 28 Jan. 1813, on board the SALSETTE 36, Capt. John Bowen, employed in the East Indies; served from 1816 until 1818 on the Home station in the ERIDANUS 36, Capt. Wm. King, and ROCHFORT 80, Capt. Sir Archibald Collingwood Dickson; then sailed for South America in the CREOLE 42, Capt. Wm. Bateman Dashwood, for the purpose of hoisting the broad pendant of Commodore Wm. Bowles; became Mate, in 1821, of the STARLING 10, Lieut.-Commander John Reeve, on the Guernsey station; and was next employed for a considerable time in the South Seas and East Indies on board the TEES 26, Capt. Thos. Coe, and LIFFEY 50, bearing the broad pendant of the same officer. After acting for some months as Lieutenant in the SOPHIE 18, Capt. Geo. Fred. Ryves, he went back to the TEES, to which vessel, commanded at the time by Capt. Fred. Marryat, he was confirmed by commission dated 17 May, 1825. He was shortly afterwards, while at Rangoon during the Burmese war, placed in command of the armed transport SATELLITE, and stationed at Panlang on the river Irawady. His succeeding appointments were—19 Aug. 1826, to the DESPATCH 18, Capt. Robt. White Parsons, with whom he chiefly served as First-Lieutenant on the African, Irish, and Lisbon stations, until paid off in 1829—in the early part of 1831, to the command of the METEOR steamer, for the purpose of escorting the Duchess and Princess of Saxe-Weimar to the Continent—20 July, 1831, to the MAGICIENNE 24, Capt. Jas. Hanway Plumridge, again in the East Indies—and, 13 April, 1835, as Senior, to the BARHAM 50, Capt. Armar Lowry Corry. In the capacity of Commander, a rank he attained 28 June, 1838, Capt. Hutton was, from 10 Dec. 1838, until finally put out of commission in Aug. 1843, re-employed in the Mediterranean and Tagus on board the VANGUARD 80, Capts. Sir Thos. Fellowes and Sir David Dunn, under the latter of whom we find him assisting at the blockade of Alexandria during the Syrian campaign. He attained his present rank 3 July, 1844; and since 12 Nov. 1846, has been employed as Governor of the Ascension and Captain of the TORTOISE store-ship.

Capt. Hutton was presented by the Queen of Portugal with the Order of the Tower and Sword, for his exertions, with a party of the VANGUARD's people, on the occasion of a fire which broke out at Lisbon in 1843, and destroyed the Military Schools. AGENTS—Messrs. Stilwell.

HYDE. (LIEUTENANT, 1815.)

GEORGE HYDE entered the Navy, 27 July, 1805, as Fst.-cl. Vol., on board the QUEEN 98, Capts. John Knight and Fras. Pender, bearing the flag afterwards of Lord Collingwood in the Mediterranean and off Cadiz. He came home in 1807 in the JUNO frigate, Capt. Hon. Granville Proby, but remained unemployed from that period until Sept. 1810, when he was ordered to the West Indies. On his return from the latter station, where he had been intermediately employed as Midshipman, in the DRAGON 74, flag-ship of Sir Fras. Laforey, and STAR sloop, Capt. Fras. Kearny White, he joined in Oct. 1811 the BELLE POULE 38, Capt. Jas. Brisbane, whom he ultimately followed into the PEMBROKE 74. He was again, in Dec. 1812, placed under the orders of Capt. White, in the THISTLE 12, in which vessel he cruized off the coast of North America until Oct. 1813. He then marched with Capt. Edw. Collier from Halifax to Kingston, in Upper Canada, and on his arrival was appointed to the CHARWELL 14, Capt. Alex. Dobbs. In Aug. 1814, having assisted in transporting the gig belonging to the latter vessel from Queenstown to Frenchman's Creek, a distance of 20 miles, and thence, with the addition of five batteaux, through the woods to Lake Erie, a further distance of eight miles, he served with a detachment of 75 seamen and marines at the capture of the *Somers* and *Ohio*, two out of three fine American schooners, whose aggregate force amounted to 92 lbs. weight of metal and 105 men, while the British were perfectly destitute of artillery. The enemy on the occasion had 1 man killed and 7 wounded; the assailants 2 killed and 4 wounded. For his gallant conduct in the attack, and the skill he displayed in afterwards navigating one of the prizes through shoals and rapids, and under a constant and heavy fire, into the river Niagara, Mr. Hyde obtained the particular mention of Capt. Dobbs.* About the same period, however, he was unfortunately taken prisoner, and he was in consequence detained in the United States until March, 1815. After he had again served for three months in the CHARWELL, commanded by Capt. Edw. Rowley, on Lake Ontario, he returned to England on board a transport, and on 20 Sept. 1815 was promoted

* *Vide* Gaz. 1814, p. 2036.

(from the Queen Charlotte 100, Capt. Edm. Boger) to the rank of Lieutenant. With the exception of a servitude of some time in the Tyne 26, commanded by his former Captain, White, on the Halifax station, Mr. Hyde has since been on half-pay.

He is married and has issue.

HYDE. (Lieutenant, 1824.)

Richard Dawbrey Hyde obtained his commission 5 Dec. 1824; and has since been on half-pay.

He holds the appointment of Dock-Master on the Glamorgan Canal. Agents—Messrs. Stilwell.

HYETT. (Lieut., 1815. f-p., 16; h-p., 26.)

Joseph Hyett entered the Navy, 28 March, 1805, as Third-cl. Vol., on board the Royal William, Capts. John Wainwright and Hon. Courtenay Boyle, bearing the flag of Admiral Montagu at Portsmouth; and after a further servitude on the Home station in the Osprey sloop, Capt. Timothy Clinch, and, as Midshipman, in the Crown 64, Lieut.-Commander Jas. Rose, sailed in March, 1809, for the West Indies in the Rhodian 10, Capt. Geo. Moubray. From May, 1812, until Aug. 1815, we find him employed with the last-mentioned officer, and with Capts. Henry Litchfield and John Moberly, on board the Moselle 18—the latter part of the time as Acting-Master, Acting-Lieutenant, and Master's Mate. He joined, therefore, in the attacks upon Norfolk and Hampton; saw a good deal of detached service in the Chesapeake; was in the boats when they cut out a 600-ton merchantman from under the forts in Charleston Bay; received, on 29 June, 1814, a musket-ball through the lower jaw in a boat-engagement with a pirate in the Gulf of Mexico; and was most severely frost-bitten in the legs during the expedition to New Orleans, where he was constantly away from his ship on boat-duty. On leaving the Moselle, as above, he took up (he had passed his examination in June, 1812) a commission dated 10 Feb. 1815; and he was lastly, from Dec. 1826, until Jan. 1831, employed as an Agent for Transports afloat. In consideration of the wound he had received in his cheek, involving the loss of hearing in one ear, and of the injuries he had sustained at New Orleans, which, after occasioning him much suffering, resulted in the amputation, 28 June, 1846, of the right leg high above the knee, Lieut. Hyett was admitted to the out-pension of Greenwich Hospital 13 Oct. following.

HYNE. (Lieutenant, 1822. f-p., 11; h-p., 25.)

Thomas Madge Hyne entered the Navy, 13 April, 1811, as Ordinary, on board the Royal George 100, Capt. John Clavell, with whom, after a brief attachment to the Lauristinus 24, he was for six years employed on the Mediterranean, North American, and East India stations, as Midshipman and Master's Mate, in the Orlando 36. He then, in 1817, returned to England with Capt. Chas. Henry Pemberton in the Melville 74; and between the month of Sept. in the following year and his official promotion, which took place 4 June, 1822, he was employed on the West India, Home, and African stations, latterly in the capacity of Acting-Lieutenant, on board the Bann 20, Capt. Andrew Mitchell, Shearwater 10, Capt. Douglas Cox, Queen Charlotte 100, Capt. Thos. Briggs, Severn 40, Coast Blockade ship, Capt. Wm. M'Culloch, and Iphigenia 42, Commodore Sir Robt. Mends, by whom he was intrusted for a short time with the command of the Snapper, a small vessel. He left the Iphigenia in the course of the month last mentioned, and (with the exception of a re-employment for about twelve months in 1829-30 in the Coast Guard as Supernumerary-Lieutenant of the Hyperion 42, Capt. Wm. Jas. Mingaye) has since been on half-pay.

HYNSON. (Lieut., 1814. f-p., 10; h-p., 33.)

Joseph Hynson entered the Navy, 10 Aug. 1804, as Midshipman, on board the Tigre 74, Capt. Benj. Hallowell, in which ship he accompanied Lord Nelson to the West Indies in his celebrated pursuit of the combined squadrons. In Nov. 1812, Capt. Hallowell having hoisted his flag as Rear-Admiral on board the Malta 84, he joined him as Master's Mate in that ship. He continued with him until made Lieutenant, 23 Dec. 1814, into the Partridge sloop, Capt. John Miller Adye; and since Sept. 1815 has been on half-pay. Agents—Coplands and Burnett.

I.

IMPEY. (Rear-Admiral of the Red, 1840.)

John Impey is son of the late Sir Elijah Impey.

This officer entered the Navy, 28 April, 1785, as Midshipman, on board the Victory 100, Capt. John Knight, bearing the flag of Lord Hood at Portsmouth; and on his return from a voyage to Otaheite, whither he had been sent for the produce of the breadfruit-tree as Master's Mate of the Providence store-ship, Capt. Wm. Bligh, was received on board the Boyne 98, lying at Spithead under the flag of Sir John Jervis. On being advanced to the rank of Lieutenant, 7 Nov. 1793, he joined the Vesuvius bomb, Capt. Chas. Sawyer, on the West India station; and he was next appointed in that capacity—17 March, 1795, to the Cumberland 74, Capt. Bartholomew Sam. Rowley, part of Admiral Hotham's fleet in the action fought off the Hyères Islands 13 July following—9 March, 1797, to the Syren frigate, Capt. Thos. Le Marchant Gosselin, employed in the Channel—and, 27 April, 1799, 4 Jan. 1800, and 21 April, 1801, to the Prince of Wales 98, bearing the flag of Admiral Harvey, Unité frigate, Capt. John Poo Beresford, and Leviathan 74, flag-ship of Sir John Thos. Duckworth, all on the West India station. He was confirmed, 15 Jan. 1802, in the command of the Fairy sloop, likewise in the West Indies; on his return whither in the Epervier 16, after having for some time commanded the Alonzo on Home service, we find him effecting the capture, 26 Jan. 1805, of *L'Elisabeth* schooner privateer, of 4 guns and 34 men. He attained Post-rank 22 Jan. 1806, and in the following Feb. was ordered to England in the *Alexandre* 80, one of the prizes taken in the action off St. Domingo. He has since been on half-pay. He became a Rear-Admiral on the Retired List 28 June, 1838; and, on 17 Aug. 1840, his name was added to the roll of active flag-officers.

IMRIE. (Lieutenant, 1811. f-p., 26; h-p., 28.)

John Imrie was born 23 Nov. 1784, at Rochester, co. Kent.

This officer entered the Navy, in March, 1793, as Boatswain's Servant, on board the Robust 74, Capts. Hon. Geo. Keith Elphinstone, Edw. Thornbrough, Geo. Countess, Wm. Brown, and Wm. Henry Jervis. Continuing in that ship for upwards of eight years he served in consequence at the occupation of Toulon in Aug. 1793—escorted to England the ships that were there taken—bore a part in Lord Bridport's action 23 June, 1795—attended the ensuing ill-fated expedition to Quiberon in support of the French Royalists—and on 12 Oct. 1798 was present as Midshipman with the force under Sir John Borlase Warren at the defeat of Commodore Bompart's squadron, when the *Hoche* 74 struck to the Robust, after a very severe action, in which the latter sustained a loss of 10 men killed and 40 wounded. In Sept. 1801 Mr. Imrie was discharged into the Edgar 74, Capt. Robt. Waller Otway, which ship being paid off on her return from the West Indies in July, 1802, he shortly afterwards, on passing his examination, joined the Port Mahon 18, Capts. Walter Grosett and Martin Neville, and, in May, 1803, as Master's Mate, the Plover 18, Capt. Rich. Turner Hancock. From April, 1804, until May, 1808, we find him serving, chiefly in the capacity last mentioned, on board the Courageux 74, Capts. Chas. Boyles, Rich. Lee, and Jas. Bissett; and participating during the period in Sir Rich. John Strachan's action 4 Nov. 1805, as also in the capture, 13 March, 1806, of the *Marengo* 80, bearing the flag of Rear-Admiral Linois, and 40-gun frigate *Belle Poule*. He then proceeded to the Mediterranean in the HYPERION 36, Capt. Thos. Chas. Brodie, through whose recommendation and that of his former Captain, Bissett, he was ordered, on his arrival home with convoy towards the close of 1809, to the West Indies for the purpose of joining Sir Alex. Cochrane as Admiralty Mate on promotion. After he had accordingly served with that officer for six months in the POMPÉE 74, and NEPTUNE 98, he was nominated, 16 July, 1810, Acting-Lieutenant of the FROLIC 18, Capt. Thos. Whinyates. It was not, however, until he had again served as Master's Mate in the DRAGON 74, flag-ship of Sir Fras. Laforey, and once more as Acting-Lieutenant in the SURINAM sloop, that he succeeded in obtaining official promotion. His commission bears date 10 Sept. 1811. After twelve months of half-pay Mr. Imrie was next, in Sept. 1812, appointed to the BOXER 12, Capt. Sam. Blyth, fitting at Portsmouth, where, in the following month, he removed to the BARHAM 74, Capt. John Wm. Spranger, with whom he cruized in the Channel until March, 1813. Joining, 1 July following, the EGMONT 74, Capt. Joseph Bingham, he was first employed at the blockade of Rochefort, and afterwards, in April, 1814, under the flag of Rear-Admiral Chas. Vinicombe Penrose, during the operations up the Gironde, where he witnessed the destruction of a French line-of-battle ship, three brigs of war, several smaller vessels, and of all the forts and batteries on the north side of the river. He left the EGMONT 28 June, 1814; and was lastly, from 13 Nov. 1841, until the early part of 1846, employed as an Agent for Transports Afloat.

Lieut. Imrie married 27 Sept. 1812; and has issue 10 children.

INCE. (COMMANDER, 1846.)

JOHN MATTHEW ROBERT INCE entered the Navy 14 Dec. 1828; passed his examination 24 April, 1835; and at the period of his promotion to the rank of Lieutenant, which took place 23 Nov. 1841, was serving in the Mediterranean as Mate of the LOCUST steamer, Lieut.-Commander John Lunn. He was appointed on 30 of the same month to the IMPLACABLE 74, Capt. Edw. Harvey, also in the Mediterranean; and from 7 March, 1842, until paid off on his return to England in 1846, was employed in the East Indies on board the FLY 18, Capt. Fras. Price Blackwood. Commander Ince, who attained his present rank on 9 Nov. in the latter year, is at present on half-pay.

INCLEDON. (COMMANDER, 1813. F-P., 17; H-P., 33.)

ROBERT INCLEDON entered the Navy, in June, 1797, as Fst.-cl. Vol., on board the SPITFIRE sloop, Capts. Michael Seymour and Robt. Keen, on the Channel station, where he continued to serve as Midshipman, latterly in the NAMUR 98, Capt. Hon. Michael De Courcy, until paid off at the peace. In the summer of 1802 he proceeded to the Mediterranean as Master's Mate in the RAVEN 18, Capt. Spelman Swaine; and on that vessel being wrecked, near Mazara, in Sicily, in Jan. 1804, he joined the KENT 74, bearing the flag of Sir Rich. Bickerton. Proceeding in the course of the same year to the East Indies in the CULLODEN 74, flag-ship of Sir Edw. Pellew, he was there, in March, 1805, appointed Acting-Lieutenant of the DUNCAN, afterwards DOVER, 38, Capts. Chas. Sibthorpe John Hawtayne, Clement Sneyd, Lord Geo. Stuart, Wm. Warden, Henry Hart, Thos. Groube, Wm. Wells, and Edw. Tucker; to which frigate (being confirmed to her by commission dated 28 Sept. 1807) he continued attached until again wrecked in Madras Roads 2 May, 1811. In Feb. 1810 Mr. Incledon, then First-Lieutenant of the DOVER, was strongly recommended by his Captain, Edw. Tucker, to the notice of the Commander-in-Chief, for the very great support he had afforded him in his operations against the island of Amboyna; and in the following Aug. he acquired the further praise of the same officer for his conduct at the reduction of the important island of Ternate.* On his arrival home in Aug. 1814, after he had been employed for a prolonged period of three years in the East Indies on board the PIEDMONTAISE and PHŒNIX frigates, Capts. Dawson, John Bowen, and Wm. Henry Webley, he found that he had been promoted to the rank of Commander on 4 May in the previous year. He is the senior officer of his rank on the List of 1813.

INGESTRIE, Viscount, C.B., K.S.L., K.S.A., K.R.G., M.P. (CAPTAIN, 1827.)

THE RIGHT HONOURABLE HENRY JOHN CHETWYND, VISCOUNT INGESTRIE, born 8 Nov. 1803, is eldest surviving son of Earl Talbot, K.G., K.P., formerly Viceroy of Ireland, by Fras. Thomasine, eldest daughter of Chas. Lambert, Esq., of Beau Parc, co. Meath. His Lordship is uncle of the Marquess of Lothian and of Viscount Lewisham.

This officer entered the Navy 6 Feb. 1817; obtained his first commission 1 Jan. 1824; joined, 7 June following, the BLONDE 42, Capt. Lord Byron; and was promoted, 18 Oct. 1826, to the command of the PHILOMEL 10. For his valiant services in the latter vessel at the battle of Navarin, with the despatches relative to which he was sent home, he was advanced to the rank of Captain,† by commission dated 22 Oct. 1827, and invested with the orders above indicated. His last appointments were, 9 and 30 Jan. 1834, to the RAINBOW and TYNE 28's, in the latter of which ships he again served in the Mediterranean. He has been on half-pay since 1837.

The Viscount, who is Lieut.-Colonel of the Queen's Own Regiment of Staffordshire Militia, formerly sat in Parliament for the borough of Hertford and the city of Dublin, and now represents South Staffordshire. He married, 8 Nov. 1828, Sarah Elizabeth, only surviving daughter of Henry, second Marquess of Waterford, and has issue three sons and four daughters. AGENTS—Messrs. Stilwell.

INGLEFIELD. (COMMANDER, 1841. F-P., 13; H-P., 2.)

EDWARD AUGUSTUS INGLEFIELD, born in March, 1820, is son of Rear-Admiral Sam. Hood Inglefield, C.B.

This officer entered the Royal Naval College 6 Oct. 1832; and embarked, 11 Oct. 1834, as a Volunteer, on board the ÆTNA 6. He removed, in the course of the following month, to the ACTÆON 26, Capt. Lord Edw. Russell; was next, from the early part of 1835 until the close of 1839, employed, chiefly as Midshipman, in the DUBLIN 50, flag-ship of Sir Graham Eden Hamond, and IMOGENE 26, Capt. Henry Wm. Bruce, on the South American station; became Mate, in March, 1840 (having passed his examination in the previous Nov.), of the THUNDERER 84, Capt. Maurice Fred. Fitzhardinge Berkeley; and after participating in the operations on the coast of Syria, where he formed one of the storming party at the capture of Sidon, and assisted at the bombardment of St. Jean d'Acre, was employed, from Oct. 1841 until June, 1842 (the last three months of the time as Acting-Lieutenant), in the ILLUSTRIOUS 72, bearing the flag of Sir Chas. Adam, and PIQUE 36, Capt. Henry Forbes, both on the West India station. He was invested (after having attended Her Majesty on the occasion of her visit to Scotland in the ROYAL GEORGE yacht, Capt. Lord Adolphus FitzClarence) with the rank of Lieutenant 21 Sept. 1842; and next appointed—25 Nov. 1842, to the SAMARANG 26, Capt. Sir Edw. Belcher, employed as a surveying-vessel in the East Indies—6 March, 1845, to the EAGLE 50, as Flag-Lieutenant to his father on the S.E. coast of America, where he removed with him to the VERNON 50—and, a few months afterwards, to the acting-command of the COMUS 16. In that vessel it was

* *Vide* Gaz. 1810, p. 1482, and Gaz. 1811, p. 1199.
† *V.* Gaz. 1827, p. 2522.

his fortune to be present in the battle of the Parana, where the combined squadrons of England and France effected the destruction, after a hard day's fighting, of four heavy batteries belonging to General Rosas at Punta Obligado, as also of a schooner-of-war mounting 6 guns, and of 24 vessels chained across the river. He was in consequence confirmed in the rank of Commander by commission dated 18 Nov. 1845.* Agents—Hallett and Robinson.

INGLEFIELD, C.B. (Rear-Admiral of the White, 1841. f-p., 28; h-p., 28.)

Samuel Hood Inglefield, born in 1783, at Singlewell, in Kent, is son of the late Capt. John Nicholson Inglefield,† R.N.; and brother-in-law of the late Admiral Sir Benj. Hallowell Carew, G.C.B.

This officer entered the Navy, 8 Sept. 1791, as Fst.-cl. Vol., on board the Medusa 50, bearing the broad pendant of his father on the coast of Africa; and from April, 1793, until Jan. 1798, served, chiefly as Midshipman, in L'Aigle 40, also commanded by Capt. Inglefield, Victory 100, flag-ship of Lord Hood, L'Aimable 32, Capt. Sir Harry Burrard, Southampton, Capt. O'Brien, Cumberland 74, Capt. Bartholomew Sam. Rowley, and again in L'Aigle, as likewise in the Zealous 74, both under the orders of Capt. Sam. Hood. He was present during the above period in L'Aimable at the reduction of Calvi, and at the capture, after a running fight, of *La Moselle* corvette of 18 guns, 23 May, 1794; and, besides being actively employed in the Zealous, off Toulon, witnessed in that ship the evacuation of St. Fiorenza, officiated as Aide-de-camp to Capt. Hood at the destruction of the tower of Mortella, and accompanied the expedition under Nelson to Teneriffe. In Jan. 1798 he was nominated by Earl St. Vincent to the command, with the rank of Acting-Lieutenant, of the Spitfire gun-vessel, in which it appears he came into very frequent and warm conflict with the enemy's flotilla off Algeciras. In Dec. 1798, having been confirmed in the rank of Lieutenant by commission dated 26 of the previous July, he was appointed to the Theseus 74, Capt. Ralph Willett Miller, under whom, during the operations connected with the defence of St. Jean d'Acre, he much distinguished himself; and on one occasion in particular, 21 March, 1799, when he shared in a gallant and sanguinary, although unsuccessful, attempt made to cut out from the port of Caiffa four djerms, or sailing lighters, which had got in there on the 18th from Alexandria, with supplies for the French army.‡ While in personal charge of the ship's boats Lieut. Inglefield had the fortune to capture a variety of vessels in the very teeth of the enemy's batteries; and when with only the barge under his command he contrived to take a French national settee, mounting 4 brass 4-pounders, and having 20 soldiers on board besides her own crew. From Sept. 1800 (in the course of which year he had also served at the siege of Genoa), until a few weeks after his advancement to the rank of Commander, which took place 29 April, 1802, we find him serving as Flag-Lieutenant to Sir Rich. Bickerton and Lord Keith in the Swiftsure and Kent 74's, Madras 54, and Foudroyant 80; and in 1801 receiving the Turkish gold medal for the part he had borne in the Egyptian campaign. Being appointed, 16 Sept. 1802, to the Hunter 18, Capt. Inglefield in the early part of 1803 was sent to Jamaica with despatches for Rear-Admiral Sir John Thos. Duckworth and Lieut.-General Nugent, the naval and military Commanders-in-Chief, announcing the renewal of hostilities with France. During his continuance in the West Indies he distinguished himself as a most zealous and active cruizer. In Aug. 1803 he accomplished the destruction of *La Mutine*, a national brig of 18 guns, which had been driven on shore in the neighbourhood of Cumberland Harbour, in the island of Cuba; and he further effected the capture of the following French and Spanish privateers:—in July, 1803, of *La Belle Vénus*, of 1 gun and 4 swivels, off Cape Dame Marie, St. Domingo, where the crew effected their escape—10 June, 1804, of *La Liberté*, of 3 guns and 37 men, off the N.E. end of Jamaica—7 March, 1805, of the *Santa Rosa*, of 3 guns and 90 men (captured in company with the Reindeer sloop), off the north side of Jamaica—5 Oct. 1805, of a schooner of 5 guns and 65 men (taken in company with the Success 32), off Point Maysi, island of Cuba—21 Sept. 1806, of the *San Jose y Animas*, of 1 gun and 13 men, off the Isle of Pines—25 Jan. 1807, of the *Isabella*, of 3 guns and 64 men (taken after an arduous chase of eight hours and much labour at the sweeps), off Negril Point, Jamaica—and, 28 July, 1807, of *L'Espérance*, armed with blunderbusses and small arms, and manned with 18 men, off Cape Dame Marie. Capt. Inglefield also, on 13 April, 1804, when off St. Jago de Cuba, chased and drove under the guns of the Moro Castle a French privateer of 14 guns, and a smaller one full of men, crippling them to such an extent in their sails and rigging as to prevent their proving of annoyance to a homeward-bound convoy then on the eve of its departure from Jamaica. On another occasion, 4 Feb. 1805, we find him capturing a Spanish frigate-built ship, the *Piedad*, of 600 tons, pierced for 24 guns, having 20 in her hold and 6 mounted, and laden with jerk beef, from Valparaiso bound to the Havana. Independently of the above capture he had the good fortune to obtain possession at different periods of 20 of the enemy's merchantmen. He once too, on 29 July, 1805, contrived to bring out an American brig, prize to a French privateer, after having silenced the fire (under which she lay) of a battery in Lagoon Harbour, near Baracoa, in the island of Cuba. During Capt. Inglefield's command of the Hunter he was twice (the first time in 1803, the next in 1807) charged with the duty of protecting the British settlements in the bay of Honduras; and for his conduct in both instances he had the satisfaction of receiving a letter of thanks from the merchants of the colony. In Aug. 1807 Capt. Inglefield was appointed by Vice-Admiral Dacres to the command of the Bacchante 20, a post-ship, to which the Admiralty confirmed him on 6 of the following Oct. Continuing his successful exertions, he took, on 13 Sept. in the same year, when in company with the Reindeer, the *Amor de la Patria* Spanish privateer, of 3 guns and 73 men, off Port Morant, Jamaica; also, on 10 Jan. 1808, off the west end of Cuba, the *El Carmen* letter-of-marque, of 9 guns and 43 men, valuably laden; next, after a spirited action fought (in company with the Elk sloop-of-war) with several gun-vessels near the Havana, of one of a convoy under their protection; and, 11 May, 1808, at the close of an action of 30 minutes, preceded by a long chase, of *Le Griffon* French national brig, of 16 guns and 105 men. In Dec. 1808, a few months after his assumption of the command of the Dædalus 32, Capt. Inglefield co-operated with a force under Capt. Chas. Dashwood in the reduction of the fort and tower of Samana, St. Domingo, almost the last port of refuge on the station for the enemy's privateers. About this period the Dædalus fell in with a Haytian squadron, consisting of the *Lord Mulgrave*, of 22 guns and 300 men, two brigs of 18 and 16 guns, and three large armed schooners; the whole under the command of an Englishman, styling himself Admiral

* *Vide* Gaz. 1846, pp. 815, 861.

† Capt. Inglefield attained the rank of Lieutenant in 1768; and that of Post-Captain in 1780. He commanded the Barfleur 98, bearing the flag of Sir Samuel Hood, in the partial action with the Comte de Grasse, 29 April, 1781; the Centaur 74, in the battle of 12 April, 1782, on which occasion he captured *Le César* 80; and subsequently the Adventure 44, Medusa 50, and Aigle 40. After he had assisted in drawing up the articles of the capitulation by which Bastia was surrendered to the British arms, he was appointed in the spring of 1794 to succeed Sir Hyde Parker as Captain of the Mediterranean fleet; and towards the close of the same year he returned to England with Lord Hood in the Victory 100. He was successively employed, from that period until the summer of 1811, as a resident Commissioner of the Navy at Corsica, Malta, Gibraltar, and Halifax.

‡ *V.* Gaz. 1799, p. 610.

Goodall, whom, with his flag-ship the *Lord Mulgrave*, Capt. Inglefield thought it his duty to detain and send to Port Royal. The ship, from motives of policy, was restored to the Haytian government, but the Admiral was taken a state-prisoner to England. For his conduct in this affair the Captain of the DÆDALUS received the approbation of the Commander-in-Chief. He was at length, in the summer of 1810, ordered home in charge of a fleet of 133 valuable merchantmen; the whole of which he conducted in perfect safety to the Channel. The DÆDALUS* being paid off in Sept. 1810, Capt. Inglefield was next, on 28 Oct. 1811, ordered to commission the MALTA 84, as Flag-Captain to his brother-in-law, Rear-Admiral Hallowell, whom he accompanied to the Mediterranean, where, during the remainder of the war, he was occasionally employed with the in-shore squadron off Toulon, and in co-operation with the British army on the east coast of Spain. When preparations were made, in June, 1813, for the investment of Tarragona, he commanded the boats' at the debarkation of the troops; and during the siege 500 seamen were put under his orders for the arduous purpose of placing the guns and howitzers in the breaching batteries, erected within 500 yards of the town works. He further assisted, in the course of the operations, in directing the fire of the gun-vessels, and on the siege being raised he was charged with the duty of bringing off the spare guns and military stores, and of re-embarking the troops. At the subsequent evacuation of the fort of St. Philippe in the Col de Balaguer, Capt. Inglefield, at the head of 1000 seamen from the fleet, was employed in dismantling and effecting the destruction of that fortification, in conjunction with the Chief Engineer of the Army, Major Thackery. For this he received the thanks in public orders both of Sir Edw. Pellew, the Commander-in-Chief, and of Rear-Admiral Hallowell. Being superseded from the MALTA in Jan. 1815, for the purpose of attending as a witness the court-martial assembled at Winchester to try Lieut.-General Sir John Murray for the failure of the attack upon Tarragona, Capt. Inglefield did not succeed in obtaining re-employment until appointed, 1 March, 1826, to the GANGES 84, flag-ship of Sir Robt. Waller Otway, Commander-in-Chief in South America. In June, 1828, the Royal Marines of the squadron present at Rio Janeiro were placed under his command and landed for the protection of the Emperor Don Pedro's person, in consequence of a serious mutiny which had broken out among the German troops (about 1700 in number, joined by nearly 2000 Irish recruits) in the service of His Imperial Majesty; who, in acknowledgment of the important part Capt. Inglefield on the occasion acted in subduing the riots, presented him with the Second Class of the Order of the Southern Cross. The GANGES, after she had completed her term of servitude, returned to England and was paid off in Sept. 1829. In 1837 the subject of the present narrative was awarded the Captain's Good-Service pension; he was nominated a C.B. 18 April, 1839; and on 23 Nov. 1841 he was advanced to the rank of Rear-Admiral. Being appointed, 5 March, 1845, to the chief command on the S.E. coast of America, he sailed thither with his flag in the EAGLE 50. He afterwards shifted it to the VERNON of similar force; and since 24 June, 1846, has had the supreme direction of naval affairs in the East Indies.

Rear-Admiral Inglefield married, 21 Oct. 1816, Priscilla Margaret, eldest daughter of the late Vice-Admiral Wm. Albany Otway. By that lady, who died 18 June, 1844, he has, with one daughter (Hannah Georgina Elizabeth, married, 5 March, 1846, to Capt. Augustus De Butts, Madras Engineers, eldest son of Lieut.-General Sir Augustus De Butts, R.E., K.C.H.), six sons, of whom the eldest, Edw. Augustus, is a Commander R.N., and the second a Lieutenant in the Royal Artillery. AGENTS—Hallett and Robinson.

* The DÆDALUS, on 3 Aug. 1809, had been dismasted in a violent hurricane off the Island off Puerto Rico, and obliged in consequence, although with great hazard and difficulty, to be taken to Port Royal, Jamaica, where she remained 16 weeks refitting, owing to the extreme weakness of the dock-yard artificers from sickness; yet during all that time, through the sanitary arrangements of Capt. Inglefield, she herself only lost 1 man and 1 boy from the fever.

INGLEFIELD. (LIEUTENANT, 1846.)

VALENTINE OTWAY INGLEFIELD obtained his commission 3 Feb. 1846; and since 16 of the following April has been attached to the VERNON 50, now flag-ship of Rear-Admiral Sam. Hood Inglefield in the East Indies.

INGLIS. (COMMANDER, 1829. F-P., 20; H-P., 20.)

CHARLES INGLIS is eldest son of Commissioner Chas. Inglis, R.N. (Captain, 1802), who distinguished himself, as Lieutenant of the JASON 38, at the capture of the French frigate *La Seine* in 1798; obtained the rank of Commander for his gallantry in the PENELOPE at the capture of the 80-gun ship *Guillaume Tell* in 1800; was afterwards for many years Flag-Captain to the late Sir Geo. Martin; and died at Ryde, in the Isle of Wight, 27 Feb. 1833. His brother, Patrick, is a Lieutenant R.N.

This officer entered the Navy, 29 May, 1807, as Fst-cl. Vol., on board the QUEEN 98, commanded by his father, with whom he continued to serve as Midshipman, chiefly under the flag of Admiral Martin, in the CANOPUS 80, IMPÉTUEUX 74, STATELY 64, and RODNEY 74, until promoted to the rank of Lieutenant, 1 July, 1814. He was in consequence stationed for a long time off Sicily and Lisbon, and was on board the CANOPUS at the pursuit and destruction, in Oct. 1809, of the French ships of the line *Robuste* and *Lion*. In Sept. 1814 Lieut. Inglis took charge of a frigate-rigged boat named the FREDERICK WILLIAM, and was sent with her as a present from the Prince Regent to the King of Prussia. He afterwards joined—18 Nov. 1814, the CHESAPEAKE frigate, Capt. Fras. Newcombe, at the Cape of Good Hope—19 Sept. 1815, the QUEEN CHARLOTTE 100, in which ship and the BOYNE 98, bearing each the flag of Sir Edw. Thornbrough, he served at Portsmouth until May, 1818—24 May, 1819, and 5 April, 1822, the LARNE 18, Capts. Henry Forbes and Robt. Tait, and ROCHFORT 80, flag-ship of Sir Graham Moore, both in the Mediterranean—22 June and 20 Sept. 1824, the CHAMPION sloop, Capt. John Fitzgerald Studdert, and VICTORY 104, bearing the flag of Sir Geo. Martin at Portsmouth—and, 7 May and 26 June, 1827, to the ROYAL CHARLOTTE and WILLIAM AND MARY yachts, both commanded by Capt. John Chambers White. He attained the rank he now holds 23 April, 1829, but has not since been employed.

Commander Inglis married, 10 April, 1828, Joanna Harriet, second daughter of the late John Chas. Lucena, Esq., Consul-General from Portugal. AGENTS—Goode and Lawrence.

INGLIS. (LIEUT., 1813. F-P., 11; H-P., 31.)

GEORGE INGLIS, born about July, 1787, is son of the late Admiral John Inglis.

This officer entered the Navy, 27 Aug. 1805, as Sec.-cl. Vol., on board the TEXEL 64, Capt. Donald Campbell, bearing the flag of Rear-Admiral Jas. Vashon, at Leith; and was soon lent, for a cruize off the coast of Norway and the Shetland islands, to the AMARANTHE 18, Capt. Edw. Pelham Brenton. Becoming Midshipman, in May, 1806, of the GANGES 74, Capt. Peter Halkett, he assisted in that ship at the capture, 27 Sept. following, of the French 44-gun frigate *Le Président*, and, after escorting General Crawford's brigade of troops to the Cape de Verde Islands, and cruizing for some time in that vicinity with a squadron commanded by Sir Sam. Hood, served under the broad pendant of Commodore Rich. Goodwin Keats in the expedition to Copenhagen. On his return to England with the 2nd battalion of the 32nd Regt., in the *Princess Sophia Frederica*, one of the Danish prizes, he joined the CAMBRIAN 40, Capts. Rich. Budd Vincent and Fras. Wm. Fane, and proceeded off the east coast of

Spain, where he was much employed in co-operation with the patriots, and assisted, on 31 July, 1808, in reducing the Castle of Mongat. Subsequently to his removal to the Colossus 74, Capt. Thos. Alexander, we find Mr. Inglis uniting, in Oct. 1809, in the chase which preceded the self-destruction, near the mouth of the Rhone, of the French ships of the line *Robuste* and *Lion*. After a servitude of more than two years at the blockade of Flushing and Brest in the Marlborough 74, Capts. Graham Moore and Matthew Henry Scott, and on the Leith station in the Clio 16, Capt. Wm. Ffarington, he successively joined, in 1812, as a passed Midshipman, the Africa 64 and St. Domingo 74, bearing the respective flags of Admirals Herbert Sawyer and Sir John Borlase Warren on the coast of North America. On 25 March, 1813, Mr. Inglis was promoted to the rank of Lieutenant, and appointed to the Royal George, Capt. Wm. Howe Mulcaster, on, we believe, Lake Erie, where he partook, soon afterwards, of an action in which two schooners were taken from the Americans. On 10 Sept. in the same year, having removed to the Detroit 19, Capt. Robt. Heriot Barclay, the senior officer of a small, miserably equipped squadron of six sail, carrying altogether 63 guns (yielding a broadside weight of 478 lbs.) and 345 men, the greater part of them nondescripts, he was further present in a most desperate action which terminated in the capture of the whole by an American force under Commodore Perry, consisting of nine excellently appointed vessels, carrying 54 guns (throwing 928 lbs. in broadside weight of metal) and 580 picked men. Shortly previous to the fatal issue of the battle, in which the British it appears lost 41 men killed and 94 wounded, and the enemy 27 killed and 96 wounded, the command, owing to the disablement of Capt. Barclay, devolved upon Lieut. Inglis, who, with a degree of calm intrepidity that reflected high credit upon him, continued the action until further resistance became impossible.* His late appointments were, for very brief periods, to the Boyne 98, Capt. Fred. Lewis Maitland, Pique 36, Capt. Hon. Anthony Maitland, and Ramillies 74, Capt. Wm. M'Culloch. Agents—Hallett and Robinson.

INGLIS. (Lieutenant, 1826.)

James Inglis entered the Navy 29 April, 1810; passed his examination in 1816; and obtained his commission 14 Dec. 1826. His appointments have since been—8 Aug. 1839, to the Edinburgh 72, Capt. Wm. Wilmott Henderson, under whom he served in the operations on the coast of Syria, and at the bombardment of St. Jean d'Acre, in 1840—30 Nov. 1841, to the Victory 104, bearing the successive flags at Portsmouth of Admiral-Superintendents Hon. Duncombe Pleydell Bouverie and Hyde Parker—and, 29 Dec. 1845, to be Admiralty-Agent in a contract mail steam-vessel, in which capacity he is now employed.

Lieut. Inglis is married, and has issue.

INGLIS. (Lieutenant, 1827.)

Patrick Inglis is brother of Commander Chas. Inglis, R.N.

This officer entered the Navy 17 Dec. 1812; passed his examination in 1819; attained the rank of Lieutenant 26 Jan. 1827; served at Portsmouth, as Lieutenant of the Victory 104, Capts. Thos. Monck Mason and John Wilson, from 23 Feb. 1828 until 30 April, 1830; and was employed for about twelve months in 1843-4 in the Coast Guard. He is now on half-pay.

Lieut. Inglis the Senior of his rank on the list of 1827—married, 24 Oct. 1833, Mary Ann, only daughter of the late J. G. Cocks, Esq., R.N. Agents—Goode and Lawrence.

INGLIS. (Lieutenant, 1821.)

Stewart Nash Inglis entered the Navy, 20 May, 1815, as a Volunteer, on board the Queen Charlotte 100, Capt. Chas. Inglis, fitting at Chatham; served from the following Sept. until Sept. 1819, on the Mediterranean and Leith stations, chiefly as Midshipman, in the Ister and Hyperion frigates, Capts. Thos. Forrest and Thos. Searle; then sailed for the East Indies on board the Leander 50, flag-ship of Hon. Sir Henry Blackwood; and on 4 June, 1821, was there confirmed a Lieutenant, if we mistake not, in the Dauntless 24, Capt. Geo. Cornish Gambier. His last appointments were, 8 Jan. 1824 and 6 Feb. 1828, to the Jupiter 60, Capts. David Dunn and Sir Wm. Saltonstall Wiseman, and Melville 74, Capts. Henry Hill, Alex. Wilmot Schomberg, and Christ. John Williams Nesham, on the Halifax and Mediterranean stations. He has been on half-pay since 29 Sept. 1831.

INGRAM. (Commander, 1841.)

Augustus Henry Ingram entered the Navy 13 Feb. 1821; passed his examination in 1827; acquired the rank of Lieutenant 10 Jan. 1837; received an appointment, two days afterwards, to the Dublin 50, flag-ship of Sir Graham Eden Hamond in South America; was employed during the earlier portion of 1839 on particular service in the Hercules 72, Capt. Edw. Barnard; and on 29 Nov. 1839, joined the Blonde 42, Capt. Thos. Bourchier. He was rewarded for his conduct in the latter ship at the taking of Canton (where, during the operations of March, he had been employed in the boats*) with a Commander's commission dated 8 June, 1841; and since 5 Nov. 1846 he has been in command of the Birkenhead steam-frigate.

Prior to the receipt of his present appointment Commander Ingram was employed as a Student at the Royal Naval College. Agents—Messrs. Stilwell.

INGRAM. (Lieutenant, 1845.)

Herbert Frederick Winnington Ingram passed his examination 12 Oct. 1840; was employed for several years in the Mediterranean as Mate of the Talbot 26 and Aigle 24, Capts. Robt. Fanshawe Stopford and Lord Clarence Edw. Paget; obtained his commission 30 Dec. 1845; and, since 12 Feb. 1846, has been serving on the south-east coast of America on board the Raleigh 50, Commodore Sir Thos. Herbert.

INGRAM. (Commander, 1829. f-p., 13; h-p., 36.)

Robert Ingram entered the Navy, 1 Sept. 1798, as Fst.-cl. Vol., on board the Formidable 98, Capt. Jas. Hawkins Whitshed, stationed in the Channel. In the following Nov. he joined the Triton 32, Capt. John Gore, with whom he continued to serve, as Midshipman, in the Medusa 32, on the Home and Mediterranean stations, until July, 1802; witnessing, in the former ship, her capture, 18 Oct. 1799, when in company off Cape Finisterre with the Naiad 38 and Alcmène 32, of the *Santa Brigida*, a Spanish 36-gun frigate, having on board 1,400,000 dollars, besides a cargo of equal value; and participating, in the Medusa, in an attack made by Lord Nelson during the year 1801 on the Boulogne flotilla. After an intermediate servitude in the Mediterranean on board the Cyclops and Termagant sloops, commanded by various officers, Mr. Ingram rejoined Capt. Gore, in Feb. 1804, in the Medusa, and on 5 Oct. following was present at the further capture of three Spanish frigates laden with treasure, and the destruction of a fourth, off Cape St. Mary. In the course of the following year he successively became Sub-Lieutenant of the Fervent and Rebuff gun-brigs, and also of the Favourite sloop, Capt. John Davie, stationed on the coast of Africa, where we find him displaying an eminent degree of zeal and perseverance in towing and sweeping the latter vessel during an arduous chase of three days, which terminated in the capture, in Dec. 1805, of *Le Général Blanchard*, privateer of 16 guns and 130 men.† He was made full Lieutenant, 1 Sept. 1806, into the Princess of Orange 74, flag-ship in the Downs of Vice-Admiral John Holloway;

* *Vide* Gaz. 1814, p. 331.

* *Vide* Gaz. 1841, pp. 1504–5. † *V.* Gaz. 1806, p. 448.

and in May, 1807, after he had been for a short time re-attached to the FAVORITE, Capt. John Nairne, on the Guernsey station, he was appointed to the MUTINE sloop, Capt. Hew Steuart, part of the force employed in the ensuing expedition to the Walcheren. Quitting the latter vessel in April, 1808, Mr. Ingram did not again go afloat until July, 1826; on 27 of which month he received an appointment to the GLOUCESTER 50, Capts. Joshua Sydney Horton and H. Steuart, with whom, it appears, he served until advanced, 28 Oct. 1829, to the command of the ÆTNA bomb. He paid that vessel off 26 May, 1830; and has not since been employed.

Commander Ingram married, 7 Sept. 1806, Miss Wilmot, of Oyster Street, Portsmouth.

INMAN. (LIEUT., 1822. F-P., 10; H-P., 23.)

ROBERT INMAN died 2 June, 1845.

This officer entered the Royal Naval College 4 Feb. 1813; and embarked, 21 May, 1815, as Midshipman, on board the ROYAL SOVEREIGN 100, Capt. Edw. Pelham Brenton, bearing the flag of Sir Benj. Hallowell, whom he soon followed into the TONNANT 80—both ships lying in Plymouth Sound. From Aug. in the same year until Dec. 1818 he served on the St. Helena and Cape stations, as Admiralty Midshipman, in the RACOON sloop, Capts. John Cook Carpenter, Geo. Fred. Rich, Robt. Worgan Geo. Festing, Jas. Wallis, and Geo. Brine; and he next, until May, 1822, officiated in the same capacity, on the Channel and Halifax stations, on board the CAMELION brig, Capt. Wm. Jas. Mingaye, PHAETON 38, Capts. Wm. Henry Dillon and Wm. Augustus Montagu, and NEWCASTLE 60, Capt. Arthur Fanshawe. He then became Acting-Lieutenant of the ATHOLL 28, Capt. Henry Bourchier, in which vessel (being confirmed to her on 29 of the following Aug.) he continued until Jan. 1823. He did not afterwards go afloat.

Lieut. Inman married, 16 June, 1839, Anne, eldest daughter of Jas. Upton, Esq., of Okey Lodge, Sedbergh, co. York.

INNES. (LIEUT., 1813. F-P., 27; H-P., 13.)

ROBERT WINTLE INNES is brother of the late Retired Commander Wm. John Innes, R.N.

This officer entered the Navy, 21 April, 1807, as Fst.-cl. Vol., on board the FAVORITE sloop, Capts. John Nairne and Fred. Hoffman, employed at first off the coast of Africa, and then in the West Indies, where he accompanied Capt. Hoffman into the GOELAN 18. Proceeding in 1808 to the East Indies in the CORNELIA frigate, Capt. Henry Folkes Edgell, he there, in 1810-11, served on shore, as Midshipman, at the taking of the Isle of France, and similarly assisted at the storming of Fort Cornelis during the operations connected with the reduction of Java. He returned home in 1812 with Capt. Edgell on board the PIEDMONTAISE 38; and on 6 Dec. 1813, after he had further served on the Home station in the THISBE 28, Capt. Thos. Dick, and SAN JOSEF and QUEEN CHARLOTTE flag-ships of Lord Keith and Sir Pulteney Malcolm, he was promoted to the rank of Lieutenant. His subsequent appointments were—22 Feb. 1814, to the HARRIER 18, Capts. Andw. Pellet Green, John Forbes, and Sir Chas. Thos. Jones, employed off the Canary Islands—in 1815, to the RIFLEMAN 18, and PIQUE 36, Capts. Henry Edw. Napier and Hon. Anthony Maitland—21 Feb. 1816, to the GLASGOW 40, Capt. Hon. A. Maitland, under whom he fought at Algiers—in April, 1821, to the command of the IONIA colonial vessel—13 Dec. 1827 and 2 March, 1829, to the INFERNAL bomb, Capts. Edm. Williams Gilbert and Brunswick Popham—and MADAGASCAR 46, Capt. Hon. Sir Robt. Cavendish Spencer, both on the Mediterranean station—for a short time in 1832 to the VERNON 50, Capt. Sir Fras. Augustus Collier, fitting at Woolwich—and 5 March, 1836, to the command of the PANDORA packet on the Falmouth station. He has been on half-pay since Jan. 1842. AGENTS—Goode and Lawrence.

INNES. (RETIRED COMMANDER, 1845. F-P., 15; H-P., 31.)

WILLIAM JOHN INNES died 24 March, 1847, at 23, Oxford-terrace, Hyde Park, in his 58th year. He was brother of the present Lieut. R. W. Innes, R.N.

This officer entered the Navy, 9 Feb. 1801, as Fst.-cl. Vol., on board the WINDSOR CASTLE 98, Capt. Jas. Oughton, bearing the flag in the Channel of Sir Andw. Mitchell; with whom, from May, 1802, until Aug. 1806, he served, as Midshipman, in the LEANDER 50, on the North American station; where, after he had been further employed on board the MILAN frigate, Capt. Sir Robt. Laurie, VESTA schooner, Lieut.-Commander Atkin Hayman, and, as Acting-Lieutenant, in the INDIAN sloop, Capt. Chas. John Austen, he was confirmed, 30 March, 1808, into the ATALANTE, Capt. Fred. Hickey. Continuing in North America until Oct. 1811, he commanded, from June, 1809, to Dec. 1810, the CHERUB schooner, and served, during the rest of the period, in the BELVIDERA frigate, Capt. Rich. Byron. His last appointments were, 30 Jan. 1812, and 6 May, 1813, to the QUEEN 74, and VOLONTAIRE 38, Capts. Lord Colville and Hon. Geo. Waldegrave, on the Home and Mediterranean stations. He was paid off from the latter ship 4 Dec. 1815; and on 18 Jan. 1845, he accepted the rank of Retired Commander. AGENTS—Case and Loudonsack.

INSKIP. (LIEUTENANT, 1834.)

PETER PALMER INSKIP entered the Navy 9 Dec. 1821; served as Midshipman on board the GENOA 74, Capt. Walter Bathurst, at the battle of Navarin, 20 Oct. 1827; passed his examination in 1828; obtained his commission 27 Aug. 1834; and (with the exception of a command from 13 June, 1839, until Oct. 1842, of the ROYAL GEORGE Revenue-vessel) has been in charge of a station in the Coast Guard since 25 Feb. 1836.

His exertions in the preservation of life from drowning have been acknowledged by the presentation of a medal from the Royal Humane Society. AGENTS—Pettet and Newton.

IRBY. (CAPTAIN, 1827. F-P., 15; H-P., 31.)

THE HONOURABLE CHARLES LEONARD IRBY was born 9 Oct. 1789, and died 3 Dec. 1845. He was youngest son of the second Lord Boston, by Christiana, only daughter of Paul Methuen, Esq., of Corsham House, Wilts; and brother of Rear-Admiral of the Red Hon. Fred. Paul Irby, C.B., who commanded the AMELIA 38 in a desperate action with the French 40-gun frigate *L'Aréthuse*, off the Iles de Los, 7 Feb. 1813, and died 24 April, 1844, aged 65.

This officer entered the Navy, 23 May, 1801, as Fst.-cl. Vol., on board the NARCISSUS 32, Capts. Percy Fraser and Ross Donnelly. In that frigate, after cruizing in the North Sea, and also in the Mediterranean, where he assisted at the capture, 8 July, 1803, of the French corvette *L'Alcion*, of 16 guns and 96 men, he accompanied the expedition to the Cape of Good Hope in 1805; on her passage whither the NARCISSUS, besides effecting the capture of *Le Prudent* privateer of 12 guns and 70 men, retook the English merchant-ship *Horatio Nelson*, mounting 22 guns, and drove on shore the *Napoléon* privateer of 32 guns and 250 men. Subsequently to the reduction of the Cape, and the capture of the 46-gun frigate *Volontaire*, Mr. Irby proceeded to the Rio de la Plata, whence we find him returning to England with the despatches announcing the conquest of Buenos Ayres. Being again ordered out, however, with Capt. Donnelly in the ARDENT 64, he joined in the operations of Feb. 1807 against Monte Video, and was slightly wounded while serving on shore in the advanced battery.* After the place had surrendered to the British, he took a passage home on board the LEDA 38, Capt. Robt. Honyman; and prior to his advancement to the rank

* *Vide* Gaz. 1807, p. 473.

of Lieutenant, 13 Oct. 1808, he was further employed for periods of a few months in the THESEUS and INVINCIBLE 74's, Capts. John Poo Beresford and R. Donnelly, off Ferrol and Flushing. He then joined the SYRIUS 36, Capt. Sam. Pym, under whom, on returning to the Cape station, he assisted at the blockade of the Mauritius, and contributed to the capture, 21 Sept. 1809, of St. Paul's, in the Ile de Bourbon. Between May, 1810, and June, 1814, we find Lieut. Irby serving on the Cape, Newfoundland, Channel, Irish, and Halifax stations, in the LEOPARD 50, Capt. Jas. Johnstone, NARCISSUS 32, Capt. Hon. Fred. Wm. Aylmer, CONQUESTADOR 74, Capt. Lord Wm. Stuart, SYBILLE 38, Capt. Clotworthy Upton, and ARMIDE 38, Capt. Sir Edw. Thos. Troubridge. On 7 of the month last mentioned our officer (who in the ARMIDE had shared in the capture of an American privateer of 17 guns and 100 men, and a French letter-of-marque of 16 guns and 60 men) was promoted to the command of the THAMES 32, *armée en flûte*, in which ship he continued (attending intermediately the expedition against New Orleans) until superseded at his own request, for the recovery of his health, in May, 1815. His next appointment was, 8 Aug. 1826, to the PELICAN 18, fitting for the Mediterranean, where he cruized with great anti-piratic activity until Sept. 1827, when (having been advanced to Post-rank on 2 of the previous July) he removed to the ARIADNE 26. He came home in the GENOA 74, which ship he paid off at Plymouth 21 Jan. 1828; and did not again go afloat.

Capt. Irby was the author, in conjunction with Mr. Jas. Mangles, of a work entitled 'Travels in Egypt, Nubia, Syria, and Asia Minor, in 1817-18,' published in 1823. He married, 8 Feb. 1825, Frances, second daughter of John Mangles, Esq., of Hurley, co. Berks, by whom he has left issue a son and daughter. AGENTS—Goode and Lawrence.

IRVINE. (RETIRED CAPTAIN, 1840. F-P., 12; H-P., 46.)

CHARLES CHAMBERLAYNE IRVINE entered the Navy, in Aug. 1789, as Midshipman, on board the ORION 74, Capt. Chas. Chamberlayne, from which ship, after having made a voyage to the West Indies, he was discharged in April, 1790. Rejoining the same officer in Oct. 1794, as Master's Mate, in the BOMBAY CASTLE 74, he proceeded to the Mediterranean, where he had an opportunity of sharing in Admiral Hotham's partial action of 13 July, 1795. On 7 Oct. following, having in the mean while removed to the CENSEUR 74, Capt. John Gore, he was in that ship when she was taken, after a gallant defence, by a French squadron under Admiral Richery. On his exchange taking place, Mr. Irvine was received, in the spring of 1796, on board the PORCUPINE, a small frigate, commanded by Capt. John Draper. In 1797, on his return from a second visit to the West Indies, during her passage whence the PORCUPINE had been dismasted in a hurricane, it was his lot to be one of the officers proscribed by the mutineers at Spithead, in opposing whom he incurred an injury which greatly crippled his right hand. During three months of the ensuing summer, Mr. Irvine, it appears, commanded a gun-brig, named the BROTHERS, lying at Plymouth. He then successively joined the POMONE frigate, Capt. Robt. Carthew Reynolds, employed in cruizing with the western squadron, and the QUEEN CHARLOTTE 100, flag-ship in the Mediterranean of Lord Keith; and on 30 Aug. 1799, he was promoted to a Lieutenancy in the PRINCESS ROYAL 98, bearing the flag of Rear-Admiral Thos. Lennox Frederick. Being next appointed to the MELPOMENE 38, Capt. Sir Chas. Hamilton, he served with the expedition to the Texel, and in April, 1800, was present at the surrender of the African island of Gorée. On the latter occasion he was placed in charge of the GORÉE schooner of 10 guns, and sent on a cruize off Senegal. This vessel, in the course of a month, being condemned as unfit for service, he obtained acting-command of the ship-sloop GORÉE of 16 guns, in which he further cruized in the same vicinity until compelled to invalid in Feb. 1801. Mr. Irvine, who also officiated for a short time as Lieut.-Governor of Gorée itself, subsequently, in Oct. 1804, assumed command of the TICKLER gun-brig, off the coast of France. Between June, 1805, and April, 1808, he served, on the West India and Mediterranean stations, in the DOLPHIN, Capt. Isaac Ferrieres, OCEAN 98, Capt. Fras. Pender, ENDYMION 40, Capt. Edw. Durnford King; and, as First-Lieutenant, in the EAGLE 74, Capt. Chas. Rowley. On the date last mentioned he became Acting-Captain of the GLATTON 54; and on 24 of the proximate month he was made Commander into the DUCHESS OF BEDFORD armed ship of 18 guns. He came home with convoy in 1809 in the LORD ELDON 18; was then paid off; and, not having since been employed, accepted his present rank 10 Sept. 1840.

Capt. Irvine married Susan, daughter of the late Sir John Reade, Bart., and aunt of the present Sir John Chandos Reade, Bart., of Shipton Court, co. Oxford.

IRVINE. (LIEUT., 1815. F-P., 8; H-P., 32.)

JAMES IRVINE entered the Navy, 17 June, 1807, as Sec.-cl. Vol., on board the CAMBRIAN 40, Capt. Hon. Chas. Paget, and, after serving at the capture of Copenhagen, removed to the ECLAIR sloop, Capt. Chas. Kempthorne Quash. From Oct. 1808 (during the three months immediately antecedent to which period he had been attached, off Flushing and the Texel, to the WARSPITE 74, Capt. Hon. Henry Blackwood) he joined L'AIMABLE 32, in which frigate, and in the HORATIO 38, both commanded by Lord Geo. Stuart, we find him continuously employed, as Midshipman, until Feb. 1811. He was in consequence present in the former ship at the blockade of the Elbe, and at the capture, 3 Feb. 1809, of *L'Iris* French national ship, pierced for 32 guns, but mounting only 24, after a short running fight, in which the latter sustained a loss of 2 men killed and 8 wounded, and L'AIMABLE (besides being materially damaged in her masts, spars, sails, and rigging) of 2 wounded; and in the HORATIO, on her return from the Cape of Good Hope to the North Sea, at the reduction of the islands of Schouwen and Tholen in Dec. 1813. In March, 1814, Mr. Irvine was transferred to the TONNANT 80, bearing the flag of Sir Alex. Cochrane on the coast of North America, where, from 1 Oct. following until 7 June, 1815, he performed the duties of Acting-Lieutenant on board the SPENCER 74, Capt. Rich. Raggett. He then took up a commission dated on 8 March in the latter year; and has since been on half-pay.

IRVINE. (LIEUT., 1813. F-P., 10; H-P., 32.)

THOMAS JOHNSON IRVINE entered the Navy, 30 Sept. 1805 (under the auspices of H.R.H. the Duke of Clarence), as Fst.-cl. Vol., on board the SUPERB 74, commanded by the late Sir Rich. Goodwin Keats, in which ship he fought under the flag of Sir John Duckworth in the action off St. Domingo, 6 Feb. 1806, and attended, in the capacity of Midshipman, the expeditions to Copenhagen and Flushing. He was also present, in Aug. 1808, at the embarkation from Nyeborg of the Spanish army under the Marquis de la Romana, to whom he acted on the occasion as Aide-de-Camp. In July, 1810, after he had cruized for a short time off Brest in the POICTIERS 74, Capt. John Poo Beresford, he rejoined Sir R. G. Keats on board the MILFORD 74, employed at the defence of Cadiz, where he assumed a command in the flotilla, and assisted in storming several of the enemy's batteries. He continued, until Nov. 1813, to serve with the last-mentioned officer on the Mediterranean, Home, and Newfoundland stations, in the HIBERNIA 120, CENTAUR 74, and as Lieutenant (commission dated 20 June, 1813) in the BELLEROPHON 74. While belonging to the HIBERNIA, Mr. Irvine twice jumped overboard, and had each time the happiness of saving the life of a man. He was lastly, from 8 Feb. 1826 until 31 Dec. 1827, employed in the Coast Blockade as Supernumerary-

Lieutenant of the HYPERION 42, Capt. Wm. Jas. Mingaye.

Lieut. Irvine has taken out a patent for certain improvements in packing-cases, boxes, trunks, portmanteaus, and other articles for containing goods, which improvements may be made applicable to the preservation of life at sea. He is married, and has issue. AGENTS—Coplands and Burnett.

IRVING. (LIEUTENANT, 1843.)

JOHN IRVING entered the Navy 25 June, 1828; passed his examination 24 June, 1834; and, at the period of his promotion to the rank of Lieutenant, which took place 23 March, 1843, had been serving for some time in the East Indies, on board the FLY surveying-vessel, Capt. Fras. Price Blackwood, and FAVOURITE 18, Capt. Thos. Ross Sulivan. His appointments have since been—10 Aug. 1843, to the VOLAGE 26, Capt. Sir Wm. Dickson, employed on Particular Service—14 Dec. 1844, to the EXCELLENT gunnery-ship at Portsmouth, Capt. Sir Thos. Hastings—and, 13 March, 1845, to the TERROR discovery-ship, Capt. Fras. Rawdon Moira Crozier, under whom he is at present engaged in a renewed attempt to explore the North-West passage through Lancaster Sound and Bering Strait.

IRWIN. (LIEUTENANT, 1827. F-P., 19; H-P., 16.)

JAMES IRWIN is son of Commander Jas. Irwin, R.N. (1802), who was a Midshipman of the ROYAL GEORGE when that ship went down at Spithead in 1782, was afterwards Flag-Lieutenant to Hon. Wm. Cornwallis, distinguished himself in 1807, as Agent for Transports before Buenos Ayres, and died in 1825. He is nephew of Capt. John Irwin who commanded the PRINCE GEORGE 98, as Flag-Captain to Rear-Admiral Wm. Parker, in the action off Cape St. Vincent 14 Feb. 1797; and cousin of Capt. Geo. Wickens Willes, R.N., now commanding the VANGUARD 80, and of Capt. Jas. Irwin Willes, R.M.

This officer entered the Navy, 13 Aug. 1812, as a Volunteer, on board the ACHILLE 74, Capt. Aiskew Paffard Hollis; became Midshipman, in April, 1813, of the MILFORD 74, bearing the flag of Rear-Admiral Thos. Fras. Fremantle; and from May, 1814, until March, 1818, served with Capt. Fras. Stanfell in the BACCHANTE, MADAGASCAR, and PHAETON frigates. While attached to the MILFORD (he had been employed in the ACHILLE at the blockade of Venice) he commanded a 10-oared cutter at the reduction of the towns of Fiumé, Bocca Rea, &c., assisted at the capture of the fort of Ragosniza, took part in a successful engagement with a battery in the neighbourhood of Capo d'Istria, and served in the batteries at the siege of Trieste. When on the American station, in the BACCHANTE, we find him present at the blockade of the American frigates *Constitution* and *Congress*, the capture of the towns of Castine and Belfast in Penobscot Bay, and the taking of Machias. In Aug. 1818, Mr. Irwin, who had passed his examination in the previous March, and had been since borne on the books of the QUEEN CHARLOTTE 100, flag-ship at Portsmouth of Sir Geo. Campbell, obtained a Mateship in the ROCHFORT 80, bearing the successive flags of Sir T. F. Fremantle and Sir Graham Moore, on the Mediterranean station; where he commanded from March, 1823, to Aug. 1825, the RACER tender; and where, until the summer of 1829, he further served (with but two slight interruptions in 1826 and again in 1827) on board the REVENGE 76, flag-ship of Sir Harry Burrard Neale, ISIS 50, Capt. Sir Thos. Staines, and, as Lieutenant (commission dated 31 Dec. 1827) in the PHILOMEL 10, Capts. Hon. Wm. Keith and Edw. Hawes. During his servitude in the ROCHFORT he had the misfortune to receive a compound fracture of the right leg; and while in command of the RACER he endured a brush with several Algerine gun-boats. His last appointment was, 11 Oct. 1834, to the Coast Guard, in which service he remained until the autumn of 1836.

IRWIN. (LIEUTENANT, 1814. F-P., 35; H-P., 6.)

JOSEPH IRWIN, born 27 Feb. 1792, is third son of the late Thos. Irwin, Esq., of Justustown, near Carlisle, by Jane, second daughter of John Senhouse, Esq., of Calder Abbey. He is brother of the present Thos. Irwin, Esq., of Justustown and Calder Abbey, a Captain on half-pay of the Enniskillen Dragoons, and a Magistrate for Cumberland, for which county he served as High Sheriff in 1836; and of Lieut. John Irwin, of the Hon. E. I. Co.'s service, who died 21 Sept. 1824.

This officer entered the Navy, 27 April, 1806, as Fst.-cl. Vol. (under the auspices of Admiral Skeffington Lutwidge), on board the THETIS 38, Capts. Wm. Hall Gage and John Miller, under whom he was actively employed, part of the time as Midshipman, on the coasts of Spain and France, and on various parts of the Mediterranean until Feb. 1808. He then became attached to the ROYAL WILLIAM, Capt. Hon. Courtenay Boyle; and in the following April he joined the UNDAUNTED 38, Capts. Thos. Jas. Maling and Geo. Chas. Mackenzie. After he had cruized for nearly three years in that ship off the Western Islands, in the West Indies, and again on the Mediterranean station, he was received, in March, 1811, on board the FAME 74, Capt. Walter Bathurst, and sent to co-operate with the patriots on the Spanish coast, where, having attained the rating of Master's Mate, he assumed command of a division of small-arm men, and frequently came into contact with the enemy, particularly at Xavia and Denia. On the issue of the unsuccessful attack made by General Donkin on the latter fortress, Mr. Irwin, who had been employed on shore throughout the operations, took charge of a boat and brought off the last half company of the 81st Regt., under a destructive fire from the French garrison, who had advanced to the very beach. So gallant was his conduct in this instance, that on reaching the FAME he was publicly thanked by Capt. Bathurst on the quarter-deck, as likewise by the General in public orders. He afterwards commanded a gun-boat with a Midshipman and 16 men under his orders at the siege of Tarragona; and it was his fortune likewise to co-operate in the reduction of the strong fort of St. Philippe in the Col de Balaquer. The representations that were in consequence made in his favour to Lord Exmouth induced the latter, in May, 1814, to afford him a berth on board his flag-ship the CALEDONIA 120. On 1 of following Sept. he had the gratification of being promoted to the rank of Lieutenant; and in the course of the next Nov. he received an appointment to the OPOSSUM 10, Capts. Sir John Chas. Richardson and Lord John Hay; in which vessel, prior to her being paid off in Sept. 1815, we find him engaged in affording assistance to the French Royalists in La Vendée. Since Dec. 1821 Lieut. Irwin has been uninterruptedly employed as an Inspecting Commander in the Coast Guard—a service from the heads of which he has had the satisfaction of eliciting strong testimonials.

He married, 1 Sept. 1826, Emily, second daughter of John Dixon, Esq., of Dublin, by whom he has issue six sons and four daughters. His second son is a Midshipmnn in the R.N. AGENTS—Messrs. Halford and Co.

ISAACSON. (LIEUTENANT, 1844.)

CHARLES AUGUSTUS ISAACSON died in Sept. 1845, on board the ECLAIR steamer sloop, a victim, with nearly all the officers and crew, to African fever of the most inveterate description.

This officer passed his examination 6 July, 1836; served for about three years in the Mediterranean as Mate of the MALABAR 72, and FORMIDABLE 84, Capts. Sir Geo. Rose Sartorius, Sir Chas. Sullivan, and Geo. Fred. Rich, latterly under the flag of Sir Edw. W. C. R. Owen; obtained his commission 10 July, 1844; became, 3 Sept. following, Additional-Lieutenant of the CALEDONIA 120, flag-ship of Sir David Milne on the Home station; and, on 21 Oct. in the same year, received his ill-fated appointment to the Eclair, Capt. Walter Grimston Bucknall Estcourt.

J.

JACK. (Retired Commander, 1840. f-p., 18; h-p., 31.)

Leigh Spark Jack entered the Navy, 7 May, 1798, as Fst.-cl. Vol., on board the Powerful 74, Capt. Wm. O'Brien Drury, employed off Cadiz and in the Mediterranean; and in the following July attained the rating of Midshipman. He continued to serve on the station last named from Jan. 1800 until Aug. 1804 in the Cyclops sloop, Capt. John Fyffe; after which we find him employed for five years on board the Pheasant 18, Capts. Robt. Paul, Robt. Henderson, and John Palmer; being during that period successively created, on 2 Nov. 1804 and 28 Aug. 1806, an acting and a confirmed Lieutenant. In the latter capacity, after he had endured a servitude of two years in the West Indies, Mr. Jack accompanied the expedition to the Rio de la Plata under Sir Sam. Achmuty, and was in consequence present at the capture of Monte Video in Feb. 1807. He then served for some time on the coast of Africa, and ultimately on the Home station; where, off the Western Islands, and at the Cape of Good Hope, he was next, from Aug. 1809 until April, 1816, employed on board the Désirée 36, and Liverpool 40, both commanded by Capt. Arthur Farquhar. In the former ship he distinguished himself by his activity as Senior Lieutenant at the blockade of the German rivers, and at the reduction of Cuxhaven and Gluckstadt, in Dec. 1813 and Jan. 1814; and when on his return to England in the Liverpool, after having been engaged at the blockade of Ile de Bourbon, he appears to have been nearly lost off Dover, in consequence of that frigate having taken the ground at the foot of Shakspeare's Cliff, from which perilous position she was only extricated by cutting away all her masts and spars, and throwing overboard her guns, provisions, and stores. Mr. Jack, who had been on half-pay since 1816, accepted his present rank 21 April, 1840.

JACKSON. (Commander, 1819. f-p., 14; h-p., 34.)

Caleb Jackson, born 3 Jan. 1791, in co. Surrey, is a younger brother of the present Capt. Geo. Vernon Jackson, R.N.

This officer entered the Navy, 5 Feb. 1799, as Fst.-cl. Vol., on board the Fame, Lieut.-Commander Witherston, lying in Portsmouth Harbour. In March, 1801, he joined the Vengeance 74, Capt. Geo. Duff; and in that ship, until paid off in July, 1802, he served in the Baltic, Bay of Biscay, and West Indies. He re-embarked, in March, 1806, as Midshipman, on board the Edgar 74, bearing the flag at first of Lord Keith in the Downs, and afterwards commanded in the Baltic by Capt. Jas. Macnamara, with whom he continued until removed, in May, 1809, to the Antelope 50, Capt. Donald M'Leod, fitting for the flag of Vice-Admiral John Holloway, Commander-in-Chief at Newfoundland, where he was soon invested with the rank of Lieutenant, and appointed, in that capacity, to the Comet sloop, Capt. Rich. Henry Muddle. On leaving the latter vessel (to which he had been confirmed by commission dated 11 Dec. 1810) Lieut. Jackson, in the early part of 1812, joined the Valiant 74, Capt. Robt. Dudley Oliver, lying at Portsmouth, and Herald 18, Capts. Geo. Jackson and Clement Milward, employed on the West India station. After serving for a short time in the Argo 44, bearing the flag at Jamaica of Rear-Admiral Wm. Brown, he became, in the autumn of 1814, Acting-Commander of the Shark receiving-ship at Port Royal. On his return to the West Indies in April, 1815, in the Warrior 74, bearing the flag of Rear-Admiral John Erskine Douglas, he rejoined the Shark, commanded at the time by Capt. Houston Stewart, and next by Capt. Alex. Campbell and himself. In Nov. of the same year and Feb. 1816 he was successively nominated to the acting-command of the Carnation 16, and Emulous 16; the latter of which sloops he brought home and paid off in June, 1816. He was not, however, officially promoted until 12 Aug. 1819; since which period he has not held any appointment.

Commander Jackson married, in 1828, Ursula, widow of Capt. Andrew Dudie, H.M. 44th Infantry.

JACKSON. (Lieut., 1842. f-p., 15; h-p., 0.)

Charles Keats Jackson is eldest son of the late Rear-Admiral Sam. Jackson, C.B., a history of whose services we have recorded in the proper place.

This officer entered the Royal Naval College 2 March, 1832; and embarked, in 1833, as a Volunteer, on board the Belvidera 42, Capt. Chas. Borough Strong. On his return home in 1837 from the West Indies, where he had been for a long time employed as Midshipman, he sailed, in the Tyne 26, Capt. John Townshend, for the Mediterranean, for the purpose of joining the Asia 84, Capt. Wm. Fisher, under whom, it appears, he shared in the operations of 1840 on the coast of Syria, and was present at the blockade of Alexandria. Proceeding next to China as Mate (he had passed his examination 12 June, 1839) in the Cornwallis 72, flag-ship of Sir Wm. Parker, he served on shore in a distinguished manner with the rocket brigade under Lieut. Jas. Fitzjames, and was wounded in the attack on the heights of Segoan and Tsekee 15 and 16 March, 1842;* and he was present, in the course of the same year, at the taking of Chapoo, the destruction of the batteries at Woosung, the storming of Chin-Kiang-Foo,† and the pacification of Nanking. Being in consequence promoted to the rank of Lieutenant by commission dated 23 Dec. 1842,‡ he was in that capacity appointed, 18 March, 1843, to the Siren 16, Capt. Wm. Smith, with whom he remained in the East Indies until ordered home to be paid off at the close of 1844. Since 9 April, 1845, he has been serving on board the Queen 110, flag-ship of Sir John West at Devonport. Agents—Messrs. Ommanney.

JACKSON. (Lieut., 1815. f-p., 16; h-p., 27.)

Charles Scott Jackson entered the Navy, 12 April, 1804, as Fst.-cl. Vol., on board the Queen 98, commanded in the Channel by Capts. Theophilus Jones and Manley Dixon; served from Aug. 1804 to Aug. 1805, on the Mediterranean station, in the Conqueror 74, Capt. Israel Pellew, and Amphitrite frigate, Capt. Hon. Courtenay Boyle; and was next employed, between June, 1806, and Dec. 1809, on board the Captain 74, Capts. Geo. Cockburn, Isaac Wolley, Jas. Athol Wood, and Christopher John Williams Nesham. In the latter ship we find him present at the capture, 27 Sept. 1806, of *Le Président* French frigate, of 44 guns; at the bombardment, in 1807, of Copenhagen; and, in 1808-9, at the reduction of Marie-galante, Martinique, and the Saintes. In Nov. 1810, after his name had been borne for nearly 12 months as a Supernumerary on the books of the Royal William, flag-ship at Spithead, he joined the Helena sloop, Capt. Henry Haynes, on the Cork station; whence, we believe, he accompanied the same officer in 1811 to the West Indies on board the Sapphire; from which vessel, in Dec. 1814, he was transferred to a Master's Mateship in the Chesapeake 38, Capt. Fras. Newcombe, at the Cape of Good Hope. He was promoted to the rank of Lieutenant 7 Dec. 1815; and afterwards appointed—in Aug. 1818 and July, 1819, to the Sapphire again, Capt. Henry Hart, and Bann 20, Capts. Jodrell Leigh, Wilson Braddyll Bigland, and John Ralph Blois, both on the Jamaica station—and, 9 Oct. 1828 and 19 Feb. 1830, to the Ramillies and Talavera Coast-Blockade ships, each commanded by Capt. Hugh Pigot. He has been on half-pay since the close of the latter year.

* *Vide* Gaz. 1842, pp. 2386, 2390, 2391.
† *V.* Gaz. 1842, p. 3405. ‡ *V.* Gaz. 1842, p. 3821.

JACKSON. (LIEUTENANT, 1836.)

CYRIL JACKSON, born 23 Feb. 1812, is son of the late Wm. Ward Jackson, Esq., of Normanby Hall, co. York (N. R.).

This officer entered the Royal Naval College in 1825; and embarked, in 1827, on board the HUSSAR 46, Capt. Edw. Boxer, bearing the flag of Sir Chas. Ogle in North America. In 1831 he became Mate of the UNDAUNTED 46, commanded at the Cape of Good Hope by Capt. Howard Harvey. On his removal from that ship, in 1833, to the BELVIDERA 42, Capt. Chas. Borough Strong, he proceeded to the West Indies; and he subsequently, we find, took an active part in quelling some disturbances which had broken out at Para, where the ringleaders were pursued into the interior of the country and captured. On obtaining his commission, 28 Nov. 1836, Mr. Jackson was appointed Additional-Lieutenant of the MELVILLE 74, flag-ship of Hon. Sir Chas. Paget on the North America and West India station. His next appointment was, 1 June, 1837, to the WOLVERENE 16, in the Mediterranean, whence he returned in 1839; and his last, for a short period in 1840, to the HOWE 120, Capt. Sir Watkin Owen Pell.

JACKSON. (LIEUT., 1815. F-P., 12; H-P., 32.)

GEORGE JACKSON died 24 Nov. 1845.

This officer entered the Navy, in Feb. 1803, as Ordinary, on board the PUISSANT 74, Capt. John Irwin, lying at Spithead; and in May, 1804, became Midshipman of the WASP 18, Capt. Hon. Fred. Wm. Aylmer; which vessel, when in convoy of a ship from Gibraltar in Feb. 1805, was attacked by a fleet of Spanish gun-boats, and only escaped capture by a breeze springing up and enabling her to bring her guns to bear on the enemy, two or three of whom were sunk. In the following Aug. the WASP was chased by the celebrated Rochefort squadron; from which however she contrived to free herself by an effort of gallant perseverance, so marked that the Captain, John Simpson (the successor of Capt. Aylmer), his officers, and crew, received the public thanks of the Commander-in-Chief, and the strong approbation of the Admiralty. In Oct. 1808, Mr. Jackson, who until then had continued to serve with the last-named Captain in the STAR and WOLVERENE sloops, on the Newfoundland and Halifax stations, obtained command of the CUTTLE schooner, and was sent to Boston to await the President's Message after the well-known affair of the LEANDER and *Chesapeake*. Joining next in the operations which led to the capture of Martinique in Feb. 1809, he was one of the first that landed on that island, where, it appears, he wrested a musket from the hands of a sentinel and hoisted the British flag. After the conquest he successively joined the MARTIN, HALIFAX, and OBSERVATEUR sloops, Capts. John Evans, Alex. Fraser, and Wm. Simpson, under the last mentioned of whom we find him sharing in an action with a French corvette, who made off during the night. Immediately on passing his examination, on which occasion, 8 Feb. 1811, he produced certificates of his having had charge of a watch three years previously, Mr. Jackson was ordered on board the AQUILON 32, Capts. Hon. Wm. Pakenham and Wm. Bowles, employed at first off Leith, and then in the Channel. Towards the close of the same year he joined the ARETHUSA 38, flag-ship of Vice-Admiral Chas. Stirling, for a passage to the West Indies; on which and the North American station he served until 1815, as Mate and Acting Lieutenant, in the THETIS 38, Capt. Wm. Henry Byam, BRAZEN sloop, Capt. Jas. Stirling, AMELIA 38, Capt. Hon. Fred. Paul Irby, RIVOLI 74, Capt. Graham Eden Hamond, NIEMEN 38, Capt. Sam. Pym, MOHAWK sloop, Capt. Henry Litchfield, and COCKCHAFER schooner, of 5 guns (4 12-pounder carronades and 1 long 12-pounder) and 22 men. While in the latter vessel, the command of which was given to him in March, 1814, he was employed in the performance of much valuable service. He was in the first place sent to Nassau, New Providence, for the purpose of affording protection to the coasting-trade, and of escorting convoys to the Havana and the Gulf of Mexico. He was also employed in negotiating with the Creek, Chocktaw, and other tribes of Indians at Pensacola, whom he induced to join the British against the Americans, conducting several of their chiefs to the officer in command at Apalatchabola, and thence back again with arms and ammunition, and a British agent appointed to organise them, to Pensacola. He was then sent with despatches for the Commander-in-Chief in the Chesapeake, and on his arrival there he was ordered up the Potomac to assist the British in their descent of that river, after the capture of Alexandria. He subsequently led the starboard division in the attack upon Baltimore, on which occasion he took the soundings that are now laid down in Anthony Demain's Chart. These operations over, Mr. Jackson returned to his station off New Providence, taking with him a brig laden with valuable government stores and presents for the Indian Chiefs. He afterwards had the good fortune, while yet in the COCKCHAFER, to effect the capture of six of the enemy's vessels, two of which were greatly his superiors, namely, the letters of marque *Aurora* of 10 long 9-pounders and 28 men, and *Java*, of 8 long nines and 22 men. In May, 1815, he took up a commission dated on 8 of the previous March, but he did not again go afloat.

Lieut. Jackson married, 15 Aug. 1839, Ann, daughter of the late John Shaw, Esq., of Idenshall Hall, co. Cheshire.

JACKSON. (LIEUTENANT, 1845.)

GEORGE MELVILLE JACKSON entered the Navy in 1831; passed his examination 21 April, 1838; served in the Mediterranean, from 1840 until paid off in 1844, as Mate on board the INDUS 78, Capt. Sir Jas. Stirling; then joined in succession the ST. VINCENT 120, QUEEN 110, and TRAFALGAR 120, flag-ships at Portsmouth and Sheerness of Sir Chas. Rowley and Sir John Chambers White; and on 24 March, 1845, was promoted to the rank of Lieutenant. He has been since serving on the S.E. coast of America in the GRECIAN 16, Capts. Alex. Leslie Montgomery and Louis Symonds Tindal.

JACKSON. (CAPT., 1841. F-P., 26; H-P., 20.)

GEORGE VERNON JACKSON, born 13 July, 1787, at Chalwood, co. Surrey, is eldest son of the late Geo. Jackson, Esq., of the Isle of Wight; and brother of the present Commander Caleb Jackson, R.N. Three of his brothers lost their lives in the service, viz., Thos. Vernon, who died Lieutenant of the ISIS in 1809, from over exertion in bringing home despatches from Portugal;—William, who was lost off the Isle of France, when Purser of the DELIGHT, in Feb. 1824;—and Chas. Reynolds, Midshipman of the REDWING, who was murdered on the coast of Africa in Nov. 1825.

This officer (whose name had been borne, since 5 May, 1795, on the books of the TRIDENT, MINERVA, PRINCESS AUGUSTA, and MAIDSTONE) first embarked, in 1801, as Midshipman, on board the TRENT 36, Capt. Sir Edw. Hamilton. After serving for some time in the LAPWING 28, Capt. Edw. Rotheram, in one of whose boats he narrowly escaped destruction, he joined, in Nov. 1802, the CARYSFORT 28, Capt. Robt. Fanshawe, who, on their arrival with convoy in the West Indies, caused a Lieutenant's commission to be made out for Mr. Jackson, but was dissuaded from handing it to him by reason of his extreme youth. In June, 1804, on leaving the hospital at Antigua, our officer—one of the only two survivors out of 14 who had entered it together—was received on board the STE. LUCIE sloop, Capt. Geo. Edm. Byron Bettesworth. When next in the BUSY 18, Capt. Wm. Henry Byam, he happened to be on duty at the fore-topmast-head of that brig when both topmasts were carried away, and again at the mast-head when she rolled her mainmast over the side. While attached, between May, 1805, and Nov. 1808, to the CLEOPATRA 32,

Capts. John Nairne, John Wight, Wm. Love, and Robt. Simpson, it was his lot to be twice sent away in prizes. On the first occasion, after having been for three days without water, the crew mutinied and attempted to throw him overboard, but his presence of mind enabled him to seize the ringleader, and subdue the remainder. When in the second vessel (on board of which were himself, two seamen, and a Lieutenant), the topmast being carried away in a heavy gale, he ascended to the masthead for the purpose of reaching the wreck, and had scarcely done so, when by a sudden jerk he was pitched into the sea, many yards to leeward. In March, 1808, we find Mr. Jackson appointed to the command, with the rank of Acting Lieutenant, of a schooner, mounting 4 guns, from which however, as he had not passed his examination, he was superseded in the next June, and sent back to the CLEOPATRA. In Nov. of the same year, in consequence of the recommendation of two captains, he was appointed by the Commander-in-Chief, Sir John Borlase Warren, Master's Mate of his flag-ship the SWIFTSURE 74. He was soon again placed in charge of a prize, a French West Indiaman; from which vessel, on her being taken in tow by the SWIFTSURE, he intrepidly jumped overboard and, nearly at the cost of his own life, rescued a seaman who had fallen from the latter. As a reward for this act of humanity Sir John Warren immediately sent him with the prize and despatches to England, and during his absence nominated him, 20 April, 1809, Second-Lieutenant of the JUNON 38—an appointment which the Admiralty confirmed by commission dated on 18 of the following Aug. It was Mr. Jackson's consequent misfortune, on 13 Dec. in the same year, to be on board the JUNON off Guadeloupe when she was captured, after an heroically desperate resistance of 45 minutes, and a loss of 20 men killed and 40 wounded, by a French squadron, consisting of the 40-gun frigates *Renommée* and *Clorinde*, and *armées-en-flûte Loire* and *Seine*, carrying each 20 guns—with the two former of whom she sustained a yard-arm and yard-arm conflict until on the verge of sinking. In Jan. 1810, he arrived a prisoner at Brest, and from that place he was sent under an escort of soldiers to Verdun. During the march he succeeded with a fellow-captive, Mr. F. Whitehurst, in effecting his escape, and after vainly endeavouring for 14 months to get off the coast, he at length, with his companion, found means of launching a flat-bottomed boat, with a sheet for a sail, in which he put to sea, followed however by some fishermen, 11 in number, who retook him. Lieut. Jackson was then imprisoned in the citadel of Verdun, whence with four others he again got away. Being discovered two days afterwards through the imprudence of his associates, he was placed in close confinement in the Porte Chaussée; from which place he twice attempted to escape, but was foiled, the first time by his companion breaking his thigh, and the second by the maladroitness of others. He was now conducted, part of the way in chains, to the strong fortress of Bitche, situate one day's journey from the Rhine. Here he remained many months a close prisoner, but, his daring spirit and ingenuity never forsaking him, he in the end formed a plan by which both himself and Lieut. L'Estrange of the 71st Regt. were enabled to break their bonds. After travelling together a distance of 40 leagues, the two, from prudential motives, parted company—Lieut. Jackson making his way to the coast of Normandy.* He there, on a Saturday in April, 1812, embarked, alone and unseen, in a small boat, and on the following Monday was picked up off the Owers in a state of great exhaustion by the MUTINE sloop. His subsequent appointments in the capacity of Lieutenant, we find, were—9 July, 1812, to the INDEFATIGABLE 44, Capt. John Fyffe, employed for nearly four years on the Home, Brazilian, and South Sea stations—3 July, 1816, as Senior, to the HECLA bomb, Capt. Wm. Popham, under whom he fought at Algiers, and continued to serve until the following Nov.—9 Oct. 1817, to the SYBILLE 38, flag-ship of Sir Home Popham in the West Indies, whence he invalided in July, 1818—and 24 Dec. in the latter year, to the command of the SERAPIS receiving-ship at Port Royal, Jamaica. During a period of nearly seven years that Capt. Jackson remained in the SERAPIS (in which he was made Commander by commission dated 13 July, 1824) he served with credit under, and occasionally bore the flags of, five successive Commanders-in-Chief, Sir Home Popham, Commodore Thos. Huskisson, Sir Chas. Rowley, Sir Edw. W. C. R. Owen, and Sir Lawrence Wm. Halsted. After his name had been borne for short periods, as Supernumerary-Commander, on the books of the PYLADES, PRIMROSE, and BRITOMART sloops, he was confirmed, 16 Sept. 1825, in the command of the PYLADES; in which vessel he was for six months Senior officer off the Havana, and in one instance gained the approbation of the Commander-in-Chief for his conduct in detaining a steam-vessel clandestinely carrying slaves. He at length, in Feb. 1828, returned to England with a valuable freight of dollars and cochineal; and on his arrival he received from the Bishop of Jamaica, to whom he had afforded a passage, a very flattering letter, accompanied by a piece of plate. He was then paid off, and has not been since able to procure employment. His advancement to the rank he now holds took place 23 Nov. 1841.

Capt. Jackson, since he has been on half-pay, has been offered the command of a line-of-battle ship in the service of the Pacha of Egypt, of which however the existing regulations prevented his acceptance. Several ingenious improvements and contrivances as connected with shipping have at various times been submitted by him to the Admiralty. He married, in 1842, Jane Oldham Johnson, of Kirby, Lancashire. AGENTS—Messrs. Stilwell.

* Lieut. L'Estrange succeeded in reaching Bordeaux, where he took a boat and got on board the HANNIBAL 74, Capt. Sir Michael Seymour, who immediately wrote a strong letter in his favour to head-quarters. On his arrival in England, three months after Lieut. Jackson, he was received at the Horse Guards by the Duke of York in the most gracious manner, was allotted three years retrospective rank as Captain, with many indulgences, and in two years attained his majority. Lieut. Jackson, however, to whose plans and exertions he had been entirely indebted for his escape, on waiting on the Port-Admiral at Portsmouth, had not the satisfaction of being greeted with even a word of approbation, nor, on repairing to the Admiralty, could he obtain either an interview with the first Lord, or the slightest notice, from any one in authority, of his manifold sufferings and privations.

JACKSON. (RETIRED COMMANDER, 1845. F-P., 20; H-P., 30.)

JOHN JACKSON (*a*) entered the Navy, in Aug. 1797, as Fst.-cl. Vol., on board the VETERAN 64, Capts. Geo. Gregory, Jas. Robt. Mosse, and Sir Archibald Collingwood Dickson, under the last mentioned of whom he was present in the action off Copenhagen 2 April, 1801. Joining next, in 1802, the CENTAUR 74, Capt. Bendall Robt. Litthales, he sailed for the West Indies, where he served for upwards of ten years—at first with Capt. Conway Shipley in the STE. LUCIE, CYANE, and HIPPOMENES—then again with Sir Sam. Hood in the CENTAUR, as also with Capt. Hon. Geo. Cadogan in the CYANE, and with Sir Alex. Cochrane in the NORTHUMBERLAND 74—for a short time with Capt. Wm. Hargrove, as Acting Lieutenant (order dated 11 Oct. 1805) in his former ship the CYANE—and finally, as Acting-Lieutenant and Lieutenant, in command, from Jan. 1806, to Oct. 1812, of the MOZAMBIQUE schooner, and NETLEY brigantine. He assisted, during the period of his original attachment to the CENTAUR, at the reduction of Ste. Lucie in June, 1803; and when in command of the MOZAMBIQUE (in which vessel, mounting 14 guns, he was confirmed a Lieutenant by commission dated 16 June, 1808) he was the gallant cause, although in company with the LILY 18, and EXPRESS 4, of the capture, on 21 April in that year, of the *Jean Jacques* French privateer of 6 guns.* His last appointments afloat were—27 July, 1813, to

* *Vide* Gaz. 1808, p. 872.

the command, at Portsmouth, of the SPRIGHTLY cutter—7 Feb. 1814, to the SPENCER 74, Capt. Rich. Raggett, off the coast of North America—and 1 Oct. 1814, and 25 Aug. 1815, to the command of the ST. LAWRENCE and WHITING schooners, on the latter and Plymouth stations. He went on half-pay in Oct. 1816, and after having been further employed in the Coast Guard from 28 Jan. 1835, until the close of 1836, was invested, 30 April, 1845, with the rank of Retired Commander. AGENTS—Messrs. Stilwell.

JACKSON. (LIEUTENANT, 1825.)

JOHN HENRY JACKSON entered the Navy 27 July, 1808; passed his examination in 1815; obtained his commission 29 July, 1825; and from 28 May, 1839, until 1846, was employed in the Coast Guard. He has since been on half-pay.

JACKSON. (LIEUTENANT, 1846.)

JOHN MILBOURNE JACKSON is son of an old Post-Captain, who died from the effects of service in the West Indies.

This officer passed a very distinguished examination, 24 July, 1840; was for some time employed, as Mate, in the EXCELLENT gunnery-ship at Portsmouth, Capt. Sir Thos. Hastings; and served from 1842, until promoted to the rank of Lieutenant 31 Jan. 1846, on board the DAPHNE 18, commanded in the Pacific by Capt. John Jas. Onslow. He was then appointed Additional of the COLLINGWOOD 80, flag-ship of Sir Geo. Fras. Seymour; but since the early part of 1847, has been on half-pay.

JACKSON. (VICE-ADMIRAL OF THE BLUE, 1847. F-P., 24; H-P., 42.)

ROBERT JACKSON entered the Navy, 20 April, 1781, as Ordinary, on board the SANTA MARGARITA 36, Capt. Elliot Salter, employed on the American station, where, in the following year, he assisted, as Midshipman, at the capture of the French frigate *Amazone*. Between March, 1784, and his promotion to the rank of Lieutenant 22 Nov. 1790, he served at Newfoundland, in the SANTA LEOCADIA, Capt. Alex. Edgar, WINCHELSEA, Capt. Edw. Pellew, and SALISBURY flag-ship of Vice-Admiral Milbanke; and he was afterwards appointed in succession—1 April, 1791, to the SAVAGE sloop, Capt. Alex. Fraser, under whom he was at the capture of the town and garrison of Ostend in April, 1793—1 July, 1793, 25 March, 1794, and 25 June, 1795, to the ROSE 18, and BEAULIEU and AIMABLE frigates, Capts. Edw. Riou and Chas. Sidney Davers, all on the West India station, where he contributed, in the ROSE, to the reduction of Martinique in 1794—in Sept. 1795, to the DORIS frigate, Capt. Lord Viscount Ranelagh, off the coast of Ireland—and in 1797-8-9, to the QUEEN CHARLOTTE 100, flag-ship of Lord Keith, FORMIDABLE 98, Capt. Jas. Hawkins Whitshed, and FOUDROYANT, BARFLEUR, and QUEEN CHARLOTTE again, each bearing the flag of Lord Keith. On the destruction of the last-mentioned ship by fire in Leghorn Roads in March, 1800, Lieut. Jackson (who in the course of the same year beheld the fall of Savona* and the surrender of Malta) assumed the acting command of the CAMELION sloop, as he did, in May following, of the BONNE CITOYENNE corvette; in which vessel he captured, 31 Dec. 1800, the Spanish privateer *Vives* of 10 guns and 80 men, and gained, in 1801, the Turkish gold medal as a reward for his services during the campaign in Egypt. Two days after his official advancement to the rank of Commander, which did not take place until 6 Oct. 1801, Capt. Jackson was appointed by the Commander-in-Chief to the TIGRE 74—an act sanctioned by the Admiralty 29 April, 1802. He returned to England in the ensuing June, and was lastly employed as Flag-Captain to Lord Keith, on the North Sea and Channel stations, from Jan. 1806 to June, 1807, in the EDGAR 74, and again (with the exception of a few months in 1814-15) from Feb. 1812, to Aug. 1815, in the SAN JOSEF, QUEEN CHARLOTTE, and VILLE DE PARIS. He became a Rear-Admiral 10 Jan. 1837; and a Vice-Admiral 8 March, 1847. AGENT—John P. Muspratt.

* *Vide* Gaz. 1800, p. 620, where it will be seen he distinguished himself by the extent of his perseverance.

JACKSON, C.B. (REAR-ADMIRAL OF THE BLUE, 1841. F-P., 31; H-P., 24.)

SAMUEL JACKSON was born in 1775, and died 16 Jan. 1845, at Bognor in Sussex.

This officer entered the Navy, 14 July, 1790, as Midshipman, on board the KITE cutter, Lieut.-Commander B. Mitchell, in which vessel he served, principally against the smugglers on the Irish station, until the commencement of the war in 1793, when he was appointed Master's Mate of the ROMULUS 36, Capt. John Sutton, and ordered to the Mediterranean. After witnessing the occupation of Toulon, commanding a boat also at the destruction of a nest of privateers in the island of Corsica, and uniting in an attack upon the forts and batteries of Bastia, he accompanied Capt. Sutton, in May, 1794, into the EGMONT 74, and was thus afforded an opportunity of sharing in Hotham's actions of 14 March and 13 July, 1795 (on the former of which occasions he was wounded), and of assisting in command of the EGMONT's barge at the cutting-out from Tunis Bay, 9 March, 1796, of the French vessels *Némésis* of 28, and *Sardine* of 22 guns, together with a polacre mounting 20 guns. On 3 Nov. 1796, Mr. Jackson, whose name had been for a short time borne on the books of the VICTORY 100, bearing the flag of Sir John Jervis, was made Lieutenant into the ALLIANCE store-ship, Capt. Wm. Cuming. Rejoining the EGMONT almost immediately afterwards, he had the singular good fortune, in Dec. of the same year, to be the means under Providence of saving the whole of the officers and crew belonging to the BOMBAY CASTLE 74, when wrecked at the entrance of the Tagus. His most extraordinary and intrepid exertions, in collecting the boats of the squadron, then in leading them to the rescue, and in finally consummating the work of humanity by jeopardising his own life, called forth the thanks of the Court-Martial which subsequently assembled to try the Captain and crew of the BOMBAY CASTLE. After sharing in the battle off Cape St. Vincent, we find Lieut. Jackson assisting in the EGMONT's barge in a gallant attack made upon the Cadiz flotilla under Don Miguel Tynason, who had come out with a large force in order to cut off the THUNDER bomb, during her retreat from before the walls of that city; on which occasion he had the honour of boarding the Don's desperately-defended vessel on one quarter, while the immortal Nelson did so on the other. On the EGMONT being paid off in the early part of 1798, Lieut. Jackson was appointed Senior of the SUPERB 74, commanded at first by Capt. Sutton and afterwards by Capt. Rich. Goodwin Keats, to whom he rendered able and active assistance in the action fought in the Gut of Gibraltar 12 July, 1801, and at its close was sent to take possession of the *St. Antoine* 74, prize to the SUPERB.* As a reward for his valour in the conflict he was advanced to the rank of Commander on 18 of the ensuing Aug. His next appointment was, 10 May, 1803, to the AUTUMN 16; and in the course of the same year, by order of Rear-Admiral Robt. Montagu, he assumed the direction of a small squadron stationed off Calais, for the purpose of preventing the gun-vessels in that port from forming a junction with the Boulogne flotilla, a service then of the utmost importance. His first operation was an attack of several hours, made on 27 Sept., upon the enemy's gunboats in Calais pier, which provoked a heavy fire from the French in all directions, and gained the high approval of the Commander-in-Chief Lord Keith.† The second affair appears to have been at the commencement of 1804, when the AUTUMN had 1 man killed and 6 others wounded, in an attempt upon a division of the enemy's flotilla, several of which, although under the protection of formi-

* *Vide* Gaz. 1801, p. 946. † *V.* Gaz. 1803, p. 1323.

dable land-batteries, were driven on the beach;—the third, on the evening of the 19th and the morning of the 20th July, when the decisive promptness exhibited by Capt. Jackson, in annoying a detachment of the enemy, and thereby preventing its reaching its destination in safety, again elicited the approbation of Lord Keith, and of the Lords of the Admiralty;*—and the last, during the celebrated catamaran expedition against the Boulogne flotilla, on which occasion he was intrusted with the charge of one of the principal explosion-vessels, and evinced a wonderful degree of gallantry and presence of mind.† During a subsequent command (which he held from Oct. 1804 until the summer of 1807) of the MOSQUITO 18, we successively discover Capt. Jackson effecting the capture, 13 April, 1805, of the French privateers *Orestes* and *Pylades*, of 1 gun, 6 swivels, and 33 men each—escorting, towards the close of the same year, a fleet of transports with 5000 troops, &c., for Lord Cathcart's army in Hanover—commanding a detachment on the Calais and Boulogne stations, where the MOSQUITO in one instance fell in with five of the enemy's armed schooners, two of which were driven on shore and destroyed—directing a number of rocket-boats in an attack made in Oct. 1806, upon the flotilla at Boulogne—and ultimately accompanying the expedition to Copenhagen, during the operations connected with which he was stationed in the Belt to prevent supplies being thrown into the island of Zealand. On the surrender of the Danish fleet, he was appointed Acting-Captain of the SURVEILLANTE 38, in which frigate he returned to England. His official promotion to Post rank taking place 5 Nov. 1807, Capt. Jackson, on 8 of the following month, was appointed to the SUPERB 74, bearing the flag of his former Commander, Rear-Admiral Keats. Continuing in that ship until paid of in Oct. 1809, he went, in consequence, to the Mediterranean in pursuit of a French squadron which had effected its escape from Rochefort—superintended the embarkation from Nyeborg, in Aug. 1808, of the Spanish army under the Marquis de la Romana‡—was in the SUPERB when, frozen up at Gottenborg in Jan. 1809, she was only extricated by a canal being cut through four miles of ice—and in the following Aug. accompanied the force sent to the Walcheren. Capt. Jackson's subsequent appointments were—14 Jan. 1812, to the POICTIERS 74, in which he prevented a French squadron from entering the port of Brest—21 Dec. 1812, to the LACEDÆMONIAN 38, stationed off the coast of North America, whence, after blockading the enemy's ports and rivers between Cape Fear and Amelia Island, co-operating in the attacks on fort St. Petre and the town of St. Mary's, and participating in the capture of property calculated at more than half a million sterling, he returned to England in June, 1815—29 Aug. 1815, to the NIGER 38, in which frigate he first conveyed Hon. Chas. Bagot as Ambassador to the United States, then escorted Sir John Sherbrooke, Governor of Canada, from Halifax to Quebec, and served as Senior officer on the coast of Nova Scotia until Sept. 1817, when, owing to her being found unserviceable, he returned home with his officers and crew in a transport—29 Oct. 1822, to a three years' command of the Ordinary at Sheerness—5 April, 1836, to the BELLEROPHON 80, fitting for the Mediterranean, where he remained for about twenty months—and 19 Feb. 1838, to the command of the ROYAL SOVEREIGN yacht, and the Superintendentship of Pembroke Dockyard. He was superseded in the latter appointment on his attainment of Flag-rank 23 Nov. 1841, and not again employed.

Rear-Admiral Jackson was nominated a C.B. 8 Dec. 1815. He married, 6 Dec. 1817, Clarissa Harriet, daughter of Capt. Madden, Agent for the Portsmouth division of Royal Marines, and niece of Major-General Sir Geo. Madden, Kt., K.T.S., by whom he has left issue two sons, Chas. Keats, a Lieutenant R.N., and Geo. Edw. Owen, Second-Lieutenant R.M., 1842. His youngest son, Outram Montagu, who had been educated at Addiscombe, died in the East Indies 17 March, 1844, a few months only after he had been appointed an Ensign of the 26th Native Infantry. AGENTS—Messrs. Ommanney.

* *Vide* Gaz. 1804, p. 890. † *V.* Gaz. 1804, p. 1237. ‡ *V.* Gaz. 1808, p. 1150.

JACKSON. (LIEUT., 1815. F-P., 18; H-P., 23.)

ROBERT ÆMILIUS JACKSON, born 29 Nov. 1793, is son of Robt. Jackson, Esq., of Hampton, Jamaica, who was Supreme Judge of the Court of Justiciary and Member of the House of Assembly, and in the Maroon war commanded a brigade of 3000 men. He is brother of Major John Serocold Jackson, late of the 22nd Regt. of Foot, and for many years Brigade-Major at Plymouth; and of Capt. Jas. Irving Jackson, of the 6th Foot, Aide-de-Camp to Prince William of Gloucester, who died in 1809.

This officer entered the Navy, 6 Aug. 1806, as Fst.-cl. Vol., on board the MALTA 84, commanded in the Mediterranean by Capts. Edw. Buller and Wm. Shield; and in Sept. 1807 attained the rating of Midshipman. Removing in Oct. 1808 to the MONTAGU 74, Capt. Rich. Hussey Moubray, he served in one of the boats of that ship at the reduction of Sta. Maura in April, 1810; after which we find him, from May, 1811, until Aug. 1815, employed, on the Home, north coast of Spain, Cork, and West India stations, latterly as Master's Mate, in the EGMONT 74, Capt. Joseph Bingham, INSOLENT 14, Capt. Edw. Brazier, and TIGRE 74, Capt. John Halliday. During the term of his attachment to the INSOLENT Mr. Jackson co-operated, in 1812, in the reduction of the Spanish town of Santander. He was frequently also placed in the command of prizes; and on one of those occasions, in Oct. 1813, while he was conducting a Norwegian boat from off Flekeroe to Gottenborg, he was benumbed in the right thigh from extreme exposure to the cold, and so injured that he was ultimately for many years rendered incapable of the least exertion, and is even now scarcely able to bend the knee—effects which we believe were accelerated, if not aggravated, by his endeavours to stop a leak in the stern-plank of a Danish sloop, with which he was shortly afterwards sent to Yarmouth. On leaving the TIGRE, as above, Mr. Jackson, who had passed his examination 7 Oct. 1812, took up a commission dated 1 March, 1815. His last appointment was to the Coast Guard, in which he served from 12 Jan. 1835, until July, 1843.

He married, 24 Dec. 1816; and has issue six children.

JACKSON. (LIEUT., 1808. F-P., 18; H-P., 29.)

THOMAS JACKSON (*a*) entered the Navy, in March, 1800, as Fst.-cl. Vol., on board the MARLBOROUGH 74, Capt. Thos. Sotheby, stationed in the Channel. In the following Nov. he removed to the SUPERB 74, commanded at first by Capt. John Sutton, next by the late Sir Rich. Goodwin Keats, and finally by Capt. Donald M'Leod, with whom he continuously served until Oct. 1807; participating during that period in Sir Jas. Saumarez' action of 12 July, 1801—in Nelson's celebrated pursuit of the combined fleets to the West Indies—in Sir John Duckworth's action off St. Domingo 6 Feb. 1806, on which occasion he was slightly wounded*—and in the expedition to Copenhagen. He then became Acting-Lieutenant of the NASSAU 64, Capt. Robt. Campbell, which ship (on being extricated with much difficulty from a mass of ice in which she had been blocked up during the whole winter) effected, in company with the STATELY 64, the capture and destruction, 22 March, 1808, on the coast of Zealand, of the Danish 74, *Prindts Christian Frederic*, after a running fight of great length and obstinacy, in which she (the NASSAU) sustained a loss of 2 men killed and 16 wounded. Mr. Jackson, whose confirmation in the rank of Lieutenant took place on 17 of the ensuing May, assumed voluntary command, 6 Sept.

* *Vide* Gaz. 1806, p. 373.

1809, of one of four boats, and assisted in boarding and carrying *Le Jean Bart*, of 4 guns and 25 men.* His succeeding appointments were—22 Nov. 1809, to the CORDELIA 10, Capt. Thos. Fortescue Kennedy, stationed in the Downs—26 April, 1811, to the COQUETTE, Capt. Geo. Hewson, with whom he served on the Leith station until paid off in Jan. 1812—and, 10 Feb. 1813, to the WASP sloop, Capts. Thos. Everard, John Fisher, and Wm. Wolrige. He served in the latter vessel, on the North American and Mediterranean stations, until put out of commission in Sept. 1818; and has since been on half-pay.

In consideration of the wound alluded to above, Lieut. Jackson received at the time a pecuniary reward from the Patriotic Society. AGENTS—Coplands and Burnett.

JACKSON. (LIEUT., 1815. F-P., 27; H-P., 14.)

THOMAS JACKSON (*b*) entered the Navy, 9 July, 1806, as Fst.-cl. Vol., on board the MAJESTIC 74, Capts. J. Hanwell, Henry Hart, Valentine Collard, Nathaniel Forster, and Fred. Watkins, in which ship, bearing the flag at first of Vice-Admiral Thos. Macnamara Russell, he witnessed the surrender of Heligoland, and continued to serve, as Midshipman, on the North Sea and Baltic stations, until March, 1809. He then joined the STANDARD 64, Capt. Aiskew Paffard Hollis, in time to participate in the reduction of the island of Anhold; and on becoming attached, in March, 1811, to the FEARLESS gun-brig, Lieut.-Commanders Geo. Le Blanc, Chas. Basden, Jas. Guy Osborn, and Henry Lord Richards, he co-operated in the defence of Cadiz and Tarifa. While next on the books of the SAN JUAN 74, bearing the flag of Rear-Admiral Sam. Hood Linzee, we find him much employed with the Gibraltar gun-boats. In 1814 he escorted convoy to the West Indies in the SULTAN 74, Capt. John West; and from March to Sept. 1815 he discharged the duties of Master's Mate in the AJAX 74, Capt. Geo. Mundy, on the Mediterranean station. Mr. Jackson then took up a commission dated 28 Feb. 1815. He obtained command, 31 March, 1829, of the DOLPHIN Revenue-vessel; and since 17 April, 1832, has been employed in the Coast Guard.

JACKSON. (LIEUTENANT, 1846.)

WILLIAM TRAVERS FORBES JACKSON served as Midshipman of the WELLESLEY and BLENHEIM 72's, during the operations on the coast of China; and was mentioned as having served on shore at the capture of Amoy and Chinghae.† He passed his examination 22 Oct. 1842; was employed for two years and a half, as Mate, in the CAMPERDOWN 104, flag-ship of Sir Edw. Brace, and INCONSTANT 36, Capt. Chas. Howe Fremantle, on the Home and Mediterranean stations; obtained his commission 15 Jan. 1846; and has been since attached, as Additional-Lieutenant, to the HIBERNIA 104, flag-ship of Sir Wm. Parker, also in the Mediterranean.

JACOBS. (LIEUT., 1813. F-P., 12; H-P., 32.)

WILLIAM JACOBS entered the Navy, in July, 1803, as Fst.-cl. Vol., on board the EMERALD frigate, Capt. Jas. O'Bryen, stationed in the West Indies; became Midshipman, in 1804, of the GALATEA 32, Capt. Henry Heathcote, whom he accompanied to the Mediterranean as Midshipman of the DÉSIRÉE 36; was transferred, in 1805, to the ORION 74, Capt. Edw. Codrington, off the port of Cadiz; joined in succession, towards the close of 1806, the ST. GEORGE and PRINCE GEORGE 98's, Capts. Thos. Bertie and Geo. Losack, on the St. Helena station; and from Feb. 1807 until confirmed in his present rank, 6 Oct. 1813, was again employed in the West Indies, occasionally as Master's Mate, Sub-Lieutenant, and Acting-Lieutenant, in the HEUREUX 24, Capt. John Ellice Watt, CIRCE and LATONA frigates, both commanded by Capt. Hugh Pigot, POMPÉE, NEPTUNE, and STATIRA, flag-ships of Sir Alex. Cochrane, DRAGON 74, bearing the flag of Sir Fras. Laforey, CASTOR 32, Capt. Chas. Dilkes, DRAGON once more, LIBERTY 14, Lieut.-Commander Geo. M'Guire, and BULWARK 74, Capt. Chas. Dashwood. He assisted in the CIRCE at the reduction of the island of Marie-galante in March, 1808; and at the capture, 31 Oct. following, under the fire of a battery which killed and wounded 2 of the British, of the *Palineur*, French national brig of 16 guns and 70 men, 7 of whom were slain and 8 wounded. In the LATONA he was severely wounded while reconnoitering, at the commencement of 1809, off Guadeloupe, the French 44-gun frigate *La Junon*, previously to her capture. His last appointments were, 24 Dec. 1813 and 13 May, 1815, to the BULWARK again, Capts. David Milne and Farmery Predam Epworth, and for a short time to the BORER, Capt. Wm. Rawlins, both on the North American station. AGENTS—Holmes and Folkard.

JACOMB. (RETIRED COMMANDER, 1842. F-P., 14; H-P., 33.)

ROBERT JACOMB entered the Navy, 3 Nov. 1800, as Fst.-cl. Vol., on board the FISGARD 36, Capts. Thos. Byam Martin and Michael Seymour, on the Home station; where, until promoted to the rank of Lieutenant, 12 March, 1807, he further served in the KITE brig, Capt. Philip Pipon, IMPÉTUEUX 84, Capts. T. B. Martin and John Erskine Douglas, and DRAGON 74, Capts. Edw. Griffith and Matthew Henry Scott. He then proceeded to the Rio de la Plata and the Cape of Good Hope in the CORMORANT, Capt. Wm. Hughes; and was afterwards, until July, 1814, employed, on the Irish, Channel, Cape, and Plymouth stations, in the DECADE, Capt. J. Stewart, DONEGAL 74, Capt. Pulteney Malcolm, SCIPION, LION, and PRESIDENT, flag-ships of Sir Robt. Stopford (under whom he co-operated in the reduction of the island of Java), and, as Flag-Lieutenant to Rear-Admiral T. B. Martin, in the PRINCE FREDERICK. The latter was his last appointment. He accepted his present rank 29 Dec. 1842. AGENTS—Halford and Co.

JAGER. (RETIRED COMMANDER, 1842. F-P., 21; H-P., 28.)

THOMAS JAGER entered the Navy, 2 Nov. 1798, as Fst.-cl. Vol., on board the SOUTHAMPTON 32, Capt. John Harvey, stationed in the West Indies, whence, after assisting as Master's Mate at the reduction of the Virgin Islands, he returned to England with the same Captain in 1801 in the AMPHITRITE. He then joined in succession the IRIS 32, Capts. Hon. Philip Wodehouse and David Atkins, and RESISTANCE 36, Capt. Hon. P. Wodehouse; and on the latter ship being wrecked off Cape St. Vincent, 31 May, 1803, he further served, until promoted to the rank of Lieutenant, 21 March, 1807, on board the TERMAGANT 18, Capt. Robt. Petler (by whom he was employed at the cutting out, near Bastia, of the national armed xebec *Podesta*), GUERRIER, bearing the flag of Rear-Admiral John Knight (during his attachment to which ship he shared, in 1805, in some gun-boat service at Gibraltar), EURYDICE frigate, Capt. Sir Wm. Bolton, and DREADNOUGHT 98, Capt. Wm. Lechmere. His succeeding appointments were, on the Home and North American stations, to the HESPER, Capt. Geo. Acklom, BARRACOUTA, Capt. Geo. Harris, AGINCOURT 64, *armée-en-flûte*, Capt. Wm. Kent, LAURESTINUS 24, Capt. Thos. Graham, NYMPHEN 36, Capt. Matthew Smith, and STATIRA 38, Capt. Spelman Swaine. Among the above ships the AGINCOURT formed part of the expedition to the Walcheren in 1809; and the LAURESTINUS and STATIRA were each wrecked; the former (after having served in the Chesapeake, and witnessed the attack upon Crany Island, &c.) off the Silver Keys, Bahama Islands, 22 Oct. 1813; and the latter on a sunken rock, off the island of Cuba, 26 Feb. 1815. In June and Aug. 1816 Lieut. Jager successively assumed command of the HAWKE and TIGER Revenue-vessels. He was superseded from the TIGER in June, 1819, and was lastly employed in the Coast Blockade, as Supernumerary-Lieute-

* *Vide* Gaz. 1809, p. 1439. † *V.* Gaz. 1842, pp. 82, 396.

nant, from June, 1828, to March, 1831, of the HYPERION 42, Capt. Wm. Jas. Mingaye. His present rank was conferred on him 19 July, 1842.

JAGO. (LIEUTENANT, 1816. F-P., 10; H-P., 30.)
JOHN SAMPSON JAGO entered the Navy, 20 April, 1807, as Fst.-cl. Vol., on board the INDEFATIGABLE 44, Capts. John Tremayne Rodd, Henry Edw. Reginald Baker, and John Broughton, in which ship, after witnessing Lord Cochrane's destruction of the French shipping in the Basque Roads, he proceeded with convoy to China. In July, 1812, having returned home, he accompanied Capt. Broughton into the CORNWALL 74, commanded subsequently by Sir Edw. Tucker; with whom, and with Sir Jas. Lucas Yeo, he served, from March, 1813, until Oct. 1815, on board the INCONSTANT 36, on the Brazilian and Portsmouth stations. He shortly afterwards joined the BOYNE 98, bearing the flag of Lord Exmouth; and, on being transferred with that gallant Admiral to the QUEEN CHARLOTTE 100, he shared as Acting-Lieutenant, and was slightly wounded, in the battle of Algiers, 27 Aug. 1816.* He was in consequence confirmed in his present rank by commission dated on 5 of the ensuing Sept.; but he has not been since employed.

JAMES. (LIEUT., 1829. F-P., 20; H-P., 15.)
HENRY JAMES was born 1 Aug. 1799.

This officer entered the Navy, 14 July, 1812, as Fst.-cl. Vol., on board the POMPÉE 74, Capt. Sir Jas. Athol Wood, with whom he served in the Mediterranean until 1815, latterly as Midshipman. He then successively joined the BERWICK and IMPREGNABLE, flag-ships of Sir John Thos. Duckworth at Plymouth, where he was further employed under the orders of Lord Exmouth, inclusive of a short period passed in the FOX and WOLF cutters, until 1818. The next four years were spent by Mr. James again in the Mediterranean, on board the RÉVOLUTIONNAIRE 46, Capt. Hon. Sir Fleetwood Broughton Reynolds Pellew. In 1822 he proceeded to the Brazils and Pacific in the TARTAR 42, Capt. Thos. Brown; and on his return in that frigate to Rio de Janeiro he removed to the flag-ship of the Commander-in-Chief, Sir Geo. Eyre. On his arrival in England in 1826 Mr. James made a trip to Lisbon with Sir Thos. Masterman Hardy. In July, 1827, he joined the VICTORY 104, lying at Portsmouth, whence he soon sailed, in the FAIRY sloop, for the West Indies, and was there, it appears, transferred to the SKIPJACK schooner. On 3 July, 1829, being at the time in the BARHAM 50, the flag-ship on the latter station of Hon. Chas. Elphinstone Fleeming, he was promoted to a Lieutenancy in the HARLEQUIN 18. He came home in the course of the same year in the DRUID 46; and he was lastly appointed, 7 Oct. 1834, as Additional-Lieutenant, to the WINCHESTER 52, flag-ship of Hon. Sir Thos. Bladen Capel, and, 7 July, 1835, to the WOLF 18, Capt. Edw. Stanley, both on the East India station. He invalided home in 1838 on board the ZEBRA sloop.

Lieut. James married, 27 Aug. 1833, Mary, daughter of the late Thos. Ridley, Esq., of Chester Square, London, by whom he has issue three children.

JAMES. (COMMANDER, 1841. F-P., 24; H-P., 19.)
HORATIO JAMES entered the Navy, 28 Dec. 1804, as Fst.-cl. Vol., on board the JASON 32, Capts. Wm. Burgundy Champain and Thos. John Cochrane; under the former of whom he assisted at the capture, 13 Oct. 1805, near Tobago, of the *Naïade* corvette of 16 guns, 4 swivels, and 170 men. Under Capt. Cochrane he was present as Midshipman off the coast of Surinam at the capture, 27 Jan. 1807, of *La Favorite* French national ship of 29 guns and 150 men; and in the course of the next Dec. he witnessed the surrender of the Danish West India islands. In the autumn of 1808, shortly after his removal with the same Captain to the ETHALION 38, he further served in an action with the French 40-gun frigate *Amphitrite*, as he did, in 1809, at the reduction of Martinique and the Saintes. The 19 months which immediately preceded his promotion to the rank of Lieutenant, 21 March, 1812, were employed by Mr. James on the Home and Brazilian stations in the DONEGAL, MARLBOROUGH, and POICTIERS 74's, Capts. Pulteney Malcolm, Graham Moore, and John Poo Beresford, and FOUDROYANT 80, flag-ship of Hon. Michael De Courcy. His subsequent appointments were—21 April, 1813, to the ROYAL SOVEREIGN 100, Capts. Jas. Bissett and Thos. Gordon Caulfeild, employed in the Channel and Mediterranean—29 March, 1814, as Senior, to the SARACEN sloop, Capts. John Harper and Alex. Dixie, in which he proceeded from the Adriatic to the Chesapeake—22 Aug. 1815, to the ANTELOPE 50, bearing the flag of Rear-Admiral John Harvey in the West Indies—9 Sept. 1822, to the EDEN, Capt. John Lawrence, on particular service—12 Nov. 1823, to the SURINAM 18, Capt. Chas. Crole, again on the West India station—29 May, 1828, to the Coast Blockade as Supernumerary-Lieutenant of the HYPERION 42, Capt. Wm. Jas. Mingaye—and 22 July, 1830, 15 June, 1831, and 27 Aug. 1834, to the command of the SURLY cutter, VIPER schooner, and TARTARUS steam-vessel. Commander James, who has not been afloat since he was paid off in the early part of 1837, assumed his present rank 23 Nov. 1841.

He is married and has issue. AGENTS—Messrs. Ommanney.

JAMES. (COMMANDER, 1828. F-P., 48; H-P., 19.)
JAMES JAMES was born, 9 Aug. 1760, at Liverpool, and died 13 Nov. 1845.

This officer entered the Navy, 14 April, 1779, as Midshipman, on board the DUKE 90, Capts. Sir Chas. Douglas, Sir Walter Stirling, and Alan Gardner, in which ship he participated in Rodney's actions of 9 and 12 April, 1782, and on one of those occasions was severely wounded in the left leg. Between June, 1783, and his promotion to the rank of Lieutenant, 16 Nov. 1790, he successively served on the Home station in the SCIPIO 64, Capt. John Nicholson Inglefield, IRRESISTIBLE, Capt. Sir Andrew Snape Hamond, SCIPIO again, DIRECTOR, Capt. Thos. West, and COURAGEUX 74, Capt. Sir A. Gardner. After an employment of three years on the coast of Ireland in the MEDUSA, Capt. Jas. Newman Newman, he obtained an appointment, in July, 1794, in the Transport service, and was sent to the West Indies. On 24 May, 1797, as a reward for the conduct he had exhibited in the PRINCE 98, flag-ship of Sir Roger Curtis, during the never-to-be-forgotten mutiny, Mr. James was nominated to the command of the HASTY gun-brig. He afterwards, in Feb. 1798, and May, 1803, assumed charge of the EAGLE and MATILDA prison and hospital ships at Gillingham and Woolwich; and, from 1 Aug. 1804 until the receipt of his second promotal commission, bearing date 1 July, 1828, he commanded the ARGONAUT hospital-ship at Chatham. The remainder of his life was passed on half-pay.

Commander James married, first, in 1789, Miss Lucy Gifford; and secondly, in 1800, Miss Margaret Copp. He has left two children by each marriage.

JAMES. (LIEUTENANT, 1821. F-P., 22; H-P., 13.)
THOMAS JAMES is son of the late John James, Esq., of Truro, Cornwall.

This officer entered the Navy, 28 May, 1812, as Fst.-cl. Vol., on board the BARHAM 74, Capt. John Wm. Spranger, stationed in the North Sea; and from the following Nov. until the conclusion of the war was employed in the Channel and West Indies, the latter part of the time as Midshipman, in the RHIN 38, Capt. Chas. Malcolm. He next served for six years on the African station in the ORONTES 36, Capt. Nathaniel Day Cochrane, PODARGUS 14, Capts. Jas. Wallis, Henry John Rous, and Jas. Cairnes, RACOON 26, Capt. Jas. Wallis, MYRMIDON 20, Capt. Henry J. Lake, TARTAR 42, Commodore Sir Geo. Ralph Collier, and PHEASANT 18, Capt. Benedictus Marwood Kelly. In Sept. 1821, after having acted

* *Vide* Gaz. 1816, p. 1792.

for six months as Lieutenant of the latter vessel, he took up a commission dated 28 of the previous April. His appointments have since been—3 May, 1833, to the Coast Guard—24 July, 1838, to the command of the PIGEON Falmouth packet—25 Jan. 1843 (after a few months of half-pay), to be Admiralty Agent in a contract mail steam-vessel—and, 26 June, 1846, to the command of the EXPRESS brig, in which he is again employed on the Falmouth station.

He married, in 1833, Emma, daughter of the late H. P. Andrews, Esq., of Bordean, Cornwall, by whom he has issue. AGENTS—Holmes and Folkard.

JAMES. (LIEUTENANT, 1815. F-P., 21; H-P., 20.)

THOMAS EDWARD JAMES entered the Navy, 3 April, 1806, as Fst.-cl. Vol., on board the HIBERNIA 120, Capt. Tristram Robt. Ricketts, in which ship he served under the flags of Earl St. Vincent, Sir Wm. Sidney Smith, and Sir Chas. Cotton, on the Channel, Lisbon, and Mediterranean stations, until Nov. 1810—nearly the whole time in the capacity of Midshipman. He had an opportunity, therefore, of witnessing, while with Sir W. S. Smith, the departure of the Royal Family of Portugal for the Brazils in 1807. In Dec. 1810, after he had further served for a short time with Sir Chas. Cotton in the SAN JOSEF 110, he joined the NAUTILUS 18, Capt. Thos. Dench, under whom, during a continued employment of nearly four years in the Mediterranean, he participated, among other performances, in the capture of three armed vessels, carrying in the whole 23 guns and 235 men. From Nov. 1814 until Aug. 1815 Mr. James, whose commission bears date 20 Feb. in the latter year, served in the North Sea and Channel as Master's Mate of the ALERT sloop, Capt. Joseph Gulston Garland. His subsequent appointments were—26 Oct. 1820, to the LEE sloop, Capt. Stewart Blacker, lying at Plymouth—17 Jan. and 22 March, 1822, to the CYRENÉ and ARAB, Capts. Percy Grace and Wm. Holmes, from the latter of which vessels he was superseded at his own request—and, 1 July, 1834, to the Coast Guard. He left that service in 1844, and has since been on half-pay.

JAMES. (LIEUTENANT, 1815. F-P., 12; H-P., 29.)

WILLIAM JAMES entered the Navy, 12 Feb. 1806, as Fst.-cl Vol., on board the EXPERIMENT packet, Capt. Jas. Manderson, on the Falmouth station. After serving off Guernsey as Midshipman of the URANIE 38, Capt. Christopher Laroche, he joined, in Aug. 1807, the BULWARK 74, Capt. Hon. Chas. Elphinstone Fleeming, off Cadiz; and he was next, from May, 1808, until March, 1814, employed in the Mediterranean on board the ESPOIR 18, Capts. Robt. Mitford and Hon. Robt. Cavendish Spencer. During that period, besides witnessing the surrender of the islands of Ischia and Procida, and participating in the capture, 26 June, 1809, of 18 French gun-boats, as also in an action with the French 40-gun frigate *Cérès*, Mr. James, on 4 April, 1810, assisted at the destruction, by the boats of the ESPOIR and SUCCESS 32, under Lieut. Geo. Rose Sartorius, of several vessels well protected on the beach abreast of Castiglione. On another occasion he contributed, in the boats of the same sloop and of the SPARTAN 38, to the capture of other craft from beneath the fire of a battery and musketry at Terracina; and, on 18 Aug. 1813, we find him serving in the boats of a small squadron under Capt. Thos. Ussher in a very gallant attack on the batteries at Cassis, where, after sustaining a loss of 4 men killed and 16 wounded, the British, in four hours, succeeded in capturing 3 heavy gun-boats and 26 vessels laden with merchandize. In March, 1814, having returned to England and removed with Capt. Spencer to the CARRON 20, Mr. James sailed for Gibraltar. In the course of the same year he further joined the CALEDONIA 120, and PRINCE FREDERICK, bearing the flags in the Mediterranean and at Hamoaze of Lord Exmouth and Rear-Admiral Thos. Byam Martin. At the period of his promotion to the rank of Lieutenant, which took place 16 Feb. 1815, he was serving as a Supernumerary on board the YORK 74, Capt. Alex. Wilmot Schomberg. He assumed charge, 30 Oct. 1824, for a short period, we believe, of the FROLIC; and he had lastly the command, from 25 Nov. 1836 until 1839, of the ECHO steam-vessel, on the North America and West India station.

JAMESON. (RETIRED COMMANDER, 1837. F-P., 18; H-P., 51.)

WALTER JAMESON entered the Navy, 25 Nov. 1778, as L.M., on board the JANUS, Capts. Bonivier Glover, — Dixon, and Horatio Nelson, on the West India station, where, and in North America and the Channel, he continued to serve, chiefly as Midshipman, in the NIGER frigate, Capt. John Brown, and again in the JANUS, Capts. W. H. O'Hara and Robt. M'Evoy, until Sept. 1783. On the renewal of hostilities in 1793, after having been for nearly 10 years employed in the merchant-service, he joined the ILLUSTRIOUS 74, Capt. Thos. Lennox Frederick, attached to the force in the Mediterranean. In the course of 1795 he there removed in succession to the WINDSOR CASTLE 98, flag-ship of Rear-Admiral Robt. Linzee, and BLENHEIM 98, commanded by his former Captain, Frederick; and in the early part of 1796 he was appointed by Sir John Jervis, in whose flag-ship, the VICTORY, he had been for a short time serving, to a Lieutenancy in a sloop under the orders at the time of Capt. Robt. Sauce. His official promotion took place on 28 July in the same year; after which period he was employed, we find, from March, 1797, to Dec. 1798, in the NAIAD and MELPOMÈNE 38's, Capts. Wm. Pierrepont and Sir Chas. Hamilton—from Nov. 1799 until July, 1800, in the THAMES 32, Capt. Wm. Lukin—from Aug. 1800 until 1802, in command of a Signal station on Black Castle Hill, Lammermuir, N. B.—and, from July, 1804, until 1808, in the Sea Fencible service in Scotland. While in command of the boats of the THAMES, and in the act of boarding two of the enemy's vessels in Quiberon Bay, Lieut. Jameson received a musket-ball in the shoulder, which, although his back has been cut open in the attempt, has never been extracted. He became a Retired Commander on the Senior List 27 Oct. 1837.

JAMISON. (LIEUTENANT, 1840.)

WILLIAM PAPILLON JAMISON entered the Navy 27 April, 1827; passed his examination in 1833; and obtained his commission 23 March, 1840. His succeeding appointments appear to have been—30 May, 1840, as Additional-Lieutenant, to the WINCHESTER 50, flag-ship of Sir Thos. Harvey in North America and the West Indies—7 March, 1841, to the PILOT 16, Capt. Geo. Ramsay, on the same station—29 Nov. 1842, to the THUNDERBOLT steam-vessel, Capt. Geo. Nathaniel Broke, under whom he served at the Cape of Good Hope, for some time as First-Lieutenant—2 Sept. 1845, to the PRESIDENT 50, fitting at Portsmouth for the flag of Rear-Admiral Jas. Rich. Dacres—and, 4 Feb. 1846, again as Senior, to the THUNDERBOLT, Capt. Alex. Boyle, in which vessel he was wrecked in Algoa Bay in Feb. 1847.

JANNS. (RETIRED COMMANDER, 1842. F-P., 11; H-P., 36.)

CHARLES JANNS entered the Navy, 29 July, 1800, as a Supernumerary, on board the PUISSANT 74, receiving-ship at Spithead, Capt. Symes; removed, in the course of the same year, to the SUFFISANT, Capts. Jonas Rose, —— Whitman, and Christopher John Williams Nesham, stationed in the Channel; served, from Oct. 1801 until Nov. 1806, at Home and in North America, on board the JAMAICA 24, Capts. Jonas Rose and John Dick; then rejoined Capt. Rose in the AGAMEMNON 64, lying at the Nore; and on 24 March, 1807, was made Lieutenant into the ALLIGATOR, Capt. Campbell. In the following Aug., having received an appointment to the INFLEXIBLE 64, Capt. Joshua Rowley Watson, he accompanied the expedition to Copenhagen. He afterwards served—from Feb. 1808 until he invalided in Jan. 1811—on the Channel, Bay of Biscay, and Mediterranean stations, in the ECLAIR sloop; which vessel, during the illness of her proper Captain, Chas. Kempthorne Quash, he personally commanded at the defence of Sicily in 1810. The latter was his last appointment. He accepted his present rank 19 July, 1842. AGENTS—Hallett and Robinson.

JAUNCEY. (COMMANDER, 1843. F-P., 23; H-P., 8.)

HORATIO JAUNCEY is eldest surviving son of Capt. Henry Fyge Jauncey, R.N.* (1821), who died in July, 1834.

This officer entered the Navy, 1 Aug. 1816, as Fst.-cl. Vol., on board the HOPE 10, commanded by his father in the Channel; and, from Oct. 1818 until July, 1822, served on the Irish and West India stations in the TRIBUNE 42, Capt. Nesbit Josiah Willoughby. He then joined the GLOUCESTER 74, flag-ship at Chatham of Sir Benj. Hallowell; and in the following Dec., after having passed his examination, he sailed for South America in the BRITON 46, Capt. Sir Murray Maxwell. Returning to England in Sept. 1826, Mr. Jauncey was next, in March, 1827, nominated to a Mateship in the HUSSAR 46, bearing the flag of Sir Chas. Ogle at Halifax, where he continued until promoted to the rank of Lieutenant 26 Feb. 1830. His appointments in the latter capacity were—10 Dec. 1833, to the ENDYMION 50, Capt. Sir Sam. Roberts, on the Lisbon and Mediterranean stations—and, 28 Dec. 1836, 3 Nov. 1840, and 17 Jan. 1843, as Senior, to the SNAKE 16, Capts. Alex. Milne and John Baker Porter Hay, VERNON 50, Capt. Wm. Walpole, and CALEDONIA 120, flag-ship of Sir David Milne, on the West India, Mediterranean, and Plymouth stations. He was advanced to his present rank in honour of a visit paid by Her Majesty to the CALEDONIA 25 Sept. 1843; and has been employed, since 16 Nov. 1846, as Second-Captain of the ALBION 90, part of the Channel squadron. AGENTS—Messrs. Halford and Co.

JAY. (COMMANDER, 1841.)

CHARLES HAWSE JAY entered the Navy, 1 May, 1801, as A. B., on board the MONMOUTH 64, Capt. Geo. Hart, under whom (we except an attachment of a few months in 1803-4 to the AMPHION 32, Capt. Sam. Sutton) he continued to serve, on the Mediterranean and North Sea stations, the greater part of the time as Midshipman, until May, 1805. He was then borne for a few months, as a Supernumerary, on the books of the WINCHELSEA frigate, Capt. Wm. Cockraft, lying at Sheerness, whence, towards the close of the same year, he returned to the Mediterranean in the STANDARD 64, Capt. Thos. Harvey. After assisting at the passage of the Dardanells in Feb. 1807, on which occasion he was slightly wounded,† Mr. Jay, on Capt. Aiskew Paffard Hollis succeeding to the command of the STANDARD, proceeded to the Baltic. Arrived on that station, he removed, in Jan. 1810, to the SNIPE cutter, Lieut.-Commander Chas. Champion, and was there actively employed until June, 1811. During the next two years he presents himself to our notice as serving at Sheerness on board the RAISONNABLE 64, Capts. Thos. New, Chas. Hewitt, and Edw. Sneyd Clay; and from July, 1813, until July, 1814, we find him in command, the last six months with the rank of Acting-Lieutenant, of the gun-boats Nos. 14 and 19, on the north coast of Spain. On his return to Sheerness Mr. Jay was received as a Supernumerary on board the NAMUR 74, flag-ship of Sir Thos. Williams. During the few months immediately antecedent to his promotion to the rank of Lieutenant 6 Feb. 1815, he served, it appears, in the VENERABLE 74, bearing the flag in the West Indies of the late Sir Philip Durham. His next appointments were—15 July, 1818, to the ONTARIO 18, Capt. Geo. Gosling, fitting at Plymouth—and, 13 Sept. 1822, and 31 May, 1823, to the SEVERN and RAMILLIES Coast-Blockade ships, Capts. Wm. M'Culloch and Hugh Pigot. He has held the office, since 26 June, 1828, of Superintendent of Semaphores at the Admiralty. The commission he at present holds bears date 22 Oct. 1841.

Commander Jay, in consideration of the wound he received at the Dardanells, obtained a pecuniary grant from the Patriotic Society. He is married, and has issue. AGENT—Fred. Dufaur.

JEAYES. (LIEUT., 1825. F-P., 25; H-P., 9.)

JOHN JEAYES, born 25 Dec. 1799, at Coventry, is son of the late Henry Jeayes, Esq., of that city; step-son of the late, and step-brother of the present Capt. John Mascal, R.M.; and brother-in-law of Rich. Rodney Bligh Hopley, Esq., Surgeon R.N.

This officer entered the Navy, in April, 1813, as Sec.-cl. Boy, on board the ASIA 74, Capts. Geo. Scott, John Wainwright, and Alex. Skene; in which ship we find him present, as Fst.-cl. Vol., in the attacks on Washington, Alexandria, Fort Bowyer, Baltimore, and New Orleans. Having attained the rating of Midshipman 1 Sept. 1815, he joined, in Feb. 1816, the RAMILLIES 74, Capt. Thos. Boys, with whom he served for two years and seven months on the Home station; after which he appears to have been employed on the coast of Africa from 28 May, 1819, until 10 Aug. 1823, nearly the whole time as Master's Mate, in the SNAPPER brig, commanded in succession by various Lieutenants. During that period Mr. Jeayes was twice in action with pirates. He assisted also at the destruction of several slave-factories in the river Pongo; and, in Aug. 1821, having volunteered his services, he succeeded, in a boat with only 14 hands, in cutting out from Duke's Town the Portuguese schooner *Conceicao* of 6 guns and 36 men, with 256 slaves on board—for his skill in navigating which vessel to Sierra Leone, although making three feet water per hour, he received the thanks of his Commander, Lieut. Christopher Knight. In Sept. 1822 Mr. Jeayes (who had passed his examination in the previous Feb.) was again sent in charge of a prize to Sierra Leone, during the last nine days of his passage whither he suffered great privations, being reduced to half a pint of water and a pint of Indian corn a-day. On the return to England of the SNAPPER in Aug. 1823, he voluntarily joined the PRINCE REGENT colonial brig, for the purpose of co-operating with the troops in the Ashantee war. Succeeding soon to the command of that vessel, Mr. Jeayes, among other important and particular services, effectually covered the retreat of Lieut. Erskine and 149 of his men, after the death of Sir Chas. M'Carthy at the battle of Assamacow, and, by his exertions in procuring fresh provisions, had the good fortune of preventing the garrison of Cape Coast Castle from delivering themselves into the hands of their ferocious enemy. He likewise on one occasion, in 1824, proceeded with the boats from Sierra Leone off the Iles de Los, a distance of about 70 miles, and captured *Les Deux Sœurs* with 136 slaves on board. In consequence, however, of the great fatigue endured by him in the performance of that service, having been exposed in an open boat for eight days and nights, he was for two months laid up with an attack of African fever. On being sent home with despatches for the benefit of his health, he was at length, through the strong recommendation of Major-General Chas. Stuart, Governor of Sierra Leone, promoted to the rank of Lieutenant by commission dated 17 Oct. 1825. Returning again to his former station, as second in command of the AFRICAN steamer, he there assumed the successive Captaincy, 3 April and 16 May, 1826, of the colonial vessels SUSAN and REVENGE. In the following Aug. Mr. Jeayes was once more compelled to invalid. His subsequent appointments were—28 Feb.

* Capt. Jauncey, when Second-Lieutenant of the ETHALION frigate, Capt. James Young, assisted, in Oct. 1799, at the capture of a Spanish galleon so valuable that his own share alone amounted to 5000*l*.

† *Vide* Gaz. 1807, p. 597

1830, to the Coast Blockade, as Supernumerary-Lieutenant of the TALAVERA 74, Capts. Hugh Pigot and David Colby—18 April, 1831, to the Coast Guard—1 Aug. 1836, to the VICTORY 104, flag-ship at Portsmouth of Sir Fred. Lewis Maitland—18 May, 1839, again to the Coast Guard—and, 4 Feb. 1840, and between Feb. 1843 and 14 Aug. 1844, to the successive command of the AFRICAN, ALBAN, PLUTO, and ALBAN steam-vessels, on the West India and Home stations. He then again invalided; but, since 29 Sept. 1846, has held a second appointment in the Coast Guard.

Lieut. Jeayes married, 8 Feb. 1826, Josephina, eldest daughter of the late John Wm. Alston, Esq., of Edinburgh, by whom he has issue a son and five daughters.

JEFFERIES. (LIEUT., 1815. F-P., 38; H-P., 3.)

JOHN HEAD JEFFERIES entered the Navy, 12 Feb. 1806, as A.B, on board the CAPTAIN 74, commanded in the Channel by Capt. Stevens. He became Midshipman, in the following July, of the OCEAN 98, bearing the flag in the Mediterranean of Lord Collingwood; removed, in July, 1809, to the MILFORD 74, Capts. Henry Wm. Bayntun and Edw. Kittoe, stationed in the Channel and off Cadiz; joined, in Aug. 1811, the FRANCHISE frigate, Capt. Rich. Buck, again in the Mediterranean; and was next, from Sept. 1814 until Aug. 1816, employed on the East India station, chiefly as Master's Mate and Acting-Lieutenant, in the FAVORITE 20, Capt. Hon. Jas. Ashley Maude, CAMELION 10, Capt. Low, LEDA 38, Capt. Geo. Sayer, and PHILOMEL 10, Capt. Jas. Hanway Plumridge. Lieut. Jefferies, whose commission bears date 8 June, 1815, has been in charge of a station in the Coast Guard ever since 17 March, 1820.

JEFFERIS. (LIEUT., 1809. F-P., 13; H-P., 33.)

CHARLES JEFFERIS entered the Navy, 19 Feb. 1801, as Fst.-cl. Vol., on board the BELLONA 74, Capts. Sir Thos. Boulden Thompson and Thos. Bertie, under the former of whom he shared in the action off Copenhagen 2 April, 1801, and then visited Cadiz and the West Indies. In the course of 1802 he successively joined the CHILDERS and DASHER sloops, both commanded by Capt. John Delafons, on whose death, in the East Indies, in 1804, he removed to the SCEPTRE 74, Capt. Joseph Bingham. Besides participating in that ship in an engagement with a French frigate and the batteries in St. Paul's Bay, Ile de Bourbon, he was frequently employed in her boats against the enemy, and was once reduced to such extremity as to be compelled to subsist for several weeks upon two ounces of bad biscuit a-day. In Nov. 1808 he was promoted from the CULLODEN 74, bearing the flag of Sir Edw. Pellew, to the rank of Acting-Lieutenant in the RATTLESNAKE 18, Capt. Jas. John Gordon Bremer—an act which the Admiralty sanctioned by commission dated 22 May, 1809. On 7 Sept. following, the firmness and humanity of Mr. Jefferis were strikingly displayed in the circumstance of his taking command, during a heavy gale, of the boats of the RATTLESNAKE, and persevering in his efforts to succour a ship under convoy, whereby 68 persons and a large amount of treasure were rescued from destruction. On that occasion he went on board and remained until every soul had been safely taken off, he himself leaving a few minutes only before the vessel foundered. A few days after the occurrence of this event we find Mr. Jefferis joining the DOVER 38, Capt. Edw. Tucker, an officer whose warm approbation it was his frequent fortune to elicit. Being on one occasion sent in command of a watering party to the island of Engano, he was there attacked by a band of armed savages, to whom, had it not been for the skill and determination he evinced, the whole of the British must have fallen a sacrifice. He afterwards saw much boat-service off the island of Java; and in Feb. 1810 he greatly signalized himself throughout the operations which led to the capture of the island of Amboyna, where, it appears, he was the senior naval officer landed from the squadron, and where, although wounded by a spent grape-shot at the storming of the second battery, he continued to afford his valuable assistance until the last.* After the surrender of the island Mr. Jefferis was often detached in the command of armed vessels for the purpose of defending it against the pirates. He also, when in charge of an armed brig, co-operated with the DOVER in the capture of the Dutch settlements of Gorontello, Manado, and Kema. In Aug. 1810, having rejoined his ship, he was again employed on shore in command of the seamen at the taking of the island of Ternate, and on his return on board, after the storming of Fort Kyo-Merah, he exerted himself, greatly to the satisfaction of his Captain, in the attack on Fort Orange and several of the enemy's batteries.† When subsequently on his way with despatches in the *Mandarin*, a captured sloop of war, from Amboyna to Madras, Lieut. Jefferis was unfortunately wrecked, by his vessel striking on an unknown reef off Red Island, in the Straits of Singapore, where, with his crew, who were saved from immediate destruction solely through the instrumentality of his own great exertions, he was picked up in a state of utter exhaustion by H.M.S. CHIFFONNE, then most providentially passing through. Lieut. Jefferis, who contrived, however, to save the despatches, was actually on board the *Mandarin* at the very moment she went down. He soon afterwards took a passage back to Amboyna in the PHŒNIX frigate, and served, *en route*, as a volunteer in a boat expedition against the Dutch settlement of Palembang. On his re-junction of the DOVER, he had the ill luck, on 2 May, 1811, to be again wrecked in Madras Roads, on which occasion, in common with the rest of the officers and crew, he endured the greatest misery, being lashed to the ship from 11 P.M. until 8 in the following morning, with a tremendous surf breaking over him at intervals of every four or five minutes. In consequence of this disaster he sustained a considerable loss of prize property, and, as he happened to be in command of the DOVER at the time, was detained in India nearly 12 months at his own expense, not being allowed any pay until after the court-martial, which took place at Portsmouth in July, 1812, and which not only fully acquitted him of all blame, but complimented him for his conduct. It had indeed been everything that could be expected from a skilful, expert, and excellent seaman. After having further served for nearly two years and a half with eminent credit, as First-Lieutenant, on the Cork, Brazilian, and West India stations, of the BACCHUS sloop, Capts. Lewis Hole, Geo. Wickens Willes, and Wm. Hilt; Mr. Jefferis was paid off in Oct. 1815. Since that period he has not been able to procure either employment or promotion.

The Lieutenant, whose testimonials of service are of a brilliant character, married, 28 Dec. 1824, Maria, daughter of the late John Pearson, Esq., of Rutland Place.

JEFFERSON. (LIEUT., 1807. F-P., 15; H-P., 33.)

FRANCIS JEFFERSON entered the Navy, in Sept. 1799, as Midshipman, on board the DIRECTOR 64, Capt. Wm. Bligh; and in Aug. 1800, on his return from a voyage to St. Helena, joined the GREYHOUND 32, Capts. Chas. Ogle, Alex. Campbell, and Wm. Hoste, stationed in the Mediterranean; where, after attending the expedition of 1801 to Egypt, he removed, as Midshipman, in Oct. 1802, to the MONMOUTH 64, Capt. Geo. Hart. From May, 1804, until his return to England in Oct. 1806, we find him serving in the West Indies, chiefly as Master's Mate, Sub-Lieutenant, and Acting-Lieutenant, on board the BEAULIEU 44, Capt. Chas. Ekins, NETLEY schooner, Lieut.-Commander Wm. Carr, and DOLPHIN 44, Capts. Thos. Tudor Tucker and Daniel Tandy. He then joined, in the capacity last mentioned, the WEYMOUTH 18, Capt. Martin White, of which vessel, successively stationed at Woolwich

* *Vide* Gaz. 1810, p. 1483.

† *V.* Gaz. 1811, p. 1196.

and Plymouth, he was confirmed a Lieutenant by commission dated 12 June, 1807. After he had been employed for a further period of two years on the Home station in the DREADNOUGHT 98, Capts. Wm. Lechmere and Geo. Burgoyne Salt, flag-ship for some time of Rear-Admiral Thos. Sotheby, he was appointed, in April, 1809, First of the CADMUS 10, Capts. E. Wynter, J. Williams, and Thos. Fife. When at Vigo, in June of the same year, Lieut. Jefferson volunteered to take command of a gun-boat, and, in unison with three others, manned by Spaniards, to attack two batteries which the French had lately erected in the vicinity.* A short time, however, after the commencement of the operations the Spaniards were observed retreating from the conflict, in consequence whereof the British were under the necessity of firing ball-cartridges over their heads, and of thus compelling them to return to their duty. Nothing, on the other hand, could exceed the valour and good conduct of the men under the command of Lieut. Jefferson, who, after they had expended all their cartridges, cut up their jackets, shirts, and stockings, for the purpose of making bags for the loose powder, and, when they victoriously rejoined their ship, were almost in a state of nudity. Struck with admiration at their conduct, the CADMUS had telegraphed to the LIVELY frigate, Commodore Geo. M'Kinley, then within signal-distance, the words—"our boat doing gloriously." Besides receiving a strong letter of approbation from the latter officer, Mr. Jefferson had the satisfaction of being mentioned in Lord Gambier's despatches as deserving his highest praise. Previously to the above affair he had volunteered to go in-shore with the boats at Corunna, and had brought off a brig from under the batteries. On 24 Dec. 1809 he effected the similar capture, with but one boat under his orders, of two of the enemy's vessels in Quiberon Bay—an exploit which obtained him a letter of thanks from the Commander-in-Chief, Rear-Admiral Hon. Robt. Stopford. On 4 Jan. 1810 he further took two vessels off the river Renerve; as, on 17 of the same month, he did three others in the Valeine. Illness at length, induced by severe duty and continual night-service in the boats, obliged him to invalid in Aug. 1810; from which period he remained on half-pay until appointed, 24 Nov. 1825, to the office of Agent for Transports Afloat. In April, 1830, on the night previous to his leaving the ship in which he had been employed as Agent, he hastened on shore, with the whole of his crew, in consequence of the danger which existed of the dockyard at Deptford being set on fire, and removed everything of a combustible nature from the threatened side. For this service he received the thanks of the Navy Board. He has had the command, since 1836, of Her Majesty's yachts on the Virginia Water, at Windsor.

Lieut. Jefferson married in 1812, and has issue six children.

* *Vide* Gaz. 1809, p. 1006.

JEFFERY. (LIEUT., 1837. F-P., 22; H-P., 5.)

BARTHOLOMEW JEFFERY is nephew of Commander John Molesworth, R.N.

This officer entered the Navy in 1820; passed his examination 1 Nov. 1826; and obtained his commission 10 Jan. 1837. His appointments have since been—8 Sept. 1837, to the THUNDER surveying-vessel, Lieut.-Commanders Bird Allen and Edw. Barnett, on the North America and West India station —27 Oct. 1838, to the MAGNIFICENT receiving-ship at Jamaica, Commodore Peter John Douglas—for a few months in 1840-1, to the Transport Service—and 3 Jan. 1846, to the Coast Guard, in which service he is now employed.

Lieut. Jeffery, who had been left a widower with three children, married, secondly, 25 April, 1845, his cousin Mary Anne, youngest daughter of the late John and Hon. Jane Stephenson, and niece of the late General Sir Benj. C. Stephenson, K.C.G.

JEFFREYS. (LIEUTENANT, 1841.)

GEORGE BARBOR JEFFREYS entered the Navy 27 March, 1828; passed his examination in 1834; and was for some time Mate of the PYLADES 18, Capt. Talavera Vernon Anson. While so attached, he shared in the principal operations in China, where (besides commanding a boat at the capture of one out of three piratical junks) he served with the flotilla at the taking of several rafts and of the last fort protecting the approaches to the city of Canton, 13 March, 1841—was similarly employed at the capture of that city on 18 of the same month—and, during the second series of operations against it, was again employed in the boats at the destruction of the whole line of defences extending about two miles from the British factory.* Being rewarded for these services by commission dated 6 May, 1841, and successively appointed to the WELLESLEY 72, Commodore Sir J. J. Gordon Bremer, and BLONDE 42, Capt. Thos. Bourchier, he further assisted at the capture of Amoy, Chusan, and Chinghae. He subsequently joined—22 Jan. 1842, the WELLESLEY again, Capt. Thos. Maitland—20 Sept. 1842, the ALFRED 50, bearing the broad pendant of Commodore John Brett Purvis on the South American station—11 May, 1844, after an interval of a few months, the same ship—1 Aug. 1844, as First-Lieutenant, the FROLIC 16, Capt. Cospatrick Baillie Hamilton, in the Pacific—and 13 June, 1846, the TALBOT 26, Capt. Sir Thos. Raikes Trigge Thompson, with whom he returned to England in 1847.

JEFFREYS. (LIEUTENANT, 1827.)

RICHARD GUNNING JEFFREYS entered the Navy 28 Nov. 1812; passed his examination in 1819; obtained his commission 30 April, 1827; served from that period until Feb. 1830, in the ALLIGATOR 28, Capts. Wm. P. Canning and Chas. Philip Yorke, on, we believe, the East India and Mediterranean stations; obtained an appointment in the Coast Guard 6 Dec. 1836; removed, 7 May, 1840, to the LUCIFER steam-vessel, Capt. Fred. Wm. Beechey, on the coast of Ireland; and went back to the Coast Guard 18 Sept. following. He has been on half-pay since the close of 1841. AGENTS—Messrs. Chard.

JENKIN. (COMMANDER, 1846.)

CHARLES JENKIN entered the Navy 7 Feb. 1814; passed his examination in 1823; and was made Lieutenant, 24 Dec. 1829, into the BARHAM 50, Capt. Sir John Louis. His subsequent appointments were, to the command—1 Nov. 1832, of a station in the Coast Guard—13 May, 1837, of the ROMNEY receiving-ship at the Havana—9 Sept. 1841, of the AVON steamer, at Woolwich—2 July, 1842, of the GRIFFON brigantine, on the North America and West India station—and 23 Dec. 1845, of the MYRMIDON steamer, employed on particular service. He attained his present rank 9 Nov. 1846; and is at present on half-pay.

Commander Jenkin married, in 1832, Henrietta Camilla, daughter of the Hon. Robt. Jackson, of the island of Jamaica. AGENTS—Messrs. Stilwell.

JENKINS. (LIEUT., 1810. F-P., 15; H-P., 28.)

HENRY JENKINS entered the Navy, 10 May, 1804, as Fst.-cl. Vol., on board the WINDSOR CASTLE 98, Capts. Davidge Gould and Chas. Boyles; under the latter of whom he participated in Sir Robt. Calder's action 22 July, 1805, witnessed the surrender of four French frigates to a squadron under Sir Sam. Hood off Rochefort 25 Sept. 1806, and passed the Dardanells in Feb. 1807. Removing in Sept. 1808 to the PALLAS 32, Capt. Geo. Fras. Seymour, he was present, in the course of the following year, at the destruction of the French shipping in Basque Roads, and also at the bombardment of Flushing; after which, it appears, he served for about 12 months with the same Captain in the MANILLA frigate, on the Lisbon and African stations. Being made Lieutenant, 27 Sept. 1810, into the

* *Vide* Gaz. 1841, pp. 1503, 1505, 2505.

Impétueux 74, Capts. John Lawford, David Milne, and Chas. Inglis, he further served in that ship off the coasts of Portugal and Africa, as also in the Baltic and Channel, part of the time under the flag of the present Sir Geo. Martin, until Dec. 1812. His subsequent appointments were—12 Nov. 1813, to the Myrmidon 20, Capts. Wm. Paterson and Robt. Gambier, with whom he cruized in the Channel and off Madeira and Teneriffe until Oct. 1815—26 Aug. 1818 and 29 March, 1820, to the Rochfort 80, bearing the flag of Sir Thos. Fras. Fremantle, and Liffey 50, Capt. Hon. Henry Duncan, both on the Mediterranean station, whence he returned in the latter ship to England in the summer of 1821—27 Feb. 1827, to the Dartmouth 42, Capt. Sir Thos. Fellowes, from which frigate he invalided in the following May—17 Sept. 1842, to the San Josef 110, flag-ship of Sir David Milne at Plymouth —and, 22 May, 1845, as Senior, to the Caledonia 120, Capt. Manley Dixon, lying at the same port. He has been on half-pay since the close of the latter year.

JENKINSON. (Captain, 1814. f-p., 11; h-p., 33.)

Henry Jenkinson is eldest son of Lieut.-General John Jenkinson.

This officer (who had been for three years a student at the Royal Naval Academy) first embarked, in Oct. 1806, as a Supernumerary Fst.-cl. Vol., on board the Royal William, flag-ship of Admiral Montagu at Spithead. He removed soon afterwards to the Décade 36, Capt. John Stuart, with whom he cruized on the Bermuda, Channel, and Irish stations, the greater part of the time as Midshipman, until June, 1809. On 11 of the following Dec., after having accompanied the expedition to the Walcheren in the Venerable 74, Capt. Andrew King, Mr. Jenkinson was promoted to the rank of Lieutenant. He was employed, during the next two years and a half, chiefly on the North Sea and Lisbon stations, in the Clyde and Inconstant frigates, bearing each the broad pendant of Commodore Edw. W. C. R. Owen, and Impétueux 74, flag-ship of Vice Admiral Geo. Martin; was made Commander, 13 Aug. 1812, into the Jasper sloop; and after commanding that vessel for nearly two years was advanced to Post-rank 7 June, 1814. His acceptance of the Retirement took place 1 Oct. 1846.

Capt. Jenkinson married, 25 Aug. 1823, Elizabeth Lucy Theresa, youngest daughter of the late Sir Thos. Dyke Acland, Bart., M.P. for North Devon.

JENNER. (Lieutenant, 1815. f-p., 9; h-p., 32.)

George Jenner was born 21 Nov. 1791, in Suffolk.

This officer entered the Navy, 18 May, 1806, as Fst.-cl. Vol., on board the Milan 38, Capt. Robt. Laurie, in which frigate he was employed in escorting convoy to Halifax, blockading the Chesapeake, and conveying troops and stores to Lisbon. On 23 Sept. 1810, a few days after he had been paid off, he became Midshipman of the Désirée 36, Capt. Arthur Farquhar, attached to the force in the North Sea, where he served for some time off the Texel, and assisted at the capture, among other vessels, of the *Vélocifère*, French privateer of 14 guns and 56 men. From the Désirée, in whose boats he had been more than once employed, Mr. Jenner removed, in Oct. 1811, to the Ajax 74, Capts. Sir R. Laurie, Robt. Waller Otway, and Geo. Mundy. Continuing in that ship until Oct. 1814, he was at first stationed off Toulon and Sicily. He afterwards cruized in the Bays of Biscay and Quiberon, and, besides witnessing the fall of St. Sebastian in Sept. 1813, was present at the taking, 17 March, 1814, of *L'Alcyon*, national brig of 16 guns and 120 men. In the boats of the Ajax he proved instrumental to the capture of several merchantmen; and on one occasion in 1812 he had the satisfaction of being complimented by his Captain, Otway, for his conduct at the capture of the *Ned* American schooner. Since the attainment of his present rank, 20 March, 1815, Lieut. Jenner (who, prior to leaving the Ajax, had made a voyage with troops to Quebec) has been on half-pay.

He married, 22 Feb. 1822, Sarah, daughter of Thos. Youngs, Esq., of Mendham, Suffolk.

JENNER. (Commander, 1847.)

Robert Jenner is third son of the Right Hon. Sir Herbert Jenner Fust, D.C.L., Dean of the Arches, and Judge of the Prerogative Court of Canterbury, by the youngest daughter of the late General Lascelles; and first-cousin and brother-in-law of the present Robt. Fras. Jenner, Esq., of Wenvoe Castle, co. Glamorgan.

This officer entered the Navy 19 June, 1826; passed his examination in 1832; obtained his first commission 26 Oct. 1840; was then appointed Additional-Lieutenant of the Princess Charlotte 104, flag-ship in the Meditereanean of Hon. Sir Robt. Stopford; and afterwards joined—17 Feb. 1841, the Thunderer 84, Capt. Dan. Pring, employed on the latter station and in attendance on the Queen off Walmer Castle—5 Dec. 1843, the St. Vincent 120, bearing the flag of Sir Chas. Rowley at Portsmouth —and, 26 Sept. 1845, the Excellent gunnery-ship, Capt. Henry Ducie Chads, of which he became First-Lieutenant. He attained his present rank 27 Jan. 1847.

The Commander married, in 1843, Selina Helen, youngest daughter of the late Jas. Jameson, Esq., of Calcutta, by whom he has issue. Agents—Messrs. Stilwell.

JENNINGS. (Lieut., 1813. f-p., 23; h-p., 19.)

Edward Jennings, born 28 Aug. 1793, at Kelvedon, co. Essex, is eldest son of David Jennings, Esq., of Ballingrove, Ireland, a Captain in the Army, by Mary, eldest daughter of Colin Campbell, Esq., of Jamaica.

This officer entered the Royal Naval College in Aug. 1805; and embarked in Jan. 1809, as Midshipman, on board the Valiant 74, Capts. John Bligh, Thos. Geo. Shortland, John Nash, and Robt. Dudley Oliver. After witnessing Lord Cochrane's destruction of the shipping in Aix Roads, sharing also in the attack upon Flushing, and serving off Rochefort and L'Orient, he successively joined, in 1811-12, the Christian VII. and Impregnable, both flag-ships in the North Sea of Admiral Wm. Young, and the Inconstant 36, bearing the broad pendant of Commodore Edw. W. C. R. Owen. During a winter-cruize of three months in the latter ship among the Western Isles, in 1812-13, Mr. Jennings, who had passed his examination in Sept. 1812, had charge of a watch, and was employed, with the Dublin 74, in search of an American squadron. On 27 May, 1813, he was appointed Acting-Lieutenant of the Calliope 10, Capt. John M'Kerlie, under whom we find him stationed in the river Elbe during the occupation of Hamburg and Cuxhaven by the French. In the following Sept. he joined the Richmond 12, Capt. Edw. O'Shaughnessy, into which vessel, it appears, he had been confirmed by commission bearing the same date as his acting order. Mr. Jennings' next appointment was, 27 March, 1814, to the Niobe 38, commanded at first by Capt. Wm. Augustus Montagu as an active frigate on the Lisbon station, and afterwards as an hospital and troop ship by Capt. Henry Colins Deacon; under whom he conveyed the sick of the Russian Imperial Guards to Cronstadt, and, independently of a participation in several particular services, assisted at the reduction of Guadeloupe in 1815. The Niobe being paid off in March, 1816, he was afterwards employed in command—from 24 Nov. 1823 until June, 1828, again from 6 June, 1834, until Feb. 1839, and from the latter date until March, 1842—of the Plover, Tyrian, and Alert packets, on the Mediterranean, North and South American, West India, and Lisbon stations.

Lieut. Jennings is the author of a nautical work of great practical utility, teeming with instruction to officers of all ages, stamped with the approbation of the Lords of the Admiralty, and adapted as well to the merchant as the naval service.* He married, 17 Dec. 1818, Mary Jane, eldest daughter of Lieut.-Col. J. C. Tufnell, of Bath, by whom he has issue three sons and two daughters.

JEPHSON. (Lieut, 1824. f-p., 12; h-p., 20.)

James Saumarez Jephson was born 15 Feb. 1802. This officer entered the Navy, 29 March, 1815, as Fst.-cl. Vol., on board the Contest 12, Capt. Jas. Rattray, on the Home station, where he continued to serve until Aug. 1818 in the Childers 16, Capts. Rattray and Rich. Wales, Madagascar and Mæander frigates, both commanded by Sir Jas. Alex. Gordon, and Impregnable 104, flag-ship of Lord Exmouth. He was then employed for nearly four years in the Mediterranean as Midshipman of the Révolutionnaire 46, Capt. Hon. Fleetwood Broughton Reynolds Pellew; and on 25 March, 1824, after having acted for several months in the Owen Glendower 42, Commodore Sir Robt. Mends, and Cyrené 20, Capt. Percy Grace, he was confirmed in the rank of Lieutenant. His last appointment was, on 18 Oct. in the latter year, to the Britannia 120, flag-ship at Plymouth of Sir Jas. Saumarez, with whom, if we mistake not, he served until paid off in 1827.

Lieut. Jephson is Secretary to the Carlton Club. He is married and has issue. Agent—J. Hinxman.

JERNINGHAM. (Commander, 1841. f-p., 22; h-p., 2.)

Arthur William Jerningham, born 26 Feb. 1807, is second son of the late Wm. Chas. Jerningham, Esq., an officer of rank in the Austrian service, by Anne, eldest daughter of Thos. Wright, Esq., of Fitzwalters, co. Essex; brother of Fred. Wm. Jerningham, Esq., late of the 29th Regt.; and nephew of the present Lord Stafford. One of his sisters is married to the eldest son of Viscount Gormanston.

This officer entered the Navy, 13 June, 1823, as Fst.-cl. Vol., on board the Mersey 26, Capt. John Macpherson Ferguson, stationed in South America, where he exchanged into the Fly 18, Capt. Wm. Fanshawe Martin. On being paid off in 1825 he became Mipshipman of the Victory 104, bearing the flag of Sir Geo. Martin at Portsmouth; and he afterwards, until Dec. 1829, served in the Channel and Mediterranean on board the Galatea 42, Capt. Sir Chas. Sullivan, and Pelican and Raleigh sloops, Capts. Alex. Wm. Baillie Hamilton, Fras. Deane Hutcheson, Geo. Haye, and Sir Wm. Dickson. In Jan. 1830 we find Mr. Jerningham, who had passed his examination in the previous Sept., joining the Britannia 120, flag-ship of Sir Pulteney Malcolm, also on the Mediterranean station, where, on 28 Feb. 1832, after having served as Mate with Capts. Hugh Berners and Wm. Smith in the Philomel 10, he was promoted to the rank of Lieutenant, while employed under Hon. Sir Henry Hotham in the St. Vincent 120. His succeeding appointments were—27 July, 1833, to the Raleigh, 16, Capt. Abraham Mills Hawkins, with whom he returned to England in the early part of 1834—17 Nov. 1835, to the Excellent gunnery-ship at Portsmouth, Capt. Thos. Hastings—and 23 June, 1837, to the Wellesley 74, bearing the successive flags of Sir Jas. John Gordon Bremer and Hon. Geo. Elliot. For his services as Gunnery and First Lieutenant in the latter ship during the early portion of the China war, he was advanced to his present rank by commission dated 22 Feb. 1841. He has been employed in the Coast Guard since 4 of the following Aug., at first as an Inspecting Commander and latterly as Inspector of small-arm exercise to that service, with his name on the books of the Excellent.

Commander Jerningham married, 19 April, 1836, Sophia Mary, eldest daughter of Rich. O'Farrell Caddell, Esq., of Harbourstown, co. Meath, by the Hon. Paulina Southwell, sister of the present Viscount Southwell. By that lady he has issue.

* 'Practical Hints addressed to Seamen, for preventing Accidents on board Ship, and especially for guarding against Hurricanes, Collision, Fire, &c.' Lond. 8vo. R. B. Bate, 1844.

JERRARD. (Lieut., 1813. f-p., 10; h-p., 32.)

Michael Jerrard entered the Navy, 1 March, 1805, as Midshipman, on board the Pluto sloop, commanded, we believe, by Capt. Rich. Gaire Janvrin, on the Channel station; whence, in 1809, he sailed for the coast of Africa in the Hawk 16, Capt. Henry Bourchier. With his name on the books of the Revenge 74, bearing the flag of Hon. Arthur Kaye Legge, we find him actively employed in command of a gun-boat at the defence of Cadiz in 1811 and 12. He afterwards served for about 12 months as Master's Mate of the same ship in the Mediterranean under Sir John Gore; and on 30 Dec. 1813 he was there made Lieutenant into the Royal George 100, bearing the flag of Vice-Admiral Fras. Pickmore. He has been on half-pay since July, 1814. Agent—J. Chippendale.

JERVIS, Bart. (Lieut., 1814. f-p., 9; h-p., 31.)

Sir Henry Meredyth Jervis White Jervis, born 20 Nov. 1793, is eldest son of the late Sir John Jervis White Jervis, by Jane, daughter of Henry Nisbett, Esq., of Ashmore, co. Longford. He succeeded his father, as second Baronet, in 1830.

This officer entered the Navy, 1 April, 1807, as Fst.-cl. Vol., on board the Kent 74, Capt. Thos. Rogers, of which ship, stationed in the Mediterranean, he became Midshipman in Jan. 1808. From Nov. 1809 until Feb. 1813 he served off Lisbon, and again in the Mediterranean, on board the Lavinia 40, Capts. Lord Wm. Stuart and Geo. Digby; and while so attached he assisted, in 1811, at the capture, under a heavy fire from a division of Suchet's army, of a well-defended island in the Bay of Rosas, which had long been a place of refuge for French privateers. On 26 Aug. 1814, after having witnessed (in the San Josef 110, flag-ship of Sir Rich. King) the two partial actions fought by Sir Edw. Pellew with the Toulon fleet, Sir Henry was confirmed a Lieutenant in the Blenheim 74, Capt. Sam. Warren, with whom he returned to England. His last appointment was, on 16 of the ensuing Sept., to the Pelorus 18, Capts. Chas. Hole and John Gourly. In that vessel he served for 12 months on the Cork and Channel stations.

He married, 16 Dec. 1818, Marian, third daughter of Wm. Campbell, Esq., of Fairfield, in Ayrshire, by Catherine, his second wife, daughter of Capt. Geo. Gunning, of the Guards. By that lady he has issue four sons and three daughters—of the former, one, Henry, is a Lieutenant in the Royal Artillery; and another, Joscelyn, a Midshipman R.N.

JERVIS. (Captain, 1846.)

William Henry Jervis entered the Navy 16 April, 1816; passed his examination in 1823; and was made Lieutenant, 2 March, 1828, into the Hussar 46, bearing the flag at Halifax of Sir Chas. Ogle, who transferred him, in the following May, to the Ringdove 18, Capt. Chas. English. After nine months of half-pay he obtained an appointment, 3 Oct. 1829, to the Winchester 52, flag-ship of Sir Edw. Griffith Colpoys on the North America and West India station. He was nominated, 25 June, 1831, Flag-Lieutenant, in the Prince Regent 120, to Rear-Admiral Wm. Parker, off Lisbon, where he continued to serve, in the same capacity, on board the Asia 84, until promoted to the rank of Commander 16 July, 1834. He was subsequently, with the exception of a few months in 1839-40, employed in the Coast Guard from 26 March, 1836, until July, 1843; and from the latter date until superseded in Oct. 1845 he commanded the Pluto 16, in the East Indies. He attained his present rank 9 Nov. 1846, and is now on half-pay.

Capt. Jervis married, 12 Jan. 1835, Susan Arabella, third daughter of the late John Starr, Esq., Member of the Provincial Parliament at Halifax for co. King's, and has issue.

JERVOIS. (COMMANDER, 1827. F-P., 18; H-P., 28.)

SAMPSON JERVOIS entered the Navy, 25 Nov. 1801, as Midshipman, on board the PRINCESS CHARLOTTE 38, Capt. Hon. Fras. Farington Gardner, bearing the flag of Lord Gardner at Cork. He subsequently cruized with the same Captain on the North Sea station in the GALYKHEID and RUBY 64's, and, on re-accompanying him in 1804 into the PRINCESS CHARLOTTE 38, sailed for the West Indies, where he assisted at the capture of several valuable Spanish merchantmen and of a French privateer brig, *Le Regulus*, of 14 guns and 84 men. Joining next, in Sept. 1805, the RAMILLIES 74, Capt. Fras. Pickmore, Mr. Jervois witnessed the capture, 13 March, 1806, of the French 80-gun ship *Marengo*, bearing the flag of Rear-Admiral Linois, and 40-gun frigate *Belle Poule*, as, in Dec. 1807, he did of the Danish islands of St. Thomas, St. John, and Sta. Croix. After a brief servitude in the BELLEISLE 74, flag-ship of Hon. Sir Alex. Cochrane, he was nominated, 16 May, 1808, Acting-Lieutenant of the DEMARARA sloop, Capt. Henry Bourchier, and in the course of the same year of the ASP 18, Capts. Robt. Preston and Wm. M'Culloch, to which vessel he was confirmed by commission dated 24 Dec. 1809. While in her he witnessed the capture, 10 Feb. 1809, of the French frigate *La Junon*, and had the command of her boats during the operations against Guadeloupe in Jan. and Feb. 1810. He returned home in June of the latter year, and was subsequently appointed—11 May, 1812, to the TALBOT 20, Capt. Spelman Swaine, in the Channel—15 Nov. 1813, to the MARTIAL sloop, Capt. Geo. Elliot—3 Jan. 1816, and 12 Feb. 1817, as First, to the PERSEUS 22, Capt. Thos. Rich. Toker, and SIR FRANCIS DRAKE 38, flag-ship of Vice-Admiral Fras. Pickmore, both at Newfoundland—18 Nov. 1818, in a similar capacity, to the DAUNTLESS 26, Capt. Hon. Valentine Gardner, fitting for the East Indies—29 Dec. 1823, three months after his return home, to the BRISK 10, Capt. Adolphus FitzClarence—and, 3 March, 1824, to the REDWING 18, commanded by the same Captain in the North Sea, where he served until paid off in 1825. He attained his present rank 26 April, 1827, but has not been since employed.

Commander Jervois married, in Oct. 1828, Elizabeth, daughter of John M'Clary, Esq., and by that lady has issue.

JESSE. (LIEUTENANT, 1841.)

RICHARD JESSE entered the Navy 12 Dec. 1826; passed his examination 7 Oct. 1835; and obtained his commission 23 Nov. 1841. His appointments have since been—18 May, 1843, to the CALEDONIA 120, flag-ship of Sir David Milne at Devonport—and, 13 Dec. 1845, to the GLADIATOR steamer, Capt. John Robb, now employed with the Channel squadron.

He married, in 1842, Emily, second daughter of the late Rev. G. C. Tenyton, D.C.L., Rector of Somersby, co. Lincoln. AGENTS—Messrs. Chard.

JESTON. (LIEUTENANT, 1825.)

HUMPHREY JESTON entered the Navy 9 June, 1808; passed his examination in 1814; was promoted to the rank of Lieutenant 10 Jan. 1825; and since 28 Sept. 1841 has been in charge of a station in the Coast Guard.

JEWELL. (LIEUT., 1812. F-P., 14; H-P., 37.)

WILLIAM NUNN JEWELL entered the Navy, in Dec. 1796, on board the GRAMPUS, Capt. Robt. Philpot, on the Jamaica station, where he served with the same officer, and with Capts. Parker and John Thicknesse, in the PELICAN sloop, until July, 1800. He re-embarked, in May, 1804, as Midshipman, on board the BRUIZER gun-brig, Lieut.-Commander Thos. Smithers, lying in the Downs; and on next joining the BELLEROPHON 74, Capts. John Loring, John Cooke, and Edw. Rotheram, sailed for the Mediterranean, and was wounded, under Capt. Cooke, at the battle of Trafalgar 21 Oct. 1805.* On his removal, in Oct. 1807, to the BEDFORD 74, Capts. Jas. Walker and Adam Mackenzie, Mr. Jewell accompanied the Royal Family of Portugal to the Brazils. In the course of 1809, 10, and 11, being still on the South American station, he was there successively appointed Acting-Sub-Lieutenant of the NANCY gun-brig, Lieut.-Commander Edw. Killwick, PORCUPINE 24, Capt. Robt. Elliot, and NANCY again, Lieut.-Commander Killwick. After a continued servitude at the Brazils as Master's Mate of the FOUDROYANT 80, flag-ship of Hon. Michael De Courcy, he was at length promoted to the full rank of Lieutenant by commission dated 6 Nov. 1812. His last appointment was, 6 Nov. 1813, to the CHATHAM 74, in which ship he served, on the Home station and among the Western Islands, under the flag of Rear-Admiral Matthew Henry Scott, until Aug. 1815.

In consideration of the wound he received at Trafalgar, the Lieutenant was presented with a pecuniary reward by the Patriotic Society. He married, 9 April, 1840, Miss Weavers. AGENT—W. H. B. Barwis.

JEWERS, K.W. (LIEUTENANT, 1809. F-P., 11; H-P., 33.)

RICHARD FRANCIS JEWERS entered the Navy, in June, 1803, as A.B., on board the MATILDA hospital-ship at Woolwich, Lieut.-Commander Jas. James; and from July, 1804, until promoted to the rank of Lieutenant 5 July, 1809, served as Midshipman and Master's Mate in the CLEOPATRA 32, and MILAN 38, both commanded by Sir Robt. Laurie, CAMBRIAN 40, Capts. John Poo Beresford and Hon. Chas. Paget, and THESEUS 74, Capt. J. P. Beresford, on the North American and Home stations. He was in consequence in the CLEOPATRA when captured, 17 Feb. 1805, after a brilliant and self-sought action of nearly three hours, and a loss of 20 killed and 38 wounded, by *La Ville de Milan*, of 46 guns and 350 men, 10 of whom were slain; and also when retaken, a few days subsequently, by the LEANDER 50, Capt. John Talbot. While on the books of the THESEUS Mr. Jewers was severely wounded in the head and hands in a fire-ship in Lord Cochrane's attack upon the French shipping in Aix Roads in April, 1809.† He continued to serve with Capt. Beresford on the stations above named in the THESEUS and POICTIERS 74's, until Feb. 1814, and was present in the latter ship at the capture of four American vessels, carrying in all 55 guns, and at the retaking of the British brig-of-war FROLIC. The Lieutenant, who has since been on half-pay, is now one of the Naval Knights of Windsor.

The wound he received in 1809 was compensated by a grant from the Patriotic Society.

JOACHIM. (LIEUT., 1815. F-P., 33; H-P., 10.)

RICHARD JOACHIM had two brothers in the Naval service, who died in the West Indies in the early part of the late war.

This officer entered the Navy, 4 Aug. 1804, as Fst.-cl. Vol., on board the ARGO 44, Capt. Geo. Parker, under whom (with the exception of about 12 months passed in 1811-12 on board the DRAGON 74, bearing the flag of Sir Fras. Laforey in the West Indies) he continued to serve, as Midshipman and Master's Mate, in the STATELY 64, and ABOUKIR and BOMBAY 74's, on the North Sea, Baltic, and Mediterranean stations, until June, 1814. When in the STATELY, in company with the NASSAU 64, we find him assisting at the capture, after an obstinate running fight, and a loss to the former of 4 men killed and 28 wounded, of the Danish 74-gun ship *Prindts Christian Frederic*, off the coast of Zealand, 22 March, 1808. He remained in the BOMBAY with Capt. John Bazely until promoted to the rank of Lieutenant 7 Feb. 1815, an event that took place rather more than three years after he had passed his examination. He joined the Coast Blockade, as Supernumerary-Lieutenant of the HYPERION 42, Capt. Wm. Jas. Mingaye, 14 Nov. 1825, and since

* *Vide Gaz.* 1805, p. 1484. † *V. Gaz.* 1809, p. 539.

its abolition in March, 1831, has been employed in the Coast Guard.

Lieut. Joachim married, 23 Aug. 1832, Elizabeth, daughter of Thos. Beard, Esq.

JOHNSON. (Lieutenant, 1840.)

Charles Richardson Johnson entered the Navy 27 Oct. 1826; passed his examination in 1834; obtained his commission 19 Feb. 1840; and on 6 of the following March joined the Princess Charlotte 104, bearing the flag of Hon. Sir Robt. Stopford, to whom he officiated as Flag-Lieutenant for a few months at the commencement of 1841. During the operations on the coast of Syria he commanded the boats in the attack upon Gebail,* served a good deal on shore, assisted at the bombardment of St. Jean d'Acre, and, subsequently to the fall of that city, was contused by the explosion of a magazine. His appointments have since been—11 May, 28 Aug., and 12 Nov. 1841, to the Ganges 84, Powerful 84, and Rodney 92, Capts. Barrington Reynolds, Geo. Mansel, and Robt. Maunsell, all in the Mediterranean —17 Oct. 1842, to the Cambridge 78, Capt. Edw. Barnard, with whom he returned to England—23 Feb. 1843, to the Coast Guard—3 Sept. 1844, as First-Lieutenant, to the Eclair steam-sloop, Capt. Walter Grimston Bucknall Estcourt, fitting for the coast of Africa—25 Jan. 1845, to the Ardent, another steamer, on the same station—21 Nov. 1845, to the Trafalgar 120, Capt. John Neale Nott, attached to the Channel squadron—and, 29 June, 1846, to the command of the Comet steamer, of 80-horse power, in which he is now employed on particular service.

He married, at Malta, 17 Oct. 1842, Julia, daughter of Major-General Bredin, of the Royal Artillery, by whom he has issue.

JOHNSON. (Commander, 1814. f-p., 19; h-p., 34.)

Edward Johnson was born, 12 Oct. 1777, at Larne, co. Antrim.

This officer entered the Navy, 1 Jan. 1794, as A.B., on board the Boyne 98, Capt. Geo. Grey, bearing the flag of Sir John Jervis in the West Indies. During the operations connected with the ensuing reduction of Martinique he was successively employed in erecting batteries on shore previously to the bombardment of Fort Bourbon—in a gun-boat under Lieut. T. Sparks at the bombardment of Fort Royal—and in personal command of a boat at the gallant cutting-out of the 28-gun frigate *Bienvenue*, the storming of Fort Royal, the debarkation of the troops at St. Pierre, and at the bringing out thence of the *Avengeur* sloop. On being transferred to the latter vessel, and placed under the command of Capt. Edw. Griffith, we find him affording assistance, as Midshipman, to the capture of Guadeloupe and Ste. Lucie. He came home with Capt. Griffith in the course of the same year in the Undaunted frigate, and was next, until promoted to the rank of Lieutenant, 4 April, 1801, employed on the North Sea, Mediterranean, and Baltic stations, in the Asia 64, bearing the flag of Rear-Admiral Thos. Pringle, Edgar 74, Capts. John M'Dougall and Edw. Buller, and San Josef 110, and St. George 98, flag-ships of Lord Nelson, under whom he served as a volunteer on board the Elephant 74, in the action off Copenhagen. He then joined the Dart 20, Capts. John Ferris Devonshire and Wm. Bolton, with whom, it appears, he further served on the Home station until Sept. 1802. In Aug. 1805, after he had been for two years attached to the Sea Fencible service in Ireland, Lieut. Johnson obtained an appointment to the London 98, Capts. Sir Robt. Barlow, Robt. Rolles, Sir Harry Burrard Neale, and Edw. Oliver Osborn, under the third-named of whom he assisted, in company with the Amazon 38, at the capture, 13 March, 1806, of the French 80-gun ship *Marengo*, bearing the flag of Rear-Admiral Linois, and 40-gun frigate *Belle Poule*, after a long running fight, in which the London sustained a loss of 10 men killed and 22 wounded. On 11 of the following June he assumed command of the Magpie 8, in which vessel he continued until driven on shore, 19 Feb. 1807, during a violent gale, on the coast of France, where himself and the whole of his crew were made prisoners-of-war. Being honourably acquitted on his return from captivity, in 1814, of all blame in the disaster, he was in consequence promoted to the rank of Commander by commission dated 27 Aug. in that year; but he has not been since able to procure employment.

He married, in Aug. 1803, Sarah, second daughter of Hugh Mountford, Esq., of Belfast, co. Antrim, by whom, who died in 1823, he had issue two sons and four daughters, now living. Agents—Messrs. Ommanney.

* *Vide* Gaz. 1840, p 2253.

JOHNSON, F.R.S. (Captain, 1838. f-p., 13; h-p., 27.)

Edward John Johnson is youngest son of the late Rev. Henry Johnson, of Bywell, Northumberland.

This officer entered the Navy, 1 May, 1807, as Fst-cl. Vol., on board the Nassau 64, Capt. Robt. Campbell. In that ship he attended the ensuing expedition to Copenhagen, and (on her subsequent extrication from a mass of ice in which she had been blocked up during the whole winter) was present, 22 March, 1808, in company with the Stately 64, at the capture and destruction, on the coast of Zealand, of the Danish 74 *Prindts Christian Frederic*, after a running fight of great length and obstinacy, in which the Nassau sustained a loss of 2 men killed and 16 (including himself slightly) wounded.* The latter vessel being paid off in Nov. 1809, he was next, until June, 1815, employed, as Midshipman and Acting-Lieutenant, in the Solebay 32, Capt. Hon. Granville Leveson Proby, Malacca 36, Capt. Wm. Butterfield, Ethalion 36, Capt. Edm. Heywood, Endymion 44, Capt. Henry Hope, St. Domingo, Asia, and Tonnant, flag-ships of Sir John Borlase Warren and Sir Alex. Cochrane, and Dragon 74, Capt. Robt. Barrie, on the Home, Baltic, and North American stations. While in the Ethalion, Mr. Johnson served in various cutting-out affairs, and on more than one occasion was sent into port as prize-master; and, when in the Tonnant, we find him co-operating on shore in the attacks upon Washington and Baltimore, and employed in the boats during the expedition against New Orleans. Being presented, on leaving the Dragon as above, with a commission dated 28 Feb. 1815, he obtained, 16 May, 1818, an appointment to the Shamrock surveying-vessel, Capt. Martin White, with whom he did duty in the Channel and off the coast of Ireland until Feb. 1820. On 4 March, 1829, shortly after he had joined the William and Mary yacht, Commodore Sir John Chambers White, he was promoted to the command of the Britomart 10, in which vessel he remained, chiefly on the Lisbon station, until paid off in 1831. He was then ordered by the Admiralty to complete the survey of the Faeröe Islands—a service he had commenced at his own expense when last on half-pay. His advancement to the rank he now holds took place 27 Dec. 1838.

Capt. Johnson, in Oct. 1835, was appointed by the Admiralty to conduct certain magnetic experiments on iron steam-vessels in the river Shannon;† and on 10 May, 1836, he was elected a Fellow of the Royal Society. He was nominated a member of the Magnetic Compass Committee of the Admiralty in 1838; and invested, 14 March, 1842, with the superintendence, which he still retains, of the Compass department of the Royal Navy. Agent—Fred. Dufaur.

JOHNSON. (Commander, 1846.)

George Johnson entered the Navy, 13 Sept. 1824; passed his examination in 1831; was pro-

* *Vide* Gaz. 1808, p. 536.

† He is the author of a paper on the above subject, published in the Philosophical Transactions of the Royal Society; and of articles in other scientific journals.

moted to the rank of Lieutenant, as a reward for his services on the coast of Syria, 4 Nov. 1840; became attached, a few weeks afterwards, to the PRINCESS CHARLOTTE 104, flag-ship in the Mediterranean of Hon. Sir Robt. Stopford; served on the East India station from 17 Sept. 1841 until his return home in 1846, chiefly as First-Lieutenant, in the NORTH STAR 26, Capt. Sir Jas. Everard Home; and on 9 Nov. in the latter year was advanced to his present rank. He is now on half-pay.

Commander Johnson married, 5 Aug. 1841, Georgiana Margaretta, daughter of Vice-Admiral Chas. Carter, but has been a widower since 6 Feb. 1842.

JOHNSON. (LIEUT., 1841. F-P., 13; H-P., 7.)
GEORGE CHARLES JEFFERYES JOHNSON was born 26 March, 1814.

This officer entered the Royal Naval College 6 Sept. 1827, and embarked, 27 June, 1829, as Fst.-cl. Vol., on board the PHILOMEL 10, Capts. Chas. Graham, Hugh Berners, and Wm. Smith, attached to the force in the Mediterranean, where he remained until the summer of 1833. In May, 1834, eight months after he had passed his examination, he returned to the latter station, as Mate, in the PORTLAND 52, Capt. David Price, under whom he served for a period of exactly four years. Joining next, in March, 1839, the IMPLACABLE 74, Capt. Edw. Harvey, he bore a part in that ship in the operations on the coast of Syria in 1840; in Dec. of which year he removed to the THUNDERER 84, Capts. Maurice Fred. Fitzhardinge Berkeley and Daniel Pring. He continued in the Mediterranean until promoted to the rank of Lieutenant 23 Nov. 1841; and has since been on half-pay. AGENT—J. Chippendale.

JOHNSON. (LIEUT., 1809. F-P., 15; H-P., 34.)
GEORGE CHILD JOHNSON entered the Navy, 28 June, 1798, as L. M., on board the NORTHUMBERLAND 74, Capt. Geo. Martin, under whom he witnessed the capture, 18 Feb. 1800, of the French 74-gun ship *Le Généreux*, served at the blockade and surrender of Malta, and attended the expedition of 1801 to Egypt. Between Sept. in the latter year and April, 1805, we find him officiating, still in the Mediterranean, as Midshipman and Master's Mate of the AGINCOURT 64, Capts. Geo. Fred. Ryves and Thos. Briggs; and afterwards joining the MEDIATOR 44, Capt. John Searle, DOLPHIN and NORTHUMBERLAND, flag-ships in the West Indies of Sir Alex. Cochrane, SEINE frigate, Capt. David Atkins, and ÆTNA bomb, Capt. Wm. Godfrey. While in the latter vessel, in which (after having officiated in her for 18 months as Sub and Acting Lieutenant) he was confirmed in his present rank 31 Jan. 1809, Mr. Johnson served under Lord Gambier at the bombardment of Copenhagen, and the destruction of the shipping in Basque Roads. He left the ÆTNA in June, 1809, and during the rest of the war was successively employed on the Mediterranean and Home stations in the AJAX 74, Capt. Robt. Waller Otway, RAVEN sloop, Capt. Geo. Gustavus Lennock, BRISTOL *armée-en-flûte*, Capt. Wm. Kent, ECHO sloop, Capt. Thos. Percival, CHRISTIAN VII. 80, Capt. Henry Lidgbird Ball, SALVADOR DEL MUNDO flag-ship of Vice-Admiral Wm. Domett, and NIOBE *armée-en-flûte*, Capt. Henry Colins Deacon. He has since been on half-pay.

JOHNSON. (LIEUT., 1815. F-P., 11; H-P., 31.)
JOHN JOHNSON entered the Navy, 12 Sept. 1805, as Third-cl. Vol., on board the SANTA MARGARITA 36, Capt. Wilson Rathborne, stationed in the Channel and off the coast of Ireland; and from Dec. 1807 until Nov. 1815 served as Midshipman and Master's Mate in the RANGER 18, Capt. Geo. Acklom, FLAMER gun-brig, Lieut.-Commanders John Cameron and Thos. Cowper Sherwin, and OBERON and DERWENT sloops, Capts. Geo. Manners Sutton and Thos. Williams, principally in the Downs, off the north coast of Spain, and at Newfoundland. He then took up a commission dated 25 Feb. 1815, and since 31 Dec. 1846 has been employed in the Coast Guard.

JOHNSON. (LIEUTENANT, 1844.)
JOHN ORMSBY JOHNSON entered the Navy 20 Sept. 1835; passed his examination 16 Nov. 1841; and while holding a Mateship in the BLONDE 42, Capt. Thos. Bourchier, was employed on shore in the operations against Tzekee in China, 15 and 16 March, 1842.* After further serving at Portsmouth and in the Mediterranean in the ST. VINCENT 120, flag-ship of Sir Chas. Rowley, and INCONSTANT 36, Capt. Chas. Howe Fremantle, he was presented with a Lieutenant's commission dated 28 June, 1844. He then became attached to the ILLUSTRIOUS 72, flag-ship of Sir Chas. Adam in North America and the West Indies; and from 16 Jan. 1845 until paid off in 1847 was employed on the same station in the HYACINTH 18, Capt. Fras. Scott.

JOHNSON. (CAPT., 1846. F-P., 16; H-P., 24.)
JOHN SAMUEL WILLES JOHNSON, born 3 July, 1793, at South Stoke, near Bath, is eldest son of the Rev. Chas. Johnson, Prebendary of Wells, Rector of South Stoke, and Vicar of South Brent and Berrow, co. Somerset, by Miss Willes, daughter of the late Archdeacon of Wells, and granddaughter of the late Bishop of Bath and Wells. He is nephew of the late Admiral Sir Davidge Gould, G.C.B.; and brother-in-law of the late Capt. Geo. Gosling, R.N.

This officer entered the Navy, 1 Feb. 1807, as Fst.-cl. Vol., on board the VESTAL 28, Capt. Edwards Lloyd Graham, in which ship he was employed for nearly two years on the Home and Newfoundland stations. In Nov. 1809, being then a Master's Mate, he was placed in charge of the *Fortitude*, a re-captured English merchantman, and sent, with the intelligence of the VESTAL having fallen in with an enemy's squadron, to Lisbon and Cadiz; on his passage whither, although without a gun on board, he succeeded by a bold *ruse-de-guerre* in inducing an enemy's armed vessel, by whom he must have been otherwise inevitably taken, to sheer off. After delivering his despatches to the flag-officer in the Tagus, Mr. Johnson proceeded to England, and on his arrival was received for three months on board the PORT MAHON sloop, Capt. Villiers Fras. Hatton. In Aug. 1810 he rejoined Capt. Graham in the PALLAS 32, then on the eve of her departure for the coast of Norway, where, it appears, he assisted at the capture of four Danish privateers and of several sail of merchantmen, one of the former of which he was ordered to conduct to Leith roads. Accompanying the same Captain in succession into the SOUTHAMPTON 32, and ALCMÈNE 38, Mr. Johnson proceeded in the latter frigate to the Adriatic, where he bore a part in several boat affairs. On one of those occasions, 22 May, 1812, a Franco-Venetian trabacolo, of 4 guns and 30 men, was captured near the island of Lessina, after a sanguinary conflict in which most of the enemy's crew were killed and all the remainder wounded; while on the part of the British 4 were slain and 22 wounded, 1 of the former and 3 of the latter in the boat commanded by Mr. Johnson, whose conduct was officially mentioned in the highest terms of commendation. On leaving the ALCMÈNE in Dec. 1813, he joined the PYLADES sloop, Capt. James Wemyss, from which vessel, on the occasion of the surrender of Genoa, 18 April, 1814, he was transferred, as Acting-Lieutenant, to the CALEDONIA 120, bearing the flag of the late Lord Exmouth—an appointment sanctioned by the Admiralty on 18 of the ensuing month. He went on half-pay in Sept. 1814, but, being again placed, in April, 1815, under the orders of the same nobleman, continued to serve with him, in the BOYNE 98, and QUEEN CHARLOTTE 100, until Oct. 1816—visiting, in the former ship, Naples, Marseilles, and the Barbary States; and participating, in the QUEEN CHARLOTTE, in the battle of Algiers. After an

* *Vide* Gaz. 1842, p. 2391.

interval of half-pay he was nominated, 13 Sept. 1817, Flag-Lieutenant to his Lordship in the IMPREGNABLE 104, at Plymouth, where he remained until promoted to the rank of Commander 6 Feb. 1821. His subsequent appointments were—22 Sept. 1835, to the Coast Guard, in which he continued for a period of nearly three years—and 16 Dec. 1841, to the command of the WOLVERENE 16, fitting for China, where he arrived in time to witness some of the closing operations of the war. Capt. Johnson, who was superseded in the latter vessel in Aug. 1842, and has not been since employed, acquired his present rank 9 Nov. 1846.

In 1827 the Captain published 'A Journal of a Tour through parts of France, Italy, and Switzerland, in the years 1823-4.' He married, 14 May, 1821, Eliza, only daughter of John De Windt, Esq., of the Island of Ste. Croix, and of Gloucester Place, London, by whom he has issue. AGENT — J. Hinxman.

JOHNSON. (LIEUT., 1810. F-P., 11; H-P., 35.)

WILLIAM JOHNSON entered the Navy, in Jan. 1801, as Fst.-cl. Vol., on board the ACHILLE 74, Capts. Geo. Murray and Edw Buller, stationed in the Channel, where he served as Midshipman until April, 1802. Re-embarking, in July, 1803, on board the CERBERUS 32, Capt. Wm. Selby, he served in that frigate at the ensuing bombardment of Granville, and was present in her as Master's Mate at the reduction of the islands of Marie-galante and Désirade, in March, 1808. In the course of the latter year he successively joined the CHEROKEE 10, Capt. Rich. Arthur, and VENERABLE 74, flag-ship of Sir Rich. John Strachan, both on the Home station; and on 10 May, 1809, he became Acting-Lieutenant of the BLAKE 74, Capt. Edw. Codrington. While in that ship, to which he was confirmed by commission dated 4 May, 1810, he accompanied the expedition to Flushing, assisted at the defence of Cadiz, and was much employed in co-operation with the patriots on the coast of Spain, particularly at Tarragona. He has been on half-pay since April, 1813.

JOHNSON. (LIEUTENANT, 1842.)

WILLIAM PONSONBY JOHNSON passed his examination 22 Aug. 1837; served during the operations on the coast of China in the BLENHEIM 72, Capts. Sir Humphrey Fleming Senhouse and Sir Thos. Herbert, and CORNWALLIS 72, flag-ship of Sir Wm. Parker; was in consequence promoted to the rank of Lieutenant 23 Dec. 1842;* and officiated in that capacity, from 11 Dec. 1844 until the early part of 1847, in the EAGLE 50, Capt. Geo. Bohun Martin, on the American station.

JOHNSON. (CAPTAIN, 1841. F-P., 25; H-P., 19.)

WILLIAM WARD PERCIVAL JOHNSON entered the Navy, 2 July, 1803, as a Supernumerary, on board the PRÉVOYANT store-ship, Master-Commander Brown, in which he took a passage to the Mediterranean for the purpose of joining the VICTORY 100, Capt. Sam. Sutton, bearing the flag of Lord Nelson, with whom he served until transferred as Midshipman, in Aug. 1804, to the CHILDERS sloop, Capt. Sir Wm. Bolton. With the latter officer he continued employed off Gibraltar, and on the Channel and Cork stations, in the GUERRIER, EURYDICE, and DRUID frigates, until promoted to the rank of Lieutenant, 18 Oct. 1809. Joining, soon afterwards, the CURAÇOA 36, Capt. John Tower, he proceeded in that frigate to the Cape of Good Hope, and then again to the Mediterranean, where he co-operated with the patriots on the coast of Catalonia, and assisted at the capture of the *Marsouin* and *Vénus* privateers, each mounting 14 guns, and carrying in the whole 127 men. In Aug. 1812, being at the time in charge of a prize, he had the misfortune to be made prisoner by the French, who detained him in captivity until the peace. His succeeding appointments were—16 Aug. 1814, to the POMPÉE 74, Capt. Sir Jas. Athol Wood, fitting for the Mediterranean, whence he returned in Nov. 1815—25 June, 1828, to the Coast Blockade, as Supernumerary-Lieutenant of the RAMILLIES 74, Capt. Hugh Pigot—28 July, 1830, as First, to the TALAVERA 74, Capts. David Colby and Thos. Brown, employed on particular service—and 26 Dec. 1831, in a similar capacity, to the MELVILLE 74, bearing the flag in the East Indies of Sir John Gore. On 19 Sept. 1835, about three months after the latter ship had been paid off, Lieut. Johnson was advanced to the rank of Commander. He obtained an appointment, 20 Feb. 1836, in the Coast Guard, from which service, on 18 March, 1839, he was removed to the Second-Captaincy of the WINCHESTER 50, flag ship of Sir Thos. Harvey, on the North America and West India station. He was superseded on the occasion of his elevation to the rank he now holds, 14 Dec. 1841, and has since been on half-pay.

Capt. Johnson married, in 1830, Elizabeth, eldest daughter of the late Rear-Admiral Thos. Harvey, C.B. AGENTS—Messrs. Halford and Co.

JOHNSTON. (COMMANDER, 1844. F-P., 31; H-P., 13.)

CHARLES ALEXANDER JOHNSTON is son of Lieut. Chas. Johnston, R.N., who died in 1804.

This officer entered the Navy, 18 Aug. 1803, as Sec.-cl. Vol., on board the TRIBUNE 36, Capts. Geo. Henry Towry and Rich. Henry Alex. Bennett, in which ship he assisted at the capture and destruction of several of the enemy's vessels, came frequently into contact with the Cherbourg batteries while employed in blockading the *Minerve* frigate in that port, and contributed at the commencement of the war with Spain to the capture of four ships laden with specie and colonial produce. Becoming Midshipman, in Sept. 1805, of the AGAMEMNON 64, Capts. Sir Edw. Berry and Jonas Rose, he had an opportunity of sharing in the battles fought off Cape Trafalgar and St. Domingo, of witnessing the capture of a national corvette (*La Lutine*) and two schooners, and (independently of a participation in various particular services) of attending the expedition to Copenhagen. On arriving with the Danish prizes at Spithead, Mr. Johnston was under the necessity of entering Haslar Hospital, in consequence of a severe injury he had received in the foot. On 20 June, 1809, having rejoined the AGAMEMNON, he had the misfortune to be wrecked in the Rio de la Plata; whereupon he was received on board the FOUDROYANT 80, flag-ship of Hon. Michael De Courcy, who retained him under his orders on the South American station until Nov. 1812. The next three years were passed by Mr. Johnston in the Baltic, West Indies, Channel, and Mediterranean, on board the VIGO 74, bearing the flag of Rear-Admiral Jas. Nicoll Morris, BENBOW 74, Capt. Rich. Harrison Pearson, SNAP 12, Capt Geo. King, and POMPÉE 74, Capt. Sir Jas. Athol Wood. On his passage to the West Indies in the BENBOW he was placed in charge of an American prize, and sent with her to Barbadoes. In Sept. 1815 he was promoted to the rank of Lieutenant by commission ante-dated to 8 Feb. in the same year; but he did not again procure employment until 8 Feb. 1825, when he joined the Coast Blockade, a service to which he continued attached, as Supernumerary-Lieutenant of the RAMILLIES and TALAVERA 74's, Capts. Wm. M'Culloch, Hugh Pigot, and David Colby, until transferred to the Coast Guard, 18 April, 1831. He twice during that period elicited the special approbation of the Lords of the Admiralty and of H. R. H. the Lord High Admiral—the first time, for the singularly gallant manner in which, with only 3 seamen, he compelled a gang of 150 armed smugglers to retreat, leaving behind them 1 of their number a prisoner, whose apprehension led to the complete suppression of the rest; and the second, for his successful intrepidity in capturing, in a small galley, with not more than 4 hands, in spite of a desperate resistance, the French lugger *La Jeune Rosalie*, of 13 men, and two tub-

* *Vide* Gaz. 1848 p. 2951.

boats. These exploits indeed were so highly estimated both by Capt. Pigot and by the Commander-in-Chief, Sir John Poo Beresford, that they each recommended him for promotion. This, however, did not take place until 5 Jan. 1844, when, after having been employed in the Coast Guard for a further period of nearly thirteen years, and been instrumental to the seizure of 50 vessels and boats, with their crews, he was at length invested with the rank of Commander. He has since been on half-pay.

JOHNSTON. (Rear-Admiral of the White, 1841. f-p., 23; h-p., 37.)

Charles James Johnston entered the Navy, about 1787, as Captain's Servant, on board the Savage sloop, Capts. Rich. R. Burgess and Dickinson, with whom he served on the Greenock station until transferred, as Midshipman, in 1790, to the Formidable 98. In the course of the same year he removed to the Scorpion sloop, Capt. Benj. Hallowell, and, after an attachment of two years to that vessel on the African and West India stations, he successively joined the Syren frigate, Stately 64, and Excellent 74, the two latter bearing the flag of Sir Rich. King and Hon. Wm. Cornwallis at Newfoundland and in the Channel. In the latter ship he continued until promoted to the rank of Lieutenant, 26 Feb. 1795; four months subsequently to which period we find him appointed to the Ruby 64, Capt. Hon. Henry Edwin Stanhope, part of the force employed at the ensuing reduction of the Cape of Good Hope. Exchanging, after that event, into the Arrogant 74, Capts. Rich. Lucas and Edw. Oliver Osborn, Lieut. Johnston witnessed the surrender of Columbo 15 Feb. 1796; and, on 9 of the following Sept., when off the coast of Sumatra, participated, in company with the Victorious 74, in a long conflict of nearly four hours with six heavy French frigates under M. Sercey, which terminated in the separation of the combatants, after each had been well crippled, and the Arrogant occasioned a loss of 7 men killed and 27 wounded. In July, 1800, our officer, who had for a long time discharged the duties of First-Lieutenant of the latter ship, and had assisted at the capture and destruction of many armed vessels and valuable merchantmen, off Batavia, and in other parts of the Java seas, joined the Suffolk 74, bearing the flag of Sir Edw. Pellew, who (besides intrusting him with the government, for a short time in 1802, of the Naval Hospital at Madras) successively appointed him to the command, between May, 1801, and June, 1805, of the Dædalus frigate, Vulcan bomb, Victor sloop, Trident 64, Dédaigneuse frigate, and Cornwallis 50. His official promotion to the rank of Commander took place while he was serving on board the Victor, 18 Jan. 1803; and to that of Captain while in the Cornwallis, 5 Sept. 1806. In the course of the latter year Capt. Johnston appears to have several times engaged the enemy's formidable batteries on the Isle of France; and on 11 Nov. he made a dash with Capt. Bingham, of the Sceptre 74, into St. Paul's Bay, Ile de Bourbon, and opened a fire upon the shipping there at anchor, consisting of the *Sémillante* French frigate, three armed ships, and 12 sail of merchantmen which had been captured from the British. Had it not been that the breeze soon subsided and impeded the manœuvres of their assailants, the enemy on this occasion would in all probability have incurred great loss. The Cornwallis was afterwards, in 1807, the first regular man-of-war that ever, we believe, passed between New Holland and Van Diemen's Land. Capt. Johnston's next and last appointments were, 18 Feb. 1808, and 23 Dec. 1813, to the Powerful and Scarborough 74's; the former of which ships, after having brought her home from India, and then accompanied the expedition to the Walcheren, he paid off 11 Oct. 1809. In the Scarborough, bearing the flag of Rear-Admiral Ferrier in the North Sea, he served until 5 May, 1814. His advancement to Flag-rank took place 23 Nov. 1841.

The Rear-Admiral is married, and has issue.

JOHNSTON. (Commander, 1846.)

Frederick Erskine Johnston is second son of the Right Hon. Sir Alex. Johnston, F.R.S., of Carnsalloch, co. Dumfries (late Chief Justice and President of Her Majesty's Council in the island of Ceylon), by Louisa, only daughter of the late Lord Wm. Campbell, Captain R.N., son of John, fourth Duke of Argyll. The Commander is nephew of Major-General Fras. Jas. Johnston, C.B.; and great-grandson of Francis Lord Napier.

This officer entered the Navy 4 Sept. 1828; passed his examination in 1834; obtained his first commission 28 June, 1838; and was successively appointed —25 July, 1838, and 6 Jan. 1841, to the Tyne 26, Capt. John Townshend, and (as Flag-Lieutenant to Sir Chas Napier) to the Powerful 84, both in the Mediterranean—28 Aug. 1841, to the Formidable 84, Capt. Sir Edw. Thos. Troubridge, fitting at Sheerness—2 Oct. 1841, and 23 April, 1844, to the Queen 110, and again to the Formidable, bearing each the flag of Sir Edw. W. C. R. Owen on the Mediterranean station—and, 18 Dec. 1845, as Senior, to the Terrible steam-frigate, Capt. Wm. Ramsay, attached to the Channel squadron. He attained his present rank 9 Nov. 1846; and has since been on half-pay.

JOHNSTON. (Lieutenant, 1841.)

Gabriel Johnston entered the Navy 12 Aug. 1826; passed his examination 1 Oct. 1832; and at the period of his promotion to the rank of Lieutenant, which took place 23 Nov. 1841, was serving at the Cape of Good Hope, as Mate, on board the Fawn brigantine, Lieut.-Commander John Foote. His appointments have since been—3 Dec. 1841, to the Southampton 50, flag-ship of Sir Edw. Durnford King on the same station—7 March, 1842, to the Acorn 16, Capt. John Adams, on the coast of Africa, whence he returned early in 1843—19 April, 1844, to the Stromboli steam-sloop, Capt. Hon. Edw. Plunkett, employed on particular service—25 Jan. 1845, to the Beacon surveying-vessel, Capt. Thos. Graves, stationed in the Mediterranean—and, 20 Feb. 1847, after a few months of half-pay, to the Volage 26, Lieut.-Commander Thos. Abel Bremage Spratt, under whom he is again engaged on surveying-duty. Agents—Messrs. Stilwell.

JOHNSTON. (Lieut., 1826. f-p., 20; h-p., 18.)

Henry Johnston, born 2 Dec. 1795, is second son of the late Henry Johnston, Esq., merchant, by his wife Henrietta Ogilvie, of Dundee, N.B.

This officer entered the Navy, 18 Feb. 1809, as Fst.-cl. Vol., on board the Nightingale 16, Capts. Wm. Wilkinson, John Eveleigh, and Christopher Nixon, stationed in the North Sea, where, and in the Baltic, he served, as Midshipman, from 1812 to 1814, in the Gloucester 74, Capt. Robt. Williams. Towards the close of the latter year, after he had been again employed for a few months under the orders of Capt. Wilkinson, in the Monmouth 64, on the Downs station, he joined the Tyne 24, Capt. John Harper, with whom, on arriving in the East Indies, he removed, as a passed Midshipman, to the Wellesley 74. Returning to England with Capt. John Bayley in the last-named ship in June, 1816, Mr. Johnston was immediately appointed Admiralty-Midshipman of the Leander 50, Capt. Edw. Chetham, and was thus afforded an opportunity of sharing in the bombardment of Algiers. He was afterwards employed, from April, 1817, until promoted to the rank of Lieutenant 27 March, 1826, in the Pactolus and Tigris frigates, commanded, on the North American and Channel stations, by Capts. Wm. Hugh Dobbie and Robt Henderson, Ramillies 74, and Queen Charlotte 100, both lying in Portsmouth harbour, and Severn and Ramillies again, each commanded, for the purposes of the Coast Blockade, by Capt. Wm. M'Culloch. His succeeding appointments were—9 Oct. 1828, to the Hyperion 42, Capt. Wm. Jas. Mingaye, under whom he served, once more on the Coast Blockade, until Dec. 1829—for a few months in 1834, as Supernumerary and First-Lieutenant, to the THALIA 46, and RALEIGH 16, Capts. Robt. Wauchope and Mich. Quin, fitting at Chatham and Sheerness—and, 9 May, 1837, to the TÉMÉRAIRE 104, Capts. Thos. Fortescue Kennedy and Sir John Hill, guard-ship at the latter place. He has been on half-pay since 1838.

Lieut. Johnston married, in 1835, Louisa Drusilla Sidney, youngest daughter of the late Jas. Cummings, Esq., R.N.

JOHNSTON. (LIEUT., 1827. F-P., 17; H-P, 13.)

JAMES CHARLES JOHNSTON, born in Nov. 1803, is maternal grandson of the late Sir Geo. Richardson, Bart.

This officer entered the Navy, in Oct. 1817, as Fst.-cl. Vol., on board the SEMIRAMIS 42, bearing the broad pendant of Sir Jas. Lucas Yeo on the coast of Africa; was next employed, between Oct. 1818 and March, 1825 (in the course of which month he passed his examination), in the VENGEUR 74, Capt. Fred. Lewis Maitland, and AURORA 46, Capt. Henry Prescott, chiefly as Midshipman, on the Home, Mediterranean, and South American stations; and, in Nov. of the latter year, became Mate of the PHILOMEL 10, Capts. Lord Wm. Paget and Viscount Ingestrie, similarly employed. He was promoted for his services in the ASIA 84, flag-ship of Sir Edw. Codrington, to the rank of Lieutenant, by commission dated 22 Oct. 1827; and was subsequently appointed—11 May, 1833, to the DONEGAL 78, Capt. Arthur Fanshawe, off Lisbon—24 Feb. 1835 (after several months of half-pay), to the WINCHESTER 52, flag-ship in the East Indies of Hon. Sir Thos. Bladen Capel—20 Oct. 1836, to the HERCULES 74, Capts. Maurice Fred. Fitzhardinge Berkeley, John Toup Nicolas, and Edw. Barnard, employed until Nov. 1839 on the Channel, Lisbon, West India, and Halifax stations—10 Oct. 1840, to the CAMPERDOWN 104, flag-ship of Sir Henry Digby at the Nore—11 Sept. 1841, as First, to the THALIA 42, Capt. Chas. Hope, fitting for Chatham—and, 13 Dec. following, to the WARSPITE 50, Capt. Lord John Hay. He invalided home from the North America and West India station in June, 1842, and has since been on half-pay.

Lieut. Johnston married, 25 April, 1843, Jane Dunlop, daughter of the late Capt. Thos. Hamilton, of Dowan, and granddaughter of the late Sir Geo. Louis Augustus Colquhoun, Bart. AGENTS—Messrs. Halford and Co.

JOHNSTON. (LIEUT., 1815. F-P., 12; H-P., 32.)

JAMES HENRY JOHNSTON entered the Navy, 16 April, 1803, as Fst.-cl. Vol., on board the SPARTIATE 74, Capts. Geo. Murray, John Manley, and Sir Fras. Laforey. In that ship, after serving, as Midshipman and Master's Mate, off Ferrol and Rochefort, he proceeded to the Mediterranean, and on 21 Oct. 1805 was present in the battle of Trafalgar. He removed, in Oct. 1809, to the OCEAN 98, bearing the flag of Lord Collingwood, who, on 4 of the next Dec., nominated him Lieutenant of the CANOPUS 80, flag-ship of Rear-Admiral Geo. Martin—an act which the Admiralty confirmed by commission dated 16 Feb. 1810. Being superseded from the CANOPUS in Nov. of the latter year, Mr. Johnston was subsequently appointed—23 Sept. 1811, to the KITE sloop, Capts Benj. Crispin and Geo. Canning, employed off the Texel and in the Mediterranean—in Jan. 1813, to the command of the QUAIL schooner, stationed in the Archipelago under the orders of Capt. John Clavell—in Aug. 1813, again to the KITE, Capts. Rowland Mainwaring and Thos. Forster, off the coast of Syria—and, 3 Dec. 1814, to the LEVERET 10, Capt. Jonathan Christian, in the Downs. He has been on half-pay since July, 1815.

JOHNSTON. (LIEUT., 1815. F-P., 9; H-P., 31.)

ROBERT JOHNSTON entered the Navy, 21 Feb. 1807, as Fst.-cl. Vol., on board the MALABAR 74, Capt. John Temple; attained the rating of Midshipman in Nov. of the same year; and, between June, 1808, when he returned home from a voyage to the Brazils and the Cape of Good Hope, and July, 1814, was successively employed, in the INVINCIBLE 74, Capt. Ross Donnelly, SEMIRAMIS 36, Capt. Wm. Granger, NORGE 74, Capts. John Sprat Rainier and Wm. Waller, and ASIA 74, flag-ship of Sir Alex. Cochrane, on the Home, Lisbon, Cadiz, Mediterranean, and Bermuda stations. He then assumed command, with the rank of Sub-Lieutenant, of the JANE advice-vessel, in which he served, on the American coast and in the West Indies, until the close of the war with the United States. He was promoted to his present rank in his former ship, the ASIA, Capt. Alex. Skene, 15 Feb. 1815; and in Feb. 1816, after having re-visited the Mediterranean and West Indies, was placed on half-pay. He has not been since employed. AGENT—Fred. Dufaur.

JOHNSTONE. (LIEUTENANT, 1818. F-P., 10; H-P., 26.)

HENRY HOPE JOHNSTONE entered the Navy, 24 June, 1811, as Fst.-cl. Vol., on board the RIFLEMAN 18, Capt. Joseph Pearce, and, after serving for some time on the Home station, proceeded to the coast of North America, where he was present with the squadron in Penobscot Bay at the capture of the town of Castine and the destruction of the U. S. frigate *John Adams*, in Sept. 1814. Becoming Midshipman, soon afterwards, of the ROYAL OAK 74, flag-ship of Sir Pulteney Malcolm, he attended in that ship the ill-fated expedition against New Orleans; and, on her return to England in the summer of 1815, he became attached, as a Supernumerary, to the PRINCE 98, Capt. Edm. Boger, lying at Spithead. In July, 1818, after he had been employed for a period of more than two years and a half in the North Sea and West Indies, in the PELICAN 18, Capts. Robt. Lisle Coulson and Edw. Curzon, he was nominated Acting-Lieutenant of the PIQUE 36, Capt. John Mackellar, to which frigate he was confirmed on 20 of the following Nov. He was paid off 21 Dec. 1818; and was lastly, from 6 Dec. 1824 until about the close of 1826, employed in the RAMILLIES 74, Coast Blockade ship, Capts. Wm. M'Culloch and Hugh Pigot.

Lieut. Johnstone is married, and has issue.

JOHNSTONE. (COMMANDER, 1841. F-P., 13; H-P., 10.)

HENRY WEDDERBURN JOHNSTONE entered the Navy 29 June, 1824; passed his examination in 1830; obtained his first commission 18 Aug. 1831; and was subsequently appointed—23 Jan. and 8 May, 1833, to the DONEGAL 78, and BRITANNIA 120, flag-ships of Sir Pulteney Malcolm in the Mediterranean—16 July, 1834, to the ENDYMION 50, Capt. Sir Sam. Roberts, with whom he returned home from Lisbon and was paid off in Nov. 1836—30 Jan. 1837, to the EXCELLENT gunnery-ship at Portsmouth, Capt. Thos. Hastings—7 Dec. 1837, as Senior-Lieutenant, to the RACEHORSE 18, Capt. Henry Wm. Craufurd, fitting for the North America and West India station, where he was superseded a few months afterwards—and, 9 Aug. 1841, in a similar capacity, to the ARDENT steam-vessel, Capt. John Russell, lying at Chatham. He was advanced to his present rank on 23 of the following Nov., but has not been since afloat.

JOHNSTONE. (LIEUTENANT, 1814. F-P., 7; H-P., 32.)

ROBERT BALLARD JOHNSTONE entered the Navy, in April, 1808, as Fst.-cl. Vol., on board the RESISTANCE 38, Capt. Chas. Adam, with whom he continued to serve, in the same ship and, as Midshipman and Master's Mate, in the INVINCIBLE 74, Capt. Chas. Adam, until Jan. 1814—witnessing, in the former, the capture, 13 March, 1806, of the *Marengo* 80, bearing the flag of Rear-Admiral Linois, and 40-gun frigate *Belle Poule;* and assisting, in the INVINCIBLE (independently of a participation in many particular services), at the defence of Tarragona, the destruction of the castle of St. Elmo, and the capture of the fort of St. Philippe, in the Col de Balaguer. He then joined in succession the QUEEN CHARLOTTE and IMPREGNABLE, flag-ships of Lord Keith and the Duke of Clarence; and, on 27 June, 1814, after having escorted the Allied Sovereigns to England, and taken part in the grand naval review held at Spithead, was promoted to the rank of Lieutenant. During the latter part of 1814, and again for some months in 1815, we find him employed, on the Downs and Irish stations, in the BERMUDA 10, Capt. Wm. Wolrige, and NYMPHEN 36, Capt. Matt. Smith. Being next, in July, 1816, appointed to the SUPERB 74, Capt. Chas. Ekins, he sailed with the expedition against Algiers, where, on the day of the bombardment, he commanded gun-boat No. 24. He soon afterwards returned to England with Lord Exmouth in the QUEEN CHARLOTTE 100, and has since been on half-pay.

JOHNSTONE. (COMMANDER, 1841. F-P., 22; H-P., 14.)

WILLIAM JOHNSTONE was born in 1795, at Edinburgh.

This officer entered the Navy, 5 Nov. 1811, as Ordinary, on board the NIGHTINGALE 16, Capt. Christopher Nixon, in which vessel he served in the North Sea and Channel, latterly as Midshipman, until Aug. 1815. He was next, between Nov. 1815 and Sept. 1818, employed in the NEWCASTLE 50, Capts. Sam. Roberts and Henry Meynell, fitting at Woolwich, and in the CYRUS 20, Capt. Wm. Fairbrother Carroll, on the coast of Ireland; after which (having passed his examination in March of the latter year) he served, from July, 1820, to Nov. 1823, part of the time as Admiralty-Midshipman, in the MARTIAL 10, Lieut.-Commander Robt. M'Kirdy, TEES 26, Capt. Thos Coe, and LIFFEY 50, Commodore Chas. Grant, on the Home and East India stations. He then officiated for about 18 months as Acting-Lieutenant and Lieutenant (commission dated 10 May, 1824) of the SATELLITE 18, and ASIA 84, both commanded by Capt. Mark John Currie, with whom he returned to England. His succeeding appointments were—24 Jan. 1827, to the ALERT 18, Capts. Sam. Burgess and John Coghlan Fitzgerald, on the South American station—13 Feb. 1832, as Senior, to the CONWAY 28, fitting for the Pacific, whence he returned home and was paid off in Oct. 1835—and, 18 Oct. 1838, in a similar capacity, to the GANGES 84, Capt. Barrington Reynolds. He served in the latter ship, on the Mediterranean station (where he was present at the blockade of Alexandria), until advanced to his present rank 23 Nov. 1841; and has not been since employed.

JOHNSTONE. (CAPTAIN, 1823.)

WILLIAM JAMES HOPE JOHNSTONE, born 28 July, 1798, is second son of the late Vice-Admiral the Right Hon. Sir Wm. Johnstone Hope,* G.C.B., M.P., Treasurer and Receiver-General of the Royal Hospital at Greenwich, by his first wife, Lady Anne Hope Johnstone, eldest daughter of James, third Earl of Hopetoun; and brother of the late Capts. Chas. Jas. Hope Johnstone and Geo. Jas. Hope Johnstone, both of the R.N. By his father's second marriage he is connected with the noble families of Athlone, Auckland, and Henley.

This officer entered the Navy, 20 June, 1811, as Sec.-cl. Vol., on board the SARPEDON brig, Capt. Jas. Green, on the Leith station, where he removed, in Sept following, to the ADAMANT 50, flag-ship of Vice-Admiral Wm. Albany Otway. Joining next, in April, 1812, the VENERABLE 74, Capt. Sir Home Popham, he assisted, in the course of that year, at the reduction of Lequeytio and Castro, on the north coast of Spain; also in the attacks made upon Puerta Galetta, Guetaria, and Santander; and at the destruction of the fortifications of Borneo, Plencia, Galea, Algorta, Begona, El Campillo las Quersas, and Xebiles. On his return to England in June, 1814, Mr. Hope Johnstone, after having escorted Earl Moira to India in the STIRLING CASTLE 74, Capt. Sir H. Popham, joined the LATONA 38, bearing his father's flag at Leith. During the three years immediately antecedent to his promotion to the rank of Lieutenant, which took place 2 May, 1818, we find him employed in the Channel, at Portsmouth, in the Mediterranean, and again at Leith, on board the ENDYMION 44, Capt. Henry Hope, TAGUS 38, Capt. Jas. Whitley Deans Dundas, SATELLITE sloop, Capt. Jas. Murray, and RAMILLIES, bearing the flag of his father. On 3 June, 1819, he obtained an appointment to the VENGEUR 74, Capt. Fred. Lewis Maitland, which ship, it appears, conveyed Lord Beresford from Rio de Janeiro to the river Tagus, and the King of the Two Sicilies from Naples to Leghorn, in 1820. Being presented on 9 Sept. in that year with a Commander's commission, which had been placed at the disposal of Sir Home Popham on his return from the chief command at Jamaica, Capt. Hope Johnstone, on 28 Feb. 1823, was invested with the command of the ECLAIR sloop, and ordered to South America, where, in the same vessel, and in the DORIS 42 (into which frigate he was posted 21 Oct. 1823), he was employed in affording protection to the British interests at Pernambuco, and on other parts of the Brazilian coast, frequently under very trying circumstances, until the close of 1824. He paid the DORIS off 12 Jan. 1825; and officiated, lastly, as Flag-Captain, from 6 June, 1828, until Oct. 1831, to Sir Pulteney Malcolm, in the ASIA 84, and BRITANNIA 120, on the Mediterranean station, and from 6 May, 1845, until 1847, to Sir Thos. John Cochrane, in the AGINCOURT 72, on the East India station. During an expedition conducted, in July, 1846, by the Commander-in-Chief against the Sultan of Borneo, Capt. Hope Johnstone assumed command of the whole of the seamen and of the field-piece and rocket-parties, and on 8 of that month assisted at the capture and destruction of the enemy's forts and batteries in the river Brune.*

He married, in 1826, Eleanor, eldest daughter of the late Sir Thos. Kirkpatrick, Bart., and has issue.

JOLLIFFE. (LIEUTENANT, 1845.)

WILLIAM KYNASTON JOLLIFFE passed his examination 20 May, 1835; and at the period of his promotion to the rank of Lieutenant, which took place 30 Dec. 1845, had been serving for about 18 months in the Mediterranean as Mate of the FLAMER steam-vessel, Lieut.-Commander Chas. Jas. Postle. He was appointed, 9 Feb. following, to the VIRAGO steam-sloop, Capt. John Lunn, on the same station; and has been there employed, since 1 Oct. 1846, as Senior of the PHŒNIX, another steamer, Capt. Jas. Sam. Akid Dennis.

JOLLY. (LIEUTENANT, 1842.)

ARCHIBALD DOUGLAS JOLLY entered the Navy 21 Aug. 1829; passed his examination 6 Dec. 1836; and, as we are informed, served as Mate in the boats of the PLUTO at the destruction of some slave-factories at the Gallianos Islands in 1842; on 23 July in which year he was promoted to the rank of Lieutenant. His succeeding appointments were—29 April, 1843, as Additional, to the ILLUSTRIOUS 72, bearing the flag of Sir Chas. Adam in North America and the West Indies—30 Dec. 1843, to the RINGDOVE 16, Capt. Sir Wm. Daniell, on the coast of Africa—and in 1844-5, to the SCYLLA 16, Capt. Robt. Sharpe, IMAUM 72, Commodores Alex. Renton Sharpe and Daniel Pring, and HYACINTH 18, Capt. Fras. Scott, all on the North America and West India station, whence he returned home and was paid off in the early part of 1847. AGENT—Joseph Woodhead.

JONES. (CAPTAIN, 1811. F-P., 19; H-P., 38.)

THE HONOURABLE ALEXANDER JONES, born 9 March, 1778, is youngest son of Charles, fourth Viscount Ranelagh, by Sarah, only daughter of Thos. Montgomery, Esq.; brother of Charles, fifth

* *Vide* Note, p. 536

* *Vide* Gaz. 1846, pp. 3441-2.

Viscount, who died a Captain R.N. in 1800; and uncle and heir-presumptive to the present nobleman. One of Capt. Jones' brothers, Benjamin, was a Lieutenant-Colonel, and two others, Richard and John, were Majors, in the Army.

This officer entered the Navy, in 1790, as Fst -cl. Vol., on board the ECHO sloop, commanded by his brother, then Hon. Chas. Jones, whom he successively followed into the KINGFISHER and ANDROMACHE, on the Channel and Newfoundland stations. Being discharged, in 1794, into the PROVIDENCE 16, Capt. Wm. Robt. Broughton, he sailed in that vessel on a voyage of discovery, and continued in her until wrecked among the Japan Islands 16 May, 1797: whereupon he took a passage home in the *Carnatic* Indiaman. On his arrival however at the Cape, he volunteered to serve with the Commander-in-Chief, Rear-Admiral Thos. Pringle, who, on the occasion of a mutiny breaking out on board his flag-ship, the TREMENDOUS 74, made him the instrument of communication between himself and the refractory seamen, by whom the Captain and all the officers had been put on shore. As a reward for this service Mr. Jones was immediately appointed, 14 Dec. 1797, Acting-Lieutenant of the SCEPTRE 64, Capt. Valentine Edwards, in which ship he remained until she was lost, with 291 of her crew, in Table Bay, 5 Nov. 1799. Joining, about the period of his official promotion, which took place 15 May, 1800, the AJAX 74, Capt. Hon. Alex. Inglis Cochrane, he attended, in the course of the same year, the expeditions to Belleisle and Ferrol; and was the means, when at the latter place, of saving H.M.S. TARTARUS, during a heavy gale, and after she had been abandoned by her officers and crew. In consideration of the intrepidity and judgment he had evinced on the occasion, Lieut. Jones was sent by his Captain to the Commander-in-Chief, Sir John Borlase Warren, and ordered to report himself as the officer who had achieved the performance. After witnessing (in the MINERVE frigate, Capt. Geo. Cockburn) the capture, 2 Sept. 1801, of the *Succès* and *Bravoure*, of 42 guns each, Lieut. Jones, until he was advanced to the rank of Commander 22 Jan. 1806, served on various stations in the CLYDE 38, Capt. John Larmour, CHAMPION 24, Capt. Robt. Howe Bromley, THISBE 28, Capt. Shephard, NAIAD 38, Capt. Jas. Wallis, and LIVELY 38, Capt. Graham Eden Hamond. In the latter frigate we find him present at the capture, 5 Oct. 1804, of three Spanish frigates, and the destruction of a fourth, off Cape St. Mary; and on 29 May, 1805, participating in her single-handed and self-sought skirmish with the Spanish 74-gun ship *Glorioso*. He was also in the LIVELY in several encounters with the enemy's gun-boats in the Gut of Gibraltar, and was further employed in her on the Italian coast. Assuming command, 6 Oct. 1807, of the TALBOT sloop, Capt. Jones, who continued in that vessel until posted, 1 Aug. 1811, assisted, during the period, at the blockade of Oporto, came also into frequent contact with the batteries on the coasts of Portugal, Spain, and Norway, and effected the capture (including the *Loven* of 2 guns and 11 men) of three privateers, besides a large number of other vessels. For his conduct at Oporto, where he was for some time employed on shore, he was placed by Sir Chas. Cotton, at the period of the Convention of Cintra, in temporary charge of a Portuguese frigate. His last appointment was to the command, for a short period in 1814, of the LEVANT 20.

Capt. Jones married, 2 Aug. 1807, Caroline, daughter of Thos. Palmer, Esq., of Hambledon, Hants, and niece of General Sir Wm. Myers, Bart., formerly Commander-in-Chief in Ireland and the West Indies, by whom he has issue three sons and two daughters. His second son, Robt. Molesworth Jones, is a Clerk in the Admiralty at Whitehall.

JONES. (RETIRED COMMANDER, 1837.)

CHARLES JONES died 19 Jan. 1847, aged 65.

This officer entered the Navy, in Nov. 1797, as Midshipman, on board the MONMOUTH 64, Capt. Jas. Walker, under whom—if we except an attachment, from Oct. 1798 until April, 1800, to the VICTOR sloop, Capt. Jas. Rennie, part of the force employed under Sir Andrew Mitchell in the expedition to the Texel—he continued to serve in the VETERAN 64, BRAAKEL 56, PRINCE GEORGE and PRINCE 98's, ISIS 50, TARTAR 32, and VANGUARD 74, until Jan. 1804. He was in consequence wounded, in the Isis, at the battle of Copenhagen 2 April, 1801;* and was on board the VANGUARD, in 1803, at the capture, besides a variety of smaller vessels, of *Le Duquesne* 74, and *La Créole* of 44 guns, with the French General, Morgan, and 530 troops on board; as also in the same ship at the surrender of the town of St. Marc, St. Domingo; the garrison of which place, amounting to about 1100 men, were brought off by the VANGUARD and her prizes to rescue them from the vengeance of the black General Dessalines. He left the VANGUARD, which had been latterly commanded by Capt. Andrew Fitzherbert Evans, in Oct. 1804; and on 5 April, 1805, after having acted for four months as Lieutenant of the GOELAN sloop, and DÉSIRÉE 36, Capts. Wm. Templar and Henry Whitby, was confirmed into the THESEUS 74, Capt. Fras. Temple. Returning to England with convoy in the following Sept., he next, between that period and Dec. 1807, served, on the Home and Baltic stations, in the POWERFUL 74, Capt. Robt. Plampin, BOADICEA 38, Capt. John Maitland, and VANGUARD 74, Capt. Alex. Fraser, under whom he accompanied Admiral Gambier's expedition against Copenhagen. He was then employed for two months in command of a cartel on the coast of Holland; after which he had charge, from May, 1808, to Feb. 1810, and from Aug. in the latter year to Aug. 1814, of the INDIGNANT and REBUFF gun-brigs, on the North Sea and Mediterranean stations—participating, in the INDIGNANT, in the operations of 1809 against Walcheren. His last appointment was, 1 April, 1822, to the Ordinary at Sheerness. The rank of Retired Commander was conferred upon him 23 Oct. 1837.

He was married, and has left issue.

JONES, Kt. (Captain, 1819. F-P., 23; H-P., 33.)

SIR CHARLES THOMAS JONES, born in 1778, is representative of the Jones' of Frontraith, co. Montgomery, a family seated there since 1608.

This officer entered the Navy, 2 May, 1791, as Captain's Servant, on board the VULCAN fire-ship, Capt. Solomon Ferris, lying at Spithead; and in the course of the same year removed, as Fst.-cl. Vol., to the ALCIDE 74, Capt. Sir Andrew Snape Douglas, stationed in Portsmouth Harbour. During the first five years of the French revolutionary war we find him serving with Lord Hugh Seymour in the LEVIATHAN 74, and SANS PAREIL 80; in the former of which ships he witnessed the occupation of Toulon in Aug. 1793, and was wounded in Lord Howe's action 1 June, 1794; and in the latter participated as Midshipman in the action fought off Ile de Groix 23 June, 1795. He was made Lieutenant, 16 Oct. 1798, into the FAIRY 18, Capt. Joshua Sydney Horton, on the coast of Africa; and was afterwards appointed—26 Aug. 1799, to the NEPTUNE 98, Capt. Jas. Vashon, flag-ship for some time of the late Lord Gambier in the Channel—in 1802, 3, and 5, to the CONCORDE, LANCASTER, and HINDOSTAN, Capts. John Wood, William Fothergill, and Alex. Fraser, all on the East India station—and 16 May, 1807, to the TRENT frigate, bearing the flag at Cork of Vice-Admiral Jas. Hawkins Whitshed. In the capacity of Commander, a rank he attained 15 Aug. 1810, Capt. Jones was employed, from 16 June, 1814, until paid off in Dec. 1818, in the HARRIER sloop, among the Canary Islands, off the coast of France, and on the Halifax station. He attained Post-rank 12 Aug. 1819, and accepted the Retirement 1 Oct. 1846.

Sir Chas. Thos. Jones, upon whom the honour of Knighthood had been conferred in 1809, mar-

* *Vide* Gaz. 1801, p. 404.

ried, in 1817, Miss Salton, daughter of Gilbert Salton, Esq., Collector of Customs at Bermuda.

JONES. (Lieutenant, 1827. f-p., 17; h-p., 17.)

Edward Leslie Jones, born 30 Dec. 1800, is fifth son of the late John Jones, Esq., of Woolley, near Bradford, Wilts; and nephew of the late Colonel Leslie Grove Jones, of the Grenadier Guards.

This officer entered the Navy, 7 July, 1813, as a Volunteer, on board the Medusa 32, Capt. Geo Bell, employed in the blockade of Cherbourg; and after conveying the 27th Regt. to Quebec in the Warspite 74, Capt. Lord Jas. O'Bryen, joined the Malta 80, Capt. Wm. Chas. Fahie, on the Mediterranean station, where he assisted, as Midshipman, at the reduction of the strong fortress of Gaeta in 1815. He served during the next three years on the coast of Africa in the 20-gun ships Bann and Cherub, Capts. Wm. Fisher and Geo. Wickens Willes; on accompanying the latter of whom into the Wye 26, commanded afterwards by Capt. Peter Fisher, he was employed for a similar period in the suppression of smuggling in the North Sea and Channel, and was for upwards of two whole months engaged in cruizing in an open boat. In Jan. 1823, having passed his examination in Feb. 1820, he rejoined Capt Willes, as Mate, in the Brazen 26, and sailed with him for the South American station, whence he returned to the coast of Africa, and was there made Lieutenant, 12 May, 1827, into the Maidstone 42, Commodore Chas. Bullen. After four years of half-pay, Mr. Jones was next, on 15 Aug. 1831, appointed to the Isis 50, Capts. Geo. Rennie and Jas. Polkinghorne, under whom he again served on the African coast until the close of 1834. His last appointment was, 19 May, 1835, to the Carron steamer, Capt. Edw. Belcher, in which vessel he was for about seven months occupied in surveying the Irish Channel. His health (impaired by his long servitude, of nine years, on the African station, where he passed a great part of the period on board slave-vessels, and underwent great hardships) has since prevented his seeking active employment.

He married, 26 May, 1840, Mary, second daughter of the late Rev. Rich. Thos. Whalley, Prebendary of Wells, and Rector of Ilchester and Yeovilton, co. Somerset, and niece of the late John Paine Tredway, Esq., M.P. for Wells. Agents—Messrs. Stilwell.

JONES. (Lieutenant, 1814.)

Henry Paget Jones was born in June, 1792.

This officer entered the Navy, 22 Jan. 1806, as Midshipman, on board the Egyptienne frigate, Capt. Hon. Chas. Paget, and on the evening of 8 March following served in the boats, under Lieut. Philip Cosby Handfield, at the cutting-out, beneath an incessant fire from two batteries, of the French frigate-built privateer *L'Alcide*, pierced for 34 guns, and moored to the beach in the harbour of Muros, in Spain. He next, in the course of 1807, joined the Hibernia 110, flag-ship of Earl St. Vincent, Donegal 74, Capt. Pulteney Malcolm, and Cambrian 40, commanded by his former Captain, Paget, under whom he accompanied the expedition against Copenhagen. In Aug. 1808, after he had been attached for a few months to the Spencer 74, flag-ship of Hon. Robt. Stopford, and Leviathan 74, Capts. Paget and Thos. Harvey, he was further received by Capt. Paget on board the Revenge, another third-rate, and was thus afforded an opportunity of sharing in the prominent part borne by that ship on the occasion of Lord Cochrane's celebrated attack on the enemy as they lay at anchor in Basque Roads in April, 1809. He continued to serve in the Revenge under the flag of Rear-Admiral Hon. Arthur Kaye Legge, latterly at the defence of Cadiz. until April, 1812, from which period until the following Oct. he acted as Lieutenant of the St. Albans 64, Capt John Ferris Devonshire. In March, 1813, we find him resuming the duties of Midshipman on board the Rippon 74, Capt. Sir Christ. Cole, stationed off Rochefort, and in about 12 months after that period transferred to the Venerable 74, bearing the flag in the West Indies of Rear-Admiral Philip Chas. Durham, who, on 19 July, 1814, caused him to be again invested with the rank of Acting-Lieutenant—an appointment which the Admiralty sanctioned by a commission dated on 26 Sept. in the same year. His succeeding appointments were—for a few months in 1815, to the Heron sloop, Capt. Fras. Chas. Annesley, in which vessel he returned to England and was paid off—13 Nov. 1821, to the Brazen 26, Capt. Wm. Shepheard, on the Irish station—11 March, 1823, to the Superb 74, Capt. Adam Mackenzie, with whom he served in the West Indies, and off Bermuda and Lisbon, until the close of 1825—and, in 1826, to the command, we believe, of the Otter steamer, which he retained until 1844.

Lieut. Jones, who is at present Commissioner of Pilotage at Holyhead, married, 13 Oct. 1837, Margaret, daughter of Norris M. Goddard, Esq., formerly Agent for conducting the Packet Service at that place. By that lady he has issue three children.

JONES. (Commander, 1846. f-p., 25; h-p., 18.)

Herbert John Jones entered the Navy, 24 March, 1804, as Fst.-cl. Vol., on board the Queen 98, Capts. Theobald Jones, Manley Dixon, and Fras. Pender, employed at first in the Channel and afterwards in the Mediterranean under the flags of Rear-Admirals John Knight and Sir Rich. Bickerton. On his return with Capt. Pender to England in Jan. 1806, as Midshipman of the Royal Sovereign 100, he joined the Renown 74, Capt. Philip Chas. Durham, with whom he continued to serve for upwards of four years off Rochefort and again in the Mediterranean, where, in Oct. 1809, he joined in the pursuit which terminated in the self-destruction of the French ships-of-the-line *Robuste* and *Lion*. After a further attachment, for very brief periods, to the St. Domingo 74, and Dictator and Ruby 64's, bearing each the flag in the Downs and Baltic of Rear-Admiral Dixon, Mr. Jones was promoted to the rank of Lieutenant by commission dated 23 Nov. 1810. His subsequent appointments were—14 Dec. 1810, to the Jasper sloop, Capt. John Eveleigh, on the Portsmouth and Lisbon stations—12 March, 1812, to the Sultan 74, Capt. John West, employed, we believe, in Basque Roads, where he continued until April, 1813—8 March, 1814, to the Conflict sloop, Capt. Abraham Mills Hawkins, which vessel, stationed off Lisbon, he left in April, 1815—1 May, 1830, and 26 Nov. 1831, to the Caledonia 120, and San Josef 110, flag-ships at the Nore of Sir Manley Dixon, under whom he served until paid off in April, 1833—12 July, 1836, to the Coast Guard—and, 22 May, 1845, again to the Caledonia 120, Capt. Manley Hall Dixon, lying at Devonport. Since the attainment of his present rank, 9 Nov. 1846, Commander Jones has been on half-pay.

He is married and has issue.

JONES. (Lieutenant, 1815. f-p., 11; h-p., 31.)

James Jones entered the Navy, 8 May, 1805, as A.B., on board the Raisonnable 64, commanded by the late Sir Josias Rowley, in which ship he served as Master's Mate in Sir Robt. Calder's action, at the reduction of the Cape of Good Hope, in all the operations in the Rio de la Plata, and at the capture of the town of St. Paul's in the Ile de Bourbon. In the course of 1810, having followed Capt. Rowley into the Boadicea 38, he was further present at the conquest of the latter island itself, the recapture of the Africaine 38, the taking, after a spirited action of 10 minutes, a loss to the Boadicea of 2 men wounded, and to the enemy of 9 killed and 15 wounded, of *La Vénus*, of 44 guns and 380 men, bearing the broad pendant of Commodore Hamelin, and of her prize the *Ceylon* 32, and the successful operations against the Isle of France. After his name had been borne for about five months on the books of the AFRICAINE and ROYAL WILLIAM, flag-ships at the Cape of Good Hope and at Plymouth of Vice-Admirals Albemarle Bertie and Sir Roger Curtis, Mr. Jones, in May, 1811, rejoined Capt. Rowley on board the AMERICA 74, and was afforded an opportunity, in consequence, of witnessing the unsuccessful attack upon Leghorn in Dec. 1813, and of participating in the ensuing capture of Genoa and its depenuencies. He continued in the Mediterranean in the QUEEN 74, and IMPREGNABLE 98, under the flags of Rear-Admirals Chas. Vinicombe Penrose and his friend Sir J. Rowley, until Aug. 1815; then took up a commission dated on 21 of the previous Feb.; and has since been on half-pay.

JONES. (RETIRED COMMANDER, 1832. F-P., 18; H-P., 35.)

JOHN JONES (*a*) entered the Navy, in Dec. 1794, as Fst.-cl. Vol., on board L'ESPIÈGLE sloop, Capt. Bartholomew Roberts, employed in the North Sea; and, from Feb. 1796 until promoted to the rank of Lieutenant 14 Oct. 1801, served as Midshipman and Master's Mate in the WINDSOR CASTLE 98, flag-ship of Admiral Robt. Mann, SATURN 74, Capt. Jas. Douglas, MONARCH 74, bearing the flag of Sir Rich. Onslow, CRESCENT 36, Capt. Wm. Grenville Lobb (under whom, when in company with the CALYPSO sloop, he assisted at the capture, 15 Nov. 1799, in sight of a Spanish line-of-battle-ship and frigate, of the corvette *El Galgo*, of 16 guns), and SANS PAREIL 80, and CARNATIC 74, bearing the flags of Lord Hugh Seymour and Admiral Robt. Montagu on the Mediterranean, Home, and Jamaica stations. He then rejoined the SANS PAREIL as Flag-Lieutenant to the last-named officer, with whom, in 1802, he returned home in a similar capacity on board the MELAMPUS frigate. Towards the close of the same year we find him appointed to the AUTUMN sloop, Capt. Richardson; and in June, 1804 (after having again officiated as Signal-Lieutenant to Admiral Montagu in various ships on the Downs station), ordered to join the ISIS 50, bearing the flag of Sir Erasmus Gower at Newfoundland. While next attached, between Feb. 1805 and April, 1811, to the POMONE 38, Capts. W. G. Lobb and Robt. Barrie, he presents himself to our notice as actively employed in the Channel and Mediterranean; and on one occasion, 5 June, 1807, displaying great judgment and gallantry in safely obtaining possession, near Sable d'Olonne, of an enemy's vessel, although his boat in the attempt was pierced through and through by grape from the shore and from three armed brigs.* His last appointments were, between Feb. 1812 and Aug. 1815, to the STROMBOLI bomb, Capt. John Stoddart, CURAÇOA frigate, Capt. John Tower, ROYAL GEORGE 100, flag-ship of Vice-Admiral Fras. Pickmore, and DRAGON 74, Capt. Robt. Barrie, again on the Mediterranean and Home stations. He accepted his present rank 2 July, 1832.

JONES. (RETIRED COMMANDER, 1835. F-P., 16; H-P., 38.)

JOHN JONES (*b*) entered the Navy, 1 July, 1793, as A.B., on board the GOELAN sloop, Capts. Thos. Wolley and Geo. Hopewell Stephens, under the former of whom he assisted in soon afterwards taking possession of Jeremie and of Cape Nicolas Mole, both on the island of St. Domingo. He next, from Sept. 1794 until Sept. 1801, served as A.B., Midshipman, Master's Mate, and Acting-Lieutenant, in the DÆDALUS, of 38 guns, Capts. Thos. Williams, Geo. Countess, Henry Ledgbird Ball, and Chas. Jas. Johnston, on the Channel, North Sea, Coast of Africa, and West and East India stations. On 9 Feb. 1799, while under Capt. Ball, he contributed to the capture, after an action of more than an hour's duration, of the French frigate *La Prudente*, of 30 guns and 301 men, 27 of whom were killed and 22 wounded, with a loss to the British, out of 212 men, of not more than 2 killed and 12 wounded.

* *Vide* Gaz. 1809, p. 838.

In the following Aug., being at the time in the Gulf of Suez, we find him participating in a three days' bombardment of the Egyptian town of Kosseir, garrisoned by a number of French troops. On leaving the DÆDALUS Mr. Jones became Acting-Lieutenant of the INTREPID 64, Capt. Wm. Hargood, to which ship, also stationed in the East Indies, he was confirmed by commission dated 27 July, 1802. In Jan. 1804, a few months after his return to England, he joined the FOUDROYANT 80, bearing the flag of Sir Thos. Graves in the Channel, where, and among the Western Islands, he served from Dec. 1805 until he invalided in Nov. 1809 on board L'IMPÉTUEUX 74, Capt. John Lawford. This was his last appointment. He accepted his present rank 6 Jan. 1835.

JONES. (LIEUTENANT, 1809. F-P., 31; H-P, 19.)

JOHN WILLIAM JONES entered the Navy, in 1797, as a Volunteer, on board the EDGAR 74, Capt. M'Dougall, with whom he served for about three years in the Mediterranean and Channel, chiefly in the capacity of Midshipman. He then removed to the ACHILLE 74, Capt. Edw. Buller; and, after a short employment under that officer on the coast of France, became Master's Mate of the IMOGENE sloop, in the West Indies. From 1802 until confirmed in his present rank, 28 Feb. 1809, he served again in the ACHILLE, as also in the MALTA 80, both commanded by Capt. Buller, and in the CONFIANCE sloop, Capt. Jas. Lucas Yeo, INDIGNANT gun-brig, Lieut.-Commander Petley, ORION 74, Capt. Sir Archibald Collingwood Dickson (part of the force employed in the expedition to Copenhagen), VICTORY 100, bearing the flag of Sir Jas. Saumarez, and, as Acting-Lieutenant, in the PROMETHEUS sloop, Capt. Thos. Forrest. He then joined the DILIGENCE 18, Capt. Abraham Lowe, employed, as had been some of the ships last named, in the Baltic. He was afterwards appointed—16 Aug. 1811, to the TIGRE 74, Capt. John Halliday, stationed off Brest and Rochefort—2 Nov. 1814, to the CRESCENT 36, Capt. John Quilliam, with whom he returned home from the West Indies and was paid off in Sept. 1815—and, 26 Jan. 1821, to the Coast Guard, in which service he continued until 1834. He has since been on half-pay.

JONES. (CAPTAIN, 1840. F-P., 30; H-P., 9.)

LEWIS TOBIAS JONES, born in Dec. 1799, is second son of Capt. L. T. Jones, formerly of the 14th Regt., who wrote and published a history of the Duke of York's campaign in Holland in 1793, 4, and 5, having served under H.R.H. during that period in the 57th Regt. His family, originally of Denbigh, in Wales, has been seated since the Commonwealth at Ardnaglass, co. Sligo.

This officer entered the Navy, 1 Jan. 1808, as Midshipman, on board the THRASHER gun-brig, Lieut.-Commander Josiah Dornford, which vessel formed part of the force sent to the Walcheren in 1809. In May, 1812, he removed to the STIRLING CASTLE 74, commanded at first by his relative Sir Jahleel Brenton off Brest, and afterwards by Capt. Augustus Brine, whom he successively followed into the BELLEROPHON and MEDWAY 74's. The latter ship, it appears, sailed in Jan. 1814 with Lord Chas. Somerset for the Cape of Good Hope, and on her arrival on that station hoisted the flag of Sir Chas. Tyler. During a subsequent cruize in the neighbourhood of St. Helena she contrived to effect the capture, after a long chase, of the American sloop-of-war SYREN, of 16 guns. On leaving her Mr. Jones, in Nov. 1815, became for a short time Acting-Lieutenant of the ARIEL sloop, Capt. Dan. Ross. He subsequently officiated for upwards of six years as Admiralty Midshipman, on the Mediterranean, Home, West India, and North American stations, of the GRANICUS 36, Capt. Wm. Furlong Wise, CYRUS 20, Capt. Wm. Fairbrother Carroll, SPARTAN frigate, Capt. W. F. Wise, NEWCASTLE 60, flag-ship of Sir Edw. Griffith Colpoys, and JASEUR sloop, Capt. Henry Edw. Napier. He received, when in the GRANICUS, a wound in each knee at the battle of Algiers, the effects of which still continue; and on his junction of the SPARTAN he accompanied the Duke of Gloucester on a trip along the coast of France from Brest to Bordeaux. Being made Lieutenant, 29 Aug. 1822, into the ATHOL 28, Capt. Henry Bourchier, Mr. Jones remained in that vessel until 1824, when he returned to England with Lord Dalhousie, Governor-General of Canada. His succeeding appointments were—3 Oct. 1827, to the CORDELIA 10, Capts. Geo. Wm. St. John Mildmay, Courtenay Edm. Wm. Boyle, and Chas. Hotham, in which vessel he served for six years, chiefly as First-Lieutenant, on the North Sea, Lisbon, West India, Newfoundland, and Mediterranean stations —and, 31 Oct. 1833 and 9 Feb. 1837, in a similar capacity, to the EDINBURGH 74, Capt. Jas. Rich. Dacres, and PRINCESS CHARLOTTE 104, flag-ship of Sir Robt. Stopford, both also in the Mediterranean. He was promoted to the Second-Captaincy of the latter ship by a commission dated 28 June, 1838; and, continuing in her until Jan. 1841, was in consequence present in the operations of 1840 on the coast of Syria, where, in the month of Sept., he landed with the Anglo-Turkish battalions at D'Journi, and served on shore, during the occupation of the encampment, as officer in charge of the beach department and of the issue of arms and ammunition to the mountaineers of Lebanon. On 4 Nov. 1840, as a reward for his services at the capture of St. Jean d'Acre, Capt. Jones was advanced to the rank he now holds. He has not, however, been afloat since the period he left the PRINCESS CHARLOTTE.

In 1844 Capt. Jones was a student at the R. N. College.

JONES. (LIEUTENANT, 1846.)

MAURICE JONES passed his examination 1 Feb. 1843; and after an intermediate servitude as Mate in the CALEDONIA 120, and COLLINGWOOD 80, flag-ships of Sir David Milne and Sir Geo. Fras. Seymour at Devonport and in the Pacific, was promoted to the rank of Lieutenant 5 Aug. 1846. He has been attached, since 12 of the following Nov., to the SAMPSON steam-frigate, Capt. Thos. Henderson, on the station last mentioned.

JONES. (LIEUTENANT, 1839.)

OLIVER JOHN JONES, born 15 March, 1813, is second son of the late Major-General Oliver Jones, who commanded the 18th Hussars under Sir John Moore in the Peninsula, by his second wife, Maria Antonia, youngest daughter of the late Henry Swinburne, Esq., of Hamsterly, co. Durham, and granddaughter of Sir John Swinburne, Bart., of Capheaton, co. Northumberland. His only brother is the present Robt. Oliver Jones, Esq., of Fonmon Castle, co. Glamorgan, a Magistrate and Deputy-Lieutenant for that shire, who served as High Sheriff in 1838.

This officer entered the Navy 7 Sept. 1826; passed his examination in 1832; and obtained his commission 21 Dec. 1839. His appointments have since been—6 July, 1840, to the SOUTHAMPTON 50, flag-ship of Sir Edw. Durnford King at the Brazils and Cape of Good Hope—8 Jan. 1842, to the CALCUTTA 84, Capt. Sir Sam. Roberts, off Lisbon—5 July, 1842, as First, to the SNAKE 16, Capt. Hon. Walter Bourchier Devereux, in the Mediterranean—21 Jan. 1843, as Additional, to the QUEEN 110, flag-ship of Sir Edw. W. C. R. Owen, on the same station—and, 11 Aug. 1843, again as Senior Lieutenant, to the PILOT 16, Capts. Wm. Henry Jervis and Geo. Knyvett Wilson, under the latter of whom he is at present employed in the East Indies. AGENTS—Messrs. Ommanney.

JONES. (LIEUTENANT, 1827.)

PHILIP BUTTON JONES passed his examination in 1820; and was made Lieutenant, 16 Nov. 1827, into the ARACHNE 18, Capt. Geo. Wm. Conway Courtenay, on the West India station, whence he soon afterwards invalided. He has not been since employed. AGENTS—Hallett and Robinson.

JONES. (COMMANDER, 1844.)

RICHARD JONES died 7 May, 1847, at Southsea.

This officer entered the Navy, in 1811, as Sec.-cl. Boy, on board the ORLANDO 36, Capt. John Clavell, in which frigate, after serving on the Mediterranean and North American stations, he proceeded, as Midshipman, to the East Indies, whence he returned to England with the same Captain, in the MALABAR 74, in 1819. In July, 1820, he assumed the duties of Master on board the MORGIANA sloop, Capt. Wm. Finlaison, on the African station, where, it appears, he subsequently officiated as Acting-Lieutenant of the same vessel, and as Admiralty-Midshipman of the OWEN GLENDOWER 42, Commodore Sir Robt. Mends, until within a short period of his being confirmed, 26 May, 1823, into the BANN 20, Capt. Chas. Phillips. He invalided home, after having acted for some months as Commander of the BANN, in Oct. 1823; and was next appointed—18 May, 1824, and 5 March, 1825, as a Supernumerary, to the RAMILLIES 74, and HYPERION 42, Coast Blockade ships, Capts. Wm. M'Culloch and Wm. Jas. Mingaye—26 June, 1829, to the Coast Guard—27 June, 1837, to the command of the DEFENCE Revenue-vessel — 11 June, 1840, again to the Coast Guard—and, 27 July, 1844, to the VICTORY 104, flag-ship of the Admiral-Superintendent at Portsmouth, Rear-Admiral Hyde Parker. Being the only Lieutenant on board the latter ship on the occasion of Her Majesty's visit, he was in consequence promoted to the rank of Commander by commission dated 22 Oct. 1844.

He has left five motherless sons in a state of destitution.

JONES. (RETIRED COMMANDER, 1844. F-P., 21; H-P., 33.)

RICHARD JONES (*a*) entered the Navy, 5 Oct. 1793, as A.B., on board the BELLONA 74, Capt. Geo. Wilson, with whom, and with Sir Thos. Boulden Thompson, he continued to serve, as Midshipman, on the Channel, West India, and Mediterranean stations, until promoted to the rank of Lieutenant 27 March, 1800. He assisted, in consequence, at the defence of Fort Matilda, Guadeloupe, in 1794; contributed, in Jan. 1795, to the capture of the French frigates *Le Ducas* of 20, and *Le Duquesne* of 44 guns; was present at an attack on a French squadron at St. Eustacia, Puerto Rico, and at the reduction of Trinidad, in 1797; commanded a tender in the course of the latter year, and fought an action against a very superior force, in which he lost an arm, and was otherwise severely wounded; and, on 19 June, 1799, witnessed the capture of Rear-Admiral Perrée's squadron of three frigates and two brigs, from Jaffa, bound to Toulon. For his services in Egypt in the FURY bomb, Capts. Rich. Curry and Hon. Fred. Wm. Aylmer, to which vessel he was attached from 6 April, 1800, until 13 July, 1802, Lieut. Jones obtained the Turkish gold medal. He was next, in March, 1803, appointed to the MALTA 80, Capt. Edw. Buller, one of Sir Robt. Calder's ships in his action with Admiral Villeneuve 22 July, 1805. He left her in April, 1806, and was lastly employed in command of a Signal station, which he held from March, 1807, to Feb. 1816. He became a Retired Commander on the Senior List 5 Nov. 1844.

He enjoys a pension for his wounds of 91*l.* 5*s.*

JONES. (LIEUT., 1812. F-P., 10; H-P., 33.)

ROBERT JONES entered the Navy, 10 Oct. 1804, as A.B., on board the SHEERNESS receiving-ship at Hull, where he was employed for a period of four years and a half under the command of Lieut. Geo. Fox, nearly the whole time in the capacity of Master's Mate. He next, in the course of 1809 and 10, joined, in succession, the ARIEL sloop, Capts. Thos. White and John and Daniel Ross, and VICTORY 100, flag-ship of Sir Jas. Saumarez, on the Baltic and Lisbon stations; after which, obtaining a commission dated 11 Feb. 1812, he was employed on Home duty, as Lieutenant, between June in the same year and Aug. 1814, in the PRINCE WILLIAM armed ship, Capt. Andw. Mott, and CEYLON and PORPOISE, both commanded by Capt. Peter Rye. Since the latter date he has been on half-pay. AGENT—J. Hinxman.

JONES. (RETIRED COMMANDER, 1840. F-P., 19; H-P., 32.)

ROBERT PARKER JONES was born 30 April, 1786.

This officer entered the Navy, 5 Nov. 1796, as a Volunteer, on board the AGINCOURT 64, Capt. John Williamson and John Lawford, under the former of whom he bore a part, as Midshipman, in the battle fought off Camperdown 11 Oct. 1797. In Feb. 1798 he removed to the NAUTILUS sloop, Capt. Henry Gunter, which vessel was wrecked, off Flamborough Head, 2 Feb. 1799. Joining then the HARPY 18, Capts. Henry Bazely, Wm. Birchall, and Chas. Worsley Boys, he was afforded an opportunity of witnessing in that vessel the capture of the French frigate *Pallas*, and of participating in the action off Copenhagen 2 April, 1801. He was next employed for a period of three years, on the Irish, African, and West India stations, in the PRINCESS CHARLOTTE frigate, Capt. Hon. Fras. Farington Gardner, PENGUIN 18, Capt. Geo. Morris, and INCONSTANT 36, Capt. Edw. Stirling Dickson; after which he proceeded in the WEYMOUTH to India, and was there (having passed his examination in July, 1803) appointed, 25 Dec. 1805, Acting-Lieutenant of the ALBION 74, Capt. John Ferrier. Being confirmed to that ship 30 Aug. 1806, he continued in her until he returned to England in June, 1809.* His succeeding appointments were, in March and Dec. 1810, and in Feb. 1812, to the EDGAR, TREMENDOUS, and CRESSY 74's, Capts. Stephen Poyntz, Robt. Campbell, Chas. Dudley Pater, and Chas. Dashwood, employed on the Baltic, Channel, and West India stations. The CRESSY, of which he had been for upwards of two years First-Lieutenant, he left in May, 1814. He accepted his present rank 9 July, 1840.

Commander Jones married, 23 July, 1819, Jane, second daughter of the late Lieut.-General Lewis, of the Royal Artillery.

JONES, M.P. (CAPT., 1828. F-P., 17; H-P., 27.)

THEOBALD JONES, born in 1790, is second son of the late Rev. James Jones, of Merrion Square, Dublin, Rector of Urney, in the diocese of Derry, by his first wife, Lydia, daughter of Theobald Wolfe; grandson of the Right Hon. Theophilus Jones, M.P., who married a daughter of the Earl of Tyrone; and nephew of the late Vice-Admiral Theophilus Jones. His father's second wife was a daughter of Sir Robt. Blackwood, Bart., by the Baroness Dufferin and Claneboye, and relict of the Very Rev. John Ryder, Dean of Lismore, son of John, Archbishop of Tuam.

This officer entered the Navy, 1 June, 1803, as Fst.-cl. Vol., on board the MELPOMENE frigate, Capt. Robt. Dudley Oliver, and in the course of the following year was twice engaged, as Midshipman, in the bombardment of Havre. In Nov. 1805 he removed to the EURYALUS 36, Capt. Hon. Henry Blackwood, with whom, on 14 Feb. 1807, he was on board the AJAX 74 when that ship took fire and blew up near the island of Tenedos. Being then received into the ENDYMION 40, Capt. Hon. Thos. Bladen Capel, he served at the ensuing passage of the Dardanells; after which, on his return to England in May, 1808, he rejoined Capt. Blackwood on board the WARSPITE 74, and continued to serve with him, as Lieutenant (commission dated 8 July, 1809), until Feb. 1814, in the North Sea and Channel, and also in the Mediterranean, where, in July, 1810, he shared in a very gallant skirmish with the Toulon fleet. In Feb. 1815, on his arrival home, after having gone with convoy to the Cape of Good Hope, in the DÉSIRÉE 36, Capt. Wm. Woolridge, Mr. Jones found that he had been promoted to the rank of Commander on 19 of the previous July. His succeeding appointments were—26 Feb. 1819, to the CHEROKEE 10, of which vessel he retained command, on the Leith station, for a period of more than three years—and, 12 May, 1827, to the Second-Captaincy of the PRINCE REGENT 120, Capts. Constantine Rich. Moorsom and Hon. Geo. Poulett, flag-ship for some time of Hon. Sir H. Blackwood at the Nore. He was advanced to his present rank 25 Aug. 1828, but has not been since afloat.

Capt. Jones has sat in Parliament for co. Londonderry since 1830.

* On her passage home the ALBION encountered a dreadful hurricane, which proved fatal to three East Indiamen under her convoy. It was with the greatest difficulty that she herself could be kept afloat during the remainder of the voyage.

JONES. (RETIRED COMMANDER, 1844. F-P., 14; H-P., 34.)

THOMAS JONES (*a*) died 27 Sept. 1845, in his 60th year, at Lewisham, in Kent.

This officer entered the Navy, in July, 1798, as Fst.-cl. Vol., on board the HORNET sloop, Capt. John Nash, stationed in the Channel, where, from 1799 until paid off in 1802, he served, part of the time as Midshipman, in LA JUSTE 80, Capts. Sir Henry Trollope. Rich. Dacres, and Sir Edm. Nagle. In 1804 he re-embarked on board the HINDOSTAN 50, Capt. Alex. Fraser, with whom he made a voyage to the East Indies; and, on 4 June, 1808, after having served for some time on the Mediterranean station, in the FORMIDABLE 98, Capt. Fras. Fayerman, he was promoted to the rank of Lieutenant. His last appointments were—25 Nov. 1808, to the ABOUKIR 74, Capt. Geo. Parker, in the North Sea—and, 2 Dec. 1809, and 27 July, 1811, to the RANGER and BRISEIS sloops, Capts. Geo. Acklom, Chas. Thurlow Smith, and John Ross, both in the Baltic. On the night of 19 June, 1812, Lieut. Jones performed a signal act of gallantry in cutting out from Pillau roads, with the pinnace of the last-mentioned vessel, containing a Midshipman and 18 men, under his orders, the (lately British) merchant-ship *Urania*, mounting 6 carriage-guns and 4 swivels, then in the possession of some French troops, who, notwithstanding a spirited resistance, were driven off the decks into their boats, which were on the opposite side, with no greater loss to the assailants than 1 man killed and the Midshipman and 1 man slightly wounded.* He went on half-pay in the early part of 1813, and retired with the rank of Commander 22 Oct. 1844.

JONES. (LIEUT., 1827. F-P., 17; H-P., 21.)

THOMAS JONES (*b*) entered the Navy, 20 July, 1809, as Fst.-cl. Vol., on board the VENERABLE 74, Capts. Andw. King and Sir Home Popham, which ship formed part of the ensuing expedition to the Walcheren. Between 1811 and 1815, in Dec. of which year he passed his examination, we find him employed, on the Mediterranean and North Sea stations, as Midshipman of the COMUS 22, Capts. Matthew Smith and Fras. Geo. Dickins, HAVRE gun-brig, and MERCURIUS 18, Capt. Thos. Renwick. The time which intervened between the latter date and that of his promotion to the rank of Lieutenant, 28 April, 1827, was passed by Mr. Jones in the capacities of Admiralty-Midshipman and Mate, on board the BULWARK 74, Capt. Geo. M'Kinley, BLOSSOM 20, Capts. Fred. Hickey, Fred. Edw. Vernon (now Harcourt), and Arch. M'Lean, BLONDE 42, Capt. Lord Byron, and ARACHNE 18, Capt. Wm. Robt. Ashley Pettman, on the Home, South American, St. Helena, Pacific, and West India stations. Since he left the ARACHNE he has been on half-pay.

JONES. (LIEUT., 1821. F-P., 27; H-P., 13.)

VALENTINE HERBERT JONES entered the Navy, 19 May, 1807, as Fst.-cl. Vol., on board the HUSSAR 38, Capt. Robt. Lloyd, under whom he assisted at the bombardment of Copenhagen, and further served, as Midshipman, in the GUERRIÈRE 38, and SWIFTSURE 74, flag-ship of Sir John Borlase Warren,

* *Vide* Gaz. 1812, p. 1364.

on the West India and North American stations, until April, 1811. He then removed to the EDINBURGH 74, Capts. Robt. Rolles and Hon. Geo. Heneage Lawrence Dundas, and, after a cruize among the Western Islands, proceeded to the Mediterranean, where, in 1813-14, he successively witnessed the capture of Port d'Anzo, the unsuccessful attack upon Leghorn, the reduction of the fortress of Santa Maria, and of the enemy's other forts and defences in the Gulf of Spezia, and the fall of Genoa. In the course of 1814 he joined the APOLLO 38, Capt. Edwards Lloyd Graham, and CONFLICT 12, Capt. Abraham Mills Hawkins, respectively employed in the Mediterranean and Channel; and he next, between Sept. 1815, and the receipt of his commission, bearing date 19 July, 1821, served, as Admiralty-Midshipman, on the Cape of Good Hope and Newfoundland stations, in the ORONTES 36, Capt. Nathaniel Day Cochrane, SIR FRANCIS DRAKE, flag-ship of Vice-Admiral Fras. Pickmore, EGERIA 26, Capt. Henry Shiffner, FAVORITE 26, Capt. Hercules Robinson, and SIR FRANCIS DRAKE again, bearing the flag of Sir Chas. Hamilton. His subsequent appointments were—27 July, 1831, to the Coast Guard—12 Oct. 1836, and 17 March, 1838, to the command of the ROSE and SPRIGHTLY Revenue-vessels—18 May, 1839, a second time to the charge of a station in the Coast Guard—6 July, 1840, to the office of Agent in a contract mail steam-vessel —and, 24 June, 1842, once more to the Coast Guard. He has been on half-pay since 1843.

JONES. (CAPTAIN, 1828. F-P., 23; H-P., 18.)

WILLIAM JONES died 24 May, 1846, at Haslar Hospital, from the effects of disease contracted on the coast of Africa.

This officer entered the Navy, 28 June, 1805, as Fst.-cl. Vol., on board the FLORA 36, Capt. Loftus Otway Bland, with whom (including two years and a half spent on the Lisbon station) he served until wrecked, as Midshipman, off the coast of Holland, where he was taken prisoner, 19 Jan. 1808. In the following July, having been released, he joined the ABOUKIR 74, bearing the flag of Hon. Alan Hyde Gardner in the North Sea and Baltic, where, from March, 1809, until promoted to the rank of Lieutenant 24 July, 1811, we find him employed, again with Capt. Bland, as also with Capts. Keith Maxwell and John Hancock, as Master's Mate, in the AFRICA 64, and NYMPHEN 36. His succeeding appointments were—16 Aug. 1811, to the PIQUE 36, Capt. Hon. Anthony Maitland, stationed in the Channel—1 June, 1812, to the COSSACK 22, Capts. Wm. King, Fras. Stanfell, Lord Algernon Percy, and Hon. Robt. Rodney, under whom he was employed in the Mediterranean and North America till July, 1815—12 Sept. 1819, to the HIND 20, Capt. Sir Chas. Burrard, lying at Portsmouth—29 June, 1821, and 20 March, 1822, to the BULWARK and GLOUCESTER 74's, bearing each the flag of Sir Benj. Hallowell in the river Medway—and 23 Nov. 1822, to the command of the MERMAID Revenue-vessel. He was made Commander into the ORESTES 18, on the Halifax station, 1 May, 1826; attained the rank of Captain 18 Aug. 1828; and was subsequently appointed—6 May, 1833, to the VESTAL 26, in which vessel he served for a period of four years and a half on the North America and West India station —and 27 June, 1843, to the PENELOPE steam-frigate. He continued in that ship on the coast of Africa, latterly with the broad pendant of Commodore, until within a short time of his death. AGENTS—Messrs. Ommanney.

JONES. (LIEUT., 1809. F-P., 10; H-P., 36.)

WILLIAM JONES (*a*), born 21 Aug. 1783, is third son of the Rev. H. Wynne Jones, Prebendary of Penymunidd, Anglesey.

This officer (who had previously been in the Hon. E. I. Co.'s service) entered the Navy, about Oct. 1801, as A.B., on board the ROMNEY 50, commanded in the East Indies by Capt. Sir Home Popham; and on next joining the SENSIBLE 36, *armée-en-flûte*, Capt. Robt. Sauce, was cast away on a quicksand off Ceylon, 2 March, 1802. On being taken off the island seven weeks afterwards by the TRINCOMALEE sloop-of-war, he became Midshipman of the VICTORIOUS 74, Capt. Pulteney Malcolm, bearing the flag of the late Vice-Admiral Peter Rainier. In Aug. 1803 he removed to the WINDSOR CASTLE 98, Capts. Albemarle Bertie, Davidge Gould, Thos. Wells, and Chas. Boyles, with the latter of whom, after enacting a part in the action off Ferrol 22 July, 1805, and witnessing Sir Sam. Hood's capture of four French frigates near Rochefort 25 Sept. 1806, he proceeded to the Mediterranean, where, having first served in a boat at the destruction of the Turkish squadron off Point Pesquies, he was slightly wounded at the repassage of the Dardanells in March, 1807.* Returning to England in April, 1808, for the purpose of passing his examination, he joined, in the ensuing Dec., the SYBILLE 44, Capt. Clotworthy Upton, stationed off the coast of Ireland. He was confirmed a Lieutenant, 16 May, 1809, in the ESPIÈGLE sloop, Capts. Henry Gage Morris and Arthur Atchison; and in the course of the same year he was transferred to the JALOUSE sloop, also commanded by Capt. Morris, with whom he was for two years employed, again on the Irish station. His last appointment was to the First-Lieutenancy, 27 Jan. 1813, of the STORK sloop, Capt. Robt. Lisle Coulson. In that vessel he continued for a period of six months. Lieut. Jones was presented with a pecuniary grant from the Patriotic Society in consideration of the wound he received at the Dardanells.

He married, 3 Nov. 1811, Maria Ellen, daughter of Major Geo. Goodman, by whom he has issue a son and nine daughters.

JONES. (LIEUTENANT, 1815.)

WILLIAM JONES (*b*) entered the Navy, 8 June, 1805, as a Volunteer, on board the CAPTAIN 74, Capts. Geo. Hopewell Stephens, Geo. Cockburn, Isaac Wolley, Jas. Athol Wood, and Christ. John Williams Nesham; and, during a period of four years and a half that he continued in that ship, assisted at the capture, 27 Sept. 1806, of the French frigate *Le Président* of 44 guns, was present in 1807 at the reduction of Copenhagen and Madeira, and served at the taking of Martinique in Feb. 1809. Removing in Dec. of the latter year to the DICTATOR 64, Capts. Rich. Harrison Pearson and Robt. Williams, he was for 16 months employed under those officers on the Baltic and Leith stations; after which, until promoted to the rank of Lieutenant 15 Feb. 1815, he served, off the coasts of France and Spain, among the Western Islands, and in North America, as Midshipman, in the SCEPTRE 74, Capt. Sam. Jas. Ballard, CONSTANT gun-brig, Lieut.-Commander John Stokes, and TONNANT 80, flag-ship of Hon. Sir Alex. Cochrane. With the exception of some time passed in the Coast Guard as Supernumerary-Lieutenant, subsequently to Nov. 1824, of the RAMILLIES 74, and HYPERION 42, Capts. Wm. M'Culloch and Wm. Jas. Mingaye, he has since been on half-pay.

JONES. (LIEUT., 1815. F-P., 9; H-P., 31.)

WILLIAM JONES (*c*) entered the Navy, 13 March 1807, as Fst.-cl. Vol., on board the SPEEDY sloop, Capt. Henry Rich. Muddle. With that officer he continued to serve as Midshipman, and for a short time as Acting-Lieutenant, in the COMET and COLUMBINE sloops, on the Newfoundland, Cadiz, Lisbon, and Leeward Island stations, until Oct. 1815. He then took up a commission bearing date 15 March in that year, and has since been on half-pay. AGENTS—Messrs. Stilwell.

JONES. (LIEUT., 1815. F-P., 9; H-P., 32.)

WILLIAM CHARLES JONES is second son of the late Rev. Rich. Jones, A.M., Rector of Charfield, Gloucestershire.

This officer entered the Navy, 12 Aug. 1806, as Fst.-cl. Vol., on board the DRAGON 74, Capt. Mat-

* *Vide* Gaz. 1807, p. 597.

thew Henry Scott, stationed in the Channel and Bay of Biscay; and, after serving for a period of more than two years in that ship, became Midshipman of the ACHILLE 74, Capt. Sir Rich. King, under whom we find him accompanying the expedition to the Walcheren, and then employed for three months in a gun-boat at the siege of Cadiz, where he co-operated in the defence of Fort Matagorda. In April, 1811, on his return from the Mediterranean, he rejoined Capt. Scott on board the MARLBOROUGH 74, off Flushing. He proceeded, in the course of the same year, to the East Indies in the ILLUSTRIOUS 74, bearing the flag of Sir Sam. Hood, whom he there followed into the MINDEN, of similar force. He was lent from the latter ship, in 1814, as Acting-Lieutenant, to the HESPER sloop, Capt. Chas. Biddulph; and on 11 Feb. 1815 he was officially constituted First of the VICTOR, Capt. Robt. Hall. He returned to England and was paid off in the following Sept., and has not been since afloat. AGENTS—Messrs. Ommanney.

JUDD. (RETIRED CAPTAIN, 1840. F.P., 19; H-P., 51.)

ROBERT HAYLEY JUDD entered the Navy, 28 Feb. 1777, as Captain's Servant, on board the BALL armed ship, Capt. Hill, on the West India station. He removed, in 1778, to a vessel commanded in the Channel by Capt. Cromwell; served next in the East Indies as Midshipman, from 1780 to 1784, of the MONMOUTH 64, Capt. Jas. Alms; and on 30 Oct. 1794, soon after he had joined the QUEEN 98, bearing the flag in the Channel of Sir Alan Gardner, was promoted to a Lieutenancy in the SANDWICH, flag-ship of Admiral Dalrymple, Commander-in-Chief at the Nore. His succeeding appointments were—24 Feb. 1795, to the FORMIDABLE 98, Capt. Hon. Geo. Cranfield Berkeley, in the Channel—3 Nov. 1797, to the BARFLEUR 98, Capt. Jas. Rich. Dacres, whom he accompanied to the Mediterranean—30 Dec. 1798, and 14 March, 1799, to the PRINCE 98, and MARS 74, flag-ships of Sir Roger Curtis and Hon. G. C. Berkeley, on the Home station—and 12 June, 1801, to the FORMIDABLE again, Capt. Rich. Grindall, in which ship he proceeded to the West Indies. He obtained a second promotal commission 29 April, 1802; and was lastly employed in command, from 3 April, 1804, until Dec. 1807, of the HEBE armed ship, on the Leith station. He retired with the rank of Captain 10 Sept. 1840.

Capt. Judd's eldest son died 13 Feb. 1835, at Sierra Leone, in his 22nd year, while serving as Midshipman of H.M. brig PELORUS, Capt. Rich. Meredith. AGENTS—Coplands and Burnett.

JULIAN. (LIEUTENANT, 1840.)

HUMPHREY JOHN JULIAN entered the Navy, 8 April, 1824; passed his examination in 1831; and was made Lieutenant, 27 April, 1840, into the WOLVERENE 16, Capt. Robt. Tucker, attached to the force on the coast of Africa, where we soon afterwards find him employed in the boats at the destruction of a slave-factory at Corisco. He returned to England and was paid off in the summer of 1841; and has been since appointed—1 Dec. 1841, to the MINDEN 20, Capt. Michael Quin, fitting for the East Indies—29 Aug. 1843, to the CORNWALLIS 72, flag-ship on that station of Sir Wm. Parker—and, 1 March, 1845, as First, to the HIBERNIA 104, bearing the flag of the same officer in the Mediterranean, where he is now serving. AGENTS—Messrs. Chard.

JULYAN. (COMMANDER, 1814. F-P., 22; H-P., 32.)

ROBERT JULYAN entered the Navy, 4 March, 1793, as a Boy, on board the DIADEM 64, Capts. Andrew Sutherland and Chas. Tyler, in which ship he served at the occupation of Toulon in the following Aug., and in Hotham's actions of 14 March and 13 July, 1795. After witnessing, in the MOSELLE sloop, Capts. Chas. Brisbane and Wm. Essington, the surrender of the Dutch squadron in Saldanha Bay 17 Aug. 1796, and serving for two years and a half in the Channel on board the ROYAL GEORGE 100, flag-ship of Lord Bridport, he became, 8 May, 1799, Acting-Lieutenant of the ROBUST 74, Capt. Geo. Countess. He was confirmed, 3 June in the same year, into the PENGUIN sloop, Capt. Bendall Robt. Littlehales, on the Irish station; and was subsequently appointed—13 Oct. 1800, to the DEFENCE 74, Capt. Lord Henry Paulet, with whom (having first shared in the action off Copenhagen 2 April, 1801) he proceeded to Cadiz and then to the West Indies—17 Oct. 1803, to the Sea Fencibles on the north coast of Cornwall, where he remained nearly six years and a half—and 11 Aug. 1810, to the SAN JUAN sheer-hulk, bearing the broad pendant at first of Commodore Chas. Vinicombe Penrose, and the flag afterwards of Hon. Arthur Kaye Legge, at Gibraltar. During three years that he was borne on the books of that ship, Lieut. Julyan held at different times the acting-command of the RICHMOND, STROMBOLI, and ONYX gun-brigs; in the boats belonging to the former of which vessels he destroyed two French privateers under a battery near Malaga in 1811. He also held a responsible appointment at the defence of Tarifa. He was promoted, 7 June, 1814, to the command of the ROLLA sloop, but was paid off, after having visited the coast of France, Halifax, and New York, 2 Dec. 1815, and has since been on half-pay.

Commander Julyan has been for some time Harbour-Master at Quebec. AGENT—Joseph Woodhead.

JUSTICE. (LIEUTENANT, 1825.)

FRANCIS WALL JUSTICE entered the Navy 13 Feb. 1811; passed his examination in 1817; and obtained his commission 4 Oct. 1825. He has not been since employed. AGENTS—Goode and Lawrence.

JUSTICE. (CAPTAIN, 1846. F-P., 18; H-P., 22.)

PHILIP JUSTICE is brother, we believe, of the present Henry Justice, Esq., of Hinstock, co. Salop, who served as High Sheriff for that shire in 1842; and also of Lieut. Robt. Justice, R.N.

This officer entered the Navy, 25 March, 1807, as Fst.-cl. Vol., on board the SHANNON 38, Capt. Philip Bowes Vere Broke, with whom he served during a period of five years and a half, and was present at the surrender of Madeira and the capture of a great number of the enemy's armed and other vessels. In Sept. 1813, rather more than two years after he had attained the rating of Midshipman, he removed, as Master's Mate to the AFRICA 64, bearing the flag of the late Sir Herbert Sawyer on the North American station. On 5 Aug. 1813, after having served for a few months in the North Sea and Mediterranean on board the SCARBOROUGH 74, and CALEDONIA 120, flag-ships of Admirals John Ferrier and Sir Edw. Pellew, Mr. Justice was nominated Acting-Lieutenant of the KITE sloop, Capt. Thos. Forster—an appointment which the Admiralty confirmed. He was afterwards, until promoted to the rank of Commander 5 Dec. 1824, employed, on the Home, Brazilian, and Mediterranean stations, in the MÆANDER and MADAGASCAR frigates, Capts. John Bastard, Arthur Fanshawe, and Wm. Augustus Baumgardt, SUPERB 74, Capt. Chas. Ekins, RALEIGH 18, Capt. W. A. Baumgardt, NAUTILUS 18, Capt. Isham Fleming Chapman, ALACRITY sloop, Capt. Henry Stanhope, ACTIVE 46, Capt. Sir Jas. Alex. Gordon, and APOLLO and ROYAL GEORGE yachts, Capts. Sir Chas. Paget and Hon. Thos. Bladen Capel. He obtained command, 11 Nov. 1841, of the PELICAN 16, on the East India station, whence he returned home with specie to the amount of 250,000*l.* on board, and was paid off, in Jan. 1845. He acquired his present rank 2 July, 1846. AGENTS—Messrs. Stilwell.

JUSTICE. (LIEUT., 1816. F-P., 12; H-P., 27.)

ROBERT JUSTICE, born 27 July, 1795, is, we imagine, brother of Capt. Philip Justice, R.N.

This officer entered the R. N. College 8 Aug. 1808, and embarked, 9 Aug. 1811, as Midshipman, on board the ELEPHANT 74, Capt. Fras. Wm. Austen. After serving for two years and four months in that ship, on the North Sea and Baltic stations, he successively joined the PRESIDENT and MÆANDER frigates, Capts. Fras. Mason, Archibald Duff, and John Bastard, under whom he served, off the coasts of Ireland and Portugal and in the East Indies, until Jan. 1816. Having passed his examination in the previous Oct., he was shortly afterwards appointed Mate of the MINDEN 74, Capt. Wm. Paterson, with whom, subsequently to the battle of Algiers, he proceeded to India, where he officiated as Signal Officer to Sir Rich. King until May, 1820. He then returned to England with a broken constitution, as Acting-Lieutenant, in the SERINGAPATAM 46, Capt. Wm. Walpole; and, on his arrival home in the following Oct., found that for his conduct at Algiers he had been promoted, four years previously, to the rank of Lieutenant, although his commission, bearing date 16 Sept. 1816, had not, in consequence of some mistake, been forwarded to him. His health has not permitted him to serve since. AGENTS—Messrs. Stilwell.

K.

KAINS. (CAPTAIN, 1846. F-P., 26; H-P., 23.)

JOHN KAINS was born 21 Jan. 1788.

This officer (whose name had been borne, since 1798, on the books of the NORTHUMBERLAND, FORTITUDE, and ST. DOMINGO 74's) embarked, in 1800, as Sec.-cl. Boy, on board the THESEUS 74, Capts. John Bligh, Edw. Hawker, Fras. Temple, and Barrington Dacres. Proceeding in that ship to the West Indies, he there, in 1803-4, assisted, as Master's Mate, at the blockade of St. François, St. Domingo —the reduction of Port Dauphin, where two forts and a 28-gun ship, *La Sagesse*, were taken from the enemy—the capture of the French squadron with the remains of General Rochambeau's army from Cape François—and the unsuccessful attempt upon Curaçoa. He was also, while at St. Domingo, employed in cutting out merchant-vessels from most of the harbours in that island. Quitting the THESEUS in Sept. 1805, he joined the RUBY 64, Capt. Chas. Rowley, stationed in the North Sea, where, with the exception of a few weeks passed as Acting-Lieutenant in the AMARANTHE 18, Capt. Edw. Pelham Brenton, he further served, from Dec. in the same year until promoted to the rank of Lieutenant 1 July, 1807, on board the MAJESTIC 74, flag-ship of Vice-Admiral Thos. Macnamara Russell. Being then appointed to the THAIS 18, Capt. Isaac Ferrieres, he was present in that sloop at the ensuing reduction of the Danish West India islands, and also, on his return from a visit to South America and the Cape of Good Hope, in the operations of 1809 against the island of Walcheren. After he had been attached for a short period, as First-Lieutenant, to the VESUVIUS bomb, Capt. Wm. Saunders, Mr. Kains joined, in a similar capacity, 5 Feb. 1810, the GRAMPUS 50, Capt. Wm. Hanwell, and sailed with a fleet of Indiamen for China. During his absence from England, and when in the Java Sea, he took command of the boats and disarmed a Malay piratical proa. His last subordinate appointment was, 23 Oct. 1811, to the Senior Lieutenancy of the WARRIOR 74, Capt. Hon. Geo. Byng, afterwards Viscount Torrington, whose highest praise, as well as that of the Commander-in-Chief, we find him eliciting by his cool and gallant conduct, on 13 July, 1813, in boarding and capturing, with the boats of the latter ship and the ÆTNA bomb under his orders, the Danish national lugger *Teigeren*, mounting 3 6-pounders, and defended by a heavy fire of musketry from the shore, whither the crew, on the approach of the British, had effected their escape. To add to the excellence of the achievement, it was performed in the proximity of three of the enemy's gun-boats, at a moment, too, when the vessel, having been fired by her crew, was in a perfect blaze, with the flames raging on her magazine-chest, and with every indication of an instant explosion. On 30 Nov. following Lieut. Kains had the honour of steering the boat which conveyed H.S.H. the Prince of Orange from the WARRIOR to the Dutch shore. He attained the rank of Commander 8 Jan. 1814, and was afterwards employed —from 6 June, 1833, until July, 1836, in the Coast Guard—from 18 April, 1837, until Feb. 1839, in the Ordinary at Chatham, as Commander of the BRUNE 22, and POICTIERS 74—and, from 5 Feb. 1839 until Oct. 1844, as Superintendent, with his name on the books of the ROYAL SOVEREIGN yacht, of the Packet Service at Holyhead. He acquired his present rank 9 Nov. 1846, and is now on half-pay.

Capt. Kains married, 2 Feb. 1814, Miss Gold, of Gillingham, co. Kent.

KANE. (LIEUTENANT, 1841.)

COLIN CAMPBELL A. KANE entered the Navy 5 Sept. 1834; passed his examination 3 Oct. 1840; and, while Mate of the CONWAY 26, Capt. Chas. Ramsay Drinkwater Bethune, was employed in the operations of May, 1841, against Canton, where he landed and assisted at the destruction of the whole line of defences, extending about two miles from the British factory, and mounting in the whole 64 pieces of cannon.* He assumed the rank of Lieutenant 8 Oct. 1841, and was afterwards appointed—22 Oct. 1842, to the CALEDONIA 120, flag-ship of Sir David Milne at Plymouth—14 Feb. 1843, to the THUNDERER 84, Capt. Dan. Pring, employed on particular service—4 May, 1843, to the LILY 16, Capt. Geo. Baker, at the Cape of Good Hope—in 1843-4, to the CORNWALLIS 72, and AGINCOURT 72, flag-ships of Sir Wm. Parker and Sir Thos. John Cochrane on the East India station—and, 9 June, 1845, as First, to the OSPREY 12, Capt. Fred. Patten, in which vessel he was wrecked on the western coast of New Zealand in March, 1846.

KATON. (VICE-ADMIRAL OF THE BLUE, 1841. F-P., 21; H-P., 42.)

JAMES KATON was born 5 July, 1770, and died 14 Dec. 1845, at Gosport. He was son of Lieut. Edw. Katon, R.N., who died in 1779, and brother-in-law of the late Capt. Henry Vaughan, R.N. Two of his brothers, both in the Royal Marines, fell victims to the yellow fever in the West Indies; and a third died a Captain of that corps and Barrack-Master of the Portsmouth division.

This officer entered the Navy, 3 July, 1783 (under the auspices of Lord Hood), as Midshipman, on board the PRINCESS ROYAL 98, Capt. Jonathan Faulknor, whom he followed into the TRIUMPH 74, both guard-ships at Portsmouth. He was next, between May, 1786, and Sept. 1791, employed, on the Newfoundland, Channel, and West India stations, in the ECHO, FALCON, and ORESTES sloops, Capts. Robt. Carthew Reynolds, Thos. Laugharne, and Thos. Revell Shivers, and MARLBOROUGH 74, Capt. Sam. Cornish. Joining Commodore Linzee, in Dec. 1792, on board the ALCIDE 74, he served in 1793 at the occupation of Toulon, and was present in the early part of the following year at the siege of St. Fiorenza, where he landed with a detachment of men under Capt. Edw. Cooke, and assisted at the storming of Convention Hill, preparatory to the evacuation of the town by the enemy's troops. On 14 March, 1794, having been promoted on 18 of the previous month to a Lieutenancy in the COURAGEUX 74, Capts. Benj. Hallowell, Wm. Waldegrave, Chas. Elphinstone, and Augustus Montgomery, he shared in the conspicuous part borne by that ship in Vice-Admiral Hotham's partial action off Genoa; after which he again served with his old Commander, then Rear-Admiral Linzee, on board the WINDSOR CASTLE 98, and VICTORY 100—also with Capt. Shuldham Peard in the ST. GEORGE 98—once more with Rear-Admiral Linzee in the PRINCESS ROYAL 98—for 20 months with Sir Roger Curtis in the PRINCE

* *Vide* Gaz. 1841, p. 2512.

98—and for two years and a half with Earl St. Vincent in the VILLE DE PARIS 110. In Jan. 1801 he was appointed by the latter nobleman Acting-Captain of the PRINCESS ROYAL, and also of the CUMBERLAND 74, from which ship, on his arrival in the following April at Jamaica, whither he had gone in quest of a French squadron under Admiral Ganteaume, he was removed by Lord Hugh Seymour to the command of the LARK sloop—an appointment which the Admiralty, we believe, ratified on 7 May. He was confirmed a Post-Captain, 23 Oct. 1801, in the CARNATIC 74, flag-ship of Rear-Admiral Robt. Montagu, with whom he soon removed to the SANS PAREIL 80. In March, 1802, previously to the departure of the latter officer from Port Royal, he presented Capt. Katon with a sword, as a token of his regard and approbation. In the same spirit Lord St. Vincent, in the preceding year, had awarded him a medal. He returned to England in June, 1803, as Captain of the TRENT frigate; and afterwards held the temporary command, from 13 Jan. 1809 to 4 May, 1810, of the MARS 74, and, from 16 April to 9 Sept. 1811, of the NIOBE 40. While in the former ship he received the thanks of the Admiralty for his protection of the Baltic trade; and when in the NIOBE he visited the coasts of Spitzbergen and Greenland, for the purpose of affording security to the British fisheries. He became a Rear-Admiral on the Retired List 22 July, 1830; was transferred to the Active List 17 Aug. 1840; and rose to the rank of Vice-Admiral 23 Nov. 1841.

He married, 28 Feb. 1804, Adeliza Arabella, second daughter of Geo. Moubray, Esq., of Cockairney, co. Fife, sister of Capt. Geo. Moubray, R.N., and cousin of the late Admiral Sir Rich. Hussey Hussey, K.C.B., by whom he has left issue a son, the present Commander J. E. Katon, R.N., and five daughters.

KATON. (COMMANDER, 1845. F-P., 21; H-P., 3.)

JAMES EDWARD KATON, born 18 Nov. 1810, is only son of the late Vice-Admiral Jas. Katon.

This officer entered the Royal Naval College 5 Nov. 1823; and embarked, 25 Sept. 1825, as Midshipman, on board the PYRAMUS 42, Capts. Robt. Gambier and Geo. Rose Sartorius. In that ship, after accompanying Mr. Morier, the British Commissioner, to Mexico, and serving for some time under the flag of Sir Thos. Masterman Hardy on the Home station, he was employed in conveying troops to Malta, Gibraltar, and also to Lisbon, where we find him present at the period of Don Miguel's first occupation of the throne. Joining next, in 1828, the PALLAS 42, Capts. Chas. Howe Fremantle, Adolphus FitzClarence, Manley Hall Dixon, and Wm. Walpole, he continued attached to her on various stations until June 1834—the last four years in the capacity of Mate. He accordingly assisted, under Capt. FitzClarence, in escorting Lord Dalhousie and the Bishop of Calcutta from Portsmouth to Bengal, General Viscount Combermere from India home, and Colonel Fox from Halifax. After a further servitude of nearly two years and a half in the OCEAN 80, and HOWE 120, flag-ships of Hon. Chas. Elphinstone Fleeming at Sheerness (where he had command for some time of a dockyard lighter), he was presented with a commission dated 15 Feb. 1837. His succeeding appointments were—4 April, 1837, to the CASTOR 36, Capt. Edw. Collier, in the Mediterranean—11 May, 1839, to the BRITANNIA 120, as Flag-Lieutenant to Hon. C. E. Fleeming at Portsmouth—1 Feb. 1840, to the CAMBRIDGE 78, Capt. Edw. Barnard, under whom he participated in the operations on the coast of Syria, and was present at the blockade of Alexandria—and, 20 Aug. 1841, to the ILLUSTRIOUS 72, bearing the flag in North America and the West Indies of Sir Chas. Adam, to whom he became Signal-Lieutenant 17 June, 1842. He was promoted to the rank of Commander on being paid off, 31 May, 1845, and has not been since afloat. AGENTS—Messrs. Halford and Co.

KAY, F.R.S. (LIEUTENANT, 1839.)

JOSEPH HENRY KAY entered the Navy 18 Dec. 1827; passed his examination in 1834; obtained his commission 6 April, 1839; and, from 15 of the following May until his return to England in 1843, was employed on an explorative mission to the Antarctic regions in the TERROR, Capt. Fras. Rawdon Moira Crozier, part of an expedition conducted under the orders of the present Sir Jas. Clark Ross.

Lieut. Kay, a Fellow of the Royal Society, is now Director of H.M. Magnetic Observatory at Hobart Town. He married, 6 Nov. 1845, Maria, daughter of Geo. Meredith, Esq., of Cambria, Great Swan Port.

KEANE. (LIEUT., 1815. F-P., 19; H-P., 22.)

EDWARD KEANE entered the Navy, 11 July, 1806, as Fst.-cl. Vol., on board the PRINCESS ROYAL 98, commanded in the Channel by Capt. Robt. Carthew Reynolds; and on removing, in 1807, to the LEYDEN 64, Capt. Wm. Cumberland, accompanied the expedition to Copenhagen. While next attached, between Nov. in the latter year and Oct. 1810, to the AMELIA 38, Capt. Hon. Fred. Paul Irby, he assisted, as Midshipman, at the destruction, 24 Feb. 1809, of three French frigates under the batteries of Sable d'Olonne, and was much employed in co-operation with the patriots on the north coast of Spain. In Nov. 1813, after he had served for three years, on the Lisbon, Home, and American stations, in the POICTIERS 74, Capt. Sir John Poo Beresford, and had aided in the capture of several of the enemy's vessels, among which were the *Wasp*, of 20 guns, and the late British brig-of-war *Frolic*, Mr. Keane became Acting-Lieutenant of the DIOMEDE troopship, Capt. Chas. Montague Fabian, whom he followed, in a similar capacity, in Aug. 1814, into the ORPHEUS 36. He left the latter vessel in the ensuing Nov., and in May, 1815, joined, again as Midshipman, the CHATHAM 74, Capt. Edw. Lloyd, on the Channel station, where he cruized for a period of three months. He then took up a commission bearing date 7 March, 1815. His appointments have since been—4 Jan. 1837, to the Coast Guard—5 Dec. 1839, 30 March, 1840, and 5 Feb. 1842, to the command of the DILIGENCE Revenue-vessel, and PROSPERO and MERLIN steam-packets—and (on leaving the latter), 6 Feb. 1847, as Additional-Lieutenant, to the REDWING, another packet, in which he is now serving at Liverpool, under the orders of Capt. Thos. Bevis.

He married, in 1834, Sarah, eldest daughter of John Peake, Esq., then Master-Shipwright at Portsmouth Dockyard, by whom he has issue.

KEANE. (COMMANDER, 1846.)

THE HONOURABLE GEORGE DISNEY KEANE, born 26 Sept. 1817, is third son of Lieut.-General Lord Keane, G.C.B., G.C.H., Colonel of the 43rd Regt., and late Commander-in-Chief in India (who was raised to the Peerage in 1839, as a reward for the brilliant expedition he had conducted against Affghanistan, and died in 1844), by his first wife, Grace, second daughter of Lieut.-General Sir John Smith, R.A. His eldest brother, the present Peer, is a Major in the Army, and Captain in the 37th Regt.; his second, also an officer in the Army; and his third, a Lieutenant R.E.

This officer entered the Navy 8 Oct. 1831; passed his examination in 1837; obtained his first commission 26 Dec. 1840; then joined the EXCELLENT gunnery-ship at Portsmouth, Capt. Sir Thos. Hastings; was next, from 25 Aug. 1841 until the close of 1843, employed in the Mediterranean, on board the FORMIDABLE 84, Capts. Sir Edw. Thos. Troubridge and Sir Chas. Sullivan; and, on 9 Nov. 1846, after having served for exactly 11 months in the Channel, as First-Lieutenant of the SCOURGE steam-sloop, Capt. Jas. Crawford Caffin, was advanced to the rank of Commander. He is at present on half-pay.

KEATLEY. (Lieutenant, 1828.)

John Savell Keatley entered the Navy 4 Feb. 1812; passed his examination in 1818; and was made Lieutenant, 9 Feb. 1828, into the Bustard 10, Capt. Geo. Sidney Smith, on the West India station, whence he invalided in the course of the same year. He was afterwards appointed—27 April, 1830, to the Coast Guard—14 Oct. 1833, to the command of the Royal Charlotte Revenue-vessel—5 Feb. 1836, again to the Coast Guard—20 June, 1836, to the command of the Royal George, another Revenue-cruizer—and, 13 June, 1839, a third time to the Coast Guard. He has been on half-pay since the early part of 1841.

Lieut. Keatley is married, and has issue.

KEATS. (Captain, 1826. f-p., 14; h-p., 28.)

William Keats is nephew of the late Admiral Sir Rich. Goodwin Keats, G.C.B.*

This officer entered the Navy, 30 Sept. 1805, as Fst.-cl. Vol., on board the Superb 74, Capt. R. G. Keats, bearing the flag at first of Sir John Thos. Duckworth, under whom he bore a part in the action off St. Domingo 6 Feb. 1806. After attending the expedition to Copenhagen in 1807, and witnessing the embarkation from Nyeborg of the Spanish troops under the Marquis de la Romana, he served until July, 1813, as Midshipman, on the Home, Cadiz, and Mediterranean stations, in the Puissant 74, Capt. Irwin, Milford 74, and Hibernia 120, bearing each the flag of Rear-Admiral Keats, and Caledonia 120, flag-ship of Sir Edw. Pellew. In Aug. of the latter year he became Acting-Lieutenant of the Partridge sloop, Capt. John Miller Adye, to which vessel (being confirmed to her by commission dated 6 of that month) he continued attached until Oct. 1814. He next, from 23 March to 9 Dec. 1815, officiated as Flag-Lieutenant to Sir R. G. Keats, in the Salisbury 50, at Newfoundland; and, on 17 April, 1816, after having been intermediately employed in the Albion 74, flag-ship of Sir Chas. Rowley at Sheerness, he was promoted to the rank of Commander. He obtained command, 7 Oct. 1822, of the Cherokee 10, on the Leith and Cork stations; but has not been since employed. His elevation to his present rank took place 27 March, 1826.

Capt. Keats married, first, 10 April, 1833, Catherine Jane, eldest daughter of Jas. Pitman, Esq., of Dunchideock House, Devon, who was drowned a few weeks after her marriage by the upsetting of a boat; and, secondly, 6 July, 1835, Augusta Maria, daughter of Giles King Lyford, Esq., of Winchester.

* Sir R. G. Keats was born 16 Jan. 1757, and entered the Navy 25 Nov. 1780, on board the Bellona 74, Capt. John Montagu. He served, at the commencement of the American war, at the burning of Norfolk, in an attack upon Hampton, Virginia, and at the capture of New York, Fort Washington, and Rhode Island. As a Lieutenant, a rank he acquired in 1777, he was on board the Ramillies in the action between Keppel and D'Orvilliers 27 July, 1778, also at the defeat of Don Juan de Langara 16 Jan. 1780, and at the ensuing relief of Gibraltar. In Jan. 1782, as a reward for the skilful manner in which he had conducted the naval part of an expedition against the enemy's small craft at New Brunswick, he was made Commander into the Rhinoceros sloop of war. In Sept. 1783, being at the time in the Bonetta, another sloop, Capt. Keats bore a conspicuous part at the capture of the French 40-gun frigate *L'Aigle*. Attaining Post-rank in 1789, he successively commanded, between that period and 1807, the Southampton 32, Niger 32, London 98, Galatea 36, Boadicea 38, and, for upwards of six years, the Superb 74. In the Galatea he attended the expedition to Quiberon, and participated in the capture and destruction of several of the enemy's frigates and other vessels. He was a long time employed, in the Boadicea, in watching the port of Brest, and on 2 July, 1799, commanded part of the force under Rear-Admiral Chas. Morice Pole in an attack on a Spanish squadron in Aix Roads; and in the Superb he acquired fame in Sir James Saumarez' action with the Franco-Spanish squadron in the Gut of Gibraltar 12 July, 1801; accompanied Lord Nelson to the West Indies, in 1805, in pursuit of the combined fleets; fought as Flag-Captain to Sir John Thos. Duckworth in the action off St. Domingo 6 Feb. 1806, and was in consequence presented with a sword valued at 100 guineas; and commanded a flying squadron of line-of-battle ships in the Bay of Biscay in the early part of 1807. In Aug. 1807, having hoisted a broad pendant on board the Ganges 74, he sailed with the expedition under Admiral Gambier against Copenhagen. In Oct. of the same year he became a Rear-Admiral; and in Aug. of the following year he was the instrument, with his flag on board his old ship, the Superb, of emancipating from French thraldom the Spanish troops stationed in the Danish provinces under the Marquis de la Romana—a service for his able management of which he was created a K.B. He afterwards held the chief command in the Baltic; served in 1809 under Sir Rich. Strachan during the operations against Walcheren; assumed charge, in 1810, of the squadron employed at the defence of Cadiz; became second in command, in 1811, of the fleet in the Mediterranean; and enjoyed, from 1813 until 1816, the government and command at Newfoundland. Sir Rich. Keats, who had been appointed to a Colonelcy in the Royal Marines in Nov. 1805, and promoted to the rank of Vice-Admiral in 1810, was nominated Major-General of Marines in 1818, and made a full Admiral in 1825. From 1821 until the period of his death, which took place 5 April, 1834, he held the Governorship of Greenwich Hospital. He died an Admiral of the White.

KEELE. (Captain, 1843. f-p., 16; h-p., 24.)

Charles Keele, born 19 Feb. 1795, at Southampton, is fourth son of John Keele, Esq., many years a surgeon at that place; and brother of Mr. Edw. Keele, R.N., who was mortally wounded on board the Java, when captured by the American ship *Constitution*, at the age of 13.

This officer entered the Navy, 1 April, 1807, as Fst.-cl. Vol., on board the Supérieure 10, commanded by his relative Capt. Edw. Rushworth, whom he accompanied with convoy to the West Indies. In the following Oct., after his name had been borne for four months on the books of the Prince George, Tisiphone, and Princess of Orange, he rejoined Capt. Rushworth, as Midshipman, in the Satellite 16, and again sailed with the West India trade. Between the latter part of 1808 and the date of his promotion to the rank of Lieutenant, 24 Sept. 1814, we find him employed on various stations in the Tisiphone, Capt. Foote, Caledonia 120, and Boyne 98, bearing each the flag of Sir Harry Neale, Barbadoes 28, Capt. E. Rushworth, Thetis 36, Capt. Wm. Henry Byam, Java of 46 guns and 377 men, Capt. Henry Lambert, and Rivoli and Edinburgh 74's, Capts. Graham Eden Hamond, Edw. Stirling Dickson, and John Lampen Manley. When in the Caledonia, Mr. Keele served in her boats at the defence of Cadiz. He was on board the Barbadoes in Sept. 1811, when, being at the time in company with the Hotspur frigate and Goshawk sloop, she made a successful attack on seven French gun-brigs in the neighbourhood of Calvados; and on 29 Dec. 1812 it was his lot to be in the Java on the occasion of her capture, after a close and dreadful action of three hours and 40 minutes, and a loss of 22 men killed and 102 (including the Captain mortally, and himself severely) wounded, by the American ship *Constitution* of 55 guns and 480 men, many of whom also suffered.* Soon after his promotion, as above, Lieut. Keele went back to the Rivoli, and was on board of her, as a Supernumerary, when she intercepted the *Melpomène* French frigate, in 1815. In the short and spirited action which preceded that event he received a severe blow in consequence of one of the gun-breechings giving way. Being paid off on his return from the Mediterranean in Feb. 1816, the Lieutenant did not again go afloat until 24 Nov. 1823, when he was appointed First of the Arachne 18, commanded by his friend Capt. Henry Ducie Chads, fitting for the East Indies. On his arrival on that station he was immediately ordered to Ava, for the purpose of co-operating in the hostilities then in force against the Burmese. On 21 and 24 Sept. 1824 we accordingly find him (the Arachne having reached Rangoon on 15 of that month) assuming command of a division of gun-vessels and row-boats, and assisting at the destruction of eight stockades, on the Panlang river. He subsequently commanded the naval part of an expedition, consisting of six gun-vessels, one mortar-boat, seven row-gun-boats, and an armed transport, sent to co-operate with a small body of troops under Lieut.-Colonel Henry Godwin in the reduction of the city of Martaban. After the destruction had been ac-

* *Vide* Gaz. 1813, p. 772.

complished of about 30 of the enemy's war-boats, the defences of the place, although of amazing strength, and resolutely defended by between 3000 and 4000 men, were stormed and carried with the most determined gallantry by not more than 220 of the British, conspicuous among whom was Lieut. Keele, who, with Capt. Borrowes of the 41st Regt., was the first on the occasion to enter a battery mounting 2 guns. His exertions throughout the whole of the affair were unremitting, and he elicited both the praise of his coadjutor and the acknowledgments of the Governor-General of India in Council. In Jan. 1825, shortly after his return from Martaban, we find him, with 48 officers and men under his command, accompanying Lieut.-Colonel Elrington to the attack of a strong hill-fort, situated on the left bank of the Pegu river, about eight miles from Rangoon, and the pagoda of Syriam, five miles in the interior. Previously to the immediate assault of the former, it was necessary for the party, soldiers and seamen, who had landed, to cross a deep unfordable nullah, the bridge over which had been removed purposely to check their progress. A new one being, however, soon constructed, under a galling fire, which killed and wounded 30 of the British, inclusive of 6 belonging to the Navy, the enemy were in an instant put to flight. In the successful attack made the next morning on the Syriam pagoda the sailors assisted in manning the scaling ladders, and Lieut. Keele was the first over the outer stockade. In the words, indeed, of Lieut.-Colonel Elrington, the naval part of this expedition he nobly conducted. The warmest thanks of Commodore Coe, the Commander-in-Chief on the station, were in consequence conveyed to him. On 6 Feb. 1825 he led one of three divisions of boats against Than-ta-bain, a large and imposing stockade, mounting 36 guns, and garrisoned by 2000 fighting men; and on that occasion he was again mentioned as being the first, with Lieut. Hall of the ALLIGATOR, to enter the enemy's position. His characteristic gallantry again obtained the applause of the Supreme Government. In the course of the same month he destroyed several boats and fire-rafts up the Lyne river; and he was afterwards attached to the light division of the flotilla in the operations against Donoobew in March, 1825.* He ultimately, on his arrival at Portsmouth with Capt. Chads, as First-Lieutenant of the ALLIGATOR 28, about Jan. 1827, found that he had been advanced to the rank of Commander by commission dated 22 July, 1826. His subsequent appointments were—26 March, 1836, to a three-years' Inspectorship in the Coast Guard—and, 13 March, 1841, to the ROVER 18, on the West India station, whither he sailed, after only 48 hours' notice, in the TWEED 20. He was promoted, a few months after he had been paid off, to the rank of Captain, 19 July, 1843. He has not been since able to procure employment.

* *Vide* Gaz. 1825, pp. 501, 690, 1434, 1967, 2277.

KEELING. (LIEUT., 1812. F-P., 32; H-P., 11.)

JOHN JAMES KEELING entered the Navy, in May, 1804, as Fst.-cl. Vol., on board the MONTAGU 74, Capt. Robt. Waller Otway. During the period he continued in that ship he was present as Midshipman in 1805 in Admiral Cornwallis' attack on the French fleet close in with Brest Harbour, on which occasion the MONTAGU exchanged fire with *L'Alexandre*, a French 80-gun ship. He also assisted at the evacuation of Scylla in 1808, and co-operated with the patriots on the coast of Catalohia. After he had further served with Capt. Otway in the MALTA 80, and with Rear-Admiral Hon. Robt. Stopford in the SPENCER 74, he joined, in Jan. 1809, the VICTORIOUS 74, Capts. Graham Eden Hamond and John Talbot. In the course of the same year we find him accompanying the expedition to the Walcheren. He was next employed on boat-service in the Faro of Messina; and on 21 Feb. 1812, the VICTORIOUS being at the time in company with the WEASEL 18, he shared, as Master's Mate, and attracted the notice of Capt. Talbot by his conduct, in a most gallant conflict of four hours and a half, which terminated in the capture, with a loss to the former ship of 27 men killed and 99 wounded, and to the enemy of 400 killed and wounded, of the French 74 *Rivoli*, whose consorts, three brigs and two gun-boats, were at the same time defeated.* Being re-appointed to the VICTORIOUS, 10 Aug. 1812, Mr. Keeling (who had left her when promoted to the rank of Lieutenant on 13 of the previous May) commanded her tender in the attacks upon Crany Island and New Hampton in 1813. From 4 Oct. 1814 until Feb. 1815, and from 27 Aug. in the latter year until he invalided 4 May, 1816, he presents himself to our notice as serving in the Channel and East Indies on board the AMARANTHE 18, and CHALLENGER 16, Capts. Rich. Augustus Yates and Henry Forbes. His appointments have since been—7 July, 1826, to the Coast Guard—29 Sept. 1832, to the command of the SHAMROCK Revenue-vessel—24 Sept. 1835, a second time to the Coast Guard—10 Oct. 1838, again to the SHAMROCK —and 20 June, 1843, once more to the Coast Guard, in which service he is at present employed.

Lieut. Keeling, we understand, enjoys a pension of 91*l*. 5*s*. AGENTS—Messrs. Stilwell.

KEITH. (CAPTAIN, 1828. F-P., 12; H-P., 22.)

THE HONOURABLE WILLIAM KEITH was born 16 Dec. 1799, and died 5 Jan. 1846, at Monkrigg, Haddington, N. B., aged 46. He was second and youngest son of William, sixth Earl of Kintore, by Maria, daughter of Sir Alex. Bannerman, Bart., of Kirkhill.

This officer entered the Navy, 14 Feb. 1812, as Fst.-cl. Vol., on board the INVINCIBLE 74, Capt. Chas. Adam, and, besides assisting in boat and other operations on the coast of Spain, was present, in June, 1813, at the reduction, after a siege of five days, of the fort of St. Philippe, in the Col de Balaguer, near Tortosa, armed with 12 pieces of ordnance, including 2 10-inch mortars and 2 howitzers, with a garrison of 101 officers and men. After he had been for a short period Midshipman of the DUBLIN 74, flag-ship at Plymouth of Lord Keith, he became attached, in April, 1814. to the ROYAL OAK 74, bearing the flag of the late Sir Pulteney Malcolm, under whom he was employed in the expeditions against Baltimore and New Orleans. From Aug. 1815 until about the commencement of 1820, Mr. Keith further served on the Home and Newfoundland stations in the TARTARUS, also the flag-ship of Sir Pulteney Malcolm, MADAGASCAR and MÆANDER frigates, both commanded by Sir Jas. Alex. Gordon (under whom, in the MÆANDER, he narrowly escaped being wrecked, off Orfordness, in Dec. 1816), and EGERIA 26, Capts. Robt. Rowley and Henry Shiffner—of which latter ship he was created a Lieutenant 10 Nov. 1819. His next appointments were to the BLONDE 42, and DARTMOUTH 42, Capts. Lord Byron and Thos. Fellowes. Under the former of those officers he accompanied from this country the remains of the late king and queen of the Sandwich Islands. He was promoted, 14 Aug. 1827, to the command of the PHILOMEL 10, one of the vessels present, on 20 of the following Oct., at the battle of Navarin. Strange to record, however, he was not permitted to join her until after the action, being compelled on the occasion to perform Lieutenant's duty on board the DARTMOUTH. He attained Post-rank 18 Aug. 1828, and remained from that period on half-pay.

Capt. Keith married, 24 June, 1830, Louisa, daughter of the late Wm. Grant, Esq., of Congalton, by whom he has left issue a son and daughter. AGENTS—Goode and Lawrence.

KELLETT. (COMMANDER, 1839.)

ARTHUR KELLETT is cousin of Capt. Henry Kellett, R.N., C.B.

This officer entered the Navy 24 June, 1811; passed his examination in 1819; and was made Lieutenant, 16 Dec. 1825, into the ESK 20, Capt.

* *Vide* Gaz. 1812, p. 852.

Wm. Jardine Purchas, on the coast of Africa, whence he returned to England in May, 1828. He attained his present rank, after having had command, from 20 Dec. 1837 until July 1839, of the BRISK brigantine, on the station last named, 7 Nov. 1839; and was lastly, from 2 Sept. 1841 until the close of 1846, employed in the Coast Guard.

He married, in 1834, Maria Lucinda, eldest daughter of the late Major Hanna, 56th Regt. AGENTS—Messrs. Chard.

KELLETT, C.B. (CAPTAIN, 1842.)

HENRY KELLETT, born 2 Nov. 1806, is cousin of Commander Arthur Kellett, R.N.

This officer entered the Navy 7 Jan. 1822, and from 1823 until 1826 served in the West Indies on board the RINGDOVE. Towards the close of the latter year, after having accompanied a body of troops to Lisbon in the GLOUCESTER 74, Capt. Joshua Sydney Horton, he joined the EDEN 26, Capt. Wm. Fitzwilliam Owen, under whom he was again employed on the coast of Africa (whither he proceeded for the colonization of Fernando Po) until his return to England in the summer of 1831—the last three years as First-Lieutenant (commission dated 15 Sept. 1828). He had command during part of that time of the CORNELIA tender, and was on board the EDEN at a period of dreadful sickness, when 46 men were laid up with fever without a surgeon, and only 2 officers besides himself were left to perform duty. Being next appointed, 7 Nov. 1831, to the ÆTNA surveying-vessel, Capts. Edw. Belcher, Wm. Geo. Skyring, and Wm. Arlett, he returned to his former station, where, at the time that Capt. Skyring was murdered, he held the post of First-Lieutenant, and was afterwards detached in charge of the RAVEN, an assistant to the ÆTNA. On 29 Oct. 1835, shortly after the latter vessel had been paid off, Lieut. Kellett assumed command of the STARLING cutter, of 105 tons, and was ordered upon surveying-service to the west coast of South America. While there, he held the acting-command, from July, 1836, until Feb. 1837, of H.M.S. SULPHUR, during the interval which elapsed between the resignation of Capt. Beechey and the advent of Capt. Belcher. He then went back to the STARLING, and in that small vessel, on his return to the Pacific after a voyage round Cape Horn, he proceeded to China, visiting *en route* the Marquesas and Tahiti, and touching at the New Hebrides, Salomon Islands, Borneo, &c. Arriving at his destination in Dec. 1840, Lieut. Kellett (whose vessel on her passage had been struck by lightning and dismasted) joined in the warfare then commencing against the Chinese, in which, as will be seen, he bore a very eminent part. On 7 Jan. 1841 we find him uniting in the operations against the enemy's forts at Chuenpee; and in the course of the same day serving with the NEMESIS and the boats of the CALLIOPE under Capt. Belcher, by whom he was spoken of in terms of high commendation, at the destruction of 11 out of 13 large war-junks, an exploit which was achieved in admirable style.* He next, on 26 Feb., acquired the thanks of Sir Gordon Bremer for his gallantry and zeal in the action which preceded the capture of the forts at the Boca Tigris.† During the operations of March against Canton he acquired every favourable consideration for his useful exertions in sounding, conjointly with Lieut. Rich. Collinson, and Mr. Rich. Browne, Master of the CALLIOPE, the various inlets through which the ships had to pass, and conducting them in safety to an anchorage off that city. In the discharge of these duties Mr. Kellett was indeed indefatigable.‡ At one period, in addition to his own vessel, the ALGERINE, and the YOUNG HEBE and LOUISA tenders, were simultaneously placed under his orders. In May, 1841, when the British renewed hostilities against Canton, our officer, whose promotion to the rank of Commander took place on 6 of that month, again found opportunity of distinction.* Proceeding afterwards to the northward, he succeeded, on the night previous to the attack upon Chapoo, 18 May, 1842, in thoroughly sounding (with the assistance of Capt. Collinson) between the anchorage of the ships and the shore, and thus enabled the CORNWALLIS, BLONDE, and MODESTE, while the troops were landing, to take up excellent positions against the sea-batteries.† In the ensuing June he appears to have again, with much zeal and perseverance, co-operated with Capt. Collinson in surveying the channel before Woosung.‡ After the fall of Shanghae, to her position in front of which place he had piloted the NORTH STAR 26, Capt. Kellett proceeded with Capt. Bourchier 30 miles up the river into the interior, and contributed to the destruction, on 20 June, of two batteries mounting 5 guns each.§ He was also present in all the operations up the Yang-tse-Kiang,|| where he led the Commander-in-Chief's ship to Nanking. As a further reward for his particularly useful services Capt. Kellett was advanced to Post-rank 23 Dec. 1842,¶ and nominated, the next day, a C.B.** He obtained leave to return to England in Aug. 1843; but since 8 Feb. 1845 has been again afloat, as Captain of the HERALD 26, now engaged in surveying the Pacific. AGENTS—Messrs. Stilwell.

* *Vide* Gaz. 1841, pp. 1162, 1222. † *V.* Gaz. 1841, p. 1408. ‡ *V.* Gaz. 1841, pp. 1504-5.

KELLOCK. (LIEUT., 1824. F-P., 23; H-P., 24.)

HENRY GRAY KELLOCK is son of an old Warrant officer who was presented with a service of plate for his distinguished conduct on board the QUEEN 98, Rear-Admiral Gardner's flag-ship in Lord Howe's action 1 June, 1794, and died Master-Rigger of Sheerness Dockyard. His grandfather and his four uncles also held warrants in the Navy. The only one of the latter now living, Robert, has retired on a pension. Mr. Kellock's elder brother, James, a Lieutenant R.N., was drowned at sea in command of a merchant-ship.

This officer entered the Navy, 15 Sept. 1800, as Third-cl. Vol., on board the ROYAL SOVEREIGN 100, Capt. Gardner, with whom he served in the Channel until April, 1802. Re-embarking, 27 Nov. 1803, on board the VILLE DE PARIS 110, Capt. Rich. Raggett, bearing the flag afterwards of Hon. Wm. Cornwallis, he was present as Midshipman in that officer's pursuit of the French fleet into Brest, and skirmish with the enemy's batteries, 22 Aug. 1805. When next in the BELLONA 74, Capt. John Erskine Douglas, we find him witnessing the destruction of the French 74-gun ship *L'Impétueux*, near Cape Henry, 14 Sept. 1806. After a servitude of three years and eight months on the Halifax, North Sea, and Baltic stations, as Midshipman, in the NEMESIS, Capt. Philip Somerville, LEVERET and KITE sloops, both commanded by Capt. Benj. Crispin, and DARING 10, Lieut.-Commander Campbell, he joined, in Feb. 1812, the RANGER sloop, Capt. Geo. Acklom, and was for some time employed at the siege of Danzig, where he was twice lent to the METEOR bomb. In Feb. 1814, having left the RANGER in the preceding June, Mr. Kellock, who shortly afterwards passed his examination, was received on board the ESPOIR sloop, Capts. Robt. Russell and Norwich Duff. During the remainder of the war with the United States he was actively employed in the Chesapeake, part of the time in a tender, in carrying troops to the attacks upon Washington and Alexandria. From 23 Sept. 1815, until promoted to the rank of Lieutenant 21 Jan. 1824, he served uninterruptedly, as Admiralty Midshipman and Chief Mate, in the ALBAN 10, and GRIPER and SCOUT Revenue-cruizers, Lieut.-Commanders Hugh Patton, Wm. Smith, Cook, and Chas. Cromer. He twice shared, during that period, in the annual bounty awarded to the vessel which had convicted

* *Vide* Gaz. 1841, p. 2510. † *V.* Gaz. 1842, p. 3692. ‡ *V.* Gaz. 1842, p. 3397. § *V.* Gaz. 1842, p. 3401. || *V.* Gaz. 1842, p. 3404. ¶ *V.* Gaz. 1842, pp. 3821-3864.
** To enable Capt. Kellett to receive Post-rank the STARLING had been rated a sloop-of-war.

the greatest number of smugglers. Since he left the SCOUT the Lieutenant has been on half-pay.

He is now Agent for Lloyd's at Southport, Ormskirk, Lancashire; and is married and has issue.

KELLY. (CAPTAIN, 1821. F-P., 17; H-P., 32.)

* BENEDICTUS MARWOOD KELLY, born 1 Sept. 1790, is second son of Benedictus Marwood Kelly, Esq., Attorney-at-law, of Holsworthy, co. Devon, by Mary, daughter of Arscott Coham, Esq., of the same place. He is brother of Commander Wm. Kelly, R.N., and of the late Lieut. John Tucker Kelly, of the Horse-Artillery at Madras; and first-cousin of the present Arthur Kelly, Esq., of Kelly, Devon. One of his uncles, Francis John, was a Captain in the 18th, or Royal Irish Regt.; another, William Hancock, died a Vice-Admiral of the Blue 2 May, 1811, aged 60, leaving a son, the late Lieut. Magnus Morton Kelly, R.N. (1808); and a third, Capt. Lewis Robertson, of the VETERAN 64, fell at the head of a brigade of seamen while serving on shore at the storming of Pointe-à-Pitre, Guadeloupe, in 1794. The eldest son of Capt. Fras. John Kelly, now deceased, was a Captain in the Royal African Corps.

This officer entered the Navy, 19 Oct. 1798, as A.B., on board the NIGER 32, Capt. Hon. Philip Wodehouse, on the Guernsey station; and in the following Nov., after having accompanied the same officer into the VOLAGE 28, joined the GIBRALTAR 80, commanded at first by his uncle, Capt. W. H. Kelly, and next by Capt. Geo. Fred. Ryves. During a continuance of nearly six years in the latter ship, he assisted at the capture, 19 June, 1799, of Rear-Admiral Perrée's squadron of three frigates and two brigs, attended the expeditions of 1800 and 1801 to Ferrol and Egypt, and was wounded while serving in the boats in a successful attack made upon the French while they were besieging the town of Porto Ferrajo in the island of Elba. In Oct. 1804, Mr. Kelly, who had been borne for short periods on the books of the ROYAL WILLIAM, flag-ship at Spithead of Admiral Geo. Montagu, and SWIFTSURE 74, Capt. Mark Robinson, rejoined his relative on board the TÉMÉRAIRE 98, in which ship he continued to be employed under Capt. Eliab Harvey, until made Sub-Lieutenant, 12 Jan. 1805, into the ELING schooner, Lieut.-Commander Wm. Archbold. Being promoted to a full Lieutenancy, 31 Jan. 1806, in the ADAMANT 50, Capt. John Stiles, he sailed with an East India convoy for the Cape of Good Hope, and on 6 of the ensuing May was present, during the passage, at the capture of the Spanish frigate-built privateer *La Reparadora*, of 30 guns and 315 men. From the ADAMANT, which ship had been latterly cruizing very productively on the coast of Guinea, and also off the Havana, where she appears to have been employed in blockading a Spanish ship of the line, Lieut. Kelly removed, in Aug. 1807, to the DÆDALUS 32, Capts. Fred. Warren, Wm. Ward, and Sam. Hood Inglefield. Under the latter officer, in company with a small squadron commanded by Capt. Chas. Dashwood, he contributed, in Dec. 1808, to the reduction of the fort and town of Samana, St. Domingo, almost the last port of refuge on the station for the enemy's privateers. The officers and crews of the latter having on the occasion effected their escape, Mr. Kelly was placed in charge of the boats of the DÆDALUS and AURORA frigates, and sent in pursuit of them. After a search of four days and nights under an incessant rain, which afterwards proved fatal to most of the persons employed, they were traced up a small river, and found in ambuscade on its banks behind a breastwork, which had been thrown up as a means of defence. This however was instantly charged in face of a galling fire of musketry, and the whole of the enemy made prisoners. In March, 1810, Mr. Kelly became First of the POLYPHEMUS 64, bearing the flag of Vice-Admiral Bartholomew Sam. Rowley; upon the occasion of whose death he was sent with despatches, in the BRAMBLE, Lieut.-Commander John Fleming, to England, where, on his arrival, he was advanced to the rank of Commander by commission dated 28 Nov. 1811. From that period, although incessant in his applications for employment, and offering to serve as a volunteer during the American war, and again with Lord Exmouth at Algiers, Capt. Kelly remained on half-pay until appointed, 28 Sept. 1818, to the command of the PHEASANT, of 22 guns. In that sloop he was employed on the coast of Africa until Feb. 1822, during the greater part of which period he was senior officer of the squadron on the station. As a reward for his zeal, activity, and vigilance, he was presented with a Post-commission dated 19 July, 1821. Since he left the PHEASANT, as above stated, in Feb. 1822, Capt. Kelly has again been on half-pay.

He married, 31 Aug. 1837, Mary Anne, only daughter and heir of Richard Price, Esq., of Highfield Park, co. Sussex, and was left a widower 14 July, 1838. 2. Juliana Boyd June 7 1855.

* Died at Salford, nr Bath, Feb. 26 1867 and was buried at Kelly.—

KELLY. (LIEUTENANT, 1825.)

EDWARD KELLY entered the Navy 2 Nov. 1810; passed his examination in 1817; and was made Lieutenant, 21 Dec. 1825, into the OWEN GLENDOWER 42, Capt. Hood Hanway Christian, stationed at the Cape of Good Hope, whence he ultimately invalided. He has since been on half-pay.

Since May, 1847, the Lieutenant has been Harbour-Master at the Mauritius. AGENTS—Messrs. Stilwell.

KELLY. (LIEUTENANT, 1812. F-P., 28; H-P., 15.)

RICHARD NUGENT KELLY entered the Navy, 14 Jan. 1804, as Fst.-cl. Vol., on board the INCONSTANT 36, Capt. Edw. Stirling Dickson, successively employed, until April, 1808, on the African, Jamaica, and Home stations—for some time under the flag of Sir Jas. Saumarez. During the earlier portion of his attachment to that frigate he witnessed the surrender of the island of Gorée, and was on one occasion taken prisoner by the Fantees, an African tribe, after a contest in which the whole of his party had been killed. In April, 1808, he became Midshipman of the BARFLEUR 98, successive flag-ship of Rear-Admirals Wm. Albany Otway, Chas. Tyler, and Sir Sam. Hood, on the Lisbon station, whence, after serving in the TRIUMPH 74, Capt. Sam. Hood Linzee, he returned home, in Jan. 1810, on board the RENOWN 74, Capt. Philip Chas. Durham, for the purpose of passing his examination. Between the following Sept. and the date of his promotion to the rank of Lieutenant, 21 March, 1812, we again find him serving on the Lisbon station, as also in the Baltic and at Spithead, in the DREADNOUGHT 98, Capt. S. H. Linzee, BARFLEUR, flag-ship of Hon. Geo. Cranfield Berkeley, DREADNOUGHT, commanded as before, and VICTORY 100, Capt. Philip Dumaresq. His appointments have since been—in March and May, 1813, to the UNION 98, Capts. S. H. Linzee, Wm. Kent, and Robt. Rolles, and SAN JUAN 74, flag-ship of Rear-Admiral S. H. Linzee, both on the Mediterranean station—20 Sept. 1813, to the office of Acting Resident-Agent for Transports and Prisoners of War at Gibraltar, where he remained until Feb. 1814—20 July, 1837, to the Coast Blockade, in which service he was employed as a Supernumerary-Lieutenant of the RAMILLIES and TALAVERA 74's, both commanded by Capt. Hugh Pigot, until Nov. 1830—and, 10 June, 1831, to a station in the Coast Guard, the command whereof, with the exception of about two years in 1838-40, he has ever since retained. AGENT—Fred. Dufaur.

KELLY. (CAPTAIN, 1844. F-P., 26; H-P., 13.)

WILLIAM KELLY entered the Navy, early in 1808, as Fst.-cl. Vol., on board the LIVELY 38, Capt. Geo. M'Kinley, in which frigate, after participating in various operations in the river Tagus, and witnessing the reduction of Vigo and Santiago, he was wrecked, as Midshipman, off the island of Malta, in Aug. 1810. From Nov. in the latter year until June, 1815, when he took up a commission dated on

8 of the previous March, we find him uninterruptedly employed as Midshipman and Master's Mate in the LEONIDAS 38,* Capts. Anselm John Griffiths, Hon. Fred. Wm. Aylmer, Geo. Fras. Seymour, and Wm. King, on the Mediterranean, Irish, West India, and North American stations. His succeeding appointments were—5 April, 1816, to the ROSARIO 10, Capt. Thos. Ladd Peake, with whom he served in the Channel until Dec. 1818—28 May and 25 June, 1822, to the JUPITER 60, Capt. Geo. Augustus Westphal, and PANDORA 18, Capts. Fred. Hunn and Wm. Gordon, in the latter of which vessels he proceeded to Newfoundland—10 Dec. 1823, to the TWEED 28, Capt Hunn—next, to the AURORA 46, Capt. Henry Prescott—23 Nov. 1826, after 21 months of half-pay, to the GLOUCESTER 74, Capt. Joshua Sydney Horton—2 May, 1828, to the PRINCE REGENT 120, Capt. Hon. Geo. Poulett—and, 11 Nov. following, to the PALLAS 42, Capt. Adolphus FitzClarence. Under the latter officer Mr. Kelly was employed in conveying the Earl of Dalhousie and the Bishop of Calcutta from Portsmouth to Bengal, General Viscount Combermere from India home, and Colonel Fox from Halifax. He obtained a second promotal commission 25 April, 1831, and was next employed—from 23 Jan. 1835 until 1838, in the Coast Guard—and from 7 March, 1842, until advanced to his present rank 5 April, 1844, as Second-Captain of the WINCHESTER 50, flag-ship of Hon. Josceline Percy at the Cape of Good Hope. He has since been in command of the CONWAY 26, on the last-named station. AGENTS—Messrs. Stilwell.

---

* KELLY. (COMMANDER, 1811. F-P., 17; H-P., 38.)

WILLIAM KELLY, born 27 Feb. 1782, is elder brother of Capt. B. M. Kelly, R.N.

This officer entered the Navy, in 1792, as Captain's Servant, on board the ST. GEORGE 98, commanded by his uncle, Capt. Wm. Hancock Kelly, with whom he continued to serve in the WINDSOR CASTLE 98, SOLEBAY 32, and VETERAN 64, until Sept. 1796—the last two years as Midshipman. While in the SOLEBAY we find him assisting at the reduction of the French West India Islands in 1794, where he was employed in the batteries as Aide-de-Camp to Lord Garlies, and to his uncle Capt. Kelly, at the siege of Fort Bourbon, and again on shore, as Aide-de-Camp to Capt. Lewis Robertson, who was killed at the storming of Pointe-à-Pitre, Guadeloupe. In March, 1798, after he had further served in the ROYAL SOVEREIGN 100, and VILLE DE PARIS 110, flag-ships of Sir Alan Gardner and Lord St. Vincent, he was nominated, by the latter nobleman, Acting-Lieutenant of the HECTOR 74, Capt. Peter Aplin, as a reward for his previous conduct at the destruction of a convoy of market-boats, together with their protectors, three gun-vessels, at the entrance of Cadiz Harbour. He was confirmed, 4 July, 1798, into the INCENDIARY fire-ship, Capts. Geo. Barker and Rich. Dalling Dunn, on the Mediterranean station, and during the latter portion of the war was there employed on board LA MINERVE 42, commanded by the present Sir Geo. Cockburn, at whose express desire he had been appointed. Besides numerous boat and other affairs he was in consequence present at the capture and destruction, 2 Sept. 1801, of *Le Succès* of 32, and *Le Bravoure* of 42 guns; on which occasion, being at the time First-Lieutenant, his Captain reported his conduct in the handsomest manner.† His subsequent appointments were—16 Dec. 1803, to the MONTAGU 74, Capt. Robt. Waller Otway, stationed in the Channel —23 Oct. 1804, to the PRINCE 98, Capts. Rich. Grindall and Wm. Lechmere, of which ship, after participating in the battle of Trafalgar,‡ he became First-Lieutenant—30 Dec. 1806, and 27 May, 1807, in the latter capacity, to the DREADNOUGHT 98, Capt. Wm. Lechmere, and VILLE DE PARIS 110, flag-ship of Lord Gardner—and, 8 Aug. 1808 and 14 May, 1811, to the CALEDONIA 120, and ROYAL GEORGE 100, bearing each the flag of Lord Gambier, to whom, subsequently to Lord Cochrane's memorable achievement in Basque Roads, on which occasion he was intrusted with the command of the CALEDONIA's boats, he became Signal-Lieutenant. He attained his present rank on Lord Gambier striking his flag, 23 Aug. 1811; and has since been on half-pay.

Commander Kelly is the only officer of his rank on the List of 1811.

* The LEONIDAS effected the capture, 23 May, 1813, of the *Paul Jones* American privateer, of 16 guns and 85 men.

† *Vide* Gaz. 1801, p. 1355.

‡ At the close of the action Lieut. Kelly was placed in charge, as Prize-Master, of the *Santissima Trinidad*, of 130 guns, in which he remained two days and nights; when, by order of Lord Collingwood, he removed his men and sank her.

* Died at Taunton August 13. 1859. —

KELSALL. (LIEUT., 1819. F-P., 10; H-P., 28.)

JOHN THEOPHILUS KELSALL entered the Navy 3 Oct. 1809, as Midshipman, on board the VALIANT 74, Capt. John Bligh. Removing in the following May to the MENELAUS 38, Capts. Sir Peter Parker and Edw. Dix, he assisted at the proximate reduction of the Isle of France, and afterwards visited the Mediterranean and Chesapeake. He was present on the former station when the MENELAUS gallantly pursued the French 40-gun frigate *Pauline* and 16-gun brig *Ecureuil* under the batteries in the neighbourhood of Toulon, and then effected a masterly retreat from the French fleet, which had come out to their protection, 28 May, 1812; and on proceeding to the Chesapeake he was on board when Sir Peter Parker was killed in a land operation at Bellair, near Baltimore, 30 Aug. 1814. Quitting the MENELAUS in May, 1815, Mr. Kelsall was next (until promoted to the rank he now holds 2 April, 1819) employed on the East India station, part of the time as Acting-Lieutenant, in the CORNWALLIS 74, Capt. Andrew King, and CHALLENGER and TRINCOMALEE, both commanded by Capt. Philip Bridges. He has since, we believe, been on half-pay.

He married, 3 March, 1827, Elizabeth Anne, daughter of the late Vice-Admiral Stephens.

KEMBALL. (LIEUT., 1815. F-P., 9; H-P., 32.)

WILLIAM HENRY KEMBALL entered the Navy, 8 Nov. 1806, as Fst.-cl. Vol., on board the NORTHUMBERLAND 74, Capt. Nathaniel Day Cochrane, bearing the flag of Hon. Sir Alex. Cochrane on the West India station; where, from June, 1807, until the close of 1810, he served with Capt. Volant Vashon Ballard, chiefly as Midshipman, in the BLONDE and STATIRA frigates, and NEPTUNE 98, assisting, during that period, at the capture of five privateers, carrying in the whole 58 guns and 515 men, as also at the destruction, previously to the fall of Guadeloupe, of the French 40-gun frigates *Loire* and *Seine*, together with a heavy battery by which they were defended, in Anse la Barque. He was next, between Dec. 1810 and Jan. 1814, employed in the Channel on board the SCEPTRE 74, Capt. Sam. Jas. Ballard, and BOYNE 98, and VILLE DE PARIS 110, both flag-ships of Sir Harry Burrard Neale. He then rejoined Sir Alex. Cochrane in the TONNANT 80, and, continuing with him until promoted to the rank of Lieutenant 18 Feb. 1815, bore an active part in consequence in the hostilities with America, and was present in the operations against New Orleans. He has not been afloat since the general peace.

KEMBLE. (COMMANDER, 1845. F-P., 16: H-P., 2.)

FREDERICK KEMBLE was born 17 Sept. 1815.

This officer entered the Navy, 29 Sept. 1829, as Midshipman, on board the GANGES 84, Capts. John Hayes, Edw. Stirling Dickson, and Geo. Burdett, on the Home station. From Feb. 1831 until Nov. 1836 he served in the Mediterranean, latterly as Mate, in the ST. VINCENT 120, and CALEDONIA 120, flag-ships of Hon. Sir Henry Hotham and Sir Josias Rowley; after which we find him, until promoted to the rank of Lieutenant 13 Nov. 1841, employed, on the South American and North America and West India stations, in the STAG 46, Commodore

Thos. Ball Sulivan, and WINCHESTER 52, bearing the flag of Sir Thos. Harvey. His succeeding appointments were—21 Jan. 1842, to the ROVER 18, Capt. Chas. Keele, on the station last named—31 Jan. 1843, to the EXCELLENT gunnery-ship at Portsmouth, Capt. Sir Thos. Hastings—and, 20 March following, to the CALEDONIA 120, as Flag-Lieutenant to Sir David Milne, Commander-in-Chief at Plymouth. He attained his present rank 29 April, 1845, and has since been on half-pay. AGENT—Joseph Woodhead.

KEMP. (LIEUTENANT, 1827.)

JAMES KEMP died in 1845.

This officer entered the Navy 1 July, 1809; passed his examination in 1815; obtained his commission 28 April, 1827; and, from 16 Nov. 1832 until the period of his death, was uninterruptedly employed in the Coast Guard.

KEMPE. (LIEUT., 1828. F-P., 21; H-P., 6.)

JOHN KEMPE is grand-nephew of the late Admiral Kempe.

This officer entered the Navy, 25 Dec, 1820, as Fst.-cl. Vol., on board the DOVER 28, Capts. Arthur Batt Bingham and Sam. Chambers, on the Leith station. Prior to his promotion to the rank of Lieutenant, which took place 13 Nov. 1828, he was further employed, as Midshipman and Mate, at home and in South America, in the MARTIAL 12, Lieut.-Commander M'Kirdy, BLONDE 42, Capt. Lord Byron (under whom he escorted from this country the remains of the late King and Queen of the Sandwich Islands), and BRITANNIA 120, and GANGES 84, flag-ships of Sir Jas. Saumarez and Sir Robt. Waller Otway. He served during the next two years, still in South America, on board the BEAGLE surveying-vessel, Capt. Robt. FitzRoy; and, from 1 Jan. 1833 until the summer of 1843, he had charge of a station in the Coast Guard. He has since been on half-pay.

He married, 23 May, 1831, Susannah Rundle, daughter of J. Prynne, Esq., of H.M. Customs, Fowey, by whom he has issue three children.

KEMPSTER. (LIEUT., 1815. F-P., 14; H-P., 28.)

RALPH RICHARD TOMKIN KEMPSTER entered the Navy, 15 Jan. 1805, as a Volunteer, on board the PRINCESS floating-battery, Capt. Sam. Martin Colquitt, lying in the River Mersey. Quitting the latter vessel in the following July, he served, during the remainder of the war, as Midshipman and Master's Mate, chiefly on the Home, West India, and Mediterranean stations, in the BOADICEA 38, Capts. John Maitland and John Hatley, SATELLITE sloop, Capts. Robt. Evans and Hon. Willoughby Bertie, DANNEMARK 74, Capt. Jas. Bissett, RODNEY 74, Capt. Edw. Durnford King, and PRINCE 98, bearing the flag of Sir Rich. Hussey Bickerton. In April, 1815 (after he had been also borne, as a Supernumerary for passage, on the books of the SNAKE, TIGRE, and TANAIS, Capts. Joseph Gape, John Halliday, and Joseph James, he was nominated Acting-Lieutenant of the ONYX 10, Capts. Smith Cobb and Chas. Strangways, then at Jamaica. On his return home for the purpose of being paid off in July, 1816, he found a commission awaiting him dated 1 Feb. 1815. His next and last appointment was, 27 Feb. 1823, to the CLIO sloop, commanded by the officer last mentioned, with whom he was for three years employed in the North Sea.

KEMPTHORN. (LIEUT., 1813. F-P., 24; H-P., 16.)

CHARLES HENRY KEMPTHORN, born 12 Oct. 1792, is son of the late Capt. T. Kempthorn.

This officer entered the Navy, 11 Nov. 1807, as Ordinary, on board the AMPHION 32, Capt. Wm. Hoste, with whom he served, nearly the whole time as Midshipman, until paid off in Aug. 1811. He was consequently present in that frigate on 12 May, 1808, in a very spirited engagement of many hours with several batteries in the bay of Rosas, in an attempt to cut out the French 800-ton store-ship *Baleine*, mounting from 20 to 30 guns, with a crew of 150 men. He also, on 23 April, 1809, served with the boats of the AMPHION, SPARTAN, and MERCURY, under Lieut. Chas. Geo. Rodney Phillott, at the capture of 13 valuable merchantmen lying in the mole of Pesaro; and on 27 Aug. following he was employed with a detachment, commanded by the same officer, at the storming of the strong fort of Cortelazzo, near Trieste, the capture of which occasioned the simultaneous surrender, within sight of the Italian squadron off Venice, of six of the enemy's gun-boats and a large convoy of merchant-trabaccolos anchored for protection under its walls.* Besides participating in similar affairs at Biseglia, Umago, and other places, it was Mr. Kempthorn's lot to be Senior Midshipman of the AMPHION in the famous action of 13 March, 1811, off Lissa, where a British squadron, carrying in the whole 156 guns and 879 men, completely routed, after a battle of six hours, and a loss to the above ship of 15 men killed and 47 wounded, a Franco-Venetian armament, whose force amounted to 284 guns and 2655 men. On leaving the AMPHION he joined the PYLADES 18, Capt. Geo. Ferguson, likewise in the Mediterranean, where, becoming Signal-Mate of the CALEDONIA 120, flag-ship of Sir Edw. Pellew, he served in that capacity in the partial action fought with the Toulon fleet 5 Nov. 1813. He attained the rank of Lieutenant on 25 Dec. in the latter year, and in the course of 1814, after having served on shore as Naval Aide-de-Camp to Major-General Sir Henry Montressor during the operations against Genoa, joined the BACCHANTE 38, Capt. Fras. Stanfell, on the North American station, whence he returned home and was paid off in July, 1815. Since 7 July, 1831, he has been in charge of a station in the Coast Guard.

KENDALL. (LIEUTENANT, 1827.)

EDWARD NICHOLAS KENDALL died 12 Feb. 1845, at Southampton, in his 45th year.

This officer entered the Navy 26 Oct. 1814; and passed his examination in 1822. He served in several expeditions to the Arctic and Antarctic Seas, including the one to the Polar Sea under Sir John Franklin in 1825-7, on which occasion he was the companion of Dr. Richardson in that branch of it which discovered and delineated the northern coast of America lying between the Mackenzie and Coppermine Rivers. He was awarded a commission dated 30 April, 1827, but does not appear to have been further officially employed.

At the period of his death Lieut. Kendall was Superintendent of the Peninsula and Oriental Steam-Packet Company. He married, in May, 1832, Mary Anne, eldest daughter of Joseph Kay, Esq., of Greenwich Hospital, and of Gower Street, Bedford Square, by whom he has left issue four children. AGENTS—Hallett and Robinson.

KENDALL. (LIEUT., 1815. F-P., 10; H-P., 32.)

THOMAS KENDALL entered the Navy, 1 April, 1805, as Fst.-cl. Vol., on board the QUEEN 98, Capt. Fras. Pender, with whom he afterwards served in the ROYAL SOVEREIGN 100, OCEAN 98, and QUEEN again, which latter ship bore the flag for some time of Rear-Admiral Geo. Martin on the Mediterranean station. Becoming Midshipman, in Oct. 1808, of the CASTOR 32, Capts. Wm. Roberts and Hon. Valentine Gardner, he proceeded to the West Indies, where, after having assisted at the capture of the French ship of the line *D'Haupoult*, and the destruction, in Anse la Barque, Guadeloupe, of the frigates *Loire* and *Seine*, he removed, in July, 1810, to the NEPTUNE 98, Capt. Volant Vashon Ballard. Between the close of the latter year and Sept. 1814 Mr. Kendall served in the Mediterranean, as Midshipman, Acting-Lieutenant, and Master's Mate, on board the STANDARD 64, and ACHILLE 74, both commanded by Capt. Aiskew Paffard Hollis, CALEDONIA 120, flag-ship of Sir Edw. Pellew, TREMENDOUS 74, Capt. Robt. Campbell, and CALEDONIA

* *Vide* Gaz. 1809, p. 1907.

120, bearing the flag, as before, of Sir E. Pellew, under whom he participated in the actions of 5 Nov. 1813 and 13 Feb. 1814 with the Toulon fleet. He was promoted (from the PRINCE FREDERICK prison-ship at Plymouth, Capt. Rich. Pridham) to the rank of Lieutenant 8 Feb. 1815; but has not been since employed.

KENDALL. (COMMANDER, 1845.)

WALTER KENDALL entered the Navy 29 Nov. 1827; passed his examinatian in 1834; and served, as Mate of the NIMROD 20, Capt. Chas. Anstruther Barlow, during the operations of March and May, 1841, against Canton, where he gained the character of being a very deserving officer, but had the misfortune to lose a leg.* Being in consequence promoted to the rank of Lieutenant, by commission dated 8 June in the latter year, he was afterwards appointed, in that capacity—10 Oct. 1842, to the EXCELLENT gunnery-ship at Portsmouth, Capt. Sir Thos. Hastings—and, 31 Jan. 1843, to the CALEDONIA 120, flag-ship of Sir David Milne at Devonport. He attained his present rank 13 March, 1845, and has since been on half-pay. AGENTS—Case and Loudonsack.

KENDERDINE. (LIEUTENANT, 1815. F-P., 7; H-P., 32.)

JOHN KENDERDINE entered the Navy, 22 July, 1808, as Fst.-cl. Vol., on board the PRINCESS CAROLINE frigate, Capt. Chas. Dudley Pater, on accompanying whom, as Midshipman, into the CRESSY 74 (commanded afterwards by Capt. Chas. Dashwood), he was in company with the ST. GEORGE and DEFENCE when those ships were lost on their passage home from the Baltic during a violent gale in Dec. 1811. He continued in the CRESSY, on the West India and Home stations, until Feb. 1814; between which period and Aug. 1815 we find him employed, at Portsmouth, in North America, and at Plymouth, part of the time as Acting-Lieutenant, in the PUISSANT 74, Capt. Benj. Wm. Page, TONNANT 80, flag-ship of Hon. Sir Alex. Cochrane, DIADEM 64, Capt. John Martin Hanchett, and ST. GEORGE 98, bearing the flag of Sir John Thos. Duckworth. He then took up a commission dated 7 March, 1815, and has since been on half-pay.

He married, in 1827, Elizabeth Harriet, daughter of Mr. Brutton, Governor of the County Prison, Stafford.

KENMURE, VISCOUNT. (LIEUTENANT, 1815. F-P., 12; H-P., 31.)

THE RIGHT HONOURABLE ADAM GORDON VISCOUNT KENMURE, born 9 Jan. 1792, at Drungan Lodge, near Dumfries, N.B., is son of the late Hon. Adam Gordon, by his first wife, Miss Harriet Davies. His eldest brother, John, died a Lieutenant in the R.N. 31 Dec. 1813; and his youngest, Edward Maxwell, a Lieutenant in the 22nd Infantry, lost his life at Jamaica 14 Dec. 1827. The Viscount succeeded his uncle in the Peerage 21 Sept. 1840.

This officer entered the Navy, 12 July, 1804, as Fst.-cl. Vol., on board the AJAX 74, Capts. Lord Garlies, Christopher Laroche, Wm. Brown, and John Pilfold, in which ship we find him sharing, in the course of 1805, in Sir Robt. Calder's action, also in Hon. Wm. Cornwallis' pursuit of the French fleet into Brest, and in the battle of Trafalgar. Removing, in April, 1806, to the SEAHORSE of 42 guns, he was present, on the night of 5 July, 1808, when that ship, with only 251 men on board, put to flight the Turkish frigate *Alis-Fezan* of 26 guns and 230 men, and captured, after a memorably furious engagement, and a loss to the British of 5 men killed and 10 wounded, her consort, the *Badere-Zaffer*, mounting 52 guns, with a complement of 543 men, of whom 170 were killed and 200 wounded. During his continuance in the SEAHORSE Mr. Gordon was often engaged with the enemy's batteries and gun-boats at Cadiz; he assisted, too, in reducing the islands of Gianuti and Pianosa;* and in one of several boat affairs on the coast of Italy he received a slight contusion. Being unfortunately, on 21 Oct. 1809, taken prisoner in a prize, off Sardinia, by the *Letteros* letter-of-marque, he was carried to Genoa, and subsequently to Verdun, where it was his lot to be detained *en parole* until 1814. He then sailed for Quebec in the PSYCHE, Capt. Peter Fisher, for the purpose of joining the Canadian Lake service, to which he continued attached, as Acting-Lieutenant and Lieutenant (order and commission respectively dated 9 April and 1 July, 1815), until he invalided in Aug. 1816. He has since been on half-pay.

Viscount Kenmure is Deputy-Lieutenant for Kirkcudbrightshire. He married, 2 Nov. 1843, Mary Anne, daughter of the late Jas. Wildey, Esq., of the Oxford Militia.

* *Vide* Gaz. 1841, pp. 1503, 1505, 2501, 2513.

* *Vide* Capt. Thos. Bennett.

KENNEDY. (COMMANDER, 1809. F-P., 16; H-P., 33.)

ALEXANDER KENNEDY (*a*) entered the Navy, 24 Oct. 1798, as Fst.-cl. Vol., on board the MAGNANIME frigate, Capt. Hon. Mich. De Courcy, with whom he served on the Irish, Channel, and Mediterranean stations, latterly as Midshipman of the CANADA 74, until April, 1800. Removing then to the THAMES 32, Capts. Wm. Lukin and Aiskew Paffard Hollis, he witnessed Sir Jas. Saumarez' action of 12 July, 1801, in the Gut of Gibraltar, and was present, in the course of the same year, at the cutting out of a gun-boat and convoy from the Bay of Estapona. The THAMES being paid off in Jan. 1803, he next, in the following April, joined the PLANTAGENET 74, Capt. Graham Eden Hamond, under whom he assisted at the capture of *Le Courier de Terre Neuve* privateer of 16 guns and 60 men, and *L'Atalante*, a beautiful corvette of 22 guns and 120 men. In 1804 we find Mr. Kennedy sailing in the ALBION 74, Capt. John Ferrier, for the East Indies, where, after an attachment of a short period to the CONCORDE 36, commanded by the present Sir Josiah Coghill, he was confirmed a Lieutenant, 2 April, 1806, in the SCEPTRE 74, Capt. Joseph Bingham; which ship, on 11 of the ensuing Nov., made a dash, with the CORNWALLIS 50, into St. Paul's Bay, Ile de Bourbon, and opened a fire upon the shipping there at anchor, consisting of the *Semillante* French frigate, three armed ships, and 12 sail of merchantmen, the whole protected by seven batteries, mounting upwards of 100 pieces of cannon. On his return home in 1808, Lieut. Kennedy was appointed to the CAPTAIN 74, Capt. Geo. Cockburn, and ordered to the West Indies; on his arrival on which station he was invested with the acting-command, on 28 Oct. in the same year, of the *Port d'Espagne* sloop, in which, we understand, he contributed to the reduction of Martinique. At the period of his official promotion to the rank he now holds, which took place 2 June, 1809, our officer had charge of the ST. PIERRE sloop. In the course of 1810 he obtained successive command of the PELORUS, SURINAM, and FORESTER, all on the Halifax station; where, and again in the West Indies, he served until April, 1814. He has since been unemployed. The FORESTER, on 5 May, 1813, assisted, in company with the SAPPHIRE sloop, in capturing the *Mary Ann* American privateer of 2 guns and 30 men. AGENTS—Hallett and Robinson.

KENNEDY. (COMMANDER, 1822. F-P., 15; H-P., 30.)

ALEXANDER KENNEDY (*b*) entered the Navy, in Nov. 1802, as Fst.-cl. Vol., on board the TONNANT 80, Capt. Sir Edw. Pellew, employed off the coast of Spain; and in 1804, on that officer hoisting his flag in the CULLODEN 74, sailed with him for the East Indies. In Dec. 1805 he became Midshipman of the CONCORDE 36, commanded by the present Sir Josiah Coghill, but, rejoining the CULLODEN in Dec. 1806, was afforded an opportunity of witnessing the destruction, 11 Dec. 1807, of the dockyard and stores at Griessee, in the island of Java, and of all the men-of-war remaining to Holland in India. Between Jan. 1808 and his promotion to the rank of Lieutenant, 25 July, 1811, Mr. Kennedy served in various ships, principally on the Home station; after which we find him, until 1815, employed in the Mediterranean, on board the CENTAUR 74, Capt. Thos. White, RAINBOW 26, Capts. Gardiner Henry Guion and Gawen Wm. Hamilton, BOYNE 98, flag-ship of Lord Exmouth, and ABOUKIR 74, Capt. Norborne Thompson. When in the RAINBOW he took command of her boats, and captured, off the island of Corsica, a lateen-rigged vessel, laden with oak-planks.* On 24 May, 1819, he assumed charge of the HOUND Revenue-cruizer, as he also did, for some time in 1821, of the SYLVIA, a similar vessel. He attained his present rank 9 Oct. 1822, and has since been on half-pay.

Commander Kennedy married, 2 Feb. 1821, Elizabeth Rolleston, niece of A. Boyd, Esq., of Gostler, co. Donegal. AGENTS—Goode and Lawrence.

KENNEDY. (COMMANDER, 1842. F-P., 23; H-P., 16.)

ANDREW KENNEDY was born 24 Aug. 1787, at Devonport. His father was 55 years in the Service.

This officer entered the Navy, 5 Jan. 1808, as a Volunteer, on board the PENELOPE 36, Capt. John Dick, under whom he served, as Midshipman, at the reduction of Martinique in Feb. 1809.† Until promoted to the rank of Lieutenant, 9 Feb. 1815, he was further actively employed on the Halifax and Newfoundland stations, chiefly as Master's Mate, in the ÆOLUS 32, Capt. Lord Jas. Townshend, and BELLEROPHON 74, flag-ship of Sir Rich. Goodwin Keats. Between April and Sept. of the latter year we find him doing duty at Portsmouth in the PRINCE 98, bearing the successive flags of Sir Rich. Bickerton and Sir Edw. Thornbrough. He next, from June, 1824, until July, 1827, served on the North American and West India stations, as First of the NIEMEN 28, Capts. Wallis, Canning, and Simeon. He was subsequently appointed to the command—in Sept. 1828, of the AFRICAN, the first Government steamer stationed between Corfu and Ancona, in which he was employed in carrying despatches relative to the war between Turkey and Russia, and also in communicating with the Pacha of Egypt on the subject of steam with India—24 June, 1830, of the HERMES, another steam-vessel, also stationed in the Mediterranean—27 Nov. 1832, and 4 June, 1834, of the ALBAN and SPITFIRE Falmouth packets—and, 27 Nov. 1838, of the ACHERON steamer. In the ALBAN, the first steam-vessel that returned to England from the West Indies, Lieut. Kennedy went 208 miles up the river Orinoco, as far as Angostura, where no British man-of-war had ever before been. He proved, in the SPITFIRE, what had been before doubted, namely, the ability on the part of a steamer to resist the effects of a hurricane; and when in the ACHERON, in which vessel he remained until Dec. 1841, he conveyed to Sir Robt. Stopford the despatches directing the attack upon St. Jean d'Acre, and afforded a passage to the British ambassador from Constantinople to Malta, and thence to Naples. He was advanced to his present rank 27 May, 1842, but has not been since employed.

Commander Kennedy married Maria, daughter of Dennis Pinnock, Esq., of the island of Jamaica, by whom he has issue six children.

KENNEDY. (LIEUT., 1838. F-P., 22; H-P., 1.)

ARTHUR KENNEDY was born in March, 1811.

This officer entered the Navy, 28 June, 1824, on board the JASEUR 18, Capt. Thos. Martin, and was soon afterwards severely hurt by a fall from aloft while on duty. The JASEUR being ordered to South America, he was afforded an opportunity of there witnessing the revolutionary proceedings in Brazil, Chili, and Peru. In 1828, on his arrival in the Mediterranean in the BLONDE 46, Capt. Edm. Lyons, he was present, it appears, at the reduction of the Morea Castle. In the course of 1830 Mr. Kennedy successively joined the DONEGAL 76, Capt. Sir Jahleel Brenton, and CORDELIA 10, Capt. Chas. Hotham, of which latter vessel, on his return to the Mediterranean, after having visited the West Indies and North America, he was created, in 1831, an Acting-Lieutenant by Sir Henry Hotham—the last appointment of the kind ever conferred by that Admiral. During this second sojourn in the Mediterranean, we find Mr. Kennedy affording protection to the trade against the pirates of Smyrna, and employed in the boats in cruizing against those in the neighbourhood of Grabusa. The CORDELIA being paid off in 1834, he was at once appointed to the EXCELLENT gunnery-ship at Portsmouth, Capt. Thos. Hastings. He next, in 1835, proceeded to South America in the BLONDE 46, Commodore Fras. Mason, who, upon the death of the Commander-in-Chief, Sir Michael Seymour, again gave him an order, as a reward for his services and conduct, to act as Lieutenant, although at the time there were 11 Mates on the station senior to him. About this period Mr. Kennedy was often engaged on shore with a party of men for the protection of British property during the civil commotions in Peru and Chili. He continued to serve in South America on board the SATELLITE 18, Capt. Robt. Smart, and again in the BLONDE, until the return of the latter ship to England in 1837, when he immediately joined the BRITANNIA 120, bearing the flag at Portsmouth of Sir Philip Chas. Durham. His appointments since his promotion to the rank of Lieutenant, which took place 6 Sept. 1838, have been—26 June, 1839, to the STAG 46, Commodore Thos. Ball Sulivan, on the South American station—25 Sept. 1839, to the CLIO 16, Capt. Stephen Grenville Fremantle, employed in cruizing for slaves off Rio de Janeiro and other places—28 April, 1841, to the ACORN 16, Capt. John Adams, on the coast of Africa, where, among a host of other captures, he assisted in taking, at the close of a running fight of nine hours, the piratical slave-brig *Gabriel*, a vessel 10 feet longer than the ACORN, noted for its injury to commerce and the frequency of its insults to the British flag; as also, after a boat-chase of seven hours, the *Minerva*, having 550 slaves on board—and, 27 May, 1842 (four months after his health had obliged him to invalid), to the command of a station in the Coast Guard, which he still retains.

Lieut. Kennedy married, 25 Dec. 1840, Miss C. Jenkins, only daughter of A. Jenkins, Esq., of Navany, co. Donegal, by whom he has issue two children. AGENTS—Messrs. Stilwell.

KENNEDY. (LIEUTENANT, 1846.)

CHARLES DOYLE BUCKLEY KENNEDY passed his examination 28 July, 1841; and served, as Mate, in the HASTINGS 72, Capt. John Lawrence, HECATE steam-vessel, Capt. Jas. Hamilton Ward, ST. VINCENT 120, flag-ship of Sir Chas. Rowley, DARING 12, Capt. Henry Jas. Matson, and LOCUST steamer, Lieut.-Commander Henry Eden, chiefly on the Mediterranean station. He obtained his commission 2 June, 1846, and has been since employed as First-Lieutenant of the CEYLON receiving-ship at Malta, Capt. Thos. Graves.

KENNEDY. (LIEUT., 1841. F-P., 14; H-P., 0.)

JOHN JAMES KENNEDY, born in April, 1821, at Waterford, is son of the Venerable Jas. Kennedy, Archdeacon of that place.

This officer entered the Royal Naval College in June, 1833, and embarked, in June, 1835, as a Volunteer, on board the MAGICIENNE 24, Capt. Geo. Wm. St. John Mildmay, employed off the coasts of Spain and Portugal. Becoming Midshipman, in Nov. 1837, of the FAVORITE 18, Capt. Walter Croker, he proceeded in that vessel to the East Indies, where, in Oct. 1839, he joined the WELLESLEY 72, Capt. Thos. Maitland. Uniting afterwards in the operations against China, Mr. Kennedy served, as Mate, either

* *Vide* Gaz. 1814, p. 1411.

† While in the PENELOPE Mr. Kennedy lost the tops of three fingers of his right hand.

in the boats or on shore, at the first capture of Chusan; the attack upon the enemy's forts at Chuenpee and the Bogue, as also upon their camp, fort, and ship *Cambridge*, bearing the Chinese Admiral's flag, below Whampoa Reach, where 98 guns were in the whole destroyed; the towing of H.M.S. SULPHUR from under the fire of a masked battery; the storming of the heights above Canton in May, 1841; and the reduction of Amoy, the recapture of Chusan, the storming of Chinghae (where he commanded the barge),* and the occupation of Ningpo. He attained his present rank 8 Oct. 1841; returned to England at the conclusion of the war in the BLENHEIM 72, Capt. Sir Thos. Herbert; and, from 12 June, 1843, until paid off in the summer of 1847, was employed at the Cape of Good Hope as Second and First Lieutenant of the CONWAY 26, Capt. Wm. Kelly.

Lieut. Kennedy holds testimonials of the highest description from Sir Gordon Bremer, Sir Thos. Maitland, and Sir Thos. Herbert, the former of whom had his broad pendant on board the WELLESLEY; and he has been awarded a first-class certificate for his proficiency in naval gunnery.

KENNEDY. (CAPT., 1813. F-P., 25; H-P., 32.)

THOMAS FORTESCUE KENNEDY was born 9 Nov. 1774, and died 15 May, 1846. He was son of the late Dr. Kennedy, Physician to George IV. when Prince of Wales, and Inspector-General of Army Hospitals, who died in April, 1795, from the effects of excessive fatigue in the performance of his duties on the Continent under the Duke of York, by the third daughter of the late Thos. Chamberlaine, Esq., of Wardington, co. Oxford. One of his brothers, a Captain in the 19th Foot, died at Ceylon in 1801; and another, Sir Robt. Hugh Kennedy, Kt., was at the head of the Commissariat department of the Army under the Duke of Wellington during the whole of the Peninsular war.

This officer entered the Navy, 12 Aug. 1789 (under the patronage of Lord Hood), as Fst.-cl. Vol., on board the COLOSSUS 74, Capts. Hugh Cloberry Christian and Henry Harvey, guard-ship at Portsmouth; and, on being lent to the POMONA frigate, Capt. Henry Savage, sailed on a voyage to Africa and the West Indies. He next, between Sept. 1790 and the commencement of the French revolutionary war, served on the Home and Newfoundland stations, as Midshipman, in the CRESCENT frigate, Capt. Wm. Young, ALCIDE 74, Capt. Sir Andrew Snape Douglas, and BONETTA sloop, Capts. Wm. Elliot and Graham Moore; after which he joined the TERRIBLE 74, Capts. Skeffington Lutwidge and Geo. Campbell, and proceeded to the Mediterranean, where he served on shore with the army during the occupation of Toulon, and obtained great praise from Sir Hyde Parker, the Captain of the fleet, for his exertions in embarking and bringing off more than 60 unfortunate emigrants, chiefly females, at the very moment when their bloodthirsty countrymen were rushing into the town. In 1794 Mr. Kennedy returned to England in LA SYBILLE frigate, Capt. Edw. Cooke. He was then detached for a short period into the LIVELY 36, Capts. Lord Garlies and Geo. Burlton, at the expiration of which he rejoined LA SYBILLE, and continued to serve in that frigate, as Lieutenant (commission dated 5 July, 1796), until April, 1798. In Jan. of the latter year he captured, with the ship's barge and only 13 men, a gun-boat, in the Bay of Manilla, carrying 5 guns, besides swivels, and a complement of 50 men. He was in consequence invested with the command of his prize, which he retained until she was broken up subsequently to an attack made a few days afterwards by LA SYBILLE, in company with the FOX frigate, on the settlement of Samboangon, in the island of Magindanao. His next appointment was, 16 Nov. 1798, to the TRIUMPH 74, Capts. Wm. Essington, Thos. Seccombe, Eliab Harvey, and Sir Robt. Barlow, under whom, and for some time under the flag of Rear-Admiral Cuthbert Collingwood, he served on the Channel and Mediterranean stations until Jan. 1803—from 5 Oct. to 15 Nov. in which year he commanded the ELIZA AND JANE tender, employed in conveying impressed men from Dublin to Plymouth. He then, at the request of Capt. Eliab Harvey, became that officer's First-Lieutenant in the TÉMÉRAIRE 98, which ship was next astern of the VICTORY, and bore a most distinguished share, in the action off Cape Trafalgar 21 Oct. 1805. As a reward for the part he had taken in the battle Lieut. Kennedy was promoted to the rank of Commander by commission dated 24 Dec. in the same year. He did not, however, again go afloat until 29 Aug. 1808, from which period until posted, 4 Dec. 1813. he had command of the CORDELIA 10. In that sloop, we understand, he accompanied the expedition to the Walcheren, effected the capture of three privateers and several merchantmen, and commanded a squadron of eight brigs at the blockade of two 40-gun frigates in the Port of Dunkerque, where he remained until the latter were dismantled and laid up. His last appointment was, 24 June, 1834, to the Superintendentship of Sheerness Dockyard, which he held, part of the time as Captain of the TÉMÉRAIRE 104, until March, 1838.

* *Vide* Gaz. 1842, p. 397.

Capt. Kennedy married, first, 2 Sept. 1806, Louisa, second daughter of Colonel Adlam, R.M.; and secondly, 2 Oct. 1834, Hannah Sarah, now deceased, daughter of Dr. Hope, and relict of Dr. Kennedy, M.D., of Gillingham, Kent. By his former wife he has left issue two sons, George, a Captain in the R.A., and Hugh, a Lieutenant in the R.M. AGENT—J. Hinxman.

KENNEDY. (COMMANDER, 1846.)

WILLIAM HUGH KENNEDY entered the Navy 27 June, 1828; passed his examination in 1834; obtained his first commission 15 Dec. 1838; and was subsequently appointed—9 March, 1839, to the SERPENT 16, Capt. Hon. Robt. Gore, employed in North America and the West Indies, whence he returned towards the close of 1840—13 Aug. 1841, to the ILLUSTRIOUS 72, flag-ship of Sir Chas. Adam, with whom he served for upwards of three years on the same station—10 Nov. 1845, to the QUEEN 110, bearing the flag of Sir John West at Devonport—and, 24 April, 1846, as First-Lieutenant, to the CONSTANCE 50, Capt. Sir Baldwin Wake Walker, fitting for the Pacific. He attained his present rank on 4 July in the latter year; and since 29 of the following Sept. has been employed in the Coast Guard.

He married, 1 April, 1841, Georgiana, fourth daughter of the late Admiral Hon. Sir Chas. Paget, and niece of the Marquess of Anglesey. AGENT—J. Hinxman.

KENNETT. (LIEUTENANT, 1839.)

EDWARD HOILE KENNETT entered the Navy 15 July, 1826; passed his examination in 1832; obtained his commission 12 Nov. 1839; and, with the exception of a few months at the commencement of 1841, was employed, from 13 Nov. 1839 until the latter part of 1846, in the SATELLITE 18, Capt. John Robb, and PIQUE 36, Capts. Rich. Augustus Yates, Henry Forbes, and Hon. Montagu Stopford, on the North America and West India station. He is now on half-pay.

KENNEY. (COMMANDER, 1841. F-P., 15; H-P., 9.)

EDWARD HERBERT KENNEY entered the Navy 1 Oct. 1823; and was promoted, immediately on passing his examination, to the rank of Lieutenant, by commission dated 30 Oct. 1829. His succeeding appointments were—16 Dec. 1831, to the MADAGASCAR 46, Capt. Edm. Lyons, in the Mediterranean—15 April, 1835, to the EXCELLENT gunnery-ship at Portsmouth, Capt. Thos. Hastings—29 July, 1836, to the MINDEN 74, Capt. Alex. Renton Sharpe, from which ship, employed on particular service, he soon afterwards invalided—8 Sept. 1837, to the HERCULES 74, Capts. John Toup Nicolas and Edw. Barnard, with whom he served, chiefly on the Lisbon station, until the close of 1839—7 Dec. 1840, as First-Lieutenant, to his old ship the EXCELLENT—and, 27 May, 1841, to the DUBLIN 50, flag-ship in the Pacific of Rear-Admiral Rich. Thomas. He was advanced to the rank of Commander on 23 of the following Nov., and has since been on half-pay.

KENNICOTT. (COMMANDER, 1846. F-P., 24; H-P., 20.)

GILBERT KENNICOTT was born in 1789.

This officer entered the Navy, 26 July, 1803, as Fst.-cl. Vol., on board the VENERABLE 74, Capt. Geo. Reynolds, bearing the flag in the Channel of his friend and patron the late Lord Collingwood, whom he successively followed, as Midshipman, into the CULLODEN 74, PRINCE 98, VENERABLE again, DREADNOUGHT 98, ROYAL SOVEREIGN 100, and OCEAN 98. In the ROYAL SOVEREIGN at Trafalgar he received nearly 40 wounds and lost the sight of his right eye;* in consequence whereof he was allowed a pension of 10*l.* so long as he should continue a petty officer, and was presented by the Patriotic Society with the sum of 50*l.* In Oct. 1807, a few months after he had been appointed Master's Mate of the HIND frigate, Capt. Fras. Wm. Fane, Mr. Kennicott had the misfortune, while in charge of a small detained Greek vessel, to be wrecked off the island of Cyprus. He fell in consequence into the hands of the Turks, and was by them held a prisoner until late in 1809. He then joined the SEAHORSE 38, Capt. John Stewart, and, on 28 Jan. 1810, he was nominated by Lord Collingwood to a Lieutenancy in his own ship, the VILLE DE PARIS—an act which the Admiralty confirmed by commission dated 22 Aug. in the same year. Removing, not long afterwards, to the MINORCA 18, Capt. Ralph Randolph Wormeley, Lieut. Kennicott, in Nov. 1810, was again placed in command of a detained (American) vessel, whose crew, of themselves equal in number to the British, conjoined with one-half of the latter, and succeeded in re-capturing and carrying her into Marseilles. A second time thus a prisoner-of-war, the Lieutenant, after he had been for some time confined in a common gaol, was conducted to Verdun, and there kept *en parole* until the conclusion of the war. His next appointments were, in April and Sept. 1815, to the MOSQUITO 18, Capts. Jas. Tomkinson and Geo. Brine, and LEVERET 10, Capt. John Theed; in the latter of which vessels he remained on the St. Helena station until obliged to invalid, for the benefit of his health, 3 June, 1817. From 17 Sept. 1836, until advanced to the rank of Commander 9 Nov. 1846, he was employed in the Coast Guard, and on more than one occasion rendered good service to the revenue. He is now on half-pay.

Commander Kennicott was re-awarded, 20 Sept. 1817, a pension for his wounds of 91*l.* 5*s.*, together with two years' arrears. He is married, and has issue two daughters, one of whom, Sophia Elizabeth, became the wife, in Nov. 1841, of Capt. W. Calder, late of the 8th Regt. AGENT—Joseph Woodhead.

KENT. (LIEUTENANT, 1847.)

CHARLES KENT passed his examination 4 June, 1845; and after serving as Mate on board the EXCELLENT gunnery-ship, Capt. Henry Ducie Chads, SPARTAN 26, Capt. Thos. Matthew Chas. Symonds, and DIDO 18, Capt. John Balfour Maxwell, on the Home and East India stations, was promoted to the rank of Lieutenant 9 June, 1847. He has been since employed as Additional of the VERNON 50, flag-ship in India of Rear-Admiral Samuel Hood Inglefield.

KENT. (COMMANDER, 1822. F-P., 22; H-P., 25.)

HENRY KENT, born at Glasgow, is youngest brother of Commander Wm. G. C. Kent, R.N.

This officer entered the Navy, in July, 1800, as Fst.-cl. Vol., on board the FORTITUDE prison-ship at Portsmouth, Lieut.-Commander John Gourly, from which he was discharged in Aug. 1801. He re-embarked, in April, 1803, on board the SALVADOR DEL MUNDO guard-ship at Plymouth, bearing the flags of Sir John Colpoys and Sir Wm. Young, under whom he continued until appointed Midshipman, in March, 1804, of the GOLIATH 74, Capts. Chas. Brisbane and Robt. Barton. In Feb. 1806, after he had been intermediately employed in the Channel and off the coast of Ireland, he joined the RÉVOLUTIONNAIRE frigate, Capt. Chas. Fielding, stationed off the coast of Spain; on his removal from which ship to a Master's Mateship in the HUSSAR 38, Capt. Robt. Lloyd, he accompanied the expedition of 1807 to Copenhagen, and then proceeded to the West Indies and North America. In June, 1809, Mr. Kent was promoted, from the SWIFTSURE 74, flag-ship of Sir John Borlase Warren, to an Acting-Lieutenancy in the HORATIO 38, Capt. Geo. Scott. He next, in Nov. 1809, and April, 1810, joined, again in the capacity of Midshipman, the POMPÉE 74, and NEPTUNE 98, flag-ships of Sir Alex. Cochrane in the Leeward Islands. On 14 March, 1811, it was Mr. Kent's fortune to be confirmed a Lieutenant in LA FANTOME sloop, Capt. John Lawrence. In that vessel, which was at first stationed in the North Sea and on the Spanish coast, he ultimately proceeded to the Chesapeake, where, in different attacks made upon the enemy's works, he distinguished himself as a brave and meritorious officer. In Jan. 1814, with a degree of zeal highly creditable to him, Lieut. Kent started from Halifax as a volunteer, at the head of upwards of 100 officers, seamen, and marines, for the purpose of proceeding to Lake Ontario, there to join the force under Sir Jas. Lucas Yeo. After traversing a distance of nearly 1000 miles across an uninhabited country, covered with snow and woods, he at length, in the month of March, reached Kingston, where he was immediately appointed First-Lieutenant of the PRINCESS CHARLOTTE frigate, Capt. Wm. Howe Mulcaster, then on the stocks, but which his officer-like, active, unremitting, and strenuous exertions were the main cause of being ready to join in the expedition of May against Oswego. On the occasion of the attack he had the personal command of the PRINCESS CHARLOTTE, owing to the absence of her Captain; and his conduct, we are informed, was zealous, brave, and intelligent in the extreme. Continuing in Canada, he assumed command, in June, 1814, of a division of the flotilla on Lake Ontario, as he did, in Aug. 1815 and Nov. 1816, of the TECUMSEH and NEWASH schooners on Lakes Erie and Huron. In June, 1817, he was appointed Superintendent of the Naval Depôt on the eve of construction at Penetenguishne, on the lake last mentioned. In 1819, in consequence of a severe attack of fever and ague, which lasted eight months, and reduced him to a mere skeleton, he removed to the establishment on Lake Champlain, where he remained until Oct. 1822. He then returned home with his officers and men after an absence of 10 years, during which period he had undergone hardships of no ordinary character; and on 26 Dec. in that year he was at last promoted to the rank of Commander. He has since been on half-pay.

In Nov. 1834 Commander Kent was appointed a Stipendiary Magistrate at Jamaica, a post he still retains. He married, 24 Aug. 1824, his first-cousin, Eliza, relict of the late Jas. Chas. Grant, Esq., of Burton Crescent, London, and eldest daughter of Capt. Wm. Kent, R.N., who died in command of the UNION 98, on the Mediterranean station. By that lady he has issue. AGENTS—Messrs. Stilwell.

KENT. (COMMANDER, 1814. F-P., 15; H-P., 34.)

WILLIAM GEORGE CARLILE KENT, born about 1788, in Lanarkshire, N.B., is second son of the late John Kent, Esq., who, after having served for upwards of 20 years as a Purser in the Navy, was appointed, in 1803, Steward of the Royal Naval Hospital at Plymouth, where he died in 1827; and brother (with the present Commander Henry Kent, R.N.) of Lieut. John Kent, R.N. (1809), formerly Senior of the THAIS 20, who died from the effects of over-exertion in his profession in Jan. 1816, as also of Commander Bartholomew Kent, R.N. (1815),

* *Vide* Gaz. 1805, pp. 1411-1484.

who served at the bombardment of Copenhagen in 1807 in the GUERRIÈRE when captured by the U.S. ship *Constitution* in Aug. 1812, and on shore at New Orleans in 1814-15, and died in Feb. 1835, aged 55. His paternal grandfather married the eldest sister of the late Vice-Admiral John Hunter, many years Governor of New South Wales, and grand-niece of the Lord-Provost Drummond, of Edinburgh. One of his father's brothers, William, died Captain of the UNION 98, off the mouth of the Rhone, in Aug. 1812; and another, Henry, Commander of the DOVER 44, *armée-en-flûte*, died on the coast of Egypt in 1801. Of his maternal uncles, one, Robt. Wright, a Colonel of the Royal Regiment of Artillery, commanded that corps in Scotland, and served as Aide-de-Camp to the Duke of Kent in Nova Scotia and at Gibraltar; a second, Peter, a Captain in the Hon. E. I. Co.'s Infantry, died of wounds received in battle at Ceylon; and a third, George, became a Colonel in the R.E. His cousins, Bartholomew and Mark Kent, were both Lieutenants in the R.N.; the former was killed in a boat affair, in 1803, while First of the GOLIATH 74, Capt. Chas. Brisbane; and the latter died at sea in 1828.

This officer entered the Navy, 2 July, 1798, as Fst.-cl. Vol., on board LE TIGRE 80, Capt. Sir Wm. Sidney Smith, under whom, after visiting Constantinople and the coast of Egypt, he served on shore at the defence of St. Jean d'Acre. In March, 1800, having previously witnessed a variety of operations on the Egyptian coast, he removed to the THESEUS 74, Capt. John Stiles, and was for some time employed at the blockade of Genoa. On his return home, towards the close of the same year, he joined the ATLAS 98, Capt. Theophilus Jones, stationed in the Channel; and we next, from Jan. 1802 until Jan. 1807, find him discharging the duties of Midshipman, Master's Mate, and Acting-Lieutenant in the BUFFALO store-ship, commanded in the East Indies and at New South Wales by Capts. Wm. Kent, Philip Gidley King, and John Houston. On the date last mentioned he became Acting-First-Lieutenant of the PORPOISE store-ship, bearing the broad pendant of Commodore Wm. Bligh, in which he continued until invested with the command of the LADY NELSON armed brig, then about to be employed in removing the settlers from Norfolk Island to the Derwent and Port Dalrymple. In April, 1808, Mr. Kent, whose confirmation in the rank of Lieutenant did not take place until 17 May, 1809, rejoined the PORPOISE in the capacity of Acting-Commander. In Jan. 1811, on his return to England, after having endured a long and rigorous imprisonment on board the PORPOISE at New South Wales by order of Commodore Bligh, he was brought to a court-martial upon certain charges preferred against him by that officer, of all of which, however, he was acquitted, being at the same time complimented for the conduct he had evinced under the extreme and extraordinary difficulties in which he had been placed. His last appointments were—25 April and 19 Dec. 1812, to the UNION 98, Capts. Sam. Hood Linzee, Wm. Kent, and Robt. Rolles, and, as First-Lieutenant, to the SPARROWHAWK sloop, Capt. Thos. Ball Clowes, both on the Mediterranean station; where, in the latter vessel, he had the misfortune to encounter an accident which caused him excruciating torture, and to be confined to his bed for a considerable length of time, blind of both eyes, and without surgical assistance. In Sept. 1814 he took up a Commander's commission dated on 15 of the previous June. He has since been on half-pay.

He married, 30 Dec. 1830, Susannah Elizabeth, third daughter of the late John Rankin, Esq., merchant, of Greenock, N.B., by whom he has issue.

KENYON. (COMMANDER, 1843. F-P., 17; H-P., 7.)

GEORGE KENYON, born 10 March, 1811, is fourth son of the Hon. Thos. Kenyon, of Pradoe, near Shrewsbury, Clerk of the Outlawries in the Court of Queen's Bench, by Louisa Charlotte, second daughter of the Rev. John Robt. Lloyd, of Aston Hall, Shropshire; and nephew of the present Lord Kenyon. His eldest brother, Lloyd, is a Captain in the Royal Horse Guards; and his next, William, is in the Hon. E. I. Co.'s military service.

This officer entered the Navy, 21 May, 1823, as Fst.-cl. Vol., on board the JASPER 10, Capt. Alex. Dundas Young Arbuthnott, whom he followed into the REDWING 18, and TERROR bomb—visiting St. Petersburg in the former vessel, and Algiers in the latter. Between Sept. 1824 and May, 1828, he served uninterruptedly, as Midshipman, on the Home, South American, and Mediterranean stations, in the BULWARK 74, Capt. Dundas, WELLESLEY 74 and SPARTIATE 76, both commanded by Capt. Graham Eden Hamond, and ARIADNE, Capt. Adolphus FitzClarence. In May, 1829, having passed the last 12 months in study on shore, he joined the VICTORY 104, Capt. Hon. Geo. Elliot; and, towards the close of the same year, he returned to South America in the VOLAGE 28, Capt. Lord Colchester. In that frigate, of which he became Mate 1 Oct. 1830, Mr. Kenyon escorted the ex-Emperor and Empress of Brazil to Cherbourg in April, 1831, and was employed during the winter of 1832 in enforcing the embargo on the coast of Holland, whence, in Dec. of that year, he brought to England, under circumstances of great difficulty, the *Ondermening*, a detained Dutch vessel. He next, until promoted to the rank of Lieutenant 1 Dec. 1837, served, off Lisbon, in the Mediterranean, at Devonport, and again off Lisbon, in the BELVIDERA 42, Capt. Hon. Rich. Saunders Dundas, SAN JOSEF and ROYAL ADELAIDE, both flag-ships of Sir Wm. Hargood, and HERCULES 74, Capts. Maurice Fred. Fitzhardinge Berkeley and John Toup Nicolas. His succeeding appointments were—15 Feb. 1838, to the SALAMANDER steamer, Capts. Sidney Colpoys Dacres and Hastings Reginald Henry, in which vessel he was at first employed on the north coast of Spain under Lord John Hay, then in cruizing after the unfortunate FAIRY, and finally in making a voyage to St. Petersburg—and 20 Oct. 1841, to the MADAGASCAR 44, Capt. John Foote, on the coast of Africa. Soon after his arrival on the latter station Lieut. Kenyon assumed the temporary command of the BONETTA brigantine. On rejoining the MADAGASCAR he assisted in capturing five slave-vessels, and in effecting the release of 1400 negroes; and on one occasion, while in command of the ship's boats, 60 miles up the Congo river, he destroyed all the baracoons on its banks, and entered into a treaty with the native chiefs for the suppression of the slave-trade. On being subsequently placed in charge of a prize, he destroyed several other baracoons, and succeeded in rescuing 120 slaves after a contest with a very superior number of the natives, and a loss to the British of 4 men killed and wounded. In Aug. 1842 Lieut. Kenyon was sent to St. Helena with a Brazilian prize, but in consequence of the leaky condition of the vessel he was under the necessity of leaving her at Fernando Po, where he took command of the SOUDAN, a small flat-bottomed steamer, built for the navigation of the Niger, and with only stowage-room for a week's fuel, in which he proceeded to Sierra Leone. Owing to the prevalence of calms, and to the cause last named, he did not reach his destination until after a lengthened voyage, during which the greatest distress was occasioned by a failure both in water and provisions. He invalided home from severe and nearly fatal illness in April, 1843, and on 1 of the following July was advanced to his present rank. He has since been on half-pay.

KEPPEL. (CAPTAIN, 1837. F-P., 18; H-P., 7.)

THE HONOURABLE HENRY KEPPEL, born 14 June, 1809, is fourth son of the Earl of Albemarle, by Hon. Elizabeth Southwell, fourth daughter of Edward Lord de Clifford.

This officer entered the Navy 7 Feb. 1822; passed his examination in 1828; obtained his first commission 29 Jan. 1829; joined, 11 Feb. 1830, and 20

July, 1831, the GALATEA 42, Capt. Chas. Napier, and MAGICIENNE 24, Capt. Jas. Hanway Plumridge —the latter on the East India station; was promoted to the rank of Commander 30 Jan. 1833; served from 16 May, 1834, until the spring of 1838, in the CHILDERS 16, in the Mediterranean and at the Cape of Good Hope; attained his present rank 5 Dec. 1837; and, from 30 Aug. 1841 until his return to England in 1845, commanded the DIDO 18. He served, in the latter vessel, at the capture of Woosung and Shanghae, and in the operations on the Yang-tse-Kiang, in 1842;* and in Aug. 1844, with only the DIDO and Hon. E. I. Co.'s steamer PHLEGETHON under his orders, he attacked a large piratical settlement on the island of Borneo; where, while the loss of the British amounted to 32 men killed and 30 wounded, the enemy had five of their towns destroyed, 250 men killed, some thousands of houses and 200 or 300 proas of various descriptions burnt, and 70 brass guns and 13 flags taken. Since he was paid off Capt. Keppel has been unemployed.

He married, 25 Feb. 1839, Katherine Louisa, daughter of the late General Sir John Crosbie, G.C.H., of Watergate, co. Sussex. AGENT—Joseph Woodhead.

* Vide Gaz. 1842, pp. 3400, 3404.

KERR, LORD. (COMMANDER, 1846.)

LORD FREDERICK HERBERT KERR, born 30 Sept. 1818, is third son of William, sixth Marquess of Lothian, K.T., by his second wife, Harriet, daughter of Henry, third Duke of Buccleuch. His lordship, who is half-uncle of the present Marquess, is brother of Lord Chas. Lennox Kerr, an officer in the 42nd Regt., and Aide-de-Camp to the late Lord Lieutenant of Ireland, and of Lord Mark Ralph Geo. Kerr, a Captain in the Army; brother-in-law both of Lord Clinton and of Sir John Stuart Forbes, Bart.; and first-cousin of Commander Hon. M. Kerr, R.N., as also of Lieut. H. A. Kerr, R.N.

This officer entered the Navy 14 June, 1831; passed his examination in 1837; and was made Lieutenant, 21 Oct. 1840, into the GORGON steamer, Capt. Wm. Honyman Henderson, on the Mediterranean station, where he removed, 16 Jan. 1841, to the BENBOW 72, Capt. Houston Stewart. The latter ship being paid off in the spring of 1842, he was next appointed, 7 Feb. 1843, and 18 April, 1844, to the THUNDERBOLT steam-sloop, Capt. Geo. Nathaniel Broke, and WINCHESTER 50, bearing the flag of Hon. Josceline Percy, in which ships he was for three years employed at the Cape of Good Hope. He attained his present rank 3 July, 1846, and has since been on half-pay. AGENTS—Hallett and Robinson.

KERR. (LIEUTENANT, 1844.)

GEORGE KERR passed his examination 22 May, 1837; and was employed as Mate in the HASTINGS 72, Capt. John Lawrence, AGINCOURT 72, and CAMPERDOWN 104, flag-ships of Sir Thos. John Cochrane and Sir Edw. Brace, and PLUTO steam-vessel, Lieut.-Commander Wm. Pearson Crozier, on the Mediterranean and Home stations. He attained his present rank 14 Aug. 1844, and on 9 of the following Sept. was appointed to the FLYING FISH 12, Capt. Robt. Harris, fitting at Portsmouth. He was almost immediately afterwards superseded, and has since been on half-pay.

KERR. (LIEUTENANT, 1845.)

GEORGE COLLIER KERR entered the Navy in 1831; passed his examination 15 Feb. 1839; and after serving for nearly three years as Mate of the AGINCOURT 72, flag-ship in the East Indies of Sir Thos. John Cochrane, was made Lieutenant, 15 Jan. 1845, into the PLOVER surveying-vessel, Capt. Rich. Collinson, with whom he returned home from the East Indies and was paid off at the close of 1846.

KERR. (LIEUTENANT, 1844.)

HENRY ASHBURTON KERR, born in 1821, is third son of the late Lord Robt. Kerr, a Lieutenant-Colonel in the Army, by Mary, daughter of the Rev. Edm. Gilbert, of Windsor House, Cornwall; and grandson of William John, fifth Marquess of Lothian. His eldest brother, Wm. Walter Raleigh, is Assistant Auditor-General at the Mauritius; and his youngest, Robt. Dundas, is an officer in the R.E. The Lieutenant (whose first-cousin, Lord Fred. Herbert Kerr, is a Commander in the Navy) is brother-in-law of Lieut.-General Sir Wm. Maynard Gomm, K.C.B., and of Lieut.-Colonel Wm. Henry Cornwall, of the Coldstream Guards.

This officer passed his examination 26 May, 1841; and from the early part of 1842 until promoted to the rank of Lieutenant, 19 Dec. 1844, was employed in the Pacific as Mate of the CARYSFORT 26, Capt. Lord Geo. Paulet. He has been serving since 16 Aug. 1845 in the PRESIDENT 50, flag-ship of Rear-Admiral Jas. Rich. Dacres, at the Cape of Good Hope.

KERR. (LIEUTENANT, 1812. F-P., 10; H-P., 31.)

JAMES KERR was born 30 March, 1791.

This officer entered the Navy, 25 April, 1806, as Fst.-cl. Vol., on board the THÉSEUS 74, Capt. Geo. Hope, employed at the Cape of Good Hope. In Nov. 1807, after he had been for a short time attached to the GANGES 74, commanded in the Baltic by Capt. Peter Halkett, he rejoined Capt. Hope as Midshipman in the POMPÉE 74, then lying at Chatham. From March, 1808, until Oct. 1811, we again find him in the Baltic on board the VICTORY 100, flag-ship of Sir Jas. Saumarez, and TARTAR frigate, Capt. Joseph Baker. He was then received into the NAMUR 74, bearing the flag at the Nore of Sir Thos. Williams; on leaving whom, in May, 1812, he went back to the VICTORY. He was confirmed a Lieutenant, 20 Nov. 1812, in the PLOVER sloop, Capt. Colin Campbell; and was subsequently, on his return from a voyage to Quebec, appointed—24 Dec. 1813, and 3 May, 1814, to the SCARBOROUGH and ACHILLE 74's, flag-ships in the North Sea and at the Brazils of Admirals John Ferrier and Manley Dixon—and, 28 Aug. 1815, to the ALERT 18, Capt. John Smith, on the Home station. He has been on half-pay since 1816.

Lieut. Kerr married, 1 Jan. 1833, Helen, eldest daughter of the late Adam Smith, Esq., of Stockbridge; and has issue one son.

KERR. (LIEUTENANT, 1830.)

JOHN JAMES KERR entered the Navy 6 July, 1813; and was Midshipman of the IMPREGNABLE 98, flag-ship of Rear-Admiral David Milne, at the battle of Algiers, 27 Aug. 1816. He passed his examination in 1819; obtained his commission 13 Aug. 1830; and, with the exception of a period of rather more than three years (from 28 Jan. 1837 until the spring of 1840) employed in the Coast Guard, has since been on half-pay. AGENTS—Messrs. Stilwell.

KERR. (COMMANDER, 1846.)

THE HONOURABLE MARK KERR, born 3 April, 1814, is second surviving son (by Charlotte, late Countess of Antrim, third daughter of Randall, late Marquess of Antrim) of the late Lord Mark Robt. Kerr, Vice-Admiral of the White.* He is grandson of Wm. John, fifth Marquess of Lothian, K.T., Colonel of the 11th Regt. of Dragoons; brother of the present Earl of Antrim; brother-in-law of the Earl of Abingdon; and first-cousin of Lord Fred. Herbert Kerr, Commander R.N.

This officer passed his examination in 1834; obtained his first commission 10 Oct. 1837; and was subsequently appointed — 29 April, 1838, to the WELLESLEY 72, Capt Thos. Maitland, in which ship

* Lord Mark Robert Kerr was born in 1776. He was Midshipman of the LION 64 in Lord Macartney's expedition to China in 1792; Lieutenant of the SANS PAREIL 80 in Lord Bridport's action in 1795; and Capt. of the CORMORANT 20 at the reduction of MINORCA in 1798. On the renewal of hostilities in 1803 his Lordship obtained command of the FISGARD frigate. He became a Rear-Admiral in 1821, attained the rank of Vice-Admiral in 1837, and died 9 Sept. 1840.

he served under Sir Gordon Bremer during the war in China—9 Feb. 1842 and 15 April, 1844, to the FORMIDABLE 84 and QUEEN 110, both commanded by Sir Chas. Sullivan on the Mediterranean station—and 21 Aug. 1845, to the PRESIDENT 50, flag-ship of Rear-Admiral Jas. Rich. Dacres at the Cape of Good Hope. He attained his present rank 12 Jan. 1846; and has since been on half-pay. AGENTS—Messrs. Halford and Co.

KERR. (LIEUT., 1823. F-P., 14; H-P., 24.)

PATRICK KERR entered the Navy, 20 Sept. 1809, as Fst.-cl. Vol., on board the DÉSIRÉE 36, Capt. Arthur Farquhar, employed off the Texel; and from Aug. 1810, until April, 1815, served on the North Sea and American stations, chiefly as Midshipman, in the SAN DOMINGO 74 and CLEOPATRA frigate, both commanded by Capt. Chas. Gill—the former as flag-ship to Sir Rich. Strachan and Sir John Borlase Warren. He then returned to England in the TONNANT 80, flag-ship of Hon. Sir Alex. Cochrane; and in Oct. 1815, after his name had been borne for short periods on the books of various ships, he removed to the TOWEY 24, Capts. Hew Steuart and Wm. Hill, fitting for the East Indies, where he was employed for a period of three years. He next, in April, 1819, joined the DOVER 28, bearing the flag at Leith of Rear-Admiral Robt. Waller Otway, with whom he remained until Nov. 1821. In the early part of 1822 we again find him sailing for the East Indies in the LIFFEY 50; of which ship, bearing the broad pendant of Commodore Chas. Grant, he was created an Acting-Lieutenant 23 Dec. in the same year. He was confirmed, 7 March, 1823, into the MADAGASCAR frigate, Capt. Evan Nepean; but since his arrival home in the following Oct. has been on half-pay.

KERR. (COMMANDER, 1838.)

ROBERT KERR entered the Navy 2 Dec. 1819; passed his examination in 1826; and on the occasion of his promotion to the rank of Lieutenant, 23 Aug. 1828, was appointed to the ARACHNE 18, in which vessel he served with Capts. Nixon, Erskine, and Deare, on the West India station, until the summer of 1830. His succeeding appointments were—17 Feb. 1832, to the CONWAY 28, Capt. Henry Eden, employed at first in the North Sea, and afterwards in the Tagus and South America—and 6 May, 1837, to the CASTOR 36, Capt. Edw. Collier, on the Mediterranean station. He attained his present rank 28 June, 1838; and since 11 Oct. 1842 has been employed in the Coast Guard.

KEVERN. (RETIRED COMMANDER, 1827. F-P., 19; H-P., 43.)

RICHARD KEVERN entered the Navy, in 1785, as Captain's Servant, on board the IRRESISTIBLE 74, Capt. Sir Andrew Snape Hamond, guard-ship at Chatham, where he served for a period of four years. He was next, until Nov. 1794, employed on the Newfoundland station, part of the time as Midshipman, in the PEGASUS, Capts. Herbert Sawyer and Wm. Domett, ASSISTANCE, flag-ship of Sir Rich. King, and TREPASSEY cutter, Lieut.-Commander Jahleel Brenton—of which latter vessel he was created a Lieutenant 24 Oct. 1793. His succeeding appointments were, on the Home station—7 Jan. 1795, to the CÆSAR 80, Capts. Chas. Edm. Nugent and Roddam Home—2 June, 1798, to the CÆSAR 80, Capt. Collis—5 April, 1799, to the ST. GEORGE 98, Capt. Sampson Edwards—in 1801, to the SAN JOSEF 110, Capt. Wm. Wolseley, which ship was paid off in the following year—6 March, 1804, to the JAMAICA 24, Capt. Jonas Rose—21 May, 1805, to the command of the EXERTION gun-brig—11 Jan. 1806, to the Sea Fencibles at Weymouth—and 26 April following, as Senior, to the SHELDRAKE 16, Capt. John Thicknesse. On 12 Oct. 1806 Lieut. Kevern took part in an action of an hour and a quarter, fought in the Bay of Erqui, between a British squadron, consisting of the SHELDRAKE, CONSTANCE 22, STRENUOUS gun-brig, and BRITANNIA cutter, on the one hand, and, on the other, a French force, amounting to the *Salamandre* of 26 guns and 80 men, a 2-gun battery planted on a hill, and one or two field-pieces, together with a few troops, on the beach; the termination whereof was the surrender of the enemy's ship, after a loss to herself of about 29 men killed, independently of several wounded, and to the British of 10 killed and 23 wounded. The assistance afforded by Lieut. Kevern on the occasion was particularly noticed by Capt. Thicknesse, who, in his letter to the Admiralty, described him as a most meritorious and able officer, and recommended him in consequence to their lordships' favourable attention.* He left the SHELDRAKE in a state of ill health in the following Nov., and accepted his present rank 3 Dec. 1827.

He is married, and has issue a son, the present Lieut. Rich. C. Kevern, R.N.

KEVERN. (LIEUTENANT, 1841.)

RICHARD CHARLES KEVERN, born 20 July, 1811, is son of Retired Commander Rich. Kevern, R.N.

This officer entered the Navy, 14 April, 1825, as Fst.-cl. Vol., on board the BRITANNIA 120, Capt. Philip Pipon, lying in Hamoaze; and after a servitude of nearly twelve months in the Channel on board the CAMELION 10, Capt. Michael Seymour, became Midshipman, in Aug. 1826, of the WINDSOR CASTLE 74, Capt. Edw. Durnford King. Removing, in Feb. 1828, to the BLONDE 46, Capt. Edm. Lyons, he was for upwards of three years employed in that ship on the Mediterranean station; after which we find him doing duty as Mate, off Lisbon, again in the Mediterranean, as also in the West Indies and in China, on board the ROMNEY troop-ship, Master-Commander Chas. Brown, THUNDERER 84, Capt. Wm. Furlong Wise, CROCODILE 28, Capt. Jas. Polkinghorne, and BLENHEIM 72, Capt. Sir Humphrey Le Fleming Senhouse. For his services in the latter ship during the early part of the hostilities with the Chinese he was promoted to the rank of Lieutenant 8 June, 1841, but he did not receive his commission until the middle of the following Oct., by which period he had further assisted at the capture of Amoy and Chinghae.† He then became First of the LARNE 18, Capt. Patrick John Blake, with whom he returned home and was paid off in July, 1842. His last appointments were for short periods—9 Sept. 1844, to the CRUIZER 16, Capt. Edw. Gennys Fanshawe, fitting at Chatham—21 Oct. 1845, as Additional, to the PENELOPE steam-frigate, Commodore Wm. Jones, on the coast of Africa—and, 3 March, 1846, to the PANTALOON 10, Capts. Edm. Wilson and Henry John Douglas. He came from the West Indies at the commencement of 1847, and has since been on half-pay.

KEY. (COMMANDER, 1845. F-P, 13; H-P., 1.)

ASTLEY COOPER KEY entered the Navy 2 Aug. 1833; passed his examination 19 Aug. 1840; and after an intermediate servitude as Mate in the EXCELLENT gunnery-ship at Portsmouth, Capt. Sir Thos. Hastings, was promoted to the rank of Lieutenant 22 Dec. 1842. His succeeding appointments were, 28 Feb. 1843 and 9 Feb. 1844, to the CURAÇOA 24, Capt. Sir Thos. Sabine Pasley, and GORGON steam-sloop, Capt. Chas. Hotham, both on the South American station. On 20 Nov. 1845 it was his lot to command the FANNY tender, and to be slightly wounded, during the battle of the Parana; on which occasion the combined squadrons of England and France effected the destruction, after a hard day's fighting, of four heavy batteries belonging to General Rosas at Punta Obligado, also of a schooner-of-war mounting 6 guns, and of 24 vessels chained across the river.‡ He was in consequence promoted to his present rank by commission dated 18 Nov. 1845;§ and since 3 May, 1847, has been in command of the BULLDOG steam-sloop, of 500 horse-power, on the coast of Portugal.

* *Vide* Gaz. 1806, p. 1364. † *V.* Gaz. 1842, pp. 82, 397.
‡ *V.* Gaz. 1846, pp. 815, 818. § *V.* Gaz. 1846, p. 861.

KEYS. (Retired Commander, 1841.)

David Keys entered the Navy, in 1786, as Ordinary, on board the Dictator 64, Capt. Wm. Parker, lying at Sheerness, where he remained but a short period. He served next, for some months in 1790, and again in 1792-3, in the Brune frigate, Capt. Davidge Gould, as also in the Centurion 50, Capt. Sam. Osborne, on the West India station; after which he was for about four years employed on the Home station, as Midshipman and Master's Mate, in the Comet, Capt. Wm. Bradley, Hero, Lieut.-Commander John Thomson, and Prince, flag-ship of Sir Roger Curtis. He was confirmed a Lieutenant, 21 July, 1798, in the Centaur 74, Capt. John Markham, under whom he was present at the surrender of the island of Minorca, the destruction of the Spanish frigate *El Guadaloupe* of 40 guns, and the capture of a French squadron of three frigates and two brigs commanded by Rear-Admiral Perrée. He left the Centaur in July 1798, and was afterwards appointed—3 April, 1804, to the Roebuck 44, flag-ship at Leith and at Plymouth of Rear-Admirals Jas. Vashon and Billy Douglas—6 Dec. 1805, for a brief period, to the Nassau 64, Capt. Robt. Campbell, lying in the river Thames—5 Sept. 1822, to the Coast Guard, in which service he continued until the close of 1833—and 3 March, 1834, to the Ordinary at Plymouth, where he remained for about three years and a half. He became a Retired Commander on the Senior List 12 Oct. 1841.

He is married and has issue.

KIDDLE. (Lieut., 1814. f-p., 26; h-p., 15.)

John Kiddle entered the Navy, 24 Dec. 1806, as Fst.-cl. Vol., on board the Mars 74, Capts. Wm. Lukin, Jas. Katon, John Surman Carden, and Henry Raper, in which ship, after attending Admiral Gambier's expedition to Copenhagen, he continued to serve as Midshipman, on the Channel and Lisbon stations, until Feb. 1813. He then joined the Bellerophon 74, bearing the flag of Sir Rich. Goodwin Keats at Newfoundland, where, shortly after his promotion to the rank of Lieutenant, which took place 29 July, 1814, he removed to the Challenger 16, Capts. Fred. Edw. Vernon and Henry Forbes. His appointments, since the paying off of the latter vessel in Sept. 1815, have been—15 Oct. 1830, to the Talavera Coast Blockade ship, Capts. Hugh Pigot and David Colby—16 April, 1831, to the Coast Guard—11 June, 1833, to the command of the Fox Revenue-vessel—22 June, 1836, to the Coast Guard—29 Jan. 1844, to the command of the Harpy, another Revenue-cruizer—and 22 April, 1847, again to the Coast Guard, in which he is at present serving.

KING, Kt., K.C.H. (Vice-Admiral of the Red, 1841. f-p., 24; h-p., 37.)

Sir Edward Durnford King is son of the late Wm. King, Esq., of Southampton, and of Harbest and Brockley, co. Suffolk, by Hannah, daughter and co-heiress of Anthony Isaacson, Esq., of Fenton, co. Northumberland; and brother of the late Capt. Andw. King, R.N.*

This officer (whose name had been borne, from 24 March, 1786, until 1788, on the books of the Irresistible 74, guard-ship at Chatham, Capt. Sir Andw. Snape Hamond) embarked, in June, 1789, as Midshipman, on board the Director 64, Capt. Thos. West, and was next, between Nov. 1790 and Feb. 1793, employed, on the Home, American, and Newfoundland stations, in the Boyne 98, Capt. Geo. Bowyer, Carnatic 74, Capt. John Ford, Bellona 74, Capt. Fras. John Hartwell, Resistance, Capt. John O'Brien, Alcide 74, Capt. Sir Andw. Snape Douglas, and Assistance, flag-ship of Sir Rich. King. He then successively joined, in the capacity of Master's Mate, the Prince, Barfleur, and Glory 98's, the latter commanded by Capt. Bourmaster, and the two former by Capt. Cuthbert Collingwood, Flag-Captain to Rear-Admiral Bowyer, through whose recommendation of his conduct on board the Barfleur in the actions of 29 May and 1 June, 1794, he was promoted, on 5 Sept. in that year, to a Lieutenancy in the Robust 74, Capt. Edw. Thornbrough. Being appointed, 30 June, 1795, to the Dryad of 44 guns and 251 men, Capts. Robt. Forbes and Lord Amelius Beauclerk, Mr. King, as First-Lieutenant to the latter officer, assisted at the capture, 13 June, 1796, after a close and spirited action of 45 minutes, attended with a loss to the British of only 2 men killed and 7 wounded, of the French frigate *La Proserpine*, of 42 guns and 348 men, 30 of whom were slain and 45 wounded. Being recommended by his Captain on the occasion as an officer truly deserving the notice of the Lords Commissioners,* and being in consequence rewarded with a Commander's commission bearing date 23 of the same month, he was appointed, 21 June, 1798, to the command of the Gaieté sloop-of-war, employed at first in the North Sea, and then in the West Indies, where he co-operated, as senior officer of a squadron in the Gulf of Paria, in the protection of Trininad, cruized with much success off the island of Guadeloupe, and was often under the fire of the enemy's batteries. On 28 Sept. 1800 Capt. King was nominated Acting-Captain of the Leviathan 74, flag-ship of Sir John Thos. Duckworth—an appointment which the Admiralty confirmed 8 Jan. 1801. In the following June, after he had assisted at the reduction of the French island of St. Martin, and of the Danish and Swedish islands of Ste. Croix, St. Thomas, and St. Bartholomew, and had gained the approbation of the Commander-in-Chief for the manner in which, in conjunction with Brigadier-Generals Maitland and Fuller, he had settled the terms of capitulation,† he removed to the Andromeda frigate, also on the West India station, whence, in Nov. of the same year, he invalided. His next appointment was, 16 April, 1805, to the Endymion 40, in which frigate we find him, until the ensuing September, employed in the blockade of Cadiz. On 19 Aug., being on the look-out off Cape St. Mary, Capt. King fell in with the combined fleets of France and Spain, consisting of 26 sail-of-the-line and nine frigates, whom, although he was chased by two of the former and one of the latter, he contrived to watch ‡ into the port of Cadiz. He then, having closely reconnoitred the enemy, repaired with the intelligence of their situations, and of their partially dismantled state, to Vice-Admiral Collingwood, at the time off the Gut of Gibraltar with only four ships-of-the-line, who thereupon immediately returned to Cadiz and resumed the blockade. Impressed with a full sense of Capt. King's zeal and ability, the Vice-Admiral afterwards selected him to follow the enemy, in the event of their quitting Cadiz, and communicate to the government at home, and the squadrons to the northward, the circumstance of their approach and probable destination—a service of the utmost importance, Napoleon being at the period in anxious expectation of their arrival in the Channel in order to enable him to carry into execution his long-projected descent upon England. The Franco-Spanish fleet, however, as is well known, remained in Cadiz until the arrival of the force under Lord Nelson, shortly after which the battle of Trafalgar for ever checked its career. At that particular epoch Capt.

* The above officer was Midshipman of the Bellerophon in the actions of 28 and 29 May and 1 June, 1794. He served as Senior Lieutenant of the Andromeda frigate at the destruction of a French squadron in Dunkerque harbour 7 July, 1799; was First also of La Désirée in the action off Copenhagen 2 April, 1801; and, as Fourth of the Victory, participated in the glories of Trafalgar 21 Oct. 1805. In 1807 he commanded the Hebe armed ship at the siege of Copenhagen; as he did the Venerable 74 in the attack upon Flushing in 1809, and the Iphigenia frigate at the reduction of Genoa in 1814. His promotion to Post-rank took place 13 Oct. 1807. He died Superintendent of the Packet Establishment at Falmouth 30 June, 1835.

* *Vide* Gaz. 1796, p. 579.

† *V.* Gaz. 1801, pp. 516, 519, 521.

‡ He even, by a *ruse de guerre*, deterred them from continuing the pursuit they had commenced of the few ships subsequently alluded to as being under the command of Vice-Admiral Collingwood.

King was absent on a special service at Gibraltar, and he was in consequence deprived of an opportunity of sharing in the triumph that was then achieved. He continued in the ENDYMION until Aug. 1806, and was subsequently appointed—23 March, 1807, to the MONMOUTH 64, in which ship, on his arrival with a valuable convoy in India, he assisted at the capture of Tranquebar—24 Sept. 1811, after three years of half-pay, to the RODNEY 74, part of the force employed at the blockade of Toulon, where he continued until Nov. 1812—14 Nov. 1814, to the CORNWALLIS 74, fitting for the East Indies, the command of which ship his health obliged him to resign 21 Dec. following—and 27 May, 1825, to the WINDSOR CASTLE 74, stationed at first as a guard-ship at Plymouth, and next attached to an expedition to Lisbon, whence he returned to England and was paid off in May, 1828. On 22 July, 1830, our officer was advanced to the rank of Rear-Admiral; and in Jan. 1833 he was knighted and created a K.C.H. He afterwards commanded-in-chief, at first on the Brazil and Cape of Good Hope stations, and then on the Cape station alone, from 29 July, 1840, until the close of 1842; and since 18 April, 1845 (his promotion to the rank of Vice-Admiral having taken place 23 Nov. 1841), he has had the chief command at the Nore. AGENTS—Messrs. Ommanney.

KING. (COMMANDER, 1814. F-P., 11; H-P., 32.)
GEORGE KING (*a*) entered the Navy, 1 May, 1804, as Midshipman, on board the UTRECHT 64, Capts. John Wentworth Loring, Fras. Pickmore, and Henry Inman, lying in the Downs; and from Jan. 1805, until his promotion to the rank of Lieutenant, 3 Sept. 1810, was employed under the present Sir Edw. W. C. R. Owen, latterly as Master's Mate, in the IMMORTALITÉ and CLYDE frigates. He was consequently present in several affairs with the enemy's flotilla; also in the attack made with Congreve's rockets on the town of Boulogne in Oct. 1806, and in the operations against Flushing in 1809. On the occasion of his promotion as above, Mr. King joined the ARIEL sloop, Capt. Daniel Ross, and sailed for the Baltic. From March, 1812, until within a few days of his attainment of the rank of Commander, 15 June, 1814, he served off the mouth of the Scheldt in the INCONSTANT 36 and CORNWALL 74, both commanded by Capt. Owen. He has since been on half-pay.
Commander King is a Magistrate at Van Diemen's Land. AGENTS—Hallett and Robinson.

KING. (COMMANDER, 1821.)
GEORGE MORISON KING entered the Navy, in June, 1807, as Midshipman, on board the THESEUS 74, commanded by the late Sir John Poo Beresford, and was for some time employed in the Channel and off Ferrol. Sailing next for the East Indies in the CLORINDE 38, Capt. Thos. Briggs, he witnessed the capture of the Isle of France in Dec. 1810; after which he returned to England in the IPHIGENIA 36, Capt. Thos. Gordon Caulfeild, and in 1812, having rejoined Sir J. P. Beresford on board the POICTIERS 74, proceeded to the Chesapeake, where he saw a good deal of boat-service and assisted at the bombardment of Louis Town. In 1813 he was promoted by Sir John Borlase Warren to a Lieutenancy in the RINGDOVE 18, Capt. Wm. Dowers, also on the North American station, whence, owing to some informality which had there occurred in his examination, he was under the necessity of returning to England, and of undergoing a second probationary ordeal. His official promotion did not in consequence take place until 22 Oct. 1814. He afterwards became Flag-Lieutenant to Lord Exmouth in the BOYNE 98, and, on accompanying that officer into the QUEEN CHARLOTTE 100, it was his fortune to participate in the same capacity in the battle of Algiers, 27 Aug. 1816, on which occasion he was wounded in the leg.* In July, 1821, after he had been for a period on half-pay, he was ordered to join the ROYAL GEORGE yacht, *on the King's staff*, two Lieutenants not being at the time allowed, and one having been already appointed. While in that vessel he attended His Majesty (George IV.) on the occasion of his visit to Ireland, and he was always present in the boat in which the royal personage landed and re-embarked. He was promoted to the rank of Commander by a commission bearing date 14 Dec. 1821; and he was lastly, from Feb. 1823 until 1832, employed in the Coast Guard; on leaving which service the officers and men late under his superintendence presented him with a handsome snuff-box "as a testimony of their respect and esteem."
He married, 27 June, 1825, Anne Sarah, relict of Fras. Hoey, Esq., of Dunganstown, co. Wicklow, and sister of Matthew Forde, Esq., M.P. for co. Down. By that lady he has issue.

* *Vide* Gaz. 1816, p. 1972.

KING. (CAPTAIN, 1841. F-P., 13; H-P., 12.)
GEORGE ST. VINCENT KING, born 15 July, 1809, is second son (by his first wife, Sarah Anne, only daughter of Admiral Sir John Thos. Duckworth, G.C.B.) of the late Vice-Admiral Sir Rich. King, Bart., K.C.B.,* whose second wife was a daughter of Admiral Sir Chas. Cotton, Bart. Capt. King is brother of the present Sir Rich. Duckworth King, Bart., of Belle Vue, co. Kent; brother-in-law of Sir Jas. S. Lake, Bart.; and nephew, by marriage, of the late Admiral Sir Chas. Rowley, G.C.B. His grandfather, Admiral Sir Rich. King, Bart., who died in 1806, distinguished himself in India during the conflicts between Sir Edw. Hughes and Admiral de Suffrein in 1782-3.
This officer entered the Royal Naval College 8 Feb. 1822, and embarked in 1824, as Midshipman, on board the REVENGE 76, Capt. Sir Chas. Burrard, bearing the flag in the Mediterranean of Sir Harry Burrard Neale, with whom he continued until 1827. In 1828 he joined the JAVA 52, flag-ship of Rear-Admiral Wm. Hall Gage in the East Indies, whence he returned to England on the occasion of his promotion to the rank of Lieutenant 15 Jan. 1830. His next appointments were, 2 June, 1830, and 29 Dec. 1831, to the COLUMBINE 18 and PALLAS 42, Capts. Jas. Wallace Gabriel, Manley Hall Dixon, and Wm. Walpole, both on the West India station. He left the PALLAS in Dec. 1833, and, obtaining a second promotal commission 8 Aug. 1834, was lastly employed in command, from 25 Jan. 1837 until paid off at the close of 1838, of the CHAMPION 18, on the West India station. He acquired his present rank 28 Aug. 1841. AGENTS—Messrs. Stilwell.

KING. (COMMANDER, 1814. F-P., 18; H-P., 34.)
HENRY KING entered the Navy, 28 Dec. 1795, as Fst.-cl. Vol., on board the NAMUR 98, Capt. Jas. Hawkins Whitshed, with whom, and latterly with Rear-Admiral Geo. Campbell, he continued to serve, as Midshipman, Master's Mate, and Acting-Lieutenant, in the BARFLEUR and TÉMÉRAIRE 98's, on the Home, Mediterranean, and West India stations, until Oct. 1802. His first commission bears date 18 of the latter month. His succeeding appointments were—13 April, 1803, to the CANOPUS 80, bearing the flag of the last-mentioned officer in the Mediterranean—27 March, 1805, to the AMBUSCADE 32, Capt. Wm. D'Urban, with whom he was for four years employed as Senior-Lieutenant on the same station—26 Sept. 1809, in a similar capacity, to the UNITÉ 36, Capts. Patrick Campbell and Edwin Henry Chamberlayne, also in the Mediterranean, whence (after having taken part in a very gallant

* Sir Rich. King was born in Nov. 1774, and in May 1794 was made a Post-Captain He commanded the SIRIUS 36 at the capture of the Dutch ships *Waakzamheid* of 26 guns and 100 men, and *Furie* of 36 guns and 153 men, 24 Oct. 1798; was in the same ship, in company with L'OISEAU 36, at the taking, 27 Jan. 1801, of the French frigate *La Dédaigneuse* of 36 guns; and commanded the ACHILLE 74 at the battle of Trafalgar. He became a Rear-Admiral in 1812; was nominated a K.C.B. in 1815; held the chief command in the East Indies from 1816 to 1820; acquired the rank of Vice-Admiral in 1821; and died Commander-in-Chief at the Nore 4 Aug. 1834.

action of an hour and a half in Sagone Bay, where that frigate, in company with the POMONE 38, and SCOUT 18, effectually destroyed the armed storeships *Giraffe* and *Nourrice*, each mounting from 20 to 30 guns, and protected by a 5-gun battery, a martello tower, and a body of about 200 regular troops) he invalided in Aug. 1811—1 May, 1812, to the TIGRE 74, Capt. John Halliday, in the Channel —and, 14 Sept. following, as First, to the SEAHORSE 38, Capt. Jas. Alex. Gordon. In Aug. 1814, Lieut. King (who had made a voyage to South America, and had been for some time actively employed in the Chesapeake) accompanied the brilliant expedition up the Potomac, where he assisted at the destruction of Fort Washington and witnessed the capitulation of Alexandria. Such was his eagerness to participate in the hardships and dangers encountered by the British during their subsequent descent of the river that he actually left a sick bed for the purpose of commanding at his quarters; and the two first guns he pointed each disabled a gun of the enemy.* Proportionately great, therefore, was the official praise bestowed upon him by Capt. Gordon. He was in consequence promoted to his present rank on 19 of the following Oct., but has not been since afloat.

Commander King is a Police Magistrate at New Zealand. AGENTS—Messrs. Stilwell.

KING. (COMMANDER, 1846.)

HENRY KING (*b*) passed his examination 18 June, 1839; served as Mate of the WELLESLEY 72, Commodore Sir J. J. Gordon Bremer, at the capture of Canton and Chinghae,† in 1841; and was for some time employed in the same capacity on board the CORNWALLIS 72, flag-ship of Sir Wm. Parker, and HERALD 26, Capt. Joseph Nias. We are informed that Mr. King, whose first commission bears date 8 Oct. 1841, was Lieutenant of the ALGERINE at the attack upon Chapoo and Woosung, and in the operations on the Yang-tse-Kiang in 1842. He afterwards, from 7 Nov. 1843 until the summer of 1845, served in the APOLLO troop-ship, Capts. Wm. Maclean and Wm. Radcliffe; and on 9 Nov. 1846 he was advanced to the rank of Commander. He has since been on half-pay. AGENTS—Messrs. Stilwell.

KING. (LIEUTENANT, 1818. F-P., 10; H-P., 28.)

HENRY KING (*a*) entered the Navy, 21 May, 1809, as Fst.-cl. Vol., on board the VENERABLE 74, Capts. Andrew King and Sir Home Popham, in which ship, after attending the expedition to the Walcheren, he served in co-operation with the patriots on the north coast of Spain until unfortunately taken prisoner in a land affair at Guetaria 17 July, 1812. On his return to liberty he joined, in May, 1814, the STIRLING CASTLE 74, commanded at first by Sir H. Popham, and afterwards by Capt. Wm. Butterfield; and in the following Aug. he removed to the MÆANDER 38, Capt. John Bastard, stationed off Lisbon and Gibraltar. From June, 1815, until May, 1816, we find him employed on board the IRIS, flag-ship in the Thames of his friend Sir Home Popham. In Oct. 1817 he accompanied that officer, in the SYBILLE frigate, to the West Indies, where, on 29 Jan. 1818, he was nominated by him to a Lieutenancy in the RIFLEMAN 18, Capt. Norwich Duff—an act which the Admiralty confirmed by a commission dated 30 April in the same year. Mr. King's next appointments were to the PRIMROSE 18, Capt. Chas. Geo. Rodney Phillott, BEAVER sloop, Capts. Wm. Popham and Rich. Saumarez, IPHIGENIA frigate, Capt. Hyde Parker, and SYBILLE again, Capt. Wm. Popham. He has been on half-pay, we believe, since 1820. AGENTS—Messrs. Ommanney.

KING. (LIEUTENANT, 1846.)

HENRY BARTLETT KING was Midshipman of the ASIA 84, Capt. Wm. Fisher, during the operations of 1840 on the coast of Syria. He passed his examination 12 April, 1842; served as Mate in the DAPHNE 18, Capt. John Jas. Onslow, EXCELLENT gunnery-ship, Capt. Sir Thos. Hastings, and CRUIZER 16, Capt. Edw. Gennys Fanshawe, on the Pacific, Home, and East India stations; obtained his commission 7 Feb. 1846; and on 11 of the same month was appointed Additional-Lieutenant of the AGINCOURT 72, flag-ship of Sir Thos. John Cochrane, also in the East Indies. While in the CRUIZER we find him assisting at the destruction, 19 Aug. 1845, by a force under Capt. Chas. Talbot, of the piratical settlement of Malloodoo, the fiercely-defended stronghold of a Borneo chieftain named Scheriff Osman.

KING. (LIEUTENANT, 1846.)

JAMES KING passed his examination 11 July, 1840; and was for several years employed on the Mediterranean, East India, and other stations, as Mate, in the BELLEISLE 72, Capt. John Toup Nicolas, DIDO 18, Capt. Hon. Henry Keppel, CHILDERS 16, Capt. Geo. Greville Wellesley, and APOLLO troop-ship, Capts. Wm. Maclean and Wm. Radcliffe. He obtained his commission 6 April, 1846, and is still serving in the APOLLO.

KING. (REAR-ADMIRAL, 1846. F-P., 17; H-P., 33.)

THE HONOURABLE JAMES WILLIAM KING is sixth son of Robert, second Earl of Kingston, by Catherine, only daughter of Rich. Fitzgerald, Esq., of Mount Ophaley, co. Kildare. He is brother of the late Capt. Edw. King, R.N., as also of the late Major-General Sir Henry King, K.C.B.; brother-in-law of the late Earl of Mountcashel; and uncle of the present Earl of Kingston. His nephew, Lieut. Rich. Fitzgerald King, R.N. (1832), died Senior of the PERSIAN sloop, on the coast of Africa, in 1840.

This officer entered the Navy, 24 Aug. 1797, as Fst.-cl. Vol., on board the SANS PAREIL 80, Capt. Wm. Browell, bearing the flag of Lord Hugh Seymour, at first in the Channel, and afterwards in the West Indies, where, subsequently to the reduction of Surinam, he became Midshipman, in 1801, of the CARNATIC 74, Capt. Chas. Vinicombe Penrose. Quitting the latter ship in 1802, he was next, until promoted to the rank of Lieutenant 3 March, 1804, employed, on the Home station, in the BITTERN sloop, Capt. Robt. Arlett, JAMAICA 24, Capt. Jonas Rose, UNICORN and ETHALION frigates, both commanded by Capt. Chas. Stewart, and MINOTAUR 74, Capt. Chas. John Moore Mansfield. In the following April he joined the VANGUARD 74, Capts. Andrew Fitzherbert Evans and Jas. Newman Newman, with whom he served, again in the West Indies, until 1805. In Dec. of that year we find him appointed to the ÆOLUS 32, Capt. Lord Wm. FitzRoy, on the Irish station. Being advanced, 15 Aug. 1806, to the command of the MELVILLE sloop, Capt. King was once more ordered to the West Indies, where, in Dec. 1807, he assisted at the reduction of the Danish islands. While on the same station he was removed, 29 July, 1808, to the PELORUS 18, and was posted, 18 Jan. 1809, into the ALCMÈNE frigate. His last appointment was, on 2 June in the latter year, to the JASON 32; which frigate, after having been employed at Newfoundland and off Flushing, bore the flag of the Duke of Clarence when H.R.H. escorted Louis XVIII. to the French shore in April, 1814. Capt. King subsequently conveyed the Emperor Alexandria, the King of Prussia, and the Duchess of Oldenburgh to Calais, on their return from England. He paid the JASON off 14 Nov. 1814; and acquired his present rank 9 Nov. 1846.

The Rear-Admiral married, 28 Nov. 1815, Caroline, second daughter of the late Most Rev. Euseby Cleaver, Archbishop of Dublin, and has issue two sons and three daughters. AGENTS—Messrs. Stilwell.

KING. (COMMANDER, 1825. F-P., 17; H-P., 24.)

JOHN KING was born 12 Sept. 1793. He belongs to an old and very respectable family.

This officer entered the Navy, 26 Dec. 1806, as

* *Vide* Gaz. 1814, p. 2081. † *V.* Gaz. 1842, p. 396.

Fst.-cl. Vol., on board the PRINCESS OF ORANGE 74, Capts. Joshua Sydney Horton and Fras. Beauman, on the Downs station; served in the Channel and Mediterranean, from Aug. 1808 until July, 1810, as Midshipman of the SPARROWHAWK 18, Capt. Jas. Pringle; and then joined the ALCESTE 38, Capt. Murray Maxwell. While in the latter ship he aided, in company with the BELLE POULE 38, in destroying, 5 May, 1811, a French national brig lying in the harbour of Parenza, and defended by a galling cross-fire from two batteries; and, independently of many dashing boat-services, he bore a part, 29 Nov. 1811, in an action of two hours and 20 minutes, fought with consummate gallantry, between the ALCESTE and the ACTIVE 38 on one side, and the French 40-gun frigates *Pauline* and *Pomone* on the other, which terminated in the capture of the *Pomone* and escape of the *Pauline*, after a loss had been occasioned to the ALCESTE of 7 men killed and 13 wounded. Removing with Capt. Maxwell, in Sept. 1812, to the DÆDALUS 38, Mr. King continued to serve with that officer until wrecked, off Ceylon, 2 July, 1813. He then joined the MINDEN 74, flag-ship in the East Indies of Sir Sam. Hood, who, in Oct. 1814, sent him to England in charge of the *Hunter*, of Boston, a valuable American prize. On his arrival, in May, 1815, he was received on board the RAMILLIES 74, Capts. Sir Thos. Masterman Hardy and Chas. Ogle; and in the following Aug. he took up a commission dated on 3 of the preceding March. Unable to procure immediate employment in his profession, Lieut. King soon afterwards assumed command of a merchant-vessel trading to the coast of Africa, where it was his fortune on more than one occasion to prove of service to Sir Geo. Collier and other officers by affording them information relative to the Bights of Benin and Bianfra; in consideration whereof, we understand, he was brought under the favourable notice of the Admiralty. On 19 Nov. 1821 he at length succeeded in procuring an appointment, as Senior-Lieutenant, to the DRIVER sloop, Capts. Thos. Wolrige and Chas. Bowen. Continuing in that vessel on the African station throughout the whole period of her being in commission, he had constant charge of her boats, and conducted them up nearly all the rivers on the coast. On one occasion he contrived, with only two of them, to cut out a Portuguese brig mounting 6 guns, and having on board a crew of 38 men, together with a cargo of 189 slaves. In July, 1823, when the King of Ashantee was advancing with his hosts upon the British settlements at Cape Coast, Lieut. King volunteered to serve on shore with Major Chisholm, the Governor, who accordingly placed under his orders a body of 3000 men, consisting of the militia, troops in the employ of the native chiefs connected with British interests, and volunteers. Marching with these into the interior of the country, where he remained four months, the Lieutenant succeeded, in unison with a force under Capt. Laing, of the Royal Cape Coast Light Infantry, distant two or three days' march on his right, in cutting the enemy off from all communication with the sea, and in obliging them to retreat to their capital. In the execution of the duties he had thus of his own accord brought upon himself, he underwent all the hardships and privations attendant upon a campaign carried on in the midst of a barbarous people, under a tropical sun, and in a climate notoriously ruinous. He had the misfortune, too, to receive a severe wound in the calf of the right leg, which entailed so much pain as to produce an attack of the fever common to the country. He was therefore under the necessity of returning to Cape Coast Castle for the benefit of medical aid. Reinforcements having by that time arrived from England, and the DRIVER being on the eve of her departure for Rio de Janeiro, Lieut. King resumed his avocations afloat. On the return, however, of his ship in May, 1824, he again joined the army, and on 21 of that month was twice wounded in a great battle, in which, although the enemy were repulsed, the British and their black allies had 88 men killed, 678 wounded, and 88 missing.* He was promoted for his services to the rank of Commander 25 April, 1825; and from 13 July, 1838, until 5 July, 1843, was employed in the Coast Guard. He has since been on half-pay.

Commander King is a Magistrate and Deputy-Lieutenant for co. Monmouth. He married, 5 April, 1831, Margaret, daughter of the late Joseph Harrisson, Esq., of Tydd Mansion, Cambridge, and sister of Everson Harrisson, Esq., of Tolethorpe Hall, Rutlandshire; and was left a widower 25 Nov. 1841.

KING, F.R.S., F.L.S. (CAPTAIN, 1830. F-P., 19; H-P., 21.)

PHILIP PARKER KING, born 13 Dec. 1793, in Norfolk Island, in the Pacific, is son of Capt. Philip Gidley King, R.N., many years Lieutenant-Governor, and for six years Governor, of New South Wales, who died 3 Sept. 1808, at Lower Tooting, co. Surrey.

This officer entered the Navy, in Nov. 1807, as Fst.-cl. Vol., on board the DIANA frigate, Capt. Chas. Grant; whose First-Lieutenant, the late Capt. Robt. Heriott Barclay, he well supported in an attack made by the ship's boats in the following year upon a French convoy passing between Nantes and Rochefort. On the night of 2 Dec. 1809 he was again noticed for his gallantry in the boats under Lieut. Daniel Miller at the cutting-out of three schuyts moored to the shore at Odenskirk, and provided with heavy ordnance.† In Sept. 1810 (he had attained the rank of Midshipman 18 May, 1808) he proceeded, as Master's Mate of the HIBERNIA 110, Capt. John Chambers White, to the Mediterranean, where he followed the latter officer into the CENTAUR 74, and joined, in Aug. 1811, the CUMBERLAND 74, Capts. Robt. Waller Otway and Thos. Baker. Towards the close of the same year he was received on board the ADAMANT 50, flag-ship at Leith of Admiral Wm. Albany Otway. After he had again served for 18 months with Capt. Grant in the ARMADA 74, on the Mediterranean station, he was there, in Jan. 1814, transferred to the CALEDONIA 120, flag-ship of Sir Edw. Pellew, through whom he was promoted, 28 Feb. following, to a Lieutenancy in the TRIDENT 64, guard-ship at Malta, bearing the flag of Rear-Admiral Laugharne. He next, from July, 1814, until July, 1815, served on board the ELIZABETH 74, Capt. Edw. Leveson Gower, flag-ship part of the time of Rear-Admiral Chas. Elphinstone Fleeming at Gibraltar, and in Feb. 1817 he was intrusted with the conduct of an expedition having for its object a survey of the coasts of Australia; a service on which he continued employed, in the MERMAID cutter and BATHURST sloop (to the command whereof he was promoted by commission dated 17 July, 1821), until his return to England in 1823. The results of the undertaking are contained in a 'Narrative of the Survey of the Intertropical and Western Coasts of Australia,' and in an Atlas, both compiled by Capt. King, and published, the former by Murray, and the latter by the Hydrographical Office at the Admiralty. In Sept. 1825, from the feeling of confidence with which he had impressed the Admiralty in the discharge of his late duties, he was appointed to the ADVENTURE sloop, and ordered to survey the southern coast of America, from the southern entrance of the Rio Plata round to Chiloe, and of Tierra del Fuego. He was paid off on his arrival in England, 16 Nov. 1830, and has not been since employed. His Post-commission bears date 25 Feb. 1830.

In 1832 Capt. King published, as the partial fruit of his recent voyage, a volume entitled 'Sailing Directions to the Coasts of Eastern and Western Patagonia, including the Straits of Magalhaen and the Sea-Coast of Tierra del Fuego.'‡ Besides being a F.R.S. and a F.L.S., the Captain is a Member of the Royal Asiatic Society of London, and a Corresponding Member of the Zoological Society. He married Harriet, daughter of Christopher Lethbridge, Esq.,

* *Vide* Gaz. 1824, pp. 1011, 1273. † *V.* Gaz. 1809, p. 2057.
‡ *V.*, also, Capt. Robert FitzRoy, note, p. 365.

of Launceston, co. Cornwall, by whom he has numerous issue. AGENTS—Messrs. Stilwell.

KING. (CAPTAIN, 1839. F-P., 21; H-P., 21.)

RICHARD HENRY KING is sixth son of the late Rev. John King, A.M., Rector of Witnesham, near Ipswich, by Elizabeth Sarah, only daughter of the Rev. Thos. Bishop, Rector of Trimley St. Martin and Ash-by-Campsey in Suffolk, and Perpetual Curate of St. Mary-at-Tower and St. Mary-at-Elms in Ipswich.

This officer entered the Navy, in May, 1805, as Fst.-cl. Vol., on board the DRUID 32, Capt. Philip Bowes Vere Broke, employed on the Irish station, where he assisted, we find, at the capture of *Le Prince Murat* privateer of 18 guns, and *Le Pandour* national brig of similar force. Following Capt. Broke, in Sept. 1806, into the SHANNON frigate, he continued to serve uninterruptedly with him on the Downs, Greenland, and Halifax stations until 8 March, 1813. He then became Acting-Lieutenant of the SYLPH sloop, Capt. Browne. He was confirmed into his old ship the SHANNON 12 July, 1813, and was afterwards appointed—25 Feb. 1814, to the ALERT 18, Capt. Joseph Gulston Garland, in the Downs—13 Oct. 1815, to the BERMUDA 10, Capt. John Pakenham, on the Jamaica station, whence he returned in the early part of 1817—28 June, 1820, to the FORTE 44, Capt. Sir Thos. John Cochrane, under whom he served at Halifax and in the West Indies, attended George IV. to Scotland, and brought home a large amount of specie from Vera Cruz and the Havana—and 5 Nov. 1824, to the OWEN GLENDOWER 42, bearing the broad pendant at the Cape of Good Hope of Commodore Hood Hanway Christian. On the return of the latter ship to England in 1828, Lieut. King was promoted to the rank of Commander by a commission bearing date 27 Aug. in that year. His last appointment was, 12 Feb. 1838, to the CRUIZER 16, fitting for the East Indies, where he attended an expedition to the mouths of the Indus, and assisted at the capture of Aden. He was advanced, as a reward for his conduct on the latter occasion, to the rank he at present holds 1 May, 1839; but he has not been since afloat.

Capt. King married, 4 May, 1830, Mary, daughter of the late Sam. Twyford, Esq., of Trotton, co. Sussex.

KING. (COMMANDER, 1834.)

WILLIAM GEORGE NASH KING embarked (we presume from the R. N. College) 12 March, 1823; passed his examination in 1828; and was made Lieutenant, 15 Feb. 1830, into the TRIBUNE 42, Capt. John Alex. Duntze, stationed in the Pacific, whence he returned to England, in the course of the same year, in the SAPPHIRE 28, Capt. Henry Dundas. His next appointments were, 28 Feb. and 29 July, 1831, to the WINDSOR CASTLE 76, Capt. Hon. Duncombe Pleydell Bouverie, and DUBLIN 50, Capt. Lord Jas. Townshend, in which ships he served in the Mediterranean and again in South America until ordered home for the purpose of being paid off in 1834. He was promoted to his present rank on 13 Oct. in that year; and has since been on half-pay.

Commander King married, in 1837, Sarah, daughter of the late T. Bulkeley, Esq., of Montagu Square. AGENTS—Hallett and Robinson.

KINGCOME. (CAPTAIN, 1838.)

JOHN KINGCOME entered the Navy, 28 May, 1808, as Sec.-cl. Vol., on board the EMERALD 36, Capt. Fred. Lewis Maitland, with whom he continued to serve as Midshipman, on the Channel, Irish, and Cape of Good Hope stations, until Dec. 1813. He was in consequence present at the destruction of the French shipping in Aix Roads in April, 1809; and had an opportunity of witnessing the capture of a large number of the enemy's vessels, armed and otherwise. On leaving the EMERALD, as above, he was received on board the TIGRE 74, Capt. John Halliday, stationed in the Channel, where he remained until again placed, in May, 1813, under the orders of Capt. Maitland, at that time commanding the GOLIATH 74, on the coast of North America. In July, 1814, he became Master's Mate of the ST. LAWRENCE, bearing the broad pendant on Lake Ontario of Sir Jas. Lucas Yeo, who nominated him, 9 March, 1815, Acting-Lieutenant of the PRINCESS CHARLOTTE, Capt. Rich. O'Connor — an appointment which the Admiralty confirmed by commission dated 1 July in the same year. In Oct. 1815, after having served for some time with Capt. Peter Sampson Hambly in the STAR sloop, he obtained command of the CONFIANCE schooner on Lake Huron; and from Oct. 1816 until July, 1817, he was again employed on Lake Ontario, in the NETLEY 10, Capt. Fras. Brace. His next appointment was, 29 July, 1822, to the TEES 26, Capts. Thos. Coe and Fred. Marryat, the former of whom, on becoming Senior officer in India, appointed him to the command, in 1824, of the LARNE sloop; which vessel, he being at the time engaged in the Burmese war, and she at New South Wales, he was not able to join until 15 April, 1825. While in her, we find him conveying Lady Brisbane (wife of Commodore Sir Jas. Brisbane) and her two daughters from Madras to Pinang, and the Archdeacon Scott from Sydney to Van Diemen's Land; and afterwards visiting New Zealand, Norfolk and Melville Islands, Batavia, and Singapore. Being superseded on his return to Madras in the following July, Lieut. Kingcome was next appointed to the PANDORA sloop, Capt. Wm. Clarke Jervoise. From that vessel, he removed, in 1826, to the WARSPITE 76, bearing the broad pendant of Sir Jas. Brisbane. Attaining the rank of Commander 8 Jan. 1828, Capt. Kingcome served in that capacity in the Coast Guard from 24 Oct. 1835 until appointed, 18 June, 1837, to the WELLESLEY 74, bearing the flag of Sir F. L. Maitland on the East India station, whence he returned on attaining his present rank 28 June, 1838. On 23 Oct. 1841 it was his fortune to be appointed to the BELLEISLE troop-ship, in which he sailed for China, and arrived there in time to witness the closing operations on the Yang-tse-Kiang.* He paid the BELLEISLE off at the close of 1843, but since 24 March, 1846, has again had the command of her.

One of Capt. Kingcome's children was drowned while serving with him as a Midshipman in Jan. 1847. AGENTS—Messrs. Stilwell.

KINGDON. (LIEUT, 1812. F-P., 18; H-P., 33.)

JOHN KINGDON entered the Navy, 9 March, 1796, as L.M., on board the SHANNON 32, Capt. Alex. Fraser, stationed in the North Sea; and from Aug. 1798 until Sept. 1801 was employed, chiefly as Midshipman and Master's Mate, in the CHAPMAN armed ship, Capts. Robert Keen and Thos Browne, at Newfoundland and in the Downs. During the next three years we find him discharging the duties of Acting-Master in the ROSARIO sloop, Capts. Rich. Byron and Wm. Mounsey, on the West India, Home, Mediterranean, and Irish stations. After a further servitude of some months, as Master's Mate, in the HIBERNIA 110, flag-ship in the Channel of Lord Gardner, he was successively appointed Sub-Lieutenant, 21 Sept. 1805, and 1 April, 1806, of the PICKLE and INVETERATE gun-brigs, Lieut.-Commanders John Richards Lapenotière, Daniel Callaway, and Geo. Norton; the former of which vessels had the fortune, while participating in the battle of Trafalgar, to save a great part of the crew of the French 74-gun ship *L'Achille* when in flames, and was afterwards sent home with the despatches announcing the victory. The INVETERATE being wrecked near St. Valery-en-Caux 18 Feb. 1807, Mr. Kingdon had the misfortune to be detained a prisoner in France until the peace of 1814. He has not been since afloat. His commission bears date 20 Nov. 1812.

* *Vide* Gaz. 1842, p. 3404.

KINGSTON. (LIEUTENANT, 1840.)

ARTHUR BURRARD KINGSTON entered the Navy 19 July, 1827; passed his examination in 1833; and was made Lieutenant, 3 July, 1840, into the WOLVERENE 16, Capt. Wm. Tucker, on the coast of Africa. Since the paying-off of the latter vessel in 1841 (with the exception of a short time passed towards the close of 1843 in the VOLAGE 26, Capt. Sir Wm. Dickson) he has not been employed. AGENTS—Coplands and Burnett.

KINGSTON. (LIEUT., 1820. F-P., 11; H-P., 27.)

JAMES KINGSTON entered the Navy, 25 Nov. 1809, as Fst.-cl. Vol., on board the MUROS brig, Capt. Clement Sneyd, on the Guernsey station; removed, in Aug. 1810, to the HIBERNIA 110, Capt. John Nash, lying in Portsmouth Harbour; and from the close of the same year until April, 1812, was employed at the defence of Cadiz in the REVENGE 74, flag-ship of Hon. Arthur Kaye Legge. He then joined the MYRTLE sloop, commanded at first by Capt. Sneyd, and afterwards by Capt. Henry Bourchier, off Lisbon, whence, on his removal with the latter officer, in 1813, to the MEDINA 20, he proceeded to Newfoundland. Returning home in Jan. 1816, he next, in April, 1817, joined the ROCHFORT 80, Capt. Sir Archibald Collingwood Dickson. In Oct. 1818 he was placed on board the IPHIGENIA 42, Capt. Hyde Parker, of which ship he was created a Lieutenant 25 July, 1820. While in her he visited Jamaica, and was employed in the North Sea and Mediterranean. He was paid off 12 June, 1821; and has not been since afloat.

KINGSTON. (LIEUT., 1811. F-P., 13; H-P., 29.)

ROBERT KINGSTON entered the Navy, 3 Aug. 1805, as Fst.-cl. Vol., on board the AURORA 28, Capt. Hon. Geo. Elliot, with whom, after having intermediately served in the Mediterranean, he removed, in Oct. 1806, to the MODESTE 36, and sailed for the East Indies; where, in Oct. 1808, he assisted at the capture of *La Jena* French national corvette of 18 guns and 150 men, at the end of a running fight of nearly an hour, in which the MODESTE had her Master killed and 1 man wounded. On his return to Europe in 1809, in the ALBION 74, Capt. John Ferrier, he joined the ACTIVE of 46 guns and 300 men, Capt. Jas. Alex. Gordon, under whom he saw much service in the Adriatic. In March, 1811, in particular, having been left in charge of one of two prizes in the port of Lissa, he actually, in conjunction with Mr. Jas. Lewe, a Midshipman, who had been placed in command of the other, successfully summoned a body of 200 French seamen and troops to surrender, who had escaped thither after the famous battle of the 13th of that month. These two spirited young men also at the same time rescued from capture a Sicilian privateer brig of 14 guns, besides beating off a Venetian schooner of 1 gun, and preserving the British and Venetian vessels in the bay from being destroyed by her.* After a servitude of nearly three months with the late Sir Wm. Hoste, in the AMPHION 32, Mr. Kingston was promoted to the rank of Lieutenant by a commission bearing date 17 Sept. in the same year. His succeeding appointments were—23 Oct. 1811, and 30 Jan. 1813, to the IMPÉRIEUSE 38, and REPULSE 74, Capts. Hon. Henry Duncan and Rich. Hussey Moubray, both in the Mediterranean, where, in the former ship, he witnessed the destruction of a French convoy under the batteries of Languelia and Alassio, and shared in a spirited skirmish with a powerful Neapolitan squadron in the Bay of Naples —and, in Nov. 1815, to the VENGEUR 74, Capt. Thos. Alexander, lying at Portsmouth. While in the latter ship, Lieut. Kingston was for some time employed in cruizing in the Channel in command of her tender, the HAWK. He has been on half-pay since Sept. 1818. AGENTS—Messrs. Stilwell.

KINSMAN. (LIEUTENANT, 1841.)

HUGH MALLETT KINSMAN is son of the late Major Kinsman, R.M.

* *Vide* Gaz. 1811, p. 897.

This officer passed his examination 10 Dec. 1833; served for some time, as Mate, in the BELLEISLE 72, Capt. John Toup Nicolas; obtained his commission 23 Nov. 1841; and, from Dec. 1841 until paid off in 1846, was employed in the Mediterranean, on board the WARSPITE 50, Capt. Provo Wm. Parry Wallis. Since 30 April, 1847, he has been First-Lieutenant of the AVENGER steam-frigate of 650 horse-power, Capt. Sidney Colpoys Dacres.

He married Josephine, daughter of Capt. John Pasco, R.N.

KINSMAN. (LIEUTENANT, 1846.)

JAMES BYRN KINSMAN, whose commission bears date 21 Jan. 1846, was appointed, on 25 March in that year, to the WANDERER 12, Capt. Philip Hodge Somerville, on the African station. He has been attached, since 14 Feb. 1847, to the TORTOISE store-ship at the Ascension, Capt. Fred. Hutton.

KIRBY. (LIEUT., 1811. F-P., 10; H-P., 33.)

THOMAS KIRBY, born 2 Nov. 1790, is third son of the Rev. John Kirby, Vicar of Mayfield, co. Sussex. His younger brother, William, was promoted for his services as Acting-Lieutenant of the CHERUB at the capture of the American frigate *Essex* in 1814, and afterwards died from the effects of the fatigue he had undergone in bringing some prizes home from the South Sea.

This officer entered the Navy, 14 May, 1804, as Fst.-cl. Vol., on board the REPULSE 74, Capts. Hon. Arthur Kaye Legge and John Halliday, in which ship he was employed for upwards of seven years, chiefly as Midshipman and Master's Mate. He was, in consequence, present in Sir Robt. Calder's action 22 July, 1805; at the capture of the *Marengo* of 80 guns, bearing the flag of Admiral Linois, and 40-gun frigate *Belle Poule*, 13 March, 1806; at the taking, 27 Sept. following, of *Le Président* French frigate; at the passage of the Dardanells, and destruction of the Turkish squadron at Point Pesquies, in Feb. 1807; at the siege of Flushing in Aug. 1809; and, on 30 Aug. 1810, when the REPULSE, in gallant style, rescued the PHILOMEL sloop from capture, by interposing herself between that vessel and an advanced division of the Toulon fleet, which she compelled to put back. In Aug. 1811 Mr. Kirby became Acting-Lieutenant of the IMOGENE 16, Capt. Wm. Stephens, with whom (the appointment being confirmed on 17 of the following Oct.) he continued to serve until 30 Nov. 1813—witnessing in the interim the reduction of the islands of Angusta and Curzola. He has since been on half-pay.

He married, in Jan. 1831, Louisa, eldest daughter of Robt. Becher, Esq., of Tunbridge Wells, by whom he has issue two sons and two daughters. AGENTS—Case and Loudonsack.

KIRBY, K.H. (COMMANDER, 1830. F-P., 17; H-P., 7.)

WALTER KIRBY, born 14 Nov. 1791, is son of the late W. Kirby, Esq., M.D., F.L.S., and belongs to a respectable Norfolk family.

This officer entered the Navy, 23 Oct. 1823, as Fst.-cl. Vol., on board the DART sloop, Capts. W. C. Brownrigg, Thos. Tudor Tucker, Mich. De Courcy, and Joseph Spear; and, until the early part of 1805, was constantly employed with the inshore squadron on the coast of France, where he came into frequent collision with the enemy at Boulogne and Calais, and was engaged in the celebrated catamaran expedition of Oct. 1804. In March, 1807, the DART being at the time in the West Indies, he there removed to the VENUS 32, Capt. Henry Matson. On next joining the ASTRÆA 32, Capt. Edm. Heywood, he had the misfortune to be wrecked, near the island of Anagada, 24 May, 1808. During the 12 ensuing months we find him serving with the present Sir Thos. John Cochrane, in the JASON 32, and ETHALION 38; and, while in the latter of those ships, sharing in a skirmish with the French 40-gun frigate *Amphitrite*, employed on shore at the storming of Fort Edward, Martinique, and affording his aid to the capture of the Saintes and the French 74-gun ship *D'Haupoult*. In June, 1809, he joined the UNDAUNTED 38, Capt. Thos. Jas. Malony, under whom he took part, in the following year, in the defence of Cadiz. Returning to the West Indies in the DRAGON 74, flag-ship of Sir Fras. Laforey, he was promoted on that station to a Lieutenancy, 6 Feb. 1811, in the FROLIC 18, Capt. Thos. Whinyates; in command of the boats of which sloop he succeeded, in the course of the same year, in bringing out a French schooner from off the shoals of Cuba. Lieut. Kirby, who left the FROLIC in March, 1812, was subsequently appointed—2 Nov. in that year, to the SATELLITE 18, Capt. John Porteous, in South America—9 Feb. 1814, after nine months of half-pay, to the BENBOW 74, Capt. Rich. Harrison Pearson, attached to the force in the West Indies, whence he returned in the ensuing Nov.—28 July, 1815, for a few weeks, to the ROTA 38, Capt. John Pasco, on the Home station—10 June and 12 Aug. 1825, to the GLOUCESTER and WINDSOR CASTLE 74's, Capts. Joshua Sydney Horton and Edw. Durnford King, employed at Sheerness, at Plymouth, and off Lisbon—and (the latter ship having been paid off in May, 1828), 22 Jan. 1829, as First, to the WARSPITE 76, bearing the flag of Rear-Admiral Thos. Baker in South America. He attained his present rank 22 July, 1830; and has since been on half-pay.

In Jan. 1828, being at the time in the WINDSOR CASTLE, Commander Kirby elicited the approbation of the Lord High Admiral for the manner in which, on 12 of that month, he effected the preservation of the UNION 104, when adrift and on shore during a violent storm. On 13 Jan. 1835 he was nominated a K.H. He married, 24 Dec. 1814, Hannah, daughter of Jas. Smith, Esq., of Langford, co. Essex, by whom he has had issue two sons and two daughters. His second son, Sidney, died, while a Gentleman Cadet, at the Royal Military Academy at Woolwich. AGENTS—Pettet and Newton.

KIRKES. (LIEUTENANT, 1840.)

MARTIN STOCKDALE KIRKES died 9 Feb. 1845, at Glasgow, aged 31.

This officer entered the Navy 17 April, 1829; passed his examination in 1835; and was promoted to the rank of Lieutenant, as a reward for his services on the coast of Syria and at the bombardment of St. Jean d'Acre, 4 Nov. 1840. He did not afterwards go afloat. AGENTS—Messrs. Ommanney.

KIRKWOOD. (LIEUT., 1810. F-P., 13; H-P., 31.)

CHARLES KIRKWOOD entered the Navy, 19 Aug. 1803, as Fst.-cl. Vol., on board the TRIBUNE frigate, Capts. Geo. Henry Towry and Rich. Henry Alex. Bennett; in which ship, and in the FAME 74, commanded at first by Capt. Bennett, and afterwards by Capts. Hornby and Ferris, he continued to serve, as Midshipman and Master's Mate, on the Home and Mediterranean stations, until promoted to the rank of Lieutenant 14 Aug. 1810. He was then employed for several months in the gun-boat service at the defence of Cadiz and Tarifa; and, on 8 Sept. 1811, having joined the HOTSPUR 36, Capt. Hon. Josceline Percy, he was present in an attack made by that officer on seven of the enemy's gun-brigs off Calvados, on which occasion the HOTSPUR took the ground, lay exposed for four hours to a heavy fire from the vessels, a battery, and some field-pieces, and sustained a loss of 5 men killed and 22 wounded. He has been on half-pay since Nov. 1815, when the HOTSPUR was put out of commission. AGENTS—Coplands and Burnett.

KISBEE. (LIEUTENANT, 1826.)

THOMAS KISBEE entered the Navy 22 June, 1808; passed his examination in 1815; obtained his commission 27 March, 1826; and on 7 of the following July was appointed to the Coast Guard, in which service he was employed for a period of 15 years. Being nominated, 7 Sept. 1841, First-Lieutenant of the DRIVER steam-sloop, of 280 horse-power, Capts. Sam. Fielding Harmer and Courtenay Osborn Hayes, he continued so to officiate on the East India station until the early part of 1847, when he returned home and was paid off. He is now unemployed.

KITCHEN. (LIEUTENANT, 1825.)

HENRY KITCHEN entered the Navy 17 Sept. 1807; passed his examination in 1814; obtained his commission 10 Jan. 1825; and was for some time employed in the Coast Blockade, as Supernumerary-Lieutenant of the HYPERION 42, Capt. Wm. Jas. Mingaye. Since he left that service he has been on half-pay. AGENTS—Messrs. Chard.

KITCHEN. (CAPTAIN, 1846. F-P., 31; H-P., 17.)

WILLIAM HEWGILL KITCHEN was born in June, 1787.

This officer entered the Navy, 3 Feb. 1799, as Fst.-cl. Vol., on board the MONARCH 74, Capt. Jas. Robt. Mosse, and, on 2 April, 1801, after having served for some time in the North Sea, under the flag of Sir Arch. Dickson, was present in the action off Copenhagen. During the remainder of the war we find him employed with Sir Hyde Parker, as Midshipman, in the LONDON 98. Joining next, in Sept. 1802, the ARGO 44, Capt. Benj. Hallowell, he commanded a tender belonging to that ship at the reduction of Ste. Lucie and Tobago in 1803. On becoming Master's Mate of the SPEEDY sloop, Capt. Jas. Gifford, he received, in 1804, a contusion of the right knee while firing at the enemy's flotilla off Ostend; and in 1805, being at the time in command of a rocket-boat under Sir Sidney Smith off Boulogne, he was severely burnt in both hands. Prior to the receipt of his first commission, which bears date 12 May, 1808, he was for nearly two years employed, chiefly as Sub and Acting Lieutenant, in the DAUNTLESS 20, Capts. Hugh Pigot and Chas. Jones, SPARKLER 12, Lieut.-Commander Jas. Sam. Akid Dennis, ALLIGATOR, Capt. Hugh Pigot, NORTHUMBERLAND 74, flag-ship of Sir Alex. Cochrane, DOMINICA 16 (commanded at first by Lieut. Wm. Dean, and then by himself), and MELVILLE 18, Capt. Hon. Jas. Wm. King. While Sub-Lieutenant of the DOMINICA, Mr. Kitchen, with her gig and cutter under his orders, captured, on 4 Oct. 1806, the French national schooner *La Chiffonne*, carrying 17 men, and having on board a French General and his suite on their passage from Guadeloupe to Martinique. On another occasion, during his attachment to the same vessel, he was slightly wounded in the leg at the cutting-out of four of the enemy's vessels from under a battery on the former island. When in the MELVILLE, Mr. Kitchen assisted at the reduction of the Danish West India islands in Dec. 1807. Between the date of his promotion, as above, and Jan. 1813, we find him serving, on the West India, Home, and Lisbon stations, in the WOLVERENE, ASP, and BEAGLE sloops, Capts. Fras. Augustus Collier, Robt. Preston, Wm. M'Culloch, and Wm. Brooking Dolling, BELLONA 74, Capt. John Erskine Douglas, and ZENOBIA 16, Capt. R. Mackenzie. As Senior of the ASP, he served, in 1809-10, at the taking of Martinique, the capture of the French frigate *La Junon*, and in the boats at the destruction of the forts and magazines of Port St. Louis, Guadeloupe. Under Capt. Dolling of the BEAGLE he was employed in the dangerous service of landing papers on the French coast. His appointments, after leaving the ZENOBIA, were, in the capacity of First-Lieutenant—8 Oct. 1813, to the TYRIAN 10, Capts. Augustus Baldwin and Wm. Popham, with whom he was for five years employed in the Channel and West Indies—16 Jan. 1819, to the WYE 26, Capts. Geo. Wickens Willes and Peter Fisher, on the Home station—11 Nov. 1820, to the FORTE 44, Capt. Sir Thos. John Cochrane, fitting for the West Indies, whence he invalided in 1822—and, 13 April, 1824, to the TERROR bomb, Capt. Alex. Dundas Young Arbuthnott, part of the force employed in the ensuing expedition against Algiers. On 13 April, 1825, he assumed command of the

NIGHTINGALE cutter in the Channel, where he cruized until some time in 1826. Obtaining a second promotal commission 2 March, 1827, Capt. Kitchen, on 6 July, 1830, was appointed to a three-years' Inspectorship in the Coast Guard at Harwich. In the following winter he so distinguished himself by his exertions in suppressing riots and extinguishing incendiary fires, that he elicited the thanks of the Secretary of State for the Home Department, of the Duke of Grafton, Lord-Lieutenant of Suffolk, of Lord Maynard, Lord-Lieutenant of Essex, and of the Magistrates of Suffolk and Essex. The Duke of Grafton, indeed, and Lord Maynard were so impressed with the value of his services, that they strongly recommended him to the notice of Lord Minto, then First Lord of the Admiralty; who, however, retired from office without conferring upon Capt. Kitchen the promotion which, we understand, he had been in consequence induced to promise. His last appointments were—9 March, 1842, to the Second-Captaincy of the QUEEN 110, bearing the flag of Sir Edw. W. C. R. Owen in the Mediterranean—and, 17 Feb. 1844, to the command of the DEVASTATION steam-sloop on the same station, whence he returned home and was paid off at the close of 1845. He acquired his present rank 9 Nov. 1846, and is now unemployed.

He married, in 1820, Miss Bell, of Shields, co. Durham. AGENT—Joseph Woodhead.

KNAPMAN. (LIEUT., 1812. F-P., 22; H-P., 22.)

EDWARD KNAPMAN, born in 1794, is brother of Lieut. John Knapman, R.N.

This officer entered the Navy, in Sept. 1803, as Fst.-cl. Vol., on board the MAGNANIME 44, Capt. John Broughton. In 1804, after he had assisted at the bombardment of Havre de Grace, he removed, as Midshipman, to the SPARTIATE 74, Capt. Sir Fras. Laforey, under whom he fought and bled at Trafalgar, being there wounded in the leg and arm, and in consequence presented with a gratuity from the Patriotic Fund.* With the exception of a few months passed, in 1810-11, in the DICTATOR 64, Capts. Rich. Harrison Pearson and Robt. Williams, on the Baltic station, where he served in the boats at the capture of three Danish luggers, Mr. Knapman continued with Sir F. Laforey in the SPARTIATE, and in the DRAGON, another 74, until promoted to the rank of Lieutenant, 21 March, 1812, latterly in the West Indies; previously, however, to proceeding whither he assisted, in the former ship, at the reduction of the islands of Ischia and Procida in 1809. His appointments have since been —11 Feb. 1813, to the ROYAL SOVEREIGN 100, Capts. Jas. Bissett and Thos. Gordon Caulfeild, by the former of whom he was placed in command of gun-boat No. 16, and sent to co-operate in the siege of St. Sebastian—11 April, 1814, to the ACHATES sloop, Capts. Isaac Hawkins Morrison and Thos. Lambe Polden Laugharne, with whom he cruized in the Bay of Biscay and Channel until paid off in Nov. 1815—5 Dec. 1826, to the WINDSOR CASTLE 74, guard-ship at Plymouth, Capt. Edw. Durnford King, of whose tender, the LEVERET 10, he was intrusted with the charge—20 Dec. 1827, to the EREBUS steamer, Capt. Geo. Haye, from which vessel, stationed in the Mediterranean, he was superseded at his own request—7 July, 1836, to the Ordinary at Plymouth, where he was for three years employed with his name on the books of the SAN JOSEF 110, Capts. Rich. Thomas, John Hancock, and Joseph Needham Tayler—and, 6 April, 1841, to the Coast Guard, in which service he is now employed.

He married, 22 Aug. 1822, the second daughter of R. Burgoyne Watts, Esq., of Treburifoot, co. Cornwall, by whom he has issue five sons and three daughters.

KNAPMAN. (LIEUTENANT, 1809.)

JOHN KNAPMAN is brother of Lieut. Edw. Knapman, R.N.

This officer entered the Navy, 1 Jan. 1801, as Midshipman, on board the PRINCE OF WALES 98, Capt. Wm. Prowse, bearing the flag of Sir Robt. Calder in the Channel, where, in 1802, he joined the SIRIUS 36, also commanded by Capt. Prowse. In 1803 he removed to the TÉMÉRAIRE 98, Capt. Eliab Harvey, and from that ship, after he had fought at Trafalgar, he was draughted, in March, 1806, into the ACHILLE 74, Capt. Rich. King. On 25 of the following Sept. we find him present at the capture, off Rochefort, of four heavy French frigates by a squadron under the orders of Sir Sam. Hood. He was next, between 1807 and his promotion to the rank of Lieutenant 14 Sept. 1809, employed, off Cape Finisterre, Cadiz, and Toulon, in the TONNANT 80, and OCEAN 98, flag-ships of Admirals E. Harvey and Lord Collingwood. During the remainder of the war he served on the Mediterranean and Home stations in the NETTUNO (afterwards CRETAN), FAVOURITE, ELECTRA, and ALBACORE sloops, and CRESSY 74, Capts. Chas. Fred. Payne, Benj. Clement, H. Gregory, Henry Thos. Davies, and Chas. Dashwood. Under Capt. Davies of the ALBACORE, Lieut. Knapman took part, 18 Dec. 1812, in a gallant action, in which that vessel, when in company with the 14-gun schooner PICKLE, 12-gun sloop BORER, and 4-gun cutter LANDRAIL, beat off the French 40-gun frigate *La Gloire*, with a loss to herself of 1 Lieutenant killed and 6 or 7 men wounded. Through the influence of his late Majesty he obtained, 20 Nov. 1827, an appointment in the Coast Guard, which he retained until 18 Dec. 1832. He has since been on half-pay.

He is married and has issue.

KNEVITT. (LIEUT., 1815. F-P., 18; H-P., 25.)

THOMAS LEPARD KNEVITT was born 16 Feb. 1790. His only brother, a Midshipman of the BULWARK 74, was drowned in Cawsand Bay in 1813.

This officer entered the Navy, 15 Aug. 1804, as Fst.-cl. Vol., on board the PENGUIN 18, Capt. Geo. Morris, with whom he continued to serve in the ELK, RENARD, and MAGNET sloops, on the Jamaica and Baltic stations, nearly the whole time as Midshipman and Master's Mate, until wrecked on the ice, 11 Jan. 1809. He then joined the SCEPTRE 74, Capts. Joseph Bingham and Sam. Jas. Ballard, and while in that ship was employed in the expedition to the Walcheren, where, in a gun-boat, he assisted at the landing of the troops. Proceeding next to the West Indies, he there, on 18 Dec. 1809, served in the boats of a squadron under Lieut. John Wyborn at the destruction of the two French 40-gun frigates *Loire* and *Seine*, and of the batteries in L'Anse la Barque, Guadeloupe, by which they had been protected. During the operations which led to the reduction of the latter island Mr. Knevitt landed with 100 seamen under the orders of Lieut. Elliot; but that officer being killed at the onset, the command devolved upon him, and he retained it until the island was thoroughly conquered. In March, 1811, a few months after he had passed his examination, he removed to the VENGEUR 74, flag-ship of Sir Joseph Sydney Yorke off Cherbourg; and in the following Dec. we find him joining the BULWARK 74, bearing at first the broad pendant of Sir Rich. King, and afterwards the flag of Rear-Admiral Philip Chas. Durham, on the Home station. On 16 and 20 Jan. 1814, being at the time on his passage to the West Indies with the last-mentioned officer in the VENERABLE 74, we find him contributing to the capture, not without opposition, of the French frigates *Iphigénie* and *Alcmène*, of 44 guns each.* On the latter occasion he led the boarders, and received the French Captain's sword; and on 28 of the ensuing month, as a reward for his distinguished conduct, he was promoted to an Acting-Lieutenancy in the PALMA 38, Capt. Jas. Andrew Worth. He was officially promoted 1 Feb. 1815, and was afterwards appointed—19 Oct. 1824, to the Coast Blockade, in which service he continued, as Supernumerary-Lieutenant of the RAMILLIES 74, and HYPERION 42, Capts. Wm. M'Culloch and Wm.

* *Vide* Gaz. 1805, p. 1484.

* *Vide* Gaz. 1814, p. 440.

Jas. Mingaye, until superseded in Sept. 1826, in consequence of a wound he had received from a spring-gun when in pursuit of a party of smugglers —and, 8 March, 1827, to the command of the Semaphore station at Holder Hill. He has been on half-pay since March, 1832.

Lieut. Knevitt's testimonials are of a very flattering character, proving his gallantry to have been most exemplary, and his conduct at all times worthy of the highest commendation. He married, first, in Jan. 1820, Amelia, daughter of Capt. Thos. Morris; and secondly, in Dec. 1822, Miss Elizabeth Williams Price. He has issue nine sons and two daughters.

KNIGHT, K.H. (Commander, 1822. f-p., 20; h-p., 21.)

Christopher Knight entered the Navy, 25 Dec. 1806, as Fst.-cl. Vol., on board the Minotaur 74, Capt. Chas. John Moore Mansfield, successive flag-ship of Admirals Sir Chas. Cotton and Wm. Essington, under the latter of whom he served as Midshipman in the expedition of 1807 against Copenhagen. Joining next the Foudroyant 80, bearing the flag of Sir Wm. Sidney Smith, he was present under that officer off Lisbon when the Royal Family of Portugal took its flight to the Brazils. He afterwards proceeded himself to South America, and continued there, in the President 38, Capt. Chas. Marsh Schomberg, until ordered home in 1810 in the Elizabeth 74, Capt. Hon. Henry Curzon. Towards the close of the same year, having rejoined Capt. Schomberg on board the Astræa, of 42 guns and 271 men, he proceeded to the Cape of Good Hope; and, on 20 May, 1811, when in company, off Madagascar, with the Phœbe and Galatea frigates, similar in force to the Astræa, and 18-gun brig Racehorse, he assisted, after a long and warmly-contested action with the French 40-gun frigates *Renommée*, *Clorinde*, and *Néréide*, and a loss to the Astræa of 2 killed and 16 wounded, at the capture of the *Renommée*, and, on 25 of the same month, of the *Néréide* and the settlement of Tamatave. On the former of those occasions Mr. Knight received two contusions. Returning to England, in Sept. 1812, on board the Galatea 36, Capt. Woodley Losack, he was employed during the next two years on the Home and Canadian stations in the Thisbe 28, flag-ship of Sir Chas. Hamilton, El Corso 12, Lieut.-Commander Curry Wm. Hillier, Queen Charlotte 100, flag-ship of Lord Keith, and Princess Charlotte 42, Capt. Edw. Collier. In Sept. 1814, being still in Canada, he was nominated Acting-Lieutenant of the Prince Regent 56, Capt. Davies —an appointment which the Admiralty confirmed on 19 Dec. in the same year. In the summer of 1815 he came home with Capt. Wm. Walpole in the Thames 32; and in July, 1816, after he had been for nearly 12 months on half-pay, he became attached to the Impregnable 104, bearing the flag of Rear-Admiral David Milne. Continuing in that ship for a period of nearly four months, he was in consequence present in the battle of Algiers, and on that occasion he had the misfortune to be contused in three places. Being next, in June 1818, appointed to the Tartar 42, Capt. Sir Geo. Ralph Collier, the Lieutenant sailed for the coast of Africa, where, on 8 June, 1821, he assumed command of the Snapper gun-brig, in which vessel he proceeded, without a pilot, 60 miles up the old Calabar river in search of slave-vessels—a greater distance, we believe, than accomplished by any other man-of-war before or since. In Nov. 1822, having been promoted to the command of the Morgiana sloop on 3 of the previous June, he returned home and paid that vessel off. His last appointments were, 1 Sept. 1828, and 18 March, 1834, to the Coast Guard, in which service he was each time employed for a period of three years. While so engaged he was very successful in the capture of smuggling-vessels and their crews; and in one instance, when in the execution of his duty, he broke his collar-bone. For his singular exertions on the occasion of the wreck of the Hound Revenue-cruizer, in Weymouth Bay, when by his own act he saved the whole of the crew, consisting of 40 persons, he was nominated a K.H. 1 Jan. 1837. Agents—Messrs. Ommanney.

KNIGHT. (Lieut., 1815. f-p., 27; h-p., 13.)

John Ellis Knight was born 11 Sept. 1791.

This officer entered the Navy, 8 March, 1807, as Fst.-cl. Vol., on board the Trompeuse corvette, Capt. Wm. Brooking Dolling, successively employed in the North Sea, off Lisbon, and in the Downs. During the expedition of 1809 to the Scheldt we find him engaged on shore in the defence of the fort of Balthz, when in vain attacked by a flotilla under the orders of the French Rear-Admiral Massiessy. Previously to the evacuation of the Walcheren he accompanied Capt. Dolling into the Beagle sloop, commanded afterwards by Capt. John Smith, with whom he continued until Oct. 1813, assisting during that period at the cutting out of two gun-boats under Cape Grisnez, the destruction of part of a convoy near Calais, the capture of three armed and other smugglers (services for which Capt. Dolling and a Master's Mate were each promoted), and the reduction and fortification, during the investment of St. Sebastian, of the important island of Sta. Clara. From Nov. 1813 until Aug. 1815 Mr. Knight was further employed, as Midshipman and Master's Mate, in the Lightning 20, Capts. Bentinck Cavendish Doyle and Geo. Rennie, on the Channel and Cork stations. Being then awarded a commission dated on 1 of the previous March, he was appointed, 5 Jan. 1827, to the Coast Blockade, as Supernumerary-Lieutenant of the Ramillies 74, Capt. Hugh Pigot, from which, however, he was obliged, in Oct. 1829, to retire, in consequence of a severe rupture of the left groin, received in the execution of his duty, but for which he has never been able to obtain remuneration. Since 22 April, 1831 (unable to procure other employment), Lieut. Knight has been in command of a station in the Coast Guard. His exertions in that service, as exhibited by numerous strong testimonials, have been most successessful. On 8 of the Oct. following his appointment he had the good fortune, at Atherfield, in the Isle of Wight, to save the lives of 19 of the crew and passengers belonging to the ship *Bainbridge*, of Halifax, which had been wrecked in a heavy gale.

He married, 7 Aug. 1816, Miss S. Mason, of Yealmpton.

KNIGHT. (Retired Commander, 1844.)

William Knight died 6 May, 1846.

This officer entered the Navy, 1 March, 1790, as a Boy, on board the Arrogant 74, Capt. John Harvey, from which ship, lying at Portsmouth, he was paid off in the following year. Rejoining Capt. Harvey, in 1793, on board the Brunswick 74, he took part, we believe, in the action of 1 June, 1794; after which he served for five years as Midshipman in the Robust 74, Capt. Edw. Thornbrough, and was ultimately promoted from the Royal George 100, flag-ship of Lord Bridport, to a Lieutenancy, 26 Aug. 1799, in the Fanny 18, Capt. Joshua Sydney Horton. While in the Robust Mr. Knight, besides accompanying the unfortunate expedition of 1795 to Quiberon, was present with the force under Sir John Borlase Warren at the defeat of Commodore Bompart's squadron 12 Oct. 1798, on which occasion that ship compelled the *Hoche* 74 to strike, and sustained a loss of 10 men killed and 40 wounded. On 6 Feb. 1800, being then in the Fairy, and in company with the Loire 38, Danaé 20, Harpy 18, and Railleur 16, we find him witnessing the capture, 6 Feb. 1800, of the *Pallas*, of 46 guns and 362 men, with which frigate the Fairy and Harpy had previously sustained a very warm and spirited action of an hour and three-quarters, attended with a loss to the former of 4 men killed and 8 wounded. His subsequent appointments were —in 1800, to the Cambridge 74, flag-ship of Sir Thos. Pasley, and Naiad 38, Capt. Philip Wilkinson, both on the Home station—in Jan. 1802, to the command, for three months, of the TICKLER gun-brig—in April, 1803, to the Impress service at Lynn, in Norfolk, where he remained until Nov. 1812—in April, 1813, to the EXPERIMENT receiving-ship at Falmouth, Capt. Jas. Slade—and subsequently to the Ordinary at Chatham. He became a Retired Commander on the Junior List 28 Nov. 1833, and on the Senior 6 Feb. 1844.

KNIGHT. (LIEUT., 1811. F-P., 10; H-P., 34.)

WILLIAM KNIGHT (c) entered the Navy, in Dec. 1803, as Fst.-cl. Vol., on board the GALGO 16, Capt. Michael Dod, stationed in the North Sea. Joining next, in Nov. 1804, the ATLAS 74, Capt. Sam. Pym, he served in that ship in the action off St. Domingo 6 Feb. 1806; after which we find him employed for upwards of four years in the Channel and Mediterranean on board the COLOSSUS 74, Capt. Jas. Nicoll Morris, and, on 28 Nov. 1810, promoted from the VILLE DE PARIS 110, flag-ship on the latter station of Rear-Admiral Thos. Fras. Fremantle, to an Acting-Lieutenancy in the ALFRED 74, commanded off Cadiz by Capt. Joshua Rowley Watson. He was confirmed in his present rank 19 Jan. 1811, and between the close of the same year and April, 1814, he endured a further servitude in the DEVASTATION bomb, Capt. Wm. Taylor, CALLIOPE 10, Capt. John M'Kerlie, YORK 74, Capt. Alex. Wilmot Schomberg, and RAPID sloop, Capt. John Foote, chiefly on the Home station. He has since been on half-pay. AGENT—J. Hinxman.

KNIGHTON. (RETIRED COMMANDER, 1843. F-P., 21; H-P., 34.)

CHARLES KNIGHTON is a near relative of Lieut. C. Knighton, R.N.

This officer entered the Navy, 28 Nov. 1792, as A.B., on board the FURY bomb, Capt. Hon. Wm. Paget, attached to the force in the Mediterranean. Removing as Midshipman, in March, 1794, to the CENTURION 50, Capt. Sam. Osborne, he witnessed, we believe, the capture, 5 May following, of the French 74-gun ship *Duguay Trouin*, off the Isle of France. He also, on 22 of the next Oct., partook of a stiff action fought in the same neighbourhood between the CENTURION and DIOMÈDE 44 on the one side, and, on the other, a French squadron consisting of the 40-gun frigate *Cybèle*, 36-gun frigate *Prudente*, 20-gun corvette *Jean Bart*, and 14-gun brig-corvette *Courier*, terminating in the flight of the enemy, with a loss to the CENTURION of 3 men killed and 24 wounded. In 1797, after he had further contributed to the reduction of Trincomalee and of the islands of Amboyna and Banda, Mr. Knighton was nominated Acting-Lieutenant of the VICTORIOUS 74, Capt. Wm. Clark. He was confirmed, while officiating in a similar capacity on board the CARYSFORT frigate, 27 March, 1799; and was afterwards appointed—11 Aug. 1800, and 14 July, 1803, to the CUMBERLAND and LEVIATHAN 74's, Capts. Thos. Graves and Henry Wm. Bayntun, on the Channel, West India, and Mediterranean stations—in Sept. 1805, to the Sea Fencible service in Ireland, where he continued until the corps was disbanded in May, 1810—24 Feb. 1813, to the command of a Signal station, which he retained until June, 1814—and 26 March, 1823, for three years, to the Ordinary at Plymouth. He became a Retired Commander on the Senior List 7 April, 1843.

KNIGHTON. (LIEUTENANT, 1841.)

CHARLES KNIGHTON (b) is closely related to Retired Commander Charles Knighton, R.N.

This officer entered the Navy 29 Nov. 1826; passed his examination 5 June, 1833; and at the period of his promotion to the rank of Lieutenant, which took place 23 Nov. 1841, was serving, on the Brazils and Cape of Good Hope station, as Mate of the GRECIAN 16, Capt. Wm. Smyth. His succeeding appointments were—15 Dec. 1841, as Additional, to the CALEDONIA 120, flag-ship at Plymouth of Sir Graham Moore—next, to the JASEUR 16, Capt. Wm. Alex. Willis, on the Mediterranean station—17 July, 1843, again as Additional, to the WINCHESTER 50, bearing the flag at the Cape of Hon. Josceline Percy—and 6 March, 1844, to the CONWAY 26, Capt. Wm. Kelly, with whom he continued employed on the station last named until ordered home, for the purpose of being paid off, in 1847. AGENTS—Messrs. Stilwell.

KNOCKER. (LIEUT., 1813. F-P., 9; H-P., 32.)

JOHN BEDINGFIELD KNOCKER, born 1 April, 1793, at Dover, co. Kent, is brother of Lieut. Wm. Knocker, R.N.

This officer entered the Navy, 27 Jan. 1806, as Fst.-cl. Vol., on board the POMPÉE 74, Capt. Rich. Dacres, bearing the flag in the Mediterranean of Sir Wm. Sidney Smith; and in the following July, having removed to the AURORA 28, Capt. Hon. Geo. Elliot, was present at the bombardment and capture, notwithstanding a very firm resistance, of a battery mounted on Cape Licosa, in Spain. Rejoining the POMPÉE soon afterwards, he served in that ship under the flag of Hon. Henry Edwin Stanhope in the expedition of 1807 to Copenhagen, whence he assisted in bringing home the *Christian VII.* 80, one of the Danish prizes. In Nov. of the latter year he obtained a berth on board the DIANA 38, Capts. Chas. Grant and John Cramer, under whom, on his return from a visit to the Brazils, we find him, from Oct. 1809 until the commencement of 1810, employed with the advanced squadron up the Scheldt. During that particular period he was constantly absent on boat service, and on the night of 2 Dec. assisted, with much gallantry, in cutting out three schuyts, moored to the shore at Odenskirk, and provided with heavy ordnance.* In Nov. 1810 he participated, as Master's Mate, in an attack made on the two French frigates *Amazone* and *Eliza*, lying aground under the protection of several strong batteries in the neighbourhood of La Hogue. On 23 of the ensuing month the latter vessel (the other having effected her escape) was effectually destroyed by two of the DIANA's boats—one of them commanded by Mr. Knocker, to whom a Lieutenant's commission was in consequence sent, but which, as he had not served his time, he was of course unable to retain. During his attachment to the DIANA, he was once struck with violence by a splinter on the occasion of a vessel being driven under the fire of some batteries on the French coast; and in Aug. 1811 he was sent home in charge of a fine schooner, of which he had himself effected the capture under the walls of St. Sebastian while in command of the ship's boats. With the exception of a few months, from Nov. 1812 to March, 1813, during which he was confined to the Naval Hospital at Port Mahon, Mr. Knocker continued to serve with Capt. Grant in the ST. ALBAN'S 64, and ARMADA 74, off Cadiz and Toulon, until nominated Acting-Lieutenant, 9 April, 1813, of the ROYAL GEORGE 100, Capt. Thos. Fras. Chas. Mainwaring. He was confirmed to that ship 10 July following, and was lastly, in Nov. of the same year, appointed to the HIBERNIA 120, flag-ship of Sir Wm. Sidney Smith. He returned home from the Mediterranean and was paid off in July, 1814.

He married, 14 Oct. 1822, Elizabeth, daughter of Anthony Cox, Esq., Banker, of Harwich, co. Essex, by whom he has issue 14 children.

KNOCKER. (LIEUT., 1815. F-P., 11; H-P., 30.)

WILLIAM KNOCKER was born 18 Dec. 1794. He is brother of Lieut. John B. Knocker, R.N.

This officer entered the Navy, 23 Aug. 1806, as Fst.-cl. Vol., on board the GLORY 98, Capt. Wm. Albany Otway, employed in the Channel and off Cadiz; removed, in July, 1807, to the NIGER 32, Capt. Jas. Hillyar, on the Mediterranean station; and in April, 1808, became Midshipman of the BARFLEUR 98, Capts. Donald M'Leod and Sam. Hood Linzee. While in that ship we find him, after the convention of Cintra, escorting the Russian Rear-

* *Vide* Gaz. 1809, p. 2057.

Admiral Seniavin's squadron from Lisbon to England, then visiting Vigo, and, in Jan. 1809, assisting at the embarkation of Sir John Moore's army after the battle of Corunna. In the course of the latter year, having joined the THALIA 36, Capt. Jas. Giles Vashon, Mr. Knocker made a voyage to Quebec, and accompanied, as Midshipman, the expedition to the Walcheren. He next, it appears, joined the PRINCESS OF ORANGE 74, commanded in the Downs by Capt. Fras. Beauman, and TARTAR 32, Capt. Jos. Baker, on the Baltic station. On the occasion of the latter ship being wrecked, 18 Aug. 1811, it was Mr. Knocker's fortune to be absent in a prize. He was afterwards, until Aug. 1815, employed in the NAIAD 38, Capt. Philip Carteret, IMPREGNABLE 98, flag-ship of Admiral Wm. Young, BARROSA 36, Capt. Wm. Henry Shirreff, AMARANTHE 18, Capt. Rich. Augustus Yates, and ASTRÆA 36, Capt. Edw. Kittoe. He served, during that period, with Admiral Young, at the blockade of the Scheldt—was present with Capt. Shirreff in many active operations in the Chesapeake, and went with him to the West Indies, where, while on duty aloft, he met an accident from the effects of which he has never recovered—and was sent in the ASTRÆA to France, during the war of 100 days, on a mission of peculiar delicacy and hazard. On the date above mentioned Mr. Knocker, who then took up a commission dated 8 March, 1815, received an appointment to the HERON 18, Capts. Timothy Scriven, Geo. Bentham, and Herbert Brace Powell, under the second of whom he fought at Algiers 27 Aug. 1816. He was superseded at his own request in Feb. 1817, for the purpose of recruiting his health, and has since been on half-pay.

From 1819 until 1832 Lieut. Knocker had command, on the Harwich station, of the DOVER packet, under the direction of the Post-office. He has been in charge, since, of different private steamers.* He married, 10 Sept. 1821, Augusta Ann, daughter of Capt. Thos. Bridge, and by that lady, who died in 1839, has issue nine children.

* In one way or another, Lieut. Knocker, with the short exception of eighteen months in 1817-18, has been constantly afloat ever since he first went to sea in 1803.

KNOLLES, K.T.S. (LIEUTENANT, 1824.)

HENRY KNOLLES entered the Navy in 1808; and served for nearly four years with Admiral Hon. Michael De Courcy, under whom, in the TONNANT 80, he assisted in embarking the army after the battle of Corunna, and was for a long time employed, in the FOUDROYANT 80, on the Brazilian station. In Sept. 1813 we find him employed at the siege of St. Sebastian in the RÉVOLUTIONNAIRE 38, Capt. John Chas. Woolcombe. He passed his examination in 1814; and after an intermediate servitude in various ships, part of the time on the Cape station, was promoted, 3 June, 1824, to a Lieutenancy in the WINDSOR CASTLE 74, Capt. Chas. Dashwood, at the particular request of Don John of Portugal, upon whose fugitive family, while Mate of that ship, he had been in especial attendance during the height of the rebellion. As a further mark of favour, the same monarch created him a K.T.S. He has been on half-pay since 1825. AGENT—J. Hinxman.

KNOTT. (LIEUTENANT, 1838.)

NATHANIEL SYDENHAM KNOTT passed his examination in 1828; obtained his commission 28 June, 1838; and was subsequently appointed—20 Nov. 1839, to the PRESIDENT 50, flag-ship in the Pacific of Rear-Admiral Chas. Bayne Hodgson Ross—26 Feb. 1841, to the ACTÆON 26, Capt. Robt. Russell, with whom he returned home from the latter station and was paid off in the summer of 1842—and 22 March, 1845, to the VERNON 50, flag-ship of Rear-Admiral Sam. Hood Inglefield on the south-east coast of America. Since 1846 he has again been on half-pay.

KNOTT. (COMMANDER, 1846.)

OWEN PHIBBS KNOTT entered the Navy 1 Sept. 1823; passed his examination in 1830; and on the occasion of his promotion to the rank of Lieutenant, 26 Oct. 1840, was appointed to the SOUTHAMPTON 50, flag-ship of Sir Edw. Durnford King on the Brazils and Cape of Good Hope station, whence he returned to England and was paid off towards the close of 1842. On 5 July, 1843, he became Additional of the DUBLIN 50, bearing the flag of Rear-Admiral Rich. Thomas in South America, where, from 29 Nov. 1843, until promoted to the rank of Commander 9 Nov. 1846, he officiated as First-Lieutenant of the CURAÇOA 24, Capts. Sir Thos. Sabine Pasley and Wm. Broughton. He is now on half-pay.

KNOX. (REAR-ADMIRAL, 1846. F-P., 12; H-P., 30.)

THE HONOURABLE EDMUND SEXTON PERY KNOX, born in 1787, is second son of Thomas, first Earl of Ranfurly, by Diana Jane, eldest daughter and co-heir of Edmund Viscount Pery, Speaker of the Irish House of Commons in the Parliaments of 1771, 1776, and 1783. He is brother of the present Earl of Ranfurly.

This officer entered the Navy, in Nov. 1799, as Fst.-cl. Vol., on board the ETHALION 38, Capt. John Clarke Searle, and on 25 of the following Dec. was wrecked on the Penmarck rocks. In May, 1800, he joined the SEAHORSE 38, Capt. Edw. Jas. Foote, under whom we find him escorting Rear-Admiral Sir Rich. Bickerton and General Sir Ralph Abercromby to the Mediterranean, the latter back again to England, and 10 sail of Indiamen to Calcutta, besides being for some time employed in attendance upon the King and Queen off Weymouth. From Oct. 1802 until Feb. 1806 Mr. Knox served in the Mediterranean as Midshipman of the JUNO 32, Capt. Henry Richardson. He then became attached for short periods to the HALCYON 16, Capt. Henry Whitmarsh Pearse, QUEEN 98, flag-ship of Lord Collingwood, and ENTREPRENANTE cutter, Lieut.-Commander Robt. Benj. Young; and on 1 Sept. in the same year, 1806, he was made Lieutenant into the ACASTA 40, Capts. Rich. Dalling Dunn and Philip Beaver, lying at Plymouth. His succeeding appointments were—on 18 of the latter month, to the NARCISSUS 32, Capt. Chas. Malcolm, stationed in the Channel—16 Jan. 1808, to the PRINCESS CHARLOTTE 38, Capt. Geo. Tobin, with whom he was for eight months employed on the coast of Ireland—and 5 July, 1809,* to the acting-command of the PULTUSK sloop in the West Indies, whence he invalided in the ensuing Aug. On 24 Feb. 1810 Capt. Knox, who had been confirmed in the rank of Commander by commission dated 2 June, 1809, was appointed to the CASTILIAN sloop off Deal. Continuing but two months in that vessel, he next, on 3 Aug. 1810, obtained command of the ST. FIORENZO troop-ship. He attained Post-rank 28 Feb. 1812; and was lastly, from 22 March until 21 June, 1814, employed as Flag-Captain to Rear-Admirals Hon. Chas. Elphinstone Fleeming and Sam. Hood Linzee, in the EUROTAS 38, off Cadiz and Gibraltar. He accepted his present rank 1 Oct. 1846.

The Rear-Admiral married, 3 July, 1813, Jane Sophia, fifth daughter of Wm. Hope Vere, Esq., and sister of Jas. Hope, Esq., of Craigie Hall, West Lothian, N. B. By that lady he has issue one son (an officer in the Army) and three daughters.

KNOX. (LIEUTENANT, 1840.)

MARCUS KNOX entered the Navy 1 Sept. 1824; passed his examination in 1831; and, including the civil war in 1834, was for many years employed on the north coast of Spain in the CASTOR 36, and NORTH STAR 28, both commanded by Lord John Hay. He obtained his commission 1 Aug. 1840; served for nearly two years as Lieutenant in the

* He had been appointed Supernumerary-Lieutenant, a few weeks previously, of the NEPTUNE 98, flag-ship of Sir Alex. Cochrane.

PHŒNIX steamer, Capt. John Richardson, on the Mediterranean station; and since 22 Nov. 1842 has been in charge of a station in the Coast Guard.

KNOX. (CAPTAIN, 1842.)

THOMAS OWEN KNOX entered the Navy 14 Feb. 1816; and was made Lieutenant, 24 April, 1824, into the SPARTIATE 76, flag-ship of Sir Geo. Eyre in South America. His next appointments were—5 June, 1824, to the ECLAIR 18, Capt. Thos. Bourchier, on the same station—7 July, 1828, to the PYRAMUS 42, Capt. Geo. Rose Sartorius—30 Aug. 1828, to the PALLAS 42, Capts. Adolphus FitzClarence and Manley Hall Dixon, under the former of whom we find him accompanying Lord Dalhousie and the Bishop of Calcutta from Portsmouth to Bengal, General Viscount Combermere from India home, and Col. Fox from Halifax—and 10 Aug. 1831, as First, to the MAGICIENNE 24, Capt. Jas. Hanway Plumridge, on the East India station, whence he returned to England and was paid off in March, 1835. Attaining the rank of Lieutenant 15 Feb. following, he was successively nominated, 29 March, 1836, and 13 May, 1840, Second-Captain of the MINDEN 72 and RODNEY 92, Capts. Alex. Renton Sharpe and Robt. Maunsell, both on the Mediterranean station. He has been on half-pay since the receipt of his Post-commission, which bears date 14 June, 1842. AGENTS—Messrs. Stilwell.

KOOYSTRA. (LIEUTENANT, 1841.)

JUSTUS BARTHOLOMEW KOOYSTRA entered the Navy 25 July, 1812; passed his examination 8 Jan. 1819; obtained an appointment in the Coast Guard 9 Oct. 1840; and was promoted to the rank of Lieutenant 23 Nov. 1841. His appointments have since been—2 Aug. 1842, as Additional, to the MADAGASCAR 44, Capt. John Foote, on the coast of Africa—2 Nov. 1842, to the PERSIAN 16, Capt. Thos. Rodney Eden, on the same station—22 June, 1843, again to the MADAGASCAR—7 Feb. 1844, to the HYDRA steam-sloop, Capt. Horatio Beauman Young, also on the African coast—2 Dec. 1844, to the TORTOISE store-ship at the Ascension, Capt. Arthur Morrell—18 Dec. 1845, to the BITTERN 16, Capt. Thos. Hope, stationed as were the above vessels—and 16 Sept. 1846, to the Coast Guard, in which service he has been nearly ever since employed. AGENTS—Messrs. Chard.

KORTRIGHT. (LIEUTENANT, 1828.)

ALFRED KORTRIGHT entered the Navy 18 May, 1822; and obtained his commission 11 Sept. 1828. His appointments have since been—28 Nov. 1828, to the Coast Blockade, as Supernumerary-Lieutenant of the HYPERION 42, Capt. Wm. Jas. Mingaye—22 Nov. 1831, to the ÆTNA surveying-vessel, Capt. Edw. Belcher, employed on the coast of Africa, whence he returned in Aug. 1832—for a few months in 1835, to the SAN JOSEF 110, and ROYAL ADELAIDE 104, bearing each the flag of Sir Wm. Hargood at Plymouth—4 May, 1842, to the command of the COLUMBIA surveying-vessel, on the North American station, where he was superseded in Oct. of the same year—and 28 April, 1845, to the VINDICTIVE 50, bearing the flag of Sir Fras. Wm. Austen, under whom he is now employed on surveying service on the North America and West India station.

Lieut. Kortright is married and has issue. AGENT—Joseph Woodhead.

KUPER, C.B. (CAPTAIN, 1841. F-P., 17; H-P., 7.)

AUGUSTUS LEOPOLD KUPER, born 16 Aug. 1809, is son of the Rev. Wm. Kuper, D.D. and K.H., Chaplain to Her Majesty the Queen Dowager.

This officer entered the Navy, 19 April, 1823, as Fst.-cl. Vol., on board the ISIS 50, flag-ship of Sir Geo. Eyre in South America, where he continued to serve until the summer of 1827, the greater part of the time as Midshipman, in the SPARTIATE 76, Capt. Thos. Gordon Falcon, MERSEY 26, Capt. John Macpherson Ferguson, and CAMBRIDGE 80, Capt. Thos. Jas. Maling. He was then, until within a short period of his promotion to the rank of Lieutenant, which took place 20 Feb. 1830, employed on the Channel and Mediterranean stations, in the ROYAL SOVEREIGN yacht, Capt. Sir Wm. Hoste, ISIS again, Capt. Sir Thos. Staines, and RALEIGH 18, Capt. Sir Wm. Dickson. His succeeding appointments were—17 Oct. 1831, to the SAVAGE 10, Capt. Lord Edw. Russell, on the Irish station—9 April, 1832, to the NIMROD 20, Capts. Lord E. Russell and John M'Dougall, employed off the coasts of Spain and Portugal—30 March, 1836, to the MINDEN 74, fitting for service off Lisbon—and 12 July, 1837, as Senior Lieutenant, to the ALLIGATOR 28, Capt. Sir Jas. John Gordon Bremer, whom he aided in forming the settlement of Port Essington in North Australia. On 27 July, 1839, Mr. Kuper was nominated to the acting-command of the PELORUS 18,* an appointment which the Admiralty afterwards confirmed. He became Acting-Captain of the ALLIGATOR 5 March, 1840; and from 14 June, 1841 (on 8 of which month he was officially posted), until 15 March, 1843, he commanded the CALLIOPE 26. In the former ship it appears he obtained mention for his zeal and alacrity at the capture of Chusan in July, 1840.† In Feb. 1841 it was his fortune to elicit the thanks of the Commander-in-Chief for his conduct in the action with the Bogue forts; as he again did for the gallant and able support he afforded Capt. Thos. Herbert in an attack upon the enemy's camp, fort, and ship *Cambridge*, bearing the Chinese Admiral's flag, at their position below Whampoa Reach, when 98 guns were in the whole destroyed.‡ On 13 March Capt. Kuper was once more mentioned in terms of praise for the assistance he rendered at the capture of the last fort protecting the approaches to Canton.§ At the taking, a few days afterwards, of the city itself, he commanded the investing force on the east side, and by his unremitting attention effectually guarded the approaches in that quarter.‖ During the second series of operations against Canton his prompt and decisive conduct had the happy result of repelling an attack made by the Chinese with fire-rafts, chained in pairs, upon the ALLIGATOR, as she lay off Howqua's Folly.¶ In July, 1842, being then in the CALLIOPE, Capt. Kuper accompanied Sir Wm. Parker up the Yang-tse-Kiang.** As a reward for his services he was nominated a C.B. 21 Jan. 1842.

He married, 19 June, 1837, Emma Margaret, eldest daughter of Commodore Sir J. J. G. Bremer, K.C.B. AGENT—Joseph Woodhead.

KYLE. (RETIRED COMMANDER, 1837. F-P., 19; H-P., 32.)

GEORGE KYLE entered the Navy, 22 June, 1796, as Midshipman, on board the VIPER sloop, Capts. John Scoffin and H. H. Parker, on the Cork station; and from Sept. in the same year until Oct. 1800 was employed on Channel service, the last three years as Master's Mate, in the CHAPMAN armed ship, Capts. Wm. Cumberland, Robt. Keen, and Thos. Browne. He then joined the ELEPHANT 74, Capts. Thos. Foley and Geo. Dundas, in which ship, after participating under Lord Nelson in the action off Copenhagen, 2 April, 1801, he proceeded to the West Indies, where, in 1803, he assisted at the blockade of Cape François, St. Domingo, and witnessed the capture of a squadron with the remains of General Rochambeau's army on board. Removing next to the HERCULE 74, bearing the flag of Sir John Thos. Duckworth, Mr. Kyle, in Jan. 1804, served on shore with the seamen and marines in the unsuccessful attempts upon Curaçoa. On 7 of the following July, after having acted for nearly

* While Capt. Kuper was in the PELORUS that vessel was driven high and dry on her beam-ends during a violent hurricane in Port Essington; and it was only after she had been for 86 days on shore that she was with difficulty hove off.

† *Vide* Gaz. 1840, p. 2991.

‡ *V.* Gaz. 1841, pp. 1498, 1500, 1501.

§ *V.* Gaz. 1841, p. 1503.

‖ *V.* Gaz. 1841, p. 1504.

¶ *V.* Gaz. 1841, p. 2502.

** *V.* Gaz. 1842, p. 2504.

four months as Lieutenant, he was confirmed in that rank in the VIGILANTE *alias* SUFFISANTE sloop, Capts. Wm. Croft and Henry Laroche. His last appointments were, 16 Jan. 1806 and 24 Oct. 1811, to the KANGAROO sloop, Capts. H. Laroche, John Baker, John Bradley, and John Lloyd, and ABOUKIR 74, Capts. Geo. Parker, Thos. Browne, and Norborne Thompson. During his attachment to the KANGAROO, besides cruizing in the Channel, he attended the expedition to the Walcheren, and was employed in escorting convoys to Spain, Portugal, and the West Indies; and while in the ABOUKIR he commanded a gun-boat on the rivers Dwina and Aa during the defence of Riga in 1812, and was present at the siege and capture of Genoa in 1814. He went on half-pay in Sept. 1815, and accepted the rank he now holds 25 Jan. 1837.

Commander Kyle married, 4 Nov. 1817, Miss Mary Irwin, and has issue two children.

KYNASTON. (LIEUTENANT, 1842.)

AUGUSTUS FREDERICK KYNASTON entered the Navy 30 Sept. 1830; passed his examination 27 April, 1837; and served as Mate in the VANGUARD 80, Capt. Sir David Dunn, PHŒNIX steamer, Capt. John Richardson, AGINCOURT 72, flag-ship of Sir Thos. John Cochrane, EXCELLENT gunnery-ship, Capt. Sir Thos. Hastings, and SHEARWATER steamer, Capt. John Washington, on the Mediterranean and Home stations. He obtained a commission 10 Nov. 1842; was appointed, on 28 of the same month, to the MADAGASCAR 44, Capt. John Foote, on the African station; and since 24 July, 1844, has been employed in the Pacific on board the COLLINGWOOD 80, flag-ship of Sir Geo. Fras. Seymour. AGENTS—Hallett and Robinson.

L.

LACON. (COMMANDER, 1842. F-P., 19; H-P., 5.)

HENRY JAMES LACON, born 27 Nov. 1810, is third son of the late Sir Edm. Knowles Lacon, Bart., of Ormesby House, near Great Yarmouth, Norfolk, by Elinor Dixon, eldest daughter and co-heir of Thos. Beecroft, Esq., of Saxthorpe Hall, co. Norfolk.

This officer entered the Royal Naval College 5 Nov. 1823; and embarked, 22 June, 1825, as a Volunteer, on board the DORIS 42, Capt. Sir John Gordon Sinclair, with whom he was for four years employed, part of the time as Midshipman, on the South American station. He then joined the CHILDERS 18, Capt. Wm. Morier, attached to the force in the North Sea, where he cruized until Nov. 1829, in the course of which month he passed his examination. Between Jan. 1830 and his promotion to the rank of Lieutenant 21 March, 1835, Mr. Lacon served on the West India, Home, and Mediterranean stations, in the NORTH STAR 28, Capt. Lord Wm. Paget, FIREFLY schooner, Lieut.-Commander John M'Donell, SHANNON 46, Capt. Benj. Clement, CONWAY 28, Capt. Henry Eden, VESTAL 26, Capt. Wm. Jones, and PORTLAND 52, Capt. David Price. His succeeding appointments were—28 Sept. 1835 and 20 Jan. 1837, to the CASTOR 36 and NORTH STAR 28, both commanded by Lord John Hay, under whom he served for five years on the north coast of Spain, and was constantly employed on shore with the Naval Brigade—5 April, 1841, to the CORNWALLIS 72, fitting for the flag of Sir Wm. Parker, Commander-in-Chief in the East Indies—and, 22 Jan. 1842, as Senior, to the BLONDE 42, Capt. Thos. Bourchier. For his services in the latter ship at the capture of Chapoo and in all the operations to the northward of that place he was advanced to the rank he now holds 23 Dec. 1842.* He has officiated, since 13 Nov. 1846, as Second-Captain of the VANGUARD 80, Capt. Geo. Wickens Willes, and is at present in the Mediterranean.

Commander Lacon married, 9 July, 1844, Carolina Louisa Bartlett, second daughter of the late J. Roberts, Esq., of Buckingham. AGENTS—Messrs. Ommanney.

* *Vide* Gaz. 1843, p. 2950.

LACY. (LIEUTENANT, 1845.)

EDWARD LACY entered the Navy in 1833; passed his examination 5 June, 1839; and served as Mate in the HASTINGS 72, Capt. John Lawrence, CALCUTTA 84, Capt. Geo. Fred. Rich, EXCELLENT gunnery-ship, Capt. Sir Thos. Hastings, and for two years and a half in the CORMORANT steam-sloop, Capt. Geo. Thos. Gordon, on the Mediterranean, Home, and South American stations. He obtained his commission 13 Dec. 1845, and has been ever since attached to the COLLINGWOOD 80, flag-ship in the Pacific of Sir Geo. Fras. Seymour.

LADD. (LIEUTENANT, 1815. F-P., 25; H-P., 17.)

CHARLES PYBUS LADD, born 17 June, 1790, at Dover, co. Kent, is son of the late Edw. Ladd, Esq., who, in conjunction with his brother Henry, raised, during the first American war, and partly equipped, a volunteer corps of Light Artillery for the defence of their native town. The latter gentleman (who was for many years Captain of Archcliffe Fort, and died at the age of 93) received a silver salver from the then Duke of Richmond, as an acknowledgment of the services he rendered on the occasion.

This officer entered the Navy, 1 Sept. 1805, as Fst.-cl. Vol., on board the UTRECHT 64, Capt. Thos. Seccombe, bearing the flag in the Downs of Vice-Admiral John Holloway; and, from May, 1806, until Oct. 1809, was employed on the Channel and Mediterranean stations, chiefly as Midshipman, in the GLATTON 50, commanded at first by Capt. Seccombe, and afterwards by Capts. John Clavell, Henry Hope, and Geo. Miller Bligh. We next find him, until confirmed in his present rank 7 Feb. 1815, serving in 12 different vessels on the Home station; during which period he six times performed the duties of Acting-Lieutenant. His succeeding appointments were—5 Aug. 1831, to the SKYLARK packet, the command of which he retained, on the Falmouth station, for upwards of nine years—8 Sept. 1841, to the REDWING steam-packet, Capt. Thos. Bevis, under whom he was for three years and a half employed at Liverpool—and, 21 May, 1845, to the command of the ZEPHYR steamer, in which vessel, stationed as a packet between Holy-Head and Kingstown, Dublin, he still serves.

Lieut. Ladd married in 1823, and has issue.

LAFARGUE. (LIEUTENANT, 1845.)

CHARLES AUGUSTUS LAFARGUE passed his examination 4 July, 1821; obtained an appointment in the Coast Guard 2 June, 1842; and was advanced to the rank of Lieutenant 25 June, 1845. He has since been on half-pay.

LAFFER. (RETIRED COMMANDER, 1847. F-P., 15; H-P., 34.)

NATHANIEL LAFFER was born in 1781.

This officer entered the Navy, 1 July, 1798, as Second-cl. Boy, on board the CAMBRIDGE 80, guard-ship at Plymouth, Capt. Boger. Removing in April, 1799, to the MELPOMÈNE 38, Capt. Sir Chas. Hamilton, he served in that ship in the ensuing expedition to the Helder, and was present in her at the capture of the African island of Gorée in April, 1800. In the course of the latter year he successively became Midshipman of a schooner and armed ship, bearing each the name of GORÉE, and commanded, the first by Lieut. Chas. Chamberlayne Irvine, and the second by Capt. Thos. Tidy, with whom he served on the coast of Africa and in the West Indies until Dec. 1801. During the next seven years he presents himself to our notice as employed on the Home and South American stations in the PUISSANT 74, Capt. Wm. Syme, CLYDE 38, Capt. John Larmour, REINDEER 18, Capt. John Fyffe, LAPWING 28, Capt. Clotworthy Upton, and LONDON 98, Capts. Sir Harry Neale and Thos. Western. While in the latter ship he contributed, in company with the AMAZON 38, to the capture, 13

March, 1806, of the *Marengo* of 80 guns, bearing the flag of Admiral Linois, and 40-gun frigate *Belle Poule*, after a long running fight in which the LONDON sustained a loss of 10 men killed and 22 wounded. He also, in 1807-8, escorted the Royal Family of Portugal to the Brazils. On leaving the LONDON, as above, Mr. Laffer was nominated Acting-Lieutenant of the AGAMEMNON 64, Capt. Jonas Rose, from which ship he was confirmed, 10 May, 1809, into the PRESIDENT 38, Capt. Chas. Marsh Schomberg. He invalided home from South America in April, 1810, and was next appointed—8 April, 1811, to the PLANTAGENET 74, Capt. Thos. Eyles, under whom, during a servitude of 21 months in the Baltic, he came frequently into contact with the Danish gun-boats—and, 22 Nov. 1813 and 26 Sept. 1814, to the ROYAL SOVEREIGN 100, and GOLDFINCH 10, Capts. Thos. Gordon Caulfeild and John Foote, on the Mediterranean and Channel stations. He went on half-pay in May, 1815, and accepted his present rank in July, 1847. AGENTS—Messrs. Stilwell.

LAKE. (COMMANDER, 1841. F-P., 20; H-P., 7.)

EDWARD LAKE is second son of the late Sir Jas. Sam. Wm. Lake, Bart., by Maria, daughter of Sam. Turner, Esq.; and nephew of the late Admiral Sir Willoughby Thos. Lake, K.C.B. His brother, the present Sir Jas. Samuel Lake, married the eldest daughter of the late Vice-Admiral Sir Rich. King, Bart., K.C.B.

This officer entered the Navy, 6 April, 1820; passed his examination in 1826; obtained his first commission 20 Aug. 1827; and was subsequently appointed—24 June and 29 Sept. 1828, to the GLOUCESTER 74, and MADAGASCAR 46, Capts. Henry Stuart and Hon. Sir Robt. Cavendish Spencer, both in the Mediterranean—1 March, 1829, to the RATTLESNAKE 28, Capts. Sir Thos. Sabine Pasley and Chas. Graham, on the South American station—1 Aug. 1831, to the BLANCHE 46, bearing the broad pendant in the West Indies of Commodore Arthur Farquhar, to whom he acted for some time as Flag-Lieutenant—12 June, 1833, to the CALEDONIA 120, Capt. Thos. Brown, attached to the force in the Mediterranean—2 June, 1835, after 12 months of half-pay, to the CANOPUS 84, Capt. Hon. Josceline Percy, also on the latter station, whence he returned in the early part of 1837—and 27 June, 1839, to the Coast Guard. He attained his present rank 23 Nov. 1841; and from 3 July, 1844, until the summer of 1847 was again employed in the Coast Guard.

Commander Lake married, in Sept. 1839, Clara, third daughter of the late Sir Wm. Johnston, Bart., of Hilltown House, near Aberdeen. AGENTS—Messrs. Stilwell.

LAKE. (COMMANDER, 1827. F-P., 14; H-P., 23.)

WILLOUGHBY LAKE is son of the late Admiral Sir Willoughby Thos. Lake, K.C.B.

This officer entered the Royal Naval College 18 Aug. 1810; and embarked, 5 April, 1813, as Midshipman, on board the MAGNIFICENT 74, commanded by his father, whom he accompanied to the West Indies. He afterwards, between Aug. 1815 and Feb. 1821, served, latterly as Acting-Lieutenant, in the TAGUS 38, Capt. Jas. Whitley Deans Dundas, and SUPERB 78, Commodore Sir Thos. Masterman Hardy, on the Mediterranean and South American stations. He was officially promoted 18 May, 1821, and was lastly employed, from 14 April, 1824, until within a few days of his advancement to the rank of Commander 20 Aug. 1827, as Flag-Lieutenant to his father, in the SUPERB 74, on the Halifax station. He has since been on half-pay. AGENTS—Messrs. Stilwell.

LAKE. (LIEUTENANT, 1840.)

WILLOUGHBY J. LAKE entered the Navy 3 April, 1829; passed his examination in 1835; and for his services on the coast of Syria, and at the bombardment of St. Jean d'Acre, was promoted to the rank of Lieutenant 4 Nov. 1840. His appointments have since been—10 May and 25 Oct. 1841, to the BITTERN 16, Capt. Hon. B. C. F. P. Cary, and ALFRED 50, Commodore John Brett Purvis, on the African and Brazilian stations, from the latter of which he returned home in the early part of 1845—and 21 Jan. 1847, to a station in the Coast Guard, the command whereof he still retains. AGENTS—Messrs. Stilwell.

LAKE, K.C.B. (ADMIRAL OF THE WHITE, 1841. F-P., 29; H-P., 38.)

SIR WILLOUGHBY THOMAS LAKE was born about 1773, and died 18 Feb. 1847, at Blackheath, co. Kent. He was second son of Sir Jas. Winter Lake, Bart., by Joyce, daughter of John Crowther, Esq., of Bow; and uncle of the present Commander Edw. Lake, R.N.

This officer entered the Navy, 1 Sept. 1780, as Captain's Servant, on board the ROEBUCK 44, Capt. Andrew Snape Hamond, under whom and the late Sir Andrew Snape Douglas he continued to serve (with the exception of an interval between May, 1783, and Dec. 1785) in the CHATHAM and IRRESISTIBLE 74's, SOUTHAMPTON 32, and GOLIATH, BEDFORD, and VANGUARD 74's, on the North American, Mediterranean, and Home stations, chiefly as Midshipman, until promoted to the rank of Lieutenant 22 Nov. 1790. In Sept. 1793, after he had been for a short time attached to the RUSSEL 74, Capt. John Willet Payne, he was invested with the command of the CHARLOTTE armed cutter, employed off Ostend and Flushing. On leaving that vessel in the following Nov., Mr. Lake officiated for four months as Flag-Lieutenant to Rear-Admiral John Macbride in the FLORA, CUMBERLAND, EURYDICE, and FORMIDABLE, on the Home station, where, in March, 1794, he became his First-Lieutenant in the MINOTAUR 74. On 25 Nov. in the same year he was promoted to the command of the WEASEL sloop, stationed between Yarmouth and Flamborough Head; and in April, 1795, he removed to the RATTLER 18, employed as a Channel cruizer. Being made Post, 11 Jan. 1796, into the PROSERPINE 28, Capt. Lake, while in that frigate, succeeded in capturing, 3 Aug. 1797, the Dutch privateer *Unity*, of 10 guns and 50 men, in the neighbourhood of Shetland. He went on half-pay a short time afterwards, and was subsequently appointed—4 April, 1803, to the TOPAZE 38, on the Irish station, where he took the privateers *Napoléon*, of 14 guns and 180 men, *Minerve*, of 14 guns and 111 men, *Général Augereau*, of 14 guns and 88 men, and *El Fenin*, of 14 guns and 85 men—16 June, 1806, to the GIBRALTAR 80, in which ship he was intrusted with the command of a small squadron off L'Orient, for the purpose of watching the enemy's vessels then ready for sea in that port—3 April, 1807, to the Sea Fencibles on the coast of Sussex, where he continued until the corps was disbanded in 1810—and, 29 Feb. 1812, to the MAGNIFICENT 74. While in the latter ship Capt. Lake, being ordered to co-operate with the force under Sir Home Popham on the north coast of Spain, assisted at the reduction of Castro, and in the attacks upon Puerta Galletta, Guetaria, &c. He also commanded a detachment of seamen and marines, to which was added the Guerilla regiment of Campillo, landed to act against the castle of St. Ano. During his pursuit of the French from that place to Santander, on their road whither the British were exposed to an incessant and galling fire from numerous small houses, walls, and hedges, Capt. Lake received a musket-ball in his right arm; and on his way back he was further wounded in the head, and for a time deprived of his senses. In consequence of these severe injuries he was for four months unable to discharge the active duties of his profession. He at length, however, rejoined his ship, which had been commanded, *pro tem.*, by Capt. John Hayes, and continued in her until paid off 8 Aug. 1815. During that period he effected the capture, 30 Oct. 1813, of an American letter-of-marque, the *Amiable*, of 6 guns and 21 men, and was sent with the trade to the West Indies, where he arrived at the period Sir Alex. Cochrane was proceeding on the expedition against New Orleans, and was left by him to carry on the duties of Senior officer on the Jamaica station. In 1815 the MAGNIFICENT returned with another convoy to England. On 12 Aug. 1819 Capt. Lake, who had been appointed a Colonel of Marines 4 June, 1814, and nominated a C.B. 2 Jan. 1815, was advanced to the rank of Rear-Admiral. He commanded-in-chief, subsequently, on the Halifax station, with his flag in the SUPERB 74, from 18 May, 1824, until 15 Aug. 1827; became a Vice-Admiral 27 May, 1825; was created a K.C.B. 17 Nov. 1830; and attained the rank of full Admiral 23 Nov. 1841.

Sir Willoughby Thos. Lake married, in 1795, Charlotte, daughter of Admiral Macbride, by whom, who died 5 Sept. 1836, he has left, with other issue, a son, the present Commander Willoughby Lake, R.N., and a daughter, Emily, married to Capt. Wm. Webb, R.N. His third son, Edward, now deceased, was a Major in the Madras Engineers, and had distinguished himself in India, where he had been twice wounded. AGENTS—Messrs. Stilwell.

LAMB. (LIEUTENANT, 1815. F-P., 11; H-P., 28.)

JAMES THOMAS LAMB entered the Navy, 22 Dec. 1808, as Fst.-cl. Vol., on board the AMETHYST, of 42 guns and 222 men, Capt. Michael Seymour; and on 6 April, 1809, took part in a severe intermittent action of about four hours, which terminated in the capture, with a loss to the AMETHYST of 8 men killed and 37 wounded, of the French frigate *Le Niemen*, of 46 guns and 339 men, of whom 47 were slain and 73 wounded. After attending the expedition to Flushing he accompanied Capt. Seymour into his prize, which had been added to the Navy as a 38-gun frigate. He continued with him in that ship, on the Channel and Irish stations, until the spring of 1812, when he again followed him, as Midshipman, into the HANNIBAL 74. In March, 1814, being then on a cruize off Cherbourg, Mr. Lamb was present at the capture of the 40-gun frigate *Sultane*. We then find him proceeding to the West Indies, where, in the course of the same year, he successively joined the BEDFORD and VENERABLE 74's, Capts. Jas. Walker and Geo. Pringle—the latter bearing the flag of Sir Philip Chas. Durham, by whom he was at first sent on a cruize in the ADAMS tender, and then nominated Acting Sub-Lieutenant of the GRECIAN schooner. He was made Lieutenant, 1 March, 1815, into the FAIRY 18, Capt. Henry Loraine Baker, part of the force present at the ensuing surrender of Guadeloupe, with the despatches relative to which she returned to England; and he was next, from 29 of the following Sept. until superseded at his own request 27 March, 1817, employed on the Irish station in the HELICON and MARTIN sloops, both commanded by Capt. Andrew Mitchell. His last appointment was, 29 Aug. 1833, to the Coast Guard, in which service he remained until the early part of 1836.

We understand that on one occasion, while in command of a merchant-ship, Lieut. Lamb performed service which was acknowledged by a reward from Lloyd's.

LAMB. (RETIRED COMMANDER, 1846. F-P., 12; H-P., 34.)

JOHN LAMB entered the Navy, in 1801, as Fst.-cl. Vol., on board the PORT MAHON sloop, Capt. Wm. Buchanan, on the Mediterranean station, where, in the course of the same year, he became Midshipman of the NORTHUMBERLAND 74, Capt. Geo. Martin. Between 1803 and the date of his promotion to the rank of Lieutenant 20 June, 1808, he presents himself to our notice as serving in the Channel and off the coast of Ireland in the ST. ALBAN'S 64, Capt. John Temple, WARRIOR 74, Capts. Wm. Bligh, Sam. Hood Linzee, and Michael Seymour, and AMETHYST, of 42 guns and 261 men, Capt. M. Seymour. While in the latter ship we find him contributing to the capture, 11 Nov. 1808, off L'Orient, of the French frigate *La Thétis*, of 44 guns and 436 men, including troops, which was boarded and carried at the close of a furious contest of more than three hours, in which the British lost 19 men killed and 51 wounded, and the enemy 135 killed and 102 wounded. His last appointments were—23 June, 1808, to the LEVIATHAN 74, Capt. John Harvey, under whom, after serving off Flushing and Cadiz, he witnessed the self-destruction, in Oct. 1809, of the French ships of the line *Robuste* and *Lion*, off Cape Cette—in 1810, to the PERLEN frigate, Capt. Norborne Thompson, in the West Indies—11 Oct. 1811, to the FANTOME brig, Capt. John Lawrence—27 April, 1812, to the UNION 98, Capts. Sam. Hood Linzee, Wm. Kent, and Robt. Rolles, in which ship he witnessed Sir Edw. Pellew's partial actions of 5 Nov. 1813, and 13 Feb. 1814, with the Toulon fleet—and, 29 March, 1814, to the HIBERNIA 120, bearing the flag of Sir Wm. Sidney Smith. He returned to England in the following Aug., and accepted his present rank 7 May, 1846.

During his servitude afloat Commander Lamb was presented, we are informed, with a gratuity from the Patriotic Fund. He married, in March, 1823, Emma, daughter of J. Robinson, Esq., of Holloway, co. Middlesex.

LAMBART. (LIEUT., 1844. F-P., 10; H-P., 0.)

THE HONOURABLE OLIVER WILLIAM MATTHEW LAMBART, born 26 Aug. 1822, is youngest son of Richard, seventh Earl of Cavan, K.C., a general officer in the Army, and Colonel of the 45th Regt. of Foot, by his second wife, Lydia, second daughter of Wm. Arnold, Esq., of Slatswood. He is half-uncle of the present Earl of Cavan.

This officer entered the Navy, 11 June, 1837, as Fst.-cl. Vol., on board the HAZARD 18, Capt. Jas. Wilkinson. In that vessel, after visiting the coast of Africa, he proceeded to the Mediterranean, where, until 1839, he served as Midshipman in the RODNEY 92, Capt. Hyde Parker, TALAVERA 74, Capt. Wm. Bowen Mends, and WASP 16, Capt. Hon. Dudley Worsley Anderson Pelham. Sailing then for China in the BLONDE 42, Capt. Thos. Bourchier, he took part in the chief operations of the war, including the first and second attacks upon Canton, the reduction of Amoy, the re-taking of Chusan, the capture of Chinghae, Ningpo, and Chapoo,* the battle of Woosung,† the storming of Chin-Kiang-Foo,‡ and the various hostilities on the Yang-tse-Kiang terminating with the pacification of Nanking. At Chin-Kiang-Foo, 21 July, 1842, Mr. Lambart was employed in the boats under Lieut. Edw. Crouch when they sustained, in an attempt to land the artillery-guns, a loss of 17 out of 24 persons wounded, including the officer last mentioned, whom he consequently succeeded in the command. In March, 1843, on his return to England, he joined the ST. VINCENT 120, flag-ship of Sir Chas. Rowley at Portsmouth, where he passed his examination 6 Sept. following, and was for some time employed as Mate in the VICTORIA AND ALBERT yacht, Capt. Lord Adolphus FitzClarence. He obtained his commission 11 Oct. 1844, and since 19 Feb. 1845 (a few days previously to which period he had been appointed to the RODNEY 92, Capt. Edw. Collier) has been serving in the VANGUARD 80, Capt. Geo. Wickens Willes, on the Home and Mediterranean stations.

Lieut. Lambart married, 26 Nov. 1844, Anne Elizabeth, second daughter of Capt. G. W. Willes, R.N.

LAMBERT. (LIEUT., 1813. F-P., 11; H-P., 32.)

CHARLES LAMBERT was born 28 June, 1790.

This officer entered the Navy, 1 July, 1804, as Fst.-cl. Vol., on board the NEMESIS 28, Capt. Philip Somerville, stationed in the Channel. In the course of 1805 he successively joined the DREADNOUGHT 98, and ROYAL SOVEREIGN 100, bearing each the flag of Lord Collingwood, under whom, after serving at the blockade of Cadiz, he fought in the latter ship at the battle of Trafalgar. From Nov. in the same

* *Vide* Gaz. 1842, pp. 396, 2388, 3694.

† *V.* Gaz. 1842, p. 3400. ‡ *V.* Gaz. 1842, p. 3405.

year, 1805, until the spring of 1810, we find Mr. Lambert employed on the Channel and Cape of Good Hope stations, principally as Midshipman, in the BELLEROPHON 74, and LEOPARD 50, flag-ships of the late Sir Albemarle Bertie. He then became attached to the NEREIDE 36, Capt. Nesbit Josiah Willoughby, under whom, we are informed, he took part in the boats in a gallant attack made on the enemy's batteries and troops at Jacotel, in the Mauritius. He also assisted, in July, 1810, at the capture of Ile de Bourbon; and on 17 Aug. he landed, we believe, at the storming of a fort on Pointe du Diable, in the Isle of France. He witnessed, next, the capture of Ile de la Passe; was on board the NEREIDE when she compelled the enemy's sloop *Victor* to surrender, and exchanged broadsides with the 40-gun frigate *Minerve;* and was slightly wounded during a series of unhappy although heroic operations, which, by 28 Aug., terminated in the self-destruction, in Port Sud-Est, of the British frigates MAGICIENNE and SIRIUS, and the capture, by a French squadron, of the NEREIDE and IPHIGENIA—the former after being reduced to a mere wreck, and incurring a loss of nearly her whole crew. Being restored to liberty on the fall of the Isle of France in the following Dec., Mr. Lambert returned to England in LA MANCHE frigate, Lieut.-Commander Edw. Grimes. In Nov. 1812, having been for the last 15 months employed in the FAVORITE and STORK sloops, Capts. Robt. Forbes and Robt. Lisle Coulson, on the Plymouth and Cork stations, he was nominated Acting-Lieutenant of the PEACOCK, of 18 guns and 122 men, Capt. Wm. Peake; which sloop (of whose crew 5, including the Commander, were killed, and 33 wounded) was sunk, at the close of a desperate action of 25 minutes, by the American ship *Hornet*, of 20 guns and 165 men, 1 only of whom was killed and 2 wounded. On his release from captivity in May, 1814, Mr. Lambert found that he had been promoted to a Lieutenancy in the EURYALUS 36, Capt. Chas. Napier, by commission dated 6 Dec. 1813. In the following Aug., being still in that ship, he accompanied Capt. Jas. Alex. Gordon's brilliant expedition up the Potomac, and was in consequence present at the capture of Fort Washington, the capitulation of Alexandria, and the destruction of the American batteries on the banks of the river. During these operations he was again slightly wounded. He invalided from the EURYALUS in the month ensuing, and was lastly, from July to Sept. 1815, employed on the Leith station in the PINCHER 12, Capt. T. Smith.

He married 24 March, 1816, and has issue six children. AGENTS—Holmes and Folkard.

LAMBERT. (LIEUTENANT, 1846.)

EDWARD HENRY GAGE LAMBERT passed his examination 7 Sept. 1844; and at the period of his promotion to the rank of Lieutenant, which took place 9 Nov. 1846, was serving on the south-east coast of America as Mate of the RALEIGH 50, Commodore Sir Thos. Herbert. He is now on half-pay.

LAMBERT. (CAPT., 1825. F-P., 15; H-P., 23.)

GEORGE ROBERT LAMBERT, a son of Robt. Lambert, Esq., many years a Captain R.N., is brother of the late Vice-Admiral Robt. Lambert,* and the late Capt. Henry Lambert, R.N.,† and of two gentlemen holding high rank in the Army.

This officer entered the Navy, in April, 1809, as Fst.-cl. Vol., on board the EAGLE 74, Capt. Chas. Rowley. Continuing in that ship for a period of five years, he attended in consequence the expedition to the Walcheren, co-operated in the defence of Cadiz in 1810, assisted at the capture, 27 Nov. 1811, of *La Corceyre* frigate, carrying 28 guns, together with 170 seamen and 130 soldiers, and beheld the fall, in 1813, of Fiumé, Trieste, and other places in the Adriatic. After a further servitude of eleven months in the GLASGOW 50, Capt. Hon. Henry Duncan, on the Channel station, he was promoted to the rank of Lieutenant 5 May, 1815, and appointed to the ISTER 36, Capt. Thos. Forrest. Quitting the latter frigate in Jan. 1817, he next, from 1 Jan. 1820, until within a few days of his promotion to the rank of Commander, 19 Jan. 1822, officiated as Flag-Lieutenant, in the VIGO 74, to his brother, Rear-Admiral Robt. Lambert, on the St. Helena station. On 23 Feb. 1824 Capt. Lambert was awarded command of the CAMELION sloop, in which we find him employed on particular service until advanced to Post-rank, 8 Aug. 1825. His appointments have since been—23 Sept. 1831, to the ALLIGATOR 28, fitting for the East Indies, whence he returned home and was paid off 27 Aug. 1835—8 Dec. 1845, to the ENDYMION 44, on the North America and West India station—and 23 Jan. 1847, to be Commodore at Jamaica, where he is now serving with his broad pendant in the IMAUM 72. AGENTS—Messrs. Chard.

* Vice-Admiral Lambert attained the rank of Lieutenant in 1791, and served in that capacity on board the BARFLEUR 98 in Lord Howe's action 1 June, 1794. In 1795-6 he acted as Flag-Captain to Rear-Admiral Rainier, in the SUFFOLK 74, at the reduction of Ceylon, Amboyna, Banda, &c.; and in 1801, being at the time in the SATURN 74, he accompanied the expedition under Sir Hyde Parker to the Baltic. He became a Rear-Admiral 12 Aug. 1819; commanded in chief on the St. Helena station, for the secure detention of Buonaparte, from 1820 to 1822; was constituted a Vice-Admiral 22 July, 1830; and died about Sept. 1836.

† A partial sketch of the services of Capt. Henry Lambert may be found in our memoir of Capt. Hen. Ducie Chads.

LAMBERT. (RETIRED COMMANDER, 1845. F-P., 11; H-P., 36.)

WILLIAM LAMBERT was born in the early part of 1788, and died at the commencement of 1847.

This officer entered the Navy, 6 Feb. 1800, as A. B., on board the FURIOUS gun-brig, Lieut.-Commander Wm. Froth, with whom he served in the North Sea and Baltic until April, 1802. From Jan. 1803 until May, 1804, we find him employed as Fst.-cl. Vol. and Midshipman, in the PRINCESS CHARLOTTE 38, and RUBY and GALYKHEID 64's, all commanded by Capt. Hon. Fras. Farington Gardner, on the Irish and North Sea stations. During the next three years he presents himself to our notice as again attached to the PRINCESS CHARLOTTE, commanded at first by Capt. Gardner, but afterwards by Capt. Geo. Tobin, under whom, besides being occasionally employed in escorting convoys, he saw a good deal of boat service on the coast of Cuba, and took part, as Master's Mate, 5 Oct. 1805, in a severe action of an hour, near Tobago, with *La Cyane* of 26 and *La Naïade* of 16 guns, the former of which then surrendered. In the course of 1807 Mr. Lambert successively joined the HIBERNIA 110, Capt. Wm. Bedford, VILLE DE PARIS 110, bearing the flag of Lord Gardner, and, as Acting-Lieutenant, the DREADNOUGHT 98, Capts. Wm. Lechmere and Geo. Burgoyne Salt, to which ship he was confirmed by commission dated 7 May, 1808. His subsequent appointments were—1 Sept. 1810, to the MUTINE 18, Capts. Chas. Montagu Fabian and Nevinson De Courcy, on the Brazilian station, whence he invalided 18 Feb. 1811—20 Jan. 1812, for three months, to the CONQUESTADOR 74, Capt. Lord Wm. Stuart, employed on the coast of France—29 April, 1813, to the MEDWAY 74, Capt. Augustus Brine, with whom he proceeded to the Cape of Good Hope—22 May, 1814, to the HARPY 18, commanded by Capt. Thos. Griffith Allen, and also, for five months, by himself, off the Isle of France—and lastly, 7 Feb. 1815, again to the MEDWAY, bearing the flag of Sir Chas. Tyler at the Cape, whence he returned to England in April, 1816. In July, 1814, while First of the HARPY, Mr. Lambert took command of her boats and, at great peril, rescued the crew of *L'Eugénie* schooner, who had been wrecked, on 19 of the previous April, on Sandy Island, while on their passage from the Seychelles to the Mauritius. The Master and one seaman belonging to the HARPY were on the occasion drowned by the upsetting of a boat. The subject of the foregoing narrative accepted the rank of Retired Commander 30 April, 1845.

He was in the commission of the peace for co. Cork; and married, 29 March, 1832, Anne, daughter of the late Adam Carr, Esq. By that lady he has left issue.

LAMBERT. (Lieutenant, 1842.)

William Leigh Lambert entered the Navy 12 Sept. 1828; passed his examination 10 May, 1837; served for some time as Mate on the Mediterranean and North America and West India stations, in the Tyne 26, Capt. John Townshend, and Illustrious 72, flag-ship of Sir Chas. Adam; and was made Lieutenant, 19 June, 1842, into the Volage 22, Capt. Sir Wm. Dickson. His appointments have since been—13 Oct. 1843, as Additional, to the Cornwallis 72, flag-ship of Sir Wm. Parker in the East Indies—5 Nov. 1844, and 2 April, 1845, to the Driver steam-sloop and Vestal 26, Capts. Courtenay Osborn Hayes and Chas. Talbot, both on the same station—and 13 Nov. 1846, to the Castor 36, Capt. Chas. Graham, in which frigate he is still serving in the East Indies.

LAMBRICK. (Retired Commander, 1837. f-p., 15; h-p., 49.)

John Lambrick entered the Navy, in 1783, as Fst.-cl. Vol., on board the Fairy sloop, Capt. W. Thomas, and was for three years employed in that vessel in the Channel. For several months in 1788, and from 1790 until the commencement of the French revolutionary war, we find him serving on the Newfoundland and Home stations, as A. B. and Midshipman, in the Echo, Capt. Robt. Carthew Reynolds, Termagant, commanded by an officer whose name has escaped us, Nymphe, Capt. Geo. Campbell, and Spider, a small vessel commanded by a Lieutenant. During the next four years Mr. Lambrick was uninterruptedly employed in the Mediterranean on board the Leda, Berwick, and Terrible, all under the orders of Capt. Campbell, Britannia 100, flag-ship of Admiral Hotham, Dolphin, Capt. Rich. Retalick, and Inconstant, Capts. Thos. Fras. Fremantle and G. Oakes. Of the Dolphin he was confirmed a Lieutenant 23 May, 1796. After serving for two years on the North Sea station in the Agamemnon, Capt. Fancourt, he obtained command of the Signal station at the Lizard; and he was lastly, between the years 1801 and 1803, employed off Cadiz and in the Channel on board the Audacious 74, Capt. Shuldham Peard, and Royal Sovereign 100, Capt. Rich. Curry. He became a Retired Commander on the Junior List 26 Nov. 1830, and on the Senior 4 July, 1837.

LAMONT. (Retired Commander, 1838. f-p., 10; h-p., 39.)

James Lamont entered the Navy, 28 Dec. 1798, as Fst.-cl. Vol., on board the Repulse 64, Capt. Jas. Alms, lying at Portsmouth; and in the course of 1799 joined the Queen Charlotte 100, bearing the flag of Sir Chas. Thompson, and Charon 44, Capt. John Mackellar; in which latter ship, on his return from a visit to the Mediterranean, he assisted at the evacuation of the Helder. Becoming Midshipman, in Jan. 1800, of the Hebe, Capts. Wm. Birchall and Geo. Reynolds, he accompanied the expedition of 1801 to Egypt; after which he was for more than two years employed in the North Sea in the Clyde 38, flag-ship of Sir John Borlase Warren, and for nearly one, as Master's Mate, in the Mediator and Renommée, both commanded by Sir Thos. Livingstone on the Channel station. He was then, in Aug. 1805, appointed Sub-Lieutenant of the Staunch gun-brig, Lieut.-Commander Benj. Street; and on 16 of the following Oct. he was confirmed a full Lieutenant of the Moselle 18, Capts. John Surman Carden and Alex. Gordon, employed at first in the Mediterranean and next in the West Indies. In 1808 it was Mr. Lamont's lot to be very severely wounded while boarding an enemy's vessel in the Gulf of Mexico, for which he received a gratuity of 80*l.* 11*s.* 6*d.* He was obliged in consequence to invalid in June of that year. Unable to procure further employment, he accepted his present rank 18 April, 1838.

LANCASTER. (Lieutenant, 1813. f-p., 10; h-p., 32.)

Henry Lancaster, born 12 May, 1791, is youngest son of the Rev. Thos. Lancaster, Rector of Merton, co. Surrey.

This officer entered the Navy, 14 Sept. 1805, as Fst.-cl. Vol., under the especial patronage of Lord Nelson, on board the Victory 100, Capt. Thos. Masterman Hardy, bearing the flag of that distinguished nobleman, under whom he was present in the ensuing action off Cape Trafalgar. After a servitude of two years with Lord Collingwood as Midshipman in the Ocean 98, he joined the Thames 32, in which frigate and the Apollo 38, both commanded by Capt. Bridges Watkinson Taylor, we find him employed, chiefly on the Mediterranean station, until promoted to the rank of Lieutenant, 20 Oct. 1813. While in the latter ship Mr. Lancaster served in her boats, with those of a squadron under Lieut. John Tailour, on the night of 31 Oct. 1809, at the capture and destruction, notwithstanding a fearful struggle and a loss to the British of 15 men killed and 55 wounded, of the French store-ship *Lamproie* of 16 guns and 116 men, bombards *Victoire* and *Grondeur*, and armed xebec *Normande*, with a convoy of seven merchant-vessels, defended by numerous strong batteries in the Bay of Rosas.* He assisted also in capturing, 13 Feb. 1812, the French frigate-built store-ship *Mérinos*, of 20 guns and 26 men, under the batteries of Corsica, and, on 20 of the following Sept., the national xebec *Ulysse* of 6 guns.† He was further, it appears, present at the reduction, in Jan. and Feb. 1813, of the islands of *Augusta* and *Curzola*, as well as on shore, as a volunteer, in 1813, at the siege of Trieste, where he was slightly wounded, and, by his conduct, obtained the thanks of Rear-Admiral Thos. Fras. Fremantle, and a particular letter of introduction from that officer to Sir Sidney Smith, to whose flag-ship he had been appointed. During the term of his attachment to the Apollo Mr. Lancaster, we must too record, was twice the instrument of preserving life by his intrepidity in jumping overboard, once in the Adriatic, and another time, at night, near Malta. In Nov. 1813, a short time after he had joined Sir Sidney Smith, our officer found himself appointed to the Prince of Wales 98, Capt. John Erskine Douglas; in which ship he had an opportunity of sharing in Sir Edw. Pellew's second partial action with the Toulon fleet, and of witnessing the fall of Genoa and Savona. His last appointment was, 10 Sept. 1814, to the Myrtle 18, Capt. Arthur Batt Bingham, with whom he served at Cork until 30 Nov. 1815.

He married, in May, 1823, and has issue. Agents—Case and Loudonsack.

LANCASTER. (Lieut., 1805. f-p., 20; h-p., 31.)

Robert Daniell Lancaster was born 6 Oct. 1783 or 1784.

This officer entered the Navy, 22 Aug. 1796, as Fst.-cl. Vol., on board the Duke 98, Capt. John Holloway, and was afterwards, until Sept. 1802, employed with the same Captain and with Capts. Sampson Edwards, Geo. Parker, Erasmus Gower, and Bridges Watkinson Taylor, chiefly as Midshipman, in the St. George 98, Santa Margarita 36, and Porcupine 22, on the Channel, Mediterranean, and West India stations. He next, in April, 1803, and Nov. 1804, joined the San Josef 110, bearing the flag off Brest of Sir Chas. Cotton, and Nimrod 18, Capt. Orde, attached to the force in the West Indies, where, on 26 Feb. 1805, he was promoted to the rank of Lieutenant, and appointed to the command of the Nelly schooner, in which vessel he was shortly afterwards sent home with despatches. His succeeding appointments were—10 April, 1805, to the

* *Vide* Gaz. 1809, p. 1907.

† In Jan. 1812 Mr. Lancaster narrowly escaped drowning, being on board a prize that foundered an hour after her capture.

Malabar 50, Capts. Robt. Hall, John Ayscough, and Geo. Scott, stationed in the North Sea and West Indies—16 Aug. 1806 and 27 Feb. 1809, to the command of the Phosphorus fire-brig, and Lyra Impress-tender, employed off Boulogne and at North Shields and Sheerness—in 1812 or 13, to the Basilisk 12, Capt. Geo. French, lying at Hamoaze—21 June, 1814, and 27 Nov. 1818, to the command of the Landrail schooner and Serapis convalescent ship—and, lastly, 26 March, 1819, to the Ordinary at Plymouth, where he remained until April, 1822. While in the Malabar, Mr. Lancaster served, in the boats of that ship and the Wolf 18, at the destruction, on the coast of Cuba, 2 Jan. 1806, of the two French privateers *Le Régulateur* and *Napoléon*, of 5 guns each, and a crew united of 146 men, after a well-contested action of an hour and three-quarters. During his command of the Lyra he made suggestions to the Admiralty relative to the Impress service which caused a saving in one port alone of 3000*l*. per annum, and for which he obtained their Lordships' thanks. On 12 July, 1814, being then in the Landrail, which vessel carried only 4 12-pounder carronades and 19 men, Mr. Lancaster had the misfortune to be captured by the American privateer-schooner *Syren* (mounting 1 long 18-pounder on a travelling-carriage, 4 long 6-pounders and 2 18-pounder carronades, with a crew of 75 men), at the end of a running fight of one hour and 10 minutes, and a close action, within pistol-shot, of 40 minutes, in all 2 hours. This strenuous and most gallant resistance on the part of the Landrail was the occasion of a loss to herself of 7 men wounded, and to her antagonist of 3 men killed and 15 wounded. Her brave commander was in consequence detained a captive in America until the conclusion of the war.

Mr. Lancaster is the Senior Lieutenant of 1805. His eldest son, John James Lancaster, Esq., M.D., is a Surgeon in the R.N. (1835). Agents—Hallett and Robinson.

LANE. (Lieutenant, 1841.)

Dennys Lane died in 1846. He was third son of the Rev. Rich. Lane, of Coffleet and Bradley, co. Devon, by Lucy, daughter of Nicholas Dennys, Esq., of Ashley, near Tiverton; and brother-in-law of Samborne Stuckley Palmer, Esq., of Timsbury House, co. Somerset.

This officer entered the Navy 24 May, 1832; passed his examination 11 Aug. 1838; attained the rank of Lieutenant, while serving as Mate on board the Cornwallis 72, flag-ship of Sir Wm. Parker in the East Indies, 27 Oct. 1841; and was appointed, 31 March and 17 Nov. 1842, to the Modeste 18, and North Star 26, Capts. Rundle Burges Watson and Sir Jas. Everard Home, both on the same station, whence he returned home and was paid off in the summer of 1846.

LANE. (Lieut., 1811. f-p., 17; h-p., 29.)

John Edward Lane entered the Navy, in 1801, as Fst.-cl. Vol., on board the Cambridge 74, Capt. Lane, lying at Hamoaze, where, in May, 1802, he joined the Centaur 74, bearing the flag of Rear-Admiral Jas. Rich. Dacres. Between June in the same year and June, 1807, we find him serving, as Midshipman, on the Mediterranean and Home stations, in the Spider, Lieut.-Commander Harding Shaw, Triumph 74, Capt. Sir Robt. Barlow, Dryad 36, Capt. Adam Drummond, Barfleur 98, Capt. Jos. Sydney Yorke, and Success 32, Capt. John Ayscough. During the next two years he acted as Lieutenant of the Belle Poule 38, Capt. Jas. Brisbane, under whom, besides contributing to the capture of other smaller vessels, he assisted in taking, 13 Feb. 1809, *Le Var* of 26 guns, laden with corn for the relief of the French garrison at Corfu. From the following July until Sept. 1810 he again served as Midshipman in the Ville de Paris and San Josef 110's, flag-ships of Lord Collingwood and Sir Chas. Cotton. He was then a second time invested with the rank of Lieutenant, in the Volontaire 38, Capts. Chas. Bullen, Abel Ferris, Henry Evelyn Pitfield Sturt, and Joseph Nourse, in which frigate he continued, co-operating intermediately with the patriots on the coast of Spain, until at length confirmed, 17 Jan. 1811, into the Trident 64, Capt. Rich. Budd Vincent, stationed at Malta. His last appointments were—4 Nov. 1811, to the Frederickstein frigate, Capt. Fras. Beaufort, also in the Mediterranean, whence he returned in Oct. 1812—8 Oct. 1813, to the Telegraph 12, Capt. Timothy Scriven, in which vessel he was for nearly two years employed on the Channel and North American stations—and 25 June, 1831, to the command of the Swan cutter of 10 guns, on the Home station, where he remained until paid off in 1835. He has not been since afloat.

He married, 16 May, 1832, Lauretta Maude, daughter of the late W. Blewett, Esq., of Halton Court, Cornwall.

LANE. (Lieutenant, 1828.)

John William Lane entered the Navy 8 June, 1809; and from that period until Dec. 1814 was employed on the Home and American stations in the Agincourt 64, Capt. Wm. Kent, Unicorn 32, Capt. Alex. Robt. Kerr, Amethyst 36, Capt. Mich. Seymour, Venerable 74, Capt. Andw. King, San Domingo 74, Capt. Chas. Gill, Cæsar 80, Capt. Chas. Richardson, Namur 74, Capt. Alex. Shippard, Chanticleer 10, Capt. Rich. Spear, Paz schooner, Lieut.-Commander Dan. Pring, Ephira 10, Capt. John Strutt Peyton, and Edinburgh 74, Capts. Robt. Rolles, Rowland Mainwaring, Hon. Geo. Heneage Lawrence Dundas, and John Lampen Manley. During his attachment to the Venerable he accompanied the expedition to the Walcheren in Aug. 1809; and when in the Edinburgh he witnessed, in 1813-14, the capture of Port d'Anzo, the unsuccessful attack on Leghorn, the reduction of the fortress of Santa Maria and of the enemy's other forts and defences in the Gulf of Spezia, and the fall of Genoa. On 17 June, 1815, being then in the Pilot 18, Capt. John Toup Nicolas, Mr. Lane, who had previously served for a short time in the Boyne 98, Capts. Fred. Lewis Maitland and Jas. Brisbane, contributed to the defeat, near Cape Corse, of the French corvette *Légère*, of 28 guns, who made off at the close of a gallant conflict in which the British vessel sustained a loss, besides being otherwise disabled, of 1 man killed and 15 wounded, and the Frenchman of 22 killed and 79 wounded. He left the Pilot in June, 1816, and, passing his examination in the following Oct., was afterwards, between Jan. 1821 and 13 Dec. 1828, employed, as Admiralty-Midshipman, Acting-Lieutenant, and Admiralty-Mate, in the Medina 20, Capts. Robt. Hockings, the Earl of Huntingdon, R. Anderson, and Patrick Duff Henry Hay, Tweed 24, Capt. Fred. Hunn, Semiramis 42, bearing the flag of Vice-Admiral Robt. Plampin, Badger 10, Capt. Chas. Crowdy, Despatch 18, Capt. Robt. White Parsons, and Tribune 42, Capt. John Wilson, on the Mediterranean, Cork, Lisbon, and South American stations. He was then made Lieutenant into the Thetis 46, Capt. Arthur Batt Bingham, also in South America, whence he invalided 17 Aug. 1829. He has since been on half-pay.

LANE. (Lieut., 1815. f-p. 25; h-p., 17.)

William Lane (*b*) entered the Navy, 13 Aug. 1805, as Fst.-cl. Vol., on board the Wolverene sloop, Capts. Thos. Smith and Fras. Augustus Collier, with the latter of whom he further served in the Circe 32, Star sloop, and Pelorus 18, on the West India station, until July, 1809. He assisted, in consequence, at the capture of several of the enemy's privateers and armed vessels, took part also in a successful attack made in Dec. 1808 by the Cyane and a small squadron on some batteries, a corvette, and two schooners near the town of St. Pierre, Martinique, and co-operated in the Star in the reduction of the latter island in Feb. 1809. During the remainder of the war we find Mr. Lane employed, latterly as Acting-Lieutenant, in the GUACHAPIN, Lieut.-Commander Wm. Weoland, ELIZABETH 74, Capts. Hon. Henry Curzon and Thos. Scarle, THESEUS 74, Capt. Wm. Prowse, NARCISSUS 32, Capt. John Rich. Lumley, TRIBUNE 36, flag-ship of Sir Fras. Laforey, and GRAMPUS 50, Capt. F. A. Collier, on the Home, West India, and China stations. On leaving the latter ship in Aug. 1815, he took up a commission dated on 13 of the previous March. His appointments have since been—8 Nov. 1815, to the ALBAN 12, Capt. Hugh Patton, from which vessel, employed in the Solway Frith, he was superseded at his own request 29 Jan. 1817—17 Jan. 1828, and 29 March, 1829, to the WASP and RALEIGH sloops, Capts. Hon. Wm. Wellesley, Thos. Edw. Hoste, and Sir Wm. Dickson, attached to the force in the Mediterranean, whence he returned home, and was paid off in Dec. 1829—19 June, 1833, to the Coast Guard, in which he continued for a period of 11 years—and 8 June, 1846, to the CALEDONIA 120, Capt. Manley Hall Dixon, with whom he is now serving in the Channel.

LANG. (LIEUTENANT, 1842.)

EDWARD WOLLASTON LANG entered the Navy (from the Royal Naval College) 13 Jan. 1833; passed his examination 5 April, 1837; and was promoted to the rank of Lieutenant while serving as Mate in the SOUTHAMPTON 50, flag-ship at the Cape of Good Hope of Sir Edw. Durnford King, 12 May, 1842. He was then appointed to the FANTOME 16, Capt. Philip Geo. Haymes, on the South American station; and since 16 May, 1843, has been employed in the Pacific on board the FISGARD 42, Capt. John Alex. Duntze. AGENTS—Messrs. Halford and Co.

LANGDON. (LIEUT., 1811. F-P., 10; H-P., 33.)

WILLIAM LANGDON was born 6 Nov. 1790, at Montacute Vicarage, co. Somerset.

This officer entered the Navy, 13 April, 1804, as Fst.-cl. Vol., on board the WEYMOUTH 44, Capt. John Draper, and after serving for a year and a half, the chief part of the time as Midshipman, on the East India and Brazilian stations, removed, in April, 1806, to the MONARCH 74, Capts. John Clarke Searle and Rich. Lee. On 15 of the following July we find him employed with a detachment of boats at the cutting out, in face of a desperate and well-concerted resistance, at the entrance of the river Gironde, of the French corvette *Le César*, mounting 16 guns, with a complement of 86 men, who, with a loss to themselves of 14 killed and wounded, occasioned the British one altogether of 9 killed and 39 wounded. He was also, on 25 Sept. in the same year, present at the capture, by a squadron under Sir Sam. Hood, of four heavy French frigates off Rochefort; on which occasion the MONARCH enacted a very conspicuous part, compelled *La Minerve*, of 44 guns and 650 men, to surrender, and experienced a total loss of 4 killed and 25 wounded. In the CHAMPION 24, Capts. Jas. Coutts Crawford and Robt. Henderson, to which vessel he removed in Aug. 1807, Mr. Langdon came frequently into contact with the batteries on the coast of France, and contributed to the capture of a French privateer near St. Maloes. Removing, as Master's Mate, in Jan. 1810, to the BADGER 10, Capt. John Lampen Manley, he served for 14 months in that vessel in the North Sea and in the rivers Elbe, Ems, and Weser. In Aug. 1811, after he had been for five months borne as a Supernumerary on the books of the DRAGON 74, bearing the flag in the West Indies of Sir Fras. Laforey, he became Acting-Lieutenant of the RINGDOVE 18, Capt. Wm. Dowers—to which vessel he was confirmed by commission dated 29 of the ensuing Oct. He invalided in May, 1812, and was lastly, from the next Oct. until Sept. 1814, employed in the BERMUDA 10, Capts. Jas. John Gordon Bremer and Wm. Wolrige, on the Downs station (where he was often in action with the Boulogne batteries, and assisted in making several captures), and also off Gottenborg and the north coast of Sweden.

Lieut. Langdon married Anne, daughter of Wm. Elliott, Esq., of co. Somerset, by whom, who died 20 May, 1844, he has issue an only child, Anne Elliott, now the wife of Sir Thos. Howland Roberts, Bart., of Brightfieldstown, co. Cork. AGENTS—Pettet and Newton.

LANGFORD. (COMMANDER, 1829.)

THOMAS NETHERTON LANGFORD, born in 1805, is second son of Edw. Langford, Esq., of Trungle, co. Cornwall, Captain in the Royal Cornwall Militia, and late of H.M. 49th Regt. of Foot, by Mary, eldest daughter of Henry Whitmarsh, Esq., of Batt's Place, near Taunton, J. P.

This officer entered the Navy 3 Oct. 1818; passed his examination in 1824; obtained his first commission 30 Nov. 1826; and was successively appointed —15 Feb. 1827, to the BADGER 10, Capt. Chas. Crowdy, in the North Sea—18 March, 1828, to the SAPPHIRE 28, Capt. Henry Dundas, in South America—and, 13 Nov. 1828, to the GANGES 84, as Flag-Lieutenant to Sir Robt. Waller Otway, on the same station. He was promoted, on being paid off, to his present rank 19 Sept. 1829; and has since been on half-pay.

Commander Langford married, 11 Feb. 1835, Caroline, eldest daughter of the late Hon. and Rev. Jas. St. Leger, brother of Viscount Doneraile, and by that lady has issue. AGENTS—Hallett and Robinson.

LANGLEY. (LIEUT., 1815. F-P., 10; H-P., 32.)

WILLIAM LANGLEY entered the Navy, 2 April, 1805, as Master's Mate, on board the SIR EDWARD HUGHES 38, Capts. Hood Hanway Christian, Gilbert Heathcote, and Edw. Ratsey, attached to the force in the East Indies. Removing, in Oct. 1807, to the CUMBERLAND 74, he was for five years employed in that ship on the Mediterranean and North Sea stations under the orders of Capts. Hon. Philip Wodehouse, Eliab Harvey, Robt. Clephane, Robt. Waller Otway, and Thos. Baker; after which we find him, from Oct. 1812 until promoted to the rank of Lieutenant 3 Feb. 1815, serving on board the IMPÉTUEUX 74, flag-ship off Lisbon of the late Sir Geo. Martin, MAGICIENNE 36, Capt. Hon. Wm. Gordon (under whom he witnessed the fall of St. Sebastian in Sept. 1813), and PRINCE 98, and MONTAGU 74, commanded at Spithead and Cork by Capts. Geo. Fowke and Peter Heywood. He has since been on half-pay.

LANGTON. (LIEUT., 1823. F-P., 24; H-P., 15.)

THOMAS WILLIAM LANGTON was born in the autumn of 1796 at Leicester.

This officer entered the Navy, 23 Dec. 1808, as Fst.-cl. Vol., on board the AMPHION 32, Capt. Wm. Hoste, stationed in the Adriatic. While in that frigate, besides participating in much boat-service, it was his fortune to be present, 13 March, 1811, in the celebrated action off Lissa, where a British squadron, carrying in the whole 156 guns and 879 men, completely routed, after a battle of six hours, and a loss to the AMPHION of 15 killed and 47 wounded, a Franco-Venetian armament, whose force amounted to 284 guns and 2655 men. On that occasion Mr. Langton was one of only three out of 10, composing the Midshipman's berth, who escaped without injury. When subsequently with the same Captain in the BACCHANTE 38, he commanded a boat under Lieut. Silas Thomson Hood, and was spoken of in the highest possible terms for his conduct at the capture, 12 June, 1813, from under the town of Gela-Nova, on the coast of Abruzzo, of seven large gun-boats mounting each 1 long 18-pounder in the bow, 3 smaller gun-vessels with a 4-pounder in the bow, and 14 sail of merchantmen, four of which also had guns in the bow. The British, as they advanced, were exposed to a heavy fire of grape and musketry; and it was not until they were fairly alongside the gun-boats that the crews of the latter slackened their fire: they were then driven from their vessels with great loss—one, the largest of them, falling a prize to Mr. Langton. The shore astern of the assailed was at the commencement lined with 100 troops, who, however, fled on the first fire, leaving two field-pieces behind them.* Our officer, who afterwards landed with Capt. Hoste near Trieste, under a tremendous fire from the citadel, continued in the BACCHANTE, which was latterly commanded by Capt. Fras. Stanfell, until July, 1815; in the course of which year we find him passing his examination, and successively joining the SEAHORSE 38, Capt. Sir Jas. Alex. Gordon, and BULWARK 74, flag-ship of Sir Chas. Rowley at Chatham. In May, 1818, he removed as Admiralty Midshipman to the LIFFEY 50, Capt. Hon. Henry Duncan, in which ship he was for nearly three years and a half employed in the Channel. He next, in Oct. 1821, joined the HIND 20, Capts. Sir Chas. Burrard and Hon. Henry John Rous, with the latter of whom he ultimately went to the Mediterranean, where, after having acted for three months, he was confirmed a Lieutenant, 25 April, 1823, in the CHANTICLEER 10, Capt. Burton Macnamara. In the following June he invalided. His appointments have since been—10 June, 1825, to the GLOUCESTER 74, Capt. Joshua Sydney Horton, lying at Sheerness—in Nov. 1825, to the Coast Guard in Scotland, in which service he continued until Oct. 1830—and 8 April, 1843, to be Admiralty Agent in a contract mail steam-vessel, a capacity in which he is now employed.

Lieut. Langton, while in the Coast Guard, was presented with a silver medal by the Royal Humane Society, and with a stock of wine by the owners, for his exertions in saving a vessel which had struck on the sands near Aberdeen. He married, in 1826, a daughter of the late Walter Mansell, Esq., of Woodperry House, Oxfordshire. AGENTS—Messrs. Chard.

* *Vide* Gaz. 1813, p. 1795.

LANGTRY. (COMMANDER, 1842. F-P. 21; H-P., 8.)

JOSEPH MILLAR LANGTRY is third son of the late Joseph Langtry, Esq., of Bishop's Waltham, Hants, and of Townabrache, co. Antrim; and elder brother of the late Wm. Henry Langtry, Esq., Master R.N. (1842), who entered the Navy in 1825, served as Master's Assistant of the DARTMOUTH 42 at the battle of Navarin, was for five years and three months Acting-Master and Master of the CLIO sloop on the East India station, took part during that period in the operations on the coast of China and up the Yang-tse-Kiang, and died in 1846.

This officer entered the Navy, 7 Nov. 1818, as Fst.-cl. Vol., on board the SLANEY 20, Capts. Donat Henchy O'Brien and Henry Stanhope, in which vessel and the AURORA 46, Capt. Henry Prescott, he served on the South American station, part of the time as Midshipman, until Feb. 1822. He then became Mate of the ALBION 74, Capts. Sir Wm. Hoste and John Acworth Ommanney; and, on proceeding to the Mediterranean, took part in the battle of Navarin 20 Oct. 1827. On that occasion he boarded and hauled down the colours of an Egyptian frigate, but was soon afterwards under the necessity, from her having caught fire, of cutting her cables for the purpose of allowing her to drift clear of the ALBION, a work in which he was assisted by Rich. Harris, A.B. As a reward for his conduct, Mr. Langtry, on the recommendation of his Captain, was promoted to the rank of Lieutenant by commission dated 22 Oct. 1827. He then served for nearly four months in the LYRA 10, Capt. John Harvey Boteler, off Lisbon; and was afterwards appointed—10 Oct. 1829, and 19 Feb. 1830, to the RAMILLIES and TALAVERA 74's, Coast Blockade ships, both commanded by Capt. Hugh Pigot—5 April, 1831, to the Coast Guard service, in which he continued until March, 1833—7 Aug. 1835, to the PYLADES 18, Capt. Wm. Langford Castle, fitting at Plymouth, where he soon afterwards invalided—25 March, 1836, to the HERCULES 74, Capt. Maurice Fred. Fitzhardinge Berkeley, which ship, stationed in the Channel, his health, in the following Oct., also obliged him to leave—2 Oct. 1837, and 13 Oct. 1840, to the DONEGAL 78, and, as Flag-Lieutenant, to the BRITANNIA 120, bearing each the flag of Sir J. A. Ommanney on the Lisbon and Mediterranean stations—and 23 Sept. 1841, to the POWERFUL 84, Capt. Michael Seymour, with whom he returned home in Dec. of the same year. He attained his present rank 4 Jan. 1842; and since 8 May, 1847, has been employed in the Coast Guard. AGENTS—Messrs. Ommanney.

LANGWORTHY. (LIEUTENANT, 1832.)

JOHN LANGWORTHY entered the Navy 14 April, 1811; passed his examination in 1822; and obtained his commission 27 March, 1832. He has since been on half-pay.

He married Mary, daughter of —Langworthy, Esq., of Exeter.

LANPHIER. (RETIRED COMMANDER, 1846. F-P., 13; H-P., 35.)

VERNON LANPHIER entered the Navy, in the spring of 1799, as Midshipman, on board the TERRIBLE 74, Capt. Wm. Wolseley, in which ship he went to the Mediterranean and back in pursuit of a French fleet. He was next, between Feb. 1800, and Nov. 1801, employed off the coasts of France and Spain in the TRITON 32, Capts. Sir John Gore and Robt. Lewis Fitzgerald, and SAN JOSEF 110, Capts. W. Wolseley and Jas. Carpenter; after which we find him, from June, 1803, until Aug. 1808, serving on board the SPARTIATE 74, Capts. John Manley and Sir Fras. Laforey. During that period he assisted in chasing a French squadron to the West Indies, returned with Lord Nelson to Europe in quest of the combined fleets of France and Spain, aided in blockading the enemy in Cadiz harbour, and shared in the glories of Trafalgar. On leaving the SPARTIATE, as above, Mr. Lanphier was nominated Acting-Lieutenant of the LEONIDAS 38, Capts. Jas. Dunbar and Anselm John Griffiths; in which frigate (being confirmed to her by commission dated 26 Nov. 1808) he continued to serve, off Toulon, in the Adriatic, and on the Irish station, until May, 1812. While in the Adriatic he saw a good deal of boat-service, contributed to the capture of a variety of vessels, and co-operated in the reduction, in Oct. 1809 and April, 1810, of Cephalonia and Santa Maura, on which latter occasion he was slightly wounded.* His last appointment was, 1 Dec. 1813, to the VENGEUR 74, Capt. Tristram Robt. Ricketts, with whom he served on the coasts of France and America until Oct. 1814, when his health obliged him to invalid. He accepted his present rank 13 April, 1846. AGENTS—Messrs. Ommanney.

LAPENOTIERE. (LIEUTENANT, 1827.)

JOHN GOOD LAPENOTIERE entered the Navy 5 Aug. 1819; passed his examination in 1825; and was made Lieutenant, 17 March, 1827, into the PYLADES 18, Capt. Geo. Vernon Jackson, on the Jamaica station, whence he returned to England in Feb. 1828. Since 21 April, 1847, he has been employed in the Coast Guard.

Having lost his first wife, 8 Feb. 1840, Mr. Lapenotiere married, secondly, 12 Dec. following, Harriette Maria, daughter of John Booth, Esq., of Whitchurch.

LAPIDGE. (LIEUTENANT, 1824.)

CHARLES HORACE LAPIDGE was promoted, 31 Aug. 1824, to a Lieutenancy in the SCOUT 18, Capt. Jas. Wigston, which vessel returned home from the West Indies and was paid off in the summer of 1825. His subsequent appointments were—19 Dec. 1837, as First, to the LILY 16, Capt. John Reeve, on the African station—10 July, 1838, as Additional, to the STAG 46, Capt. Thos. Ball Sulivan, employed in South America, where he continued until 1839—and 24 Nov. 1841, to the command of

* *Vide* Gaz. 1810, p. 1137.

the PANTALOON 10, on the coast of Africa, whence he returned in 1844. He has not been since afloat.

He was left a widower 21 June, 1846. AGENT—J. Chippendale.

LAPIDGE, K.I.C., K.S.F. (CAPTAIN, 1837. F-P., 32; H-P., 12.)

WILLIAM FREDERICK LAPIDGE entered the Navy, 10 Nov. 1803, as Fst.-cl. Vol., on board the PLANTAGENET 74, Capts. Hon. Michael De Courcy, Fras. Pender, and Wm. Bradley, in which ship, with the exception of a voyage to St. Helena, he served on the Channel station until July, 1807. After attending the expeditions to Copenhagen and the Walcheren as Midshipman of the DICTATOR 64 and AUDACIOUS 74, both commanded by Capt. Donald Campbell, he joined, in Nov. 1809, the IMPÉRIEUSE 38, Capts. Thos. Garth and Hon. Henry Duncan, and proceeded to the Mediterranean, where he remained employed, chiefly as Master's Mate, Acting-Master, and Acting-Lieutenant of the same ship, and as Lieutenant (commission dated 9 April, 1814) of the FRANCHISE 36, and FLORIDA 20, until the summer of 1816. He was on board the IMPÉRIEUSE at the destruction, 27 June, 1812, of a French convoy under the batteries of Languelia and Alassio; and he was in her, on 17 of the ensuing Aug., in a spirited skirmish with a Neapolitan squadron in the Bay of Naples. After he left the FLORIDA, Mr. Lapidge's appointments in the capacity of Lieutenant were—23 Oct. 1819, to the RALEIGH 18, Capt. Wm. Augustus Baumgardt, whom he accompanied to the West Indies—27 June, 1822, and 23 Oct. 1823, to the SUPERB 74, and OCEAN 80, guard-ships at Plymouth, Capts. Adam Mackenzie, Lucius Ferdinand Hardyman, and John Sykes—9 Jan. 1827, to the SPARTIATE 78, Capt. Fred. Warren—and in 1830-1, to the successive command of the MESSENGER and CARRON steamers, VIGILANT ketch, and LEVERET brig. In the last vessel he appears to have been employed during the civil war in Portugal. Being awarded a second promotal commission 2 Oct. 1833, Capt. Lapidge, on 21 of the following Nov., obtained command of the RINGDOVE 16. The services performed by him in that vessel on the north coast of Spain, particularly at the defence of Portugalete and the siege of Bilbao in Nov. and Dec. 1836, were acknowledged by the Queen Regent, who created him a Commander of Isabella la Catolica, and presented him with the second class of San Fernando. He attained Post-rank 6 Jan. 1837, but did not leave the RINGDOVE until the following April. His last appointment was, 23 Nov. 1843, to the CYCLOPS steam-frigate, in which we find him employed on particular service, and on the S.E. coast of America and Channel stations, until paid off at the commencement of 1847.

Capt. Lapidge married, in 1817, a sister of the late Capt. Sir Wm. Elliott, R.N., C.B. AGENTS—Messrs. Stilwell.

LARCOM. (CAPTAIN, 1841. F-P., 20; H-P., 19.)

JOSEPH PAFFORD DICKSON LARCOM, born 14 Sept. 1795, is son of Commissioner Joseph Larcom, of Malta Dockyard, who had been promoted to the rank of Commander for his conduct as First of the THUNDERER 74 in Lord Howe's action 1 June, 1794, and died at Gibraltar, on his way to England, 17 Feb. 1818; and nephew of the present Vice-Admiral Geo. M'Kinley, and of the late Vice-Admiral A. P. Hollis, and the late Capt. Thos. Larcom, R.N., who commanded the RUSSEL 74 in Lord Bridport's action in 1795, and was afterwards Flag-Captain to Rear-Admirals Sir Chas. Cotton and Cuthbert Collingwood, in the PRINCE 98, and TRIUMPH 74.

This officer entered the Royal Naval College 13 Feb. 1808; and embarked, 22 June, 1810, as a Supernumerary, on board the SAN JOSEF 110, Capt. R. J. Neve, bearing the flag of Sir Chas. Cotton, Commander-in-Chief in the Mediterranean; where, from the following Sept. until the close of 1817, he was successively employed on board the VILLE DE PARIS 110, Capt. Fras. Beaufort, SATELLITE sloop, Capt. Walter Bathurst, FREDERICKSTEIN frigate, Capt. F. Beaufort, THAMES 32, and EURYALUS 36, both commanded by Capt. Chas. Napier, CALEDONIA 120, flag-ship of Lord Exmouth, CASTOR 32, Capt. Chas. Dilkes, ABOUKIR 74, Capt. Norborne Thompson, PAULINA sloop, Capt. Rowland Mainwaring, WOODLARK 10, Capt. Wm. Cutfield, SATELLITE again, Capt. Jas. Murray, and ALBION 74, bearing the flag of Sir Chas. Vinicombe Penrose. In May, 1813, being then Midshipman of the EURYALUS, Mr. Larcom served in the boats of that ship, and the BERWICK 74, at the capture and destruction of *La Fortune* xebec of 10 guns, 4 swivels, and 95 men, and of 22 vessels collected under the batteries in the harbour of Cavalacie. The 26 Sept. 1814 was marked by his promotion to a Lieutenancy in the CASTOR. His appointments, after he left the ALBION, were—28 Nov. 1820, to the ATHOLL 28, Capt. Henry Bourchier, fitting for the Halifax station, whence he returned in 1824—7 March, 1825, to the AURORA 46, Capts. John Maxwell and Chas. John Austen, employed off Lisbon and in the West Indies—and, in 1828-9, to the DRUID 46, MERSEY 26, and ICARUS 10, Capts. Williams Sandom, Geo. Wm. Conway Courtenay, and Hon. Thos. Best, all on the Jamaica station. He was there promoted, 8 Aug. 1829, to the command of the HARPY 10, which vessel he paid off 11 June, 1831; and from 10 June, 1841, until advanced, 23 Nov. following, to Post-rank, he had command of the SCOUT 18, on the Mediterranean station. He has since been on half-pay.

Capt. Larcom married, 17 Sept. 1844, his cousin, Westmoreland Jane, youngest daughter of Vice-Admiral M'Kinley. AGENT—J. Hinxman.

LARKE. (RETIRED COMMANDER, 1834. F-P., 18; H-P., 33.)

WILLIAM LARKE entered the Navy, 10 Jan. 1796, as A.B., on board the HEBE 38, Capt. Matt. Henry Scott, and sailed for the West Indies, where, in the course of the same year, he assisted, as Midshipman, at the re-conquest of Ste. Lucie, and the suppression of an insurrection in the islands of St. Vincent and Grenada. On his return to Europe, in the following Nov., he joined the PRINCE GEORGE 98, successive flag-ship of Admirals Wm. Parker and Sir Chas. Thompson, under the former of whom he took part in the action off Cape St. Vincent 14 Feb. 1797. After a servitude of four years with Earl St. Vincent and Hon. Wm. Cornwallis, as Master's Mate, in the VILLE DE PARIS 110, and of two months with Capt. John Wm. Spranger, as a Supernumerary, in the ÆOLUS, on the Mediterranean, Channel, and West India stations, Mr. Larke was nominated, 2 March, 1802, Acting-Lieutenant of the BRUNSWICK 74, Capt. Geo. Hopewell Stephens. He was officially promoted 1 July following, and, in May, 1804, after an intermediate employment, for short periods, in the MAGNIFICENT 74, Capt. Wm. Henry Jervis, and in the Sea Fencibles at Cromer, in Norfolk, he was invested with the Governorship of the R.N. Hospital at North Yarmouth, where he continued until 30 Sept. 1814. He accepted his present rank 7 July, 1834.

LAROCHE. (CAPTAIN ON RETIRED HALF-PAY, 1800. F-P., 22; H-P., 43.)

CHRISTOPHER LAROCHE is second son of the late Henry Laroche, Esq., of Halburton, Devon.

This officer entered the Navy, 22 Feb. 1782, as Captain's Servant, on board the TRUSTY 50, Capt. Jas. Bradley, on the Home station, where, and in the West Indies and Mediterranean, he further, until Sept. 1793, served, as Midshipman and Master's Mate, in the ALEXANDER and POWERFUL 74's, both commanded by Capt. Thos. Fitzherbert, EUROPA 50, flag-ship of Admirals Gambier and Innes, PORCUPINE sloop, Capt. Herbert Sawyer, ORION, POWERFUL, and ORION again, Capts. Hyde Parker, Andw. Sutherland, and Chas. Chamberlayne, BERWICK 74, Capts. H. Parker and Roger Curtis, and VICTORY 100, bearing the flag of Lord Hood. While in the latter ship, Mr. Laroche, whose promotion to the rank of Lieutenant took place 11 Sept. 1793, was intrusted, during the investment of Toulon, with the command of a floating battery, in which, rendering intermediately the most important services, he remained until that implement of destruction was nearly knocked to pieces, and he himself severely wounded. He was then sent to direct a battery on shore. His appointments, subsequently to the evacuation of Toulon, appear to have been—in Jan. 1794, to the POULETTE 28—in April following and Jan. 1796, to the ST. GEORGE 98, and BRITANNIA 100, bearing each the flag of Sir Hyde Parker, under whom he took part in Hotham's partial actions in 1795—30 Aug. 1796, as First, to the SATURN 74, Capt. Jas. Douglas—in Jan. 1797, to the PROSELYTE 32, Capt. John Loring, for passage to the West Indies—in April following, again as Senior, to the QUEEN 98, bearing the flag on that station of his friend Sir H. Parker—and in the course of 1798 (so great was the confidence reposed in him by the latter officer) to the acting-command of the DRAKE 16, PELICAN 18, PROSELYTE 32, SWALLOW 18, ADVENTURE 44, and STORK 18. From the last-mentioned vessel (to which he had been confirmed by commission dated 18 Aug. 1798) Capt. Laroche was promoted, 11 Nov. 1799, to the acting-captaincy of the ABERGAVENNY 64, on the Jamaica station, where, on 29 Jan. 1800, he was officially posted into the SURPRISE 32. He returned to England in June, 1801, and was afterwards appointed—25 Aug. 1804, to the TEXEL 64, flag-ship at Leith of Rear-Admiral Jas. Vashon—24 Nov. in the same year (during the temporary absence of Capt. Robt. Dudley Oliver), to the MELPOMÈNE 38, in which ship, while commanding a squadron of observation off Havre de Grace, he received the thanks of Lord Keith for effecting the capture of two privateers, each of 17 guns, which had hitherto, to the great prejudice of trade, baffled the vigilance of the British cruizers—1 March, 1805, for a very short period, to the AJAX 74, in which ship he proceeded to join Sir Robt. Calder off Ferrol—and, 27 Dec. following, to the URANIE 38. In that frigate, an old one of very inferior pretensions, whose long 18-pounders had been exchanged for a battery of long 12-pounders, Capt. Laroche was at first employed in cruizing among the Channel islands and on the north-west coast of France. It being afterwards understood that the enemy had fitted out at Cherbourg and equipped for sea a frigate, *La Manche*, rated at 40, and a brig-corvette, *Le Cigne*, mounting 16 guns, our officer was deputed, on 30 April, 1807, to keep a rigid blockade on that dangerous and intricate port. Such were the energy and perseverance he evinced in the execution of this onerous and responsible duty, that he frustrated every attempt on the part of the French to escape, nor would they ever allow him to entice them out of the reach of their batteries. Nevertheless, on returning to Spithead in July, to report, the officers applied for a court-martial on their Captain, on the ground that he had not done his utmost to bring the enemy to action, particularly on 15 May and 22 June. In regard to the former of those days, 15 May, it was asserted that *La Manche*, with the brig and five launches, had been discovered *standing out and steering towards the* URANIE. Although, however, Capt. Laroche protested that he never saw the vessels, —notwithstanding, too, that the ship at the time was enveloped in fog, and in spite of very conflicting evidence on the side of his accusers—the court was of opinion that the charge had been in part proved, and in consequence sentenced him to be dismissed from the command of his ship. Now, as far as concerns the charge we have here detailed, it very fortunately happens that we have it in our power to refute the whole of it on the authority of two official documents which have passed through our hands, the first, bearing date Cherbourg, 23 March, 1841, signed by M. Redon, surveyor of the port, and authenticated both by the Rear-Admiral Superintendent, Martineng, and the French Minister of Marine, Admiral Duperré, declaring the fact that the frigate *La Manche* (so far from making towards the URANIE) was lying in the roads of Cherbourg on 15 May, 1807, and did not sail until 15 of the following Nov.; and the second (dated Cherbourg, 21 July, 1842, and authenticated by the signature of M. Parsenof, then Rear-Admiral Superintendent) proving, from further research into the archives of the port, that not only was the French frigate in the roads on the day in question, but that a man was actually sent on shore to the hospital, and that several embarkations and debarkations took place. It thus is manifest that, unless Capt. Laroche had had the rashness to enter Cherbourg, it was perfectly impossible for him to have come to an engagement. The light now therefore thrown on the testimony by which the gallant officer was convicted of the first part of the charge brought against him gives so very doubtful an appearance to all the consecutive evidence, that, had the fact been earlier known, he would neither, we may presume, have been suffered to pass the remainder of his days in inactivity, nor have been deprived of his flag.

In 1841 (prior, unfortunately, to the arrival of the documents above quoted) Capt. Laroche's case was brought before Parliament by the then Member for Hertford; but so strong were the objections entertained by Ministers to any control being exercised in the House over the decisions of courts-martial, especially after such a lapse of time, that the motion was withdrawn. Capt. Laroche served as an Esquire at the installation of Sir Thos. Graves, 16 May, 1803. While afloat, we may add, he made capture of a more than ordinary number of privateers and other vessels. AGENTS—Messrs. Stilwell.

LASCELLES. (LIEUTENANT, 1828. F-P., 16; H-P., 20.)

JOHN LASCELLES, born 25 Aug. 1798, is son of the late Colonel, and grandson of the late General, Lascelles.

This officer entered the Navy, in July, 1811, as a Volunteer, on board the ULYSSES 44, Capt. Henry Edw. Reginald Baker, stationed off Jersey. He afterwards followed the same Captain, as Midshipman, into the DANNEMARK 74, in which ship, and in the SAN JOSEF 110, and FLORIDA 20, Capts. Jeffry Raigersfeld and Wm. Elliott, he continued employed, as Midshipman, until the spring of 1816. He then served for nearly three years and a half in the West Indies, latterly as Mate, in the SCAMANDER 36, also commanded by Capt. Elliott; and he afterwards joined—8 Sept. 1819, the Coast Blockade, as Midshipman of the SEVERN 40, Capt. Wm. M'Culloch—8 April, 1822, the BRITANNIA 100, flag-ship of Sir Alex. Cochrane at Plymouth—23 May, 1824, as Acting-Lieutenant (a rank he held for more than three years), the BLANCHE 46, Capt. Wm. Bowen Mends, in South America—and, 12 July and 13 Aug. 1827, as Admiralty-Mate, the ASIA 84, flag-ship of Sir Edw. Codrington, and BRISK 10, Capt. Bruce, both in the Mediterranean. He was confirmed a Lieutenant, 19 April, 1828, in the CAMELION 10, also on that station, but was superseded, at his own request, in the following Sept., and has not been since employed.

Since he has been on half-pay, Lieut. Lascelles has for upwards of three years had command of a steam-packet.

LASCELLES. (COMMANDER, 1814. F-P., 12; H-P., 35.)

JOHN FRANCIS LASCELLES, born 22 March, 1787, at Northallerton, co. York, is second surviving son of the Rev. Lascelles Sturdy Lascelles, by Jane, eldest daughter of Simon Butterwick, Esq., of Thirsk, in that county. His father was the sole heir and representative of the late Colonel Thos. Lascelles, Chief Engineer of Great Britain.

This officer entered the Navy, in April, 1800, as Fst.-cl. Vol., on board the SYREN 32, Capt. Thos. Le Marchant Gosselin, and, after being for some time in attendance on George III. off Weymouth, accompanied the same Captain to the West Indies with convoy as Midshipman of the MELAMPUS 36, which frigate returned home and was paid off 23 June, 1802. In the following Nov. he joined the LEDA 38, Capts. Jas. Hardy and Robt. Honyman, under whom he served as Midshipman, Master's Mate, Acting-Lieutenant, and Lieutenant (order and commission respectively dated 27 Sept. 1806 and 28 April, 1807), until wrecked, near the entrance of Milford Haven, 31 Jan. 1808. He consequently, during that period, came into frequent contact with the Boulogne flotilla—assisted at the reduction of the Cape of Good Hope in Jan. 1806—was present at the capture, 21 Feb. and 4 March following, of the *Rolla* brig and *Volontaire* frigate, in Table Bay—attended Sir Home Popham's ensuing expedition to the Rio de la Plata—served in the same year with the boats at the destruction of a brigantine off Monte Video—participated in the operations of 1807 against Copenhagen—and was at the taking of *L'Apropos* French privateer of 16 guns and 70 men. In May, 1808, Mr. Lascelles received an appointment to the VENERABLE 74, Capt. Andrew King, lying in the Downs. He was next, for several months of 1810, employed in the SATURN 74, Capt. Wm. Cumberland, on the Baltic station, whence excessive fatigue obliged him to invalid; and he lastly, from 10 Sept. 1812, until advanced to the rank of Commander 27 Aug. 1814, served in the Channel and Mediterranean on board the MULGRAVE 74, Capt. Thos. Jas. Maling.

He married, 30 Nov. 1830, Henrietta, second daughter of Sam. Higham, Esq., of Torrington Square, London, by whom he has issue one daughter.

LASH. (LIEUTENANT, 1828.)

JAMES LASH entered the Navy 31 Jan. 1810; passed his examination in 1817, and obtained his commission 29 Jan. 1828. He has since been on half-pay.

He married, 28 Dec. 1839, Elizabeth Sarah, daughter of the late J. Harris, Esq., of Pentonville, and was left a widower 27 June, 1841.

LASTON. (LIEUT., 1815. F-P., 25; H-P., 16.)

SAMUEL HORNIGOLD LASTON entered the Navy, in Sept. 1806, as Midshipman, on board the SPARTAN 38, Capts. Geo. Castle and Jahleel Brenton. Continuing in that ship until April, 1809, he served in her boats at the cutting out of a vessel under the batteries of Civita Vecchia, participated in an attempt made to cut off a convoy under the batteries of Leghorn, and was present in an attack upon a disguised armed polacre off Nice, on which occasion he brought off the barge and pinnace with only three men, and received a severe contusion. On leaving the SPARTAN Mr. Laston became Master's Mate of the BUSTARD 10, Capts. John Duff Markland, Chas. Borough Strong, and Lord John Hay, with whom, it appears, he was for a period of six years employed on the Mediterranean, West India, and Lisbon stations. While so attached he assisted, as Acting-Lieutenant, at the capture and destruction of some gun-boats under the Castle of Duino, cooperated in the defence of Sicily, and was often engaged with enemy's gun-vessels in the Faro of Messina. His official advancement to the rank he now holds took place 15 Feb. 1815. He shortly afterwards joined the BOMBAY 74, flag-ship in the Mediterranean of Sir Chas. Vinicombe Penrose; and in the following year, we are informed, he was present at the bombardment of Algiers. His last appointments were—in 1824 and 1830, as a Supernumerary, to the RAMILLIES and TALAVERA, Coast Blockade ships, Capts. Wm. M'Culloch and Hugh Pigot—and, 18 April, 1831, to the Coast Guard, in which he remained until the close of 1839. AGENTS—Coplands and Burnett.

LA TOUCHE. (LIEUTENANT, 1840.)

ASHLEY LA TOUCHE is one of the 14 children of the late Peter La Touche, Esq., of Bellevue, co. Wicklow, by the Hon. Charlotte Maude, daughter of Cornwallis Viscount Hawarden. His grandfather, the Right Hon. David La Touche, of Marlay, co. Dublin, was for many years Member in the Irish Parliament for his own borough of Newcastle and other places.

This officer entered the Navy 3 Feb. 1825; served as Midshipman of the BLONDE 46, Capt. Edm. Lyons, at the bombardment of the Morea Castle in 1828; and passed his examination in 1832. Becoming Mate of the IMOGENE 28, Capt. Price Blackwood, he proceeded in that ship to China, where he assisted, in 1834, in forcing the passage of the Boca Tigris. For his services on the coast of Syria and at St. Jean d'Acre in the REVENGE 76, Capt. Hon. Wm. Waldegrave, Mr. La Touche was promoted to the rank of Lieutenant 4 Nov. 1840. His appointments have since been, on the North America and West India station—21 April, 1841, as Additional, to the WINCHESTER 50, flag-ship of Sir Thos. Harvey—27 Aug. 1841, to the VESTAL 26, Capt. John Parker, with whom he returned home and was paid off in 1842—19 Sept. 1843, again as Additional, to the ILLUSTRIOUS 72, bearing the flag of Sir Chas. Adam—1 Jan. 1844, as First, to the SCYLLA 16, Capt. Robt. Sharpe—and, 17 Nov. 1844, in a similar capacity, to the IMAUM 72, bearing the broad pendants of Commodores Alex. Renton Sharpe, Dan. Pring, and Geo. Robt. Lambert at Jamaica, where he is still employed. AGENTS—Messrs. Stilwell.

LAUGHARNE. (CAPT., 1832. F-P., 24; H-P., 25.)

THOMAS LAMB POLDEN LAUGHARNE was born in June, 1786.

This officer entered the Navy, 8 April, 1798, as Fst.-cl. Vol., on board the VAN TROMP 50, Capt. Rich. Hill, on the Irish station; removed as Midshipman, in March, 1799, to the AGINCOURT 64, flag-ship at Newfoundland of Hon. Wm. Waldegrave; and, from 1800 until April, 1805, served on the Home and Halifax stations in the ACTIVE 38, Capt. John Giffard, THESEUS 74, Capt. John Bligh, and CAMBRIAN 40, Capts. Wm. Bradley and John Poo Beresford. He then became Acting-Lieutenant of the BERMUDA 10, Capt. Keilly, and, after a servitude of seven months in that vessel, proceeded in the DRIVER sloop, Capt. John Simpson, to the West Indies, where, on joining the NORTHUMBERLAND 74, flag-ship of Hon. Alex. Cochrane, he took part in the action off St. Domingo 6 Feb. 1806. In the course of the following month he received an order to act as Lieutenant of the UNICORN 32, Capt. Lucius Ferdinand Hardyman, in which frigate (being confirmed to her on 8 of the following Aug.) he continued to serve until June, 1809, witnessing during that period the siege of Monte Video, the embarkation of the army after the battle of Corunna, and the destruction of the French shipping in Basque Roads. Sailing next for the Cape of Good Hope in the CAMEL store-ship, Mr. Laugharne there, in Nov. 1809, joined the NEREIDE 36, Capt. Nesbit Josiah Willoughby, under whom, it appears, he was present in a dashing attack made on the enemy's batteries and troops at Jacotel, in the Mauritius, 1 May, 1810, as also at the capture, in the following July, of the Ile de Bourbon. On 13 Sept. 1810, being then Senior of the BOADICEA 38, Capt. Josias Rowley, we find him recommended to the favourable notice of the Commander-in-Chief for the steadiness and zeal he manifested at the re-capture of H.M.S. AFRICAINE in the presence of two French frigates; and on 21 of the same month he presents himself to our notice as contributing to the capture, after a spirited action of 10 minutes, and a loss to the BOADICEA of 2 men wounded, and to the enemy of 9 killed and 15 wounded, of *La Vénus*, of 44 guns and 380 men, bearing the broad pendant of Commodore Hamelin, and of her prize the CEYLON 32. Being again strongly recommended for his able assistance in taking charge of and conducting into port both the AFRICAINE and *La Vénus*, Lieut. Laugharne was promoted, 11 Oct. 1810, to the acting-command of the OTTER sloop, and ordered to England with despatches announcing Vice-Admiral Bertie's intention of resuming the blockade of Port Louis. His advancement to the rank of Commander took place 12 Feb. 1811. After nearly 12 months of half-pay Capt. Laugharne was next, 6 Feb. 1812, appointed to the ALERT sloop (formerly a Newcastle collier), mounting 14 18-pounder carronades and 2 long sixes, with a complement of 86 men. On 13 of the ensuing Aug. this vessel, at the time in search of the U.S. ship *Hornet*, fell in with and most gallantly bore down upon the *Essex* frigate, of 46 guns and 328 men, by whom, however, she was in 15 minutes unfortunately taken captive, with seven feet water in her hold and three of her men wounded. By a court-martial which, on 8 of the proximate Oct., assembled at Newfoundland, Capt. Laugharne was of course most honourably acquitted of all blame in the loss of his ship. His last appointment afloat was to the ACHATES 18, in which sloop he cruized in the Channel until Nov. 1815. He became an Inspecting-Commander in the Coast Guard in Nov. 1823, and on 4 April, 1832, as a reward for his exertions in that service, he was advanced to Post-rank. He has since been on half-pay.

Capt. Laugharne has had his skull severely fractured and trepanned in two places—the first time through a fall in a gale of wind when Midshipman of the THESEUS 74, in Aug. 1802; and the second, in the same part of the head, when cutting out, with the UNICORN's boats, in July, 1808, an armed schooner from the harbour of St. Sebastian, on the north coast of Spain. On the latter occasion he also lost a great portion of the upper jaw. Among the numerous other boat affairs in which Capt. Laugharne took part, we may instance his capture of a French national schooner when in command of the boats of the BOADICEA. In consideration of his wounds he is allowed a pension of 91*l.* 5*s.* He married, in Feb. 1820, Mary Amelia, eldest surviving daughter of Sir Stewkely Shuckburgh, Bart., of Shuckburgh Park, co. Warwick, by whom he has issue two children.

LAUGHARNE. (COMMANDER, 1814. F-P., 16; H-P., 33.)

WILLIAM LAUGHARNE, born 21 Dec. 1785, at Poole, co. Dorset, is son of the late Capt. Thos. Laugharne, R.N., and nephew of the late Vice-Admiral John Laugharne. His only brother, Lieut. Thos. Laugharne, perished in the JASEUR brig when crossing the Bay of Bengal, on his way to China, in Aug. 1809.

This officer entered the Navy, 6 Jan. 1798, as Fst.-cl. Vol., on board the BARFLEUR 98, Capt. Jas. Rich. Dacres, with whom he removed as Midshipman, in the following Sept., to the FOUDROYANT 80, commanded afterwards by Capts. Wm. Brown, Thos. Masterman Hardy, and Sir Edw. Berry. While in the latter ship, besides witnessing the surrender of Naples, we find him, while at the blockade of Malta, assisting at the capture, 18 Feb. 1800, of *Le Généreux* 74, and *Ville de Marseilles* armed store-ship, and on 31 March, after a desperate conflict, in which the FOUDROYANT (then in company with the LION 64, and PENELOPE 36) sustained a loss of 8 men killed and 64 wounded, of *Le Guillaume Tell*, of 84 guns and 1000 men, bearing the flag of Rear-Admiral Decrès. From Nov. 1800 until April, 1802, Mr. Laugharne further served with Sir Edw. Berry and Capt. Henry Hill in the PRINCESS CHARLOTTE 38, and RUBY 64, in the Mediterranean and in the North Sea and Baltic. He then, in the CONCORDE 36, Capts. Robt. Barton and John Wood, proceeded to the Cape of Good Hope, where, in Feb. 1803, he joined the TREMENDOUS 74, Capt. John Osborne. In March, 1805, being at the time in the CULLODEN 74, flag-ship in the East Indies of Sir Edw. Pellew, he was nominated Acting-Lieutenant of the CORNWALLIS frigate, Capt. Wm. Jones Lye. Being confirmed, 14 Nov. 1806, into the RUSSELL 74, bearing the flag of Rear-Admiral Wm. O'Brien Drury, he was present in that ship at the ensuing destruction of the Dutch force in Batavia Roads. His subsequent appointments were—27 Sept. 1809, to the RATTLESNAKE 18, Capt. Jas. John Gordon Bremer, with whom he returned to England—2 Nov. 1810, to the SOUTHAMPTON 32, Capts. Edwards Lloyd Graham and Jas. Lucas Yeo, stationed in the Channel —31 Jan. 1811, to the ALCMÈNE 38, Capt. E. L. Graham, in which frigate he again went to the Mediterranean—and, 3 Dec. 1813 and 19 July, 1814, to the TRIDENT 64, and SWIFTSURE 74, as Flag-Lieutenant at Malta to his uncle Rear-Admiral Laugharne. He was advanced to his present rank 23 Sept. 1814, and has since been on half-pay.

Commander Laugharne married, first, in Nov. 1818, Louisa, daughter of Retired Commander Peter Tait (1800); and secondly, in June, 1825, Mary Emilia, daughter of the late Sam. Rawlings, Esq., of Charlton, co. Kent.

LAURIE, Bart., K.C.B. (ADMIRAL OF THE BLUE, 1846. F-P., 30; H-P., 37.)

SIR ROBERT LAURIE, born 25 May, 1764, is son of the late Lieut.-General Sir Robt. Laurie, Bart., Knight-Marshal of Scotland, and for upwards of 30 years M.P. for co. Dumfries, by Mary Elizabeth, daughter of the sixth Lord Ruthven, and niece of the Earl of Bute. He succeeded his father as sixth baronet in 1804.

This officer entered the Navy, 24 April, 1780, as Captain's Servant, on board the SURPRIZE, Capt. Sam. Reeve, in which ship, and, as Midshipman, in the CROWN, he served with the same officer on the Newfoundland and Home stations until the autumn of 1783. He afterwards, until confirmed in the rank of Lieutenant 12 Nov. 1790, served at Newfoundland and Jamaica, part of the time as Acting-Lieutenant, in the SALISBURY 50, flag-ship of Admiral Campbell, EDGAR 74, Capt. Adam Duncan, EXPEDITION and EUROPA, bearing each the broad pendant of Commodore Alan Gardner, and ALERT sloop, Capt. Geo. Burdon. In Jan. 1793 he rejoined Commodore (then Rear-Admiral) Gardner, on board the QUEEN 98, in which ship he fought and was wounded in Lord Howe's action 1 June, 1794.* Being made Commander, 25 June, 1795, into the ZEPHYR sloop, Capt. Laurie was for some time employed in that vessel on the North Sea station, whence he ultimately returned to the West Indies, capturing on his passage out, 8 Jan. 1797, *La Réfléchie*, French privateer of 12 guns and 67 men, and assisting, on his arrival, at the reduction of Trinidad. On 17 July in the same year Capt. Laurie was advanced to Post-rank. His next appointment, we therefore find, was to a frigate, the ANDROMACHE 32, the command of which he retained, on the West India and American stations, from Nov. 1798 until Feb. 1804. On one occasion during that period, 22 March, 1801, while cruizing off Punta de Mulas, on the north-east coast of the island of Cuba, in company with the CLEOPATRA 32, Capt. Israel Pellew, he took charge of the boats of both ships for the purpose of capturing or destroying 25 Spanish vessels, richly laden, and lying at anchor in the bay of Levita under the protection of three armed galleys or gun-vessels, armed with long 24 and 18 pounders. Soon after midnight the boats arrived within gunshot of the galleys, and were received, quite unexpectedly, with a heavy and destructive fire of grape, langridge, and musketry. In spite of this opposition the British gallantly pushed on, and boarded several vessels, but from the heavy loss they sustained (9 killed and 12 wounded) were only able to bring off one of the galleys. Obtaining command, 9 July, 1804, of the CLEOPATRA, of 38 guns and 200 men, Sir Robt. Laurie continued in that frigate until 17 Feb. 1805; on which date he had the misfortune to be captured, after a brilliant and self-sought action of nearly three hours and a loss to his own ship of 20 killed and 38 wounded, by *La Ville de Milan*, of 46 guns and 350 men, 10 of whom appear to have been slain. The latter frigate being however so shattered in the combat as to be scarcely able to protect herself, the two, on falling in, six days afterwards, with the 50-gun ship LEAN-

* *Vide* Gaz. 1794, p. 557.

DER, Capt. John Talbot, became easy prizes to that officer.* In the following April Sir Robt. Laurie had the satisfaction of being appointed to his late antagonist, which had been added to the British Navy as a 38-gun frigate, and named the MILAN. He continued in her until the summer of 1810, and was lastly, towards the close of 1811, intrusted with the successive command of the BRUNSWICK and AJAX 74's; in the latter of which ships he served in the Mediterranean until superseded 26 July, 1813. He became a Rear-Admiral 19 July, 1821; a Vice-Admiral 10 Jan. 1837; and a full Admiral 9 Nov. 1846.

In consideration of the wound he received in Lord Howe's action, Sir Robt. Laurie was at the time rewarded with a pecuniary grant from the Patriotic Fund. AGENTS—Case and Loudonsack.

LAUZUN. (LIEUT., 1811. F-P., 14; H-P., 33.)

FRANCIS DANIEL LAUZUN entered the Navy, 14 Oct. 1800, as Midshipman, on board the PRINCE 98, commanded by the Earl of Northesk, with whom he served in the Channel until April, 1802. In June, 1803, after he had been for nearly five months employed on the Guernsey station in the ALCMÈNE 32, Capt. John Stiles, he rejoined the same nobleman on board the BRITANNIA, and for his subsequent conduct as one of his Aides-de-Camp at the battle of Trafalgar he had the satisfaction of receiving his Lordship's thanks. On the last-mentioned ship being paid off in June, 1806, Mr. Lauzun joined the LAVINIA 40, Capts. Lord Wm. Stuart and John Hancock, under whose orders he remained until Nov. 1808. During that period, it appears, he was much employed with the in-shore squadrons off Brest and Toulon, saw a good deal of arduous boat-service on the shores of France, Spain, and Italy, and was twice taken prisoner in a prize, the first time by a Spanish privateer, and the second by a national brig. Removing next to the NORGE 74, Capt. John Sprat Rainier, Mr. Lauzun in Jan. 1809 proceeded to Corunna for the purpose of assisting at the embarkation of the army under the late Sir John Moore. While there, the pinnace, of which our officer had the charge, was sunk by a gun-shot at a moment when she was crowded with soldiers, women, and baggage. Luckily, owing to his presence of mind, and to the manner in which he preserved his authority in the midst of so much peril, not a soul was lost, the whole being rendered able to get on board a neighbouring frigate, the UNICORN 32. A full share of credit was of course awarded to Mr. Lauzun for his conduct under such very trying circumstances. In the following year we find him employed on shore at Ferrol, and receiving in common with others the thanks of the Regency for his exertions in equipping several Spanish men-of-war lying there dismantled, and in also removing the naval stores to prevent their falling into the hands of the French. In April, 1810, being then at Lisbon, he was nominated Acting-Lieutenant of the ULYSSES 44, Capt. Henry Edw. Reginald Baker, flag-ship afterwards of the Duc de Bouillon off Guernsey. Owing to some informality in the appointment, the Admiralty, although requested by the latter officer, refused to confirm it, and in Nov. of the same year Mr. Lauzun was accordingly superseded. He was however made Lieutenant, 2 Feb. 1811, into the DIADEM *armée-en-flûte*, Capt. John Phillimore, and was afterwards appointed—19 Sept. 1811, again to the ULYSSES, at first employed as before, but afterwards commanded, in the Baltic, by Capt. Thos. Browne—and, 15 Jan. 1814, to the DANNEMARK 74, Capt. H. E. R. Baker, which ship, after having escorted an East India convoy to the Cape of Good Hope, returned home and was paid off 29 April, 1815. He has not been since afloat.

LAVIE. (LIEUT., 1830. F-P., 15; H-P., 10.)

AUGUSTUS LAVIE, born 6 April, 1805, is brother of Commander Geo. Lavie, R.N.

This officer entered the Navy, 5 Jan. 1822, as Fst.-cl. Vol, on board the SPENCER 74, Capt. Thos. Dundas, lying at Plymouth, where he followed the same officer into the BULWARK 74. From Sept. 1823 until Feb. 1827 we find him employed in South America as Midshipman of the SPARTIATE 76, and WELLESLEY 74, flag-ships of Sir Geo. Eyre. During the next seven months he was again stationed at Plymouth, in the BRITANNIA 120, and OCEAN 80, Capts. Philip Pipon and Patrick Campbell. He then joined the TALBOT 28, Capt. Hon. Fred. Spencer, attached to the force in the Mediterranean, where, from July, 1828, until advanced to the rank of Lieutenant 6 April, 1830, he discharged the duties of Mate on board the ASIA 84, Capts. Edw. Curzon and Wm. Jas. Hope Johnstone. His succeeding appointments were—9 May, 1832, and 6 Jan. 1834, to the ARIADNE 28, and COMUS 18, Capts. Chas. Phillips and Wm. Price Hamilton, both on the West India station, whence he invalided in May, 1835—27 Oct. 1836, to the SAMARANG 28, Capt. Wm. Broughton, with whom he served in South America until Nov. 1839—20 Dec. 1841, to the VINDICTIVE 50, Capt. John Toup Nicolas, lying at Portsmouth—and 26 May, 1842, to the CALCUTTA 84, Capt. Sir Sam. Roberts. He returned home from Quebec in Nov. of the latter year, and has since been on half-pay.

* *Vide* Gaz. 1805, p. 540.

LAVIE. (COMMANDER, 1846. F-P., 17; H-P., 4.)

GEORGE LAVIE, born 24 July, 1813, is son of the late Sir Thos. Lavie, K.C.B., who received the honour of Knighthood in 1806, as a reward for his conduct in having in the BLANCHE, of 46 guns and 265 men, effected the capture of the French frigate *Guerrière* of 50 guns and 317 men. He is brother of Lieut. Augustus Lavie, R.N.

This officer entered the Royal Naval College in Nov. 1826; and embarked in Nov. 1828, as a Volunteer, on board the MADAGASCAR 46, Capt. Hon. Sir Robt. Cavendish Spencer. Proceeding in that ship to the Mediterranean, he there became Midshipman, in Nov. 1830, of the WINDSOR CASTLE 76, Capt. Hon. Duncombe Pleydell Bouverie; and he was afterwards, until promoted to the rank of Lieutenant 15 Dec. 1834, employed on the Home and South American stations, latterly as Mate, in the REVENGE 78, Capt. Jas. Hillyar, ALLIGATOR 28, Capt. Geo. Robt. Lambert, ALGERINE 10, Capt. Hon. John Fred. Fitzgerald de Roos, and EXCELLENT gunnery-ship, Capt. Thos. Hastings. His succeeding appointments were—26 Aug. 1835, again to the EXCELLENT—30 Dec. 1836, to the SCYLLA 16, Capt. Hon. Joseph Denman, on the Lisbon station—11 May, 1839, to the REVENGE again, Capt. Hon. Wm. Waldegrave, in the Mediterranean—12 July, 1842, as Senior, to the ISIS 44, Capt. Sir John Marshall, at the Cape of Good Hope, whence he returned in Jan. 1845—and, 31 Dec. in the latter year, to the FLAMER steam-vessel, stationed in the Mediterranean. He was advanced to his present rank 9 Nov. 1846, and still commands the FLAMER.

LAVINGTON. (LIEUTENANT, 1827.)

THOMAS LAVINGTON entered the Navy, 31 Jan. 1812, as Fst.-cl. Vol., on board the ROYAL SOVEREIGN 100, Capt. Wm. Bedford, employed in blockading Basque Roads and Brest. Removing as Midshipman, in Nov. 1813, to the MELPOMÈNE troop-ship, Capt. Robt. Rowley, he proceeded to North America, where he commanded a boat up the Patuxent at the destruction of Commodore Barney's flotilla, was present at the capture of Washington, served on shore in the attack upon Baltimore, and had charge of one of the boats of a squadron at the capture, 14 Dec. 1814, on Lake Borgne, of five American gun-boats under Commodore Jones, which did not surrender until the British, after a fierce contest, had been occasioned a loss of 17 men killed and 77 wounded. During the first three years of the general peace Mr. Lavington was stationed in South America on board the HYACINTH 20, Capt. Alex. Renton Sharpe. He then, in Oct. 1818, passed his examination, and between that period and 1822 became in succession attached to the SEVERN Coast-Blockade ship, Capt. Wm. M'Culloch, and QUEEN CHARLOTTE 100, and VICTORY 104, commanded at Portsmouth by Capts. John Baker Hay and Chas. Inglis. On leaving the latter ship, he proceeded, as Admiralty Midshipman of the DRIVER sloop, Capt. Thos. Wolrige, to the coast of Africa, but, being soon compelled to invalid, he next, in 1823, joined, in a similar capacity, the NAIAD 46, Capt. Hon. Robt. Cavendish Spencer, and sailed for the Mediterranean. Arrived on that station, he contributed, 31 Jan. 1824, to the complete defeat of the *Tripoli* Algerine corvette of 18 guns and 100 men; and on the night of 23 May following, he aided in the boats under Lieut. Michael Quin at the valiant destruction of a 16-gun brig moored in a position of extraordinary strength alongside the walls of the fortress of Bona, in which was a garrison of 400 soldiers, who, from cannon and musket, kept up a tremendous fire almost perpendicularly on the deck. We subsequently find him ordered to the East Indies in the WARSPITE 76, in which ship, bearing the flag at first of Rear-Admiral Wm. Hall Gage, he ultimately returned to the Mediterranean, where, after the battle of Navarin, he was promoted from the ASIA 84, bearing the flag of Sir Edw. Codrington, to a death-vacancy in the ROSE 18, Capt. Hon. Wm. Wellesley. His commission bears date 17 Dec. 1827. He returned to England in 1828; and with the exception of a period of nearly three years, between 1835 and 1838, has been in the Coast Guard since 1 Dec. 1829.

Lieut. Lavington married, 25 May, 1830, Anne, eldest daughter of Wm. Ferris, Esq., of Lymington, Hants, by whom he has issue six children.

LAWLESS. (LIEUT., 1814. F-P., 18; H-P., 22.)

HENRY LAWLESS entered the Navy, in May, 1807, as Fst.-cl. Vol., on board the PROCRIS 18, Capt. Fras. Beauman, attached to the force in the North Sea; and between the close of the same year and the date of his promotion to the rank of Lieutenant, 27 April, 1814, was successively employed, chiefly as Midshipman, in the INFLEXIBLE 64, Capt. Joshua Rowley Watson, ECLAIR sloop, Capt. Chas. Kempthorne Quash, PRINCESS OF ORANGE 74, flag-ship of Vice-Admiral Campbell, PERLEN 38, and BOMBAY 74, both commanded by Capt. Norborne Thompson, BARHAM 74, Capt. John Wm. Spranger, and ARGO 44, Capts. Wm. Browne and Wm. Fothergill, on the Home and West India stations. He then joined the STATIRA frigate, Capt. Spelman Swaine, and, continuing in that ship until Jan. 1815, was present in her in the expedition against New Orleans. His next appointments were—17 Feb. and 26 Nov. 1830, to the RAMILLIES and TALAVERA Coast Blockade ships, both commanded by Capt. Hugh Pigot—and 15 April, 1831, to the Coast Guard, in which he remained until the commencement of 1833. Since 7 March, 1843, he has been again employed in the latter service.

He married, 17 Jan. 1825, Miss Catherine Gask, of Bury Street, St. James's. AGENT—J. Chippendale.

LAWRANCE. (RETIRED COMMANDER, 1836. F-P., 13; H-P., 37.)

GEORGE BELL LAWRANCE died 9 April, 1846.

This officer entered the Navy, 1 March, 1797, as Master's Mate, on board the EL CORSO 18, Capt. Bartholomew James, with whom he served, in the same vessel and the CANOPUS 80, on the Mediterranean and Lisbon stations, until Sept. 1799. During the next three years and a half he was employed off St. Helena and in the Downs and West Indies on board the DIRECTOR 64, Capt. Wm. Bligh, and LEVIATHAN 74, flag-ship of Sir John Thos. Duckworth. He then, in March, 1803, became Acting-Lieutenant of the RACOON 18, Capt. Austen Bissell, and while in that sloop, to which he was confirmed by commission dated 8 Sept. following, we find him in the course of the same year participating in a very warm action of 40 minutes, which terminated in the capture, in Leogane Roads, of the French corvette *Le Lodi*, of 10 guns and 61 men—contributing, also, to the destruction, off the island of Cuba, of the national brig *La Mutine*, of 18 guns—and further present, with distinction, in an action in which the RACOON, with only 42 men on board, most gallantly took, notwithstanding a long and desperate resistance on the part of the enemy, a French gun-brig, cutter, and schooner, carrying altogether between 300 and 400 men.* In 1805, Lieut. Lawrance—who had for some time had command of the GIPSY schooner of 10 guns, and been also employed in the ECHO sloop, Capt. Edmund Boger—successively joined the ACASTA 40, Capt. Rich. Dalling Dunn, HERCULE 74, flag-ship of Rear-Admiral Jas. Rich. Dacres, and THESEUS 74, Capt. Fras. Temple, all on the West India station; and he next, from 10 July 1806 until 15 July, 1808, served with the late Sir Sam. Hood on board the CENTAUR 74. While in the ECHO he cut out a brig from the Bight of Leogane; he captured, in the GIPSY, a privateer of 4 guns off Trinidad; and, when in the CENTAUR, he assisted, in company with the MARS and MONARCH 74's, at the defeat, 25 Sept. 1806, of four heavy French frigates off Rochefort, on which occasion Sir Sam. Hood lost his arm—accompanied, in Aug. and Sept. 1807, the expedition to Copenhagen, where he was employed in taking soundings during the siege—and was present in Dec. of the same year at the surrender of Madeira. His last appointment was, 5 June, 1810, to the CADMUS 10, Capt. Thos. Fife, with whom he served on the coast of France until 17 Dec. 1811. He retired with the rank of Commander 4 May, 1836.

Commander Lawrance married, in 1814, a daughter of Rich. Bennett, Esq., of Lostwithiel, co. Cornwall, by whom he has left, with one daughter, a son, the present Lieut. Geo. Bennett Lawrance, R.N.

LAWRANCE. (LIEUTENANT, 1843.)

GEORGE BENNETT LAWRANCE is only surviving son of the late Retired Commander Geo. Bell Lawrance, R.N.

This officer entered the Navy 19 June, 1829; passed his examination 6 Jan. 1836; and since his promotion to the rank of Lieutenant, 15 Feb. 1843, has been in command, on the North America and West India station, of the LARK surveying-vessel, in which he had been previously employed for many months in the capacity of Mate.

LAWRANCE. (LIEUT., 1826. F-P., 34; H-P., 5.)

HENRY LAWRANCE was born 4 Aug. 1789.

This officer entered the Navy, 10 June, 1808, as Ordinary, on board the VAN TROMP, Lieut.-Commander Michael M'Carthy, lying at Falmouth; and from Feb. 1809 until June, 1816, was employed, on the Home and Mediterranean stations, as Midshipman and Master's Mate, in the NONPAREIL 12, Lieut.-Commander Jas. Dickinson, ARGO 44, Capt. Fred. Warren, EURYALUS 36, Capt. Hon. Geo. Heneage Lawrence Dundas, and TRIDENT 64, Capt. Rich. Budd Vincent. While in the latter ship, in Aug. 1815, he passed his examination. Until promoted to the rank of Lieutenant 27 June, 1826, he appears to have further served, on the same stations as above, as Admiralty Midshipman and Mate, in the CALYPSO 18, Capt. Sam. Sison, FLORIDA 20, Capt. Chas. Sibthorpe John Hawtayne, WYE 26, Capt. Geo. Wickens Willes, HIND 20, Capts. Sir Chas. Burrard, Hon. Henry John Rous, and Lord John Churchill, and REVENGE 76, flag-ship of Sir Harry Burrard Neale. He then joined the SERINGAPATAM 46, Capt. Chas. Sotheby, also in the Mediterranean, whence he returned in Dec. 1827; and since 1 Jan. 1833 he has been employed in the Coast Guard.

He married, in Jan. 1837, Mary, daughter of Pierce Chute, Esq., of Tralee, co. Kerry.

---

* *Vide* Gaz. 1804, p. 162.

LAWRENCE. (Captain, 1816. F-P., 17; H-P., 32.)

Daniel Lawrence has two brothers, we believe, in the Royal Marines, both of whom served with great credit during the late war with America.

This officer entered the Navy in March, 1798, as a Volunteer, on board the Grand Falconer hired cutter, Lieut.-Commander John Chilcott, stationed off the coast of France; and on removing to the Cynthia sloop, Capt. Micajah Malbon, was employed as Midshipman and Master's Mate in the expeditions to Holland, Quiberon, Ferrol, and Egypt. He continued to serve with Capt. Malbon in the Aurora 28, and Hebe 32, on the Newfoundland, Home, and African stations, until April, 1806, and, while in the latter ship, was often engaged with the enemy's flotilla and batteries near Boulogne. Proceeding next to the West Indies, Mr. Lawrence, after he had been there borne for short periods as a Supernumerary on the books of the Dolphin, Canada, and Northumberland, flag-ships of Hon. Sir Alex. Cochrane, was successively nominated, in June, 1806, and Jan. 1807, Sub and Acting Lieutenant of the Orinoco, Lieut.-Commander Geo. Alex. Briarly, and Heureux 16, Capts. Wm. Coombe and John Watt. Being confirmed to the latter vessel by commission dated 19 May, 1808, we find him, on 28 of the following Nov., accompanying three boats under the personal command of Capt. Coombe in an attempt to cut out seven vessels lying under the protection of two batteries in the harbour of Mahaut, Guadeloupe. Having arrived at their destination after a row of about six hours, Lieut. Lawrence —while Capt. Coombe, in the barge with 19 men, was boarding a schooner of 2 guns and 39 men— landed with the remainder of the party, amounting to about 44 officers and men, and spiked the two 24-pounders upon the nearest battery. He then succeeded in boarding a brig; but, before either the schooner or the brig could be got off, the shore was lined with musketry, and 3 field-pieces were brought to bear upon the two captured vessels. These, having the misfortune to ground on their way out, became fixed objects for the enemy's fire, and were ultimately abandoned, but not until Capt. Coombe had been killed, and Lieut. Lawrence wounded by a musket-ball just above the wrist. Having distinguished himself in various other boat attacks, our officer (to whom the Patriotic Society awarded a gratuity for the injury we have alluded to) was permitted, as soon as he had served the necessary time, to ascend the next step in his profession, and his commission as Commander accordingly bears date 19 May, 1810. Previously, however, to his promotion, Capt. Lawrence appears to have been in acting-command of the Wanderer sloop at the reduction of Guadeloupe. His next and last appointments were, 28 May, 1814, and 21 Oct. 1815, to the Alceste and Weser troop-ships, in the former of which he attended the expedition to New Orleans. He acquired his present rank 2 Sept. 1816, and accepted the Retirement 1 Oct. 1846.

LAWRENCE. (Lieut., 1815. F-P., 22; H-P., 19.)

James Lawrence entered the Navy, 22 July, 1806, as Fst.-cl. Vol., on board the Colossus 74, Capts. Jas. Nicoll Morris and Thos. Alexander, in which ship he was for upwards of six years employed off Lisbon and in the Channel and Mediterranean —the last four as Midshipman. He next, in the course of 1812-13, became in succession attached, on the Channel, Baltic, and Irish stations, to the Surprise 38, Capt. Sir Thos. John Cochrane, Vigo, flag-ship of Rear-Admirals J. N. Morris and Graham Moore, and Ethalion 36, Capts. Edm. Heywood and Wm. Hugh Dobbie. He obtained his commission 18 March, 1815, and was afterwards employed— from March to Aug. 1819, and again from 18 April, 1825, to May, 1828, in the Coast Blockade, as Supernumerary-Lieutenant of the Severn 40, and Ramillies 74, Capts. Wm. M'Culloch and Hugh Pigot— and, from 31 Oct. 1828 until the early part of 1838, in the Coast Guard. He has since been on half-pay.

The Lieutenant married, 5 Oct. 1816, Mary Eliza, daughter of Christopher Jennings, Esq., Clerk in H. M. Dockyard at Portsmouth, by whom he has issue seven children.

LAWRENCE. (Lieut., 1821. F-P., 17; H-P., 18.)

James Ross Lawrence entered the Navy, 17 July, 1812, as Midshipman, on board the Bittern sloop, Capt. Geo. Augustus Hire, and was employed in that vessel, on Impress service, until Dec. 1815. Joining next, in July, 1816, the Leander 50, Capt. Edw. Chetham, he had an opportunity of participating in the ensuing bombardment of Algiers. After a further servitude in the same ship, on the Halifax station, he became, in Sept. 1819, Master's Mate of the Owen Glendower 42, Capt. Hon. Robt. Cavendish Spencer, and sailed for South America. He left the Owen Glendower in Feb. 1822, having been advanced to the rank of Lieutenant on 30 of the previous Nov.; and he was lastly, from 30 April, 1825, until the commencement of 1833, employed in the Coast Guard.

LAWRENCE, C.B. (Captain, 1817. F-P., 28; H-P., 26.)

John Lawrence entered the Navy, 18 Feb. 1793, as Fst.-cl. Vol., on board the Berwick 74, Capts. Sir John Collins and Wm. Shield, and in the following Aug. was present at the occupation of Toulon. Accompanying Capt. Shield as Midshipman, in May, 1794, into the Sincere 20, he served in that vessel at the sieges of Bastia and Calvi; after which, on joining the Windsor Castle 98, flag-ship of the late Admiral Robt. Linzee, he took part in Hotham's actions of 14 March and 13 July, 1795. Towards the close of the same year, being then with Capt. Jas. Macnamara in the Southampton 32, Mr. Lawrence assisted in compelling *La Vestale* of 36 guns, one of several French men-of-war that had just come out of the port of Genoa, to strike her colours. Between April, 1796, and Feb. 1799, we find him serving on the Mediterranean, Home, and Cadiz stations, in the Egmont 74 and Princess Royal 98, flag-ships of Admiral Linzee, Prince 98, bearing the flag of Sir Roger Curtis, Lively 32, Capt. Benj. Hallowell, Ville de Paris 110, bearing the flag of Earl St. Vincent, Romulus frigate, Capt. Geo. Hope, and Lively again, Capt. Jas. Nicoll Morris. He then became Acting-Lieutenant of the Alexander 74, Capts. Alex. John Ball and Manley Dixon, in which ship (being confirmed to her by commission dated 28 June in the same year) he continued until Oct. 1802. He was in consequence present at the capture, 18 Feb. 1800, of *Le Généreux* 74 and *Ville de Marseilles* store-ship; and he served also on shore at the sieges of Malta and the Castle of St. Elmo, at Naples. His after-appointments, as Lieutenant, were, on the North American station—4 Feb. and 6 Oct. 1803, to the Lapwing and Boston frigates, Capts. Alex. Skene and John Erskine Douglas—30 June, 1804 and 19 Aug. 1806, to the Leander and Leopard 50's, Capts. A. Skene, John Talbot, and Salusbury Pryce Humphreys—and, 17 Sept. 1807, to the Bellona 74, Capt. J. E. Douglas. Of the Lapwing Mr. Lawrence was Senior when she effected an escape from a French squadron: he was present, in the Leander, at the capture, 23 Feb. 1805, of the *Ville de Milan* of 46 guns, and retaking of her prize the Cleopatra 32; and, when in the Leopard, he witnessed the surrender to that ship of the U. S. frigate *Chesapeake*, 22 June, 1807. In Jan. 1808 our officer was nominated Acting-Commander of the Observateur sloop, to which it was his fortune to be confirmed on 30 of the ensuing March. In 1809 he removed to the Driver, another sloop, in which, when in company with the Melampus 36, he assisted in taking the French 20-gun ship *Fantôme*. Being placed, in Aug. 1810, in command of the prize, Capt. Lawrence, who continued in her until Oct. 1814, was for some time, we understand, employed at the defence of Cadiz. In the early part of May, 1813, having returned to America, he took charge, at the particular request of Rear-Admiral Cockburn, of an expedition against the town of Havre de Grace, at the entrance of the Susquehanna river, and by the able and judicious manner in which he there silenced a heavy battery, as well as by the gallantry, zeal, and attention he showed at the destruction of a neighbouring cannon-foundry, one of the most valuable works of the kind in America, he called forth the Admiral's highest encomiums and acknowledgments.* From the FANTÔME, which for a short time bore the flag of the latter officer, and proved the captor, 5 Oct. 1813, of a privateer, the *Portsmouth Packet*, of 5 guns and 45 men, Capt. Lawrence removed to the RECRUIT 16. He came home and was paid off in June, 1815; and on 8 Dec. in that year, as a reward for his services, was nominated a C.B. As a Post-Captain, a rank he attained 1 Jan. 1817, his appointments appear to have been—31 Aug. 1822, to the EDEN 26, fitting for the West Indies, where, we believe, he remained the usual period—and 4 June, 1839, to the HASTINGS 72, part of the force employed during the operations on the coast of Syria in 1840. Since the commencement of 1842, at which period the HASTINGS was put out of commission, Capt. Lawrence has been on half-pay.

His eldest daughter, Margaret Frances, was married, in 1840, to Rich. S. Bunce, Esq., First-Lieutenant R.M. (1839). AGENTS—Messrs. Ommanney.

LAWRENCE. (RETIRED COMMANDER, 1845. F-P., 23; H-P., 30.)

PAUL SANDBY LAWRENCE has lost two brothers in the Naval Service of their country.

This officer entered the Navy, 14 Sept. 1794, as Fst.-cl. Vol., on board the CAMBRIDGE 80, bearing the flag at Plymouth of Sir Rich. King. He was employed as Midshipman, during the five following years, in various ships, on the Home and Mediterranean stations; was confirmed a Lieutenant (after having acted for several months as such) in the RESOLUTION 74, Capt. Hon. Alan Hyde Gardner, 6 May, 1801; and served during the whole of the late war, under different officers, in the MALTA 80, ASTREA frigate, CENTURION 50, PRIMROSE sloop, ZEALOUS 74, BARFLEUR 98, and RAMILLIES and SCEPTRE 74's, on the Channel, Baltic, Mediterranean, Lisbon, and American stations. By periling his existence, Mr. Lawrence was the means, on one occasion, of saving one of H.M. ships from destruction. His last appointment was, 5 June, 1833, to the Ordinary at Plymouth, where he remained until 13 July, 1836. He became a Retired Commander on the Senior List 25 Dec. 1845. AGENTS—Messrs. Halford and Co.

LAWRENCE. (LIEUT., 1813. F-P., 10; H-P., 31.)

THOMAS LAWRENCE entered the Navy, 29 Jan. 1806, on board the CENTAUR 74, bearing the broad pendant of Sir Sam. Hood. While in that ship he assisted, in company with the MARS and MONARCH 74's, at the capture, 25 Sept. 1806, of four heavy French frigates from Rochefort, after an action in which Sir Sam. Hood lost his arm. He also attended, in Aug. and Sept. 1807, the expedition to Copenhagen; beheld, in Dec. of the same year, the surrender of Madeira—aided, in conjunction with the IMPLACABLE 74, at the taking, 26 Aug. 1808, in sight of the whole Russian fleet near Rogerswick, of the 74-gun ship *Sewolod*, at the end of a close and furious conflict, in which the CENTAUR lost 3 killed and 27 wounded, and the enemy 180 killed and wounded—and, in Aug. 1809, was engaged, under Capt. Wm. Henry Webley, in the attack upon Walcheren, where he had charge of a gun-boat. Between Nov. 1810 and Aug. 1812 Mr. Lawrence officiated as Midshipman, in the Mediterranean, of the HIBERNIA 120, flag-ship of Sir S. Hood and Sir Rich. Goodwin Keats. He then came home in the INVINCIBLE 74, Capt. Watson; and on 29 Dec. in the same year, 1812, being then on his passage to the East Indies as a Supernumerary (for the purpose of there joining Sir Sam. Hood) of the JAVA of 46 guns and 377 men, he had the misfortune to be captured by the American ship *Constitution*, of 55 guns and 480 men, after a desperate struggle and a loss to the JAVA of 22 killed and 102 (including her Captain, Henry Lambert, mortally) wounded. Mr. Lawrence, whose commission bears date 29 Dec. 1813, ultimately reached India in the ACORN 20, Capt. Geo. Henderson, in the early part of 1814. He remained on that station with Sir S. Hood in the MINDEN 74, and with Capts. Robt. O'Brien and John Harper in the DORIS 36, until 1816; since which period he has been on half-pay.

* *Vide* Gaz. 1814, p. 1331.

LAWS. (CAPTAIN, 1833. F-P., 19; H-P., 19.)

JOHN MILLIGEN LAWS, born 14 Feb. 1799, is son of the late G. Laws, Esq., of Waltington, co. Norfolk, by Lydia, eldest daughter of the late Robt. Seppings, Esq., and sister of the late Sir Robt. Seppings, Surveyor of the Navy, and of the late Lieut. John Milligen Seppings, for a long time Comptroller of Revenue-cruizers.

This officer entered the Navy, 19 Dec. 1809, as Fst.-cl. Vol., on board the SOPHIE 18, Capt. Nicholas Lockyer, in which vessel he was for nearly two years employed in the Channel. In Oct. 1812 he became Midshipman of the RAMILLIES 74, Capts. Sir Thos. Masterman Hardy and Chas. Ogle, attached to the force on the coast of North America, where, besides participating in many boat affairs, and being frequently invested with the charge of a prize, he landed, it appears, at Washington, Baltimore, and Moose Island, and was wounded at New Orleans. After a brief servitude in the IPHIGENIA 36, Capt. Andrew King, lying at Chatham, Mr. Laws, in Oct. 1815, joined the ANTELOPE 50, bearing the flag of Rear-Admiral John Harvey in the West Indies; whence, in 1818, he came home as Acting-Lieutenant of the SCAMANDER 36, Capt. Wm. [illegible]ott. On his arrival in England he was confirmed by commission dated 11 Nov. in that year. His succeeding appointments were—14 Oct. 1819, to the SPARTAN 46, Capt. Wm. Furlong Wise, whom he accompanied to the West Indies and South America—in 1821, to the PYRAMUS 42, VALOROUS 26, and AURORA 46, Capts. Fras. Newcombe, Jas. Murray, and Henry Prescott, employed at Home and again in South America—7 May, 1824, to the command of the FALMOUTH mortar-vessel, in which he joined Sir Harry Neale off Algiers—and, next, to the WELLESLEY 74, Capt. Graham Eden Hamond, under whom he accompanied Lord Stuart de Rothesay to the Brazils. Attaining the rank of Commander, 1 July, 1825, Capt. Laws was next, 22 Nov. 1826, appointed in that capacity to the SATELLITE 18, employed at first as an experimental cruizer, and then on service in the East Indies. While on the latter station we find Capt. Laws affording relief to some settlers in New Holland who had been hemmed in by the natives, and discharging for fourteen months the duties of Senior officer at Sydney. He also effected the capture of a band of convicts who had turned pirates, and, besides making a survey of the Society Islands and New Zealand, demonstrated the necessity of frequent visits to those parts. In Jan. 1831, after he had extensively examined the east coast of the Bay of Bengal, Capt. Laws was removed to the CRUIZER 18, and sent to Pondicherry for the purpose of acknowledging the government of Louis Philippe. On 17 of the following April he became Acting-Captain of the SOUTHAMPTON 52, bearing the flag on the same station of Sir Edw. W. C. R. Owen, with whom he returned to England towards the close of 1832. He was then sent to join the fleet employed under Sir Pulteney Malcolm off Antwerp during the period of General Gérard's attack on the citadel of that place. On 7 Jan. 1833, in the course of which month the SOUTHAMPTON was paid off, Capt. Laws was confirmed in his present rank. He has not been since employed.

Capt. Laws is the Senior Officer of his rank on the List of 1833. He married, 26 June, 1836, Mary, only daughter of Chas. Mathias, Esq., of Lamphey Court, co. Pembroke, by whom he has issue two sons.

LAYE. (Lieutenant, 1836.)

Henry Thomas Laye entered the Navy, 26 April, 1823, as Fst.-cl. Vol., on board the Trinculo 18, Capt. Rodney Shannon, on the Irish station; and was afterwards, until 1829, employed, as Midshipman, in the Jasper 10, Capt. Henry Martin Blackwood, Jupiter 60, flag-ship at Halifax of Rear-Admiral Willoughby Thos. Lake, and Wellesley 74, Capt. Fred. Lewis Maitland—which latter ship, when in company with a French 74, enforced the evacuation of two places in the Mediterranean. During the period which elapsed between the date last mentioned and that of his promotion to the rank of Lieutenant, 10 Sept. 1836, we find him serving in the Mediterranean, North Sea, and East Indies, as Mate, on board the Donegal 78, Capts. John Dick and Arthur Fanshawe, and Jupiter again, employed at first as a troop-ship, under Master-Commander Richmond Easto, and then in escorting, under Capt. Hon. Fred Wm. Grey, the Earl of Auckland as Governor-General to India. The Donegal, we may add, bore the flag of Sir Pulteney Malcolm during the siege of Antwerp. As Lieutenant, Mr. Laye's only appointments appear to have been—12 Jan. 1837, to the Stag 46, bearing the broad pendant of Commodore Thos. Ball Sulivan in South America, where he was superseded in the early part of the following year—and 4 Nov. 1840, to the Endymion 44, commanded by his former Captain, Hon. F. W. Grey, with whom he continued until paid off at the close of 1843. During that period he visited the Persian Gulf, the Red Sea, and China, and was in the Yang-tse-Kiang previously to the pacification of Nanking. While there he commanded a detached force that escaladed the walls of Chin-Kiang-Foo, and, owing to the illness of the commanding officer, brought the Rattlesnake 28 down the river.

LAYTON. (Lieut., 1815. f-p., 11; h-p., 32.)

Buxton Layton entered the Navy, 27 May, 1804, as Fst.-cl. Vol., on board the Ethalion frigate, Capts. Chas. Stuart and Joseph Spear, employed at first in the North Sea, and then in the West Indies, where, in March, 1806, he became Midshipman of the Amelia 38, Capt. Wm. Champain. From the following Aug. until Dec. 1810, he appears to have been again stationed in the North Sea, as also in the Baltic, on board the Nassau 64, Capt. Robt. Campbell, Edgar 74, Capt. Stephen Poyntz, and Stately 64, Capt. R. Campbell. While in the Nassau, which ship was for a long time employed in blockading the Texel, and formed part of the expedition to Copenhagen in Aug. and Sept. 1807, Mr. Layton (on her being extricated from a mass of ice in which she had been blocked up during the whole winter) assisted, 22 March, 1808, in company with the Stately 64, at the capture and destruction, on the coast of Zealand, of the Danish 74-gun ship *Prindts Christian Frederic*, after a running fight of great length and obstinacy, in which the Nassau sustained a loss of 2 men killed and 16 wounded. In Dec. 1810 he accompanied Capt. Campbell into the Tremendous 74, and sailed for the Mediterranean, where he remained with that officer until May, 1815, participating intermediately in a variety of important services. He then took up a commission dated 10 Feb. 1815, and has since been on half-pay.

LAYTON. (Captain, 1846. f-p., 16; h-p., 19.)

Henry Layton, born 2 Feb. 1799, at Chigwell, co. Essex, is second son of the Rev. Thos. Layton, M.A., Vicar of that place and of Theydon Bois, and a magistrate for the above co.

This officer entered the Navy, 3 May, 1812, as Fst.-cl. Vol., on board the Barfleur 98, Capt. Sir Thos. Masterman Hardy, whom he followed as Midshipman in the ensuing Sept. into the Ramillies 74. While in that ship, besides serving at the capture of Washington, Baltimore, and Stonington, and participating in the operations against New Orleans, he assisted in the boats of a squadron at the taking, 14 Dec. 1814, on Lake Borgne, of five American gun-boats under Commodore Jones, which did not surrender until the British, after a violent conflict, had been occasioned a loss of 17 men killed and 77 wounded. From Nov. 1815, when he left the Ramillies, until Dec. 1818, Mr. Layton was employed on the Home station in the Malta 80, and Rivoli 74, both commanded by the present Sir Chas. Ogle, and Rosario 10, Capt. Thos. Ladd Peake. He shortly afterwards passed his examination; and was then for nearly three years and a half stationed in South America, once more under Sir T. M. Hardy, in the Superb 78, Creole 42, and again in the Superb. He was during that period promoted to the rank of Lieutenant by commission dated 2 Nov. 1821. His next appointment was, 9 June, 1824, to the Bulwark 76, Capt. Thos. Dundas, guard-ship at Plymouth, where he was paid off 28 Feb. 1825. Attaining the rank of Commander 10 June following, Capt. Layton was in that capacity employed in the Coast Guard at Killybegs and Gosport from 30 June, 1834, until 26 July, 1837; and on 19 April, 1844, appointed to the Cygnet 6, in which sloop he sailed for the suppression of the slave-trade on the coast of Africa, carrying out Mr. Duncan, the African traveller, to Cape Coast, on his way to the Niger, together with presents for the chiefs of the Cameroon river. He was superseded in Feb. 1846; was advanced to his present rank on 9 Nov. in the same year; and since 12 of that month has been in command of the Belvidera store-ship.

Capt. Layton married, 16 May, 1839, Charlotte Elizabeth, second daughter of the Rev. Edw. Barnard, Rector of Alverstoke, Hants.

LEACH. (Commander, 1841. f-p., 21; h-p., 12.)

Charles Leach was born 12 Sept. 1800.

This officer entered the Navy, 23 June, 1814, as Fst.-cl. Vol., on board the Monmouth 64, Capt. Wm. Wilkinson, flag-ship in the North Sea of the late Sir Thos. Foley. In the following month he removed to the Forester 18, Capt. Wm. Hendry, lying at Portsmouth; and during the next seven years we find him employed, on the Cape of Good Hope, Home, African, and South American stations, principally as Midshipman, in the Harpy 16, Capt. Geo. Tyler, Malta 80, Capt. Thos. Gordon Caulfeild, Inconstant and Semiramis frigates, bearing each the broad pendant of Sir Jas. Lucas Yeo, and Alert 18, and Myrmidon 20, both commanded by Capt. Henry John Leeke. He then, in Nov. 1821, passed his examination, but it was not until 9 April, 1828, that he succeeded in obtaining a commission. By that time he had further served, almost without interruption, in the Fly 18, Capts. Geo. Tyler and Edw. Curzon, Doris 42, Capts. Thos. Bourchier and Wm. Jas. Hope Johnstone, Prince Regent 120, bearing the flag of Sir Robt. Moorsom at Chatham, and Ranger 28, Capt. Lord Henry Fred. Thynne—all which ships, excepting the Prince Regent, were stationed in South America, where, from the date of his promotion, as above, until the early part of 1830, and again from 6 Oct. 1832, until he invalided in March, 1834, he was further employed on board the Cadmus 10, Capt. Sir Thos. Raikes Trigge Thompson, and Spartiate 76, bearing the flag of Sir Michael Seymour. His last appointment was 28 July, 1834, to the Winchester 52, flag-ship of Hon. Sir Thos. Bladen Capel in the East Indies, whence he returned home and was paid off in June, 1838. He attained his present rank 23 Nov. 1841.

LEAN. (Lieutenant, 1810. f-p., 18; h-p., 31.)

James Sedgwick Lean entered the Navy, in July, 1798, as Fst.-cl. Vol., on board the Kangaroo 18, Capt. Edw. Brace; and in the following Oct. was twice engaged, in a very gallant manner, with *La Loire* of 46 guns (part of a force originally under the orders of Commodore Bompart, and destined for the invasion of Ireland), previously to the surrender of that ship to the KANGAROO and her consort the ANSON 44. He continued in the same vessel until the close of 1800; and in Sept. 1804, after an intermediate servitude in the Channel and North Sea on board the CLYDE 38, Capts. Chas. Cunningham and John Larmour, he joined, as Midshipman, the CAMEL store-ship, Capts. Thos. Garth and John Joyce, under the latter of whom, having first visited the Mediterranean and Cape of Good Hope, he commanded a gun-boat during the unfortunate attempt made to recover Buenos Ayres in July, 1807. In the course of 1808 Mr. Lean became in succession Master's Mate, on the Home station, of the INVINCIBLE 74, Capt. Ross Donnelly, and REDPOLE 10, Capts. John Joyce and Colin M'Donald. While in the latter of those vessels we find him serving in the ZEPHYR fire-ship on the occasion of Lord Cochrane's memorable attack on the enemy's squadron in Aix Roads in April, 1809; and, among other services, commanding a boat on the river Scheldt during the siege of Flushing. Attaining the rank of Lieutenant 4 Jan. 1810, he served from that period until Dec. 1813 in the THRACIAN 18, Capts. Jas. Grant, John Lawson, Henry Hart, Joseph Symes, and John Carter, on the Channel and Baltic stations. His next appointment was, 4 Sept. 1826, to the Coast Blockade, in which service he continued for two years as Supernumerary-Lieutenant of the HYPERION 42, Capt. Wm. Jas. Mingaye.

Lieut. Lean at present holds the appointment of Emigration Agent in London.

LEARY. (LIEUT., 1821. F-P., 21; H-P., 17.)

GEORGE ALEXANDER LEARY died 31 Jan. 1845, a victim to the climate of Sierra Leone.

This officer entered the Navy, 1 Aug. 1807, as Schoolmaster, on board the DICTATOR 64, Capt. Donald Campbell; on accompanying whom, after he had attended the expedition to Copenhagen, into the AUDACIOUS 74, he took part, as Midshipman, in the operations of 1809 against Walcheren. From the period of his quitting the latter ship, in Dec. 1811, until May, 1814, Mr. Leary, with the exception of four months passed in 1813 on board the REDWING 18, Capt. Sir John Gordon Sinclair, served continuously with Capt. John Erskine Douglas in the PRINCE OF WALES 98, on the Mediterranean station, where he beheld Sir Edw. Pellew's two partial actions with the Toulon fleet, and the fall, in April of the latter year, of Genoa. During the short period of his attachment to the REDWING, Mr. Leary, besides sharing in a hostile operation under the batteries of Morgean, near Marseilles, assisted, we understand, in capturing, beneath those of Cassis, a convoy of 26 sail, together with 2 heavy gun-boats, after an opposition had been encountered which occasioned the British a loss of 4 men killed and 16 wounded. Removing, in May, 1814, to the FURIEUSE 36, Capt. Wm. Mounsey, he served during the next 15 months in that frigate on the coast of North America; after which we find him, until promoted to the rank of Lieutenant 19 July, 1821, employed on the West India, Mediterranean, and Home stations, in the PRIMROSE 18, Capt. Chas. Geo. Rodney Phillott, LANDRAIL 4, Master-Commander Anthony De Mayne (under whom he was for a considerable time occupied among the Bahama Islands as Assistant-Surveying Master), SALISBURY 50, flag-ship of Rear-Admiral Donald Campbell, FLY 18, Capt. Jas. Tomkinson, ROCHFORT 80, bearing the flag of Sir Graham Moore, GLASGOW 50, Capt. Hon. Anthony Maitland, QUEEN CHARLOTTE 100, Capt. John Baker Hay, and ROSE 18, Capt. Thos. Ball Clowes. His subsequent appointments were—8 Oct. 1830, for six months, to the Coast Blockade, as Supernumerary-Lieutenant of the TALAVERA 74, Capt. Hugh Pigot—31 May, 1831, to the Coast Guard, which he left at the close of 1832—16 Aug. 1837, to the HERCULES 74, Capt. John Toup Nicolas, off Lisbon—16 June, 1838, to the command of the BULLFROG schooner on the Lakes of Canada—next, as Senior, to the NIAGARA 20, commanded there by Capt. Williams Sandom, under whom he assisted, 16 Nov. 1838, in defeating a band of rebels, on which occasion he was sent with a flag of truce, and induced them to surrender—13 Jan. 1840 (having been superseded from the latter ship in the previous Oct.), to the command of the ASP, a Portpatrick steamer, wherein he remained until May, 1841—and 28 Jan. 1843, to the office (which he retained until his death) of Agent on board the GLEN HUNTLEY emigration transport.

LEATHART. (LIEUT., 1833. F-P., 13; H-P., 11.)

ALFRED LEATHART entered the Navy, 13 June, 1823, as Fst.-cl. Vol., on board the WINDSOR CASTLE 74, Capts. Chas. Dashwood, Hugh Downman, and Edw. Durnford King, employed at first in the Channel and off Lisbon, and then as a guard-ship at Plymouth. In July, 1827 (he had attained the rating of Midshipman in 1824) he removed to the VIGILANT 10, Lieut.-Commander Meredith; and he was next, between July and Aug. 1828, employed, again in the WINDSOR CASTLE, Capt. Hon. Duncombe Pleydell Bouverie, on the Mediterranean station; where, in the Downs, and on the coast of Portugal during the Pedro and Miguel disputes, he further, until promoted to the rank of Lieutenant 27 Aug. 1833, served on board the RAMILLIES and TALAVERA 74's, and CALEDONIA 120, Capts. Hugh Pigot, David Colby, and Thos. Brown. Mr. Leathart, who had passed his examination 7 Oct. 1829, was subsequently appointed—21 Feb. 1834, to the Coast Guard—and (on leaving the latter service) 13 Oct. 1836, to the WOLVERENE 16, Capt. Hon. Edw. Howard. He invalided home from the Mediterranean about June, 1837, and has since been on half-pay. AGENTS—Coplands and Burnett.

LECHMERE. (LIEUTENANT, 1815.)

EDMUND LECHMERE died 30 Jan. 1841, at Hereford. He was a relative of the present Lieut. John Lechmere, R.N.

This officer entered the Navy, 1 Feb. 1806, as Midshipman, on board the PRINCE 98, Capt. Wm. Lechmere, stationed off Cadiz. Removing, in the following Dec., to the ACASTA 40, Capt. Philip Beaver, he was for nearly three years employed in that ship on the West India station, where, in Feb. 1809, he witnessed the reduction of Martinique. After a short servitude in the Basque Roads on board the SCIPION 74, flag-ship of Hon. Robt. Stopford, he rejoined Capt. Beaver, in May, 1810, in the NISUS 38, and in the following Dec. was present, as Master's Mate, at the capture of the Isle of France, as also, in 1811, in the operations against Java. Quitting the NISUS, which had been latterly commanded by Capt. Chas. Marsh Schomberg, in May, 1813, Mr. Lechmere next, for a few months in 1814, served off Lisbon in the RODNEY 74, flag-ship of Vice-Admiral Geo. Martin. He attained the rank of Lieutenant 3 Feb. 1815, and was lastly, from April in that year until July, 1816, and from April, 1828, until March, 1829, employed in the Mediterranean in the SPARTAN 38, Capt. Phipps Hornby, and in the Coast Blockade as Supernumerary-Lieutenant of the RAMILLIES 74, Capt. Hugh Pigot.

LECHMERE. (LIEUT., 1815. F-P., 11; H-P., 31.)

JOHN LECHMERE, born 9 Jan. 1793, is eldest surviving son of the late Vice-Admiral Wm. Lechmere, of Steeple Aston, co. Wilts, by Elizabeth Dashwood, youngest daughter of Sir John Dashwood King, Bart., of West Wycombe, co. Bucks; younger brother of Commander Chas. Lechmere, R.N. (1815), who died on board H.M.S. LEVEN 9 Nov. 1822; brother-in-law of the present Lord de Saumarez; and a distant cousin of the late Lieut. Edm. Lechmere, R.N.

This officer entered the Navy, in April, 1805, as Midshipman, on board the THUNDERER 74, commanded by his father; after serving in which ship in Sir Robt. Calder's action he was lent, in time to participate in the battle of Trafalgar, to the ORION 74, Capt. Edw. Codrington. In Sept. 1806, having during the last few months been again employed with Capt. Lechmere in the PRINCE 98, and with Capt. Rich. Dalling Dunn in the ACASTA 40, he joined the ROYAL GEORGE 100, flag-ship of Sir John Thos. Duckworth, with whom, in Feb. 1807, he passed the Dardanells. In May, 1809, he followed the same Admiral into the SAN JOSEF 110; and between Oct. in that year and Dec. 1811 he served, we find, on the Cape of Good Hope, Lisbon, and Baltic stations, in the INCONSTANT 36, Capt. Edw. Stirling Dickson, FORMIDABLE 98, Capt. Jas. Nicoll Morris, and CRESSY 74, Capt. Chas. Dudley Pater. On 24 of the month last mentioned Mr. Lechmere was on board the GRASSHOPPER 18, Capt. Henry Fanshawe, when that vessel, to avoid being lost, as was her consort the HERO 74, surrendered to the Dutch fleet in the Texel. He accordingly remained a prisoner until the peace of 1814, when he returned to England, and, on 3 Feb. 1815, was promoted to the rank of Lieutenant. During the Hundred Days' War we find him employed on board the ASTRÆA 36, Capt. Edw. Kittoe, in which frigate he escorted to La Vendée the celebrated Larochejaquelin, with whom, owing to his knowledge of the French language, he was afterwards made the constant medium of communication. Three days before his death that personage did Mr. Lechmere the honour of extracting from him a musket-ball with his own hands; and he actually, in the presence of General Roget and other of his officers, promised him the Cross of St. Louis—an intention his premature death unfortunately prevented him from realizing. On one occasion, relying upon an assurance conveyed to him from his Admiral, to the effect that the latter would do all in his power towards procuring him his promotion, Mr. Lechmere, although warned from the same source that in so doing he exposed himself to the probability of being hanged by the Republicans as a spy, volunteered to land for the purpose of ascertaining the correctness of a report that the Royalist party had been surprised and entirely cut off. He accordingly went on shore, and, having satisfied himself that such was not the fact, returned on board with the pleasing intelligence. He still, however, remains a Lieutenant. His last appointment was, 19 Jan. 1816, to the DEE 24, Capt. Sam. Chambers, with whom he served on the Halifax station until Aug. 1817, when he invalided.

Lieut. Lechmere is a Deputy-Lieutenant for co. Oxford. He married, 3 March, 1823, Anna Maria, youngest daughter of the late Hon. Andrew Foley, M.P., of Newport House, co. Hereford, and Hately Court, Oxon, and cousin of the present Lord Foley. AGENT—J. Hinxman.

LECKIE. (LIEUTENANT, 1845.)

CHARLES TAYLOR LECKIE is nephew of Vice-Admiral Sir Chas. Malcolm.

This officer entered the Navy in 1834; passed his examination 14 Dec. 1840; served as Mate, from 1842 until 1844, in the THALIA 42, Capt. Chas Hope, on the Pacific station; and next joined, in that capacity, the HIBERNIA 104, bearing the flag in the Mediterranean of Sir Wm. Parker, who promoted him, 12 Nov. 1845, to a death vacancy in the INCONSTANT 36, Capt. Chas. Howe Fremantle, and, on presenting him with his commission on the quarter-deck of the HIBERNIA, informed him that he did so on account of his invariably good conduct, and because he possessed qualities which would do honour to the service. The INCONSTANT returned home and was paid off in 1847.

LECOUNT, F.R.A.S. (LIEUTENANT, 1827. F-P., 18; H-P., 20.)

PETER LECOUNT was born 25 May, 1794.

This officer entered the Navy, 29 Dec. 1809, as L.M., on board the THUNDER bomb, Capt. Wm. Shepheard, under whom he continued to serve, as Midshipman, in the COLUMBINE and COMET sloops until 1812. While in the THUNDER at the siege of Cadiz in 1810 he appears to have been not less than 45 times in action with the enemy, witnessing, during that period, the destruction of Fort Matagorda—sharing, also, in an engagement with Fort Napoléon, when one of the prison-ships, filled with *détenus*, had broken from her moorings and drifted under the enemy's fire, as likewise with Fort Catalina in an attempt to afford assistance to a Spanish 74 which had grounded near it—serving, too, in the boats when they were thrice beaten off in an effort to board the *Argonaut* 80, another prison-ship (ultimately burnt), which had got under the French batteries—engaging the enemy, next, while they were erecting a battery on the Trocadero—contributing, further, to the bringing out of the American schooner *Priscilla*, after the latter had been deserted by her crew under Catalina—and present in an attack made by the British flotilla on a strong detachment of gun-vessels on their way from Rota to Port Santa Maria. Among the numerous (many of them fierce) cutting-out affairs in which Mr. Lecount took part when in the COLUMBINE, was the capture, by three boats, after 40 had failed, of the *Guadalquiver* privateer, near San Lucar, on which occasion he lost the sight of his right eye and was slightly wounded in the right foot and left arm. In a previous expedition of the same nature every man in his boat had been either killed or knocked overboard. From 1812 until Feb. 1816, in the course of which month he passed his examination, Mr. Lecount (who had co-operated, we should state, in the defence of Tarifa, and been present at the battle of Barrosa) served with activity on the Home, Jamaica, and Newfoundland stations, in the CIRCE 32, Capt. Edw. Woolcombe, FYLLA 22, Capt. Wm. Shepheard (in which ship he assisted at the capture, in Jan. 1814, of *L'Inconnu* French privateer, of 15 guns and 109 men), HARLEQUIN 18, Capt. Wm. Kempthorne, and AFRICAINE 38, Capt. Hon. Edw. Rodney. He was subsequently appointed Admiralty-Midshipman—in April, 1816, of the MÆANDER 38, Capts. John Bastard and Arthur Fanshawe, stationed in the Channel—next, of the INFERNAL bomb, Capt. Hon. Geo. Jas. Percival, under whom he served at the bombardment of Algiers—in Oct. 1816, of the CONQUEROR 74, bearing the flag of Rear-Admiral Robt. Plampin at St. Helena—and, in Dec. 1820, of the QUEEN CHARLOTTE 100, Capts. Thos. Briggs, John Baker Hay, and J. Nash, lying at Portsmouth. On quitting the latter ship in April, 1824, Mr. Lecount became Admiralty-Mate of the PRINCE REGENT 120, bearing the flag at the Nore of Sir Robt. Moorsom, who, at the expiration of his command, most unexpectedly presented him, 6 Aug. 1827, with the hauling-down commission at his disposal. He has since been on half-pay.

Lieut. Lecount, a Civil Engineer, is the author, among other works, of a pamphlet entitled 'A Practical Treatise on Railways,' being an article which originally appeared under that head in the seventh edition of the *Encyclopædia Britannica;* also of three treatises on railway bearings; and of one on the polarization and inflection of light. An important dissertation, published by him in 1820, on Variable Magnetism, led to his being elected a Fellow of the Royal Astronomical Society while yet a Midshipman, the only instance of the kind known. He held an appointment for some time on the London and Birmingham Railway.

LEE. (LIEUTENANT, 1845.)

WILLIAM ALFRED ROSE LEE entered the Navy in 1828; passed his examination 26 Dec. 1837; and served as Mate, between 1840 and the early part of 1845, in the TWEED 20, Capt. Hugh Donald Cameron Douglas, EXCELLENT gunnery-ship, Capt. Sir Thos. Hastings, and HECLA steam-sloop, Capt. John Duffill, on the North America and West India, Home, and Mediterranean stations. He obtained his commission 30 Aug. 1845; and, from 3 of the following Sept. until the commencement of 1847, was employed in the KINGFISHER 12, Capts. Chas. Foreman Brown and Fred. Wilmot Horton, on the coast of Africa.

LEE. (LIEUTENANT, 1827. F-P., 16; H-P., 10.)

WILLIAM VALENTINE LEE, born 14 Feb. 1806, at Reculvers, co. Kent, is son of Lieut. Wm. Lee, R.N. (1796), who died 24 Feb. 1817, at the Telegraph, West Square.

This officer entered the Navy, 22 June, 1821, as Schoolmaster, on board the WYE 26, Capt. Peter Fisher, stationed in the North Sea; and, on removing with that officer to the RANGER 28, visited North America and the West Indies, and then the Mediterranean, where, in 1824, we find him employed as Midshipman under Sir Harry Neale at the blockade of Algiers. During the three following years he presents himself to our notice as serving at Sheerness, and again in the Mediterranean, on board the GLOUCESTER 74, Capts. Sir Edw. W. C. R. Owen and Joshua Sydney Horton, PHILOMEL 10, Capts. Wm. Paget and Viscount Ingestrie, and ASIA 84, bearing the flag of Sir Edw. Codrington. For his conduct as Mate of the HIND, tender to the latter ship, Lieut.-Commander John Robb, at the battle of Navarin, where he lost a leg, Mr. Lee was advanced to his present rank by commission dated 22 Oct. 1827. His next appointment was, 25 Oct. 1836, to the VICTORY 104, Capts. Thos. Searle, Fras. Erskine Loch, and Wm. Wilmott Henderson, under whom, in succession, he was for nearly six years and a half employed at Portsmouth. He has had charge, since 20 June, 1844, of the Semaphore station at Chelsea.

Lieut. Lee is in the receipt of a pension for his wound of 45*l.* 10*s.* He married, 4 Dec. 1828, Harriet, youngest daughter of John Pearce, Esq., of Haslar Hospital, by whom he has issue six children.

LEECH. (LIEUT., 1811. F-P., 12; H-P., 32.)

ROBERT LEECH entered the Navy, 9 March, 1803, on board the ETHALION 36, Capts. Chas. Stewart and Hon. Michael De Courcy, and, after serving for some time in the North Sea, proceeded to the West Indies; where, from March, 1806, until she was captured by two French privateers in April, 1807, he served, as Master's Mate and Acting-Master, in the ST. LUCIA 16, commanded at first by Capt. De Courcy and next by Capt. Chas. Gordon. Personally, Mr. Leech escaped falling into the hands of the enemy on the latter occasion through the providential circumstance of his having been placed, the night before, in charge of a prize.* Although still clinging to the rating of Midshipman, he further acted (on an assurance from the Commander-in-Chief, Sir Alex. Cochrane, that he would receive him as such on board his flag-ship as soon as he had served his time) as Master, for two years and three months, of the PULTUSK 16, Capts. Chas. Napier, Geo. Pringle, and David Sloan. During that period he assisted, it appears, at the reduction of the Danish islands of St. Thomas and Ste. Croix, was present in many gallant boat affairs under Capt. Napier (whom he aided in destroying a garda-costa on the Spanish main), and co-operated in the capture of Martinique. On one occasion, too, 12 Feb. 1809, he contrived, with two small boats, to cut out a French letter-of-marque brig, of 8 guns and 20 men, from under a battery on the island of Guadeloupe; an exploit which induced his Captain, Pringle, to forward a recommendation in his favour to Sir Alex. Cochrane. In the following July, as had been agreed, he at length joined that officer, as a Supernumerary-Midshipman, on board the POMPÉE 74; and on 14 Sept. in the same year he passed his examination. After witnessing the destruction, in L'Ance la Barque, of the 40-gun frigates *Loire* and *Seine*, Mr. Leech, in Feb. 1810, united in the operations against Guadeloupe, where he served on shore in command of a party of seamen, and was present at the storming of the forts of Matuba. In July, 1810, at the request of his former Captain, Sloan, our officer, who had accompanied Sir Alex. Cochrane into the NEPTUNE 98, was nominated Acting First-Lieutenant of the BELLETTE 18; from which sloop, on her sailing, in the ensuing Oct., for England, he was removed, in a similar capacity, to the AMARANTHE 18, commanded by another of his old Captains, Geo. Pringle. The state of discipline into which he soon brought that vessel was such that, on the occasion of a visit of inspection from Sir Francis Laforey, the new Commander-in-Chief, he had the satisfaction of receiving the thanks of that Admiral—his Captain generously acknowledging that to him alone was the credit due. Continuing in the AMARANTHE until superseded in April, 1811, he proved himself a second time worthy of a strong recommendation from Capt. Pringle for his behaviour during the latter month in an arduous five days' chase of a national brig, who had hitherto been the destruction of British trade, but who, although she effected her escape, was so battered as to be afterwards incapable of further mischief. On leaving the AMARANTHE, as above, Mr. Leech returned, at his own expense, to England, and on his arrival was immediately promoted to the rank of Lieutenant by commission dated 26 July, 1811. His next appointment was, 21 Sept. following, to the EDINBURGH 74, Capts. Robt. Rolles, Rowland Mainwaring, Hon. Geo. Heneage Lawrence Dundas, and John Lampen Manley, with whom he continued to serve, in the North Sea and Mediterranean, until the close of 1814. While under Capt. Dundas, we find him, in 1813, commanding the EDINBURGH's boats at the capture of Port d'Anzo, and of a large convoy under its batteries; and also at the destruction of the batteries at Via Reggio, the reduction of Lucca, and the unsuccessful attack on Leghorn, where, after landing the troops, he took command of the EDINBURGH's small-arm men. In 1814, being again in charge of the boats of the same ship, Lieut. Leech destroyed all the batteries and towers along the coast of Italy from Via Reggio to the Gulf of Spezia. He next, when at Lerici, took possession of the castle at that place, and successfully defended it against a party of French troops, having previously blown up a large fort and destroyed the arsenal. At the subsequent siege of the fortress of St. Mary, the Lieutenant was there invested with the command of a battery, and had the honour of opening the first fire. On the advance of the squadron towards Genoa, Mr. Leech, owing to the absence of Capt. Dundas and the First and Second Lieutenants, was left in sole charge of the ship, and while so intrusted waited upon Lord Wm. Bentinck, the military Commander-in-Chief, at the time on board the AMERICA 74, Capt. Josiah Rowley. For this he obtained the thanks of Capt. Dundas in his public despatches.* The EDINBURGH returned to England after the fall of Genoa, and was put out of commission in Dec. 1814; since which period, unable to procure employment, Lieut. Leech has been on half-pay.

* He had, however, left all his effects behind him.

* *Vide* Gaz. 1814, p. 180.

LEEKE, Kt., K.H. (CAPTAIN, 1826. F-P., 17; H-P., 27.)

SIR HENRY JOHN LEEKE is son of Sam. Leeke, Esq., a Magistrate and Deputy-Lieutenant for co. Hants, who lost his life from the effects of over-exertion in the suppression of a riot; and brother-in-law of Rear Admiral Sir Edw. Tucker, K.C.B., and of Capt. W. B. Bigland, R.N., K.H. One of his brothers was killed in command of a gun-boat at the defence of Cadiz; and another carried the colours of the 52nd Light Infantry at the battle of Waterloo.

This officer entered the Navy, 28 Sept. 1803 (under the auspices of his godfather Lord Henry Paulet), as Fst.-cl. Vol., on board the ROYAL WILLIAM, Capt. John Wainwright, bearing the flag of Admiral Montagu at Spithead. In the course of 1806 he successively joined the IRIS 32, Capt. John Tower, VILLE DE PARIS and ROYAL SOVEREIGN, both commanded by Capt. Henry Garrett, and TERRIBLE 74, Capt. Lord Henry Paulet; as Midshipman of which latter ship, and the VOLONTAIRE 38, Capt. Chas. Bullen, we find him continuously employed off Cadiz and in the Mediterranean until January, 1810. Previously to leaving the VOLONTAIRE, he had an opportunity, besides commanding one of her boats at the destruction of a French vessel near Marseilles, of serving with those of a squadron which, on the night of 31 Oct. 1809, captured and destroyed, after a fearful struggle and a loss to the British of 15 men killed and 55 wounded, the French store-ship *Lamproie*, of 16 guns and 116 men, bombards *Victoire* and *Grondeur*, and armed xebec *Normande*, with a convoy of seven merchant-vessels, lying under the protection of numerous strong batteries in the Bay of Rosas.* Between the period of his advancement to the rank of Lieutenant, which took place while he was serving with Capt. Sam. Martin Colquitt on board the PERSIAN sloop, 24 Nov. 1810, and the receipt of his second promotal commission, bearing date 15 June, 1814, he was again employed in the Mediterranean, and also at the Cape of Good Hope, in the VOLONTAIRE and CAMBRIAN frigates, each under the orders of Capt. Chas. Bullen, LION 64, flag-ship of the late Sir Chas. Tyler, HARPY sloop, Capt. Allen, and MEDWAY 74, bearing the flag of Sir C. Tyler. On one occasion, while the PERSIAN, with a host of French prisoners on board, was off Cape Trafalgar on her passage home, the latter, availing themselves of the absence of the crew (who, worn out by fatigue, had all, with the exception of Mr. Leeke, the Quartermaster, and two men, gone below), assembled on the deck, and were in the act of making a rush aft, when Mr. Leeke seized a cutlass, threw another to the Quartermaster, and with much gallantry succeeded in keeping them off until the alarm had brought the ship's company to his assistance. On 26 March, 1819, after he had had the command for about six months of the ALERT sloop, and had served as the senior officer of a small squadron ordered to escort the Grand Duke Michael to Calais, Capt. Leeke was appointed to the MYRMIDON 20, on the western coast of Africa, where he cruized with great activity against the slave-trade, and either liberated, or contributed to the release of, upwards of 3000 human beings. In May, 1820, having the command at the time of H.M. ships MYRMIDON, MORGIANA, THISTLE, and SNAPPER, he landed at the Pongas, in the neighbourhood of Sierra Leone, and, at the head of only 170 seamen and marines, added to 180 black soldiers of the 2nd West India Regt., contrived to burn eight towns, to demolish a battery, and to effect the utter defeat of a barbarian force of 5000 men, commanded by King Munga-Brama, a ruffian who had murdered an officer and several men belonging to the THISTLE, and had retained three others as prisoners. The combination, indeed, of skill, perseverance, prudence, and bravery exhibited by Capt. Leeke, proved the means of not only recovering the captives, but of saving the colony itself from much anarchy and bloodshed. Correspondent, therefore, with the importance of the exploit were the terms of gratitude on the one hand, and of admiration on the other, with which its achievement was hailed by Brigadier-General Sir Chas. M'Carthy, the Governor of Sierra Leone, and Sir Geo. Ralph Collier, the Commodore of the squadron employed on that station. In Sept. 1820 Capt. Leeke suppressed a mutiny which had broken out on board a Brazilian sloop-of-war, *Les Trois Royaumes Unis*, and then restored the vessel to her Commander. He next succeeded by his exertions in saving a Portuguese schooner from being wrecked in the Sierra Leone river; and on a subsequent occasion he carried the MYRMIDON over the fearful bar of the river Dunny for the purpose of attacking two slave-vessels who had beaten off his boats and had wounded two officers and several men. After he had accomplished their capture, he compelled the King of that part of the country to enter into a treaty fixing the duty to be paid by British merchants trading to the river for palm-oil—an arrangement which in particular saved many thousands per annum to the importers of Liverpool. During the three years that he remained on the African station, Capt. Leeke surveyed the coast to the extent of 600 miles. When afterwards in the HERALD yacht, to which vessel he was appointed 31 May, 1824, he made a voyage to St. Petersburg, conveyed the Bishops of Jamaica and Barbadoes to their respective sees, brought upwards of a million of dollars home from the Havana, took the Earl of Dalhousie out to Quebec, and landed the Marquess of Hastings at Malta. He attained his present rank 27 May, 1826; and, on 18 Oct. 1845, after having held for a short period the command of the CALLIOPE 26, was appointed to the QUEEN 110, in which ship, now bearing the flag of Sir John West, Commander-in-Chief at Devonport, he has repeatedly cruized with experimental squadrons.

* *Vide* Gaz. 1809, p. 1908.

Sir H. J. Leeke, a Magistrate for cos. Hants and Sussex, and a Deputy-Lieutenant for the former, received the honour of Knighthood, as a reward for his eminent services on the coast of Africa, 1 April, 1835, and was nominated a K.H. 25 Jan. 1836. In acknowledgment of some good offices he had the fortune to render the King of the French when a Midshipman, he has been presented by that monarch with a gold medal; as he has also been by the King of Prussia. Sir Henry married, 13 Nov. 1818, the second daughter of Jas. Dashwood, Esq., of Parkhurst, co. Surrey. AGENTS—Messrs. Stilwell.

LEFEBVRE. (COMMANDER, 1838. F-P., 19; H-P., 17.)

NICHOLAS LEFEBVRE entered the Navy, 18 Jan. 1811, as a Volunteer, on board the VICTORY 100, Capt. Philip Dumaresq, bearing the flag of Sir Jas. Saumarez in the Baltic; and in the following Dec. was on his passage home in company with the ST. GEORGE and DEFENCE when those ships were lost. Becoming Midshipman, in July, 1812, of the ETHALION 36, Capts. Edm. Heywood and Wm. Hugh Dobie, he was, for some time prior to Dec. 1814, employed on the North American and Irish stations. He then removed, as Master's Mate, to the ZENOBIA sloop, Capt. Nicholas Chas. Dobree, and while in that vessel had the misfortune, during the war of a hundred days, to be taken prisoner by the French. Contriving soon to effect his escape, he rejoined the ZENOBIA, and was in her when she escorted Napoleon Buonaparte to St. Helena. Previously to the return of the latter vessel to England he landed, it appears, at Ascension with a party of marines from the flag-ship, and was for some length of time employed on shore. We subsequently, from April, 1816, until Sept. 1818, and from Feb. 1819, to Jan. 1822, find Mr. Lefebvre serving on the Leith and North American stations on board the DRIVER 18, Capts. John Ross and Chas. Hope Reid, and NEWCASTLE 60, flag-ship of the late Sir Edw. Griffith Colpoys. He next, in July, 1823, joined the SPARTIATE 76, and, in Aug. 1825, the WELLESLEY 74, bearing each the flag of Sir Geo. Eyre in South America; whence, in the following Nov., he returned to England on board the TARTAR 42, Capt. Thos. Brown. On 3 Jan. 1826, nearly nine years after he had passed his examination, Mr. Lefebvre was promoted to the rank of Lieutenant. In the course of the ensuing month he obtained an appointment to the BRITANNIA 120, flag-ship of Sir Jas. Saumarez at Plymouth, where he remained until April, 1827; and he was lastly, from 9 June, 1834, until paid off in Oct. 1838, employed, as First-Lieutenant, in the ZEBRA 16, commanded by Capt. Robt. Contart M'Crea (whom see), on the East India and South Sea stations. For his gallant conduct during that period, and more especially for the zealous perseverance he exhibited in the boats when in quest of pirates, Mr. Lefebvre, on the earnest recommendation of the Commander-in-Chief, Sir Thos. Bladen Capel, was promoted to the rank of Commander by commission dated 27 Dec. 1838.

Commander Lefebvre has been presented by the Royal Humane Society with a medal as a reward for his conduct in having frequently saved the lives of seamen.

LE FEUVRE. (Retired Commander, 1839. F-P., 14; H-P., 34.)

John Le Feuvre was born 16 April, 1786.

This officer (whose name had been borne, from 24 April, 1794, to 3 Dec. 1795, on the books of the Royal William, flag-ship at Portsmouth of Sir Peter Parker) embarked, 12 July, 1799, as a Volunteer, on board La Juste 80, Capt. Sir Henry Trollope; and in July of the following year, being then in the Andromeda 32, Capt. Henry Inman, witnessed the capture of the French frigate *La Désirée;* to which, on her being soon afterwards added to the British Navy, he was transferred, as Midshipman, with Capt. Inman, under whom he took a warm part, 2 April following, in the action off Copenhagen. Continuing to serve in La Désirée, with Capts. Rich. Dacres, Chas. Bayne Hodgson Ross, and Henry Whitby, until 1804, Mr. Le Feuvre (besides assisting in the ship's barge at the capture, on 21 Feb. in the latter year, of a French armed row-boat) was present, in 1803, at the blockade of Cape François, the reduction of Port Dauphin, where two forts and a 28-gun ship, *La Sagesse*, were taken from the enemy, and the capture of the French squadron with the remains of General Rochambeau's army on board from Cape François. Previously to the surrender of *La Sagesse* he appears to have accompanied the First-Lieutenant on board that vessel in the capacity of interpreter. In July, 1804, we find him transferred to the Theseus 74, bearing the flag of Vice-Admiral Jas. Rich. Dacres; and, in the following Sept., present in a violent hurricane in which the latter ship lost her three lower masts and tiller, sprang her bowsprit, had all her boats stove or washed away, parted with 13 of her guns, and sprang so bad a leak that the officers even were obliged to work at the pumps. On 7 Oct. 1805, being then with Admiral Dacres in the Hercule 74, Mr. Le Feuvre was appointed Sub-Lieutenant of the Pitt schooner, Lieut.-Commander Michael Fitton; from which vessel, however, he removed as Acting-Lieutenant, on 30 of the same month, to the Veteran 64, Capt. Andw. Fitzherbert Evans. Being confirmed in the rank of Lieutenant by commission dated 31 March, 1806, he was subsequently appointed, in that capacity—13 June, 1806, to the Fisgard 36, Capt. Sir Wm. Bolton, still in the West Indies, where, immediately prior to the brilliant capture of Curaçoa, he was sent for (having been at the island before) by Capt. Brisbane, and interrogated as to the strength of Fort Amsterdam—10 Dec. 1807 (after rather more than seven months' half-pay), to the Ranger 18, Capt. Geo. Acklom, under whom he assisted at the reduction of the island of Anholdt in May, 1809—30 Nov. 1809 and 14 May, 1810, to the Clio 10, Capt. Thos. Folliott Baugh, and Adamant 50, flag-ship of Rear-Admirals Sir Edm. Nagle and Wm. Albany Otway, both on the Leith station—and, lastly, 6 July, 1813, to the Severn 40, Capt. Joseph Nourse, which frigate he left, after having made a voyage from Deptford to Portsmouth, in the following Nov. He accepted his present rank, 15 July, 1839.

LEGARD, K.T.S. (Commander, 1838.)

James Anlaby Legard passed his examination in 1825; and for his services at the battle of Navarin was made Lieutenant, 22 Oct. 1827, into the Brisk 10, Capt. Thos. Smith. His succeeding appointments were—2 March, 1829, to the Infernal bomb, Capts. Popham and Orlando Geo. Sutton Gunning, on the Mediterranean station—30 Aug. 1832 (after two years of half-pay) to the Ætna 6, Capt. Edw. Belcher, employed in the river Douro for the protection of British property during the civil war—14 May, 1833, as Senior, to the Volage 28, Capts. Geo. Bohun Martin and Peter Richards, in which ship, with the exception of a short time passed at the close of 1835 in the Caledonia 120, under the flag of Sir Josias Rowley, he served in the Mediterranean for three years and a half—and, 18 Jan. 1837, in a similar capacity, again to the Caledonia. He was paid off in the following summer; and on 28 June, 1838, was advanced to his present rank. He has since been on half-pay.

Commander Legard, in 1844, obtained the royal permission to accept and wear the insignia of a K.T.S.

LE GEYT, C.B. (Rear-Admiral, 1846. F-P., 21; H-P., 35.)

George Le Geyt, born 20 March, 1777, at Canterbury, co. Kent, is son of the late Robt. Le Geyt, Esq., of that place (first-cousin of the late Vice-Admiral d'Auvergne, Prince de Bouillon), by Jane, daughter of the Rev. Wm. Byrch, Rector of St. Mary's, Dover, and of Mongham, also in co. Kent. His grandfather and great-grand-uncle both held the office of Chief Civil Magistrate of the Royal Court and President of the States of Jersey.

This officer entered the Navy, in March, 1791, as Captain's Servant, on board the Colossus 74, Capt. Henry Harvey, lying at Spithead. Being discharged in the following Aug., he next, in March, 1792, joined the Hussar 28, Capt. Rupert George, and sailed for the Halifax station, where he assisted at the capture of the two privateers *Républicain* and *Jou-jou.* On the former of those vessels being brought into the service, named the Prince Edward, and the command given to Lieut. John G. Saville, we find Mr. Le Geyt appointed to her as Master's Mate, and in that capacity witnessing, 17 May, 1795, the capture, by a force under the orders of Capt. Hon. Alex. Cochrane, of two French ships, *La Prévoyante* of 24, and *La Raison* of 18 guns. After their surrender, he went on board *La Prévoyante*, and aided in fitting her with jurymasts. That frigate being subsequently added to the British Navy, Mr. Le Geyt continued in her under the command of Capt. John Poo Beresford, until the spring of 1796, and was twice sent into port in charge of detained vessels. He then removed to the Resolution 74, bearing the flag of Vice-Admiral Geo. Murray, under whom he was further present, 28 Aug. 1796, at the capture of the French frigate *Elisabeth.* On 5 of the following Nov. Mr. Le Geyt was nominated Acting-Lieutenant of the Rover 16, Capt. Geo. Irvine, in which vessel (being confirmed to her 27 Jan. 1797) he remained, assisting intermediately at the taking of *Le Jean Bart*, a noted privateer, until wrecked in a fog in the Gulf of St. Lawrence in Aug. 1798. On his return, immediately afterwards, to England in the Resolution, Capt. Wm. Lechmere, our officer, who had then been for upwards of six years on the Halifax station, was at once, at the request of Capt. John Holloway, of the St. George 98, appointed to that ship. Removing as Second-Lieutenant, in March, 1799, to the Tamar, of 46 guns and 281 men, Capt. Thos. Western, he proceeded soon with the flag of Lord Hugh Seymour, to the West Indies, where, besides contributing to the reduction of Surinam, he served at the capture, among numerous other vessels, of *La Républicaine* French national corvette, of 32 guns and 175 men (after a close action of about 10 minutes, a loss to the enemy of 9 killed and 12 wounded, and to the British of only 2 wounded); also of *Le Général Masséna*, ship privateer, of 16 guns (pierced for 18) and 150 men; and of a schooner privateer of 10 guns and 50 men. Towards the close of 1801 (he had been the last year and a half First-Lieutenant of the Tamar) Mr. Le Geyt joined the Leviathan 74, bearing the flag at Jamaica of Sir John Thos. Duckworth, who promoted him, 28 May, 1803, to the command of the Stork 18—an act which the Admiralty approved. While in that sloop, in which he continued upwards of nine years, Capt. Le Geyt effected the capture, 24 Feb. 1804, of the French national schooner *Coquette* of 2 guns and 95 men, after a chase of 265 miles,* and, on 30 of the ensuing month, of *L'Hirondelle* privateer, of 3 guns and 44 men. In Aug. 1806 he was sent with a small squadron, consisting, besides his own vessel, of the Supérieure sloop, and Flying-Fish and Pike schooners, to attack a number of small vessels lo-

* *Vide* Gaz. 1804, p. 518.

cated at Batabano, in the island of Cuba. Although the STORK, from her draught of water, was unable to approach within 30 leagues of the place, the objects of the expedition were nevertheless fully accomplished by the other vessels, aided by her boats, under the command of Capt. Edw. Rushworth.* In 1807 Capt. Le Geyt was ordered with convoy to England, whence, in 1808, after he had been for some months employed on the Guernsey station, he took out the Pope's Nuncio to the Brazils. Returning next to the West Indies, he united in the blockade of Martinique, and was so employed until its surrender. While off that island, on 12 Dec. 1808, he co-operated with the CIRCE 32, Capt. Fras. Augustus Collier, and MORNE FORTUNÉE gun-brig, and displayed much coolness and intrepidity, in silencing the fire of two batteries and of a body of troops which protected an enemy's schooner aground between the Pearl Rock and the town of St. Pierre; and he then, in company with the CIRCE and EXPRESS schooner, commenced an action with four adjoining batteries, under which lay two other vessels, one of whom, *Le Cygne* corvette, 16 guns, was in the end destroyed.† In April, 1809, being on a cruize with the CIRCE, then commanded by Capt. Edw. Woollcombe, the STORK fell in with a French squadron of three line-of-battle ships and two frigates, steering for the Saintes. With the intelligence of this she was instantly despatched to the Commander-in-Chief; the result whereof was the capture of the 74-gun ship *D'Haupoult*. On 12 Aug. 1812, Capt. Le Geyt, at that time on the Cork station, was at length advanced to Post-rank. Unable, however, to procure further employment, he accepted, 1 Oct. 1846, the rank he now holds.

The Rear-Admiral was nominated a C.B. 4 July, 1840. He married, in 1812, Rose Marie, daughter of the late Rear-Admiral Heath, by whom he has issue 11 children. AGENTS—Messrs. Stilwell.

* *Vide* Gaz. 1806, p. 1537. † *V.* Gaz. 1809, p. 146.

LE HARDY, K.S.F., K.I.C. (COMMANDER, 1837. F-P., 20; H-P., 9.)

THOMAS PHILIP LE HARDY, born 1 May, 1803, is a native of Jersey, where his family for many centuries past has occupied a prominent position. Three of his ancestors attained Flag-rank. One of them was Sir Thos. Hardy, whose decisive conduct, when in command of H M.S. PEMBROKE, led to the action off Vigo under Sir Geo. Rooke 11 Oct. 1702; and another, Sir Chas. Hardy, who commanded the Channel fleet, and died Governor of Greenwich Hospital about 1780.

This officer entered the Navy, 1 Aug. 1818, as Fst.-cl. Vol., on board the CONFIANCE 18, Capt. Alex. Montgomerie; and sailed for the West Indies, where, until 1823, he served, the last three years as Midshipman, in the SYBILLE 48, Capt. Wm. Popham, ONTARIO 18, Capt. Jodrell Leigh, and SYBILLE again, Capt. Joshua Ricketts Rowley. From Dec. 1823 until May, 1827, we find him employed on the South American, Irish, and Jamaica stations, as Midshipman, Mate, and Acting-Lieutenant (he passed his examination in April, 1825), on board the TWEED 28, Capt. Fred. Hunn. He was then for four months engaged on home duty in the MELVILLE 74, Capt. Henry Hill; and at the expiration of that period he proceeded to the coast of Africa as Mate of the PRIMROSE 18, Capt. Thos. Saville Griffinhoofe. On his removal there, in Jan. 1829, to his old ship the SYBILLE, bearing the broad pendant at the time of Commodore Fras. Augustus Collier, Mr. Le Hardy was sent to cruize, as Senior Mate, in the BLACK JOKE tender, mounting but 1 gun, a long 18-pounder on a pivot, with a crew of 34 men, Lieut.-Commander Henry Downes. In that vessel it was soon his fortune to participate in a most brilliant exploit; nothing less than the capture of the Spanish slaver *El Almirante*, of 14 guns (10 eighteens and 4 long nines) and 80 men, after 11 hours had been absorbed in sweeping up, and a close action endured of 80 minutes, in which the British had 3 men killed and 7 wounded, and the enemy 15 killed and 13 wounded. Mr. Le Hardy, who was himself wounded, and who appears to have shared in two other engagements, was rewarded for his valour on the occasion by a commission dated 2 May, 1829. He did not, however, succeed in obtaining a fresh appointment until Nov. 1833; on 20 of which month he assumed command of the SARACEN brig, of 10 guns. Being ordered at first to the coast of Portugal, we find him serving for some time at Lisbon and off Oporto during the contest between Pedro and Miguel; and afterwards sent to the north coast of Spain, where he was actively employed with the squadron under Lord John Hay, particularly on the Bilboa river. For his conduct at the relief of that city in Dec. 1836, he not only received, in common with others, the thanks of the Admiralty, but was promoted to the rank of Commander 6 Jan. 1837, and presented by the Queen of Spain with the Third Class of the Order of San Fernando, as also with the Companionship of the Order of Isabella la Catolica, and a decoration commemorative of the event. He left the SARACEN in April, 1837; was employed, next, in the Coast Guard, from 13 July, 1838, until July, 1843; and since 4 June, 1846, has been in command of the FANTOME 16, in the Mediterranean.

Commander Le Hardy married, in Nov. 1833, Louisa Jane, second daughter of Chas. de la Garde, Esq., of Jersey. AGENTS—Coplands and Burnett.

LE HUNTE, K.F.M. (COMMANDER, 1814. F-P., 11; H-P., 36.)

FRANCIS LE HUNTE entered the Royal Naval Academy 1 Nov. 1800, and, after a course of more than four years' study at that institution, embarked, 18 April, 1805, as a Volunteer, on board the NEMESIS 28, Capt. Philip Somerville, stationed in the Channel, where, from Sept. 1806 to April, 1808, he cruized as Master's Mate in the NARCISSUS 32, Capt. Chas. Malcolm. The next nine months were employed by this officer in the PALLAS 32, Capt. Geo. Fras. Seymour, on the coast of Spain. In July, 1811, exactly two years after he had passed his examination, he received, with the rank of Acting-Lieutenant, an appointment to the Sicilian flotilla at Messina. His confirmation took place 26 Sept. following; and on 15 Feb. 1813 we find him serving on shore in command of a party of seamen, and co-operating with the troops under Brigadier Hall, in an attack upon a strong body of the enemy, consisting of a complete battalion, with two troops of cavalry and two pieces of artillery, located at Pietra Nera, on the Calabrian coast. On that occasion he stormed and carried, in a very gallant style, several obstinately defended batteries, and by his exemplary conduct attracted as well the admiration of the Brigadier as the observation both of soldiers and sailors.* He was afterwards sent with a division of gun-boats to guard the island of Ponza; and in March and April, 1814, being attached to the expedition against Genoa and its dependencies, he particularly distinguished himself by his gallant and able conduct at the reduction of the enemy's forts in the Gulf of Spezia.† During the short war of 1815, Commander Le Hunte, who had been advanced to his present rank on 15 June in the preceding year, was selected to serve in the river Scheldt with a brigade of seamen under the orders of Capt. Chas. Napier. After the overthrow of Napoleon he assumed command, 20 June, 1815, of the EREBUS 16, and retained it, in the Downs, until 4 Sept. following. He has since been on half-pay.

In consideration of the valour and intrepidity he had displayed at Pietra Nera, Commander Le Hunte was presented by the King of the Two Sicilies with the insignia of the Small Cross of the Order of St. Ferdinand and of Merit. AGENT—Joseph Woodhead.

* The enemy at Pietra Nera had upwards of 150 men killed and wounded, and 163 taken prisoners. The loss of the British was very trifling.—*Vide* Gaz. 1813, p. 726.

† *V.* Gaz. 1814, p. 984.

LEIGH. (Retired Commander, 1833. f-p., 24; h-p., 40.)
Benjamin Leigh died 22 Feb. 1846.

This officer entered the Navy, in 1782, as Fst.-cl. Boy, on board La Fortunée, Capt. Hugh Cloberry Christian, and cruized, until the peace of 1783, on the coast of North America. He served next, from 1786 to 1792, part of the time as Midshipman, in the Atalante sloop, Capts. Delgano, Schomberg, Halsted, Foote, and Elphinstone, on the East India station; and after a further attachment to the Alcide 74, and, as Acting-Lieutenant, to the Spitfire sloop, was confirmed, 10 March, 1795, into the Hornet sloop, Capts. Wm. Lukin and Robt. Larkan, in which vessel he made a voyage to St. Helena. His subsequent appointments were—27 Dec. 1796, to the Minerva frigate, Capt. Thos. Peyton, in the Channel—28 Sept. 1797, to the Inflexible, Capt. Ferris, on the Downs station—28 June, 1799, to La Juste 80, Capt. Sir Henry Trollope, which ship a serious injury compelled him to leave in the following year—for a short time in 1801, to the command of the Crown prison-ship at Portsmouth—and, in 1804, to the charge of a signal station in the Isle of Wight, where he remained until 1814. He became a Retired Commander, on the Senior List, 10 Jan. 1833.

He was father-in-law of the present Commander Geo. Caswell, R.N.

LEIGH. (One of the Junior Lieutenants.)
Frederick George Leigh entered the Navy 16 Sept. 1831; passed his examination 2 Dec. 1835; and, after having served as Mate in the Medea steamer, commanded in the Mediterranean by Capt. Fred. Warden, and Caledonia 120, flag-ship of Sir Graham Moore at Plymouth, was promoted to the rank of Lieutenant 7 Feb. 1842. His succeeding appointments were—16 March, 1842, as Additional, to the Driver steam-vessel, Capt. Sam. Fielding Harmer, in the East Indies—25 Aug. 1842, to the Apollo troop-ship, Capt. Chas. Frederick, with whom he returned to England in 1843—and, 5 Feb. 1845, to the Stromboli steam-sloop, Capt. Thos. Fisher. On 25 Sept. following he was dismissed his ship by sentence of court-martial, and placed for two years at the bottom of the List of Lieutenants, for having over abused and punished the stoker. Agents—Goode and Lawrence.

LEIGH. (Captain, 1829. f-p., 20; h-p., 26.)
Jodrell Leigh, baptized 27 Feb. 1790, at Goosetrey, is third son of the late Egerton Leigh, Esq., of the West Hall, High Leigh, co. Cheshire, by Elizabeth, daughter and co-heiress of Fras. Jodrell, Esq., of Yeardsley and Tremlow, in the same co. He is brother-in-law of Lord Dunfermline, formerly the Hon. Jas. Abercromby, M.P., Speaker of the House of Commons; and also of John Smith, Esq., of Dale Park, co. Sussex, youngest brother of Lord Carrington, and M.P., in 1833, for Buckinghamshire.

This officer entered the Navy, 14 July, 1801, as Fst.-cl. Vol., on board the Malta 80, Capt. Albemarle Bertie, attached to the Channel fleet. Becoming Midshipman, in 1802, of the Leander 50, he continued to serve in that ship on the Halifax station under Capts. Jas. Oughton, Fras. Wm. Fane, Alex. Skene, John Talbot, and Salusbury Pryce Humphreys, until Aug. 1806; and was in consequence present with Capt. Talbot at the taking, 23 Feb. 1805, of *La Ville de Milan* French frigate, of 46 guns, and the simultaneous recapture of her prize the Cleopatra 32. In Aug. 1806 Mr. Leigh followed Capt. Humphreys into the Leopard 50; and in April, 1807, he was nominated Acting-Lieutenant of the Bermuda 18, Capt. Wm. Henry Byam; in which vessel (being confirmed to her 29 Feb. following) he continued until wrecked on the Memory Rock, Little Bermuda, 22 April, 1808. His next appointment was, 22 Aug. in the same year, to the Melampus 36, Capt. Edw. Hawker, under whom, during a servitude of three years and a half, we find him assisting at the capture of the French ships of war *Le Colibri*, of 16 guns and 92 men, and *Le Beauharnais*, of 16 guns and 109 men, and co-operating in the reduction of Guadeloupe Quitting the Melampus in Feb. 1812, Mr. Leigh further served, between that period and March, 1820, on the Channel, Newfoundland, Cork, St. Helena, and Jamaica stations, in the Mars 74, Capt. Henry Raper, Dryad 36, Capt. Edw. Galwey, Bonne Citoyenne 20, Capts. Pitt Burnaby Greene and Augustus Wm. Jas. Clifford, Falmouth 20, Capts. Robt. Worgan Geo. Festing and Geo. Fred. Rich, and Sybille 44, bearing the flag of Sir Home Popham. He then assumed the acting-command of the Bann 20, also in the West Indies, where, soon after his official promotion, which took place 12 June following, he removed to the Ontario 18. He returned to England, after a dreadfully tempestuous passage, in Dec. 1821; and was lastly appointed, 28 Feb. 1829, to the Royal Charlotte yacht, Capt. Hon. Josceline Percy. He attained his present rank 2 June in the same year.

LEIGH. (Commander, 1835. f-p., 22; h-p., 21.)
Thomas Leigh died in 1846.

This officer entered the Navy, 3 June, 1803, as a Volunteer, on board the Conqueror 74, Capts. Thos. Louis and Israel Pellew; under the latter of whom, after pursuing the combined squadrons of France and Spain to the West Indies and back, he shared in the action off Cape Trafalgar 21 Oct. 1805. Being discharged from the Conqueror in Jan. 1806, he served during the next eight years, as Midshipman and Master's Mate, in the Melampus 36, Capts. Stephen Poyntz and Edw. Hawker, Porgey schooner, Lieut.-Commander Hugh Goold, Bellona 74, Capt. John Erskine Douglas, Pilot 18, Capt. John Toup Nicolas, Royal George 100, flag-ship of Rear-Admiral Fras. Pickmore, and Impétueux, Stately, and Rodney, bearing each the flag of Vice-Admiral Geo. Martin, on the North American, Home, Mediterranean, and Lisbon stations. While in the Pilot, Mr. Leigh served, 25 July, 1810, in her boats, with those of the Thames 32, and Weasel 18, and was officially alluded to for his conduct, at the very gallant capture and destruction, near Amanthea, notwithstanding a most spirited opposition, of 31 transports, seven large gun-boats, and five armed vessels.* He was confirmed a Lieutenant, 26 Jan. 1814, in the Bristol troop-ship, Capt. Geo. Wyndham, employed in the Channel and off Lisbon, and was subsequently appointed—in the course of 1815, to the Havock 12, Capt. Geo. Truscott, Rifleman 16, Capts. Henry Edw. Napier and Geo. Bennet Allen, and Vengeur 74, Capt. Thos. Alexander, all on the Home station, where he served, until superseded from ill health in May, 1818—and, 4 Dec. 1827, to the Coast Guard. He left that service, on attaining the rank of Commander, 23 June, 1835; and remained thenceforward on half-pay. Agents—Coplands and Burnett.

LEITH. (Captain, 1825. f-p., 20; h-p., 24.)
John Leith, born at Leith Hall, co. Aberdeen, the seat of his father, is second son of the late General Alex. Leith Hay, by Mary, daughter of Chas. Forbes, Esq., of Ballogie; brother of the present Sir Andw. Leith Hay, Kt., of Rannes and Leith Hall, a Lieut.-Colonel in the Army, and M.P. for the Elgin district of burghs; and nephew of Lieut.-General Sir Jas. Leith, G.C.B., K.T.S., Grand Cordon of the Order of Merit of France, Governor of Barbadoes, and Commander-in-Chief of the forces in the Windward and Leeward Islands, who died 16 Oct. 1816.

This officer entered the Navy, 11 June, 1803, as Fst.-cl. Vol, on board the Lapwing 28, Capt. Alex. Skene, which vessel, when soon afterwards off the banks of Newfoundland, was so closely chased for three days by the French 74-gun ship *Duguay Trouin* and 40-gun frigate *Guerrière*, that, in order to effect her escape, she was under the ne-

* *Vide* Gaz. 1810, p 1860.

cessity of throwing overboard her guns, boats, all her anchors and cables but one, and all but one week's provisions and water. In Oct. of the same year he removed with Capt. Skene to the LEANDER 50, commanded next by Capts. John Talbot, Henry Whitby, and Salusbury Pryce Humphreys; and, on 23 Feb. 1805, he was present, under Capt. Talbot, at the capture of *La Ville de Milan* French frigate of 46 guns, and re-capture of her prize the CLEOPATRA 32. Following Capt. Humphreys, in Aug. 1806, into the LEOPARD 50, Mr. Leigh was in that ship on 22 June, 1807, when she compelled the U. S. frigate *Chesapeake* to surrender, in consequence of a refusal on the part of the latter to allow the British to search her for deserters. In April, 1808, he joined the TRIUMPH 74, Capt. Sir Thos. Masterman Hardy, and after serving, as Master's Mate, in the North Sea and at the blockade of L'Orient, became attached with that officer to the BARFLEUR 98, bearing the flag off Lisbon of Hon. Geo. Cranfield Berkeley, who, on 26 June, 1809, nominated him Acting-Lieutenant of the NORGE 74, Capts. Edm. Boger and John Sprat Rainier. In the course of the same summer we find Mr. Leith engaged in fitting out some Spanish men-of-war at Ferrol, then threatened by the French. In the following Oct., on 10 of which month he was confirmed a Lieutenant, he went back to the BARFLEUR, and on the promotion, in Dec. 1810, of the present Capt. Berkeley, succeeded him in the office of Flag-Lieutenant. Previously, however, to that event, he had been invested with the command (which he retained until the final expulsion of the French army under Masséna from Portugal) of the telegraph posts on the lines of Torres Vedras. During the last siege of Badajos Mr. Leith, it appears, was present at the head-quarters of Lord Wellington; and in April, 1811, he was there when it was stormed and carried. The BARFLEUR being ordered home in 1812, he was next (after an interval of a few months, the first he had enjoyed since his entrance into the Navy) appointed, in April, 1813, to the SCEPTRE 74, Capt. Chas. Bayne Hodgson Ross, flag-ship of Rear-Admiral Geo. Cockburn; previously to accompanying whom into the ALBION 74, he took part in the attack upon Hampton, the capture of Ocracoke and Portsmouth islands (whence were brought off the *Anaconda* of 20, and *Atlas* of 12 guns), the occupation of Kent Island, and other services. In June, 1814, he returned to England on board the ST. DOMINGO 74. He attained the rank of Commander 13 June, 1815, but was not again employed until Sept. 1822, on 4 of which month we find him appointed to the BELLETTE 18, fitting for the West Indies, where he removed, 28 June, 1825, to the PYLADES 18, was appointed, 28 June following, Acting-Captain of the ISIS 50, and was confirmed, 11 Nov. in the same year, into the RATTLESNAKE 28. Being paid off on his return home with the Duke of Manchester, late Governor of Jamaica, in Sept. 1827, Capt. Leith remained on half-pay until appointed, 6 Feb. 1837, to the SERINGAPATAM 46, in which frigate he was again ordered to the West Indies, there to take charge of the Barbadoes station. On his passage out he took with him the ROMNEY 50, destined to form a *dépôt* for liberated negroes at the Havana, where he succeeded in installing her after encountering much opposition from the governor. With the exception of a visit to Jamaica, on the occasion of Sir John Strutt Peyton being sent home in 1838, he remained senior officer at Barbadoes until July, 1841, when he sailed for Halifax to recruit his own health and that of his crew. Before his departure, however, he had the satisfaction of being presented with an address and a piece of plate by the inhabitants. He invalided at last from Halifax in Oct. 1841; and has since been on half-pay.

Capt. Leith is married, and has issue.

LEITH. (LIEUTENANT, 1815. F-P., 10; H-P., 33.)

LOCKHART LEITH entered the Navy, 24 July, 1804, as Midshipman, on board the DEVASTATION bomb, Capt. Alex. Milner, and, until discharged in the following Dec., was employed off Boulogne and in the Downs. Re-embarking, in July, 1806, on board the MONARCH 74, Capt. Rich. Lee, we find him, in company with a squadron under Sir Sam. Hood, at the capture, 25 Sept. following, of four heavy French frigates from Rochefort, on which occasion the above ship enacted a very conspicuous part, compelled *La Minerve*, of 44 guns and 650 men, to surrender, and sustained a loss of 4 men killed and 25 wounded. The MONARCH, it appears, was afterwards employed in blockading the Tagus, in escorting, towards the close of 1807, the Royal Family of Portugal to the Brazils, and in the expedition to the Walcheren in Aug. 1809. In Dec. 1811 Mr. Leith removed to the MARLBOROUGH 74, Capt. Matt. Henry Scott, stationed off Flushing and in the Channel, where he served until Aug. 1812. In the following month, the latter officer having hoisted his flag in the CHATHAM 74, he rejoined him on board that ship, in which he continued employed, under Capts. Wm. Lukin and David Lloyd, on the Home and Cork stations, until July, 1815. He then took up a commission dated on 10 of the previous March; and has not been since afloat.

LEITH. (COMMANDER, 1814. F-P., 16; H-P., 35.)

WILLIAM FORBES LEITH entered the Navy, 18 Dec. 1796, as A.B., on board the PRINCE GEORGE 98, Capt. Wm. Bowen, bearing the flag of Rear-Admiral Wm. Parker, with whom he continued to serve, in the Channel, off Cadiz and Lisbon, and in the Mediterranean, as Midshipman of the BLENHEIM 98, and again of the PRINCE GEORGE, until Sept. 1799. During the next three years and a half we find him employed, on the Home station, in the AMETHYST frigate, Capts. Cook, Glynn, and Campbell; and, on 7 May, 1804, after having for a few months acted as Lieutenant of the MALTA 80, and GANGES 74, Capts. Edw. Buller and Thos. Fras. Fremantle, formally promoted to that rank. His succeeding appointments were—19 June, 1804, to the NEMESIS 28, Capt. Philip Somerville, lying at Plymouth—16 April, 1805, to the DRUID 32, in which frigate, commanded by Capts. Broke, Astley, Bennett, Mackay, Bolton, and Louis, he served for nearly six years on the Cork and Cadiz stations, and assisted at the capture of *Le Pandour* national brig of 18 guns and 114 men—and 30 Sept. 1811, to the REPULSE 74, Capt. Rich. Hussey Moubray, attached to the force in the Mediterranean, whence he invalided in Jan. 1813. He attained his present rank 15 June, 1814; and has since been on half-pay.

LE MESURIER. (LIEUTENANT, 1815. F-P., 10; H-P., 30.)

EDWARD LE MESURIER entered the Navy, in Sept. 1807, as Fst.-cl. Vol., on board the INCONSTANT 36, Capt. Edw. Stirling Dickson, in which ship and in the DIOMEDE 50, and VICTORY 100, all flag-ships of Sir Jas. Saumarez, he continued to serve as Midshipman, on the Guernsey station, until April, 1810. He then joined the EURYALUS 36, commanded off Toulon by Hon. Geo. Heneage Lawrence Dundas, and after a short attachment to the VILLE DE PARIS 110, Capt. John Duff Markland, was received, in March, 1811, on board the UNITÉ 36, Capt. Edwin Henry Chamberlayne; under whom, on 1 of the following May, he assisted, in company with the POMONE 38, and SCOUT 18, at the destruction, after a gallant action of an hour and a half in Sagone Bay, of the store-ships *Giraffe* and *Nourrice*, each mounting from 20 to 30 guns, and both protected by a 5-gun battery, a martello tower, and a body of about 200 regular troops. On 29 May in the same year we find him further contributing to the capture, at the close of a severe running fight of four hours, of the 26-gun store-ship *La Persanne*, supposed, until the moment of her capture, to be a fully armed frigate. Removing, in July, 1814, to the UNDAUNTED 38, Capt. Chas. Thurlow Smith, Mr. Le Mesurier was present, in that ship, during the war of 100 days, at the reduction of the Tremiti islands and the cutting out of a convoy from Barletta. On being paid off in Oct. 1815, he took up a commission dated on 24 of the preceding March. His last appointment was, 19 March, 1816, to the FLORIDA 24, Capts. Wm. Elliott and Chas. Sibthorpe John Hawtayne, stationed in the North Sea, where he was superseded at his own request 16 Oct. 1817. AGENT—J. Hinxman.

LE MESURIER. (LIEUTENANT, 1824. F-P., 16; H-P., 22.)

FREDERICK HENRY LE MESURIER, born 1 Sept. 1795, is brother of Lieut.-General Le Mesurier, late Governor of Alderney.

This officer entered the Navy, 13 Jan. 1809, as Fst.-cl. Vol., on board the DAPHNE 20, Capt. Philip Pipon, stationed in the Baltic, where, in the same ship, and as Midshipman in the VICTORY 100, bearing the flag of Sir Jas. Saumarez, he served until March, 1812. He then sailed for the East Indies in the THEBAN 36, Capt. Stephen Thos. Digby, which frigate, when in the China Sea in the following Sept., had the misfortune to be dismasted in a typhoon. On his return to England with Capt. Digby in the CORNWALLIS 74, Mr. Le Mesurier, in Oct. 1813, joined the AMPHION 32, Capts. Jas. Pattison Stewart and John Brett Purvis, and, until the close of the American war, was employed at Bermuda. For a short period in the summer of 1815, in May of which year he passed his examination, we find him on duty at Portsmouth in the PRINCE 98, Capt. Edm. Boger. Being appointed, in July, 1816, Admiralty-Midshipman of the FURY bomb, Capt. Constantine Rich. Moorsom, he assisted in that vessel at the bombardment of Algiers; after which, and until confirmed in his present rank, 12 Nov. 1824, he served in the same capacity, and also as Acting-Lieutenant, in the SEVERN 40, Capt. Hon. Fred. Wm. Aylmer, MYRMIDON 20, Capt. Robt. Gambier, VENGEUR 74, Capt. Fred. Lewis Maitland, NIEMEN 28, Capt. Edw. Reynolds Sibley, RAMILLIES 74, Capt. Edw. Brace, ANDROMACHE frigate, Capt. Joseph Nourse, and ESPIÈGLE 18, Capt. Isham Fleming Chapman—on the Home, Mediterranean, American, and Cape of Good Hope stations. He continued to officiate as Lieutenant of the latter vessel until July, 1825, when. being at the time at the Mauritius, he was compelled to invalid and return to England in consequence of the repeated attacks of a severe complaint which for the last ten years has completely laid him up. From 10 April, 1826, until May, 1827, Mr. Le Mesurier served at Plymouth in the BRITANNIA 120, flag-ship of Sir Jas. Saumarez.

He married, 11 Sept. 1828, Jane Catherine, only daughter of the late Thos. Cecil Maunsell, Esq., of Thorpe Malsor, co. Northampton, by whom he has issue five sons.

LEMPRIERE. (Captain, 1825.)

GEORGE OURRY LEMPRIERE obtained his first commission 25 May, 1807; was advanced to the rank of Commander 30 Jan. 1813; procured an appointment to the TRENT hospital and receiving ship at Cork 7 May, 1814; acquired the rank of Captain 27 May, 1825; and accepted the Retirement 1 Oct. 1846.

Capt. Lempriere has been twice married—the second time, 10 Aug. 1833, to Frances, daughter of Wm. Dumaresq, Esq., of Pelham Place, Hampshire. He has issue.

LE NEVE. (LIEUT., 1814. F-P., 9; H-P., 32.)

ANSELM PETER LE NEVE entered the Navy, 25 Dec. 1806, as L. M., on board the MAJESTIC 74, Capts. Geo. Hart, Valentine Collard, Matthew Forster, Fred. Watkins, and Thos. Harvey. While in that ship, which bore the flag of Vice-Admiral Thos. Macnamara Russell, we find him present as Midshipman at the surrender of Heligoland in Sept. 1807, and afterwards employed in escorting the trade through the Great Belt, where he constantly came into collision with the Danish gun-boats. Removing, in Feb. 1810, to the GRAMPUS 50, Capt. Wm. Hanwell, he accompanied a convoy in that ship to China; on his return whence, in Dec. 1811, he joined the MAIDSTONE 36, Capts. Geo. Burdett and Wm. Skipsey, with whom, until Dec. 1814, he served as Master's Mate on the North American station. He then took up a commission bearing date 25 July in the latter year; and was lastly, from 24 Nov. 1815 until 6 June, 1816, employed with Capts. Wm. Skipsey and Edw. Chetham, in the LEANDER 50, on Home service. AGENT—Joseph Woodhead.

LENNOCK. (RETIRED COMMANDER, 1845. F-P., 19; H-P., 35.)

CHARLES ADAM LENNOCK entered the Navy, in May, 1793, as Fst.-cl. Vol., on board the VETERAN 64, Capt. Chas. Edm. Nugent; and sailed, towards the close of the same year, with the expedition intended for the reduction of the French West India Islands. In Aug. 1794, being at the time in the SANTA MARGARITA 36, Capt. Eliab Harvey, we find him assisting at the apparent destruction, near the Penmarcks, of the French 36-gun frigate *Volontaire*, and corvettes *Espion* and *Alert*. After again serving with Capt. Nugent, as Midshipman, in the CÆSAR 80, and POMPÉE 74, and with Capt. Fras. Pickmore in the ROYAL WILLIAM, Mr. Lennock, in March, 1796, joined the ASSISTANCE 50, Capt. Henry Mowat, on the North American station, where he witnessed the capture, 28 Aug. following, of the French frigate *Elisabeth* of 36 guns, and where he continued to serve as Master's Mate in the ASIA 64, Capt. Robt. Murray, and as Acting-Lieutenant and Lieutenant (order and commission respectively dated 16 April and 29 Nov. 1800), in the ST. ALBANS 64, Capt. John Okes Hardy, until the peace of Amiens. His subsequent appointments were—28 Oct. 1802, to the Sea Fencibles—14 Sept. 1804, to the ST. ALBANS again, Capt. John Temple, on the Home station—22 Aug. 1805, to the STANDARD 64, Capts. Thos. Harvey, Aiskew Paffard Hollis, and Joshua Sydney Horton, in which ship, during a continuance of five years and a half, he assisted at the passage of the Dardanells, and the reduction of the island of Anholdt—22 April, 1811, to the BULWARK 74, also commanded by Capt. Horton, and employed at the defence of Cadiz—and 7 Dec. following, to the COURAGEUX 74, Capt. Philip Wilkinson, stationed in the Baltic, where he remained until May, 1813. He was placed on the Junior List of Retired Commanders 26 Nov. 1830; and on the Senior 11 Sept. 1845.

LENNOCK. (Captain, 1814. F-P., 29; H-P., 29.)

GEORGE GUSTAVUS LENNOCK entered the Navy, in April, 1789, as Captain's Servant, on board the BLANCHE frigate, Capt. Robt. Murray, with whom he was for three years employed in the West Indies, latterly in the capacity of Midshipman. Returning to the same station (after he had been for a short time attached on Home service to the JUNO 32, Capt. Sam. Hood) in the VETERAN 64, Capt. Chas. Edm. Nugent, he there co-operated in the reduction of the French Islands, and afterwards joined the BOYNE 98, flag-ship of Sir John Jervis. He was made Lieutenant, 8 May, 1795, into the SHARK sloop, Capt. John O'Brien, at Newfoundland; and was subsequently appointed—11 Nov. 1795, to the ASSISTANCE 50, Capt. Henry Mowat, under whom he witnessed the capture, 28 Aug. 1796, of the French 36-gun frigate *Elisabeth*, off Cape Henry—21 April, 1798, to the RESOLUTION 74, bearing the flag at Halifax of Vice-Admiral Vandeput—11 Aug. following, to the ASIA 64, Capts. Robt. Murray and John Dawson, employed, until the peace, on the same station and in the Baltic and North Sea—28 Sept. 1802, to the AMBUSCADE *alias* SEINE 36, Capts. Hon. John Colville and David Atkins, in one of whose boats, on his return to the West Indies, he was severely wounded in an attempt to cut a privateer out from St. Jago*—and in 1805-6, to the

* He obtained, in consequence, a gratuity from the Patriotic Society.

acting-command of the SHARK, DRAKE, and MIGNONNE sloops, on the Jamaica station. While in the latter vessel Mr. Lennock was confirmed a Commander by commission dated 6 Aug. 1806. He returned to England, after having further had command of the MUSETTE and MOSELLE sloops, in Feb. 1809; and was next, in Oct. of that year, appointed to the RAVEN 16, attached to the force in the North Sea. On 3 July, 1812, in face of the enemy's fleet at Flushing, and under the very guns of that enemy's forts, Capt. Lennock made a dashing attack on 14 brigs (each armed with 3 or 4 long 24-pounders) and drove three of them on shore. His quickness, indeed, in deciding upon this exploit, and his skill and spirit in executing it, obtained him very high approbation.* His last appointment was, 21 Jan. 1814, to the ESK corvette, of 20 guns; in which vessel we find him continuously employed off the Canary Islands, and in the Channel and South America, until paid off in Dec. 1818. During the earlier part of that period Capt. Lennock (whose Post commission bears date 4 June, 1814) effected the capture of the *Sine-quâ-non* American privateer, of 7 guns and 81 men, and fought a smart action, off Teneriffe, with two other American vessels, the *Grampus* and *Terpsichore*. He accepted the Retirement 1 Oct. 1846.

Capt. Lennock married, in 1829, Anna, eldest daughter of J. Walker, Esq., of Crawford Town, by whom he has issue.

* *Vide* Gaz. 1812, p. 1319.

LEROUX. (RETIRED COMMANDER, 1844. F-P., 17; H-P, 37.)

FREDERICK JAMES LEROUX entered the Navy, in Nov. 1793, as Fst.-cl. Vol., on board the CHARON hospital-ship, Capt. Geo. Countess, whom, after sharing in Lord Howe's action 1 June, 1794, he successively followed as A.B., Midshipman, and Master's Mate, into the PEGASUS 28, DÆDALUS 32, ETHALION 38, and ROBUST 74. In those ships he served on the North Sea, West India, Channel, and Cork stations until the commencement of the year 1800; and, while in the ETHALION, was present, on the coast of Ireland, at the capture, 12 Oct. 1798, of the French 40-gun frigate *La Bellone*, after a sharp conflict and a trifling loss to the British. On 25 April, 1800, being at the time a Supernumerary of the ROYAL GEORGE 100, flag-ship of Lord Bridport, Mr. Leroux was promoted to a Lieutenancy in the ASTRÆA *armée-en-flûte*, Capts. Peter Ribouleau and Alex. Campbell, under the former of whom he won the Turkish gold medal for his services in Egypt. Quitting the ASTRÆA in Dec. 1801, he was subsequently appointed—12 March, 1803, to the UTRECHT 64, flag-ship on the Home station of Admirals Montagu, Patton, and Holloway—31 Dec. 1804, to the RAMILLIES 74, Capt. Fras. Pickmore, in which ship he beheld the capture, 13 March, 1806, of the *Marengo* 80, bearing the flag of Admiral Linois, and 40-gun frigate *Belle Poule*—17 Sept. and 3 Oct. 1808 (having invalided from the RAMILLIES in June, 1806), to the CORDELIA 10, and BOMBAY 74, Capts. Thos. Fortescue Kennedy and Wm. Cuming, on the Home and Mediterranean stations—5 Nov. 1809, to the FAME 74, Capts. Bennett, Hornby, Ferris, and Bathurst, also in the Mediterranean—and, lastly, 19 Nov. 1811 (eight months after his return to England), to the command (which he retained until 6 June, 1814) of the GANGES prison-ship at Plymouth. He became a Retired Commander on the Junior List 26 Nov. 1830; and on the Senior 15 Nov. 1844.

LESLIE. (REAR-ADMIRAL, 1846. F-P., 32; H-P., 22.)

SAMUEL LESLIE, born in March, 1779, at Rockfield, co. Antrim, is son of the late Ven. Edm. Leslie, Archdeacon of Down, by his second wife, Eleanor, daughter of Geo. Portis, Esq., of London; and descends from a noble Hungarian family who settled in North Britain in 1067. His grand-aunt, Penelope, wife of E. F. Stafford, Esq., was mother of the first Viscountess Dungannon, and grandmother of the late Countess of Mornington, mother of the Duke of Wellington.

This officer entered the Navy, in May, 1793, as Ordinary, on board the POMONA 28, Capt. Henry d'Esterre Darby; and until the early part of 1794 was employed, chiefly in the capacity of Midshipman, in annoying the enemy's coasting-trade, a service which frequently brought him under fire of the batteries on the French shore. During the next three years we find him cruizing, at first with Capt. Darby, and then with Capt. Wm. Hotham, in the ADAMANT 50, on the West India, Newfoundland, and Lisbon stations. On next joining the IMPÉTUEUX 74, Capt. John Willett Payne, Mr. Leslie served for many months at the blockade of Brest; after which, on being again placed under the orders of Capt. Darby in the BELLEROPHON 74, he fought as Master's Mate at the battle of the Nile 1 Aug. 1798. In the summer of 1799, as soon as he had passed his examination, he was received on board the FOUDROYANT 80, bearing the flag of Lord Nelson, who, as a reward for his conduct in having volunteered in a heavy gale of wind to recover one of the ship's boats which had broken adrift in Palermo Bay, nominated him, in the following Nov., Acting-Lieutenant of the SUCCESS 32, Capt. Shuldham Peard. While in that frigate, to which he was not confirmed until 16 Oct. 1800, Mr. Leslie served at the blockade of Malta, assisted at the capture, on 18 Feb. and 24 Aug. in the latter year, of the French 74-gun ship *Le Généreux*, and 40-gun frigate *La Diane*, and was on board her when she was herself taken, 13 Feb. 1801, by a French squadron under M. Ganteaume. Being soon exchanged, he joined, in the ensuing May, the HAERLEM 64, Capts. Geo. Burlton, John Stuart, John Geo. Saville, and — Northey, with whom he continued in the Mediterranean until the close of 1802. After a servitude of two years and five months at Newfoundland and among the Western Islands, in the CAMILLA 20, Mr. Leslie, in Sept. 1805, was appointed to LA CHIFFONNE 36, Capts. Patrick Campbell and John Wainwright; which frigate was at first employed in attendance on George III. off Weymouth, and afterwards at the blockade of Cadiz, and in the Mediterranean and East Indies. Previously to his departure for the latter station, Mr. Leslie, it appears, took part in many cutting-out affairs, and on one occasion had 2 men killed and 3 wounded in a boat under his immediate orders. In Nov. 1809, being then Senior of LA CHIFFONNE, he accompanied an expedition conducted by Capt. Wainwright and Lieut.-Colonel Lionel Smith against the pirates of the Persian Gulf. During the attack which was there made upon Ras-al-Khyma, the stronghold of the freebooters, he distinguished himself in a very remarkable manner. In the first place, he burnt, within twice her own length of the shore, the *Minerva*, an English ship, which had some time before fallen into their hands.* Besides being very active in the cannonade of the place, he also, with excellent judgment and gallantry, executed, on the northern end of the town, a feint, which had the effect of facilitating the main attack on the southern end; and he then, while the operations of the troops were in progress, performed much valuable service with the gun-boats attached to his ship. In the course of the same day, Nov. 13, he set fire to all the dows which were afloat in the harbour, and was of further essential assistance in the re-embarkation of the military. The active and unwearied nature of Mr. Leslie's services, indeed, was such as to call forth, together with a warm recommendation on his behalf for promotion, the strongest expressions of admiration and gratitude from the Lieutenant-Colonel, and a most glowing panegyric from his own Captain. He was not, however, in any way rewarded until Jan. 1811, when at length the Commander-in-Chief promoted him into the WILHELMINA hospital-ship at Poulo-Pinang — an appointment which the Admiralty confirmed 1 March following. On 31 July, 1812, exactly four months after he had been nominated Acting-Captain

* *Vide* Gaz. 1810, p.1022.

of the SIR FRANCIS DRAKE frigate, Capt. Leslie, who afterwards assumed command of the MALACCA 36, VOLAGE 22, and THEBAN 36, was officially advanced to Post-rank. While in the VOLAGE we find him heading a party of seamen belonging to H.M.S. HUSSAR, and co-operating, 28 June, 1813, with a detachment of troops under Colonel Watson, in an attack upon the defences of Sambas, a piratical state on the western coast of Borneo, where, after six hours' march in an almost impenetrable jungle, five batteries were in succession assaulted and carried with the utmost intrepidity. His zeal and gallantry in this instance also obtained for him the congratulations of his senior officer, Capt. Geo. Sayer, and the thanks of the Commander-in-Chief, Sir Sam. Hood. He was slightly wounded on the occasion in each leg. In Sept. of the same year the Captain, then under the orders of Hon. Geo. Elliot of the HUSSAR, with whom was employed a body of troops under Lieut.-Colonel Macgregor, proved a chief instrument to the re-establishment of the Nagor Ordeen on the throne of Palambang, precluding, by the greatness of his expedition and efforts, and the completeness of the surprise he produced on the enemy, the possibility of resistance. Proportionate, of course, were the acknowledgments of Sir Sam. Hood; to whom, on removing, in Jan. 1814, to the THEBAN, he became Flag-Captain. He subsequently commanded a squadron in the Java seas. He paid the THEBAN off in April, 1816; and was lastly, from April, 1823, until April, 1832, employed as an Inspecting Commander in the Coast Guard. His advancement to the rank he now holds took place 1 Oct. 1846.

The Rear-Admiral is a Magistrate for co. Down. He married, in Sept. 1817, Martha, only daughter of the late Geo. Vaughan, Esq., the descendant of an old English family.

LESLIE. (LIEUT., 1814. F-P., 17; H-P., 27.)

WALTER LESLIE entered the Navy, 1 Oct. 1803, as Fst.-cl. Vol., on board the HAZARD sloop, Capt. R. J. Neve, stationed in the Channel; and, in Nov. 1804, removed to the NIOBE 40, Capts. Matthew Henry Scott and John Wentworth Loring, under the latter of whom, on 28 March, 1806, he witnessed the capture of the French corvette *Le Néarque* of 16 guns and 97 men. Rejoining Capt. Scott, in the following July, as Midshipman, in the DRAGON 74, he sailed in that ship for the West Indies; on his return whence, in Dec. 1808, he was received on board the ACHILLE 74, Capt. Sir Rich. King. After co-operating in the defence (during the siege of Cadiz) of Fort Matagorda, where he was wounded, Mr. Leslie, in July, 1810, became Acting-Lieutenant of the TÉMÉRAIRE 98, bearing the flag on that station of Rear-Admiral Fras. Pickmore. He went back, however, in the following Oct., to a Midshipman's berth in the ACHILLE; and he was next, from Feb. 1811 until March, 1813, employed in the North Sea as Master's Mate of the MARLBOROUGH 74, Capt. M. H. Scott, and CHRISTIAN VII. 80, and IMPREGNABLE 98, flag-ships of Admiral Wm. Young, by whom, for a few weeks in the former year, he was lent, as Acting-Lieutenant, to the BRITOMART sloop, Capt. Wm. Buckley Hunt. He then repaired to the Canadian lakes, where he joined in an attack on the enemy's army and flotilla, and continued to serve as Lieutenant (commission dated 24 Aug. 1814) of the PRINCE REGENT and ST. LAWRENCE, bearing the broad pendants of Commodore Sir Jas. Lucas Yeo and Edw. W. C. R. Owen, until Sept. 1815. His last appointment was to the PENGUIN, a Falmouth packet, the command of which he retained from 5 Nov. 1841 until Nov. 1846.

LESTER. (RETIRED COMMANDER, 1846. F-P., 30; H-P., 17.)

WILLIAM LESTER is brother of Lieut. Jas. Lester, R.N. (1827), who died in 1844, while commanding the LAPWING Revenue-vessel.

This officer entered the Navy, 20 April, 1800, as Fst.-cl. Vol., on board the WINDSOR CASTLE 98, Capts. Albemarle Bertie and Jas. Oughton, bearing the flag for some time of Sir Andrew Mitchell in the Channel, where he served until April, 1802—the last seven months in the capacity of Midshipman. Re-embarking, in the following June, on board the BITTERN 18, Capt. Robt. Corbet, he was at first employed in that vessel in cruizing against the smugglers on the Yorkshire coast; after which he proceeded to the Mediterranean, and there assisted at the capture, 10 Sept. 1803, and 28 April, 1804, of the French privateers *La Caille*, of 6 guns and 60 men, and *L'Hirondelle*, of 14 guns and 80 men—the latter at the close of an arduous chase with the sweeps during a calm of nearly two days. After further serving for a short time with Capt. Corbet in the AMPHITRITE frigate, he removed with him, in June, 1805, to the SEAHORSE, of 42 guns and 281 men, commanded subsequently by Capt. John Stewart, under whom, on the night of 5 July, 1808, we find him contributing to the capture, after a signally furious engagement, and a loss to the SEAHORSE (30 of whose crew were absent) of 5 men killed and 10 wounded, of the Turkish man-of-war *Badere Zaffer*, mounting 52 guns, with a complement of 543 men, of whom 170 were killed and 200 wounded. The *Alis Fezan*, of 26 guns and 230 men, a ship which had been also opposed to the SEAHORSE, was at the same time put to flight. Being declared by his Captain very worthy of promotion for his conduct on the occasion,* Mr. Lester was accordingly awarded a commission bearing date 6 of the same month, and appointed to the NETTUNO 18, Capt. Chas. Fred. Payne. In the early part of 1809, however, he rejoined the SEAHORSE, and while in that ship, in which he remained until 1811, assisted in taking several privateers, co-operated in the reduction of the islands of Gianuti and Pianoza, and commanded the boats at the capture of a large armed merchant-ship on the Roman coast. When afterwards in the FURIEUSE 36, Capt. Wm. Mounsey, he witnessed the conquest of the island of Ponza 26 Feb. 1813—commanded her boats (having gallantly volunteered to do so), in conjunction with Lieut. Walter Croker, at the cutting out, 4 Oct. following, with a loss to the British of 2 men killed and 10 wounded, of 14 out of a convoy of 19 vessels, protected, in the harbour of Marinelo, by the galling fire of 2 gun-boats, a fort of 2 long 24-pounders, and a strong fortified tower and castle†—destroyed a privateer under the batteries of Orbitello—was again in charge of the boats during the unsuccessful attack upon Leghorn—beheld the occupation of Santa Maria and of the enemy's other forts in the Gulf of Spezia—and aided at the reduction of Genoa and its dependencies in March and April, 1814. He left the FURIEUSE in Aug. 1815; and was lastly, from 24 June, 1824, until Jan. 1839, employed as an Agent for Transports afloat. He accepted his present rank 6 Feb. 1846.

When Commander Lester was a Midshipman of the BITTERN, that sloop had her main-topmast and mizen top-gallantmast carried away in a squall in the Faro of Messina, in clearing away the wreck of which he sustained an injury that procured him on his arrival in England a pension of 4*l*. This ceased on his promotion to the rank of Lieutenant, but was restored to him in 1843. We may add that when in the FURIEUSE he was on one occasion left at the island of Milo in charge of 14 sail of prizes. He is married.

LETCH. (RETIRED COMMANDER, 1837. F-P., 16; H-P., 33.)

CHARLES LETCH was born in Nov. 1782.

This officer entered the Navy, 8 July, 1798, as Fst.-cl. Vol., on board the DRAGON 74, Capts. Geo. Campbell, Fred. Lewis Maitland, John Aylmer, and Edw. Griffith, in which ship he continued to serve, as Midshipman and Master's Mate, in the Channel and also in the Mediterranean (where he attended the expedition of 1801 to Egypt), until nominated, in Jan. 1805, Sub-Lieutenant of the DARING gun-

* *Vide* Gaz. 1808, p. 1438. † *V.* Gaz. 1814, p. 123.

brig, Lieut.-Commander Chas. C. Ormsby, then at Portsmouth. He was made Lieutenant, 19 March, 1805, into the ALBACORE sloop, Capt. Major Jacob Henniker, but, exchanging back a few months afterwards into the DRAGON, continued in that ship, which was latterly commanded by Capt. Matthew Henry Scott, until paid off at the close of 1808. He then became First-Lieutenant of the PLOVER 18, Capt. Philip Browne, with whom (following him in July, 1811, into the HERMES 20) we find him employed, on the Home and South American stations, until the end of the war. He assisted during that period at the capture of many privateers, and was in the PLOVER in the expedition to the Walcheren, where he served under the broad pendant of the present Sir Geo. Cockburn, who, both personally and by letter, expressed his acknowledgments for the meritorious conduct he had displayed. He accepted his present rank 15 July, 1837. AGENTS—Messrs. Chard.

LETHBRIDGE. (LIEUTENANT, 1827. F-P., 19; H-P., 19.)

JOHN LETHBRIDGE was born 24 Nov. 1793.

This officer entered the Navy, 11 Feb. 1809, as Fst.-cl. Vol., on board the FREDERICKSTEIN 32, Capt. Joseph Nourse, on the Mediterranean station, where he followed the same Captain as Midshipman into the VOLONTAIRE 38, and continued, latterly in the HIBERNIA 120, Capt. Edw. Kittoe, until Aug. 1811. He then returned to England with Capt. Robt. Waller Otway in the CUMBERLAND 74; and towards the close of the year, having been received on board the ANDROMACHE 38, Capt. Geo. Tobin, proceeded off the north coast of Spain. While there he served at the blockade of St. Sebastian, preparatory to its reduction, and, on 23 Oct. 1813, assisted at the capture of *La Trave*, of 44 guns and 321 men, which ship surrendered, after a short but smart action, and a loss of 1 man killed and 28 wounded. In the spring of 1814 Mr. Lethbridge participated in the operations up the Gironde, where, on shore and afloat, we find him concerned in the destruction of a French line-of-battle-ship, three brigs of war, several smaller vessels, and all the forts and batteries on the north side of the river. In July, 1814, he removed to the TANAIS 38, Capt. Joseph James, and during the two following years was stationed in the West Indies. Having passed his examination 3 July, 1815, he was next, between Oct. 1816 and the period of his advancement to the rank of Lieutenant 28 April, 1827, employed at Portsmouth, Plymouth, and the Cape of Good of Hope, and again on the Home station, as Admiralty-Midshipman and Mate, in the QUEEN CHARLOTTE 100, Capt. Edm. Boger, SUPERB 74, Capt. Chas. Ekins, TEES 26, Capt. Geo. Rennie, SEVERN 40, Capt. Wm. M'Culloch, RACEHORSE 18, Capt. Wm. Benj. Suckling (under whom he was wrecked on a reef of rocks, off Langness Point, Isle of Man, 14 Dec. 1822), GANNET 18, Capt. Wm. Simpson, and RAMILLIES 74, Capt. Hugh Pigot. At the period of his promotion Mr. Lethbridge, who has since been on half-pay, was the oldest Mate, as to age, in the service.

LETHBRIDGE. (LIEUTENANT, 1811. F-P., 11; H-P., 33.)

ROBERT LETHBRIDGE entered the Navy, 5 Dec. 1803, as Fst.-cl. Vol., on board the PRINCESS ROYAL 98, Capts. Jas. Vashon, Herbert Sawyer, and Robt. Carthew Reynolds; of which ship, stationed in the Channel, he became Midshipman 7 April, 1804. Removing, in May, 1805, to the UNITÉ 36, Capts. Chas. Ogle and Pat. Campbell, he was for five years and a half employed under those officers on the Mediterranean station, where—besides assisting, in May, 1808, at the taking of *Il Ronco* brig of war, of 16 guns and 100 men, and, in June following, at the simultaneous capture of the *Nettuno* and *Toulie*, of similar force—he commanded one of six boats belonging to the UNITÉ and TOPAZE in an affair near Toulon, and was officially commended for his conduct in defending, in a 10-oared cutter, four prizes, taken on the occasion, against the subsequent attacks of six armed boats. On 29 Oct. 1810, and 17 Jan. 1811, he was successively appointed an acting and a confirmed Lieutenant of the YORK 74, Capts. Robt. Barton and Alex. Wilmot Schomberg, with whom we find him successively employed in the Mediterranean and North Sea until May, 1813. His last appointment was, on 9 Nov. in the latter year, to the CONQUESTADOR 74, Capt. Lord Wm. Stuart, stationed at first in the Channel and then in the West Indies, whence he returned in Sept. 1814. AGENTS—Pettet and Newton.

LETT. (LIEUTENANT, 1826.)

STEPHEN JOSHUA LETT was born 2 Nov. 1801, at Enniscorthy, co. Wexford.

This officer entered the Navy 15 July, 1815; passed his examination in 1821; and, as a reward for his meritorious services as Mate of the ARACHNE 18, Capt. Henry Ducie Chads, during the war in Ava, was made Lieutenant, 26 Dec. 1826, into the LARNE sloop, Capt. Wm. Burdett Dobson, with whom he returned home and was paid off in April, 1827. He has been in charge, since 3 April, 1837, of a station in the Coast Guard.

LEVELL. (RETIRED COMMANDER, 1847. F-P., 14; H-P., 33.)

THOMAS LEVELL was born 19 Jan. 1788, at Bildeston, in Suffolk.

This officer entered the Navy, 25 Oct. 1800, as Fst.-cl. Vol., on board the EXCELLENT 74, Capts. Hon. Robt. Stopford, Robt. Tucker, and John Nash, with whom he served in the Channel and West Indies until May, 1803—the last two years in the capacity of Midshipman. After a short attachment to the TOPAZE frigate, Capt. Willoughby Thos. Lake, he rejoined Capt. Stopford, in the course of the latter year, on board the SPENCER 74, in which ship, commanded subsequently by Capt. John Quilliam, he was for upwards of five years employed. During that period we find him assisting at the blockade of Ferrol, Corunna, and Toulon; uniting in Lord Nelson's pursuit of the combined fleets to the West Indies and back; participating in Sir John Duckworth's search after the celebrated Rochefort squadron; present, 6 Feb. 1806, in the action off St. Domingo; escorting General Crawford and a body of troops to the Cape of Good Hope; and serving on shore, in the erection of batteries, at the siege of Copenhagen. Having passed his examination 1 July, 1807, Mr. Levell was nominated, 14 Sept. 1808, Sub-Lieutenant of the ATTACK gun-brig, Lieut.-Commander Thos. Swain; and on 27 Jan. 1809 was promoted to the full rank of Lieutenant. Being then appointed to the LITTLE BELT of 20 guns and 121 men, Capts. John Crispo and Arthur Batt Bingham, it was his fortune, on 16 May, 1811, to be on board that sloop in the furious and well-known action fought between her and the American 44-gun frigate *President*, whose fire in half an hour killed and wounded 32 of the British. He was paid off from the LITTLE BELT in Sept. 1811; and was afterwards appointed—25 Jan. 1812, to the OSPREY 18, Capt. Tim. Clinch, in the boats of which sloop he was occasionally employed up the river Elbe—12 Jan. and 28 June, 1813, to the FERVENT 12, Capt. Chas. Hope Reid, and FLAMER, of similar force, Capts. John Baldwin and Job Hanmer, with whom he served until put out of commission in Aug. 1814—and, lastly, 8 May, 1815, to the command of a Telegraph station in the county of Surrey, where he was relieved in the following March. While in the FLAMER, Mr. Levell was engaged in escorting convoys to Gottenborg; and on one occasion, when off the Skawe, took command of her boats, and drove a Danish privateer cutter on shore. He accepted the rank he now holds 3 Feb. 1847.

Commander Levell is married, and has issue three sons and two daughters.

LEVEN AND MELVILLE, Earl of, formerly Viscount Balgonie. (Rear-Admiral, 1846.)

The Right Honourable David Earl of Leven and Melville, born 22 June, 1785, is eldest son (by Jane, daughter of John Thornton, Esq., of London) of the late Earl, whom he succeeded, as eighth Earl of Leven and seventh Earl of Melville, 22 Feb. 1820.

This officer attained the rank of Lieutenant 8 Aug. 1806; and, while attached to the Ville de Paris 110, bearing the flag of Lord Collingwood, was mentioned for his conduct in her boats with those of a squadron under Lieut. John Tailour, at the capture and destruction, on the night of 31 Oct. 1809, of the French armed store-ship *Lamproie* of 16 guns and 116 men, bombards *Victoire* and *Grondeur*, armed xebec *Normande*, and seven merchant-vessels, defended by numerous strong batteries in the Bay of Rosas, after a desperate struggle, and a loss to the British of 15 killed and 55 wounded.* Although not aware, we believe, of the circumstance, his Lordship had been awarded a second promotal commission on 16 of the preceding Sept. He was posted, after having for some time had command of the Delight sloop in the Mediterranean, 28 Feb. 1812; and advanced to his present rank 1 Oct. 1846.

The Earl married, 21 June, 1824, Elizabeth Anne, daughter of Sir Archd. Campbell, Bart, by whom he has issue three sons and four daughters.

LE VESCONTE. (Commander, 1828.)

Henry Le Vesconte is brother of Commander Philip Le Vesconte.

This officer entered the Navy, 5 June, 1790, as Fst.-cl. Vol., on board the Cambridge 74, Capt. Boger, bearing the flag at Plymouth of Admiral Graves. He was discharged in the following Jan.; but re-embarked, in March, 1793, on board the Duke 98, bearing the broad pendant in the West Indies of Commodore Geo. Murray, and between the close of that year and the receipt of his first commission, bearing date 27 Oct. 1800, was employed on the Home, North American, and Cape of Good Hope stations, in 12 different ships, in the capacities of Volunteer, Midshipman, and Acting-Lieutenant. Joining, then, the Jamaica 24, Capts. John Mackellar and Jonas Rose, he shared in that vessel in the action off Copenhagen 2 April, 1801; and on 21 of the following Aug. took command, in conjunction with Lieut. Jas. John Chas. Agassiz, of the boats of a squadron, and gained the praise of Lord Nelson for his gallantry and zeal at the capture and destruction, with but slight loss to the British, of six flat-bottomed gun-vessels which had been driven on shore near St. Valery, and were protected by the fire of a body of military and five field-pieces.† He invalided from the Jamaica in Jan. 1804, and was subsequently appointed — 16 June following, to the Naiad 38, Capts. Jas. Wallis and Thos. Dundas, under the latter of whom he fought at Trafalgar, and on that occasion assisted in extricating the Belleisle 74 from a perilous position near the shoals, whither she was fast drifting —5 July, 1808, after seven months of half-pay, to the Raven sloop, Capt. Jas. Grant, on the Mediterranean station—1 Feb. 1809, and 18 March and 1 Aug. 1811, to the Ville de Paris 110, and, as First-Lieutenant, to the Rodney and Milford 74's, flag-ships in the Mediterranean of Admirals Lord Collingwood and Thos. Fras. Fremantle—1 Feb. 1812, to the acting-command, for a few weeks, of the Epervier sloop, on the same station—and, afterwards, to the Queen 74, bearing the flag, also in the Mediterranean, of the late Sir Chas. Vinicombe Penrose. He attained his present rank 5 Jan. 1828; and has since been on half-pay.

Commander Le Vesconte is Senior of 1828. Agents—Messrs. Stilwell.

---

* *Vide* Gaz. 1809, p. 1907. † *V.* Gaz. 1801, p. 1037.

LE VESCONTE. (Lieutenant, 1841.)

Henry Thomas Dundas Le Vesconte entered the Navy 19 May, 1829; passed his examination in 1836; and, joining (as Mate of the Calliope) in the China war, assisted at the destruction of a 20-gun battery at the back of the island of Anunghoy, 23 Feb. 1841*—served in the boats, on 13 March, at the capture of several rafts and of the last fort protecting the approaches to Canton†—was similarly employed at the capture of that city on 18 of the same month‡—and, during the second series of hostilities against it, was afresh engaged in the boats at the destruction, 26 May, of the whole line of defences, extending about two miles from the British factory. In consequence of these performances he was promoted to the rank of Lieutenant by commission dated 8 June, 1841.§ His appointments have since been—16 Oct. following, to the Hyacinth 18, Capt. Geo. Goldsmith, in the East Indies —15 June, 1842, to the Clio 16, Capts. Edw. Norwich Troubridge and Jas. Fitzjames, under whom he was for upwards of two years employed on the same station and off the coast of Africa—17 Dec. 1844, as Senior, to the Superb 74, Capt. Armar Lowry Corry, attached to the Channel squadron—and, 4 March, 1845, to the Erebus discovery-ship, Capt. Sir John Franklin, in which he is at present concerned in a renewed attempt to explore the North-west Passage through Lancaster Sound and Bering Strait. Agents—Messrs. Stilwell.

LE VESCONTE. (Commander, 1816. f-p., 21; h-p., 32.)

Philip Le Vesconte is son of Philip Le Vesconte, Esq., who lost a leg in Earl Howe's action 1 June, 1794, and died Purser of the Royal William, flag-ship at Spithead, 25 May, 1807. He is brother of Commander Henry Le Vesconte, R.N.

This officer entered the Navy, in 1794, as Fst.-cl. Vol., on board the Saturn 74, Capt. Jas. Douglas, and on 13 July, 1795, was present as Midshipman in Hotham's partial action with the French fleet off the Hyères Islands. He removed, in 1797, to the St. Alban's 64, Capt. Fras. Pender, and, after serving for two years in that ship on the Channel and Halifax stations, joined the Lynx sloop, Capt. Alex. Skene, attached to the force in the North Sea. On being received into the Monarch 74, Capt. Jas. Robt. Mosse, Mr. Le Vesconte bore a part and was wounded in the battle of Copenhagen, 2 April, 1801;‖ in consequence whereof he was promoted, 23 May following, to a Lieutenancy in the Glatton 50, Capts. Wm. Birchall, Wm. Nowell, and John Ferris Devonshire, stationed in the Baltic, where he remained until April, 1802. His next appointment was, 6 Sept. 1803, to the Magnificent 74, Capt. Wm. Henry Jervis, in which ship, when forming part of the in-shore squadron off Brest, it was his misfortune to be wrecked, during a gale of wind, 25 March, 1804. On being restored to liberty after seven years of captivity, we find him joining, in the course of 1811, the Leopard 50, *armée en flûte*, Capt. Wm. Henry Dillon, and Elephant 74, Capt. Fras. Wm. Austen. With the latter officer he served in the North Sea and Baltic until May, 1814; in Aug. of which year he obtained an appointment to the Queen 74, Capts. Lord John Colville and John Coode, flag-ship for some time of Rear-Admiral Chas. Vinicombe Penrose. He returned home from the Mediterranean in Dec. 1815; and has since been on half-pay. His promotion to the rank he now holds took place 7 Nov. 1816.

Commander Le Vesconte is at present Vice-Consul at L'Orient. He is married and has issue. Agents—Pettet and Newton.

LEVINGE. (Commander, 1845.)

Reginald Thomas John Levinge, born 20 Oct. 1813, is third son of Sir Rich. Levinge, Bart., of Knockdrin Castle, co. Westmeath, by Elizabeth

* *Vide* Gaz. 1841, p. 1497. † *V.* Gaz. 1841, p. 1503. ‡ *V.* Gaz. 1841, p. 1505. § *V.* Gaz. 1841, p. 2512. ‖ *V.* Gaz. 1801, p. 404.

Anne, eldest daughter of Thos. Boothby, first Lord Radcliffe. One of his brothers, Richard, the eldest, is a Captain in the Army; another, George, a Lieutenant in the Royal Horse Artillery; a third, Augustus, a Lieutenant in the 71st Infantry; a fifth, Charles, also in the Army; and, a sixth, Vere Henry, in the Hon. E. I. Co.'s service.

This officer entered the Navy 7 Jan. 1827; passed his examination in 1832; obtained his first commission 18 Oct. 1839; and was afterwards appointed—24 Oct. 1839, as Additional Lieutenant, to the MELVILLE 72, flag-ship of Hon. Geo. Elliot in the East Indies—12 Feb. 1840, to the WOLVERENE 16, Capt. Wm. Tucker, on the coast of Africa—25 Aug. following, to the command of the BUZZARD brigantine, on the same station, whence he returned in 1842—17 Jan. 1844, as Senior, to the VOLAGE 26, Capt. Sir Wm. Dickson, employed on particular service—and 7 Feb. 1845, to the command of the DOLPHIN brigantine, of 3 guns, on the south-east coast of America. On 20 Nov. in the latter year we find him present in the battle of the Parana, where a hard day's fighting terminated in the destruction, by the combined squadrons of England and France, of four heavy batteries belonging to General Rosas at Punta Obligado, as also of a schooner-of-war mounting 6 guns, and of 24 vessels chained across the river. The little DOLPHIN on that day occupied a berth better suited to a frigate, and was so much exposed that the Commodore, the present Sir Chas. Hotham, declared in his public despatch that he sometimes trembled when he beheld the shower of shot, shell, grape, and rockets flying over her. The gallantry of Mr. Levinge was in consequence rewarded with a Commander's commission dated 18 Nov. 1845.* He has since been on half-pay.

LEWIN. (LIEUTENANT, 1830.)

ELISHA LEWIN entered the Navy 19 April, 1807; passed his examination in 1815; and obtained his commission 22 July, 1830. He has since been on half-pay.

LEWIN, Kt. (LIEUT., 1814. F-P., 11; H-P., 28.)

SIR GREGORY ALLNUTT LEWIN died 12 Oct. 1845, at Exeter, aged 51. He was son of Rich. Lewin, Esq., of Eltham, co. Kent.

This officer entered the Navy, 24 March, 1808, as Fst.-cl. Vol., on board the TIGRE 74, Capt. Benj. Hallowell, with whom, on the latter hoisting his flag, he removed, in Aug. 1811, to the MALTA 80, and continued to serve, as Midshipman and as an Acting and a confirmed Lieutenant (order and commission respectively dated 7 Sept. and 23 Dec. 1814), until Feb. 1815. In the former of those ships, after having served in the North Sea, he united, in Oct. 1809, in the chase which preceded the self-destruction, near the mouth of the Rhone, of the French ships-of-the-line *Robuste* and *Lion*; and on becoming attached to the MALTA we find him co-operating with the patriots on the east coast of Spain, where he assisted at the siege of Tarragona, and at the capture of the fort of St. Philippe, in the Col de Balaguer. On his return to England in 1815, Mr. Lewin attended as a witness the court-martial assembled at Winchester to try Sir John Murray for the failure of the attack upon Tarragona. He was lastly, from April in the same year until paid off in March, 1818, employed in the ROYAL SOVEREIGN 100, and TONNANT 80, as Flag-Lieutenant to Sir Benj. Hallowell, during that period Commander-in-Chief at Cork.

Sir G. A. Lewin, who was knighted while in the TONNANT by the Viceroy of Ireland, Earl Talbot, on the occasion of that nobleman visiting the naval establishment at Cork, afterwards went to the bar, and became a Queen's Counsel. He married, in 1824, Elizabeth Caroline, daughter of Wm. Buller, Esq., of Maidwell Hall, Northamptonshire, and has left issue two sons and three daughters. AGENT—F. Dufaur.

---

* *Vide* Gaz. 1846, pp. 815, 817, 861.

LEWIS. (LIEUT., 1813. F-P., 9; H-P., 32.)

BENJAMIN LEWIS entered the Navy, 15 Dec. 1806, as A.B., on board the MELEAGER 36, Capts. John Broughton and Fred. Warren, employed at first in the North Sea and off Greenland, and then on the Jamaica station, where he was wrecked, while holding the rating of Master's Mate, 30 July, 1808. After serving for nearly five years as Midshipman, in the West Indies and at Newfoundland, of the POLYPHEMUS 64, flag-ship of Vice-Admiral Bartholomew Sam. Rowley, HYPERION 36, Capt. Wm. Pryce Cumby, and ANTELOPE 50, and BELLEROPHON 74, bearing the flags of Sir John Thos. Duckworth and Sir Rich. Goodwin Keats, he was nominated, 7 June, 1813, Acting-Lieutenant of the MUROS 12, Capts. Thos. Saville Griffinhoofe, H. E. Gordon, Fras. Wemyss, and Geo. Gosling, to which vessel (being confirmed to her 19 July following) he continued attached on the South American and Leeward Island stations until Dec. 1815. He has since been on half-pay.

LEWIS. (CAPTAIN, 1830. F-P., 29; H-P., 29.)

FRANCIS JAMES LEWIS is son of the late Lieut.-General Lewis.

This officer entered the Navy, in 1789, as Lieutenant's Servant, on board the ANDROMEDA frigate, Capt. Salusbury, on the books of which ship he was borne until 1790. Becoming Midshipman, in 1793, of the HECTOR 74, Captain, afterwards Rear-Admiral, Geo. Montagu, he took part in the unsuccessful attack made, in June of that year, on the island of Martinique. In July, 1794, we find him joining the LONDON 98, bearing the flag of the late Sir John Colpoys, under whom he was still serving at the period of the Spithead mutiny. After an attachment to various other ships, he was nominated, in April, 1804, Acting-Lieutenant of the WASP 18, Capts. Hon. Fred. Wm. Aylmer and John Simpson; on board which vessel it was his fortune to be present in Aug. 1805, when she effected a most gallant escape from the celebrated Rochefort squadron, compelling, on the occasion, by the excellent fire of the only six guns her perilous position had not compelled her to throw overboard, a large frigate and brig, who for 40 minutes had been engaging her on each quarter, to give up the pursuit. He was confirmed a Lieutenant on 11 of the ensuing month; and between that period and May, 1814, he was in succession employed, on the Home, East India, and North American stations, in the HIBERNIA 120, flag-ship of Admiral Douglas, MARS 74, Capts. Robt. Dudley Oliver and Wm. Lukin, ÆOLUS 32, Capt. Lord Wm. FitzRoy, DECADE frigate, Capt. Stuart, PALLAS 32, Capts. Geo. Fras. Seymour and Hon. Geo. Cadogan, ARGUS sloop, Capts. Stuart and Bott, MALACCA 36, Capts. Wm. Butterfield and Sam. Leslie, MODESTE 36, Capt. Jas. Coutts Crawford, and SATURN 56, Capt. Jas. Nash. While in the MARS, he contributed to the capture, 28 July, 1806, of *Le Rhin*, of 44 guns and 318 men, and was with Sir Sam. Hood's squadron on 25 Sept. in the same year at the taking, off Rochefort, of four heavy French frigates, two of which, the *Gloire* 46, and *Infatigable* 44, struck to the MARS. During his servitude in the PALLAS he witnessed Lord Cochrane's destruction of the French shipping in Basque Roads, and co-operated in the siege of Flushing. In Aug. 1814 he obtained an appointment to the ALBION 74, flag-ship in the Chesapeake of the present Sir Geo. Cockburn; upon being appointed Signal-Lieutenant to whom in the NORTHUMBERLAND 74, we find him escorting Napoleon Buonaparte to St. Helena; where, from March to Aug. 1816, he held the acting-command of the JULIA 14. He next, in Nov. 1819, joined the VIGO 74, flag-ship on the Leith and St. Helena stations of Rear-Admirals Robt. Waller Otway and Robt. Lambert, with whom he continued until advanced to the rank of Commander 29 Jan. 1821. His last appointment was, 12 May, 1827, to the OCEAN 80, Capt. Patrick Campbell, then stationed as a guard-ship at Plymouth, but afterwards employed in withdrawing the

British troops from Portugal, and finally attached to the force in the Mediterranean, whence he returned home and was paid off in May, 1830. Capt. Lewis was advanced to Post-rank 22 July following.

He married, 3 Feb. 1831, Anne, second daughter of the late Wm. Land, Esq., of Hayne House, Silverton.

LEWIS. (RETIRED COMMANDER, 1839. F-P., 19; H-P., 30.)

FREDERICK LEWIS entered the Navy, 28 July, 1798, as Fst.-cl. Vol., on board the DISCOVERY bomb, Capt. John Dick, lying at Sheerness; and on removing, in the following Dec., to the CHAMPION 24, Capt. Graham Eden Hamond, was for some time most actively employed in the North Sea, where he assisted at the capture, 28 June, 1799, of *L'Anacréon*, a notorious French privateer, of 16 guns and 125 men. In Dec. of the latter year he became Midshipman of the POMPÉE 74, Capt. Chas. Stirling, under whom he was afforded an opportunity of sharing in the action off Algeciras 6 July, 1801. He was next, for several months of 1802, stationed in the West Indies on board the MAGNIFICENT 74, Capt. John Giffard; after which we find him, in 1803, proceeding to the East Indies in the RUSSELL 74, Capt. Robt. Williams, and on 9 March, 1805, promoted, from the TRIDENT 64, flag-ship of Rear-Admiral Peter Rainier, to an Acting-Lieutenancy in the WILHELMINA frigate, Capts. Hon. Alex. Cochrane and Chas. Foote. From that vessel, to which he had been confirmed 29 Jan. 1806, he followed Capt. Foote, in May, 1808, into the PIÉMONTAISE 38. He invalided from India in Dec. 1809; and was subsequently appointed—27 April, 1811, and 3 Feb. 1812, to the HANNIBAL 74, and CHRISTIAN VII. 80, flag-ships in the Baltic and North Sea of Rear-Admiral Philip Chas. Durham—17 April, 1813, to the ULYSSES 44, Capt. Thos. Browne, under whom he escorted the army under Sir Thos. Graham to the Scheldt and a convoy to Jamaica—8 Oct. 1814, to the SYBILLE 44, Capt. Thos. Forrest, employed among the Western Islands—in June, 1815, to the direction of the Telegraph at the Admiralty—and, in May, 1816, to the command of the HOUND Revenue-vessel, in which he remained until superseded in May, 1819. He accepted his present rank 4 April, 1839.

The Commander is married, and has issue.

LEWIS. (LIEUTENANT, 1832.)

GEORGE WENHAM LEWIS entered the Navy in 1815, on board the SWIFTSURE 74; passed his examination in 1823; and was promoted to the rank he now holds 8 Jan. 1832. He has not been since employed.

Lieut. Lewis is Senior of 1831. AGENT—John P. Muspratt.

LEWIS. (LIEUTENANT, 1810. F-P., 13; H-P., 33.)

HENRY LEWIS (*a*) entered the Navy, 24 Sept. 1801, as A.B., on board the DIANA 38, Capts. John Poo Beresford and Thos. Jas. Maling, of which frigate, successively stationed in the Mediterranean, Channel, and West Indies, he became Midshipman in the following Oct., and Master's Mate in May, 1805. On 3 Feb. 1806, being at the time prize-master on board a detained American brig, he had the misfortune to be taken prisoner by a French privateer off the Scilly islands, and carried to France. He effected his escape in Dec. 1809, and, attaining the rank of Lieutenant 10 Feb. 1810, was afterwards appointed in that capacity—in the course of the same month, to the RESOLUTION 74, Capt. Hardy, stationed in the Baltic—12 Jan. 1811, to the CONQUESTADOR 74, Capt. Lord Wm. Stuart, with whom he was for two years employed in the North Sea and Channel—and, 8 Oct. 1813, to the ORONTES 36, Capt. Nathaniel Day Cochrane. In the latter ship he served on the Irish and West India stations, and again in the Channel, until Sept. 1815. He has since been on half-pay.

LEWIS. (LIEUTENANT, 1815. F-P., 12; H-P., 32.)

HENRY LEWIS (*b*) entered the Navy, 27 April, 1803, as Fst.-cl. Vol., on board the AMETHYST frigate, Capts. Alex. Campbell and John Wm. Spranger, employed in the North Sea and Baltic; and in May, 1805, became Midshipman of the DIOMEDE 50, Capts. Hugh Downman and Joseph Edmonds. On his return to England in the summer of 1807, after having witnessed the reduction of the Cape of Good Hope and the operations against Buenos Ayres and Monte Video, he joined the BRUNSWICK 74, Capt. Thos. Graves, and forthwith accompanied the expedition to Copenhagen under Admiral Gambier. Between Dec. of the same year and the date of his promotion to the rank of Lieutenant, 6 Feb. 1815, Mr. Lewis was successively employed, the latter part of the time as Master's Mate, on board the MINOTAUR 74, flag-ship of Sir Wm. Sidney Smith, AFRICA and STATELY 64's, Capts. Loftus Otway Bland, Geo. Fred. Ryves, Edw. Stirling Dickson, and Chas. Bateman, IMPÉTUEUX 74, Capt. Bateman, ERIDANUS 36, Capt. Henry Prescott, CERES 32, Capt. Jas. Prevost, and SCAMANDER 36, Capt. Gilbert Heathcote. The STATELY was attached to the force engaged in the defence of Cadiz; the other ships occupied on the Home station. Since his promotion Mr. Lewis has been on half-pay.

LEWIS. (LIEUT., 1838. F-P., 28; H-P., 13.)

RICHARD FELLOWES LEWIS, born 16 March, 1799, is nephew of the late Lieut. John Lewis, R.N., a *protégé* of the Duke of Kent, who was First-Lieutenant of H. M. S. ARIADNE in 1806, and lost his life in the service of his country.

This officer entered the Navy, 11 Jan. 1806, as Fst.-cl. Vol., on board the BARFLEUR 98, Capts. Joseph Sydney Yorke, Donald M'Leod, Sam. Hood Linzee, and Sir Thos. Masterman Hardy. During an attachment of nearly six years to that ship we find him serving at the blockade of Lisbon, escorting the Russian Rear-Admiral Seniavin's squadron to England after the convention of Cintra, assisting as Midshipman at the embarkation of the army after the battle of Corunna, and employed on boat-duty in the river Tagus during the occupation of the lines of Torres Vedras by Lord Wellington's army. He was next, between June, 1812, and Dec. 1815, stationed at the Cape of Good Hope and St. Helena on board the MINDEN 74, Capt. Alex. Skene, LION 64, Capt. Henderson Bain, and MEDWAY 74, Capt. Augustus Brine; and while in the last-mentioned ship he assisted at the capture, after an eight hours' chase, of the United States brig *Syren* of 18 guns. In Jan. 1816 Mr. Lewis was appointed Chief Clerk to the Master Attendant at the Naval Arsenal at the Cape of Good Hope; in which capacity and that of Chief Clerk to the Comptroller of Customs he continued to officiate until Nov. 1820. Re-embarking in Feb. 1822, he served for four years and ten months, on the Home and South American stations, in the PIONEER schooner, Lieut.-Commander Thos. Favill, NORTHUMBERLAND 74, SPARTIATE 76, and CAMBRIDGE 82, all commanded by Capt. Thos. Jas. Maling, and GLOUCESTER 74, Capt. Joshua Sydney Horton. He left the latter ship in Dec. 1827, and, having passed his examination in Jan. 1823, was employed during the ten following years as Chief Mate in the TARTAR and CAMELION Revenue-cruizers; in which he proved instrumental to the capture of 967 tubs of spirits and to the destruction of 2917 tubs, as also of eight vessels and boats. When in pursuit, on one occasion, of a smuggler, he was severely wounded in the right hand. His zeal and activity at length procuring him a commission dated 29 Jan. 1838, he was appointed, on 25 May in that year, to a Lieutenancy in the TRIBUNE 24, Capt. Chas. Hamlyn Williams, and ordered to the Mediterranean, where he had the misfortune to be wrecked, near Tarragona, 28 Nov. 1839. He then returned home on board the MINDEN 74, Capt. Alex. Renton Sharpe; and was lastly, from 2 March, 1840, until superseded at his own request in 1841, employed in the Coast Guard. When in the CAMBRIDGE, on the South American station, he saved at different times the lives of two seamen, although at the hazard of his own.

From every Captain with whom he served Lieut. Lewis had the satisfaction of receiving the most flattering testimonials. He married, 12 June, 1830, Miss Eliza Watson, and by that lady has issue a son and three daughters.

LEWIS. (LIEUT., 1821. F-P., 23; H-P., 15.)

THOMAS ARUNDEL LEWIS entered the Navy, 13 June, 1809, as Fst.-cl. Vol., on board the NEMESIS 28, Capt. Wm. Ferris, stationed in the Baltic; and on becoming Midshipman of the PALLAS 32, Capt. Geo. Paris Monke, was wrecked in that frigate, off St. Abb's Head, 18 Dec. 1810. He then joined the LAUREL 38, Capt. Sam. Campbell Rowley, with whom he served until again wrecked, on the Govivas Rock, in the Teigneuse passage, 31 Jan. 1812. After an attachment of two years to the POMONE frigate, Capts. Fras. Wm. Fane and Philip Carteret, on the Newfoundland and Lisbon stations, Mr. Lewis, in Feb. 1814, was received on board the VILLE DE PARIS 110, flag-ship in the Channel of Sir Harry Burrard Neale; and towards the close of the same year, having removed to the BEDFORD 74, Capt. Jas. Walker, he accompanied the expedition to New Orleans. He was next, from Sept. 1815 to Aug. 1818, employed on the coast of Africa in the INCONSTANT and SEMIRAMIS frigates, bearing each the broad pendant of Sir Jas. Lucas Yeo. During the two years which immediately succeeded his promotion to the rank of Lieutenant, 23 June, 1821, we find him borne on the books of the BULWARK 74, commanded in the river Medway by Capt. Warren, and SEVERN 40, Capt. Wm. M'Culloch, lying in the Downs. His appointments have since been—9 April, 1823, again to the BULWARK, Capt. Thos. Dundas, stationed at the time at Plymouth—27 Dec. 1825 and 31 March, 1826, to the SUPERB 78, and MELVILLE 74, guard-ships at Portsmouth, both commanded by Capt. Henry Hill—12 Sept. 1826, to the GALATEA 42, Capt. Sir Chas. Sullivan, with whom, until paid off in Jan. 1829, he participated in various services—and 9 May, 1842, to the command (which he still retains) of the CRANE 6, on the Falmouth station. AGENT—Fred. Dufaur.

LEWIS. (RETIRED COMMANDER, 1837.)

WILLIAM LEWIS (*b*) entered the Navy, in the summer of 1796, as A. B., on board the OVERYSSEL 64, commanded in the Downs by Capt. Wm. Bowen, with whom, until the peace of Amiens, he further served, as Midshipman and Master's Mate, in the VILLE DE PARIS 110, BLENHEIM and PRINCE GEORGE 98's, flag-ships of Sir Wm. Parker, and CAROLINE frigate, on the Lisbon and Mediterranean stations. After an employment of exactly two years, at home and on the north coast of Spain, in EL CORSO, Lieut.-Commander Joshua Kneeshaw, ILLUSTRIOUS 74, Capt. Sir Chas. Hamilton, and NORTHUMBERLAND 74, flag-ship of Hon. Alex. Inglis Cochrane, he was made Lieutenant, 23 March, 1805, into the ST. GEORGE 98, Capts. Hon. Michael De Courcy and Thos. Bertie, with whom he was employed, it appears, in the Channel until Jan. 1808. From the following May until Jan. 1815 he officiated as Agent for Transports Afloat on the Lisbon Embassy station; and he afterwards discharged the duties of Agent at Cork. In 1809 Mr. Lewis assisted in fitting out the fire-ships intended for the destruction of the French squadron in Basque Roads. He accepted the rank of Commander 23 Oct. 1837. AGENTS—Messrs. Stilwell.

LEWIS. (LIEUTENANT, 1826.)

WILLIAM LEWIS (*b*) entered the Navy 5 Dec. 1810; passed his examination in 1817; and was promoted, 18 Oct. 1826, into the MENAI 26, Capt. Houston Stewart, on the Halifax station, whence he returned to England and was paid off in the following Dec. On 18 Nov. 1833 he became Additional Lieutenant of the BRITANNIA 120, bearing the flag of Sir Josias Rowley in the Mediterranean; and he was lastly, from 10 July, 1834, until the early part of 1837, employed on that station in the THUNDERER 84, Capt. Wm. Furlong Wise.

LEWORTHY. (LIEUT., 1816. F-P., 35; H-P., 9.)

HENRY LEWORTHY was born 23 Feb. 1793.

This officer entered the Navy, 20 July, 1803, as Ordinary, on board the GRAPPLER gun-brig, Lieut.-Commander Abel Wantner Thomas; and on 31 of the following Dec. was wrecked on the Iles de Chausey, near Granville; after sustaining a desperate engagement with an overwhelming force sent from which place to effect their capture, Mr. Leworthy and his companions were compelled to surrender and were taken prisoners to Verdun. In consideration of the distinguished bravery they had shown on the occasion, Napoleon Buonaparte in the course of a short time ordered the swords of all the officers to be restored to them, and that they should be allowed to wear them during the remainder of their captivity. After he had been for more than ten years in bondage, and had undergone inconceivable hardships in three thwarted attempts at escape, Mr. Leworthy at length, in the early part of 1814, succeeded in accomplishing a flight. He was then for upwards of two years employed on the American and Home stations in the AKBAR 50, Capts. Jas. John Gordon Bremer and John Pasco; and on 14 Nov. 1816 he was promoted to the rank of Lieutenant. His appointments have since been—21 Oct. 1825, to the Coast Blockade, as Supernumerary-Lieutenant of the HYPERION 42, Capt. Wm. Jas. Mingaye—11 July, 1831, to the command of the HAWKE Revenue-vessel—and 30 June, 1834, to the Coast Guard Service, in which he still continues. On 7 Dec. 1840, at the hazard of his life and of his boat's crew, the Lieutenant rescued 8 persons from the French brig *L'Espérance*, which vessel was in fifteen minutes dashed to pieces against the rocks at the entrance of Salcombe Harbour. AGENTS—Goode and Lawrence.

LEY. (LIEUTENANT, 1813.)

GEORGE LEY entered the Navy, in July, 1806, as Fst.-cl. Vol., on board the BARFLEUR 98, Capt. Joseph Sydney Yorke, attached to the Channel fleet. Removing as Midshipman, in June, 1807, to the BRUNSWICK 74, Capt. Thos. Graves, he attended the ensuing expedition to Copenhagen, and then returned to the Channel; where, and in the North Sea, he served from May, 1808, until promoted to the rank of Lieutenant, 6 Dec. 1813, on board the CHRISTIAN VII. 80, and IMPREGNABLE 98, flag-ships of Sir Edward Pellew and Admiral Wm. Young. While in the CHRISTIAN VII., during the years 1809-10, we find him assisting at the destruction of several convoys under the batteries on the coast of France. His next appointments were—14 Feb. 1814, to the HOPE 10, Capts. Edward Saurin and Henry Fyge Jauncey, with whom he was employed on home service until paid off in Oct. 1818—and 18 April, 1829, to the Ordinary at Sheerness, where he remained until July, 1831. He is now on Quarantine duty.

LEYCESTER. (LIEUTENANT, 1841.)

EDMUND MORTIMER LEYCESTER is third son of Geo. Hanmer Leycester, Esq., of White Place, co. Berks, by Charlotte Jemima, youngest daughter of the late Hans Wintrop Mortimer, Esq., of Caldwell, co. Derby, M.P. for Shaftesbury, who married a granddaughter of the Duke of Hamilton.

This officer entered the Navy 9 Oct. 1825; passed his examination 2 July, 1834; and at the period of his promotion to the rank of Lieutenant, which took place 23 Nov. 1841, was serving in the Mediterranean as Mate on board the VANGUARD 80, Capt. Sir David Dunn. His appointments have since been, on the same station—30 Nov. 1841, to the INDUS 78, Capt. Sir Jas. Stirling—21 Dec. 1843, to the ORESTES 18, Capt. Edw. St. Leger Cannon—13 Dec. 1845, as Additional, to the HIBERNIA 104, flag-ship of Sir Wm. Parker—and, 4 June, 1846, to the BONETTA surveying-vessel, Capt. Thos. Saumarez Brock, under whom he is now employed. AGENTS—Messrs. Chard.

LIARDET. (CAPTAIN, 1840. F-P., 25; H-P., 13.)

FRANCIS LIARDET, born 14 June, 1798, at Chelsea, co. Middlesex, is eldest son of John Liardet, Esq., by the Lady Perpetue Catherine de Paul de Lamanon d'Albe; and brother of Lieut. Wm. Liardet, R.N.

This officer entered the Navy, 14 June, 1809, as Sec.-cl. Vol., on board the MERCURY 28, Capt. Hon. Henry Duncan, with whom he sailed for the Mediterranean. On next joining, in March, 1810, the BELVIDERA 36, Capt. Rich. Byron, he cruized for some time off the coast of Africa; and on being then ordered to North America, was slightly wounded, as Midshipman, on the occasion of the BELVIDERA's celebrated escape from a powerful squadron under Commodore Rodgers, after a long running fight and a loss of 2 men killed and 22 wounded, 23 June, 1812. Besides participating in much active boat-service he beheld the subsequent capture and destruction of the privateers *Bunker's Hill* of 7, and *Mars* of 15 guns; and from the paying off of the BELVIDERA in Oct. 1814 until Oct. 1816, he served in the West Indies as Midshipman and Master's Mate of the WARRIOR 74, flag-ship of Rear-Admiral John Erskine Douglas, and FORESTER 16, Capt. Wm. Hendry. After an unemployed interval of three years and a half, Mr. Liardet, in May, 1821, joined the HYPERION 42, Commodore Jas. Lillicrap, fitting for the Cape of Good Hope; whence he ultimately returned to the West Indies, and was there appointed, 30 Jan. 1823, Senior Mate of the UNION schooner, commanded at first by Lieuts. Jas. Marriott and Wm. Henderson, and then by himself. During the next 15 months we find Mr. Liardet evincing a conspicuous degree of bravery, skill, and perseverance in the suppression of piracy, and on one occasion, 25 July, 1823, receiving two severe gun-shot wounds; long before his recovery from which he resumed the active duties of his profession. As a reward for these services he was officially promoted to the rank of Lieutenant 18 March, 1824, and appointed to the command of the LION, another schooner. Continuing his zealous exertions in that vessel, he succeeded in destroying several piratical establishments on the coast of Cuba—retook (at the same time that he captured nine piratical vessels) the French ship *Calypso*, which was loaded and brought off the shoals, under circumstances of the greatest difficulty—and made prize of a slaver. He was afterwards, as First-Lieutenant, appointed—28 Feb. 1827, to the PROCRIS 10, Capt. Hon. Wm. Waldegrave, in which sloop he appears to have been in attendance on the Duke of Clarence during two successive summers—24 Sept. 1828, to the JASEUR 18, Capts. John Lyons, Fras. Harding, and Archibald Sinclair, under whom he served for four years at the Cape of Good Hope—16 March, 1833, to the SNAKE 16, Capt. Wm. Robertson, employed for the suppression of slavery on the South American station—and 12 Aug. 1835, to the CLEOPATRA 26, Capt. Hon. Geo. Grey, in which he escorted the Countess of Durham and suite to St. Petersburg, then returned to South America, and eventually conveyed the Marquess of Clanricarde as Ambassador to the former court. Having attained the rank of Commander 28 June, 1838, Capt. Liardet, who did not take up his commission until paid off in the following Nov., was next, 12 Jan. 1839, appointed to the Second-Captaincy of the POWERFUL 84, Capt. Chas. Napier. For his services during the war in Syria, where he was in command of the POWERFUL during the period of Sir C. Napier's absence on shore, and assisted in the bombardment of St. Jean d'Acre, he was promoted to Post-rank 4 Nov. 1840. He has been on half-pay since Jan. 1841.

The heroism displayed by Capt. Liardet in frequently perilling his existence for the preservation of others—a quality as indicative of a chivalrous spirit as the proudest deed of arms—has rendered him an ornament and a boast even to his own noble profession. We offer no apology, therefore, for pausing to record the following facts:—It was late on an evening in Aug. 1816, the FORESTER being at the time in Portsmouth Harbour, that the cry was raised of "A man overboard!" The next instant, Mr. Liardet, plunging in, was by the side of the drowning man: but so strong was the tide then running, that 20 minutes elapsed before a boat could reach them, by which time they had both been carried under the side of a distant vessel, and were on the verge of sinking. On another occasion, 12 Jan. 1829, being on his passage to the Cape of Good Hope in the JASEUR, he again, in a fresh breeze and heavy sea, sprang overboard, and snatched from the deep a seaman who had fallen from the maintopsail-yard. In the following Sept., the same ship being 150 miles off the east coast of Africa, going at the rate of seven knots an hour, with studding-sails set, Mr. Liardet, although the JASEUR had been surrounded with sharks during the whole day, a third time dashed into the sea, to the rescue of a Midshipman. A fourth, a fifth, and even a sixth time, did this meritorious officer equally distinguish himself. He was also in 1830, as on other similar occasions, the chief instrument, by his nautical skill and intrepid conduct, of saving a French merchant-brig from almost inevitable destruction, near Tamatave, in the island of Madagascar. It is needless to add that his gallantry has been deservedly rewarded by several medallions from the Royal Humane Society; and that he has received the thanks of those who have benefited by his single-minded and generous exertions. Capt. Liardet married, 11 Oct. 1842, Caroline Anne, widow of the late Lieut. John Jervis Gregory, R.N., and sister of the present Sir Edm. Filmer, Bart., M.P. for the Western Division of Kent, by whom he has issue two daughters and one son. AGENTS—Messrs. Ommanney.

LIARDET. (LIEUT., 1814. F-P., 12; H-P., 29.)

WILLIAM LIARDET, born 29 Sept. 1794, is brother of Capt. Fras. Liardet, R.N.

This officer entered the Navy, 22 Nov. 1806, as Fst.-cl. Vol., on board the REDWING 18, Capts. Thos. Ussher, Edw. Augustus Down, and Sir John Gordon Sinclair, under whom he successively served, on the Mediterranean station, a great part of the time as Midshipman and Master's Mate, until Aug. 1814. During that period he took part, 20 April, 1807, in a very spirited action with a division of Spanish gun-boats and several batteries near Cabritta Point, in which the British lost 3 men killed and 4 wounded; and while absent, on one occasion, in a detained vessel, he was taken prisoner. On 31 March, 1813, having rejoined the REDWING, he witnessed the capture and destruction of two strong batteries and 14 sail of vessels at Morjean; where, in charge of a cutter, he subsequently, on 2 May, co-operated with the boats of the UNDAUNTED, VOLONTAIRE, and REPULSE, in cutting out a well-protected convoy. In the course of the following summer he commanded one of four boats at the capture of a merchantman under some batteries near Marseilles; and he also, on 18 Aug., served, with the REDWING's two cutters under his orders, in a brilliant attack on the batteries at Cassis, where, after sustaining a loss of 4 men killed and 16 wounded, the British succeeded in capturing two heavy gun-boats and 26 vessels laden with merchandize, two of which were brought out by Mr. Liardet himself. Indeed, during the whole term of his attachment to the REDWING, the last two years of which he had charge of a watch, Mr. Liardet proved instrumental to the capture of a large number of merchantmen and privateers, was engaged in nearly every boat and battery affair in which that ship was concerned, and, in whatever service employed, always distinguished by a "degree of zeal and activity highly creditable." We may add that, including the occasion above alluded to, he twice fell into the hands of the enemy, although in both instances he was speedily released. After he had further served, still in the Mediterranean, as Admiralty Midshipman of the GRANICUS 36, Capt. Wm. Furlong Wise, and ELIZABETH 74, Capt. Gardner Henry Guion, he there became, 31 Oct. 1814, Acting-Lieutenant of the JASPER 10, Capt. Thos. Carew, to which vessel he was confirmed 23 Dec. following. Invaliding home in Feb. 1815, he was next, from 5 Jan. 1816 until 3 Oct. 1818, employed, latterly as First-Lieutenant, on board the PERSEUS 22 and TAMAR 26, both commanded by Capt. Thos. Rich. Toker, on the Newfoundland station. He has been in charge since 29 Sept. 1846 of a station in the Coast Guard.

He married, 13 Oct. 1836, Adeline Eliza, youngest daughter of the late Thos. Pinnock, Esq., of Jamaica, and has had issue two sons and one daughter. The eldest son, William Francis, died at the Royal Naval School, 22 April, 1846, in his ninth year. AGENTS—Goode and Lawrence.

LIBBY. (RETIRED COMMANDER, 1839. F-P., 13; H-P., 45.)

EDWARD LIBBY entered the Navy, 21 May, 1789, as a Volunteer, on board the CUMBERLAND 74, Capt. John Macbride, and was employed, until Sept. 1791, on the Home and West India stations, chiefly in the capacity of Midshipman. Re-embarking, 19 Dec. 1792, on board the LOWESTOFFE frigate, he was for three years and a half in that vessel on the Mediterranean station, under Capts. Wolseley, Cunningham, Middleton, and Plampin; after which he joined the VICTORY 100, bearing the flag of Sir John Jervis, and on 8 Feb. 1797 was appointed Acting-Lieutenant of the BLENHEIM 98, Capt. Thos. Lennox Frederick. For his conduct in the latter ship in the action off Cape St. Vincent, where he was wounded,* he was confirmed a Lieutenant, 22 March following, in the DOLPHIN 44, Capts. Rich. Retalick, Robt. Williams, Josiah Nisbet, Jas. Bayley, Philip Beaver, and Jas. Dalrymple, with whom he served on the Lisbon, Mediterranean, and Home stations, until Dec. 1800. He then joined the ATHÉNIENNE 64, Capt. Sir Thos. Livingstone, in which ship he returned to England from the Mediterranean at the peace; and he was lastly, from Nov. 1804, until the close of 1805, employed in the Channel and North Sea on board the SULPHUR bomb, Capt. Matthews, and NAMUR 74, Capt. Lawrence Wm. Halsted. In compensation of his wound the Commander was presented with a grant from the Patriotic Fund. He was placed on the Junior List of Retired Commanders 26 Nov. 1830; and on the Senior 20 March, 1839.

LIDDELL. (LIEUT., 1822. F-P., 13; H-P., 22.)

JAMES LIDDELL entered the Navy, 23 July, 1812, as Fst.-cl. Vol., on board the CLARENCE 74, Capts. Henry Vansittart and Fred. Warren, attached to the Channel Fleet; and in Oct. 1814 became Midshipman of the QUEEN 74, bearing the flag of the late Sir Chas. Vinicombe Penrose in the Mediterranean; where, until May, 1819, he continued to serve, in the PARTRIDGE sloop, Capt. John Miller Adye, and ALBION 74, Capt. John Coode. In the last-mentioned ship he assisted at the bombardment of Algiers 27 Aug. 1816, and was again employed under the flag of Sir C. V. Penrose. In the summer of 1821, after he had been for 18 months borne on the books of the BULWARK 74, commanded at Chatham by Capts. Sam. Warren, Fras. Newcombe, and Alex. Skene, Mr. Liddell sailed for South America in the AURORA 46, Capt. Henry Prescott. On his arrival on that station he was nominated, in the following Sept., Acting-Lieutenant of the ALACRITY sloop, Capt. Hon. Fred. Spencer; of which vessel, in April, 1822, he became Acting-Master. He went back, a few weeks afterwards, to the AURORA, in the capacity of Acting Second-Master; was awarded a commission on 26 of the ensuing Aug.; and, with the exception of three months in the same year, during which period he officiated as Flag-Lieutenant to Sir Thos. Masterman Hardy, remained in the AURORA until her return to England in Feb. 1825. He has since been on half-pay.

* *Vide* Gaz. 1797, p. 212.

LIDDON. (COMMANDER, 1821. F-P., 16; H-P., 27.)

MATTHEW LIDDON entered the Navy, 3 May, 1804, as Fst.-cl. Boy, on board the LILY 18, Capts. Geo. Morrison and Donald Campbell, and sailed for the West Indies, where, when Midshipman in charge of a prize, he had the misfortune to be captured by two French privateers, and taken to Cumana. From that place, however, he contrived in the dead of night to effect his escape by swimming off with 10 or 12 companions to a schooner in the harbour, the crew of which, after a struggle, were secured. Having returned to England, and been, in Aug. 1806, received on board the PHEASANT 18, Capt. John Palmer, Mr. Liddon accompanied the expedition under Sir Sam. Auchmuty to the Rio de la Plata, where, in Feb. 1807, he served on shore at the storming of Monte Video. While next attached, between Dec. 1808 and Feb. 1811, to the THAMES 32, Capt. Hon. Granville Geo. Waldegrave, on the Mediterranean station, he participated in a variety of detached operations, and, on 25 July, 1810, was officially alluded to for his conduct in her boats, with those of the PILOT and WEASEL sloops, at the very gallant capture and destruction, notwithstanding a most spirited opposition, of 31 transports, 7 large gun-boats, and 5 armed vessels.* On leaving the THAMES we find him acting for two months as Lieutenant of the HERALD 20, Capt. Geo. Jackson, and during that period commanding her boats in an expedition on the coast of Italy conducted under the directions of Capt. John Toup Nicolas of the PILOT. On the day on which the latter occurrence took place Mr. Liddon saved the life of a man by jumping overboard after him. Being confirmed in the rank of Lieutenant 3 May, 1811, he took a passage home, as soon as he had received his commission, on board the CUMBERLAND 74, Capt. Robt. Waller Otway, from the poop of which ship, while passing rapidly through the water, with all her canvass spread, he again dashed into the sea for the same humane purpose as before. On 6 of the following Nov. he obtained an appointment to the MAIDSTONE 36, Capt. Geo. Burdett, with whom he served at first in the Channel and then in North America. On 8 Feb. 1813, being at the time in the Chesapeake, he took command of the MAIDSTONE's barge, and assisted the boats of a squadron under Lieut. Kelly Nazer in capturing, after a most determined resistance, the *Lottery* letter-of-marque, of 6 12-pounder carronades and 28 men—an exploit which was acknowledged by the especial thanks of Rear-Admiral Cockburn. He next, on 3 April following, accompanied a brilliant boat expedition 15 miles up the Rappannock river, where, acting, in the MAIDSTONE's launch, in conjunction with Lieut. Geo. Bishop in the STATIRA's large cutter, he most gallantly boarded and carried the *Dolphin* schooner, of 12 guns and 98 men.† On 8 April, 1814, having further accompanied a detachment of six boats under Capt. Rich. Coote to the neighbourhood of Pettipague Point, on the river Connecticut, he there contributed to the destruction of 27 of the enemy's vessels, three of which were heavy privateers, and the aggregate burden of the whole upwards of 5000 tons. From the MAIDSTONE, while in which ship he had a third time intrepidly rescued a man from drowning, Mr. Liddon exchanged, 11 Aug. 1814, into LA HOGUE 74, Capt. Hon. Thos. Bladen Capel, with whom he soon returned to England and was paid off. His subsequent appointments were—in 1815-16, to the ALBION, QUEEN, and NORTHUMBERLAND 74's, all commanded by Capt. Jas. Walker at Sheerness, where he served until paid off in Sept. 1818—and, 29 Jan. 1819, to the command of the GRIPER brig. In the latter vessel he accompanied an expedition to the Arctic regions under the present Sir Edw. Parry. He paid the GRIPER off 21

* *Vide* Gaz. 1810, p. 1860. † *V.* Gaz. 1813, p. 995.

Dec. 1820, and has not been since employed. His commission as Commander bears date 8 Nov. 1821.

He married, in 1827, Anne, only daughter of the late Sam. Bilke, Esq., Stamford Street, Blackfriars.

LIDDON. (Lieutenant, 1828.)

Matthew John Liddon entered the Navy 13 July, 1815; passed his examination in 1822; and obtained his commission 23 May, 1828. His appointments have since been—16 Sept. 1828, to the Victor 18, Capt. Rich. Keane, on the Jamaica station, whence he returned to England in 1830 in the Fairy 10, Capt. Fras. Blair—and 14 July, 1838, to the Coast Guard, in which service he still continues.

LILBURN. (Lieut., 1829. f-p., 21; h-p., 6.)

James Robert Roddam Lilburn, born 1 April, 1807, is son of Commander Jas. Lilburn, R.N. (who was killed in a cutting-out affair under the Molehead batteries in the port of Malaga 29 April, 1812), by Phillis, youngest daughter of Gilbert Selby, Esq., of Holy Island. He is brother of the present Lieut. Selby Lilburn, R.N.; and nephew of Lieut. Robt. Lilburn, R.N., who died while commanding a schooner in the West Indies.

This officer entered the R.N. College 3 Feb. 1820; embarked 7 Feb. 1822, as a Volunteer, on board the Active 46, Capt. Andrew King, lying at Portsmouth; and in the following Nov., after having been borne as a Supernumerary on the books of various ships, joined the Martin 20, Capts. Christ. Crackenthorp Askew and Henry Eden, on the Mediterranean station. He next, from Feb. 1825 until Oct. 1826, served in South America as Midshipman on board the Doris and Thetis frigates, Capts. Sir John Gordon Sinclair and Sir John Phillimore; and he was then for two years and a half employed as Mate, at home and in the Mediterranean, in the Herald yacht, Capts. Henry Eden and Edw. Wm. Corry Astley, Prince Regent 120, flag-ship of Sir Robt. Moorsom, Pearl 20, Capt. Geo. Chas. Blake, and Asia 84, flag-ship of Sir Pulteney Malcolm. On 9 July, 1829, he was made Lieutenant into the Wellesley 74, Capt. Fred. Lewis Maitland, also on the Mediterranean station, whence he returned in Sept. 1830. His appointments have since been—6 April, 1831, for a few months, to the Savage 10, Capt. Lord Edw. Russell, employed at Lisbon and at Cork—15 April, 1835, to the Magicienne 24, Capt. Geo. Wm. St. John Mildmay, stationed off the coasts of Spain and Portugal—19 Nov. 1838, and 3 Nov. 1839, to the Daphne 18, and Vanguard 80, Capts. John Windham Dalling and Sir Thos. Fellowes, again in the Mediterranean—and 6 Dec. 1841, to the Coast Guard, in which service he continues.

When in the Doris, Wellesley, and Magicienne, Lieut. Lilburn distinguished himself by thrice jumping into the sea after persons who had fallen overboard. He married, 19 Sept. 1843, Christian, daughter of G. Markwell, Esq., of Holy Island, by whom he has issue. Agents—Messrs. Stilwell.

LILBURN. (Lieutenant, 1845.)

Selby Lilburn is brother of Lieut. J. R. R. Lilburn, R.N.

This officer passed his examination 11 Nov. 1834; and at the period of his promotion to the rank of Lieutenant, which took place 13 Aug. 1845, had been serving for several years on the East India and African stations in the Camelion 10, Lieut.-Commander Geo. Martin Hunter, and Prometheus steam-sloop, Capt. John Hay. He was appointed, a few days afterwards, Additional-Lieutenant of the Penelope steam-frigate, Commodore Wm. Jones; with whom he returned home in the spring of 1846. He has since been on half-pay.

LILLICRAP. (Rear-Admiral, 1846. f-p., 36; h-p., 31.)

James Lillicrap, a native of Plymouth, is uncle of Jas. Lillicrap Marchant, Esq., Purser and Paymaster R.N., one of whose brothers died a Midshipman, and another a Lieutenant, R N.

This officer entered the Navy, 5 Sept. 1780, as Captain's Servant, on board the Cambridge 74, Capt. Fras. John Hartwell, lying at Plymouth, where his name, during several months in 1782-3, was borne on the books of the Dunkirk, Capt. Milligan. Joining, in Sept. 1784, the Racehorse sloop, Capt. Thos. Wilson, he was for two years and a half employed in that vessel on the Halifax station, and in the suppression of smuggling on the coast of Scotland. On leaving her he became for a short period attached to the Termagant, another sloop, Capt. Rowley Bulteel; and he was next, between 1788 and 1793, stationed at Home and in the Mediterranean, as Midshipman, in the Cumberland 74, Capt. John Macbride, Syren 32, Capt. John Manley, St. George and Windsor Castle 98's, flag-ships of Rear-Admiral Phillips Cosby, and Victory 100, bearing the flag of Lord Hood. On 30 Oct. in the year last mentioned, after having served on shore at the occupation of Toulon, Mr. Lillicrap was promoted to a Lieutenancy in La Moselle 20, Capt. Rich. Henry Alex. Bennett; in which vessel he continued until 7 Jan. 1794, when he had the misfortune to be taken prisoner in the jolly-boat while voluntarily reconnoitring the harbour at the above place subsequently to its evacuation by the British. Being exchanged in 1795, he embarked at Marseilles, and proceeded to Genoa, whence he returned overland to England *viâ* Cuxhaven, bringing with him despatches from Mr Drake, the British Minister at Genoa. On his arrival he was appointed, 12 Oct. in the same year, to the Trusty 50, Capts. John Osborne and Andrew Todd; under the former of whom he partook of a variety of services in the North Sea and Channel, and assisted in conveying Lord Macartney to the Cape of Good Hope. During the mutiny which broke out on that station in 1797, Mr. Lillicrap was placed by Rear-Admiral Pringle in charge of the Rattlesnake sloop; which vessel he succeeded in placing so close under the guns of the Amsterdam battery, in Table Bay, that the ringleaders were obliged to surrender. Returning to England in the early part of 1799 on board the Trusty, he next, in the following April, joined the Venerable 74, Capts. Sir Wm. Geo. Fairfax and Sam. Hood, and was thus afforded an opportunity of sharing in an attack which was soon afterwards made by Rear-Admiral Chas. Morice Pole on a Spanish squadron in Aix roads, and of also participating in Sir Jas. Saumarez' actions of 6 and 13 July, 1801, off Cadiz and in the Gut of Gibraltar. In consideration of his distinguished conduct as the Venerable's First-Lieutenant on the latter occasion, and of the most able manner in which he supported Capt. Hood,* Mr. Lillicrap was rewarded with a Commander's commission dated 18 Aug. 1801. His first appointment in his new rank was, 2 April, 1804, to the Vesuvius bomb, employed under Sir Wm. Sidney Smith on the Boulogne station; where, in Nov. 1805, he had 1 man killed and several wounded in an attack upon the enemy's flotilla. While next in the Despatch 18, to which sloop he removed 25 Sept. 1806, Capt. Lillicrap, in the course of 1807, sailed from the Downs in command of a light squadron and with a large fleet of transports under his protection, having on board two divisions of the King's German Legion. These his indefatigable exertions and active measures enabled him to land in safety on the island of Rugen, at a time when the French army was besieging Stralsund, the capital of Swedish Pomerania. After he had for some time discharged the duties of Senior officer in Pert Bay, Capt. Lillicrap conducted the last division of troops under Lord Rosslyn from Rugen to Zealand, where he rendered good service by the mode in which he superintended their disembarkation in Kioge Bay. During the operations against Copenhagen he was the Senior Commander employed in the in-shore squadron under Capt. Paget, and, until its surrender, was in constant action with the enemy. Although,

* *Vide* Gaz. 1801, p. 1104.

in the general promotion which followed the capture of the Danish fleet, 17 Commanders, all junior to him, attained superior rank, Capt. Lillicrap, notwithstanding that the important nature of his services was set forth in the strongest manner by Lord Cathcart, the Earl of Rosslyn, Sir Chas. Morice Pole, and the commanding officers of the German Legion, was passed over, and not promoted until three years afterwards; two of which he spent, generally in command of a detached squadron, on the West India station, on his passage whither he effected the capture, 2 Oct. 1808, of *La Dorade* French privateer, of 1 gun and 20 men. On 24 Jan. 1815, Capt. Lillicrap, whose advancement to Post-rank had at length taken place by a commission dated 21 Oct. 1810, assumed command of the HYPERION 42; in which frigate he visited Lisbon and escorted a large fleet of merchantmen home from Oporto. Subsequently to his appointment, 8 April following, to the EUROTAS 38, we find him, while lying in Plymouth Sound, invested by Lord Keith with the command of the boats of the fleet, for the purpose of nightly guarding Napoleon Buonaparte, at the time on board the BELLEROPHON. On his return to Plymouth, after witnessing the ex-Emperor's removal to the NORTHUMBERLAND off Berry Head, he was ordered to Malta, there to deliver Generals Savary and Lallemand, with three Colonels and several other officers, late belonging to Buonaparte's suite, into the hands of Sir Thos. Maitland. The EUROTAS being paid off 22 Jan. 1816, Capt. Lillicrap did not again go afloat until re-appointed, 6 April, 1821, to the HYPERION. In the following Sept. he sailed with Lord Chas. Somerset for the Cape of Good Hope, where he had no sooner arrived than he hoisted a broad pendant. He continued for about 12 months to fill the post of Commodore on the same station; during which period, 10 June, 1822, the officers and seamen under his orders were so thoroughly the means of saving the *Albion*, an Indiaman of immense value, from being lost in a gale in Simon's Bay, that the Hon. Company awarded the sum of 500*l.* to be distributed among them. Capt. Lillicrap was himself presented with the same amount.* Proceeding, next, to the West Indies, he cruized for a time off Cuba with a detachment under his orders for the suppression of piracy, and on 24 Oct. 1823 was appointed to the GLOUCESTER 74, bearing the broad pendant of Sir Edw. W. C. R. Owen. He returned home with the latter officer in March, 1824, and was lastly, from 6 April, 1830, until 4 June, 1833, employed as Captain-Superintendent of the Ordinary at Portsmouth. He was admitted to the out-pension of Greenwich Hospital 17 Feb. 1837; and advanced to his present rank 1 Oct. 1846.

Rear-Admiral Lillicrap, while in the Ordinary at Portsmouth, transmitted to the Admiralty a model for rendering the numerous warping or transporting buoys available to the preservation of life. The plan was at once adopted; and the Royal Humane Society, to mark their appreciation of its utility and excellence, forwarded him their medallion. He married, 30 Dec. 1811, Frances Adams, youngest daughter of Giles Welsford, Esq., of Plymouth, by whom he has issue six sons and three daughters. One of the former, Walter Welsford, is a First-Lieutenant R.M. (1838).

LINCOLN. (LIEUT., 1837. F-P., 12; H-P., 11.)

HENRY LINCOLN was born 26 July, 1811.

This officer entered the Navy, 18 March, 1824, as Fst.-cl. Vol., on board the LIVELY 46, Capt. Wm. Elliott, employed at first off Lisbon (where his participation, as Midshipman, in the operations against Don Miguel procured him the medal of the Tower and Sword of Portugal), and afterwards on the West India, African, and Channel stations. Having left the LIVELY in Dec. 1826, he next, in March, 1827, joined the WELLESLEY 74, Capts. Fred. Lewis Maitland and Sam. Campbell Rowley, attached to the force in the Mediterranean, on which station (with the exception of an interval between Jan. 1832 and Nov. 1833) he served, in the capacity of Mate, from 1830 until within a short period of his promotion to the rank of Lieutenant 26 Dec. 1837, in the same ship and in the FAVOURITE 18, Capt. Geo. Rodney Mundy, and MALABAR 74, Capts. Henry Shovell Marsham and Wm. Augustus Montagu. His commission was awarded to him while an invalid at Plymouth Hospital, whither he had been sent in consequence of illness contracted in the performance of duty at Cadiz; and which, having produced lameness, has since kept him on half-pay.

* Two Russian men-of-war were rescued from danger during the same gale; a service for which Capt. Lillicrap received letters of thanks from their Captains.

LIND. (LIEUTENANT, 1815. F-P., 15; H-P., 32.)

JAMES LIND died 17 July, 1847.

This officer entered the Navy, 17 Feb. 1800, as Sec.-cl. Vol., on board the CANADA 74, Capts. Hon. Michael De Courcy and Joseph Sydney Yorke, stationed in the Channel, where he attained the rating of Midshipman 2 July, 1801. Removing, in March, 1802, to the DONEGAL 74, Capt. Sir Rich. John Strachan, he was for upwards of three years employed in that ship, chiefly at the blockade of Cadiz; after which we find him, from Aug. 1804 until June, 1809, and from Aug. in the latter year until April, 1815, serving, on the Mediterranean and Home stations, part of the time as Master's Mate, in the AMBUSCADE 32, Capt. Wm. D'Urban, and BOMBAY 74, Capts. Wm. Cuming, Norborne Thompson, Geo. Parker, and Henry Bazely. He then took up a commission bearing date 7 Feb. 1815; and remained thenceforward on half-pay. AGENT—Joseph Woodhead.

LINDSAY. (LIEUTENANT, 1837.)

COLIN WILLIAM LINDSAY passed his examination in 1827; obtained his commission 10 Jan. 1837; and was afterwards appointed—8 Feb. 1837, to the RUSSELL 74, Capt. Sir Wm. Henry Dillon, employed in the Mediterranean and off Lisbon—8 April, 1839, to the CURAÇOA 24, Capt. Jenkin Jones, fitting for the South American station, whence he returned home and was paid off at the close of 1842—and, 23 Feb. 1844, to the AMERICA 50, Capt. Hon. John Gordon, attached to the force in the Pacific. He left the latter ship on her arrival in England in 1846; and is at present on half-pay.

LINDSAY. (LIEUT., 1815. F-P., 12; H-P., 30.)

JAMES LINDSAY died 18 Sept. 1845.

This officer entered the Navy, 22 Aug. 1803, as A.B., on board the SNAKE 18, Capt. Wm. Roberts, on the West India station, whence he returned to England with the same Captain in the summer of 1804, as Midshipman of LA VERTU. He was then, until Dec. 1810, employed on board the MARS 74, Capts. Geo. Duff, Robt. Dudley Oliver, Wm. Lukin, Jas. Katon, and John Surman Carden; and while so attached he took part, as Acting Second-Mate, in the battle of Trafalgar 21 Oct. 1805—assisted in taking, 28 July, 1806, *Le Rhin*, of 44 guns and 318 men—was present, 25 Sept. following, with Sir Sam. Hood's squadron, at the capture, off Rochefort, of four heavy French frigates, two of which, the *Gloire* 46 and *Infatigable* 44, struck to the MARS—attended the expedition of 1807 to Copenhagen—and was actively employed in affording protection to the Baltic trade. On leaving the MARS, Mr. Lindsay joined the BARFLEUR 98, bearing the flag in the Thames of Hon. Geo. Cranfield Berkeley, with whom he served for a period of 13 months. He then, in Jan. 1812, became Acting-Sub-Lieutenant of the HERRING, Lieut.-Commander John Murray, and sailed for Halifax, where in July, 1813, he followed the latter officer into the MUSQUEDCHET 12. He came home in April, 1814; obtained his commission 13 Feb. 1815; and was lastly, from 27 March, 1828, until April, 1829, employed in command of the STORK Revenue-vessel. AGENTS—Coplands and Burnett.

LINDSEY. (Commander, 1814. f-p., 11; h-p., 33.)

John Lindsey entered the Navy, 1 Nov. 1803, as Fst.-cl. Vol., on board the San Josef 110, Capt. John Tremayne Rodd, bearing the flag in the Channel of Sir Chas. Cotton; and from Dec. 1806 until promoted to the rank of Lieutenant 1 June, 1810, was employed off L'Orient, and on the Lisbon, Cork, and Mediterranean stations, as Midshipman, in the Pallas 32, Capts. Geo. Miller, Henry Manaton Ommanney, and Geo. Fras. Seymour, Hibernia 120, flag-ship of Sir C. Cotton, Virginie 38, Capt. Edw. Brace, and again in the San Josef. He was then appointed to the Achille 74, Capt. Sir Rich. King, and he afterwards joined—5 Jan. 1811, the Impérieuse 38, Capt. Hon. Henry Duncan, also in the Mediterranean—1 May, 1812 (after an interval of four months), the Coquette 20, Capt. John Simpson, on the West India station—23 Oct. 1813, the Jason 32, Capt. Hon. Jas. Wm. King, employed off Helvoetsluys—and 22 June, 1814, the Impregnable 104, bearing the flag of H.R.H. the Duke of Clarence, whom he accompanied to Bordeaux. He was advanced to his present rank 27 Aug. following; and has since been on half-pay. Agents—Hallett and Robinson.

LIPSCOMB. (Lieut., 1826. f-p., 16; h-p., 25.)

Edwin Lipscomb, born 24 Aug. 1796, is son of the late Rev. W. Lipscomb, Rector of Welbury, Yorkshire; and nephew of the gallant Capt. John Cooke, R.N., who fell at Trafalgar, in command of the Bellerophon 74.

This officer entered the Navy, 10 May, 1806, as Fst.-cl. Vol., on board the Avenger 16, Capt. Thos. White, part of the force on the Newfoundland station. Becoming attached, in March, 1811, to the Elizabeth 74, Capts. Edw. Leveson Gower and Gardiner Henry Guion, he was for upwards of four years employed as Midshipman and Master's Mate of that ship off Lisbon, and also in the Mediterranean and Adriatic, where he served in the boats at the capture and destruction of many of the enemy's armed vessels, and was present at the reduction, in June and July, 1813, of the towns of Omago, Dignano, and Fiumé. He next, in Oct. 1815, joined the Active 46, Capt. Philip Carteret, on the Jamaica station, whence he returned to England in Sept. 1817; and he was afterwards (he had passed his examination in Aug. 1816) employed, between Jan. 1819 and his promotion to the rank of Lieutenant 3 May, 1826, on board the Newcastle 60, flag-ship of Rear-Admiral Edw. Griffith, Albion 74, Capt. Sir Wm. Hoste, and Revenge 76, bearing the flag of Sir Harry Burrard Neale—on the North American, Home, and Mediterranean stations. He then obtained an appointment to the Isis 50, flag-ship at Jamaica of Sir Lawrence Wm. Halsted, with whom he returned to England in June, 1827. He has since been on half-pay.

He married, 16 July, 1846, Mary, eldest daughter of the late Dansey Dansey, Esq., of Brincep Court, Herefordshire.

LIPSON. (Commander, 1819. f-p., 23; h-p., 31.)

Thomas Lipson entered the Navy, in 1793, as Fst.-cl Vol., on board the Windsor Castle 98, Capt. Sir Thos. Byard, with whom he served in that ship at the reduction of Corsica; in the Bedford 74 in the action off Camperdown 11 Oct. 1797, and in the Foudroyant 80 at the capture, in Oct. 1798, of a French squadron under M. Bompart, destined for the invasion of Ireland. He continued in the last-mentioned ship under the flags of Lord Keith and Nelson until 1799—latterly on the Mediterranean station; where, and in the North Sea, he was during the rest of the war employed, as Midshipman and Master's Mate, in the Princess Charlotte 38, Ruby 64, and Isis 50, Capts. Sir Edw. Berry and Thos. Masterman Hardy. In 1803, after his name had been borne for short periods on the books of the Neptune 98, Capt. Fras. Wm. Austen, Amphion 32, Capt. T. M. Hardy, and Hydra 38, Capt. Geo. Mundy, he joined the Montagu 74, Capt. Robt. Waller Otway. During his continuance in that ship he assisted at the blockade of the enemy's ports from Brest to the Dardanells; and was present, 22 Aug. 1805, in Adm. Hon. Wm. Cornwallis' attack on the French fleet close in with Brest Harbour, on which occasion the Montagu exchanged broadsides with *L'Alexandre* of 80 guns. On 24 Jan. 1808 Mr. Lipson was nominated Acting-Lieutenant of the Sabrina 18, Capt. Edw. Kittoe, then off Cadiz. He was officially promoted 29 June, 1809, and was subsequently appointed—29 Jan. 1810, as Senior, to the Bonne Citoyenne corvette, Capt. Pitt Burnaby Greene, in South America—1 March, and 21 Sept. 1812, to the Laurestinus 24, and Barfleur 98, Capts. Hon. Wm. Gordon and Sir Edw. Berry, on the Brazilian and Mediterranean stations—in 1814-15, as First, to the Iphigenia 36, Capt. Andrew King, Tonnant 80, flag-ship of Hon. Sir Alex. Cochrane, and Royal Sovereign 100, Capt. Wm. Robt. Broughton, employed on the coast of North America and at home—and, 20 Nov. 1816 (after several months of half-pay), to the command of the Lapwing Revenue-cutter, which vessel, in Jan. 1817, was driven from her anchorage in Mill Bay, Plymouth, and went ashore high and dry, over a ridge of rocks, with comparatively little injury. He attained his present rank 4 March, 1819; and has not been since afloat.

Commander Lipson is now Harbour-Master at Adelaide, South Australia. He married, 30 July, 1812, Elizabeth, daughter of Wm. Took, Esq., of Weymouth. Agent—Joseph Woodhead.

LITCHFIELD. (Captain, 1826. f-p., 23; h-p., 24.)

Henry Litchfield was born 7 Oct. 1786, at Great Torrington, co. Devon.

This officer entered the Navy, 1 May, 1800, as Midshipman, on board the Impétueux 74, Capt. Sir Edw. Pellew, under whom he assisted in blowing up *L'Insolente* in the Morbihan river, and accompanied the expeditions to Quiberon, Ferrol, and Vigo. While at the latter place, we find him, on the night of 29 Aug. 1800, aiding in the boats of a squadron, 20 in number, commanded by Lieut. Henry Burke, at the cutting-out, close in with the enemy's batteries, of *La Guêpe* privateer, of 18 guns and 161 men, which vessel, 25 of whose people were killed and 40 wounded, was in 15 minutes boarded and carried, with a loss to the British of 3 seamen and 1 marine killed, 3 Lieutenants, 12 seamen, and 5 marines wounded, and 1 seaman missing. In the course of 1802 Mr. Litchfield successively joined the Courageux 74, Capt. Thos. Sotheby, and Pique 36, Capts. Wm. Cumberland and Chas. Bayne Hodgson Ross; under the latter of whom he was employed, in 1803-4, at the blockade of Aux Cayes and Cape François, St. Domingo, and on shore in the unsuccessful attack on Curaçoa. On the occasion of General Rochambeau's evacuation of Cape François, he served, it appears, in a boat, and assisted the present Sir Nesbit Josiah Willoughby in rescuing the French 40-gun frigate *La Clorinde*, and 900 souls who were on board, from the destruction with which they were threatened by the blacks under General Dessalines, at the time in possession of Fort St. Josef, on the rocks immediately beneath which *La Clorinde* had grounded. On leaving the Pique in Dec. 1804, Mr. Litchfield joined Le Renard, of 18 guns and 121 men, Capt. Jeremiah Coghlan; as Acting-Master of which vessel he contributed, 20 March, 1805, to the annihilation, after a brisk action of 35 minutes, of *Le Général Ernouf* French privateer of 20 guns and 160 men; as also, in May, 1806, to the capture, at the end of a chase of three days and nights, of *La Diligente* national brig, of 16 guns and 125 men. On 12 Oct. 1806 Mr. Litchfield was nominated Sub-Lieutenant of the Ferret 18, Capt. Hon. Geo. Cadogan; and on 24 March, 1807, he became Acting First-Lieutenant of the Reindeer 18, Capts. John Fyffe and Peter John Douglas.

In the latter sloop, to which he was confirmed 29 June following, he participated in the Walcheren operations of 1809. After again serving in the West Indies, chiefly as Senior Lieutenant, in the ELK 18, Capts. J. Coghlan and Clement Milward, POLYPHEMUS 64, flag-ship of Vice-Admiral Bartholomew Sam. Rowley, THETIS 38, Capt. Wm. Henry Byam, BRAZEN sloop, Capt. Jas. Stirling, and SHARK, bearing the flag of Vice-Admiral Chas. Stirling, he was there appointed, in March, 1813, Acting-Commander of the MOSELLE 18. Being confirmed in the command, on 12 July in the same year, of the MOHAWK sloop of 8 guns, Capt. Litchfield, who continued in her until Oct. 1814, was during that period most actively employed in the Chesapeake; where, besides co-operating in the attacks upon Crany Island and Hampton, he commanded his own gig, at the capture, by the boats of the MOHAWK and CONTEST, under the orders of Capt. Jas. Rattray, of the United States gun-vessel *Asp*, of 3 guns and 25 men, hauled up close to the beach, under the protection of a large body of militia, after an action in which the British had 2 killed and 6 wounded, and the enemy 10, including their Commander, killed and wounded. His next appointment was, 10 Oct. 1817, to an Inspecting-Commandership in the Coast Guard; in which service he continued until invested, 1 June, 1824, with the command of the ORONTES 18, employed at first as an experimental vessel, and subsequently on the Halifax station; whence he returned on being promoted, as a reward for his long and active services, to Post-rank, 20 Nov. 1826. He accepted the Retirement 1 Oct. 1846.

Capt. Litchfield, in 1815-16, was Acting-Postmaster at Norwich. He married, 1 Jan. 1831, Louisa Elizabeth, only daughter of Henry Chas. Litchfield, Esq., of the Treasury. AGENTS—Hallett and Robinson.

LITTLE. (COMMANDER, 1846.)

ALEXANDER LITTLE passed his examination in 1834; obtained his first commission 26 Dec. 1837; and was afterwards appointed—14 Feb. and 22 Aug. 1838, to the MALABAR 74 and RACEHORSE 18, Capts. Edw. Harvey and Henry Wm. Craufurd, both on the North America and West India station, whence he returned in 1839—1 Feb. 1840, to the THUNDERER 84, Capt. Daniel Pring, employed in the Mediterranean and in attendance on the Queen at Walmer Castle—and 19 Oct. 1843, as Senior, to the IRIS 26, commanded in the East Indies by Capt. Geo. Rodney Mundy. He was superseded from the latter ship on attaining his present rank 9 Nov. 1846; and has since been on half-pay. AGENTS—Hallett and Robinson.

LITTLE. (COMMANDER, 1846.)

EDWARD LITTLE passed his examination in 1832; and on the occasion of his promotion to the rank of Lieutenant, 30 Dec. 1837, was ordered to join the DONEGAL 78, Capt. John Drake, on the Lisbon station. His appointments have since been—1 Oct. 1840, to the BRITANNIA 120, flag-ship in the Mediterranean of Sir John Acworth Ommanney—2 March, 1842, to the VINDICTIVE 50, Capt. John Toup Nicolas, in South America—and 4 March, 1845 (after 18 months of half-pay), to the TERROR discovery-ship, Capt. Fras. Rawdon Moira Crozier, now employed on a north-west passage explorative mission. He acquired the rank he now holds 9 Nov. 1846.

LITTLEHALES. (VICE-ADMIRAL OF THE RED, 1840. F-P., 26; H-P., 43.)

BENDALL ROBERT LITTLEHALES died in Aug. 1847, at Compton Bishop, Somersetshire, aged 82. He was second son of Baker John Littlehales, Esq., of Moulsey House, Surrey, by Maria, daughter and sole heiress of Bendall Martyn, Esq. His brother, Sir Edw. Baker, Bart., a Lieutenant-Colonel in the Army, married a daughter of the second Duke of Leinster.

This officer entered the Navy, 25 June, 1778, as Captain's Servant, on board the VIGILANT 64, Capts. Robt. Kingsmill and Sir Digby Dent; and on 27 of the ensuing month was present in the action between Keppel and d'Orvilliers. Accompanying Sir Digby Dent, as Midshipman, into the ROYAL OAK 74, he next, 6 July, 1799, took part in Byron's action off Grenada; after which we find him, until promoted to the rank of Lieutenant, 21 Sept. 1790, employed, on the Channel and Newfoundland stations, on board the CUMBERLAND and REPULSE 74's, both commanded by Sir D. Dent, and PORTLAND and SALISBURY, flag-ships of Admirals John Campbell and John Milbanke. His succeeding appointments were—16 April, 1791, for a short period, to the DUKE 98, Capt. R. Kingsmill—22 June, 1793, and 25 March, 1794, as Senior, to the ROSE and BEAULIEU frigates, both commanded by Capt. Edw. Riou—in May and July, 1795, as First and Flag-Lieutenant, to the MAJESTIC 74 and BLANCHE frigate, bearing each the flag of Vice-Admiral Benj. Caldwell in the Leeward Islands—and 21 Nov. 1795, again as Senior, to the AMAZON 36, Capt. Robt. Carthew Reynolds. Attending, in the ROSE, the expedition of 1794 against the French West India islands, Mr. Littlehales was much employed there both on shore and afloat, particularly at the reduction of Martinique, where he served in one of the batteries on Pointe Carrière, and assisted in storming Fort Louis, opposite to which they had been erected. His gallantry, when in the BEAULIEU, in voluntarily boarding and destroying a French ordnance store-ship, mounting 18 guns, under a battery at St. François, Guadeloupe, won the admiration of every beholder, and led to his being appointed by Vice-Admiral Caldwell, under whose eye the exploit was achieved, to his own flag-ship the MAJESTIC, on promotion; although, unfortunately, no vacancy occurred prior to the Admiral's supersession. In the AMAZON, when that frigate, in company at the time with the INDEFATIGABLE 46, Capt. Sir Edw. Pellew, sustained a loss of 3 men killed and 15 wounded in an action of 10 hours with *Les Droits de l'Homme* 74, and was at its close wrecked, near Ile Bas, 14 Jan. 1797, Mr. Littlehales again distinguished himself, and was in consequence recommended by his Captain to the notice and patronage of the Admiralty; who, on his returning from captivity, promoted him, 27 Sept. following, to the rank of Commander, and soon afterwards, 8 Nov., invested him with the command of the PENGUIN sloop. In the latter vessel Capt. Littlehales served on the Irish station until about two months subsequently to his attainment of Post-rank, 15 May, 1800. Being next, 14 Jan. 1801, appointed, *pro tempore*, to the CENTAUR 74, in the command of which ship he was ultimately confirmed, he cruized during the remainder of the war off Brest and Rochefort, then hoisted the flag of Vice-Admiral Dacres at Plymouth, and was afterwards ordered to the West Indies, where he conveyed Lieut.-General Grinfield, the military Commander-in-Chief, on a tour of inspection to the different islands. In the summer of 1803, after having displayed much assiduity and attention in the attack upon Ste. Lucie,* on which occasion the CENTAUR bore the broad pendant of Sir Sam. Hood, Capt. Littlehales was sent home by that officer with his despatches announcing the conquest, in the MORNE FORTUNÉE brig. Incapacitated at first from accepting, in consequence of illness contracted during his sojourn in the West Indies, and lacking the power afterwards to obtain, active employment afloat, his only other appointments were—6 May, 1808, to the Sea Fencibles at Liverpool, where he remained until the corps was disbanded in 1810—and 23 Aug. 1811, to the superintendence of ship-payments at Plymouth, the duties attached to which office he continued to discharge until the peace. He became a Rear-Admiral 22 July, 1830, and a Vice-Admiral 17 Aug. 1840.

Vice-Admiral Littlehales married, in Aug. 1803, Mary Anna, daughter of Thos. Cleather, Esq., of Plymouth, by whom he has left, with other issue,

* *Vide* Gaz. 1803, p. 918.

a son, the present Commander Edw. Littlehales, R.N.

LITTLEHALES. (COMMANDER, 1841.)

EDWARD LITTLEHALES is second son of the late Vice-Admiral Littlehales.

This officer entered the Navy, 3 Dec. 1818; served for some time in the Mediterranean as Midshipman of the REVENGE 76, flag-ship of Sir Harry Burrard Neale; passed his examination in 1825; and was made Lieutenant, 11 March, 1828, into the SUCCESS 28, Capts. Jas. Stirling and Wm. Clarke Jervoise. In Nov. 1829 the latter ship was all but lost on a reef, while making for Cockburn Sound, in Western Australia; on which occasion Mr. Littlehales' exemplary conduct was of so signal a nature that he not only received the warmest thanks of Capt. Jervoise, but was permitted by the Lords of the Admiralty to succeed the present Captain Edmund Yonge, whose own conduct on the occasion procured him promotion, in the post of First-Lieutenant, and to retain it until paid off 16 Dec. 1831. His subsequent appointments were—8 April, 1834, as Senior, to the HASTINGS 74, Capt. Henry Shiffner, bearing the flag afterwards of Sir Wm. Hall Gage on the Lisbon station, whence he returned at the close of 1837—and, 2 March, 1840, to the command of the DOLPHIN brigantine on the coast of Africa. He attained the rank he now holds 23 Nov. 1841; and since Jan. 1842 has been on half-pay. AGENTS—Messrs. Halford and Co.

LITTLEWORT. (LIEUT., 1817. F-P., 20; H-P., 19.)

RICHARD JOHN PIKE LITTLEWORT, born 5 Nov. 1792, is son of Lieut. Rich. Littlewort, R.N. (1777), who was on board the SALISBURY 50, in 1779, lost an eye in the service of his country, and died on full-pay in 1798.

This officer entered the Navy, 25 May, 1808, as Fst.-cl. Vol., on board the LEVIATHAN 74, commanded in the North Sea and Mediterranean by his friend and patron Capt. John Harvey; with whom, after having witnessed, as Midshipman, the destruction of the two French line-of-battle ships *Robuste* and *Lion* near Cape Cette, he removed in March, 1811, in the capacity of Master's Mate, to the ROYAL SOVEREIGN 100. On leaving the last-mentioned ship, which had been recently commanded by Capt. Wm. Bedford, Mr. Littlewort was successively employed between Aug. 1812 and Aug. 1815, part of the time as Acting-Master, in the HELENA 18, Capt. Henry Montresor, INDUS 74, Capt. Wm. Hall Gage, COSSACK 22, Capts. Hon. Algernon Percy and Hon. Robt. Rodney, and DRIVER sloop, Capt. Hon. A. Percy—on the Cork, North Sea, Mediterranean, Halifax, and Portsmouth stations. He then joined the ANTELOPE 50, bearing the flag in the West Indies of his former Commander, Rear-Admiral Harvey, who procured him a commission dated 1 Jan. 1817. He continued in the ANTELOPE until paid off in April, 1819; and since 12 March, 1838, has been in command of a station in the Coast Guard.

Previously to the receipt of his present appointment Lieut. Littlewort (who is Senior of 1817) was for a long time employed in the Merchant service, in which, we understand, he endured the heaviest misfortunes. His eldest and only surviving son was drowned in his arms when wrecked off the coast of Portugal in 1831. He has one daughter now living. He had married in May, 1823. AGENTS—Messrs. Ommanney.

LIVINGSTONE, BART. (VICE-ADMIRAL OF THE RED, 1838. F-P., 25; H-P., 40.)

SIR THOMAS LIVINGSTONE is son of the late Sir Alex. Livingstone, Bart., by his first wife, Anne, daughter of John Atkinson, Esq., of London. He succeeded his father, as 10th Baronet, in 1795; and is heir and representative of the attainted Earl of Linlithgow.

This officer entered the Navy, 17 Sept. 1782, on board the BRUNE frigate, Capt. Rich. Hussey Bickerton, on the Home station; where, and in the West Indies, he served, until promoted to the rank of Lieutenant 22 Nov. 1790, in the DÆDALUS 32, Capt. Thos. Pringle, DICTATOR 64, Capt. Wm. Parker, IRRESISTIBLE 74, Commodore Sir Andrew Snape Hamond, SYBIL frigate, Capt. R. H. Bickerton, and BOYNE 98, Capt. Geo. Bowyer. His succeeding appointments were—for a few months in 1791, to the CAMEL store-ship, Capt. Chas. Paton—16 Jan. 1793, to the MONARCH 74, commanded by the late Sir Jas. Wallace, under whom he witnessed the unsuccessful attack made in the following June upon Martinique—and in April, 1795, and April, 1796, to the ASIA and TREMENDOUS 74's, flag-ships of Rear-Admiral Thos. Pringle in the North Sea and at the Cape of Good Hope. On 26 Dec. 1796, after having acted for four months on the latter station as Commander of the ECHO sloop, Sir Thos. Livingstone was confirmed in his appointment to that vessel. In Feb. 1797, in consequence of her being condemned as unfit for service, he took a passage home, and was next, 2 June, 1798, appointed to the EXPEDITION 44, *armée-en-flûte*, in which vessel we find him, in 1799, employed in conveying part of the Russian contingent from Revel to England. He was posted, 13 Jan. 1800, into the DIADEM 64, employed as a troop-ship in the expeditions to Quiberon and Belleisle; and he was subsequently invested with the command—10 Dec. 1800, of the ATHÉNIENNE 64, in which vessel, prior to her being paid off in Oct. 1802, he accompanied Sir John Borlase Warren to the coast of Egypt in quest of a French squadron under M. Ganteaume—17 July, 1804, and 23 Jan. 1805, of the MEDIATOR and RENOMMÉE frigates, stationed at first in the Downs and off Boulogne, for the purpose of watching the enemy's flotilla, and then in the Mediterranean, where the RENOMMÉE, in effecting the capture, 4 April, 1806, under the fire of Fort Callaretes, of the *Vigilante* Spanish brig of war of 18 guns and 109 men, sustained a loss of 2 wounded, and occasioned her antagonist one of 4 killed and wounded*—and lastly, 3 Oct. 1821 (not having been afloat since the RENOMMÉE was put out of commission in June, 1808), of the GENOA 74, on the Lisbon station. He became a Rear-Admiral 22 July, 1830; and a Vice-Admiral 28 June, 1838.

Sir Thos. Livingstone, a Deputy-Lieutenant for co. Linlithgow, is Keeper of the Royal Palace of Linlithgow and of the Castle of Blackness. He married, in 1809, Janet, daughter of the late Sir Jas. Stirling, Bart., of Mansfield, and was left a widower in 1831. AGENTS—Hallett and Robinson.

LLOYD, K.H., F.R.S. (CAPTAIN, 1821. F-P., 15; H-P., 34.)

EDWARD LLOYD entered the Navy, in Sept. 1798, as Midshipman, on board the DICTATOR 64, Capt. Jas. Hardy, under whom, besides sharing in a multiplicity of particular services, he attended the expedition of 1801 to Egypt, where he commanded a boat at the debarkation of the troops in Aboukir Bay on 8 March, witnessed the battles fought on 13 and 21 of the same month, and had the subsequent charge of a djerm employed on the river Nile in keeping up a communication between Rosetta and the Anglo-Turkish shipping. While on the latter service he was intrusted with the care of Madame Menou, who was going to join her husband, the French Commander-in-Chief, at Alexandria. He continued in his djerm on Lake Mareotis until compelled to return to the DICTATOR by the effects of a severe contusion, which his zeal had prevented his attending to when it first occurred. In March, 1802, Mr. Lloyd joined, for a short period, the HERMES sloop, Capt. Jas. Watson; and in the following Oct. he became Master's Mate of the LEDA 38,† Capts. Jas. Hardy and Robt. Honyman. At the commencement of the late war we find him in

* *Vide* Gaz. 1806, p. 601.

† Mr. Lloyd had charge of a Lieutenant's watch during nearly the whole period of his servitude in the LEDA.

the constant voluntary command of a boat near Boulogne, and on the night of 29 July, 1804, distinguishing himself, under Lieut. Neil M'Lean, who was killed, in a most gallant but unsuccessful attempt to cut a mortar-vessel, on which occasion only 14 out of 38 of the British succeeded in effecting their escape. Fortunately for him, Mr. Lloyd, although wounded, was among the number that got off. In consideration of the injury he received, and of his gallant conduct, the Patriotic Society voted him a pecuniary reward, and presented him with an honorary testimonial. Among numerous other affairs with the enemy's flotilla in which he took part, we may instance the capture, 24 April, 1805, of seven schuyts, armed with 18 guns and 1 howitzer, and having on board 168 men. About the same period, too, he volunteered his services in a *catamaran* expedition, and placed one of the explosion machines in the precise position he had been directed. On 1 Nov. 1805 Mr. Lloyd, as officer of the middle watch, had the fortune, by means of a careful look-out and timely exertion, of saving the Leda from destruction, at a moment when the *King George* transport and *Britannia* Indiaman were both totally lost by striking on the Roccas, near Fernando Norunha. After assisting at the reduction, in Jan. 1806, of the Cape of Good Hope, where he was employed in bringing forward the field-pieces and howitzer belonging to the division of the army that first effected a landing under Brigadier-General Ferguson, he removed to the Diadem 64, bearing the broad pendant of Sir Home Popham, who, on 10 of the ensuing March, nominated him Acting-Lieutenant of the Volontaire frigate, Capt. Hon. Josceline Percy. Exchanging soon afterwards, in a similar capacity, into the Raisonnable 64, Capt. Josias Rowley, to which ship he was confirmed 14 Jan. 1808, Mr. Lloyd displayed, during an attachment to her of four years, a considerable degree of zeal, courage, and ability, and was foremost to volunteer his services on every occasion of difficulty or danger. Landing at first in the Rio de la Plata in command of a detachment of seamen styled the "Royal Blues," he assisted in the attacks upon Monte Video and Buenos Ayres, and partook, latterly as Aide-de-Camp to Capt. Rowley, in every military operation which preceded the final evacuation of Spanish America in the summer of 1807. When next at the blockade of the Isles of France and Bourbon, he frequently accompanied the present Sir Nesbit Josiah Willoughby in boat expeditions alongshore; and was frequently employed in reconnoitring the strength of the enemy's positions. He once, while so engaged, in a ten-oared cutter, boarded, carried, and brought out, under a heavy cross fire from two batteries, a large armed ship named the *Tady Bar*, although moored with springs and fully prepared for defence. Thirty-two of the enemy were on the occasion taken prisoners. On 21 Sept. 1809 Mr. Lloyd had the misfortune to be a second time severely wounded, when serving on shore as a volunteer in command of the Raisonnable's small-arm men, at the capture of St. Paul's, in the Ile de Bourbon.* In July, 1810, having followed Capt. Rowley into the Boadicea frigate, he united in the attack upon Bourbon itself, where his conduct obtained him the thanks of Lieut.-Colonel Keating,† and had confided to him the difficult task of placing a transport as a breakwater to facilitate the landing of the troops. After the conquest of the island he was left in charge of the Signal-posts for the purpose of reporting the motions of a French squadron then blockading it; an arrangement which led to the recovery of H. M. ships Africaine and Ceylon, and the capture of *La Vénus* of 44 guns, bearing the broad pendant of Commodore Hamelin, senior officer of the enemy's force in the Indian Ocean. On 28 Nov. 1810, being at the time First-Lieutenant of the Africaine, flag-ship of Vice-Admiral Bertie, Mr. Lloyd, previously to the first debarkation of the army at the Mauritius, landed by himself, with the view of ascertaining whether there lay any hostile force concealed behind the sea-wall that girted the island. During the operations that followed he joined the naval brigade under Capt. Wm. Augustus Montagu; and was directed, in addition to his other duties, to communicate the movements of the troops, by telegraph, to the Admiral. In the advance on Port Louis, Mr. Lloyd, who received the first flag of truce sent out by Governor-General De Caen, had charge of the guns with the leading column; and so signalized himself by his zeal, ability, and gallantry, that he drew forth the high encomiums of Capt. Montagu and the military Commander-in-Chief, and was warmly recommended by Vice-Admiral Bertie to the notice of the Admiralty. Being invested, 6 Dec. 1811, with the acting-command of the Hesper sloop, he was immediately selected by Major-General Abercromby to convey him and his staff to Bombay; on his arrival at which place he had the mortification to find himself superseded by the present Capt. Barrington Reynolds, who had been appointed by the then recently deceased Vice-Admiral Drury. Unwilling to return home, he continued as a passenger on board the Hesper until her arrival at Malacca, where, meeting with Lieut.-General Sir Sam. Auchmuty, he volunteered to serve under him during the Javese campaign. Landing accordingly with that officer's staff at Chillingching, he bore a part in the skirmish between the advanced divisions of the British and Dutch armies, which ended in the defeat of the latter and the capture of the important post of Weltervreeden. He was also present when the enemy made a sortie from Meester Cornelis; where, it appears, he assisted in storming their entrenched camp. On his arrival home in Dec. 1811, in the Caroline frigate, Capt. Christ. Cole, Capt. Lloyd had the satisfaction of finding that he had been confirmed a Commander on 9 of the previous May. His next appointment was, 21 Jan. 1814, to the Raven 16, in which vessel, prior to her being paid off in Oct. 1815, he served at the blockade of the enemy's flotilla at Ter Veere during the occupation of the East Scheldt by the fleet under Admiral Wm. Young—witnessed the operations against Balthz—encountered on his passage to Halifax a hurricane, which compelled him to throw half his guns overboard—received the public thanks of Sir Ralph Woodford, Governor of Trinidad, for his exertions in obtaining some exclusive and important privileges for British merchants trading to the Spanish Main—and succeeded, while in charge of the Gulf of Paria, in putting a stop to a system of bloodshed which political animosity, prior to his arrival, had carried to a frightful extent. From the period the Raven was put out of commission, Capt. Lloyd remained on shore until appointed, 9 Aug. 1820, to the Esk 20, fitting for the Leeward Islands. He was superseded on being advanced to his present rank 19 July, 1821; since which period, unsuccessful in his applications for employment, he has remained on half-pay.

Capt. Lloyd was nominated a K.H. 1 Jan. 1834. He married, in Aug. 1816, Colin Campbell, youngest daughter of the late Jas. Baillie, Esq., of Ealing Grove, co. Middlesex, formerly M.P. for Horsham, in Sussex; by whom he has issue. Agents—Hallett and Robinson.

LLOYD. (Lieutenant, 1842.)

Edward Alexander Tylden Lloyd entered the Navy 7 June, 1833; passed his examination 20 Jan. 1841; served, as Mate, on the Mediterranean and Home stations, in the Rodney 92, Capt. Robt. Maunsell, Madagascar 44, Capt. John Foote, and Queen 110, bearing the flag of Sir Edw. W. C. R. Owen; and, in honour of Her Majesty's visit to the latter ship when lying at Spithead, was promoted to the rank of Lieutenant 7 March, 1842. His succeeding appointments were, again in the Mediterranean—16 March, 1842, as Additional, to the Queen—31 Oct. 1842, to the Vernon 50, Capt. Wm. Walpole—23 March, 1844, as Additional, to the Geyser steam-sloop, Capt. Edw. John Carpenter—and, 31 Dec. 1844, to the Orestes 18, Capt. Edw. St. Leger Cannon. He became attached, 3 Oct.

* *Vide* Gaz. 1810, p. 215. † *V.* Gaz. 1810, p. 1683.

1845, to the EXCELLENT gunnery-ship at Portsmouth, Capt. Henry Ducie Chads; and, since 5 May, 1847, has been serving in the DRAGON steam-frigate, Capt. Wm. Hutcheon Hall, now on the Lisbon station.

LLOYD. (CAPTAIN, 1828. F-P., 13; H-P., 30.)

GEORGE LLOYD, born 13 Oct. 1793, is third son of John Lloyd, Esq. (Major in the 46th Regt., and Aide-de-Camp to Sir Henry Clinton during the American war, in which he received three wounds, the ultimate cause of his death), by Corbetta, daughter of the Rev. Geo. Holcombe, Archdeacon of Caermarthen, and Rector of Pwllcrochon, in Pembrokeshire. He is brother (with Major Wm. John Lloyd, R.A., who died at Brussels, 29 July, 1815, of a wound received at Waterloo) of the present John Wm. Lloyd, of Dan-yr-allt, co. Caermarthen, and South Park, Penshurst, Kent, and also of Lieut. Vaughan Lloyd, R.N. Capt. Lloyd, a distant relative of the late Admiral Wm. Lloyd, is nephew, by marriage, of the late Admiral Sir Herbert Sawyer, K.C.B.

This officer entered the Navy, in the spring of 1804, as Fst.-cl. Vol., on board the PRINCESS ROYAL 98, Capts. Herbert Sawyer, Gardiner Henry Guion, and Robt. Carthew Reynolds, stationed in the Channel, where, until Feb. 1808, he continued to serve, as Midshipman, in the SAN JOSEF* and HIBERNIA, flag-ships of Sir Chas. Cotton and Earl St. Vincent, and PLOVER sloop, Capt. Philip Browne. While next employed, between the latter date and Jan. 1812, in the VOLONTAIRE 38, and CAMBRIAN 40, each commanded by Capt. Chas. Bullen, we find him coming into frequent contact with the enemy both on board those frigates and in their boats, particularly at the defence of Tarragona, the destruction of the batteries at Palamos, the capture of 19 merchantmen at Cadaqués and of others at Selva, and the cutting out of a French vessel from under the Medas Islands. After he had been for some time Master's Mate of the AFRICA 64, bearing the flag in North America of Rear-Admiral Herbert Sawyer, and had for a short period acted as Lieutenant of the RATTLER sloop, Capts. Alex. Gordon and John Thomson (under whom, it appears, he assisted at the capture of many vessels off New York and up the Chesapeake), Mr. Lloyd was confirmed to the latter vessel by commission dated 3 Nov. 1812. His next appointment was, 7 Dec. 1813, to the TRENT 32, flag-ship on the Cork station of his friend Admiral Sawyer, who, on different occasions, allowed him to act as Commander of the CASTILIAN 18, PELICAN 18, and also of the TRENT. On 1 Sept. 1814 Capt. Lloyd, then in command of the CASTILIAN, fell in with the U. S. sloop *Wasp* of 22 guns, just as the latter had reduced H.M. brig AVON to the necessity of striking her colours. Having driven the American off the field, he immediately, in consequence of her repeated signals of distress, stood towards the British vessel, who, such had been her gallant resistance, went down almost before her crew could be removed.† Being officially promoted to the rank of Commander 8 Nov. 1815, Capt. Lloyd was in that capacity appointed, 22 Aug. 1827, to the VICTOR 18, fitting for the Jamaica station, where he made prize of *Las Damas Argentinas*, a notorious piratical schooner of 2 guns and 40 men, 28 of whom were hanged at St. Kitt's. Since the receipt of his Post-commission, which bears date 26 Aug. 1828, he has been on half-pay. AGENTS—Goode and Lawrence.

LLOYD. (LIEUTENANT, 1846.)

GRUFFYD CLAYTON LLOYD passed his examination 8 April, 1844; served, as Mate, from Feb. 1845 until Aug. 1846, in the EXCELLENT gunnery-ship at Portsmouth, Capt. Henry Ducie Chads; then joined the VICTORIA AND ALBERT steam-yacht, Capt. Lord Adolphus FitzClarence; and on 7 Oct. in the same year was promoted to the rank of Lieutenant. He has been serving, since 30 of the following Dec., in the TERRIBLE steam-frigate of 800 horse-power, Capt. Wm. Ramsay, and is now on the coast of Portugal.

LLOYD. (LIEUTENANT, 1841.)

HENRY LLOYD entered the Navy 3 Feb. 1828; passed his examination 26 Sept. 1834; and obtained his commission 23 Nov. 1841. His succeeding appointments were—in the course of 1842, to the ILLUSTRIOUS 72, flag-ship of Sir Chas. Adam, THUNDER surveying-vessel, Capt. Edw. Barnett, and ELECTRA 18, Capt. Arthur Darley, all attached to the force in North America and the West Indies—17 Feb. 1844, again to the THUNDER, as Senior-Lieutenant—11 Dec. 1844, as Additional, to the CALEDONIA 120, flag-ship at Devonport of Sir David Milne—11 Jan. 1845, to the WATERWITCH 10, Capt. Thos. Fras. Birch, on the coast of Africa—and, 24 Aug. 1845, as only Lieutenant, to the STAR 6, commanded on the same station by Capts. Robt. John Wallace Dunlop and Fred. Leopold Augustus Selwyn. He returned to England and was paid off in 1847.

LLOYD. (LIEUT., 1814. F-P., 11; H-P., 33.)

JOHN LLOYD entered the Navy, 17 Sept. 1803, as Fst.-cl. Vol., on board the MONARCH 74, Capt. Stewart, bearing the flag on the Downs of Lord Keith, whom he followed, in Aug. 1805, into the EDGAR 74. From Feb. 1806 until June, 1809, he again served in the MONARCH, commanded during that period by Capts. John Clarke Searle and Rich. Lee; under the latter of whom (besides assisting, as Midshipman, at Sir Sam. Hood's capture, 25 Sept. 1806, of four heavy French frigates, on which occasion the MONARCH acted a very prominent part, compelled *La Minerve* of 44 guns and 650 men to surrender, and sustained a loss of 4 men killed and 25 wounded) he was employed in blockading the Tagus, and in escorting, towards the close of 1807, the Royal Family of Portugal to the Brazils. Joining, next, the ALFRED 74, Capt. Joshua Rowley Watson, in which ship he continued until Sept. 1810, Mr. Lloyd, previously to making a voyage to the West Indies, accompanied the expedition to the Walcheren. In June, 1811, he was received on board the SAN JUAN 74, Capt. Chas. Vinicombe Penrose, lying at Gibraltar, where, and off Lisbon, he served, until Jan. 1814, in the SABRINA 20, Capt. Mackenzie, and STATELY 64, flag-ship of Vice-Admiral Geo. Martin. He was confirmed a Lieutenant, 22 July following, in the SAN JUAN, bearing the flag at the time of Hon. Chas. Elphinstone Fleeming; and he was lastly, from Aug. to Nov. in the same year, employed on gun-boat service in the Straits and at Cadiz. AGENTS—Pettet and Newton.

LLOYD. (LIEUTENANT, 1831.)

JOHN HUGHES LLOYD, born 7 July, 1803, is second son of the late Rich. Hughes Lloyd, Esq., of Plymog, Gwerclas, and Bashall, Major of the Royal Merioneth Militia, by Caroline, daughter of Henry Thompson, Esq. This gentleman, whose family is of illustrious Welsh extraction, and who is a collateral descendant of King Henry VII., is brother of Capt. Edw. Salubury and Hugh-Hughes Lloyd, both of the Hon. E. I. Co.'s service.

This officer entered the Navy 13 June, 1815; passed his examination in 1822; obtained his commission 12 Sept. 1831; and, with the exception of a servitude, from 23 Sept. 1834 until paid off 3 Oct. 1835, in the ÆTNA surveying-vessel, commanded on the coast of Africa by Lieut. Wm. Arlett, has since been on half-pay.

He married, 13 Feb. 1843, Mary, only child of Lucas Yeo Ward, Esq., a scion of the Wards of Northamptonshire. AGENTS—Hallett and Robinson.

* The SAN JOSEF formed part of the fleet under Admiral Cornwallis when that gallant officer pursued the French into Brest 22 Aug. 1805.

† Mr. James, in his 'Naval History,' and Lieut. Marshall, in his 'Naval Biography,' erroneously represent the CASTILIAN to have been commanded, on the occasion, by Capt. David Braimer.

LLOYD. (Lieut., 1810. f-p., 19; h-p., 29.)

Rickard Lloyd, born in Sept. 1790, is third son of the late Rickard Lloyd, Esq., of Ballincollig Castle, co. Cork; and a near relative of Lieut.-Colonel Lloyd, who fell at the head of his regiment, the 84th, at the battle of the Nive, 6 Dec. 1813. Lieut. Lloyd, whose uncle was a Captain in the Navy, has a brother in the Army, who has seen nearly 30 years' full-pay service in every climate.

This officer entered the Navy, 22 Sept. 1799, as Fst.-cl. Vol., on board the Pomone 40, Capts. Robt. Carthew Reynolds and Edw. Leveson Gower. Continuing in that ship until 1803, he served in her in the expedition to the Helder under Sir Andw. Mitchell; and was present, on proceeding to the Mediterranean, at the capture, 3 Aug. 1801, after a stiff action of 10 minntes, in which the British endured a loss of 2 killed and 4 wounded, of the *Carrère* of 40 guns and 320 men; as also, on 2 of the following Sept., of the frigates *Succès* and *Bravoure*. During a subsequent attachment to the Pique 36, Capts. Wm. Cumberland and Chas. Bayne Hodgson Ross, we find him witnessing the evacuation of Aux Cayes, St. Domingo, the capture, with other vessels, of *Le Goelan* 18, and the surrender of three French frigates with the remains of General Rochambeau's army from Cape François on board. He was also, in Jan. 1804, a participator in the unsuccessful attack on the island of Curaçoa; and in Dec. 1804 and Feb. 1805 he assisted at the capture of the Spanish ships of war *Diligentia* and *Orquijo*. On 26 March, 1806, he further contributed to the taking of the French corvettes *Phaëton* and *Voltigeur*, of 16 guns and 115 men each; the former of which vessels offered so fierce a resistance, that 9 of the British were killed and 14 of them wounded while in the act of boarding. For their gallantry on the occasion the officers were each presented by the Patriotic Society with the sum of 100*l*. for the purchase of a sword, and the men with 20*l*. a-piece. Becoming Midshipman, in Aug. 1806, of the Pelican sloop, Capts. Ward and Morrison, Mr. Lloyd, while in that vessel, accompanied the expedition against Copenhagen, where, it appears, he was lent to the gun-boat service. In March, 1808, being then Acting-Lieutenant of the Pelican, he landed and carried the colours with the naval brigade at the reduction of the island of Descada; and in the course of the same year he presents himself to our notice as cutting out, with only two boats, a heavily-laden merchant-brig, lying under the batteries of Omoa, in the Bay of Honduras. Prior to the receipt of his commission, which bears date 22 Sept. 1810, Mr. Lloyd further acted for several months as Lieutenant in the Dart and Surinam sloops, Capts. Bertie and Hodge, and Alfred 74, Capt. Joshua Rowley Watson. In the Surinam he officiated as her Senior Lieutenant at the reduction of Martinique and Guadeloupe; and, with her boats under his orders, he cut out an armed schooner from beneath the batteries of St. Eustatius. During the remainder of the war Mr. Lloyd served on the Home, Jamaica, and American stations, in the Neptune 98, Capt. Volant Vashon Ballard, Sceptre 74, Capt. Jas. Ballard, Fawn 20, Capt. Thos. Fellowes, Alert 18, Capt. Joseph Gulston Garland, Rippon 74, Capt. Sir Christopher Cole, and Norge 74, Capt. Chas. Dashwood. While in the Sceptre, besides assisting at the blockade of the French fleet in Aix Roads, he was frequently employed on boat-service, and on one occasion obtained the thanks of Sir Harry Neale, the Commander-in-Chief, for cutting off from an armed convoy a chasse-marée, notwithstanding a heavy fire which had been opened upon him from the batteries at Belleisle. Among the other ships above alluded to, the Fawn appears conspicuous for her activity and success as a cruizer, and the Alert for the frequency of her engagements with the batteries in the neighbourhood of Dunkerque and Calais. Accompanying the Norge on the New Orleans expedition, Mr. Lloyd, in command of her barge, aided, with the boats of a squadron, in capturing, on Lake Borgne, 14 Dec. 1814, a flotilla of five American gun-vessels under Commodore Jones, which did not surrender until they had inflicted on the British a loss of 17 men killed and 77 wounded. The casualties in Mr. Lloyd's boat alone amounted to 2 of the former and 3 of the latter. He was afterwards employed on shore with the army in all its operations. The Lieutenant, who had been on half-pay since 1815, was lastly, from 15 March, 1827, until March, 1830, employed in the Ordinary at Portsmouth.

He married, 2 May, 1816, Susan, second daughter of the late Edw. Heard, Esq., of Patna, co. Cork, a Major in the Hon. E. I. Co.'s Service, by whom he has issue two sons and two daughters. The eldest son is a Lieutenant in H.M. 36th Regt.

LLOYD. (Vice-Admiral of the White, 1837. f-p., 24; h-p., 43.)

Robert Lloyd was born 24 March, 1765, and died 17 Jan. 1846, at his seat, Tregayan, co. Anglesey. He was eldest son of Robt. Lloyd, Esq., of Gunys, co. Caernarvon, by Margaret Edmunds, of Tregayan, only daughter of the Rev. Dr. Edmunds, Rector of Aber, in the same shire.

This officer entered the Navy, 31 March, 1779, as Captain's Servant, on board the Valiant 74, Capt. Goodall; on removing from which ship to a Midshipman's berth in the Fairy 18, Capts. Berkeley, Keppel, and Brown, he was wounded in a sharp action which preceded the capture of that sloop by the French frigate *Madame*. After a captivity of some time in France, he was exchanged about March, 1781, and on his return to England was received on board the Medway 74, Capts. Harwood and Edgar. He next, between May, 1782, and July, 1787, served on the Channel station in the Hebe frigate, Capts. Keppel and Edw. Thornbrough, and on 22 Nov. 1790, he was promoted to the rank of Lieutenant. Obtaining an appointment, in Dec. 1792, to the Latona 38, Capts. Thornbrough and Hon. Arthur Kaye Legge, Mr. Lloyd fought under the former of those officers in the action of 1 June, 1794; and on rejoining him as Senior Lieutenant in the Robust 74, he served in Lord Bridport's action, and was severely wounded in the expedition to Quiberon. On 6 Dec. 1796 we find him promoted to the command of the Racoon sloop in the North Sea; where, after a short running fight, in which the Racoon had 1 person, the Master, killed, and 4 wounded, he succeeded in taking, 11 Jan. 1798, *Le Policrate* French privateer, of 16 guns and 72 men;* and, on 22 of the same month, *La Pensée*, of 2 guns, 9 swivels, and 32 men. Capt. Lloyd, who had previously captured *Les Amis*, of 2 guns, 6 swivels, and 31 men, made further prize, 20 Oct. following, at the end of a running action of two hours, of *La Vigilante*, of 14 guns and 50 men.† Prior to his attainment of Post-rank 6 Dec. 1799, he had the increased good fortune to sink a French lugger, and to effect the capture of the privateers *Le Vrai Décidé*, of 14 guns, 4 swivels, and 41 men, and *L'Intrépide*, of 16 guns and 60 men, 13 of whom were killed and wounded.‡ On the latter occasion he unfortunately received a wound in the head from a half-pike. His last appointments were—12 Jan. 1801, to the Mars 74, bearing the flag of Rear-Admiral Thornbrough in the Channel, where he remained until April, 1802—25 March, 1807, to the Hussar 38, in which ship, after assisting at the reduction of Copenhagen, he visited North America and the West Indies—31 May, 1809, and 25 Sept. 1810, to the Guerrière 40, and Swiftsure 74, flagship of Sir John Borlase Warren, both on the North American station—and, 11 Feb. 1812 (after ten months of half-pay), to the Plantagenet 74. Continuing in the latter vessel until paid off in April, 1815, Capt. Lloyd was at first employed in the Baltic, and afterwards again in North America, where he captured a large number of coasters,§ and accompanied the expeditions against Washing-

* *Vide* Gaz. 1798, p. 35. † *V.* Gaz. 1798, p. 1026.
‡ *V.* Gaz. 1799, p. 1256.
§ Between 8 Sept. and 17 Dec. 1813, Capt. Lloyd took not less than 20 sail of vessels, measuring, in the whole, about 1250 tons.—*Vide* Gaz. 1814, p. 512.

ton and New Orleans. On his return to England he brought with him the bodies of Generals Gibbs and Pakenham. He became a Rear-Admiral 22 July, 1830; and a Vice-Admiral 10 Jan. 1837.

In 1790 Vice-Admiral Lloyd was High Sheriff for Caernarvon; as he was, in 1820, for Anglesey. At the period of his death he was a Deputy-Lieutenant for the latter county, and a Magistrate for both. He married, first, in 1789, Elizabeth Charlotte, daughter of Henry Gibbs, Esq., of Portsmouth, Surveyor-General of Customs; and secondly, 28 Nov. 1839, Ellen, daughter of the late Thos. Roberts, Esq., Surgeon, of Garth View, Bangor, North Wales. His only daughter was the wife of the late Capt. Thos. Parry Jones Parry, R.N.

LLOYD. (Lieut., 1815. f-p., 11; h-p., 27.)

Vaughan Lloyd, born 29 Jan. 1795, is brother of Capt. Geo. Lloyd, R.N.

This officer entered the Navy, 10 June, 1809, as Fst.-cl. Vol., on board the Ajax 74, Capt. Robt. Waller Otway; previously to accompanying whom, in the summer of 1811, into the Cumberland 74, he participated, as Midshipman, in a very gallant skirmish in which the British with a slender force beat back a powerful division of the French Toulon fleet; witnessed a disastrous yet most valorous attack made by Capt. Fras. Wm. Fane on the enemy's shipping in the mole of Palamos; and contributed to the capture, 31 March, 1811, of *Le Dromadaire* store-ship, of 20 guns and 150 men. On leaving the Cumberland, in which ship, commanded the greater part of the time by Capt. Thos. Baker, he had escorted convoy to the West Indies and back, Mr. Lloyd, in June, 1813, rejoined the Ajax, then again under the orders of Capt. Otway, with whom he served at the reduction, in the following Sept., of the town of St. Sebastian, and at the capture, 17 March, 1814, of *L'Alcyon* French corvette, of 16 guns and 120 men. After cruizing for ten months on the Irish station as Master's Mate of the Tiber 38, Capt. Jas. Rich. Dacres, and for two more as Acting-Lieutenant of the Eurydice 24, Capt. Rich. Spencer, he was confirmed in his present rank by commission dated 20 Sept. 1815. His last appointments were, in 1816-17, to the Eurydice again, Capt. Robt. Wauchope, Leveret 10, Capt. John Theed, and Conqueror 74, flag-ship of Rear-Admiral Robt. Plampin—all on the St. Helena station, whence he returned in Sept. 1820.

Lieut. Lloyd married Augusta, daughter of John Adams, Esq., of Lydstep House, co. Pembroke.

LLOYD. (Retired Commander, 1840. f-p., 17; h-p., 33.)

William Lloyd (*a*) entered the Navy, 1 May, 1797, as Fst.-cl. Vol., on board the Montagu 74, Capt. John Knight, stationed in the North Sea; served as Midshipman, from Jan. 1798, until wrecked 4 Nov. 1800, in the Marlborough 74, commanded in the Channel and Mediterranean by Capts. Joseph Ellison and Thos. Sotheby; and in Jan. 1801 joined the Superb 74, Capts. John Sutton and Rich. Goodwin Keats. While under the latter officer we find him sharing in Sir Jas. Saumarez' action in the Gut of Gibraltar 12 July, 1801, accompanying Lord Nelson to the West Indies and back in 1805 in pursuit of the combined squadrons of France and Spain, and on 6 Feb. 1806 enacting a part in the action off St. Domingo. Immediately after the latter event he returned to England as Acting-Lieutenant of the Jupiter, Capt. Chas. Gill; and on 9 June in the same year he was officially promoted. His succeeding appointments were—25 July, 1806, to the Ardent 64, Capts. Geo. Eyre, Ross Donnelly, and Edwin Henry Chamberlayne, in which ship he beheld the attack on Monte Video in Feb. 1807—28 April, 1808 (he had left the Ardent in the preceding Dec.), and 7 Jan. 1809, to the Zebra and Cruizer sloops, Capts. Geo. Barne Trollope and Thos. Rich. Toker, employed on the Baltic and North Sea stations—and lastly, 12 Sept. 1814, after 10 months of half-pay, to the Kangaroo, Capt. Hall, with whom he cruized in the Channel and on the American coast until his return home in Aug. 1815. He accepted his present rank 19 Aug. 1840.

Commander Lloyd is a Police-Magistrate at Port Elizabeth, Cape of Good Hope.

LLOYD. (Lieutenant, 1827.)

William Lloyd (*b*) died 12 July, 1847, at Montreal, of typhus fever, contracted while ministering to the wants of the sick and destitute Irish immigrants.

This officer passed his examination in 1826; and for his conduct as Mate of the Albion 74, Capt. John Acworth Ommanney, at the battle of Navarin, where he was wounded, was promoted to the rank of Lieutenant 22 Oct. 1827. He remained thenceforward on half-pay.

LLOYD. (Lieut., 1815. f-p., 24; h-p., 18.)

William Hayman Lloyd, born in July, 1792, is son of Wm. Lloyd, Esq., Surgeon, of London.

This officer entered the Navy, in Dec. 1805, as Fst.-cl. Vol., on board the Cæsar 80, Capt. Thos. Geo. Shortland, to which ship, bearing the successive flags of Rear-Admirals Sir Rich. John Strachan, Hon. Robt. Stopford, and Wm. Albany Otway, he continued attached as Midshipman and Master's Mate until June, 1811. He was in consequence present, during the year 1809, at the destruction of three French frigates under the batteries of Sable d'Olonne, in the attack also on the enemy's shipping in Aix Roads, and in the operations against Walcheren, where he served in an armed transport at the bombardment of Flushing, and commanded a gun-boat until its final evacuation by the British. On leaving the Cæsar, Mr. Lloyd successively joined the Venerable and Tigre 74's, Capts. Sir Home Popham and John Halliday; by the latter of whom, during Lord Wellington's occupation of the lines of Torres Vedras, he was there intrusted with the command of a signal station for five months. The ship into which he was next received was the Pembroke 74, Capt. Jas. Brisbane, under whom, it appears, he beheld the fall of Genoa in April, 1814. In the ensuing summer he went on a timber-getting voyage to South America, as Second-Master of the Serapis store-ship, Master-Commander Wm. Lloyd; and on his return to England, in Aug. 1815, he found that he had been awarded a commission dated 6 Feb. in that year. From Dec. 1822 until the close of 1833, and from 13 May, 1841, until the summer of 1844, Lieut. Lloyd held appointments in the Coast Guard. He is now on half-pay.

He married the only daughter of Lieut. Jas. Nichols, formerly Resident Agent of Transports at Gibraltar, by whom he has issue two sons and five daughters.

LOCH. (Captain, 1814. f-p., 27; h-p., 21.)

Francis Erskine Loch, born in April, 1788, is youngest son of Geo. Loch, Esq., of Drylaw, co. Edinburgh, by Mary, daughter of John Adam, Esq., of Blair, co. Kinross, sister of the Right Hon. Wm. Adam, Lord Chief Commissioner of the Scotch Jury Court, and aunt of the present Vice-Admiral Sir Chas. Adam, K.C.B., Governor of Greenwich Hospital. Capt. Loch (whose grandmother was herself the grand-daughter of David, fourth Earl of Buchan) is uncle of Capt. Granville Gower Loch, R.N., and of Lieut. Geo. John Loch, R.N.

This officer entered the Navy, 1 Sept. 1799, as Fst.-cl. Vol., on board the Queen Charlotte 100, Capt. Andrew Todd, bearing the flag of Lord Keith; and on 17 of the following March narrowly escaped involvement in the destruction of that ship, being on board when she took fire in Leghorn Roads. After he had further served with Lord Keith, as Midshipman, in the Audacious and Minotaur 74's, and Foudroyant 80, and had assisted in the Minotaur at the blockade of Genoa, he removed to the Mondovi 14, Capt. John Stewart,

While under that officer he landed as his Aide-de-Camp at the island of Rhodes for the purpose of accelerating the fitting out of the numerous gun-boats intended for the conveyance of troops to Egypt; was employed in a boat at the debarkation in Aboukir Bay; assisted in cutting out a Greek vessel from under the guns of the castle at that place; was present in the battles of 13 and 21 March; and was for a long time again Aide-de-Camp to his Captain on Lake Mareotis. In the course of the same year Mr. Loch successively joined the Africaine and Pearl frigates; the former commanded by Capt. Stewart, and the latter by Capt. Sam. Jas. Ballard; under whom, while at the blockade of Malta, he beheld the capture of *La Carrère*, of 40 guns, and was serving on shore with the seamen and marines belonging to Sir John Borlase Warren's squadron when they were repulsed at Porto Ferrajo. On leaving the Pearl, in Nov. 1801, he returned, as Signal-Midshipman, to the Foudroyant, still on the Mediterranean station, whence, in 1802, he came home in the Princess Augusta yacht, Capt. Hon. Geo. Grey. Being discharged, in May, 1803, into La Chiffonne 36, commanded by his cousin, Capt. Adam, he cruized with much success in that ship in the North Sea and Channel until the summer of 1805; on 10 June in which year La Chiffonne (the Falcon sloop, Clinker gun-brig, and Frances armed-cutter in company) drove on shore under the batteries of Fécamp a division of the French flotilla, consisting of two corvettes and 15 gun-vessels, carrying in all 51 guns, 4 8-inch mortars, and 3 field-pieces, accompanied by 14 transports. In Dec. 1805, after he had been for a short time stationed with Capt. Adam off the mouth of the Scheldt in the Resistance 38, Mr. Loch was nominated Sub-Lieutenant of the Seagull 16, Capt. Robt. Cathcart. His appointments in the capacity of Lieutenant, a rank he attained 22 Jan. 1806, were, it appears—5 Aug. 1806, to the Diadem 64, bearing the flag of Rear-Admiral Chas. Stirling—11 Aug. 1808, to the Semiramis 36, Capts. Wm. Granger and Chas. Richardson—8 May, 1811, to the Caledonia 120, flag-ship of Sir Edw. Pellew—and, in 1812, to the San Josef 110, and Queen Charlotte 100, bearing each the flag of Lord Keith. During the operations of 1807 in the Rio de la Plata, Mr. Loch, then in the Diadem, commanded a party of seamen attached to the guns under Brigadier-General Auchmuty and Lieut.-General Whitelocke at the capture of Monte Video and in the unsuccessful attack upon Buenos Ayres. On the fall of the former place he was intrusted with the charge of 60 prizes taken in the harbour, many of them vessels-of-war. When in the Semiramis, in 1808, we find him escorting to Corunna Mr. Frere, the British Minister, together with the patriot general the Marquis de la Romana; and, on his appointment to the Caledonia, participating in a skirmish between the British and French fleets off Cape Sepet. While Flag-Lieutenant in 1812 of the Queen Charlotte, he was sent in the hired-cutter Fanny to reconnoitre Brest Roads; and so well did he carry out his instructions, that he succeeded in making a sketch of the position of each of the enemy's vessels; not however without much peril, as the Fanny was at first nearly sunk by the batteries in Le Goulet, and next all but captured by a ship of the line. As a reward for this service, Mr. Loch was, in Oct. 1812, invested by Lord Keith with the acting-command of the Rover sloop, and ordered to cruize between Ushant and Ile de Bas, where he forced an armed convoy to seek protection among the rocks. Prior to his official promotion to the rank of Commander, which took place 6 Jan. 1813, he had the fortune to capture the *Experiment* American letter-of-marque, of 6 guns and 17 men, laden with cotton and rice, from Charlestown bound to Bourdeaux—the first vessel of the kind that had attempted a voyage to Europe since the declaration of war. On then leaving the Rover (although he had been in her so short a period) the officers and crew united in presenting him with an elegant sword, accompanied by an equally handsome complimentary address. Being next appointed, 16 Aug. 1813, to the Sparrow 16, Capt. Loch was for some time stationed at the mouth of the river Bidasoa; and on 10 of the following Nov., while Lord Wellington's army was forcing the French lines along the coast to St. Jean de Luz, we find him assisting in a naval demonstration in the rear of Socoa, where the Sparrow sustained some slight damage in her hull and sails, and had 1 man wounded.* On 26 March, 1814, the latter vessel, when off Brest, fell in during thick weather with the two French frigates *Etoile* and *Sultane;* in closely reconnoitring which she sustained further injury, and had her Master killed and 1 man wounded. The Hebrus 36 heaving in sight while she was so engaged, and the Hannibal 74 soon joining in the chase, the enemy's ships were fortunately both captured. Capt. Loch's conduct in this affair procured him the thanks of the Admiralty. In the ensuing summer the Sparrow was employed in bringing to England some of the Generals (among whom were the famous Barclay de Tolly and Hetman Platoff) attached to the suites of the Allied Sovereigns. On the occasion of the grand naval review her Captain was directed by the Admiral of the Fleet to superintend the procession of boats which attended the embarkation of the Prince Regent and his royal visitors on board the Impregnable. He was then despatched to Genoa, in convoy of several transports with Sardinians discharged from the British army; and on 29 Sept. 1814, as soon as he had accomplished the mission, he was made Post into the Minstrel 26. In that ship, which he paid off in Dec. 1815, Capt. Loch was employed, during the war of a hundred days, in conveying arms and ammunition to the adherents of the Duc d'Angoulême on the coast of Spain; and in blockading, previously to the surrender of the island of Elba, the harbour of Porto Ferrajo, where lay the French frigate *Alcmène* and several gun-boats. Obtaining command, 21 March, 1818, of the Eden 26, he equipped and sailed for the East Indies, and on his arrival on that station was appointed, 16 Oct., Senior officer in the Persian Gulf, in which capacity he contrived to capture or destroy nine piratical vessels. In Nov. 1819 he became second in command of an expedition sent under the orders of Capt. Fras. Augustus Collier to act against the head-quarters and principal resort of the freebooters at Ras-al-Khyma. At the commencement of the operations Capt. Loch conducted the debarkation of the troops, 3000 in number; and he then, landing in person, performed the duties of Beach-Master, and served in one of the breaching batteries. When the bulk of the armament returned, he remained with Major Colebrook to arrange any differences that might afterwards arise. His conduct throughout the whole proceedings, we may add, afforded the highest satisfaction both to the Admiralty and to the Government of India.† The Eden being paid off in Aug. 1821, Capt. Loch did not again go afloat until Jan. 1838; on 31 of which month he received an appointment to the Hastings 72. In the following April that ship took the Earl of Durham to Quebec. On her return to England she sailed, in the early part of Oct., for the Mediterranean with the Queen Dowager, whom, after visiting Gibraltar, Naples, Messina, and Syracuse, she landed at Malta on 1 Dec. In April, 1839, Capt. Loch again had the honour of receiving Her Majesty on board, and of being ordered to conduct her to England, where, having been driven back to Palermo by stress of weather, and having touched on his passage at Lisbon and Vigo, he arrived 24 May. His health obliging him almost immediately to invalid, he was appointed, 19 Sept. following, to the Victory 104, ordinary guard-ship at Portsmouth. Since Sept. 1841, about which period he left the Victory, he has been Superintendent of Quarantine at Standgate Creek, in the river Medway.

On 4 May, 1847, Capt. Loch was appointed a Naval Aide-de-Camp to Her Majesty. He married, 17 June, 1822, Jesse, daughter of Major Robertson,

* *Vide* Gaz. 1813, p. 2406. † *V.* Gaz. 1820, p. 1672.

Barrack-Master-General for North Britain, and niece of General Robertson, of Lawyers, Perthshire, N.B., and by that lady has several children, of whom two are in the Bombay Cavalry and one in the Royal Navy. AGENTS—Messrs. Stilwell.

LOCH. (LIEUTENANT, 1846.)

GEORGE JOHN LOCH is son of John Loch, Esq., formerly M.P. for Hythe, a Director of the East India Company, by Marion, daughter of Archibald Cullen, Esq., K.C.; and nephew of Capt. Fras. Erskine Loch, R.N.

This officer passed his examination 16 April, 1842; and served as Mate, on the East India, Home, North America and West India, and African stations, in the ENDYMION 44, Capt. Hon. Fred. Wm. Grey, EXCELLENT gunnery-ship, Capt. Sir Thos. Hastings, ILLUSTRIOUS 72, flag-ship of Sir Chas. Adam, and BITTERN 16, Capt. Thos. Hope. He obtained his commission 15 Jan. 1846; and since 20 of that month has been serving, still on the coast of Africa, in the NIMROD 20, Capt. Jas. Rich. Dacres.

LOCH. (CAPTAIN, 1841. F-P., 15; H-P., 6.)

GRANVILLE GOWER LOCH, born in 1813, is second son of Jas. Loch, Esq., of Drylaw, co. Edinburgh, an Advocate at the Scottish bar, and M.P. for Kirkwall, &c., by Ann, youngest daughter of P. Orr, Esq., of Kincardineshire; and nephew of Capt. Fras. Erskine Loch, R.N.

This officer entered the Navy 23 Feb. 1826; passed his examination in 1832; obtained his first commission 23 Oct. 1833; was appointed, 21 Aug. 1834 and 27 Aug. 1835, to the OCEAN 80 and HOWE 120, as Flag-Lieutenant at the Nore to Hon. Chas. Elphinstone Fleeming; joined, 18 March, 1836, the VANGUARD 80, Capt. Hon. Duncombe Pleydell Bouverie, fitting for the Mediterranean; ascended the next step in his profession 28 Feb. 1837; and was invested, 12 July, 1838, and 26 Dec. 1840, with the command of the FLY 18 and VESUVIUS steamer, in which vessels (with the exception of a short period which intervened between his paying off the one and his appointment to the other) he served, on the South American and Mediterranean stations, until advanced to his present rank 26 Aug. 1841.

On his return to England on the occasion of his last promotion, Capt. Loch volunteered to join the expedition in China, where, it appears, he acted as extra Aide-de-Camp to Sir Hugh Gough at the storming of Chin-Kiang-Foo 21 July, 1842,* and was present with Sir Henry Pottinger in his negociations with the natives. In the course of 1842 he published an able and very interesting work entitled 'The closing Events of the War in China.' AGENT—John P. Muspratt.

LOCK. (COMMANDER, 1828. F-P., 10; H-P., 31.)

CAMPBELL LOCK is son, we understand, of the late Vice-Admiral Walter Lock (who served as Lieutenant of the QUEEN CHARLOTTE in Lord Howe's action, commanded the CHARON hospital-ship in the affair off Ile de Groix, and was for some time Agent for Prisoners of War), by a sister of Capt. Michael Head, R.N. His brother James, a Lieutenant in the R.N., fell a victim to the climate of the West Indies in 1808.

This officer entered the Navy, 11 Nov. 1806, as Third-cl. Boy, on board the PUISSANT 74, Capt. John Irwin, lying at Spithead; and from 14 Dec. 1808 until 19 Jan. 1811 served as Midshipman and Master's Mate in the ARETHUSA 38, Capt. Robt. Mends; under whom he witnessed the capture, 6 April, 1809, of the French 40-gun frigate *Le Niemen*, and actively co-operated with the patriots on the north coast of Spain, where, with the exception of Castro, he assisted at the destruction, during the summer of 1811, of all the batteries from St. Sebastian to St. Andero, upon which were found altogether about 100 pieces of cannon. On leaving the ARETHUSA we find him successively joining, on the Home and North American stations, the POMPÉE 74, Capt. Sir Jas. Athol Wood, SPARTAN 38, Capt. Edw. Pelham Brenton, and PLANTAGENET 74, Capt. Robt. Lloyd. He was confirmed a Lieutenant, 30 May, 1814, in the MORGIANA sloop, Capts. David Scott and Vincent Newton, stationed, until July, 1815, at Halifax and Bermuda; and he was lastly, from 1 Feb. 1827, until promoted to the rank of Commander 17 July, 1828, employed in the VICTORY 104, guard-ship at Portsmouth, Capt. Hon. Geo. Elliot.

Commander Lock is married, and has issue. AGENT—J. Hinxman.

LOCKYER, C.B. (CAPTAIN, 1815. F-P., 26; H-P., 22.)

NICHOLAS LOCKYER died 27 Feb. 1847, while in command of H.M.S. ALBION, at Malta, aged 65. He was brother of the present Colonel H. F. Lockyer, K.C., commanding H.M. 90th Regt., now in garrison at that place.

This officer (whose name had been borne from 1790 to 1792 on the books of the SYREN 32, Capt. John Manley) embarked, in 1799, as Master's Mate, on board the VOLTIGEUR sloop, Capts. Thos. Geo. Shortland and Lennox Thompson, with whom he served until 1801 in the Channel and at Newfoundland. He then joined in succession LA CONSTANCE 24, and BLANCHE 36, both commanded by Capt. Zachary Mudge; and on 17 Dec. 1803, after having been for some time actively employed on the Lisbon and West India stations, especially at the blockade of St. Domingo, he was promoted to a Lieutenancy in the TARTAR 32, Capts. John Perkins, Keith Maxwell, Edw. Hawker, and Stephen Poyntz. While with Capt. Maxwell, Mr. Lockyer assisted, as second in command of three boats under Lieut. Henry Mullah, in boarding and carrying, on a reef of rocks midway between the islands of Saona and St. Domingo, *L'Hirondelle* privateer, of 10 long 4-pounders and 50 men, notwithstanding that the British in their advance, besides having to pull against a strong sea-breeze, were assailed by a heavy fire of grape and musketry, and on reaching the vessel found the whole crew drawn up round the deck. Although the victors in this very gallant affair had but 2 men hurt, their opponents sustained a loss of 9 killed and 6 wounded. The undaunted spirit and perseverance of the former were most highly eulogized by Capt. Maxwell, who, in regard in particular to Lieuts. Mullah and Lockyer, declared himself unable to express the sense he entertained of their brave and intrepid conduct.* Obtaining a second promotal commission 25 Sept. 1806, the subject of the present narrative assumed command, 25 March, 1807, of the HOUND bomb; which vessel, in Aug. 1808, bore the flag of Rear-Admiral Rich. Goodwin Keats, and assisted in embarking the Spanish troops under the Marquis de la Romana from the vicinity of Nyeborg.† On 26 Oct. 1809 Capt. Lockyer removed to the SOPHIE 18 and in her he continued most actively and successfully employed on the Channel and Halifax stations for more than five years; effecting the capture or destruction during that period of one privateer (the *Pioneer*) of 320 tons, 17 guns, and 170 men, of another of 2 guns and 25 men, and of a merchant-ship, two brigs, 10 schooners, and two sloops. The SOPHIE also, while attached to the Chesapeake squadron, proved instrumental to the taking of numerous merchantmen; and, on 15 Sept. 1814, forming part at the time of a small force under Capt. Hon. Wm. Henry Percy, she endured a loss of 6 men killed and 16 wounded in an attack on Fort Bowyer. In command, 14 Dec. 1814, of the boats of a squadron, 45 in number, containing altogether about 980 persons, Capt. Lockyer, after a tedious row of 36 hours on Lake Borgne, attacked a flotilla of five gun-vessels, under the American Commodore Jones, with such judgment and determination,‡ that, in spite of the enemy's formidable force (consisting of 16 long guns, 14 carronades, 2 howitzers, 12 swivels, and 245 men), their advantage of a chosen position, and their studied and deliberate preparation, they were all cap-

* *Vide* Gaz. 1842, p. 3414.

* *Vide* Gaz. 1801, p. 1282. † *V.* Gaz. 1808, p. 1150. ‡ *V.* Gaz. 1815, p. 446.

tured in so serviceable a state as to afford the most essential aid to the operations connected with the expedition against New Orleans.* On at first closing with the enemy, Capt. Lockyer made for the Commodore's vessel, in boarding which it was his lot to be dangerously wounded. So stern was the general resistance offered by the Americans, that, before they were finally subdued, their own loss amounted to not less than 6 killed and 35 wounded, nor that of the British to less than 17 killed and 77 wounded. The prizes being collectively placed upon the establishment of a 36-gun frigate, the command of them was at once given to Capt. Lockyer by Sir Alex. Cochrane, who in his public despatch declared him justly entitled to the protection of the Admiralty. On 29 March, 1815, he was in consequence confirmed in Post-rank. His subsequent appointments, it appears, were—26 June, 1816, to a command on Lake Ontario, which he retained until 18 June, 1817—17 Dec. 1824, to the Romney 50, *armée-en-flûte*, variously employed, until paid off 12 Oct. 1827, in passages to Quebec, the Tagus, the Mediterranean, and Sierra Leone—12 Oct. 1832, to the Stag 46, stationed off the coast of Portugal, whence he returned in Dec. 1835—and 10 Nov. 1843, to the Albion 90. In that ship, in which he continued until the period of his death, Capt. Lockyer served at first as Flag-Captain to Sir David Milne at Devonport, then on the Lisbon station, and finally with the Channel squadron.

He had been nominated a C.B. 4 June, 1815; and awarded, about the same period, a gratuity for his wounds of 301*l.* 2*s.* 6*d.* Agents—Messrs. Ommanney.

* An armed sloop was on the same occasion taken by a division of Capt. Lockyer's boats under the present Sir Samuel Roberts.

LOCKYER. (Lieutenant, 1845.)

William Nicholas Love Lockyer entered the Navy in 1832; passed his examination 2 Nov. 1838; and after having been for some time attached, as Mate, to the Excellent gunnery-ship at Portsmouth, Capt. Sir Thos. Hastings, was employed in that capacity in the Aigle 24, Capt. Lord Clarence Edw. Paget, on the Mediterranean station, from the close of 1841 until promoted to the rank of Lieutenant 1 Sept. 1845. His appointments have since been—on 15 of the latter month, as Additional, to the Penelope steam-frigate, bearing the broad pendant on the coast of Africa of Commodore Wm. Jones—26 Dec. 1845, to the Albion 90, Capt. Nicholas Lockyer, part of the Channel squadron—and 6 May, 1847, again to the Excellent, Capt. Henry Ducie Chads, under whom he is at present serving.

LODDER. (Lieutenant, 1846.)

Charles Arthur Lodder served as Midshipman of the Powerful 84, Commodore Chas. Napier, during all the operations on the coast of Syria, including the bombardment of St. Jean d'Acre. He passed his examination 7 July, 1842; was employed in the Mediterranean, as Mate, from the close of that year until promoted to the rank of Lieutenant 26 June, 1846, of the Orestes 18, Capt. Hon. Swynfen Thos. Carnegie, and Virago steam-sloop, Capts. Geo. Graham Otway and John Lunn; and since 22 Oct. in the latter year has been serving in the Sidon steam-frigate, Capt. Wm. Honyman Henderson, now on the coast of Portugal.

LODWICK. (Commander, 1845.)

John Lodwick died in the summer of 1845.

This officer passed his examination in 1831; obtained his first commission 19 Jan. 1837; and was appointed—20 Jan. 1837, to the Phœnix steam-vessel, Capts. Wm. Honyman Henderson and Anthony Wm. Milward, with whom he was employed on particular service until paid off at the close of 1838—22 May, 1839, as Senior Lieutenant, to the Dee steamer, Capt. Joseph Sherer, attached to the force in North America and the West Indies—7 March, 1841, to the Winchester 50, flag-ship of Sir Thos. Harvey on the same station—and, 19 March, 1842, again as First, to the Growler steam-sloop, Capt. Claude Henry Mason Buckle, on the coast of Africa, where he remained until promoted to the rank of Commander 1 May, 1845.

LOFTUS. (Lieut., 1813. f-p., 8; h-p., 33.)

Arthur Loftus is second son of the Rev. Arthur Loftus, by Ellen, daughter of Sir Duke Gifford, Bart., of Castle Jordan, co. Meath; and brother of the late Major Henry Duke Loftus, and the late Capt. Wm. Loftus, both in the Army. One of his uncles, Thos. Loftus, was a M.P. and a Captain in the 1st Horse Guards; and another, Wm. Loftus, of Kilbride, co. Wicklow, many years a Member of the Irish and English Parliaments, was a General Officer in the Army, Colonel of the 2nd Dragoon Guards, and Lieutenant of the Tower of London. Lieut. Loftus—a first-cousin of the present Major-General Loftus of Kilbride—is a direct descendant of Adam Loftus, Archbishop of Dublin in the reign of Queen Elizabeth, and Chancellor of Ireland, who had (with seven daughters, all married to Knights) a family of five sons; three of whom received the honour of Knighthood. One of the Prelate's two other sons, Adam, a Captain in the Army, was killed in action with the O'Byrnes of co. Wicklow 29 May, 1599.

This officer entered the Navy, 28 March, 1806, as Fst.-cl. Boy, on board the Milan 38, Capt. Sir Robt. Laurie; and from 5 of the following April until 5 Oct. 1810 was employed, chiefly as Midshipman, in the Quebec 32, Capts. Geo. M'Kinley, Lord Viscount Falkland, Hon. Geo. Poulett, and Chas. Sibthorpe John Hawtayne. He assisted during that period at the cutting-out (he had not at the time been a fortnight in the service) of several vessels on the coast of Holland—made two voyages to the shores of Greenland—witnessed the surrender, in Sept. 1807, of the island of Heligoland—was twice nearly wrecked, on the coasts of Norway and Denmark (on the first occasion during a tremendous gale which lasted three days)—joined (after having been blocked up for a whole winter in the ice at Gottenborg) in the Quebec's gallant pursuit of the Danish 74 *Prindts Christian Frederic*, a pursuit that led to the capture of that ship, 22 March, 1808, by the Nassau and Stately 64's—accompanied the expedition of 1809 to the Scheldt, where he obtained the thanks of Sir Rich. Strachan for his conduct in command of a launch, armed with a 12-pounder carronade, in an attack on the island of South Beveland—served at the blockade of an enemy's force in Cherbourg—and co-operated in the defence of Cadiz. Becoming attached, in Feb. 1811, to the Scipion 74, bearing the flag of Hon. Robt. Stopford, Mr. Loftus contributed, in the course of the same year, to the conquest of the island of Java. In April, 1812, having returned to England, he passed his examination; but he was not promoted to the rank of Lieutenant until 14 June, 1813; prior to which period he had been further employed in the Scipion, under Capt. Henry Heathcote, on the Mediterranean station. After he had been lent for brief periods to the Ocean 98 and Mulgrave 74, Mr. Loftus received an appointment, 7 Oct. 1813, to the Royal George 100, Capt. Thos. Francis Chas. Mainwaring; under whom, it appears, he beheld Sir Edw. Pellew's two partial actions with the Toulon fleet, and saw some boat-service. Since the paying-off of the Royal George, in Aug. 1814, he has not been afloat.

Lieut. Loftus, now a widower, married Anne Abigail, only child and heiress of John Grey, Esq., a lady belonging to a junior branch of the family of Lord Grey de Groby, by whom he has issue a son and daughter. The former is a Lieutenant in the 10th Hussars.

LONEY. (Lieut., 1807. f-p., 25; h-p., 31.)

John Jenkins Loney, born 8 Dec. 1783, is son of the late Mr. J. Loney, a warrant-officer in the Royal Navy, who served his country with credit for nearly 50 years.

This officer entered the Navy, early in 1791, as Captain's Servant, on board the THORN sloop, Capt. Taylor, on the Leith station. In the course of the same year he became attached to the PROSERPINE frigate, commanded in the West Indies by Capt. Jas. Alms; and on joining, for a short time in 1794, the LATONA 38, Capt. Edw. Thornbrough, he fought and was severely wounded in Lord Howe's famous action. With the exception of a few months in 1796-7, during which we find him serving at Home on board the CARNATIC, COLOSSUS, and RUSSELL 74's, all commanded by Capt. Rich. Grindall, he did not again go afloat until May 1803, on 5 of which month he was received into the WINDSOR CASTLE 98, Capts. Philip Chas. Durham, Albemarle Bertie, and Davidge Gould. With those officers Mr. Loney was for two years employed in the Channel, principally in the capacity of Midshipman. He then in succession joined the THUNDERER 74, Capt. Wm. Lechmere, and DART sloop, Capt. Brownrigg; and on 6 Feb. 1806, having returned to the West Indies, it was his fortune to be present in the action off St. Domingo on board the NORTHUMBERLAND 74, flag-ship of the late Sir Alex. Cochrane; by whom he was nominated, 5 May, 1807, Acting-Lieutenant of the CHICHESTER store-ship, Capt. Tait. On leaving that vessel, to which he had been confirmed 11 Aug. in the same year, Mr. Loney was appointed, 26 April, 1808, to the THISBE 28, bearing the flag in the Thames of Hon. Henry Edwin Stanhope. Removing, a month afterwards, to the THRUSH 18, Capt. Chas. Webb, he was again ordered to the West Indies, where, in July, 1809, he witnessed the surrender of St. Domingo. About the early part of 1810, being at the time engaged in the defence of Cadiz, he was placed by Sir Rich. Goodwin Keats in acting-command of the THUNDER bomb, in which vessel he remained until superseded on the arrival from England of a Captain appointed by the Admiralty. While next in command (from Nov. 1810 until compelled by illness to resign in March, 1811) of the DART cutter, Mr. Loney was employed in the conveyance of despatches between Cadiz and Lord Wellington's army in Portugal. His subsequent appointments were—12 Dec. 1811, to the SPIDER 16, Capt. Frank Gore Willock, on the West India station, whence he invalided 6 Feb. 1813—4 Sept. 1826, to be Agent for Transports afloat, which service a severe injury received in the head during a heavy gale obliged him to quit in the ensuing March—and 2 April, 1827, and 6 Feb. 1837, to the command, for a period each time of five years, of the Semaphores at Beacon Hill and Portsmouth. He has been on half-pay since 1 April, 1842.

Lieut. Loney married, 20 April, 1808, the daughter of a respectable Government Contractor, by whom he has issue ten children. One of his sons, John Felix, a Master in the R. N. (1845), is now serving in that capacity on board the POICTIERS 72, guard-ship at Chatham.

LONEY. (COMMANDER, 1837. F-P., 24; H-P., 26.)

ROBERT LONEY entered the Navy, in Sept. 1797, as a Boy, on board the ATLAS 98, Capts. Matthew Squire and Theophilus Jones, with whom he served in the Channel until March, 1801. In March, 1803, he became Fst.-cl. Vol. of the SALVADOR DEL MUNDO, bearing the flags of Admirals Sir John Colpoys and Wm. Young at Plymouth, where he continued to officiate as Midshipman, until transferred, in Feb. 1806, to L'AIGLE 36, Capt. Geo. Wolfe. In March, 1808, we find him participating in a very gallant engagement fought by L'AIGLE with two French frigates and the enemy's batteries at Ile de Groix, where, besides having 3 of her guns split and dismounted, a bower-anchor cut in two, and her mainmast and bowsprit irreparably injured, the former ship had 22 of her people more or less severely wounded. One of her antagonists was compelled to take refuge under a fort, and the other to run on shore on Pointe des Chats. In April, 1809, immediately prior to the destruction of the shipping in Aix Roads, Mr. Loney served in the boats under Lieut. Rich. Devonshire at the destruction of the works on the Boyart Rock, a hazardous achievement which elicited the thanks of Lord Gambier; and he subsequently, on becoming attached to the Walcheren armament, assisted in forcing the passage between Flushing and Cadsand; on which occasion L'AIGLE, in consequence of a shell bursting in her after gun-room, sustained a loss of 5 men wounded and had her stern-frame greatly damaged. After a servitude of three months in the West Indies on board the PERT sloop, Capt. Wm. Hall, Mr. Loney, in Aug. 1810, rejoined the SALVADOR DEL MUNDO, bearing the flag of Sir Robt. Calder at Plymouth, where he remained a few weeks, and had command during the period of the Admiral's tender. Joining, then, the SCIPION 74, he served as Second-Master of that ship, under the flag of Hon. Robt. Stopford, at the reduction of Java in Sept. 1811; immediately after which event he was nominated Acting-Lieutenant of the MADAGASCAR frigate, Capt. Chas. Sullivan. He was confirmed a Lieutenant 8 May, 1812; and on 16 of the ensuing Oct. was appointed to the REINDEER 18, Capt. Wm. Manners, with whom he cruized until compelled from ill health to invalid 21 June, 1814. His subsequent appointments were to the command—16 Dec. 1825, of the NIMBLE Revenue-cutter—12 Aug. 1829 (four months after he had left the latter vessel), of the VIGILANT ketch, on the Plymouth station, where we find him employed until paid off 21 Nov. 1831—and 1 Nov. 1832, of the SAVAGE 10, which vessel was put out of commission 23 July, 1836. For his services in the SAVAGE off Oporto during the civil war in Portugal, and the protection he afforded to British interests during the revolution in Venezuela, Lieut. Loney was rewarded with the rank of Commander 10 Jan. 1837. He has since been on half-pay.

LONG. (RETIRED COMMANDER, 1842. F-P., 20; H-P., 30.)

JAMES LONG was born 17 April, 1774.

This officer entered the Navy, 1 Feb. 1797, as A.B., on board the SYBILLE, of 48 guns, Capts. Edw. Cooke, Wm. Waller, and Chas. Adam; and was a Midshipman of that ship in Jan. 1798, when, in company with the FOX 32, she entered the Spanish harbour of Manilla under French disguise, although three sail of the line and three frigates belonging to the enemy were lying there, and succeeded, besides eliciting much information, in capturing seven boats, about 200 men, numerous implements of war, and a large quantity of ammunition. In the course of the same month, he joined in an attack made by the SYBILLE and FOX on the settlement of Samboangon in the island of Magindanao, where, in an action with a fort and battery, the two ships sustained a loss of 6 men killed and 16 wounded. On 1 March, 1799, we find him present, off the sand-heads of Bengal River, in a most furious engagement of two hours and a half, which terminated in the SYBILLE's capture of the French frigate *La Forte*, of 52 guns and 370 men, after a loss to the latter of 65 (including her Captain) killed, and 80 wounded, and to the British, out of 371 men, of 5 killed and 17 (Capt. Cooke himself being mortally) wounded. The damage done to each ship was in proportion to her loss. Independently of a participation in other services, Mr. Long assisted, while under Capt. Adam, at the capture and destruction, 23 Aug. 1800, of five Dutch armed vessels and 22 merchantmen in Batavia Roads. He further contributed, in the following Oct., to the making prize of 24 Dutch proas, four of which mounted 6 guns each; and on 19 Aug. 1801 (when off Mahé, the principal of the Seychelle Islands) he aided in taking, with a loss to the SYBILLE (out of 300 men) of 2 killed and 1 wounded, of *La Chiffonne* of 42 guns and 296 men, 23 of whom were killed and 30 wounded. This action, a very gallant one of 20 minutes, was attended with the disadvantage to the British of being fought among rocks and shoals, and under the fire of an enemy's battery. Following Capt. Adam, on his return to England in 1803, into his prize LA CHIFFONNE, which had been added to the British Navy as a 36-gun frigate, Mr. Long proceeded on a cruize to the North Sea, where he next, it appears, joined the MONARCH 74, bearing the flag of Lord Keith, and EDGAR 74, Capts. John Clarke Searle and Robt. Jackson. He attained the rank of Lieutenant 7 Nov. 1806; and was subsequently appointed —26 Dec. 1806, to the OTTER sloop, Capts. John Davis and Nesbit Josiah Willoughby, in which vessel he witnessed the evacuation of Monte Video in 1807, and the capture of St. Paul's, Ile de Bourbon, in Sept. 1809—21 Nov. in the latter year, to the SAPPHIRE sloop, Capt. Hon. Wm. Gordon, with whom he returned to England—18 Dec. 1810, and 25 June, 1811, to the PHIPPS 14, and MOSQUITO 18, Capts. Christopher Bell and Jas. Tomkinson, stationed in the Downs and North Sea, where he cruized until superseded in April, 1813—8 March, 1837, to the command of the Semaphore on Portsdown Hill—and 25 Oct. 1841, to a Rendezvous for seamen in the Isle of Man, which closed a month afterwards. He accepted his present rank 11 Feb. 1842.

Commander Long married, 27 Oct. 1827, Jacobina, youngest daughter of Jas. Young, Esq., of Lanark, N.B., by whom he has issue five children.

LONGCHAMP. (COMMANDER, 1822. F-P., 34; H-P., 16.)

JOHN LONGCHAMP entered the Navy, 18 July, 1797, as Midshipman, on board L'ESPOIR sloop, Capt. Henry Inman; continuing to serve with whom in the BELLIQUEUX 64, ANDROMEDA 32, and DÉSIRÉE 36, he witnessed, in the ANDROMEDA, an attack made on a French squadron in Dunkerque Roads 7 July, 1800, and was present, we believe, in the DÉSIRÉE in the action off Copenhagen 2 April, 1801. In the course of the latter and the following year he successively removed to the PRINCESS OF ORANGE 74 and LEDA 38, both commanded by Capt. Geo. Hope, ACASTA 40, Capt. Jas. Athol Wood, and PRINCESS ROYAL 98, Capts. Jas. Vashon, Herbert Sawyer, and Robt. Carthew Reynolds. He made a voyage, in the LEDA, to the Mediterranean; and served on the Channel station, in the PRINCESS ROYAL, until promoted to the rank of Lieutenant 5 Dec. 1806. He then joined the FURY bomb, Capt. John Sanderson Gibson, attached to the force in the Baltic, where he was taken prisoner in Oct. 1807; and he was subsequently appointed—3 Jan. 1809 (three months after he had been exchanged), to the CORDELIA 10, Capt. Thos. Fortescue Kennedy, lying in the Downs—29 May following, to the PUISSANT 74, guard-ship at Spithead, Capts. Irwin, Hall, and Patterson—2 Nov. 1811, as Senior, to the TYRIAN 10, Capts. Fred. Burgoyne and Augustus Baldwin, employed in the Channel—18 Nov. 1814, to the BOYNE 98, Capt. Fred. Lewis Maitland, on the Irish station—25 Aug. 1815, to the IPHIGENIA 36, Capt. Andrew King, with whom he cruized for exactly three months in the North Sea—in July and Oct. 1816, to the command of the INDUSTRY and WATCHFUL Revenue-vessels — and 27 March, 1819, to the Coast Guard, in which service he continued to discharge the duties of Inspecting Commander until the early part of 1832. He has since been on half-pay. The commission he at present holds bears date 26 Dec. 1822. AGENTS—Messrs. Ommanney.

LORD. (LIEUTENANT, 1835.)

WILLIAM LORD passed his examination in 1829; obtained his commission 11 Aug. 1835; and has since been on half-pay.

The Lieutenant, who has been for a considerable period Inspector of the River Mersey, married, 22 Nov. 1840, Fairlina Euphemia, only daughter of Lieut. T. Anderson, of Stromness.

LORING. (COMMANDER, 1845. F-P., 14; H-P., 12.)

HECTOR LORING, born in Aug. 1808, at Fareham, co. Hants, is second and only surviving son of Capt. John Loring, R.N., who commanded the BELLEROPHON 74 at the blockade of St. Domingo in 1803, and died 9 Nov. 1808; and first-cousin of the present Vice-Admiral Sir John Wentworth Loring, K.C.B., K.C.H. His elder brother, John, a passed Midshipman in the R.N., died of yellow fever at Bermuda on board the EURYALUS frigate, about 1820.

This officer entered the Navy, 8 Aug. 1821, as Fst.-cl. Vol., on board the QUEEN CHARLOTTE 100, Capt. John Baker Hay, bearing the flag at Plymouth of Sir Jas. Hawkins Whitshed. Proceeding towards the close of the same year to the East Indies in the LIFFEY 50, Commodore Chas. Grant, he was afforded an opportunity, during the Burmese war, of witnessing the capture of Rangoon, and of participating, as Midshipman, in much boat-service on the river Irawady. On his return to England in Jan. 1826 he joined the VICTORY 104, flag-ship of Sir Geo. Martin at Portsmouth, where he remained until the following Dec.; in the course of which month he was received on board the CHALLENGER 28, Capts. Hayes, Joseph Harrison, and Adolphus FitzClarence. After a further servitude on the Home station in the latter ship and in the GLOUCESTER 76, Capt. Henry Stuart, Mr. Loring (whose examination was passed in Sept. 1827) again, in 1829, sailed for the East Indies, as Mate of the SOUTHAMPTON 50, bearing the flag of Sir Edw. W. C. R. Owen, who appointed him Acting-Lieutenant, in 1831-2, of his own ship, and of the SATELLITE 18, Capt. Marcus Theodore Hare, CRUIZER 18, Capt. John Parker, and CURAÇOA 26, Capt. David Dunn. He continued to officiate in the capacity last mentioned for upwards of four years; and on 23 June, 1835, was at length confirmed in the rank of Lieutenant, a few weeks only before the CURAÇOA was paid off. His next appointments were—4 Oct. 1835, to the ÆTNA bomb, Capt. Alex. Thos. Emeric Vidal, fitting for the coast of Africa—13 Nov. 1835, as Additional, to the PRESIDENT 52, flag-ship of Sir Geo. Cockburn in North America and the West Indies—25 Jan. 1836, to the NIMROD 20, Capt. John Frazer, of which vessel, employed on the same station, he soon became First-Lieutenant—1 Feb. 1840, to the THUNDERER 84, Capts. Maurice Fred. Fitzhardinge Berkeley and Daniel Pring, under the former of whom he discharged the duties of Second-Lieutenant in the operations on the coast of Syria, including the storming of Sidon and bombardment of St. Jean d'Acre—and 1 Feb. and 19 July, 1844, and 30 Jan. 1845, as First-Lieutenant (a post he had for a long time held in the THUNDERER), to the CAMPERDOWN 104, QUEEN 110, and TRAFALGAR 120, flag-ships of Sir John Chambers White at the Nore. He attained his present rank 25 July, 1845, and since 30 April, 1847, has been serving as Second-Captain of the HOWE 120, Capt. Sir Jas. Stirling.

Commander Loring married, in May, 1841, Charlotte Jessy, daughter of the late Jas. Jameson, Esq., of the Bengal Medical Service, by whom he has issue. AGENTS—Messrs. Stilwell.

LORING, K.C.B., K.C.H. (VICE-ADMIRAL OF THE WHITE, 1846. F-P., 46; H-P., 12.)

SIR JOHN WENTWORTH LORING, born 13 Oct. 1775, in America, is son of the late Joshua Loring, Esq., permanent High Sheriff of the province of Massachusetts previously to the Transatlantic War of Independence; grandson of Commodore Loring, who commanded on the Lakes of Canada, also prior to the struggle with America; and first-cousin of the present Commander Hector Loring, R.N. One of his brothers, Henry Lloyd, died Archdeacon of Calcutta in 1822; another, William, a Captain in the Horse Artillery, served under Sir John Moore during his celebrated retreat, from the fatigues of which he never recovered, dying at Madeira in 1809; and a third, a Major in the Army, was Military Secretary to Lieut.-General Sir Gordon Drummond, G.C.B., Governor of the Canadas during the late war with America.

This officer, whose name had been borne from 24 April, 1783, until 13 Dec. 1785, on the books of the SALISBURY 50, embarked, in June, 1789, on board that ship, then bearing the flag of Vice-Admiral Milbanke at Newfoundland, whence he returned in Dec. 1791. He then in succession became Midshipman, on the Home and Mediterranean stations, of the ALCIDE 74, Capt. Sir Andrew Snape Douglas, ROMNEY 50, flag-ship of Rear-Admiral Sam. Cranston Goodall, ORESTES 18, Capt. Lord Augustus FitzRoy, CONFLAGRATION fire-vessel, Capts. Thos. Freeman, Edw. Brown, and John Loring, and VICTORY 100, flag-ship of Lord Hood. While with the latter nobleman at the occupation of Toulon, Mr. Loring served as a volunteer at Fort Mulgrave, where, on the night of its assault and capture by the republican troops, 17 Dec. 1793, he received a severe wound by a musket-ball just below the knee, which obliged him to proceed in the DOLPHIN hospital-ship to Gibraltar for recovery.* Rejoining the VICTORY while yet lame, he again acted as a volunteer at the reduction of Bastia, and was intrusted during the operations with the command of a gun-boat, in which he was every night employed, from dark till dawn, in watching the Mole-head. On the surrender of that place, Mr. Loring was promoted, 24 May, 1794, to a Lieutenancy in LA FLÈCHE 16, Capt. John Gore. Being soon afterwards transferred, at the request of Sir Hyde Parker, to his flag-ship, the ST. GEORGE 98, he had an opportunity of sharing in Hotham's actions of 14 March and 13 July, 1795. In the early part of 1796 we find him accompanying the same Admiral into the BRITANNIA 100; and towards the close of that year taking a passage to the West Indies in the COMET fire-ship, Capt. Edw. Hamilton, for the purpose of there rejoining him in the QUEEN 98. In June, 1798, Lieut. Loring was advanced to the acting-command of the RATTLER of 16 guns; in which sloop he so ably co-operated with Brigadier Sir Brett Spencer in superintending the evacuation of the Cayemites Islands, near St. Domingo, that he had the gratification of finding himself removed, in the ensuing Sept., to the LARK 18, a vessel superior to any other of her class on the station. The appointment being confirmed, 3 Jan. 1799, Capt. Loring succeeded, during the period of his command, in taking as many as 8 privateers and 27 merchant-vessels; and on one occasion, the LARK having been totally dismasted in a hurricane, he re-equipped her with such remarkable expedition, and in face of so many difficulties, that Lord Hugh Seymour, the new Commander-in-Chief, not only returned him his public thanks, but successively appointed him, in April and Oct. 1801, to the ABERGAVENNY of 54, and the SYREN of 32 guns. In March, 1802, while cruizing alone off Cape François, Capt. Loring, with a degree of coolness that called forth the highest admiration and applause of Sir John Thos. Duckworth (who had succeeded Lord Hugh Seymour), contrived to quell a most dangerous mutiny that had broken out on board the SYREN, the crew having combined to seize their Captain and take possession of the ship. The strong manner in which he was in consequence recommended to the Admiralty caused their Lordships, on receipt of the intelligence, to confirm him in Post-rank by a commission ante-dated to 28 April, 1802, the day prior to the general promotion which had taken place in honour of the peace. The SYREN being paid off in the following Oct., Capt. Loring's after-appointments afloat, it appears, were—14 Sept. 1803, to the UTRECHT 64, flag-ship in the Downs of Rear-Admirals Robt. Montagu, Philip Patton, and John Holloway—5 Jan. 1805, to the AURORA 28, in which frigate he made a voyage to Bermuda and back—13 Nov. 1805, to the NIOBE 40, an active cruizer—and, 19 July, 1813, to the IMPREGNABLE 98, flag-ship of Admiral Wm. Young, employed in blockading the Scheldt. On 28 March, 1806, being in the NIOBE off L'Orient, Capt. Loring observed three large French frigates and a corvette standing out to sea. Notwithstanding the great superiority of the enemy, he immediately made sail in pursuit, and in the course of the night, which fortunately proved dark and rainy, contrived to come up with the sternmost of their vessels, *Le Néarque*, of 16 guns and 97 men; of which, by running close alongside and dropping two boats' full of men from her quarters, the NIOBE took silent possession. This neat action, as termed by Earl St. Vincent,* will be further alluded to in our memoir of Capt. Barrington Reynolds, the boarding officer. On 20 Oct. 1810 Capt. Loring captured *L'Hirondelle* privateer of 4 guns and 30 men; and in the course of the following month he received the approbation of the Admiralty for his zeal and gallantry in an attack made in company with the DIANA 38, Capt. Chas. Grant, upon the two French 40-gun frigates *Amazone* and *Eliza*, who were driven under the batteries of La Hogue, where the latter was ultimately burnt.† While employed in alone watching the port of Havre, whither the *Amazone* had effected her escape, the NIOBE made prize, 4 March, 1811, of *Le Loup Marin* privateer of 16 guns and 64 men. Towards the close of the same month the *Amazone*, having slipped in the night, was forced on shore near Cape Barfleur by a squadron under the orders of Capt. Jas. Macnamara of the BERWICK 74, whom the NIOBE, with much judgment, there led in an attack which ended with the self-destruction of the French ship. From 21 March, 1816, until he resigned, 14 Oct. following, Capt. Loring was Superintendent of the Ordinary at Sheerness. He became Lieutenant-Governor of the Royal Naval College 4 Nov. 1819, and continued in discharge of the duties of that post until his attainment of Flag-rank 10 Jan. 1837. He was promoted to the rank of Vice-Admiral 9 Nov. 1846.

Sir John Wentworth Loring, who had been nominated a C.B. 4 June, 1815, and a K.C.H. 30 April, 1837, was created a K.C.B. 4 July, 1840. He married, 18 July, 1804, Anna, second daughter of Vice-Admiral Patton, who then held a seat at the Board of Admiralty; and by that lady has issue three sons (the second, William, a Commander in the R.N.) and three daughters.

* *Vide* Gaz. 1791, p. 44.

* *Vide* Gaz. 1806, p. 422. † *V.* Gaz. 1810, p. 1840.

LORING. (COMMANDER, 1841.)

WILLIAM LORING is second son of Vice-Admiral Sir John Wentworth Loring, K.C.B., K.C.H.

This officer entered the Navy, in July, 1826, on board the UNDAUNTED 46, employed on particular service; was afterwards stationed in the Mediterranean, at Home, and in the East Indies, in the ALLIGATOR 28, BRITANNIA 120, MELVILLE 74, and WOLF 18; obtained (having passed in 1832) his first commission 26 Feb. 1836; and from 22 of the following Nov. until promoted to his present rank, 27 Aug. 1841, was again employed in the Mediterranean, latterly as First-Lieutenant, in the CARYSFORT 26, Capt. Henry Byam Martin. He has been in command, since 5 Jan. 1846, of the SCOUT 14, on the East India station.

LORY. (LIEUT., 1821. F-P., 25; H-P., 13.)

WILLIAM LORY was born 24 Dec. 1794, in the parish of St. Keverne, co. Cornwall, where his father was the principal resident freeholder and agriculturist.

This officer entered the Navy, 1 Feb. 1809, as Fst.-cl. Vol., on board the UNICORN 32, Capt. Lucius Ferdinand Hardyman; with whom, after having witnessed Lord Cochrane's destruction of the French shipping in Aix Roads, he removed, 30 Aug. following, to the ARMIDE 38; in the boats of which ship we find him frequently engaged in cutting out the enemy's vessels and storming their batteries off Rochefort, Rochelle, and the Ile de Rhé. With an interval between March, 1812, and Feb. 1813, during which he served with Capt. Edw. Galwey in the DRYAD 36, Mr. Lory was employed under Capt.

Hon. Fred. Wm. Aylmer from Oct. 1810 to June, 1816, in the NARCISSUS 32, FORTUNÉE 36, PACTOLUS 38, and SEVERN 40. Participating, in the PACTOLUS, in the operations on the coast of America, he there commanded a boat at the capture and destruction of many vessels, and assisted at the bombardment of Stonington. In the summer of 1815, being still in the same ship, he accompanied a most successful expedition sent up the Gironde in support of the French king. In Nov. 1818 Mr. Lory, who had passed his examination in the summer of 1815, re-joined the SEVERN, then commanded by Capt. Wm. M'Culloch as a Coast Blockade ship; on the books of which, it appears, his name was borne as Admiralty-Midshipman, Admiralty-Mate, and Lieutenant (commission dated 14 Nov. 1821), until Oct. 1822. His commission was given him as a reward for his conduct, on 10 Nov. 1821, in an affray on shore with a large body of armed smugglers, from whom he took a boat and part of her cargo, killing and wounding at the same time several of their number. On the occasion, however, it was his lot to be himself severely hurt by a ball through the right thigh, and a painful contusion in the left breast, the effects of which still continue. During a three-years' command of the STORK Revenue-vessel, to which he was appointed 11 July, 1831, Lieut. Lory, at the time of the Dutch embargo, although he had only 2 guns and 25 men on board, detained on her passage from the East Indies the Dutch ship *Prince of Orange* of 1200 tons, armed with 12 guns and 48 men, which he conducted from off Beachy Head to Portsmouth. In Feb. 1833 he captured the *Sarah* of London, a smuggling smack that had been for years successfully engaged in bringing over contraband goods to the coasts of Kent and Sussex. The manner in which the latter exploit was achieved afforded the Inspecting-Commander of the district to which Lieut. Lory was attached an opportunity of reporting him to the Comptroller-General as "one of the most zealous and best officers in His Majesty's service." He subsequently, from 3 May, 1837, until Feb. 1842, had charge of the DELIGHT Falmouth packet; as, since 9 Jan. 1847, he has had of the SWIFT, a similar description of vessel.

We understand that before he joined the STORK Lieut. Lory had for four years and a half been in command of a station in the Coast Guard. He married, 3 Sept. 1823, Miss Pearce, a lady belonging to the same place as himself, by whom he has had a family of 15 children, seven of whom are still living.

LOUDON. (LIEUT., 1812. F-P., 10; H-P., 23.)

WILLIAM LOUDON entered the Navy, 25 June, 1804, as a Volunteer, on board the ADAMANT 50, Capt. Geo. Burlton, stationed off Boulogne; where, and in the Baltic, he served, from the following Sept. until July, 1809, chiefly as Second-Master, in the WRANGLER, Lieut.-Commanders Chas. Burlton and John Bentinck Pettet. After discharging for twelve months the duties of Master's Mate in the TÉMÉRAIRE 98, Capts. Clay and Chamberlayne, he was successively appointed Acting-Lieutenant, in July, 1810, and Feb. and April, 1811, of the HOUND bomb, Capt. John Williams, and BULWARK 74, and STANDARD 64, each commanded by Capt. Hon. Chas. Elphinstone Fleeming. During his attachment to those ships he co-operated in the defence of Cadiz and made a voyage to Lima. He was confirmed in his present rank 18 Aug. 1812; and was lastly, from July, 1813, to Oct. 1814, and from Jan. to July, 1815, employed in the VENGEUR 74, commanded off Brest by Capts. Thos. Dundas and Tristram Robt. Ricketts, and ELIZABETH 74, flag-ship at Gibraltar of Hon. C. E. Fleeming.

LOUIS, Bart. (REAR-ADMIRAL OF THE RED, 1838. F-P., 30; H-P., 22.)

SIR JOHN LOUIS is eldest son of the late Rear-Admiral Sir Thos. Louis, Bart., K.F.M.,* by Jacquetta, daughter of Sam. Belfield, Esq.; and brother of the present Lieut.-Colonel Matthew Louis, R.A., and the late Commander Chas. Belfield Louis, R.N. (1819), who died in Dec. 1834, at Chelston, near Torquay. His nephew, Belfield Woolcombe, is a Lieutenant in the R.N.

This officer entered the Navy, in Sept. 1795, as Fst.-cl. Vol., on board the MINOTAUR 74, commanded by his father in the Channel; and, from Feb. 1797 until Aug. 1800, served as Midshipman in the INDEFATIGABLE 46 and IMPÉTUEUX 74, each under the orders of Capt. Sir Edw. Pellew, whom, in June of the latter year, he accompanied in an expedition to Quiberon. After an attachment of a few months to the AJAX 74, Capt. Hon. Alex. Inglis Cochrane, and CAMBRIAN 40, Capt. Fred. Lewis Maitland, he again, in Feb. 1801, joined the MINOTAUR, of which ship, still commanded by his father, he was created a Lieutenant 21 April, 1801. While in her Mr. Louis was employed in the expedition to Egypt. Being next, in 1802, appointed to the NAIAD 38, Capt. Jas. Wallis, he took command, jointly with Lieut. Wm. Dean, of the boats of that frigate, and on the evening of 4 July, 1803, assisted in cutting out the French national schooner *La Providence*, of 2 guns and 22 men, laden with timber and cannon, and lying near Brest—a service which was effected without casualty, notwithstanding a great rapidity of tide and the difficulties offered by a number of rocks and shoals with which the enemy's vessel was surrounded. On 14 Dec. 1804, 12 months after he had joined the ROYAL GEORGE 100, flag-ship in the Mediterranean of Sir Rich. Bickerton, Mr. Louis was there promoted to the acting-command of the CHILDERS sloop. He was confirmed a Commander 28 Feb. 1805; and on 22 Jan. 1806, several months subsequent to his removal to the BITTERN, he was promoted to Post-rank. His succeeding appointments, it appears, were—1 Aug. 1810, to the DRUID frigate, employed off the coast of Ireland and the port of Cadiz—in April, 1811, to L'AIGLE 36, stationed in the Mediterranean and West Indies—26 Aug. 1815, to the SCAMANDER 36, lying at Sheerness—19 Feb. 1816, to the FORTH 40, fitting for the North American station, whence he returned home and was paid off in July, 1819—and, 30 Aug. 1826, to the BARHAM 50, in which ship (put out of commission 12 Aug. 1830) he served in the West Indies as Flag-Captain to Hon. Chas. Elphinstone Fleeming. During his command of L'AIGLE Sir John Louis earned a very high character, and was in particular mentioned for the manner in which he placed his ship, and the precision of her fire, on the occasion of the capture and destruction of a French convoy under the guns of Porto Maurizio, 11 April, 1814. On 6 Jan. 1838 he was appointed Superintendent, with the rank of Commodore, of Malta dockyard, where he continued during the usual period of five years. Since 16 Dec. 1846 (he had acquired Flag-rank 28 June, 1838) he has been in discharge of the duties of Admiral-Superintendent at Plymouth.

During the reign of William IV. Sir John Louis was one of His Majesty's Naval Aides-de-Camp. He married, 15 Oct. 1807, the eldest daughter of Lieut.-Colonel Wm. Kirkpatrick, 8th Regt. Bengal Native Infantry, by whom he has a son, William, a Captain in the R.N.; and a daughter, Clementina, married to Capt. Robt. Spencer Robinson, R.N. AGENT—Joseph Woodhead.

---

* Sir Thos. Louis entered the Navy in 1770; was Lieutenant of the BIENFAISANT in Keppel's action with the Comte d'Orvilliers in 1778; and in 1780 fought in the same ship in the action with Don Juan de Langara, of whose flag-ship he was constituted Prize-Master. Obtaining Post-rank in 1783, and the command, subsequently, of the MINOTAUR 74, it was his fortune to be present in that ship at the battle of the Nile 1 Aug. 1798. In 1804 he was advanced to the rank of Rear-Admiral: and in April, 1806, as a reward for his conduct under Sir John Duckworth in the action off St. Domingo, he was raised to the dignity of a Baronet. In Feb. 1807 Sir Thomas Louis was the companion of the latter officer in the passage of the Dardanells. He died 17 May following on board the CANOPUS 80, while in command of the naval portion of the Egyptian expedition.

LOUIS. (Captain, 1846. f-p., 15; h-p., 9.)

William Louis, born 21 May, 1810, is son of Rear-Admiral Sir John Louis, Bart.

This officer entered the Royal Naval College 1 May, 1823, and embarked, 7 Dec. 1824, as a Volunteer, on board the Boadicea 46, Commodore Sir Jas. Brisbane, previously to accompanying whom into the Warspite 76 he took part in some of the operations connected with the Burmese war. On his return to England in 1827 he became for a short period Midshipman of the Victory 104, guard-ship at Portsmouth, Capt. Hon. Geo. Elliot; after which, and until promoted to the rank of Lieutenant 30 May, 1829, we find him employed on the African, Home, and West India stations, in the Primrose 18, Capt. Thos. Saville Griffinhoofe, Galatea 42, Capt. Sir Chas. Sullivan, Shannon 46, Capt. Benj. Clement, and Barham 50, commanded by his father as Flag-Captain to Hon. Chas. Elphinstone Fleeming. He continued to serve in the West Indies, until the close of 1832, in the Ranger 28, Capt. Wm. Walpole, Barham again, Grasshopper 18, Capts. Chas. Deare and John Elphinstone Erskine, Winchester 52, flag-ship of Sir Edw. Griffith Colpoys, and Hyacinth 18, Capt. Wm. Oldrey; and he was next appointed – 5 July, 1833, to the Revenge 78, Capts. Donald Hugh Mackay and Wm. Elliott, stationed off Lisbon and in the Mediterranean—and, 6 Jan. 1838 (after six months of half-pay), to the command of the Ceylon receiving-ship, as Flag-Lieutenant to his father at Malta. He was presented with a second promotal commission 28 June, 1838; appointed, 11 June, 1841, to the command (which he retained until June, 1843) of the Stromboli steam-vessel, in the Mediterranean; and advanced to his present rank 9 Nov. 1846.

Capt. Louis married, 11 July, 1843, Mary, daughter of J. Daniel, Esq., of Parson's Green, co. Middlesex. Agent—Joseph Woodhead.

LOVE. (Captain, 1837. f-p., 14; h-p., 28.)

Henry Ommanney Love, born 1 March, 1793, is eldest son of the late Commander Wm. Love, R.N.,* by Harriet, youngest daughter of Gabriel Acworth, Esq., Purveyor of the Navy, nephew of Sir Jacob Acworth, Surveyor of the Navy from March, 1715, until the period of his death in March, 1749. His grandfather, Mr. Thos. Lovell, also in the R.N., married a sister of Lovell Pennell, Esq., whose granddaughter became the wife of the Right Hon. John Wilson Croker, M.P., late Secretary to the Admiralty. One of Capt. Love's uncles, Thomas, was Master's Mate of the Berwick 74 in Keppel's action with D'Orvilliers, and Master of the Alfred 74 on the glorious 1 June, 1794.

This officer entered the Royal Naval Academy 21 May, 1805, and embarked, 23 Dec. 1808, as Midshipman, on board the Dannemark 74, Capt. Jas. Bissett, part of the force employed in the expedition to the Walcheren. He removed, in Sept. 1809, to the Tisiphone sloop, commanded by his father off Lymington, where he remained until June, 1810. After serving for 18 months on the North American and Leith stations in the Venus 32, Capts. Jas. Coutts Crawford and Kenneth Mackenzie, he rejoined the Tisiphone, but had not been long in that vessel before he was transferred to the Boyne 98, bearing the flag in the Channel of Sir Harry Burrard Neale, who, as a reward for his conduct in having jumped overboard under very perilous circumstances and saved the life of a young Midshipman, and "as an encouragement to enterprise and humanity," successively nominated him Acting-Lieutenant of the Tigre 74, Capt. Halliday, Boyne and Ville de Paris, his own flag-ships, and Sparrow sloop, Capt. Fras. Erskine Loch. He was not, however, confirmed until the Allied Sovereigns visited the fleet at Spithead, when, being the Senior passed Midshipman present (he had undergone his examination in 1812), he received a commission dated 27 June, 1814. His succeeding appointments were—11 April, 1821, to the Hyperion 42, Capt. Jas. Lillicrap, fitting for the Cape of Good Hope, where, previously to proceeding to the West Indies, he assisted in saving from destruction the *Albion*, an Indiaman of immense value, which had broken from her moorings during a gale, and had drifted to within a few feet of the rocks—13 May, 1824, to the Pyramus 42, Capt. Fras. Newcombe, on the Jamaica station—and, towards the close of the same year, to the command of the Union and Renegade schooners, also in the West Indies, whence he invalided in the summer of 1825. He obtained a second promotal commission 10 July, 1826; and was lastly, from 2 July, 1831, until paid off 12 March, 1834, employed in command, again on the West India station, of the Columbine 18. During the whole of that period Capt. Love did not lose a single man through sickness. When at Barbadoes, in Jan. 1833, he had succeeded in getting a ship off shore after 48 hours of incessant labour—an achievement which every experienced person in the island had considered impracticable. On the Columbine being put out of commission, the officers gave their Commander a parting dinner, as "a token of their respect and esteem." He was advanced to Post-rank 5 Dec. 1837.

Capt. Love lays claim to having suggested the use of paddles, instead of wheels, for steam-vessels. He is at present Sub-Commissioner of Pilotage for the Port of Southampton and Superintendent of Lights, Buoys, and Beacons for the Isle of Wight district, between Portland and Beachy Head, under the Trinity Corporation. The Captain has been three times Mayor of Yarmouth. Agents—Messrs. Ommanney.

* Commander Wm. Love, a most meritorious officer, was born in April, 1764. Entering the Navy in 1778 on board the Havana 24, he witnessed in that vessel the close of Byron's action with D'Estaing in 1779; accompanied Sir George B. Rodney to the relief of Gibraltar in 1780, and was present at the defeat of Don Juan de Langara. On the memorable 12 April, 1782, he was serving on board the Prothée 64, and was wounded. He obtained his first commission in 1794; was made Commander in 1807; had charge, during the after part of the war, of the Driver and Tisiphone sloops; was admitted to the out-pension of Greenwich Hospital in 1830; and died at Yarmouth 17 April, 1839. His father, Mr. Thos. Lovell, alluded to above, was Master of the Prothée, and lost a leg, in the action of 12 April, 1782.

LOVELESS. (Lieut., 1811. f-p., 13; h-p., 33.)

Bassett Jones Loveless was born, 19 Feb. 1785, at Swansea, Glamorganshire.

This officer entered the Navy, in April, 1801, as A.B., on board the Audacious 74, Capt. Shuldham Peard, and on 6 and 12 July following was present in the actions fought under Sir Jas. Saumarez off Algeciras and in the Gut of Gibraltar. The Audacious being paid off on her return from the West Indies in Sept. 1802, Mr. Loveless next, in March, 1803, joined the Gannet 16, Capts. Edw. Bass and Jas. Robt. Phillips, after cruizing for three years and four months in which vessel on the Channel station, he removed with Capt. Phillips, in July, 1806, to the Bonetta 18, and proceeded to the Baltic, where, during the operations of 1807 against Copenhagen, he came into frequent contact, as Master's Mate, with the enemy's block-ships. On leaving the Bonetta, which had been latterly commanded by Capt. Jas. Pringle, Mr. Loveless became in succession attached to the Nautilus 18, Capt. Matthew Smith, Astræa 32, Capt. Edm. Heywood, and Belleisle 74 and Neptune 98, flag-ships of Hon. Sir Alex. Cochrane. Being wrecked in the Astræa (at the time under the command of Lieut. Edm. Potenger Greenlaw) on a coral reef off Anegada 24 May, 1808, he was reduced to the necessity of remaining for three months on that barren and swampy island, where he endured many privations from the want of clothing and wholesome food. While acting as Lieutenant, from Jan. 1809 to Oct. 1810, of the Fawn 18, Capt. Hon. Geo. Alfred Crofton, we find him assisting at the reduction of Martinique and Guadeloupe; and on one occasion (with but two small boats under his orders, carrying each 5 men) effecting the capture, off Basseterre, of an armed row-boat, manned with 21 men, together with her prize. In Nov. 1810 he was again ordered to perform Midshipman's duty in the DRAGON 74, flag-ship of Sir Fras. Laforey. He was, however, confirmed a Lieutenant 2 Feb. 1811, in the ROSAMOND sloop, Capt. Dan. Campbell, also in the West Indies, whence, on being appointed, 3 May following, to the CASTOR 32, Capt. Chas. Dilkes, he proceeded to the Mediterranean. On 23 June, 1813, being off the coast of Catalonia, Lieut. Loveless took command of the CASTOR'S boats, in conjunction with the present Sir Edwyn Fras. Stanhope, and, after having had 4 of his men killed and 9 wounded, succeeded in bringing out from under the Castle of Mongat the French privateer *La Fortune*, of 2 guns, 2 swivels, and 48 men. The vessel had been moored in a very strong manner to the shore, and, when attacked, was lying within pistol-shot distance of a 5-gun battery, of another mounting 2 howitzers, and of a body of about 200 soldiers drawn up on the beach for her protection. On 15 Jan. 1814 Lieut. Loveless succeeded in the large cutter with 15 men in making prize, off Barcelona, and close under the guns of Monjui, of *L'Heureux* privateer, of 1 12-pounder and 25 men. In this affair, however, besides having 1 of his men mortally wounded, he had the misfortune to lose an arm at the shoulder-joint,* and he was in consequence obliged to invalid. Owing to an unsound cure he was for four years subjected to severe suffering, and was under the necessity of submitting to three painful operations. Being compelled to retire from active service, he was appointed, 8 May, 1844, to the Royal Hospital at Greenwich. In addition to a pension from Government of 91*l.* 5*s.*, the Patriotic Society voted him a gratuity.

The benevolent and humane exertions of Lieut. Loveless in allaying the ravages of cholera at Swansea in 1832 were acknowledged in the presentation to him of a piece of plate by the inhabitants.

LOVELESS. (LIEUT., 1815. F-P., 21; H-P., 22.)

JAMES LOVELESS was born 12 Nov. 1791, at Portsmouth.

This officer entered the Navy, 28 Nov. 1804, as Fst.-cl. Vol., on board the ST. GEORGE 98, Capts. Hon. Mich. De Courcy, Thos. Bertie, and Edw. Sneyd Clay; in which ship he went, as Midshipman, to the West Indies in pursuit of a French squadron, and on his return to Europe, after having been all but lost in a hurricane, was employed, until July, 1808, on the Channel station. While attached, from the latter date until March, 1811, to the TONNANT 80, commanded during that period by various officers, he assisted in embarking the army after the battle of Corunna, was engaged in numerous cutting-out affairs under the enemy's batteries on the coast of France, twice returned to Plymouth in the capacity of Prize-Master, served for a month on board the *Nettuno* Spanish block-ship at the siege of Cadiz (where he nearly lost his right eye by the bursting of a shell while voluntarily assisting on shore at the defence of Fort Matagorda, and where he was afterwards employed in a gun-boat), and had charge, we believe, of the ship's pinnace in the river Tagus for about two months prior to the departure of the French from Santarem. After serving for nine months, as Master's Mate, in the VESTAL troop-ship, Capts. Maurice Fred. Fitzhardinge Berkeley and Sam. Bartlett Deeckar (by the former of whom he was recommended for promotion, and on one occasion sent in charge of an American brig into Portsmouth), and for a short period, as a Supernumerary, in the ROYAL WILLIAM, Capt. Robt. Hall, Mr. Loveless, in Feb. 1812, joined the VIGO 74, Capts. Henry Manaton Ommanney and Thos. White. During the period of his stay in that ship we find him escorting a Russian squadron to England; and, on his return to the Baltic, intrusted with the personal conveyance of despatches from Malmo to Gottenborg. Previously to quitting her in April, 1813, he joined, further, in an attack on Elsineur castle, and accompanied an immense fleet of merchantmen through the Sound. He then returned to England on board the COURAGEUX 74, Capt. Philip Wilkinson; and was next, from June, 1813, until Sept. 1814, actively employed in the ALBION and SCEPTRE 74's, Capts John Ferris Devonshire and Wm. Waller, chiefly on the North American station, where he assisted in blockading the U. S. frigate *President* in Rhode Island, and was again invested with the charge of a captured vessel. At the period of his promotion to the rank of Lieutenant, which took place 8 Feb. 1815, Mr. Loveless had been for upwards of four months a Supernumerary of the NAMUR 74, guard-ship at the Nore. His next appointment being, 13 Aug. 1827, to the RAMILLIES Coast Blockade ship, Capt. Hugh Pigot, he was allowed, until paid off in March, 1830, to command the ANTELOPE tender, for the purpose of raising volunteers for the service, and for the suppression of smuggling. He rejoined the Blockade Service 26 Nov. 1830, as Supernumerary-Lieutenant, for a few months, of the TALAVERA 74, Capt. Hugh Pigot; and, with the omission of an interval between Oct. 1839 and April, 1842, has been employed in the Coast Guard since 26 Aug. 1834.

Lieut. Loveless married, first, in Oct. 1815, Miss Osborn, of Deptford, who died in Jan. 1829; and, secondly, Mrs. Quik, widow, of Gloucester. By his former marriage he has issue a son and two daughters.

LOVELL, formerly BADCOCK, K.H. (Captain, 1815. F-P., 16; H-P., 32.)

WILLIAM STANHOPE LOVELL, born about 1788, is second son of the late Thos. Stanhope Badcock, Esq., of Little Missenden and Maplethorpe Halls, a Magistrate and Deputy-Lieutenant, and formerly High Sheriff, for co. Buckingham, by Anne, daughter of Wm. Buckle, Esq., of the Mythe House, Tewkesbury, co. Gloucester; and brother of Lieut.-Colonel Benj. Lovell, commanding the 15th Hussars, an officer who served with distinction in the 14th Dragoons in France, Spain, and Portugal, and was wounded at the battle of Fuentes d'Onor. His father was a Lieutenant in the 6th Regt. of Foot during the war between Great Britain and her colonies, and served as such in America and the West Indies; he afterwards held a commission in the Royal Bucks Militia, and was with that corps in Ireland during the rebellion of 1798. Capt. Lovell, who is brother-in-law of Major-General Sir Jasper Nicolls, K.C.B., assumed his present surname, in lieu of his patronymic, in 1840. He is a descendant of Sir Salathiel Lovell, one of the Barons of the Exchequer.

This officer entered the Navy in May, 1799, on board the ROYAL WILLIAM, Capt. Fras. Pickmore, lying at Spithead; and in the following Oct. joined the RENOWN 74, bearing the flag of Sir John Borlase Warren. Continuing in that ship until 1804, he saw much active service on the Home and Mediterranean stations, particularly in 1800; in June and July of which year he assisted in the boats of a squadron at the capture and destruction of *La Thérèse* national ship of 20 guns, seven other armed vessels, nine sail of merchantmen laden with government supplies, three land-batteries, and the same number of magazines. On the night of 29 Aug. following he further (after having attended the expedition to Ferrol) contributed in the boats, 20 in number, commanded by Lieut. Henry Burke, to the cutting-out, close to the batteries in Vigo Bay, of *La Guêpe* privateer, of 18 guns and 161 men, which vessel, 25 of whose people were killed and 40 wounded, was in 15 minutes boarded and carried, with a loss to the British of 3 seamen and 1 marine killed, 3 Lieutenants, 12 seamen, and 5 marines wounded, and 1 seaman missing. On leaving the RENOWN, Mr. Lovell (as we shall for convenience name him) successively joined the KENT 74, Capt. John Chambers White, and BARFLEUR and NEPTUNE 98's, Capts. Geo. Martin and Thos. Fras. Fremantle. On 2 Nov. 1805, 12 days after the battle of Trafalgar, in which he had had the fortune

* *Vide* Gaz. 1814, p. 483.

to be present, he was nominated Acting-Lieutenant of the MELPOMÈNE 38, Capt. Peter Parker. While in that frigate, to which the Admiralty confirmed him 29 Jan. 1806, he was struck by lightning in a tempest almost fatal to the ship; co-operated in the defence of Gaeta, when besieged by 30,000 troops under Marshal Masséna; made prize, in a six-oared cutter (although with only four cutlasses and two pistols among the nine persons under his orders) of a French row-boat, whose crew, 16 in number, and well-armed, rose and re-took their vessel;* participated in various particular services; commanded the MELPOMÈNE's boats on numerous successful occasions; and assisted at Malta in re-capturing Fort Ricozali, when in possession of Fubourg's mutinous regiment. In 1807 Mr. Lovell rejoined Sir John Borlase Warren in the SWIFTSURE 74, on the Halifax station, where he continued until Feb. 1811; encountering during that period, 4 May, 1810, a very severe accident, which deprived him, while doing duty as First-Lieutenant, of five teeth, and caused him a fracture of the jaw. In the course of 1811, having been sent to Lisbon on promotion, he was there placed by Admiral Berkeley in command of the TOPAZE hospital-ship. He chanced, shortly afterwards, to be present on shore at the siege of Badajos. On 11 June, 1812, he received an order to act as Commander of the BRUNE 38, *armée en flûte*; and, on 13 of the ensuing Aug., he had the satisfaction of finding the appointment confirmed. While employed, at first, in the Mediterranean, Capt. Lovell prevented a French foraging party, 300 strong, from levying contributions on the inhabitants of Altea; drove a small privateer on shore near the town of Denia; was mentioned for the assistance he afforded while attached to the army at the siege of the Col de Balaguer; and conveyed Sir John Murray to Palermo after his retreat from before Tarragona. The meritorious nature of his conduct, indeed, throughout the whole of the operations on the coast of Catalonia had the effect of procuring him the public thanks of Sir Edward Pellew, Rear-Admiral Benj. Hallowell, and the present Sir Chas. Adam. On his return with Lord Mahon to England, Capt. Lovell was ordered with a large body of troops to Holland, and then sent to North America; where, among different services incidental to a troop-ship, we find him blockading Commodore Barney's flotilla up the Patuxent—commanding a subdivision of boats in the expedition to Washington, which occasioned his being 18 days and nights absent from his ship—serving also on shore in the attack upon Baltimore, on the failure whereof, and the death of General Ross, he conveyed in his own boat the body of that distinguished officer on board the TONNANT—accompanying Capts. Robt. Barrie and C. B. H. Ross, subsequently, in expeditions up the Rapahannock and St. Mary's rivers—and contributing to the destruction of the enemy's works on the coast of Georgia. The activity, gallantry, and ability manifested on every occasion by Capt. Lovell procured him the warm acknowledgments of Rear-Admiral Cockburn. He was promoted to Post-rank, on paying off the BRUNE, 21 Aug. 1815; was nominated a K.H. 25 Jan. 1836; and accepted the Retirement 1 Oct. 1846.

Capt. Lovell married, 2 Jan. 1822, Selina, youngest daughter of the late Sir Henry Harpur Crewe, Bart., of Calke Abbey, by whom, who died 30 March, 1838, he has issue a son, a Lieutenant in the 16th Regt., and three daughters. AGENTS—Burnett and Holmes.

* In this affair, which took place 18 May, 1806, Mr. Lovell was wounded in the hand and stunned in the head. He was exchanged three months afterwards.

LOWCAY. (COMMANDER, 1813. F-P., 22; H-P., 34.)

HENRY LOWCAY is son of Mr. Henry Lowcay, a veteran warrant-officer, who was Master's Mate of the SWALLOW sloop of war in a voyage of discovery to the South Seas in 1766-9, and died 5 Feb. 1827, at Portsmouth, aged 87; and brother of Retired Commander William, and Lieut. Robt. Lowcay, R.N. He had three other brothers, one of whom died a Lieutenant R.N.; a second, a First-Lieutenant R.M., from the effects of fever caught at the Brazils; and the third, from the sufferings he had endured when cast away, as Midshipman, on the coast of Africa.

This officer entered the Navy, 2 April, 1791, as Midshipman, on board the DUKE 98, Capts. Robt. Kingsmill, Robt. Calder, and John Knight, flag-ship for some time of Admirals Roddam and Lord Hood in the Channel. Removing, in Aug. 1792, to the JUNO 32, Capt. Sam. Hood, he assisted at the commencement of the war at the capture of many of the enemy's vessels, and was on board that frigate in Jan. 1794, when she effected an extraordinary escape from the inner harbour of Toulon, into which she had entered in ignorance of the previous evacuation of the British. After witnessing the surrender of the tower of Mortella and the capture of Fornelli, in the island of Corsica, he followed Capt. Hood, in March, 1794, into L'AIGLE 36, and in the course of the same year was present at the sieges of Bastia and Calvi. When next with the same Captain, in the ZEALOUS 74, Mr. Lowcay united in Nelson's attack upon Santa Cruz, Teneriffe, 24 July, 1797. At the commencement of the operations he took voluntary command of a boat, but had not been long in her before she was sunk, and had 1 of her men killed, by the enemy's shot. In consequence of this disaster he was obliged to swim on shore under a tremendous fire of round, grape, and musketry, and through a very high surf. On landing he joined Capt. Hood, and continued by him as his Aide-de-Camp during the remainder of the proceedings. In Dec. 1797, a few weeks after his removal to the VILLE DE PARIS 110, flag-ship of Earl St. Vincent, he was nominated Acting-Lieutenant of the CULLODEN 74, Capt. Thos. Troubridge, then off Cadiz, where, while engaged one night in rowing guard, he pursued, and, notwithstanding some resistance, captured an armed brig. On 1 Aug. 1798 it was Mr. Lowcay's fortune to be present at the battle of the Nile; subsequently to which we find him making prize, with the ship's boats under his orders, of a vast number of laden market-boats between Alexandria and Rosetta, and at the same time intercepting a large quantity of church-plate taken at Malta. Being confirmed a Lieutenant of the CULLODEN by commission dated 7 Jan. 1799, he officiated in the course of that year as Aide-de-Camp to Capt. Troubridge, and gained great praise for his meritorious conduct, at the sieges of St. Elmo and Capua, and in the various operations which terminated with the expulsion of the French from the Roman territory.* He was then sent in an open country boat from Naples to Palermo with despatches for Lord Nelson, and in charge of all the colours that had been taken from the enemy. The latter his Lordship deputed him to present to the Sicilian King, who in return gave him a valuable diamond ring, and made him the bearer of another, as also of a snuff-box, for Capt. Troubridge. After passing a fortnight as a guest at Lord Nelson's house, Lieut. Lowcay went back to the CULLODEN; prior to the return of which ship to England in the summer of 1800 he came into further boat-contact with the enemy in the vicinity of Cadiz, and saw good service along the Egyptian and Italian shores. With the exception of a few months in 1802-3, during which he served on board the PIQUE 36, Capt. Wm. Cumberland, he presents himself to our notice as attached, between Sept. 1800 and Feb. 1806, to the PRINCE OF WALES 98, bearing the flag of Sir Robt. Calder, under whom he shared in the action off Cape Finisterre 22 July, 1805. He then performed the duties of Flag-Lieutenant for upwards of two years to the late Sir Geo. Martin, in the GLADIATOR, MONTAGU, QUEEN, and CANOPUS, on the Portsmouth and Mediterranean stations. In the summer of 1808, having returned to England in the BITTERN sloop, Capt. Thos. Ussher, he obtained an appointment to the Sea

* *Vide* Gaz. 1799, p. 873.

Fencibles in the river Medway; where he remained until ordered, in June, 1809, to join the NAMUR 74, Capt. Rich. Jones, part of the force employed in the ensuing expedition to the Scheldt. In June, 1810, he was again (in the SALVADOR DEL MUNDO) placed under the orders of Sir Robt. Calder, then Commander-in-Chief at Plymouth, who successively invested him, 9 Nov. 1812, and 20 Jan. and 29 March, 1813, with the charge of the FAVORITE, SEALARK, and ACHATES sloops. In the first-mentioned of those vessels he retook a West Indiaman that had been only the night before captured by a French frigate; and conducted safely into Bristol and Liverpool a convoy for which he had been sent to cruize between the 44th and 47th degrees of West longitude. He was confirmed in his present rank on the occasion of Sir Robt. Calder hauling down his flag 29 Oct. 1813; and has since been on half-pay.

During his career afloat Commander Lowcay was at times employed at the blockade of Brest, Rochefort, Ferrol, Corunna, Cadiz, Minorca, Genoa, Toulon, Alexandria, and Smyrna. He was for 11 months off Rochefort, without once returning to port. He married, 3 May, 1836, Miss E. B. Steere, of Plymouth.

LOWCAY. (LIEUTENANT, 1815.)

ROBERT LOWCAY is brother of Commander Henry Lowcay, R.N.

This officer entered the Navy, 13 Jan. 1806, as Fst.-cl. Vol., on board the PRINCE OF WALES 98, commanded in the Channel by Capts. Inglis and Bedford; and in the course of the same year became Midshipman of the PROTHEUS and PEARL, Lieut.-Commanders Todman and Woodger, lying at Portsmouth. He next, from Feb. 1807 to Sept. 1810, served on board the DREADNOUGHT 98, Capts. Wm. Lechmere, Geo. Burgoyne Salt, and Valentine Collard, also on the Home station; where, during a period of nearly three years, he was further employed in the VENERABLE 74, Capt. Sir Home Popham, UNICORN 32, Capt. G. B. Salt, FAVORITE sloop, commanded by his brother, Capt. Henry Lowcay, and SALVADOR DEL MUNDO, flag-ship of Sir Robt. Calder. Proceeding then to the Cape of Good Hope in the LION 64, bearing the flag of the late Sir Chas. Tyler, he was by that officer nominated Acting-Lieutenant, 8 Feb. 1814, of the HARPY sloop, Capt. Allen, and on the occasion of his official promotion, 7 Feb. 1815, received as his Signal-Lieutenant into the MEDWAY 74. He returned home in April, 1816; and was afterwards appointed—5 Feb. 1820, to the EGERIA 28, Capt. John Toup Nicolas, fitting for the Newfoundland station—11 Sept. 1823, to the CAMBRIDGE 80, Capt. Thos. Jas. Maling, lying at Sheerness—16 Dec. 1823 and 31 Jan. 1824, to the QUEEN CHARLOTTE and VICTORY, Capts. Jas. Nash and Chas. Inglis, both at Portsmouth—next, to the Preventive Service—25 April, 1834, to the Ordinary at Portsmouth—1 Aug. 1836, again to the VICTORY, Capt. Thos. Searle—13 Feb. 1837, to the command of the SPARROW 10, in South America, where he was superseded in Oct. 1839—27 Aug. 1841, as Senior-Lieutenant, to the POICTIERS 72, Capt. Wm. Henry Shirreff, guard-ship at Chatham—and, 16 March, 1844, in a similar capacity, to the BONETTA surveying-vessel, Capt. Thos. Saumarez Brock, on the Mediterranean station. Lieut. Lowcay has been on half-pay since 20 Oct. in the latter year.

His eldest daughter is the wife of Commander John H. Norcock, R.N.

LOWCAY. (RETIRED COMMANDER, 1847. F-P., 25; H-P., 26.)

WILLIAM LOWCAY, born 21 Sept. 1787, at Chatham, co. Kent, is brother of Commander Henry Lowcay, R.N.

This officer entered the Navy, 22 Aug. 1796, as Sec.-cl. Vol., on board the DUKE 98,* Capt. John Holloway, under whom he continued to serve as Midshipman, on the Channel station, until April, 1798. He re-embarked, in July, 1802, as Master's Mate, on board the PIQUE 36, Capt. Wm. Cumberland; and, in July, 1804, after having been for 12 months attached to the DEFIANCE 74, Capt. Philip Chas. Durham, he joined the AJAX 74, Capts. Lord Viscount Garlies, Christopher Laroche, Wm. Brown, and John Pilfold. He was in consequence present, during the year 1805, in Sir Robt. Calder's action, also in Admiral Cornwallis' pursuit of the French fleet into Brest, and in the battle of Trafalgar. After further serving with Capt. Laroche in the URANIE 38, and with Capt. Thos. Le Marchant Gosselin in the AUDACIOUS 74, he was appointed, 21 Sept. 1807, and 3 March, 1808, Sub-Lieutenant of the CONTEST and ENCOUNTER gun-brigs, Lieut.-Commanders John Gregory and Jas. Hugh Talbot. In the boats belonging to the former of those vessels Mr. Lowcay was engaged in frequent attacks on the enemy's convoys on the French coast; and on one occasion he was slightly wounded. Being created a full Lieutenant, 25 March, 1809, of the PRINCESS OF ORANGE 74, Capt. Fras. Beauman, he accompanied the ensuing expedition to the Walcheren, where he was lent to the gun-boat service. On his return he was successively, until the peace of 1814, employed, always on the Home station, in the CRANE 18, Capt. D. Winter, SALVADOR DEL MUNDO, flag-ship of Sir Robt. Calder, CLARENCE 74, Capt. Henry Vansittart, GLADIATOR 44, flag-ship of Rear-Admiral Wm. Hargood, and TEAZER 14, Capt. Hargrave. He served next, from 27 April to 15 June, 1815, in the ROLLA 10, commanded at Plymouth by Capt. Robt. Julyan; and from 29 Nov. 1820 until 5 July, 1833, had charge of a station in the Coast Guard. He accepted his present rank 9 April, 1847.

Commander Lowcay married, 14 June, 1814, Mary Anne, sister of Capt. John Lawrence, R.N., C.B., and by that lady, who died 1 Dec. 1844, has issue two sons and one daughter.

* The DUKE was one of the refractory ships during the mutiny at Spithead.

LOWE. (Captain, 1814. F-P., 20; H-P., 36.)

ABRAHAM LOWE was born in July, 1771.

This officer (whose name had been borne from 1777 to 1779 on the books of the LEVANT, Capt. Geo. Murray) embarked, in Jan. 1791, as Midshipman (under the auspices of the late Sir Erasmus Gower), on board the LONDON 98, Capt. Geo. Blagden Westcott, bearing the flag of Rear-Admiral Sam. Cranston Goodall in the Channel. In the following Oct. he joined the EDGAR 74, Capts. Anthony Jas. Pye Molloy and Albemarle Bertie; and on becoming Master's Mate, in 1792, of the LION 64, commanded by his patron Sir E. Gower, he sailed with Lord Macartney on his embassy to China, and while there was intrusted with the charge of the JACKAL tender. Being promoted, on his return home, to a Lieutenancy, 24 Nov. 1794, in the TRIUMPH 74, Capt. Sir E. Gower, he was present in that ship, which bore the brunt of the enemy's attack, in Cornwallis' celebrated retreat of 16 and 17 June, 1795. His succeeding appointments, it appears, were—22 June, 1797, to the DIAMOND 38, Capt. Sir Rich. John Strachan, on the Channel station—18 Dec. following to the NEPTUNE 98, Capts. Sir E. Gower and Jas. Vashon, in which ship he proceeded to the Mediterranean—31 July, 1800, as Senior, to the THAMES 32, Capts. Wm. Lukin and Aiskew Paffard Hollis, under the latter of whom (after having witnessed the capture of two privateers carrying between them 32 guns and 287 men, and of *L'Aurore* national corvette of 16 guns) he bore a part in Sir Jas. Saumarez' action of 12 July, 1801, in the Gut of Gibraltar—in Oct. of the latter year, to the PRINCESS ROYAL 98, bearing the flag of Sir E. Gower in the Channel—31 Jan. 1804 (he had been for nearly two years on half-pay), to the command of the CONFLICT gun-brig in the North Sea—22 May, 1804, to the ISIS 50, flag-ship at Newfoundland of Sir E. Gower, who in 1806 authorized him to act as Magistrate and Surrogate for that island—and in July, 1807, to the PRINCE OF WALES 98, bearing the flag of the late Lord Gambier. Being First of the latter ship in the ensuing attack upon Copenhagen, Lieut. Lowe, at the conclusion of the operations, was nominated by his Admiral to the command, 13 Oct. 1807, of the CURLEW sloop. This appointment the Admiralty confirmed. From Dec. in the same year, however, until June. 1809, Capt. Lowe remained unemployed. He then volunteered to serve in the expedition against Walcheren, and his offer being accepted he was intrusted by Sir Rich. Strachan with the command of a division of the light flotilla engaged at the bombardment of Camvere, and by his conduct won the admiration of that officer. After the surrender of Camvere and the reduction of the fort of Rammekens, we find him employed in cutting off the communication between Flushing and Cadsand; and then assisting Sir Home Popham in sounding and buoying the channels of the West Scheldt for the purpose of enabling the line-of-battle ships and frigates to advance, and of thus aiding the ulterior objects of the expedition—a service performed with much judgment and correctness. During his stay in the Scheldt,* Capt. Lowe was invested by Rear-Admiral Wm. Albany Otway with the charge, in Nov. 1809, of the SABRINA sloop. His next appointments were—12 Jan. 1810, to the DILIGENCE 16, attached to the force in the Baltic, where he was most actively employed, and effected the capture of three or four Danish privateers—and 12 Aug. 1812, to the JALOUSE 18. He served in the latter vessel on the Cork and Jamaica stations until posted 7 June, 1814; and with the exception of a few months during the summer of 1815, had command, from 12 Jan. in that year until paid off 19 Jan. 1819, of the LARNE 20, among the Western Islands, and in the Channel and West Indies. He accepted the Retirement 1 Oct. 1846.

Commander Lowe married, in 1802, a daughter of R. Rogers, Esq., of Beaulieu, near Southampton; by whom he has had, with other issue, two sons, the present Commander Gower Lowe, R.N., and the late Lieut. W. H. J. Lowe, R.N. AGENT—J. Hinxman.

* *Vide* Gaz. 1809, p. 1298.

LOWE. (CAPTAIN, 1845. F-P., 18; H-P., 2.)

ARTHUR LOWE, born 26 July, 1814, at Corfton, co. Salop, is third son of the Rev. Thos. Hill Peregrine Furye Lowe, D.D. (of Court of Hill, Salop, and Norbiton House, Surrey), Dean of Exeter, by Ellen Lucy, eldest daughter of Geo. Pardoe, Esq., of Nash Court, Salop; and nephew, by marriage, of Capt. Sir Thos. Hastings, R.N., Kt.

This officer entered the Navy, 25 April, 1827, as Fst.-cl. Vol., on board the VICTORY 104, Capt. Chas. Inglis, bearing the flag at Portsmouth of Sir Geo. Martin; sailed soon afterwards for the Lisbon station in the MELVILLE 74, Capt. Henry Hill; was employed in the Mediterranean as Midshipman, from 1828 to 1832, in the FERRET 10, Capt. Thos. Hastings, and DONEGAL 78, Capt. John Dick; then rejoined Capt. Hastings in the EXCELLENT gunnery-ship at Portsmouth, where he passed his examination in July, 1833; and after a servitude of about three years in the East Indies and on the north coast of Spain in the ANDROMACHE 28, Capt. Henry Ducie Chads, and PHŒNIX steamer, Capt. Wm. Honyman Henderson, was promoted to the rank of Lieutenant 3 Sept. 1837. On 28 of the following Nov. he obtained an appointment to the VOLAGE 28, Capt. Henry Smith, fitting at Chatham; and on 2 Feb. 1838 he joined the HASTINGS 72, Capts. Fras. Erskine Loch and John Lawrence. In that ship he served in the Mediterranean until advanced to the rank of Commander 28 Aug. 1841. His last appointment was, 3 June, 1842, to the Second-Captaincy of the EXCELLENT, still commanded by his uncle, with whom he continued until promoted to his present rank 30 Aug. 1845. AGENTS—Messrs. Ommanney.

LOWE. (LIEUT., 1837. F-P., 21; H-P., 1.)

FREDERICK LOWE, born 30 Oct. 1811, is son of Wm. Lowe, Esq., of the firm of J. and W. Lowe, Attorneys, 2, Tanfield Court, Temple.

This officer entered the Royal Naval College 3 March, 1825; and embarked, 2 Dec. 1826, as a Volunteer, on board the COLUMBINE 18, Capts. Wm. Symonds, Chas. Crole, and John Townshend, stationed at first in the Channel, and afterwards in North America, where, in Sept. 1828, he removed for a short time, as a Supernumerary, to the HUSSAR 46, flag-ship of Sir Chas. Ogle. From the early part of 1829 until 1831, in the course of which year he passed his examination, we find him employed in the Mediterranean on board the MADAGASCAR and BLONDE frigates, Capts. Hon. Sir Robt. Cavendish Spencer, Edm. Lyons, and Sir Thos Sabine Pasley. He then proceeded to South America in the SAMARANG 28, Capt. Chas. Henry Paget; and in Aug. 1834, on the departure of that ship for England, he accompanied an expedition sent from Lima to Para under the orders of Lieutenant Smyth for the purpose of exploring the Pachitea, Marañon, and Ucayali rivers. On his arrival in England in the spring of 1835, Mr. Lowe found that his name had been allowed to remain until then on the books of the SAMARANG. Sailing soon afterwards for the East Indies in the JUPITER 38, Capt. Hon. Fred. Wm. Grey, which ship carried out Lord Auckland as Governor-General, he there joined the WINCHESTER 52, bearing the flag of Hon. Sir Thos. Bladen Capel, by whom he was presented with a commission dated 17 Nov. 1837. He came home in June, 1838; and was next appointed—14 Sept. following, as Additional, to the CORNWALLIS 74, flag-ship of Hon. Sir Chas. Paget in North America and the West Indies—28 March, 1839, to the DEE steam-vessel, Capt. Joseph Sherer, with whom he served for two years on the same station, half the time as First-Lieutenant—and in Aug. and Sept. 1841, in the latter capacity, to the STYX and DEVASTATION steamers, commanded by Capt. Hastings Reginald Henry at Home and in the Mediterranean. On leaving the last-mentioned vessel, he assumed command, 23 Feb. 1843, of the PROMETHEUS, as he has since done, 10 Aug. 1844 (after nearly 12 months of half-pay), and 21 June, 1845, of the ALBAN and PLUTO—all of them steamers. He is now employed on particular service. AGENTS—Messrs. Stilwell.

LOWE. (COMMANDER, 1840. F-P., 23; H-P., 8.)

GOWER LOWE is son of Capt. Abraham Lowe, R.N.

This officer entered the Navy, 12 April, 1816, as Fst.-cl. Vol., on board the LARNE 20, commanded by his father, with whom he served in the Channel until Feb. 1817, in the course of which month he entered the Royal Naval College. He re-embarked, in April, 1819, as Midshipman, on board the HIND 20, Capt. Sir Chas. Burrard, and during the next three years was actively employed in the suppression of smuggling. He then joined the RANGER 28, Capts. Peter Fisher and Lord Henry Fred. Thynne, successively stationed at Newfoundland, and in the North Sea, West Indies, Mediterranean, and Channel; and in July, 1825, having passed his examination in 1823, he became Mate of the HARLEQUIN 18, Capts. Jas. Scott and Chas. Elliot. Of that vessel, on her arrival in the West Indies, he was appointed, in Feb. 1816, Acting First-Lieutenant. Being confirmed to her, 2 Dec. following, he continued in the HARLEQUIN until transferred, in Jan. 1829, in a similar capacity, to the HARPY 10, Capts. Chas. Rich and Joseph Pafford Dickson Larcom, also on the West India station; where, in the summer of 1830, he removed to the SLANEY 20, Capt. Chas. Parker. Returning to England in Jan. 1831, he was next, 7 July, 1834, appointed First-Lieutenant of the ROSE 18, Capt. Wm. Barrow, with the boats of which sloop under his orders he was twice, it appears, engaged with pirates in the Straits of Malacca. In the autumn of 1837, Capt. Barrow having invalided at the Cape of Good Hope, Mr. Lowe was sent home in personal command of the ROSE. After eight months of half-pay he became in succession Senior, 11 July, 1838, and 11 May, 1839, of the TRIBUNE 24 and REVENGE 76, Capts. Chas. Hamlyn

Williams and Hon. Wm. Waldegrave, employed on the Lisbon and Mediterranean stations. For his conduct in the latter ship during the operations on the coast of Syria, where he commanded her boats at the landing of the troops at Gebail, again had charge of them at the capture of Sidon, and served at the bombardment of St. Jean d'Acre, he was advanced to his present rank by commission dated 4 Nov. 1840. He continued in the REVENGE, in discharge of the duties of Second-Captain, until paid off in Feb. 1842; and since 21 Nov. 1846 has been in command of the RESISTANCE 42, troop-ship.

LOWE. (LIEUT., 1815. F-P., 25; H P., 13.)

JOSEPH LOWE died in 1845, in the Coast Guard.

This officer entered the Navy, 14 March, 1807, as Clerk, on board the SHARPSHOOTER 14, Lieut.-Commander John Goldie; of which vessel, successively employed on the Guernsey, Halifax, and Downs stations, he became Midshipman, in July, 1809, and Acting-Master in Nov. 1814. He continued in her until Sept. 1815, and, while so attached, was twice, in the course of 1808, engaged with the enemy's gun-brigs and luggers in the vicinity of Granville—assisted, on one occasion, in saving a merchant-ship from destruction, a service for which Lloyds' bestowed a reward of 800*l.*—was instrumental to the cutting-out, in 1810, of the *Alcide* of 4 guns, although lying under the protection of the enemy's batteries—took part in other affairs of the same description—and was on board the SHARPSHOOTER when sent home from New London with the duplicate despatches of the peace. In Nov. 1815, being at the time Midshipman of the HOPE 10, Capt. Henry Fyge Jauncey, Mr. Lowe was presented with a commission bearing date 15 March in that year. With the exception of a few months in 1829, he served in the Coast Blockade, as Supernumerary-Lieutenant of the RAMILLIES and TALAVERA 74's, Capts. Wm. M'Culloch and Hugh Pigot, from 21 March, 1825, until the spring of 1831; and he was lastly, from 13 Dec. 1834 until the period of his death, employed in the Coast Guard. In 1829 he won the thanks of the Corporation of the City of London Insurance Office for saving the brig *London Packet* of London; he was nearly drowned, in Feb. 1830, in rendering assistance to the ship *Huskisson* when on shore in a heavy gale; and in the following Nov. he afforded every aid to the bewrecked crew and passengers of the *Surprize* of Plymouth. In 1831 we find his exertions towards the preservation of life obtaining him the thanks of the Royal Humane Society, the National Shipwreck Institution, and the French Government. AGENTS—Messrs. Chard.

LOWE. (LIEUTENANT, 1841.)

WILLIAM HENRY JOHN LOWE died in 1847. He was son of Capt. Abraham Lowe, R.N.

This officer entered the Navy 6 Sept. 1821; passed his examination 15 Dec. 1828; and at the period of his promotion to the rank of Lieutenant, 23 Nov. 1841, was serving in the Mediterranean as Mate of the BRITANNIA 120, flag-ship of Sir John Acworth Ommanney. His succeeding appointments were—11 Jan. 1842, to the MINDEN Hospital-ship, Capt. Michael Quin, stationed in the East Indies, whence he returned at the close of 1844—and, 9 Oct. 1845, to the ALARM 26, Capts. Chas. Colville Frankland and Granville Gower Loch, with whom he served in North America and the West Indies until the period of his death. AGENT—J. Hinxman.

LOWRY. (COMMANDER, 1822. F-P., 26; H-P., 36.)

JAMES LOWRY was born 18 April, 1773.

This officer entered the Navy, in 1785, as Ordinary, on board the SPRIGHTLY, Lieut.-Commander Swan, with whom and with Capt. Salusbury of the TERMAGANT sloop, he served on the Falmouth station until 1787. In Dec. 1795 he re-embarked, as Midshipman, on board the CASTOR 32, Capt. Rowley Bulteel; and he was next, from Sept. 1796 until Feb. 1806, uninterruptedly employed under the orders of the late Sir Thos. Louis in the MINOTAUR 74 (of which ship he became an acting and a confirmed Lieutenant 10 Oct. 1798 and 28 Jan. 1802), CONQUEROR 74, LEOPARD 50, AMBUSCADE 32, and CANOPUS 80. During the term of his attachment to the MINOTAUR he had charge of her forecastle at the battle of the Nile 1 Aug. 1798—witnessed the evacuation of Genoa by the French in June. 1800—commanded the ship's launch at the first debarkation of the troops, and participated in all the after-operations of the campaign, in Egypt in 1801—and on 3 Sept. 1800 had under his orders one of eight boats which brought out from Barcelona Roads, after having sustained a loss of 3 men killed and 5 wounded, the Spanish corvettes *Esmeralda* and *Paz*, of 22 guns each, although defended by a heavy fire from four strong batteries, 10 gun-boats, two schooners, armed between them with 4 long 36-pounders, and a fort upon Mount Ioni which threw shells. In this affair the enemy had 3 men killed and 21 wounded.* Besides being employed, while on the books of the LEOPARD, in charge of a fire-vessel in an attack on the Boulogne flotilla in Oct. 1804,† Lieut. Lowry was present, when in the CANOPUS, in Nelson's pursuit of the combined squadrons to the West Indies, and also in Sir John Duckworth's action off St. Domingo 6 Feb. 1806. On leaving the CANOPUS he joined the NORTHUMBERLAND 74, bearing the flag in the West Indies of Hon. Alex. Cochrane, who, in Aug. 1806, sent him home in charge of a schooner with despatches. From May, 1807, until Oct. 1811, we find him employed, chiefly as First-Lieutenant, in the MONTAGU 74, MALTA 80, and AJAX and CUMBERLAND 74's, all commanded by Capt. Robt. Waller Otway, who publicly acknowledged the assistance he derived from him in the AJAX on the occasion of a gallant affair in which the British with a slender force beat back a powerful division of the French Toulon fleet, 20 July, 1810.‡ His subsequent appointments were—in April, 1812, to the Transport service, in which he was for seven years employed—31 Jan. 1821, to the command of the CAMELION Revenue-vessel—and, 21 Feb. 1822, as First-Lieutenant, to the APOLLO yacht, Capt. Hon. Sir Chas. Paget, under whom he had the honour of escorting George IV. to Scotland. He was in consequence promoted to his present rank 12 Sept. 1822, but has not been since afloat.

Commander Lowry married, 29 May, 1802, Miss Jennings, by whom he has issue. His only son, James, died a Lieutenant in the R.N.

LOWRY. (LIEUTENANT, 1837.)

JAMES LOWRY died 6 Feb. 1846. He was only son of Commander Jas. Lowry, R.N.

This officer passed his examination in 1827; obtained his commission 30 March, 1837; and was afterwards appointed—4 April, 1837, to the SPARROWHAWK 16, Capt. John Shepherd, on the Brazils and Cape of Good Hope station, whence he returned at the close of 1840—6 April, 1841, to the IMPREGNABLE 104, commanded in the Mediterranean by Capt. Thos. Forrest—and, 18 Jan. 1842, 8 July, 1843, and 28 Feb. 1844, as First-Lieutenant, to the STROMBOLI steamer, EURYDICE 26, and ELECTRA 18, Capts. Wm. Louis, Geo. Elliot, and Arthur Darley, employed on the Mediterranean, and North America and West India stations. The ELECTRA was paid off in 1845.

LOWRY. (LIEUTENANT, 1819. F-P., 8; H-P., 34.)

WILLIAM LOWRY is fifth and youngest son of the late Robt. Lowry, Esq., of Pomeroy House, co. Tyrone, by Eliza, daughter of Major Tighe; and grand-nephew of Galbraith Lowry, Esq., of Ahenis, M.P. for Tyrone, father of Armar Lowry Corry, first Earl of Belmore. Three of his brothers were in the Army; a fourth is the present Robt. Wm.

* *Vide* Gaz. 1800, p. 1156. † *V.* Gaz. 1804, p. 1237. ‡ *V.* Gaz. 1810, p. 1510.

Lowry, Esq., of Pomeroy House, a Magistrate and Deputy-Lieutenant, and in 1812 High-Sheriff, for the above county, who married the only daughter of Admiral Graves.

This officer entered the Navy, 24 Dec. 1805, as Fst.-cl. Vol., on board the Ramillies 74, Capts. Fras. Pickmore and Robt. Yarker. Continuing in that ship for nearly three years, he was in consequence present, as Midshipman, at the capture, 13 March, 1806, of the *Marengo* 80, bearing the flag of Admiral Linois, and 40-gun frigate *Belle Poule;* and at the reduction, in Dec. 1807, of the Danish islands of St. Thomas and Ste. Croix. He fell on one occasion from the ship's side, and was so seriously injured that for many years he felt the effects. Towards the close of 1808 we find him proceeding in the Cornelia frigate, Capt. Henry Folkes Edgell, to the Cape station, where, in Dec. 1810, he co-operated in the reduction of the Isle of France. Returning home in the early part of 1811, in consequence of ill health, in the Actæon 16, commanded by Capt. Bertie Cornelius Cator, who was charged with the despatches announcing the conquest, Mr. Lowry did not again go afloat until July, 1813; between which period and Dec. 1815, he served on the Home and Mediterranean stations, part of the time as Admiralty Midshipman, in the Blenheim, Namur, and Bombay 74's, and Malta 80, Capts. Sam. Warren, Chas. John Austen, Geo. M'Kinley, Henry Bazely, and Wm. Chas. Fahie. From the date last mentioned until July, 1819, he remained a second time on shore. It was his fortune to be then appointed Admiralty Midshipman of the Royal George yacht, Capt. Hon. Chas. Paget; during the presence of the Prince Regent on board which vessel, he appears to have had the care of the royal barge, and to have had the honour of steering the Duke of York. He was promoted to the rank of Lieutenant by a commission dated 11 Oct. 1819; and has since been on half-pay.

One of his sons, Wm. J. Lowry, is a Midshipman in the R.N.; and another is Lieutenant in the 47th Regt. of Foot.

LOWTHER. (Lieutenant, 1844.)

Marcus Lowther entered the Navy in 1830; passed his examination 8 June, 1838; and after serving as Mate of the Hastings 72, Capt. John Lawrence, on the Mediterranean station, was employed in that capacity, from 1842 until promoted to the rank of Lieutenant 9 Aug. 1844, on board the Agincourt 72, bearing the flag in the East Indies of Sir Thos. John Cochrane. He was then re-appointed to the same ship and continued attached to her until her return to England in 1847. On 19 Aug. 1845 he appears to have had charge of a gun-boat, and to have served with the boats of a squadron, carrying altogether 530 officers, seamen, and marines, at the destruction, under Capt. Chas. Talbot, of the piratical settlement of Malloodoo, on the north end of the island of Borneo, where the British encountered a desperate opposition, and sustained a loss of 6 men killed and 15 wounded.* We also, in July, 1846, on the occasion of an expedition conducted by the Admiral against the Sultan of Borneo, find him commanding the third company of small-arm men, and assisting at the capture and destruction of the enemy's forts and batteries up the river Brune.†

LOWTHIAN. (Commander, 1813. f-p., 20; h-p., 34.)

Robert Lowthian entered the Navy, 30 June, 1793, as A.B., on board the Queen Charlotte 100, Capt. Hugh Cloberry Christian, bearing the flag in the Channel of Lord Hood. Removing, in March, 1794, to the Royal George 100, flag-ship of the late Lord Bridport, he was afforded an opportunity of sharing in the ensuing action of 1 June, and of also participating in the one fought off the Ile de Groix 23 June, 1795. In Jan. 1797 he sailed for the West Indies as Master's Mate of the York 74, Capt. John Ferrier. While in that ship, of which he was confirmed a Lieutenant, after having acted for 12 months as such, 2 Nov. 1799, we find him engaged in numerous cutting-out affairs at the islands of St. Domingo and Cuba. On his return to the Downs he was the Senior Lieutenant, it appears, employed from her in the boats in the attack made by Lord Nelson on the Boulogne flotilla in Aug. 1801. The York being put out of commission in April, 1802, he was next, 3 June, 1803, appointed to the Colossus 74, Capts. Geo. Martin and Jas. Nicoll Morris, with whom he served for two years and 10 months in the Channel. He afterwards became Senior Lieutenant—22 April and 2 Sept. 1805, of the Trusty 50, and Inconstant 36, commanded in the Downs and off Guernsey by Capts. Geo. Argles and Edw. Stirling Dickson—25 June, 1808, and 16 Aug. 1810, of the Brazen 18, and Helder 32, Capts. Lewis Shepheard and John Serrell, both on the Jamaica station—and, 15 Feb. 1811 and 29 Jan. 1813, of the Bellerophon and Scarborough 74's, bearing each the flag off Flushing of Rear-Admiral John Ferrier. He went on half-pay in Jan. 1814, having been advanced to his present rank on 4 of the previous month, and has not been since able to procure employment.

* *Vide* Gaz. 1845, p. 6536. † *V.* Gaz. 1846, p. 3442.

LUARD. (Lieutenant, 1841.)

William Garnham Luard entered the Navy 8 Feb. 1833; passed his examination in 1840; and was about the same period appointed Mate of the Samarang 26, Capt. Jas. Scott. Joining soon afterwards in the operations on the coast of China, he there, by his zealous and promising conduct, drew forth the repeated commendations of his Captain —particularly by his gallantry at the storming of the fort of Tycocktow 7 Jan. 1841, and by his subsequent behaviour during the celebrated forced passage, effected, between 3 a.m. on 13, and 4 p.m. on 15 March, by the Nemesis and the Samarang's boats up the inner channel from Macao to Whampoa, a navigation never before traversed by European boat or vessel, in the course of which were destroyed five forts, one battery, two military stations, and nine man-of-war junks, in which collectively were 115 guns and 8 ginjalls.* As a reward for his services he was promoted to the rank of Lieutenant 6 May, 1841. His appointments have since been—13 Sept. 1841, to the Belleisle 72, Capt. John Toup Nicolas, lying at Plymouth—16 Nov. 1841, to the Isis 44, Capt. Sir John Marshall, with whom he was for three years employed at the Cape of Good Hope—14 March, 1845, to the Melampus 42, Capt. John Norman Campbell, fitting at Devonport—and 14 April following, as First, to the Grecian 16, Capt. Louis Symonds Tindal, in which vessel he is now serving on the S.E. coast of America.

LUCE. (Lieut., 1814. f-p., 20; h-p., 20.)

William Luce entered the Navy, in Aug. 1807, as A.B., on board the Pluto sloop, Capt. Rich. Gaire Janvrin, stationed in the Channel; and in Aug. 1808 joined the Christian VII. 80, Capt. Joseph Sydney Yorke. In that ship, which shortly afterwards hoisted the flag of Sir Edw. Pellew, and (with the same Admiral) in the Caledonia 120, he continued to serve as Midshipman and Master's Mate, on the North Sea and Mediterranean stations, until nominated, after having shared in a skirmish with the French Toulon fleet, Acting-Lieutenant, in Jan. 1814, of the Prince of Wales 98, Capt. John Erskine Douglas, part of the force employed in a second encounter with the enemy. He was confirmed a Lieutenant 16 March, 1814, and was subsequently appointed—16 Dec. 1814, to the Bonne Citoyenne 20, Capt. Augustus Wm. Jas. Clifford, on the Irish station—for a few months in 1815 to the Favorite 20 and Curaçoa 36, Capts. Hon. Jas. Ashley Maude and John Tower, both employed on Home service—25 June, 1828, and 19 Feb. 1830, as a Supernumerary, to the Ramillies

* *Vide* Gaz. 1841, pp. 1164, 1509.

and TALAVERA Coast Blockade ships, Capt. Hugh Pigot—11 July, 1832 (after 15 months of half-pay), as sole Lieutenant, to the ASTRÆA 6, Capts. Wm. and Andrew King, on the Falmouth station—and 11 Sept. 1835, 22 Dec. 1836, and 24 July, 1838, to the successive command of the PLOVER, PIGEON, and PENGUIN, all Falmouth packets. He has been on half-pay since Nov. 1841.

He married, 1 June, 1840, the widow of Lieut. John Downey, R.N., formerly Commander of H.M. packet BRISEIS. AGENTS—Messrs. Chard.

LUCKRAFT, K.L.H., K.R.G. (CAPTAIN, 1838. F-P., 24; H-P., 24.)

ALFRED LUCKRAFT, born 2 April, 1792, is brother of the present Capt. William, and half-brother of the late Lieut. John Luckraft, R.N.

This officer, whose name had been borne since 25 July, 1799, on the books of the MONARCH 74, Capt. Jas. Robt. Mosse, embarked in that ship in Jan. 1801, and on 2 of the following April was present, as Fst.-cl. Vol., in the action off Copenhagen. After a servitude of 19 months in the BLENHEIM 74, bearing the flag of Sir Archibald Dickson, OISEAU frigate, Capt. Phillips, and COURAGEUX 74, Capt. John Okes Hardy, he joined, in April, 1803, the MARS 74, Capts. John Sutton, Geo. Duff, Robt. Dudley Oliver, and Wm. Lukin. While in that ship, in which he soon attained the rating of Midshipman, we find him present and slightly wounded in the leg at the battle of Trafalgar 21 Oct. 1805*—contributing, next, to the capture, 28 July, 1806, of *Le Rhin*, of 44 guns and 318 men—assisting also, 25 Sept. in the same year, at the taking, by a force under Sir Sam. Hood, of four heavy French frigates, two of which, the *Gloire* 46 and *Infatigable* 44, struck to the MARS—and accompanying, in 1807, the expedition to Copenhagen. In consideration of the wound he received at Trafalgar he was presented with a gratuity from the Patriotic Fund. He became Sub-Lieutenant, in March, 1808, of the STEADY gun-brig, Capt. Arthur Stow, and in the course of the same year sailed for South America, where, in Jan. and Feb. 1809, and May, 1810, he was in succession nominated Acting-Lieutenant of the AGAMEMNON 64, Capt. Jonas Rose, HYACINTH 18, Capt. John Carter, and PRESIDENT 38, Capt. Adam Mackenzie. On his return to England he was confirmed, 3 Sept. 1810, to a Lieutenancy in the BELLEROPHON 74, bearing the flag in the North Sea of Rear-Admiral John Ferrier, with whom he continued to serve in the SCARBOROUGH 74 until May, 1814. From the following Sept. until Sept. 1815 we find him employed on the Home station as Senior of the FOXHOUND sloop, Capts. John Parish and Thos. Warrand. Being next, 4 Feb. 1828, appointed First to the BLONDE 46, Capt. Edm. Lyons, he very highly distinguished himself, in Oct. of the same year, during the operations conducted, in unison with the French, against Morea Castle, the last stronghold of the Turks in the Peloponnesus. On that occasion, landing with a party of seamen, he assumed command, supported by the present Capt. Sidney Colpoys Dacres, of the central of five breaching batteries, named *George the Fourth's Battery*. He remained in the trenches 12 days and nights, during the three last of which he worked his only 4 guns with such effect as to expend upwards of 1000 18-pound shot, and 6000 lbs. weight of powder. The greatness indeed of Lieut. Luckraft's exertions not only procured a strong recommendation in his behalf from his own Commander-in-Chief Sir Pulteney Malcolm, but had the effect of eliciting the loud praise of the French Admiral De Rigny, and of obtaining for him the insignia of the Legion of Honour and of the Redeemer of Greece.† His promotion to the rank of Commander did not, however, take place until 28 Oct. 1829; at which period he was invested with the command of the PROCRIS sloop. He was afterwards appointed—30 Nov. 1829, to the CAMELION 10, attached to the force in the Mediterranean, whence he returned in March, 1830—20 June, 1831, to the REVENGE 78, Capts. Jas. Hillyar and Donald Hugh Mackay, employed, until March, 1834, on the Lisbon station—and 13 July, 1835, to the RUSSELL 74, Capt. Sir Wm. Henry Dillon, again in the Mediterranean. He was superseded from the latter ship on being advanced to his present rank 28 June, 1838, and has since been on half-pay.

During the late war Capt. Luckraft was never a single day on shore. He is married and has issue two sons and two daughters. One of his sons, Alfred, is a Lieutenant R.N.

* *Vide* Gaz. 1805, p. 1411. † *V.* Gaz. 1828, p. 2201.

LUCKRAFT. (LIEUTENANT, 1846.)

ALFRED LUCKRAFT is son of Capt. Alfred Luckraft, R.N.

This officer passed his examination 21 April, 1841; and from that period until promoted to the rank of Lieutenant, 15 Jan. 1846, was employed as Mate, on the Mediterranean, Home, Brazilian, and Pacific stations, in the WEASEL 10, Capt. Wm. Edmondstone, EXCELLENT gunnery-ship, Capt. Sir Thos. Hastings, and FROLIC 16, Capts. Wm. Alex. Willis and Cospatrick Baillie Hamilton. He was then re-appointed to the FROLIC, in which vessel he returned to England and was paid off in 1847.

LUCKRAFT. (LIEUTENANT, 1845.)

CHARLES MAXWELL LUCKRAFT is son of the late Lieut. John Luckraft, R.N.

This officer passed his examination 8 June, 1837; and at the period of his promotion to the rank of Lieutenant, which took place 28 May, 1845, had been serving for several years on the Mediterranean and Home stations, as Mate of the CAMBRIDGE 78, Capt. Edw. Barnard, RODNEY 92, Capt. Robt. Maunsell, and CALEDONIA 120, flag-ship of Sir David Milne. He was then appointed to the SIREN 16, Capt. Harry Edm. Edgell, fitting for the Mediterranean, where he is now serving as First of the HARLEQUIN 12, Capt. John Moore.

LUCKRAFT. (LIEUT., 1802. F-P., 18; H-P., 42.)

JOHN LUCKRAFT was born 23 April, 1775, at Milbrook, in Cornwall, and died in 1846. He was half-brother of the present Capts. Alfred and Wm. Luckraft, R.N. One of his own brothers, Adrian, died Purser of H.M.S. WOLVERENE in the West Indies in 1806; another, Frederick, also in the R.N., was drowned at sea; and a third, Robert, at one time in the Navy, died in civil service in the West Indies in 1823.

This officer entered the Navy, in Oct. 1786, as Captain's Servant, on board the LEANDER 50, Capt. Sir Jas. Barkley, bearing the broad pendant of Commodore (afterwards Rear-Admiral) Herbert Sawyer, on the Halifax station, where, in the following year, that ship was nearly lost by striking on a sunken reef near Cape Despair. During the heaving-down process which was in consequence rendered necessary on her reaching port, Mr. Luckraft had the misfortune to lose the total use of the index finger of his left hand. The LEANDER being afterwards ordered to the Mediterranean, he continued in her on that station until April, 1791. He next, in July and Dec. 1793, joined the FURY 16, and OISEAU 36, Capts. Frank Sotheron and Robt. Murray, under whom he was for two years and seven months employed on the Home and Halifax stations. Becoming attached, in July, 1796, to LA NYMPHE 36, Capts. John Cooke and Percy Fraser, he assisted, as Midshipman of that vessel, at the capture, when in company with the SAN FIORENZO 36, of the French frigates *La Résistance* of 48, and *La Constance* of 24 guns, 9 March, 1797. Being immediately appointed second in command of the former ship, he had the fortune to be the chief instrument of her preservation under circumstances of a very trying nature, in which he displayed so much ability that he was greeted with the high encomiums both of Capt. Cooke and the late Sir Harry Neale. In the following month Mr. Luckraft was present in the mutiny at Spithead. He was afterwards, in April,

1798, in company with the MARS 74, at the famous capture of *L'Hercule*, a ship of similar force, on which occasion he was sent on board the prize in order to assist in clearing her decks of the dead, the dying, and the general wreck. On leaving LA NYMPHE in April, 1799, he was placed by his friend, Admiral Sir Thos. Pasley, in command, with the rating of Master's Mate, of the CAROLINE gun-vessel; and in the course of the same and the two following years was successively appointed by him, with the rank of Acting-Lieutenant, to the TERPSICHORE 32 and SEAGULL 18, Capts. Wm. Hall Gage and Thos. Lavie, to the command of the SWAN hired-cutter (in which vessel he captured the lugger-privateer *Vengeance*), and to the SAN FIORENZO 36, Capt. Wm. Chas. Paterson. While the latter ship was on one occasion becalmed and engaged with 12 or 14 Spanish gun-vessels off Cabritta Point, Mr. Luckraft was despatched in a boat to Gibraltar for assistance, and in executing this mission he was exposed, in going and returning, to the whole fire of the enemy. In July, 1801, although he had been performing First-Lieutenant's duty, and was strongly recommended, as he had frequently been before, for promotion, he was superseded from the SAN FIORENZO, and again ordered to serve as Midshipman and Master's Mate, at first in command of the EXPERIMENT fire-vessel, and then on board the ROYAL SOVEREIGN 100, flag-ship of Sir Henry Harvey. On 29 March, 1802, however, at the joint instance of the last-mentioned officer and of Sir Thos. Pasley, he was at length officially promoted to a Lieutenancy in the RANGER sloop, Capts. Rich. Goddard and Chas. Coote.* In that vessel he served in the North Sea and off Boulogne until Sept. 1803; and in June, 1804, after having been for a few months employed in the METEOR bomb, Capt. Jas. Master, and TIGRE 80, Capt. Dacres, he obtained command of the PHŒBE hired cutter, of 12 guns. In the following Nov. his intrepidity in giving chase to the notorious privateer *Le Contre Amiral de Magon*, of 17 guns and 84 men, was the fortunate means of the latter being captured by the CRUIZER 18, Capt. John Hancock. When next, in the early part of 1805, in the HARPY 18, Capt. Edm. Heywood, Mr. Luckraft was in almost daily collision with the enemy's flotilla in the neighbourhood of Boulogne, where, in an action with seven of their schuyts, he boarded and carried one of them at the head of a few men from the main chains of the HARPY, who then proceeded in pursuit of the remainder. On 30 May in the same year, a few weeks previously to which he had joined the FLORA 36, Capt. Loftus Otway Bland, we find him assuming command of the PIGEON schooner. He shortly afterwards received from on board H.M.S. TRIBUNE the Earl of Harrowby, at the time on an embassy to Berlin, and conveyed his Lordship and suite up the Elbe to Hamburgh. Towards the close of Nov. 1805, the PIGEON, through the ignorance of her pilot, was unfortunately lost off the Texel, while on her passage with despatches for General Don at Bremerlehe, and her Commander and crew in consequence became prisoners to the Dutch. Being set at liberty in 1806, Mr. Luckraft soon proceeded for the benefit of his health to the Mediterranean, where, although on half-pay, he cruized for some time as a Supernumerary in various ships. In Nov. 1808, while on his passage home for the purpose of taking up an appointment awarded to him, he fell into the hands of the Turks, among whom he remained a captive until enabled, at the end of 1809, to effect his escape. With the exception of a few months passed in 1815 in the Impress service at Deal, the Lieutenant was not again employed until 1825, in April of which year he was appointed to the office of Agent on board the VIBILIA transport, and ordered to Janeiro. During the voyage, and when off the Cape de Verde Islands, the latter vessel was fallen in with and chased by a powerful pirate, who, however, notwithstanding her overwhelming force, was foiled in every attempt to board, and ultimately compelled to strike her colours, although she contrived to effect her escape. Not long after this gallant affair Mr. Luckraft was thrown by a roll of the ship down the after-hatchway, and fractured his right leg. There being no surgeon on board, the wound was so badly treated as to be the cause of eventual paralysis of the leg and thigh. He was discharged on the return home of the transport in Dec. 1825, and did not again go afloat.

* The magazine of the RANGER having in one instance caught fire by the ignition of some loose powder, Lieut. Luckraft, in the most undaunted manner, and with the greatest presence of mind (while the major part of the crew was hastening away), rushed into the flames, removed all the powder casks with his own hands, and saved the ship from destruction.

Lieut. Luckraft married, 30 April, 1800, Miss Martha Wilson, of Torpoint, Cornwall, by whom he has left issue (with one daughter married to Lieut. Wm. Geo. Pearne, R.N.) two sons, the elder, John Pasley, a Master R.N., and the other, Chas. Maxwell, a Lieutenant.

LUCKRAFT. (CAPT., 1840. F-P., 28; H-P., 23.)

WILLIAM LUCKRAFT is an elder brother of Capt. Alfred Luckraft, R.N.

This officer entered the Navy, 25 June, 1796, as a Volunteer, on board the ASIA 64, Capt. Robt. Murray, and was for upwards of four years employed in that ship on the Halifax station, part of the time in the capacity of Midshipman. He then joined the ASSISTANCE 50, Capt. Rich. Lee, under whom he was wrecked between Dunkerque and Gravelines 29 March, 1802. Being set free after 10 days of captivity, he became in succession attached, in the course of the same year, to the BRILLIANT 28, Capt. Adam Mackenzie, SUFFISANTE 14, Capt. Christopher John Williams Nesham, and CONCORDE 36, Capt. John Wood. In the latter ship we find him proceeding to the East Indies, where, in 1805, having previously assisted at the capture of *La Fortune*, a very heavy privateer, he removed to the CULLODEN 74, bearing the flag of Sir Edw. Pellew, and was by him appointed Acting-Lieutenant of the SCEPTRE 74, Capt. Joseph Bingham, and RATTLESNAKE 18, commanded by Capts. John Bastard and Wm. Warden, and for a short time by himself. As a reward for the manner in which he subsequently, with the sloop's boats under his orders, boarded and carried *Les Deux Sœurs* privateer, of 14 guns and 76 men, Mr. Luckraft, who had witnessed the capture of *La Bellone*, a similar vessel, mounting 30 guns, with a complement of 194 men, was confirmed a Lieutenant 11 Dec. 1807. Having, however, several months prior to the receipt of his commission, rejoined the CULLODEN, he contributed on the date last mentioned, as it chanced, to the destruction at Griessee, in the island of Java, of the dockyard and stores, and of all the men-of-war remaining to Holland in the East Indies. Returning to Europe in 1809, he was next, in Nov. of that year, in Nov. 1811, and in March, 1814, appointed to the SHELDRAKE 16, METEOR bomb, and BOMBAY 74, Capts. Jas. Pattison Stewart, Peter Fisher, and Henry Bazely—the two former on the Baltic, the latter on the Mediterranean station, where he served until Aug. 1816. In March, 1811, he officiated as First-Lieutenant of the SHELDRAKE at the defence of Anholdt, when attacked by a powerful Danish flotilla, and on that occasion was instrumental to the capture of two of the enemy's largest gun-boats. He was Senior of the METEOR in the operations against South Beveland, at the siege of Danzig, and at the blockade of the Scheldt. During the six years immediately antecedent to his promotion to the rank of Commander, which took place 27 July, 1825, he was employed in the Channel and West Indies as First of the SPARTAN 46, and PYRAMUS 42, Capts. Wm. Furlong Wise and Fras. Newcombe. His last appointment was, 17 July, 1838, to the Second-Captaincy of the BELLEROPHON 80, Capt. Chas. John Austen, for his conduct under whom in the operations on the coast of Syria, including the bombardments of Beyrout and Acre, he was advanced to the rank he now holds 4 Nov. 1840.

Capt. Luckraft married, in 1815, Charlotte, only daughter of J. Camsell, Esq., of H.M. Brewery at Weovil, near Gosport. He was left a widower in Oct. 1827.

LUGG. (Retired Commander, 1845. f-p., 22; h-p., 29.)

William Lugg was born 17 March, 1774.

This officer entered the Navy, 25 April, 1796, as Master's Mate, on board the Star 18, Capts. Hon. John Colville and David Atkins. On his arrival in that ship at the Cape of Good Hope he was appointed, in June, 1797, Acting-Master of the Hope 14, Capt. Wm. Granger, in which capacity, and until his return to England in 1804, he continued to officiate, on the same station and in the East Indies, in the Rattlesnake 16, also commanded by Capt. Granger, and in the Sphynx 18, Capt. Thos. Alexander, Braave 40, Capts. Josias Rowley, Lord Augustus FitzRoy, and T. Alexander, Diomede 50, Capts. Hon. Chas. Elphinstone Fleeming and Sam. Mottley, and Tremendous 74, Capt. John Osborn. Joining next, in April, 1805, the Medusa frigate, Capt. Sir John Gore, he again sailed for the East Indies with the late Marquis Cornwallis; and on his passage out and home, although without the rating of Master's Mate, he performed all the duties of Lieutenant, having confided to him the management of the chronometers and the lunar observations. Rejoining Sir John Gore (after a short attachment to the Hibernia 110, flag-ship off Ushant of Earl St. Vincent) in June, 1806, as Acting-Lieutenant, on board the Revenge 74, he was afforded an opportunity, on 25 of the following Sept., of witnessing the capture of four French frigates by a squadron under Sir Sam. Hood off Rochefort. He was confirmed a Lieutenant, 8 Nov. in the same year, in the Hyacinth 18, Capt. John Davie, stationed in the North Sea; and was subsequently appointed—10 June, 1807, to the Bulwark 74, Capt. Hon. C. E. Fleeming, employed off Cadiz and in the Mediterranean, whence he invalided in March, 1809—4 Oct. and 1 Dec. following, to the Rapid 10, Capt. Mathew, and Namur 74, bearing the flags at the Nore of Vice-Admirals Hon. Sir Henry Edwin Stanhope and Thos. Wells—6 Feb. 1811, to the Princess Caroline 74, Capt. Hugh Downman, under whom he escorted convoy to Madeira, and then cruized off Cherbourg until compelled by ill health to resign, 23 Jan. 1813—and, 6 Aug. in the latter year, to the Queen 74, Capt. Lord Colville, which ship, on her return with the flag of Sir Fras. Laforey from the West Indies, he left in June, 1814. From Oct. 1835 until May, 1836, again, from March, 1838, until May, 1839, and from the following Oct. until Sept. 1843, Lieut. Lugg served as Agent for Transports afloat. He was the Senior Agent employed under Sir Wm. Parker during the campaign in China, where we find him landing the troops at Amoy and Chusan. He accepted his present rank 10 March, 1845.

From Oct. 1826 until May, 1831, Commander Lugg had charge of the hired packet *Lady Wellington*, under the control of the Post-office. He married in May, 1813, and has issue three sons and two daughters.

LUNN. (Commander, 1844.)

John Lunn served as Midshipman of the Phœbe, of 46 guns and 300 men, Capt. Jas. Hillyar, and was in company with the Cherub 18 at the capture, 28 March, 1814, off Valparaiso, of the American frigate *Essex*, of 46 guns and 265 men, who struck her colours at the close of a warm action of two hours, in which the Phœbe lost 4 men killed and 7 wounded, and herself 24 killed and 45 wounded. In 1821, having passed his examination in 1817, and been appointed Mate of the Révolutionnaire 46, Capt. Hon. Fleetwood Broughton Reynolds Pellew, he assisted in the boats of that ship at the capture of several pirates in the Mediterranean. His appointments in the capacity of Lieutenant, a rank he attained 12 June, 1829, were—29 Nov. 1831, to the Caledonia 120, Capts. Jas. Hillyar, Thos. Brown, and Geo. Bohun Martin, in which ship he was for nearly six years employed in the Mediterranean, half the time under the flags of Sir Josias Rowley and Hon. Sir Robt. Stopford—and, 10 Aug. 1838, and 12 Oct. 1840, to the command of the Pluto and Locust steamers. In those vessels, with the exception of a short period which intervened between the paying off of the one and the commissioning of the other, he served uninterruptedly on the North America and West India and Mediterranean stations, until advanced to his present rank 19 Dec. 1844. Since 20 May, 1846, he has been in command of the Virago steam-sloop, of 300 horse-power, again in the Mediterranean. Agent—Joseph Woodhead.

LUSCOMBE. (Lieut., 1810. f-p., 13; h-p., 30.)

Edward Luscombe, born 6 Aug. 1791, at Efford House, in the parish of Holbeton, Devon, is second son of the Rev. John B. Luscombe.

This officer entered the Navy, 12 Sept. 1804, as Fst.-cl. Vol., on board the Hazard sloop, Capt. Robt. Jenner Neve, employed on the Home station, where he became Midshipman, in May, 1806, of the San Josef 110, flag-ship of Sir Chas. Cotton and Sir Jas. Saumarez, and, in June, 1807, joined the Prince of Wales 98, bearing the flag of Admiral Jas. Gambier. After sharing in the hostilities against Copenhagen, where he was frequently employed in the boats, he removed to the Implacable 74, Capt. Thos. Byam Martin, under whom we find him taking part, 26 Aug. 1808, in a gallant action of 20 minutes with the Russian 74-gun ship *Sewolod*, which was completely silenced, and in the end, with the assistance of the Centaur 74, flag-ship of Sir Sam. Hood, captured and burnt, in sight of the whole Russian fleet near Rogerswick, after a total loss to the enemy of 303 men, and to the Implacable, individually of 6 killed and 26 wounded. He continued in the same ship, participating intermediately in much boat-service in the Baltic, until 1810; in Feb. and April of which year he joined the Scipion 74, Capt. Chas. Philip Butler Bateman, and Victory 100, bearing the flag of Sir Jas. Saumarez. Attaining the rank of Lieutenant by virtue of a commission dated 3 Dec. 1810, he was next, from Jan. 1811 until March, 1815, employed in that capacity, on the Home and Mediterranean stations, in the Cadmus 10, Capt. Thos. Fife (in a boat belonging to which vessel he was severely frost-bitten on the coast of France), Leopard 50, Capts. Wm. Henry Dillon and Edw. Crofton, Horatio 38, Capt. W. H. Dillon, Namur 74, flag-ship of Sir Thos. Williams, and Granicus 36, Capt. Wm. Furlong Wise. His last appointments were, 13 April, 1818, and 20 Sept. 1819, to the Topaze 38, Capt. John Rich. Lumley, and Minden 74, flag-ship of Sir Rich. King, both on the East India station, whence he invalided in June, 1820.

Lieut. Luscombe married, 23 Nov. 1836, Emily, relict of Chas. Murly, Esq., Solicitor, and youngest daughter of Abraham Tucker, Esq.

LUSHINGTON, K.S.L., K.R.G. (Captain, 1829. f-p., 14; h-p., 17.)

Stephen Lushington, born 12 Dec. 1803, is second son of Sir Henry Lushington, Bart., of South-Hill Park, co. Berks, by Fanny Maria, eldest daughter of Matthew Lewis, Esq., Under-Secretary at War; and nephew of Stephen Lushington, Esq., D.C.L., the eminent civilian.

This officer entered the Navy, 17 Oct. 1816, as Fst.-cl. Vol., on board the Tagus 38, Capt. Jas. Whitley Deans Dundas, stationed in the Mediterranean; where and in South America he appears, from the spring of the following year until 1821, to have served as Midshipman in the Ganymede 26 and Owen Glendower 42, both commanded by Hon. Robt. Cavendish Spencer. He then returned to the Mediterranean in the Hind 20, Capt. Hon. Henry John Rous, in the boats belonging to which vessel we find him actively employed in the suppression of piracy in the Archipelago until promoted to the rank of Lieutenant 13 July, 1824. His next appointments were—5 Feb. and 7 Dec. 1825, to the ZEBRA 18 and CAMBRIAN 48, Capts. Edw. Rich. Williams and Gawen Wm. Hamilton, both in the Mediterranean, where he again performed good service against the pirates—and, 24 Oct. 1827, to the ASIA 84, flag-ship of Sir Edw. Codrington on the same station. Being advanced, 13 May, 1828, to the command of the ÆTNA bomb, Capt. Lushington united in the following Oct. in the operations against Morea Castle, and so distinguished himself by his exertions and skill as to obtain the orders of St. Louis of France and the Redeemer of Greece. On 28 Oct. 1829 he was further rewarded with a Post-commission. His next appointment was, 19 Jan. 1839, to the CLEOPATRA 26, fitting for the West Indies, whence, after nine months of severe illness, he was ordered by Sir Thos. Harvey, the Commander-in-Chief, to be invalided, in Nov. 1840. He has been in command, since 11 Oct. 1845, of the RETRIBUTION steam-frigate and VENGEANCE 84, on the Home station.

Capt. Lushington married, 5 July, 1841, Henrietta, eldest daughter of Rear-Admiral Henry Prescott, C.B., now a Lord of the Admiralty, by whom he has issue. AGENT—Joseph Woodhead.

LUTMAN. (LIEUT., 1815. F-P., 16; H-P., 27.)

CHARLES WILLIAM LUTMAN was born 20 Oct. 1790.

This officer entered the Navy, in June, 1804, as Midshipman, on board the ROYAL GEORGE 100, Capt. Joseph Sydney Yorke, and in 1806 removed to the NARCISSUS 32, Capt. Chas. Malcolm, both ships stationed in the Channel. Joining, next, the TARTARUS 18, Capt. Thos. Fras. Chas. Mainwaring, he served in that sloop at the bombardment of Copenhagen in 1807; and on 25 April, 1808, he assisted in her boats, with those of the DAPHNE 20, commanded by Lieut. Wm. Elliott, at the cutting out, with a loss to the British of only 5 persons wounded, of a convoy of 10 deeply-laden vessels, moored close under the fort of a castle mounting 10 guns, in the harbour of Fladstrand, near the Skawe, defended also by a heavy fire from another battery, as well as from the crews of the vessels assembled on the beach, and made fast to the shore by hawsers. While attached as Master's Mate, between July, 1809, and July, 1811, to the SHELDRAKE 16, Capts. John Thicknesse and Jas. Pattison Stewart, we find him commanding a boat, in open day, at the capture of a galliot under a fire of field-pieces and musketry from the sand-hills on the Jutland beach; and also contributing in a very eminent manner, when in the boats under Lieut. Watson, to the preservation from capture of a valuable convoy of transports. On one occasion, while endeavouring to cut several vessels out from the coast of Jutland, the boat he was in upset, and 5 men, with their commanding officer, Lieut. Watson, were unfortunately drowned. Mr. Lutman, who had supported the latter until he was himself nearly exhausted, afterwards succeeded, by swimming to the boat, in saving three of his companions. Being all in the end thrown on shore by the surf, they were made prisoners, but were released on surrendering their prizes. During the period which intervened between his discharge from the SHELDRAKE, as above, and his confirmation in his present rank 18 Feb. 1815, Mr. Lutman was employed at Home and in South America, for some time as Sub and Acting Lieutenant, on board the ARGONAUT hospital-ship, Lieut.-Commander Jas. James, MONTAGU 74, flag-ship of Rear-Admiral Manley Dixon, NANCY 12, Lieut.-Commander Wm. D'Aranda, NEREUS 42, Capt. Manley Hall Dixon, CERES 32, Capt. Wm. Bowles, and AJAX 74, Capt. Rich. Hussey Moubray. His succeeding appointments were—31 March, 1815, to the BERWICK 74, Capt. Edw. Brace, employed at the siege of Gaeta, where for nearly 10 weeks he had charge of a division of Sicilian gun-boats—4 July, 1816, for four months, to the IMPREGNABLE 98, also commanded by Capt. Brace, under whom he was slightly wounded at the battle of Algiers—and, 20 June, 1823, and 23 March, 1827, to the GANGES 74 and OCEAN 80, Capts. Brace and Patrick Campbell, principally employed on the Home station. He has been on half-pay since April, 1828.

Independently of the instance above alluded to, this officer has not less than five times displayed the intrepid humanity of his nature by his exertions in rescuing others from a watery grave. The first example of the kind was in 1810, when, chancing to be on board the HERO 74, he dashed into the sea and saved the life of Mr. Self, the Captain's Clerk; the second and third, in the course of the same year, on which occasions, being Sub-Lieutenant of the NANCY in South America, he similarly preserved from destruction the lives of the Assistant-Surgeon (Mr. Bryson) and the Captain of the fore-top, by jumping overboard after them at night; the fourth, while in the GANGES at Portsmouth, where, in his anxiety to save a drowning seaman, he broke his arm; and the last, during his servitude in the OCEAN. He plunged from that ship when at sea, but, although he succeeded in his generous efforts and preserved the life of another man, Jas. Leary, he underwent so much exertion that the result was a severe attack of illness, which reduced him to the necessity of invaliding. He married 12 Nov. 1838.

LUTWIDGE. (RETIRED COMMANDER, 1845. F-P., 22; H-P., 31.)

HENRY THOMAS LUTWIDGE is third son of the late Henry Lutwidge, Esq., of Holm Rook, co. Cumberland, by Jane, daughter of Rigby Molineux, Esq., of Preston; and nephew of Admiral Skeffington Lutwidge, who commanded the TERRIBLE at the occupation of Toulon in 1793, and had his flag on board the same ship at the reduction of Corsica in 1794. His grandfather, Thos. Lutwidge, Esq., an officer in King William's army, and High-Sheriff for Cumberland in the 12th of George I., married Lucy, daughter of Sir Chas. Hoghton, Bart., of Hoghton Tower, by his wife, Lady Mary Skeffington, eldest daughter of Viscount Massereene. The Commander's eldest surviving brother, the present Skeffington Lutwidge, Esq., of Holm Rook, is a Magistrate and Deputy-Lieutenant for Cumberland.

This officer entered the Navy, in June, 1794, as Captain's Servant, on board the TERRIBLE 74, bearing the flag in the Mediterranean of his uncle, Rear-Admiral Lutwidge. Becoming Midshipman, in March, 1795, of the BARFLEUR 98, Capt. Jas. Rich. Dacres, he served under that officer in the actions fought, 23 June, 1795, and 14 Feb. 1797, off Ile de Groix and Cape St. Vincent; after which, joining the ENDYMION 40, Capt. Sir Thos. Williams, he co-operated with the King's troops in an attack made in June, 1798, upon the town of Wexford, where were destroyed 100 large boats and vessels, which the rebels had collected for their escape. He continued in the ENDYMION, cruizing intermediately with much activity, until July, 1800; and on 6 of the following Sept., being at the time on board the ROYAL WILLIAM, flag-ship of Admiral Milbanke at Spithead, he was made Lieutenant into the PRÉVOYANTE store-ship, Capt. John Seater. His next appointments were, in the following Oct., and in May, 1801, and July, 1802, to the LAPWING, RESISTANCE, and HUSSAR frigates, Capts. Edw. Rotheram, Henry Digby, and Philip Wilkinson, all on the Home station; where, in the early part of 1804, he was wrecked, off the coast of France. He was in consequence detained a prisoner of war until May, 1814; on 4 Aug. in which year he joined the TIBER 38, Capt. Jas. Rich. Dacres. He left that frigate, after having served on the Irish and Lisbon stations, in Oct. 1814, and was lastly, from 2 Aug. 1821 until 31 Aug. 1822, employed in the Water Guard. He became a Retired Commander on the Junior List 26 Nov. 1830, and on the Senior 27 March, 1845.

Commander Lutwidge married Mary, daughter of —— Taylor, Esq., of Osbaston Hall, co. Leicester.

LYALL. (Lieut., 1825. f-p., 13; h-p., 21.)

George Lyall, born 6 Jan. 1799, is second son of the late Capt. Wm. Lyall, R.N., who fell into the hands of the enemy during his passage home in a packet from Halifax, suffered a consequent captivity of eight years, and died in June, 1814, three days only after his return to England. His brother, James, is a Purser and Paymaster R.N. (1833).

This officer entered the Royal Naval College 9 Dec. 1813; and embarked, 10 Dec. 1816, as Midshipman, on board the Larne 20, Capt. Abraham Lowe, under whom he was for two years employed in the West Indies, and was often sent away in the boats for the purpose of cruizing after pirates and slavers. Joining, in Jan. 1819, the Active 46, to which ship, commanded by Capts. Sir Jas. Alex. Gordon and Andrew King, he continued attached, in the capacity of Admiralty-Midshipman, until Sept. 1824, he partook of much special service, and was for several months engaged at the blockade of Algiers. On the date last mentioned (having passed his examination in 1822) he removed, as Mate, to the Dartmouth 42, Capts. Hon. Jas. Ashley Maude and Henry Dundas, and was again ordered to the West Indies, where his conduct in boarding and carrying, in a boat with only 11 men, a piratical schooner off the north coast of Cuba, on which occasion he was slightly wounded in the left leg, procured him a commission dated 1 July, 1825. He remained in the Dartmouth until the following Dec.; and was then received as a Supernumerary into the Eden 26, Capt. John Lawrence. He has not been afloat since July, 1826.

The Lieutenant married, 6 Nov. 1827, Catherine, youngest daughter of the late Robt. Lindsay, Esq., of Almericcloss, Forfar, N.B., by whom he has issue five children.

LYDE. (Lieutenant, 1814. f-p., 11; h-p., 33.)

George Lyde entered the Navy, 1 Nov. 1803, as Midshipman, on board the Prince of Wales 98, Capt. Wm. Cuming, bearing the flag of Sir Robt. Calder. After sharing in the action fought off Cape Finisterre 22 July, 1805, he successively followed Capt. Cuming, in 1806, into the Isis 50, and Sampson 64—escorting Rear-Admiral Chas. Stirling, in the latter ship, to the Rio de la Plata, and a convoy thence to the Cape of Good Hope. Returning to Europe in the early part of 1807, he served from May in that year until promoted to his present rank 9 Sept. 1814, chiefly as Master's Mate, although for a short time as Acting-Lieutenant, in the Inflexible 64, Capt. Joshua Rowley Watson, Eclair 18, Capt. Chas. Kempthorne Quash, Bombay 74, Capts. Wm. Cuming, Norborne Thompson, and Geo. Parker, and Caledonia 120, flag-ship of Lord Exmouth, on the Home, Baltic, and Mediterranean stations. He has since been on half-pay. He had served in the Bombay from 19 Oct. 1808 until 20 April, 1814, and had passed his examination in 1809.

Lieut. Lyde married, 14 Dec. 1830, Catherine, youngest daughter of Commander Wm. West, R.N., who died in 1811. He has issue six children.

LYDIARD. (Captain, 1842.)

George William Charles Lydiard entered the Royal Naval College 22 Sept. 1815; and embarked, 17 Jan. 1818, as Fst.-cl. Vol., on board the Queen Charlotte 100, Capt. Edm. Boger, bearing the flag of Sir Edw. Thornbrough at Portsmouth; whence, after having been for a short time borne on the books of the Drake sloop, Capt. Henry Shiffner, he proceeded to the Mediterranean in the Spey 20, commanded at first by Capt. Jas. Kearney White, and next by Capts. Jas. Barnwell Tattnell and John Donaldson Boswall. In May, 1821, and Aug. 1822, being still on the station last named, he was there received in succession into the Rochfort 80, flag-ship of Sir Graham Moore, and Larne sloop, Capt. Robt. Tait. His appointments in the capacity of Lieutenant, a rank he attained 20 March, 1823, appear to have been—2 Sept. 1824, to the Owen Glendower 42, Capt. Hood Hanway Christian, fitting for the Cape of Good Hope, whence he obtained leave to return—18 Sept. 1829, to the Ganges 84, Capts. John Hayes, Edw. Stirling Dickson, and Geo. Burdett, again in the Mediterranean—7 Nov. 1833, as Senior, after 20 months of half-pay, to the Blonde 46, Capt. Fras. Mason, fitting for South America—7 Oct. 1834, to the acting-command of the Satellite 18, on the latter station—and, 19 Feb. 1835, again to the Blonde. He was promoted to the rank of Commander, on that ship being put out of commission, 5 Dec. 1837; and was lastly, from 31 July, 1838, until paid off at the close of 1841, employed as Second-Captain of the Donegal 78, and Britannia 120, flag-ships of Sir John Acworth Ommanney on the Lisbon and Mediterranean stations. He was posted 30 Aug. 1842.

LYE. (Rear-Admiral of the Blue, 1841. f-p., 18; h-p., 33).

William Jones Lye was born 9 June, 1783, and died 7 March, 1846, at Bath. He was brother of Capt. Leigh Lye, who served throughout the Peninsular war and at Waterloo in the 11th Dragoons.

This officer entered the Navy, 5 Aug. 1795, as Fst.-cl. Vol., on board the Formidable 98, Capts. Berkeley and Murray, bearing the flag in the Channel of Sir Roger Curtis. In 1799, after he had cruized with that Admiral off the coast of Ireland, and off Cadiz and Gibraltar, as Midshipman of the Prince 98, he sailed with him in the Lancaster 64, for the Cape of Good Hope, where, on 12 Sept. 1801, he was nominated Acting-Lieutenant of the Tremendous 74, Capt. John Osborn. While in that ship, to which he was confirmed 15 Jan. 1802, we find him commanding a boat at the destruction of a vessel under the enemy's forts on the Isle of France. On 19 March and 26 May, 1805, Mr. Lye successively assumed the acting-command of the Cornwallis 44, and Rattlesnake 18; and on 22 May, 1806 (having been officially appointed to the latter vessel on 31 of the preceding Jan), he was posted into the Bombay, *alias* Ceylon, 32.* Removing, in April, 1810, to the Doris 36, he was intrusted, in the course of that year, with the conduct of two expeditions that sailed from Madras and Bombay for the Mauritius and Bourbon; and he afterwards, in Dec. 1810 and Sept. 1811, took part in the operations which led to the reduction of the islands of France and Java. On the former occasion he commanded a division of boats at the landing of the army. At Java he had charge, at first, of a small blockading squadron. After its subjugation he was for some time Senior officer at Batavia. He returned to England with Sir Sam. Hood's despatches (having been upwards of 13 years absent on the Cape of Good Hope and East India stations), and was paid off in Dec. 1812. The latter was Capt. Lye's last appointment. He attained Flag-rank 23 Nov. 1841.

The Rear-Admiral married, 29 Jan. 1817, Eliza, daughter of Benjamin Cobb, Esq., of New Romney, co. Kent, by whom he has left issue four children. His two eldest sons are in the East India Service.

LYELL. (Lieutenant, 1824.)

Thomas Lyell is second son of Chas. Lyell, Esq., of Kinnordy, co. Angus, a Magistrate and Vice-Lieutenant of that shire, by Frances, only daughter of Thomas Smith, Esq., of Maker Hall, Swaledale, co. York; and elder brother of Capt. Henry Lyell, of the 43rd Bengal Light Infantry. One of his aunts married Capt. Gilbert Heathcote R.N., brother of the present Admiral Sir Henry Heathcote, Kt.

This officer entered the Navy 14 July, 1813; obtained his commission 8 July, 1824; and was subse-

* The Bombay made prize, 10 July, 1807, of the French national brig *Le Jaseur* of 12 guns and 55 men, after a chase of nine hours.—*Vide* Gaz. 1808, p. 71.

quently appointed—2 July, 1825, to the DESPATCH sloop, Capt. Robt. White Parsons—14 Jan. 1826, to the MAIDSTONE 42, bearing the broad pendant of Commodore Chas. Bullen on the coast of Africa—for a short time in the spring of 1830, to the post of Flag-Lieutenant to the Earl of Northesk at Plymouth—20 May, 1831, to the TWEED 20, Capt. Allan Bertram, in the West Indies—22 Feb. 1832, as First-Lieutenant, to the GANNET 18, Capt. Mark Halpen, on the same station—and, 6 June, 1834, in a similar capacity (after several months of half-pay), to the WINCHESTER 52, Capt. Edw. Sparshott, fitting at Chatham. He was superseded from the latter ship in the following July, and has since been on half-pay. AGENT—J. Hinxman.

LYNE. (RETIRED CAPTAIN, 1840. F-P., 16; H-P., 45.)

THOMAS LYNE was born 17 Nov. 1768, at Ringwood.

This officer entered the Navy, 8 April, 1786, on board the THISBE 28, Capts. Isaac Coffin and Sam. Hood, stationed at Halifax; where, from 1789 until 1791, he served, as Midshipman, in the DIDO 28, Capt. Edw. Buller. After an attachment for short periods to various ships, he sailed for the Mediterranean in the ALCIDE 74, Capt. Robt. Linzee, and was present at the occupation of Toulon; while in command of a gun-boat at which place he was promoted to the rank of Lieutenant 12 Oct. 1793. His succeeding appointments were—29 Dec. in the latter year, for seven months, to the GORGON, Capt. Jas. Wallis, also in the Mediterranean—16 Dec. 1794, to the CULLODEN 74, Capt. Thos. Troubridge, under whom he bore a part in the actions of 13 July, 1795, and 14 Feb. 1797, off the Hyères islands and Cape St. Vincent—and, 15 March, 1797, as Senior, to the ARGO 44, Capt. Jas. Bowen. In Nov. 1798 he was present in the latter ship at the reduction of Minorca; and on 6 Feb. 1799 he assisted in taking the Spanish frigate *Santa Teresa* of 42 guns and 530 men, including 250 soldiers. During the chase which preceded the surrender of the enemy Mr. Lyne, as officially declared by his Captain, displayed great merit in keeping sight, and observing the different shifts, of the enemy, whereby great advantage accrued to the ARGO. Much commendation was also bestowed on his professional skill and great exertions, after possession had been taken of the prize, in saving the tottering mast from tumbling overboard. The ARGO, it appears, subsequently brought Earl St. Vincent home from the Mediterranean, conveyed nine homeward-bound Indiamen from St. Helena, and was for some time employed on the coast of Africa. Her First-Lieutenant attained the rank of Commander 29 April, 1802; and accepted that of Captain, on the Retired List, 10 Sept. 1840.

LYON. (LIEUT., 1814. F-P., 20; H-P., 22.)

FRANCIS LYON was born 24 Aug. 1794.

This officer entered the Navy, 1 July, 1805, as Fst.-cl. Vol., on board the ROMULUS frigate, *armée en flûte*, Capt. Thos. Burton, stationed in the Channel; and from Aug. 1806, until wrecked on Sable Island 3 Aug. 1812, was employed in the West Indies and on the coast of America, nearly the whole time as Midshipman, in the EMULOUS 18, Capts. Gustavus Stupart and Wm. Howe Mulcaster. He assisted, during that period, in beating off, when in the neighbourhood of Puerto Rico, 9 Nov. 1809, a French frigate mounting 32 guns, after an action, fought within pistol-shot, of an hour and 40 minutes, in which the EMULOUS was cut to pieces, and sustained a loss of 10 killed and 20 wounded; and, on 26 Aug. 1811, and 30 July, 1812, he contributed to the capture of *L'Adèle* French letter-of-marque, laden with cotton, and the *Gossamer* American privateer of 14 guns and 100 men. During the whole term of Capt. Mulcaster's command, a period of nearly two years, he was in constant charge of a watch, and was intrusted with the conduct into port of every prize of the least value. On the occurrence of the catastrophe above alluded to, he was turned over with his Captain to the NAUTILUS brig, in which vessel, it appears, he cruized with great activity and success. In April 1813, being then Master's Mate, although performing the duties of Lieutenant, of the STATIRA 38, Capt. Hassard Stackpoole, we find him commanding one of the boats of a squadron, containing 105 men, under the orders of Lieut. Jas. Polkinghorne, at the dashing capture, 15 miles up the Rappahannock river, of four schooners, carrying in the whole 31 guns and 219 men, an exploit which was productive of a loss to the British of 2 killed and 11 wounded, and to the enemy of 6 killed and 10 wounded. After serving for a few months in the ST. DOMINGO 74, flag-ship of Sir John Borlase Warren, and PRINCE REGENT 56, bearing the broad pendant of Sir Jas. Lucas Yeo on Lake Ontario, he was, in June, 1814, nominated, at the earnest recommendation of his friend Capt. Mulcaster, Acting-Lieutenant of the PRINCESS CHARLOTTE 42, commanded at first by that gallant officer, and next by Capts. Edw. Collier and Rich. O'Conor, also on the Canadian station; where, being confirmed by a commission dated 18 of the following Nov., he continued employed, in the same ship and the PSYCHE 32, Capt. Peter Fisher (participating in the mean while in much valuable and important service), until ordered home, in July, 1815, in the CALLIOPE 10, Capt. Alex. Maconochie. From the latter date, unable to procure an appointment, Lieut. Lyon remained on half-pay until 1837; since 8 Feb. in which year he has been in command of a station in the Coast Guard.

He married, 17 Feb. 1817, Miss Eliza Fawcett, of Portarlington, and by that lady has issue five children.

LYON. (LIEUTENANT, 1846.)

HENRY THOMAS LYON, born 28 Oct. 1825, is second son of Thomas Lyon, Esq., of Appleton Hall, co. Chester, a Magistrate and Deputy-Lieutenant for cos. Lancaster and Chester, by Eliza, youngest daughter of Geo. Clayton,* Esq., of Lostock Hall, Lancashire. One of his uncles, John Lyon, also in the R. N., died in 1821, at the Cape of Good Hope, aged 24.

This officer passed his examination 9 June, 1845; was appointed Mate, 19 Feb. 1846, of the EXCELLENT gunnery-ship at Portsmouth, Capt. Henry Ducie Chads; attained his present rank 29 June, 1846; and, since 6 of the following Aug., has been serving on board the COLUMBINE 16, Capts. Jas. Rich. Booth and Chas. Conrad Grey, now on the East India station.

LYONS, Bart., G.C.B., K.C.H., K.S.L., K.C.R.G., (CAPTAIN, 1814. F-P., 19; H-P., 27.)

SIR EDMUND LYONS, born 21 Nov. 1790, is second surviving son of the late John Lyons, Esq., of Antigua, and of St. Austen's House, Lymington, Hants, by Catherine, daughter of Joseph Walrond, Esq., of Mountrath, co. Devon, and brother of Capt. John Lyons, R.N.

This officer entered the Navy, in June, 1801, as Fst.-cl. Vol., on board the ROYAL CHARLOTTE yacht, Capt. Sir Harry Burrard Neale. In Jan. 1802 he removed to the MAIDSTONE frigate, Capt. Rich. Hussey Moubray, with whom, in Aug. 1803, he was transferred to the ACTIVE 38. After sharing in much service on the Mediterranean station, and enacting a Midshipman's part in Sir John Duckworth's expedition to the Dardanells, where he assisted in demolishing the formidable redoubt on Point Pesquies, he returned to England in 1807 on board the BERGÈRE sloop, Capt. G. B. Winyates. Sailing towards the close of the same year for the East Indies in the MONMOUTH 64, Capt. Edw. Durnford King, he was there, in June, 1808, three months after he had joined the RUSSELL 74, flag-ship of Rear-Admiral Wm. O'Brien Drury, appointed Acting-

* By Dorothea, sister of Admiral the first Lord Gardner, and widow of Robert Barrie, Esq., by whom she was mother of Rear-Admiral the late Sir Robert Barrie, K.C.B., K.C.H.

Lieutenant of the CAROLINE 36, Capt. Henry Hart. In the following Aug. he became attached, in a similar capacity, to the BARACOUTA brig; and to that vessel, commanded by Capts. Wm. Wells and Wm. Fitzwilliam Owen, he was confirmed by commission dated 22 Nov. 1809. At the celebrated capture, in Aug. 1810, of the island of Banda Neira, Mr. Lyons obtained mention as being among the foremost to escalade the walls of the castle of Belgica, an achievement for boldness in the design and conduct in the execution rarely paralleled.* In Dec. following, on the arrival of the BARACOUTA with the news of the conquest at Madras, we find him immediately appointed Flag-Lieutenant to Rear-Admiral Drury in the MINDEN 74. Continuing, on the death of the Commander-in-Chief, to serve in the same ship under Capt. Edw. Wallis Hoare, he proceeded in the spring of 1811 to the coast of Java, there to await the arrival of an expedition fitting out at the different ports of India for the subjugation of that island. While stationed in the Sunda Strait, Mr. Lyons' extreme zeal for the service, and the gallantry of his nature, led him to the performance of an exploit which so far surpassed all his Captain's ideas of possibility as to elicit from him a declaration that it was beyond all comment. This was nothing less than the storming and capture, on the night of 30 July, 1811, with not more than 35 men, and with but trifling loss, of the strong fortress of Marrack, mounting 54 guns and garrisoned by 180 soldiers and the crews of two boats.† Previously to the latter event Mr. Lyons had been of material assistance to Capt. Geo. Sayer, of the LEDA frigate, in reconnoitring and procuring information relative to the force and position of the enemy. During the operations which were shortly afterwards regularly commenced, he was at first intrusted with the command of a flotilla of five gunboats recently captured by Capt. Robt. Maunsell (*whom see*); and was then allowed to serve in the batteries opposed to Fort Cornelis. After the glorious assaults on that stronghold his health became so impaired from the exertions he had undergone that he felt himself under the necessity of invaliding; and he accordingly returned home in the CAROLINE 36, Capt. Christ. Cole. Being awarded, on his arrival, a second promotal commission, dated 21 March, 1812, Capt. Lyons was next, 5 April, 1813, appointed to the command of the RINALDO 10; in which vessel, it appears, he escorted Louis XVIII. to France and the Allied Sovereigns to England, besides affording a passage to Mr. Planta, the bearer of the treaty of Paris. Although advanced to Post-rank 7 June, 1814, he was not again employed until 1828; on 18 Jan. in which year he obtained command of the BLONDE 46, fitting for the Mediterranean. In the following Oct., after having for some time blockaded the port of Navarin, we find him directing the movements of the naval part of an expedition ordered to co-operate with the French in the siege of Morea Castle, the last hold of the Turks in the Peloponnesus.‡ During an arduous service of twelve days and nights, in very unfavourable weather, which preceded its unconditional surrender, he distinguished himself in an especial manner, and, having landed, was almost constantly in the trenches, exposed to a tremendous fire of great guns and musketry. The greatness, indeed, of Capt. Lyons' exertions, added to the satisfaction afforded to the French by his cordial behaviour towards them, led to his being invested with the insignia of the order of St. Louis of France and of a Knight Commander of the Order of the Redeemer of Greece. In the summer of 1829 the BLONDE conveyed Sir Robt. Gordon as Ambassador to Constantinople. She was afterwards the first British man-of-war that ever entered the Black Sea; and in Jan. 1831 she took Sir John Malcolm from Alexandria to Malta. Removing about the latter period to the MADAGASCAR 46, Capt. Lyons was afforded an opportunity, in May, 1832, of witnessing Ibrahim Pacha's bombardment of St. Jean d'Acre; and, in the early part of 1833, of attending King Otho and the Bavarian Regency from Trieste to Greece. He paid the MADAGASCAR off 17 Jan. 1835, and has not been since afloat. In the course of the month last mentioned he was nominated a K.C.H., and received the honour of Knighthood.

Sir Edm. Lyons, who has filled the office of Minister Plenipotentiary at the court of Athens since July, 1835, was created a Baronet for his civil services in 1840, and a G.C.B. 10 July, 1844. He married, 18 July, 1814, Augusta, second daughter of the late Capt. Josias Rogers, R.N., who commanded the QUEBEC frigate at the capture of the French West India islands in 1794, and niece of the late Rear-Admiral Thos. Rogers. By that lady he has issue with two daughters (the one married to the Baron Philip de Wurtzburg, the other to the Earl of Arundel and Surrey) two sons, the elder of whom, Rich. Bickerton Pemell, is an *attaché* to the embassy in Greece, and the younger, Edm. Moubray, a Commander in the R.N. AGENT—Joseph Woodhead.

* *Vide* Gaz. 1811, p. 1196. † *V.* Gaz. 1811, p. 2407. ‡ *V.* Gaz. 1828, p. 2201.

LYONS. (COMMANDER, 1846.)

EDMUND MOUBRAY LYONS, born 27 June, 1819, is second and youngest son of Capt. Sir Edm. Lyons, Bart., G.C.B., K.C.H.

This officer entered the Royal Naval College 10 July, 1829; passed his examination in 1838; obtained his first commission 11 June, 1841; and was subsequently appointed, always on the Mediterranean station—in the course of the same year, as Additional, to the HOWE 120, flag-ship of Sir Fras. Mason—1 March, 1842, to the RODNEY 92, Capt. Robt. Maunsell—11 Jan. 1844, again as Additional, to the QUEEN 110, bearing the flag of Sir Edw. W. C. R. Owen—15 April, 1844, to the AIGLE 24, Capt. Lord Clarence Edw. Paget—19 June, 1845, to the TYNE 26, Capt. Wm. Nugent Glascock—and, 10 April, 1846, as First, to the SIREN 16, Capt. Harry Edm. Edgell. He attained his present rank 9 Nov. 1846; and is now on half-pay. AGENT—Joseph Woodhead.

LYONS. (CAPTAIN, 1830. F-P., 17; H-P., 32.)

JOHN LYONS is brother of Capt. Sir Edm. Lyons, Bart., G.C.B., K.C.H.

This officer entered the Navy, 20 Sept. 1798, as Midshipman, on board the ST. GEORGE 98, Capts. John Holloway, Sampson Edwards, Henry Nichols, and Wm. Grenville Lobb; in which ship, bearing the flag for some time of Admirals Lord Nelson and Chas. Morice Pole, he bore a part (previously to visiting the Mediterranean) in the action off Copenhagen 2 April, 1801. He served during the peace of Amiens, on the West India and Home stations, in the EDGAR 74, Capt. Robt. Waller Otway, CHILDERS sloop, Capt. Delafons, and AFRICAINE 38, Capt. Thos. Manby; and on the renewal of hostilities in 1803 he joined the MAGNIFICENT 74, Capt. Wm. Henry Jervis, under whom, while attached to the in-shore squadron off Brest, he was wrecked, on the Black Rocks, in March, 1804. Being received, in the following Sept. (after three months' servitude with Capt. Jervis on board the TONNANT 80), into the VICTORY 100, flag-ship of Lord Nelson, he was afforded an opportunity, 21 Oct. 1805, of sharing in the glories of Trafalgar. He was in consequence promoted, while with Lord Collingwood in the QUEEN 98, to the rank of Lieutenant, 24 Dec. in the same year; and he was afterwards appointed—17 Feb. 1806, to the EAGLE 74, Capt. Chas. Rowley, in which ship, we understand, he witnessed the reduction of the island of Capri—18 Aug. 1806, to the QUEEN 98, Capt. Fras. Pender, stationed off Cadiz —18 June, 1807, to the MONTAGU 74, Capts. Robt. Waller Otway and Rich. Hussey Moubray, again on the Mediterranean station, where he assisted at the evacuation of Scylla in the winter of 1807, and commanded a detachment of seamen at the reduction of Santa Maura in April, 1810*—23 Feb. and 1 Sept. 1811, to the REPULSE 74, Capt. R. H. Moubray, and BOMBAY 74, Capts. Wm. Cuming and Norborne

* *Vide* Gaz. 1810, p. 1136.

Thompson, principally employed off Toulon—24 May, 1813, after six months of half-pay, to the ANACREON sloop, Capt. John Davis, which vessel, attached to the force on the Plymouth station, his health obliged him to leave in the ensuing Aug.—and, 29 Jan. 1814, to the VILLE DE PARIS 110, bearing the flag in the Channel of Sir Harry Burrard Neale. He attained the rank of Commander 27 June in the latter year; and from 26 Aug. 1828 until posted, 22 July, 1830, was employed in that capacity at the Cape of Good Hope on board the JASEUR 18. He has since been on half-pay.

Capt. Lyons, we believe, has been for some time employed by the Government in Egypt. AGENT—Joseph Woodhead.

LYONS. (LIEUTENANT, 1825.)

WILLIAM LYONS entered the Navy 20 March, 1810; passed his examination in 1820; obtained his commission 20 July, 1825; was appointed, 31 Oct. following, to the BEAVER sloop, Capt. Wm. Geo. Hyndham Whish; and since 18 March, 1834, has been employed in the Coast Guard.

LYS. (LIEUTENANT, 1818. F-P., 12; H-P., 25.)

MATTHEW LYS entered the Royal Naval College 20 Oct. 1810; and embarked, 24 June, 1812, as A.B., on board the NEREUS 36, Capt. Peter Heywood. With that officer he continued to serve in the MONTAGU 74, on the South American and Home stations until Nov. 1814; assisting as Midshipman, during the latter year, in the conveyance of the British army from Bordeaux to England, and particularly in the grand naval review held at Spithead. He then sailed for the East Indies in the CORNWALLIS 74, flag-ship of Sir Geo. Burlton; and on his return to England in 1816 in the THEBAN 36, Capt. Sam. Leslie, joined the MINDEN 74, Capt. Wm. Paterson. After assisting at the bombardment of Algiers he again proceeded to India, where, in March, 1817, he was nominated by Sir Rich. King Acting-Lieutenant of the MELVILLE 74, Capt. Henry Chas. Pemberton. He was confirmed by the Admiralty on his arrival home, 20 Jan. 1818, and was subsequently appointed—29 Dec. 1820, to the MEDINA 20, Capt. Robt. Hockings, on the Mediterranean station—22 March, 1821, to the DORIS frigate, Capts. Thos. Graham and Fred. Edw. Venables Vernon, fitting for the Brazils, whence he invalided—and 2 Dec. 1823, to the OCEAN 80, Capts. Lucius Ferdinand Hardyman and John Sykes, flag-ship for some time of Lord Amelius Beauclerk in the river Tagus. He was paid off we believe in 1827, and has not been since afloat.

LYSAGHT. (REAR-ADMIRAL OF THE WHITE, 1841. F-P., 14; H-P., 38.)

ARTHUR LYSAGHT belongs to the family of Lord Lisle.

This officer entered the Navy, 30 June, 1795, as Fst.-cl. Vol., on board LA SYBILLE of 48 guns, Capts. Edw. Cooke and Lucius Ferdinand Hardyman, stationed at first in the Channel and afterwards in the East Indies; where, in Jan. 1798, he was Midshipman of that vessel when, in company with the Fox 32, she entered the Spanish harbour of Manilla (notwithstanding that there were lying there three ships of the line and three frigates), and captured seven boats, 200 men, and a large quantity of ammunition and implements of war. In the course of the same month he was present in an action with the enemy's batteries at Samboangon in the island of Magindanao, whose fire occasioned the two ships a collective loss of 6 killed and 16 wounded; and on the night of 28 Feb. 1799 he contributed to the capture, at the mouth of the Bengal River, of the French frigate *La Forte* of 52 guns and 370 men, after a deadly action of two hours and a half, in which the enemy had 65 of their number (including the Captain) killed and 80 wounded, and the British, out of 371 men, 5 killed and 17 (among whom was Capt. Cooke mortally) wounded. On the prize being added to the British Navy and placed under the orders of Capt. Hardyman, Mr. Lysaght joined her, in May, 1799, in the capacity of Master's Mate. He continued in her until she was wrecked, in the Red Sea, about June 1801; and then removed to the Fox 32, Capt. Henry Stuart, whom, in the following Oct. he accompanied, as Acting-Lieutenant, into LA CHIFFONNE 36. Invaliding home in March, 1802, Mr. Lysaght, whose official promotion took place 3 Aug. in that year, was next, 23 March, 1803, and 5 July, 1805, appointed to the MELPOMÈNE 38, and MALABAR 74, Capts. Robt. Dudley Oliver and Robt. Hall, on the Channel and West India stations. He obtained a second promotal commission 22 Jan. 1806; assumed command, 8 Feb. following of the GOELAN sloop, also in the East Indies; acquired Post-rank 25 Sept. in the same year; and was lastly, from 20 May, 1807, until 19 Nov. 1810, employed as Captain of the JAMAICA 24, on the Channel, Lisbon, and Newfoundland stations. He was advanced to Flag-rank 23 Nov. 1841.

The Rear-Admiral married, first, in 1813, Caroline, daughter of Thos. Cuming, Esq., of Camden Place, Bath; and, that lady dying in 1825, secondly, 22 Aug. 1831, Eliza Dorothy, eldest daughter of the late Henry Percy Pulleine, Esq., of Crake Hall, co. York, by whom he has issue three sons.

LYSAGHT. (LIEUTENANT, 1841.)

THOMAS HENRY LYSAGHT entered the Navy (from the Royal Naval College) 11 Feb. 1830; passed his examination in 1835; and, participating, while Mate of the SAMARANG 26, Capt. Jas. Scott, in the operations on the coast of China, was in particular mentioned for his gallantry and zeal at the forcing of the inner passage from Macao to Whampoa; during their advance on which place the boats of that ship, in conjunction with the NEMESIS steamer, destroyed, between 3 A.M. on 13 and 4 P.M. on 15 March, 1841, five forts, one battery, two military stations, and nine war-junks, in which collectively were 115 guns and 8 ginjalls.* He obtained a commission 8 June following; served, from 23 Aug. in the same year until superseded in 1844, in the SPARTAN 26, Capt. Hon. Chas. Gilbert John Brydone Elliot, on the North America and West India station; and since 10 Nov. 1846 has been in command of the GRAPPLER steamer, of 220 horse-power, on the coast of Africa.

LYSTER. (CAPTAIN, 1845. F-P., 25; H-P., 11.)

HENRY LYSTER entered the Navy, 28 Nov. 1811, as Fst.-cl. Vol., on board the MERCURY, Capt. Clement Milward, with whom he continued to serve as Midshipman and Master's Mate in the PERUVIAN 16, and HERALD 20, on the West India and North American stations until Oct. 1815. He was then for two years and a half employed on the coast of Africa in the INCONSTANT and SEMIRAMIS frigates, bearing each the broad pendant of Sir Jas. Lucas Yeo. On his arrival home in the autumn of 1818 he became for a few weeks attached to the SEVERN Coast Blockade ship, Capt. Wm. M'Culloch; after which he sailed for South America, and was there retained on service in the SLANEY 20, Capts. Donat Henchy O'Brien and Henry Stanhope, until transferred, in June, 1822, to the JUPITER 60, Capt. Geo. Augustus Westphal, fitting for the conveyance of Lord Amherst to Bengal. After having acted for six months as Lieutenant, he was confirmed in that rank, on the return of the JUPITER to England, 20 Jan. 1824; and he was next appointed—towards the close of the same year, to the FERRET sloop, Capt. Wm. Hobson, on the Jamaica station, whence he invalided in March 1826—4 July, 1831, as Senior, to the IMOGENE 28, Capt. Price Blackwood, in which vessel, on proceeding to China, he assisted in forcing the passage of the Boca Tigris 9 Sept. 1834—18 March, 1836, to the CORNWALLIS 74, Capt. Robt. Worgan Geo. Festing, fitting at Plymouth—12 July, 1836, as First, to the ROYAL ADELAIDE 104, flag-ship at that port of Lord Amelius Beauclerk, under

* *Vide* Gaz. 1841, p. 1509.

whom he served for a period of nearly three years—and 2 April, 1840, in a similar capacity, to the VANGUARD 80, Capt. Sir David Dunn, on the Mediterranean station. Obtaining a second promotal commission 23 Nov. 1841, he was appointed, 3 March, 1842, to the Second-Captaincy of the AGINCOURT 72, fitting for the flag of Sir Thos. John Cochrane, Commander-in-Chief in the East Indies. On 10 Aug. 1845, being at the time Acting-Captain of that ship, he assumed charge, as second in command under Capt. Chas. Talbot, of the boats of a squadron carrying altogether 530 officers, seamen, and marines, and by his valorous conduct materially contributed to the destruction of the piratical settlement of Malloodoo, on the north end of the island of Borneo, where the British, owing to a desperate opposition, experienced a loss of 6 men killed and 15 wounded. During the operations he was for upwards of an hour undauntedly engaged, under a well-sustained fire from 11 of the enemy's guns, not 200 yards distant, in endeavouring to effect an opening through a remarkably well-constructed boom which had been placed across the river to obstruct the progress of the British; and in which he ultimately succeeded. He was in consequence confirmed in his present rank by a commission dated back to 30 of the previous June. He returned home in 1846, and has since been on half-pay.

Capt. Lyster married, in April, 1831, at Wexford, Elizabeth, second daughter of the late General Hatton.

LYSTER. (LIEUTENANT, 1845.)

WILLIAM DURHAM LYSTER passed his examination 4 May, 1836; and after having been for some time employed on the Mediterranean and East India stations, as Mate, in the GEYSER steam-vessel, Capt. Edw. John Carpenter, RODNEY 92, Capt. Robt. Maunsell, and IRIS 26, Capt. Geo. Rodney Mundy, was promoted, 13 Dec. 1845, to the rank of Lieutenant, and appointed Additional of the AGINCOURT 72, bearing the flag of Sir Thos. John Cochrane. He continued attached to the latter ship until her return home from the East Indies in 1847.

M.

M'CLEVERTY. (COMMANDER, 1842. F-P., 17; H-P., 7.)

JAMES JOHNSTONE M'CLEVERTY, born 21 June, 1810, is third and youngest son of Major-General Sir Robt. M'Cleverty, Kt., C.B., K.C.H., formerly Colonel-Commandant of the Royal Marines at Woolwich, who died in 1838, by Elizabeth, youngest daughter of Daniel Maude, Esq., of Wakefield, co. York, and first-cousin of the present John Maude, Esq., of Moor House, near Wakefield. The Commander's two brothers, William Anson and Robert, are both in the Army, the one a Major in the 48th, the other a Captain in the 79th Regt. His paternal grandfather, Wm. M'Cleverty, was a Captain in the R.N.

This officer entered the Navy, 6 July, 1823, as Fst.-cl. Vol., on board the HUSSAR 46, Capt. Geo. Harris, employed at first on the Home, and then on the West India station, where, it appears, he shared, as Midshipman, in the capture of numerous piratical vessels. Becoming attached in Nov. 1826, to the ASIA 84, successive flag-ship in the Mediterranean of Sir Edw. Codrington and Sir Pulteney Malcolm, he was afforded an opportunity of sharing, under the former Admiral, in the action fought at Navarin 20 Oct. 1827. He continued with Sir Pulteney Malcolm in the BRITANNIA 120, until promoted to the rank of Lieutenant 1 Nov. 1831; and was next appointed—2 May, 1832, to the CASTOR 36, Capts. Sir Rich. Grant and Lord John Hay, with whom he served at home and off the coast of Portugal until Sept. 1834—and 4 Oct. 1835, as First, to the ÆTNA 6, Capt. Alex. Thos. Emeric Vidal, employed as a surveying vessel on the coast of Africa, whence he returned to England and was paid off in Nov. 1838. In Aug. 1841 Lieut. M'Cleverty obtained command of the Hon. E. I. Co.'s war-steamer PHLEGETHON of 2 guns; his services in which vessel, as they led to his advancement to the rank he now holds, we shall here state:—On 26, then, of the month last-mentioned, he presents himself to our notice as assisting at the capture of Amoy.* He contributed, next, to the reduction of Chusan, 1 Oct. following; and on 10 of the same month we find him lauded in the despatches of Sir Wm. Parker for the spirit of enterprise and zeal he displayed at the taking of Chinghae.† He subsequently, 10 March, 1842, obtained the thanks of Capt. Rundle Burges Watson of the MODESTE, the senior officer present, for the valuable assistance he afforded on the occasion of a night attack made by the Chinese upon the British at Ningpo.‡ In the previous Jan. he had conjoined with the NEMESIS steamer in effecting the destruction of the government buildings belonging to the town of Fungwah. Preparatory to the attack made in the ensuing May upon the enemy's fortifications at Chapoo, he was employed with the same vessel in making a very satisfactory reconnoissance of that city.§ During the celebrated operations against Woosung, the PHLEGETHON, having first towed the COLUMBINE to her proper position abreast of the Chinese batteries, again united with the NEMESIS, and had the fortune to prove instrumental to the annihilation of 13 war-junks, each mounting 3 guns.‖ The activity of her Commander on the occasion was exhibited as in all his other performances. He afterwards beheld the fall of Chin-Kiang-Foo; and, prior to the pacification of Nanking, at which he was also present, he was concerned in enforcing (in company with the STARLING sloop and MEDUSA steamer) the silence of a 12-gun battery in the Yang-tse-Kiang river.¶ As a reward for the above and other services, Mr. M'Cleverty, as already intimated, was rewarded with a Commander's commission dated 23 Dec. 1842.** Subsequently to his return to England he was permitted by the Admiralty to study at the R.N. College. He has been in command, since 23 April, 1846, of the POLYPHEMUS steam-sloop, and is now on the coast of Portugal.

Commander M'Cleverty married, 2 June, 1846, Sophia, relict of Commander R. F. Cleveland, R.N., and fifth daughter of the Rev. Hubert Oakeley, D.D., of Oakeley, Shropshire.

M'CLINTOCK. (LIEUTENANT, 1845.)

FRANCIS LEOPOLD M'CLINTOCK is second son of the late Henry M'Clintock, Esq , formerly in the 3rd Dragoon Guards, Collector of Dundalk, by Elizabeth Melisina, daughter of the late Venerable Geo. Fleury, D.D., Archdeacon of Waterford; first-cousin of Commander W. B. M'Clintock Bunbury, R.N., whose memoir immediately follows; and brother-in-law of the late Capt. Chas. Henry Paget, R.N.

This officer entered the Navy in 1831; passed his examination 23 Oct. 1838; and after having been for several years employed as Mate in the EXCELLENT gunnery-ship at Portsmouth, Capt. Sir Thos. Hastings, and GORGON steamer, commanded on the south-east coast of America by Capt. Chas. Hotham, was promoted to the rank of Lieutenant 29 July, 1845. Being appointed, 16 Aug. following, to the FROLIC 16, Capt. Cospatrick Baillie Hamilton, he continued to serve in that vessel in the Pacific until 1847, in the course of which year he returned home and was paid off.

M'CLINTOCK, M.P., now BUNBURY. (COMMANDER, 1835.)

WILLIAM BUNBURY M'CLINTOCK BUNBURY, born in 1800, is second son of John M'Clintock, Esq., of Drumcar, co. Louth, Chief Serjeant-at-Arms for Ireland since a period antecedent to the legislative

* *Vide* Gaz. 1842, p. 83. † *V.* Gaz. 1842, pp. 394, 396.
‡ *V.* Gaz. 1842, p. 2389. § *V.* Gaz. 1842, p. 3692.
‖ *V.* Gaz. 1842, p. 3309. ¶ *V.* Gaz. 1842, p. 3402.
** *V.* Gaz. 1842, p. 3821.

Union, and formerly M.P. for the borough of Athlone, and for co. Louth, by his first wife, Jane, only daughter of the late Wm. Bunbury, Esq., of Moyle, M.P. for co. Carlow, and sister of the late Thos. Bunbury, Esq., also M.P. for that co. The Commander, a first-cousin of Lieut. F. L. M'Clintock, R.N., is connected with the noble houses of Anglesey and Beaufort, and nearly allied to many others of distinction. One of his half-brothers, Charles, died a Captain in the 74th Regt.; another, George, is at present an officer in the 37th Regt. He assumed the name of Bunbury, in addition to his patronymic, on the death of his uncle, Thos. Bunbury, Esq., M.P., in 1846.

This officer entered the Navy, in July, 1813, as Fst.-cl. Vol., on board the AJAX 74, Capts. Robt. Waller Otway and Geo. Mundy, under the former of whom we find him co-operating in the siege of St. Sebastian and contributing, 17 March, 1814, to the capture of *L'Alcyon* French corvette, of 16 guns and 120 men. Towards the close of the year last mentioned, after he had been for a short time employed on the American coast, he sailed for the Cape of Good Hope in the NIGER 38, Capt. Peter Rainier. Quitting that ship in 1815, he next, until promoted to the rank of Lieutenant 12 Sept. 1822, served on the Home, Mediterranean, Brazilian, and Newfoundland stations, chiefly as Midshipman, in the PACTOLUS 38 and SEVERN* 40, both commanded by Capt. Hon. Fred. Wm. Aylmer, BRITOMART sloop, Capt. Hon. Geo. Jas. Perceval, FAVORITE 20, Capt. Hercules Robinson, GRASSHOPPER sloop, Capt. David Buchan, QUEEN CHARLOTTE 100, bearing the flag of Sir Jas. Hawkins Whitshed, and APOLLO and ROYAL GEORGE yachts, each under the orders of Hon. Sir Chas. Paget. His subsequent appointments were—11 Sept. 1823, to the TAMAR 26, Capt. Sir Jas. John Gordon Bremer, fitting in the river Thames—2 Feb. 1824, to the SAMARANG 28, Capts. Sir Wm. Saltonstall Wiseman and David Dunn, employed at Halifax and the Cape of Good Hope—21 Aug. 1828, to the PROCRIS 10, Capts. Chas. Henry Paget and Sir Thos. Sabine Pasley, stationed off Cork and in the Mediterranean—and, 3 June, 1831, again to the SAMARANG, Capt. C. H. Paget, in which vessel he officiated for three years as First-Lieutenant in South America. He was promoted to the rank of Commander, on being paid off, 9 Feb. 1835, and has since been on half-pay.

In July, 1846, on the death of his uncle, Commander Bunbury was elected M.P. for co. Carlow. He was again returned in 1847. He married, 3 Nov. 1842, Pauline, second daughter of Sir Jas. Matthew Stronge, Bart., of Tynan Abbey, co. Armagh.

M'CLURE. (LIEUTENANT, 1837.)

ROBERT JOHN LE MESURIER M'CLURE passed his examination in 1830; and obtained his commission 30 Nov. 1837. His appointments have since been—1 Feb. 1838, to the HASTINGS 74, Capt. Fras. Erskine Loch, fitting at Portsmouth—16 June following, to the NIAGARA 20, Capt. Williams Sandom, on the Lakes of Canada—17 Aug. 1839, as First-Lieutenant, to the PILOT 16, Capt. Geo. Ramsay, attached to the force in North America and the West Indies—18 June, 1842, to the command of the ROMNEY receiving-ship at the Havana, where he remained until the early part of 1846—and, 29 Dec. in the latter year, to the Coast Guard, in which service he is now employed.

M'CORMICK. (COMMANDER, 1841. F-P., 12; H-P., 32.)

SHEPHERD M'CORMICK was born in Jan. 1794.

This officer entered the Navy, 17 Sept. 1803, as Fst.-cl. Vol., on board the REPULSE 74, Capts. Hon. Arthur Kaye Legge and John Halliday, to which ship he continued attached in the capacities of Midshipman and Master's Mate until Feb. 1811. It was his fortune to be present, in consequence, in Sir Robt. Calder's action 22 July, 1805; at the capture of the *Marengo* of 80 guns, bearing the flag of Admiral Linois, and 40-gun frigate *Belle Poule*, 13 March, 1806; at the taking, 27 Sept. following, of *Le Président* French frigate; at the passage of the Dardanells, and the destruction of the Turkish squadron at Point Pesquies, in Feb. 1807; at the siege of Flushing in Aug. 1809; and on 30 Aug. 1810, when the REPULSE gallantly rescued the PHILOMEL sloop from capture, by interposing herself between that vessel and an advanced division of the Toulon fleet, which she compelled to put back. In Oct. 1811, after he had been for eight months employed with Capts. Halliday and Joseph Bingham in the MONTAGU and EGMONT 74's, he joined the SWIFTSURE of similar force; in the boats belonging to which ship, when off the island of Corsica, we find him assisting at the capture of a privateer, whose resistance occasioned her assailants a heavy loss. Being appointed Acting-Lieutenant, in March, 1813, of the VOLCANO bomb, Capts. Wm. Fairbrother Carroll, David Price, and John Wyat Watling, Mr. M'Cormick (whose promotion was confirmed 25 June following, and who continued in the same vessel until Aug. 1815) was at first very actively employed in co-operation with the army on the coast of Catalonia, where he frequently landed and was wounded during the arduous investment of the fort of St. Philippe in the Col de Balaguer, mounting 12 pieces of ordnance, with a garrison of 101 officers and men. Proceeding subsequently to the coast of America, he was afforded an opportunity, previously to participating in the operations against New Orleans, of serving with the boats of a squadron at the capture, on Lake Borgne, 14 Dec. 1814, of five American gun-vessels, after a very desperate struggle in which the British sustained a loss of 17 men killed and 77 wounded. On 31 of the preceding Oct., the VOLCANO, at the time in charge of a transport, had succeeded, with a loss to herself of 2 persons killed, in beating off the U. S. privateer *Saucy Jack*, a vessel of far superior force, 7 of whose people were slain and 14 wounded. During the insurrection of 1837 in Canada, Mr. M'Cormick received five balls through the body and a sabre-cut across the right loin while effecting the capture of a piratical steamer, the *Caroline*. This led to his promotion to the rank he now holds, 23 Nov. 1841. He is at present on half-pay.

Commander M'Cormick is in the receipt of a pension of 91*l.* 5*s.* for his wounds. He married, in Dec. 1821, Miss Charlotte Roe, a lady by whom he has issue six children. AGENTS—Burnett and Holmes.

* In the SEVERN he fought at Algiers.

M'CORNISH. (LIEUTENANT, 1827.)

JAMES M'CORNISH died in the early part of 1846.

This officer entered the Navy, 10 Jan. 1810, as Fst.-cl. Vol., on board the RHIN 38, Capt. Chas. Malcolm. Continuing in that ship until paid off in Aug. 1815, he co-operated with the patriots on the north coast of Spain, was for some time employed in the West Indies, and cruized off the coast of France during the war of 100 days. He passed his examination 7 Feb. 1816, and between that period and the date of his advancement to the rank of Lieutenant, 21 Nov. 1827, was employed in vessels of different descriptions—from 1817 to 1820, as chief officer, in a Revenue-cruizer. At the period of his promotion he was with Capt. Malcolm in the ROYAL CHARLOTTE yacht. He did not afterwards go afloat.

M'COY. (COMMANDER, 1814. F-P., 20; H-P., 33.)

ROBERT M'COY is son of Daniel M'Coy, Esq., Master R.N. (1788), who died in April, 1835, at Southsea, aged 75.

This officer entered the Navy, in Nov. 1794, as Captain's Servant, on board the HANNIBAL 74, Capt. John Colpoys, attached to the force in the Channel, whence, in 1794, he sailed for the West Indies in the GANGES 74, Capt. Wm. Truscott. Quitting that ship in June, 1795, he next, between 1797 and Oct. 1801, served on the Home and Mediterranean stations as Midshipman in the JUSTE 80, Capt. Hon. Thos. Pakenham, ROYAL WILLIAM, bearing the flag of Sir Peter Parker, SNAKE sloop, Capt. John Mason Lewis, PEARL 32, Capt. Sam. Jas. Ballard, and FOUDROYANT 80, flag-ship of Lord Keith, under whom he took part in the operations connected with the expedition to Egypt. Being confirmed a Lieutenant (after having acted for six months as such in the West Indies on board the DEFENCE 74, Capt. Lord Henry Paulet) by commission dated 3 July, 1802, Mr. M'Coy was subsequently appointed in that capacity—22 Nov. 1803, to the RAISONNABLE 64. Capts. Wm. Hotham, Robt. Barton, Chas. Malcolm, and Josias Rowley, in which ship, prior to serving on shore at the reduction of the Cape of Good Hope, he fought in Sir Robert Calder's action 22 July, 1805—in Feb. 1806, to the NARCISSUS 32, Capt. Ross Donnelly, under whom he witnessed the fall of Buenos Ayres —17 July, 1807 (after nine months of half-pay), to the RESOLUTION 74, Capts. Geo. Burlton and Temple Hardy, part of the force employed in 1809 at the destruction of the French shipping in Basque Roads and at the capture of Flushing—14 Aug. 1811, to the SWIFTSURE 74, Capts. T. Hardy, Andrew King, Wm. Stewart, Jeremiah Coghlan, and Edw. Stirling Dickson, stationed in the Mediterranean, where he shared in one of Sir Edw. Pellew's partial actions with the Toulon fleet—and, 16 July, 1814, to the TREMENDOUS 74, Capt. Robt. Campbell. In the following Nov. Mr. M'Coy, who had been altogether upwards of seven years First-Lieutenant of the NARCISSUS, RESOLUTION, SWIFTSURE, and TREMENDOUS, took up a Commander's commission dated 15 of the previous June. With the exception of an appointment held in the Coast Guard from 6 April, 1831, until the commencement of 1834, he has since been on half-pay.

His only daughter is the wife of Capt. W. L. Castle, R.N.

M'CREA. (CAPTAIN, 1837. F-P., 18; H-P., 26.)

ROBERT CONTART M'CREA was born 13 Jan. 1793.

This officer entered the Navy, 23 Nov. 1803, as Sec.-cl. Vol., on board the DÉCADE frigate, commanded at the blockade of Cherbourg by Capt. Wm. Geo. Rutherford; on accompanying whom as Midshipman into the SWIFTSURE 74, he went with Lord Nelson in pursuit of the Franco-Spanish fleet to the West Indies, and took part, 21 Oct. 1805, in the battle of Trafalgar. After again serving for a few months off Cherbourg in the THALIA 36, Capt. Thos. Manby, he successively joined, in March and July, 1808, the VICTORY 100, flag-ship in the Baltic of Sir Jas. Saumarez, and SALSETTE 36, Capt. Walter Bathurst. In the latter ship Mr. M'Crea saw much active service, passed through scenes of a very trying nature, and assisted, in 1809, at the reduction of Flushing. He continued with Capt. Bathurst in the FAME 74, latterly on the Mediterranean station, until April, 1811; and in Jan. 1812 he was a second time placed under the orders of Sir Jas. Saumarez in the VICTORY, of which ship it was his fortune to be confirmed a Lieutenant, after having acted for five months in that capacity, 20 Nov. following. While next attached, between 6 May, 1813, and 27 April, 1815, to the AMPHION 32, Capt. Jas. Pattison Stewart, we find him on one occasion, with two boats under his orders, cutting off two sloops laden with provisions for the relief of Fort Balthz, and driving a third on shore under the enemy's batteries, in the East Scheldt; and, on another, officiating as third in command of five boats in a desperate attempt made to cut out five French brigs from under the walls of Fort Lillo. Assuming charge, in the early part of 1818, of the SCOURGE Revenue-cruizer, Mr. M'Crea, who continued in that vessel until 1821, succeeded in effecting the capture of not less than 13 smuggling luggers, sloops, and cutters. On 4 June, 1824, 10 weeks after he had been nominated Flag-Lieutenant, in the BRITANNIA 120, to Sir Jas. Saumarez, Commander-in-Chief at Plymouth, he was awarded a second promotal commission; but he did not again go afloat until 1834—on 1 June in which year he obtained an appointment to the ZEBRA 16. When subsequently on the coast of New Holland that sloop, it appears, was thrown on her beam-ends and compelled to part with her guns; and she was also, when in the Straits of Malacca, struck with lightning and dismasted. In April, 1837, her Commander, who had been advanced to Post-rank on 10 of the previous Jan., succeeded in forcibly removing the ex-Rajah of Quedah from his abode at Bruas, on the coast of Perak, in the Straits of Malacca, and carrying him a prisoner to Pinang. In the performance of this service the boats of the ZEBRA, under the personal direction of Capt. M'Crea, had had to sustain a severe action of an hour and a half with a brig and a powerful stockade, defended by a numerous band of Malays, more than 60 of whom are reported to have been killed and wounded. The loss of the British was also very severe. Before they could reach the stockade it had been necessary for them to ascend a narrow, tortuous river, enfringed with jungle on both sides; where, had a few trees been felled and allowed to fall across, they would have been perfectly hemmed in, and their destruction have been inevitable. To mark their estimation of Capt. M'Crea's conduct, the East India Company presented him with a piece of plate of the value of 100 guineas. He paid the ZEBRA off in Oct. 1838; and has not been since employed.

He married, 10 April, 1822, Charlotte, elder daughter of the Rev. W. P. Dobree, Rector of a place in Guernsey, by whom he has issue eight children.

M'DANIEL. (LIEUT., 1814. F-P., 8; H-P., 32.)

JEREMIAH M'DANIEL entered the Navy, 29 April, 1807, as Fst.-cl. Vol., on board the FRANCHISE 36, Capt. Chas. Dashwood, with whom until Jan. 1814 he continued most actively employed as Midshipman and Master's Mate in the PYRAMUS 38, and CRESSY 74, on the Baltic, West India, and Mediterranean stations. In the FRANCHISE, in particular, he was present at the bombardment of Copenhagen, and at the capture of the town of Samana, St. Domingo, almost the last port of refuge on the station for the enemy's privateers. Joining, in July, 1814, the TONNANT 80, bearing the flag of Hon. Sir Alex. Cochrane, he served, while in that ship, on shore at the battle of Bladensburg, and was severely wounded in the attack upon Washington.* He was in consequence nominated Acting-Lieutenant, 2 Sept. in the same year, of the MAJESTIC 56, Capt. John Hayes; and on 19 of the following Oct. was confirmed into the DISPATCH 16, Capt. Wm. Cobbe. He went on half-pay in April, 1815, and has not been since afloat.

MACDONALD. (RETIRED COMMANDER, 1842.)

ARCHIBALD MACDONALD, born in Nov. 1786, in co. Linlithgow, N.B., is a younger son of John Macdonald Kinneir, of Sander and Kinneir, and is descended in a direct line from the second son of John, Lord of the Isles. His brother, Sir John Macdonald Kinneir, was Envoy in Persia.

This officer entered the Navy, 8 March, 1798, as Midshipman, on board the ARDENT 64, Capt. Thos. Bertie; previously to accompanying whom into the BELLONA 74, he attended the expedition of 1799 to the Helder, and was wounded in the action off Copenhagen 2 April, 1801.† In Feb. 1802, being then in the West Indies, he removed to the BELLEROPHON 74, Capt. John Loring; and during his attachment to that ship he assisted at the capture, among other vessels, of *Le Duquesne* 74, and *La Créole* of 44 guns, with the French General Morgan and 500 troops on board. After he had for a short time served in the CUMBERLAND 74, Capt. John Serrell, Mr. Macdonald was transferred, in July, 1803, to LA CRÉOLE, which had been added to the British Navy and placed under the orders of Capt. Austin Bissell. In Jan. 1804, however, the latter ship, during her passage to England, unfortunately foundered, and would have carried all on board to destruction had

* *Vide* Gaz. 1814, p. 1942.

† The Patriotic Society presented him, in consequence, with a gratuity.

not the CUMBERLAND miraculously hove in sight at the eleventh hour, and with great difficulty effected their rescue. In the following May (he had been intermediately employed in the MONTAGU 74, Capt. Robt. Waller Otway, and VILLE DE PARIS 110, flag-ship of Hon. Wm. Cornwallis) Mr. Macdonald was placed, with the rank, we believe, of Acting-Lieutenant, in command of the CAPELIN schooner, on the Newfoundland station, where he remained until Feb. 1807. He was then (having been officially promoted on 22 of the preceding Dec.) appointed a Lieutenant of the TRIBUNE frigate, Capts. Thos. Baker and Geo. Reynolds, with whom, until he invalided in Nov. 1812, he served in the Channel, Baltic, and West Indies. In April, 1807, we find him assisting, when in company with the ISIS, at the destruction of the greater part of a convoy of 30 vessels passing from Ferrol to Bilbao under the protection of several gun-boats. He was also present, in 1809, in an action with some Danish gun-boats in the Belt; and in the course of the same year he chanced to be on board the CHARGER gun-brig, in the Malmo Channel, when that vessel preserved a convoy from capture. He had previously, we understand, been sent by Sir Rich. Keats with despatches from off Gottenborg to England in a small prize-boat of so crazy a description that it was with the greatest difficulty he succeeded in keeping her afloat, encountered as he was by four days of the most desperate weather. On 12 May, 1810, being again on board the TRIBUNE, Mr. Macdonald partook of a gallant action of two hours and a quarter, in which the latter, with a loss of 9 men killed and 15 wounded, beat off, on the coast of Norway, four Danish brigs-of-war, carrying altogether 74 guns. From Sept. 1813 to June, 1814, he had charge of the BIENFAISANT prison-ship at Plymouth. Entering the Transport service in Jan. 1815, he superintended the debarkations of the troops before and after the battle of Waterloo; and when at Antwerp in the following winter he alone despatched upwards of 90 vessels with army ordnance and stores to England. His last appointment afloat was to the command, in 1823, of the HARPY Revenue-vessel, in which he cruized with much success for a period of three years. He accepted his present rank 26 Jan. 1842.

Commander Macdonald has been for many years employed in the Quarantine service at Liverpool. He married Miss Cox, of St. John's, Newfoundland, and by that lady has had issue a large family.

MACDONALD, C.B. (Captain, 1814. F-P., 20; H-P., 34.)

COLIN MACDONALD is second son of Colin Macdonald, second Laird of Boisdale, by his second wife, Isabella, daughter of Capt. Robt. Campbell, of Glenfalloch, whose family are next in succession to the Breadalbane titles and estates. One of his half-brothers, Alexander, served as Captain in the 71st Regt during the American war; and another, Donald, on attaining, in 1796, the rank of Colonel, raised a regiment of the line, called the Macdonald Regiment, of which he was Colonel-Commandant. Capt. Colin Macdonald is a younger brother of the late Sir Reginald Macdonald, an Advocate and H.M. Sheriff Depute for co. Stirling, and also of the present Lieut.-Colonel Robt. Macdonald, C.B., of Inchkenneth and Gribune, co. Argyle. He is uncle of Sir Henry Jas. Seton Steuart, Bart., of Allanton, co. Lanark, and of Lieut. Jas. Archibald Macdonald, R.N.

This officer entered the Navy, 2 April, 1793, as Ordinary, on board the SOUTHAMPTON 32, Capt. Hon. Robt. Forbes, which vessel was attached to the fleet under Lord Howe in the action of 1 June, 1794. In April, 1795, Mr. Macdonald, who on that occasion had performed the duties of Midshipman, removed to the DRYAD, of 44 guns and 251 men, commanded at first by Capt. Forbes, and afterwards by Lord Amelius Beauclerk, on the coast of Ireland, where he took part, 13 June, 1796, in a close and spirited engagement of 45 minutes, which resulted in the capture, with a loss to the British of 2 killed and 7 wounded, and to the enemy of 30 killed and 45 wounded, of the French frigate *La Proserpine*, of 42 guns and 348 men. On 3 June, 1799, at which time he was serving on board the ANDROMACHE 32, Capt. Robt. Laurie, Mr. Macdonald was made Lieutenant into the BEAVER sloop, Capt. C. B. Jones. His next appointments were—4 Jan. 1800, to the NEPTUNE 98, Capt. Jas. Vashon—17 Nov. 1800, to the RESOLUTION 74, Capt. Hon. Alan Hyde Gardner, whom he accompanied to the West Indies—15 Jan. 1803 (after six months of half-pay), to the CONSTANCE 24, Capt. Anselm John Griffiths, employed in the North Sea—19 Oct. 1803, to the HERO 74, Capt. Hon. A. H. Gardner, also on the Home station—and, 8 June, 1804, and 3 Aug. 1805, to the MONARCH and EDGAR 74's, flag-ships, again in the North Sea, of Admiral Lord Keith. Obtaining a second promotal commission 4 June, 1807, Capt. Macdonald successively assumed command, 8 Aug. in that year and 13 Aug. 1812, of the REDPOLE 10 and SCYLLA 18. In the former of those vessels, after having co-operated in the reduction of Flushing, he made prize, 9 Dec. 1809, at the end of an action of half an hour, fought off Beachy Head, of *Le Grand Rodeur* French privateer, of 16 guns and 80 men, 1 of whom was killed and 2 wounded;* and on 21 Sept. 1811 he contributed, in a very zealous manner, to the capture, in the course of a valiant contest with a division of the Boulogne flotilla, of *La Ville de Lyons* praam, of 12 long 24-pounders and 112 men.† When in the SCYLLA, and in company with the ROYALIST 18, Capt. Macdonald, after a long chase, commenced a spirited action, which lasted 1 hour and 40 minutes, and terminated in the surrender, 21 Oct. 1813, on the approach of the RIPPON 74, of the French frigate *Le Weser*, of 40 guns and 340 men, at the time under jury main and mizen masts. The loss of the enemy appears to have been 4 killed and 15 wounded; and that of the sloops, united, of 2 killed and 11 wounded.‡ Capt. Macdonald attained Post-rank 7 June, 1814; was nominated a C.B. 4 June, 1815; and accepted the Retirement 1 Oct. 1846.

MACDONALD. (CAPTAIN, 1846.)

GORDON GALLIE MACDONALD entered the Navy 21 July, 1809; and was made Lieutenant, 15 Dec. 1824, into the RATTLESNAKE 28, Capts. Hugh Patton and John Leith. His succeeding appointments were—20 Dec. 1825, to the PRINCE REGENT 120, flag-ship at the Nore of Sir Robt. Moorsom—13 Nov. 1828, to the CHILDERS 18, Capts. Wm. Morier and Robt. Deans, in which vessel, employed on various services, he continued, latterly as First-Lieutenant, until paid off in the early part of 1833—3 April, 1835, to the command (which he retained for nearly four years) of the BASILISK ketch, on the South American station—and 31 Oct. 1840, as Senior, to the MONARCH 84, Capt. Sam. Chambers, fitting for the Mediterranean. He returned to England on the receipt of his second promotal commission, bearing date 23 Nov. 1841; and was lastly, from 28 Nov. 1842 until paid off in 1845, employed as Second-Captain of the DUBLIN 50, flag-ship in the Pacific of Rear-Admiral Rich. Thomas. He attained his present rank 9 Nov. 1846.

Capt. Macdonald married, 13 Dec. 1842, Maria, relict of Wm. Gray, Esq., of the Inner Temple, and daughter of the Rev. Wm. Oddie, M.A. He was left a widower 4 Jan. 1846. AGENTS—Messrs. Ommanney.

MACDONALD. (LIEUTENANT, 1827.)

JAMES ARCHIBALD MACDONALD, born 18 Jan. 1808, is third son of Lieut.-Colonel Robt. Macdonald, C.B., of Inchkenneth and Gribune, co. Argyle, a Magistrate and Deputy-Lieutenant for that shire, by Mary, third daughter of Thos. Douglas, Esq., of Grantham. He is a younger brother of Capt. Robt. Douglas Macdonald, late of the 42nd Highlanders, and of Capt. Chas. Kerr Macdonald, late

* *Vide* Gaz. 1809, p. 1973. † *V.* Gaz. 1811, p. 1862. ‡ *V.* Gaz. 1813, p. 2102.

of the 42nd Regt.; and a nephew of the present Capt. Colin Macdonald, R.N., C.B.

This officer was promoted to the rank of Lieutenant, immediately on passing his examination, 8 Sept. 1827. His appointments have since been—30 May, 1834, to the WOLF 18, Capt. Edw. Stanley, fitting for the East Indies, where, in command of the boats of that ship, he came into contact in 1836 with 18 Malay piratical vessels of 2 guns each, and where in 1837 (being at the time First-Lieutenant) he destroyed several others off the island of Poulo Linghy—30 Jan. 1839 (a few months after the WOLF had been paid off) to the Coast Guard—4 April, 1842, to the command (which he retained for nearly 12 months) of the CHARYBDIS brigantine in North America and the West Indies—30 Oct. 1844, again to the Coast Guard—and 15 March and 12 June, 1845, to the successive command of the LIZARD and METEOR steamers, in the latter of which vessels, of 140-horse power, he is now serving in the Mediterranean.

Lieut. Macdonald married, in 1837, Martha, daughter of — Greig, Esq., and niece of Lady Rollo, by whom he has issue three daughters. AGENTS—Hallett and Robinson.

MACDONALD. (RETIRED COMMANDER, 1829. F-P., 31; H-P., 37.)

JOHN MACDONALD died in 1845.

This officer entered the Navy, 3 Aug. 1777, as Midshipman, on board the CULLODEN 74, Capt. Geo. Balfour, and in 1780-1 was present in that ship in several engagements with the French fleet in the West Indies. Removing, in the course of the latter year, to the BEDFORD 74, Commodore Affleck, he was afforded an opportunity of sharing in Rodney's action, 12 April, 1782. During the peace he was employed, chiefly in the capacity of Master's Mate, in the EDGAR, Capt. Adam Duncan, PÉGASE, Capts. Marshall and Rich. Rodney Bligh, ADVENTURE, Capts. Fras. Perry and John Nicholson Inglefield, FAIRY, Capt. Thos. Spry, ELEPHANT, Capt. Chas. Thompson, and BARFLEUR, flag-ship of Admiral John Elliot. On 29 Nov. 1793, a few days after he had joined Lord Hood in the VICTORY off Toulon, Mr. Macdonald found himself promoted to a Lieutenancy in an armed ship, commanded by Capt. Walter Serocold. His subsequent appointments were—15 Dec. 1794, to the WINDSOR CASTLE 98, flag-ship of Admirals Philip Cosby, Robt. Linzee, and Robt. Mann, under the second-named of whom he shared in Hotham's actions 14 March and 13 July, 1795—23 March and 10 Nov. 1797, to the DEFIANCE 74, Capt. Theophilus Jones, and MONARCH 74, flag-ship of Admirals Sir Rich. Onslow and Arch. Dixon, both on the Home station—19 May, 1800 (after eight months of half-pay), to the Impress service at Exeter, where he remained until Oct. 1801—in 1804-5, to the successive command of the CHANCE, NANCY, and VIGILANT, in which vessels we find him employed, on the Mediterranean and Home stations, until Jan. 1806—and, 8 Aug. 1807, to the Transport service, in which he continued upwards of eight years. He became a Retired Commander on the Senior List 14 Feb. 1829.

MACDONALD. (LIEUTENANT, 1842.)

REGINALD JOHN JAMES GEORGE MACDONALD is eldest son of Reginald Geo. Macdonald, Captain and Chief of Clanranald, a Deputy-Lieutenant for Inverness, by Lady Caroline Anne Edgcumbe, second daughter of Richard, second Earl of Mount Edgcumbe. One of his sisters is married to Hon. Chas. Cust, second son of the Earl of Brownlow; and another to the Hon. and Rev. Alfred Wodehouse, youngest son of Lord Wodehouse.

This officer entered the Navy 11 May, 1833; passed his examination 8 May, 1839; and, after having served in the Mediterranean, as Mate of the HOWE 120, Capts. Sir Watkin Owen Pell and Robt. Smart, flag-ship latterly of Sir Fras. Mason, was promoted to the rank of Lieutenant 14 Dec. 1842. His appointments have since been—15 Feb. 1843, again to the HOWE, commanded at the time by Capt. Thos. Forrest—3 Nov. 1843, to the ALBION 90, Capt. Nicholas Lockyer, off Lisbon—and, 30 May, 1844, to the COLLINGWOOD 80, Capt. R. Smart, bearing the flag in the Pacific of Sir Geo. Fras. Seymour, to whom he became Signal-Lieutenant 20 Jan. 1847. AGENTS—Messrs. Stilwell.

M'DONELL. (CAPT., 1846. F-P., 25; H-P., 11.)

JOHN M'DONELL entered the Navy, 10 Feb. 1811, as Fst.-cl. Vol., on board the LEVERET brig, Capt. Geo. Wickens Willes, stationed at first in the North Sea, and afterwards in the Mediterranean; where, on becoming attached to the UNITÉ 36, Capt. Edwin Henry Chamberlayne, he was wounded in the boats of that frigate at the capture of two of the enemy's vessels in 1812. Removing, as Midshipman, in Oct. 1814, to the PHŒNIX 36, Capt. Chas. John Austen, he continued to serve in the Mediterranean until wrecked in a hurricane near Smyrna, 20 Feb. 1816; after which, and until promoted to the rank of Lieutenant, 6 Sept. 1823, we find him employed, six years of the time as a passed Midshipman, in the BULWARK 74, Capt. Geo. M'Kinley, MÆANDER 38, Capt. Sir Jas. Alex. Gordon, EGERIA 24, Capt. Robt. Rowley, ACTIVE 38, Capt. Sir I. A. Gordon, ALBION 74, Capt. Rich. Raggett, and APOLLO and ROYAL GEORGE yachts, Capts. Hon. Sir Chas. Paget and Hon. Thos. Bladen Capel—on the Home and Newfoundland stations. His succeeding appointments were—9 Dec. 1824, to the PANDORA 18, Capts. Wm. Gordon, Wm. Clarke Jervoise, and Hon. John Fred. Gordon, with whom, until paid off in Feb. 1830, he served at Newfoundland and in the East Indies—9 Nov. 1830, as First, to the ARIADNE 28, Capt. Chas. Phillips, employed on particular service—9 Sept. 1831, in a similar capacity, to the CURAÇOA 26, Capt. David Dunn, on the East India station—26 June, 1832, again as Senior, to the CRUIZER 18, Capt. John Parker, with whom he returned home in the early part of 1833—25 March, 1836, still as First, to the HERCULES 74, Capt. Maurice Fred. Fitzhardinge Berkeley, on the Lisbon station—and, 24 Jan. 1837, as only Lieutenant, to the ROYAL GEORGE yacht, Capt. Lord Adolphus FitzClarence. He continued in the latter vessel until promoted to the rank of Commander 28 June, 1838; and he afterwards, from 24 Aug. 1841 until put out of commission in 1844, officiated as Second-Captain of the MALABAR 72, Capt. Sir Geo. Rose Sartorius, on the Mediterraneon station. He was advanced to his present rank 9 Nov. 1846, and is now on half-pay. AGENTS—Burnett and Holmes.

M'DONELL. (COMMANDER, 1846.)

JOHN JULIUS M'DONELL entered the Navy 16 Jan. 1816; and while Midshipman of the CAMBRIAN frigate was intrusted with the charge of a merchantman, in which he succeeded in beating off two piratical boats in the Negropont. He passed his examination in 1823; obtained his first commission 13 Sept. 1826; and was afterwards appointed—3 Oct. 1829, to the WINCHESTER 52, flag-ship of Sir Edw. Griffith Colpoys in North America and the West Indies—8 Dec. 1830, to the command of the FIREFLY schooner, which vessel, employed on the station last mentioned, he had the misfortune to lose in 1835—8 July, 1844, to the Coast Guard—and 1 July, 1845, to the command of the NAUTILUS 10. He was employed in the latter vessel on Home service until advanced to his present rank 9 Nov. 1846; and is now on half-pay.

He married, in 1841, Louisa, relict of the late H. Hyde, Esq., of London. AGENTS—Messrs. Chard.

M'DONELL. (LIEUT., 1810. F-P., 9; H-P., 34.)

THOMAS M'DONELL entered the Navy, 4 March, 1804, as Fst.-cl. Vol., on board the VETERAN 64, Capts. Sir Rich. King, Jas. Newman Newman, and Andrew Fitzherbert Evans, employed on the Home and West India stations. On his return to England in 1807, as Midshipman of the HERCULE 74, Capt. Barrington Dacres, he cruized for several months in the NARCISSUS 32, Capt. Chas. Malcolm, and then rejoined Capt. Newman, as Master's Mate, on board the HERO 74. In Aug. 1809 he was sent in command of a gun-boat to co-operate in the attack upon Flushing. He attained the rank of Lieutenant 18 July, 1810, and was employed, during the last three years of the war, in the OPOSSUM 10, Capt. Thos. Wolrige, and VALIANT 74, Capt. Robt. Dudley Oliver, on the West India and North American stations. He has since been on half-pay. AGENTS—Pettet and Newton.

M'DOUALL. (COMMANDER, 1814. F-P., 21; H-P., 30.)

JAMES M'DOUALL died 30 Dec. 1845.

This officer entered the Navy, 27 July, 1795, as A.B., on board the ZEBRA sloop, Capts. Norborne Thompson, David M'Iver, and John Hurst, in which vessel, stationed in the West Indies, he continued to serve, in the capacities of Midshipman, Master's Mate, and Acting-Lieutenant, until transferred, 25 April, 1797, to a Master's Mateship in the INTREPID 64, Capts. Robt. Parker and Wm. Hargood. In Sept. 1801, after having again acted as Lieutenant in the ship last mentioned, Mr. M'Douall, then in the East Indies, became Master's Mate of the ARROGANT 74, Capt. Edw. Oliver Osborne; and on 11 of the following month he was appointed, a third time, to the post of Acting-Lieutenant in the TRIDENT 64, Capts. Thos. Surridge, Chas. Jas. Johnston, Peter Rainier, and Benj. Wm. Page, bearing the flag for a period of Vice-Admiral Rainier. Being confirmed to the TRIDENT by commission dated 22 April, 1802, he continued attached to her, on the East India station, until Oct. 1805. While cruizing next, for a few months in 1806, in the BELLEISLE 74, Capt. Wm. Hargood, we find him assisting at the destruction, off Cape Henry, on the American coast, of the French 74-gun ship *L'Impétueux*. Between Aug. 1807 and his advancement to the rank of Commander 12 Oct. 1814, he served on the West India, Mediterranean, and Home stations, in the YORK 74, Capt. Robt. Barton, VILLE DE PARIS 110, flag-ship of Lord Collingwood, NORTHUMBERLAND 74, Capts. Wm. Hargood and Hon. Henry Hotham, ASIA and BARHAM 74's, both commanded by Capt. John Wm. Spranger, and SAN JOSEF and QUEEN CHARLOTTE, flag-ships of Lord Keith. His last employments were, from 15 Nov. 1814 to 6 Sept. 1815, as Regulating Officer and Commandant of gun-boats at Greenock—and, from 21 March 1816 to 25 March, 1819, as Superintendent of the Ordinary at Portsmouth.

M'DOUGALL. (RETIRED COMMANDER, 1844. F-P., 20; H-P., 34.)

JOHN M'DOUGALL entered the Navy, 1 April, 1793, as Captain's Servant, on board the VESTAL 28, Capt. John M'Dougall, attached to the force on the Home station, where he further, until the receipt of his first commission, bearing date 26 April, 1800, served as Midshipman and Acting-Lieutenant in the ASIA 64, Capt. J. M'Dougall, SAVAGE sloop, Capt. G. Winckworth, and EDGAR 74, Capts. J. M'Dougall and Edw. Buller. He was then employed for several months at the blockade of Dunkerque in the ATALANTE sloop, Capt. Anselm John Griffiths; on leaving which vessel he proceeded to the West Indies, and there cruized, during the remainder of the war, in the CRESCENT 36, Capts. Wm. Grenville Lobb and Jas. Carthew. In July, 1804, after he had been for 14 months employed in the Sea-Fencibles at Southend in Essex, Mr. M'Dougall obtained an appointment to the HECLA bomb, in which vessel, commanded by Capts. Sykes and Scott, we find him assisting at the bombardment of Havre in July and Aug. 1804. Joining next the CÆSAR 80, Capt. (afterwards Rear-Admiral) Sir Rich. John Strachan, he was afforded an opportunity of participating in that ship in the action off Ferrol 4 Nov. 1805. In Dec. 1806, his health compelling him to invalid, he sailed from Halifax, Nova Scotia, in a merchant-vessel, carrying with him Sir R. J. Strachan's despatches. It was his misfortune however, on 13 of the following month, to fall, when off Scilly, into the hands of a French privateer, by whom he was taken a prisoner to France, where he remained in captivity until April 1814. Returning then to England, he assumed, 11 May, 1815, the command, which he held until 23 March, 1816, of the Telegraph station at Beacon Hill in Kent. He became a Retired Commander on the Junior List 1 Dec. 1830; and on the Senior 9 Dec. 1844.

M'DOUGALL. (CAPTAIN, 1836. F-P., 19; H-P., 26.)

JOHN M'DOUGALL, born in 1790, at Edinburgh, is eldest surviving son of the late Patrick M'Dougall, Esq., of Dunolly Castle, co. Argyle, by Louisa Maxwell, youngest daughter of John Campbell, Esq., of Achalader, in Perthshire, and sister of the late Generals Sir Alex. Campbell, Commander-in-Chief at Madras, and Archibald Campbell, Governor of Fort Augustus, N.B. His elder brother, Alexander, a Captain in the 5th Regt. of Foot, was killed at the storming of Ciudad Rodrigo in Jan. 1812; and his next, Patrick, is now a Lieutenant-Colonel in the Army. Capt. M'Dougall's family are the undisputed lineal representatives of the M'Dougalls Lords of Lorn, or of Argyle, and are the admitted chiefs of that name.

This officer entered the Navy, 16 Dec. 1802, as Fst.-cl. Vol., on board the CRUIZER 18, Capt. John Hancock, and in the course of the following year was five times in action with the enemy between Calais and Flushing, once in particular, 14 June, when the CRUIZER, in company with the IMMORTALITÉ 36 and JALOUSE 18, assisted at the capture of the French gun-brigs *L'Inabordable* and *La Commode*, after an hour's engagement with the batteries on the east part of Cape Blanc-nez. In June, 1804, after having been in frequent contact with the enemy in the DORIS 36, Capt. Patrick Campbell, he became Midshipman of the FOUDROYANT 80, bearing the flag in the Channel of Rear-Admiral Thos. Graves. He went back, however, in the following Dec. to the DORIS, and was in that frigate in Jan. 1805 when she was set on fire and abandoned near the mouth of the Loire, in consequence of her having struck upon a sunken rock in the vicinity of Quiberon, and sustained so much damage as to render her preservation impossible. Joining then the HERO 74, Capt. Hon. Alan Hyde Gardner, he shared in the action fought by Sir Robt. Calder with the combined fleets of France and Spain off Cape Finisterre 22 July, 1805; after which he joined the CHIFFONNE 36, Capt. P. Campbell, DONEGAL 74, Capt. Pulteney Malcolm, and, in June, 1806, the UNITÉ 36, Capt. P. Campbell. He commanded, during his attachment to the latter ship, a boat at the destruction of five vessels under a battery near the town of Omago, in the Adriatic, 18 Oct. 1806; assisted, ten days afterwards, at the storming of a battery and the capture of several sail of merchantmen near Point Salvooy; was present at the reduction, 28 April, 1807, of the island of St. Piedro de Niembo; had charge, 12 June following, of a division of boats at the capture of several vessels in the river Po, and the annihilation of two signal posts; participated, in command of a boat, in a successful attack made upon a French privateer near Ancona, 12 Jan. 1808; contrived, in an eight-oared cutter, to take possession, 24 March in the same year, after a sharp engagement, of another privateer, carrying 2 guns and 36 men; contributed, 2 May ensuing, to the capture of the Italian brig-of-war *Il Ronco*, of 16 guns and 100 men; aided, three days later, in cutting out several vessels from under the batteries at Paran; enacted a part, on 1 June, at the simultaneous capture of the *Nettuno* and *Toulie* brigs, equal in force to *Il Ronco*; took command of the boats on 4 of the same month, and succeeded in making prize, notwithstanding a desperate and mutually destructive conflict, of three Turkish ships and several coasting-vessels under Cape Palero; was on board the UNITÉ when she beat off, 18 Dec.

1808, a flotilla of 12 gun-boats, by whom she had been attacked during a calm; conducted, 12 Jan. 1809, a virtually successful attack made on six vessels lying under the protection of two batteries in the harbour of Vieste, and secured by cables from their mast-heads to the shore; had charge of the boats, on 23 April, in an attempt to cut off some vessels full of troops from the island of Fano, near Corfu, under a heavy fire of musketry from the shore; was similarly employed at the bringing out, 30 July ensuing, of two large merchantmen from under a fort at Citta Nuova, where the boats suffered considerably; and, on the night of 31 Oct., had command of one of the boats of a squadron under Lieut. John Tailour at the capture and destruction, after a violent struggle, and a loss to the British of 15 killed and 55 wounded, of the French armed store-ship *Lamproie*, of 16 guns and 116 men, bombards *Victoire* and *Grondeur*, with a convoy of seven sail, defended by numerous strong batteries in the Bay of Rosas.* For his conduct in the latter affair, in which he was wounded, Mr. M'Dougall, on the earnest recommendation of his Captain, was nominated by Lord Collingwood to a Lieutenancy, 25 Nov. 1809, in his own flag-ship the VILLE DE PARIS 110—an act sanctioned at home by a commission dated 3 Jan. 1810. In March, 1811, having been latterly under the flag of Rear-Admiral Thos. Fras. Fremantle, he removed to the TIGRE 74, Capt. Benj. Hallowell, but he had not been long in that ship before he again, in the month of May, joined the UNITÉ, then commanded by Capt. Edwin Henry Chamberlayne. On 4 of the ensuing July we once more find him serving in the boats, and co-operating with Lieut. Joseph Wm. Crabb, at the cutting out, from under a shower of grape from a 2-gun battery near Port Hercule, on the Roman coast, of the *St. François de Paule*, a vigorously-defended brig, mounting 8 six and three-pounders. Towards the close of the next Nov., while in charge of a large detained Austrian ship, and on his way to Malta, Lieut. M'Dougall fell in with three French men-of-war, on perceiving whom he immediately, with a judgment and zeal which did him infinite credit,† put back for the purpose of communicating the intelligence to the Senior officer in the Adriatic, Capt. Murray Maxwell of the ALCESTE. The result was the capture, by the latter ship, of the *Pomone*, of 44, and, by the UNITÉ, of *La Persanne*, of 26 guns. On 16 June, 1812, Lieut. M'Dougall, who had rejoined his ship previously to the last-mentioned event, presents himself to our notice as effecting, with the boats of a frigate squadron under his orders, the capture and destruction of three vessels and several field-pieces in a small port near Cape Otranto. He invalided from the UNITÉ in Sept. 1812, and was next appointed—22 Dec. 1813, as Senior, to the LEANDER 50, Capts. Gordon Thos. Falcon and Sir Geo. Ralph Collier, under the latter of whom he came several times into action with the enemy on the coast of North America—12 Dec. 1815, to the SUPERB 74, Capt. Chas. Ekins, in which ship he received two wounds at the bombardment of Algiers 27 Aug. 1816‡—23 June, 1818, as First (after ten months of half-pay), to the TARTAR frigate, fitting for the broad pendant of Sir G. R. Collier—and, 4 Aug. following, as Flag-Lieutenant, in the SALISBURY 50, to Rear-Admiral Donald Campbell on the West India station, where his conduct in 1819, in saving, during a hurricane at the island of St. Thomas, the crew of a Danish vessel, after numerous unavailing efforts had been made from the shore, procured him the thanks of the King of Denmark, conveyed through the Lords of the Admiralty. Obtaining a second promotal commission 9 Feb. 1820, Capt. M'Dougall did not again go afloat until Aug. 1833, on 27 of which month he assumed command of the NIMROD 20. In that vessel he served in the river Douro and on the coast of Spain and Portugal during the revolutionary commotions, and ultimately accompanied the STAG frigate, with Don Miguel on board, from the neighbourhood of Lisbon to Genoa. He continued in the NIMROD* until 1835; and on 16 Aug. 1836, within a short period of his appointment to the SALAMANDER steamer, was advanced to Post-rank. Since 15 Feb. 1845, he has been in command of the VULTURE steam-frigate, of 470 horse-power, on the East India station.

Capt. M'Dougall is a Magistrate and Deputy-Lieutenant for Argyleshire. He married, 22 Aug. 1826, Elizabeth Sophia, only daughter of the late Retired Commander Chas. Sheldon Timins, R.N., of Oriel Lodge, Cheltenham, by whom he has issue six sons and three daughters. AGENTS—Collier and Snee.

MACDOUGALL. (COMMANDER, 1846.)

JOHN MACDOUGALL passed his examination in 1831; obtained his first commission 30 April, 1837; assumed command, 12 Sept. following, of the DOLPHIN 3, on the coast of Africa; and served from 18 July, 1838, until paid off in the summer of 1846, the last five years as First-Lieutenant, in the PIQUE 36, Capts. Edw. Boxer, Rich. Augustus Yates, Henry Forbes, and Hon. Montagu Stopford, on the North America and West India, Mediterranean, and again on the North America and West India stations. During the Syrian operations of 1840 he assisted at the capture of the towns of Caiffa and Tsour (at the former of which places he was severely wounded by the discharge of one of the enemy's guns at the moment he was in the act of striking it†), and was also present at the bombardment of St. Jean d'Acre. He attained the rank of Commander 28 July, 1846.

M'FARLAND. (RETIRED CAPTAIN, 1840. F-P., 28; H-P., 38.)

JAMES M'FARLAND entered the Navy, 2 Dec. 1781, as Fst.-cl. Vol., on board the UNION 98, Capt. John Dalrymple, attached to the Channel fleet; and in the following Aug. became Midshipman of the HARPY fire-ship, Capt. Sir Jas. Barclay. After a short servitude in the DILIGENTE, flag-ship at Spithead of Sir Thos. Pye, he joined, in Aug. 1783, the SALISBURY 50, bearing the flag of Admiral Campbell at Newfoundland, where he continued until Dec. 1785. He served during the remainder of the peace on the Home station in the DRUID 36, Capt. Joseph Ellison, POWERFUL and ORION 74's, both commanded by Capt. Andw. Sutherland, WINDSOR CASTLE and LONDON 98's, flag-ships of Rear-Admirals Herbert Sawyer and Sam. Cranston Goodall, and ALCIDE and HECTOR 74's, Capts. Sir Andw. Snape Douglas and Geo. Montagu. In March, 1793, Mr. M'Farland joined the QUEEN CHARLOTTE 100, bearing the flag in the Channel of Earl Howe; for his conduct as Acting-Lieutenant of which ship on the memorable 1 June, 1794, he obtained a commission dated 23 of that month. Continuing in her under the orders of Sir A. S. Douglas until July, 1797, he was in consequence present in the action fought by Lord Bridport with the French fleet off the Ile de Groix. We afterwards find him appointed in succession to the MONARCH 74, PRINCE 98, and LANCASTER 64, flag-ships at Home and at the Cape of Good Hope of Rear-Admiral Sir Roger Curtis. On 12 Sept. 1800, at which period he was Senior of the LANCASTER, he received a compound fracture of the right arm, and was officially commended for his conduct at the cutting-out, by the boats of that vessel and the ADAMANT 50, of a ship lying under the fire of two heavy batteries at Port Louis in the Isle of France. He was confirmed in the rank of Commander, after having had charge for 10 months of the PENGUIN sloop at the Cape, 18 June, 1803; and was lastly, from the following July until March, 1810, employed in the Sea Fencible service. He accepted the rank of Captain 10 Sept. 1840.

* *Vide* Gaz. 1809, p. 1908. † *V.* Gaz. 1812, p. 566. ‡ *V.* Gaz. 1816, p. 1792.

* In Jan. 1834 the boatswain and twelve of the NIMROD's crew were swamped in the barge while Capt. M'Dougall was endeavouring, with the rest of his boats, to save the Spanish frigate *Lealtad* from being lost off Santander.

† *Vide* Gaz. 1840, p. 2601.

MACFARLANE. (LIEUTENANT, 1815.)

WILLIAM MACFARLANE died 14 Feb. 1846.

This officer entered the Navy, 9 March, 1805, as A.B., on board the SALVADOR DEL MUNDO, Capt. Cooke, flag-ship at Plymouth of Admiral Young; and, between the following July and Feb. 1806, was employed in the Channel as Master's Mate of the CAPTAIN 74, Capt. Geo. Hopewell Stephens. He joined, next, the MERLIN sloop, Capts. Wm. Standway Parkinson, Buckland Stirling Bluett, and Wm. Fisher, with whom he cruized for some time on the West India and Home stations. In 1807 he returned to the West Indies in the DRAGON 74, Capt. Matthew Henry Scott; and he afterwards, from 1808 until the autumn of 1815, served on the Home, North American, and Mediterranean stations, latterly in the capacity of Master, in the IMPÉTUEUX 74, Capt. John Lawford (part of the Walcheren expeditionary force), MARLBOROUGH 74, Capt. M. H. Scott, CHATHAM of similar force, bearing the flag of the last-named officer, and ZEALOUS and POMPÉE 74's, Capts. Jas. Anderson and Sir Jas. Athol Wood. He then took up a commission dated 24 Feb. 1815. His last appointment was, 6 April, 1844, to the post, which he retained until the autumn of 1845, of Agent in a contract mail steam-vessel. AGENTS—Coplands and Burnett.

M'GLADERY. (LIEUT., 1811. F-P., 43; H-P., 10.)

JOHN M'GLADERY was born in Dec. 1776, near Dungannon, co. Tyrone.

This officer (who had been seven or eight years in the Merchant service) was impressed, 28 Nov. 1794, into the Navy, from the wreck of the ship *Wildman*, of London, and rated A.B., on board the CULLODEN 74, Capt. Thos. Troubridge; under whom, it appears, he was successively present in Hotham's action 13 July, 1795, in the battle off Cape St. Vincent 14 Feb. 1797, at the ensuing attack upon Santa Cruz, Teneriffe, in the action off the Nile 1 Aug. 1798, and at the capture of Naples, Rome, Genoa, &c. He received a splinter-wound in the right eye in Hotham's affair; experienced a similar injury in the St. Vincent achievement; and, being one of the landed party at Santa Cruz, was so severely hurt by a sabre-cut in the head as to be reported among the slain. Removing in Aug. 1800 to LA VICTORIEUSE 12, Capt. John Richards, he took part, in the capacity we believe of Quartermaster, in most of the operations connected with the campaign of 1801 in Egypt, from the landing of the troops in Aboukir Bay until the fall of Alexandria, including the reduction of Marabout Castle and a variety of boat skirmishes. In March, 1803, Mr. M'Gladery, who had previously attained the rating of Midshipman, was transferred to the FOUDROYANT 80, in which ship, bearing the flags of Admirals Sir Thos. Graves, Sir John Borlase Warren, Albemarle Bertie, and Sir Wm. Sidney Smith, he served for upwards of five years, on the Home, North American, Lisbon (whence he witnessed the flight of the Royal Family of Portugal), and Brazilian stations. He was present, 13 March, 1806, at the capture of the *Marengo* 80, bearing the flag of Admiral Linois, and 40-gun frigate *Belle Poule*. In Sept. 1808, on his arrival at the Cape of Good Hope in the SYLVIA cutter, Lieut.-Commander Augustus Vere Drury, he was nominated, having passed his examination 5 Oct. 1805, Acting-Lieutenant of the LEOPARD 50, flag-ship of the above-named Admiral Bertie. Exchanging, in May, 1810, into the OTTER sloop, Capt. Jas. Tomkinson, he witnessed, in the following Sept., the re-capture of H. M. S. AFRICAINE, and the capture of the French frigate *La Vénus* and her prize the CEYLON 32; and on rejoining Admiral Bertie, shortly afterwards, in the AFRICAINE, he co-operated in the reduction of the Isle of France and its dependencies, being on the occasion allowed to superintend the debarkation of the troops. Having unluckily mislaid his passing certificate, he was not confirmed in the rank of Lieutenant until 24 April, 1811; from which period he remained unemployed until the receipt of his present appointment in the Coast Guard 1 Nov. 1821. AGENTS—Hallett and Robinson.

M'GOWAN. (LIEUTENANT, 1827.)

THOMAS M'GOWAN entered the Navy 11 Nov. 1809; passed his examination in 1815; and obtained his commission 28 April, 1827. We are not aware that he has been since employed.

M'GREGOR. (LIEUTENANT, 1838.)

FITZJAMES STEWART M'GREGOR entered the Navy 19 Nov. 1830; and was Midshipman of the ANDROMACHE 28, Capt. Henry Ducie Chads, when that vessel, in company with the IMOGENE 28, forced the passage of the Boca Tigris, in China, 7 and 9 Sept. 1834. He obtained a commission 14 Aug. 1838; and was afterwards appointed—29 June, 1839, to the HYDRA steamer, Capt. Anthony Wm. Milward, in the Mediterranean—21 Oct. 1839, to the BELLEROPHON 80, Capt. Chas. John Austen, under whom he took part in the different operations on the coast of Syria, terminating with the bombardment of St. Jean d'Acre—17 Sept. 1841, 21 Feb. and 26 March, 1842, and 5 April, 1843, to the NORTH STAR 26, Capt. Sir Jas. Everard Home, VINDICTIVE 50, Capt. John Toup Nicolas, AGINCOURT 72, flag-ship of Sir Thos. John Cochrane, and BELLEISLE troop-ship, Capt. John Kingcome, all on the East India station—23 May, 1844, as Senior Lieutenant, to the PROMETHEUS steam-sloop, Capt. John Hay, on the coast of Africa—24 Aug. 1844, to the TORTOISE store-ship at the Ascension, Capt. Arthur Morrell—and, 2 Dec. 1844, again as Senior, to the HYDRA steam-sloop, Capt. Horatio Beauman Young, also on the African station. He has been on half-pay since the commencement of Jan. 1846. AGENTS—Messrs. Chard.

M'GRIGOR. (LIEUTENANT, 1846.)

CHARLES GRAEME M'GRIGOR passed his examination 16 July, 1840; served as Mate, on the East India, Home, and Pacific stations, in the CONWAY 26, Capt. Chas. Ramsay Drinkwater Bethune, CALEDONIA 120, flag-ship of Sir David Milne, CYCLOPS steam-frigate, Capt. Wm. Fred. Lapidge, and AMERICA 50, Capt. Hon. John Gordon; obtained his commission 4 May, 1846; was then appointed Additional-Lieutenant of the COLLINGWOOD 80, flag-ship of Sir Geo. Fras. Seymour in the Pacific; and since 30 Jan. 1847 has been employed on the coast of Africa in the MARINER sloop, Capt. Chas. Mitchell Mathison.

M'GWIRE. (RETIRED CAPTAIN, 1840. F-P., 32; H-P., 36.)

WILLIAM M'GWIRE, born 10 June, 1766, is third son of the late Arthur M'Gwire, Esq., of Dawson Street, Dublin, and Clonrea Castle, co. Waterford.

This officer entered the Navy, 14 April, 1779, as Captain's Servant, on board the EGMONT 74, Capts. John Carter Allen and Robt. Fanshawe, under whom he served as Midshipman until the close of 1781, witnessing during that period a hurricane that spread desolation over the whole of the Caribbean Islands and Jamaica, and totally dismantled the EGMONT. In 1782 he joined the PROSELYTE frigate, Capt. John Brown, attached to the force on the Home station; and he was next, between 1783 and 1786, employed on the African and American coasts, and also in the North Sea, on board the RACEHORSE sloop, Capt. Thos. Wilson. In Jan. 1792, after he had been for nearly three years on the Jamaica station in the CENTURION 50, flag-ship of Rear-Admiral Philip Affleck, he was there nominated to the command, with the rank of Acting-Lieutenant, of the ADVICE cutter. He was confirmed a Lieutenant, 18 March, 1793, in the HELENA sloop, Capt. Wm. Charlton; and on 18 of the following July he was transferred, from the VESTAL 32, Capt. John M'Dougall, in which ship he had been again serving in the North Sea, to the INVIN-

CIBLE 74, Capt. Hon. Thos. Pakenham; whom, after having participated in the actions of 29 May and 1 June, 1794, and risen to the post of First-Lieutenant, he followed in that capacity, in Sept. 1795, into the JUSTE 80. From the period of his promotion to the rank of Commander 22 May, 1797, until the peace of Amiens, Capt. M'Gwire appears to have had under his orders the whole of the gun-boats employed in protecting the coast of Ireland; where he further, from Sept. 1803 until 1810, served in the Sea-Fencible establishment between Cork Head and Youghal. In Aug. of the latter year he was appointed to the superintendence (which he retained until Sept. 1814) of the Impress service at Waterford. He accepted his present rank 10 Sept. 1840.

Capt. M'Gwire married, in Nov. 1802, Mary, eldest daughter of Sam. Hobson, Esq., Barrister-at-Law, of Waterford and co. Cork, and sister of the late Capt. Wm. Hobson R.N., by whom he has three sons and one daughter living. His eldest son died of yellow fever at Jamaica, while serving with Capt. Hobson as Midshipman in the FERRET sloop of war.

M'HARDY. (CAPTAIN, 1840. F-P., 22; H-P., 13.)

JOHN BUNCH BONNEMAISON M'HARDY was born 3 Dec. 1801.

This officer entered the Navy, 25 May, 1812, as Fst.-cl. Vol., on board the TARTARUS 32, Capt. John Pasco, in which frigate, and in the ROTA 38, also commanded by Capt. Pasco, he served as Midshipman on the American, Irish, North Sea, and Lisbon stations until paid off in Aug. 1815. Proceeding next to the West Indies in a merchant-vessel at his own expense, he there, in Nov. 1816, succeeded in obtaining a vacancy in the BERMUDA 10, Capt. John Pakenham, under whom however he was almost immediately wrecked near Tampico Bar. He then successively joined the ESK 20, Capt. Geo. Gustavus Lennock, and LANDRAIL and KANGAROO surveying-vessels, Master-Commander Anthony De Mayne, all too on the West India station, where he remained until the early part of 1821, at which period he returned home for the purpose of passing his examination. As soon as that ordeal had been gone through he was ordered a passage back in the PYRAMUS 42, Capt. Fras. Newcombe, and on his arrival was received, first on board the NAUTILUS 18, Capt. Isham Fleming Chapman, and next on board the SYBILLE 46, flag-ship of Sir Chas. Rowley. On 23 Feb. 1823 we find him nominated Second in command, with the rating of Master's Mate, of the LION schooner, of 1 gun, Lieut.-Commander Wm. Hobson, in order to assist in the suppression of piracy on the coast of Cuba, where, it appears, he participated in the capture of three schooners, and came into contact with a very superior force on shore. Towards the close of the same year, after having been for a time attached to the GLOUCESTER 74, Commodore Sir Edw. W. C. R. Owen, and been allowed to reside for the benefit of his health in America, he joined the ICARUS 10, Capt. John Geo. Graham. As a reward for his services both in that sloop and in her boats, particularly in an affair off the Isle of Pines, Mr. M'Hardy, in Feb. 1824, was ordered by his Captain to act in the room of Lieut. Laton, who, with 4 seamen, had been recently murdered by the pirates. He continued to officiate as Acting-Lieutenant of the ICARUS until 19 Aug. 1824; and he was then, as an acknowledgment for his exertions on the above occasion, as well as at the subsequent capture of two schooners, two feluccas, and four row-boats, confirmed by the Admiralty. Previously however to the receipt of his commission he took command of the boats, carrying 34 men, under Lieut. Chas. Croker, and contributed, on 20 of the month last mentioned, to the capture, off the Havana, of, among other vessels, the notorious piratical schooner *Diableto*, mounting 6 guns, with a complement of 55 men—an exploit for which, as we should have recorded in our memoir of the now Commander Croker, those who achieved it received the official approbation of the Board. Being placed on half-pay in consequence of his promotion, Lieut. M'Hardy, although the Commodore had recommended his being further employed in the West Indies, did not succeed in obtaining an appointment until Oct. 1827, on 18 of which month he received instructions to proceed, in the VICTOR 18, Capt. Geo. Lloyd, to Jamaica, there to join the BARHAM 50, flag-ship of Hon. Chas. Elphinstone Fleeming, who, on 1 Jan. 1828, invested him with the command of the PICKLE schooner, of 3 guns, 30 men, and 6 boys. In that vessel it was his fortune to effect the capture, 6 June, 1829, after a severe action of an hour and 20 minutes, fought within pistol-shot, of the famous slaver *Bolodera* of 235 tons, pierced for 16 guns, mounting 2 long 18-pounders and 2 long 12's, and manned, exclusive of armed negroes, with a crew of 60 men, 10 of whom were killed and 14 wounded—the loss of the PICKLE being confined to 1 person killed, and 10, three of them mortally, wounded. For this very gallant performance Lieut. M'Hardy deservedly received, a second time, the official acknowledgments of the Admiralty. On the PICKLE being paid off at Plymouth in Oct. 1830, the state of discipline and efficiency in which she was found so attracted the attention of the Commander-in-Chief Sir Manley Dixon, that he was induced to bring his name in a most favourable manner under the notice of their Lordships; and on 20 of the following Dec. he was specially rewarded "for his meritorious services" with the rank of Commander. On 8 March, 1831, Capt. M'Hardy was appointed Inspecting-Commander, for three years, of the Burnham (Norfolk) district of Coast Guard; on leaving which service in 1834, the Lieutenants who had been employed under his superintendence gave him a farewell dinner "in testimony of their esteem for so active and enterprising an officer." He was re-appointed, 19 March, 1835, to the Cromer district, also on the coast of Norfolk, whence he was removed, 1 July, 1836, to the Deal district. Owing to the increase of smuggling in the Isle of Wight, Capt. M'Hardy, in the ensuing Oct., was transferred to the district at Ryde; to which, on the expiration of his term of command, he was again appointed 22 March, 1838. He was selected, 1 Jan. 1840, to become the recipient of the Captain's commission annually granted for good service in the Coast Guard; and has since been on half-pay.

Capt. M'Hardy, who is Senior of 1840, was elected Chief Constable for co. Essex 11 Feb. in that year. He married, 11 Dec. 1830, Horatia Victoria Elizabeth Aitchison, daughter of the present Rear-Admiral Pasco, the officer under whose orders he first went to sea. By that lady he has issue four sons and three daughters. AGENTS—Messrs. Stilwell.

M'ILWAINE. (COMMANDER, 1838.)

WILLIAM M'ILWAINE entered the Navy 4 Jan. 1811, and, being made Lieutenant, 20 Aug. 1824, into the LIFFEY 50, Capts. Chas. Grant and Thos. Coe, was employed in that ship during the Burmese war. His succeeding appointments were—11 May, 1827, to the WELLESLEY 74, stationed off Lisbon—6 July, 1832, to the Coast Guard—17 May, 1833, to the CALEDONIA 120, flag-ship of Sir Josias Rowley in the Mediterranean—and 1 Nov. 1834 and 6 Dec. 1836, to the command of the PORTSMOUTH yacht and VOLCANO steamer, in which vessels he continuously served (in the former as Flag-Lieutenant to the Admiral Superintendent at Portsmouth, Sir F. L. Maitland, and in the latter on the Mediterranean station) until advanced to his present rank 28 June, 1838. He was employed as an Inspecting Commander in the Coast Guard from 4 July, 1839, until July, 1844; and since 13 Feb. 1845 has again been in that service.

Commander M'Ilwaine married, 14 April, 1842, Cecilia, youngest daughter of the late Chas. Lambert, Esq., of Fitzroy Square.

MACKAY. (Rear-Admiral of the Red, 1838. f-p., 20; h-p., 35.)

The Honourable Donald Hugh Mackay, born 31 Dec. 1780, is second surviving son of Hon. Geo. Mackay, of Skibo, M.P., in 1754, for co. Sutherland, and afterwards Master of the Mint of Scotland, by Anne, third daughter of Eric Sutherland, only son of the attainted Lord Duffus, who was at first a Captain in the British, and then a Flag-officer in the Russian Navy. He is nephew of Lieut.-General Hon. Alex. Mackay, appointed in 1780 Commander-in-chief of the Forces in Scotland; and brother of the present Lord Reay.

This officer entered the Royal Naval Academy in Jan. 1792; and embarked, in Oct. 1794, as Midshipman, on board the Dædalus 32, Capt. Thos. Williams; on accompanying whom into the Unicorn of 38 guns, he assisted at the capture of the Dutch brig of war *Comet* of 18 guns, as also, we are informed, after a severe action, of the French frigate *La Tribune* of 44 guns and 339 men, 37 of whom were killed and 15 wounded, with impunity to the British. After an active servitude of more than 18 months with Sir Rich. Strachan, in the Melampus and Diamond frigates, on the Home station, he was made Lieutenant, 27 March, 1798, into the Ariadne 20, Capt. Jas. Bradley, in which ship, it appears, he accompanied an expedition under Sir Home Popham having for its object the destruction of the locks and sluice-gates of the Bruges Canal. He removed, towards the close of the same year, to the Melpomène 38, Capt. Sir Chas. Hamilton; and on next, in 1799, joining the Isis 50, flag-ship of the late Sir Andw. Mitchell, he witnessed the fall of the Helder fortress and the surrender of the Texel squadron, and commanded a tender at the capture of four Dutch gun-vessels forming part of the flotilla collected for the protection of Amsterdam. Prior to his advancement to the rank of Commander, 29 April, 1802, Mr. Mackay further served with the Channel fleet, in the Formidable 98, Capt. Edw. Thornbrough, and, again with Sir A. Mitchell, in the Windsor Castle of similar force. His ensuing appointments were, 20 April and 26 Sept. 1804, to the command of the Prince William armed ship (employed in the escort of North Sea convoys) and Scout sloop, on the Mediterranean station. He attained Post-rank 22 Jan. 1806, and was afterwards invested with the Captaincy—20 June, 1807, of the Druid frigate, on the coast of Ireland—9 Aug. 1808, for three months, of the Inflexible 64, fitting for Halifax—20 Sept. 1811, 13 Sept. 1812, and 4 Jan. 1815, of the Volage 26, Malacca 42, and Minden 74, all on the East India station, whence he returned about April, 1816—and, 7 Nov. 1831, of the Revenge 78, which ship, after having been intermediately attached to the force off Lisbon, was put out of commission in the early part of 1834. During his command of the Volage, Capt. Mackay conveyed Sir Evan Nepean, Bart., to his government at Bombay, and was actively employed, under the orders of Sir Sam. Hood, in the Eastern Archipelago and China Seas, where his duties were of a very arduous character. In the Malacca he cooperated with a squadron under Capt. Geo. Sayer in a serious attack made in June, 1813, upon the piratical settlement of Sambas, in the island of Borneo. He attained Flag-rank 28 June, 1838. Agent—John P. Muspratt.

MACKELLAR. (Lieut., 1816. f-p., 11; h-p., 28.)

Duncan Mackellar entered the Navy, 1 June, 1808, as Fst.-cl. Vol., on board the Porpoise store-ship at New South Wales, Capts. Wm. Geo. Carlile Kent and John Porteous. On his return to England, at the close of 1810, he became Midshipman, a rating he had previously attained, of the Guadeloupe of 16 guns and 102 men, Capts. Joseph Swabey Tetley and Geo. Rose Sartorius, fitting for the Mediterranean; where he took part, 27 June, 1811, in a close and spirited action of an hour and 35 minutes, fought by that vessel, off the town of Vendré, with the French corvette *Tactique* of 18 guns and at least 150 men, and armed xebec *Guêpe* of 8 guns and 65 or 70 men; both of whom were in the end beaten off with great slaughter to themselves, and with a loss to the British (who for some time had been simultaneously opposed by the fire of two heavy batteries) of 1 man killed and 12 or 13 wounded. In Dec. 1811 Mr. Mackellar rejoined Capt. Tetley on board the Perlen 38, in which frigate, on Capt. John Allen succeeding to the command, he returned to England, in April, 1812. Becoming attached, then, to the Magnificent 74, Capt. Willoughby Thos. Lake, he was at first employed in active co-operation with the patriots on the north coast of Spain, and next on the West India station, where he removed, in Aug. 1815, to the Salisbury 50, Capt. John Mackellar, and obtained, 10 May, 1816, a Lieutenancy in the Variable 8, Capt. John Sykes. He came home in the following Aug., and has since been on half-pay. Agents—Case and Loudonsack.

MACKELLAR. (Admiral of the Blue, 1847. f-p., 25; h-p., 41.)

John Mackellar, born about 1768, at Minorca, is eldest son (by Miss Elizabeth Basaline, of that island) of the late General Patrick Mackellar, a Colonel of the Royal Engineers, who served as Chief Engineer under General Wolfe at Quebec, assisted, in a similar capacity, at the reduction of Martinique, Guadeloupe, and the Havana, and closed a most honourable and valuable life as Chief Engineer, at Minorca, in 1779. The Admiral's only brother, Neil, also attained high rank in the Army.

This officer entered the Navy, 6 Jan. 1781, as A.B., on board the Romney 50, Capt. Roddam Home, bearing the broad pendant of Commodore Johnstone; and in the course of the same year was wounded in the leg during an action with a French squadron under M. de Suffrein, in Porto Praya Bay. Removing, in April, 1782, to the Enterprize 28, Capts. John Willet Payne and Hon. Wm. Carnegie, he assisted, as Midshipman of that vessel, at the capture or destruction, in the West Indies, of two valuable Spanish polacres, a privateer of 16 guns and 70 men, six other armed vessels, the *Comte de Grasse* of 20 guns and 120 men, and the *Mohawk* of 22 guns and 125 men. He was on one occasion sent up a river in charge of one of several boats, which effected the annihilation, after a party of native militia had been defeated, of the store-houses belonging to two plantations; and on another, he took command of one of two boats, and aided in destroying a privateer of 16 guns, notwithstanding the resistance offered by her crew, supported by some military, and the presence of several French men-of-war lying in Boston harbour. Subsequently to the general peace we find the Enterprize taking formal possession of Montserrat, Nevis, St. Kitt's, and Dominica, in consequence of those islands having been restored to Great Britain by the treaty of Versailles. Between Sept. 1784 and the date of his promotion to the rank of Lieutenant 22 Nov. 1790, Mr. Mackellar was employed, on the Home and Newfoundland stations, in the Edgar 74, Capt. Adam Duncan, Hebe and Phœnix frigates, Capts. Edw. Thornbrough and John Willet Payne, Alcide 74, Capt. Benj. Caldwell, and Barfleur 98, Salisbury 50, and Victory 100, flag-ships, the first and last of Lord Hood, and the second of Vice-Admiral Milbanke. His next appointments were—22 April, 1791, to the Circe, Capt. Geo. Oakes, under whom he cruized, in the Channel and off Cork, until the following Oct.—19 June, 1793, to the Assistance 50, Capts. Sir Rich. Bickerton and Henry Mowat, in which ship, after having visited the Cape of Good Hope, he contributed to the capture, 28 Aug. 1796, of the French 36-gun frigate *Elisabeth*, off Cape Henry—and, 28 Jan. 1797, to the acting-command of the Rover sloop. Being superseded in the latter vessel in the ensuing May, he returned home a passenger in the St. Albans 64, but had the satisfaction on his arrival of being confirmed by a commission dated 5 July in the same year. In Feb.

1798 Capt. Mackellar obtained an appointment to the MINERVA frigate, *armée en flûte*, part of the force sent three months afterwards, under Sir Home Popham, to destroy the locks and sluice-gates of the Bruges Canal. In the execution of that service he distinguished himself in a very remarkable manner, and obtained the particular commendation of the military Commander-in-Chief, Major-General Coote; with whom, and the troops under his orders, he had the misfortune to be taken prisoner, owing solely to the circumstance of his having voluntarily remained on shore for the purpose of assuming command of a detachment of seamen who had unavoidably been left without an officer of sufficient rank to direct them, at a moment when the presence of one was absolutely necessary. Regaining his liberty in the course of the next Dec., Capt. Mackellar was rewarded for his conduct—after having held command for 14 weeks of the WOLVERENE sloop and CHARON 44, on the Home and Mediterranean stations—by advancement to Post-rank 27 April, 1799. He continued some months in the ship last mentioned, performing during that period various particular services, and assisting at the evacuation of the Helder; and he was next, in Sept. 1800 and March, 1801, appointed to the JAMAICA 26 and TERPSICHORE 32. In the former of those vessels he escorted a fleet of merchantmen to and from the Baltic, made one or two captures, and compelled a large privateer, commanded by the famous Blackeman, to lighten herself of her guns, &c., in order to effect her escape. On his removal to the TERPSICHORE, Capt. Mackellar was at first employed at the blockade of Boulogne and Calais, and then in the East Indies. While on that station in Dec. 1801, he volunteered, at a period when the TERPSICHORE was in a dismantled state, to take charge of an expedition, consisting of the MARQUIS CORNWALLIS of 48 guns, and several of the Hon. Company's vessels, for the purpose of conveying a reinforcement of 1000 troops to the Portuguese settlements of Demaun and Diu. The able and successful manner in which he accomplished the objects of the mission elicited the high approbation and thanks of the Bombay Government. His exertions in subsequently conveying a body of 3000 men from Goa to the relief of the Governor of that Presidency, Hon. Jonathan Duncan, when surrounded by his enemies at Surat, again procured him similar acknowledgments. He returned to England in 1802, having been latterly employed at the blockade of Goa, and was afterwards appointed—in May, 1804, to the agency for prisoners of war and transports, and the Governorship of the Naval Hospital at Halifax, Nova Scotia, where he remained about six years—2 Aug. 1815, to the ROMNEY 50, lying at Chatham—11 Dec. following, to the SALISBURY 58, bearing the flag at Jamaica of Rear-Admiral John Erskine Douglas—and, 14 March, 1817, to the PIQUE 36, on the same station, whence he returned home (encountering on his passage an almost fatal hurricane) and was paid off in Dec. 1818. Previously to his departure, Capt. Mackellar received an address signed by the Mayor and the heads of 49 commercial houses, expressive of the sense they entertained of the solicitude he had always evinced for the welfare of the trade of the island. He became a Rear-Admiral 27 May, 1825; a Vice-Admiral 10 Jan. 1837; and a full Admiral.

He is married, and has issue.

MACKENZIE. (LIEUTENANT, 1811. F-P., 10; H-P., 33.)

ALEXANDER MACKENZIE was born 30 June, 1790.

This officer entered the Navy, in May, 1804, as Fst.-cl. Vol., on board the REVENGE 74, Capt. Robt. Moorsom, stationed in the Channel; and on becoming Midshipman of the NEPTUNE 98, Capt. Thos. Fras. Fremantle, took part, 21 Oct. 1805, in the battle of Trafalgar. In Nov. 1806 he removed to the PHŒBE 36, Capt. Jas. Oswald, in the boats of which frigate, it appears, he was frequently employed in destroying the enemy's trade and signal-posts along the French shores, and also saw much service on the coast of Portugal. At the expiration of two years he next, in Nov. 1808, joined the LAVINIA 40, Capt. Lord Wm. Stewart, under whom, during the expedition of 1809 to the Walcheren, he assisted in forcing the passage between the batteries of Flushing and Cadsand, and participated in all the boat operations on the East and West Scheldt. After an attachment of 14 months to the THAMES 32, Capt. Hon. Wm. Waldegrave, and CUMBERLAND 74, Capt. Hon. Philip Wodehouse, on the Mediterranean station, where in the boats of the last-mentioned ship he served for two months in the Faro of Messina, and contributed to the capture and destruction of a large convoy in face of a body of troops in the Bay of St. Eufemia, Mr. Mackenzie was nominated, in Jan. 1811, Acting-Lieutenant of the WARRIOR 74, Capt. John Wm. Spranger, and was for some time employed with the flotilla at the defence of Cadiz. He was officially promoted 27 April following, and was subsequently appointed—24 Aug. and 25 Sept. in the same year, to the DISPATCH 18 and COLOSSUS 74, Capts. Aberdour and Thos. Alexander, both on the Home station—and 4 March, 1814, as Senior, after an interval of six months, to the CYANE of 32 guns and 171 men, Capt. Gordon Thos. Falcon. On 20 Feb. 1815 it was his fate to be on board the latter vessel when taken, together with her consort, the LEVANT of 20 guns and 131 men, by the U. S. frigate *Constitution* of 54 guns and 469 men, at the end of a fierce conflict in which the CYANE, besides being cut to pieces, sustained a loss of 6 men killed and 13, including himself severely, wounded. We may add, that the captives, after having been plundered of all they possessed, were put on shore at Maranham, on the coast of Brazil, and there left to find their way home as best they could. Lieut. Mackenzie has since been on half-pay.

He married a daughter of J. Worth, Esq., of Worth House, co. Devon, and has issue two children.

M'KENZIE. (LIEUT., 1799. F-P., 22; H-P., 32.)

CHARLES M'KENZIE was born 1 Aug. 1773.

This officer entered the Navy, 23 Aug. 1793, as A.B., on board the QUEBEC 32, Capt. Josias Rogers, and, after visiting the coast of Holland, accompanied the expedition under Vice-Admiral Sir John Jervis and General Sir Chas. Grey against the French West India islands, where he was wounded in the left shoulder during the landing at Fort Royal, Martinique. On his removal as Midshipman, in April, 1794, to the VESUVIUS bomb, Capt. Thos. Rogers, he co-operated in the reduction of Ste. Lucie and Guadeloupe, and then returned with convoy to England. He was next, for a period of nearly two years, employed in the Channel, off the coast of Africa, and again in the West Indies, on board L'ESPIÈGLE 16, Capt. Benj. Roberts, and SHEERNESS 44, Capt. Simon M'Kenzie; after which we find him, from Sept. 1796 until advanced to his present rank 9 Dec. 1799, commanding, with the rating of Master's Mate, the SUCCESS gun-brig, on the Plymouth station. He joined, on the occasion of his promotion, the CAMBRIDGE 80, bearing the flag in the Mediterranean of Sir Thos. Pasley; and was subsequently appointed—15 Sept. 1800, to the PIQUE 36, Capts. Jas. Young and Wm. Cumberland, under the former of whom he assisted at the landing of the troops in Egypt in 1801—29 Oct. 1803, nine months after he had left the PIQUE, to the MALTA 80, Capts. Edw. Buller, Wm. Shield, and Robt. Waller Otway, to which ship (with the exception of a short time passed in 1807 with Capt. Shield, as First-Lieutenant, in the QUEEN 98) he continued attached until Nov. 1808, participating during that period, and receiving a wound, in Sir Robt. Calder's action—on 16 of the month last-mentioned, as Senior, to the IMPLACABLE 74, Capts. Geo. Chas. M'Kenzie and Thos. Byam Martin, part of the force employed in embarking the army after the battle of Corunna—for a few months in 1814 (he had not been afloat since Dec. 1809), to the SPARROW 16 and MINSTREL 26, both commanded by Capt. Fras. Erskine Loch in the Mediterranean, and, 21 Oct. in the same year, to the charge of the SAN JUAN guard-ship at Gibraltar, where he remained until 6 Nov. 1816. Lieut. M'Kenzie was admitted into Greenwich Hospital 19 Dec. 1844.

He married 22 June, 1826, and has issue two sons and four daughters. AGENT—Joseph Woodhead.

M'KENZIE. (LIEUTENANT, 1841.)

DONALD M'LEOD M'KENZIE entered the Navy (from the Royal Naval College) 25 June, 1830; passed his examination 24 Oct. 1834; and at the period of his promotion to the rank of Lieutenant, 23 Nov. 1841, was serving on the coast of Africa as Mate of the IRIS 26, Capt. Wm. Tucker. His appointments have since been—18 Oct. 1842, to the EXCELLENT gunnery-ship at Portsmouth, Capt. Sir Thos. Hastings—and, 3 May, 1843, to the CASTOR 36, Capt. Chas. Graham, now in the East Indies.

MACKENZIE. (COMMANDER, 1847. F-P., 15; H-P., 9.)

JAMES GEORGE MACKENZIE entered the Navy 23 Dec. 1823; served as Midshipman of the PHILOMEL 10, Capt. Lord Viscount Ingestrie, at the battle of Navarin 20 Oct. 1827; and was promoted, soon after passing his examination, to the rank of Lieutenant, 15 May, 1830. His succeeding appointments were—19 July, 1833, to the CALEDONIA 120, Capt. Thos. Brown, on the Mediterranean station—5 Feb. 1834, to the command (as Flag-Lieutenant to Sir Thos. Briggs, Admiral-Superintendent of Malta) of the CEYLON receiving-ship, in which he remained until the summer of 1837—and, 31 Oct. 1840, to the INDUS 78, Capt. Sir Jas. Stirling, fitting for the Mediterranean, whence, after having officiated for two years and a half as First-Lieutenant, he came home and was paid off in 1844. He attained his present rank 29 April, 1847; and has been employed, since 12 of the following May, as Second-Captain of the CALEDONIA 120, Capt. Manley Hall Dixon, at Devonport.

Commander Mackenzie married, 24 Sept. 1831, Martha Catherine, third daughter of the late John Kearney, Esq., of co. Kilkenny, Ireland, and sister-in-law of Lieut. Wm. Breedon, R.N., by whom he has issue. AGENTS—Messrs. Stilwell.

MACKENZIE. (LIEUTENANT, 1846.)

JOHN FRANCIS CAMPBELL MACKENZIE passed his examination 30 Aug. 1841; was employed for a few months in 1843 on particular service in the THUNDERER 84, Capt. Daniel Pring; then became attached for a period of two years to the EXCELLENT gunnery-ship at Portsmouth, Capts. Sir Thos. Hastings and Henry Ducie Chads; and after having further served for a short time in the QUEEN 110, bearing the flag of Sir John West at Devonport, was awarded a commission dated 26 June, 1846. He has been borne as Additional-Lieutenant, since 9 April, 1847, on the books of the VINDICTIVE 50, flag-ship in North America and the West Indies of Sir Fras. Wm. Austen.

MACKENZIE. (LIEUTENANT, 1810. F-P., 20; H-P., 27.)

THOMAS HENRY MACKENZIE, born 1 Nov. 1782, is son of His Excellency Sir Thos. Henry Mackenzie, Kt., Rear-Admiral, and Commander-in-Chief of all her Imperial Majesty Catherine the Second's forces by land and sea in the Crimea.

This officer entered the Navy, 13 Nov. 1800, as Midshipman, on board the CAMEL store-ship, Capt. Matthew Buckle, on the Jamaica station, where he continued to serve as Midshipman of the JUNO frigate, Capts. Dundas and Manby, until ordered home at the peace of Amiens. In Oct. 1803 he re-embarked on board the DIAMOND 38, Capt. Thos. Elphinstone, attached to the force in the Channel; and he was next, from Feb. 1804, until May, 1809, employed, both on the Home and Jamaica stations, in the BACCHANTE 20, Capts. Chas. Dashwood, Macdonald, Jas. Ward, Jas Rich. Dacres, Bell, and Sam. Hood Inglefield. During that period, besides contributing to the capture of a variety of the enemy's armed and other vessels, including the *Dauphin* of 3, and the *Griffon* of 16 guns, he assisted in gallantly storming the forts of Rio de la Hacha and Samana (*see* Capt. Dacres), on the north side of the island of St. Domingo. In the execution of the latter service Mr. Mackenzie was unfortunately very severely wounded in the face, and suffered a fracture of the jaw; in consequence whereof he was presented with a gratuity from the Patriotic Fund. On leaving the BACCHANTE, as above, he joined the REPULSE 74, Capts. Hon. Arthur Kaye Legge and John Halliday; on board which ship we find him present 30 Aug. 1810 when she intrepidly rescued the PHILOMEL sloop of war from capture by interposing herself between that vessel and an advanced division of the Toulon fleet, whom she compelled to put back. He was promoted (after having taken part in several cutting-out affairs) to a Lieutenancy, 18 Aug. 1810, in the BOMBAY 74, Capts. Wm. Cuming and Norborne Thompson; and was subsequently appointed—in the course of 1812, to the CROCUS brig, Capt. Arden Adderley, BOMBAY again, and THUNDER bomb, Capt. Watkin Owen Pell, all on the Mediterranean station—23 Dec. 1813, to the REYNARD 10, Capt. David Latimer St. Clair, under whom he served on the north coast of Spain, and in all the operations of 1814 up the river Gironde, where he witnessed the destruction of a French line-of-battle ship, three brigs of war, several smaller vessels, and of the forts and batteries on the north side of the river—26 June, 1815, as Senior, to the BUCEPHALUS 32, Capt. Amos Freeman Westropp, in which ship he served off St. Helena and at the Cape of Good Hope until Aug. 1816—and, lastly, 8 March, 1827, to the command, for five years, of the Semaphore station at Pewley Hill, Guildford.

He married 29 June, 1814, and has issue a son and daughter. AGENT—J. Hinxman.

M'KERLIE. (REAR-ADMIRAL, 1846. F-P., 20; H-P., 33.)

JOHN M'KERLIE, born 7 June, 1774, is descended from a Scottish warrior, who resided at Cruggleton Castle, co. Wigton, and was thence expelled by the English for his faithful adherence to the renowned Sir Wm. Wallace, who in consequence undertook an expedition for the purpose of reinstating him.

This officer entered the Navy, 23 April, 1794, as A.B., on board the ARETHUSA 38, Capt. Sir Edw. Pellew; under whom, when in company with other ships, he successively witnessed the capture of *Le Babet* of 22 guns and 178 men, *L'Engageante* of 38 guns and 300 men, and *La Révolutionnaire* of 44 guns and 351 men. On his removal with the same officer to the INDEFATIGABLE of 46 guns, he further assisted, as Midshipman, at the taking of *L'Unité* of 38 guns and 265 men, and *La Virginie* of 44 guns and 340 men; besides contributing, in company with the AMAZON 36, to the destruction, with a loss to the INDEFATIGABLE of 19 men wounded, of *Les Droits de l'Homme* 74. On the latter occasion Mr. M'Kerlie lost his right arm, and received a wound in the thigh. Following Sir Edw. Pellew, next, into the IMPÉTUEUX 74, he accompanied in 1800 an expedition sent to co-operate with the Royalists in Quiberon Bay; and, on the occasion of a successful attack made, 6 June in that year, upon the enemy's shipping in the Morbihan River, he aided in the boats, under Lieut. John Pilfold, in boarding and blowing up *L'Insolente*, an 18-gun corvette. We may add that in services of a similar nature he was always a volunteer. Three weeks after the latter event he was nominated Acting-Lieutenant of the THAMES 32, Capt. Wm. Lukin. He was confirmed, 18 Aug. in the same year, in the MEGÆRA fire-ship, Capts. Henry Hill and John Newhouse, with the former of whom, during the peace of Amiens, he served at Newfoundland in the CAMILLA 24. Being appointed First-Lieutenant, 13 March, 1804, of the Spartiate 74, Capt. Sir Fras. Laforey, Mr. M'Kerlie in the year following went with Lord Nelson to the West Indies in pursuit of the combined fleets of France and Spain, and on his return shared in the battle of Trafalgar. Although advanced in consequence to the rank of Commander, 24 Dec. 1805, he did not succeed in procuring another appointment until 1808, in June and Aug. of which year we find him assuming successive command of the Diligence 12, fitting for service in the straits of Gibraltar, and Calliope of 10 guns (8 18-pounder carronades and 2 long sixes) and 75 men, destined for the North Sea station. In that vessel Capt. M'Kerlie accompanied the expedition to the Scheldt, where, after the fall of Flushing, he was invested with the charge of a division of gun-brigs, and gave so much satisfaction that Sir Rich. Strachan gave him the north coast of Holland and the neighbourhood of Heligoland for a cruizing-ground. On 25 Oct. 1810 he contrived, at the end of a running fight of an hour and a half, fought with much spirit, and attended with a loss to the British of 3 persons wounded, to make prize of a large privateer, the *Comtesse d'Hambourg* schooner of 14 guns (8 12-pounders and 6 8-pounders) and 51 men. In March, 1813, after having driven another privateer of 16 guns into the Vlie passage, Capt. M'Kerlie was appointed to the command of the naval force stationed at Heligoland; and in the ensuing April he was directed to employ the sloops, gun-brigs, and other vessels at his disposal as much in co-operation as possible with the Allies in the rivers Ems, Elbe, Weser, and Jade. In the month of May he was the senior officer off Cuxhaven when that place was re-occupied by the French. He continued to command the Heligoland squadron until Oct. 1813, when he was superseded by Capt. Arthur Farquhar, who, it appears, directed him soon afterwards to proceed, with a gun-boat and a strong division of row-boats, up the Weser as far as Braak, for the purpose of there seizing two 20-gun corvettes building, as well as all other vessels, naval stores, &c., which could be found, belonging to the enemy.* These orders he fully executed; and when the corvettes were ready for sea he was sent with them to England; on his arrival where, at the close of Dec. 1813, he had the satisfaction of learning that he had been promoted to Post-rank on 4 of that month. Capt. M'Kerlie's last appointments were, 14 Feb. and 27 Aug. 1834, to the President 52 and Vernon 50. In the former of those ships he conveyed Sir Colin Campbell, K.C.B., Governor-General of Nova Scotia, to Halifax; and in the latter, an experimental ship, he served for two years and a half in the Mediterranean, outsailing and beating during that period every vessel that competed with him. He accepted his present rank 1 Oct. 1846.

In 1806 Rear-Admiral M'Kerlie (who is a Magistrate for Wigtonshire, and is in the receipt of a pension of 300*l.* for the loss of his arm) was instructed by the Admiralty to assist Mr. T. Telford, a Civil Engineer, in making a survey of the line of communication between the north of England and the north of Ireland, and also in surveying the harbours on each side of the Channel. He married Harriet, second daughter of Patrick Stewart, Esq., of Cairnsmore and Burness, by whom he has issue one daughter. Agents—Messrs. Halford and Co.

M'KILLOP. (Lieut, 1812. f-p., 9; h-p., 34.)

John M'Killop, born in March, 1788, at Glenarm, co. Antrim, is son of the late David M'Killop, Esq., 50 years a Lieutenant in the R.N., and brother of the late Rich. M'Killop, who held the same rank for a period of 18 years.

This officer entered the Navy, 10 Oct. 1804, as Fst.-cl. Vol., on board the Loire 46, Capt. Fred. Lewis Maitland, with whom he continued almost uninterruptedly to serve, in the same ship, and in the Volontaire 38 and Emerald 36, until Sept. 1810. He was under the fire, during that period, of the batteries in Muros Bay, when they were gallantly stormed and carried, and the privateers *Confiance* and *Bélier* taken, by the boats under the late Sir Jas. Lucas Yeo, 4 June, 1805; assisted, on 25 of the same month, in capturing *Le Vaillant* of 30 guns; was in company, 24 Dec. following, with L'Egyptienne frigate, at the capture, after an obstinate resistance, of *La Libre* of 40 guns; conveyed, in July, 1806, to Sir Rich. Keats, off L'Orient, intelligence which led to the capture of *Le Rhin* of 44 guns; contributed further, in the course of 1807, to the capture of many other vessels and the blockade of Rochefort; witnessed, on the night of 13 March, 1808, the destruction, in Vivero harbour, in face of a desperate opposition, of a large French schooner, *L'Apropos*, of 8 guns and 70 men; and was present, as Midshipman, in April, 1809, at the destruction of the French shipping in Basque Roads. Becoming Master's Mate, in Sept. 1810, of the Astræa of 42 guns and 271 men, Capt. Chas. Marsh Schomberg, Mr. M'Killop proceeded to the Cape of Good Hope; and on 20 May, 1811, when in company, off Madagascar, with the Phœbe and Galatea frigates, similar in force to the Astræa, and 18-gun brig Racehorse, he assisted—after a long and warmly-contested action with the French 40-gun frigates *Renommée*, *Clorinde*, and *Néréide*, and a loss to the Astræa of 2 killed and 16 wounded—at the capture of the *Renommée*, and, on 25 of the same month, of the *Néréide* and the settlement of Tamatave. As a reward for his conduct on the occasion he was nominated, 30 June following, Acting-Lieutenant of the Astræa. He was confirmed to her 8 May, 1812, but went on half-pay on her return, under Capt. John Eveleigh, to England in Sept. 1813, and has not been since afloat.

He married Anne, eldest daughter of the late Thos. Dickey, Esq., of Ballymena, co. Antrim, by whom he has issue five children.

MACKINNON. (Lieutenant, 1842.)

Lauchlan Bellingham Mackinnon, born 21 April, 1815, is second son of Wm. Alex. Mackinnon, Esq., a Magistrate and Deputy-Lieutenant for cos. Middlesex, Hants, and Essex, M.P. for Lymington, and Chief of the Clan Mackinnon in the Western Highlands of Scotland, by Emma, daughter and sole heiress of Joseph Palmer, Esq., of Rush House, co. Dublin, and Palmerstown, co. Mayo. He is nephew of Col. Dan. Mackinnon, of the Coldstream Guards, and grand-nephew of Major-General Henry Mackinnon, of the same corps, who fell at Ciudad Rodrigo 19 Feb. 1812, and to whom a tablet has been erected by the country in St. Paul's Cathedral.

This officer entered the Navy, 1 Oct., 1829, on board the Prince Regent 120, lying at Chatham, and was afterwards employed, as Midshipman and Mate, in the Columbine 18, Belvidera 42, Arrow 6, and Vanguard 80, on the West India, North and South American, and Mediterranean stations. When in the Belvidera in the West Indies, under Capt. Chas. Borough Strong, he was lent in 1834 for a period of 12 months to H.M. steam-vessel Flamer, and was the only person on board during that time who was not attacked by the yellow fever. In Nov. 1835, having made himself thoroughly acquainted with the theory of the steam-engine, he volunteered and took charge, in the capacity of engineer, of the Meteor steamer, which he conducted from the island of St. Thomas to English Harbour, Antigua, and thence to Carlisle Bay, Barbadoes—again escaping the ravages of the yellow fever, although most fatal in its effects to the officers and crew. Having passed his examination in Feb. 1836, he was promoted, 10 Feb. 1842, to the rank of Lieutenant. His appointments have since been—17 March, 1842, for a few months, to the St. Vincent 120, flag-ship of Sir Edw. Codrington at Portsmouth—22 Aug. 1844, as Additional-Lieutenant, to the Formidable 84, bearing the flag of Sir Edw. W. C. R. Owen in the Mediterranean—17 Dec. 1844, to the Superb 80, Capt. Armar Lowry Corry, fitting at Devonport—12 Nov. 1845, to the Alecto steam-sloop, Capt.

* *Vide* Gaz. 1813, p. 2302.

Fras. Wm. Austen, stationed on the south-east coast of America—and, 1 Feb. 1847, to the MASTIFF surveying-vessel, Capt. Alex. Bridport Becher, now employed in surveying the Orkneys. In June, 1846, during an action which took place between the combined squadrons of England and France and the formidable batteries erected by General Rosas on the heights of San Lorenzo, in the river Parana, Lieut. Mackinnon obtained the particular mention of Commodore Sir Chas. Hotham for the skill he exemplified in the command of a rocket-party, which had been obliged to remain two days and nights concealed under the enemy's nose.*

He married, 9 Aug. 1842, Augusta, daughter of the late John Entwisle, Esq., of Foxholes, M.P. for Rochdale, by whom he has issue.

* *Vide* Gaz. 1846, p. 3355.

M'KINLEY. (VICE-ADMIRAL OF THE WHITE, 1841. F-P., 38; H-P., 36.)

GEORGE M'KINLEY, born at Devonport, is the son of a Lieutenant in the R.N. One of his brothers, Samuel, commanded the COMET galley, and died on the American station; and another, John, who served as a Lieutenant under the late Sir Chas. Morice Pole at the capture of the *Santa Catalina* Spanish frigate, died off St. Domingo in 1782.

This officer entered the Navy, 5 Aug. 1773, as Captain's Servant, on board the ALBION 74, Capts. Hon. Jas. Barrington and Hon. John Leveson Gower, to which ship, lying at Portsmouth, he continued attached until 1777. In Jan. 1778 he rejoined the former officer, then a Rear-Admiral, on board the PRINCE OF WALES 98, and sailed for the West Indies, where, on being discharged at the close of the same year into the CERES sloop, Capt. Jas. Rich. Dacres, he was captured, while holding the rating of Midshipman, by the French frigate *Iphigénie*. Regaining his liberty in the early part of 1779, he served during the next three years, still on the West India station, in the SURPRIZE, ALCMÈNE frigate (which vessel he had assisted in taking from the French), and BELLIQUEUX 64, all commanded by Capt. Jas. Brine (whom he fought under in the latter ship in the actions of 29 April and 5 Sept. 1781, off Martinique and the Chesapeake), and also in the BARFLEUR 98, bearing the flag of Sir Sam. Hood. On 14 Jan. 1782 Mr. M'Kinley was made Lieutenant into the STORMONT sloop, but that vessel being captured before he could join her he went back to the BARFLEUR, and was in consequence present in the actions of 9 and 12 April, and at the capture, on 19 of the same month, of the enemy's ships *Jason*, *Caton*, *Aimable*, and *Ceres*, in the Mona passage. On the date last mentioned he removed to the CHAMPION 24, Capt. Alex. Hood, with whom, in July, 1783, he returned home from America in L'AIMABLE frigate. We next, between April, 1784, and Aug. 1791, find him serving on the Newfoundland and Home stations in the THORN sloop, Capt. Wm. Lechmere, EDGAR 74, Capt. Adam Duncan, TRIMMER 16, Capt. Chas. Tyler, and ILLUSTRIOUS 74 and FORMIDABLE 98, bearing each the flag of Hon. J. L. Gower. When in the TRIMMER in 1787, Mr. M'Kinley was sent in pursuit of a smuggler in the jolly-boat, and during an absence of 30 hours without food was caught in a heavy gale and all but lost. His first appointment, on leaving the FORMIDABLE, was, 1 Dec. 1792, to the ALCIDE 74, Captain (afterwards Commodore and Rear-Admiral) Robt. Linzee; previously to accompanying whom, in 1794, into the WINDSOR CASTLE 98, he participated (the second time on board the FORTITUDE 74, Capt. Wm. Young) in two unsuccessful attacks upon the tower of Mortella in the island of Corsica. Assuming command, in March, 1795, after four months of half-pay, of the LIBERTY cutter, he cruized for upwards of three years in that vessel on the Channel station, and on 17 March, 1796, gained the particular notice of Sir Wm. Sidney Smith by the gallant and judicious manner in which, having entered the harbour of Herqui in company with the DIAMOND frigate and ARISTOCRAT lugger, he went into action with the corvette *Etourdie*, of 16 guns, preparatory to her destruction.* On 16 May, 1798, Mr. M'Kinley was promoted to the command of the OTTER fire-ship. In the following year, being ordered to accompany the expedition to Holland, he witnessed the surrender of Rear-Admiral Storey's squadron in the Texel, and was placed in charge, with a detachment of marines, of the town of Enkuysen, where he remained until the evacuation of the Helder and the removal of the British naval force from the Zuyder Zee. On 2 April, 1801, immediately after the battle of Copenhagen, on which occasion the OTTER had formed part of the light squadron attached to Lord Nelson's division, Capt. M'Kinley was nominated to the temporary command of the BELLONA 74, whose Captain, Sir Thos. Boulden Thompson, had lost a leg in the action. As soon as he had refitted that ship he was superseded and sent in charge of the ARDENT 64 to England, whence, on 20 of the ensuing Oct., the very day he was confirmed in Post-rank, he sailed for the West Indies in the PELICAN sloop with despatches relative to the treaty of Amiens. He removed, immediately on his arrival, to the ABERGAVENNY 54, and was subsequently appointed—23 July, 1802, to the GANGES 74, in which ship he returned home *viâ* Halifax—11 July, 1803, to the ROEBUCK 44, employed at first as a guard-ship at Leith (where the explosion of a powder-horn, while on duty, deprived him of sight for several weeks), and then as flagship to Rear-Admiral Billy Douglas in Yarmouth Roads—23 Jan. 1806, to the QUEBEC 32, stationed off the coast of Holland—20 May following, to the LIVELY 38—19 April, 1811, to the SAN JOSEF 110, bearing the flag in the Mediterranean and Channel of Sir Chas. Cotton, with whom he continued until his death in Feb. 1812—5 May in the latter year, to the BELLONA 74, in which ship he cruized off the Scheldt, made a voyage to St. Helena, and served with the Channel fleet—and (after an interval of nine months), 21 Nov. 1814, and 26 Aug. 1815, to the NAMUR and BULWARK 74's, as Flag-Captain to Sir Chas. Rowley in the River Medway. During his command of the LIVELY, Capt. M'Kinley was for some time Senior officer on the Lisbon station, where he rendered an essential service in bringing away the British factory and all the English merchant-vessels lying in the Tagus, at a time when General Junot was rapidly approaching with a powerful French army to take possession of the Portuguese capital. His conduct, indeed, afforded so much satisfaction to the merchants that they united in presenting him with a piece of plate. In Jan. 1808 the LIVELY conveyed Rear-Admiral Wm. Albany Otway to the squadron employed in the blockade of Lisbon; and then went on a cruize off the Western Islands. After the convention of Cintra her Captain was sent into the Tagus, with orders to take charge of the naval arsenal, which he retained until it was delivered over to the Portuguese authorities. He subsequently cruized off Oporto, and received the thanks of the merchants there for his exertions in clearing the river Douro of all the British shipping previously to the French entering that city. In March, 1809, his assistance being solicited by the inhabitants of Galicia, he repaired thither, and took an active part in the operations which led to the capture of Vigo and Santiago.† On the advance of Marshal Soult towards St. Payo, Capt. M'Kinley was the means of saving it from capture by effectually destroying the bridge. In July, 1809, he convoyed a fleet from Lisbon to England; and on 18 Sept. in the same year he contributed to the capture of *L'Aurore* French lugger-privateer, of 16 guns and 69 men. After lying for a time in the Downs as flag-ship of the late Sir Geo. Campbell, the LIVELY, in April, 1810, conveyed Sir Chas. Cotton to Cadiz. On her return she was ordered to escort the outward-bound trade to Portugal and the Mediterranean. After executing that service she was unfortunately wrecked, 10 Aug. 1810, on a reef of rocks near Point Coura, in the

* *Vide* Gaz. 1796, p. 277.

† *V.* Gaz. 1809, pp. 404, 490, 1006.

island of Malta; a disaster of any share in which Capt. M'Kinley was by court-martial fully acquitted. On afterwards leaving the BULWARK, he was appointed, 16 Jan. 1818, a Captain of the Royal Hospital at Greenwich; and in April, 1821, he was nominated Superintendent of the Royal Naval Asylum on the occasion of its incorporation with the former institution. His services in the latter capacity were acknowledged in 1828 by a special increase of 100*l*. per annum to his salary. He became a Rear-Admiral 22 July, 1830; and attained his present rank 23 Nov. 1841.

Vice-Admiral M'Kinley married a sister of the late Vice-Admiral Aiskew Paffard Hollis, by whom he has issue. AGENT—J. Chippendale.

M'KIRDY. (RETIRED COMMANDER, 1837. F-P., 16; H-P., 34.)

JOHN M'KIRDY entered the Navy, in March, 1797, as L.M., on board the GLENMORE frigate, Capt. Geo. Duff, employed off the coast of Ireland; and in 1798 became Midshipman of the HYÆNA 24, Capts. Hon. Courtenay Boyle and David Lloyd, stationed at first in the Channel, and then in the Mediterranean; where, in 1799, he joined the SANTA TERESA 32, Capt. Robt. Campbell. While in that ship he commanded a boat under Lieut. John Chiene, and had two of his men killed, in cutting out a vessel from under a battery on the coast of Catalonia. He assisted likewise at the capture, 19 June, 1799, of Rear-Admiral Perrée's squadron of three frigates and two brigs, and served at the blockade of Malta and in the operations on the coasts of Genoa and Egypt. When next in the West Indies in the BLENHEIM 74, flag-ship of Sir Archibald Dickson, we find him present, as Master's Mate, in one of two boats commanded by Lieut. Thos. Furber, and aiding, in a most spirited manner, at the boarding and carrying, after a pull of an hour and a half in the heat of the sun, and under a fire of grape and musketry, of *La Fortune* French privateer, of 2 guns, 6 swivels, and 29 men, 15 Sept. 1803. On 16 of the following Nov. he participated in another gallant exploit of the same nature, also conducted by Lieut. Furber, namely, the cutting out from the harbour of Marin, Martinique, with loss to both parties, of the *Harmonie*, a notorious privateer of 8 guns and 66 men. He was confirmed a Lieutenant, after having acted for nearly five months as such, in the HEUREUX 24, Capts. Loftus Otway Bland, Geo. Younghusband, and John Morrison, 8 May, 1804. He continued actively employed in that vessel in the West Indies until she was lost in 1806; and was subsequently appointed—4 Feb. 1807, to the MALABAR 74, Capt. John Temple, stationed in the North Sea—14 May, 1808, to the ARDENT 64, flag-ship at Leith of Vice-Admiral Jas. Vashon—20 Jan. and 16 Nov. 1809, to the ALCMÈNE 32* and MUROS brig, Capts. Wm. Henry Brown Tremlett and Clement Sneyd, both on the Channel station—27 Aug. 1810, to the HIBERNIA 120, Capt. John Nash, lying at Portsmouth—14 Nov. following, to the REVENGE 74, flag-ship of Hon. Arthur Kaye Legge, under whom he officiated as First-Lieutenant at the defence of Cadiz—and, 23 Dec. 1811, to the CUMBERLAND 74, Capt. Thos. Baker. He served in the ship last mentioned in the North Sea and Channel until 22 April, 1814; and on 28 Feb. 1837, not having been further employed, he accepted his present rank. AGENTS—Burnett and Holmes.

M'KIRDY. (LIEUTENANT, 1814.)

ROBERT M'KIRDY died about the commencement of 1847.

This officer entered the Navy (into which he was impressed), 16 April, 1806, on board the ENTERPRIZE receiving-ship at the Tower. In the following June, after he had for a short time been attached to the ZEALAND, commanded at the Nore by Capt. Henry Lidgbird Ball, he became Midshipman of the THESEUS 74, Capts. Geo. Hope and John Poo Beresford, in which ship and the POICTIERS 74, also under the orders of Capt. Beresford, we find him serving on the Home station, in the capacities of Master's Mate and Second-Master, until July, 1812. He was in consequence present, in the THESEUS, at the destruction of the enemy's shipping in Basque Roads in April, 1809. On leaving the POICTIERS he sailed for the East Indies in the MINDEN 74, flag-ship of Sir Sam. Hood, who nominated him, 2 May, 1813, Acting-Lieutenant of the CORNWALLIS 74, Capt. Stephen Thos. Digby. He went on half-pay in Aug. 1814, having been officially promoted on 4 of the preceding Feb.; and he was afterwards employed, for a long time, in command of the TICKLER cutter and MARTIAL gun-brig. In the former vessel he was engaged in superintending the herring-fishery on the N.W. coast of Scotland.

* The ALCMÈNE was wrecked off Nantes, while blockading two of the enemy's frigates, 29 April, 1809.

MACKWORTH. (LIEUTENANT, 1811. F-P., 15; H-P., 29.)

HERBERT MACKWORTH, born 1 Oct. 1791, is second son of the late Sir Digby Mackworth, Bart., by his first wife, Jane, only daughter of the Rev. Matthew Deere; and brother of the present Sir Digby Mackworth, Bart., K.H., a Lieut.-Colonel in the Army, who served in the Peninsula, in France, and at Waterloo, and was lately Aide-de-Camp to Lord Hill, Commander-in-Chief. His father's second wife was a daughter of General Sir Jas. Affleck, Bart.

This officer entered the Navy, 13 Dec. 1803, as Fst.-cl. Vol., on board the EURYALUS 36, Capt. Hon. Henry Blackwood, and after a servitude of 17 months, on the Channel and Irish stations, was transferred, in May, 1805, to the PEARL, Lieut.-Commander Woodger, lying at Portsmouth. Proceeding in the summer of 1806 to the Mediterranean in the ROYAL GEORGE 100, bearing the flag of Sir John Thos. Duckworth, he there, in Oct. of that year, rejoined Capt. Blackwood in the AJAX 74; on the destruction of which ship by fire near the island of Tenedos, 14 Feb. 1807, he was received into the TIGRE 74, Capt. Benj. Hallowell, under whom he took part in the ensuing operations on the coast of Egypt. In April, 1808, he was again placed under the orders of Capt. Blackwood in the WARSPITE 74, also attached to the force in the Mediterranean. He was confirmed a Lieutenant in the MUTINE brig, Capt. Nevinson De Courcy, on the Brazilian station, 29 April, 1811; and between Aug. 1812 and Nov. 1818 was successively employed in the PRINCE OF WALES 98, Capt. John Erskine Douglas, HIBERNIA 120, flag-ship of Sir Wm. Sidney Smith, ROYAL SOVEREIGN 100, Capt. Chas. Thurlow Smith, EURYDICE 24, Capt. Hon. Valentine Gardner, SCAMANDER 36, Capts. Sir John Louis, Chas. Sibthorpe John Hawtayne, and Wm. Elliott, BRAZEN 18, Capt. Jas. Stirling, and SEVERN, Coast Blockade-ship, Capt. Wm. M'Culloch—on the Mediterranean, Cork, West India, and Home stations. He has since been on half-pay.

Lieut. Mackworth was lately High Sheriff for Trinidad. He married Miss Jesse Anderson, and by that lady has issue two sons and four daughters. AGENTS—Messrs. Ommanney.

M'LEAN. (LIEUTENANT, 1826.)

CHARLES CLAYTON M'LEAN entered the Navy 24 March, 1810; passed his examination in 1818; obtained his commission 6 Dec. 1826; and since 2 Aug. 1833 has been employed in the Coast Guard service.

MACLEAN. (COMMANDER, 1823. F-P., 18; H-P., 31.)

RAWDON MACLEAN entered the Navy, 24 Oct. 1798, as Fst.-cl. Vol., on board the TERPSICHORE 32, Capt. Wm. Hall Gage, employed in the Mediterranean and then in the Channel, where, from Oct. 1800 until April, 1802, he served as Midshipman in the ATLAS 98, Capt. Theophilus Jones. In Oct. 1803 he re-embarked on board the LEOPARD 50, Capt. Jas. Nicoll Morris; on accompanying whom into the COLOSSUS 74, he received, in the battle of Trafalgar, a wound so severe that he still feels its effects.* A gratuity from the Patriotic Fund was his consequent reward. He removed, in Dec. 1805, to the CAMILLA 20, Capt. John Tower, but had not been many months in that vessel before he was promoted, 7 July, 1806, to the rank of Lieutenant, and re-appointed to the COLOSSUS, commanded at first by Capt. Morris, and subsequently by Capt. Thos. Alexander. In Nov. 1808 we find him serving on shore under the present Earl of Dundonald, at the celebrated defence of the fortress of Rosas, on the north-eastern extremity of Spain. He commanded a gun-boat also during the siege of Cadiz by the French; and on 1 Dec. 1811 he assisted at the capture and destruction of part of an enemy's convoy, protected by several armed vessels, near Rochelle. His health at length obliging him to leave the COLOSSUS in Sept. 1813, after he had been altogether for nearly nine years attached to her, he was next appointed—31 Jan. and 31 Oct. 1814, to the ROYAL SOVEREIGN 100, Capts. Thos. Gordon Caulfeild, Chas. Thurlow Smith, and Robt. Lambert, and STORK sloop, Capt. Robt. Lisle Coulson, in which vessels he served in the Mediterranean and North Sea until 18 Sept. 1815—and, 26 Nov. 1822, as Senior, to the GLOUCESTER 74, bearing the broad pendant of Sir Edw. W. C. R. Owen in the West Indies. He was there promoted to the command, 1 July, 1823, of the BUSTARD 10. He removed, in the following Oct., to the CARNATION 18, and after cruizing with activity in the suppression of piracy, returned home and was paid off in July, 1825. He has not been since employed.

From 1 Oct. 1841 until 1 Dec. 1843, Commander Maclean was Superintendent of the Royal Mail Steam Packet Company in the West Indies. He married in Sept. 1829, and has issue one son and a daughter. AGENTS—Messrs. Ommanney.

MACLEAN. (CAPTAIN, 1846. F-P., 16; H-P., 8.)

WILLIAM MACLEAN is ninth son of Colonel Alex. Maclean, of Ardgour, by the Lady Margaret Hope, daughter of John, second Earl of Hopetoun, and granddaughter of Alexander, fifth Earl of Leven and Melville. One of his brothers, Archibald, a Captain in the R.N. (1822), died in 1832.

This officer entered the Navy, early in 1823, as a Volunteer, on board the BRITON 46, Capt. Sir Murray Maxwell, and sailed for South America, where, at home, and in India, he continued to serve as Midshipman in the same frigate, and in the PRINCE REGENT 120, Capt. Constantine Rich. Moorsom, THETIS 46, Capt. Arthur Batt Bingham, RANGER 28, Capt. Lord Henry Fred. Thynne, and PRINCE REGENT again and SOUTHAMPTON 52, flag-ships of Sir Henry Blackwood and Sir Edw. W. C. R. Owen, until promoted, 10 Feb. 1830, to a Lieutenancy in the SUCCESS 28, Capt. Wm. Clarke Jervoise, also on the East India station, whence he came home in Oct. 1831 in the CALCUTTA 84, Capt. Peter Fisher. His succeeding appointments were—7 Nov. 1833, to the BLONDE 46, Capt. Fras. Mason, fitting for South America—5 April, 1836 (soon after his return to England), to the BRITANNIA 120, flag-ship of Sir Philip Chas. Durham at Portsmouth, where he remained a period of three years—and, 27 Aug. 1841, to the HOWE 120, as Flag-Lieutenant to Sir Fras. Mason in the Mediterranean. He attained the rank of Commander 23 Nov. following; served in that capacity, from 28 Sept. 1843 until Feb. 1845, on board the APOLLO troop-ship; obtained command, 22 Dec. in the latter year, of the CRUIZER 16, on the East India station; and acquired his present rank 9 Nov. 1846. He has since been on half-pay.

Capt. Maclean married, 30 Aug. 1838, Elizabeth, only daughter of the late T. Melet Charter, Esq., of Lynchfield House, co. Somerset, and granddaughter of the late Mrs. Freke Gunston, of Frethey Cottage, near Taunton, by whom he has issue. AGENTS—Hallett and Robinson.

* *Vide* Gaz. 1805, p. 1484.

M'LEOD. (RETIRED COMMANDER, 1824. F-P., 24; H-P., 46.)

ALEXANDER M'LEOD (*a*) entered the Navy, 11 Nov. 1777, as Captain's Servant, on board the VALIANT 74, Capts. Hon. John Leveson Gower and Sam. Cranston Goodall, attached to the Channel fleet. Between Sept. 1779 and May, 1783, he served under various officers, chiefly in the capacity of Midshipman, in the AJAX, VENGEANCE, DILIGENTE, and ARGO, on the West India and Home stations; where, and in the Mediterranean, he was further, until promoted to the rank of Lieutenant, 20 Nov. 1790, employed on board the SOLITAIRE, Capt. Robt. Montagu, EDGAR 74, Capt. Adam Duncan, KINGFISHER sloop, Capt. Geo. Lumsdaine, MAGNIFICENT 74, Capt. Rich. Onslow, and PRINCESS ROYAL 98, flag-ship of Rear-Admiral Wm. Hotham. During the French revolutionary war we find him in succession appointed to the BEAULIEU, Capts. Hon. Wm. Carnegie and John Salisbury, ROSE, Capt. Robt. Faulknor, ULYSSES, Capt. Rich. Morris, HECTOR, Capt. Cuthbert Collingwood, SAMPSON, Capt. Thos. Lewis, WEYMOUTH armed transport, DIADEM, Capt. John Dawson, CYNTHIA, Capt. Micajah Malbon, and CARYSFORT, Capts. Adam Drummond and Geo. Mundy. The CYNTHIA formed part of the expeditions to Holland and Vigo in 1799 and 1800; the other ships appear to have been chiefly employed in the West Indies; where, at the commencement of 1794, Mr. M'Leod, we believe, assisted at the reduction of the French islands. After having had command for upwards of three years of the SULTAN and SUFFOLK, on the Home station, and been deprived of part of his right hand, he was admitted an out-pensioner of Greenwich Hospital 22 Sept. 1806. He accepted the rank he now holds 4 Oct. 1824. AGENT—J. Hinxman.

M'LEOD. (LIEUT., 1823. F-P., 15; H-P., 23.)

ALEXANDER M'LEOD (*c*) died 8 March, 1846.

This officer entered the Navy, 27 July, 1808, as Fst.-cl. Vol., on board the SNAKE sloop, Capts. Thos. Young and Wm. Hellard, on the Leith station; and in Oct. 1811, while holding the rating of Master's Mate, was driven in a prize into Norway during a gale of wind, and there taken prisoner. On being restored to liberty in 1812, he again (after he had been for a short time borne as a Supernumerary on the books of the DICTATOR 64 and ADAMANT 50, Capts. Wm. Autridge and Matthew Buckle) joined the SNAKE; in which vessel he continued to serve, under the orders of Capts. Hellard and Joseph Gape, on the West India, Cork, and Channel stations, until Oct. 1815. He subsequently became attached—15 Dec. 1815, to the PHAETON 46, Capt. Fras. Stanfell, on the St. Helena station—20 March, 1818, as Admiralty-Midshipman, to the VENGEUR 74, commanded in the Channel by Capt. Thos. Alexander—and 3 Oct. following, and 26 Sept. 1822, in the same capacity and as Admiralty-Mate, to the SEVERN and RAMILLIES, Coast Blockade ships, each under the orders of Capt. Wm. M'Culloch. He obtained his commission 19 July, 1823; and (with the exception of a few weeks again passed, in 1824, in the RAMILLIES) remained thenceforward on half-pay.

Lieut. M'Leod married, 19 Jan. 1841, Sarah Elizabeth, second daughter of B. Alder, Esq., of Brixton.

MACLEOD. (LIEUTENANT, 1841.)

ROBERT BRUCE ÆNEAS MACLEOD is eldest son of Roderick Macleod, Esq., Lord Lieutenant of co. Cromarty, Deputy-Lieutenant of Rosshire, and late M.P. for co. Sutherland, by Isabella, daughter of Wm. Cunninghame, Esq., of Lainshaw, in Ayrshire; and grandson of the present Robt. Bruce Æneas Macleod, Esq., of Cadboll, co. Cromarty, and of Invergordon Castle, in Rosshire.

This officer entered the Navy, 4 Feb. 1831; passed his examination 19 Aug. 1837; and at the period of his promotion to the rank of Lieutenant, 26 Aug. 1841, was serving in the Mediterranean as Mate of the THUNDERER 84, Capt. Maurice Fred. Fitzhardinge Berkeley. His appointments have since been

—26 Feb. 1842, to the VANGUARD 80, Capt. Sir David Dunn, on the Lisbon station, whence he returned home and was paid off in the summer of 1843—10 Jan. 1844, to the RESISTANCE troop-ship, Capt. Chas. Geo. Edw. Patey—and 3 Jan. 1846, after a few months of half-pay, to the CALYPSO 20, Capt. Henry John Worth, now in the Pacific. AGENTS—Messrs. Ommanney.

M'LEOD. (LIEUT., 1811. F-P., 13; H-P., 32.)

WILLIAM M'LEOD entered the Navy, 18 June, 1802, as Third-cl. Boy, on board the BLENHEIM 74, Capts. Peter Turner Bover, Henry Matson, and Thos. Graves, on the Leeward Island station, where he removed, in March, 1804, to the ULYSSES 44, Capt. Edwin Henry Chamberlayne. In Aug. 1806, after he had been for ten months attached to the ROYAL WILLIAM, bearing the flag of Admiral Montagu at Spithead, he became Midshipman of the PIGMY 14, Lieut.-Commander Geo. Montagu Higginson, under whom it was his fate to be wrecked, off the Ile d'Oléron, and taken prisoner, 2 March, 1807. Being restored to liberty in Dec. 1809, he next, during several months of 1810, served in the West Indies on board the NEPTUNE and STATIRA, flag-ships of Hon. Sir Alex. Cochrane. He was there, in April, 1811, nominated Acting-Lieutenant of the PERLEN 38, Capts. Norborne Thompson, Joseph Swabey Tetley, and John Allen; in which vessel, on proceeding to the Mediterranean, he took part, under Capt. Tetley, in a very gallant skirmish, which terminated in her repulse, 22 Nov. 1811, of a French ship-of-the-line and two frigates belonging to the Toulon fleet. Mr. M'Leod, whose official promotion had taken place on 10 of the preceding Sept., was next, 26 Aug. 1812, appointed to the SNAP 16, Capts. Geo. Rose Sartorius, Wm. Bateman Dashwood, and Geo. King. While with Capt. Dashwood he assisted in capturing, 1 Nov. 1813, *Le Lion* privateer of 16 guns and 69 men, after a close action of 10 minutes, fought off the coast of France. In Jan. 1815 he rejoined Capt. Sartorius on board the SLANEY 20. He cruized in that vessel until the following Sept., and has since been on half-pay. AGENT—J. Hinxman.

M'MILLAN. (LIEUT., 1810. F-P., 20; H-P., 36.)

ALLAN M'MILLAN entered the Navy, 25 Sept. 1791, as a Boy, on board the BEDFORD 74, Capt. Sir Andw. Snape Hamond, in which ship, with the exception of an interval between Nov. 1795 and Jan. 1797, he continued to serve, under Capts. Robt. Mann, Davidge Gould, Augustus Montgomery, and Sir Thos. Byard, on the Home and Mediterranean stations, until May, 1798—latterly in the capacity of Midshipman. He was in consequence present in 1795 in Hotham's partial actions, and in company with the CENSEUR 74, when that ship was taken by a French squadron under M. Richery. On finally leaving the BEDFORD, he joined the FOUDROYANT 80, bearing the successive flags of Lords Nelson and Keith, and commanded, among other Captains, by Sir Edw. Berry, under whom, while at the blockade of Malta, he assisted at the capture, 18 Feb. 1800, of *Le Généreux* 74 and *Ville de Marseilles* armed store-ship, and, 31 March following, after a desperate conflict in which the FOUDROYANT (in company at the time with the LION 64 and PENELOPE 36) sustained a loss of 8 men killed and 64 wounded, of *Le Guillaume Tell*, of 84 guns and 1000 men, bearing the flag of Rear-Admiral Decrès. Continuing in the same ship until the peace of Amiens, Mr. M'Millan was afforded an opportunity of sharing in the operations in Egypt in 1801. Between Feb. 1803 and the date of his official promotion, 31 Oct. 1810, he served, occasionally as Acting-Lieutenant, in 13 different ships, under various distinguished officers, on the Home and Baltic stations—commanding during that period the CONVULSION mortar-vessel, off Boulogne, for nearly 12 months in 1805-6, and accompanying, in the SKYLARK sloop, Capt. Jas. Boxer, the expedition to the Walcheren in 1809. His last appointments were—12 Jan. 1811, for nine months, to the SCYLLA 16, Capt. Arthur Atchison, attached to the force in the Channel—and, 20 April, 1812, to the CALLIOPE 10, Capt. John M'Kerlie. In that vessel, which he left in Jan. 1814, Lieut. M'Millan was actively employed off Flushing, Heligoland, and the German rivers.

M'MURDO. (COMMANDER, 1843. F-P., 17; H-P., 6.)

ARCHIBALD M'MURDO, born 24 Sept. 1812, is son of Lieut.-Colonel M'Murdo, who lost his eyesight, and in the end his life, from the effects of a wound received in action in the West Indies.

This officer entered the Navy, 6 Oct. 1824, as Fst.-cl. Vol., on board the PYLADES 18, Capts. Fras. Fead, Geo. Vernon Jackson, and John Leith, stationed in the West Indies, where he removed, in Sept. 1825, to the BELLETTE 18, Capt. Chas. Croker. After serving for nearly two years at home, as Midshipman of the SUPERB and MELVILLE 74's, both commanded by Capt. Henry Hill, and BRITOMART 10, Capt. Russell Henry Manners, he proceeded in 1828 to the Mediterranean in the BLONDE 46, Capt. Edm. Lyons, under whom, in Oct. of that year, he co-operated in the reduction of Morea Castle, the last hold of the Turks in the Peloponnesus. He had been previously employed at the blockade of Navarin. The BLONDE being put out of commission in June, 1831, Mr. M'Murdo (who had passed his examination in the preceding Nov.) was appointed Mate, a few months afterwards, of the ALLIGATOR 28, Capt. Geo. Robt. Lambert, and ordered to the East Indies, whence he returned home and was paid off in Aug. 1835. For the services he had during that period performed in recovering the crew of a wrecked whaler from the natives of New Zealand, he was promoted to the rank of Lieutenant 15 Feb. 1836. His succeeding appointments were—23 May, 1836, to the TERROR bomb, Capt. Geo. Back, whom he accompanied on a disastrous voyage of discovery to the northward of Charles Island, in Hudson's Bay, returning to England in the autumn of 1837—2 Feb. 1838, to the VOLAGE 28, Capt. Henry Smith, from which vessel, on her arrival in the East Indies, his health obliged him to invalid, 27 Oct. in the same year—and, 23 Aug. 1839, again, as First-Lieutenant, to the TERROR, Capt. Fras. Rawdon Moira Crozier, fitting for an explorative mission to the Antarctic regions, where he remained until illness compelled him to return in Aug. 1842. He was advanced, in consequence, to his present rank, 4 Oct. 1843; and since 11 June, 1846, has been in command of the CONTEST 12, on the coast of Africa. AGENTS—Messrs. Chard.

M'NAGHTEN. (LIEUTENANT, 1845.)

ALEXANDER M'NAGHTEN passed his examination 6 Sept. 1837; and served as Mate, on the East India, Mediterranean, and Home stations, in the BLENHEIM 72, Capt. Sir Humphrey Fleming Senhouse, FORMIDABLE 84, Capts. Sir Chas. Sullivan and Geo. Fred. Rich (flag-ship for some time of Sir Edw. W. C. R. Owen), WATERWITCH 10, Capt. Thos. Fras. Birch, and SUPERB 80, Capt. Armar Lowry Corry. He obtained his commission 1 Sept. 1845; and since 8 of the following Oct. has been serving in North America and the West Indies in the ALARM 26, Capts. Chas. Colville Frankland and Granville Gower Loch.

MACNAMARA, Kt. (CAPTAIN, 1833. F-P., 18; H-P., 21.)

SIR BURTON MACNAMARA, born in 1794, is sixth son of the late Fras. Macnamara, Esq., of Doolen, co. Clare, by Jane, daughter of Geo. Stamer, Esq., of Carnelly, in the same county; and brother of the present Wm. Nugent Macnamara, Esq., of Doolen, a Major of Militia, and M.P., since 1830, for co. Clare. He is a descendant of the ancient Admirals of Munster, whose office is said to have originated the name "Mac-na-mara," or "Son of the Sea."

This officer entered the Navy, 26 July, 1808, as Fst.-cl. Vol., on board the EDGAR 74, Capt. Jas. Macnamara; previously to accompanying whom, as

Midshipman, in March, 1810, into the BERWICK 74, he witnessed the embarkation from Nyeborg of the Marquis de la Romana and his patriot army, and the capture, which attended it, of the Danish vessels *Fama* of 18, and *Salorman* of 12 guns. After assisting, in the BERWICK, in causing the self-destruction, near Barfleur, 25 March, 1811, of the French 40-gun frigate *L'Amazone*, Mr. Macnamara successively joined, in the course of that and the following year, the SAN FIORENZO *armée-en-flûte*, Capt. Hon. Edm. Sexton Pery Knox, SAN DOMINGO 74, bearing the flag of Sir Rich. Strachan, and STATIRA 38, Capt. Hassard Stackpoole. While attached to the last-mentioned ship we find him frequently employed in her boats on the coast of North America, particularly on one occasion, 3 April. 1813, when he served with those of a squadron, containing 105 men, under the orders of Lieut. Jas. Polkinghorne, at the dashing capture, 15 miles up the Rappahannock river, of four schooners, carrying in the whole 31 guns and 219 men—an exploit whose achievement proved inflictive of a loss to the British of 2 killed and 11 wounded, and to the enemy of 6 killed and 10 wounded. In May, 1813, Mr. Macnamara commanded a boat, under Rear-Admiral Cockburn, in an attack upon the town of Havre-de-Grace, at the entrance of the Susquehanna river, and assisted in destroying a valuable cannon-foundry in its immediate vicinity. He was similarly employed in an expedition against Frenchtown. In Aug. 1814, having returned to England and passed his examination, he volunteered his services on the Canadian lakes. Proceeding thither accordingly, he continued on that station until Dec. 1815—the last nine months as Acting-Lieutenant of the PRINCE REGENT, Capt. Henry Thos. Davies, and NIAGARA, Capt. Edw. Collier. He then took up a commission bearing date 1 of the previous July; but he did not again go afloat until July, 1820, on 25 of which month he received an appointment to the CAMBRIAN 48, Capt. Gawen Wm Hamilton, fitting for the Mediterranean, where he was advanced, 19 July, 1822, to the command of the CHANTICLEER 10. During his continuance in that sloop, a period of two years, Capt. Macnamara was actively employed, owing to the revolution in Greece, in protecting the British and Ionian trade in the Archipelago against the violence of the contending parties. His exertions procured him the thanks of the Commander-in-Chief, Sir Graham Moore. His last appointment was, 1 June, 1825, to the Coast Guard, in which service he remained, stationed we believe in co. Clare, until the summer of 1832. In 1830, at a period of great disturbance, he appears to have been very active in the restoration of tranquillity. His Post-commission bears date 16 Nov. 1833.

Sir Burton Macnamara (who was knighted in 1839 by the Lord-Lieutenant of Ireland, the Marquess of Normanby) is a Magistrate for Clare, and in 1841 was a candidate for the representation of the borough of Ennis in Parliament. He married, 1 March, 1832, Jane, daughter of Daniel Gabbett, Esq., of Strand, Limerick. AGENTS—Messrs. Halford and Co.

MACNAMARA. (LIEUT., 1821. F-P., 21; H-P., 17.)

TIMOTHY MACNAMARA entered the Navy, 26 April, 1809, as Fst.-cl. Vol., on board the EDGAR 74, Capt. Jas. Macnamara, stationed in the Baltic, where he saw much boat-service. Removing, as Midshipman, in March, 1810, to the BERWICK 74, commanded by the same officer, he took part, 25 March, 1811, in the operations which led to the self-destruction, near Barfleur, of the French 40-gun frigate *L'Amazone*. In the following Oct. he joined the TIGRE 74, Capt. John Halliday, under whom, it appears, he served on the West India, St. Helena, and Home stations, until Aug. 1815, and coalesced at one time with the troops in an attack upon Bergen-op-Zoom. During the first three years of the peace Mr. Macnamara was employed on the Irish station in the FLY sloop, Capt. John Baldwin, and TONNANT 80, flag-ship of Sir Benj. Hallowell. He then, in Nov. 1818, joined the Coast Blockade, as Midshipman of the SEVERN 40, Capt. Wm. M'Culloch, and while in that service, in which he continued until promoted to the rank of Lieutenant 29 Jan. 1821, he received, in 1819, a severe contusion in an encounter with a band of smugglers. He has had charge, since 1 March, 1838, of a station in the Coast Guard.

Lieut. Macnamara has received a gold medal from the Royal National Shipwreck Institution. He was left a widower 18 Aug. 1838. AGENTS—Hallett and Robinson.

M'NEALE. (LIEUTENANT, 1825.)

MALCOLM M'NEALE entered the Navy 1 April, 1814; passed his examination in 1821; and in the following year, while Mate of the CYRENÉ 20, Capt. Percy Grace, assisted in the boats of that vessel in an attack on a slave-factory on the coast of Africa. He obtained his commission 4 Oct. 1825, and was subsequently appointed—5 Oct. 1832, as Additional-Lieutenant, to the ISIS 50, Capt. Jas. Polkinghorne, at the Cape of Good Hope—27 June, 1833, to the CURLEW 10, Capt. Henry Dundas Trotter, on the same station—and, after he had been a few months on half-pay, 22 Dec. 1834 and 1 Sept. 1835, to the VICTORY 104, and BRITANNIA 120, flag-ships of Sir Thos. Williams at Portsmouth, where he remained until 1836. AGENT—John P. Muspratt.

MACNEVIN. (LIEUTENANT, 1810.)

JOHN MACNEVIN entered the Navy, 10 Aug. 1797, as Fst.-cl. Vol., on board the SHANNON 32, Capt. Alex. Fraser, on the coast of Ireland. He served, between 1799 and Aug. 1808, on the Mediterranean and Home stations, chiefly in the capacity of Midshipman, in the DIANA frigate, Capts. John Poo Beresford and Thos. Jas. Maling, and HERCULE, SUPERB,* ROYAL GEORGE, and BELLEISLE, flag-ships of Admirals Dacres, Sir John Thos. Duckworth, and Sir Alex. Cochrane; and on 31 Aug. 1810, after having intermediately acted as Lieutenant of the WOLVERENE and SUPÉRIEURE sloops, he was confirmed in that rank. His next appointments were —24 Oct. 1810, to the DEFIANCE 74, Capt. Rich. Raggett, off the Texel—9 Dec. 1811, to the SPIDER brig, Capt. Frank Gore Willock, in the West Indies —3 Nov. 1813, to the command of the BALLAHOU schooner, on the same station—and, 22 April, 1814, to the CHARYBDIS 16, Capt. Jas. Clephan, under whom he accompanied the expedition against New Orleans. He was paid off from the last-mentioned vessel in Aug. 1815; and, since 27 Nov. 1822, has been in command of a station in the Coast Guard.

He married, in Jan. 1836, Eliza, second daughter of John M'Mahon Blackhall, of Kilcard, co. Clare, Ireland. AGENT—J. Hinxman.

MACONOCHIE, K.H. (COMMANDER, 1815. F-P., 12; H-P., 32.)

ALEXANDER MACONOCHIE entered the Navy, in Aug. 1803, as Fst.-cl. Vol., on board the NORTHUMBERLAND 74, Captain (afterwards Rear-Admiral) Hon Alex. Cochrane, under whom he was for some time employed off Ferrol, and then proceeded to the West Indies in pursuit of a French squadron escaped from Rochefort. In Sept. 1805 he removed as Midshipman (a rating he had attained in March, 1804) to the SEINE 36, Capt. David Atkins, also on the West India station, where, in Sept. 1806, he again joined Sir A. Cochrane in the BELLEISLE 74. During the next two years we find him chiefly serving on board the DISPATCH, tender to the ship last mentioned. He then became attached to the ARDENT 64, bearing the flag of Vice-Admiral Jas Vashon in Leith Roads; but, being a third time, in March, 1809, placed under the orders of Sir A. Cochrane, in the POMPÉE 74, was by that Admiral nominated Lieutenant, 15 Sept. following, of the ETHALION frigate, Capt. Thos. John Cochrane, stationed at first among the Leeward Islands and then off Cadiz—an act which the Admiralty confirmed. In Nov. 1810 Mr. Maconochie obtained an

* Part of the force employed in the action off St. Domingo 6 Feb. 1806.

appointment to the GRASSHOPPER 18, Capt. Henry Fanshawe, in which vessel he continued until, in order to avoid being lost, as was her consort the HERO 74, she surrendered to the Dutch fleet in the Texel 24 Dec. 1811. The peace of 1814 restoring him to liberty, he once more, in the course of the same year, joined, on board the TONNANT 80, his friend and patron Sir A. Cochrane, who, in Jan. 1815, invested him with the command of the CALLIOPE 10. He was officially promoted to the rank he now holds 8 Sept. in the same year, and has since been on half-pay.

Commander Maconochie was nominated a K.H. 4 May, 1836. He was formerly Secretary to the London Geographical Society, and is now Secretary to the Lieutenant-Governor of Van Diemen's Land.* He is married, and has issue.

M'QUHAE. (CAPTAIN, 1835. F-P., 18; H-P., 26.)

PETER M'QUHAE entered the Navy, 22 Sept. 1803, as Fst.-cl. Vol., on board the EXCELLENT 74, Capt. Frank Sotheron. In that ship, in which he soon attained the rating of Midshipman, he served for nearly three years in the Mediterranean, where he took part in the defence of the Bay of Naples. He was next, from Aug. 1806 until Nov. 1808, employed, chiefly on the Home station, in the PHŒBE 36, Capt. Jas. Oswald; after which, becoming Master's Mate of the LAVINIA 40, Capt. Lord Wm. Stuart, he assisted, previously to the fall of Flushing, in forcing a passage between the batteries of that place and Cadsand. In Jan. 1810, having attained the rank of Lieutenant 7 Oct. 1809, and been for a short time attached to the APELLES sloop, Capt. Thos. Oliver, he joined the PYRAMUS frigate, Capts. Chas. Dashwood and Jas. Whitley Deans Dundas, under whom he served with activity in the Baltic and Mediterranean, among the Western Islands, and along the coast of France, until within a short time of his advancement to the rank of Commander, 15 June, 1814. From the latter date Capt. M'Quhae did not again go afloat until Sept. 1831; on 17 of which month we find him appointed to the FLY 18, fitting for the West Indies, whence he returned home and was paid off in Oct. 1835. He was advanced to the rank he now holds 10 Dec. following; and since 11 Oct. 1844 has been in command of the DÆDALUS 20, in the East Indies.

Capt. M'Quhae married (a second time), 19 Oct. 1831, Caroline, relict of S. Bloss Copping, Esq., of Harleston, co. Norfolk, by whom he has issue. AGENTS—Hallett and Robinson.

MADDEN. (COMMANDER, 1829. F-P., 20; H-P., 16.)

CHARLES MADDEN is fifth son of the late Capt. Wm. John Madden, R.M. (1780), Agent for the Royal Marines at Portsmouth; brother of Sir Fred. Madden, Kt., Keeper of MSS. in the British Museum; nephew of the late Major-General Sir Geo. Madden, Kt., C.B., K.T.S.; and brother-in-law of the late Rear-Admiral Sam. Jackson, C.B.

This officer entered the Navy, 1 Feb. 1811, as Third-cl. Vol., on board the VENERABLE 74, Capts. Sir Home Popham, Jas. Whitley Deans Dundas, and David Milne; under the first-named of whom he assisted at the blockade of Brest, L'Orient, and Cherbourg, and was actively employed in co-operation with the patriots on the north coast of Spain, where, it appears, he witnessed, as Midshipman, the reduction of Lequeytio and Castro, the attacks upon Puerta Galetta, Guetaria, and Santander, and the destruction of the fortifications of Bermeo, Plencia, Galea, Algorta, Begona, El Campillo las Quersas, and Xebiles. Rejoining Sir Home Popham in Feb. 1813 in the STIRLING CASTLE 74, he sailed soon afterwards with the Earl of Moira for Calcutta; on his return whence in the summer of 1814 he removed to the MAGNIFICENT 74, Capt. Willoughby Thos. Lake, and proceeded to the West Indies. On that ship being paid off in Aug. 1815 Mr. Madden became in succession attached to the LACEDÆMONIAN and NIGER frigates, in the latter of which (they were both commanded by Capt. Sam. Jackson) he escorted Hon. Chas. Bagot as Ambassador to the United States, and Sir John Sherbrooke, Governor of Canada, from Halifax to Quebec. In Sept. 1818, after he had been for a period of 17 months on shore, and had passed his examination, he joined the TARTAR 42, fitting for the broad pendant of Sir Geo. Ralph Collier, Commander-in-Chief on the coast of Africa. On his return home in June, 1819, he was transferred to the SYBILLE frigate, bearing the flag at Jamaica of his early friend Sir Home Popham, who promoted him, 23 Sept. following, to a death-vacancy in the WASP 18, Capt. Thos. Wren Carter. That sloop being paid off in Aug. 1820, Mr. Madden's next appointments were, again on the West India station—3 Dec. 1822, to the RINGDOVE 18, Capts. Geo. Frederick, and Edwin Ludlow, Rich, in which vessel he was present at Demarara during an insurrection of the negroes in Aug. 1823—8 June, 1826, to the VALOROUS 26, Capt. the Earl of Huntingdon—29 Jan. 1828, to the MAGNIFICENT 74, receiving-ship, Capts. Wm. Robt. Ashley Pettman, Henry Gosset, Williams Sandom, and Geo. Wm. Conway Courtenay—in Nov. 1828, to the temporary command of the VICTOR 18—14 Jan. 1829, to the MERSEY 26, Capt. G. W. C. Courtenay—and 1 June and 13 July following, to the acting command of the SPEEDWELL schooner and HARLEQUIN 18. He came home in the ensuing Sept. on board a transport, and on his arrival was confirmed in his present rank by a commission bearing date 30 March, 1829. His last appointment was, 13 Nov. 1840, to the Coast Guard; in which service he remained, as an Inspecting Commander, until 5 Jan. 1846.

MADGE. (LIEUT., 1815. F-P., 11; H-P., 31.)

ROBERT PEPPEREL MADGE entered the Navy, 1 Nov. 1805, as Fst.-cl. Vol., on board the ADAMANT 50, Capt. Geo. Burlton, lying in the Downs; and from 27 of the same month until Nov. 1810, served in the Bay of Biscay and Mediterranean, the greater part of the time as Midshipman, in the FAME 74, Capts. Graham Moore, Rich. Henry Alex. Bennett, Phipps Hornby, and Abel Ferris. After a prolonged servitude on the same station in the SALSETTE 36, Capt. John Hollinworth, and VOLAGE 22, Capt. P. Hornby, he proceeded in the latter vessel, under Capt. Hon. Donald Hugh Mackay, to the East Indies, where, from Sept. 1812 until 1815, he performed the duties of Master's Mate and Acting-Master in the MALACCA 36, Capts. Mackay and Geo. Henderson. In Aug. 1815, at which period he was officiating at Spithead as a Supernumerary of the PRINCE 98, Capt. Edm. Boger, we find him presented with a commission dated 21 Feb. in that year. He last appointment was, 16 Dec. 1817, to the FLORIDA 24, Capt. Chas. Sibthorpe John Hawtayne, with whom he served on the Home station until paid off in Dec. 1818. AGENTS—Burnett and Holmes.

MAGAN. (LIEUT., 1814. F-P., 7; H-P., 33.)

ARTHUR MAGAN entered the Navy, 14 Nov. 1807, as Fst.-cl. Vol., on board the PEARL, Lieut.-Commander Woodriff, lying at Spithead; cruized, from May 1808 to July 1809, in the North Sea and Channel, in the WARSPITE 74, Capt. Hon. Henry Blackwood; and, between the latter date and Sept. 1814, served with Capt. Geo. Burlton, chiefly in the capacities of Midshipman and Master's Mate, in the RESOLUTION and RODNEY 74's, VILLE DE PARIS 110, and BOYNE 98, on the Home and Mediterranean stations. The RESOLUTION formed part of the force employed at the destruction of the French shipping in Basque Roads and at the siege of Flushing in 1809; and the BOYNE, of the armament under Sir Edw. Pellew in his partial actions of 5 Nov. 1813 and 13 Feb. 1814 with the Toulon fleet. On leaving that ship Mr. Magan took up a commission

* In 1818 he published a work entitled 'A Summary View of the Statistics and existing Commerce of the Principal Shores of the Pacific Ocean,' &c.

dated 16 June, 1814. He has since been on half-pay.

MAGIN. (Retired Commander, 1844. f-p., 13; h-p., 34.)

Joseph Magin, born about Christmas 1785, is brother of Wm. Magin, Esq., First-Lieutenant R.M. (1805), who fought in that capacity on board the Tonnant 80, at the battle of Trafalgar; and nephew of Dr. John Magin, Surgeon R.N., who served in the Monarch 74, flag-ship of Sir Rich. Onslow, in the action off Camperdown 11 Oct. 1797, and died Head Surgeon of the Royal Marine Infirmary at Stonehouse, Plymouth, in 1812.

This officer entered the Navy, 30 April, 1800, as Fst.-cl. Vol., on board the Princess Royal 98, Capt. Thos. Macnamara Russell, of which ship, stationed in the Channel, his uncle was at the time Surgeon. In the course of 1801 he successively joined the Alkmaar, Capt. Rich. Poulden, and Blenheim 74, bearing the flag in the North Sea of Sir Archibald Dickson; and on becoming, in 1803, attached, as Midshipman, to the Seagull 18, Capt. Henry Burke, he took part in a running fight of 12 hours which terminated in the capture, although not without loss, of the *Lord Nelson* East Indiaman. Removing, in Dec. 1804, to the Amphion 32, Capts. Sam. Sutton and Wm. Hoste, Mr. Magin was on board that frigate when, in Nov. 1805, she effected the defeat, notwithstanding that she was simultaneously opposed by the fire of an immense battery, of a division of about 30 Spanish gun-boats, which had come out of Algeciras in the hope of capturing a British convoy. On 25 Sept. 1806, a few months after he had passed his examination and been transferred to the Repulse 74, Capt. Hon. Arthur Kaye Legge, he witnessed the capture of *Le Président* French frigate; and in Feb. 1807 we find him present, in the same ship, at the passage of the Dardanells. On the occasion of the attack made upon the Turkish squadron at Point Pesquies, Mr. Magin volunteered and proceeded with two boats under the orders of Lieut. Kidd for the purpose of setting fire to the Admiral's ship. During the stay of the party between decks, the boats, owing to the blaze which had speedily resulted from their exertions, were under the necessity of putting off; in consequence whereof, the Lieutenant and his companions were compelled to jump overboard, and were picked up when the ship exploded. On his arrival home Mr. Magin, in consideration of a wound he had received in the operations, was presented by the Patriotic Society with a gratuity of 30*l*. He was promoted (while serving in the Atlas 74, flag-ship of Rear-Admiral John Child Purvis, off Cadiz) to a Lieutenancy, 4 Jan. 1808, in the Gazi Musrett 36, Capt. Geo. M. Honey, one of the prizes recently taken at Alexandria. His succeeding appointments were—6 Oct. 1808, as Senior, to the Apelles sloop, Capt. Thos. Oliver, under whom he accompanied the expedition to the Walcheren, and commanded the boats at the cutting-out of a vessel from under a very severe fire of the enemy's batteries at Etaples —13 Jan. 1810, to the Scipion 74, flag-ship of Hon. Robt. Stopford, in which he co-operated in the reduction of Java—and, 24 Nov. 1812, again as First-Lieutenant (after six months of half pay) to the Griffon sloop, Capt. Geo. Barne Trollope, stationed in the Downs, where he cruized until Dec. 1813. He accepted his present rank 13 Sept. 1844.

Commander Magin married, 6 April, 1815, Elizabeth, daughter of Rich. Magin, Esq., of Greenhill House, co. Down, by whom he has issue five children. Agent—J. Hinxman.

MAGUIRE. (Lieutenant, 1840.)

Rochfort Maguire entered the Navy (from the Royal Naval College) 12 Nov. 1830; passed his examination in 1835; and in consideration of his services as Mate of the Wasp 16, Capt. Geo. Mansel, during the operations on the coast of Syria, where he was severely wounded at the capture of Sidon, and behaved most gallantly,* was promoted to the rank of Lieutenant 28 Sept. 1840. His appointments have since been—23 Jan. 1841, to the Vernon 50, Capt. Wm. Walpole, stationed in the Mediterranean, whence he returned in the early part of 1844—30 Nov. in the latter year, as Additional, to the Agincourt 72, flag-ship of Sir Thos. John Cochrane in the East Indies—and 10 Feb. 1845, as Senior, to the Herald 26, Capt. Henry Kellett, now employed on Surveying-service in the Pacific. Agents—Messrs. Ommanney.

MAINGAY. (Commander, 1821. f-p., 19; h-p., 28.)

Henry Maingay was born 26 Oct. 1785, in Guernsey, and died 22 Aug. 1846, at Stoke, Devonport. He was first son of the late John Maingy, Esq., of the island of Guernsey, and cousin of the present Commander Peter Maingay, R.N.

This officer entered the Navy, in the summer of 1799, as Fst.-cl. Vol., on board the Cæsar 80, Capt. Jahleel Brenton, bearing the flag of Sir Jas. Saumarez, under whom he fought in the actions of 6 and 12 July, 1801, off Algeciras and in the Gut of Gibraltar. The Cæsar being paid off in Aug. 1802, he next, between the following Oct. and Feb. 1806, served as Midshipman, in the Mediterranean and Channel, on board the Révolutionnaire and Decade frigates, Capts. Walter Locke and Wm. Geo. Rutherford, Speedwell, Lieut.-Commander Wm. Robertson, and Charwell, Capt. Dumaresq. He was confirmed a Lieutenant (after having acted for some months as such in the Cerberus, Tourterelle, and Squirrel, Capts. Selby, Marshall, and Shortland, on the West India and Halifax stations) 17 Sept. 1806; and was subsequently appointed—in the course of 1807, to the Mermaid 32, Capts. Aiskew Paffard Hollis, and, as First-Lieutenant, to the Primrose and Racehorse sloops, Capts. Jas. Mein and Wm. Fisher—28 March, 1808, to the Victory 100, flag-ship of Sir Jas. Saumarez in the Baltic—15 Jan. and 9 June, 1813, again as Senior, to the Fylla 20 and Eridanus 36, Capts. Henry Prescott and Wm. Paterson, with whom he served in the Channel until paid off in Oct. 1815—8 March, 1816, in a similar capacity, to the Spencer 76, which ship, commanded at Plymouth by Capt. Wm. Robert Broughton, was put out of commission 31 Aug. 1818—and, 5 July, 1821, still as First-Lieutenant, to the Royal George yacht, Capt. Hon. Sir Chas. Paget. On 14 of the ensuing Dec. Mr. Maingay, after having accompanied Geo. IV. on his visits to Ireland and Hanover, was promoted to the rank of Commander. He did not again go afloat.

He married, 26 Oct. 1818, Harriet, fourth daughter of the Rev. W. Smith, formerly Rector of Meavy, Devon.

MAINGAY. (Commander, 1815. f-p., 14; h-p., 33.)

Peter Maingay, born 16 Dec. 1784, at Newton Bushel, co. Devon, is son of Peter Maingy, Esq., of the island of Guernsey; and first-cousin of the late Commander Jas. Maingay, R N.

This officer entered the Navy, 1 Sept. 1800, as Midshipman, on board L'Impétueux 74, Capt. Sir Edw. Pellew, in which ship he accompanied an expedition to Vigo, and was employed off Brest and Rochefort until April, 1802; during the latter months of which year we find him serving in the Channel with Capt. Edw. Bass, of the Gannet sloop. In March, 1803, he rejoined Sir E. Pellew on board the Tonnant 80, and in the following year, after having been engaged in the blockade of Ferrol, he sailed with him in the Culloden 74 for the East Indies, whence in 1805 he returned to England in the Trident 64, flag-ship of Vice-Admiral Peter Rainier. He then became attached in succession to the San Josef 110, bearing the flag in the Channel of Sir Chas. Cotton, Audacious 74, Capt. Thos. Le Marchant Gosselin (under whom he

* *Vide* Gaz. 1840, p. 2604.

went in pursuit of Jerome Buonaparte to the West Indies, and was present in a hurricane which dismasted the ship), and San Josef again, commanded by Capt. John Conn as Flag-Captain to Sir Jas. Saumarez off Guernsey. In April and July, 1807, Mr. Maingay was nominated Acting-Lieutenant of the Barfleur and Dreadnought 98's, Capts. Sir Joseph Sidney Yorke and Wm. Lechmere; and on 11 Sept. in the same year he was confirmed into the Racehorse 18, Capt. Wm. Fisher, stationed, as were the two ships last named, in the Channel. His succeeding appointments were—24 Dec. 1807, a second time to the Audacious, in which ship he escorted the army under Sir John Moore to and from Gottenborg, accompanied that officer and Lieut.-Generals Sir Harry Burrard and Sir John Hope to the shores of Portugal, and assisted in embarking the army after the battle of Corunna —21 April, 1809, as Senior, to La Nymphe 36, Capts. Hon. Josceline Percy and Edw. Sneyd Clay, under the latter of whom he was wrecked in a gale at the entrance of the Frith of Forth, 18 Dec. 1810—1 May, 1811, to the Argo 44, Capt. Fred. Warren, lying at Spithead—27 July following, and for a short time in 1812, to the Swiftsure 74, and Rainbow 26, Capts. Temple Hardy and Gardiner Henry Guion, both in the Mediterranean—4 Sept. in the latter year, to the Success 32, *armée-en-flûte*, Capt. Thos. Barclay, stationed at first on the coast of Spain, and then in the Chesapeake, where he had command of the boats on an occasion in which they were cut up by the musketry of the enemy, whose fire killed the coxswain in his (Mr. Maingay's) own boat—24 Nov. 1813, to the Harlequin 18, Capt. Wm. Kempthorne, employed at Sheerness—20 April, 1814, to the Hermes 20, Capt. Hon. Henry Wm. Percy, which vessel, after 25 of her men had been killed and 24 wounded in an unsuccessful attack upon Fort Bowyer, Mobile, was set on fire and destroyed in order to prevent her falling into the hands of the Americans, 15 Sept. 1814—and 11 May, 1815 (having previously united in the operations against New Orleans), to the Vengeur 74, Capt. Tristram Robt. Ricketts, attached to the force off Brest. He was advanced to the rank he at present holds on 13 of the ensuing June; and was next, from 6 July, 1830, until 1833, employed as an Inspecting Commander in the Coast Guard. He has not been since able to procure an appointment.

Commander Maingay married, in March, 1818, Emeline, fourth daughter of the late John Carne, Esq., of Falmouth, co. Cornwall. Agents—Messrs. Chard.

MAINWARING. (Lieutenant, 1814. f-p., 17; h-p., 26.)

Benjamin Mainwaring, born 5 April, 1794, is brother of Capt. Edw. R. P. Mainwaring, R.N.

This officer entered the Navy, 21 Sept. 1804, as A.B., on board the Téméraire 98, Capt. Eliab Harvey, and on 21 Oct. 1805 was present in the action off Cape Trafalgar, where that ship occupied a position next astern of the Victory, and enacted a most distinguished part. In March, 1806, he became Midshipman of the Tonnant 80, bearing the flag of the last-named officer, and afterwards of Hon. Michael de Courcy, off Cadiz; and he next, between July 1808 and May 1814, served in the St. George 98, successive flag-ship in the Baltic and Channel of Rear-Admirals E. Harvey, Fras. Pickmore, and Robt. Carthew Reynolds, Cordelia 10, commanded by Capt. Thos. Fortescue Kennedy on the Downs station, and Revenge 74, bearing the flag in the Mediterranean of Sir John Gore. During the period he continued in the latter ship he served in her boats and assisted in cutting out two privateers from under the enemy's batteries on the coast of Catalonia.* He was confirmed a Lieutenant (after having acted for a few weeks as such) in the Trident receiving-ship at Malta, Capts. Rich. Budd Vincent and Chas. Hope Reid, 19 July, 1814. He came home in the early part of 1816, and was lastly, from 26 July, 1831, until 1836, employed in the Coast Guard.

Lieut. Mainwaring married, 6 Jan. 1819, Miss Mary Milbon.

* *Vide Gaz.* 1814, p. 124.

MAINWARING. (Captain, 1841. f-p., 33; h-p., 15.)

Edward Reeves Philip Mainwaring, born 16 June, 1788, is eldest son of the late Edw. Mainwaring, Esq., who served as an officer during the first American war, and who eventually obtained a considerable grant of land as an acknowledgment for the services he had rendered in raising a company of loyalists at his own expense. His family is a branch of that of Mainwaring of Whitmore, co. Stafford, now represented by Capt. Rowland Mainwaring, R.N. He is brother of Lieut. Benj. Mainwaring R.N. Another of his brothers, Senior Major of the 51st Regt., served in most of the Peninsular actions and was present at Waterloo; a third, a Captain in the 22nd Regt., saw much service in the Persian Gulf, in Ava, and at Hyderabad, and was twice wounded; a fourth, Charles, a Captain in the 47th Regt., died, from the effects of cholera, at Calcutta; and a fifth, Edwin, a Lieutenant in the 1st Regt., died at Madras. One of his uncles, Capt. Jemmett Mainwaring, R.N., commanded the Babet 20 when that vessel foundered with all on board in the West Indies in 1801; and another, Lieut.-General Mainwaring, who died in 1842, served in 1809 at the siege of Flushing, where, with two companies of the 51st and two of the 82nd Regt., he repulsed the French on the occasion of a *sortie* made by them, taking 600 of their number prisoners, and capturing 2 9-pounders.

This officer entered the Navy, in the summer of 1799, as Fst.-cl. Vol. on board the Roebuck 44, Capt. Wm. Buchannan, and after accompanying the expedition to Egypt, where he was employed at the landing of the troops, removed as Midshipman, in Nov. 1801, to the Haerlem 64, commanded at first by Capt. Buchannan and next by Capts. Jas. Murray Northey and John G. Saville. He subsequently, between Jan. 1803 and Aug. 1806, served on the North Sea and Mediterranean stations in the Caroline 36, Capt. Benj. Wm. Page, Raisonnable 64, Capt. Wm. Hotham, and Queen 98, Capts. Manley Dixon and Fras. Pender, bearing the flag latterly of Lord Collingwood. He then became Acting-Lieutenant of the Espoir sloop, Capt. Henry Hope, also in the Mediterranean; and on 11 June, 1807, he was confirmed into the Plantagenet 74, Capts. Thos. Eyles and Robt. Lloyd. Continuing in that ship until paid off in April, 1815, he served in her in the Baltic, and on the North American and West India stations; and on one occasion, when off New York, was sent with two boats in pursuit of a letter-of-marque, the *Rapid*, carrying 1 long 24-pounder, with small arms and a crew of 40 men, which vessel, after pulling for 11 hours in a calm, he succeeded in capturing in so gallant a manner as to elicit the thanks of the Commander-in-Chief Sir John Borlase Warren. His succeeding appointments were—4 Nov. 1818,* as a Supernumerary, to the Severn Coast Blockade ship, Capt. Wm. M'Culloch, under whom he served until Sept. 1820—1 Aug. 1821, as First, to the Ramillies 74, Capt. Edw. Brace, lying at Portsmouth—and 31 May, 1823, to the Ganges 84,† to which ship (at the particular request of her successive Captains, E. Brace and Patrick Campbell, and of Rear-Admiral Robt. Waller Otway, who hoisted his flag on board her) he continued attached, in the capacity last mentioned, on the West India, Home, and Brazilian stations, until advanced to the rank of Commander 27 May, 1826. He was afterwards employed—from June 1827 until 1830, and again from 20 March, 1832, until 1835, in the Coast Guard ser-

* For some time prior to the above date he had had command of a West Indiaman.

† The Ganges, through Mr. Mainwaring's exertions, was got ready for sea with so much rapidity, that Capt. Brace was induced to bring his name in an especial manner under the notice of the First Lord of the Admiralty.

vice—and from 7 April, 1839, until paid off in June, 1841, in command of the ELECTRA 18, in South America. He attained his present rank 23 Nov. 1841, but has not been since able to procure an appointment.

Capt. Mainwaring married, 1 Oct. 1827, Elizabeth, daughter of the Rev. M. Hill, Rector of Snailwell, Cambridgeshire, and a descendant of the Right Rev. Dr. Edm. Gibson, Lord Bishop of London, by whom he has issue two sons and one daughter.

MAINWARING. (CAPTAIN, 1830. F-P., 20; H-P., 32.)

ROWLAND MAINWARING, born 31 Dec. 1783, is eldest surviving son of Rowland Mainwaring, Esq., of Four Oaks, co. Warwick, a Field Officer, by Jane, daughter of Capt. Latham, R.N. He is a cousin of the present Rear-Admiral Mainwaring; and is the representative of an ancient Staffordshire family, settled for many centuries at Whitmore Hall, near Newcastle-under-Lyne.

This officer entered the Navy, in May, 1795, on board the JUPITER, Capt. Wm. Lechmere, lying at Sheerness; and in the course of the same year became Midshipman of the SCIPIO 64, Capt. Robt. M'Doual, on the West India station, where, after serving for a short time with Capt. Fras. Laforey in the BEAULIEU frigate and GANGES 74, he joined, in the early part of 1796, the MAJESTIC 74, Capts. Geo. Blagden Westcott and Robt. Cuthbert, bearing the flag at first of Sir John Laforey. Subsequently to the battle of the Nile, on which occasion Capt. Westcott was killed, Mr. Mainwaring, in Oct. 1798, removed to the THALIA 36, Capt. Lord Henry Paulet, under whom he was further employed in the DEFENCE 74 on different European stations, until within a short period of his being made Lieutenant, 7 Dec. 1801, into the HARPY sloop, Capts. Chas. Worsley Boys and Edm. Heywood. His succeeding appointments were—4 Aug. 1802, to the LEDA 38, Capts. Geo. Hope, Jas. Hardy, and Robt. Honyman, by the latter of whom he was intrusted with the command of a boat charged with an explosion-machine in an attack upon the Boulogne flotilla—8 Nov. 1804, to the TERRIBLE 74, Capt. Lord Henry Paulet, which ship was totally dismasted in a hurricane while in pursuit, in the West Indies, of a French squadron under Jerome Buonaparte—7 Oct 1806, as First-Lieutenant, to the NARCISSUS 32, Capts. Chas. Malcolm and Hon. Fred. Wm. Aylmer—and 16 Aug. 1811, in a similar capacity, after nearly eight months of half-pay, to the MENELAUS 38, Capt. Sir Peter Parker. In the NARCISSUS Mr. Mainwaring assisted at the capture, 18 Aug. 1807, of the Spanish national ship *Cantela*, pierced for 12 guns, besides witnessing the reduction in April 1809 of the Saintes, near Guadeloupe, and co-operating in 1810 with the patriots on the north coast of Spain. During his servitude in the MENELAUS we find him repeatedly, in the course of 1812, obtaining the official notice of Sir Peter Parker—first, by the judgment and ability he exhibited in capturing, without loss, the *St. Josef*, a beautiful French brig, pierced for 16 guns, lying within pistol-shot of one battery, flanked by another, and also by musketry from the shore, near the Bay of Frejus*—next, by the attention and assistance he afforded on the occasion of the MENELAUS (together with the HAVANNAH and FURIEUSE frigates and PELORUS brig) being chased by the French Toulon fleet—a third time, by his admirable gallantry and good conduct when the MENELAUS, having pursued the French 40-gun frigate *Pauline* and 16-gun brig *Ecureuil* under the batteries in the vicinity of Toulon, once more effected a masterly retreat from the fleet that had come out to their protection, by passing through its line ahead of one 74, and astern of another—again, by the manner in which, under circumstances peculiarly honourable to him, he boarded and brought out the French xebec *La Paix*, mounting 2 long 6-pounders, with a complement of 30 men, from within pistol-shot of the towers of Terracina, under a galling fire—a fifth time, by his highly creditable behaviour in cutting out, under a heavy fire from the batteries in the river Mignone, near Civita Vecchia, the French letter-of-marque *St. Esprit*, pierced for 12 guns, but with only 2 6-pounders mounted*—and lastly, by his conspicuous gallantry in burning the enemy's vessels in the port of Méjan, Marseilles. In acknowledgment of his valour on so many occasions Mr. Mainwaring was awarded a second promotal commission dated 13 Aug. 1812, but he did not leave the MENELAUS until the commencement of the following Oct.; between which period and the autumn of 1813 he was successively invested by Sir Edw. Pellew with the command of the EDINBURGH 74, GORGON 44, hospital-ship at Malta, UNDAUNTED 38, EURYALUS 36, CALEDONIA 120, bearing that officer's own flag, and KITE and PAULINA sloops. While in command of the KITE he was stationed for the protection of British trade in the Archipelago, where he destroyed a French privateer, rescued a valuable merchantman which she had captured, and obtained from the Bey of Salonica a promise that in future no vessels of the same description should be equipped in his harbours. During his command of the PAULINA Capt. Mainwaring chased a large fast-sailing American privateer into the harbour of Tripoli, and effectually prevented her escape for a period of six weeks, until, indeed, the ratification of the treaty of peace with the United States had placed it out of her power to do further mischief. For this service he elicited the thanks of Rear-Admiral Sir Chas. Vinicombe Penrose. He was paid off in Nov. 1815, and has not been since afloat. On the accession of William IV. to the throne he was selected by Lord Melville as one of the old war-officers deserving of promotion, and he was accordingly posted by commission dated 22 July, 1830.

Capt. Mainwaring (a Magistrate and Deputy-Lieutenant for Staffordshire) married first, 31 Dec. 1810, Sophia Henrietta, only daughter of Major Duff, of the 26th Regt., and step-daughter of Rear-Admiral Geo. Tobin, by whom he had issue seven sons and two daughters; secondly, 15 Nov. 1826, Mary Ann, second daughter of John W. Clark, Esq., of Preshute, Wilts, who (at her death in 1834) left an only daughter; and thirdly, 11 Nov. 1836, Laura Maria Julia Walburga, only child of Colonel Florian Chevillard, formerly in the service of Napoleon Buonaparte, who died of wounds received in the battle of Leipzig. By the last-mentioned lady he has issue four sons. His eldest son, Rowland, died Midshipman of the WARSPITE 76, at Port Jackson, 27 Oct. 1826; and his next, Edward Pellew, is married to a sister-in-law of the Duke of Calabritto, and the Hon. Constantine Dillon, brother of Viscount Dillon.

MAINWARING. (REAR-ADMIRAL, 1846. F-P., 17; H-P., 37.)

THOMAS FRANCIS CHARLES MAINWARING, born in 1780, is eldest son of the late Chas. Henry Mainwaring, Esq., by Julia, daughter of the Rev. Philip Wroughton; and grand-nephew of Edw. Mainwaring, Esq., of Whitmore Hall, co. Stafford, whose grandson is the present Capt. Rowland Mainwaring, R.N. His only brother, George, an officer in the Royal Artillery, died in 1838.

This officer entered the Royal Naval Academy in Feb. 1793; and embarked, 5 Nov. 1796, as a Volunteer, on board the CLYDE 38, Capt. Chas. Cunningham. After serving for three years on the Home station he proceeded as Midshipman of the LANCASTER 64, flag-ship of Sir Roger Curtis, to the Cape of Good Hope, where, having previously acted for several months as Lieutenant, he was confirmed to that rank, 11 July, 1800, in the ADAMANT 50, Capt. Wm. Hotham. On his return to England about Dec. 1801, he joined the FISGUARD 38, Capts. Michael Seymour and Jas. Wallis; the latter of

* *Vide* Gaz. 1812, p. 781.

* *Vide* Gaz. 1812, p. 2017.

whom, in Sept. 1802, he accompanied into the NAIAD 38, commanded subsequently by Capt. Thos. Dundas, and employed as one of Lord Nelson's repeaters in the battle of Trafalgar. Being awarded a second promotal commission 21 Jan. 1806, Capt. Mainwaring assumed command, 23 Dec. following, of the TARTARUS fire-ship; and in Aug. 1807 was charged with the landing of the troops under Sir Arthur Wellesley in Wibeck Bay, preparatory to the investment of Copenhagen. In the early part of 1808 he removed to the VANGUARD 74, the first ship of her class that ever wintered in the Baltic. After he had commanded her for a period of six months he went back to the TARTARUS, in which vessel we find him, in 1810, sinking two French privateers off Pillau,* and then conveying Gustavus, the ex-King of Sweden, from Riga to England, under circumstances of a particularly difficult and singular nature. He was promoted for the latter service to the rank of Captain 27 Nov. 1810; and was intrusted, during the last two years of the war, with the command of the ROYAL GEORGE 100, on the Mediterranean station. He accepted his present rank 1 Oct. 1846.

Rear-Admiral Mainwaring married, first, in 1811, Mary Anne, daughter of Bacon Frank, Esq., of Campsall, near Doncaster; and (having been left a widower in 1840) secondly, 14 Dec. 1841, Cecilia Charlotte, only daughter of the late Dean of Durham and the Hon. Mrs. Hall. By his first wife he has issue.

MAITLAND, K.C.M.G., C.B. (REAR-ADMIRAL OF THE WHITE, 1841. F-P., 19; H-P., 33.)

THE HONOURABLE SIR ANTHONY MAITLAND, born 10 June, 1785, is second son of James, eighth Earl of Lauderdale, K.T., by Eleanor, only daughter of Anthony Todd, Esq.; brother (with Colonel Hon. John Maitland, who died in 1839) of the present Earl; nephew of Lieut.-General Hon. Sir Thos. Maitland, G.C.B., Governor of Malta and the Ionian Islands, who died in 1824; and cousin of the present Capt. Sir Thos. Maitland, R.N., Kt, C.B., and of Commanders James, Lewis, and William Heriot, Maitland, R.N.

This officer entered the Navy, 2 Oct. 1795, as Admiral's Servant, on board the VICTORY 100, Capt. Hon. Geo. Grey, on the books of which ship, bearing the flag in the Mediterranean of the late Earl St. Vincent, his name was borne until June, 1796. In Oct. 1798 he became Midshipman, under the same nobleman, in the VILLE DE PARIS 110; and he next, from Jan. 1801 until Dec. 1803, served with Capt. Sir John Gore in the TRITON and MEDUSA frigates. In the latter vessel, which bore the flag at the time of Lord Nelson, we find him particularly distinguishing himself and severely wounded in an attack made in Aug. 1801 on the Boulogne flotilla.† On leaving the MEDUSA he rejoined his Lordship, as a Supernumerary, on board the VICTORY, then again in the Mediterranean, where, in Aug. 1804, he was nominated Acting-Lieutenant of the CHILDERS sloop, Capt. Sir Wm. Bolton. He was confirmed a Lieutenant 2 Feb. 1805, and after officiating for some months in that capacity in the BLENHEIM 74, flag-ship in the East Indies of Sir Thos. Troubridge, was made Commander, 6 May, 1806, into the ARROGANT guard-ship at Bombay. He attained Post-rank 25 Sept. in the same year; and was next appointed—1 Aug. 1811, to the PIQUE 36, in which ship he was for four years and a half employed on the Downs, Lisbon, Brazilian, and West India stations, capturing, during that period, the *Hawk* American privateer, of 5 guns and 68 men—and 19 Feb. 1816, to the GLASGOW 50, part of the force engaged under Lord Exmouth at the bombardment of Algiers.‡ On 21 Aug. 1817, Capt. Maitland, who had paid the GLASGOW off in the preceding Nov., recommissioned that ship. He served in her in the Mediterranean until March, 1821, and has since been on half-pay. He acquired flag-rank 23 Nov. 1841.

The Rear-Admiral, who was nominated a C.B. for his conduct at Algiers, 19 Sept. 1816, and in 1832 created a Knight of the Order of St. Michael and St. George, sat for some time in Parliament as member for co. Berwick; of which shire he is now a Deputy-Lieutenant. In Aug. 1830 he was appointed a Naval Aide-de-Camp to King William IV.; and he continued to hold the same office under her present Majesty until the date of his promotion.

* *Vide* Gaz. 1810, p. 1663.

† *V.* Gaz. 1801, p. 1006. ‡ *V.* Gaz. 1816, p. 1792.

MAITLAND. (COMMANDER, 1836. F-P., 16; H-P., 13.)

JAMES MAITLAND, born 18 April, 1806, is second surviving son of the late Chas. Maitland, Esq., of Rankeilour, co. Fife, by Mary, eldest daughter of David Johnston, Esq., of Latheisk, in the same shire. He is brother of Commander Lewis Maitland, R.N.; nephew of the late Rear-Admiral Sir Fred. Lewis Maitland, K.C.B.,* who made him his heir; first-cousin of the present Commander Wm. Heriot Maitland, R.N.; and cousin also of Rear-Admiral Hon. Sir Anthony Maitland, C.B., K.C.M.G., and Capt. Sir Thos. Maitland, R.N., Kt., C.B. His grandfather, Hon. Fred. Lewis Maitland, a Captain in the R.N., was son of Charles, sixth Earl of Lauderdale, and had one brother, Richard, a Colonel in the Army, and another, John, a Lieutenant-Colonel in the R.M. He commanded the ELIZABETH 74 in Keppel and Rodney's actions, and afterwards captured a French 64-gun ship.

This officer entered the Navy, 22 Dec. 1818, as Fst.-cl. Vol., on board the VENGEUR 74, Capt. Fred. Lewis Maitland, and during the two following years was employed on the North Sea, South American, and Mediterranean stations. He then, until promoted to the rank of Lieutenant 10 July, 1826, served as Midshipman and Mate, again in South America, as also at Portsmouth and in the West Indies, in the AURORA 46, Capt. Henry Prescott, GANGES 84, Capt. Patrick Campbell, and ALLIGATOR 28. He next cruized for some months on the station last mentioned in the FERRET 10, Capt. Henry Gosset, and was subsequently appointed—18 Jan. 1828, to the TRIBUNE 42, Capts. John Wilson and John Alex. Duntze, attached to the force in the Pacific, whence he returned home at the close of 1831—17 Oct. 1832, to the PORTSMOUTH yacht, as Flag-Lieutenant to his uncle, Sir F. L. Maitland, Admiral-Superintendent at that port—and 2 Sept. 1834, in a similar capacity, to the THALIA 46, bearing the flag at the Cape of Good Hope of Rear-Admiral Patrick Campbell. He went on half-pay in the summer of 1835, and has not been since afloat. He acquired his present rank 9 May, 1836.

Commander Maitland (the Senior of his rank on the List of 1836) married, first, in March, 1836, Emma, daughter of Thos. Magne Willing, Esq., of Philadelphia; and (that lady dying in June, 1838) secondly, 20 Aug. 1840, Frances Harriet, daughter of the late Rich. Sam. Short, Esq., of Edlington Grove, Lincolnshire. AGENTS—Messrs. Stilwell.

MAITLAND. (COMMANDER, 1841. F-P., 19; H-P., 3.)

LEWIS MAITLAND, born 12 April, 1811, is brother of Commander Jas. Maitland, R.N.

* Sir Fred. Lewis Maitland was born in 1776. He served as Midshipman of the SOUTHAMPTON 32 in Lord Howe's action 1 June, 1794; was employed, while holding the rank of Commander, in the expedition to Egypt in 1801; attained Post-rank in the course of that year; and had commanded, during the late war, of the LOIRE and EMERALD frigates (*see* Capt. Charles Bertram), GOLIATH 58, BOYNE 98, and BELLEROPHON 74. In the ship last mentioned he had the honour of receiving Napoleon Buonaparte when he surrendered after the battle of Waterloo. During the peace he commanded the VENGEUR, GENOA, and WELLESLEY 74 s. He was nominated a C.B. in 1815; advanced to Flag-rank in July, 1830; and created a K C.B. in the following November. He filled the office of Admiral-Superintendent at Portsmouth from June, 1832, until July, 1837; and that of Commander-in-Chief in the East Indies from the latter period until the date of his death, 30 Nov. 1839.

This officer entered the Royal Naval College 23 Dec. 1825; and embarked, in March, 1827, as a Volunteer, on board the WELLESLEY 74, commanded by his uncle, Capt. Fred. Lewis Maitland, at first on the Lisbon, and then on the Mediterranean station, where, in July, 1830, two years after he had attained the rating of Midshipman, he removed to the WASP 18, Capt. Brunswick Popham. Towards the close of 1831, after he had served for a few months in the Channel and North Sea in the IMOGENE 28, Capt. Price Blackwood, he sailed for the East Indies in the MELVILLE 74, flag-ship of Sir John Gore. On his return in 1832 with the flag of Sir Edw. W. C. R. Owen in the SOUTHAMPTON 52, Capt. John Milligan Laws, we find him employed off Antwerp during the period of General Gérard's attack on the citadel of that place. He next, in Jan. 1833 (in March of which year he passed his examination), joined the CASTOR 36, Capt. Lord John Hay, with whom he served off Lisbon and on the north coast of Spain until Jan. 1836. On leaving the latter vessel Mr. Maitland was placed under the orders of Capt. Peter John Douglas in the MELVILLE 74, bearing the flag of Sir Peter Halkett in North America and the West Indies; and on again proceeding to the East Indies in the WELLESLEY 72, flag-ship of his relative Sir F. L. Maitland, he was by him nominated Lieutenant, in June, 1838, of the FAVORITE 18, Capt. Walter Croker—an act which the Admiralty sanctioned 15 Feb. 1839. Rejoining the WELLESLEY in the course of the same year in the capacity of Additional-Lieutenant, he served in her, under the broad pendant of Sir Gordon Bremer, at the capture of Chusan in July, 1840; after which, on becoming attached to the SAMARANG 28, Capt. Jas. Scott, he assisted in reducing the forts of the Boca Tigris, and in demolishing the works on the Canton river. He was also present, and gained the public acknowledgments of his Captain for the gallantry and zeal he displayed, at the forcing, by the NEMESIS steamer and the boats of the SAMARANG, of the inner passage from Macao to Whampoa; during their advance on which latter place the British, between 3 A.M. on 13 and 4 P.M. on 15 March, 1841, destroyed five forts, one battery, two military stations, and nine war-junks, in which collectively were 115 guns and 8 ginjalls.* On his return to England in the following summer he took up a Commander's commission dated 15 Feb. 1841. He has been employed, since 3 July, 1844, in the Coast Guard service.

He married, 23 Nov. 1841, Henrietta Louisa, widow of the late W. Northage, Esq., jun., and second daughter of the late Sir John H. Newbolt, Chief Justice of Madras. AGENTS—Messrs. Stilwell.

MAITLAND, Kt., C.B. (CAPTAIN, 1837.)

SIR THOMAS MAITLAND, born in 1803, is only son of Hon. Wm. Mordaunt Maitland, a General in the Army, by his first wife, Mary, widow of John Travers, Esq., of Fir Grove, co. Cork, and daughter of the Rev. Rich. Orpen, of Killowen. He is grandson of James, seventh Earl of Lauderdale, a Lieutenant-Colonel in the Army; and first-cousin of Rear-Admiral Hon. Sir Anthony Maitland, C.B., K.C.M.G.

This officer entered the Navy 22 Sept. 1816, and was made Lieutenant, 16 May, 1823, into the EURYALUS 42, Capt. Augustus Wm. Jas. Clifford. His next appointments were, 20 Dec. 1825, and 1 March, 1826, to the SUPERB 78, Capt. Henry Hill, guard-ship at Portsmouth, and GANGES 84, fitting for the flag of Sir Robt. Waller Otway, Commander-in-Chief in South America. Obtaining a second promotal commission 30 April, 1827, he successively assumed command, 14 June, 1832, and 4 April, 1835, of the SPARROWHAWK 18 and TWEED 20. In the former vessel, which he paid off 7 May, 1833, Capt. Maitland brought home 589,405 Mexican dollars and 42 bales of cochineal; in the TWEED, the command whereof he retained until posted, 10 Jan. 1837, he served during the civil war on the north coast of Spain, and was in consequence presented with the Cross of Charles III. On 19 June in the year last mentioned we find him nominated Captain of the WELLESLEY 72, in which ship he continued employed under the flags of Sir Fred. Lewis Maitland and Sir Gordon Bremer, until paid off in the summer of 1842. In 1838 he commanded the seamen and marines landed for the purpose of quelling an insurrection on the coast of Malabar; he participated, in 1839, in the operations on the coast of Sinde and in the Persian Gulf; and during the hostilities in China he obtained mention for his zeal and alacrity at the capture of Chusan in July, 1840, and for the valuable assistance he afforded Sir Gordon Bremer at the reduction of Tycocktow, 7 Jan. 1841*—was present with H.M. Plenipotentiary at a formal meeting which was held with the Chinese Commissioner on 26 of the same month†—again acquired the public thanks of Sir G. Bremer for the cordial aid he afforded him in the action which preceded the capture of the Bogue Forts, 26 Feb.‡—had charge of the WELLESLEY's boats during the original advance of the British towards Canton§—commanded the first naval battalion, consisting of 11 officers and 172 of other ranks, at the storming of the heights in the vicinity of that city during the operations which led to its re-capture‖—elicited notice for the admirable manner in which he placed the WELLESLEY (within 400 yards of the principal battery) in the attack upon Amoy, 26 Aug.¶—and in Oct. of the same year (1841) was further praised for his skill, zeal, and ability at the reduction of Chusan and Chinghae.** For these services Capt. Maitland was nominated a C.B. 29 June, 1841; and in 1843 invested with the honour of Knighthood. He has been in command, since 10 Nov. 1846, of the AMERICA 50, on the coast of Portugal.

Sir Thos. Maitland is a Deputy-Lieutenant for co. Berwick. He married, 7 Feb. 1828, at Rio Janeiro, Amelia, daughter of the late Wm. Young, Esq., and by that lady has issue. AGENTS—Messrs. Stilwell.

MAITLAND. (COMMANDER, 1840.)

WILLIAM MAITLAND died in Oct. 1846, in command of H.M. steam-sloop SPITEFUL.

This officer entered the Navy 4 Feb. 1819; passed his examination in 1825; obtained his first commission 13 June, 1827; and was appointed, on the Mediterranean station—16 March, 1831, to the BARHAM 50, Capt. Hugh Pigot—21 March, 1834, to the BRITANNIA 120, Capt. Peter Rainier, which ship was paid off in the early part of 1835—and, 12 April, 1839, as First-Lieutenant, to the BENBOW 72, Capt. Houston Stewart. For his services in the latter ship, at the attack upon Tortosa (where he landed and obtained warm praise for his very gallant conduct††) and the bombardment of St. Jean d'Acre, he was promoted to the rank of Commander 4 Nov. 1840. On 14 Dec. 1842 he assumed command of the SPITEFUL steam-sloop, which vessel, in July, 1846, bore the flag of Rear-Admiral Sir Thos. John Cochrane during an expedition against the Sultan of Borneo, whose forts and batteries in the river Brune were all destroyed.‡‡ AGENTS—Hallett and Robinson.

MAITLAND. (COMMANDER, 1842. F-P., 12; H-P., 3.)

WILLIAM HERIOT MAITLAND, born 3 July, 1819, is second son of Jas. Maitland, Esq., of Ramorny, by Margaret, daughter of Wm. Dalgleish, Esq., of Scots-craig; and first-cousin of Commander Jas. Maitland, R.N.

This officer entered the Navy, 16 Oct. 1832, as Fst.-cl. Vol., on board the CASTOR 36, Capt. Lord John Hay, and in July, 1836, after having been employed on the Home station and off the north coast of Spain during the civil war, removed as Midship-

* *Vide* Gaz. 1841, pp. 1507, 1509.

* *Vide* Gaz. 1840, p. 2991, and Gaz. 1841, p. 1162.
† *V.* Gaz. 1841, p. 1496.
‡ *V.* Gaz. 1841, p. 1498.
§ *V.* Gaz. 1841, p. 1501.
‖ *V.* Gaz. 1841, p. 2496.
¶ *V.* Gaz. 1842, p. 82.
** *V.* Gaz. 1842, p. 293-6.
†† *V.* Gaz. 1840, p. 2605.
‡‡ *V.* Gaz. 1846, p. 3438.

man to the Vanguard 80, commanded in the Mediterranean by Capts. Hon. Duncombe Pleydell Bouverie and Sir Thos. Fellowes. Joining next, in June, 1837, the Wellesley 72, bearing the flag of his uncle, Sir Fred. Lewis Maitland, he served as Mate of that ship at the taking of Currachee in Feb. 1839, and in her boats in a skirmish at Bushehr, in the Persian Gulf, in April of the same year. His appointments as Lieutenant, a rank he attained on 6 of the month last mentioned, appear to have been —10 July, 1839, to the Hyacinth 18, Capt. Wm. Warren—23 June, 1840, again to the Wellesley, Capt. Thos. Maitland—16 Oct. 1841, to the command of the Algerine 10—and, 20 Sept. 1842, to the Blonde 42, Capt. Thos. Bourchier. In the Hyacinth Mr. Maitland was in action with the enemy's junks at Chuenpee; and, when in the Wellesley, he assisted in demolishing the enemy's fortifications at the latter place—landed, during the attack on the Bogue forts, in command, with Mr. W. H. Hall of the Nemesis, of a party of seamen and marines, and took possession of Little Tycocktow, spiking at the same time its guns, and destroying a neighbouring encampment—and united in the operations against Canton, Amoy, Chusan, Chinghae,* and Ningpo. In the attack upon Amoy his skull was fractured and he was otherwise much injured. During his command of the Algerine we find him particularly mentioned for his conduct at the capture of Chapoo, where, after he had assisted in landing the troops, he accompanied them on their advance, and with his own hands slew two mandarins.† He was also employed in the same vessel in surveying the Yang-tse-kiang, and was present in action with the Woosung batteries, and at the pacification of Nanking.‡ On his return to England in the Blonde in March, 1843, Mr. Maitland found that his services had procured him a Commander's commission dated 23 Dec. 1842. His last appointment was, 31 Jan. 1846, to the command of the Electra 14, fitting for the North America and West India station, where he remained until his health obliged him to invalid, in March, 1847. Agents—Messrs Stilwell.

MALCOLM, Kt. (Vice-Admiral of the Blue, 1847. f-p., 26; h-p., 30.)

Sir Charles Malcolm, born 5 Sept. 1782, is tenth and youngest son of the late Geo. Malcolm, Esq., of Burnfoot, co. Dumfries (a descendant of the Malcolms of Lahore and Innertiel), by Margaret, sister of Admiral Sir Thos. Pasley, who held a Rear-Admiral's command, and was raised to the dignity of a Baronet for his gallantry, in the action of 1 June, 1794. He is brother of Sir Jas. Malcolm, K.C.B., Colonel of Marines, who was with Lord Howe at the relief of Gibraltar, and earned distinction during the late war in Spain and North America—of Admiral Sir Pulteney Malcolm, G.C.B., G.C.M.G.,§—and of the late Sir John Malcolm, G.C.B., a General Officer in the Army, who died in 1833. Another of his brothers, George, a Lieutenant in the R.N., died at St. Domingo in 1794. Sir Charles is first-cousin of Vice-Admiral Sir Thos. Briggs, G.C.M.G.

This officer (whose name had been borne from 10 Sept. 1791 until Aug. 1792 on the books of the Vengeance 74, bearing the broad pendant of his uncle, Commodore Pasley, and from April to Dec. 1793 on those of the Penelope 32, Capt. Bartholomew Sam. Rowley) embarked, in April, 1795, as Midshipman, on board the Fox 32, commanded by his brother, Capt. Pulteney Malcolm, and fitting for the East India station;* where, in Jan. 1798, he was Master's Mate of that vessel, when, in company with La Sybille 38, she entered the Spanish harbour of Manilla under French disguise, and (notwithstanding that there were lying there three ships of the line and three frigates) assisted in capturing seven boats, 200 men, and a large quantity of ammunition and implements of war. In the course of the same month we find Mr. Malcolm present in an action with the enemy's batteries at Samboangon, in the island of Magindanao, in which the loss sustained by the two ships amounted to 6 killed and 16 wounded. Accompanying his brother in June, 1798, into the Suffolk 74, bearing the flag of Vice-Admiral Peter Rainier, he was promoted, 12 Jan. 1799, to a Lieutenancy in that ship. He continued in her until nominated Acting-Commander, 3 Oct. 1801, of the Albatross sloop—an appointment which the Admiralty confirmed 28 May, 1802. On his arrival home in the spring of 1803, as Acting-Captain of the Eurydice 24, he found that he had been officially posted on 29 of the preceding Dec. His succeeding appointments were—6 April, 1804, for four months, to the Raisonnable 64, stationed in the North Sea—17 Sept. 1806, to the Narcissus 32—17 June, 1809, to the Rhin 38, in which ship he continued until Aug. 1815—15 Sept. 1817, to the Sybille 44, fitting for the flag of Sir Home Popham, Commander-in-Chief in the West Indies, whence he invalided in Feb. 1819—and 8 July, 1822, and 30 June, 1826, to the William and Mary and Royal Charlotte yachts, lying at Dublin for the purpose of attending on the Lord Lieutenant, the Marquess Wellesley, a service on which he continued until 28 Nov. 1827. On the night of 30 Oct. 1807 Capt. Malcolm, then in the Narcissus, made a desperate attack with four boats on a convoy of 30 sail, lying in Couquet Roads, near Brest, under the protection of several heavy batteries, a cutter, and two gun-brigs, but was eventually obliged to retire with a loss of 7 men killed, and 16, including himself slightly, wounded. Towards the close of the same year it was his fortune to be the chief instrument, as testified by an address from the merchants, of preserving the property of the British at Oporto from falling into the hands of the French. So great was his anxiety on the occasion to afford whatever assistance he could, that, although on the point of starting on a cruize which promised to be most productive, he relinquished that intention, and, when ordered to England with a convoy of 49 sail, not only received on board the plate and other valuable property belonging to the merchants, but actually took charge of 180 pipes of wine—a service of which the Admiralty

* *Vide* Gaz. 1842, p. 396.

† In allusion to the conduct of Lieut. Maitland on the occasion, Sir Wm. Parker, in his despatch, expresses himself thus:—"He bids fair to rival the gallantry of his lamented uncle, that bright ornament of his profession, the late Sir Frederic Maitland."—*Vide* Gaz. 1842, p. 3693.

‡ *Vide* Gaz. 1842, pp. 3397, 3404.

§ Sir Pulteney Malcolm was born 20 Feb. 1768, and entered the Navy, 20 Oct. 1778, on board the Sybil frigate, commanded by his uncle, Capt. Pasley. He was promoted (after having shared in an action between Commodore Johnstone and a French squadron under M. de Suffrein in Porto Praya Bay) to the rank of Lieutenant 3 March, 1783; was made Commander 3 April, 1794; and posted 22 Oct. in the same year. Between the latter period and that of his advancement to Flag-rank, 4 Dec. 1813, he held command in succession of the Fox 32, Suffolk and Victorious 74's, flag-ships of Vice-Admiral Rainier, Royal Sovereign 100, Kent, Renown, Donegal, and Royal Oak 74's, and San Josef 110. In those ships his general activity, and the skill and judgment he exhibited on all occasions, gained him much distinction. He commanded the Donegal in Nelson's pursuit of the combined squadrons to the West Indies; also in Sir John Duckworth's action (for which he obtained a gold medal and a vase from the Patriotic Society, valued at 100*l*.); and at the destruction of the French shipping in Aix Roads. In the Kent he officiated as Captain of the Fleet under Lord Keith. During the latter portion of the operations on the Coast of North America he held a Rear-Admiral's command, and was employed in that capacity in the attack upon New Orleans. In the summer of 1815, Sir Pulteney (who had been nominated in 1812 a Colonel of Royal Marines, and in Jan. 1815 a K.C.B.) was appointed to the command of a Naval force ordered to co-operate with the Duke of Wellington and the allied armies. He next, from the spring of 1816 until the close of 1817, commanded in chief on the St. Helena station; and, attaining the rank of Vice-Admiral 19 July, 1821, was further employed as Commander-in-Chief in the Mediterranean from June, 1828, until June, 1831, in the Downs and on the coast of Holland with the combined fleets of France and Spain under his orders in 1832, and again in the Mediterranean from May, 1833, until April, 1834. He was created a G.C.M.G. in 1829, a G.C.B. in 1833, and a full Admiral 10 Jan. 1837. He died 20 July, 1838.

* The Fox, in Nov. 1796, conveyed the present Duke of Wellington, then Colonel Wellesley, of the 33rd Regt., from the Cape of Good Hope to India.

marked its approbation. After much active employment in the Channel he sailed, in the early part of 1809, for the West Indies, with intelligence for Sir Alex. Cochrane of a French squadron having proceeded thither; and in April of that year he gained the warmest acknowledgments of Major-General Maitland for his conduct on shore at the capture of the Saintes islands.* After their subjugation the NARCISSUS returned home with General Maitland, Governor of Grenada, and General Montgomery, Governor of Dominica. In 1812-13, at which time he had command of the RHIN, Capt. Malcolm was employed in active co-operation with the patriots on the north coast of Spain, under the orders of Sir Geo. Collier and Sir Home Popham; particularly at the attack upon Lequeytio, during which he had command of the island of St. Nicholas, situated near that town;† at Guetaria, where he landed for the purpose of reducing the town, but was compelled, by the sudden appearance of more than 2000 French troops, to retire, with the loss of 3 Midshipmen and 29 men taken prisoners;‡ also at Santander, where he again went on shore, took possession of a fort, and rendered much important service; and at the defence of Castro. In the spring of 1813 he was ordered with convoy to the West Indies; and in the course of the following year he was sent, with the PIQUE 36 and MOSQUITO brig under his orders, to cruize after an American squadron on the Brazilian station. On 18 July, 1815, Capt. Malcolm, who was at that time Senior officer on the coast of Bretagne, and had been joined by the MENELAUS and HAVANNAH frigates, performed a very neat exploit in landing at the head of a body of seamen and marines from the three ships at Corrijou, near Abervrach, where he stormed and carried a fort, and, with the assistance of the FLY and FERRET sloops, who had followed, effected the capture of an armed cutter, a praam-brig, and a gun-vessel, together with a convoy reposing in the harbour under their protection. This affair was the last of the sort achieved during the war. While in the NARCISSUS and RHIN, Capt. Malcolm, who appears to have been in frequent command of small flying squadrons, contrived to take, independently of a whole host of merchantmen, upwards of 20 privateers and other armed vessels, carrying 168 guns and 1059 men.§ On leaving the ROYAL CHARLOTTE as above, Sir Chas. Malcolm (he had received the honour of Knighthood at the hands of the Irish Viceroy) was appointed Superintendent of the Bombay Marine; the duties of which important post he continued to discharge for ten years, faithfully and zealously watching over and advancing the interests of the honourable and scientific corps under his command, and ably assisting Government in his station. During that period, as we gain from the general order issued by the Governor in Council on the occasion of his being succeeded by the present Sir Robt. Oliver, he proved eminently successful in elevating the character of the service, instituted many extensive and important surveys, was the means by his judicious instructions and suggestions of making numerous interesting and valuable additions to geography and navigation, and rendered himself conspicuous by his exertions in the introduction and establishment of steam-navigation in the Red Sea. Indeed he effected a complete revulsion in the administration of naval affairs, converting the system as it had pre-existed into what is now recognised as the Indian Navy, a name he was himself the first to impart. His promotion to the rank of Rear-Admiral took place 10 Jan. 1837, and to that of Vice-Admiral 28 April, 1847.

Sir Chas. Malcolm married, first, 4 June, 1808, his cousin, Magdalene, daughter of Chas. Pasley, Esq.; and, secondly, 11 April, 1829, Elmira Riddell, youngest daughter of Major-General Shaw. By his first marriage he has issue one daughter, and by his second three sons—the eldest of whom, George John, a Midshipman R.N., entered the service in June, 1842, and was in the FIREBRAND with the present Capt. Jas. Hope in the expedition up the Parana in Nov. 1845. AGENTS—Messrs. Stilwell.

* *Vide* Gaz. 1809, p. 780. † *V.* Gaz. 1812, p. 1278.

‡ *V.* Gaz. 1812, p. 1441.

§ Including the *Cantela* Spanish man-of-war schooner, pierced for 12 guns, but carrying only 6, with 25 men, captured 19 Aug 1807 (*Vide* Gaz. 1807, p. 1125); the *Aventura* letter-of-marque of 10 guns and 43 men; and the privateers *Navarrois* of 16 guns and 132 men, *San Joseph* of 14 guns and 68 men, *La Comtesse de Montalivet* of 14 guns and 57 men, *La Courageuse* of 14 guns and 70 men, and *Decatur* of 223 tons.

MALDEN. (LIEUT., 1818. F-P., 14; H-P., 24.

CHARLES ROBERT MALDEN was born, 9 Aug. 1797, at Putney, co. Surrey. His father, a medical man and general practitioner of repute, resided at Malden, in Essex, a place from which his family, who had been seated there for many generations, derives its name.

This officer entered the Navy, 22 June, 1809, as a Supernumerary, on board the DILIGENCE Navy transport, Master-Commander Alex. Black, in order to await an opportunity of joining the ACASTA 40, Capt. Philip Beaver, from which latter vessel he eventually, in Oct. of the same year, removed to the SCIPION 74, bearing the flag in the Bay of Biscay of Rear-Admiral Hon. Robt. Stopford. Being again, in June, 1810, placed under the orders of Capt. Beaver in the NISUS 38, and awarded the rating of Midshipman, he sailed for the Cape of Good Hope and the East Indies, and assisted, while on those stations, at the reduction of the Mauritius and the island of Java. Soon after the commencement of the war with the United States, he was sent home in a captured American Indiaman. On the NISUS being paid off in May, 1814,* Mr. Malden (he had only rejoined her a short time previously, having been intermediately employed on board the PRINCE 98, guard-ship at Spithead) became attached to the TRAAVE 38, *armée en flûte*, Capts. Rowland Money and John Codd. In the following Sept. we find him serving on shore as Aide-de-Camp to Capt. Money in the attack upon Baltimore; and in Dec. of the same year accompanying the expedition against New Orleans, where he suffered much from exposure in open boats, and was for three weeks deprived by the frost of the use of his feet—an infliction of which he still feels the effects. We may add that during a portion of the operations he again officiated as Aide-de-Camp to Capt. Money. Quitting the TRAAVE in Aug. 1816, Mr. Malden (who about that period passed his examination) next, in March, 1817, joined the TAGUS 38, Capt. Jas. Whitley Deans Dundas, on the Mediterranean station, where the favourable report made by that officer to the Admiralty of his proficiency in the science of surveying led to his being confirmed a Lieutenant (after he had acted for a few weeks as such on board the ALBION 74, flag-ship of Sir Chas. Vinicombe Penrose) in the AID surveying-vessel, Capt. Wm. Henry Smyth, 1 Sept. 1818. He continued under the latter officer until Jan. 1821, and was lastly appointed—14 Sept. 1823, to the SHAMROCK, another surveying-vessel, commanded in the Channel and on the coast of Ireland by Capt. Martin White—and in the summer of 1824 (in the capacity of Supernumerary-Lieutenant and Head-Surveyor), to the BLONDE 42, Capt. Lord Byron, fitting for the Pacific, whither he escorted the remains of the late King and Queen of the Sandwich Islands. During the voyage an island was discovered in lat. 4° 0′ S., long. 155° 0′ W., to which Lord Byron gave the name of *Malden*, in compliment to the subject of the present memoir; who, pending his sojourn among the Sandwich Islands, surveyed the south coast and harbour of Honorura, and also an important harbour in the island of Ha-wai-i (or Owhyhee) capable of containing five or six sail-of-the-line in perfect security, which had entirely escaped the observation both of Cook and Vancouver, and to which he affixed the name of *Byron's Bay*. He was discharged on the return of the BLONDE to England in the spring of 1826.

Lieut. Malden is the present proprietor and con-

* She was at the time commanded by Capt. Chas. Marsh Schomberg.

ductor of a respectable educational establishment in Montpellier Road, Brighton. He married, 8 April, 1828, Frances, eldest daughter of the Rev. Wm. Hodgson Cole, Rector of West Clandon, and Vicar of Wonersh, near Guildford, Surrey, by whom he has issue seven sons and one daughter.

MALING. (Lieutenant, 1829.)

Irwin Maling died 26 March, 1845, at sea, on board the brig Royalist, from Sierra Leone, aged 32, having invalided at that place from H.M. steam-frigate Penelope on 8 of the previous Feb.

This officer entered the Navy 2 Feb. 1823; passed his examination in 1831; obtained his commission 16 Dec. 1839; and was appointed—on 20 of the same month, as Additional, to the Princess Charlotte 104, flag-ship in the Mediterranean of Hon. Robt. Stopford—14 March, 1840, to the Hydra steamer, of which vessel (commanded in the Mediterranean and in North America and the West Indies by Capts. Robt. Spencer Robinson and Alex. Murray) he became First-Lieutenant—and, 1 July, 1843, to the Penelope steam-frigate, bearing the broad pendant of Commodore Wm. Jones on the coast of Africa.

Agents—Messrs. Halford and Co.

MALING. (Vice-Admiral of the Red, 1841. f-p., 27; h-p., 29.)

Thomas James Maling, born 15 July, 1778, is son of Christopher Thompson Maling, Esq., J. P., of Hendon Lodge, co. Durham; and brother-in-law of the late Earl of Mulgrave, G.C.B., a General Officer in the Army, and Colonel of the 31st Regt., father of the present Marquess of Normanby.

This officer entered the Navy, 13 June, 1791, as Captain's Servant, on board the Duke 98, Capt. Robt. Kingsmill, lying at Spithead; joined, next, the Alcide 74, and Niger 32, Capts. Sir Andw. Snapê Douglas and Rich. Goodwin Keats; and in Aug. 1792 became attached to the Penelope 32, Capt. Bartholomew Sam. Rowley, on the Jamaica station, where he assisted at the capture, 16 April, 1793, of *Le Goelan* 14, the first republican vessel taken during the war. In Dec. of the latter year he became Midshipman of the Swiftsure 74, bearing the flag at Cork of Rear-Admiral Kingsmill; and on being again, in the spring of 1795, placed under the orders of Capt. Rowley in the Cumberland 74, he took part, 13 July in that year, in the partial action fought by Admiral Hotham with the French fleet off the Hyères Islands. In the course of the ensuing Oct. Mr. Maling removed to the Victory 100, bearing the flag of Sir John Jervis, by whom, after having officiated as his Aide-de-Camp and Signal-Mate in the action off Cape St. Vincent, he was nominated, in Feb. 1797, Lieutenant of La Minerve frigate, Capt. Geo. Cockburn. Previously to his confirmation in the rank of Lieutenant, which took place 6 Oct. following, we find him serving in the boats of the last-mentioned ship and the Lively, and particularly distinguishing himself at the capture, close to the town of Santa Cruz, after a loss to the British of 15 men wounded, of *La Mutine* French national corvette of 14 guns, which was brought out, notwithstanding a smart fire of musketry from the crew, 113 in number, and a heavy discharge of artillery and small-arms from the shore, as also the fire of a large ship at anchor in the road.* Attaining the rank of Commander 24 Dec. 1798, Capt. Maling was immediately appointed, in that capacity, to La Bonne Citoyenne 20; in which vessel he had charge for many months of the blockade of Malta, and was present at the capture of *Le Généreux* 74, *La Ville de Marseilles* armed store-ship, and *Le Guillaume Tell* of 84 guns and 1000 men. He was nominated Acting-Captain of Le Guillaume Tell 11 April, 1800; was officially posted, on 6 of the next Sept., into the Alkmaar 54; and was subsequently appointed—10 Oct. 1801 (after seven months of half-pay), to the Diana 38, actively employed, during six years, on the Mediterranean, Cork, and North and South American stations—27 Oct. 1807, to the Undaunted 38, attached to the force in the West Indies and Channel, where he served until June, 1810—1 Sept. 1812, for two years, to the Mulgrave 74, in the Mediterranean—and, 31 July, 1821, and 31 May and 23 June, 1823, to the Northumberland 78, Spartiate 76, and Cambridge 82, the two former on the Home, the latter on the South American station, whence he returned in 1827. It was his fortune, when in command of the Diana, and in company with the Pique 36, to effect the capture, in Dec. 1804, of the Spanish ship of war *Diligentia* of 28 guns; as also, 18 Feb. 1807, of the French privateer *La Charlotte* of 14 guns, pierced for 20, with a complement of 118 men. He conducted for a long time, too, the blockade of Curaçoa, and, by taking possession of the island of Oruba, whence it had drawn its supplies, succeeded in reducing it to the state in which it was found by the late Sir Chas. Brisbane previously to its surrender. The Undaunted proved the captor, 12 Feb. 1809, of the *San Josephe* privateer of 14 guns and 96 men, and was for a time engaged at the defence of Cadiz: the Mulgrave, besides capturing two martello towers, was very successful against the enemy's trade, and formed part of the force under Sir Edw. Pellew in his action of 5 Nov. 1813 with the Toulon fleet. The subject of the present narrative became a Rear-Admiral 22 July, 1830; and attained the rank he now holds 23 Nov. 1841.

The Vice-Admiral is a Magistrate for cos. Durham and Worcester, and a Deputy-Lieutenant for the latter. He married, first, 2 Dec. 1811, Harriet, youngest daughter of the late celebrated Dr. Darwin, of the Priory, near Derby; and, secondly, 29 July, 1828, Jemima, second daughter of the late Colonel Bromley, of Abberley Lodge, co. Worcester, by whom he has issue a son and two daughters.

* *Vide* Gaz. 1797, p. 614.

MALLARD. (Lieut., 1821. f-p.,14; h-p., 26.)

Charles Mallard entered the Navy, 13 Nov. 1807, as Fst.-cl. Vol., on board the Neptune 98, Capt. Sir Thos. Williams, attached to the Channel fleet; and from Nov. 1808 until March, 1815, was employed as Midshipman in the Ethalion frigate, Capt. Thos. John Cochrane (under whom he shared in a slight encounter with the French 40-gun frigate *Amphitrite*, and assisted at the reduction of Martinique and the Saintes), Hannibal 74, Royal George 100, and Hibernia 120, flag-ships of Admirals Sir Thos. Williams, Fras. Pickmore, and Sir Wm. Sidney Smith, Blake and Rippon 74's, Capts. Edw. Codrington and Sir Christopher Cole, and Tonnant 80, bearing the flag of Sir Alex. Cochrane on the West India, Lisbon, Mediterranean, Home, and North American stations. In the Rippon he witnessed the capture, 21 Oct. 1813, of the French 44-gun frigate *Le Weser*. He returned home from America (after having acted for a short time as Lieutenant of the President frigate) in Sept. 1815 on board the Vengeur 74; and between that period and the date of his promotion to the rank of Lieutenant, 29 Jan. 1821, served as Admiralty Midshipman, chiefly on the South American station, in the Hyacinth 20, Capt. Alex. Robt. Sharpe, Lee 20, Capt. Stewart Blacker, and Superb 78, Commodore Sir Thos. Masterman Hardy. He has since been on half-pay. Agents—Messrs. Stilwell.

MALLOCK. (Lieut., 1830. f-p., 18; h-p., 16.)

Thomas Mallock, born 11 June, 1799, is second son of Rawlin Mallock, Esq., of Axminster, co. Devon; and is closely related to the Mallocks of Cockington Court. His family had the honour of representing the borough of Lyme Regis in Parliament in the reigns of Edward I., Mary, and Elizabeth. One of its members, a daughter of John Mallock, Esq., of Axmouth, was the wife of the first Baron Mountflorence.

This officer entered the Navy, 15 July, 1813, as Fst.-cl. Vol., on board the Ajax 74, Capts. Robt. Waller Otway and Geo. Mundy, in which ship he served in the Channel, and on the North American and Mediterranean stations, part of the time as Midshipman, until April, 1816. He then joined the ERNE 20, Capt. Rich. Spencer, also in the Mediterranean; as he afterwards did—in 1818, the BULWARK 74, flag-ship at the Nore of Sir John Gore—in the course of the same year, the VENGEUR 74, bearing the flag at first of Rear-Admiral W. Otway at Leith, but afterwards commanded by Capt. Fred. Lewis Maitland in South America and the Mediterranean—in 1821, the GENOA 74, Capt. F. L. Maitland, lying at Chatham—in 1822, as Mate (having passed his examination 21 Dec. 1819), the JUPITER 50, Capt. Geo. Augustus Westphal, under whom he escorted Lord Amherst, Governor-General of India, to Bengal—in 1823 and 1827, the MINAI 26, Capt. Houston Stewart, and (as Admiralty Mate) the HUSSAR 46, flag-ship of Sir Chas. Ogle, both on the North American station—and, in 1830 (in the capacity last mentioned), the ROYAL GEORGE yacht, Capts. Geo. Mundy and Lord Adolphus FitzClarence. During his attachment to the JUPITER Mr. Mallock jumped overboard and had the good fortune to save the life of a boy, the son of the Purser, Mr. Davies. In March, 1825, he was sent with a party of seamen from the MENAI, then at Halifax, to Liverpool, Nova Scotia, for the purpose of affording assistance to the CHEBUCTOO Colonial Government brig, which had been driven on shore during a heavy gale and bilged. After contending for three weeks with the greatest difficulties he succeeded in lifting the vessel from off the rocks and floating her between two schooners over the bar into the harbour. This service had scarcely been performed, when, another gale arising, the American schooner *Billow* was seen fast drifting towards the very spot on which the CHEBUCTOO had been bilged; but she was luckily saved from wreck by the prompt and decisive conduct of Mr. Mallock, who instantly took a cable and anchor in boats across the bar to her succour. In 1829 he was selected by Sir C. Ogle to aid in fixing the geographical position of the most prominent points in the Bay of Fundy. He was promoted from the ROYAL GEORGE to the rank of Lieutenant 31 Dec. 1830; and was lastly, from 8 July, 1836, until paid off in the early part of 1838, employed in the MALABAR 74, Capt. Sir Wm. Augustus Montagu, off Lisbon.

He married, in 1838, Edith Stiles Paterson, daughter of the late D. Goddard, Esq., and grand-niece of the late Arthur Mills Raymond, Esq., of Norfolk Street, Park Lane, London, and of the Manor House, Ealing, co. Middlesex, by whom he has issue four children. AGENTS—Messrs. Halford and Co.

MALONE. (LIEUT., 1809. F-P., 39; H-P., 8.)

EDMUND MALONE was born in 1786, in co. Westmeath.

This officer entered the Navy, in Sept. 1800, as Fst.-cl. Vol., on board the PRINCE 98, Capt. Sam. Sutton, bearing the flag in the Channel of Sir Chas. Cotton, under whom he continued to serve, in the capacity of Midshipman, until May, 1801. Proceeding in 1803 to the East Indies in the ALBION 74, Capt. John Ferrier, he there in succession removed to the RUSSELL 74, bearing the flag of Rear-Admiral Wm. O'Brien Drury, ARROGANT 74, Capt. Wm. Flint, and CEYLON of 40 guns, Capts. Wm. Jones Lye and Chas. Gordon—in which latter ship he was confirmed a Lieutenant 18 Sept. 1809. In May, 1803, we find him assisting at the capture, by the ALBION and other vessels, of the French frigate *La Franchise* of 36 guns; and, in 1808, witnessing, as Mate of the RUSSELL, the surrender of the Danish settlement of Tranquebar. He was also, when in the CEYLON, present, 18 Sept. 1810, in a fierce intermittent night-action of four hours, which terminated in the capture of that frigate (after she had incurred a loss, out of 295 men, of 10 killed and 31 wounded) by the French ships *Vénus* of 44 guns and 380 men, and *Victor* of 16 guns. The CEYLON being, however, retaken in the course of the same day, Mr. Malone was afforded an opportunity of officiating as her First-Lieutenant at the ensuing reduction of the Mauritius. He invalided home in Feb. 1811; and was next appointed, on the Home station—24 July following, to the COLOSSUS 74, Capt. Thos. Alexander, in the boats of which ship he was frequently employed under the enemy's batteries on the coast of France in operations against their trade—30 May, 1814, to the TEAZER 14, Capt. Thos. Prickett—3 May, 1815, to the QUEEN CHARLOTTE 100, Capt. Chas. Inglis—and 9 Oct. 1815, to the VENGEUR 74, Capt. Thos. Alexander. On leaving the ship last mentioned Mr. Malone obtained an appointment, 2 March, 1818, to the Royal Naval College at Portsmouth, where he remained for a period of 19 years. He has been attached, since 8 March, 1842, to the Royal Hospital at Plymouth.

His son, Robt. Edmund Malone, is at present acting as Purser and Paymaster of the STROMBOLI steam-sloop.

MANCHESTER, DUKE OF, formerly VISCOUNT MANDEVILLE. (COMMANDER, 1822. F-P., 11; H-P., 24.)

HIS GRACE GEORGE, DUKE OF MANCHESTER, born 9 July, 1799, is eldest son of William, fifth Duke of Manchester (Governor of Jamaica, Collector of the Customs for the port of London, and Lord-Lieutenant and Custos Rotulorum of co. Huntingdon), by Lady Susan Gordon, third daughter of Alexander, fourth Duke of Gordon. The Duke, who succeeded his father 18 March, 1843, is brother-in-law of the Marquess of Tweeddale, a General Officer in the Army.

This officer entered the Navy, 19 Feb. 1812, as a Volunteer, on board the ANTELOPE 50, Capt. Jas. Carpenter, bearing the flag at Newfoundland of Sir John Thos. Duckworth. In Feb. 1813 he joined the SAN JOSEF 110, flag-ship of Sir Rich. King in the Mediterranean, where, in Jan. 1814, he became Midshipman of L'AIGLE 36, Capt. Sir John Louis, with whom, it appears, he continued to serve in the SCAMANDER and FORTH frigates, on the Home and Halifax stations, until transferred, in Sept. 1818, to the LARNE 20, Capt. Abraham Lowe, then at Jamaica. He was promoted, 20 Nov. 1818, to a Lieutenancy in the CONFIANCE sloop, Capt. Alex. Montgomerie, also in the West Indies, on which station he removed, 2 Feb. 1819, to the SYBILLE 44, flag-ship of Sir Home Popham. His last appointments were, 22 March and 30 Oct. 1821, to the MEDINA 20 and ROCHFORT 80, Capts. Robt. Hockings and Chas. Marsh Schomberg. He attained his present rank 19 July, 1822.

Prior to his accession to the Dukedom his Grace (who is Deputy-Lieutenant for co. Armagh) sat in the House of Commons for Huntingdonshire. He married, 8 Oct. 1822, Mellicent, only daughter and heir of the late General Robt. Bernard Sparrow, of Brampton, in Northamptonshire, by his wife, the Lady Olivia Acheson, eldest daughter of Arthur, first Earl of Gosford, and has issue four sons. AGENTS—Messrs. Chard.

MANGIN. (REAR-ADMIRAL OF THE BLUE, 1841. F-P., 10; H-P., 42.)

REUBEN CAILLAUD MANGIN was born 1 Nov. 1780, in Dublin, and died 20 July, 1846, at Kingstown, near that city. He was son of Lieut.-Colonel Sam. Henry Mangin, of the 12th Dragoons, and grand-nephew of Brigadier-General John Caillaud, of Aston House, co. Oxford.

This officer entered the Navy, 24 Oct. 1794, as Midshipman, on board the IMPREGNABLE 98, Capt. Sir Chas. Cotton; and from the following Dec. until promoted to the rank of Lieutenant, 3 Dec. 1800, served (with the exception of a short attachment in 1799 to the NAIAD frigate, Capt. Wm. Pierrepont) in LA POMONE 44, CANADA 74, TÉMÉRAIRE 98, and RENOWN 74, all under the orders of his patron Sir John Borlase Warren. He was a participator, during that period, in the capture of an extraordinary number of vessels; was in the POMONE in the expedition to Quiberon in 1795; and was present in the CANADA at the defeat of Commodore Bompart's squadron, off the coast of Ireland, 12 Oct. 1798. His succeeding appointments were, 16 July, 1801, 19 May, 1802, and 16 July, 1803, to the MINERVE,* SAN FIORENZO, and VIRGINIE frigates, Capts. Geo. Cockburn, Joseph Bingham, and John Poo Beresford, employed on the Mediterranean, East India, and Home stations. Obtaining a second promotal commission 8 May, 1804, Capt. Mangin was invested, 26 March, 1807, with the command of the VALOROUS praam. In that vessel he co-operated in the defence of Danzig, and was honoured with the thanks of the King of Prussia for the assistance he afforded in rescuing the garrison of Fort Weeickselmunde at the very moment it was about to be occupied by a division of Marshal Lefebvre's troops. He was advanced, at the recommendation of Admiral Gambier, to Post-rank for his conduct off Copenhagen, 13 Oct. 1807; and from March to May, 1811, he held temporary command of the SALDANHA frigate on the Irish coast. This was the last appointment he was able to procure. He acquired Flag-rank 23 Nov. 1841.

The Rear-Admiral married, 11 April, 1803, Magdalene, daughter of the Rev. H. D'Abzac, formerly Senior Fellow of Trinity College, Dublin, by whom, who died 13 Aug. 1840, he had issue four sons and two daughters. AGENTS—Messrs. Halford and Co.

MANGLES, F.R.S. (COMMANDER, 1815. F-P., 15; H-P., 32.)

JAMES MANGLES entered the Navy, in March, 1800, as Fst.-cl. Vol., on board the MAIDSTONE frigate, Capt. Ross Donnelly; previously to following whom as Midshipman, in Nov. 1801, into the NARCISSUS 32, he served off the coast of France, escorted convoy home from Oporto, and made a voyage to Quebec. In the NARCISSUS, after cruizing in the North Sea and also in the Mediterranean, where he assisted at the capture, 8 July, 1803, of the French corvette *L'Alcion*, of 16 guns and 96 men, he accompanied the expedition to the Cape of Good Hope; on her passage whither the NARCISSUS, besides effecting the capture of *Le Prudent* privateer, of 12 guns and 70 men, retook the English merchant-ship *Horatio Nelson*, mounting 22 guns, and drove on shore the *Napoléon* privateer, of 32 guns and 250 men. Subsequently to the reduction of the Cape and the capture of the 46-gun frigate *Volontaire*, Mr. Mangles, who had been invested with the rank of Acting-Lieutenant, proceeded to the Rio de la Plata, whence we find him returning to England with the despatches announcing the conquest of Buenos Ayres. He had previously, 11 July, 1804, served with the boats of the NARCISSUS, SEAHORSE, and MAIDSTONE, 10 in number, under the orders of Lieut. John Thompson, at the capture and destruction of 12 settees, lying at La Vandour, in the Bay of Hières, where the British, encountered by a tremendous fire of grape-shot and musketry, as well from the vessels themselves as from a battery and the houses of the town, sustained a loss of 4 men killed and 23 wounded. His appointments, after he left the NARCISSUS, were—26 Sept. 1806, to the PENELOPE 36, Capts. Wm. Robt. Broughton and John Dick, employed at first on the coast of Spain and at Halifax, and then on the West India station, where he aided at the reduction of Martinique in Feb. 1809—in 1811-13, to the BOYNE 98, and VILLE DE PARIS 110, flag-ships in the Channel of Sir Harry Burrard Neale, under whom he was latterly in discharge of the duties of Signal-Lieutenant, and was present at the grand naval review held at Spithead —5 Sept. 1814, as First, to the DUNCAN 74, bearing the flag in South America of Sir John Poo Beresford—and, in Jan. 1815, to the acting-command of the RACOON sloop, in which he returned to Plymouth, after escorting part of the Brazilian trade to Bristol. He was confirmed in his present rank 13 June, 1815, but has not been since afloat.

* The MINERVE effected the capture and destruction, 2 Sept. 1801, of the *Succès* of 32, and *Bravoure* of 42 guns.

Commander Mangles published in Aug. 1823, in conjunction with the late Capt. Hon. Chas. Leonard Irby, R.N., a work entitled 'Travels in Egypt, Nubia, Syria, and Asia Minor, in 1817-18.' He is a F.R.S., and a Member of the London Geographical Society. AGENTS—Goode and Lawrence.

MANICO. (LIEUT., 1814. F-P., 13; H-P., 28.)

PETER SMITH MANICO entered the Navy, 26 March, 1806, as Fst.-cl. Vol., on board the OCEAN 98, Capt. Rich. Thomas, bearing the flag of Lord Collingwood in the Mediterranean, where he soon attained the rating of Midshipman, and continued to serve, until Nov. 1815, in the CAMBRIAN 40, Capts. Fras. Wm. Fane and Chas. Bullen, UNDAUNTED 38, Capts. Rich. Thomas and Thos. Ussher, CALEDONIA 120, flag-ship of Sir Edw. Pellew, and UNDAUNTED again, Capts. T. Ussher and Chas. Thurlow Smith, of which latter ship he was confirmed a Lieutenant 16 March, 1814, after having for nearly three months acted in that capacity. On 13 Dec. 1810, being at the time in the CAMBRIAN, he witnessed the destruction of a large convoy protected by two batteries in the Mole of Palamos, at which place the British, out of 600 officers and men, who had been employed in the boats of a squadron, sustained a loss of upwards of 200 killed, wounded, and taken prisoners. He was otherwise much engaged in the same ship in co-operation with the patriots on the coast of Catalonia; and, when Lieutenant of the UNDAUNTED, assisted in conveying Napoleon Buonaparte from Frejus to Elba, and was present at the capture of the Tremiti islands. His last appointments were—6 July, 1821, to the PERSEUS receiving-ship off the Tower, Capt. Jas. Couch—and, 13 Jan. 1824, to the GRIPER discovery-ship, Capt. Geo. Fras. Lyon. In the course of the latter year he joined in a disastrous attempt made to reach Repulse Bay—an enterprise whose harassing and distressing nature nearly ruined the constitutions of all connected with it. He was paid off in Dec. 1824, and has not been since afloat.

MANN. (LIEUTENANT, 1827.)

ADRIAN THOMAS MANN entered the Navy 11 Feb. 1814; served as Midshipman of the SWINGER 12, in action with an American privateer off Surinam in 1815; passed his examination in 1820; was employed in a boat of the CAMBRIAN frigate at the capture of a pirate in the Archipelago in 1826; and in 1827 (on 24 April in which year he attained his present rank) took command of the boats of the CAMELION, and cut out a similar description of vessel. His appointments, since his promotion, have been—20 June, 1831, to the Coast Guard—26 Sept. 1837, to the command of the STORK Revenue-vessel—6 Oct. 1840, again to the Coast Guard —30 Dec. 1844, to the post of Agent on board a contract mail steam-vessel—19 June, 1846, to the REDWING steam-packet, Capt. Thos. Bevis, lying at Liverpool—and, 5 Feb. 1847, to the command of the MERLIN, another steam-packet, of 312 horse-power.

Lieut. A. Mann married, in 1829, Sarah, daughter of Mr. Pearce, at that time chief officer of the Coast Guard station at Hope, near Kingsbridge, by whom he has issue.

MANN. (LIEUTENANT, 1845.)

JAMES SAUMAREZ MANN entered the Navy in 1835; passed his examination 8 June, 1842; and after serving as Mate of the EXCELLENT gunnery-ship at Portsmouth, Capt. Sir Thos. Hastings, and PANTALOON 10, commanded on the coast of Africa by Capt. Edm. Wilson, was promoted to the rank of Lieutenant 21 Oct. 1845, and appointed Additional of the PENELOPE steam-frigate, bearing the broad pendant on the latter station of Commodore Wm. Jones. He has been attached, since 15 Sept. 1846, to the RODNEY 92, Capt. Edw. Collier, now in the Mediterranean.

MANN. (Commander, 1845. f-p., 33; h-p., 4.)

Robert Mann* is first-cousin of Commander H. W. Scott, R.N., Lieut. R. Y. M. Darracott, R.N., and R. M. Read, Esq., Purser and Paymaster, R.N. (1812.) His 11 paternal uncles (sons of Robert Mann, Esq., of Barton, near Plympton, Devon, a gentleman of property) were all swept away in the Naval and Military service of their country.

This officer entered the Navy, 16 May, 1810, as a Supernumerary (under the auspices of Vice-Admiral Robt. Man, a distant relative), on board the Salvador del Mundo, bearing the flag at Plymouth of Admiral Wm. Young, for the purpose of awaiting an opportunity to join the Royal George 100, commanded by Capt. Geo. Burgoyne Salt, with whom, in April, 1811, he removed as Midshipman to the Unicorn 32. Continuing in that frigate under the orders of Capts. Wm. Hext and Sam. Geo. Pechell until Oct. 1814, he served at the blockade of Basque Roads, L'Orient, and Brest, co-operated much with the patriots on the north coast of Spain, was stationed off the coast of Holland during the severe winter of 1813-14, escorted the Duke of Cambridge from Hanover to England, and cruized for some time off the coast of Norway. While on the latter service he was sent in charge of a prize from Christiansand to Leith, but was compelled, in consequence of the springing of a timber-head during a gale of wind off Rattray Head, to run the vessel ashore. On leaving the Unicorn we find him successively joining—11 Nov. 1814, the Goldfinch 10, Capt. John Foote, whom he accompanied to the West Indies—13 Feb. 1816, the Malta 84, from which ship, commanded at Plymouth by Capt. Thos. Gordon Caulfeild, he was lent, from April to Aug. 1816, to the Traave 38, *armée-en-flûte*, Capt. John Codd—23 Feb. 1818 (after he had been for 12 months on shore), the Harlequin 18, Capts. Bennett, Parker, and Weeks, employed on the coast of Ireland, where he served upwards of six years—and, 16 June, 1824, the Ocean 80, bearing the flag in the Tagus of Lord Amelius Beauclerk, who, in Oct. 1824, and again in June, 1825, nominated him (solely for conduct) Lieutenant of the Superb 74, Capt. Sir Thos. Staines. His promotion being confirmed by commission dated 6 July, 1825, he was next, 28 Dec. 1829, appointed to the Coast Guard, in which service he remained (stationed for two years in Ireland, and for 14 at Hastings) until advanced, as a reward for meritorious behaviour, to his present rank 16 Jan. 1845. Since 3 July following he has been employed as Inspecting Commander of the Coast Guard at Kilrush—an appointment he received at the special recommendation of the Board of Customs.

Commander Mann married, 21 Dec. 1826, Julia, second daughter of Joseph Motton, Esq., of Teignmouth, by whom he has issue one son.

MANNERS. (Captain, 1829. f-p., 14; h-p., 20.)

Russell Henry Manners entered the Royal Naval College 6 May, 1813; and embarked, 6 March, 1816, as a Volunteer, on board the Minden 74, Capt. Wm. Paterson, in which ship, after assisting we believe at the bombardment of Algiers, he proceeded to the East Indies, where he served, under the flag of Sir Rich. King, until nominated Midshipman, 1 July, 1818, of the Orlando 36, commanded by Capt. John Clavell, with whom, in 1819, he returned to England in the Malabar 74. After an intermediate employment on the Channel and West India stations in the Spartan and Pyramus frigates, Capts. Wm. Furlong Wise and Fras. Newcombe, he became, 29 July, 1822, Acting-Lieutenant of the Tyne 26, Capt. John Edw. Walcott, to which vessel the Admiralty confirmed him 19 Oct. following. In May, 1823, he rejoined the Pyramus, still commanded by Capt. Newcombe, under whom he continued until awarded a second promotal commission 16 Aug. 1825. His last appointment was, 21 Oct. 1827, to the command of the Britomart 10, at Plymouth. He attained his present rank 4 March, 1829.

Capt. Manners married, 3 July, 1834, Louisa Jane, daughter of Le Comte de Noé, a Peer of France, by whom he has issue. Agents—Messrs. Ommanney.

* The Commander's name, although spelt as above in his baptismal certificate, is correctly 'Man.'

MANNING. (Lieutenant, 1824.)

George Manning is eldest son of Henry Manning, Esq., of Wonford House, co. Devon.

This officer entered the Navy 6 May, 1814; obtained his commission 20 Aug. 1824; and was appointed—30 March, 1826, to the Spartiate 76, Capt. Fred. Warren, employed off Lisbon and in the Mediterranean—and, 30 Sept. 1831, to the Melville 74, bearing the flag of Sir John Gore in the East Indies. He has been on half-pay since June, 1833.

He married, 9 Dec. 1834, Emma Jane, daughter of the late W. H. Jones, Esq., of Ashurst Park, co. Kent. Agents—Messrs. Ommanney.

MANSEL, K.L.H. (Captain, 1840. f-p., 17; h-p., 22.)

George Mansel entered the Navy, 30 May, 1808, as Fst.-cl. Vol., on board the Venerable 74, Capts. Andw. King and Sir Home Popham, in which ship, bearing the flag of Sir Rich. John Strachan, he accompanied the expedition of 1809 to the Walcheren. After cruizing for some time in the Eliza tender, Lieut.-Commander Nicholas Kortwright, he became attached, in July, 1811, to the Surveillante 38, Capt. Sir Geo. Ralph Collier, under whom he served, in co-operation with the patriots on the north coast of Spain, until transferred, as Midshipman, about March, 1812, to the San Domingo 74, successive flag-ship of Sir R. J. Strachan and Sir John Borlase Warren in the North Sea and North America. He continued on the latter station in the Colibri sloop, Capt. John Thomson, Nymphe 38, Capt. Farmery Predam Epworth, and Albion 74 and Tonnant 80, bearing the flags of Admirals Geo. Cockburn and Hon. Sir Alex. Cochrane, until the summer of 1815; and he then, for a few weeks, joined the Royal Sovereign 100, Capt. Wm. Robt. Broughton, on the Channel station. In July, 1816, he sailed for the Mediterranean in the Queen Charlotte 100, bearing the flag of Lord Exmouth, who, on their arrival, nominated him Lieutenant of the Minden 74, Capt. Wm. Paterson, a capacity in which he took part in the bombardment of Algiers. He returned home shortly afterwards in the Queen Charlotte, and was paid off; but he did not succeed in obtaining his official promotion until 29 Jan. 1821. His next appointment was, 24 July, 1824, to the Valorous sloop, Capt. the Earl of Huntingdon, fitting for the Jamaica station, where it was his fortune, 2 Dec. 1826, to be made Commander into the Magnificent hospital and store-ship at Port Royal. Returning home about the commencement of 1828, Capt. Mansel, on a subsequent occasion, proceeded to the Mediterranean, and there, during the operations of the French against Algiers, performed such good service as to lead to his being invested, 14 Nov. 1831, with the order of the Legion of Honour. He afterwards, 20 April, 1840, assumed command of the Wasp 16; and on 28 Sept. in that year, as a reward for his services at the capture of Sidon* he was advanced to Post-rank. In the following Nov. he witnessed the fall of St. Jean d'Acre. His appointments have since been—9 Jan. 1841, to the Powerful 84, also in the Mediterranean, whence he came home in the following Sept.—and, 14 Dec. 1844, to the Actæon 26, in which ship he is now on the coast of Africa.

Agent—John Chippendale.

MANSEL. (Captain, 1834. f-p., 19; h-p., 30.)

Thomas Mansel entered the Navy, in 1798, as Fst.-cl. Vol, on board the Hyæna 24, Capts. Hon. Courtenay Boyle and David Lloyd, stationed at

* *Vide* Gaz. 1840, p. 2603.

first in the North Sea and afterwards in the Mediterranean. Removing as Midshipman, in 1800, to the ELEPHANT 74, Capts. Thos. Foley and Geo. Dundas, he served in that ship under Lord Nelson at the battle of Copenhagen 2 April, 1801, and on proceeding to the West Indies took part in the operations of 1803 against the French at St. Domingo. Between the summer of 1804, on 16 Sept. in which year he was confirmed a Lieutenant, and the date of his promotion to the rank of Commander, 15 June, 1814, we find him serving, in every quarter of the globe, in the PORT MAHON sloop, Capt. Sam. Chambers, BARRACOUTA schooner, commanded by himself, RACOON 18, Capt. Edw. Crofton, AVON 18, Capt. Mauritius Adolphus Newton De Starck, DREADNOUGHT 98, Capt. Wm. Lechmere, VOLONTAIRE 38, Capt. Chas. Bullen, HIBERNIA 110, Capt. R. J. Neve, TROUBRIDGE armed ship, under his own orders, DRAGON 74, bearing the flag of Sir Fras. Laforey, and BARHAM 74, Capt. John Wm. Spranger. He was wounded, during that period, in the boats of the RACOON at the recapture of a merchant-vessel off Cuba—was present in the AVON (after having escorted a Russian ship of the line to the Baltic, and Mr. Erskine, H. M. Minister, to the United States) in a gallant escape made by that vessel from the French 74-gun ship *Regulus*—aided, when in the VOLONTAIRE, in conveying the present King of the French to Malta, as also in capturing the island of Pomégue, near Marseilles, and in destroying Fort Rioux, mounting 14 guns, near Cape Croisette—and commanded the TROUBRIDGE at the reduction of the Isle of France. His last appointment was, 13 April, 1831, to the Coast Guard, in which service he continued until posted 12 Feb. 1834.

MANSELL. (LIEUTENANT, 1841.)

ARTHUR LUKIS MANSELL is son of Capt. Sir Thos. Mansell, R.N., Kt., K.C.H.

This officer entered the Navy from the Royal Naval College 8 Sept. 1831; passed his examination in 1835; obtained his commission 14 Dec. 1841; and from 23 March, 1842, until 1846, was employed in the Mediterranean as Additional-Lieutenant of the BEACON surveying-vessel, Capt. Thos. Graves.

MANSELL. (RETIRED COMMANDER, 1847. F-P., 14; H-P., 33.)

BONAMY MANSELL, born 13 Oct. 1786, at Guernsey, is brother of Capt. Sir Thos. Mansell, R.N., Kt., K.C.H.

This officer entered the Navy, 1 Jan. 1800, as Fst.-cl. Vol., on board the LONDON 98, commanded in the Channel by Capt. John Child Purvis, whom he there followed as Midshipman, in April, 1801, into the ROYAL GEORGE 100. Joining next, in 1802, LA DÉDAIGNEUSE 36, Capts. Thos. Geo. Shortland, Peter Heywood, and Chas. Jas. Johnston, he sailed for the East Indies, where, in June, 1805, he accompanied the last-mentioned officer into the CORNWALLIS 50. After participating, 11 Nov. 1806, in a gallant attack made by that vessel, in company with the SCEPTRE 74, on the *Sémillante* French frigate, three armed ships, and 12 sail of merchantmen, the whole protected by seven batteries, mounting upwards of 100 pieces of cannon, in St. Paul's Bay, Ile de Bourbon, Mr. Mansell, in Jan. 1807, joined the CULLODEN 74, bearing the flag of Sir Edw. Pellew; under whom, on 11 of the ensuing Dec., he witnessed the destruction of the dockyard and stores at Griessee, in the island of Java, and of all the men-of-war remaining to Holland in India. Being successively, 28 May, 1808, and 7 March, 1809, constituted an acting and a confirmed Lieutenant of the SAPPHIRE sloop, Capts. George Davies and Bertie Cornelius Cator, we find him, on 1 May in the latter year, uniting with the NEREIDE frigate, Capt. Robt. Corbett, in a successful engagement with two batteries near St. Rose, in the Ile de Bourbon, where he was severely hurt in the leg by the premature explosion of a magazine containing 100 barrels of powder, which took place while he was in the act of pulling off from the shore with a message to Capt. Corbett from Lieut. Arthur Batt Bingham of the NEREIDE, with whom he had landed. He was subsequently concerned in the capture of the French frigate *Caroline* and of other vessels in St. Paul's Bay, Ile de Bourbon; and he was then removed with Capt. Cator to the OTTER sloop. His last appointments were—23 May, 1810, for passage home, to the LEOPARD 50, Capt. Jas. Johnstone—20 Dec. 1810, to the TYRIAN 10, Capt. Henry Thos. Davies, attached to the force in the Channel—6 Sept. 1811 (having left the TYRIAN in the previous May), to the HELDER 36, Capt. John Serrell, stationed in the Baltic—13 Sept. 1813 (after eight months of half-pay), to the SALVADOR DEL MUNDO, flag-ship at Plymouth of Vice-Admiral Wm. Domett—and 21 Nov. following, as First-Lieutenant, to the SATURN 56, Capts. Jas. Nash and Thos. Brown, in which ship, until 30 Nov. 1814, he was most actively employed on the coast of North America. During the year 1812 Mr. Mansell, at the time in the HELDER, succeeded, in the presence of a convoy of 300 sail, in setting fire, at noonday, to a galliot, defended, on the beach, in the Great Belt, by a sharp fire from 3 or 4 field-pieces and musketry—an enterprise which occasioned the boats under his orders a loss of 2 Midshipmen and of at least 10 or 12 men killed and wounded. He had also the good fortune, in a boat of the same ship, in conjunction with another belonging to the BELLETTE, to effect the capture of a valuable merchantman laden with linen, and afterwards sold we believe for 11,000*l*. He accepted his present rank 9 April, 1847.

MANSELL, Kt., K.C.H., K.S.S. (Captain, 1814. F-P., 20; H-P., 34.)

SIR THOMAS MANSELL, born 9 Feb. 1777, is third son of the late Thos. Mansell, Esq., of Guernsey; and brother of Retired Commander Bonamy Mansell, R.N.

This officer entered the Navy, 20 Jan. 1793, as Midshipman, on board the CRESCENT, Capt. Jas. Saumarez, of 42 guns and 257 men, and on 20 of the following Oct. assisted at the capture, after a close action of two hours, of the French frigate *La Réunion*, of 36 guns and 320 men, 120 of whom were either killed or wounded, without any casualty whatever to the British.* He afterwards accompanied an expedition sent under the orders of Earl Moira and Rear-Admiral M'Bride to co-operate with the French Royalists on the coasts of Normandy and Brittany; and on 8 June, 1794, he was present when the CRESCENT, by a bold and masterly manœuvre, effected her escape from a French squadron, consisting of two cut-down 74's, each mounting 54 guns, two frigates, and a brig. Following Sir Jas. Saumarez, in March, 1795, into the ORION 74, Mr. Mansell was afforded an opportunity of sharing in that ship in Lord Bridport's action, as Master's Mate in the battle fought off Cape St. Vincent (where he was wounded †), and in a similar capacity in the victory of the Nile. On 22 Oct. 1798, owing to the strong manner in which he was recommended by his Captain to Lord Nelson, he found himself nominated Acting-Lieutenant of L'AQUILON 74, Capt. Thos. Bowen. He was confirmed a Lieutenant 17 April, 1799, and was subsequently appointed—12 Aug. following, to the IMPREGNABLE 98, Capt. Jonathan Faulknor, under whom he was wrecked between Langstone and Chichester 19 Oct. in the same year—11 Dec. 1799 and 5 Feb. 1801, to the LONDON 98 and ROYAL GEORGE 100, in the former of which ships (they were both commanded by Capt. John Child Purvis) he accompanied the expedition to Ferrol in Aug. 1800—5 April, 1803, after nearly 12 months of half-pay, to the CERBERUS 32, Capt. Wm. Selby, on the Guernsey station, where, during an attack made in the month of Sept. on the town of Granville, he took command of the carronade launch, and elicited the applause of his Admiral for the manner in which

* As a reward for this achievement Capt. Saumarez received the honour of Knighthood.

† *Vide* Gaz. 1797, p. 212.

he assisted in silencing the fire of nine gun-vessels by whom the CERBERUS had been assailed when for three hours aground on a sand-bank *—8 June, 1804, to the DIOMEDE 50, Capts. Hugh Downman and Joseph Edmunds, in which ship, bearing the flag at first of Sir Jas. Saumarez, he superintended the landing of the troops under Major-General (now Lord) Beresford in the operations against the Cape of Good Hope, and had charge of the seamen attached to that officer's brigade at Saldanha Bay—27 Jan. 1806, as First, to the DIADEM 64, bearing the broad pendant of Sir Home Popham—11 March ensuing, to the command of an armed transport, for the purpose of conveying home intelligence of a French squadron under Jerome Buonaparte having arrived in the vicinity of the Cape—and, 29 Aug. in the same year, to the post of Flag-Lieutenant under Sir Jas. Saumarez, with whom he successively served in the Channel and Baltic on board the DIOMEDE, HIBERNIA, and VICTORY. Being confirmed, 17 Sept. 1808, in the command of the ROSE sloop, Capt. Mansell, while in that vessel, assisted at the capture of the island of Anholdt, 18 May, 1809, and succeeded, with much gallantry and good conduct, in beating off, near the Skawe, 28 April, 1810, a Danish flotilla, consisting of four gun-vessels, with other rowing-boats, whose fire, although it but slightly wounded five of the ROSE's people, proved nevertheless, during upwards of an hour's continuance, most destructive to her sails and rigging, carrying away also the wheel, besides lodging 19 shot in the hull, and rendering the mainyard and mainmast unserviceable. In 1812 Capt. Mansell was presented by Viscount Cathcart, the British Ambassador at St. Petersburg, with a valuable diamond ring, which his Lordship had been directed by the Emperor Alexander to forward to him as a mark of the high sense that monarch entertained of his services, especially in safely conducting through the Belt a Russian squadron under Vice-Admiral Crown; and in the course of the same year he was honoured by King Charles XIII. with the insignia of a Knight of the Royal Military Order of the Sword, in testimony of the esteem in which his services were likewise held by his Swedish Majesty. The ROSE being paid off in April, 1813, he was next, 23 Aug. following, appointed to the PELICAN brig, of 18 guns, in which vessel we find him serving on the Irish station and off the north coast of Spain until his promotion to Post-rank, 7 June, 1814. During the period he commanded the ROSE and PELICAN, Capt. Mansell evinced a degree of zeal and activity that did not fail to procure him the approbation of every officer under whom he was employed. He contrived, indeed, to make prize of at least 170 vessels of various descriptions, and among them, 13 June, 1814, the *Siro*, American letter-of-marque of 225 tons, pierced for 16 guns, mounting 12 long nine-pounders, with a complement of 49 men.† Unsuccessful, after his advancement to Post-rank, in his applications for further employment, he accepted the Retirement 1 Oct. 1846.

Sir Thos. Mansell (whom William IV. nominated a K.C.H., and invested with the honour of Knighthood, in 1837) married, in Nov. 1806, Catherine, daughter of John Lukis, Esq., merchant, of Guernsey, by whom he has issue four sons and four daughters. Of the former, the eldest, a M.D., is a Surgeon R.N. (1840); the second, Arthur Lukis, a Lieutenant R.N.; the third, William Mansell, First-Lieutenant R.M. (1846); and the fourth, George Hope, a Mate R.N. (1847).

MANSELL. (LIEUT., 1821. F-P., 13; H-P., 25.)

WILLIAM MANSELL is son of the late Walter Mansell, Esq., of Woodbury House, co. Oxford.

This officer entered the Navy, in June, 1809, as Sec.-cl. Vol., on board the VENERABLE 74, Capts. Sir Home Popham and Andrew King, in which ship he accompanied the ensuing expedition to the Walcheren, escorted the Earl of Chatham thence to England, and was all but lost during a gale off the coast of Holland. Between 1810 and Aug. 1815 we find him serving, part of the time as Midshipman, in the ORION and SULTAN 74's, Capts. Sir Archibald Collingwood Dickson and John West, and DÉSIRÉE 36, Capt. Wm. Woolridge. The two former ships were employed in the Baltic, Channel, and West Indies; the DÉSIRÉE in endeavouring to intercept Napoleon Buonaparte after the battle of Waterloo. After an employment of nearly three years on the Home station in the SCAMANDER 36, Capts. Chas. Sipthorpe John Hawtayne and Wm. Elliott, and FLORIDA 24, also commanded by Capt. Hawtayne, Mr. Mansell, having passed his examination in Dec. 1816, was appointed, in Jan. 1819, Admiralty Midshipman of the MORGIANA sloop, Capts. Chas. Borough Strong, Alex. Sandilands, and Wm. Finlaison, in which vessel he sailed for the coast of Africa, where, on 10 of the following Dec., he took command of the gig and assisted at the capture by boarding, in open day, of the Spanish armed slave-schooner *Esperança*, of greatly superior force. On that occasion Mr. Mansell, followed by a marine named Lord, was the first on the enemy's deck. For the space of two minutes he and his brave companion, from unavoidable circumstances, were left unsupported in the presence of very fearful odds, but they made ample use of their time, the former attacking, wounding, and overcoming the Captain of the slaver and another person; and the marine killing the man at the wheel. The loss of the assailed in the affair amounted altogether to 2 men killed and 6 wounded: that of the British to 3 slightly wounded. Among the latter was Mr. Mansell, who had been previously severely bruised by cold shot thrown into the boats with a view of sinking them during their approach. In consideration of his gallant behaviour on the occasion he was so strongly recommended in the despatches to the Admiralty, and his claim to promotion so warmly pressed by the late Mr. Wilberforce, that, on 14 Sept. 1821, he was promoted to the rank of Lieutenant. Prior, however, to that event he appears, in May, 1820, to have landed at the Pongas, near Sierra Leone, and to have united in a series of operations conducted by the present Sir Henry John Leeke, at the head of 170 seamen and marines and 180 black soldiers of the 2nd West India Regt.; the result whereof was the destruction by fire of eight towns, the demolition of a strongly stockaded battery, mounting four guns, and the defeat of a body of 5000 men commanded by King Munga Brama, a barbarian who had murdered an officer and several men belonging to H.M.S. THISTLE, and had retained 3 as prisoners. On this, as on other occasions, Mr. Mansell again distinguished himself. He continued in the MORGIANA as her First-Lieutenant until Feb. 1822; and was lastly, from 2 Dec. 1825 until Aug. 1827, employed on the Coast Blockade service as a Supernumerary of the RAMILLIES 74, Capt. Hugh Pigot.

In 1838 Lieut. Mansell was appointed Secretary to the Metropolitan Public Carriage Office; and in 1843, Deputy-Registrar of Metropolitan Public Carriages. He married, first, 9 Dec. 1830, Phillis, only daughter of Joseph Horsford, Esq., of Weymouth; and, that lady dying in 1834, secondly, 10 Aug. 1836, Susannah Maria, only daughter of John Surman, Esq., of the Lodge, Malvern, co. Worcester.

MANSFIELD. (LIEUTENANT, 1845. F-P., 14; H-P., 1.)

WALTER GEORGE MANSFIELD, born about 1818, is son of Walter H. Mansfield, Esq., of Yeomanstown House, co. Kildare.

This officer entered the Navy, in May, 1832, as Fst.-cl. Vol., on board the VERNON 50, Capt. Sir

* *Vide* Gaz. 1803, p. 1273. Mr. Mansell, who was for some time First-Lieutenant of the CERBERUS, had, in the preceding Aug., commanded her boats in two cutting-out affairs. He brought out, on the first occasion, a large fishing-vessel from Concalle Bay, and on the second he captured, with but two boats, not less than seven smacks, mounting from 16 to 18 guns each, in St. Cas Bay.—*Vide* Gaz. 1803, p. 1050.

† *V.* Gaz. 1814, p. 232.

Fras. Augustus Collier, and in the course of the same year was employed with the squadron on the coast of Holland. In 1833 he sailed for the West Indies, where, it appears, he continued to serve in the VERNON, and in the PRESIDENT 52, PICKLE schooner, and SNAKE 16, until 1839, in July of which year he returned to England and passed his examination at the R. N. College. He had passed for seamanship 17 Sept. 1838. Joining next, in July, 1840, the VANGUARD 80, Capt. Sir David Dunn, he proceeded to the Mediterranean, where he was afforded an opportunity of sharing in the ensuing operations on the coast of Syria. In 1843, being at the time off Lisbon, Mr. Mansfield landed with a party of seamen from the VANGUARD and assisted in subduing an alarming fire and disturbance which had there simultaneously broken out. For this service he was presented by the Queen of Portugal with the Order of the Tower and Sword. After an attachment of 12 months to the QUEEN 110 and TRAFALGAR 120, both commanded by Capt. Wm. Fanshawe Martin, whom he accompanied in various experimental cruizes, he was promoted to the rank of Lieutenant by commission dated 1 Sept. 1845, and appointed, a few days afterwards, Additional of the PENELOPE steam-frigate, bearing the broad pendant of Commodore Wm. Jones on the coast of Africa. He has been serving since 26 of the following Dec. on the same station, in the WATERWITCH 10, Capt. Thos. Fras. Birch.

MANT. (RETIRED COMMANDER, 1837. F-P., 15; H-P., 51.)

JOSEPH BINGHAM MANT was born 15 July, 1768, at Havant, in Hants, and died 2 March, 1845, at Padstow, co. Cornwall. He was brother-in-law, we believe, of General Miller, R.M.

This officer entered the Royal Naval Academy 3 Feb. 1779, and continued a student at that institution until Sept. 1782; on 12 of which month he embarked as Midshipman on board the ATLAS 98, Capt. Geo. Vandeput, and proceeded off Gibraltar. He next, from 1783 to 1786, and for a short time in 1791, served on the Halifax and Channel stations in the MERCURY and MARLBOROUGH, Capts. Stanhope and Bazely; and in 1794-5 he became in succession attached to the VICTORY 100, flag-ship of Lord Hood, and ARETHUSA and PHAETON frigates, Capts. Mark Robinson and Hon. Robt. Stopford. On 6 Sept. 1796, Mr. Mant, who had acted for a period as Lieutenant of the ARETHUSA, was confirmed to that rank in the FIRM gun-vessel. His succeeding appointments were, chiefly on the Home station, to the CUMBERLAND 74, Capt. Rowley, SHANNON frigate, Capt. Alex. Fraser, POWERFUL 74, Capt. Wm. O'Brien Drury, DROMEDARY store-ship, Capt. Thos. Leith, VALIANT 74, Capt. John Cochet, RUBY 64, Capt. Hon. Alan Hyde Gardner, ATLAS 98, Capt. Theophilus Jones, and COURAGEUX 74, Capt. Chas. Boyles. He left the ship last mentioned in 1804 in consequence of ill health, and did not again go afloat. He accepted the rank of Retired Commander on the Senior List 26 Dec. 1837.

From 9 Oct. 1804 until July, 1812, Commander Mant was a Poor Knight of Windsor. He married, 14 Jan. 1813, Miss Jane Osborne, and by that lady had issue three sons and two daughters. His eldest son was drowned in the merchant-service in 1834; and his next, George, at present holds an appointment in the Excise.

MANTON. (RETIRED COMMANDER, 1839. F-P., 19; H-P., 32.)

JOHN MANTON was born 14 May, 1782, in London, and died in July, 1846. He was son of John Manton, Esq., of co. Lincoln.

This officer entered the Navy, 1 Jan. 1796, as Fst.-cl. Vol., on board the AGINCOURT 64, Capt. John Williamson, and after enacting a Midshipman's part in the action off Camperdown 11 Oct. 1797, removed to the ROMNEY 50, Capts. John Lawford and Sir Home Popham. Being lent on his arrival in that ship at the Cape of Good Hope to the SPITFIRE tender, it was his lot, after conveying despatches to Bombay, to be wrecked in 1801 on a coral-reef in the Indian Ocean; in consequence whereof he was subjected, with the rest of the ship's company, to the severest privations for nearly a whole month, each person's allowance of water, during that period, being restricted to half-a-pint a-day. The advent of a vessel sent to their assistance at length enabling them to be rescued, Mr. Manton rejoined the ROMNEY, in which vessel he continued until May, 1803. Prior to the latter date he appears, on the occasion of a visit to the Red Sea, to have landed, for the purpose of procuring a supply of water, in the neighbourhood of Mount Felix, where his party, 11 in number, was suddenly attacked by a body of the natives, lying in ambush, who murdered all but himself and a Midshipman, the present Commander Wm. Savage. That officer was severely wounded in the head, and only escaped by being forcibly dragged to a boat by Mr. Manton, who succeeded in keeping the enemy at bay until they were both out of danger. In June, 1803, having returned to England,* he was received on board the COLOSSUS 74, Capt. Geo. Martin; and on 17 March, 1806, after a servitude of 18 months off the port of Cadiz and in the Channel in the POLYPHEMUS 64, and AUDACIOUS and IMPÉTUEUX 74's, each under the orders of Capt. John Lawford, he was promoted to the rank of Lieutenant and appointed to the command of the ALPHEA schooner on the Bermuda and Newfoundland stations, where he continued until Feb. 1808. During the remainder of the war we find him employed, with intervals, in the REDPOLE 10, Capt. John Joyce, IMPÉTUEUX 74, Capt. John Lawford, and AMELIA and NIGER 38's, Capts. Hon. Fred. Paul Irby and Peter Rainier. He was wounded, in the REDPOLE, in an action with a French brig-of-war off Bordeaux; accompanied, in the IMPÉTUEUX, the expedition to the Walcheren; and when Senior of the NIGER, and in company with the TAGUS 38, assisted, 6 Jan. 1814, at the capture, among the Cape de Verde Islands, of the French 40-gun frigate *Cérès*. His conduct on the latter occasion afforded Capt. Rainier, who sent him home in command of the prize, an opportunity of recommending him to the notice of the Admiralty as a deserving officer.† During a subsequent cruize off the coast of Africa, Lieut. Manton was placed in charge of a Portuguese slaver, whose crew, with 50 of the negroes, rose in the night, and, after inflicting on him eight wounds in the head and hands, retook their vessel and carried the British prisoners to Pernambuco, where they were for a short time confined. His last appointment was, 7 April, 1820, to the Coast Guard, in which service he remained for a period of 21 months. He retired with the rank of Commander 15 July, 1839.

He married, in 1808, Elizabeth, daughter of John Wills, Esq., Government Contractor, of Plymouth, by whom he has issue two daughters.

MAPLES, C.B. (REAR-ADMIRAL, 1846. F-P., 29; H-P., 36.)

JOHN FORDYCE MAPLES died 12 May, 1847, at the Priory, Kilburn, aged 79.

This officer entered the Navy, 5 Oct. 1782, as Captain's Servant, on board the TRIUMPH 74, Capt. Peter Affleck, lying at Portsmouth; served, from Sept. 1784 to April, 1789, in the HEBE frigate, commanded in the Channel by Capt. Edw. Thornbrough; and after an intermediate attachment, as Master's Mate, on the West India station, to the BLONDE 32, Capt. Wm. Affleck, CENTURION 50, flag-ship of Rear-Admiral P. Affleck, and PENELOPE 32, Capt. Bartholomew Sam. Rowley, was there nominated, 7 May, 1794, Acting-Lieutenant of the EUROPA 50, bearing the broad pendant of Commodore Ford. On 16 April, 1793, at which period he was belonging to the PENELOPE, we find

* Before he left the East Indies Mr. Manton had the misfortune to receive a *coup-de-soleil*.

† *Vide* Gaz. 1814, p. 881.

him assisting at the capture of *Le Goelan* 14, the first republican vessel taken during the war, and in the following Sept. present at the occupation of Jeremie, St. Domingo, and at the capture of about 2000 tons of shipping laden with colonial produce, two neutral vessels with cargoes, and an armed schooner, in the bays near St. Louis. He also, when in company with the IPHIGENIA 32, took part, 25 Nov. in the same year, in a warm action of half an hour, which terminated in the capture, with a loss to the PENELOPE of 1 man killed and 7 wounded, of the French 36-gun frigate *L'Inconstante.* At the commencement of 1794 the PENELOPE was employed in the blockade of Port-au-Prince, and soon afterwards in covering the debarkation of the troops under Lieut.-Colonel Whitelocke, near Cape Tiburon. She subsequently engaged the batteries of Aux Cayes, and brought out thence several loaded merchantmen. On his removal to the EUROPA Mr. Maples served for several weeks in a fort at St. Nicolas Mole. After witnessing the subjugation of Port-au-Prince, 4 June, 1794, he removed (he had been confirmed a Lieutenant on 16 of the preceding May) to LA MAGICIENNE 32, Capts. Geo. Martin, Rich. Hussey Moubray, Wm. Henry Ricketts, and Wm. Ogilvy, and was for some time employed in co-operating with the army in a vain attempt to complete the conquest of the French posts in St. Domingo. Continuing in LA MAGICIENNE for a period of nearly five years, he assisted in consequence at the capture of a variety of the enemy's vessels, and, among these, of *Le Cerf Volant* corvette of 18 guns, *La Fortune* privateer of 8 guns and 74 men, *Le Poisson Volant*, of 12 guns and 80 men, and two Spanish brigs laden with cocoa. In Jan. and Feb. 1797, with the boats of the same ship under his orders, Mr. Maples cut out two privateers and a Spanish armed brig from different anchorages at the west end of Puerto Rico; and on 6 of the ensuing April, in conjunction with those of the REGULUS 74, he effected the destruction of 11 sail of merchantmen in the harbour of Cape Roxo, spiked 4 guns on shore, and brought out two vessels, without the loss of a man. On the occasion of a spirited and well-timed attack made on 23 of the latter month on the enemy in Carcasse Bay by LA MAGICIENNE and the REGULUS and FORTUNE schooner, Mr. Maples, who had become Senior Lieutenant of the first-named ship, boarded a 6-gun sloop and took her in tow under a tremendous fire of round-shot, grape, and musketry—a service in the performance of which his boat sustained a loss of 4 men killed, and Mr. Morgan, Master's Mate, and 10 men wounded. On 28 Sept. he had 2 men badly wounded in an unsuccessful attack upon two small privateers at Porto Paix. He further, on 22 Dec. in the same year, 1797, commanded the boats at the capture of a privateer mounting 2 guns near Cape Causedo; and on 27 he was present with a small squadron at the taking, in Guadilla Bay, Puerto Rico, of *Le Brutus*, of 9 guns, a merchant-ship, three brigs, and a schooner. LA MAGICIENNE and her consorts were next employed in dislodging a large body of brigands who had established themselves in Platform Bay. On 19 March, 1798, Mr. Maples landed with 100 seamen under his orders to do garrison-duty at Irois; on returning whence to the ship he was slightly wounded by a musket-ball in the right leg, and had one of his party killed close to him. In the early part of 1799 he was again intrusted with the conduct of several boat enterprises, and contrived to make many prizes. In the course of that and the following year we find him joining the QUEEN 98, ROYAL GEORGE 100, and LONDON 98, flag-ships in the West Indies, Channel, and Baltic of Sir Hyde Parker. On 2 April, 1801, he served as a volunteer with Nelson's division in the action off Copenhagen; and during the four following months he had charge of the OTTER fire-brig, also stationed in the Baltic. His subsequent appointments, in the capacity of Lieutenant, were to the GANGES 74, Capts. Thos. Fras. Fremantle, Joseph Baker, and Geo. M'Kinley, PRINCE GEORGE 98, Capt. Joseph Sydney Yorke, DEFENCE 74, Capt. Geo. Hope, TIGRE 80, Capt. Benj. Hallowell, NAIAD 38, Capt. Thos. Dundas, MARS 74, Capts. Wm. Lukin and Jas. Katon, and ATLAS 98; in which ships he was principally employed on the Jamaica, Halifax, Home, and Mediterranean stations. He fought in the NAIAD at Trafalgar, 21 Oct. 1805; and during the 16 months which preceded his advancement to the rank of Commander 21 Oct. 1810, was First-Lieutenant of the MARS and ATLAS. Obtaining command, 30 Aug. 1811, of the ÆTNA bomb, Capt. Maples was for some time employed in that vessel at the defence of Isla de Leon—a service of a very harassing nature. In Oct. 1812 he removed to the PELICAN, of 18 guns, yielding a broadside weight of 262 lbs.; and on 14 of the following Aug. he had the good fortune, during a cruize on the Cork station, to capture, after a spirited and highly-creditable action of 45 minutes, the American sloop *Argus*, of 20 guns and 122 men, throwing a weight in broadside of 228 lbs., whose resistance occasioned a loss to themselves of 6 killed and 18 wounded, and to the British, out of 101 men, of 2 killed and 5 wounded.* As a reward for his promptitude, skill, and gallantry in this affair, Capt. Maples was deservedly advanced to Post-rank by a commission dated 23 Aug. 1813. His last appointment was, 14 Dec. 1814, to the command of the LARNE 20, which however he only retained until 15 of the ensuing month. He was nominated a C.B. 4 June, 1815; and accepted the rank of Retired Rear-Admiral 1 Oct. 1846.

He married, in 1814, the widow of John Carthew, Esq., Solicitor, of Woodbridge, co. Suffolk, and niece of Vice-Admiral Jas. Carthew. AGENTS—Messrs. Chard.

MAPLETON. (COMMANDER, 1846.)

DAVID ROBERT BUNBURY MAPLETON, born 4 Feb. 1810, is son of the late Commander David Mapleton, R.N.,† of Newton Abbots, co. Devon.

This officer entered the Royal Naval College in 1822, and embarked in 1824, as a Volunteer, on board the ATHOLL 28, Capt. Jas. Arthur Murray, fitting at Portsmouth. After serving for some time in the CHANTICLEER 10, BOADICEA 46, and PARTHEAN 10, Capts. Hope Johnstone, Sir Jas. Brisbane, and Hon. Geo. Barrington, he became Midshipman of the DIAMOND 46, Capt. Lord Napier, and sailed for South America, where he continued, in the THETIS and BRITON frigates, Capts. Arthur Batt Bingham and Hon. Wm. Gordon, until 1828. In the following year, having returned to England and passed his examination, he again proceeded to Southern America in the WARSPITE 76, flag-ship of the late Sir Thos. Baker, who, we believe, nominated him Lieutenant of the TALBOT 28, Capt. Rich. Dickinson. He was not, however, officially promoted until 10 Jan. 1837; previously to which period he had been re-employed as Mate in the REINDEER packet, Lieut.-Commander Henry Percy Dicken, and WANDERER 16, commanded on the North America and West India station by Capt. Thos. Dilke. His succeeding appointments were—28 Feb. 1837, to the MALABAR 74, Capt. Sir Wm. Augustus Montagu, fitting for the Lisbon station—24 March, 1838, to the FAIRY 10, Capt. Wm. Hewett, engaged in the survey of the North Sea—9 May, 1839, to the command (which he retained until 17 June, 1841) of the RAVEN cutter, employed on particular service—4 May, 1842, to the Coast Guard—31 May, 1843, to the command of the AVON steam-

* *Vide* Gaz. 1813, p. 1664.

† Commander Mapleton entered the Navy in 1797, and obtained his first commission 10 May, 1804. He served for a long time as Second and First Lieutenant under Lord Cochrane (whose high official praise he repeatedly elicited) in the PALLAS and IMPÉRIEUSE frigates; was in upwards, during the term of his career afloat, of 100 engagements with the enemy—principally in cutting out vessels and storming forts; and was on several occasions wounded, especially at the taking of Genoa, where he was the only officer mentioned by Lord Wm. Bentinck. He attained the rank of Commander 17 May, 1814; and died 22 March, 1842, aged 61.

vessel, on the North America and West India station, whence he returned in the following Sept.—and, 27 April, 1844, and 1 Sept. 1846, to that of the SYDENHAM and TORCH steamers, on the Mediterranean and Home stations. He attained his present rank 9 Nov. 1846.

Commander Mapleton married, first, in Jan. 1837, Elizabeth, daughter of Capt. David Braimer, R.N. (1817); and, that lady dying in March, 1838, secondly, 21 July, 1840, Ann, daughter of David Compigné, Esq., of Gosport, Hants, by whom he has issue a son and two daughters. AGENT—Joseph Woodhead.

MARCH. (LIEUTENANT, 1816. F-P., 9; H-P., 31.)

CHARLES MARCH entered the Navy, 23 Dec. 1807, as Fst.-cl. Vol., on board the HINDOSTAN store-ship, Capt. Lewis Hole; and in the following April, on his return from a visit to the Tagus, became Midshipman of the EGERIA sloop, also commanded by Capt. Hole, with whom he continued to serve in the Channel, off the coasts of Spain and Portugal, and in the North Sea (assisting intermediately at the capture of the *Næsois* privateer of 10 guns and 26 men, *Aalborg* cutter of 6 guns and 25 men, and *Alvor* privateer of 14 guns and 38 men), until transferred, 1 Aug. 1812, to the CORNWALL 74, Capts. John Broughton, Edw. Tucker, and Edw. W. C. R. Owen, employed off Flushing and with the Brest fleet. In June, 1813, he rejoined Capt. Hole on board the BACCHUS 16; and in Feb. and April, 1814, he became in succession attached to the SALVADOR DEL MUNDO, flag-ship at Plymouth of Vice-Admiral Wm. Domett, and WOODLARK 10, commanded in the Channel and Mediterranean by Capts. Robt. Balfour and Wm. Cutfield. Of the latter vessel he was for a short time Acting-Lieutenant. Removing as Admiralty-Midshipman, in July, 1816, to the SUPERB 74, Capt. Chas. Ekins, Mr. March was afforded an opportunity of sharing in that ship in the battle of Algiers. He was in consequence advanced to his present rank by commission dated 16 Sept. in the same year; but has not been since afloat.

Lieut. March married, first, Mary, only daughter of the late J. Byles, Esq., of Stow Market, co. Suffolk; and (having been left a widower 22 Jan. 1842) secondly, 11 June, 1843, Emma, daughter of T. Ebbs, Esq., of Beccles, in the same shire.

MARCH. (LIEUTENANT, 1815. F-P., 10; H-P., 31.)

JEREMIAH MARCH entered the Navy, 13 Sept. 1806, as Ordinary, on board the ESCORT gun-brig, to which vessel, commanded by Lieuts. Wm. Smith and Geo. Vandeput Crosbe, he continued attached on the North Sea, Channel, and North American stations, until July, 1815—the last five years and a half in the capacity of Midshipman. In the following Oct., after having been intermediately borne, at Sheerness and Portsmouth, on the books of the NAMUR 74, QUEEN CHARLOTTE 100, and WASP 16, Capts. Geo. M'Kinley, Edmund Boger, and Wm. Woolridge, he took up a commission bearing date 11 March in the same year, 1815. He has not been since employed. AGENTS—Coplands and Burnett.

MARCUARD. (LIEUTENANT, 1840.)

CHARLES RICHARD MARCUARD entered the Navy 19 Dec. 1828; passed his examination in 1835; obtained his commission 23 March, 1840; was then appointed Additional-Lieutenant of the PRESIDENT 50, Capt. Wm. Broughton, as he subsequently was, 26 Dec. 1841, of the DUBLIN 50, flag-ship of Rear-Admiral Rich. Thomas, both on the South American station, whence he returned at the close of 1842; and on 7 Nov. 1843, and 2 April, 1845, joined the VESTAL 26, and DRIVER steam-sloop, commanded in the East Indies by Capts. Chas. Talbot and Courtenay Osborn Hayes. The latter vessel was paid off in 1847. AGENTS—Messrs. Chard.

MARKETT. (LIEUTENANT, 1833.)

JOHN MARKETT entered the Navy 12 April, 1814; passed his examination in 1822; acquired the rank of Lieutenant 31 May, 1833; was appointed, 1 June, 1837, to the MAGNIFICENT receiving-ship at Jamaica, Capt. John Paget; and since 14 July, 1838, has been in command of a station in the Coast Guard.

MARKHAM. (LIEUT., 1824. F-P., 11; H-P., 26.)

JOHN MARKHAM, born 6 June, 1797, is second son of the late Wm. Markham, Esq., of Becca Hall, near Aberford, co. York, private Secretary to Warren Hastings, by Elizabeth, daughter of the late Oldfield Bowles, Esq., of North Aston, co. Oxford. He is brother (with the Rev. David Fred. Markham, Canon of Windsor, and Rector of Great Horkesley, co. Essex) of the present Wm. Markham, Esq., of Becca Hall, Colonel of the West York Militia, and a Magistrate and Deputy-Lieutenant for the West Riding; also of Capt. Warren Markham of the 72nd Highlanders, who died at the Cape of Good Hope 15 Nov. 1831; and of Lieut.-Colonel Chas. Markham, of the 60th Rifles, who died at Jamaica 2 April, 1842. His eldest sister, Laura, is married to Wm. Mure, Esq., of Caldwell, Colonel of the Renfrewshire Militia.

This officer entered the Navy, in 1810, as Fst.-cl. Vol., on board the GALATEA frigate, Capt. Woodley Losack; and on his arrival in the following year at the Cape of Good Hope in the CURAÇOA 36, Capt. John Tower, joined the SCIPION 74,* bearing the flag of Hon. Robt. Stopford; with whom he removed to the LION 64, and in 1812 returned to England in the PRESIDENT 50. He afterwards, until 1819, served on the Home, Mediterranean, St. Helena, and Jamaica stations, chiefly in the capacity of Midshipman, in the ALBION 74, flag-ship of Sir Roger Curtis, BELLONA and DEVONSHIRE 74's, Capts. Geo. M'Kinley and Ross Donnelly, EUROTAS 38 and ELIZABETH 74, bearing each the flag of Hon. Chas. Elphinstone Fleeming, VOLONTAIRE 38, Capt. Hon. Geo. Granville Waldegrave, and NEWCASTLE and SYBILLE flag-ships of Sir Pulteney Malcolm and Sir Home Popham. Returning home then as Acting-Lieutenant, in the ESK 20, Capt. Geo. Gustavus Lennock, he next, after an interval of three years, joined, in Dec. 1822, and June, 1823, the TARTAR 42, Capt. Thos. Brown, and CREOLE, of similar force, bearing the broad pendant of Sir Thos. Masterman Hardy, both on the Brazilian station, where he was confirmed a Lieutenant, 30 Jan. 1824, in the DORIS 42, Capts. Thos. Bourchier and Wm. Jas. Hope Johnstone. He invalided home in the following Aug. on board the BRAZEN sloop; and has not been since afloat.

He married Miss Marianne Wood, and by that lady has issue five sons. AGENTS—Messrs. Halford and Co.

MARKLAND, C.B., K.L.A. (REAR-ADMIRAL, 1846. F-P., 19; H-P., 33.)

JOHN DUFF MARKLAND, born 14 Sept. 1780, at Leeds, is son of Edw. Markland, Esq., of that place (a descendant of the Marklands of Wigan, co. Lancaster, located there as far back as the reign of Edw. III.), by Elizabeth Sophia, second daughter of Josiah Hardy, Esq., H.M. Consul at Cadiz, and formerly Governor of the Jerseys in North America. He is nephew, by marriage, of Capt. John Cooke, R.N., who fell in command of the BELLEROPHON 74 at Trafalgar; first-cousin of Capts. G. W. H. D'Aeth and J. H. Godby, also of the R.N.; and a relative of Commander T. P. Le Hardy, R.N.

This officer entered the Navy, 27 May, 1795, as Fst.-cl. Vol., on board the HEBE frigate, Capt. Paul Minchin, stationed in the Channel; and in the following July became Midshipman of LA TOURTERELLE 28, commanded by his uncle Capt. Cooke; whom, after cruizing for eight months on the Cork station in the SEAHORSE 38, Capts. John Peyton

* We believe he was present, in the SCIPION, at the reduction of the island of Java.

and Robt. Dudley Oliver, he rejoined, in Aug. 1796, on board La Nymphe 36. On 9 of the following March we find him assisting, in company with the San Fiorenzo 36, at the capture of the French frigates *La Résistance* of 48, and *La Constance* of 24 guns. On leaving La Nymphe, which ship had been latterly commanded by Capt. Percy Fraser, Mr. Markland, in April, 1798, joined the Royal George 100, bearing the flag at Portsmouth of Lord Bridport, with whom he remained until again placed, in April, 1799, under the orders of Capt. Cooke on board the Amethyst 38. While cruizing in that vessel in the Bay of Biscay and off the north coast of Spain, he was afforded an opportunity of contributing to the capture of *L'Aventure* French privateer of 14 guns and 75 men, *Le Vaillant* cutter of 15 guns and 131 men, and *Le Mars* ship of 22 guns and 100 men; and of witnessing the surrender of *La Dédaigneuse* frigate of 36 guns and 300 men. On 8 Jan. 1801 he was made Lieutenant into the Malta 80, Capt. Albemarle Bertie, on the Channel station, where he served until April 1802. His next appointment was, 29 Nov. in the latter year, to the Albion 74, Capt. John Ferrier, under whom, it appears, he aided in taking, off Brest, 28 May, 1803, *La Franchise* French frigate, and, in the Bay of Bengal, in the following Jan., *La Clarisse* corvette. In Dec. 1805, after he had been for nearly two years First-Lieutenant of the Albion, he invalided home on board the Tremendous 74, Capt. John Osborne; and on his arrival he had the satisfaction of finding that he had been promoted to the rank of Commander by commission dated 22 Jan. 1806. Obtaining an appointment, 12 April, 1808, to the Bustard 16, Capt. Markland was at first employed in that vessel off Boulogne and was then ordered to the Mediterranean. On 29 July, 1809, being at the time in the Adriatic, he coalesced with the Acorn sloop, and the boats of the Excellent 74, and elicited the highest admiration of Capt. John West, the senior officer on the station, by the masterly manner in which he led into the little-known harbour of Duino, near Trieste, and by his well-directed fire assisted in capturing six heavy gun-boats belonging to the Italian marine, and 10 coasting traders, laden with brandy, flour, rice, and wheat.* At the commencement of July, 1810, the Bustard took and destroyed nine of the enemy's vessels in a harbour on the east side of Calabria; and during the next three months her Captain was intrusted with the command of the sloops of war stationed in the Faro of Messina for the purpose of protecting Sicily from the threatened invasion of Joachim Murat, whose army, consisting of nearly 40,000 men, was encamped on the opposite shore, and who had collected more than 80 gun and mortar boats between Scylla and Reggio. He was thrown in consequence into frequent action with the enemy's land-batteries and flotilla, and rendered such good service† that he not only obtained the repeated thanks of Rear-Admiral Geo. Martin, but, on 5 Feb. 1811, a few days after his removal to the Eclair 18, was nominated by the Commander-in-Chief, Sir Chas. Cotton, although personally unknown to him, Captain of the Ville de Paris 110, flag-ship of Rear-Admiral Thos. Fras. Fremantle, whom he followed, in the course of the same year, into the Rodney and Milford 74's. Capt. Markland's confirmation to Post-rank took place while he was in the Rodney, 18 April, 1811. Joining in all the operations of 1813 in the Adriatic, he assisted in reducing the town of Fiumé, where, as soon as the batteries had been silenced, he proceeded with the armed boats and dislodged the enemy from their last stronghold. He also landed at Porto Ré;‡ was very active in exciting a spirit of revolt against their oppressors among the inhabitants of the different islands at the head of the Adriatic; beheld the fall of Rovigno, Piran, and Capo d'Istria; landed, with Capt. Jas. Black of the Weasel sloop, and, by a *coup-de-main*, took possession of the arsenal at Trieste, destroying its guns, and sawing into many pieces the keel and stern-post of a large frigate; and, during the operations which led to the surrender of the citadel at the latter place, was again employed on shore, and called forth the thanks of Rear-Admiral Fremantle for having in every way exerted himself, particularly in the arrangements of stores and provisions.* Resigning command of the Milford 31 Oct. 1813, Capt. Markland, in the ensuing Dec., returned to England with despatches from the last-mentioned officer. He was rewarded for his services by being nominated a C.B. 4 June, 1815; and in 1816, "in testimony of his Imperial Majesty's approbation of the distinguished services rendered by him at the capture of Trieste, and the other operations in Italy during the campaign of 1813," he was presented with the Cross of the Order of Leopold of Austria. His last appointment was, 28 April, 1830, to the command (which he retained until paid off in Jan. 1833) of the Briton 46, employed on particular service. He obtained the Captains' Good Service pension 19 Feb. 1842, and accepted his present rank 1 Oct. 1846.

The Rear-Admiral married, 8 March, 1814, Helen Ellery, eldest daughter of Lewis Dymocke Grosvenor Tregonwell, Esq., of Cranbourn Lodge, co. Dorset, by whom he has issue one son and three daughters. Agents—Messrs. Halford and Co.

* *Vide* Gaz. 1809, p. 1931.

† During his command of the Bustard Capt. Markland took, in the whole, 25 vessels, and destroyed 39, including some armed feluccas, which, with the assistance of the Halcyon sloop, were altogether annihilated under Cape del Arme, where they were for a long time defended by their crews, some soldiers, and the neighbouring peasantry.—*V.* Gaz. 1810, p. 1859.

‡ *V.* Gaz. 1813, p. 2009.

* *Vide* Gaz. 1813, p. 2478.

MARLEY. (Lieut., 1809. f-p., 21; h-p., 34.)

Robert Roper Marley entered the Navy in 1792, as an Officer's Servant, on board the Powerful 74, in which ship, commanded by Capts. Thos. Hicks, Wm. Albany Otway, Fisher, and Wm. O'Brien Drury, he served, on the St. Helena, West India, Channel, North Sea, and Mediterranean stations, until 1800—the last five years in the capacity of Midshipman. On 11 Oct. 1797 he was present in the action off Camperdown. After a servitude of 20 months in the Proselyte, Capt. Geo. Fowke, Mr. Marley, towards the close of 1802, at which period he was in the West Indies, became attached to the Leviathan 74, bearing the flag of Sir John Thos. Duckworth, with whom and with the late Vice-Admiral Jas. Rich. Dacres he continued employed in the same ship and in the Hercule 74 until 1806; during which period he took part in the operations against the French at St. Domingo, and was for a time detached in the Gracieuse tender of 12 guns, commanded by Mr. T. B. Smith, Midshipman. In that vessel, after having assisted at the capture of a large Spanish schooner, and exchanged fire with a French sloop within gun-shot of the forts of the city of St. Domingo, he shared in a very gallant conflict which terminated in the destruction, 11 April, 1805, of a schooner carrying 1 long brass 12-pounder, mounted on a circle amidships, 2 long brass 4-pounder carriage-guns, and 4 brass 3-pounder swivels, with a crew of 96 men. A wound he received on the occasion† procured him a grant from the Patriotic Society. In April 1806 and Jan. 1807 he was successively nominated Acting Sub-Lieutenant of the Pelican sloop, Capt. Wm. Ward, and Pike schooner, Lieut.-Commander John Ottley, also in the West Indies, where, after he had again served for nine months as Midshipman in the Veteran 64, flag-ship of Vice-Admiral Dacres, he became Acting-Lieutenant of the Drake sloop, Capt. John Fleming. He removed in a similar capacity, in the following July, to the Jasper 10, Capt. Wm. Westcott Daniel, stationed on the coasts of Spain, France, and Portugal; and on 31 Dec. 1809 he was confirmed a Lieutenant in the Alfred 74, Capts. Joshua Rowley Watson and Joshua Sydney Horton. Being subsequently, on his return from a second visit to the West Indies, ordered off Cadiz, he was there, in Feb. 1812, placed in command of

† *V.* Gaz. 1805, p. 901.

gun-boat No. 7, and employed in the defence of that place. He went back to the ALFRED in the ensuing April, but left her in Sept. of the same year; and was lastly, from 6 Aug. 1813 to 7 July, 1814, stationed off the coast of Ireland in the AVON sloop, Capt. Geo. Rose Sartorius.

He is in the receipt, for his wounds, of a pension of 91*l.* 5*s.*

MARRETT. (RETIRED CAPTAIN, 1845. F-P., 16; H-P., 38.)

JOSEPH MARRETT entered the Navy, 23 Jan. 1793, as Midshipman, on board the CRESCENT of 42 guns and 257 men, Capt. Jas. Saumarez; and on 20 of the following Oct. was present at the capture of the French frigate *La Réunion* of 36 guns and 320 men, 120 of whom were either killed or wounded, without however any casualty to the British. In Dec. of the same year he accompanied an expedition under Earl Moira and Rear-Admiral M'Bride to the coasts of Normandy and Brittany; and on 8 June, 1794, we find him in action with an enemy's squadron of very superior force, from which the CRESCENT escaped by the most bold and masterly manœuvres. On afterwards accompanying Sir Jas. Saumarez (who had been knighted for the capture of *La Réunion*) into the ORION 74, he shared in Lord Bridport's action, in the battle off Cape St. Vincent, and in the victory of the Nile. He was confirmed a Lieutenant of the CANOPUS 80, Capt. Bartholomew James, after having acted for nearly five months in that capacity, 5 April, 1799; and was subsequently appointed—12 Aug. 1799, to the ROYAL SOVEREIGN 100, flag-ship of Lord Gardner and Sir Henry Harvey in the Channel, where he served until Oct. 1801—19 Sept. 1803, to the EURUS sloop, Capt. Alex. Innes, on the Cork station—24 Nov. 1804, and 8 April, 1805, to the successive command of two gun-brigs, in the latter of which, the MARTIAL, he served in the Channel and off the coast of Spain until compelled by ill health to invalid in Nov. 1809—and, 29 Sept. 1810, to the ULYSSES 44 as Flag-Lieutenant, on the Guernsey station, to the Duc de Bouillon. He was made Commander 26 May, 1812; and accepted his present rank 20 Oct. 1845.

Capt. Marrett's eldest daughter was the wife of the late Lieut. Wakeman Edwards, R.N. (1810). AGENT—Fred. Dufaur.

MARRIOTT. (LIEUT, 1842. F-P., 14; H-P., 2.)

GEORGE MARRIOTT entered the Navy 5 Aug. 1831; served for nearly six years and a half as Volunteer and Midshipman on the West India station; passed his examination 5 Dec. 1837; and during the next four years and a half was employed in the capacity of Mate on the coast of Africa, where the valour he exhibited in command of a boat belonging to the ROLLA 10, Lieut.-Commander Chas. Hall, procured him a commission dated 15 Aug. 1842. His appointments have since been—20 Oct. 1843, to the ST. VINCENT 120, flag-ship at Portsmouth of Sir Chas. Rowley—9 March, 1844, to the PENELOPE steam-frigate, bearing the broad pendant of Commodore Wm. Jones on the coast of Africa, whence he returned in the summer of 1845—and 26 May, 1846, to the TRAFALGAR 120, Capt. John Neale Nott, now employed on particular service. AGENT—Joseph Woodhead.

MARRYAT, C.B., F.R.S., F.L.S. (CAPTAIN, 1825. F-P., 15; H-P., 26.)

FREDERICK MARRYAT, born 10 July, 1792, in London, is second son of the late Joseph Marryat, Esq., M.P. for Sandwich, Chairman of the Committee at Lloyd's, and Colonial Agent for the island of Grenada, by Charlotte, third daughter of the late Fred. Geyer, Esq., a distinguished American loyalist, who suffered much from the fervency of his attachment to the Throne at the period of the separation of Great Britain from her colonies. He is brother of Joseph Marryat, Esq., formerly M.P. for Sandwich; and a descendant of Le Sieur Thos. Marriatte, a Protestant native of Normandy, and an officer in the Huguenot army, who, having escaped the massacre of St. Bartholomew, 24 Aug. 1572, fled to England with the loss of all his property. His grandfather, Thos. Marryat, Esq., M.D., was the author of a work entitled 'Therapeutics, or the Art of Healing.'

This officer entered the Navy, 23 Sept. 1806, as a Volunteer, on board the IMPÉRIEUSE, 38, Capts. Lord Cochrane and Thos. Garth, in which ship he remained until Oct. 1809. While under the gallant Cochrane he contributed to the capture and destruction, within one month, of three French national transports and 12 merchant-vessels, and also to the demolition of Fort Roquette, at the entrance of Arcasson; served in the boats when they incurred a loss of 16 men killed and wounded in effecting the capture of a Maltese privateer, supposed until the moment of her surrender to be an enemy's vessel, 15 Nov. 1807; was present at the cutting-out of a Turkish ship from Port Valona, on the coast of Dalmatia; assisted, in the year 1808, during a cruize of four months off the coast of Catalonia and among the Balearic islands, in taking and destroying one national brig, six gun-vessels, one privateer, and about 50 sail of merchantmen; aided, 31 July, 1808, in reducing and levelling the castle of Mongat, by which the road from Barcelona to Gerona, besieged at the time by the French, had been completely commanded; participated in a variety of dashing operations on the coast of France during the ensuing months of Aug. and Sept.; landed on returning to the shores of Catalonia, and was particularly mentioned for his conduct at the defence of Trinidad Castle, attached to the fortress of Rosas, against a whole French army, 1000 of whose picked men were completely repulsed by 80 of the British, supported by an equal number of Spaniards, on the occasion of an assault made by the former, 30 Nov. 1808;* aided, 30 Dec. following, in obtaining possession, in the harbour of Cadaqués, after a short action, of the enemy's batteries, two national vessels, and 12 merchantmen, laden with wheat for the garrison of Barcelona; and, besides acting a part in other affairs of an equally spirited character, served with credit in an explosion-vessel under Lieut. Urry Johnson in the memorable attack made upon the French shipping in Aix Roads 11 April, 1809, and was on board the IMPÉRIEUSE the next day, when, unsupported, she approached the *Calcutta* of 56 guns, and compelled that ship to strike her colours. In Oct. 1809, at which period he was with the Flushing expedition, Mr. Marryat took a passage to England in the VICTORIOUS 74, and on his arrival joined the CENTAUR 74, flag-ship of Sir Sam. Hood, with whom he soon again sailed for the Mediterranean. He returned towards the close of the following year in the ATLAS 74, Capt. Jas. Sanders; and was next, until promoted to the rank of Lieutenant, 26 Dec. 1812, employed, on the Home, West India, and North American stations, in the NAMUR 74, Capt. Alex. Shippard, AFRICA 64, Capt. John Bastard, CHUB schooner, Lieut.-Commander Jas. Nisbett, ÆOLUS and SPARTAN frigates, Capts. Lord Jas. Townshend and Edw. Pelham Brenton, and ROYAL WILLIAM, Capt. Geo. Fowke. On 30 Sept. 1811 we find him earning the general admiration of the ship's company, and the high approval of his Captain, for his courageous conduct, when no other person would attempt it, in leading the way aloft during a tremendous gale from the S.E., which had laid the ÆOLUS on her beam-ends, and had literally blown away her topmasts and mizenmast, for the purpose of cutting away the mainyard, as the only means left of saving the mainmast and righting the ship. In Aug. 1812, a few days prior to his discharge from the SPARTAN, he appears to have been engaged in two boat-attacks in Haycos Harbour and Little River, the result of which was the capture of six American armed vessels. In the capacity of Lieutenant, Mr. Marryat was appointed—8 Jan. 1813, to the ESPIÈGLE sloop, Capt. John Taylor, on the West India station, whence he returned in the next April—and 31 Jan. 1814, to

* *Vide* Gaz. 1809, p. 307.

the NEWCASTLE 58, Capt. Lord Geo. Stuart. In that ship he lent his aid to the capture of the privateers *Ida* of 10 guns and 65 men, and the *Prince de Neufchâtel* of 18 guns and 135 men; and on 19 Dec. 1814 he took command of her barge and cut out four vessels from Boston Bay, an exploit which occasioned him a loss of 11 men killed and wounded. Illness compelling him to leave the NEWCASTLE in Feb. 1815, he returned home a passenger in the CONWAY 26; and on 13 of the following June was promoted to the rank of Commander. His succeeding appointments were—13 June, 1820, to the BEAVER sloop, in which vessel, after visiting Madeira, Teneriffe, St. Jago, Trinidad on the Main, Tristan de Cunha, and the Cape of Good Hope, he proceeded off St. Helena, where, on the morning after the decease of Napoleon Buonaparte, 6 May, 1821, he formed one of the three Naval Captains admitted to view the body of the unfortunate Emperor*—7 July, 1821, to the ROSARIO 10, part of the squadron selected to escort the remains of Queen Caroline from Harwich to Cuxhaven—and, 31 March, 1823 (having paid the latter vessel off 7 Feb. 1822), to the LARNE 20, fitting for the East Indies. Joining, in May, 1824, in the hostilities against Ava, Capt. Marryat continued from that period until the following Sept. to officiate as senior Naval Officer in co-operation with the expedition under Major-General Sir Archibald Campbell, K.C.B., and won considerable fame by the able, gallant, and zealous manner in which he discharged the duties of that conspicuous and responsible post. He subsequently, during the months of Feb. and March, 1825, commanded an armament sent in conjunction with a military force under Major Sale up the Bassein River, where the services he rendered materially operated in the general results of the campaign.† His conduct from first to last, indeed, was so marked that it procured him the repeated acknowledgments of the Supreme Government and other high authorities in India, and was the means of his being included in a vote of thanks from both Houses of Parliament, his rank proving the only obstacle to his being personally named. In April, 1825, Capt. Marryat assumed acting-command of the TEES 26, owing to a death vacancy; but his Post-commission was not signed until 25 July following. In the early part of 1826 he returned to England and paid the TEES off. He was nominated a C.B. 26 Dec. in the same year; and was lastly, from 10 Nov. 1828 until Nov. 1830, employed in the ARIADNE 28 on diplomatic service at Madeira and the Western Islands, and in searching for supposed dangers in the Atlantic.

In addition to the productions which have rendered him famous as a novelist, Capt. Marryat is the author of a work, published in 1822, entitled 'Suggestions for the Abolition of the present System of Impressment in the Naval Service,' a volume in which he so clearly demonstrated the propriety of all merchant-vessels carrying apprentices in proportion to their tonnage, instead of West Indiamen only, as was then the case, that in a few months Government adopted his views. He had previously invented a code of signals for vessels in the merchant-service, including a cipher for secret correspondence, now in general use by our own and all foreign navies.‡ On their being translated into French, and supplied by *ordonnance* to the French marine and merchant service, the King of the French sent him the Croix d'Officier of the Légion d'Honneur. In Dec. 1847 Capt. Marryat was awarded the Good Service pension. He married, 21 Jan. 1819, Catherine, youngest daughter of Sir Stephen Shairp, of Russell Place, formerly Chargé d'Affaires at the Court of Russia, by whom he has, with other issue, two sons, both in the R.N.—the elder, Frederick, a Lieutenant.

* *Vide* Gaz. 1821, p. 1409.

† *V.* Gaz. 1824, pp. 1957, 1965; and Gaz. 1825, pp. 325, 327, 498, 1494, 2277.

‡ Not less than five times has Capt. Marryat generously hazarded his existence for the preservation of others. The first instance of the kind occurred in 1807, when he jumped from the IMPÉRIEUSE and saved a midshipman, Mr. Henry Cobbett; the second in 1810, in the course of which year, belonging at the time to the CENTAUR he effected the rescue of a man named Thomas Moubray, who had fallen from the main-yard, while cruizing off Toulon; the third in 1811, when, running down the Trades at the rate of seven knots an hour, he leaped from the AFRICA after another seaman, James Walker, whom, however, his humane efforts failed to benefit, being left nearly two miles astern of the ship, and upwards of thirty minutes in the water before a boat arrived to his assistance; the fourth in the same year, when he saved one of the crew of the ÆOLUS; and the last in Feb. 1813, on 8 of which month, although his efforts were unfortunately not successful, he dashed from L'ESPIÈGLE in a heavy sea, in the hope of succouring a sailor, Jacob Small, and was picked up a mile and a half distant from the sloop in an exhausted and nearly senseless state. His gallant and benevolent exertions could not, of course, do otherwise than elicit the warmest thanks of the Royal Humane Society, with whose medal he was subsequently presented for his invention of a life-boat, described in its 47th Report.

MARRYAT. (LIEUTENANT, 1845.)

FREDERICK MARRYAT is eldest son of Capt. Fred Marryat, R.N., C.B.

This officer entered the Navy in 1830; passed his examination 8 Jan. 1841; and after a servitude of more than three years in the East Indies as Mate of the CAMBRIAN 36, Capt. Henry Ducie Chads, was promoted to the rank of Lieutenant 1 Sept. 1845. His appointments have since been—5 Oct. 1846, to the SPHYNX steam-sloop, Capt. John Bettinson Cragg, his exertions in rescuing which vessel, when aground in Brixstone Bay in Jan. 1847, procured him the thanks of the Admiralty, but nearly cost him his life—and, 9 April, 1847, to the AVENGER steam-frigate of 650 horse-power, Capt. Sidney Colpoys Dacres, now on the Lisbon station. On two consecutive evenings in the month of Oct. 1847 Lieut. Marryat intrepidly plunged into the sea after a man who had each time fallen overboard. On the last occasion, the drowning person having convulsively clasped him round the neck, he would have been inevitably lost had it not been for the presence of mind of the First-Lieutenant, Hugh Mallett Kinsman, who, observing the danger in which his shipmates were placed, instantly jumped in himself and was the means of their both being saved.

MARSH. (CAPTAIN, 1842. F-P., 21; H-P., 20.)

DIGBY MARSH is third son of the Rev. Jeremy Marsh, Rector of Rosenallis, Queen's County, by Rachel, daughter of Colonel Montgomery, who was murdered during the rebellion of 1798. He is a direct descendant of Francis and Narcissus Marsh, Lords Primate of Ireland and Dublin; as also of the celebrated Jeremy Taylor. Among his professional relatives are the present Capt. Joseph and Lieut. Edw. Digby, R.N.

This officer entered the Navy, 10 Jan. 1806, as Fst.-cl. Vol., on board the EURUS store-ship, Capt. Ennis; and on 15 of the following month removed to the MINERVA frigate, commanded by the late Sir Geo. Ralph Collier; with whom he continued to serve as Midshipman, Master's Mate, and for a short time as Acting-Lieutenant, in the SURVEILLANTE 38, until Nov. 1813. He assisted, in the MINERVA, at the capture of Copenhagen in Sept. 1807; and was actively employed, in the SURVEILLANTE, in co-operation with the patriots on the north coast of Spain, where he was severely wounded in a breaching battery at the siege of St. Sebastian in Aug. and Sept. 1813.* On the occasion of the second assault on that place he volunteered to conduct a column of Portuguese infantry over the breach; as he also did to recross it under a heavy fire for the purpose of conveying a pencil despatch from the commander of the storming party, ordering a reinforcement. This service was handsomely and warmly acknowledged by the late Sir Alex. Dixon, then in command of the Artillery. Mr. Marsh had previously served in a boat belonging to the SURVEILLANTE at the capture of a French merchant-brig between the batteries of St. Guildas and St. Jacques, in Quiberon Bay, 5 Sept. 1810;†

* *Vide* Gaz. 1813, pp. 1606, 1856.

† *V.* Gaz. 1810, p. 1488.

and had commanded one of two boats under Lieut. O'Reilly at the capture of a French gun-vessel carrying troops to the relief of St. Antonio; besides having so successfully contributed to the defence of two valuable prizes against the attacks of a French and American privateer as to have induced Sir Edw. Tucker, at the time in temporary command of the SURVEILLANTE, to present him with a sum of money for the purchase of a sword. On leaving the SURVEILLANTE as above he became Acting-Lieutenant of the CHALLENGER 18, Capts. Fred. Edw. Vernon (now Harcourt) and Henry Forbes; to which vessel (being confirmed to her by commission dated 24 Dec. 1813) he continued attached until Sept. 1815—commanding her boats, during that period, at the destruction, by a force under Rear-Admiral Chas. Vinicombe Penrose, of a French squadron and flotilla in the river Gironde. He appears to have been in the same sloop when she brought the Prince of Orange over to this country on the eve of his intended marriage with the Princess Charlotte. His next appointment was, 25 July, 1818, to the TARTAR 42, fitting for the broad pendant of his friend Sir G. R. Collier, Commander-in-Chief on the coast of Africa; where his conduct, in twice preserving life under circumstances of a very trying and hazardous nature, procured him a strong recommendation to the Admiralty. On the first occasion, a boat he had entered and had been hastening to lower having broken at one end from her holdings, he was precipitated into the water, and in his endeavour to save himself lost all the flesh off the inside of his hand. During his continuance in the TARTAR (he did not leave her until 8 Oct. 1821) Lieut. Marsh succeeded in her boats in capturing several heavy-armed vessels, and in one instance was nearly killed while in the act of firing a brass 4-pounder, which broke from its carriage, struck him on the head, and, passing over, severely wounded 2 of his men. He attained the rank of Commander 5 Jan. 1822; but was not again employed until 6 June, 1833, when he received a three years' appointment in the Coast Guard. He went back to that service 11 July, 1837, and continued in it until posted, 1 Jan. 1842. In admiration of his intrepidity in putting off in a boat during a dark and stormy night in Nov. 1840, and rescuing the crew of the brig Otterton of Sunderland, wrecked on the beach between Blarshide and Black Rock, co. Cornwall, the Royal Humane Society presented Capt. Marsh with a gold medal. On the occasion of his last promotion he was requested by the officers of the Brighton district, over which he had been latterly presiding, to accept at their hands a pair of epaulettes, a compliment the existing regulations of the service compelled him to decline. He has since been on half-pay.

Capt. Marsh (the Senior of 1842) married Adelaide, youngest daughter of John Rowley, Esq., of the island of Tobago, by whom he has issue five children. AGENTS—Collier and Snee.

MARSH. (COMMANDER, 1844.)

JOHN BARLING MARSH passed his examination in 1828; and was made Lieutenant, 2 Feb. 1830, into the WARSPITE 76, flag-ship of Sir Thos. Baker on the South American station, whence he returned to England and was paid off in the summer of 1833. His succeeding appointments were—6 Dec. 1834, as Senior, to the PELICAN 16, Capt. Brunswick Popham, under whom he was for three years employed at the Cape of Good Hope and on the coast of Africa—and, 4 Nov. 1840, in a similar capacity, to the ENDYMION 44, Capt. Hon. Fred. Wm. Grey. In that ship, which was put out of commission at the close of 1843, he took part in the hostilities against China. He attained his present rank 20 May, 1844; but has not been since afloat. AGENT—Joseph Woodhead.

MARSH. (LIEUTENANT, 1824.)

RICHARD JOHN MARSH obtained his commission 12 Nov. 1824; and, from 21 Dec. 1825 until paid off, served in the ESPIÈGLE 18, Capt. Rich. Augustus Yates, on the Jamaica station. He has not been since employed.

The Lieutenant is married and has issue.

MARSHALL. (LIEUTENANT, 1843.)

EDWARD MARSHALL entered the Navy 3 Jan. 1829; passed his examination 19 Dec. 1836; and was for several years employed on the North America and West India and Home stations as Mate of the SAPPHO 16, Capt. Edw. Iggulden Parrey, and CALEDONIA 120, flag-ship of Sir David Milne. His appointments (since his promotion to the rank of Lieutenant, which took place 7 July, 1843) have been, on the Cape of Good Hope station—29 July, 1843, as Additional, to the WINCHESTER 50, flag-ship of Hon. Josceline Percy—16 June, 1845, to the CONWAY 26, Capt. Wm. Kelly—and 1 May, 1847, to the NIMROD 20, Capt. Jas. Rich. Dacres, with whom he is now serving.

MARSHALL. (COMMANDER, 1825. F-P., 21; H-P., 25.)

GEORGE EDWARD MARSHALL is the son of an old Commander in the R.N., who lost his health on the coast of Africa, and was from that cause, as well as from the effect of wounds, obliged to retire from active service. His brother, Lieut. Thos. Marshall, R.M., was killed in the REPULSE 74, Capt. Hon. Arthur Kaye Legge, at the passage of the Dardanells, in Feb. 1807.

This officer entered the Navy, 16 Feb. 1801, on board the INVINCIBLE 74, Capt. John Rennie, bearing the flag of Rear-Admiral Thos. Totty in Yarmouth Roads; and became Midshipman, soon afterwards, of the ASSISTANCE 50, Capt. Rich. Lee, under whom he was wrecked, between Dunkerque and Gravelines, 29 March, 1802. During the five years which preceded his promotion to the rank of Lieutenant, Mr. Marshall, it appears, was employed on the Newfoundland and Channel stations in the FALCON sloop, Capt. Henry Manaton Ommanney, GOLIATH 74, Capt. Chas. Brisbane, and PHŒNIX and TRIBUNE frigates, both commanded by Capt. Thos. Baker. In the FALCON, at the commencement of the war, he assisted in taking possession of the islands of St. Pierre and Miquelon; and in the PHŒNIX he was present, as Master's Mate, in Sir Rich. Strachan's action, 4 Nov. 1805; on which occasion he was sent on board one of the prize-ships to aid in navigating her into port. While serving in the TRIBUNE, we find him contributing, 29 April, 1807, to the destruction, by that ship and the IRIS, of the greater part of a convoy of 30 vessels, passing from Ferrol to Bilboa under the protection of several gun-boats. He was also a participator in many boat affairs on the coast of France. On being promoted, as above, he joined the NEPTUNE 98, Capt. Sir Thos. Williams, at the time in the Channel; and he was afterwards appointed—18 Nov. 1808, to the ACASTA 40, Capt. Philip Beaver, under whom he served as First-Lieutenant at the capture of Martinique and the Saintes in 1809—25 June, 1810 (after seven months of half-pay), to the AMELIA 38, Capt. Hon. Fred. Paul Irby, attached to the force in the Channel—17 Aug. following, and 27 April, 1811, to the HANNIBAL 74* and ROYAL GEORGE 100, flag-ships of Sir Thos. Williams off Lisbon and in the Channel—2 Jan. 1812, to the NAMUR 74, as Signal-Lieutenant to the same officer as Sheerness—4 April, 1813, to the acting-command, for nearly six weeks, of the HASTY 14, on the Baltic station—5 Jan. 1814, again to the NAMUR, in his former capacity—9 March ensuing, to the HORATIO 38, Capt. Wm. Henry Dillon, in which ship he was for about twelve months employed off Newfoundland—and, 4 June, 1821, as Senior, to the GLASGOW 50, Capt. Bentinck Cavendish Doyle. In the last-mentioned ship, which was paid off in Nov. 1824, Mr. Marshall

* During the term of his servitude in the HANNIBAL, and while acting as Flag-Lieutenant to Sir Thos. Williams, he was sent up the Tagus in command of a division of boats, and was on that river when Lord Hill crossed it in sight of the French army at Santarem.

assisted in conveying the remains of the late Queen from Harwich to Cuxhaven; Sir Edward Paget and family from Portsmouth to the East Indies; and the Marquess of Hastings from Calcutta to Gibraltar. He attained his present rank 27 May, 1825; and from 15 June, 1832, until the summer of 1835, was employed in the Coast Guard in Ireland. He has since been on half-pay. AGENTS—Hallett and Robinson.

MARSHALL. (COMMANDER, 1814. F-P., 19; H-P., 33.)

HENRY MASTERMAN MARSHALL, born 15 June, 1784, at St. Stephen's, near Saltash, co. Cornwall, is son of the late Rev. — Marshall, of Saltash; grandson of Mr. Masterman, many years a Purser and Secretary in the R.N.; nephew of the late Superannuated Rear-Admiral Thos. Gaberion; and first-cousin of the present Lieut. Chas. Henry Masterman, R.N. One of the Commander's brothers, Thomas Gaberion, a Lieutenant R.N., served as Midshipman and Master's Mate of the CULLODEN 74 under the late Sir Thos. Troubridge; was present in that ship in the famous actions of 1 June, 1794, 14 Feb. 1797, and 1 Aug. 1798; and was eventually killed in action in South America. Another of his brothers, John, died a Midshipman in the service.

This officer entered the Navy, in Jan. 1795, as A.B., on board the CAMEL store-ship, Capts. Edw. Rotheram, Rich. Raggett, Thos. Gordon Caulfeild, and John Lee; and was present in that vessel at the detention of five Dutch men-of-war and a large convoy in Plymouth Sound, and also in the operations which preceded the surrender to the British of St. Fiorenza, in the island of Corsica. Removing, some months after he had attained the rating of Midshipman, to the SWIFTSURE 74, Capt. Benj. Hallowell, Mr. Marshall, who continued in the same ship under the flag of Sir Rich. Bickerton until the early part of 1801, saw a vastitude of active service. While stationed at first off Cadiz (in the vicinity of which place he came into frequent contact with the enemy's gun-vessels) he so distinguished himself by the alacrity he exhibited in being the first with his boat to take in tow the THALIA frigate and ALEXANDER 74, when those ships lay becalmed under a torrent of shot and shells from the enemy's flotilla and batteries, that Earl St. Vincent was impelled to thank him on the quarter-deck of his flag-ship, the VILLE DE PARIS, and to make him a promise of early promotion. After sharing in the battle of the Nile, and assisting at the capture of *La Fortune* corvette of 16 guns and 70 men, we find him serving on shore as Aide-de-camp to Capts. Hallowell and Troubridge at the capture of Naples and its dependencies; during the proceedings connected with which he was constantly employed, under a heavy fire, in carrying the despatches of Lord Nelson and Capt. Alex. John Ball, the second in command, to and from Naples and the head-quarters before St. Elmo. He was not unfrequently, too, selected to receive and re-conduct a flag-of-truce. Besides participating in a variety of boat-services along the Egyptian and Italian shores, and lending his aid to the capture, 5 April, 1800, of the two Spanish 36-gun frigates *El Carmen* and *Florentina*, each laden with 1500 quintals of silver, he was made, we may add, the bearer of the celebrated coffin constructed out of the mainmast of *L'Orient*, the French Commander-in-Chief's ship in the battle of the Nile, sent by Capt. Hallowell as a present to Lord Nelson, whose thanks Mr. Marshall had had the fortune of previously eliciting. Following Sir Rich. Bickerton into the KENT 74, he was afforded an opportunity, during the expedition to Egypt, of being present at the landing of the troops, 8 March, 1801, and in the actions of 13 and 21 of the same month. For the important service he afterwards rendered in piloting a number of frigates, brigs, and smaller vessels into the western harbour of Alexandria, where, it appears, he was intrusted with the charge of all the prizes, he was nominated Acting-Lieutenant of the MADRAS 54, into which ship Sir Rich. Bickerton had shifted his flag. He was not, however, confirmed a Lieutenant until 30 Aug. 1803, by which period he had again served with the last-mentioned officer in the KENT 74, and with Capts. Wm. Hancock Kelly and Geo. Fred. Ryves in the GIBRALTAR 80. We must not omit to record here that his Egyptian services had procured him the superior Turkish gold medal; and that for his official promotion he was indebted to the early promise of Lord St. Vincent. He continued in the GIBRALTAR until Aug. 1804; then joined the DREADNOUGHT 98, bearing the flag in the Channel of Vice-Admiral Collingwood; and was subsequently appointed—27 July, 1805, to the HIND 28, in which ship, successively commanded by Capts. Fras. Wm. Fane and Rich. Budd Vincent, for four months by himself, and by Capts. John Simpson and Geo. Miller Bligh, he returned to the Mediterranean—18 Nov. 1808, to the WOOLWICH 44, Capt. Fras. Beaufort, on the same station—9 Aug. 1809, to the command of the VETERAN prison-ship at Portsmouth—and 23 Nov. 1812, and 27 July, 1813, to the ROYAL WILLIAM and, as First-Lieutenant, to the PRINCE 98, flag-ships at Spithead of his old friend Sir R. Bickerton. During the operations of 1807 in Egypt, Mr. Marshall, then in the HIND, was very actively employed; and on the final evacuation of Alexandria was ordered by the senior naval officer, Capt. Hallowell, to sink several ships laden with stores, for the purpose of destroying the entrance into the harbour. He soon afterwards volunteered to land at the island of Cyprus, for the purpose of conveying letters to the Acting-Consul, instructing him to prevent the further transmission of supplies to Egypt—a most perilous service, in the performance of which he was compelled to use every precaution to avoid falling into the hands of the Turks, and was for three days under the necessity of lying concealed. On one occasion, while cruizing in the Archipelago he contrived, with the HIND's jolly-boat and only four unarmed men under his orders, to board and make prize of a Turkish brig of 4 guns, having on board the Governor of Candia and his body-guard, armed in the usual manner with sabres, pistols, muskets, and dirks; and on another he succeeded, in a punt belonging to a one-masted felucca in which he had been sent to Majorca for the purpose of effecting an exchange of prisoners, in capturing a large three-masted felucca, carrying, in addition to her crew and 4 guns, a valuable cargo, and as many as 50 refugees proceeding from Tarragona to Palma. In the achievement of the latter exploit Mr. Marshall's boat was again manned with but four persons, natives of Gibraltar, commonly called "Rock Scorpions," and was totally destitute of arms. In 1808 he assisted, and was second in command under Capt. Trollope, at the evacuation of Scylla, where, as had been the case during the last series of operations on the coast of Egypt, he was wounded by a musket-ball in the left leg. He was advanced to his present rank in honour of the grand naval review held before the Allied Sovereigns at Spithead, 27 June, 1814, and has since been on half-pay.

Commander Marshall is the author of 'An Appeal to the British Nation on behalf of the Mercantile Marine,' published by Ridgway in 1836. He married, first, 21 May, 1805, Ann, niece of the late Sir Walter Ferguson, and also of Capt. Jas. Ferguson, R.N., who died Lieutenant-Governor of Greenwich Hospital, 14 Feb. 1793. By that lady he had issue seventeen children, six only of whom, three sons and three daughters, are now living. He married a second time, 14 Feb. 1839, Ann, only daughter of the late J. C. Bright, Esq., of Plaistow, Essex.

MARSHALL, Kt., C.B., K.C.H., K.S.G., K.S.S. (CAPTAIN, 1814.)

SIR JOHN MARSHALL, born in 1785, is descended from a family of considerable antiquity.

This officer entered the Navy, 13 Feb. 1800, as Fst.-cl. Vol., on board the AURORA 28, Capt. Thos.

Gordon Caulfeild; and in the course of the next month attained the rating of Midshipman. Removing in March, 1802, after an intermediate servitude on the Lisbon and Mediterranean stations, to the LATONA 38, Capt. Frank Sotheron, he was for seven months employed in that ship in the Channel and Baltic. Being again, in April, 1803, placed under the orders of Capt. Caulfeild in the GRAMPUS 50, he cruized for some time on the Guernsey station, and then sailed for the East Indies, where, in Dec. 1805, he followed the same officer, as Master's Mate, into the RUSSEL 74. In Oct. 1806 Mr. Marshall was nominated by Sir Edw. Pellew Acting-Lieutenant of his flag-ship the CULLODEN 74, in which, on 27 of the ensuing month, he contributed to the capture and destruction of a Dutch frigate, seven brigs of war, and about 20 armed and other merchant-vessels in Batavia Roads. In the spring of 1807 he went back, in the capacity last mentioned, to his former ship the RUSSEL, still commanded by Capt. Caulfeild, with whom he continued, latterly under the flag of Rear-Admiral Wm. O'Brien Drury, until compelled by ill health to invalid in Feb. 1809. His next appointment we find was, 24 Oct. in the latter year, to the ABOUKIR 74, Capt. Geo. Parker, then attached to the Walcheren expedition. On 24 Oct. 1812, up to which period he had been serving in the North Sea and Baltic, part of the time under the flag of Rear-Admiral Thos. Byam Martin, and latterly in charge of a gun-boat at the defence of Riga, Mr. Marshall was promoted to the command of the PROCRIS sloop, on the East India station, whither he took a passage in the JAVA of 46 guns and 377 men, Capt. Henry Lambert. It was his consequent misfortune to be present on board that frigate 23 Dec. 1812, when she was captured, after a close and terrific action of three hours and 40 minutes, and a loss of 22 men killed and 102 (including the Captain mortally) wounded, by the American ship *Constitution* of 55 guns and 480 men, many of whom suffered. His exertions and the advice he afforded throughout the contest were particularly acknowledged in the despatches of the senior surviving officer, the present Capt. Henry Ducie Chads.* On 11 Nov. 1813 Capt. Marshall was invested with the command of the SHAMROCK brig; and on joining that vessel off Cuxhaven he was ordered higher up the Elbe, with a detachment of gun-boats under his orders, for the purpose of watching the enemy at Gluckstadt until the arrival there of the Swedish troops under the Baron de Boyé. The zeal he subsequently displayed in the arduous operations which terminated in its surrender to the allied forces called forth the official thanks of the late Sir Arthur Farquhar, who commanded the naval force employed in the attack.† On 9 Jan. 1814, four days after the event last mentioned had taken place, the SHAMROCK entered the haven of Gluckstadt, and took possession of the Danish flotilla found in it, consisting of one brig and seven gunboats. Her commander was then despatched to Kiel, in order to establish the claims of the British squadron to the enemy's vessels, naval stores, &c., taken in the Elbe. He next assisted at the blockade of Hamburg and Haarburg. The importance indeed of Capt. Marshall's services on the German rivers was fully acknowledged by his being advanced to Post rank 7 June, 1814; created, in the early part of 1815, a Knight of the highest Russian Military Order of St. George and of the Swedish Military Order of the Sword, and a C.B. 4 June in the same year. In Jan. 1826 he was selected to fill the office of Superintendent of Lazarettos at Milford; and, about Jan. 1827, of the Quarantine establishment at Standgate Creek. William IV., in June, 1832, invested him with the insignia of a K.C.H., and also conferred on him the honour of Knighthood. His last appointment was, 18 Aug. 1841, to the ISIS 44, fitting for the Cape of Good Hope, whence he returned home and was paid off at the commencement of 1845; in April of which year he had the satisfaction of receiving a letter of thanks from the Committee at Lloyd's for the great attention he had paid during his recent command to the interests of the mercantile community generally, but especially for the arrangements he had made for the preservation of peace and the furtherance of trade at Icheboe.

Sir John Marshall married, a second time, 17 Sept. 1828, Augusta Eliza, youngest daughter of John Wynne, Esq., of Garthmeillo, co. Denbigh, and grand-daughter of the Rev. S. Parr, D.D., Prebendary of St. Paul's. His eldest daughter, Frances Orris, is married to Martin Hadsley Gosselin, Esq., only son of Admiral T. Le M. Gosselin; and his third, Louisa Phillips, to Capt. Geo. Black, of the Royal Canadian Rifles. AGENTS—Burnett and Holmes.

* *Vide* Gaz. 1813, p. 774.

† *V.* Gaz. 1814, p. 126.

MARSHALL. (RETIRED COMMANDER, 1844.)

JOHN MARSHALL (*a*)—whose name had been borne in 1790 on the books of the MARLBOROUGH 74, Capt. Cornish, and QUEEN CHARLOTTE 100, bearing the flag of Lord Howe—embarked, in 1793, as A.B., on board the EGMONT 74, Capts. Archibald Dickson and John Sutton; in which ship he cooperated in the reduction of Corsica, and was present in Hotham's actions of 14 March and 13 July, 1795, and in the battle fought off Cape St. Vincent 14 Feb. 1797. He also, in 1796, assisted at the evacuation of the island above named. At the close of 1799, after having further served with Capt. Sutton in the SUPERB 74, with Lord Bridport in the ROYAL GEORGE 100, and with Sir Thos. Boulden Thompson as Acting-Lieutenant in the BELLONA 74, on the Home station, Mr. Marshall was unfortunately obliged to be invalided and sent to the hospital at Plymouth. Being, however, officially promoted, 18 Feb. 1800, to a Lieutenancy in the RENOMMÉE frigate, Capt. M'Kellar, he was employed in the course of that year in the expedition to Egypt. His next appointment was, 17 Sept. 1802, to the PORT MAHON brig, Capts. Walter Grosett, — Neville, — M'Donald, — Murray, and Sam. Chambers, on the Jamaica station; where, under Capt. Chambers, he assisted at the capture, recapture, and destruction of at least fifty vessels; among which were *El Galgo* Spanish packet, the *Amaranza* letter-of-marque, and *El Courier* privateer. He further, 25 June, 1806, united in chasing the *San Josef* letter-of-marque brig (armed with 1 long 18-pounder on a pivot amidships, and 4 12-pounder carronades and 2 long 4-pounders on her sides, with swivels, pikes, and muskets, and 30 men), into the intricate harbour of Banes, in the island of Cuba; and then, taking command of the boats of the PORT MAHON, succeeded with the utmost gallantry in cutting her out without the loss of a man; although the vessel was protected by the fire from, and moored by a line to, a tower mounting 2 heavy guns, and notwithstanding too that in endeavouring to conduct her out of the harbour she grounded within pistol-shot of the battery, and was struck by several shot from it.* He left the PORT MAHON, of which he appears to have been for some time in charge, in 1807; and was afterwards employed in the Impress service at Poole, and in visiting Quebec and other parts of North America in the WOOLWICH 44, *armée-en-flûte*, Capt. Thos. Ball Sulivan. Ill health, again, in Aug. 1813, compelled him to leave his ship and to enter the hospital at Bermuda. He became a Retired Commander on the Junior List 26 Nov. 1830; and on the Senior 30 July, 1844.

MARSHALL. (COMMANDER, 1845.)

WILLIAM MARSHALL (*b*) was born in Jan. 1796.

This officer entered the Navy, 3 Sept. 1805, as a Volunteer, on board the TARTAR 32, Capt. Edw. Hawker, employed on the Halifax station; where he continued to serve, until the conclusion of hostilities, in the MELAMPUS 36, also commanded by Capt. Hawker, and in the INDIAN 18, Capt. Chas. John Austen, HORATIO 38, Capt. Geo. Scott, RUBY

* *Vide* Gaz. 1806, p. 1537.

64, Capt. Ferrier, GUERRIÈRE of 48 guns and 244 men, Capt. Jas. Rich. Dacres, BELVIDERA 36, Capt. Rich. Byron, MEROPE 10, Capt. Wm. Benj. Suckling, and WASP sloop, Capts. Peter Fisher and Wm. Woolridge. He was on board the HORATIO at the capture, 21 Feb. 1810, after a long chase and a running fight of one hour, of *La Nécessité*, pierced for 40 guns, but not mounting more than 28, with a complement of 186 men; and, as Midshipman, on board the GUERRIÈRE, when taken, 19 Aug. 1812, notwithstanding a struggle of nearly an hour and three-quarters, attended with a loss of 15 killed and 63 wounded, by the United States ship *Constitution*, of 56 guns and 460 men, 7 of whom at least were killed and as many wounded. While attached to the BELVIDERA he was afforded an opportunity of seeing much boat-service. He remained in the WASP, on the Mediterranean station, latterly in the capacity of Acting-Master, until the summer of 1818; and between that period and his promotion to the rank of Lieutenant, 29 July, 1825, was employed in the Coast Blockade as Midshipman and Mate of the SEVERN 40, Capt. Wm. M'Culloch. He left the latter service, after having been further borne on the books of the RAMILLIES and TALAVERA 74's, Capts. M'Culloch and Hugh Pigot, in April, 1831; and was subsequently appointed—15 April, 1831, to the Coast Guard—30 June, 1834, to the command of the NIMBLE Revenue-vessel—27 June, 1837, again to the Coast Guard—and 22 Dec. 1841, to the command of the ADELAIDE, another Revenue-cruizer. He acquired the rank he now holds 16 Jan. 1845, and has since been on half-pay.

He married in 1821, and has issue five children. AGENT—J. Hinxman.

MARSHALL. (LIEUT., 1815. F-P., 15; H-P., 33.)

WILLIAM MARSHALL (*a*) entered the Navy, in 1799, as Fst.-cl. Vol., on board the WRANGLER gun-brig, commanded in succession by two Lieutenants, under whom he was for three years employed on the Leith station. In 1802 he proceeded to the West Indies in the REYNARD sloop, Capt. Peter Spicer; and he was next, between 1803 and 1807, employed on the St. Helena and Home stations, chiefly we believe in the capacity of Second Master, in the EGYPTIENNE frigate and REVENGE 74, both commanded by Hon. Chas. Elphinstone Fleeming; assisting, in the EGYPTIENNE, at the capture of *L'Epervier* of 16 guns and 90 men, *L'Actéon* of 16 guns and 126 men, and *La Chiffonette* privateer of 14 guns and 80 men; and sharing, in the same ship, in Sir Robert Calder's action 22 July, 1805. In June, 1807, he removed to the EDGAR 74, Capts. Jas. Macnamara and Stephen Poyntz; in which ship, it appears, he served off Rochefort, in the Baltic, and off Flushing, until Dec. 1810. During his stay in the Baltic we find him witnessing the embarkation, from Nyeborg, of the Spanish General the Marquis de la Romana, and his patriot troops. On leaving the EDGAR he joined the TREMENDOUS 74, Capt. Robt. Campbell. With that officer he continued to serve, again in the Baltic, and also in the Mediterranean, until May, 1815. He then took up a commission dated on 10 of the previous Feb., and has since been on half-pay. AGENTS—Goode and Lawrence.

MARSHALL. (LIEUTENANT, 1845.)

WILLOUGHBY CHARLES MARSHALL passed his examination 30 Aug. 1837; and for several years prior to his promotion to the rank of Lieutenant, which took place 1 Sept. 1845, was employed on the South American station, as Mate, in the ACTÆON 26, Capt. Robt. Russell, CRESCENT receiving-ship, Lieut.-Commander Malachi Donellan, and GORGON steam-sloop, Capt. Chas. Hotham. He was on board the latter vessel when she was driven on shore in a hurricane at Colonia, and was concerned in the long and arduous operations which preceded her being got off. For several months of 1846 Lieut. Marshall was employed in the East Indies on board the DIDO 18, Capt. John Balfour Maxwell.

MARSHAM. (CAPTAIN, 1833. F-P., 20; H-P., 20.)

HENRY SHOVELL MARSHAM entered the Navy, 17 May, 1807, as Fst.-cl. Vol., on board the SUPERB 74, Capts. Donald M'Leod and Sam. Jackson, bearing the broad pendant of Commodore Rich. Goodwin Keats. In that ship he went to the Mediterranean in pursuit of a French squadron which had effected its escape from Rochefort, witnessed the embarkation from Nyeborg of the Spanish troops under the Marquis de la Romana, and, previously to accompanying the expedition to the Walcheren, was in her when she was frozen up at Gottenborg and only extricated by a canal being cut through four miles of ice. After a servitude of three months at Spithead in the PUISSANT 74, Capt. Robt. Hall, he became Midshipman, in March, 1810, of the DEFIANCE 74, commanded by Capt. Hon. Henry Hotham, with whom he continued employed in the NORTHUMBERLAND 74 until Jan. 1813; being in consequence afforded an opportunity, in the latter ship, of assisting, 22 May, 1812, when in company with the GROWLER gun-brig, at the gallant destruction, at the entrance of L'Orient, of the French 40-gun frigates *L'Arienne* and *L'Andromaque*, and 16-gun-brig *Mamelouck*, whose united fire, conjointly with that of a destructive battery, killed 5 of the NORTHUMBERLAND'S people and wounded 28. He obtained his first commission while serving with Sir John Borlase Warren on the coast of North America in the SAN DOMINGO of 74 guns, 30 June, 1813; and was subsequently appointed — 1 July, 1813, to the RAMILLIES 74, Capt. Sir Thos. Masterman Hardy, engaged in the blockade of New London—2 Sept. 1814, again to the SUPERB, bearing the flag of Hon. H. Hotham on the coasts of America and France—26 Aug. 1818 (two years and seven months after he had left the SUPERB), to the ROCHFORT 80, Capts. Andrew Pellet Green and Chas. Marsh Schomberg, to which ship, bearing the flags in the Mediterranean of Sir Thos. Fras. Fremantle and Sir Graham Moore, he continued attached for upwards of five years and a half—and 6 July, 1824, as senior, to the CAMBRIAN 46, Capt. Gawen Wm. Hamilton, on the same station, where, in command, in the Negropont Channel, of the boats of his own ship and the SERINGAPATAM, he contrived to board and carry, in the most gallant manner, notwithstanding a desperate resistance, two piratical vessels, each with 1 gun and about 30 men, 31 Jan. 1825.* The terms of high commendation in which his conduct on the occasion was reported procured him a Commander's commission dated 21 of the following April. His next appointments were—10 Sept. 1829 and 25 Feb. 1831, to the BRITANNIA 120, Capt. Geo. Burdet, and ST. VINCENT 120, Capt. Humphrey Fleming Senhouse, stationed in the Mediterranean, where, at the period of his official advancement to the rank of Captain, 24 Dec. 1833, he was acting as such in the MALABAR 74. Since the paying off of the MALABAR in July, 1834, he has been on half-pay.

Capt. Marsham married, in 1838, Maria, daughter of W. Jones, Esq., of Ballinamore, co. Leitrim, and Hayle Place, co. Kent. AGENTS — Messrs. Ommanney.

MARSINGALL. (RETIRED COMMANDER, 1843. F-P., 13; H-P., 36.)

SAMUEL MARSINGALL entered the Navy, 20 Jan. 1798, as Fst.-cl. Vol., on board LA LUTINE, Capt. John Monckton; whom he followed as Midshipman, in April, 1799, into the MARS 74, bearing the flag in the Channel of Hon. Geo. Cranfield Berkeley. In Jan. 1801 he removed to the ST. FIORENZO of 42 guns and 253 men, Capts. C. W. Paterson and Joseph Bingham; and in June, 1803, on his arrival in the East Indies, he joined the WILHELMINA *armée-en-flûte*, Capt. Henry Lambert, carrying 21 guns and 134 men. In that ship it appears

* *Vide* Gaz. 1825, p. 698.

he took part, 11 April, 1804, in a very gallant conflict of an hour and a half, which terminated in her beating off, with a loss to herself of 10 men wounded, the French frigate-built privateer *Psyché* of 36 guns and 250 men, 11 of whom were killed and 33 wounded. Returning subsequently with Capt. Lambert to the St. Fiorenzo he assisted, 14 Feb. 1805, at the capture, after a desperate action of several hours, of the above named *Psyché*, which had been since added to the French navy, and whose loss on the present occasion amounted, out of 252 men, to 57 killed and 70 wounded, while that of the British did not exceed 12 killed and 36 (including himself) wounded. On 12 March, 1806, at which time he had been for nine months attached to the Culloden 74, bearing the flag, still on the East India station, of Rear-Admiral Sir Edw. Pellew, Mr. Marsingall was nominated Acting-Lieutenant of the Grampus 50, Capt. Jas. Haldane Tait, to which ship the Admiralty confirmed him 20 Aug. 1807. His last appointments were—3 Nov. 1807, to the Camel store-ship, Capt. John Joyce, for passage to England—14 May, 1808, to the Triumph 74, Capt. Sir Thos. Masterman Hardy, part of the Channel fleet—and 14 May and 4 Nov. 1809, to the Barfleur 98, flag-ship of Hon. Geo. Cranfield Berkeley, and Myrtle sloop, Capt. Thos. Innes, both on the Lisbon station. He invalided home in March, 1810; and accepted his present rank 1 Nov. 1843.

The wound received by Commander Marsingall at the capture of the *Psyché* was rewarded with a gratuity by the Patriotic Society. Agents—Messrs. Stilwell.

MARTEN. (Lieutenant, 1844.)

Francis Marten, born in 1814, is eldest son of the late Geo. Sulivan Marten, Esq., of Marshals Wick near St. Alban's, Herts, by his second wife, Charlotte, daughter of Col. Tucker. He is half-brother of the present Geo. Robt. Marten, Esq., of Marshals Wick, a Magistrate and Deputy-Lieutenant for co. Herts.

This officer passed his examination 28 Aug. 1837; and between 1840 and his promotion to the rank of Lieutenant 20 Nov. 1844, was employed as Mate in the Ferret 10, Lieut.-Commander Wm. Sidney Thomas, and Siren 16, Capt. Wm. Smith, on the African and East India stations. His appointments have since been—18 Dec. 1844, to the Persian 16, Capt. Henry Coryton, from which vessel, fitting at Devonport, he was shortly afterwards superseded —and 16 Aug. 1845, to the President 50, now flag-ship of Rear-Admiral Jas. Rich. Dacres at the Cape of Good Hope.

MARTIN. (Lieut., 1811. f-p., 19; h-p., 33.)

Alexander Martin entered the Navy, in June, 1795, as Fst.-cl. Vol., on board the Triumph 74, Capts. Sir Erasmus Gower and Wm. Essington, under the latter of whom he fought in the action off Camperdown 11 Oct. 1797. In Jan. 1799 he removed to the Formidable 98, Capts. Jas. Hawkins Whitshed, Edw. Thornbrough, and Rich. Grindall; and in that ship he served in the Channel, Mediterranean, and West Indies until Sept 1802—towards the close of the period in the capacity of Midshipman. Rejoining Capt. Grindall, in 1803, on board the Prince 98, he was for upwards of three years employed with him in the Channel and off the Port of Cadiz, and was afforded an opportunity of sharing in the battle of Trafalgar 21 Oct. 1805. After an attachment of some months to the Glory 98, Capt. Wm. Albany Otway, and Prince 98, flag-ship of Rear-Admiral John Child Purvis, both stationed off Cadiz, he was nominated, about Dec. 1807, Acting-Lieutenant of the Terrible 74, Capt. Lord Henry Paulet, part of the force employed in the Mediterranean, where, in Feb. 1810, he joined, in a similar capacity, the Alacrity 18, Capt. Nesbit Palmer. In May, 1811, that vessel was unfortunately captured by the enemy, a catastrophe, however, Mr. Martin escaped, from the circumstance of his being at the time absent in charge of a Greek prize. He was confirmed a Lieutenant 29 Oct. in the same year; and was lastly, from 2 of the ensuing month until 18 Jan. 1815, employed on the Leith station in the Nightingale 16, Capt. Christopher Nixon.

MARTIN, G.C.B., G.C.M.G., K.S.J. (Admiral of the Fleet. f-p., 32; h-p., 39.)

Sir George Martin died 28 July, 1847, at his house in Berkeley Square, in the 83rd year of his age. He was third and youngest son of the late Capt. Wm. Martin, R.N., by Arabella, daughter of Sir Wm. Rowley, K.B., Admiral of the Fleet, and sister of Rear-Admiral Sir Joshua Rowley, the first Baronet of that name, father of the late Admiral Sir Chas. Rowley, Bart., G.C.B., G.C.H., and father-in-law of Admiral Sir Chas. Cotton, Bart. His grandfather, Bennet Martin, was a M.D.; one of his grand-uncles, Wm. Martin, died Admiral of the Fleet in 1756; and another, Roger Martin, also an Admiral, died in 1780. Sir George was brother of the present Wm. Martin, Esq., of Hemingston, co. Suffolk; and uncle of the present Capt. Geo. Bohun Martin, R.N., C.B. His mother married, a second time, Colonel Gibbs, of Horseley Park, Sussex, father of Major-General Sir Sam. Gibbs, K.C.B., who fell at New Orleans 8 Jan. 1815, and of Major-General Sir Edw. Gibbs, Governor of Jersey, and Colonel of the 68th Regt.

This officer (whose name had been borne from 13 Dec. 1771 until 30 April, 1774, on the books of the Mary yacht) embarked, 20 Nov. 1776, as Captain's Servant, on board the Monarch 64, commanded by his uncle Capt. Joshua Rowley, and was present as Midshipman of that ship in Keppel's action with the Comte d'Orvilliers 27 July, 1778. On next joining the Suffolk 74, Capt. Hugh Cloberry Christian, he was afforded an opportunity of sharing in Byron's action with d'Estaing 6 July, 1779; and on 16 July, 1780, after having participated in three actions fought in the preceding months of April and May between Rodney and De Guychen, and been for short periods employed in the Camelion, Rover, and Alert sloops, Capts. Thos. Watson, John Thos. Duckworth, and Jas. Vashon, he was made Lieutenant into the Russel 74, Capt. Robt. Hanwell. His succeeding appointments, it appears, were, to the Princess Royal 98, Capt. J. T. Duckworth, Ulysses 44, Capt. John Thomas, and Sandwich, Capt. Silverius Moriarty. He was promoted, 9 March, 1782, to the command of the Tobago sloop; and on 17 March, 1783, was posted into the Preston 50. In April, 1784, Capt. Martin, whose services had hitherto been on the West India station, returned to England. He was subsequently appointed—9 July, 1789, to the Porcupine 24, employed off the coast of Ireland until Aug. 1792—12 March, 1793, to the Magicienne 32, in the West Indies—9 Nov. 1795, to the Irresistible 74—15 July, 1798, to the Northumberland 74—and (after eight months of half-pay) 22 May, 1803, and 24 April and 21 Nov. 1804, to the Colossus 74, and Glory and Barfleur 98's, on the Channel station. In the Irresistible Capt. Martin bore a conspicuous part in the battle off Cape St. Vincent 14 Feb. 1797, and towards the close of the action hoisted the broad pendant of Commodore Nelson, whose ship, the Captain, was completely disabled.* His conduct on the occasion procured him a gold medal and the thanks of Parliament. On 26 April in the same year the Irresistible, in company with the Emerald 36, pursued into Conil Bay, near Trafalgar, and, at the end of an hour's engagement, succeeded in effecting the capture of the Spanish frigates *Ninfa* and *Santa Elena* of 34 guns and 320 men each. The latter vessel, as soon as she had struck, cut her cable and ran on shore; her crew effecting their escape. Although eventually got off, she was found in too damaged a state to be kept afloat; and she accordingly went down. Part of the *Ninfa's* crew also effected their escape to the shore. The loss sustained by the two frigates amounted to about 18 killed and 30 wounded: that

* *Vide* Gaz. 1797, p. 212.

of the IRRESISTIBLE to 1 man killed and 1 wounded. The skill exhibited by Capt. Martin in having rounded a dangerous reef of rocks, called the Laja de Cape Rocha, a little to the northward of Conil, and his decision in the ensuing attack, were declared by Earl St. Vincent to have displayed one of the most notable actions that had ever come under his observation.* In Feb. 1800 we find Capt. Martin, then in command of the NORTHUMBERLAND, acquiring the approbation of Lord Nelson for his alacrity and good conduct at the capture of the French 74-gun ship *Généreux*; † and in the ensuing May succeeding Capt. Troubridge in the command of the blockading squadron before Malta. In the month of Aug. the *Diane* and *Justice* frigates made their escape from the harbour of Valetta, but not unperceived by the NORTHUMBERLAND, who, joining the SUCCESS 32, went in immediate chase and contrived to capture the *Diane*.‡ On 5 Sept. in the same year Capt. Martin, whose perseverance in the discharge of his blockading duties had been unremitting, had the honour of signing the capitulation in virtue of which the important island of Malta became annexed to the Crown of England.§ He afterwards, in 1801, accompanied the expedition under Lord Keith and Sir Ralph Abercromby to Egypt, where his activity and exertions a second time caused his being included in the thanks of Parliament. In April 1804 he was nominated a Colonel of Marines; and on 22 July, 1805, at which period, as above shown, he was in command of the BARFLEUR, he distinguished himself in Sir Robt. Calder's action with Admiral Villeneuve.|| Attaining Flag-rank 9 Nov. 1805, Rear-Admiral Martin, on 17 Jan. 1806, was appointed second in command at Portsmouth, where, with his flag in the GLADIATOR 50, he remained for a period of 10 months—during, we believe, the absence of Sir Isaac Coffin on Admiralty leave. In May 1807 he proceeded, in the CUMBERLAND 74, off Cadiz, for the purpose of watching the enemy's ships in the harbour; after which, entering the Mediterranean, he continued on that station, with his flag in the MONTAGU 74, QUEEN 98, and CANOPUS 80, until some months subsequent to his promotion, 31 July, 1810, to the rank of Vice-Admiral. At first, he was employed off the coast of Italy, and in protecting Sicily from the hostile designs of the French; and in June, 1809, he took possession of the islands of Ischia and Procida.¶ On the night of 23 Oct. 1809, being at the time off Cape St. Sebastian in the CANOPUS, the Rear-Admiral was detached by Lord Collingwood with eight of his best sailing ships (two of which accidentally parted company) in pursuit of a division of the enemy's fleet, consisting of three ships of the line and two frigates. By noon on the 25th his intrepid perseverance had compelled the *Robuste* 80 and *Lion* 74, to run themselves on shore, within pistol-shot of each other, at a spot about six miles north-east of the harbour of Cette, and near to the village of Frontignan; and had induced the *Borée* 74, and *Pauline* frigate to seek refuge in Cette harbour, although it scarcely contained depth sufficient to float them. The two former ships were fired and blown up by their own crews.** In the summer of 1810, Vice-Admiral Martin returned to his station off Sicily, and while there was presented with the Order of St. Januarius by the King of Naples, as a mark of his Majesty's approbation of the essential and zealous services rendered by him to that kingdom. We may add that the cordial and friendly co-operation he at all times afforded the troops, did not fail to call forth the public thanks of the military commander Lieut.-General Sir John Stuart, K.B.†† In May, 1812, being appointed to the chief command on the Lisbon station, he hoisted his flag on board the IMPÉTUEUX 74, and sailed for his destination, where he remained, latterly with his flag in the SABRINA frigate and RODNEY 74, until June, 1814; about which period he received the honour of knighthood in commemoration of the King's visit to the fleet at Spithead.* In Jan. 1815, he was created a K.C.B.; in Feb. 1821, a G.C.B.; and on 19 July in the latter year an Admiral of the Blue. His last appointment was, 27 March, 1824, to the post of Commander-in-Chief at Portsmouth; where his flag, which had been flying the whole time in the VICTORY, was struck 30 April, 1827. Sir Geo. Martin was raised to the dignity of Admiral of the Fleet 9 Nov. 1846. He had been successively constituted Rear and Vice-Admiral of the United Kingdom in Jan. 1833 and April, 1834; † and a G.C.M.G. in 1836.

He married, first, 3 April, 1804, the youngest daughter of the late Capt. John Albert Bentinck, R.N. (by Renira, Baroness de Twyell de Ceroos-kerken), sister of Vice-Admiral Wm. Bentinck (who married the only daughter of the first Earl Manvers and died 21 Feb. 1813), sister-in-law of Sir Jas. Hawkins Whitshed, Bart., G.C.B., Admiral of the Fleet, and grand-niece of the first Duke of Portland. That lady dying 15 Oct. 1806, he married a second time, 2 June, 1815, Miss A. Locke, daughter of Wm. Locke, Esq. of Norbury Park, co. Surrey. He was again left a widower 1 Mar. 1842.

* *Vide* Gaz. 1797, p. 446. † *V.* Gaz. 1800, p. 297. ‡ *V.* Gaz. 1800, p. 1156. § *V.* Gaz. 1800, p. 1155. || *V.* Gaz. 1805, p. 982. ¶ *V.* Gaz. 1809, pp. 1410, 1437. ** *V.* Gaz. 1809, pp. 1901-2. †† *V.* Gaz. 1810, p. 1834.

* *Vide* Gaz. 1814, pp. 1320–3.

† He was re appointed Vice-Admiral of the U. K. 21 July, 1837.

MARTIN, C.B., K.S.L., K.S.A., K.R.G. (CAPTAIN, 1828. F-P., 21; H-P., 14.)

GEORGE BOHUN MARTIN is third and youngest son of the late Henry Martin, Esq., of Colston Basset, Notts, a Magistrate for the co., M.P. for Kinsale, and one of the Masters in Chancery, by Maria Elizabeth, daughter of Fras. Edmunds, Esq., of Worsborough, co. York. He is nephew of the late Sir Geo. Martin, G.C.B., G.C.M.G., Admiral of the Fleet.

This officer entered the Royal Naval College, 3 April, 1812; and embarked, 11 April, 1815, as Midshipman, on board the IMPREGNABLE 98, Capt. Sam. Campbell Rowley, bearing the flag of Sir Josias Rowley in the Mediterranean; where, in the following Oct., he removed to the SPARTAN 38, Capt. Phipps Hornby. Quitting that ship in July, 1816, he next, until the receipt of his first commission, dated 17 March, 1821, served on the Channel, Mediterranean, and Cork stations, in the MADAGASCAR and MÆANDER ‡ frigates, both commanded by Capt. Sir Jas. Alex. Gordon, GANYMEDE 26, Capts. Wm. M'Culloch and Hon. Robt. Cavendish Spencer, WASP sloop, Capt. Wm. Woolridge, HYPERION 42, Capt. Thos. Searle, NEWCASTLE 60, Capt. Arthur Fanshawe, CADMUS and BRISK sloops, each under the orders of Capt. Jas. Montagu, SPENCER 74, flag-ship of Sir Josias Rowley, and, as Acting-Lieutenant, in the SAPPHO sloop, Capt. Jas. Hanway Plumridge. On the date of his official promotion, as above, Mr. Martin was nominated Flag-Lieutenant, in the QUEEN CHARLOTTE 100, to Admiral Sir Jas. Hawkins Whitshed, Commander-in-Chief at Portsmouth. Obtaining a second promotal commission in consequence, 24 April, 1824, he assumed command, 17 April, 1827, of the MUSQUITO 10, and, returning to the Mediterranean, was afforded an opportunity of sharing, 20 Oct. following, in the battle of Navarin. His conduct on that occasion procured him the honours above indicated, and was the cause of his being advanced (as soon as he had served the necessary time as Commander) to Post-rank, 19 April, 1828. His next appointments were, 17 April, 1833, and 31 Oct. 1835, to the VOLAGE 28, and CALEDONIA 120, flag-ship of Sir Josias Rowley, both in the Mediterranean, whence he returned in the autumn of 1837. He has been in command, since 4 Nov. 1844, of the EAGLE 50; in which ship he at first conveyed Rear-Admiral Sam. Hood Inglefield to the south-east coast of America, was then employed in North America and the West Indies, and is now engaged in the performance of a particular service.

‡ The MÆANDER, during a violent gale, struck upon a shoal off Orfordness, and was all but lost, 19 Dec. 1816.

Capt. Martin married Isabella Harriett, daughter of Vice-Admiral Sir Thos. Briggs, G.C.M.G., by whom he has issue. AGENTS—Messrs. Chard.

MARTIN, C.B. (CAPTAIN, 1827. F-P., 16; H-P., 15.)

HENRY BYAM MARTIN is second son of Admiral Sir Thos. Byam Martin, G.C.B.

This officer entered the Royal Naval College, 8 Oct. 1816; and embarked, in Oct. 1818, as Midshipman, on board the LIFFEY 50, Capt. Hon. Henry Duncan, with whom he was employed in the Channel and on particular service, until transferred, in April, 1820, to the ROCHFORT 80; from which ship, bearing the flag of Sir Graham Moore in the Mediterranean, he was lent for several months in 1821-2 to the SERINGAPATAM 46, Capt. Sam. Warren, CHANTICLEER sloop, Capt. Henry Eden, and EURYALUS 42, Capt. Augustus Wm. Jas. Clifford. In Feb. 1823, he joined the RAMILLIES 74, Capt. Edw. Brace, lying at Portsmouth; and on 20 of the ensuing month he was promoted to the rank of Lieutenant; his appointments in which capacity, it appears, were, 1 July, 1823, and 26 Dec. 1824, to the SYBILLE frigate, Capt. John Brooke Pechell, and REVENGE 76, flag-ship of Sir Harry Burrard Neale, on the Jamaica and Mediterranean stations. He attained the rank of Commander 8 April, 1825; and, after he had had command for about 12 months of the PARTHIAN 10, in the Mediterranean, was advanced, 28 April, 1827, to Post-rank. From the latter date Capt. Martin did not again go afloat until appointed, 21 Nov. 1836, to the CARYSFORT 26, in which vessel he was for nearly five years again employed in the Mediterranean, where his services on the coast of Syria, including the attacks upon Tortosa and St. Jean d'Acre, procured his enrolment among the Companions of the Bath, 18 Dec. 1840. On the former occasion he received the grateful acknowledgments of Capt. Houston Stewart, of the BENBOW, the senior officer present, for the support and assistance he afforded him, as well as for the astonishing precision of his fire in covering the boats and men employed on shore.* He has been in command, since 15 Nov. 1845, of the GRAMPUS 50, in the Pacific. AGENTS—Messrs. Halford and Co.

MARTIN. (LIEUT., 1814. F-P., 8; H-P., 33.)

JOSEPH WINTHROP MARTIN entered the Navy, 28 Nov. 1806, as Fst.-cl. Vol., on board the SYBILLE frigate, Capt. Robt. Winthrop, and after cruizing among the Western Islands, six months in the capacity of Midshipman, removed, in July, 1807, to the TÉMÉRAIRE 98, Capts. Sir Chas. Hamilton, Edw. Sneyd Clay, Edwin Henry Chamberlayne, Joseph Spear, and Sam. Hood Linzee. In that ship, which for some time bore the flags of Rear-Admirals Manley Dixon and Fras. Pickmore, he was for four years and eight months employed in the Channel and Baltic, off Cadiz, in the Mediterranean, and at Plymouth. He then followed Capt. Linzee into the UNION 98, but had not been long in her before he was transferred to the NARCISSUS 32, Capt. John Rich. Lumley; with whom, it appears, he served in the West Indies and North America until May, 1813. He obtained a commission 27 May, 1814; and was lastly, from Oct. in the same year until Aug. 1815, employed in the TAMAR 24, Capt. Chas. Sotheby, and VALIANT 74, flag-ship of Rear-Admiral Manley Dixon, on the North and South American stations. AGENTS—Messrs. Stilwell.

MARTIN. (COMMANDER, 1825.)

NATHANIEL MARTIN died in 1847.

This officer entered the Navy, 17 Feb. 1799, as Fst.-cl. Vol, on board the DIAMOND 38, Capt. Sir Rich. John Strachan; under whom, on being removed to the CAPTAIN 74, he assisted at the capture, 19 June, 1799, of Rear-Admiral Perrée's squadron of three frigates and two brigs, and attended, as Midshipman, the expeditions of 1800 to Quiberon and Ferrol. In May, 1802, at which period the CAPTAIN, in command of Capt. Chas. Boyles, was at Jamaica, he took a passage home in the VENGEANCE 74, Capt. Geo. Duff; rejoining Sir R. J. Strachan, on his arrival, in the DONEGAL 80. Previously to leaving that ship, Mr. Martin was for some time employed in blockading the port of Cadiz, and contributed to the capture, 25 Nov. 1804, of the Spanish frigate *Amfitrite* of 44 guns. When subsequently with Sir Richard in the CÆSAR 80, we find him enacting a part in the action off Ferrol 4 Nov. 1805. On 1 July, 1806, he was nominated Acting-Lieutenant of the TRIUMPH 74, Capt. Sir Thos. Masterman Hardy, and again ordered to the West Indies; after cruizing for three or four months on which station, he went back to the CÆSAR in the capacity last-mentioned, and continued in her (his promotion to the rank of Lieutenant being confirmed 19 March, 1807) under the flags of Rear-Admirals Sir R. J. Strachan, Hon. Robt. Stopford, and Wm. Albany Otway, under the command of Capts. Chas. Richardson and Wm. Granger, until May, 1811. He was in consequence present, during the year 1809, at the destruction of three French frigates near the batteries of Sable d'Olonne, in Lord Cochrane's attack upon the French shipping in Basque Roads, and in the expedition to the Walcheren. His last appointments were—3 Oct. 1811, to the LYRA 10, Capt. Robt. Bloye, under whom he saw much active service on the north coast of Spain—12 Aug. 1812 and 2 Feb. 1813, to the VENERABLE and STIRLING CASTLE 74's, in the latter of which ships (the VENERABLE had been employed as the LYRA) he escorted Earl Moira to India—7 Nov. 1814, to the MARTIN sloop, Capt. Hon. Jas. Arbuthnot, stationed, until Oct. 1815, on the coast of Ireland—18 Aug. 1818, to the command of the GRECIAN cutter, in the Channel—and, 26 Sept. 1822, to the Ordinary at Portsmouth. The rank of Commander was conferred on him 27 July, 1825.

He had been left a widower in March, 1820. AGENTS—Holmes and Folkard.

MARTIN. (CAPTAIN, 1826. F-P., 17; H-P., 31.)

THOMAS MARTIN, born 11 Dec. 1787, is only surviving son of the late John Nickleson Martin, Esq., of Wollaton, co. Nottingham, a Captain in the Army, by Elizabeth, daughter and heiress of John Hutchinson, Esq., of Skirsgill, near Penrith, and of Crossfield House, near Kirkoswald, co. Cumberland. His grandfather, George Martin, Esq., was Surgeon of St. Thomas's Hospital, London; and his maternal uncle, John Hutchinson, who died on board the EDGAR 74, off Madras Roads, in 1783, was a Lieutenant in the Royal Marines. Capt. Martin is a descendant of Harold de Vaux, Lord de Vaux, who at a very early period crossed over from Normandy and settled in England.

This officer entered the Navy, in March, 1799, as Midshipman, on board the SUPERB 74, Capt. John Sutton, whom, after an intermediate servitude in the Channel and Mediterranean, he followed, in March, 1801, into the VILLE DE PARIS 110, flag-ship of Hon. Wm. Cornwallis. In Dec. 1801, he removed to the IMMORTALITÉ 36, commanded in the Channel by Capts. Hon. Henry Hotham and Edw. W. C. R. Owen; and in the summer of 1805 (having been latterly employed, still on the Home station, in the MARS 74, Capt. John Sutton, and, as Master's Mate, in the RÉVOLUTIONNAIRE 44, Capt. Hon. Henry Hotham) he was successively nominated Acting-Lieutenant of the HIBERNIA 110, Capt. Wm. Bedford, and AUDACIOUS 74, Capts. John Lawford and Jas. Bissett. He was confirmed a Lieutenant 22 Jan. 1806, and was subsequently appointed Senior—27 March, 1806, of the PENELOPE 36, Capts. Wm. Robt. Broughton and John Dick, stationed for some time on the coast of North America, as also in the West Indies, where he served on shore with a party of seamen at the capture of Fort Trinité, prior to the surrender of Martinique in Feb. 1809—3 Dec. 1810, of the WOLVERENE brig, Capt. Chas. Julius Kerr, attached to the force in the Channel—and, in

* *Vide* Gaz. 1840, p. 2607.

1811-12-13, of the DRAGON 74, and TRIBUNE 36, flag-ships of Sir Fras. Laforey, and GRAMPUS 50, Capt. Fras. Augustus Collier, in the West Indies. He was promoted, 10 Aug. 1813, to the command of the SURINAM sloop, in which vessel he returned home with convoy and was paid off in the following Oct.; and he was lastly, from 3 June, 1824, until Jan. 1827, employed on the Jamaica station in command of the JASEUR 18. His Post-commission bears date 2 Aug. 1826.

Capt. Martin married, 5 Aug. 1828, Ann, daughter of John Miles, Esq., of London; and by that lady has had issue five sons and two daughters. AGENTS—Case and Loudonsack.

MARTIN, G.C.B., K.S.S. (ADMIRAL OF THE RED, 1830. F-P., 27; H-P., 35.)

SIR THOMAS BYAM MARTIN is third son of the late Sir Henry Martin, Bart., Comptroller of the Navy, and M.P. for Southampton, by Eliza Anne, daughter of Harding Parker, Esq., of Hilbrook, co. Cork, and relict of Hayward Gillman, Esq., of Gillmanville, in the same co. His half-uncle, Sam. Martin, Esq., M.P., several years Joint Secretary to the Treasury, and Treasurer to the Princess Dowager of Wales, died in Nov. 1789; and his own uncle, Josiah Martin, Esq., a Colonel in the Army, who died in 1786, was Governor of North Carolina in 1770. One of her cousins, Sam. Martin, Esq., Colonel in the 1st Regt. of Guards, was killed at St. Sebastian; and another, Wm. Byam Martin, Esq., was for some time Governor of Amboyna. His father's grandmother, Lydia, daughter of Colonel George Thomas, of Antigua (who commanded the Barbadoes Regiment, and greatly distinguished himself at the capture of St. Christopher's in 1690), married, a second time, Edw. Byam, Esq., Governor of the Leeward Islands.

This officer, whose name had been borne from 23 June, until 31 Dec. 1782, on the books of the FOUDROYANT 80, Capt. John Jervis, entered the Royal Naval Academy in Aug. 1785, and embarked, in March, 1786, as Captain's Servant, on board the PEGASUS 28, commanded by H. R. H. Prince William Henry, with whom he continued to serve in that vessel, and, as Midshipman, in the ANDROMEDA frigate, on the North American and West India stations, until July, 1789. He was then in succession employed, chiefly on Channel service, in the COLOSSUS 74, Capt. Hugh Cloberry Christian, SOUTHAMPTON 32, Capt. Rich. Goodwin Keats, and BARFLEUR 98 and ROYAL GEORGE 100, flag-ships of Admiral Barrington; and on 22 Oct. 1790, he was made Lieutenant into the CANADA 74, Capts. Lord Hugh Seymour and Erasmus Gower. After serving for two years in the capacity last-mentioned on board the INCONSTANT and JUNO frigates, commanded in the Channel by Capts. Geo. Wilson and Sam. Hood, he was promoted, in May, 1793, to the command of the TISIPHONE 12, fitting for the Mediterranean, where, on 5 of the ensuing Nov., having witnessed Lord Hood's occupation of Toulon, he was made Post into the MODESTE frigate. His ensuing appointment was to the ARTOIS, in which vessel, we believe, he co-operated in the reduction of Bastia. Obtaining command, next, of the SANTA MARGARITTA, of 40 guns and 237 men, Capt. Martin, besides making prize, in that ship, of *Le Jean Bart* corvette of 18 guns, and the privateers *Le Buonaparte* of 16 guns and 137 men, and *Le Vengeur* of 18 guns and 110 men, succeeded, 8 June, 1796, in effecting the capture, after a close and gallant action of 20 minutes, of the *Tamise*, of 40 guns and 306 men, of whom 32 were killed and 19 wounded, with a loss to the British of only 2 slain and 3 wounded.* In Dec. 1796, he removed to the TAMAR 38, and, being ordered to the West Indies, was present, in April, 1797, in the unsuccessful attack on Puerto Rico. During the five following months he had the fortune to capture not less than nine privateers, carrying in the whole 58 guns and 519 men.† In Oct. 1798, at which period he had had command for 10 months of the DICTATOR 64, Capt. Martin removed to the FISGARD of 46 guns and 281 men. Continuing in that frigate on the Channel station until Dec. 1801, he contrived, 20 Oct. 1798, when off Brest, to capture the French ship *Immortalité* of 42 guns and 580 men, including troops, at the close of an obstinate conflict of great length, productive of a loss to the enemy of 54 killed and 61 wounded, and to the FISGARD of 10 killed and 26 wounded.* To add to the merit of Capt. Martin in possessing himself of the *Tamise* and *Immortalité*, we may record the fact that in both instances his own ship was manned with a young, raw, and inexperienced crew; but in neither case did his valour meet with the least reward. On the night of 23 June, 1800, we find him, in personal command of the boats of a squadron, entering the Quimper river, and effecting, on its banks, the destruction of three batteries, mounting seven 24-pounders, together with their magazines.† Prior to leaving the FISGARD he further took *La Venus* of 32 guns and 200 men, *Le Dragon* corvette of 14 guns, *La Gironde* privateer of 16 guns and 141 men, *L'Alerte* privateer of 14 guns and 84 men, *El Vivo* national vessel of 14 guns and 100 men, and three others mounting 18 guns. His succeeding appointments were—in March, 1803, to the IMPÉTUEUX 84, in which ship he served in the Channel until 22 Dec. 1805—in 1807 to the PRINCE OF WALES 98, and IMPLACABLE 74, on the Home and Baltic stations—2 Sept. 1808, to the VICTORY 100, as Captain of the Fleet under Sir Jas. Saumarez, Commander-in-Chief in the Baltic—a short time afterwards, again to the IMPLACABLE—and, about Aug. 1810, to the ROYAL SOVEREIGN yacht. On 26 Aug. 1808, Capt. Martin, at the time in the IMPLACABLE, fell in with, and, after a long chase, brought to close action, in a most brave and gallant manner, the Russian 74-gun ship *Sewolod*, whose fire he silenced in about 20 minutes, being only prevented from capturing her by the approach of the whole Russian fleet, which bore up to her support. She soon, however, grounded on a shoal at the entrance of the port of Rogerswick and in that position was attacked by Rear-Admiral Sir Sam. Hood, in the CENTAUR, who, although that ship herself took the ground, compelled her to surrender, after an obstinate defence, in which and in her engagement with the IMPLACABLE (6 of whose people were slain and 26 wounded) she had 303 men killed, wounded, and missing. She was then set on fire and destroyed; the CENTAUR having been previously hove off by the exertions of Capt. Martin, who displayed so much professional ability on the occasion as to call forth the thanks of Sir Sam. Hood. In alluding to the conduct of the IMPLACABLE in her antecedent action, Sir Samuel, in his official letter, declares himself unable by any words of his to enhance the "merit of her brave, worthy, and excellent commander;" ‡ upon whom the King of Sweden, as an acknowledgment, conferred the insignia of a Knight of the Order of the Sword. On 6 July, 1809, Capt. Martin, in company with the MELPOMÈNE frigate, entered the Gulf of Narva, and captured nine merchant-vessels § Being advanced to the rank of Rear-Admiral 1 Aug. 1811, he hoisted his flag, in April, 1812, on board the ABOUKIR 74, and returned to the Baltic, where he took an energetic part in the defence of Riga, and co-operated with the Russian army under Prince Bagration against the French troops under Davoust. In the course of the same year he was appointed second in command at Plymouth; at which port he continued (with the exception of a short time, passed in the CREOLE 36, and AKBAR 50, on the coast of Spain and off the Scheldt) until 1815; his flag flying during the period in the PRINCE FREDERICK 74, IMPREGNABLE 98, and GANGES 74. In 1814 he re-

* *Vide* Gaz. 1796, p. 577.

† *Le Poisson Volant* of 4 guns and 40 men, *La Jalouse* of 4 guns and 45 men, *La Galatée* of 8 guns and 55 men, *L'Heureuse* of 2 guns and 26 men, *Le Poisson Volant* of 4 guns and 38 men, *La Barbarossa* of 8 guns and 61 men, *Le Pont d'Arcole* of 4 guns and 48 men, *Le Renard* of 10 guns and 71 men, and *L'Utile* of 14 guns and 135 men.

* *Vide* Gaz. 1798, p. 1012.

† *V.* Gaz. 1800, p. 749.

‡ *V.* Gaz. 1808, p. 1282.

§ *V.* Gaz. 1809, p. 1209.

ceived the honour of Knighthood. He was created a K.C.B. 2 Jan. 1815; a Vice-Admiral 12 Aug. 1819; a G.C.B. 3 March, 1830; a full Admiral 22 July following; and Vice-Admiral of the United Kingdom in 1847.

In Jan. 1815, Sir Thos. Byam Martin was appointed Deputy-Comptroller of the Navy, and in the following year he succeeded Sir T. B. Thompson as Comptroller of the Navy; the duties of which post he continued to discharge for many years. From 1818 until 1831 he sat in Parliament as Member for Plymouth. He is now one of the Elder Brethren of the Trinity House; and has been a Director of Greenwich Hospital, a Commissioner of the Board of Longitude, &c. At the funerals of George IV. and William IV. the Admiral acted as an assistant supporter of the canopy over the royal body. He married Catherine, daughter of Capt. Robt. Fanshawe, R.N.,* Resident Commissioner of Plymouth Dockyard, sister of the present Capt. Arthur Fanshawe, R.N., C.B., and sister-in-law of Admirals Wm. Bedford, Sir John Chambers White, K.C.B., and Hon. Sir Robt. Stopford, G.C.B., by whom he has had issue three sons and three daughters. His two elder sons, Wm. Fanshawe and Henry Byam, are both Captains in the R.N. His youngest, Lieut.-Colonel Robt. Fanshawe Martin, Deputy-Adjutant-General of the Queen's Forces at Bombay, died at Poonah 13 July, 1846. One of his daughters is married to her cousin, Sir Henry Martin, Bart., of Lockynge, co. Berks.

MARTIN. (COMMANDER, 1821. F.-P., 17; H-P., 31.)

WILLIAM MARTIN, born 3 Dec. 1783, at Glanmire, co. Cork, is third son of the late Thos. Martin, Esq., of Springmount, near that place, who, as a Magistrate and the Commander of a corps of Yeomanry, rendered good service in the rebellion of 1798. One of his brothers, an officer in the 19th Light Dragoons, was for a long time employed in India as Aide-de-Camp to Lord Lake.

This officer entered the Navy, 15 Oct. 1799, under the auspices of General Myers, as Fst.-cl. Vol., on board the DRYAD 36, Capt. Chas. John Moore Mansfield, with whom he served until transferred, in June, 1802, to the HERCULE 74, Capt. Solomon Ferris, lying at Portsmouth; assisting, during that period, at the capture of *Le Premier Consul* privateer, of 14 guns (pierced for 24) and 150 men, and of a Swedish frigate mounting 34 guns. Rejoining Capt. Mansfield, in 1803, on board the MINOTAUR 74, he witnessed the surrender, on 28 May in that year, of *La Franchise*, French frigate of 36 guns, and was present in the same ship in the battle of Trafalgar, 21 Oct. 1805. On Aug. 1806, at which period he was serving with Lord Collingwood in the OCEAN 98, Mr. Martin was made Lieutenant to the SATURN 74, Capt. Lord Amelius Beauclerk, under whom he was for nearly 18 months employed in the Mediterranean. His succeeding appointments were—18 Jan. 1808, to the LION 64, Capt. Henry Heathcote, in command of the launch of which ship he succeeded, in the vicinity of Manilla, in defeating five large piratical boats, carrying between them 20 small guns and about 200 men, after a desperate action of two hours, in which himself and the greater part of his crew, only 20 in number, were wounded—20 March, 1810, to the MAGNET sloop, Capt. John Smith (*a*), stationed, for the protection of the trade, off Heligoland and the German rivers—13 Dec. 1810, to the ABOUKIR 74, Capt. Geo. Parker, employed in the blockade of Flushing—11 Feb. 1812, to the CALLIOPE 10, Capt. John M'Kerlie, lying at Chatham—16 April following, to the ARDENT 64, *armée-en-flûte*, Capt. Geo. Bell, under whom, after conveying troops to Bermuda, he was nearly lost in an awful gale in the Bay of Biscay, during which his presence of mind and courage were most conspicuous, leading him aloft when no other person on board could be found to attempt it—3 March, 1813 to the ALBION 74, Capt. John Ferris Devonshire, fitting for service on the coast of North America—29 Jan. 1814, as First-Lieutenant, to the SCEPTRE 74, in which ship, commanded by the same officer, he returned home in time to participate in the grand naval review held at Spithead—29 July, 1818, in a similar capacity, to the CREOLE 36, Capt. Wm. Bateman Dashwood, with whom he proceeded to the Rio de la Plata, where his nautical skill in a great measure saved the ship from wreck—8 Jan. 1819 (on the latter vessel receiving the broad pendant of Commodore Wm. Bowles, although he had been given by the Admiralty to understand that he was not to have been superseded), to the AMPHION 32, Capt. W. B. Dashwood, a leaky old vessel, whose hand-pumps were obliged to be kept going during the whole of her passage home—and, 18 Nov. 1819, to the command (six months after the AMPHION had been paid off) of the CLINKER gun-brig. While in that vessel on the Newfoundland station, Lieut. Martin was in discharge, from Oct. 1820 to April, 1821, of the important duties of Surrogate at Harbour Grace, where his impartial administration of justice in more than 300 cases that came before him for adjudication, gave so much satisfaction, that on his departure he was presented with a most flattering address signed by all the principal inhabitants. In the following summer he was ordered by Sir Chas. Hamilton, Governor of Newfoundland, to explore the Grand Esquimaux Inlet, and then to proceed to the northward in order to find out and communicate with the different stations of the Moravian missionaries on the coast of Labrador. These instructions he carried into effect in a complete and most successful manner. His conduct on arriving among the missionaries, after encountering many dangers and hardships, was such as to endear him greatly to them, and to elicit the earnest thanks of the "Church of the United Brethren" in England. His advent took place during their jubilee-year; and the occasion was the first of their having been visited by a man-of-war. He returned home in May, 1822, having been advanced to his present rank on 19 of the previous July; and has not been since able to procure employment.

Commander Martin married first, in 1816, the daughter of Robt. Henning, Esq., of Compton Bishop, co. Somerset; and (that lady dying in 1825), secondly, 19 Feb. 1829, at Bristol, Anna Maria, eldest daughter of B. O. Donnoghue, Esq. By his first wife he has issue.

MARTIN. (CAPTAIN, 1824. F-P., 18; H-P., 16.)

WILLIAM FANSHAWE MARTIN is eldest son of Admiral Sir Thos. Byam Martin, G.C.B.

This officer entered the Navy, 15 June, 1813, as Fst.-cl. Vol, on board the PRINCE FREDERICK 74, Capt. Rich. Pridham, in which ship, and in the IMPREGNABLE 98, and AKBAR 50, each bearing the flag of his father, he served at Plymouth and off the Scheldt until April, 1815. He then became in succession attached, for short periods, to the GLASGOW 50, Capt. Hon. Henry Duncan, SPENCER 74, Capt. Richard Raggett, ROCHFORT 74, Capt. Sir Archibald Collingwood Dickson, and ERIDANUS 36, Capt. Wm. Paterson, all on the Channel station; and on next, in Jan. 1816, joining the ALCESTE 38, Capt. Murray Maxwell, he sailed in that ship with Lord Amherst for China—continuing in her until wrecked in the Straits of Gaspar, on her passage home, 18 Feb. 1817. In the following Aug. Mr. Martin was rated Midshipman of the PRINCE REGENT yacht, Capt. Sir Edw. Hamilton. He was promoted (after nearly three years' servitude in the Mediterranean in the GLASGOW 50, Capt. Hon. Anthony Maitland) to a Lieutenancy, we believe, in the FORTE 44, Capt. Sir Thos. John Cochrane, 15 Dec. 1820; and, on 7 April, 1821, he joined the AURORA frigate, Capt. Henry Prescott, fitting for South America; where, on 8 Feb. 1823, he was made Commander into the FLY sloop. He attained Post-rank 5 June, 1824; and was subsequently appointed—15 Nov. 1826, to the SAMARANG 28, on the Mediterranean station, whence he returned in

* *Vide* Note, p. 347.

the summer of 1831—and, 19 July, 1844, and 30 Jan. 1845, to the QUEEN 110, and TRAFALGAR 120, flag-ships of Sir John Chambers White and Sir Edw. Durnford King, at Sheerness. He has been on half-pay since Oct. 1845.

Capt. Martin married, first, 24 July, 1826, Hon. Anne Best, daughter of the late Lord Wynford, Lord Chief Justice of the Court of Common Pleas, and sister of Capt. Hon. Thos. Best, R.N. That lady dying in 1836, he married, a second time, 21 May, 1838, Sophia, second daughter of Rich. Hurt, Esq., of Wirksworth, Derbyshire. He has issue by both marriages. AGENT—J. Chippendale.

MARTIN. (LIEUTENANT, 1821.)

WILLIAM HENRY MARTIN entered the Navy, 26 May, 1809, as Fst.-cl. Vol., on board the ANTELOPE 50, Capt. Donald M'Leod, bearing the flag at Newfoundland of Admiral John Holloway; and in the following Sept. became a Supernumerary Midshipman of the POMPÉE 74, flag-ship of Hon. Sir Alex. Cochrane in the West Indies; where he continued employed, until the following July, in the PULTUSK and WELLINGTON, both commanded by Capt. John M'George. During the next four years and nine months we find him serving on the Cadiz and Lisbon stations in the PAPILLON sloop, Capt. Jas. Hay. He was then, in 1815, borne for a short time on the books of the NAMUR 74, flag-ship of Sir Chas. Rowley at the Nore; after which he was successively, between May, 1816, and Dec. 1820, nominated Admiralty Midshipman of the CADMUS 10, Capt. John Gedge, PIQUE 36, Capts. Jas. Haldane Tait and John Mackellar, IPHIGENIA 42, Capt. Hyde Parker, and SYBILLE 44, Capt. Joshua Ricketts Rowley, on the Home and Jamaica stations. He was confirmed a Lieutenant (after having acted for a brief period as such in the EURYALUS 42, Capts. Isham Fleming Chapman and Wilson Braddyll Bigland) 6 March, 1821; and was subsequently appointed—22 March, 1822, to the ALBION 74, Capts. Rich. Raggett and Sir Wm. Hoste, lying at Portsmouth—and, 15 Nov. 1826, to the THETIS 46, Capts. Arthur Batt Bingham and Sam. Burgess, under the latter of whom he was, we presume, wrecked near Cape Frio, 5 Dec. 1830. He has not been since afloat. AGENTS—Messrs. Chard.

MASON, K.C.B. (REAR-ADMIRAL OF THE RED, 1838. F-P., 24; H-P., 30.)

SIR FRANCIS MASON was born 10 Feb. 1779.

This officer entered the Navy, 23 May, 1793, as A.B., on board the RUSSEL 74, Capts. John Willet Payne and Thos. Larcom, part of the force employed in the actions of 28 and 29 May and 1 June, 1794, and 23 June, 1795. Previously to the latter affair he had been lent to the JUPITER 50, on board which ship his friend Capt. Payne had hoisted a broad pendant, for the purpose of escorting H.S.H. the Princess Caroline of Brunswick from Cuxhaven to England. In the summer of 1796 he removed to the IMPÉTUEUX 74, commanded at first by Capt. Payne, and next by Capt. Sampson Edwards; and, on 8 July, 1799, at which period he had been for ten months attached, as Master's Mate, still in the Channel, to the PHAETON 38, Capt. Hon. Robt. Stopford, he was made Lieutenant into the ALECTO sloop, Capt. Lennox Thompson, stationed off Lymington. After a servitude of three years in the North Sea, Baltic, Red Sea (where he was much employed in surveying), and East Indies, in the BEAVER sloop, Capt. Jones, and ROMNEY 50, Capts. John Lawford and Sir Home Popham, he took up in Nov. 1802 a Commander's commission, bearing date 29 of the preceding April. On 30 Dec. 1803, Capt. Mason received an appointment to the RATTLER sloop, mounting 24 guns; in which vessel he came into very frequent and warm contact with the enemy in the vicinity of Flushing. On one occasion in particular, 16 May, 1804, he united with the CRUIZER 18, Capt. John Hancock, and by his conduct gained the highest praise of Sir Wm. Sidney Smith, in a gallant attack upon a flotilla of praams, schooners, &c., in all 59 sail, passing along shore from the above place to Ostend.* Besides having the whole of her lower masts disabled by shot, and her yards, sails, and rigging much injured, the RATTLER in the action sustained a loss of 2 men killed and 10 wounded. On 23 of the ensuing June she received further damage while engaged with her consorts, the GALGO and INSPECTOR, in close conflict with 27 schuyts, whose fire was strengthened by that of several land-batteries and a body of artillery; and in Oct. of the same year she was thrice in action with the enemy's flotilla at Dieppe, and again, each time, much exposed to the batteries. After having twice visited Newfoundland, and been for a whole winter frozen up in St. John's Harbour, Capt. Mason, in July, 1806, was superseded from the RATTLER, in consequence of his promotion to Post-rank, which had taken place on 22 of the preceding Jan. Being soon appointed to the DAPHNE 20, he served in that vessel at the capture of Monte Video, and in all the operations which had preceded the evacuation of Spanish America. He afterwards proceeded to the Baltic, where, among other vessels, he took, in Aug. 1807, the Danish national schooner *Acertif*, pierced for 12 guns, but mounting only 8, and at the same time drove on shore a cutter of 4 guns. Resigning command of the DAPHNE soon afterwards from ill health, he remained on half-pay until Oct. 1809, in the course of which month he was appointed to the FISGARD 38, part of the force employed at the mouth of the Scheldt, where his conduct obtained him the fullest confidence of Sir Rich. Strachan, the Commander-in-Chief, and induced the latter to intrust him with the bringing off of the rear-guard on the occasion of the evacuation of the Walcheren.† Continuing in the FISGARD until paid off in July, 1812, Capt. Mason was for several months Senior officer off the Scheldt, and succeeded at different times in effecting the capture, with the aid of his boats, of a large number of vessels, among which were the *Juliana* Danish privateer of 6 guns, a schooner of 1 gun, and a French privateer of 2 guns, together with 56 sail of merchantmen. He also destroyed the *Ziska* Danish privateer of 6 guns and 40 men. In Feb. 1811 he accompanied a squadron under Sir Joseph Sydney Yorke to the Tagus; and, after conveying a Portuguese Ambassador to Revel, he cruized for some time off Cherbourg. While next in command, from 27 March, 1813, until 5 May, 1814, of the PRESIDENT 38, we find him present at the storming of St. Sebastian, and employed on the Cork station. On 4 June, 1815, Capt. Mason was nominated a C.B.; and in Oct. and Nov. 1833 he was successively appointed to the BLANCHE and BLONDE, each of 46 guns. In Feb. 1834 he sailed for Port Royal, Jamaica, with the broad pendant flying of a Commodore of the Second Class. Having landed the Marquis of Sligo and family at that place, he proceeded to South America, where, in the month of July, owing to the death of Sir Mich. Seymour, he assumed the duties of Commander-in-Chief, and hoisted the red pendant; which, on being superseded by Rear-Admiral Sir Graham Eden Hamond, he exchanged, in Feb. 1835, for his former or the blue pendant. He ultimately, in Oct. 1837, returned to England, and in the following month paid the BLONDE off. Attaining Flag-rank 28 June, 1838, Rear-Admiral Mason was next, 23 Aug. 1841, appointed second in command on the Mediterranean station, whither, on 8 Oct., he proceeded with his flag in the IMPREGNABLE 104. Previously to his departure he was raised, 24 Aug., to the dignity of a K.C.B. On his arrival in the Mediterranean, 31 Oct., Sir Fras. Mason found himself invested with the temporary command of the fleet, consisting of 12 sail of the line, which he retained until the advent, in April, 1842, of Vice-Admiral Sir Edw. Owen. He returned to England, in consequence of a reduction in the Mediterranean force, in May, 1843; and has since been on half-pay.

Previously to the receipt of his flag, Sir Fras. Mason had been, in 1833 and 1837, nominated extra

* *Vide* Gaz. 1804, p. 640. † *V.* Gaz. 1809, p. 2056.

Naval Aide-de-Camp to his late, and to her present Majesty; and he had likewise, in the year last mentioned, been awarded the Captains' Good-service Pension. He married, 16 April, 1805, Selina, youngest daughter of Henry, second Viscount Hood, and sister of Lieut.-Col. Fras. Wheler Hood, who was killed in action on the heights of Aire, 2 March, 1814. By that lady, a near connexion of Admiral Sir Graham Eden Hamond, Bart., K.C.B., Sir Francis has had issue twelve children, nine of whom are still living. His eldest son, Charles, a Midshipman R.N., was lost in the ARAB sloop of war in Dec. 1823. One of his daughters, Charlotte Susannah, married, 14 April, 1832, Capt. Hood Richards, h-p. 6th Dragoon Guards.

MASON. (LIEUTENANT, 1827.)

GEORGE MASON entered the Navy 1 Oct. 1809; and was present, we are informed, at the reduction of Guadeloupe (where he had previously witnessed the destruction of the French frigates *Loire* and *Seine*), and also in the operations against New Orleans. He passed his examination in 1815; obtained his commission 28 April, 1827; was appointed, 19 June, 1828, and 19 Feb. 1830, Supernumerary-Lieutenant of the RAMILLIES and TALAVERA Coast Blockade ships, both commanded by Capt. Hugh Pigot; obtained charge of a station in the Coast Guard 4 April, 1831; and was removed, 21 Jan. 1847, to the command of a Revenue-vessel, the STAG, in which he is now serving

Lieut. Mason married, 1 June, 1831, Ann, eldest daughter of W. Whitehead, Esq., of Teynham, co. Kent.

MASON. (COMMANDER, 1815. F-P., 11; H-P., 33.)

HENRY BROWNE MASON, born 26 April, 1791, is descended from Daniel Finch, second Earl of Nottingham and Winchelsea.

This officer entered the Navy, 6 Dec. 1803, as Fst.-cl. Vol., on board the PRINCE 98, Capt. Rich. Grindall, stationed in the Channel and off Cadiz. After sharing in the battle of Trafalgar he removed, in Nov. 1805, to the AMPHION 32, Capt. Wm. Hoste, on the Mediterranean station, where, in May, 1809, he was captured in a prize by two French privateers, and carried to Ancona. From that place he was marched to Briançon, and subsequently to Verdun. In Aug. 1810, owing to misconduct on the part of other midshipmen, he was deprived of his parole, and placed in close confinement in the citadel prison. Thence, in the following Nov., after many ineffectual attempts, he contrived to escape; and on 1 Jan. 1811, having traversed Holland, he had the good fortune to reach England. He was in consequence promoted, on 2 Feb. in the same year, to a Lieutenancy in the DREADNOUGHT 98, Capt. Sam. Hood Linzee, off Lisbon; and he was next appointed—3 May and 18 Dec. 1811, to the AMERICA and KENT 74's, Capts. Josias Rowley and Thos. Rogers, on the Mediterranean station—and, 28 June, 1813 (after six months of half-pay), to the FORTH 40, Capt. Sir Wm. Bolton. He acquired his present rank 13 June, 1815, but has not been since employed.

Commander Mason, for upwards of 13 years, has been in the Commission of the Peace for co. Southampton. He was left a widower, with six children, 29 Oct. 1843.

MASON. (LIEUT., 1815. F-P., 11; H-P., 30.)

HENRY WILLIAM MASON entered the Navy, 5 Nov. 1806, as Fst.-cl. Vol., on board the TERRIBLE 74, Capt. Lord Henry Paulet. In that ship, which was at first employed off Cadiz, he saw a good deal of active service in the Mediterranean, where he assisted, as Midshipman, in driving two French ships on shore, and commanded the jolly-boat at the cutting-out of an enemy's vessel. He left the TERRIBLE in June, 1810, and between that period and Aug. 1815 was employed on the Lisbon, North American, Mediterranean, Home, and Bermuda stations in the MACEDONIAN 38, Capts. Lord Wm. Fitzroy, Hon. Wm. Waldegrave, and John Surman Carden, CONQUESTADOR 74, Capt. Lord Wm. Stuart, RESISTANCE 38, Capts. Chas. Hole, Wm. Hamilton, and Fleetwood Broughton Reynolds Pellew, THISBE 28, Acting-Capt. Rich. Weymouth, and SCAMANDER 36, Capt. Gilbert Heathcote. He then took up a commission, bearing date 27 Feb. 1815; and was afterwards, from 5 Oct. in that year until 9 Oct. 1817, employed on the Home, Jamaica, and South American stations, in the DÉSIRÉE and ACTIVE frigates, both commanded by Capt. Philip Carteret. During the term of his attachment to the ship last mentioned Lieut. Mason was placed in charge of the SPEEDWELL tender, and employed on the eastern coast of England. Since he left the ACTIVE he has been on half-pay.

In 1829 Lieut. Mason was Sheriff for Buckinghamshire. He is now a Magistrate and Deputy-Lieutenant for that co. He married first, in 1822, Mary, niece of the late Sir Wm. Heathcote, Bart.; and (that lady dying in 1825), secondly, in 1826, Horatia, fourth daughter of Geo. Matcham, Esq., of Ashford Lodge, Sussex, by Catherine, sister of the immortal Nelson. By his second wife (who is sister-in-law of Lieuts. John Bendyshe and John Davies, and of the late Capt. Edw. Blanckley, R.N.), the Lieutenant has had issue two sons and five daughters. AGENTS—Messrs. Ommanney.

MASON. (COMMANDER, 1841.)

THOMAS HENRY MASON entered the Navy 7 Nov. 1822; passed his examination in 1830; obtained his first commission 21 July, 1837; and was appointed—29 of the same month, as Additional Lieutenant, to the WINCHESTER 52, flag-ship in the East Indies of Hon. Sir Thos. Bladen Capel—11 March, 1838, to the WELLESLEY 72, bearing the flag of Sir Fred. Lewis Maitland on the same station—and, 26 March, 1839, to the command of the ALGERINE 10. In that vessel he obtained mention for his zeal and alacrity at the capture of Chusan in July, 1840;* after which he was sent, in company with the CONWAY 28, and YOUNG HEBE tender, to examine the entrance of the Yang-tse-Kiang. In the attack made upon Canton in March, 1841, we find him enacting a very conspicuous part;† as he subsequently did in the operations renewed in the following May against that place. Having, in the words of Sir Humphrey Le Fleming Senhouse, won his promotion by a series of gallant and brave services,‡ he was accordingly, 8 June, 1841, advanced to the rank of Commander. Continuing, however, in the ALGERINE until Sept. 1842, he was afforded an opportunity of aiding in the capture of Amoy.§ He has been in command, since 25 Jan. 1847, of the MEDEA steam-sloop of 350 horse-power, in the East Indies.

Commander Mason married, 14 July, 1846, Isabella Susanna, third daughter of the late Edw. Frere, Esq., of Bitton, Gloucestershire.

MASSEY. (LIEUT., 1810. F-P., 10; H-P., 34.)

JOHN MASSEY entered the Navy, 3 Nov. 1803, as Fst.-cl. Vol., on board the PLANTAGENET 74, Capts. Hon. Michael De Courcy, Fras. Pender, and Wm. Bradley. After a servitude of four years in the Channel and among the Western Islands, half the time in the capacity of Midshipman, he joined, in Nov. 1807, the TONNANT 80, bearing the flag of his friend Hon. M. De Courcy; whom, in March, 1809 (having previously assisted in embarking the remains of Sir John Moore's army at Corunna), he followed, as Master's Mate, into the FOUDROYANT 80, of which ship he was successively created an acting and a confirmed Lieutenant 3 Nov. 1809 and 9 April, 1810. He continued in her on the Brazilian station until Nov. 1812; and was next, from Nov. 1813 until Nov. 1814, employed off New York in the SATURN 56, Capt. Nash. He has not been since afloat.

* *Vide* Gaz. 1840, p. 2991. † *V.* Gaz. 1841, p. 1565. ‡ *V.* Gaz. 1841, p. 2519. § *V.* Gaz. 1842, p. 83.

MASSIE. (Retired Commander, 1840. f-p., 15; h-p., 35.)

Henry George Massie entered the Navy, 15 Jan. 1797, as A.B, on board the Nassau 64, Capts. Herbert Sawyer and Edw. O'Bryen; on accompanying the latter of whom, as Midshipman, into the Monarch 74, he was afforded an opportunity of sharing, under the flag of Vice-Admiral Rich. Onslow, in the action off Camperdown, 11 Oct in the same year, 1797. He continued in the Monarch with Vice-Admiral Archibald Dickson, on the North Sea station until March, 1800, and then joined the Hebe frigate, Capts. Wm. Birchall and Geo. Reynolds, attached to the force in the Mediterranean, where, on his removal to the Foudroyant 80, bearing the flag of Lord Keith, he took part in the operations of 1801 on the coast of Egypt. In Dec. 1803, nearly five months after he had left the ship last named, he was received on board the Neptune 98, Capts. Wm. O'Brien Drury and Sir. Thos. Williams; in which ship, and in the Monarch and Edgar 74's, bearing the flag of Lord Keith, we find him continuously employed, in the Channel, until there nominated, 7 July, 1806, Acting-Lieutenant of the Daphne, Lieut.-Commander Price. He was officially promoted 9 Sept. following; and was subsequently appointed — 13 Nov. 1806, to the Flying Fish, Lieut.-Commander Goodwin, from which vessel, after witnessing the unsuccessful attack upon Buenos Ayres, he invalided in Sept. 1807—17 March, 1809, to the Africa 64, Capts. Loftus Otway Bland and Geo. Fred. Ryves, stationed in the Baltic—14 Jan. 1811, to the Royal William flag-ship at Spithead of Sir Roger Curtis and Sir Rich. Bickerton—and, 6 Feb. 1813, to the Prospero sloop, Capt. John Hardy Godby, in the North Sea. He went on half-pay in the following Sept., and accepted his present rank 5 Oct. 1840. Agent—J. Hinxman.

MASSIE. (Lieutenant, 1838. f-p., 22; h-p., 2.)

John Bevis Massie, born 5 Sept. 1809, is brother of Capt. Thos. L. Massie, R.N.

This officer entered the Navy, 26 July, 1823, as Fst.-cl. Vol., on board the Queen Charlotte 100, commanded at Portsmouth by Capt. J. Nash; and from the following Nov. until Oct 1825 was employed on particular service in the Phaeton 46, Capt. Hon. Evelyn Pitfield Sturt. He then became Midshipman of the Icarus 10, Capt. Hon. Wm. Waldegrave, lying at Portsmouth; but had not been many weeks in that vessel before he was transferred to the Procris 10, commanded at first by Capt. Waldegrave and next by Capts. Chas. Henry Paget, Sir Thos. Sabine Pasley, and John Thos. Talbot; with whom, it appears, he served on the North Sea, Cork, and Mediterranean stations until July, 1832—the last three years in the capacity of Mate. Being next, in April, 1833, received on board the Malabar 74, Capt. Hon. Josceline Percy, he returned to the Mediterranean, where he continued employed under that officer in the Canopus 84, until Feb. 1837. In the ensuing Oct. we find him joining the Donegal 78, flag-ship at Lisbon of Sir John Acworth Ommanney. He attained the rank of Lieutenant 28 June, 1838; and has been since appointed—15 Nov. 1838, to the Daphne 18, Capt. John Windham Dalling, under whom he partook of the operations of 1840 on the coast of Syria—15 July, 1842, and 15 April, 1844, to the Queen 110, and, as Senior Lieutenant to the Formidable, 84, bearing each the flag of Sir Edw. W. C. R. Owen in the Mediterranean, whence he returned and was paid off at the close of 1845—and 22 Jan 1846, also as First, to the Grampus 50, Capt. Henry Byam Martin, now in the Pacific. Agent—Joseph Woodhead.

MASSIE. (Captain, 1841. f-p., 20; h-p., 9.)

Thomas Leeke Massie entered the Navy 28 Oct. 1818, as Midshipman, on board the Rochfort 80, Capt. Andrew Pellet Green, bearing the flag of Sir Thos. Fras. Fremantle and Sir Graham Moore in the Mediterranean; where he continued, until the spring of 1828, to serve in the Redpole 10, Capt. R. Anderson, Rochfort again, Capt. Chas. Marsh Schomberg, Columbine 18, Capt. Hon. Chas. Abbot, Martin 18, Capt. Henry Eden, Rose 18, Capts. Hon. C. Abbot and Lewis Davies, and Asia 84, Capt. Sir Edw. Codrington. While in the Columbine, which vessel was totally lost off Sapienza, nea the Morea, 25 Jan. 1824; we find him employed in several boat-attacks on the pirates in the vicinity ot Cape Matapan; particularly on one occasion, when he took command of the pinnace and assisted in capturing one vessel and destroying another. He was present in the Martin, in Sir Harry Neale's demonstration before Algiers: and when in the Rose during the Greek revolution, he was again anti-piratically employed, and obtained mention for his conduct in an attack upon several vessels at Samothracia As a reward for his behaviour in the Asia at the battle of Navarin, Mr. Massie was promoted to a death-vacancy in that ship, and his commission dated 11 Nov. 1827. His subsequent appointment, in the capacity of Lieutenant were—25 June, 1828, and 19 Feb. 1830, as a Supernumerary, to the Ramillies and Talavera Coast Blockade ships, Capts. Hugh Pigot and David Colby—7 April, 1831, to the Prince Regent 120, Capt. Jas. Whitley Deans Dundas, employed in the Channel and under the flag of Rear-Admiral Wm. Parker off Lisbon—27 June, 1832, as Senior, for the purposes of a trial-cruize, to the Vernon 50, Capt. Sir Fras. Augustus Collier—8 Jan. 1833, in a similar capacity, to the Satellite 18, Capt. Robt. Smart, stationed in the North Sea with the force off Antwerp, and in South America, where he remained three years—7 June, 1836, to the Vanguard 80, Capt. Hon. Duncombe Pleydell Bouverie, part of an experimental squadron—and, 22 Nov. 1836, again as First, to the Carysfort 26, Capt. Henry Byam Martin, in the Mediterranean. He attained the rank of Commander 28 June, 1838; and, being appointed Second-Captain, 7 March, 1840, of the Thunderer 84, Capt. Maurice Fred. Fitzhardinge Berkeley, was present in the course of that year at the camp at D'Journi, and at the bombardment of Beyrout, the storming of Sidon, and the capture of St. Jean d'Acre. On the fall of Sidon Capt. Massie went on shore, and assisted in organizing the police, and putting the place in a state of defence—a service that procured him the approbation of Capt. Berkeley. For his conduct at Acre he was advanced (as soon as he had completed his term of servitude as Commander) to Post-rank, by commission dated 17 March, 1841. He has since been on half-pay.

In 1839, Capt. Massie and several other officers were sent out to assist in reconstructing the Turkish fleet; but, in consequence of some political change, they were under the necessity of returning at the end of six months. Capt. Massie married, 8 Feb. 1844, Charlotte Hester, only daughter of E. V. Townshend, Esq., of Wincham Hall, Cheshire.

MASSINGBERD. (Commander, 1842. f-p., 18; h p., 7.)

Vincent Amcotts Massingberd is a relative of Algernon Langton Massingberd, Esq., of Gunby Hall, co. Lincoln, whose maternal grandfather, Henry Massingberd, Esq., was a son (with Capt. Thos. Massingberd, R.N., of Candlesby House, co. Lincoln) of Thos. Massingberd, Esq., by Elizabeth Emerson, sister of Sir Walter Amcotts, Bart.

This officer entered the Navy, 21 June, 1822, as Fst.-cl. Vol., on board the Ariadne 28, Capt. Constantine Rich. Moorsom, and sailed for the Cape of Good Hope, where, in 1824, he exchanged, with the same Captain, into the Andromache 46. In Sept. 1825, having returned to England, he followed Capt. Moorsom, as Midshipman, into the Prince Regent 120, bearing the flag of Sir Robt. Moorsom at Chatham. In the summer of 1826 he was discharged into the Jasper 10, fitting for the Mediterranean, on which station he continued employed, under Capts. Henry Martin Blackwood and Leonard Chas. Rook, until wrecked, off Santa Maura, 11 Oct. 1828. Mr. Massingberd had been previously, 11 Oct. 1827, wounded in a boat engagement with pirates. Having passed his examination 20 June, 1828, he was successively nominated Mate — in Feb. 1829, of the PRINCE REGENT, flag-ship at the time of Hon. Sir Henry Blackwood at Chatham—in Nov. 1829 of the VOLAGE 28, Capt. Lord Colchester, under whom he escorted the ex-Emperor and Empress of Brazil to Cherbourg, and was employed during the winter of 1832 in enforcing the Dutch embargo —in Feb. 1834 (he had been on shore since Jan. 1833) of the SALAMANDER steamer, Capt. Wm. Langford Castle, engaged on Home service—and in Sept. 1835 (six months after the latter vessel had been paid off), of the RODNEY 92, Capt. Hyde Parker, stationed in the Mediterranean, whence he invalided in June, 1836. Being at length promoted to the rank of Lieutenant, 10 Jan. 1837, Mr. Massingberd, on 21 of the same month, obtained an appointment in that capacity to the PELORUS 16, Capt. Fras. Harding; which vessel, after a very useful career in the East Indies, had the misfortune to be wrecked, at Port Essington, 25 Nov. 1839. For his subsequent services in China, as Senior-Lieutenant of the BLENHEIM 72, Capt. Sir Thos. Herbert, Mr. Massingberd, who remained in that ship from 20 June, 1841, until paid off in March, 1843, was promoted to the rank of Commander by commission dated 23 Dec. 1842.* He has been in command, since 17 Nov. 1846, of the ALECTO steam-sloop, of 200 horse-power, on the south-east coast of America.

He married, 3 Sept. 1844, Julia, eldest daughter of Moses Gutteres, Esq., of Belmont, near Sidmouth, Devon. AGENTS—Messrs. Stilwell.

MASTERMAN. (LIEUTENANT, 1815. F-P., 9; H-P., 31.)

CHARLES HENRY MASTERMAN was born 20 Nov. 1791, at Chepstow, co. Monmouth. He is first-cousin of Commander Henry Marshall, R.N.; and has lost three brothers in the service of their country.

This officer entered the Navy, 21 May, 1807, as Sec.-cl. Vol., on board the CAMBRIAN 40, Capt. Hon. Chas. Paget, lying at Portsmouth; and on becoming Midshipman, soon afterwards, of the ZEBRA bomb, Capt. Wm. Bowles, accompanied the expedition to Copenhagen, where he was for nearly two months employed with the in-shore squadron. In Nov. of the same year he rejoined Capt. Paget on board the CAMBRIAN, commanded next by Capts. Rich. Budd Vincent and Fras. Wm. Fane. After serving in the Channel and Mediterranean, in that vessel and also in the HIND 28, Capts. R. B. Vincent and Geo. Miller Bligh, and WOOLWICH 44, Capt. Fras. Beaufort, he returned to England in May, 1809, and in the course of the next month was received into the ROYAL OAK 74, Capt. Lord Amelius Beauclerk, and STATELY 64, bearing the flag in the Baltic of Rear-Admiral Thos. Bertie. In the latter ship, when commanded, in 1811, by Capt. Edw. Stirling Dickson, we find Mr. Masterman cooperating in the defence of Cadiz, and assisting in landing the troops previous to the battle of Barossa. From Aug. in that year until his return home in July, 1814, he again served with Capt. Bowles in the AQUILON and CERES frigates, on the Baltic and South American stations. In the boats of the former vessel, commanded by Lieut. Sam. Sparshott, he aided in destroying a convoy off the island of Rugen. On leaving the CERES, he successively joined, on the Home and West India stations, the NYMPHEN 36, Capt. Matt. Smith, MONTAGU 74, Capt. Peter Heywood, WARRIOR 74, flag-ship of Rear-Admiral J. E. Douglas, SHARK sloop, Capt. Alex. Campbell, and DRAKE 10, Capt. Gregory Grant. The DRAKE, of which vessel he had been constituted an acting and a confirmed Lieutenant 26 May and 14 July, 1815, he left in Sept. of that year. With the exception of a short time passed about 1825 in the Coast Blockade, as Supernumerary-Lieutenant of the HYPERION 42, Capt. Wm. Jas. Mingaye, he has not been since employed.

Lieut. Masterman is married, and has two sons living. His third son, Samuel, died at the Upper School, Greenwich, in 1839, aged 13.

* *Vide* Gaz. 1843, p. 2950.

MASTERS. (RETIRED COMMANDER, 1841. F-P., 15; H-P., 33.)

JAMES MASTERS entered the Navy, 23 Aug. 1799, as Fst.-cl. Vol., on board the DEFIANCE 74, Capt. Thos. Revell Shivers, attached to the Channel fleet; with which he continued to serve, as Midshipman of the WINDSOR CASTLE 98, flag-ship of Sir Andw. Mitchell, and MALTA 84, Capt. Albemarle Bertie, until April, 1802; when he again joined Sir A. Mitchell in the CAMBRIAN 40, at Newfoundland. In the following Dec. he removed to the LEANDER 50, Capts. Jas. Oughton, John Talbot, Alex. Skene, and Henry Whitby; and while in that ship, under Capt. Talbot, he assisted at the taking, 23 Feb. 1805, of *La Ville de Milan* French frigate of 46 guns, and the simultaneous recapture of her prize, the CLEOPATRA 32. He was confirmed a Lieutenant, after having acted for four months as such, in the HALIFAX sloop, Capt. Jas. Townshend, 22 Sept. 1806; and was subsequently appointed—19 Nov. 1808, to the BELLONA 74, Capt. John Erskine Douglas, employed on the Home station, where, in April, 1809, he witnessed the destruction of the shipping in Aix Roads—and, 21 Nov. 1810 and 14 April, 1813, as Senior, to the LAVINIA and NIOBE frigates, Capts. Geo. Digby and Wm. Augustus Montagu. In those vessels he served in the Mediterranean and off Cadiz and Lisbon until June, 1814 He accepted his present rank 29 Jan. 1841.

MASTERS. (LIEUT., 1809. F-P., 9; H-P., 35.)

THOMAS JAMES POOLE MASTERS is son of Wm. Masters, Esq., Solicitor, of Hampstead, co. Middlesex.

This officer entered the Navy, 3 Oct. 1803, as Sec.-cl. Vol., on board the REPULSE 74, Capt. Hon. Arthur Kaye Legge; and was employed during the two following years, the greater part of the time as Midshipman, in the North Sea and off Rochefort and Ferrol, being afforded an opportunity during that period of sharing in Sir Robt. Calder's action, 22 July, 1805. In Jan. 1806 he removed to the IRIS 32, commanded by Capt. Thos. Lavie; on accompanying whom into the BLANCHE of 46 guns and 265 men, he assisted, 19 July in the same year, at the capture, off the Faeroe Islands, of the *Guerrière* French frigate of 50 guns and 317 men, after a severe action, in which the British had but 4 men wounded, and the enemy 50 killed and wounded. For his gallantry in achieving this exploit Capt. Lavie received the honour of Knighthood. Mr. Masters continued in the BLANCHE until wrecked, off Ushant, on the night of 4 March, 1807; on which occasion, after floating for many hours on a spar, he was washed on shore, and taken prisoner. At first he was placed *en parole* at Verdun; whence, owing to his having taken part with a British seaman, he was removed to Givet, and there kept for many months in solitary confinement, subjected the whole time to very cruel treatment. He at length, however, 25 Nov. 1808, contrived to make his escape from the Porte Chaussée, Verdun; and in Jan. 1809 he had the good fortune to reach Trieste; having in the meanwhile travelled not less than 1800 miles on foot, and in disguise, through France, Germany, Switzerland, Italy, and a small part of Austria. He had also crossed the Alps, and had all but perished in the snows on Mount St. Gothard; and, having no passport, had been twice taken up on suspicion. On setting out he had but 18 Napoleons in his possession; and he accomplished the last 500 miles with but 25 francs; eating bread but once a-day, sleeping often in woods among the wolves, and enduring all kinds of hardships and privations. On arriving at Trieste, as above, he contrived to get on board the UNITÉ 36, Capt. Pat.

Campbell; and in the boats of that ship, in which he continued a period of nine months, he assisted, it appears, at the destruction of a convoy under the protection of the enemy's batteries. He was made a Lieutenant, 4 Nov. 1809, into the NEPTUNE 98, commanded in the West Indies by Sir Jas. Athol Wood, with whom he removed, in March, 1810, to the POMPÉE 80. In the ensuing Sept. he became Second Lieutenant of the HORATIO 38, Capt. Lord Geo. Stuart, on the North Sea station; and on 2 Aug. 1812 we find him serving with four boats under Lieut. Abraham Mills Hawkins, whom he supported in the most spirited and able manner in a sanguinary combat, which terminated in the capture (with a loss to the British, out of about 80 officers and men, of 9 killed and 16 wounded, and to their opponents of 10 killed and 13 wounded) of a Danish schooner and cutter, carrying between them 10 6-pounders and 52 men, lying at anchor in a position of extraordinary strength near a village on an arm of the sea, 35 miles inland, on the coast of Norway.* So severely was Lieutenant Masters on the occasion wounded, that he for ever lost the use of his right hand, and was under the necessity of being sent to Yarmouth Hospital. His highly-praised gallantry and the sufferings he endured obtained him a pension of 91*l.* 5*s.* and a reward of 50 guineas from the Patriotic Fund. He has not, however, been since employed. AGENTS—Pettet and Newton.

MATHEWS. (LIEUTENANT, 1840.)

EDWARD MORRELL MATHEWS died about the close of 1846, on board H.M.S. IRIS. He was son of C. Mathews, Esq., of Wargrave, Henley-on-Thames.

This officer entered the Navy 16 Nov. 1828; passed his examination in 1834; and, after much creditable service, was made Lieutenant, 14 Oct. 1840, into the MODESTE 18, Capts. Harry Eyres and Rundle Burges Watson, under whom, prior to the return of that ship to England in 1843, he took part, if we mistake not, in all the operations on the coast of China, including the storming of Chinghae.† His last appointment was, 19 Oct. 1843, to the IRIS 26, Capt. Geo. Rodney Mundy, fitting for the East Indies, where, in July, 1846, on the occasion of an expedition conducted by Sir Thos. John Cochrane against the Sultan of Borneo, he took command of the 5th company of small-arm men, and assisted at the capture and destruction of the enemy's forts and batteries up the river Brune.‡ In the course of the same month we find him, with 136 seamen belonging to the IRIS and ROYALIST under his orders, accompanying Capt. Mundy and a detached force up different branches of the Borneo river, and then penetrating deep into the country, in a fruitless pursuit of the Sultan, supposed to be at a place called Damuan. During nearly the whole period of their march, which lasted several days, the British were under a torrent of rain, and were plunged knee-deep in swamp at every step. The exertions, however, of Lieut. Mathews throughout were such as to obtain him the thanks of Capt. Mundy.§

MATHEWS. (LIEUT., 1810. F-P., 27; H-P., 21.)

ROBERT BATES MATHEWS was born 5 June, 1785.

This officer entered the Navy, in Dec. 1799, as Fst.-cl. Vol., on board the HARPY 18, Capts. Henry Bazely and Wm. Birchall; under the former of whom, when in company with the FAIRY 18, he took part, 6 Feb. 1800, in a very gallant action of an hour and three-quarters, which terminated in the repulse, with a loss to the HARPY of 1 killed and 3 wounded, of the French frigate *Pallas* of 46 guns and 362 men. In the evening of the same day he was present in a second action, the upshot of which was the surrender of the *Pallas* to the above named sloops and their consorts, the LOIRE 38, DANAE 20, and RAILLEUR 16. At the commencement of 1801 Mr. Mathews became Midshipman of the BRUNSWICK 74, Capt. Geo. Hopewell Stephens; and, on his return from the West Indies in 1802, he successively joined the NEPTUNE 98, flag-ship of Admiral Milbanke at Spithead, and APOLLO 36, Capt. John Wm. Taylor Dixon. In the latter vessel it was his misfortune to be wrecked, off the coast of Portugal, 1 April, 1804; on which occasion the Captain and 60 of the crew were lost; himself and the remainder being left for three days on the wreck without sustenance, and only partially clothed. So great was the shock to his constitution that he has never recovered its effects. Joining next, as Master's Mate, the MACKEREL 4, Lieut.-Commander R. Williams, he proceeded to Bermuda; where, in 1805, while in the act of protecting an American vessel, on the rocks, he received a wound which greatly weakened his right hand, and disabled its fore-finger. In 1806, having removed to the MERCURY 28, Capt. Chas. Pelly, Mr. Mathews was placed in charge of a re-captured merchantman, which he carried in safety to Lisbon, although surrounded and chased on the passage by four Spanish privateers. His conduct indeed was such as to procure him mention in his Captain's official letter to Sir Erasmus Gower, the Commander-in-Chief at Newfoundland. Having passed his examination, 5 June, 1806, and been intermediately employed in the Mediterranean on board the COLOSSUS 74, Capt. Jas. Nicoll Morris, and ROYAL SOVEREIGN 100, bearing the flag of Vice-Admiral Edw. Thornbrough, Mr. Mathews was promoted, 4 May, 1810, to the rank of Lieutenant, and appointed to the HIBERNIAN 110, which ship the state of his health, however, deprived him of the possibility of joining. He was afterwards employed—from July to Sept. 1811, in the IMPREGNABLE 98, in which ship he proceeded from Sheerness to Portsmouth—from 23 March, 1812, to 31 Jan. 1816, in command of the Signal Station at Barry's Head, co. Cork—and from 14 Feb. 1820 until, we believe, 1831, in the Coast Guard. During the latter period he received a gold medal from the Royal National Shipwreck Institution, in acknowledgment of his exertions in having saved 31 persons from shipwreck. His resignation of his appointment was induced by extreme ill health; a complaint contracted in the Coast Guard having caused him to undergo two surgical operations. On leaving that service, however, he accepted the appointment of Harbour Master at Lowestoft, in Suffolk; the duties of which office he continued to fill until Oct. 1843, when he relinquished it, in consequence of the sale of the navigation by the Exchequer Loan Commissioners.

Lieut. Mathews (who receives a pension of 4*l.* per annum for the wound he received at Bermuda) married Elizabeth, sister of Retired Commander Thos. Jager, by whom he had issue 12 children. AGENTS—Hallett and Robinson.

MATHIAS. (COMMANDER, 1837. F-P., 25; H-P., 12.)

THOMAS MATHIAS entered the Navy, 19 Nov. 1810, as Fst.-cl. Vol., on board the COURAGEUX 74, Capt. Philip Wilkinson, stationed in the Baltic; where, in May, 1813, 12 months after he had attained the rating of Midshipman, he removed to the AMPHION 32, Capt. Jas. Pattison Stewart; under whom, in the following Dec., he assisted in reducing the islands of Schouwen and Tholen. Towards the close of 1814, after having visited Madeira, in the BOMBAY 74, Capt. Henry Bazely, he sailed for the East Indies in the CORNWALLIS 74, flag-ship of Sir Geo. Burlton. In Aug. 1818 (he had returned to England in Nov. 1816) he joined the ONTARIO 18, Capt. Geo. Gosling, lying at Plymouth; and he next, between Sept. in the same year and June, 1823, served, principally as Acting Second Master and Admiralty-Midshipman, in the SLANEY 20, Capts. Donat Henchy O'Brien and Henry Stanhope, NIMROD sloop, Capt. Wm. Rochfort, BRAZEN 26, Capt. Geo. Wickens Willes, and DORIS frigate, Capt. Fred. Edw. Vernon (now Harcourt). The NIMROD was employed in 1822 in sub-

* *Vide* Gaz. 1812, p. 1760.

† *V.* Gaz. 1842, p. 396. ‡ *V.* Gaz. 1846, p. 3412.

§ *V.* Gaz. 1846, pp. 3444-6-7.

during some serious riots among the keelmen on the river Tyne: the other vessels were all stationed in South America; where, on the date above mentioned, Mr. Mathias was nominated Acting-Lieutenant of the TARTAR 42, bearing the broad-pendant of Sir Thos. Masterman Hardy. He was officially promoted 22 Oct. 1823; and was afterwards appointed—23 March, 1824, again to the DORIS, Capts. Vernon, Thos. Bourchier, and Wm. Jas. Hope Johnstone, in which vessel he returned home and was paid off in Jan. 1825—12 March, 1830, to the TALAVERA 74, Capts. Hugh Pigot, David Colby, and Thos. Brown, on the Home and Lisbon stations —and, 17 May, 1833, as First, to the CALEDONIA 120, commanded in the Mediterranean, part of the time a flag-ship to Sir Josias Rowley, by Capts. T. Brown and Geo. Bohun Martin. He was superseded on being advanced to his present rank 10 Jan. 1837; and he was next, from 22 March, 1838, until 1843, employed in the Coast Guard. He has since been on half-pay.

Commander Mathias married, first, 14 July, 1838, Emily, fourth daughter of the late Rev. John Taylor, Rector of Stainford; and (that lady dying 19 Feb. 1839), secondly, in 1840, Lydia Charlotte, eldest daughter of R. Moyle, Esq., of Penzance, Cornwall. AGENTS—Hallett and Robinson.

MATHISON. (COMMANDER, 1843.)

CHARLES MITCHELL MATHISON entered the Navy 5 Aug. 1819; passed his examination in 1825; and was made Lieutenant, 12 May, 1827, into the ALACRITY 10, Capt. Geo. Jas. Hope Johnstone, on the Mediterranean station. His succeeding appointments were—12 March, 1830, to the SCYLLA 18, Capts. John Hindmarsh and Hon. Geo. Grey, also in the Mediterranean, whence he returned in the early part of 1834—31 Jan. 1835, as a Supernumerary, to the DUBLIN 50, Capt. Chas. Hope, fitting at Plymouth—10 April, 1835, 2 Nov. 1836, and 18 May, 1837, to the BARHAM 50, THUNDERER 84, and MINDEN 72, Capts. Armar Lowry Corry, Wm. Furlong Wise, and Alex. Renton Sharpe, all in the Mediterranean, where he remained until the commencement of 1840—20 Aug. 1841, to the MALABAR 72, Capt. Sir Geo. Rose Sartorius, on the South American station—and, 2 Jan. 1843, to the ST. VINCENT 120, as Flag-Lieutenant to Sir Chas. Rowley at Portsmouth. He attained the rank he now holds 25 Sept. in the latter year; and since 28 Jan. 1847 has been in command of the MARINER 16, on the coast of Africa.

MATSON. (COMMANDER, 1830. F-P., 22; H-P., 20.)

GEORGE WILLIAM MATSON was born 10 Aug. 1794.

This officer entered the Navy, 12 June, 1805, as Fst.-cl. Vol., on board the GLORY 98, Capt. Sam. Warren, and on 22 July following was present, under the flag of Rear-Admiral Chas. Stirling, in Sir Robt. Calder's action with the combined squadrons of France and Spain off Cape Finisterre. Quitting the GLORY in July, 1806, he was next, until March, 1814, employed, chiefly in the capacity of Midshipman, in the SAMPSON 64, bearing the flag of Rear-Admiral Stirling. DIADEM 64, BELLEROPHON 74, and PRESIDENT 38, all commanded (the two former as flag-ships of Rear-Admirals Stirling and Gardner) by Capt. Sam. Warren, PRINCE 98, bearing the flag of Sir Rich. Bickerton, ARDENT 64, Capt. John Cochet, NORTH STAR 20, Capt. Thos. Coe, SHARK sloop, Capt. John Gore, and ARGO 44, Capts. Cornelius Quinton and Wm. Fothergill. He served in the DIADEM at the reduction of Monte Video in Feb. 1807; assisted, 7 July, 1809, in the boats of the BELLEROPHON and other ships, at the capture of a Russian flotilla and convoy in the Baltic (an exploit more particularly alluded to in our memoir of Capt. Chas. Allen); and was present, in the PRESIDENT, at the taking of Java in Sept. 1811. On 25 March, 1814, at which time he was serving in the ARGO in the West Indies, he was nominated Acting-Lieutenant of the BONNE CITOYENNE 20, Capts. Pitt Burnaby Greene and Augustus Wm. Jas. Clifford. He obtained official promotion 1 Feb. 1815; and was afterwards appointed —29 April, 1815, to the gun-boat service at Deal—5 Nov. following, to the HARRIER sloop, Capt. Sir Chas. Thos. Jones, on the Halifax station, where he continued, the last two years and a half as First-Lieutenant, until the close of 1818—about Dec. 1820, in the capacity last mentioned, to the SOPHIE 18, Capts. Geo. French, Robt. Graham Dunlop, and Geo. Fred. Ryves, fitting for the East Indies, whence he invalided 28 Aug. 1823—14 Sept. 1824, again as Senior, to the ESK 20, Capt. Wm. Jardine Purchas, whom he accompanied to the coast of Africa—and, 21 Nov. 1825 and 1 Nov. 1826, to the command, on that station, of the SWINGER and CLINKER gun-brigs. On paying the SWINGER off at Portsmouth, 26 July, 1826, Lieut. Matson was presented by the crew with a dress-sword, belt, and epaulette, in token of their very great esteem. He was advanced to his present rank soon after his return to England in the CLINKER (in which vessel he had effected the emancipation of 1400 slaves) 22 Oct. 1830; and has since been on half-pay.

Commander Matson married, 7 Oct. 1835, Jane Newman, eldest daughter of the late Wm. Walter Yea, Esq., of Pyrland, co. Somerset, and sister of the present Sir Wm. Walter Yea, Bart. AGENTS—Holmes and Folkard.

MATSON. (COMMANDER, 1843. F-P., 22; H-P., 2.)

HENRY JAMES MATSON, born 5 April, 1810, is son of Chas. Matson, Esq., Paymaster and Purser, R.N. (1793); nephew of Admiral Rich. Matson; grand-nephew of the late Admiral Sir Henry Harvey, K.B., who commanded the RAMILLIES 74 in the action of 1 June, 1794, and also of the gallant Capt. John Harvey, R.N., who was mortally wounded in command of the BRUNSWICK 74 on the same occasion; and second-cousin of Commander G. W. Matson, R.N.

This officer entered the Navy, 10 July, 1823, as Fst.-cl. Vol., on board the SERINGAPATAM 46, Capt. Sam. Warren, stationed in the Channel; and in the early part of the following year proceeded in the SAMARANG 28, Capt. Sir Wm. Saltonstall Wiseman, to North America; where, in Dec. 1824, he joined the JUPITER 60, bearing the flag of Rear-Admiral Willoughby Thos. Lake. In Sept. 1827, having attained the rating of Midshipman some time previously, he joined the REVENGE 76, Capts. Norborne Thompson and Hon. Chas. Orlando Bridgeman, in which ship, stationed in the Mediterranean, he continued until Oct. 1830. In the course of the ensuing month (he had passed his examination 12 Aug. 1829) he became Mate of the UNDAUNTED 46, Capt. Edw. Harvey, fitting for the Cape of Good Hope; and in Feb. 1833 he was transferred from that frigate to the CURLEW 10, Capt. Henry Dundas Trotter, and placed in charge of a watch. For his subsequent conduct at the capture of some pirates on the west coast of Africa, Mr. Matson, who left the CURLEW in June, 1834, was promoted, 8 April, 1835, to the rank of Lieutenant, and appointed, a week afterwards, to the PEARL 20, Capts. Hugh Nurse and Lord Clarence Edw. Paget, employed at first on the Lisbon and then on the North America and West India station. The latter vessel, of which he had been for eighteen months First-Lieutenant, being put out of commission 2 Jan. 1839, he obtained command, 2 March following, of the WATERWITCH 10, and was again ordered to the west coast of Africa; where four years of the most successful exertion in suppression of the slave trade resulted in his advancement to the rank of Commander, 17 July, 1843. His last appointment was to the command, 7 Sept. 1844, of the DARING 12, in which sloop he served on the Home and North America and West India stations until superseded in Feb. 1847.

Commander Matson married, 12 June, 1837, Philadelphia Stephens, daughter of Thos. Josling, Esq., of Lisbon, by whom, who died 23 Oct. 1845, he had issue one daughter. AGENTS—Messrs. Stilwell.

MATSON. (ADMIRAL OF THE BLUE, 1847. F-P., 21; H-P., 43.)

RICHARD MATSON is son of the late John Matson, Esq., Chief Justice and Governor of Dominica; uncle of Commander Henry Jas. Matson, R.N.; and cousin of Commander Geo. Wm. Matson, R.N.

This officer entered the Navy, 20 March, 1783, as Fst.-cl. Vol., on board the IRRESISTIBLE 74, bearing the broad pendant at Chatham of Sir Andrew Snape Hamond; and was afterwards, between 1786 and Jan. 1793, employed, in the capacities of Midshipman and Master's Mate, in the SOLEBAY 32, Capt. John Holloway, JUPITER 50, Commodore Wm. Parker, SOLEBAY again, Capt. Wm. Squire, and HERMIONE 32, Capt. John Hills, on the West India and Home stations. He then joined the BRITANNIA 100, bearing the flag of Vice-Admiral Wm. Hotham in the Mediterranean; where, in the course of the same and the following year, he served on shore at the occupation of Toulon, was publicly thanked by Sir Wm. Sidney Smith for his conduct at the destruction of the arsenal and fleet in the harbour of that place,* and was present at the sieges of St. Fiorenza and Bastia. Being made Lieutenant, 15 Oct. 1794, into the BEDFORD 74, Capts. Davidge Gould and Augustus Montgomery, he was afforded an opportunity of sharing, under the former of those officers, in Hotham's partial actions of 14 March and 13 July, 1795. After a servitude of nearly two years on the Lisbon, Mediterranean, Cape of Good Hope, and West India stations, in the SYBILLE and DAPHNE frigates, Capts. Edw. Cooke and Jas. Brisbane, TAMAR 38, Capt. Thos. Byam Martin, and PRINCE OF WALES 98, flag-ship of Vice-Admiral Henry Harvey, he was promoted, 22 Sept. 1797, to the command of the BEAVER sloop, also in the West Indies; where he removed, in May, 1798, to the CYANE 18, and was posted, 22 March, 1799, into the DAPHNE 20. He returned to England in April, 1802; and was subsequently appointed—2 Sept. 1807 and 9 April, 1808, to the SAN YSIDORO and BRAAVE 40, lying at Plymouth—and 16 June, 1808, to the Sea Fencible service between North Shields and St. Abb's Head. He has been on half-pay since Feb. 1810. He became a Rear-Admiral 27 May, 1825; a Vice-Admiral 10 Jan. 1837; and a full Admiral 26 June, 1847. AGENTS—Hallett and Robinson.

MATTHEWS. (COMMANDER, 1822. F-P., 15; H-P., 29.)

ALFRED MATTHEWS, born 26 Jan. 1792, is fifth son of the late John Matthews, Esq., of Belmont, co. Hereford, Colonel of the Local Militia, and several years M.P. for that shire, by Elizabeth, daughter of Mr. Arthur Ellis, of Much Marcle. He is brother of the present John Holder Matthews, a Magistrate and Deputy-Lieutenant for co. Hereford: also of the Rev. Arthur Matthews, Canon of Hereford and Vicar of Linton, who died in Sept. 1842; and of Henry Matthews, Esq., author of the well known 'Diary of an Invalid,' who died soon after his elevation to the Bench in the island of Ceylon.

This officer entered the Navy, 31 Jan. 1803, as Fst.-cl. Vol., on board the CULLODEN 74, Capts. Chas. Henry Lane and Bartholomew Dacres, flag-ship for some time, in the Channel, of Rear-Admiral Geo. Campbell; whom, in the course of the same year, he accompanied to the Mediterranean in the CANOPUS 80. Removing as Midshipman, in April, 1804, to the TIGRE 80, Capt. Benj. Hallowell, Mr. Matthews, who continued in that ship until Feb. 1808, was for a long period employed at the blockade of Cadiz, and, besides accompanying Lord Nelson to the West Indies and back in pursuit of the combined fleets of France and Spain, served throughout the second Egyptian campaign, from the capture of Alexandria to its evacuation. In June, 1808, we find him joining the IPHIGENIA 36, Capt. Henry Lambert, under whom, after making a voyage to Quebec, he proceeded to the Cape of Good Hope station, where he witnessed the conquest of Ile de Bourbon in July, 1810, and, in the course of the following month, assumed a share in a series of gallant but unfortunate operations, which, by the 28th, terminated in the self-destruction of the British frigates, SIRIUS, bearing the broad pendant of Commodore Sam. Pym, and MAGICIENNE, the capture of the NÉRÉIDE, and the surrender to a powerful French squadron of the IPHIGENIA herself, after incurring an individual loss of at least 5 men killed and 13 wounded, at the entrance of Port Sud-Est, Isle of France. He remained in consequence in captivity until released at the reduction of the Mauritius, when he was again placed on board the IPHIGENIA, under the orders of Capt. Thos. Gordon Caulfeild. He next, between July and Oct. 1811, served in the SCIPION 74, flag-ship of Hon. Robt. Stopford at the Cape; and on 11 Feb. 1812 he was there made Lieutenant into the ASTREA frigate, Capt. Chas. Marsh Schomberg. He returned to England in Sept. 1813; and was subsequently appointed—18 April, 1814, to the HERMES 20, Capt. Hon. Henry Wm. Percy, which vessel, after 25 of her men had been killed and 24 wounded, in an unsuccessful attack upon Fort Bowyer, Mobile, was set on fire and destroyed in order to prevent her falling into the hands of the Americans, 15 Sept. 1814*—10 June, 1816, as Senior, to the ALERT sloop, Capt. John Smith, stationed in the North Sea, where, in one of the vessel's galleys, he captured a smuggling lugger—and, 24 April, 1817, to the command of the DRAKE Revenue cruizer, in which he appears to have been for three years very actively and successfully employed off the Land's End and Scilly. He attained the rank of Commander 19 July, 1822, and between that period and April, 1823, was employed on the Jamaica station in the SURINAM and ICARUS sloops. He has since been on half-pay.

He married, 26 Oct. 1833, Emily Rosetta, youngest daughter of the late Rev. Jas. Bernard, Rector of Combe Flory, co. Somerset.

MATTHEWS. (COMMANDER, 1815. F-P., 17; H-P., 31.)

MICHAEL MATTHEWS is son of F. Matthews, Esq., formerly in the Ordnance Department at Portsmouth.

This officer entered the Navy, in Aug. 1799, as Fst.-cl. Vol., on board the SANS PAREIL 80, Capts. Chas. Vinicombe Penrose, Jas. Katon, and Wm. Essington, successive flag-ship of Admirals Lord Hugh Seymour and Robt. Montagu in the Channel and West Indies, where he served until Sept. 1802, latterly in the capacity of Midshipman. In Feb. 1803, he joined the VENERABLE 74, bearing the flag, on the former station, of the late Lord Collingwood; whom, in the course of 1804, he followed into the COLOSSUS and CULLODEN 74's, and PRINCE and ST. GEORGE 98's. He was made Lieutenant, 15 Oct. 1806, into the PRINCE OF WALES 98, Capt. Wm. Bedford, flag-ship for some time of Sir Jas. Saumarez in the Baltic; and he was next, between Aug. 1807, and July, 1813, employed, on the latter and on the West and East India stations, in the CAPTAIN 74, Capt. Isaac Wolley, MELVILLE sloop, Capt. Hon. Jas. Wm. King, CORNELIA frigate, Capt. Henry Folkes Edgell, RUSSEL 74, bearing the flag of Vice-Admiral Wm. O'Brien Drury, and MINDEN 74, Capts. Edw. Wallis Hoare, Alex. Skene, and Jos. Prior, flag-ship latterly of Sir Sam. Hood. In the RUSSEL he took part in the earlier portion of the operations that preceded the fall of the Isle of France; and in the MINDEN he saw much active service on the coast of Java. On leaving that ship he was nominated Lieutenant-Governor of the Na-

* *Vide* Gaz. 1794, p. 44.

* After the destruction of the HERMES he volunteered to serve with the army against New Orleans, and assisted in a successful dash across the Mississippi, 8 Jan. 1815.

val Hospital, and Superintendent of the Impress, at Bombay. He continued in discharge of the duties thus imposed upon him until Feb. 1815; and on 20 of the following Sept., after having acted in command of the WELLESLEY 74, he was confirmed in that of the HESPER sloop. He returned to England about Aug. 1816 in the HECATE 16; and has since been on half-pay.

He is married, and has issue. AGENTS—Messrs. Ommanney.

MAUDE. (COMMANDER, 1827. F-P., 13; H-P., 23.)

THE HONOURABLE FRANCIS MAUDE, born in 1798, is fifth and youngest son of the first Viscount Hawarden, by his third wife, Anne Isabella, daughter of Thos. Monck, Esq., barrister-at-law, and niece of Viscount Monck; and brother (with Capt. Hon. Sir Jas. Ashley Maude, R.N., C.B., K.C.H. (1814), who died 23 Oct. 1841) of the present Viscount. He is brother-in-law of Lord Wm. Stuart, Lord Robt. Ponsonby Tottenham, Bishop of Clogher, Lord Lifford, and Lord Dunalley.

This officer entered the Royal Naval College 20 Nov. 1811; and embarked, 24 April, 1814, on board the PRINCE 98, Capt. Geo. Fowke, bearing the flag of Sir Rich. Bickerton at Spithead. In the course of the same year he joined the AMPHION 32, Capt. Jas. Pattison Stewart, and also the FAVORITE 20, commanded by his brother, Capt. Hon. Jas. Ashley Maude. In that vessel, after having brought home from America the ratification of the treaty of Ghent, he proceeded to the East Indies; where, in Dec. 1816, 20 months after he had attained the rating of Midshipman, he removed to the MAGICIENNE 36, Capt. John Brett Purvis. In Aug. 1819, he became Admiralty-Midshipman of the SUPERB 78, bearing the broad pendant in South America of Sir Thos. Masterman Hardy; who, on 24 May, 1820, nominated him Lieutenant of that ship. He was confirmed, 7 Oct. following, in the ICARUS 10, Capt. Henry Algernon Eliot; and returning home about June, 1821, was next, from 13 Dec. 1823, until promoted to the rank of Commander, 30 April, 1827, employed in the GRASSHOPPER 18, Capts. John Geo. Aplin and another. He has not been since afloat.

Commander Maude married, 4 Sept. 1827, Frances, second daughter of Hon. A. H. Brooking, Collector of His Majesty's Customs at St. John's, Newfoundland, and Member of the Council for that island. By that lady, who died in 1832, he had issue a son and two daughters. AGENTS—Messrs. Stilwell.

MAUDE. (RETIRED COMMANDER, 1840. F-P., 9; H-P., 45.)

WILLIAM GEORGE MAUDE (*a*) was born at York.

This officer entered the Navy, 28 Jan. 1793, as Captain's Servant, on board the LEOPARD 50, Capt. John Maude, flag-ship of Rear-Admirals John Macbride and John Peyton; and in the following Nov., on his return from a voyage to St. Helena, joined the THETIS frigate, Capt. Hon. Alex. Inglis Cochrane; with whom he continued employed as Midshipman, on the Home and North American stations, until transferred, in Jan. 1796, to the ESPERANCE sloop, Capt. Jonas Rose. Towards the close of 1797 we find him sailing for the Cape of Good Hope in the GARLAND frigate, Capt. John Clarke Searle; and in May, 1798, following that officer into the TREMENDOUS 74, bearing the flag of Sir Hugh Cloberry Christian. On 23 Feb. 1799, at which period he was serving, still on the Cape station, in the RAISONNABLE 64, Capt. Chas. Boyles, Mr. Maude was nominated Acting-Lieutenant of the DÆDALUS 32, Capt. Henry Lidgbird Ball. Being confirmed to that ship 24 July, 1799, he continued in her on the East India station, in the capacity of First-Lieutenant, until 1801; in April of which year, owing to a liver complaint and an attack of yellow fever, he invalided. He was admitted to the out-pension of Greenwich Hospital 7 Nov. 1823; and invested with the rank of Commander on the Retired List 20 Oct. 1840.

He married Mary, daughter of the late Geo. Hebden, Esq., and sister of the present Jas. Hebden, Esq., of Appleton, co. York, as also of Henry Hebden, Esq., a Captain in the Army. His eldest son, William George, is a Commander R.N.; and his second, a Midshipman R.N., was drowned by the upsetting of a boat while belonging to the SALISBURY, flag-ship at Bermuda of Rear-Admiral Wm. Chas. Fahie. AGENTS—Hallett and Robinson.

MAUDE. (COMMANDER, 1846.)

WILLIAM GEORGE MAUDE (*b*) is eldest son of Retired Commander Wm. Geo. Maude, R.N.

This officer entered the Navy 2 June, 1821; passed his examination in 1827; and obtained his first commission 20 May, 1833. His succeeding appointments were—26 March, 1834, to the NORTH STAR 28, Capt. Octavius Vernon Harcourt, fitting for South America, whence he returned at the close of 1836—1 June, 1837, as Senior Lieutenant, to the WOLVERENE 16, Capts. Hon. Edw. Howard and Wm. Tucker, under whom he was for about two years employed on the Mediterranean and Cape of Good Hope stations—31 Oct. 1840, to the INDUS 78, Capt. Sir Jas. Stirling, fitting at Portsmouth—6 Jan. 1841, as First, to the PHŒNIX steamer, Capt. John Richardson, in which vessel he served in the Mediterranean until ordered home for the purpose of being paid off at the end of 1842—and, 23 May, 1845, as Additional Lieutenant, to the CALEDONIA 120, Capt. Manley Hall Dixon, stationed at Devonport. He attained his present rank 9 Nov. 1846; and is now on half-pay.

Commander Maude married, 7 Aug. 1839, Fanny Anne, only daughter of Rear-Admiral Wm. Maude (1841), who assisted, when in command of the JASON, in capturing the French frigate *Topaze*, in 1809, and died in 1843. AGENTS—Hallett and Robinson.

MAUGER. (RETIRED COMMANDER, 1845. F-P., 15; H-P., 39.)

NICHOLAS MAUGER was born 17 July, 1773.

This officer entered the Navy, in June, 1793, as Midshipman, on board the MAGICIENNE frigate, Capt. Geo. Martin, employed at first in the North Sea and then in the West Indies, where he assisted at the capture of St. Marc's, St. Domingo, and served in the boats, under Lieut. Thompson, at the boarding and capture of a French privateer of 12 guns and 40 men. Removing, in July, 1794, to the SCEPTRE 64, Capts. Jas. Rich. Dacres, Wm. Essington, and Thos. Alexander, he assisted in that ship at the capture of eight Dutch Indiamen off St. Helena (in one of which he was sent as Prize-Master to Ireland), and witnessed the surrender of the Dutch squadron in Saldanha Bay, 17 Aug. 1796. In the course of the ensuing month he was successively nominated Acting-Lieutenant of the DAPHNE and SYBILLE frigates, Capts. Jas. Brisbane and Edw. Cooke; under the latter of whom, in Jan. 1798, he entered, in company with the FOX 32, the Spanish harbour of Manilla (notwithstanding that there were lying there three ships-of-the-line and three frigates), and assisted in capturing seven boats, 200 men, and a large quantity of ammunition and implements of war. He was also, during the same month, present in an action with the enemy's batteries at Samboangon, in the island of Magindanao, whose fire occasioned the two ships a collective loss of 6 men killed and 16 wounded; and on the night of 28 Feb. 1799, he contributed to the capture, at the mouth of the Bengal river, by the SYBILLE alone, whose force consisted of 48 guns, of the French frigate *La Forte*, of 52 guns and 370 men, after a dreadful action of two hours and a half, in which the enemy had 65 of their number (including the Captain) killed and 80 wounded, and the British, out of 371 men, 5 killed and 17 (among whom was Captain Cooke mortally) wounded. On the surrender of the enemy's ship, Mr. Mauger, who during the conflict had commanded the SYBILLE's main-deck, was sent to take possession of her. On 17 June, 1800, 12 months after he had risen to the post of Acting-Lieutenant, he was at length confirmed in his appointment to the SYBILLE, commanded at the time by Capt. Chas. Adam. Among other services in which he participated under that officer, was the capture and destruction, 23 Aug. 1800, of five Dutch armed vessels and 22 merchantmen in Batavia roads. He further, in the following Oct., aided in making prize of 24 Dutch proas, four of which mounted 6 guns each; and on 19 Aug. 1801 (when off Mahé, the principal of the Seychelle Islands) was instrumental to the taking, with a loss to the SYBILLE (out of 300 men) of 2 killed and 1 wounded, of *La Chiffonne*, of 42 guns and 296 men, 23 of whom were killed and 30 wounded. This action, a very gallant one of 20 minutes, was attended with the disadvantage to the British of being fought among rocks and shoals, and under the fire of an enemy's battery. As soon as the vessel had struck her colours, Mr. Mauger was placed in charge of her as Prize-Master. On leaving the SYBILLE in Oct. 1801, he joined the SUFFOLK 74, Capts. Wm. Clark and Curtis; and in that ship, in the spring of 1802, he returned to England. His next appointment was, 16 June, 1803, to LA CHIFFONNE, then a British 36-gun frigate, commanded by his former Captain, Adam; whom, in Sept. 1805, he accompanied, as Senior Lieutenant, into the RESISTANCE 38. In the former ship, when in company with the FALCON sloop, CLINKER gun-brig, and FRANCES armed-cutter, we find him assisting, 10 June, 1805, in driving on shore under the batteries of Fécamp a division of the French flotilla, consisting of 2 corvettes and 15 gun-vessels, carrying in all 51 guns, 4 8-inch mortars, and 3 field-pieces, accompanied by 14 transports. While attached to the RESISTANCE, he beheld Sir John Borlase Warren's capture, 13 March, 1806, of the *Marengo* 80, flag-ship of Rear-Admiral Linois, and 40-gun frigate *Belle Poule*, aided in the transport home from Vera Cruz of a considerable quantity of freight, was at the taking of *L'Aigle* privateer of 14 guns and 66 men, and escorted a large body of General Officers to the coast of Portugal. He left the RESISTANCE in Dec. 1808; and was next, from 3 May to 25 Aug. 1815, employed in the QUEEN CHARLOTTE 100, flag-ship of Sir Geo. Martin, with whom he went from Chatham to Portsmouth. He became a Retired Commander on the Junior List 15 Dec. 1830; and on the Senior 17 Feb. 1845.

Commander Mauger married, in 1802, Miss Margaret Allez, and by that lady has issue four sons and two daughters. One of his sons, Charles, is a Captain in the 17th Regt. Bombay Native Infantry; and another, John, was a Lieutenant in the Royal Marines.

MAUNSELL. (LIEUTENANT, 1846.)

EDWARD EYRE MAUNSELL is, we believe, eldest son of the Rev. Edw. Eyre Maunsell, A.M., of Fort Eyre, co. Galway, by Eliza Maria, daughter of Rich. Studdert, Esq., of Bunratty Castle, co. Clare.

This officer passed his examination 21 Aug. 1839; and after having served for some time as Mate on board the ST. VINCENT 120, flag-ship at Portsmouth of Sir Chas. Rowley, was promoted, 23 March, 1846, to a Lieutenancy in the FERRET 8, Capt. Geo. Sprigg, on the coast of Africa. Since 5 July, 1847, he has been attached, in the capacity of Additional Lieutenant, to the PRESIDENT 50, flag-ship of Rear-Admiral Jas. Rich. Dacres, at the Cape of Good Hope.

MAUNSELL, C.B. (CAPTAIN, 1812. F-P., 22; H-P., 25.)

ROBERT MAUNSELL was born, in May, 1786, at Limerick, and died 31 Aug. 1845. He was third son of the Rev. Wm. Maunsell, Archdeacon of Limerick, by Lucy, daughter and co-heir of Philip Oliver, Esq., M.P., of Castle Oliver, co. Limerick; and a near relative of Admiral Robt. Dudley Oliver. His eldest brother, the present Thos. Philip Maunsell, Esq., of Thorpe Malsor, Northamptonshire, is M.P. for the northern division of that co., Colonel of the Northampton Militia, and Captain of the Kettering Yeomanry Cavalry: his second, the Rev. Wm. Wray Maunsell, Archdeacon of Limerick, married the eldest daughter of the Right Rev. Chas. Warburton, Bishop of Cloyne.

This officer entered the Navy, in Feb. 1799, as Fst.-cl. Vol., on board the MERMAID 32, Capt. Robt. Dudley Oliver, fitting for the Mediterranean; where he attained the rating of Midshipman in July, 1800, removed in 1801 to the MAIDSTONE 32, Capts. Rich. Hussey Moubray and Hon. Geo. Elliot, and continued most actively employed until the end of 1804. It was his fortune during that period to be made a participator in many cutting-out affairs; but particularly on 11 July, 1804, when, holding the rating of Master's Mate, he served with the boats of the MAIDSTONE, NARCISSUS, and SEAHORSE, 10 in number, under the orders of Lieut. John Thompson, and assisted at the capture of 12 settees, lying at La Vandour, in the Bay of Hières, after a conflict, in which the British, encountered by a tremendous fire of grape-shot and musketry, as well from the vessels themselves as from a battery and the houses of the town, sustained a loss of 4 men killed and 23 (including himself, severely) wounded.* So great were the coolness and perseverance developed on the occasion by Mr. Maunsell, that he was promoted, as soon as he had accomplished his time, to a Lieutenancy, 7 March, 1805, in the PRINCESS ROYAL 98, Capt. Robt. Carthew Reynolds, attached to the Channel fleet.† Being next, 26 May, 1807, appointed to the BLANCHE 28, Capt. John Edgcumbe, on the East India station, he took a passage thither in, we believe, the ST. ALBAN's 64, and, soon after his arrival, had the satisfaction of being advanced, by a commission dated 15 Feb. 1808, to the command of the PROCRIS 18. Among the numerous prizes made by Capt. Maunsell in that sloop, we may include the capture, in 1809, of the Dutch company's brig *Wagsted* of 8 guns, 4 swivels, and 86 men.‡ On the morning of 31 July, 1811, being off the mouth of the Indramargu River, coast of Java, he took personal command of the boats of the PROCRIS, together with two flat-boats, carrying an officer and 20 men of H.M.'s 14th Regt., and an officer and the same number of men from H.M.'s 89th Regt., and with a degree of skill and ability that called forth the after-thanks of Commodore Broughton, led them ashore to the attack of six of the enemy's gun-boats; each mounting 1 brass 32-pounder carronade forward and 1 18-pounder aft, both on pivots, with a crew of more than 60 men, in convoy of 40 or 50 proas. Although the latter contrived to escape by hauling through the mud up the river, yet were five of the armed vessels irresistibly boarded and carried, and the remaining one destroyed; this, too with a loss of only 11 men wounded, notwithstanding that the enemy, in addition to the fire of their guns, kept up a constant discharge of musketry.§ As a reward for his meritorious conduct in achieving so gallant an exploit, Capt. Maunsell was almost immediately placed in acting-command of the ILLUSTRIOUS 74, bearing the Commodore's broad pendant. Prior to the event we have just recorded he had been ordered to take charge of a transport with 400 troops in the Sunda Strait, for the purpose of joining the expedition then daily expected off Batavia. Owing to the reluctance felt by the Master of the transport to run during the night, Capt. Maunsell, fearing that the delay thereby occasioned would prevent their arriving at the appointed rendezvous in time to assist in the landing, took the whole 400 men on board his own vessel, and by his promptitude in so doing was enabled to reach his destination two days previous to the debarkation, whereas the transport did not arrive until nearly a month afterwards. During his command of the ILLUSTRIOUS, a period of about two months, Capt. Maunsell served on

* In consideration of the injury he received the Patriotic Society voted him a gratuity.

† He had often, previously, had charge of a watch.

‡ *Vide* Gaz. 1810, p. 388. § *V.* Gaz. 1811, pp. 2409-11

shore throughout all the operations which terminated in the fall of Java; where he enacted a distinguished part on shore at the head of a body of seamen, and aided in the bombardment and storming of Fort Cornelis 26 Aug. 1811.* On the night of 10 of the ensuing month, we further discover him, with a division of boats under his orders, taking captive, in the neighbourhood of Samarang, a large sloop-rigged gun-boat, mounting 4 heavy guns and 2 brass swivels, a Malay-rigged gun-boat, carrying 1 12-pounder carronade, and a despatch-boat.† In the early part of 1812, on 7 Feb. in which year he was confirmed to Post-rank, Capt. Maunsell, in consequence of an attack of Batavian fever, returned to England; and on 24 of the ensuing Aug. was appointed to the CHATHAM 74, bearing the flag in the North Sea of Rear-Admiral Matthew Henry Scott, with whom he continued until 26 May, 1814. After 16 years' incessant application for employment, he was next, 22 Feb. 1831, placed in command of the ALFRED 50, and sent to the Mediterranean; where, during a servitude of three years, he witnessed the establishment of King Otho on the throne of Greece, and was selected to watch the movements of the hostile fleets of Turkey and Egypt. His last appointment afloat was, 13 May, 1840, to the RODNEY 92. On his arrival in that ship off Alexandria, 22 Nov. in the same year, he was instructed by Commodore Napier to open a direct communication between him and Mehemet Ali. Landing, accordingly, close to his Highness' palace, he managed to pass the guards unmolested, and, entering the presence-chamber, without introduction, had the good fortune to obtain a very flattering audience, and fully to carry out the object of his mission. The next day he landed, with the Commodore, and, we believe, remained with him until the conclusion of the celebrated convention between him and the Egyptian potentate. The RODNEY, it appears, was the means of afterwards, in Nov. 1842, rescuing the FORMIDABLE 84, when on shore near Barcelona; and in the course of the ensuing month was present at the reduction of that city by the force under Espartero. In the spring of 1843, having returned to England, she was despatched to the Cape of Good Hope with the 7th Dragoon Guards, a company of the 45th Regt., another of Artillery, and 150 men, on board. In Oct. 1843 she was paid off.

On 20 July, 1838, Capt. Maunsell was nominated a C.B.; and in April, 1844, as a tribute to "his high personal character, and his eminent professional service," he was spontaneously appointed by Sir Robt. Peel a Commissioner of Greenwich Hospital. AGENTS—Messrs. Chard.

MAURICE. (REAR-ADMIRAL, 1846. F-P., 21; H-P., 37.)

JAMES WILKES MAURICE was born 10 Feb. 1775, at Devonport. His twin brother, Ferdinand Moore Maurice, was lost in command of the MAGNET sloop in the autumn of 1811.

This officer (whose name had been borne in 1783-4 on the books of the MONKEY, Lieut.-Commander Jas. Glassford) embarked, in Aug. 1789, as A.B., on board the INSPECTOR sloop, Capts. Alex. Mackey and Jas. Leakey, and was employed in that vessel on the Channel station until Oct. 1791. Becoming Midshipman, in Dec. 1792, of the POWERFUL 74, Capts. Thos. Hicks and Wm. Albany Otway, he escorted a fleet of outward-bound Indiamen, at the commencement of hostilities with France, to the Cape of Good Hope, and on his return he successively, in Jan. and May, 1794, joined the CAMBRIDGE 74, Capt. Rich. Boger, and LA CONCORDE 36, Capts. Sir Rich. John Strachan and Anthony Hunt. In Aug. 1795, after having participated in Lord Bridport's action, he was nominated by Sir John Borlase Warren Lieutenant of the THUNDERER 74, Capt. Albemarle Bertie; but the appointment not being confirmed, he went back, about Jan. 1796, to LA CONCORDE, and continued in that ship, under Capts. Hunt and Rich. Bagot (witnessing intermediately the capture, among other vessels, of the French frigates *Unité* and *Virginie*, and the destruction of *La Volage* corvette, of 26 guns), until transferred, in Feb. 1797, to the ROYAL GEORGE 100, flag-ship in the Channel of Lord Bridport, who, on 17 of the ensuing month, promoted him into the GLORY 98, Capt. Jas. Brine—the Admiralty confirming the appointment by a commission dated 3 April, 1797. In Jan. 1799 Mr. Maurice removed to the CANADA 74, Capts. Hon. Michael De Courcy and Sir Joseph Sydney Yorke, in which ship, bearing the flag for some time of Sir John Borlase Warren, he served in the Channel and Mediterranean until May, 1802. Obtaining an appointment, in the following Sept., to the CENTAUR 74, bearing the broad pendant of Commodore Sam. Hood, he aided in that ship at the capture of Ste. Lucie, Tobago, Demerara, and Essequibo, and on 26 Nov. 1803 he landed at the head of 40 seamen, with the greater part of the marines under Capt. Crozier, at Petite Ance d'Arlette, Martinique, and assisted in destroying a battery of 6 24-pounders.* In the performance, however, of this service he received a wound, occasioned by the explosion of the magazine, and was in consequence presented by the Patriotic Society with a sword valued at 50*l*. On 3 Feb. 1804, after nearly a month had been expended in planting 5 guns (3 24-pounders and 2 long 18's), and placing provisions, stores, &c., upon an all but inaccessible eminence, situated in the sea near the south-west end of Martinique, and called the Diamond Rock, the rating was assigned it of a sloop-of-war, and the command given to Lieut. Maurice, as a reward for the arduous and prominent part he had borne in the equipment. Being confirmed in his new appointment, 7 May in the same year, he continued to hold it until 2 June, 1805, when, owing to a want of ammunition and water, he was under the necessity of surrendering to a French squadron of 2 sail-of-the-line, 1 frigate, 1 brig, a schooner, and 11 gun-boats, together with 1500 troops, after sustaining a three days' attack with a degree of gallantry that had the effect of subsequently procuring him not only the honourable acquittal but the high admiration of a Court-Martial, and the warm applause of Lord Nelson. The enemy, during the operations, appear to have had about 30 killed and 40 wounded on shore, independently of their ships and boats, and to have lost 3 gun-boats and 2 row-boats. The British, of whom there were in the whole not more than 107, had but 2 killed and 1 wounded. Capt. Maurice arrived in England with despatches from Rear-Admiral Hon. Alex. Cochrane 3 Aug. 1805, and in less than a fortnight was appointed to the command of the SAVAGE, a new 18 gun-brig. In that vessel he appears, until June, 1807, to have been employed in convoying the trade from different ports in St. George's Channel and the Downs. He next escorted a fleet of merchantmen from Cork to the West Indies; and in Dec. 1807 contrived, while cruizing on the Jamaica station, to capture the *Don Quixote*, Spanish privateer, of 8 guns and 99 men. In the autumn of 1808 Capt. Maurice was nominated by Sir Alex. Cochrane Governor of Marie-Galante, a post appointment, which the Admiralty sanctioned with its approbation 18 Jan. 1809. After having administered the affairs of the colony for 12 months under circumstances of a very trying character, but in a manner that gained him a most flattering address from the legislative body and the principal inhabitants, he found himself, in Oct. 1809, compelled, from the effects of intermittent fever, to invalid. His next appointment, we find, was to the Governorship, 30 July, 1810, of the island of Anholdt, where, in March, 1811, he rendered his name for ever famous by the brilliant manner in which he defeated an attempt made to reduce it by a Danish flotilla and army, consisting in all of nearly 4000 men, who, after a close combat of four hours and a half, were driven back to their ports, with the loss of 3 pieces of cannon, 14 shells, 484 muskets, 470 swords, 16000 musket-ball cartridges,

* *Vide* Gaz. 1811, p. 2404. † *V.* Gaz. 1812, p. 116.

* *Vide* Gaz. 1804, p. 109

and upwards of 500 prisoners—a greater number by 150 than the garrison itself. Although the loss of the assailants was most severe, that of the British was confined to 2 killed and 30 wounded.* The glorious defence of Anholdt, indeed, became the universal theme of praise, and its gallant conductor, as a matter of course, received the warm plaudits of the Admiralty. His second in command, Lieut. H. L. Baker, was promoted to superior rank; and, as a compliment to himself, his brother, the gentleman alluded to at the commencement of the present narrative, was placed in command of a sloop-of-war. Capt. Maurice, whom the garrison of Anholdt united in presenting with a valuable sword "in token of their admiration of his personal bravery in the battle of 27 March, and as a grateful memorial for his liberal, forbearing, and kind consideration of their feelings during his government," remained in that island until Sept. 1812, and has not been since employed. He accepted his present rank 1 Oct. 1846.

He married, 5 Oct. 1814, Miss Sarah Lyne, of Plymouth, and was left a widower in June, 1815. Agents—Hallett and Robinson.

* Vide Gaz. 1811, p. 649.

MAW. (Lieutenant, 1825.)

Henry Lister Maw has lost two brothers in the military service of their country.

This officer entered the Navy 11 May, 1818; and was for some time Midshipman of the Liffey 50, bearing the broad pendant in the East Indies of Commodore Chas. Grant, by whom, during the expedition to Ava, he was allowed to act as Naval Aide-de-Camp to Sir Alex. Campbell, Commander-in-Chief of the troops. While officiating in that capacity he appears to have been employed in surveying the Rangoon river, and to have effected, 25 June, 1824, the destruction of two fire-rafts. In an attack subsequently made on a strong stockade on the Dalla river, it was his misfortune, while cheering on his men, to receive a ball in the head—a circumstance which obliged him to return to England for the benefit of his health. Having all along, however, distinguished himself by "a series of gallantry" exhibitive of the "most conspicuous and forward bravery," and being recommended in the strongest terms by Capt. Marryat, the senior naval officer on the station, he was rewarded with a Lieutenant's commission dated 25 July, 1825. His succeeding appointments were—2 Feb. 1826, to the Harrier sloop, Capt. John Pakenham, on the coast of Ireland—7 Jan. 1827 and 2 Oct. 1829, to the Menai 26, and Volage 28, Capts. Michael Seymour and Lord Colchester, both on the South American station—and, 3 Dec. 1832 and 16 July, 1834, as Second-Lieutenant, to the Vernon 50, and President 52, flag-ships of Sir Geo. Cockburn in North America and the West Indies. He has not been employed since 30 Aug. 1834.

In 1830 Lieut. Maw was presented with the large silver medal of the "Society for the Encouragement of Arts, Manufactures, and Commerce," for fragments, &c. collected by him in South America; and in July, 1831, he took out a patent for an invention of an improved method of using fuel, so as to burn smoke. In 1832 he published a "Memoir of the Early Operations of the Burmese War." He married, 21 March, 1839, Sarah Anne, only daughter of the late Cornelius Peacock, Esq. Agents—Messrs. Ommanney.

MAW. (Lieutenant, 1807. f-p., 17; h-p., 32.)

Richard Stovin Maw had three brothers, who were either killed or wounded in their country's service.

This officer entered the Royal Naval Academy in Aug. 1798, and embarked, in May, 1802, as a Volunteer, on board the Resistance 36, Capt. Hon. Philip Wodehouse, under whom he was wrecked off Cape St. Vincent, 31 May, 1803. After serving for a few months in the Termagant 18, Capt. Robt. Pettet, he joined the Weazle 14, Capt. Wm. Layman, and in that vessel was again wrecked, near Cabritta Point, Gibraltar Bay, 1 March, 1804. Becoming Midshipman, in the following July, of the Glory 98, successive flag-ship of Admirals Sir John Orde and Chas. Stirling, he shared in Sir Robert Calder's action, 22 July, 1805; after which we find him following the last-mentioned officer into the Sampson and Diadem 64's. In the early part of 1807, on 8 Oct. in which year he was confirmed a Lieutenant in the Diadem, Mr. Maw was for three weeks employed on shore with the army at the siege of Monte Video; and in the ensuing July, it appears, he assisted in landing the troops during the unsuccessful attempt upon Buenos Ayres. His succeeding appointments were—2 June, 1808, to the Oberon 16, Capt. Geo. Manners Sutton, attached to the force in the Channel—21 Feb. 1809, as Senior, to the Rose 18, Capt. Thos. Mansell, in which sloop he participated in the capture of more than 100 of the enemy's vessels, and aided in the land operations at the taking of Anholdt—25 Jan. 1810, to the Bellerophon 74, Capt. Sam. Warren, employed in the North Sea—and, 14 Feb. 1811, 26 Feb. 1813, and 2 Aug. 1815, as First, to the Cyane 22, Capts. Fras. Augustus Collier and Thos. Forrest, Lacedæmonian 38, Capt. Sam. Jackson, and Ister 36, Capt. Thos. Forrest, on the Mediterranean, West India, North American, and Home stations. On the evening of 5 Oct. 1814 Mr. Maw, then in the Lacedæmonian, was sent with the boats of that frigate, carrying two other Lieutenants, several Midshipmen, and upwards of 100 men under his orders, in pursuit of three American gun-boats and a convoy of about 36 sail, which had been discovered passing between Cumberland and Jekyll islands. After rowing a distance of 30 miles the British succeeded in coming up with some of the vessels, and the result of their attack was the capture of one of the gun-boats, No. 160 (which Mr. Maw himself was the first to board), and four merchantmen; the loss to the assailants being 4 officers and men wounded, and to their opponents 1 man killed, 4 wounded, and several driven overboard.* Debilitated from the effects of the exposure and hardships attendant upon continual boat-service, Mr. Maw, in Jan. 1815, found himself under the necessity of invaliding from the Lacedæmonian; and in June, 1817, a recurrence of bad health when on board the Ister again obliged him to seek half-pay. Notwithstanding the very neat exploits we have above recorded, and the fact that for upwards of six years he filled the important post of First-Lieutenant, he has never been able to procure that rank for which he had so earnestly striven. Agents—Messrs. Ommanney.

* Vide Gaz. 1815, p. 454.

MAWBEY. (Lieut., 1815. f-p., 16; h-p., 33.)

John Mawbey was born 6 May, 1781.

This officer entered the Navy, 9 April, 1798, as Midshipman, on board the Romney 50, Capt. John Lawford. In the following summer he witnessed the capture of a Swedish convoy laden with naval and military stores for the use of the French; and, on 30 Aug. 1799, having accompanied the expedition to Holland, he was present at the surrender of the Dutch squadron under Admiral Storey. He afterwards served with Capt. Lawford, in the Polyphemus 64, at the battle of Copenhagen, 2 April, 1801; and between Dec. 1802 and the date of his promotion to the rank of Lieutenant, 8 Feb. 1815, was employed on the Home, West India, and Mediterranean stations, chiefly in the capacity of Midshipman, in the Calcutta 50, Capt. Daniel Woodriff, Puissant 74, Capt. Jas. Bowen, Windsor Castle 98, flag-ship of Admiral Montagu, Spartiate 74, Capt. Sir Fras. Laforey, Neptune 98, bearing the flag of Hon. Sir Alex. Cochrane, Abercromby 74, Capt. Wm. Chas. Fahie, Leyden 64, Capts. Edw. Chetham and John Davie, Barfleur 98, Capt. Sir Thos. Masterman Hardy, Blake 74, Capt. Edw. Codrington, Blenheim 74, Capt. Sam. Warren, and Caledonia 120, Prince Frederick 74, and Impregnable 98, flag-ships of Sir Edw. Pellew,

Sir Thos. Byam Martin, and Sir John Thos. Duckworth. Besides participating in much arduous blockade-service, Mr. Mawbey, when in the SPARTIATE, went to the West Indies in pursuit of the celebrated Rochefort squadron, and on his return thence with Lord Nelson was afforded an opportunity of sharing in the action off Cape Trafalgar, 21 Oct. 1805. He was in the same ship at the reduction of the islands of Ischia and Procida in 1809; and, during the term of his attachment to the LEYDEN and BARFLEUR, was employed (part of the time as commanding officer) in a flat boat in co-operation with the British army in the Tagus, where the excessive fatigue he underwent produced an attack of fever, which rendered necessary his return for four months to England. In the CALEDONIA he beheld the fall of Genoa. Since his promotion, which did not take place until more than six years after he had passed his examination, he has not been afloat.

Lieut. Mawbey married, 20 Feb. 1819, Miss Mary Ann Lancaster, and by that lady has issue two sons and two daughters. AGENTS—Messrs. Stilwell.

MAX. (LIEUTENANT, 1806. F-P., 13; H-P., 36.)

JOHN GEORGE MAX entered the Navy, 16 Nov. 1798, as Midshipman, on board the EL CORSO, Capt. Lord Wm. Stuart, on the Mediterranean station, where he continued, until Sept. 1802, to serve in the GOLIATH 74, Capt. Thos. Foley, and in the LION and CHAMPION, both commanded by the above-named nobleman. After a further employment, on Home service (particularly off Boulogne), in the HARPY sloop, Capts. Edm. Heywood and Chas. Pelly, and with Lord Wm. Stuart and Capt. Jas. Carthew in the CRESCENT frigate, he was promoted, 6 Feb. 1806, to the rank of Lieutenant, and appointed to the ALBACORE sloop, on the Guernsey station. He remained in that vessel a period of two years and a half; and was next, between Feb. 1811 and April, 1814, employed, at Home and in the Baltic, on board the BRISEIS 10, Capts. Chas. Thurlow Smith and John Halsted, BELLEROPHON 74, Capt. Augustus Brine, ANTELOPE 50, Capt. Sam. Butcher, and REYNARD sloop, Capt. David Latimer St. Clair. He has since been on half-pay. AGENT—Joseph Woodhead.

MAXEY. (LIEUT., 1814. F-P., 12; H-P., 31.)

EDWARD MAXEY, born 5 Feb. 1790, is second son of the Rev. Lewis Maxey, of Byford Rectory, co. Hereford.

This officer entered the Navy, 2 Nov. 1804, as Fst.-cl. Vol., on board the UTRECHT 64, Capt. John Holloway, lying in the Downs; and in the following year joined the INTREPID 64, Capt. Hon. Philip Wodehouse, on the Mediterranean station; where, on removing, after the capture of Capri and the siege of Gaeta, to the AMPHION 32, Capt. Wm. Hoste, he came into daily collision, either in that ship or her boats, with the enemy on the coast of Calabria. After serving for short periods in the BERGÈRE sloop, Capt. Thos. Whinyates, ATLAS 74, Capt. Sam. Pym, and GLORY 98, Capt. Wm. Albany Otway, he was received, about 1808, on board the NORGE 74, Capt. John Sprat Rainier. Continuing in that ship until 1 May, 1814, he assisted, as Master's Mate, at the embarkation of the army after the battle of Corunna, co-operated in the defence of Cadiz, aided in fitting out a Spanish fleet at Friedland and in escorting it to Minorca, and visited the latitude of Greenland in pursuit of the American frigate *President*, Commodore Rodgers. He was promoted (having passed his examination in 1809) to the rank of Lieutenant while serving with the Duke of Clarence in the ROYAL CHARLOTTE yacht, 27 May, 1814; and was next appointed, on the American, Home, and West India stations, to the JASEUR 16, Capt. Nicholas Pateshall, FORTH 40, Capt. Sir Wm. Bolton, DÉSIRÉE 36, Capt. Wm. Woolridge, ACTIVE 38, Capt. Philip Carteret, and ROYALIST 18, Capt. Geo. Bennett Allen. He has been on half-pay since Oct. 1816.

Lieut. Maxey married, 2 Oct. 1829, Eliza, daughter of Joseph Edye, Esq., Alderman of the city of Bristol.

MAXWELL. (LIEUT., 1811. F-P., 15; H-P., 33.)

FRANCIS MAXWELL was born in Feb. 1789, at Bromyard, in Herefordshire.

This officer entered the Navy, in March, 1799, as Clerk, on board the REDBRIDGE schooner, Lieut.-Commander Geo. Lempriere, in which vessel, stationed off Jersey, he continued employed until taken off Toulon by four French frigates, 4 Aug. 1803. In Sept. 1807, having succeeded after many hardships in effecting his escape from France, he was received as Midshipman on board the ESCORT gun-brig, Lieut.-Commander Wm. Smith (2), on the Mediterranean station; where he was subsequently, for nearly three years, employed in the OCEAN 98 and VILLE DE PARIS 110, flag-ships of Admirals Lord Collingwood and Thos. Fras. Fremantle. Being nominated, 12 Aug. 1811, Acting-Lieutenant of the TUSCAN sloop, Capt. Geo. Matthew Jones, Mr. Maxwell, whose promotion was confirmed 26 Sept. following, served for some time in that vessel at the defence of Cadiz. In the following Dec. he removed to the BUSTARD 16, Capt. Chas. Burrough Strong; and in the course of the next few months, while in command of the boats in shore, he had the good fortune to capture several of the enemy's vessels. On one occasion he landed and intercepted a quantity of flour intended for the fortress of Barcelona. He remained in the BUSTARD, part of the time as First-Lieutenant, until compelled by ill health to invalid, in Aug. 1812; and he was lastly, from 6 Aug. 1813 until June, 1814, employed on the Cork station in the AVON 18, Capt. Geo. Rose Sartorius. Sickness then again reduced him to the necessity of seeking half-pay. AGENTS—Messrs. Chard.

MAXWELL. (CAPT., 1830. F-P., 16; H-P., 35.)

GEORGE BERKELEY MAXWELL entered the Navy, 2 July, 1796, as Fst.-cl. Vol., on board the ROYAL WILLIAM, Capt. Fras. Pickmore, successive flag-ship of Admirals Sir Peter Parker and Mark Milbanke at Portsmouth, where he remained until Oct. 1801. In Dec. 1804 he joined the AMPHION 32, Capts. Sam. Sutton and Wm. Hoste, on the Mediterranean station; and on 22 Sept. 1807 he was made Lieutenant into the BULWARK 74, flag-ship of Hon. Chas. Elphinstone Fleeming, lying at Spithead. His succeeding appointments were—26 Oct. 1807, to the ASTRÆA 32, Capt. Edm. Heywood, in the West Indies; where, while under the temporary command of Lieut. Edm. Potenger Greenlaw, he was wrecked on a coral reef off the island of Anagada 24 May, 1808—13 Feb. 1809, to the VICTORY 100, bearing the flag of Sir Jas. Saumarez, in the Baltic—and 4 May, 1810, and 11 Jan. 1813, to the SAN JOSEF 110 and QUEEN CHARLOTTE 100, flag-ships of Sir Chas. Cotton and Lord Keith, in the Mediterranean and Channel. He acquired the rank of Commander 15 June, 1814, but did not again go afloat until April, 1829; on 7 of which month we find him receiving an appointment to the HERALD yacht. In that vessel, it appears, he conveyed Lady Heytesbury to St. Petersburg; Wm. Turner, Esq. (Envoy Extraordinary), to Carthagena; Lord Aylmer to Quebec; and Lieut.-General Sir James Kempt thence to England. Since his promotion to Post-rank 20 Nov. 1830, Capt. Maxwell has been on half-pay.

He married, 10 May, 1821, Lætitia, daughter of John Clerk, Esq., of Downham House, co. Gloucester, and by that lady has issue.

MAXWELL. (CAPT., 1837. F-P., 18; H-P., 17.)

JOHN BALFOUR MAXWELL, born in 1799, is only son of the late Capt. Sir Murray Maxwell,* R.N., Kt., C.B., F.R.S.; nephew of the late Capts. Keith

* Sir Murray Maxwell attained the rank of Lieutenant, in 1796; was promoted, in Dec. 1802, to the command of the

Maxwell* and John Maxwell,† R.N., of Major Stuart Maxwell, R.A., and of Lieut.-Colonel Montgomery Maxwell, 36th Regt.; and brother-in-law of Capt. Chas. Hallowell Carew, R.N. He is a relative of the present Sir Wm. Maxwell, Bart., of Monreith, co. Wigtoun, Captain unattached, late of the 14th Light Dragoons.

This officer entered the Navy, 15 Nov. 1812, as Fst.-cl. Vol., on board the DÆDALUS 38, commanded by his father, Capt. Murray Maxwell, under whom he was wrecked, off Ceylon, 2 July, 1813. After an attachment of a few months, as a Supernumerary, to the MINDEN 74, bearing the flag of Sir Sam. Hood, he returned to England, as Midshipman, in the early part of 1814, in the CORNWALLIS 74, Capt. Stephen Thos. Digby. During the next two years we find him joining in succession, on the Home station, the STIRLING CASTLE 74, Capt. Wm. Butterfield, GLASGOW 50, Capt. Hon. Henry Duncan, BULWARK 74, Capt. Geo. M'Kinley, and ALCESTE 38, commanded by his father. In the ship last mentioned Mr. Maxwell, after accompanying Lord Amherst in his expedition to China, was again wrecked, in the Straits of Gaspar, 18 Feb. 1817. He afterwards, from June in the same year until Dec. 1818, served on the St. Helena station in the FALMOUTH 20 and RACOON 18, Capts. Robt. Worgan Geo. Festing, Jas. Wallis, and Geo. Brine; and, attaining the rank of Lieutenant 6 April, 1820, was successively appointed in that capacity—30 June following, to the Ordinary service on Lake Ontario, whence he returned in June, 1821—and 6 Sept. and 30 Nov. 1822, to the EGERIA 28 and BRITON 46, Capts. John Toup Nicolas and Sir Murray Maxwell, on the Home and South American stations. On 28 April, 1827, seven months after the BRITON had been paid off, Lieut. Maxwell was promoted to the command of the CHANTICLEER 10, in the Mediterranean, where he remained for a period of eight months. His next appointment was, 6 June, 1833, to the GANNET 16, the command of which vessel he retained in the West Indies until posted, 10 Jan. 1837. His appointments have since been—19 June, 1845, to the CROCODILE 26, flag-ship of Sir Hugh Pigot at Cork—and 9 May, 1846, to the DIDO 18, now in the East Indies.

Capt. Maxwell is a widower, with one daughter. AGENTS—Messrs. Ommanney.

CYANE sloop, part of the squadron employed under Commodore Hood, at the ensuing reduction of Ste. Lucie; and was posted 4 Aug. 1803. He commanded the CENTAUR 74, bearing the broad pendant of Commodore Hood, at the capture of Tobago, Demerara, and Berbice; and while in the same ship, in 1824, bore a very distinguished part in the operations which led to the fall of Surinam. When Capt., subsequently, of the ALCESTE 38, he rendered his name conspicuous by the dashing nature of his services in the Mediterranean; where, in company with the ACTIVE 38, he fought, 29 Nov. 1811, a most gallant action with the French 40-gun frigates *Pauline* and *Pomone*. Capt. Maxwell afterwards commanded the DÆDALUS 38, ALCESTE again, BULWARK 74, and BRITON 46. In the ALCESTE, as above recorded, he took out Lord Amherst on the occasion of that nobleman's embassy to China, for his services as connected with which the East India Company, in May, 1819, presented him with the sum of 1500*l.* He had been nominated a C.B. in 1815, and in May, 1818, awarded the honour of knighthood.

* Capt. Keith Maxwell obtained his first commission in 1794: and as a reward for his heroic conduct in cutting out, with the boats of a squadron under his orders, the French corvette *La Chevrette*, of 20 guns and 350 men, was promoted to the rank of Commander in July, 1801. Attaining Post-rank 1 May, 1804, Capt. Maxwell was subsequently employed in command of the TARTAR and NYMPHEN frigates; in the latter of which, during the expedition of 1809 to the Walcheren, he assisted in forcing the passage between the batteries of Flushing and Cadsand. He died 22 April, 1823.

† Capt. John Maxwell was made a Lieutenant in 1808; a Commander 22 Jan. 1806; and a Post-Captain 15 June, 1810. When in command of the ROYALIST 18, he contrived, between May, 1809, and 24 Feb. 1810, to capture as many as five French privateers, carrying, altogether, 64 guns and 255 men. During the last two years of the war he served on the coast of Africa in the FAVOURITE 20; and he afterwards commanded the BARROSA 42, and AURORA 46; on board which latter ship he died 31 May, 1826.

MAXWELL, Bart. (LIEUTENANT, 1828.) F-P., 15; H-P., 11.)

SIR JOHN HERON MAXWELL, born 7 March, 1808, is third and eldest surviving son of Sir John Maxwell, Bart., of Springkell, Dumfriesshire, by Mary, only surviving child and heir of Patrick Heron, Esq., of Heron, in the Stewartry of Galloway, M.P., whose wife, Elizabeth, was the only daughter of the eighth Earl of Dundonald. He succeeded his elder brother, the late Sir Patrick Heron Maxwell, as sixth Baronet, 27th Aug. 1844.

This officer entered the Navy 1 Feb. 1821; passed his examination in 1827; obtained his commission 17 Sept. 1828; and was subsequently appointed—11 Jan. 1832, to the STAG 46, Capt. Sir Edw. Thos. Troubridge, on the Cork station—21 Oct. following, to the BRITANNIA 120, Capt. Peter Rainier, employed off Lisbon, whence he returned in 1833—11 Dec. 1838, to the command of a station in the Coast Guard—and 17 Sept. 1842, to the SAN JOSEF 110, bearing the flag of Sir Sam. Pym, Admiral Superintendent at Devonport. Since the paying off of the latter ship, in 1845, Sir John has been on half-pay.

He married, 7 Nov. 1833, Caroline, sixth daughter of the Hon. Montgomery J. G. Stewart, and niece of the late Earl of Galloway, by whom he has issue a son and three daughters.

MAXWELL. (LIEUT., 1820. F-P., 34; H-P., 3.)

WILLIAM MAXWELL entered the Navy, in May, 1810, as Fst.-cl. Vol., on board the DIANA 38, Capt. Chas. Grant; and, on 15 of the following Nov., was present in an attack made on the two French frigates *Amazone* and *Eliza*, as they lay aground under the protection of several strong batteries in the neighbourhood of La Hogue. In April, 1811, he became Midshipman of the HANNIBAL 74, bearing the flag in the North Sea of Rear-Admiral Philip Chas. Durham; whom, in June, 1813, after a servitude of four months off Flushing in the CHRISTIAN VII. 80, Capts. Thos. Browne and Henry Lidgbird Ball, he rejoined, on board the BULWARK 74, off Rochefort. Following the same officer into the VENERABLE 74, Mr. Maxwell, during the passage of that ship to the West Indies, assisted, when in company with the CYANE sloop, at the well-resisted capture, 16 and 20 Jan. 1814, of the French 44-gun frigates *Iphigénie* and *Alcmène*. He continued to serve on the station last mentioned in the HERON sloop, Capt. Geo. Luke, VENERABLE again, and BARROSA 42, Capts. Wm. M'Culloch and John Maxwell, until the close of 1815; and then proceeded to the East Indies; where, with Capts. Andrew King and John Reynolds, he was for nearly two years employed, latterly as Master's Mate and Acting-Master, in the IPHIGENIA 36, CONWAY 24, and VOLAGE 22. At the end of 1817 he went back to the West Indies in the SYBILLE 44, flag-ship of Sir Home Popham; who, on 6 Nov. 1819, nominated him Lieutenant of the ONTARIO 18, Capt. Geo. Gosling. In the boats of that vessel Mr. Maxwell contributed to the capture of one, and the destruction of another, piratical schooner. Quitting her about the period of his official promotion, which took place 9 June, 1820, he was next, 23 May, 1823, appointed to the CAMELION 10, Capts. Jas. Ryder Burton, Geo. Robt. Lambert, and Michael Seymour; under the first of whom, when in company with the NAIAD frigate, he took part, 31 Jan. 1824, in a close and gallant action, which terminated in the boarding and capture, under the very batteries of Algiers, of the corvette *Tripoli* of 18 guns and 100 men. On 18 Aug. 1826, a few days after the CAMELION (whose services had chiefly been of the class termed "Particular") had been paid off, he received an appointment to the HYPERION 42, Coast Blockade ship, Capt. Wm. Jas. Mingaye; on the books of which he continued borne, as a Supernumerary, until 30 Dec. 1830. He has been in command, since 16 March, 1831, of a station in the Coast Guard. AGENTS—Hallett and Robinson.

MAY. (LIEUTENANT, 1838.)

AUGUSTUS CHARLES MAY passed his examination in 1830; and obtained his commission 28 June, 1838. His succeeding appointments were—5 July, 1838, as Additional Lieutenant, to the CORNWALLIS 74, flag-ship of Hon. Sir Chas. Paget—27 Oct. following, to the THUNDER surveying-vessel, Capt. Edw. Barnett—16 Feb. 1840, again as Additional, to the WINCHESTER 50, bearing the flag of Sir Thos. Harvey—25 Sept. 1840, to the PILOT 16, Capt. Geo. Ramsay—2 March, 1841, to the command of the SKIPJACK schooner—11 Jan. 1842, as First-Lieutenant, after an interval of half-pay, to his former ship the THUNDER, still commanded by Capt. Barnett—5 Dec. 1843, in a similar capacity, to the LARNE 18, Capt. John Wm. Douglas Brisbane—and, 19 Nov. 1845, again as Senior, to the ALARM 26, Capts. Chas. Colville Frankland and Granville Gower Loch. With the exception of the LARNE, which formed part of the force on the coast of Africa, the above ships were all employed on the North America and West India station. Lieut. May has been on half-pay since April, 1847. AGENTS—Messrs. Stilwell.

MAY. (LIEUTENANT, 1843.)

CHARLES HENRY MAY entered the Navy 17 Aug. 1829; passed his examination 27 July, 1836; became Mate, in 1841, of the FORMIDABLE 84, Capt. Sir Chas. Sullivan, on the Mediterranean station; and was promoted, 7 March, 1843, to the rank of Lieutenant. His appointments have since been—29 June, 1843, to the EURYDICE 26, Capt. Geo. Elliot, under whom he was for about three years employed on the North America and West India station—and, 14 July, 1846, to the SUPERB 80, Capt. Armar Lowry Corry, now in the Mediterranean. AGENTS—Messrs. Stilwell.

MAY. (LIEUTENANT, 1815. F-P., 22; H-P., 21.)

CHRISTOPHER MAY entered the Navy, 3 Oct. 1804, as a Volunteer, on board the SALVADOR DEL MUNDO, flag-ship at Plymouth of Admirals Sir John Colpoys and Wm. Young. Removing, in June, 1809, to the RALEIGH 18, Capts. Geo. Sayer, John Sheridan, and Geo. Wastell Hooper, he accompanied, under the first named of those officers, the ensuing expedition to the Walcheren; assisted at the capture, in Feb. 1810, off Beachy Head, of *La Modeste*, French privateer, of 4 guns (pierced for 18) and 43 men; participated, 23 May following, when in company, near the Skawe, with the ALBAN and PRINCESS OF WALES cutters, in an engagement with seven Danish gun-vessels, one of which was blown up and the remainder dispersed, greatly damaged; and contributed, 2 Nov. in the same year, to the capture of the *Admiral Neil Sieul*, Danish privateer, pierced for 16 guns but with only 10 mounted, and a complement of 28 men. After a servitude of eight months, as Midshipman, in the BRAAVE, prison-ship at Plymouth, Capt. Edw. Hawkins, Mr. May, in Sept. 1812, joined the FAIRY 18, Capts. Edw. Grey and Henry Loraine Baker; in which vessel, after visiting the coast of Brazil, he partook of the various arduous operations on the river Potomac connected with the expedition of 1814 against the city of Alexandria; and was present, in 1815, at the surrender of Guadeloupe. He attained the rank he now holds 2 Nov. 1815; and since 12 July, 1836, has been in command of a station in the Coast Guard.

MAY. (LIEUTENANT, 1845.)

PHILIP WILLIAM MAY entered the Navy in 1831; passed his examination 27 Sept. 1838; and, in 1842, after having gone through a course of study at the Royal Naval College, was successively appointed Mate of the CARYSFORT 26, Capt. Lord Geo. Paulet, and AGINCOURT 72, bearing the flag of Sir Thos. John Cochrane. While in the latter ship, on the East India station, we find him serving, 19 Aug. 1845, with the boats of a squadron, carrying altogether 530 officers, seamen, and marines, at the destruction, under Capt. Chas. Talbot, of the piratical settlement of Malloodoo, on the north end of the island of Borneo, where the British encountered a desperate opposition, and sustained a loss of 6 men killed and 15 wounded. He was rewarded for his conduct on the occasion by a commission bearing date the day of the occurrence; and continued attached to the AGINCOURT, in the capacity of Additional Lieutenant, until paid off in the summer of 1847.

MAYNARD. (COMMANDER, 1825. F-P., 22; H-P., 17.)

JOSEPH MAYNARD entered the Navy, 20 Dec. 1808, as Fst.-cl. Vol., on board the FREDERICKSTEIN 32, Capts. Thos. Searle and Joseph Nourse, on the Mediterranean station, where he was very actively employed, and assisted at the capture of two privateers. In Dec. 1810, previously to which period he had attained the rating of Midshipman, he removed to the SALSETTE 36, Capt. John Hollinworth; and on again, in 1811, joining Capt. Nourse in the VOLONTAIRE 38, he served at the defence of Tarragona. Between the close of the year last mentioned and Jan. 1815, we find him employed on the Mediterranean, Home, and East India stations, in the ROYAL SOVEREIGN 100, Capt. John Harvey, DIANA 38, Capt. Wm. Ferris, COLOSSUS 74, Capt. Thos. Alexander, and MINDEN 74, flag-ship of Sir Sam. Hood. He then returned to England in the MALACCA 42, Capt. Geo. Henderson; and, on his arrival, was once more placed under the orders of Capt. Nourse, in the SEVERN 40. In July, 1815, Mr. Maynard took up a commission dated 4 of the preceding March. His succeeding appointments were—2 Oct. 1815 and 20 May, 1817, to the GANYMEDE 20 and SEVERN again, both commanded by Capt. Wm. M'Culloch, on the Home station, where, while in chase of a smuggler in a boat belonging to the latter ship, he had the misfortune to lose the fore-finger and part of the thumb of the right hand—17 May, 1819 (sickness having compelled him to leave the SEVERN in the preceding Sept.), to the BRISK 10, Capts. John Wm. Montagu and Edw. Stewart, stationed in the Channel—and, 1 Nov. 1821, to the ANDROMACHE frigate, fitting for the broad pendant of his friend Commodore Nourse, Commander-in-Chief at the Cape of Good Hope, where he had command, for two years, of the WIZARD colonial brig. He attained his present rank 4 Oct. 1825; and was lastly, from 22 March, 1838, until 1844, employed in the Coast Guard as Inspecting Commander of the Stranraer district, on the west coast of Scotland.

Commander Maynard had charge for some time of the Duke of Portland's Harbour at Troon, Ayrshire, N.B. He married, in 1828, Harriet, eldest daughter of Clark Hillyard, Esq., of Thorpelands, co. Northampton, by whom he has issue seven children. AGENTS—Messrs. Ommanney.

MAYNARD. (RETIRED CAPTAIN, 1840. F-P., 22; H-P., 45.)

THOMAS MAYNARD entered the Navy, 11 May, 1780, as First-Lieutenant's Servant, on board the MEDEA 28, Capt. Jas. Montagu, and, until discharged towards the close of the same year, was employed on the Guernsey station. Rejoining Capt. Montagu in 1781, on board the JUNO 32, he cruized for a few months off the coast of Ireland, and then proceeded to the East Indies, where he arrived in time to participate in the last of Sir Edw. Hughes's actions with M. de Suffrein, 20 June, 1783. Returning to Europe in 1785, he served during the six following years on the Home station, chiefly as Midshipman, in the CULLODEN 74, Capts. Rowland Cotton and Sir Thos. Rich, ARDENT 64, Capt. Sir Fras. Hartwell, and COLOSSUS 74, Capts. Henry Harvey and Hugh Cloberry Christian. He next, at the commencement of the French revolutionary war, became Master's Mate of the SAMPSON 64, Capt. Robt. Montagu, lying at Plymouth; and in Jan. 1794 and Jan. 1795, he was successively constituted Master of the AMPHION 32, and NASSAU 64, commanded, on the Newfoundland and North Sea stations, by Capt. Herbert Sawyer. He was made Lieutenant, 5 July, 1796, into the SEAGULL sloop, Capt. Henry Wray, attached to the force in the North Sea; and was afterwards appointed—8 Sept. 1798, to the BOSTON 32, Capt. John Erskine Douglas, under whom, besides serving off Havre and visiting the West Indies, he was for a whole year employed in blockading the *Sémillante*, a French frigate of far superior force, in the Chesapeake—in 1802-3, to the RESEARCH 18 and CHICHESTER 44, the latter commanded by Capt. Joseph Spear, under whom he brought troops home from Halifax—and, in 1804, to the CRESCENT frigate, Capt. Lord Wm. Stuart, employed off Flushing, in attendance upon the King off Weymouth, and off the Black Rocks at Brest. In all the above ships Mr. Maynard filled the post of Lieutenant. He acquired the rank of Commander 12 Jan. 1805; and retired with that of Captain 17 Oct. 1840.

Capt. Maynard is a Commissioner of Lighthouses. His third daughter, Charlotte, is the wife of Lieut. Walter F. Robinson, R.N. AGENTS—Messrs. Stilwell.

MAYNARD. (LIEUTENANT, 1828.)

THOMAS BURTON MAYNARD entered the Navy 10 May, 1810; passed his examination in June, 1816; and while Mate, we believe, of the SPEY 20, Capt. Hon. Fred. Noel, was second in command of the boats of that vessel, under Lieut. Wm. Hobson, at the capture of a noted piratical vessel at Smyrna in 1820. He obtained his commission 20 Dec. 1828; and has since been on half-pay.

He married, first, 14 Sept. 1830, Henrietta Frank, eldest daughter of Colin Chisholm, Esq., M.D.; and (that lady dying 27 Feb. 1839) secondly, 30 March, 1841, Louisa Francis, eldest daughter of the present Capt. Edw. Wallis Hoare, R.N. He has issue by both marriages.

MAYNE. (COMMANDER, 1829. F-P., 20; H-P., 15.)

DAWSON MAYNE, born 24 Dec. 1799, in Dublin, is seventh son of the Hon. Mr. Justice Mayne, of the Court of Queen's Bench in that city; and cousin of the late Retired Commander Robert Mayne, R.N.

This officer entered the Navy, 18 Nov. 1812 (under the auspices of Admiral Sir John Colpoys), as Fst.-cl. Vol., on board the VILLE DE PARIS 110, Capt. Geo. Burlton, lying at Portsmouth; and in the following March sailed with a large convoy for the East Indies and China, in the DORIS 36, Capt. Robt. O'Brien. While in that frigate he was employed blockading several American merchantmen in the harbour of Whampoa; during his stay off which place, having landed on an island with a party of four boys, he was attacked by a body of Chinese, who dragged him up a hill with a rope round his neck, and were only prevented from carrying him off through a feeling of alarm, induced by the appearance of the DORIS and another frigate in the offing. Removing, in Jan. 1815, as Midshipman (a rating he had attained more than twelve months previously), to the MALACCA 36, Capts. Donald Hugh Mackay and Geo. Henderson, he returned soon to England; and in the course of the same year was successively received on board the TRENT, flag-ship at Cork of Sir Herbert Sawyer, and LEANDER 60, Capts. Wm. Skipsey and Edw. Chetham. After assisting, 27 Aug. 1816, in the bombardment of Algiers, where a slight wound in the foot and a severe one in the thigh procured him a grant from the Patriotic Fund, and a pension which lasted until his promotion to the rank of Lieutenant, Mr. Mayne proceeded with the flag of Sir David Milne to North America, where, in July, 1817, he joined the HARRIER 18, Capt. Sir Chas. Thos. Jones, and, in Jan. 1819, the NEWCASTLE 60, flag-ship of Rear-Admiral Edw. Griffith, under whom he continued employed as an Acting and confirmed Lieutenant (order and commission respectively dated 16 Oct. 1820 and 5 Feb. 1821) until Jan. 1822. His next appointments were, 26 July, 1825, and 18 May, 1828, to the DRUID 46, Capt. Sam. Chambers, and BARHAM 50, bearing the flag of Hon. Chas. Elphinstone Fleeming; in the former of which ships (they were both stationed in the West Indies) we find him escorting General Bolivar and suite from La Guiara to Carthagena. On 14 Aug. 1829 he was promoted to the command of the ICARUS 10, also in the West Indies; where, on 22 July, 1830, he was transferred to that of the SPARROWHAWK 18. He was nominated, 28 Oct. 1831, Acting-Captain of the MAGNIFICENT receiving-ship at Port Royal, Jamaica, in which he continued until Feb. 1832, when she was reduced to a Lieutenant's command. He was afterwards employed as an Inspecting Commander in the Coast Guard at Sheerness, Hastings, and Brighton, from 25 Sept. 1834 until Oct. 1837; and on the north coast of Ireland and again at Hastings from 2 May, 1839, until Feb. 1840.

Commander Mayne has filled the post, since 6 Feb. 1840, of Chief Constable of the Rural Police for co. Salop. He married, 14 May, 1840, Elizabeth Mary, youngest daughter of the late Wm. Hewitt, Esq., of the island of Jamaica, and cousin of Viscount Hill. AGENTS—Hallett and Robinson.

MAYNE. (RETIRED COMMANDER, 1842. F-P., 18; H-P., 31.)

ROBERT MAYNE died, 19 Jan. 1846, at Jersey, aged 63. He was cousin of the present Commander D. Mayne, R.N.

This officer entered the Navy, 3 March, 1798, as Fst.-cl. Vol., on board the ROMNEY 50, commanded in the North Sea by Capt. John Lawford; on accompanying whom as Midshipman into the POLYPHEMUS 64, he fought in the action off Copenhagen 2 April, 1801. He was next, between May, 1802, and the receipt of his commission, 2 Oct. 1804, employed on the West India station, latterly as Acting-Lieutenant, in the BLENHEIM 74, under the command of various officers; and was subsequently appointed—on 22 of the month last mentioned, again to the POLYPHEMUS, Capts. J. Lawford, Robt. Redmill, Wm. Robt. Broughton, and Peter Heywood, during his attachment to which ship he served at the battle of Trafalgar, 21 Oct. 1805, and was attached, when under the flag of Rear-Admiral Geo. Murray, to the naval brigade in the operations of 1807 against Copenhagen—1 June, 1808, to the command of a Signal station at Cork—16 March, 1813, to the SAN JOSEF 110, Capts. Henry Bourchier and Stewart, lying in Hamoaze—and, 22 Dec. 1813, to the office of Agent for Transports, which he continued to fill in Portugal, Spain, France, Canada, America, Ireland, the West Indies, and Flanders, until 1816. He retired with the rank of Commander 22 Dec. 1842. AGENTS—Burnett and Holmes.

MEADE. (COMMANDER, 1812. F-P., 16; H-P., 35.)

JOHN MEADE, born 2 March, 1782, is son of the Rev. Rich. Meade, by Hon. Mary De Courcy, daughter of John, 25th Lord Kinsale, and sister of Admiral Hon. Michael De Courcy.

This officer entered the Navy, 1 Sept. 1796, as Midshipman, on board the MAGNANIME of 48 guns, commanded by his uncle, Capt. Hon. M. De Courcy, under whom, besides contributing to the capture of several privateers, he assisted at the taking, off Cape Finisterre, 24 Aug. 1798, of *La Décade* French frigate of 36 guns, and at the defeat, 12 Oct. following, of the squadron under Commodore Bompart intended for the invasion of Ireland. Removing, as Master's Mate, in the early part of 1799, to the CANADA 74, commanded at first by Capt. De Courcy and next by Capt. Joseph Sydney Yorke, he was on board that ship in the winter of 1800-1, when she had the fortune, at much risk to herself, of saving the MARS 74, bearing the flag of Rear-Admiral Edw. Thornbrough, from being wrecked on the rocks to the eastward of Ushant. On 20 Nov. 1802, a few months previously to which period he had joined the LEANDER 50, bearing the flag at Halifax of Sir Andrew Mitchell, Mr. Meade was there nominated Acting-Lieutenant of the CAMBRIAN 40, Capts. Jas. Bradley and John Poo Beresford; to which ship he was confirmed 19 April, 1803. After he had again, for fifteen months, served under Sir A. Mitchell in the LEANDER, he obtained, 19 Aug. 1806, an appointment to the LEOPARD 50, Capt. Salusbury Pryce Humphreys, also on the Halifax station; where, on 22 June, 1807, he assisted in enforcing the surrender of the U.S. frigate *Chesapeake*, in consequence of a refusal on the part of the latter to allow the British to search her for deserters. He subsequently, from May, 1808, until advanced to his present rank, 4 Nov. 1812, officiated as Flag-Lieutenant to his uncle in the TONNANT 80, DIANA 38, and FOUDROYANT. He assisted, in the TONNANT, at the embarkation of the army after the battle of Corunna in Jan. 1809; and was employed in the other ships on the Brazilian station.

Commander Meade married, 19 Sept. 1814, Miss Elizabeth Hutchinson Quin, and by that lady has issue ten children.

MEADOWS. (LIEUT., 1810. F-P., 13; H-P., 31.)

WILLIAM MEADOWS entered the Navy, 11 Oct. 1803, as A.B., on board the PRINCE GEORGE 98, Capts. Joseph Sydney Yorke and Geo. Losack. After a servitude of three years on the Channel station, latterly in the capacity of Midshipman, he sailed, towards the close of 1806, for South America in the AFRICA 64, Capt. Henry Wm. Bayntun, under whom he shared in the operations connected with the unfortunate attempt made in 1807 to effect the re-capture of Buenos Ayres. On leaving the latter ship he joined, in Feb. 1808, the SALSETTE 36, Capt. Walter Bathurst, employed at first in the Baltic, where, it appears, he assisted at the capture, 23 June, 1808, of the Russian cutter *Apith*, of 14 guns and 61 men, 4 of whom were killed and 8 wounded, with a loss to the British of 1 man killed. He afterwards accompanied the expedition to the Scheldt, and while there was actively employed in the gun-boat service. He was promoted to the rank of Lieutenant 1 March, 1810, while borne as a Supernumerary on the books of the NAMUR 74, flag-ship at the Nore of Vice-Admiral Thos. Wells; and was subsequently appointed—15 of the same month, to the BEAVER sloop, Capt. Edw. O'Brien Drury—and, 1 May following, 18 Jan. 1811, and 8 Nov. 1812, to the BARBADOES 24, Capt. Brian Hodgson, BUCEPHALUS 32, Capts. Chas. Pelly and Joseph Drury, and AFRICAINE 38, Capt. Hon. Edw. Rodney, all on the East India station; where, under Capt. Pelly, he assisted at the reduction of Java, and took part in a very long and gallant chase made by the BUCEPHALUS alone after the two French 40-gun frigates *Nymphe* and *Méduse*. He has not been since afloat.

Lieut. Meadows was Assistant-Astronomer at the Cape of Good Hope in 1834.

MEDLEY. (LIEUT., 1807. F-P., 35; H-P., 11.)

EDWARD MEDLEY was born in Aug. 1789 or 90.

This officer entered the Navy, in April, 1801, as Fst.-cl. Vol., on board the BRUNSWICK 74, Capt. Geo. Hopewell Stephens; and in Aug. 1802, on his return from a voyage to Jamaica, joined the ESCORT gun-brig, Lieut.-Commander Wm. Peake. Between the following May and Nov. 1807, we find him employed on the Home station, chiefly in the capacity of Midshipman, in the EGYPTIENNE 40, Capt. Hon. Chas. Elphinstone Fleeming, ENTREPRENANTE cutter, Lieut.-Commanders Brown and Robt. Benj. Young, REGULUS 44, Capt. Chas. Worsley Boys, CAPTAIN 74, Capt. G. H. Stephens (part of the force under Admiral Hon. Wm. Cornwallis in his attack on the French fleet close in with Brest Harbour 22 Aug. 1805), and QUEBEC 32, Capts. Geo. M'Kinley and Viscount Falkland. In the latter ship he assisted at the capture of Heligoland 5 Sept. 1807; and in her boats he contributed to the cutting out of several vessels on the coast of Holland. He was confirmed a Lieutenant (after having acted for about a month as such) in the WANDERER 18, Capt. Edw. Crofton, on the West India station, 22 Dec. 1807; and was next appointed—23 Jan. 1809, to the STANDARD 64, Capt. Thos. Harvey, lying at Chatham—22 Feb. following, and 7 March, 1810, to the RHODIAN 10, Capt. Geo. Moubray, and DÆDALUS 32, Capt. Sam. Hood Inglefield, both on the Jamaica station—25 Aug. 1810, and 15 March, 1811, to the REYNARD 10, and CRESSY 74, commanded in the Baltic by Capts. Hew Steuart and Chas. Dudley Pater—15 Nov. 1811 (having invalided from the CRESSY in the preceding June), to the CHANTICLEER 10, Capt. Rich. Spear—18 Aug. 1812, to the DIOMEDE 50, Capt. Chas. Montagu Fabian, under whom he was employed in the conveyance of troops to Spain and Portugal until April, 1813—and, 16 Sept. 1815, for two months, to the ALBAN schooner, Capts. David Boyd and Hugh Patton. In July, 1808, Mr. Medley, then in the WANDERER, was severely wounded in the neck and taken prisoner while officiating as second in command of a party of 135 men, belonging to that sloop and to the SUBTLE and BALLAHOV schooner, in a gallant but sanguinary and unsuccessful attack made under the orders of Lieut. Geo. Augustus Spearing (who was killed) on the French island of St. Martin. On being exchanged he took a passage home on board a merchant-brig, the *Mary Ann*, carrying 10 guns in addition to her cargo, in which vessel, when off the Lizard, 1 Jan. 1809, he materially aided in beating off a French privateer of 16 guns. When First-Lieutenant, afterwards, of the REYNARD, he appears to have been engaged in her boats in two cutting-out affairs; the result of the first being the capture of a vessel from Claysholm; and of the second, that of three row-boat privateers, carrying 1 gun each, with, in the whole, 50 or 60 men, by the gig and cutter manned with only 26 men under the command of Capt. Steuart and himself. His appointments, since he left the ALBAN, have been—8 Nov. 1823, to the Preventive Water-Guard Service on the coast of Cornwall, where he remained until 1826—6 July, 1827, to the command of the PLUMPER gun-brig, then on the eve of her departure for the coast of Africa, whence, on account of her defective condition, she was ordered home in Dec. 1828, with 40 persons on board under charge of piracy, and was paid off in March, 1829—22 April, 1831, to the Ordinary at Sheerness, during his stay at which place, a period of three years, he rendered himself conspicuous by his exertions in procuring the erection, for the first time, of a church and school, and also by his conduct in performing, at the time of the cholera, duties which a fear of infection had caused to be withholden from the very convicts—and, 26 Aug. 1834, to the Coast Guard. In that service, of which he is now an Inspecting-Lieutenant, Mr. Medley has been successively employed at Cromarty, at West Haven, on the banks of the Tay (where his judicious arrangements were to a great extent the means of preserving property and preventing shipwreck), and at Freswick and Staxigoe, N.B.

He married, in 1811, a daughter of Mr. Story, King's Pilot, of Sheerness Yard, who had served in that capacity on board the VENERABLE 74, in the action off Camperdown 11 Oct. 1797. By that lady he has surviving issue two sons and four daughters, one of whom is married to Lieut. W. H. Woodham, R.N., and another to Jas. Jeffery, Esq., Master R.N. (1841), now serving on board the AVON steamer, Capt. Henry C. Otter. One of his sons, a Midshipman of the VESTAL 26, Capt. Wm. Jones, died on board that ship in 1835. He had previously distinguished himself while surveying the coast of Africa under Capts. Edw. Belcher and Wm. Geo. Skyring; and had been on shore with the latter officer when killed by the natives at Cape Roxo; on which occasion, after carrying his Captain in his arms to a boat, he was under the necessity of making a precipitate flight in order to avoid sharing the same fate.

MEE. (Lieutenant, 1815. f-p., 12; h-p., 31.)

John Mee entered the Navy, in Feb. 1804, as Fst.-cl. Vol., on board the Santa Margarita 36, Capt. Wilson Rathborne, in which frigate he participated in Sir Rich. Strachan's action 4 Nov. 1805, and continued employed as Midshipman in the Bay of Biscay and off the coast of Ireland until April, 1808. During the next two years we find him coming into frequent contact, in the Talbot sloop, Capt. Hon. Alex. Jones, with the batteries on the coasts of Portugal, Spain, and Norway. He then, in 1810, joined the San Josef 110, successive flag-ship of Sir Chas. Cotton and Lord Keith off Toulon and Brest; and he was afterwards employed, in the Baltic and North America, on board the Victory 100, bearing the flag of Sir Jas. Saumarez, Orion 74, Capt. Sir Archibald Collingwood Dickson, and Tonnant 80, flag-ship of Hon. Sir Alex. Cochrane, whom he accompanied in the expedition against New Orleans. He was made Lieutenant, 9 Feb. 1815, into the Narcissus 32, Capt. Hon. Geo. Alfred Crofton; and since his return to England in May, 1816, has been on half-pay. Agents—Burnett and Holmes.

MEECH. (Lieut., 1810. f-p., 10; h-p., 34.)

Radford Gundry Meech entered the Navy, 25 Sept. 1803, as Fst.-cl. Vol., on board the Britannia 100, Captain (afterwards Rear-Admiral) the Earl of Northesk, employed at first in the Channel and then in the Mediterranean; where, after enacting a Midshipman's part in the action off Cape Trafalgar 21 Oct. 1805, he removed to the Royal George 100, flag-ship of Sir John Thos. Duckworth, whom he accompanied in Feb. 1807 in the expedition to the Dardanells. During the next three years we find him serving in the North Sea and Baltic, at the Nore, and in the West Indies, on board the Brunswick 74, Capt. Thos. Graves, Owen Glendower 36, Capt. Chas. Selby, Namur 74, Capt. Alex. Shippard, and Neptune 98, Capt. Sir Jas. Athol Wood. In March, 1810, he became Acting-Lieutenant of the Freija frigate, Capt. John Hayes, also in the West Indies; where he remained until three months after his official promotion, which took place 15 June following. His last appointments were—17 Nov. in the same year, to the Orion 74, Capt. Sir Archibald Collingwood Dickson, with whom he served in the Baltic until Jan. 1813—and, 19 May, 1815, as Senior, to the Weser 44, Capts. Bartholomew Kent and Dan. Lawrence, on the North American station, whence he returned in the following Nov.

MEGGISON. (Lieut., 1811. f-p., 11; h-p., 33.)

William Henry Meggison entered the Navy, 12 Sept. 1803, as Fst.-cl. Vol., on board the Indefatigable 46, Capt. Graham Moore; and on 5 Oct. 1804, was present in that ship off Cape St. Mary in an action which terminated in the capture of three Spanish frigates laden with treasure, and the destruction of a fourth. In Nov. 1805 he removed, as Midshipman, to the Fame 74, commanded at first by Capt. Moore and next by Capt. Rich. Henry Alex. Bennett on the Channel and Mediterranean stations, where he continued until May, 1810. He was made Lieutenant, 16 March, 1811, into the Eurydice 24, Capt. Jas. Bradshaw, on the Halifax station; and was lastly, from April, 1812, until Sept. 1815, employed in the North Sea and South America on board the Inconstant 36, Capts. Edw. W. C. R. Owen and Sir Edw. Tucker. Agent—J. Hinxman.

MEHEUX. (Lieutenant, 1825.)

Archibald Bryan Meheux entered the Navy 26 Oct. 1811; passed his examination in 1818; and was made Lieutenant, 28 Feb. 1825, into the Tweed 28, Capt. Fred. Hunn, on the Jamaica station. He has been on half-pay since 1827.

MEHEUX. (Lieutenant, 1836.)

Thomas Charles Meheux passed his examination in 1826; and obtained his commission 12 April, 1836. His appointments have since been—18 May following, as Additional-Lieutenant, to the Melville 74, flag-ship of Sir Peter Halkett in North America and the West Indies—3 Dec. in the same year, to the Rainbow 28, Capt. Thos. Bennett, on the same station, whence he returned in 1838—20 June and 21 Sept. 1839, to the Gorgon steamer and Carysfort 26, Capts. Wm. Honyman Henderson and Henry Byam Martin, with whom he continued (participating intermediately in the operations on the coast of Syria) until 1841—9 Aug. 1843, as Senior, to the Alert 6, Capt. Chas. John Bosanquet, on the African station—7 Dec. 1844, in a similar capacity, to the Tartarus steamer, Capt. Jas. Wolfe, employed in surveying the coast of Ireland—and, 5 Feb. 1847, to the command of the Crescent receiving-ship at Rio de Janeiro, where he is at present serving.

MEIN. (Lieutenant, 1812. f-p., 14; h-p., 34.)

John Mein entered the Navy, 10 June, 1799, as Fst.-cl. Vol., on board Le Caton, Lieut.-Commander R. Brown, lying at Plymouth; on the books of which vessel he continued until Oct. 1800. Re-embarking, 28 Nov. 1804, on board the St. George 98, Capts. Hon. Michael de Courcy and Thos. Bertie, he served during the two following years in the Channel and West Indies; and on being then transferred, as Midshipman, to the Néréide 36, Capt. Robt. Corbet, he proceeded first to the Cape of Good Hope and next to the Rio de la Plata, where, in 1807, he took part in the unsuccessful attempt upon Buenos Ayres. After a further attachment, on the Cape, Home, and East India stations, to the Grampus 50, Capt. Jas. Haldane Tait, Raisonnable 64, Capt. Josias Rowley, St. Fiorenzo 36, Capt. John Bastard, Plover sloop, Capt. Philip Browne, Hesper, Blanche, Cornwallis, and Russell, all commanded by Capt. Edw. Wallis Hoare, and Africaine 38, Capt. Philip Beaver, he was nominated, 19 Nov. 1810, Acting-Lieutenant of the Ceylon 32, Capts. Jas. Tomkinson and Wm. Paterson, under the former of whom we find him employed on shore at the ensuing capture of the Isle of France. With the exception of a short servitude as Midshipman (from 3 Aug. to 30 Nov. 1811) in the Barfleur 98, off Lisbon, he continued to act as Lieutenant in the Ceylon, also in the Néréide under Capt. Geo. Henderson, and in the Myrtle sloop, Capt. Clement Sneyd, until Feb. 1812. He then again, in the same capacity as before, joined the Barfleur, commanded at the time by Sir Thos. Masterman Hardy. He was within a few weeks, however, officially promoted to his present rank, by a commission bearing date 21 March, 1812; and was subsequently appointed—14 Aug. in the same year, to the Talbot 20, Capt. Spelman Swaine, on the Irish station—30 April and 11 Nov. 1814, to the Warspite 74, and Orpheus 36, Capts. Lord Jas. O'Bryen and Chas. Montagu Fabian, with whom he served on the coasts of North and South America until June, 1816—and, 24 May, 1821, to the Martin 20, Capt. Christopher Crackenthorp Askew, fitting for the Mediterranean, where he invalided. He has since been on half-pay.

Lieut. Mein is married, and has issue.

MELLERSH. (Lieutenant, 1837.)

Arthur Mellersh passed his examination in 1831; and on being advanced to his present rank, 24 Oct. 1837, was appointed Additional-Lieutenant of the Cornwallis 74, flag-ship of Hon. Sir Chas. Paget on the North America and West India station; where he removed, 8 March, 1838, to the Serpent 16, Capt. Rich. Laird Warren. On 22 July, 1839, a few months after his return to England, he joined the Phœnix steamer, Capt. Robt. Spencer Robinson, fitting for the Mediterranean. His appointments since he left that vessel have been, always in the capacity of First-Lieutenant—1 March, 1840, and 6 May, 1841, to the Hydra steamer, and Tyne 26, Capts. Alex. Murray and John Townshend, likewise in the Mediterranean—9 Feb. 1842, to the Minden Hospital-ship in the East Indies, Capt.

Michael Quin—and, 22 March, 1845, to the VERNON 50, bearing the flag of Rear-Admiral Sam. Hood Inglefield, at first on the S.E. coast of America, and then in the East Indies, where he is now serving. AGENTS—Messrs. Stilwell.

MENDS. (COMMANDER, 1841.)

GEORGE CLARKE MENDS is son of the late Commodore Sir Robt. Mends, Kt., G.C.C.,* by a daughter of the late Jas. Butler, Esq., of Bagshot, co. Surrey; brother of Commander Jas. Augustus Mends, R.N.; and nephew of Capt. Wm. Bowen Mends, R.N. His eldest brother, Robert Butler Mends, Midshipman of the OWEN GLENDOWER 42, died on board that ship off Sierra Leone, 5 Dec. 1823, from the effects of illness contracted in the preceding June, while employed in her boats in the Bight of Biafra.

This officer entered the Navy, 21 Feb. 1821, on board the QUEEN CHARLOTTE 100, flag-ship at Portsmouth; served, from Sept. in the same year, until Sept. 1823, under his father's broad pendant, on the coast of Africa; passed his examination in 1827; and was made Lieutenant, 24 Jan. 1829, into the MAIDSTONE 42, bearing the broad pendant of Commodore Chas. Marsh Schomberg at the Cape of Good Hope; where he removed, 9 March following, to the JASEUR 18, Capts. John Lyons and Fras. Harding. His succeeding appointments were—27 Dec. 1831, to the UNDAUNTED 46, Capt. Edw. Harvey, in the East Indies—16 Sept. 1834, to the ÆTNA surveying-vessel, Capt. Rich. Laird Warren, fitting at Portsmouth—17 Dec. following, to the CHAMPION 18, Capt. Robt. Fair, on the North America and West India station, whence he returned in 1835—10 April, 1839, as First, to the BLENHEIM 72, Capt. Sir Humphrey Fleming Senhouse, attached to the force off Lisbon—and, 12 Feb. 1840, to the CAMBRIDGE 78, Capt. Edw. Barnard, in the Mediterranean. He acquired his present rank 23 Nov. 1841; and since 25 Feb. 1843 has been employed as an Inspecting-Commander in the Coast Guard. AGENTS—Messrs. Ommanney.

MENDS. (LIEUTENANT, 1841.)

GEORGE PECHELL MENDS is son of Capt. Wm. Bowen Mends, R.N.

This officer entered the Navy 9 Feb. 1824; passed his examination 1 April, 1834; and at the period of his promotion to the rank of Lieutenant, which took place 30 Aug. 1841, was serving in the Mediterranean as Mate of the LOCUST steamer, Lieut.-Commander John Lunn. His appointments have since been—3 Sept. 1841, to the MALABAR 72, Capt. Sir Geo. Rose Sartorius, also in the Mediterranean—5 Oct. 1844, as Senior, to the MUTINE 12, Capt. Rich. Borough Crawford, attached to the force at the Cape of Good Hope—and 17 Oct. 1846, in a similar capacity, to the EURYDICE 22, Capt. Talavera Vernon Anson, on the same station, where he is now serving. AGENTS—Messrs. Ommanney.

MENDS. (COMMANDER, 1846.)

JAMES AUGUSTUS MENDS is brother of Commander Geo. Clarke Mends, R.N.

This officer passed his examination in 1829; and on attaining the rank of Lieutenant, 28 Nov. 1836, was nominated Additional-Lieutenant of the CALEDONIA 120, bearing the flag of Sir Josias Rowley in the Mediterranean. His subsequent appointments were—19 June, 1837, to the DONEGAL 78, Capt. John Drake, fitting at Plymouth—14 Aug. 1838, to the ACTÆON 26, Capt. Robt. Russell, on the Brazil and Cape of Good Hope station—26 Feb. 1841 and 11 Jan. 1842, to the PRESIDENT 50, Capt. Wm. Broughton, and DUBLIN 50, flag-ship of Rear-Admiral Rich. Thomas, both in South America, whence he returned in 1845—and 15 June, 1846, to the TRAFALGAR 120, Capt. John Neale Nott, attached to the Channel squadron. On 27 Nov. 1846, at which period he had become First-Lieutenant of the latter ship, Mr. Mends was promoted to the rank of Commander. He is at present on half-pay.

MENDS. (LIEUTENANT, 1846.)

ROBERT HAMILTON HANDFIELD MENDS is son of Capt. Wm. Bowen Mends, R.N.

This officer passed his examination 12 Dec. 1843; served for some time on board the EXCELLENT gunnery-ship at Portsmouth, Capt. Sir Thos. Hastings; and from 28 Feb. 1844, until promoted to the rank of Lieutenant, 9 Nov. 1846, was employed in the East Indies as Mate of the FOX 42, Commodore Sir Henry Martin Blackwood.

MENDS. (CAPTAIN, 1814. F-P., 24; H-P., 29.)

WILLIAM BOWEN MENDS, born 27 Jan. 1781, in Pembrokeshire, is brother of the late Commodore Sir Robt. Mends, Kt., G.C.C.

This officer entered the Navy, in Nov. 1794, as A.B., on board LA POMONE 40, Commodore Sir John Borlase Warren; on following whom, as Midshipman (after sharing in Lord Bridport's action, attending also the expedition in support of the French royalists to Quiberon, and participating in a variety of boat and other service on the coast of France), into the CANADA 74, he witnessed the defeat, 12 Oct. 1798, of a French squadron under Commodore Bompart, intended for the invasion of Ireland. In Feb. 1799 he became Midshipman of L'IMPÉTUEUX 74, Capt. Sir Edw. Pellew; and in the course of the same year he again joined Sir J. B. Warren in the TÉMÉRAIRE 98, and RENOWN 74. On the night of 29 Aug. 1800, immediately subsequent to the Ferrol expedition, we find him serving with the boats of a squadron, 20 in number, commanded by Lieut. Henry Burke, at the cutting-out, close to the batteries in Vigo Bay, of *La Guèpe* privateer, of 18 guns and 161 men; which vessel, 25 of whose people were killed and 40 wounded, was in 15 minutes boarded and carried, with a loss to the British of 3

* Sir Robert Mends entered the Navy 1 Jan. 1779, on board the CULLODEN 74, in which ship he assisted at the defeat of Don Juan de Langara 16 Jan. 1780. He was afterwards, 16 March, 1781, present in the GUADALOUPE in the action between Admiral Arbuthnot and M. Destouches; and, from the following April until taken prisoner with Lord Cornwallis and his army, was employed on shore with a detachment of seamen throughout all the operations of the campaign in Virginia. On the last-mentioned occasion his right arm was shot off by a cannon-ball, and his left knee slightly wounded by a shell. He had the further misfortune, while sharing, in the CONQUEROR, in the glories of 9 and 12 April, 1782, to receive a splinter-wound in the head, and to sustain a fracture of the right jaw. In 1789, at the especial command of George III., Mr. Mends was presented with a Lieutenant's commission. After witnessing the evacuation of Toulon, and being severely burnt and bruised in the COLOSSUS in Lord Bridport's action, he was promoted, in 1796, to the command of the DILIGENCE sloop of 16 guns; and on 2 May, 1800, having previously effected the capture of *La Nativetas* Spanish ship of 500 tons, 16 guns, and 50 men, he was advanced to Post-rank. During the remainder of the French revolutionary war he had command of the ABERGAVENNY 54, THUNDERER 74, QUEBEC 32, and NÉRÉIDE 36. In 1805 he was placed over the Malahide district of Sea Fencibles in Ireland; and in 1808, as a reward for the manner in which he had for some time discharged the duties of Regulating Officer at Liverpool, he was appointed to the ARETHUSA of 46 guns. In that frigate, in 1809–10, Capt. Mends rendered himself conspicuous by a system of the most active co-operation with the patriots on the north coast of Spain; where, in the summer of the latter year, a squadron under his orders effected the destruction of all the batteries (with the exception of Castro) from St. Sebastian to St. Andero, mounting in the whole about 100 pieces of cannon. For these services the Order of the Cross of Victory of Asturias, and the rank of Major-General in the Spanish army, were conferred on him, and he was recommended in the strongest manner to his Majesty's Government by the Regency of Spain, and by the Captain-General of the Junta of Gallicia. He had previously, while assisting at the capture of the French frigate, *Le Niemen*, of 46 guns and 339 men, been struck by a splinter in the forehead, the effects of which he seriously felt during the remainder of his life. From 1811 until 1814 we find him superintending the prison-ships in Portsmouth Harbour. He received, in 1815, the honour of Knighthood, together with the insignia of the Order of Charles III. of Spain; and in 1816 a pension of 300*l.* was settled upon him in consideration of his wounds. In June, 1821, Sir Robert Mends hoisted a broad pendant in the IPHIGENIA 42, as Commodore of the squadron employed on the western coast of Africa, where he died, on board the OWEN GLENDOWER frigate, 4 Sept. 1823.

seamen and 1 marine killed, 3 lieutenants, 12 seamen, and 5 marines wounded, and 1 seaman missing. For his conduct in this affair Mr. Mends had the honour of being publicly thanked by the Commander-in-Chief; who, although he had not completed his time, at once ordered him to act as Lieutenant-Commander of the St. Vincent gun-brig. Being officially promoted 9 April, 1801, and appointed to the command of the Ferreter, another gun-brig, he was afforded an opportunity, in the course of the same year, of enacting a part in Lord Nelson's attack on the Boulogne flotilla, on which occasion, it appears, he served in his own boat, and had 4 persons, out of 9, either killed or wounded. He paid the Ferreter off in Sept. 1802; and was next in succession appointed—4 July, 1803, to the Foudroyant 80, bearing the flag of Sir Thos. Graves in the Channel—19 March, 1805, to the Surinam 18, Capt. Alex. Shippard, whom he accompanied to Gibraltar—about March, 1806, again to the Foudroyant, flag-ship of Sir J. B. Warren on the West India, North American, and Home stations—13 April, 1807, to the Goliath 74, Capt. Peter Puget, under whom he served with the advanced squadron at the siege of Copenhagen, and so distinguished himself that a strong recommendation in his favour was forwarded to the Commander-in-Chief—and 29 Oct. 1807, to the Swiftsure 74, bearing the flag of Sir J. B. Warren at Halifax, where, from June, 1808, until Oct. 1809, and from May to Sept. 1810, he was allowed to act as Commander of the Vesta schooner and Indian sloop. On leaving the Swiftsure, Mr. Mends was presented with a second promotal commission, dated 26 Feb. 1811. After exactly two years of half-pay, he obtained command, 26 Feb. 1811, of the Loup Cervier 18; and on 23 March, 1814, having been intermediately employed at the blockade of New London, he was nominated Acting-Captain of the Terpsichore frigate, which ship he brought home and paid off 27 June following. His promotion had in the mean while been confirmed by a commission dated 26 May, 1814. His last appointments were—24 Jan. 1824, to the Blanche 46, in which frigate he conveyed Vice-Admiral Lord Amelius Beauclerk to the Tagus, and then proceeded to South America, whence, after having been for some time Senior officer off the coast of Peru, he returned with nearly 800,000 dollars to England, 28 Sept. 1827—and 26 Nov. 1836, to the Talavera 74. In that ship Capt. Mends was employed at first on the Lisbon station; then in affording co-operation, with a large squadron under his orders, to the Queen's forces during the civil war on the south-east coast of Spain; next in transporting the 73rd Regt. from Gibraltar to Halifax, and the 11th from that place to St. John's, New Brunswick; and, finally, in the Mediterranean, on the Greek portion of which he was for six months Senior officer. The Talavera was put out of commission 3 Jan. 1840.

Capt. Mends has three sons in the Navy—William Robert, a Commander; and George Pechell and Robert Hamilton Handfield, Lieutenants. Agents—Messrs. Ommanney.

MENDS. (Commander, 1846. f-p., 21; h-p., 1.)

William Robert Mends, born 27 Feb. 1812, is eldest son of Capt. Wm. Bowen Mends, R.N.

This officer entered the Royal Naval College 7 May, 1825; and embarked, 21 Dec. 1828, as a Volunteer, on board the Challenger 26, Capt. John Hayes. In the ensuing Jan. he removed to the Thetis 46, Capts. Arthur Batt Bingham and Sam. Burgess, with whom he continued to serve on the South American station, latterly in the capacity of Midshipman, until wrecked off Cape Frio 5 Dec. 1830; and he was next, between April, 1831, and his promotion to the rank of Lieutenant, 11 Aug. 1835, employed as Mate in the Actæon 26 and Pique 36, Capts. Hon. Fred. Wm. Grey and Hon. Henry John Rous, in the Mediterranean and on particular service. His succeeding appointments were—30 Dec. 1835, 29 Nov. 1836, and 17 Jan. 1837, to the Vernon 50, Capt. John M'Kerlie, Caledonia 120, flag-ship of Sir Josias Rowley, and Rodney 92, Capt. Hyde Parker, all on the Mediterranean station—between 28 July, 1838, and June, 1843, to the Ceylon 2, Benbow 74, and Ganges 84, as Flag-Lieutenant to Sir John Louis, Admiral Superintendent at Malta—and 3 Nov. 1843, as Senior, to the Fox 42, bearing the broad pendant of Sir Henry Martin Blackwood in the East Indies. He returned to England on the occasion of his advancement to the rank of Commander, 9 Nov. 1846; and is at present unemployed.

Commander Mends married, 6 Jan. 1838, Melita, third daughter of Joseph Stilon, Esq., M.D., Surg. R.N. (1815).

MENZIES. (Retired Commander, 1816.)

Duncan Menzies was born in March, 1759, and died, 20 Dec. 1846, at 4, Park-place, George-square, Edinburgh. He was uncle by marriage of Capt. Nicholas Lockyer, R.N., C.B.

This officer entered the Navy in 1770, as Midshipman, on board the Hazard sloop, Capt. Ford; and was afterwards, until promoted to the rank of Lieutenant, 1 April, 1781, employed in the Emerald 32, Capt. Moutray, Culloden and Resolution 74's, Capts. Dundas and Ogle, Culloden again, Capt. Balfour, Sandwich 90, Capt. Young, and Formidable of similar force, flag-ship of Sir Geo. Rodney; assisting during that period at the capture of Ste. Lucie in 1778, in the action off Cape St. Vincent 16 Jan. 1780, and as Aide-de-Camp to the last-mentioned officer at the reduction of St. Eustatius in Feb. 1781. On the occasion of his promotion, as above, Mr. Menzies joined the Alfred 74, Capt. Bayne, in which ship it was his fortune to be present in the memorable action of 12 April, 1782. On that occasion he was one of the officers sent on board the Ville de Paris to receive the sword of the Comte de Grasse. In the course of the same year we find him present at the relief of Gibraltar. He subsequently, during the French revolutionary war, served on board the Belligerent and Inflexible 64's, Capts. Brine and Jervis, on the West India station; also in the Caton 64; and in command of the Piercer gun-brig. In the latter vessel he accompanied the expedition to Holland in 1799, and assisted at the debarkation of the troops under Sir Ralph Abercromby. During the late war Lieut. Menzies was employed in the Impress service at Falmouth, and in command of the Firm prison-ship at Plymouth. He retired with the rank of Commander 1 Jan. 1816.

Commander Menzies married, in Jan. 1808, Miss Elizabeth Grove, of Falmouth, and by that lady has left issue a son and two daughters.

MERCER. (Commander, 1824. f-p., 14; h-p., 35.)

John Davis Mercer entered the Navy, in 1798, as Midshipman, on board the Perdrix 22, Capt. Wm. Chas. Fahie, on the books of which ship, stationed in the Leeward Islands, his name was borne until the following year. We next, in 1801, find him on board the Berschermer 54, Capt. Alex. Fraser, off Harwich; and, in 1805, rejoining Capt. Fahie in the Amelia frigate, on the West India station; where, on following him into the Ethalion, he assisted at the capture of the Danish islands of St. Thomas and Ste. Croix in Dec. 1807. In 1808 he returned to England in the Ramillies 74, Capt. Robt. Yarker, but, being soon ordered back in the Gloire 38, Capt. Jas. Carthew, was again, in the course of the same year, placed under the orders of Capt. Fahie as Master's Mate on board the Belleisle 74—following him afterwards into the Pompée and Abercromby of similar force. The Belleisle, we may here observe, formed part of the squadron employed at the reduction of Martinique in Feb. 1809; and, in the ensuing April, the Pompée, with a loss to herself of 9 men killed and 30 wounded, proved the captor, when in company with the Castor 32, of the French 74-gun ship *d'Haupoult*, between 80 and 90 of whose people were killed and wounded. Attaining the rank of Lieutenant 8 Dec. 1809, Mr. Mercer continued employed in that capacity in the West Indies for a further period of nearly four years in the PULTUSK sloop, Capts. Wm. Elliott and John M'George, PELORUS 18, Capt. Thos. Huskisson, ABERCROMBY again, Capt. W. C. Fahie, CYGNET sloop, commanded by various officers, DRAGON 74 and GRAMPUS 50, flag-ships of Sir Fras. Laforey, and CLEOPATRA frigate, Capt. Chas. Gill. His next appointments were, 18 March, 1821, to the SALISBURY 50, Capt. John Wilson, on the Leeward Island station, and 5 Aug. in the same year to the FORTE 44, as Flag-Lieutenant to the late Sir Edw. Griffith Colpoys, Commander-in-Chief at Halifax, where he afterwards, in the SALISBURY, filled the like post under his early friend Rear-Admiral Fahie. He acquired his present rank 9 Sept. 1824, and has since been on half-pay. AGENTS—Hallett and Robinson.

MERCER. (COMMANDER, 1838. F-P., 19; H-P., 6.)

SAMUEL MERCER entered the Navy, 20 Jan. 1822, as Midshipman, on board the LEVEN 26, Capt. Wm. Fitzwilliam Owen, in which vessel, until Sept. 1826, he was employed in surveying the east and west coasts of Africa. In Feb. 1827, after he had been for about two months attached to the CHALLENGER 28, Capt. John Hayes, on the Home station, he again joined Capt. Owen on board the EDEN 26. Continuing with him until June, 1830, he was in consequence afforded an opportunity of assisting in the colonization of Fernando Po, and had the satisfaction during the period of being awarded a Lieutenant's commission dated 12 Jan. 1829. His next appointments were—23 June, 1831, to the BLOSSOM 16, Capt. Rich. Owen, employed on surveying-service in the West Indies, where he remained, part of the time in command of the MONKEY tender, until Oct. 1832—and 11 Jan. 1834, to the command of the CHARYBDIS 3. While in that vessel, which he paid off in Sept. 1837, Lieut. Mercer was again stationed on the African coast, and succeeded in capturing not less than 14 slave-vessels. Attaining his present rank 28 June, 1838, he officiated, from 17 Aug. 1841, until Aug. 1846, as Superintendent of the Packet service at Dover, with his name on the books of the OCEAN 80, guard-ship at Sheerness. He is now on half-pay.

Commander Mercer married, 20 Feb. 1839, Fanny, eldest daughter of Lieut. Josiah Durnford, R.N., by whom he has issue. AGENTS—Hallett and Robinson.

MEREDITH. (CAPT., 1837. F-P., 21; H-P., 27.)

RICHARD MEREDITH, whose name had been borne in 1799 on the books of the POLYPHEMUS 64, Capt. Geo. Lumsdaine, embarked, in Oct. 1800, as Fst.-cl. Vol., on board the PHŒBE of 44 guns, Capts. Robt. Barlow, Thos. Baker, Jas. Keith Shepard, Hon. Thos. Bladen Capel, and Jas. Oswald. Under the first-named of those officers he contributed, 19 Feb. 1800, to the capture of the French frigate *Africaine* of 44 guns and 715 men (including 400 troops and artificers), after a close and desperate night-action of two hours, attended (although the British, out of 239 men, had but 1 killed and 12 wounded) with the awful loss to the enemy of at least 200 killed and 143 wounded, the greatest part of them mortally. For his gallantry in achieving this exploit, Capt. Barlow was rewarded with the honour of Knighthood. Continuing in the PHŒBE on the Mediterranean and Home stations until April, 1806, Mr. Meredith, in addition to much cutting-out work, had the fortune to enact a part, 21 Oct. 1805, in the action off Cape Trafalgar, on which occasion he was sent to take possession of the *Monarca* Spanish 74-gun ship. We may add that he remained on board the prize until she took the ground seven days after the battle, when, with her crew and the few British who had followed him, only 39 in number, he was rescued by the LEVIATHAN 74. On his return in the summer of 1806 to the Mediterranean in the DIANA 38, Capt. Thos. Jas. Maling, he rejoined Capt. Capel on board the ENDYMION 40. In that ship we find him accompanying the expedition to the Dardanells, and assisting at the destruction of the Turkish shipping off Point Pesquies, in Feb. 1807; in the course of which month he had the satisfaction of receiving a Lieutenant's commission bearing date 15 Aug. 1806. He took a passage home in consequence in the AMPHION 32, Capt. Wm. Hoste; and was next, during upwards of six years, employed on the Baltic, Mediterranean, Home, West India, Cadiz, and Newfoundland stations, in the VULTURE sloop, Capt. Jos. Pearce, HYPERION 36, Capt. Thos. Chas. Brodie, INTREPID 64, Capt. Andrews, IMPLACABLE 74, Capts. Thos. Byam Martin, Geo. Cockburn, and Joshua Rowley Watson, and SYBILLE 44, Capts. Clotworthy Upton and Jas. Sanders. After assisting, in the VULTURE, at the reduction of Copenhagen in 1807, Lieut. Meredith was sent home in charge of one of the 18-gun brigs taken on the occasion, the *Nyd Elven*, mounting, however, only 4 guns, with a crew of 22 men, and laden with a large quantity of stores. During the passage, and when on the Dogger Bank, he was attacked at night by a privateer, but succeeded at the end of an action of 45 minutes in beating her off. While attached, in 1810, to the IMPLACABLE, Lieut. Meredith had command for six weeks of the gun-boats employed at the defence of Cadiz. Being obliged to invalid from the SYBILLE in consequence of an injury sustained by the fall of a block on his head, he did not again go afloat until 10 Aug. 1821; between which period and his promotion to the rank of Commander, 16 March, 1824, he served at home, and on the east and west coasts of South America, in the NORTHUMBERLAND 78, SPARTIATE 76, and CAMBRIDGE 82, all under the orders of Capt. Thos. Jas. Maling. He then returned to England with despatches across the Isthmus of Panama; and was, lastly, from 26 Sept. 1831, until paid off at the close of 1835, employed on the coast of Africa in command of the PELORUS 16—the last two years as Senior officer. He attained Post-rank 6 June, 1837.

Exclusive of the time he was at Cadiz, where he was almost constantly under fire, Capt. Meredith during the war was not less than 35 times in actual combat with the enemy, including ship actions, attacks upon batteries, and boat affairs. He married, 2 Sept. 1844, Marian D'Oyley, widow of the late Jas. Barlow Hay, Esq., of Thornhite Park, South Hants. AGENTS—Messrs. Stilwell.

MEREDITH. (COMMANDER, 1828. F-P., 24; H-P., 15.)

SAMUEL MEREDITH entered the Navy, 8 May, 1808, as a Volunteer, on board the CADMUS 10, Capt. Delamere Wynter, attached to the force in the Channel. After serving off Greenwich in the THISBE 28, flag-ship of Hon. Sir Henry Edwin Stanhope, and in the North Sea and off Greenland in the BELVIDERA 36, Capt. Rich. Byron, he became Midshipman, 22 Sept. 1810, of the MALACCA 36, Capts. Wm. Butterfield and Sam. Leslie, with the latter of whom he continued employed on the East India station in the VOLAGE 22, and THEBAN 36, until April, 1816. In the VOLAGE he witnessed an attack made, 28 June, 1813, upon the defences of Sambas, a piratical state on the western coast of Borneo, as he also did, in Sept. of the same year, the restoration of the Sultan of Palambang to his throne. Of the THEBAN, Mr. Meredith, who had been acting in her for nine months, was confirmed a Lieutenant 24 Nov. 1815. His appointments after he left her were—6 Sept. 1816, to the LARNE 20, Capt. Abraham Lowe, employed in the Channel and West Indies, whence he returned in Jan. 1819—11 July, 1820, to the SEVERN 40, Capt. Wm. M'Culloch, lying in the Downs for the purposes of the Coast Blockade—6 Dec. 1822, to the PRINCE REGENT 120, flag-ship of Sir Benj. Hallowell at Chatham—11

April, 1823, and, again, 4 Sept. 1824, to the post of Agent for Transports Afloat—and, 8 April, 1825, to the command of the VIGILANT cutter of 12 guns, on the Plymouth station. He was advanced to his present rank 7 May, 1828; and was subsequently, from 6 July, 1830, until 1833, and, again, from 20 March, 1835, until 1838, employed as an Inspecting Commander in the Coast Guard.

The Commander, who is Chief Constable for co. Wilts, married, 21 June, 1819, Lydia, third daughter of John Dyer, Esq., Secretary of Greenwich Hospital. AGENTS—Messrs. Stilwell.

MERRIMAN. (LIEUT., 1815. F-P., 8; H-P., 33.)

CHARLES MERRIMAN entered the Navy, 9 Oct. 1806, as Third-cl. Vol., on board the PHEASANT 18, Capt. John Palmer; and in the course of 1807 was present at the storming of Monte Video, and in all the operations which preceded the evacuation of Spanish America by the British. He was employed during the next four years on the Home station, as Midshipman and Master's Mate, under Lord Amelius Beauclerk, in the SATURN and ROYAL OAK 74's; and in the latter ship, in 1809, he accompanied the expedition to the Walcheren. He afterwards, until May, 1814, served, chiefly off the coasts of France, Spain, and Holland, in the TIGRE and RIVOLI 74's, Capts. John Halliday and Graham Eden Hamond, CHALLENGER 16, Capt. Fred. Edw. Vernon (now Harcourt), and LEVERET sloop, Capt. Jonathan Christian. In the CHALLENGER, Mr. Merriman, in 1813, co-operated in the attack upon St. Sebastian, and assisted at the capture of *Le Flibustier* French national brig, mounting 16 guns, a brass howitzer, and 4 swivels, and laden with treasure, arms, ammunition, and salt provisions. His last appointment was to the Coast Guard, in which service he continued from 27 Nov. 1821 until 17 Oct. 1822. He attained the rank of Lieutenant 27 Feb. 1815. AGENTS—Goode and Lawrence.

METCALFE. (COMMANDER, 1841.)

WILLIAM CHARLES METCALFE entered the Navy 7 Oct. 1824; served as Midshipman of the ASIA 84, flag-ship of Sir Edw. Codrington, at the battle of Navarin, 20 Oct. 1827; passed his examination in 1832; and obtained his first commission 7 March, 1837. His succeeding appointments were—24 of the same month, to the MALABAR 74, Capts. Sir Wm. Augustus Montagu and Edw. Harvey, with whom he served, on the Lisbon and North America and West India stations, until paid off in the following year—and 7 Nov. 1839, to the BLONDE 42, Capt. Thos. Bourchier. For his conduct in that ship during the campaign in China, where he witnessed the first and second capture of Canton, he was advanced to his present rank 8 Oct. 1841. He has since been on half-pay. AGENTS—Messrs. Ommanney.

METHERELL. (LIEUT., 1823. F-P., 25; H-P., 12.)

RICHARD ROE METHERELL entered the Navy, in May, 1810, as Fst.-cl. Vol., on board the ARETHUSA 38, Capts. Robt. Mends and Fras. Holmes Coffin, with whom he continued actively employed on the north coast of Spain, and on the African and West India stations, until July, 1813—the last two years and two months in the capacity of Midshipman. He then removed to the CYDNUS 38, Capts. Fred. Langford and Hon. Robt. Cavendish Spencer; and, after an intermediate servitude on the Home, West India, and Halifax stations, was next, from May to Oct. 1816, attached to the IMPREGNABLE 104, and BERWICK 74, flag-ships at Plymouth of Sir John Thos. Duckworth. Between May, 1818, and Oct. 1819, we find him officiating as Master's Mate, in the East Indies and at the Cape of Good Hope, of the PHAETON 46, Capt. Wm. Henry Dillon. He subsequently, in Nov. 1820, joined the SURINAM 18, Capts. Wm. M'Kenzie Godfrey, Alfred Matthews, and Chas. Crole, employed at first on the Barbadoes, and then on the Jamaica station; where he was confirmed a Lieutenant, 27 March, 1823, in the TYNE 26, Capts. John Edw. Walcott and John Walter Roberts. He left that vessel in Jan. 1824; and was afterwards appointed—25 Oct. 1827, to the BRITOMART 10, Capts. Russell Henry Manners and Edw. John Johnson, employed on the Plymouth and Lisbon stations—22 Aug. 1831 and 29 Feb. 1832, as Senior, to the ARIADNE 28, and COLUMBINE 18, Capts. Chas. Phillips and Henry Ommanney Love, both in the West Indies, whence he returned in March, 1834—and 18 Nov. 1835, to the Coast Guard, in which service he remained until 1843. He has since been on half-pay. AGENTS—Messrs. Ommanney.

MEYNELL (LIEUTENANT, 1846.)

FRANCIS MEYNELL served as Midshipman, during the campaign in China, on board the CALLIOPE 26, Capt. Thos. Herbert, and was mentioned for the assistance he rendered at the capture, 13 March, 1841, of the last fort protecting the approaches to the city of Canton.* He passed his examination 17 Dec. 1842; and after having served for upwards of two years on the coast of Africa, as Mate, in the PENELOPE steamer, Commodore Wm. Jones, RAPID 10, Lieut.-Commander Edw. Chas. Earle, and STAR 6, Capt. Robt. John Wallace Dunlop, was presented with a commission dated 15 Jan. 1846, and re-appointed, in the capacity of Additional-Lieutenant, to the PENELOPE. He went on half-pay soon afterwards, and has not been since employed.

MEYNELL. (CAPT., 1816. F-P., 12; H-P., 32.)

HENRY MEYNELL is second son of the late Hugo Meynell, Esq., of Hoar Cross, by Hon. Elizabeth Ingram, daughter and co-heiress of Viscount Irwin, whose elder daughter married the second Marquess of Hertford. Capt. Meynell is next brother of the present Hugo Chas. Meynell-Ingram, of Temple Newsam, co. York, and Hoar Cross, co. Stafford, a Magistrate and Deputy-Lieutenant for the latter shire, and High Sheriff in 1826; and brother-in-law of Wm. Beckett, Esq., of Kirkstall Grange, co. York, M.P. for Leeds, and Lieut.-Colonel of the Yorkshire Hussars.

This officer entered the Navy, 24 June, 1803, as Fst.-cl. Vol, on board the ISIS 50, Capts. Wm. Grenville Lobb and John Acworth Ommanney, bearing the successive flags of Vice-Admirals Jas. Gambier and Sir Erasmus Gower at Newfoundland, where he remained until Feb. 1805. Between the following month and July, 1806, we again find him serving with Capt. Lobb, chiefly in the capacity of Midshipman, in the POMONE 38 and CAPTAIN 74, on the Lisbon and Home stations. Towards the close of the year last mentioned he joined, first the BOREAS 22, Capt. Robt. Scott, and then the LAVINIA 40, Capt. Lord Wm. Stuart, in which frigate, it appears, he continued employed at Home and in the Mediterranean until promoted to the rank of Lieutenant 8 Nov. 1809. He witnessed in consequence the surrender of a frigate and store-ship, contributed to the cutting-out of several vessels from under the enemy's batteries, carried a prize on one occasion to Malta, and assisted, we believe, in forcing the passage between the batteries of Flushing and Cadsand during the expedition to the Walcheren. Obtaining an appointment, 16 Jan. 1810, to the THEBAN 36, Capt. Stephen Thos. Digby, Mr. Meynell, after cruizing for a considerable time in the Channel (where he commanded the boats at the capture, 2 Feb. 1811, of a French merchant-brig lying aground under two batteries near Dieppe†), sailed with convoy for the East Indies and China;‡

* *Vide* Gaz. 1841, p. 1503. † *V.* Gaz. 1811, p. 205.

‡ The following is an extract from a letter addressed to the author by an officer who was on board the THEBAN at the period to which it refers —"On 18 March, 1811, the THEBAN, having been ordered to Portsmouth to refit, entered the harbour under royals, let go the anchor off the PERSEVERANCE hulk at half-past eleven o'clock; and by half-past twelve—that is to say in one hour—the ship was secured to the hulk and completely stripped to the lower masts, the sails and rigging made up, with the yards and small spars on board the hulk. Capt. H. Meynell was the Senior Lieutenant then doing duty."

on her passage whither the THEBAN had the misfortune, at noon on 8 Sept. 1812, to be caught in a typhoon, which before midnight left her nothing standing but her foremast and bowsprit. In the early part of 1813 Mr. Meynell was nominated Acting-Commander of the ARROGANT at Bombay; and, on 24 Aug. in the same year, he was there officially promoted into the CORNWALLIS. Quitting that vessel in the ensuing Oct., he was next, 23 Aug. and 24 Nov. 1815, appointed Acting-Captain of the 50-gun ships JUPITER and NEWCASTLE; to the latter of which, bearing the flag of Sir Pulteney Malcolm at St. Helena, the Admiralty confirmed him 10 April, 1816. He was paid off 10 Sept. 1817, and has not been since afloat.

From 22 March, 1820, until the death of George IV., Capt. Meynell (who is Senior of 1816) filled the post of Gentleman Usher Quarterly Waiter to that monarch; as he also did to William IV. from 24 July, 1830, until 23 March, 1831, when he resigned. He was returned to Parliament in 1826 for the borough of Lisburn, which he continued to represent until 1847. For some time prior to April, 1845, Capt. Meynell held the office of Groom in Waiting on her present Majesty. AGENTS—Hallett and Robinson.

MIALL. (COMMANDER, 1838. F-P., 24; H-P., 23.)

GEORGE GOVER MIALL entered the Navy. 24 Feb. 1800, as Third-cl. Vol., on board the ACHILLE 74, Capts. Geo. Murray and Edw. Buller, bearing the flag in the Channel of Earl St. Vincent; and from June, 1802, until Oct. 1806, was employed on the North American station, chiefly in the capacity of Midshipman, in the 50-gun ships LEANDER and LEOPARD, Capts. Jas. Oughton, Fras. Wm. Fane, Alex. S. Kene, Wm. Lyall, John Talbot, Henry Whitby, and Salusbury Pryce Humphreys. In the LEANDER, under Capt. Talbot, he assisted at the capture, 23 Feb. 1805, of the French frigate *La Ville de Milan*, of 48 guns, and the simultaneous re-capture of her prize, the CLEOPATRA 32. On leaving the LEOPARD as above he was appointed to the command, with the rank of Sub-Lieutenant, of the CHEBUCTOO schooner, also on the American station, where, in April, 1807, he was ordered to act as Lieutenant-Commander of the BREAM, another schooner, to which he was confirmed by a commission dated 11 April, 1808. His succeeding appointments were, to the command—1 June and 25 July, 1809, of the DUGUAY TROUIN and VESTA schooners, in the latter of which we find him employed until Sept. 1815 in carrying despatches to the West Indies, the coast of Africa, the Mediterranean, Newfoundland, and the coasts of Portugal, France, and Spain—5 April, 1826, for three years, of the ROYAL CHARLOTTE Revenue-vessel—1 Nov. 1832, of the MINX 3, on the Jamaica station, where he remained until the following Aug.—and, 6 Sept. 1833, of the FORESTER 3, in which vessel, attached to the force on the African coast, he had the fortune, in the course of three years and a half, to effect the capture of five slavers, having on board 1115 negroes, and to make prize of two others fully equipped. During the nine months immediately antecedent to his promotion to the rank of Commander, 28 June, 1838, Lieut. Miall officiated as Admiralty Agent on board a contract mail steam-vessel. He has since been on half-pay. AGENT—Joseph Woodhead.

MICHELL. (CAPTAIN, 1830. F-P., 23; H-P., 24.)

FREDERICK THOMAS MICHELL, born 8 April, 1788, is son of Sampson Michell, Esq., Lieutenant R.N., who by permission entered the Naval service of the late Queen of Portugal, and died an Admiral at Rio de Janeiro in Jan. 1809. He is the only brother of Lieut.-Colonel C. C. Michell, Surveyor-General at the Cape of Good Hope.

This officer entered the Royal Naval Academy 27 April, 1800, and embarked, 17 Sept. 1803, as Midshipman, on board the EURYDICE 24, Capts. John Nicholas and Wm. Hoste, employed at first in the Channel and off the coast of Africa, and then in the Mediterranean, where, on 6 Oct. 1805, we find him serving with the boats under Lieut. Andrew Pellet Green at the capture of the *Mestuo la Solidad* Spanish privateer of 6 guns, and a convoy of which the latter had charge. In the ensuing Nov., having followed Capt. Hoste into the AMPHION 32, he assisted at the defeat, although simultaneously opposed by the fire of an immense battery, of a division of about 30 Spanish gun-boats, which had come out of Algesiras in the hope of capturing a British convoy. He was afterwards present in the operations against the French on the coast of Calabria; and in the course of 1806 he became in succession attached to the TERMAGANT 18, Capt. Robt. Pettet, MORGIANA sloop, Capt. Wm. Landless, and OCEAN 98, flag-ship of Lord Collingwood—all, too, in the Mediterranean, on which station he continued until promoted to the rank of Lieutenant, 29 May, 1807. Obtaining an appointment, in the following Oct., to the ACTIVE 38, Capts. Rich. Hussey Moubray and Jas. Alex. Gordon, he aided in that ship at the capture, 26 March, 1808, of the *Friedland* brig-of-war, of 16 guns, having on board the Commander-in-Chief of the Italian marine; and was wounded in two successful boat expeditions on the coast of Albania. On the first of those occasions he was in sole charge of the boats, and evinced so much zeal, professional ability, and gallantry, that his name was brought under the special notice of the Commander-in-Chief. We may add that, out of seven casualties that occurred, his own boat sustained the loss of 1 killed and 5 wounded. The injuries he himself received were rewarded by a gratuity from the Patriotic Fund. During a subsequent servitude of five years and nine months, from June, 1809, to March, 1815, in the RHIN 38, Capt. Chas. Malcolm, Mr. Michell, as may be seen by a reference to our memoir of the latter officer, was most actively employed on the Home, West India, and Brazilian stations, assisting during the period at the capture of nine privateers (of one of which he took possession in a heavy gale), carrying altogether 103 guns and 735 men, and co-operating extensively, in 1812-13, with the patriots on the north coast of Spain. When the LAUREL frigate, in Jan. of the former year, was cast away in the Teigneuse passage, he made one trip more than any other officer to the wreck, although under fire of the enemy, and brought off the Captain and the last of the crew. On leaving the RHIN as above he joined, first the BOYNE 98, and then the QUEEN CHARLOTTE 100, bearing each the flag of Lord Exmouth, who, on the day preceding the battle of Algiers, placed him in charge, with the rank of Commander, of the whole of the battering flotilla attached to his squadron. During the ever-memorable bombardment Capt. Michell, in execution of the duty with which he had been intrusted, went on board the Dutch Admiral and every British ship engaged in the line of battle. In the midst of the conflict, when, as it was supposed, the Captain of the QUEEN CHARLOTTE had been mortally wounded, he was sent for by the Commander-in-Chief, and directed to act in his stead. He was removed from the command of the flotilla to that of the BEELZEBUB bomb, 1 Sept. 1816; and on 16 of the same month he was officially promoted. Quitting the BEELZEBUB on 21 of the ensuing Oct., Capt. Michell did not again go afloat until Dec. 1826. On 27 of that month he obtained an appointment to the RIFLEMAN 18, fitting for the Mediterranean, where, it appears, he was attached to the commissariat of the French army in the Morea, and was recommended to the consideration of the Admiralty by Sir Edw. Codrington and Sir Pulteney Malcolm, the successive Commanders-in-Chief, and by H.M. Ambassador at the Porte, in a manner that procured him a Post-commission, dated 22 Feb. 1830. His last appointments were, 23 April, 1840, and 4 Aug. 1841, to the MAGICIENNE 24, and INCONSTANT 36, in the former of which ships he united in the operations on the coast of Syria; and in the latter saved, by his zeal and promptitude, the SCOUT sloop-of-war from being lost, after she had been a week on shore on the island of Cyprus. The INCONSTANT was paid off 30 March, 1843.

Capt. Michell, whose person bears the marks of not less than eight wounds, married the youngest daughter of the late Mr. Prideaux, of Wadebridge House, near Truro, co. Cornwall. AGENT—Joseph Woodhead.

MICHELL. (COMMANDER, 1843. F-P., 19; H-P., 6.)

REYNELL CHARLES MICHELL entered the Navy 7 Feb. 1822; and, while Midshipman of the ARACHNE 18, bore an active part in the hostilities in Ava, where his conduct procured him the highest encomiums of his Captain, Henry Ducie Chads.* He was made Lieutenant, 11 Nov. 1829, into the SATELLITE 18, Capt. John Parker, attached to the force in the East Indies; and was afterwards appointed —22 Aug. 1831, to the CHALLENGER 28, Capt. Chas. Howe Fremantle, on the same station, whence he returned in 1833—15 June, 1835, as Senior, to the RALEIGH 18, Capt. Michael Quin, also in the East Indies—30 Oct. 1838, in a similar capacity, to the TYNE 26, commanded in the Mediterranean by Capt. John Townshend—6 May, 1841, still as Senior, to the HYDRA steamer, Capt. Alex. Murray, on the North America and West India station—and, 20 March and 29 July, 1842, to the MAGNIFICENT and IMAUM, receiving-ships at Jamaica, each bearing the broad pendant of Hon. Henry Dilkes Byng. He was promoted to his present rank, after having been for a few months on half-pay, 19 July, 1843; and, since 15 Sept. 1847, has been in command of the DEVASTATION steam-sloop, of 400 horse-power, on the coast of Africa. AGENTS—Holmes and Folkard.

* *Vide* Gaz. 1825, p. 1493.

MICKLETHWAIT. (LIEUTENANT, 1842.)

HENRY SHARNBORNE NATHANIEL MICKLETHWAIT, born 12 Aug. 1814, is second son of Nathaniel Micklethwait, Esq., of Taverham and Beeston Halls, co. Norfolk, by his second wife, Lady Charlotte Rous, second daughter of the first Earl of Stradbrooke; half-brother of Lieut.-Colonel Nathaniel Waldegrave Micklethwait, of the Scots Fusileer Guards; and nephew of Sir S. B. Peckham Micklethwait, some time a Captain in the 3rd Dragoon Guards, who was created a Baronet 27 July, 1838, for a personal service rendered to Her Majesty and the Duchess of Kent at St. Leonard's, co. Sussex, in Nov. 1832. His father's first wife was the Lady Maria Waldegrave, daughter of George, fourth Earl of Waldegrave.

This officer entered the Navy, from the Royal Naval College, 11 Feb. 1830; passed his examination 3 June, 1835; and, after serving for a short time as Mate of the DUBLIN 50, flag-ship in the Pacific of Rear-Admiral Rich. Thomas, was promoted to the rank of Lieutenant 3 Feb. 1842. His succeeding appointments were—on 7 of the same month, again to the DUBLIN—and, 1 Oct. 1844, and 15 April, 1845, to the ALFRED 50, Commodore John Brett Purvis, and CURAÇOA 24, Capt. Wm. Broughton, both on the south-east coast of America, whence he returned in 1847.

MIDDLETON, LORD. (RETIRED CAPTAIN, 1840.)

THE RIGHT HONOURABLE DIGBY WILLOUGHBY, LORD MIDDLETON, born 6 Nov. 1769, is only surviving son (by Octavia, daughter and co-heir of Fras. Fisher, Esq., of the Grange, Grantham, Lincolnshire) of Fras. Willoughby, Esq., of Hasseley, Notts, brother of Henry, fifth Lord Middleton. He succeeded to the peerage, as seventh Baron, on the death of his cousin, 19 June, 1835. His Lordship is a distant relative of the present Rear-Admiral Sir Nesbit Josiah Willoughby, Kt., C.B., K.C.H.

This officer entered the Navy 20 May, 1782; obtained his first commission 10 Jan. 1794; served on board the CULLODEN 74, Capt. Isaac Schomberg, in the ensuing action of 1 June; was advanced to the rank of Commander 7 May, 1802; and retired with that of Captain 10 Sept. 1840. AGENTS—Case and Loudonsack.

MIDDLETON. (LIEUT., 1811. F-P., 12; H-P., 31.)

JOHN MIDDLETON entered the Navy, 5 Feb. 1804, as Fst.-cl. Vol., on board the MONTAGU 74, Capt. Robt. Waller Otway; and on 22 Aug. 1805 was present, as Midshipman, in Admiral Hon. Wm. Cornwallis' pursuit of the French fleet into Brest, on which occasion the MONTAGU exchanged fire with the French 80-gun ship *L'Alexandre*. After assisting at the evacuation of Scylla, and further serving with Capt. Otway on board the MALTA 80, he became attached as a Supernumerary, in Nov. 1808, to the SALVADOR DEL MUNDO, flag-ship at Plymouth of Admiral Young. Joining next, in Jan. 1809, the TRIBUNE 36, Capt. Geo. Reynolds, he shared, in the course of that year, in an action fought with several Danish gun-boats in the Belt; and, on 12 May, 1810, he was afforded an opportunity of participating in a gallant conflict of two hours and a quarter, in which the same frigate, with a loss of 9 men killed and 15 wounded, beat off, on the coast of Norway, four Danish brigs-of-war, carrying altogether 74 guns. As a reward for his conduct in the latter affair, Mr. Middleton, on proceeding to the West Indies, was appointed, 28 April, 1811, Admiralty-Midshipman of the DRAGON 74, flag-ship of Sir Fras. Laforey, who, on 5 of the ensuing month, nominated him Lieutenant of the ARACHNE 18, Capt. Sam. Chambers—an act which was sanctioned by a commission bearing date 29 Oct. in the same year. He served last, from 10 April, 1812, until 5 July, 1813, and from 19 Nov. following until Jan. 1816, in his former ship the TRIBUNE, still commanded by Capt. Reynolds, and in the MEDINA 20, Capt. Henry Bourchier, on the West India and Newfoundland stations.

The Lieutenant married, 11 April, 1822, a daughter of — Scott, Esq., of Parliament Street, London.

MILDMAY. (CAPTAIN, 1828. F-P., 22; H-P., 22.)

GEORGE WILLIAM ST. JOHN MILDMAY is third son of the late Sir Henry Paulet St. John Mildmay, Bart., by Jane, eldest daughter and co-heir of Carew Mildmay, Esq., of Shawford House, co. Hants; brother of the present Sir Henry Carew St. John Mildmay, Bart.; brother-in-law of Lord Methuen, the Viscount Bolingbroke, and the Earl of Radnor; and uncle of Lieut. H. G. St. J. Mildmay, R.N. One of his brothers, Humphrey, married the eldest daughter of Lord Ashburton, and another, Carew, in Holy Orders, the youngest sister of Rear-Admiral Lord Radstock, C.B.

This officer entered the Navy, 14 Sept. 1803, as Fst.-cl. Vol., on board the ARDENT 64, Capt. Robt. Winthrop; and on 28 of the following Nov. was present, as Midshipman, at the destruction of *La Bayonnaise* French frigate of 32 guns and 200 men, in Finisterre Bay. He continued to serve in the ARDENT, also in the REVENGE 74, Capt. Robt. Moorsom, and again with Capt. Winthrop in the SYBILLE 44, on the Home station, until June, 1807; and between that period and April, 1812, was employed, chiefly in the Mediterranean, on board the CANOPUS 80, flag-ship of Rear-Admiral Geo. Martin, FAME 74, Capt. Walter Bathurst, and MENELAUS 38, Capt. Sir Peter Parker. In the CANOPUS we find him uniting, in Oct. 1809, in a chase which led to the self-destruction of the French ships-of-the-line *Robuste* and *Lion* off Cape Cette. He was confirmed a Lieutenant (after having acted for a few weeks as such) in the TRIDENT 64, bearing the flag at Malta of Rear-Admiral John Laugharne, 19 May, 1812, and was subsequently appointed—5 Aug. 1813, for passage home, to the KINGFISHER sloop, Capt. Ewell Tritton—17 Dec. following, to the LEANDER 50, Capt. Sir Geo. Ralph Collier, under whom he saw much active service on the coast of America—18 Sept. 1815, to the EUPHRATES 36, Capt. Robt. Preston, lying at Sheerness—24 Nov. 1818 (having left the last-mentioned ship in April, 1816), to the

WASP 18, Capt. Thos. Wren Carter, fitting for the West Indies, where he assisted at the capture of the Venezuelan sloop-of-war *El Libertador*, bearing the broad pendant of Commodore Chitty, and a Spanish brigantine, her prize—and, 2 July, 1821 (11 months after the WASP had been paid off), to the IPHIGENIA 42, equipping for the broad pendant of Sir Robt. Mends, Commodore of the African squadron. In command of the boats of that frigate, and of the MYRMIDON 20, Mr. Mildmay won distinction by the gallant manner in which, overcoming a desperate resistance, he effected, off the river Bonny, the capture of five vessels having on board upwards of 1800 negroes. As a reward he was promoted to the rank of Commander 10 Aug. 1822. He obtained command of the CORDELIA sloop, of 10 guns, 15 Nov. 1826; acquired Post-rank 16 Aug. 1828; and was lastly, from 14 April, 1835, until paid off at the close of 1838, employed on the Home station in the MAGICIENNE 24.

Capt. Mildmay married, 28 April, 1832, Mary, widow of John Morritt, Esq., of Rokeby, co. York, by whom he has issue. AGENTS—Hallett and Robinson.

MILDMAY. (LIEUTENANT, 1844.)

HERVEY GEORGE ST. JOHN MILDMAY is second son of Paulet St. John Mildmay, Esq., by Anna Maria, youngest daughter of the Hon. Bartholomew Bouverie; and nephew of Capt. G. W. St. John Mildmay, R.N.

This officer entered the Navy 6 Jan. 1832; passed his examination 15 March, 1838; served as Mate of the TALBOT 26, Capt. Robt. Fanshawe Stopford, at the bombardment of St. Jean d'Acre, 3 Nov. 1840; and, while on the North America and West India station, in the PIQUE 36, Capt. Hon. Montagu Stopford, was promoted to the rank of Lieutenant, 24 Feb. 1844. His appointments have since been—1 March, 1844, as Additional, to the ILLUSTRIOUS 72, bearing the flag of Sir Chas. Adam, Commander-in-Chief in North America and the West Indies—16 Oct. following, again to the PIQUE—and, 14 Oct. 1846 (soon after the latter ship had been paid off), to the THETIS 36, Capt. Henry John Codrington, now in the Mediterranean.

MILES. (COMMANDER, 1846. F-P., 18; H-P., 18.)

ALFRED MILES was born 31 Dec. 1796.

This officer entered the Navy, 21 Sept. 1811, as Fst.-cl. Boy, on board the ULYSSES 44, Capts. Henry Edw. Reginald Baker and Wm. Fothergill, flag-ship of the Prince d'Auvergne, on the Jersey station. Rejoining Capt. Baker, as Midshipman, in Sept. 1812, on board the DANNEMARK 74, he served for a time with the fleet in the North Sea, and afterwards escorted convoy to and from the Cape of Good Hope; on his return whence he became attached, in April, 1815, to the IMPREGNABLE 98, bearing the flag of Sir Josias Rowley in the Mediterranean. After a servitude of three years at Plymouth, in the SPENCER 74, Capt. Wm. Robt. Broughton, and again in the IMPREGNABLE, under the flag of Lord Exmouth, he successively joined, in the capacities of Admiralty Midshipman and Mate —9 Nov. 1818, the SEVERN Coast Blockade ship, Capt. Wm. M'Culloch, by whom he was employed at Dungeness and in the neighbourhood of New Romney—23 Feb. 1821 and 20 Dec. 1823, the CHANTICLEER 10, Capts. the Earl of Huntingdon, Henry Eden, and Burton Macnamara, and ADVENTURE 6, Capt. Wm. Henry Smyth, both on the Mediterranean station, where, in the vessel last mentioned, he aided in surveying the coast of Sardinia—17 Feb. 1825 (for a passage to the West Indies), the FERRET 10, Capt. Wm. Hobson—and 21 June, 1825, the KANGAROO, Master Commander Anthony De Mayne. Under the latter officer we find him for upwards of two years employed on Surveying service in the Crooked Passage, Bahamas, and on the coast of Cuba. In Sept. 1827, owing to his Commander having been accidentally left behind, Mr. Miles, who during the last three months had filled the post of Assistant-Surveyor, brought the KANGAROO home and paid her off. He was promoted to the rank of Lieutenant 8 Nov. following; and was afterwards appointed, in the capacity of Assistant-Surveyor—27 May, 1830, to the ÆTNA 6, Capt. Edw. Belcher, stationed on the west coast of Africa, whence he returned in Oct. 1831—and 9 Jan. 1842, and 1 Jan. 1843, to the FEARLESS 1, and TARTARUS 2, both commanded by Capt. Fred. Bullock, with whom he served on the river Thames until 11 Feb. in the latter year. He attained his present rank 15 Jan. 1846.

From Feb. 1833 until June, 1842, Commander Miles was employed as an Assistant in the Hydrographic Office at the Admiralty, to which he was reappointed 12 Feb. 1843. He married, 13 Aug. 1833, Sibilla Elizabeth, daughter of John Westby Hatfield, Esq., of Penzance, co. Cornwall, authoress of 'The Wanderer of Scandinavia,' and other poems, by whom he has issue. AGENTS—Burnett and Holmes.

MILES. (LIEUT, 1815. F-P., 10; H-P., 32.)

EDMUND MILES was born 5 Aug. 1788, at Fellrigg, co. Norfolk.

This officer entered the Navy, 25 Aug. 1805, as L. M., on board the SATURN 74, Capt. Lord Amelius Beauclerk, of which ship, on her arrival in the Mediterranean in the following Oct., he was constituted Midshipman. With the exception of three short intervals (from 10 Feb. to 5 March, 1812, from 8 Feb. to 2 May, 1814, and from 29 Sept. 1814 to 20 Jan. 1815), during which we find him serving in the HANNIBAL 74, Capt. Thos. Geo. Shortland, and acting as Lieutenant of the GOLDFINCH 10 and REGULUS 44, Capts. Edm. Waller and Robt. Ramsey, he continued employed, from April, 1809, until March, 1815, in the ROYAL OAK 74, under Lord A. Beauclerk and the late Sir Pulteney Malcolm, on the Home and North American stations, chiefly in the capacity of Master's Mate. He landed, during that period, with the small-arm men in the attack upon Walcheren in 1809; and, besides participating in much boat-service in Basque Roads and on the coast of France, witnessed, in 1814, the destruction of Commodore Barney's flotilla up the river Patuxent, and joined in the expedition against Baltimore. While attached to the REGULUS he commanded her boats at the capture of the town of St. Mary's, on the coast of Georgia. In April, 1815, at which period he had been acting for upwards of five weeks as Lieutenant of the THAMES 32, *armée-en-flûte*, Capt. Hon. Chas. Leonard Irby, he took up a commission bearing date 8 Feb. in that year. He has since been on half-pay.

MILES. (LIEUTENANT, 1825.)

LAWFORD MILES entered the Navy 4 Aug. 1806; and while serving as Midshipman of the AMETHYST, of 42 guns and 261 men, assisted at the capture, 11 Nov. 1808, off L'Orient, of the French frigate *La Thétis*, of 44 guns and 436 men, including troops, which was boarded and carried at the close of a furious conflict of more than three hours, in which the British had 19 men killed and 51 (including himself severely) wounded, and the enemy 135 killed and 102 wounded.* The injury he sustained on the occasion was at first rewarded by a gratuity from the Patriotic Fund, and subsequently by a pension of 6*l*. On 6 April, 1809, he was further present in a severe intermittent action of about four hours, which terminated in the capture, with a loss to the AMETHYST of 8 men killed and 37 wounded, of another of the enemy's frigates, *Le Niémen*, of 46 guns and 339 men, of whom 47 were slain and 73 wounded. During his stay in the AMETHYST Mr. Miles also served in the boats at the capture and destruction of a convoy off Chasseron Tower; and was a participator in the operations connected with the expedition to the Walcheren. In Aug. 1816 (he had passed his examination in the course of the preceding year) we find him on board the QUEEN CHARLOTTE 100, flag-ship of Lord Exmouth, at the

* *Vide* Gaz. 1808, p. 1555.

battle of Algiers. He was made Lieutenant, 4 April, 1825, into the MENAI 26, Capt. Houston Stewart, on the Halifax station, whence he invalided in the following April; and, since 19 Oct. 1846, has been serving as Agent on board a contract mail steam-vessel.

MILLER. (LIEUT., 1812. F-P., 13; H-P., 33.)
ALEXANDER MILLER entered the Navy, 9 March, 1801, as Fst.-cl. Vol., on board the ATLAS 98, Capt. Theoph. Jones, with whom he served off Brest until April, 1802, the greater part of the time in the capacity of Midshipman. Re-embarking, 30 July, 1803, on board the PRINCESS ROYAL 98, Capt. Jas. Vashon, he made a voyage in that ship to St. Helena; on his return whence, he removed, in Jan. 1804, to the PRINCE GEORGE 98, Capts. Joseph Sydney Yorke and Geo. Losack, attached to the fleet in the Channel. After a servitude of three years and a half on the West India and Home stations in the FORTUNÉE 36, Capt. Henry Vansittart, he was nominated, 1 Aug. 1809, Acting-Lieutenant of the BRISK 18, Capt. John Coode. Rejoining Capt. Vansittart in Feb. 1810, as Master's Mate, on board the FORTUNÉE, he sailed with him in the course of that year for the Mediterranean in escort of Rear-Admiral Thos. Fras. Fremantle; under whose personal orders he was afterwards employed in the VILLE DE PARIS 110, RODNEY 74, and as Acting-Lieutenant in the MILFORD 74. Mr. Miller (whose commission bears date 27 July, 1812) was next, 28 Aug. 1813, appointed to the VESUVIUS bomb, Capt. Wm. Hext; in which vessel he shared in the operations of 1814 in the river Gironde and assisted in throwing shells into the fortress of Blaye. He was paid off in Sept. of the latter year, and has not been since afloat.

MILLER. (LIEUTENANT, 1840.)
DAVID MILLER entered the Navy 5 Aug. 1831; passed his examination in 1839; obtained his commission 25 June, 1840; and was successively appointed—6 July, in the same year, to the RODNEY 92, Capt. Robt. Maunsell, under whom he served at the blockade of Alexandria, witnessed the siege of Barcelona, and escorted troops to the Cape of Good Hope—and, 3 Nov. 1843, to the VESTAL 26, Capt. Chas. Talbot, on the East India station, whence he returned home, as First-Lieutenant, and was paid off, in 1847.

MILLER. (LIEUTENANT, 1826.)
EDWARD CHARLES MILLER died 29 Sept. 1845, at Malta, in command of the VOLCANO steam-sloop.
This officer entered the Navy 16 June, 1808; passed his examination in 1815; was slightly wounded on board the SEVERN 40, Capt. Hon. Fred. Wm. Aylmer, at the battle of Algiers, 27 Aug. 1816; and obtained his commission 27 March, 1826. His succeeding appointments were—28 April, in the latter year, to the Coast Blockade, as Supernumerary Lieutenant of the HYPERION 42, Capt. Wm. Jas. Mingaye—27 Dec. 1831, as Senior, to the VICTOR 18, Capt. Robt. Russell, on the West India station, whence he returned at the close of 1832—and, 6 April, 1844, to the command (which he retained until the period of his death) of the VOLCANO steamer. AGENTS—Messrs. Stilwell.

MILLER. (LIEUTENANT, 1837.)
ROBERT BOYLE MILLER entered the Navy 1 Nov. 1821; passed his examination in 1827; and obtained his commission 10 Jan. 1837. His appointments have since been—8 Feb. in the latter year, to the SNAKE 16, Capt. Alex. Milne, attached to the force in North America and the West Indies, where he was superseded in March, 1838—9 March, 1839, to the command of the HORNET brigantine 6, on the same station—and, 26 April, 1845, as Senior (a few months after the HORNET had been paid off) to the MELAMPUS 42, Capt. John Norman Campbell, now in the East Indies. AGENTS—Messrs. Halford and Co.

MILLER. (LIEUTENANT, 1844.)
THOMAS MILLER entered the Navy in 1833; passed his examination 7 June, 1839; and after serving as Mate on the Mediterranean, Home, and East India stations, in the BRITANNIA 120, flag-ship of Sir John Acworth Ommanney, POWERFUL 84, Capt. Mich. Seymour, and AGINCOURT 72, bearing the flag of Sir Thos. John Cochrane, was promoted to the rank of Lieutenant 22 July, 1844. His appointments have since been—30 Aug. 1844, again to the AGINCOURT, in which ship he returned home and was paid off in 1846—and 1 Jan. 1847, to the CALEDONIA 120, bearing the flag of Sir John Louis, Admiral Superintendent at Portsmouth, where he is at present employed.

MILLER. (LIEUTENANT, 1825.)
WILLIAM DUNCAN MILLER entered the Navy 5 Nov. 1811; and was made Lieutenant, 17 Oct. 1825, into the PRIMROSE 18, Capt. Octavius Vernon (now Harcourt), on the West India station, whence he returned in July, 1827. He has been serving, since 8 Feb. 1843, as Admiralty Agent on board a contract mail steam-vessel.

MILLER. (LIEUTENANT, 1841.)
WILLIAM STEWART MILLER entered the Navy 16 May, 1831; passed his examination 2 Aug. 1837; and was for some time Mate of the CRUIZER and COLUMBINE sloops, Capts. Henry Wells Giffard and Thos. Jordaine Clarke. In the former vessel he took part in the capture of Aden in 1839; and in the COLUMBINE (of which, for his China services, he was created a Lieutenant 8 Oct. 1841*) he assisted at the first and second capture of Canton,† the reduction of Amoy and Chinghae, the destruction of the Chinese fire-rafts, and the attacks on Tsekee,‡ Woosung, and Shanghae. When next in the CHILDERS 16, Capt. Geo. Greville Wellesley, we find him participating in the operations of 1842 in the Yang-tse-Kiang. He returned to England in that vessel in the summer of 1844, and was subsequently appointed—31 May, 1845, to the VERNON 50, flag-ship of Rear-Admiral Sam. Hood Inglefield, on the south-east coast of America—and, 31 July, 1846, to the command, on the same station, of the DOLPHIN brigantine of 3 guns, which he brought home and put out of commission in 1847. AGENT—J. Hinxman.

MILLETT. (LIEUT., 1815. F-P., 19; H-P., 22.)
JOHN MILLETT entered the Navy, 19 Feb. 1806, as Midshipman, on board the EXPERIMENT receiving-ship at Falmouth, Lieut.-Commanders Jas. Manderson and Jas. Fagan; and in the course of the same year, after having cruized for a short time in the GIBRALTAR 80, Capt. Wm. Lukin, joined the MARS 74, commanded at first by the same officer, and next by Capts. Jas. Katon, John Surman Carden, and Henry Roper. Continuing in that ship until April, 1812, he served with a squadron under Sir Sam. Hood at the capture, off Rochefort, 25 Sept. 1806, of four heavy French frigates, two of which, the *Gloire* 46 and *Infatigable* 44, struck to the MARS—accompanied the expedition of 1807 to Copenhagen, where, throughout the siege, he was actively employed in command of the boats—was much engaged in affording protection to the Baltic trade—and when at Lisbon, in 1810, was sent on shore on detached service at Fort St. Juliaõ. After a short attachment at Portsmouth to the GOLIATH 74, Capt. Edw. Leveson Gower, he removed in June, 1812, to the COSSACK 22, Capt. Wm. King, off Cadiz; and in Dec. of the same year he became Master's Mate of the ABOUKIR 74, Capts. Geo. Parker and Norborne Thompson. In that ship, in April 1814, Mr. Millett witnessed the fall of Genoa. He took up, in May, 1815, a commission bearing date 15 Feb. in that year; was next, from 22 Jan. 1825 until May, 1827, employed in the Coast Blockade as Supernumerary-Lieutenant of the RAMILLIES 74, Capts. Wm. M'Cul-

* *Vide* Gaz. 1841, p. 2539. † *V.* Gaz. 1841, pp. 1505, 2505. ‡ *V.* Gaz. 1842, p. 2391.

loch and Hugh Pigot; and since 24 Oct. 1840 has been in command of a station in the Coast Guard.

He married, 16 April, 1832, a daughter of — Cole, Esq., Purser and Paymaster R.N.

MILLS. (LIEUTENANT, 1827.)

HENRY FORSTER MILLS entered the Navy 23 Aug. 1814; passed his examination in 1821; and obtained his commission 30 April, 1827. His appointments have since been—27 June, 1829, to the ALGERINE 10, on the South American station, where he continued, part of the time as First-Lieutenant, under Capt. Hon. John Fred. Fitzgerald De Roos, until the close of 1833—6 Jan. 1837, in the capacity last mentioned, to the TRINCULO 16, Capt. Henry Edw. Coffin, attached to the force off Lisbon, with which he served until superseded in May, 1838—and, 17 April, 1847, to the VICTORY 104, Capt. John Pasco, guard-ship at Portsmouth, where he is now employed. AGENTS—Messrs. Halford and Co.

MILNE. (CAPTAIN, 1839. F-P., 22; H-P., 8.)

ALEXANDER MILNE, born in Nov. 1806, is second and youngest son of the late Admiral Sir David Milne, G.C.B., by his first wife, Grace, daughter of Sir Alex. Purves, Bart.

This officer entered the Royal Naval College 8 Feb. 1817; and embarked in 1819 on board the LEANDER 50, Capt. Edw. Chetham, bearing his father's flag in North America. In June, 1820, we find him joining the CONWAY 26, Capt. Basil Hall; in which vessel, and in the RAMILLIES 74, and GANGES 84, both commanded by Capt. Edw. Brace, ALBION 74, Capt. Sir Wm. Hoste, and GANGES again, Capts. Pat. Campbell and Sam. Hood Inglefield, bearing the flag for some time of Sir Robt. Waller Otway, he continued employed on the South American, West India, Home, and Brazilian stations, latterly as Mate and Acting-Lieutenant, until June, 1827. He then removed, in the capacity last mentioned, to the CADMUS 10, Capts. Chas. Gordon and Sir Thos. Raikes Trigge Thompson, also on the coast of Brazil; where he further served in that vessel (being confirmed to her by commission dated 8 Sept. 1827) until her return to England in April, 1830; on 25 Nov. in which year he was advanced to the rank of Commander. Obtaining an appointment, 26 Dec. 1836, to the SNAKE 16, Capt. Milne, on his arrival in that sloop in the West Indies, had the good fortune, during a cruize off the island of Cuba, to effect the capture, 23 Nov. 1837, of the Portuguese brigantine *Arrogante*, having on board 406 slaves, and, 5 Dec. following, of the *Matilda* Spanish schooner, laden with 259 slaves. He was made Post, 30 Jan. 1839, into the CROCODILE 26; and, in Nov. 1840, after having served in various parts of the North America and West India station (where he made prize of the Spanish slaver *Mercedita*, and had for some months charge of the Newfoundland and Labrador fisheries), he removed to the CLEOPATRA 26. In that vessel, when in the West Indies, he took, 27 Jan. 1841, the *Secundo Rosario* Spanish schooner, carrying 284 slaves. Returning, in the ensuing March, to the CROCODILE, Capt. Milne continued in her, affording protection in the mean while to the fisheries in the river St. Lawrence, until paid off in Nov. of the same year. He was next, from 27 April, 1842, until April, 1845, employed in the CALEDONIA 120, as Flag-Captain to his father, Commander-in-Chief at Devonport; and from 7 Oct. 1846 until Dec. 1847 he officiated, in the ST. VINCENT 120, in a similar capacity under Sir Chas. Ogle, Port-Admiral at Portsmouth. Since the date last mentioned Capt. Milne has filled a seat at the Board of Admiralty. AGENTS—Messrs. Halford and Co.

MILNE, G.C.B., K.S.J., K.W.N. (ADMIRAL OF THE WHITE, 1841. F-P., 30; H-P., 36.)

SIR DAVID MILNE was born in May, 1763, at Musselburgh, near Edinburgh, and died 5 May, 1845, while on his passage, in the CLARENCE steamer, from London to Granton Pier, in Scotland. He was son of David Milne, Esq., merchant, of Edinburgh, by a daughter of —— Vernor, Esq., of Musselburgh.

This officer entered the Navy, 26 May, 1779, as Midshipman, on board the CANADA 74, Capts. Hugh Dalrymple, Sir Geo. Collier, and Hon. Wm. Cornwallis. While in that ship, in which he continued until the close of 1782, he accompanied Admiral Darby to the relief of Gibraltar in 1780; assisted, after having been repeatedly engaged with the Spanish gun-boats and batteries, at the capture, despite a brave defence, of the *Santa Leocadia* Spanish frigate of 44 guns; was with the fleet under Sir Sam. Hood when thrice attacked, in Jan. 1782, by the Comte de Grasse at St. Kitt's; enacted a warm part in Rodney's famous actions of 9 and 12 April (for his conduct on the latter of which occasions he was awarded the rating of Master's Mate); and was present in the ensuing Sept. in a dreadful hurricane, which only allowed the CANADA and JASON, out of 10 ships of war, all homeward bound, to reach their destination. On leaving the CANADA, as above, Mr. Milne was received on board the ELIZABETH 74, Capt. Kingsmill, fitting for the East Indies; but being in a few weeks paid off, and having no immediate prospect of employment in his own profession, he entered the merchant service, in which he continued, part of the time in the East Indies, until the renewal of war with France in 1793, when he was afforded an opportunity of joining the BOYNE 98, bearing the flag of Sir John Jervis, who, on his arrival in the West Indies, promoted him, 13 Jan. 1794, to a Lieutenancy in the BLANCHE of 38 guns, Capts. Christopher Parker, Robt. Faulknor, and Chas. Sawyer. Under the second-named of those officers we find him actively employed in the proximate operations against the French islands, particularly in an attack upon one of the Saintes, where he landed and assisted in taking the enemy by a *coup-de-main*. On her return to the West Indies, after conveying H.R.H. the Duke of Kent to Halifax, the BLANCHE was stationed off Guadeloupe, the whole of which island, with the exception of Fort Matilda, had again fallen into the hands of the French; and Lieut. Milne was in consequence repeatedly employed on detached service. On one occasion he so distinguished himself by the manner in which he boarded and brought a vessel out from under a pelting fire from the batteries in Mahout Bay, that Capt. Faulknor, on being presented by him with the French commander's sword, returned it to him with many flattering compliments; and on another, 30 Dec. 1794, with an equal degree of gallantry, he cut out a large armed schooner of 8 guns from beneath a destructive fire from a fort and a body of troops, not fifty yards distant, in the island of Deseada. On 5 Jan. 1795 it was his fortune to be Second-Lieutenant of the BLANCHE when, after a deadly action of nearly four hours and a half, and a loss to herself, out of 198 men, of 8 persons (including Capt. Faulknor) killed and 21 wounded, she effected the capture of the French frigate *La Pique*, of 38 guns and about 279 men, of whom 76 were killed and 110 wounded. As the boats of both ships, at the end of the conflict, were either completely destroyed or unable to float, Mr. Milne, followed by 10 seamen, swam to the conquered vessel, and took possession of her.* As a reward for his valour on so dashing an occasion, he was promoted, as soon as the intelligence reached the Admiralty, to the command of the INSPECTOR sloop; but, prior to the receipt of his commission, he appears to have been further present in the BLANCHE in the unsuccessful attack on Ste. Lucie, and, until the troops were obliged to re-embark and return to Martinique, to have been constantly employed in her boats. When at length apprized of his promotion, the INSPECTOR being on a distant service, Capt. Milne was successively nominated Acting-Captain of the QUEBEC 32 and ALARM 32; in the latter of which frigates, having previously escorted convoy to the northward of the islands, he destroyed, in the neighbourhood of

* *Vide* Gaz. 1795, p. 148.

Puerto Rico, 30 May, 1795, the French corvette *La Liberté* of 20 guns, with clothing and ammunition on board for the French army at Guadeloupe. On the departure of the INSPECTOR, shortly after he had joined her, for England, he was induced, by an offer from Sir John Laforey, the Commander-in-Chief, of the first Post vacancy that should occur, to take charge of the transport department under him; a service in which, by collecting a great number of transports from all parts of the West Indies, which had been uselessly lying there at a great expense, and sending them to England, he saved an immense sum to the nation. He was also employed at Martinique, which was daily threatened with an attack from Guadeloupe and Ste. Lucie; and had the satisfaction, while there, of witnessing the perpetual repulse of the enemy. On 2 Oct. 1795, as had been promised, he was made Post into the MATILDA frigate; but so necessary did the Commander-in-Chief find it to have by him an officer of his experience and active disposition, that he ordered that ship to cruize under her First-Lieutenant. At the close of the year, however, the command of LA PIQUE, the frigate he had so materially contributed to capture, becoming vacant, he solicited the Admiral for the appointment with claims that were not to be denied; and he accordingly, in Jan. 1796, joined her at Barbadoes. On 9 of the ensuing March, being on a cruize in the neighbourhood of that island in quest of a part of the convoy which had been dispersed in the memorable gales under Sir Hugh Cloberry Christian, Capt. Milne succeeded in making prize of the *Lacédémonien* French privateer of 14 guns and 90 men, and in chasing a ship of 20 guns, a brig, and a schooner off the station. He next, in April, 1796, accompanied the expedition against the Dutch colonies of Demerara, Essequibo, and Berbice; and in the course of the same year, feeling himself justified by circumstances, although without any orders to do so, he took charge of a valuable convoy and returned to England—a step, however, which the Admiralty sanctioned with its approbation. After the general mutiny at Spithead, and a second exhibition of insubordination on board LA PIQUE in particular, which was completely subdued by a mixture of intrepidity, firmness, and clemency on the part of Capt. Milne, he continued attached to the force on the coast of France, until there wrecked at the capture, 29 June, 1798, of the French frigate *La Seine* of 42 guns and 610 men (including troops), after a running action of about five hours, in which the enemy sustained a loss of 170 killed and 100 wounded, and the British (whose force consisted, in addition to LA PIQUE, of the JASON 38, and MERMAID 32) of 9 killed and 18 wounded.* Being acquitted by court-martial of all blame in the loss of his ship, Capt. Milne was soon afterwards appointed to the command of LA SEINE, whose armament, upon her being added to the British Navy, had been increased to 48 guns, and her complement of men fixed at 281. In Oct. 1799 he sailed with the annual store-ship for the coast of Africa, whence, at the end of four months, during which period he had gallantly gone in pursuit of three French frigates, and had lost, owing to the sanitory nature of his arrangements, but one man from the unhealthiness of the climate, he proceeded with convoy to the West Indies; subsequently to his arrival on which station, and when in the Mona Passage, he had the good fortune to effect, 21 Aug. 1800, the capture of *La Vengeance* of 52 guns and 326 men, an achievement which was the result of a brilliant action of two hours and a half, attended with a loss to LA SEINE of 13 men killed and 29 wounded, and to her opponent of more than twice that number. Notwithstanding that the performance was highly and justly lauded in the despatches of the Commander-in-Chief, Lord Hugh Seymour,† and that it was allowed to glitter among the brightest exploits of the war, Capt. Milne received neither honour nor reward. After passing some time in the blockade of the Mississippi, where he made prize of several vessels, he returned to England, and in April, 1802, was paid off. Resuming command of LA SEINE in April of the following year, he joined the force under Admiral Thornbrough in the North Sea; where, on 21 July, 1803, while proceeding to blockade the Texel, he had the misfortune, owing to the ignorance of his pilots, to be wrecked, by running on a sandbank off Schelling Island. In 1811, having been for about six years very efficiently employed in command of the Frith of Forth district of Sea Fencibles, he obtained an appointment to the IMPÉTUEUX 74; in which ship, and in the DUBLIN 74, ROYAL CHARLOTTE yacht, and VENERABLE and BULWARK 74's, he served with activity on the Baltic, North Sea, Lisbon, Channel, and North American stations until informed of his advancement to Flag-rank, which took place 4 June, 1814. While in the last-mentioned ship, he had command of a squadron in Boston Bay, and was engaged in blockading the different harbours and rivers along that part of the American coast, where he destroyed so many of the enemy's vessels that their trade was totally ruined. He also served at the capture of Castine, in the Penobscot; and when afterwards, in Oct. 1814, at Halifax, there being at the time no line-of-battle ship off Boston, he volunteered and was sent thither for the purpose of watching such vessels as might be in the port fitting for sea. He continued on this service (capturing intermediately the *Harlequin* privateer, of 300 tons, 10 long 12-pounders, and 115 men) until the close of the month; and then, having been superseded in the BULWARK in consequence of his promotion, returned to England a passenger in the LOIRE frigate. On 2 May, 1816, Rear-Admiral Milne (who, to his mortification, had been omitted in the extension of the Order of the Bath in the preceding year) hoisted his flag on board the LEANDER 50, as Commander-in-Chief in North America and on the Lakes of Canada. At his urgent request, however, he was allowed, previously to his departure, to join, as second in command, the expedition fitting out under Lord Exmouth against Algiers; where, on the memorable 27 Aug., with his flag in the IMPREGNABLE 104, he afforded his Lordship such honourable and cordial support, that he was induced to send him home in charge of the despatch announcing the glorious result of the battle.* Owing to the dilapidated condition of his own ship, the LEANDER, the Rear-Admiral was under the necessity of returning to England in the GLASGOW 50. Subsequently to his arrival he had the gratification, as well for the brilliancy of his former services as for his recent meritorious conduct, of being nominated a K.C.B., with additional armorial bearings, 19 Sept. 1816. He was voted also the thanks of both Houses of Parliament; obtained the Royal permission to accept and wear the insignia of the Orders of Wilhelm of the Netherlands and St. Januarius of Naples, conferred upon him by the Sovereigns of those countries; received from the city of London its freedom, accompanied by a handsome sword; and was presented by Lord Exmouth with a gold snuff-box, having on it a device expressive of the effects resulting from the ever-famous battle in which they had fought. In 1817 Sir David Milne proceeded to Halifax for the purpose of assuming command, as originally intended, of the British squadron in North America, whence he returned in the summer of 1819—receiving, previously to his departure, a very flattering address from the merchants at Bermuda. He attained the rank of Vice-Admiral 27 May, 1825; was created a G.C.B. 4 July, 1840; and became a full Admiral 23 Nov. 1841. From 21 April, 1842, until within a few days of his decease, he filled the post of Commander-in-Chief at Devonport, with his flag on board the CALEDONIA 120.

Sir David Milne, who was a Magistrate and Deputy-Lieutenant for co. Berwick, was returned to Parliament in 1820 as Member for the town of

* *Vide* Gaz. 1798, p. 630. † *V.* Gaz. 1800, p. 1256.

* *Vide* Gaz. 1816, p. 1790. During the conflict Rear-Admiral Milne received a severe contusion in consequence of a large round shot passing between his thighs. Although so serious as to occasion lameness for several months, he would not allow it to be reported.

Berwick-upon-Tweed. He married, first, in 1804, Grace, daughter of Sir Alex. Purves, Bart.; and (that lady dying in 1814), secondly, 28 Nov. 1819, a daughter of the late Geo. Stephen, Esq., of the island of Grenada. By his former marriage he had issue two sons, the younger of whom, the present Capt. Alex. Milne, R.N., is a Lord of the Admiralty. AGENTS—Messrs. Halford and Co.

MILNE. (RETIRED COMMANDER, 1844. F-P., 16; H-P., 32.)

WILLIAM MILNE entered the Navy, in Jan. 1799, as Midshipman, on board the SWINGER gun-brig, Lieut.-Commander John Lucas, part of the force employed in the ensuing expedition to Holland, where he served on shore at a battery in the first engagement fought after the landing of the troops. Joining next, in Feb. 1800, the ELEPHANT 74, Capts. Thos. Foley and Geo. Dundas, he served for some time at Portsmouth and in the Channel under the flags of Sir Rich. Bickerton and Sir Chas. Cotton, and on 2 April, 1801, was present under Lord Nelson in the action off Copenhagen. Proceeding subsequently to the West Indies, he there, in the course of 1803, witnessed the capture of *Le Duquesne* 74, and of *La Créole* of 44 guns, with the French General Morgan and 530 troops on board; assisted at the boarding and carrying, by night, of a war-schooner under Cape François; and beheld, with the evacuation of the latter place, the surrender of a French squadron with the remains of General Rochambeau's army. At the commencement of 1805, about which period he passed his examination, he removed to the RUBY 64, Capt. Chas. Rowley, stationed at first in the Channel and then in the North Sea; where, while Master's Mate of the MAJESTIC 74, flag-ship of Vice-Admiral Thos. Macnamara Russell, he was allowed, from 25 March to 10 April, 1806, to act as Lieutenant of the AIMABLE frigate, Capt. Clotworthy Upton. Being successively nominated, 28 March and 7 July, 1807, Acting-Sub-Lieutenant and Sub-Lieutenant of the CARRIER 4, Lieut.-Commander Robt. Ramsey, he served, in the capacity last mentioned, at the capture of Heligoland, and in the expedition against Copenhagen; after the fall of which place he was promoted, 3 Oct. 1807, to the acting-command of the CARRIER, and sent home in charge of despatches from Admiral Gambier, Lord Cathcart, and Mr. Pierrepont, British Minister in Sweden. During the passage, Mr. Milne, on 14 Nov., had the good fortune to fall in with and capture the French privateer cutter *L'Actif*, pierced for 8 guns, but carrying only 2, with 16 brass musketoons mounted on swivels, and manned with a crew of 32 men, all trained marksmen from the camp at Boulogne.* His conduct on the occasion being highly approved by the Admiralty, he was confirmed in the rank of Lieutenant, and in the command of the CARRIER, by commission dated 19 Nov. 1807. In the following year we find him present in the same vessel in an attack made on the town of Boulogne. It was his lot, however, on 5 Feb. 1809, after an action with two batteries near Etaples, in which he had been twice wounded, to be wrecked and taken prisoner with the whole of his crew; but so strenuous were his exertions to avoid the catastrophe, that they had the effect of eliciting a strong testimonial from the French General Lorcet, to whom the surrender was made. On his release from captivity at the end of the war, he was fully acquitted by court-martial, and was immediately, 27 July, 1814, appointed First-Lieutenant of the GALATEA 36, Capt. Woodley Losack, with an assurance from Sir Joseph Yorke, then a Lord of the Admiralty, of being sent out on promotion to the East Indies. The destination of the ship being unfortunately for him changed to Newfoundland, he was compelled, in Oct. 1814, within a short time of his arrival on that station, to invalid in consequence of an inflammation in the lungs produced by the climate. During the rebellion of 1837-8, in Upper Canada, Lieut. Milne, at the period a resident there, raised about 700 men for its defence, and, as Major of Volunteers under Colonel Sir Allan MacNab, rendered very important and efficient service on the frontier and in the London district. He also distinguished himself by his conduct under the present Capt. Andw. Drew, R.N., at the reduction of Navy Island, in the river Niagara, where he commanded a division of boats; and, besides having for some time charge of the naval brigade at Chippewa, he so signalized himself by his exertions on Lake Erie, especially by his efforts in rescuing the COLBORNE hired armed steamer from an attempt made by the insurgents to destroy her, that he was appointed a Captain of the Provincial Navy, and placed in command of that vessel. He accepted his present rank 24 July, 1844. AGENTS —Messrs. Ommanney.

* *Vide* Gaz. 1807, p. 1555.

MILWARD. (REAR-ADMIRAL, 1846. F-P., 19; H-P., 35.)

CLEMENT MILWARD entered the Navy, 26 Oct. 1793, as A.B., on board the ALARM 32, Capt. Lewis Robertson; and in the following year was severely wounded, as Midshipman of that frigate, in an attack upon Pointe-à-Pitre, Guadeloupe. After two years of servitude, still on the West India station, in the VETERAN 64, and SOLEBAY 32, both commanded by Capt. Wm. Henry Bayntun, and, as Master's Mate, in the ETRUSCO, Capt. Jas. Hanson, he joined, in Aug. 1796, the PRINCE OF WALES 98, flag-ship of Rear-Admiral Henry Harvey, under whom, in Feb. 1797, he beheld the surrender of Trinidad. In Oct. of the latter year he became Acting-Lieutenant of the FAVORITE sloop, Capt. Lord Camelford;* and in Aug. 1799, being then again in the PRINCE OF WALES, under Lord Hugh Seymour, he assisted, as Midshipman, at the capture of Surinam. On that occasion he was again invested with the rank of Acting-Lieutenant, and appointed to the SURINAM, a prize-corvette of 20 guns; to which vessel, commanded by Capt. Christopher Cole, the Admiralty confirmed him by commission dated 8 July, 1800. Invaliding home from the West Indies in Oct. 1802, he subsequently joined—12 July, 1803, the PHAETON 38, Capts. Geo. Cockburn and John Wood, in which frigate, after serving off Havre de Grace, and conveying Mr. Merry, the British Minister Plenipotentiary, to the United States, he proceeded to the East Indies, and was afforded, we believe, an opportunity of participating, when in company with the HARRIER sloop, in an action of two hours, fought, 2 Aug. 1805, with the French 36-gun frigate *Sémillante* and several batteries at the entrance of the Straits of St. Bernardino, Philippine Islands—3 April, 1807, the RUSSELL 74, Capt. Thos. Gordon Caulfeild, also in the East Indies—19 Feb. 1808, for a passage home, the MONMOUTH 64, Capt. Edw. Durnford King—and in Sept. 1808, and March, 1809, the POMPÉE and BELLEISLE 74's, both commanded by Capt. Cockburn, under whom, in the POMPÉE, he assisted at the reduction of Martinique. On his return to England in the BELLEISLE with the surrendered Governor and garrison of the latter island, he was presented with a Commander's commission dated 14 June, 1809. He was next, 28 Dec. 1810, and 8 Nov. 1811, appointed to the ELK and MERCURY sloops, on the West India station; where, on 1 Jan. 1813, he was nominated Acting-Captain of the HERALD 20. Being confirmed to that vessel 28 May following, and continuing in her until 11 Oct. 1815, he succeeded in effecting the capture of several of the enemy's vessels, and took an active part in the expedition against New Orleans. Not having been further employed, he accepted his present rank 1 Oct. 1846. AGENTS—Messrs. Halford and Co.

MINCHIN. (COMMANDER, 1821. F-P., 18, H-P., 38.)

WILLIAM MINCHIN died 7 Sept. 1845.

This officer entered the Navy, 15 Jan. 1790, as A.B., on board the ADVICE cutter, Lieut.-Com-

* Mr. Milward was the officer from whom Lord Camelford took the pistol on the well known occasion on which he shot Lieut. Chas Peterson, of H.M.S. WOOLWICH, for mutinous conduct at English Harbour, Antigua, 13 Jan. 1798.

mander Henry Wray, attached to the force at Jamaica; and, between March of the following year and April, 1794, was employed on the Home and Mediterranean stations, the last 16 months as Master's Mate, in the SCOUT and ORESTES sloops, Capts. Rich. Runwa Bowyer, Sir Harry Burrard, Graham Moore, Solomon Ferris, and Lord Augustus Fitz-Roy; with the latter of whom he further, until Feb. 1796, served in the POMONA, AMPHITRITE, and IMPÉRIEUSE frigates. Being promoted (from the ROMNEY 50, flag-ship at Newfoundland of Sir Jas. Wallace) to a Lieutenancy, 27 Dec. 1796, in the STAR sloop, Capt. David Atkins, he served in that vessel in the Channel and at the Cape of Good Hope until Feb. 1799; and he was next, between July, 1800, and Oct. 1803, employed, on the Java, Baltic, and West India stations, in the CAMEL store-ship, Capt. John Lee, SCOUT again, Capt. Geo. Ormsby, MONARCH 74, Capts. Jas. Robt. Mosse and Wm. Bligh, BLENHEIM 74, Capt. Peter Turner Bover, and EMERALD 36, Capt. Jas. O'Bryen. In the MONARCH he fought and bled at Copenhagen * He afterwards served on the Home and Newfoundland stations—from Sept. 1804, to May, 1807, in the WARRIOR 74, Capts. Wm. Bligh and Sam. Hood Linzee, TISIPHONE sloop, Capt. Wm. Williams Foote, and DIANA 38, Capt. Thos. Jas. Maling—from Sept. 1815 to Aug. 1816, in the ALBION and QUEEN 74's, each under the orders of Capt. Jas. Walker—and from Nov. 1819, until awarded a second promotal commission, 19 July, 1821, in command of the PELTER gun-brig. He did not afterwards go afloat.

MINGAYE. (CAPT., 1822. F-P., 24; H-P., 25.)

WILLIAM JAMES MINGAYE entered the Navy, 16 Sept. 1798, as a Volunteer, on board the ANSON of 46 guns, Capt. Philip Chas. Durham; and in the course of the ensuing month was present, we believe, at the defeat of the squadron under Commodore Bompart, carrying troops for the invasion of Ireland, and (in company with the KANGAROO 18) at the capture, with a loss to the ANSON of 2 killed and 13 wounded, of *La Loire* of 46 guns and 664 men (including troops), 46 of whom were killed and 71 wounded. After an attendance of some time upon the King off Weymouth, he accompanied Capt. Durham, in Feb. 1801, into the ENDYMION 40, in which ship, besides assisting at the capture of *La Furie* privateer of 14 guns, he escorted a convoy of 10 Indiamen home from St. Helena. In 1802 he became in succession attached to the ALARM and AMAZON frigates, both commanded by Capt. Wm. Parker: and on next joining the MAGNIFICENT 74, Capt Wm. Henry Jervis, he was wrecked on the Black Rocks off Brest, in March, 1804. On 8 Feb. 1805, having in the interim served with Capt. Jervis on board the TONNANT 80, he was nominated Sub-Lieutenant of the TICKLER gun-brig, Lieut.-Commander John W. Skinner, stationed off Boulogne, where he remained until presented with a Lieutenant's commission dated 6 July following. Joining then the BELLIGERENT 64, Capt. Hon. Geo. Byng, he served on shore with the naval brigade under that officer at the capture of the Cape of Good Hope in Jan. 1806;† after which he was, it appears, appointed—10 June, 1806, to the BOMBAY *alias* CEYLON 32, Capt. Wm. Jones Lye, on the East India station, whence he invalided 10 Aug. 1809—19 March and 31 Dec. 1812, to the COSSACK 22 and DRUID frigate, both commanded in the Mediterranean by Capt. Wm. King, with whom he continued until 5 July, 1813—and 5 March, 1816, and 21 July, 1817, as Senior, to the ERIDANUS 36, and ROYAL GEORGE yacht, Capts. Wm. King and Hon. Chas. Paget, each employed on Home Service. As Commander, a rank he attained 2 Oct. 1817, Capt. Mingaye served, from 1 Oct. 1818 until paid off in Jan. 1822, in the CAMELION 10, on the Portsmouth station. He was advanced to Post-rank on 29 of the month last mentioned; became Acting-Captain, 23 July ensuing, of the ROYAL GEORGE yacht: obtained command, in July, 1824, of the ROMNEY 50, *armée-en-flûte*, fitting at Chatham; and, from 8 Jan. 1825 until the abolition of the Service in 1831, was in command of the HYPERION 42, lying in Newhaven Harbour, on the establishment of a third-rate, for the purposes of the extended Coast Blockade.

* *Vide* Gaz. 1801, p. 404.

† *V.* Gaz. 1806.

MITCHELL. (LIEUT., 1815. F-P., 16; H-P., 27.)

GEORGE MITCHELL entered the Navy, 27 April, 1804, as Midshipman, on board the EAGLE 74, Capts. David Colby and Chas. Rowley, in which ship he continued to serve until 30 Aug. 1811. At first he was employed in the North Sea under the flags of Admirals Edw. Thornbrough and Thos. Macnamara Russell; he afterwards, in May, 1806, assisted at the capture of the island of Capri, on the coast of Italy; and in 1810, having previously taken part in the gun-boat service in the expedition to the Walcheren, he aided in conveying powder to Fort Matagorda, when attacked by the French during the siege of Cadiz. Joining next, in Jan. 1812 (he had passed his examination 15 Jan. 1811), the SAPPHO sloop, Capt. Hayes O'Grady, he served for two years in that vessel on the Jamaica station, and was often employed in her boats in effecting the well-resisted capture of slave-vessels and other contraband traders. In Nov. 1815, after he had been attached for three months as a Supernumerary to the NAMUR 74, flag-ship of Sir Thos. Williams at Sheerness, and for 14 as Master's Mate and Acting-Lieutenant to the TANAIS 38, Capt. Jos. James, on the Jamaica station, he took up a commission dated 3 March in that year. His next and last appointment was, 27 Dec. 1825, to the Coast Blockade, in which service he continued, with his name on the books of the RAMILLIES 74, Capt. Hugh Pigot, until March, 1830.

MITCHELL. (LIEUT., 1817. F-P., 22; H-P., 14.)

LEWIS DUNBAR MITCHELL, born 3 Dec. 1796, is a relative of Admiral Sir Robt. Calder, Bart., K.C B, who died in 1818.

This officer entered the Navy, 28 March, 1811, as Fst.-cl. Vol, on board the THESEUS 74, Capt. Wm. Prowse. After a servitude of more than two years in the North Sea—a great part of the time in the capacity of Midshipman—and a voyage to St. Helena for the purpose of convoying home a large China fleet, he removed, in Dec. 1813, to the GRANICUS 36, Capt. Wm. Furlong Wise. In that ship, which was at first employed off the coasts of Spain and Portugal, he had charge of the signals, and was severely wounded in the leg at the bombardment of Algiers 27 Aug. 1816.* In Jan. and April, 1817, he successively joined, at Plymouth, the IMPREGNABLE 104, flag-ship of Sir John Thos. Duckworth, and the LEE 20, Capt. John Pasco; and on 29 Sept. in the same year, at which period he was serving in the West Indies on board the PRIMROSE 18, Capt. Chas. Geo. Rodney Phillott, he was promoted to a Lieutenancy in the LARNE 20, Capt. Abraham Lowe. He went back to the PRIMROSE in Oct. 1818; and (that vessel being paid off on 19 of the ensuing month) was afterwards appointed—29 Nov. 1825, to the Coast Blockade, as Supernumerary-Lieutenant of the RAMILLIES 74, Capt. Hugh Pigot—19 Nov. 1828, to the Coast Guard—3 Oct. 1831, to a three years' command of the GREYHOUND Revenue-cruizer—and 22 Dec. 1837, to the office of Admiralty Agent on board a contract mail steam-vessel. From the aggravated effects of the wound he had received at Algiers, Lieut. Mitchell was under the necessity, in June, 1842, of resigning the situation last named. Although prevented, from the same cause, from resuming the active duties of his profession, he has hitherto been unsuccessful in his endeavours to obtain a pension.

MITCHELL. (LIEUT., 1813. F-P., 23; H-P., 49.)

RICHARD MITCHELL entered the Navy, about 1775, as Gunner's Servant, on board the ANTELOPE

* *Vide* Gaz. 1816, p. 1793.

50, Capt. Dixon, in which ship, bearing the flag of Admiral Gayton, he was for four years employed in the West Indies. In 1781 he joined the DRAGON 74, receiving-ship at Portsmouth, Capt. Osborn; and he next, between 1782 and the commencement of the French revolutionary war, served, as Midshipman, on the East India, Newfoundland, Mediterranean, and Home stations, in the DEFENCE 74, and ISIS 50, both commanded by Capt. Thos. Newnham, MERLIN sloop, Capt. Edw. Pakenham, BEDFORD 74, Capt. Robt. Mann, AQUILON 32, Capt. Robt. Montagu, FORMIDABLE 98, bearing the flag of Admiral Leveson Gower, and EDGAR 74, Capt. Albemarle Bertie. He was made Lieutenant, about 1796, into the TOURTERELLE, Capts. Cook and Fellows; was subsequently, from the same year until the peace of Amiens, employed in the CHAPMAN armed ship, Capts. Cumberland and Keen, PYLADES sloop, Capt. M'Kenzie, and MONMOUTH 64, Capts. Deans and Hart; and, during the late war, became attached for short periods, to the EXPERIMENT 44, Capt. Geo. Chas. Mackenzie, COMUS 32, Capt. Conway Shipley, HYACINTH sloop, Capt. John Davie, LATONA 38, Capt. Sotheby, and DEVASTATION bomb, Capt. Thos. Alexander. He accompanied, in the MONMOUTH, the expedition to Egypt in 1801; and in the other ships he appears to have been chiefly engaged on Home service. The commission he at present holds bears date 18 Dec. 1813.

MITCHELL. (RETIRED COMMANDER, 1838. F-P., 17; H-P., 34.)

SPALDING MITCHELL entered the Navy, 28 Nov. 1796, as Fst.-cl. Vol., on board the HARPY sloop, Capt. Henry Bazely, on the Home station; where, from July, 1797, until May, 1801, he served with Capt. Fras. Fayerman in the BEAULIEU 40 and TERRIBLE 74, and with Capt. Stephen Poyntz again in the BEAULIEU; in which ship, under the former officer, he fought as Midshipman in the action off Camperdown 11 Oct. 1797. Being nominated in March, 1803, Master's Mate (after a servitude of eight months as Admiralty-Midshipman in the SIRIUS frigate, Capt. Wm. Prowse) of the MALTA 80, Capt. Edward Buller, he served in that ship in Sir Robt. Calder's action with the combined fleets of France and Spain, 22 July, 1805. He became Sub-Lieutenant, 21 Sept. following, of the SPRIGHTLY cutter, Lieut.-Commander Sam. Gordon; and, being awarded a full Lieutenant's commission, 22 Jan. 1806, was next, from 14 April in that year until 18 July, 1810, employed, in that capacity, in the CHARWELL sloop, Capts. Philip Dumaresq, Edwin Henry Chamberlayne, Robt. Lisle Coulson, Hon. Wm. Gordon, and Henry Thompson. He was in consequence present in the operations of 1807 against Monte Video and Buenos Ayres; he also, in 1809, being at the time First-Lieutenant, took command of the boats, and brought off a vessel which the CHARWELL had driven ashore on the Ile de Bourbon; and in the course of the same year he had the misfortune to be severely wounded by the explosion of a powder-horn while in the act of pointing a gun for the purpose of covering the retreat of a party that had been sent on shore for water in the neighbourhood of St. Denis. In consideration of his sufferings the Patriotic Society voted him a gratuity. His last appointments were, 15 March, 1811, and 2 July, 1813, to the SCEPTRE and MARLBOROUGH 74's, Capts. Sam. Jas. Holland, Thos. Harvey, and Robt. Honyman, on the North American and West India stations. When Second-Lieutenant of the former ship in 1812, he jumped overboard and saved the life of a seaman. He was paid off from the MARLBOROUGH in March, 1814; and accepted his present rank 13 Oct. 1838.

MITCHELL. (COMMANDER, 1842. F-P., 23; H-P., 13.)

THOMAS MITCHELL is son of Major Mitchell, R.M.

This officer entered the Navy, 31 Aug. 1811, as Sec.-cl. Vol., on board the AMERICA 74, Capt. Josias Rowley, attached to the force in the Mediterranean; where, until Oct. 1816, he continued to serve, in the CENTAUR 74, Capt. John Chambers White, EDINBURGH 74, Capts. Robt. Rolles and Hon. Geo. Heneage Lawrence Dundas, FURIEUSE 36, Capt. Wm. Mounsey, EDINBURGH again, Capt. Dundas, REPULSE 74, Capt. Rich. Hussey Moubray, and BERWICK 74, and IMPREGNABLE 104, both commanded by Capt. Edw. Brace. He was present, as Midshipman of the FURIEUSE, at the reduction of the island of Ponza in Feb. 1813. In the EDINBURGH he witnessed, in the course of the same year, the storming of the batteries of d'Anzo, and the capture of a convoy of 29 vessels anchored for protection under the walls; also the surrender of Via Reggio; and the unsuccessful attack on Leghorn. In 1815 it was his lot to be on board the BERWICK at the taking of Gaeta; and on 27 Aug. 1816 he assisted in the IMPREGNABLE, under the flag of Rear-Admiral David Milne, at the bombardment of Algiers. From Jan. 1817 until Oct. 1823, we find him in succession employed, on the Home, St. Helena, and West India stations, in the ISTER 42, Capt. Thos. Forrest, ALBION 74, Capt. Rich. Raggett, VIGO 74, flag-ship of Rear-Admiral Robt. Lambert, and GLOUCESTER 74, Commodore Sir Edw. W. C. R. Owen. He was then, as a reward for his conduct in having twice in one day gone off in the quarter-boat during a heavy sea for the purpose of rescuing a man who had fallen overboard, placed on the Admiralty List for promotion, and appointed Mate of the ICARUS 10, Capt. John Geo. Graham; of which vessel (having passed his examination in April, 1819) he was nominated Acting-Lieutenant 10 March, 1824. After three months of very active boat-service against the pirates on the coast of Cuba, he was placed as Mate, in July of the latter year, on board the SERAPIS receiving-ship at Port Royal, Capt. Geo. Vernon Jackson. He was confirmed a Lieutenant, 10 Dec. following, in the CARNATION 18; and, that sloop being paid off in July, 1825, was subsequently appointed Senior—27 March, 1828, of the ADVENTURE 6, Capt. Philip Parker King, employed, until her return to England in the autumn of 1830, in surveying the neighbourhood of Cape Horn—20 Aug. 1831, of the ÆTNA 6, Capt. Edw. Belcher, during a servitude of three years in which vessel he assisted in surveying part of the coast of Africa and the Mediterranean, and was stationed in the river Douro during the hostilities between Pedro and Miguel, by a sentry belonging to the latter of whom he was fired at and struck while on the quarter-deck—20 Nov. 1834, for a few weeks, of the EXCELLENT gunnery-ship at Portsmouth, Capt. Thos. Hastings—18 March, 1836, of the MINDEN 74, Capt. Alex. Renton Sharpe, fitting for the Mediterranean, where, prior to his return in Feb. 1840, he received the thanks of the Admiralty (in conjunction with Lieut. Roberts) for having again gone off in the quarter-boat during a hard gale to pick up a man who had fallen into the sea—and 3 Sept. 1841, of the FORMIDABLE 84, Capts. Sir Edw. Thos. Troubridge and Sir Chas. Sullivan, fitting at Sheerness. He attained his present rank 28 Jan. 1842, and has since been on half-pay.

Commander Mitchell married, 22 Nov. 1842, Caroline, daughter of the late T. W. Pink, Esq., of Portsea.

MITCHELL. (RETIRED COMMANDER, 1834. F-P., 18; H-P., 34.)

THOMAS MITCHELL entered the Navy, 8 Nov. 1795, as Midshipman, on board the ADVENTURE 44, Capt. Wm. Geo. Rutherford; and for upwards of three years was employed in the West Indies in the same vessel, and in the DICTATOR 64, also commanded by Capt. Rutherford, BRUNSWICK 74, flag-ship of Rear-Admiral Rich. Rodney Bligh, and CERES 32, Capt. Rich. Harrison Pearson. Joining then the AMETHYST 36, Capts. John Cooke and Henry Rich. Glynn, he accompanied the expedition of 1800 to Ferrol, was much employed in the conveyance of royal and diplomatic personages, and contributed to the capture, 28 Jan. and 9 April, 1801, of the French 36-gun frigate *La Dédaigneuse*, and national corvette *Le Général Brune* of 14 guns. He attained the rank of Lieutenant 29 April, 1802; and was subsequently appointed—16 Nov. 1803, to the SCOURGE sloop, Capt. Wm. Wooldridge, stationed in the Channel—23 Oct. 1804, and 21 Aug. 1806, to the HARRIER 18, and MACASSAR 36, Capts. W. Wooldridge, Edw. Ratsey, Edw. Thos. Troubridge, and Wm. Wilbraham, both in the East Indies, whence he returned in Sept. 1807—in the course of 1809, to the ZEBRA bomb, Capt. Geo. Barne Trollope, HELDER 36, Capt. John Serrell, and SALSETTE 36, Capts. Walter Bathurst, John Hollinworth, and Henry Hope, all on the Home station—and 14 July, 1813, to the AJAX 74, Capts. Robt. Waller Otway and Geo. Mundy, with whom he served, part of the time in the Mediterranean, until paid off in July, 1816. When Senior of the HARRIER, and in company with the PHAETON 38, Lieut. Mitchell was present, 2 Aug. 1805, in a severe action of two hours and a half with the French 36-gun frigate *Sémillante*, and several batteries, at the entrance of the Straits of St. Bernardino, Philippine Islands; on which occasion the HARRIER, besides being much cut up, sustained a loss of 2 men wounded. He was afterwards mentioned for the great assistance he afforded his Captain (Troubridge) in an action of an hour with a Dutch squadron, which terminated in the surrender, near Java, 26 July, 1806, of the 36-gun frigate *Pallas*, and armed ships *Vittoria* and *Batavia*, to the HARRIER, and her consort the GREYHOUND 32.* During his servitude in the SALSETTE, of which he was also First-Lieutenant, we find him, while attached to the Walcheren expedition, commanding two divisions of boats in an attack on 13 of the enemy's gun-vessels; and presented in consequence with the thanks of the late Admiral Sir Rich. Keats. He accepted the rank of Commander on the Retired List 25 March, 1834.

MITCHELL. (LIEUT., 1829. F-P., 30; H-P., 9.)

WILLIAM MITCHELL, born 19 Oct. 1799, is son of Lieut.-Col. Thos. Mitchell, R.M., who died in Oct. 1829.

This officer entered the Navy, 4 May, 1808, as Sec.-cl. Boy, on board the WARSPITE 74, Capt. Hon. Henry Blackwood, with whom he served in the Mediterranean until Oct. 1812—the greater part of the time in the capacity of Midshipman. He re-embarked, 12 June, 1818, on board the ISTER 42, Capt. Thos. Forrest; and on 26 Oct. 1820, after he had been for rather more than three years employed on the Newfoundland station, in the SIR FRANCIS DRAKE frigate, Capt. John Bowker, CARNATION 18, Capt. Wm. Nugent Glascock, and DRAKE 10, Capt. Octavius Vernon Harcourt, he passed his examination. During the next eight years and a half we find him serving as Admiralty Midshipman, Mate, and Admiralty Mate, in the SEVERN 40, and RAMILLIES 74, both commanded by Capt. Wm. M'Culloch, RAINBOW 28, Capt. Hon. Henry John Rous, LARNE 20, Capt. Wm. Burdett Dobson, PRINCE REGENT 120, Capt. Constantine Rich. Moorsom, and ISIS 50, Commodore Sir Thos. Staines, on the Downs, East India, Chatham, and Mediterranean stations. He was then, 25 Aug. 1829, promoted to a Lieutenancy in the SAMARANG 28, Capt. Wm. Fanshawe Martin, also in the Mediterranean; whence, in Nov. 1830, he returned to England in the RIFLEMAN 18, Capt. Rich. Shepheard Triscott. He has been in command, since 18 March, 1834, of a station in the Coast Guard.

Lieut. Mitchell married, 18 Aug. 1842, Frances Heassey, eldest daughter of Lieut. W. Ashby, R.N., then of Bexhill.

---

* *Vide* Gaz 1807, p. 423, where it will be seen that, among other vessels, he contributed to the capture of the *Belgica* of 12 guns.

MITFORD. (REAR-ADMIRAL, 1846. F-P., 18; H-P., 35.)

ROBERT MITFORD, born 26 Jan. 1781, is second son of the late Bertram Mitford, Esq., of Mitford Castle, co. Northumberland, by Tabitha, daughter of Fras. Johnson, Esq., M.D., of Newcastle. The Rear-Admiral, who belongs to an old baronial family celebrated in earlier days as border chieftains, is uncle of Lieut. B. M. Atherton, R.N., and a relative of Miss Mary Russell Mitford, the admired authoress of 'Our Village.'

This officer entered the Navy, 8 Oct. 1794, as Fst.-cl. Vol., on board the SAN FIORENZO of 42 guns, Capts. Sir Harry Burrard Neale and Wm. Chas. Paterson. While in that ship, besides being much in attendance on the King off Weymouth, he assisted, in company with LA NYMPHE 36, at the capture of *La Résistance* of 48 and *La Constance* of 24 guns, 9 March, 1797—passed, soon afterwards, through the mutinous fleet at the Nore—took part in a very warm action of nearly two hours, which terminated in the defeat, by the SAN FIORENZO, and her consort the AMELIA 38, of a French squadron, consisting of three frigates and a gun-vessel, 9 April, 1799—and, we believe, was present, 2 July following, in an attack made by Rear-Admiral Chas. Morice Pole on a Spanish squadron lying in Aix Roads. After serving for some time with Capt. Philip Chas. Durham in the ANSON and ENDYMION frigates, and with Capt. Bendall Robt. Littlehales in the CENTAUR 74, he was promoted, 13 Jan. 1802, to a Lieutenancy in the RESISTANCE 36, Capts. Henry Digby and Hon. Philip Wodehouse. Invaliding from that ship in the ensuing Sept., he was next, 28 Jan. 1804 and 30 Oct. 1806, appointed to the CERBERUS 32 and INDEFATIGABLE 44, Capts. Wm. Selby and John Tremayne Rodd, both employed, as had been the other ships, on the Home station. On 16 Feb. 1807 he was advanced to the command of the DUCHESS OF BEDFORD armed ship; and on 24 May, 1808, after having been attached to the force off Cadiz and Gibraltar, he assumed that of the ESPOIR 18. In that sloop we find him, in June, 1809, assisting at the capture of the islands of Ischia and Procida and of 18 gun-boats;* and on 25 April, 1810, uniting with the SPARTAN and SUCCESS frigates in an attack upon the enemy at Terracina; on which occasion, previously to the bringing off of several vessels by the boats of the three ships, he distinguished himself by his great energy and judgment in running in and sounding under the various batteries. He was nominated, 2 Feb. 1813, Acting-Captain of the MINSTREL 24, and, in that vessel, to which he was confirmed 31 March following, he continued employed, still in the Mediterranean, until Aug. 1814, when he invalided. He accepted his present rank 1 Oct. 1846.

Rear-Admiral Mitford married, in Dec. 1830, Margaret, daughter of Jas. Dunsmure, Esq., of Edinburgh, by whom he has issue one daughter.

MOBERLY. (Captain, 1815. F-P., 14; H-P., 32.)

JOHN MOBERLY entered the Navy, 20 Aug. 1801, as Fst.-cl. Vol., on board the TRIUMPH 74, Capt. Sir Robt. Barlow. After rather more than three years' servitude in that ship in the Mediterranean, chiefly in the capacity of Midshipman, he became in succession attached, between Dec. 1804 and his attainment of the rank of Lieutenant, 14 Oct. 1807, to the BARFLEUR 98, Capt. Geo. Martin, TRIUMPH 74, Capt. Henry Inman (part of the force engaged in Sir Robt. Calder's action, 22 July, 1805), LONDON and BARFLEUR 98's, both commanded by Sir Robt. Barlow, EDGAR 74, flag-ship of Lord Keith, NAMUR 74, Capt. Lawrence Wm. Halsted, and ELIZABETH 74, Capt. Hon. Henry Curzon—all on the Home station. In July, 1808, having been intermediately employed in the CUMBERLAND 74, Capt. Hon. Philip Wodehouse, and as Flag-Lieutenant to Sir John Borlase Warren, in the SWIFTSURE 74, in the North Sea and North America, he obtained an appointment to the MELAMPUS 36, Capt. Edw. Hawker. In that frigate, besides assisting in making prize of

* *Vide* Gaz. 1809, p. 1437.

several privateers, we find him, in the course of 1809-10, escorting a fleet of transports from Halifax to Barbadoes, lending his aid to the capture of *Le Colibri* French brig-of-war of 16 guns and 92 men, and co-operating in the reduction of Guadeloupe. Removing, in June, 1811, to the LITTLE BELT, Capt. Arthur Batt Bingham, he served as Senior of that vessel in the furious and well-known action fought between her and the American 44-gun frigate *President*, whose fire in half an hour not only greatly damaged her opponent in masts, sails, rigging, and hull, but killed and wounded 32 of her crew. In a gale which arose after the battle, Mr. Moberly, who had proved himself in every respect a most excellent officer, afforded his Captain very great assistance by personally stopping the leaks, securing the masts, and doing everything in his power.* On leaving the LITTLE BELT he made a voyage it appears to St. Helena in the IPHIGENIA 36, Capt. Lucius Curtis, and again officiated as Flag-Lieutenant to Sir J. B. Warren, in the SAN DOMINGO 74, on the North American station. He attained the rank of Commander 29 May, 1813; was appointed, in the following July, to the MOSELLE sloop, at Jamaica; and on 26 Aug. 1815 was posted. He accepted the Retirement 1 Oct. 1846.

Capt. Moberly is at present Inspector of Licences at Simcoe, Upper Canada.

* *Vide* Gaz. 1811, p. 1296.

MOFFATT. (LIEUT., 1811. F-P., 22; H-P., 23.)

JOHN MOFFATT is son of a Surgeon in the R.N., who served in various frigate actions, and was on board the AMPHION in the battle off Lissa, 13 March, 1811. The united services of himself and his family extend over a period of considerably more than a hundred years, and include the action of 1 June, 1794, the capture of the Dutch squadron in Saldanha Bay in 1796, the action under Sir Robt. Calder in July, 1805, and the battle of Trafalgar.

This officer entered the Navy, 30 Dec. 1802, as Fst.-cl. Vol, on board the HERCULE 74, Capt. Solomon Ferris; in which ship, while under the temporary command of Lieut. John B. Hills, he was present as Midshipman at the capture, between 28 June and 1 July, 1803, of *La Mignonne* corvette of 16 guns, and 40-gun frigate *La Créole*, having on board the French General Morgan and 530 troops, and participated in a severe running action with *La Poursuivante* of 44 guns These occurrences took place in the West Indies, whence, on removing, in July, 1803, to the LEVIATHAN 74, Capt. Henry Wm. Bayntun, Mr. Moffatt proceeded to the Mediterranean. In Nov. 1804 he there became Master's Mate of the ÆTNA bomb, Capts. Rich. Thomas, John Quilliam, and John Yule; under the latter, we believe, of whom, when off Cape Finisterre in 1806, he jumped overboard during a gale, and was nearly lost in an endeavour to save the life of the Gunner's Mate. In Dec. 1807, at which period he had been serving for about 14 months in the CRESCENT frigate, Capt. Jas. Carthew, he joined the VANGUARD 74, Capts. Alex. Fraser, Thos. Fras. Chas. Mainwaring, and Henry Rich. Glynn. Continuing in that ship (of which he was nominated Acting-Lieutenant 28 May, 1809) until Feb. 1810, he came into frequent contact with the Danish gun-boats and batteries, while affording protection to convoys through the Sound; and assisted on one occasion in driving a man-of-war schooner on the rocks between Elsineur and Copenhagen. On another, having been the first to board a Prussian ship which the Danes had taken and run on shore, he succeeded, although under a heavy fire of field-pieces, in driving the enemy out of her, and in then setting her on fire. In Aug. 1810 he became Acting-Lieutenant of the ACORN sloop, Capt. Robt. Clephane; as at the close of the same year (after he had served for a short time as Mate and Midshipman of the AMPHION 32, Capt Wm. Hoste) he further did of the CERBERUS 32, Capt. Henry Whitby. In the boats of the two last-mentioned ships we find him taking part in many important affairs, and in particular at the capture of a convoy under a severe cross fire from the enemy's musketry at Pesaro. In the CERBERUS it was his lot to be present, 13 March, 1811, in the celebrated action off Lissa, where a British squadron, carrying in the whole 156 guns and 879 men, completely routed, after a conflict of six hours, and a loss to the CERBERUS of 13 killed and 41 wounded, a Franco-Venetian armament consisting of 284 guns and 2655 men. His conduct on the occasion procured him a commission bearing date the day of the battle. The appointments he next received were, on the Home station —4 Sept. 1811, to the ZEPHYR 16, Capt. Thos. Cuthbert Hichens—13 Feb. 1812, to the CHRISTIAN VII., 80, Capts. Jas. Andrew Worth and Henry Lidgbird Ball—23 April following, to the BULWARK 74, flag-ship of Rear-Admiral Philip Chas. Durham -and, 24 Dec. 1813, as Senior, to the MYRTLE 20, Capt. Arthur Batt Bingham, with whom he continued until Sept. 1814. While attached in 1813 to the BULWARK, Lieut. Moffatt, in cutting out a French vessel, was attacked and all but cut off by the boats of a squadron; who, however, on his being reinforced, were in their turn driven back and compelled to take refuge under the shelter of their own guns. In Nov. 1820 he obtained charge of a Coast Guard station in Yorkshire; on his removal whence to the Isle of Wight he had the good fortune to prevent the revenue from being defrauded to a considerable amount, and was often in consequence recommended to the notice of the Admiralty. His last appointments were to the command—in 1827, of the STARLING 14, stationed in the Channel—18 July, 1828, of the SPARROW 14, employed, until 1830, in protecting the Jersey fisheries—and, 9 Nov. 1832, for nine months, of the MAGPIE 4, on the North Sea, Channel, and Lisbon stations.

Lieut. Moffatt is married, and has issue seven children. AGENT—J. Hinxman.

MOLESWORTH. (COMMANDER, 1814. F-P., 16; H-P., 33.)

BOURCHIER MOLESWORTH is fifth son of the late Robt. Molesworth, Esq., and great-grandson of the first Viscount Molesworth. One of his brothers, Arthur, a Major-General in the E. I. Co.'s service, died 7 Jan. 1843; and another, Bysse Cole, a Major in the Army, died 4 Dec. 1819. He is second-cousin of the present Commander John Molesworth, R.N.

This officer entered the Navy, 5 July, 1798, as Midshipman, on board the EXCELLENT 74, commanded in the Mediterranean by Capt. Cuthbert Collingwood; and from the early part of the following year until Jan. 1805 was employed, at first under the flag of the same officer, in the TRIUMPH 74, Capts. Thos. Seccombe, Eliab Harvey, and Sir Robt. Barlow, on the Channel and Mediterranean stations. He was then nominated Sub-Lieutenant of the HARDY gun-brig, Lieut.-Commander Rodney Augustus Reid, lying at Portsmouth; and on 14 of the following Oct. he was promoted to a full Lieutenancy in LA CHIFFONE 36, Capts. Patrick Campbell and John Wainwright, again in the Mediterranean; where, and on the West India, Home, and Lisbon stations, he further, from April, 1808, until advanced to his present rank, 16 May, 1814, served in the EAGLE 74, Capt. Chas. Rowley, DAUNTLESS sloop, Capt. Josias Wittman, SCEPTRE 74, Capt. Sam. Jas. Ballard (under whom, antecedently to a participation in the operations against Guadeloupe, he witnessed the destruction, 18 Dec. 1809, of the French 40-gun frigates *Loire* and *Seine*, lying under the protection of several strong batteries in L'Ance la Barque), STAR sloop, Capt. Wm. Paterson, ORPHEUS 36, Capt. Robt. Preston, DRAGON 74, flag-ship of Sir Fras. Laforey, THETIS and TRIBUNE frigates, Capts. Wm. Henry Byam and Geo. Reynolds, STIRLING CASTLE and BELLEROPHON 74's, both commanded by Capt. Brine, RIPPON 74, Capt. Sir Christ. Cole, STATELY 64, flag-ship of Rear-Admiral Geo. Martin, and ROYAL CHARLOTTE yacht, Capt. Thos. Eyles. He has since been on half-pay.

MOLESWORTH. (COMMANDER, 1821. F-P., 18; H-P., 29.)

JOHN MOLESWORTH, born in July, 1789, is second son of the late Rich. Molesworth, Esq. (brother of the fifth Viscount Molesworth, and many years Accountant in the Army Pay Office), by Catherine, daughter of Fras. Cobb, Esq., of Twickenham; and is grandson of Capt. Wm. Molesworth, who figured in the wars with Spain, and was afterwards M.P. for Philipstown, and a Commissioner of Trade and Plantations. The Commander (a brother of the present Viscount Molesworth and of Capt. Anthony Oliver Molesworth, R.A.) is uncle of Lieut. Bartholomew Jeffery, R.N., and second-cousin of Commander Bourchier Molesworth, R.N. His cousin, the sixth Viscount Molesworth, a Major-General in the Army, and Lieut.-Colonel of H.M.'s 9th Regiment, was lost in the *Armston* transport, near the Cape of Good Hope, 30 May, 1815.

This officer entered the Navy, in April, 1800, as Fst.-cl. Vol., on board the PLOVER 18, Capts. Edw. Galwey and Matthew Forster, with whom he served in the Channel and West Indies until Sept. 1802, latterly in the capacity of Midshipman. In July, 1803, after he had been for six months attached to the CULLODEN 74, Capts. Chas. Henry Lane, John Conn, and Bartholomew Dacres, he joined the CANOPUS 80; in which ship, bearing the successive flags of Rear-Admirals Geo. Campbell, Sir Thos. Louis, and Geo. Martin, he continued until Feb. 1808; assisting during that period in the action off St. Domingo, at the capture of the French frigate *Le Président*, in the passage of the Dardanells, and in the expedition to Egypt. On 7 March, 1808, he was promoted, from the OCEAN 98, flag-ship of Lord Collingwood, to an Acting-Lieutenancy in the MALTA 80, Capt. Wm. Shield; and on 24 of the ensuing month he was confirmed into the IMPÉRIEUSE 38, Capt. Lord Cochrane. On 28 Jan. 1809, while in charge of a prize belonging to the latter frigate, he landed near Tarragona, in ignorance of the proximity of the French, by whom he was unfortunately taken prisoner. In Sept. of the same year, having regained his liberty, he joined the PARTRIDGE sloop, Capts. Wm. Williams Foote and John Miller Adye, under whom he continued employed in the Channel, West Indies, and North Sea, until May, 1811. While next attached, from 26 Aug. in the latter year until 8 Oct. 1814, to the AMERICA 74, commanded by the late Sir Josias Rowley, it was his fortune to see much service in the Mediterranean; where, on 19 May, 1812, he creditably aided, in the boats of that ship and of the LEVIATHAN 74 and ECLAIR sloop, at the capture of 16 and destruction of two deeply laden vessels, which had taken shelter under the town and batteries of Languelia, on the coast of Italy, and had been secured by various contrivances to the houses and beach—an exploit that occasioned the British a loss of 16 men killed and 20 wounded.* Besides enacting a part in the operations against Leghorn and Genoa, he aided in reducing the enemy's defences in the Gulf of Spezia, and was in particular commended for the manner in which he directed the batteries at the siege of the fortress of Santa Maria.† His last appointments were—27 March, 1815, to the IMPREGNABLE 104, flag-ship in the Mediterranean of Sir Josias Rowley, with whom he remained for a period of eight months, part of the time as Signal-Lieutenant—and, 6 May, 1818, again as Flag-Lieutenant to the same officer at Cork. He was advanced to his present rank on the Admiral striking his flag, 14 Dec. 1821; and has not been since afloat.

Commander Molesworth married, 6 Feb. 1828, Louisa, daughter of the late Rev. Dr. Tomkyns, of Buckenhill Park, co. Hereford, by whom he has issue a son and two daughters.

MOLYNEUX. (LIEUTENANT, 1846.)

THOMAS HOWARD MOLYNEUX passed his examination 9 Oct. 1843; and at the period of his promotion to the rank of Lieutenant, which took place 23 June, 1846, had been serving for a considerable time as Mate in the EXCELLENT gunnery-ship at Portsmouth, Capts. Sir Thos. Hastings and Henry Ducie Chads. He has been employed, since 27 July, 1846, in the SPARTAN 22, Capt. Thos. Matthew Chas. Symonds, on the Mediterranean station.

MOLYNEUX. (COMMANDER, 1833. F-P., 16; H-P., 19.)

WILLIAM MOLYNEUX died 18 July, 1847. He was third son of the late Lieut.-General Sir Thos. Molyneux, Bart., by Elizabeth, daughter of Thos. Perrin, Esq.; and brother-in-law of Lord Wm. G. Henry Somerset.

This officer entered the Navy, 9 Aug. 1812, as Fst.-cl. Vol., on board the NORGE 74, Capts. John Sprat Rainier and Chas. Dashwood, under the latter of whom, on proceeding to North America, he served as Midshipman (a rating he had attained in Nov. 1812) in the expedition of 1814 against New Orleans. Joining, in Nov. 1815, the LYRA 10, Capt. Basil Hall, he accompanied Lord Amherst in the ensuing year in his embassy to China. He returned to England in Nov. 1817; and was next, between March, 1818, and Oct. 1821, employed on the Home and West India stations, in the SPENCER 74, Capt. Wm. Robt. Broughton, TONNANT 80, and WINDSOR CASTLE 74, both commanded by Capt. Thos. Gordon Caulfeild, RALEIGH 18, Capt. Wm. Augustus Baumgardt, SALISBURY 50, flag-ship of Rear-Admiral Wm. Chas. Fahie, and PYRAMUS 42, Capt. Fras. Newcombe. He was then nominated Acting-Lieutenant of the FALMOUTH 20, Capt. Edw. Purcell; in which vessel (being confirmed to her by commission dated 21 Feb. 1822) he continued employed, still in the West Indies, until 11 July, 1823. His succeeding appointments were, on the Jamaica station—15 May, 1824, to the DARTMOUTH 42, Capt. Hon. Jas. Ashley Maude—7 Jan. and 9 March, 1826, to the SERAPIS and MAGNIFICENT convalescent and store-ships, Capts. Chas. Elliot, Jas. Cooper Bennett, and Geo. Mansel—23 March, 1829, to the BARHAM 50, bearing the flag of Hon. Chas. Elphinstone Fleeming—and, 10 March, 1830, to the acting-command of the FAIRY sloop. He returned to England in the following June; but was not officially promoted until 12 March, 1833. He did not again go afloat.

MOLYNEUX. (COMMANDER, 1841. F-P., 15; H-P., 21.)

WILLIAM HARGRAVES MOLYNEUX entered the Navy, 23 Nov. 1811, as Fst.-cl. Vol., on board the DAPHNE 20, Capts. Philip Pipon and Jas. Green, fitting for the Baltic, where he served at the siege of Danzig, and came into boat-contact with the enemy's privateers off the island of Rugen. Rejoining Capt. Pipon, in Sept. 1813, on board the TAGUS 38, he assisted, on 6 of the ensuing Jan., while cruizing among the Cape de Verde Islands, in company with the NIGER 38, at the capture of the French 40-gun frigate *Cérès;* and he subsequently, on visiting the Pacific, fell in with Pitcairn's Island —the first time it had been touched at since settled on by the mutineers of the BOUNTY. In the early part of 1816 we find him sailing in the MAGICIENNE 36, Capt. John Brett Purvis, for the East Indies, with the flag of Sir Rich. King, whom he there followed, in Oct. 1817, into the MINDEN 74. He was promoted, on his return home, to the rank of Lieutenant, by commission dated 31 Oct. 1820; and was subsequently appointed—7 Nov. 1822, to the JUPITER 60, Capt. Geo. Augustus Westphal, under whom he escorted Lord Amherst, Governor-General of India, to Bengal—4 June, 1824 (six months after the latter ship had been paid off), to the NIEMEN 28, Capts. Provo Wm. Parry Wallis, Wm. Pitt Canning, and Chas. Simeon, in which vessel he was for three years employed on the Halifax station—19 Jan. 1836, as First, to the MINDEN 74, fitting for the flag of Sir Peter Halkett, Commander-in-Chief in North America and the West Indies, whence he returned to

* *Vide* Gaz. 1812, p. 1395. † *V.* Gaz. 1814, p. 984.

England and was paid off in Aug. 1837—and, 1 Nov. 1841, in a similar capacity, to the ALFRED 50, equipping at Sheerness for the broad pendant of Commodore John Brett Purvis. He was advanced to his present rank on 23 of the month last mentioned; and has since been on half-pay.

Commander Molyneux married, 8 June, 1837, Martha Maria, only daughter of the late Admiral Sir Andw. Mitchell, K.B., by whom he has issue two sons and a daughter.

MONDAY. (COMMANDER, 1846. F-P., 17; H-P., 32.)

EDWARD MONDAY was born 13 May, 1782.

This officer entered the Navy, 7 Dec. 1798, as Ordinary, on board the HAZARD sloop, Capts. Wm. Butterfield and R. J. Neve; and while in that vessel, in which he remained until Aug. 1805, he was continuously employed on the Irish and Channel stations—chiefly in the capacities of Midshipman and Master's Mate; in which latter he assisted, in June, 1803, in cutting out a French brig and chasse-marée from under a heavy fire from the enemy's batteries and musketry in Hodierne Bay. After serving for short periods, as Midshipman, in the VILLE DE PARIS and HIBERNIA, flag-ships of Hon. Wm. Cornwallis and Earl St. Vincent, as Acting-Lieutenant in the LONDON 98, Capt. Thos. Western, and again, as Midshipman, in the HIBERNIA, he was nominated, in Oct. 1806, Acting-Lieutenant of the PHŒNIX 36, Capts. Zachary Mudge, Jas. Bowen, Wm. Henry Webley, and Chas. John Austen; under whom, the appointment being confirmed on 7 of the following month, he continued (with the exception of a brief attachment, from Dec. 1808 until March, 1809, to the ALERT sloop, Capt. Williams) to serve, until wrecked, during a hurricane near Smyrna, 20 Feb. 1816. He commanded her boats, during that period, at the capture of *El Cupido* Spanish schooner from Buenos Ayres, bound to Corunna, carrying 1 large gun on a circular slide and 17 men, in Dec. 1806; in conjunction with those of the JALOUSE, at the very gallant capture, with a loss to the British of 1 man killed and another wounded, of *Le Charles* French brig privateer of 14 guns and 90 men, under a heavy fire of grape and musketry, 29 Jan. 1810;* at the reduction of Fort Pulo Kissa, in the Eastern Archipelago, in March, 1811; together with the boats of a squadron, in an attack on Sambas, a piratical settlement on the coast of Borneo, in Jan. 1813; and at the capture of two piratical proas in the Grecian Archipelago in 1815. He also, in 1811, took, by escalade, with a party of seamen and marines, Fort Concordia, on the island of Timor, mounting 26 pieces of cannon; and in 1812 he was employed in the boats of a squadron at the reduction of Palambang. During four months of 1812-13 Mr. Monday (by whom all the above services, with the exception of the capture of *El Cupido*, were performed in the capacity of First-Lieutenant) acted as Captain of the PHŒNIX. After nearly 32 years of half-pay he was advanced to the rank of Commander 9 Nov. 1846!

Commander Monday is married, and has issue six children.

MONDAY. (CAPTAIN, 1838. F-P., 20; H-P., 21.)

JOHN MONDAY entered the Navy, 15 March, 1806, as Clerk, on board the BUSTLER gun-brig, Lieut.-Commander Richard Welsh. Although present, as we are informed, in the FOUDROYANT at the capture, in the following month, of the *Marengo* 80, bearing the flag of Rear-Admiral Linois, and 40-gun frigate *Belle Poule*, his name, we believe, continued borne on the books of the above vessel, chiefly as Midshipman and acting Sub-Lieutenant, until Jan. 1809, during which period he saw much boat-service on the Downs station. After an employment of two years and a half, as Master's Mate, in the DIOMEDE 50, flag-ship off Guernsey and in the East Indies of Admirals D'Auvergne and Wm. O'Brien Drury, he became attached, in Oct. 1811, to the QUEEN 74, Capts. Lord Colville and John Coode; under the former of whom he was landed in 1812 for the purpose of co-operating with the patriots on the north coast of Spain. He continued to serve in the QUEEN, as an acting and confirmed Lieutenant (order and commission respectively dated 30 Jan. and 27 June, 1814), until Dec. 1815, part of the time in the West Indies and Mediterranean, under the flags of Rear-Admirals Sir Fras. Laforey and Chas. Vinicombe Penrose; and was next appointed, in the capacity of First-Lieutenant —1 Sept. 1821, to the SEMIRAMIS 42, flag-ship of Lord Colville at Cork, where he remained until paid off in April, 1825—14 April, 1826, to the CLIO 18, Capt. Robt. Aitchison, stationed in the North Sea —and, 3 Aug. following, to the GLASGOW 50, Capt. Hon. Jas. Ashley Maude. For his conduct in the latter ship at the battle of Navarin he was presented with a second promotal commission dated 22 Oct. 1827. He afterwards, 28 Sept. 1832, obtained a three years' appointment in the Coast Guard, and from 12 Dec. 1836, until advanced to his present rank 27 Dec. 1838, he commanded the STAG 46, bearing the broad pendant of Commodore Thos. Ball Sulivan in South America. He has since been on half-pay.

Capt. Monday is married, and has issue.

MONEY, C.B. (Captain, 1815. F-P., 15; H-P., 36.)

ROWLAND MONEY, born 28 April, 1782, is son of the late Wm. Money, Esq., of Horn House, co. Hereford, by Mary, daughter of Wm. Webster, Esq., of Stockton-on-Tees; and brother (with Geo. Money, Esq., late Master in Equity, Accountant-General, and Keeper of the Records in the Supreme Court of Judicature at Calcutta) of the Rev. Wm. Money Kyrle, the present possessor of Horn House. His eldest brother, Sir Jas Kyrle Money, Bart., was a Major-General in the army, and died 26 June, 1843; another, the Rev. Kyrle Ernle Money, M.A., was Prelector and Prebendary of Hereford Cathedral; and a third, John, a Commander in the Indian Navy, died 6 Aug. 1825.

This officer entered the Navy, 21 April, 1796, as a Volunteer, on board the ST. FIORENZO 36, Capt. Sir Harry Burrard Neale, attached to the force in the Channel; where, and on the Halifax and Mediterranean stations, we find him, from March, 1798, until Aug. 1802, serving, as Midshipman (a rating he had attained in April, 1797) and Master's Mate, in the ST. ALBANS 64, Capt. Fras. Pender, THETIS 36, Capt. Hon. Alex. Cochrane, NAIAD 38, Capt. Wm. Pierrepont, AJAX 74, Capt. Hon. A. Cochrane, and MAIDSTONE and NARCISSUS frigates, both commanded by Capt. Ross Donnelly. Towards the close of 1804 he joined the ROYAL SOVEREIGN yacht, Capt. Sir Harry Burrard Neale, off Weymouth. He attained the rank of Lieutenant 12 Jan. 1805; and in the course of that and the following year was successively appointed to the VALOROUS, Capt. Geo. Nicholas Hardinge, VESTAL 28, Capt. Stephen Thos. Digby, and LIVELY 38, Capt. Geo. M'Kinley. In March, 1806, Mr. Money, then in the VESTAL, was the means, under very hazardous circumstances, of saving the crew of a merchant-brig, the *Friendship*, of Hull, which had grounded on the Gunfleet, near Harwich, in a heavy gale of wind. On the evening of 19 Nov. 1807, after having escorted the troops under Lord Cathcart to Copenhagen, and when in lat. 47° 10′ N., long. 16° W., he again manifested the intrepid benevolence of his disposition by volunteering in the jolly-boat (although it was thought that no boat could live in the sea then running) to rescue the crew of a foundering merchantman to leeward. He made, notwithstanding, three successive trips to the distressed vessel, and had the happiness of saving every soul. On ultimately regaining the LIVELY, the jolly-boat, so tempestuous was the weather, was cut adrift, it being found impossible to preserve her. On leaving the LIVELY, Mr. Money, in Aug. 1809, rejoined the ROYAL SOVEREIGN yacht, commanded at the time by Capt. Hen.

* *Vide* Gaz. 1810, p. 178.

Hume Spence, with whom he continued until presented, 9 Nov. following, with a second promotal commission. His next appointment was, 16 April, 1814, to the TRAAVE 36, *armée-en-flûte;* in which ship he conveyed part of the 4th Regiment of infantry from the river Garonne to North America. In Aug. of the same year he had charge of a subdivision of boats at the destruction of Commodore Barney's flotilla up the Patuxent.* He commanded, too, a party of seamen, and obtained the thanks of Rear-Admiral Geo. Cockburn for his exertions and steady gallantry, in the attacks upon Washington and Baltimore;† and for his conspicuous conduct in the operations against New Orleans, where he was similarly employed, and had both bones of the right leg broken by a musket-shot at the storming of a battery on the Mississippi 8 Jan. 1815, he was highly lauded by Colonel Thornton, commanding the 85th Regiment, and most strongly recommended by Sir Alex. Cochrane to the protection of the Admiralty, and intrusted by him with the conveyance of his despatches to England.‡ He was in consequence promoted to Post-rank by commission dated 29 March, 1815; nominated a C.B. 4 June following; and awarded, 16 Feb. 1816, a pension of 250*l*. His last appointment was to an Inspecting Command in the Water Guard in the Isle of Wight, where he remained from 1822 until 1825. He accepted the Retirement 1 Oct. 1846.

Capt. Money married, 13 Sept. 1805, Maria, fifth daughter of the late Wm. Money, Esq., of Walthamstow, co. Essex, one of the Elder Brethren of the Trinity House, and a Director of the East India Company, and sister of the late Wm. Taylor Money, Esq., K.H., formerly H.M. Consul-General at Venice and Milan, and M.P. successively for Wotton Basset and St. Michael's. By that lady, who died 6 Feb. 1847, he had issue four sons and five daughters. Of the latter, the eldest, Maria Rowlanda, married, in 1830, the Rev. Sam. Jas. Gambier, nephew of Admiral Lord Gambier, G.C.B.; the second, Amelia Mary, in 1841, the Hon. H. F. Pery, brother of the present Earl of Limerick; and the third, Angelica Mary, in 1844, Geo. Selby, Esq., of the Madras Artillery. AGENTS—Messrs. Stilwell.

* *Vide* Gaz. 1814, p. 1941. † *V.* Gaz. 1814, p. 1938, 2074.
‡ *V.* Gaz. 1815, p. 440, 450.

MONK. (LIEUTENANT, 1812.)

GEORGE MITFORD MONK entered the Navy, 29 Jan. 1805, as Fst.-cl. Vol., on board the RAMILLIES 74, Capts. Fras. Pickmore and Robt. Yarker; and, on 13 March, 1806, while cruizing with a squadron under the orders of Sir John Borlase Warren, was present at the capture of the *Marengo* 80, bearing the flag of Rear-Admiral Linois, and 40-gun frigate *Belle Poule*. In Oct. and Nov. 1808 (he had attained the rating of Midshipman in April, 1807) he successively joined the PRINCESS OF ORANGE 74, Capt. Fras. Beauman, and RESISTANCE 38, Capts. Chas. Adam, John Hollinworth, and Philip Rosenhagen; and on 23 Jan. 1812, on his return home from the Mediterranean in the TOPAZE 36, Capt. Edw. Harvey, he was promoted to the rank of Lieutenant. Being ordered back in the ARMADA 74, Capt. John Ferris Devonshire, he joined, on his arrival off Toulon, the EDINBURGH 74, Capt. Robt. Rolles. He was subsequently, during five months of the same year, 1812, again employed, under Capt. Devonshire, in the ST. ALBANS 64, at the defence of Cadiz. From Feb. 1813 until Nov. 1814 we find him attached to the NIOBE 40, Capts. Wm. Augustus Montagu and Henry Colins Deacon, stationed at first on the coasts of America and Portugal, and then engaged in conveying the staff of the Russian Imperial Guards to Cronstadt. His last appointments were —2 Dec. 1814, to the NIGER 38, Capt. Peter Rainier, with whom he remained for about nine months at the Cape of Good Hope—3 July, 1816, to the LÆANDER 50, Capt. Edw. Chetham, in which ship he assisted at the bombardment of Algiers—and, 27 Jan. 1817, to an Inspecting Command in the Water Guard. Lieut. Monk's services afloat extend to a period of ten years.

MONK. (LIEUT., 1814. F-P., 11; H-P., 30.)

JOHN MONK entered the Navy, 5 July, 1806, as A. B., on board the DICTATOR 64, Capts. Jas. Macnamara and Donald Campbell; under the latter of whom he enacted a Midshipman's part in the expedition of 1807 against Copenhagen; whence he returned to England in charge of one of the enemy's captured vessels. In Aug. 1808, having rejoined Capt. Macnamara on board the EDGAR 74, he served in a boat under that officer at the capture of the forts of Nyeborg, on the occasion of the embarkation thence of the Spanish General the Marquis de la Romana and his patriot troops; whom, in command of the Danish man-of-war prize *Fama*, he assisted in convoying as far as Gottenborg. After the operations against Flushing, where he received a wound in the left hand and had two of his fingers broken, he followed Capt. Macnamara, as Master's Mate, in Feb. 1810, into the BERWICK 74; in which ship he continued employed, under Capts. Sir Robt. Laurie and Edw. Brace, until July, 1816. At first he was very actively engaged in the vicinity of Cherbourg, and while so stationed was present, 25 March, 1811, at the self-destruction of the French 40-gun frigate *L'Amazone*. Proceeding next to the Mediterranean, he there participated in much boat-service on the coasts of Spain, France, and Italy. On 16 May, 1813, we find him aiding, in the boats of his own ship and the EURYALUS 36, under Lieut. Henry Johnston Sweedland, and mentioned for his conduct, at the capture and destruction of *La Fortune* xebec of 10 guns, 4 swivels, and 95 men, and of 22 vessels collected under the enemy's batteries (which were likewise taken) in the harbour of Cavalarie.* On the evening of 11 Dec. following, with a view to the capture of a convoy in the port of Negaye, he landed at that place at the head of a party of seamen, and, assisted by a body of marines, succeeded, without the loss of a man, in obtaining possession of a martello tower, and of the enemy's castle and forts. This part of the business being accomplished, and the concerted signal being made for the boats to advance, he received orders from the First-Lieutenant, Sweedland, to take charge of the launch and second barge, and proceed to the attack of the vessels. Being unexpectedly met by a terrific fire from two national schooners, Lieut. Sweedland gave orders for a retreat; heedless, however, of which, Mr. Monk and his party with three cheers dashed alongside the first schooner, and, after a bloody struggle, carried her. She was found to be armed with long 18-pounders, and to have on board 200 barrels of powder and 1400 stand of arms. Her guns being immediately turned against her consort, the latter, we believe, was sunk. Unfortunately, at this juncture a heavy and unaccountable fire was opened by those who had been left in the batteries; in consequence of which Mr. Monk was under the necessity of ordering the cable of his prize to be cut, and of making the best of his way out of the harbour. On his road he picked up the gig with Lieut. Sweedland and the whole of her crew killed! In the second barge the loss was also most fearful, two-thirds of the crew being either slain or wounded, including, among the former, Mr. Jas. Hawkins Whitshed, Midshipman, son of the present Admiral of the Fleet. The captured vessel, we may add, was commanded by a son of the celebrated French General, Bertrand, whose life Mr. Monk had the good fortune on three occasions to save. He afterwards acted as Flag-Officer to Lord Wm. Bentinck in the operations against Naples, Leghorn, and Genoa; and in March, 1814, commanded a party of seamen with scaling ladders at the reduction of the forts in the Gulf of Spezia. In consequence of his Lordship's strong recommendation he was nominated, on 24 of the ensuing month, Acting-Lieutenant of the BERWICK—an appointment to which the Admiralty accorded its sanction 13 June in the same year.

* *Vide* Gaz. 1813, p. 1805.

After further serving at the bombardment of Gaeta in 1815, and accompanying Lord Exmouth in the early part of 1816 in his visits to Algiers, Tunis, and Tripoli, Lieut. Monk was appointed with Capt. Brace, in July, 1816, to the IMPREGNABLE 104; in which ship, on 27 of the proximate Aug., he bore a warm part under the flag of Rear-Admiral David Milne in the bombardment of Algiers; where he was wounded and burnt, and sustained serious injury in the eyes, resulting in the loss of the sight of one of them. He was discharged from the BERWICK in Oct. 1816; and has since been on half-pay.

Although their efforts were not attended with success, it may be as well here to record the fact, that after the battle of Algiers a memorial praying for Lieut. Monk's promotion was drawn up by the Mayor and Corporation of Chester for presentation to the Lords of the Admiralty; and others, with the same intent, by the Mayor, Corporation, and Merchants of Liverpool, to Mr. Canning, Lord Sandon, and Mr. Huskisson; by the last-mentioned of whom he was personally introduced to H.R.H. the Lord High Admiral. From 1818 until 1844 Lieut. Monk was employed in command of his own ships in trading to all parts of the globe.

MONTAGU. (LIEUTENANT, 1814.)

EDWARD PROUDFOOT MONTAGU, born 23 April, 1791, is eldest son of the late Gerard Montagu, Esq., formerly of Burlingham, co. Norfolk (a direct descendant of Henry, first Earl of Manchester, ancestor of the present Duke of that name), by Mary Anne, daughter of Geo. Doughty, Esq., of Theberton Hall, co. Suffolk. He is brother-in-law of Capts. Sir David Dunn and Robt. Hockings, R.N.; and second-cousin of Capt. John Wm. Montagu, R.N.

This officer entered the Navy, in Feb. 1805, as Fst.-cl. Vol., on board the ROYAL WILLIAM, Capt. John Wainwright, bearing the flag at Spithead of his relative Admiral Geo. Montagu. On his return from a voyage to the East Indies in the LION 64, Capt. Robt. Rolles, he became Midshipman, about Jan. 1808, of the PROSERPINE 32, Capt. Chas. Otter; in which ship it was his misfortune, on the night of 28 Feb. 1809, to be captured, while off the port of Toulon, by the French 40-gun frigates *Pénélope* and *Pauline*, despite a noble resistance on the part of the British, whose loss extended to 1 man killed and 10 wounded. On his restoration to liberty, after four years of captivity, Mr. Montagu was successively received, in the course of 1813, into the SOLEBAY 32, flag-ship at Yarmouth of Rear-Admiral Geo. Murray, and, on the North American station, into the HOGUE 74, Capts. Hon Henry Hotham and Hon. Thos. Bladen Capel, SAN DOMINGO 74, bearing the flag of Sir John Borlase Warren, and ORPHEUS 36, Capt. Hugh Pigot. He was confirmed a Lieutenant of the last-mentioned ship 1 July, 1814, but left her in the following Oct., and has not been since afloat.

He married, in 1817, Mary Anne, daughter of Capt. Everard, and by that lady has had issue ten sons and three daughters. His eldest son, Gerard, is a First-Lieutenant R.M. (1843); and his second, Jas. Van Harthals, an officer in the 10th Foot. AGENTS—Messrs. Ommanney.

MONTAGU. (Captain, 1824. F-P., 14; H-P., 30.)

JAMES MONTAGU, born 10 April, 1791, is brother of Capt. John Wm. Montagu, R.N.

This officer entered the Navy, in 1803, as Fst.-cl. Vol., on board the PRINCESS ROYAL 98, Capt. Jas. Vashon, bearing the flag at Portsmouth of his father, Admiral Geo. Montagu; under whom, from 1804 to 1806, he served in the ROYAL WILLIAM. He then joined the MEDUSA 32, Capt. Hon. Duncombe Pleydell Bouverie, in which frigate he participated, as Midshipman, in all the operations (including the capture of Maldonado and the island of Gorriti) that took place in the Rio de la Plata between Oct. 1806 and her return to England, in Sept. 1807, with Lieut.-General Whitelocke. After having further, in company with the THALIA 36, gone in fruitless pursuit of two French frigates to the latitude of Greenland, and endured three months of great privation on the coast of Labrador, he removed, in 1808, to the AFRICAINE 38, Capt. Rich. Raggett, and sailed for the Mediterranean, where, in Jan. 1809, he was received on board the TIGRE 74, Capt. Benj. Hallowell. On the night of 31 Oct. following we find him serving in the boats of a squadron under Lieut. John Tailour at the capture and destruction, after a desperate struggle and a loss to the British of 15 killed and 55 wounded, of the French store-ship *Lamproie* of 16 guns and 116 men, bombards *Victoire* and *Grondeur*, and armed xebec *Normande*, with a convoy of seven merchant-vessels, defended by numerous strong batteries in the Bay of Rosas. He had, a few days previously, assisted in causing the self-destruction of the French ships-of-the-line *Robuste* and *Lion*.* On 17 Aug. 1810 he was confirmed a Lieutenant (having been ordered to act as such on 21 of the preceding June) in the VILLE DE PARIS 110, Capt. Rich. Thomas; and he was next, 29 Sept. following, appointed to the ALCESTE 38, Capt. Murray Maxwell. In that ship he aided, in company with the BELLE POULE 38, in destroying, 5 May, 1811, a French national brig lying in the harbour of Parenza and defended by a galling cross fire from two batteries. He also took part, 29 Nov. 1811, and obtained mention for the admirable manner in which he directed the main-deck guns, in an action of two hours and a half, fought with consummate gallantry, between the ALCESTE and ACTIVE 38 on one side, and the French 40-gun frigates *Pomone* and *Pauline* on the other, which terminated in the capture of the *Pomone* and escape of the *Pauline*, after a loss had been occasioned to the ALCESTE of 7 men killed and 13 wounded.† At the end of a period of two years passed as Lieutenant of the SCEPTRE and ALBION 74's, flag-ships of Rear-Admiral Geo. Cockburn on the North American station, Mr. Montagu was awarded a second promotal commission 7 June, 1814, and on 23 of the same month appointed to the command of the THISTLE 12, which sloop he brought home and paid off in Sept. 1815. His last appointment was, 9 April, 1823, to the RIFLEMAN 18, fitting for the Halifax station, where he remained until posted, 17 July, 1824. He accepted the Retirement 1 Oct. 1846. AGENTS—Messrs. Ommanney.

MONTAGU. (Captain, 1820. F-P., 18; H-P., 26.)

JOHN WILLIAM MONTAGU, born 18 Jan. 1790, is second son of the late Admiral Sir Geo. Montagu, G.C.B.,‡ by Charlotte, daughter and co-heir of

* *Vide* Gaz. 1809, p 1907. † *V.* Gaz. 1812, p. 567.

‡ Sir Geo. Montagu was born 12 Dec. 1750; entered the R. N. Academy in 1763; and first went to sea in the PRESIDENT 50, Capt. (afterwards Lord) Gardner. He was promoted in 1770 to the rank of Lieutenant; was made Commander into the KINGFISHER sloop; and in 1773 was posted into the FOWEY 20. In that ship, during the first American war, he covered the retreat and embarkation of the army under Sir Wm. Howe, at the evacuation of Boston, and was present at the siege of New York. He subsequently, assuming command (after two years of servitude in the ROMNEY 50, his father's flag-ship) of the PEARL of 32 guns, 700 tons, and 220 men, effected the capture, 14 Sept. 1799, of the *Santa Monica* of 32 guns, 900 tons, and 280 men, 38 of whom were killed and 45 wounded, with a loss to the British of 12 killed and 19 wounded. In Dec of the same year he accompanied Sir Geo. Rodney to the relief of Gibraltar; and on 8 of the ensuing month he assisted at the capture of the Caraccas convoy, with which he returned to England in company with the AFRICA 64. On 30 Sept. in the latter year it was his fortune to make prize, after a long and obstinate battle (attended with a loss to the PEARL of 6 killed and 10 wounded, and to the enemy of 20 killed and 24 wounded), of *L'Espérance*, a French frigate of about equal force. On 16 March, 1781, he was in company with the squadron under Vice-Admiral Arbuthnot in a partial action fought with the French under M. de Ternay. The PEARL being paid off in 1782, Capt. Montagu, in 1790, obtained command of the HECTOR 74; in which ship, in June, 1793, he was employed, under Rear-Admiral Gardner, in the unsuccessful attack on Martinique. Attaining the rank of Rear-Admiral 12 April, 1794, he was ordered, in the early part of the following month, to escort the outward-bound East India fleet, and other convoys, amounting in

Geo. Wroughton, Esq.; and grandson of Admiral John Montagu,* himself the great-grandson of Hon. Jas. Montagu, third son of Henry, first Earl of Manchester, ancestor of the present Duke of that name. He is brother of Lieut.-Colonel Geo. Wroughton Wroughton, of Wilcot, co. Wilts, and of Capt. Jas. Montagu, R.N.; and brother-in-law of the late Vice-Admiral Sir John Gore, K.C.B., by the marriage to that officer of his eldest sister, Georgiana, now a Bedchamber Woman to Queen Adelaide. One of his uncles, James, was killed in command of the MONTAGU 74 in the action of 1 June, 1794; and another, Edward, Lieut.-Colonel of Artillery, Hon. E. I. Co.'s service, fell at the storming of Seringapatam in 1799. Capt. Montagu is second-cousin of the present Lieut. E. P. Montagu, R.N.

This officer entered the Royal Naval Academy in 1803; and embarked, about 1806, as Midshipman, on board the CAPTAIN 74, Capt. Geo. Cockburn; in which ship, on 27 Sept. in that year, he witnessed the capture, in the Bay of Biscay, of the French frigate *Le Président* of 44 guns. In Feb. 1807 he became Master's Mate of the FAME 74, Capt. Rich. Henry Alex. Bennett; and on 9 Oct. 1809, after having been employed off Cadiz and on boat-service at the defence of Rosas, he was promoted to the rank of Lieutenant. His succeeding appointments were—31 March, 1810, to the STANDARD 64, Capt. Aiskew Paffard Hollis, attached to the force in the Baltic—29 Oct. following, to the EMERALD 36, Capt. Fred. Lewis Maitland, under whom he served off the coast of Ireland and made a voyage to the Cape of Good Hope—and, 18 Dec. 1811, 14 June, 1812, and 29 March, 1814, to the EDINBURGH 74, Capt. Robt. Rolles, CERBERUS 32, Capt. Thos. Garth, and REVENGE 74, flag-ship of Sir John Gore, all stationed in the Mediterranean. On 29 Jan. 1813 he commanded one of the boats of the CERBERUS at the capture of a trabaccolo, armed with 2 guns, and deeply laden with corn and flour for the garrison of Corfu: he assisted, in the following May, in bringing out from under a martello tower, to the southward of Brindisi, a vessel mounting 1 6-pounder, from Otranto bound to Ancona; and on 28 of the same month, taking charge of two boats belonging to the CERBERUS, he participated, in conjunction with two others under the orders of Lieut. Wm. Henry Nares of the APOLLO 38, in a most determined and gallant attack upon a convoy protected by 11 gun-boats near Otranto, where the cliffs were covered with French troops.† In the REVENGE Lieut. Montagu served at the blockade of Venice and at the capture of Corfu. Attaining the rank of Commander 31 May, 1814, he was successively, 1 and 31 March, 1819, appointed in that capacity to the CADMUS and BRISK sloops; in the latter of which, until posted, 30 Nov. 1820, we find him actively employed in the suppression of smuggling. He assumed command, 7 June, 1828, of the CROCODILE 28, fitting for the East Indies, whence he returned in the summer of 1832; and he was lastly, from 23 Nov. 1839 until March, 1841, employed in the BRITANNIA 120 and QUEEN 110, as Flag-Captain to Sir Edw. Codrington, Commander-in-Chief at Portsmouth. He accepted the Retirement 1 Oct. 1846.

Capt. Montagu married, 12 March, 1840, Isabella Elizabeth, daughter of Chas. Geo. Beauclerk, Esq., of St. Leonard's Forest, Sussex, by whom he has issue.

the whole to about 800 sail, as far to the southward as Cape Finisterre. Immediately on the arrival of the intelligence of Lord Howe's victory of 1 June, he was again ordered to sea in search of a valuable French convoy expected from America; and on 9 of that month, with eight 74-gun ships, one 64, and several frigates under his command, he fell in with the enemy's fleet, consisting of 14 effective line-of-battle ships, and of 5 others which had been disabled in the recent battle. In the face of a force so superior the Rear-Admiral, of course, could only act on the defensive. After a few days' further cruize he returned to Cadsand Bay and struck his flag. He was advanced to the rank of Vice-Admiral 1 June, 1795; and on 1 Jan. 1801 to that of full Admiral From June, 1803, until Jan. 1809, he held the office of Commander-in-Chief at Portsmouth; and so highly did he acquire the respect and esteem of the Captains who during that period fitted out at the port, that in Aug. 1810 he was presented, by a large body of them, with a superb piece of plate. He was nominated a G.C.B. in 1815; and died an Admiral of the Red in 1829.

* Admiral John Montagu served his country with zeal and fidelity for 63 years. He commanded the squadron employed on the coast of North America previous to the colonial war; was afterwards appointed Governor of Newfoundland; and held the chief command at Portsmouth subsequent to the peace of 1783. He died in 1795.

† *Vide* Gaz. 1813, p. 1791.

MONTAGU. (COMMANDER, 1841. F-P., 16; H-P., 12)

JOHN WILLIAM MONTAGU is son of the late Admiral Robt. Montagu;* and a descendant of Admiral Sir Henry Montagu, M.P., who was created Earl of Sandwich as a reward for his loyalty in inducing the fleet to declare in favour of King Charles II. Commander Montagu's grandfather, John, fourth Earl of Sandwich, was First Lord of the Admiralty in 1763, and again from 1771 to 1782.

This officer entered the Navy, 4 Dec. 1819, as Midshipman, on board the PHAETON 46, Capt. Wm. Augustus Montagu. After serving for two years and a half in that frigate on the coast of North America, he was next, from July, 1822, until Dec. 1825, employed in the ESPIÈGLE sloop, and colonial brig WIZARD, in surveying the west coast of Africa, in cruizing in suppression of the slave-trade, and in civilizing the natives of Madagascar. Between 1 Jan. 1826, in the course of which year he passed his examination, and 3 Aug. 1827, Mr. Montagu appears to have been attached, at Portsmouth and on the coast of Ireland, to the VICTORY 104, WILLIAM AND MARY yacht, TIGER cutter, and ROYAL CHARLOTTE yacht; the latter under the command of the present Sir Chas. Malcolm, by whom we find him officially described as a young officer of high promise, "zealous, manly, and steady in the performance of his duty." He obtained a Lieutenant's commission on 18 Sept. in the year last mentioned; and was subsequently appointed—25 Aug. 1828, to the BRITOMART 10, Capts. Russell Henry Manners and Edw. John Johnson, employed on the coast of Portugal—26 Oct. 1830, to the REVENGE 78, Capts. Jas. Hillyar and Donald Hugh Mackay, in which ship he continued for about three years on the Home station—16 Aug. 1834, as Second-Lieutenant (a rank he had for some time held in the REVENGE), to the MALABAR 74, Capt. Sir Wm. Augustus Montagu, with whom he served for two years, chiefly in the Mediterranean and off Lisbon—20 Aug. 1839, for 12 months, to the Coast Guard in Norfolk and Kent—and 19 Aug. 1841, as Senior, to the ISIS 44, Capt. Sir John Marshall, fitting at Chatham. He attained his present rank 23 Nov. 1841; and has since been on half-pay.

Commander Montagu is married and has issue. AGENT—Frederick Dufaur.

MONTAGU. (COMMANDER, 1815. F-P., 14; H-P., 34.)

MONTAGU MONTAGU entered the Navy, 6 April, 1799, as Fst.-cl. Vol., on board the DRYAD 36, Capts. Chas. John Moore Mansfield and Robt. Williams; with whom he continued employed on the

* Admiral Robt. Montagu was confirmed a Post-Captain in the SEAHORSE of 20 guns, 3 March, 1781 He commanded the EXETER 64 in the action between Sir Edw. Hughes and M. de Suffrein, off Negapatnam, 6 July, 1782; and was afterwards appointed to the FLORA 38, AQUILON 32, SAMPSON 64, and HECTOR and CUMBERLAND 74's. In consideration of his having, when in the SAMPSON in the autumn of 1794, convoyed 19 of the Hon. Co.'s ships home from the East Indies, in company with the LION 64 (on board of which was Lord Macartney returning from his embassy to China), Capt. Montagu was presented, by the Court of Directors, with the sum of 350 guineas. In the HECTOR he served in Hotham's partial action of 13 July, 1795. Being advanced to the rank of Rear-Admiral 14 Feb. 1799, he was subsequently, in 1801-2, employed in the chief command on the Jamaica station, vacant by the death of Lord Hugh Seymour; and, after the renewal of hostilities, in command of a part of the North Sea fleet under Lord Keith. He became a Vice-Admiral 9 Nov. 1805; and a full Admiral 31 July, 1810.

Home station in the same vessel, and in the RUSSELL and MINOTAUR 74's, until May, 1805, nearly the whole time in the capacity of Midshipman. In the ship last mentioned, under Capt. Mansfield, he assisted, we believe, at the capture, 28 May, 1803, of the French 36-gun frigate *Franchise*. Being nominated, 3 Dec. 1805, Acting-Lieutenant of the SUPERB 74, he was afforded an opportunity of participating, under the flag of Sir John Thos. Duckworth, in the action off St. Domingo 6 Feb. 1806, and was in consequence officially promoted by a commission dated 5 of the ensuing month. His succeeding appointments were—5 Aug. 1806, to the ROYAL GEORGE 100, bearing the flag of the same officer, with whom he passed the Dardanells in Feb. 1807, and afterwards served in the West Indies and Channel—13 May, 1809, to the SAN JOSEF 110, also flag-ship of Sir J. T. Duckworth, lying at Spithead—in the course of the latter year and of 1810, to the HYPERION 36, Capt. Thos. Chas. Brodie, SHARK sloop, Capt. Edm. Denman, GARLAND 22, Capts. Charlton and Graves, and AVON sloop, Capt. Henry Tillieux Fraser, all on the Jamaica station, whence he invalided in March, 1811—29 Oct. 1812, to the BARROSA 36, Capt. Wm. Henry Shirreff, attached to the force on the coast of North America—31 Dec. 1813 (seven months after he had left the BARROSA), to the PUISSANT 74, Capt. Benj. Wm. Page, at Spithead—and, in the early part of 1815, to the IMPREGNABLE 98, YORK 74, and ST. GEORGE 100, as Flag-Lieutenant to Sir J. T. Duckworth at Plymouth. Since his attainment of the rank of Commander, 13 June, 1815, he has been on half-pay. AGENTS—Messrs. Stilwell.

MONTAGU, Kt., C B., K.C.H. (REAR-ADMIRAL OF THE WHITE, 1841. F-P., 23; H-P., 28.)

SIR WILLIAM AUGUSTUS MONTAGU entered the Navy, 4 Sept. 1796, as Fst.-cl. Vol., on board the GLATTON 50, Capt. Henry Trollope; under whom he continued employed on the Home station, as Midshipman, in the RUSSELL 74 (part of the victorious fleet in the action off Camperdown 11 Oct. 1797), and JUSTE 80, until transferred, about the close of 1800, to the SIRIUS 36, Capt. Sir Rich. King. In that ship he witnessed, 27 Jan. 1801, the surrender of the French 36-gun frigate *La Dédaigneuse*. After a servitude of four years in the East Indies on board the DASHER, of which sloop (commanded at first by Capt. Delafons) he was successively confirmed Lieutenant and Commander by commissions dated 14 Nov. 1804 and 31 Oct. 1805, he was there nominated, 8 June, 1807, Acting-Captain of the TERPSICHORE frigate—an appointment sanctioned, 8 Dec. following, by the approval of the Admiralty. In March of the following year Capt. Montagu, whose ship mounted but 28 guns and had only 180 men on board, fell in with, fought, and (with a loss to himself of 21 men killed and 22 wounded) fairly beat off the French frigate *Sémillante* of 40 guns and a crew of at least 300 men. Being soon afterwards appointed to the CORNWALLIS of 50 guns and 335 men, he assisted, in the early part of 1810, at the reduction of the island of Amboyna, where he elicited from Capt. Edw. Tucker, the senior officer present, the greatest praise for the able nature of his support in the different actions with the enemy's batteries and forts, and for the judgment he displayed in the navigation of his ship amidst baffling winds and strong currents.* About the same period Capt. Montagu succeeded in effecting the capture of the Dutch corvettes *Mandarin* and *De Ruyter*. In the following Nov. he was intrusted with the command of the naval brigade landed to assist at the reduction of the Isle of France; during the operations connected with which, particularly on the occasion of the defeat of the French troops before St. Louis, 1 Dec., his zeal and exertions were such as to call forth the sincere acknowledgments of Major-General Abercromby. His last appointments were—8 Sept. 1812, to the NIOBE 40, employed until June, 1814, on the Channel, American, and Lisbon stations—29 Oct. 1819, to the PHAETON 46, which ship he commanded on service at Halifax until put out of commission in Sept. 1822—and 25 July, 1834, to the MALABAR 74, fitting for the Mediterranean, where, and off Lisbon, he continued until ordered home at the close of 1837 for the purpose of being paid off. He attained Flag-rank 23 Nov. 1841.

The Rear-Admiral (a Deputy-Lieutenant for co. Huntingdon) was nominated a C.B. 8 Dec. 1815; a K.H. 5 Oct. 1830; and a K.C.H. (accompanied with the honour of Knighthood) in Jan. 1832. He married, 26 Aug. 1823, Anne, third daughter of the late Sir Geo. Wm. Leeds, Bart., of Croxton Park, Cambridgeshire.

* *Vide* Gaz. 1810, p. 1482.

MONTGOMERIE. (Captain, 1820. F-P., 15; H-P., 30.)

ALEXANDER MONTGOMERIE is second son of the late Alex. Montgomerie, Esq., of Annick Lodge, co. Ayr (brother of Hugh, twelfth Earl of Eglinton, and grand-uncle of the present Peer), by Elizabeth, daughter of Dr. Taylor; and brother-in-law of the Right Hon. David Boyle, Lord Justice-Clerk. His brother, Hugh, married a daughter of Lieut.-General Rumley, E. I. Co.'s service; and his grand-uncle, James, died a Lieut.-General in the Army 13 April, 1829. His eldest brother, the present Wm. Eglinton Montgomerie, Esq., of Annick Lodge, is a Magistrate and Deputy-Lieutenant, and Lieut.-Colonel Commandant of the Ayrshire Yeomanry Cavalry.

This officer entered the Navy, 27 June, 1802, as Fst.-cl. Vol., on board the HAZARD sloop, Capt. R. J. Neve, lying at Portsmouth; and from the following Aug. until Aug. 1808, was employed as Midshipman and Master's Mate in the ARGO 44, and TIGRE 74, both commanded by Capt. Benj. Hallowell. In the ARGO, after visiting the coast of Africa, he assisted at the reduction of Ste. Lucie and Tobago; and when in the TIGRE, besides accompanying Lord Nelson to the West Indies in pursuit of the combined fleets of France and Spain, he participated in the operations of 1807 in Egypt, was present at the capture of Alexandria, and saw much boat service on Lake Mareotis. In Sept. 1809, on passing his examination, he joined the ORPHEUS 36; and from that ship he was soon transferred to the SCEPTRE 74, Capt. Sam. Jas. Ballard, for a passage to the West Indies; where, on 18 of the ensuing Dec., we find him contributing, in the boats of a squadron under the personal command of Capt. Hugh Cameron, who was killed, to the destruction, in L'Ance la Barque, Guadeloupe, of the 40-gun frigates *Loire* and *Seine*, laden with stores, and protected by numerous strong batteries. As a reward for his conduct on the occasion, which was officially reported, he was nominated, the next day, Acting-Lieutenant of the FREIJA frigate, Capt. John Hayes—an appointment the Admiralty confirmed by a commission dated 4 May, 1810. Previously to that event Mr. Montgomerie, during the operations which led to the reduction of Guadeloupe, had been employed in the boats of his own ship and the SCEPTRE in destroying the various batteries erected on the island. After three months' command of the MAGNANIME at Sheerness, he was appointed, 28 Jan. 1811, to the AQUILON 32, Capts. Wm. Bowles and Jas. Boxer, under whom he served for upwards of three years and a half on the North Sea, Baltic, and South American stations. When in the Baltic in 1812, and engaged with the boats under his orders in an attempt to bring some vessels off from the island of Rugen, he greatly distinguished himself by his conduct in capturing a temporary fort occupied by a superior number of troops, whom, on their being reinforced and endeavouring to recover their loss, he several times repulsed. On his return from the Rio de la Plata in Sept. 1814, Mr. Montgomerie, who had been latterly First-Lieutenant of the AQUILON, found that he had been promoted to the rank of Commander on 7 of the preceding June, and appointed to the RACOON sloop, which vessel, however, being at the time on the coast of Brazil, he never joined. He afterwards, 21 March, 1818, assumed command of the CONFIANCE 18, fitting for the West Indies, where he became, 13 July, 1820, Acting-Captain of the SAPPHIRE 26. He was confirmed 3 Oct. following; and in Sept. 1821 he returned to England and was paid off. He accepted the Retirement 1 Oct. 1846. AGENT—John P. Muspratt.

MONTGOMERY. (CAPTAIN, 1846.)

ALEXANDER LESLIE MONTGOMERY, born 15 March, 1807, is second son (by Sarah Mercer, daughter of Leslie Grove, Esq., of Grove Hall, co. Donegal) of the late Sir Henry Cunningham Montgomery, Bart., M.P. for St. Michael's and the borough of Yarmouth, who, during the war with Tippoo Sultan, won distinction at the head of three battalions of infantry and 5000 cavalry, and was afterwards, in 1803, appointed Inspecting Field-Officer of Yeomanry and Volunteers in co. Donegal, with the rank of Lieutenant-Colonel in the Army. Capt. Montgomery's eldest brother, the present Sir Henry Cunningham Montgomery, Bart., is in the civil service of the East India Company at Madras; his next, Hugh, is an officer in the Madras Army; and his youngest, Arthur, is married to a daughter of Colonel Wyndham, of Petworth House, co. Sussex. His eldest sister is the wife of the Hon. and Rev. Grantham Munter Yorke, youngest son of the late Admiral Sir Joseph Sydney Yorke, K.C.B., and brother of the Earl of Hardwicke, Captain R.N.

This officer entered the Royal Naval College 7 Oct. 1819; embarked in Oct. 1821; and, on passing his final examination, was made Lieutenant, 30 Aug. 1828, into the HELICON 10, Capt. Robt. Henry Stanhope, at the Cape of Good Hope. His succeeding appointments were—26 Feb. 1830, to the ALLIGATOR 28, Capt. Chas. Philip Yorke (now Earl of Hardwicke), with whom he served in the Mediterranean until paid off in the summer of 1831—9 May, 1833, to the ORESTES 18, Capts. Wm. Nugent Glascock and Sir Wm. Dickson, in which vessel he continued, chiefly on the Lisbon station, until put out of commission in the spring of 1834—and 16 July, 1836, to the INCONSTANT 36, Capt. Dan. Pring, also attached to the force off Lisbon. He was promoted from the latter ship to the rank of Commander 28 June, 1838; and from 12 March, 1845, until advanced to the rank he now holds, 2 July, 1846, was employed on the south-east coast of America in the GRECIAN 16. He has since been on half-pay.

Capt. Montgomery married, 30 June, 1840, Caroline Rose, daughter of Jas. Campbell, Esq., of Hampton Court, co. Middlesex. AGENT—J. Hinxman.

MONTGOMERY. (COMMANDER, 1815. F-P., 22; H-P., 27.)

THOMAS MONTGOMERY, born 10 March, 1786, is son of the Rev. Robt. Montgomery, Rector of Monaghan, whose family for many generations represented co. Monaghan in Parliament.

This officer entered the Royal Naval Academy in July, 1798; embarked, in May, 1802, as Fst.-cl. Vol., on board the AURORA 38, Capt. Micajah Malbon; and in the course of the following year was present, as Midshipman, at the surrender of the islands of St. Pierre and Miquelon. From Feb. 1804 to March, 1806, he served, chiefly at the blockade of Brest, in the PLANTAGENET 74, Capts. Hon. Michael De Courcy, Fras. Pender, and Wm. Bradley. He then removed to the FORWARD gun-brig, Lieut.-Commander Dan. Shiels, and on 1 Oct. following he was made Lieutenant into the URANIE 38, Capts. Christopher Laroche and Thos. Manby, also on the coast of France. His succeeding appointments were—13 Oct. 1807, to the HYACINTH sloop, Capt. John Davie, whom he accompanied to the Brazils—12 Dec. 1808, to the MARLBOROUGH 74, Capt Graham Moore, employed at first on the latter station, and then in the North Sea, where, in 1809, he commanded a division of boats at the bombardment of Flushing, and continued attached to the gun-boat service on the river Scheldt until the evacuation of Walcheren—at the close of 1811 (after about 12 months of half-pay) to the AFRICAINE 38, Capt. Hon. Edw. Rodney, for passage on promotion to the East Indies—in 1812 to the HECATE 18, Capt. Joseph Drury, the boats of which sloop he commanded in Jan. 1813, at the storming of the works of Sambas, a piratical settlement on the coast of Borneo—and 13 Jan. 1814, to the CLORINDE 38, Capt. Thos. Briggs, with whom he returned home and was paid off in Sept. of the same year. He was advanced to his present rank 13 June, 1815; and was subsequently employed for a period of seven years in the Coast Guard in Ireland. AGENT—Joseph Woodhead.

MONTRESOR. (COMMANDER, 1843.)

FREDERICK BYNG MONTRESOR entered the Navy 27 June, 1823; passed his examination in 1829; and obtained his first commission 30 July, 1835. His succeeding appointments were, on the North America and West India station—30 Dec. 1835, as Additional-Lieutenant, to the PRESIDENT 52, flag-ship of Sir Geo. Cockburn—24 March, 1836, to the FORTE 44, Capt. Watkin Owen Pell—3 Feb. 1837, again as Additional, to the MELVILLE 74, bearing the flag of Sir Peter Halkett—13 July, 1837, to the CHAMPION 18, Capt. Geo. St. Vincent King—18 March, 1839 (a few months after the latter vessel had been paid off), to the WINCHESTER 50, flag-ship of Sir Thos. Harvey—and 12 Dec. 1840, to the command of the PICKLE schooner. He acquired the rank he now holds 12 Jan. 1843; and has been in command, since 20 April, 1846, of the CYGNET 6, and WANDERER 12, on the coast of Africa. His appointment to the latter vessel took place 14 Feb. 1847.

MONYPENNY. (COMMANDER, 1841. F-P., 17; H-P., 7.)

WILLIAM BACKHOUSE MONYPENNY, born 13 Dec. 1808, is fourth son of the late Thos. Monypenny, Esq., by Catherine, daughter of Isaac Rutton, Esq., of Ospringe and Whitehills, co. Kent; and brother of the present Thos. Gybbon Monypenny, Esq., of Hole House, Rolvenden, a Magistrate and Deputy-Lieutenant for cos. Kent and Sussex, and late M.P. for Rye. His youngest brother, Robert Honywood, died a Captain in the 4th Infantry 8 March, 1839.

This officer entered the Navy, 29 April, 1823, as Fst.-cl. Vol., on board the RAMILLIES 74, Capt. Edw. Brace, with whom, until Nov. 1824, he served on the Home and West India stations, part of the time as Midshipman of the GANGES 84. He was then for three years and a half employed in the GANNET 18, Capt Fras. Brace, on the coast of Ireland, and also in the Mediterranean; where he further, from 1828 until 1830, served on board the GLOUCESTER 74, Capt. Houston Stewart, and PELICAN 18, Capt. Fras. Deane Hutcheson. Joining next, 9 Nov. 1831, in the capacity of Mate (he had passed his examination 4 July, 1829), the ÆTNA surveying-vessel, Capt. Edw. Belcher, he proceeded to the coast of Africa, and was afterwards, previously to his return to the Mediterranean, employed on the river Douro for the protection of British property during the hostilities between Pedro and Miguel. While in charge, in 1833, of one of the ÆTNA's decked boats, manned with but 4 hands, he accidentally lost sight of the ship off the Straits of Gibraltar, but providentially succeeded in reaching Portsmouth in his flimsy tenement after a passage of 19 days, arriving there on 18 Sept. Towards the close of the same year he again sailed for the African coast in the ÆTNA, with Capt. Wm. Geo. Skyring. He continued in that vessel under the command of Lieut. Wm. Arlett and Capt. Alex. Thos. Emeric Vidal (10 months of the time as Acting-Lieutenant) until Oct. 1835; and on 30 Sept. 1837 (having further served as Mate, in the Channel, off Lisbon, in the Mediterranean, and at Plymouth, in the PEMBROKE 74, Capts. Sir Thos. Fellowes and Fairfax Moresby, and DONEGAL 78, Capts. Fras.

Brace and John Drake) he was promoted to the rank of Lieutenant. His succeeding appointments were—3 Nov. 1837, as Additional, to the PRESIDENT 52, flag-ship of Rear-Admiral Chas. Bayne Hodgson Ross in South America—and 16 June, 1838, as Senior, to the SULPHUR surveying-vessel, commanded by his old Captain, Belcher. On his subsequent arrival in China from the Pacific, we find him assisting, in the early part of 1841, at the capture of Chuenpee, Tycocktow, and the Bogue; uniting, also, in an attack made by a squadron under Capt. Herbert on the enemy's camp, fort, and ship *Cambridge*, bearing the Chinese Admiral's flag, at their position below Whampoa Reach, where 98 guns were in the whole destroyed;* and participating in the operations against Canton. As a reward for his exertions he was promoted to the rank of Commander by commission dated 8 June, 1841. He left the SULPHUR in the following Nov., and has since been on half-pay.

* *Vide* Gaz. 1841, p. 1501.

MOODIE. (LIEUT., 1816. F-P., 7; H-P., 32.)

DONALD MOODIE entered the Navy, 15 Dec. 1808, as Fst.-cl. Vol., on board the ARDENT 64, Capt. Jas. Vashon, bearing the flag of Sir Edm. Nagle at Leith. He removed in March, 1809, to the SPITFIRE sloop, Capt. John Ellis; and after serving for two years and a half in that vessel in the North Sea and Channel, at Quebec, and on the Spanish coast, he became Midshipman, in Sept. 1811, of the AMERICA 74, Capt. Josias Rowley, on the Mediterranean station; where, in 1813-14, he witnessed the unsuccessful attack upon Leghorn, the reduction of Santa Maria and the enemy's forts and defences in the Gulf of Spezia, and the fall of Genoa. Quitting the AMERICA in Oct. 1814, he next, until Dec. 1815, served off Ushant and Madeira, and again in the Mediterranean, in the GLASGOW 50, Capt. Hon. Henry Duncan, and IMPREGNABLE 104, flag-ship of Sir Josias Rowley. His commission bears date 9 Dec. 1816. He has since been on half-pay.

Lieut. Moodie has been for some time Acting-President of the Government Bank at the Cape of Good Hope. AGENT—J. Hinxman.

MOONEY. (LIEUTENANT, 1844.)

WILLIAM MOONEY passed his examination 22 Oct. 1836; and has been serving since 1841 on the North America and West India station, as Mate and Lieutenant of the THUNDER surveying-vessel, Capt. Edw. Barnett. His commission bears date 26 Aug. 1844.

MOOR. (LIEUT., 1815. F-P., 9; H-P., 32.)

PHILIP MOOR was born 2 June, 1793. His brother James, a Lieutenant R.M., died in the island of Marie-galante in 1808.

This officer entered the Navy, 30 Aug. 1806, as Fst.-cl. Vol., on board the WINDSOR CASTLE 74, Capt. Chas. Boyles, in which ship, after witnessing Sir Sam. Hood's destruction of four heavy French frigates off Rochefort, he passed the Dardanells with Sir John Duckworth, and was present at the destruction of the Turkish squadron off Point Pesquies. Joining next, in Oct. 1808, the UNICORN 32, Capts. Lucius Ferdinand Hardyman and Alex. Robt. Kerr, he assisted, as Midshipman, in embarking the army after the battle of Corunna in Jan. 1809, and in the ensuing April beheld Lord Cochrane's brilliant attack on the French shipping in Aix Roads. In Sept. of the same year he rejoined Capt. Hardyman on board the ARMIDE 38; but, previously to doing so, he appears to have attracted the notice of Lord Gambier by his gallant defence of the UNICORN's launch against nine of the enemy's gun-boats after his commanding-officer, Lieut. Hamilton, had been killed. On leaving the ARMIDE, in May, 1810, he became in succession attached to the DREADNOUGHT 98, flag-ship of Rear-Admiral Thos. Sotheby, and to the IMPÉRIEUSE 38, LIVELY 38, and TRIDENT 64, bearing each the flag of Rear-Admiral Boyles, to whom he acted as aide-de-camp. In the LIVELY, commanded by Capt. Geo. M'Kinley, it was Mr. Moor's misfortune to be wrecked, 10 Aug. 1810, on a reef of rocks near Point Coura, in the island of Malta. During an after servitude of 13 months in the SCOUT sloop, Capt. Alex. Renton Sharpe, he had charge for some time of a watch, carried two prizes safely into port, and aided, in company with the POMONE 38, and UNITÉ 36, at the destruction, 1 May, 1811, after a gallant action of an hour and a half, in Sagone Bay (where the SCOUT incurred a loss of 3 men killed and 9 wounded), of the two armed store-ships *Giraffe* and *Nourrice*, each mounting from 20 to 30 guns, and protected by a 5-gun battery, a martello-tower, and a body of about 200 regular troops. In Dec. 1811, three months after he had returned to the TRIDENT, he was received on board the THAMES 32, Capt. Chas. Napier, by whom he was soon awarded the rating of Master's Mate. While in that ship, besides being thrice deputed to perform the duties of prize-master, he had command of a tender, and came into frequent contact with the enemy on the Calabrian coast. He once, when on shore on impress service at Malta, received a very severe wound in the under-jaw, and had five of his teeth knocked out, the remainder being so broken and displaced as to be afterwards rendered unserviceable. He was on two other occasions also slightly wounded, and (a fact well attested) had a piece of his hat in one instance shot away by a cannon-ball while in charge of a boat. During the two years which preceded his attainment of the rank of Lieutenant, 16 Feb. 1815, he served, as Midshipman and Master's Mate, in the BELLEROPHON 74, Capt. Edw. Hawker, flag-ship of Sir Rich. Goodwin Keats at Newfoundland. In Dec. 1814, having volunteered his services, he took charge of a recaptured vessel, deeply laden with crockery-ware, and, after a desperate passage of 11 days, succeeded in carrying her into Plymouth. During eight days of the time the sea was perpetually washing over, and, as there existed no possibility of opening the hatches or of going below, those on board were reduced to the necessity of subsisting entirely upon raw meat. The conduct exhibited by Mr. Moor on this, as on a previous occasion, afforded Capt. Hawker an opportunity of recommending him to the Admiralty as an officer most fully deserving promotion. Since the receipt of his commission he has been on half-pay.

MOORE. (COMMANDER, 1817.)

CHARLES MOORE (*a*) entered the Navy, in Jan. 1806, as Midshipman, on board the EAGLE 74, commanded by the late Sir Chas. Rowley; and, while in that ship (of which he was created a Lieutenant 26 Jan. 1813), he accompanied the expedition of 1809 to the Walcheren, co-operated in the defence of Cadiz in 1810, assisted at the capture, 27 Nov. 1811, of *La Corceyre* frigate, carrying 28 guns, together with 170 seamen and 130 soldiers, and beheld the fall, in 1813, of Fiumé, Trieste (where he served on shore, and by his courage and activity elicited the admiration of Rear-Admiral Fremantle*), and other places in the Adriatic. Being subsequently nominated Flag-Lieutenant to the above officer, on his assuming the chief command at the Nore, he served in that capacity both in the NAMUR and BULWARK 74's. In the spring of 1817 he was lent to the ROYAL SOVEREIGN yacht, Capt. Sir Edw. W. C. R. Owen, for the purpose of escorting the King of the French from England to Calais; off which place he so distinguished himself by his heroic intrepidity in a boat in saving the lives of part of the crew of a vessel which had been driven on shore during a strong north-west gale, that he was promoted to the rank of Commander 24 June in the same year. His last appointment was to the Coast Guard, in which service he remained from 18 March, 1834, until 1837.

Commander Moore married, in 1819, at Grantham, co. Lincoln, Elizabeth Anne, second daughter of the late Rich. Palmer, Esq. AGENTS—Messrs. Chard.

* *Vide* Gaz. 1813, p. 2478.

MOORE. (Lieutenant, 1841.)

Charles Moore entered the Navy 23 Nov. 1825; passed his examination in 1833; and obtained his commission 15 March, 1841. His succeeding appointments were—17 March, 1841, as Additional-Lieutenant, to the Southampton 50, bearing the flag of Sir Edw. Durnford King, Commander-in-Chief at the Brazils and Cape of Good Hope—25 Nov. 1841, to the Pearl 20, Capt. Rich. Henry Stopford, on the South American station, whence he returned to England and was paid off in 1844—and, 11 March, 1845, to the Canopus 80, Capt. Fairfax Moresby, with whom he was for about 12 months employed on Home service. Agents—Messrs. Stilwell.

MOORE. (Lieut., 1815. f-p., 11; h-p., 32.)

Edward Moore entered the Navy, 5 Nov. 1804, as Fst.-cl. Vol., on board the Neptune 98, Capts. Sir Thos. Williams and Thos. Fras. Fremantle, stationed in the Channel and off Cadiz; and from Dec. 1806 until Jan. 1812 was employed, as Midshipman (a rating he had attained in Dec. 1805) and Master's Mate, in the Dreadnought 98, Capts. Wm. Lechmere, Geo. Burgoyne Salt, Valentine Collard, and Sam. Hood Linzee (flag-ship for some time of Rear-Admiral Thos. Sotheby), in the Channel, off Rochefort and Lisbon, and in the Baltic. During the next two years and seven months we find him serving on the Home and Brazilian stations, in the Bulwark 74, bearing the broad pendant of Sir Rich. King, Montagu 74, flag-ship of Rear-Admiral Manley Dixon, and Nereus 42, Capt. Manley Hall Dixon. He was then, 2 Sept. 1814, appointed to the Albacore sloop, Capt. Joseph Patey, in which vessel he continued, still at the Brazils, until July, 1815; at which period he took up a commission bearing date 13 of the preeding March. He has since been on half-pay.

MOORE. (Lieut., 1814. f-p., 10; h-p., 33.)

Howard Moore entered the Navy, in Jan. 1804, as Midshipman, on board the Renard 14, Lieut.-Commander Rich. Spencer, stationed in the Mediterranean; where, from Oct. 1805 until Oct. 1812, he served, as Acting-Master, in the Spider 16, Lieut.-Commanders Wm. Stewart and Wm. Sandford Oliver, Herald 20, Capt. Geo. Jackson, Weasel sloop, Capt. Henry Prescott, and Alceste 38 Capt. Murray Maxwell. In the Herald we find him, in 1810, employed in the defence of Sicily against Murat, and in constant action with the enemy's gun-boats and batteries in the Faro of Messina. When in company, in the Alceste, with the Belle Poule 38, he landed, 5 May, 1811, and aided in destroying a French national brig lying in the harbour of Parenza, and defended by a galling cross fire from four batteries. On 29 of the ensuing month it was his fortune to be present in an action of 2 hours and 20 minutes, fought with consummate gallantry, between the Alceste and the Active 38 on one side, and the French 40-gun frigates *Pauline* and *Pomone* on the other, and which terminated in the capture of the *Pomone* and escape of the *Pauline*, after a loss had been occasioned to the Alceste of 7 men killed and 13 wounded. While engaged, in Feb. 1812, in protecting the island of Lissa, Mr. Moore was sent by Capt. Maxwell with two barges under his orders to the coast of Dalmatia, for the purpose of preventing the enemy from conveying supplies to the governor of Ragusa. In carrying out his instructions he fell in with five armed feluccas, and succeeded in effecting the capture of the whole of them, at the end of a desperate struggle, in which he was most gallantly supported by the present Commanders Chas. Croker and John King.* In attempting to board one of the vessels he was very severely wounded by a musket-ball passing through his lungs. For this he was awarded, 29 June, 1816, a pension of 91*l.* 5*s.* He left the Alceste, as above, in Oct. 1812; and was afterwards employed—from July to Nov. 1813, in the Raisonnable 64, Capt. Edw. Sneyd Clay, at Sheerness—and, from 1 Jan. until 16 Jan. 1814, in the Rodney 74, flag-ship of Vice-Admiral Geo. Martin off Lisbon. He has not been since afloat. His commission bears date 27 June, 1814.

* When recording the services of Commanders Croker and King we were not aware of the above circumstance.

MOORE. (Commander, 1843. f-p., 10; h-p., 3.)

John Moore is son of the late Admiral Sir Graham Moore,* G.C.B., G.C.M.G., by Dora, daughter of Thos. Eden, Esq., of Wimbledon, Deputy-Auditor of Greenwich Hospital, sister of Capt. Henry Eden, R.N., and niece of William, first Lord Auckland. He is nephew of the gallant Lieut.-General Sir John Moore, who fell at Corunna in Jan. 1809, and of the late Fras. Moore, Esq., Under Secretary at War. He descends from Capt. Chas. Moore, an officer in the army, who served in the wars of William III.

This officer entered the Navy 7 Feb. 1834; passed his examination 10 March, 1841; and, on 22 Sept. following, after serving at Plymouth, as Mate, on board the Caledonia 120, his father's flag-ship, was promoted to the rank of Lieutenant. On 30 Oct. in the same year he was nominated Additional-Lieutenant of the Queen 110, fitting at Portsmouth for the flag of Sir Edw. W. C. R. Owen; and he was next, from 26 July, 1842, until advanced to his present rank 22 Nov. 1843, employed on the Mediterranean station in the Aigle 24, Capt. Lord Clarence Edw. Paget. He has had command, since 12 Nov. 1846, of the Harlequin 12, again in the Mediterranean.

MOORE. (Retired Commander, 1846. f-p., 18; h-p., 36.)

John Moore entered the Navy, 14 Feb. 1793, as A.B., on board the Brazen cutter, Lieut.-Commander Jas. Fegen; removed, in the following April, to the Colossus 74, Capts. Chas. Morice Pole and John Monckton, successively employed in the Mediterranean and Channel; served next, from Feb. 1796 to May 1797, in the Carnatic 74, flag-ship of Rear-Admiral C. M. Pole; and then became Midshipman (a rating he had attained in the preceding Oct.) of the Ambuscade of 40 guns, Capt. Henry Jenkins. On 14 Dec. 1798 he was Master's Mate of that frigate when captured, in the Bay of Biscay, by the French ship *Baionnaise* of 32 guns, 8 swivels, and at least 250 men, after a severe conflict, in which the British sustained a loss, out of 190 men, of 10 killed and 36 wounded, and the enemy of 30 killed and 30 badly wounded. Being received, in March, 1799, on board the Russel 74, Capts. Herbert Sawyer and Wm. Cuming, he served in that ship in the action off Copenhagen 2 April, 1801, and on 27 and 24 of the ensuing June and July was successively constituted an acting and a

* Sir Graham Moore commanded the Bonetta sloop of war in 1793. He attained Post-rank 2 April, 1794; and was afterwards Captain of the Syren 32, Melampus of 42 guns and 267 men, Indefatigable 44, Marlborough 74, Royal Sovereign yacht, and Chatham 74. In the Melampus he succeeded, after having taken part in the action between Sir John Borlase Warren and Commodore Bompart, in effecting the capture, 14 Oct. 1798, of the French frigate *La Résolue* of 40 guns and 500 men, including troops; and in the Indefatigable he commanded a squadron at the capture of three Spanish frigates laden with treasure, and the destruction of a fourth, off Cape St. Mary, 5 Oct. 1804. In the Marlborough, with several other ships of the line under his orders, he escorted the royal family of Portugal on the occasion of its flight from Lisbon to the Brazils in 1807. For this service he was created a Knight of the Tower and Sword. When the Walcheren was evacuated in 1809, being still in the Marlborough, he was intrusted with the duty of destroying the basin, arsenal, and sea defences of Flushing. Attaining Flag-rank 12 Aug. 1812, he assumed, soon, the chief command on the Baltic station; and was next employed as Captain of the North Sea fleet under Lord Keith. After filling, for four years, a seat at the Board of Admiralty, he was appointed, in 1820, Commander-in-Chief in the Mediterranean, where he continued until 1823. He was nominated a K.C.B. in 1815, a G.C.M.G. in 1832, and a G.C.B. in 1836; became a Vice-Admiral 12 Aug. 1819, and a full Admiral 10 Jan. 1837; and from April, 1839, until April, 1842, was Commander-in-Chief at Plymouth. He died an Admiral of the White at the close of 1843.

confirmed Lieutenant in her. He went on half-pay in Oct. 1801; and was subsequently appointed—7 Jan. 1804, to the Sea Fencibles in Galway—18 May, 1805, to the TRITON, Capt. Wm. Cashman, at Waterford, where he remained until May, 1810—and, 5 March, 1812, to the Impress service at Dublin, in which he was employed for upwards of two years. He became a Retired Commander on the Junior List 25 July, 1831, and on the Senior 23 June, 1846. AGENTS—Hallett and Robinson.

MOORE. (LIEUT., 1814. F-P., 11; H-P., 32.)
JOHN MOORE entered the Navy 7 Nov. 1804, as Sec.-cl. Vol., on board the MATILDA, Lieut.-Commander Thos. Dorsett Birchall, bearing the flag of Hon. Henry Edwin Stanhope in the Thames; where, in Sept. 1806, on his return from a visit made to the Mediterranean as Midshipman of the SERAPIS, Master-Commander Wm. Lloyd, he joined the MAGNIFICENT 74, Capt. Geo. Eyre. After a servitude of two years and eight months on the Baltic, Lisbon, South American, and Channel stations, in the SOLEBAY 32, Capts. Robt. Howe Bromley, Thos. Brown, and Edw. Henry Columbine, he was received, in Sept. 1809, on board the ORPHEUS 32, Capts. Pat. Tonyn, Robt. Preston, and Hugh Pigot, attached to the force in the West Indies, whence, in 1812, he came home as Master's Mate of the GLOIRE frigate, Capt. Jas. Carthew. Joining then the SEAHORSE 38, Capt. Jas. Alex. Gordon, he ultimately, after cruizing in the Channel, proceeded to North America, and in Aug. 1814 accompanied the brilliant expedition up the Potomac, where he witnessed the capture of Fort Washington and the surrender of Alexandria. For his services during the operations connected therewith he obtained the official eulogiums of his Captain, and was in consequence promoted to the rank of Lieutenant 19 Oct. in the same year. He was afterwards, we believe, present in the attack upon New Orleans. He has been on half-pay since 1815. AGENTS—Messrs. Stilwell.

MOORE. (LIEUT., 1815. F-P., 13; H-P., 28.)
JOHN ARTHUR MOORE entered the Navy, 22 July, 1806, as a Supernumerary, on board the ROYAL GEORGE 100, Capt. Thos. Gill, bearing the flag of Sir John Thos. Duckworth; and on 21 Oct. following joined, off Cadiz, the AJAX 74, Capt. Hon. Henry Blackwood; which ship, when near the island of Tenedos, accidentally caught fire and blew up 14 Feb. 1807. Being in consequence received as Midshipman on board the THUNDERER 74, Capt. John Talbot, he was present at the ensuing passage of the Dardanells, and at the destruction of the Turkish squadron off Point Pesquies. During these operations he was slightly wounded.* He was next, from Sept. 1808 to June, 1813, again employed, under the orders of Capt. Blackwood, in the WARSPITE 74, on the Home station, and also in the Mediterranean; where, on 20 July, 1810, he participated in a very gallant skirmish, in which the British with a slender force beat back a powerful division of the French fleet. In Nov. 1813 he became Master's Mate of the ORONTES 36, Capt. Nathaniel Day Cochrane; with whom he served, on the coast of Ireland and in the West Indies, until promoted to the rank of Lieutenant 18 Feb. 1815. From 24 Nov. 1823 until the early part of 1829 Mr. Moore commanded the RINALDO Falmouth packet. This was his last appointment.

MOORE. (LIEUTENANT, 1845.)
JOHN GEORGE SARSFIELD MACNAMARA MOORE passed his examination 16 April, 1830; served in the Coast Guard from 23 March, 1841, until the attainment of his present rank 16 Jan. 1845; and since 1 Nov. following has been again employed in that department.

MOORE. (LIEUT., 1809. F-P., 12; H-P., 32.)
JOHN JAMES MOORE entered the Navy, 7 Nov. 1803, as Fst.-cl. Vol., on board the CULLODEN 74, Capt. Barrington Dacres, bearing the flag in the Channel of Rear-Admiral Collingwood; and from July, 1804, until promoted to the rank of Lieutenant 7 Nov. 1809, was employed on the Jamaica station, chiefly as Midshipman, in the THESEUS and HERCULE 74's, and VETERAN 64, flag-ships of Rear-Admiral Jas. Rich. Dacres, ARGO 44, Capt. Stephen Thos. Digby, and POLYPHEMUS 64, bearing the flag of Vice-Admiral Bartholomew Sam. Rowley; in the boats of which vessel, under Lieut. Chas. Fraser, he assisted, and obtained high praise for his conduct, at the boarding and capture, 9 March, 1809, with a loss to the British of 7 wounded, of the notorious French national felucca *Joseph*, of 3 guns and 53 men, and defended by a heavy fire of musketry and grape, as well from the vessel herself as from a whole range of batteries on the island of St. Domingo.* He then joined the ELK sloop, Capt. Jeremiah Coghlan, also in the West Indies, whence, in 1810, he returned to England on board the NEPTUNE 98, Capt. Volant Vashon Ballard. He next, from March to Dec. 1811, served off the coast of France in the POMPÉE 80, Capt. Sir Jas. Athol Wood; and while attached, between Jan. 1812 and Oct. 1815, to the IPHIGENIA 36, Capts. Lucius Curtis, Hon. Fleetwood Broughton Reynolds Pellew, and Andw. King, he made a voyage to St. Helena, assisted at the reduction of Genoa in 1814, and visited the shores of North America. Since the date last mentioned he has been on half-pay. AGENTS—Messrs. Halford and Co.

MOORE. (LIEUT., 1815. F-P., 11; H-P., 32.)
JOSEPH HENRY MOORE was born 16 June, 1791, at Bath.

This officer entered the Navy, 15 Dec. 1804, as Sec.-cl. Vol., on board the EURYALUS 36, Capts. Hon. Henry Blackwood and Hon. Geo. Heneage Lawrence Dundas; in which frigate he took part in the battle of Trafalgar, 21 Oct. 1805, and was employed on various particular services. After an attachment of nearly 12 months to the NAIAD 38, Capts. Geo. Cox and Henry Hill, he became Midshipman, in July, 1810, of the RUBY 64, and then of the VIGO 74, flag-ships of Rear-Admirals Manley Dixon and Jas. Nicoll Morris on the Baltic station, where for more than two years he endured much fatigue in the escort of convoys, and in the performance of other harassing duties. On his removal to the SHAMROCK brig, Capts. Andw. Pellet Green and John Marshall, he assisted at the capture, in Nov. 1813, of two strong batteries at Cuxhaven, and, in Jan. 1814, of the redoubtable fortress of Glückstadt. In consideration of his services on the latter occasion, he was invested with the command, in the following April, of a division of gun-boats, and was directed to co-operate in the reduction of Hamburgh and Harburgh; off which places, as officially testified, he continued very creditably employed, until compelled to invalid from the effects of a severe wound in the left hand, of which he has since lost the use. Prior to that unfortunate event he had been sent on shore for the purpose of seizing, and selling by public auction for the use of the British, all confiscated goods belonging to the Danish Government. Between July, 1814, and Aug. 1815, he served, on the Home and Irish stations, in the TAMAR 24, Capt. Chas. Sotheby, HAVOCK 12, Capt. Geo. Truscott, and, the last seven months as Acting-Lieutenant, in the TRENT, flag-ship of Sir Herbert Sawyer. He then took up a commission dated 13 Feb. 1815; and has since been on half-pay.

Lieut. Moore, in compensation for his wound, was granted, 22 Sept. 1818, a pension of 91*l.* 5*s.* He married, in Jan. 1815; and has issue nine children. AGENTS—Messrs. Ommanney.

MOORE. (LIEUTENANT, 1822. F-P., 8; H-P., 29.)
PAUL WOLLOND MOORE died at the close of 1846.
This officer entered the Navy, 13 Feb. 1810, as Fst.-cl. Vol., on board the POICTIERS 74, Capt. (afterwards Admiral) Sir John Poo Beresford, in

* *Vide* Gaz. 1807, p. 597.

* *Vide* Gaz. 1809, p. 787.

which ship he was four years employed off Brest and Lisbon, in Basque Roads, off Flushing and the Texel, and on the coast of America—assisting, as Midshipman, during that period, at the capture, among other vessels, of the U.S. ship *Wasp*, of 20 guns, and the late British brig-of-war *Frolic*. He next, from Feb. 1814, until May, 1816, served on the American, Mediterranean, and Home stations in the TONNANT 80 and ASIA 74, both commanded by Capt. Alex. Skene, GRANICUS 36, Capt. Wm. Furlong Wise, and ST. GEORGE and IMPREGNABLE 98's, each under the orders of Capt. Jas. Nash. From the period he left the last-mentioned vessel he did not again go afloat until appointed, 4 Feb. 1822, Admiralty Midshipman of the DIVER 28, bearing the flag of Sir J. P. Beresford at Leith. He was promoted to the rank of Lieutenant 10 Oct. following, and remained thenceforward on half-pay. AGENT—Frederick Dufaur.

MOORE. (LIEUTENANT, 1841.)

ROBERT SEPPINGS MOORE entered the Navy 26 Dec. 1826; passed his examination in 1833; obtained his commission 23 Nov. 1841; had command, from 27 Feb. 1843, until the early part of 1844, of the WILBERFORCE steamer, on the coast of Africa; and, since 18 Dec. 1844, has been serving, the latter part of the time as First-Lieutenant, in the COMUS 18, Capts. Thos. Sparke Thompson and Edwin Clayton Tennyson D'Eyncourt, on the south-east coast of America.

MOORE. (LIEUTENANT, 1843.)

THOMAS EDWARD LAWS MOORE entered the Navy 19 Oct. 1832; passed his examination 15 Feb. 1839; and, from that year until his return to England in 1843, was employed on board the TERROR, Capt. Fras. Rawdon Moira Crozier, part of an expedition sent under the orders of Capt. Jas. Clarke Ross to the Antarctic Ocean for the purposes of magnetic research and geographical discovery. He was promoted to the rank of Lieutenant by commission dated 4 Oct. 1843; and was subsequently appointed —11 Nov. 1843, to the CALEDONIA 120, flag-ship at Devonport of Sir Alex. Milne—4 Sept. 1844, as Additional, to the WINCHESTER 50, bearing the flag of Hon. Josceline Percy at the Cape of Good Hope, whence he came home at the close of 1845—and, 20 May, 1846, in a similar capacity, to the WILLIAM AND MARY yacht, Capt. Houston Stewart, on the books of which vessel his name continued to be borne until the ensuing Dec. Since 17 Nov. 1847 he has been in command of the PLOVER, a vessel now engaged in search of the Polar expedition under Sir John Franklin.

MOORE. (LIEUTENANT, 1828.)

THOMAS NORRIS MOORE entered the Navy 5 Feb. 1813; passed his examination in 1820; obtained his commission 19 April, 1828; and, from 31 Dec. 1835 until the close of 1840, was employed in command of a station in the Coast Guard. He has since been on half-pay.

MOORE. (LIEUTENANT, 1814. F-P., 11; H-P., 31.)

WILLIAM MOORE was born 13 Oct. 1792.

This officer entered the Navy, 25 April, 1805, as Fst.-cl. Vol., on board the ISIS 50, Capts. John Acworth Ommanney, Wm. Cuming, and John Laugharne, successive flag-ship at Newfoundland of Vice-Admirals Sir Erasmus Gower and John Holloway. In Dec. 1807, upwards of 18 months after he had attained the rating of Midshipman, he removed to the CONFIANCE 22, commanded by the late Sir Jas. Lucas Yeo, in which vessel he first visited Lisbon, and then proceeded to the coast of Brazil. At the reduction of Cayenne, in Jan. 1809, he was intrusted with the charge of a gun-boat, and for his services was presented, in common with the other Midshipmen of the CONFIANCE, with a sword and medal by the Prince Regent of Portugal. Being paid off in the early part of 1810, he next, in Oct. of that year, joined the SALVADOR DEL MUNDO, bearing the flag of Sir Robt. Calder at Plymouth, and very soon afterwards the SCEPTRE 74, Capt. Sam. Jas. Ballard, employed off Brest. Transferred by Admiralty order, at the commencement of 1811, to the SOUTHAMPTON, of 38 guns and 212 men, commanded by his former Captain, Yeo, he sailed forthwith for the Jamaica station, and, on 3 Feb. 1812, assisted at the capture of the Haytian frigate *Améthyste*, of 44 guns and 700 men, at the close of a sharp conflict, in which the enemy sustained a loss of 105 men killed and 120 wounded, and the British of only 1 man killed and 10, including himself, wounded. On 23 of the same month Mr. Moore passed his examination. In the following Aug. an attack of yellow fever rendered it necessary for him to be sent to the hospital at Port Royal, on being discharged from which he was successively placed, as a Supernumerary, on board the GARLAND 20, Capt. Rich. Plummer Davies, and SHARK sloop, bearing the flag of Vice-Admiral Chas. Stirling. He returned home with Capt. Yeo, in Feb. 1813, in the BRAZEN 18, Capt. Jas. Stirling, but, from the state of his health, was not able to seek further employment until the ensuing Aug., about which period he became attached, as Supernumerary-Mate, on promotion, to the MEDWAY 74, and PRINCE 98, flagships of Sir Rich. Bickerton at Spithead. Proceeding in a few weeks to the Cape of Good Hope in the LAUREL 38, Capt. Hon. Granville Leveson Proby, he there, in the month of Dec., rejoined the MEDWAY, of which ship, bearing the flag of Sir Chas. Tyler, he was created a Lieutenant 12 July, 1814. He returned to England and was paid off in April, 1816; and was lastly, from 23 Oct. 1817 until Sept. 1818, employed on the coast of Africa in the SEMIRAMIS 42, bearing the broad pendant of his friend, Sir J. L. Yeo, at whose request he had obtained the appointment.

MOORE. (LIEUTENANT, 1815. F-P., 16; H-P., 29.)

WILLIAM HENRY MOORE was born 27 June, 1790. His elder brother, Mr. J. H. Moore, was at one time a Midshipman in the service.

This officer entered the Navy, 1 Jan. 1802, as Fst.-cl. Vol., on board the SPITFIRE 18, Capt. Robt. Keen, with whom he served in the St. George's Channel until Aug. 1804. Becoming Midshipman, in April, 1805, of L'IMPÉTUEUX 74, Capts. Thos. Byam Martin and John Lawford, he witnessed, 22 Aug. following, Admiral Hon. Wm. Cornwallis' pursuit of the French fleet into Brest harbour, and was subsequently, in 1810, employed in that ship's boats on the river Tagus. In May, 1811, he was appointed, on promotion, to the ANTELOPE 50, bearing the flag of Sir John Thos. Duckworth at Newfoundland, where he remained until the ensuing Dec.; and he was next, in Oct. 1813, received on board the HEBRUS, of 42 guns and 284 men, Capt. Edm. Palmer, in which ship we find him assisting, under Cape La Hogue, at the capture, 27 March, 1814, of the French frigate *L'Etoile*, of 44 guns and 315 men, after a close and obstinate engagement of two hours and a quarter, in which the British had 13 men killed and 25 wounded, and the enemy 40 killed and 73 wounded. In April of the year last mentioned he was appointed, again on promotion, to the BELLEROPHON 74, flag-ship at Newfoundland of Sir Rich. Goodwin Keats, under whose orders he continued until at length advanced to the rank of Lieutenant, 8 Feb. 1815. He afterwards, from 25 April, 1834, until May, 1837, served in the Ordinary at Sheerness, latterly on board the TÉMÉRAIRE 104, Capt. Thos. Fortescue Kennedy. He has been employed, since 26 Sept. 1845, in the CALEDONIA 120, Capt. Manley Hall Dixon, on the Home station.

Lieut. Moore married, 5 April, 1826, Miss Mary Horsford.

MOORMAN, K.F.M. (COMMANDER, 1814. F-P., 15; H-P., 34.)

RICHARD MOORMAN (*a*), born 22 July, 1784, is uncle of Commander Richard Moorman (*b*), R.N.

One of his brothers was killed on board the MONARCH 74, Vice-Admiral Onslow's flag-ship, in the action off Camperdown, 11 Oct. 1797, and was buried with the honours of war at Minster Church, near Sheerness, where a monument was erected to his memory by his brother officers. A brother-in-law of the Commander was killed in action while defending H.M. packet MONTAGU, of 6 guns and 30 men, against the American privateer *Globe*, of 16 guns and 160 men, which vessel was in the end beaten off.

This officer entered the Navy, 25 May, 1798, as Midshipman, on board the MONARCH 74, Capt. Edw. O'Brien, bearing the flag of Sir Rich. Onslow in the North Sea. In Nov. 1800 he joined the RÉVOLUTIONNAIRE 38, Capt. Thos. Twysden, on the Cork station; and he next, from Sept. 1801 until Feb. 1806, served, chiefly in the capacity of Mate, on board the DONEGAL 74, Capts. Sir Rich. John Strachan and Pulteney Malcolm. He assisted during that period at the capture, in 1804, of the Spanish 44-gun frigate *Amfitrite*, and of a ship with a cargo on board worth 200,000*l.*—accompanied Lord Nelson in pursuit of the combined fleets to the West Indies and back in 1805—contributed, in the same year, to the capture of *El Rayo*, of 100 guns, one of the ships previously defeated at Trafalgar—and participated in the victory gained by Sir John Thos. Duckworth off St. Domingo, 6 Feb. 1806. On 14 of the latter month, as a reward for the conduct he had exhibited in the recent action, he was nominated Acting-Lieutenant of LE JUPITER 74, Capt. Chas. Gill, one of the ships taken from the French; and in the ensuing months of July and Feb. he was successively appointed Midshipman, on promotion, of the ROYAL GEORGE 100, and OCEAN 98, flag-ships in the Mediterranean of Sir J. T. Duckworth and Lord Collingwood. He was confirmed a Lieutenant, 14 April, 1807, in the QUEEN 98, bearing the flag, also in the Mediterranean, of Rear-Admiral Geo. Martin, whom, in the course of the same year, he followed into the CANOPUS 80. He afterwards commanded the boats of a squadron at the capture of a French flotilla of 12 gun-boats from Gaeta, bound to Naples; and in Oct. 1809 joined in the pursuit which led to the self-destruction, off Cette, of the French ships-of-the-line *Robuste* and *Lion*. He also, in July, 1809, commanded the flotilla employed at the taking of Ischia and Procida. Being appointed Senior Lieutenant, in April, 1810, of the TERMAGANT 18, Capts. Henry Evelyn Pitfield Sturt, Rich. Buck, Chas. Squire, and Gawen Wm. Hamilton, he commanded the boats of that sloop, and received a musket-ball in the body, in a cutting-out affair during the defence of Messina against the French. For this service he was created a Knight of the Order of St. Ferdinand and of Merit by the King of the Two Sicilies, was presented with a gratuity from the Patriotic Fund, and was awarded a pension, subsequently increased to 150*l.* per annum. During his stay in the TERMAGANT, of which he held for three months the acting command, he succeeded in one morning (22 July, 1812) in cutting out two privateers, one of which was *L'Intrépide*, of 3 guns and 40 men, taken near Malaga. He invalided home in Sept. 1812, and afterwards commanded the transports at the embarkation of the British army at Bourdeaux. Since his promotion to the rank of Commander, 15 June, 1814, he has been on half-pay.

Commander Moorman has been four times wounded. He married, 12 April, 1820, Miss Catherine Hill Millett, and by that lady has issue one son and three daughters. The son, a Midshipman R.N., was lately serving in the West Indies on board the SPARTAN 26, Capt. Hon. C. G. J. B. Elliot. AGENTS—Pettet and Newton.

MOORMAN. (COMMANDER, 1845. F-P., 18; H-P., 6.)

RICHARD MOORMAN (*b*), born 19 April, 1810, at Tregony, co. Cornwall, is fourth and youngest son of Wm. Moorman, Esq., of Falmouth; and nephew of Commander Rich. Moorman (*a*), R.N.

This officer entered the Navy, 27 Nov. 1823, as Fst.-cl. Vol., on board the SEMIRAMIS 42, Capt. Peter Ribouleau, bearing the flag of Lord Colville at Cork; and, from Aug. 1825 until Nov. 1831 (in the course of which month he passed his examination), was employed, chiefly as Midshipman, in the PANDORA 18 and SUCCESS 28, both commanded by Capt. Wm. Clarke Jervoise, and CALCUTTA 84, Capt. Peter Fisher, on the East India station. In Nov. 1829 the SUCCESS was all but lost on a reef, while making for Cockburn Sound, Western Australia. Five days elapsed before she could be got off, and then only by dint of the most determined exertions. The spirited and undaunted manner in which Mr. Moorman and his brother Midshipmen performed the very arduous duties that fell to their lot had the effect of officially eliciting the warmest praise and admiration on the part of Capt. Jervoise. In Feb. 1832 he was appointed Mate of the PIGEON, and in Sept. 1834 (after an interval of 15 months) of the SEAGULL, Falmouth packets, Lieut.-Commanders John Binney and John Parsons. On leaving the latter vessel, in Sept. 1835, he took command of a Liverpool West Indiaman, and continued trading from that port for a period of two years. In April, 1838, he joined the EXCELLENT gunnery-ship at Portsmouth, Capt. Sir T. Hastings; and, on 1 June, 1839, he entered the Royal Naval College, on the occasion of its being opened for the instruction of Mates and half-pay officers. He removed, in the capacity of Gunnery-Mate, to the CALCUTTA 84, Capt. Sir Sam. Roberts, 26 Sept. 1840; and, on 28 Sept. 1841, owing to the strong recommendation of Sir Thos. Hastings, and as a mark of the especial importance attached by their Lordships to the cultivation of gunnery, he was promoted to the rank of Lieutenant. On his return to England from the Mediterranean he was reappointed, 7 Dec. 1841, to the EXCELLENT, in which ship he continued employed, in the capacity of Gunnery-Lieutenant, until advanced to the rank of Commander, 30 Aug. 1845. He has been in command, since 14 Sept. 1847, of the HECATE steam-sloop, of 240-horse power.

MOORSOM. (CAPTAIN, 1818. F-P., 18; H-P., 25.)

CONSTANTINE RICHARD MOORSOM, born 22 Sept. 1792, is son of the late Admiral Sir Robt. Moorsom, K.C.B.,* by Eleanor, daughter of Thos. Scarth, Esq., of Stakesby, near Whitby. One of his brothers, Robert, died in command of the JASPER sloop in 1826; and another was a Captain in the Army.

This officer (whose name had been borne, between Oct. 1804 and Jan. 1806, on the books of the MAJESTIC and REVENGE 74's, both commanded by his father) entered the Royal Naval College 21 July, 1807, and (after having carried off three mathematical prizes, together with the first medal) embarked, 13 Nov. 1809, on board the REVENGE, commanded at first by Capt. Hon. Chas. Paget, and subsequently by Capts. John Nash and Chas. Philip Butler Bateman, under whom he served at the defence of Cadiz —latterly as Signal-Mate to Rear-Admiral Hon. Arthur Kaye Legge—until May, 1812. He then

* Sir Robert Moorsom was born in June, 1760, and embarked, in 1777, on board the ARDENT 64, commanded by the late Lord Mulgrave. Removing with the same officer to the COURAGEUX 74, he was afforded an opportunity of participating, as Midshipman, in the battle off Ushant, under Admiral Keppel; the relief of Gibraltar, under Admiral Darby, and also under Lord Howe; and the action off Cape Spartel, and the capture, by Admiral Kemperfelt, of part of a convoy going to the West Indies with Admiral de Guichen. Attaining Post-rank in 1790, he commanded, during the war of 1793, the NIGER and ASTREA frigates, and HINDOSTAN 50; and during that of 1803, the MAJESTIC and REVENGE 74's. In the latter ship he served at the battle of Trafalgar 21 Oct. 1805. In the course of 1809 he was successively appointed a Colonel of Marines, a Lord of the Admiralty, and Master-General of the Ordnance. He became a Rear-Admiral in 1810, a Vice-Admiral in 1814, a K.C.B. in 1815, and a full Admiral in 1830. He commanded in chief at Chatham from 1824 to 1827; and died about April, 1835.

returned to England in the WARSPITE 74, Capt. Hon. Henry Blackwood; and, attaining the rank of Lieutenant on 6 of the ensuing month, was next appointed, 30 July and 19 Oct. 1812, to the ST. ALBAN'S 64, Capt. John Ferris Devonshire (also on the Cadiz station), and SUPERB 74, Capts. Hon. Chas. Paget and Alex. Gordon. In the latter ship he continued employed in Basque Roads, on the coast of Brazil, and, under the broad pendant of Hon. Henry Hotham, on the coast of North America, until made Commander, 19 July, 1814, into the GORÉE sloop, at Bermuda. His succeeding appointments were—16 June, 1815, to the TERROR bomb, in which he returned from Bermuda to England in the following Aug.—2 July, 1816, to the FURY bomb, part of the force employed at the bombardment of Algiers,* where that vessel, in the course of nine hours, threw 318 shells, nearly double the number ejected by any other of her class †—and, 4 Oct. and 15 Nov. 1816, to the BRITOMART 10, and PROMETHEUS 22, both on the Home station, where he served until paid off in Aug. 1818. He was advanced to Post-rank 7 Dec. following; and was afterwards nominated Captain—2 April, 1822, and 29 Dec. 1824, of the ARIADNE 28, and ANDROMACHE 42, attached to the squadron at the Cape of Good Hope—and, 19 Dec. 1825, of the PRINCE REGENT 120, bearing his father's flag at Chatham. The ARIADNE, originally built as a corvette, had been raised, when commissioned by Capt. Moorsom, by the addition of a quarter-deck and 6 more guns, after the fashion of the VALOROUS, a ship which had not however been found to answer. By a different method of stowage, and with only 75 tons of ballast instead of the established proportion, 120 tons, Capt. Moorsom succeeded in making the ARIADNE sail as fast, work as well, and prove as good a seaboat as could possibly be expected. He took command of the ANDROMACHE on the death of Commodore Joseph Nourse, and, hoisting a broad pendant, continued in personal discharge of the duties of Commodore, until the arrival at the Cape of Good Hope of the present Rear-Admiral Christian, when he returned to England and paid the ANDROMACHE off. Since 1827, in the summer of which year the PRINCE REGENT was put out of commission, Capt. Moorsom has not been afloat.

He married, 12 March, 1822, Mary, daughter of Jacob Maude, Esq., of Silaby Hall, co. Durham, by whom he has issue five sons and three daughters. AGENTS—Case and Loudonsack.

* *Vide* Gaz. 1816, p. 1792.

† An inquiry into the cause of the difference was set on foot by the Admiralty, and the result was, the adoption of an entirely new description of bomb-vessel, founded on the plan acted upon by Capt. Moorsom.

MOORSOM. (LIEUTENANT, 1842.)

WILLIAM MOORSOM entered the Navy 28 June, 1830; passed his examination 16 June, 1835; and at the period of his promotion to the rank of Lieutenant, which took place 29 March, 1842, had been serving for some time in the East Indies as Mate on board the ENDYMION 40, Capt. Hon. Fred. Wm. Grey. His appointments have since been—22 April, 1842, as Additional, to the CORNWALLIS 72, bearing the flag of Sir Wm. Parker in the East Indies—12 Sept. 1842, to the VIXEN steam-sloop, Capt. Geo. Giffard, on the same station—29 March, 1845, to the EXCELLENT gunnery-ship at Portsmouth, Capt. Sir Thos. Hastings—19 Sept. 1845, to the RODNEY 92, Capt. Edw. Collier, attached to the Channel squadron—and, 9 May, 1846, to the ST. VINCENT 120, flag-ship of Sir Chas. Ogle at Portsmouth, where he is now employed.

MORESBY, C.B., K.M.T. (CAPTAIN, 1814. F-P., 25; H-P., 23.)

FAIRFAX MORESBY, born at Calcutta, is son of Fairfax Moresby, Esq., of Stow House, Lichfield, co. Stafford, formerly Lieutenant-Colonel of the 2nd Staffordshire Militia, and Colonel-Commandant of the Lichfield Volunteer Yeomanry. He descends from the Moresbys of Moresby, co. Cumberland.

This officer entered the Navy, 21 Dec. 1799, as A.B., on board the LONDON 98, Capt. John Child Purvis, with whom, after having taken a Midshipman's part in Sir John Borlase Warren's expedition to Ferrol, he removed to the ROYAL GEORGE 100. In March and Nov. 1802 he successively joined the ALARM 32, and AMAZON 38, both commanded by Capt. Wm. Parker. In the former ship he escorted a body of German troops to Holland; and in the AMAZON, besides accompanying the Duke of Kent from Gibraltar home, and participating in much general service, he went with Lord Nelson to the West Indies in pursuit of the combined fleets of France and Spain. Previously to the latter event he had been frequently placed in charge of captured vessels, and had had the misfortune on one occasion, while so employed, to fall into the hands of the enemy, by whom he was detained a prisoner at Malaga until released through the interference of the immortal hero. In Dec. 1805 Mr. Moresby became Master's Mate of the PUISSANT 74, at Portsmouth; and on 10 April, 1806, at which period he was serving with Lord St. Vincent in the HIBERNIA 110, off Ushant, he was made Lieutenant into the VILLE DE PARIS 110, Capt. Geo. Aldham. Being next, in the course of the ensuing summer, appointed to the KENT 74, Capt. Thos. Rogers, he was at first employed in that ship at the blockade of Rochefort, and afterwards in her boats and tenders in various parts of the Mediterranean; where, on 1 Aug. 1808, he distinguished himself by his conduct at the capture, by the boats of the KENT and WIZARD sloop, of a convoy of 10 deeply-laden coasters lying at anchor, under protection of a gun-boat, close to the beach abreast of the town of Noli, on the coast of Italy, fastened to the shore by ropes from their keels and mast-heads, and further defended by the fire of two adjacent field-pieces, of a heavy gun in front of the town, and of a volley of musketry kept up by a considerable body of regular troops, whom the resistless impetuosity of the British quickly put to flight.* So repeated and favourable was the mention made of Lieut. Moresby's name, that on the return of the KENT to England, in Dec. 1809, he was immediately ordered back to the Mediterranean on promotion in the REPULSE 74, Capt. John Halliday. On his arrival he was at once appointed to the SULTAN 74, Capt. John West, and in that ship he remained until invested, 5 Feb. 1811, with the acting-command of the ECLAIR 18. Removing in a few days to the ship-sloop ACORN, he was for a short time employed in the Adriatic in alone watching the remains of the Franco-Venetian squadron so memorably defeated by Capt. Hoste off Lissa; and he was next concerned in a variety of operations against the enemy's trade, which resulted in the speedy capture of more than 60 of their vessels. Although superseded in the ACORN, on the receipt of his Commander's commission, bearing date 18 April, 1811, and placed in consequence on half-pay, Capt. Moresby was forthwith appointed by the Commander-in-Chief, Sir Chas. Cotton, to the WIZARD 16, and sent to repress the piracies then so frequent in the Grecian archipelago; where his exertions in enforcing the restitution of plunder, in effecting the capture of three privateers (one of them the *Corcira*, of 8 guns and 60 men), and in performing other important services, led to his obtaining high official encomium, and to his being presented with a valuable sword by the mercantile body at Malta. After conveying important despatches from Constantinople to England, Capt. Moresby returned with a valuable convoy to the Mediterranean, and, having deposited his charge at Valetta, proceeded to join Sir Edw. Pellew off Toulon. Being sent, next, to the Adriatic, he made prize, during his passage thither, of *Le Petit Chasseur* French privateer; after which, volunteering his services, he took command, 18 Aug. 1813, of the boats of his own vessel and of the SARACEN and WEASEL brigs, and, landing under a heavy fire of round shot and musketry, stormed, carried, and assisted in destroying two strong batteries at the entrance of the Boco di Cattaro. This

* *Vide* Gaz. 1809, p. 15.

exploit was happily performed without loss, owing solely to the conduct of Capt. Moresby; whose order in advancing, judgment in landing, and determination of manner in leading the men up to the batteries, so intimidated the enemy, that they did not wait for the charge, but hastily fired and fled. During the proximate siege of Trieste, he served on shore in command, from 16 to 24 Oct., of one of the batteries; he was then ordered to form one with 4 32-pounders, within breaching distance; and this, in the course of 56 hours, under all the disadvantages of weather, &c., he contrived, with 50 men from the Milford and 20 from the Wizard, to complete without assistance of any kind.* For the above and other important services performed in co-operation with the Austrian troops on the coasts of the Adriatic, Capt. Moresby obtained permission, 23 May, 1814, to accept and wear the insignia of a Knight of the Imperial Military Order of Maria Theresa; and being moreover strongly recommended to the consideration of the Admiralty, he was advanced, 7 June following, to Post-rank; besides being nominated, 4 June, 1815, a C.B. His next appointment was, 26 April, 1819, to the Menai 24; in which ship, after visiting St. Helena, then the abode of Napoleon Buonaparte, he proceeded as Senior officer to the Cape of Good Hope. In 1820 he undertook the survey of Algoa Bay and its vicinity, as also the landing of the settlers, in number 2000, and the other duties connected with the first establishment of a colony at that place, the whole of which, notwithstanding their arduous nature, he discharged in a manner in the highest degree creditable to his sagacity and benevolence. In Feb. 1821 Capt. Moresby assumed the chief command at the Mauritius, with a view to the suppression of the slave-trade, which, up to the period of his arrival, had been carried on to a very great extent. Within a short time, however, the more notorious vessels were either captured or destroyed; prosecution was commenced against the owners and captains; and a complete stop put to other adventurers. For the purpose of preventing a recurrence of what he had so successfully demolished, Capt. Moresby then entered into a treaty with the Imaum of Muscat, afterwards confirmed by the British government, upon whom it conferred the right of exerting itself to the utmost for the abolition of the nefarious traffic. At the expiration of the Menai's term of service, in the spring of 1822, the Admiralty, on the application of Lord Bathurst, Secretary of State for the Colonies, and at the solicitation of Mr. Wilberforce and others, was induced to prolong the period of Capt. Moresby's command at the Mauritius; and he accordingly continued there until June, 1823. He then embarked the Governor, Sir Robt. Farquhar, and, after arranging a treaty with the King of Madagascar for the suppression of the slave-trade in his dominions, returned to England and was paid off in the month of Sept. To such an extent had his health become impaired while in command of the Menai, particularly in the extensive surveys he had made of the Ethiopian archipelago and of the African coast, that for five years he was subject to attacks which reduced him each time to the lowest state of debility. Although the vigour of his constitution was at length restored, he did not succeed in procuring fresh employment until Jan. 1837, on 25 of which month he was selected to succeed Sir Thos. Fellowes in the command of the Pembroke 74, on the Mediterranean station, whence he came home and was put out of commission in Feb. 1840. He has been in command, since 1 March, 1845, of the Canopus 84, employed chiefly on particular service.

Capt. Moresby married, 6 Aug. 1814, at Malta, Eliza Louisa, youngest daughter of John Williams, Esq., of Bakewell, Derbyshire, by whom he has issue three sons and two daughters—the elder married to Commander J. C. Prevost, R.N. His eldest son, Fairfax, now a Mate R.N. (1845), was born in Dec. 1826, and served as Midshipman of the Pique 36, Capt. Edw. Boxer, throughout all the operations on the coast of Syria, including the bombardment of Acre, as also of the Cornwallis 72, Sir Wm. Parker's flag-ship, during the war in China. Capt. Moresby's youngest son, John, born in March, 1830, was lately serving as a naval cadet on board the America 50, Capt. Hon. John Gordon. Agents—Messrs. Ommanney.

* *Vide* Gaz. 1813, p. 2478.

MORGAN. (Lieutenant, 1845.)

Edward Edwin Morgan passed his examination 10 Sept. 1836; and after having served for several years as Mate, on the South American and East India stations, in the Rose 18 and North Star 26, Capts. Peter Christie and Sir Jas. Everard Home, was promoted, 20 Jan. 1845, to the rank of Lieutenant, and appointed, 13 Feb. following, Additional of the Agincourt 72, flag-ship on the latter station of Sir Thos. John Cochrane. Being next, 17 Dec. in the same year, appointed to the Hazard 18, Capt. Fras. Philip Egerton, he accompanied, in July, 1846, an expedition conducted by Sir T. J. Cochrane against the Sultan of Borneo, where, on 8 of that month, he commanded the eighth company of small-arm men at the capture of the enemy's forts and batteries on the river Brune. On the ensuing ascent of a branch of the latter stream by a force under Capt. Geo. Mundy, and its debarkation, after struggling for many hours against an almost impenetrable navigation, at the village of Mallout, Mr. Morgan, while the main body marched on to Damuan, in the hope of there capturing the Sultan's person, was left behind in partial charge of a flotilla of seven gun-boats under Lieut. Geo. Edwin Patey, and was mentioned for the cheerful assistance he afforded on the occasion.* The Hazard was paid off in 1847.

MORGAN. (Captain, 1836. f-p., 25; h-p., 24.)

James Morgan is son of the late Rev. Patrick Morgan, Rector of Killybegs, co. Donegal; and brother of Lieut. Wm. Moore Morgan, R.M., who fell at the battle of Algiers while serving on board the Granicus 36, Capt. Wm. Furlong Wise. Another brother, Hugh, was an officer in the Royal Artillery.

This officer entered the Navy, 1 Nov. 1798, as Fst.-cl. Vol., on board the Savage 16, Capts. Norborne Thompson, Wm. Henry Webley, and John Tower, stationed in the Downs; where, in March, 1803, nearly two years and a half after he had attained the rating of Midshipman, he accompanied Capt. Tower into the Lark sloop. In Feb. 1805, at which period he was serving on board the Fury bomb, he was appointed Sub-Lieutenant of the Flamer gun-brig, Lieut.-Commander Jas. Storey; and on 30 Jan. 1806, as a reward for meritorious conduct he had displayed off Boulogne, he was promoted, on the recommendation of Lord Keith, to a full Lieutenancy in the Lynx sloop, Capt. John Willoughby Marshall, attached to the force in the North Sea. Quitting that vessel in the summer of 1807, he served, during the next four years, on the St. Helena, Home, and West India stations, in the Agincourt 64, Capt. Henry Hill, Resolution 74, Capt. Geo. Burlton, Nymphe 38, Capt. Hon. Joscelinc Percy, Neptune 98, Capt. Jas. Athol Wood, Elk sloop, Capt. Jeremiah Coghlan, Hyperion 36, Capts. Thos. Chas. Brodie and Wm. Pryce Cumby, and Polyphemus 64, flag-ship of Vice-Admiral Bartholomew Sam Rowley. In 1811, owing to the circumstance of Capt. Brodie and two of his officers having been taken captive in their boats by the black commandant at Gonaives, St. Domingo, in consequence of protection afforded by the former to an English merchant who had been detained a prisoner for an alleged breach of blockade, Lieut. Morgan, then Senior of the Hyperion, anchored the ship as soon as possible with one broadside to the batteries and the other to a Haytian frigate, and succeeded by his threatening demeanour in forthwith obtaining their release. In April, 1812, nine months after the state of his health had obliged

* *Vide* Gaz. 1846, pp 3442, 3446.

him to invalid from the West Indies, he assumed command of the BARBARA schooner, of 111 tons, 10 12-pounder carronades, and 50 men; and in that vessel he continued employed for upwards of two years on the Irish, Downs, Baltic, and Plymouth stations. He contrived, during the period, to beat off, 11 Feb. 1813, a detachment of seven luggers, carrying from 8 to 14 guns each, after more than an hour's close action, fought in the neighbourhood of Boulogne. On the following day he drove a lugger on shore and destroyed her; and he subsequently, among a host of dashing affairs, cut out a ship of 400 tons, two galliots, and a sloop, laden with corn, from the harbour of Aalbourg, although hotly pursued by nine Danish armed vessels 13 April, 1813—brought to and examined, 18 June following, a licensed Danish merchantman, under the fire of three national brigs and five gun-boats, close inshore off Christiansand—engaged, 3 July, the *Norge*, a cutter-rigged praam, mounting 2 long 32-pounders and 6 18-pounder carronades, with a complement of 80 men, supported by several other armed vessels, near Fladstrand — and on 11 Aug. came a second time into action with the *Norge*, through whose fire, and that of nine gun-boats in her company, the BARBARA sustained severe damage. On 6 Oct. in the same year, 1813, a very gallant exploit was performed a few miles to the southward of Wingo Sound, where, by a five-oared boat under the command of Lieut. Rich. Banks of the FORWARD gun-brig, and by the BARBARA's four-oared gig under Lieut. Morgan, a Danish cutter, mounting one howitzer, with a complement of 25 men, was boarded and carried in spite of a fierce resistance, in which the enemy sustained a loss of 5 men killed and their commander badly wounded, and the British of 2 killed and 3 (including Lieut. Morgan severely) wounded. During her stay in the Baltic, a period of nine months, the BARBARA captured and destroyed not less than 2544 tons of the enemy's shipping, navigated by 136 seamen; and, in conjunction with the *Hawke* privateer, of Hastings, made prize of a Danish privateer, and re-took a ship from under the batteries on Lessoe Island and the fire of 13 gun-boats and 10 privateers.* So much activity and gallantry on the part of Lieut. Morgan could not do otherwise than elicit strong expressions of approbation from his successive Commanders-in-Chief, the late Admirals Sir Geo. Hope and Sir Graham Moore. Quitting the BARBARA about June, 1814, he was next employed in command, from April to Sept. 1815, and from the latter date until Feb. 1818, of the AGGRESSOR gun-brig and PICTON schooner, on the Irish station. He obtained a second promotal commission 19 July, 1821; and afterwards officiated as an Inspecting-Commander of the Coast Guard at Whitby and Newhaven, from 1827 to 1830, and from 16 March, 1831, until promoted to Post-rank 15 Jan. 1836. On leaving the Whitby district in June, 1830, he was presented by his officers with a handsome piece of plate "as a grateful testimony of his kind and gentlemanly conduct towards them." He has not been employed since his last promotion.

Capt. Morgan is a Knight of the Royal Hanoverian Guelphic Order, and is the Senior Captain of 1836. He married, 24 July, 1833, Eliza, daughter of T. C. Faulconer, Esq., of Newhaven.

MORGAN. (CAPTAIN, 1846.)

JAMES WILLIAM MORGAN was born in 1802.

This officer entered the Navy, 19 May, 1814, as Fst.-cl. Vol., on board the LEYDEN 64, Capt. John Davie, attached to the force in the North Sea; and between 1815 and 1822 was employed as Midshipman, on the Cape of Good Hope, Home, North American, and St. Helena stations, in the CENTAUR 74 and MALTA 84, both commanded by Capt. Thos. Gordon Caulfeild, ROCHFORT 80, Capt. Sir Arch. Collingwood Dickson, CARNATION 18 and TAMAR 26, each under the orders of Capt. Hon. John Gordon, and VIGO 74, bearing the flag of Rear-Admiral Robt. Lambert. He then, having passed his examination in 1821, became Mate of the WINDSOR CASTLE 74, Capt. Chas. Dashwood; a capacity in which he further, from 1823 until promoted to the rank of Lieutenant 2 March, 1833, served in South America on board the TARTAR 42, Capt. Thos. Brown, GANGES 84, flag-ship of Sir Robt. Waller Otway, and DRUID 46, Capt. Gawen Wm. Hamilton. His succeeding appointments were—23 March, 1833, to the MADAGASCAR 46, Capt. Edm. Lyons, on the Mediterranean station, whence he returned to England and was paid off in the early part of 1835—and 22 Sept. in the latter year, 18 April, 1836, and (after about 12 months of half-pay) 8 April, 1839, to the HARRIER 18, Capt. Wm. Henry Hallowell Carew, DUBLIN 50, bearing the flag of Sir Graham Eden Hamond, and, as First-Lieutenant, to the CURAÇOA 24, Capt. Jenkin Jones, all in South America. He came home on the occasion of his promotion to the rank of Commander 23 Nov. 1841; and was next, from 1 Feb. 1844, until posted 9 Nov. 1846, employed on Home service as Second-Captain of the CAMPERDOWN 104, QUEEN 110, and TRAFALGAR 120, Capts. Wm. Fanshawe Martin and John Neale Nott. He is not at present afloat.

He married, 11 June, 1838, Caroline Dorothea, eldest daughter of Rear-Admiral Thos. Brown.

MORGAN. (COMMANDER, 1837.)

JOHN MORGAN was born 29 Jan. 1794.

This officer entered the Navy, 11 July, 1807, as Midshipman, on board the URANIE 38, Capts. Christopher Laroche and Thos. Manby, on the Guernsey station; joined, next, the HORATIO 38, and ROYAL WILLIAM, Capts. Geo. Scott and Hon. Courtenay Boyle, lying at Portsmouth; and from the close of the same year until May, 1811, was employed in the East and West Indies and at the Cape of Good Hope in the SAPPHIRE 18, Capts. Geo. Davies and Bertie Cornelius Cator, CHARWELL 16, Capt. Hon. Wm. Gordon, and SAPPHIRE again, Capts. B. C. Cator, Wm. Fitzmaurice, Hon. W. Gordon, Geo. Davies, and Henry Montresor. The ensuing three years and ten months were passed by Mr. Morgan on the West India, Portsmouth, Mediterranean, and Irish stations, in the HELENA sloop, Capt. H. Montresor, GLADIATOR 44 and SAN JOSEF 110, flag-ships of Rear-Admirals Wm. Hargood and Sir Rich. King, and BONNE CITOYENNE 20, Capt. Aug. Wm. Jas. Clifford. He was then promoted to the rank of Lieutenant by commission dated 17 Feb. 1815; and was subsequently appointed to the command—4 Aug. 1826, for two years, of the SPRIGHTLY Revenue-cruizer—and 2 June and 28 Aug. 1832, of the CRACKER and SEAFLOWER cutters, in which vessels he served until paid off in 1835. Prior to joining the CRACKER, Mr. Morgan commanded for some time the SYLVIA cutter. He obtained a second promotal commission 10 Jan. 1837; and was lastly, from 22 March, 1838, until 1842, employed as an Inspecting Commander in the Coast Guard. AGENT—Frederick Dufaur.

MORGAN. (COMMANDER, 1834. F-P., 22; H-P., 20.)

RICHARD MORGAN entered the Navy, 15 April, 1805, as Fst.-cl. Vol, on board the PRÉVOYANTE store-ship, Master-Commander Dan. M'Coy, and, after serving for a few months off Gibraltar and Cadiz in that vessel and the COLOSSUS 74, Capt. Jas. Nicoll Morris, joined the CANOPUS 80, successive flag-ship of Rear-Admirals Sir Thos. Louis, Geo. Martin, and Chas. Boyles. Under the first-mentioned of those officers he accompanied Lord Nelson to the West Indies in pursuit of the combined fleets of France and Spain, enacted a part in the action off St. Domingo 6 Feb. 1806, assisted as Midshipman at the capture, 27 Sept. following, of the French frigate *Le Président*, and, after attending Sir John Duckworth's expedition to Constantinople in Feb. 1807, assumed a share in the ensuing operations in Egypt. Under Rear-Admiral Martin, he joined, in Oct. 1809, in the pursuit which led to the self-destruction, off Cette, of the French ships-of-the-

* *Vide* Gaz. 1813, p. 2167.

line *Robuste* and *Lion*. Removing, in Sept. 1811, to the ACHILLE 74, Capt. Aiskew Paffard Hollis, he was for about 18 months employed in that ship in the Adriatic, where he aided in blockading the French and Venetian squadrons at Venice, consisting of three line-of-battle ships and a frigate ready for sea, and several of each class fitting in the arsenal. In Feb. 1814, having returned with convoy to England, and been for a short time engaged at the blockade of Cherbourg, he became Master's Mate of the QUEEN CHARLOTTE 100, bearing the flag of Lord Keith in the Channel, whence, in the course of the same year, he sailed for North America with Rear-Admiral Pulteney Malcolm in the ROYAL OAK 74. After witnessing, as Supernumerary-Midshipman on promotion of the TONNANT 80, flag-ship of Hon. Sir Alex. Cochrane, the attack on New Orleans, he was nominated, 19 May, 1815, Acting-Lieutenant of the BELLE POULE troop-ship, Capt. Fras. Baker. On his arrival home in the ensuing summer he found that he had been officially advanced to the rank of Lieutenant on 6 of the preceding Feb. His succeeding appointments were—19 May, 1818, to the QUEEN CHARLOTTE 100, flag-ship of Sir Geo. Campbell at Portsmouth, where he served until paid off in 1821—30 April, 1827, to the BRITANNIA 120, bearing the flag of the Earl of Northesk at Plymouth—22 Sept. 1828, and 28 April, 1830, to the ASIA 84, and BRITANNIA aga[illegible], in which ships he continued employed in the Mediterranean and North Sea, under the flag of Sir P. Malcolm, until the close of 1831—and, 8 March, 1833, a third time, to the BRITANNIA, as Flag-Lieutenant to the last-mentioned officer in the Mediterranean. He attained his present rank 23 April, 1834; and, from 29 March, 1837, until the spring of 1840, officiated as an Inspecting-Commander in the Coast Guard. He has since been on half-pay. AGENTS—Hallett and Robinson.

MORGAN. (LIEUT., 1815. F-P., 12; H-P., 32.)

ROBERT MORGAN (*a*) entered the Navy, 18 May, 1803, as L.M., on board the TERMAGANT sloop, Capt. Robt. Pettet, attached to the force in the Mediterranean; where, from May, 1805, until Aug. 1808, he served as Midshipman and Master's Mate in the BITTERN 18, Capts. John Louis, Edw. Aug. Down, and Thos. Ussher. He then proceeded to the Brazils in the BRILLIANT, Capt. Thos. Smyth, and next to the Cape of Good Hope in the INCONSTANT 36, Capt. Edw. Stirling Dickson. In July, 1810, he joined the HANNIBAL 74, bearing the flag of Sir Thos. Williams off Lisbon; and after a servitude of two years and nine months on that station, he removed, in April, 1811, to the DRAGON 74, flag-ship of Sir Fras. Laforey in the West Indies; where, between Oct. 1812 and May, 1813, he acted as Master of the SWAGGERER gun-brig, Lieutenant-Commander Chas. Dayman Jermy. In Oct. of the latter year he arrived in England in the SURINAM sloop, Capt. Thos. Martin; in which vessel, since the date last mentioned, he had been officiating as Acting-Lieutenant. On 22 June, 1814, after he had been for six months borne as Supernumerary-Midshipman and Master's Mate on the books of the ASIA 74 and TONNANT 80, flag-ships of Hon. Sir Alex. Cochrane in North America, he was there again ordered to act as Lieutenant in the HEBRUS frigate, Capt. Edm. Palmer; as he was subsequently, in April and May, 1815, in the GORÉE and PYLADES sloops, both commanded by Capt. Edw. Stone Cotgrave. On his return to England in the ensuing July he took up a commission bearing date 9 Feb. 1815. He has since been on half-pay. AGENTS—Hallett and Robinson.

MORGAN. (LIEUT., 1815. F-P., 12; H-P., 35.)

ROBERT MORGAN (*b*) is third son of the late Thos. Morgan, Esq., Recorder of Clonekilty, co. Cork.

This officer entered the Navy, 15 Feb. 1800, as Ordinary (after seven years' employment in the merchant-service, latterly in the capacity of Mate), on board the INFLEXIBLE 64, *armée-en-flûte*, Capt. Benj. Wm. Page, under whom he took part in the operations in Egypt in 1801. Returning to England in the early part of 1802, he next, in May, 1804, joined the LOIRE 38, Capt. Fred. Lewis Maitland; on leaving which ship in the following July he was received on board the TRITON frigate, Capt. Wm. Cashman, off Waterford. In Aug. 1806 he became Master's Mate of the ACTIVE 38, Capts. Rich. Hussey Moubray and Jas. Alex. Gordon; under the former of whom, in Feb. 1807, he accompanied Sir John Duckworth past the Dardanells, and on that occasion was so stunned by the explosion of a gun that the blood gushed out of both ears, and he ultimately lost all sense of hearing, although, from the accident not being properly reported, he was never able to procure compensation. While attached, from May, 1809, to April, 1811, to the ALFRED 74, Capt. Joshua Rowley Watson, he witnessed the capture of Flushing and Guadeloupe, and was also present at the defence of Cadiz, where he commanded a gun-boat, and had every oar shot away while retreating from under a battery, without, fortunately, any of his crew being touched.* After further serving with Capt. Watson in the IMPLACABLE 74, with Admirals Sir Robt. Calder and Lord Keith in the SALVADOR DEL MUNDO and QUEEN CHARLOTTE (of which latter ship he officiated as Second-Master from 26 March, 1813, to 30 Aug. 1814), with Capts. J. Richards and Geo. M'Kinley in the NAMUR 74, and with Capt. Nathaniel Day Cochrane in the ORONTES 36 on the Mediterranean and Home stations, he took up, in Nov. 1815, a commission bearing date 15 of the preceding March. He has since been on half-pay.

Lieut. Morgan married, first, in 1804 or 1805; and, again, in 1830. By his first wife he has living two sons (both of whom, educated at the Naval School at Greenwich, are now in the merchant-service) and one daughter.

MORIARTY. (LIEUT., 1814. F-P., 9; H-P., 31.)

MERION MARSHALL MORIARTY is brother of Commander Wm. Moriarty, R.N.

This officer entered the Navy, 18 Feb. 1807, as Fst.-cl. Vol., on board the MINOTAUR 74, Capt. Chas. John Moore Mansfield, successive flag-ship of Admirals Wm. Essington and Sir Chas. Cotton, with the latter of whom, after assisting at the reduction of Copenhagen, he removed, as Midshipman, in Jan. 1808, to the HIBERNIA 110, and proceeded off Lisbon. In Nov. 1812, up to which period he had been further employed under the orders of Sir C. Cotton, and also of Lord Keith, in the SAN JOSEF 110, on the Mediterranean and Channel stations, he joined the RÉVOLUTIONNAIRE 38, Capt. John Chas. Woolcombe, cruizing among the Western Islands. He removed, in Aug. 1814, to the CYDNUS 38, Capt. Fred. Langford, attached to the Channel fleet, where he served until Feb. 1814. In the following summer he proceeded to the West Indies as Acting-Lieutenant of the HAZARD sloop, Capt. John Cookesley, in which vessel, being confirmed to her 26 Sept. following, he afterwards visited Newfoundland. He invalided home in Sept. 1815; and has since been on half-pay.

Lieut. Moriarty, who had previously had command for several years of the Bristol Company's steam-ship QUEEN, has filled the appointment, since

* On resigning his command in the Cadiz flotilla, Mr. Morgan received from Commodore Hall, under whose orders he had been serving, a certificate couched in so peculiar and original a style that we cannot resist affording it insertion.—

" Mr. Morgan, it seems, having now bid adieu
To the gun-boat that lately was called 'Twenty-two,'
And having determined to serve us no more,
A certificate wants from his old Commodore.
Now what can I say but he commanded her well,
And escaped twice or thrice from the verges of hell,—
That I wish him success, tho' he quits my pennant,
And hope from my heart he'll be made Lieutenant?
His merits are great—to enumerate all
Would worry the patience of Commodore Hall;
But I trust that his services, merits, and feats,
Will merit the attention of Admiral Keats."

1842, of Port Officer at Sydney, New South Wales. He married Anne, daughter of the late Major Edw. Orpen, of Killowen, co. Kerry, by whom he has issue four sons (the eldest a Barrister-at-law) and seven daughters. AGENT—J. Hinxman.

MORIARTY. (LIEUT, 1812. F-P., 15; H-P., 28.)
REDMOND MORIARTY is the eldest brother of Commander Wm. Moriarty, R.N.

This officer entered the Navy, 27 May, 1804, as Midshipman, on board the ROMULUS 36, Capt. Thos. Burton, stationed in the North Sea. In Aug. 1806 he removed to the ARDENT 64, Capt. Geo. Eyre, with whom, in the course of the same year, he proceeded, in the MAGNIFICENT 74, to the Mediterranean, where, besides serving at the blockade of Cadiz, Toulon, and Corfu, he assisted at the defence of Rosas in Nov. 1808, united in the reduction of Zante, Cephalonia, &c., in Oct. 1809, and was employed on shore in co-operation with the army at the taking of Sta. Maura in March, 1810. Removing in May, 1811, to the ACTIVE, of 46 guns, Capt. Jas. Alex. Gordon, he served in the boats of that ship, four in number, at the capture and destruction, 27 July following, of 28 sail of merchantmen, defended, in a creek of the island of Ragosniza, by three gun-vessels and a body of 300 troops;* as a reward for his conduct on which occasion he was nominated, 1 Sept. in the same year, Acting-Lieutenant of the ACTIVE. On 29 of the ensuing Nov. we find him sharing in a hard-fought action of an hour and a half, which, in rendering the latter ship captor of the *Pomone*, of 44 guns and 332 men, 50 of whom were killed and wounded, produced a loss to her of 8 killed and 27 wounded, including Capt. Gordon (whose warmest praise he had the fortune to elicit), and the First and Second Lieutenants.† After saving a boat's crew from being drowned, Mr. Moriarty, officiating at the time as Third Lieutenant, was placed in charge of the prize, and, although she was in a nearly sinking state, he succeeded in carrying her safe into Lissa (where he received the thanks of Capt. Murray Maxwell, the Senior officer on the station), and thence to Malta. He was confirmed a Lieutenant 7 Jan. 1812; and was subsequently appointed—in the course of the same year, to the command of No. 5 gun-boat, in which he was for upwards of two years employed at the defence of Cadiz, and between that port and Gibraltar—27 Sept. 1814, for passage home, to the EDINBURGH 74, Capt. John Lampen Manley—6 Dec. following, to the ROVER sloop, Capt. Wm. Henry Bruce, with whom he served on the Brazilian, West India, and Home stations until Sept. 1815—and, 8 June, 1824, to the Coast Blockade, in which he remained as Supernumerary-Lieutenant of the RAMILLIES 74, and HYPERION 42, Capts. Wm. M'Culloch and Wm. Jas. Mingaye, until compelled by illness to resign in 1828. He has not been since employed.

He married, first, Dorcas Helena, daughter of Major Edw. Orpen, of Killowen, co. Kerry; and, secondly, Rachael Ann, daughter of John Mayberry, Esq., of Green Lane, in the same co. By his first marriage he has issue a son and daughter; and, by his last, a daughter. AGENTS—Hallett and Robinson.

MORIARTY. (COMMANDER, 1822. F-P., 16; H-P., 28.)
WILLIAM MORIARTY is son of the late Vice-Admiral Sylverius Moriarty, Flag-Captain to Rear-Admiral Thos. Graves in the RAMILLIES 74, prior to the commencement of the French revolutionary war; and brother-in-law of Capt. Peter John Douglas, R.N. He is brother of Lieuts. Redmond and Merion Marshall Moriarty, R.N.; and also of the late Messrs. Peter, Sylverius, and Martin Moriarty, all in the R.N.—the first of whom died a Lieutenant of fever in the West Indies, the second was lost with the QUEEN CHARLOTTE in 1800, and the third died of cold caught while extinguishing a fire on board the CAPTAIN 74, at Plymouth.

* *Vide* Gaz. 1811, p. 2193. † *V.* Gaz. 1812, p. 566.

This officer entered the Royal Naval Academy 26 Sept. 1803; and embarked, 17 Aug. 1807, as Midshipman, on board the NYMPHE 36, Capts. Conway Shipley, Geo. Pigot, Hon. Josceline Percy, and Edw. Sneyd Clay; under the first of whom, who was killed, he was wounded in the boats in a desperate but unsuccessful attack made on the night of 23 April, 1808, on a French corvette, *La Gavotte*, of 22 guns and 150 men, lying at anchor in a bight above Belem Castle, in the river Tagus. He had previously enacted a part at the siege of Copenhagen; and he subsequently, when under Capt. Percy, escorted General Junot to Rochelle after the convention of Cintra. Quitting the NYMPHE in Dec. 1810, he next, for about three years, served, on the Home, North American, Baltic, and Mediterranean stations, in the CONQUESTADOR 74, Capt. Lord Wm. Stuart, SEINE frigate, Capt. John Hatley, PRINCE OF WALES 98, Capt. Thos. Burton, VICTORY 100, flag-ship of Sir Jas. Saumarez, and, as Master's Mate and Acting-Lieutenant, in the PARTRIDGE 16, Capt. John Miller Adye. Having passed his examination in the summer of 1811 he was confirmed a Lieutenant 13 Oct. 1813. His succeeding appointments were—29 March, 1814, to the CERBERUS 32, Capt. Thos. Garth, also in the Mediterranean—19 Sept. following, to the TYRIAN sloop, Capt. Augustus Baldwin, in which vessel, stationed in the Channel, he served until Oct. 1815—and, 15 April, 1818, to the TOPAZE frigate, Capt. John Rich. Lumley, fitting for the East Indies. In 1820 he accompanied an expedition sent to the Persian Gulf for the purpose of obtaining redress for injuries which the British interests had suffered from the officers of the Imaum of Senna; and in Dec. of that year he was wounded at the head of a party of seamen while storming a fort during a series of operations against the city of Mokha. Although the attack was not crowned with the success it deserved, yet the daring intrepidity displayed by Lieut. Moriarty, exposed as he was to a heavy and galling fire of musketry, met its due reward in his being advanced, 1 Nov. 1822, to the rank he now holds.*

Commander Moriarty has been for many years Port Officer at Hobart Town, Van Diemen's Land. He married Aphra, daughter of the late and sister of the present Dr. Crump, of Tralee, co. Kerry. AGENT—J. Hinxman.

MORIENCOURT. (RETIRED COMMANDER, 1827. F-P., 14; H-P., 46.)
JOSEPH SALVADOR MORIENCOURT entered the Navy, in Feb. 1787, as Midshipman, on board the ADVENTURE 44, Capts. Fras. Parry and John Nicholson Inglefield, on the African station; and between July, 1790, and his promotion to the rank of Lieutenant, 12 Sept. 1793, was employed in the Channel, off the coast of Africa, at Portsmouth, and in the Mediterranean, in the EXCELLENT 74, Capt. John Gell, MEDUSA frigate, Capt. J. N. Inglefield, BARFLEUR 98, flag-ship of Vice-Admiral Roddam, and ROMNEY 50, and PRINCESS ROYAL 98, bearing each the flag of Rear-Admiral Sam. Cranston Goodall. He was then, being at the siege of Toulon, placed in command of a floating battery, which suffered much from the enemy's batteries. He went on half-pay in Dec. 1793; but was afterwards, between July, 1794, and July, 1801, afforded an opportunity of serving on the Home station in the SEAHORSE frigate, Capt. John Peyton, NEPTUNE 98, Capts. Hon. Henry Edwin Stanhope and Sir Erasmus Gower, ARETHUSA 38, Capt. Thos. Wolley, NEPTUNE again, Capts. Sir E. Gower and Jas. Vashon, and TRITON 32, Capt. Fitzgerald. His last appointment, we believe, was, for a short time in the summer of 1803, to L'ARGUS, Capt. Hon. Edw. Rodney. He retired with the rank of Commander, on the Senior List, 1 Sept. 1827. AGENT—Fred. Dufaur.

MORIER. (CAPTAIN, 1830. F-P., 15; H-P., 29.)
WILLIAM MORIER entered the Navy, in Nov. 1803, as Fst.-cl. Vol., on board the ILLUSTRIOUS 74,

* *Vide* Gaz. 1821, pp. 939, 2029.

Capt. John Giffard, lying at Woolwich, and after cruizing for nine months on the Irish station in the DRYAD 36, Capt. J. Giffard, was constituted Midshipman, in Jan. 1805, of the AMBUSCADE 32, Capt. Wm. D'Urban, attached to the force in the Mediterranean, where it was his fortune to participate in much boat service. Quitting the last-mentioned ship in March, 1807, he was next, until April, 1810, employed on the Mediterranean and Lisbon stations in the MINORCA sloop, Capt. Hon. Granville Geo. Waldegrave, INTREPID 64, Capt. Hon. Philip Wodehouse, ALFRED 74, Capt. John Bligh, and THAMES 32, Capt. Hon. G. G. Waldegrave. He was then nominated Acting-Lieutenant of the ZEALOUS 74, Capt. Thos. Boys; and on 4 of the following month (having intermediately taken part in the defence of Cadiz, and assisted in setting fire to a prison-ship driven on shore by the French prisoners) he was confirmed into the COLOSSUS 74, Capt. Thos. Alexander. In Nov. of the same year he returned to the THAMES, still commanded by Capt. Waldegrave, although afterwards by Capts. Chas. Napier and John Strutt Peyton. In that ship he contributed to the reduction of the island of Ponza in Feb. 1811, and, among other boat affairs performed on the coast of Calabria, displayed characteristic zeal at the destruction, 16 June following, of 10 large armed feluccas, on the beach, near Cetraro, in the gulf of Policastro. After a servitude of 20 months in the PACTOLUS 38, Capt. Hon. Fred. Wm. Aylmer, during which period he had escorted, we believe, the Duke of Cambridge to Cuxhaven and his late Majesty to the Scheldt, and had witnessed the bombardment of Stonington in America, he was presented with a Second promotal commission dated 13 June, 1815. His last appointments were—12 Oct. 1826 and 17 Sept. 1828, to the HARRIER and CHILDERS sloops, of 18 guns each; which vessels he successively commanded on the North Sea station until the close of 1829. He attained his present rank 18 Jan. 1830.

Capt. Morier married, in 1841, Fanny, daughter of D. Bevan, Esq., of Belmont, Herts. AGENTS—Hallett and Robinson.

MORLEY. (LIEUT., 1824. F-P., 26; H-P., 13.)

ARTHUR THOMAS MORLEY entered the Navy, in May, 1808, as Fst.-cl. Vol., on board the KANGAROO 18, Capt. John Baker, under whom he assisted at the capture, 20 Nov. following, of *L'Egayant* privateer, of 14 guns and 31 men, and continued actively employed in the Channel and off the coasts of Spain and Portugal until Nov. 1810. During the next four years we find him serving as Midshipman, off Cadiz and in various parts of the Mediterranean, in the ST. ALBAN'S 64, and BERWICK 74, both commanded by Capt. Edw. Brace. In the former ship he appears to have been in co-operation with the British army at the battle of Barrosa; and, in the BERWICK, to have witnessed the fall of Genoa. He then, in Dec. 1814, joined the ST. LAWRENCE 98, Capt. Chas. Fred. Payne, on Lake Ontario, where, after an attachment of a few months to the PRINCE REGENT 56, Capt. Wm. Fitzwilliam Owen, he acted, from March, 1816, until July, 1817, as Master of the NETLEY 10, Capt. Fras. Brace. In Dec. 1818 he became Master's Mate of the LEVEN 24; and in that vessel, successively commanded by Capts. David Ewen Bartholomew and Robt. Baldey, he was for two years and a half employed in surveying the Azores, part of the African coast, and some of the Cape de Verde Islands. He was next, in Aug. 1821, appointed to the Coast Blockade as Admiralty-Midshipman of the SEVERN 40, Capt. Wm. M'Culloch; from which service, in Dec. 1822, he was removed, in a similar capacity, to the GLOUCESTER 74, bearing the broad pendant in the West Indies of Commodore Sir Edw. W. C. R. Owen. He attained his present rank 21 Jan. 1824; and was afterwards employed, from 15 April in the same year until superseded at his own request 8 Nov. 1825, again in the Coast Blockade, as Supernumerary-Lieutenant of the RAMILLIES 74, and HYPERION 42, Capts. Wm. M'Culloch and Wm. Jas. Mingaye, and, from 20 March, 1835, until the close of 1844, in the Coast Guard.

MORLEY. (LIEUT., 1815. F-P., 12; H-P., 29.)

WILLIAM MORLEY was born in Jan. 1791, at St. John's, Newfoundland.

This officer entered the Navy, 20 March, 1806, as Fst.-cl. Vol., on board the RATTLER sloop, Capts. Fras. Mason and Jas. John Chas. Agassiz, on the Newfoundland station; where, from Dec. 1808 until July, 1811, he served, part of the time as Midshipman, in the ADONIS 10, Lieut.-Commander David Buchan. He then joined the MINERVA 32, Capt. Rich. Hawkins, with whom, during a continuance of nearly three years, he saw service at Halifax and also in the West Indies. After he had been for four months borne, as a Supernumerary, on the books of the NAMUR 74, Capt. Chas. John Austen, he joined, about Oct. 1814, the CYANE, of 32 guns, Capt. Gordon Thos. Falcon; and, next, the TRITON, prison-ship at Newfoundland, Lieut.-Commander Thos. Bishop. He took up, in June, 1815, a commission bearing date 6 Feb. in that year; and he was, lastly, from April, 1816, until paid off in Nov. 1817, employed on the coast of North America and in the Leeward Islands in the PIKE 12, and HYDRA troop-ship, Capts. D. Buchan and Dan. Roberts.

He married, in 1829, Eleanor, daughter of Thos. Sutton, Esq., of Scarborough, co. York, and by that lady has issue 10 children.

MORRELL. (COMMANDER, 1823. F-P., 24; H-P., 22.)

ARTHUR MORRELL is son of the late Lieut. Morrell, R.N.; and brother of the late Commander John Arthur Morrell, R.N.

This officer entered the Navy, 6 Aug. 1801, as Fst.-cl. Vol., on board the DORIS 38, Capts. Chas. Brisbane and Wm. Cumberland, with whom he served in the Channel until June, 1802—latterly in the capacity of Midshipman. Joining, in the ensuing August, LA PIQUE 36, also commanded by Capt. Cumberland, he proceeded to the West Indies, where he continued uninterruptedly employed for a period of nine years in the same ship and in the SUFFISANTE, Capt. Henry Laroche, REDBRIDGE 12, Lieut.-Commander Edw. Burt, POLYPHEMUS 64, Capt. Wm. Pryce Cumby, flag-ship for some time of Vice-Admiral Bartholomew Sam. Rowley, AVON 18, Capt. Henry Tillieux Fraser, SPARROW sloop, Capts. Edw. Burt, Joshua Ricketts Rowley, Edmund Denman, and Joseph Needham Tayler, THALIA 36, Capt. Jas. Giles Vashon, and ELK sloop, Capt. Clement Milward. Independently of numerous boat services performed during that period, and many engagements fought with privateers, he witnessed, in LA PIQUE, in 1803, the evacuation of Aux Cayes and of other places in St. Domingo, and also the surrender, with the remains of General Rochambeau's army from Cape François on board, of the three French frigates *Surveillante*, *Vertu*, and *Clorinde*—the last mentioned of which he assisted in conducting, under the present Sir Nesbit Josiah Willoughby, to Jamaica. In the following year he took part, likewise in LA PIQUE, in the unsuccessful attack upon Curaçoa. In the REDBRIDGE, of which vessel he was Master's Mate, he was wrecked off Nassau, New Providence, 4 Nov. 1806; and, when holding the same post on board the POLYPHEMUS, he commanded the pinnace belonging to that ship at the capture of the French schooner *Calibre*. After acting for three months as Lieutenant of the AVON, he was confirmed, 28 July, 1809, into the SPARROW. Having paid off the ELK as Senior Lieutenant at the close of 1811, he was next in succession appointed—3 Feb. 1812, to the OCEAN 98, Capt. Robt. Plampin, attached to the force off Toulon, and, as First Lieutenant—13 Nov. following, to the TERMAGANT sloop, Capts. John Lampen Manley and Chas. Shaw, stationed at first in the Mediterranean (where he beheld the fall of Genoa), and afterwards in the East Indies, whence he returned to England and was paid off in Oct. 1816—

14 Jan. 1818, to the DOROTHEA hired-ship, Capt. David Buchan, whom he accompanied on a perilous voyage of discovery to the neighbourhood of Spitzbergen (*vide note*, p. 67)—19 Jan. 1820 (the DOROTHEA had been put out of commission in Nov. 1818), to the REVOLUTIONNAIRE 46, Capt. Hon. Fleetwood Broughton Reynolds Pellew, in which ship he was for about two years and a half employed in the Mediterranean—and, 11 Nov. 1822, to the TARTAR 42, Capt. Thos. Brown, fitting for South America. While in the REVOLUTIONNAIRE, Mr. Morrell, with her barge and pinnace under his orders, succeeded, on the night of 18 May, 1821, in effecting the capture, in the harbour of St. Jean, in the gulf of Patras, of two Greek pirate-boats, after a hard struggle, in which his party sustained a loss of 1 man killed and 3 slightly wounded. He himself received several sabre-cuts in the face; but he was not advanced to the rank of Commander until 18 April, 1823. He had then, as we have shown, been eight years First-Lieutenant of various ships. His next appointment, it appears, was, 2 June, 1841, after 18 years of solicitation, to the CALCUTTA 84, Capts. Sir Sam. Roberts and Geo. Fred. Rich; of which ship, stationed in the Mediterranean, we find him, during the illness of the former officer, acting for a short time as Captain. The CALCUTTA being paid off in the latter part of 1842, he obtained, 25 May, 1843, command of the ESPOIR 10, equipping for the coast of Africa; where it was his fortune to make prize of two slave-vessels, one of them laden with 546 negroes. From the ESPOIR Commander Morrell was transferred, 6 Dec. 1844, to the TORTOISE store-ship, and nominated Governor of Ascension. Although the latter appointment, we understand, had been conferred upon him as a permanence, he was superseded without compensation, in Nov. 1846, by an officer holding Post-rank. He came home in command of the HYDRA steam-sloop at the commencement of 1847, and has since been on half-pay.

He married, 6 Feb. 1820, a daughter of Mr. Wm. Reid, First Pay-Clerk for Wages at Devonport Dockyard, and by that lady has issue. AGENTS—Messrs. Chard.

MORRES. (LIEUTENANT, 1816. F-P., 8; H-P., 30.)

ELLIOT MORRES entered the Navy, 26 May, 1809, as Fst.-cl. Vol., on board the MEDUSA 32, Capt. Hon. Duncombe Pleydell Bouverie; in which ship, during a servitude of four years on the Home station, he assisted, as Midshipman, at the capture, 6 and 14 Jan. 1810, of the privateers *L'Aventure*, of 14 guns and 82 men, and *L'Hirondelle*, of 14 guns and 72 men, and co-operated much with the patriots on the north coast of Spain. In June, 1813, and Sept. 1815, he successively joined the RIVOLI 74, Capts. Graham Eden Hamond and Edw. Stirling Dickson, both attached to the force in the Mediterranean; where, on being appointed Admiralty-Midshipman of the GLASGOW 40, Capt. Hon. Anthony Maitland, he took part in the bombardment of Algiers 27 Aug. 1816. He was promoted in consequence to the rank of Lieutenant 16 Sept. following. He left the GLASGOW 31 Oct. in the same year; and has since been on half-pay.

He is married and has issue.

MORRIES. (RETIRED COMMANDER, 1841.)

ANDREW MORRIES had a brother a Major in the Army.

This officer entered the Navy, 6 Feb. 1796, as Fst.-cl. Vol., on board the ANDROMEDA 32, Capts. Wm. Taylor and Henry Inman; under the latter of whom, after serving some time on the coast of North America, he witnessed, 8 July, 1800, the capture, in Dunkerque Roads, of the French 40-gun frigate *Désirée*. On next joining the POLYPHEMUS 64, Capts. Geo. Lumsdaine and John Lawford, he fought in the action off Copenhagen 2 April, 1801. In 1803 he was received on board the MONARCH 74, flag-ship in the Downs of Lord Keith, who, in the course of the same year, placed him in command, with the rank of Lieutenant, of the LORD KEITH cutter. In the course of 1805 he was successively nominated Acting-Flag-Lieutenant to Sir Wm. Sidney Smith and Lord Keith in the ANTELOPE 50, and EDGAR 74; in the latter of which ships, being confirmed to her by commission dated 25 Aug. 1806, he continued employed until the summer of 1807. During the remainder of the war we find him serving on the Leith and Baltic stations in the TEXEL and ARDENT 64's, Capts. Jas. Giles Vashon and Robt. Honyman, flag-ships for some time of Rear-Admiral Jas. Vashon, COURAGEUX 74, Capt. Philip Wilkinson, and STORK sloop, Capt. Robt. Lisle Coulson. He retired with the rank of Commander 5 May, 1841.

The Commander is in possession of high recommendatory letters from Lord Keith, Sir Wm. Sidney Smith, and Admiral Billy Douglas.

MORRIS. (LIEUTENANT, 1842. F-P., 15; H-P., 0.)

FREDERICK MORRIS, born 25 Jan. 1819, is third son of Sir John Morris, Bart., of Sketty Park and Clasemont, co. Glamorgan, by Lucy Juliana, youngest daughter of John, fifth Viscount Torrington, and sister of the late Vice-Admiral Viscount Torrington.

This officer entered the Navy, in Oct. 1832, as Fst.-cl. Vol., on board the LARNE 18, Capt. Wm. Sidney Smith, employed at first in the North Sea and off the coast of North America, and afterwards in the West Indies, where he served his time as Midshipman in the FORTE 44, Capt. Watkin Owen Pell, and SATELLITE 18, Capt. John Robb. He returned to England in 1839 as Mate of the RACEHORSE 18, Capt. Henry Wm. Craufurd; and on his arrival he was appointed to the EXCELLENT gunnery-ship at Portsmouth, Capt. Sir Thos. Hastings. Joining, next, the PIQUE 36, Capt. Edw. Boxer, he took part in the operations of 1840 on the coast of Syria, and, prior to assisting in the bombardment of St. Jean d'Acre, obtained mention for his conduct at the taking of Caiffa and Tsour. While serving subsequently on the North America and West India station in the ILLUSTRIOUS 72, flag-ship of Sir Chas. Adam, he was promoted, 3 Oct. 1842, to a Lieutenancy in the TWEED 20, Capt. Hugh Donald Cameron Douglas. His appointments, since he left that vessel, have been—19 July, 1844, as Additional-Lieutenant, to the FORMIDABLE 84, bearing the flag of Sir Edw. W. C. R. Owen in the Mediterranean—next, to the SNAKE 16, Capt. Hon. Walter Bourchier Devereux, in which vessel he returned to England and was paid off in Oct. 1845—2 Feb. 1846, to the CYCLOPS steam-frigate, Capt. Wm. Fred. Lapidge, attached to the Channel squadron—and, 11 Feb. 1847, to the CANOPUS 84, Capt. Fairfax Moresby, now employed on particular service. AGENTS—Messrs. Stilwell.

MORRIS. (REAR-ADMIRAL, 1846. F-P., 19; H-P., 39.)

GEORGE MORRIS, born 7 Oct. 1778, is son of the late Wm. Morris, Esq., Master R.N.; and brother of Commander John R. Morris, R.N.

This officer entered the Navy, in Oct. 1789, as Master's Servant, on board the VICTORIOUS 74, commanded by his father, then Master Superintendent of Ordinary. In Jan. 1793 he removed, as A.B., to the AUDACIOUS 74, Capt. Wm. Parker, under whom, while holding the rating of Midshipman, he lost a leg in Lord Howe's action, 28 May, 1794. After serving a year and ten months at the Nore in the SANDWICH 90, Capt. Jas. Robt. Mosse, he was made Lieutenant, 2 June, 1796, into the ARDENT 64, Capts. Rich. Rundell Burgess and Thos. Bertie, attached to the force on the North Sea station, where, under Capt. Burgess, who was killed, he fought, as Second Lieutenant, in the action off Camperdown, 11 Oct. 1797. During the expedition to Holland, in 1799, being still in the same ship, he assisted at the debarkation of the troops, and was present at the surrender of the Dutch squadron in the Texel, whence, it appears, he brought the *Admiral De Ruyter*, one of the prizes, to England. Assuming command, 22 March, 1800, of the LADY CHARLOTTE, hired armed brig, Lieut. Morris, who continued in that vessel until Oct. 1801, succeeded, while cruizing between Start Point and Portland, in capturing *L'Espoir* and *Le Petit Pirate*, small privateers (the former carrying 6 carriage-guns and 23 men*), and in retaking several British merchantmen. Attaining the rank of Commander, 14 April, 1802, he was successively appointed, in that capacity—6 Oct. 1803, 15 June, 1806, and 2 April, 1807, to the PENGUIN, ELK, and RENARD sloops, on the African and Jamaica stations—3 Dec. 1807, to the MAGNET 18, in the Baltic—11 April, 1809, for 12 months, to the Sea Fencibles at Lynn—and, 23 Sept. 1811, to the VULTURE 16, employed off Jersey and Guernsey. In the PENGUIN, aided by his boats, he effected the destruction, on the bar of Senegal river, of the French privateer *La Renommée*, of 14 guns and 87 men, supported by two other vessels, 24 March, 1804;† he destroyed and took, in the ELK, the French and Spanish privateers *Alliance*, of 5 guns and 75 men, and *Cacila*, of 4 guns and 20 men; and, in the MAGNET, after intercepting the Danish privateer *Paulina*, of 10 guns and 42 men, he was wrecked on the ice near Malmo, 11 Jan. 1809. After that catastrophe he marched with his ship's company to Göttenborg, for the purpose of joining Sir Rich. Keats, then lying in Wingo Sound. On the breaking up of the ice he was sent home with despatches in the CENTINEL gun-brig, Lieut.-Commander Wm. Elleston King. He left the VULTURE, on attaining Post-rank, 1 Feb. 1812; and, on 1 Oct. 1846, he accepted the rank he now holds.

For the loss of his leg Rear-Admiral Morris was awarded, 4 April, 1816, a pension of 300*l.* per annum. He married, 10 Nov. 1807, Sarah, daughter of B. Bentham, Esq., of Sheerness, by whom he has issue two sons and three daughters. AGENT—Frederick Dufaur.

MORRIS. (LIEUTENANT, 1823.)

GEORGE MORRIS entered the Navy, 4 March, 1808, as Sec.-cl. Boy, on board the PUISSANT 74, Capts. John Irwin, Robt. Hall, and Wm. Paterson, in which ship he was for nearly four years employed at Spithead. In March, 1812, he joined, as Fst.-cl. Vol., the SCEPTRE 74, Capts. Thos. Harvey and Robt. Honyman, stationed at first in the North Sea, and next on the coast of North America, where, from July, 1813, until Feb. 1814, he served with the last-mentioned officer in the MARLBOROUGH 74. He then obtained a Midshipman's berth on board the PERSEUS 22, Capt. Edw. Henry A'Court, at Newfoundland; and he afterwards became attached in succession—in Sept. 1815, to the ANTELOPE 50, flag-ship of Rear-Admiral John Harvey in the Leeward Islands—and (after an interval of 10 months), in May, 1819, and Nov. 1821, to the SUPERB 74, and CREOLE 36, bearing each the broad pendant of Sir Thos. Harvey in South America, where, having held for 12 months the rating of Admiralty Midshipman on board the latter ship, he was nominated, 16 Nov. 1822, Acting-Lieutenant of the CONWAY 26, Capt. Basil Hall. On his return to England he was confirmed by commission dated 15 Feb. 1823. His appointments have since been—26 Nov. 1823, as a Supernumerary, to the RAMILLIES 74, Coast Blockade ship, Capt. Wm. M'Culloch—8 Dec. 1827, to the EREBUS bomb, Capt. Philip Broke, on the Mediterranean station, where he remained about two years—29 May, 1833, to the REVENGE 78, Capts. Donald Hugh Mackay and Wm. Elliott, of which ship, employed on the Lisbon and Home stations, he became First-Lieutenant—16 April, 1834, to the Coast Guard—25 May, 1843, to the command (on leaving the latter service) of the SKYLARK brig, of 4 guns, which vessel, on her return from the coast of Scotland, was lost in a fog off the Isle of Wight 25 April, 1845—and, 23 Nov. 1846, to the command of the TORCH steamer, of 150-horse power, now engaged on particular service.

Lieut. Morris is Senior of 1823. He married, 12 Jan. 1841, Harriet, daughter of W. Smith, Esq., of the Customs, West Cowes, Isle of Wight. AGENTS—Messrs. Halford and Co.

* *Vide* Gaz. 1801, p. 190. † *V.* Gaz. 1804, p. 890.

MORRIS. (REAR-ADMIRAL, 1846. F-P., 31; H-P., 40.)

HENRY GAGE MORRIS, born 27 March, 1770, at New York, is only surviving son (by Mary, daughter of Fred. Philipse, Esq., of that place) of the late Hon. Lieutenant-Colonel Roger Morris, a member of the Governor's Council at New York, who served with distinction in the first American war; was wounded in the celebrated battle of the Monongahela river, in which General Braddock was killed, with most of his officers; assisted at the taking of Quebec; and was Aide-de-Camp at other periods to General Gage and Lord Amherst. Rear-Admiral Morris, whose family sustained immense loss by its adherence to the Crown, had an elder brother, Amherst, who was rewarded with the rank of Commander for his conduct as First-Lieutenant of the NYMPHE frigate, Capt. Edw. Pellew (whose own gallantry procured him the honour of Knighthood), at the capture of the French ship *La Cléopatre*, of 40 guns and 320 men, 18 June, 1793, and died 29 April, 1802.

This officer (whose name had been borne from 1776 to 1778 on the books of the MAIDSTONE frigate, Capt. Alan Gardner) embarked, 22 Jan. 1782, as A.B., on board the CENTURION 50, Capts. Sam. W. Clayton and Jas. Cotes, and in Jan. of the following year was present, in company with the HUSSAR 28, at the capture, on the North American station, of the French 36-gun frigate *La Sybille*. During the peace he was successively employed, as Midshipman and Master's Mate, on the Home and Jamaica stations, in the PRINCESS ROYAL 98, Capt. Jonathan Faulknor, CAMILLA 20, Capt. John Hutt, POWERFUL 74, Capt. Andrew Sutherland, DRAKE 14, Capt. Geo. Countess, COURAGEUX 74, Capt. Alan Gardner, LIZARD 28, Capt. J. Hutt, NIGER 32, Capt. Rich. Goodwin Keats, MARTIN 16, Capt. Geo. Duff, and QUEEN 98, flag-ship of Rear-Admiral Gardner. Being made Lieutenant, 2 April, 1793, into the DUKE 98, Commodore Geo. Murray, he shared, in the ensuing June, in the unsuccessful attack upon Martinique. He was afterwards appointed, on the Home station—23 Oct. 1793, to the GLORY 98, bearing the broad pendant of Commodore Murray—24 July, 1794, to the PROSERPINE 28, Capts. Alex. Fraser and Willoughby Thos. Lake—and, 8 Dec. 1796, to the ROYAL SOVEREIGN 100, bearing the flag of his friend and patron, then Sir Alan Gardner, under whom, with the exception of a brief interval during the peace of Amiens, he continued employed in various ships, a great part of the time as Flag-Lieutenant, until presented by him with a commission, dated 8 May, 1804. In the following June he obtained command of the ESPIÈGLE 16, and in that sloop, and the JALOUSE 18, to which vessel he removed 30 June, 1809, he was almost incessantly engaged for eight years in escorting convoys to and from Ireland, the British Channel, Lisbon, and the West Indies. It is worthy of remark, that on no occasion did any of the numerous vessels placed during that period under his charge either endure capture or part company. He attained Post-rank 12 Aug. 1812, but was not able to procure further employment. The rank he at present holds was conferred on him 1 Oct. 1846.

The Rear-Admiral married, 31 Jan. 1804, Rebecca Newenham Millerd, third daughter of the late Rev. Fras. Orpen, B.A., of Trinity College, Dublin, Vicar of Kilgarvan, co. Kerry, and Rector of Dangorney and Douglas, co. Cork. By that lady he has issue six sons and four daughters. His eldest son, the Rev. Fras. Orpen Morris, B.A., of Worcester College, Oxford, is Vicar of Nafferton, in the East Riding of Yorkshire, and Chaplain to His Grace the Duke of Cleveland; his second son, Henry Gage, is a Commander R.N.

MORRIS. (COMMANDER, 1846.)

HENRY GAGE MORRIS, born 20 Nov. 1811, is second son of Rear-Admiral Henry Gage Morris.

This officer served as Midshipman of the GLASGOW 50, Capt. Hon. Jas. Ashley Maude, at the battle of Navarin, 20 Oct. 1827. Passing his examination in 1830, he obtained a commission 19 April, 1837; and he was afterwards appointed—20 April, 1837, as Additional, to the HASTINGS 74, flag-ship of Sir Wm. Hall Gage, off Lisbon—25 May, 1838, to the HERALD 26, Capt. Joseph Nias, of which vessel, stationed in the East Indies, he became First-Lieutenant—31 Oct. 1840, to the ENDYMION 38, Capt. Hon. Fred. Wm. Grey, lying at Plymouth—10 June and 28 Aug. 1841, as Senior, to the CHAMPION 18 and HARLEQUIN 16, Capts. Rich. Byron and Hon. Geo. Fowler Hastings, in the latter of which vessels he returned to the East Indies, and shared in the operations on the coast of China—15 Aug. 1842, to the acting-command, which he retained until March, 1844, of the WOLVERENE 16, also in the East Indies—5 Sept. 1845, again as First, to the JUNO 26, fitting at Sheerness—and, 17 Nov. 1845, to the ST. VINCENT 120, bearing the flag at Portsmouth of Sir Chas. Ogle, to whom he became Signal-Lieutenant 16 Jan. 1846. He attained his present rank 25 June following; and since 20 Oct. 1847 has been in command, again in the East Indies, of the CAMBRIAN 40, Commodore Jas. Hanway Plumridge.

MORRIS. (COMMANDER, 1814. F-P., 37; H-P., 23.)

JOHN ROW MORRIS is brother of Rear-Admiral Geo. Morris.

This officer entered the Navy, in April, 1787, as Ordinary, on board the NARCISSUS frigate, Capts. Philip D'Auvergne, John Salisbury, and Paul Minchin, stationed in the Channel; where, from Aug. 1791 until Jan. 1795, he served, as Midshipman, in the ALFRED 74, Capt. John Bazely, and was afforded an opportunity of sharing in the action of 1 June, 1794. After a brief attachment to the SANDWICH 90, Capt. Jas. Robt. Mosse, he was promoted, 20 May, 1795, to a Lieutenancy in the SCOURGE sloop, Capt. Wm. Stapp, stationed in the North Sea. His succeeding appointments were—21 Sept. 1795, to the DORIS 36, Capt. Lord Ranelagh, employed off the coast of Ireland—16 Aug. 1797, to the ST. ALBANS 64, Capts. Fras. Pender and John Okes Hardy, with whom he served on the Halifax and West India stations until June, 1801—14 March, 1803, to the RAISONNABLE 64, Capt. Wm. Hotham, attached to the force in the North Sea—and 19 Oct. 1803, and (after five months of half-pay) 24 April, 1810, to the command of the INSOLENT gun-brig and PIONEER schooner, on the Home and Mediterranean stations. In the INSOLENT he assisted at the destruction of the French shipping in Basque Roads in April, 1809, and in the PIONEER he contributed, in company with the DECOY cutter, to the capture, 9 May, 1812, of the *Infatigable* French lugger-privateer, of 29 men, 10 of whom (including their Commander) were killed and wounded.* He attained the rank he now holds 15 June, 1814; and was lastly, from 31 Dec. 1820 until the spring of 1832, employed as an Inspecting-Commander in the Coast Guard. AGENT—Fred. Dufaur.

MORRIS. (LIEUT., 1815. F-P., 10; H-P., 32.)

PETER MORRIS entered the Navy, 19 Aug. 1805, as A. B., on board the CAPTAIN 74, Capt. Geo. Hopewell Stephens, stationed in the Channel. In March, 1806, he removed as Midshipman, a rating he had previously attained, to the OCEAN 98, bearing the flag of Lord Collingwood off Cadiz; and after an attachment of nine months to the HINDOSTAN 50, Capt. Lewis Hole, off Lisbon, he served as Master's Mate, from Jan. 1809 to May, 1814, in the Bay of Biscay, on board the GOLDFINCH of 10 guns and 75 men, Capts. Fitzherbert Geo. Skinner and Arden Adderley, under the former of whom he assisted in beating off, 18 May, 1809, the French corvette *Mouche*, of 16 guns and 180 men, at the close of an action of four hours, in which the British vessel, besides being much cut up, sustained a loss of 3 men killed and 3 severely wounded. After attending, in the ALCESTE troop-ship, Capt. Dan. Lawrence, the expedition to New Orleans, he was promoted to the rank of Lieutenant 10 March, 1815. His last appointment was, 4 Nov. in the latter year, to the WESER, another troop-ship, also commanded by Capt. Lawrence, in which he remained until paid off on his return from a voyage to the West Indies, 16 Aug. 1816. AGENTS—Holmes and Folkard.

* *Vide* Gaz. 1812, p. 888.

MORRIS. (LIEUTENANT, 1846.)

WALTER WINDYER MORRIS passed his examination 24 Feb. 1834; and from 24 Oct. 1840 until promoted to the rank of Lieutenant, 3 July, 1846, was employed in the Coast Guard. His appointments have since been—30 Nov. 1846, to the PENELOPE steam-frigate of 650-horse power, bearing the broad pendant of Sir Chas. Hotham, on the coast of Africa—and, 14 Feb. 1847, as Senior, to the WANDERER 12, Capt. Fred. Byng Montresor, on the same station, where he is at present serving.

MORRIS. (COMMANDER, 1841. F-P., 20; H-P., 22.)

WILLIAM MORRIS (*a*), born in Oct. 1792, is son of the late Capt. Robt. Morris, who represented the city of Gloucester in four successive Parliaments, from 1805 to 1817, and who, at a time when the country was menaced with invasion, raised and for many years supported at his own expense a corps of yeomanry cavalry.

This officer entered the Navy, 4 Nov. 1805, as Fst.-cl. Vol., on board the KENT 74, Capts. Henry Garrett and Thos. Rogers, in which ship, employed in the Channel and off Lisbon, he assisted at the capture, 28 July, 1806, of the French frigate *Le Rhin* of 44 guns. From Nov. in the latter year until Jan. 1812 he served in the Mediterranean, chiefly at the blockade of Toulon, in the ROYAL SOVEREIGN 100, Capts. David Colby, Abel Ferris, Henry Whitmarsh Pearse, Joseph Spear, John Harvey, and Wm. Bedford. On his arrival in the East Indies in the VOLAGE 26, Capt. Hon. Donald Hugh Mackay, he was received, in Sept. 1812, on board the ILLUSTRIOUS 74, bearing the flag of Sir Sam. Hood, who, on 12 Jan. 1813, nominated him Acting-Lieutenant of the ARROGANT sheer-hulk at Bombay, Capt. Chas. Biddulph. Accompanying the latter officer in a similar capacity, shortly afterwards, into the HESPER sloop, he accompanied an expedition against the pirates of Ras-al-Khyma in the Persian Gulf. He was confirmed a Lieutenant while serving, still in the East Indies, in the CORNWALLIS *armée-en-flûte*, Capt. Stephen Thos. Digby, 24 Aug. 1813; and he was subsequently appointed—in Dec. 1814, to the CLORINDE 40, Capt. Sam. Geo. Pechell, employed in the Mediterranean in attendance upon her late Majesty Queen Caroline until the summer of 1816*—1 July and 28 March, 1822, to the BULWARK and GLOUCESTER 74's, flag-ships of Sir Benj. Hallowell at the Nore—11 March, 1823, to the GENOA 74, Capts. Wm. Cumberland and Walter Bathurst, during his attachment to which ship he had command for some time of the RAYMOND tender, and was afforded an opportunity of sharing in the battle of Navarin, 20 Oct. 1827—and, 8 Jan. 1838, to the command of the PARTRIDGE brig of 10 guns. In the latter vessel he was at first employed in protecting the fisheries on the coast of Scotland; he then proceeded to the coast of Africa with presents for King Trassar; and, when afterwards on the Brazilian station, he effected the capture of two slave-vessels, the *Asseisceira* and *San Antonio*. He continued in the PARTRIDGE until promoted to his present rank, 23 Nov. 1841; and has since been on half-pay. AGENTS—Messrs. Halford and Co.

---

* Lieut. Morris was subpœnaed on the trial of that unfortunate Princess in the House of Lords.

MORRIS. (COMMANDER, 1846.)

WILLIAM MORRIS (*b*) entered the Navy 26 July, 1823; and served as Midshipman of the GENOA 74, Capt. Walter Bathurst, at the battle of Navarin, 20 Oct. 1827. He passed his examination in 1829; obtained his first commission 28 June, 1838; and was afterwards appointed—17 Jan. 1839, to the TRINCULO 16, Capt. Henry Edward Coffin, on the Lisbon station—6 Aug. 1841, to the IMPREGNABLE 104, Capt. Thos. Forrest, in the Mediterranean—19 Oct. 1843, to the HYACINTH 18, Capt. Fras. Scott, employed on particular service—9 March, 1844, as Senior, to the TORTOISE store-ship at the Ascension, Capt. Arthur Morrell—and, 16 Dec. 1844, in a similar capacity, to the ARDENT steam-sloop, Capt. John Russell, stationed on the coast of Africa, whence he returned to England and was paid off at the close of 1845. He acquired his present rank 28 May, 1846; and, since 28 Aug. 1847, has been in command of the ARAB 16, at the Cape of Good Hope. AGENTS—Hallett and Robinson.

MORRISH. (LIEUTENANT, 1841.)

SAMUEL MORRISH entered the Navy 11 Dec. 1828; passed his examination 22 Jan. 1835; and at the period of his promotion to the rank of Lieutenant, 23 Nov. 1841, was serving in South America as Mate of the PRESIDENT 50, Capt. Wm. Broughton. His appointments have since been—15 Sept. 1842, as Additional, to the ILLUSTRIOUS 72, flag-ship of Sir Chas. Adam, in North America and the West Indies—17 Feb. 1844, to the ELECTRA 18, Capt. Arthur Darley, on the same station—25 June, 1845, to the Coast Guard—and, 14 Sept. 1847, to the ASIA 84, bearing the flag of Rear-Admiral Phipps Hornby, in the Pacific, where he is now serving.

He married, 1 July, 1845, Mary Elizabeth, daughter of the late Capt. John Mackeson, of the Hon. E. I. Co.'s service, and of the island of Jamaica. AGENT—Joseph Woodhead.

MORRISON. (Captain, 1814. F-P., 22; H-P., 30.)

ISAAC HAWKINS MORRISON entered the Navy, 8 June, 1795, as Fst.-cl. Vol., on board the MALABAR 54, Capt. John Parr, and in April and May, 1796, was present at the surrender of the Dutch settlements of Demerara, Essequibo, and Berbice. Following Capt. Parr, as Midshipman, in Dec. of the latter year into the STANDARD 64, and next into the ZEALAND, he continued with him in those ships until Feb. 1801, on the Home station; where he further, until May, 1804, served, part of the time as Master's Mate and Admiralty-Midshipman, in the FORTUNÉE 36, Capt. Lord Amelius Beauclerk, RAVEN and GANNET sloops, Capts. Jas. Sanders and Edw. Bass, and TONNANT 80, Capt. Sir Edw. Pellew. While in the ZEALAND, he had been lent to the TISIPHONE sloop, Capt. Robt. Honyman, and ANDROMEDA 32, Capt. Henry Inman. Being advanced to the rank of Lieutenant, 1 May, 1804, he was subsequently appointed in that capacity—21 July, 1804, to the command, at Newfoundland, of the QUEEN CHARLOTTE hired cutter—25 Oct. following to the CAMILLA 20, Capt. Bridges Watkinson Taylor, on the same station—25 Feb. 1805, to the AMARANTHE 18, Capt. Edw. Pelham Brenton, employed in the North Sea and Channel—26 June, 1806, to the TRUSTY 50, Capt. Brian Hodgson, attached to the force in the Downs—16 April, 1807, to the URANIE 38, Capt. Christ. Laroche, off Cherbourg—and, 28 Nov. 1807, to the ADAMANT 50, Capt. Micajah Malbon, at Jamaica. After having acted for a short time as Commander of the PELICAN sloop, he was confirmed to that rank in the SHARK receiving-ship at Port Royal 10 June, 1808. He invalided home in Feb. 1809, and was next, 31 May, 1813, appointed to the ACHATES brig of 16 guns. In that vessel, with much injury to her sails and rigging, Capt. Morrison fought, off the coast of France, 21 Oct. following, a very gallant running action of several hours' duration with *La Trave*, a French frigate of 44 guns and 321 men, which had been previously dismasted in a gale of wind, and which was captured two days afterwards by the ANDROMACHE 38, Capt. Geo. Tobin. He also, 25 Feb. 1814, witnessed the surrender, to the EUROTAS of 46 guns and 320 men, of another French frigate, *La Clorinde*, mounting 44 guns and 12 brass-swivels, with a complement of 360 picked men. He attained Post-rank 7 June in the latter year; and was lastly, from 25 Oct. 1824 until the close of 1831, employed as an Inspecting Commander in the Coast Guard at Tralee, co. Kerry. He accepted the Retirement 1 Oct. 1846.

Capt. Morrison married, 16 July, 1823, Louisa Adams, daughter of John Powell Smith, Esq., of Upper Berkeley Street, Portman Square, London.

MORRISON. (LIEUT., 1815. F-P., 11; H-P., 30.)

RICHARD JAMES MORRISON, born 15 June, 1795, is son of the late Rich. Caleb Morrison, Esq., who for 27 years was a Gentleman Pensioner under King George III. His grandfather, Rich. Morrison, was a Captain in the Hon. E. I. Co.'s service.

This officer entered the Navy 30 Sept. 1806, as Fst.-cl. Vol., on board the SPARTAN of 46 guns and 258 men, Capts. Geo. Astle, Jahleel Brenton, and Edw. Pelham Brenton. Under Capt. Jah. Brenton, he saw much boat service in the Adriatic, participated as Midshipman in various attacks upon Pesaro and Ceseratico, and assisted at the capture of Lissa, Zante, Cephalonia, and Cerigo. He also, 3 May, 1810, shared in a brilliant and single-handed victory gained by the SPARTAN, in the Bay of Naples (after a contest of more than two hours, in which the British sustained a loss of 10 men killed and 22 wounded), over a Franco-Neapolitan squadron, carrying altogether 95 guns and about 1400 men. He continued in the same ship until Dec. 1810; and was subsequently, between Aug. 1811 and July, 1815, employed, part of the time as Master's Mate, in the ELIZABETH 74 and MYRTLE 20, Capts. Fras. Wm. Austen and Arthur Batt Bingham, on the North Sea, Baltic, and Cork stations. In the latter vessel he appears to have likewise performed the duties of Lieutenant and Master. He took up, on leaving her, a commission bearing date 3 March, 1815. His last appointment was to the Coast Guard, in which he served from April, 1827, until Oct. 1829, when he was under the necessity of resigning from the effects of ill health, induced by the exposure he had suffered in rescuing 4 men and a boy from wreck in the month of Feb. 1828. His exertions on the occasion were acknowledged by a medal from the "Society for the Preservation of Life from Shipwreck." We may add that his commission had been presented to him in less than six months after he had passed his examination, as a reward for the conduct he had exhibited during the action in the Bay of Naples.

On 22 April, 1824, Lieut. Morrison presented a plan to the Admiralty "for registering merchant seamen"—since adopted in principle. He also, 24 Jan. 1827, proposed another "for propelling ships of war in a calm;" and on 6 March, 1835, he further suggested to the Board "a plan for providing an ample supply of seamen for the fleet without impressment." In reference to the latter scheme he received the thanks of their Lordships, and had the gratification of not only hearing his arguments immediately employed in the House of Commons by Sir Jas. Graham, then First Lord of the Admiralty, but of likewise seeing them partially enforced, by the addition of a thousand boys to the naval force of the country. He married, 23 Aug. 1827, Miss Sarah Mary Paul, of Waterford, and by that lady has issue nine children. AGENTS—Burnett and Holmes.

MORRISS. (LIEUT., 1815. F-P., 33; H-P., 7.)

EDWARD JOHN MORRISS entered the Navy, 1 Jan. 1807, as Fst.-cl. Vol., on board the ORION 74, Capt. Sir Arch. Collingwood Dickson, with whom he continued to serve in the Baltic, where he assisted at the siege of Copenhagen, and in the North Sea, until March, 1813—the last four years and a half in the capacity of Midshipman. He was then for 18 months employed in the Mediterranean as Master's Mate of the San Josef 110, flag-ship of Rear-Admirals Edw. Jas. Foote and Sir Rich. King; and, after a further attachment to the Plissant 74, Capt. Benj. Wm. Page, at Spithead, and, as Admiralty-Mate, to the Statira 38, Capt. Spelman Swaine, in which ship he accompanied the expedition against New Orleans, and was wrecked on a rock off the island of Cuba, 26 Feb. 1815, he was awarded a commission dated 17 of that month. His appointments have since been—6 June, 1815, for three months, to the Plissant, commanded as before—3 July, 1816, for an equally brief period, to the Belzebub bomb, Capts. Wm. Kempthorne and Fred. Thos. Michell, part of the force employed at the bombardment of Algiers—17 Jan. 1817, to the Alban 12, Capt. Hugh Patton, which vessel, employed for some time off Holyhead, was paid off in Oct. 1818—and, 26 April, 1825, to the command, which he still retains, of a station in the Coast Guard.

MORRITT. (Commander, 1845.)

George Morritt entered the Navy 21 Aug. 1816; passed his examination in 1823; and obtained his first commission 10 Jan. 1837. His succeeding appointments were—12 Jan. and 20 April, 1837, as Additional-Lieutenant, to the Melville and Hastings 74's, flag-ships of Hon. Sir Chas. Paget and Sir Wm. Hall Gage on the North America and West India and Lisbon stations—7 Sept. 1837 and 1 Oct. 1840, to the Minden 72 and Howe 120, Capts. Alex. Renton Sharpe and Thos. Forrest, both attached to the force in the Mediterranean—and, 6 Dec. 1843, as Senior, to the Vestal 26, Capt. Chas. Talbot, fitting for the East Indies. For his conduct in command of the barge belonging to the latter ship, at the capture and destruction, 19 Aug. 1845, of Maloodoo, a strong fortification in the possession of Scheriff Osman, a rebel Borneo chieftain, he was promoted to the rank of Commander by commission dated back to the day of the achievement.* He has been employed, since 30 June, 1847, as an Inspecting Commander in the Coast Guard. Agents—Messrs. Stilwell.

MORSHEAD. (Lieut., 1836. f-p., 21; h-p., 5.)

John Morshead was born in 1806.

This officer entered the Navy, 17 Nov. 1821, as a Volunteer, on board the Iphigenia 42, bearing the broad pendant of Commodore Mends on the coast of Africa; where, on following his chief, as Midshipman, into the Owen Glendower 42, he served on shore at Cape Coast Castle, during the Ashantee war. In the spring of 1825, a few months after he had returned to England and been received on board the Prince Regent 120, flag-ship at Chatham of Sir Benj. Hallowell, he again sailed for the coast of Africa in the Redwing 18, Capt. Douglas Chas. Clavering; and, on his arrival, was transferred to the Maidstone 42, Commodore Chas. Bullen. Invaliding home in Dec. of the same year, he next joined in succession—in March, 1826, the Britannia 120, Capt. Philip Pipon, lying at Plymouth—between Feb. 1828 and June, 1830, the Erebus and Infernal bombs, Capts. Geo. Haye, Edm. Wm. Gilbert, and Brunswick Popham, both in the Mediterranean—and, in June, 1831, the Imogene 28, Capt. Price Blackwood, whom he accompanied, first to the East Indies, and then to China, where, in Sept. 1834, he commanded a division of guns at the forcing of the passage of the Boca Tigris. He returned to England in Aug. 1835; and on 24 May, 1836, nearly eight years after he had passed his examination, he was promoted to the rank of Lieutenant. His appointments have since been—in 1836-7, to the Dublin 50, Harrier 18, and Blonde 42, Capts. Chas. Eden, Wm. Henry Hallowell Carew, and Sir Fras. Mason, all on the South American stations, whence he returned in Nov. 1837—21 July, 1838, to the Hastings 74, Capts. Fras. Erskine Loch and John Lawrence, under the latter of whom, during the Syrian war, he was employed in the boats in a successful attempt to remove a quantity of powder from the castle of Beyrout*—6 Nov. 1843 (he had left the Hastings in Feb. 1842), to the Albion 90, Capt. Nicholas Lockyer, from which ship, employed on the Home station, he invalided in Sept. 1845—and, 19 Nov. 1846, as Additional, to the Caledonia 120, bearing the flag of Sir John Louis, Admiral-Superintendent at Plymouth, where he is at present serving.

* Vide Gaz. 1845, p. 6536.

MORSHEAD, C.B. (Captain, 1842.)

William Henry Anderson Morshead entered the Navy 4 Sept. 1823; passed his examination in 1830; and obtained his first commission 21 Sept. 1832. His succeeding appointments were—2 April, 1833, as Additional-Lieutenant, to the St. Vincent 120, Capt. Humphrey Fleming Senhouse, in the Mediterranean—29 July following, and 30 May and 16 Dec. 1834, to the Malabar 74, Capts. Hon. Josceline Percy and Henry Shovell Marsham, Talavera 74, Capt. Edw. Chetham, and Edinburgh 74, Capt. Jas. Rich. Dacres, on the same station, whence he returned in the early part of 1837—28 Sept. in the latter year, as Senior, to the Favourite 18, Capt. Walter Croker, whom he accompanied to the East Indies—and, 1 June, 1838, in a similar capacity, to the Hyacinth 18, Capt. Wm. Warren. On 13 and 18 March, 1841, we find him commanding the boats of the latter vessel at the capture of the last fort protecting the approaches to Canton, and also of the city itself.† During the second series of operations against it, it was his lot to be slightly wounded, and to perform service which gained him the public mention of Sir Humphrey Fleming Senhouse.‡ Being rewarded with the rank of Commander 8 June, 1841, and appointed, 16 Oct. following, to the Columbine 16, he further distinguished himself by the manner in which, with his own boats and those of the Hon. Co.'s war-steamer Queen, he destroyed a large number of fire-junks intended for the destruction of Her Majesty's shipping in the neighbourhood of Ningpo, 10 March, 1842.§ In the course of the same year he participated in the attacks upon Chapoo and Woosung, and in the operations on the Yang-tse-Kiang.‖ For these services he was recompensed with a Post-commission dated 23 Dec. 1842, and, the next day, with the Companionship of the Bath. He paid the Columbine off in the early part of 1843, and has not been since employed. Agent—John P. Muspratt.

MORTIMER. (Lieut., 1813. f-p., 12; h-p., 30.)

George Mortimer, born 16 Dec. 1792, at Bideford, co. Devon, is son of the late Commander John Mortimer, R.N. (1797); and brother of the late Lieut. Mortimer and nephew of the late Major Mortimer, both of the R.M. Another uncle, Mr. Porrett, was Ordnance Storekeeper at the Tower; as was also a cousin, bearing the same name.

This officer (whose name had been previously borne as a Supernumerary on the books of the Cæsar 80, Capt. Sir Rich. John Strachan, Nimble 14, Lieut.-Commander Thos. Delafons, and Audacious 74, and Barfleur 98, which latter ship, commanded by Capt. Geo. Martin, formed part of the force under Admiral Hon. Wm. Cornwallis when he pursued the French fleet close in with Brest harbour) became Midshipman, in the summer of 1805, of the Warrior 74, Capts. Sam. Hood Linzee, Michael Seymour, and John Wm. Spranger, with whom he continued employed in the Channel and Mediterranean until Feb. 1811. Towards the close of the former year, having fallen in with the Victory at sea, he assisted in towing that ship, with the body of Lord Nelson on board, into Spithead. In 1809 he co-operated in the reduction of the islands of Ischia, Procida, Zante, Cephalonia, and Cerigo; and he next commanded a mortar-boat at the defence of Sicily. In 1811 (in the course of which year he successively removed to the San Juan and

* Vide Gaz. 1840, p. 2610. † V. Gaz. 1841, pp. 1503, 1505.
‡ V. Gaz. 1841, pp. 2502, 2504. § V. Gaz. 1842, p. 2388.
‖ V. Gaz. 1842, pp. 3092, 3399, 3404.

NEPOMUCENO 74's, bearing each the broad pendant of Commodore Chas. Vinicombe Penrose, and, as Acting-Lieutenant, to the COLUMBINE and SWALLOW sloops, Capts. Wm. Shepheard and Edw. Reynolds Sibly) we find him employed in the gun-boat service at Gibraltar and Tarifa. After performing for 19 months the duties of Master's-Mate in the CALEDONIA 120, and PRINCE 98, flag-ships in the Mediterranean and at Portsmouth of Sir Edw. Pellew and Sir Rich. Bickerton, he was advanced, 17 Dec. 1813, to a Lieutenancy in the VENERABLE 74, bearing the flag of Rear-Admiral Philip Chas. Durham, in which, when on his passage to the West Indies, and in company with the CYANE sloop, he contributed to the capture, not without opposition, of the French 40-gun frigates *Iphigénie* and *Alcmène*, 16 and 20 Jan. 1814. His last appointments were—12 March, 1814, to the VESTAL 36, Capt. Sam. Bartlett Deeckar, which vessel was paid off three months afterwards at Barbadoes—and, 4 Feb. 1815, to the MALTA 80, Capts. Wm. Chas. Fahie, Thos. Boys, Chas. Ogle, and Thos. Gordon Caulfeild. Under Capt. Fahie, besides witnessing the surrender of Naples, he took part in the reduction of Gaeta in 1815, and commanded a division of boats at the cutting out of a large Russian ship from under its batteries. For those services he received, in common with the other officers employed, the thanks of the Neapolitan and British ministers. The MALTA was put out of commission in Feb. 1817, and Lieut. Mortimer, rendered incapable of further employment from the effects of injuries he had received during his career afloat, was admitted to the out-pension of Greenwich Hospital 9 Dec. 1831.

He married, 8 Sept. 1835, Miss Prideaux, eldest daughter of the late John James, Esq., of Sidmouth, by whom he has issue one son.

MORTON. (COMMANDER, 1827. F-P., 13; H-P., 27.)

CHARLES MORTON, born in the vicinity of London, is member of a family seated for some centuries in the West Riding of Yorkshire.

This officer entered the Navy, 30 Oct. 1807, as Fst.-cl. Vol., on board the VOLONTAIRE 38, Capt. Chas. Bullen, whom he followed as Midshipman, in Feb. 1811, into the CAMBRIAN 40. In the former frigate he escorted the Duke of Orleans and his brother, Count Beaujolois, to Malta, served for some time with the in-shore squadron off Toulon, witnessed in 1809 the capture of the island of Pomégue, near Marseilles, and the destruction, near Cape Croisette, of Fort Rioux, mounting 14 guns, was present at an attack made, 31 Oct. in the latter year, on a large French convoy in the Bay of Rosas, and co-operated in 1810 with the patriots on the coast of Catalonia. In the CAMBRIAN we find him assisting, in the course of 1811, at the reduction of the towns of St. Philon and Palamos, whose batteries were destroyed and guns embarked; also at the capture of 19 merchant-vessels at Cadaqués, and at the defence of Tarragona. In Nov. 1814, after he had been for nearly three years employed on the Home and Mediterranean stations in the BULWARK and POMPÉE 74's, Capts. Thos. Brown and Sir Jas. Athol Wood, he rejoined Capt. Bullen on board the AKBAR 50, of which ship, having first conveyed despatches from Flushing to Antwerp, he was created an Acting-Lieutenant by Rear-Admiral Sir Thos. Byam Martin, 13 April, 1815. He was confirmed on the return of the AKBAR from the Halifax station 10 Dec. 1816; and he was next, 11 Dec. 1823, appointed First of the MAIDSTONE 42, fitting for the broad pendant of his friend Commodore Bullen, who had been nominated to the chief command on the coast of Africa. While on that station Lieut. Morton was most actively employed in the suppression of the slave-trade. He was promoted to the rank of Commander 6 Oct. 1827, a few weeks after the MAIDSTONE had been paid off, and has not been since afloat.

Commander Morton is the author of "An Essay on the Electrical Formation of Hailstones, in opposition to the absurd Theories of the learned Philosophers," and is the inventor of a plan for increasing the power and rapidity used in the art of swimming. He married, 23 Sept. 1829, Eliza, only daughter of the late John Thompson, Esq., of Hanover, Jamaica.

MORTON. (LIEUT., 1812. F-P., 12; H-P., 33.)

THOMAS CONSTANT PAGGETT MORTON entered the Navy, 2 Sept. 1802, as Sec.-cl. Boy, on board the ARGO 44, Capts. Benj. Hallowell and Geo. Parker, employed in succession on the coast of Africa, and in the West Indies, Mediterranean, and North Sea. While in the West Indies, in 1803, he co-operated in the reduction of the islands of Ste. Lucie and Tobago. Becoming Midshipman, in Oct. 1804, of the PROSELYTE 28, Capts. Geo. Nich. Hardinge, Geo. Sayer, and John Chas. Woolcombe, he again, in the early part of 1805, sailed for the West Indies in escort of a large convoy. From Nov. in the latter year until Oct. 1811 we find him serving in the ILLUSTRIOUS 74, Capts. Wm. Shield, Wm. Robt. Broughton, Robt. Worgan Geo. Festing, and Robt. Maunsell, at first off Cadiz, and then in the East Indies, where, having assisted at the capture of Java, he removed to the DASHER sloop, Capt. Wm. Kelly. On his return to England in March, 1812, he became Master's Mate of the THISBE 28, bearing the flag of Sir Chas. Hamilton at Deptford; and in the following June he was received, in a similar capacity, on board the IMPÉTUEUX 74, flag-ship off Lisbon of the late Sir Geo. Martin. He was confirmed a Lieutenant, 15 Oct. in the same year, in the SAN JUAN 74, successive flag-ship of Rear-Admirals Sam. Hood Linzee and Hon. Chas. Elphinstone Fleeming at Gibraltar, whence, in the summer of 1814, he returned home in the SHEARWATER 10, Capt. John Townsend Coffin. He has since been on half-pay.

MOSS. (LIEUTENANT, 1825.)

CHARLES MOSS entered the Navy 1 Sept. 1808, and was for some time Master's Mate of the SHELDRAKE 16, Capt. Jas. Pattison Stewart, in which vessel he came into frequent contact with the Danish flotillas in the Baltic, co-operated, in 1811, in the brilliant defence of Anholdt, and was severely wounded in boarding a Danish sloop on the coast of Jutland. He passed his examination in 1814; obtained his commission 27 May, 1825; and was subsequently appointed—2 Nov. 1825, as a Supernumerary, to the HYPERION 42, Coast Blockade ship, Capt. Wm. Jas. Mingaye—6 July, 1832, to the Coast Guard, which he left in the early part of 1834—2 July, 1840, to the same service—and, 15 Oct. 1841, to the command of the WICKHAM Revenue cruizer. He continued in the latter vessel until the end of 1846, and is now again in the Coast Guard. AGENTS—Hallett and Robinson.

MOSS. (LIEUTENANT, 1822. F-P., 13; H-P., 23.)

SIDNEY MOSS entered the Navy, in Sept. 1811, as a Boy, on board the BERWICK 74, Capts. Sir Robt. Laurie and Edw. Brace, in which ship, with the exception of a few months passed in 1814 in the EDINBURGH 74, Capt. John Lampen Manley, he continued employed, the greater part of the time in the capacity of Midshipman, until July, 1816. He saw much service during that period on the coast of Spain, and assisted at the blockade of Toulon, the reduction of Genoa and Gaeta, and the capture of a host of the enemy's vessels. He also, at the commencement of 1816, accompanied Lord Exmouth to Algiers, Tunis, and Tripoli for the accomplishment of objects connected with the abolition of Christian slavery. On leaving the BERWICK he served for several months on Lake Ontario in the MONTREAL, Commodore Sir Robt. Hall; after which, returning to England in the PACTOLUS 38, Capt. Nich. Lockyer, he was for upwards of three years employed on the Home station in the SYBILLE 44, Capt. Chas. Malcolm, QUEEN CHARLOTTE 100, bearing the flags of Sir Edw. Thornbrough and Sir Geo. Campbell, and, as Admiralty-Midshipman, in the SEVERN, Coast Blockade ship, Capt. Wm. M'Culloch. After an attachment of two years to the SURINAM 18, Capts. Wm. M'Kenzie Godfrey, Chas. Crole, and Alfred Matthews, on the West India station, he was there, 25 Nov. 1822, promoted to a death vacancy in the ICARUS 10, commanded at first by Capts. Crole and Matthews, and afterwards by Capts. Thos. Stopford and John Geo. Graham. He has been on half-pay since 31 Jan. 1824.

Lieutenant Moss is married. AGENTS—Messrs. Chard.

MOTTLEY. (COMMANDER, 1843.)

JOSEPH MARTIN MOTTLEY entered the Navy 9 Oct. 1812; passed his examination in 1821; and was made Lieutenant, 11 Feb. 1829, into the NORTH STAR 28, Capt. Septimus Arabin, on the coast of Africa. He was afterwards appointed—5 March, 1830, as a Supernumerary, to the HYPERION 42, Coast Blockade ship, Capt. Wm. Jas. Mingaye—16 March, 1831, to the Coast Guard—5 Oct. 1832, to the UNDAUNTED 46, Capt. Edw. Harvey, employed in the East Indies, whence he returned in the early part of 1834—7 Nov. 1835, as First, to the TWEED 20, Capt. Thos. Maitland, stationed off Lisbon—19 Jan. 1837, to the command, for Home service, of the SPEEDY cutter, of 8 guns—10 March, 1838, as Senior, to the DEE steamer, Capt. Joseph Sherer, fitting for the North America and West India station, where he continued until superseded in May, 1839—7 Aug. 1839, to the REVENGE 76, Capt. Hon. Wm. Waldegrave, of which ship, attached to the force in the Mediterranean, he became First-Lieutenant—and, 27 April and 26 July, 1842, in the latter capacity, to the CALEDONIA 120, flag-ship at Portsmouth of Sir David Milne, and IMAUM receiving-ship at Jamaica, Commodore Hon. Henry Dilkes Byng. He attained his present rank 24 Jan. 1843; and, since 29 Oct. 1845, has been employed as an Inspecting-Commander in the Coast Guard.

He married, in 1838, Eliza, youngest daughter of W. Stone, Esq., builder, of Chatham Dockyard. AGENT—Joseph Woodhead.

MOTTLEY. (RETIRED COMMANDER, 1845.)

SAMUEL MOTTLEY died in 1845. He was brother of the late Admiral Mottley.

This officer entered the Navy, in Feb. 1800, as Fst.-cl. Vol., on board the PRINCE 98, Capt. Sam. Sutton, flag-ship in the Channel of Sir Chas. Cotton, whom he followed into the PRINCE GEORGE 98. Becoming Midshipman, in Feb. 1801, of the CÆSAR 80, bearing the flag of Sir Jas. Saumarez, he took part in the actions fought, 6 and 12 July following, off Algeciras and in the Gut of Gibraltar. In the course of 1802 he successively joined the LEDA frigate, Capt. Hardy, and RAMBLER sloop, Capt. Thos. Innes; and on 2 July, 1803, he was on board LA MINERVE, of 48 guns, Capt. Jahleel Brenton, when that ship took the ground under the batteries of Cherbourg, and was compelled, in spite of a desperate and sanguinary resistance, to strike her colours. Being restored to liberty in Oct. 1806, he was appointed (after a brief attachment, on the Home and West India stations, to the ROYAL WILLIAM, Capt. Hon. Courtenay Boyle, PRINCE GEORGE 98, Capt. Geo. Losack, NORTHUMBERLAND 74, flag-ship of Hon. Sir Alex. Cochrane, and HEUREUX 24, Capt. John Ellis Watt) to the command, with the rank of Acting-Lieutenant, of the ALLIANCE schooner, 5 March, 1807. In the ensuing Dec. he removed, with the rank last mentioned, to the HAUGHTY gun-brig, Lieut.-Commander John Mitchell. He was confirmed a Lieutenant 20 May, 1808, and was afterwards appointed—28 of the same month, to the CHRISTIAN VII. 80, Capt. Sir Joseph Sydney Yorke, in the Channel—12 July, 1810, to the MACEDONIAN, of 48 guns and 254 men, Capts. Lord Wm. FitzRoy and John Surman Carden, off Lisbon—26 Nov. 1813, to the BULWARK 74, Capt. David Milne, on the North American station—in Nov. 1814, for passage home, to the LOIRE 38, Capt. John Nash—and, 6 June, 1815, to the ALBION 74, Capt. Philip Somerville. As Second-Lieutenant of the MACEDONIAN, Mr. Mottley elicited the highest acknowledgments of Capt. Carden for his conduct, on 25 Oct. 1812, in a desperate action of 2 hours and 10 minutes, which rendered that frigate a shattered prize, after experiencing a loss of 36 men killed and 68 wounded, to the American ship *United States*, of 56 guns and 474 men, 12 of whom only appear to have been killed and wounded.* In the BULWARK, besides sharing in other operations, he commanded a boat, in a manner that obtained him much praise, at the destruction, up the Penobscot, of the American frigate *Adams*, 3 Sept. 1814.† Quitting the ALBION in Sept. 1815, Lieut. Mottley's next appointments were—in the summer of 1815, and in July, 1823, and March, 1825, to the command of the HARDWICKE, BAT, and CAMELION Revenue-cruizers—25 April, 1834, to the Ordinary at Portsmouth, where he remained, latterly as Senior of the VICTORY 104, Capt. Thos. Searle, until the spring of 1837—and, 30 Dec. 1837, to the Coast Guard, in which service he continued nearly six years and a half. He accepted the rank of Commander on the Retired List 30 April, 1845, a short time only prior to his death.

Commander Mottley married, 3 Aug. 1819, Maria Dundas Beatson, of Campbell Town, by whom he has left issue. AGENT—J. Hinxman.

MOTTLEY. (LIEUTENANT, 1841.)

WILLIAM MOTTLEY died 13 July, 1845, as related beneath, aged 27. He was son of Geo. Henry Mottley, Esq., of Portsmouth, the talented editor of the 'Hampshire Telegraph.'

This officer entered the Navy 14 April, 1830; passed his examination 5 July, 1837; and at the period of his promotion to the rank of Lieutenant, 30 Aug. 1841, was serving as Mate of the WASP 16, Capt. Hon. Henry Anthony Murray, in which sloop he had assisted, under Capt. Geo. Mansel, at the capture of St. Jean d'Acre. His succeeding appointments were—2 Sept. 1841, again to the WASP—21 June, 1842 (soon after his return from the Mediterranean), to the THUNDER surveying-vessel, Capt. Edw. Barnett, on the North America and West India station—10 Jan. 1844, to the PENELOPE steam-frigate, bearing the broad pendant of Commodore Wm. Jones on the coast of Africa—and, 27 Sept. 1844, a third time, to the WASP, then commanded by Capt. Sidney Henry Ussher. He died of fever at Ascension, as above, on board the PENELOPE, while on his passage to rejoin the WASP, after having taken to Sierra Leone a slave-brig captured by her. AGENTS—Messrs. Ommanney.

MOUAT. (LIEUTENANT, 1815. F-P., 20; H-P., 23.)

JOHN ALEXANDER MOUAT, born about 1793, is son of Commander Alexander Mouat, R.N., who was a Midshipman with Capt. Cook during his voyages, and died fom fever while in command of the RATTLESNAKE sloop, in the West Indies, in 1793; and grandson of Capt. Patrick Mouat, R.N., who commanded the TAMER on a voyage of discovery with Admiral Byron. One of his uncles died in the ASSISTANCE while in command of the North American station; and two others were killed in action in the LONDON, off St. Domingo.

This officer entered the Navy, in Aug. 1804, as Fst.-cl. Vol., on board the ZEBRA bomb, Capt. Wm. Standway Parkinson, with whom he continued to serve, as Midshipman, in the MERLIN, WASP, and FAVORITE sloops, on the Home and West India stations, until 1808—assisting, when in the FAVORITE, at the capture of the Danish islands of St. Thomas and Ste. Croix. He then returned home in the THAIS 20, Capt. Wm. Ferris; and in Dec. 1808, after having served for seven months in the ISIS 50, flag-ship at Newfoundland of Vice-Admiral John Holloway, he joined the AFRICAINE 38, Capt. Rich. Raggett, under whom we find him employed in escorting Lord Hill's brigade from Cork to Lisbon, the Duke of Orleans from Portsmouth to Malta, Mr. Jackson, the British Ambassador, to the

* *Vide* Gaz. 1812, p. 2595. † *V.* Gaz. 1814, p. 2031.

United States, and the Hon. Mr. Erskine thence to England. With the exception of an interval passed in the summer of 1810 on board the SALVADOR DEL MUNDO, flag-ship at Plymouth of Admiral Young, he continued under Capt. Raggett in the AFRICAINE and DEFIANCE 74, latterly in the North Sea, until Jan. 1813. He was then sent out to India on promotion in the DÆDALUS 38, Capt. Murray Maxwell; and on that frigate being wrecked off Ceylon in the following July, he was received on board the MINDEN 74, of which ship, bearing the flag of Sir Sam. Hood, he was nominated Acting-Lieutenant 23 Sept. in the same year. In the early part of 1814 he successively removed, in the latter capacity, to the HECATE and SPHYNX sloops, Capts. John Hill and Hon. Arthur Turnour. He was confirmed to the SPHYNX 11 Feb. 1815, and, being paid off in the ensuing Dec., was afterwards appointed—in Nov. 1818, to the NEWCASTLE 60, bearing the flag of the late Sir Edw. Griffith Colpoys at Halifax, whence he returned in 1821—6 Nov. 1828, as First-Lieutenant (a rank he had held the last 12 months on board the NEWCASTLE), to the CHALLENGER 28, Capt. Chas. Howe Fremantle, under whom, after taking possession of the colony at Swan River, he proceeded to the East Indies, whence his health obliged him to invalid in Oct. 1829—and, 7 Oct. 1833, to the Coast Guard, in which service he remained until superseded, at his own request, in the autumn of 1838. He has since been on half-pay.

He married, in 1828, Maria Janetta, daughter of the Rev. John Mudge, Vicar of Brampfordspeke, and Rector of Lustleigh, co. Devon.

* MOUBRAY. (CAPTAIN, 1812. F-P., 21; H-P., 37.)

GEORGE MOUBRAY, born 9 Feb. 1773, is son of the late Geo. Moubray, Esq., of the ancient family of Moubray of Cockaidnie, co. Fife; brother-in-law of the late Vice-Admiral Jas. Katon; and cousin of the late Vice-Admiral Sir Rich. Hussey Hussey, K.C.B., G.C.M.G.

This officer entered the Navy, 1 Feb. 1789, as Midshipman, on board the BELLONA 74, Capt. Fras. John Hartwell, on the Home station; and in June of the same year removed to the ADAMANT 50, bearing the flag of Sir Rich. Hughes at Halifax, where he remained until June, 1792. He then joined in succession the HANNIBAL 74, Capt. John Colpoys, and JUNO 32, Capt. Sam. Hood; and in Jan. 1794 he was acting as Master's Mate of the latter ship when she effected an extraordinary escape from the harbour of Toulon, into which she had entered in ignorance of the evacuation of the British. Being shortly afterwards received on board the VICTORY 100, flag-ship of Lord Hood, he served in the boats at the sieges of St. Fiorenzo and Bastia. He was promoted, 27 May, 1794, to a Lieutenancy in LA MOSELLE sloop, Capts. Percy Fraser, Chas. Dudley Pater, and Chas. Brisbane, under the latter of whom he was hotly engaged and all but captured in Hotham's first partial action, 14 March, 1795; and he was subsequently appointed—19 Aug. 1796, to LA VIRGINIE 40, Capt. Anthony Hunt, in which frigate, after the Spithead mutiny, he escorted the Duke and Duchess of Wurtemberg to Cuxhaven, Rear-Admiral Sir Hugh Cloberry Christian to the Cape of Good Hope, and Lord Mornington to Calcutta, and then cruized in the East Indies until the peace of Amiens—7 May, 1803, as Senior, to the SEAHORSE 38, Capt. Hon. Courtenay Boyle, fitting for the Mediterranean—4 Nov. 1804, to the ROYAL SOVEREIGN 100, bearing the flag of Sir Rich. Bickerton off Toulon—and, 5 Oct. 1805, as First, to the POLYPHEMUS 64, Capt. Robt. Redmill, part of the victorious fleet employed in the ensuing action off Cape Trafalgar. Succeeding to the command of the latter ship immediately after the action, owing to the serious illness of his Captain, Lieut. Moubray had the good fortune, during the gale that followed, to regain possession of the *Argonauta* Spanish 80, and deliver her over to Admiral Collingwood off Cadiz. He afterwards took in tow the VICTORY, with the body of Lord Nelson on board, and conducted her to the mouth of the Straits of Gibraltar; and he also, in spite of her mutinous crew, carried the *Swiftsure* French 74, in a similar manner, from the neighbourhood of Cadiz to Gibraltar. On 24 Dec. 1805 he was promoted to the rank of Commander; and he was next, 27 Jan. 1809 and 27 March, 1812, appointed in that capacity to the RHODIAN 10, and MOSELLE 18; in which vessels he served in the West Indies, the chief part of the time with a small squadron under his orders for the protection of the Bahamas, until 31 March, 1813. Capt. Moubray, whose promotion to Post-rank had taken place 12 Aug. 1812, was not again employed until 23 Sept. 1844, when he obtained command of the VICTORY 104, at Portsmouth, which he retained until admitted into Greenwich Hospital 25 March, 1846.

He married, 14 June, 1812, Eliza Pellew, eldest daughter of A. N. Yates, Esq., Naval Storekeeper at Jamaica, by whom he has issue five sons and three daughters.

MOUBRAY. (LIEUTENANT, 1845.)

ROBERT HUSSEY MOUBRAY passed his examination 13 March, 1837; and from 1841 until promoted to the rank of Lieutenant, 1 Dec. 1845, was employed in the East Indies as Mate of the HAZARD 18, Capts. Chas. Bell and Fras. Philip Egerton. He served during several months of 1847 on board the TERRIBLE steam-frigate, of 800-horse power, Capt. Wm. Ramsay.

MOUBRAY. (LIEUT., 1843. F-P., 14; H-P., 2.)

WILLIAM HOBSON MOUBRAY, born 28 Aug. 1818, is third son (by Laura, fourth daughter of Wm. Hobson, Esq., of Markfield, co. Middlesex) of Sir Robt. Moubray, Kt, K.H., of Cockaidnie, co. Fife, a Deputy-Lieutenant and Magistrate for that shire, and a Lieutenant-Colonel in the Army, who was for 10 years employed in India, and for eight in the Mediterranean, where, as Captain in the 80th Regt. of Foot, he served in Egypt under Sir Ralph Abercromby. His eldest brother, Robert, is a Captain in the Fifeshire Militia; his second, Richard, a Captain in the 1st Madras Light Cavalry, died 20 April, 1843; and his youngest, Edward, is now a Lieutenant in the Royal Artillery. Lieut. Moubray, a descendant of the family of William the Conqueror, is nephew of the late Vice-Admiral Sir Rich. Hussey Hussey, K.C.B., G.C.M.G.,* who assumed the name of Hussey by sign-manual on inheriting the estates of his cousin Admiral Sir Rich. Hussey Bickerton, Bart., K.C.B.

This officer entered the Navy, 18 April, 1831, on board the BARHAM 50, Capt. Hugh Pigot, fitting for the Mediterranean, where he was present at the restoration of Athens and the Negropont to the Greeks. After a servitude of three years in South America in the NORTH STAR 28, Capt. Octavius Vernon Harcourt, and HARRIER 18, Capt. Wm. Henry Hallowell Carew, he became Mate, about Jan. 1838, of the HASTINGS 72, Capts. Fras. Erskine Loch and John Lawrence. In that ship he escorted

* Sir Rich. Hussey Hussey was born 16 Mar. 1776; and embarked, in 1789, on board the IMPREGNABLE 98. He served in the EUROPA 50, Commodore Ford, at the capture, in Sept. 1793, of Jeremie and St. Nicholas Mole, St. Domingo; and, being shortly afterwards promoted to the rank of Lieutenant, was present as First of the same ship at the reduction of Port-au-Prince. He was advanced, in June, 1794, to the command of the FLY sloop, in which vessel he assisted at the detention of five Dutch men-of-war, and of a large convoy in Plymouth Sound, 19 Jan. 1795. He attained Post-rank 10 April, 1797; and after serving as a volunteer under Capt. Sir R. Bickerton on board the RAMILLIES and TERRIBLE 74's, was appointed to the successive command, between 1801 and 1814, of the MAIDSTONE and ACTIVE frigates, and MONTAGU and REPULSE 74's. During the whole of that period (thirteen years) he was never absent from his duty for a single day, even on leave. In the ACTIVE he passed the Dardanells with Sir John Duckworth in Feb. 1807; and in the MONTAGU he played an important part at the reduction of Sta. Maura in March, 1810. He was created a C.B in June, 1815; a Rear-Admiral in July, 1821; a K.C.B. in April, 1833; and a G C.M.G. and a Vice Admiral in 1837. He died a Vice-Admiral of the Red 6 Nov. 1842.

the Earl of Durham to Quebec and Her Majesty the Queen Dowager to and from the Mediterranean, besides assisting, in 1840, in the attack upon Beyrout. He subsequently joined the DUBLIN 50, fitting at Portsmouth for the flag of Rear-Admiral Rich. Thomas, and the CALEDONIA 120, flag-ship of Sir David Milne at Devonport; and on 16 Feb. 1843 he was promoted to the rank of Lieutenant. His succeeding appointments were—9 Nov. 1843, to the VESTAL 26, Capt. Chas. Talbot, equipping at Sheerness—13 Jan. 1844, to the ALBION 90, Capt. Nicholas Lockyer, employed as an experimental ship—and, 7 Nov. 1845, to the ST. VINCENT 120, flag-ship of Sir Chas. Ogle at Portsmouth, and of Sir Fras. Augustus Collier in the Channel. He has been on half-pay since the close of 1846.

Lieut. Moubray married, 16 Dec. 1846, Selina Mary Anna, daughter of J. B. Rooper, Esq., of Abbots Ripton Hall, Huntingdonshire, late M.P. and High-Sheriff for that co. AGENTS—Hallett and Robinson.

MOULD. (RETIRED COMMANDER, 1843. F-P., 14; H-P., 34.)

RICHARD COTTON MOULD is second-cousin of Lieut. Wm. Mould, R.N.

This officer entered the Navy, 16 Dec. 1799, as Fst.-cl. Boy, on board the RÉVOLUTIONNAIRE 38, Capts. Thos. Twysden and Hon. John Murray, stationed off the coast of Ireland; and between July, 1800, and Jan. 1806, was employed as Midshipman and Master's Mate, chiefly in the Mediterranean and at Home, on board the VIGILANT, Capt. Jas. Wood, AURORA, Capts. Thos. Gordon Caulfeild and Micajah Malbon, FALCON, Capt. Henry Manaton Ommanney, WINDSOR CASTLE, Capts. Albemarle Bertie, Thos. Wells, and Davidge Gould, and ARIADNE, Capt. Hon. Edw. King. In the latter ship, in 1805, we find him once or twice warmly engaged with the invasion flotilla. On leaving her, as above, he was nominated Acting-Lieutenant of the STARLING cutter, Lieut.-Commander Chas. Fred. Napier, in the North Sea. He was confirmed, 12 May, 1807, into the RECRUIT 18, Capt. Hon. Warwick Lake, whom he accompanied to the West Indies; and he was afterwards appointed—21 June, 1808, to the NIMROD sloop, Capt. De Courcy, in which vessel he returned to England—15 Dec. 1808, to the ST. ALBAN'S 64, Capts. Fras. Wm. Austen, Edw. Brace, Chas. Grant, and John Ferris Devonshire, employed at first in escorting convoy to the East Indies and China, and next, until Nov. 1812, at the defence of Cadiz—and, 10 July, 1813, and (after eight months of half-pay) 28 April, 1815, to the CLARENCE 74, Capts. Henry Vansittart and Fred. Warren, and SWIFTSURE 74, Capt. Wm. Henry Webley, both attached to the force in the Channel. He was paid off from the SWIFTSURE in Aug. 1815; and awarded the rank of Commander on the Retired List 10 Feb. 1843.

Commander Mould was left a widower 26 Oct. 1845.

MOULD. (LIEUTENANT, 1842. F-P., 19; H-P., 0.)

WILLIAM MOULD was born 6 April, 1814. He is second-cousin of Retired Commander R. C. Mould, R.N.

This officer entered the Navy, 13 Aug. 1828, as Fst.-cl. Vol., on board the PRINCE REGENT 120, Capt. Hon. Geo. Poulett, bearing the flag at Chatham of Sir Benj. Hallowell; and in Aug. 1829 joined the WINDSOR CASTLE 74, Capt. Hon. Duncombe Pleydell Bouverie, in the Mediterranean. In Aug. 1831 he became Midshipman of the REVENGE 78, Capts. Jas. Hillyar, Hon. Donald Hugh Mackay, and Wm. Elliott, with whom he continued employed off Lisbon and again in the Mediterranean until Nov. 1836—the last two years in the capacity of Mate. He then removed to the THUNDERER 84, Capt. Wm. Furlong Wise, on the station last named; and after further serving for four years and six months in North America and the West Indies on board the RINGDOVE 16, Capts. Horatio Stopford Nixon and Hon. Keith Stewart, and for five months in the QUEEN 110, flag-ship of Sir Edw. W. C. R. Owen in the Mediterranean, he was promoted, 7 March, 1842, to the rank of Lieutenant, and re-appointed to the latter ship. He has since become attached in succession—19 April, 1842, to the THUNDERER 84, Capt. Dan. Pring, also in the Mediterranean—6 Oct. 1843, to the EXCELLENT gunnery-ship at Portsmouth, Capt. Sir Thos. Hastings—and, 4 March, 1845, to the CANOPUS 84, Capt. Fairfax Moresby, now employed on particular service.

MOURILYAN. (RETIRED COMMANDER, 1839. F-P., 14; H-P., 35.)

EDWARD MOURILYAN entered the Navy, 29 July, 1798, as L.M., on board the TIGRE 74, Capts. Sir Wm. Sidney Smith, Wm. Mansell, Robt. Jackson, and Rich. Curry. In that ship, in which he continued until paid off in Sept. 1802, he assisted as Midshipman at the defence of St. Jean d'Acre in 1799, and took part, in 1801, in the operations in Egypt. In March, 1803, he rejoined Sir W. S. Smith, as Master's Mate, in the ANTELOPE 50, on the North Sea station, where, in 1804, he was severely wounded while in the act of boarding a Dutch gun-boat. For this he received a pecuniary reward from the Patriotic Society. After serving as Acting-Lieutenant in the ST. ALBAN'S 64, Capt. John Temple, and again with Sir W. S. Smith, as Master's Mate and Acting-Lieutenant, in the ANTELOPE 50, and POMPÉE 74, he was confirmed a Lieutenant of the latter ship by commission dated 31 Jan. 1806. In the spring of the same year, besides witnessing the surrender of the island of Capri, he joined in an attack upon the town of Scalea, where, in command of the POMPÉE's launch, he took possession of the castle, and drove the French from their guns, 2 36-pounders, which, together with 22 barrels of powder, he contrived, through great exertion, to bring off. During the remainder of the war we find him serving with his patron on the Brazilian and Mediterranean stations in the FOUDROYANT 80, and HIBERNIA 120; and also commanding, from 29 Dec. 1809 until 25 April, 1811, and from 7 Oct. 1813 until 26 March, 1814, the SWAN hired cutter, and POMPÉE armed transport. The SWAN was sunk in the Baltic in a severe action with a flotilla of Danish gun-boats. On 6 April, 1839, Lieut. Mourilyan was invested with the rank of Commander on the Retired List. He had been admitted to the out-pension of Greenwich Hospital 31 Aug. 1835.

MOWBRAY. (LIEUT., 1813. F-P., 10; H-P., 32.)

THOMAS MOWBRAY entered the Royal Naval College 15 Nov. 1805; and embarked, 23 Dec. 1808, as Midshipman, on board the BOADICEA 38, Capt. John Hatley; with whom, after serving for upwards of 12 months at the Cape of Good Hope, he returned to England, in July, 1810, in the RAISONNABLE 64. Between the latter period and the date of his promotion to the rank of Lieutenant, 2 Feb. 1813, we find him employed on the Home station in the TONNANT 80, Capt. Sir John Gore, ELIZABETH 74, Capt. Edw. Leveson Gower, ROYAL WILLIAM, flagship of Sir Roger Curtis, and TYRIAN brig, Capt. Augustus Baldwin. His last appointment was, 3 Nov. 1813, to the SURPRISE 38, Capt. Sir Thos. John Cochrane; in which ship he beheld the attacks upon Washington and Baltimore in 1814, and participated in the operations on the coast of Georgia. He was placed on half-pay 1 Sept. 1815. AGENT—Fred. Dufaur.

MOXON. (LIEUTENANT, 1813. F-P., 10; H-P., 34.)

JAMES MOXON entered the Navy, 23 Sept. 1803, as Ordinary, on board the ZEALAND 64, Capt. Wm. Mitchell, bearing the flag of Rear-Admiral Bartholomew Sam. Rowley at the Nore; served as Midshipman, from March, 1804, to May, 1805, in the VETERAN 64, Capts. Rich. King and Jas. Newman Newman, and ACHILLE 74, Capt. R. King, on the

Channel and Cadiz stations; and in Oct. of the latter year joined the CLEOPATRA 32, Capts. John Wight, Wm. Love, Robt. Simpson, and Sam. John Pechell. Under Capt. Pechell he assisted, on his arrival in the West Indies from Halifax, at the capture (the British ships JASON 32 and HAZARD 18 in company) of the French 40-gun frigate *La Topaze*, 22 Jan. 1809, after a very spirited action fought chiefly between the CLEOPATRA and the enemy; and in the ensuing month he co-operated in the reduction of Martinique. From Oct. 1810 until Nov. 1812 Mr. Moxon served, again at Halifax and also in the North Sea, the greater part of the time as Master's Mate, in the SWIFTSURE 74, flag-ship of Sir John Borlase Warren, and in the CHRISTIAN VII. 80, and IMPREGNABLE 98, bearing each the flag of Admiral Wm. Young. He was promoted, 27 March, 1813, to a Lieutenancy in the SAN DOMINGO 74, then the flag-ship of Sir J. B. Warren; and he was afterwards employed for several months in 1813-14, in the COLUMBIA sloop, Capts. John Kinsman and Henry Ducie Chads, and TERPSICHORE 32, Capt. Wm. Bowen Mends, both on the North American station. He has been on half-pay since June of the latter year.

MOYLE. (LIEUTENANT, 1842.)

GRANVILLE RICHARD MOYLE entered the Navy 10 Feb. 1830; passed his examination 10 March, 1836; and at the period of his promotion to the rank of Lieutenant, 10 Nov. 1842, had been for some time employed on the lakes of Canada, as Mate, in the NIAGARA 20, Capt. Williams Sandom. His last appointment was to the DUBLIN 50, in which ship, bearing the flag of Rear-Admiral Rich. Thomas, Commander-in-Chief in the Pacific, he served from 19 Dec. 1842 until paid off in 1845. AGENTS—Messrs. Stilwell.

MOYSES. (LIEUT., 1815. F-P., 11; H-P., 33.)

CHOYCE WILLIAM MOYSES entered the Navy, in March, 1803, as A.B., on board the UTRECHT 64, Capt. Thos. Rogers, employed in the North Sea; and in the course of the same year successively joined the GRAMPUS and DIOMEDE 50's, flag-ships of Sir Jas. Saumarez off Guernsey. Becoming Midshipman, in Jan. 1804, of the ALCMÈNE 32, Capt. John Stiles, he saw much service in the boats of that frigate off the coast of France; and on removing to the POMONE 38, Capts. Wm. Grenville Lobb and Robt. Barrie, he was employed in a similar manner off the coast of Spain, where he assisted at the boarding and capture of several of the enemy's privateers and other vessels. In the early part of 1807, having brought a prize under very perilous circumstances into Portsmouth, he took a passage on board the BLANCHE 38, Capt. Sir Thos. Lavie, for the purpose of rejoining his own ship. Before he could reach the POMONE, however, it was his misfortune to be wrecked, during a stormy night in the month of March, off the island of Ushant; on which occasion 45 of the BLANCHE's crew lost their lives. Being in consequence taken prisoner, he was doomed, notwithstanding several attempts at escape, to continue in captivity at Verdun, Givet, and Bitche, part of the time in a dungeon, until the conclusion of the war. His promotion to the rank of Lieutenant took place 11 March, 1815, but he has not been since able to procure employment.

MUDGE. (LIEUTENANT, 1815.)

ROBERT MUDGE entered the Navy, 6 July, 1806, as Midshipman, on board the PHŒNIX 36, Capt. Zachary Mudge, in which frigate (with the exception of five months, from Oct. 1808 to March 1809, passed in the NAIAD 38, Capt. Thos. Dundas) he served, on the Channel and Cork stations, until May, 1812. He then sailed, in the BUCEPHALUS 32, Capts. Joseph Drury and Barrington Reynolds, for the East Indies, where he was further, until the summer of 1814, employed in the ILLUSTRIOUS 74, flag-ship of Sir Sam. Hood, THEBAN 36, Capts. Stephen Thos. Digby and Basil Hall, and PROCRIS sloop, Capt. Hon. Thos. Roper Curzon. In June, 1815, after having served, at Sheerness, in the NAMUR 74, bearing the flag of Sir Chas. Rowley, and QUEEN CHARLOTTE 100, Capt. Chas. Inglis, he took up a commission bearing date 21 Feb. in that year. His appointments have since been, 17 Aug. 1820 and 15 Dec. 1826, to the office of Agent for Transports Afloat; and to the continuous command, 3 June, 1837, in the course of 1845, and 12 Jan. 1846, of the BEAVER, ARIEL, and ONYX steam-packets on the Dover station, where he still remains.

MUDGE. (VICE-ADMIRAL OF THE RED, 1841. F-P., 28; H-P., 39.)

ZACHARY MUDGE is son of the late John Mudge, Esq., of Plymouth, an eminent Physician.

This officer entered the Navy, 1 Nov. 1780, as Captain's Servant, on board the FOUDROYANT 84, Capt. John Jervis; and, on 21 April, 1782, assisted at the capture, after a gallant action of nearly an hour, attended, however, with no casualty to the British, of the French 74-gun ship *Pégase*, whose loss, besides being seriously damaged, amounted, out of a crew of 700 men, to 80 killed and wounded. During the next seven years we find him serving on the Home and American stations, chiefly in the capacity of Midshipman, on board the PÉGASE and another ship, both commanded by Capt. Hon. Geo. Cranfield Berkeley, SAMPSON 64, Capt. Chas. Hope, PERSEUS 22, Capt. Geo. Palmer, LEANDER 50, flag-ship of Rear-Admiral Herbert Sawyer, and BOMBAY CASTLE 74, Capt. Robt. Fanshawe. He was then, 24 May, 1789, promoted to a Lieutenancy in the CENTURION 50, bearing the flag at Jamaica of Rear-Admiral Peter Affleck; and he was next appointed —26 Nov. in the same year, to the CARNATIC 74, Capt. Ford, lying at Plymouth—20 Jan. 1790, again to the PERSEUS, Capt. John Gibson, employed on the Irish and Channel stations—and, 15 Dec. 1790 and 8 Feb. 1794, as Senior, to the DISCOVERY and PROVIDENCE, in which ships he was for six years employed on voyages of discovery under Capts. Vancouver and Broughton. When at Nootka Sound in the DISCOVERY Mr. Mudge was despatched in an open vessel to India, with a crew of only 14 men. Being awarded a second promotal commission 24 Nov. 1797, he obtained command, 8 Nov. 1798, of the FLY 16; and while in that sloop, in which he continued until posted, 15 Nov. 1800, he effected the capture of the French privateers *Le Glaneur*, of 6 guns and 32 men, and *Le Trompeur*, and was all but lost on an immense island of ice during his passage home from Halifax with despatches from H.R.H. the Duke of Kent. His subsequent appointments were—1 April, 1801, to LA CONSTANCE 24—23 Sept. 1802, to the BLANCHE of 44 guns—18 Nov. 1805, to the PHŒNIX 36—and, 4 July, 1814 (having left the PHŒNIX in May, 1810), to the VALIANT 74. In LA CONSTANCE Capt. Mudge, in the spring of 1801, received the thanks of the British merchants and consuls at Lisbon and Oporto for the service he had rendered them in safely convoying a fleet from Falmouth to Portugal, and also for the activity he had exhibited in collecting some vessels at Viana, laden with brandy, which could not have otherwise been got ready to go home under his protection. About the same period he captured the Spanish national cutter *El Duides*, of 8 guns and 69 men, and lugger privateer *Venture*, of 2 guns and 27 men. In July, 1801, with the assistance of the STORK 18, and of the boats of the two ships, we find him making prize, near Cape Ortegal, of *El Cantara*, Spanish privateer of 22 guns and 110 men, and of her consort, a vessel mounting 10 guns. LA CONSTANCE was subsequently engaged in conveying a number of disbanded foreign soldiers from Lymington to the Elbe. At the close of 1803, Capt. Mudge, then in the BLANCHE, was employed at the blockade of St. Domingo; where, in less than a month, he captured and destroyed 24 of the enemy's vessels.* In the course of 1804-5 he had the increased good fortune to take, independ-

* *Vide* Gaz. 1804, p. 162.

ently of a large number of merchantmen, the *Gracieuse* and *Amitié*, French national vessels of 14 guns each,* the Dutch schooner *Nimrod*, of 4 guns,† and the French privateer *Le Hasard*, of 3 guns and 58 men. On 19 July in the latter year, however, the BLANCHE was herself captured (after an action of 45 minutes, and a loss, out of 215 men, of 8 killed and 15 wounded, and when on the verge of sinking) by a powerful French squadron, consisting of *La Topaze* frigate, of 44 guns and 410 men, one sloop of 22 guns and 236 men, a corvette of 18 guns and 213 men, and a brig of 16 guns and 123 men.‡ Under such circumstances Capt. Mudge was of course honourably acquitted by court-martial of all blame in the loss of his ship; and not only acquitted but eulogised for his very able and gallant conduct. He afterwards served, as above, in the PHŒNIX and VALIANT, on the Bay of Biscay, Lisbon, and Brazilian stations. The latter ship he left in Aug. 1815. He became a Rear-Admiral 22 July, 1830; and a Vice-Admiral 23 Nov. 1841.

MUIR. (RETIRED COMMANDER, 1831. F-P., 29; H-P., 34.)

THOMAS MUIR (*a*) entered the Navy, in 1784, as Sec.-cl. Vol., on board the SCORPION sloop, Capt. Paget Bailey, on the West India station, where, and at Home, he afterwards, until promoted to the rank of Lieutenant 14 Aug. 1794, served as Midshipman in the BRUNE frigate, Capt. Davidge Gould, DUKE 90, bearing the flag of Lord Hood, RACEHORSE sloop, Capt. Jas. Leakey, and MAJESTIC 74, Capt. Chas. Cotton. Being then re-appointed to the latter ship, he again sailed for the West Indies, with the flag of Rear-Admiral Benj. Caldwell. His subsequent appointments (after serving for a short time under the flag of Sir Chas. Thompson in the MONTAGU 74) were, chiefly on the Home station—16 April, 1796, to the AMPHION 32, Capt. Israel Pellew—13 March, 1797, to the VESTAL 28, Capt. Chas. White, under whom, we believe, he assisted at the capture, 10 April and 13 May following, of *Le Voltigeur* privateer, of 8 guns, 8 swivels, and 40 men, and *La Jalouse* corvette of 18 guns—21 June, 1799, to the JUSTE 80, Capt. Sir Henry Trollope, which ship was paid off at the peace—5 Aug. 1803, to the Sea Fencibles at Rochester—25 June, 1804, to the AJAX 74, Capt. Lord Garlies—next to the PRINCE OF WALES 98, Capt. Sir Thos. Troubridge—18 June, 1805, to the FURY bomb, Capts. John Yelland and Thos. Searle—6 Feb. 1807 (after a few months of half-pay), to the BRUNSWICK 74, Capt. Thos. Graves—13 July, 1808, to the command of a signal station, which he retained until Feb. 1809—and, 26 July, 1810, and (having been for nine months unemployed) 30 Oct. 1812, to the Impress service at Cowes, in the Isle of Wight, and at the Tower of London. He was placed on half-pay 30 April, 1814; and on the Senior List of Retired Commanders 16 Aug. 1831. AGENT—Joseph Woodhead.

MULLER. (LIEUT., 1803. F-P., 23; H-P., 28.)

HENRY MULLER entered the Navy, 9 Oct. 1796, as Fst.-cl. Vol., on board the EDGAR 74, Capts. John M'Dougall and Edw. Buller, employed at first in the Channel, and then in the Mediterranean, where, in April, 1800, he removed as Midshipman, a rating he had attained in Dec. 1797, to the ADVENTURE 44, *armée-en-flûte*, Capts. Robt. Mansel and Chas. Carter. After a servitude of two years and eight months on the Channel and Jamaica stations in the AUTUMN sloop, Capt. Wm. Richardson, AMBUSCADE 36, Capt. Hon. John Colville, RACOON 18, Capts. Wm. Rathborne and Austin Bissell, and LEVIATHAN and HERCULE 74's, both flag-ships of Sir John Thos. Duckworth, under whom he participated in many operations off St. Domingo, he was promoted, 4 Nov. 1803, to a Lieutenancy in the TARTAR 32, Capts. John Perkins, Edw. Hawker, and Stephen Poyntz; in which ship we find him contributing to the capture, 9 June, 1806, of *L' Observateur*

* *Vide* Gaz. 1805, pp. 52, 954. † *V.* Gaz. 1804, p. 1266.
‡ *V.* Gaz. 1805, p. 1003.

French national brig of 18 guns and 104 men. On his return to England from Halifax in the following Dec. he obtained an appointment to the DREADNOUGHT 98, bearing the flag of Rear-Admiral Thos. Sotheby in the Channel. He was afterwards, from Feb. 1809 until Jan. 1815, and from Nov. 1818 until Jan. 1823, employed in command of a signal-station, and as an Inspecting Commander in the Water Guard.

MUNDY, K.C.B. (VICE-ADMIRAL OF THE RED, 1841. F-P., 27; H-P., 31.)

SIR GEORGE MUNDY is son of the late Edw. Miller Mundy, Esq., M.P. for Derbyshire; and is closely connected with the Dukes of Newcastle, Grafton, and Richmond.

This officer entered the Royal Naval Academy 9 July, 1789, and embarked, in Oct. 1792, as Midshipman, on board the BLANCHE frigate, Capt. Christ. Parker. On his return, in Jan. 1793, from the West Indies in the PERSEUS 22, Capt. Geo. Palmer, he was received on board the VICTORY 100, bearing the flag of Sir Hyde Parker, and next on board the JUNO 32, Capt. Sam. Hood, which frigate, in Jan. 1794, made a very remarkable escape from the inner harbour of Toulon, into which she had entered in ignorance of its evacuation by the British. After assisting at the capture of many of the enemy's vessels, and at the reduction of St. Fiorenzo, Mr. Mundy followed Capt. Hood into L'AIGLE 36, part of the force employed at the taking of Bastia and Calvi. He was confirmed a Lieutenant (having acted for nearly two months as such) in the ST. GEORGE 98, Capt. Sam. Peard, 11 March, 1796; and he was subsequently appointed in that capacity to the BLENHEIM 98, Capt. Thos. Lennox Frederick, VICTORY 100, Capt. Thos. Sotheby, and GOLIATH 74, Capt. Thos. Foley. In the BLENHEIM he fought in the action off Cape St. Vincent 14 Feb. 1797; and in the GOLIATH he shared in the glories of the Nile 1 Aug. 1798. In the following Oct. he was nominated Acting-Commander of the TRANSFER brig of 14 guns, in which vessel (the appointment being confirmed by commission dated 24 Dec. in the same year) we find him constantly employed on hazardous service off Cadiz and in the Mediterranean until Aug. 1800. Being advanced, while serving in the SWAN sloop, to Post-rank in the VENGEANCE of 74 guns, 10 Feb. 1801, he afterwards obtained command—7 April, 1802, of the CARYSFORT 28, in the Channel—21 Oct. 1802, of the HYDRA 38, in which frigate he continued eight years—14 Oct. 1814, of the AJAX 74, stationed, until July, 1816, in the Channel and Mediterranean—and, 27 May, 1825, and 29 Dec. 1828, of the PRINCE REGENT and ROYAL GEORGE yachts. In the HYDRA Capt. Mundy was at first employed off the coast of France, where he made prize, 25 June and 1 Aug. 1803, of the privateers *La Phœbe*, of 4 guns and 2 swivels, and *Le Favori*, of 4 guns, and, 30 Jan. 1804, of No. 51 gun-brig, of 3 guns and 56 men, and No. 411 lugger, of 1 gun and 36 men.* He was next ordered to the Mediterranean, where, during Nelson's pursuit of the combined fleets to the West Indies, he was left under the orders of the Hon. Thos. Bladen Capel to assist in protecting Sardinia, Sicily, &c , against the designs of the enemy; a service in which he acquired reputation for exemplary vigilance and activity. On 27 Feb. 1806, being off Cadiz lighthouse, he succeeded in capturing, in the presence of four French frigates, the national brig *Le Furet*, pierced for 20 guns, mounting 18, with a complement of 132 men; and, on 28 of the ensuing April, he took, after a chase of 230 miles, the Spanish war-schooner *Argonauta*, mounting 4 guns, but pierced for 12.† Subsequently to this he escorted a fleet of transports to Sicily, conveyed the British Consul to Algiers, attacked and dispersed a division of gun-boats on the coast of Granada, and captured the *Tigre* Spanish letter-of-marque. On 7 Aug. 1807 we find him, with the assistance of his boats, possessing

* *Vide* Gaz. 1804, p. 146. † *V.* Gaz. 1806, pp. 409, 619.

himself, in a very gallant manner, of three armed polacres (the *Prince Eugène* of 16 guns and 130 men, *Belle Caroline* of 10 guns and 40 men, and *Rosario* of 4 guns and 20 men) lying in the narrow harbour of Begu, on the coast of Catalonia, under the fierce defence of a battery, mounting 4 26-pounders, a tower, and of a considerable land-force.* On his return with the outward-bound trade to the Mediterranean, after having been sent with convoy to England to refit, Capt. Mundy, in the early part of 1809, took up a station on the Catalonian coast, with the LEONIDAS frigate and several smaller vessels under his orders, for the purpose of co-operating with the Spanish patriots. While on that service, on which he continued until the following Oct., he effectually blockaded Barcelona, and was constantly engaged, as were his boats, in attacking the enemy's detachments passing from the eastward to that city. His indefatigable exertions, and the union of activity and skill developed in all his operations, encountered as he frequently was by circumstances of a very trying character, were productive of the greatest benefits to the cause in which he was embarked, and procured him the warm acknowledgments of Lord Collingwood, the Commander-in-Chief. During the war of a hundred days, Capt. Mundy, then in command of the AJAX, was despatched to Marseilles, with instructions to ascertain, if possible, the sentiments of the inhabitants of that city. The discretion and good judgment he exhibited in discharge of the duties attendant on so delicate a mission were such as to demand the high approval of Lord Exmouth; under whom, in March, 1816, we find him visiting Algiers, Tunis, and Tripoli, for purposes connected with the abolition of Christian slavery. In June of the preceding year he had been nominated a C.B. He was promoted to the rank of Rear-Admiral while in command of the ROYAL GEORGE yacht, 22 July, 1830; was created a K.C.B 28 Feb. 1837; and raised to the rank he now holds 23 Nov. 1841.

Shortly after the cessation of hostilities Sir Geo. Mundy accepted command of a troop of yeomanry cavalry in Derbyshire; and in 1818 he was elected M P. for Boroughbridge, co. York. AGENTS—Messrs. Halford and Co.

MUNDY. (CAPTAIN, 1837. F-P., 19; H-P, 10.)

GEORGE RODNEY MUNDY, born 19 April, 1805, is son of General Godfrey Basil Mundy, by Hon. Sarah Brydges Rodney, youngest daughter of the celebrated Lord Rodney; and nephew of Vice-Admiral Sir Geo. Mundy, K.C.B.

This officer entered the Royal Naval College 5 Feb. 1818; and on 19 Dec. 1819, having carried off a medal and been allotted two years' service, embarked, as a Volunteer, on board the PHAETON 46, Capt. Wm. Augustus Montagu, attached to the force in North America. In April, 1824, after a period of two years passed in the Mediterranean as Midshipman of the EURYALUS 42, Capt. Augustus Wm. Jas. Clifford, and ROCHFORT 80, Capt. Chas. Marsh Schomberg, he joined the BLANCHE frigate, Capt. Wm. Bowen Mends. stationed in South America; where he continued to serve in the WELLESLEY 74, flag-ship of Sir Geo. Eyre, JASEUR sloop, Capt. Thos. Martin, THETIS transport, Capt. H. Hopkins, BLANCHE again, Capt. W. B. Mends, CAMBRIDGE 82, Capt. Thos. Jas. Maling, and ECLAIR 18, Capt. Thos. Bourchier (into which vessel he was confirmed a Lieutenant† 4 Feb. 1826), until 25 Sept. 1827. He was next, from 5 Feb. 1828 until promoted to the rank of Commander 25 Aug. following, employed at Portsmouth and off Lisbon in the VICTORY 104, Capt. Hon. Geo. Elliot, CHALLENGER 28, Capt. Adolphus FitzClarence, and PYRAMUS 42, Capt. Geo. Rose Sartorius. Obtaining command, 29 Aug. 1833, of the FAVORITE 18, he sailed in that sloop for the Mediterranean; where, during the Turkish commotions of 1836, he became Senior officer on the coast of Tripoli. He paid the FAVORITE off a few weeks after his promotion to Post-rank, which took place 10 Jan. 1837; and he was next, 4 Oct. 1842, appointed to the IRIS 26, in which vessel (with the exception of an interval in the latter part of 1843, during which he officiated as Supernumerary-Captain of the ST. VINCENT 120 and VICTORY 104) he served on the African, Irish, and East India and China stations, until finally put out of commission in Aug. 1847. In Nov. 1843, in consideration of the rapidity with which he had fitted his ship out after she had been in dock, we find him eliciting the thanks of the Board of Admiralty. On 8 July, 1846, during an expedition up the River Bruné, conducted under the personal direction of Rear-Admiral Sir Thos. John Cochrane against the Sultan of Borneo, he took command of the gun-boats employed, and, after having silenced the fire of a battery situated 100 feet up the side of a hill, landed, spiked, and threw the guns over the walls, and blew up the magazine. Towards the close of the same day, in addition to the latter, he effected the destruction of four forts, disabling at the same time 17 iron, and bringing off 3 brass, guns.* He was afterwards sent, with 19 boats and a body of 472 men under his orders, accompanied by Mr. Brooke, up different branches of the Borneo River, for the purpose of gaining certain points of debarkation, and of thence marching into the interior of the country with a view to obtaining possession, if possible, of the Sultan's person. In carrying out his instructions, which, unfortunately, were not attended with the result desired, Capt. Mundy, during an absence of six days, was assailed with difficulties of no ordinary description. Afloat he experienced an almost impenetrable navigation; on shore his men were often up to their middles in swamp, floundering in the mud, and scarcely capable of preserving their ammunition dry. As a mark of the confidence with which his conduct throughout such arduous service had impressed the Commander-in-Chief, Capt. Mundy was left in charge of the whole Borneo station † from Aug. 1846 until Feb. 1847, during which period he carried out extensive operations against the pirates, and twice received the thanks of the Admiralty.

In 1832 Capt. Mundy served on board the DONEGAL 78, as confidential agent under Vice-Admiral Sir Pulteney Malcolm on the coast of Holland, and was officially present at the siege of Antwerp. In 1833 he was employed by the First Lord of the Admiralty, Sir Jas. Graham, on a special mission to Holland and Belgium. On the suspension of hostilities he returned to England. AGENTS—Messrs. Stilwell.

MUNDY. (LIEUTENANT, 1846.)

MEYNELL HORTON MILLER MUNDY is fourth son of the late E. M. Mundy, Esq., of Shipley, in the county of Derby.

This officer passed his examination 21 March, 1843; and from 31 July, 1845, until advanced to his present rank 4 May, 1846, was employed as Mate on board the EXCELLENT gunnery-ship at Portsmouth, Capt. Henry Ducie Chads. He has been serving since 26 of the latter month in the EURYDICE 22, Capts. Geo. Elliot and Talavera Vernon Anson, now at the Cape of Good Hope.

MUNRO. (LIEUTENANT, 1815. F-P., 10; H-P., 29.)

MATTHEW MUNRO was born in 1795.

This officer entered the Navy, 29 March, 1808, as Fst.-cl. Vol., on board the RESISTANCE 38, Capt. Chas. Adam, employed in the Channel, off the coast of Portugal, and in the Mediterranean. Following Capt. Adam, as Midshipman, in April, 1810, into the INVINCIBLE 74, he joined in a series of very active co-operations with the patriots on the coast of Catalonia, where he assisted at the defence of Tarragona in May and June, 1811, and served with the boats at the reduction, in June, 1813, after a siege of five days, of the fort of St. Philippe, in the

* *Vide* Gaz. 1807, p. 1350.

† He had been acting for some time as such on board the WELLESLEY, BLANCHE, and CAMBRIDGE. He did not join the ECLAIR until June, 1826.

* *Vide* Gaz. 1846, p. 3438, 3439. † *V.* Gaz. 1846, p 3448.

Col de Balaguer, near Tortosa, armed with 12 pieces of ordnance, including 2 10-inch mortars and 2 howitzers, with a garrison of 101 officers and men. From Oct. 1809 to May, 1811, Mr. Munro, we may observe, had been allowed to serve on board the COLOSSUS 74, Capt. Thos. Alexander. On finally leaving the INVINCIBLE, in Jan. 1814, he became attached as a Supernumerary to the SALVADOR DEL MUNDO, Capt. Robt. Hall, lying at Plymouth, and next, in the course of the same year, as Master's Mate, to the LEANDER 50, Capt. Sir Geo. Ralph Collier, on the North American station. In Aug. 1815 he took up a commission dated 4 of the preceding March; and he was subsequently, 4 July and 17 Oct. 1816, appointed to the IMPREGNABLE 104 and LEANDER again, the latter bearing the flag of Sir David Milne at Halifax. While in the IMPREGNABLE he commanded a gun-boat, No. 1, at the bombardment of Algiers. He was superseded from the LEANDER 19 June, 1818, and has since been on half-pay.

Lieut. Munro married, in Feb. 1822, Philadelphia Jane Caroline, eldest daughter of the late Lieut.-General Monro, of Edmondsham House, Dorset, by whom he has issue a daughter. AGENTS —Hallett and Robinson.

MUNTON. (LIEUTENANT, 1844.)

WILLIAM ANTHONY MUNTON passed his examination 7 Oct. 1835; and was for several years employed in the Mediterranean, as Mate, in the INCONSTANT 36, Capts. Daniel Pring and Fred. Thos. Michell. On 8 Nov. 1844, while serving on board the CALEDONIA 120, flag-ship of Sir David Milne at Devonport, he was promoted to the rank of Lieutenant. He was re-appointed to the CALEDONIA, in the capacity of Additional-Lieutenant, 11 Dec. following; and he was next, from 4 Jan. 1845 until the close of 1846, stationed on the coast of Africa in the ACTÆON 26, Capt. Geo. Mansel.

MURIEL. (LIEUTENANT, 1812. F-P., 12; H-P., 30.)

WILLIAM MURIEL, born 7 May, 1794, at Ely, co. Cambridge, is son of Robt. Muriel, Esq., Surgeon.

This officer entered the Navy, 30 Aug. 1805, as Fst.-cl. Vol., on board the HERO 74, Capts. Hon. Alan Hyde Gardner and John Poo Beresford. On 4 Nov. following he fought in Sir Rich. Strachan's action with the four line-of-battle ships escaped from Trafalgar; and on 13 March, 1806, he witnessed the capture of the *Marengo* 80, bearing the flag of Rear-Admiral Linois, and 40-gun frigate *Belle Poule*. After a servitude of 17 months in the Channel on board the DRAGON 74, he rejoined his first Commander, then Rear-Admiral Gardner, in the BELLEROPHON 74; in the boats of which ship, on her arrival in the Baltic, we find him in perpetual contact with the enemy's gun-boats, batteries, &c. While next attached, between June, 1810, and Sept. 1812, to the SAN JOSEF 110, flag-ship of Sir Chas. Cotton, and ECLAIR sloop, Capts. Wm. Gregory, John Bellamy, and Fairfax Moresby, he saw much similar service in the Adriatic. On 15 of the month last mentioned he became Acting-Lieutenant of the MERMAID 32, *armée-en-flûte*, commanded by the present Sir David Dunn, with whom (the appointment being confirmed by commission dated 5 Dec. 1812) he continued until Nov. 1814. He took part, in consequence, in the siege of Trieste (where he served on shore and in the boats), also in the attack upon Leghorn, and in the capture of Genoa. His last appointment was, 2 Oct. 1817, to the BULWARK 74, Capts. Geo. M'Kinley, Sam. Warren, Fras. Newcombe, and Alex. Skene; from which ship, stationed at Sheerness, he was lent to the ROYAL SOVEREIGN yacht, Capt. Sir Edw. W. C. R. Owen, for the purpose of escorting the Duke and Duchess of Clarence from Dunkerque to England. He has been on half-pay since 1820.

Lieut Muriel married, in 1828, Miss Catherine M. Alexander, of London, and by that lady has issue a son and two daughters.

MURLEY. (COMMANDER, 1813. F-P., 13; H-P., 33.)

WILLIAM MURLEY entered the Navy, in Jan. 1801, as Fst.-cl Vol., on board the BELLEISLE 74, Capts. Wm. Domett, Chas. Boyles, John Whitby, and Wm. Hargood. In that ship, of which he was created Midshipman in the following Sept., he continued employed until Jan. 1806; serving at first in the Channel and Mediterranean, then accompanying Lord Nelson to the West Indies and back in pursuit of the combined fleets, and finally participating, as Signal-Midshipman, in the action off Cape Trafalgar 21 Oct. 1805. In Jan. 1807 he sailed for Buenos Ayres in the THISBE 28, Capt. Lewis Shepheard; and on his arrival he was received on board the DIADEM 64, flag-ship of Rear-Admiral Chas. Stirling. He was thus afforded an opportunity of witnessing, again as Signal-Midshipman, the unsuccessful attack upon Buenos Ayres, and the other operations which immediately preceded the evacuation of Spanish America. On his return to England he successively joined, in the early part of 1808, the WARSPITE 74, Capt. Hon. Henry Blackwood, and VILLE DE PARIS 110, flag-ship of Lord Gambier, both lying at Chatham. He was made Lieutenant, 29 June in the same year, into the CROCUS 14, Capts. Robt. Merrick Fowler, Hon. Wm. Walpole, Rich. Buck, and John Bellamy; and next appointed, 18 Dec. 1810 and 8 May, 1811, to the MEDUSA 32, Capt. Hon. Duncombe Pleydell Bouverie, and CALEDONIA 120, bearing the flag of Sir Edw. Pellew. When First of the CROCUS, we find him commanding a flat-bottomed gun-boat at the siege of Flushing in 1809: he served, in the MEDUSA, off Bordeaux; and in the CALEDONIA he was present in a partial action with the Toulon fleet 5 Nov. 1813. He left the last-mentioned ship in Jan. 1814, having been awarded the rank of Commander on 29 of the preceding October; and he has since been on half-pay.

He married, in June, 1815, Miss Mary Murley, a lady by whom he has issue six children.

MURRAY. (COMMANDER, 1840. F-P., 23; H-P., 5.)

ALEXANDER MURRAY entered the Navy, 26 March, 1819, as Fst.-cl. Vol., on board the CHEROKEE 10, Capt. Theobald Jones; and in the course of the same year sailed, as Midshipman of the LEANDER 60, flag-ship of Hon Sir Henry Blackwood, for the East Indies; where, in Aug. 1822, he joined the SOPHIE 18, Capts. Geo. French, Geo. Fred. Ryves, and Edw. Blanckley. Uniting, in 1824, in the hostilities against Ava, he found frequent opportunity of distinction, and was present, in the course of that year, at the occupation of Pegu and the capture and defence of Rangoon. He also, in 1825, served in the SOPHIE's boats when the British advanced up the River Irawady; and he came into contact with the enemy at Panlang, Donoobew, and Meaday. In Feb. 1826 he returned to England, as Mate, in the LIFFEY 50, Commodore Coe. After he had further served in that capacity on the Mediterranean and Home stations in the ASIA 84, flag-ship of Sir Edw. Codrington, GLOUCESTER 74, Capts. Joshua Sydney Horton and Henry Stuart, FERRET 10, Capt. Thos. Hastings, and ASIA again, bearing the flag of Sir Pulteney Malcolm, he was promoted, 6 July, 1829, to a Lieutenancy in the MASTIFF surveying-vessel, Capt. Rich. Copeland, whom he followed, early in 1830, into the METEOR. He came home in Dec. 1831, and was next appointed—2 Dec. 1834, to the EXCELLENT gunnery-ship at Portsmouth, Capt. Thos. Hastings—20 July, 1835, as Gunnery-Lieutenant, to the RUSSELL 74, Capt. Sir Wm Henry Dillon, off Lisbon—and, 11 Feb. 1837, in a similar capacity, to the PRINCESS CHARLOTTE 104, bearing the flag of Hon. Sir Robt. Stopford, again in the Mediterranean. For his services during the campaign in Syria, including the capture of St. Jean d'Acre, he was promoted to the rank of Commander 4 Nov. 1840. When off Beyrout, in the preceding Sept., he had been sent on shore, with a flag-of-truce and a letter addressed by Sir R. Stopford and the French Rear-Admiral Baudiera, to

Soliman Pasha.* He obtained an appointment, 26 Dec. 1840, to the HYDRA steamer, on the North America and West India station, whence he returned to England and was paid off about Aug. 1842; and since 13 March, 1846, he has been in command of the FAVORITE 14, on the coast of Africa. AGENTS—Messrs. Stilwell.

MURRAY. (LIEUTENANT, 1841.)

AUGUSTUS CHARLES MURRAY, born 16 Dec. 1815, is eldest son of the late Hon. Alex. Murray, a Lieutenant-Colonel in the Army, by Deborah, daughter of Robt. Hunt, Esq., Commander-in-Chief of the Bahamas; and grandson of John, fourth Earl of Dunmore, Governor, successively, of New York and Virginia, and Captain-General of the Bahama Islands. He is brother of Virginius Murray, an officer in the Army; brother-in-law of Prince Louis Stanislas Kotska de la Tremouille; and first-cousin of Commander Jack Henry Murray, R.N.

This officer entered the Navy 19 Jan. 1827; passed his examination 8 Aug. 1835; and was subsequently appointed Mate of the DOLPHIN 3, Lieut.-Commander Edw. Littlehales, on the coast of Africa; where, on the morning of 30 May, 1841, with the gig and cutter under his orders (the latter commanded by Mr. John Fletcher Rees, Second-Master), he succeeded, after a pull of two hours and a half, a fierce struggle of twenty minutes, and a loss to the British, out of 15 men, of 2 killed and 3 wounded, in capturing the *Firme* slaver, of 170 tons. Although knocked back into his boat by the butt end of a musket, which broke his collar-bone, he was the first to board the vessel, in effecting which his left hand was nearly severed at the wrist by the stroke of a cutlass; another blow was made at his head, but this he fortunately parried, hewing his opponent down. We may add that, determined not to be taken by an English man-of-war's boats, the enemy had bestowed great attention on their arms, and had adopted every precaution in the arrangement of their vessel. As a reward for his gallantry Mr. Murray was promoted to the rank of Lieutenant 1 Oct. in the same year.† His appointments have since been—14 Dec. 1842 and 17 June, 1844, to the SPITEFUL steam-sloop and PELICAN 16, Capts. Wm. Maitland and Philip Justice, both in the East Indies, whence he returned to England and was paid off in the early part of 1845—6 Dec. in the latter year, as First, to the TERRIBLE steam-frigate, of 800-horse power, Capt. Wm. Ramsay, employed on particular service—and, 20 March, 1847, as Additional, to the HIBERNIA 104, flag-ship of Sir Wm. Parker in the Mediterranean, where he continues.

Lieut. Murray, in consideration of his wounds, receives a pension of 45*l.* 12*s.* 6*d.* per annum. AGENTS—Messrs. Halford and Co.

MURRAY. (LIEUTENANT, 1846.)

AUGUSTUS GEORGE ERNEST MURRAY, born in 1823, is eldest son (by Ruperta Catherine, only child of the late Sir Geo. Wright, Bart.) of the Rev. Edw. Murray, Vicar of Northolt, co. Middlesex, grandson of John, third Duke of Atholl. He is nephew of the Bishop of Rochester, of the late Countess of Ilchester, and of Hon. Amelia Matilda Murray, Maid of Honour to the Queen; and cousin of Capt. Jas. Arthur Murray, R.N.

This officer passed his examination 21 Aug. 1844; and at the period of his promotion to the rank of Lieutenant, 9 Nov. 1846, had been serving for a few months in the Channel as Mate of the ST. VINCENT 120, Commodore Sir Fras. Augustus Collier. He has since been on half-pay.

MURRAY. (LIEUT., 1815. F-P., 9; H-P., 29.)

FRANCIS ABERDEEN MURRAY was born 21 Dec. 1795.

This officer entered the Navy, 25 June, 1809, as Fst.-cl. Vol., on board the VENERABLE 74, Capt. Andrew King, in which ship, bearing the successive flags of Admirals Sir Rich. John Strachan, Sir Thos Williams, and Philip Chas. Durham, he assisted, on arriving with the Earl of Chatham in the Scheldt, at the bombardment of Flushing, and was employed, as Midshipman, in various parts of the North Sea and Mediterranean until May, 1812. Joining then the GANYMEDE 26, Capt. John Brett Purvis, he saw much boat and other service on the east coast of Spain, and was present, in June, 1813, at the siege of Tarragona. On 21 of the month last mentioned, while attempting to cut out a French privateer, he received a ball in the left breast, which passed through the lungs, shattered the shoulder-blade, and came out at the back. On his return to England, after visiting the Adriatic and Bermuda, he followed Capt. Purvis, as Master's-Mate, into the AMPHION 32, and MAGICIENNE 36. In Oct. 1815 he took up a commission bearing date 6 of the preceding July. His last appointment was, 4 March, 1816, to the GRIFFON 14, Capts. Geo. Hewson, Jas. Arthur Murray, and Wm. Elliot Wright, fitting for the St. Helena station, whence he came home and was paid off in Sept. 1818. AGENTS—Messrs. Stilwell.

* *Vide* Gaz. 1840, p 2226. † *V.* Gaz. 1841, pp 2688–9.

MURRAY. (LIEUTENANT, 1847.)

GEORGE DON MURRAY is a relation, we believe, of Lord Elibank.

This officer, while serving as Midshipman of the NORTH STAR 26, Capt. Sir Jas. Everard Home, commanded a subdivision of seamen, and was severely wounded, in an attack made in Jan. 1846 on a pah belonging to a rebel chief named Kawiti, at Ruapikapika, in New Zealand, which was assaulted and carried in a most gallant manner, after a severe action of four hours.* As a reward for his conduct he was presented, as soon as he had passed his examination, with a commission dated 9 Nov. 1847. He has been employed, since 10 of the following Dec., in the PRINCE REGENT 90, Capt. Wm. Fanshawe Martin.

MURRAY. (CAPTAIN, 1841.)

THE HONOURABLE HENRY ANTHONY MURRAY, born 10 Jan. 1810, is third and youngest son of George, fifth Earl of Dunmore, by Lady Susan Hamilton, third daughter of Archibald, ninth Duke of Hamilton and Brandon.

This officer entered the Navy 30 Nov. 1823; passed his examination in 1829; and obtained his first commission 31 Jan. 1831. His succeeding appointments were—28 Nov. 1831, to the REVENGE 78, Capt. Hon. Donald Hugh Mackay, off Lisbon—19 July, 1833, to the ENDYMION 50, Capt. Sir Sam. Roberts, lying at Plymouth—7 Feb. 1834, to the TYNE 28, Capt. Lord Viscount Ingestre, under whom he was for three years employed in the Mediterranean—and, 6 Feb. 1838, as Senior-Lieutenant, to the MODESTE 18, Capt. Harry Eyres, on the Home station. He acquired the rank of Commander 28 June in the latter year; and, from 26 Dec. 1840, until paid off in the spring of 1842, served in that capacity, again in the Mediterranean, on board the WASP 16. He was advanced to his present rank 23 Nov. following, but has not been since afloat. AGENTS—Messrs. Chard.

MURRAY. (COMMANDER, 1841.)

JACK HENRY MURRAY, born 26 July, 1810, is eldest son of Hon. Granville Leveson Keith Murray, of the Madras Civil Service (fourth son of John, fourth Earl of Dunmore, successively Governor of New York and Virginia, and Captain-General of the Bahama Islands), by his second wife, the widow of John Thursley, Esq , also of the Civil Service at Madras. He is brother of Capt. Sam. Hood Murray, of the 67th Regt.; nephew of Capt. Hon. John Murray, who commanded the FRANCHISE 36, and died 1 July, 1805; and first-cousin of Lieut. Augustus Chas. Murray, R.N.

This officer entered the Navy 7 May, 1824; passed his examination in 1830; acquired the rank of Lieutenant 14 June, 1833; and was afterwards ap-

* *Vide* Gaz. 1846, p. 2346.

pointed—22 May, 1834, to the TRIBUNE 24, Capt. Jas. Tomkinson, fitting for the Mediterranean, whence he returned to England and was paid off in the early part of 1838—and, 28 Sept. in the latter year, as Senior, to the ROVER 18, Capts. Thos. Matthew Chas. Symonds and Chas. Keele, with whom he served in North America and the West Indies until advanced to his present rank, 23 Nov. 1841. He has since been unemployed. AGENTS—Messrs. Stilwell.

MURRAY. (LIEUT., 1802. F-P., 25;* H-P., 28.)
JAMES MURRAY entered the Navy, in 1794, as a Volunteer, on board the SEAFLOWER 16, Lieut.-Commander Jas. Murray, employed on the Home station, where, we believe, he assisted, as Midshipman, at the capture, 19 March, 1800, of the *Chaser* French privateer, of 14 guns and 37 men. Proceeding soon afterwards to the West Indies in the SEVERN 44, Capts. John Whitby and Geo. Barker, he was there, some months after his removal to the LEVIATHAN 74, flag-ship of Sir John Thos. Duckworth, promoted, 4 Dec. 1802, to a Lieutenancy in the STORK 18, Capts. Fred. Cottrell and Geo. Le Geyt. On 23 May, 1805, being sent with two boats, carrying between them 18 men, under the orders of Lieut. Geo. Robinson, into a harbour near Cape Roxo, in the island of Puerto Rico, Mr. Murray assisted in gallantly boarding and capturing a brig, together with a Dutch privateer, the *Antelope*, pierced for 5 guns, the two vessels being defended by at least 40 men.† In this affair he was slightly wounded. On 3 Sept. 1806 we find him officially mentioned for the great assistance he afforded, as chief of a detached party under the direction of Capt. Edw. Rashwork, of the SUPÉRIEURE brig, at the storming of a battery containing 6 long 18-pounders, mounted on travelling carriages, at Batabano, in the island of Cuba, and the seizure of a number of armed and other vessels there collected.‡ After serving for a few months in the INTREPID 64, Capts. Christopher John Williams Nesham and Geo. Andrews, he obtained command, 30 Dec. 1809, of the EXERTION gun-brig, in which vessel, it appears, he continued, on the North Sea station, until July, 1812, when she unfortunately took the ground in the river Elbe, and was in consequence destroyed by H.M.S. REDBREAST. Between May, 1813, and Oct. 1815, Mr. Murray was again employed in the West Indies, on board the SHARK sloop and ARGO 44, bearing each the flag of Vice-Admiral Chas. Stirling, and THRACIAN 18, Capt. John Carter. In June, 1820, he received an appointment to the Coast Guard; and, from 9 March, 1843, until 1847, he served at Sheerness in the OCEAN 80, Capts. Peter Fisher, Rich. Arthur, and David Price.

In consideration of the wound above noticed the Lieutenant was presented with a gratuity from the Patriotic Fund. AGENT—Fred. Dufaur.

MURRAY. (Captain, 1816. F-P., 16; H-P., 28.)
JAMES ARTHUR MURRAY, born 10 March, 1790, is only son of the late Lord Wm. Murray, by Mary Ann, daughter of Jas. Hodges, Esq.; grandson of John, third Duke of Atholl, who, in 1763, disposed of the sovereignty of the Isle of Man to the British Government for 70,000*l*.; and nephew of George, late Bishop of Rochester. He is cousin of Lieut.-Colonel Rich. Murray, who died in Oct. 1843; and of the present Lieuts. A. G. E. Murray and C. M. Aynsley, R.N.

This officer entered the Navy, 27 June, 1803, as Fst.-cl. Vol., on board LA CHIFFONNE 36, Capt. Chas. Adam, in which frigate, after having been for some time employed in blockading a French corvette and brig on the coast of Norway, he assisted (in company with the FALCON sloop, CLINKER gun-brig, and FRANCES armed cutter) in driving on shore under the batteries of Fécamp, 10 June, 1805, a division of the French flotilla, consisting of 2 corvettes and 15 gun-vessels, carrying in all 51 guns, 4 8-inch mortars, and 3 field-pieces, accompanied by 14 transports. In the following Sept., six months after he had obtained the rating of Midshipman, he removed with Capt. Adam to the RESISTANCE 38, and was in consequence afforded an opportunity of witnessing the surrender, 13 March, 1806, of the *Marengo* 80, bearing the flag of Rear-Admiral Linois, and 40-gun frigate *Belle Poule*. In the course of 1808 we find him engaged in escorting a large body of general officers to the coast of Portugal, in embarking the wounded at the battle of Vimeira, and in conveying the French troops to Rochefort after the Convention of Cintra. On his arrival in the West Indies in the FYLLA 20, Capt. Hon. Edw. Rodney, in March, 1809, he joined the NEPTUNE 98, bearing the flag of Hon. Sir Alex. Cochrane, under whom, in the ensuing April, he served at the capture of the Saintes Islands and the 74-gun ship *d'Hautpoult*. Being made Lieutenant, 25 Sept. in the same year, into the ST. CHRISTOPHER 12, Capt. Fras. Smith, he was subsequently appointed, in that capacity—16 May, 1810, to the UNICORN 32, Capts. Alex. Robt. Kerr and Geo. Burgoyne Salt, stationed off the north coast of Spain, where he contributed to the capture of many vessels—17 Aug. 1812 (after three months of half-pay), to the AMERICA 74, Capt. Josias Rowley, in which ship he aided at the blockade of Toulon, also in bringing off the troops from Tarragona, and in the unsuccessful attack upon Leghorn—and, 28 Dec. 1813, to the SWALLOW 18, Capt. Edw. Reynolds Sibly. On the receipt, in Feb. 1814, of his second promotal commision, bearing date 6 Dec. 1813, Capt. Murray assumed command of the SCOUT 18, likewise in the Mediterranean, on which station and in the Channel he continued until paid off 22 Sept. 1815. His next appointment was, 14 May, 1816, to the GRIFFON 16, at St. Helena. He was there nominated, 20 Sept. 1816, Acting-Captain of the SPEY 20, and in that vessel, to which he was confirmed 15 Nov. following, he continued until put out of commission 21 Nov. 1817. Being invested, 14 Aug. 1824, with the command of the ATHOLL 28, he effected the capture, on the western coast of Africa, of six slavers, carrying in the whole about 1000 negroes; and, besides serving at Rangoon during the close of the Burmese war, was employed in the suppression of piracy on the east coast of Africa. He paid the ATHOLL off 19 Oct. 1827, and accepted the Retirement 1 Oct. 1846.

Capt. Murray married, first, 13 Dec. 1821, Harriet, youngest daughter of Wm. Coupland, Esq., of St. Mary's, Shrewsbury, by whom (who died in 1829) he had issue three sons and two daughters; and secondly, 3 May, 1838, Julia, daughter of the late John Delme, Esq., of Cain's Hall, Fareham, Hants. By the latter lady he has had five other children. AGENT—John P. Muspratt.

MURRAY. (RETIRED COMMANDER, 1840. F-P., 11; H-P., 46.)
JAMES COPLAND MURRAY, born 12 May, 1774, is eldest son of Alex. Murray, Esq., proprietor of the lands of Inglosten, and feudal superior of the Lordship of that ilk.

This officer entered the Navy, in July, 1790, as a Supernumerary, on board the BERWICK 74, Capt. Benj. Caldwell, fitting at Portsmouth, and in the following Oct. removed to the HIND 28, Capt. Hon. Alex. Inglis Cochrane, attached to the force in the North Sea. Between the summer of 1793 and the date of his promotion to the rank of Lieutenant, 11 July, 1797, we find him serving as Midshipman, principally on the Home station, in the SPITFIRE sloop, Capts. Philip Chas. Durham and Jas. Cook, HIND again, Capts. P. C. Durham and Rich. Lee, and UNION 44, also commanded by Capt. Durham. In the latter ship he took part in Lord Bridport's action with the French fleet off Ile de Groix, 23 June, 1795, then accompanied the expedition sent under Sir John Borlase Warren to co-operate with the Royalists in Quiberon Bay, and witnessed the surrender, in March, 1796, of *L'Etoile* French

* Independently of the time he passed in the Coast Guard.
† *Vide* Gaz. 1805, p. 772. ‡ *V.* Gaz. 1806, p. 1537.

frigate of 30 guns. On the occasion of his promotion as above he joined the PORCUPINE 24, Capt. Chas. Dudley Pater, with whom he continued until captured, while employed, we believe, on a detached service. On his restoration to liberty in March, 1799, he was appointed to the WASSENAAR 64, commanded in the Channel and Baltic by Capt. Chas. Craven. He was next, from Jan. 1800 to Feb. 1801, employed in the Mediterranean on board the INFLEXIBLE 64, *armée-en-flûte*, Capt. Benj. Wm. Page. Unable to procure any further appointment, he accepted the rank of Retired-Commander on the Junior List 26 Nov. 1830. His promotion to the Senior took place 13 July, 1840.

Independently of many cutting-out affairs, Commander Murray, during the term of his servitude afloat, was five times in action with the enemy. He married, 9 May, 1805, his cousin Helen, eldest daughter of Thos. Hunter, Esq., of Kirkconnell, by whom he has issue seven sons and two daughters.

MURRAY. (COMMANDER, 1841.)

JOHN HALLIBURTON MURRAY entered the Navy 7 August, 1822; passed his examination in 1828; and obtained his first commission 22 March, 1832. His succeeding appointments were—8 March, 1833, to the ARIADNE 28, Capt. Chas. Phillips, on the North America and West India station—7 Aug. 1834, to the RALEIGH 16, Capt. Michael Quin, in the East Indies, where he was superseded about June, 1835—27 Oct. 1836, to the SAMARANG 28, Capt. Wm. Broughton, fitting at Portsmouth—7 Feb. 1837, to the TWEED 20, Capt. Hon. Fred. Thos. Pelham, employed on particular service—and (the latter vessel having been paid off at the close of 1838), 29 July and 1 Oct. 1840, to the HOWE 120 and CAMPERDOWN 104, as Flag-Lieutenant to Sir Henry Digby at Sheerness. Since his last promotion, which took place 14 Dec. 1841, Commander Murray has been on half-pay. AGENTS—Messrs. Chard.

MURRAY. (LIEUT., 1815. F-P., 11; H-P., 32.)

WILLIAM HAMILTON MURRAY was born 20 June, 1789.

This officer entered the Navy, 5 April, 1804, as Fst.-cl. Vol., on board LA CHIFFONNE 36, Capt. Chas. Adam; in which ship, when in company with the FALCON sloop, CLINKER gun-brig, and FRANCES armed cutter, we find him assisting at the destruction, after a chase of nine hours, attended with some loss to the British from the incessant fire of the forts along shore, of a division of the French flotilla, consisting of two corvettes and 15 gun-vessels, carrying in all 51 guns, 4 8-inch mortars, and 3 field-pieces, accompanied by 14 transports, under the batteries of Fécamp. On removing with Capt. Adam to the RESISTANCE 38, he witnessed the capture, 13 March, 1806, of the French 80-gun ship *Marengo*, bearing the flag of Rear-Admiral Linois, and 40 gun frigate *Belle Poule*. After a servitude of nearly three years as Midshipman, on the Home and Baltic stations, in the PILOT sloop, Capt. Hon. Wm. Walpole, and ARDENT 64, Capts. Jas. Giles Vashon and Robt. Honyman, Mr. Murray, in Sept. 1810, joined the IMPÉRIEUSE 38, Capt. Hon. Henry Duncan, under whom it was his fortune to see a vast deal of active service in the Mediterranean. On 2 Nov. 1811 he participated, in conjunction with the THAMES 32, in the gallant capture and destruction of 10 gun-boats and 22 richly-laden feluccas, defended by a strong tower and two batteries in the harbour of Palinuro on the coast of Calabria, at which place the British were opposed by a land-force of 700 men. He next contributed, 27 June, 1812, to the destruction of a French convoy and of the batteries at Languelia and Alassio—was also present, 17 Aug. in the same year, in a spirited skirmish with a powerful Neapolitan squadron in the Bay of Naples—and, in 1813-14, witnessed the capture of Port d' Anzo, and the operations against Leghorn and Genoa. He left the IMPÉRIEUSE about July, 1814; and was next, from that period until April, 1815, employed in the North Sea on board the LARNE 20 and DEE 24, both commanded by Capt. John Wm. Andrew. He then took up a commission bearing date 4 Feb. in the latter year, but has not been since afloat.

Lieut. Murray married 7 July, 1835, and has issue one son.

MUSTON. (RETIRED CAPTAIN, 1840. F-P., 12; H-P., 39.)

THOMAS GOLDWYER MUSTON entered the Navy 24 July, 1796, as Midshipman, on board, we believe, the IRIS 32, Capt. Thos. Surridge, with whom, after serving for 12 months in the North Sea, he sailed in 1797 for India as Master's Mate of the LEOPARD 50, and there, in May, 1802, followed him into the TRIDENT 64; of which ship, bearing for some time the flag of Admiral Rainier, he became an acting and a confirmed Lieutenant 31 March, 1803, and 4 July, 1804. His succeeding appointments were—8 Sept. 1804, to the ALBION 74, Capt. John Ferrier, also in the East Indies, where his health soon obliged him to invalid—19 Aug. and 24 Nov. 1806, to the SPARTAN 38, and AFRICA 64, Capts. Geo. Astle and Wm. Henry Bayntun, on the Home and South American stations—and, 28 Jan. and 8 Aug. 1808, to the VICTORY 100, and CALEDONIA 120, flag-ships at the Nore and in the Channel of Sir Jas. Saumarez and Lord Gambier. For the distinguished manner in which he conducted the HARMONY fire-vessel, at the destruction of the French shipping in Aix Roads, Lieut. Muston was promoted, on the recommendation of Lord Cochrane, to the command, 11 April, 1809, of the DOTEREL 18. In that sloop he served off Lisbon until the ensuing Sept. In 1810 he was again ordered to India to join Vice-Admiral Wm. O'Brien Drury on promotion. Finding, however, on his arrival that that gallant officer had just expired, he was under the necessity of returning to England without having received any appointment. It was afterwards proposed to send him on Admiralty promotion to the West Indies; but this offer the state of his health obliged him to decline. Unable subsequently to procure employment, he accepted, 10 Sept. 1840, the rank he now holds.

Capt. Muston married, in 1816, Susanna Eliza, daughter of Nathaniel Godbold, Esq., of London. AGENTS—Goode and Lawrence.

N.

NAGLE. (LIEUT., 1815. F-P., 10; H-P., 32.)

ARCHIBALD NAGLE entered the Navy, 2 Sept. 1805, as Fst.-cl. Vol., on board the ROYAL SOVEREIGN 100, Capts. Mark Robinson, John Conn, Edw. Rotheram, and Fras. Pender; and after sharing under the flag of Vice-Admiral Collingwood in the action off Cape Trafalgar, removed, in Jan. 1806, to the RENOWN 74, Capt. Philip Chas. Durham, employed at first off Rochefort and then in the Mediterranean; where, in Oct. 1809, he witnessed, as Midshipman, the self-destruction of the French ships of the line *Robuste* and *Lion*. Joining next, in March, 1810, the NISUS 38, Capt. Philip Beaver, he assisted under that officer at the reduction of the Isles of France and Java. On leaving the NISUS he served for a short time in the spring of 1813 in the LION 64, Capt. Henderson Bain, at the Cape of Good Hope. He attained the rank of Lieutenant 14 March, 1815; and was afterwards, in 1829-30, employed in the Coast Blockade as Supernumerary-Lieutenant of the RAMILLIES and TALAVERA 74's, Capt. Hugh Pigot. He has since been on half-pay. AGENTS—Goode and Lawrence.

NAPIER, K.C.B., G.C.T.S., K.M.T., K.S.G., K.R.E. (REAR-ADMIRAL OF THE BLUE. F-P., 20; H-P., 28.)

SIR CHARLES NAPIER, born 6 March, 1786, is eldest son of Hon. Chas. Napier, of Merchistoun Hall, co. Stirling, Captain R.N., who died 19 Dec. 1807, by his second wife, Christian, daughter of

Gabriel Hamilton, Esq., of Westburn, co. Lanark. He is grandson by a first marriage of Francis, fifth Lord Napier; brother of Thos. Erskine Napier, a Colonel in the Army; and cousin, with the present Capt. Henry Edw. Napier, R.N., of Lord Napier, Captain R.N., who died Chief Commissioner for regulating the trade with China 11 Oct. 1834.

This officer entered the Navy, 1 Nov. 1799, as Fst.-cl. Vol., on board the MARTIN sloop, Capt. Hon. Matthew St. Clair, employed in the North Sea. Removing in the spring of 1800 to the RENOWN 74, flag-ship of Sir John Borlase Warren, he accompanied, in the course of that year, the expedition to Ferrol, and proceeded next to the Mediterranean, where, in Nov. 1802, he became Midshipman of the GREYHOUND 32, Capt. Wm. Hoste. On his return from a visit to St. Helena in the EGYPTIENNE 40, Capt. Hon. Chas. Elphinstone Fleeming, he successively joined, in 1804-5, the MEDIATOR and RENOMMÉE frigates, commanded, the latter off Boulogne, by Capt. Sir Thos. Livingstone. He was made Lieutenant, 30 Nov. 1805, into the COURAGEUX 74, Capts. Rich. Lee and Jas. Bissett, part of the squadron under Sir J. B. Warren at the capture, 13 March, 1806, of the French 80-gun ship *Marengo*, bearing the flag of Admiral Linois, and 40-gun frigate *Belle Poule*; and in March, 1807, being then in the West Indies in the PRINCE GEORGE 98, Capt. Geo. Losack, he was nominated Acting-Commander of the PULTUSK brig; to which vessel the Admiralty confirmed him 30 Nov. following. On 17 July, 1808, we find Capt. Napier (he had previously witnessed the reduction of the Danish islands St. Thomas and Ste. Croix) assisting in the boats under the command of Lieut. Jas. Robertson (now Walker) of the FAWN sloop, to whom he had surrendered the conduct of the enterprise, at the cutting-out of a Spanish merchant-vessel lying at the N.E. end of Puerto Rico under the protection of two batteries, the guns in one of which, on the party landing, were spiked and rendered unserviceable. In Aug. of the same year he removed to the RECRUIT brig of 18 guns; in which vessel, on 6 of the ensuing month, he fought a very smart action with, and in the end put to flight, the *Diligente* French corvette of 22 guns and 140 men, after having, however, had his mainmast shot away, many of his carronades dismounted, one of his men killed, and himself* and several others wounded. In Feb. 1809 he assisted at the reduction of Martinique, where he won distinction, and considerably shortened the siege, by the manner in which, with only 5 men, he landed, scaled the walls, and, in open day, planted the union-jack on the ramparts of Fort Edward, separated about 100 yards from Fort Bourbon; and in the next April, during Sir Alexander Cochrane's pursuit of three French ships of the line, which lasted upwards of two days, and terminated in the capture of the *d'Haupoult* 74, he signalized himself by the proximity he kept to the enemy, although fired at from all their stern-chase guns, and by his efforts in doing all he could to cut away their masts and rigging.† So fully did the Commander-in-Chief appreciate the gallantry displayed by Capt. Napier, that he at once posted him into the prize, an act which the Admiralty sanctioned by a commission dated 22 May, 1809. In the following summer Capt. Napier returned with convoy to England in the JASON frigate, but he did not again go afloat until 1811, in the early part of which year he obtained an appointment to the THAMES 32.‡ On 21 of the ensuing July, uniting with the CEPHALUS brig, Capt. Augustus Wm. Jas. Clifford, he succeeded, with a degree of gallantry that reflected much honour on him, in silencing the fire of a flotilla of 11 gun-boats, together with a felucca, carrying in the whole 13 guns and 280 men, moored across the harbour of Porto del Infreschi, on the coast of Italy, and also that of a round tower, and of a body of musketry on the adjacent hills; after which the boats of the two ships, under Capt. Clifford, brought out, as well the vessels of war as a convoy of 14 merchantmen and 34 spars, the latter intended for a ship of the line and frigate at Naples.* On 1 Nov. 1811, in command of his own boats and those of the IMPÉRIEUSE 38, Capt. Napier landed with 250 men belonging to the 62nd Regt., under Major Edw. Dailey, at the back of the harbour of Palinuro, where, setting an animating example, he immediately ascended the heights and assisted in carrying them in a very gallant style, under a heavy fire from the enemy, who had assembled in force to oppose the attack, and who soon after dark endeavoured to regain their position, but were instantly compelled to retire.† The next day, returning on board his ship, he aided in effecting the capture and destruction of 10 gun-boats, of 22 richly-laden feluccas assembled on the beach, and of a battery of 24-pounders protecting them. The coolness, judgment, and intrepidity he displayed throughout the whole of the above affair met, it is scarcely requisite to add, the entire approbation of Sir Edw. Pellew, the Commander-in-Chief. He subsequently, 14 May, 1812, attacked the port of Sapri, where, previously to the capture of 28 vessels laden with oil, he contrived, supported by the PILOT sloop, to enforce the discretionary surrender of a strong battery and tower, mounting 2 32-pounders, with an officer and 38 men, whom, in consideration of their brave defence (having suffered themselves to be battered for two hours within pistol-shot), he allowed to march out with the honours of war.‡ On 26 Feb. 1813, being in company with the FURIEUSE 36, and having on board the second battalion of the 10th Regt., under Lieut.-Col. John Pine Coffin, Capt. Napier, in a most masterly manner, and without loss, took possession of the island of Ponza, notwithstanding that in the attempt he was exposed to the fire of four batteries and a tower, mounting 10 24 and 18-pounders, 2 12-pounders, and 2 9-inch mortars.§ On his removal, soon afterwards, to the EURYALUS 36, we find his judicious arrangements enabling him, with the aid of his boats, to make prize, 16 May, 1813, of *La Fortune* national xebec, carrying 10 long 9-pounders, 4 swivels, and 95 men, together with upwards of 20 merchant-vessels, lying in Cavalarie road. During the proximate winter he simultaneously drove on shore, in Calvi Bay, the *Balleine* French store-ship, of 22 guns and 120 men, and compelled a gaberre of 30 guns and 150 men, laden with stores, and a national schooner of the largest class to seek refuge under the land-batteries. After this he proceeded, in company with a squadron, under the orders of Capt. Andrew King, and a fleet of transports, to North America. On his arrival he took part in the brilliant expedition against Alexandria, and rendered such effective service that Capt. Jas. Alex. Gordon, the conducting officer, declared in his despatches "that he owed him more obligations than he had words to express."‖ In the subsequent operations against Baltimore, Capt. Napier was sent with a division of boats up the Ferry branch of the Patapsco river, for the purpose of causing a diversion favourable to the intended assault upon the enemy's entrenched camp at the opposite side of the city. The object of this mission he fully accomplished. In June, 1815, the EURYALUS was paid off; and on 4 of that month her gallant commander was nominated a C.B. He was not, however, again called into activity until 8 Jan. 1829, from which period until the early part of 1832 he was employed on particular service in the GALATEA 42. In 1833 he succeeded Admiral Sartorius in the command of

* Although his thigh was broken he refused to leave the deck.

† *Vide* Gaz. 1809, p. 711.

‡ During the interval which elapsed between his leaving the JASON and his appointment to the THAMES, Capt. Napier served a campaign with the army in Portugal, as a volunteer, and was again wounded. He was present at the battle of Busaco.

* *Vide* Gaz. 1811, p. 1863. † *V.* Gaz. 1812, p. 143.

‡ *V.* Gaz. 1812, p. 1396-7. § *V.* Gaz. 1813, p. 1146.

‖ *V.* Gaz. 1814, p. 2081.—While in the Potomac the EURYALUS, in a tremendous squall, lost her bowsprit and all her topmasts, but in twelve hours was again ready for work.

Don Pedro's fleet, and gained a signal victory over the more numerous and powerful armament of Don Miguel off Cape St. Vincent; an achievement for which he was rewarded with the title of Count Cape St. Vincent, and with the grand cross of the order of the Tower and Sword. On 1 Jan. 1839 Capt. Napier obtained command of the POWERFUL 84, fitting for the Mediterranean; where, hoisting in 1840 the broad pendant of Commodore, he became second in command, under Admiral Hon. Sir Robt. Stopford, of the force engaged on the coast of Syria, and added afresh to his already well-earned fame. On 10 Sept. in that year he there effected a landing at D'journie, at the head of a body of 1500 Turks and marines; and in this, his first important operation, he displayed such indefatigable zeal and activity as to elicit the particular praise of his Admiral.* In the course of the same month he defeated a body of the enemy at Kelbson,† and on 27, in the execution of a judicious and excellent plan he had previously formed, he bombarded and successfully stormed, with a force of not more than 900 allies and 500 Turks, the strong town of Sidon, protected by a fort and citadel and a line of wall defended by 2700 men, all of whom were made prisoners. On that occasion, at the head of the British marines, he broke into the enemy's barracks, and then obtained possession of the castle.‡ On 9 of the following Oct. he had the fortune utterly to rout an Egyptian force located, under Ibrahim Pacha, in a strong position on the mountains near Beyrout. The result of the forward movement which had immediately preceded this success was the surrender of Beyrout itself to the allies; and the effect of the victory the entire disorganization and submission of the army of Soliman Pacha. Thus, within one month from the date of the Commodore's original debarkation, had the whole nearly of Lebanon been freed from its invaders; and, notwithstanding that the small body of men with which he had at first landed had from time to time decreased to half the number of which it had then consisted, he had contrived to make about 5000 prisoners, and to gain over almost as many deserters.§ After co-operating in the memorable attack upon St. Jean d'Acre, he proceeded to take charge of the squadron off Alexandria,‖ where he landed and concluded a convention with Mehemet Ali. In acknowledgment of the distinguished part he had borne throughout the campaign he was created a K.C.B. 4 Dec. 1840; he was also included in the thanks of Parliament; and was presented, by the Emperors of Austria and Russia and the King of Prussia, with the cross of the order of Maria Theresa of Austria, the cross of the order of St. George of Russia, and the insignia of the second class of the order of the Red Eagle of Prussia. In the spring of 1841 he returned to England; and, on 30 Nov. in that year, he was appointed a Naval Aide-de-Camp to her Majesty. He had been awarded, 1 Jan. 1837, the Captains' Good Service Pension. He attained his present rank 9 Nov. 1846; and since 19 May, 1847, has been employed on particular service, with his flag in the ST. VINCENT 120.

In 1832 and 1837 Sir Chas. Napier unsuccessfully contested the representation of Portsmouth and Greenwich; but in 1841 he was returned for Marylebone. About the year 1828 he submitted to the Admiralty the model of a ship afterwards placed in the United Service Museum; and in 1846 we find him engaged in constructing the SIDON, a steam-frigate of 560-horse power. Several articles from the pen of Sir Charles have appeared in the pages of the United Service Journal; among which we may notice, as published in 1832, his 'Observations on the Construction and Qualities of the VERNON and CASTOR, and Naval Architecture in General;' together with his 'Remarks on Steam-Vessels' and his 'Remarks on the State of the Navy.' He is the author, also, of 'An Account of the War in Portugal between Don Pedro and Don Miguel,' published in 1836; and of 'The War in Syria,' published in 1842. He married Eliza, daughter of — Younghusband, Esq., and widow of Edwards Elers, Esq., Lieutenant R.N., by whom he has issue an only daughter. AGENTS—Hallett and Robinson.

* *Vide* Gaz. 1840, p. 2225. † *V.* Gaz. 1840, p. 2603.
‡ *V.* Gaz. 1840, p 2604. § *V.* Gaz. 1840, pp. 2610–11.
‖ *V.* Gaz. 1840, p. 2987.

NAPIER. (CAPTAIN, 1841.)

CHARLES GEORGE ELERS NAPIER was lost in command of the AVENGER steam-frigate, 20 Dec. 1847. He was son of the late Lieutenant Edwards Elers, R.N.; and step-son of Rear-Admiral Sir Chas. Napier, K.C.B.

This officer entered the Navy 7 Dec. 1825; passed his examination in 1831; obtained his first commission 28 Dec. 1832; joined, 26 March, 1834, the NORTH STAR 28, Capt. Octavius Vernon Harcourt, fitting at Portsmouth; and, from 4 Oct. following until paid off at the commencement of 1837, was employed in the Mediterranean in the VERNON 50, Capt. John M'Kerlie. Attaining the rank of Commander 28 June, 1838, he served as such from 30 Oct. 1840 until posted, 1 Nov. 1841, in the PELICAN 16, on the East India station. In July, 1842, being at the time in China, he assisted as a volunteer at the storming of Chin-Kiang-Foo.* He assumed command, 20 Nov. 1847, of the AVENGER steam-frigate, of 650-horse power, and perished, as above, on the Sorelle rocks, in the Mediterranean. AGENTS—Hallett and Robinson.

NAPIER. (LIEUTENANT, 1842. F-P., 15; H-P., 1.)

GERARD JOHN NAPIER was born 2 Nov. 1818.

This officer entered the Navy in Sept. 1831; served two years at the Royal Naval College, and nearly five in the West Indies on board the RACER 16, Capt. Jas. Hope; passed his examination 3 Oct. 1838; and, between that period and the date of his promotion, 28 Jan. 1842, was employed at Home and in the Mediterranean in the EXCELLENT gunnery-ship, Capt. Sir Thos. Hastings, VANGUARD 80, Capt. Sir David Dunn, BRITANNIA 120, flag-ship of Sir John Acworth Ommanney, POWERFUL 84, Capt. Geo. Mansel, and LIGHTNING steamer, Master-Commander Geo Henry Karr Bowen. His appointments have since been—27 Aug. 1842, to the ORESTES 18, Capt. Edw. St. Leger Cannon, again in the Mediterranean—10 Nov 1846 (soon after the latter vessel had been paid off), as Additional-Lieutenant, to the PRESIDENT 50, flag-ship of Rear-Admiral Jas. Rich. Dacres at the Cape of Good Hope—and, 26 April, 1847, as Senior, to the ROSAMOND steam-sloop, of 287-horse power, Capt. John Foote, on the same station, where he is now serving. AGENTS—Messrs. Halford and Co.

NAPIER. (CAPTAIN, 1830. F-P., 15; H-P., 29.)

HENRY EDWARD NAPIER, born 5 March, 1789, is fifth son of the Hon. Geo. Napier, of Mercheston Hall, N.B., a Colonel in the Army and Comptroller of Army Accounts in Ireland (who died 13 Oct. 1804), by Lady Sarah Lennox, seventh daughter of Charles, second Duke of Richmond; and grandson of Francis, fifth Lord Napier, by his Lordship's second marriage. He is brother of Lieut.-General Sir Chas. Jas. Napier, G.C B, the heroic Commander-in-Chief in Scinde; of Major-General Sir Geo. Thos. Napier, K.C.B., Governor and Commander at the Cape of Good Hope; and of Major-General Wm. Fras. Patrick Napier, C.B., Lieut.-Governor of Jersey, and author of the 'History of the Peninsular War.' One uncle, Patrick, died a Captain R.N. 15 June, 1801; and another, James John, a Lieutenant R.M, was killed on board the Fox frigate in 1776.

This officer entered the Royal Naval Academy 5 May, 1803, and embarked, 20 Sept. 1806, as Fst -cl. Vol., on board the SPENCER 74, Capts. Hon. Robt. Stopford and John Quilliam, in which ship, after visiting the Cape of Good Hope, he enacted a Midshipman's part in the expedition against Copenhagen, and assisted at the destruction of Fleckeröe Castle, on the coast of Norway. From Dec. 1808

* *Vide* Gaz. 1842, p. 3404.

until Sept. 1811 he served in the East Indies on board the CLORINDE 38, Capt. Thos. Briggs, RUSSEL 74, bearing the flag of Vice-Admiral Wm. O'Brien Drury, and DIOMEDE 50, Capt. Hugh Cook. While in the last-mentioned ship, of which he had been ordered to act as Lieutenant 31 Oct. 1809, he was officially promoted by commission dated 4 May, 1810. His next appointments were, in the course of 1812-13, to the CHATHAM 74, Capt. Graham Moore, MINERVA 32, Capt. Rich. Hawkins, and NYMPHE 38, Capt. Farmery Predam Epworth, on the North Sea and North American stations. On 7 June, 1814, he was promoted to the command of the GORÉE 18, at Bermuda; and on soon afterwards removing to the RIFLEMAN 18, he was for a considerable time intrusted with the charge of the trade in the Bay of Fundy. In Aug 1815 Capt. Napier went on half-pay, having previously, from private motives, declined accepting a piece of plate which had been voted to him for his care in the conduct of convoys between the port of St. John's, New Brunswick, and Castine. His last appointments were—23 Jan. 1821, to the JASEUR 18, on the Halifax station, whence he returned in July, 1823—and, 6 July, 1826, for a brief period, to the PELORUS 18, lying at Plymouth. He attained his present rank 31 Dec. 1830.

Capt. Napier married, 17 Nov. 1823, Miss Caroline Bennet, and by that lady, who died at Florence 5 Sept. 1836, had issue three children. AGENTS—Hallett and Robinson.

NARES. (COMMANDER, 1814. F-P., 12; H-P., 33.)

WILLIAM HENRY NARES entered the Navy, 9 June, 1802, as Fst.-cl. Vol., on board the CARYSFORT 28, Capt. Geo. Mundy, with whom he continued to serve, as Midshipman and Master's Mate, in the HYDRA 38, on the Channel and Mediterranean stations, until July, 1808. Among the numerous captures at which he assisted during that period, we may enumerate the gun-brig No. 51 of 3 guns, the lugger No. 411 of 1 gun, *Le Furet* national brig of 18 guns and 132 men (taken off Cadiz lighthouse in the presence of four French frigates 27 Feb. 1806), the Spanish war-schooner *Argonauta* pierced for 12 guns, the armed polacres *Le Prince Eugène* of 16 guns and 130 men, *Belle Caroline* of 10 guns and 40 men, and *Rosario* of 4 guns and 20 men. protected by a 4-gun battery, a tower, and a body of musketry in the harbour of Begu, on the coast of Catalonia, and numerous privateers. He was also, during Nelson's pursuit of the combined fleets to the West Indies, employed in defending Sardinia, Sicily, &c, against the designs of the enemy. In Nov. 1808 he became Acting-Lieutenant of the ROMAN 16, Capts. Sam. Fowell and Wm. Henry Whorwood, to which vessel, also stationed in the Mediterranean, he was confirmed 17 April, 1809. After again serving with Capt. Mundy in the HYDRA, we find him, in the early part of 1811, co-operating in the defence of Cadiz, with his name successively on the books of the STANDARD 64, Capt. Aiskew Paffard Hollis, HOUND, Capt. Chas. Phillips, and MILFORD 74, flag-ship of Sir Rich. Goodwin Keats. His next appointments were to the IMPLACABLE and AJAX 74's, Capts. Joshua Rowley Watson and Sir Robt. Laurie, APOLLO 38, Capt. Bridges Watkinson Taylor, and HAVANNAH 36, Capts. Edw. Reynolds Sibly and Gawen Wm. Hamilton. In the APOLLO, besides assisting at the capture of the *Ulysse* xebec of 6 guns, and at the reduction of the islands of Angusta, Curzola, and Malero, he commanded two of her boats, with two others belonging to the CERBERUS 32, in a gallant and most determined and successful attack (productive of a loss to the British of 1 officer, Mr. Suett, and 1 seaman killed, and 1 marine dangerously wounded) on a convoy protected by 11 gun-boats near Otranto, where the cliffs were covered with French troops, 28 May, 1813.* In the course of the ensuing month, with three of the APOLLO's boats under his orders, Lieut. Nares boarded and took, despite some resistance, a French gun-vessel, mounting a 12 and a 6-pounder, and having on board M. Bautrand, Chief of Engineers at Corfu. While awaiting, near Morto, in Albania, the return of a flag-of-truce sent to land the wounded enemy, nine in number, at Corfu, he was assailed, with his two remaining boats, by 6 gun-vessels, a felucca, and a row-boat, all full of troops, and compelled to run on shore upon the border of the French territory at Parga. Until his ammunition was expended he kept this large force from landing; having then no alternative, he took refuge for several days in the mountains. Before he finally left the APOLLO, Lieut. Nares was intrusted, from Jan. to April, 1814, with the command of the WEASEL 18. In the following Oct., having previously, we believe, accompanied, in the HAVANNAH, the expedition against Baltimore, he took up a Commander's commission, bearing date 1 July, 1814, appointing him to the PHILOMEL 18, which sloop, however, he never joined. He has since been on half-pay.

* *Vide* Gaz. 1813, p. 1794.

Commander Nares married, first, 26 Aug. 1820, Elizabeth, daughter of the late John Alex. Dodd, Esq., of Redbourn, co. Herts; and secondly, 24 Oct. 1844, Susan, relict of the late John Ramsay, Esq. of Barra.

NASH. (LIEUTENANT, 1826. F-P., 18; H-P., 19.)

JOHN WILLIAM CORNELIUS NASH was born 1 Nov. 1802, and died in July, 1846. He was son of the late Capt. Jas. Nash, R.N. (1802), a very distinguished officer; nephew of the late Capt. John Nash, R.N. (1802); and grandson of Mr. Rich. Nash, Purser and Paymaster R.N. (1781), who served in that capacity under Lord St. Vincent. He was the last survivor out of 14 of his family who had been all devoted to the Naval service.

This officer entered the Navy, in 1811, as Fst.-cl. Vol., on board the SALVADOR DEL MUNDO 112, commanded by his father, under whom we find him for six years employed, on the Home and North American stations, in the same ship and in the SATURN 56, LOIRE 38, IMPREGNABLE 98, ST. GEORGE 100, and BERWICK 74. After passing about three years at the Naval College at Portsmouth he became Midshipman, in 1820, of the SPARTAN 46, Capt. Wm. Furlong Wise; and next, of the SERINGAPATAM 46, Capt Sam. Warren, ISIS 50, Capt. Thos. Forrest, RENEGADE schooner, Lieut.-Commander Wm. Edw. Fiott, and PRIMROSE 18, Capt. John Stoddart, on the Home, Mediterranean, and West India stations. He was confirmed a Lieutenant, 11 Feb. 1826, into the DARTMOUTH 42, Capt. Henry Dundas, at Jamaica; and he was lastly, between 1827 and 1830, employed at Plymouth in the OCEAN 80, Capt. Patrick Campbell, BRITANNIA 120, Capt. Edw. Hawker, and CALEDONIA 120—commanding part of the time the ROYALIST tender of 10 guns.

He married, about 1830, Amelia, daughter of Hugh Stewart, Esq., R.N.

NASON. (LIEUTENANT, 1809. F-P., 9; H-P., 35.)

HENRY NASON lost a brother at the battle of Almeida.

This officer entered the Navy, 12 March, 1803, as Fst.-cl. Vol, on board the ANTELOPE 50, bearing the broad pendant of Sir Wm. Sidney Smith; and, on 16 May, 1804, was present in an attack made by a British squadron on a division of the enemy's flotilla passing alongshore between Flushing and Ostend. After a servitude of two years and a half in the North Sea and off Brest in the CRESCENT frigate, Capt. Lord Wm. Stuart, he again, in Dec. 1806, joined Sir W. S. Smith on board the POMPÉE 74, in which ship, in the course of 1807, we find him sharing in a series of operations on the coast of Calabria, and accompanying also the expeditions past the Dardanells and to Copenhagen During the 20 months which immediately preceded his promotion to the rank of Lieutenant, 28 Oct. 1809, he served on the Home and Brazilian stations in the VICTORY 100, Capt. John Serrell, and LONDON 98, FOUDROYANT 80, and DIANA 38, bearing each the flag of Sir W. S. Smith. His succeeding appointments were—18 Dec. 1809, to the ARGUS 16, Capt. Stewart, on the Irish station—11 April, 1810, to the THAIS 20, Capt. Ferrier, attached to the force in the Mediterranean, where, owing to the death of his brother, and to the necessity of attending to his family affairs, he was superseded at his own request in Jan. 1811—and, 30 April, 1813, as Senior, to the BONNE CITOYENNE 20, Capt. Pitt Burnaby Greene, in the North Sea. In 1810 he commanded the boats of the THAIS at the re-capture of two merchant-vessels under the protection of two privateers off Cape Spartivento. He invalided from the BONNE CITOYENNE from the effects of rheumatism in Nov. 1813, and has since been on half-pay.

Lieut. Nason is married and has issue.

NASON. (LIEUTENANT, 1812. F-P., 15; H-P., 31.)

RICHARD NASON entered the Navy, 3 May, 1801, as a Supernumerary, on board the VILLE DE PARIS 110, Capt. John Sutton, bearing the flag in the Channel of Hon. Wm. Cornwallis; and, after his name had been borne in a similar capacity on the books of the DE RUYTER and TEXEL 64's, Capts. Rich. Dacres and Rich. Incledon, AJAX 74, Capt. Hon. Alex. Inglis Cochrane, and CAMBRIAN and NEMESIS frigates, Capts. Bradley and Owen, all flag-ships at Spithead, became in succession Midshipman, in the course of 1802, of the CHILDERS sloop, Capt Jas. Coutts Crawford, of a vessel commanded by Capt. John G. Saville, and of the CALCUTTA 54, Capt. Dan. Woodriff. In that ship he was at first employed in the transport of convicts to Van Diemen's Land, on his return whence he proceeded for convoy to St. Helena. During her passage home the CALCUTTA, after having beaten the French 40-gun frigate *Armide*, was attacked, 26 Sept. 1805, and, at the end of a gallant action of three-quarters of an hour, productive to her of a loss, out of 343 men, of 6 killed and 6 wounded, unavoidably captured by the 74-gun ship *Majestueux*, part of a squadron under the orders of Rear-Admiral Allemand. On effecting his escape from confinement Mr. Nason was received on board the BRISEIS 10, Capt. Chas. Thurlow Smith. He attained the rank of Lieutenant 21 March, 1812, and was subsequently appointed—1 Oct. and 22 Dec. following, to the ALFRED and MARS 74's, Capts. Joshua Sydney Horton and Henry Raper, employed off the coast of Spain and at Portsmouth—2 Feb. 1813, to the VENERABLE 74, Capt David Milne, cruizing in the Channel and among the Western Islands—and, 24 Jan. and 4 June, 1814, to the CRETAN 16, Capt. Chas. Fred. Payne, and CHANTICLEER 10, Capts. Stewart Blacker, John Thompson, Geo. Tupman, and Wm. Henry Dickson. The CRETAN led a squadron of frigates and brigs through the Wielinge Passage into the West Scheldt for the purpose of co-operating with the British and Russian troops before Antwerp and Bergen-op-Zoom; and was afterwards employed in blockading Fort Bathz, in the island of South Beveland, where the enemy's deserted batteries were all dismantled. The CHANTICLEER formed part of the force employed in the reduction of Guadeloupe in 1815. Since Aug. 1816, at which period that sloop was put out of commission, Lieut. Nason has been on half-pay.

NAZER. (COMMANDER, 1828. F-P., 20; H-P., 28.)

HENRY NAZER was born at Sandwich, co. Kent, and died in 1846. He was brother of the present Retired Commander Kelly Nazer, R.N.; and also of Lieut. Wm. Nazer, R.N. (1794), who died at Jamaica in 1804, and of Lieut. John Ferrier Nazer, R.N. (1796), who died at the same place in 1798. His uncle, John Ferrier, died a full Admiral.

This officer entered the Navy, in April, 1799, as Second-Master and Pilot, on board the EAGLE receiving-vessel at Poole, in Dorsetshire, Lieut.-Commander Wm. Nazer; removed, as Master's Mate, in Sept. 1801, to the YORK 74, Capt. John Ferrier, lying in the River Thames; and from July, 1802, until March, 1807, served in the East Indies on board the CONCORDE 36, and PHAETON 38, both commanded by Capt. John Wood. In the CONCORDE he assisted at the capture, after a long chase and running fight, of a privateer mounting 30 guns; and in the PHAETON he took part, in company with the HARRIER 18, in a severe action of two hours, fought 2 Aug. 1805, with the French 36-gun frigate *Sémillante*, and several batteries at the entrance of the Straits of St. Bernardino, Philippine Islands; on which occasion the PHAETON, besides having two persons wounded, sustained damage in her sails, rigging, and masts, had three of her boats injured, and received nine shot in her hull. In the course of 1807 Mr. Nazer successively joined the SCEPTRE and ALBION 74's, Capts. Joseph Bingham and John Ferrier, also in the East Indies; where he was made Lieutenant, 2 May, 1808, into the ST. FIORENZO 36, Capt. John Bastard, and where he continued to serve, in the SAMARANG 18, Capt. Rich. Buck, CAROLINE 36, Capt. Chas. Gordon, and TERPSICHORE 32, Capt. Jas. Murray Gordon, until his return to England in July, 1809. Joining, in the following Nov., the IRIS 36, Capts. Thos. Geo. Shortland and Hood Hanway Christian, he was afforded an opportunity of actively co-operating with the patriots in the north of Spain, and of contributing to the reduction of several small towns along the coast. His last appointments were—7 Nov. 1811 and 29 Jan. 1813, to the BELLEROPHON and SCARBOROUGH 74's, flag-ships off the Scheldt of his relative Rear-Admiral J. Ferrier—24 Sept. 1814 (having left the SCARBOROUGH in the preceding May), to the MONMOUTH 64, bearing the flag of Vice-Admiral Thos. Foley in the Downs, where he remained but a few weeks—4 March, 1819, to the command (which he retained until wrecked, near Torbay, 5 Dec. ensuing) of the VIGILANT Revenue-cruizer—and, 5 Oct. 1820, to that of the BADGER, also employed in the protection of the revenue. In the latter vessel, with a loss of 1 man killed and 7, including himself, wounded, he succeeded, at the close of a running action of three hours, in making prize of a smuggling lugger, 3 of whose people were killed and 5 wounded. He left the BADGER in Dec. 1824; and on 28 Aug 1828 was presented with a second promotal commission.

Commander Nazer married Louisa, daughter of Thos. Woolnough, Esq, of Hallesley, Suffolk, by whom he has left issue two sons and one daughter.

NAZER. (RETIRED COMMANDER, 1847. F-P., 15; H-P., 33.)

KELLY NAZER was born 17 Jan. 1787.

This officer entered the Navy, 9 April, 1799, as A.B., on board the EAGLE receiving-vessel at Poole, co. Dorset, Lieut.-Commander Wm. Nazer; and in the course of the same month attained the rating of Midshipman. With the exception of a brief attachment, in the summer of 1802, to the ALARM 32, Capt. Wm. Parker, and again, towards the close of the same year, to the MAGICIENNE 36, Capt. Henry Vansittart, he served, from Sept. 1801, until June, 1809, in the YORK 74, FORTUNÉE 36, and ALBION 74, all commanded by his uncle Capt. John Ferrier, on the Home and East India stations. In the latter ship, of which he became an acting and a confirmed Lieutenant 11 Nov. 1807 and 30 Dec. 1808, he assisted at the capture of several privateers, and, in May, 1803, of *La Franchise* French frigate of 36 guns. He was also on board the ALBION in a terrific hurricane, which, during her passage home, sank three of her convoy, East Indiamen, nearly dismasted herself, and occasioned the pumps to be kept constantly going for six months. Being again, towards the close of 1809, ordered to India in the LEDA 36, Capt. Geo. Sayer, he there, in the summer of 1811, co-operated in the reduction of Java. His health obliging him soon afterwards to invalid, he was next, 8 May, 1812, appointed to the MAIDSTONE 36, Capt. Geo. Burdett. On 8 Feb. 1813, being at the time in the CHESAPEAKE, he took command of the boats of a squadron, nine in number, and, rushing through an animated fire of round and grape, boarded and, after a most obstinate resistance on the part of the enemy, succeeded in carrying the American letter-of-marque *Lottery*, of 6 12-pounder carronades and 29 men, of whom 19, including the Captain mortally, were wounded. The British had 1 man killed and 5 wounded.* Although the gallantry of the exploit was such as to obtain the especial thanks of Rear-Admiral Cockburn, an expression of approbation on the part of the Admiralty, and a certain prospect of promotion from Capt. Burdett, yet was its brave conductor suffered to pass wholly unrewarded. He subsequently, 6 May, 1814, led the second division of boats under the immediate orders of Rear-Admiral Cockburn up the Sassafras River, and, having assisted in routing a body of about 400 men, who had opened on them a fire from an entrenched position on the two opposite banks of the stream, contributed to the demolition of the settlements of Georgetown and Frederickstown. On 27 of the ensuing June he was present at the destruction of an American torpedo-boat on Long Island, sent from New York for the purpose of destroying H.M. shipping. Independently of the above, Lieut. Nazer was on many occasions in action with the enemy. He returned to England in Oct. 1814 on board LA HOGUE 74, Capt. Hon. Thos. Bladen Capel; and on 3 Feb. 1847 he accepted the rank he now holds.

At the commencement of the peace Commander Nazer took charge of a merchant-ship, and made eight voyages to Jamaica. He married, 11 July, 1821, Miss Cecilia Burlingson. AGENTS—Collier and Snee.

NEALE. (RETIRED COMMANDER, 1846. F-P., 16; H-P., 35.)

JOHN NEALE entered the Navy, 30 May, 1796, as Midshipman, on board the VENERABLE 74, Capts. Wm. Johnstone Hope and Wm. Geo. Fairfax, bearing the flag of Lord Duncan, under whom he fought as Signal-Midshipman in the action off Camperdown 11 Oct. 1797. While attached, between March, 1798, and Nov. 1804, to the KENT 74, Capts. W. J. Hope, Mansell, John Stewart, Pulteney Malcolm, and John White, successive flag-ship of Lord Duncan and Sir Rich. Bickerton, he was at first employed in the operations connected with the expedition to Holland, where he served on shore with a party of seamen and two field-pieces throughout the whole campaign. He also, in 1801, assisted in expelling the French from Egypt, after having participated, with the naval brigade under the orders of Sir Wm. Sidney Smith, in the battles of 8, 13, and 21 March. On 3 Aug. 1805, at which period he had been nine months in the North Sea on board the ADAMANT 50, Capt. Geo. Burlton, he was there nominated Sub-Lieutenant of the STARLING gun-brig, Lieut.-Commander Chas. Napier. He removed as Acting-Lieutenant, 31 Jan. 1806, to the ROMULUS 36, Capt. Burton; and on 22 Sept. in the same year he was confirmed into the ROEBUCK 44, flag-ship of Rear-Admiral Billy Douglas at Yarmouth. In 1809 he took part, in the ACUTE gun-brig, in the siege of Flushing, and was often in action with the enemy's gun-boats, privateers, &c. Assuming command, 22 March, 1810, of the ALERT cutter, he effected the capture, on one occasion, of four gun-boats, whose resistance occasioned him a loss of nearly a third of his crew; and on another, he landed on the coast of Holland, and succeeded, after overcoming severe opposition, in recovering a gentleman who had been employed on shore on secret service. He left the ALERT in Feb. 1812; and accepted his present rank 27 Oct. 1846.

NEAME. (COMMANDER, 1832. F-P., 45; H-P., 3.)

WILLIAM NEAME entered the Navy, in 1799, as Fst.-cl. Vol., on board the STEADY gun-brig; in which vessel, commanded by a Lieutenant, he served in the North Sea and West Indies until 1802—the last two years in the capacity of Midshipman. He then successively joined the HORNET sloop,

* *Vide* Gaz. 1813, p. 550.

Capt. John Nash, and EXCELLENT 74, Capts. Hon. Robt. Stopford and J. Nash; and next, in 1803, the SPENCER 74, Capt. Hon. R. Stopford. For his conduct (on his return from the Mediterranean to the West Indies) in the action off St. Domingo 6 Feb. 1806, on which occasion he was slightly wounded,* he was immediately nominated Acting-Lieutenant of the CANOPUS 80, flag-ship of Rear-Admirals Sir Thos. Louis and Geo Martin. Under the former of those officers he assisted, in 1806-7, at the capture of the French frigate *Le Président*, and was present in the expeditions to the Dardanells and Egypt. His promotion being confirmed by commission dated 28 June, 1808, he subsequently, 22 Nov. 1809 and 6 March, 1814, became Senior of the SCOUT 18, Capts. Alex. Renton Sharpe, Benj. Crispin, and Jas. Arthur Murray, and HYACINTH 24, Capt. A. R. Sharpe, on the Mediterranean and Home stations. In the SCOUT he was again (severely) wounded, while contributing, in company with the POMONE 38 and UNITÉ 36, to the destruction, 1 May, 1811, of the French store-ships *Giraffe* and *Nourrice*, each mounting from 20 to 30 guns, and both protected by a 5-gun battery, a martello-tower, and a body of about 200 regular troops, in Sagone Bay, Island of Corsica; where the service was accomplished at the close of a gallant action of an hour and a half, attended with a loss to the British of 2 men killed and 25 wounded.† Having left the HYACINTH in Sept. 1815, he was appointed, 10 Jan. 1817, a Chief Officer in the Water Guard. He removed, 28 Sept. 1818, to the command of a Revenue-vessel; and from 6 Sept. 1820 until awarded his present rank 4 April, 1832, he was employed as an Inspecting-Commander in the Coast Guard. He was re-appointed to the latter service as an Inspecting-Commander 18 March, 1834; and since 5 of the following Sept. has held in it the office of Deputy-Inspector-General.

The injuries received by Commander Neame during the war procured him gratuities from the Patriotic Fund. AGENTS—Messrs. Halford and Co.

NEED. (LIEUTENANT, 1841.)

HENRY NEED is eldest surviving son of the late Lieut.-General Sam. Need, of Fountain Dale, Notts, Colonel of H.M. 9th Lancers; and brother of Lieut. Chas. Need, of the 7th Native Infantry.

This officer entered the Navy 16 March, 1833; passed his examination 1 May, 1839; was subsequently employed, as Mate, in the MELVILLE 72, Capt. Hon. Rich. Saunders Dundas, on the East India station; and for his services in that capacity, while attached to the DRUID 44, Capt. Henry Smith, in the operations of May, 1841, against Canton, was promoted to the rank of Lieutenant 8 Oct. in the same year.‡ His appointments have since been—15 March, 1843, to the HARLEQUIN 16, Capt. Hon. Geo. Fowler Hastings, again in the East Indies, whence he returned in the early part of 1845—and, 6 Dec. in the latter year, to the TERRIBLE steam-frigate, of 800 horse-power, Capt. Wm. Ramsay, under whom he is now employed, as Senior-Lieutenant, on particular service.

He married, 23 Dec. 1845, Jane, eldest daughter of Jas. M'Dowell, Esq., of Portland Place, London, and East Bridgeford, Notts. AGENTS — Messrs. Stilwell.

NEED. (COMMANDER, 1847.)

WALTER NEED entered the Navy 11 Dec. 1824; passed his examination in 1831; and obtained his first commission 28 June, 1838. His succeeding appointments were—10 April, 1839, and 20 May, 1841, to the BELLEISLE 72, Capt. John Toup Nicolas, and MONARCH 84, Capt. Sam. Chambers, both in the Mediterranean, whence he returned to England and was paid off at the close of 1843—4 Jan. 1845, as Senior, to the ACTÆON 26, Capt. Geo. Mansel, fitting for the coast of Africa, where he was superseded in the latter part of the same year—and, 4

* *Vide* Gaz. 1806, p. 373. † *V.* Gaz. 1811, p. 1250.
‡ *Vide* Gaz. 1841, pp. 2504, 2539.

Feb. 1847, in a similar capacity, to the RODNEY 92, Capt. Edw. Collier, employed on the Home and Mediterranean stations. He attained his present rank 12 Oct. 1847.

NEILL. (COMMANDER, 1815. F-P., 13; H-P., 35.)
JOSEPH NEILL entered the Navy, 7 March, 1799, as Fst.-cl. Vol., on board the AMERICA 74, Capt. John Smith, attached to the force in the North Sea; where and in the Channel he continued employed as Midshipman of the same ship and of the BELLIQUEUX 64, Capt. Rowley Bulteel, until May, 1802. In the AMERICA he accompanied the expedition to Holland under Sir Andrew Mitchell; and in the BELLIQUEUX he assisted, while in escort of an East India convoy, at the capture of the French 40-gun frigate *La Concorde*. After a servitude of three years and nine months, still on the Home station, in L'AFRICAINE 38, Capt. Thos. Manby, and REPULSE 74, Capt. Hon. Arthur Kaye Legge, part of the force engaged in Sir Robt. Calder's action, he was promoted, 11 Nov. 1806, to a Lieutenancy in the COURAGEUX 74, Capt. Jas. Bissett, off Cadiz. He left that ship in May, 1808, and between the following Nov. and Oct. 1814 was employed, on the Downs, Channel, Lisbon, Baltic, North Sea, and West India stations, in the TRUSTY 50, Capt. Brian Hodgson, TYRIAN sloop, Capt. Henry Thos. Davies, DOLPHIN, Capt. Christopher Watson, and DICTATOR 64 and GLOUCESTER 74, both commanded by Capt. Robt. Williams. In the DICTATOR he was constantly occupied in affording protection to the British convoys in the Baltic against the frequent attacks of the Danish gun-boats. He attained the rank of Commander 26 Aug. 1815, and has since been on half-pay.

NELSON. (Captain, 1822. F-P., 12; H-P., 30.)
CHARLES NELSON is second son of the Rev. Edm. Nelson, Rector of Congham, near Lynn, co. Norfolk; and cousin of the hero of the Nile, Copenhagen, and Trafalgar.

This officer entered the Navy, 30 Sept. 1805, as Midshipman, on board the SUPERB 74, Capts. Rich. Goodwin Keats, Donald M'Leod, and Sam. Jackson; in which ship he fought in the action off St. Domingo, 6 Feb. 1806, accompanied the expedition of 1807 against Copenhagen, assisted in Aug. 1808 at the embarkation from Nyeborg of the Marquis de la Romana and his patriot troops, and passed the winter of 1808-9 at Gottenborg. In July, 1809, he was discharged into the PUISSANT sheerhulk at Spithead, Capt. Robt. Hall; and he was next, between March, 1810, and April, 1812, employed in the Mediterranean on board the EURYALUS 36, Capts. Hon. G. H. L. Dundas and Abel Ferris, and HIBERNIA 120, flag-ship of Sir R. G. Keats. Receiving, then, a commission bearing date 5 Feb. 1812, he was in the course of that year appointed, again in the Mediterranean, to the EDINBURGH 74, Capt. Robt. Rolles, SPARROWHAWK sloop, Capt. Thos. Ball Clowes, and UNION 98, Capt. R. Rolles. In the last-mentioned ship, which he left in July, 1814, he witnessed the surrender of Genoa. He attained the rank of Commander 13 June, 1815; and was lastly, from 25 June, 1819, until June, 1822, employed in the NIMROD 18, on the coast of Holland, where he made prize of two smuggling vessels. His elevation to Post-rank took place 9 Oct. 1822; and his acceptance of the Retirement 1 Oct. 1846.

NELSON. (LIEUTENANT, 1846.)
HORATIO NELSON passed his examination 28 Sept. 1844; and after serving a short time as Mate in the HEROINE 6, Capt. Chas. Edmunds, on the coast of Africa, was there, 9 Jan. 1846, nominated Acting-Lieutenant of the ROLLA 10, Capt. John Simpson; in which vessel (the appointment being confirmed 9 Nov. following) he is still employed under Capt. Hugh Myddleton Ellicombe.

NEPEAN. (CAPTAIN, 1841. F-P., 22; H-P., 27.)
EVAN NEPEAN, born 15 Aug. 1785, at Devonport, is second son of Lieut.-General Nicholas Nepean, who died in 1823, by Francina only daughter of Major Wedikind, of the 11th Hanoverian Regt.; and nephew of the Right Hon. Sir Evan Nepean, Bart., M.P., who died 2 Oct. 1822, having held the offices of Secretary to the Admiralty, Secretary of State for Ireland, a Lord of the Admiralty, and Governor of Bombay. Capt. Nepean is brother (with the present Lieut. John Nepean, R.N.) of Capt. Chas. Wedikind Nepean, of the 7th Madras Native Infantry, and also of Thos. Rudolph Nepean, Midshipman R.N., who was drowned in 1801 while serving with the late Admiral Jas. Macnamara in the CERBERUS 32.

This officer entered the Navy, 17 Jan. 1798, as Fst.-cl. Vol., on board the ANSON, of 46 guns and 327 men, Capt. Philip Chas. Durham; during a servitude of seven months in which ship he was employed cruizing in the Bay of Biscay, and participated, in company with the PHAETON 38, in a night-action with the French frigate *La Charente*. While attached next, between July, 1799, and Feb. 1802, to the PHAETON, commanded by Capt. Jas. Nicoll Morris, he went through a great variety of service, escorted Lord Elgin as Ambassador to Constantinople, assisted in landing troops at the siege of Malta, joined in the successful operations against Genoa, and aided in making prize of a large number of privateers and other vessels. He also, 28 Oct. 1800, contributed in the boats under Lieut. Fras. Beaufort to the cutting out after an obstinate engagement, of the Spanish polacre-rigged ship *San Josef*, carrying 14 brass guns, 34 seamen, and 22 soldiers, moored under the protection of 5 guns in the fortress of Fuengirola, near Malaga: a most spirited performance, in which the enemy sustained a loss of 19 men wounded, and the British of 1 man killed and 4 wounded. In March, 1802, Mr. Nepean, who had been sent home in the prize under the command of Lieut. Huish, but had again joined the PHAETON, was received as Midshipman on board the CAMBRIDGE 74, Capt. Chas. Henry Lane, lying at Plymouth; and in the course of the same year he was in succession transferred to the SALVADOR DEL MUNDO 112 and HUSSAR 38, the latter commanded by Capt. Philip Wilkinson, under whom, while returning to England from Ferrol with despatches, he had the misfortune to be wrecked on the southernmost part of the Saintes, on the night of 8 Feb. 1804. Being reduced in consequence to the necessity of surrendering with the rest of his shipmates to the French fleet in Brest Harbour, he was detained a prisoner *en parole* in France, first at Verdun and then at Arras and at Amiens, until June, 1814. On 9 of that month he was placed on board the PRINCE 98, Capt. Geo. Fowke, at Portsmouth; and in Aug. of the same year he passed his examination. In Aug. 1815, being at the time in the ALBION 74, Capt. Philip Somerville, he took up a commission dated 13 of the preceding Feb., and he was next, in July, 1821, appointed to the EURYALUS 42; in which vessel he remained as commanding officer, fitting her out intermediately for the pennant of the present Sir Augustus Wm. Jas. Clifford, until removed, in the ensuing Oct., to the LIFFEY 50, Commodore Chas. Grant. Proceeding to India, he was there, 22 Oct. 1823, advanced to the rank of Commander, and immediately sent home as Acting-Captain of the MADAGASCAR 46. During the passage he was for three weeks exposed to a furious north-wester, which entailed so much fatigue that the greater part of the crew was placed on the sick-list, and scarcely enough left to work the ship. From 10 April, 1835, until the spring of 1836, when the rotten and defective state of his vessel compelled him prematurely to return, we find Capt. Nepean commanding the SERPENT 16 in the West Indies; on which station he captured a slaver, and a vessel carrying 180 desperadoes who had been guilty of piracy. His last appointment was, 9 May, 1839, to the COMUS 18, again on the West India station, where he was principally employed in affording protection to British trade during the revolutionary movements at New Grenada. For several months after the death of Vice-Admiral Sir Thos. Harvey he performed the duties of senior officer at Jamaica. He returned home on the occasion of his elevation to Post-rank, 23 Nov. 1841.

Capt. Nepean married, 7 June, 1825, Mary, daughter of Capt. Stuart, R.N., of Montagu Square, London, by whom he has issue. AGENTS—Burnett and Holmes.

NEPEAN. (LIEUT., 1806. F-P., 19;* H-P., 30.)

JOHN NEPEAN was born 6 Jan. 1785. He is brother of Capt. Evan Nepean, R.N.

This officer entered the Navy, 3 March, 1798, as Fst.-cl. Vol., on board the CATON, Lieut.-Commander Robt. Browne, lying in Hamoaze; and between 1799 and Aug. 1803 was employed on various parts of the Home station in the SATURN 74, Capt. Thos. Foley, NEREIDE frigate, Capt. Fred. Watkins, VICTORIEUSE, Capt. Richards, AMBUSCADE 36, Capt. Hon. John Colville, GALGO sloop, Capt. Rich. Hawkins, and GALATEA and AIGLE frigates, both commanded by Capt. Geo. Wolfe. After a further servitude in the FOUDROYANT 80, bearing the flag in the Channel of Rear-Admiral Dacres, also in the QUEBEC and EURYALUS frigates, each under the orders of Capt. Hon. Geo. Heneage Lawrence Dundas (with whom he visited Cadiz and Teneriffe), and in the ACASTA 40, Capt. Rich. Dalling Dunn, he was promoted, on his return home from Gibraltar, to the rank of Lieutenant by commission dated 25 Sept. 1806; and next in succession appointed—29 of the same month, to the RAVEN sloop, Capt. Jas. Grant, stationed off Lisbon and Oporto—21 Dec. 1807, to the BELLEROPHON 74, bearing the flag of Rear-Admiral Albemarle Bertie in the Channel—8 April, 1808, to the HUMBER, Capts. John Hill and Robt. England, employed between Falmouth and the Downs—about July, 1809, to the IMPÉRIEUSE 38, Capts. Lord Cochrane, Thos. Gould, and Hon. Henry Duncan, attached to the force in the North Sea and Mediterranean—and, in 1811, to the Regulating service, which he left in 1814. While belonging to the RAVEN he was wounded in her boats in an attack upon a privateer; and when in the IMPÉRIEUSE, in 1809, he assisted at the destruction of a fort in the river Scheldt, took part in the operations connected with the siege of Flushing, and was a second time wounded in an affair with five Dutch schuyts near South Beveland. His last appointments were—26 April, 1823, to the Water Guard, in which service he continued, we believe, but a short period—28 Oct. 1841, to the post (which he retained until the close of 1843) of Admiralty Agent on board a contract mail steam-vessel—and, 4 Jan. and 22 May, 1845, to the SAN JOSEF 110, and CALEDONIA 120, both commanded by Capt. Manley Hall Dixon, at Devonport, where he is now employed.

* Independently of time passed in the Water Guard.

NESHAM. (VICE-ADMIRAL OF THE WHITE, 1846. F-P., 19; H-P., 46.)

CHRISTOPHER JOHN WILLIAMS NESHAM, born in 1771, is son of the late Christ. Nesham, Esq. (who served as Aide-de-Camp to Colonel Monson at the capture of Manilla in 1762), by Mary Williams, sister of Wm. Peere Williams Freeman, Esq., who died Admiral of the Fleet (1830), and a relative of the late Lord North.

This officer entered the Navy, 21 Jan. 1782, as Fst.-cl. Vol., on board the JUNO frigate, Capt. Jas. Montagu; and on 20 June, in the following year, was present, as Midshipman, in the action fought between Sir Edw. Hughes and M. de Suffrein off Cuddalore. On his return to England in the spring of 1785 he successively joined the EDGAR 74 and DRUID 32, Capts. Adam Duncan and Joseph Ellison, under whom he served at Portsmouth and in the Channel until March, 1788. In June, 1790, he became attached to the SALISBURY 50, bearing the flag at Newfoundland of Vice-Admiral Milbank; and on 17 of the following Nov. he was promoted to the rank of Lieutenant. His succeeding appointments were—16 July, 1791, and 1 Sept. 1792, to the DRAKE sloop, Capt. John Doling, and NIGER 32, Capts. Rich. Goodwin Keats and Robt. Moorsom, both in the Channel—and, 11 May, 1793, to the ADAMANT 50, Capts. Wm. Bentinck, Henry D'Esterre Darby, Henry Warre, and Wm. Hotham, in which ship we find him employed on the West India, Newfoundland, Lisbon, and North Sea stations. Under the officer last mentioned he was present, as First-Lieutenant, in the mutiny at the Nore, and in the action off Camperdown 11 Oct. 1797. Being awarded a second promotal commission 2 Jan. 1798, he was next, 13 April, 1801, invested with the command (which he retained until posted 29 April, 1802) of the SUFFISANTE sloop. His after-appointments were—26 Oct. 1804, to the FOUDROYANT 80, bearing the flag of Sir Thos. Graves off Rochefort, where he continued until Feb. 1805—and, 25 March, 1807, 6 July, 1808, and 21 July, 1809, to the ULYSSES 44, INTREPID 64, and CAPTAIN 74, all on the West India station, whither, in the ULYSSES, he escorted a fleet of merchantmen. In that ship Capt. Nesham also co-operated in the reduction of Marie-Galante in March, 1808. In the INTREPID he assisted, in Feb. 1809, and was mentioned in terms of high approbation for his able support of Commodore Geo. Cockburn, at the capture of Martinique; where, in command with Capt. Robt. Barton of a body of about 400 seamen and marines, he superintended (prior to the erection of batteries, whose fire he soon rendered irresistible) the transport of the heavy cannon, mortars, and howitzers up to Mount Sourier, from the eastern side of Fort Edward, a service, owing to the rains and the deepness of the roads, of the utmost labour and difficulty.* On 15 of the following April the INTREPID was severely cut up in an engagement with the French frigates *Henriade* and *Félicité*, under the guns of Fort Matilda, Guadeloupe. In Dec. 1809 Capt. Nesham returned to England and paid the CAPTAIN off, that ship being found unfit for further service. His last appointment was, 22 July, 1830, to the MELVILLE 74, in the Mediterranean, where he remained about 12 months. He became a Retired Rear-Admiral 10 Jan. 1837, but was transferred to the Active list 17 Aug. 1840, and on 9 Nov. 1846 advanced to the rank he now holds.

The Vice-Admiral married, first, in 1802, Margaret Anne, youngest daughter of the first, sister of the second, and aunt of the present Lord Graves; and (that lady dying in 1808) secondly, in July, 1833, Elizabeth, youngest daughter of Colonel Nicholas Bayly, brother of the late Earl of Uxbridge, and first-cousin of the Marquis of Anglesey, K.G., G.C.B. His only daughter by his former marriage became the wife, in Jan. 1831, of Major Lloyd, of the 73rd regt.

NETTLETON. (LIEUTENANT, 1845.)

PETER GORDON NETTLETON passed his examination 13 Feb. 1837; and between 1840 and the date of his promotion to the rank of Lieutenant, 8 Aug. 1845, was employed on the Mediterranean and African stations, as Mate, in the CAMBRIDGE 78, Capt. Edw. Barnard, MALABAR 72, Capt. Sir Geo. Rose Sartorius, and ECLAIR steam-sloop, Capt. Walter Grimston Bucknall Estcourt. He then joined the TORTOISE store-ship at Ascension, Capt. Arthur Morrell; and since 24 April, 1846, has been serving in the APOLLO troop-ship, Capt. Wm. Radcliffe.

NEVILL. (CAPTAIN, 1846. F-P., 20; H-P., 20.)

WILLIAM NEVILL is son of the late Wm. Nevill, Esq., of Easton, Hants; and brother-in-law of J. Griffith, Esq., of H.M. Ordnance.

This officer entered the Navy, 2 April, 1807, as Fst.-cl. Vol., on board the ROYAL WILLIAM, Capt. John Irwin, lying at Spithead; removed, in Feb. 1810, to the Royal Naval College at Portsmouth; and again, 30 Nov. 1812, embarked, as a Supernu-

* *Vide* Gaz. 1809, pp. 482, 488.

merary, on board the PUISSANT 74, sheerhulk, at Spithead, Capt. Benj. Wm. Page. He sailed soon afterwards for St. Helena, as a Volunteer, in the BELLONA 74, Capt. Geo. M'Kinley; and on his return successively joined, in Jan. 1814, the ROYAL SOVEREIGN 100, Capt. Chas. Thurlow Smith, and, as Midshipman, the SCAMANDER 36, Capts. Gilbert Heathcote and Sir John Louis. After serving in that ship at Bermuda, as Master's Mate in the RAMILLIES 74, and MALTA 80, commanded at Plymouth by Capt. Chas. Ogle, and as Admiralty-Midshipman in the AMPHION 32, Capt. Wm. Bowles, in South America, he joined, in March, 1816, the MAGICIENNE 36, Capt. John Brett Purvis; of which ship, stationed in the East Indies, he was created a Lieutenant 12 Dec. in the same year. Being paid off in July, 1819, he was next appointed—28 May, 1822, to the JUPITER 60, Capt. Geo. Augustus Westphall, under whom he escorted Lord Amherst and suite to Bengal—and, 14 June, 1824, to the JASEUR sloop, Capt. Thos. Martin, fitting for South America. He attained the rank of Commander 9 Feb. 1825; and was subsequently, from 27 Nov. 1841, until advanced on his return to England to Post-rank, 2 May, 1846, employed in that capacity in the SERPENT 16, again on the East India station. He has since been on half-pay.

Capt. Nevill is a Magistrate for Winchester and co. Hants.

NEVILLE. (COMMANDER, 1828. F-P., 21; H-P., 32.)

JAMES NEVILLE entered the Navy, in 1794, as Fst.-cl. Vol., on board the CERBERUS 32, Capts. John Drew and Jas. Macnamara. In that ship, besides sharing as Midshipman in many privateer actions, he took part, off Ferrol, 20 Oct. 1799, in a most gallant and all but successful attack upon one of five Spanish frigates in escort, with two armed brigs, of a large convoy of merchantmen. Becoming Master's Mate, in May, 1800, of the IPHIGENIA frigate, Capt. Hassard Stackpoole, he obtained command, on the night of 29 Aug. following, of one of the boats of a squadron, 20 in number, under the orders of Lieut. Henry Burke, and assisted in cutting out, close to the batteries in Vigo Bay, *La Guêpe* privateer, of 18 guns and 161 men, which vessel, 25 of whose people were killed and 40 wounded, was in 15 minutes boarded and carried, with a loss to the British of 3 seamen and 1 marine killed, 3 Lieutenants, 12 seamen, and 5 marines wounded, and 1 seaman missing. While Acting Senior-Lieutenant of the same ship, which was soon afterwards burnt in Aboukir Bay, Mr. Neville was present at the landing of the troops in Egypt in March, 1801. In June of that year he was again ordered to act as Lieutenant in the NORTHUMBERLAND 74, Capt. Geo. Martin, attached to the force in the Mediterranean; and on 3 Dec. 1802 he was officially promoted. His succeeding appointments were—8 April, 1803, and 21 July, 1804, to the TEXEL 64 and MALABAR 50, Capts. Hon. Geo. Byng and Robt. Hall, employed off Margate and in the North Sea—5 July, 1805, to the DART sloop, Capts. Wm. Brownrigg, Hon. Michael De Courcy, Joseph Spear, and Thos. Tudor Tucker, in the West Indies—11 April, 1807, to the VENUS 32, Capt. Henry Matson, on the same station, whence, in the ensuing June, he returned with convoy to England—8 March, 1808, to the DELPHINEA 18, Capt. Rich. Harward, which vessel was cast away five months afterwards on the coast of Holland—17 Dec. 1808, for a few weeks, to the ECLIPSE sloop, Capt. Creyke—3 Nov. and 26 Dec. 1810, to the GANYMEDE and STATIRA frigates, commanded by Capt. Hassard Stackpoole in the West Indies and on the North American station, whence he invalided in Nov. 1812—3 July, 1813, for two years, to the FORTH 44, Capt. Sir Wm. Bolton, employed at first in the North Sea, and then again on the American coast—and, 7 April, 1826, in a similar capacity, to the PERSEUS receiving-ship off the Tower, Capt Jas. Couch. On 19 Sept. 1814, being at the time Senior of the FORTH, he took command of her boats, captured by boarding, and afterwards destroyed, at the mouth of Little Egg Harbour, the American letter-of-marque brig *Regent*, of 5 guns and 35 men, 2 of whom were killed and 2 wounded, with a loss to the British of himself and 1 seaman wounded.* He attained his present rank 2 Sept. 1828; and has since been on half-pay.

He was awarded, 23 Oct. 1815, a pension of 91*l.* 5*s.* per annum for his wounds.

NEWCOMEN. (LIEUTENANT, 1842.)

GEORGE NEWCOMEN entered the Navy 5 Aug. 1831; passed his examination 27 Aug. 1838; and at the period of his promotion to the rank of Lieutenant, 29 Aug. 1842, had been serving for some time in the Mediterranean as Mate of the WEASEL 10, Lieut.-Commander Wm. Edmonstone. His succeeding appointments were—12 Sept. 1842, as Additional, to the QUEEN 110, flag-ship of Sir Edw. W. C. R. Owen, also in the Mediterranean—24 June, 1843, to the EXCELLENT gunnery-ship at Portsmouth, Capt. Sir Thos. Hastings—5 March, 1844, again as Additional, to the AGINCOURT 72, bearing the flag of Sir Thos. John Cochrane in the East Indies, whence he returned at the close of 1845—20 March, 1846, to the DEVASTATION steam-sloop, Capt. Sir Chas. Hotham, fitting for the coast of Africa—and, 3 Aug. 1846, to the SATELLITE 18, Capt. Robt. Hibbert Bartholomew Rowley, which vessel was paid off in 1847, on her arrival home from the S.E. coast of America. AGENTS—Messrs. Stilwell.

NEWELL. (CAPTAIN, 1838. F-P., 17; H-P., 22.)

JULIUS JAMES FARMER NEWELL entered the Navy, 18 May, 1808, as Fst.-cl. Vol., on board the DIANA 38, Capts. Chas. Grant and Wm. Ferris; under the former of whom, on his return from a voyage to the West Indies, he participated in an attack made in Nov. 1810 upon the two French frigates *Amazone* and *Elize*, lying aground under the protection of several strong batteries in the neighbourhood of La Hogue. In Oct. 1811 he rejoined Capt. Grant on board the ST. ALBANS 64; and, continuing to serve with him in the ARMADA 74 until Sept. 1814, was present in that ship in a partial action with the French fleet off Toulon 5 Nov. 1813, also in the unsuccessful attack upon Leghorn, and at the reduction of Genoa and Savona. Being received, next, on board the RHIN 38, Capt. Chas. Malcolm, he was afforded an opportunity, 18 July, 1815, of witnessing the capture, by the boats of a squadron, of three armed vessels and a convoy in the harbour of Corrijou, near Abervrach. He took up, in the following month, a commission bearing date 4 March, 1815; and was next appointed—23 Sept. 1817, to the PANDORA 18, Capts Geo. Matthew Jones and Chas. Grenville Randolph, in which vessel he was for nearly five years employed on the Cork station—and, 11 May, 1824, as First-Lieutenant, to the SAPPHO 18, Capts. Wm. Hotham and Wm. Pitt Canning, fitting for Halifax, where and at the Cape of Good Hope he served for about two years. Attaining the rank of Commander 20 Nov. 1828, he was appointed in that capacity, 28 Jan. 1836, to the ORESTES 18, and next, 1 Jan. 1838, to the Second-Captaincy of the ASIA 84, Capt. Wm. Fisher, both in the Mediterranean. Since his advancement to Post-rank, which took place 28 June in the latter year, he has been on half-pay. AGENTS—Messrs. Stilwell.

NEWENHAM. (LIEUT., 1810. F-P., 18; H-P., 26.)

WILLIAM PERSSE NEWENHAM, born 8 Feb. 1790, is grandson of the late Sir Edw. Newenham, three years M.P. for co. Dublin. His uncle fell in command of a fort at Toulon in 1793.

This officer entered the Navy, 18 Feb. 1803, as Third-cl. Boy, under the patronage of Admiral Lord Hood, on board the VIRGINIE 38, Capt. John Poo Beresford; in which frigate and, as Midshipman, in the CLEOPATRA of 38 guns and 200 men, Capt. Sir Robt. Laurie, he was for some time employed in

* *Vide* Gaz. 1814, p. 2466.

blockading the Dutch fleet in the Texel, and also in watching the invasion flotilla at Boulogne. On proceeding with intelligence of the war with Spain to Halifax, he was present in the latter ship when captured, 17 Feb. 1805, after a brilliant and self-sought action of nearly three hours, and a loss of 20 killed and 38 wounded, by *La Ville de Milan*, of 46 guns and 350 men, 10 of whom appear to have been slain. During the combat, although severely hurt by the wheel falling upon him, Mr. Newenham, on the ensign being shot away, ran aft and hoisted another at the mizen-top. He acted on the occasion as Aide-de-Camp to his Captain. On 23 of the same month the French ship, owing to the damage she had sustained, fell an easy capture, as did her prize, to the Leander 50, Capt. John Talbot; and being added to the British Navy as the 38-gun frigate Milan, was commissioned by Sir Robt. Laurie; under whom (with the exception of an interval in 1806 and Aug. 1807, partly spent in the Espiègle sloop, Capt. Henry Gage Morris, on the coast of Ireland) Mr. Newenham continued to serve, still on the Halifax station, until nominated, 16 June, 1810, Acting-Lieutenant of the Harpy sloop, Capts. Geo. Wm. Blamey, Edw. Henry A'Court, and Henderson Bain. In that vessel, to which he was confirmed 23 July following, he co-operated for a time with the British army in the Tagus, and then proceeded to India, where he served on shore as her Senior-Lieutenant with a party of seamen at the reduction of Java in Aug. 1811. In consequence of an attack of dysentery, there contracted, he was compelled in the ensuing Dec., a few months after his removal to the Lion 64, Capt. Henry Heathcote, to invalid home on board the Java 38, Capt. Scott. He arrived in England in March, 1812, and for four years was a martyr to the severity of his complaint. Although his health at the end of that period became re-established he did not succeed in obtaining further employment until 17 Aug. 1826, when, through the instrumentality of Sir Robt. Laurie, he was appointed to the Sussex Coast Blockade as Supernumerary-Lieutenant of the Hyperion 42, Capt. Wm. Jas. Mingaye, and was stationed at Hastings. Continuing in that service until it was broken up in 1831, he repeatedly performed the duties of Divisional-Lieutenant, and came into frequent and severe contact with armed bodies of smugglers, from whom, during the last year, he wrested two cutters and a fishing-lugger, with cargoes on board of the value of at least 2000*l.* His next appointment was, 6 Nov. 1837, to the Coast Guard, in which he remained until obliged in 1842 to resign, after having been thrice sent to Haslar Hospital, and been for 15 weeks supplied with private medical aid, from the effects of contusion of the brain and of two other accidents in the head received in the execution of his duty. He has been employed, since 6 Sept. 1845, as Admiralty-Agent on board a contract mail steam-vessel.

Lieut. Newenham married 7 March, 1826; and has issue a son and daughter. Agents—Case and Loudonsack.

NEWENHAM. (Lieutenant, 1841.)

William Thomas Newenham entered the Navy 10 Sept. 1813; and in 1814-15 was present as Fst.-cl. Vol. of the Hannibal 74, Capt. Sir Michael Seymour, at the capture of the French 40-gun frigate *La Sultane*, and, while holding the same rating on board the Statira 38, Capt. Hassard Stackpoole, in the operations against New Orleans. He afterwards, as Midshipman of the Slaney 20, Capt. Chas. Mitchell, enacted a part in the hostilities against Ava. He passed his examination 4 Dec. 1825; obtained an appointment in the Coast Guard 25 June, 1840; and acquired his present rank 23 Nov. 1841. He has been on half-pay since the commencement of 1842.

NEWLAND. (Commander, 1847.)

Charles Frankland Newland passed his examination in 1831; obtained his first commission 2 March, 1838; and was subsequently appointed—in May of the same year, as Additional-Lieutenant, to the Princess Charlotte 104, flag-ship in the Mediterranean of Hon. Sir Robt. Stopford—15 Dec. following, to the Wolverene 16, Capt. Wm. Tucker, on the African station, where he was superseded early in 1840—24 July, 1840, and 1 Jan. 1842, again as Additional, to the President 50, Capt. Wm. Broughton, and Dublin 50, flag-ship of Rear-Admiral Rich. Thomas, both in South America—and, 17 Jan. 1843, as Senior, to the Spiteful steamer, of 280 horse-power, Capts. Wm. Maitland and Sir Wm. Hoste, fitting for the East Indies. During an expedition conducted, in July, 1846, by Sir Thos. John Cochrane, against the Sultan of Borneo, we find him, on 8 of that month, commanding a party of seamen at the capture and destruction of the enemy's forts and batteries in the River Brune.* Between the 20th and the 26th he was employed under Capt. Geo. Rodney Mundy (whose thanks he obtained for his exertions) in ascending different branches of that stream and in marching, despite many impediments, into the interior of the country, again at the head of a body of seamen, in a fruitless attempt to gain possession of the Sultan's person.† He was promoted to his present rank on his return to England 30 July, 1847; and is now on half-pay. Agent—J. Hinxman.

NEWMAN. (Lieutenant, 1827.)

Robert Amyett Newman assisted, while Midshipman of the Courageux 74, Capts. Chas. Boyles and Rich. Lee, at the reduction of Ste. Lucie, in July, 1803, also in Sir Rich. John Strachan's action with the four line-of-battle ships escaped from Trafalgar 4 Nov. 1805, and at the capture, 13 March, 1806, of the *Marengo* 80, bearing the flag of Rear-Admiral Linois, and 40-gun frigate *Belle Poule.* On becoming attached to the San Domingo 74, successive flag-ship of Sir R. J. Strachan and Sir John Borlase Warren, he accompanied the expedition of 1809 to the Walcheren, and served in her boats at the capture of four privateers in the Chesapeake, and in the attack made in 1813 on Crany Island, Hampton, and other places. In charge, on one occasion, of a prize, he succeeded in taking a merchant-ship laden with valuable naval stores; and while serving in the Chesapeake in a tender he was wounded. In 1815, being then in the Phœnix 36, Capt. Chas. John Austen, he again saw much boat-service against the pirates of the Grecian Archipelago; where, we believe, he was wrecked during a hurricane, 20 Feb. 1816. On 11 Dec. 1827, eleven years after he had passed his examination, he was promoted to the rank of Lieutenant. His appointments have since been—19 Feb. 1830, to the Coast Blockade, in which service he continued, as Supernumerary-Lieutenant of the Talavera 74, Capt. Hugh Pigot, until it was broken up in 1831—10 April, 1840, to the San Josef 110, flag-ship of Rear-Admirals Fred. Warren and Sir Sam. Pym, Admiral-Superintendents at Plymouth, where he was superseded in May, 1843—and, 7 Nov. in the latter year, to the command, which he still retains, of a station in the Coast Guard.

In July, 1846, Lieut. Newman received a Silver Medal from the Royal Humane Society as a reward for the manner in which he had risked his existence by throwing himself into the water to the rescue of others. He is married and has issue.

NEWNHAM. (Lieutenant, 1815.)

Nathaniel Newnham entered the Navy, 15 May, 1807, as Fst.-cl. Vol., on board the Superb 74, Capts. Donald M'Leod and Sam. Jackson. In that ship, which bore the broad pendant and flag of the late Sir Rich. Goodwin Keats, he accompanied the expedition to Copenhagen in 1807, went to the Mediterranean in pursuit of a French squadron which had effected its escape from Rochefort, assisted at the embarkation from Nyeborg of the Spanish army under the Marquis de la Romana in Aug. 1808, was

* *Vide* Gaz. 1846, p. 3442. † *V.* Gaz. 1846, pp. 3446-47.

frozen up in Jan. 1809 at Gottenborg (whence the SUPERB was only extricated by a canal being cut through four miles of ice), and in the following Aug. co-operated in the attack upon Flushing. After a servitude of rather more than five months and a half at Spithead in the PUISSANT 74, Capt. Robt. Hall, he became Midshipman, in April, 1810, of the THEBAN 36, Capt. Stephen Thos. Digby; which frigate, at noon on 8 Sept. 1812, was caught in a typhoon in the China Sea, and before midnight was left with nothing standing but her foremast and bowsprit. On his return to England with Capt. Digby in the CORNWALLIS 74, Mr. Newnham, in Oct. 1814, joined the TYRIAN brig, Capt. Augustus Baldwin, stationed in the Channel. He was next received on board the BELLEROPHON 74 and SALISBURY 50, the latter bearing the flag of Sir R. G. Keats at Newfoundland; where, in the course of 1815, on 1 Jan. in which year he had been awarded a commission, he was appointed a Lieutenant of the HARLEQUIN 18, Capt. Wm. Kempthorne. From 12 Dec. ensuing until paid off, 17 April, 1819, he again served in the East Indies on board the TOWEY 24, Capts. Hew Steuart and Wm. Hill. His last appointments were—2 June, 1824, to the Coast Blockade, in which he was for some time employed as Supernumerary-Lieutenant of the RAMILLIES 74, Capt. Wm. M'Culloch, and HYPERION 42, Capt. Wm. Jas. Mingaye—22 Jan. 1827, as Senior, to the ALLIGATOR 28, Capt. Wm. Pitt Canning, on the Halifax station—5 March following, to the charge, for five years, of the Signal station on Kingston Hill—and, 12 Jan. 1835, to the command (which he retained until the commencement of 1841) of a station in the Coast Guard. In 1840 he received a Silver Medal from the Shipwreck Society, and the thanks of the Royal Humane Society, for his exertions in saving the crews of three vessels wrecked on the beach between Bearshide and Black Rock, co. Cornwall.

Lieut. Newnham is Senior of 1815. He married, 8 June, 1819, Mary, youngest daughter of Dr. Cooke, of Gower Street, Bedford Square, London. AGENTS—Messrs. Chard.

NEWTON. (COMMANDER, 1838. F-P., 26; H-P., 9.)

CHARLES JAMES FRANKLIN NEWTON was born in 1799.

This officer entered the Navy, 4 March, 1812, as Fst.-cl. Vol, on board the EGMONT 74, Capt. Joseph Bingham, in which ship, during a servitude of seven months and a half, part of the time in the capacity of Midshipman, he was employed at the blockade of Flushing, the Texel, and Cherbourg, and in cruizing among the Western Islands. Joining next, in Dec. 1813, the NIGER 38, Capt. Peter Rainier, he visited the Cape of Good Hope, the Brazils, and coast of Africa, and, among other vessels, assisted, in company with the TAGUS 36, at the capture of the French 40-gun frigate *Cérès*, off the Cape de Verde Islands, 6 Jan. 1814. In Sept. 1815 he removed to the VENGEUR 74, Capt. Thos. Alexander, at Portsmouth; and he subsequently, between March, 1816, and the date of his promotion to the rank of Lieutenant, 4 May, 1821, served, on the Home station, in the PELICAN 16, Capt. Robt. Lisle Coulson, and GANYMEDE 20 and SEVERN 40, both commanded by Capt. Wm. M'Culloch. His commission was presented to him at the instance of the Commander-in-Chief at Chatham, as a reward for his conduct in having, on 21 of the preceding Feb., attacked, with the present Lieut. Edw. Digby, an overwhelming body of armed smugglers at Brookland, in Kent, and captured two of the principal among them, one of whom was executed. In the course of the same year Mr. Newton, who had been wounded, was presented with a sword by the committee at Lloyd's for saving the crew of a vessel wrecked on Dungeness beach. His appointments as Lieutenant were—22 Sept. 1821, to the BRISK 10, Capts. Edw. Stewart and Adolphus FitzClarence, on the Home station—12 April, 1824, for a few months, to the INFERNAL bomb, Capt. Robt. Heriott Barclay, part of the time under Sir Harry Burrard Neale, in his demonstration before Algiers, where he had charge of a rocket-boat—10 April, 1826, to the PRINCE REGENT 120, successive flag-ship of Sir Robt. Moorsom and Hon. Sir Henry Blackwood, at Chatham—11 May, 1832 (two years after he had left the PRINCE REGENT), and 12 July, 1833, as a Supernumerary, to the SPARTIATE 76, Capt. Robt. Tait (flag-ship for some time of Sir Michael Seymour), and DUBLIN 50, Capt. Lord Jas. Townshend, both in South America—and, 25 Feb. 1834, to the CHALLENGER 28, Capt. Michael Seymour, on the same station, whence he returned in 1835. He attained his present rank 28 June, 1838, and was afterwards employed, from 4 July, 1839, until the summer of 1844, in the Coast Guard; and from 14 Dec. in the latter year until paid off in July, 1847, in command of the LILY 16, on the coast of Africa.

Commander Newton married, in 1830, the only daughter of D. H. Day, Esq, of Wilmington Hall, co. Kent, by whom he has issue two children.

NEWTON. (LIEUT., 1815. F-P., 13; H-P., 27.)

JAMES NEWTON died 29 July, 1845.

This officer entered the Navy, 15 June, 1805, as Third-cl. Vol., on board the PUISSANT 74, Capt. John Irwin, lying at Spithead. Removing, as Fst.-cl. Vol., in July, 1807, to the HORATIO of 46 guns and 270 men, Capt. Geo. Scott, he visited Quebec and Halifax, and then proceeded to the West Indies, where, in company with the LATONA 38, and SUPÉRIEURE and DRIVER sloops, he assisted at the capture, 10 Feb. 1809, of *La Junon* French frigate, of 46 guns and 323 men, after a close and sanguinary action of three hours, attended with a loss to the HORATIO of 7 killed and 33 wounded, to her antagonist of 130 killed and wounded. On 21 Feb. 1810, having attained the rating of Midshipman, he further aided in making prize, at the close of a long chase, and of a running fight of one hour, of *La Nécessité*, pierced for 40 guns, but not mounting more than 28, with a complement on board of 186 men, and laden with naval stores and provisions from Brest, bound to the Isle of France. Between the following Oct. and June, 1815, he was employed on the Home, Baltic, West India, and North American stations, in the AIMABLE 32, Capt. John Chas. Woolcombe, THISBE 28, Capt. Wm. Rogers, BELLETTE 18, Capt. David Sloane, and ASIA 74 and TONNANT 80, flag-ships of Hon. Sir Alex. Cochrane, whom he accompanied in the expedition against New Orleans. On leaving the TONNANT, as above, he took up a commission bearing date 2 March, 1815. His last appointment was, 3 Sept. 1818, to the DRIVER 18, Capt. Chas. Hope Reid, in which vessel he served for about three years on the Leith station.

NEWTON. (LIEUT., 1815. F-P., 12; H-P., 32.)

ROBERT NEWTON entered the Navy, 28 Nov. 1803, as A. B., on board the NEPTUNE 98, Capts. Wm. O'Brien Drury, Sir Thos. Williams, and Thos. Fras. Fremantle, in which ship he served in the Channel, at the blockade of Cadiz, and at Trafalgar. From Feb. 1806 until Feb. 1812 we find him employed as A. B., Quartermaster, and Midshipman, in the DREADNOUGHT 98, Capts. Wm. Lechmere and Sam. Hood Linzee (flag-ship for some time of Rear-Admiral Thos. Sotheby), on the Baltic and Channel stations. He then joined the OCEAN 98, Capt. Robt. Plampin, attached to the force in the Mediterranean, where he shared in a partial action fought 13 Feb. 1814 with the Toulon fleet; and in June, 1815, after having served a short time as Mate, again in the Channel, of the MULLET, Lieut.-Commander Crosby, and for seven months on the Cork station as Second-Master of the MARTIAL 12, Capt. Jas. Leach, he took up a commission dated 3 Feb. in that year. He has since been on half-pay. AGENTS—Holmes and Folkard.

NIAS, C.B. (CAPTAIN, 1835. F-P., 25; H-P., 15.)
JOSEPH NIAS entered the Navy 19 Nov. 1807, as Fst.-cl. Vol., on board the NAUTILUS sloop, Capt. Matthew Smith, with whom he continued employed, as Midshipman and Master's Mate, in the COMUS 22 and NYMPHEN 36, on the Lisbon, Mediterranean, North Sea, and Channel stations, until Aug. 1815. Between Oct. in the latter year and Jan. 1818 he served at Plymouth and Portsmouth as Master's Mate and Admiralty-Midshipman in the RAMILLIES 74, MALTA 80, and RIVOLI 74, Capts. Chas. Ogle and Aiskew Paffard Hollis, also in the QUEEN CHARLOTTE 100, flag-ship of Sir Edw. Thornbrough, and in the VENGEUR 74, Capt. Thos. Alexander. He then joined the ALEXANDER brig, in which vessel, commanded by the present Sir Edw. Wm. Parry, he accompanied an expedition sent under the orders of Capt. John Ross to ascertain the existence of a North-West Passage. In Feb. 1819, three months after his return to England, he was again placed under the orders of Capt. Parry, in the HECLA bomb, and in the following May sailed on another mission to the frozen regions, where he penetrated to long. 113° 54′ 43″ W., within the Arctic Circle, and became thereby entitled to a portion of a Parliamentary reward of 5000*l.* On his arrival home he was presented with a commission dated 26 Dec. 1820. Being next, 1 Jan. following, appointed to the HECLA bomb, also commanded by Capt. Parry, he sailed with that enterprising officer, 8 May, 1821, on a third voyage of discovery to the Polar Sea, whence he returned in Nov. 1823. On 6 Jan. 1826 we find him appointed First of the ASIA 84, flag-ship of Sir Edw. Codrington in the Mediterranean; and on 11 Nov. 1827, as a reward for his conduct at the battle of Navarin, promoted to the rank of Commander; in which capacity he was further, from 8 Jan. 1828 until 1830, employed in the Mediterranean on board the ALACRITY 10. He attained Post-rank 8 July, 1835, but he did not succeed in again procuring employment until 24 May, 1838, when he received instructions to commission the HERALD 26 for service in the East Indies. While in that ship, in which he continued a period of five years, Capt. Nias bore a very distinguished part, and was warmly mentioned for the able conduct he displayed, during the campaign in China, particularly in the action with the Bogue forts, 26 Feb. 1841, in the attack made the next day upon the enemy's camp, fort, and ship *Cambridge*, bearing the Chinese Admiral's flag, at their position below Whampoa Reach, where 98 guns were in the whole destroyed, and in the operations of the ensuing March against Canton.* As a reward for his services, he was nominated a C.B. 29 June, 1841. AGENTS—Messrs. Stilwell.

NICHOLAS. (LIEUT., 1815. F-P., 16; H-P., 25.)
JOHN NICHOLAS entered the Navy, 1 Jan. 1806, as Fst.-cl. Vol., on board the ACHILLE 74, Capts. Sir Rich. King, Hon. Geo. Heneage Lawrence Dundas, and Aiskew Paffard Hollis; in which ship he continued to serve, as Midshipman and Master's Mate, on the Home, Mediterranean, and Brazilian stations, the latter part of the time under the flag of Vice-Admiral Manley Dixon, until July, 1815. Besides accompanying the expedition of 1809 to the Walcheren, he co-operated in the defence of Sicily, and was for a considerable period employed in blockading the French and Venetian squadrons in Venice, consisting of three line-of-battle ships and a frigate ready for sea, and several of each class fitting in the arsenal. On leaving the ACHILLE, as above, he took up a commission dated 15 Feb. 1815. His subsequent appointments were—9 May, 1837, to the SAN JOSEF 110, flag-ship at Plymouth of Admiral-Superintendent Fred. Warren—10 April, 1840, for a brief period, to the Coast Guard—and 22 May, 1843, and 22 May, 1845, to the SAN JOSEF again and CALEDONIA 120, both commanded at Devonport by Capt. Manley Hall Dixon. He has been on half-pay since the spring of 1846.

* *Vide* Gaz. 1841, pp 1498, 1501, 1505.

NICHOLLS. (LIEUT., 1815. F-P., 23; H-P., 19.)
JAMES THOMAS NICHOLLS entered the Navy, 1 Sept. 1805, as Fst.-cl. Vol., on board the GLORY 98, Capts. Sam. Warren, Wm. Albany Otway, and Donald M'Leod, and was for upwards of two years employed in that ship in the Channel and off Cadiz —part of the time as Midshipman under the flag of Rear-Admiral Chas. Stirling. From Dec. 1807 until Nov. 1811 he was occupied on Home service in the BARFLEUR 98, Capt. Donald M'Leod, BUSTARD 16, Capt. John Duff Markland, OBERON sloop, Capts. Geo. Manners Sutton and Jas. Murray, and ROYAL WILLIAM, flag-ship of Sir Rich. Bickerton. He then joined the DOMINICA schooner, mounting 12 12-pounder carronades, 2 sixes, and a 32-pounder on a traversing carriage, with a complement of 66 men, Capts. Robt. Hockings and Geo. Wilmot Barretté, which vessel, after having had all but one of her crew either killed or wounded in a determined resistance of nearly an hour, was boarded and taken, 5 Aug. 1813, by the Franco-American privateer *Decatur*, carrying 6 12-pounder carronades and 1 long 18-pounder traversing carriage, together with a crew of at least 120 men, 4 of whom were slain and 15 wounded. On his release from captivity in July, 1814, Mr. Nicholls became attached to the ARGO 44, flag-ship at Jamaica of Rear-Admiral Wm. Brown. He was next received on board the PRINCE 98, bearing the flag at Spithead of Sir Edw. Thornbrough, and EURYALUS 36, Capts. Chas. Napier and Thos. Huskisson; and in Aug. 1815 he took up a commission dated 24 of the preceding Feb. He was afterwards employed in the Coast Guard from 5 April, 1831, until the spring of 1844, and has since been on half-pay.

NICHOLLS. (RETIRED COMMANDER, 1843. F-P., 14; H-P., 36.)
THOMAS WILLCOCKS NICHOLLS died in 1847.
This officer entered the Navy, 1 Sept. 1797, as L.M., on board the VIPER gun-brig, Lieut.-Commander John Pengelly, on the Channel station, where, and on the coast of Spain, he continued employed, the greater part of the time in the capacity of Midshipman, in the HAERLEM 64, Capt. Geo. Burlton, AJAX 74, Capts. Hon. Alex. Inglis Cochrane and John Pakenham, INDEFATIGABLE 46, Capts. Hon. Henry Curzon and Matthew Henry Scott, and AGGRESSOR gun-brig, Lieut.-Commander Thomson, until 1802. Joining next the AFRICAINE 38, Capt. Thos. Manby, he served for some time at the blockade of Helvoetsluys and the Texel, and was on board that ship in a gale in which she was totally dismasted. On arriving with convoy in the West Indies in 1805, he was received as a Supernumerary on board the NORTHUMBERLAND 74, bearing the flag of Hon. Alex. Cochrane, who, on 18 Nov. in the same year, appointed him Sub-Lieutenant of the PERT, Capt. Pringle. In the ensuing Dec., and in March, 1806, and Feb. 1807, he was successively nominated, also in the West Indies, Acting-Lieutenant of the DOLPHIN, HIPPOMENES, and CANADA, to which latter ship, commanded by Capt. John Harvey, the Admiralty confirmed him 13 Aug. 1807. His last appointments were—1 Aug. 1808 (seven months after he had left the CANADA), to the LEVIATHAN 74, commanded by Capt. Harvey in the Mediterranean, where he remained for a period of two years—and, 28 April, 1814, to the command (which he retained until 9 Sept. 1815) of the BRAMBLE 8, on the American station. He was placed on the list of Retired Commanders 19 Oct. 1843.

NICHOLS. (LIEUT., 1812. F-P., 10; H-P., 36.)
THOMAS GEORGE NICHOLS entered the Navy, 27 June, 1801, as Midshipman, on board the SCOURGE gun-vessel, Lieut.-Commander Chas. Rundle, lying in the river Medway, where he served until April, 1802. In May, 1804, he rejoined the same officer in the TRIAL cutter, off Woolwich; and in Sept. of the same year he was transferred to the MERCURY 28, Capt. Hon. Duncombe Pleydell Bouverie, under whom he escorted the outward-bound trade to the

Mediterranean, and, after assisting at the capture of the Spanish national vessel *El Fuerte de Gibraltar*, of 4 guns and 59 men, proceeded to the West Indies. After passing a few weeks off Lisbon in the POMONE 38, Capt. Wm. Grenville Lobb, he was again, in Sept. 1805, placed under the orders of the Hon. D. P. Bouverie in L'AIMABLE 32. Following the same Captain, as Master's Mate, in Feb. 1806, into the MEDUSA 32, he took part in that frigate in all the operations in the Rio de la Plata, from Oct. 1806 until her return to England with Lieut.-General Whitelocke in Sept. 1807, including the capture of Maldonado and the island of Gorriti. Besides assisting at the capture of several privateers, we find him, in 1808, ordered to the coast of Labrador in fruitless pursuit, jointly with the THALIA 36, Capt. Thos. Manby, of two French frigates, and experiencing in consequence three months of great privation and hardship. On his subsequent arrival at the Cape of Good Hope in the SCIPION 74, flag-ship of Hon. Robt. Stopford, he was nominated, 5 April, 1811, Acting-Lieutenant of the RACEHORSE 18, Capt. Jas. De Rippe, a circumstance which afforded him an opportunity, 20 May following, when in company off Madagascar with the 36-gun frigates ASTRÆA, PHŒNIX, and GALATEA, of assisting, after a long and warmly-contested action with the French 40-gun frigates *Renommée*, *Clorinde*, and *Néréide*, at the capture of the *Renommée*, and, on 25 of the same month, of the *Néréide* and the settlement of Tamatave. He was confirmed a Lieutenant of the RACEHORSE 2 Jan. 1812, but was superseded in Nov. of the same year, and has not since been afloat.

Lieut. Nichols is Senior of 1812.

NICHOLSON. (LIEUTENANT, 1845.)

FREDERICK FALKINER NICHOLSON passed his examination 29 March, 1843; served as Mate on board the VOLAGE 26, Capt. Sir Wm. Dickson, and DOLPHIN brigantine, Lieut.-Commander Reginald Thos. John Levinge; and for his conduct in the action of the Parana, detailed in our memoir of the latter officer, was promoted to the rank of Lieutenant 18 Nov. 1845. His appointments have since been—26 June, 1846, to the VERNON 50, bearing the flag of Rear-Admiral Sam. Hood Inglefield on the south-east coast of America—and, 4 Nov. 1846, to the COMUS 18, Capt. Edwin Clayton Tennyson D'Eyncourt, on the same station, where he is still employed.

NICHOLSON. (LIEUT., 1815. F-P., 18; H-P., 24.)

RICHARD ADAMS NICHOLSON entered the Royal Naval College 14 May, 1805; and embarked, 23 Dec. 1808, on board the ORION 74, Capt. Sir Archibald Collingwood Dickson, employed in the Baltic and North Sea. In Dec. 1813 he removed to the ROYAL SOVEREIGN 100, Capts. Thos. Gordon Caulfeild and Chas. Thurlow Smith, on the Mediterranean station; and in May, 1815, after having there served for 12 months as Master's Mate in the ALCMÈNE 38, Capt. Jeremiah Coghlan, he took up a commission dated 18 of the preceding Feb. He has been in command, since 27 June, 1839, of a station in the Coast Guard.

He married, 9 April, 1839, Miss Catherine Strong, of Fratton, daughter of the late Mr. Rich. Strong, R.N.

NICKOLL. (LIEUT., 1815. F-P., 17; H-P., 32.)

EDWARD NICKOLL entered the Navy, 2 Nov. 1798, as Fst.-cl. Vol., on board the SOUTHAMPTON 32, Capt. John Harvey, and in the following Dec. attained the rating of Midshipman. After assisting at the reduction of the Virgin Islands he followed Capt. Harvey, in June, 1801, into the AMPHITRITE frigate, in which ship he continued to serve with Capt. Fred. Warren off Lymington until the ensuing Oct. In Feb. 1803 he joined the HUSSAR 38, Capt. Philip Wilkinson, under whom, while returning with despatches from Ferrol, he was wrecked on the southernmost part of the Saintes, on the night of 8 Feb. 1804. In consequence of this misfortune he remained a prisoner in France until May, 1814. Returning then to England, he was employed for five months off Deal in the MONMOUTH 64, Capt. Wm. Wilkinson. He served next, from May to Aug. 1815, in the HERON sloop, Capt. Fras. Annesley, off Dungeness; and at the end of that period he took up a commission dated 27 of the preceding Feb. He has since been on half-pay. AGENT—J. Hinxman.

NICKOLL. (LIEUT., 1815. F-P., 26; H-P., 17.)

JAMES HARVEY NICKOLL entered the Navy, 2 Sept. 1804, as Fst.-cl. Vol., on board the AGAMEMNON 64, Capt. John Harvey, previously to accompanying whom, in Sept. 1805, into the CANADA 74, he fought in Sir Robt. Calder's action with the combined fleets off Cape Finisterre. In Dec. 1807, on his return in the CANADA from the West Indies, he joined the ECLAIR sloop, Capt. Chas. Gordon; and on subsequently proceeding with the latter officer, in the CAROLINE 36, to the East Indies, he assisted at the destruction, during the month of Nov. 1809, of more than 80 piratical vessels at Ras-al-Khyma and other ports in the Persian Gulf. On 18 Sept. 1810, having followed Capt. Gordon into the CEYLON, of 40 guns and 295 men, he was captured in that frigate off the Isle of France, after a violent intermittent night action of three hours, and a loss of 10 killed and 31 wounded, by the French ships *Vénus* of 44 guns and 380 men, and *Victor* of 16 guns. The CEYLON being retaken in the course of the same day by the BOADICEA 38, in company with the OTTER brig, Mr. Nickoll, who continued in her under the orders of Capts. Jas. Tomkinson and Wm. Paterson until May, 1811, was afforded an opportunity of co-operating in the reduction of the Mauritius. From the date last mentioned until July, 1815, we find him employed on the North American and Brazilian stations in the VALIANT 74, Capts. Robt. Dudley Oliver and Zachary Mudge. He then found that he had been promoted to the rank of Lieutenant by a commission bearing date 6 Feb. 1815. His next appointment was, 18 Sept. 1820, to the WYE 26, Capt. Peter Fisher, on the Home station, where he served for some months. He has been in command, since 3 April, 1833, of a station in the Coast Guard.

NICOLAS, C.B., K.H., K.F.M. (CAPTAIN, 1815. F-P., 29; H-P., 21.)

JOHN TOUP NICOLAS, born 22 Feb. 1788, is eldest son of the late Retired Commander John Harris Nicolas, R.N.,* of East Looe, co. Cornwall, by Margaret, youngest daughter and co-heir of John Blake, Esq., and granddaughter of the Rev. John Keigwin, Vicar of Landrake. He is brother of Paul Harris Nicolas, Esq., First-Lieutenant R.M., who served on board the BELLEISLE 74 at the battle of Trafalgar; of Lieut. Wm. Keigwin Nicolas, R.N.; and of Sir Nicholas Harris Nicolas, G.C.M.G., K.H., Lieutenant R.N. One of his uncles, Paul Harris Nicolas, an Alderman of East Looe, was father of the late Capt. Nicholas Harris Nicolas of the Royal Artillery; and another, the late Major Nicholas Harris Nicolas (who died in Nov. 1816), after having held a commission in the Royal Marines, and been severely wounded at the battle of Bunker's Hill, removed into the line, became a Captain in the 44th and 89th regts, and, subsequently to the peace

* Commander J. H. Nicolas was born in 1758. He entered the Navy in 1772; served in the ORPHEUS 32 at the blockade of Boston, New York, and Philadelphia; attained the rank of Lieutenant in 1779; and between that period and 1786 was employed in the OCEAN 90, as senior in the BUFFALO 60, and in command, for two years, of the SPRIGHTLY cutter. From 1792 until 1798 he regulated the Impress service at Dartmouth in a manner most creditable to himself and satisfactory to the inhabitants. His prudent and spirited conduct on one occasion saved the town from being destroyed by fire. In 1798 he was appointed to command the Sea Fencibles on the coast of Devon; and from 1803 until 1810 he commanded the RESOLUE guard-ship at Plymouth. He was placed on the list of Retired Commanders 17 March, 1814, and died 12 July, 1844.

of 1783, Major of the Royal Cornwall Fencible Dragoons.

This officer entered the Navy, in 1797, as Fst.-cl. Vol., on board the ATTACK gun-vessel, in which, and in the FORESTER and NIMBLE, commanded by Lieuts. Hinton, Allen, and Lloyd, he served on the Dartmouth station, until received as Midshipman, in Sept. 1799, into the EDGAR 74, under the orders of his patron, Capt. Edw. Buller, whom, in the spring of 1801, he accompanied into the ACHILLE 74, attached, as had been the EDGAR, to the force in the Channel. In April, 1803, having passed some months in the NAIAD frigate, Capt. Jas. Wallis, he again joined Capt. Buller on board the MALTA 80. In that ship, of which he was created a Lieutenant 1 May, 1804, he fought in Sir Robt. Calder's action with the combined fleets off Cape Finisterre 22 July, 1805. In June and Oct. 1807 he became Flag-Lieutenant, in the QUEEN 98 and CANOPUS 80, to Rear-Admiral Geo. Martin, on the Mediterranean station; where, 12 Oct. 1809, he was ordered to act as Commander of the REDWING 18. In the following Dec., finding that he had been officially promoted to the command of the PILOT brig of 18 guns, by a commission bearing date 26 of the preceding Aug., he returned to England, and in April, 1810, joined that vessel at Portsmouth. Returning soon with convoy to the Mediterranean, he commenced a series of operations against the enemy along the Italian shores, unsurpassed for activity and success, the principal of which we shall now proceed to record. His first act was the destruction, when in company with the ORTENZIA schooner, of five out of a convoy of 51 sail, protected, near the town of St. Lucido, on the coast of Calabria, by a battery, 16 armed vessels, and a body of musketeers, whose fire killed 3 of the British. This event took place 24 June, 1810; and on 8 of the ensuing month we find him earning the high admiration of Rear-Admiral Martin by the manner in which he took, near the same place, and destroyed two gun-boats, three armed scampavias, and 17 sail of transport-vessels, laden with stores and ammunition for Murat's army at Scylla. Seventeen days afterwards, being in company with the THAMES 32 and WEASEL 18, the zeal and gallantry of Capt. Nicolas were again displayed at the capture and destruction, under the batteries of Amantea, of a convoy of 31 vessels, also laden for the army of Murat, together with seven large gun-boats and five scampavias; a service which procured him the acknowledgments as well of the Admiralty as of his Commander-in-Chief.* Independently of many gallant exploits performed by her boats at Monasteracci, Riacci, Strongoli, Castellar,† Policastro,‡ and other places, in which she herself more or less participated, the PILOT, in company with the THAMES 32, Capt. Chas. Napier, came into action, 4 April, 1812, with a Neapolitan flotilla, consisting of a brig, three schooners, and 14 gun-vessels, whom an unfortunate calm enabled to escape under the strong batteries of Salerno. On 14 of the ensuing month the two ships attacked the port of Sapri, and, after having battered for two hours its defences (a strong battery and tower mounting 2 32-pounders), compelled it to surrender at discretion. The support afforded by Capt. Nicolas on the occasion was great; he flanked the battery in a most judicious manner, and afterwards commanded the launching of 28 vessels laden with oil.§ In June, 1812, uniting with the EURYALUS 36 and CEPHALUS 18, the PILOT suffered severely in her sails and rigging while engaged in a five hours' attempt to destroy a large convoy at Dino, protected by three batteries, several gun-boats, and a large body of troops. Between April, 1810, and July, 1812, she effected, we may add, the unassisted capture, with a loss of but 8 of her people killed and 24 wounded, of not less than 130 of the enemy's vessels. In the course of the month last mentioned she was ordered to the Adriatic; and while next cruizing between Sicily and the African coast, she succeeded in taking, among other prizes, the French armed-brig *Harp*, with a valuable cargo on board, at the close of a long and anxious chase, 4 June, 1813. At the commencement of the peace of 1814 her Commander was sent by Lord Exmouth to Murat, then King of Naples, to inquire into a supposed insult offered by a Neapolitan frigate to H.M. sloop PYLADES; which, however, in a personal interview with Joachim, was proved to him to have originated in mistake. Towards the close of 1814, having returned with convoy to England, Capt. Nicolas applied to the Admiralty for leave to have the PILOT altered agreeably to a plan he had formed, by which a shot-hole between wind and water, in any part of the ship, could be immediately stopped, an object hitherto impracticable from the arrangements of the bread and store rooms. His request was at once granted, and the suggestions he had made ordered to be carried out in regard to all the 18-gun brigs then under repair at Portsmouth. On the escape of Napoleon Buonaparte from Elba, Capt. Nicolas was again sent to the Mediterranean, where he was intrusted with the important duty of opening a communication with Marseilles and the coast adjacent, for the purpose of assuring those who adhered to the royal cause of the assistance of Great Britain. On 17 June, 1815, being off Cape Corse, he achieved an exploit of much gallantry in effecting the defeat of the French corvette *Légère* of 28 guns; which vessel made off at the end of a close and obstinate combat of nearly two hours, attended with a loss to herself of 22 men killed and 79 wounded, and to the British, with damage to their sails and rigging, of 1 man killed and 15 wounded. To mark the sense they entertained of his conduct on the occasion, the Admiralty promoted Capt. Nicolas to Post-rank by a commission dated 26 Aug. 1815. On 4 of the preceding June he had formed one of the six Commanders nominated to the C.B. on the extension of the order of the Bath. In the following Oct. he was presented, in compliment to his distinguished services, with the Small Cross of the Order of St. Ferdinand and of Merit by the King of the Two Sicilies; who, on 26 April, 1816, as an additional mark of favour, conferred on him the Cross of a Knight Commander of the same Order. After accompanying Lord Exmouth on his visits to Algiers and Tunis, Capt. Nicolas returned to England, and, in July, 1816, was paid off. During the time he had been employed in the Mediterranean he had frequently attracted the notice of the Admiralty by the valuable additions he had made to hydrographic knowledge. Obtaining command, 5 Jan. 1820, of the EGERIA 28, Capt. Nicolas was forthwith despatched to Newfoundland, where it was his lot for some months to discharge the anomalous duties of a naval surrogate. A better proof of the satisfactory manner in which he acquitted himself cannot be adduced than the fact that out of more than a thousand cases in which he adjudicated at St. John and Harbour Grace only three appeals were made, and in each of these his decision was confirmed by the Supreme Court. A gratifying testimony, too, of the general esteem in which he was held, was afforded him by the spontaneous manner in which the chief inhabitants of the latter place came forward, on the publication of a libel against him, and subscribed the sum of 400*l.* towards the conviction of the offender. In May, 1822, he returned to England; and in Nov. of that year, in consequence of a dispute which had arisen between the keelmen and the shipmasters and owners at Newcastle, he was deputed with a small squadron to the river Tyne, to aid the civil power in subduing the alarming insubordination displayed. By a union of firmness, decision, and forbearance, he succeeded in six weeks, without the occurrence of a single casualty, in fully restoring order; and in such a manner as to elicit the marked approbation of the Mayor, Magistrates, and merchants belonging to the town of Newcastle, of the Commander-in-Chief at the Nore, Sir Benj. Hallowell, and of the present Sir Robt. Peel, then Secretary of State for the Home Department. The EGERIA being put out of commission in the early part of 1823, Capt. Nicolas, notwithstanding many

* *Vide* Gaz. 1810, p. 1860. † *V.* Gaz. 1811, p. 2193.
‡ *V.* Gaz. 1812, p. 1396. § *V.* Gaz. 1812, pp. 1396-7.

applications for employment, remained on half-pay for a period of 14 years. His appointments have since been—16 Aug. 1837, to the HERCULES 74, on the Lisbon station, whence his health obliged him to return in Jan. 1839—10 April, in the latter year, to the BELLEISLE 72, employed on the Mediterranean and Home stations—30 Sept. 1841 (on leaving the BELLEISLE, which, not being found effective as an active man-of-war, had been paid off, and, at his suggestion, fitted for the conveyance of troops), to the VINDICTIVE 50—and, 1 Sept. 1847, to the Superintendentship of the Victualling Yard at Plymouth, where he is now serving. During the three years he commanded the VINDICTIVE, Capt. Nicolas was chiefly employed on the East India station. On touching, on his passage home, at Tahiti, circumstances arose which called for his interference, and afforded him occasion for the display of much zeal, ability, and firmness, in resisting the aggressions of the French on that island.

In reference to the success which had attended the efforts of the American navy, Capt. Nicolas, towards the end of 1814, published a pamphlet entitled 'An Inquiry into the Causes which have led to our late Naval Disasters, by an Officer in the Navy, in a Series of Letters addressed to a Friend.' He was nominated a K.H. 1 Jan. 1834; and on 9 Nov. 1846 awarded the Good Service Pension. He married, 1 Aug. 1818, Frances Anna, daughter of Nicholas Were, Esq., of Landcox, near Wellington, co. Somerset, by whom he has issue four sons and two daughters. His third son, Beville Granville Wyndham, is in the Royal Navy.

NICOLAS, G.C.M.G., K.H. (LIEUTENANT, 1815. F-P., 7; H-P., 32.)

SIR NICHOLAS HARRIS NICOLAS, born 10 March, 1799, is brother of Capt. John Toup Nicolas, R.N., C.B.

This officer entered the Navy, 27 Oct. 1808, as Fst.-cl. Vol., on board the SALVADOR DEL MUNDO 112, Capt. Thos. Wolley, bearing the flag of Admiral Wm. Young at Plymouth; where he continued employed in the RÉSOLUE and PRINCE FREDERICK 74's, flag-ships of Sir Edw. Buller, until April, 1811; in the course of which month he sailed in the CEPHALUS 18, Capt. Aug. Wm. Jas. Clifford, for the Mediterranean, and there joined the PILOT 18, commanded by his brother, Capt. J. T. Nicolas. In that vessel (of which he was nominated Midshipman 31 March, 1812) he served for a period of four years and a half, and was frequently engaged in her boats at the capture and destruction of armed vessels and convoys on the Calabrian coast. After a servitude of six months at Plymouth and again in the Mediterranean (whither he proceeded in the SPARROWHAWK 18, Capt. Fred. Wm. Burgoyne), in the IMPREGNABLE and BOYNE 98's, flag-ships of Sir John Thos. Duckworth and Lord Exmouth, he was promoted, 20 Sept. 1815, to the rank of Lieutenant. He then went back to the PILOT, and served in her as an Extra-Lieutenant until the early part of 1816. Since that period he has been on half-pay.

Unsuccessful in his efforts to obtain employment, Lieut. Nicolas adopted the profession of the law, and in May, 1825, was called to the Bar by the Society of the Inner Temple. In Oct. 1831 he was nominated a K.H. and a K.C.M G.; and in Oct. 1840 a G.C.M.G. He was appointed Secretary of the Knight Commanders and Companions of the Bath 10 April, 1832; and he was subsequently selected to fill the office (which he still holds) of Chancellor of the Order of St. Michael and St. George. Sir N. H. Nicolas, whose prolific writings, too numerous to enumerate here,* have rendered him eminent as a literary genius, has received the large Silver Medal of the 'Society for the Encouragement of Arts, Manufactures, and Commerce,' for telegraphic improvements; among which are the numerical code of flags now used by the Royal Yacht Squadron, and submitted by him to the Admiralty in March, 1819. He married, 28 March, 1822, Sarah, youngest daughter of John Davison, Esq., of Loughton, co. Essex, by whom he has issue four sons and four daughters. AGENTS—Messrs. Stilwell.

* We may however mention, as among his recent productions, 'The Letters and Despatches of Admiral Lord Viscount Nelson,' and 'A History of the Royal Navy from the earliest period to the Wars of the French Revolution.'

NICOLAS. (LIEUT., 1809. F-P., 14; H-P, 30.)

WILLIAM KEIGWIN NICOLAS was born 23 April, 1792. He is brother of Capt. J. T. Nicolas, R.N., C.B.

This officer entered the Navy, 16 March, 1803, as Fst.-cl. Vol., on board the MALTA 80, Capts. Edw. Buller, Wm. Shield, and Robt. Waller Otway, under the first-mentioned of whom he fought as Midshipman in Sir Robt. Calder's action with the combined fleets off Cape Finisterre 22 July, 1805. In Nov. 1808, on his return from the Mediterranean, he joined the DEFIANCE 74, Capt. Hon. Henry Hotham, attached to the force employed on the coast of France, where, under the batteries of Sable d'Olonne, he contributed, 24 Feb. 1809, to the destruction of three French frigates, after a contest in which the DEFIANCE, added to severe damage experienced in her sails and rigging, sustained a loss of 2 men killed and 25 wounded. He was made Lieutenant, 15 April following, into the CROCODILE, Capt. Edwin Henry Chamberlayne, employed off Shetland and in the Arctic Sea; and he was next in succession appointed—4 Dec. 1809, to the RAPID sloop, Capt. Wm. Mather, in the Channel—26 Jan. 1811, and 8 March, 1813, to the BOYNE 98 and VILLE DE PARIS 110, flag-ships of Sir Harry Burrard Neale on the Home station—and, 11 Jan. 1815, as Senior, to the PILOT 18, commanded by his brother, Capt. John Toup Nicolas. In the VILLE DE PARIS, which ship he paid off as First-Lieutenant in Aug. 1814, he took part in the grand naval review held at Spithead at the close of the war; and in the PILOT he was warmly recommended to the notice of the Admiralty for his conduct in the gallant victory gained by that vessel over the French corvette *Légère* of 28 guns, 17 June, 1815. Although his Captain, under whose name we have more fully alluded to the action, was deservedly rewarded with a Post commission, the valour displayed by Lieut. Nicolas was allowed to pass unnoticed, nor has it yet been regarded. The PILOT being put out of commission in Aug. 1816, he did not succeed in procuring fresh employment until 16 July, 1847. Since that period he has been serving as First-Lieutenant of the OCEAN 80, Capt. David Price, guard-ship at Sheerness.

NICOLSON, Bart. (CAPTAIN, 1846.)

SIR FREDERICK WILLIAM ERSKINE NICOLSON, born 22 April, 1815, is son of the late Major-General Sir Wm. Nicolson, Bart., by Mary, daughter of John Russell, Esq., and granddaughter of Dr. Robertson, the celebrated historian. He succeeded his father, as 10th Baronet, 5 Aug. 1820.

This officer entered the Navy (from the Royal Naval College) 24 Nov. 1829; passed his examination in 1834; obtained his first commission 2 Jan. 1837; served during the two following years on the Lisbon station in the TRINCULO 16, Capt. Henry Edw. Coffin; and on 7 Nov. 1839 was appointed to the BLONDE 42, Capt. Thos. Bourchier. For his services in the latter ship in the operations of May, 1841, against Canton (where he well played his part),* and the meritorious and valuable assistance he afforded as her Senior Lieutenant in those of the ensuing Aug. and Oct. against Amoy and Chinghae,† he was rewarded with a Commander's commission dated 26 Aug. in the same year. Obtaining command, 14 Dec. 1844, of the FANTOME 16, he sailed, in the early part of the following year, for the Mediterranean, where, in personal command of the boats of that vessel, he was for many hours, 12 May, 1846, engaged in a desperate affray with a large force of Moorish pirates on the coast of Barbary in a successful attempt to recover the merchant-brig *Ruth*, of which they had obtained possession. The British on the

* *Vide* Gaz. 1841, p. 2510. † *V.* Gaz 1842, pp 84, 396.

occasion sustained a loss of a Midshipman (Mr. Rich. Boys) killed, and 8, including the First-Lieutenant, John Sanderson, wounded. Sir Frederick himself suffered a narrow escape : while in the midst of the fire, encouraging and cheering his men, two bullets went through his hat; another caught the heel of his boot, and a stone grazed his lip. For his gallant conduct he was advanced to his present rank by a commission bearing date the day of the action. He returned in consequence to England, and has since been on half-pay.

He married, 26 May, 1847, Mary Clementina Marion, only daughter of Jas. Loch, Esq., M.P. for Wick, N. B., and niece of Capt. Fras. Erskine Loch, R.N.

NIGHTINGALE. (LIEUTENANT, 1812. F-P., 10 ;* H-P., 32.)

DAVID THOMAS NIGHTINGALE died 22 Dec. 1844.

This officer entered the Navy, 14 Sept. 1803, as Ordinary, on board the MAGNANIME frigate, Capt. John Broughton; and in May, 1804, after having cruized in the Bristol Channel, removed as Midshipman to the ATLAS 74, Capts. Wm. Johnstone Hope and Sam. Pym. In March, 1806, on his return from the West Indies, where he had been serving a short time in the BEAULIEU 44, Capt. Chas. Ekins, he became attached to the CLYDE 38, Capt. Edw. W. C. R. Owen, off Boulogne. Rejoining Capt. Ekins, in Feb. 1807, on board the DEFENCE 74, he witnessed, during Admiral Gambier's ensuing operations against Copenhagen, the surrender to the COMUS 22, Capt. Edm. Heywood, of the Danish frigate *Fredericscoarn*. After this he visited Lisbon, and then, a second time, the West Indies; on which station he was successively received on board the BELLEISLE 74, NEPTUNE 98, and POMPÉE 80, all flag-ships of Hon. Sir Alex. Cochrane; by whom, subsequently to the reduction of Martinique, we find him nominated, 18 Dec. 1809, Acting-Lieutenant of the ST. CHRISTOPHER sloop, Capts. Michael Head, Henry Nathaniel Rowe, and Wm. M'Culloch, part of the force employed at the taking of Guadeloupe in Feb. 1810. On 27 Jan. 1811, at which period he was serving as a Supernumerary in the DRAGON 74, flag-ship of Sir Fras. Laforey, he was placed in command, with the rank of Acting-Sub-Lieutenant, of the ORANGE schooner. He left that vessel in Jan. 1812; and was next, between the following Sept. (on 21 of which month he was officially advanced to the rank of Lieutenant) and Nov. 1814, employed on the West India, North American, and Home stations, in the NARCISSUS 32, Capt. John Rich. Lumley, STATIRA 38, Capt. Hassard Stackpoole, NEGRO prison-ship, Lieut.-Commander Isaac Strutt, and FAVORITE 22, Capt. Hon. Jas. Ashley Maude. His last appointment was, 26 Nov. 1823, to the Coast Blockade, in which he served some time as Supernumerary-Lieutenant of the RAMILLIES 74, Capts. Wm. M'Culloch and Hugh Pigot.

* Independently of the time he passed in the Coast Blockade.

NIND. (COMMANDER, 1844. F-P., 32 ; H-P., 12.)

PHILIP PITT NIND was born 14 Dec. 1788.

This officer entered the Navy, 8 Dec. 1803, as Midshipman, on board the UTRECHT 64, Capt. John Wentworth Loring, bearing the flag in the Downs of Rear-Admiral Philip Patton. With the exception of a few months in 1805-6, during which he was borne at Plymouth on the books of the SALVADOR DEL MUNDO, Capt. John Loring, he continued employed with Capt. J. W. Loring in the AURORA 28, and NIOBE 40, chiefly on the Home station, until promoted to the rank of Lieutenant 17 March, 1810; assisting, in the latter ship, at the capture, 28 March, 1806, of *Le Néarque* French national vessel of 16 guns and 97 men. Being next, 21 March, 1810, appointed to the ALERT of 16 guns and 84 men, Capts. Alex. Renny, Geo. Barne Trollope, and Thos. Lamb Polden Langharne, he was on board that sloop on the Newfoundland station when captured, 13 Aug. 1812, by the U. S. frigate *Essex* of 46 guns and 328 men, after a most gallant resistance of 15 minutes, in which the British vessel had 3 of her people killed, and received seven feet water in her hold. While attached, from May, 1813, until Jan. 1814, to the BULWARK 74, flag-ship of Rear-Admiral Philip Chas. Durham, Mr. Nind was frequently employed in command of the boats against the enemy in Basque Roads. His last appointments were—27 Oct. 1814, to the SPARROWHAWK 18, Capts. Thos. Ball Clowes and Fred. Wm. Burgoyne, under whom he served for upwards of 12 months on the Leith and Mediterranean stations—30 Aug. 1822, to the Coast Guard—in the early part of 1824, to the command of the DEFENCE Revenue cruizer—15 Nov. 1827, again to the Coast Guard—and 9 April, 1840, to the command of the PRINCE ALBERT, another Revenue vessel. On 6 Jan. 1823, it was his fortune to save the crew of the *Little Mary* of London; a service for which he was honoured with the commendation of the Board of Admiralty and with the thanks of the Committee at Lloyd's; who presented him with the sum of 50*l.* for distribution among those of his men who had put off with him in the boats to the rescue. As a reward for his conduct during 21 years' continuous employment in the Revenue service he was promoted to the rank of Commander 5 Jan. 1844.

Commander Nind, who is Senior of 1844, married, 17 Feb. 1811, Miss Mary Chanly White, a lady by whom he has issue five sons and three daughters.

NIXON. (LIEUTENANT, 1812. F-P., 12 ; H-P., 33.)

JAMES NIXON died in 1847.

This officer entered the Navy, 1 May, 1802, as Fst.-cl. Vol., on board the AURORA 28, Capt. Thos. Gordon Caulfeild, lying at Spithead; and in the following month removed to the DIAMOND 38, Capt. Thos. Elphinstone, in the Channel. In March, 1803, he rejoined Capt. Caulfeild as Midshipman on board the GRAMPUS 50, on the Guernsey station, whence he ultimately proceeded to the East Indies, and there accompanied the same Captain into the RUSSELL 74. Between Sept. 1807 and May, 1809, we find him alternately serving in the SIR FRANCIS DRAKE and PHAETON frigates, Capts. Fleetwood Broughton Reynolds Pellew, Clement Sneyd, and Geo. Harris; and on 11 Dec. in the former year contributing in the boats of the SIR FRANCIS DRAKE to the destruction at Griessee, in the island of Java, of the dockyard and stores, and all the men-of-war remaining to Holland in the East Indies. After again serving for 10 months with Capt. Caulfeild in the RUSSELL, he was nominated, 15 March, 1810, Acting-Lieutenant of the HESPER sloop, Capts. Henry Drury, David Paterson, Edw. Lloyd, and Barrington Reynolds. Continuing in that vessel until Sept. 1811, he succeeded, in command of her cutter, in boarding and carrying, 15 Nov. 1810, with a loss to the British of himself and 2 men wounded, the French national schooner *La Mouche*, bound to the Isle of France with despatches, 2 of whose people were killed, and 5, including their Commander, wounded;* and he assisted also at the reduction of Java, where he was employed on shore at the storming of Fort Cornelis. On his arrival home in the CAROLINE 36, Capt. Christopher Cole, he was confirmed in the rank of Lieutenant by a commission bearing date 3 Jan. 1812. Being next, 10 Sept. following, appointed to the PEMBROKE 74, Capt. Jas. Brisbane, he was afforded an opportunity of sharing in a partial action fought with the French fleet off Toulon, 5 Nov. 1813, and of witnessing the fall of Genoa in April, 1814. He was placed on half-pay in Aug. of the latter year, and did not afterwards go afloat. AGENTS—Burnett and Holmes.

NOAD. (LIEUTENANT, 1838. F-P., 16 ; H-P., 8.)

ARTHUR MAYNE NOAD entered the Navy, 19 Dec. 1823, as Fst.-cl. Vol., on board the TWEED 28, Capts. Fred. Hunn and Lord Hen. John Spencer Churchill; in which ship he was for upwards of seven years employed, the greater part of the time as Midshipman, on the South American, Irish, North America

* *Vide* Gaz. 1811, p. 297.

and West India, and Cape of Good Hope stations. In April, 1831, having passed his examination in July, 1830, he was appointed Mate of the RATTLESNAKE 28, Capt. Chas. Graham, fitting for the Pacific, whence he returned in Nov. 1833. He next, in May, 1834, joined the CHILDERS 18, Capt. Hon. Henry Keppel, with whom he served on the Mediterranean and African stations (nearly four months of the period as Acting-Lieutenant) until May, 1838. On 28 of the following June he was officially advanced to the rank he at present holds. His last appointments were—7 May, 1839, to the SERINGAPATAM 42, Capts. John Leith and Wm. Ward Percival Johnson, which ship was paid off on her return from the North America and West India station in Nov. 1841—and 22 Feb. 1842, to the ISIS 44, Capt. Sir John Marshall, at the Cape of Good Hope. On 19 July in the latter year, while engaged in hoisting out the launch at Port Natal, preparatory to the embarkation of the 25th Regiment, Lieut. Noad sustained a dreadful accident in consequence of the hook of the boat's purchase giving way. He suffered a dislocation of the right hip, had both bones of his leg fractured, and received such severe contusions of the right shoulder and arm that mortification was apprehended. After being buffeted in this lamentable condition at sea for 12 days in very hard weather, he was put on shore and sent to the hospital at Simon's Bay. In the following Dec. he invalided; and on 2 Oct. 1843 he was awarded a pension. AGENT—Joseph Woodhead.

NOBLE. (LIEUTENANT, 1815. F-P., 8; H-P., 33.)

GEORGE NOBLE was born 11 Oct. 1791, at Glasgow, and died in 1847.

This officer entered the Navy, 24 July, 1806, as Midshipman, on board the FRANCHISE 36, Capt. Chas. Dashwood, in which ship he escorted home from Jamaica a convoy of 10 sail under circumstances of great difficulty, accompanied the expedition of 1807 against Copenhagen, returned with the trade in 1808 to the West Indies, and witnessed the capture, in Dec. of that year, of the town of Samana, St. Domingo, almost the last port of refuge on the station for the enemy's privateers. After a further servitude in the West Indies on board the POLYPHEMUS 64, Capt. Wm. Pryce Cumby, and DÉCOUVERTE 10, Capts. Joshua Ricketts Rowley and Jas. Oliver, he came home in May, 1811, in the SAVAGE 16, Capt. Wm. Ferrie. With the exception of a short time passed in 1813 in the KINGFISHER 18, Capt. Ewell Tritton, he was next, until 1814, employed on board the MILFORD 74, flag-ship of Sir Thos. Fras. Fremantle in the Adriatic, where he assisted in wresting several towns from the enemy. We may here allude to a very narrow escape from destruction experienced by Mr. Noble. On 10 Oct. 1813, while the MILFORD was lying at anchor a few miles below Trieste, a howitzer and several pieces of cannon were brought into a neighbouring wood, and a fire immediately opened upon her. At a moment when Mr. Noble was standing on the quarter-deck receiving instructions from the commanding officer, a 5½-inch shell struck the deck at his feet, tearing off one of his coat-pockets in its descent, and scattering its contents in all directions. The remains of a silver snuff-box, which happened to be in it, were subsequently found in the main-chains, and are still in his possession. After this freak, the shell rebounded and, without injuring a soul, burst over the poop, where were assembled upwards of a hundred of the officers, seamen, and marines. On 16 March, 1815, Mr. Noble, who had acted as Lieutenant both in the KINGFISHER and MILFORD, was awarded a commission. He did not again go afloat.

He has left a widow and a large family.

NOBLE. (VICE-ADMIRAL OF THE WHITE, 1846. F-P., 13; H-P., 47.)

JAMES NOBLE, descended from a respectable mercantile family settled at Bristol, co. Somerset, is second and only surviving son of a distinguished loyalist, who sacrificed considerable property in the royal cause during the war with America, where, after raising an independent corps, consisting chiefly of Germans employed at the iron-works on his estate in the Bergen County, East Jersey, he received a bayonet wound in his right eye and had his skull fractured in an affair with the Republicans (a calamity which deprived him for upwards of 18 months of the use of his reason, and caused a majority to which he had been nominated to be conferred on another), and was afterwards killed by a party of rebels while holding the appointment of Assistant-Commissary under Sir Henry Clinton. The Vice-Admiral's eldest brother, Richard, was drowned in *La Dorade*, a French privateer, prize to the CLYDE frigate; and his youngest, Dejoncourt, a Midshipman of the VANGUARD 74, fell a victim to the yellow fever in the West Indies.

This officer entered the Navy, in July, 1787, as Fst.-cl. Vol., on board the IMPREGNABLE 98, Capt. Sir Thos. Byard, flag-ship at Plymouth of Admiral Graves; and served, between Sept. 1788 and Nov. 1791, latterly in the capacity of Midshipman, in the TERMAGANT sloop, Capt. John Salisbury, IMPREGNABLE again, bearing the flag of Sir Rich. Bickerton, and FERRET sloop, Capt. Wm. Nowell, on the Home station. Joining next, in Jan. 1793, the BEDFORD 74, Capts. Robt. Mann and Davidge Gould, he assisted, and was employed on shore with a party of small-arm men, at the occupation of Toulon, and shared also in the partial actions of 14 March and 13 July, 1795, with the French fleet; on the former of which occasions the BEDFORD came into close contact with the *Censeur* 74, and *Ça Ira* 80, whose fire killed 9 and wounded 17 of her people. After serving a short period with Admiral Hotham in the BRITANNIA 100, he was nominated, 5 Oct. 1795, Acting-Lieutenant of the AGAMEMNON 64, Commodore Horatio Nelson; to which ship the Admiralty confirmed him by a commission bearing date 9 March, 1796. A short time prior to the latter event he had been taken prisoner while conveying despatches to the Austrian camp near Savona. On 25 of the following April, having rejoined his ship, we find him serving in her boats, with those of the MELEAGER, DIADEM, and PETEREL, at the bringing off of four vessels, laden with corn, rice, wine, powder, 8 brass guns, and 1600 stand of arms, from under a heavy fire from the enemy's batteries and musketry at Loano. "It is with the greatest grief I have to mention," says Nelson, in his report of this affair to the Commander-in-Chief, Sir John Jervis, "that Lieutenant James Noble, a most worthy and gallant officer, is, I fear, mortally wounded."* In July of the same year, Lieut. Noble, who had by that time recovered, and had been transferred with the Commodore to the CAPTAIN 74, was invested with the temporary command of *La Genie* otherwise *Vernon* gun-brig. Rejoining his heroic chief in the ensuing Oct., he continued to serve with him as his Flag-Lieutenant in the CAPTAIN, MINERVE of 42 guns and 286 men, CAPTAIN again, and IRRESISTIBLE 74, until 20 March, 1797. In the MINERVE, besides witnessing, among other services, the capture of Porto Ferrajo and the island of Capraja, together with the evacuation of Corsica, he assisted, 20 Dec. 1796, at the capture and defeat, in presence of the Spanish fleet, of the *Sabina* of 40 and *Matilda* of 34 guns. The former ship struck her colours, after a combat of three hours; and a loss, out of 286 men, of 14 killed and 44 wounded; the other was compelled to wear and haul off at the close of a sharp action of half an hour; the collective loss of the MINERVE on both occasions amounting to 7 men killed and 44 wounded. Among the latter was Lieut. Noble severely, in regard to whom Commodore Nelson, in his letter to Sir John Jervis, thus a second time expressed himself:—"You will observe, too, I am sure with regret, amongst the wounded, Lieut. Jas. Noble, who quitted the CAPTAIN to serve with me; and whose merit and repeated wounds, received in fighting the enemies of our country, entitle him to every reward

* *Vide* Gaz. 1796, p. 614.

which a grateful nation can bestow."* In the action fought off Cape St. Vincent 14 Feb. 1797, being again in the CAPTAIN, he occupied a conspicuous position in the brilliant part enacted by Nelson and his gallant companions; with whom he boarded and assisted in carrying in succession the *San Nicolas* of 80 and *San Josef* of 112 guns. On 27 of the same month his continued meritorious conduct was rewarded with a Commander's commission. His last appointment was to the Sea Fencible Service in Sussex, in which he remained from 29 May, 1798, until Nov. 1802. His promotion to Post-rank took place 29 April in the latter year. He was placed on the Retired List of Admirals 10 Jan. 1837, but was removed to the Active List 17 Aug. 1840, and on 9 Nov. 1846 advanced to the rank he now holds.

Vice-Admiral Noble married, first, in 1801, Sarah, daughter of Jas. Lamb, Esq., of Rye, co. Sussex, by whom, who died in 1818, he had issue seven sons and three daughters; secondly, in 1820, Dorothy, daughter of the late — Halliday, Esq., M.D.; and, that lady dying in Aug. 1840, thirdly, 2 Feb. 1842, Jane Anne, widow of Edm. Spettigue, Esq. One of his sons, Jeffery Wheelock, is a Captain R.N.; and another, Edward Meadows, a Lieutenant in the same service (1841), died 22 Jan. 1843, at Amoy, in China, while belonging to the SERPENT 16, Capt. Wm. Nevill. AGENT—Joseph Woodhead.

NOBLE. (CAPTAIN, 1846.)

JEFFERY WHEELOCK NOBLE is son of Vice-Admiral Jas. Noble.

This officer entered the Navy 5 Nov. 1816; passed his examination in 1824; served as Mate of the BOADICEA frigate during the Burmese war; and was made Lieutenant, 11 Oct. 1826, into the TAMAR 26, Capt. Jas. John Gordon Bremer. His appointments after he left that ship were, in the capacity of Senior Lieutenant—17 April, 1831, to the PALLAS 42, Capts. Manley Hall Dixon and Wm. Walpole, under whom he was for three years employed on the North America and West India station—19 May, 1834, to the TRIBUNE 24, Capt. Jas. Tomkinson, fitting for the Mediterranean, whence he returned to England and was paid off in the early part of 1838—and, 29 Nov. in the latter year, to the INCONSTANT 36, Capts. Dan. Pring and Fred. Thos. Michell. In the last-mentioned ship, until promoted to the rank of Commander, 23 Nov. 1841, he was again employed on the Mediterranean station; where, and in North America and the West Indies, he officiated, from 4 Jan. 1842 until paid off in 1844, and from 5 March, 1845, until advanced to his present rank, 9 Nov. 1846, as Second Captain of the INDUS 78, Capt. Sir Jas. Stirling, and VINDICTIVE 50, flag-ship of Sir Fras. Wm. Austen. He is now on half-pay. AGENTS—Holmes and Folkard.

NOBLE. (LIEUT., 1814. F-P., 12; H-P., 32.)

WILLIAM BLACKMORE NOBLE entered the Navy, 18 Aug. 1803, as Fst.-cl. Vol., on board the ROEBUCK 44, Capt. Geo. M'Kinley, with whom, as Midshipman of the same ship, and of the QUEBEC 32, and LIVELY 38, he continued very actively employed, as shown in the memoir of that officer, until wrecked off the island of Malta 10 Aug. 1810. In the following Dec. he joined the SAN JOSEF 110, bearing the flag of Sir Chas. Cotton in the Mediterranean and Channel; and in June, 1812, he accompanied Capt. M'Kinley, who had latterly had command of that ship, into the BELLONA 74. After a servitude of 20 months in the North Sea and again in the Channel, he proceeded in the early part of 1814 to Lake Ontario, where he was received on board the PRINCE REGENT 56, bearing the broad pendant of Commodore Sir Jas. Lucas Yeo, by whom he was nominated Lieutenant of the CHARWELL schooner, Capt. Edw. Rowley. He was confirmed to that vessel 27 Aug. 1814. In Sept. 1815 he returned to England, and he has since been on half-pay. AGENTS—Holmes and Folkard.

* *Vide* Gaz. 1797, p. 200.

NOLLOTH. (LIEUTENANT, 1845.)

CHARLES NOLLOTH passed his examination 6 June, 1838; and was for several years employed in the East Indies as Mate in the DRUID 44, Capt. John Smith, PYLADES 18, Capt. Louis Symonds Tindal, APOLLO troop-ship, Capts. Chas. Frederick and Wm. Maclean, and DÆDALUS 20, Capt Peter M'Guhae. On 19 Aug. 1845, he had charge of the pinnace belonging to the latter ship, and served with the boats of a squadron, carrying altogether 530 officers, seamen, and marines, at the destruction, under Capt. Chas. Talbot, of the piratical settlement of Malloodoo, on the north end of the island of Borneo, where the British encountered a desperate opposition, and had 6 men killed and 15 wounded.* As a reward for his conduct he was presented with a commission bearing date the day of the occurrence. He was appointed, 3 Dec. following, Additional-Lieutenant of the AGINCOURT 72, flag-ship of Sir Thos. John Cochrane, also on the East India station; where, since 28 Aug. 1846, he has been serving in the RINGDOVE 16, Capts. Sir Wm. Hoste, Wm. John Cavendish Clifford, and Edw. Augustus Inglefield.

NOLLOTH. (LIEUTENANT, 1828.)

HENRY OVENDEN NOLLOTH entered the Navy 15 Aug. 1818; passed his examination in 1825; obtained his commission 18 Sept. 1828; and was employed for several months in 1831, in the GALATEA 42, Capt. Chas. Napier, on particular service, and, from 10 April, 1839, until the close of 1840, in the BELLEISLE 72, Capt. John Toup Nicolas, on the Mediterranean station. Since the latter date he has been on half-pay.

NOLLOTH. (COMMANDER, 1846.)

MATTHEW STAINTON NOLLOTH entered the Navy 27 Aug. 1824; passed his examination in 1830; and obtained his first commission 28 June, 1838. His succeeding appointments were—16 May, 1839, to the CHILDERS 16, Capts. Edw. Pellew Halsted and Geo. Greville Wellesley, in which vessel, paid off in 1844, he participated in the operations of 1842 in the Yang-tse-Kiang, and served for some time as First-Lieutenant—and, 22 Nov. 1845, in the capacity last mentioned, to the BITTERN 16, Capt. Thos. Hope, fitting for the coast of Africa. Since his attainment of the rank he now holds, 12 March, 1846, he has been on half-pay.

NOPS. (LIEUT., 1810. F-P., 24; H-P., 28.)

JOHN GEORGE NOPS entered the Navy, in Sept. 1795, on board the JUSTE 84, Capt. Hon. Thos. Pakenham, with whom he served in the Channel until the mutiny of 1797 at Spithead. He then became Midshipman of the GIBRALTAR 80, Capt. Wm. Hancock Kelly, off Cadiz; and, on 10 April, 1802, after a servitude of three years on the Irish station in the HUSSAR 38, Capts. Lord Viscount Garlies and Wm. Brown, he was advanced to the rank of Lieutenant. Being next, in Sept. of the latter year, appointed to LA DÉTERMINÉE frigate, *armée-en-flûte*, Capt. Alex. Becher, he was wrecked in that vessel, off Jersey, 24 March, 1803. He served during the 18 following months in the Channel on board the DREADNOUGHT 98, flag-ship of Hon. Wm. Cornwallis, and NEPTUNE 98, Capts. Edw. O'Brien Drury and Sir Thos. Williams; and he afterwards, between 25 Oct. 1804 and 11 Sept. 1810 (at which period the date of his commission was altered), held successive command of the DEFENDER gun-brig, PRINCESS AUGUSTA cutter, TURBULENT gun-brig, POLL cutter, DEFENDER again, and HARDY gun-brig, on the Home, Baltic, and Cadiz stations. During his original command of the DEFENDER he was wounded on the coast of France in 1806, and in consequence presented with a gratuity from the Patriotic Fund. His succeeding appointments were —7 Nov. 1810, for three years, to the Impress service in London—18 Feb. 1814, to the ACHILLE 74, Capt. Aiskew Paffard Hollis, on the Brazilian station, whence he returned in Oct. 1815—for a few

* *Vide* Gaz. 1846, p. 6536.

days in Dec. 1817, to the CADMUS 10, Capt. John Gedge, lying at Sheerness—and, 19 March, 1822, to the command, which he retained until 5 March, 1827, of the Signal station on Kingston Hill. He was admitted to the out-pension of Greenwich Hospital 9 July, 1842.

Lieut. Nops is at present employed in the Excise service. AGENT—Fred. Dufaur.

NORCOCK. (LIEUTENANT, 1841.)

GEORGE LOWCAY NORCOCK entered the Navy 10 May, 1830; passed his examination in 1836; and, on the occasion of his promotion to the rank of Lieutenant, 15 March, 1841, was appointed to the command of the FORESTER brigantine, on the coast of Africa. His next appointments were—23 Dec. 1841, to the WARSPITE 50, Capt. Lord John Hay, employed on particular service—23 Oct. 1843, to the ST. VINCENT 120, flag-ship of Sir Chas. Rowley at Portsmouth—22 Jan. 1846, as Senior, to the RINGDOVE 16, Capt. Sir Wm. Hoste, on the East India station—and, 28 Aug. following, to the VESTAL 26, Capt. Chas. Talbot, with whom he returned to England and was paid off in July, 1847. During an expedition conducted, in July, 1846, by Rear-Admiral Sir Thos. John Cochrane against the Sultan of Borneo, we find him commanding the 7th company of small-arm men, together with half the men belonging to the ROYALIST brig, and assisting at the capture and destruction, on 8 of that month, of the enemy's forts and batteries on the river Brune. On the ensuing ascent of a branch of the latter stream by a force under Capt. Geo. Rodney Mundy, and its debarkation, after struggling for many hours against an almost impenetrable navigation, at the village of Mallout, Mr. Norcock, while the main body marched on to Damuan, in the hope of there capturing the Sultan's person, was left in partial charge of a flotilla of seven gun-boats, and was mentioned for the cheerful assistance he afforded on the occasion.*

He married, 4 Nov. 1843, Isabella, daughter of the late Major Jenkins, of the 11th Hussars. AGENTS—Case and Loudonsack.

NORCOCK. (COMMANDER, 1846. F-P., 23; H-P., 3.)

JOHN HENRY NORCOCK was born 1 Feb. 1809.

This officer entered the Navy, 30 Dec. 1821, as Fst.-cl. Vol., on board the LIFFEY 50, bearing the broad pendant of Commodore Chas. Grant in the East Indies; where, in May, 1824, while engaged in the expedition to Ava, he was discharged as Midshipman into the LARNE 20, Capts. Fred. Marryat and John Kingcome. On 8 Aug. in the same year we find him assisting, with a detachment of 400 men under Lieut.-Col. Kelly, at the capture of two strong stockades in the Dallah creek, an enterprise of great gallantry, in which the British sustained a loss of 4 men killed, and 15, including himself slightly, wounded.† He also, 6 Feb. 1825, united with a force under Lieut.-Col. Godwin and Capt. Henry Ducie Chads, R.N., in effecting the reduction of a 36-gun stockade at Than-ta-bain, on the Lyne river, garrisoned by 2000 fighting men, together with the destruction of an immense number of fire-rafts and canoes filled with combustibles; and, in the course of the following month, having accompanied, in the SATELLITE transport, an armament under the orders of Capt. Marryat and Major Sale up the Bassein river, he contributed, in a manner that obtained him high commendation, to the capture of the town of Thingang and the village of Pumkayi.‡ Removing in Aug. 1826 to the WARSPITE 76, he served in that ship, at first under the broad pendant of Sir Jas. Brisbane, and next under Capts. Hon. Rich. Saunders Dundas and Wm. Parker, on the East India, South American, Lisbon, Mediterranean, and Home stations, until Jan. 1829. Having passed his examination 21 April, 1828, he was then appointed Mate of the KENT 78, Capt. John Ferris Devonshire, lying at Plymouth. He was subsequently, from Nov. in the latter year until paid off in Nov. 1833, employed in North America and the West Indies on board the WINCHESTER 50, flag-ship of Sir Edw. Griffith Colpoys, COLUMBINE 18, Capt. Thos. Metcalfe Currie, WINCHESTER again, RACEHORSE 18, Capt. Fras. Vere Cotton, and BLANCHE 46, Commodore Sir Arthur Farquhar; and in the early part of 1835, after a servitude of 14 months at Portsmouth in the EXCELLENT gunnery-ship, Capt. Thos. Hastings, he returned to the East Indies in the RATTLESNAKE 28, Capt. Wm. Hobson. Attaining the rank of Lieutenant 10 Jan. 1837, he was next appointed—28 Nov. following to the VESTAL 26, Capts. Thos. Wren Carter and John Parker, with whom he was for four years and a half employed on the North America and West India station—15 Nov. 1843 to the CALEDONIA 120, flag-ship of Sir David Milne at Plymouth—17 March, 1845, for a few weeks, to the MELAMPUS 42, Capt. John Norman Campbell, fitting at that port—and, 2 Jan. 1846, as Senior, to the CANOPUS 80, Capt. Fairfax Moresby, attached to the Channel squadron. He was advanced to his present rank 9 Nov. 1846, and is now on half-pay.

Commander Norcock married, 5 Oct. 1837, Jane Money, eldest daughter of Lieut. Robt. Lowcay, R.N., by whom he has issue. AGENTS—Case and Loudonsack.

NORCOTT. (COMMANDER, 1838. F-P., 20; H.P., 22.)

EDMUND NORCOTT entered the Navy, 15 July, 1805, as Sec.-cl. Vol., on board the BELLIQUEUX 64, commanded by the late Viscount Torrington, in which ship, after witnessing the reduction of the Cape of Good Hope, he assisted, 27 Nov. 1806, at the capture and destruction of a Dutch frigate, seven brigs of war, and about 20 armed and other merchant-vessels, in Batavia Roads. In Aug. 1810, two years after he had attained the rating of Midshipman, he removed to the SIR FRANCIS DRAKE frigate, Capt. Geo. Harris; and on next joining the MINDEN 74, Capt. Edw. Wallis Hoare, he co-operated in the reduction of Java, and was wounded in an affray with the Malay pirates. After a short servitude in the ILLUSTRIOUS 74, Commodore Wm. Robt. Broughton, he returned, in Sept. 1812, to England in the AKBAR 50, Capt. Henry Drury. Rejoining Lord Torrington in Feb. 1813 on board the WARRIOR 74, he escorted the Prince of Orange in the following Nov. to Holland, and then sailed for the West Indies; where, in Nov. 1814, at which period he was serving with Rear-Admiral Wm. Brown in the ARGO 44, he was nominated Acting-Lieutenant of the ARACHNE 16, Capt. Wm. M'Kenzie Godfrey. He was confirmed a Lieutenant 10 Feb. 1815, and subsequently appointed—10 Oct. 1825, to the ALBION 74, Capt. John Acworth Ommanney, part of the force engaged at the battle of Navarin, 20 Oct. 1827—15 Oct. 1828, to the Coast Blockade, as Supernumerary-Lieutenant of the HYPERION 42, Capt. Wm. Jas. Mingaye—20 Nov. 1829, to the TRINCULO 18, Capt. Sam. Price, on the Cork station—30 April, 1831, as Senior, to the DRUID 46, Capts. Gawen Wm. Hamilton and Sam. Roberts, with whom he served in South America and off Lisbon until paid off in 1833—4 Oct. 1834, to the Coast Guard—and, 21 April, 1835, to the command of the CURLEW 10, on the coast of Africa, whence he returned soon after his promotion to the rank of Commander, 28 June, 1838.

He was nominated Governor of the settlements on the Gambia 20 Nov. 1843. AGENTS—Messrs. Chard.

NORIE. (RETIRED COMMANDER, 1840. F-P., 20; H-P., 33.)

EVELYN NORIE is brother of Mr. John Wm. Norie, author of 'The Naval Gazetteer,' 'A Complete Epitome of Practical Navigation,' &c., and late of the firm of J. W. Norie and Wilson, Publishers, of 157, Leadenhall Street, London.

This officer entered the Navy, 1 June, 1794, as

* *Vide* Gaz. 1846, pp. 3442, 3446.

† *V.* Gaz. 1825, p. 1494. ‡ *V.* Gaz. 1825, p. 2278.

Ordinary, on board the GLORY 98, Capt. Bourmaster, attached to the Channel fleet. Removing, in Dec. of the same year, to the PRINCE OF WALES 98, bearing the flag of Rear-Admiral Henry Harvey, he served in that ship in the action off Ile de Groix 23 June, 1795, and also at the reduction of Trinidad in Feb. 1797. On his return to England in Jan. 1800 in the CONCORDE 36, Capt. Robt. Barton, he was received on board the ROYAL WILLIAM, Capt. Fras. Pickmore, lying at Spithead. Being soon again ordered to the West Indies in the JUNO 32, Capt. Geo. Dundas, he there, 11 April, 1800, joined the BUSY 18, Capts. John Acworth Ommanney, Lord Viscount Falkland, Wm. Henry Byam, Michael Spencer, and Timothy Clinch; in which vessel he assisted at the capture of a Spanish letter-of-marque, and continued employed, as Midshipman, Master's Mate, and Acting-Master, until Oct. 1803. In Jan. 1804 he became Master's Mate of the VOLCANO bomb, on the coast of France; where, from Jan. 1805 until presented with a full commission bearing date 12 Sept. 1806, he officiated as Sub-Lieutenant on board the THRASHER, CLINKER, and SPARKLER gun-brigs. His subsequent appointments were—14 Oct. 1806, to the MARS 74, Capt. Wm. Lukin, in which ship he was slightly wounded during the attack of 1807 upon Copenhagen—in Sept. and Oct. 1809, to the TRINCULO and GOLDFINCH sloops, the latter commanded by Capt. Arden Adderley—and, for a few months in 1815, to the CHEROKEE 10, Capt. Wm. Ramage, and, as Senior, to the CYRUS 20, Capt. Wm. Fairbrother Carroll. From May, 1810, to May, 1814, Lieut. Norie was a prisoner of war in France. He accepted his present rank 13 Oct. 1840.

NORMAN. (COMMANDER, 1845.)

CHARLES SPRY NORMAN entered the Navy 6 Jan. 1829; passed his examination in 1835; and as a reward for his services as Mate of the EDINBURGH 72, Capt. Wm. Wilmott Henderson, during the war in Syria, where on the night of 2 Oct. 1840 he assisted in the boats under Capt. Fras. Decimus Hastings in removing a quantity of powder from the castle of Beyrout,* was promoted to the rank of Lieutenant 4 Nov. 1840. His succeeding appointments were—28 May, 1841, as Additional, to the CORNWALLIS 72, flag-ship of Sir Wm. Parker during the latter part of the hostilities with China—22 Jan. and 29 Aug. 1842, to the CRUIZER 16, and NIMROD 20, Capts. Joseph Pearse and Fred. Henry Hastings Glasse, both in the East Indies, whence he returned to England and was paid off at the close of 1844—and, 25 Feb. 1845, as Senior, to the COMUS 18, Capt. Thos. Sparke Thompson. For his conduct in the latter ship during the warfare carried on against General Rosas in the Parana, he was advanced to the rank he now holds 18 Nov. 1845. Since the receipt of his commission he has been on half-pay. AGENT—Joseph Woodhead.

NORMAN. (LIEUT., 1841. F-P., 11; H-P., 5.)

HENRY ANNE NORMAN, born 14 Jan. 1816, is son of Rich. Norman, Esq., by the Lady Elizabeth Isabella Manners, eldest daughter of Charles, fourth Duke of Rutland, K.G., who died Lord-Lieutenant of Ireland 24 Oct. 1787. He is nephew of his Grace the present Duke; and also of Lord Chas. Henry Somerset Manners, K.C.B., M.P., a General officer in the Army, and Colonel of the 11th Dragoon Guards.

This officer entered the Navy, 13 Feb. 1831, as Fst.-cl. Vol., on board the SAPPHIRE 28, Capts. Hon. Wm. Wellesley and Hon. Geo. Rolle Walpole Trefusis, employed in North America and the West Indies; where, in Jan. 1833, he rejoined Capt. Wellesley as Midshipman on board the WINCHESTER 52. Returning home in the following June he was received, in Nov. of the same year, on board the EDINBURGH 74, Capt. Jas. Rich. Dacres, fitting for the Mediterranean; on which station he continued to serve in the ORESTES 18, Capts. Henry John Codrington, Julius Jas. Farmer Newell, and Wm. Holt, until April, 1838—the last 12 months in the capacity of Mate. In the summer of 1809 Mr. Norman was successively appointed to the EXCELLENT gunnery-ship at Portsmouth, Capt. Sir Thos. Hastings, and BLENHEIM 72, Capts. Sir Humphrey Le Fleming Senhouse and Sir Thos. Herbert. Participating in the latter ship in the operations in China, he assisted, in 1841, at the attack on Chuenpee, the capture of the Bogue forts, the second series of operations against Canton (during which he served with Sir H. Le F. Senhouse as part of the staff belonging to Major-General Sir Hugh Gough),* the storming of Amoy, the re-taking of Chusan, the assault upon Chinghae,† and the occupation of Ningpo. On hearing of his promotion to the rank of Lieutenant, which had taken place 3 Sept. 1841, Mr. Norman, in May, 1842, returned to England a passenger in the HYACINTH 18, Capt. Geo. Goldsmith. His last appointment was, 17 Sept. 1846, to the RODNEY 92, Capt. Edw. Collier, in which ship he was for some months employed in the Channel and Mediterranean.

He married, 10 May, 1843, Helen, daughter of the late T. C. Worsley, Esq., of Platt Hall, Lancashire, by whom he has issue.

NORMAN. (LIEUTENANT, 1842.)

JOHN NORRIS NORMAN is son of the Rev. J. H. Norman, of Deal, co. Kent.

This officer entered the Navy 3 April, 1829; passed his examination 26 April, 1836; and at the period of his promotion to the rank of Lieutenant, which took place 18 Nov. 1842, had been serving for some months in North America and the West Indies as Mate of the RACER 18, Capt. Thos. Harvey. His appointments have since been—4 July, 1843, to the WINCHESTER 50, flag-ship of Hon. Josceline Percy at the Cape of Good Hope—5 Feb. 1845, to the HELENA 16, Capt. Sir Cornwallis Ricketts, on the same station—and, 30 Oct. 1847, as First (soon after the latter vessel had been paid off), to the ALERT 6, Capt. Hugh Dunlop, fitting for the coast of Africa, where he is at present employed.

NORMAN. (LIEUT., 1814. F-P., 17; H-P., 31.)

MASTERS NORMAN was born 30 March, 1784, at Portsea, co. Hants. His eldest brother, James, died First-Lieutenant of the PRINCE GEORGE 98; the second, William, after having fought as Second-Lieutenant of the THUNDERER 74, at Trafalgar, was killed (before he had received a Commander's commission which had been made out for him) while leading, as Senior of the SIRIUS 36, Capt. Sam. Pym, the party which stormed and took the Ile de la Passe, in the Isle of France, 13 Aug. 1810; and the third, Chas. Rice, a Lieutenant of the ROTA 38, Capt. Philip Somerville, was killed in the boats in a sanguinary attack on the *General Armstrong* American privateer, in Fayal Roads, 26 Sept. 1814. His uncle, Capt. Jas. Norman, R.N., died in 1807.

This officer entered the Navy, 3 Sept. 1799, as Fst.-cl. Vol., on board the CORMORANT 24, Capt. Hon. Courtenay Boyle; in which ship, after having assisted at the capture of *El Batador* Spanish privateer of 14 guns, he was wrecked, while in the conveyance of despatches from Lord Keith to Sir Wm. Sidney Smith, off Damietta, 20 May, 1800. On being exchanged after a few months of cruel captivity, he joined in succession the MERCURY 28, TIGRE 74, Capt. Sir W. S. Smith, KING GEORGE transport, and PENELOPE and DIANE frigates. In the latter ship, commanded by Capt. Stevenson, he shared as Midshipman in the operations of 1801 in Egypt, whence, at the peace, he returned to England. In March, 1803, he re-embarked on board the ALCMÈNE 32, Capt. John Stiles, attached to the force in the Channel, on which station he cruized with much activity until transferred, in June, 1805, to the ZEALOUS 74, Capts. John Okes Hardy and John Giffard, employed for some time off Cadiz,

* *Vide* Gaz. 1840, p. 2610.

* *Vide* Gaz. 1841, p. 2508. † *V.* Gaz. 1842, p. 396.

where, in March, 1807, he joined the QUEEN 98, Capt. Fras. Pender. Removing, in July following, to the SAN JUAN 74, guard ship at Gibraltar, Lieut.-Commander Thos. Spence, he was there for some months engaged on gun-boat service. On his arrival home in April, 1808, he was received as a Supernumerary on board the ROYAL WILLIAM, Capt. Hon. Courtenay Boyle, guard-ship at Spithead. In the summer of the same year he sailed for the West Indies in the FLYING FISH schooner, Lieut.-Commander Jas. Glassford Gooding, under whom he continued until the ensuing Nov., when a fall from the rigging obliged him to invalid. So serious was the injury he sustained on the occasion, that it was not until March, 1811, that he was again enabled to go afloat. He then joined the AQUILON and SALDANHA frigates, Capts. Wm. Bowles and Hon. Wm. Pakenham; from the latter of which vessels, stationed on the coast of Ireland, he was sent in the following Oct. to England for the purpose of passing his examination, a short time only before she was lost with nearly the whole of her officers and crew. Proceeding next, in Feb. 1812, to the Mediterranean, on board the GORGON 44, *armée-en-flûte*, Capt. Alex. Milner, he was nominated, in May of that year, Master's Mate of the ROYAL GEORGE 100, Capt. Thos. Fras. Chas. Mainwaring, stationed off Toulon, where he witnessed the partial actions of 5 Nov. 1813 and 13 Feb. 1814 with the French fleet. On 6 March, 1814, he became Acting-Lieutenant of the BARFLEUR 98, Capt. John Maitland; he was confirmed, while again in the ROYAL GEORGE, 5 April following; and in the next July he returned to England, in the BARFLEUR, and was paid off. His last appointment was, 1 Nov. 1820, to the Coast Guard, in which service he continued a period of five years and three months.

Lieut. Norman married in April, 1817, and has issue five sons and one daughter. One of the former, Wm. Henry, Purser and Paymaster, R.N. (1841), is at present serving at the Cape of Good Hope in the ROSAMOND steam-sloop, of 287 horse-power. AGENT—J. Hinxman.

NORRIS. (LIEUTENANT, 1812. F-P., 9: H-P., 33.)

JOSEPH NORRIS was born 16 Aug. 1789.

This officer entered the Navy, 10 Nov. 1805, as Midshipman, on board the APOLLO 38, Capt. Edw. Fellowes, with whom he removed, in July, 1808, to the CONQUEROR 74, and continued to serve, chiefly in the Mediterranean, until made Lieutenant, 22 Feb. 1812, into the POLYPHEMUS 64, Capt. Peter John Douglas, on the West India station, whither he proceeded in the JASON 32, Capt. Hon. Jas. Wm. King. While in the APOLLO, besides assisting at the cutting out of many of the enemy's vessels on the coast of Calabria, he was present in 1807 at the landing of the troops under Major-General Fraser in Egypt, where he witnessed the surrender of Alexandria, and had command of a boat on Lake Etko at the reduction of Rosetta. During the term of his servitude in the CONQUEROR he came into frequent contact with the enemy in the neighbourhood of Toulon; on one occasion in particular, 20 July, 1810, when that ship, in company with the WARSPITE and AJAX 74's, rescued in a most gallant manner the EURYALUS frigate and SHEARWATER brig from being captured by a powerful division of the enemy's fleet, consisting of six sail of the line and four frigates. We also find him, 11 Sept. 1811, commanding one of three boats under the orders of Lieut. Rich. Howell Fleming, at the destruction, in noon day, of an armed vessel chained from her masts to the shore, at Aras, in the gulf of Genoa, where the British encountered so fierce an opposition that 2 of their number were killed and 9 wounded. During the passage home of the POLYPHEMUS with convoy in the autumn of 1812, Lieut. Norris was placed in command, as Prize-Master, of the *James Maddison* captured American schooner, of 12 guns. In that vessel, on the merchantmen being dispersed in a gale, he succeeded in re-collecting 20 of them; the whole of which, after having beaten off an American privateer of superior force, he conducted in safety to England, receiving, on his arrival, the thanks of the Committee at Lloyd's. His last appointments were, 2 Feb. 1813 and 17 Oct. 1814, to the PERSIAN and MERCURIUS sloops, Capts. Chas. Bertram and Thos. Renwick. In the PERSIAN he was wrecked, as detailed in our memoir of Capt. Bertram, on the Silver Keys, in the West Indies, 16 June, 1813: and in the MERCURIUS he was actively employed off the coast of France during the war of a hundred days. He has been on half-pay since 18 Sept. 1815.

He married, 1 Jan. 1818, Ann Grigg, sister of Jas. Cassell, Esq., First-Lieutenant R.M., and niece of Lieut.-Colonel Cassell, of the same corps, by whom he has issue four children.

NORTHUMBERLAND, DUKE OF, formerly LORD PRUDHOE, F.R.S., F.S.A. (CAPTAIN, 1815. F-P., 11; H-P., 31.)

HIS GRACE ALGERNON DUKE OF NORTHUMBERLAND, born 15 Sept. 1792, is second and youngest son of Hugh, second Duke of Northumberland, K.G., by Frances Julia, third daughter of Peter Burrell, Esq., of Beckenham, co. Kent, and sister of Peter, late Lord Gwydir. His brother, Hugh, third Duke, K.G., whom he succeeded in 1847, assisted, as His Britannic Majesty's Envoy Extraordinary, at the coronation of CHARLES X., King of France, became subsequently Lord-Lieutenant of Ireland, and held the office of Vice-Admiral of co. Northumberland, and of the town and co. of the town of Newcastle-upon-Tyne.

This officer (then Lord Algernon Percy*) entered the Navy, in March, 1805, as Fst.-cl. Vol., on board the TRIBUNE frigate, Capt. Rich. Henry Alex. Bennett, whom he followed, as Midshipman, in the ensuing Sept., into the FAME 74. In those ships he served, off Shetland, Rochefort, and Cadiz, and in various parts of the Mediterranean, until 1810. He then joined the HYDRA 38, Capt. Geo. Mundy, and after having commanded a gun-boat in co-operation with the patriots on the coast of Andalusia, he became attached, in Jan. 1811, to the CHRISTIAN VII. 80, bearing the flag off the Scheldt of Sir Edw. Pellew; under whom, when again serving in the Mediterranean on board the CALEDONIA 120, he was confirmed in the rank of Lieutenant by a commission bearing date 16 Dec. 1811. Prior to the receipt of the intelligence of his official advancement to the rank of Commander, which took place 8 March, 1814, his Lordship occasionally acted as Captain of the SCOUT and PELORUS sloops, and also of the CALEDONIA herself, in which ship he fought in a partial action with the French fleet off Toulon, and witnessed the fall of Genoa. He subsequently officiated for some months as Acting-Captain of the COSSACK 22, on the coast of North America; and at the period of his elevation to Post-rank, 19 Aug. 1815, was serving at Portsmouth on board the DRIVER sloop. He has since been on half-pay.

The Duke was elected a F.R.S. 9 April, 1818. He married, 25 Aug. 1842, Lady Eleanor, eldest daughter of Earl Grosvenor. AGENT—John P. Muspratt.

NORTON. (RETIRED CAPTAIN, 1840. F-P., 21; H-P., 35.)

JOHN NORTON was born 24 May, 1771, and died 26 Sept. 1845.

This officer entered the Navy, about 1789, as A.B., on board the PHŒNIX 36, Capts. Byron and Sir Rich. John Strachan; under the latter of whom, while cruizing off the coast of Malabar in company with the PERSEVERANCE frigate, he took part, 19 Nov. 1791, in an obstinate action (produced by a resistance on the part of the French Captain to a search being imposed by the British upon two merchant-vessels under his orders) with *La Résolue*, of 46 guns, whose colours were not struck until she had herself sustained a loss of 25 men killed and 40 wounded, and had occasioned one to the PHŒNIX

* He was raised to the peerage as Lord Prudhoe in 1816.

of 6 killed and 11 wounded. Removing, in Nov. 1793, to the ALEXANDER 74, Capt. Rich. Rodney Bligh, he was on board that ship when captured, off Scilly, 6 Nov. 1794, after a glorious resistance of more than two hours, and a loss in killed and wounded of 40 men, by five French 74's and three frigates under Rear-Admiral Nielly. On his release from French prison in Aug. 1795, he joined the TOPAZE 36, Capt. Stephen Geo. Church, and sailed for the Halifax station, where he witnessed, 28 Aug. 1796, the surrender of the French 36-gun frigate *Elisabeth*. He was confirmed a Lieutenant of the TOPAZE, after having acted for four months as such, 8 Jan. 1799; and he was subsequently appointed—about 1801, to the RESOLUTION 74, Capt. Hon. Alan Hyde Gardner, which ship was paid off on her return from the West Indies 15 July, 1802—22 Sept. 1803, to the TRENT 36, bearing the flag of Lord Gardner at Cork—14 Dec. 1804 and 24 Aug. 1805, to the command of the MARIE tender and FRISK cutter, on the Home station—and (having left the latter vessel in Sept. 1816), 30 April, 1807, as Senior, to the FAME 74, Capt. Rich. Henry Alex. Bennett, in the Mediterranean. In the FRISK he assisted, in April, 1806, at the capture and destruction of a battery, of 3 long 36-pounders, with a garrison of 50 men,* situated on Pointe d'Equillon, in the Pertuis Breton, and was highly commended by Lord Cochrane for his zeal on the occasion. He continued in the FAME until Feb. 1811; he then took up a commission bearing date 21 of the preceding Oct.; and on 10 Sept. 1840 he accepted the rank of Captain on the Retired List.

We may add, that, when in the TOPAZE, Capt. Norton had been severely wounded by an explosion of powder while clearing for action. He married 16 Sept. 1803, and had issue one daughter.

NORTON. (RETIRED COMMANDER, 1846. F-P., 15; H-P., 34.)

NATHANIEL NORTON, born in July, 1787, at Leatherhead, co. Surrey, is second son of the late John Norton, Esq., of Hurstperpoint, co. Sussex. His elder brother, John, a Lieutenant R.N., was lost on board the HERO 74, during the disastrous winter of 1811.

This officer entered the Navy, 6 Jan. 1798, as Third.-cl. Boy, on board the BUSY 18, Capt. John Acworth Ommanney, in which vessel, when in company with the SPEEDWELL brig, he assisted, in Aug. 1799, in taking possession, off the island of Gorée, of a fleet of merchantmen under the convoy of a Swedish frigate. He afterwards joined in the expedition against the Helder; and on 16 Sept. 1799 he contributed to the capture of *Le Dragon*, French lugger privateer, of 16 guns. In July, 1800, being at the time in the West Indies, he removed to the UNITÉ frigate, Capt. Thos. Harvey, under whom, in March, 1801, he was present, as Midshipman, at the reduction of the Danish and Swedish islands. The latter ship being paid off in April, 1802, he was next, from June, 1803, until Oct. 1807, employed off Harwich and on the Irish station in the ROMULUS 36, and HELENA 18, Capts. Woodley Losack and Jas. Andrew Worth. In the HELENA he aided in effecting the capture, 5 June, 1805, of the *Santa Leocadia*, Spanish privateer, pierced for 20 guns, mounting 14 nine-pounders, with a complement of 114 men. After serving nearly three months as Acting-Lieutenant in the DRYAD 36, Capt. Adam Drummond, he was nominated, in Jan. 1808, Master's Mate of LA VIRGINIE, of 46 guns and 281 men, Capt. Edw. Brace; and on 19 May following he shared in that ship, and was mentioned for his conduct, in an obstinate conflict of an hour and a half, which terminated in the surrender, with a loss to the British of not more than 1 man killed and 2 wounded, of the Dutch frigate *Guelderland*, of 36 guns and 253 men, 25 of whom were slain and 50 wounded.† Eight days after this exploit Mr. Norton, as a reward for his conduct, was again ordered to act as Lieutenant in the BRISK sloop, Capt. John Coode, and on 3 June in the same year his promotion was sanctioned by the Admiralty. Obtaining an appointment, 29 July ensuing, to the ILLUSTRIOUS 74, commanded by the late Commodore Wm. Robt. Broughton, he witnessed, in April, 1809, the famous attack made by Lord Cochrane on the enemy's shipping in Basque Roads, and, after enacting a part in the proximate operations in the Scheldt, sailed for the East Indies. On 6 Feb. 1812, having previously assisted at the conquest of the Mauritius and of the island of Java, he was appointed by Commodore Broughton to the command of the PROCRIS sloop, of 18 guns. After a servitude of nearly 23 months in that vessel, on the Indian station, he had the mortification, in Dec. 1813, to be superseded, without confirmation, and placed on half-pay. His last appointment was, 30 May, 1815, to the TIGRE 74, Capt. John Halliday, with whom he cruized in the Channel until paid off in the following Aug. He accepted his present rank 9 March, 1846.

Commander Norton married, 4 March, 1841, Miss Ellen Barker. He has been residing for many years near Sydney, N. S. W. AGENTS—Holmes and Folkard.

* *Vide* Gaz. 1806, p. 684. † *V.* Gaz. 1808, p. 750.

NORWAY. (LIEUT., 1838. F-P., 13; H-P., 11.)

NEVIL NORWAY was born 20 April, 1807. He is nephew maternally of Commander Rich. Moorman (*a*), R.N., K.F.M.

This officer entered the Navy, 18 May, 1823, as Fst.-cl. Vol., on board the HUSSAR 46, Capt. Geo. Harris. After a servitude of three years and a half in the West Indies, part of the time in the capacity of Midshipman, he joined, towards the close of 1826, the PRINCE REGENT 120, bearing the flag of Sir Robt. Moorsom at Chatham; and he was next, from July, 1827, until June, 1829 (in the course of which month he passed his examination), employed, chiefly on the Mediterranean station, in the ISIS 50, Capt. Sir Thos. Staines, and BRISK 10, Capt. Smith. He then became Mate of the VICTORY 104, Capt. Hon. Geo. Elliot, lying at Portsmouth, as he subsequently did, in March, 1830, of the ASIA 84, Capts. Hyde Parker and Peter Richards, on the Lisbon station—in Oct. 1833, for a few weeks, of the SAN JOSEF 110, Capt. Gordon Thos. Falcon, at Plymouth—and, in Oct. 1837, of the RODNEY 92, Capt. Hyde Parker, in the Mediterranean. Attaining the rank of Lieutenant 28 June, 1838, he was successively appointed in that capacity, on the Lisbon and Mediterranean stations—18 Oct. 1838, to the GANGES 84, Capt. Barrington Reynolds—and, in 1839-40, to the HYDRA and PHŒNIX steamers, Capts. Anthony Wm. Milward and Robt. Fanshawe Stopford. In the latter vessel he was present throughout the operations on the coast of Syria, including the bombardment of St. Jean d'Acre. He has been on half-pay since Dec. 1840.

He married, 15 June, 1843, Judith Catherine, only child of the late N. Cole, Esq., of Trebyan. AGENTS—Messrs. Stilwell.

NOTT. (COMMANDER, 1846.)

EDWARD BUNBURY NOTT entered the Navy 17 June, 1815; passed his examination in 1821; and obtained his first commission 12 May, 1829. His succeeding appointments were—in the course of the latter year, to the SYBILLE 48, Capt. Fras. Augustus Collier, on the coast of Africa, whence he returned in 1830—16 Nov. 1832, to the Coast Guard, which service he left in the spring of 1835, but rejoined 15 June, 1838—18 Aug. 1841, as Senior, to the SIREN 16, Capt. Wm. Smith (*b*), under whom he was for three years employed in the East Indies —and, 4 March, 1845, in a similar capacity, to the CANOPUS 84, Capt. Fairfax Moresby, attached to the force on the Home station. He attained his present rank 8 June, 1846; and, since 6 Feb. 1847, has been officiating as an Inspecting-Commander in the Coast Guard.

Commander Nott married, in Oct. 1829, at St.

Helena, Sarah Elizabeth, eldest daughter of Thos. Reid, Esq. Agents—Goode and Lawrence.

NOTT. (Captain, 1842.)

John Neale Nott, born in 1800, at Reading, co. Berks, is eldest son of the Rev. Edw. Nott, more than a quarter of a century Rector of Weeke, co. Hants; and grandson of Capt. John Neale Pleydell Nott, who fell in command of the Centaur 74 in an action between Sir Sam. Hood's squadron and the French fleet in the West Indies, 29 April, 1781.

This officer entered the Navy, in Oct. 1812, as Fst.-cl. Vol., on board the San Josef 110, Capt. Robt. Jackson, in which ship and the Queen Charlotte 100, each bearing the flag of Lord Keith in the Channel, he served until Aug. 1814. Between that period and 1820, in Aug. of which year he passed his examination, we find him employed on the Brazilian, East India, Home, and Mediterranean stations, in the Duncan and Cornwallis 74's, flag-ships of Sir John Poo Beresford and Sir Geo. Burlton, Tyne 24, Capt. John Allen, Theban 36, Capt. Sam. Leslie, Rivoli 74, Capt. Chas. Ogle, and Racehorse 18, Capt. Hon. Geo. Pryse Campbell. After a further attachment, latterly in the West Indies, to the Active 46, Capts. Sir Jas. Alex. Gordon and Andrew King, and Valorous 28, Capt. the Earl of Huntingdon, he was promoted, 25 Aug. 1826, to the rank of Lieutenant, and next, 16 April, 1832, and 18 Dec. 1833, appointed to the Excellent gunnery-ship at Portsmouth, Capt. Thos. Hastings, and Edinburgh 74, Capt. Jas. Rich. Dacres. On the paying off of the last-mentioned ship Mr. Nott, having been three years her Gunnery-Lieutenant in the Mediterranean, was presented with a second promotal commission bearing date 10 Jan. 1837. He subsequently obtained command—14 Feb. 1838, of the Medea steamer, in which vessel he served in the river St. Lawrence and on other parts of the North American station until paid off in Nov. 1839—7 Aug. 1840, as Second Captain, of the Excellent, Capt. Sir Thos. Hastings, employed as before at Portsmouth—and, 1 Jan. 1842 (with his name on the books of the William and Mary yacht), of the Firebrand (now the Black Eagle) steam-yacht. In the latter vessel, which he left in the following month, he conveyed the King of Prussia from Ostend to England, and again from England to Ostend. He was advanced in consequence to Post rank by commission dated 28 Jan. 1842. From 18 Aug. 1845 until Nov. 1847 he was variously employed in the Trafalgar 120, part of the time as Flag-Captain to Sir Edw. Durnford King at Sheerness. He is now on half-pay.

Capt. Nott married, first, in May, 1827, Elizabeth Anne Bennet, eldest daughter of the late Thos. Calley, Esq., M.P., of Burderop Park and Overton House, Wilts, a Magistrate and Deputy-Lieutenant for that county; and, that lady dying three months afterwards, secondly, 18 Feb. 1840, Mary, eldest daughter of Sir Wm. Burnett, Kt., M.D., K.C.H., F.R.S., Director-General of the Medical Department of the Navy. Agents—Goode and Lawrence.

NOTT. (Commander, 1846. f-p., 17; h-p., 29.)

John Thomas Nott entered the Navy, 23 Jan. 1801, as Fst.-cl. Vol., on board the Clyde 38, Capt. Chas. Cunningham, attached to the force in the Channel. In the course of 1802 (he had previously attained the rating of Midshipman) he successively joined the Achille 74, Capts. Edw. Buller and John Okes Hardy, and Rosario sloop, Capt. Wm. Mounsey; and he was next, between April, 1803, and June, 1807, employed in the Channel and off Cadiz and Ferrol in the Malta 84, Capt. Edw. Buller, under whom he bore a warm part in Sir Robt. Calder's action with the combined fleets of France and Spain, 22 July, 1805. After a servitude of 15 months in the Mediterranean on board the Queen 98, flag-ship of Real-Admiral Geo. Martin, he proceeded, towards the close of 1808, to the West Indies in the Subtle, Lieut.-Commander Chas. Brown, and on his arrival on that station was nominated, first in Jan. 1809, and then in the ensuing Dec., Acting-Lieutenant of the Port d'Espagne and Curieux sloops, Capts. Alex. Kennedy, Sam. Geo. Pechell, and Colin Campbell In the Port d'Espagne he assisted, we believe, at the reduction of Martinique. Being confirmed, 18 Oct. 1810, into the Perlen 38, Capts. Norborne Thompson, Joseph Swabey Tetley, and John Allen, he was in that vessel, off Toulon, when she effected, 22 Nov. 1811, a gallant escape from a French line-of-battle ship and frigate with whom she had for several hours endured a close running fight. In 1812-13-14 we find him employed on the Mediterranean and North American stations in the Thames 32, Capt. Chas. Napier, Pilot 18, Capt. John Toup Nicholas, Ocean 98, Capt. Robt. Plampin, and Iphigenia 36, Capt. Andrew King. In the Pilot he was present, 14 May, 1812, in an attack made, in company with the Thames, on the port of Sapri, where a strong battery and tower, mounting two 32-pounders, were surrendered at discretion, after having been battered for two hours within pistol-shot. From 8 Dec. 1841 until the spring of 1843, and from 7 Sept. in the latter year until the close of 1845, Lieut. Nott commanded the Partridge 10, and Lynx brigantine—the former in South America, the latter on particular service. He was advanced to the rank he now holds 9 Nov. 1846.

NOURSE. (Lieutenant, 1841.)

Joseph Nourse entered the Navy 3 Jan. 1825; passed his examination 2 Jan. 1832; and, at the period of his promotion to the rank of Lieutenant 23 Nov. 1841, was serving at the Cape of Good Hope in the Southampton 50, flag-ship of Sir Edw. Durnford King. His succeeding appointments were —3 Dec. following, again to the Southampton, in the capacity of Additional-Lieutenant—8 Feb. 1842, to the command, which he retained for 12 months, of the Fawn brigantine, on the Cape station—6 Feb. 1845, to the Rodney 92, Capt. Edw. Collier, fitting at Portsmouth—and, 6 May following, to the Rattler steam-sloop, Capts. Henry Smith (*b*) and Rich. Moorman, with whom he was for two years employed on Home service, the greater part of the time as First-Lieutenant. Agents—Messrs. Ommanney.

NOWELL. (Lieut., 1812. f-p., 14; h-p., 30.)

William Nowell was born 20 Sept. 1788.

This officer entered the Navy, 25 March, 1803, as L.M., on board the Prince Frederick, Lieut.-Commander Sam. Gordon, lying at Plymouth, where he attained the rating of Midshipman in Feb. 1804, and continued until transferred, in July, 1805, to the Captain 74, Capt. Geo. Hopewell Stephens. In that ship he witnessed, 22 Aug. following, Admiral Hon. Wm. Cornwallis' pursuit of the French fleet into Brest, and was on one occasion very nearly lost. After cruizing for 12 months with Capts. Wm. Lukin and Willoughby Thos. Lake in the Gibraltar 80, he joined, in Feb. 1807, the Sprightly cutter, in which vessel (part of the force engaged in the expedition of 1809 to the Walcheren) and in the Dwarf, of 10 guns, he was for four years employed in the Channel and Downs, again under the orders of Lieut. Gordon. In the summer of 1808, during a dead calm and thick hazy weather, he contrived, in the Sprightly's small boats, with only four hands, to recapture the American brig *Washington*, laden with a valuable cargo, although in tow, at the moment he boarded her, of a French lugger privateer, rowing 13 sweeps on each side. The next day he carried his prize in safety into Dartmouth harbour. In 1811, after his name had been borne for a short period as a Supernumerary on the books of the Princess Caroline, Royal William, and Despatch, he joined the Milford 74, bearing the flag of Sir Rich. Goodwin Keats at the defence of Cadiz; where, in the Devastation and Thunder bombs, Capts. Taylor and Watkin Owen Pell, and in command of gun-boats Nos. 1 and 12, he remained until Nov. 1812. He then (he had been promoted to the rank of Lieutenant on 21 of the preceding March) took a passage in the BRISTOL 50, *armée-en-flûte*, Capt. John Thompson, for the purpose of joining the BARFLEUR 98, Capt. Sir Edw. Berry, off Toulon. During a subsequent cruize off the coast of Catalonia as Supernumerary-Lieutenant of the POMPÉE 74, Capt Sir Jas. Athol Wood, we find him detached in command of a tender. On 13 March, 1813, having removed to the SCIPION 74, Capt. Henry Heathcote, he took command of the launch belonging to that ship, and had the good fortune to rescue H.M. gun-brig CONFOUNDER from what had appeared inevitable destruction. Before, however, he had had time to regain his own vessel he was driven in a squall to sea, where he remained four days and three nights without either provisions or water. In the end he was picked up by a merchantman, and carried into Port Mahon, but so great had been the sufferings undergone, that 8 of his crew died from the effects. As to himself, he ultimately lost the sight of the right eye, and was injured in the other to an extent that he has ever since continued to feel. He was afterwards present in the SCIPION in the partial action fought with the French fleet off Toulon, and in Nov. 1814 was paid off. His last appointments were, in 1823-4, to the OCEAN 80, Capt. Lucius Ferdinand Hardyman, BRITANNIA 120, flag-ship of Sir Jas. Saumarez, and WINDSOR CASTLE 74, Capts. Hugh Downman and Edw. Durnford King, all stationed at Plymouth, where, in July, 1825, he was superseded at his own request.

Lieut. Nowell married, 27 June, 1816, Mary Ann Sutherland, eldest daughter of the late Mr. A. Vine, of Stonehouse, Devon, and sister of the late Lieut. Wm. Vine, R.N. (1812), of Darland, near Chatham, co. Kent. By that lady he has issue nine children.

NOWELL. (LIEUTENANT, 1828.)

WILLIAM CALMADY NOWELL entered the Navy 5 Feb. 1813; passed his examination in 1820; and obtained his commission 8 Aug. 1828. His appointments have since been—15 March, 1831, to the PALLAS 42, Capts. Manley Hall Dixon and Wm. Walpole, fitting for the West Indies, whence he returned to England and was paid off in 1834—13 Oct. 1836, to the VANGUARD 80, Capts. Hon. Duncombe Pleydell Bouverie and Sir Thos. Fellowes, under whom he was for upwards of three years and a half employed in the Mediterranean—14 Jan. 1841, to the POWERFUL 84, Capts. Geo. Mansel and Michael Seymour, on the same station—and, 16 March, 1842, and 15 April, 1844, as Senior-Lieutenant, to the FORMIDABLE 84 and QUEEN 110, commanded, also in the Mediterranean, by Capt. Sir Chas. Sullivan. He was paid off from the QUEEN in the summer of the latter year; and he has been in command, since 9 Oct. 1847, of the ARDENT steam-sloop of 200 horse-power, again on the station last named.

He married, 9 April, 1839, at Malta, Catanna, daughter of the Marquis of Testaferrata.

NUGENT. (COMMANDER, 1841. F-P., 48; H-P., 6.)

JOHN NUGENT, born in March, 1782, is second son of the late Jas. Nugent, of Ballynacorr, co. Westmeath, a Count of the Germanic or Holy Roman Empire, by his second wife, Matilda, daughter of Con O'Donel, Esq., of Larkfield, co. Leitrim, and neice, maternally, of Sir Neale O'Donnel, Bart. One of his brothers, Constantine, a Lieutenant in the 64th Regt. of Foot, was wounded at the capture of the Virgin Islands in 1801, and died soon afterwards at St. Christopher's; and another, Thos. D'Alton, entering the Austrian service in 1819, under the auspices of his kinsman, Field-Marshal Prince Nugent, as Lieutenant in the 4th Imperial Guards, became a Captain in Prince Nugent's own Regiment of Foot. The eminent family to which Commander Nugent belongs is closely connected with most of the chief houses in Ireland, and in its history is identified with the principal events in the annals of that country. His father's first wife was a niece of the Marchioness of Buckingham and of Robt. Nugent Lord Clare; and he had inherited his title in right of his mother, a sister of Christopher, Count D'Alton, Field-Marshal in the service of Austria. Commander Nugent is uncle of the present Count Nugent.

This officer entered the Navy, 25 April, 1793, as Captain's Servant, on board the RAISONNABLE 64, Capt. Lord Cranstoun; and in the following month joined the INVINCIBLE 74, commanded at first by his patron, Capt. Hon. Thos. Pakenham, and next by Capt. Lawrence Wm. Halsted. In the course of the same year he assisted at the destruction of a convoy under the batteries at Barfleur; he was present, in 1794, in Lord Howe's actions of 28 and 29 May and 1 June; and, in 1795, after participating in Lord Bridport's action, he accompanied an expedition sent to co-operate with the Royalists in Quiberon Bay. Between Oct. in the latter year and Oct. 1799 he became in succession attached, chiefly in the capacity of Midshipman, to the JUSTE 80, Capts. Hon. T. Pakenham, John Lawford, and Wm. Hancock Kelly, LATONA 38, Capt. Hon. Arthur Kaye Legge, PRINCESS ROYAL 98, flag-ship of Rear-Admirals Sir John Orde and Thos. Lennox Frederick, and VILLE DE PARIS 110 and QUEEN CHARLOTTE 100, bearing the flags of Earl St. Vincent and Lord Keith. In the boats of the PRINCESS ROYAL we find him frequently engaged with the enemy's gun-boats off Cadiz; and in the VILLE DE PARIS present as Signal-Midshipman at the capture, 19 June, 1799, of Rear-Admiral Perrée's squadron of three frigates and two brigs. We may here observe that he had been appointed Signal-Midshipman of the latter ship on promotion by Lord St. Vincent as a reward for the promptitude with which on a certain occasion he had repeated that nobleman's signals in the PRINCESS ROYAL. During the term of his servitude in the QUEEN CHARLOTTE Mr. Nugent was often employed in the boats under Lord Cochrane in action with Spanish gun-vessels; and he was in her when the combined fleets of France and Spain were pursued into Brest. Towards the close of 1799 he was invested with the rank of Acting-Lieutenant and the command of the WELKIN gun-boat. In that vessel he succeeded soon afterwards in recapturing a Danish brig from two French privateers, under the batteries of Ceuta, and behaved in a manner so extremely gallant that his conduct was reported to Lord Keith in the most flattering manner by Capt. Jas. Newman Newman of the LOIRE frigate, an eyewitness of the exploit, in which, it must be added, Mr. Nugent was slightly wounded. Being confirmed in the rank of Lieutenant by commission dated 15 Jan. 1800, he was successively appointed in that capacity—14 Sept. following, for two years, to the PHŒNIX 36, Capt. Lawrence Wm. Halsted—between Aug. 1803 and March, 1805, to the command of the TRIAL, STAG, INDUSTRY, FOX, and NILE cutters—on 1 of the month last mentioned, to the AGINCOURT 64, Capt. Thos. Briggs—13 July, 1805, to the command, which he retained for nine years, of the STRENUOUS brig of 14 guns—and 4 Nov. 1814, as First, to the CORNWALLIS 74. In the PHŒNIX, besides commanding her boats, in conjunction with the present Admiral Christian, at the cutting out of several vessels under a battery near Piombino, he accompanied the expedition of 1801 to Egypt, and assisted at the capture, 3 Aug. and 2 Sept. in that year, of the French frigates *Carrère*, *Succès*, and *Bravoure*. During his command of the FOX and NILE he effected several recaptures, drove on shore and destroyed three lugger privateers, and was slightly wounded while cutting out a richly-laden vessel from under the batteries at Dieppe. In the STRENUOUS Lieut. Nugent performed many dashing services. On 12 Oct. 1806 he took part in an action of an hour and a quarter, fought in the Bay of Erqui, between a British squadron, consisting, with the STRENUOUS, of the CONSTANCE 22, SHELDRAKE 16, and BRITANNIA cutter, on the one hand, and, on the other, of the *Salamandre* of 26 guns and 80 men, a 2-gun battery planted on a hill, and one or two field-pieces, together with a few troops on the beach; the result whereof was the surrender of the enemy's ship, after a loss to herself of about 29 men killed, independently of several wounded, and to the British of 10 killed and 23 wounded. The letter which apprized the Admiralty of the achievement we have here detailed also bore testimony to the zeal and bravery of Lieut. Nugent, declaring him, on the present, as well as on former occasions, to have shown himself a gallant and anxious officer.* In the following year he retook the *Lord Middleton*, a rich West Indiaman, and another vessel, the *Fame*, of Dublin, and, after a long chase, drove on shore, on the Ile de Bas, the French schooner privateer *Étoile*, by whom the two former had been originally captured. In 1808 the Lieutenant performed a very neat exploit. A French frigate being in the act of fitting out at St. Maloes, he disguised his brig and stood into that harbour. Shortly after he had entered it he was approached by a cutter, rowing 12 oars, under the orders of the First-Lieutenant. Of this boat, and of all who were in her, he took instant possession; he then poured three broadsides into the frigate; and before either she or the batteries could bring a gun to bear upon him he was off and again at sea. In 1809 he brought out a vessel laden with oak timber from under the batteries at Cherbourg. On the next night, while engaged in a similar affair, he had several men killed and wounded in his boats; and on the following morning he captured a valuable American brig. In Sept. of the same year he made prize, off the Naze, of the *Dorothea Catharina* Danish privateer, of 6 guns and 35 men. He subsequently, in 1810, chased the French brig-of-war *Le Cygne* into Cherbourg, seizing, simultaneously, one of her boats, commanded by a Lieutenant; and, on 10 Aug. in that year, he attacked and drove on the rocks, on the coast of Norway, although under the protection of a three-masted schooner and another armed vessel, a convoy of 10 sail, two of which his boats succeeded in bringing off.† A few weeks afterwards he chased on shore and destroyed, on different occasions, the Danish privateers *Aelbergh* of 8 guns and 30 men, and *Popham* of 3 guns and 10 men, together with the *Troforte*, a brig laden with rye and barley.‡ Independently of many other affairs equally creditable to his zeal and activity, we find him, in 1813, capturing another privateer (the *Dansbergh* of 4 guns and 24 men §), driving three gun-boats on shore, and recapturing and destroying a Swedish galliot frozen up at Carlscrona. We are informed that he also assisted in reducing the Danish island of Udsire. On becoming, as above, First-Lieutenant of the CORNWALLIS, Mr. Nugent fitted that ship for the flag of Sir Geo. Burlton; finding then, however, that the Admiral intended taking a follower and an officer junior to him in rank as his First-Lieutenant, he resigned his appointment, but had the satisfaction, in doing so, of receiving very high testimonials as well from Sir Geo. Burlton himself as from the Flag-Captain. He next, 22 Nov. 1816, obtained command of the GREYHOUND Revenue-cruizer; in which vessel, during the three years and upwards that he continued in her, he made an unprecedented number of seizures. Since 11 Oct. 1823 he has been employed under the Treasury as an Inspecting-Commander of the Coast Guard in the North-West district of Ireland. Notwithstanding the long train of valuable services we have above recorded, added to others performed in the situation he at present fills, he was not advanced to the rank of Commander until 23 Nov. 1841!

We may add that, when in the STRENUOUS in 1807, Commander Nugent jumped overboard in the Race of Alderney and saved the life of a Gunner's Mate, Mr. Jas. Sinnott. In 1818 he rescued the lives of a Coast Guard crew and also of two excisemen; and in 1827 he saved, in co. Mayo, the lives of the crew of the *Maria* of Galway. On two occasions, when in the GREYHOUND, it fell to his lot to be desperately assaulted and beaten by smugglers—once at Hastings in Sussex, and once at Portland in Dorset. Although reduced in each instance to the necessity of being long under medical treatment, he never received the least compensation. His humane exertions in the cause of others, however, have been acknowledged by the presentation to him of a medal and several small pieces of plate. A sword, during the war, was voted to him by the Patriotic Society in consideration of his wounds. AGENTS—Burnett and Holmes.

* *Vide* Gaz. 1806, p. 1364.—In the preceding month he had assisted, in company with the CONSTANCE and SHARPSHOOTER gun-brig, in driving the *Salamandre* on shore, and by his exertions had excited (*Vide* Gaz. 1806, p. 1235) the highest approbation of Sir James Saumarez.

† *V.* Gaz. 1810, p. 1285. ‡ *V.* Gaz. 1810, p. 1582. § *V.* Gaz. 1813, p. 2406.

O.

OAKE. (CAPTAIN, 1846. F-P., 22; H-P., 19.)

JOSIAH OAKE entered the Navy, 14 July, 1806, as Fst.-cl. Vol., on board the SAMPSON 64, Capt. Wm. Cuming, in which ship and the DIADEM, of similar force, he continued employed in South America (where he witnessed the capture of Maldonado and Monte Video) and at the Cape of Good Hope until the spring of 1808—the latter part of the time in the capacity of Midshipman. He then joined the SALVADOR DEL MUNDO, flag-ship at Plymouth of Admiral Young; and next, in Dec. 1808, July 1810, and May 1811, the BELLEROPHON 74, Capt. Sam. Warren, CORMORANT, Master-Commander Josiah Oake, and AIGLE 36, Capt. Sir John Louis. In those ships he served on the Baltic, Lisbon, Mediterranean, and West India stations for a period of six years and a half. He assisted, in the AIGLE, at the capture and destruction of a French convoy under the guns of Porto Maurizio, 11 April, 1814. In March, 1815, he took up a commission bearing date 2 of the preceding March; and he was subsequently, 23 Jan. 1821 and 10 Feb. 1825, appointed to the ADVENTURE surveying-vessel, and ZEBRA 18, Capts. Wm. Henry Smyth and Edw. Rich. Williams, both in the Mediterranean. Being awarded a second promotal commission 28 April, 1827, he served as an Inspecting-Commander in the Coast Guard from 24 June, 1836, until the summer of 1839, and in command, on the coast of Africa, of the FERRET 6, from 1 Dec. 1841 until 1845. He attained his present rank 9 Nov. 1846. AGENTS—Hallett and Robinson.

OAKELEY (LIEUTENANT, 1843.)

HENRY OAKELEY is fifth son of the late Rev. Herbert Oakeley, D.D., of Oakeley, Salop, Rector of Lydham, and Prebendary of Worcester.

This officer entered the Navy 6 Nov. 1830; passed his examination in 1837; obtained his commission 4 Oct. 1843; and from 2 May, 1844, until paid off in 1847, served on the coast of Africa in the CYGNET 6, Capts. Henry Layton, Fred. Wilmot Horton, and Fred. Byng Montresor.

He married, 1 June, 1847, Emily Letitia, third daughter of the late Colonel Hamelin Trelawny, R.A., and niece of Sir Wm. Lewis Salusbury Trelawny, Bart.

OAKES. (COMMANDER, 1828. F-P., 14; H-P., 20.)

ORBELL OAKES, born in 1800, is second son of the late Orbell Ray Oakes, Esq., of Nowton Court, a Magistrate and Deputy-Lieutenant for co. Suffolk, and a Magistrate for Bury St. Edmunds, by Elizabeth Francis, daughter of John Plampin, Esq., of Chadacre Hall, Simpling. His youngest sister, now deceased, married Lieut.-Colonel Astley, of the Royal Engineers.

This officer entered the Navy, 6 Aug. 1813, as Fst.-cl. Vol., on board the BOYNE 98, Capt. Geo. Burlton, stationed in the Mediterranean; where, in the following month, he removed to the OCEAN 98, Capt. Robt. Plampin. From July, 1814, until Jan. 1820, he served at Plymouth, and on the Irish, Newfoundland, and St. Helena stations, in the SALVADOR DEL MUNDO, Capt. Robt. Hall, TIBER 38,

Capt. Jas. Rich. Dacres, and CONQUEROR 74, bearing the flag of Rear-Admiral Plampin. He was then nominated Acting-Lieutenant of the ROSARIO 10, Capt. Wm. Hendry; from which vessel, in three months, he returned in a similar capacity to the CONQUEROR. Being confirmed by commission dated 14 Oct. 1820, he was next, from 15 March, 1825, until advanced to his present rank 19 May, 1828, employed in the TWEED and SEMIRAMIS frigates, as Flag-Lieutenant to Rear-Admiral Plampin at Cork. On 28 March, 1839, he received an appointment to the Coast Guard. He left that service in the spring of 1841; but since 31 March, 1845, has again been engaged in it.

Commander Oakes married, at Florence, 3 March, 1832, Caroline, youngest daughter of Wm. Bryan, Esq. AGENTS—Goode and Lawrence.

O'BRIEN. (LIEUT., 1807. F-P., 17; H-P., 32.)

ANDREW O'BRIEN entered the Navy, 10 March, 1798, as a Boy, on board the ROMNEY 50, Capt. John Lawford; and in the summer of the same year was present at the detention of a large convoy laden with naval and military stores for France, and under the protection of a Swedish frigate. After accompanying the expedition against the Helder, and witnessing the surrender of Rear-Admiral Story's squadron, he followed Capt. Lawford, as Midshipman, in Aug. 1800, into the POLYPHEMUS 64, which ship formed part of Lord Nelson's division in the attack upon the Danish line of defence before Copenhagen, 2 April, 1801. In the course of 1803 he became in succession attached to the ACHILLE and COURAGEUX 74's, both commanded, the latter in the West Indies, by Capt. John Okes Hardy; and he next, between 1803 and the close of 1807, served, principally on the Home station, in the BRITANNIA 100, Captain (afterwards Rear-Admiral) the Earl of Northesk, AVON sloop, Capt. Fras. Jackson Snell, and AUDACIOUS 74, Capts. John Lawford and Thos. Le Marchant Gosselin. Of the latter ship he was created a Lieutenant 25 April, 1807. His succeeding appointments were—24 Dec. in that year, to the RACEHORSE 18, stationed at first off Guernsey, and then at the Cape of Good Hope, whence he invalided in July, 1810—6 March, 1811, for a few weeks, to the RECRUIT sloop, Capt. Humphrey Fleming Senhouse, at Newfoundland—28 Sept. following, to the BRISK 16, Capt. Eyles Mounsher, on the Irish station—and, 28 June, 1813, to the FORTH 40, Capt. Sir Wm. Bolton, employed in the North Sea and North America. He returned to England in May, 1815; and has since been on half-pay.

O'BRIEN. (LIEUTENANT, 1840.)

CHARLES DOUGLAS O'BRIEN died about the commencement of 1846.

This officer entered the Navy 29 March, 1823; passed his examination in 1830; and, as a reward for his services during the operations on the coast of Syria, was promoted to the rank of Lieutenant 4 Nov. 1840. His succeeding appointments were—15 Dec. 1840, 13 Sept. 1841, and 17 Oct. 1842, to the BENBOW 72, CAMBRIDGE 78, and RODNEY 92, Capts. Houston Stewart, Edw. Barnard, and Robt. Maunsell, all in the Mediterranean—1 Feb. 1844, to the Coast Guard—11 Dec. following, as Additional-Lieutenant, to the CALEDONIA 120, flag-ship of Sir David Milne at Devonport—and 11 Jan. and 6 May, 1845, to the RANGER 6, and PROMETHEUS steam-sloop, Capts. Jas. Anderson and John Hay, both on the coast of Africa, where he continued employed as First-Lieutenant of the latter vessel until the period of his death.

O'BRIEN. (CAPTAIN, 1821. F-P., 20; H-P., 31.)

DONAT HENCHY O'BRIEN was born in March, 1785. He is descended from one of the ancient monarchs of Ireland.

This officer entered the Navy, 16 Dec. 1796, as Ordinary, on board the OVERYSSEL 64, Capts. John Young and John Bazely, bearing the successive flags of Admirals Joseph Peyton and Skeffington Lutwidge on the Home station. Continuing in that ship until Jan. 1800, he accompanied, in the capacity of Master's Mate, the expedition of 1799 against the Helder, where, in command of a flat-bottomed boat, he assisted at the landing of the army. After this he was placed in charge of a merchantman laden with Portland stone, intended to be sunk, with others, at the entrance of Goree harbour, for the purpose of preventing the egress of three Dutch line-of-battle ships. Before, however, an opportunity had presented itself for the execution of the plan, the vessel was caught in a gale of wind and went down, three minutes only after Mr. O'Brien had been rescued from his perilous situation through the intrepid humanity of a boat's crew belonging to the LION armed-cutter under the orders of Lieut. Tatham. In Jan. 1800, as above mentioned, he was directed to act as Lieutenant of the ATALANTE 16, Capt. Anselm John Griffiths, in which sloop, owing to the absence of her own Lieutenant, and of the Master, Boatswain, and Gunner, he was for three months most harassingly employed off the Flemish banks, Dunkerque, and Gravelines, being, during the whole of that period, compelled, with the present Capt. Jas. Couch, to keep six hours' alternate watch. He then went back to the OVERYSSEL; and he next, in Dec. 1801, Feb. 1802, and Feb. 1803 (in the course of which month he passed his examination), became in succession attached, again as Master's Mate, to the BERSCHERMER 54, Capt. Alex. Fraser, AMPHION 32, Capts. Rich. Henry Alex. Bennett, Alex. Fraser, and Thos. Masterman Hardy, and HUSSAR 38, Capt. Philip Wilkinson. In the latter frigate it was his lot, during a passage home with despatches from Ferrol, to be wrecked, 8 Feb. 1804, on the southernmost part of the Saintes; a misfortune which in a few days rendered him a prisoner to the French at Brest. After three attempts at escape, which had entailed on him privations and hardships not to be imagined, and had all ended in his re-capture, he at length, 14 Sept. 1808, succeeded in effecting a flight, truly wonderful in its history, from the famed fortress of Bitche.* Reaching Trieste in the following Nov., he contrived, with two friends (one of them the present Lieut. Maurice Hewson), to get on board a boat belonging to the AMPHION 32, Capt. Wm. Hoste, which had been sent inshore on the look-out under the command of Lieut. Geo. Matthew Jones. Under that officer, before his return to the frigate, we find him afforded an opportunity of participating in a desperate attack on two powerful vessels, whose successful resistance killed 2 and wounded 5 of the British, including himself severely through the right arm. Proceeding soon to Malta in H.M. brig SPIDER, he was there received on board the OCEAN 98, flag-ship of Lord Collingwood, who promoted him, 29 March, 1809, to a Lieutenancy in the WARRIOR 74, Capt. John Wm. Spranger. After assisting at the reduction of the islands of Ischia and Procida, and of those of Zante, Cephalonia, Ithaca, and Cerigo, he again, in March, 1810, joined the AMPHION, still commanded by Capt. Hoste. On 29 of the ensuing June, with the boats of the latter frigate and the CERBERUS under his orders, he covered the landing of a body of seamen and marines commanded by Lieut. Wm. Slaughter, near the town of Grao, where the gallantry and exertion of the British enabled them to defeat a numerous body of French troops, and to effect the capture and destruction of a large convoy laden with naval stores for the arsenal at Venice.† Besides many other dashing services, Mr. O'Brien was subsequently, 13 March, 1811, present, as Second-Lieutenant of the AMPHION, in the celebrated action

* We are relieved, even had we space, from the necessity of entering at large into the history of Capt. O'Brien's captivity, it being already familiar to the public through the medium of the 'Narrative,' &c., published by him in 1814, and re-produced in 1839, in two volumes, under the title of 'My Adventures during the late War; comprising a Narrative of Shipwreck, Captivity, Escapes from French Prisons, &c., from 1804 to 1827.'

† *Vide* Gaz. 1810, p. 1857.

fought off Lissa; on which occasion a British squadron, carrying in the whole 156 guns and 879 men, completely routed, after a battle of six hours and a loss to the above ship of 15 men killed and 47 wounded, a Franco-Venetian armament, whose force amounted to 284 guns and 2655 men. On the victory being accomplished he was sent to Malta in charge of *La Bellona*, one of the captured French frigates. Accompanying Capt. Hoste as his First-Lieutenant, in Nov. 1811, into the BACCHANTE 38, he continued, in that frigate also, to share in a great variety of service in the Adriatic. On the night of 31 Aug. 1812, having been detached in command of the boats, he cut out from the port of Lema seven vessels laden with ship-timber for the Venetian government, together with *La Tisiphone* French national xebec, of 1 6-pounder, 2 3-pounders, and 28 men, one gun-boat, with a 9-pounder, 2 3-pounders, and 24 men, and another of 1 9-pounder and 20 men, intended for the protection of the trade on the coast of Istria, from Pola to Trieste. This service was fortunately executed without any loss, owing chiefly to the arrangements of Lieut. O'Brien, the gallantry and promptitude with which he led the boats to the attack, and the brave and determined support he received from those under his orders.* On 18 of the ensuing Sept. he was again sent, with the boats, six in number, containing 72 officers and men, to effect the capture of eight armed-vessels, carrying in the whole 8 long 12-pounders, 6 swivels, and 104 men, and a convoy of 18 sail, laden chiefly with oil and almonds, which the BACCHANTE had chased between Tremiti and Vasto on the coast of Apulia. Leading to the attack with his accustomed valour, Lieut. O'Brien's fearless exertions were again crowned with success; the enemy, notwithstanding a heavy fire of grape and musketry, were impetuously assailed, and driven in every direction from their vessels; while a party of marines, under Lieut. Wm. Haig, landing, forced the fugitives from a neighbouring wood, and thereby gave the *coup-de-grace* to the affair. "I want words," says Capt. Hoste in his report to Rear-Admiral Fremantle, "to convey to you my admiration of the determined manner in which this service was performed."† Its brave conductor was in consequence promoted to the rank of Commander 22 Jan. 1813; but before the receipt of his commission he appears to have been concerned in the achievement of two other exploits deserving of notice; the first in Nov. 1812, when, with the boats of the BACCHANTE, and EAGLE and ACHILLE 74's, he brought off a large quantity of government oak-timber from the beach near Fesano, a small town in the vicinity of Pola, in face of 300 soldiers; and the second in Jan. 1813, on 6 of which month his prompt and judicious measures enabled him, after a good deal of firing and much resistance, to board, near Otranto, a gun-boat carrying 2 pivot-guns and 36 men, and then to pursue and capture two other vessels of a similar description.‡ In April, 1813, Capt. O'Brien left the BACCHANTE, receiving at the same time, for the cordial co-operation he had at all times afforded, the sincere and public thanks of Capt. Hoste, who availed himself of the opportunity of proclaiming "that his promotion, as it had been gained entirely by his own exertions, unassisted by interest, held to the remaining officers a striking example that meritorious service would meet its own reward." He shortly afterwards returned to England a passenger in the THUNDER bomb, Capt. Watkin Owen Pell; but it was not until 1818 that he again succeeded in procuring employment. Obtaining command, in Aug. of that year, of the SLANEY 20, he sailed in the ensuing Dec. for the South American station, and in May, 1819, he reached Valparaiso. During his stay in the Pacific, a period of more than 12 months, it was Capt. O'Brien's fortune to render many essential services to British commerce on the coasts of Chili and Peru. On his subsequent arrival in the Rio de la Plata, we find him hoisting for a short time the broad pendant of Sir Thos. Masterman Hardy; by whom, on his departure on service round Cape Horn, he was left Senior officer at Buenos Ayres. This happened at a very critical period, just as the latter state had been involved in war with the neighbouring provinces; and Capt. O'Brien had in consequence many harassing and perplexing duties to perform. One result, we may here observe, of the opening hostilities had been a manifesto published by the Buenos Ayrean government for the purpose of compelling all the British residents to organize themselves into a regiment. This measure, attended as it was likely to be with a large sacrifice of property, demanded of course strenuous opposition on the part of Capt. O'Brien; who, after a long and painful discussion, succeeded in extracting from the authorities a document, exempting every British resident from being drawn for military service, or in any way required to act hostilely against its recently-declared enemies. In Oct. 1821, having been advanced to Post-rank on 5 of the preceding March, he was superseded in the command of the SLANEY. He took a passage home in the OWEN GLENDOWER frigate, and has not been since able to procure employment.

* *Vide* Gaz. 1813, p. 163. † *V.* Gaz. 1813, p. 164. ‡ *V.* Gaz. 1813, p. 627.

Capt. O'Brien married, 28 June, 1825, Hannah, youngest daughter of the late John Walmsley, Esq., of Castle-Meer, in Lancashire, and sister of Geo. Walmsley, Esq., of Bolesworth Castle, co. Chester, by whom he has had issue seven children. AGENTS—Hallett and Robinson.

O'BRIEN. (CAPTAIN, 1829. F-P., 16; H-P., 24.)

JOSEPH O'BRIEN entered the Navy, 25 June, 1807, as Fst.-cl. Vol., on board the EDGAR 74, Capts. Jas. Macnamara and Stephen Poyntz, employed off Rochefort and in the Baltic and North Sea. In Aug. 1808 he was present, as Midshipman, at the embarkation of the Spanish troops under the Marquis de la Romana; and in March, 1810, he removed to the BERWICK 74, Capts. Jas. Macnamara, Sir Robt. Laurie, and Edw. Brace, stationed at first off Flushing and Cherbourg, and then in the Mediterranean. In the latter ship, of which he was created a Lieutenant 1 Oct. 1814, he witnessed the fall of Genoa, and was present in 1815 at the siege of Gaeta. While next attached, between July and Nov. 1816, to the IMPREGNABLE 98, also commanded by Capt. Brace, Mr. O'Brien fought under the flag of Rear-Admiral David Milne at the bombardment of Algiers. His succeeding appointments were, on the West India station—11 Dec. 1822, to the GLOUCESTER 74, bearing the broad pendant of Sir Edw. W. C. R. Owen—29 Dec. 1823, to the PYRAMUS 42, Capt. Fras. Newcombe—10 Oct. 1824, to the command of the RENEGADE schooner—and, 1 Nov. following, to the RATTLESNAKE 28, Capts. Hugh Patton and John Leith. He was advanced (from the ISIS 50, flag-ship of Sir Lawrence Wm. Halsted) to the command of the BEAVER sloop 3 May, 1826; and next appointed (still in the West Indies)—24 April, 1828, to the ESPIÈGLE 18—and, 5 Jan. 1829, to the SLANEY 20. Since his Post-promotion, which took place 8 Aug. in the latter year, the Captain has been on half-pay. AGENTS—Messrs. Halford and Co.

O'BRIEN. (LIEUT, 1838. F-P., 18; H-P., 8.)

ROBERT O'BRIEN, born 17 Aug. 1808, at Ardfry, co. Galway, is third son of Retired Rear-Admiral Robt. O'Brien (1837), of co. Clare, who commanded the DORIS 42, in the East Indies, at the close of the war, and died about Jan. 1838, at Cheltenham, by his first-cousin Anne O'Brien, herself a first-cousin of the present Earl of Charlemont. He is grandson of the late, and first-cousin of the present, Sir Lucius O'Brien, Bart., of Dromoland, co. Clare.

This officer entered the Royal Naval College 7 June, 1821; and embarked, in June, 1823, as Midshipman, on board the RANGER 28, Capt. Peter Fisher, employed at first in the Channel, and then in the Mediterranean. Between June, 1825, and March, 1828, in the course of which month he passed his examination, he served, on the South American station, in the DORIS 42, Capt. Sir John Gordon Sinclair, and JASEUR 18, Capt. Edw. Handfield; and he next, from June, 1828, until Oct. 1832, and from June, 1834, until he invalided in Sept. 1837, officiated as Mate, in the East Indies and Mediterranean, of the CROCODILE 28 and CHILDERS 18, Capts. John Wm. Montagu and Hon. Henry Keppel. His appointments, since his promotion to the rank of Lieutenant, which took place 28 June, 1838, have been—22 May, 1839, as Additional, to the WINCHESTER 50, fitting at Chatham for the flag of Sir Thos. Harvey—7 Sept. following, to the CROCODILE 26, Capt. Alex. Milne, on the North America and West India station, whence he invalided in Aug. 1840—26 May, 1841, to the BELLEISLE 72, Capt. John Toup Nicolas, which ship, in the following Oct., was paid off at Plymouth, where she had been for some time stationary—3 March, 1842, as Additional, for a few months, to the ILLUSTRIOUS 72, bearing the flag of Sir Chas. Adam in North America and the West Indies—and, 4 Sept. 1844, to the command, which he still retains, of a station in the Coast Guard.

In 1825 Lieut. O'Brien, then belonging to the DORIS, received the thanks of the Admiralty for his conduct in having saved the life of a man who had fallen overboard. During his servitude in the WINCHESTER he had the misfortune to dislocate his shoulder-joint, and also to receive much injury by a block falling on his head. AGENTS—Hallett and Robinson.

O'CALLAGHAN. (CAPTAIN, 1846. F-P., 16; H-P., 6.)

GEORGE WILLIAM DOUGLAS O'CALLAGHAN was born 15 Aug. 1811.

This officer entered the Navy, 28 May, 1825, as Fst.-cl. Vol., on board the CAMELION 10, Capts. Geo. Robt. Lambert and Mich. Seymour, stationed in the Channel. In July, 1826, he became Midshipman of the RAMILLIES 74, Capt. Hugh Pigot, lying in the Downs for the purposes of the Coast Blockade; and he was next, from Feb. 1827 until July, 1831, employed in the West Indies in the BARHAM 50, flag-ship of Hon. Chas. Elphinstone Fleeming, DRUID 46, Capt. Williams Sandom, GRASSHOPPER 18, Capt. Chas. Deare, and MERSEY 26, Capt. Geo. Wm. Conway Courtenay. Prior to his examination, which he passed 8 Sept. 1831, he served for a short period also in the ISIS 50, Capt. Geo. Rennie. In the early part of 1831 he sailed for the East Indies as Mate of the HARRIER 18, Capt. Spencer Lambert Hunter Vassall; in command of one of the boats belonging to which vessel we find him on two occasions engaged in attacks upon the Malay pirates. Being advanced to the rank of Lieutenant 6 June, 1834, and appointed, a few months afterwards, to the ANDROMACHE 28, Capt. Henry Ducie Chads, also on the East India station, he was slightly wounded, while in that frigate, in endeavouring to effect the suppression of piracy in the straits of Malacca, and for his services was presented, in common with the other officers employed, with a sword by the merchants, &c., of Bombay, besides receiving the thanks of the Admiralty and of the Chambers of Commerce at Calcutta and Madras. He returned to England in Sept. 1837; and was afterwards appointed, on the Mediterranean station—24 April, 1838, to the TALBOT 28, Capt. Henry John Codrington—25 Oct. following, to the ASIA 84, Capt. Wm. Fisher—29 Jan. 1839, as First, to the RHADAMANTHUS steamer, Capt. Arth. Wakefield, which vessel he left in July, 1840—and in June, 1841, in a similar capacity, to the IMPLACABLE 74, Capt. Edw. Harvey. He obtained a second promotal commission 11 Aug. 1841; and from 22 March, 1845, until advanced to his present rank, 30 Nov. 1846, had command of the VESUVIUS steam-sloop of 280 horse power on the North America and West India station. He has since been on half-pay.

Capt. O'Callaghan married, 25 Aug. 1840, Miss Harriet Graves Barton, and by that lady has issue. AGENTS—Messrs. Halford and Co.

O'CALLAGHAN. (LIEUTENANT, 1815.)

HENRY JOHN O'CALLAGHAN obtained his commission 25 Feb. 1815. He has since been on half-pay. AGENT—Frederick Dufaur.

O'CONNELL. (LIEUT., 1815. F-P., 21; H-P., 20.)

MAURICE FITZGERALD O'CONNELL entered the Navy, 1 Jan. 1806, as Fst.-cl. Vol., on board the AMETHYST 36, Capts. John Wm. Spranger and Mich. Seymour, on the Cork station; where, in the following Aug., he removed to the DRUID 32, Capts. Bennett, Hon. Donald Hugh Mackay, and Sir Wm. Bolton. In Nov. 1809, being at the time in the Bay of Biscay, he participated in an unsuccessful attack made by the boats of the latter frigate on two French national vessels; the result of which was the slaughter of two Lieutenants and several men, and the capture of himself and 20 others. Being retaken in a few days by the DRUID, he continued in that ship until Sept. 1810, when he followed Sir Wm. Bolton into the ENDYMION 40, a very active cruizer. Joining next, in May, 1812, the IRIS 36, Capt. Hood Hanway Christian, he served for some time in co-operation with the patriots on the north coast of Spain, where, among other places, he beheld the capture of Castro. On one occasion he was sent to assist in cutting out an American brig which had been chased into Vivero harbour. On the return of the party with their prize, a gale arose which caused two boats with 3 men to become detached, and drift towards an inaccessible rock. In this emergency Mr. O'Connell volunteered to go with another boat to their rescue, and in his humane efforts he happily succeeded. The gale, however, continuing, he was obliged to put into Vivero, and thence to travel with his men, 13 in number, overland to Corunna—10 weeks elapsing before he was enabled to rejoin his ship. During that period we find him serving (as Supernumerary of the LYRA 10, Capt. Robt. Bloye) in a battery at the defence of Castro, when attacked and stormed by a very superior French force. On leaving the IRIS in July, 1813, he rejoined Sir Wm. Bolton, as Master's Mate, on board the FORTH 40. In March, 1814, he was present in that ship when sent, with the ANTELOPE 50, Capt. Sam. Butcher, and a Russian frigate, to reinforce a squadron stationed in the West Scheldt. While in the act, for this purpose, of forcing the Hondt passage, the ANTELOPE unfortuately grounded within shell-range of Flushing; and in consequence he was at night ordered to assist in bringing several schuyts down the river to lighten her. When afterwards on the coast of North America he served at the blockade of New York, and was engaged at the attack and capture of an American brig chased into Egg harbour, an exploit in the achievement of which the First-Lieutenant of the FORTH was severely wounded. In Aug. 1815, having passed his examination at the commencement of 1812, Mr. O'Connell took up a commission bearing date 14 of the preceding Feb. He has been employed in the Coast Guard since 12 Jan. 1836.

He married Agnes, daughter of the late Geo. Gorham, Esq., of Obrennan, co. Kerry, by whom he has issue four sons and one daughter. AGENTS—Messrs. Halford and Co.

O'CONOR, K.C.H. (Captain, 1814. F-P., 14; H-P., 35.)

RICHARD O'CONOR is second son of the late Sir Pat. O'Conor, of Cork, by Miss Terry, of Castle Terry, in that co.

This officer entered the Navy, in Sept. 1798, as Fst.-cl. Vol., on board the DRYAD 36, Capt. Lord Amelius Beauclerk, employed on the Cork station, where, in 1799, he removed to the DORIS 36, Capt. Lord Ranelagh. In 1801 he again joined Lord Amelius Beauclerk, as Midshipman, on board the FORTUNÉE frigate, attached to the Channel fleet, with which he continued to serve, until Aug. 1805, in the PLANTAGENET and MAJESTIC 74's, Capts. Graham Eden Hamond and Lord A. Beauclerk, and HIBERNIA 110, flag-ship of Lord Gardner. He was then nominated Sub-Lieutenant of the ATTACK gun-brig; and on 1 Feb. 1806 he was made full Lieutenant into the CONFIANCE sloop, Capt. Jas. Lucas Yeo. After further serving in the ROYAL WILLIAM, flag-ship of Admiral Montagu at Spithead, in the THALIA 36, commanded on the Guernsey station by Capt. Jas. Walker, and for two years as Flag-Lieutenant to Sir Edm. Nagle in the ARDENT 64, at Leith, he was promoted, 17 Aug. 1810, to the rank of Commander. In 1813 we find him superintending the naval yards on the Canadian lakes; and on 6 May, 1814, performing, in the PRINCE REGENT, the duties of Flag-Captain to Commodore Sir Jas. Lucas Yeo at the capture of Oswego, where he was intrusted with the direction of the boats and gun-vessels employed in landing the troops.* In 1815, having been advanced to Post-rank 16 Aug. in the preceding year, he returned to England. He was nominated a K.C.H. 25 Jan. 1836; and accepted the Retirement 1 Oct. 1846.

Capt. O'Conor married Miss Hannah Ross, daughter of an eminent merchant and East India Director, by whom he has issue a son (an officer in the Hon. E. I. Co.'s service) and three daughters, the eldest of whom is married to a Swiss nobleman. AGENTS—Messrs. Ommanney.

* *Vide* Gaz. 1814, p. 1367.

OGILVIE. (LIEUT., 1812. F-P., 12; H-P., 31.)

HENRY OGILVIE was born 1 Sept. 1791.

This officer entered the Navy, 23 March, 1804, as Fst.-cl. Vol., on board the BACCHANTE 20, Capt. Chas. Dashwood, stationed in the Channel; he removed, in the following Aug., to the CANOPUS 80, bearing the flag of Rear-Admiral Geo. Campbell in the Mediterranean; and, from March, 1805, until Dec. 1810, he served on board the DONEGAL 94, Capt. Pulteney Malcolm. He accompanied Lord Nelson, in the latter ship, in his pursuit of the combined squadrons to the West Indies and back—participated in the capture of *El Rayo* of 100 guns, one of the ships recently defeated at Trafalgar—was wounded in the action off St. Domingo 6 Feb. 1806, for which he received a gratuity of 40*l.* from the Patriotic Fund—escorted Sir Arth. Wellesley's army from Cork to Portugal in 1808—witnessed the destruction, 24 Feb. 1809, of three French frigates under the batteries of Sable d'Olonne—was present in the ensuing April at Lord Cochrane's destruction of the enemy's shipping in Basque Roads—and on 15 Nov. 1810 assisted in an attack made, by Capt. Chas. Grant of the DIANA, on the two French frigates *Amazone* and *Eliza*, protected by the fire of several strong batteries, near Cherbourg. On leaving the DONEGAL he became attached to the ILLUSTRIOUS 74, bearing the broad pendant of Commodore Wm. Robt. Broughton in the East Indies; where, on his removal, as Master's Mate, to the AKBAR 50, Capt. Hen. Drury, he aided in effecting the conquest of Java. He was confirmed a Lieutenant (after having acted four months as Mate) in the DORIS 36, Capt. Wm. Jones Lye, 7 Feb. 1812; and, returning to England in the following Dec., was next appointed—2 June, 1813, to the PRESIDENT 38, Capts. Fras. Mason and Arch. Duff, for some time employed off the north coast of Spain, where he served, under Lieut. Dowell O'Reilly of the SURVEILLANTE, in the breaching batteries at the siege of St. Sebastian—12 July, 1815 (he had invalided from the PRESIDENT in Aug. 1814), to the NIGHTINGALE 16, Capt. Christopher Nixon, in which vessel, stationed in the Downs, he remained but a few weeks—and, 2 April, 1816, to the NEWCASTLE 50, bearing the flag at St. Helena and the Cape of Good Hope of his former Captain, Sir Pulteney Malcolm, to whom he became Signal-Lieutenant 20 Sept. following. He has been on half-pay since 16 Aug. 1817.

OGILVIE. (LIEUT., 1816. F-P. 8; H-P., 31.)

SIMON TAYLOR OGILVIE entered the Navy, 3 Aug. 1808, as Sec.-cl. Vol., on board the ROVER brig, Capt. Fras. John Nott, with whom during the remainder of the year he cruized in the North Sea. Becoming Midshipman, in April, 1809, of the HEROINE 32, Capt. Hood Hanway Christian, he accompanied the ensuing expedition to the Walcheren, and was present, under Lord Wm. Stuart, at the forcing of the passage between the batteries of Flushing and Cadsand. In Nov. of the same year he joined the CASTILIAN 18, Capts. Robt. Brown Tom and David Braimer; and in the course of 1811 he commanded the cutter belonging to that vessel at the cutting-out of a brig from under a heavy fire of musketry near Dieppe In July of the same year we again find him placed under the orders of Capt. Christian in the IRIS 36, in which ship, after co-operating with the patriots on the north coast of Spain, and witnessing the capture of Castro, he sailed for the Brazils, whence, in May, 1814, he returned home as a Supernumerary in the AKBAR 50, Capt. Arch. Dickson. Between the following July and Oct. 1815 he served on the Home station in the MARTIAL 12, Capts. Hen. Forbes and Jas. Leach, CHALLENGER 16, Capt. Hen. Forbes, and, as Admiralty Midshipman, in the ORLANDO 36, Capt. John Clavell. He was then transferred, in the capacity last mentioned, to the HEBRUS 36, Capt. Edm. Palmer; and for his services in that frigate at the bombardment of Algiers he was promoted to the rank of Lieutenant 16 Sept. 1816. He has since been on half-pay.

OGILVIE. (RETIRED COMMANDER, 1846. F-P., 16; H-P., 37.)

WILLIAM OGILVIE entered the Navy, in July, 1794, as Fst.-cl. Vol., on board the TREMENDOUS 74, Capts. John Aylmer, Geo. Hopewell Stephens, and Chas. Brisbane; in which ship he continued employed in the Channel and at the Cape of Good Hope, part of the time as Midshipman under the flag of Rear-Admiral Thos. Pringle, until his return with that officer to England in the CRESCENT frigate in 1798. After serving three years in the North Sea and Baltic on board the ST. GEORGE 98, Capts. John Holloway, Sampson Edwards, and Thos. Masterman Hardy, flag-ship latterly of Lord Nelson, and participating in the attack upon the Danish line of defence before Copenhagen, he was made Lieutenant, 27 June, 1801, into the RUSSEL 74, Capt. Wm. Cuming, with whom he proceeded off Cadiz. He left the RUSSEL in Nov. 1801, and was afterwards appointed—11 June, 1803, to the WINDSOR CASTLE 98, Capts. Albemarle Bertie, Thos. Wells, Davidge Gould, and Chas. Boyles, stationed in the Channel—about July, 1805, to the SAMPSON 64, employed at first in South America and then at the Cape of Good Hope, whence he returned in May, 1806—21 May, 1807, to the BANTERER 22, Capt. Alex. Shiphard, under whom he was wrecked in the river St. Lawrence 29 Oct. 1808, suffering on the occasion many hardships—and, 29 April, 1809, to the VENERABLE 74, Capt. Sir Home Popham, in which ship he accompanied the expedition to the Walcheren, and served in the Channel until March, 1812. He became a Retired Commander on the Junior List 11 Aug. 1832; and on the Senior, 9 March, 1846. AGENT—Joseph Woodhead.

OGILVY. (COMMANDER, 1841.)

GEORGE KEITH OGILVY died 20 Sept. 1846, at Wyndham Place. He was son of the late Rear-Admiral Sir Wm. Ogilvy, Bart.,* by the eldest daughter of the late Jas. Morley, Esq.

* Sir Wm. Ogilvy entered the Navy in 1773. He served, as Lieutenant of the POLYPHEMUS 64, in the partial action with the combined fleets off Cape Spartel 20 Oct. 1782; acted as Captain of the ROBUST 74 at the occupation of Toulon in 1793; and was presented with a second promotal commission for his conduct as First of the GLORY 98, in Lord Howe's action 1 June, 1794. As Commander of the LARK sloop, he distinguished himself during Sir John Warren's expedition to Quiberon in 1795, and was present, in 1796, at the unsuccessful attack upon the town and fort of Leogane, in the island of St. Domingo. He afterwards, until the peace of Amiens, commanded the THUNDERER 74, in which he caused the self-destruction of the *Harmonie*, a French frigate of the largest class, and *Magicienne* 32. His Post-commission bore date 5 July, 1797. He was placed on the list of Superannuated Rear-Admirals 6 Dec. 1821.

This officer entered the Navy 31 May, 1824; passed his examination in 1830; and obtained his first commission 1 May, 1834. His subsequent appointments were—21 Nov. 1834, as Additional-Lieutenant, to the THALIA 46, bearing the flag of Rear-Admiral Patrick Campbell at the Cape of Good Hope—1 March, 1835, to the JUPITER 38, Capt. Edw. Henry A'Court, fitting at Woolwich—18 May following, to the BARHAM 50, Capt. Armar Lowry Corry, on the Mediterranean station—29 Nov. 1836, and 29 July, 1837, to the VICTORY 104 and WELLESLEY 72, in which ships, stationed at Portsmouth and in the East Indies, he served as Flag-Lieutenant to Sir Fred. Lewis Maitland until the death of that officer in Nov. 1839—27 Oct. 1840, to the IMPREGNABLE 104, Capt. Thos Forrest, fitting at Plymouth—and, 6 Aug. 1841, to the ILLUSTRIOUS 72, equipping for the flag of Sir Chas. Adam, Commander-in-Chief in North America and the West Indies. He attained the rank of Commander 23 Nov. 1841. AGENTS—Messrs. Stilwell.

OGLE, Bart. (ADMIRAL OF THE RED, 1841. F-P., 31; H-P., 28.)

SIR CHARLES OGLE, born 24 May, 1775, is eldest son of Sir Chaloner Ogle (who received the honour of Knighthood and was created a Baronet for his professional services, and died Senior Admiral in the British Navy 27 Aug. 1816) by Hester, youngest daughter and co-heir of the Right Rev. John Thomas, Lord Bishop of Winchester. He is brother of Major Thos. Ogle, of the 58th Regt., who was killed in the boats at the landing in Egypt in 1801; brother-in-law of the present Lord Dacre; uncle of Commander Graham Ogle, R.N.; and a relative of Sir Chaloner Ogle, Kt., who died Admiral of the Fleet in 1751. One of his father's sisters was mother of the present Rear-Admiral De Starck; and another grandmother of the late Earl Grey.

This officer entered the Navy about 1788, as Captain's Servant, on board the ADVENTURE 44, Capt. John Nicholson Inglefield, with whom, in the same ship and the MEDUSA 50, he made three trips to the coast of Africa. In Sept. 1791 he became Midshipman of the ALCIDE 74, Capt. Sir Andrew Snape Douglas, lying at Portsmouth; and he was next for two years employed, at Halifax and at Home, in the WINCHELSEA frigate, Capt. Fisher, EDGAR 74, Capt. Albemarle Bertie, and BOYNE 98, Capt. Wm. Albany Otway. On 14 Nov. 1793 he was made Lieutenant into the WOOLWICH 44, Capt. Craven, attached to the force in the West Indies; on which station, in the ensuing Dec. and Jan., he successively joined the VENGEANCE 74, Commodore Chas. Thompson, and, a second time, the BOYNE, bearing the flag of Sir John Jervis. During the proximate operations against the French islands he commanded a boat at the capture, under a heavy fire of great guns and musketry, of two schooners lying at anchor, with others, near Maran, Martinique; where he assisted at the taking of Pigeon Island, was intrusted with the command of a party of seamen landed at Point Negro to co-operate with the army, and remained on shore until after the surrender of Fort Bourbon. At the siege of Guadeloupe he again commanded a division of seamen, and greatly distinguished himself by his conduct at the storming of Fort Fleur d'Epée. Towards the close of May, 1794, he was nominated Acting-Captain of the ASSURANCE 44. He was made Commander, 21 May following, into the AVENGER sloop; appointed next to the PETEREL; and, on 11 Jan. 1796, posted into LA MINERVE frigate, in the Mediterranean. During the after part of the French revolutionary war he commanded the MELEAGER and GREYHOUND, of 32 guns each, and EGYPTIENNE 40, on the Jamaica station, and again in the Mediterranean. While in the MELEAGER off Cadiz he acquired the approbation of Sir John Jervis by the manner in which he repeated that officer's signals. In the GREYHOUND we find him effecting the capture of a Genoese privateer mounting 10 guns, also of a Spanish armed polacre, and of other vessels; and, in the EGYPTIENNE, earning the Turkish gold medal for his services during the Egyptian campaign. His subsequent appointments were—1 April, 1805, to the UNITÉ frigate, fitting for the Mediterranean—19 June, 1806, to the PRINCESS AUGUSTA yacht, in which he remained a period of exactly nine years—26 Aug. 1815, to the RAMILLIES 74, stationed in the Channel—and, 20 Nov. following and 20 Jan. 1816, to the MALTA 84 and RIVOLI 74, lying at Plymouth and Portsmouth. The latter ship he left in the following Sept. As Rear-Admiral, a rank he attained 12 Aug. 1819, Sir Chas. Ogle commanded-in-chief on the North American station from 27 April, 1827, until 14 July, 1830. He became a Vice-Admiral 22 July, 1830; rose to the rank of full Admiral 23 Nov. 1841; and since 30 Sept. 1845 has held the chief command at Portsmouth. Sir Chas. Ogle is President of the Royal Naval Benevolent Society.

He married, first, 22 April, 1802, Charlotte Margaret, sister of Henry, third Viscount Gage, and of the present Admiral Sir Wm. Hall Gage, G.C.H., and daughter of the late General Hon. Thos. Gage, Commander-in-Chief of his Majesty's forces in North America during the first American war. By that lady, who died in 1814, he had issue one son, Chaloner, formerly a Captain in the Army, and two daughters. He married, secondly, 4 Sept. 1820, Letitia, daughter of Sir Wm. Burroughs, Bart., by whom he had issue another son. Being again left a widower 13 Nov. 1832, he married a third time, 10 April, 1834, Mary-Anne, daughter of Geo. Cary, Esq., of Tor Abbey, co. Devon, and relict of John Dalton, jun., Esq., of Thurnham Hall, co. Lancaster, and of Sir John Hayford Thorold, Bart. The last Lady Ogle died 4 Feb. 1842. AGENTS—Messrs. Halford and Co.

OGLE. (COMMANDER, 1846.)

GRAHAM OGLE, born 27 Sept. 1814, is second son of the Rev. Jas. Ogle, M.A., Rector of Bishop's Waltham, and Vicar of Crondall, by Elizabeth, daughter of the Rev. Edm. Poulter, Prebendary of Winchester. He is nephew of Admiral Sir Chas. Ogle, Bart.; and brother-in-law of the Marquis Gentili, of Naples. His youngest brother, Edmund, is in the Royal Engineers.

This officer entered the Navy 28 May, 1827; passed his examination in 1834; and obtained his first commission 6 Sept. 1838. His succeeding appointments were—26 Jan. 1839, as Additional-Lieutenant, to the PRINCESS CHARLOTTE 104, bearing the flag of Hon. Sir Robt. Stopford in the Mediterranean—9 March, 1840, to the EDINBURGH 72, Capt. Wm. Wilmott Henderson, by whom, prior to witnessing the bombardment of St. Jean d'Acre, he was highly lauded for the bravery he evinced in partial command of the boats in a successful attempt made, 2 Oct., to remove a quantity of powder from the castle of Beyrout*—22 Sept. 1841 (soon after the latter ship had been paid off) to the CAMBRIAN 36, Capt. Henry Ducie Chads, fitting for the East Indies—and, 11 April, 1844, to the command, on that station, of the ROYALIST brig. He attained his present rank 8 June, 1846; and since 15 Jan. 1847 has been officiating as Second-Captain of the ST. VINCENT 120 and VICTORY 100, flag-ships at Portsmouth of his uncle Sir Chas. Ogle.

OGLE (CAPTAIN, 1838. F-P., 25; H-P., 13.)

THOMAS OGLE entered the Navy 25 Jan. 1809, as Fst.-cl. Vol., on board the SATURN 74, Capt. Lord Amelius Beauclerk, to whom, on removing to the ROYAL OAK 74, he officiated as Aide-de-Camp during the operations connected with the Walcheren expedition. With the exception of a few weeks passed in the early part of 1812 in the HANNIBAL 74, also commanded by Lord Beauclerk, he continued to serve with that nobleman and the late Sir Pulteney Malcolm in the ROYAL OAK until June, 1815. He was often in consequence detached against the enemy on the coast of France, and was

* *Vide* Gaz. 1840, p. 2610.

constantly employed in a tender from the capture of Washington until the attack on New Orleans. In Sept. 1815, at which period he was serving at Portsmouth on board the BRUNE troop-ship, Capt. Wm. Stanhope Badcock, he was nominated Admiralty Midshipman of the CHEROKEE 10, Capt. Wm. Ramage, on the Leith station; and, on 25 July, 1816, while filling the same rank at St. Helena in the NEWCASTLE 50, flag-ship of Sir P. Malcolm, he received an order to act as Lieutenant of the JULIA 14, Capt. Jenkin Jones. He was confirmed a Lieutenant 20 Aug. 1817, a few weeks after he had rejoined the NEWCASTLE; and subsequently appointed—in Dec. 1821, to the ACTIVE 46, Capts. Andrew King and Hon. Robt. Rodney, engaged on particular service—18 Oct. 1824, to the OCEAN 80, bearing the flag of Lord A. Beauclerk in the Tagus—and, 9 Jan. 1827, to the SPARTIATE 76, Capt. Fred. Warren, on the same station. Being re-appointed to the last-mentioned ship on the occasion of his promotion to the rank of Commander, 26 May, 1828, he continued in her, as Second-Captain, until 1830. We next find him employed—from 6 Aug. 1831 until Dec. 1834, in the ISIS 50, flag-ship of Rear-Admiral Fred. Warren at the Cape of Good Hope—from 21 March, 1836, until April, 1837, in the CORNWALLIS 74, Capts. Robt. Worgan Geo. Festing and Sir Joshua Ricketts Rowley, on the Lisbon station—and, from 31 Aug. 1837 until June, 1839 (during which period he was advanced, 28 June, 1838, to Post-rank), in the PRESIDENT 52, flag-ship of Rear-Admiral Chas. Bayne Hodgson Ross in the Pacific. His last appointment was, 11 Oct. 1841, to the SOUTHAMPTON 50, fitting for the flag of Sir Edw. Durnford King, Commander-in-Chief at the Cape of Good Hope. While in that ship, in which he remained until Dec. 1842, he forced the entrance into Port Natal, and, by landing a body of troops, rescued a detachment surrounded at the time by a host of hostile tribes.

Capt. Ogle is a Knight of the Brazilian order of the Southern Cross. He married Mary, eldest daughter of John Garth, Esq., of Preston, Lancashire, by whom he has issue one son and two daughters. AGENTS—Messrs. Stilwell.

O'GRADY. (CAPTAIN, 1814.)

HAYES O'GRADY is son of the late Darby O'Grady, Esq., of Mount Prospect, co. Limerick, by Mary, daughter of Jas. Smyth, Esq., and brother of the late and uncle of the present Viscount Guillamore. He is uncle also of Lieut. Hon. John O'Grady, R.N.

This officer was educated at the Royal Naval College, and embarked, 4 Dec. 1802, as Fst.-cl. Vol., on board the LEDA 38, Capts. Jas. Hardy and Robt. Honyman; in which ship, after contesting with the enemy off Boulogne, and serving for some months under the flag of Rear-Admiral Edw. Thornbrough, he assisted as Midshipman at the reduction of the Cape of Good Hope, and then accompanied the expedition to the Rio de la Plata; where we find him employed in the boats as Master's Mate at the destruction of an armed brigantine off Monte Video 9 Sept. 1806.* On 21 March, 1807, he was confirmed a Lieutenant, nearly six months after he had been ordered to act as such, in the HOWE *alias* DROMEDARY storeship, Capt. Edw. Killwick. He was sent in the course of the same year to England in charge of a prize; and he was subseqnently appointed—28 Dec. 1807, to the THETIS 38, Capts. Wm. Hall Gage and Geo. Miller, employed on the St. Helena, Channel, Leeward Island, and Halifax stations—22 Aug. 1809, to the COMET sloop, Capt. Rich. Henry Muddle, attached to the force on the coast of North America—and, 15 Sept. following, to the ANTELOPE 50, bearing the flag of Admiral Holloway at Newfoundland. He attained the rank of Commander 15 June, 1810, and between that period and April, 1814, was employed in the SHARK receiving-ship at Jamaica, and for three years in the SAPPHO brig in various parts of the West Indies. Since his promotion to Post-rank, which took place 7 June, 1814, he has been on half-pay.

* *Vide* Gaz. 1807, p. 126.

Capt. O'Grady married, in July, 1831, Susan, daughter of Jas. Finucane, Esq., and granddaughter of the late Mr. Justice Finucane. AGENTS—Hallett and Robinson.

O'GRADY. (LIEUTENANT, 1831.)

THE HONOURABLE JOHN O'GRADY is sixth son of the late Viscount Guillamore, several years Chief Baron of the Exchequer in Ireland, by Katherine, second daughter of the late John Thos. Waller, Esq., of Castletown, co. Limerick. He is brother of the present Viscount; brother-in-law of Viscount Gort; and nephew of Capt. Hayes O'Grady, R.N.

This officer entered the Navy, 13 July, 1822, as Fst.-cl. Vol., on board the GENOA 74, lying at Sheerness. He served next in the CLIO 18 on the coast of Scotland, and in the RAINBOW 28 and FLY 18 in the East Indies; and on his return to England at the close of 1828 in the BOMBAY 84 he passed his examination. After a further attachment, on the Home and West India stations, to the VICTORY 104, BLOSSOM 24, PINCHER schooner, and FALCON 10, he was promoted to the rank of Lieutenant 17 Feb. 1831. His last appointment was, 19 Nov. 1834, to the SCYLLA 16, Capt. Edw. John Carpenter, in which vessel, until paid off in 1836, we find him employed, as sole Lieutenant, in North America and the West Indies. AGENTS—Hallett and Robinson.

O'HEA. (LIEUT., 1815. F-P., 10; H-P., 32.)

MATTHEW O'HEA is brother of Lieut. Dan. O'Hea, R.N. (1805), who died about the commencement of 1835; and nephew of the late Capt. Henry Power, R.N. This officer entered the Navy, 20 Oct. 1805, as L.M., on board the SOPHIE 18, Capts. Philip L. J. Rosenhagen and Wm. Mansell; in the boats of which sloop, and of the LONDON 98, he distinguished himself at the cutting-out from Algeciras of two Spanish gun-vessels strongly defended. In March, 1807, at which period he had been serving for two months in the river Thames on board the HINDOSTAN 50, he joined the BEDFORD 74; and in that ship, commanded by Capt. Jas. Walker, and for a short time by Capt. Adam Mackenzie, he continued employed for upwards of eight years. While stationed at first off Lisbon he assisted in destroying two forts at the entrance of the Tagus. He next escorted the Royal Family of Portugal in its flight to the Brazils; and when afterwards on the coast of North America he served with the boats of a squadron at the capture on Lake Borgne, 14 Dec. 1814, of five American gun-vessels under Commodore Jones, whose resistance was prolonged until the British had sustained a loss of 17 men killed and 77 wounded. He also took an active part in the operations against New Orleans, where he saw much arduous boat-service, and was severely wounded in the thigh and hand. The injuries he sustained not being, from some unaccountable reason, reported, he never received any compensation. In Feb. 1815 we find him present in the attack on Fort Bowyer, Mobile. He took up in the following June a commission bearing date 4 Feb. 1815; and has since been on half-pay.

Lieut. O'Hea married, in July, 1818, Miss Margaret Fitzgerald, and by that lady has issue two sons.

OKE. (LIEUTENANT, 1825.)

WILLIAM WALTER OKE entered the Navy 2 April, 1808; passed his examination in 1814; obtained his commission 10 Jan. 1825; and from 10 Oct. in that year until, we believe, 1827, was employed in the Coast Blockade as Supernumerary-Lieutenant of the RAMILLIES 74, Capt. Hugh Pigot. He has been in command, since 3 May, 1841, of the ASP steam-packet, of 50-horse power, on the Portpatrick station.

He is Senior of 1825.

OKES, K.W. (LIEUT., 1807. F-P., 14; H-P., 33.)

CHARLES OKES entered the Navy, 17 Oct. 1800, as Fst.-cl. Vol., on board the PRINCE GEORGE 98, bearing the flag of Sir Chas. Cotton in the Channel, where he served until April, 1802. In the following Aug. he joined the RANGER, Capt. Chas. Coote, lying at Deptford; and he was next, for nearly four years, employed in the Mediterranean and West Indies, off Cadiz, and in the Downs, as Midshipman, in the SEAHORSE 38, Capts. Hon. Courtenay Boyle, Robt. Corbet, and John Stewart, and DEFENCE 74, Capt. Chas. Ekins. He was then, 18 Feb. 1807, promoted to a Lieutenancy in the INDEFATIGABLE 46, Capts. John Tremayne Rodd, Henry Edw. Reginald Baker, and John Broughton, in which frigate he was for three years and a half chiefly stationed off Bordeaux and the north coast of Spain. He subsequently, from 3 Aug. 1810 until 25 Feb. 1811, had command of a gun-boat attached to the division under the present Sir Thos. Fellowes at the defence of Cadiz; where he was next for 15 months attached to the ST. ALBANS 64, Capts. Edw. Bruce, Chas. Grant, and John Ferris Devonshire. His last appointment afloat was, 8 Aug. 1812, to the SAN DOMINGO 74, flag-ship in North America of Sir John Borlase Warren, with whom he continued until 3 June, 1814.

Lieut. Okes has for many years formed one of the Naval Knights of Windsor, of which respectable body he is now Governor.

OLDMIXON. (COMMANDER, 1847. F-P., 13; H-P., 26.)

GEORGE OLDMIXON is son of the late Sir John Oldmixon, and brother of Lieuts. John William and William Henry Oldmixon, R.N. A third brother, Edward, having fought and bled on the Canadian lakes without reward, entered the service of the United States.

This officer entered the Navy, 23 June, 1808, as Fst.-cl. Vol., on board the BELLONA 74, Capt. John Erskine Douglas, with whom he continued to serve, as Midshipman and Master's Mate, in the same ship and in the PRINCE OF WALES 98, on the Halifax, Home, and Mediterranean stations, until July, 1814. In the BELLONA he witnessed Lord Cochrane's destruction of the French shipping in Basque Roads, and was present at the siege of Flushing in 1809; and, when in the PRINCE OF WALES, he served on shore at the reduction of Genoa in April, 1814. After cruizing six months in the Channel on board the HOPE 10, Capt. Henry Fyge Jauncey, he sailed for Jamaica as a Supernumerary in the WARRIOR 74, bearing the flag of his former Captain, then Rear-Admiral Douglas. He was promoted, on his arrival, to a Lieutenancy, 1 June, 1815, in the TANAIS 38, Capt. Joseph James, in which frigate he remained until June, 1816; and he was subsequently appointed—10 Nov. 1842, to the command of the MEGÆRA steamer, which vessel he unfortunately lost off Port Royal, Jamaica, in March, 1843—12 Jan. 1844, as Senior, to the HECATE steam-sloop, Capts. Jas. Paterson Bower and Joseph West, employed at first on particular service, and next on the coast of Africa—and 11 June, 1846, to the acting command of the FLYING FISH sloop, on the station last mentioned. He was advanced to his present rank soon after his return to England, 27 Sept. 1847.

Commander Oldmixon is married to a sister of Sir Wm. Scott, Bart., of Ancrum, Roxburghshire. AGENTS—Messrs. Chard.

OLDMIXON. (LIEUT, 1812. F-P., 12; H-P., 32.)

JOHN WILLIAM OLDMIXON was born in 1788. He is eldest brother of Commander Geo. Oldmixon, R.N.

This officer entered the Navy, in Oct. 1803, as Ordinary, on board the PHAETON 38, Capts. Geo. Cockburn, John Wood, Pownoll Bastard Pellew, and Fleetwood Broughton Reynolds Pellew. In that ship, after escorting Mr. Merry, the British Minister Plenipotentiary, to the United States, he assisted, as Midshipman, at the blockade of the Isle of France, where he came into frequent collision with the enemy's batteries. He was subsequently absent for a whole month in a prize, which, after braving many dangers, was wrecked on the coast of China; and while detached for a short period in the HARRIER sloop, Capt. Edw. Ratsey, he aided in forcing the batteries at the Boca Tigris. During the operations which led to the reduction of Java we find him present at the storming of the fortress of Samanap, and mentioned as an "intelligent young officer."* On 10 Oct. 1811, a few days after his removal to the ILLUSTRIOUS 74, Commodore Wm. Robt. Broughton, he was nominated Acting First-Lieutenant of the HECATE 18, Capt. Hon. Henry John Peachey; to which vessel he was confirmed 11 Feb. 1812. In the following Aug. he invalided home on board the MODESTE 36, Capt. Jas. Coutts Crawford; and he was next, from Aug. 1813 until July, 1816, employed on the Home, West India, and Mediterranean stations, in the LEVIATHAN 74, Capts. Patrick Campbell, Adam Drummond, and Thos. Briggs. Although constant in his applications, he has not been able to procure any further appointment.

The Lieutenant married, in 1830, Anne, daughter of Mr. Barrington and Lady Mary Price. AGENTS—Hallett and Robinson.

OLDMIXON. (LIEUT., 1815. F-P., 14; H-P., 27.)

WILLIAM HENRY OLDMIXON entered the Navy, 14 Oct. 1806, as Fst.-cl. Vol., on board the TARTAR 32, Capts. Edw. Hawker and Stephen Poyntz, on the Halifax station. In the following Jan., after he had been for a brief period attached to the MELEAGER frigate, Capt. John Broughton, fitting at Chatham, he became Midshipman of the AGAMEMNON 64, Capt. Jonas Rose; under whom he was at first employed off Lisbon, then with the expedition against Copenhagen, and ultimately on the Brazilian station; where, in June, 1809, he removed to the FOUDROYANT 80, Capt. Rich. Turner Hancock. Joining, next, the RÉVOLUTIONNAIRE 38, Capt. John Chas. Woolcombe, he served for some time in that ship on the north coast of Spain, and in Aug. and Sept. 1813 was employed in the batteries at the siege of St. Sebastian. From Dec. in the latter year until Aug. 1815, we find him officiating as Master's Mate of the COLUMBIA sloop, Capt. Henry Ducie Chads, and SHARK receiving-ship at Port Royal, Jamaica, Capts. Jackson and Campbell. He was then (he had been promoted to the rank of Lieutenant by commission dated 24 Feb. 1815) appointed to the ONYX 10, Capt. Chas. Strangways, also on the West India station; whence, in April, 1816, he returned to England in the NORTH STAR 20, Capt. Geo. Bentham. His last appointment was, 18 Dec. 1841, to the office of Admiralty Agent on board a contract mail steam-vessel, which he retained until the spring of 1847. AGENTS—Messrs. Chard.

OLDREY. (CAPTAIN, 1838. F-P., 14; H-P., 29.)

WILLIAM OLDREY entered the Navy, 22 June, 1804, as Fst.-cl. Vol., on board the WARRIOR 74, Capts. Wm. Bligh and Sam. Hood Linzee, attached to the Channel fleet. In the summer of 1805 (he had attained the rating of Midshipman in July, 1804) he sailed in the PORPOISE for New South Wales; whence, in Dec. 1807, he returned to England in the BUFFALO. He then joined the DIOMEDE 50, flag-ship of Sir Jas. Saumarez and Sir Edm. Nagle off Guernsey and Cherbourg; and after a servitude of three years and a half on the Home and Lisbon stations in the DOTEREL sloop, Capts. Anthony Abdy, Thos. Goldwire Muston, and Cohen (part of the force employed at the destruction of the French shipping in Basque Roads), and BARFLEUR 98, flag-ship of Hon. Geo. Cranfield Berkeley, he was made Lieutenant, 7 July, 1812, into the UNION 98, commanded in the Mediterranean by Capts. Wm. Kent and Robt. Rolles. Being next, 9 April, 1813, appointed to the UNDAUNTED 38, Capt. Thos. Ussher, he took command, 3 May following,

* *Vide* Gaz. 1812, p. 120.

of a boat belonging to that ship, and in the most gallant manner boarded and carried an enemy's brig under a furious cannonade from the batteries at Marseilles. On 7 of the same month he attacked a French national schooner of the largest class, with a fleet of coasting vessels under her protection: two of the latter were taken, and several driven on shore; but unfortunately, just as he was about to board the schooner, a squall of wind arose, and she was enabled to effect her escape, notwithstanding that he made every effort again to close with her, and resolutely continued the chase as long as the most distant hope remained of doing so, although his boat had already suffered a severe loss, and he himself had had his thigh-bone fractured. In consequence of his wound, for which he now receives a pension of 91*l*. 5*s*., he was under the necessity, in the ensuing July, of invaliding. His next appointments were—6 June, 1815, for a few months, to the Albion 74, Capts. Philip Somerville and Jas. Walker, employed at Portsmouth and Sheerness—and 16 Dec. 1818, to the command, which he retained for about three years, of the Pioneer 10, on the Home station. As Commander, a rank he attained 24 April, 1828, Capt. Oldrey, from 14 March, 1831, until paid off at the close of 1832, served in the West Indies on board the Hyacinth 18. He attained his present rank 28 June, 1838, but has not been since afloat.

OLIVER. (Lieut., 1815 f-p., 14; h-p., 27.)

George Colin Oliver entered the Navy, in May, 1806, as a Supernumerary, on board the Milan 38, Capt. Sir Robt. Laurie, then on the point of sailing for Newfoundland, where, in the course of the same year, he successively joined the Leander 50 and Leopard 50, both commanded by Capt. Salusbury Pryce Humphreys. On 22 June, 1807, he was present, we believe, in the latter ship when she compelled the U.S. frigate *Chesapeake* to surrender, in consequence of a refusal on the part of the American Captain to allow her to be searched by the British for deserters. Between 1808 and the date of his promotion to the rank of Lieutenant, 3 March, 1815, we find him employed on the Halifax, Mediterranean, and Home stations, as Midshipman and Master's Mate, in the Swiftsure 74, flag-ship of Sir John Borlase Warren, Laurestinus 24 and Orlando 36, both commanded by Capt. John Clavell, and Nautilus 18, Capts. Thos. Dench and John Bradley. His succeeding appointments were —17 Oct. 1818, to the Rochfort 80, flag-ship of Sir Thos. Fras. Fremantle and Sir Graham Moore in the Mediterranean—7 Nov. 1821, to the Racehorse 18, Capt. Hon. Chas. Abbot (now Lord Colchester), on the same station, whence he returned to England and was paid off about Feb. 1822—and, 23 Dec. 1825, to the Spartiate 74, Capt. Fred. Warren, lying at Portsmouth. Since the close of 1826, at which period he was superseded from the last-mentioned ship at his own request, Lieut. Oliver has been on half-pay. Agents—Messrs. Chard.

OLIVER. (Commander, 1813.)

James Oliver entered the Navy, in 1782, as Sec.-cl. Vol., on board the Otter sloop, Capt. Eliab Harvey, stationed in the Baltic. From 1783 until 1785, and from 1788 until 1790, he served at Newfoundland and Gibraltar in the Merlin, Capt. Geo. Lumsdaine, and Mercury, Capt. Montgomery; and on 8 June, 1797, he was promoted to a Lieutenancy in the Alcmène 32, Capts. Wm. Brown, Geo. Hope, Henry Digby, and John Tremayne Rodd. Continuing in that ship for a period of nearly four years, he contributed to the capture, 26 June, 1799, after a long chase and running fight, of the French privateer *Courageux*, of 28 guns and 253 men. He also, 18 July following, assisted, in partial command of the Alcmène's boats, at the capture (although protected by two forts and a detached gun in Vivero harbour, on the north coast of Spain) of *La Felicidad*, a ship of about 800 tons, pierced for 22 guns, with a cargo of hemp, lower masts, and ship timber;* and of *El Bisarro* brig, laden with timber and iron. His appointments, after he left the Alcmène, were —for a few months in 1801, to the Vlieter 44, Capt. Wm. Birchall, off Harwich—2 Dec. 1803 and 27 Feb. 1807, to the Bacchante 20 (which ship he left in April, 1806) and Franchise 36, both commanded by Capt. Chas. Dashwood—24 Sept. 1809, to the Polyphemus 64, flag-ship at Jamaica of Vice-Admiral Bartholomew Sam. Rowley—26 Jan. 1810, to the command of the Découverte schooner, on the same station, whence he invalided in Dec. 1810 —in Oct. 1811, to the Hibernia 120, flag-ship of Sir Edw. Pellew in the Mediterranean—in the following month, to the command of the Carlotta brig—and, 29 Oct. 1813, as Senior, to the Sultan 74, Capt. John West, attached to the force in the Channel. On 3 April, 1805, being at the time First-Lieutenant of the Bacchante, Mr. Oliver assisted at the capture of the Spanish war-schooner *Elizabeth*, of 10 guns and 47 men. Two days afterwards he was sent with two boats, containing about 35 seamen and marines, to cut out three notorious French privateers reported to be in the harbour of Mariel, near the Havana, the entrance to which was defended by a round tower nearly 40 feet high, armed at the top with 3 long 24-pounders, surrounded with numerous loop-holes for musketry, and garrisoned by a Spanish Captain and 30 soldiers. Being discovered during his approach, Lieut. Oliver, who was in the foremost boat, immediately landed, and, with a degree of gallantry as irresistible as it was heroic, rushed, through a tremendous fire that badly wounded 1 of the only 13 men with him, to the foot of the tower, which, without further loss, he scaled and carried. Having performed this noble exploit, left a Sergeant of Marines and 6 men as a guard at the fort, and been joined by his other boat, under the orders of Lieut. John Campbell, he proceeded in search of the privateers, but to his mortification found that they had sailed the day before on a cruize. Although thus disappointed, he contrived nevertheless to obtain possession of, and bring off, two schooners laden with sugar, notwithstanding that they were lying alongside a wharf, under repeated discharges of musketry from the troops and militia, who were pouring down in numbers from the adjacent country.† In spite, however, of the glowing terms in which his conduct on this occasion was reported by Capt. Dashwood, Lieut. Oliver was suffered to remain unpromoted for upwards of eight years. During that period he was present, in the Franchise, at the bombardment of Copenhagen in Sept. 1807, and at the capture, in Dec. 1808, of the town of Samana, St. Domingo, almost the last port of refuge on the station for the enemy's privateers. In the Découverte he sustained so serious an injury in the left eye, from arduous and active service, as to be obliged, as above stated, to invalid; and, in April, 1812, he had the misfortune to lose the Carlotta on the coast of Sicily, on which occasion, through exertion and fatigue in saving a quantity of specie, he again lost the use of his eye. His advancement to the rank of Commander at length took place 4 Dec. 1813, since which period, however, he has not been able to procure employment.

His son, Wm. Browne Oliver, is a Commander R.N.

OLIVER. (Commander, 1844.)

Richard Aldworth Oliver is son of Admiral Oliver.

This officer entered the Navy (from the Royal Naval College) 26 April, 1825; passed his examination in 1830; and obtained his first commission 28 June,

* *Vide* Gaz. 1799, p. 984. The part taken in the above affair by the subject of the present narrative has been erroneously attributed by Mr. James, in his 'Naval History,' to the late Retired-Commander Wm. Sandford Oliver.

† *V.* Gaz. 1805, pp. 772-3. The conduct of this achievement, too, is by Mr James ascribed, in error, to the late Commander Thos. Oliver.

1838. His succeeding appointments were—25 July, 1838, to the ASIA 84, Capt. Wm. Fisher, attached to the force in the Mediterranean, whence he returned in the spring of 1841—2 Sept. 1841, to the THALIA 42, Capt. Chas. Hope, fitting at Chatham—and, 30 Oct. following, to the QUEEN 110, in which ship he was for upwards of two years again employed in the Mediterranean under the flag of Sir Edw. W. C. R. Owen, and the command of Capt. Sir Chas. Sullivan. He attained his present rank 23 Sept. 1844; and, since 11 Oct. 1847, has been in command of the FLY 18 in the East Indies. AGENTS—Messrs. Chard.

OLIVER, Kt. (CAPT., 1834. F-P., 23; H-P., 24.)
SIR ROBERT OLIVER is uncle of Lieut. Geo. Cleaveland, R.N.

This officer entered the Navy, 23 May, 1800, on board the FORMIDABLE 98, commanded by the late Sir Edw. Thornbrough, with whom he continued for eight years employed as Midshipman and Master's Mate in the MARS 74, GALYKHEID 64, RUBY 64, EAGLE and KENT 74's, and ROYAL SOVEREIGN 100, on the Home and Mediterranean stations, where, during the remainder of the war, he served (his promotion to the rank of Lieutenant took place 22 Feb. 1810) in the OCEAN 98, flag-ship of Lord Collingwood, ESPOIR sloop, Capt. Robt. Mitford, MENELAUS 38, Capt. Sir Peter Parker, BANTERER sloop, Capt. Chas. Warde, and GLASGOW 50, Capt. Hon. Henry Duncan. On 4 April, 1810, he commanded the boats of the ESPOIR, in unison with those of the SUCCESS 32, under Lieut. Geo. Rose Sartorius, and was particularly mentioned for his conduct at the destruction, under a heavy fire of great guns and musketry, of several vessels on the beach near Castiglione, on the coast of Calabria.* He assisted soon afterwards at the destruction of an armed ship and three barks under the castle of Terracina. His appointments after he left the GLASGOW were—4 March, 1823, to the ISIS 50, Capt. Gordon Thos. Falcon, lying at Chatham—23 June following and 21 Aug. 1825, to the SPARTIATE 76 and WELLESLEY 74, flag-ships of Sir Geo. Eyre in South America—and, 30 April, 1827, to the VICTORY 104, Capt. Hon. Geo. Elliot, lying at Portsmouth. Obtaining a second promotal commission 29 Oct. 1827, he was successively invested with the command—30 May, 1831, of the ASIA 84, flag-ship off Lisbon of Rear-Admiral Wm. Parker—and, 9 June, 1832, and 6 Nov. 1833, of the DEE and PHŒNIX steamers. The DEE served with the North Sea squadron during the blockade of the Dutch ports, and afterwards conveyed Vice-Admiral Sir Pulteney Malcolm to Lisbon. The PHŒNIX attended Queen Adelaide to Rotterdam in the summer of 1834. On 28 Aug. in the latter year Capt. Oliver was advanced to Post-rank: and since 1837 he has been in discharge of the duties attached to the office of Superintendent of the Indian Navy. The honour of Knighthood was conferred on him 20 April, 1843, as a reward for services he had rendered during the war in China. AGENTS—Messrs. Ommanney.

OLIVER. (COMMANDER, 1814. F-P., 15; H-P., 34.)
ROBERT OLIVER (*a*) entered the Navy, 28 Nov. 1798, as Midshipman, on board LA SEINE, of 43 guns and 281 men, Capt. David Milne, employed at first in the Channel and off the coast of Africa, and then in the West Indies, where, 21 Aug. 1800, he assisted at the capture, in the Mona Passage, of *La Vengeance*, of 52 guns and 326 men, at the close of a brilliant action of two hours and a half, in which the British lost 13 men killed and 29 wounded, and the French more than twice that number. After a servitude of three years and four months in the North Sea and Channel, nearly the whole time as Master's Mate, in the AMETHYST 36, Capts. Henry Rich. Glynn, Alex. Campbell, and John Wm. Spranger, and PENELOPE 36, Capt. Wm. Robt. Broughton, he was nominated, 14 Nov. 1805, Sub-Lieutenant of the LIBERTY 14, Lieut.-Commander John Codd. He was made full Lieutenant, 30 Jan. 1806, into the CAPTAIN 74, Capt. Geo. Hopewell Stephens, lying in Portsmouth Harbour; and subsequently appointed—18 Feb. 1806, to the CHAMPION 24, Capts. Robt. Howe Bromley, Kenneth Mackenzie, and Jas. Coutts Crawford, in which vessel he visited Halifax and Quebec—26 May, 1808, to the ROVER sloop, Capt. Fras. John Nott, attached to the force in the North Sea, where he remained a year and eight months—towards the close of 1810, to the TONNANT 80, Capt. Sir John Gore, off Lisbon—in May, 1811, to the gun-boat service at Cadiz—21 Sept. following, to the QUEEN 74, Capt. Lord Colville, in the Channel—and, in Jan. and March, 1813, to the VILLE DE PARIS 110 and BOYNE 98, both commanded by Capt. Geo. Burlton. Prior to joining the TONNANT Lieut. Oliver had been the means, in 1810, of rescuing from destruction a Spanish frigate from Cadiz bound to Ferrol, together with the whole of her crew, upwards of 200 soldiers, and a large quantity of specie. For his signal exertions on the occasion he was earnestly recommended by the Spanish to the British Government. When Second of the BOYNE he was present, 13 Feb. 1814, in a partial action fought with the Toulon fleet, in which that ship bore the brunt and greatly distinguished herself. In the ensuing April Lieut. Oliver (who, we may here observe, had been often employed on detached service and had participated in various cutting-out affairs) witnessed the fall of Genoa. His promotion to the rank of Commander took place 27 Aug. in the same year, and since that period he has been on half-pay.

During his career afloat Commander Oliver received not less than five wounds in the head, in addition to one in the right arm and other grievous injuries, which have had the effect for many years past of incapacitating him from great exertion. AGENT—John P. Muspratt.

OLIVER. (ADMIRAL OF THE RED, 1841. F-P., 26; H-P., 42.)
ROBERT DUDLEY OLIVER was born 31 Oct. 1766.

This officer entered the Navy, 13 May, 1779, on board the PRINCE GEORGE 98, Capts. Philip Patton, Wm. Fox, and Jas. Williams, bearing the flag of Rear-Admiral Digby; and in the following Dec. sailed with Sir Geo. Rodney for the relief of Gibraltar. During the passage he assisted at the capture of a 64-gun ship (afterwards named the PRINCE WILLIAM, in honour of His late Majesty, who was on board the PRINCE GEORGE), six armed vessels belonging to the Royal Caraccas Company, and 14 sail of transports from St. Sebastian, bound to Cadiz, laden with naval stores, provisions, &c.; and also at the defeat of the armament under Don Juan de Langara 16 Jan. 1780. Gibraltar having been placed in a state of perfect security, he was next, while returning to England, present, 23 Feb. 1780, at the capture of the *Prothée*, a French 64-gun ship, and three vessels, forming part of a convoy bound to the Mauritius, laden with naval and military stores. Towards the close of 1782, having participated, as Midshipman, in the relief of St. Kitts, and shared in Rodney's celebrated action of the 12th of April, Mr. Oliver successively joined the VIXEN galley, Lieut.-Commander John White, and, as Master's Mate, the ALBACORE sloop, Capts. Geo. Oakes and Edm. Crawley, both on the North American station; where, from June, 1783, until July, 1785, he acted as Lieutenant in the ARIADNE, Capt. Sam. Osborne. He then came home as a Supernumerary of the HERMIONE, Commodore Sir Chas. Douglas; and in 1789 he again received an order to act as Lieutenant in the RACEHORSE sloop, Capt. Thos. Foley, in the North Sea. Being officially promoted by a commission bearing date 21 Sept. 1790, he was successively appointed Senior Lieutenant—26 April and 11 Sept. 1791, of the AQUILON 32 and SQUIRREL, Capts. Hon. Robt. Stopford and Wm. O'Brien Drury, employed on the Channel and Irish stations—and 24 Jan. 1793, and 23 July, 1794, of the ACTIVE frigate and ARTOIS of 44 guns and 281 men, both com-

* *Vide* Gaz. 1810, p. 1138.

manded by Capt. Edm. Nagle. For his conduct in the latter ship during an action of 40 minutes which preceded the surrender of *La Révolutionnaire* of 44 guns and 351 men, 8 of whom were killed and 5 wounded, with a loss to the British of 3 killed and 5 wounded, Mr. Oliver was made Commander, 21 Oct. 1794 (the date of the occurrence), into the Terror bomb, at Portsmouth. He removed, 3 Nov. following, to the Hazard sloop; and, after a servitude of a year and five months in that vessel on the coast of Ireland, he was posted, 30 April, 1796, into the Nonsuch, lying in the river Humber. His subsequent appointments were—2 Feb. 1798, to the Nemesis 28—26 March, 1799, to the Mermaid 32—23 March, 1803 (having left the Mermaid in the preceding July), to the Melpomène 38—22 Oct. 1805, for twelve months, to the Mars 74—and, 2 May, 1810, to the Valiant 74. In the Nemesis Capt. Oliver escorted convoy to Quebec; and in the Mermaid he made a voyage to the Mediterranean; where, previously to his return with Lord Hutchinson, the conqueror of Egypt, to England, he effected the capture of three corvettes and upwards of 70 sail of vessels, and chased the largest frigate in the possession of France into Toulon.* While in command of the Melpomène † we find him in 1804-5 engaged in blockading the French coast, and on two occasions conducting the bombardment of Havre de Grace.‡ On 28 July, 1806, being at the time in the Mars, he made prize, off the coast of France, after a chase of more than 150 miles, and in presence of three other heavy French frigates, of *Le Rhin* of 44 guns and 318 men.§ While in the Valiant, the command of which ship he resigned in July, 1814, Capt. Oliver cruized in the North Sea, Channel, and West Indies, assisted at the capture, 17 June, 1813, of the *Porcupine* letter-of-marque, of 20 guns and 72 men, and was a considerable time employed at the blockade of New York, New London, and other places on the American coast. He became a Rear-Admiral 12 Aug. 1819; a Vice-Admiral 22 July, 1830; and a full Admiral 23 Nov. 1841.

He married, 19 June, 1805, Mary, daughter of the late Sir Chas. Saxton, Bart., Commissioner of the Royal Dockyard at Portsmouth, by whom he has issue five sons and one daughter. One of the sons, Richard Aldworth, is a Commander R.N. Agents—Messrs. Chard.

OLIVER. (Commander, 1841. f-p., 26; h-p., 7.)

William Browne Oliver, born 12 March, 1802, is son of Commander Jas. Oliver, R.N.

This officer entered the Royal Naval College 1 Aug. 1814, and embarked, 21 June, 1817, as a Volunteer, on board the Tamar 26, Capts. Thos. Rich. Toker and Hon. John Gordon, attached to the force at Newfoundland. In Dec. 1819 he removed, as Midshipman, to the Redpole 10, Capts. Wm. Devereux Evance, Patrick Duff, Henry Hay, and Rich. Anderson, employed at first in the Channel and then in the Mediterranean; whence, in the summer of 1822, he returned to England in the Larne 20, Capt. Robt. Tait. After a servitude of four years in South America as a passed Midshipman and Mate in the Tartar 42, Capt. Thos. Brown, and Diamond 46, Capt. Lord Napier, he joined, in Dec. 1826, the Pyramus 42, Capt. Geo. Rose Sartorius, on the Channel station; and he was next, in Jan. 1828, appointed to the Terror bomb, Capt. David Hope. For his exertions in saving that vessel when shortly afterwards cast away on the coast of Portugal, and the great assistance he afforded throughout the laborious operations which took place before she was rendered fit to return to England, he was sent in the following summer to the Mediterranean on promotion in the Meteor bomb, also commanded by Capt. Hope (*whose Memoir see*). He was there made Lieutenant, 25 Aug. 1829, into the Erebus bomb, Capt. Philip Broke; and he was subsequently appointed—in July, 1830, as a Student, to the Royal Naval College at Portsmouth, where he remained one year—11 Oct. 1832, to the Serpent 16, Capts. John Chas. Symonds, Mark Halpen Sweny, and Evan Nepean, of which sloop, stationed for upwards of three years in the West Indies, he was for a long time First-Lieutenant and twice Acting-Commander—and 3 April, 1837, to the command (as a reward for meritorious conduct) of the Fair Rosamond schooner of 2 guns, fitting for the coast of Africa. In the latter vessel, in which he continued until 1 Oct. 1840, Lieut. Oliver, who went through scenes of great mortality, was most active in his efforts in the cause of freedom, and captured not less than nine slavers. He was in consequence advanced to his present rank 23 Nov. 1841. Since 18 July, 1845, he has been employed as an Inspecting-Commander in the Coast Guard. We may add that he has thoroughly qualified himself in the art of steam navigation.

OLIVER. (Retired Commander, 1844. f-p., 18; h-p., 35.)

William Sandford Oliver died in 1845.

This officer entered the Navy, 15 Jan. 1793, as a Supernumerary, on board the Polyphemus 64, employed in the North Sea; and from the following Oct. until June, 1799, served as Midshipman and Master's Mate in the Cerberus 32, Capts. John Drew and Jas. Macnamara, on the Irish station; where, in Nov. 1797, he assisted at the capture of the privateers *Epervier* of 16 guns and 145 men, and *Rénard* of 18 guns and 189 men, besides sharing in an action with the *Buonaparte*, another privateer of 32 guns and 250 men. After acting for a short time in the Channel as Lieutenant of the Bellona and Russel 74's, he was confirmed, 26 Sept. 1799, into the Seagull, Capts. Henry Wray and Thos. Lavie, on the Guernsey station. His succeeding appointments were—24 Nov. 1800, to the Royal George 100, in the Channel—3 Jan. 1801, to the Hussar 38, Capts. Lord Viscount Garlies and Wm. Brown, on the Irish station, where he remained until July, 1802—27 Sept. 1803, to the Terrible 74, Capt. Lord Henry Paulet, attached to the Channel Fleet—8 Nov. 1804, to the Severn 40, bearing the flag of the Prince de Bouillon off Jersey—in April, 1805, for a passage to Gibraltar, to the Queen 98, flag-ship of Rear-Admiral John Knight—in May following, to the San Juan 74, as Flag-Lieutenant to the latter officer at the place last mentioned—and 14 May, 1806, and 6 Dec. 1811, to the command of the Spider and Martial brigs in the Mediterranean and North Sea. He went on half-pay in March, 1812; became a Retired Commander on the Junior List 26 Nov. 1830; and was transferred, 3 May, 1844, to the Senior List.

OMMANNEY. (Captain, 1846.)

Erasmus Ommanney is son of the late Sir Fras. Molyneux Ommanney, Kt., M.P. for Barnstaple, the well-known Navy Agent; and nephew of Vice-Admiral Sir John Acworth Ommanney, K.C.B.

This officer entered the Navy 15 July, 1826; passed his examination in 1833; and obtained his first commission 10 Dec. 1835. His succeeding appointments were—28 Dec. 1835, to the Cove, Capt. Jas. Clark Ross, employed on particular service—7 Oct. 1836, to the Pique 36, Capt. Henry John Rous, attached to the force off Lisbon—and, 18 Oct. 1837, to the Donegal 78, as Flag-Lieutenant to his uncle Sir J. A. Ommanney, on the station last named, where he continued during a further period of three years. He was advanced to the rank of Commander 9 Oct. 1840; and from 28 Aug. 1841 until paid off at the close of 1844, was employed in that capacity

* He also made prize, 1 June, 1800, of *La Cruelle* brig, of 6 guns and 43 men.—*Vide* Gaz. 1800, p. 784

† The Melpomène happening to be in dock at Portsmouth on the eve of Lord Nelson's final departure from England, Capt. Oliver repaired to the George Hotel for the purpose of there taking leave of his Lordship, and of expressing his regret that the repairs required by his ship would prevent his accompanying him. In reply to Captain Oliver's observation his Lordship exclaimed,—"I hope you will come in time to *tow some of the rascals*." The words were prophetic, for the Melpomène actually joined the fleet the morning after the battle of Trafalgar, and had the good fortune to rescue one of the captured ships of the line, by towing her off the land.

‡ *Vide* Gaz. 1804, pp. 898, 938. § *V.* Gaz. 1806, p. 1009.

in the Mediterranean on board the VESUVIUS steam-sloop. He has since been on half-pay. His promotion to the rank he now holds took place 9 Nov. 1846.

Capt. Ommanney married, 27 Feb. 1844, Amelia Mary, eldest daughter of Sam. Smith, Esq., of H. M. Dockyard, Malta. AGENTS—Messrs. Ommanney.

OMMANNEY. (REAR-ADMIRAL OF THE RED, 1840. F-P., 19; H-P., 41.)

HENRY MANATON OMMANNEY is a younger brother of Vice-Admiral Sir John Acworth Ommanney, K.C.B.

This officer entered the Navy, in June, 1787, as Fst.-cl. Vol., on board the COLOSSUS 74, Capt. Hugh Cloberry Christian, lying off Woolwich. He removed, in June, 1788, to the ARROGANT 74, commanded in the river Medway by Capt. John Harvey; and after a servitude of four years and ten months on the Newfoundland and Channel stations as Midshipman in the ROSE frigate and CHILDERS sloop, Capts. Jacob Waller and Robt. Barlow, and QUEEN CHARLOTTE 100, flag-ship of Earl Howe, was made Lieutenant, 10 April, 1794, into the HAZARD sloop, Capt. John Loring, at Sheerness. During the atter part of the French revolutionary war he was employed in the Channel and West Indies, off Lisbon and Cadiz, and in the North Sea and Mediterranean, on board the AQUILON 32, Capt. Robt. Barlow, RAISONNABLE 64 and SWIFTSURE 74, flag-ships of the late Sir Wm. Parker, VILLE DE PARIS 110, Commodore Robt. Calder, BLENHEIM 98, bearing the flag of Sir W. Parker, ALLIANCE, Capt. Geo. Davies, CÆSAR 80, Capts. Roddam Home and Sir Jas. Saumarez, WAAKZAMKEIDT, Capt. Robt. Hall, and ACTIVE frigate, Capt. Chas. Sydney Davers. For his services in the last-mentioned ship during the campaign of 1801 in Egypt, he obtained the Turkish gold medal. Being awarded the rank of Commander 29 April, 1802, he served in that capacity from the following May until March, 1804, in the FALCON sloop, on the Newfoundland station, and from Jan. to Dec. 1805 in the THAMES, attached to the force in the North Sea. He acquired Post-rank 22 Jan. 1806; and afterwards, from 17 Sept. 1807, until 20 March, 1808, and from 29 Jan. 1812 until 12 Jan. 1813, commanded the PALLAS frigate off L'Orient, and the VIGO 74, flag-ship of Rear-Admiral Jas. Nicoll Morris. in the Baltic. He was placed on the Retired List of Rear-Admirals 28 June, 1838; and on the Active, 17 Aug. 1840.

Rear-Admiral Ommanney is a Deputy-Lieutenant for co. Banff. AGENTS—Messrs. Ommanney.

OMMANNEY, K.C.B., K.S.L., K.S.V., K.R.G. (VICE-ADMIRAL OF THE RED, 1841. F-P., 24; H-P., 43.)

SIR JOHN ACWORTH OMMANNEY is eldest son of Rear-Admiral Cornthwaite Ommanney, who died in 1801; brother of the present Rear-Admiral H. M. Ommanney; and uncle of Capt. Erasmus Ommanney, R.N. One of his brothers, Cornthwaite, was a Captain in the 24th Light Dragoons; and another, Montagu (who died on service in the West Indies in 1796), a Lieutenant in the Royal Artillery.

This officer (whose name had been borne, from 11 June, 1780, until Nov. 1781, on the books of the AJAX, SANDWICH, and GIBRALTAR, all commanded by Capt. John Symons, and who had served from April to Aug. 1783 in the POWERFUL, Capt. Thos. Fitzherbert, at Plymouth) joined, in May, 1786, the ROSE frigate, Capt. Henry Harvey, on the Newfoundland station. He was next, from Dec. 1788 until April, 1792, employed in the Mediterranean (the chief part of the time as Midshipman) on board the LEANDER 50, flag-ship of Rear-Admiral Peyton, AQUILON 32, Capt. Robt. Montagu, and ZEBRA sloop, Capt. Wm. Brown; and in July of the latter year, after having been for a few weeks attached to one of the royal yachts, commanded in the Thames by Sir G. Young, he joined Sir Erasmus Gower in the LION 64. In that ship, of which he was confirmed a Lieutenant 20 May, 1793, Mr. Ommanney accompanied Lord Macartney in his embassy to China. On his return to England he was appointed, 18 Oct. 1794, First of his former ship the AQUILON, then commanded by Sir Robt. Barlow, with whom he continued cruizing in the Channel until transferred, 27 March, 1795, to the QUEEN CHARLOTTE 100, Capt. Sir Andrew Snape Douglas, part of the force under Lord Bridport in his ensuing action with the French fleet off the Ile de Groix. During the mutiny of 1797 at the Nore, Capt. Ommanney (he had been advanced to the rank of Commander 6 Dec. 1796) volunteered his services towards its suppression; and his offer being accepted, he was for six weeks employed for that purpose in a gun-brig, No. 28. He was afterwards sent with two other Captains to Deal with the view, in the event of circumstances justifying the measure, of assuming command of some vessels lying in the Downs, whose crews still evinced disrespect towards their officers. The return, however, of the men to their duty happily rendered the step unnecessary. In Dec. 1797 Capt Ommanney obtained an appointment to the BUSY 18, fitting for service in the North Sea, where he soon obtained a high character for activity. In Aug. 1799, being off Goree in company with the SPEEDWELL brig, he intercepted a fleet of merchantmen under convoy of a Swedish frigate; the whole of which he sent for examination to the Downs; displaying throughout all the details of the affair a degree of promptitude and firmness that elicited the particular approbation of the Admiralty. After attending the expedition against the Helder, and effecting, with his usual alacrity, the capture of *Le Dragon*, a noted French privateer, of 16 guns,* Capt. Ommanney, in Jan. 1800, proceeded to the Leeward Islands; whence, in the following July, the debilitated state of his health compelled him to return. Within a few weeks of his arrival in England he had the satisfaction of being presented by Earl Spencer (who had but just given him a temporary appointment to the GARLAND frigate) with a Post-commission dated 16 Oct. 1800. During the last year of the French revolutionary war Capt. Ommanney successively commanded, in the Channel, the HUSSAR 38, ROBUST 74, and BARFLEUR 98—the latter bearing the flag of Rear-Admiral Collingwood. He next, between May, 1804, and March, 1806, officiated as Flag-Captain to Sir Erasmus Gower in the ISIS 50, at Newfoundland; but from the latter date he did not again go afloat until June, 1825. Obtaining command, on 7 of that month, of the ALBION 74, he sailed first for the Lisbon station, and afterwards joined the fleet in the Mediterranean under Sir Edw. Codrington. Continuing there until 1828, he was afforded an opportunity of sharing in the battle of Navarin 20 Oct. 1827. For his conduct on the occasion he was nominated a C.B. by his own sovereign ; and by those of France. Russia, and Greece, was presented with the Cross of St. Louis, the insignia of the Third Class of St. Vladamir, and the insignia of the Redeemer of Greece. He subsequently, in the capacity of Rear-Admiral, a rank he attained 22 July, 1830, commanded in chief, from 16 Oct. 1837 until the summer of 1840, and from 24 Sept. in the latter year until Oct. 1841, on the Lisbon and Mediterranean stations, with his flag in the DONEGAL 78 and BRITANNIA 120. He became a Vice-Admiral 23 Nov. 1841; was awarded the honour of Knighthood 20 May, 1835; and created a K.C.B. 20 July, 1838.

Sir John Acworth Ommanney is a Deputy-Lieutenant in co. Southampton. He married, in Oct. 1803, Frances, daughter of Rich. Ayling, Esq., of Slindham, co. Sussex, by whom he has issue. AGENTS—Messrs. Ommanney.

OMMANNEY. (One of the JUNIOR-LIEUTENANTS. F-P., 8; H-P., 17.)

JOHN COLPOYS OMMANNEY was born 9 Aug. 1809. This officer entered the Royal Naval College in

* *Vide* Gaz. 1799, p. 954.

April, 1822; and, after having carried off the French and mathematical prizes, together with the second medal, embarked, in March, 1824, as a Volunteer, on board the BLANCHE 46, Capt. Wm. Bowen Mends, fitting for the South American station, whence he returned, as Midshipman, in Oct. 1827. In Jan. and Feb. 1828 he successively joined the WASP 18, Capt. Dickenson, and ASIA 84, Capt. Edw. Curzon —the latter stationed in the Mediterranean, where, in March, 1829, he was lent, as Mate (he had passed in the preceding April), to the METEOR bomb, Capt. David Hope. He was promoted to the rank of Lieutenant 12 Aug. 1829; and was lastly, 18 Aug. 1836, appointed to the MINDEN 74, Capt. Alex. Renton Sharpe, on the Lisbon station. In April, 1837, he was dismissed by sentence of court-martial, and placed at the bottom of the list.

He married, 7 Sept. 1841, and has issue. AGENTS —Holmes and Folkard.

ONSLOW. (CAPTAIN, 1834. F-P., 19; H-P., 18.)

JOHN JAMES ONSLOW is second surviving son of the late Admiral Sir Rich. Onslow, Bart., G.C.B.,* by Anne, daughter of Commodore Matthew Mitchell, of Chiltern, co. Wilts. He is brother of the present Sir Henry Onslow, Bart., a Captain in the Royal Artillery; and brother-in-law of Admiral Sir Hyde Parker, who died 16 March, 1807.

This officer entered the Navy, 19 April, 1810, as Fst.-cl. Vol., on board the SURVEILLANTE 38, Capt. Sir Geo. Ralph Collier, under whom he was for some time actively employed on the north coast of Spain, particularly in the boats at the capture of Bermeo and Deba. He continued in the SURVEILLANTE, in the capacity of Midshipman, until April, 1812; and between that period and the date of his promotion to the rank of Lieutenant, 5 Sept. 1816, was employed on the Brazilian, Jamaica, and Home stations in the MONTAGU 74, flag-ship of the late Sir Manley Dixon, AQUILON and CERES frigates, both commanded by Capt. Wm. Bowles, ARAXES 38, Capt. Geo. Miller Bligh, and BOYNE 98, Capt. Edmund Boger. He joined soon afterwards the CONQUEROR 74, bearing the flag of Rear-Admiral Robt. Plampin at St. Helena; whence, at the close of 1817, he returned to England in the IPHIGENIA 42. From Sept. 1818 until superseded at his own request in Sept. 1819, he served in the Downs on board the ALERT sloop, Capts. Henry John Leeke and Chas. Farwell; and, on 23 April, 1822, he attained the rank of Commander. His next appointments were —22 July, 1824, to the BEAVER 8, on the Jamaica station, where he remained about two years—and, 30 April, 1830, to the CLIO 18, fitting for South America. While on that station Capt. Onslow was sent by Rear-Admiral Sir Thos. Baker to reclaim possession of the Falkland Islands, which lapse of time had encouraged the Buenos Ayreans and other foreigners to consider as absolutely abandoned by the British. Arriving, in Dec. 1832, at Port Egmont (West Falkland), he exercised the rights of sovereignty, and employed his boats in examining Brett's Harbour, Byron's Sound, and other anchorages as far to the westward as Point Bay, a distance of 60 miles from the place at which the CLIO lay. He then proceeded to Berkeley Sound (East Falkland), anchored at Port Louis, and ejected a Buenos Ayrean force stationed there under the protection of a schooner-of-war. He returned to Portsmouth from Rio de Janeiro with upwards of 880,000 dollars, 3 June, 1833; and on 17 of the same month was paid off. He was advanced to Post-rank 27 Aug. 1834; and was lastly, from 23 July, 1842, until put out of commission in the early part of 1847, employed in the Pacific on board the DAPHNE 18.

Capt. Onslow is married and has issue. AGENT— J. Hinxman.

* Sir Rich. Onslow (son of Lieutenant-General Onslow, Governor of Plymouth, and grand-nephew of Admiral Sir George Walton) was born 23 June, 1711. He obtained his first commission 17 Dec. 1758; acquired the rank of Commander 11 Feb. 1761; and was made Post 14 April, 1762, into the HUMBER of 40 guns. He afterwards commanded the AQUILON frigate, DIANA 32, ST. ALBAN'S 64, and BELLONA and MAGNIFICENT 74's. In the ST. ALBAN'S, in 1778, he served in Admiral Barrington's attack upon Ste. Lucie, and in the same officer's encounters with the Comte d'Estaing; and in the BELLONA, prior to accompanying Lord Howe to the relief of Gibraltar, he effected the capture, after a sharp action, of the Dutch ship *Princess Caroline* of 54 guns He became a Rear-Admiral 1 Feb. 1793, and a Vice-Admiral 4 July, 1794; was appointed, in March, 1796, Commander-in-Chief at Plymouth; and hoisted his flag shortly afterwards as second in command of the fleet under Admiral Duncan. For his distinguished conduct in the action off Camperdown he was raised to the dignity of a Baronet 30 Oct. 1797, voted the thanks of Parliament, and presented by the City of London with its freedom and a sword worth 100*l*. He was advanced to the rank of full Admiral 14 Feb. 1799, and was afterwards appointed a Lieutenant General of Marines, and nominated a G.C.B. He died at Southampton 3 Jan. 1818.

O'REILLY. (LIEUT., 1815. F-P., 18; H-P., 21.)

JOHN O'REILLY (*a*), born 9 April, 1794, is third son of the late Thos. O'Reilly, Esq., of Beltrasna, co. Meath, by Margaret, daughter of Hon. Justice Robt. Sibthorpe, of Duncanny, co. Louth, and grand-niece of the Earl of Dundonald. His brother, Anthony Alexander, is a Major in the Army.

This officer entered the Navy, 2 Oct. 1808, as Fst.-cl. Vol., on board the WARSPITE 74, Capt. Hon. Henry Blackwood, successively employed in the North Sea, at the blockade of Cherbourg, and in the Mediterranean. Removing as Midshipman, in Sept. 1810, to the COLOSSUS 74, Capt. Thos. Alexander, he was for some time engaged in that ship at the defence of Cadiz, where he constantly volunteered his services, and was on several occasions in action with the enemy's gun-boats, under a heavy fire from the batteries on shore. In April, 1811, he joined the SALDANA 36, Capt. Hon. Wm. Pakenham, from which ship he was fortunately detached in charge of a captured privateer, the *Amiral Martin*, a few days only before she was entirely lost, with all her crew, off Lough Swilly. In March, 1812, Mr. O'Reilly was received on board the HAZARD sloop, Capt. John Cookesley, off Newfoundland; and in Jan. 1814, after having acted for upwards of 12 months as Master of that vessel, he was transferred to the ASIA 74, flag-ship of Hon. Sir Alex. Cochrane; whom, in the following July, after a servitude of two months with Capt. Rich. Byron as Acting-Lieutenant in the BELVIDERA 36, he rejoined on board the TONNANT 80. In the course of the same summer he was present in the boats at the destruction of Commodore Barney's flotilla up the Patuxent, and on shore at the battle of Bladensburg, the taking of Washington, and the attack upon Baltimore; and on 14 of the following Dec. we find him commanding one of the boats of a squadron at the capture, on Lake Borgne, of five American gun-boats under Commodore Jones, whose desperate resistance occasioned the British a loss of 17 men killed and 77 wounded. Among the latter was Mr. O'Reilly,* who had the misfortune to sustain the loss of his right eye, for which he now receives a pension of 91*l*. 5*s*. His promotion to the rank of Lieutenant took place 2 Nov. 1815. His appointments have since been—26 Aug. 1834, to the Coast Guard—4 Nov. 1835, to the command, which he retained for six years, of the SPIDER brigantine of 6 guns, on the South American station—and, 29 Aug. 1843, again to the Coast Guard, in which service he continues. It has been Mr. O'Reilly's good fortune to rescue many persons from shipwreck.

The Lieutenant is the inventor of an illuminated shell, which supplies the desideratum required in Capt. Manby's apparatus. He married, 22 Oct. 1821, Anna, third daughter of Geo. Snart, Esq., of Sutton House, co. Middlesex, by whom he has issue an only daughter, married to Commander Albert Heseltine, R.N. AGENTS—Messrs. Stilwell.

O'REILLY. (LIEUTENANT, 1828.)

JOHN O'REILLY (*b*) entered the Navy 25 March, 1812; and passed his examination in 1818. In the following year, while at Calais in the PIONEER

* *Vide* Gaz. 1815, p. 448.

schooner, Capt. Wm. Oldrey, he had the good fortune, by his presence of mind, to save H.R.H. the Duke of Kent from an impending accident. He was afterwards employed in the Coast Blockade. He obtained his commission 18 Sept. 1828; and since 16 March, 1831, has been in charge of a station in the Coast Guard. The important nature of his services in cases of shipwreck has had the effect of eliciting the acknowledgments of Lloyd's, of the Royal Humane Society, and of various merchants and shipowners.

Lieut. O'Reilly's testimonials of conduct are of a high order. His son, Montagu Frederic, is a Lieutenant R.N.

O'REILLY. (LIEUT., 1845. F-P., 11; H-P., 1.)

MONTAGU FREDERIC O'REILLY, born 17 Feb. 1822, is the only child of Lieut. John O'Reilly (*b*), R.N.

This officer entered the Royal Naval College in Feb. 1835; and embarked, in Feb. 1837, as a Volunteer, on board the PELORUS 16, Capt. Fras. Harding; in which vessel he was wrecked at Port Essington, Australia, while holding the rating of Midshipman, 25 Nov. 1839. Joining next, in 1841, the DRUID 44, Capt. Henry Smith, he took part in the hostile operations then in progress in China, where, in Aug. of that year, he assisted at the capture of Amoy and Golongsoo, and was intrusted with the charge of a Signal station at the latter place. On the DRUID being paid off in the spring of 1843, having passed his examination 14 July, 1842, he was appointed Mate of the EXCELLENT gunnery-ship at Portsmouth, Capt. Sir Thos. Hastings. After a servitude of three months off Lisbon in the ALBION 90, Capt. Nicholas Lockyer, he sailed, at the commencement of 1845, for the coast of Africa, in the ACTÆON 26, Capt. Geo. Mansel. Volunteering to remain on that unhealthy station, although offered an appointment in the Mediterranean, he was nominated, 15 Aug. following, Acting-Lieutenant of the LILY 16, Capt. Chas. Jas. Franklin Newton; to which sloop he was confirmed 12 Dec. in the same year. Since 23 Sept. 1847 (shortly previous to which date the LILY had been put out of commission) he has been employed on particular service in the BELLEROPHON 78, Capt. Robt. Lambert Baynes.

ORLEBAR. (COMMANDER, 1845.)

JOHN ORLEBAR, born in 1810, is third son of the late Rich. Orlebar, Esq., of Hinwick House, co. Bedford, who served as High Sheriff of that co. in 1808, by Maria, fourth daughter of Benj. Longuet, Esq., of Bath. He is brother of the late Alex. Orlebar, Esq., an officer in the Royal Engineers; and nephew of the present Lieut. Orlando Orlebar, R.N.

This officer entered the Navy 16 March, 1824; passed his examination in 1831; obtained his first commission 10 Sept. 1832; and from May, 1833, until the close of 1835, was employed in North America and the West Indies on board the LARNE 18, Capt. Wm. Sidney Smith, and FORTE 44, Capt. Watkin Owen Pell. For his services as a Surveyor he was advanced to his present rank 6 Feb. 1845. His name, since 28 April in the latter year, has been borne on the books of the VINDICTIVE 50, flag-ship of Sir Fras. Wm. Austen on the North America and West India station, where he is still surveying.

He married, at Quebec, 5 Feb. 1838, Harriet, youngest daughter of John Hale, Esq, Receiver-General of Lower Canada, by Elizabeth, sister of the present Earl Amherst, and daughter of the late Lieut.-General Wm. Amherst, Aide-de-Camp to the King, Lieut.-Governor of Portsmouth, Governor of St. John's, Newfoundland, and Adjutant-General of H.M. Forces. AGENTS—Hallett and Robinson.

ORLEBAR. (LIEUT., 1811. F-P., 14; H-P., 33.)

ORLANDO ORLEBAR, born in 1786, is fourth son of the late Rich. Orlebar, Esq., of Hinwick House, co. Bedford, one of the clerks extraordinary of the Privy Council, by his second wife Charlotte, daughter of Robt. Willing, Esq., of London. He is brother of the late Henry Orlebar, Esq., R.N.; and uncle of Commander John Orlebar, R.N.

This officer entered the Navy, 15 Oct. 1800, as Fst.-cl. Vol., on board the JAMAICA 26, commanded in the North Sea by Capt. John Mackellar; with whom, and with Capts. Walter Bathurst, Fleetwood Broughton Reynolds Pellew, Wm. Wells, Geo. Bell, Wm. Augustus Montagu, and Jas. Murray Gordon, we find him, from March, 1801, to Oct. 1808, serving, as Midshipman and Master's Mate, in the TERPSICHORE 32, on the Cape of Good Hope and East India stations. In 1805 he was wounded while assisting in a boat which was sunk at the capture, after a desperate resistance, of the French corvette *Tourterelle*, under the batteries of St. Denis, Ile de Bourbon. He was present in the course of the same year in another boat which was sunk in effecting the destruction of a French brig off the Isle of France; and in Nov. 1806 he was engaged in the headmost boat at the annihilation, in Batavia Roads, of a Dutch frigate, seven brigs-of-war, and about 20 armed and other vessels. On his arrival home in 1809 in the ALBION 74, Capt. John Ferrier, he rejoined Capt. Bathurst on board the SALSETTE 36, and, accompanying the ensuing expedition to the Walcheren, was there intrusted with the command of a gun-boat. In Oct. 1809 he left the SALSETTE; and in Oct. 1810 he was received on board the VILLE DE PARIS 110, bearing the flag of Rear-Admiral Thos. Fras. Fremantle in the Mediterranean; where he was nominated, 25 Jan. 1811, Acting-Lieutenant of the BLAKE 74, Capt. Edw. Codrington. His official promotion took place 14 March following. He invalided in Aug. of the same year, and was next, from Dec. 1811 until Aug. 1815, employed on the Channel, North American, and West India stations, in the WOLVERENE sloop, Capts. Chas. Kerr and Geo. Grey Burton. Since he left that vessel, in which it appears he was present in the attack upon Baltimore, he has been on half-pay.

Lieut. Orlebar (who was left a widower 15 Nov. 1831) married, 24 April, 1824, Helen Maria, only daughter of the late Admiral Aplin, and sister of the present Capt. J. G. Aplin. His eldest daughter is the wife of Lieut. Augustus John Burton, R.N.

ORMOND. (COMMANDER, 1825. F-P., 15; H-P., 28.)

FRANCIS ORMOND entered the Navy, 18 Sept. 1804, as Fst.-cl. Vol., on board the IMPÉTUEUX 74, Capt. Thos. Byam Martin, attached to the Channel fleet; and, between Oct. 1805 and the date of his promotion to the rank of Lieutenant 3 Dec. 1810, was employed on the Home and Baltic stations, as Midshipman and Master's Mate, in the SAN JOSEF 110, bearing the flag of Sir Chas. Cotton, PRINCE OF WALES 98, Capts. T. B. Martin and Sir Home Popham, IMPLACABLE 74, Capts. T. B. Martin, Philip Pipon, and Geo. Chas. Mackenzie, and SCIPION 74 and VICTORY 100, flag-ships of Hon. Sir Robt. Stopford and Sir Jas. Saumarez. He was present in the PRINCE OF WALES under the flag of Admiral Gambier at the bombardment of Copenhagen in Sept. 1807; in the IMPLACABLE he took part, 26 Aug. 1808, in a gallant action of 20 minutes with the Russian 74-gun ship *Sewolod*, which was completely silenced, and in the end, with the assistance of the CENTAUR 74, flag-ship of Sir Sam. Hood, captured and burnt in sight of the whole Russian fleet near Rogerswick, after a total loss to the enemy of 303 men, and to the IMPLACABLE, individually, of 6 killed and 25 wounded; and on 7 July, 1809, he assisted, in the IMPLACABLE's boats, in a brilliant attack on a Russian flotilla, described in our memoir of Capt. Chas. Allen. His appointments in the capacity of Lieutenant (after a brief servitude as such in the ALEXANDER 74, Capts. John Quilliam and Robt. Cathcart) were—18 March, 1811, to the CHEROKEE sloop, Capt. Wm. Ramage, on the coast of Norway—2 March, 1812, to the DICTATOR 64, Capts. Robt. Williams and Wm. Autridge, in the Baltic—25 May following, for four months, to the

Aboukir 74, as Flag-Lieutenant, on the latter station, to Rear-Admiral T. B. Martin—19 May, 1813, to the Endymion of 48 guns, Capt. Henry Hope, on the coast of North America, whence he returned in Sept. 1815—25 July, 1816, to the Impregnable 98, in which ship, bearing the flag of Rear-Admiral David Milne, he remained until the following Oct. —15 March, 1818, to the Iphigenia 42, Capt. Hyde Parker, under whom he escorted the Duke of Richmond as Governor-General to Canada, and then made a voyage to Jamaica, whence, in Aug. 1819, he invalided—towards the close of 1820, to the Atholl 28, Capt. Henry Bourchier—and, after about two years of half-pay, to the Victory 104, flag-ship of Sir Geo. Martin at Portsmouth. In 1812 Mr. Ormond, at that time a Lieutenant of the Aboukir, was attached to the flotilla at the defence of Riga. While serving in the Endymion he commanded a division of gun-boats, under the orders of Capt. Robt. Barrie, in an expedition up the Penobscot river, on which occasion he contributed, and was honourably mentioned for the able assistance he afforded, at the capture of the towns of Castine, Hamden, and Bangor, and the destruction, by the Americans, of the U.S. corvette *Adams*, a brig pierced for 18 guns, a large privateer, and eight merchant-vessels.* He was also present in the Endymion's boats in an unsuccessful attack upon the American privateer *Prince de Neufchâtel*, whose opposition occasioned the assailants a loss of 28 killed and 37 badly wounded; and, on 15 Jan. 1815, he contributed in that ship to the memorable capture, after a close action of two hours and a half, a loss to the British, out of 319 men, of 11 killed and 14 wounded, and to the enemy of 35 killed and 70 wounded, of the *President* American frigate of 56 guns and 465 men. He was Second-Lieutenant of the Impregnable at the battle of Algiers, 27 Aug. 1816. Since his last promotion, which took place 27 May, 1825, he has been on half-pay.

Commander Ormond married, 20 June, 1822, Fanny, daughter of J. Hedges, Esq., of Wallingford.

* *Vide* Gaz. 1814, p. 2031.

OSBORN. (Retired Commander, 1838. f-p., 19; h-p., 35.)

John Osborn was born 17 Feb. 1775.

This officer entered the Navy, 22 Aug. 1793, as A.B., on board the Irresistible 74, Capt. John Henry; and in the early part of the following year was present at the reduction of the French islands in the West Indies, where, at Port-au-Prince, he was employed on shore with the army. Joining next the Bombay Castle 74, Capts. Chas. Chamberlayne, Jas. Macnamara, and Thos. Sotheby, he was afforded an opportunity of sharing, as Midshipman, in Hotham's second partial action, 13 July, 1795. In Dec. 1796, when the latter ship was wrecked in the river Tagus, Mr. Osborn was struck by lightning while in the act of cutting away the masts, and greatly injured in the head. On his return to England in charge of a prize at the commencement of 1797, he was ordered to join the Ville de Paris 110, bearing the broad pendant at first of Sir Robt. Calder, and the flag, next, of Earl St. Vincent, off Cadiz and in the Mediterranean, where from June, 1799, until May, 1803, he served, as Master's Mate and Acting-Master, in the Vincejo sloop. Capts. Geo. Long, Robt. Yarker, Geo. Chas. Mackenzie, Jas. Murray Northey, and Jas. Prevost. While in that vessel, besides participating in a variety of cutting-out affairs, he was present at the blockade and surrender of Malta, at the capture of *Le Guillaume Tell* of 84 guns and 1000 men, and in the operations against the French in Egypt. He was also severely wounded by the passage of a ball through his right arm in an action fought between the Vincejo and two Greek vessels; and in Oct. 1801 he was again wounded while serving on shore in a partially successful attack on the enemy's batteries at Porto Ferrajo, where the British sustained a loss of 15 (including Capt. Long) killed, 33 wounded, and 77 missing. In Oct. 1803 Mr. Osborn became Master's Mate of the Repulse 74, Capt. Hon. Arthur Kaye Legge, under whom he witnessed the capture, 13 March, 1806, of the French 80-gun ship *Marengo*, bearing the flag of Admiral Linois, and 40-gun frigate *Belle Poule*. His appointments as Lieutenant, a rank he had attained 22 Jan. preceding, were—26 May, 1806, to the Lucifer bomb, Capt. Robt. Elliot, in the North Sea, where he was superseded from ill health in the ensuing Sept.—30 Jan. 1807, to the Prince of Orange 74, flag-ship in the Downs of Vice-Admirals Bartholomew Sam. Rowley and Geo. Campbell—and, 18 March, 1808, to the command of the Quail 4. In the latter vessel, until he invalided in Feb. 1813, he was employed in escorting convoys to different places, and in bearing despatches to Sir Edw. Pellew off Toulon. He accepted his present rank 13 Oct. 1838.

Commander Osborn married, 6 Nov. 1806, Miss Johannah Catmore, of Aldborough, by whom he has issue three children.

OSBORN. (Lieutenant, 1846.)

Sherard Osborn was Midshipman of the Hyacinth 18, Capt. Wm. Warren, at the reduction of Canton in 1841, and of the Clio 18, Capt. Edw. Norwich Troubridge (with whom he served on shore), at the capture of the batteries of Woosung, 16 June, 1842.* He passed his examination 6 Dec. 1843; served as Mate on board the Excellent gunnery-ship at Portsmouth, Capt. Sir Thos. Hastings, and Collingwood 80, bearing the flag in the Pacific of Sir Geo. Fras. Seymour; and obtained his commission 4 May, 1846. He was then re-appointed to the Collingwood, in which ship he is still employed.

OTTER. (Commander, 1844.)

Henry Charles Otter entered the Navy 12 Jan. 1822; passed his examination in 1828; obtained his first commission 5 Dec. 1831; was employed at Sheerness, from 15 Aug. 1833 until the close of 1835, as Supernumerary-Lieutenant, in the Ocean 80 and Howe 120, Capts. Sam. Chambers, Edw. Barnard, and Alex. Ellice; assumed command, 5 March, 1844, of the Sparrow surveying-vessel, on the coast of Scotland; acquired his present rank 26 Aug. following; and, since 1 Jan. 1847, at which period he left the Sparrow, has been in command, on the same station, of the Avon steam surveying-vessel, of 160-horse power.

When a Midshipman, Commander Otter's heroic exertions saved the lives of a boat's crew; and in 1845 he again displayed the intrepid humanity of his disposition by jumping overboard from the Sparrow for the purpose of affording assistance to some of his crew who had been capsized.

OTTY. (Commander, 1815. f-p., 14; h-p., 30.)

Allen Otty entered the Navy, 15 Aug. 1803, as A.B., on board the Helder, guard-ship in the river Humber, Capts. Edw. Hawkins and Benj. Walker. From April, 1806, until promoted to the rank of Lieutenant 14 April, 1810, he served, chiefly in the capacity of Master's Mate (a rating he had attained 9 May, 1805), in the San Josef and Ville de Paris of 110 guns, Caledonia 120, and Barfleur 98, flag-ships on the Channel and Lisbon stations of Sir Chas. Cotton, Lords Gardner and Gambier, and Hon. Geo. Cranfield Berkeley. His succeeding appointments were to the Impétueux 74, Capt. John Lawford, Phipps gun-brig, Capt. Christopher Bell, and Goshawk sloop, Capts. Jas. Lilburn, Thos. Ball Clowes, and Hon. Wm. John Napier; to the gun-boat service on the river St. Lawrence; and to the Confiance 18 and Minstrel 20, both commanded by Capt. Peter Fisher. On the night of 29 April, 1812, we find him serving with the boats of the Goshawk and of a squadron under the orders of Capt. Thos. Ussher, and acquiring the greatest praise for his undaunted courage, in a brilliant attack on the enemy's privateers and batteries in

* *Vide* Gaz. 1842, p. 2400.

the Mole of Malaga, an enterprise which, although partially successful, terminated in a loss to the British, out of 149 officers and men, of 15 (including Capt. Lilburn) killed and 53 wounded. After having acted for a period as Commander of the STAR sloop in North America, Mr. Otty was confirmed in his present rank by a commission bearing date 1 July, 1815. During the two following years he appears to have had command of the MONTREAL and CHARWELL on the lakes of Canada. He has since been on half-pay.

OTWAY, Bart. (CAPTAIN, 1846.)

SIR GEORGE GRAHAM OTWAY, born in Sept. 1816, is eldest surviving son of the late Admiral Sir Robt. Waller Otway, Bart., G.C.B., whom he succeeded 12 May, 1846.

This officer entered the Navy 15 July, 1828; and on the occasion of his promotion to the rank of Lieutenant, 10 Oct. 1838, was appointed Additional of the PRINCESS CHARLOTTE 104, bearing the flag of Hon. Sir Robt. Stopford in the Mediterranean, where he removed, 21 Feb. 1839, to the HAZARD 18, Capt. Jas. Wilkinson. His succeeding appointments were—8 Nov. 1839, to the VANGUARD 80, Capt. Sir Thos. Fellowes, with whom he returned to England—5 June, 1840, to the SOUTHAMPTON 50, Capt. Wm. Hillyar, fitting at Chatham—and, 13 Aug. following, to the MEDEA steamer, Capt. Fred. Warden, in the Mediterranean. Being awarded a second promotal commission 25 Jan. 1841, he was next—from 25 May, 1843, until advanced, in compliment to his father's memory, to Post-rank, 18 May, 1846—employed in command of the VIRAGO steam-sloop, of 300-horse power, again in the Mediterranean. He has since been on half-pay. AGENTS—Hallett and Robinson.

OTWAY. (COMMANDER, 1837. F-P., 13; H-P., 29.)

ROBERT OTWAY entered the Navy, 10 Jan. 1805, as Midshipman, on board the PALLAS 32, Capt. Lord Cochrane. Under that gallant officer he assisted, in March, 1805, at the capture of a galleon, *Il Fortuna*, laden with specie to the amount of 150,000*l.*, and with merchandize of nearly equal value; he witnessed also, in May, 1806, the destruction of the semaphores along the French coast; and, in the course of the same month, he was present, under a heavy fire from the batteries on Ile d'Aix, in a single-handed attack made by the PALLAS on the French 40-gun frigate *La Minerve*, in company with three 18-gun brigs. On the latter occasion the British ship, while preparing to board, unfortunately ran foul of her opponent, and by the tremendous shock was reduced to a complete wreck. Between June, 1806, and Feb. 1812, Mr. Otway was successively employed, on the West India and Home stations, part of the time as Master's Mate, in the NORTHUMBERLAND and BELLEISLE 74's, both flag-ships of Hon. Sir Alex. Cochrane, ETHALION 36, Capt. Wm. Chas. Fahie, BELLEISLE again, bearing the broad pendant of Commodore Geo. Cockburn, NEPTUNE 98, Capt. W. C. Fahie, ABERCROMBY 74, Capt. Sir Jas. Athol Wood, DRAGON 74, flag-ship of Sir Fras. Laforey, WANDERER sloop, Capt. Frank Gore Willock, DRAGON a second time, NAYADEN frigate, Capt. Robt. Merrick Fowler, HELENA sloop, Capt. Henry Montresor, and again in the DRAGON. In the ETHALION we find him aiding, as Master's Mate, at the reduction, in Dec. 1807, of the Danish islands of St. Thomas and Ste. Croix; and in the BELLEISLE, in 1809, at the capture of Martinique and Flushing. He was confirmed in the rank of Lieutenant (after having acted for three months as such in the DEMERARA, Capt. W. Smith, on the West India station) 14 May, 1812; and was subsequently appointed—for a few months in 1813, to the BOYNE 98 and VILLE DE PARIS 110, flag-ships of Sir Harry Burrard Neale in the Channel—17 Sept. 1822, to the BULWARK 76, Capt. Thos. Dundas, lying at Plymouth, where he remained upwards of 12 months—22 July, 1830, to the command (which he retained until the close of 1833) of the ECHO steam-vessel—and, 23 April, 1836, to the command (with his name on the books of the WILLIAM AND MARY yacht) of the COMET, another steamer. As an especial mark of the approbation entertained by the Admiralty of his services in the ECHO and COMET on the coasts of Spain and Portugal during the civil war, he was advanced to his present rank 6 Jan. 1837. He has since been on half-pay.

In 1838 Commander Otway published 'An Elementary Treatise on Steam.' He is married and has issue. AGENT—Joseph Woodhead.

OTWAY. (COMMANDER, 1846. F-P., 19; H-P., 7.)

ROBERT JOCELYN OTWAY is youngest son of the Rev. J. Sam. Otway; and nephew of the late Admiral Sir Robt. Otway, Bart., G.C.B.

This officer entered the Navy 3 May, 1821; passed his examination in 1827; and was made Lieutenant, 13 Nov. 1828, into the SAPPHIRE 28, Capt. Henry Dundas, on the South American station, whence he returned home and was paid off in 1830. His succeeding appointments were—8 Oct. 1832, for nearly three years, to the SPARTIATE 76, Capt. Robt. Tait, successive flag-ship of Sir Michael Seymour and Sir Graham Eden Hamond, again in South America—22 Aug. 1840, to the CALCUTTA 84, Capts. Sir Sam. Roberts and Geo. Fred. Rich, with whom he served, in the Mediterranean and off Lisbon, until paid off at the close of 1842, the chief part of the time as First-Lieutenant—and, 16 May, 1843, in the latter capacity, to the CASTOR 36, Capt. Chas. Graham, fitting for the East Indies. In Dec. 1845, being at the time at New Zealand, Lieut. Otway landed in command of 188 officers, seamen, and marines belonging to the latter ship, and on 11 of the following month, after having most usefully participated for three weeks in a series of trying operations (more particularly alluded to in our memoir of Capt. Graham), assisted, and was officially mentioned for his conduct, at the storming and capture, notwithstanding a desperate resistance of four hours, of a strongly fortified pah belonging to a rebel chieftain named Kawiti. He was in consequence promoted to the rank of Commander by commission bearing date the day of the occurrence.* He returned to England in the course of the same year, and is now on half-pay.

Commander Otway married, 17 Aug. 1836, Anne Digby, youngest daughter of the late Sir Hugh Crofton, Bart., of Mohill House, co. Leitrim, by whom he has issue. AGENTS—Hallett and Robinson.

OTWAY, Bart., G.C.B. (ADMIRAL OF THE WHITE, 1841. F-P., 36; H-P., 26.)

SIR ROBERT WALLER OTWAY was born in April, 1772, and died suddenly 12 May, 1846. He was second son of Cooke Otway, Esq., of Castle Otway, co. Tipperary, an old officer of dragoons, by Elizabeth, daughter of Sam. Waller, Esq., of Lisbrian, in the same co., sister of Sir Robt. Waller, Bart., and niece of Sir Robt. Jocelyn, Bart., who, after filling the office of Lord Chancellor of Ireland, was created Baron Newport and Viscount Jocelyn. Sir Robt. Otway (whose family, a branch of the Otways of Middleton and Ingmire Hall, co. Westmoreland, had been seated in Ireland since the days of Cromwell) was brother (with Major Geo. Otway of the 85th Regt., who died at Jamaica in 1804) of Sir Loftus Wm. Otway, C.B., a Lieutenant-General in the Army and Colonel of the 84th Regt., and uncle of the late Hon. Robt. Otway Cave, M.P., and the present Commander Robt. Jocelyn Otway, R.N.

This officer entered the Navy, 15 April, 1784, as Midshipman, on board the ELIZABETH 74, Capt. Robt. Kingsmill, and after a servitude of three years in the Mediterranean on board the PHAETON frigate, and a further attachment, in the West Indies, to the BLONDE, was made Lieutenant, 8 Aug.

* *Vide* Gaz. 1846, pp. 2345, 2346, 2348.

1793, into the FALCON brig. Being appointed, next, to the IMPREGNABLE 98, bearing the flag of Rear-Admiral Benj. Caldwell, he was afforded an opportunity of participating in that ship in Lord Howe's actions of 28 and 29 May and 1 June, 1794. On the last-mentioned occasion, although but a Junior Lieutenant, he contrived greatly to distinguish himself by his alacrity in going aloft, with the late Sir Chas. Dashwood, then a Midshipman, and lashing the foretopsail-yard, which had been shot in the slings, to the cap; by which means the ship was enabled to wear in pursuit of the enemy. So well pleased was the Rear-Admiral at the performance of this essential service, without which the topsail could not have been again set, that he returned him his thanks publicly on the quarter-deck; and, on shortly afterwards shifting his flag to the MAJESTIC 74, took him with him as his First-Lieutenant—a post which, with a degree of modesty and good feeling highly creditable to him, Mr. Otway had declined filling on board the IMPREGNABLE, from a fear of creating jealousies, detrimental to the service, among his messmates, all of whom were senior to himself. His personal as well as his professional merit having thus strongly recommended him, he was in the course of the same year appointed by Rear-Admiral Caldwell, who had been directed to assume the control of naval affairs in the Leeward Islands, Commander of the THORN sloop of 16 6-pounders. In that vessel Capt. Otway, in April, 1795, had the good fortune to capture *La Belle Créole*, a large schooner, sent by the notorious Victor Hugues, from Guadeloupe, to assist in carrying into execution a plan that had been concerted between himself and the disaffected inhabitants of St. Pierre, Martinique, for the burning of that town and the massacre of all those who were inimical to them. The detection thus afforded of the diabolical conspiracy was considered of such importance that the French Royalists united in presenting Capt. Otway with a gold-hilted sword, valued at 200 guineas. On 25 of the following month he fell in with, and after a spirited night action of 35 minutes, during which the enemy made two ineffectual attempts to board the THORN, succeeded, much to his praise, in capturing, the French corvette *Le Courrier National*, of 18 guns (8 and 6 pounders) and 119 men, 7 of whom were killed and 20 wounded, with a loss to the British of their Commander and 5 out of 80 men wounded.* During the Carib war in the island of St. Vincent, Capt. Otway was actively employed in co-operation with the army, particularly in an attack made upon Owia, which place was surprised and taken by the THORN and a party of soldiers belonging to the 60th Regt. He afterwards landed his crew, and, in conjunction with a detachment of troops, stormed the strong post of Château Bellair, the loss of which obliged the enemy to retire into the interior of the country. His abilities and zeal having already attracted the attention of Sir John Laforey, the new Commander-in-Chief, Capt. Otway (who on the occasion last named had been slightly wounded, and had had 25 of his people killed and wounded) was by him promoted, 30 Oct. 1795, to a Post-vacancy in the MERMAID 32. While cruizing soon afterwards off Lebaye, in the island of Grenada, in company with the FAVORITE sloop, Capt. Jas. Athol Wood, he landed with a party of seamen and marines from both vessels, and, under the covering fire of the latter, stormed, carried, and levelled with the ground a battery which had been erected by the revolutionary enemy in a position for scouring the beach and intercepting all communication between the shipping and a body of English troops who lay pent up in a block-house. Not long after this affair several regiments arrived from England, and were disembarked in the neighbourhood of the same place; but scarcely had they commenced operations, when the appearance of two French vessels, having on board considerable reinforcements, induced the General in command of the British forces to decide upon immediately re-embarking. Perceiving, however, that the result of this measure would be the total loss of the island, Capt. Otway peremptorily refused his acquiescence in it, observing "that he had landed the troops at a great risk* by the General's desire, and that *they must now fight it out, as he would not embark a man*." Having thus taken upon himself an awful amount of responsibility, he galloped up a height on which were posted some field-pieces under the command of an artillery officer, ordered their fire to be opened on the enemy's vessels, and by that means compelled them to cut their cables and stand out to sea with the soldiers still on board. They were pursued with great promptitude by Capt. Wood, but escaped in consequence of the FAVORITE unfortunately losing her foretopmast. A general attack was then made by the British troops, led on by Brigadier-General Campbell, who charged the enemy on Pilot Hill, and gained a thorough victory. Thus to the resolution and intrepidity, and the judgment and exertions,† of one man was Great Britain in the main indebted for the preservation of the island of Grenada. Capt. Otway's next exploit was the defeat, 8 Aug. 1796, under the batteries of Basse-terre, Guadeloupe, of *La Vengeance*, a French frigate mounting 52 guns, sent by Victor Hugues for the express purpose of either capturing or sinking the MERMAID. The action, which lasted upwards of three hours, although attended with no casualty whatever to the British, was productive of a loss to their opponent of at least 12 killed and 26 wounded; and so exasperated was Victor Hugues at its result, that, on the return of the beaten *Vengeance* to her anchorage, he broke the French Captain's sword, and deprived some English prisoners at Basse-terre, who had cheered on witnessing the issue of the combat, of water for the space of 24 hours. In the month of April, 1797, the MERMAID, in company with the HERMIONE, QUEBEC, and PENELOPE frigates, had a smart affair with the forts at Jean Rebel, St. Domingo, and aided in a manner that obtained her Commander the thanks of his senior officer at the cutting out of 12 sail of merchantmen.‡ Exchanging soon afterwards into the CERES 32, Capt. Otway captured, in the boats of that frigate, *La Mutine* French privateer of 18 guns and 90 men, lying at anchor in a creek at Puerto Rico, and drove on shore and burnt another vessel of the same name and force. When in chase, in the early part of 1798, of a guarda-costa, the CERES, with her consort the TRENT 36, unfortunately took the ground near the Havana, a circumstance which enabled the hostile vessel to place herself in a very annoying posture. The advantage she had thus gained was however brief; for Capt. Otway, throwing himself into one of the boats sent by the squadron to their assistance, made instantly towards her, followed by five others, and in a few minutes boarded, carried, and burnt her. She mounted 6 long 24-pounders and 4 smaller guns, and bore the broad pendant of a Commodore of flotilla. The CERES, being almost immediately afterwards got afloat, assisted in extricating the TRENT, the command of which frigate, on the proximate death of her Captain, was bestowed upon the gallant subject of the present narrative, as a reward for the great exertions he had displayed in rescuing her from her perilous position. At the commencement of 1799 Capt. Otway landed on the south side of the island of Puerto Rico, and surprised a battery of 6 24-pounders, under the protection of which lay an enemy's schooner, whose capture was in consequence secured. In the execution of this service he displayed his accustomed tact, and, although he had but 1 man killed, was under the necessity of putting 20 of the enemy to the sword. A few weeks subsequently, being in the same vicinity, in company with the SPARROW cutter, he discovered two French privateers, each mounting 18 guns, together with a Spanish brig of 10 guns and some coasting

* *Vide* Gaz. 1795, p. 804.

* The *Pontsborn* East-Indiaman was lost that night, in consequence of being detained after landing the soldiers embarked in her.

† *Vide* Gaz. 1796, p. 719. ‡ *V.* Gaz. 1797, p. 517.

vessels, at anchor under a small battery within the Dead Man's Chest. The enemy's guns on shore were soon silenced by the TRENT, and her boats sent under cover of the SPARROW to attack the vessels. On their approach each of the privateers hoisted the bloody (red) flag, as an indication that no quarter would be given; but notwithstanding this they resolutely pushed on, and, after a smart action carried the whole without losing a man, while the enemy had not less than 50 killed and wounded. In the following July Capt. Otway formed a plan for cutting out the late British frigate *Hermione*, whose crew had mutinied, and carried her, as reported, into the port of Laguira. For this purpose he left the TRENT with two boats; and at one A.M. on the 8th, after a fatiguing row of many hours, entered the enemy's anchorage, but, to his mortification, found that the object of his search was not there. Resolved, however, to effect something, he made a dash at a vessel, apparently a corvette, which his pilot informed him had lately arrived from Spain. Although knocked back, while in the act of boarding, by the discharge of a musket, whose contents passed close along his cheek, his determined spirit was not to be daunted; and in a few minutes he and his brave followers were in full possession of their trophy. By break of day they had succeeded in towing her clear of a heavy fire which had been opened upon her from the batteries; but, as the sun rose, a flotilla of gun-boats was observed coming out of the harbour in pursuit. As a dead calm had by this time set in, and as it was perfectly impossible to compete with a force so overwhelming, the only question that remained was as to how they should themselves avoid falling into the enemy's hands. With that coolness and presence of mind which never forsook him, Capt. Otway instructed the Lieutenant who was with him, the late Sir Thos. Ussher, to place double sentinels over the prisoners, to point two of the guns (Spanish 12-pounders), treble-shotted, down the main hatchway, and upon the arrival of the flotilla within grape-range to fire them through the bottom. These directions were strictly followed, and on the approach of the enemy they found full employment in saving their countrymen from going down with the sinking vessel—the adventurous British being thereby suffered to accomplish their escape without further molestation. Capt. Otway continued to command the TRENT until Sept. 1800, when he sailed for England with the flag of Sir Hyde Parker. During the six years that he had then served in the West Indies, he was supposed to have captured and destroyed 200 of the enemy's privateers and merchantmen, mounting in the whole upwards of 500 guns. He had, besides, assisted at the siege of Morne Fortuné, in Ste. Lucie, and of Fort Matilda, in Guadeloupe. On his arrival home he resigned the command of the TRENT for the purpose of assuming that of the ROYAL GEORGE 100, bearing the flag of his friend Sir Hyde Parker, with whom he soon removed into the LONDON 98, and in March, 1801, sailed with the fleet destined to act against the northern confederacy. On the expedition reaching the Kattegat, a consultation, as is well known, was held between the Flag Officers, the Captain of the Fleet, and some of the Senior Captains, as to the best means of carrying its main object into effect; and it was decided that the advance should be made through the Belt. On this arrangement being brought to the knowledge of Capt. Otway he at once perceived the fatal difficulties that would result; he lost not a moment therefore in explaining his views to the Commander-in-Chief; and so manifest was his reasoning that immediate measures were taken for rectifying the error, and the plan adopted which was afterwards followed. Owing to the LONDON not forming a part of the division engaged, Capt. Otway had but slender hopes, at the commencement of the battle, of being enabled to obtain any share in it. As the conflict, however, progressed, and the critical position of the squadron under Lord Nelson grew apparent, it became a subject of consideration between Sir Hyde Parker and the Captain of the Fleet whether or not the signal should be made for discontinuing the action. At this juncture Capt. Otway, by whom the step had been strongly opposed, was despatched in a boat to his Lordship in order to ascertain the state of affairs. Before he reached the ELEPHANT the signal to leave off action was made; it was, however, disregarded by Nelson; and as Capt. Otway had *verbal authority from Sir Hyde Parker that the battle should continue if he saw any probability of success*, the action was maintained until the enemy announced his submission. Capt. Otway, we may add, remained on board the ELEPHANT until that happy consummation of the struggle. On the following day he was deputed, at the suggestion of Lord Nelson, to perform a service of the utmost importance; one indeed of which he acquitted himself in a manner that redounded beyond measure to his character for judgment and ingenuity. The achievement we allude to was nothing less than that of procuring the surrender (after two other officers had failed in their attempts to effect it) of the *Holstein*, a 60-gun ship, which, although she had actually struck, the Danes refused to give up, upon the plea that the colours had been merely shot away in the action, and that, as a proof, her pendant still remained flying. This subterfuge Capt. Otway effectually removed by proceeding with a flag of truce on board the disputed ship, and enabling his coxswain, at a moment when the attention of the whole crew was directed towards himself, to ascend unperceived through the mainchains into the maintop, haul down the pendant, and convey it into his boat. Having thus far succeeded, and been referred by the Danish Captain (who, in ignorance of what had occurred, still persisted in the old excuse) to his Commodore, Capt. Otway forthwith repaired to that authority, who met him with the same objection, and was in the act of pointing in proof to the pendant, when, finding it to his astonishment gone, he was forced to acknowledge the ship a lawful prize, and to issue an order for its immediate delivery.* Immediately after this Capt. Otway was sent home with Sir Hyde Parker's despatches.† He then rejoined the LONDON in the Baltic, where he remained until appointed to the EDGAR 74; which ship, after serving with the Channel fleet and visiting the West Indies, he paid off in July, 1802. On the renewal of hostilities in 1803 he was selected to command the CULLODEN 74; but ill health and a severe domestic calamity prevented him from joining her. While serving next in the MONTAGU 74, he assisted in blockading the enemy's ports from Brest to the Dardanells; and was present, 22 Aug. 1805, in Admiral Hon. Wm. Cornwallis' attack on the French fleet close in with Brest harbour, on which occasion the MONTAGU poured a destructive broadside into *L'Alexandre* 80. He also accompanied Sir Rich. Strachan to the West Indies in pursuit of a French squadron; conducted, in Feb. 1808, the evacuation of Scylla, a fortified rock in the Faro of Messina, the garrison of which was embarked under a smart fire from the Calabrian shore;‡ and was for some time intrusted with the command of a squadron employed in co-operation with the patriots on the coast of Catalonia, where he received the thanks of the Junta of Gerona for the assistance afforded by him during the siege of that city, and for taking possession of the fortress of Rosas,§ by which measure the French troops were compelled to retire from Castalon, a town of some importance, situated five miles from the coast. Towards the close of 1808 he returned to England in the MALTA 80; and in 1809 he again sailed for the Mediterranean with convoy in the AJAX 74. During the greater part of the following winter he cruized with a small

* Clarke and McArthur, in their 'Life of Nelson,' and also Mr. Southey, have erroneously mentioned the *Zealand* as being the ship in dispute, and have, as mistakenly, attributed the recovery to the diplomatic dexterity of the immortal hero The Danes, in their printed account of the battle, assert "that an officer *with a flag of truce* came the morning after and *stole a seventy-four from them.*"

† *Vide* Gaz. 1801, p. 401. ‡ *V.* Gaz. 1808, p. 503

§ *V.* Gaz. 1808, p. 1322.

squadron under his orders off the island of Sardinia, and made many captures. He was afterwards employed with the in-shore squadron at the blockade of Toulon; and on 20 July, 1810, while so stationed, he displayed a high degree of gallantry, and was in particular lauded for his promptitude and good judgment, in interposing the AJAX between the SHEARWATER brig and a pursuing French force, consisting of 6 sail of the line and 4 frigates, whom the bold front maintained by himself and his consorts, the CONQUEROR and WARSPITE 74's and EURYALUS frigate, induced to put back.* On 31 March, 1811, we find him effecting, in company with the UNITÉ frigate, the capture, off the island of Elba, of *Le Dromédaire* store-ship of 800 tons and 20 guns, laden with 15,000 shot and shells and 90 tons of gunpowder. His health being much impaired, Capt. Otway returned in the course of the same year to England in the CUMBERLAND 74, and from that period remained on half-pay until May, 1813. Being then re-appointed to the AJAX, he at first joined the Channel fleet; in the following autumn he was employed in covering the siege of St. Sebastian; he made prize, 17 March, 1814, off Scilly, of *L'Alcyon*, a French corvette of 16 guns and 120 men;† and he next convoyed a squadron of transports from Bordeaux to Quebec, having on board 5000 troops destined to reinforce the English army in Canada; where, it appears, he assisted in equipping the flotilla on Lake Champlain. Attaining Flag-rank 4 June, 1814, Rear-Admiral Otway was next, from 3 Aug. 1818 until 24 Nov. 1821, employed as Commander-in-Chief at Leith; prior to his relinquishment of which post he was presented with the freedom of the city of Edinburgh, and entertained at a public dinner given by the noblemen and gentlemen of the club in St. Andrew's Square, as a testimony of their respect for his public and private character. At the commencement of 1826 he was offered, but declined, the chief command in the East Indies. In June of the same year, however, he accepted the chief command on the South American station, where he remained until the summer of 1829. On 22 July, 1830, Sir Robt. Otway (he had been nominated a K.C.B. 8 June, 1826) attained the rank of Vice-Admiral; and on 15 Sept. 1831 he was raised to the dignity of a Baronet. His last appointment was to the chief command at the Nore, which he held from 23 Feb. 1837 until July, 1840. His promotion to the rank of full Admiral took place 23 Nov. 1841; and his investiture with the G.C.B. 8 May, 1845. He had been presented, while on the South American station, with the insignia of the Brazilian Order of the Southern Cross. In Dec. 1830 and July, 1837, he was successively appointed a Groom of the Bedchamber to his late and her present Majesty.

Sir Robt. Waller Otway during the term of his career afloat had been not less than one hundred times engaged with the enemies of his country. He married, 15 Aug. 1801, Clementina, daughter and co-heir of Admiral John Holloway, of Wells, co. Somerset, by whom he has left issue three sons (the eldest, the present Sir Geo. Graham Otway, a Captain R N.) and six daughters. His eldest son, Robt. Waller Otway, a Commander R.N. (1839), was killed by a fall from his horse in Hyde Park in May, 1840; and his second, Chas. Cooke Otway, holding the same rank, was lost in command of the VICTOR sloop during a hurricane in the West Indies in Sept. 1842. AGENTS—Hallett and Robinson.

OVEREND. (RETIRED COMMANDER, 1844. F-P., 13; H-P., 35.)

HENRY OVEREND entered the Navy, 2 Aug. 1799, as Third-cl. Boy, on board the CERBERUS 32, Capt. Jas. Macnamara; and on 20 of the following Oct., while cruizing off Ferrol, was present in a very gallant attack made by that ship on one of five Spanish frigates in escort of a large convoy. In July, 1803, soon after his return from a visit to the West Indies, he became Midshipman (a rating he had attained in Aug. 1801) of the SUFFISANTE sloop, Capt. Gilbert Heathcote, lying at Plymouth; and he next, in Jan. 1804 and Nov. 1805, joined in succession the FRANCHISE 36, and, as Master's Mate, the BACCHANTE 20, Capts. Hon. John Murray, Randall Macdonnell, and Jas. Rich. Dacres, both on the Jamaica station; where, after a servitude of 12 months in the VETERAN 64, Capt. Andrew Fitzherbert Evans, he was nominated, 3 Dec. 1807, Acting-Lieutenant of the ARETHUSA 38, Capt. Sir Chas. Brisbane. On the morning of 30 Aug. 1806, being then in the BACCHANTE, Mr. Overend served with the boats under Lieut. Geo. Norton at the cutting out of an armed brig and two armed feluccas, under a tremendous fire from them and from several batteries and field-pieces on the beach in the harbour of Santa Martha, on the Spanish Main.* On leaving the ARETHUSA, of which frigate he had been confirmed a Lieutenant 9 Jan. 1808, he followed Sir C. Brisbane, in Sept. of that year, into the BLAKE 74, commanded subsequently by Capt. Edw. Codrington in the Downs. His last appointments were—16 June, 1809 (three months after he had left the BLAKE), to the MERMAID 32, Capt. Major Jacob Henniker, whom he accompanied with convoy to Quebec—12 Jan. 1810, to the GRAMPUS 50, Capt. Wm. Hanwell, in which ship he sailed with the trade for China—and 30 Nov. 1812, to the PRIMROSE 18, Capt. Chas. Geo. Rodney Phillott, employed off Flushing. He went on half-pay in Aug. 1812; and accepted the rank he now holds 19 Oct. 1844.

OWEN. (LIEUTENANT, 1811. F-P., 22; H-P., 21.)

BELL ROBERT OWEN entered the Navy, 8 April, 1804, as Fst.-cl. Vol., on board the ATHÉNIENNE 64, Capt. Fras. Fayerman; with whom, on his return from a voyage to China, he removed, in Oct. 1805, to the FORMIDABLE 98. After a servitude of more than five years in that ship on the Channel, Mediterranean, and Baltic stations, latterly under the command of Capt. Jas. Nicoll Morris, and nearly the whole time as Midshipman and Master's Mate, he was received as a Supernumerary, in March, 1811, on board the STATELY 64, Capt. Edw. Stirling Dickson, employed at the defence of Cadiz. Attaining the rank of Lieutenant 1 Aug. following, he was successively appointed in that capacity—6 Dec. in the same year, to the TWEED sloop, Capts. Thos. Edw. Symonds and Wm. Mather, in which vessel he served in the North Sea, visited the coast of Africa, and was wrecked, 5 Nov. 1813, in Shoal Bay, Newfoundland, where only 52 of the crew were saved—11 May, 1816, for nearly eight months, to the CADMUS 10, Capt. John Gedge, again in the North Sea—and 3 April, 1827, to the Coast Blockade, as Supernumerary of the HYPERION 42, Capt. Wm. Jas. Mingaye. He left the latter service on its abolition in 1831; and, since 31 Dec. 1838, has been employed in the Coast Guard.

OWEN. (COMMANDER, 1815. F-P., 14; H-P., 32.)

CHARLES CUNLIFFE OWEN, the representative of the ancient family of Cunliffe of Wycoller, is eldest surviving son of the late Chas. Owen, Esq., in the commission of the peace for co. Middlesex. He is nephew of the late Henry Owen Cunliffe, Esq., of Wycoller Hall, Lancashire; and of Joseph Owen, Esq., Captain in H.M. 77th Regt., who was killed at the storming of Seringapatam in 1799.

This officer entered the Navy, 6 March, 1801, as Midshipman, on board the VENGEANCE 74, Capts. Geo. Mundy and Geo. Duff, in which ship he was for about sixteen months employed in the Baltic and West Indies. He served next, until 1806, in the Channel and Mediterranean, in the VENERABLE 74, bearing the flag of Rear-Admiral Collingwood, NIOBE 40, Capt. Matthew Henry Scott, and WIZARD sloop, Capt. Edm. Palmer; and he then in succession joined the NORTHUMBERLAND and BELLEISLE 74's, flag-ships in the West Indies of Hon. Sir Alex. Cochrane; who, on 10 Aug. 1807, the very day he

* *Vide* Gaz 1810, p. 1509. † *V.* Gaz. 1814, p. 628.

* *Vide* Gaz. 1806, p. 1535.

had accomplished his time, nominated him Lieutenant of the NORTHUMBERLAND, commanded at the period by Capt. Wm. Hargood. Being confirmed, after his return to England, into the DREADNOUGHT 98, by a commission dated 13 Feb. 1808, he continued in that ship, as Acting Flag-Lieutenant to Rear-Admiral Thos. Sotheby, until 1809; in the course of which year he had the misfortune to be taken prisoner, while engaged, under Lieut. John Foreman, in a desperate and unsuccessful attempt to cut a French brig out from under the batteries of Ile d'Aix. After three years of captivity he at length, in 1812, contrived to effect his escape under circumstances of a peculiarly difficult and hazardous character. In the spring of 1813, having been, on his arrival in England, sent out on promotion to the Lakes of Canada, Lieut. Owen there joined the WOLFE 24, bearing the broad pendant of Sir Jas. Lucas Yeo, by whom he was intrusted with the command of a division of boats, and employed on shore in an attack made in May of that year on Sackett's Harbour. In the following month we find him assuming charge of the SIR SIDNEY SMITH schooner of 12 32-pounder carronades and 86 men; in which vessel, it appears, he was concerned in every engagement that took place during the remainder of the year on Lake Ontario. In the action fought on 28 Sept. at the head of the lake, with a squadron of superior force under Commodore Chauncey, the SIR SIDNEY SMITH, whose loss amounted to 3 men killed and 5 wounded, won distinction by the very gallant manner in which she supported the ROYAL GEORGE 20, Capt. Wm. Howe Mulcaster, and assisted in covering the retreat of the WOLFE, the Commodore's ship, after that vessel had lost her main and mizen topmasts. On 2 Nov. also, Lieut. Owen served with a force under the immediate orders of Capt. Mulcaster in a successful attack upon an armament assembled, for the invasion of Lower Canada, at French Creek in the river St. Lawrence; where he contrived, with much ability and courage, to place his schooner in an excellent position for annoying the enemy. On 29 March, 1814, a few weeks after he had been placed in acting-command of the ROYAL GEORGE, he was invested with the charge of the flotilla of gun-boats on the river St. Lawrence, for the purpose of conveying specie, stores, provisions, &c., for the Army and Navy, and of affording a channel of communication between the Upper and Lower Provinces. So great were the judgment, zeal, and talent, evinced by Commander Owen in the performance of the duties allotted to him, that, although the scene of his operations extended along more than 60 miles of the enemy's frontier, not a single boat belonging to the British was captured during the whole term of his command, a period of 10 months. The fatigue, indeed, and the privations endured by himself and his companions appear to have been of a more trying description than experienced by any other branch of the Canadian Service. Yet, as we have said, were his exertions unremitting and ardent in the extreme; and the judicious and energetic manner in which he afforded co-operation to the military whenever an opportunity offered was exhibited in the warm acknowledgments of General Sir Gordon Drummond, Colonel Morrison of the 44th Regt., &c. As may be presumed he obtained the high applause of Sir J. L. Yeo, and was by him recommended in the strongest manner to the notice and favourable consideration of the Admiralty. He was appointed Acting-Commander of the STAR sloop, on Lake Ontario, 1 Dec. 1814; but, owing to some informality in his original acting order, he was not confirmed in his present rank until 28 Feb. 1815; about which period he returned home with his friend Sir J. L. Yeo. He has since been on half-pay.

Commander Cunliffe Owen married, 9 Jan. 1821, Mary, only daughter of the late Sir Henry Blosset, Kt., Chief Justice of Bengal, and grandniece of the Countess de Salis, by whom, who died 3 May, 1841, he had issue three sons and one daughter. The eldest son, Henry Charles, a Captain in the Royal Engineers, was recently serving with credit on the Caffre frontier; and the youngest, Francis Philip, a Midshipman R.N., was lately serving in the SUPERB 80, Capt. A. L. Corry. The second son, Robert Julius, distinguished himself as Midshipman of the EDINBURGH 72, Capt. W. W. Henderson, during the operations on the coast of Syria (*vide* Gazette, 1840, p. 2601), and died on board that ship 9 April, 1841. AGENTS—Goode and Lawrence.

OWEN. (LIEUT., 1815. F-P., 9; H-P., 31.)

EDWARD OWEN entered the Navy, 19 May, 1807, as Fst.-cl. Vol., on board the HUSSAR 38, Capt. Robt. Lloyd, under whom he accompanied the expedition to Copenhagen, and continued to serve, as Midshipman, in the GUERRIÈRE 40 and SWIFTSURE 74, on the West India and North American stations, until April, 1811. During the next three years and three months we find him employed in the Channel and Mediterranean, in the EDINBURGH 74 and UNION 98, both commanded by Capt. Robt. Rolles. In the latter ship he witnessed Sir Edw. Pellew's partial actions of 5 Nov. 1813 and 13 Feb. 1814 with the Toulon fleet. After again serving in the West Indies and North America in the DOVER troop-ship, Capt. Robt. Henley Rogers, and on the Home station in the SNAP 12, Capt. Geo. King, he was advanced to the rank of Lieutenant 19 Sept. 1815. He has since been on half-pay.

Lieut. Owen married Harriet Juliana, fourth daughter of the late Rev. Edm. Sharington Davenport, of Davenport House, co. Salop, Vicar of Worfield. AGENTS—Messrs. Ommanney.

OWEN, G.C.B., G.C.H. (ADMIRAL OF THE BLUE, 1846. F-P., 50; H-P., 22.)

SIR EDWARD WILLIAM CAMPBELL RICH OWEN is son of Capt. Wm. Owen, R.N., a gentleman of high Welsh extraction, who lost his right arm, when a Midshipman, at the taking of Pondicherry from the French in 1760, and who, after assisting in command of the CORMORANT at the second capture of that town, was accidentally killed at Madras, while returning to England with despatches, in 1778. Sir Edward is brother of the present Rear-Admiral Wm. Fitzwilliam Owen; and first-cousin of Sir Arthur David Owen, Kt., of Glan Severn, a Deputy-Lieutenant for co. Montgomery, and High Sheriff in 1814, who for many years prior to his death, which took place in 1816, commanded the Montgomeryshire Yeomanry Cavalry under the Right Hon. Chas. W. W. Wynn.

This officer entered the Navy, 11 Aug. 1775, as Captain's Servant, on board the ENTERPRIZE, commanded in the Mediterranean by Capt. Sir Thos. Rich, with whom, from 1780 until 1782, he served in the West Indies in the PRINCESSA, SANDWICH, and PRINCESS ROYAL. In July, 1786, he rejoined the same Captain, as Midshipman, on board the CULLODEN 74, lying at Plymouth; and while on the books of that ship he was on two occasions lent to the FAIRY sloop, Capt. Isaac Geo. Manley, and LEANDER 50, bearing the broad pendant at Halifax of Commodore Herbert Sawyer. In the early part of 1790, after a servitude of two years on the Channel and Mediterranean stations in the LOWESTOFFE frigate, Capt. Edm. Dod, he passed his examination. He then became in succession attached to the THISBE 28, Capt. Rupert George, DIDO frigate, Capt. Edw. Buller, VENGEANCE 74, Capt. Sir Thos. Rich, HANNIBAL 74, Capt. John Colpoys, PORCUPINE 24, Capt. Edw. Buller, and CULLODEN again, Capt. Sir Thos. Rich; in which ships he served on the North American, Home, and West India stations, until made Lieutenant, 6 Nov. 1793, into the FORTUNÉE 36, Capt. Wooldridge, off Cadiz; where he soon removed to the HANNIBAL, still commanded by Capt. Colpoys. His next appointments were, 22 July and 15 Dec. 1794, to his old ship the CULLODEN, and to the LONDON 98, bearing the flags in the Channel of Admirals Sir Thos. Rich and J. Colpoys; by the latter, we believe, of whom he was nominated, after having enacted a part in Lord Bridport's action, Acting-Captain, in March and May, 1796, of the IMPREGNABLE 98, and QUEEN CHARLOTTE 100. Being awarded a second promotal commission, bearing date 19 Sept. 1796, Capt. Owen, in Jan. 1797, rejoined his friend Admiral Colpoys, as a Volunteer, on board the LONDON; on leaving which ship in the ensuing May he was for two months employed in command of the gun-brigs stationed in the river Thames and at the Nore, under the orders of Commodore Sir Erasmus Gower. He obtained Post-rank, 23 April, 1798, in the NORTHUMBERLAND 74, lying at Sheerness; and he was subsequently appointed—for a short period in the summer of the same year, to the IRRESISTIBLE 74, stationed in the river Medway—1 Jan. 1801, to the NEMESIS 28—11 May, 1802, to the IMMORTALITÉ 36—21 March, 1806, to the CLYDE 38—6 Dec. 1810, to the INCONSTANT 36—17 Feb. 1813, to the CORNWALL 74—30 July, 1814, to the DORSET yacht, off Deptford—12 Dec. 1814, to the chief command on the lakes of Canada—6 Feb. 1816, for six years, to the ROYAL SOVEREIGN yacht—and 25 Nov. 1822, to the GLOUCESTER 74. In the NEMESIS Capt. Owen commanded a detachment of vessels off the Scheldt and in the neighbourhood of Dunkerque; and in the IMMORTALITÉ he was at first employed, as Senior Officer, during the peace of Amiens, of a squadron of frigates lying in readiness for service in the Downs. On the renewal of hostilities we find him stationed with several sloops and smaller vessels under his orders on the coast of France, where his activity and zeal kept the enemy in a constant state of alarm. In June, 1803, he drove on shore, near Cape Blanc-nez, *Le Commode* and *L'Inabordable*, a French brig and schooner, each mounting 4 guns.* On 14 Sept. following he bombarded with effect the towns of Dieppe and St. Valery-en-Caux;† and in July, 1804, he directed an attack upon a powerful division of the French invasion flotilla, consisting of 45 brigs and 43 luggers, part of which was endeavouring to effect a passage from Boulogne to Etaples.‡ In Aug. of the same year he was for several days engaged with the enemy, particularly on the 25th and 26th, when the interchange of fire with their vessels and batteries in the vicinity of Boulogne was frequent and heavy. On 23 Oct. 1804 the IMMORTALITÉ and her consorts sustained a running action of an hour, between Capes Blanc-nez and Gris-nez, with three praams, seven brigs, and fifteen luggers,§ and in July, 1805, they took part in a very smart affair with the enemy near Ambleteuse. On the latter occasion the IMMORTALITÉ had her foremast, maintopmast, spanker-boom, and three boats shot through, her rigging and sails much cut, her hull struck in several places, 2 carronades disabled, and 4 men killed and 12 wounded, several of them severely. She had previously, 7 March, 1805, captured *El Entrepeda Corune* Spanish privateer of 44 guns and 66 men. On his removal (after having had command of a squadron stationed in the rivers Elbe and Weser, for the purpose of embarking the troops under Lord Cathcart) to the CLYDE, Commodore Owen (he had been ordered to hoist a broad-pendant) superintended, in Oct. 1806, a decisive and very successful experiment made with Congreve's rockets on the town of Boulogne, where many of the buildings and several vessels were destroyed.‖ Accompanying the expedition of 1809 to the Walcheren, the Commodore throughout the operations which there took place distinguished himself in a high degree by his gallant and animated conduct, and obtained warm commendation for the manner in which he discharged the various arduous duties he had to perform. His skill and judgment were in particular demonstrated in the position he assigned to the bomb and other vessels under his orders in the attack upon Flushing, and his activity and zeal in the assistance he afforded the ST. DOMINGO, the flag-ship of the Commander-in-Chief, when aground under the enemy's fire, which, through his exertions, was speedily slackened.* In the INCONSTANT Commodore Owen made a voyage to Vera Cruz and back, and was for some time attached to the fleet off the Scheldt; where, on his appointment to the CORNWALL, he assumed command of the advanced portion of the shipping. At the close of 1813 he rendered himself conspicuous by his exemplary conduct at the head of a body of seamen and marines landed to co-operate with the Dutch royalists in the defence of the island of South Beveland.† While in command of the ROYAL SOVEREIGN yacht he had the honour of conveying to this country the present Queen Dowager, the Dukes and Duchesses of Kent, Cumberland, Cambridge, and Hesse Homburg, and the Grand Duke Michael of Russia. With the exception of some months in 1823-4, Sir Edw. Owen (who had been nominated a K.C.B. 2 Jan. 1815, invested with the honour of Knighthood 14 May, 1816, and appointed a Colonel of Royal Marines 19 July, 1821) continued in the GLOUCESTER, on the West India station (where the House of Assembly at Jamaica passed a vote of thanks to him for his prompt attention to commercial and naval interests), from the date above mentioned until that of his promotion to Flag-rank 27 May, 1825. On 20 Dec. 1828 he was appointed to the chief command on the East India station, whence he returned in Oct. 1832; and he was next, from 14 Oct. 1841 until Feb. 1845, intrusted with the chief command (he had attained the rank of Vice-Admiral 10 Jan. 1837) in the Mediterranean, with his flag successively in the QUEEN 110 and FORMIDABLE 84. His nomination to the G.C.H. took place 24 Oct. 1832; and to the G.C.B. 8 May, 1845.

Sir Edw. W. C. R. Owen sat in Parliament in 1826 as Member for Sandwich. In May, 1827, he was appointed Surveyor-General of the Ordnance; he was selected, in March, 1828, to form a member of the Council of the Lord High Admiral; and in Dec. 1834 he was called to office as Clerk of the Ordnance. He married, in 1829, Miss Selena Hey. AGENTS—Hallett and Robinson.

* *Vide* Gaz. 1803, p. 711. † *V.* Gaz. 1803, p. 1273.
‡ *V.* Gaz. 1804, p. 891. § *V.* Gaz. 1804, p. 1320.
‖ Commodore Owen had very zealously and usefully co-operated in the famous Catamaran display made in Oct. 1804 against the enemy's flotilla.—*Vide* Gaz 1804, p. 1237.

* *Vide* Gaz. 1809, p. 1325, 2006, 2055.
† *V.* Gaz. 1813, p. 2676-77.

OWEN. (CAPTAIN, 1837.)

RICHARD OWEN is the son of a clergyman in co. Wexford.

This officer entered the Navy, 30 May, 1811, and was employed during the remainder of the war in the SCIPION 74 and LION 64, flag-ships of Hon. Robt. Stopford at the Cape of Good Hope, and in the BLENHEIM 74, Capt. Sam. Warren, in the North Sea and Mediterranean. In July, 1817, after a servitude of three years on the coast of Africa and in the West Indies in the ULYSSES 44, Capt. Thos. Browne, and PRIMROSE 18, Capt. Chas. Geo. Rodney Phillott, he passed his examination; and on 16 Feb. 1821, while attached to the KANGAROO surveying vessel, he was promoted to a Lieutenancy in the EURYALUS 42, Capt. Wilson Braddyll Bigland, on the Jamaica station. His next appointment was, 14 Nov. 1821, to the LEVEN 24, Capt. Wm. Fitzwilliam Owen, employed on a surveying expedition to the coast of Africa, where, during a continuance of nearly five years, he was for some time intrusted with the command of the COCKBURN and ALBATROSS schooners. In the ALBATROSS it was his fortune, during the Ashantee war, to obtain the best thanks of Major-General Chas. Turner for his unceasing and successful exertions in getting his vessel up the river, and for his forwardness both in the boats and on shore in an attack made, 19 Feb. 1826, on the town of Maccaba.‡ As a reward for his services, he was promoted to the rank of Commander 30 Sept. 1826. In 1828 he was employed by the Admiralty in surveying on the south coast of Wales, in connection with the Ordnance Survey; and on 9 May, 1829, he commissioned the BLOSSOM 16, for the purpose of conducting a survey in the West Indies.

‡ *V.* Gaz. 1826, p. 1159.

On the latter vessel from her defective condition being paid off, Capt. Owen obtained command, 25 March, 1833, of the THUNDER 6. He continued employed as before in the West Indies until advanced to his present rank 10 Jan. 1837; and has since been on half-pay.

Capt. Owen * was lately employed as Auditor of the Poor-Law Commissioners. He married, 4 July, 1837, Susannah Charlotte, eldest daughter of John Walker, Esq., Ordnance Storekeeper at the Bahamas.

* See Rear-Admiral W. F. Owen.

OWEN. (REAR-ADMIRAL OF THE BLUE, 1847. F-P., 34; H-P., 25.)

WILLIAM FITZWILLIAM OWEN is brother of Admiral Sir Edw. W. C. R. Owen, G.C.B., G.C.H.

This officer entered the Navy, 4 June, 1788, as Midshipman, on board the CULLODEN 74, Capt. Sir Thos. Rich, attached to the force on the Home station; where, and for a short time in the West Indies, he continued to serve in the ZEBRA sloop, Capts. Chas. Boyles and Hon. Robt. Forbes, ASSISTANCE 50, Capt. Lord Cranstoun, VENGEANCE 74, Capt. John Ford, HANNIBAL 74, Capt. John Colpoys, and CULLODEN again, Capts. Sir T. Rich, Isaac Schomberg, and Rich. Randell Burgess, until the close of 1794. In the last-mentioned ship he fought under Capt. Schomberg in the famous action of 1 June. On his return to England from the Cape of Good Hope, whither he had gone in the RUBY 64, Capt. Hon. Henry Edwin Stanhope, he joined, in Nov. 1795, the LONDON 98, bearing the flag in the Channel of Vice-Admiral John Colpoys. For his conduct during the mutiny at Spithead he was promoted, 12 June, 1797, to the rank of Lieutenant; and at the same time placed in command of the FLAMER gun-vessel. He was next, between Dec. 1798 and Oct. 1801, employed, principally in the Channel, on board the CHARON 44, Capt. John M'Kellar, GORGON, Capt. Robt. Williams, and NAMUR, flag-ship of Earl St. Vincent, and for seven months in command of the NANCY fire-vessel. Assuming command, 8 July, 1803, of the SEA FLOWER brig of 14 guns, Lieut. Owen, after serving for a time on the French coast, sailed for the East Indies, where he effected the capture, 15 July, 1806, of *Le Charles* French national ketch. In the following Sept. he explored part of the Maldiva Islands, and their separating channels, which had never been investigated; and on 10 Nov. in the same year he discovered an excellent channel, now bearing the name of his brig, situated between the islands of Sai Berout and Poulo Pora, near the west coast of Sumatra. On 27 of the latter month, having conducted Sir Edw. Pellew's squadron through a very intricate navigation into Batavia Roads, he there distinguished himself by his gallantry in command of a division of boats at the capture and destruction of a Dutch frigate, seven brigs-of-war, and about 20 armed and other merchant-vessels. We subsequently, 11 Dec. 1807, find him contributing to the destruction of the dockyard and stores at Griessee, in the island of Java, and of all the men-of-war remaining to Holland in India. In Sept. 1808 Lieut. Owen had the misfortune to be taken captive by the French, who detained him in the Mauritius until June, 1810; from Aug. to Nov. in which year he was employed, we believe, in superintending the transports sent from Madras to the Isle of France. He then, having been awarded a second promotal commission bearing date 20 May, 1809, obtained command of the BARRACOLTA 18, part of the force employed in the summer of 1811 at the reduction of the island of Java, where he assisted at the debarkation of the troops at Chillingching, and continued attached to the army until after the surrender of Batavia. In Dec. 1811 Capt. Owen, who had been advanced to Post-rank on 2 of the preceding May, and had held for a short time the command of the PIÉMONTAISE frigate at Bombay, was appointed to the CORNELIA 32. In 1812 he took possession, with a squadron under his orders, of the island of Palembang. He returned to England with a China convoy in June, 1813; and was subsequently appointed—27 March, 1815, to the Surveying service on the lakes of Canada, whence he came home in May, 1816—10 Aug. 1821, to the LEVEN 24, in which vessel he was for upwards of four years employed in conducting a survey of the coast of Africa*—2 Feb. 1827, to the EDEN 26, fitting for another expedition to the African coast, where, prior to his departure for South America, he was engaged in forming a settlement at Fernando Po—and (having paid the last-mentioned ship off at the close of 1831), 22 April, 1847, to the COLUMBIA steam surveying-vessel, of 100 horse-power, stationed in North America. Since 21 Dec. 1847, the date of his elevation to Flag-rank, he has been on half-pay.

Assisted by various officers, Rear-Admiral Owen, during his command of the LEVEN, constructed the following charts and views: viz. 22 of the West Coast of Africa, 31 of the East Coast of Africa, 12 of the East Coast of Madagascar, 17 of the West Coast of Madagascar, and 1 of the Harbour of Grand Port, in the Mauritius. He also, we understand, surveyed the coast of Asia from Cape Comorin, along the shores of Malabar and Surat, together with the whole extent of the sea-side of Persia and Arabia. In 1828 he constructed two charts of the Seychelles, and one of the port and bay in the island of Mahé. He has executed a chart of the mouth of the river Demarara, and published, in conjunction with Capt. Rich. Owen, 'Tables of Latitudes and Longitudes by Chronometers of Places in the Atlantic and Indian Oceans, with an Essay on the Management and Use of Chronometers.' AGENTS—Hallett and Robinson.

OXENHAM. (LIEUTENANT, 1826.)

JUSTUS OXENHAM entered the Navy 8 Jan. 1812; passed his examination in 1821; and on the occasion of his promotion to the rank of Lieutenant, 14 April, 1826, assumed command of the SPEEDWELL schooner, on the Jamaica station; where he was next, 5 Sept. 1828 and 4 July, 1829, appointed to the SLANEY 20, Capts. Henry Gosset and Chas. Parker, and MAGNIFICENT receiving-ship, Capts. Robt. Milborne Jackson and John Paget. He returned to England in the early part of 1832, and was subsequently, from 27 Feb. 1841 until paid off in 1845, employed on the Brazilian station in command of the COCKATRICE schooner. He has since been on half-pay.

He married, 15 June, 1835, Mary, only daughter of the late Mr. Peter, of Kelso, N.B., and niece of Sir John Peter, formerly H.M. Consul for the Netherlands. AGENT—J. Hinxman.

OXFORD. (LIEUT., 1821. F-P., 22; H-P., 18.)

JOHN OXFORD entered the Navy, 6 April, 1807, as Fst.-cl. Vol., on board the MAIDA 74, Capt. Sam. Hood Linzee; and in the following Nov., after having witnessed the fall of Copenhagen, became Midshipman of the NEPTUNE 98, Capt. Sir Thos. Williams, attached to the Channel fleet. From Nov. 1808 until Nov. 1815 he served on the West India, Home, Mediterranean, Brazilian, and African stations, in the BELLEISLE 74, Commodore Geo. Cockburn, TYRIAN 10, Capt. Henry Thos. Davies, HANNIBAL 74 and ROYAL GEORGE 100, both flag-ships of Sir Thos Williams, RODNEY 74, Capt. Edw. Durnford King, ROYAL WILLIAM, Capt. Geo. Fowke, and PORCUPINE 24, Capts. Robt. Elliot and John Coode. In the BELLEISLE he assisted at the reduction of Martinique and Flushing in 1809; and in the PORCUPINE he was present at the memorable entrance into the Adour of the flotilla under Rear-Admiral Chas. Vinicombe Penrose, and at the forcing of the Gironde. After a servitude of two years at Plymouth in the MALTA 80, Capt. Thos. Gordon Caulfeild, and, as Admiralty-Midshipman,

* During the Ashantee war he found opportunity of eliciting the grateful acknowledgments of Major-General Charles Turner for his manly co-operation, and the zeal he evinced for the public service, in a land attack made 19 Feb. 1826 on the town of Maccaba.—*Vide* Gaz. 1826, p. 1158.

in the SUPERB 74, Capt. Chas. Ekins, he sailed in 1818 for the East Indies, in the latter capacity, on board the TOPAZE frigate, Capts. John Rich. Lumley and Chas. Richardson. He returned to England in May, 1822, having been advanced to the rank of Lieutenant 19 July, 1821; and since 4 April, 1840, has been employed in the Coast Guard.

P.

PACE. (LIEUT., 1821. F-P., 15; H-P., 23.)

EDMUND HOWARD PACE is nephew of the late Rear-Admiral John Hayes, C.B.

This officer entered the Navy, in Sept. 1809, as Fst.-cl. Vol., on board the FREIJA 38, commanded in the West Indies by his uncle Capt. John Hayes; and was next, from Sept. 1810 to Nov. 1815, employed on the Home and North American stations as Midshipman, in the VENGEUR 74, flag-ship of Sir Joseph Sydney Yorke, BULWARK 74, bearing the broad pendant of Sir Rich. King, LOIRE 38, Capt. Thos. Brown, MAJESTIC 56, Capt. John Hayes, and FLY and MUSQUITO sloops, Capts. John Baldwin, Robt. Tomlinson, and Geo. Brine. In the FREIJA he served at the reduction of Guadeloupe in Feb. 1810; he escorted, in the VENGEUR, a large body of troops intended as a reinforcement to the Duke of Wellington's army in Portugal; and in the MAJESTIC, previously to witnessing the surrender of the American ship PRESIDENT, he assisted at the capture, 3 Feb. 1814, after a running action of two hours and a half, of the *Terpsichore* French frigate of 44 guns. In the FLY he was present, 18 July, 1815, at the cutting-out of several vessels from the harbour of Corrijon—an exploit more fully alluded to in our history of Sir Chas. Malcolm. Between Feb. 1816 and May, 1821, Mr. Pace became in succession attached as Admiralty-Midshipman, on the Home, Mediterranean, West India, and St. Helena stations, to the GANYMEDE 26, Capt. Wm. M'Culloch, GLASGOW 40, Capt. Hon. Anthony Maitland (part of the force engaged at the battle of Algiers), HERON 18, Capt. Herbert Brace Powell, TIGRIS 36, Capt. Robt. Henderson, SPARTAN 38, Capt. Wm. Furlong Wise, and VIGO 74, flag-ship of Rear-Admiral Robt. Lambert. He then returned to England as Master's Mate of a store-ship, Master-Commander Thompson; and in Aug. of the same year, 1821, took up a commission bearing date 29 of the preceding Jan. His next appointment was, 2 June, 1824, to the CHAMPION 18, Capt. John Fitzgerald Studdert, fitting for the East Indies; whence, in 1826, he came home as First-Lieutenant of the ARACHNE 18, Capt. And. Baird. With the exception of a short period passed in the Coast Guard about 1831, he has since been on half-pay. AGENTS —Messrs. Ommanney.

PADDON. (COMMANDER, 1826. F-P., 23; H-P., 31.)

SILAS HISCUTT PADDON was born 12 May, 1774, at Abotasham, near Bideford.

This officer entered the Navy, at the close of 1793, as A.B., on board the ISCA hired-vessel, Lieut.-Commander Philip Jones, employed, until 1797, in the conveyance of men from Bristol, Swansea, and Appledore to Plymouth. Joining, in the course of the latter year, the VIPER cutter of 12 guns, Lieut.-Commanders John Pengelly, Nathaniel Foster, and Jeremiah Coghlan, he made a voyage in that vessel to Sierra Leone, and during a term of nearly four years was actively employed as Midshipman on the coast of France. Under Lieut. Pengelly he assisted at the capture, 26 Dec. 1799, of *Le Furet* French privateer of 14 guns and 57 men; and under Lieut. Coghlan he contributed, on the night of 29 July, 1800, to the cutting-out, by a single boat containing 20 men, of a fully-prepared and desperately-defended gun-brig, *La Cerbère* of 7 guns and 87 men, moored with springs on her cables in a naval port of difficult access, within pistol-shot of three batteries, surrounded by several armed craft, and not a mile distant from a 74, bearing an Admiral's flag, and two frigates. The enemy in this brilliant exploit had 6 men killed, and 20 (including every officer) wounded; and the British, who were twice beaten back in their endeavours to board, 1 killed and 10 wounded. Among the latter was Mr. Paddon,* who received two pike-wounds under the ribs of his right side, also two in his left side and through his left leg, and two sword-wounds, one in the left hand and the other on the head. So long was he confined to his cot by these severe injuries that he lost the opportunity of appearing before the Board at Greenwich for the purpose of passing the examination necessary to entitle him to the receipt of a pension. On being paid off, after having further aided at the capture of *Le Héro* privateer of 14 guns and 73 men, and the defeat of the *Tapageur* corvette of 16 guns, he was received, at the close of 1801, on board the CAMBRIDGE 74, flag-ship of Sir Thos. Pasley at Plymouth; and in the course of 1802 he became in succession attached to the CENTAUR 74, bearing the flag of Vice-Admiral Jas. Rich. Dacres, DIAMOND frigate, Capt. Edw. Griffith, and NIMBLE cutter, Lieut.-Commander Jeremiah Coghlan. In Dec. 1803 he sailed for the Mediterranean on promotion in the HINDOSTAN store-ship, Capt. John Le Gros. Being accidentally burnt out of that vessel in the Bay of Rosas, 2 April, 1804, he was under the necessity of joining for short periods, in the course of the same year, the JUNO and SEAHORSE frigates, TRIUMPH and SUPERB 74's, Capts. Sir Robt. Barlow and Rich. Keats, MADRAS 54, Capt. Chas. Marsh Schomberg, and THISBE 28, Capt. Lewis Shepheard. In the latter vessel Mr. Paddon, whose advancement to the rank of Lieutenant had taken place on 20 of the month last mentioned, returned to England; joining, on his arrival, the ZEALAND 64, flag-ship at the Nore of Rear-Admiral Bartholomew Sam. Rowley. In May, 1806, he obtained command of the CUCKOO schooner, in which vessel we find him accompanying the expedition of 1809 to the Walcheren, and employed on the Channel and North Sea stations until wrecked, near Haarlem, 4 April, 1810. On that occasion he received several severe contusions in the back and chest, broke his right shoulder-blade and two of his ribs (the effects of which continue to this hour), and, worse than all, was doomed to experience the anguish of witnessing his infant son perish at his side. On his return to England, after a few months of captivity, he was appointed, 29 Oct. 1810, to the PRINCE FREDERICK, flag-ship of Sir Edw. Buller and Sir Thos. Byam Martin at Plymouth, where he remained until paid off in Feb. 1815. He was afterwards, in 1815–16, intrusted with the command of a Signal-station; and on 27 March, 1826, having memorialized George IV., he was advanced to the rank he now holds. He has since been on half-pay.

Commander Paddon is at present a Commissioner of Pilotage at Padstow. He has been twice married—the second time, 19 Feb. 1833, to Miss P. Richards, of Padstow. By his first marriage, which took place in 1802, he had issue four children, all of whom, including the one above alluded to, are since dead. In Nov. 1840 he was admitted to the out-pension of Greenwich Hospital.

PAGE. (ADMIRAL OF THE BLUE, 1841. F-P., 27; H-P., 40.)

BENJAMIN WILLIAM PAGE was born, 7 Feb. 1765, at Ipswich, co. Suffolk, where he died 3 Oct. 1845.

This officer entered the Navy, 20 Nov. 1778, as Fst.-cl. Vol., on board the SUPERB 74, bearing the flag in the East Indies of his patron Sir Edw. Hughes, under whom, in the course of 1782, he fought in four general actions with the French fleet under M. de Suffrein, and on one occasion received a severe wound in the leg. Being nominated, 27 Dec. in the latter year, Acting-Lieutenant of the EXETER 64, Capt. John Sam. Smith, he was afforded an opportunity of enacting a part in Sir Edw. Hughes' fifth and last engagement with the

* *Vide* Gaz. 1800, p. 897-8.

enemy, off Cuddalore, 20 June, 1783. He then in succession joined, in the capacity last mentioned, the WORCESTER 64, and LIZARD 18, Capts. Chas. Hughes and Donald Campbell; and on his return to England, as only Lieutenant, in the EURYDICE 24, Capt. Geo. Wm. Augustus Courtenay, was presented, about July, 1785, with a commission bearing date 20 Nov. 1784. His next appointments were—19 Oct. 1786 and 26 June, 1790, to the ASTREA 32, and MONARCH 74, both commanded by Capt. Peter Rainier on the Jamaica and Channel stations—23 Dec. 1790, to the MINERVA 38, Capt. Robt. Manners Sutton, fitting for the East Indies—in Aug. 1791, to the CROWN 64, Commodore Hon. Wm. Cornwallis, with whom he returned to England in July, 1792—and, 9 Jan. 1793, as First, to the SUFFOLK 74. On again visiting the East Indies in the latter ship, with a large convoy, under the broad pendant of Commodore Peter Rainier, he was nominated by that officer, after having for a time acted as his Flag-Captain, to the command, in Sept. 1795, of the HOBART 18—an appointment which the Admiralty confirmed by a commission bearing date 12 April, 1796. Previously to joining that vessel Capt. Page had assisted at the reduction of the Dutch settlements in the island of Ceylon. He subsequently united with a detachment of troops under the Hon. Capt. Monson in taking possession of the Dutch factory of Molletive;* and in Jan. 1796, he accompanied an expedition against the Moluccas. Owing to his great knowledge of the Indian Seas he was selected to conduct the fleet through the difficult passages leading to those islands; but being sent back to Madras with important despatches previously to their capture, he was prevented from sharing in the large sums of prize-money arising therefrom. For his services in Dec. 1796, in escorting a valuable convoy of China traders from Prince of Wales Island to Bombay, he received the thanks both of the government and merchants, together with a present from the latter of 500 guineas. On 27 Feb. 1797, he was nominated Acting-Captain of the ORPHEUS 32; and in the following Aug., having been advanced by the Admiralty to Post-rank on 22 of the preceding Dec., he returned to England. He was subsequently appointed —21 Jan. 1800, to the INFLEXIBLE 64, *armée-en-flûte* —9 Nov. 1802 (after nine months of half-pay) to the CAROLINE 36—26 Feb. 1805, to the TRIDENT 64, bearing the flag of Vice-Admiral Rainier in the East Indies—10 May, 1809, to the Sea Fencibles at Harwich, where he remained until the corps was disbanded in 1810—and 21 Aug. 1812, to the PUISSANT 74, stationed as a guardship at Spithead. In the INFLEXIBLE, Capt. Page was twice sent with troops to the Mediterranean. On the first occasion he was for a short time employed at the blockade of Genoa; whence he was unfortunately sent, the day before its surrender, on special service to Leghorn, and was thereby again deprived of a share in the spoils. During the period of his second sojourn he assisted at the debarkation of the army in Aboukir Bay, 8 March, 1801, and was then attached to the blockading force before Alexandria. On the surrender of Cairo he was ordered to convey the French troops to Marseilles; but not being able to return prior to the close of the campaign he was a third time prevented from participating in the profits of victory. He was, however, presented with the Turkish gold medal. On his return to England he brought with him Sir Eyre Coote, second in command of the British army, and the 3rd Regiment of Guards. Being sent on the renewal of hostilities to India, Capt. Page, then in the CAROLINE, contrived during his passage to capture several French vessels and to detain two others belonging to the Batavian republic. On board one of these, the *De Haasje* brig-of-war,† were found despatches from Buonaparte, containing information which led to the detention of some Dutch ships at St. Helena, and prevented the English merchantmen going there from being allowed to depart without convoy. On reaching his destination, Capt. Page's local knowledge of the Bay of Bengal, where he found himself senior officer, enabled him to convoy the Company's ships in safety for several months. On 5 Jan. and 4 Feb. 1804, he had the good fortune to make prize of two privateers, *Les Frères Unis* of 16 guns (mounting 8) and 134 men, and *Le Général de Caen* of 22 guns and 200 men; the capture of which vessels immediately on their arrival from France, and before they had committed any depredations on our commerce, was considered of such importance, that the merchants of Bombay and Madras each voted him the sum of 500 guineas. Capt. Page, after this, received instructions from Admiral Rainier to take under his orders the GRAMPUS 50, DÉDAIGNEUSE 38, and DASHER 18, for the purpose of protecting a valuable convoy to and from China, it being anticipated that the French Admiral Linois, in the *Marengo* of 80 guns, with several frigates, would have made an attack upon them, as he had previously done on the East India fleet under Commodore Dance. On the paying-off of the TRIDENT in Oct. 1805, Capt. Page, who had conducted home in that ship a convoy of 44 vessels, was again presented, by the Court of Directors, with the sum of 500 guineas. He left the PUISSANT in Sept. 1815, and did not afterwards go afloat. He became a Rear-Admiral 12 Aug. 1819; a Vice-Admiral 22 July, 1830; and a full Admiral 23 Nov. 1841.

Admiral Page married Elizabeth, only child of John Herbert, Esq., of Totness, Devon, and was left a widower, without children, in 1834. AGENTS—Goode and Lawrence.

* *Vide* Gaz. 1796, p. 310.

† Taken 2 Aug. 1803. *V.* Gaz. 1803, p. 1554.

PAGE. (LIEUTENANT, 1845.)

HENRY HOTHAM M'RODEN PAGE entered the Navy in 1830; passed his examination 6 March, 1839; and was for several years employed on the coast of Africa, as Mate, in the ACORN 16, Capt. John Adams, PROMPT schooner, and FERRET 6—the latter commanded by Capt. Josiah Oake. He obtained his commission 1 Dec. 1845; and, since 27 of the same month, has been serving on the Channel and Lisbon stations in the CANOPUS 84, Capt. Fairfax Moresby.

PAGET. (CAPTAIN, 1829. F-P., 16; H-P., 10.)

CHARLES HENRY PAGET was born in 1806, and died 26 May, 1845, at Portsmouth. He was eldest son of the late Hon. Sir Chas. Paget, Kt., G.C.H.,* by Elizabeth Araminta, daughter and co-heir of Henry Monk, Esq.; brother of Lieut. Brownlow Henry Paget, R.N. (1838), who died in South America in 1843, on board the CHAMPION 18; and nephew of the Marquis of Anglesey.

This officer entered the Navy 6 May, 1819; passed his examination in 1825; obtained his first commission, while serving in the ROYAL GEORGE yacht, 3 Jan. 1826; became Flag-Lieutenant, in the GANGES 84, to Rear-Admiral Robt. Waller Otway, on the South American station, 20 Feb. following; acquired the rank of Commander 21 Feb. 1828; and on 12 of the ensuing Aug. was appointed to the PROCRIS 10, at Cork. He attained Post-rank 28 Oct. 1829; and was afterwards employed, from 3 June, 1831, until

* The Hon. Sir Chas. Paget was born 7 Oct. 1778. He commanded the MARTIN sloop in the action off Camperdown 11 Oct. 1797; and on 17 of the same month was advanced to Post-rank. He afterwards commanded the BRILLIANT, HYDRA, ENDYMION, and EGYPTIENNE frigates, REVENGE and SUPERB 74's, and PRINCE REGENT and ROYAL GEORGE yachts. In the BRILLIANT he accompanied Sir John Borlase Warren in the expedition to Ferrol in 1800; he contrived, in the ENDYMION, to effect a large number of captures; and in the SUPERB, during the war with the United States, he commanded a squadron at the blockade of New London. He received the honour of Knighthood and the insignia of a K.C.H. in Oct. 1819; became a Rear-Admiral in April, 1823, and a Vice-Admiral in Jan. 1837; was nominated a G.C.H. in March, 1832; and was for many years M.P. for Carnarvon. In 1822 he had been appointed Groom of the Bedchamber to George IV. He commanded in chief at Cork in 1829; and from 11 Feb. 1837 until the period of his death, which took place 27 Jan. 1839, he held the supreme direction of Naval affairs in North America and the West Indies.

paid off in the early part of 1835, in command of the SAMARANG 28, in South America, and from 24 Feb. 1837 until superseded in June, 1839, as Flag-Captain, in the HOWE 120, to Sir Robt. Waller Otway, Commander-in-Chief at the Nore.

Capt. Paget married, first, in 1836, Elizabeth, daughter of Mr. Annals; and secondly, 20 Jan. 1840, Emily Caroline, daughter of Henry M'Clintock, Esq., Collector of the Customs at the port of Dundalk, and sister of Lieut. Fras. Leopold M'Clintock, R.N. AGENTS—Messrs. Stilwell.

PAGET, LORD, M.P. (CAPTAIN, 1839.)

THE RIGHT HONOURABLE LORD CLARENCE EDWARD PAGET, born 17 June, 1811, is eldest son of Field-Marshal the Marquis of Anglesey, K.G., G.C.B., by his second wife, Lady Charlotte Cadogan, sister of Rear-Admiral Earl Cadogan, C.B. He is brother of Lord Alfred Henry Paget, M.P. for Lichfield, and of Lord Geo. Augustus Fred. Paget, both officers in the army; half-brother of Lord Wm. Paget, Captain R.N.; and brother-in-law of Viscount Sydney and the Earl of Sandwich.

This officer entered the Navy 29 May, 1823; served as Midshipman of the ASIA 84, flag-ship of Sir Edw. Codrington, at the battle of Navarin, 20 Oct. 1827; passed his examination in 1830; and obtained his first commission 14 May, 1831. His succeeding appointments were—11 Aug. 1831, to the WARSPITE 76, flag-ship of Sir Thos. Baker in South America—27 Feb. 1832, as Supernumerary-Lieutenant, to the ST. VINCENT 120, Capt. Humphrey Fleming Senhouse, stationed off Lisbon, whence he returned in the early part of 1833—and, 7 June, 1834, to the WINCHESTER 52, Capt. Edw. Sparshott, fitting at Chatham. Being advanced to the rank of Commander 25 Sept. in the year last mentioned, he obtained command, 17 Jan. 1837, of the PEARL 20, on the North America and West India station. He paid that vessel off within a short period of his elevation to Post-rank, which took place 26 March, 1839; and he was next appointed—26 June following, to the HOWE 120, flag-ship of Sir Robt. Waller Otway at the Nore, where he remained until July, 1840—and, 23 Aug. 1841, to the AIGLE 24, fitting for the Mediterranean. He returned to England in the summer of 1845, and has since been on half-pay.

In July, 1846, his Lordship was appointed Secretary to the Board of Ordnance; and in 1847 he was returned to Parliament as Member for Sandwich. AGENTS—Hallett and Robinson.

PAGET. (COMMANDER, 1837. F-P., 19; H-P., 28.)

JOHN PAGET entered the Navy, 4 March, 1800, as A.B., on board the MINORCA sloop, Capt. Geo. Miller, under whom we find him in the course of the following year employed as Midshipman and Master's Mate in the operations against the French in Egypt. Quitting the MINORCA in Oct. 1801, he served during the next five years, on the Mediterranean and Home stations, in the GREYHOUND 32, Capts. Chas. Ogle and Wm. Hoste, DIOMEDE 50, Capts. Thos. Larcom and Hugh Downman, UNITÉ 38, Capt. Chas. Ogle, and PRINCE 98, Capt. Wm. Lechmere. Being appointed, on the occasion of his promotion to the rank of Lieutenant, which took place 20 Dec. 1806, to the OLYMPIA sloop, Capt. Wm. Taylor, he sailed in that vessel for the Rio de la Plata. He invalided home in July, 1807; and was next, between Nov. 1808 and Feb. 1809, employed under Capt. John Surman Carden in the VILLE DE PARIS 110. During that period he assisted in embarking the army after the battle of Corunna. From the date last mentioned Lieut. Paget did not again go afloat until nominated, 22 Jan. 1828, First of the HARPY 10, Capt. Chas. Rich, on the West India station. On 11 Jan. 1829 he was removed to the MAGNIFICENT, receiving-ship at Jamaica, of which vessel, it appears, he retained command from 19 Dec. 1831 until May, 1839. He was re-appointed to her 24 Feb. 1842; and on 26 of the following July was transferred to the IMAUM, also a receiving-ship. He has been on half-pay since 1843. His present commission bears date 1 April, 1837.

Commander Paget married, 15 Sept. 1834, at St. Ann's, Jamaica, Anna, daughter of Jas. Lawrence Hilton, Esq. AGENTS—Messrs. Stilwell.

PAGET, LORD. (CAPT., 1826. F-P., 16; H-P., 14.)

THE RIGHT HONOURABLE LORD WILLIAM PAGET, born 1 March, 1803, is second son of Field-Marshal the Marquis of Anglesey, K.G., G.C.B., by his first wife, Caroline Elizabeth, daughter of George, fourth Earl of Jersey. His Lordship is half-brother of Lord Clarence Edw. Paget, Captain R.N.; brother-in-law of the Duke of Richmond, the Marquis Conyngham, and the Lords Crofton and Templemore; and nephew of Capt. Hon. Wm. Paget, R.N., who died in 1795—of Hon. Sir Edw. Paget, G.C.B., a General Officer in the army and Colonel of the 28th Regt. of Foot—of the late Vice-Admiral Hon. Sir Chas. Paget, Kt., G.C.H.—of the Earls of Galloway and Enniskillen—and of the late Lord Graves. He is also connected with the noble houses of Argyll, Westmoreland, Dartmouth, Ormonde, Guillamore, and Essex.

This officer entered the Navy, 1 April, 1817, as Fst.-cl. Vol., on board the GLASGOW 50, Capts. Hon. Robt. Cavendish Spencer, Hon. Anthony Maitland, and Bentinck Cavendish Doyle, employed at first in the Mediterranean and then on the Home station, where, and in the West Indies, he served from 26 April, 1821, until promoted to the rank of Lieutenant 18 April, 1823, as Midshipman in the DORIS 42, Capt. Thos. Graham, ROYAL GEORGE yacht, Capt. Hon. Sir Chas. Paget, ALBION 74, Capt. Rich. Raggett, PHAETON 46, Capt. Wm. Augustus Montagu, and ACTIVE, of similar force, Capt. Andrew King. His next appointments were, to the TARTAR 42, Capt. Thos. Brown, AURORA 46, Capt. Henry Prescott, FLY 18, Capt. Wm. Fanshawe Martin, and SPARTIATE 76, Capt. Gordon Thos. Falcon, all in South America, on which station he was made Commander, 20 April, 1825, into his former ship the FLY. He removed, 23 Dec. following, to the PHILOMEL 10, fitting for the Mediterranean; and on 18 Oct. 1826 was advanced to Post-rank. His succeeding appointments were—6 Nov. 1827, to the ROYAL CHARLOTTE yacht, lying at Dublin, where he remained until Feb. 1829—12 Dec. 1828, to the NORTH STAR 28, in which vessel he returned to the West Indies—18 May, 1831, to the WINCHESTER 52, bearing the flag of Sir Edw. Griffith Colpoys, Commander-in-Chief on the North America and West India station—and, 24 Sept. 1832, again to the NORTH STAR, which ship he brought home and paid off in the summer of 1833. He has not been since employed.

Lord Wm. Paget sat in Parliament for the borough of Andover from 1841 until 1846. He married, 22 Jan. 1827, Frances, only daughter of Lieut.-General Francis, Baron de Rottenburg, by whom he has issue three children.

PAIN. (LIEUTENANT, 1815. F-P., 21; H-P., 23.)

MARTIN PAIN entered the Navy, 4 June, 1803, as Midshipman, on board the SULPHUR bomb, Capt. Daniel M'Leod; and while in that vessel was frequently in action with the enemy's gun-boats and batteries in the neighbourhood of Boulogne, was engaged in an attempt to sink two stone-ships at the entrance of the harbour at that place, and united in the bombardment of Granville. After a servitude of nine months in the UTRECHT 64, commanded in the Downs by Capts. Fras. Pickmore and Henry Inman, he joined, in April, 1805, the HEBE 32, Capt. Micajah Malbon, with whom he continued actively employed in the ADAMANT 50, at first off Boulogne, and then on the West India station, until Oct. 1808. In May and June of the latter year we find him acting as Prize-Master of the Spanish schooners *Galna* and *Magdalena*. On quitting the ADAMANT he became in succession attached to the PRINCESS OF ORANGE 74, Capt. Fras.

Beauman, AGINCOURT 64, Capt. Wm. Keat, and MONMOUTH 64, Capts. Hyde Parker and Wm. Wilkinson. In the course of 1814 he was nominated Acting-Lieutenant of the GRIFFON brig, Capt. Geo. Barne Trollope, Midshipman of his former ship the MONMOUTH, Acting-Lieutenant and Commander of the VIPER cutter, and Master's Mate of the IMPREGNABLE 98, Capts. Chas. Adam and John Wentworth Loring. In the VIPER he was sent by H.R.H. the Duke of Clarence to Calais with despatches, and was employed by Rear-Admiral Foley in escorting convoys from Deal to St. Helen's. In the IMPREGNABLE, after conveying Marshal Blücher from Boulogne to England, and taking part in the grand naval review held at Spithead, he proceeded to Bordeaux for the purpose of bringing home the first and second battalions of the German Legion. While attached, in the early part of 1815, to the BOMBAY 74, Capt. Henry Bazely, he cruized among the Western Islands, in company with the CHATHAM 74 and LARNE 20, in quest of two American frigates. He took up in April of that year a commission bearing date 7 of the preceding Feb., and, since 12 May, 1837, has been employed in command of a station in the Coast Guard. AGENT—J. Chippendale.

PAKENHAM. (Captain, 1826. F-P., 13; H-P., 30.)

JOHN PAKENHAM, born 18 Oct. 1790, is fourth son of the late Admiral Hon. Sir Thos. Pakenham, G.C.B.* (second son of the first Lord Longford), by Louisa, daughter of the Right Hon. John Staples; and brother (with Lieut. Henry Pakenham, R.N. (1827), who died in April, 1839) of the present Edw. Michael Conolly, Esq., D.C.L., Captain R.A., and M.P. for Donegal. Capt. Pakenham is first-cousin of the gallant Major-General Hon. Sir Edw. Michael Pakenham, G.C.B., who fell at New Orleans 8 Jan. 1815; of Lieut.-General Hon. Sir Hercules Robt. Pakenham, K.C.B., a distinguished Peninsular officer; of Capt. Hon. Wm. Pakenham, R.N., who was lost in the SALDANHA frigate in 1811; and of the late Duchess of Wellington.

This officer entered the Navy, 22 April, 1804, as Fst.-cl. Vol., on board the REPULSE 74, Capts. Hon. Arthur Kaye Legge and John Halliday, under the former of whom he took part, as Midshipman, in Sir Robt. Calder's action, 22 July, 1805, and accompanied the expeditions of 1807 and 9 to the Dardanelles and the Scheldt. In the course of 1810, after a short servitude in the Mediterranean on board the WARSPITE 74, Capt. Hon. Henry Blackwood, he was nominated, on that station, Acting-Lieutenant of the VILLE DE PARIS 110, bearing the flag of Rear-Admiral Thos. Fras. Fremantle. In Oct. of the same year he went back, in a similar capacity, to the WARSPITE, still commanded by Capt. Blackwood, although subsequently by Capt. Henry Edw. Reginald Baker. While in that ship, to which he was confirmed by commission bearing date 16 July, 1811, we find him participating in a very gallant skirmish, in which the British, with a slender force, beat back a powerful division of the French Toulon fleet. In Aug. 1812 Mr. Pakenham joined the MAGICIENNE 36, Capt. Hon. Wm. Gordon; and on 15 June, 1814, after having witnessed the fall of St. Sebastian, he was advanced to the rank of Commander. His next appointment was, 21 June, 1815, to the BERMUDA 10, which vessel, on her arrival in the West Indies, was unfortunately lost near Tampico Bar, 16 Nov. 1816. From the latter date Capt. Pakenham did not again go afloat until invested, 16 Aug. 1825, with the command of the HARRIER 18, on the Cork station. He acquired his present rank 26 Aug. 1826; and on 1 Oct. 1846 he accepted the retirement.

He married, 3 Nov. 1817, Caroline Emily, third daughter of the late Rear-Admiral Sir Home Riggs Popham, K.C.B., by whom (who died 2 Aug. 1844) he had issue a son and three daughters. AGENTS—Hallett and Robinson.

PAKENHAM. (LIEUTENANT, 1844.)

THE HONOURABLE THOMAS ALEXANDER PAKENHAM, born 3 March, 1820, is third son of the late Earl of Longford, by Georgiana Emma Charlotte, daughter of William, first Earl of Beauchamp. His eldest brother, the present Earl of Longford, is an officer in the Second Life Guards; and three other of his brothers are also in the army.

This officer entered the Navy, from the Royal Naval College, 14 April, 1835; passed his examination 2 May, 1840; was for some time attached, as Mate, to the EXCELLENT gunnery-ship at Portsmouth, Capt. Sir Thos. Hastings; and, after a servitude of nearly three years in that capacity on board the WARSPITE 50, Capts. Lord John Hay and Provo Wm. Parry Wallis, on the North America and West India and Mediterranean stations, was promoted to the rank of Lieutenant 10 June, 1844. His appointments have since been—9 Sept. 1844, to the MUTINE 12, Capt. Rich. Borough Crawford, at the Cape of Good Hope—and, 2 Sept. 1845, to the PRESIDENT 50, flag-ship of Rear-Admiral Jas. Rich. Dacres, on the same station, where he is now employed.

PALK. (RETIRED COMMANDER, 1831. F-P., 19; H-P., 32.)

ROBERT PALK died 12 May, 1845.

This officer entered the Navy, in Dec. 1794, as Fst.-cl. Vol., on board the DROMEDARY store-ship, Capts. Rich. Hill and Jas. Harrison. On his arrival at Gibraltar, after having visited the West Indies, he removed, in May, 1795, to the CAMEL, another store-ship, commanded by Capt. Edw. Rotheram. Becoming Midshipman, in the following July, of the ARDENT 64, Capts. Rich. Rundell Burgess and Thos. Bertie, he fought in that vessel in the action off Camperdown, 11 Oct. 1797, and, besides accompanying the expedition of 1799 to Holland, was present, 2 April, 1801, in the attack made on the Danish line of defence before Copenhagen. After a servitude of a few weeks on board the LONDON and ST. GEORGE 98's, flag-ships of Sir Hyde Parker and Lord Nelson, he was made Lieutenant, 23 June, 1801, into the BELLONA 74, Capt. Thos. Bertie. His succeeding appointments were—16 Nov. 1802, to the COURAGEUX 74, Capt. John Okes Hardy, part of the force employed at the reduction of Ste. Lucie in June, 1803—19 Dec. 1803, 24 Sept. 1804, and 12 May, 1806, as First, to the DOLPHIN and TROMPEUSE sloops, and LIVELY 38, Capts. John Shortland, Wm. Brooking Dolling, and Geo. M'Kinley, with whom he served until March, 1807, on the Home, African, and Lisbon stations—and, 1 April, 1812, to the command of the SYLVIA cutter, in which vessel he cruized in the Downs and Channel, and assisted at the siege of St. Sebastian. He went on half-pay 5 Sept. 1814; and accepted the rank of Retired Commander 22 April, 1831.

PALLISER. (LIEUTENANT, 1847.)

WRAY RICHARD GLEDSTANES PALLISER is son, we believe, of Colonel Wray Palliser, of Derryluskan, co. Tipperary.

This officer passed his examination 13 May, 1845; and, after having served as Mate in the EXCELLENT

* The Hon. Sir Thos. Pakenham was born in 1757, and first went to sea in 1770 on board the SOUTHAMPTON frigate, Captain M'Bride. He attained the rank of Lieutenant in 1776; of Commander in 1779; and of Post-Captain (as a reward for his distinguished services as Acting-Captain of the BRISTOL, under Commodore Cornwallis) 2 March, 1780. When in command of the CRESCENT of 28 guns and 198 men, he accompanied Admiral Darby to the relief of Gibraltar in 1781; and on 29 May in that year maintained a brilliant action of two hours and a half with the Dutch 36-gun frigate *Brill*, to whom he did not strike until he had had 103 of his people killed and wounded, and further opposition was impossible. He afterwards commanded the MINERVA 38, INVINCIBLE 74, and JUSTE 84. In the INVINCIBLE he bore a conspicuous part in the battle of 1 June, 1794, and for his conduct on the occasion was presented with a gold medal. He was nominated a Colonel of Marines in 1795, a Rear-Admiral in Feb 1799, a Vice-Admiral in April, 1804, a full Admiral in July, 1810, and in May, 1820, a G.C.B. He was for some time Master-General of the Ordnance in Ireland, and died Senior Admiral of the Red 2 Feb. 1836.

gunnery-ship at Portsmouth, Capts. Sir Thos. Hastings and Henry Ducie Chads, and in the VANGUARD 80, Capt. Geo. Wickens Willes, on the Channel station, was advanced to the rank of Lieutenant 28 Feb. 1847. He has been since employed as Additional of the HIBERNIA 104, flag-ship of Sir Wm. Parker in the Mediterranean.

PALMER. (LIEUT., 1820. F-P., 13; H-P., 25.)

CHARLES PALMER was born 27 Dec. 1792.

This officer entered the Navy, in Aug. 1809, as Fst.-cl. Vol., on board the GIBRALTAR 80, Capts. Hen. Lidgbird Ball and Robt. Plampin, stationed in the Channel, where in the following month he attained the rating of Midshipman, and in Feb. 1812 removed to the STIRLING CASTLE 74, Capts. Sir Jahleel Brenton and Augustus Brine. With Capt. Brine he continued employed in the VENERABLE, BELLEROPHON, and MEDWAY 74's (the latter bearing the flag of Rear-Admiral Chas. Tyler at the Cape of Good Hope), until nominated, 27 Dec. 1815, Acting-Lieutenant of the TAMAR 24, Capt. Chas. Sotheby. He returned to England in Feb. 1816; and between Aug. of that year and the date of his promotion to the rank of Lieutenant, which took place 26 Dec. 1820, was in succession appointed Admiralty-Midshipman of the GANYMEDE 26, Capt. Wm. M'Culloch, ERNE 20, Capt. Rich. Spencer, IMPREGNABLE 104, flag-ship of Lord Exmouth, DOROTHEA hired-ship, Capt. David Buchan, and HECLA bomb, Lieut.-Commander Wm. Edw. Parry. In the GANYMEDE, ERNE, and IMPREGNABLE he was employed on the Downs, Mediterranean, and Plymouth stations; he took part, in the DOROTHEA, in a perilous voyage of discovery to the neighbourhood of Spitzbergen; and in the HECLA he penetrated to long. 113° 54′ 43″ W. within the Arctic Circle, and thereby became entitled to a portion of a Parliamentary reward of 5000*l*. Being re-appointed, 8 Jan. 1821, to the HECLA, then commanded by Capt. Geo. Fras. Lyon, he sailed in the following May with Capt. Parry's second expedition in quest of a North-west passage. He returned to England in the autumn of 1823, and has since been on half-pay.

Lieut. Palmer married, 29 May, 1828, Miss Sarah C. Yorke.

PALMER. (LIEUT., 1809. F-P., 36; H-P., 8.)

EDWARD GASCOIGNE PALMER entered the Navy, 20 June, 1803, under the auspices of H. R. H. the Duke of Kent, as Fst.-cl. Vol., on board the DONEGAL 74, Capts. Sir Rich. John Strachan and Pulteney Malcolm. In the following year he was present, we believe, at the capture of the Spanish 44-gun frigate *Amfitrite*, and of a ship with a cargo on board worth 200,000*l*.; and in 1805 he accompanied Lord Nelson to the West Indies and back in pursuit of the combined fleets. On 6 Feb. 1806, after having assisted at the capture of *El Rayo* of 100 guns, one of the ships recently defeated at Trafalgar, he took part with Sir John Thos. Duckworth in the action off St. Domingo. On leaving the DONEGAL, of which ship he had been constituted Midshipman in July, 1805, he became, 7 July, 1806, Master's Mate of the KINGFISHER 18, Capt. Geo. Fras. Seymour; whom, in Jan. 1807, he followed into the AURORA 28. In that frigate, and in the KINGFISHER, to which vessel, commanded by Capts. Wm. Hepenstall and Ewell Tritton, he returned in June, 1808, Mr. Palmer saw much boat-service in the Mediterranean, and was on one occasion wounded by the fire of a polacre near Corfu. He obtained his commission 19 Oct. 1809, and was subsequently appointed, chiefly in the capacity of First-Lieutenant—28 Oct. 1809, and 1 June, 1810, to the RINALDO 10, and OBERON 16, Capts. Jas. Anderson and Jas. Murray, both in the Downs—14 Dec. 1811, to the WARRIOR 74, Capt. Hon. Geo. Byng, off Flushing—12 Feb. 1813, to the COSSACK 22 Capt. Fras. Stanfell, on the Jamaica station—7 March, 1814, to the CALEDONIA 120, flag-ship of Lord Exmouth, under whom he beheld the fall of Genoa—and, 23 Oct. 1815 (after a few months of half-pay), to the ESK 20, Capt. Geo. Gustavus Lennock, fitting for the West Indies, whence he invalided in 1817. In the RINALDO, whose force consisted of 8 18-pounder carronades and 2 long sixes, with a complement of 65 men, Mr. Palmer led the boarders, and was badly wounded in the leg, at the capture, 7 Dec. 1809, after some resistance, of *Le Maraudeur* French privateer, of 14 guns and 66 men, 5 of whom were wounded. His appointments, since he left the ESK, have been—in 1824, for three years, to the Ordinary at Sheerness—24 Nov. 1827, and 19 Feb. 1830, as a Supernumerary, to the RAMILLIES and TALAVERA Coast Blockade Ships, both commanded by Capt. Hugh Pigot—15 Jan. 1831, to the Coast Guard—14 Oct. 1831, to a three-years' command of the CHEERFUL Revenue-vessel—and, 11 June, 1835, again to the Coast Guard, in which service he continues.

Lieut. Palmer married, 3 Aug. 1831, Harriet, relict of the late Diggles Bayley, Esq., of Cape Coast Castle, by whom he has issue one child.

PALMER. (COMMANDER, 1840. F-P., 25; H-P., 17.)

GEORGE PALMER entered the Navy, 22 Jan. 1805, as Fst.-cl. Vol., on board the PLUTO sloop, Capt. Rich. Gaire Janvrin, employed on the Home station; where, and in the Baltic, he continued employed, as Midshipman and Master's Mate, in the ROYAL WILLIAM, Capt. John Irwin, PANDORA 18, Capts. R. G. Janvrin and John Macpherson Ferguson, NAMUR 74, Capt. Shepheard, and BRISEIS 10, Capts. Chas. Thurlow Smith and John Ross, until promoted to the rank of Lieutenant 20 Nov. 1812. In the PANDORA he assisted at the capture, 31 Dec. 1810, of *Le Chasseur* privateer of 16 guns and 36 men; and while in the BRISEIS he served, 29 June, 1812, in the pinnace belonging to that vessel, containing 18 men, under the orders of Lieut. Thos. Jones, at the cutting-out from Pillau Roads the (lately British) merchant ship *Urania*, mounting 6 carriage-guns and 4 swivels, in the possession of some French troops, who, notwithstanding a spirited resistance, were driven off the decks into their boats, which were on the opposite side, with no greater loss to the assailants than one man killed and himself slightly wounded.* Being re-appointed to the BRISEIS in Sept. 1813, Lieut. Palmer continued attached to that sloop (with the exception of an interval between Oct. 1814 and May, 1815, occasioned by ill health), under the command of Capts. Wm. Rush Jackson and Geo. Domett, until Jan. 1816. His last appointments were—12 Sept. 1825, to the Coast Blockade, as Supernumerary-Lieutenant of the HYPERION 42, Capt. Wm. Jas. Mingaye—5 April, 1831 (on the latter service being abolished), to the Coast Guard—11 Oct. 1834, to the command of the SKYLARK Revenue-vessel—and, 26 Sept. 1837, again to the charge (which he retained until advanced, as a reward for his services, to the rank he now holds 1 Jan. 1840) of a station in the Coast Guard. Commander Palmer is Senior of 1840.

PALMER. (LIEUTENANT, 1841.)

JOHN PALMER entered the Navy 24 Nov. 1825; passed his examination 6 Jan. 1832; and at the period of his promotion to his present rank, which took place 26 Aug. 1841, was serving, as Mate, in the SOUTHAMPTON 50, flag-ship of Sir Edw. Durnford King at the Cape of Good Hope. His appointments have since been—30 Aug. 1841, again to the SOUTHAMPTON—10 March, 1843, to the ROSE 18, Capts. Henry Rich. Sturt and Rich. Wilson Pelly, fitting for the North America and West India station, whence he returned home and was paid off at the close of 1846—and, 12 Oct. 1847, as Additional-Lieutenant, to the VINDICTIVE 50, bearing the flag of Sir Fras. Wm. Austen, Commander-in-

* *Vide* Gaz. 1812, p. 1364.—Mr. James, in his 'Naval History,' has erroneously attributed the part borne in the affair by the subject of the present narrative to Mr. Wm. Palmer.

Chief in North America and the West Indies, where he is now employed on Surveying-service.

PALMER. (LIEUTENANT, 1843.)

JOHN JERVIS PALMER passed his examination 7 Oct. 1840; and between that date and the period of his promotion to the rank of Lieutenant, 23 Jan. 1843, was employed in the East Indies and China, as Mate, on board the ENDYMION 44, Capt. Hon. Fred. Wm. Grey, and CORNWALLIS 72, flag-ship of Sir Wm. Parker, who noticed him as having served in the boats which covered the assault on the town of Chin-Kiang-Foo 21 July, 1842.* On leaving the CORNWALLIS he joined the SERPENT 16, Capt. Wm. Nevill, also in the East Indies, where, in Sept. 1843, he removed to the CAMBRIAN 36, Capt. Henry Ducie Chads. His appointments since his return to England in the summer of 1845 have been, on the Mediterranean station—1 Dec. in that year to the HIBERNIA 104, flag-ship of Sir Wm. Parker—24 Dec. 1846, to the GLADIATOR steam-vessel of 430 horse-power, Capt. John Robb—and, 26 Oct. 1847, to the Acting-command, which he yet retains, of the MUTINE 12.

PALMER. (LIEUT., 1813. F-P., 12; H-P., 31.)

WILLIAM PALMER, born 9 April, 1789, at Monkwearmouth, co. Durham, is son of Mr. Wm. Palmer, shipowner, of that place.

This officer entered the Navy, 12 Nov. 1804, as A.B., on board the INCONSTANT 36, Capt. Edw. Stirling Dickson, flag-ship for some time of Sir Edm. Nagle and Sir Jas. Saumarez on the coast of France. On his removal, as Master's Mate, in April, 1808, to the BELLE POULE 38, Capt. Jas. Brisbane, he sailed for the Mediterranean, where he was for nearly two years very actively employed, and assisted, in the course of 1809, at the capture of *Le Var* of 26 guns, laden with corn for the relief of the French garrison at Corfu, and at the reduction of the islands of Zante, Cephalonia, and Cerigo. Returning in the spring of 1810 to England in the EXCELLENT 74, Capt. Edw. Griffith, he joined the VICTORY 100: in which ship, besides being for a long time stationed in the Baltic under the flag of Sir Jas. Saumarez, he escorted a body of troops sent in 1811 to the coast of Portugal under Sir Joseph Sydney Yorke. After serving for a few months off Cherbourg in the LACEDÆMONIAN 38, Capt. Sam. Jackson, and again in the Baltic on board the DEFIANCE 74, flag-ship of Rear-Admiral Geo. Hope, Mr. Palmer was promoted, 17 Aug. 1813, to a Lieutenancy in the ROLLA 10, Capts. Wm. Hill and Robt. Julyan; under the former of whom we find him present, in Feb. 1814, at the celebrated passage of the flotilla under Rear-Admiral Chas. Vinicombe Penrose across the bar of the Adour; on which occasion he had the good fortune to save the lives of two persons, whose boat had capsized. His last appointment was, 17 Dec. 1814, to the AMELIA 38, Capt. Hon. Granville Leveson Proby, with whom he served in the Mediterranean until the summer of 1816. On 15 July, 1815, while engaged in the AMELIA's pinnace in an attempt to capture a French vessel of very superior force at Campo, in the island of Elba, he was wounded by a musket-ball, which entered his right side above the hip-joint, and has never been extracted. He was at the same time made prisoner, but shortly afterwards exchanged.

Lieut. Palmer married, in 1830, Elizabeth, third daughter of the late Mr. Kingswood Greenwell, shipowner, and grand-daughter of the late Dr. Greenwell, of Scot's House. He was left a widower, with one daughter, in Jan. 1844.

PALMES. (LIEUTENANT, 1842.)

JOHN PHILIP PALMES is third son of Geo. Palmes, Esq., of Naburn, co. York, by Margaret Isabella, daughter of Wm. Lindsay, Esq., of Oatlands, near Glasgow. His eldest brother, Bryan, a Captain in the 57th light infantry, died at Barbadoes in 1839.

This officer entered the Navy 2 Dec. 1830; passed his examination 10 Nov. 1838; served for some time at Portsmouth, as Mate, in the QUEEN 110, flag-ship of Sir Edw. Codrington; and was promoted to the rank of Lieutenant, while in the ROYAL GEORGE yacht, Capt. Lord Adolphus FitzClarence, 7 March, 1842. His succeeding appointments were —29 March, 1842, to the THUNDERER 84, Capt. Dan. Pring, employed, until the close of 1843, in the Mediterranean and on particular service — 11 Dec. 1844, as Additional, to the HYDRA steam-sloop, Capt. Horatio Beauman Young, on the coast of Africa—2 April, 1845, to the PENELOPE steam-frigate, Commodore Wm. Jones, on the same station, whence he returned towards the close of the year—31 March, 1846, to the BELLEISLE 24, troop-ship, Capt. John Kingcome—and, 30 April, 1847, for a few months, to the HOWE 120, Capt. Sir Jas. Stirling, fitting at Portsmouth. AGENTS—Messrs. Stilwell.

PANTON. (LIEUT., 1812. F-P., 13; H-P., 30.)

PAUL GRIFFITH PANTON, born 31 Oct. 1795, is second son of Jones Panton, Esq., of Plusgurm, co. Anglesey.

This officer entered the Navy, 19 July, 1804, as Fst.-cl. Vol., on board the HYDRA 38, Capt. Geo. Mundy; and on being lent, after cruizing for some time in the Mediterranean, to the CANOPUS 80, flag-ship of Rear-Admiral Thos. Louis, fought in the action off St. Domingo 6 Feb. 1806. On finally leaving the HYDRA, of which ship he had been created a Midshipman in April, 1807, he joined, in Oct. 1810, the ULYSSES 44, bearing the flag at Jersey of Vice-Admiral D'Auvergne. In March and July, 1811, he was successively nominated Acting-Lieutenant and Master's Mate of the MARLBOROUGH 74, and ÆOLUS 32, Capts. Matthew Henry Scott and Lord Jas. Townshend; and on 7 Feb. 1812, at which period he was again acting as Lieutenant in the MORGIANA sloop, Capt. David Scott, he was officially advanced to the rank he now holds. His last appointments were—on 25 of the month last mentioned, to the COLIBRI 18, Capt. John Thompson, under whom he was wrecked in Port Royal, Jamaica, 22 Aug. 1813—2 Sept. following, to the PLANTAGENET 74, Capt. Robt. Lloyd, which ship he left in Jan. 1814—and, 5 June, 1818, to the BELLETTE 20, Capt. Geo. Rich. Pechell, fitting for the Halifax station, whence he returned in 1821.

Lieut. Panton married 3 Oct. 1826, and has issue. AGENTS—Messrs. Halford and Co.

PARDOE. (RETIRED COMMANDER, 1839. F-P., 17; H-P., 40.)

WILLIAM PARDOE entered the Navy, 15 July, 1790, as A.B., on board the TREMENDOUS 74, Capt. Hon. Geo. Cranfield Berkeley, lying at Chatham; where, in the following Nov., he attained the rating of Midshipman. After a servitude of two years in the PILOTE, PIGMY, and SULTANA cutters, Lieut.-Commanders Henry Gunter, Henry Inman, and Digby Dent, he became successively attached, in the early part of 1798, to the WINDSOR CASTLE and ST. GEORGE 98's, both commanded by Capt. Hancock Kelly, and, as Master's Mate, to the MARLBOROUGH 74, Capt. Hon. G. C. Berkeley. While participating, in the latter ship, in the glories of 1 June, 1794, he had the misfortune to have his skull fractured, his nose materially injured, and several parts of his body contused.* The effects he still feels. In March, 1795, he followed Capt. Berkeley into the FORMIDABLE 98, commanded next by Capt. Geo. Murray; and on leaving that ship in Feb. 1797 he joined the ROYAL GEORGE 100, flag-ship of Lord Bridport, and GLORY 98, Capt. Geo. Brine. On being advanced, 12 April following, to the rank of Lieutenant, he was appointed First of the CHARON 44, *armée-en-flûte*, Capt. Thos. Manby, and was for some time employed in the Channel and on the coast of Ireland. His last appointments were—29 Nov. 1798, to the command (which he retained until 14 June, 1802) of the FEARLESS gun-brig, attached to the force in the Channel—20 July, 1803,

* *Vide* Gaz. 1842, p. 3405.

* *Vide* Gaz. 1794, p. 556.

to the Sea Fencibles on the coast of Lincolnshire—20 May, 1805, as Senior, to the BRILLIANT 28, Capt. Robt. Barrie, employed on the Irish station, whence he invalided 31 March, 1806—and, 7 Jan. 1808, to the Impress service in Kent. In June, 1810, he was placed on half-pay. He accepted the rank of Retired Commander, on the Junior List, 24 Dec. 1830; and, on the Senior, 16 April, 1839. AGENT—Fred. Dufaur.

PARISH. (LIEUTENANT, 1846.)

JOHN EDWARD PARISH passed his examination 11 July, 1842; and from the close of that year until advanced to his present rank, 4 May, 1846, was employed on the Mediterranean and Home stations as Mate in the INDUS 78, Capt. Sir Jas. Stirling, EXCELLENT gunnery-ship, Capts. Sir Thos. Hastings and Henry Ducie Chads, and ST. VINCENT 120, flag-ship of Sir Chas. Ogle. He has been since serving, again in the Mediterranean, on board the VANGUARD 80, Capts. Geo. Wickens Willes and Geo. Fred. Rich.

PARK. (LIEUTENANT, 1815. F-P., 8; H-P., 32.)

JOHN STEELE PARK was born 3 June, 1791.

This officer entered the Navy, 1 April, 1807, as Fst.-cl. Vol., on board the ROSAMOND 18, Capt. Jas. Whitley Deans Dundas, fitting at Chatham. In the course of the same year he sailed for the East Indies as Midshipman in the MONMOUTH 64, Capt. Edw. Durnford King; and on his return to England in Sept. 1808 he successively joined the STATELY 64, Capt. Wm. Cumberland, and PRINCESS CAROLINE 38, Capts. Chas. Dudley Pater and Hugh Downman. While in the latter ship we find him, 25 July, 1809, commanding one of the boats of a squadron under Capt. Thos. Forrest, in a long and desperate action with a Russian flotilla, near Fredericksham, in the Gulf of Finland, which, with a loss to the British of 60 men killed and wounded, terminated in the total defeat of the enemy, 87 of whom met a similar fate. He continued in the PRINCESS CAROLINE, the last four months in the capacity of Acting-Lieutenant, until Sept. 1814; and after an intermediate servitude at Sheerness and Portsmouth as Master's Mate, in the NAMUR 74, flag-ship of Sir Thos. Williams and Sir Chas. Rowley, and LEVEN 20, Capt. Buckland Stirling Bluett, was officially advanced to his present rank 16 Feb. 1815. He has since been on half-pay.

Lieut. Park married, 23 Aug. 1827, Sarah, eldest daughter of W. Clark, Esq., of the Triangle, Hackney.

PARKER. (COMMANDER, 1829. F-P., 18; H-P., 17.)

CHARLES PARKER is son of the late Admiral Sir Hyde Parker, Kt., by his second wife, Frances, daughter of Admiral Sir Rich. Onslow, Bart.; brother of Rich. Parker, Esq., Capt. in the Life Guards; and half-brother of the present Rear-Admiral Hyde Parker, C.B.

This officer entered the Navy, 16 July, 1812, as Fst.-cl. Vol., on board the TENEDOS 38, commanded by his half-brother, under whom he was for three years very actively employed on the North American station, where he witnessed the surrender, in Jan. 1815, of the U.S. frigate *President*. From Aug. in the latter year until Oct. 1818 he served at Halifax, as Midshipman, in the SCAMANDER 36, EUROTAS 38, and FORTH 40, all commanded by Capt. Sir John Louis. On 30 March, 1819, he rejoined Capt. Parker, as Acting-Lieutenant, in the IPHIGENIA 42, on the Jamaica station; and in the following June he was transferred, in a similar capacity, to the SPARTAN 46, Capt. Wm. Furlong Wise. After again acting as Lieutenant in the IPHIGENIA, and also in the SAPPHIRE 26, Capt. Henry Hart, he was confirmed in that rank 20 Jan. 1820, and re-appointed to the IPHIGENIA. He subsequently joined—8 Dec. 1821, the FLY 18, Capts. Geo. Tyler and Edw. Curzon, employed on the Mediterranean and Cork stations—21 Feb. 1823, the EGERIA 24, Capt. Sam. Roberts, whom he accompanied to Newfoundland—28 May, 1825, the VICTORY 104, flag-ship of Sir Geo. Martin at Portsmouth—8 May, 1826, the AURORA 46, Capt. Chas. John Austen, in the West Indies—and, 23 May, 1828, as First, the BARHAM 50, bearing the flag at Jamaica of Hon. Chas. Elphinstone Fleeming. On 8 Sept. 1829 he was advanced to the command of the SLANEY sloop. He paid that vessel off 29 Jan. 1831; and has not been since afloat.

Commander Parker married, 16 June, 1835, Kate, widow of the Rev. Hely Hutchinson Smith, and third daughter of the late John Williams, Esq., of Elm Grove, Southsea, by whom he has issue. AGENTS—Messrs. Chard.

PARKER. (LIEUT., 1812. F-P., 14; H-P., 34.)

CHARLES PARKER (*a*) entered the Navy, in Nov. 1799, as Fst.-cl. Vol., on board the HINDOSTAN 50, Capts. Mulloch, Mottley, and John Le Gros; in which ship he continued employed as Midshipman until transferred, in May, 1803, to the TRIBUNE frigate, Capt. Rich. Henry Alex. Bennett. On 13 March, 1804, he had the misfortune to fall into the hands of the enemy, who carried him a prisoner to France. He there remained, we believe, until the close of 1810; when, being restored to liberty, he joined the VICTORY 100, flag-ship in the Baltic of Sir Jas. Saumarez. He attained the rank of Lieutenant 21 March, 1812; and was afterwards employed, on Home service—from Jan. to Aug. 1813, in the CADMUS 10, Capt. Thos. Fife, and IMPREGNABLE 98, flag-ship of Admiral Wm. Young and of H.R.H. the Duke of Clarence—and, from April to Sept. 1815, in the PRESIDENT 38, Capt. Archibald Duff. He has since been on half-pay. We are informed that during part of 1813 he commanded a gun-boat on the River Elbe. AGENTS—Messrs. Ommanney.

PARKER. (LIEUT., 1816. F-P., 12; H-P., 27.)

CHARLES PARKER (*b*) was born 31 March, 1794.

This officer entered the Navy, 20 Jan. 1808, as Fst.-cl. Vol., on board the CHILDERS sloop, of 14 12-pounder carronades and 65 men; and on 14 March following was present in a gallant action of six hours, which terminated in that vessel beating off, on the coast of Norway, with a loss to the British of 2 men killed and 8 (including himself in the hand and stomach) wounded, the Danish man-of-war brig *Longen*, of 20 18-pounder guns and 160 men. In consideration of the injury he sustained on the occasion he was voted by the Patriotic Society a sum of 15 guineas. In Nov. of the same year, after he had been for six months borne as a Supernumerary on the books of the TEXEL 64 and ROYAL WILLIAM, flag-ships of Admirals Vashon and Montagu at Leith and Spithead, he became Midshipman of the DOTTEREL sloop, successively commanded, on the Channel and Lisbon stations, by Capts. Anthony Abdy, Thos. Goldwire Muston, John Smith Cowan, A. Abdy, Thos. Hanloke, and Wm. Westcott Daniel. In that vessel, in 1809, he witnessed the destruction of three heavy French frigates under the batteries of Sable d'Olonne, and also of the shipping in Basque Roads. Quitting her in Dec. 1811 he served during the next three years off the Western Islands and in the West Indies on board the PIQUE 36, Capt. Hon. Anthony Maitland. On his return to England in the spring of 1815 in the PALMA 38, Capt. Jas. Andrew Worth, he was received first on board the PRINCE 98, flag-ship of Sir Edw. Thornbrough at Portsmouth, and then on board the BOYNE 98, flag-ship of Lord Exmouth in the Mediterranean; where, on following that nobleman, as Master's Mate, into the QUEEN CHARLOTTE 100, he was afforded an opportunity of assisting in the bombardment of Algiers 27 Aug. 1816; for his conduct on which occasion, particularly in steering the explosion vessel under the lighthouse battery, he was rewarded with a commission bearing date 17 Sept. in the same year. His last appointments were—4 Oct. 1817, for a few months, to the CADMUS 10, Capt. John Gedge, on the Yarmouth station—and,

8 Dec. 1821, as Senior-Lieutenant, to the REDWING 18, Capt. Hon. Geo. Rolle Walpole Trefusis, with whom, until superseded at his own request in March, 1814, he served off Milford, made a voyage to the Havana, and was employed off Jersey and Yarmouth.

Lieut. Parker married 3 Dec. 1827, and has issue one daughter.

PARKER, Bart. (CAPTAIN, 1822. F-P., 13; H-P., 30.)

SIR CHARLES CHRISTOPHER PARKER, born 16 June, 1792, is third and only surviving son of the late Christ. Parker, Esq., Vice-Admiral of the Blue,* by Augusta Barbara Charlotte, daughter of Admiral Hon. John Byron, granddaughter of the fourth Lord Byron, and aunt of the poet. Sir Charles is grandson of the late Sir Peter Parker, Bart., Admiral of the Fleet;† great-grandson of Rear-Admiral Christ. Parker (1749), who entered the Navy towards the close of the seventeenth century, commanded the SPEEDWELL in 1712, and the TORBAY 80 in 1739, and died in 1763; and cousin of the late Admiral Sir Geo. Parker, K.C.B. His eldest brother, Sir Peter Parker, Bart., after a gallant career, was killed on shore, while Captain of the MENELAUS 38, in a sanguinary affair with the Americans at Bellair, near Baltimore, 30 Aug. 1814; and his second brother, John Edm. Geo., whom he succeeded in the Baronetcy 18 Nov. 1835, was a Captain in the Royal Artillery. His nephew, Sir Peter Parker, Bart., only son of the last-mentioned Sir Peter, was a Commander R.N. (1834), and died 17 March, 1835. Sir Charles is brother-in-law of Colonel Chas. Parker Ellis, late of the Grenadier Guards.

This officer entered the Navy, 18 June, 1804, as Sec.-cl. Vol., on board the GLORY 98, Capt. Geo. Martin, whom he accompanied, towards the close of the same year, into the BARFLEUR 98. In those ships he served with the Channel Fleet until June, 1805. Being then received on board the WEASEL 18, commanded by his brother, Capt. Peter Parker, he proceeded, after having narrowly escaped shipwreck, to join Lord Nelson off Cadiz. On the departure of the enemy's fleet from that harbour immediately prior to the battle of Trafalgar, the WEASEL was the first vessel that observed their outward movement; and she was only prevented from acting a part in the glorious scene that followed by the mortifying circumstance of being forthwith despatched to communicate the event to the ships at Gibraltar. So chagrined was her brave Commander at this disappointment that he actually shed tears on the quarter-deck. Mr. Parker continued to serve with his brother in the MELPOMÈNE 38 until March, 1806; in the course of which month he was transferred, as Midshipman, to the EAGLE 74, Capt. Chas. Rowley. He had been previously present in a violent storm, which had left the MELPOMÈNE for five days without a rudder. On joining the EAGLE, he soon became engaged in a variety of operations on the coast of Italy, where, in May, 1806, it was his fortune to witness the capture of the island of Capri and the defence of the fortress of Gaeta. On the return home of the EAGLE in the spring of 1809, Mr. Parker obtained a berth on board the ST. GEORGE 98, bearing the flag in the Baltic of Rear-Admiral Fras. Pickmore, under whom during the remainder of the year he was arduously employed. We may observe too that he suffered very severely from the effects of the climate, and that on one occasion while at the main-top he was so stiffened by the cold as to render it necessary for him to be lowered by a rope. In the early part of 1810 he returned with Sir Chas. Cotton to the Mediterranean in the SAN JOSEF 110; and in June of that year he accomplished his probationary term of servitude as Midshipman. Owing, however, to a recent Order in Council, retrospective in its operation, by virtue of which it was settled that no officer should be considered eligible for the receipt of a commission until he had attained the age of 19, Mr. Parker, being then only 18, was obliged to submit to the delay of another year before he could obtain leave to pass his examination. During the greater part of that period, although only holding the rating of Midshipman, he was allowed nevertheless to perform the duties of Lieutenant on board the UNITÉ 36, Capt. Patrick Campbell. While so attached, we find him frequently employed on boat-service on the coast of France and Italy, particularly on one occasion, when he took part, and gained the warmest approbation of his Captain for his conduct, in an attack upon a convoy under the batteries of Cape Talliat. At another time, while the UNITÉ was working in for the purpose of lowering her boats during some hostile operations against the town of Cotrone, he fell from the quarter-deck into the gun-room, and sustained so much injury in the head that the effects have since materially debilitated his constitution. On at length passing his examination, 17 June, 1811, Mr. Parker, then on board the TÉMÉRAIRE 98, bearing the flag of his friend Rear-Admiral Pickmore, was by Sir Chas. Cotton made, the same day, Lieutenant into his own flag-ship the SAN JOSEF. In the following Aug. he went on half-pay for the recovery of his health; but in the spring of 1812 he resumed the active duties of his profession, and again joined his brother on board the MENELAUS 38; in which ship it appears he was present when, having pursued the French 40-gun frigate *Pauline* and 16-gun brig *Ecureuil* under the batteries of Toulon, she effected a masterly retreat from the fleet that had come out to their protection, by passing through its line ahead of one 74 and astern of another. This affair took place in May, 1812; and about the same period Mr. Parker removed to the MALTA 80, flag-ship of Rear-Admiral Benj. Hallowell. In 1813 he assisted at the siege of Tarragona. He was next advanced to the rank of Commander 5 April, 1815, having been nominated by Admiral Pickmore to one of his hauling-down vacancies; and he was afterwards, from 17 July, 1819, until promoted to his present rank, 23 April, 1822, employed in the HARLEQUIN 18, on the Irish station. He has since been on half-pay.

Sir Chas. Christ. Parker married, 19 Sept. 1815, Miss Georgiana Ellis Parker. AGENTS—Hallett and Robinson.

---

* Vice-Admiral Christopher Parker, when commanding the LOWESTOFFE frigate, led the squadron, and distinguished himself in a successful attack made about 1778, in pursuance of a plan conceived by his father, Sir Peter, on the formidable fortress of St. Fernando de Omoa, on the Coast of South America. Towards the close of the French revolutionary war his own flag and that of his father were flying at the same time at Spithead—the only instance of the kind, we believe, on record. He died 26 May, 1804.

† Admiral Sir Peter Parker was born in 1721. He was made a Lieutenant in 1743, and a Post-Captain in 1749. In the latter capacity he commanded the MARGATE frigate, WOOLWICH 44, BRISTOL 50, MONTAGU 64, BUCKINGHAM 70, TERRIBLE 74, and BARFLEUR 90. For services rendered previously to the year 1772, he received the honour of Knighthood. Being appointed in 1775 to the command on the North American station, he hoisted a broad pendant on board his former ship, the BRISTOL, and sailed with a squadron to co-operate with the loyalists in South Carolina. On 28 June, 1776, Sir Peter made a tremendous attack upon the batteries of Charlestown, which was as furiously resisted. The conflict continued throughout the day, and the enemy's firing was at times silenced, but as the troops, commanded by General Clinton, were unable from some cause to effect a landing, the expedition failed. The carnage on board the ships was terrific in the BRISTOL alone the loss amounted to 40 killed and 70 wounded. In the course of the same year Sir Peter Parker co-operated in an attack upon Long Island, and reduced Rhode Island. In 1777, on his promotion to flag-rank, he was promoted to the chief command on the Jamaica station, where he remained until 1782 In Dec. of that year he was created a Baronet of Great Britain. He became a Vice-Admiral in 1779, and a full Admiral in 1787: he was appointed Commander-in-Chief at Portsmouth in 1793; and on the death of Earl Howe in 1779, he was made Admiral of the Fleet and a General of Marines. For some years prior to the commencement of the French revolutionary war Sir Peter sat in Parliament as M.P. for the borough of Maldon. We may add, that when in command at Jamaica he was the first to discern the merits of Nelson and Collingwood, who, to the liberal patronage he in consequence afforded them, were solely indebted for their advancement in early life. The Admiral died 21 Dec. 1811.

PARKER. (COMMANDER, 1814. F-P., 14; H-P., 34.)

FREDERICK AUGUSTUS HARGOOD PARKER entered the Navy, 18 March, 1799, as A.B., on board the PRINCE GEORGE 98, Capt. Joseph Bingham, bearing the flag of Sir Wm. Parker in the Mediterranean; whence, on removing with the same officer to the AMERICA 64, he proceeded to Halifax and the West Indies. In Dec. 1800, the AMERICA having struck upon the Formigas rocks and been rendered unfit for further service, he joined the ST. ALBANS 64, the new flag-ship of Sir Wm. Parker; on leaving which, in June, 1801, he was received as Midshipman on board the ANDROMACHE 32, Capt. Robt. Laurie. After a servitude of more than two years and a half in that frigate on the West India and North American stations, he removed, in Feb. 1804, to the TÉMÉRAIRE 98, Capt. Eliab Harvey, attached to the fleet in the Channel, where he remained until May, 1805. He was confirmed, 22 Jan. 1806, to the post of First-Lieutenant in the NIGHTINGALE sloop, Capt. Wm. Wilkinson; and was afterwards appointed—8 Dec. 1808, to the TARTAR 32, Capt. Joseph Baker, which ship he left in Oct. 1809—16 June, 1810, again as First, to the ROLLA 10, Capt. Sam. Clarke—19 March, 1811, to the DICTATOR 64, Capt. Robt. Williams—and 5 Dec. 1811, a third time as Senior Lieutenant, to the ALEXANDRIA 32, Capt. Robt. Cathcart. In the five ships last mentioned Mr. Parker was employed on the Home and Baltic stations. On 15 July, 1809, he commanded the boats of the TARTAR, in conjunction with Lieut. Thos. Sykes, at the capture, near Felixberg, on the coast of Courland, of a Danish privateer of 4 guns, whose crew, 24 in number, had landed with their muskets, and, being joined by the country people, had posted themselves behind the sandhills close to the beach;* and in July, 1813, he was present on board the ALEXANDRIA when, in company with the SPITFIRE 16, she drove from off her cruizing-ground, after a chase of 91 hours, the powerful U. S. frigate *President*, together with her consort the *Scourge* privateer, and thereby saved a large and valuable convoy from capture. He attained the rank of Commander 15 June, 1814; and has since been on half-pay.

* *Vide* Gaz. 1809, p. 867.

PARKER, K.C.B. (ADMIRAL OF THE RED, 1837. F-P., 34; H-P., 40.)

SIR GEORGE PARKER was born in 1767, and died 24 Dec. 1847. He was son, by Miss Gore, of the late Geo. Parker, Esq., elder brother of Admiral Sir Peter Parker, Bart.; and was cousin of the present Sir Chas. Christ. Parker, Bart., Captain R.N. His ancestor, the Rev. Dr. Parker, was Archbishop of Canterbury in the reign of Queen Elizabeth.

This officer entered the Navy, 21 Dec. 1773, under the patronage of his uncle Sir Peter Parker, who promoted him, 13 March, 1782, to the rank of Lieutenant. He had then served throughout the whole of the American war. In 1786 he obtained an appointment to the WASP sloop, on the Downs station; and on his removal, in 1788, to the PHŒNIX 36, Capts. Geo. Byron and Rich. John Strachan, he sailed for the East Indies. While on that station he was actively employed, in the boats and on shore, in co-operation with the army under Sir Robt. Abercrombie during the war with Tippoo Saib; and he was also, 19 Nov. 1791, present, in company with the PERSEVERANCE frigate, in an obstinate action (produced by a resistance on the part of the French Captain to a search being imposed by the British upon two merchant-vessels under his orders) with *La Résolue* of 46 guns, whose colours were not struck until she had herself sustained a loss of 25 men killed and 40 wounded, and had occasioned one to the PHŒNIX of 6 killed and 11 wounded. In Oct. 1792, having been sent home in charge of the despatches of Commodore Hon. Wm. Cornwallis, Mr. Parker, who on the occasion last named had played the part of First-Lieutenant, was appointed, in a similar capacity, to the CRESCENT of 36 guns and 257 men, Capt. Jas. Saumarez; under whom, whose gallantry in the affair procured him the honour of Knighthood, he assisted, 20 Oct. 1793, at the capture of the French frigate *La Réunion* of 40 guns and 300 men, of whom 120 were killed and wounded, without any casualty whatever to the British. For his own conduct on the occasion Lieut. Parker was promoted, 4 Nov. in the same year, to the command of the ALBACORE sloop, on the North Sea station, where he was posted, 7 April, 1795, into the SQUIRREL 20. Removing, towards the close of 1796, to the SANTA MARGARITA 36, he contrived, during a cruize off the coast of Ireland and in the West Indies, to effect the capture of a variety of the enemy's vessels, particularly of *L'Adour* of 16 guns, pierced for 20, and 147 men, and of *La Victorine* of 16 guns and 82 men, the *San Francisco* of 14 guns and 53 men, and *Le Quatorze Juillet* of 14 guns and 65 men. He was also much employed in convoying the trade to Quebec, the Mediterranean, and (the East India ships) past the Canary Islands; and on one occasion he received a letter of thanks from the masters and owners of a convoy, transmitted through the Admiralty, for his care and attention to them. At the close of the war, at which period the SANTA MARGARITA was serving on the Leeward Island station, Capt. Parker's health obliged him to invalid. His next appointments were, in 1804-5, to the ARGO 44 and STATELY 64, both attached to the force in the North Sea; where, in the STATELY, he was for a time employed in blockading the enemy's squadron in the Texel. Being sent, in Jan. 1808, on a particular service to the Baltic in command of three ships of the line, it was his fate, on reaching Gottenborg, to be frozen up in the ice; through which, however, in the ensuing March, he caused a canal to be cut, and thus extricated as well his own squadron as a large convoy of merchantmen bound to England. On 22 of the same month Capt. Parker, then in company with the NASSAU 64, had the good fortune to fall in with, and, after an obstinate running fight, attended with a loss to the STATELY of 4 men killed and 28 wounded, to enforce the surrender, on the coast of Zealand, of the Danish 74-gun ship *Prindts Christian Frederic*. The NASSAU's loss in the engagement did not exceed 2 killed and 16 wounded; while that of the enemy (whose ship, having taken the ground, was fired and blown up by her captors) extended to as many as 55 killed and 88 wounded.* Not long after this Capt. Parker was succeeded in his command by Rear-Admiral Sir Sam. Hood, who expressed his entire approbation of all the arrangements he had made, and of the able conduct he had manifested on every occasion. On the return of the STATELY to England he was appointed to the ABOUKIR 74, in which ship (part of the Walcheren expeditionary force) he continued employed in the North Sea and Mediterranean until the end of 1813. He then returned home in the BOMBAY 74, and did not again go afloat. He became a Rear-Admiral 4 June, 1814; a Vice-Admiral 19 July, 1821; and a full Admiral 10 Jan. 1837. His nomination to the K.C.B. took place 6 June, 1833.

Sir Geo. Parker married a daughter of the late Peter Bult, Esq. AGENTS—Hallett and Robinson.

* *Vide* Gaz. 1808, p. 536.

PARKER. (COMMANDER, 1814. F-P., 13; H-P., 33.)

HENRY PARKER entered the Navy, 27 Jan. 1801, as Fst.-cl. Vol., on board the BELLEISLE 74, Capts. Wm. Domett, Chas. Boyles, John Whitby, and Wm. Hargood; in which ship he continued for a period of six years and a half. At first he was stationed in the Channel; he afterwards accompanied Lord Nelson to the West Indies and back in pursuit of the combined squadrons of France and Spain; and on 21 Oct. 1805 he was present as Midshipman (a rating he had attained in June, 1801) at the battle of Trafalgar. He next, 14 Sept. 1806, witnessed the destruction, off Cape Henry, of the French 74-gun ship *L'Impétueux;* and in Nov. 1807, on his return from a second visit to the West Indies, where he had removed with Capt. Hargood to the NORTHUMBERLAND 74, he was ordered to join the SWIFTSURE 74, bearing the flag at Halifax of Sir

John Borlase Warren. Under that officer (with the exception of an interval between Nov. 1811 and May, 1813, passed on board the DRAGON 74, Capts. Thos. Forrest, Fras. Aug. Collier, and Robt. Barrie) Mr. Parker, whose first commission bears date 28 April, 1808, continued almost uninterruptedly employed in the same ship and in the SAN DOMINGO 74, part of the time as Flag-Lieutenant, until advanced to his present rank, 27 June, 1814. His last appointment was to the Coast Guard, in which service he remained from 3 Feb. 1832 until the early part of 1835.

Commander Parker married, 10 April, 1822, Lady Frances Theophila Anne Hastings, eldest daughter of the late and sister of the present Earl of Huntingdon. AGENTS—Messrs. Chard.

PARKER. (RETIRED COMMANDER, 1836. F-P., 19; H-P., 34.)

HENRY DICKSON PARKER was born in 1778.

This officer entered the Navy, in Nov. 1794, as Midshipman, on board the STATELY 64, Capt. Billy Douglas, and in the summer of the following year was present at the reduction of the Cape of Good Hope, where he served on shore with the second battalion of seamen under Capt. Temple Hardy. After co-operating in the capture of the island of Ceylon, and witnessing the surrender of the Dutch squadron in Saldanha Bay, he became Master's Mate, in Sept. 1796, of the CRESCENT 36, Capts. John Wm. Spranger and Chas. Brisbane, flag-ship for some time of Rear-Admiral Thos. Pringle at the Cape. In the following Dec. he was detached in command, as Acting-Lieutenant, of the EUPHROSYNE cutter, employed as a cartel, for the purpose of conveying some prisoners taken at Foul Point, Madagascar, to the Isle of France; where, for the want of hands to assist in navigating his vessel back to the Cape of Good Hope, he was retained until Oct. 1797. On the return of the CRESCENT to England in the summer of 1798, Mr. Parker was ordered to join the KENT 74, flag-ship of Lord Duncan, in the North Sea. During the expedition of 1799 to Holland we find him employed on shore with a party of seamen under Lieut. Chas. Richardson, and attached to the army of Sir Ralph Abercromby. After the surrender of Admiral Story's squadron he returned to England in one of the Dutch 68's. In Dec. 1800 he was received on board the FOUDROYANT 80, bearing the flag in the Mediterranean of Lord Keith; and, on 10 Feb. 1801, he was nominated Acting-Lieutenant of the PEGASUS 28, *armée-en-flûte*, Capt. John Pengelley. While in that ship, of which, in Jan. 1802, he became Acting-First-Lieutenant, he was present at the landing of the troops in Aboukir Bay, 8 March, 1801, and during the subsequent operations in Egypt was employed in a Turkish gun-boat and on shore. Being confirmed in the rank of Lieutenant 11 April, 1803, he removed in that capacity, in the course of the following month, to the TRIUMPH 74, Capt. Sir Robt. Barlow, with whom he cruized for 18 months off Toulon. From Dec. 1804 to May, 1805, Mr. Parker remained on half-pay in consequence of a severe liver complaint. He then joined the ELEPHANT 74, Capt. Geo. Dundas, in the North Sea; and he was afterwards appointed, on the Home and Baltic stations—21 May, 1806, to the NASSAU 64, Capt. Robt. Campbell, part of the force employed in the attack upon Copenhagen—6 Oct. 1807, to the PRINCE OF WALES 98, bearing the flag of Admiral Jas. Gambier—21 Jan. and 14 May, 1808, to the HYPERION 36, and VENERABLE 74, Capts. Thos. Chas. Brodie and Andrew King—5 Feb. 1810 (after nine months of half-pay) to the SCIPION 74, Capt. Chas. Philip Butler Bateman—and, 17 March and 27 Nov. following, as Senior-Lieutenant, to the STATELY 64 and TREMENDOUS 74, both commanded by Capt. Robt. Campbell. From June, 1811, to Nov. 1814, Mr. Parker had charge of a signal-station in the counties of Essex and Kent. He accepted his present rank 23 Jan. 1836.

The Commander married, 4 May, 1839, Josephine Maria, eldest daughter of Capt. Rich. Lyle Hornbrook, R.M. (1833.) He had had a daughter by a former marriage.

PARKER, C.B. (REAR-ADMIRAL OF THE WHITE, 1841. F-P., 31; H-P., 20.)

HYDE PARKER is son of the late Admiral Sir Hyde Parker, Kt.,* by his first wife, Anne, daughter of John Palmer Boteler, Esq., of Henley; half-brother of Commander Chas. Parker, R.N.; and grandson of the late Vice-Admiral Sir Hyde Parker, Bart.† One of his brothers, John, a Colonel in the Army, married a daughter of the late Rear-Admiral Sir Home Popham, K.C.B.; and another, Harry, a Lieutenant in the Guards, was killed at Talavera. The Rear-Admiral is uncle of Capt. Harry Eyres, R.N., C.B.

This officer entered the Royal Naval Academy 5 Feb. 1796; and embarked, in Sept. 1799, as a Volunteer, on board the CAMBRIAN 40, Capts. Hon. Arthur Kaye Legge and Geo. Henry Towry, employed at first in the Channel and then in cruizing among the Western Islands. In Nov. 1801 he re-

* Admiral Sir Hyde Parker was born in 1739. After serving with his father (the late Vice-Admiral Sir Hyde Parker, Bart.) as Midshipman in the LIVELY, SQUIRREL, and BRILLIANT, he was promoted, 25 Jan. 1758, to the rank of Lieutenant. Accompanying his parent, subsequently, into the NORFOLK, GRAFTON, and PANTHER, he was present, in the GRAFTON, at the siege of Pondicherry, and in the expedition of 1762 against the Manilla Islands; and in the PANTHER, at the capture of the *Santissima Trinidad* galleon. He attained Post-rank 18 July, 1763, and he afterwards, between 1770 and 1790, commanded, in succession, the BOSTON 32, PHŒNIX 44, LATONA 38, and GOLIATH, ORION, and BRUNSWICK 74's. For his services in the PHŒNIX during the war with America, where he took part in the attack upon New York, accompanied the expedition against Philadelphia, and conducted the naval part of the operations on the Coast of Georgia, he was rewarded with the honour of Knighthood 21 April, 1779. In the GOLIATH Sir Hyde sailed with Lord Howe, in 1782, for the relief of Gibraltar, and in the action with the combined forces which followed the accomplishment of that object, had the honour of leading the van division of the fleet. In 1790 he was nominated a Colonel of Marines. On attaining, in 1793, the rank of Rear-Admiral, he became Captain of the Mediterranean fleet under Lord Hood, with whom he served in that capacity at the occupation of Toulon, and at the reduction of Corsica. In 1795, having in the preceding year acquired the rank of Vice-Admiral and hoisted his flag on board the ST. GEORGE 98, he was afforded an opportunity of sharing in Admiral Hotham's two partial actions with the French. He was afterwards, for three years, Commander-in-Chief on the Jamaica station; and on his return to England he was appointed to the chief command of the Channel fleet. He had risen to the rank of full Admiral in Feb. 1799. He closed his naval career by commanding in chief the famous expedition which, in the battle of 2 April, 1801, broke the Northern Confederacy. For that service he received the thanks of both Houses of Parliament. He died an Admiral of the Red 16 March, 1807.

† Vice-Admiral Sir Hyde Parker, Bart., served as Midshipman under Commodore Anson in 1739-40, was made a Lieutenant about 1744, and a Post-Captain in the LIVELY frigate about 1747. Between 1757 and the period of his promotion to Flag rank, which took place 23 Jan. 1778, he commanded the SQUIRREL, BRILLIANT, NORFOLK, GRAFTON, PANTHER, and INVINCIBLE. In the BRILLIANT he served under Rear-Admiral Rodney at the destruction of Havre-de-Grace in 1759; in the NORFOLK he assisted at the siege of Pondicherry, and at the capture of the Manilla Islands in 1762; and in the PANTHER, in Nov. of the latter year, he made prize, after a close action of two hours, of the *Santissima Trinidad* Spanish galleon, pierced for 60 guns, carrying between 700 and 800 men, and valued at upwards of 500,000*l.* In 1778 Rear-Admiral Parker succeeded to the chief command in the West Indies, where his exertions in protecting the commerce of England, and in distressing that of the enemy, were highly successful. On 17 April, 1780, he bore a distinguished part in Sir George Rodney's partial engagement with the French fleet under Admiral de Guichen, off Ste. Lucie; and in the following Sept. he was advanced to the rank of Vice-Admiral. Being soon afterwards invested with the chief command in the North Sea, he there, on 5 Aug. 1781, with 7 sail of the line, 4 frigates, and a cutter, fell in, near the Doggerbank, with a Dutch squadron, under Admiral Zoutman, consisting of 6 line of battle ships, two of 44 guns each, and 4 frigates: the whole of which, after a brilliant and most obstinate conflict of three hours and forty minutes, were compelled to retire into the Texel, with the loss of one ship of the line. On 13 Oct. 1782, Sir Hyde sailed for the East Indies with his flag in the CATO 50, but he was never heard of after leaving Rio de Janeiro on 12 Dec.

moved as Midshipman to the NARCISSUS 32, Capt. Ross Donnelly; and while in that frigate, of which he was created an acting and a confirmed Lieutenant 6 Oct. 1803 and 24 Sept. 1804, he saw much active service. On 11 July in the latter year, in particular, he assisted with the boats of his own ship and of the MAIDSTONE and SEAHORSE, 10 in number, under the orders of Lieut. John Thompson, and was highly spoken of for his conduct at the capture and destruction of 12 settees, lying at La Vandour, in the Bay of Hyères, after a conflict, in which the British, encountered by a tremendous fire of grape-shot and musketry, as well from the vessels themselves as from a battery and the houses of the town, sustained a loss of 4 men killed and 23 wounded.* In the following year Mr. Parker, who in July, 1803, had contributed to the capture of *L'Alcyon*, of 16 guns and 96 men, accompanied the expedition to the Cape of Good Hope; on her passage whither the NARCISSUS, besides making prize of *Le Président* privateer, of 12 guns and 70 men, retook the English merchantship *Horatio Nelson*, mounting 22 guns, and drove on shore the *Napoléon* privateer, of 32 guns and 250 men. Subsequently to the reduction of the Cape, Mr. Parker, on the surrender there of the 46-gun frigate *Volontaire*, was placed on board that ship under the orders of Capt. Hon. Josceline Percy. In June, 1806, having been advanced to the rank of Commander on 22 of the preceding Jan., he went on half-pay. His next appointment was, in March, 1807, to the PROMETHEUS sloop; from which vessel, for his services during the expedition to Copenhagen, he was promoted, 13 Oct. following, to Post-rank. He afterwards obtained command—11 March, 1811, of the MONMOUTH 64, bearing the flag in the Downs of Rear-Admiral Thos. Foley—15 April, 1812, of the TENEDOS 38, attached to the force on the coast of North America, whence he returned in Aug. 1815—15 March, 1818, of the IPHIGENIA 46, which ship was paid off 12 June, 1821—1 May, 1830, of the ST. VINCENT 120, bearing the flag of Sir Thos. Foley at Portsmouth—16 Feb. 1831, of the ASIA 84, on the Lisbon station—19 Dec. following, again of the VICTORY, employed, as before, at Portsmouth, where he remained until Feb. 1833—and, 29 Aug. 1835, for upwards of four years and a half, of the RODNEY 92, on the Mediterranean station. While in the TENEDOS Capt. Parker was engaged, in company with the SHANNON 38, Capt. Philip Bowes Vere Broke, in blockading, during the month of April, 1813, the port of Boston, in which lay the American frigates *President* and *Congress*;† he afterwards, in April, 1814, united with the JUNON 38, Capt. Clotworthy Upton, in chasing the *Constitution* frigate into Marblehead Harbour, whither he was only prevented from following her by a signal of recall from the JUNON;‡ and, on 15 Jan. 1815, he witnessed the surrender of the above-named *President* to the British frigate ENDYMION, Capt. Henry Hope.§ In the IPHIGENIA, after having conveyed the Duke of Richmond to Quebec, he proceeded to the West Indies, where the fever in a few weeks carried off 84 of his officers and men. On 5 Sept. 1831 Capt. Parker was nominated an Extra Naval Aide-de-Camp to King William IV. He attained flag-rank 23 Nov. 1841; and, from 4 Aug. 1842 until the close of 1847, he held the appointment of Admiral Superintendent at Portsmouth. In 1845 he commanded an experimental squadron. He was nominated a C.B. 18 April, 1839.

Rear-Admiral Parker married, 16 July, 1821, Caroline, daughter of the late Sir Fred. Morton Eden, Bart., and sister of Capt. Chas. Eden, R.N. By that lady he has issue. AGENTS—Messrs. Chard.

* *Vide* Gaz. 1804, p. 1239.

† On 21 of the following month, being in company with the CURLEW brig, he took the *Enterprize* American schooner privateer of 4 guns (pierced for 18) and 91 men.

‡ In Sept. 1814 he commanded the squadron employed in co-operation with the troops under Lieut.-Colonel Pilkington at the reduction of Machias, the last post possessed by the enemy between the Penobscot and Passamaquoddy Bay.—*Vide* Gaz. 1814, pp. 2026, 2121.

§ *Vide* Gaz. 1815, p. 281.

PARKER. (COMMANDER, 1847.)

HYDE PARKER obtained his first commission 5 April, 1844; and, from 15 May, 1846, until advanced to his present rank 4 Aug. 1847, was employed in the Pacific on board the CONSTANCE 50, Capt. Sir Baldwin Wake Walker. He is now on half-pay.

PARKER. (CAPTAIN, 1838. F-P., 32; H-P., 10.)

JOHN PARKER entered the Navy, 1 May, 1805, as A.B., on board the UTRECHT 64, Capt. Thos. Seccombe, bearing the flag in the Downs of Rear-Admiral John Holloway; and in the course of the same year was present, we are informed, as Midshipman, in the boats of the VESUVIUS bomb, in an attack upon the Boulogne flotilla. While serving next with Capt. Seccombe in the GLATTON 50, he assisted in the boats of that ship at the cutting out, 1 March, 1807, of a Turkish corvette of 10 guns, lying at anchor in the port of Sigri, in the Grecian archipelago, where the resistance encountered by the British killed their commanding officer, Lieut. Edw. Watson, and 4 men, and wounded 9, including Mr. Parker, whom, in the course of the same year, we find employed in a gun-boat on Lake Mareotis, in co-operation with the army during the expedition to Egypt. On 30 Jan. 1808 he chanced, with Capt. Seccombe, to be on board the DELIGHT 16, Capt. Philip Cosby Handfield, when that vessel, in an endeavour to re-capture four Sicilian gun-vessels, took the ground near Reggio, and was obliged to surrender, after losing, from an exposure of 15 hours to a galling fire from the enemy's batteries and troops, two-thirds of her crew, together with her Commander and Capt. Seccombe. In the following May he became attached to the STANDARD 64, Capt. Thos. Harvey; previously to accompanying whom, in March, 1809, into the MAJESTIC 74, he aided in cutting out an armed schooner near Otranto, and in spiking the guns of a battery at Cape St. Mary's. While serving as Master's Mate in the MAJESTIC Mr. Parker was wounded in her boats in escorting a convoy through the Great Belt; and on his removal in 1810 to the SOLEBAY 32, Capt. Hon. Granville Leveson Proby, he beat off, in a prize, a Danish privateer. On his arrival in the East Indies in the MALACCA 36, Capt. Wm. Butterfield, he was nominated, 9 June, 1812, Acting-Lieutenant of the PHŒNIX 36, Capt. Jas. Bowen; under whom, it appears, he accompanied an expedition against the pirates of Sambas, in the island of Borneo. After a servitude of 20 months, the chief part of the time as a Supernumerary, in the ILLUSTRIOUS 74, Capt. Joseph Prior, BARRACOUTA sloop, Capt. Chas. Hawkey, MINDEN 74, flag-ship of Sir Sam. Hood (by whom he was employed in surveying the neighbourhood of Trincomalee), STIRLING CASTLE, and CORNWALLIS, of similar force, Capts. Sir Home Popham and Stephen Thos. Digby, and MONMOUTH 64, Capt. Wm. Wilkinson, he was made Lieutenant, 29 Nov. 1814, into the SPENCER 74, Capts. Rich. Raggett and Wm. Robt. Broughton, stationed at first on the coast of North America, and then at Plymouth, where, for nine months, he had command of a tender. We may here mention that on leaving the STIRLING CASTLE he received from Sir Home Popham a very flattering letter for the zeal and exertions he had exhibited while under his orders. The SPENCER being paid off in Aug. 1818 he was next in succession appointed—3 Dec. 1822, to the NORTHUMBERLAND 78, Capt. Thos. Jas. Maling, lying at Sheerness—27 Feb. 1823, as First, to the ECLAIR 18, Capts. Wm. Jas. Hope Johnstone and Thos. Bourchier, fitting for South America—5 June, 1824, to the SPARTIATE 76, Capt. Gordon Thos. Falcon, on the latter station—and, 13 Sept. 1825, as Senior, to the VOLAGE 28, Capts. Hon. Rich. Saunders Dundas, Robt. Tait, and Michael Seymour. Attaining the rank of Commander 26 Feb. 1829, Capt. Parker was nominated, 12 March following, Second-Captain of the SOUTHAMPTON 52, flag-ship of Sir Edw. W. C. R. Owen, in the East Indies; where he was placed in command, 12 May, 1831, of the CRUIZER 18.* That vessel being paid off about Jan. 1834, he was appointed, 11 April, in the same year, to the HASTINGS 74, bearing the flag at Lisbon of Sir Wm. Hall Gage, under whom he served for a period of three years and nine months. He attained his present rank 28 June, 1838, and was afterwards, 18 March, 1839, and 18 Aug. 1841, placed in command of the WINCHESTER 50, flag-ship of Sir Thos. Harvey, and VESTAL 26, both on the North America and West India station. Since the autumn of 1842, at which period the latter vessel was put out of commission, Capt. Parker has been on half-pay. AGENTS—Goode and Lawrence.

* Prior to joining the CRUIZER Capt. Parker commanded for a time the SATELLITE 18.

PARKER. (LIEUT., 1815. F-P., 13; H-P., 26.)

ROBERT BROCKHOLES PARKER, born 19 Aug. 1790, is eldest son of the late Edw. Parker, Esq., of Clithero, by Sarah, daughter of John Leaper, Esq., of Kellet House, co. Lancaster.

This officer entered the Navy, 22 Sept. 1808, as L.M., on board the SEMIRAMIS 36, Capt. Wm. Granger, attached to the force on the Lisbon station, where he attained the rating of Midshipman in Sept. 1809, and in April, 1810, followed the same Captain into the CÆSAR 80. Removing, in May, 1811, to the VENERABLE 74, Capt. Sir Home Popham, he assisted in that ship, in the course of 1812, at the reduction of Lequeytio and Castro, on the north coast of Spain; also in the attacks made upon Puerta Galetta, Guetaria, and Santander; and at the destruction of the fortifications of Bermeo, Plencia, Galea, Algorta, Begona, El Campillo las Quersas, and Xebiles. In Aug. 1814, after having escorted Earl Moira to India in the STIRLING CASTLE 74, also commanded by Sir H. Popham, he joined the VALIANT 74, Capt. Zachary Mudge, stationed in the Channel; whence, in the ensuing month, he sailed for North America, as a Supernumerary, in the LIVERPOOL 50, Capt. Arthur Farquhar. Being nominated, on his arrival, Master's Mate of the TONNANT 80, flag-ship of Hon. Sir Alex. Cochrane, he was afforded an opportunity, in consequence, of sharing in the operations against New Orleans. He returned to England in March, 1815, in the ARMIDE 38, Capt. Sir Edw. Thos. Troubridge; attained his present rank 20 Sept. following; was subsequently, between Feb. 1825 and the early part of 1827, employed in the AURORA 46, and, as First-Lieutenant, in the ARIADNE 26, Capts. John Maxwell and Adolphus FitzClarence; and since 21 June, 1843, has been officiating as Admiralty Agent in a contract mail steam-vessel.

Lieut. Parker married, 19 June, 1816, Sarah, daughter of John Cundale, Esq., of Snab Green, near Lancaster, by whom he has issue two sons and two daughters. AGENTS—Messrs. Ommanney.

PARKER. (LIEUT., 1815. F-P., 12; H-P., 31.)

WALTER TURNER PARKER was born 5 Feb. 1793.

This officer entered the Navy, 2 Sept. 1804, as Third-cl. Vol., on board the INSOLENT gun-brig, Lieut.-Commander John Row Morris, under whom he was for three years actively employed, part of the time as Midshipman, on the Channel and Mediterranean stations. On his removal, in Aug. 1807, to the DESPERATE, another gun-brig, commanded in succession by Lieuts. John Price, Jas. Leach, Joshua Birks, Thos. Ellery, and Geo. Green, he was at first engaged in attendance on the Copenhagen expedition, and next in blockading the enemy's ports and in destroying their trade on the coast of France; where, it appears, he took part in many hazardous cutting-out affairs, was on one occasion wounded in the head, and at times landed in charge of secret papers. After witnessing the operations in the Scheldt, whence he brought a gun-boat, No. 31, to England, Mr. Parker was received, in March, 1810, on board the GRAMPUS 50, Capt. Wm. Hanwell. On his return home with convoy from China, whither he had also escorted the trade, he joined, in Nov. 1811, the RAVEN 16, Capt. Geo. Gustavus Lennock; in which vessel, on 3 July, 1812, we find him, in face of the enemy's fleet at Flushing, and under the very guns of that enemy's forts, assisting in a dashing attack made by her on 14 brigs (each armed with 3 or 4 long 24-pounders), three of which were driven on shore. In Dec. of the same year he was sent in charge of a prize to North Yarmouth; but the vessel on her passage taking fire, he was under the necessity of abandoning her, and of remaining in consequence exposed, until picked up, to several hours of intense hardship. He afterwards went back to the RAVEN, and continued in her until Sept. 1813. Becoming attached, in Feb. 1814, to the DIOMEDE 50, *armée-en-flûte*, Capt. Chas. Montagu Fabian, he sailed in that ship for Quebec; from which place, in the ensuing June, he proceeded as a Volunteer to Lake Ontario, and there joined the PRINCE REGENT 56, bearing the broad pendant of Sir Jas. Lucas Yeo, by whom he was in succession transferred to various vessels, and for a time entrusted with the command of a gun-boat. On his arrival home in a transport in Dec. 1815, he was promoted for his services to the rank of Lieutenant by a commission bearing date 17 of the preceding March. His last appointment was, 31 Jan. 1833, to the Coast Guard, in which he remained nearly two years.

Lieut. Parker married, 3 Oct. 1819, Rachel, daughter of Wm. Smith, Esq., of Wickford Hall, co. Essex, by whom he has issue three children. AGENTS—Messrs. Chard.

PARKER, Bart., G.C.B. (VICE-ADMIRAL OF THE WHITE, 1841. F-P., 30; H-P., 24.)

SIR WILLIAM PARKER is immediately descended from a younger son of Sir Thos. Parker, Kt., who held the office of Lord Chief Baron of the Exchequer for a period terminating in Oct. 1772; and is a relative of the present Thos. Hawe Parker, Esq., of Park Hall, co. Stafford, a Deputy-Lieutenant for that shire. He is nephew of the late Earl St. Vincent.

This officer entered the Navy, 5 March, 1793, as Captain's Servant, on board the ORION 74, Capt. John Thos. Duckworth; in which ship he served for some time in the West Indies, and was present, as Midshipman, in the actions of 28 and 29 May and 1 June, 1794. Following Capt. Duckworth, in March, 1795, into the LEVIATHAN 74, he soon again sailed for the West Indies, where, besides assisting at the capture of a large number of the enemy's vessels, he took part in the unsuccessful attack made in March, 1796, on the town of Leogane, St. Domingo. On 6 May and 24 June, 1798, he was successively nominated (after an unemployed interval of 18 months) Acting-Lieutenant, on the Jamaica station, of the MAGICIENNE frigate, Capts. Wm. Henry Ricketts and Wm. Ogilvy, and QUEEN 98, flag-ship of Sir Hyde Parker; by whom, from 29 April, 1799, until the receipt of his first Admiralty commission bearing date 5 Sept. in the same year, he was entrusted with the command of the VOLAGE 22, and of the AMARANTHE and PELICAN sloops. Attaining the rank of Commander 10 Oct. 1799, Capt. Parker, after intermediately commanding the ABERGAVENNY 54, was appointed, 11 Nov. following, to the STORK 18; in which vessel, employed in the West Indies, North Sea, and Channel, he made prize of *La Légère* French packet, of 14 guns and 50 men, laden with a valuable cargo, and contributed, in company with LA CONSTANCE 24, Capt. Zachary Mudge, to the capture of *El Cantara* Spanish privateer of 22 guns and 110 men, and of her consort a lugger mounting 10 guns. On the occasion of his promotion to Post rank, 9 Oct. 1801, Capt. Parker was appointed to L'OISEAU 36; and on 8 Nov. 1802, after having held command for eight months of the ALARM 32, and conveyed a body of German troops to Holland, he joined the AMAZON 38. In that ship, at the commencement of the late war with France, he brought the Duke of Kent home from Gibraltar; and, on his return to the Mediterranean, so distinguished himself on several occasions, particularly by his spirited conduct in chasing a French frigate into Toulon, that he excited the admiration and secured the friendship of the immortal Nelson; with whom, in 1805, we find him pursuing the combined squadrons to the West Indies and back. Previously to the latter event Capt. Parker had had the fortune, 16 July, 1803, to effect the capture of *Le Félix* privateer of 16 guns and 96 men. He afterwards, 12 Sept. 1805, took the *Principe de la Paz* Spanish privateer, mounting 24 9-pounders and 4 brass swivels, with a complement of 160 men; and on 13 March, 1806, he signalized himself by his meritorious and gallant behaviour throughout a long running fight, which terminated in the surrender to the London 98, and to the Amazon, whose loss extended to 4 men killed and 5 wounded, of the *Marengo* 80, bearing the flag of Rear-Admiral Linois, and 40-gun frigate *Belle Poule*.* In the summer of 1809, Capt. Parker was employed in active co-operation with the patriots on the coast of Galicia, especially at Ferrol, where he landed at the head of a party of seamen.† On 23 March, 1811, he captured *Le Cupidon* French privateer of 14 guns and 82 men. Quitting the Amazon in Feb. 1812, he was next, 11 Oct. 1827, appointed to the Warspite 76; from which ship, stationed in the Mediterranean, he was transferred, 29 Dec. 1828, to the Prince Regent yacht. On 1 May, 1831, Rear-Admiral Parker (who had attained Flag rank 22 July, 1830, and been nominated a C.B. 4 June, 1815) was invested with the chief command on the Lisbon station, which he continued to hold—occasionally commanding an experimental squadron—until 11 July, 1834.‡ On 16 of that month he was created a K.C.B. He became, 10 days later, a Lord of the Admiralty; and on resigning that appointment was constituted, 12 May, 1841, Naval Commander-in-Chief in the East Indies; whither he sailed with his flag in the Cornwallis 72. As a reward for the brilliancy and importance of his ensuing services in China, where he superintended all the operations from the taking of Amoy in Aug. 1841 to the pacification of Nanking in 1842,§ and was often personally engaged both afloat and on shore, he was nominated a G.C.B. 2 Dec. 1842, and raised, on his return to England in 1844, to the dignity of a Baronet. Since 27 Feb. 1845, Sir Wm. Parker (he had become a Vice-Admiral 23 Nov. 1841) has been in chief command on the Mediterranean station with his flag in the Hibernia 104. He was awarded the Good Service pension of 300*l.* per annum 26 April, 1844; and appointed, 19 Dec. 1846, First and Principal Aide-de-Camp to the Queen.

He married, 7 June, 1810, Frances Anne, youngest daughter of Sir Theophilus Biddulph, Bart., by whom he has issue.

* *Vide* Gaz. 1806.
† *V.* Gaz. 1809, p. 1010.
‡ His flag, during the period, was flying in the Asia 84.
§ *Vide* Gaz. 1842, *passim*.

PARKER. (Lieutenant, 1801.)

William Parker entered the Navy, in March, 1793, as A.B., on board the Diadem 64, Capt. Andw. Sutherland, with whom, after witnessing, as Midshipman, the occupation of Toulon, he removed, in Aug. 1794, to the Berwick 74. On leaving that ship, which for a time was commanded by Capt. Chas. Tyler, he successively joined the St. George 98, Britannia 100, and Goliath 74, all under the orders, the two former as flag-ships of Sir Hyde Parker, of Capt. Thos. Foley. In the St. George he fought in Hotham's two actions with the French fleet in 1795; he took part, in the Britannia, in the battle off Cape St. Vincent, 14 Feb. 1797; and in the Goliath he shared in the glories of the Nile 1 Aug. 1798. He was confirmed a Lieutenant (after having acted for 12 months as such) in the Druid 32, Capt. Chas. Apthorp, 16 March, 1801; and he was subsequently (having first obtained the Turkish gold medal for his services during the campaign in Egypt) appointed—2 Nov. 1801, to the Champion 24, Capt. Lord Wm. Stuart, attached to the force in the Mediterranean, whence he returned in Sept. 1802—16 Nov. 1803, and 13 Sept. 1806, to the command of the Cleveland and Neptune hired vessels, in which he served in the Channel until Dec. 1809—16 May, 1810, for four months, to the Savage sloop, Capt. Wm. Ferrie, on the West India station—18 March, 1811, to the Hebe hired armed ship, commanded at first by Capt. Edw. Elliott, next by himself, and then again by Capt. Elliott, in the North Sea and Baltic—17 Dec. 1812, to the charge, which he retained until May, 1814, of a Signal-station on the north coast of Ireland—3 July, 1817, to the command of the Neptune, for the purpose of superintending a division of the Plymouth Ordinary—in 1824, to the office of Agent for Transports Afloat—25 April, 1834, again to the Ordinary at Plymouth, where he became, 1 Aug. 1836, Senior of the San Josef 110, Capts. Rich. Thomas and John Hancock—and, towards the close of 1837, to an Admiralty Agency on board a contract mail steam-vessel. He has held an appointment, since 26 Nov. 1838, in the R.N. Hospital at Haslar.

Lieut. Parker is married, and has issue. One of his daughters, Mary, is the wife of John Brickwood, Esq., Purser and Paymaster R.N. (1840), now serving on board the Odin steam-frigate of 560 horse-power.

PARKER. (Lieut., 1815. f-p., 11; h-p., 29.)

William Frederick Parker entered the Navy, 27 July, 1807, as Fst.-cl. Vol., on board the Royal George 100, Capt. Rich. Dalling Dunn, bearing the flag in the Channel of Vice-Admiral Sir John Thos. Duckworth. From March, 1809, until March, 1814, he served, on the Mediterranean, West India, and Home stations, chiefly in the capacities of Midshipman and Master's Mate, in the Spider, Lieut.-Commander Wm. Sandford Oliver, Pylades 18, Capt. Geo. Ferguson, Spider again (commanded at first by Lieut. Oliver, and next by Capt. Frank Gore Willock), Elizabeth, Lieut.-Commander Dwyer, Demerara, Capt. Wm. Henry Smith, and Cressy and Egmont 74's, Capts. Chas. Dashwood and Joseph Bingham. Being then nominated Acting-Lieutenant of the Porcupine 22, Capt. John Coode, he took part in the ensuing operations on the Gironde, where he witnessed the destruction of a French line-of-battle ship, 3 brigs of war, several smaller vessels, and of all the forts and batteries on the north side of the river. After again serving as Master's Mate in the Egmont, and also in the Queen 74, the flag-ship of Rear-Admiral Chas. Vinicombe Penrose, he took up, in June, 1815, a commission bearing date 3 of the preceding March. His succeeding appointments were—6 July, 1816, to the Hecla bomb, Capt. Wm. Popham, whom he accompanied in the ensuing expedition against Algiers—2 Nov. following, and 3 July, 1817, to the Conqueror 74, flag-ship of Rear-Admiral Robt. Plampin, and, as First-Lieutenant, to the Griffon 16, Capt. Wm. Elliot Wright, both on the St. Helena station, whence he returned in Sept. 1818—and, in July, 1824, for a short period, to the Beaver 10, Capt. John Jas. Onslow, attached to the force in the West Indies. Since he left the latter vessel he has been on half-pay. Agents—Messrs. Stilwell.

PARKER, Bart. (Captain, 1814. f-p., 14; h-p., 39.)

Sir William George Parker was born 19 Aug. 1787, and died 24 March, 1848, at Plymouth. He was eldest son of the late Vice-Admiral Sir Wm. Parker, Bart.,* by Jane, eldest daughter of Edw.

* Sir Wm. Parker was born in Kent in 1743. Prior to 1778, in which year he was advanced to Post-rank, he served, we believe, under Lord Shuldham and Admiral Byron. During the war with America he commanded the Deal Castle, Maidstone, and Iphigenia frigates; as he subsequently did the Dictator 64, Jupiter 50, Formidable 98, and Audacious 74. In the Jupiter he was for three years Commodore and Commander in-Chief on the Leeward Island station; and in

Collingwood, Esq., of Greenwich. One of his sisters, Jane, married the late Capt. Geo. Cook, R.N.; a second, Sarah, the late Rear-Admiral Joseph Bingham; a third, Susannah, the late Capt. Wm. Hawkwell Bowen, R.N.; and a fourth, Mary, Colonel Peter Roberton. Sir W. G. Parker was uncle of the present Commander Parker Duckworth Bingham, R.N., and also of Lieut. A. F. J. Bowen.

This officer entered the Navy, in Oct. 1794, on board the RAISONNABLE 64, Capt. Rich. Parker, fitting for the flag of his father, Rear-Admiral Wm. Parker; with whom, in Feb. 1795, he sailed for the West Indies, and in July, 1796, returned to England in the SWIFTSURE 74. Rejoining the Rear-Admiral, in the following Dec., on board the PRINCE GEORGE 98, he fought with him in the action off Cape St. Vincent 14 Feb. 1797; shortly after which event he left the PRINCE GEORGE. He rejoined her, however, in Oct. 1798; and after serving for a time with his father off Cadiz, and with him in the AMERICA 74 at Halifax, was received on board the BOSTON 32, Capt. John Erskine Douglas. On 10 Oct. and 9 Nov. 1802 he was successively nominated Acting-Lieutenant of the CUMBERLAND and LEVIATHAN 74's, Capts. Wm. Henry Bayntun and Rich. Dalling Dunn; to the latter of which ships, bearing the flag of Sir John Thos. Duckworth at Jamaica, he was confirmed 2 Feb. 1803. His succeeding appointments were—2 April, 1803, to the DE RUYTER 68, Capt. Volant Vashon Ballard, cruizing in the Atlantic—14 Oct. following and 25 Jan. 1805, to L'AIMABLE and LA RENOMMÉE frigates, Capts. Wm. Bolton and Sir Thos. Livingstone, employed off Flushing and Boulogne, and in the Mediterranean—25 Nov. 1806, to the ROYAL GEORGE 100, flag-ship of Sir John Thos. Duckworth, whom he accompanied in the expedition to the Dardanells—and, 1 May, 1810, after two years of half-pay, to the ANTELOPE 50, as Flag-Lieutenant to the same officer at Newfoundland. While attached to LA RENOMMÉE, Sir Wm. Parker assisted at the capture, 4 April, 1806, under the fire of Fort Callaretes, of the *Vigilante* Spanish brig-of-war, of 18 guns and 109 men. He next, on 4 of the ensuing May, with the boats of the same ship and of the NAUTILUS 18 under his orders, boarded, carried, and brought out from under the fire of the guns of the town and Torre de Vieja, and also from under the fire of more than 100 musketeers, the Spanish schooner *Giganta*, of 9 guns and 38 men. "When it is considered," says the official report of his Captain, addressed to Lord Collingwood, "that this schooner was moored with a chain within half-pistol shot of the shore, that she had boarding nettings up, and was in every way prepared to receive our boats, as were also the batteries and musketeers, too much praise cannot be given to the officers and men employed; and I am confident their conduct will meet your Lordship's approbation." * On the night of 21 Oct. following the boats of LA RENOMMÉE, under the direction of Sir Wm. Parker, entered the port of Colon, in the island of Majorca, and, in the face of a fire from the vessels lying there, and of one from the town of Falconara, gallantly boarded and took a Spanish tartan, mounting 4 guns, and two settees, deeply laden with grain, one of them armed. The latter were with great difficulty brought out; but the tartan, having got on shore, was set fire to and destroyed. In the execution of this enterprise the British had only one man wounded. During the ensuing night Sir Wm. Parker brought off, from under the guns of Falconara, a settee, carrying 2 guns. On the occasion he was much annoyed by a fire of musketry from behind the bushes, which wounded one of his men; and in order to put a stop to the mischief he landed with a few sailors and marines, killed 1 Spaniard, and drove away the remainder.* Being awarded a second promotal commission dated 29 Nov. 1810, he succeeded, 1 Feb. 1812 and 21 May, 1813, in obtaining command of the RINALDO 10 and FLY 16. In the former vessel he contributed, 4 May, 1812 (in a manner that procured him the official thanks of the Senior officer present, Capt. A. Cunningham, of the BERMUDA sloop), to the capture, under the fire of a battery near Boulogne, of the *Apelles* brig-of-war;† and in the FLY he made a voyage to Brazil. He acquired Post-rank 6 June, 1814; and accepted the Retirement 1 Oct. 1846.

Sir Wm. Geo. Parker married, 29 Aug. 1808, Elizabeth, daughter of Jas. Chas. Still, Esq., of East Knoyle, Wilts, and has left a large family.

the AUDACIOUS he distinguished himself by the gallant manner in which, during Lord Howe's action of 28 May, 1794, he defeated the French 110-gun ship *Révolutionnaire*, after a close and furious engagement of nearly two hours. As a reward for his valour he was presented, in the course of the same year, with a gold medal, was promoted to Flag-rank, and appointed Commander-in Chief at Jamaica. Being subsequently sent to reinforce the fleet under Sir John Jervis, he fought with that officer in the action off Cape St. Vincent 14 Feb 1797, and in acknowledgment of his services on the occasion, was raised, 24 June following, to the dignity of a Baronet, besides being presented by the King with a gold medal and chain, and by the City of London with its freedom in a gold box His last appointment was on the Halifax station, where he commanded in chief from March 1800 until some time in the following year. He died of apoplexy at Ham, near Richmond, co. Surrey, 31 Dec. 1802.

* *Vide* Gaz. 1806, p. 828.

* *Vide* Gaz. 1806, p. 1558. † *V.* Gaz. 1812, p. 853.

PARKHURST. (LIEUTENANT, 1841.)

PERCY PARKHURST died in Nov. 1846 on board the ROSE, and was buried at sea.

This officer entered the Navy 6 Nov. 1829; passed his examination in 1836; and, participating in the operations on the coast of China, was in particular mentioned for his gallantry and zeal at the forcing of the inner passage from Macao to Whampoa; during their advance on which place the boats of the SAMARANG 28, in conjunction with the NEMESIS steamer, destroyed, between 3 A.M. on 13 and 4 P.M. on 15 March, 1841, five forts, one battery, two military stations, and nine war-junks, in which collectively were 115 guns and 8 ginjalls ‡ For the above and other services, including the capture of Canton, he was promoted to the rank of Lieutenant 8 June, 1841. His succeeding appointments were—17 Sept. 1841, to the STYX steam-vessel, Capt. Alex. Thos. Emeric Vidal, fitting for service at the Azores—20 Dec. 1842, to the CAMBRIDGE 78, Capt. Edw. Barnard, lying at Plymouth—and, 16 May, 1843, to the ROSE 18, Capts. Henry Rich. Sturt and Rich. Wilson Pelly, on the North America and West India station, where he died. AGENTS—Messrs. Stilwell.

‡ *V.* Gaz. 1841, p 1599.

PARKIN. (COMMANDER, 1837. F-P., 22; H-P., 16.)

JAMES LAMPORT PARKIN entered the Navy, 13 April, 1809, as Fst.-cl. Vol., on board the ACHILLE 74, Capts. Sir Rich. King, Hon. Geo. Heneage Lawrence Dundas, and Aiskew Paffard Hollis. During his attachment to that ship he accompanied the expedition to Flushing, cruized off Cherbourg and Cadiz, and was for a time employed, in the capacity of Midshipman, in blockading the French and Venetian squadrons at Venice, consisting of three line-of-battle ships and a frigate ready for sea, and of several of each class fitting in the arsenal. After a servitude of three years and a half on the Mediterranean, North American, and St. Helena stations in the HAVANNAH 36, Capts. Hon. Geo. Cadogan, Jas. Black, Edw. Reynolds Sibly, and Gawen Wm. Hamilton, he was received, in July, 1816, as Master's Mate, on board the MINDEN 74, Capt. Wm. Paterson, under whom he took part in the bombardment of Algiers, and then sailed for the East Indies; where he became, 11 March, 1817, Acting-Lieutenant of the ORLANDO 36, flag-ship of Sir Rich. King, and, 12 Feb. and 1 May, 1818, Acting-Second-Master and full Lieutenant of the MINDEN, then the flag-ship of Sir Rich. King. The latter vessel being paid off about 1820 he was subsequently appointed—23 Oct. 1823, to the OCEAN 80, flag-ship of Lord Amelius Beauclerk off Lisbon, where he remained three years—22 Oct. 1828, as First, to the CRUIZER 18, Capts. John Edw. Griffith Colpoys and John Parker, with whom he served in the East Indies until 1832—and, 3 May, 1834, to the HASTINGS 74, as Flag-Lieutenant to Sir Wm. Hall Gage at Lisbon. While attached to the CRUIZER, of which vessel he held the command for a short period, Lieut. Parkin was actively employed on the Swan River. He was advanced to his present rank, on the return home of the HASTINGS, 23 Dec. 1837; and has since been on half-pay. AGENTS—Messrs. Stilwell.

PARKIN. (CAPTAIN, 1841. F-P., 16; H-P., 26.)
JOHN PENGELLY PARKIN entered the Navy, 31 March, 1805, as Fst.-cl. Vol., on board the ACHILLE 74, commanded by the late Sir Rich. King; and on 21 of the following Oct. was present as Midshipman in the action off Cape Trafalgar. He was afterwards in the same ship at the blockade of Ferrol and Cherbourg, and at the defence of Cadiz. In March, 1811, he followed Sir Rich. King into the SAN JOSEF 110, flag-ship of Sir Chas. Cotton in the Mediterranean; on his return whence he joined, in March, 1812, the HERMES 20, Capt. Philip Browne. He removed, in the following Oct., to the SALVADOR DEL MUNDO, bearing the flag of Sir Robt. Calder at Plymouth, where he remained until March, 1813. Being then again placed under the orders of Sir Rich. King, whose flag was flying in the Mediterranean on board the SAN JOSEF, he continued employed with him, alternately in the capacities of Master's Mate and Acting-Lieutenant, until again transferred, in Aug. 1814, to the SALVADOR DEL MUNDO, flag-ship at the time of Admiral Wm. Domett. On 15 Sept. in the latter year he was confirmed in the rank of Lieutenant. His next appointments were—25 Oct. and 8 Dec. 1815, to the ST. GEORGE and IMPREGNABLE 98's, flag-ships of Sir John Thos. Duckworth at Plymouth—and, 6 March, 1816, to the MAGICIENNE 36, as Flag-Lieutenant to Sir Rich. King in the East Indies; on which station he was made Commander, 12 Dec. 1816, into the BACCHUS 18. He returned to England about 1820; and was lastly, from 11 Feb. 1840 until advanced to his present rank 28 Aug. 1841, employed as Second-Captain in the CAMBRIDGE 78, Capt. Edw. Barnard; under whom he took part in the operations on the coast of Syria and was present at the blockade of Alexandria. He has since been on half-pay. AGENTS—Messrs. Stilwell.

PARKINSON. (LIEUTENANT, 1842.)
WILLIAM FREDERICK W. PARKINSON passed his examination 2 March, 1837; was for some time Mate of the CALEDONIA 120, flag-ship of Sir Graham Moore at Plymouth; and for his services in that capacity in China on board the CAMBRIAN 36, Capt. Henry Ducie Chads, was promoted to the rank of Lieutenant 23 Dec. 1842.* His next and last appointment was, 20 Jan. 1844, to the VOLAGE 26, Capt. Sir Wm. Dickson; under whom he was employed on particular service until paid off in 1845. He was awarded a pension for wounds 22 Dec. 1846.

PARKMAN. (LIEUT., 1812. F-P., 19; H-P., 34.)
JOHN PARKMAN, born at Portsea, co. Hants, is son of the late Mr. John Parkman, an old and well-known Pilot for the coast of France.
This officer entered the Navy, 11 Nov. 1794, as Fst.-cl. Vol., on board the ROBUST 74; in which ship, successively commanded by Capts. Edw. Thornbrough, Geo. Countess, Wm. Brown, John Acworth Ommanney, and Wm. Henry Jervis, he continued until July, 1802. In 1795 he was present in Lord Bridport's action, and in the expedition to Quiberon; he assisted afterwards at the blockade of Brest, L'Orient, and La Rochelle; and on 12 Oct. 1798 he contributed, off the coast of Ireland, to the capture, with a loss to the ROBUST of 10 killed and 40 wounded, of the French 74-gun ship *Le Hoche*, one of a squadron commanded by Commodore Bompart. Previously to the latter affair he had aided in landing a body of troops at Wexford. At the commencement of 1802 he made a voyage to the West Indies. After an attachment of a few months, as Admiralty-Midshipman, to the DIAMOND 38, Capt. Thos. Elphinstone, he was nominated, in June, 1803, Master's Mate of the MAGNIFICENT 74, commanded by his former Captain W. H. Jervis; under whom he was wrecked during a gale of wind off Brest 25 March, 1804. He was in consequence detained a prisoner in France until the end of the war. His promotion to the rank of Lieutenant took place 20 Nov. 1812.
He married, 10 Aug. 1810, at Verdun, and has issue 12 children. AGENTS—Pettett and Newton.

* *Vide* Gaz. 1843, p. 2950.

PARKS. (LIEUTENANT, 1815. F-P., 21; H-P., 20.)
ABRAHAM PARKS entered the Navy, 24 Dec. 1806, as Clerk, on board the SANDWICH, Lieut.-Commander Emanuel Hungerford, lying in the River Medway, where he attained the rating of Midshipman in April, 1808, and in the following Sept. removed to the IRRESISTIBLE prison-ship, Lieut.-Commander Poynter Crane. Becoming attached, in Jan. 1809, to the SIRIUS 36, Capt. Sam. Pym, he assisted in that vessel at the reduction, in the ensuing Sept., of the town of St. Paul's, in the Ile de Bourbon. On his return to England in July, 1810, in the RAISONNABLE 64, Capt. John Hatley, he joined the MELPOMÈNE troop-ship, Capts. Hon. Wm. Waldegrave, Gordon Thos. Falcon, and Robt. Rowley; under whom he continued employed until Feb. 1815 on the Lisbon and Mediterranean stations, and also in the Chesapeake, where he was severely burnt by an explosion of gunpowder. On 7 of the month last mentioned he was nominated Acting-Lieutenant of the PORTIA 14, Capt. Henry Thomson; and in the following Nov., after having again served on board the MELPOMÈNE as Master's Mate, and as Admiralty-Midshipman in the JULIA 14, Capt. John Wyatt Watling, he took up a commission bearing date 15 March in the same year. His appointments have since been—18 May, 1835, to the Coast Guard—7 Feb. 1839, to the VICTORY 104, flag-ship of Hon. Duncombe Pleydell Bouverie, Admiral-Superintendent at Portsmouth—and, 24 July, 1839, 3 Sept. 1841, and 20 Oct. 1847, to the successive command of the PIKE, CUCKOO, and DASHER steam-packets. AGENTS—Messrs. Ommanney.

PARLBY. (COMMANDER, 1836. F-P., 26; H-P., 11.)
JAMES EDWARD PARLBY entered the Navy, 27 Aug. 1810, as Sec.-cl. Vol., on board the ARMIDE 38, Capt. Rich. Dalling Dunn, attached to the force on the Home station; where he continued employed as Midshipman, until Aug. 1815, in the DUBLIN 74, Capts. R. D. Dunn and Thos. Elphinstone, CENTAUR 74, Capts. John Chambers White and Thos. Gordon Caulfeild, and RHIN 38, Capt. Chas. Malcolm. While on board the latter ship he witnessed the cutting out of several vessels from the harbour of Corrijou, near Abervrach, 18 July, 1815. On leaving her he joined the SUPERB 74, Capt. Chas. Ekins; under whom, in Aug. 1816, he accompanied the expedition against Algiers. He continued to serve in the SUPERB at Plymouth until Oct. 1818; and he was next, between that date and March, 1823, employed as Admiralty-Midshipman in the RÉVOLUTIONNAIRE 46, Capt. Hon. Fleetwood Broughton Reynolds Pellew, IMPREGNABLE 104, flag-ship of Lord Exmouth, RÉVOLUTIONNAIRE again, Capt. Pellew, ALBION 74, Capt. Sir Wm. Hoste, and CREOLE 42, Commodore Sir Thos. Masterman Hardy, on the Mediterranean, Home, and South American stations. He was then nominated Acting-Lieutenant of the DORIS 42, Capt. Fred. Edw. Vernon (now Harcourt); and on 7 June following he was confirmed into his former ship the CREOLE. His succeeding appointments were—in Feb. 1824, to the ALBION 74, Capts. Sir Wm. Hoste and John Acworth Ommanney, in which ship he remained until Sept. 1825—25 May, 1830, to the DRYAD 42, Capt. John Hayes, fitting for the coast of Africa—and, 11 Oct. 1832, to the command (a short time after the DRYAD had been paid off) of the GRIFFON brigan-

tine, on the same station, where he remained nearly four years. He attained his present rank 28 Oct. 1836; and was lastly, from 22 March, 1838, until 1843, employed as an Inspecting-Commander in the Coast Guard.

Commander Parlby married, 14 Feb. 1825, Sophia Sylvester, daughter of the late Capt. Holland, 44th Regt. AGENTS—Messrs. Halford and Co.

PARR. (LIEUTENANT, 1806. F-P., 34; H-P, 17.)

ALEXANDER FORSYTH PARR was born 7 Oct. 1786. His father, a veteran Gunner, entered the service in 1777 and died in 1840 at the advanced age of 85. He had served in seven ships of war under 30 different Admirals and Captains: he had been on board the SWIFTSURE 74 when captured by the French in June, 1801; and on board the VENERABLE 74 when wrecked in Torbay in Nov. 1804. One of Lieut. Parr's brothers died a Midshipman at Guadeloupe in 1790; two others were also in the R.N.—the first a Commander, the second a Lieutenant; and a fourth died as Deputy-Assistant-Commissary-General in the Army at George Town, Demerara.

This officer entered the Navy, 20 Oct. 1796, as Third-cl. Vol., on board the SWIFTSURE 74; in which ship (of which his father was at the time Gunner) he continued employed under Capts. Arthur Phillip, John Irwin, and Benj. Hallowell, until May, 1801. After participating in a slight engagement with a fort at Teneriffe during an attempt made to cut some merchant-vessels out from that place, he proceeded off Lisbon and then to the Mediterranean. While on that station he shared as Midshipman in the glories of the Nile 1 Aug. 1798, and assisted in expelling the French from Naples, where he united in the siege of Fort St. Elmo. He was subsequently present off Cabritta Point, in the Gut of Gibraltar, when the SWIFTSURE, being becalmed, was attacked, severely cut up in her sails and rigging, and subjected to a loss of 2 men killed and 3 wounded, by a flotilla of 40 Spanish gun-boats. On 8 March, 1801, we find him aiding at the debarkation of the troops in Aboukir Bay. On leaving the SWIFTSURE as above, Mr. Parr joined the PENELOPE 36, Capt. Hon. Henry Blackwood, with whom he returned home from the Mediterranean and was paid off in May, 1802. Being next, in June, 1803, received on board the WASP 18, Capts. Hon. Fred. Wm. Aylmer, John Packwood, and John Simpson, he twice escorted convoy in that vessel to the coast of Portugal, served for some time off the port of Cadiz, and cruized in various parts of the Mediterranean, until his return to England in July, 1805, when he was discharged for the purpose of passing his examination. In the following Oct. he became attached to the AGAMEMNON 64, Capts. Sir Edw. Berry, Joseph Spear, and Jonas Rose; under the first-mentioned of whom, after having narrowly escaped capture by the enemy, he had the good fortune to enact a part in the action off Cape Trafalgar. Subsequently to the battle he was sent on board the COLOSSUS 74, to ascertain the state of that ship, and so dilapidated did it prove to be that the AGAMEMNON was under the necessity of taking her in tow. During the long and disastrous gale which shortly afterwards arose, the rope that connected the two vessels unfortunately broke, and the COLOSSUS was in imminent danger of being driven on shore and utterly lost. In order to prevent if possible a catastrophe so awful, it was determined by Sir Edw. Berry, notwithstanding the risk, that a boat should be lowered for the purpose of passing a fresh rope to the distressed ship, and of thus again taking her in tow. We have only to add that the execution of the hazardous enterprise was confided to, and most ably accomplished by, Mr. Parr. Continuing in the AGAMEMNON, we find him, besides sharing in various pursuits after the enemy's squadrons, present, 6 Feb. 1806, in the action off St. Domingo (for his conduct on which occasion he was promoted to the rank of Lieutenant 2 April following), and next at the capture of *La Lutine* national corvette, and in the operations connected with the expedition to Copenhagen. On the fall of the latter place (previously to which event he had assisted in escorting a large convoy home from the West Indies) Mr. Parr aided in navigating to England, as second in command, the Danish 74-gun ship *Princess Caroline*, with the 95th Regiment on board. On again joining the AGAMEMNON, he sailed for South America, where, while filling the post of First-Lieutenant, he was wrecked, in the Rio de la Plata, 20 June, 1809. So great were the exertions he underwent on the occasion, that, on being received on board the BEDFORD 74, he sank into a state of complete exhaustion, and, from the effects of inflammation produced in the eyes, was for eighteen days deprived of the power of sight. Mr. Parr's next appointment was, 26 Dec. 1809, to the ARGO 44, Capt. Fred. Warren; which ship, however, he did not join until July, 1810. Becoming soon her First-Lieutenant, he was employed in that capacity in protecting convoys to the river St. Lawrence, to the coasts of Spain and Portugal, and to the Mediterranean, also in conveying an ambassador to Constantinople and Algiers, and in accompanying another convoy from Malta to England. Being superseded from the ARGO at his own request in Nov. 1813, he was nominated, 18 May, 1814, Senior of the ALPHEUS 36, Capt. Geo. Langford, fitting for the East Indies; whence he returned in Dec. 1816. Since 27 April, 1831, the Lieutenant has been attached to the Royal Hospital at Haslar.

When on board the SWIFTSURE, in 1798, Mr. Parr fell and broke the small bone of his left leg; while belonging, in Nov. 1804, to the WASP, and on duty aloft, his right leg was so severely lacerated that he was for two months on the doctor's list; and in 1803 an explosion of powder on board the AGAMEMNON occasioned him a severe wound in the forehead. He married 21 April, 1821.

PARREY. (CAPTAIN, 1843.)

EDWARD IGGULDEN PARREY is a relative of Lieut. Robt. Parrey, R.N.

This officer entered the Navy 20 Feb. 1809; and in the following summer was present, in the ROYAL OAK 74, Capt. Lord Amelius Beauclerk, in the expedition to the Walcheren. He was subsequently employed in the same ship on the coast of North America; where, on becoming attached to the SHANNON of 50 guns, throwing a broadside weight of 538 lbs., and 306 men, Capt. Philip Bowes Vere Broke, he assisted, 1 June, 1813, at the capture of the American ship *Chesapeake*, of 50 guns, yielding a broadside of 590 lbs, and 376 men—an exploit achieved after a close and desperate action of 15 minutes, a loss to the British of 24 killed and 59 wounded, and to the enemy of 47 killed and 115 wounded. At the close of 1819, while acting as Lieutenant of the LIVERPOOL 50, Capt. Fras. Aug. Collier, he accompanied an expedition sent to the Persian Gulf for the purpose of crushing a race of notorious pirates whose head-quarters lay at Ras-al-Khyma, which place was in a short time destroyed, and all the vessels lying in its vicinity burnt or sunk. In an attack made on one of the latter in the LIVERPOOL's barge, Mr. Parrey was severely wounded. He was confirmed a Lieutenant in the same ship 28 Nov. 1820, and, returning home in 1822, was afterwards appointed, in the capacity of Senior Lieutenant—20 Sept. 1824, to the CHANTICLEER 10, Capt. Chas. Jas. Hope Johnstone, fitting for the Mediterranean—and 9 Aug. 1827, to the PRIMROSE 18, Capt. Thos. Saville Griffinhoofe, with whom he sailed for the coast of Africa. In the early part of 1829 Mr. Parrey, in command of a boat belonging to the latter vessel, boarded and took a Portuguese vessel (formerly the *Saucy Jack* American privateer) of 4 guns and 40 men, with 225 slaves. On proceeding up the river Noonaz he found two schooners, one French and one Spanish, quite ready for slaves; and he also discovered, in the same stream, an English brig, the *Lochiel* of Liverpool, without a living soul on board, the Captain, Mate, and all the crew being found dead below. With much praiseworthy exertion he brought the vessel down the river, a very dangerous one, to the PRIMROSE, by whom she was carried to Sierra Leone, where her Agent allotted a salvage of 190*l*. Mr. Parrey subsequently made prize, in the pinnace, of a galliot (at one time a yacht belonging to Alderman Sir Wm. Curtis) with 38 slaves on board, lying in the river Cachao. On 10 Feb. 1830 he was advanced to the rank of Commander. He afterwards, from 26 June, 1835, until 1838, and from 4 July, 1839, until Dec. 1841, officiated as an Inspecting-Commander in the Coast Guard. On 22 of the month last mentioned he obtained command of the SAPPHO on the North America and West India station, whence, in the summer of the following year, he returned to England and was paid off. He has since been on half-pay. His advancement to Post-rank took place 7 July, 1843.

Capt. Parrey married, 7 Dec. 1830, at Abbot's Rippon, Huntingdonshire, Miss Burn.

PARREY. (LIEUT., 1829. F-P., 28; H-P., 3.)

ROBERT PARREY is son of the late Commander Robt. Parrey, R.N.;* and a relative of Capt. E. I. Parrey, R.N.

This officer entered the Navy, 15 May, 1816, as Fst.-cl. Vol., on board the SCAMANDER 42, Capt. Wm. Elliott, under whom he was for two years and a half employed in the West Indies, and suffered much from yellow fever. Becoming Midshipman, in Nov. 1818, of the HYPERION 42, Capt. Thos. Searle, he made a voyage in that frigate to Leith, and was then ordered to South America; whither, after having conveyed a large freight to England, he returned in 1821 in the DORIS 42, Capts. Thos. Graham and Jas. Henderson; the latter of whom, in May, 1822, he accompanied into the BLOSSOM 24, commanded next by Capts. Thos. Bourchier and Arch. Maclean. On the arrival home of the BLOSSOM with a considerable amount of specie in the middle of 1824, Mr. Parrey (who had passed his first examination two years previously) was received on board the WELLESLEY 74, Capt. Graham Eden Hamond. In that ship he again sailed, as Mate, for South America, with the present Lord Stuart de Rothesay, then recently appointed Ambassador at the court of Brazil; whence at the close of 1825 he came home with the same officer in the SPARTIATE 74. After a servitude of nearly three years in the East Indies on board the WARSPITE 76, bearing the flag of Rear-Admiral Wm. Hall Gage, TAMAR 26, Capt. Jas. John Gordon Bremer, and JAVA 52, also the flag-ship of Rear-Admiral Gage, he was promoted, 27 March, 1829, to a Lieutenancy in the PANDORA 18, Capt. Hon. John Fred. Gordon (now Lord Hallyburton), with whom he returned to England and was paid off in Feb. 1830. His next appointments were—for a short time, to the HYPERION 42, Coast Blockade ship, Capt. Wm. Jas. Mingaye—and 19 Dec. 1831, to the ASIA 84, bearing the flag of Rear-Admiral Wm. Parker at Lisbon, where he remained until Oct. 1832. He has been in command, since 13 Dec. 1834, of a station in the Coast Guard—a service in which, in the execution of his duty, he has been severely wounded and otherwise injured.

* Commander Robt. Parrey entered the Navy in 1778, and was present on board the YARMOUTH, commanded by his relative, Capt. Anthony Parrey, in Rodney's celebrated action 12 April, 1782. Between 1793 and the date of his promotion to the rank of Commander, 26 Aug. 1808, he served as First Lieutenant in the MODESTE frigate, Capt. Thos. Byam Martin, as also in the DUKE and ST. GEORGE 98's, and SAN JOSEF 110; and officiated for several years as Flag-Lieutenant to Admiral John Holloway. He afterwards, during the expedition of 1809 to the Walcheren, acted as an agent for transports; and in the course of the following year he served in a similar capacity at the reduction of Guadeloupe. In 1814 he was nominated Flag-Captain to Rear-Admiral Rolles, who had been recently selected to fill the office of Commander-in-Chief at Jamaica; but as the Admiral never sailed, he of course lost the appointment. In early life he had been a messmate of his late Majesty, King William IV., through whose recommendation his son was eventually promoted to the rank of Lieutenant. He died in 1832.

Lieut. Parrey married, 20 Dec. 1831, Eliza, youngest daughter of the late J. B. Stone, Esq., Comptroller of Customs at Newhaven, by whom he has issue.

PARRY. (LIEUT., 1811. F-P., 29; H-P., 19.)

HENRY PARRY entered the Navy, in 1799, as a Volunteer, on board the BLANCHE troop-ship, Capt. John Ayscough; under whom, after having attended the expedition to the Helder, he was wrecked in the Texel 28 Sept. in the same year. Joining then the EURUS, Capt. Dan. Oliver Guion, he was afforded an opportunity of participating, in 1800-1, in the operations against the enemy at Ferrol and Cadiz and in Egypt. He returned to England with Capt. Guion, as Midshipman, in the TRUSTY 50, in April, 1802; and he was next, between March, 1803, and June, 1809, employed, on the Home, East India, and Mediterranean stations, in the GRAMPUS 50, flag-ship of Lord Gardner, ARROGANT 74, Capt. Lord Geo. Stuart, FOX 32, Capt. Wm. Hugh Dobbie, TREMENDOUS 74, Capt. John Osborn, BLONDE frigate, Capt. Volant Vashon Ballard, and PORCUPINE and MERCURY, both commanded by Capt. Hon. Henry Duncan. While acting as First-Lieutenant of the FOX, Mr. Parry, in 1805-6, officiated as Second in command of an expedition sent against the pirates near the Indus, and at the bombardment of the Temple of Somnauth. As Master's Mate of the PORCUPINE and MERCURY he served in the boats in a variety of cutting-out affairs. On leaving the vessel last mentioned he was successively nominated, between June and Nov. 1809, Acting-Lieutenant of the TRIDENT 64, flag-ship of Sir Alex. John Ball, SPARTAN 38, Capt. Jahleel Brenton, TRIDENT again, and KINGFISHER sloop, Capt. Ewell Tritton. Under Capt. Brenton he aided in effecting the capture of several islands in the Bay of Naples; and in the KINGFISHER he contributed to the reduction of the Ionian Islands. He had previously served on shore at the capture of Capri. Rejoining Capt. Duncan, in Sept. 1810, on board the IMPÉRIEUSE 38, Mr. Parry again saw much boat service, particularly in the neighbourhood of Toulon; where he was confirmed, 16 Aug. 1811, to a Lieutenancy in the LEVIATHAN 74, Capts. Patrick Campbell, Adam Drummond, and Thos. Briggs. In the course of 1812 he lent his aid to the cutting-out of a brig from under the batteries in the same vicinity; and also to the capture of some batteries and of 18 sail of vessels near Genoa. He returned home from a visit to Jamaica in Oct. 1814; and was afterwards employed—from 19 Oct. 1825 until 1831, in the Coast Blockade, as Supernumerary-Lieutenant of the HYPERION 42, Capt. Wm. Jas. Mingaye, and RAMILLIES and TALAVERA 74's, both commanded by Capt. Hugh Pigot—and from 14 Oct. 1836 until the early part of 1847, in charge of a station in the Coast Guard.

PARRY. (COMMANDER, 1832. F-P., 15; H-P., 29.)

HOWARD LEWIS PARRY entered the Navy, 23 Aug. 1803, on board the NIOBE 40, Capt. Matthew Henry Scott, stationed in the Channel. He removed, in Dec. 1804, to the HIBERNIA 110; and he next, from Feb. 1805 until March, 1806, served on the Home and Mediterranean stations in the TONNANT 80, Capt. Chas. Tyler. In Nov. 1809 he became Midshipman of the DOLPHIN 44, *armée-en-flûte*, Capts. Christopher Watson and Alex. Milner, with whom he served until transferred, in Feb. 1811, to the GRASSHOPPER 18, Capt. Henry Fanshawe. In the following Dec. he was on board the latter vessel when, in order to avoid sharing the fate of the unfortunate HERO, she was under the necessity of surrendering to the Dutch fleet in the Texel. He was in consequence taken prisoner and detained in captivity until the peace of 1814. He then successively joined the AMPHION 32, Capt. Jas. Pattison Stewart, and PANDORA 16, Capts. Jas. Kearny White, Sam. Malbon, Wm. Popham, and Hon. Fred. Noel; and in those vessels we find him employed on the North American, West India, and Home stations, until presented, in Oct. 1815, with a commission bearing date 10 of the preceding March. His next appointments were—10 Sept. 1825, to the RAMILLIES 74, Coast Blockade ship, Capts. Wm. M'Culloch and Hugh Pigot—and, 22 July, 1831, to the Coast Guard. "For gallant conduct and severe wounds" received in the latter service he was advanced to his present rank 10 Feb. 1832. He has since been on half-pay.

In consideration of his wounds Commander Parry was awarded, 19 April, 1833, a pension of 91*l*. 5*s*. per annum. He is the senior Commander on the list of 1832. AGENTS—Hallett and Robinson.

PARRY. (RETIRED CAPTAIN, 1840. F-P., 15; H-P., 34.)

THOMAS PARRY JONES-PARRY was born 14 April, 1784, and died 26 May, 1845. He was of very ancient Welsh extraction—was the son of Thos. Parry Jones-Parry, Esq., of Llwynon, co. Denbigh, by Margaret, daughter and co-heiress of Love Parry, Esq., M.P., of Peniarth and Madryn, co. Caernarvon—and brother (with Lieut.-Colonel Wm. Parry Jones-Parry) of the present Major-General Sir Love Parry Jones-Parry, K.H., of Madryn Castle, formerly M.P. for Horsham, in Sussex, and also for Caernarvonshire. One of his sisters was the wife of the late Robt. Browne Macgregor, Esq., Lieut.-Colonel of the 88th Regt.; and another, of Major-General Clapham, of Widcombe House, co. Somerset.

This officer entered the Navy, 29 Oct. 1796, as Midshipman, on board the TRIUMPH 74, Capts. Sir Erasmus Gower and Wm. Essington, under the latter of whom he fought in the action off Camperdown, 11 Oct. 1797. In Feb. 1798 he rejoined Sir E. Gower on board the NEPTUNE 98, in which ship, commanded afterwards by Capts. Jas. Vashon, Herbert Sawyer, and Edw. Brace, he continued employed in the Channel and Mediterranean until transferred, in Nov. 1801, to the THESEUS 74, Capt. John Bligh, fitting for the Jamaica station, where, after having acted as Lieutenant in the GANGES 74, Capt. Geo. M'Kinley, and RACOON 18, Capt. Austin Bissell, he was confirmed by commission dated 28 Jan. 1803, and appointed First of the ECHO sloop, Capts. Edm. Boger and Rich. Henry Muddle. In that vessel he assisted, 1 Oct. 1804, at the capture of the *Hazard*, French privateer, of 16 guns and 50 men. Returning to Europe in 1807, he was next, in the course of that and of the following year, appointed to the PORCUPINE and LEVERET, Capts. Hon. Henry Duncan and Robt. Evans. In the LEVERET he was for several months employed in the Baltic. He was promoted (while again serving in the West Indies on board the GARLAND) to the command, 27 Dec. 1808, of the MUSETTE sloop, in which he remained until Sept. 1810. His last appointment was, 7 June, 1814, to the ROYALIST 16, lying at Plymouth. He went on half-pay in the following Nov., and accepted the rank of Captain on the retired list 10 Sept. 1840.

Capt. Jones-Parry was a Magistrate for cos. Denbigh and Caernarvon, and a Deputy-Lieutenant for Caernarvonshire, for which county he served the office of High Sheriff in 1836. He married, 19 April, 1811, Margaret, only child of the late Vice-Admiral Robt. Lloyd, of Tregayan, co. Anglesey, by whom he has left issue three sons and five daughters.

PARRY, Kt., LL.D., F.R.S, L. & E. (CAPTAIN, 1822. F-P., 32; H-P., 12.)

SIR WILLIAM EDWARD PARRY, born 19 Dec. 1790, at Bath, is fourth and youngest surviving son of the late Dr. Caleb Hillier Parry, F.R.S., an eminent physician in that city, by Miss Rigby, of Norwich, sister of the late Dr. Rigby. His brother-in-law, the Rev. Thos. Garnier, Dean of Winchester, is uncle of the present Lieut. Brownlow North Garnier, R.N.

This officer entered the Navy, 30 June, 1803, as Fst.-cl. Vol., on board the VILLE DE PARIS 110, Capt. Tristram Robt. Ricketts, bearing the flag of Hon. Wm. Cornwallis, in the Channel; where, and in the Baltic, he continued employed as Midshipman and Master's Mate on board the TRIBUNE 36 and VANGUARD 74, Capts. Thos. Baker and Henry Rich. Glynn, until promoted to the rank of Lieutenant 6 Jan. 1810. In the VANGUARD he commanded a gun-boat attached to the ship, and came into frequent action with the Danish flotilla. His first appointment after his promotion was, 9 Feb. 1810, to the ALEXANDRIA 32, Capts. John Quilliam and Robt. Cathcart; in which vessel, besides affording protection to the Spitzbergen whale fishery, he was much employed in making astronomical observations, and in preparing for the Admiralty charts, which were much prized, of Balta Sound, of the Voe, a harbour in the north-eastern part of the Shetland islands, and of various places on the coasts of Denmark and Sweden. At the commencement of 1813 Lieut. Parry proceeded in the SCEPTRE 74, Capt. Robt. Honyman, to North America, for the purpose of joining LA HOGUE 74, Capt. Hon. Thos. Bladen Capel. On 8 April, in the following year, having accompanied a detachment of boats under the orders of Capt. Rich. Coote, to the neighbourhood of Pettipague Point, on the river Connecticut, we there find him contributing to the destruction of 27 of the enemy's vessels, three of which were heavy privateers, and the aggregate burden of the whole upwards of 5000 tons. In the course of 1814 Lieut. Parry furnished many of the junior officers on the Halifax station with copies of his 'Practical Rules for observing at Night by the Fixed Stars,' a treatise which was afterwards published in order to "facilitate the acquisition of a species of knowledge highly conducive to the welfare of the naval service." In Aug. 1814 he exchanged into the MAIDSTONE 36, Capt. Wm. Skipsey; and he next, in July, 1815, and Jan. and June, 1816, became in succession attached to the ARDENT 64, Capt. Sir Wm. Burnaby, and CARRON 20, and NIGER 38, Capts. Nicholas Lechmere Pateshall and Saml. Jackson, all on the North American station, whence, in March, 1817, he returned to England. On 14 Jan. 1818 he obtained command of the ALEXANDER brig, hired for the purpose of accompanying an expedition to the Arctic Regions under Capt. John Ross, with whom he returned home in the following Nov. Owing to the failure of the enterprize, a new one was determined on and the conduct of it intrusted to Lieut. Parry, who was consulted in the choice both of his ships and officers. He accordingly assumed command, 16 Jan. 1819, of the HECLA bomb, and in the early part of the ensuing May sailed from Deptford in company with the GRIPER gun-brig, Lieut.-Commander Matt. Liddon, for the purpose of carrying out the object of his mission—the discovery of a north-west passage. In the course of the voyage, which, although not thoroughly successful, exceeded in its general results the most sanguine expectations of its projectors, Lieut. Parry penetrated to long. 113° 54′ 43″ W., within the Arctic circle, and thereby obtained for the expedition the sum of 5000*l*., the amount of a parliamentary reward which had been promised to such as should cross the meridian of 110° W. from Greenwich, in the latitude of 74° 44′ 20″. A full narrative of his proceedings will be found in a volume, published by him in 1822, entitled 'Journal of a Voyage for the Discovery of a North-West Passage in 1819-20.'* The HECLA and GRIPER re-entered the Thames about the middle of Nov. 1820, and were paid off at Deptford on 21 of the ensuing Dec. On 4 of the former month Lieut. Parry was advanced to the rank of Commander; and on 19 Dec. the Bedfordean gold medal of the Bath and West of England Society for the Encouragement of Arts, Manufactures, and Commerce was unanimously voted to him. With the sum of 500 guineas subscribed for the purpose, "the Explorer of the Polar Sea" was afterwards presented with a silver vase highly embellished with devices emblematic of the arctic voyages; and on 24 March, 1821, the city of Bath presented its freedom to him in a box of oak, highly and appropriately ornamented. Encouraged by the discoveries made during the late expedition, and by the presumption it

* *Vide* also Gaz. 1820, p. 2064.

afforded of the existence of a north-west passage, the Admiralty soon made preparations for another; the command of which was again confided to Capt. Parry, who, on 30 Dec. 1820, received a commission for the Fury bomb, with which vessel and the Hecla, commanded by Capt. Geo. Fred. Lyon, he sailed from the Nore 8 May, 1821. After having passed two winters in the polar regions, the first to the northward of Southampton Island, and the second at Ingloolik, a small island in lat. 69° 21′, long. 81° 44′, the expedition, with its grand object still unattained, but with the acquisition of much important geographical knowledge,* returned to Deptford, where the two vessels were paid off 14 Nov. 1823. On 1 of the following month Capt. Parry (whose valuable services had been rewarded with a Post-commission bearing date 8 Nov. 1821) was appointed Acting-Hydrographer to the Admiralty; and, on 26 he was presented with the freedom of the city of Winchester. Being selected, 17 Jan. 1824, to take charge of a fresh expedition to the frigid zone, Capt. Parry, on 8 of the following May again sailed from Deptford, with the same ships as on the last occasion—the Hecla, however, being commanded by himself, and the Fury by Capt. Henry Parkyns Hoppner. The following winter was spent at Port Bowen, in Prince Regent's Inlet, where the two vessels remained, from 28 Sept. 1824 until 20 July, 1825. The Fury being shortly afterwards wrecked in lat. 72° 42′ 30″, long. 91° 50′ 5″, the Hecla was unfortunately reduced to the necessity of forthwith returning, with a double ship's company, to England. She arrived, accordingly, in the middle of Oct. On 22 Nov. in the same year, Capt. Parry (to whom the freedom of the borough of Lynn was voted a month afterwards in testimony of the high sense entertained by the corporation of his meritorious and enterprising conduct) was formally appointed Hydrographer to the Admiralty, which office he continued to hold until 10 Nov. 1826. At the end of that period, having proposed and obtained sanction for a plan of reaching the North Pole, from the northern shores of Spitzbergen, by travelling with sledge-boats over the ice, or through any spaces of open water that might occur, he was again appointed to the Hecla. Sailing from Deptford 25 March, 1827, he left the Hecla in Treurenburg Bay, lat. 79° 55′ 20″, long. 16° 48′ 45″ E., 21 June following, and then took to his sledge-boats, with which he contrived, by 23 July, to reach a little beyond 82° 45′, a latitude more northern than had been ever yet attained. He then retraced his steps to the Hecla, which he brought home and paid off at Deptford 1 Nov. 1827.† On the following day he resumed his duties as Hydrographer to the Admiralty, where he remained until 13 May, 1829 —a fortnight prior to which period he had received the honour of Knighthood.‡ He was subsequently employed—from 1829 until 1834 as Commissioner to the Australian Company in New South Wales—from 7 March, 1835, until 3 Feb. 1836, as Assistant Poor-Law Commissioner in co. Norfolk—and, from 19 April, 1837, until Dec. 1846, as Comptroller of the Steam Department of the Navy. He has filled, since the latter date, the post of Captain-Superintendent of the Royal Hospital at Haslar.

Sir W. E. Parry (who is an LL.D. of Oxford, an F.R.S. of Lond. and Edin., and a Member of the Imperial Academy of Sciences at St. Petersburg) is the author of a small work entitled 'Thoughts on the Parental Character of God.' He married, first, 23 Oct. 1826, Isabella Louisa, fourth daughter of Lord Stanley, of Alderley, by whom, who died 13 May, 1839, he had issue two sons and two daughters, now living. He married, a second time, 29 June, 1841, Catherine Edwards, daughter of the Rev. Robt. Hankinson, of Walpole, co. Norfolk, and relict of Sam. Hoare, jun., Esq., of Hampstead. By that lady he has had issue two daughters.

* Detailed in Capt. Parry's 'Journal of a Second Voyage, &c. in 1821-3,' published in 1824.

† *See* a 'Narrative of an Attempt to reach the North Pole in the year 1827,' published by Capt. Parry in 1828.

‡ *Vide* Gaz. 1829, p. 798.

PARSON. (Captain, 1837. f-p., 19; h-p., 28.)

John Parson died 29 Nov. 1847, at St. Helier's, Jersey, aged 62.

This officer entered the Navy, in the spring of 1800, as Fst.-cl. Vol., on board the Leviathan 74, Capt. Jas. Carpenter, bearing the flag in the West Indies of Sir John Thos. Duckworth; with whom he continued employed as Midshipman in the Hercule 74, until Feb. 1805. He was in consequence present in the latter ship at the unsuccessful attack upon Curaçoa in 1804, and in various other operations. After sharing, we believe, as Master's Mate of the Acasta 40, Capt. Rich. Dalling Dunn, in the battle fought off Cape St. Domingo, and serving for a short time as a Supernumerary on board the Dolphin, bearing the flag of Hon. Sir Alex. Cochrane, he was constituted, 6 May, 1806, Sub-Lieutenant of the Pert sloop, Capt. Jas. Pringle. He was nominated Acting-Lieutenant, 20 Jan. 1807, of the St. Christopher, Capts. Andrew Hodge and John Tancock; was confirmed, 1 Nov. following, into the Alexandria 32, Capt. Nathaniel Day Cochrane; and was subsequently (after cruizing for two years in the North Sea) appointed—29 Jan. and 4 May, 1810, to the San Josef and Hibernia, of 110 guns each, Capts. R. D. Dunn and John Nash, stationed off Gibraltar and Cadiz—8 Nov. following, to the Armide 38, Capts. R. D. Dunn, Fras. Temple, and Sir Edw. Thos. Troubridge, employed, until May, 1815, in the Channel and off the coast of North America—and, in July, 1816, to the Granicus 36, Capt. Wm. Furlong Wise, under whom he fought as First-Lieutenant at the battle of Algiers. For his conduct on that occasion he was advanced to the rank of Commander by commission bearing date 16 Sept. 1816. He subsequently, from 14 Oct. 1833 until advanced to Post-rank 10 Jan. 1837, officiated as Second-Captain of the Thunderer 84, Capt. W. F. Wise, on the Mediterranean station. He did not again go afloat.

Capt. Parson was married and has left issue.

PARSONS. (Lieut., 1802. f-p., 19; h-p., 33.)

George Samuel Parsons entered the Navy, in July, 1795, as Fst.-cl. Vol., on board the Barfleur 98, Capt. Jas. Rich. Dacres, under whom he fought as Midshipman in the action off Cape St. Vincent, 14 Feb. 1797. Removing, in April, 1798, to the Foudroyant 80, he acted as Signal-Midshipman of that ship under Lord Nelson at the capture, 18 Feb. 1800, of *Le Généreux* 74 and *Ville de Marseilles* armed store-ship, and, on 31 March following, after a desperate action, in which the Foudroyant (in company at the time with the Lion 64 and Penelope 36) sustained a loss of 8 men killed and 64 wounded, of *Le Guillaume Tell*, of 84 guns and 1000 men, flag-ship of Rear-Admiral Decrès. After officiating in a like capacity under Lord Keith during the expedition to Egypt, where he was intrusted with the command of a gun-boat on Lake Mareotis, he was nominated, 6 Aug. 1801, Acting-Lieutenant of El Carmen, Capt. Wm. Selby: in which ship, the bearer of Sir Wm. Sidney Smith, he returned, towards the close of the same year, to England. For his services in Egypt Mr. Parsons was presented with a gold medal by the Turkish government. He was confirmed a Lieutenant, 25 March, 1802, into the Batavier, Capt. Wm. Robt. Broughton, but continued only a few weeks in that ship, and was subsequently appointed—9 Sept. 1803, to the Ganges 74, Capt. Thos. Fras. Fremantle, employed off the coasts of Ireland and Spain—3 Feb. and 1 April, 1805, as First, to the Racoon and Elk sloops, Capts. Jas. Alex. Gordon, Rundel M'Donnel, and Jas. Rich. Dacres, both in the West Indies—8 Feb. 1806, for passage home, to the Malabar 74, Capt. Geo. Scott—13 Sept. following, to the Texel 64, flag-ship of Vice-Admiral Jas. Vashon at Leith—27 Feb. 1807, to the Orion 74, Capt. Sir Archibald Dickson, part of the force employed in the attack upon Copenhagen—and, 14 May, 1809 (after five months of half-pay, caused by indisposition), as Senior, to the Valiant 74, Capts. Thos. Geo. Shortland, John

Bligh, and Robt. Dudley Oliver. In the RACOON and ELK Lieut. Parsons served at the blockade of St. Domingo and Curaçoa; and in the latter vessel, under Capt. Dacres, he fought in an action with 11 Spanish gun-boats on the Spanish Main. While attached to the VALIANT he commanded her boats at the cutting out of a convoy from Basque Roads; besides contributing, under Capt. Bligh, to the capture, near Belleisle, 3 Feb. 1810, of the French 40-gun frigate *Cannonière*, laden with the spoil of the principal prizes which the enemy had taken in the East Indies during the three preceding years. The state of his health obliging him to seek half-pay in Dec. 1810, he was not again officially employed until 1841. Since 1 Nov. in that year he has been in discharge of the duties of Admiralty agent on board a contract mail steam-vessel, and has been once wrecked.

Lieut. Parsons is the author of an interesting work, entitled 'Nelsonian Reminiscences,' published in 1843 by Saunders and Otley. The volume contains a more elaborate statement of his services than we have been able to find space for. He married in 1812, and has a family of eight children now living.

PARSONS. (LIEUT., 1815. F-P., 24; H-P., 20.)

JOHN PARSONS, born 7 Oct. 1791, at Portsmouth, is brother of Lieut. Wm. Parsons, R.N., and of Geo. Parsons, Esq., Master R.N. (1825); nephew of the late Retired Commander Wm. Parsons, R.N.; and cousin of Capt. Sam. Hellard, R.N. Two other of his relatives, an uncle and a cousin, were present at the battle of Trafalgar, where the former was killed.

This officer entered the Navy, 29 May, 1803, as Fst.-cl. Vol., on board the DEFIANCE 74, Capts. Philip Chas. Durham and Hon. Henry Hotham; under the former of whom he fought, in 1805, in Sir Robt. Calder's action and in the battle of Trafalgar. In July, 1808, after having been for six months attached as Midshipman (a rating he had attained 22 Oct. 1805) to the GLADIATOR 44, flag-ship of Sir Isaac Coffin at Portsmouth, he joined the PODARGUS 14, Capt. Wm. Hellard; in which vessel, in the course of the following month, he witnessed the surrender of the Russian squadron in the River Tagus, and assisted, agreeably to the convention of Cintra, in embarking for France the French army defeated at Vimeira. On the night of 15 Aug. 1809, while engaged in landing papers for distribution along the French coast, Mr. Parsons fell into the hands of the enemy, who marched him in chains to Havre-de-Grace, where he was for three months confined to a dungeon, with no other sustenance than bread and water, and in the hourly expectation of being shot. Pardoned at length in consideration of his youth, he was sent, still in chains, to Arras; in the gaol at which place, owing to a subsequent attempt at escape, he was for four months imprisoned. He was then ordered to Verdun, where he remained until Dec. 1813. On 25 of that month, favoured by fortune, he succeeded in accomplishing a flight, in the course whereof, concealed in a cart under a heap of crockery ware, he passed through the centre of the French army on its road to Russia. On reaching the island of South Beveland, after traversing Belgium and Holland, he was taken by the Dutch, but was released the next day in consequence of the latter having declared for the Prince of Orange. Arriving at last in England he was received, in April, 1814, as Master's Mate, on board the WOLVERENE 16, Capts. Chas. Kerr and Geo. Guy Burton; in the launch of which vessel, armed with a carronade, he co-operated in the attack upon Baltimore. In Dec. of the same year he removed to the VENERABLE 74, bearing the flag in the West Indies of Rear-Admiral Durham, his former Captain; and while detached, shortly afterwards, in the FLYING FISH tender, he aided in beating off a large American schooner. His promotion to the rank of Lieutenant took place 3 Feb. 1815; from May to Sept. in which year we find him employed, on the same station, in the CRESCENT 38, Capt. John Quilliam. He subsequently commanded, for upwards of two years, the *Duke of Bedford* Indiaman, of 720 tons. His last appointments appear to have been—5 Jan. 1829, as Senior-Lieutenant, for nine months, to the ALLIGATOR 28, Capt. Chas. Philip Yorke, on the Leith station—14 Feb. 1831, in a similar capacity, to the NORTH STAR 28, Capts. Lord Wm. Paget and Hon. Geo. Rolle Walpole Trefusis, with whom he served in the West Indies until the close of 1833—6 June, 1834, to the command, which he retained until 15 March, 1842, of the SEAGULL Falmouth-packet—and, 28 June, 1847, to that, which he still holds, of the CRANE, another Falmouth packet.

Lieut. Parsons married, 27 Feb. 1834, Miss Anne Rebecca Read, of Norfolk Street, Southsea; and has issue one daughter.

PARSONS. (CAPTAIN, 1828. F-P., 21; H-P., 29.)

ROBERT WHITE PARSONS entered the Navy, in the summer of 1797, as Midshipman, on board the MARLBOROUGH 74, Capts. Joseph Ellison and Thos. Sotheby. In Jan. 1801, after having been for three years and a half employed, part of the time as Midshipman, on the Channel and Mediterranean stations, he joined the TOPAZE frigate, Capts. Stephen G. Church and Robt. Honyman, attached to the force in the West Indies. Removing with Capt. Honyman, in Dec. 1802, to the LEDA 38, he served in that vessel during 18 months in the North Sea and off Boulogne. He then sailed in the CULLODEN 74, flag-ship of Sir Edw. Pellew, for the East Indies; where he was nominated, 20 March, 1805, Acting-Lieutenant of the VICTOR sloop, Capts. Geo. Bell, Wm. Wells, and Thos. Groube. While in the latter vessel, to which he was confirmed 11 April, 1806, he fought in an action with a body of Malay pirates, and, we believe, contributed to the annihilation, in Dec. 1807, of the dockyard and stores at Griessee, in the island of Java, and of all the naval force remaining to Holland in the East Indies. His appointments, after he left the VICTOR, were—9 Aug. 1808, to the TERPSICHORE frigate, Capt. Jas. Murray Gordon, also on the Indian station—6 Nov. 1809, to the DANNEMARK 74, Capt. Jas. Bissett, in the West Indies—27 Dec. 1810, to the DIANA 38, Capts. Chas. Grant and Wm. Ferris, employed in the Channel and off the coast of France—12 Oct. 1812, after six months of half-pay, to the ARMADA 74, Capt. Chas. Grant, attached to the force in the Mediterranean, whence he returned in Sept. 1814—and, 25 March, 1815, to the BOYNE 98, bearing the flag of Lord Exmouth on the same station. On 25 Aug. 1811, being then in the DIANA under Capt. Ferris, he headed the boarders of that ship, and was mentioned for the great assistance he afforded his Captain, at the capture, in the mouth of the River Gironde, of the (lately British) gun-brig *Teazer*, mounting 12 18-pounder carronades and 2 long 18-pounders, with 85 men.* In Dec. 1813 Mr. Parsons, while serving in the ARMADA, commanded the boats of that ship in the unsuccessful attempt made by Sir Josias Rowley to obtain possession of Leghorn.† Attaining the rank of Commander 7 Nov. 1816, he served in that capacity, from 2 July, 1825, until posted 11 Nov. 1828, on board the DISPATCH 18, on the Irish station, where he captured a smuggling lugger, under French colours, with 400 bales of tobacco on board. He has since been on half-pay.

Capt. Parsons married, 28 Sept. 1829, Frances, daughter of the late Fras. Adams, Esq., of Norton Malreward and Stockwood House, Somerset.

PARSONS. (LIEUT., 1815. F-P., 26; H-P., 18.)

TIMOTHY PARSONS entered the Navy, 21 Oct. 1803, as Third-cl. Boy, on board the BUSY sloop, Capt. Timothy Clinch, fitting for the West Indies; where, on following the same officer into the OSPREY 18, he assisted at the capture, 17 May, 1805, of the *Teaser* French privateer, of 7 guns and 51 men. He continued to serve in the OSPREY, under Capt. Rich.

* *Vide* Gaz. 1811, p. 1752. † *V.* Gaz. 1813, p. 1827.

Walter Wales, on the Home station, until Dec. 1812 —the last four years and a half in the capacity of Midshipman; and he was next, until Aug. 1815, when he took up a commission bearing date 2 March in that year, employed in the BELLONA 74, Capt. Geo. M'Kinley, HORATIO 38, Capt. Wm. Henry Dillon, and LEVEN 20, Capt. Buckland Stirling Bluett. In the BELLONA he made a voyage to St. Helena; in the HORATIO he was engaged in protecting the Greenland whale-fishery against the American cruizers; and in the LEVEN he co-operated in 1815 with the royalists on the coast of La Vendée. He has been in charge, since 29 Aug. 1833, of a station in the Coast Guard.

PARSONS. (RETIRED COMMANDER, 1836. F-P., 20; H-P., 40.)

WILLIAM PARSONS died in 1846. He was uncle of the present Lieuts. John and Wm. Parsons, R.N.

This officer entered the Navy, in 1787, as Fst.-cl. Boy, on board the DILIGENTE, Capt. Anthony Hunt, lying at Portsmouth. After serving for two years with Capt. Sir Fras. Hartwell in the BELLONA 74, and for a short time with Capt. Geo. Brisac in the SCOURGE sloop, which vessel was compelled to throw part of her guns overboard in a gale of wind off Cape Clear, he became, in 1792, Midshipman of the TERRIBLE 74, Capt. Skeffington Lutwidge, under whom we find him, in the following year, present at the occupation of Toulon. On next joining the MODESTE frigate, Capt. Thos. Byam Martin, he assisted at the reduction, in 1794, of the island of Corsica; after which he removed to the PROSERPINE 28, Capt. Alex. Fraser, and was on board that vessel when she took the ground on the Haak Sands, and was obliged, before she could be hove off, to have her mainmast cut away and every moveable thing thrown overboard. He was made Lieutenant, 18 Feb. 1796, into the VENUS 32, Capt. Thos. Graves, at Newfoundland; and was afterwards appointed— 6 Feb. 1797, to the SHARK sloop, Capts. John O'Brien and Fred. Warren, on the same station—25 Jan. 1799, to the VENERABLE 74, Capt. Sir Wm. Geo. Fairfax, attached to the Channel fleet—in March, 1801, as Senior, to the DRUID frigate, Capt. Chas. Apthorp, under whom he partook of the ensuing operations in Egypt—21 March, 1804 (after two years of half-pay), to the CHICHESTER 44, Capt. Joseph Spear, on the Home station—16 Aug. 1805, to the FAVORITE 18, Capt. John Davie, on the coast of Africa—29 May, 1806, for six months, to the COURAGEUX 74, Capt. Jas. Bissett, in which ship he visited the West Indies and North America—and, in Nov. 1807, to the Sea Fencibles in Ireland. Mr. Parsons was serving on board the VENUS when the French Admiral Richery appeared off St. John's, Newfoundland; where, in expectation that the enemy would land, he was intrusted with a command on shore. When Senior of the FAVORITE he distinguished himself, 28 Dec. 1805, by his zeal and perseverance, at the capture, after an action of 20 minutes, of *Le Général Blanchard* French privateer, of 16 guns and 130 men, 11 of whom were killed and 25 wounded;* and on 6 of the following month he was in the same vessel when taken by a French squadron under M. L'Hermite. He was immediately, however, sent in a cartel to England; during the whole period of his passage whither, two months and two days, he was limited, with the rest, to half a pint of water a-day. He left the Sea Fencibles, on the occasion of the corps being disbanded in 1810, and was not afterwards employed. He accepted the rank of Retired Commander on the Junior List 26 Nov. 1830; and on the Senior 1 Dec. 1836.

PARSONS. (LIEUT., 1815. F-P., 18; H-P., 23.)

WILLIAM PARSONS (*b*) was born 12 Aug. 1794, at Portsea, co. Hants. He is brother of Lieut. John Parsons, R.N.

This officer entered the Navy, 18 Dec. 1806, as L.M., on board the MILBROOK 16, Lieut.-Commander Jas. Leach; which vessel, until wrecked in a storm 26 March, 1808, was very actively employed off the coasts of Spain and Portugal; where she captured a Spanish polacca ship, retook the *Badger* brig, of London, drove on shore a Spanish gun-boat and her prize, and was on one occasion totally dismasted and compelled to part with her guns. After serving for short periods on board the HIBERNIA 110, flag-ship of Sir Chas. Cotton, MEDIATOR 44, Capt. Geo. Wm. Blamey, and DESPERATE bomb, Lieut.-Commanders Jas. Leach and Robt. Ellary, Mr. Parsons (who had been engaged, in the boats of the DESPERATE, on secret service on the coast of France) joined, in March, 1809, the PODARGUS 14, Capt. Wm. Hellard; under whom, while holding the rating of Midshipman, he aided, at different times, in driving on shore, on the French coast, a lugger privateer, a schooner with naval stores on board, and another privateer, together with her prize an English ship. In effecting the latter service he was for an hour and a-half under fire of the batteries at Dieppe. Following Capt. Hellard, in Nov. 1810, into the SNAKE 18, he was soon afterwards involved in that vessel in a running action, on the coast of Norway, with five Danish brigs-of-war, from which, however, although at one time completely surrounded, she effected a very gallant escape. In Nov. 1811, the SNAKE, being caught in a gale of wind, drifted as far to the northward as lat. 73° 38′. When subsequently, in the early part of 1812, on a cruize between the Orkney and Shetland islands, Mr. Parsons, during another gale, volunteered in the most handsome manner to put off in a boat to the assistance of a vessel in distress. He accordingly made two trips, and had the good fortune to rescue the whole of the crew, consisting of 11 persons; although, on reaching the SNAKE the second time, the boat was stove and lost. Continuing in the same sloop, with Capts. Geo. Robbin and Joseph Gale, until July, 1815, at which period he was presented with a commission, bearing date 21 of the preceding Feb., Mr. Parsons was afforded an opportunity of making a voyage to the West Indies, and of cruizing for some time on the coast of Ireland and in the Downs. In the winter of 1814 he intrepidly jumped overboard at night and saved the life of a seaman; and on 15 Dec. in the same year he was washed in a gale of wind out of the fore-rigging, and fractured his left arm. After having been for several years employed in the East India trade, Lieut. Parsons succeeded, 3 Jan. 1838, in obtaining the command, which he still holds, of a station in the Coast Guard. Since he has been in that service he has been the means of convicting 12 smugglers, three of whom he captured with his own hands. He has also received an English silver and a French gold medal for his exertions in having saved the crew, eight in number, of a French vessel on shore in a gale of wind under St. Alban's Head; together with a letter of thanks for the rescue of 12 Englishmen wrecked at the same place.

The Lieutenant married, 26 Aug. 1822, Eliza, daughter of Mr. Goble, a Master in the merchant service, by whom he has issue eight children. His eldest son, William F. Parsons, is a Second-Master in the R.N. (1845). AGENTS—Hallett and Robinson.

PARTRIDGE. (LIEUTENANT, 1846.)

FREDERICK JOHN PARTRIDGE, born 21 Nov. 1821, is third son of John Partridge, Esq., of Bishop's Wood, co. Hereford, a Magistrate and Deputy-Lieutenant for that shire, and in the commission of the Peace for Monmouthshire, of which county he was High Sheriff in 1824, by Elizabeth, eldest daughter of Edw. Ives, Esq., of Titchfield House, Hants. His eldest brother, William, a barrister-at-law, is also a Magistrate and Deputy-Lieutenant for co. Hereford.

This officer served on board the PIQUE 36, Capt. Edw. Boxer, and was mentioned for his conduct during the operations of 1840 on the coast of Syria.* He passed his examination 16 Dec. 1844; officiated

* *Vide* Gaz. 1806, p. 448.

* *Vide* Gaz. 1840, p. 2601.

as Mate, from that period until March, 1846, of the EXCELLENT gunnery-ship at Portsmouth, Capts. Sir Thos. Hastings and Henry Ducie Chads; then joined the ST. VINCENT 120, successive flag-ship of Sir Chas. Ogle and Sir Fras. Augustus Collier; and on 26 June, 1846, was advanced to the rank of Lieutenant. Since 20 July in the latter year Mr. Partridge has been serving on board the SUPERB 80, Capt. Armar Lowry Corry.

PARTRIDGE. (LIEUTENANT, 1844.)

WILLIAM LUKE PARTRIDGE is sixth son of Henry Sam. Partridge, Esq., of Hockham Hall, co. Norfolk, a Magistrate and Deputy-Lieutenant, by Mary Frances, daughter of the Venerable Luke Heslop, D.D., Rector of Marylebone, London, and Archdeacon of Buckinghamshire. His eldest brother, Henry Champion Partridge, Esq., of Snare Hill, likewise a Magistrate and Deputy-Lieutenant for Norfolk, married, in Aug. 1834, Ftheldred Frances, the eldest daughter of Lieut.-General Birch Reynardson, of Holywell, co. Lincoln; and another brother, the Rev. Walter John Partridge, married, in Aug. 1842, Maria Agnes, fifth daughter of Sir Chas. Mansfield Clarke, Bart., of Dunham Lodge, co. Norfolk, M.D.

This officer entered the Navy 15 Sept. 1833; passed his examination 28 Oct. 1839; and was for several years employed on the Mediterranean and East India stations in the DIDO 18, Capts. Lewis Davies and Hon. Henry Keppel. Under the latter he served at the capture of Woosung and Shanghae, and in the operations on the Yang-tse-Kiang in 1842; as also, we believe, in an attack made in Aug. 1844, on a piratical settlement in the island of Borneo. His promotion to the rank he now holds took place 1 July in the latter year; he joined, not long afterwards, in the capacity of Additional Lieutenant, the AGINCOURT 72, flag-ship of Sir Thos. John Cochrane; and since 11 March, 1846, he has been serving on the south-east coast of America in the GRECIAN sloop, Capts. Alex. Leslie Montgomery and Louis Symonds Tindal.

PASCO. (LIEUTENANT, 1843.)

CRAWFORD AITCHESON DENHAM PASCO is second son of Rear-Admiral Pasco.

This officer entered the Navy 1 Jan. 1830; passed his examination 25 Feb. 1837; and was for a long time employed in Australia as Mate of the BEAGLE surveying-vessel, Capts. John Clements Wickham and John Lort Stokes. His appointments, since his promotion to the rank of Lieutenant, which took place 20 Nov. 1843, have been—13 Dec. in that year, as Additional, to the CALEDONIA 120, bearing the flag at Cork of Rear-Admiral Wm. Bowles—and 13 Jan. 1844 and 28 Aug. 1846, to the VESTAL 26, and VULTURE steam-frigate, of 470 horse-power, Capts. Chas. Talbot and John M'Dougall, both in the East Indies, where he is now serving. In charge of the VESTAL's pinnace, Mr. Pasco assisted at the capture and destruction, 19 Aug. 1845, of Maloodoo, a strong fortification in possession of Scheriff Osman, a rebel Borneo chieftain.*

* *Vide* Gaz. 1845, p. 6576.

PASCO. (REAR-ADMIRAL OF THE BLUE, 1847. F-P., 32; H-P., 31.)

JOHN PASCO was born 20 Dec. 1774.

This officer entered the Navy, 4 June, 1784, as Captain's Servant, on board the DRUID 32, Capts. Geo. Anson Byron and Joseph Ellison, lying at Plymouth. In 1786 he joined the PEGASUS 28, commanded by H. R. H. the Duke of Clarence, with whom he served for about 12 months in the West Indies and on the coast of North America. He then became attached to the IMPREGNABLE 98, flagship at Plymouth of Admiral Graves, and to the PENELOPE 32, Capt. John Linzee, on the Halifax station; and he was next, between 1790 and 1795, employed as Midshipman and Master's Mate, principally in the Channel and West Indies, on board the SYREN 32, Capt. John Manley, ORION 74, Capt. John Thos. Duckworth, LONDON 98, Capt. Rich. Goodwin Keats, CÆSAR 80, Capt. Anthony Jas. Pye Molloy, ORION again, Capt. J. T. Duckworth, MINOTAUR 74, and AIMABLE 32, flagships of Admirals John Macbride and Sir John Laforey, and BEAULIEU 38, Capt. Francis Laforey. Attaining the rank of Lieutenant 15 July, 1795, he was subsequently appointed in that capacity—in 1795-6, to the MAJESTIC 74, flag-ship of Sir J. Laforey, again to the BEAULIEU, Capt. Lancelot Skynner, and to the MINOTAUR 74, Capt. Thos. Louis, all in the West Indies—27 Sept. 1796, to the RAISONNABLE 64, Capt. Chas. Boyles, employed at the Cape of Good Hope and in the Channel—27 Dec. 1799, as First, to the IMMORTALITÉ 36, Capts. Hon. Henry Hotham and Edw. W. C. R. Owen, on the latter station—and 7 April, 1803 (after six months of half-pay) to the VICTORY 100, flag-ship of Lord Nelson. When Senior Lieutenant, in 1796, of the BEAULIEU, Mr. Pasco landed with a battalion of seamen, and assisted at the reduction of Ste. Lucie; and in 1801, at which period he belonged to the IMMORTALITÉ, he volunteered and was appointed to cut out from Camaret Bay the French corvette *La Chevrette*, but was prevented from carrying his plans into execution by the circumstance of his ship being ordered on a cruize before the weather had proved sufficiently favourable. The glory of achieving the exploit fell in consequence to the lot, as is well known, of the late Capt. Keith Maxwell. On his passage to the Mediterranean in May, 1803, Mr. Pasco, then in the VICTORY, contributed to the capture of the French 32-gun frigate *Embuscade*. He afterwards went in pursuit of the combined squadrons to the West Indies; and on his return he shared, 21 Oct. 1805, in the battle of Trafalgar. It being Lord Nelson's practice to make the officer first on his list for promotion do the duty of Signal-Officer, and the Junior that of First-Lieutenant, Mr. Pasco, although Senior of the VICTORY in the action, was obliged to submit to the regulation enforced by his Lordship, through whose death he in consequence lost that promotion to which his rank entitled him. He had thus the mortification of only receiving a Commander's commission, dated 24 Dec. 1805; while Mr. Quilliam, the Sixth-Lieutenant, was at once advanced to Post-rank. During the battle he had the misfortune to be very severely wounded by a grape-shot in the right side and arm;* for which he now receives a pension of 250*l.* per annum, besides having at the time obtained a grant from the Patriotic Fund.† After he left the VICTORY, Capt. Pasco remained on half-pay until May, 1808. He then at length succeeded in procuring command of the MEDIATOR 32; in which vessel he served for three months off Cadiz and Lisbon. In the following Nov. he joined the HINDOSTAN 50, *armée-en-flûte*, fitting for a voyage to New South Wales; on his return whence he was appointed, in Nov. 1810, to the TARTARUS 20. In that ship, in which he was made Post by commission bearing date 3 April, 1811, Capt. Pasco continued employed, on the Channel, American, and Cork stations, until May, 1815. In the ensuing June he assumed command, at Lisbon, of the ROTA 38; and he next, from 20 Aug. 1815 until paid off 2 Sept. 1818, served in the LEE 20, on the Channel station; where he made prize of several smuggling vessels. On 18 March, 1846, he was admitted into the Royal Hospital at Greenwich; but, resigning the appointment almost immediately, he was placed, 1 April following, in command of his old ship the VICTORY, stationed at Portsmouth. He had been previously, 19 Feb. 1842, selected as a recipient for the Captain's Good Service Pension. He attained his present rank 22 Sept. 1847.

Rear-Admiral Pasco married, first, 1 Sept. 1805, Rebecca, daughter of J. L. Penfold, Esq., of the

* *Vide* Gaz. 1805, p. 1484.

† In conveying the memorable injunction to the fleet, "England expects every man to do his duty," the word "England" was substituted for "Nelson," at the suggestion of Lieut. Pasco. That officer having remarked to Lord Nelson that, as it would take some time to spell the word "Nelson," it might be better to say "England," which was in the vocabulary, his Lordship replied, "Right, right; make it England!"

Royal Dockyard at Plymouth; and, secondly, 22 July, 1843, Eliza, relict of Capt. John Weaver, R.M. (1826). By his first wife he had issue three sons and two daughters. Of the former, the eldest, William, is a Commander, and the second, Crauford, a Lieutenant, in the R.N. The youngest son, George Magrath Ley Pasco, was a Second Lieutenant, R.M. (1841). One of the Rear-Admiral's daughters is married to Capt. J. B. B. M'Hardy, R.N.; the other to Lieut. H. M. Kinsman, R.N. AGENTS—Messrs. Stilwell.

PASCO. (COMMANDER, 1846.)

WILLIAM MONTAGU ISAACSON GEORGE PASCO is eldest son of Rear-Admiral Pasco.

This officer entered the Navy 3 Feb. 1820; passed his examination in 1826; and obtained his first commission 8 Jan. 1830. His succeeding appointments were—5 May, 1831, to the DUBLIN 50, Capt. Lord Jas. Townshend, fitting for South America, whence he returned in the summer of 1834—5 Feb. 1835, to the ROVER 18, Capt. Chas. Eden, under whom he was employed for a further period of three years in South America, part of the time as First Lieutenant —8 Oct. 1838, to the Coast Guard—18 May, 1842, to the command of the KITE steamer, equipping for the coast of Africa, whence he returned to England and was paid off in 1843—and 7 April, 1845, to that of the JACKAL, another steamer, stationed in the Mediterranean. He attained his present rank 9 Nov. 1846. AGENTS—Case and Loudonsack.

PASCOE. (LIEUT., 1815. F-P., 10; H-P., 32.)

JOHN EYRE PASCOE entered the Navy, 18 Aug. 1805, as Midshipman, on board the WARRIOR 74, Capts. Sam. Hood Linzee, Michael Seymour, and John Wm. Spranger, attached to the Channel fleet. He removed, in Dec. 1807, to the INDEFATIGABLE 46, Capts. John Tremayne Rodd, Henry Edw. Reginald Baker, and John Broughton, stationed off the coast of France; and he was next, between Aug. 1810 and Sept. 1815, employed, off Lisbon, at Portsmouth, on the north coast of Spain, and in the Mediterranean, on board the DREADNOUGHT 98, Capt. Sam. Hood Linzee, PLOVER sloop, Capt. Colin Campbell, HANNIBAL 74, Capt. King, UNION 98, Capt. Geo. Burgoyne Salt, VESUVIUS bomb, Capt. Wm. Hext, and CLORINDE 40, Capt. Sam. Geo. Pechell. He then took up a commission bearing date 7 March, 1815; and has since been on half-pay.

Lieut. Pascoe married, at Plymouth, in 1839, Sarah, third daughter of S. Kerswell, Esq.

PASLEY. (RETIRED COMMANDER, 1845. F-P., 18; H-P., 35.)

JAMES PASLEY entered the Navy, 17 June, 1794, as Ordinary, on board the SPITFIRE sloop, Capt. Clements, attached to the force in the Channel, where he joined, in the following Sept., the MINOTAUR 74, flag-ship of Rear-Admiral John Macbride, and, in July, 1795, the RATTLER sloop, Capts. Willoughby Thos. Lake, John Cochet, J. Hall, W. Duncombe, John Hayes, and John Wentworth Loring. After assisting, as Midshipman, at the capture, in May, 1796, of the French privateer *Le Pichegru* of 10 guns and 34 men, he sailed for the West Indies; on which station he witnessed the evacuation of the Cayemites Islands, near St. Domingo, and in Sept. 1799 accompanied Capt. Loring, as Acting-Lieutenant, into the LARK 18, commanded subsequently by Capts. Caton, Tippet, New, and Jas. Johnstone. While in that vessel he appears to have been most actively employed, and to have contributed to the capture of a large number of armed and other vessels.* On 13 Sept. 1801, in particular, with two of her boats under his orders, each carrying 16 men, he attacked, in face of a heavy fire, boarded, and gallantly took, within the Portillo reefs, in the island of Cuba, the Spanish privateer-schooner *Esperanza* of 1 long 8 and 2 4-pounders and 45 men, 21 of whom were killed and 6 wounded, with a loss to the British of 1 man killed and 13 wounded.* He had previously, we are informed, while serving, *pro tem.*, on board the BEAULIEU 38, Capt. Steph. Poyntz, assisted in the boats of that ship and of the DORIS and URANIE frigates, commanded by Lieut. Keith Maxwell, at the cutting-out, on the night of 21 July, 1801, of *La Chevrette* corvette of 20 long 9-pounders and 350 men, under the batteries in Camaret Bay, a position deemed almost impregnable, after a deadly conflict, in which the enemy lost their Captain, 6 other officers, and 85 men killed, and 1 Lieutenant, 4 Midshipmen, and 57 men wounded, and the British 1 Lieutenant R.M., 1 Midshipman, and 9 men slain, and 2 Lieutenants, 1 Master's-Mate, 3 Midshipmen, and 51 men wounded.† In June, 1802, he rejoined Capt. Caton on board the TRENT 36, in which ship he continued for about 12 months on the West India station. His subsequent appointments were—5 April, 1804, to the Sea Fencibles in Ireland—8 June, 1805 (having left the latter service in the preceding Feb.), to the ARGUS sloop, Capts. Edw. Kittoe and Jas. Stewart, off Cork—and, 19 June, 1807, to the command, which he retained until 28 May, 1813, of the ENCHANTRESS, at Bristol. He became a Retired Commander on the Junior List 26 Nov. 1830; and on the Senior 17 Feb. 1845. AGENTS—Burnett and Holmes.

PASLEY, Bart. (CAPT., 1831. F-P., 15; H-P., 15.)

SIR THOMAS SABINE PASLEY, born 26 Dec. 1804, is only son of the late Major John Sabine, of the Grenadier Guards, by Maria, eldest daughter of the late Admiral Sir Thos. Pasley, Bart.;‡ in pursuance of whose will he assumed, in 1809, the surname and arms of Pasley, instead of those of his paternal family, Sabine. One of the Baronet's maternal grand-aunts was the mother of the present Vice-Admiral Sir Chas. Malcolm, Kt., and another of Vice-Admiral Sir Thos. Briggs, G.C.M.G.

This officer entered the Royal Naval College, 7 Aug. 1817; and embarked, 20 Dec. 1818, as a Volunteer, on board the ROCHFORT 80, Capts. Andrew

* On 14 March, 1800, the boats, under Lieut. Lane, who was killed, having been repulsed in an endeavour to obtain possession of a privateer lying under the protection of two heights at the entrance of a bay in the island of Cuba, Mr. Pasley landed with a party of men at a place ten miles distant, and advanced on the enemy's rear with so much expedition and judgment, that, on the arrival of Capt. Loring in the boats to renew the attack, he found nothing left for him to do than to witness, and bestow his commendation on, the successful issue of the steady and good conduct which had been displayed.—*Vide* Gaz. 1800, p. 825.

* *Vide* Gaz. 1802, p. 115. † *V.* Gaz. 1801, p. 919.

‡ Sir Thos. Pasley was born 2 March, 1734. After having served his time as Midshipman in various parts of the globe under Capts. Willett, Cockburn, Webber, and Digby, he was invested with the rank of Acting-Lieutenant, and sent with Capt. Digby on the unfortunate expedition against Rochefort. Being confirmed in the rank of Lieutenant on his return to England, he was next, until 1762, employed in that capacity on board the ROMAN EMPEROR fire-ship, and HUSSAR and ÆOLUS frigates. In the latter vessel he distinguished himself at the capture, 19 March, 1759, of *La Mignonne* of 20 guns; and also, when in company with the BRILLIANT and PALLAS of 36 guns each, at the taking, 28 Feb. 1760, after a fierce contest, of the French frigates *Belleisle, Blonde,* and *Terpsichore.* On leaving the ÆOLUS, as above, he was advanced to the rank of Commander; and in 1771, after having had command of the ALBANY and WEASEL sloops, he attained Post-rank. He subsequently served in the SEAHORSE 20, GLASGOW, SIBYLLE 28, JUPITER 50, and BELLEROPHON 74. In the JUPITER he was present, in 1781, in the encounter between Commodore Johnstone and M. de Suffrein in Porto Praya Bay. From 1788 until his appointment to the BELLEROPHON in 1793, Capt. Pasley held the chief command, with the rank of Commodore, of the ships lying in the river Medway Being advanced, in April, 1794, to the rank of Rear-Admiral, and appointed to a command in Lord Howe's fleet, he enacted, with his flag in the BELLEROPHON 74, a very signal and important part in the famous actions of 28 and 29 May and 1 June. On the latter occasion he lost a leg. He had the satisfaction, however, of being raised for his services to the dignity of a Baronet, and of receiving, with the thanks of Parliament, a pension of 1000*l* a-year He was also presented, by the Patriotic Society, with a pair of goblets valued at 500*l.* He became a Vice-Admiral 1 June, 1795; was afterwards, in 1798 and 1799, appointed Commander in-Chief in the Medway, and Port-Admiral at Plymouth; and died an Admiral of the White 29 Nov. 1808.

Pellett Green and Chas. Marsh Schomberg, successive flag-ship of Vice-Admirals Sir Thos. Fras. Fremantle and Sir Graham Moore in the Mediterranean; where, in June, 1821, and Oct. 1822, he was lent, as Midshipman, for a few months, to the LARNE 20, Capt. Robt. Tait, and EURYALUS 42, Capt. Augustus Wm. Jas. Clifford. He left the ROCHFORT in Oct. 1823; and, after having intermediately served on board the REDPOLE 10, Capt. Rich. Anderson, and ARACHNE 18, Capt. Henry Ducie Chads, he was advanced, 16 March, 1824, to the rank of Lieutenant. His succeeding appointments were—17 April, 1824, to the TWEED 28, Capt. Fred. Hunn, with whom he sailed for South America—25 Aug. following, as Senior, to the ECLAIR 18, commanded on that station by Capt. Thos. Bourchier—13 June, 1827 (having been on half-pay since July, 1825), to the FAIRY 10, Capt. Geo. Wm. Conway Courtenay, fitting for the West Indies—and, 6 June, 1828, to the ASIA 84, as Flag-Lieutenant to Sir Pulteney Malcolm in the Mediterranean. Being awarded a second promotal commission, dated 17 Sept. 1828, he successively assumed command, also on the Mediterranean station—31 Oct. following, of the CAMELION 10—30 Nov. 1829, of the PROCRIS 10—in May, 1830, as Acting-Captain, of the RATTLESNAKE 28—and in Nov. 1830, in a similar capacity, of the BLONDE 46. On the paying off of the latter ship he was confirmed in his present rank 24 May, 1831. His next and last appointment was, 22 Feb. 1843, to the CURAÇOA 24, in which vessel he served on the S.E. coast of America, until superseded in Jan. 1846.

Sir Thos. Sabine Pasley married, 10 June, 1826, Jane Matilda Lilly, eldest daughter of the Rev. Montagu John Wynyard, rector of Wesh Rounton, and of St. Martin's, Micklegate, Yorkshire, by whom he has issue seven sons and two daughters. AGENTS—Messrs. Stilwell.

PATERSON. (LIEUTENANT, 1841.)

GEORGE YATES PATERSON entered the Navy 17 June, 1828; passed his examination in 1834; served for some time in the Mediterranean as Mate of the BRITANNIA 120, flag-ship of Sir John Acworth Ommanney; and was advanced to his present rank 23 Nov 1841. He was next, 7 Jan. 1842, appointed to the EXCELLENT gunnery-ship at Portsmouth, Capt. Sir Thos. Hastings; and from 16 May, 1843, until paid off on his return to England at the close of 1847, was employed in the Pacific on board the FISGARD 42, Capt. Jas. Alex. Duntze. AGENTS—Messrs. Stilwell.

PATERSON. (RETIRED COMMANDER, 1847. F-P., 19; H-P., 32.)

WILLIAM LOVE PATERSON was born 17 March, 1781, at Doneraile, co. Cork. His brother, Thos. Paterson, Master's Mate of H. M. S. ARROW, was killed in a boat affair in the Gulf of Venice 4 June, 1804, aged 21.

This officer entered the Navy, 6 Oct. 1796, as a Volunteer, on board the TERPSICHORE 32, Capts. Rich. Bowen and Wm. Hall Gage. On 13 of the same month he assisted at the capture, off the port of Carthagena, of the *Mahonesa* Spanish frigate of 34 guns and 275 men, after a spirited contest of an hour and 20 minutes, in which the enemy sustained a loss of 30 men killed and as many wounded, and the British, out of 182 men, of only 4 wounded; and on 13 of the ensuing Dec. he was present, off Cadiz, in another most determined action of an hour and forty minutes, which terminated in the surrender to the TERPSICHORE (whose loss on the occasion amounted, out of 166 men, to 4 killed and 18 wounded) of the French frigate *La Vestale* of 36 guns and at least 270 men, 30 of whom were killed and 37 wounded. In the summer of 1797 we find Mr. Paterson co-operating in the bombardment of Cadiz, and employed, as Midshipman, in the TERPSICHORE's barge, in Lord Nelson's attack upon Santa Cruz, Teneriffe, where Capt. Bowen was killed. Quitting the TERPSICHORE in Jan. 1800, he served, during the five following years, chiefly on the Home station, in the TRITON 32, Capt. John Gore, MAJESTIC 74, Capt. Davidge Gould, PORT MAHON 18, Capts. Walter Grosett and Ralph Neville, and IMPÉTUEUX 74, Capts. Thos. Byam Martin and John Erskine Douglas. He was then, in Jan. and Sept. 1805, and July, 1806, successively nominated Sub-Lieutenant of the BORER gun-brig, Lieut.-Commander Rich. Wilbraham, PEGASUS, Capt. John Pengelly, and TICKLER gun-brig, Lieut.-Commander Skinner; on leaving the latter of which vessels he was constituted, 6 Sept. 1806 (although the date of his commission was subsequently altered to 20 Jan. 1809), full Lieutenant of the SURINAM 18, Capt. John Lake. Becoming attached next, 6 Feb. 1807, to the TARTARUS 20, Capts. Thos. Fras. Chas. Mainwaring and John Pasco, Mr. Paterson accompanied in that vessel the expedition sent in the course of the same year against Copenhagen; and on 25 April, 1808, he assisted in her boats, with those of the DAPHNE 20, commanded by Lieut. Wm. Elliott, at the cutting-out, with a loss to the British of only 5 persons wounded, of a convoy of 10 deeply-laden vessels, moored close under the foot of a castle mounting 10 guns, in the harbour of Fladstrand, near the Skawe, defended also by a heavy fire from another battery, as well as from the crews of the vessels assembled on the beach, and made fast to the shore by hawsers.* With the exception of a short command, held between June and Nov. 1811, of the CUTTLE schooner, at Halifax, he continued employed in the TARTARUS, on the American, West India, and Cork stations, until May, 1815. Not having been since afloat, he accepted his present rank 3 Feb. 1847.

Commander Paterson married, 9 April, 1811, Miss Priscilla Blight, of Plymouth.

PATESHALL. (Captain, 1815. F-P., 19; H-P., 33.)

NICHOLAS LECHMERE PATESHALL, born 13 Sept. 1782, is fourth son of the late Edm. Pateshall, Esq., of Allensmore House, co. Hereford, by Ann, daughter and heiress of Wm. Burnam, Esq., of Wellington Court, in the same co.; and brother of Capt. Edwyn Sandys Pateshall, Hon. E. I. Co.'s service, who died at Ceylon in 1819.

This officer entered the Navy, in Aug. 1795, as Fst.-cl. Vol., on board the INDEFATIGABLE 46, Capt. Sir Edw. Pellew, with whom he continued to serve, in the same frigate and in the IMPÉTUEUX 78, on the Home and Mediterranean stations, until June, 1801, the greater part of the time as Midshipman and Master's Mate. In the former ship he assisted, in April, 1796, at the capture of a fleet of French merchantmen, the destruction of *La Volage* of 26, and the further capture of *L' Unité* of 38 guns and 255 men, and, after a chase of 15 hours and a close action of an hour and 45 minutes, of *La Virginie* of 44 guns and 340 men. He was also, on 13 Jan. 1797, present, in company with the AMAZON 36, in a very gallant engagement of 10 hours, which terminated in the destruction, with a loss to the INDEFATIGABLE of 19 men wounded, of the French 74-gun ship *Les Droits de l' Homme*. The IMPÉTUEUX formed part, in June and Aug. 1800, of the expeditions to Quiberon and Ferrol. At Quiberon, where he was wounded in blowing up a battery, Mr. Pateshall was actively employed with the boats of the squadron, and at Ferrol he landed with the naval brigade. During the term of his attachment to the INDEFATIGABLE and IMPÉTUEUX he contributed to the capture and destruction, including the vessels already mentioned, of as many as 20 ships of war, carrying in the whole, we are informed, 468 guns and 3937 men.† In June and Sept. 1801 we find him successively joining the ROBUST 74, Capt. Wm. Henry Jervis, and VILLE DE PARIS 110; of which

* *Vide* Gaz. 1808, p. 697.

† Among them were *L'Insolente* and (*vide* Gaz. 1800, p. 898) *La Cerbère*, captured, as detailed in our Memoirs of Rear-Admiral McKerlie and Commander Paddon. He commanded one of the boats of the VIPER cutter on the latter occasion, and was afterwards placed in charge of the prize.

latter ship, bearing the flag in the Channel of Hon. Wm. Cornwallis, he was created a Lieutenant 20 Nov. in the same year. His succeeding appointments were—6 Nov. 1802 (after six months of half-pay) to the CALCUTTA 50, Capt. Dan. Woodriff, with whom he visited Botany Bay, and circumnavigated the globe—6 Sept. 1804, again to the VILLE DE PARIS, still bearing the flag of Hon. Wm. Cornwallis —12 June, 1806, as Senior, to the KENT 74, Capt. Thos. Rogers, under whom, during a servitude of three years and nine months, he was frequently employed in the cutting-out of convoys in the Mediterranean—in Nov. 1809, to the HYPERION 36, Capt. Thos. Chas. Brodie, in which ship he proceeded to the West Indies—2 March, 1810, to the SAPPHO 18, Capt. Thos. Graves, on that station—and, 8 July following, to the POLYPHEMUS 64, as Flag-Lieutenant at Jamaica to Vice-Admiral Bartholomew Sam. Rowley. On 24 July, 1811, he was advanced to the command of the SHARK sloop; from which vessel, in the ensuing Oct., he was transferred to the Acting-Captaincy of the POLYPHEMUS, then bearing the broad pendant of Commodore Jas. Giles Vashon. Returning to England in the course of the following month, he was subsequently, 7 Oct. 1813 and 7 June, 1814, appointed to the ADDER 12 and JASEUR 16, stationed chiefly on the coast of North America; where he was made Post, 18 Feb. 1815, into the CARRON 20. He paid that ship off, on her arrival home from the West Indies, in Aug. 1816; and did not afterwards go afloat. He accepted the Retirement 1 Oct. 1846.

Capt. Pateshall, we understand, has filled the office of Mayor of Hereford.

PATEY. (RETIRED COMMANDER, 1825. F-P., 40; H-P., 28.)

CHARLES PATEY, born 31 Dec. 1770, is brother of Commander Joseph Patey, R.N.

This officer entered the Navy, in 1779, as Captain's Servant, on board the OCEAN 98, Capt. Geo. Ourry, stationed in the Channel; where, in 1781, he joined the NONSUCH 64, Capt. Wm. Truscott. Becoming attached, next, to the WARRIOR 74, Capts. Sir Jas. Wallace and John Symonds, he served in that ship in Rodney's actions of 9 and 12 April, 1782, and was present in her at the ensuing capture, by Sir Sam. Hood, of the *Caton, Jason*, &c., in the Mona Passage. Paid off at the peace in 1783, he did not go afloat until 1785; between which period and the date of his promotion to the rank of Lieutenant, 22 Nov. 1790, we find him alternately employed, at Plymouth, in the CROWN 64 and BOMBAY CASTLE 74, under Capts. Sam. Reeve, Robt. Fanshawe, Chas. Morice Pole, Anthony Jas. Pye Molloy, and John Thos. Duckworth. His succeeding appointments were—6 Sept. 1791, to the CARNATIC 74, Capt. John Ford, lying at the port last mentioned—22 Dec. 1792, to the TERRIBLE 74, Capts. Skeffington Lutwidge, Geo. Campbell, and Sir Rich. Hussey Bickerton—27 Sept. 1797, to the ZEALAND 64, bearing the flag of Vice-Admiral Lutwidge at the Nore—29 June, 1798, to the command of the GEORGE cutter of 14 guns, employed, until Dec. 1800, on the Home and West India stations—and, in May, 1801, to the Semaphore service, in which he continued (with the exception of an interval between March, 1802, and May, 1803) until Nov. 1814. In 1793 Lieutenant Patey, then belonging to the TERRIBLE, was present at the occupation and evacuation of Toulon; on the latter of which occasions he very narrowly escaped destruction, the boat he commanded being blown to pieces.* He afterwards took part, in the same ship, in the reduction of Bastia and Calvi; and also in Hotham's partial engagements of 14 March and 13 July, 1795. During his command of the GEORGE he fought an action of two hours with a French cutter, whom he at length compelled to take refuge in the port of Cherbourg. In the same vessel he captured, 19 Nov. 1798, after a chase of four hours, the French privateer lugger *Enterprise*, mounting two swivels, with muskets, pistols, swords, half-pikes, &c., and carrying 16 men.* The British on this occasion sustained a loss of 2 men killed and 2 wounded. From Jan. 1820 until 1830 Commander Patey (who was advanced to his present rank 20 July, 1825) officiated as a chief officer in the Coast Guard.

One of his sons, Chas. G. E. Patey, is a Captain, and another, George Edwin, a Commander, in the R.N.

* *Vide* Gaz. 1794, p. 43.

PATEY. (CAPTAIN, 1846.)

CHARLES GEORGE EDWARD PATEY is son of Retired Commander Chas. Patey R.N.

This officer entered the Navy 20 Jan. 1824; passed his examination in 1830; and obtained his first commission 6 Dec. 1836. His succeeding appointments were—6 May and 16 Aug. 1837, to the CALEDONIA 120 and PRINCESS CHARLOTTE 104, flag-ships in the Mediterranean of Sir Josias Rowley and Hon. Sir Robt. Stopford—and, 22 Feb. 1840, as First-Lieutenant, to the CASTOR 36, Capt. Edw. Collier. Uniting, in the latter ship, in the operations on the coast of Syria, he found opportunity of highly distinguishing himself by his officer-like, cool, and steady conduct, at the capture both of Caiffa and Tsour. On the fall of Caiffa he planted the Ottoman flag upon the ramparts; and in a day or two afterwards, with the marines and a few seamen belonging to the CASTOR and PIQUE under his orders, destroyed a castle mounting 5 guns, in full view of 500 of the Egyptian army.† At Tsour, as soon as the enemy had been put to flight, he landed and took possession of the town; in the immediate vicinity of which he contrived, although in the presence of 800 infantry and 60 cavalry, to get into his possession 40 prisoners and deserters.‡ On 4 Nov. 1840, the day after the bombardment of St. Jean d'Acre, he was advanced to the rank of Commander. He served next, from 5 March, 1842, until posted, 27 June, 1846, in the RESISTANCE 42, troop-ship; and is now on half-pay.

PATEY. (LIEUTENANT, 1813. F-P., 12; H-P., 32.)

GEORGE EDWARD PATEY, born in 1789, is only son of Lieut. Wm. Patey R.N., who lost his life while employed in embarking troops on the coast of Spain in 1810; and nephew of Commander Joseph Patey R.N. Two other uncles died Lieutenants in the service.

This officer entered the Navy, 7 April, 1803, as Fst.-cl. Vol., on board the MARS 74, Capts. John Sutton, Geo. Duff, Wm. Hennah, and Robt. Dudley Oliver, stationed at first off Brest and then off the port of Cadiz. After sharing as Midshipman and Aide-de-Camp to Capts. Duff and Hennah in the battle of Trafalgar, he removed, in Jan. 1806, to the CRESCENT 36, Capt. Jas. Carthew; under whom he was for two years employed, chiefly at the blockade of the Texel. He then proceeded to the Mediterranean, where, in the BOMBAY 74, he was for a further period of three years engaged in watching the port of Toulon. In April, 1811, and March, 1812, Mr. Patey became in succession Master's Mate of the VIGO and MONTAGU 74's, bearing each the flag of Rear-Admiral Manley Dixon in the Baltic and South America. He was confirmed to the rank of Lieutenant, after having twice acted in that capacity, 20 July, 1813; and from the latter date until Feb. 1815 was employed, on the station last named, in the NEREUS 36, Capt. Manley Hall Dixon, and ALBACORE 18, Capt. Joseph Patey. In the ALBACORE he assisted, as First-Lieutenant, in chasing into St. Salvador, and in there detaining, a notorious American privateer, the *True-Blooded Yankee*, of equal force. In 1831 he was appointed Senior of the PALLAS 42, Capt. M. H. Dixon; but a nearly fatal illness deprived him of the possibility of joining. He has not been since able to procure employment.

We are told that during the war Lieut. Patey was

* *Vide* Gaz. 1798, p. 1109. † *V.* Gaz. 1840, p. 2601.
‡ *V.* Gaz. 1840, pp. 2602, 2608.

captured in a transport-brig by two privateers after an honourable defence. He married, in Feb. 1817, Lucy, only child and heiress of the late Thos. Macnamara Russell, Esq., Admiral of the White, formerly Commander-in-Chief in the North Sea; by whom he has had issue four sons. One of them, the eldest, Russell, is a Lieutenant R.N.; a second, Macnamara, was a Lieutenant R.M. (1843); and the two others are in the Church and Army. AGENT—John P. Muspratt.

PATEY. (COMMANDER, 1846.)

GEORGE EDWIN PATEY is son of Retired Commander Chas. Patey, R.N.

This officer passed his examination in 1833; was promoted, for his services on the coast of Syria, to the rank of Lieutenant 4 Nov. 1840; and was subsequently appointed—15 Dec. 1840, to the CARYSFORT 26, Capt. Henry Byam Martin, attached to the force in the Mediterranean—9 Dec. 1841, to the CALEDONIA 120, flag-ship of Sir Graham Moore at Plymouth—14 June, 1842, to the WOLF 18, Capt. Courtenay Osborn Hayes, fitting for the East Indies—and 18 March, 1843, and 1 April, 1845, as Senior, to the WOLVERENE 16, Capts. Henry Gage Morris, Chas. Foreman Brown, and Wm. John Cavendish Clifford, and AGINCOURT 72, flag-ship of Sir Thos. John Cochrane, both on the same station. As a reward for his highly lauded exertions as second in command, under Capt. Geo. Rodney Mundy, of the force employed during the operations on the island of Borneo, detailed in our memoir of that officer, Lieut. Patey was advanced to the rank of Commander 8 July, 1846.* He has been officiating, since 26 Jan. 1848, as Second-Captain of the RODNEY 92, Capt. Edw. Collier, on the Mediterranean station.

PATEY. (COMMANDER, 1815. F-P., 22; H-P., 35.)

JOSEPH PATEY, born 20 Sept. 1780, is brother of Retired Commander Chas. Patey, R.N.; and uncle of Lieut. Geo. Edw. Patey, R.N.

This officer entered the Navy, 1 June, 1790, as Gunner's Servant, on board the ROYAL SOVEREIGN 100, bearing the flag in the Channel of Lord Hood, with whom he remained until the following Dec. Re-embarking, in July, 1793, on board the PORCUPINE 24, commanded by Capt. Manley Dixon, he successively followed that officer, as Midshipman, in June, 1795, and July, 1797, into the ESPION 38 and LION 64. In the ESPION he assisted at the capture, in the North Sea, 14 Feb. 1797, of *Le Buonaparte* French privateer of 17 guns and 110 men. On 15 July, 1798, being off Carthagena, he took part in a brilliant action between the LION and four Spanish frigates of 42 guns each, which terminated in the surrender of one of the latter, the *Santa Dorothea*;† and when subsequently in company with the FOUDROYANT 80 and PENELOPE 36 at the blockade of Malta, he was present as Acting-First-Lieutenant, and rendered the greatest possible assistance to his Captain, at the capture, 31 March, 1800, of the French 80-gun ship *Guillaume Tell*, after a tremendous conflict productive of a loss to the LION of 8 men killed and 38 wounded.‡ On leaving the LION, which had been latterly commanded by Lord Wm. Stuart, he was again, in July, 1800, placed under the orders of Capt. Dixon on board LE GÉNÉREUX 74; in which ship, in the course of the ensuing Aug. and Sept., we find him present, still as Acting-Lieutenant, at the capture of *La Diane* of 42 guns, and the surrender of the island of Malta. He continued in LE GÉNÉREUX under Capt. Velterers Cornewall Berkeley until within a few weeks of his confirmation in the rank of Lieutenant, 6 Sept. 1802.§ His succeeding appointments were—14 Sept. 1803, to the CRESCENT frigate, Capts. Lord Wm. Stuart and Jas. Carthew, employed in the North Sea, off the Western Islands, and in the Channel—in Nov. 1807, to the acting command, for a short time, of the RAILLEUR 18, in the North Sea—30 May, 1808, and 22 April, 1809, to the ROYAL GEORGE 100 and SAN JOSEF 110, flag-ships in the Channel of Sir John Thos. Duckworth—in July, 1809, to the RUBY 64, as Flag-Lieutenant in the Baltic to his former Captain, then Rear-Admiral Dixon, whom he accompanied, in the same capacity, into the VIGO* and MONTAGU 74's, the latter on the South American station—22 Sept. 1812, to the acting command of the BENJAMIN, in which vessel (a corvette borrowed from the Brazilian Government) he remained for three months—at the expiration of that time, to the MONTAGU and INDEFATIGABLE, again as Flag-Lieutenant to Admiral Dixon—and in the early part of 1814 to the acting command, in succession, of the CERES and AQUILON frigates, and ALBACORE 18. In the latter vessel it was Commander Patey's good fortune, in Dec. 1814, to chase the *True-Blooded Yankee*, a mischievous privateer of 18 guns, into St. Salvador, where he kept her closely blockaded until she was sold to defray the expenses of her stay. He was thus the means of saving two of the king's packets from capture, as well as many valuable merchantmen. He was officially promoted to the rank he now holds 19 July, 1815; and with the exception of a few months in 1835, from Feb. to Sept., during which he officiated as Supernumerary-Commander of the SAN JOSEF 110, flag-ship of Sir Wm. Hargood at Plymouth, has since been on half-pay.

Commander Patey, including the occasion above alluded to, has been thrice wounded. In March, 1841, he was admitted into the Royal Hospital at Greenwich. He married, 31 Jan. 1803, Miss Grigg, by whom he has two daughters living; the younger of whom became the wife, in March, 1841, of Thos. Corral, Esq., Surgeon R.N. (1841). A son of the Commander died on the coast of North America while serving under the flag of Sir Chas. Ogle.

PATEY. (LIEUTENANT, 1844.)

RUSSELL PATEY is eldest son of Lieut. Geo. Edw. Patey, R.N.

This officer entered the Navy in 1831; passed his examination 14 April, 1838; and after having served in South America on board the PRESIDENT 50, Capt. Wm. Broughton, and at Portsmouth in the EXCELLENT gunnery-ship, Capt. Sir Thos. Hastings, was promoted to the rank of Lieutenant 20 Nov. 1844. His appointments have since been —18 Dec. 1844, to the CRUIZER 16, Capts. Edw. Gennys Fanshawe, Wm. Maclean, and Edw. Peirse, on the East India station—and, 27 Oct. 1847, to the NERBUDDA 12, commanded by the last-mentioned officer at Bombay, where he is now employed.

PATRIARCHE. (RETIRED COMMANDER, 1844. F-P., 14; H-P., 40.)

CHARLES PATRIARCHE entered the Navy, 30 Aug. 1793, as A.B., on board the CONCORDE 36, Capts. Thos. Wells and Sir Rich. John Strachan; on rejoining the former of whom, in April, 1794, in the MELAMPUS 36, he assisted, when in company with a squadron under Sir John Borlase Warren, at the capture of *La Pomone* of 44 guns and 341 men, *Le Babet* of 22 guns and 178 men, and *L'Engageante* of 38 guns and 300 men. On quitting the MELAMPUS, which frigate had been latterly commanded by Sir R. J. Strachan, he was received as Midshipman, in Oct. 1794, on board the DEFENCE 74, and in that ship he continued employed, under the orders of

* *Vide* Gaz. 1846, pp. 3438, 3441, 3442, 3444, 3445, 3447, 3767.

† Although slightly wounded in the shoulder, Mr. Patey would not leave his quarters, but from first to last was particularly active.—*V.* Gaz. 1798, p 880.

‡ *Vide* Gaz. 1800, p. 575.

§ Mr. Patey had passed his examination in 1799, but, his certificate being mislaid at the Admiralty, he was compelled to undergo a second probatory ordeal, which, however, he was not afforded an opportunity of doing until his return from the Mediterranean in Aug. 1802. He lost, in consequence, the promotion which would otherwise have been his reward for the part he acted at the capture of *Le Guillaume Tell.* We may here add, that in April, 1799, the LION made prize, off Alexandria, of the *Chasseur*, a corvette of 16 guns.

* While borne on the books of the VIGO he acted for a brief period as Commander of the FLY 16.

Capts. Wells, Wm. Brown, John Peyton, Jas. Stevenson, and Lord Henry Paulet, until confirmed in the rank of Lieutenant, after having acted for 12 months in that capacity, 26 Nov. 1799. He was in consequence present in Hotham's second partial action 13 July, 1795; also at the blockade of the Texel; and as Master's Mate at the battle of the Nile 1 Aug. 1798. His last appointments were —30 Nov. 1799, to the PYLADES 18, Capt. Jas. Boorder, employed in the North Sea—10 Jan. 1801, to the SUPERB 74, Capts. John Sutton and Rich. Goodwin Keats, under the latter of whom he fought in Sir Jas. Saumarez' action in the Gut of Gibraltar 12 July, 1801, accompanied Lord Nelson to the West Indies in pursuit of the combined fleet in 1805, and was so severely wounded in the battle off St. Domingo 6 Feb. 1806, as to be reduced, in the following June, to the necessity of invaliding*—and, 28 Sept. 1812, to the VULTURE sloop, Capt. Henry Baugh, in which vessel he cruized in the Channel until June, 1813, when the effects of his wound again compelled him to seek half-pay. He became a Retired Commander on the Junior List 26 Nov. 1830; and on the Senior 16 May, 1844.

In consideration of his sufferings Commander Patriarche, besides receiving a grant from the Patriotic Society, was allotted, 9 Aug. 1806, a pension of 91*l.* 5*s.* He is married. AGENTS—Messrs. Ommanney.

* *Vide* Gaz. 1806, p. 373.

PATTEN. (COMMANDER, 1837. F-P., 25; H-P., 8.)

FREDERICK PATTEN entered the Navy, 31 Jan. 1814, as Fst.-cl. Vol., on board the ROYAL SOVEREIGN 100, Capts. Thos. Gordon Caulfeild and Chas. Thurlow Smith, stationed in the Mediterranean; where, in the course of the same year, he followed the latter officer, as Midshipman, into the DUNCAN 74, and also into the UNDAUNTED 38; in which frigate he witnessed, in 1815, the capture of the Tremiti Islands. In Feb. 1816, three months after he had left the UNDAUNTED, he joined the RAMILLIES 74, bearing the flag of Sir Wm. Johnstone Hope on the Leith station; and he was next, between Nov. 1818 and the date of his promotion to the rank of Lieutenant 19 July, 1822, employed in South America, at Plymouth, and in the Mediterranean, on board the VENGEUR 74, Capt. Fred. Lewis Maitland, BLOSSOM 24, Capt. Fred. Edw. Vernon (now Harcourt), IMPREGNABLE 104, flag-ship of Lord Exmouth, CHANTICLEER sloop, Capt. the Earl of Huntingdon, and REVOLUTIONNAIRE 46, Capt. Hon. Fleetwood Broughton Reynolds Pellew. His succeeding appointments were—16 Oct. 1822, to the CAMBRIAN 48, Capt. Gawen Wm. Hamilton, also in the Mediterranean, whence he returned in July, 1824—in March, 1825, to the RANGER 28, Capt. Lord Henry Fred. Thynne, fitting for South America—24 June, 1828, for a few months, to the GLOUCESTER 74, Capt. Henry Stuart, lying at Sheerness —26 June, 1830, as First, to the GANNET 18, Capt. Mark Halpen Sweny, on the West India station—30 July, 1832, in a similar capacity (after a brief interval of half-pay), to the BLONDE 46, Capt. John Duff Markland, attached to the force off Lisbon—and, 14 July, 1833 (the latter ship having been put out of commission in the preceding Jan.), to the command, which he retained for three years, of the RAPID 10, in South America. On 10 Jan. 1837, as a reward for the manner in which, during his servitude in the RAPID, he had discharged various responsible duties, he was promoted, on the recommendation of Sir Graham Eden Hamond, the Commander-in-Chief, to the rank he at present holds. We may here mention that he had twice when belonging to the CAMBRIAN, and once when in the BRITON, jumped overboard and succeeded in saving life. His last appointments were—13 Aug. 1838, to the Coast Guard, in which service he continued until the early part of 1843—and, 7 Sept. 1844, to the command of the OSPREY 12. While in that vessel he was on several occasions intrusted with the command of squadrons of sloops varying from four to seven in number. Towards the close of 1845, in consequence of the unsettled state of New Zealand, Commander Patten was selected by Sir Thos. John Cochrane, Commander-in-Chief in the East Indies, to act as senior officer on that station, in which capacity he continued to officiate until the arrival of Capt. Chas. Graham in the CASTOR 36. He remained, however, at New Zealand, engaged with success in the performance of many delicate and arduous services, until at length unavoidably wrecked, in March, 1846, on the western part of the coast at a place called False Hokianga, which had never been surveyed. Determined upon saving all that they could from the ship, Commander Patten and his crew remained for two months in the vicinity of the spot on which the catastrophe had occurred, and then commenced a march of 110 miles overland to the opposite side of the island, where, at the expiration of five days, during which, with but three days' provisions, they had traversed, through rivers and forests, an almost unknown country, in the most inclement weather, they embarked on board H.M. sloop RACEHORSE.* On his arrival home in Dec. 1846, Commander Patten had the satisfaction of not only receiving the full acquittal of a court-martial for the loss of his ship, but of being complimented for the exertions he had made on the disastrous occasion. He is now on half-pay.

He married, 3 April, 1829, Alicia Cavendish, daughter of Wm. Hillier, Esq., of Boley Hill, Rochester.

PATTERSON. (LIEUT., 1815. F-P., 11; H-P., 32.)

WILLIAM PATTERSON entered the Navy, 1 July, 1804, as Fst.-cl. Vol., on board the MONMOUTH 64, Capt. Geo. Hart, bearing the flag in Yarmouth Roads of Rear-Admiral Thos. Macnamara Russell. In May, 1805, nine months after he had attained the rating of Midshipman, he removed to the STATELY 64, Capt. Geo. Parker; under whom we find him, when in company with the NASSAU 64, present, 22 March, 1808, at the capture, off the coast of Zealand, of the Danish 74-gun ship *Prindts Christian Frederic*, whose surrender was accomplished at the close of an obstinate running fight in which the STATELY sustained a loss of 4 men killed and 28 wounded. Following Capt. Parker, in the ensuing May, into the ABOUKIR 74, he accompanied in that ship the expedition of 1809 to the Walcheren. He afterwards, in Sept. 1811, joined the HANNIBAL 74, and, in the course of 1812-13, the CHRISTIAN VII., BULWARK, and VENERABLE 74's, all bearing the flag of Rear-Admiral Philip Chas. Durham. In the HANNIBAL and CHRISTIAN VII. he was successively employed in the Baltic, Channel, and North Sea; in the BULWARK, of which ship he was for a short time Acting-Lieutenant, he served in Basque Roads; and in the VENERABLE, on his passage to the Leeward Islands, he contributed, in company with the CYANE sloop, to the well-resisted capture, 16 and 20 Jan. 1814, of the French 40-gun frigates *Iphigénie* and *Alcmène*. On the latter being added to the British Navy under the name PALMA, Mr. Patterson, by virtue of an order dated 28 Feb. 1814, was nominated one of her Acting-Lieutenants. He was confirmed a Lieutenant 21 Feb. 1815, but has not been since employed.

PATTON. (Captain, 1819. F-P., 18; H-P., 25.)

HUGH PATTON is son of the late Colonel Patton, Governor of the island of St. Helena; nephew of the late Philip Patton, Esq., Admiral of the Red;†

* The fatigue endured by Commander Patten revived the painful effects of a serious injury he had sustained when on duty in the RAPID.

† Admiral Patton was an officer highly esteemed and justly respected. His last employment afloat was as Commander-in-Chief in the Downs. When Lord Barham presided over naval affairs, he filled a seat at the Board of Admiralty. He was the author of a work entitled 'The Natural Defence of an Insular Empire earnestly recommended.' He died 31 Dec. 1815, at Fareham, Hants, aged 76.

first-cousin of the present Capt. Robt. Patton, R.N.; and brother-in-law of the late Major-General Sir Henry Torrens, K.C.B.

This officer entered the Navy, in Oct. 1804, as Fst.-cl. Boy, on board the PUISSANT 74, Capt. John Irwin, lying at Portsmouth. Becoming attached, shortly afterwards, to the BELLEROPHON 74, Capts. John Loring, John Cooke, and Edw. Rotheram, he fought as Midshipman of that ship in the action off Cape Trafalgar 21 Oct. 1805. At the commencement of 1806 he joined the NIOBE 40, Capt. John Wentworth Loring, in time, we believe, to assist at the capture of *Le Néarque* corvette of 16 guns. After a servitude of 12 months on the Jamaica station in the POLYPHEMUS 64, Capt. Wm. Pryce Cumby, he was nominated, 25 Oct. 1810, Acting-Lieutenant of the THALIA 36, Capt. Jas. Giles Vashon; to which ship the Admiralty confirmed him 1 Feb. 1811. Invaliding home in the ensuing Oct., he was next in succession appointed—16 March, 1812, to the SYBILLE 44, Capt. Clotworthy Upton, on the Irish station—in the early part of 1813, to the ABOUKIR and GLADIATOR, as Flag-Lieutenant to Rear-Admiral Edw. Jas. Foote at Portsmouth—and, 24 Aug. in the same year, to the ASTREA 36, Capt. John Eveleigh. In the latter ship he shared, we understand, in a yard-arm-and-yard-arm conflict of upwards of an hour with the French 40-gun frigate *Etoile*, which terminated in a drawn battle, wherein the British lost 9, including their Captain, killed, and 37 wounded, and the enemy 20 killed and 30 wounded. On leaving the ASTREA in Sept. 1814 he took up a Commander's commission bearing date 6 Dec. 1813. He subsequently, from 6 Sept. 1815 until 22 Oct. 1818, commanded the ALBAN 12, on the Plymouth station, and on 12 Aug. 1819 was advanced to the rank of Captain. His last appointments were—28 Nov. 1823, to the RATTLESNAKE 28, fitting for the West Indies—and, 16 Sept. 1825, to the ISIS 50, bearing the flag of Sir Lawrence Wm. Halsted at Jamaica, whence he returned in 1827. He accepted the Retirement 1 Oct. 1846. AGENTS—Pettet and Newton.

PATTON. (Captain, 1827. F-P., 12; H-P., 31.)

ROBERT PATTON, born in 1791, is son of the late Retired Captain Chas. Patton, R.N.;* and first-cousin of Capt. Hugh Patton, R.N.

This officer entered the Navy, 1 Feb. 1804, as Fst.-cl. Vol., on board the UTRECHT 64, Capt. John Wentworth Loring, bearing the flag in the Downs of his uncle Vice-Admiral Philip Patton. In the following June he removed as Midshipman to the PUISSANT 74, Capt. John Irwin, lying at Portsmouth; and on being received, next, into the BELLEROPHON 74, Capts. John Loring, John Cooke, and Edw. Rotheram, he was afforded an opportunity of participating, 21 Oct. 1805, in the battle of Trafalgar. After having served for three years and nine months in the NIOBE 40, commanded by his old Captain, J. W. Loring, under whom, during that period, he had assisted at the capture of *Le Néarque* corvette of 16 guns, he became Master's Mate, in Nov. 1809, of the POLYPHEMUS 64, Capts. Wm. Pryce Cumby and Thos. Graves, of which ship, stationed at Jamaica, he was nominated, 26 Aug. 1810, an Acting-Lieutenant. He was confirmed 13 Nov. following, and was subsequently appointed—26 April, 1811, for five months, to the DISPATCH sloop, Capt. Jas. Aberdour, also in the West Indies—29 July, 1812, to the DOTEREL 18, Capt. Wm. Westcott Daniel, successively employed in the Channel, the West Indies, and North America—and, in April, 1813, and Nov. 1814, to the LOIRE 40 and JUNON 38, Capts. Thos. Brown and Clotworthy Upton, both on the station last named, where he performed, in both ships, the duties of First-Lieutenant. Attaining the rank of Commander 13 June, 1815, he served in that capacity from 3 May, 1826, until posted, 30 April, 1827, in the TRINCULO 18, on the Cork station. The latter was his last appointment. He accepted the Retirement in 1847.

Capt. Patton was presented with the honorary medallion of the Royal Humane Society 13 April 1826.

* Capt. Chas. Patton was made a Lieutenant 17 Feb. 1780, a Commander 25 Sept. 1781, and a Post-Captain 30 May, 1795. During the whole of the late war he was in superintendence of the Transport department at Plymouth, and acquitted himself of his duties in a manner that gained him the esteem of all who were employed under him, at the same time that it yielded unqualified satisfaction to the Board of Admiralty and the Commander-in-Chief at the port. He was the author of a work entitled 'An Attempt to establish the Basis of Freedom on simple and unerring Principles,' 8vo., published in 1793; and of another called 'The Effects of Property upon Society and Government;' to which was added, by his brother, Admiral Philip Patton, 'An Historical Review of the Monarchy and Republic of Rome,' 8vo. 1797.

PATTON. (LIEUT., 1812. F-P., 10; H-P., 32.)

THOMAS PATTON entered the Navy, in Sept. 1805, as Fst.-cl. Vol., on board the OTTER sloop, Capts. John Davies and Nesbit Josiah Willoughby, under the latter of whom, in the same vessel and the NÉRÉIDE 36, he saw a great deal of active service. He was present in the NÉRÉIDE in particular at the capture of Ile de Bourbon in July, 1810; also when she compelled the enemy's sloop *Victor* to surrender, and exchanged broadsides with the 40-gun frigate *Minerve;* and again during a series of unhappy although heroic operations, which, by 28 Aug. 1810, terminated in the self-destruction, in Port Sud-Est, Isle of France, of the French frigates *Magicienne* and *Sirius*, and the capture by a French squadron of the NÉRÉIDE and IPHIGENIA—the former after being reduced to a mere wreck, and incurring a loss of nearly her whole crew. On the reduction of the Mauritius in the following Dec. Mr. Patton was sent home in the MINERVA frigate, Capt. Robt. Tom Blackler. On his arrival he successively joined the ANN tender, Lieut.-Commander John Turner, lying at Swansea, and the SALVADOR DEL MUNDO 112, commanded at Plymouth by Capt. John Nash. He attained the rank of Lieutenant 21 March, 1812. His last appointments were—11 July and 3 Aug. following, to the EGERIA and FORESTER sloops, Capts. Lewis Hole and Alex. Kennedy, on the Home station—21 April, 1813, to the BENBOW 74, Capt. Rich. Harrison Pearson, in the West Indies—and, 26 Oct. 1814, to the LYRA 10, Capt. Dowell O'Reilly, attached to the force in the Mediterranean, whence he returned in Aug. 1815.

PAUL. (COMMANDER, 1841.)

ALFRED JOHN PAUL was born 11 Jan. 1811, and died 18 Aug. 1845.

This officer entered the Navy, 11 Jan. 1824, as Fst.-cl. Vol., on board the TAMAR 26, Capt. Jas. John Gordon Bremer, under whom he witnessed the establishment of a colony on Melville Island, Australia. In Sept. 1825 he removed to the LIFFEY 50, bearing the broad pendant in the East Indies of Commodore Thos. Coe; and in June, 1826, five months after he had left the latter ship, he became Midshipman of the VICTORY 104, Capt. Chas. Inglis, lying at Portsmouth. Joining next, in April, 1827, the DARTMOUTH 42, Capt. Thos. Fellowes, he served for nearly three years in that ship on the Mediterranean station, where it was his fortune to act a part in the battle of Navarin. In Oct. 1830 Mr. Paul, at that time in the PRINCE REGENT 120, Capt. Jas. Whitley Deans Dundas, passed his examination. He was subsequently employed on the Mediterranean, African, South American, Lisbon, and East India stations, as Mate, in the GANGES 84, Capt. Geo. Burdett, LYNX 3, Lieut.-Commander Henry Vere Huntley, ROVER 18, Capt. Chas. Eden, DUBLIN 50, Capts. Wm. David Puget and Geo. Wickens Willes, MINDEN 74, Capt. Alex. Renton Sharpe, and ALLIGATOR 28, Capt. Sir J. J. G. Bremer. While in the latter ship, in which he served from Sept. 1837 until Jan. 1840, he was present at the formation of a colony at Port Essington, and was advanced to the rank of Lieutenant by a commission bearing date 28 June 1838. On quitting her he removed to the WELLESLEY 72, on board which ship Sir Gordon Bremer (to whom, in the following June, he became

Flag-Lieutenant) had hoisted a broad pendant. He assisted in consequence at the capture of Chusan and of several batteries in the Canton river.* His promotion to the rank of Commander took place 14 June, 1841.

PAULET, Lord. (Capt., 1833. f-p., 18 ; h-p., 12.)

The Right Honourable Lord George Paulet, born 12 Aug. 1803, is third son of Chas. Ingoldsby, 13th Marquis of Winchester ; brother of Lord Wm. Paulet, Lieut.-Colonel 68th Regt., and of Lord Fred. Paulet, an officer in the Coldstream Guards ; and brother-in-law of Capt. Wm. Ramsden, R.N., and Sir Chas. Des Vœux, Bart.

This officer entered the Royal Naval College 6 Feb. 1817 ; and embarked, 18 Dec. 1819, as Midshipman, on board the Liffey 50, Capt. Hon. Henry Duncan, stationed in the Channel. From Oct. 1820 until Jan. 1824 he served in the Mediterranean and again in the Channel in the Cambrian 48, Capt. Gawen Wm. Hamilton, Racehorse 18, Capt. Hon. Chas. Abbot, and Active 46, Capt. Andrew King. He then passed his examination ; and on 9 Feb. 1825, at which period he had been serving for upwards of six months in South America on board the Blanche 46, Capt. Wm. Bowen Mends, he was made Lieutenant into the Jaseur 18, Capts. Thos. Martin and Edw. Handfield. Attaining the rank of Commander 28 Feb. 1828, he was next, from 4 March, 1830, until paid off 2 Jan. 1834, employed in that capacity on board the Nautilus 10, in which vessel, after having served in the Channel and off the coast of Ireland, we find him stationed in and off the rivers Douro and Tagus during the whole of the civil war in Portugal, from July, 1832, to Oct. 1833 ; and subsequently off the north coast of Spain at the commencement of the hostilities in that country. His Lordship, prior to the Nautilus being put out of commission, had been advanced, 18 Nov. 1833, to the rank he now holds. His last appointment was, 28 Dec. 1841, to the Carysfort 26, fitting for the Pacific, where, in Feb. 1843, certain indignities having been offered by the King of the Sandwich Islands, Kamehameha III., to Her Majesty's subjects resident in his dominions, Lord George felt it his duty to institute demands, which led to the whole of the group being provisionally ceded to him. He accordingly retained possession of them, in the name of Queen Victoria, until 31 July following, when, by order of Rear-Admiral Thomas, the Commander-in-Chief, they were restored to their former government. The Carysfort afterwards conveyed Queen Pomare, with 50 of her relatives and suite, from Tahiti to Raiatea, one of the leewardmost of the Society Islands. She returned to England and was paid off in June, 1845.

Lord Geo. Paulet married, 11 July, 1835, Georgina, daughter of the late Major-General Sir Geo. Wood, K.C.B., of Ottershaw Park, co. Surrey, and niece of the late Sir Mark Wood, Bart., by whom he has issue two children.

PAULSON. (Commander, 1842. f-p., 20; h-p., 15.)

John Thomas Paulson entered the Navy, 16 March, 1812, as Fst.-cl. Vol., on board the Barham 74, Capt. John Wm. Spranger, employed at first in the Channel, and afterwards among the Western Islands and in the West Indies. In July, 1814, he removed as Midshipman to the Cordelia 10, Capt. Wm. Sargent, attached to the force on the Home station ; and he next, in April and Aug. 1816, joined the Newcastle 60, flag-ship of Sir Pulteney Malcolm, and Spey 20, Capts. John Lake and Jas. Arthur Murray, both at St. Helena, whence, in Nov. 1817, he returned to England. From Feb. 1818 to April, 1819, he again served on board the Spey, under Capts. White and Tattnall, on the Mediterranean station. In the following Aug., having passed his examination, he joined the Leander 60, Capts. Chas. Richardson and Robt. Gore, in which ship, bearing the flag in the East Indies of Hon. Sir Henry Blackwood, he continued employed, as Midshipman, Master's Mate, Second-Master, and Acting-Lieutenant, until transferred with Capt. Gore, about Nov. 1822, in the capacity last mentioned, to the Satellite 18. In that vessel he visited New South Wales. He was confirmed a Lieutenant 29 March, 1822 ; and was subsequently appointed—30 June following, to the Sophie 18, Capts. Geo. French, Robt. Graham Dunlop, and Geo. Fred. Ryves, in which vessel, prior to his return to England in July, 1824, he was afforded an opportunity of sharing, as First-Lieutenant, in the opening operations against the Burmese—7 Feb. 1829, to the Seringapatam 46, Capt. Hon. Wm. Waldegrave, fitting for service in South America, whence he came home and was paid off at the close of 1832—15 Jan. 1838, to the command, which he retained for nearly four years, of the Espoir 10, on the Lisbon station—and, 8 March, 1842, to the Royal George yacht, Capt. Lord Adolphus FitzClarence. He attained his present rank in honour of the Queen's visit to Scotland 21 Sept. 1842 ; and has since been on half-pay.

* During the operations against Canton in March, 1841, he appears to have been attached to the person of Capt. Herbert, of H.M.S Calliope.—*Vide* Gaz 1841, p 1505.

PAYNE. (Lieutenant, 1848.)

Charles Bradney Payne is nephew of Retired Commander Wm. Payne, R.N.

This officer passed his examination 1 Sept. 1847 ; was appointed Mate, 16 Oct. following, of the Excellent gunnery-ship at Portsmouth, Capt. Henry Ducie Chads ; and since his promotion to the rank of Lieutenant, 4 March, 1848, has been serving on board the Havannah 19, Capt. John Elphinstone Erskine.

PAYNE. (Captain, 1814. f-p., 21 ; h-p. 33.)

Charles Frederick Payne, born in 1779, at Weymouth, co. Dorset, is son of the late Rev. Sam. Payne, Rector of Weymouth, Wyke, and Portland ; and brother of Retired Commander Wm. Payne, R.N.

This officer entered the Navy, 1 March, 1793, as L.M., on board the Culloden 74, Capts. Sir Thos. Rich, Isaac Schomberg, and Thos. Troubridge ; in which ship, on his return from a voyage to the West Indies, we find him present as Midshipman in the battle of 1 June, 1794. On subsequently joining the London 98, he served, under the flag of Sir John Colpoys, in Lord Bridport's action with the French fleet off Ile de Groix 23 June, 1795. In the course of 1797 he was transferred in succession to the Révolutionnaire 38 and Nymphe 36, Capts. Fras. Cole and Percy Fraser ; and on 18 April, 1799, after having acted for some time as Lieutenant in the latter frigate, he was confirmed into the Cambridge 74, bearing the flag of Sir Thos. Pasley at Plymouth. On his removal, in the following Nov., to L'Aimable 32, Capt. Henry Raper, he sailed in company with the Glenmore 44 and a fleet of merchantmen for the West Indies. On 17 Dec., having fallen in with *La Sirène*, a heavy French frigate, *La Bergère* corvette, and the *Calcutta*, an extra East-Indiaman, which the enemy had just captured, L'Aimable, while the Glenmore was engaged in re-capturing and retaining possession of the Indiaman, went in pursuit of the men-of-war, with whom, although they contrived in the end to make off, she maintained for 35 minutes a very spirited action. Some time afterwards Lieut. Payne was sent into Aguada Bay, Puerto Rico, for the purpose of cutting out a large schooner at anchor there. On the vessel being boarded, the enemy, who had just before discharged a broadside of grape, jumped out of her and made good their escape. The British, however, had scarcely commenced towing their prize when a heavy fire from a battery on shore was opened upon them, which killed and wounded almost every man in the barge. The other boats not being able to make any progress with the schooner, she was in consequence abandoned ; it being the next day ascertained that she had been secured to the shore by hawsers under water. On leaving L'Aimable in April, 1801, Lieut. Payne assumed command of the Tromp at Martinique ; he next, from Aug. in the same year until Aug. 1802, served, likewise in the West Indies, on board the

GAIÉTÉ, Capts. Fanshawe and Briggs; and in April, 1803, and March, 1806, he became Senior of the IMMORTALITÉ and CLYDE frigates, both commanded by the present Sir Edw. Wm. Campbell Rich Owen. During his servitude in the IMMORTALITÉ he assisted at the bombardment of Dieppe and St. Valery-en-Caux 14 Sept. 1803;* and on that and other occasions displayed so much merit that he was the constant theme of his Captain's praise. Independently of being slightly wounded at the boarding and capture of one of the enemy's vessels, we may mention that he commanded a division of rocket-boats sent in to attempt the destruction of the tower and flotilla at Boulogne, also one of the store-ships ordered to be sunk at the entrance of the harbour at that place, and, 2 Oct. 1804, one of the principal explosion vessels employed in a renewed attack upon the flotilla there stationed.† In an action fought on 23 of the latter month with the enemy's flotilla between Capes Blanc Nez and Gris Nez, Mr. Payne, although ill, stuck to his quarters, and by his zealous exertions attracted much attention.‡ Attaining the rank of Commander 26 Dec. 1806, he was in that capacity appointed to the ADELPHI rocket-ship, and, after 12 months of half-pay, to the CRETAN 16. In the ADELPHI, we understand, he passed the Dardanells with Sir John Thos. Duckworth in Feb. 1807; and in the CRETAN, to which vessel he was appointed 26 Sept. 1809, he was highly eulogised for the manner in which he led a squadron of frigates and sloops through the Wielinge Passage, past the fortifications of Flushing and Breskens, to a safe anchorage off Cadsand. On leaving the CRETAN, Capt. Payne (who had captured in her, 28 Oct. 1810, the *Neptune* Danish privateer of 5 guns and 24 men) was promoted, 7 June, 1814, to Post-rank. In the following Dec. he proceeded to the Canadian lakes, for the purpose of assuming command of the ST. LAWRENCE 98 as Flag-Captain to Sir Edw. W. C. R. Owen, then on the eve of opening a campaign against the American Commodore Chauncey. The intelligence of peace, however, arriving before the ice had broken up, he was ordered to superintend the dismantling of the squadron and the placing of their stores and guns in a state of readiness for immediate use. He returned to England in Dec. 1815; and, not having been since afloat, was induced, 1 Oct. 1846, to accept the Retirement.

Capt. Payne married in July, 1817, and has issue seven children.

PAYNE. (LIEUTENANT, 1815. F-P., 16; H-P., 32.)

RICHARD PAYNE entered the Navy, 26 Feb. 1799, as Sec.-cl. Boy, on board the CÆSAR 80, Capt. (afterwards Rear-Admiral) Sir Jas. Saumarez; under whom, in July, 1801, he fought in the actions off Algeciras and in the Gut of Gibraltar. In Aug. 1802 he left the CÆSAR. He was next, between Sept. 1803 and Dec. 1812, employed in the Channel and Baltic on board the SAN JOSEF 110, HIBERNIA 110, DIOMEDE 50, and VICTORY 100, flag-ships of Sir Chas. Cotton, Earl St. Vincent, and Sir Jas. Saumarez; he then joined the VILLE DE PARIS 110, Capt. Geo. Burlton, lying at Portsmouth; and in March, 1814, after having again served for 12 months in the Baltic, part of the time as Acting-Lieutenant, in the ARIEL sloop, Capt. Dan. Ross, he was nominated Acting-Master (he had been for three months Second-Master of the VICTORY) of the HARRIER 16, Capts. Andrew Pellet Green, John Forbes, and Sir Chas. Thos. Jones. In the latter vessel he took part in the grand naval review held before the Allied Sovereigns at Portsmouth, and was afterwards sent on a cruize among the Canary Islands. He was advanced to his present rank 13 Feb. 1815; and has since been on half-pay.

PAYNE. (RETIRED COMMANDER, 1835. F-P., 20; H-P., 38.)

WILLIAM PAYNE, born in Oct. 1773, is brother of Capt. C. F. Payne, R.N.; and uncle of Capts. P. T. M. and G. B. Payne, both of the R.M., also of W. C. H. Payne, Esq., Second-Master R.N. (1845), and of Lieut. C. B. Payne, R.N.

This officer entered the Navy, 29 Sept. 1789, as Midshipman, on board the FALCON sloop, Capt. Laugharne, on the Home station, where he next, in succession, joined the RESISTANCE 44, Capt. Hewit, FALCON again, Capts. Bligh and Eastwood, and ALCIDE and BEDFORD 74's, Capts. Sir And. Snape Douglas and Sir And. Snape Hamond. Rejoining Sir And. Snape Douglas, in Jan. 1792, on board the PHAETON 38, he assisted in that ship at the capture, in the course of the following year, of *Le Général Dumourier* of 22 guns and 196 men, having on board 2,040,000 dollars; her prize, the *St. Jago*, laden with a cargo worth nearly 300,000*l.*; *La Prompte* frigate of 28 guns and 180 men; another privateer of 16 guns and 60 men; and *La Blonde* national corvette of 24 guns. After sharing, under the command of Capt. Wm. Bentinck, in the action of 1 June, 1794, he removed to the QUEEN CHARLOTTE 100, commanded by his old Captain, Sir A. S. Douglas; at whose recommendation, for his conduct in Lord Bridport's rencontre with the French fleet off Ile de Groix, he was nominated, 6 July, 1795, Acting-Lieutenant of the SANS PAREIL 80, Capt. Lord Hugh Seymour. He was confirmed (as soon as he had passed his examination) into the AQUILON 32, Capt. Cracraft, 9 Oct. following; and was subsequently appointed—15 Dec. 1797, to the MAIDSTONE 32, Capts. Matthews, Ross Donnelly, Rich. Hussey Moubray, and Hon. Geo. Elliot—17 Dec. 1804, to the Sea Fencibles at Weymouth—11 Dec. 1806, to the MODESTE 36, Capt. Hon. G. Elliot—20 Feb. 1808, to the CULLODEN 74, bearing the flag of Sir Edw. Pellew—and, 25 Jan. 1809, again to the MODESTE, still commanded by Capt. Elliot. While stationed, in the AQUILON, in the West Indies, Mr. Payne was severely attacked by the yellow fever. In 1798, during his homeward passage in the MAIDSTONE, Capt. Matthews died; but, notwithstanding he was at the time First-Lieutenant, he received neither additional pay nor promotion. Continuing in the MAIDSTONE until appointed, as above, to the Sea Fencibles, he was in consequence in that ship when she was sent with the treaty of peace to the Mediterranean. Although, in 1807, at which period he was Senior of the MODESTE, he escorted the Governor-General of India to the seat of his government, he was again disappointed of the promotion which had always been customary on occasions of the kind. He was, however, appointed First of the CULLODEN; but the latter being ordered to England before an opportunity of effecting his advancement had occurred, he went back to the MODESTE, in command of the boats of which ship and the BARRACOUTA he succeeded, 15 July, 1810, in cutting out, from under the protection of two batteries and five armed vessels, in a bay in the Straits of Sunda, the Dutch schooner *Tuyncelaar* of 8 guns and 22 men.* A slight attack of liver-complaint, added to the disappointments he had experienced, induced him, in Dec. 1809, to invalid. He did not again go afloat, but accepted, 26 Nov. 1830, the rank of Retired Commander on the Junior List. He was transferred to the Senior List 23 Dec. 1835.

At the close of the French revolutionary war Commander Payne suggested to Lord St. Vincent, then First Lord of the Admiralty, the necessity of placing the surplus stores of ships under the charge of their respective warrant officers. On the paying off of the fleet the plan was carried into execution, and a great saving to the country thereby effected. The Commander married, in 1841, Cecilia, only child of J. Glendinning, Esq., by whom he has issue a son. An only child by a former marriage is the wife of the Rev. Wm. H. Gorton.

PAYNE. (LIEUTENANT, 1845.)

WILLIAM HENRY PAYNE passed his examination 5 Dec. 1837; and, after having served for some years on the Mediterranean and Home stations, as Mate, in the GORGON steamer, Capt. Wm. Honyman

* *Vide* Gaz. 1803, p. 1273. † *V.* Gaz. 1804, p. 1237. ‡ *V.* Gaz. 1804, p. 1320.

* *Vide* Gaz. 1810, p. 787.

Henderson, CAMPERDOWN 104, flag-ship of Sir Edw. Brace, and BLAZER steam surveying-vessel, Capt. John Washington, was promoted to the rank of Lieutenant 1 Sept. 1845. He was then appointed to the HEROINE 6, Capt. Chas. Edmunds, fitting for the coast of Africa, whence, in 1847, he returned to England.

PAYNE. (LIEUTENANT, 1834.)

WILLIAM ROUSSEAU PAYNE entered the Navy 30 July, 1823; passed his examination in 1829; obtained his commission 2 April, 1834; and was afterwards appointed—29 Aug. 1835, to the RODNEY 92, Capt. Hyde Parker, on the Mediterranean station —10 May, 1837, to the CHILDERS 16, Capt. Hon. Henry Keppel, attached to the force on the coast of Africa, whence he returned to England at the close of the same year—and, 1 Nov. 1838 and 1 Oct. 1840, to the HOWE 120 and CAMPERDOWN 104, bearing the flags of Sir Robt. Waller Otway, Sir Henry Digby, and Sir Edw. Brace at the Nore. Of the latter ship he was for some time First-Lieutenant. He has been on half-pay since Nov. 1843.

PAYNTER. (LIEUT., 1814. F-P., 12; H-P., 32.)

CHARLES PAYNTER, born in Jan. 1791, is second son of the late Chas. Paynter, Esq., of Penzance, co. Cornwall, himself the son of Fras. Paynter, Esq., of Boskenna, near that place. An heiress of the house of Paynter, Margaret Paynter, of Trelissick, became the wife of John Hearle, Esq., and was the mother of three daughters, co-heiresses, who allied themselves to families of eminence, one espousing Commissioner Wallis, the circumnavigator, another Henry Hawkins Tremayne, Esq., of Heligan, and the third Col. Fras. Rodd, of Trebartha. Lieut. Paynter is cousin of Commander John Pender Paynter, R.N.; and a distant relation of Capt. Wm. Pender Roberts, R.N.

This officer entered the Navy, 12 July, 1803, as Fst.-cl. Vol., on board the SAN JOSEF 110, Capts. John Tremayne Rodd and Tristram Robt. Ricketts, bearing the flag in the Channel of Sir Chas. Cotton. On leaving that ship, of which he had been nominated Midshipman in Oct. 1803, he was again, in Jan. 1806, placed under the orders of Capt. Rodd on board the INDEFATIGABLE 44, commanded afterwards by Capt. Hen. Edw. Reginald Baker. Uniting, 15 July following, with the boats of a squadron under Sir Sam. Hood, he assisted at the cutting-out, in face of a desperate and well-concerted resistance, at the entrance of the river Gironde, of the French corvette *Le César*, mounting 16 guns, with a complement of 86 men, who, with a loss to themselves of 14 killed and wounded, occasioned one to the British of 9 killed and 39 wounded. In April, 1809, we find the INDEFATIGABLE forming part of the force employed in Lord Cochrane's operations against the French fleet in Aix Roads, where, on 12 of that month, she was for upwards of 10 hours exposed to the fire of the enemy's batteries, and was for 50 minutes engaged in close action with *La Ville de Varsovie* of 80 guns, which ship, during the preceding night, had run on shore. The only injury sustained by the INDEFATIGABLE on the occasion was the loss of her maintopmast. On 15 Jan. 1810, having been placed in charge of a schooner captured on the coast of Spain, Mr. Paynter had the misfortune to be wrecked on the Penmarck rocks and taken prisoner. The hardships he at first experienced were such as to throw him on a bed of sickness. In the course of time, however, he recovered; but it was not until the month of Dec. 1813 that he was restored to liberty. He then, having effected his escape, made the best of his way to Holland, whence he embarked for England. On his arrival in Feb. 1814 he was ordered on board the PRINCE 98, flag-ship of Sir Rich. Bickerton at Portsmouth, where, in the course of the following month, he passed his examination. He was promoted to the rank of Lieutenant 27 June in the same year; and was lastly, from the ensuing Nov. until paid off in Sept. 1815, employed with Capt. J. T. Rodd on board the WARRIOR 74. During the passage home of that ship from the West Indies, in the summer of the latter year, she was caught in a violent hurricane, was totally dismasted, received 11 feet water in her hold, and all but foundered.

PAYNTER. (COMMANDER, 1846.)

JAMES AYLMER DORSET PAYNTER entered the Navy 1 Jan. 1826; passed his examination 11 Feb. 1833; and at the period of his promotion to the rank of Lieutenant, 23 Nov. 1841, was serving in the Mediterranean, as Mate, on board the VERNON 50, Capt. Wm. Walpole. His succeeding appointments were—5 Feb. 1842, to the AGINCOURT 72, fitting for the flag of Sir Thos. John Cochrane, Commander-in-Chief in the East Indies—and, 6 July, 1846, to the command, on that station, of the ROYALIST brig. On 19 Aug. 1845, assuming charge of the AGINCOURT's barge, he served with the boats of a squadron, carrying altogether 530 officers, seamen, and marines, at the destruction, under Capt. Chas. Talbot, of the piratical settlement of Malloodoo, on the north end of the island of Borneo, where the British encountered an earnest opposition, and sustained a loss of 6 men killed and 15 wounded.* In July, 1846, during an expedition conducted by Sir Thos. Cochrane against the Sultan of Borneo, he contributed, as officer in command of the field-piece and rocket brigade, to the capture and destruction, on 8 of that month, of the enemy's forts and batteries on the river Brune. While ascending that stream he appears to have been lent to the PHLEGETHON steamer, and to have so astonished and dismayed the enemy assembled on the banks by the admirable nature of the fire he kept up that they precipitately fled.† As a reward for his meritorious conduct he was advanced to his present rank by a commission bearing date 8 July, 1846. He was in consequence superseded in the command of the ROYALIST, to which he had been appointed as above, and is now on half-pay. AGENTS —Messrs. Halford and Co.

PAYNTER. (LIEUT., 1814. F-P., 21; H-P., 20.)

JOHN MEYRICK PAYNTER entered the Navy, 25 June, 1806, as Fst.-cl. Vol., on board the SUPERB 74, Captain (afterwards Rear-Admiral Sir) Rich. Goodwin Keats; and while in that ship, commanded for some time by Capts. Donald M'Leod and Sam. Jackson, was present, as Midshipman, at the bombardment of Copenhagen, the embarkation from Nyeborg of the Spanish General the Marquis de la Romana and his patriot troops, and the capture of Flushing. After a servitude of eight months at Spithead and Plymouth in the PUISSANT 74, Capts. Robt. Hall and John Irwin, and MENELAUS 38, Capt. Sir Peter Parker, he joined, in July, 1810, the MILFORD 74, bearing the flag, at the defence of Cadiz, of his old Captain, Sir R. G. Keats, whom, in Aug. 1811, he followed into the HIBERNIA 110. Being again, in Aug. 1812, placed under the orders of Sir Peter Parker on board the MENELAUS, he sailed in that ship for the coast of North America; where, on being nominated, 27 July, 1814, Acting-Lieutenant of the WESER troop-ship, Capts. Thos. Ball Sulivan, Bartholomew Kent, and Dan. Lawrence, he witnessed the destruction of Commodore Barney's flotilla up the Patuxent, and took part in the unsuccessful attack made upon Baltimore. His appointment to the WESER being confirmed by commission dated 11 Oct. 1814, he continued in that vessel until Nov. 1815, and was in consequence present in the expedition against New Orleans. Since 20 March, 1835, he has been in command of a station in the Coast Guard.

PAYNTER. (COMMANDER, 1816. F-P., 13; H-P., 30.)

JOHN PENDER PAYNTER, born 1 Nov. 1788, is a cousin of Lieut. Chas. Paynter, R.N. His brother,

* *Vide* Gaz. 1845, p. 6536.

† *V.* Gaz. 1846, pp. 3139, 3441, 3442, 3767.

Edw. Wm. Paynter, a Midshipman R.N., died in 1810 on board the IMPLACABLE 74, Capt. Geo. Cockburn.

This officer entered the Navy, 12 Feb. 1804, as Fst.-cl. Vol., on board the SAN JOSEF 110, Capts. John Tremayne Rodd and Tristram Robt. Ricketts, bearing the flag of Sir Chas. Cotton, under whom he attained the rating of Midshipman in Aug. of the same year. In Jan. 1806, up to which period he had been employed in the blockade of Brest, he rejoined Capt. Rodd on board the INDEFATIGABLE 44, in which ship, participating, in April, 1809, in Lord Cochrane's attack upon the French fleet in Aix Roads, he was, on 12 of that month, for upwards of 10 hours under fire of the enemy's batteries, and for 50 minutes engaged in close action with the *Ville de Varsovie* 80, which ship had run on shore during the preceding evening. He continued in the INDEFATIGABLE with Capt. Henry Edw. Reginald Baker until Feb. 1810; and on 1 Aug. in that year, after having been again employed, under the command of Capt. Rich. Dalling Dunn and the flag of Sir Chas. Cotton, on board the SAN JOSEF, was made Lieutenant into the EURYALUS 36, Capts. Geo. Heneage Lawrence Dundas, Abel Ferris, Thos. Ussher, Jeremiah Coghlan, and Chas. Napier. Under Capt. Dundas he took part in several battery actions on the coast of Calabria; and under Capt. Napier, besides contributing to the capture, 16 May, 1813, of *La Fortune* national xebec, of 10 guns, 4 swivels, and 95 men, together with upwards of 20 sail of merchantmen lying in the harbour of Cavalarie, he assisted in the following winter in simultaneously driving on shore, in Calvi Bay, the *Balleine* French store-ship of 22 guns and 120 men, and compelling a gaberre of 30 guns and 150 men, laden with stores, and a national schooner of the largest class, to seek refuge under the land batteries. In 1814 Mr. Paynter, having accompanied a fleet of transports to North America, was further present at the capture, up the Patuxent river, of Fort Washington, and the capitulation of Alexandria. Becoming, 25 March, 1815, Flag-Lieutenant to Lord Exmouth in the BOYNE 98, he beheld, in the course of that year, the surrender of Naples, and afterwards visited the Barbary States for the purpose of endeavouring to procure the release of Christian slaves. At Algiers, being sent on shore to demand the release from custody of the English Consul, Colonel Macdonald, he was himself seized by the Dey, and lodged in the Black Hole. The menacing aspect subsequently assumed by the British fleet procured his enlargement; and on his return to England he was advanced to the rank of Commander 7 Nov. 1816. He has since been on half-pay.

PEACE. (LIEUT., 1811. F-P., 18; H-P., 25.)

RICHARD PEACE was born 25 Sept. 1790.

This officer entered the Navy, 6 Feb. 1804, as Midshipman, on board the DOLPHIN 44, Capt. John Shortland, with whom he continued employed in the TROMPEUSE 18 and SQUIRREL 24, on the Irish, African, and Halifax stations, until Nov. 1808. Joining next, in Jan. 1809, the SUCCESS 32, Capt. John Ayscough, he commanded a boat belonging to that ship at the reduction of Ischia and Procida, and co operated in the defence of Sicily against the threatened invasion of Murat. On 30 July, 1809, we find him serving in the boats, as Master's Mate, at the capture, off Cerigo, of two French privateers, one carrying 9 guns, 4 swivels, and 78 men, the other 1 gun and 20 men. He shortly afterwards commanded a boat, one of two under the orders of Lieut. Geo. Rose Sartorius, at the taking of a ship of 6 guns and 30 men. On 4 April, 1810, he was reported in the highest terms for his conduct at the destruction (by the boats of the SUCCESS and ESPOIR sloop, commanded by the same officer) of several vessels well protected on the beach abreast of Castiglione;* and on 25 of the same month he had charge of a boat at the capture of an armed ship and three barks under the castle of Terracina. In the following Oct. he assisted, on the coast of Naples, in destroying 2 gun-boats and 34 sail of troop-ships. He was confirmed a Lieutenant of the TRIDENT 64, Capt. Rich. Budd Vincent, after having acted for a short time as Mate, 22 April, 1811; and was next, between Dec. of the same year and Oct. 1815, employed, on the Mediterranean, Home, and Barbadoes stations, in the ECLAIR sloop, Capt. John Bellamy, TRIDENT again, Capt. R. B. Vincent, MINORCA 18, Capt. Ralph Randolph Wormeley, APOLLO troop-ship, Capt. Anthony Blagrave Valpy, and, as Senior Lieutenant, in the RAVEN 16, Capt. Edw. Lloyd. His last appointments were, in the capacity last mentioned—19 Aug. 1818, to the REDWING 18, Capt. Fred. Hunn, stationed, until her return to England in the autumn of 1821, off St. Helena for the purpose of watching Napoleon Buonaparte—and, 18 May, 1827, to the TWEED 28, Capt. Lord Henry John Spencer Churchill, fitting for the Cape of Good Hope, whence he came home in Feb. 1831. AGENTS—Goode and Lawrence.

* *Vide* Gaz. 1810, p. 1138.

PEACOCKE. (VICE-ADMIRAL OF THE BLUE, 1841.)

RICHARD PEACOCKE died 24 April, 1846, at Aix-la-Chapelle, of disease of the heart.

This officer entered the Navy, 9 March, 1781, as Captain's Servant, on board the EUROPA 50, Capt. John Thos. Duckworth, stationed in the Channel, where, in 1782, he followed the same Captain into the SALISBURY 50. From 1783 to 1786 he served in the West Indies, as Midshipman and Master's Mate, in the CAMILLA 20, Capt. Hutt; he next, in 1793, joined the SUFFOLK 74, bearing the broad pendant of Commodore Peter Rainier in the East Indies; and on 22 Jan. 1796 he was confirmed a Lieutenant, after having acted for six months as such, in the RESISTANCE 44, Capt. Edw. Pakenham. In that ship he co-operated in the reduction, in Aug. 1795, of Malacca; and, as Senior-Lieutenant, in the capture, in March, 1796, of Amboyna and Banda. Invaliding home in the following Nov., he was appointed, 13 Oct. 1797, to the LEVIATHAN 74, commanded by his old Captain, Duckworth; under whom, when in company with the ARGO 44, he assisted, again as First-Lieutenant, at the capture, 6 Feb. 1799, of the Spanish frigate *Santa Teresa*, of 42 guns. Previously to that event he had been serving, for a few months in 1798, on board the PRINCE 98, flag-ship of Sir Roger Curtis off Cadiz. On leaving the LEVIATHAN in 1799 he was appointed, for a short time, Acting-Captain of the POWERFUL 74. On 28 Jan. 1801, four months previously to which period he had rejoined the LEVIATHAN, he was promoted to the command of the GAIÉTÉ sloop in the West Indies; where he was made Post, 4 June, 1801, into the ARAB. He subsequently, in 1802-3, served in the CASTOR frigate on the same station, and in 1806-7 in the FOUDROYANT 80 in the Channel. He became a Rear-Admiral on the Retired List 22 July, 1830; on the Active 17 Aug. 1840; and a Vice-Admiral 23 Nov. 1841.

He married, 27 Feb. 1821, Martha Louisa, fourth daughter of the late Geo. Dacre, Esq., of Marwell House, Hants. AGENTS—Hallett and Robinson.

PEAKE. (LIEUTENANT, 1814. F-P., 10; H-P., 30.)

CHARLES PEAKE was born 25 July, 1793, and died 2 Jan. 1847.

This officer entered the Navy, 26 Jan. 1807, as Fst.-cl. Vol., on board the VESTAL 28, Capt. Edwards Lloyd Graham; under whom, until paid off in April, 1810, he was constantly employed in the Channel and North Sea, among the Western Islands, and at Newfoundland. He assisted during that period at the capture, with a large number of merchant-vessels, of *L'Intrépide* privateer of 20 guns and 125 men, and was on several occasions intrusted with the charge of a prize. In May, 1810, he became Midshipman (a rating he had attained in June, 1809) of the PALLAS 32, commanded at first by Capt. Graham, and subsequently by Capts. Pringle

Stoddart and Geo. Paris Monke. In command of one of the boats belonging to that ship Mr. Peake, while cruizing on the coast of Norway, assisted in taking, at one time, two Danish privateers, mounting respectively 6 and 5 guns; and, at another, two Danish cutters. The PALLAS being wrecked off St. Abb's Head 18 Dec. 1810, he again, in the following Feb., joined Capt. Graham on board the ALCMÈNE 38, fitting for the Mediterranean station, where he was soon afforded an opportunity of participating in much detached service. On 22 May, 1812, in particular, we find him (the ALCMÈNE being at the time on a cruize to the Adriatic) present, in command of the Captain's 6-oared gig, in a most gallant but sanguinary attack made by four boats, under Lieut. Edw. Saurin, upon an enemy's armed convoy, the result of which was the capture of one of their principal vessels, after nearly the whole of the crew had been either killed or wounded. The slaughter on the part of the British was likewise dreadful—the pinnace alone sustaining a loss of at least 20 officers and men killed and wounded. Mr. Peake afterwards assisted at the cutting out of a vessel from under a battery; at the capture of a French national schooner, *La Flêche*, of 12 guns; and at the further cutting out, on the coast of Corsica, of two polacres and a xebec. On leaving the ALCMÈNE, which ship had been latterly commanded by Capt. Jeremiah Coghlan, he was received, 6 March, 1814, on board the CALEDONIA 120, bearing the flag of Sir Edw. Pellew, by whom, after witnessing the fall of Genoa, he was nominated, 27 April in the same year, Acting-Lieutenant of a 74-gun ship of that name, commanded by Capt. Arthur Stow. On 1 July following his promotion was confirmed. He went on half-pay in Nov. 1814; and was next, 3 July, 1818, appointed to the EURYALUS 42, Capts. Thos. Huskisson and Wilson Braddyll Bigland. On 27 Sept. 1820, having risen to the post of First-Lieutenant, Mr. Peake was appointed by the former officer, who had become Commodore on the Jamaica station, to the command of the BANN sloop, rendered vacant by the death of Capt. Stow of the TAMAR, and the removal to that ship of the commander of the BANN. On the arrival, however, of the latter vessel at Halifax, Rear-Admiral Griffith, the Commander-in-Chief, also thought proper to fill up the vacancy. This fact being communicated to the Commodore, he forthwith wrote to the Admiralty, requesting that their Lordships would not suffer him to be deprived of the patronage which so justly belonged to him, the vacancy having occurred while the TAMAR was within the limits of his station. Unwilling to grant the request, the Board superseded all the appointments that had taken place, and gave the command of the TAMAR to an officer then in England; at the same time paying off the sloop he commanded, in order to avoid promoting either of the Lieutenants selected by the Commodore and Rear-Admiral. Mr. Peake subsequently commanded the EURYALUS for a short period; and on the paying off of that ship in Aug. 1821 was presented by the crew with a handsome silver vase and cover, together with a sword and belt, as a testimony of their "gratitude and esteem." Unsuccessful in his endeavours to procure employment, he remained thenceforward on half-pay.

The Lieutenant,* whose wife, Margaret Peake, had died 3 May, 1840, has left issue a son (educated at the Royal Naval School) and a daughter.

* He was the author of several popular works, and a contributor to many of the periodicals of the day.

PEAKE. (COMMANDER, 1838. F-P., 19; H-P., 17.)

HENRY FREDERICK PEAKE is brother of Capt. Thos. Ladd Peake, R.N.

This officer entered the Navy, 8 Feb. 1811, as Fst.-cl. Vol., on board the DEFIANCE 74, Capt. Rich. Raggett. In the course of the following month he was placed at the Royal Naval College at Portsmouth, where he remained until 17 June, 1813. He then again embarked, on board the RIVOLI 74, Capts. Graham Eden Hamond and Edw. Stirling Dickson; under the latter of whom we find him, 30 April, 1815, assisting as Midshipman at the capture, on the Mediterranean station, after a brave defence of 15 minutes, of the French frigate *La Melpomène*. Joining next, in 1816, the MADAGASCAR and MÆANDER frigates, both commanded by Sir Jas. Alex. Gordon, he was present in the latter ship when nearly lost, in Dec. of the same year, off Orfordness. In Feb. 1817 he became Admiralty-Midshipman of the ROSARIO 10, commanded by his brother, Capt. Thos. Ladd Peake, at Portsmouth; where (with the exception of the following summer, which he passed in the Mediterranean on board the GANYMEDE 26, Capt. Hon. Robt. Cavendish Spencer, and of a subsequent unemployed interval of a few months) he continued to serve until Aug. 1820, in a similar capacity, in the CAMELION 10, Capt. Wm. Jas. Mingaye, and ACTIVE 46, Capt. Sir J. A. Gordon. He then sailed for the West Indies in the SYBILLE 44; of which ship, bearing the flag of Sir Chas. Rowley, he was created a Lieutenant 5 Feb. 1821. He returned home in the following June, and was afterwards appointed—26 Nov. 1823 and 5 March, 1825, as a Supernumerary-Lieutenant, to the RAMILLIES and HYPERION Coast-Blockade ships, Capts. Wm. M'Culloch and Hugh Pigot—and, 2 Dec. 1828, as Senior, to the COMET 18, Capt. Alex. Albert Sandilands, fitting for the East Indies, whence he returned at the close of 1832. He has since been on half-pay. His promotion to the rank of Commander took place 28 June, 1838.

With the permission of the Admiralty, Commander Peake was for some time employed under the Spanish and Portuguese Governments.

PEAKE. (Captain, 1822. F-P., 24; H-P., 25.)

THOMAS LADD PEAKE is son of the late Sir Henry Peake, Kt., who filled the office of Surveyor of the Navy from 27 June, 1806, until 25 Feb. 1822; and brother of Commander Wm. Peake, who was killed, and his ship, the PEACOCK of 18 guns and 122 men, sunk, in a desperate action with the American sloop *Hornet* of 20 guns and 165 men, 24 Feb. 1813. Capt. Peake's youngest brother, James, is married to a sister of the present Commander Henry Eden, R.N.

This officer entered the Navy, towards the close of 1798, on board the REDBRIDGE schooner, Lieut.-Commander Geo. Hayes. He next, in the course of 1799, joined the CANADA 74, Capt Hon. Michael De Courcy, and RENOWN of similar force, bearing the flag of Sir John Borlase Warren; under whom, in the following year, he accompanied the expedition to Ferrol, and in 1801 that to Egypt. At the former place he served on shore with the army under Sir Jas. Pulteney. On his return to England at the close of 1804, in the KENT 74, with Capt. John Chambers White, who had latterly had command of the RENOWN, he was received as a Supernumerary on board the ZEALAND 64, flag-ship at the Nore of Admiral Douglas. He was nominated, 4 Jan. 1805, Sub-Lieutenant of the BLOODHOUND 12, Lieut.-Commander Henry Richardson; was made a full Lieutenant, 8 May following, into the MAJESTIC 74, flag-ship of Admiral Thos. Macnamara Russell in the North Sea; and was subsequently, in 1807 and 1809, appointed to the CLIO 18, Capt. Thos. Folliott Baugh, and VICTORIOUS 74, Capts. Graham Eden Hamond and John Talbot. In the latter ship he participated in the Walcheren operations of 1809; and on 21 Feb. 1812, the VICTORIOUS being at the time in company with the WEASEL 18, he shared as First-Lieutenant in a most gallant conflict of two hours and a half, which terminated in the capture, with a loss to the former of 27 men killed and 99 wounded, and to the enemy of 400 killed and wounded, of the French 74 *Rivoli*, whose consorts, three brigs and two gun-boats, were at the same time defeated.* He was in consequence ad-

* In the early part of the action Capt. Talbot, being severely wounded, was placed *hors de combat*. "The exertions, however, of Mr. Peake," he informs us in his official despatch, "prevented his inability from proving of any detriment to his Majesty's service."—*Vide* Gaz. 1812, p. 852.

vanced to the rank of Commander by commission bearing date 8 May following, a few weeks after he had been placed in charge of the prize, for the purpose of conducting her to England. His last appointments were—7 June, 1813, to the ROSARIO 10, on the Home station, where he served until paid off in Dec. 1818—and, 31 Aug. 1820, to the post, which he retained for nearly five years, of Inspecting-Commander in the Coast Guard. He attained his present rank 1 March, 1822; and accepted the Retirement 1 Oct. 1846.

Capt. Peake (who was for four years a Special Magistrate at the Cape of Good Hope) has been twice married: the first time to a daughter of Sir Jas. Brabazon Urmston, Superintendent of Cargoes at Canton. By both marriages he has issue. AGENTS—Messrs. Stilwell.

PEARCE. (COMMANDER, 1842. F-P., 22; H-P., 12.)

EDWARD STOKES PEARCE entered the Navy, 29 Oct. 1813, as Fst.-cl. Vol., on board the SULTAN 74, Capt. John West. In March, 1815, after having served on the coast of France and in the West Indies, he joined the AJAX 74, Capt. Geo. Mundy, on the Mediterranean station; where, and at Halifax and in the North Sea, he continued employed as Midshipman and Master's Mate in the same ship and in the DEE 24, WYE 28, and ALERT 18, Capts. Sam. Chambers, John Harper, and Chas. Farwell, until Jan. 1821. In the following month (he had passed his examination 11 April, 1820) he returned to the Mediterranean in the DISPATCH 18, Capts. Wm. Clarke Jervoise and Edw. Hinton Scott; he was next, from Nov. 1824 until May, 1831, borne on the books of the HYPERION 42, Coast Blockade ship, Capt. Wm. Jas. Mingaye; and he was then for a few weeks employed in the SAMARANG 28, Capt. Chas. Henry Paget. During six years of the period he belonged to the HYPERION he commanded her tender the HIGHFLYER. His sole appointments as Lieutenant, a rank he attained 25 June, 1831, were —2 March, 1837, to the PRINCESS CHARLOTTE 104, bearing the flag in the Mediterranean of Hon. Sir Robt. Stopford, under whom he assisted at the bombardment of St. Jean d'Acre—and 8 Feb. 1842, after six months of half-pay, to the command of the LIGHTNING steamer. Since his promotion to his present rank, 7 May, 1842, he has been on half-pay.

PEARNE. (LIEUT., 1824. F-P., 37; H-P., 2.)

WILLIAM GEORGE PEARNE was born 12 May, 1795.

This officer entered the Navy, 1 Feb. 1808, as Fst.-cl. Vol., on board the EREBUS 18, Capt. Wm. Autridge, stationed in the Baltic; where, in June, 1812, he became Midshipman of the DICTATOR 64, Capt. Jas. Pattison Stewart. In 1809 a prize-sloop of which he had charge was run over in a snow-storm, on her passage from Carlskrona to Hull, by a timber-laden brig, and immediately went down, barely allowing him to effect his escape; and in 1811, while acting as Master of another prize, he had the misfortune to be captured by four Danish gun-boats on the coast of Norway; in consequence whereof he was detained a prisoner for a period of nearly 12 months, and underwent great privations. On leaving the DICTATOR in Oct. 1812, he joined the PELICAN 18, Capts. John Fordyce Maples and Thos. Mansell; in which vessel, and in the SATURN 56, Capts. Jas. Nash and Thos. Brown, FERRET 14, Capt. Jas. Stirling, and ERNE 20, Capt. Hon. Wm. John Napier, we find him, until Aug. 1815, employed on the West India, American, and Home stations. While attached to the SATURN, Mr. Pearne assisted at the blockade of New York, and was frequently sent with prizes into port; and when in the FERRET he contributed to the capture, 18 July, 1815, of an armed cutter, a praam-brig, and a gun-vessel, together with a convoy reposing under the protection of a fort, which the British destroyed, in the harbour of Corrijou—an exploit detailed in our memoir of Vice-Admiral Sir Chas. Malcolm. With his name, from Aug. 1815 until Aug. 1818, on the books of the ROCHFORT 74, Capt. Sir Archibald Collingwood Dickson, Mr. Pearne was actively employed as Master's Mate in a variety of tenders and boats in the protection of the revenue. On one occasion he possessed himself, off the Start, of a smuggler, the *Charles*, of Morlaix, having on board a hundred tubs of contraband spirits. After a servitude of two years and eight months on the Channel and Irish stations, as Admiralty-Midshipman in the PIGMY cutter, Lieut.-Commander Wentworth Parsons Croke, as Second-Master in the FALMOUTH 20, Capt. Henry Theodosius Browne Collier, and again as Admiralty-Midshipman in the SPENCER 74, flag-ship of Sir Josias Rowley, he was appointed, 31 May, 1821, Chief Mate of the VANDELEUR Revenue-cruizer, Lieut.-Commander Chas. Fred. Napier. In the following Nov., the VANDELEUR being at the time at anchor in a disabled state off Kilrush, Mr. Pearne, acting upon information he had received, proceeded with the crew to a place called Kilkee, 13 miles distant, where he arrived in time to seize a boat with 13 bales of tobacco and a chest of tea belonging to a smuggling lugger. Another part of the cargo, amounting to 437 bales, was afterwards landed on the island of Arran, and secreted in caves underground. These being, however, discovered through the exertions of Mr. Pearne, he succeeded with only 24 men, in capturing the whole of the property, notwithstanding that several hundred persons had assembled for the purpose of rescuing it. He had the gratification in consequence of receiving a flattering letter of approbation from the Commander-in-Chief, Sir J. Rowley. After having had command for a long time of the VANDELEUR owing to the illness of Lieut. Napier, he was promoted to his present rank 21 Jan. 1824. His appointments have since been—21 Oct. 1826 and 19 Feb. 1830, to the RAMILLIES and TALAVERA Coast Blockade ships, both commanded by Capt. Hugh Pigot—15 April, 1831, to the Coast Guard at Walmer, in Kent—11 Oct. 1834, to the command of the DOVE Revenue-cruizer—and 26 Sept. 1837, again to the Coast Guard, in which service he still continues. In command of the ANTELOPE, tender to the RAMILLIES, he piloted a Russian squadron from the Texel to the Downs in Aug. 1827; and in the DOVE he had the good fortune to make prize, among other vessels, of a yawl, a schooner of 65 tons, a sloop of 39 tons, and a Cawsand boat of 20 tons. His efforts in staying the progress of a fire which broke out on one occasion in the citadel at Plymouth obtained for him the thanks of Sir Willoughby Cotton, who at the time held command of that place.

Lieut. Pearne married, in May, 1827, Julia Edgecombe, daughter of the late Lieut John Luckraft, R.N., by whom he has issue a son and three daughters.

PEARS. (LIEUT., 1829. F-P., 20; H-P., 7.)

CHARLES WETHERED PEARS entered the Royal Naval College 3 Feb. 1820; and embarked 20 Feb. 1822, as a Volunteer, on board the RANGER 28, Capt. Peter Fisher; under whom, in 1824, he served at the blockade of Algiers. Joining, in Nov. of that year, the BOADICEA frigate, Commodore Sir Jas. Brisbane, he united, in Sept. 1825, in the hostilities in progress against the Burmese, and until the end of the war was employed in command of a gun-boat on the river Irawady. On leaving the BOADICEA he was received, in Aug. 1826, on board the WARSPITE 76; in which ship, in the summer of the following year, he returned to England. After having further served, as Mate, in the ECLAIR 18, Capt. Spencer Lambert Hunter Vassall, VICTORY 104, Capt. Hon. Geo. Elliot, ASIA 84, Capt. Edw. Curzon, and RALEIGH 18, Capts. John Burnet Dundas, Geo. Haye, and Sir Wm. Dickson, he was promoted to the rank of Lieutenant 27 June, 1829, and appointed to the ALACRITY 10, Capt. Joseph Nias, on the Mediterranean station. He afterwards joined—30 April, 1830, the TALBOT 28, Capt. Rich. Dickinson, fitting for the Cape of Good Hope, whence he returned at the close of 1831—1 May, 1832, the VERNON 50, Capt. Sir Francis Augustus Collier, employed, until the close of the same year, on particular service—28 Oct. 1833, a second time, the VERNON, bearing then the flag of Sir George Cockburn in North America and the West Indies—29 April, 1834, as First-Lieutenant, the ARACHNE 16, Capts. Jas. Burney and John Sam. Foreman, on the same station, where he remained until 1835—1 Feb. 1838, the HASTINGS 72, Capts. Francis Erskine Loch and John Lawrence, under the former of whom he escorted the Earl of Durham to Quebec, and the Queen Dowager to the Mediterranean and back—and, 17 Sept. 1845, after five years of half-pay, to the command, which he still retains, of a station in the Coast Guard. AGENTS—Messrs. Stilwell.

PEARSE. (COMMANDER, 1825. F-P., 23; H-P., 31.)

JOHN PEARSE was born 17 May, 1780. His only brother, a Lieutenant in the service, died in the East Indies in 1809.

This officer entered the Navy, at the commencement of 1793, on board the MYRMIDON, slop-ship at Plymouth, Lieut.-Commander John Burrows; and, between June, 1794, and the date of his promotion to the rank of Lieutenant 29 Dec. 1800, was employed as Midshipman in the GIBRALTAR 80, Capt. John Pakenham, BOMBAY CASTLE 74, Capts. Jas. Macnamara, Wm. Shield, and Thos. Sotheby, CULLODEN 74, Capt. Sir Thos. Troubridge, PRINCESS ROYAL 98, Capt. Thos. Macnamara Russell, and VILLE DE PARIS 110, flag-ship of Earl St. Vincent. He officiated for some time, too, as Acting-Lieutenant of the NEPTUNE and TÉMÉRAIRE 98's. In the GIBRALTAR he fought in Hotham's action 13 July, 1795; in the BOMBAY CASTLE, in which ship he was wrecked in Dec. 1796, he witnessed the capture, in Tunis Bay, of the *Nemesis* of 28, the *Sardine* of 22, and a polacre of 20 guns, as likewise the evacuation of the island of Corsica; and in the CULLODEN he was present in the action off Cape St. Vincent, at the bombardment of Cadiz, in the expedition against Teneriffe, and at the battle of the Nile. He served also on shore at the sieges of Naples and Capua, at the capture of Civita Vecchia and Rome, and at the bombardment, in 1799, of Alexandria. With the colours taken at Capua Mr. Pearse was sent by Lord Nelson to the Queen of Naples, by whom he was presented, in return, with a diamond ring. His appointments, subsequently to his promotion, were—in Jan. 1801, to the SPITFIRE 18, Capt. Robt. Keen, employed on the Channel and Irish stations, where he saw much boat-service—18 Sept. 1804, after three months of half-pay, to the ARGO 44, Capt. Geo. Parker—in Oct. following, as Senior, to the CRUIZER 18, Capts. John Hancock, Pringle Stoddart, and Geo. Chas. Mackenzie, with whom he served in the Downs, North Sea, and Baltic until Jan. 1809—and 17 Nov. in the latter year, and 24 April, 1810, to the command of the SAFEGUARD gun-brig and DECOY cutter. During the period of his attachment to the CRUIZER we find him concerned in the capture of five privateers, 12 smuggling cutters and luggers, and many other vessels; besides participating in a warm action with the Crown batteries and Danish gunboats during the siege of Copenhagen in 1807. In command of the boats he succeeded in making prize of a variety of merchantmen, one of which, a galliot, laden with brandy and wine, he carried off from the beach near Blaukenburg after considerable difficulty, although 2 field-pieces were brought to the water's edge to protect her. He also, with much judgment and resolution, possessed himself, at the same place, of a 14-gun privateer, notwithstanding that the crew, 50 in number, attempted to defend her, and that a body of the enemy had assembled on the sandhills for a similar purpose. While absent in Jan. 1806 in a captured smuggling cutter with only 8 men, very indifferently equipped, he fell in with three large smuggling luggers, and, although one was armed, contrived by stratagem to seize upon two of them, carrying 24 men, together with 1700 casks of spirits and 300 bales of dry goods. In a small tender fitted out by the CRUIZER in 1808, Mr. Pearse attacked a Danish convoy, and, in face of a schooner of five times his own force, captured one galliot laden with wheat, drove two others on shore, and dispersed the rest. He afterwards captured a schuyt laden with wheat, another laden with iron and deals, and two small packet-boats, and destroyed 14 other vessels. During his command of the DECOY, stationed for four years in the Downs, he boarded and carried one privateer, chased on shore and destroyed another near Gravelines, induced a third, from a fear of being boarded, to cut her cable and run on the rocks in Boulogne Bay, destroyed a large gun-boat after chasing her on shore near Nieuport, captured 10 smuggling vessels of various descriptions laden with 4000 gallons of spirits and a considerable quantity of light goods, sunk a lugger with 20,000 guineas on board by running her over, and burnt a sloop in ballast taken at the entrance of Gravelines harbour. From May, 1817, to May, 1820, Mr. Pearse commanded the WICKHAM Revenue-cutter on the Irish station. He attained his present rank 27 May, 1825, and has since been on half-pay. We may add that in the course of his career afloat he was twice wounded.

Commander Pearse has laboured for upwards of a quarter of a century in scientifically examining various nautical questions, and has published much useful and interesting matter on the mechanical properties of an anchor, on the formation of cutters' jibs and the setting and standing of sails in general, and on the stowage and sailing of ships, &c. His remarks on the jib-sails of cutters called forth in 1829 the thanks of the Society of Arts, and were ordered for publication in the 47th volume of its 'Transactions.' He has also very elaborately investigated the theory of naval architecture—that part of it in particular that bears reference to the way in which the motions and evolutions of ships are performed; and has demonstrated by numerous experiments that a ship performs its motions about an axis passing through the *metacentre* or *point of stability*, and that the theory which determines the centre of gravity of a ship to be the centre of motion, and which has existed ever since naval architecture was first considered as a science, is erroneous. Much has been published by Commander Pearse on the subject, but we refer our readers especially to a small pamphlet published by him in 1836 at Plymouth under the title of 'Reflections on the present State of the Theory of Naval Architecture, exhibiting at the same time some of the Errors which, from time immemorial, have existed;' and also to papers from his pen inserted in the numbers of the United Service Journal for March, May, and October, 1842, and March, 1843. Commander Pearse was one of the first to invent and propose a plan for naval gun-sights.

PEARSE. (CAPTAIN, 1846. F-P., 33; H-P., 8.)

JOSEPH PEARSE was born 17 June, 1794. He is first-cousin of Capt. John Banks, R.N.

This officer entered the Navy, 17 April, 1806, as Fst.-cl. Vol., on board the DEFIANCE 74, Capt. Hon. Henry Hotham, with whom he continued to serve as Midshipman and Master's Mate in the same ship and in the NORTHUMBERLAND 74, on the Channel station, until Jan. 1813. In the DEFIANCE he was present, 24 Feb. 1809, at the destruction of three French frigates under the batteries of Sable d'Olonne, where that ship, besides being much cut up in her masts and rigging, sustained a loss of 2 men killed and 25 wounded; and in the NORTHUMBERLAND he contributed, in company with the GROWLER gun-brig, to the gallant destruction, near L'Orient, of the French 40-gun frigates *L'Arienne* and *L'Andromaque*, and 16-gun brig *Mamelouck;* whose united fire, conjointly with that of a heavy battery, killed 5 and wounded 28 of the NORTHUMBERLAND'S people. On 3 April, 1813, having removed to the SAN DOMINGO 74, flag-ship of Sir John Borlase Warren on the coast of North America, we find Mr. Pearse serving with the boats of a squadron containing 105 men, under the orders of Lieut. Jas. Polkinghorne, at the capture, 15 miles up the Rappahannock river, of four schooners, carrying in the whole 31 guns and 219 men—an exploit whose achievement inflicted on the British a loss of 2 killed and 11 wounded, and on the enemy of 6 killed and 10 wounded. He was made Lieutenant 22 July, 1813, into the BARROSA 36, Capts. Wm. Henry Shirreff, Wm. M'Culloch, and John Maxwell, with the latter of whom he returned home from the West Indies in Oct. 1815; and was subsequently appointed—in the course of 1818, to the CYRUS 20, Capt. Wm. Fairbrother Carroll, SPENCER 74, Capt. Sam. Campbell Rowley, and TONNANT 80 and WINDSOR CASTLE 74, both commanded by Capt. Thos. Gordon Caulfeild, with whom he served at Plymouth until May, 1821—on 18 of the latter month, as Senior, to the GANNET 18, Capt. Wm. Simpson, stationed on the coast of Ireland, where he remained until Sept. 1824, and made prize, in the boats, of a large smuggling lugger, carrying 10 guns—15 March, 1825, 21 Oct. 1828, and 25 Feb. 1831, in a similar capacity, to the RANGER 28, Capt. Lord Henry Fred. Thynne, MELVILLE 74, Capts. Alex. Wilmot Schomberg, Henry Hill, and Christopher John Williams Nesham, and ST. VINCENT 120, Capt. Humphrey Fleming Senhouse, in which ships, the latter bearing the flag of Hon. Sir H. Hotham, he was continuously employed, with the exception of a few months in 1828, on the South American and Mediterranean stations, until May, 1834—17 Nov. following, and, after eight months of half-pay, 14 June, 1836, to the command of the BLAZER and FIREFLY steamers, both also in the Mediterranean, whence he returned in Sept. 1839—and, 6 Jan. 1840, as First, to the BLENHEIM 72, Capt. Sir H. F. Senhouse. For his services in the latter ship during the campaign in China, where he had charge of the rocket-boats* at the capture of the Bogue forts, and was mentioned for his conduct at the head of a division of seamen at the capture of the forts above Canton,† he was advanced to the rank of Commander 8 June, 1841, and appointed to the NIMROD 20; from which vessel, after having effected the destruction of four batteries and a war-junk in the harbour of Kelon, in the island of Formosa, he was transferred, 16 Oct. in the same year, to the CRUIZER 16. Since his arrival home from the East Indies in March, 1843, he has been on half-pay. His elevation to Post-rank took place 8 Jan. 1846. AGENTS—Messrs. Ommanney.

* Which were admirably placed and served.—*Vide* Gaz. 1841, p. 1498; where, it will be perceived, he was strongly recommended for promotion.

† *Vide* Gaz. 1841, p. 2510.

PEARSE. (LIEUT., 1807. F-P., 38; H-P., 21.)

THOMAS PEARSE died 16 July, 1846. He was son of Mr. Thos. Pearse, Master's Mate of H.M.S. APOLLO, who was killed in action with the French frigate *Oiseau* at the close of the first American war, by Mary Elizabeth, fourth daughter of Geo. Wm. Hambly, Esq., of Stonehouse, Devon.

This officer entered the Navy, about 1787, as Captain's Servant, on board the PEGASUS 28, commanded by H. R. H. Prince William Henry, with whom he served for a short time in the West Indies. Re-embarking, 26 May, 1793, on board the LONDON 98, Capt. Rich. Goodwin Keats, he cruized in that ship on the Channel station until transferred as Midshipman, in March, 1794, to the EURYDICE 24, Capt. Fras. Cole. On 8 of the following month we find him present, in company with the CRESCENT 36 and DRUID 32, the former commanded by Sir Jas. Saumarez, in an action fought off Guernsey with a powerful French squadron, from whom the British contrived in a very skilful manner to effect their escape. While attached, next, from Sept. 1794 until Dec. 1801, to the GALATEA 36, Capts. Rich. Goodwin Keats and Hon. Geo. Byng, he took part in Lord Bridport's action, 23 June, 1795, was wounded during the ensuing expedition to Quiberon, and assisted at the capture or destruction of, among other vessels, *La Révolutionnaire* of 44 guns and 351 men, *Le Jean Bart* of 18 guns, *L'Expédition* of 16 guns, *L'Eveille* of 18 guns, *L'Etoile* of 30 guns (one of five French frigates in escort of a provision fleet of 70 sail), *La Proserpine* of 42 guns and 348 men, *L'Andromaque* of 44 guns and 300 men, and *Le Ranger* of 14 guns. From Jan. to Oct. 1802 Mr. Pearse served in the West Indies as Master's Mate of the MAJESTIC 74, Capt. Davidge Gould. In the early part of the following year he successively joined the PENELOPE 36, Capt. Wm. Broughton, and VICTORY 100, flag-ship of Lord Nelson; by whom he was nominated, 12 Aug. in the same year, Acting-Lieutenant of the HALCYON 16, Capts. Henry Whitmarsh Pearse and Thos. Stamp—the first promotion made by his Lordship out of the VICTORY; in which ship, during her passage to the Mediterranean, Mr. Pearse had aided in making prize of the French 32-gun frigate *Embuscade*. Continuing in the HALCYON until the peace, he took part in numerous engagements with the gun-boats in the Gut of Gibraltar, and saw a vast deal of other active service. In Sept. 1804 he assisted at the capture of *L'Espérance* French privateer of 10 guns and 54 men; and in the summer of 1806 he contributed, after the battle of Maida, to the destruction of the enemy's batteries along the coast of Calabria, and the reduction of the town of Reggio. On 13 Dec. in the same year it was his lot to be again wounded in an action fought with great spirit for three hours, between the HALCYON, singly, and three Spanish vessels of far superior force, which terminated in the capture of one of the latter, the *Neptuno* of 14 guns and 72 men—the other two, *La Virgine de Solidad* brig of 14 guns and 78 men, and *El Vives* xebec of 12 guns and 65 men, being put to flight.* In consideration of the part taken by him in the affair, Mr. Pearse was presented with a sword by the Patriotic Society, and on 1 Aug. 1807 was confirmed in his appointment to the HALCYON. He afterwards accompanied Admiral Gambier in the expedition against Copenhagen; assisted, in Sept. 1808, in capturing, in Diamante Bay, a flotilla of 38 vessels; commanded the HALCYON's boats at the destruction, in May, 1809, of the enemy's forts on the small islands of Gianuti and Pianosa; and in 1810 co-operated in the defence of Messina and in the second capture of the town of Reggio. His last appointments afloat were—30 July, 1812, to the PRIMROSE 18, Capt. Chas. Geo. Rodney Phillott, with whom he served on the North Sea and North American stations until Dec. 1813—and 10 Feb. 1814, to the SYBILLE 44, Capts. Jas. Sanders and Thos. Forrest, which frigate, after having made a voyage to Spitzbergen, his health obliged him to leave in the following Oct. In 1825 he was placed in command of the Ordinary at Woolwich; in 1828 he was nominated Warden of Deptford Dockyard; and from 6 April, 1830, until 1841, he was again employed at Woolwich as Warden and Director of Police. He was admitted to the out-pension of Greenwich Hospital 25 June, 1841.

PEARSE. (LIEUTENANT, 1833.)

WILLIAM PEARSE entered the Navy, 28 Feb. 1815, as Midshipman, on board the ABUNDANCE store-ship, Master Commander Josiah Oake, with whom he visited North America, the West Indies, and Mediterranean. Between 1817 and 1824 we find him serving, the last two years as a passed Midshipman, in the PRÉVOYANTE 10, Master Commander Stokes, HYPERION 42, Capt. Thos. Searle, and VALOROUS 26, Capt. Jas. Murray, on the Home, North and South American, and West India stations. He then became in succession attached, in the capacity of Mate, to the EDEN 26, Capt. John Lawrence, and HUSSAR 46 and BARHAM 50, flag-ships of Sir Chas. Ogle and Hon. Chas. Elphinstone Fleeming. In the EDEN he made a second voyage to the Mediterranean; and in the HUSSAR and BARHAM he was again em-

* *Vide* Gaz. 1807, p. 52.

ployed in North America and the West Indies. After serving for a short time in the SPEEDWELL schooner, he was nominated, in 1830, Acting First-Lieutenant of the VICTOR 18, Capt. Rich. Keane. On the paying-off of that sloop in 1831, his promotion not being confirmed, he was appointed Mate of the SAN JOSEF 110, flag-ship of Sir Manley Dixon at Plymouth; where he remained until presented by Sir Jas. Graham with a commission bearing date 30 July, 1833, as "a reward for long services and good conduct, and, especially, for the zeal and exertions he had displayed on the occasion of a recent fire on board the SAN JOSEF." His last appointment was, 26 Feb. 1834, to the RACEHORSE 18, Capt. Sir Jas. Everard Home, in which vessel he remained until 1836, when he was compelled to invalid in consequence of an injury he had received while engaged in the boats in suppressing an insurrection at Para on the coast of Brazil.

PEARSE. (LIEUTENANT, 1841.)

WILLIAM ALFRED RUMBULOW PEARSE passed his examination 2 May, 1839; and was afterwards, until paid off at the commencement of 1843, employed as Mate and Acting-Lieutenant in the MODESTE 18, Capts. Harry Eyres and Rundle Burges Watson. In the former capacity he assisted, during the war in China, in boarding, 27 Feb. 1841, the ship *Cambridge*, bearing the Chinese Admiral's flag, at the enemy's position below Whampoa Reach, where he also landed and contributed to the destruction, in the whole, of 98 guns.* On 13 of the following month he served in the boats at the capture of several rafts and of the last fort protecting the approaches to Canton; and on 18 he was similarly employed at the capture of the city itself.† During the series of operations against it we find him commanding the MODESTE's cutter, under the present Sir Edw. Belcher, in an affair up a creek on the western side, where 28 vessels were destroyed.‡ In a day or two afterwards he had the misfortune to be wounded.§ In Aug. and Oct. he co-operated in the reduction of Amoy and Chinghae. As Acting-Lieutenant, Mr. Pearse, on 10 March, 1842, succeeded with two boats in towing four fire-rafts clear of the shipping off Ningpo.‖ On 15 and 16 of the same month he was employed on shore under Capt. Thos. Bourchier in an attack on the enemy's camp at Tsekee.¶ On the paying off of the MODESTE as above, he was confirmed a Lieutenant by commission bearing date 8 June, 1841. His appointments have since been—28 May, 1843, to the CYCLOPS steamer, Capt. Horatio Thos. Austin, under whom he was employed for about six months on particular service—9 Sept. 1844, as Senior, to the OSPREY 12, Capt. Fred. Patten, fitting at Portsmouth, where he was shortly afterwards superseded—19 May, 1845, as Additional, to the PENELOPE steam-frigate, bearing the broad pendant of Commodore Wm. Jones on the coast of Africa—20 Feb. 1846, to the RALEIGH 50, in which ship, bearing the broad pendant of Sir Thos. Herbert, he sailed for the south-east coast of America, and there became First-Lieutenant—and 8 June, 1847, to the command, which he still retains, of the LIZARD steam-vessel, of 150 horse-power, on the latter station.

PEARSON. (COMMANDER, 1820. F-P., 18; H-P., 30.)

ALEXANDER STEVENSON PEARSON (whose name had been borne from 12 April, 1799, until Oct. 1801, on the books of the ROYAL WILLIAM, flag-ship at Portsmouth of Admirals Sir Peter Parker and Mark Milbanke) embarked, in Jan. 1803, as Midshipman, on board the GARLAND 28, Capts. John Serrell and Fred. Cottrell. Removing, in the following Sept., to the THESEUS 74, Capt. John Bligh, he served in that ship at the capture of the French squadron with the remains of General Rochambeau's army from Cape François on board, and also in the unsuccessful attempt upon Curaçoa. While attached next, between Oct. 1805 and June, 1808, to the POWERFUL 74, Capts. Robt. Plampin, Rich. Buck, Hon. Fleetwood Broughton Reynolds Pellew, and Chas. Jas. Johnston, he assisted at the capture of the privateers *La Henriette* of 20 guns and 124 men, and *La Bellone* of 30 guns and 194 men; at the capture and destruction, 27 Nov. 1806, of a Dutch frigate, seven brigs-of-war, and about 20 armed and other merchant-vessels lying in Batavia Roads; and at the destruction, at Griessee, 11 Dec. 1807, of the dockyard and stores, and of all the men-of-war remaining to Holland in the East Indies. *La Bellone* was not taken until after a running-fight of considerable length, in which the enemy sustained a loss of 1 man killed and 6 or 7 wounded, and the British of 2 killed and 11 wounded. Mr. Pearson continued employed in the East Indies in the SAN FIORENZO 36, Capt. John Bastard, until Jan. 1809. From that period he did not again go afloat until May, 1812. He then joined in succession the UNION and OCEAN 98's, Capts. Sam. Hood Linzee, Wm. Kent, and Robt. Plampin, both on the Mediterranean station; whence, in Sept. 1813, he returned to England. Proceeding, in the early part of 1814, to Canada in the CEYLON troop-ship, Capt. Arthur Philip Hamilton, he was very actively employed from the following June until Aug. 1815, on the river St. Lawrence and on Lake Ontario, in the flotilla under Capt. Chas. Cunliffe Owen, and as Lieutenant (commission dated 14 Dec. 1814) in the NIAGARA 20 and PRINCE REGENT 56, Capts. Edw. Collier and Henry Thos. Davies. He afterwards, from 7 Nov. 1816 until promoted to his present rank 3 Oct. 1820, served, latterly as Flag-Lieutenant, under Rear-Admiral Robt. Plampin in the CONQUEROR 74 on the St. Helena station; and from 24 June, 1836, until the summer of 1839, discharged the duties of an Inspecting-Commander in the Coast Guard. He has since been on half-pay.

PEARSON. (CAPTAIN, 1837. F-P., 21; H-P., 26.)

CHARLES PEARSON entered the Navy, 12 July, 1800, as Fst.-cl. Vol., on board the PRINCE GEORGE 98, Capt. Jas. Walker, whom he successively followed into the PRINCE 98, ISIS 50, TARTAR 32, and VANGUARD 74. In the ISIS he fought at Copenhagen 2 April, 1801; and in the VANGUARD he assisted, in 1803, at the capture, besides a variety of smaller vessels, of *Le Duquesne* 74, and *La Créole* of 44 guns, with the French General Morgan and 530 troops on board. He was also present at the surrender of the town of St. Marc, St. Domingo; the garrison of which place, amounting to about 1100 men, were brought off by the VANGUARD and her prizes to rescue them from the vengeance of the black General, Dessalines. After a further servitude of six months with Capt. Walker, as Midshipman, in the DUQUESNE, he joined, in the autumn of 1804, the AMPHION 32, Capts. Sam. Sutton and Wm. Hoste; under the latter of whom, in 1805, he accompanied Lord Nelson to the West Indies and back in pursuit of the combined squadrons. He served subsequently in the Mediterranean in the SAN ILDEFONSO, Capt. John Quilliam, AMPHION again, Capt. Hoste, and OCEAN 98, flag-ship of Lord Collingwood; was made Lieutenant, 8 Nov. 1808, into the METEOR bomb, Capt. Jas. Collins; and was next consecutively appointed—11 July, 1810, to the COLUMBINE sloop, Capts. Jas. Collins and Wm. Shepheard—in May, 1811, to the LEYDEN 64, *armée-en-flûte*, Capt. Edw. Chetham—20 Feb. 1812, after five months of half-pay, to the TONNANT 80, Capt. Sir John Gore—and, 20 Aug. following, to the PHŒBE of 46 guns and 300 men, Capt. Jas. Hillyar. In command of the boats of the METEOR Mr. Pearson cut out one privateer on the coast of Dalmatia, and another (although protected by batteries and a large detachment of French troops) from the Bay of Almeria, on the coast of Spain—the British on both occasions sustaining loss. He served in the boats of the same vessel also at the defence of Rosas; and was employed in her at the siege of

* *Vide* Gaz. 1841, p. 1501. † *V.* Gaz. 1841, pp. 1503–5.
‡ *V.* Gaz. 1841, p. 2504. § *V.* Gaz. 1841, p. 2513.
‖ *V.* Gaz. 1842, p. 2388. ¶ *V.* Gaz. 1842, p. 2391.

Cadiz. In the PHŒBE he contributed, 28 March, 1814, in the capacity of Second-Lieutenant, to the capture, off Valparaiso, of the American frigate *Essex* of 46 guns and 265 men, after a warm action of 2 hours, productive of a loss to the British of 4 men killed and 7 wounded, and to the enemy of 24 killed and 45 wounded. The Senior Lieutenant, Wm. Ingram, being killed during the battle, Mr. Pearson, whose conduct on the occasion obtained him a strong recommendation to the notice of the Admiralty, succeeded to that post, and was sent in charge of the prize to England, where he arrived in company with the PHŒBE 13 Nov. following.* He was promoted to the rank of Commander by commission bearing date 29 July, 1814; and was subsequently employed, from 6 July, 1830, until 1833, in the Coast Guard at North Yarmouth; and, from 9 Nov. 1833 until 4 Feb. 1837, in the SPARROWHAWK 18, in South America. His advancement to Post-rank took place 3 April in the latter year; since which period he has been on half-pay.

Capt. Pearson married, 3 Jan. 1826, Maria, daughter of the late J. Sayers, Esq., of North Yarmouth. AGENT—Fred. Dufaur.

* *Vide* Gaz. 1814, p. 1485.

PEARSON. (RETIRED COMMANDER, 1846. F-P., 12; H-P., 34.)

CHARLES PEARSON is brother of Lieut.-General Sir Thos. Pearson, Kt., C.B., K.C.H., Colonel of the 85th Regt.; another brother, George, who had been severely wounded in the BELLEROPHON at Trafalgar, and had been subsequently employed under Sir Sam. Hood, died a Lieutenant in India towards the close of the war.

This officer entered the Navy, about Feb. 1801, as Fst.-cl. Vol., on board the ST. GEORGE 98, Capts. Thos. Masterman Hardy and Wm. Grenville Lobb; in which ship, bearing at first the flag of Lord Nelson, he served in the Baltic, off Cadiz, and in the West Indies, until July, 1802. Joining next, in Aug. 1803, the SPENCER 74, Capt. Hon. Robt. Stopford, he fought and was wounded in the action off St. Domingo 6 Feb. 1806, and in 1807 accompanied the expedition against Copenhagen, where, during an attack upon the in-shore squadron, the boat he commanded was sunk. In consideration of the wound he received at St. Domingo, Mr. Pearson was presented with a grant from the Patriotic Fund. On 21 May, 1808, a short time after he had been removed to the VICTORY 100, flag-ship in the Baltic of Sir Jas. Saumarez, he was nominated Acting-Lieutenant of the THUNDER bomb, Capt. Jas. Caulfeild; under whom we find him, 9 June following, present (while in charge of a homeward-bound convoy, and in company with the CHARGER, PIERCER, and TURBULENT gun-brigs, the latter of which was captured) in a very severe running action of four hours with 25 Danish gun-boats off the island of Saltholm. Being confirmed a Lieutenant, 8 Nov. in the same year, in the ORION 74, Capt. Sir Arch. Dickson, he sailed in the year following with the armament destined to act against Flushing, during the operations against which place he was intrusted with the charge of an armed brig. In Sept. 1809, on the application of Rear-Admiral Stopford, he was appointed to that officer's flag-ship, the SCIPION 74; and in Jan. 1812, after having co-operated in the reduction of Java, he was selected to officiate as his Flag-Lieutenant; a post which, on the eve of the SCIPION's return from the Cape of Good Hope to England, he was induced by the Admiral to resign for the purpose of effecting the advancement of a near connexion of the latter, a Midshipman, but upon the understanding that it was not to interfere with his promotion on the flag being hauled down. He was doomed, however, to disappointment. He served from 1813 to 1815 in the PRESIDENT 38, Capts. Sam. Warren, Fras. Mason, and Arch. Duff; and has since been on half-pay. Under Capt. Mason he was employed on shore in the batteries at the siege of St. Sebastian. He accepted his present rank 27 Jan. 1846.

Commander Pearson married, in 1831, a niece of Col. Knight, of Coolrass, co. Limerick, and has issue three children. AGENTS—Hallett and Robinson.

PEARSON. (LIEUTENANT, 1832.)

CHARLES PEARSON (*b*) entered the Navy 31 July, 1819; passed his examination in 1829; and obtained his commission 31 July, 1832. His appointments have since been—28 Dec. 1833 and 20 Aug. 1834, to the ENDYMION 50 and BRITANNIA 120, Capts. Sir Sam. Roberts and Peter Rainier, both in the Mediterranean, whence he returned home and was paid off in the early part of 1835—12 Sept. in the latter year, to the HOWE 120, flag-ship at the Nore of Hon. Chas. Elphinstone Fleeming—and, 6 Jan. 1837, to the Coast Guard, in which service he continues.

He married, 31 Oct. 1835, Emma, third daughter of Wm. Rowes, Esq., of Elm Grove, Southsea, formerly Assistant Master-Attendant of Portsmouth Dockyard. AGENTS—Messrs. Stilwell.

PEARSON. (LIEUT., 1815. F-P., 32; H-P., 8.)

THOMAS PEARSON was born 8 Dec. 1792.

This officer entered the Navy, 9 April, 1807, as Fst.-cl. Vol., on board the ALFRED 74, Capts. John Bligh, John Hayes, and Joshua Rowley Watson; removed as Midshipman, in Oct. 1809, to the NARCISSUS 32, Capt. Hon. Fred. Wm. Aylmer; and from March, 1812, to Aug. 1815, was employed in the ROYAL SOVEREIGN 100, Capts. Wm. Bedford and Jas. Bissett, TELEGRAPH 12, Capt. Timothy Scriven, CLARENCE 74, Capt. Fred. Warren, and TAY 24, Capts. Wm. Robilliard and Robt. Bloye. While in the ALFRED he accompanied Admiral Gambier in the expedition to Copenhagen, served under Sir Chas. Cotton at the blockade of the Russian squadron in the TAGUS prior to the convention of Cintra, landed and assisted in taking possession of the town of Figueira, and aided in disembarking the army under Sir Arthur Wellesley in Mondego Bay. Being lent, in 1809, to the SAN DOMINGO 74, flag-ship of Sir Rich. Strachan, he took part in the reduction of Flushing, and was employed in a gun-boat during the after-operations in the Scheldt. In the NARCISSUS, in 1810, Mr. Pearson, besides witnessing the capture of two privateers carrying between them 28 guns and 180 men, was engaged in active co-operation with the patriots on the north coast of Spain. He afterwards, in the same ship, visited the latitude of Greenland. In the ROYAL SOVEREIGN he was for nearly sixteen months stationed in Basque Roads; and in the TELEGRAPH he was also employed on the coast of France, where he cut out a great number of the enemy's vessels, and on 13 Oct. 1813, shared, in sight of the French and British armies, and under the fire of some batteries in the neighbourhood of Bayonne, in a spirited action of 15 minutes with the French corvette *Flibustier* of 16 guns, whose crew, after having effectively set her on fire, took to their boats and escaped. Within view of the TELEGRAPH were the 18-gun sloop CHALLENGER and 12-gun brig CONSTANT. On leaving the TAY in Aug. 1815, Mr. Pearson, whose zeal and good conduct in the action had gained him the official thanks of his Captain,* took up a commission bearing date 27 Feb. in that year. He has been in command, since 2 Dec. 1823, of a station in the Coast Guard, and has rendered much valuable service to the revenue.

Lieut. Pearson has been twice married, the first time in Sept. 1819, the second in Aug. 1842. By his former marriage he has issue nine children.

PEAT. (CAPTAIN, 1847. F-P., 21; H-P., 16.)

DAVID PEAT was born 21 June, 1795, at Kirkaldy, in Scotland.

This officer entered the Navy, 2 April, 1810, under the auspices of the late Admiral Sir Philip Durham, as L.M., on board the ARCHER gun-brig,

* *Vide* Gaz. 1813, p. 2205.

Lieut.-Commanders Lawrence Smith, Michael Fitton, Jas. Lindsay, and Wm. Carnegie. After sharing, as Midshipman, in an affair with some Danish gun-boats, he removed, in Jan. 1812, to the MOSQUITO sloop, in which vessel, commanded by Capts. Christopher Bell and Jas. Tomkinson, he came into frequent contact with the enemy's batteries and made a voyage to the West Indies and Brazil. In Sept. 1814 (he had been employed during the three preceding months in the DUNIRA 18, Capt. Edw. Boys, on the Leeward Island station) he again joined Lieut. Fitton on board the CRACKER gun-brig: he served next, from the following Dec. until June, 1816, in the Mediterranean, on board the AJAX 74, Capt. Geo. Mundy; and, in the ensuing Oct. and May, he became attached to the GANYMEDE 26 and SEVERN 40, both commanded by Capt. Wm. M'Culloch. While engaged in the two latter ships in the Coast Blockade, on which service he was the first officer ever sent, he encountered several desperate affrays with the Deal smugglers, and gave occasion for so many letters of approbation from the Admiralty and his various superiors that he was advanced to the rank of Lieutenant 24 Nov. 1817. Being re-appointed to the SEVERN in June, 1818, he was stationed by Capt. M'Culloch at Dungeness, where, among other affairs with illicit traders in which life was lost, he was once attacked singly, in open day, by three desperadoes, against whom he successfully defended himself, killing one on the spot, and, although possessed of no weapon but his regulation-sword, compelling the remainder to fly. While employed next at Folkstone he received two pistol-balls on one occasion through his thigh; and on another, 9 June, 1821, when on the cliffs to the eastward with only three men, he was attacked by a numerous gang of ruffians, not less than 60 of whom were armed. In the unequal conflict that ensued he received two musket-balls, six pistol-balls, and ten slugs; one of his small party, a quartermaster, was shot through in five places, and fell dead at his side; and the other two were also brought to the ground, the one by a ball in the groin, the second by a shot in the knee. For his conduct and sufferings Lieut. Peat was advanced to the rank of Commander by commission bearing date the day of the occurrence; and awarded, 29 July, 1822, a pension of 91*l*. 5*s*. per annum. He was afterwards employed as an Inspecting Commander in the Coast Guard, from 5 July, 1836, until 1839, and again from 30 March, 1840, until promoted to his present rank, 1 Jan. 1847. AGENTS—Hallett and Robinson.

PEAT. (LIEUTENANT, 1815. F-P., 10; H-P., 32.)

JOHN GREEN PEAT was born 1 Nov. 1789.

This officer entered the Navy, 29 Nov. 1805, as Fst.-cl. Vol., on board the FAME 74, Capts. Graham Moore, Rich. Henry Alex. Bennett, Phipps Hornby, and Abel Ferris, employed at first off Rochefort and afterwards in the Mediterranean; where, in Nov. 1810 and March, 1811, he became in succession Midshipman (a rating he had attained in July, 1806) of the SALSETTE frigate, Capt. John Hollinworth, and PYLADES 18, Capt. Geo. Ferguson. In March, 1813, after he had been for eight months borne as a Supernumerary on the books of the ROYAL WILLIAM, flag-ship at Spithead of Sir Rich. Bickerton, he joined the SAN DOMINGO 74, bearing the flag of Sir John Borlase Warren in North America; on which station, with the exception of an interval of six months occasioned by ill health, he continued employed as Master's Mate in the DIADEM 64, Capt. John Martin Hanchett, until nominated, 24 Sept. 1814, Acting-Master of the WOLVERENE 16, Capt. Geo. Guy Burton. On his return home from the West Indies, for the purpose of being paid off, in Aug. 1815, he found that he had been advanced to the rank of Lieutenant by commission bearing date 17 March in that year. He has since been on half-pay. AGENTS—Messrs. Ommanney.

PECHELL. (LIEUTENANT, 1844.)

CHARLES PECHELL is son of Capt. Sam. Geo. Pechell, R.N. (1810), who commanded the CLORINDE 40 in attendance upon the unfortunate consort of George IV. during her visit to the Mediterranean in 1815-16, and died 30 Dec. 1840, by Caroline, second daughter of Wm. Thoyts, Esq., of Sulhampstead House, Herts. His grandfather, Augustus Pechell, Receiver-General of the Post Office in 1785, and of the Customs in 1790, was uncle of the present Rear-Admiral Sir Sam. John Brooke Pechell, Bart., C.B., K.C.H., and also of Capt. Geo. Rich. Pechell, R.N., M.P.

This officer entered the Navy in 1833; passed his examination 14 Aug. 1840; served as Mate on the East India, North America and West India, and Home stations in the CONWAY 26, Capt. Chas. Ramsay Drinkwater Bethune, PIQUE 36, Capt. Hon. Montagu Stopford, and EXCELLENT gunnery-ship, Capt. Sir Thos. Hastings; obtained his commission 5 Dec. 1844; and from 27 of that month until paid off at the commencement of 1848 was employed, again in North America and the West Indies, on board the PERSIAN 16, Capt. Henry Coryton.

PECHELL, M.P. (CAPTAIN, 1822. F-P., 15; H-P., 29.)

GEORGE RICHARD PECHELL, born 30 June, 1789, is brother of Rear-Admiral Sir Sam. John Brooke Pechell, Bart., C.B., K.C.H.

This officer entered the Navy, in Sept. 1803, as Sec.-cl. Vol., on board the NEMESIS 28, Capt. Philip Somerville, lying at Weymouth; and in March, 1804, removed to the TRIUMPH 74, Capt. Sir Robt. Barlow, part of the force stationed under Lord Nelson at the blockade of Toulon. While attached next, between Sept. in the latter year and July, 1808, to the MEDUSA 32 and REVENGE 74, both commanded by Sir John Gore, he went through much active service. In the former ship he contributed to the capture of three Spanish frigates laden with treasure, and the destruction of a fourth, near Cape St. Mary, 5 Oct. 1804; as also to the detention, in the ensuing Nov., of the *Matilda* 36, a ship laden with a cargo of quicksilver worth 200,000*l*. In the early part of 1805 we find the MEDUSA conveying the Marquis Cornwallis as Governor-General to India, whence she effected her passage home, a distance of 13,831 miles, in the extraordinarily short period of 82 days. During his servitude in the REVENGE Mr. Pechell was employed off Brest and L'Orient, and for nine months at the blockade of Rochefort, where he witnessed, 25 Sept. 1806, the capture of four French frigates by a squadron under the orders of Sir Sam. Hood. On the return of the REVENGE to England with the Commissioners appointed by the Supreme Council of Seville to treat with the British Cabinet he removed (he had been engaged for the long period of 18 months blockading the port of Cadiz) to the VENUS 32, Capt. Jas. Coutts Crawford, under whom, while co-operating with the Spanish patriots, and performing the duties of Lieutenant, he landed, in March, 1809, and took possession of the citadel of Vigo, in which he continued until the besieging enemy was defeated at the bridge of San Payo, and obliged to retreat towards Lugo. In the course of the same year Mr. Pechell was received, on promotion, on board the BARFLEUR 98, flag-ship of Hon. Geo. Cranfield Berkeley in the river Tagus, where he was confirmed a Lieutenant, 25 June, 1810, in the CÆSAR 80, Capt. Wm. Granger. Being next, 3 July, 1811, appointed to the MACEDONIAN 38, Capt. John Surman Carden, he proceeded in that ship on special service to the United States, and on his return was attached to the blockading force off Rochefort under Rear-Admiral Philip Chas. Durham. While stationed there he assisted in destroying the enemy's coasting-trade, in face of many startling difficulties; and on one occasion, 7 Aug. 1812, captured a French lugger lying aground within musket-shot of the formidable batteries of La Rochelle, an exploit which was communicated to the squadron by the following telegraphic message:—

"*None killed; drove on shore by ship last night, and gallantly brought from under batteries by Lieut. Pechell.*" On 25 Dec. 1812, five months after he had joined the San Domingo 74, flag-ship of his uncle Sir John Borlase Warren, Mr. Pechell was placed in temporary command of the Colibri brig, in which vessel he cruized until the following Feb. off New York, and aided in making a number of prizes. He then returned to the San Domingo; and in May of the same year (1813) was placed in acting-command of the Recruit, another sloop, carrying 18 guns, with a crew reduced by sickness to only 80 men. Continuing in that vessel until confirmed in the rank of Commander 30 May, 1814, he contrived, notwithstanding, to capture and destroy a great variety of vessels, including the *Inca* American letter-of-marque of 6 guns and 35 men, which was driven on shore in the neighbourhood of Charleston 2 Nov. 1813. Capt. Pechell's next appointment was, 26 May, 1818, to the Bellette 18, fitting for the Halifax station, where he was actively employed in enforcing the stipulations of the treaty of Ghent in regard to the fisheries and trade of Nova Scotia and New Brunswick, a service which occasioned his obtaining possession of about 20 vessels of different descriptions. In Oct. 1820 he received directions from Rear-Admiral Griffith to assume command of the Tamar 26, which ship had just arrived from Jamaica with scarcely a sufficent number of men on board to navigate her even in the finest weather; her Captain, Arthur Stow, and 75 of her crew having died since her departure from the West Indies. This appointment gave rise to an official correspondence, which terminated in the Admiralty superseding all the officers whom the Commanders-in-Chief on the Halifax and Jamaica stations, each claiming the patronage, had intended to raise to superior ranks. Capt. Pechell was in consequence under the necessity of returning to the Bellette. During six months, however, that he had had command of the Tamar he had succeeded in obtaining the authority of the Haytian Government for putting a stop to the numerous acts of piracy which had been recently committed between Jamaica and St. Domingo; and had procured an order to the Commandants of the several ports in Hayti to permit the Tamar to search every suspected vessel;* in the execution of which service, although with not more that 80 men on board, he had fallen in with and captured, after a long chase in the Mona Passage, a large brigantine pierced for 20 guns, with forged commissions from the different independent states of South America, and a crew of 98 men, desperadoes of every nation. On his passage in the Speedy schooner to rejoin the Bellette at Bermuda, we may here mention that Capt. Pechell encountered off the east end of the island of Cuba a squadron of four large piratical vessels, from under whose broadsides the schooner fortunately escaped with very little damage. The Bellette returned to England and was paid off about Christmas 1821; and on 26 Dec. 1822 Capt. Pechell was advanced to Post-rank. He has since been on half-pay.

In July, 1830, Capt. Pechell was nominated Gentleman Usher of the Privy Chamber, and in April, 1831, Equerry, to Queen Adelaide. In July, 1837, he was gazetted as one of the Grooms-in-Waiting to Her present Majesty; but this appointment his sense of duty to the Queen Dowager induced him to decline. He has acted, since 1827, as a Magistrate for co. Sussex; and has sat in Parliament, since Jan. 1835, as Member for Brighton. In the latter capacity, on subjects connected with the Navy, Capt. Pechell has ever steered a zealous, straightforward, and independent course, and has at all times proved the unbending advocate of those classes and individuals in it whose grievances have appeared to demand his attention. We would gladly, had we space, afford our readers a sketch of his political career; as it is, we must be contented with alluding to his exertions during the sessions of 1838, 1840, and 1842, in obtaining the introduction (into Acts 1 and 2 Vict. cap. 47, 3 and 4 Vict. cap. 67, and 5 and 6 Vict., relating to the abolition of the traffic in slaves) of the several clauses for granting bounty on the tonnage of vessels captured; for the abolition of all Treasury and Exchequer fees on bounties for slaves and for tonnage of vessels; and for providing for the payment of the net proceeds of vessels and cargoes to the Captain, instead of the moiety of the same. In the session of 1836, we may add, he carried a bill through the House for the preservation of the brood of fish and the better regulation of the Channel fisheries; and in the session of 1839 he successfully contended for the restoration of the Good-Service Pension to those officers who had been deprived of it on their appointment to a ship; as he also did for the allowance of half-pay to the Lieut.-Governor of Greenwich Hospital, which had been withheld from him, although enjoyed by the Governor of Greenwich, the officers of Chelsea, and the Lords of the Admiralty. Through his exertions Capt. Pechell proved of material assistance to Lord Palmerston in obtaining from France, by a Special Convention, the recognition of the claims of Great Britain to an exclusive right of fishing within three miles of her own shores—a right which had been in dispute for upwards of a century; and in providing against the recurrence of those collisions between the French and English fishermen which had led to such serious consequences. Capt. Pechell married, 1 Aug. 1826, the Hon. Katherine Annabella Bisshopp, daughter (and co-heiress with her sister, the present Baroness De la Zouche) of the late Lord De la Zouche, by whom he has issue a son and two daughters. Agents—Messrs. Burnett and Holmes.

* See 'Narrative of a Visit to the Island of St. Domingo,' published by Capt. Pechell in 1824.

PECHELL, Bart., C.B., K.C.H., F.R.S. (Rear-Admiral of the White, 1846. f-p., 21; h-p., 30.)

Sir Samuel John Brooke Pechell, born 1 Sept. 1785, is eldest son of the late Major-General Sir Thos. Brooke Pechell, Bart., M.P. for Downton, in Wiltshire, and a Gentleman of the Privy Chamber to the consort of George III., by Charlotte, second daughter of Lieut.-General Sir John Clavering, Bart., K.B., who died Commander-in-Chief in India. He is brother of the present Capt. G. R. Pechell, R.N.; grandson of Lieut.-Colonel Sir Paul Pechell, who was created a Baronet for his services 1 May, 1797; great-grandson of John, first Earl of Delawarr; nephew of Admiral Sir John Borlase Warren, Bart., G.C.B., who died 27 Feb. 1822; and first-cousin of the late Capt. Sam. Geo. Pechell, R.N. His grand-uncle, Geo. Pechell, a Lieutenant in the Royal Marines, was killed in Carthagena. Sir Samuel succeeded his father as third Baronet 18 June, 1826.

This officer entered the Navy, in July, 1796, as Fst.-cl. Vol., on board La Pomone 40, commanded by his relative Sir John Borlase Warren; and, from Aug. 1797 until nominated, 28 Feb. 1803, Acting-Lieutenant of the Active 38, Capts. Chas. Sidney Davers and Rich. Hussey Moubray, was employed as Midshipman and Master's Mate, under the late Sir Robt. Barlow, in the Phœbe 44 and Triumph 74. In La Pomone he saw much service on the coast of France; and in the Phœbe he assisted at the capture of two French frigates (*La Néréide* of 36 guns and 330 men, and *L'Africaine* of 44 guns and 715 men, including 400 troops and artificers), one large corvette, *L'Heureux*, of 22 guns and 220 men, three privateers, carrying in the whole 58 guns and 455 men, and a letter-of-marque, *L'Hazard*, of 10 guns and 60 men, laden with spices, ivory, and gum, from Senegal, valued at 10,000*l.* *La Néréide* did not surrender until after a close action of 45 minutes, productive of a loss to herself of 20 killed and 55 wounded, and to the British, out of 261 men, of 3 killed and 10 wounded; and the resistance of *L'Africaine* was protracted until, in the course of a desperate night action of two hours, she had sustained (although the Phœbe, out of 239 men, had but 1 killed and 12 wounded) the terrific loss of at least 200 killed and 143 wounded, the greater part of them mortally. For his gallantry in the latter exploit, which was achieved 19 Feb. 1801, Capt. Barlow was rewarded with the honour of knighthood. On leaving the ACTIVE, to which frigate, employed on the Mediterranean, North Sea, and Cork stations, he had been confirmed 1 April, 1803, Mr. Pechell, in Jan. 1806, joined the FOUDROYANT 80, bearing the flag at the time of Sir J. B. Warren, under whom we find him, on 13 of the following March, witnessing the capture of the *Marengo* 80, bearing the flag of Rear-Admiral Linois, and 40-gun frigate *Belle Poule.* He was made Commander, 23 March, 1807, into the FERRET sloop-of-war on the Jamaica station; was advanced to Post-rank in the CLEOPATRA of 38 guns, at Halifax, 16 June, 1808; and was subsequently appointed—25 Sept. 1810, to the GUERRIÈRE of 48 guns, also on the Halifax station—in July, 1811, again to the CLEOPATRA, employed off Cherbourg, in the North Sea, and at Gibraltar—20 Oct. 1812, to the SAN DOMINGO 74, bearing the flag of Sir J. B. Warren in North America, where he remained until Aug. 1814—and, 1 July, 1823, to the SYBILLE 48, stationed at first in the West Indies and afterwards in the Mediterranean. In the CLEOPATRA Capt. Pechell, on being sent to the West Indies, fought, 22 Jan. 1809, a close action of 40 minutes, reflective of credit on his intrepidity and judgment, as well as on the high discipline and steadiness of his crew, with the French frigate *La Topaze*, of 48 guns, anchored, with springs on her cable, under a small battery to the southward of Pointe-Noire, Guadeloupe. At the expiration of 50 minutes from the commencement of the conflict, the JASON 32 and HAZARD 18 having come up, the enemy surrendered. The CLEOPATRA, the only British ship that suffered loss, had 2 seamen killed and 1 wounded; the *Topaze*, on the other hand, out of a complement, including 100 soldiers, of about 430 men, incurred a loss of 12 men killed and 14 wounded. She had on board 1100 barrels of flour.* As a mark of the sense entertained by the Admiralty of the CLEOPATRA's conduct, her First-Lieutenant, Mr. Wm. Simpson, was promoted to the rank of Commander. A few days after the exploit Capt. Pechell, although still belonging to the Halifax squadron, joined the expedition proceeding against Martinique, during the siege of which island he distinguished himself by working into Fort Royal Bay, previously to the surrender of Pigeon Island; thereby cutting off the retreat of the enemy, and compelling them to destroy all the shipping at that anchorage; among which was the *Amphitrite*, another frigate of the largest class. When subsequently in the same ship on the Gibraltar station Capt. Pechell made a survey of the harbour of Ceuta, and drew up a plan of the fortifications, together with remarks on the navigation of the Gut. In June, 1813, being then in the SAN DOMINGO, and under the immediate orders of Rear-Admiral Cockburn, we find him uniting in the attack on Crany Island and the destruction of the enemy's camp at Hampton; on which latter occasion he commanded the boats and tenders detached to cover the landing of the troops under Sir Sydney Beckwith.† During his command of the SYBILLE Capt. Pechell was actively employed in the suppression of piracy and the protection of the Ionian Islands for a period of three years, during which his boats were frequently involved in sanguinary actions with the freebooters. The judgment, firmness, and promptitude with which he discharged a delicate and important duty confided to him, pending a serious discussion which took place in 1824 with the Greek government, had the effect of procuring him the congratulations of his Commander-in-Chief, Vice-Admiral Sir Harry Burrard Neale, and a strong expression of approbation on the part of Earl Bathurst, H.M. Secretary of State for Foreign Affairs, and the Lords of the Admiralty. He paid the SYBILLE off in Nov. 1826; and has since been on half-pay. He attained Flag-rank 9 Nov. 1846.

Sir Sam. John Brooke Pechell was nominated a C.B. 4 June, 1815, and a K.C.H. 6 Jan. 1833. He sat in Parliament for Hallestone in 1830, and for Windsor in 1833; was a Lord of the Admiralty from 1830 until 1834, and again from 1839 until 1841; and from 1831 until 1846 filled the post of Naval Aide-de-Camp to his late and her present Majesty. Sir John, who bears a high reputation for his thorough knowledge of the art of naval gunnery, is the author of a valuable pamphlet on the subject (the first edition of which was published in 1812, the second in 1824, and the third in 1828), entitled 'Observations upon the Defective Equipment of Ships' Guns.' He married, 15 April, 1833, Julia Maria, only surviving daughter of Robt. Edw., ninth Lord Petre, and was left a widower 6 Sept. 1844.

* *Vide* Gaz. 1809, p. 403. † *V.* Gaz. 1813, p. 1576.

PEDDER. (LIEUT., 1809. F-P., 14; H-P., 33.)

GEORGE MURRAY M'KINLEY PEDDER died 26 Aug. 1847, at St. Simon's Bay, Simon's Town, Cape of Good Hope.

This officer entered the Navy, in Jan. 1800, as Fst.-cl. Vol., on board the ACHILLE 74, Capt. Geo. Murray, with whom he continued employed on the Home and Baltic stations as Midshipman in the EDGAR 74, part of Lord Nelson's fleet in the action off Copenhagen, and LONDON 98, until transferred, in May, 1802, to the PENELOPE 36, Capt. Wm. Robt. Broughton. In Sept. 1804, on his return from a voyage to the Mediterranean, he joined the MONMOUTH 64, bearing the flag at North Yarmouth of Rear-Admiral Thos. Macnamara Russell. He next, in April, 1805, sailed in the BLENHEIM 74, flag-ship of Sir Thos. Troubridge, for the East Indies; where, on 1 April, 1806, he was nominated Acting-Lieutenant of the CAROLINE of 42 guns, Capt. Peter Rainier. In that ship, on 18 Oct. 1806, he contributed, in a manner that won his Captain's highest approbation, to the capture, near the island of Java, of the Dutch 14-gun brig *Zeerop*, and, in the course of the same day, after an action of half an hour, of the *Maria-Riggersbergen* of 40 guns and 270 men, 50 of whom were killed and wounded, with a loss to the CAROLINE, out of 204 men, of 3 killed and 18 wounded. In company with the *Maria-Riggersbergen* were the *William* 14, *Patriot* 18, and *Zee-Ploeg* 14, together with some gun-boats who partially assisted her; 30 other gun-boats lay in-shore, but did not attempt to come out.* On 27 Jan. 1807 Mr. Pedder was further present at the capture of the *St. Raphael* Spanish register-ship, mounting 16 guns, with a complement of 97 men, having on board 500,000 dollars in specie, and 1700 quintals of copper, besides a valuable cargo. In securing this rich prize the CAROLINE had 7 men wounded; the enemy's vessel, before she surrendered, incurred a loss of 27 killed and wounded. Mr. Pedder was confirmed a Lieutenant 30 Sept. 1809, and was subsequently, until Aug. 1813, employed in the GANGES 74, Capts. Peter Halkett and Geo. Dundas, ARGO 44, Capts. Fred. Warren and Cornelius Quinton, and NIEMEN 38, Capt. Sam. Pym, on the Baltic, Lisbon, Mediterranean, and Cape of Good Hope stations. At the period of his death he was Port-Captain at St. Simon's Bay.

PEDDER. (LIEUTENANT, 1824.)

WILLIAM PEDDER entered the Navy 5 April, 1814; obtained his commission 21 June, 1824; held an appointment in the Coast Guard from 28 Oct. 1834 until the early part of 1839; and, as second in command of the Hon. E. I. Company's war-steamer *Nemesis*, participated in the China services detailed in our memoir of Capt. Wm. Hutcheon Hall. At the storming, 27 Feb. 1841, of the enemy's works at their position below Whampoa Reach, he formed one of the landing party;† and for the able and gallant manner in which he supported the boats during the expedition up the inner passage to Canton he obtained the thanks of

* *Vide* Gaz. 1808, p. 569. † *V.* Gaz. 1841, p. 1501.

Capt. Jas. Scott.* He was appointed Harbour-Master at Hong Kong 9 Feb. 1844.

He is married and has issue.

PEDLAR. (COMMANDER, 1814. F-P., 18; H-P., 35.)

GEORGE PEDLAR entered the Navy, in April, 1794, as Sec.-cl. Boy, on board L'ESPION 18, Capt. Wm. Hugh Kiltoe; and on 22 of the following July was captured off Falmouth by a squadron of French frigates. Being restored to liberty by exchange in Nov. 1795, he again, in Jan. 1796, embarked on board the KINGFISHER 18, Capts. Edw. Marsh, John Bligh, Hon. Chas. Herbert Pierrepont, and Fred. Lewis Maitland; in which vessel, prior to being wrecked on the bar of Lisbon in Dec. 1798, he assisted in making prize of the *Betsey* French privateer, of 16 guns and 118 men, after a very creditable action productive of a loss to the enemy of 1 man killed and 8 wounded, and to the British of only 1 man, out of 120, slightly wounded. Being received next, as Master's Mate, on board the SPEEDY, of 14 guns and 60 men, Capt. Jahleel Brenton, he was present in that vessel, 6 Nov. 1799, when she singly defeated, near Gibraltar, and put to flight two Spanish schooners, each carrying 2 long 24-pounders and 50 men; 10 other vessels of 1 24-pounder and 40 men each; and a French xebec privateer, of 8 guns. In April, 1800, Mr. Pedlar followed Capt. Brenton into the GÉNÉREUX 74. After the surrender of Genoa he rejoined Capt. Maitland on board the CAMELION sloop, commanded subsequently by Capt. Edw. O'Bryen. On 20 March, 1801, having assisted at the debarkation of the troops in Aboukir Bay, he removed on promotion to the FOUDROYANT 80, flag-ship of Lord Keith, by whom he was nominated, 16 Aug. 1801, Acting-Lieutenant of the MUTINE 18, Capts. Wm. Hoste and Lord Wm. FitzRoy. He was confirmed a Lieutenant 7 Jan. 1802; and was subsequently appointed—1 March, 1802, to the LOIRE 38, Capt. F. L. Maitland—11 Nov. 1803, again to the FOUDROYANT, bearing the flag of Sir Thos. Graves in the Channel—26 March, 1806, to the BRILLIANT 28, Capts. Robt. Barrie, Rich. Budd Vincent, and Thos. Smyth, from which vessel, employed on the Cork and Channel stations, he invalided in Dec. 1808—and, 18 Aug. 1812, and 12 April, 1813, as First, to the GRAMPUS 50 and DRAGON 74, both commanded by Capt. Robt. Barrie, with whom he visited Cadiz, the West Indies, and North America. While in the last-mentioned ship he witnessed the surrender of the town of Castine, and was in meritorious command of the boats of a squadron employed up the Penobscot at the taking of Hamden and Bangor, and the destruction, by the enemy, of the U.S. corvette *Adams*, a brig pierced for 18 guns, a large privateer, and eight merchant-vessels.† On a previous occasion, 5 Nov. 1813, with the boats of the DRAGON and SOPHIE under his orders, he had brought three American vessels out from a creek in the river Potomac.‡ He went on half-pay in April, 1815, having been rewarded for his services with a Commander's commission bearing date 12 Oct. 1814; and has not been since able to procure employment.

He married, in 1811, a daughter of Addis Archer, Esq., of Leigham, by whom he has an only son in Holy Orders. AGENTS—Messrs. Stilwell.

PEEL. (COMMANDER, 1841.)

EDMUND PEEL is second son of Edmund Peel, Esq., of Church Bank, Lancashire. His paternal and maternal grandfathers, Wm. Peel, Esq., of Church Bank and Peel Fold, and Jonathan Peel, Esq., of Accrington, were brothers of the late Sir Robt. Peel, Bart., and uncles of the present Right Hon. Sir R. Peel, Bart., M.P.

This officer entered the Navy, 3 March, 1814; obtained his first commission 21 Dec. 1824; and was subsequently appointed—4 March, 1825, for a short time, to the FLY 18, Capt. Lord Wm. Paget, on the South American station—8 Jan. 1829, to the GALATEA 42, Capt. Chas. Napier, under whom he was for two years and a half employed on particular service—and, 25 Oct. 1841, as First-Lieutenant, to the VOLAGE 26, Capt. Sir Wm. Dickson, fitting for North America and the West Indies. He was promoted to the command, 21 Dec. following, of the RACEHORSE 18, on the latter station, whence he returned at the close of 1842; and he afterwards, from 1 July, 1843, until paid off in 1845, commanded the BITTERN 16, at the Cape of Good Hope.

Commander Peel married, in Dec. 1832, Lucy, daughter of Rich. Meek, Esq., of Fetlow Fold. AGENT—W. H. B. Barwis.

PEEL. (COMMANDER, 1846. F-P., 9; H-P., 0.)

WILLIAM PEEL, born 2 Nov. 1824, is third son of the Right Hon. Sir Robt. Peel, Bart., M.P., by Julia, youngest daughter of General Sir John Floyd, Bart.

This officer entered the Navy, 7 April, 1838, as Midshipman, on board the PRINCESS CHARLOTTE 104, Capt. Arthur Fanshawe, bearing the flag in the Mediterranean of Hon. Sir Robt. Stopford, under whom, in Nov. 1840, he witnessed the fall of St. Jean d'Acre. Towards the close of 1841, after having been further employed on the Mediterranean station in the MONARCH 84, Capt. Sam. Chambers, he successively joined the WILLIAM AND MARY yacht, Capt. Phipps Hornby, and CAMBRIAN 36; in which latter ship, commanded by Capt. Henry Ducie Chads, we find him, until April, 1843, attached to the force in China. On his return home in the following Sept. in the BELLEISLE troop-ship, Capt. John Kingcome, he was received on board the CAMPERDOWN 104, bearing the flag of Sir Edw. Brace at the Nore; and in the following Nov. he joined the EXCELLENT gunnery-ship at Portsmouth, Capt. Sir Thos. Hastings. On 13 May, 1844, a week after he had passed his examination—an examination so brilliant that it called forth a public eulogium of Sir Thos. Hastings, and a very flattering notice from Sir Chas. Napier in the House of Commons—Mr. Peel was promoted to the rank of Lieutenant. His succeeding appointments appear to have been—15 May, 1844, to the WINCHESTER 50, flag-ship of Hon. Josceline Percy at the Cape of Good Hope—13 June following, as Additional, to the CORMORANT steam-sloop, Capt. Geo. Thos. Gordon, in the Pacific—29 Aug. in the same year, to the THALIA 42, Capt. Chas. Hope, similarly stationed—next, we believe, to the AMERICA 50, Capt. Hon. John Gordon, by whom he was sent in charge of dispatches from San Blas to Vera Cruz—27 Feb. 1846, after a brief interval of half-pay, to the DEVASTATION steam-sloop, Capt. Edw. Crouch, equipping at Woolwich—and, 15 May ensuing, to the CONSTANCE 50, Capt. Sir Baldwin Wake Walker, lying at Devonport. He attained his present rank 27 June, 1846; and, since 11 Feb. 1847, has been in command of the DARING 12, on the North America and West India station.

PEIRSE. (COMMANDER, 1842.)

EDWARD PEIRSE entered the Navy 24 April, 1827; passed his examination in 1833; obtained his first commission 22 April, 1834; and was subsequently appointed—24 May, 1834, to the SPARTIATE 76, flag-ship of Sir Graham Eden Hamond in South America—6 March, 1835, to the DUBLIN 50, Capt. Chas. Hope, lying at Plymouth—21 Sept. 1835, to the NIMROD 20, Capt. John Frazer, on the North America and West India station, where he became First-Lieutenant, and was superseded in Aug. 1836—14 Sept. 1837, for a short time, to the TYNE 28, Capt. John Townshend, equipping at Portsmouth—8 Oct. 1838, as Additional, to the STAG 46, bearing the broad pendant of Commodore Thos. Ball Sulivan in South America, whence he returned in the summer of 1839—and, 18 May, 1842, to the INDUS 78, Capt. Sir Jas. Stirling, in the Mediterranean. He acquired the rank of Commander 10 Nov. 1842; and since 12 Nov. 1846, has been serving in the East Indies in the CRUIZER 16 and NERBUDDA 12. His appointment to the latter vessel took place 27 Oct. 1847.

* *Vide* Gaz. 1841, p. 1509. † *V.* Gaz. 1814, p. 2031. ‡ *V.* Gaz. 1814, p. 232.

PELHAM. (CAPTAIN, 1840. F-P., 12; H-P., 10.)
THE HONOURABLE DUDLEY WORSLEY ANDERSON PELHAM, born 20 April, 1812, is second son of the late Earl of Yarborough, by Henrietta Anna Maria Charlotte, second daughter of Hon. John Bridgman Simpson, and granddaughter of Henry, first Baron Bradford. He is brother-in-law of Sir Joseph Wm. Copley, Bart.

This officer entered the Navy 4 Aug. 1825; served as Midshipman on board the DARTMOUTH 42, Capt. Thos. Fellowes, at the battle of Navarin, 20 Oct. 1827; obtained his first commission 28 Sept. 1831; and was subsequently appointed—17 Sept. 1832, to the CONWAY 28, Capt. Henry Eden, from which vessel, employed on particular service, he was superseded in Feb. 1833—7 Nov. in the latter year, to the BLONDE 46, Capt. Fras. Mason, fitting for South America—and, 21 Aug. 1835, to the JUPITER 38, Capt. Hon. Fred. Wm. Grey, under whom he accompanied Lord Auckland as Governor-General to India. Attaining the rank of Commander 15 Feb. 1836, he served in that capacity, from 21 Oct. 1837, until superseded in April, 1840, in the WASP 16, in the Mediterranean. He was advanced to the rank he now holds 26 Oct. 1840; and has since been on half-pay.

Capt. Pelham married, 15 Oct. 1839, Madalena, second daughter of Sir John Gordon Sinclair, Bart., Capt., R.N. AGENTS—Messrs. Ommanney.

PELHAM, K.S.F. (CAPTAIN, 1840. F-P., 15; H-P., 9.)
THE HONOURABLE FREDERICK THOMAS PELHAM, born 2 Aug. 1808, is second son of Thomas, second Earl of Chichester (who filled the office of Secretary to Lords Northington and Camden, when Lord-Lieutenants of Ireland, and was afterwards Secretary of State for the Home Department and Post-master-General) by Henrietta Juliana, daughter of Fras. Godolphin, fifth Duke of Leeds. His brother, the present Earl of Chichester, is married to a sister of the Earl of Cardigan.

This officer entered the Navy 27 June, 1823; and while attached, as Midshipman, to the SYBILLE 48, Capt. Sam. John Pechell, was present in 1826 in an attack on the pirates in the Grecian Archipelago. He passed his examination in 1829; acquired the rank of Lieutenant 22 Feb. 1830; served as First of the FERRET 10, Capt. Edw. Wodehouse, on the Mediterranean station, from 28 April following until paid off at the commencement of 1832; and between 2 May in the latter year and the date of his promotion to the rank of Commander, 21 Sept. 1835, was employed on the north coast of Spain in the CASTOR 36, Capt. Lord John Hay. For services performed while in command, from 17 Jan. 1837 until the autumn of 1838, of the TWEED 20, on the Lisbon station, Capt. Pelham was presented, 9 Aug. 1839, with the cross of San Fernando. He attained Post-rank 3 July, 1840; and since 24 May, 1847, has been in command, in the Mediterranean, of the ODIN steam-frigate, of 560 horse-power.

He married, in July, 1841, Ellen Kate, daughter of Rowland Mitchell, Esq., of Upper Harley Street, by whom he has issue. AGENT—Joseph Woodhead.

PELL, Kt. (CAPTAIN, 1813. F-P., 23; H-P., 25.)
SIR WATKIN OWEN PELL, born in 1788, is son of Sam. Pell, Esq., of Sywell Hall, co. Northampton, by the daughter of Owen Owen, Esq., of Llaneyher, co. Denbigh.

This officer entered the Navy, in April, 1799, as Fst.-cl. Vol., on board the LOIRE 38, Capt. Jas. Newman Newman; and on 6 Feb. 1800 was deprived of his left leg while assisting, in company with the DANAE 20, and FAIRY, HARPY, and RAILLEUR sloops, at the capture of the French 38-gun frigate *Pallas*, under the heavy fire of a battery on one of the Seven Islands.* Being in consequence obliged to leave his ship, he did not again go afloat until Jan. 1802. He then rejoined Capt. Newman, as Midshipman, on board the LOIRE; and on 11 Nov. 1806, after a servitude of four years and a half on the Home and West India stations in the ACASTA 40, Capt. Jas. Athol Wood, VETERAN 64, and VANGUARD 74, both commanded by Capt. J. N. Newman, POMPÉE 74, Capt. Rich. Dacres, and VIRGINIE 38, Capt. Edw. Brace, he was made Lieutenant into the MERCURY 28, Capts. Chas. Pelly, Jas. Alex. Gordon, and Hon. Henry Duncan, employed at first at Bermuda and Newfoundland, and afterwards in the Mediterranean. On 4 April, 1808, being then First of the MERCURY, we find him commanding the boats of that vessel, in company with those of the ALCESTE 38, under Lieut. Allen Stewart, at the capture of seven Spanish tartans under the very muzzles of the guns in the batteries at Rota, and in the presence of numerous armed barges and pinnaces sent from Cadiz to assist in their defence. The prizes had formed part of a fleet of merchantmen originally under the protection of 20 gun-boats, whom the MERCURY, with her consorts, the ALCESTE and GRASSHOPPER 18, had defeated in the teeth of 11 French and Spanish ships-of-the-line.* The next exploit recorded of Lieut. Pell was the capture by him in the boats, 1 April, 1809, of a Venetian gun-boat, *La Leda*, of 1 long 24-pounder and 6 large swivels, lying in the harbour of Rovigno, under a very heavy fire of great guns and musketry. "More bravery," says Capt. Duncan, "I do not think was ever displayed than by the officers, seamen, and marines employed on this occasion. They were commanded and led on in the most gallant manner by the First-Lieutenant, Watkin Owen Pell, who received two severe wounds in boarding, and has before lost a leg in the service of his country." The wounds alluded to were inflicted, as suggested, while Mr. Pell was endeavouring to get through *La Leda*'s boarding-nettings—he received the contents of a blunderbuss in his right hand and arm, and had them perforated by not less than seven balls. On the night of 7 Sept. 1809, being off the harbour of Barletta, he again took command of the boats of the MERCURY, and, in the most gallant style, boarded and carried, near that place, the French schooner-of-war *La Pugliése*, pierced for 10 guns, but carrying only 5 6-pounders and 2 18's, commanded by an *Enseigne de Vaisseau*, and having on board 31 out of a complement of 50 men, who were so prepared for the attack as to be able to fire twice before the boats got alongside.† "It gives me sincere pleasure," Capt. Duncan reports in his official account of the affair, "to add, that this service has been performed without a man being hurt on our side; and as, besides her own means of defence, the vessel was moored with eight cables inside, and almost touching a mole lined with musketry, and within musket-shot of a castle mounting 8 guns, and two armed feluccas, from under which fire she was towed without rudder or sails, I must principally attribute this good fortune to the judicious and prompt manner in which the attack was made, which strongly marks the judgment and gallantry of the First Lieutenant, Pell, who directed it." For his conduct on the two occasions last mentioned Lieut. Pell had the satisfaction of receiving the thanks of his Commander-in-Chief. In Aug. 1809 he was voted 80*l*. for the purchase of a sword by the Patriotic Society; he was subsequently presented with one by Capt. Duncan; and on 29 March, 1810, he was promoted to the rank of Commander. Being next, 22 Oct. 1810, appointed to the THUNDER bomb, Capt. Pell was in that vessel actively employed at the defence of Cadiz from 11 of the following month until 5 Dec. 1811. He was then detached, in company with the STATELY 64, DRUID frigate, and several gun-boats, to co-operate with the garrison of Tarifa, then besieged by 10,000 French troops under Marshal Victor. He afterwards resumed his former station before Catalina; and continued to protect Isla de Leon until the whole of the enemy's works were abandoned in

* *Vide* Gaz. 1800, p. 155, where he is styled, in error, "Watkins Oliver Pell."

* *Vide* Gaz. 1808, p. 570.

† *V.* Gaz. 1809, p. 2006.—Here again Mr. Pell is misnamed "Pall."

Aug. 1812. On 9 Oct. 1813, on her return from the coast of Valencia, and while proceeding from Portsmouth to Woolwich for the purpose of being paid off, the THUNDER was attacked and boarded by *Le Neptune* privateer, of 16 guns and 65 men; the enemy, however, were driven back, and their own vessel boarded in return and captured.* Capt. Pell's Post commission bears date 1 Nov. 1813. His succeeding appointments were—4 Oct. 1814, to the MENAI 24, in which vessel, prior to being paid off in Feb. 1817, he served on the Irish station, cruized with a small force under his orders in the Bay of Fundy, and was employed off the Chesapeake and in visiting different American ports—6 May, 1833, to the FORTE 44, fitting for the West Indies, where he had command of the Jamaica station from Dec. following until ordered home in March, 1837, a period rendered important by the emancipation of the slaves—1 Oct. 1840, to the HOWE 120, equipping for service in the Mediterranean—24 Aug. 1841, to the Superintendentship of Deptford Victualling Yard—next, to that of the Dockyard at Sheerness—and, 17 Dec. in the same year, 1841, to the command of the ROYAL SOVEREIGN yacht, and the office of Superintendent of Pembroke Dockyard. While in command of the FORTE, Capt. Pell had the honour of receiving on board Her present Majesty, then the Princess Victoria, together with the Duchess of Kent, and the Earls of Yarborough and Durham, and of making an excursion with them to view the Eddystone. He resigned his appointment at Pembroke on being appointed a Commissioner of Greenwich Hospital 18 Feb. 1845.

During his command of the THUNDER, Capt. Pell received the thanks of the Admiralty for his services at Cadiz and Tarifa, and also for the capture of *Le Neptune.* In Jan. 1813, the Duke of Wellington addressed a letter to Lord Melville, from which the following is an extract:—"I enclose a letter from General Cooke, in regard to the services of Capt. Pell of the THUNDER bomb during the late blockade of Cadiz. I assure your Lordship that when I was at Cadiz all descriptions of persons concurred in their praises of that officer, and of those under his command; and I therefore take the liberty of drawing your attention to his merits during a most harassing service of nearly three years' duration." In April, 1837, Capt. Pell received from Sir Herbert Taylor a notification of his late Majesty's intention of conferring upon him the honour of Knighthood and the insignia of a K.C.H. The King's illness and death prevented the royal wish from being carried into effect; but upon the accession of Queen Victoria to the throne, Capt. Pell had the gratification of being the first naval Knight created by her Majesty. The K.C.H. was also conferred upon him by the King of Hanover. Sir Watkin is in the receipt of a pension of 300*l.* per annum for the loss of his leg. AGENTS—Messrs. Stilwell.

PELLEW, Kt., C.B., K.C.H. (REAR-ADMIRAL OF THE BLUE, 1846. F-P., 18; H-P., 30.)

The HONOURABLE SIR FLEETWOOD BROUGHTON REYNOLDS PELLEW, born 13 Dec. 1789, is second son of the late Admiral Viscount Exmouth, G.C.B.,† by Susannah, second daughter of Jas. Frowde, Esq., of Knoyle, co. Wilts; brother of Pownoll Bastard, second Viscount, a Captain R.N. (1806), who died 2 Dec. 1833; and uncle of the present Peer. One of his sisters was the wife of the late Admiral Sir Lawrence Wm. Halsted, G.C.B.; and another of the late Capt. Rich. Haward, R.N. Sir Fleet-

* *Vide* Gaz. 1813, p. 2011.

† Lord Exmouth, originally Mr. Edward Pellew, was born at Dover 19 April, 1757. He entered the Navy in 1770 on board the JUNO frigate, Capt. Stott; served in the CARLETON schooner in the battle fought on Lake Chaplain 11 Oct. 1776; was present with General Burgoyne's army at the convention of Saratoga 17 Oct. 1777; obtained, soon afterwards, his first commission; and for his gallant conduct as senior of the APOLLO frigate, commanded by Capt. Philomen Pownoll, who was killed, in an action with a letter of marque of 32 guns, on the Flemish coast, was made Commander into the HAZARD sloop For services he performed on his removal to the PELICAN, another sloop, particularly in driving on shore several privateers inside the Ile de Bas, he was advanced to Post-rank 31 May, 1782. He afterwards commanded the ARTOIS 64, WINCHELSEA 32, SALISBURY 50, NYMPHE of 40 guns and 240 men, ARETHUSA of 44 guns and 277 men, INDEFATIGABLE 46, IMPÉTUEUX 74, and TONNANT 80. His valour in the NYMPHE, in effecting the capture, 18 June, 1793, of the *Cleopâtre* of 40 guns and 320 men, procured Capt. Pellew the honour of knighthood. In the ARETHUSA he occasionally commanded a squadron of frigates, and either took, or assisted in taking, among other vessels, *La Pomone* of 44 guns and 341 men, *Le Babet* of 22 guns and 178 men, *L'Engageante* of 38 guns and 300 men, *La Félicité*, alias *Volontaire*, of 40 guns and about 300 men, *L'Espion* and *Alert* corvettes of 18 guns and 140 men each, and *La Revolutionnaire* of 44 guns and 351 men. The wonderful heroism and humanity displayed by Sir Edward Pellew, when on shore at Plymouth at the commencement of 1796, in permitting himself to be hauled, during a violent storm, on board an Indiaman, which had been driven under the citadel, and was fast going to pieces, whereby he was enabled to send a hawser to the shore and save the crew, had the effect of obtaining for him the freedom of the borough of Plymouth, and the dignity of a Baronet of the United Kingdom During his command of the INDEFATIGABLE, Sir Edward was present at the capture or destruction of *La Volage* of 26 guns, *L'Unité* of 38 guns and 255 men, and *La Virginie* of 44 guns and 339 men; and on 13 Jan. 1797, participated, in company with the AMAZON 36, in a very gallant engagement with the French 74-gun ship *Les Droits de l'Homme*, which, together with the AMAZON, was in the end wrecked in Hodierne Bay. In the summer of 1800, Sir Edward Pellew, then in the IMPÉTUEUX, was sent with a squadron consisting of seven ships of the line, one of 50 guns, nine frigates, a sloop of war, and a cutter, having on board a detachment of troops under the command of Major-General Maitland, to co-operate with the French Royalists and Chouans, in Quiberon Bay and the Morbihan; and in the following autumn he accompanied Sir John Borlase Warren in an expedition against Ferrol. In 1801 he was nominated a Colonel of Marines, and in 1802 elected M.P. for Barnstaple in Devon. Attaining flag-rank in April, 1804, he proceeded in the course of the same year as Commander-in-Chief to the East Indies, where he succeeded in obliterating from the Indian seas the tricoloured flag of Holland, by destroying, first at Onrust, in Batavia Roads, the *Phœnix* frigate and several smaller vessels; and next, at Griessee, two 70's and one 68-gun ship, the *Revolutie*, *Pluto*, and *Kortenaar*. On 28 April, 1808, Sir Edward Pellew was advanced to the rank of Vice-Admiral, and in the following year he returned to England. He was next, in 1810, employed, with his flag in the CHRISTIAN VII. 80, in the blockade of Flushing. In April, 1811, he succeeded Sir Chas. Cotton in command of the Mediterranean Fleet; during his tenure of which he fought two partial actions with the Toulon fleet, 5 Nov. 1813 and 13 Feb. 1814, and proved a constant source of annoyance to the enemy. His flag during the period was flying in the CALEDONIA 120. On 1 June, 1814, as a reward for his long and valuable services, he was raised to the peerage, as Baron of Exmouth, of Cannonteign, co. Devon, and granted at the same time a pension of 2000*l.* per annum. On 4 of the following month he became an Admiral of the Blue; in Jan. 1815 a K.C.B; and in March, 1816, a G.C.B. On the escape of Buonaparte from Elba, his Lordship, with his flag in the BOYNE 98, was immediately ordered back to the Mediterranean, where he materially contributed to the restoration of the legitimate government of Naples, and to the support of the royalist cause along the southern coast of France. In March, 1816, he had the satisfaction of concluding treaties with the Deys of Tunis and Tripoli relative to the abolition of Christian slavery, in virtue whereof 1792 persons were released from bondage. He also entered into arrangements with the Dey of Algiers, but the atrocities perpetrated by that potentate subsequently to his Lordship's return to England, being such as to induce Great Britain to inflict upon him a signal mark of her displeasure, a fresh armament was equipped, and the command of it again given to the noble Admiral. He accordingly hoisted his flag on board the QUEEN CHARLOTTE 100, and on 27 Aug. reappeared, with, including his own, five ships of the line, one 50, four frigates, five sloops, and four bombs, accompanied by five Dutch frigates and a corvette, before the colossal fortifications of Algiers. The result of the awful conflict that ensued who but knows? It is sufficient for us to record, that the gallant and veteran Baron became a Viscount, that he received the thanks of both Houses of Parliament, a sword from the City of London, and a piece of plate, valued at 1400 guineas, from his officers, that he was created a Knight of various foreign orders, and beyond all, that he secured for ever the admiration and gratitude of the Christian world. He had been previously presented by the flag officers and captains who had served with him in the Mediterranean, with a table ornament worth 500 guineas, as a token of their respect and regard From the autumn of 1817 until Feb. 1821, he held the chief command at Plymouth. He was appointed Vice-Admiral of the United Kingdom 15 Feb. 1832, and died an Admiral of the Red 23 Jan. 1833.

wood is a nephew of the late Admiral Sir Israel Pellew, K.C.B.*

This officer entered the Navy, in March, 1799, as Fst.-cl. Vol., on board the IMPÉTUEUX 74, commanded by his father, then Sir Edw. Pellew, under whom, with the exception of an interval occasioned by the peace of Amiens, he continued employed, as Midshipman, in the same ship and the TONNANT 80, on the Channel and Mediterranean stations, until May, 1804. He next, in April, 1805, joined the CULLODEN 74, Capt. Christopher Cole, on the East India station; where he was made Lieutenant, 8 Sept. in the same year, into the SCEPTRE 74, Capt. Joseph Bingham. He shortly afterwards went back to the CULLODEN 74, flag-ship at the time of his father, by whom he was successively placed in command, 25 July and 18 Sept. 1806, and 30 March, 1807, of the RATTLESNAKE 18, TERPSICHORE 32, and PSYCHE 36. While in the TERPSICHORE he commanded the boats of a squadron, and exhibited much gallantry, at the capture and destruction, 27 Nov. 1806, of a Dutch frigate, 7 brigs of war, and about 20 armed and other merchant vessels, in Batavia Roads.† He also had charge of the boats of a squadron at the destruction of several piratical proas on the coast of Java. In the PSYCHE he made prize, in the port of Samarang, 31 Aug. 1807, of a schooner of 8 guns, in company with a large merchant brig; and the next day he took, with two other vessels (the *Resolutie* armed merchant ship of 700 tons, richly laden, and the *Ceres*, a remarkably fine brig, in the Dutch Company's service, of 12 guns and 70 men), the *Scipio* corvette of 24 guns.‡ In Oct. 1807, on 12 of which month he was confirmed in the rank of Commander, we find him nominated Acting-Captain of the POWERFUL 74; in which ship he was present, 11 Dec. following, at the annihilation, at Griessee, of the docks and stores, and of all the men-of-war remaining to Holland in the East Indies.‖ On 18 Feb. and 5 July, 1808, Capt. Pellew, whose Post commission bears date 14 Oct. in that year, was invested with the command, first of the CORNWALLIS, *alias* AKBAR 50, and then of the PHAETON 38. In the latter frigate, which during two whole days in 1808 lay in the harbour of Nagasaki in the island of Japan, he accompanied the expedition of 1810 against the Isle of France, and in 1811 co-operated in the reduction of the island of Java. On his arrival at Java in charge of a division of transports, he took command of the boats employed in protecting the debarkation of the troops. During the operations which preceded its final surrender he landed, 31 Aug., on the neighbouring island of Madura, in command, with Capt. Geo. Harris, of the SIR FRANCIS DRAKE, his senior officer, of a body of seamen and marines, and assisted in the most gallant manner in storming the strong fortress of Samanap, mounting 16 6-pounders; immediately after which he attacked from one point, as did Capt. Harris from another, and utterly routed a force of about 2000 men, protected by 4 field-pieces in their front, on a bridge possessing every advantage of situation. "I gladly acknowledge," says Capt. Harris, in his official account of this proceeding, "the assistance and advice I have received from Capt. Pellew, who aided every point of service with his well-known zeal, ability, and bravery."* In Aug. 1812 the PHAETON returned to England in escort of 16 Indiamen; for his care and attention to which Capt. Pellew received the thanks of the Court of Directors, accompanied by a present of 500 guineas. Being next, 23 Oct. 1812, appointed to the IPHIGENIA 36, he proceeded to the Mediterranean; on his arrival on which station he removed, in Jan. 1813, to the RESISTANCE of 46 guns. On 5 Oct. following he aided, in company with the EDINBURGH 74, IMPÉRIEUSE 38, and SWALLOW, ECLAIR, and PYLADES sloops, in silencing the fire of several batteries at Port d'Anzo, where a convoy of 29 vessels fell into the hands of the British. In Feb. 1814 Capt. Pellew left the RESISTANCE. His last appointment was, 25 Aug. 1818, to the RÉVOLUTIONNAIRE 46, again in the Mediterranean, whence he returned in June, 1822. He attained Flag-rank 9 Nov. 1846.

In June, 1815, the Rear-Admiral was nominated a C.B.; and in Jan. 1836 he received, with the honour of Knighthood, the insignia of a K.C.H. He was appointed a Naval Aide-de-camp to the Queen 4 July, 1842. He married, 5 June, 1816, Harriet, only daughter of the late Sir Godfrey Webster, Bart., by whom he has issue an only daughter, the wife of Lord Walpole, eldest son of the Earl of Orford. AGENT—John P. Muspratt.

* Sir Israel Pellew was born at Dover 25 Aug. 1758, and entered the Navy in 1771, on board the FALCON sloop. After serving in the ALBION and witnessing, in the FLORA, the capture of the frigate *Fox*, he joined the ROYAL GEORGE 100, and in 1779 was promoted to the rank of Lieutenant. In Jan. 1783, in command of the RESOLUTION cutter, of 12 guns and 75 men, he took, after a chase of 14 hours and a smart action of about an hour and a quarter, the *Flushinger* Dutch privateer, pierced for 14 guns, mounting twelve 14-pounders, with a complement of 68 men. He was advanced to the rank of Commander 22 Nov. 1790; and on 25 June, 1793, having been a volunteer with his brother on board the NYMPHE at the capture of *La Cleopâtre*, he was presented with a Post commission. He afterwards commanded, until the peace of Amiens, the SQUIRREL 20, and AMPHION, GREYHOUND, and CLEOPATRA frigates; and was on board the AMPHION when she blew up in Plymouth Sound 22 Sept. 1796. Being appointed, in 1804, to the CONQUEROR 74, he served in that ship at the battle of Trafalgar, and was employed, previously to the convention of Cintra, in blockading the Russian fleet in the Tagus. Prior to the action off Cape Trafalgar he had accompanied Lord Nelson to the West Indies and back, in quest of the combined squadrons. In July, 1810, at which period he had been for upwards of a year in superintendence of the ships afloat at Plymouth, he attained the rank of Rear-Admiral. In 1811 he became Captain of the Mediterranean fleet, under his brother, Sir Edward Pellew, with whom he remained until 1815. He was created a K.C.B. in Jan. of the latter year; a Vice-Admiral in Aug. 1819; and an Admiral in July, 1830. He died at Plymouth 19 July, 1832, after a protracted and severe illness.

† *Vide* Gaz. 1807, p. 894. ‡ *V.* Gaz. 1808, p. 537.

‖ Immediately prior to the above event, Capt. Pellew and one or two others, who had been sent on shore with a flag of truce, were detained by the Dutch Commodore and placed under arrest they were soon, however, released.

* *Vide* Gaz. 1812, pp 116, 120.

PELLEW. (LIEUTENANT, 1843.)

The HONOURABLE POWNOLL FLEETWOOD PELLEW, born 26 July, 1823, is eldest son of Pownoll Bastard, second Viscount Exmouth, Captain R.N. (1806), who died 2 Dec. 1833, by his second wife, Georgina Janet, eldest daughter of Mungo Dick, Esq.; half-brother of the present Viscount; and nephew of Rear-Admiral Hon. F. B. R. Pellew, Kt., C.B., K.C.H.

This officer entered the Navy 18 Aug. 1836; passed his examination 8 Aug. 1842; and after serving, as Mate, in the CORNWALLIS 72, Capt. Peter Richards, CONWAY 26, Capt. Robt. Fair, and VICTORIA AND ALBERT steam-yacht, Capt. Lord Adolphus FitzClarence, was promoted to the rank of Lieutenant 30 Dec. 1843. His appointments have since been—2 Feb. 1844, as Additional, to his former ship the CORNWALLIS—2 July, 1844, in a similar capacity, to the COLLINGWOOD 80, bearing the flag of Sir Geo. Fras. Seymour in the Pacific—and, 8 Oct. 1847, to the HOWE 120, Capt. Sir Jas. Stirling, now employed on Particular Service.

PELLY. (COMMANDER, 1844.)

RICHARD WILSON PELLY, born 1 Nov. 1814, is fifth son of Sir John Henry Pelly, Bart., of Upton, co. Essex, by Emma, sixth daughter of Henry Boulton, Esq., of Thorncroft, co. Surrey; and nephew of the late Capt. Chas. Pelly, R.N.†

† Capt. Chas. Pelly was wounded, when a Lieutenant, in a sanguinary attack, made in Aug. 1801, on the French invasion flotilla. In March, 1804, at which time he commanded the BEAVER 14, he served with the boats of that vessel and the SCORPION 18, under Capt. Geo. Nicholas Hardinge, at the cutting out, in the Vlie passage, after a most spirited and determined conflict, of the Dutch brig *Atalante*, of 16 long 12-pounders and 76 men When Captain of the BUCEPHALUS 36, he co-operated in the reduction of the island of Java in 1811, and displayed much gallantry in pursuing for several days the French 40-gun frigates *Nymphe* and *Meduse*.

This officer entered the Navy 27 June, 1828; obtained his first commission 20 July, 1836; and was afterwards appointed—5 Oct. 1836, as Additional-Lieutenant, to the WINCHESTER 52, flag-ship of Hon. Sir Thos. Bladen Capel in the East Indies—20 June, 1837, to the VICTOR 16, Capt. Rich. Crozier, on the same station, whence he returned in 1839—and, 30 Jan. 1840, to the ANDROMACHE 26, Capt. Robt. Lambert Baynes, at the Cape of Good Hope. He was advanced to the rank he now holds 10 Feb. 1844, nearly 12 months after the ANDROMACHE had been paid off. His last appointment was to the ROSE 18, which vessel he commanded on the North America and West India station from 13 Dec. 1844, until put out of commission at the close of 1846.

PENFOLD. (LIEUT., 1823. F-P., 36; H-P., 1.)

GEORGE PENFOLD was born, 19 July, 1798, at Plymouth, co. Devon.

This officer (who had previously served as a Volunteer, in the IRIS 36, Capt. John Tower, and had assisted, when in company, in 1807, with the TRIBUNE 36 and MARTIAL gun-brig, in beating off a large flotilla of Spanish gun-boats near Ferrol) entered the Navy, 26 Jan. 1810, as Fst.-cl. Vol., on board the SOLEBAY 32, Capt. Hon. Granville Leveson Proby, employed in the North Sea and Baltic. In Nov. 1810 he removed to the KRON PRINCESS, Lieut.-Commander Thos. Spearing Osmer, lying in the river Medway; and in Sept. 1812, after having again served, for 12 months, in the SOLEBAY, under the flag, at North Yarmouth, of Rear-Admiral Robt. Murray, he became Midshipman of the HORATIO 38, Capt. Lord Geo. Stuart; under whom, in Dec. 1813, on his return from the Cape of Good Hope to the North Sea, he contributed to the reduction of the islands of Schouwen and Tholen. Following Lord Geo. Stuart, in March, 1814, into the NEWCASTLE 50, he continued employed in that ship, under the command of Capts. Sam. Roberts and Henry Meynell, in North America and the West Indies, until transferred, 16 April, 1816, to the PACTOLUS 38, Capt. Wm. Hugh Dobbie. On leaving the latter ship, in which he had been again serving on the North American station, Mr. Penfold, in Sept. 1817, passed his examination. He was subsequently, between Aug. 1818 and Oct. 1823, employed a second time in the West Indies, on board the ONTARIO 18, Capt. Geo. Gosling, CONFIANCE 18, Capts. Alex. Montgomerie and Robt. Gordon, SERAPIS receiving-ship, Lieut.-Commander Geo. Vernon Jackson, and ESK 20, Capt. Arthur Lee Warner. He was created a Lieutenant of the vessel last mentioned 15 Feb. 1823; and since 15 Nov. in the same year has been in command of a station in the Coast Guard.

In Jan. 1837 his name, at the recommendation of the Lord-Lieutenant of Ireland, was placed on the Admiralty list for promotion, for services rendered to the Government of that country. The Lieutenant, who was formerly for nine years in the Commission of the Peace, married, 3 March, 1824, Mary, daughter of John and Bridget Collier, of Balbiggan, co. Dublin, by whom he has had issue seven children. AGENT—J. Chippendale.

PENGELLEY. (COMMANDER, 1814. F-P., 16;* H-P., 35.)

CHARLES PENGELLEY entered the Navy, in 1796, as Fst.-cl. Vol., on board the ATLAS 98, Capts. Edm. Dod and Matthew Squire, stationed in the Channel; where, and in the Mediterranean, he served, as Midshipman, from 1798 until 1802, in the POMONE 40, Capt. Robt. Carthew Reynolds, and IMMORTALITÉ 36, Capt. Hon. Henry Hotham. He then, in succession, joined the SAN JOSEF 110, Capts. Wm. Wolseley and Jas. Carpenter, and TONNANT 80, Capt. Sir Edw. Pellew, both attached to the Channel fleet; and on 16 Feb. 1805 he was made Lieutenant into the THISBE 28, Capt. Lewis Shepheard, employed at first in the Mediterranean, and then on the Guernsey station. He invalided in the following Sept.; and was afterwards appointed—27 June and 28 July, 1806, to the WINDSOR CASTLE 98, Capt. Chas. Boyles, and ROYAL GEORGE 100, Capt. Rich. Dalling Dunn, under whom, after having served with Sir John Thos. Duckworth at the passage of the Dardanells, he sailed for the West Indies—29 July, 1809, to the FYLLA 22, Capt. Hon. Edw. Rodney, employed off Oporto, Guernsey, and Jersey—1 May, 1810, to the HAMADRYAD 36, Capt. Sir Thos. Staines, in which ship, until April, 1812, when his health again obliged him to invalid, we find him engaged in cruizing off the Western Islands, escorting troops to the mouth of the Tagus, accompanying a fleet of Indiamen from St. Helena to the Downs, and serving off the coast of Ireland—5 Jan. 1813, to the SAN JOSEF 110, flag-ship of Sir Rich. King in the Mediterranean—and, 6 July following, to the flotilla service in the Faro of Messina. For his conduct in leading a division of the flotilla in the attack upon Genoa,† he was nominated, 18 April, 1814, Acting-Commander of the GUADELOUPE 16, in which sloop he remained for a period of three months. He was confirmed in his present rank 20 Sept. in the same year; and was afterwards employed for same time in the Water and Coast Guard.

Commander Pengelley's eldest son, Charles William, married in 1839 the only surviving child of Capt. Wm. Rogers, of the Holyhead station.

* Apart from his servitude in the Revenue.

† *Vide* Gaz. 1814, p. 980.

PENGELLEY. (LIEUTENANT, 1815. F-P., 11; H-P., 32.)

JOHN PENGELLEY is son of the late Capt. John Pengelley, R.N., who, when commanding the VIPER cutter, of 14 4-pounders and 48 men, distinguished himself by his gallantry in effecting the capture, 13 March, 1797, and 26 Dec. 1799, of the privateers *Piteous Virgin Maria*, carrying 10 4 and 6-pounders, 8 swivels, and 42 men, and *Furet*, of 14 4-pounders and 57 men.

This officer entered the Navy, in Jan. 1804, as Midshipman, on board the PEGASUS 28, commanded by his father, with whom he was stationed off Harwich until June, 1806. In Feb. 1807 he became a Student at the Royal Naval College; and in Feb. 1810 he again embarked, on board the PHEASANT 18, Capt. John Palmer, attached to the force in the Channel; where, and off Flushing and the coast of North America, he served, from June, 1812, until promoted to the rank of Lieutenant, 8 Feb. 1815, in the YORK 74, Capts. Robt. Barton and Alex. Wilmot Schomberg. He has since been on half-pay. AGENTS—Messrs. Stilwell.

PENGELLY. (LIEUTENANT, 1812. F-P., 10; H-P., 32.)

HENRY PENGELLY entered the Navy, 30 Aug. 1805, as L.M., on board the PRINCE FREDERICK, Lieut.-Commander Jas. Leach, lying in Plymouth Harbour; removed, in Feb. 1806, to the DIAMOND 38, Capt. Thos. Elphinstone, attached to the Channel Fleet; and from the following Aug. until promoted to the rank of Lieutenant, 21 March, 1812, was employed as Midshipman and Master's Mate, on the Home, Baltic, and American stations, in the SOLEBAY, IRIS, and SPARTAN frigates, Capts. John Tower, Hon. Granville Leveson Proby, Thos. Geo. Shortland, and Edw. Pelham Brenton. With the exception of an interval, between Sept. 1812 and Feb. 1813, he continued to serve on the coast of America in the ÆOLUS 32, Capt. Lord Jas. Townshend, LOIRE 38, Capt. Thos. Brown, and BULWARK 74, Capt. Farmery Predam Epworth, until May, 1815, since which period he has been on half-pay.

Lieut. Pengelly married, at Jamaica, in 1834, Charlotte, youngest daughter of J. Heriott, Esq., formerly of Mexican Estate, in that island.

PENGELLY. (LIEUTENANT, 1826.)

ROBERT LAMPORT PENGELLY entered the Navy 27 June, 1809; passed his examination in 1817; and while serving in 1826 in a tender belonging to the

Maidstone frigate, Commodore Chas. Bullen, was wounded at the capture of the *Prince of Guinea* slave-brig of 10 guns. He was made a Lieutenant 9 Dec. in the same year; and was afterwards, from 6 Oct. 1832 until paid off in 1834, employed on the Lisbon station in the Asia 84, flag-ship of the present Sir Wm. Parker. He has not been since afloat.

PENNEFATHER. (Lieutenant, 1821. f-p., 23; h-p., 16.)

William Westby Pennefather is second son of the late Rev. John Pennefather, Rector of St. John parish, in the diocese of Cashel, co. Tipperary, by Elizabeth, daughter of Major Percival; and grandson of Kingsmill Pennefather, Esq., M.P. in 1753, 1761, and 1771 for Cashel. One of his brothers, Kingsmill, was a Major in the Limerick Militia; another, John Lysaght, a Major in the 22nd Regt.; and a third, Robt. Percival, a Lieutenant and Adjutant in the 3rd Regt. of Native Cavalry, in Bengal. The Lieutenant, a near relative of the Lord Chief Justice of the Court of Queen's Bench, in Ireland, is brother-in-law of the late Vice-Admiral Henry Vansittart, and the present Lieut. Thos. Pearce Evans, R.N. His first-cousin, Matthew Pennefather, of New Park, co. Tipperary, is now representative of the family.

This officer entered the Navy, in July, 1808, as Fst.-cl. Vol., on board the Fortunée 36, Capt. Henry Vansittart, stationed on the coast of Ireland. In the summer of 1809 he removed to the Paulina brig, Capt. Westby Percival, attached to the force in the Mediterranean; where, and on the Lisbon, Cape of Good Hope, Home, and Newfoundland stations, he served, from May, 1811, to Oct. 1815, as Midshipman, in the Leviathan 74, Capt. Patrick Campbell, Andromeda 24, Capt. Rich. Arthur, Stag 36, Capt. Phipps Hornby, Procris and Pilot sloops, Capts. Curzon and John Toup Nicolas, and Bellerophon 74, and Salisbury 58, flag-ships of Sir Rich. Goodwin Keats. He was next, between Oct. 1816 and July, 1817, employed as Admiralty-Midshipman in the Granicus 36, Capt. Wm. Furlong Wise, and Martin sloop, Capt. Andrew Mitchell—the latter stationed on the coast of Ireland. After a further servitude, chiefly in the West Indies, on board the Nautilus 18, Capt. Isham Fleming Chapman, Sybille 44, Capt. Joshua Ricketts Rowley, Surinam 18, Capt. Wm. M'Kenzie Godfrey, and Confiance 18, Capt. Robt. Gordon, he was confirmed a Lieutenant, 22 Aug. 1821, into the Surinam, still commanded by Capt. Godfrey, although subsequently by Capt. Chas. Crole. His last appointments were—12 Nov. 1823, to the Eden 26, Capt. John Lawrence, likewise in the West Indies, whence he returned soon afterwards—28 Sept. 1830, to the Coast Guard, in which service he continued until the close of 1837—and 10 May, 1839, for three years, to the Victory 104, bearing the flag at Portsmouth of Hon. Duncombe Pleydell Bouverie, Admiral-Superintendent. Agents—Messrs. Stilwell.

PENNELL. (Captain, 1828. f-p., 14; h-p., 15.)

Follett Walrond Pennell, born 4 Feb. 1804, is sixth son of Wm. Pennell, Esq., formerly H.B.M.'s Consul-General at Rio de Janeiro. One of his sisters is the wife of the Right Hon. John Wilson Croker, LL.D., many years First Secretary of the Admiralty; and another, of Geo. Barrow, Esq., eldest son of Sir John Barrow, Bart., the late Second Secretary; a third sister is married to Sir Anthony Perrier, Kt., H.B.M.'s Consul at Brest.

This officer entered the Navy, in Feb. 1818, as Fst.-cl. Vol., on board the Impregnable 104, Capt. Hon. Pownoll Bastard Pellew, bearing the flag at Plymouth of Viscount Exmouth. After a servitude of about three years in the Mediterranean as Midshipman in the Révolutionnaire 46, Capt. Hon. Fleetwood Broughton Reynolds Pellew, and of some months on the Home station in the Phaeton 46, and Apollo yacht, Capts. Wm. Aug. Montagu and Hon. Sir Chas. Paget, he joined, in 1823-4, the Gloucester 74, Commodore Sir Edw. W. C. R. Owen, and Bustard 10, Capt. Rawdon Maclean, both in the West Indies, where he was made Lieutenant, 1 Sept. 1824, into the Pyramus 42, Capt. Fras. Newcombe. On 19 Dec. 1825, having previously filled the post of Flag-Lieutenant to Rear-Admiral Bingham in the Warspite 76, at Portsmouth, he was appointed to the Cyrené 20, Capt. Alex. Campbell, on the East India station. He was there promoted to the command, 13 Nov. 1826, of the Fly 18. He attained Post-rank 14 July, 1828; and was afterwards, from 31 May, 1834, until paid off in July, 1837, employed in South America in the Talbot 28. He has not been since afloat.

Capt. Pennell married, in 1838, Catherine Anna, daughter of the late Colonel M'Murdo, of Lotus, Dumfriesshire, by whom he has issue one daughter.

PENRUDDOCK. (Commander, 1814. f-p., 16 h-p., 33.)

George Penruddock is youngest son of the late Chas. Penruddock, Esq., of Compton, M.P. for co. Wilts; and brother of the present John Hungerford Penruddock, Esq., Colonel Commandant of the 3rd Wilts Local Militia.

This officer entered the Navy, 28 July, 1798, as Fst.-cl. Vol., on board the Adamant 50, Capt. Wm. Hotham; in which ship, while cruizing off the Isle of France in company with the Tremendous 74, he assisted as Midshipman, 11 Dec. 1799, in driving on shore the French frigate *La Preneuse*, under a heavy fire from the batteries in the neighbourhood of Port Louis. Quitting the Adamant in Dec. 1801, he served during the next four years on the Home and West India stations, in the Braak, Naiad frigate, Raisonnable 64, Capt. Wm. Hotham, Royal William, flag-ship of Admiral Geo. Montagu, Triumph 74, Capt. Henry Inman, and Wolf and Elk sloops, Capts. Geo. Chas. Mackenzie and Jas. Rich. Dacres. On 7 April, 1806, he was nominated Sub-Lieutenant of the Peterel sloop, Capt. John Lamborn, also in the West Indies; where, after again serving as Midshipman in the Cuba, Capt. Fred. Langford, and Bacchante 20, Capt. J. R. Dacres, he was made Full Lieutenant, 28 July, 1807, into the ship last mentioned, which was subsequently commanded by Capts. Sam. Hood Inglefield and Wm. Ward. Under Capt. Inglefield Mr. Penruddock was often in close action with the enemy, from whom he aided in wresting, 11 May, 1808, at the close of an action of 30 minutes, preceded by a long chase, *Le Griffon* French national brig, of 16 guns and 105 men. Being next, 21 June, 1809, appointed to the Pilot 18, Capt. John Toup Nicolas, we find him present, in company with the Ortenzia schooner, at the destruction, 24 June, 1810, of 5 out of a convoy of 51 sail, protected, near the town of St. Lucido, on the coast of Calabria, by a battery, 16 armed vessels, and a body of musketeers, whose fire killed three of the British. The vessels in question were destroyed by the shot of the Pilot and Ortenzia; the boats under Lieut. Penruddock having been received on their approach by so heavy a fire that Capt. Nicolas was induced to make the signal of recall. On 8 of the following month, being in the vicinity of the same place, Lieut. Penruddock, who was then Senior of the Pilot, handsomely volunteered, with Lieut. Fras. Chas. Annesley, to bring out two gun-boats from a secure position they had taken behind a small island—a service which was fortunately accomplished, although the vessels were well fastened to the shore, and a number of soldiers and people with musketry kept up the whole time a heavy fire on the British. The Pilot herself, on the occasion, destroyed three armed scampavias and 17 sail of transport-vessels, laden with stores and ammunition for Murat's army at Scylla; and 17 days afterwards, acting in unison with the Thames 32 and Weazle 18, she contributed to the capture and destruction, under the batteries of Amantea, of a convoy of 31 vessels, also laden for the army of Murat, together with 7 large gun-boats and 5 scampavias. In the latter affair Lieut. Penruddock was again employed in the boats, and, in common with the others employed, was exposed to a galling fire from the enemy while endeavouring to launch some of the vessels which had been hauled high on the beach and lay flanked by two small batteries.* In Jan. 1811 he returned to England in the WARRIOR 74, Capt. John Wm. Spranger; but in the following summer, being appointed to the FAME 74, Capt. Walter Bathurst, he again sailed for the Mediterranean. Co-operating afterwards with the Spanish patriots, he landed in command of a party of small-arm men, and in conjunction with the troops under General Donkin took part in the unsuccessful attack upon the fortress of Denia, where, on the defeat of the British, he greatly distinguished himself by the gallant manner in which, under a heavy fire from the French garrison, who had advanced close to the beach, he exerted himself in carrying the wounded soldiers into the boats. We believe that he was subsequently present at the siege of Tarragona and at the reduction of the strong fort of St. Philippe in the Col de Balaguer. He was advanced to the rank of Commander 15 June, 1814; and has since been on half-pay. AGENT—J. Hinxman.

* *Vide* Gaz. 1810, p. 1860.

PENTLAND. (LIEUT., 1824. F-P., 17; H-P., 18.)

JAMES MURRAY PENTLAND is son of the late Geo. Pentland, Esq., of Black Hall, co. Louth, many years Solicitor of the Excise in Dublin.

This officer entered the Navy, in 1812, on board the RAMILLIES 74, Capt. Sir Thos. Masterman Hardy, for the purpose of joining the present Sir Geo. Cockburn, with whom, during the war with the United States, he served as Fst.-cl. Vol. and Midshipman in the MARLBOROUGH, SCEPTRE, and ALBION 74's. He was in consequence present in the operations against Crany Island, Hampton, Washington, and Baltimore, and in various hostile operations of minor note. Following Sir G. Cockburn, in 1815, into the MARLBOROUGH 74, he sailed in that ship with Napoleon Buonaparte for St. Helena, where, in 1816, he joined the LEVERET 10, Capt. John Theed. In 1818 he returned to England. He was subsequently, until advanced to his present rank 13 July, 1824, employed at home and in North America in the BULWARK 74, flag-ship of Sir John Gore, MERSEY 26, Capt. Edw. Collier, EGERIA 28, Capt. John Toup Nicolas, RANGER 28, Capt. Peter Fisher, and SIR FRANCIS DRAKE frigate, flag-ship of Sir Chas. Hamilton. From 1826 to 1829 he filled an appointment in the Coast Guard. He has since been on half-pay. AGENTS—Messrs. Ommanney.

PEPPIN. (LIEUTENANT, 1837.)

MATTHEW PEPPIN entered the Navy 29 Nov. 1812; passed his examination in 1819; and obtained his commission 10 Jan. 1837. His succeeding appointments were—28 March, 1837, to the FAIRY surveying-vessel, Capt. Wm. Hewett, with whom he served until the commencement of 1838—and, 13 Dec. 1838, to the WILLIAM AND MARY yacht, Capt. Phipps Hornby. He has not been employed since July, 1840.

PERCEVAL. (LIEUT., 1845. F-P., 12; H-P., 1.)

MICHAEL HENRY PERCEVAL is third son of the late Michael Henry Perceval, Esq., of Spencer Wood, Lower Canada, Collector of H.M. Customs at the port of Quebec, and Member of the Executive and Legislative Assemblies of that city, by Anne Mary, eldest daughter of Sir Chas. Flower, Bart., of Mill Hill, co. Middlesex, and Lobb Farm, co. Oxford. He is first-cousin of Alex. Perceval, Esq., of Temple House, co. Sligo, Lieut.-Colonel of the Sligo militia, many years M.P. for that co., and now Serjeant-at-Arms to the House of Lords.

This officer entered the Navy, 2 Jan. 1834, as Fst.-cl. Vol., on board the ORESTES 18, Capt. Sir Wm. Dickson, employed off Lisbon; and on becoming attached, in the following June, to the DEE steamer, Capt. Wm. Ramsay, sailed for the North America and West India station, where he became Midshipman, in Sept. 1836 and Dec. 1837, of the SKIPJACK schooner, Lieut.-Commander John Jas. Robinson, and VESTAL 26, Capt. Thos. Wren Carter. In the summer of 1841, having passed his examination 21 May, 1840, he was appointed Mate of the INDUS 78, Capt. Sir Jas. Stirling, in which ship he remained for a period of three years in the Mediterranean. Previously to joining her he served a few months, we believe, in the QUEEN 110. Obtaining, in May, 1845, an appointment to the EXCELLENT gunnery-ship at Portsmouth, Capts. Sir Thos. Hastings and Henry Ducie Chads, he continued there employed, as Mate and Gunnery-Lieutenant (his commission bears date 8 Aug. 1845), until May, 1847. He has been serving since in the HOWE 120, again with Sir Jas. Stirling.

PERCEVAL. (LIEUT., 1815. F-P., 24; H-P., 18.)

RICHARD PERCEVAL entered the Navy, 15 Nov. 1805, as Midshipman, on board the STEADY gun-brig, Lieut.-Commander Arthur Stow, stationed at first in the Rio de la Plata and on the coast of Brazil, and afterwards in the Mediterranean, where, in Feb. 1812, he removed to the OCEAN 98, Capt. Robt. Plampin. In Sept. 1814 he became Master's Mate of the PICKLE schooner, Lieut.-Commander Wm. Figg, attached to the force in the Channel; and in Oct. 1815, at which period he had been just nominated Admiralty-Midshipman of the LEE 20, Capt. John Pasco, he was presented with a commission dated back to 6 of the preceding April. His appointments have since been—19 June, 1833, to the Coast Guard—17 March, 1838, to the command, for upwards of four years, of the BADGER revenue-vessel—19 July, 1842, again to the Coast Guard, which he left at the close of 1844—and, 4 July, 1845, to the office of Admiralty Agent on board a contract mail steamer. He is still employed in the latter capacity.

PERCY, C.B. (REAR-ADMIRAL OF THE RED, 1841. F-P., 26; H-P., 24.)

THE HONOURABLE JOSCELINE PERCY, born 29 Jan. 1784, is fourth son of Algernon, first Earl of Beverley, by Isabella Susannah, second daughter of Peter Burrell, Esq., of Beckenham, in Kent, and sister of Peter, first Lord Gwydyr. One of his brothers, Algernon, Minister Plenipotentiary to the Swiss Cantons, died 10 Aug. 1833; another, Hugh, present Bishop of Carlisle, is married to a daughter of the late Vice-Admiral Sir Wm. Johnstone Hope, G.C.B.; a third, Henry, having served as Aide-de-Camp to Sir John Moore at Corunna and to the Duke of Wellington at Waterloo, became a Lieutenant-Colonel and died a C.B. in 1825; a fourth, William Henry, is now a Rear-Admiral; and a fifth, Francis John, died a Captain in the 23rd regt. in 1812. The Rear-Admiral (whose eldest brother, the Earl of Beverley, holds the appointment of Captain of the Queen's Yeomen of the Guard) is grandson of the first Duke of Northumberland.

This officer entered the Navy, 23 Feb. 1797, as a Volunteer, on board the SANS PAREIL 80, Capts. Wm. Browell and Chas. Vinicombe Penrose, in which ship, bearing for some time the flag of Lord Hugh Seymour, he witnessed an attack made in July, 1799, on a Spanish squadron in Aix Roads. In 1801, being then in the West Indies, he removed as Midshipman to the AMPHION 32, Capts. Rich. Henry Alex. Bennett, Alex. Fraser, and Thos. Masterman Hardy. He next, on his arrival in 1803 off Toulon, joined the VICTORY 100, flag-ship of Lord Nelson. On 1 Aug. in the same year he was nominated Acting-Lieutenant of the MEDUSA 32, Capt. John Gore; and on leaving that ship,* to which he had been confirmed 30 April, 1804, he was appointed, 31 Dec. following, to the DIADEM 64,

* The MEDUSA formed one of a squadron which effected the capture of three Spanish frigates laden with treasure, and the destruction of a fourth, off Cape St. Mary, 5 Oct. 1804. On 8 of the following month she intercepted the MATILDA Spanish register ship, having on board a cargo of quicksilver worth 200,000*l*.

bearing the broad pendant of Sir Home Popham. Subsequently to the reduction of the Cape of Good Hope, at which he was present, Mr. Percy was ordered, 11 Jan. 1806, to assume command of the ESPOIR brig. Before he had time, however, to join her he was sent to Simon's Bay for the purpose of taking possession of the *Bato*, a Dutch 68; but the latter, as he found on his arrival, had been unfortunately reduced by the enemy to a complete wreck; in consequence whereof, and of the ESPOIR having during his absence sailed with despatches for England, he was under the necessity of rejoining the DIADEM in the capacity of a Volunteer. An opportunity, notwithstanding, was soon afforded him of obtaining another command. In ignorance of the colony having changed masters, the French frigate *Volontaire*, of 46 guns, on 4 of the ensuing March, entered Table Bay; she was compelled forthwith to strike her colours, and Capt. Percy, who was sent on board to take possession of her, placed in charge of her.* Shortly after this he was sent to St. Helena to afford protection to the homeward-bound Indiamen. His promotion to the ranks of Commander and Post-Captain being confirmed at the Admiralty by commissions dated 22 Jan. and 25 Sept. 1806, he was subsequently appointed—7 Sept. 1807, to the COMUS 22—24 April, 1808, to LA NYMPHE 36—5 Nov. 1810, to the HOTSPUR 36, in which frigate he continued five years—27 Jan. 1829, for two years, to the ROYAL CHARLOTTE yacht, stationed at Dublin, in attendance upon the Duke of Northumberland, then Lord-Lieutenant of Ireland—and, 16 Oct. 1832 and 25 Nov. 1833, to the MALABAR 74 and CANOPUS 84, both in the Mediterranean, whence he returned in the early part of 1837. In Dec. 1807 Capt. Percy, at that time in the COMUS, was present with Sir Sam. Hood at the occupation of Madeira; and in 1808 we find him, in LA NYMPHE, conveying General Junot from the coast of Portugal to Rochelle, in compliance with the stipulations of the convention of Cintra. On 1 Sept. 1811, with the HOTSPUR under his orders, he contrived, with much zeal and ability, to decoy the French squadron at Cherbourg nearly into mid-Channel, in the hope of keeping it in play until the arrival of the blockading force under Capt. Pulteney Malcolm. On the occasion he allowed himself to be so closely approached that the first shot from the bow-chaser of the HOTSPUR, fired when the pursuit was surrendered, passed through the mainsail of the enemy's centre ship, whom he continued to harass until they had regained their anchorage, a quarter of an hour only before the British squadron came up with him. On 8 of the same month Capt. Percy, in company with the BARBADOES 28 and GOSHAWK brig, made an attack upon seven French brigs, each mounting 3 long 24-pounders and 1 mortar, with a complement of 75 men, near the Calvados rocks, on the coast of Normandy. In endeavouring to near them the HOTSPUR unfortunately took the ground, and lay for four hours exposed to a heavy fire from the vessels, a battery, and some field-pieces, which inflicted on her a loss, besides considerable damage in her hull, sails, and rigging, of 2 Midshipmen and 3 seamen killed, and 22 seamen and marines wounded. One of the brigs, however, was sunk, and two driven on shore.† While on the Channel station the HOTSPUR made prize, 13 May and 26 Oct. 1813, of the French ship letter-of-marque *Impératrice Reine* of 12 guns, pierced for 20, and 50 men, and the American schooner *Chesapeake* of 5 guns and 29 men. She was afterwards employed for two years on the coast of South America. On 23 Nov. 1841 (he had been nominated a C.B. 26 Sept. 1831) Capt. Percy attained Flag-rank. His last appointment was to the chief command at the Cape of Good Hope, which he held, with his flag in the WINCHESTER 50, from 17 Dec. 1841 until the spring of 1846.

The Rear-Admiral, a Deputy-Lieutenant for the West Riding of Yorkshire, retained a seat in Parliament, in 1806, 1807, 1812, and 1818, for Beeralston, in Devonshire. He married, in Dec. 1820, Sophia Elizabeth, third daughter of Morton Walhouse, Esq., of Hatherton, co. Stafford, by whom he has issue a son and three daughters. His eldest daughter, Sophy Elizabeth, was married, in July, 1846, to Lieut.-Colonel Chas. Bagot, eldest son of the late Right Hon. Sir Chas. Bagot, G.C.B. AGENT—Joseph Woodhead.

* *Vide* Gaz. 1806, p. 602. † *V.* Gaz. 1811, p. 1774.

PERCY. (REAR-ADMIRAL, 1846. F-P., 11; H-P., 35.)

THE HONOURABLE WILLIAM HENRY PERCY was born 24 March, 1788. He is a younger brother of Rear-Admiral Hon. Josceline Percy, C.B.

This officer entered the Navy, 1 May, 1801, as Fst.-cl. Vol., on board the LION 64, Capt. Henry Mitford, and on his return from a voyage with convoy to Canton, became Midshipman, in Nov. 1802, of the MEDUSA 32, Capt. John Gore. In that ship, after participating in the service mentioned in the note attached to our memoir of his brother, he sailed with the Marquis Cornwallis for India, and returned from the Ganges to the Lizard, a distance of 13,831 miles, in the surprisingly short period of 84 days. After serving for some months on the Home station in the TRIBUNE 36, Capts. Rich. Henry Alex. Bennett and Thos. Baker, ROYAL WILLIAM flag-ship of Admiral Geo. Montagu, and FAME 74, Capt. R. H. A. Bennett, he was made Lieutenant, 6 July, 1807, into the DÉCADE frigate, Capt. John Stuart, on the coast of Ireland. His next appointment was, 15 Nov. 1809, to the HIBERNIA 110, Capt. Robt. Jenner Neve, in the Mediterranean. Being advanced to the rank of Commander, 2 May, 1810, Capt. Percy, from 28 Dec. following until Posted 21 March, 1812, served in that capacity in the MERMAID 28, *armée-en-flûte*, employed in the conveyance of troops to Portugal and Spain. His only other appointment appears to have been, 4 April, 1814, to the HERMES 20, which vessel, after 25 of her men had been killed and 24 wounded in an unsuccessful attack upon Fort Bowyer, Mobile, was set on fire and destroyed to prevent her falling into the hands of the Americans, 15 Sept. in the same year. Capt. Percy had under his orders at the time, besides his own ship, the CANON 20, and SOPHIE and CHILDERS of 18 guns each. Of all blame in the loss of the HERMES he was by Court-martial honourably acquitted 18 Jan. 1815. On 9 March following he arrived at the Admiralty, with despatches from Sir Alex. Cochrane, reporting the defeat of the British army before New Orleans. He accepted his present rank 1 Oct. 1846.

Rear-Admiral Percy has been for some years a Commissioner of Excise. He sat in Parliament as Member for Stamford, co. Lincoln.

PERKINS. (LIEUT., 1814. F-P., 12; H-P., 29.)

HENRY AUGUSTUS PERKINS entered the Navy, 26 June, 1806, as Fst.-cl. Vol., on board the CANOPUS 80, Capts. Thos. Geo. Shortland and Chas. Inglis, successive flag-ship of Rear-Admirals Sir Thos. Louis and Geo. Martin; under the former of whom he served as Midshipman at the passage of the Dardanells and in the expedition to Egypt. Quitting the CANOPUS in March, 1809, he was next, between the following Aug. and Dec. 1813, employed, on the Home and Mediterranean stations, in the SAN JOSEF 110, Capt. Rich. Dalling Dunn, THAMES 32, Capt. Hon. Granville Geo. Waldegrave, RENOWN 74, Capt. Philip Chas. Durham, ECHO 16, Capt. Robt. Keen, and DRUID and AIGLE frigates, both commanded by Sir John Louis. On 6 of the month last mentioned he was nominated Acting-Lieutenant of the SWALLOW 18, Capts. Edw. Reynolds Sibly, Arthur Stow, and James; to which vessel, also in the Mediterranean, he was confirmed 16 March, 1814. In the following month he went on half-pay. He was subsequently appointed to the PHILOMEL 16, Capt. Jas. Hanway Plumridge, POMPÉE 74, Capt. Sir Jas. Athol Wood, GRANICUS 36, Capt. Wm. Furlong Wise, and

* *Vide* Gaz. 1816, p. 1703.

IMPREGNABLE 98, flag-ship of Lord Exmouth. In the GRANICUS, which frigate he left in Oct. 1816, he was wounded at the battle of Algiers;* and in the IMPREGNABLE he served at Plymouth from 16 May, 1818, until 1820. He has not been since afloat.

PERRIER. (LIEUTENANT, 1846.)

WILLIAM PERRIER is son of Sir Anthony Perrier, Kt., H. B. M.'s Consul at Brest, by a sister of Capt. F. W. Pennell, R.N.

This officer passed his examination 2 May, 1842; obtained his commission 10 March, 1846; and was then appointed to the EXCELLENT gunnery-ship at Portsmouth, Capt. Henry Ducie Chads. He has been serving, since 26 March, 1847, in the SIDON steam-frigate, of 500 horse-power, Capt. Wm. Honyman Henderson, in the Mediterranean.

PERRY. (LIEUT., 1828. F-P., 17; H-P., 20.)

JAMES CLEWLOW PERRY was born in 1798.

This officer entered the Navy, 2 July, 1810, as Fst.-cl. Boy, on board the TALBOT 18, Capts. Hon. Alex. Jones and Spelman Swaine, employed off the coast of Ireland; removed, in Aug. 1812, to the WARSPITE 74, commanded in the Channel by Capts. Hon. Henry Blackwood and Lord Jas. O'Bryen; became Midshipman, in Oct. 1814 and Aug. 1815, of the PRESIDENT 38, Capt. Archibald Duff, and TRENT 36, both on the Irish station; joined, in April, 1818, after two years of non-servitude, the EDEN 26, Capt. Fras. Erskine Loch, in the East Indies; was there transferred, in 1820, to the LEANDER 60, flag-ship of Hon. Sir H. Blackwood; invalided home in 1821; and from 1823 until paid off in 1830 served, at first at home and afterwards in South America, on board the QUEEN CHARLOTTE 100, flag-ship at Portsmouth, RIFLEMAN 18, Capt. Jas. Montagu, SPARTIATE 76, and WELLESLEY 74, bearing each the flag of Sir Geo. Eyre, GANGES 84, DORIS frigate, Capt. Sir John Gordon Sinclair, and FORTE 44, Capt. Jeremiah Coghlan. Having accompanied, in the EDEN, an expedition against the pirates of the Persian Gulf, he there, in Jan. 1820, assisted, as a passed Midshipman, at the bombardment of Ras-al-Khyma, their principal resort and head-quarters, where the fortifications were all destroyed, their vessels burnt, and a large quantity of treasure seized. He was confirmed a Lieutenant of the FORTE 3 March, 1828; and since that vessel was put out of commission has been on half-pay.

In 1837 he was appointed Inspector of the Gaol at Cork, where he continues.

PETCH. (LIEUTENANT, 1828.)

CHARLES ADOLPHUS PETCH, born about 1797, is brother of Lieut. Wm. Tatton Petch, R.N.

This officer entered the Navy 8 Feb. 1810; and on 13 Dec. in the same year was present in the KENT 74, Capt. Thos. Rogers, at the destruction of a large convoy protected by two batteries in the Mole of Palamos, at which place the British, out of 600 officers and men, who had been employed in the boats of a squadron, sustained a loss of upwards of 200 killed and wounded. Joining, subsequently, the THAMES 32, Capt. Chas. Napier, he assisted in that ship at the capture, 26 Feb. 1813, of the island of Ponza. On 16 May following, being then with Capt. Napier in the EURYALUS 36, we find him contributing to the capture of *La Fortune* national xebec, of 10 guns, 4 swivels, and 95 men, together with upwards of 20 merchant-vessels, lying in Cavalarie Road. In 1814 he accompanied, in the same ship, the brilliant expedition sent up the Potomac under Capt. Jas. Alex. Gordon to effect the capture of Alexandria. In 1815, while in charge of a prize to Bermuda, he fell into the hands of the enemy. Being made Lieutenant, 13 June, 1828 (11 years after he had passed his examination), into the ALACRITY 10, Capt. Joseph Nias, he was present in the following year, in the Mediterranean, at the capture of a pirate by the boats of that vessel. His appointments, since his return to England in 1830, have been, in succession—5 April, 1831, to the Coast Guard—20 June, 1836, to the command of the GREYHOUND Revenue-vessel—in 1839, to the office of Agent in a contract mail steam-vessel on the Liverpool and Kingstown station—and, 28 Aug. 1841 and 26 Jan. 1843, to the command of the WILDFIRE and ADVICE steam-packets, in the latter of which he is still serving. AGENTS—Hallett and Robinson.

* *Vide* Gaz. 1816, p. 1793.

PETCH. (LIEUT., 1814. F-P., 16; H-P., 32.)

WILLIAM TATTON PETCH was born 22 Sept. 1790. He is brother of Lieut. Chas. Adolphus Petch, R.N.

This officer entered the Navy, 15 March, 1799, as Third-cl. Boy, on board the NEPTUNE 98, Capts. Erasmus Gower, Jas. Vashon, Edw. Brace, and Fras. Wm. Austen; in which ship, bearing the flag in the Channel of Vice-Admiral Jas. Gambier, he continued employed as Midshipman until paid off in April, 1802. Joining next, in March, 1805, after having been for a time attached to the merchant-service, the BELLIQUEUX 64, Capt. Hon. Geo. Byng, he assisted on shore as Aide-de-Camp to that officer at the reduction of the Cape of Good Hope in Jan. 1806; and on 27 of the following Nov. commanded a launch at the capture and destruction of a Dutch frigate, seven brigs of war, and 20 armed and other merchant-vessels in Batavia Roads. On his return to England in 1813 he followed Capt. Byng, as Master's Mate, into the WARRIOR 74, and in Nov. of the same year sailed with the Prince of Orange for Holland. In the ensuing Dec. he removed to the IMPREGNABLE 98, successive flag-ship of Admiral Wm. Young and H.R.H. the Duke of Clarence; as Aide-de-Camp to the latter of whom we find him escorting the allied sovereigns from Calais to Dover. He was advanced in consequence (he had passed in 1808) to the rank of Lieutenant 27 June, 1814. With the exception of a short time passed in 1826-7 in the Coast Blockade as Supernumerary-Lieutenant of the RAMILLIES 74, Capt. Hugh Pigot, he has since been on half-pay.

Lieut. Petch married, 18 April, 1816, Hannah, daughter of Thos. Stapleton, a Master in the merchant-service, by whom he has issue 9 children. His eldest son, Wm. Henry Petch, Second-Master R.N. (1844), has been acting, since Aug. 1844, as Master of the PROMETHEUS steamer, and SEALARK sloop, on the coast of Africa. AGENTS—Messrs. Ommanney.

PETLEY. (RETIRED COMMANDER, 1843. F-P., 21; H-P., 33.)

JOHN PETLEY entered the Navy, 4 Feb. 1793, as Midshipman, on board the SUFFOLK 74, Capts. Robt. Lambert and Pulteney Malcolm, employed at first in the Channel and afterwards in the East Indies; where he was nominated, 21 Aug. 1798, Acting-Lieutenant of the CENTURION 50, Capt. John Sprat Rainier. Under Capt. Lambert he assisted, in 1795-6, at the reduction of Ceylon, Amboyna, Banda, &c. He was confirmed a Lieutenant, 4 Aug. 1799, into the INTREPID 64, Capt. Wm. Hargood, also in the East Indies; and subsequently appointed—28 June, 1801, to the DÆDALUS 36, Capt. Wm. Waller, with whom he returned to England in 1803—16 Nov. in that year, to the ATALANTE 16, Capt. Joseph Ore Masefield, with whom he cruized in the Channel until Oct. 1805, when a wound he had received in the eye obliged him to be sent to the Hospital at Plymouth—4 Feb. 1806, to the command of a Signal station in co. Waterford, which he retained until Oct. 1809—and, in Feb. 1810, to the Impress service at Gravesend. In April, 1814, he was placed on half-pay. He became a Retired Commander on the Junior List 30 July, 1840; and on the Senior 23 Dec. 1843.

PETRIE. (LIEUT., 1816. F-P., 9; H-P., 31.)

PETER PETRIE was born 14 Oct. 1789, in Fifeshire, N.B.

This officer entered the Navy, 16 Nov. 1807, as Fst.-cl. Vol., on board the CAPTAIN 74, Capts. Isaac

Wolley, Jas. Athol Wood, and Christopher John Williams Nesham; during his servitude in which ship he commanded a boat, as Midshipman, at the landing of the troops at Madeira in Dec. 1807, served on shore with the small-arm men and had charge of an outpost at the capture of Marie-Galante in March, 1808, and in Feb. 1809 co-operated in the reduction of Martinique. During the operations connected with the latter affair he had command of a boat, served in a battery, and was wounded in the ankle. In April, 1809, he witnessed the capture of the Saintes Islands and the surrender of the French 74-gun ship *D'Haupoult*. In the following Dec., having returned to England, he was received on board the Espiègle 16, Capt. Donald Campbell, fitting for the West Indies, where he continued employed with the same officer in the Port d'Espagne 14 and Rosamond 18, until transferred, in Jan. 1814, to the Tonnant 80, flag-ship of Sir Alex. Cochrane in North America—part of the time as Acting-Lieutenant. While borne on the books of the Rosamond he appears, at the commencement of the war with the United States, to have conducted two valuable prizes, the *Friendship* and *Dolphin*, into Plymouth, and to have carried two American vessels from the Gulf of Paria into Grenada. He was also intrusted with the charge of a boat and employed in the suppression of smuggling on the Spanish main. In the Tonnant we find him present at the capture of Washington, at the unsuccessful attack upon Baltimore, and in the expedition against New Orleans. In command of one of the same ship's boats he served, with those of a squadron, and was slightly wounded in the fingers, at the capture, on Lake Borgne, 14 Dec. 1814, of five American gun-vessels, after a very desperate struggle, in which the British sustained a loss of 17 men killed and 77 wounded. In the Tonnant's barge he aided in covering the retreat of the army from New Orleans. Being nominated, 13 March, 1815, Acting-Lieutenant of the Arab 16, Capt. Henry Jane, he was employed in that vessel, after Buonaparte's escape from Elba, in blockading a heavy French frigate in New York. Since he was confirmed in his present rank, 30 July, 1816, he has been on half-pay. He has, however, had command of ships in the merchant service, and has visited in them most parts of the world.

He married, in Jan. 1819, Elizabeth, eldest daughter of Walter Grindlay, Esq., a ship-owner, by whom he has issue three sons and five daughters.

PETTET. (Lieutenant, 1828.)

John Pettet was born 13 May, 1796. He had a relative in the service, Mark Pettet, who was wounded at New Orleans; and also a brother and brother-in-law, both of whom died Lieutenants.

This officer entered the Navy, 27 Oct. 1810, as a Volunteer, on board the Monarch 74, Capt. Rich. Lee; in which ship, and in the Bellerophon and Scarborough 74's, the former bearing the flag of Rear-Admiral John Ferrier, and the latter commanded by Capts. John Halsted and Chas. Jas. Johnston, he served in the North Sea, part of the time as Midshipman, until May, 1814. After a further employment of eight months on the same station in the Mercurius 16 and Plumper 12, Capts. Thos. Renwick and Geo. Domett, he joined, in Sept. 1815, the Romney 50, Capt. John Mackellar, fitting for the West Indies; where he continued, in the Salisbury 58, flag-ship of Rear-Admiral John Erskine Douglas, Rifleman 18, Capts. Robt. Rochfort Felix and Norwich Duff, and again, as Master's Mate, in the Salisbury, until the spring of 1818. Prior to joining the Rifleman he appears to have been lent to the Briseis 10, Capt. Geo. Domett, and to have been wrecked in that vessel on a desolate part of the island of Cuba 5 Nov. 1816; from which period, until picked up 11 weeks and a half afterwards by the Landrail, he remained exposed, with his fellow-sufferers, to the greatest hardships, being nearly destitute the whole time of provisions and clothing. In March, 1819, having passed his examination in the preceding Nov., he was received, as Admiralty-Midshipman, on board the Severn 50, Capt. Wm. M'Culloch, lying in the Downs, for the purposes of the Coast Blockade. He left that service in Feb. 1820; and during the nine following years was employed, on the Jamaica, Home, and African stations, in the Tribune 42, Capt. Nesbit Josiah Willoughby, Euryalus 42, Capt. Thos. Huskisson, Nautilus 18 and Bann 22, both commanded by Capt. John Ralph Blois, Scout 18, Capts. John Theed and Jas. Wigston, Pheasant 18, Capt. Douglas Chas. Clavering, Prince Regent 120, Capt. Wm. Henry Webley Parry, Conflict 12, Lieut.-Commander Christie, Maidstone 42, Commodore Chas. Bullen, Esk 20, Capt. Wm. Jardine Purchas, Sybille 48, Commodore Fras. Augustus Collier, and Plumper 12, Lieut.-Commander Edw. Medley. In the Bann and Pheasant he performed the duties of Second-Master and Master; and, while serving in the Sybille, he was promoted to the rank of Lieutenant, by commission bearing date 14 July, 1828. During his sojourn on the coast of Africa where he saw much detached service, he had the good fortune to participate in the capture of a large number of slaves. He returned home in the Plumper in the early part of 1829, with at least 40 persons charged with piracy under his care; and has since been on half-pay.

We had nearly omitted to record that, while attached, in 1819, to the Coast Blockade, he had very materially contributed to the rescue of the Dawn brig, by getting her off the rocks near Dover, and conducting her thence to Ramsgate, although she had lost her rudder and had six feet water in the hold.

PETTMAN. (Lieut., 1810. f-p., 12; h-p., 33.)

Richard Pettman entered the Navy, in Dec. 1802, as Fst.-cl. Vol., on board the Albion 74, Capt. John Ferrier, with whom he continued employed, as Midshipman and Master's Mate, on the Channel and East India stations, until the summer of 1809. In Nov. of that year, after having been for a few months borne as a Supernumerary on the books of the Sceptre 74, Capt. Joseph Bingham, he was nominated Acting-Lieutenant of the Jalouse 18, Capt. Henry Gage Morris, attached to the force on the coast of Ireland, where, in March, 1810, he joined the Trent 36, flag-ship of Vice-Admiral Jas. Hawkins Whitshed. He was officially promoted 15 Aug. following; and subsequently appointed—15 Sept. 1810, to the Portia 14, Capts. Joseph Symes and John Thomson, at North Yarmouth—29 Jan. 1813, to the Vigo 74, flag-ship in the Baltic of Rear-Admiral Jas. Nicoll Morris—and, 19 April, 1814, after nearly four months of half-pay, to the Levant 20, Capts. Hon. Alex. Jones and Hon. Geo. Douglas, stationed off Madeira. He invalided in Jan. 1815; and has not been since afloat.

PEW. (Lieutenant, 1816. f-p., 8; h-p., 30.)

George Pew is brother of the late Major Pew.

This officer entered the Navy, 22 March, 1809, as Fst.-cl. Vol., on board the Pheasant 18, Capt. John Palmer, stationed in the Channel, where, during a servitude of three years and a half, he assisted at the capture of three privateers, carrying in the whole 25 guns and 155 men. Becoming Midshipman, in Sept. 1812, of the Surprise 38, Capt. Sir Thos. John Cochrane, he witnessed in that ship the capture, 16 Jan. 1813, of the *Decatur* American privateer of 12 guns and 82 men, and was in her during the attacks on Washington and Baltimore, and throughout the operations on the coast of Georgia. In July, 1816, after a servitude of nine months at Plymouth as Master's Mate of the Spencer 74, Capt. Wm. Robt. Broughton, he removed in that capacity to the Beelzebub bomb, Capt. Wm. Kempthorne; and on 16 of the following Sept., as a reward for his services at the bombardment of Algiers, he was promoted to the rank of Lieutenant. He has since been on half-pay.

In 1817 Lieut. Pew obtained permission from the

Admiralty to command a West Indiaman, in which he traded to Jamaica until 1838. He had frequently during the war had charge of a prize. AGENTS—Messrs. Stilwell.

PHELPS. (LIEUTENANT, 1842.)

HENRY PHELPS entered the Navy, 18 April, 1832; passed his examination 4 June, 1838; and while serving, as Mate, on board the POWERFUL 84, Commodore Chas. Napier, was present at the bombardment of St. Jean d'Acre 3 Nov. 1840. On 21 July, 1842, being then Mate of the CORNWALLIS 72, flagship of Sir Wm. Parker, he assisted in the boats in covering the assault made on the city of Chin-Kiang-Foo.* For his services in China he was promoted to the rank of Lieutenant 23 Dec. 1842.† His appointments have since been—18 March, 1843, again to the CORNWALLIS, in which ship he continued until her return to England in 1844—15 April, 1845, to the MELAMPUS 42, Capt. John Norman Campbell, with whom he again sailed for the East Indies—and, 2 June, 1847, to the ST. VINCENT 120, as Flag-Lieutenant to Sir Chas. Napier.

PHEPOE. (RETIRED COMMANDER, 1848. F-P., 12; H-P., 34.)

JOHN PHEPOE, born 10 Aug. 1786, is son of John Phepoe, Esq., of Dublin, Colonel of a regiment of the Irish Volunteers of 1782.

This officer entered the Navy 15 May, 1801, as Fst.-cl. Vol., on board the ATLAS 98, Capt. Theophilus Jones, attached to the Channel fleet, with which he served until April, 1802. In the following Oct. he joined the GALGO 16, Capt. Michael Dodd, stationed on the coast of Ireland; he next, in May, 1803, became Midshipman of the MINOTAUR 74, Capt. Chas. John Moore Mansfield, again in the Channel; and in Aug. 1805 he was received on board the AJAX 74, Capts. Wm. Brown, John Pilfold, and Hon. Henry Blackwood. He was in the latter ship when she caught fire and was burnt off the island of Tenedos 14 Feb. 1797; on which occasion he was obliged, in order to save his life, to plunge into the sea, and to support himself, by dint of swimming, until picked up by a boat belonging to H.M.S. CANOPUS. Being at once received into the THUNDERER 74, Capt. John Talbot, he served with Sir John Duckworth at the ensuing passage of the Dardanells, and then accompanied the expedition to Egypt, where he landed and co-operated with the army in the two unsuccessful attacks on Rosetta. From the THUNDERER Mr. Phepoe, in Sept. 1808, was transferred to the WARSPITE 74, commanded by his former Captain, Blackwood, with whom he continued employed on Home service until promoted to the rank of Lieutenant 13 June, 1809. In the following Sept., after having been attached to the flotilla in the operations against Walcheren, he obtained an appointment to the ARMIDE 38, Capts. Lucius Ferdinand Hardyman, Rich. Dalling Dunn, Fras. Temple, and Sir Edw. Thos.Troubridge; in the boats of which ship, aided by those of the CADMUS sloop and MONKEY and DARING gunbrigs, we find him, 4 May, 1811, contributing to the destruction of 13 out of a convoy of 17 sail, defended, at the Ile de Ré, by batteries on shore, two armed luggers, and several pinnaces—the loss of the British amounting, on the occasion, to 3 killed and 3 wounded, all belonging to the ARMIDE. In command, 19 Oct. following, of two boats, carrying 22 men, Mr. Phepoe, in company with two other boats under the orders of Lieut. Jas. Couch of the ACASTA 40, captured in a calm on the coast of France an American schooner, the *Trojan*, pierced for 18 guns, but carrying only 4 12-pounder carronades and 2 swivels, with a crew of 22 men. From March, 1813, to March, 1814, he served on the Newfoundland station in the SYBILLE 44, Capts. Clotworthy Upton and Jas. Sanders. The latter was his last appointment. He accepted his present rank 5 Jan. 1848. AGENTS—Messrs. Ommanney.

* *Vide* Gaz. 1842, p. 3405. † *V.* Gaz 1842, p. 3821.

PHILIPPS. (LIEUTENANT, 1844.)

GRIFFITH GRISMOND PHILIPPS is son of Commander John Henry Philipps, R.N.

This officer served as Midshipman of the DARTMOUTH 42, Capt. Thos. Fellowes, at the battle of Navarin 20 Oct. 1827. He passed his examination in 1831; and obtained, 28 June, 1838, a commission, the date of which was afterwards altered to 7 Feb. 1844. His appointments have since been—5 July, 1838, as Additional Lieutenant, to the CORNWALLIS 72, bearing the flag of Sir Thos. Harvey in North America and the West Indies—28 March, 1839, to the SERINGAPATAM 42, Capts. John Leith and Wm. Ward Percival Johnson, on the same station, whence he returned to England and was paid off in Nov. 1841—9 March, 1842, as First, to the RINGDOVE 16, Capt. Sir Wm. Daniell, with whom he served in the West Indies until Feb. 1844—2 June, 1845, to the HECATE steam-sloop, of 240-horse power, Capt. Joseph West, fitting for the coast of Africa—and, 23 Nov. 1847, after a brief interval of half-pay, to the ACHERON steam surveying-vessel, of 160-horse power, Capt. John Lort Stokes, now in the East Indies. AGENTS—Messrs. Halford and Co.

PHILIPPS. (COMMANDER, 1814. F-P., 18; H-P., 33.)

JOHN GEORGE PHILIPPS was born in Sept. 1783. His father, the late J. Y. Philipps, Esq., was many years M.P. for the borough of Caermarthen.

This officer entered the Navy, in May, 1796, as a Vol., on board the RUSSEL 74, Capt. Thos. Larcom, bearing the flag of Vice-Admiral John Macbride in the North Sea. Removing, in the following Sept., to the MINOTAUR 74, Capt. Thos. Louis, he served in that ship, as Midshipman, at the battle of the Nile 1 Aug. 1798; and, continuing in her until March, 1802, was present on shore at the capture of Naples, Civita Vecchia, Rome, &c., co-operated in the siege of Genoa, and took part in the operations of 1801 in Egypt. He also, 3 Sept. 1800, served in one of eight boats which brought out from Barcelona Roads, after having sustained a loss of 3 men killed and 5 wounded, the Spanish corvettes *Esmeralda* and *Paz* of 22 guns each, although defended by a heavy fire from four strong batteries, 10 gunboats, two schooners, armed between them with 4 long 36-pounders, and a fort upon Mount Ioni, which threw shells. The enemy in the affair had 3 men killed and 21 wounded. On leaving the MINOTAUR, as above, Mr. Philipps joined the ARDENT 64, Capt. Wm. Nowell, on the Home station; where, and on the coast of North America, we find him, until March, 1806, employed in succession, the greater part of the time as Acting-Lieutenant and Lieutenant, in the ARGONAUT and LEANDER, flagships of Admiral Bartholomew Samuel Rowley and Sir Andrew Mitchell, CAMBRIAN 40, Capt. Wm. Bradley, and AVENGER sloop, Capt. Thos. White. His official promotion took place while he was in the latter vessel, 8 Feb. 1805. His subsequent appointments were—in March, 1806, to the LAVINIA 40, Capt. Lord Wm. Stuart, employed in the Channel and on the north coast of Spain—8 Dec. 1807, to the PILOT 18, Capt. Hon. Wm. Walpole, lying at Portsmouth—25 March, 1808, to the SPEEDY sloop, Capt. Rich. Henry Muddle, at Newfoundland—in March, 1809, to the MAJESTIC 74, Capt. Thos. Harvey, in the Baltic—and, in Jan. 1810, and April, 1811, to the REDPOLE 10, Capt. Colin Macdonald, and MONMOUTH 64, bearing the flag of the late Sir Thos. Foley, both in the Downs. Becoming, in May, 1814, Signal-Lieutenant to the officer last mentioned, he was lent soon afterwards to the ROYAL SOVEREIGN yacht, Capt. Sir John Poo Beresford, to assist in escorting Louis XVIII. from Dover to Calais. He was advanced to his present rank 22 Oct. following; and has since been on half-pay.

Commander Philipps is a Magistrate and Deputy-Lieutenant for co. Caermarthen. He married, in Feb. 1808, and has issue nine children. One of his sons, Griffith Grismond, is a Lieutenant, and another, Geo. Vaughan, a Midshipman in the R.N.

PHILIPPS. (Lieut., 1815. f-p., 15; h-p., 25.)

John Philipps Philipps entered the Navy, 26 May, 1807, as Fst.-cl. Vol., on board the Temeraire 98, Capts. Sir Chas. Hamilton and Edw. Sneyd Clay; the former of whom, after having been for three years and a half employed in the Channel and Baltic, part of the time under the flag of Rear-Admiral Manley Dixon, he rejoined, as Midshipman, in Dec. 1809, on board the Tonnant 80, commanded subsequently, off Cadiz and Lisbon, by Capts. Hassard Stackpoole and Sir John Gore. He next, from June, 1812, until May, 1815, served, in the Channel, at St. Helena and the Cape of Good Hope, on the coast of North America, and in the West Indies, in the Niemen 38, Capt. Sam. Pym. In the following Aug., being then at Plymouth in the San Josef 110, he was presented with a commission bearing date 6 of the preceding March. His last appointments were, 27 June, 1837, and 8 Aug. 1839, to the command of the Lucifer and Medusa steam-packets, in which he served until July, 1844. Agent—W. H. B. Barwis.

PHILIPS. (Rear-Admiral of the Red, 1841. f-p., 17; h-p., 45.)

James Robert Philips, a native of Scarborough, is son of the late Mr. Alex. Philips, Master R.N.; and brother of Major John Alex. Philips, of the Royal Marines, who, prior to joining that service, served as Midshipman of the Belleisle 74 in the action off Cape Trafalgar.

This officer entered the Navy, 4 Oct. 1785, as A.B., on board the Resolution, Capt. Israel Pellew, with whom he was for two years employed on the coast of Ireland. Between 1789 and April, 1796, he served on the Home and West India stations in the Swallow sloop, Capts. Wm. Hargood and Jas. Bissett, Inconstant 36, Capt. Geo. Wilson, Camel store-ship, commanded by his father, Cambridge 74, Capt. Rich. Boger, Sampson 64, Capt. Robt. Montagu, Bellona 74, Capt. Geo. Wilson, Woolwich 44, Capt. Wm. Chas. Fahie, and Majestic 74, bearing the flag of Sir John Laforey. Of the latter ship he was created a Lieutenant 10 Dec. 1795. He had previously, in 1794, when Midshipman of the Bellona, assisted at the defence of Fort Matilda, Guadeloupe. On leaving the Majestic, as above, he joined the Beaulieu 40, Capts. Lancelot Skynner and Fras. Fayerman; during his servitude in which ship we find him employed on shore at the capture of Ste. Lucie in May, 1796, and present, 11 Oct. 1797, in the action off Camperdown. At the close of that conflict Lieut. Philips took charge of the *Mounikendam*, a Dutch 40; wherein he had the misfortune to be wrecked on a sand near West Capel. He fell, on the occasion, into the hands of the enemy, and remained for some time in captivity. On his restoration to liberty he went back to the Beaulieu, and proceeded in her to the Mediterranean. Invaliding thence in March, 1800, he joined, in the following July, the Princess Royal 98, flag-ship in the Channel of Sir Erasmus Gower, with whom he remained until April, 1802. His next appointments were—19 July, 1803, and 30 July, 1804, to the Russel 74, Capt. Robt. Williams, and Centurion 50, Capts. Jas. Lind and John Sprat Rainier. In the latter ship, of which he was First-Lieutenant, he assisted, 18 Sept. 1804, in gallantly beating off, in Vizagapatam Roads, a French squadron, by whom she had been vigorously attacked, consisting of the *Marengo* 80, bearing the flag of Admiral Linois, and 40-gun frigates *Atalante* and *Sémillante*. At the commencement of the action, which was long maintained, Mr. Philips, owing to the absence of his Captain, was in sole command of the Centurion. "I had been on shore," says Capt. Lind at the beginning of his official narrative addressed to Vice-Admiral Rainier, "and was not present in the early part of the action, for, till now, the Centurion had been under the direction of the First-Lieutenant, Mr. Jas. Robt. Philips; and before I proceed any further in this account, permit me to notice the judicious conduct of this deserving and old officer, and his gallant defence of the ship against so superior a force as that of the enemy. I hope, Sir, his conduct will be thought worthy of a reward, and that he will be esteemed deserving of promotion." * He was, in consequence, advanced to the rank of Commander 15 March, 1805; and on 28 May, 1806, he was appointed to the Bonetta 14, and ordered, until the arrival of that vessel in port, to act as Commander of the Gannet 16. Joining the Bonetta in the following June, he was employed, during the remainder of the year, in escorting merchantmen to and from the German rivers, and in 1807 in affording protection to the trade in the Baltic; where he took part, under Admiral Gambier, in the operations against Copenhagen. He attained Post-rank 13 Oct. 1807; and has since been on half-pay. His promotion to Flag-rank took place 23 Nov. 1841.

PHILLIMORE. (Lieutenant, 1845.)

Augustus Phillimore entered the Navy in 1835; passed his examination 17 May, 1842; and at the period of his promotion to the rank of Lieutenant, 7 Sept. 1845, was serving as Mate on board the Hibernia 104; in which ship, bearing the flag of Sir Wm. Parker in the Mediterranean, he still continues.

PHILLIPPS. (Lieutenant, 1814.)

Henry Cranmer March Phillipps, born 23 March, 1793, is fifth son of the late Thos. March Phillipps, Esq., of More Critchell, co. Dorset, and Garendon Park and Grace Dieu Manor, co. Leicester, by Susan, daughter of Chas. Lisle, Esq., of Moyles Court, co. Hants. He is brother-in-law of the late Bishop of Lichfield and Coventry.

This officer entered the Navy, 18 Aug. 1806, as a Supernumerary, on board the Theseus 74, Capt. Geo. Hope, lying in Cawsand Bay; and in the course of the same year joined the Royal George 100, flag-ship of Sir John Thos. Duckworth, Sophie sloop, Capt. Wm. Mansell, and Seahorse of 42 guns and 281 men, Capt. John Stewart. Continuing in the latter ship until June, 1811, he was employed during that period in attendance on many diplomatic personages, and was afforded an opportunity of participating in numerous important services. On the night of 5 July, 1808, in particular, he contributed to the capture, after a furious engagement and a loss to the Seahorse (30 of whose crew were absent) of 5 men killed and 10 wounded, of the Turkish man-of-war *Badere Zaffer*, mounting 52 guns, with a complement of 543 men, of whom 170 were slain and 200 wounded. The *Alis Fezan*, of 26 guns and 230 men, a ship which had been also opposed to the Seahorse, was at the same time put to flight. After a servitude of two years as Midshipman in the Valiant 74, Capt. Robt. Dudley Oliver, Mr. Phillipps, in July, 1813, being then on the North American station, became Acting-Lieutenant of the Wasp sloop, Capt. Thos. Everard. He was confirmed a Lieutenant 10 March, 1814. At the commencement of the peace he was serving on board the Eridanus 36, Capts. Henry Prescott, Wm. Paterson, and Wm. King. Since he left that frigate he has been on half-pay. Agents—Messrs. Chard.

PHILLIPPS. (Lieutenant, 1830.)

Robert Phillipps, born 6 Aug. 1807, is fifth and youngest son of the late Rev. John Phillipps, of Lower Eaton, co. Hereford, Rector of Stoke St. Milborough, co. Salop, by Anne, fourth daughter of Chas. Pye, Esq., of Wadley, in Berkshire. Two of his brothers, Charles and Henry, were lately Captains in the 3rd Light Dragoons.

This officer entered the Navy 10 Aug. 1820; passed his examination in 1827; obtained his commission 26 Feb. 1830; served from 15 June, 1837

* *Vide* Gaz. 1805, p. 334.

until paid off at the close of 1840, as First-Lieutenant, in the SPARROWHAWK 16, Capt. John Shepherd (*b*), on the Brazils and Cape of Good Hope stations; and since 18 July, 1845, has been in command of the BLOODHOUND steamer of 150 horse-power. AGENTS—Messrs. Ommanney.

PHILLIPS. (COMMANDER, 1848.)

CHARLES GERRANS PHILLIPS entered the Navy 25 Nov. 1820; passed his examination in 1827; and obtained his first commission 28 June, 1838. His succeeding appointments were—21 Sept. 1839, to the TERROR, Capt. Fras. Rawdon Moira Crozier, in which vessel he sailed with an expedition under Capt. Jas. Clarke Ross, for the purposes of magnetic research and geographical discovery in the Antarctic Ocean—and, 23 Nov. 1843, as First-Lieutenant, to the HELENA 16, Capt. Sir Cornwallis Ricketts, fitting for the Cape of Good Hope, whence he returned to England and was paid off in 1847. He was advanced to the rank of Commander 31 Jan. 1848. AGENTS—Messrs. Chard.

PHILLIPS. (LIEUT., 1812. F-P., 15; H-P., 31.)

EDWARD PHILLIPS was born 22 Aug. 1790. His grandfather, Lieut. Rich. Lang, was nearly 50 years a commissioned officer in the service.

This officer entered the Navy, 15 July, 1801, as Fst.-cl. Vol., on board the GOLIATH 74, Capts. Wm. Essington, Chas. Brisbane, and Robt. Barton, employed in the Channel and West Indies—for some time under the flag of Sir John Thos. Duckworth. In Feb. 1806 he removed as Midshipman (a rating he had attained in June, 1802) to the ST. GEORGE 98, flag-ship in the Baltic and Channel of Rear-Admirals Eliab Harvey and Fras. Pickmore; he next, from Nov. 1809 until Oct. 1812, served, in the North Sea and Baltic, on board the HEARTY 14, Lieut.-Commander Wm. Wickham, CRESSY 74, Capt. Chas. Dudley Pater, and VICTORY 100, flag-ship of Sir Jas. Saumarez; and on 20 Nov. in the latter year he was confirmed a Lieutenant in the ROSE sloop, Capt. Thos. Mansell. In the GOLIATH, Mr. Phillips witnessed the capture, 28 June, 1803, and 11 and 18 Aug. 1805, of *La Mignonne* of 16 guns and 80 men, *La Faune* of 16, and *La Torche* of 18 guns. While attached to the HEARTY he retook a galliot, and cut out a Danish privateer, *The Quick Huntsman;* and when in the CRESSY, besides making prize of another privateer, he came into contact, in 1811, with a flotilla of 40 gun-boats. Although the latter had been the aggressors, several of them were taken by the CRESSY. When afterwards in charge of a Russian brig, Mr. Phillips was cast away and taken prisoner on the coast of Lapland. During the winter of 1812, at which time he was serving on board the ROSE, he assisted at the capture by that sloop of every vessel that came out from Norway or Jutland. Lieut. Phillips' last appointment was to the CALLIOPE 10, Capts. John M'Kerlie, John Codd, and Alex. Maconochie, with whom he continued from 25 May, 1813, until paid off in Sept. 1815. On 8 July, 1813, he was for two hours in action with the enemy's naval force at Cuxhaven; and on 31 of the following Oct., having been sent up the river Weser in charge of the boats of the CALLIOPE and WRANGLER, he passed the strong batteries of Bremerlehe and Blexen (at the surrender of which he was shortly afterwards present), and succeeded in capturing two row-boats, one carrying 16 the other 12 men, together with four sail of merchantmen, lying off Braak, where he also aided in taking possession of two 20-gun corvettes that were building. During the expedition against New Orleans Lieut. Phillips, with the CALLIOPE's cutter in charge, co-operated with the small-arm men under Capt. Rowland Money, and the troops under Colonel Thornton, at the storming of a battery on the Mississippi, 8 Jan. 1815.

He married, 28 Nov. 1825, Miss Mary Clapshaw.

PHILLIPS. (LIEUT., 1815. F-P., 33; H-P. 9.)

FREDERICK PHILLIPS entered the Navy, 28 Aug. 1805, as Fst.-cl. Vol., on board the BELLONA 74, Capts. Chas. Dudley Pater and John Erskine Douglas; under the latter of whom we find him present, as Midshipman, at the destruction of the French 74-gun ship *Impétueux*, off Cape Henry, 14 Sept. 1806, also in the attack upon the enemy's fleet in Basque Roads and in the expedition to the Walcheren in 1809, and at the capture, 18 Dec. 1810, of *Le Héros du Nord* privateer of 14 guns and 44 men. On 22 June, 1807, he chanced to be, as a Supernumerary, on board the LEOPARD 50, Capt. Salusbury Pryce Humphreys, when that ship compelled the U. S. frigate *Chesapeake* to surrender, in consequence of a refusal on the part of the latter to allow the British to search her for deserters. Following Capt. Douglas from the BELLONA, in May, 1812, into the PRINCE OF WALES 98, he sailed with him soon afterwards for the Mediterranean, where, in April, 1814, he beheld the fall of Genoa. On his return to England in April, 1815, from the West Indies, whither he had gone with convoy in the SWIFTSURE 74, Capt. Wm. Henry Webley Parry, Mr. Phillips found that he had been promoted to the rank of Lieutenant 7 Feb. preceding. From May, 1824, until March, 1831, he served in the Coast Blockade as a Supernumerary of the RAMILLIES 74 and HYPERION 42, Capts. Wm. M'Culloch and Wm. Jas. Mingaye. He has been since serving in the Coast Guard.

PHILLIPS. (LIEUT., 1815. F-P., 9; H-P., 31.)

WILLIAM PHILLIPS entered the Navy, 12 April, 1807, as Fst.-cl. Vol., on board the SHELDRAKE 16, Capt. John Thicknesse, employed on the Jersey and Guernsey station, where he came into frequent contact with the enemy's gun-brigs and batteries, and was more than once engaged in cutting out their vessels. In 1809, having removed as Midshipman to the DIOMEDE 50, Capt. Hugh Cook, he sailed with Vice-Admiral Wm. O'Brien Drury for the East Indies, whence, in March, 1811, we find him escorting several of the Hon. Co.'s ships by St. Helena. In the following Sept. Mr. Phillips was received on board the ULYSSES 44, in which ship he continued to serve under the flags, off Jersey and Cherbourg, of Admirals D'Auvergne and Wm. Brown, until Sept. 1812. During the next 12 months he was employed at the blockade of the Texel, as Master's Mate, in the DANNEMARK 74, Capt. Henry Edw. Reginald Baker. He then joined the MEDWAY 74, bearing the flag of Sir Chas. Tyler at the Cape of Good Hope. In Nov. 1815, having been awarded a commission dated 6 of the preceding March, he returned to England. He has since been on half-pay. He married in 1817, and has issue one son and seven daughters.

PHILLOTT. (Captain, 1818. F-P., 24; H-P., 29.)

CHARLES GEORGE RODNEY PHILLOTT entered the Navy, 27 Jan. 1794, as Captain's Servant, on board the VANGUARD 74, Capt. John Stanhope, then on the eve of her departure for the West Indies; and was afterwards, until advanced to the rank of Lieutenant, 1 July, 1801, employed on various stations in the AVENGER sloop, Capt. Chas. Ogle, RUBY 64, Capt. Henry Edwin Stanhope, AMERICA 64, Commodore John Blanket, NEPTUNE 98, bearing the broad pendant of Sir Erasmus Gower, ACHILLE 74, Capts. H. E. Stanhope and Geo. Murray, and AGINCOURT 64, flag-ship of Rear-Admiral Chas. Morice Pole. As Midshipman of the RUBY, we find him present at the detention of five Dutch men-of-war, together with a large convoy, in Plymouth Sound, 19 Jan. 1795; and, in the course of the same year, assisting at the reduction of the Cape of Good Hope. In the AMERICA he witnessed the surrender of the Dutch squadron in Saldanha Bay, 17 Aug. 1796. On the occasion of his promotion, as above, Mr. Phillott joined the TERROR bomb, Capt. Sam. Campbell Rowley, with whom he continued cruizing in the Baltic until the close of the following Oct. Being next, 31 Aug. 1802, appointed to the AMPHION 32, Capts. Thos. Masterman Hardy, Sam. Sutton, and Wm. Hoste, he sailed in that ship for the Mediterranean, in the early part of 1803, with the flag on board of Lord Nelson, and was afterwards afforded an opportunity of participating, more or less prominently, in a train of valuable and distinguished services. On 5 Oct. 1804 he contributed to the capture of three Spanish frigates, and the destruction of a fourth, off Cape St. Mary; in the summer of 1805 he accompanied Lord Nelson to the West Indies and back, in pursuit of the combined squadrons of France and Spain; he assisted, in the following Nov., at the defeat, although supported by the fire of an immense battery, of a division of about 30 Spanish gun-boats, which had come out of Algeciras in the hope of capturing a British convoy; and in the summer of 1806 he was present at the debarkation of the troops immediately prior to the battle of Maida, as also at the capture of the town of Reggio, and of the important fortress of Cotrone, with all its stores and magazines, and upwards of 600 troops. He next, 12 May, 1808, shared in a very spirited engagement of many hours with several heavy batteries in the Bay of Rosas, in an attempt to cut out the French frigate-built 800-ton store-ship *Baleine*, mounting from 26 to 30 guns, with a crew of 150 men. In command, 8 Feb. 1809, of the boats of the AMPHION and REDWING, he landed on the island of Melida, in the Gulf of Venice, brought off 3 guns, and destroyed two large stores of oil and wine.* He also, 23 April following, with a division of the boats of the AMPHION, SPARTAN, and MERCURY under his orders, behaved in an exemplary manner at the capture of 13 valuable merchantmen lying in the mole of Pesaro;† and, on 27 Aug. in the same year, he signalized himself by his gallant attack on the strong fort of Cortelazzo, near Trieste, which he stormed and carried at the head of a detachment of 70 officers, seamen, and marines—occasioning the simultaneous surrender, within sight of an Italian squadron off Venice, of six of the enemy's gun-boats, and a convoy of merchant-trabaccolos anchored for protection under its walls.‡ In Jan. 1810, having been rewarded for his conspicuous conduct on the latter occasion by a commission bearing date the same day, Capt. Phillott left the AMPHION; and, on 25 Oct. following, assumed command of the PRIMROSE 18, in which vessel, besides accompanying Sir Joseph Sydney Yorke with a body of troops to Lisbon, he served in the Scheldt and North Sea, twice escorted convoy to North America, and was for some time stationed on the coast of Spain.§ He was engaged also in conveying troops from the river Garonne to Bermuda; and on 25 Aug. 1814 he effected the destruction, off the Savannah river, of the American privateer *Pike*, of 13 guns and a complement of 85 men, 47 of whom were on board.* In Feb. 1815, in command of a division of boats belonging to the squadron under Sir Geo. Cockburn at Cumberland Island on the coast of Georgia, he proceeded up St. Mary's river to a considerable distance for the purpose of surprising a detachment of the enemy; but finding the attempt impracticable, and having been for many hours exposed to a galling fire from the heights along both banks of the stream, during which 3 men were killed and 15 wounded, including himself, in five places, by a rifle-ball and buck-shot, he found it imperative on him to return. On their way back, the boats behaved with the greatest coolness and order.† In Aug. 1815 the PRIMROSE was paid off. She was, however, immediately re-commissioned, on the peace establishment, by Capt. Phillott, who continued to command her, on the Jamaica station, until again paid off, 19 Dec. 1818. His promotion to Post-rank took place on 7 of that month. He accepted the Retirement 1 Oct. 1846.

* *Vide* Gaz. 1809, p. 622. † *V.* Gaz. 1809, p. 1257.
‡ *V.* Gaz. 1809, p. 1906.
§ The following is taken from Marshall's 'Naval Biography,' Supplement, Part IV., pp. 193-5:—
"On the 12th of March, 1814, being then in lat. 43° 16′ N., long. 10° 56′ W., he discovered and made sail after a strange brig on his lee bow, running nearly before the wind. Observing that she altered her course to avoid him, that she frequently yawed about as the PRIMROSE approached (with a large red ensign at the peak), and that she had neither lower studding-sail nor royals set, he supposed her to be an English vessel in the hands of a prize crew. Unfortunately her real character was not discovered nor even suspected, until after much mischief had been done. It may here be as well to state that the stranger was a King's Packet named the DUKE OF MARLBOROUGH, commanded by Capt. John Bull, and employed in conveying a mail from Falmouth to Lisbon. On observing the PRIMROSE bear up and make sail, Capt. Bull suspected her to be an American cruizer, and made the private signal, in order to ascertain whether she was an enemy or not; the end on position of the two brigs, however, together with their distance from each other, and the circumstances of his flags being only half the established size, prevented the possibility of making it out. At 7 55 P.M., it being then too dark for flags of any size to be distinguished, the Packet, after an ineffectual attempt to make the private night-signal, opened her stern chasers (long brass nines), shot away most of the supposed American's headgear, including jib and flying jib-stays, and continued firing them with considerable precision for about 20 minutes. The PRIMROSE then ranged up on her larboard quarter and hailed three times, but was only answered by as many single guns, followed by a whole broadside. Upon this Capt. Phillott gave her a gun or two, and endeavoured to lay her on board, but his head-braces being shot away, he failed in the attempt, and some little time elapsed before he could again overtake her. The PRIMROSE then commenced firing in earnest. The Packet was, of course, soon silenced, and upon her being once more hailed the painful truth came out. Her damages proved to be of a very serious nature; two 32-pound shot had passed through just below the water's edge. She had between three and four feet water in her hold, and the leak was fast increasing; her masts were much injured, and her standing and running rigging nearly all cut away. Her loss consisted of two passengers killed and ten or twelve other persons wounded. The PRIMROSE had one man slain, her Master (Mr. Andrew Leach), one petty officer and twelve men wounded; but, with the exception of a shot in the mainmast, and her sails been much cut by those fired at her during the chase, she sustained no other damage than what has been stated above."

* *Vide* Gaz. 1814, p. 2123. † *V.* Gaz. 1815, p. 871.

PHILLPOTTS. (LIEUTENANT, 1841.)

GEORGE PHILLPOTTS died in 1845, on board the HAZARD sloop.

This officer entered the Navy 5 Sept. 1827; passed his examination 26 Nov. 1833; obtained his commission 12 Nov. 1841; and was successively, 8 Feb. and 15 Dec. 1842, appointed to the VIXEN steamer and HAZARD 18, Capts. Henry Boyes and Fras. Philip Egerton, both on the East India station, where he died. AGENT—Joseph Woodhead.

PHIPPS. (Captain, 1814.)

WESTON PHIPPS died in 1847, at Barnstaple.

This officer entered the Navy, in 1798, as Fst.-cl. Vol., on board the SCORPION sloop, in which vessel and the SNAKE, both commanded by Capt. Chas. Tinling, he was, until 1800, actively occupied on the Home and West India stations. After again serving for about two years in the West Indies, as Midshipman, in the CASTOR frigate, Capts. Robt. Fanshawe and Rich. Peacocke, he successively, in April, 1803, and April, 1805, joined the THUNDERER 74, Capt. Wm. Bedford, and HIBERNIA 110, flag-ship of Lord Gardner, both in the Channel, where he became Sub-Lieutenant, 14 Oct. in the latter year, of the SURINAM sloop, Capts. Alex. Shippard and John Lake, Acting-Lieutenant, in July, 1806, of the HIBERNIA, bearing the flag of Lord St. Vincent, and full Lieutenant, 4 Aug. 1806, of the AIGLE 36, Capt. Geo. Wolfe. He was next, until advanced to the rank of Commander, 30 April, 1810, employed, still on Home service, in the IMPLACABLE 74, Capt. Thos. Byam Martin, and MINERVE frigate, Capt. Rich. Hawkins. He attained the rank of Captain 7 June, 1814; and accepted the Retirement 1 Oct. 1846.

PHIPPS. (LIEUT., 1810. F-P., 10; H-P., 34.)

WILLIAM PHIPPS entered the Navy, 21 June, 1803, as Fst.-cl. Vol., on board the SAN JOSEF 110, Capts. John Tremayne Rodd and Tristram Robt. Ricketts, bearing the flag of Sir Chas. Cotton in the Channel. In March, 1806, he rejoined Capt. Rodd, as Midshipman (a rating he had attained in Aug. 1804) on board the INDEFATIGABLE 44; in which ship, commanded subsequently by Capts. Henry Edw. Reginald Baker and John Broughton, he continued for four years employed in the Bay of Biscay and on the north coast of Spain. On 11 Sept. 1810, at which period he was again serving under Sir Chas. Cotton in the SAN JOSEF on the Mediterranean station, he was made Lieutenant into the ÆTNA bomb, Capt. John Fordyce Maples, lying in Cadiz Bay. His name was next, from 9 Nov.

1813 until 2 Feb. 1814, borne on the books of the BREVDRAGEREN 12. He has since been on half-pay. He had been superseded from the ÆTNA in Dec. 1812. AGENTS—Messrs. Chard.

PHIPPS. (LIEUTENANT, 1846.)

WILLIAM HUGH PHIPPS passed his examination 8 Oct. 1844; served as Mate, from 16 Dec. 1845, until promoted to the rank of Lieutenant 9 Nov. 1846, in the RATTLER steam-sloop, of 200 horse-power, Capt. Henry Smith (*b*); became, 31 Dec. following, Additional-Lieutenant of the CALEDONIA 120, flag-ship of Sir John West at Devonport; and since 12 April, 1847, has been attached, in a similar capacity, to the COLLINGWOOD 80, bearing the flag of Sir Geo. Fras. Seymour in the Pacific. While on the books of the CALEDONIA he was employed in her tender the AVENGER steam-frigate of 650 horse-power.

PICKARD. (LIEUTENANT, 1843.)

BENJAMIN SPENCER PICKARD is son of Commander Jas. Pickard, R.N.

This officer obtained his commission 10 Aug. 1843; was appointed, 15 March, 1845, Additional-Lieutenant of the VINDICTIVE 50, fitting for the flag of Sir Geo. Fras. Seymour; and, from 5 April following until 1847, was employed in the MELAMPUS 42, Capt. John Norman Campbell, on the East India station.

PICKARD. (COMMANDER, 1814. F-P., 18; H-P., 33.)

JAMES PICKARD, born 28 June, 1781, at Birmingham, is son of the late Mr. Jas. Pickard, of that town, who succeeded in effecting many great improvements in the steam-engine.

This officer entered the Navy, 5 Aug. 1796, as A.B., on board the DIANA 38, Capt. Jonathan Faulknor, stationed off the coast of Ireland. While serving next as Midshipman, between Aug. 1797 and March, 1801, in the BOADICEA 38, Capts. Rich. Goodwin Keats and Chas. Rowley, he was long and arduously employed with the in-shore squadron at the blockade of Brest, assisted at the capture of many of the enemy's privateers and merchantmen, and was present in an attack made 2 July, 1799, by Rear-Admiral Chas. Morice Pole on a Spanish squadron in Aix Roads. Rejoining Capt. Keats as Master's Mate, in March, 1801, on board the SUPERB 74, he continued actively occupied in that ship on the Lisbon and Mediterranean stations until nominated by Lord Nelson, 2 April, 1805, Acting-Lieutenant of the CANOPUS 80, Capt. Thos. Geo. Shortland, bearing the flag of the late Sir Thos. Louis. While in that ship, to which he was confirmed by commission dated 11 Oct. 1805, he visited various parts of the Mediterranean, and accompanied the hero to the West Indies and back in pursuit of the combined squadrons of France and Spain. He also enacted a part in the action off St. Domingo 6 Feb. 1806, and, after assisting at the capture on the coast of France of the French 40-gun frigate *Le Président*, returned to the Mediterranean, where, in 1807, the CANOPUS formed the van-ship of Sir John Duckworth's squadron at the passage and re-passage of the Dardanells, and then proceeded to join the force engaged in the expedition to Egypt. On her arrival at Alexandria, Lieut. Pickard, with the launches of several transports under his orders, was sent up the river Nile for the purpose of carrying provisions for the use of the troops employed against Rosetta; on the failure of the attack on which place we find him bringing down many of the wounded soldiers. The siege being shortly afterwards renewed, he was placed in command of a party of 50 seamen attached to the naval brigade under Capt. Benj. Hallowell; with whom he continued for three weeks under the walls of Rosetta. The British were then again reduced to the necessity of retiring—six of the CANOPUS' people falling, during the retreat, into the hands of the enemy. Subsequently to the death of Sir Thos. Louis, which took place 17 May, 1807, Lieut. Pickard was intrusted with the command of the gun-boats employed on the Egyptian lakes. In the following Aug. he removed with Capt. Shortland to the QUEEN 98; and he was afterwards appointed—14 Oct. 1808, to the ONYX 10, Capt. Chas. Gill, lying at the Nore—29 of the same month, to the NAIAD 38, Capts. Thos. Dundas, Geo. Cocks, Henry Hill, and Philip Carteret, stationed chiefly off the coast off France—and 17 April, 1812, as Senior, to the TENEDOS 38, Capt. Hyde Parker. In the NAIAD, under Capt. Carteret, he shared, 20 and 21 Sept. 1811, in two actions with divisions of the Boulogne flotilla. On the last-mentioned occasion the NAIAD sustained a loss of 2 men killed and 14 wounded, but succeeded in taking one of the enemy's praams, *La Ville de Lyon;* which vessel had upwards of 30 of her people either killed or wounded. As Senior of the TENEDOS Lieut. Pickard was most actively employed on the coast of North America, where he assisted in making a large number of prizes, and in blockading in the port of Boston the U. S. frigates *President* and *Congress*. He invalided home from the effects of the climate in May, 1814, and found on his arrival that he had been promoted, 7 June, 1814, to the command of the ROVER sloop. The state of his health at the time did not permit of his joining, and although constant in his applications he has not been since able to procure employment.

Commander Pickard married, in March, 1815, Jane, only surviving child (she had had two brothers, one of whom, Benjamin Spencer, Lieut. R.M., had fallen on board the EDGAR 74, at Copenhagen, 2 April, 1801) of the Rev. Benj. Spencer, LL.D., who was for 52 years Vicar of Aston, near Birmingham, for 44 years Rector of Wotton, in Lincolnshire, and for 42 years a Magistrate for cos. Warwick and Stafford, in which latter capacity he rendered essential service to Government during the great Birmingham riots. With two daughters, Commander Pickard has issue three sons, two of them, Benj. Spencer and Spencer Hicks, Lieutenants R.N., and the other, James, a First-Lieutenant R.M. (1845). AGENTS—Messrs. Ommanney.

PICKARD. (LIEUTENANT, 1845.)

SPENCER HICKS PICKARD is son of Commander Jas. Pickard, R.N.

This officer passed his examination 3 Nov. 1837; and after having served as Mate on the Mediterranean and East India stations in the CALCUTTA 84, Capts. Sir Sam. Roberts and Geo. Fred. Rich, and SPITEFUL steam-sloop, Capt. Wm. Maitland, was promoted to the rank of Lieutenant 1 Sept. 1845. He was then appointed Additional of the AGINCOURT 72, flag-ship of Sir Thos. John Cochrane, also in the East Indies, whence he returned in 1847. He has been serving, since 28 Jan. 1848, at Devonport, in the SAN JOSEF 110, Capt. Sir Henry John Leeke.

PICKERNELL. (COMMANDER, 1810. F-P., 19; H-P., 38.)

PETER GILES PICKERNELL was born 15 Feb. 1772.

This officer entered the Navy, in Oct. 1790, as a Volunteer, on board the MELEAGER, Capt. Nathaniel Brenton, lying in the river Medway, where he removed shortly afterwards to the LEVIATHAN 74, Capt. Lord Mulgrave, and in Nov. of the same year was paid off. Re-embarking, in Nov. 1793, on board the MAGICIENNE 32, Capt. Geo. Martin, he sailed for the West Indies, and was there for nearly two years most actively employed. While at anchor in 1794 at Port-au-Prince, St. Domingo, we find him serving with the boats under Acting-Lieut. Forbes in an unsuccessful attempt made to cut a privateer of 6 or 8 guns out from a small bay on the north side of the Bight of Leogane; and subsequently present, with the BELLIQUEUX, SCEPTRE, and HERMIONE, in a severe action with a battery on Pointe Leogane. On his return to England, after having gone through scenes of great mortality, Mr. Pickernell was transferred, in Sept. 1795, to the PRINCE of Wales 98, bearing the flag on the coast of France of the late Sir Henry Harvey, by whom, having again sailed for the West Indies, he was placed, at the close of 1796, in command of the Alexandria tender, carrying 8 4-pounders, with a crew of 30 men. During a continuance of nearly four years in that vessel he was constantly engaged in carrying to different parts of the station the despatches of Admiral Harvey and his successor Lord Hugh Seymour. He very often, too, came into contact with the enemy's privateers, six or seven of which he had the good fortune to capture. One of these, mounting 8 guns, with a crew of 70 men, he made prize of, after an action of three-quarters of an hour, 9 Oct. 1799—the very day that an order he had received, in May, 1798, from Admiral Harvey to act as Lieutenant had been confirmed by the new Commander-in-Chief. We are informed that Mr. Pickernell was the only Acting-Lieutenant whom Lord Hugh Seymour on his arrival did not supersede. During his command of the Alexandria it must be recorded that he witnessed the capture of Trinidad, the unsuccessful attack upon Puerto Rico, and the reduction of Surinam. His appointments, after the Prince of Wales had been paid off, were—5 Sept. 1800, to the Royal Sovereign 100, bearing the flag of Sir H. Harvey, with whom he served, principally off Brest, until the peace of Amiens—30 Aug. 1803, to the Severn 44, commanded by the Duke de Bouillon off Jersey—21 Aug. 1804, to the Galykheid 64, Capt. Isaac Wolley, lying in the river Humber—9 April, 1805, to the Revenge 74, Capts. Robt. Moorsom and Sir John Gore, in which ship he served as Second Lieutenant at the battle of Trafalgar, 21 Oct. 1805, and as First at the capture, by Sir Sam. Hood, of four French frigates off Rochefort, 25 Sept. 1806—22 Jan. 1807, to the Excellent 74, Capt. John West, fitting at the Nore—and 13 July, 1808, to the command of the 12-gun brig Gallant. In the latter vessel, after cruizing in the Downs, and previously to being sent to the coast of Scotland, he accompanied the expedition to the Walcheren, and assisted in destroying the enemy's batteries on South Beveland. He attained his present rank 4 July, 1810. The only active appointment he could ever afterwards succeed in obtaining was to the Ordinary at Sheerness, where he served for a period of three years, dating from 22 Oct. 1823. He was admitted to the out-pension of Greenwich Hospital 11 Dec. 1846.

Commander Pickernell married, 7 Feb. 1807, and has issue six children. Agent—Wm. H. B. Barwis.

PICKTHORN. (Lieutenant, 1808. f-p., 18; h-p., 33.)

John Pickthorn is a native of Devonport, co. Devon.

This officer entered the Navy, 12 Oct. 1796, as Ordinary, on board the Alexander 74, Capts. Joseph Bullen, Alex. John Ball, and P. Ormsby; in which ship he came into frequent action with the enemy's gun-boats and batteries in the neighbourhood of Cadiz, and took part in the battle of the Nile, in the blockade of Malta, and in various operations along the coast of Italy. Quitting the Alexander in Sept. 1800, he was next, until April, 1802, employed on the Mediterranean and Home stations as Midshipman (a rating he had previously attained) in the Guillaume Tell 84, Capt. Thos. Elphinstone, flag-ship of Admiral Milbank, Alkmaar, Capt. Fred. Lewis Maitland, and Malta 84, Capt. Albemarle Bertie. In March, 1803, he returned to the latter ship, commanded at the time by Capt. Edw. Buller on the coast of Spain; and, from July, 1804, until Oct. 1806, he served in the West Indies and Channel on board the Eagle and Kent 74's, and Ville de Paris 110, all flag-ships of Sir Edw. Thornbrough; whom, in Feb. 1807, after having been for about three months attached to the Acasta 40, Capt. Philip Beaver, he again joined in the Royal Sovereign 100, on the Mediterranean station. On 3 March, 1808, he was made Lieutenant into the Eagle 74, Capt. Chas. Rowley, also in the Mediterranean; where, from the following July until Jan. 1812, and from May in the latter year until Oct. 1814, we find him employed a second time in the Royal Sovereign 100, Capts. Henry Garrett, David Colby, Abel Ferris, Henry Whitmarsh Pearse, Joseph Spear, John Harvey, and Wm. Bedford, and Unicorn 32, Capts. Geo. Burgoyne Salt and Sam. Geo. Pechell. During the first four months of his last servitude in the Royal Sovereign he officiated as Flag-Lieutenant to Sir E. Thornbrough. Since he left the Unicorn he has not been afloat.

In the winter of 1840-1 Lieut. Pickthorn appears to have been engaged in raising men for the Navy at Aberdeen. He married the only daughter of Jas. Russell, Esq., Master-Attendant at North Yarmouth.

PIERCE. (Commander, 1823. f-p., 22; h-p., 22.)

George Pierce entered the Navy, 5 Aug. 1803, as Fst.-cl. Vol., on board the Thunderer 74, Capt. Wm. Bedford, employed at first on the Irish station and afterwards in the Channel; where, and in the Baltic, North Sea, and West Indies, he served from Feb. 1805, until promoted to the rank of Lieutenant, 21 March, 1812, as Midshipman and Master's Mate, in the Hibernia 110, flag-ship of Lord Gardner, Ville de Paris 110, Capt. Geo. Aldham, Prince of Wales 98, and Ville de Paris again, bearing the flags of Admirals Edw. Thornbrough, Sir Jas. Saumarez, and Lord Gambier, Apelles sloop, Capt. Thos. Oliver, Neptune 98, and Statira 38, flag-ships of Hon. Sir Alex. Cochrane, Dragon 74, bearing the flag of Sir Fras. Laforey, Ganymede and Barbadoes frigates, Capts. Robt. Preston and Edw. Rushworth, and a second time in the Dragon under Sir F. Laforey. In the Prince of Wales he accompanied the expedition of 1807 to Copenhagen; and, while attached to the Apelles, he commanded a gun-boat in the attack upon Walcheren in 1809. His appointments in the capacity of Lieutenant (prior to his attainment of which rank he had been upwards of two years on the list for promotion) were—1 Oct. 1812, to the Mulgrave 74, Capt. Thos. Jas. Maling, stationed in the Mediterranean, where he partook of much boat-service, and was present in the partial action fought with the Toulon fleet 5 Nov. 1813—1 Oct. 1814, to the Comus 22, Capt. John Tailour, under whom, while employed on the coast of Africa, he ascended the new Calabar river as high as Duke's Town (the Comus was the first man-of-war that ever did so) and assisted in the boats at the capture of several slavers —3 July, 1816, as Senior, after eight months of half-pay, to the Beelzebub bomb, Capts. Wm. Kempthorne and Fred. Thos. Michell, in which vessel he served at the bombardment of Algiers—18 Dec. 1816, to the Madagascar 46, Capt. Wm. Aug. Baumgardt, lying at Sheerness—13 May, 1817, to the Tonnant 80, flag-ship of Sir Benj. Hallowell at Cork—7 Dec. 1818, to the Windsor Castle 74, Capt. Thos. Gordon Caulfeild at Plymouth—and, 29 June, 1821, and 28 March and 6 Dec. 1822, to the Bulwark 76, Gloucester 74, and Prince Regent 120, flag-ships of Sir B. Hallowell in the river Medway. The day preceding his promotion to the rank of Commander, 5 Sept. 1823, he officiated as Aide-de-Camp to Viscount Melville at the opening of the new basin and dock at Sheerness. He was afterwards, from 15 June, 1832, until 1835, employed as an Inspecting-Commander in the Coast Guard.

Commander Pierce, during the last nine years, has filled the office of Secretary to the "Sailor's Home," in Wells Street, London Docks. In 1843 he was examined before the House of Commons on the state of the Merchant Seamen's Fund. He is married and has issue.

PIERCE. (Lieut, 1807. f-p., 15; h-p., 33.)

Thomas Pierce entered the Navy, 1 March, 1799, as Fst.-cl. Vol., on board the William, Capt. Robinson, lying at Woolwich; removed, in the following Sept., to the ZEALAND 64, Capt. Parr, flag-ship at the Nore; served, from Dec. in the same year, until July, 1802, part of the time as Midshipman, in the RESOLUTION 74, Capts. Wm. Mitchell and Hon. Alan Hyde Gardner, on the Home and West India stations; and in March, 1803, joined the ANTELOPE 50, Commodore Sir Wm. Sidney Smith. On 16 May, 1804, we find him present in a gallant attack made by a squadron under the orders of the latter officer upon a division of the enemy's flotilla passing alongshore from Flushing to Ostend. Accompanying Sir W. S. Smith subsequently to the Mediterranean in the POMPÉE 74, he was there, 24 June 1806, nominated Acting-Lieutenant of the SIRIUS 36, Capt. Wm. Prowse; to which vessel he was confirmed by the Admiralty 1 Sept. 1807. He returned home in May, 1808; and while next attached, between Aug. of that year and Dec. 1813, to the ACHILLE 74, Capts. Sir Rich. King, John Hayes, Hon. Geo. Heneage Lawrence Dundas, and Aiskew Paffard Hollis, was employed in the Channel, in the expedition to the Walcheren and off the port of Cadiz, and in the Adriatic, where he aided in blockading the French and Venetian squadrons in Venice, consisting of three line-of-battle ships and a frigate ready for sea, and several of each class fitting in the arsenal. From May, 1815, to Jan. 1816, Lieut. Pierce was engaged at Cork in impressing and raising seamen for the service. He has since been on half-pay. AGENTS—Pettet and Newton.

PIERSON, Kt. (CAPTAIN, 1838. F-P., 22; H-P., 29.)

SIR WILLIAM HENRY PIERSON was born in 1782.

This officer entered the Navy, 27 May, 1796, as A.B., on board the ASIA 64, Capt. Robt. Murray, bearing the flag of Admiral Vandeput, Commander-in-Chief in North America, where, in May, 1798, he attained the rating of Midshipman. In Dec. 1800 he removed to the BELLEISLE 72, Capts. Wm. Domett, Chas. Boyles, John Whitby, and Wm. Hargood; with the last-mentioned of whom, after cruizing with the Channel fleet, he proceeded to the Mediterranean, and next to the West Indies and back in pursuit of the combined squadrons of France and Spain. For his conduct as Master's Mate in the action off Cape Trafalgar, 21 Oct. 1805, on which occasion he was wounded,* Mr. Pierson was promoted, 24 Dec. in that year, to a Lieutenancy in the CONQUEROR 74, Capts. Israel Pellew and Edw. Fellowes, employed both on the Home and Mediterranean stations; where, from April, 1810, until July, 1815, we find him in succession serving in the NORTHUMBERLAND 74, Capts. Wm. Hargood and Hon. Henry Hotham, CALEDONIA 120, flag-ship of Sir Edw. Pellew, MENELAUS 38, Capt. Sir Peter Parker, VILLE DE PARIS 110, and BOYNE 98, each under the orders of Capt. Geo. Burlton, FYLLA 22, Capt. Wm. Shepheard, and AMPHION 32, Capt. Jas. Pattison Stewart. While First of the FYLLA, he was slightly wounded, as was a marine, at the capture, 30 Jan. 1814, of the French lugger privateer *L'Inconnu* of 15 guns (pierced for 20) and 109 men, 5 of whom were killed and 4 wounded.† He was often during the above period engaged in cutting out the enemy's vessels, and in co-operating with the patriots on the coast of Catalonia. Between 30 March, 1824, and 16 Aug. 1825, Lieut. Pierson served, as Senior, on board the WELLESLEY 74, Capt. Graham Eden Hamond, stationed at first as a guard-ship at Portsmouth, and engaged next in conveying the present Lord Stuart de Rothesay to the Brazils; whence, in Dec. 1825, he returned home with Capt. Hamond in the SPARTIATE 76. Attaining the rank of Commander 27 March, 1826, he did not again go afloat until appointed, 11 June, 1836, to the MADAGASCAR 46, Capt. Sir John Strutt Peyton, fitting for the West Indies. In the following Oct., while lying, prior to her final departure, in Kingstown, Dublin, the MADAGASCAR was visited by the Lord-Lieutenant, the Marquis of Normanby; and Capt. Pierson on the occasion received the honour of knighthood. He was advanced to his present rank 28 June, 1838—two months after the ship had been paid off; and has not been since employed.

* *Vide* Gaz. 1805, p. 1484. † *V.* Gaz. 1814, p. 280.

Sir W. H. Pierson married, in July, 1826, Jane, daughter of Edw. Daun, Esq., of Warblington, co. Hants, by whom he has issue two sons and one daughter.

PIGOT. (LIEUTENANT, 1842.)

GEORGE PIGOT died at the commencement of 1846.

This officer entered the Navy 26 July, 1827; passed his examination 1 Sept. 1835; served for some time in the Mediterranean as Mate of the ACHERON steamer, Capt. Andrew Kennedy; obtained his commission 7 Feb. 1842; and from 18 of that month until paid off in 1844 was employed in the East Indies on board the VINDICTIVE 50, Capt. John Toup Nicolas.

PIGOT, K.C.B., K.C.H. (VICE-ADMIRAL OF THE BLUE, 1847. F-P., 35; H-P., 24.)

SIR HUGH PIGOT is a near relative of Lieut.-General Sir Robt. Pigot, Bart. (who commanded the left wing of the British army at the battle of Bunker's Hill, in North America, and was presented by George III. with the Colonelcy of the 38th regt., as a reward for his distinguished conduct on that occasion).

This officer entered the Navy, 1 May, 1788, on board the SALISBURY 50, Capt. Erasmus Gower, bearing the flag of Rear-Admiral Elliot at Newfoundland, where he removed, in the course of the same year, to the MERLIN sloop, Capt. Edw. Pakenham. After having served for three years at Home with Capt. Andrew Snape Douglas, as Midshipman, in the SOUTHAMPTON 32, and GOLIATH and ALCIDE guard-ships, he sailed in 1792 for the Mediterranean in the ROMNEY 50, flag-ship of Rear-Admiral Sam. Cranston Goodall, whom he accompanied, in May, 1793, into the PRINCESS ROYAL 98. In 1794, subsequently to the evacuation of Toulon, he was nominated Acting-Lieutenant of the BERWICK 74, Capt. Andrew Sutherland; but it was not until he had again, for a short period, performed the duties of Midshipman in the PRINCESS ROYAL and in the BRITANNIA 100, the flag-ship of Admiral Wm. Hotham, that he was officially promoted, 12 Nov. in the same year, into LA FLÈCHE sloop, Capts. Hon. Henry Hotham, Shuldham Peard, and Edwards. His next appointments were to the GLADIATOR, Capt. John Pakenham, SURPRISE 32, Capts. Ralph Willett Miller and Edw. Hamilton, MONARCH 74, bearing the flag of Sir Rich. Onslow, and ÆOLUS, Capt. John Wm. Spranger. In those ships he served on the Mediterranean, Newfoundland, North Sea, Baltic, and Jamaica stations. Attaining the rank of Commander 29 April, 1802, he was employed in that capacity off Seaford, in the SPEEDY sloop, from 24 Aug. 1803 until made Post 8 May, 1804. His succeeding appointments were—27 March, 1805, for three months, to the DAUNTLESS, lying at Sheerness—7 Feb. and 28 June, 1806, to the ALLIGATOR 28 and CIRCE 32, both in the West Indies—towards the close of 1808, to the CAPTAIN 74 and LATONA 38, on the same station—1 Nov. 1810, to the ORPHEUS 36, in which ship he was for four years stationed in the West Indies and at Halifax—and, at the end of 1814, to the DIOMEDE 50 and NYMPHE 38, also on the coast of North America, whence he returned to England and was paid off in Aug. 1815. On 5 April, 1807, Capt. Pigot, then in the CIRCE, made prize of *L'Austerlitz* French privateer of 18 guns and 125 men. On 2 March, 1808, he took possession, in the same ship, of the island of Marie-Galante;* and on 31 Oct. following he captured in her, near Martinique, the *Palineur* national brig of 16 guns and 79 men, 7 of whom were killed and 8 wounded, with a loss to the CIRCE, occasioned by a battery on the Diamond Rock, of 2 men killed and wounded.†

* *Vide* Gaz. 1808, p. 604. † *V.* Gaz. 1809, p. 15.

On 10 Feb. 1809, at the commencement of which year, being in the LATONA, he commanded the blockading squadron off Guadeloupe, we find him assisting at the capture of *La Junon* French frigate of 46 guns and 323 men, whose fire wounded 6 of the LATONA's crew. The exertions and activity he displayed in erecting jury-masts, &c., and putting the prize in a sea-worthy state, procured him the warm official thanks of the senior officer present, Capt. Geo. Scott, of the HORATIO 38.* On 17 April following Capt. Pigot witnessed (and was much praised for his spirited exertions during the chase which preceded) the surrender of the *D'Hautpoult* 74; † and on 18 June in the same year he captured *La Félicité*, pierced for 42 guns, but having only 14 of her main-deckers mounted, with a complement of 174 men, and a cargo of sugar, coffee, &c.‡ In the ORPHEUS, besides effecting the destruction, 28 April and 11 May, 1813, of the *Wampoe* letter-of-marque of 8 guns, and the *Holkar* privateer of 20 guns, he captured, 20 April, 1814, the U. S. ship *Frolic*, of 20 32-pounder carronades, 2 long 18's, 539 tons, and 171 men.§ On 3 Nov. 1825 Capt. Pigot was appointed Superintendent of the Coast Blockade and Captain of the RAMILLIES 74, in which ship, and the TALAVERA of similar force (he was transferred to her 15 Sept. 1829), he continued, on the Downs station, until placed in command, 9 March, 1831, of the BARHAM 50, fitting for the Mediterranean, where he continued the usual period of three years. He was nominated a C.B. 26 Sept. 1831, and a K.C.H., accompanied with the honour of Knighthood, in 1834; created a Rear-Admiral 10 Jan. 1837, and a Vice-Admiral 6 Aug. 1847; and raised, 10 July in the latter year, to the dignity of a K.C.B. From 16 May, 1844, until 1 July, 1847, Sir Hugh Pigot commanded-in-chief on the Cork station.

PIGOT. (COMMANDER, 1814. F-P., 17; H-P., 34.)

RICHARD HENRY HOLLIS PIGOT, born 20 July, 1787, is son of the late John Hollis Pigot, Esq., M.D., of Derby.

This officer entered the Navy, 20 June, 1796, as Fst.-cl. Vol., on board LA POMONE 40, Commodore Sir John Borlase Warren, under whom, while cruizing with a squadron on the coast of France, he aided at the capture of many of the enemy's armed and other vessels, particularly of the frigates *Andromaque* and *Calliope*. Continuing employed with Sir J. B. Warren until Sept. 1800, he successively followed him, during that period, into the CANADA 74, TÉMÉRAIRE 98, and RENOWN 74. In the CANADA he witnessed the defeat, 12 Oct. 1798, of a French squadron under Commodore Bompart, intended for the invasion of Ireland; and when Midshipman of the RENOWN, having first accompanied the expedition to Ferrol, he assisted, 29 Aug. 1800, in the boats of a squadron, 20 in number, commanded by Lieut. Henry Burke, at the cutting out, close to the batteries in Vigo Bay, of *La Guêpe* privateer, of 18 guns and 161 men; which vessel, 25 of whose people were killed and 40 wounded, was, in 15 minutes, boarded and carried, with a loss to the British of 3 seamen and 1 marine killed, 3 Lieutenants, 12 seamen, and 5 marines wounded, and 1 seaman missing. On leaving the RENOWN in Sept. 1800, Mr. Pigot removed to the CYNTHIA 18, Capt. Jas. Hawes. He went back to the former ship in the following Nov., but, rejoining Capt. Hawes, in Aug. 1801, on board the CAMELION 18, continued to serve with him in that vessel and the ROEBUCK 44, on the Mediterranean station, until April, 1802. After an attachment of three years and a half, on Home service, to the CLYDE 38, Capt. John Larmour, WINCHELSEA, Lieut.-Commander D. Pope, and MOUCHERON 16, Capt. Jas. Hawes, he was nominated, 13 March, 1806, Sub-Lieutenant of the ADDER gun-brig, Lieut.-Commander Molyneux Shuldham. He was made full Lieutenant, 22 Oct. in the latter year, into the KANGAROO 18, Capt. John Baker, lying in the Downs; and subsequently appointed—14 Nov. 1807, to the SWIFTSURE 74, bearing the flag of Sir J. B. Warren at Halifax—27 May, 1811, as Senior, to the DRUID frigate, Capts. Thos. Searle and Fras. Stanfell, in which ship he served at the sieges of Cadiz and Tarifa—31 Dec. 1812, as a Supernumerary, to the SAN JUAN 74, bearing the broad pendant of Commodore Chas. Vinicombe Penrose at Gibraltar—and, 31 March, 1814, after 12 months of half-pay, to the SAN DOMINGO 74, as Flag-Lieutenant to Sir J. B. Warren on the coast of North America. Since the attainment of his present rank, 31 May, 1814, he has been on half-pay.

During the war Commander Pigot was often engaged in cutting out the enemy's vessels. He married, in 1838, Catherine, daughter of the Rev. J. Parsons, Rector of Cossington, Derby, by whom he has had issue one daughter.

* *Vide* Gaz. 1809, p. 543. † *V.* Gaz. 1809, p. 712.
‡ *V.* Gaz. 1809, p. 1384. § *V.* Gaz. 1814, p. 1415.

PIGOTT. (LIEUTENANT, 1844.)

LEIGHTON PRICE PIGOTT is fourth son of the Rev. John Dryden Pigott, of Edgmond, co. Salop, Rector of that place and of Habberley, by Frances, second daughter and co-heir of Henry Bevan, Esq., of Shrewsbury.

This officer entered the Navy in 1834; passed his examination 6 July, 1840; and, after having served on the Mediterranean and Home stations as Mate in the IMPREGNABLE 104, Capt. Thos. Forrest, ST. VINCENT 120, flag-ship of Sir Chas. Rowley, and VICTORIA AND ALBERT yacht, Capt. Lord Adolphus Fitz-Clarence, was promoted to the rank of Lieutenant 22 Oct. 1844. He has been again employed in the Mediterranean since 18 Nov. 1844, in the AMAZON 26, Capt. Jas. John Stopford.

PIKE. (RETIRED COMMANDER, 1847. F-P., 25; H-P., 29.)

THOMAS PIKE was born in 1782 at Exeter, co. Devon. His nephew, Thomas W. R. Pike, is a Master R.N. (1842.)

This officer entered the Navy, 14 Sept. 1793, as Captain's Servant, on board the LONDON 98, Capt. Rich. Goodwin Keats, on the Home station, where he continued employed, latterly as a Volunteer of the first class, in the VALIANT 74, Capt. Thos. Pringle (part of Lord Howe's fleet in the action of the 1st of June), and again with Capt. Keats in the GALATEA 32, until Nov. 1794. Re-embarking, 6 July, 1799, in the TÉMÉRAIRE 98, Capt. Peter Puget, he served in that ship with Rear-Admirals Sir John Borlase Warren, Jas. Hawkins Whitshed, and Geo. Campbell, in the Channel, off the coast of Ireland, and in the West Indies, until Oct. 1802. On the renewal of hostilities in 1803 he became Midshipman of the CULLODEN 74, flag-ship in the Channel of Lord Keith. Removing shortly afterwards to the CANOPUS 80, bearing the flags of Rear-Admirals Geo. Campbell and Sir Thos. Louis, he accompanied the latter officer in 1805 in Lord Nelson's pursuit of the combined squadrons of France and Spain to the West Indies, and back. In July, 1805, he returned from the Mediterranean to England in the PRÉVOYANTE store-ship, Master-Commander Daniel M'Coy, for the purpose of passing his examination. That ordeal having been gone through, he next in succession joined the SUPERB 74,* flag-ship of Sir John Thos. Duckworth, TÉMÉRAIRE 98 and AUDACIOUS 74, Capts. Eliab Harvey and John Larmour, and TONNANT 80; of which latter ship, bearing the flag of Rear-Admiral E. Harvey, he was confirmed a Lieutenant 25 March, 1807. His succeeding appointments were—29 July, 1807, to the THESEUS 74, Capt. John Poo Beresford, off Ferrol—30 June and 22 Oct. 1808, to the BRISEIS 10, Capt. John Pettet, and ST. GEORGE 98, flag-ship of Rear-Admirals E. Harvey and Fras. Pickmore, stationed in the Channel and Baltic—in Nov. 1809, to the AVENGER 18, Capt. Thos. White, also in the Baltic—13 March, 1811, to the MONMOUTH 64, as Flag-

* He was sent on board the SUPERB for the purpose of joining the VICTORY, but, the battle of Trafalgar intervening, an opportunity of doing so did not occur.

Lieutenant, in the Downs, to Vice-Admiral Thos. Foley—26 Aug. 1813, to the post of Agent for Transports Afloat, which he retained until 31 Oct. 1814—26 April, 1815, for five months, to the ACTÆON 16, Capt. John Ross, employed in cruizing to the westward—in 1821, to the Coast Guard—23 Nov. 1822, to a four-years' command of the DILIGENCE Revenue-cruizer—and, 18 Dec. 1826, to the charge, which he retained until 23 Dec. 1831, of the Semaphore station at Lump's Fort. While he was in the ST. GEORGE he succeeded, with a detachment of boats, covered by the guns of the STANDARD 64, in bringing off a large Swedish vessel which had drifted within range of a battery in the Great Belt. Unsuccessful, after he left the Semaphore service, in his efforts to procure employment, he accepted, 14 Jan. 1847, the rank he now holds.

We cannot close the present narrative without alluding to one or two severe disappointments experienced by the subject of it during the term of his professional career. While Flag-Lieutenant to Vice-Admiral Foley he had the honour of steering the barge of H.R.H. the Duke of Clarence on the occasion of his reviewing the North Sea fleet in the Downs; a circumstance which would have been followed by his immediate promotion to the rank of Commander, had not H. R. H., considering that the post he then filled would ensure him that boon, suggested that the service he had performed should, on his obtaining it, be made a recommendation for an appointment. After he had been, however, nearly two years and a half Flag-Lieutenant, he found himself under the necessity of resigning in order to make room for another upon whom Vice-Admiral Foley wished to confer the commission at his disposal! He married in 1808, and has issue five sons and one daughter.

PIKE. (RETIRED COMMANDER, 1840. F-P., 17; H-P., 32.)

WALTER PIKE was born 11 March, 1785.

This officer entered the Navy, 4 July, 1798, as A.B., on board the ACHILLE 74, Capts. Hon. Henry Edwin Stanhope, Geo. Murray, and Edw. Buller, with whom he continued employed in the Channel, principally in the capacity of Midshipman, until transferred, in April, 1802, to the ENDYMION 40, Capts. Philip Chas. Durham and John Larmour, lying at Portsmouth. After a servitude of two years as Master's Mate in the ISIS 50, flag-ship at Newfoundland of Vice-Admiral Jas. Gambier, he became successively attached, in the course of 1804, to the ROYAL WILLIAM, SWIFTSURE 74, and GLORY 98, bearing the flags at Spithead and at Cadiz of Admirals Geo. Montagu and Sir John Orde. Of the ship last mentioned he was confirmed a Lieutenant 20 Feb. 1805. His succeeding appointments were—22 June, 1805, to the WOLVERENE sloop, Capt. Thos. Smyth, at Plymouth—3 Sept. following, to the EURYALUS 36, commanded in the Mediterranean by Capts. Hon. Henry Blackwood and Hon. Geo. Heneage Lawrence Dundas, under the former of whom he took part in the battle of Trafalgar—25 Feb. 1809, as First-Lieutenant, to the MERMAID 32, Capt. Major Jacob Henniker, in which ship he visited Lisbon and Quebec—and 8 May, 1810, with similar rank, to the ACHATES of 16 guns, Capts. John Davies, Isaac Hawkins Morrison, and Thos. Lamb Polden Laugharne. Under Capt. Morrison he shared, 21 Oct. 1813, in a very gallant running action of several hours' duration, fought off the coast of France between the ACHATES, whose sails and rigging suffered much, and *La Trave*, a French frigate of 44 guns and 321 men, which had been previously dismasted in a gale of wind, and which was captured two days afterwards by the ANDROMACHE 38, Capt. Geo. Tobin. He also, in the same vessel, witnessed the surrender, to the EUROTAS of 46 guns and 320 men, of another French frigate, *La Clorinde*, mounting 44 guns and 12 brass swivels, with a complement of 360 picked men, 25 Feb. 1814. The ACHATES was paid off in Nov. 1815; and Mr. Pike, who did not again go afloat, accepted, 12 Aug. 1840, the rank he now holds.

PILCH. (COMMANDER, 1813. F-P., 25; H-P., 39).

ROBERT PILCH died in 1846.

This officer entered the Navy, in 1783, as Captain's Servant, on board the THETIS frigate, Capt. John Blankett, with whom he was for four years employed in the Mediterranean. With the exception of a brief attachment, in 1790, to the PRINCE 98, bearing the flag of Sir John Jervis in the Channel, he did not again go afloat until 1794. He then joined the VICTORIOUS and VENERABLE 74's, both under the orders of Sir John Orde; whom, in 1795, he followed as Master's Mate into the PRINCE GEORGE 98, commanded subsequently by Capt. Wm. Edge. Becoming attached next to the GLORY 98 and THUNDERER 74, each bearing the flag of Sir Hugh Cloberry Christian, he assisted, in the latter ship, at the reduction of Ste. Lucie in May, 1796. Being confirmed a Lieutenant in the THUNDERER by commission dated 22 Dec. 1796, he continued to serve in her on the Jamaica station, under Capts. Jas. Bowen, Wm. Ogilvie, John Loring, John Cochet, John Crawley, Temple Hardy, Robt. Mends, Wm. Henry Bayntun, and Henry Vansittart, until June, 1801. His subsequent appointments were—20 July, 1801, to the BELLEROPHON 74, Capts. Lord Garlies and John Loring, employed at first in the Channel and afterwards in the West Indies, where, in command of the launches of that ship and the ELEPHANT 74, he captured, 23 Nov. 1803, under a very smart fire from the enemy's great guns and musketry, the French national schooner *La Découverte*, mounting 6 long 6-pounders and 6 swivels, with a complement of 52 men, lying in the Caracol Passage, near Cape François, St. Domingo—1 Nov. 1804, to the GLORY 98, flag-ship of Rear-Admirals Sir John Orde and Chas. Stirling off Cadiz and in the Channel, and, under the latter officer, part of Sir Robt. Calder's fleet in the action off Cape Finisterre 22 July, 1805—22 July and 7 Dec. 1806, to the SAMPSON and DIADEM 64's, each bearing the flag of Rear-Admiral Stirling, with whom, subsequently to the capture of Monte Video in Feb. 1807, he proceeded to the Cape of Good Hope—13 June, 1808, again to the BELLEROPHON 74, Capt. Sam. Warren, stationed in the North Sea and Baltic, on which latter station, after having taken possession, with the boats, of three vessels, he made a dash at, and in the most gallant manner carried, 19 June, 1809, one of four batteries by which they had been covered, mounting 4 24-pounders and garrisoned by 103 men, a service that elicited the acknowledgments of the Admiralty*—and 4 Sept. 1810, and 17 June, 1813, to the PRESIDENT 38 and BLENHEIM 74, likewise commanded by Capt. Warren, the former at the reduction of Java, the latter in the North Sea. He was advanced to the rank of Commander 4 Dec. 1813, and not afterwards employed. AGENTS—Messrs. Ommanney.

PILCH, K.W. (LIEUTENANT, 1814. F-P., 31; H-P., 12.)

WILLIAM PILCH entered the Navy, 4 Oct. 1804, as Fst.-cl. Vol., on board the BELLEROPHON 74, Capts. John Loring, John Cooke, and Edward Rotheram. In Dec. 1805, after having shared in the battle of Trafalgar, he removed to the GLORY 98, bearing the flag of Rear-Admiral Chas. Stirling, with whom he continued employed in the SAMPSON and DIADEM 64's, on the Home, North American, and Cape of Good Hope stations, until April, 1808. In the ship last mentioned he served as Midshipman at the capture of Monte Video in Feb. 1807. On leaving her he joined the DEFIANCE 74, Capt. Hon. Henry Hotham; previously to following whom, in Sept. 1810, into the NORTHUMBERLAND 74, we find him present with a squadron under Rear-Admiral Hon. Robt. Stopford, at the destruction, 24 Feb. 1809, of three French frigates under

* *Vide* Gaz. 1809, p. 1101.

the batteries of Sable d'Olonne, on the coast of France, after a contest in which the DEFIANCE, added to severe damages experienced in her sails and rigging, sustained a loss of 2 men killed and 25 wounded. In the NORTHUMBERLAND he assisted, 22 May, 1812, in company with the GROWLER gun-brig, in destroying, at the entrance of L'Orient, the French 40-gun frigates *L'Arienne* and *L'Andromaque*, and 16-gun brig *Mamelouck;* whose united fire, conjointly with that of a heavy battery, killed 5 and wounded 28 of the NORTHUMBERLAND'S people. In Jan. 1813 Mr. Pilch removed to the VALIANT 74, Capt. Robt. Dudley Oliver. Rejoining Capt. Hotham, however, in the following March, he continued to serve with him from that period until April, 1815, on the coast of North America, in the SAN DOMINGO and ASIA 74's and TONNANT 80, flag-ships of Sir John Borlase Warren and Hon. Sir Alex. Cochrane, FORTH 40, and SUPERB 74. His promotion took place 24 Sept. 1814; and from 28 Feb. 1827 until appointed, in 1848, a Naval Knight of Windsor, he held command of a station in the Coast Guard.

PILKINGTON. (COMMANDER, 1830. F-P., 19; H-P., 11.)

EDWARD WILLIAMS PILKINGTON, born 14 Dec. 1803, is second son of the late Rev. Chas. Pilkington, Canon Residentiary of Chichester, by Harriet Elizabeth, daughter of the late Wm. Williams, Esq.; and nephew, maternally, of the late Vice-Admiral Sir Geo. Murray, K.C.B., who commanded the EDGAR 74, and led the fleet under Lord Nelson into action in the attack on the Danish line of defence before Copenhagen 2 April, 1801.

This officer entered the Royal Naval College 7 Aug. 1817, and in Dec. 1818, having carried off the Silver Medal, embarked on board the NEWCASTLE 60, Capt. Arthur Fanshawe, bearing the flag of the late Sir Edw. Griffith Colpoys, on the North American station, whence he returned home and was paid off in Jan. 1822. Joining next the ACTIVE and PHAETON of 46 guns each, Capts. Andrew King and Wm. Aug. Montagu, he escorted George IV. in the latter ship on the occasion of his visit to Scotland, and then sailed, under Capt. Henry Evelyn Pitfield Sturt, for the West Indies, where he was soon actively employed in the suppression of piracy and the slave-trade. In Dec. 1823 he became attached, as a passed Midshipman, to the CAMELION 10, Capt. Geo. Robt. Lambert, also on the West India station; and on being subsequently, 22 Oct. 1824, appointed Mate of the BOADICEA 46, Commodore Sir Jas. Brisbane, he proceeded to the East Indies. Uniting, on his arrival, in the hostilities in force against the Burmese, he took command, with the rank of Acting-Lieutenant (order dated 22 Oct. 1825), of the BOADICEA'S barge and a division of gun-boats; and was present at the storming of Nepadee, the capture of Meaday, Melloone, Pagahmmew, &c., and in the various operations on the river Irawady. On the ratification of peace he was intrusted with the duty of protecting the rear of the army in its retrograde movement towards Rangoon—a service of no small difficulty, as the enemy, either in ignorance of the treaty, or with the view of plundering, never lost an opportunity of attacking the boats of the Commissariat, the merchants, and others. Mr. Pilkington's vigilance and exertions, however, had the effect of saving a considerable amount of property, and were so fully estimated that they procured him the thanks of a large body of British, Bengalee, and Armenian traders. On leaving the BOADICEA, to which frigate he had been confirmed by commission dated 29 April, 1826, he was turned over, in Aug. of that year, to the WARSPITE 76, Capts. Hon. Rich. Saunders Dundas and Wm. Parker; under whom, having returned through the Pacific to Europe, we find him employed in the Tagus and at the blockade, against the Egyptians, of the Greek ports in the Mediterranean; where, while off the harbour of Navarin, he contributed to the capture of a corvette and sloop of-war who had endeavoured to force a passage with provisions and specie for the army under Ibrahim Pacha. Being next, 1 Dec. 1829, appointed Flag-Lieutenant, in the WINCHESTER 52, to Sir E. G. Colpoys, then again Commander-in-Chief in North America and the West Indies, he was by him promoted, 16 Aug. 1830, to a death-vacancy in the ROSE 18. In that sloop Commander Pilkington was at first engaged in protecting the North American fisheries and the settlements of the Hudson's Bay Company in Labrador against the encroachments of the United States, and afterwards in conducting the naval operations at Black River, Jamaica, during the insurrection in 1831 and 1832. Prior to the departure thence of the ROSE, the command of which vessel he resigned in April, 1832, Commander Pilkington had the gratification of receiving an animated acknowledgment of his services in the shape of an address signed by Major-General Robertson, the officers of the Militia, and the proprietors and inhabitants of the district of St. Elizabeth. He subsequently, from 13 July, 1838, until 1841, officiated as an Inspecting-Commander in the Coast Guard; in which service, since 29 Sept. 1846, he has been again employed.

He married, 29 April, 1835, at Chichester, Louisa Frances, only daughter of the Rev. W. S. Bayton, of Eastergate, by whom he has issue five children. AGENTS—Messrs. Stilwell.

PINHORN. (LIEUT., 1818. F-P., 19; H-P., 17.)

WILLIAM PINHORN died 23 July, 1845, at Sunderland, in his 48th year.

This officer entered the Navy, 21 Nov. 1809, as Fst.-cl. Vol., on board the LEDA 36, Capt. Geo. Sayer, with whom he continued actively employed in the East Indies as Midshipman, and the last nine months as Acting-Lieutenant, until Dec. 1816—assisting during that period at the reduction of Java and in a desperate attack made upon the pirates of Sambas in the island of Borneo. From March, 1817, until promoted to the rank of Lieutenant, 20 Jan. 1818, he served with Capt. Hon. Robt. Cavendish Spencer in the SEVERN 40 and GANYMEDE 26, on the Home and Mediterranean stations. In 1827-8 he held an appointment in the Coast Blockade as Supernumerary-Lieutenant of the RAMILLIES 74, Capt. Hugh Pigot; and from 18 May, 1835, until the period of his death he commanded, with the exception of a short interval in 1842, a station in the Coast Guard. AGENTS—Messrs. Chard.

PINTO. (RETIRED CAPTAIN, 1840. F-P., 14; H-P., 38.)

THOMAS PINTO was born 5 March, 1772.

This officer entered the Navy, 5 Sept. 1795, as A.B., on board the POWERFUL 74, Capt. Wm. O'Brien Drury, lying at Spithead; and in the course of the same year joined the MAGICIENNE 32, Capt. Geo. Martin, under whom, deducting a short time passed in 1798 on board the PALLAS troop-ship, Capt. Joseph Edmonds, he continued to serve as Midshipman and Master's Mate for about six years in the IRRESISTIBLE and NORTHUMBERLAND 74's. In the IRRESISTIBLE he fought in the action off Cape St. Vincent, 14 Feb. 1797; and on 26 April following contributed, in company with the EMERALD 36, to the capture, after a smart contest of an hour, of the *Ninfa* and *Santa Elena* Spanish frigates, which had been pursued into Conil Bay, near Cape Trafalgar. In the NORTHUMBERLAND he witnessed the capture of the 74-gun ship *Le Généreux* and frigate *La Diane*, assisted at the blockade of Malta, and participated in the operations of 1801 in Egypt. After further serving on the Mediterranean and Home stations in the FOUDROYANT 80, flag-ship of Lord Keith, AFRICAINE 38, Capt. Thos. Manby, and COLOSSUS 74 and GLORY 98, both commanded by Capt. Geo. Martin, as Acting-Lieutenant in the FAVORITE sloop, Capt. Wm. Williams Foote, and again as Master's Mate in the GLORY, under the flag of Sir John Orde, he was officially promoted, 20 Feb. 1805, into the AGAMEMNON 64, Capts. John

Harvey, Sir Edw. Berry, and Jonas Rose, part of the force employed in the actions off Capes Finisterre and Trafalgar and the island of St. Domingo, 22 July and 21 Oct. 1805, and 6 Feb. 1806. On 8 Dec. 1807, four months after he had been removed to the ULYSSES 44, Capt. Christopher John Williams Nesham, he was nominated Acting-Commander of the DART sloop on the West India station, where he was confirmed by commission dated 9 Feb. 1808; and next, towards the close of the same year, appointed to the NEPTUNE 98, flag-ship of Hon. Sir Alex. Cochrane, and ACHATES 14. The latter vessel he had the misfortune to lose in Feb. 1810. He accepted his present rank 10 Sept. 1840. AGENTS—Messrs. Stilwell.

PIPER. (LIEUTENANT, 1812. F-P., 8; H-P., 33.)

EDMUND JOHN PIPER entered the Navy, 5 April, 1806, as Fst.-cl. Vol., on board the BELLEISLE 74, Capt. Wm. Hargood; and on 14 Sept. following was present at the destruction, off Cape Henry, of the French 74-gun ship *L'Impétueux*. After visiting the West Indies he accompanied Capt. Hargood as Midshipman, in July, 1807, into the NORTHUMBERLAND 74, commanded subsequently by Capt. Hon. Henry Hotham, under whom, while cruizing off L'Orient, we find him assisting, in company with the GROWLER gun-brig, at the gallant destruction, 22 May, 1812, of the French 40-gun frigates *L'Arienne* and *L'Andromaque*, and 16-gun brig *Mamelouck*, whose united fire, conjointly with that of a heavy battery, killed 5 and wounded 28 of the NORTHUMBERLAND'S people. He had previously, in 1809, lost a leg in an attack upon a large convoy in the Adriatic. Proceeding in the summer of 1812 to the Cape of Good Hope, as a Supernumerary, in the MINDEN 74, Capt. Alex. Skene, he was there made Lieutenant, 21 Nov. in the same year, in the HARPY sloop, Capt. Henderson Bain. He invalided home in May, 1813, and has since been on half-pay. In consideration of his wound he received a pecuniary grant from the Patriotic Fund, and was awarded, 28 May. 1816, a pension of 91*l.* 5*s.* per annum.

PITFIELD. (LIEUTENANT, 1824.)

JACOB PITFIELD obtained his commission 6 Dec. 1824; served in the Coast Blockade as Supernumerary-Lieutenant of the RAMILLIES 74, Capt. Hugh Pigot, from 22 Dec. 1826 until 1829; and from 15 Dec. 1830 until 1838 held command of a station in the Coast Guard. He has not been since employed.

PITFIELD. (LIEUT., 1815. F-P., 12; H-P., 28.)

JOSEPH EDWARD CHILCOTT PITFIELD entered the Navy, 8 Nov. 1807, as Master's Mate, on board the PROSERPINE 32, Capt. Chas Otter, which ship, despite a noble resistance, productive of a loss to her of 1 man killed and 10 wounded, was captured off the port of Toulon, on the night of 28 Feb. 1809, by the French 40-gun frigates *Pénélope* and *Pauline*. Regaining his liberty early in 1811, he served from that period until promoted to the rank of Lieutenant 9 Jan. 1815, on the Home station, in the BOYNE 98, VILLE DE PARIS 110, and IMPREGNABLE 104, flag-ships of Sir Harry Burrard Neale and Sir Wm. Domett. His last appointments were—3 April, 1815, to the HYACINTH 24, Capt. Alex. Renton Sharpe, in the North Sea—22 Nov. following, to the SUPERB 74, Capt. Chas. Ekins, under whom he fought at Algiers 27 Aug. 1816, and continued to serve until paid off in Oct. 1818—and, 28 Dec. 1820, to the GRASSHOPPER 18, Capt. David Buchan, on the Newfoundland station, where he remained about 12 months.

PITMAN. (COMMANDER, 1842.)

JOHN CHARLES PITMAN, born 22 March, 1814, is fourth son of Jas. Pitman, Esq., of Dunchideock House, co. Devon, Major of the 1st or East Devon Militia, and a Magistrate and Deputy-Lieutenant for that shire, by Catherine, eldest daughter of John Harris, Esq., of Radford, co. Devon. His eldest sister, drowned by the upsetting of a boat, was wife of the present Capt. Wm. Keats, R.N.; and a younger one, also deceased, of the late Sir Edw. Wm. Corry Astley, Kt., Capt R.N. (1829).

This officer entered the Navy 8 Jan. 1827; served on board the ROSE 18, Capt. Lewis Davies, at the battle of Navarin, 20 Oct. 1827, and in the TALBOT 28, Capt. Hon. Fred. Spencer, in co-operation with the French, at the reduction of Morea Castle in Oct. 1828; passed his examination in 1833; obtained his first commission 3 July, 1840; and was employed during the operations in China in the MELVILLE 72, flag-ship of Hon. Geo. Elliot, BLENHEIM 72, Capt. Sir Humphrey Le Fleming Senhouse, and DRUID 44, Capt. Henry Smith. In 1841 he officiated as Aide-de-Camp to Sir Hugh Gough and Sir H. Le F. Senhouse on the heights of Canton.* He was rewarded for his services with a Commander's commission bearing date 7 Dec. 1842; and, since 28 Feb. 1846, has been in command of the CHILDERS 12, in the East Indies.

Commander Pitman married, 5 Oct. 1843, Elizabeth, daughter of the gallant Sir Humphrey Le Fleming Senhouse, Kt., C.B., K.C.H., Capt. R.N. (1814), who died in command of the BLENHEIM, in China, in 1841.

PITMAN. (LIEUT., 1806. F-P., 21; H-P., 31.)

WILLIAM PITMAN entered the Navy, 19 April, 1795, as a Volunteer, on board the MARS 74, Capt. Sir Chas. Cotton; and on 16 and 17 June following was present in Cornwallis' celebrated retreat. From July, 1796, until Dec. 1800, he served on the Home and Cape of Good Hope stations, as Midshipman and Master's Mate, in the STAR sloop, Capts. Hon. John Colville, David Atkins, and John Gardner. He was then made Prize-Master of the *Guadeloupe* in the West Indies, whence, in Oct. 1801, he returned to England in the MORGIANA sloop. In the course of 1802-3 we find him joining in succession the CAMBRIDGE 74, FALCON sloop, Capt. Henry Manaton Ommanney, PUISSANT 74, Capt. John Irwin, and EXCELLENT of similar force, Capt. Frank Sotheron. In the FALCON he visited Newfoundland; and in the EXCELLENT he was employed in the Mediterranean from Aug. 1803 to Aug. 1806. His appointments in the capacity of Lieutenant, a rank he had attained 31 Jan. in the latter year, were—3 Nov. 1806, to the CURLEW sloop, Capt. Thos. Young, lying at Sheerness—28 April, 1807, to the HERCULE 74, Capt. Hon. J. Colville, part of the force employed in the expedition against Copenhagen—and, 7 Feb. 1808, to the Impress service at Folkestone, where, and at Bristol, he remained until 31 May, 1816. He has since been on half-pay. He was admitted to the out-pension of Greenwich Hospital 1 Jan. 1845.

He married, in 1833, Anne, daughter of Mr. Wm. Abraham, Landing-Waiter at the port of Liverpool, by whom he has issue. AGENT—J. Hinxman.

PITT. (LIEUTENANT, 1809. F-P., 25; H-P., 21.)

EDWARD WILLIAM PITT, born 14 Jan. 1790, at Ealing, co. Middlesex, is eldest son of Joseph Pitt, Esq., Surgeon, by Elizabeth Browne, co-heiress of the late Thos. Browne, Esq., of Drayton Green, in the parish of Ealing.

This officer entered the Navy, 29 May, 1801, on board the THESEUS 74, Capt. John Bligh, with whom, after serving in the North Sea and Channel, he proceeded to the West Indies, where he was present as Midshipman, in 1803-4, at the blockade of Cape François, St. Domingo; the capture, with Port Dauphin, of two forts and a 28-gun ship *La Sagesse*; the surrender of the French squadron with the remains of General Rochambeau's army from Cape François; and the unsuccessful attempt upon Curaçoa. Continuing with Capt. Bligh in the SURVEILLANTE 38, on the West India station, until 1806, he saw much other active service, and assisted at the reduction of the Spanish island of St. Andreas. After an attachment of some months to

* *Vide* Gaz. 1841, p. 2508.

the MAGNIFICENT 74, commanded in the Channel by Capt. Geo. Eyre, we again, in May, 1807, find him joining his former Captain in the ALFRED 74. Uniting in that ship with the force employed in the expedition against Copenhagen, he displayed much zeal at the debarkation of the troops, came likewise into frequent contact in her boats with the Danish gun-vessels and praams, and on the surrender of the enemy's fleet aided in fitting out the 74-gun ship *Syren*. When subsequently on the Lisbon station Mr. Pitt was placed in command of the ALFRED's launch, fitted as a gun-boat, and was sent up the Mondego river to assist in landing a body of 300 marines. On the arrival of the troops under Sir Arthur Wellesley from England he was ordered on similar duty. During the battle of Vimeira he was employed in serving the army with ammunition, and after it in embarking the artillery captured. He was also present at the surrender of the Russian fleet in the Tagus. Attaining the rank of Lieutenant 11 March, 1809, he served during the rest of the war in that capacity on board the SCEPTRE 74, Capts. Joseph Bingham and Sam. Jas. Ballard, WELLINGTON 18, Capt. John M'George (which vessel was sent to Laguira for the purpose of bringing General Bolivar to England), ROYAL OAK 74, Capts. Lord Amelius Beauclerk and Pulteney Malcolm, QUEBEC 32, Capt. Chas. Sibthorpe John Hawtayne, MARS 74, Capt. Henry Raper, and LAUREL and AMELIA 38's, both commanded by Capt. Hon. Granville Leveson Proby, the former at the Cape of Good Hope. In the SCEPTRE, after having accompanied the expedition to the Scheldt (where he co-operated in the siege of Flushing, served with the flat-bottomed boats off Bathz, and participated in an attack made upon some Dutch gun-vessels), he again sailed for the West Indies, and was there, 18 Dec. 1809, present at the destruction of the French 40-gun frigates *Loire* and *Seine*, lying under the protection of several strong batteries in L'Ance la Barque, Guadeloupe. On 30 Jan. 1810 he landed on the latter island with a brigade of seamen and marines under the orders of Capt. Ballard, and continued acting in unison with the army until its final subjugation, the latter part of the time in command of the Sailors' Battery. The ROYAL OAK formed part of the fleet under Lord Gambier at the destruction of the French shipping in Basque Roads. In her boats Mr. Pitt often attacked the enemy's convoys on the French coast; as he also, when belonging to the MARS, appears to have done in the Baltic. From 1815 he remained on half-pay until appointed, 22 Dec. 1836, to the VICTORY 104, Capt. Thos. Searle, ordinary guard-ship at Portsmouth, where he soon succeeded to the post of First-Lieutenant. He has filled the office, since Dec. 1838, of Resident Agent of Transports at Leith.

All Lieut. Pitt's certificates concur in proving him a most zealous, active, enterprising, intelligent, and excellent officer. Capt. Searle's testimonial strongly recommends him to the notice of the Admiralty. He married, 6 Feb. 1817, Emma, second daughter of John Clarke, Esq., of Ealing, by whom he has issue two sons and one daughter.

PITT. (LIEUTENANT, 1814. F-P., 10; H-P., 31.)

WILLIAM PITT (*b*) was born 16 Oct. 1793. His brother, John Pitt, while serving as Midshipman in the East Indies in the VICTOR sloop, was placed in charge of a prize brig taken from the Dutch at Java, and never heard of afterwards.

This officer entered the Navy, 9 May, 1806, as Fst.-cl. Vol., on board the HOWE store-ship, Capt. Edw. Killwick, and in July and Aug. following was received on board the MEDUSA 32, Capt. Hon. Duncombe Pleydell Bouverie, and LION 64, Capt. Robt. Rolles. On his arrival in India he joined, in Oct. of the same year, the BLENHEIM 74, flag-ship of Sir Thos. Troubridge; on leaving which, in Jan. 1807, he became in succession attached, in the capacity of Midshipman, to the DASHER sloop, Capt. Augustus Montagu, POWERFUL 74, Capt. Robt. Plampin, PHAETON 38, Capts. Pownoll Bastard Pellew and Fleetwood Broughton Reynolds Pellew (under the latter of whom he co-operated in the reduction of Java in 1811), and ILLUSTRIOUS 74, bearing the broad pendant at first of Commodore Wm. Robt. Broughton, and the flag subsequently of Sir Sam. Hood. He returned home in Aug. 1813 in the BUCEPHALUS 32, Capt. Barrington Reynolds; and after serving for a time in the SALVADOR DEL MUNDO flag-ship at Plymouth of Admiral Wm. Domett, and CALEDONIA 120, flag-ship of Sir Edw. Pellew in the Mediterranean (whither he proceeded in the INDUS 74), Capt. Wm. Hall Gage, was made Lieutenant, 29 Jan. 1814, into the RIVOLI 74, Capts. Graham Eden Hamond and Edw. Stirling Dickson. Under the latter officer he continued to serve in the Mediterranean until Feb. 1816, and assisted at the capture, 30 April, 1815, after a brave defence of 15 minutes, of the French frigate *La Melpomène* of 44 guns. He has since been on half-pay.

Lieut. Pitt is married.

PITTS, K.T.S. (COMMANDER, 1830. F-P., 14; H-P., 25.)

EDWARD PITTS, born 7 Oct. 1795, is eldest surviving son of John Pitts, Esq., Lieutenant-Colonel and Commandant of the Bridlington Light Infantry and Artillery from the commencement of the French Revolution until the year 1809, by Frances, eighth daughter of Jas. Heblethwayte, Esq., of Bridlington. His eldest brother, Thos. Jas. Heblethwayte Pitts, Captain and commanding officer of the Royal Engineers attached to the 4th division of the army in the Peninsula under Sir Lowry Cole, was killed in Feb. 1814; and his second, Wm. Pitts, was drowned in 1806 off Dungeness in one of the boats of the POMONE frigate, Capt. Robt. Barrie. His maternal uncle, Edw. St. Quintin Heblethwayte, First-Lieutenant of the ARROGANT 74, having been mortally wounded in an action fought between that ship and the VICTORIOUS 74 on one side and six heavy French frigates under M. Sercey on the other, died and was buried at sea 21 Sept. 1796.

This officer entered the Navy, 4 May, 1808, as Fst.-cl. Vol., on board the LEOPARD 50, Capt. Jas. Johnstone, bearing the flag of Vice-Admiral Albemarle Bertie at the Cape of Good Hope; became Midshipman, in Sept. 1810, of the VENGEUR 74, Capt. Thos. Brown, lying at Sheerness; and, from 10 Nov. following until Oct. 1815, was employed, again at the Cape and on the West India and Newfoundland stations, in the GALATEA 42, Capt. Woodley Losack. While cruizing in the latter ship off Madagascar, in company with the ASTREA and PHŒBE, frigates about equal in force to the GALATEA, and 18-gun brig RACEHORSE, we find him participating, 20 May, 1811, in a long and trying action with the French 40-gun frigates *Renommée*, *Clorinde*, and *Néréide*, in which the GALATEA, besides being much damaged in her hull, masts, and rigging, sustained a loss of 16 men killed and 46 wounded. He took up, on leaving the GALATEA, a commission bearing date 7 March, 1815; and was subsequently appointed —11 March, 1823, to the WINDSOR CASTLE 74, Capts. Chas. Dashwood, Hugh Downman, and Edw. Durnford King, on the Lisbon and Home stations—15 Nov. 1825, as First, to the NIMROD 18, Capts. Rich. Pridham and Sam. Sparshott, attached to the force on the coast of Ireland, where he remained until that vessel, by the breaking of her anchor, was driven on the rocks in Holyhead Bay 17 Jan. 1827 —4 Nov. 1828, in a similar capacity, to the DISPATCH 18, Capt. Wm. Bohun Bowyer—and, on 10 of the same month, again as First, to the ARIADNE 28, Capt. Fred. Marryat, employed on general service. He was advanced to his present rank 22 July, 1830; and has since been on half-pay.

In commemoration of John VI. of Portugal having taken shelter on board the WINDSOR CASTLE when off Lisbon in 1824, the order of the Tower and Sword was by that sovereign conferred upon the subject of the present narrative in common with the other officers of the ship. Commander Pitts was left a widower 16 Feb. 1847.

PLACE. (Lieutenant, 1842.)

Lionel Read Place entered the Navy 31 Oct. 1829; passed his examination 5 July, 1836; served in the East Indies as Mate in the Melville 72, Capt. Hon. Rich. Saunders Dundas; and was promoted to the rank of Lieutenant 29 March, 1842, in honour of a visit paid by her Majesty to the Queen 110, on the eve of the departure of that ship for the Mediterranean, with the flag of Sir Edw. W. C. R. Owen. His appointments have since been—5 April, 1842, again to the Queen, in which ship he returned to England under the command of Sir Chas. Sullivan, and was paid off in 1844—4 Dec. 1846, to the Amphion steam-frigate, of 300-horse power, Capt. Woodford John Williams, fitting at Devonport—and, 8 Feb. 1847, to the President 50, flag-ship of Rear-Admiral Jas. Rich. Dacres at the Cape of Good Hope, where he is now serving.

PLUMRIDGE. (Captain, 1822. f-p., 28; h-p., 20.)

James Hanway Plumridge entered the Navy, 6 Sept. 1799, as Fst.-cl. Vol., on board the Osprey sloop, Capt. Watts, on the Home station; where, and in the Mediterranean, he served as Midshipman, Master's Mate, and for a short time as Acting-Lieutenant, in the Leda 38, Capts. Geo. Hope and Robt. Honyman, Defence 74, Capt. G. Hope, Melpomène 38, Capt. Peter Parker, and Theseus 74, Capt. G. Hope, from Dec. 1800 until presented, 20 Aug. 1806, with his first commission. The Leda formed part of the force engaged in the expedition to Egypt in 1801; and the Defence of the victorious fleet at the battle of Trafalgar 21 Oct. 1805. For upwards of seven years after his promotion Mr. Plumridge was employed on the Home, West India, Baltic, Cape of Good Hope, and Mediterranean stations, chiefly as First-Lieutenant, in the Repulse 74, Capt. Hon. Arthur Kaye Legge, Zealous 74, Capts. John Giffard and Pierrepont, Melpomène again, Capt. P. Parker, Tartar 32, Capt. Joseph Baker, Menelaus 38, Capt. Parker, Tonnant 80, Capt. Sir John Gore, Tremendous 74 and Hibernia 120, flag-ships of Sir Wm. Sidney Smith, Resistance 36, Capt. Fleetwood Broughton Reynolds Pellew, Royal Sovereign 100, Capt. Thos. Gordon Caulfeild, and Caledonia 120, bearing the flag of Sir Edw. Pellew. On 1 May, 1809, we find him commanding the Melpomène's boats and effecting the destruction, with admirable gallantry, of a Danish cutter-of-war of 6 guns and several merchantmen lying under the protection of a tremendous fire in the harbour of Huilbo, on the coast of Jutland, where the British sustained a loss of 1 Lieutenant, George Rennie, and 5 men severely wounded;* and, not long afterwards, contributing to the repulse, by the same ship, of a flotilla of 20 gun-boats, whose fire in the course of a vigorous action killed and wounded 34 of her people, besides inflicting considerable damage on her hull, sails, and rigging. In Dec. 1810 he assisted in the Menelaus at the reduction of the Isle of France; on 5 Oct. 1813 he commanded the boats of the Resistance at the destruction of the enemy's batteries and the capture of a convoy in Port d'Anzo; and, in April, 1814, he officiated as Aide de Camp to Sir Edw. Pellew at the reduction of Genoa. He was made Commander, 7 June, 1814, into the Crocus sloop; and on 6 of the following month was appointed to the Philomel 18. Proceeding, in that vessel, to the East Indies, he was there, 29 April, 1816, nominated Acting-Captain of the Amphitrite 38, in which frigate, in Feb. 1817, he returned to England. While commanding next, from 10 Feb. 1818 until 15 March, 1821, the Sappho 18, he visited St. Helena, and made prize, on the Irish station, of three American smugglers, one of which had on board 400 bales of tobacco. His appointments since his promotion to Post-rank, which took place 9 Oct. 1822, have been—18 July, 1831, to the Magicienne 24, on the East India station, whence he returned in the early part of 1835—7 April, 1837, to the Superintendentship (which, with his name on the books of the Astræa 6, he retained until 1841) of the Packet establishment at Falmouth—and, 5 Aug. 1847, to the Cambrian 40, again in the East Indies, where, since 13 Oct. following, he has had a broad pendant flying as second in command.

From 1841 until 1847 Capt. Plumridge sat in Parliament as Member for Falmouth. On 23 June, 1842, he was appointed Storekeeper of the Ordnance; and, on 29 June, 1847, awarded the Good Service Pension. His first wife having died 31 July, 1827, he married, a second time, in 1835, Harriet Agnes, daughter of the Right Hon. H. Elliot, by whom he has issue. He was again left a widower 17 April, 1845. Agent—Joseph Woodhead.

* *Vide* Gaz. 1809, p. 690.

PLUNKETT. (Captain, 1846.)

The Honourable Edward Plunkett, born 29 Nov. 1808, is second son of Lord Dunsany, by his first wife, Charlotte Louisa, youngest daughter of Nicholas, first Lord Cloncurry; and nephew, by marriage, of Capt. Jas. Ryder Burton, R.N.

This officer entered the Navy 4 Oct. 1823; served as Midshipman in the boats of the Sybille 48, Capt. Sam. John Brooke Pechell, in a severe encounter with the pirates in the Grecian Archipelago in 1826; passed his examination in 1830; and obtained his first commission 24 Aug. 1834. His succeeding appointments were, 10 Sept. 1834, to the Castor 36, Capts. Lord John Hay and Wm. Robertson, and, 19 Jan. 1837 and 16 July, 1838, to the command of the 10-gun brigs Royalist and Savage. In the three vessels last mentioned he served on the coast of Spain during the civil war from 1835 until promoted to the rank of Commander 1 Aug. 1840. He was subsequently, from 9 Oct. 1843 until June, 1845, employed on particular service in the Stromboli steamer; and, on 9 Nov. 1846, was advanced to his present rank.

Capt. Plunkett, in 1846, published a pamphlet much prized, entitled 'The Past and Future of the British Navy.' Agent—Joseph Woodhead.

POAD. (Lieut., 1812. f-p., 23; h-p, 21.)

James Poad was born 11 Jan. 1789 at Devonport.

This officer entered the Navy, 14 June, 1803, as Third-cl. Vol., on board the Conqueror 74, Capts. Thos. Louis and Israel Pellew, stationed at first in the Channel and afterwards in the Mediterranean. Removing as Midshipman, in March, 1805, to the Victory 100, bearing the flag of Lord Nelson, he accompanied the hero in his celebrated pursuit of the combined squadrons to the West Indies and back, and fought under him in the action off Cape Trafalgar. From 16 Jan. 1806 until May, 1812, he served on the Mediterranean and Lisbon stations, part of the time in the capacity of Master's Mate, in the Ocean 98, Ville de Paris 110, and Barfleur 98, flag-ships of Lord Collingwood, Rear-Admiral Thos. Fras. Fremantle, and Hon. Geo. Cranfield Berkeley. He was then nominated Acting-Lieutenant of the Mermaid troop-ship, Capt. David Dunn, on the eve, at the time, of her departure for England; where on his arrival, 12 days afterwards, he had the mortification to be superseded. Being, however, 5 July following, appointed Admiralty Midshipman of the Impétueux 74, bearing the flag of Vice-Admiral Geo. Martin off Lisbon, he was again, 31 of that month, ordered to assume the rank of Lieutenant, and, with it, the command of No. 7 gun-boat at Cadiz. On 24 Aug. in the same year his promotion received official sanction. He was next, from 14 Dec. 1812, until paid off in Nov. 1814, employed in the Mediterranean on board the Union 98, Capt. Robt. Rolles, and Leviathan and Scipion 74's, Capts. Patrick Campbell and Henry Heathcote; and was subsequently appointed —in 1829, to the office of Agent for Transports Afloat, in which service he continued until wrecked in 1830 on the coast of Sicily *—9 March, 1837, to the charge of the Semaphore station on Haste Hill —in Oct. 1841, to the Rendezvous established at Sunderland for the raising of seamen—and 7 Dec. following, to the Semaphore on Pewley Hill, where he remained upwards of six years.

POATE. (Retired Commander, 1845. f-p., 17; h-p., 46.)

James Poate is nephew of Capt. Jas. Colnett, R.N., who went round the world with Capt. Cook, and afterwards circumnavigated it several times by himself.

This officer entered the Navy, 28 Dec. 1784, as Lieutenant's Servant, on board the Pégase sloop, Capt. Marshall, lying in Portsmouth Harbour, where he remained until Aug. 1786. On 14 June, 1796, he again embarked, on board the York 64, Capt. John Ferrier; and in the following Oct., after having been borne on the books of the Ardent 64, Capt. Rich. Rundell Burgess, and Arrow sloop, Capt. Nathaniel Portlock, he was received by his uncle, Capt. Colnett, on board the Hussar 28. In that ship, in which he had attained the rating of Midshipman, it was his lot to be wrecked, 27 Dec. in the same year, on the coast of France; where he was for six months detained a prisoner of war, subject, nearly the whole time, to very great privations. In June, 1797, having regained his liberty, he rejoined Capt. Portlock on board the Arrow, then at Spithead; and in the ensuing Jan. he removed to the Impétueux 74, Capts. John Willet Payne, Sampson Edwards, and Sir Edw. Pellew. While at anchor off Belleisle in 1799 Mr. Poate was sent in the barge of the latter ship to endeavour to obtain possession of a coasting vessel which had run on shore in Quiberon Bay: he had scarcely, however, succeeded in boarding her, when an attack from 80 French soldiers compelled him to take to his boat and return to the Impétueux. After the expedition to Ferrol we find him present, 29 Aug. 1800, at the cutting-out, close to the batteries in Vigo Bay, of *La Guêpe* privateer of 18 guns and 161 men—an exploit more fully alluded to in our narrative of the services of Capt. Geo. Hills. He was made Lieutenant, 22 Dec. 1800, into the Raven 18, Capt. Jas. Sanders, lying in the Downs; and subsequently appointed—15 Sept. 1801, for nine months, to the Donegal 74, Capt. Sir Rich. John Strachan, attached to the Channel fleet—20 Aug. and 19 Dec. 1804, to the Hindostan 54, Capt. Alex. Fraser, and Glatton 50, Capt. Jas. Colnett—2 March, 1805, to the Helder guard-ship in the river Humber, Capt. Benj. Walker—and 15 Nov. following, to the Minerva frigate, Capts. Sir Geo. Fielding, Geo. Ralph Collier, and Rich. Hawkins, of which he was for seven years First-Lieutenant. While the latter ship was fitting out in Jan. 1806 in the river Thames, Mr. Poate had the honour of attending the funeral of Lord Nelson; on which occasion he was present in the headmost boat, bearing the hero's flag, during the advance of the procession from Greenwich to the Admiralty, and as a supporter to Capt. Philip Durham on its route thence to St. Paul's. During the years 1807-8 Mr. Poate saw much boat service on the coast of France, where he contributed to the capture and destruction of 36 of the enemy's vessels, and on one occasion boarded and carried, with the two cutters, although five miles away from the ship and close in-shore, the *Epervier* French letter-of-marque, of 8 guns and 35 men. Having conducted his prize to London, and rejoined the Minerva, he was on board of her in Sept. 1808 when she fell in with a brig, the *Josephina* letter-of-marque, of 8 guns, pierced for 18, and 50 men, which overset and went down just as the British frigate, after a chase of 75 miles, had arrived within gun-shot of her—barely allowing time for rescue to 16 out of her unfortunate crew. In Jan. 1809 Mr. Poate was sent with the Minerva's boats to assist in bringing off the wounded after the battle of Corunna. He subsequently witnessed the destruction of the French frigate *Amphitrite*, and saw service in the West Indies and at Newfoundland. In Aug. 1813 he invalided home from Halifax, bringing with him a high testimonial of conduct from Capt. Hawkins. He accepted his present rank 25 Sept. 1845.

Commander Poate married 20 Jan. 1810; and has issue one son (educated at the Upper School at Greenwich) and four daughters.

* The vessel he was in had on board a detachment of the 90th regiment, consisting of about 320 men; all of whom, together with 40 women and children, and the greater part of the government stores, were landed in safety.

PODMORE. (Lieut., 1815. f-p., 9; h-p., 40.)

John George King Podmore entered the Navy, 17 Aug. 1798, as Fst.-cl. Vol., on board the Prompte 20, Capts. Thos. Dundas, Matthias Spread, and Robt. Philpot, in which ship we find him serving until Oct. 1800 in the West Indies, and there assisting at the destruction of a Spanish vessel-of-war, pierced for 26 guns, but with only 12 mounted. From the date last mentioned he did not again go afloat until Dec. 1807. Returning, then, to the West Indies as Midshipman in the Variable, Lieut.-Commander Robt. Ballard Yates, he continued employed on that station in the Sandwich, Lieut.-Commander Edw. Kingston Foley, and Musette sloop, Capt. Thos. Parry Jones Parry, until transferred, in July, 1810, to the Fawn 18, Capts. Hon. Geo. Alfred Crofton and Thos. Fellowes, attached to the force in the Channel; where he assisted at the capture, 11 Oct. following, of *Le Téméraire* privateer, of 10 guns, 6 large swivels, and 35 men; and, in April and May, 1812, removed to the Oberon and Griffon sloops, Capts. Jas. Murray and Geo. Barne Trollope. In April, 1813, after he had been for three months borne as Master's Mate on the books of the Ceres, flag-ship at Chatham of Rear-Admiral Thos. Surridge, he sailed for Canada in the Niobe 40, Capt. Wm. Augustus Montagu; and on his arrival in the ensuing June joined the Naval Establishment on Lake Ontario, under the orders of Commodore Sir Jas. Lucas Yeo. In a gallant but unsuccessful endeavour made, 30 May, 1814, by a detachment of 180 seamen and marines, under Capts. Stephen Popham and Francis Brockell Spilsbury, to cut out 18 American gun-boats lying at Sandy Creek under the protection of a powerful land force, Mr. Podmore fell into the hands of the enemy, by whom 18 of his companions had been killed and 50 wounded. He was promoted to the rank of Lieutenant 14 March, 1815, but has not been since afloat. Agents—Hallett and Robinson.

POGSON. (Commander, 1819. f-p., 28; h-p., 29.)

Henry Freeman Young Pogson entered the Navy, in the spring of 1790, as A.B., on board the Romulus 36, Capt. Thos. Lennox Frederick, and, until the following year, was employed, latterly with the rating of Midshipman, in watching the port of Brest. After a servitude of five years and four months on the Mediterranean and Channel stations in the Terrible 74, Capts. Skeffington Lutwidge, Geo. Campbell, and Sir Rich. Bickerton (under the first and second of whom he assisted at the occupation of Toulon in 1793, at the reduction of Corsica in 1794, and in Hotham's partial actions in 1795), he was made Lieutenant, 28 April, 1798, into the Espiègle sloop, Capt. Jas. Broodler, employed as a cruizer in the North Sea. His succeeding appointments were—26 Dec. 1799, to the Neptune 98, Capt. Jas. Vashon, attached to the Channel fleet—18 Aug. 1801, to the Téméraire 98, in which ship, bearing the flag of Rear-Admiral Geo. Campbell, he made a voyage to the West Indies—8 April, 1803 (after six months of half-pay), to the Canopus 80, bearing the flag of the same officer in the Mediterranean, where he remained until Aug. 1805, officiating part of the time as First-Lieutenant—3 June, 1807, to the Majestic 74, flag-ship of Vice-Admiral Thos. Macnamara Russell in the Downs, where he became Signal-Lieutenant, and witnessed the surrender of Heligoland—17 March,

1808, and 7 Nov. 1810, to the PRINCE OF ORANGE 74, and MONMOUTH 64, flag-ships in the Downs of Admirals G. Campbell and Thos. Foley—and 17 July and 26 Aug. 1812, 28 June, 1814, and 7 June, 1816, to the command of the BOLD, BRAMBLE, RACER, and EAGLE. In the BRAMBLE and RACER (which latter vessel was wrecked in the Gulf of Florida 10 Oct. 1814) he was employed in carrying despatches to the coasts of Spain and North America; and in the EAGLE he cruized in protection of the revenue until promoted to his present rank 4 March, 1819. His last appointment was, 6 April, 1830, to the Coast Guard, in which service he continued, as an Inspecting-Commander, for nearly three years.

POLLARD. (LIEUT., 1806. F-P., 27; H-P., 23.)

JOHN POLLARD was born 27 July, 1787.

This officer entered the Navy, 1 Nov. 1797, as Fst.-cl. Vol., on board the HAVICK 16, Capt. Philip Bartholomew; in which sloop, after having chased a large convoy and three armed vessels under the batteries of St. Maloes, and been there for some time warmly engaged with the enemy, he was wrecked, 9 Nov. 1800, in St. Aubin's Bay, Jersey. He was then received as a Supernumerary on board the CAMBRIDGE 74, Capt. Thos. Wolley; and next, in Sept. 1801, on board the HERCULE 74, Capt. Wm. Luke, with whom he cruized in the Channel until paid off in April, 1802. Joining in succession, in April, 1803, the CULLODEN 74 and CANOPUS 80, both commanded by Capt. John Conn, he sailed in the latter ship with the flag of Rear-Admiral Geo. Campbell for the Mediterranean, where, in March, 1805, he removed on promotion to the VICTORY 100, bearing the flag of Lord Nelson. On the return of the fleet from its pursuit of the combined squadrons to the West Indies, Mr. Pollard was afforded an opportunity of participating, as Signal-Midshipman, in the action off Cape Trafalgar On that occasion, while standing on the poop, he was struck by a splinter on the right arm, and chanced to be the first officer who was there touched. A musket-ball next passed through the shell of his spy-glass, about a foot above the hand that held it; and a second one shattered the watch in his pocket. Some time after the VICTORY had been in action with the French 74-gun ship *Redoutable*, the officers and men around him beginning to fall fast, the attention of Mr. Pollard was arrested by a number of soldiers whom he perceived crouching in the tops of the *Redoutable*, and directing a destructive fire on the poop and quarter-deck of the VICTORY. He immediately seized a musket, and, being supplied by the Signal-Quartermaster, King, with ball-cartridges from two barrels kept on the after-part of the poop for the use of the marines (who at the time were elsewhere engaged), continued firing at the soldiers every time they rose breast-high in the tops, until not one was to be seen. In the act of handing the last parcel of ball-cartridges, the Quartermaster was shot through the forehead, and fell lifeless on the spot. When the action terminated Mr. Pollard was the only officer left alive of those who had been originally stationed on the poop; and thus, in the manner we have described, originated the belief that it was he who had shot the man who killed Lord Nelson. On leaving the VICTORY in Nov. 1805, he joined, first the QUEEN 98, and then the DREADNOUGHT of similar force, and HIBERNIA 110, bearing the respective flags of Lords Collingwood, Northesk, and St. Vincent. He was made Lieutenant, 14 Nov. 1806, into the DÉCADE 36, Capt. John Stuart, in the Channel; and was subsequently appointed—25 Dec. 1807, to the BRUNSWICK 74, Capt. Thos. Graves, stationed in the Baltic, where, prior to the embarkation from Nyeborg of the Spanish troops under the Marquis de la Romana, he served in the boats at the attack and capture of the Danish brig *Fama* of 18, and her consort the *Salorman* cutter (which he was among the first to board) of 12 guns—14 June 1810, after 16 months of half-pay, to the NORTH STAR 20, Capt. Thos. Coe, with whom he cruized in the Channel until May, 1811—4 Jan. 1812, to the MERCURIUS sloop, Capt. Thos. Renwick, employed in the North Sea and Baltic—9 May, 1814 (having left the MERCURIUS in the preceding Nov.), to the WOODLARK 10, Capt. Wm. Cutfield, on the north coast of Spain, whence he returned sick in the following Sept.—and 19 April, 1828, for three years, to the Ordinary at Chatham. He has been in charge, since 2 Aug. 1836, of a station in the Coast Guard.

Lieut. Pollard married, in Aug. 1822, Miss Matilda Trevethan, a lady by whom he has issue six children.

POLLARD. (LIEUTENANT, 1843.)

WALTER JAMES POLLARD is third son of the late Wm. Dutton Pollard, Esq., of Kintuck, Castle Pollard, co. Westmeath, a Magistrate and Deputy-Lieutenant, and High Sheriff for the co. in 1811, whose first wife, Frances, was third daughter of Gustavus Hume Rochfort, Esq., of Rochfort, M.P. for co. Westmeath; and whose second, Louisa Anne, was eldest daughter of the late Admiral Hon. Sir Thos. Pakenham, G.C.B.

This officer entered the Navy 21 Dec. 1830; passed his examination 7 April, 1837; and, between 1840 and the date of his promotion to the rank of Lieutenant, 19 July, 1843, was employed as Mate on the African, Home, and North America and West India stations, in the BUZZARD brigantine, MEGÆRA steamer, and GRIFFON brigantine, Lieut.-Commanders Reginald Thos. John Levinge, Geo. Oldmixon, and Chas. Jenkin. His appointments have since been—9 March, 1844, as Additional Lieutenant, to the PENELOPE steam-frigate, Capt. Wm. Jones, on the coast of Africa—17 Aug. 1844, to the LARNE 18, Capt. John Wm. Douglas Brisbane, on the same station—16 April, 1845, to the PROMETHEUS steam-sloop, of 200 horse-power, of which vessel, also stationed on the African coast, he became First-Lieutenant—17 Nov. 1847, as Additional, to the VINDICTIVE 50, bearing the flag of Sir Fras. Wm. Austen in North America and the West Indies—and 11 Feb. 1848, in a similar capacity, to the HAVANNAH 19, Capt. John Elphinstone Erskine, fitting at Devonport. AGENTS—Hallett and Robinson.

PONSONBY. (LIEUTENANT, 1827.)

THOMAS CARRIQUE PONSONBY entered the Navy 1 March, 1815; passed his examination in 1822; obtained his commission 30 April, 1827; and served in the Coast Guard from 9 Nov. 1831 until 1836. His appointments have since been—10 Oct. 1840, to the LUCIFER steamer, Capt. Fred. Wm. Beechey, on the coast of Ireland, where he was superseded in Feb. 1841—26 April, 1847, to the POICTIERS 72, Capt. Sir Thos. Bourchier, lying at Chatham—and, 24 Nov. following, to the command of the FIREFLY steamer, of 220 horse-power, now on the coast of Africa. AGENTS—Messrs. Stilwell.

POOLE. (LIEUTENANT, 1825.)

ROBERT POOLE entered the Navy 14 May, 1808; passed his examination in 1814; attained the rank of Lieutenant 10 Jan. 1825; served for three years (dating from 23 Nov. 1827) in the Coast Blockade as Supernumerary-Lieutenant of the RAMILLIES and TALAVERA 74's, both commanded by Capt. Hugh Pigot; had charge of a station in the Coast Guard from 7 June, 1831, until Sept. 1847; and has since been in command of the ACTIVE and EAGLE Revenue-vessels.

POOLEY. (LIEUT., 1820. F-P., 19; H-P., 15.)

GEORGE POOLEY entered the Navy, 1 May, 1813, as Fst.-cl. Vol., on board the ALBION 74, Capt. John Ferris Devonshire, with whom he continued to serve, as Midshipman, in the SCEPTRE 74, on the North American station until June, 1814. In the following Sept., after he had been for two months borne at Portsmouth as a Supernumerary on the books of the PRINCE 98, flag-ship of Sir Rich.

Bickerton, and CENTAUR 74, Capt. White, he joined the BEDFORD 74, Capt. Jas. Walker, whom he accompanied in the expedition against New Orleans. Returning to England in July, 1815, he served during the next five years, at Portsmouth and at Plymouth, in the PUISSANT 74, NYMPHE 38, Capt. Hugh Pigot, VENGEUR 74, Capt. Thos. Alexander, DWARF, Lieut.-Commander Gordon, ERIDANUS 42, Capt. Wm. King, IMPREGNABLE 104, flag-ship of Lord Exmouth, and SPARTAN 46, Capt. Wm. Furlong Wise. He then, in June and Oct. 1820, joined in succession the RALEIGH sloop, Capt. Geo. Blackman, and EURYALUS 42, Capt. Thos. Huskisson, both on the Jamaica station; where he was nominated, 5 Nov. following, Acting-Lieutenant of the ONTARIO 18, Capt. Joddrell Leigh. His official promotion took place 27 Dec. 1820, but he did not again go afloat until Feb. 1824. On 28 of that month he received an appointment to the MEDINA 20, Capts. Chas. Montagu Walker and Timothy Curtis, under whom he was for nearly two years employed in the Mediterranean. He has had command, since 20 Sept. 1837, of a station in the Coast Guard.

Lieut. Pooley married, 7 Nov. 1837, Frances Anne, second daughter of John Vigars, Esq., Surgeon, of Falmouth.

POORE. (LIEUT., 1815. F-P., 8; H-P., 31.)

JOHN POORE is brother of Retired Commander Wm. Poore, R.N.

This officer entered the Navy, 15 May, 1808, as Fst.-cl Vol., on board the FISGARD 38, Capts. Wm. Bolton and Fras. Mason; under the latter of whom we find him performing the duties of Midshipman in the attack of 1809 upon Flushing, and otherwise actively employed until Aug. 1810. During the four following years he served uninterruptedly in the VILLE DE PARIS 110, and RODNEY and MILFORD 74's, all flag-ships of Rear-Admiral Thos. Fras. Fremantle on the Mediterranean station; where, in the Adriatic portion of it, he co-operated in the reduction of Fiumé, witnessed the fall of Rovigno, Piran, and Capo d'Istria, and assisted at the capture of Trieste. From Sept. 1814 to Aug. 1815 Mr. Poore cruized off the coast of Ireland in the PRESIDENT 38, Capt. Norwich Duff. He then took up a commission dated 25 Feb. in the latter year; and has since been on half-pay.

He married Miss Martha Midlane.

POORE. (RETIRED COMMANDER, 1847. F-P., 21; H-P., 26.)

WILLIAM POORE was born 21 Aug. 1789. He is brother of Lieut. John Poore, R.N.

This officer entered the Navy, 15 Sept. 1800, as Fst.-cl. Vol., on board the GANGES 74, Capts. Thos. Fras. Fremantle and Joseph Baker, in which ship he was employed, until June, 1802, off Brest, in the Baltic (where he fought at the battle of Copenhagen), and in watching the French at St. Domingo. He then returned to England as a Midshipman in LA DÉCADE frigate, Capt. Wm. Geo. Rutherford. During the first six years of the war we find him serving in succession on the Channel, Mediterranean, and Cork stations, in the AMPHION 32 and VICTORY 100, both flag-ships of Lord Nelson, CAMELION sloop, Capt. Thos. Staines, VICTORY again, bearing the flag of Lord Nelson, and EURYDICE and DRUID frigates, both commanded by Sir Wm. Bolton. In the AMPHION he was present at the capture of the *Orion* Dutch Indiaman, the first enemy's vessel taken after the renewal of hostilities; in the VICTORY he assisted at the blockade of Toulon; and in the EURYDICE he was often in action with gun-boats and batteries. In the CAMELION's boats he partook of much detached service on the coasts of Genoa and France; and on one occasion in particular, 11 Aug. 1805, brought off the ship's cutter after an unsuccessful attack upon an armed convoy, consisting of seven sail of feluccas, in which the British had their commanding officer and 3 men killed, 1 man wounded, and another taken prisoner. On 2 March, 1809, he was made Lieutenant into the HINDOSTAN 50, *armée-en-flûte*, Capt. John Pasco, fitting for a voyage to New South Wales, where he took charge of the DROMEDARY store-ship when on fire, and personally assisted in extinguishing the flames. His last appointments were—28 Jan. 1811, as First, to the RAINBOW 28, Capts. Jas. Wooldridge and Gardiner Henry Guion, employed in co-operation with the patriots on the coast of Catalonia—2 Dec. 1812, in a similar capacity (having invalided from the RAINBOW in May, 1812), to the CHANTICLEER 10, Capts. Rich. Spear, Stewart Blacker, John Thomson, Geo. Tupman, and Wm. Henry Dickson, in which vessel he served at the capture of Guadeloupe in 1815, and continued employed until paid off in Aug. 1816—29 Oct. 1822, to the command of the LION, a most active and successful Revenue cruizer—31 May, 1825, to the ASTREA packet, Capt. Wm. King, stationed at Falmouth—and 22 Dec. following, to the KINGFISHER, another Falmouth packet, the command of which he was induced from ill health and impaired vision to resign in Dec. 1828. He was admitted to the out-pension of Greenwich Hospital 3 March, 1834; and invested with his present rank 9 April, 1847.

Commander Poore married, 10 June, 1817, Marianne, daughter of Rich. Jeffreys, Esq., of Basingstoke, co. Hants, by whom he has issue two sons and one daughter. AGENT—John P. Muspratt.

POPE. (LIEUTENANT, 1826.)

EDMUND POPE entered the Navy 16 May, 1807; passed his examination in 1815; and obtained his commission 27 March, 1826. He has since been on half-pay. AGENTS—Messrs. Chads.

POPHAM. (CAPTAIN, 1838. F-P., 18; H-P., 12.)

BRUNSWICK POPHAM is brother of Capt. Wm. Popham, R.N.; and second son of the late Rear-Admiral Sir Home Riggs Popham, K.C.B.

This officer entered the Navy, 4 Dec. 1817, as Fst.-cl. Vol., on board the ANDROMACHE 44, Capt. Wm. Henry Shirreff, fitting for the South American station, whence he returned to England in Aug. 1821. In Jan. 1822 he was received as Midshipman (a rating he had previously attained) on board the LIFFEY 50, bearing the broad pendant of Commodore Chas. Grant in the East Indies. He next, in July, 1825, joined the GANGES 84, Capt. Patrick Campbell, lying at Portsmouth; and, on 3 Jan. 1826, having passed his examination in April, 1824, he was promoted to the rank of Lieutenant. In the following Feb. he received an appointment to the GLASGOW 50, Capt. Hon. Jas. Ashley Maude, employed at first off the coast of Portugal, and then in the Mediterranean; where, after acting a part in the battle of Navarin, he removed to the PELORUS 18, Capt. Peter Richards, and in Jan. 1828 became Flag-Lieutenant, in the ASIA 84, to Sir Edw. Codrington. On 2 March in the latter year he was made Commander into the ZEBRA 18. His subsequent appointments in that capacity were—30 Oct. 1828 and 20 April, 1830, to the INFERNAL bomb and WASP 18, both stationed in the Mediterranean, whence he returned home and was paid off in June, 1831—and, 3 Dec. 1834, to the PELICAN 16, in which vessel he served at the Cape of Good Hope and on the east and west coasts of Africa until May, 1839. He has since been on half-pay. His Post-commission bears date 28 June, 1838.

Capt. Popham married, 26 Oct. 1841, Susan, eldest daughter of Patrick Murray, Esq., of Arthurstone, Perthshire, N.B. AGENTS—Collier and Snee.

POPHAM. (Captain, 1819. F-P., 14; H-P., 28.)

WILLIAM POPHAM, born in April, 1791, is eldest son of the late Rear-Admiral Sir Home Riggs Popham,* K.C.B.; brother of Capt. Brunswick Popham,

* Sir Home Riggs Popham was born at Gibraltar in 1762. For some years previous to the late war he was employed in surveys on the coast of Africa and in the East Indies, and rendered services for which he was thanked by the Government and the Court of Directors of the East India Company.

R.N.; nephew of Capt. Joseph Lamb Popham, R.N. (1806), who died in 1833; and brother-in-law of Capt. John Pakenham, R.N.

This officer entered the Navy, in May, 1805, as Fst.-cl. Vol., on board the DIADEM 64, commanded by his father, under whom, while holding the ratings of Midshipman and Master's Mate, he assisted at the reduction of the Cape of Good Hope, and served on shore with the naval brigade at the capture of Buenos Ayres. Between 1807 and the date of his promotion to the rank of Lieutenant 14 Feb. 1812, he was employed on the St. Helena, Baltic, Brazilian, Home, and Mediterranean stations, in the SAMPSON 64, Capt. Wm. Cuming, SURVEILLANTE 38, Capt. Geo. Ralph Collier (part of the force attached to the Copenhagen expedition), VENERABLE 74, Capt. Sir H. R. Popham, CALEDONIA 120, Capt. Jas. Nash, ROYAL GEORGE 100, Capt. Andrew King, and CALEDONIA again, flag-ship of Sir Edw. Pellew. He next, from June, 1812, until advanced to the rank of Commander 23 Dec. 1814, served in the West Indies and on the coast of North America in the NARCISSUS 32 and LOIRE 38, Capts. John Rich. Lumley and Jas. Nash. In the former ship he saw much boat-service; and on one occasion in particular, 24 Nov. 1812, assisted, under Lieut. John Cririe, in boarding and carrying, under a shower of grape and langridge, productive to the British of a loss of 1 man killed and another wounded, the *Joseph and Mary*, a mischievous privateer, mounting 4 guns, with a complement of 73 men, on a cruize between St. Domingo and Cuba. Capt. Popham's last appointments were—on his promotion, as above, to the PANDORA 16, lying in the Downs—27 July, 1816 (12 months after he had left the PANDORA), to the HECLA bomb, in which vessel he served under Lord Exmouth at the battle of Algiers*—4 Oct. following, to the CORDELIA 10, at Sheerness—1 Jan. 1817 and 9 Oct. 1818, to the TYRIAN and BEAVER of 10 guns each, both on the West India station—and, 2 Feb. 1819, as Acting-Captain, to the SYBILLE 44, bearing his father's flag at Jamaica. In the ship last mentioned, to which he was confirmed 19 May following, he continued until Aug. 1820. He accepted the retirement 1 Oct. 1846.

He married in Aug. 1843, and has issue two children. AGENTS—Collier and Snee.

POPPLEWELL. (LIEUTENANT, 1842.)

GEORGE OTWAY POPPLEWELL entered the Navy 14 Feb. 1832; passed his examination 14 June, 1836; and on his return from South America (where he had been serving for some time as Mate) in the CURAÇOA 24, Capt. Jenkin Jones, was promoted to the rank of Lieutenant 18 Nov. 1842. His appointments have since been—24 May, 1843, to the EXCELLENT gunnery-ship at Portsmouth, Capt. Sir Thos. Hastings—and, 22 Oct. 1844, to the DÆDALUS 19, Capt. Peter M'Quhae, fitting for the East Indies, where he is now employed.

In 1798 he commanded, in conjunction with Major-General Coote, an expedition sent to destroy the locks and sluice-gates of the Bruges Canal; in 1799 he accompanied Sir Andrew Mitchell to the Coast of Holland; and in 1801 he assisted, from the Red Sea, in driving the French out of Egypt. In 1802 Sir Home was returned to Parliament as Member for the Borough of Yarmouth. Through Lord Melville's patronage he was appointed to the superintendence of a scheme for destroying a fleet by means never before heard of. This experiment was ludicrously called the 'Catamaran expedition,' and two vessels were destroyed by it off Boulogne in 1804. An attack on a larger scale was subsequently attempted at Fort Conge, but did not succeed. In the course of 1806 we find Sir Home Popham commanding the naval force employed at the reduction of the Cape of Good Hope and the capture of Buenos Ayres. He afterwards joined in the expedition of 1809 to the Scheldt; and in 1812 commanded a squadron employed in co operation with the patriots on the North coast of Spain. From 1817 to 1820 he commanded in chief at Jamaica. Devoted to the service of Government for forty years in the East and West Indies, Africa, America, and several parts of Europe, and worn out by the indefatigable and intense anxiety of his mind, he died at Cheltenham 11 Sept. 1820. Sir Home Popham was the inventor of a code of signals adopted in the navy.

* *Vide* Gaz. 1816, p. 1792.

POPPLEWELL. (COMMANDER, 1813. F-P., 16; H-P., 35.)

MATTHEW JAMES POPPLEWELL is son of the late Mr. Thos. Popplewell, Master R.N. (1793).

This officer entered the Navy, 2 May, 1796, as a Volunteer, on board the FLORA 36, Capt. Robt. Gambier Middleton, in which ship he served on the Lisbon and Cadiz stations until Oct. 1799. In July, 1801, he re-embarked on board the GOLIATH 74, Capt. Wm. Essington, whom, in April, 1802, being at the time in the West Indies, he followed as Midshipman into the SANS PAREIL 80. He next, in Sept. of the latter year, joined L'OISEAU, Capt. John Phillips, lying at Plymouth; and, after serving for two years on the Mediterranean, Baltic, and Home stations in the WILLIAM store-ship and ORESTES 14, both commanded by Capt. Thos. Brown, and ROYAL SOVEREIGN 100, Capt. Sir Harry Burrard Neale, was successively, in Jan. and Oct. 1805, nominated Sub-Lieutenant of the SAFEGUARD, Lieut.-Commander Robt. Balfour, and RAVEN brig, Capt. Thos. Brown. On 22 Jan. 1806 he was promoted to the full rank of Lieutenant. In the course of the same year he was appointed to the ÆOLUS 32, Capt. Lord Wm. FitzRoy, and GLORY 98, commanded by the late Vice-Admiral Wm. Albany Otway, under whom, from Jan. 1808 until officially advanced to his present rank 6 Nov. 1813, we find him filling the post of Flag-Lieutenant in the LIVELY 38, GANGES 74, BARFLEUR 98, GLADIATOR 50, MONARCH 74, CÆSAR 80 (the two latter forming part of the Walcheren expeditionary force), GLADIATOR again, THISBE 28, and ADAMANT 50, on the Lisbon, Portsmouth, and Leith stations. During that period, besides having brought the VENTEUR home from Flushing, he was at times intrusted with the command, on the coast of Norway, of the CLIO, NIGHTINGALE, and SARPEDON. Since the date last mentioned he has been on half-pay.

Commander Popplewell is married and has issue.

PORCHER. (LIEUTENANT, 1846.)

EDWIN AUGUSTUS PORCHER is second son of the Rev. Geo. Porcher, of Maiden Erlegh, Berks, by Amelia, daughter of John Chamier, Esq., and sister of Commander Frederick Chamier, R.N. His grandfather, Josias Dupré Porcher, Esq., of Winslade House, co. Devon, many years M.P. for Old Sarum, married a daughter of Admiral Sir Wm. Burnaby, Bart.; and his uncle, Henry Porcher, Esq., of Arborfield, Berks, was lately M.P. for Clitheroe.

This officer passed his examination 8 June, 1844; obtained his commission 9 Nov. 1846; and since 18 of that month has been serving in the SIDON steam-frigate, of 560 horse-power, Capt. Wm. Honyman, now on the Mediterranean station.

PORTEOUS. (LIEUTENANT, 1842.)

FRANCIS PENDER PORTEOUS entered the Navy 2 Aug. 1827; and on 20 Oct. following was present in the GENOA 74, Capt. Walter Bathurst, at the battle of Navarin. He passed his examination 4 June, 1834; and, after serving for a time at Plymouth and in the Mediterranean, in the CALEDONIA 120, flag-ship of Sir Graham Moore, and MALABAR 72, Capt. Sir Geo. Rose Sartorius, was promoted to the rank of Lieutenant 29 March, 1842. His appointments have since been—5 April, 1842, to the QUEEN 110, bearing the flag of Sir Edw. W. C. R. Owen in the Mediterranean—23 Feb. 1843, to the DEVASTATION steamer, Capts. Hastings Reginald Henry, Hon. Swynfen Thos. Carnegie, and Wm. Hewgill Kitchen, on the same station, whence he returned at the close of 1845—8 April, 1846, as Additional, to the VERNON 50, bearing the flag of Rear-Admiral Sam. Hood Inglefield on the south-east coast of America—1 July following, as First, to the RACER 16, Capt. Archibald Reed, similarly stationed—and, 10 Dec. 1847, to the PRINCE REGENT 92, Capt. Wm. Fanshawe Martin, lying at Portsmouth.

PORTER. (COMMANDER, 1822. F-P., 15; H-P., 25.)

THOMAS PORTER entered the Navy, 14 Nov. 1807, as Fst.-cl. Vol., on board the POMPÉE 74, Capt. Rich. Dacres, attached to the Channel fleet; removed, in Jan. 1808, to the ECLIPSE sloop, Capt. Geo. Adey Creyke, employed on the Lisbon, West India, and Home stations; served from June, 1810, to Feb. 1813 in the ARMADA 74, Capts. Adam Mackenzie, John Ferris Devonshire, and Chas. Grant, in the North Sea and Mediterranean; then joined the HIBERNIA 120, bearing the flag of Sir Wm. Sidney Smith off Toulon; and on 27 July, 1814, was advanced to the rank of Lieutenant. His succeeding appointments were—7 Sept. 1814, to the CRESCENT 38, Capt. John Quilliam, in the West Indies—29 Sept. 1815, to the TYRIAN 10, Capt. Augustus Baldwin, in the Channel—5 Sept. 1817, after nearly 12 months of half-pay, to the ANDROMACHE 44, Capt. Wm. Henry Shirreff, fitting for South America—and, 10 May 1821, to the SUPERB 78, bearing the broad pendant of Sir Thos. Masterman Hardy on that station. On 26 Aug. 1822 he was made Commander into the ALACRITY sloop, in which vessel, in July, 1823, he returned to England with 1,000,000 dollars. He has not been since afloat. AGENTS—Hallett and Robinson.

PORTER. (LIEUT., 1814. F-P., 10;* H-P., 33.)

WILLIAM PORTER entered the Navy, in Nov. 1804, as L.M., on board the MONARCH 74, Capt. John Clarke Searle, bearing the flag of Lord Keith in the Downs. From Feb. 1805 until Feb. 1810 he served in the Channel, Baltic, and North Sea, chiefly in the capacity of Midshipman, in the CONSTANT 12, Lieutenant-Commander John Stokes; he then joined the NAUTILUS 18, Capt. Thos. Dench, attached to the force in the Mediterranean; and in March, 1813, after a servitude of two years on that and the Home stations, part of the time as Second Master, in the SAN JOSEF 110, and QUEEN CHARLOTTE 100, flag-ships of Sir Chas. Cotton and Lord Keith, was again placed under the orders of Lieut. Stokes in the CONSTANT. From the following April until confirmed in his present rank 10 Aug. 1814, he was a second time employed, as Master's Mate and Acting Lieutenant, in the SAN JOSEF, under the flag, in the Mediterranean, of Sir Rich. King. Subsequently to Feb. 1820 he held an appointment in the Water Guard.

* Apart from the time he passed in the Water Guard.

PORTMAN. (LIEUTENANT, 1826.)

WYNDHAM BERKELEY PORTMAN, born 4 June, 1804, is third son of Edw. Berkeley Portman, Esq., of Bryanston, co. Dorset, and Orchard Portman, co. Somerset, by Lucy, daughter of the Rev. Thos. Whitby, of Creswell Hall, Staffordshire; and brother of the present Lord Portman.

This officer entered the Navy 7 Aug. 1817; passed his examination in 1823; and was made Lieutenant, 26 Jan. 1826, into the BRISK 10, Capt. Hon. Wm. Anson, on the Mediterranean station; where we find him, in 1827-8, serving in the TALBOT 28, Capt. Hon. Fred. Noel. Since the year last mentioned he has been on half-pay.

He married, in Oct. 1829, Sarah, only daughter of Thos. Thornhill, Esq., of Riddlesworth Hall, co. Norfolk, by whom he has issue.

POSTLE. (COMMANDER, 1845.)

CHARLES JAMES POSTLE passed his examination in 1831; and on the occasion of his promotion to the rank of Lieutenant, 6 July, 1836, was appointed Additional of the CALEDONIA 120, flag-ship of Sir Josias Rowley on the Mediterranean station, where he next, 7 Jan. and 1 Nov. 1837, joined the BELLEROPHON 80 and PORTLAND 52, Capts. Sam. Jackson and David Price. His succeeding appointments were—4 Aug. 1838, to the PILOT 16, Capt. Geo. Ramsay, on the North America and West India station, where he was superseded in Aug. 1839—20 April, 1840, for a few months, to the VANGUARD 80, Capt. Sir David Dunn, again in the Mediterranean—30 July, 1841, to the Coast Guard—and, 12 Jan. 1842 and 6 Oct. 1843, to the command of the LIZARD and FLAMER steam-vessels, the former of which was run down and sunk by the French steamer *Véloce* 24 July, 1843. Preparatory to his return to England Lieut. Postle had the gratification, in Dec. 1845, of receiving a most complimentary and flattering address, signed by the Chairman, Deputy-Chairman, and members of the Exchange Committee of Gibraltar, expressive of the deep sense they entertained of the numerous obligations they owed him for the prompt and efficient manner in which he had at all times, both in the LIZARD and FLAMER, rendered protection to the trade of the place; and of their admiration of the spirited manner in which he had, when occasion offered, exacted a proper respect for the British flag. The humane and devoted nature of the exertions he afforded, in the course of the same month, to the crew of the French steamer *Pepin*, wrecked between Azamoor and Mazagan, on the coast of Barbary, had the effect of eliciting a glowing letter of thanks as well from the Consul-General for France in Morocco as from the Consul of France at Gibraltar. The King of the French, too, being desirous of publicly testifying his appreciation of the noble conduct exhibited by Lieut. Postle, expressed his intention of conferring upon him the Cross of the Legion of Honour. The regulations of the British service, however, not permitting him to accept it, His Majesty presented him instead with a pair of valuable pistols, appropriately inscribed. He was promoted to the rank of Commander 12 Dec. 1845; and has been employed since 15 Aug. 1846 as an Inspecting-Commander in the Coast Guard at Dundalk, where, on 28 Jan. 1846, he again found means of rendering himself conspicuous by the services he performed on the occasion of the wreck of the cutter *Lord Nelson*, the owners of which, Messrs. Horsfall and Sons, of Liverpool, presented him with a silver box of great intrinsic value and of exquisite workmanship. AGENTS—Messrs. Stilwell.

POTBURY. (COMMANDER, 1844.)

JOHN MOON POTBURY died at the commencement of 1848.

This officer entered the Navy, 1 Nov. 1805, as Second-cl. Vol., on board the ACASTA 40, Capt. Rich. Dalling Dunn, under whom he fought in the action off St. Domingo, 6 Feb. 1806. Between Dec. in the latter year and July, 1808, he served on the Plymouth station, part of the time as Midshipman, in the PORCUPINE 24, Capt. Hon. Henry Duncan, in another ship, the name of which has escaped us, and in the EL FIRME, Capt. Wells. He was next, from June, 1810, to March, 1811, employed in the North Sea on board the CHRISTIAN VII. 80; and in May, 1812, he joined the NAMUR 74, stationed at first on the coast of North America, and then in the West Indies; where, prior to his return to England in April, 1817, we find him serving for two years and 10 months in the EMULOUS 16, Capt. Rich. John Lewin, SHARK sloop, ELECTRA 14, Capt. R. J. Lewin, EMULOUS again, Capt. Thos. Wren Carter, a second time in the SHARK, Capt. Hunter, PIQUE 36, Capt. Jas. Haldane Tait, SALISBURY 50, flag-ship of Rear-Admiral John Erskine Douglas, and PRIMROSE 18, Capt. Chas. Geo. Rodney Phillott. In May, 1822, until within a few weeks of which period he had been further employed, on Home service, in the IMPREGNABLE 104, flag-ship of Sir John Thos. Duckworth, NORTHUMBERLAND 74, Capt. Sir Michael Seymour, and, for two years and five months as Admiralty Midshipman, in the LEE and REDWING sloops, Capts. Stewart Blacker and Hon. Geo. Rolle Walpole Trefusis, he was appointed, in the capacity last mentioned, to the ALLIGATOR 28, Capt. Thos. Alexander, fitting for the East Indies. Being there confirmed a Lieutenant 22 Oct. 1823—six months and 17 days after he had been ordered to act as such—in the TEES 26, Capt. Thos. Coe, he was afforded an opportunity, both in that vessel and in the LIFFEY 50, commanded by the same officer, of participating in the hostilities against the King of Ava. His appointments, after he left the LIFFEY, were—24 April, 1827, to the CADMUS 10, Capts. Chas. Gordon and Sir Thos. Raikes Trigge Thompson, on the South American station, whence he returned in May, 1830—26 Jan. 1831, to the command of the NIMBLE schooner, at Jamaica, where he was superseded in Feb. 1833—13 Nov. 1835, to the FLAMER steamer, which vessel, deducting a few months in 1836, he commanded for three years and a half on the Home and North America and West India stations—10 Aug. 1841, to the command of the SPY brigantine, at Sheerness—and 22 Dec. following to the SAN JOSEF 110, Flag-Lieutenant to Sir Sam. Pym, Admiral-Superintendent at Devonport. On 16 Sept. 1844 he was advanced to the rank of Commander. His last appointment was, 30 March, 1847, to the GROWLER steam-sloop of 280 horse-power.

POTTS. (LIEUT., 1808. F-P., 13; H-P., 34.)

JOHN POTTS died in 1847.

This officer entered the Navy, 7 Oct. 1800, as Fst.-cl. Vol., on board the ASSISTANCE 50, Capt. Rich. Lee in which ship (he had attained the rating of Midshipman) he was wrecked between Dunkerque and Gravelines 29 March, 1802. Joining next, in March, 1803, the CONQUEROR 74, Capts. Thos. Louis and Israel Pellew, he served, under the latter officer, in Nelson's pursuit of the combined squadrons to the West Indies and back, and at the battle of Trafalgar. On 7 May, 1808, a few days after his removal to the HIBERNIA 120, flag-ship of Sir Chas. Cotton at Lisbon, he was made Lieutenant into the ECLIPSE sloop; and in that vessel, commanded in succession by Capts. Geo. Adey Creyke, Thos. Ball Sulivan, Geo. Henderson, and Henry Lynne, he was employed, on the Channel, East and West India, and Cape of Good Hope stations, until July, 1814. He remained thenceforward on half-pay.

POULDEN. (REAR-ADMIRAL OF THE RED, 1840. F-P., 28; H-P., 41.)

RICHARD POULDEN died 16 March, 1845.

This officer entered the Navy, 22 July, 1776, as Captain's Servant, on board the HECTOR 74, Capt. Sir John Hamilton, on the Home station, where he continued employed as Midshipman in the CAMBRIDGE 74, Capt. Francis John Hartwell, and DILIGENTE sloop, Capt. Anthony Hunt, until transferred, in Oct. 1780, to the BARFLEUR 90, fitting for the flag of Sir Sam. Hood, under whom, on arriving in the West Indies, he fought in a partial action with the Comte de Grasse 29 April, 1781. On 8 Jan. 1782 he was nominated, by the officer last mentioned, Acting-Lieutenant of the ALFRED 74, Capts. Bain, Barber, and Thos. Dumaresq; to which ship the Admiralty confirmed him, 12 Feb. 1783. He returned to England in the following July, and was subsequently appointed, on the Home and Mediterranean stations—in March, 1788, to the THORN sloop, Capts. W. Taylor and John Woodley—27 Sept. 1791 and 11 Feb. 1793, to the SPITFIRE and NEMESIS, both commanded by Capt. Woodley—in Sept. of the latter year, to the ALCIDE 74, successive flag-ship of Admirals Robt. Linzee and Philip Cosby, under the former of whom he co-operated in the reduction of Corsica—and 21 Jan. 1795, to the IRRESISTIBLE 74, Capts. John Leigh Douglas and Rich. Grindall, part of Lord Bridport's fleet in the action off the Ile de Groix. On that occasion, Capt. Grindall having been wounded, the charge of the ship devolved upon Mr. Poulden; whose promotion to the rank of Commander was in consequence effected by a commission bearing date 29 of the same month, June, 1795. In the ensuing Oct. he was sent as Principal Agent for Transports to the river Elbe, for the purpose of embarking the foreign corps, with which he afterwards accompadied Sir Hugh Cloberry Christian to the West Indies. Being next, in Nov. 1797, appointed to the CALCUTTA 24, Capt. Poulden was present in that ship, again in the capacity of Principal Transport Agent, at the reduction of the island of Minorca, where he remained, in charge of the dockyard at Port Mahon, until the arrival of Commissioner Coffin. Quitting the CALCUTTA in Aug. 1799, he assumed command, 12 March, 1801, of the ALKMAAR 50; in which ship we find him, until Sept. 1802, employed on the Home, Baltic, and West India stations. Having attained Post rank 29 April in the latter year, he was afterwards appointed—23 March, 1803, to the Superintendence of the Rendezvous for seamen at Whitby, in Yorkshire—19 Sept. 1805, to the Sea Fencible service—and, 14 July, 1810, to the office of Principal Agent for Transports at Lisbon, where he remained until April, 1815. He became a Rear-Admiral on the Retired List 10 Jan. 1837; and on the Active 17 Aug. 1840.

POULETT. (REAR-ADMIRAL OF THE RED, 1841. F-P., 13; H-P., 37.)

THE HONOURABLE GEORGE POULETT, born 10 May, 1786, is second son of John, fourth Earl Poulett, by Sophia, daughter and heir of Admiral Sir Geo. Pocock, K.B. He is brother of the present Earl Poulett; and brother-in-law of the Duke of Cleveland. His youngest brother, William, an Ensign in the 4th Foot, died in 1812.

This officer entered the Navy, 2 Aug. 1797, as A.B., on board the PRINCESS AUGUSTA yacht, Capt. Riou, lying in the River Thames; served in the Channel as Midshipman, from Nov. 1798 until April, 1802, in the SAN FIORENZO 36, Capts. Sir Harry Burrard Neale and Chas. Wm. Paterson, and MALTA 80, Capt. Albemarle Bertie; and from July in the latter year until promoted to the rank of Lieutenant 3 April, 1804, cruized on the Downs station, the latter part of the time in the LARK sloop. He was present in the SAN FIORENZO, and in company with the AMELIA 38, at the defeat, by those ships, of three heavy French frigates and a gun-vessel, after a warm action of an hour and 55 minutes, fought within the jaws of one of the enemy's ports, 9 April, 1799; and also, 2 July following, in an attack made by Rear-Admiral Chas. Morice Pole on a Spanish squadron lying in Aix Roads. Mr. Poulett's appointments, in the capacity of Lieutenant, were—16 July, 1804, to the MONMOUTH 64, bearing the flag of Rear-Admiral Thos. Macnamara Russell at North Yarmouth—and, in March and June, 1805, to the VALOROUS and ROYAL SOVEREIGN, Capts. Geo. Nicholas Hardinge and Sir Harry Burrard Neale, employed in the Downs and off Weymouth. He attained the rank of Commander 12 Oct. 1805; was appointed, 14 Jan. 1806, to the ORESTES sloop, in the North Sea; acquired Post-rank 31 July following; was employed from 14 Nov. 1807, until 16 April, 1810, on the Home station, in the QUEBEC 32; and, on 24 July, 1827, became Flag-Captain, in the PRINCE REGENT 120, to Hon. Sir Henry Blackwood, Commander-in-Chief at the Nore, where he remained until July, 1830. He was advanced to his present rank 23 Nov. 1841.

From Aug. 1830 until his attainment of Flag-rank, the Rear-Admiral acted as a Naval Aide-de-Camp to his late and her present Majesty. He had been previously appointed Receiver-General of the Land and Assessed Taxes in Somersetshire. He married, 9 Dec. 1811, Catherine Sophia, eldest daughter of Sir Geo. Dallas, Bart., by whom, who died 11 April, 1831, he has issue three sons—the eldest, George, a Lieutenant in the 54th Regt.

POWELL. (LIEUTENANT, 1838.)

CÆSAR COTTRELL POWELL is fourth son of the late John Folliott Powell, Esq., at one time of Sandy Brook, co. Derby, and afterwards of Leamington, co. Warwick, by Frances, eldest daughter of Chas. Arnett, Esq., of the Low, in Cheshire, and of Toft, co. Stafford, niece of Sir Joseph Scott, Bart., of Great Barr. The Lieutenant is first-cousin of the present Henry Folliott Powell, Esq., of Brandlesome Hall, co. Lancaster; and a near connexion of

Capt. Wm. Burnaby Greene, R.N., and Lieut. John Wainwright, R.N. His grand-uncle, John Powell, an officer in the R.N., died 15 Jan. 1789.

This officer entered the Navy 14 Sept. 1824; passed his examination in 1830; and obtained his commission 28 June, 1838. His appointments have since been—17 Aug. 1838, to the NIAGARA 20, Capt. Williams Sandom, with whom he served on the Lakes of Canada until the early part of 1842—29 Nov. 1842, as First-Lieutenant, to the FROLIC 16, Capt. Wm. Alex. Willis, fitting for the Brazilian station, where he was superseded at the end of 1843—and, 24 March, 1846, in a similar capacity, to the BELLEISLE troop-ship, Capt. John Kingsome, now employed on particular service. AGENTS—Messrs. Stilwell.

POWELL. (COMMANDER, 1841. F-P., 19; H-P., 22.)

GEORGE EYRE POWELL, born in 1790, is fifth son of the late Eyre Powell, Esq., of Great Connel, co. Kildare. Two of his brothers fell in the service of their country.

This officer entered the Navy, 19 Jan. 1806, as Fst.-cl. Vol., on board the WIZARD sloop, of 16 guns and 95 men, Capts. Edm. Palmer and Abel Ferris. Attaining soon the rating of Midshipman, he served in that capacity in the expedition to Egypt in 1807. A wound he received in the course of the same year at the cutting-out of a vessel from under the protection of a martello tower on the coast of Calabria had the effect of procuring him a grant from the Patriotic Fund. He subsequently, by jumping overboard, proved of material assistance in saving the life of the Captain's coxswain, a man named Wm. Johnstone, who had been upset in the jolly-boat; and in May, 1808, he was on board the WIZARD when she fell in with, chased for 88 hours, and, after having run a distance of 369 miles, and once beaten her opponent in an action of one hour and a half, compelled the French brig-corvette *Le Requin*, of 18 guns and 110 men, to seek refuge in the neutral port of Tunis. Removing in the following June to the AMPHION 32, Capt. Wm. Hoste, he was placed a short time afterwards in command of a tender, with the rating of Master's Mate, and detached on a cruize in the Adriatic, where he succeeded in capturing many of the enemy's vessels. In March, 1809, he was sent in charge of a heavily-laden prize, accompanied by another one intrusted to the care of the present Commander Henry Browne Mason, to Malta, for the purpose of obtaining stores for the use of the AMPHION. At day-break on the 6th, observing the approach of two privateers (the one carrying a long 22-pounder in the bow, a carronade in the stern, and 38 men, and the other a 22-pounder in the bow and 28 men), Mr. Powell, concentrating the force of the two prizes on board his own, made all the opposition that could be expected from 2 one-pounder swivels and 6 muskets in the hands of 14 men. The enemy at length boarded on each quarter; and the British, having no alternative, surrendered. Mr. Powell, with his companions, was carried to Zara, thence taken to Ancona, and ultimately marched across the Alps to Briançon and Verdun. Escaping, in the autumn of 1810, with two other Midshipmen, Messrs. Burbidge and Thomas, he traversed Holland under great privations, and on reaching its shores embarked in a fishing-boat, in which he had the good fortune to be picked up by the IDAS cutter, Lieut.-Commander Duncan. In that vessel, after he had been conveyed on board the CHRISTIAN VII., flag-ship of Sir Edw. Pellew in the North Sea, and been by him highly complimented, he was sent to England. Reporting himself, on his arrival, at the Admiralty, he was at once ordered to join the THISBE 28, Capt. Wm. Rogers, guard-ship at Woolwich. Soon after this, while absent on leave, he was attacked by the Walcheren fever, and for several weeks incapacitated from exertion. On his return to the THISBE he was removed, in Dec. 1810, to the PRIMROSE 18, Capt. Chas. Geo. Rodney Phillott, under whom we find him, during the next 12 months, employed in escorting troops to Lisbon, protecting the trade to Quebec, and cruizing off Flushing. Rejoining Capt. Hoste at the end of that period as Master's Mate on board the BACCHANTE 38, he accompanied him a second time to the Adriatic, and again acted a part in more than one animated scene. On the night of 31 Aug. 1812, receiving charge of the BACCHANTE's launch, he served with a detachment of boats under the command of Lieut. Donat Henchy O'Brien, and assisted in cutting out from the port of Lema seven vessels laden with ship-timber for the Venetian Government, together with *La Tisiphone* French national xebec of 1 six-pounder, 2 three-pounders, and 28 men; one gun-boat with a nine-pounder, 2 three-pounders, and 24 men; and another of 1 nine-pounder and 20 men, intended for the protection of the trade on the coast of Istria from Pola to Trieste. On 6 Jan. 1813 Mr. Powell, with the same launch under his orders, united in a successful attack made by the boats of the BACCHANTE and WEASEL sloop on five of the enemy's gun-vessels in the neighbourhood of Otranto. While in command, previously to the latter affair, of the above-named *Tisiphone*, which had been converted into a tender and named the AMPHION, he had fallen in, 2 Sept. 1812, with a convoy of 11 sail under the escort of two gun-boats; one of which, carrying 1 long 28-pounder in the bow, 1 22-pounder in the stern, together with 6 brass swivels and 38 men, he had succeeded, although with but 1 Midshipman, 13 seamen, and 5 marines on board, in driving on the rocks, after a running action of 35 minutes, in so shattered a condition that she soon went down. The other gun-boat was driven off the field. As a reward for his frequently distinguished conduct Mr. Powell was made Lieutenant, 22 Jan. 1813, into the TREMENDOUS 74, Capt. Robt. Campbell. While in that ship he assisted at the reduction of the Castle of Trieste, and commanded a battery and a division of seamen at the taking of Rovigno, and in other operations on the coast of Istria. In charge of the flotilla employed in co-operation with the Austrians under Marshal Belgrade, he ascended the Po as far as the river Mincio, and aided at the blockade of Mantua, displaying in his exertions so much zeal, alacrity, and perseverance, that he elicited the thanks of the Marshal, and induced the late Sir Chas. Rowley, then commanding the EAGLE 74, to mention him in a very warm manner in his despatches to Rear-Admiral Thos. Fras. Fremantle, the chief naval authority in the Adriatic. On the restoration of Naples to its ancient sovereign, and the surrender to Capt. Campbell of the shipping and arsenal, Mr. Powell was sent on shore to act as Commissioner, and remained there until the arrival of Lord Exmouth. He then escorted the ex-Queen to Trieste, and was by her presented with a valuable diamond ring. On the paying off of the TREMENDOUS he was appointed, 29 Nov. 1815, Senior of the CORDELIA 10, Capts. Wm. Sargent and Wm. Popham, under the former of whom he took part in the bombardment of Algiers, 27 Aug. 1816. He served next, from 18 Jan. 1817 until Oct. 1822, on the Home, St. Helena, and Cape stations, as First-Lieutenant in the HERON 18, Capts. Herbert Brace Powell and Job Hanmer, and was on board that vessel when she brought home the despatches announcing the death of Napoleon Buonaparte. He returned from the Cape of Good Hope with Capt. Hanmer, in the LEANDER 60, in Jan. 1823, from which period he remained on half-pay until appointed, 4 Feb. 1840, First of the VICTORY 104, Capts. Fras. Erskine Loch and Wm. Wilmott Henderson, ordinary guard-ship at Portsmouth. He attained his present rank 23 Nov. 1841.

Commander Powell married Catherine, youngest daughter of the late Joseph Kingdon, Esq., Comptroller of the Customs for Exeter, and sister of Wm. Page Kingdon, Esq., late Mayor of Exeter, by whom he has had issue seven children.

www.ingramcontent.com/pod-product-compliance
Ingram Content Group UK Ltd.
Pitfield, Milton Keynes, MK11 3LW, UK
UKHW012145240726
13966UKWH00001B/160